INFORMATION
PLEASE
ALMANAC®
ATLAS & YEARBOOK

1997

50TH EDITION

HOUGHTON MIFFLIN COMPANY
BOSTON & NEW YORK

1997

Executive Editor
Otto Johnson

Senior Editor
Borgna Brunner

Managing Editor
Tasha M. Vincent

Associate Editors
Vera Dailey, Natalie Aust

Production Editor
Christine Frantz

Contributing Editors
Arthur Reed, Jr. (Current Events)
Thomas Nemeth, Ph.D. (World Countries)
Christine Frantz and Dennis M. Lyons
(Sports)

Proofreading and Fact-checking:
Susan Chicoski, Ann-Marie Imbornoni,
Erik T. Johnson, Nicholas A. Kosar,
Javier Mateu, Steven C. Thomas

The *Information Please Almanac*® invites comments and suggestions from readers. Because of the many letters received, however, it is not possible to respond personally to every correspondent. Nevertheless, suggestions are welcome, and the editors will consider them carefully. (Information Please Almanac does not rule on bets or wagers.)

Information Please Almanac
Editorial Office

Inso Corporation
31 St. James Avenue
Boston, MA 02116-4101
E-mail: IPA@inso.com

ISBN (Paperback): 0-395-82858-9
ISBN (Hardcover): 0-395-82859-7
ISSN: 0073-7860

Previous editions of the *Information Please Almanac* were published from 1984–1995 by Houghton Mifflin Company, in 1982 by A&W Publishing Company, from 1979–1981 by Simon & Schuster, in 1978 and 1977 by Information Please Publishing, Inc., and from 1947–1976 by Dan Golenpaul Associates.

HOW TO ORDER BY MAIL

Copies of the *Information Please Almanac* may be ordered directly by mail from: Customer Service Department, Houghton Mifflin Company, 181 Ballardvale Road, Wilmington, MA 01887. FAX 800-634-7568. Phone toll-free, (800) 225-3362 for price and shipping information.

Information Please and *Information Please Almanac* are registered trademarks of Inso Corporation.

Printed in the United States of America

WP Pa   BP Hbd 10 9 8 7 6 5 4 3 2 1

QUICK CONTENTS

Also *see* Contents, pages 4–5, and Comprehensive Index, pages 6–32.

CONTENTS

SPORTS CONTENTS

SPECIAL FEATURES

4

SPECIAL SECTIONS

WE'RE FIFTY YEARS OLD NOW

When the almanac was first published in 1947, there were no personal computers, microwave ovens, VCRs, CDs, or video games. The transister had just been invented and the long-playing record was the latest audio development. Vinyl records had been invented the year before and the solid electric guitar (Fender) was just around the corner in 1948.

Fifty years ago, listening to the radio was the most popular form of home entertainment, and although television had arrived, only 14,000 homes owned sets. One of the most successful radio shows in that golden era was a quiz program on NBC called "Information Please," created in 1938. During the show, a panel of experts answered questions on a wide range of topics from queries sent in by listeners. If the experts were stumped by a question, the sender received ten dollars and a set of encyclopedias.

Because the show received a tremendous number of questions from listeners who were mainly seeking information, the producers decided to publish an almanac that was more than a book of dry statistics. In 1947 the first edition of the *Information Please Almanac* appeared on the nation's retail bookshelves.

Substantial changes have been made in the almanac since its inception, but the goal remains the same: to attempt to provide the general readers with answers to all the questions they may ask. Although this is impossible to achieve, we assure our readers that we'll keep on trying.—*Ed.*

COMPREHENSIVE INDEX

J

K

ELECTIONS

The Hundred and Fifth Congress
The 1996 elections took place on Tuesday, November 5, 1996.

The Senate

The senior senator is listed first. Dates in left column indicate term in office; birthdates are given in parentheses after name and party affiliation. All terms are for six years and expire in January. Mailing address: The Senate, Washington, DC 20515.

ALABAMA
1987–99   Richard Shelby (R) (1934)
1997–2003   Jeff Sessions (R) (1946)

ALASKA
1970–2003   Ted Stevens (R) (1923)
1981–99   Frank H. Murkowski (R) (1933)

ARIZONA
1987–99   John McCain (R) (1936)
1995–2001   Jon Kyl (R) (1942)

ARKANSAS
1975–99   Dale Bumpers (D) (1925)
1997–2003   Tim Hutchinson (R) (1949)

CALIFORNIA
1993–2001   Dianne Feinstein (D) (1933)
1993–99   Barbara Boxer (D) (1940)

COLORADO
1993–99   Ben Nighthorse Campbell (R) (1933)
1997–2003   Wayne Allard (R) (1943)

CONNECTICUT
1981–99   Christopher J. Dodd (D) (1944)
1989–2001   Joseph I. Lieberman (D) (1942)

DELAWARE
1971–2001   William V. Roth, Jr. (R) (1921)
1973–2003   Joseph R. Biden, Jr. (D) (1942)

FLORIDA
1987–99   Bob Graham (D) (1936)
1989–2001   Connie Mack III (R) (1940)

GEORGIA
1993–99   Paul Cloverdell (R) (1939)
1997–2003   Max Cleland (D) (1942)

HAWAII
1963–99   Daniel K. Inouye (D) (1924)
1990–2001   Daniel K. Akaka (D) (1924)

IDAHO
1991–2003   Larry E. Craig (R) (1945)
1993–99   Dirk Kempthorne (R) (1951)

ILLINOIS
1993–99   Carol Mosely Braun (D) (1947)
1997–2003   Richard J. Durbin (D) (1944)

INDIANA
1977–2001   Richard G. Lugar (R) (1932)
1989–99   Dan Coats (R) (1943)

IOWA
1981–99   Charles E. Grassley (R) (1933)
1985–2003   Tom Harkin (D) (1939)

KANSAS
1997–2003   Sam Brownback (R) (1956)
1997–2003   Pat Roberts (R) (1936)

KENTUCKY
1974–99   Wendell H. Ford (D) (1924)
1985–2003   Mitch McConnell (R) (1942)

LOUISIANA
1987–99   John B. Breaux (D) (1944)
1997–2003   Mary L. Landrieu (D) (1955)

MAINE
1995–2001   Olympia J. Snowe (R) (1947)
1997–2003   Susan M. Collins (R) (1952)

MARYLAND
1977–2001   Paul Sarbanes (D) (1933)
1987–99   Barbara A. Mikulski (D) (1936)

MASSACHUSETTS
1962–2001   Edward M. Kennedy (D) (1932)
1985–2003   John Kerry (D) (1943)

MICHIGAN
1979–2003   Carl Levin (D) (1934)
1995–2001   Spencer Abraham (R) (1952)

MINNESOTA
1991–2003   Paul Wellstone (D) (1944)
1995–2001   Rod Grams (R) (1948)

MISSISSIPPI
1978–2003   Thad Cochran (R) (1937)
1989–2001   Trent Lott (R) (1941)

MISSOURI
1987–99   Christopher S. "Kit" Bond (R) (1939)
1995–2001   John Ashcroft (R) (1942)

MONTANA
1978–2003   Max Baucus (D) (1941)
1989–2001   Conrad Burns (R) (1935)

NEBRASKA
1989–2001   Robert Kerrey (D) (1943)
1997–2003   Chuck Hagel (R) (1946)

NEVADA
1987–99   Harry M. Reid (D) (1939)
1989–2001   Dick Bryan (D) (1937)

NEW HAMPSHIRE
1991–2003   Robert C. Smith (R) (1941)
1993–99   Judd Gregg (R) (1947)

NEW JERSEY
1982–2001   Frank R. Lautenberg (D) (1924)
1997–2003   Robert G. Torricelli (D) (1951)

NEW MEXICO
1973–2003   Pete V. Domenici (R) (1932)
1983–2001   Jeff Bingaman (D) (1943)

NEW YORK
1977–2001   Daniel P. Moynihan (D) (1927)
1981–99   Alfonse M. D'Amato (R) (1937)

NORTH CAROLINA
1973–2003   Jesse Helms (R) (1921)
1993–99   Lauch Faircloth (R) (1928)

NORTH DAKOTA
1993–2001   Kent Conrad (D) (1948)
1987–99   Byron Dorgan (D) (1942)

OHIO
1974–99   John H. Glenn, Jr. (D) (1921)
1995–2001   Mike DeWine (R) (1947)

OKLAHOMA
1989–99   Don Nickles (R) (1948)
1994–2003   James M. Inhofe (R) (1934)

OREGON
1996–99   Ron Wyden (D)
1997–2003   Gordon Smith (R) (1952)

PENNSYLVANIA
1981–99   Arlen Specter (R) (1930)
1995–2001   Rick Santorum (R) (1958)

RHODE ISLAND
1976–2001   John H. Chafee (R) (1922)
1997–2003   Jack Reed (D) (1949)

SOUTH CAROLINA
1957–2003   Strom Thurmond (R) (1902)
1966–99   Ernest F. Hollings (D) (1922)

SOUTH DAKOTA
1987–99   Thomas A. Daschle (D) (1947)
1997–2003   Tim Johnson (D) (1946)

TENNESSEE
1995–2003   Fred Thompson (R) (1942)
1995–2001   Bill Frist (R) (1952)

TEXAS
1985–2003   Phil Gramm (R) (1942)
1995–2001   Kay Bailey Hutchison (R) (1943)

UTAH
1977–2001   Orrin G. Hatch (R) (1934)
1993–99   Robert Bennett (R) (1933)

VERMONT
1975–99   Patrick J. Leahy (1940)
1989–2001   James M. Jeffords (R) (1934)

VIRGINIA
1979–2003   John W. Warner (R) (1927)
1989–2001   Charles Robb (D) (1939)

WASHINGTON
1989–2001   Slade Gorton (R) (1928)
1993–99   Patty Murray (D) (1950)

WEST VIRGINIA
1959–2001   Robert C. Byrd (D) (1917)
1985–2003   John D. "Jay" Rockefeller IV (D) (1937)

WISCONSIN
1989–2001   Herbert Kohl (D) (1935)
1993–99   Russell D. Feingold, Jr. (D) (1953)

WYOMING
1995–2001   Craig Thomas (R) (1933)
1997–2003   Michael B. Enzi (R) (1944)

House of Representatives

The numeral indicates the Congressional District represented; AL is for representatives At Large. All terms expire January 1999. Mailing address: House of Representatives, Washington, DC 20515. Election results as of 4 p.m., Nov. 6, 1996.

ALABAMA
1. Sonny Callahan (R)
2. Terry Everett (R)
3. Bob Riley (R)
4. Robert Aderholt (R)
5. Robert E. "Bud" Cramer (D)
6. Spencer Bachus (R)
7. Earl F. Hilliard (D)

ALASKA
AL Don Young (R)

ARIZONA
1. Matt Salmon (R)
2. Ed Pastor (D)
3. Bob Stump (R)
4. John Shadegg (R)
5. Jim Kolbe (R)
6. J.D. Hayworth (R)

ARKANSAS
1. Marion Berry (D)
2. Vic Snyder (D)
3. Tim Hutchinson (R)
4. Jay Dickey (R)

CALIFORNIA
1. Frank Riggs (R)
2. Wally Herger (R)
3. Vic Fazio (D)
4. John T. Doolittle (R)
5. Robert T. Matsui (D)
6. Lynn Woolsey (D)
7. George Miller (D)
8. Nancy Pelosi (D)
9. Ronald V. Dellums (D)
10. Ellen O. Tauscher (D)
11. Richard W. Pombo (R)
12. Tom Lantos (D)
13. Pete Stark (D
14. Anna G. Eshoo (D)
15. Tom Campbell (R)
16. Zoe Lofgren (D)
17. Sam Farr (D)
18. Gary A. Condit (D)
19. George P. Radanovich (R)
20. Cal Dooley (D)
21. Bill Thomas (R)
22. Walter Holden Capps (D)
23. Elton Gallegly (R)
24. Brad Sherman (D)

25. Howard P. "Buck" McKeon (R)
26. Howard L. Berman (D)
27. James E. Rogan (R)
28. David Dreier (R)
29. Henry A. Waxman (D)
30. Xavier Becerra (D)
31. Matthew G. Martinez (D)
32. Julian C. Dixon (D)
33. Lucille Roybal-Allard (D)
34. Esteban E. Torres (D)
35. Maxine Waters (D)
36. Jane Harman (D)
37. Juanita Millender-McDonald (D)
38. Steve Horn (R)
39. Ed Royce (R)
40. Jerry Lewis (R)
41. Jay C. Kim (R)
42. George E. Brown, Jr. (D)
43. Ken Calvert (R)
44. Sonny Bono (R)
45. Dana Rohrabacher (R)
46. Robert K. Dornan (R)
47. Christopher Cox (R)
48. Ron Packard (R)
49. Brian P. Bilbray (R)
50. Bob Filner (D)
51. Randy "Duke" Cunningham (R)
52. Duncan Hunter (R)

COLORADO
1. Diana DeGette (D)
2. David E. Skaggs (D)
3. Scott McInnis (R)
4. Bob Schaffer (R)
5. Joel Hefley (R)
6. Dan Schaefer (R)

CONNECTICUT
1. Barbara B. Kennelly (D)
2. Sam Gejdenson (D)
3. Rosa DeLauro (D)
4. Christopher Shays (R)
5. James H. Maloney (D)
6. Nancy L. Johnson (R)

DELAWARE
AL Michael N. Castle (R)

FLORIDA
1. Joe Scarborough (R)
2. Allen Boyd (D)

3. Corrine Brown (D)
4. Tillie Fowler (R)
5. Karen L. Thurman (D)
6. Cliff Stearns (R))
7. John L. Mica (R)
8. Bill McCollum (R)
9. Michael Bilirakis (R)
10. C.W. Bill Young (R)
11. Jim Davis (D)
12. Charles T. Canady (R)
13. Dan Miller (R)
14. Porter J. Goss (R)
15. Dave Weldon (R)
16. Mark Foley (R)
17. Carrie P. Meek (D)
18. Ileana Ros-Lehtinen (R)
19. Robert Wexler (D)
20. Peter Deutsch (D)
21. Lincoln Diaz-Balart (R)
22. E. Clay Shaw, Jr. (R)
23. Alcee L. Hastings (D)

GEORGIA
1. Jack Kingston (R)
2. Sanford D. Bishop, Jr. (D)
3. Mac Collins (R)
4. Cynthia A. McKinney (D)
5. John Lewis (D)
6. Newt Gingrich (R)
7. Bob Barr (R)
8. Saxby Chambliss (R)
9. Nathan Deal (R)
10. Charlie Norwood (R)
11. John Linder (R)

HAWAII
1. Neil Abercrombie (D)
2. Patsy T. Mink (D)

IDAHO
1. Helen Chenoweth (R)
2. Michael D. Crapo (R)

ILLINOIS
1. Bobby L. Rush (D)
2. Jesse Jackson, Jr. (D)
3. William O. Lipinski (D)
4. Luis V. Gutierrez (D)
5. Rod R. Blagojevich (D)
6. Henry J. Hyde (R)

7. Danny K. Davis (D)
8. Philip M. Crane (R)
9. Sidney R. Yates (D)
10. John Edward Porter (R)
11. Jerry Weller (R)
12. Jerry F. Costello (D)
13. Harris W. Fawell (R)
14. Dennis Hastert (R)
15. Thomas W. Ewing (R)
16. Donald Manzullo (R)
17. Lane Evans (D)
18. Ray LaHood (R)
19. Glenn Poshard (D)
20. John M. Shimkus (R)

INDIANA
1. Peter J. Visclosky (D)
2. David M. McIntosh (R)
3. Tim Roemer (D)
4. Mark Souder (R)
5. Steve Buyer (R)
6. Dan Burton (R)
7. Edward A. Pease (R)
8. John Hostettler (R)
9. Lee H. Hamilton (D)
10. Julia M. Carson (D)

IOWA
1. Jim Leach (R)
2. Jim Nussle (R)
3. Leonard L. Boswell (D)
4. Greg Ganske (R)
5. Tom Latham (R)

KANSAS
1. Jerry Moran (R)
2. Jim Ryun (R)
3. Vince Snowbarger (R)
4. Todd Tiahrt (R)

KENTUCKY
1. Edward Whitfield (R)
2. Ron Lewis (R)
3. Anne Meagher Northup (R)
4. Jim Bunning (R)
5. Harold Rogers (R)
6. Scotty Baesler (D)

LOUISIANA
1. Robert L. Livingston (R)
2. William J. Jefferson (D)
3. "Billy" Tauzin (R)
4. Jim McCrery (R)
5. John Cooksey (R)
6. Richard H. Baker (R)
7. Chris John (D)

MAINE
1. Thomas H. Allen (D)
2. John Baldacci (D)

MARYLAND
1. Wayne T. Gilchrest (R)
2. Robert Ehrlich, Jr. (R)
3. Benjamin L. Cardin (D)
4. Albert R. Wynn (D)
5. Steny H. Hoyer (D)
6. Roscoe G. Bartlett (R)
7. Elijah E. Cummings (D)
8. Constance A. Morella (R)

MASSACHUSETTS
1. John W. Olver (D)
2. Richard E. Neal (D)
3. James P. McGovern (D)
4. Barney Frank (D)
5. Martin T. Meehan (D)
6. John F. Tierney (D)
7. Edward J. Markey (D)
8. Joseph P. Kennedy II (D)
9. Joe Moakley (D)
10. William D. Delahunt (D)

MICHIGAN
1. Bart Stupak (D)
2. Peter Hoekstra (R)

3. Vernon J. Ehlers (R)
4. Dave Camp (R)
5. James A. Barcia (D)
6. Fred Upton (R)
7. Nick Smith (R)
8. Debbie Stabenow (D)
9. Dale E. Kildee (D)
10. David E. Bonior (D)
11. Joe Knollenberg (R)
12. Sander M. Levin (D)
13. Lynn Rivers (D)
14. John Conyers, Jr. (D)
15. Carolyn Cheeks Kilpatrick (D)
16. John D. Dingell (D)

MINNESOTA
1. Gil Gutknecht (R)
2. David Minge (D)
3. Jim Ramstad (R)
4. Bruce F. Vento (D)
5. Martin Olav Sabo (D)
6. William P. "Bill" Luther (D)
7. Collin C. Peterson (D)
8. James L. Oberstar (D)

MISSISSIPPI
1. Roger Wicker (R)
2. Bennie Thompson (D)
3. Charles W. "Chip" Pickering, Jr. (R)
4. Mike Parker (R)
5. Gene Taylor (D)

MISSOURI
1. William L. Clay (D)
2. James M. Talent (R)
3. Richard A. Gephardt (D)
4. Ike Skelton (D)
5. Karen McCarthy (D)
6. Pat Danner (D)
7. Roy Blunt (R)
8. Jo Ann Emerson (I)
9. Kenny Hulshof (R)

MONTANA
AL Rick Hill (R)

NEBRASKA
1. Doug Bereuter (R)
2. Jon Christensen (R)
3. Bill Barrett (R)

NEVADA
1. John Ensign (R)
2. Jim Gibbons (R)

NEW HAMPSHIRE
1. John E. Sununu (R)
2. Charles Bass (R)

NEW JERSEY
1. Robert E. Andrews (D)
2. Frank A. LoBiondo (R)
3. H. James Saxton (R)
4. Christopher H. Smith (R)
5. Marge Roukema (R)
6. Frank Pallone, Jr. (D)
7. Bob Franks (R)
8. William J. Pascrell, Jr. (D)
9. Steven R. Rothman (D)
10. Donald M. Payne (D)
11. Rodney Frelinghuysen (R)
12. Mike Pappas (R)
13. Robert Menendez (D)

NEW MEXICO
1. Steven H. Schiff (R)
2. Joe Skeen (R)
3. Bill Richardson (D)

NEW YORK
1. Michael P. Forbes (R)
2. Rick A. Lazio (R)
3. Peter T. King (R)
4. Carolyn McCarthy (D)
5. Gary L. Ackerman (D)
6. Floyd H. Flake (D)

7. Thomas J. Manton (D)
8. Jerrold Nadler (D)
9. Charles E. Schumer (D)
10. Edolphus Towns (D)
11. Major R. Owens (D)
12. Nydia M. Velazquez (D)
13. Susan Molinari (R)
14. Carolyn B. Maloney (D)
15. Charles B. Rangel (D)
16. Jose E. Serrano (D)
17. Eliot L. Engel (D)
18. Nita M. Lowey (D)
19. Sue W. Kelly (R)
20. Benjamin A. Gilman (R)
21. Michael R. McNulty (D)
22. Gerald B.H. Solomon (R)
23. Sherwood Boehlert (R)
24. John M. McHugh (R)
25. James T. Walsh (R)
26. Maurice D. Hinchey (D)
27. Bill Paxon (R)
28. Louise M. Slaughter (D)
29. John J. LaFalce (D)
30. Jack Quinn (R)
31. Amo Houghton (R)

NORTH CAROLINA
1. Eva Clayton (D)
2. Bob Etheridge (D)
3. Walter B. Jones, Jr. (R)
4. David E. Price (D)
5. Richard M. Burr (R)
6. Howard Coble (R)
7. Mike McIntyre (D)
8. W.G. "Bill" Hefner (D)
9. Sue Myrick (R)
10. Cass Ballenger (R)
11. Charles H. Taylor (R)
12. Melvin Watt (D)

NORTH DAKOTA
AL Earl Pomeroy (D)

OHIO
1. Steve Chabot (R)
2. Rob Portman (R)
3. Tony P. Hall (D)
4. Michael G. Oxley (R)
5. Paul E. Gillmor (R)
6. Ted Strickland (D)
7. David L. Hobson (R)
8. John A. Boehner (R)
9. Marcy Kaptur (D)
10. Dennis J. Kucinich (D)
11. Louis Stokes (D)
12. John R. Kasich (R)
13. Sherrod Brown (D)
14. Tom Sawyer (D)
15. Deborah Pryce (R)
16. Ralph Regula (R)
17. James A. Traficant, Jr. (D)
18. Bob Ney (R)
19. Steven C. LaTourette (R)

OKLAHOMA
1. Steve Largent (R)
2. Tom Coburn (R)
3. Wes Watkins (I)
4. J.C. Watts (R)
5. Ernest Istook (R)
6. Frank D. Lucas (R)

OREGON
1. Elizabeth Furse (D)
2. Bob Smith (R)
3. Earl Blumenauer (D)
4. Peter A. DeFazio (D)
5. Darlene Hooley (D)

PENNSYLVANIA
1. Thomas M. Foglietta (D)
2. Chaka Fattah (D)
3. Robert A. Borski (D)
4. Ron Klink (D)
5. John E. Peterson (R)

6. Tim Holden (D)
7. Curt Weldon (R)
8. James C. Greenwood (R)
9. Bud Shuster (R)
10. Joseph M. McDade (R)
11. Paul E. Kanjorski (D)
12. John P. Murtha (D)
13. Joseph M. Hoeffel (D)[1]
13. Jon D. Fox (R)[1]
14. William J. Coyne (D)
15. Paul McHale (D)
16. Joseph R. Pitts (R)
17. George W. Gekas (R)
18. Mike Doyle (D)
19. Bill Goodling (R)
20. Frank R. Mascara (D)
21. Phil English (R)

RHODE ISLAND
1. Patrick J. Kennedy (D)
2. Robert A. Weygand (D)

SOUTH CAROLINA
1. Mark Sanford (R)
2. Floyd D. Spence (R)
3. Lindsey Graham (R)
4. Bob Inglis (R)
5. John M. Spratt, Jr. (D)
6. James E. Clyburn (D)

SOUTH DAKOTA
AL John R. Thune (R)

TENNESSEE
1. William L. "Bill" Jenkins (R)
2. John J. "Jimmy" Duncan, Jr. (R)
3. Zach Wamp (R)
4. Van Hilleary (R)
5. Bob Clement (D)
6. Bart Gordon (D)
7. Ed Bryant (R)

8. John Tanner (D)
9. Harold E. Ford, Jr. (D)

TEXAS
1. Max Sandlin (D)
2. Jim Turner (D)
3. Sam Johnson (R)
4. Ralph M. Hall (D)
5. Pete Sessions (R)
6. Joe L. Barton (R)
7. Bill Archer (R)
8. Kevin Brady (R)
9. Steve Stockman (R)
10. Lloyd Doggett (D)
11. Chet Edwards (D)
12. Kay Granger (R)
13. William M. "Mac" Thornberry (R)
14. Ron Paul (R)
15. Ruben Hinojosa (D)
16. Silvestre Reyes (D)
17. Charles W. Stenholm (D)
18. Sheila Jackson Lee (D)
19. Larry Combest (R)
20. Henry B. Gonzalez (D)
21. Lamar Smith (R)
22. Tom DeLay (R)
23. Henry Bonilla (R)
24. Martin Frost (D)
25. Ken Bentsen (D)
26. Dick Armey (R)
27. Solomon P. Ortiz (D)
28. Frank Tejeda (D)
29. Gene Green (D)
30. Eddie Bernice Johnson (D)

UTAH
1. James V. Hansen (R)
2. Merrill Cook (R)
3. Christopher B. Cannon (R)

VERMONT
AL Bernard Sanders (I)

VIRGINIA
1. Herbert H. Bateman (R)
2. Owen B. Pickett (D)
3. Robert C. Scott (D)
4. Norman Sisisky (D)
5. Virgil H. Goode, Jr. (D)
6. Robert W. Goodlatte (R)
7. Thomas J. Bliley, Jr. (R)
8. James P. Moran, Jr. (D)
9. Frederick C. "Rick" Boucher (D)
10. Frank R. Wolf (R)
11. Thomas M. Davis III (R)

WASHINGTON
1. Rick White (R)
2. Kevin Quigley (D)
3. Brian Baird (D)
4. Richard "Doc" Hastings (R)
5. George Nethercutt (R)
6. Norm Dicks (D)
7. Jim McDermott (D)
8. Jennifer Dunn (R)
9. Adam Smith (D)

WEST VIRGINIA
1. Alan B. Mollohan (D)
2. Bob Wise (D)
3. Nick J. Rahall II (D)

WISCONSIN
1. Mark W. Neumann (R)
2. Scott L. Klug (R)
3. Ron Kind (D)
4. Gerald D. Kleczka (D)
5. Thomas M. Barrett (D)
6. Tom Petri (R)
7. David R. Obey (D)
8. Jay Johnson (D)
9. F. James Sensenbrenner, Jr. (R)

WYOMING
AL Barbara Cubin (R)

1. Recount.

The Governors of the Fifty States

State	Governor	Current term[1]	State	Governor	Current term[1]
Ala.	Fob James, Jr. (R)	1995–1999	Mont.	Marc Racicot (R)	1997–2001
Alaska	Tony Knowles (D)	1994–1998[2]	Neb.	Ben Nelson (D)	1995–1999
Ariz.	Fife Symington (R)	1995–1999	Nev.	Bob Miller (D)	1995–1999
Ark.	Mark Huckabee (R)	1996–1999	N.H.	Jeanne Shaheen (D)	1997–1999
Calif.	Pete Wilson (R)	1995–1999	N.J.	Christine Todd Whitman (R)	1994–1999
Colo.	Roy Romer (D)	1995–1999	N.M.	Gary Johnson (R)	1995–1999
Conn.	John Rowland (R)	1995–1999	N.Y.	George E. Pataki (R)	1995–1999
Del.	Thomas R. Carper (D)	1997–2001	N.C.	James B. Hunt, Jr. (D)	1997–2001
Fla.	Lawton Chiles (D)	1995–1999	N.D.	Edward T. Schafer (R)	1997–2001
Ga.	Zell Miller (D)	1995–1999	Ohio	George V. Voinovich (R)	1995–1999
Hawaii	Benjamin Cayetano (D)	1994–1998[2]	Okla.	Frank Keating (R)	1995–1999
Idaho	Philip E. Batt (R)	1995–1999	Ore.	John Kitzhaber (D)	1995–1999
Ill.	Jim Edgar (R)	1995–1999	Pa.	Tom Ridge (R)	1995–1999
Ind.	Frank O'Bannon (D)	1997–2001	R.I.	Lincoln C. Almond (R)	1995–1999
Iowa	Terry Branstad (R)	1995–1999	S.C.	David Beasley (R)	1995–1999
Kan.	Bill Graves (R)	1995–1999	S.D.	William J. Janklow (R)	1995–1999
Ky.	Paul E. Patton (D)	1995–1999[2]	Tenn.	Don Sundquist (R)	1995–1999
La.	Murphy J. "Mike" Foster (R)	1996–2000	Texas	George W. Bush (R)	1995–1999
Me.	Angus King (Ind.)	1995–1999	Utah	Michael O. Leavitt (R)	1997–2001
Md.	Parris N. Glendening (D)	1995–1999	Vt.	Howard Dean (D)	1997–1999
Mass.	William F. Weld (R)	1995–1999	Va.	George Felix Allen (R)	1994–1999
Mich.	John Engler (R)	1995–1999	Wash.	Gary Locke (D)	1997–2001
Minn.	Arne H. Carlson (R)	1995–1999	W. Va.	Cecil H. Underwood (R)	1997–2001
Miss.	Kirk Fordice (R)	1996–2000	Wis.	Tommy G. Thompson (R)	1995–1999
Mo.	Mel Carnahan (D)	1997–2001	Wyo.	Jim Geringer (R)	1995–1999

1. Except where indicated, all terms begin in January. 2. December.

Presidential Election of 1996

Principal Candidates for President and Vice President
Democratic: William J. Clinton; Albert A. Gore, Jr.
Republican: Robert J. Dole; Jack F. Kemp
Independent: H. Ross Perot; Pat Choate

	William J. Clinton		Robert J. Dole		H. Ross Perot		Electoral Votes		
	Popular Vote	%	Popular Vote	%	Popular Vote	%	D	R	I
Alabama	664,503	43	782,029	51	92,010	6		9	
Alaska	66,508	34	101,234	51	21,536	11		3	
Arizona	612,412	47	576,126	44	104,712	8	8		
Arkansas	469,164	54	322,349	37	66,997	8	6		
California	4,639,935	51	3,412,563	38	667,702	8	54		
Colorado	670,854	44	691,291	46	99,509	7		8	
Connecticut	712,603	52	481,047	35	137,784	10	8		
Delaware	140,209	52	98,906	36	28,693	11	3		
D.C.	152,031	86	16,637	9	3,479	2	3		
Florida	2,533,502	48	2,226,117	42	482,237	9	25		
Georgia	1,047,214	46	1,078,972	47	146,031	6		13	
Hawaii	205,012	57	113,943	32	27,358	7	4		
Idaho	165,545	34	256,406	52	62,506	13		4	
Illinois	2,299,476	54	1,577,930	37	344,311	8	22		
Indiana	874,668	42	995,082	47	218,739	10		12	
Iowa	615,732	50	490,949	40	104,462	9	7		
Kansas	384,399	36	578,572	54	92,093	9		6	
Kentucky	635,804	46	622,339	45	118,768	9	8		
Louisiana	928,983	52	710,240	40	122,981	7	9		
Maine	311,092	52	185,133	31	85,290	14	4		
Maryland	924,284	54	651,682	38	113,684	7	10		
Massachusetts	1,567,223	62	717,622	28	225,594	9	12		
Michigan	1,911,553	52	1,413,812	38	326,751	9	18		
Minnesota	1,096,355	51	751,971	35	252,986	12	10		
Mississippi	385,005	44	434,547	50	51,500	6		7	
Missouri	1,024,817	48	889,689	41	217,103	10	11		
Montana	167,169	41	178,957	44	55,017	14		3	
Nebraska	231,906	35	355,665	53	76,103	11		5	
Nevada	203,388	44	198,775	43	43,855	10	4		
New Hampshire	245,260	49	196,740	40	48,140	10	4		
New Jersey	1,599,932	53	1,080,041	36	257,979	9	15		
New Mexico	252,215	50	210,791	41	30,978	6	5		
New York	3,513,191	59	1,861,198	31	485,547	8	33		
North Carolina	1,099,132	44	1,214,399	49	165,301	7		14	
North Dakota	106,405	40	124,597	47	32,594	12		3	
Ohio	2,100,690	48	1,823,859	41	470,680	11	21		
Oklahoma	488,102	40	582,310	48	130,788	11		8	
Oregon	326,099	47	256,105	37	73,265	11	7		
Pennsylvania	2,206,241	49	1,793,568	40	430,082	10	23		
Rhode Island	220,592	60	98,325	27	39,965	11	4		
South Carolina	495,878	44	564,856	50	63,324	6		8	
South Dakota	139,295	43	150,508	47	31,248	10		3	
Tennessee	905,599	48	860,809	46	105,577	6	11		
Texas	2,455,735	44	2,731,998	49	377,530	7		32	
Utah	220,197	33	359,394	54	66,100	10		5	
Vermont	138,400	54	80,043	31	30,912	12	3		
Virginia	1,070,990	45	1,119,974	47	158,707	7		13	
Washington	899,645	51	639,743	36	161,642	9	11		
West Virginia	324,394	51	231,908	37	70,853	11	5		
Wisconsin	1,071,859	49	845,172	39	227,426	10	11		
Wyoming	77,897	37	105,347	50	25,854	12		3	
Total US	**45,599,094**	**49**	**37,842,270**	**41**	**7,866,627**	**8**	**379**	**159**	

Source: News Election Service, New York, N.Y. Note: Unofficial results as of 4:00 p.m., Nov 6, 1996.

Senate and House Standing Committees, 104th Congress

Committees of the Senate

Agriculture, Nutrition, and Forestry (18 members)
Chairman: Richard G. Lugar (Ind.)
Ranking Dem.: Patrick J. Leahy (Vt.)
Appropriations (28 members)
Chairman: Mark O. Hatfield (Ore.)
Ranking Dem.: Robert C. Byrd (W. Va.)
Armed Services (21 members)
Chairman: Strom Thurmond (S.C.)
Ranking Dem.: Sam Nunn (Ga.)
Banking, Housing, and Urban Affairs (16 members)
Chairman: Alfonse D'Amato (N.Y.)
Ranking Dem.: Paul S. Sarbanes (Md.)
Budget (24 members)
Chairman: Pete V. Domenici (N.M.)
Ranking Dem.: J. Jim Exon (Neb.)
Commerce, Science, and Transportation
  (21 members)
Chairman: Larry Pressler (S.D.)
Ranking Dem.: Ernest F. Hollings (S.C.)
Energy and Natural Resources (20 members)
Chairman: Frank H. Murkowski (Alaska)
Ranking Dem.: J. Bennett Johnston (La.)
Environment and Public Works (18 members)
Chairman: John H. Chafee (R.I.)
Ranking Dem.: Max Baucus (Mont.)
Finance (20 members)
Chairman: William V. Roth, Jr. (Del.)
Ranking Dem.: Daniel Patrick Moynihan (N.Y.)
Foreign Relations (18 members)
Chairman: Jesse Helms (N.C.)
Ranking Dem.: Claiborne Pell (R.I.)
Governmental Affairs (15 members)
Chairman: Ted Stevens (Alaska)
Ranking Dem.: John Glenn (Ohio)
Judiciary (18 members)
Chairman: Orrin G. Hatch (Utah)
Ranking Dem.: Joseph R. Biden, Jr. (Del.)
Labor and Human Resources (16 members)
Chairman: Nancy Landon Kassebaum (Kan.)
Ranking Dem.: Edward M. Kennedy (Mass.)
Rules and Administration (16 members)
Chairman: John W. Warner (Va.)
Ranking Dem.: Wendell H. Ford (Ky.)
Small Business (19 members)
Chairman: Christopher S. Bond (Mo.)
Ranking Dem.: Dale Bumpers (Ark.)
Veterans' Affairs (12 members)
Chairman: Alan K. Simpson (Wyom.)
Ranking Dem.: John D. Rockefeller IV (W. Va.)

Select and Special Committees

Aging (21 members)
Chairman: William S. Cohen (Maine)
Ranking Dem.: David Pryor (Ark.)
Ethics (6 members)
Chairman: Mitch McConnell (Ky.)
Ranking Dem.: Byron L. Dorgan (N.D.)
Indian Affairs (16 members)
Chairman: John McCain (Ariz.)
Ranking Dem.: Daniel K. Inouye (Hawaii)
Intelligence (17 members)
Chairman: Arlen Specter (Pa.)
Ranking Dem.: Bob Kerrey (Neb.)

Committees of the House

Agriculture (48 members)
Chairman: Pat Roberts (Kan.)
Ranking Dem.: E. "Kika" de la Garza (Texas)
Appropriations (58 members)
Chairman: Robert L. Livingston (La.)
Ranking Dem.: David R. Obey (Wis.)
Banking and Financial Services (52 members)
Chairman: Jim Leach (Iowa)
Ranking Dem.: Henry B. Gonzalez (Texas)
Budget (42 members)
Chairman: John R. Kasich (Ohio)
Ranking Dem.: Martin Olav Sabo (Minn.)
Commerce (49 members)
Chairman: Thomas J. Bliley, Jr. (Va.)
Ranking Dem.: John D. Dingell (Mich.)
Economic and Educational Opportunities
  (43 members)
Chairman: Bill Goodling (Pa.)
Ranking Dem.: William L. Clay (Mo.)
Government Reform and Oversight (52 members)
Chairman: William F. Clinger, Jr. (Pa.)
Ranking Dem.: Cardiss Collins (Ill.)
House Oversight (12 members)
Chairman: Bill Thomas (Calif.)
Ranking Dem.: Vic Fazio (Calif.)
International Relations (45 members)
Chairman: Benjamin A. Gilman (N.Y.)
Ranking Dem.: Sam Gejdenson (Conn.)
Judiciary (36 members)
Chairman: Henry J. Hyde (Ill.)
Ranking Dem.: John Conyers, Jr. (Mich.)
National Security (55 members)
Chairman: Floyd D. Spence (S.C.)
Ranking Dem.: Ronald V. Dellums (Calif.)
Resources (49 members)
Chairman: Don Young (Alaska)
Ranking Dem.: George Miller (Calif.)
Rules (13 members)
Chairman: Gerald B.H. Solomon (N.Y.)
Ranking Dem.: John J. Moakley (Mass.)
Science (50 members)
Chairman: Robert S. Walker (Pa.)
Ranking Dem.: George E. Brown, Jr. (Calif.)
Small Business (43 members)
Chairman: Jan Meyers (Kan.)
Ranking Dem.: John J. LaFalce (N.Y.)
Standards of Official Conduct (10 members)
Chairman: Nancy L. Johnson (Conn.)
Ranking Dem.: Jim McDermott (Wash.)
Transportation and Infrastructure (64 members)
Chairman: Bud Shuster (Pa.)
Ranking Dem.: James Oberstar (Minn.)
Veterans' Affairs (33 members)
Chairman: Bob Stump (Ariz.)
Ranking Dem.: G.V. "Sonny" Montgomery
  (Miss.)
Ways and Means (39 members)
Chairman: Bill Archer (Texas)
Ranking Dem.: Sam M. Gibbons (Fla.)

Speakers of the House of Representatives

Dates served	Congress	Name and State	Dates served	Congress	Name and State
1789–1791	1	Frederick A. C. Muhlenberg (Pa.)	1869–1869	40	Theodore M. Pomeroy (N.Y.)[5]
1791–1793	2	Jonathan Trumbull (Conn.)	1869–1875	41–43	James G. Blaine (Me.)
1793–1795	3	Frederick A. C. Muhlenberg (Pa.)	1875–1876	44	Michael C. Kerr (Ind.)[6]
1795–1799	4–5	Jonathan Dayton (N.J.)[1]	1876–1881	44–46	Samuel J. Randall (Pa.)
1799–1801	6	Theodore Sedgwick (Mass.)	1881–1883	47	J. Warren Keifer (Ohio)
1801–1807	7–9	Nathaniel Macon (N.C.)	1883–1889	48–50	John G. Carlisle (Ky.)
1807–1811	10–11	Joseph B. Varnum (Mass.)	1889–1891	51	Thomas B. Reed (Me.)
1811–1814	12–13	Henry Clay (Ky.)[2]	1891–1895	52–53	Charles F. Crisp (Ga.)
1814–1815	13	Langdon Cheves (S.C.)	1895–1899	54–55	Thomas B. Reed (Me.)
1815–1820	14–16	Henry Clay (Ky.)[3]	1899–1903	56–57	David B. Henderson (Iowa)
1820–1821	16	John W. Taylor (N.Y.)	1903–1911	58–61	Joseph G. Cannon (Ill.)
1821–1823	17	Philip P. Barbour (Va.)	1911–1919	62–65	Champ Clark (Mo.)
1823–1825	18	Henry Clay (Ky.)	1919–1925	66–68	Frederick H. Gillett (Mass.)
1825–1827	19	John W. Taylor (N.Y.)	1925–1931	69–71	Nicholas Longworth (Ohio)
1827–1834	20–23	Andrew Stevenson (Va.)[4]	1931–1933	72	John N. Garner (Tex.)
1834–1835	23	John Bell (Tenn.)	1933–1934	73	Henry T. Rainey (Ill.)[7]
1835–1839	24–25	James K. Polk (Tenn.)	1935–1936	74	Joseph W. Byrns (Tenn.)[8]
1839–1841	26	Robert M. T. Hunter (Va.)	1936–1940	74–76	William B. Bankhead (Ala.)[9]
1841–1843	27	John White (Ky.)	1940–1947	76–79	Sam Rayburn (Tex.)
1843–1845	28	John W. Jones (Va.)	1947–1949	80	Joseph W. Martin, Jr. (Mass.)
1845–1847	29	John W. Davis (Ind.)	1949–1953	81–82	Sam Rayburn (Tex.)
1847–1849	30	Robert C. Winthrop (Mass.)	1953–1955	83	Joseph W. Martin, Jr. (Mass.)
1849–1851	31	Howell Cobb (Ga.)	1955–1961	84–87	Sam Rayburn (Tex.)[10]
1851–1855	32–33	Linn Boyd (Ky.)	1962–1971	87–91	John W. McCormack (Mass.)[11]
1855–1857	34	Nathaniel P. Banks (Mass.)	1971–1977	92–94	Carl Albert (Okla.)[12]
1857–1859	35	James L. Orr (S.C.)	1977–1987	95–99	Thomas P. O'Neill, Jr. (Mass.)[13]
1859–1861	36	Wm. Pennington (N.J.)	1987–1989	100–101	James C. Wright, Jr. (Tex.)[14]
1861–1863	37	Galusha A. Grow (Pa.)	1989–1994	101–103	Thomas S. Foley (Wash.)
1863–1869	38–40	Schuyler Colfax (Ind.)	1995–	104–	Newt Gingrich (Ga.)

1. George Dent (Md.) was elected Speaker pro tempore for April 20 and May 28, 1798. 2. Resigned during second session of 13th Congress. 3. Resigned between first and second sessions of 16th Congress. 4. Resigned during first session of 23rd Congress. 5. Elected Speaker and served the day of adjournment. 6. Died between first and second sessions of 44th Congress. During first session, there were two Speakers pro tempore: Samuel S. Cox (N.Y.), appointed for Feb. 17, May 12, and June 19, 1876, and Milton Sayler (Ohio), appointed for June 4, 1876. 7. Died in 1934 after adjournment of second session of 73rd Congress. 8. Died during second session of 74th Congress. 9. Died during third session of 76th Congress. 10. Died between first and second sessions of 87th Congress. 11. Not a candidate in 1970 election. 12. Not a candidate in 1976 election. 13. Not a candidate in 1986 election. 14. Resigned during first session of 101st Congress. *Source: Congressional Directory.*

Floor Leaders of the Senate

Democratic	Republican
Gilbert M. Hitchcock, Neb. (Min. 1919–20)	Charles Curtis, Kan. (Maj. 1925–29)
Oscar W. Underwood, Ala. (Min. 1920–23)	James E. Watson, Ind. (Maj. 1929–33)
Joseph T. Robinson, Ark. (Min. 1923–33, Maj. 1933–37)	Charles L. McNary, Ore. (Min. 1933–44)
Alben W. Barkley, Ky. (Maj. 1937–46, Min. 1947–48)	Wallace H. White, Jr., Me. (Min. 1944–47, Maj. 1947–48)
Scott W. Lucas, Ill. (Maj. 1949–50)	Kenneth S. Wherry, Neb. (Min. 1949–51)
Ernest W. McFarland, Ariz. (Maj. 1951–52)	Styles Bridges, N. H. (Min. 1951–52)
Lyndon B. Johnson, Tex. (Min. 1953–54, Maj. 1955–60)	Robert A. Taft, Ohio (Maj. 1953)
Mike Mansfield, Mont. (Maj. 1961–77)	William F. Knowland, Calif. (Maj. 1953–54, Min. 1955–58)
Robert C. Byrd, W. Va. (Maj. 1977–81, Min. 1981–86, Maj. 1987–88)	Everett M. Dirksen, Ill. (Min. 1959–69)
George John Mitchell, Me. (Maj. 1989–1994)	Hugh Scott, Pa. (Min. 1969–1977)
Thomas A. Daschle, S.D. (Min. 1995–)	Howard H. Baker, Jr., Tenn. (Min. 1977–81, Maj. 1981–84)
	Robert J. Dole, Kan. (Maj. 1985–86, Min. 1987–94, Maj. 1995–96)
	Trent Lott, Miss. (Maj. 1996–)

NOTE: Min. = Minority Leader; Maj. = Majority Leader. *Source:* United States Senate, Secretary for the Majority.

Black Elected Officials

Year	U.S. and State Legislatures	City and County Offices	Law Enforcement	Education	Total
1970 (Feb.)	182	715	213	362	1,472
1975 (Apr.)	299	1,878	387	939	3,503
1980 (July)	326	2,832	526	1,206	4,890
1981 (July)	343	2,863	549	1,259	5,014
1982 (July)	342	2,951	563	1,259	5,115
1983 (July)	366	3,197	607	1,369	5,559
1984 (Jan.)	396	3,259	636	1,363	5,654
1985 (Jan.)	407	3,517	661	1,431	6,016
1986 (Jan.)	420	3,824	676	1,504	6,424
1987 (Jan.)	440	3,966	728	1,547	6,681
1988 (July)	436	4,105	738	1,550	6,829
1989 (Jan.)	448	4,406	759	1,612	7,225
1990 (Jan.)	447	4,499	769	1,655	7,370
1991 (Jan.)	484	4,508	847	1,638	7,480
1992 (Jan.)	510	4,569	847	1,623	7,549
1993 (Jan.)	571	4,825	923	1,694	8,016

Source: Joint Center for Political and Economic Studies, Washington, D.C., *Black Elected Officials: A National Roste* Copyright. Data is most recent available.

1997 Annual Salaries of Federal Officials

President of the U.S.	$200,000[1]	Senators and Representatives	$133,600
Vice President of the U.S.	171,500[2]	President Pro Tempore of Senate	148,400
Cabinet members	148,400	Majority and Minority Leader of the Senate	148,400
Deputy Secretaries of State, Defense, Treasury	133,600	Majority and Minority Leader of the House	148,400
Deputy Attorney General	133,600	Speaker of the House	171,500
Secretaries of the Army, Navy, Air Force	133,600	Chief Justice of the United States	171,500
Under secretaries of executive departments	123,100	Associate Justices of the Supreme Court	164,100

1. Plus taxable $50,000 for expenses and a nontaxable sum (not to exceed $100,000 a year) for travel expenses. 2. Plus taxable $10,000 for expenses. NOTE: All salaries shown above are taxable; 1997 fiscal year began Oct. 1, 1996. *Source* Office of Personnel Management.

Projected Voting Age Population, November 1996—Sex, Race, and State[1]

	Total	Male	Female	White	Black	His-panic[2]		Total	Male	Female	White	Black	His-panic[2]
Voted in 1992	61.3%	60.2%	62.3%	63.6%	54.0%	28.9%	Voted in 1992	61.3%	60.2%	62.3%	63.6%	54.0%	28.9%
U.S.	196,509	94,296	102,213	165,225	22,857	18,609	Mo.	3,980	1,893	2,087	3,527	397	4
Ala.	3,218	1,526	1,692	2,438	744	20	Mont.	647	311	336	609	2	
Alaska	425	221	294	332	17	14	Neb.	1,208	578	630	1,147	41	3
Ariz.	3,094	1,478	1,616	2,795	85	602	Nev.	1,180	580	600	1,032	72	14
Ark.	1,860	875	985	1,583	253	18	N.H.	860	416	444	843	5	
Calif.	23,133	11,357	11,774	18,447	1,716	6,323	N.J.	6,005	2,867	3,138	4,917	819	63
Colo.	2,843	1,385	1,458	2,642	113	251	N.M.	1,210	578	632	1,078	22	50
Conn.	2,468	1,180	1,288	2,223	199	173	N.Y.	13,579	6,445	7,135	10,614	2,292	1,61
Del.	547	261	286	443	92	15	N.C.	5,499	2,648	2,851	4,249	1,126	6
D.C.	435	206	230	157	269	20	N.D.	473	229	244	451	3	
Fla.	11,043	5,130	5,913	9,467	1,375	1,409	Ohio	8,358	3,980	4,378	7,387	866	11
Ga.	5,396	2,605	2,791	3,937	1,368	101	Okla.	2,419	1,159	1,260	2,044	164	6
Hawaii	882	427	455	378	24	69	Ore.	2,396	1,149	1,247	2,247	37	10
Idaho	845	407	437	819	4	49	Pa.	9,196	4,366	4,831	8,241	814	19
Ill.	8,764	4,217	4,547	7,219	1,245	728	R.I.	750	358	392	702	29	3
Ind.	4,369	2,097	2,271	3,987	331	81	S.C.	2,777	1,325	1,452	1,978	771	2
Iowa	2,138	1,022	1,116	2,073	38	30	S.D.	530	253	277	492	3	
Kan.	1,898	917	981	1,739	107	75	Tenn.	4,021	1,917	2,104	3,390	589	2
Ky.	2,924	1,400	1,525	2,700	201	15	Tex.	13,622	6,612	7,011	11,670	1,564	3,73
La.	3,137	1,485	1,653	2,183	902	75	Utah	1,323	638	685	1,259	10	6
Maine	939	449	489	925	4	6	Vt.	441	213	228	435	2	
Md.	3,811	1,825	1,987	2,676	982	110	Va.	5,089	2,468	2,621	3,992	924	13
Mass.	4,623	2,210	2,413	4,252	234	229	Wash.	4,122	2,004	2,119	3,720	111	19
Mich.	7,067	3,374	3,693	5,956	972	159	W. Va.	1,414	671	743	1,364	40	
Minn.	3,412	1,647	1,765	3,247	65	44	Wis.	3,824	1,839	1,986	3,571	180	7
Miss.	1,961	925	1,036	1,311	632	12	Wyo.	352	172	180	339	3	2

1. In thousands. Population 18 years and over. Includes Armed Forces in each state. 2. Persons of Hispanic origin may be of any race.

Robert Joseph Dole

Republican Presidential Candidate

In April 1995 Bob Dole began his fourth run in presidential politics—twice before as a candidate and once as the vice-presidential nominee in 1976—running on his experience, conservatism, and character. Dole has served in government for 45 years, 35 of which were spent in Congress, making him the second longest-serving Republican and one of the most influential senators of the twentieth century. His belief in reducing government, cutting taxes, balancing the budget, and his consistent opposition to liberal social causes identified him as a classic conservative. Dole's small-town beginnings in the American heartland, heroism in World War II, and triumph over physical disabilities earned him a reputation for integrity and perseverance.

After winning in the primaries against Pat Buchanan, Steve Forbes, and Lamar Alexander, Dole's campaign faltered somewhat, lacking focus and organization. But in May he dramatically resigned from the Senate to shed his Washington insider image and campaign as "just a man," recognizing that the legislative skills he was famous for were not the same strengths that would elect him president. Throughout his campaign, Dole struggled unsuccessfully with his reputation for being a "legislative mechanic," as Lamar Alexander called him, a pragmatist without a coherent vision. His difficulty in communicating an overarching ideology was further hindered by his stoic reserve, which contrasted with Clinton's famous warmth and empathy.

The G.O.P. convention in San Diego in August nominated him enthusiastically after adopting a platform more conservative even than Dole's own views on many issues. The Republican plank supported a ban on abortion under all circumstances, whereas Dole contended there should be exceptions—an important distinction if Dole were not to alienate Republican moderates. Dole laid out his economic program in a hard-hitting speech in Chicago just before the convention, proposing to stimulate the economy with a 15 percent tax reduction, to overhaul the education system, and to balance the budget within five years. Although a long-time skeptic of Ronald Reagan's supply-side economics, Dole pledged to "finish the job Ronald Reagan started so brilliantly." Dole also promised to get tough on drugs and crime, and condemned the immorality of the entertainment industry, repeating the Republican refrain of family values.

The two presidential debates in October did not lessen Clinton's consistent two-digit lead over Dole. Although Dole was able to convey an uncharacteristic ease and optimism in the first debate that voters reacted favorably to, Clinton was declared the winner. Dole's attacks on Clinton's character in the second debate were ignored by the President, who instead emphasized his accomplishments and concentrated on the issues. In a final effort to turn the tide of what for months had seemed an inevitable Clinton victory, Dole intensified his negative campaigning, portraying the President as slippery and unethical. The tactic was ineffectual; Clinton continued to appear presidential and above the fray, whereas Dole came across as mean-spirited, a trait that has periodically surfaced throughout his career. More damagingly, Dole's focus on Clinton's shortcomings squandered his opportunity to put forth a compelling argument for a Dole presidency.

Dole was born July 22, 1923, in Russell, Kansas, and as a teenager distinguished himself as an athlete and hard worker. He joined the army at 18, where he was wounded on a battlefield in Northern Italy during World War II and narrowly escaped death. He lost a kidney, use of his right arm, and most of the feeling in his left, and endured three years of surgery and rehabilitation. He attended the University of Kansas before the war, then switched to Washburn University in Topeka, from which he received a B.A. and a law degree magna cum laude. He began his long career of public service: Kansas State Legislature (1951–53); Russell County Attorney (1953–61), U.S. Representative (1961–69), Senator (1969–96), Senate Minority Leader (1986–94), Senate Majority Leader (1984–86 and 1994–96). A protégé of Richard Nixon, he served as chairman of the Republican National Committee (1971–73) and was a nominee for vice president on Gerald Ford's ticket in 1976.

In 1975 Dole married Elizabeth Hanford, a highly respected and prominent public figure whose most recent office was president of the Red Cross. He has a daughter, Robin (born in 1954), from a previous marriage that ended in divorce.

Jack French Kemp

Republican Vice-Presidential Candidate

Congressional veteran and a Republican party favorite, Jack Kemp brought wide name recognition, charisma, and an optimistic outlook to the 1996 Republican ticket. Dole/Kemp was hailed by some as an ideal partnership, though initially most were astonished at Dole's choice: the pair had a long history of legislative antagonism and ideological incompatibility, with Kemp a fervent advocate of supply-side economics and Dole labeling himself a "deficit hawk." And just months earlier, Kemp's endorsement of Steve Forbes in the primaries had been a significant blow to the Dole campaign.

Kemp was born on July 13, 1935, in Los Angeles. As a youth he worked part-time in his father's trucking concern to pay his way through Occidental College, where he became a football star. He then played professionally (1957–70), becoming quarterback for the San Diego Chargers and then the Buffalo Bills. He developed a taste for politics as a volunteer for the Goldwater and Nixon presidential campaigns, and for then–California governor Ronald Reagan. He served as a U.S. Representative from upstate New York between 1971 and 1989, and later became Secretary of Housing and Urban Development under George Bush (1989–92). His political career has been distinguished by its independence: an arch-conservative in many respects, Kemp has liberal leanings on some social issues, referring to himself as a "compassionate conservative." Kemp married Joanne Main in 1958. They have two sons and two daughters.

—A.P.R., Jr.

See page 672 for a biography of President Bill Clinton.

TAXES

History of the Income Tax in the United States

Source: Deloitte & Touche LLP

The nation had few taxes in its early history. From 1791 to 1802, the United States Government was supported by internal taxes on distilled spirits, carriages, refined sugar, tobacco and snuff, property sold at auction, corporate bonds, and slaves. The high cost of the War of 1812 brought about the nation's first sales taxes on gold, silverware, jewelry, and watches. In 1817, however, Congress did away with all internal taxes, relying on tariffs on imported goods to provide sufficient funds for running the Government.

In 1862, in order to support the Civil War effort, Congress enacted the nation's first income tax law. It was a forerunner of our modern income tax in that it was based on the principles of graduated, or progressive, taxation and of withholding income at the source. During the Civil War, a person earning from $600 to $10,000 per year paid tax at the rate of 3%. Those with incomes of more than $10,000 paid taxes at a higher rate. Additional sales and excise taxes were added, and an "inheritance" tax also made its debut. In 1866, internal revenue collections reached their highest point in the nation's 90-year history—more than $310 million, an amount not reached again until 1911.

The Act of 1862 established the office of Commissioner of Internal Revenue. The Commissioner was given the power to assess, levy, and collect taxes, and the right to enforce the tax laws through seizure of property and income and through prosecution. His powers and authority remain very much the same today.

In 1868, Congress again focused its taxation efforts on tobacco and distilled spirits and eliminated the income tax in 1872. It had a short-lived revival in 1894 and 1895. In the latter year, the U.S. Supreme Court decided that the income tax was unconstitutional because it was not apportioned among the states in conformity with the Constitution.

In 1913, the 16th Amendment to the Constitution made the income tax a permanent fixture in the U.S. tax system. The amendment gave Congress legal authority to tax income and resulted in a revenue law that taxed incomes of both individuals and corporations. In fiscal year 1918, annual internal revenue collections for the first time passed the billion-dollar mark, rising to $5.4 billion by 1920. With the advent of World War II, employment increased, as did tax collections—to $7.3 billion. The withholding tax on wages was introduced in 1943 and was instrumental in increasing the number of taxpayers to 60 million and tax collections to $43 billion by 1945.

In 1981, Congress enacted the largest tax cut in U.S. history, approximately $750 billion over six years. The tax reduction, however, was partially offset by two tax acts, in 1982 and 1984, which attempted to raise approximately $265 billion.

On October 22, 1986, President Reagan signed into law The Tax Reform Act of 1986, one of the most far reaching reforms of the United States tax system since the adoption of the income tax. In an attempt to remain revenue neutral, the Act called for a $120 billion increase in business taxation and a corresponding decrease in individual taxation over a five-year period.

Following what seemed to be a yearly tradition of new tax acts which began in 1986, the Revenue Reconciliation Act of 1990 was signed into law on November 5, 1990. As with the '87, '88, and '89 acts, the 1990 act, while providing a number of substantive provisions, was small in comparison with the 1986 act. The emphasis of the 1990 act was increased taxes on the wealthy.

On August 10, 1993, President Clinton signed the Revenue Reconciliation Act of 1993 into law. The Act's purpose was to reduce by approximately $496 billion the federal deficit that would otherwise accumulate in fiscal years 1994 through 1998. Approximately $241 billion of the deficit reduction will be accomplished through tax increases.

In recent years, the tax system has come under increased scrutiny leading to proposals for tax reform. Many policy makers in Washington have advocated some form of flat tax, a value added tax, or a retail sales tax—or a combination of these. Because any new tax law would have to be considered and passed by the president and both branches of Congress before a transition would take place, it is unlikely that a radically changed tax system would become fully effective prior to the year 2000.

Internal Revenue Service

The Internal Revenue Service (IRS), a bureau of the U.S. Treasury Department, is the federal agency charged with the administration of the tax laws passed by Congress. The IRS functions through a national office in Washington, 4 regional offices, 63 district offices, and 10 service centers.

Operations involving most taxpayers are carried out in the district offices and service centers. District offices are organized into Resources Management, Examination, Collection, Taxpayer Service, Employee Plans and Exempt Organizations, and Criminal Investigation. All tax returns are filed with the service centers, where the IRS computer operations are located.

IRS service centers are processing an ever increasing number of returns and documents. In 1995 the number of returns and supplemental documents processed totaled 205.75 million.

Prior to 1987, all tax return processing was performed by hand. This process was time consuming and costly. In an attempt to improve the speed and efficiency of the manual processing procedure, the IRS began testing an electronic return filing system beginning with the filing of 1985 returns.

The two most significant results of the test were that refunds for the electronically filed returns were issued more quickly and the tax processing error rate was significantly lower when compared to paper returns.

Internal Revenue Service

	1995	1994	1993	1992	1991	1970
U.S. population (in thousands)	263,730	261,698	259,015	256,219	252,901	204,878
Number of IRS employees	112,023	110,665	113,352	116,673	115,628	68,683
Cost to govt. of collecting $100 in taxes	$0.55	$0.58	$0.60	$0.58	$0.56	$0.45
Tax per capita	$5,216.44	$4,878.00	$4,543.33	$4,374.38	$4,343.84	$955.31
Collections by principal sources (in thousands of dollars)						
Total IRS collections	$1,375,731,835	$1,276,466,776	$1,176,685,625	$1,120,799,558	$1,086,851,401	$195,722,096
Income and profits taxes						
Individual	$675,779,337	$619,819,153	585,774,159	557,723,156	546,876,876	103,651,585
Corporation	$174,422,173	$154,204,684	131,547,509	117,950,796	113,598,569	35,036,983
Employment taxes	$465,405,305	$443,831,352	411,510,516	400,080,904	384,451,220	37,449,188
Estate and gift taxes	$15,144,394	$15,606,793	12,890,965	11,479,116	11,473,14	3,680,076
Alcohol taxes	NOTE 2	NOTE 2	NOTE 2	NOTE 2	NOTE 2	4,746,382
Tobacco taxes	NOTE 2	NOTE 2	NOTE 2	NOTE 2	NOTE 2	2,094,212
Manufacturers' excise taxes	NOTE 1	NOTE 1	NOTE 1	NOTE 1	NOTE 1	6,683,061
All other taxes	44,980,627	$43,004,794	34,962,476	33,565,587	30,451,596	2,380,094

NOTE: For fiscal year ending September 30th. NOTE 1: Manufacturers' excise taxes are included in the "All other taxes" amount. NOTE 2: Alcohol and tobacco tax collections are now collected and reported by the Bureau of Alcohol, Tobacco, and Firearms. *Source:* IRS 1995 Annual Report.

Electronic filing of individual income tax returns became an operational program in selected areas for the 1987 processing year. In 1994 13,510,000 individual returns were filed electronically, compared to 11,143,000 in 1995.

In addition to the program for the electronic filing of individual returns, the IRS has also implemented programs for the electronic filing of partnership, fiduciary, and employee benefit plan returns.

Auditing Tax Returns

Most taxpayers' contacts with the IRS arise through the auditing of their tax returns. The Service has been empowered by Congress to inquire about all persons who may be liable for any tax and to obtain for review the books and/or records pertinent to those taxpayers' returns. A wide-ranging audit operation is carried out in the 63 district offices by 16,078 revenue agents and 2,831 tax auditors.

Selecting Individual Returns for Audit

The primary method used by the IRS in selecting returns for audits is a computer program that measures the probability of tax error in each return. The higher the score, the greater the tax change potential. Other returns are selected for examination on the basis of claims for refund, multi-year audits, related return audits, and other audits initiated by the IRS as a result of

informants' information, special compliance programs, and the information document matching program.

In 1995, the IRS recommended additional tax and penalties on 1,919,437 individual returns, totaling $7.8 billion.

The Appeals Process

The IRS attempts to resolve tax disputes through an administrative appeals system. Taxpayers who, after audit of their tax returns, disagree with a proposed change in their tax liabilities are entitled to an independent review of their cases. Taxpayers are able to seek an immediate, informal appeal with the Appeals Office. If, however, the dispute arises from a field audit and the amount in question exceeds $10,000, a taxpayer must submit a written protest. Alternatively, the taxpayer can wait for the examiner's report and then request consideration by the Appeals Office and file a protest if necessary. Taxpayers may represent themselves or be represented by an attorney, accountant, or any other advisor authorized to practice before the IRS. Taxpayers can forego their right to the above process and await receipt of a deficiency notice. At this juncture, taxpayers can either (1) not pay the deficiency and petition the Tax Court by a required deadline or (2) pay the deficiency and file a claim for refund with the District Director's office. If the claim is not allowed, a suit for refund may be brought either in the District Court or the Claims Court within a specified period.

Federal Individual Income Tax

The federal individual income tax is levied on the world-wide income of U.S. citizens and resident aliens and on certain types of U.S. source income of non-residents. For a non-itemizer, "tax table income" is adjusted gross income (*see* below) less $2,550 for

each personal exemption and the standard deduction (*see* below). If a taxpayer itemizes, tax table income is adjusted gross income minus total itemized deductions and personal exemptions. In addition, individuals may also be subject to the alternative minimum tax.

Tax Brackets—1996
Taxable Income

Joint return	Single Taxpayer	Rate
$0–$40,100	$0–$24,000	15%
40,101–96,900	24,001–58,150	28%
96,901–147,700	58,151–121,300	31%[2]
147,701–263,750	121,301–263,750	36%[2]
263,751 and up[1]	263,751 and up[1]	39.6%[2]

1. The deduction for personal exemptions is phased out as the taxpayer's gross income exceeds $176,950 for a joint return and $117,950 for single taxpayers. 2. The tax rate is effectively increased because total otherwise allowable itemized deductions are reduced by 3% of the taxpayer's adjusted gross income in excess of $117,950.

Who Must File a Return[1]

You must file a return if you are:	and your gross income is at least:
Single (legally separated, divorced, or married living apart from spouse with dependent child) and are under 65	$6,550
Single (legally separated, divorced, or married living apart from spouse with dependent child) and are 65 or older	$7,550
A person who can be claimed as a dependent on your parent's return, and who has taxable dividends, interest, or other unearned income	$650
Head of household under age 65	$8,450
Head of household over age 65	$9,450
Married, filing jointly, living together at end of year (or at date of death of spouse), and both are under 65	$11,800
Married, filing jointly, living together at end of year (or at date of death of spouse), and one is 65 or older	$12,600
Married, filing jointly, living together at end of year (or at date of death of spouse), and both are 65 or older	$13,400
Married, filing separate return, or married but not living together at end of year over age 65	$2,550

1. In 1996.

Adjusted Gross Income

Gross income consists of wages and salaries, unemployment compensation, tips and gratuities, interest, dividends, annuities, rents and royalties, up to 85% of Social Security Benefits if the recipient's income exceeds a base amount, and certain other types of income. Among the items excluded from gross income, and thus not subject to tax, are public assistance benefits and interest on exempt securities (mostly state and local bonds).

Adjusted gross income is determined by subtracting from gross income: alimony paid, penalties on early withdrawal of savings, payments to an I.R.A. (reduced proportionately based upon adjusted gross income levels if taxpayer is an active participant in an employer maintained retirement plan), payments to a Keogh retirement plan, and self-employed health insurance payments and moving expenses.

Itemized Deductions

Taxpayers may itemize deductions or take the standard deduction. The standard deduction amounts for 1996 are as follows: Married filing jointly and surviving spouses, $6,700; Heads of household, $5,900; Single, $4,000; and Married filing separate returns, $3,350. Taxpayers who are age 65 or over or are blind are entitled to an additional standard deduction of $1,000 for single taxpayers and $800 for a married taxpayer.

In itemizing deductions, the following are major items that may be deducted in 1996: state and local income and property taxes, charitable contributions, employee moving expenses, medical expenses (exceeding 7.5% of adjusted gross income), casualty losses (only the amount over the $100 floor which exceeds 10% of adjusted gross income), mortgage interest, and miscellaneous deductions (deductible only to the extent by which cumulatively they exceed 2% of adjusted gross income).

Personal Exemptions

Personal exemptions are available to the taxpayer for himself, his spouse, and his dependents. The 1996 amount is $2,550 for each individual. No exemption is allowed to a taxpayer who can be claimed as a dependent on another taxpayer's return.

Credits

Taxpayers can reduce their income tax liability by claiming the benefit of certain tax credits. Each dollar of tax credit offsets a dollar of tax liability. The following are a few of the available tax credits:

Certain low-income households may claim an Earned Income Credit. The maximum Earned Income Credit is $323 for taxpayers with no qualifying children, $2,152 for taxpayers with one qualifying child and $3,556 for taxpayers with two or more qualifying children. This maximum credit will be reduced if earned income or adjusted gross income exceeds $11,610, or $5,280 for taxpayers with no qualifying children. For families with one qualifying child, the credit will be zero if earned income or adjusted gross income exceeds $25,078; for families with two or more qualifying children the credit will be zero if income exceeds $28,495, and for families with no qualifying children, the credit will be zero if income exceeds $9,500. The earned income credit is a refundable credit.

A credit for Child and Dependent Care Expenses is available for amounts paid to care for a child or other dependent so that the taxpayer can work. The credit is between 20% and 30% (depending on adjusted gross income) of up to $2,400 of employment-related expenses for one qualifying child or dependent and up to $4,800 of expenses for two or more qualifying individuals.

The elderly and those under 65 who are retired under total disability may be entitled to a credit of up to $750 (if single) or $1,125 (if married and filing jointly). No credit is available if the taxpayer is single and has adjusted gross income of $17,500 or more. Similarly, the credit is unavailable to a married couple filing jointly if their adjusted gross income exceeds $25,000.

Federal Income Tax Comparisons

Taxes at Selected Rate Brackets After Standard Deductions and Personal Exemptions[1]

Adjusted gross income	Single return listing no dependents				Joint return listing two dependents			
	1996	1995	1994	1975	1996	1995	1994	1975
$ 10,000	$ 518	$ 540	$ 563	$ 1,506	$ –3,556	$ –3,110[2]	$–2,527[2]	$ 829
20,000	2,018	2,040	2,063	4,153	–1,324	–773	–358	2,860
30,000	3,518	3,573	3,693	8,018	1,965	2,018	2,078	5,804
40,000	6,246	6,373	6,493	12,765	3,465	3,518	3,578	9,668
50,000	9,046	9,173	9,293	18,360	4,965	5,018	5,078	14,260

1. For comparison purposes, tax rate schedules were used. 2. Refund based on a basic earned income credit for families with dependent children.

Federal Corporation Taxes

Corporations are taxed under a graduated tax rate structure as shown in the chart. If a corporation has taxable income in excess of $100,000, the amount of tax shall be increased by the lesser of five percent of such excess or $11,750. When a corporation has taxable income in excess of $15,000,000 the amount of tax shall be increased by an additional amount equal to the lesser of three percent of such excess or $100,000.

If the corporation qualifies, it may elect to be an S corporation. If it makes this election, the corporation will not (with certain exceptions) pay corporate tax on its income. Its income is instead passed through and taxed to its shareholders. There are several requirements a corporation must meet to qualify as an S corporation including having 35 or fewer shareholders, and having only one class of stock (35-

shareholder limit for S corporations will increase to 75 shareholders in 1997).

Tax Brackets—1996

Taxable income	Tax rate
$0–$50,000	15%
$50,001–$75,000	25%
$75,001–$100,000	34%
$101,000–$335,000	39%
$335,001–$10,000,000	34%
10m–15m	35%
15m–18.3m	38%
18.3m and up	35%

State Corporation Income and Franchise Taxes

All states except Texas, Nevada, South Dakota, Washington, and Wyoming impose a tax on corporation net income. The majority of states impose the tax at flat rates ranging from 2.3% to approximately 10.75%. Several states have adopted a graduated basis of rates for corporations.

Nearly all states follow the federal law in defining net income. However, many states provide for varying exclusions and adjustments.

A state is empowered to tax all of the net income of

its domestic corporations. With regard to non-resident corporations, however, it may only tax the net income on business carried on within its boundaries. Corporations are, therefore, required to apportion their incomes among the states where they do business and pay a tax to each of these states. Nearly all states provide an apportionment to their domestic corporations, too, in order that they not be unduly burdened. Several states tax unincorporated businesses separately.

Federal Estate and Gift Taxes

A Federal Estate Tax Return must generally be filed for the estate of every U.S. citizen or resident whose gross estate, adjusted taxable gifts, and specific exemption exceed $600,000. An estate tax return must also generally be filed for the estate of a non-resident, if the value of his gross estate in the U.S. is more than $60,000 at the date of death. The estate tax return is due nine months after the date of death of the decedent, but a reasonable extension of time to file may be obtained for good reason.

Under the unified federal estate and gift tax structure, individuals who made taxable gifts during the calendar year are required to file a gift tax return by April 15 of the following year.

A unified credit of $192,800 is available to offset both estate and gift taxes. Any part of the credit used to offset gift taxes is not available to offset estate taxes. As a result, although they are still taxable as gifts, lifetime transfers no longer cushion the impact of progressive estate tax rates. Lifetime transfers and transfers made at death are combined for estate tax rate purposes.

Gift taxes are computed by applying the uniform

rate schedule to lifetime taxable transfers (after deducting the unified credit) and subtracting the taxes payable for prior taxable periods. In general, estate taxes are computed by applying the uniform rate schedule to cumulative transfers and subtracting the gift taxes paid. An appropriate adjustment is made for taxes on lifetime transfers—such as certain gifts within three years of death—in a decedent's estate.

Among the deductions allowed in computing the amount of the estate subject to tax are funeral expenditures, administrative costs, claims and bequests to religious, charitable, and fraternal organizations or government welfare agencies, and state inheritance taxes. For transfers made after 1981 during life or death, there is an unlimited marital deduction.

An annual gift tax exclusion is provided that permits tax-free gifts to each donee of $10,000 for each year. A husband and wife who agree to treat gifts to third persons as joint gifts can exclude up to $20,000 a year to each donee. An unlimited exclusion for medical expenses and school tuition paid for the benefit of any donee is also available.

Federal Estate and Gift Taxes

Unified Transfer Tax Rate Schedule, 1996[1]

If the net amount is:		Tentative tax is:		
From	To	Tax +	%	On excess over
$ 0	$ 10,000	$ 0	18	$ 0
10,001	20,000	1,800	20	10,000
20,001	40,000	3,800	22	20,000
40,001	60,000	8,200	24	40,000
60,001	80,000	13,000	26	60,000
80,001	100,000	18,200	28	80,000
100,001	150,000	23,800	30	100,000
150,001	250,000	38,800	32	150,000
250,001	500,000	70,800	34	250,000
500,001	750,000	155,800	37	500,000
750,001	1,000,000	248,300	39	750,000
1,000,001	1,250,000	345,800	41	1,000,000
1,250,001	1,500,000	448,300	43	1,250,000
1,500,001	2,000,000	555,800	45	1,500,000
2,000,001	2,500,000	780,800	49	2,000,000
2,500,001	3,000,000	1,025,800	53	2,500,000
3,000,001 and up	—	1,290,800	55	3,000,000

1. The estate and gift tax rates are combined in the single rate schedule effective for the estates of decedents dying, and for gifts made, after Dec. 31, 1976. 2. The tentative tax determined above is increased by an amount equal to 5% with respect to cumulative taxable transfers between $10,000,000 and $21,040,000.

Rising Payroll Taxes Push Federal Tax Load Higher

Source: Tax Features, June 1996, Tax Foundation

According to the latest federal data, while personal income taxes as a percent of GDP have risen about 8 percent over the past 40 years, and excise and corporate income taxes have fallen, payroll taxes (also called social insurance taxes) have more than tripled.

In all, federal taxes rose from 17.9 percent of GDP in 1956 to 19.4 percent this year. Federal individual income taxes remained stable in that time, climbing from 7.7 percent to 8.6 percent. Federal corporate in-come taxes dropped from 5 percent to 2.3 percent of GDP over the last 40 years, and federal excise taxes fell from 2 percent to about 0.9 percent in that time frame.

On the other hand, social insurance taxes—originally earmarked solely for Social Security and Medicare—have gone from 2.2 percent of GDP to 6.9 percent since 1956, and are apparently the driving force behind the climb in the federal tax burden. □

State General Sales and Use Taxes[1]

State	Percent rate	State	Percent rate	State	Percent rate
Alabama	4	Louisiana	4	Ohio	5
Arizona	5	Maine	6	Oklahoma	4.5
Arkansas	4.5	Maryland	5	Pennsylvania	6
California	6	Massachusetts	5	Rhode Island	7
Colorado	3	Michigan	6	South Carolina	5
Connecticut	6	Minnesota	6.5	South Dakota	4
D.C.	5.75	Mississippi	7	Tennessee	6
Florida	6	Missouri[2]	4.225	Texas	6.25
Georgia	4	Nebraska	5	Utah	4.875
Hawaii	4	Nevada	6.5	Vermont	5
Idaho	5	New Jersey	6	Virginia[3]	3.5
Illinois	6.25	New Mexico	5	Washington	6.5
Indiana	5	New York	4	West Virginia	6
Iowa	5	North Carolina	4	Wisconsin	5
Kansas	4.9	North Dakota	5	Wyoming	4
Kentucky	6				

1. Local and county taxes, if any, are additional. 2. State use tax 5.725% in areas where local tax and state meet or exceed 5.725%. In areas that do not meet or exceed 5.725%, the use tax rate is 4.225%. 3. Local rate 1%. NOTE: Alaska, Delaware, Montana, New Hampshire, and Oregon have no state-wide sales and use taxes. *Source: Information Please Almanac* questionnaires to the states.

Tax Freedom Day

Tax Freedom Day—the day the average American can expect to quit working for Uncle Sam and his counterparts at the state and local level and begin

FY 96 Federal Tax Burden by State

State	Per capita burden	State	Per capita burden
Connecticut	8,096	Nebraska	4,866
D.C.	7,518	Missouri	4,842
New Jersey	7,159	Indiana	4,829
Massachusetts	6,409	Georgia	4,744
New York	6,352	Texas	4,689
Delaware	6,179	Iowa	4,684
Illinois	6,046	Vermont	4,674
Nevada	5,965	Tennessee	4,606
Maryland	5,958	South Dakota	4,573
Alaska	5,939	North Carolina	4,464
New Hampshire	5,836	North Dakota	4,443
Minnesota	5,556	Arizona	4,369
Michigan	5,539	Idaho	4,270
Colorado	5,532	Maine	4,242
Washington	5,519	Montana	4,168
Rhode Island	5,437	Alabama	4,105
Pennsylvania	5,340	Louisiana	4,104
Hawaii	5,337	Kentucky	4,028
Virginia	5,334	Arkansas	4,007
Florida	5,218	South Carolina	4,000
California	5,212	Oklahoma	4,000
Wyoming	5,115	New Mexico	3,904
Ohio	5,076	Utah	3,823
Wisconsin	5,037	West Virginia	3,702
Kansas	4,963	Mississippi	3,413
Oregon	4,916	**U.S. Average**	**$5,225**

Source: Tax Foundation

working for him or herself—arrived on May 7, 1996, according to the Tax Foundation. At 128 days into the year, it was the latest national Tax Freedom Day ever.

Since 1992, the total tax burden borne by the average American has jumped a full week, and according to Tax Foundation economist Patrick Fleenor, this trend is likely to continue.

The residents of Connecticut bear the heaviest tax burdens in 1996 ($8,096). After Connecticut, residents of New Jersey are the hardest hit by federal taxes, with an average tax bill of $7,159. The average resident of Massachusetts will pay $6,409 in 1996, the third highest federal tax burden in the nation.

At the other end of the spectrum, residents of Mississippi ($3,413), West Virginia ($3,702), and Utah ($3,823), have the lightest federal tax loads in the country.

The variation in the per capita tax burden by state is primarily due to differences in per capita income among the states. Because the federal government's primary sources of revenue—individual income and payroll taxes—are levied as a percentage of income, states with high per capita income will also tend to have high per capita federal tax collections.

According to the Washington, D.C.–based Tax Foundation, a nonprofit, nonpartisan research organization, in 1996 the average American will have to work roughly 42 days to pay his or her personal income taxes, and another 39 days to pay payroll taxes, which fund social insurance programs such as Social Security and Medicaid. In addition, it will take the average American 18 days to pay for sales and excise taxes, another 15 days to pay for property taxes, and about 12 days to pay his or her share of corporate income taxes. Another 2 days will be spent working to pay miscellaneous taxes.

FY 95 Federal Tax Burden v. FY 95 Federal Expenditures by State

	Tax burden per capita	Expenditures per capita	Expenditures per dollar of taxes[1]		Tax burden per capita	Expenditures per capita	Expenditures per dollar of taxes[1]
Alabama	$3,919	$5,314	$1.35	Nebraska	$4,631	$4,673	$1.00
Alaska	5,786	6,887	1.18	Nevada	5,875	4,541	0.77
Arizona	4,256	5,050	1.18	New Hampshire	5,614	4,225	0.75
Arkansas	3,818	4,725	1.23	New Jersey	6,821	4,692	0.68
California	5,040	4,810	0.95	New Mexico	3,765	7,060	1.86
Colorado	5,328	5,200	0.97	New York	6,041	5,089	0.84
Connecticut	7,699	5,270	0.68	North Carolina	4,289	4,289	0.99
Delaware	5,930	4,585	0.77	North Dakota	4,212	5,826	1.38
Florida	5,063	5,336	1.05	Ohio	4,828	4,488	0.92
Georgia	4,577	4,650	1.01	Oklahoma	3,817	4,872	1.27
Hawaii	5,135	6,318	1.22	Oregon	4,715	4,406	0.93
Idaho	4,104	4,646	1.13	Pennsylvania	5,076	5,257	1.03
Illinois	5,746	4,272	0.74	Rhode Island	5,183	5,700	1.09
Indiana	4,596	3,937	0.85	South Carolina	3,840	4,806	1.24
Iowa	4,439	4,516	1.01	South Dakota	4,357	5,235	1.19
Kansas	4,735	4,807	1.01	Tennessee	4,406	4,996	1.13
Kentucky	3,836	5,152	1.34	Texas	4,523	4,490	0.99
Louisiana	3,891	5,119	1.31	Utah	3,693	4,427	1.19
Maine	4,057	5,206	1.28	Vermont	4,476	4,548	1.01
Maryland	5,717	7,279	1.27	Virginia	5,128	7,748	1.50
Massachusetts	6,102	5,854	0.95	Washington	5,325	5,359	1.00
Michigan	5,267	4,087	0.77	West Virginia	3,504	5,399	1.53
Minnesota	5,312	4,071	0.76	Wisconsin	4,806	3,848	0.80
Mississippi	3,257	5,260	1.61	Wyoming	4,854	5,185	1.06
Missouri	4,617	5,873	1.26	Dist. of Columbia	7,090	37,533	5.26
Montana	3,980	5,545	1.39	**United States**	**$5,006**	**$5,035**	**$1.00**

1. When calculating these ratios, expenditures by state were adjusted downward to account for deficit spending.
Source: Tax Foundation; Census Bureau.

Four Tax Laws Add Up to Big Changes

Source: Tax Features, August 1996, Tax Foundation

When viewed in their entirety, the four bills that Congress passed prior to closing for the August recess—health care reform, a provision to more effectively protect taxpayers against IRS actions, welfare reform, and a combination minimum wage increase/small business tax relief/miscellaneous provisions bill—make 170 changes to the tax code. These changes either directly affect taxes owed or tax administration, according to an analysis by the Tax Foundation.

In his latest Special Report, "Analysis of the Four New Tax Laws," Tax Foundation executive director and chief economist J.D. Foster provides a summary of the fiscal impact of this summer's tax policy changes. In purely dollar terms, he calculates, the small business tax relief bill is the largest of the four bills, involving over $25 billion in tax increasing provisions and $21 billion in tax reducing provisions over the 1996 to 2006 time period. Together, the four bills include $52.9 billion in tax increases, $41.5 billion in tax reductions, and represent a net reduction in the budget deficit of $11.4 billion over the period.

Welfare Reform Legislation

The welfare reform bill represents a major shift in the federal government's approach to assisting those in need, while reducing the federal budget deficit by over $6.9 billion over the next six years. Only the bill's provisions relating to the Earned Income Tax Credit (EITC) affect tax policy.

The EITC is a refundable credit of up to $3,560 annually for a family with two or more children (lesser amounts for single workers and families with one child). A family with two children qualifies for the EITC by having wage income of no more than $28,524. The changes to the EITC, which yield $3.2 billion in savings over six years, include establishing that the credit could only be claimed by individuals with valid taxpayer identification numbers, thereby excluding illegal aliens from the benefits; and requiring taxpayers to include previously excluded elements of capital income such as net capital gains.

Health Care Reform Legislation

The health care reform bill will include important changes in the nation's health care system, particularly if the bill's most contentious provision, the medical savings accounts (MSAs), works as advertised in instilling greater market discipline in the health care system. The health care reform bill raises $20.4 billion in new revenues while providing about the same amount of tax relief, for a net of $12 million in deficit reduction over the next six years.

The MSA program is experimental and temporary. The bill directs the Treasury to monitor the development and use of MSAs. Under the bill, after December 31, 2000, no new MSA policies may be written, though individuals with MSA policies may continue to make tax-deferred contributions. The expectation is that the Congress and the president will re-evaluate the program in the year 2000 to determine whether the program should be continued and, if so, whether changes are in order.

Minimum Wage and Small Business Tax Relief Legislation

This bill could more accurately be called the Minor Omnibus Tax and Minimum Wage Act of 1996, as it includes tax provisions relating to small businesses, pensions, reforms of the Subchapter S rules, international tax provisions, previously expired provisions, miscellaneous issues, and revenue-raising provisions, all in addition to the minimum wage increase. On balance, the bill offers $21 billion in tax relief over 10 years, offset by $25 billion in tax increases, for a net of $4 billion in deficit reduction.

The minimum wage increases from $4.25 an hour to $4.75 effective October 1, 1996, and to $5.15 an hour effective September 1, 1997. The bill increases the limit on expensing for small businesses to $25,000, phased in over eight years. Also, the bill allows owners to use the 15-year depreciation schedule for convenience stores, fast-food stores, and other structures installed at gasoline stations. And the bill extends the credit retroactively to off-premises employees.

The bill also includes important changes to the rules relating to Subchapter S corporations. For tax purposes, the income of an S corporation is subject to a single level of tax at the ownership level, in contrast to the double level of tax associated with a C corporation. The S corporation reforms generally relax some of the strictures on ownership and activities that previously applied.

Taxpayer Bill of Rights 2 (H.R. 2337)

The first Taxpayer Bill of Rights was enacted in 1988 and was championed by Senator David Pryor (D-AR). T2, as the 1996 version is called, also originated through Senator Pryor's efforts. The total cost of the taxpayer provisions is $138 million over the fiscal years 1996 to 2000.

Most important, the bill replaces the taxpayer ombudsman with a newly created "taxpayer advocate." The taxpayer advocate will be at the same level in the sense of rank as the IRS chief counsel and will be appointed by the Commissioner. The taxpayer advocate will, among other things, assist taxpayers in resolving problems with the IRS and write reports to the congressional taxwriting committees proposing administrative and legislative changes to address these problems. □

Free Tax Assistance

While taxpayers are encouraged to use these alternative sources, free tax help will still be available both by phone and in person. Recorded tax information on 148 topics is available 24 hours a day using a touch-tone phone; call 1-800-829-4477. Automated refund information is available from 7:00 a.m. to 11:30 p.m. weekdays; call 1-800-729-4477. Tax help is available on-line from Internal Revenue Information System (IRIS) at FedWorld http://www.irs.ustreas.gov. IRS telephone assistors are available at 1-800-829-1040. Volunteer programs are set up in shopping centers, libraries, churches or community centers; call 1-800-829-1040. Walk-in help, including tax law information, tax return preparation, and forms and publications, is available at more than 400 IRS offices nationwide. Tax forms are available by phone Monday through Friday during normal business hours by calling IRS at 1-800-TAX-FORM (1-800-829-3676). These are also available by fax, 7 days a week, 24 hours a day using the voice unit of a fax machine to dial (703) 487-4160.

BUSINESS & ECONOMY

The Job Outlook Through 2005

Every two years, the Bureau of Labor Statistics (BLS) publishes its latest projections on the structure of the economy, labor force demographics, and future job growth. The following is a summary of the most recent BLS projections that were released at the end of 1995. They focused on occupational changes over the period 1994–2005.

Labor Force

The projected growth of the labor force during the 1994–2005 period is 16 million. This is 3.5 million less than it was during the previous 11 years. Its growth is slowing because growth of the civilian non-institutional population 16 years of age and older is declining.

The number of Hispanics, Asians, and others in the labor force will continue to increase much faster than white non-Hispanics, due primarily to immigration. However, white non-Hispanics will still account for the vast majority of workers in 2005.

The number of blacks in the labor force will grow slightly faster than the labor force as a whole.

The rate at which women enter the labor force will continue to be much faster than the rate for men, and women's share of the labor force will increase to 48%.

The rapid rate of increase of women and minority groups into the labor force has been widely discussed. But, another important change in labor force activity has continued for a very long period and has received much less attention: the long-term decline in labor force participation rates of virtually all age groups of men.

Reasons behind this trend have not been fully explored, but a contributing factor includes the increase in the number of men who report that they are unable to work. Also, the structural changes in the U.S. economy have clearly left many men ill-prepared for the direction job growth has taken during the last two decades, particularly men with the least education or training who worked in manufacturing or mining industries. Consequently, many men displaced by structural adjustments in the economy left the labor force permanently because they had insufficient education or training for the available jobs.

Gross Domestic Product

Exports will grow very rapidly, but employment will grow little in most industries producing goods for export because of rising productivity. Foreign trade is expected to continue to play an increasing role in the U.S. economy. The real GDP is expected to increase 2.3% per year over the 1994–2005 period according to the BLS moderate projections. This is lower than the 2.9% annual growth over the previous period 1983–1994.

Industry and Employment Projections

Employment shows a slower growth rate than it did in the previous period. However, it is still expected to expand by 17.7 million by 2005, of which 16.8 million are nonfarm wage and salary jobs.

Industry employment will be very concentrated. The services and retail trade industry divisions will account for 16.2 million new wage and salary jobs, about 96% of the total. Most of the growth will be in just four areas: health, education, business services, and eating and drinking places. On the other hand, manufacturing will have 1.3 million fewer workers in 2005 than in 1994.

Within retail trade, employment of salespersons, cashiers, waiters and waitresses, food preparation workers, marketing and salesworker supervisors, and food service and lodging managers is expected to grow substantially.

Although retail trade will increase by 2.7 million jobs, self-employed workers in the industry will continue to decline as small, independent retail establishments have difficulty competing with large establishments and retail chains.

Fastest Growing Occupations, 1994–2005

Occupation	Growth, %
Personal and home care aides	119
Home health aides	102
Systems analysts	92
Computer engineers	90
Physical and corrective therapy assistants and aides	83
Electronic pagination systems workers	83
Occupational therapy assistants and aides	82
Physical therapists	80
Residential counselors	76
Human services workers	75
Occupational therapists	72
Manicurists	69
Medical assistants	59
Paralegals	58
Medical records technicians	56
Teachers, special education	53
Amusement and recreation attendants	52
Correction officers	51
Operations research analysts	50
Guards	48
Speech-language pathologists and audiologists	46
Detectives, except public	44
Surgical technologists	43
Dental hygienists	42
Dental assistants	42
Adjustment clerks	40
Teacher aides and educational assistants	39
Data processing equipment repairers	38
Nursery and greenhouse managers	37
Securities and financial services sales workers	37

Source: U.S. Department of Labor. Latest data.

Employment in transportation, communications, and utilities is projected to increase 7%, slower than average. Half of the growth will be in trucking and warehousing. Transportation is expected to add more than 476,000 jobs over the 1994–2005 period. The future shape of the communications industry is highly uncertain. Employment reached a 1.4 million peak in 1982 mostly in telecommunications (1.1 million). Since then, it has declined to 903,000.

Jobs in the financial, insurance, and real estate sector are expected to increase except in depository institutions (banks, credit unions, savings and loans) because their growth will be dampened as banks continue to consolidate and restructure. Additionally, banks will continue to extend the use of automatic tellers and other computerized means of providing services to customers, instead of hiring additional employees.

Employment for insurance carriers is expected to grow by 82,000 to slightly more than 1.6 million in 2005. Employment for agents, brokers, and service will increase slightly for a gain of only 16,000.

The real estate sector is projected to increase from 1.3 million in 1994 to 1.5 million by 2005.

Wholesale trade will grow slowly. Business consolidation and direct selling of goods from manufacturers to retail establishments will reduce growth compared to that of recent years.

In the public sector, state and local government employment (excluding education and hospitals) will increase by 450,000 jobs. Much of the projected increase is related to law enforcement. Federal government positions will decline by more than 200,000 jobs, largely due to the decline in defense-related jobs.

Total employment in all divisions in the goods-producing sector will decline, except for construction. Construction will increase at a slower rate than previously because of significant overbuilding of office buildings and other types of construction in the past.

Agriculture, forestry, fishing, and related occupations are projected to decline by 112,000 jobs. They will only account for 2.5% of all jobs by 2005.

Mining, the smallest industry division, is projected to decline by 162,200 wage and salary jobs, led by a decline of nearly 100,000 jobs in oil and gas extraction.

Because of the close relationship between industries and occupations, most health occupations, which are concentrated in the rapidly growing health services industry, will grow faster than average. Health occupations will increase by 2.7 million jobs or 15% of total employment growth, in large part because of the need to care for an aging population with a longer life expectancy.

There will be numerous opportunities for registered nurses, licensed practical nurses, nursing aides, orderlies and attendants, health care orderlies, and personal and home care aides.

Education-related occupations will increase by nearly 2 million and account for 11% of employment growth over the 1994–2005 period. These occupations accounted only for 6% in 1994. Public and private elementary and secondary school teachers are expected to experience the most growth and special education teachers are projected to grow fastest because of legislation emphasizing training and employment for individuals with disabilities and a growing public interest in people with special needs.

Engineers, scientists, and workers in related fields numbered 4.6 million in 1994, or 4% of total employment, but are expected to account for 7% of total employment growth over the 1994–2005 period.

Because of the continuing spread of computer technology, employment in the computer sector will account for 60% of the overall growth. Within this field, there will be slower growth for computer programmers due to improved software and programming techniques that simplify or eliminate some programming tasks.

Employment in administrative support occupations including clerical numbered 22.2 million in 1994, more than any occupational cluster, and accounted for about 18% of all workers. However, this cluster will account for only a small share of employment growth and is projected to grow by only 4% or 994,000 jobs through 2005.

Office automation is expected to have a large impact on many of the individual occupations in this group. For example, the demand for typists and bookkeeping, accounting, and auditing clerks will be held down by advances in computer technology.

Top Declining Occupations, 1994–2005

Occupation	Proj. employment decline in thousands
Farmers	−273
Typists and word processors	−212
Bookkeeping, accounting and auditing clerks	−178
Bank tellers	−152
Sewing machine operators, garment	−140
Cleaners and servants, private household	−108
Computer operators, except peripheral equipment	−98
Billing, posting, and calculating machine operators	−64
Duplicating, mail, and other office machine operators	−56
Textile draw-out and winding machine operators and tenders	−47
File clerks	−42
Freight, stock, and material movers, hand	−36
Farm workers	−36
Machine tool cutting operators and tenders, metal and plastic	−34
Central office operators	−34
Central office and PBX installers and repairers	−33
Electrical and electronic assemblers	−30
Station installers and repairers, telephone	−26
Personnel clerks, except payroll and timekeeping	−26
Data entry keyers, except composing	−25
Bartenders	−25
Inspectors, testers, and graders, precision	−25
Directory assistance operators	−24
Lathe and turning machine tool setters and set-up operators, metal and plastic	−22
Custom tailors and sewers	−21
Machine feeders and offbearers	−20
Machinists	−20
Service station attendants	−20
Machine forming operators and tenders, metal and plastic	−19
Communication, transportation, and utilities operations managers	−19

Source: U.S. Department of Labor. Latest data.

Poverty and Income in the United States

Source: Current Population Reports, "Consumer Income," Bureau of the Census, issued May 1996.

Poverty Thresholds

The poverty thresholds in 1994 were as follows: one person under 65: $7,710; age 65 and over: $7,108; two persons: householder under 65, $9,976; householder 65 and over, $8,967; three persons, $11,821; four persons, $15,141; five persons, $17,900; six persons, $20,235; seven persons, $22,923; eight persons, $25,427; and nine or more persons, $30,300.

The number of persons below the official government poverty level was 38.1 million in 1994, representing 14.5% of the nation's population. Both the number of poor and the poverty rate showed a significant decline from the 1993 figure of 39.3 million and a poverty rate of 15.1 percent.

Age

In 1994, the poverty rate for all persons under 18 years old was 21.8%. Higher than the percentage for other age groups, this was significantly lower than the 1993 rate of 22.7%. Half of the nation's poor in 1994 were either under 18 years of age or 65 and over (50%).

The elderly are underrepresented in the poverty population. These persons 65 and over are approximately 12% of the total population but make up only 10% of the poor. However, a higher proportion of elderly (7%) than nonelderly (4%) were concentrated just over their respective poverty thresholds (between 100% and 125% of their thresholds); 18% of the nation's 12.3 million "near poor" persons were elderly.

Persons under age 18 continue to represent a very large segment of the poor (40%) even though they are only a little more than one-fourth of the total population.

Children under age sex have been particularly vulnerable to poverty. In 1994, the overall poverty rate for related children under six years of age was 24.5%. Of related children under six years old living in families with a female householder, no spouse present, 63.7% were poor, compared to 12.3% of such young children in married-couple families.

Race and Hispanic Origin

In 1994, the poverty rate was 11.7% for whites, 9.4% for non-Hispanic whites, and 30.6% for blacks. For persons of Hispanic origin (who may be of any race) the poverty rate was 30.7 percent. For Asians and Pacific Islanders, the largest component of persons of other races, the poverty rate was 14.6% in 1994.

Even though the poverty rate for whites was lower than that for the other racial and ethnic groups, the majority of poor persons in 1994 were white (67%), and 48% were non-Hispanic white.

Blacks showed a decrease in poverty between 1993 and 1994 in both the poverty rate and the number living below poverty. The last time blacks showed a significant year-to-year decline in the poverty rate was in 1985.

While the poverty rate for whites decreased with no significant change in the number of poor, persons of Hispanic origin showed an increase in the number living in poverty, but not in the rate. The poverty rate for Asians and Pacific Islanders did not change significantly between 1993 and 1994.

Families

There was a significant decrease in both the number of poor families and in their poverty rate between 1993 and 1994. The poverty rate for families was 11.6% in 1994 compared with 12.3% in 1993. The decline in poverty for families, as was true for family income, was mainly attributable to declines for married couples, with a 1994 poverty rate of 6.1%, down from 6.5% in 1993.

Black families followed the same pattern, showing a decline from 31.3% in 1993 to a 27.3% poverty rate in 1994, with poverty for black married couples declining from 12.3% in 1993 to 8.7% in 1994. There was no significant change in poverty from 1993 to 1994 for white families.

For families with a female householder, no spouse present, the poverty rate was 34.6%. Female-householder families were overrepresented among the poor. While 53% of all poor families had a female householder with no spouse present, only 18% of all families in the United States had a female householder. Neither of these figures was statistically different from their respective 1993 estimates.

Persons Below the Poverty Level, 1975–1994

(in thousands)

Year	All persons	White	Black	Hispanic origin[1]	Year	All persons	White	Black	Hispanic origin[1]
1975	25,877	17,770	7,545	2,991	1985	33,064	22,860	8,926	5,236
1976	24,975	16,713	7,595	2,783	1986	32,370	22,183	8,983	5,117
1977	24,720	16,416	7,726	2,700	1987	32,221	21,195	9,520	5,422
1978	24,497	16,259	7,625	2,607	1988	31,745	20,715	9,356	5,357
1979	26,072	17,214	8,050	2,921	1989	31,528	20,785	9,302	5,430
1980	29,272	19,699	8,579	3,491	1990	33,585	22,326	9,837	6,006
1981	31,822	21,553	9,173	3,713	1991	35,708	23,747	10,242	6,339
1982	34,398	23,517	9,697	4,301	1992[2]	38,014	25,259	10,827	7,592
1983	35,303	23,984	9,882	4,633	1993	39,265	26,226	10,877	8,126
1984	33,700	22,955	9,490	4,806	1994	38,059	25,379	10,196	8,416

1. Persons of Hispanic origin may be of any race. 2. Revised. *Source:* U.S. Department of Commerce, Bureau of the Census.

INCOME

The real median income of households in the United States showed no statistically significant change between 1993 and 1994. Median household income in 1994 was $32,264. Although the most recent recessionary period ended in March 1991, household income has not recovered to its 1989 prerecessionary peak of $34,445 (in 1994 dollars). Real median household income in 1994 is 6.3% below its 1989 level.

Race and Hispanic Origin

Among the race and Hispanic origin groups, Asian and Pacific Islander households had the highest median household income in 1994 ($40,482), and black households had the lowest ($21,027). Households maintained by white persons had a median income of $34,028, and those maintained by Hispanic-origin persons had a median income of $23,421.[1]

Black households were the only racial group to experience a significant increase in real income between 1993 and 1994. Black households experienced a 5.0% increase, from $20,032 to $21,027, the first significant annual increase in income since 1989.

The increase in the income of black households overall can be attributed to the increase in the income of married-couple households and households maintained by women with no husband present. The median income of black married-couple households increased by 11.3% between 1993 and 1994, going

1. At least part of the difference between white and Asian and Pacific Islander household income is attributable to the larger size of Asian and Pacific Islander households.

from $36,316 to $40,432.

For households maintained by black women with no husband present, the increase was 15.0%, going from $12,741 to $14,650. The income of black households maintained by men with no wife present was unchanged at $23,073.

Year-Round, Full-Time Workers

The real median earnings of year-round, full-time workers 15 years old and over declined for males and remained unchanged for females between 1993 and 1994. This is the second consecutive year that male, year-round, full-time workers experienced a decline in their earnings. Between 1993 and 1994, the median earnings of male, year-round, full-time workers declined by 1.1% from $31,186 to $30,854. The median earnings of female, year-round, full-time workers in 1994 was $22,205. The female-to-male earning ratio in 1994 was unchanged at .72, remaining comparable with the all-time high reached in 1990.

Per Capita Income

Overall, per capita income increased by 2.3% between 1993 and 1994, after adjusting for inflation, to $16,555. Increases in per capita income were also evident for the white ($17,611) and black ($10,650) populations, 2.2% and 5.3% respectively. The per capita income for Asian and Pacific Islander and Hispanic-origin populations remained unchanged, $16,902 and $9,435, respectively. This is the second consecutive year that the overall population and the white population have experienced significant annual increases in real per capita income. Blacks had not experienced a significant annual increase since 1988. □

Percent of Persons in Poverty, by State: 1991–1994

State	1994 Percent	1993 Percent	1992[r] Percent	1991[1] Percent	State	1994 Percent	1993 Percent	1992[r] Percent	1991[1] Percent
Alabama	16.4	17.4	17.3	19.0	Montana	11.5	14.9	13.8	15.5
Alaska	10.2	9.1	10.2	12.0	Nebraska	8.8	10.3	10.6	9.8
Arizona	15.9	15.4	15.8	15.5	Nevada	11.1	9.8	14.7	11.6
Arkansas	15.3	20.0	17.5	17.4	New Hampshire	7.7	9.9	8.7	7.4
California	17.9	18.2	16.4	16.3	New Jersey	9.2	10.9	10.3	10.0
Colorado	9.0	9.9	10.8	10.6	New Mexico	21.1	17.4	21.6	23.0
Connecticut	10.8	8.5	9.8	9.0	New York	17.0	16.4	15.7	15.7
Delaware	8.3	10.2	7.8	7.7	North Carolina	14.2	14.4	15.8	14.6
D.C.	21.2	26.4	20.3	18.6	North Dakota	10.4	11.2	12.1	14.7
Florida	14.9	17.8	15.6	15.7	Ohio	14.1	13.0	12.5	13.5
Georgia	14.0	13.5	17.7	17.1	Oklahoma	16.7	19.9	18.6	17.2
Hawaii	8.7	8.0	11.2	7.8	Oregon	11.8	11.8	11.4	13.6
Idaho	12.0	13.1	15.2	14.1	Pennsylvania	12.5	13.2	11.9	11.2
Illinois	12.4	13.6	15.6	13.8	Rhode Island	10.3	11.2	12.4	10.7
Indiana	13.7	12.2	11.8	15.8	South Carolina	13.8	18.7	19.0	16.5
Iowa	10.7	10.3	11.5	9.8	South Dakota	14.5	14.2	15.1	14.3
Kansas	14.9	13.1	11.1	12.4	Tennessee	14.6	19.6	17.0	15.5
Kentucky	18.5	20.4	19.7	18.8	Texas	19.1	17.4	18.3	18.0
Louisiana	25.7	26.4	24.5	19.2	Utah	8.0	10.7	9.4	13.0
Maine	9.4	15.4	13.5	14.2	Vermont	7.6	10.0	10.5	12.7
Maryland	10.7	9.7	11.8	9.3	Virginia	10.7	9.7	9.5	10.0
Massachusetts	9.7	10.7	10.3	11.3	Washington	11.7	12.1	11.2	9.7
Michigan	14.1	15.4	13.6	14.2	West Virginia	18.6	22.2	22.3	17.9
Minnesota	11.7	11.6	13.0	13.1	Wisconsin	9.0	12.6	10.9	10.0
Mississippi	19.9	24.7	24.6	23.8	Wyoming	9.3	13.3	10.3	9.9
Missouri	15.6	16.1	15.7	14.9					

r. Revised, based on 1990 census population controls. 1. 1991 poverty estimates were adjusted using a ratio of 1992 estimates with 1980 and 1990 census population controls. *Source:* "Income, Poverty, and Valuation of Noncash Benefits 1994," *Current Population Reports,* U.S. Bureau of the Census, published May 1996, latest data.

Gap Widens Between High- and Low-Income Households

Are the rich getting richer and the poor getting poorer?

Source: U.S. Census Bureau, Current Population Reports, June 1996

The most commonly used measure of income inequality, the Gini index (also known as the index of income concentration) indicated a decline in family income inequality of 7.4% from 1947 to 1968. Since 1968, there has been an *increase* in income inequality, reaching its 1947 level in 1982 and increasing further since then. The increase was 16.1% from 1968 to 1992, and 22.4% from 1968 to 1994.

The Gini index for households indicates that inequality grew slowly in the 1970s and rapidly during the early 1980s. From about 1987 through 1992, the growth in measured inequality seemed to taper off, reaching 11.9% above its 1968 level. This was followed by a large apparent jump in 1993, partly due to a change in survey methodology. The Gini index for households in 1994 was 17.5% above its 1968 levels.

Why Is Income Inequality Growing?

The long-run increase is related to changes in the nation's labor market and its household composition. The wage distribution has become considerably more unequal, with more highly skilled, -trained, and -educated workers at the top experiencing real wage gains, and those at the bottom real wage losses.

One factor is the shift in employment from those goods-producing industries that have disproportionately provided high-wage opportunities for low-skilled workers, toward services that disproportionately employ college graduates, and toward low-wage sectors such as retail trade. But the within-industry shifts in labor demand away from less-educated workers is perhaps a more important explanation of eroding wages than the shift out of manufacturing.

Other factors putting downward pressure on the wages of less-educated workers are intensifying global competition and immigration, the decline of the proportion of workers belonging to unions, the decline in the real value of the minimum wage, the increasing need for computer skills, and the increasing use of temporary workers.

At the same time, long-run changes in living arrangements have taken place that tend to exacerbate differences in household incomes. For example, divorces, and separations, births out of wedlock, and the increasing age at first marriage have led to a shift away from married-couple households and toward single-parent and nonfamily households, which typically have lower incomes. Also, the increasing tendency over the period for men with higher-than-average earnings to marry women with higher-than-average earnings has contributed to widening the gap between high-income and low-income households.

NOTE: The Census Bureau focused mainly on demographic and survey-related changes to explain the growing income inequality. However, fiscal and monetary policy changes, particularly in the 1980s, would obviously havae contributed to the widening gap.

Share of Aggregate Income Received by High- and Low-Income Households

Year	Number (thous.)	Income at selected positions (dollars) Upper limit of each fifth ($)					Percent distribution of income	
		Lowest fifth	Second	Third	Fourth	Highest fifth	Lowest fifth	Top 5 percent
1994	98,990	13,426	25,200	40,100	62,841	109,821	3.6	21.2
1993	97,107	13,299	25,311	39,786	61,844	107,318	3.6	21.0
1992	96,426	13,309	25,499	40,034	61,273	104,596	3.8	18.6
1990	94,312	14,174	26,830	41,047	62,597	107,434	3.9	18.6
1988	92,830	14,259	26,934	41,975	63,380	107,285	3.8	18.3
1986	89,479	13,856	26,503	41,132	62,176	104,262	3.8	18.0
1985	88,458	13,692	25,761	39,908	60,021	99,173	3.9	17.6
1984	86,789	13,551	25,361	39,073	59,023	97,706	4.0	17.1
1982	83,918	13,022	24,766	37,841	56,428	93,146	4.0	17.0
1980	82,368	13,466	25,253	38,716	56,687	91,227	4.2	16.5
1975	72,867	13,185	24,746	37,393	53,690	84,725	4.3	16.6
1974	71,163	13,878	25,742	38,038	55,205	87,378	4.3	16.5
1973	69,859	13,872	26,353	39,091	56,470	89,513	4.2	16.6
1972	68,251	13,518	26,035	38,485	55,074	88,653	4.1	17.0
1970	64,374	13,230	25,348	36,874	52,609	83,171	4.1	16.6
1968	61,805	13,063	24,766	35,497	49,877	78,031	4.2	16.6
1967	60,446	12,248	23,883	33,910	48,343	77,570	4.0	17.5

NOTE: Households as of March of the following year. Income in CPI-U-X1 adjusted dollars.

Consumer Price Indexes

(1982–84 = 100)

Year	All items	En-ergy	Food	Shel-ter	Apparel[1]	Trans porta-tion	Medical care	Fuel oil	Electric-ity	Utility (gas)	Tele-phone	Com-modi-ties
1960	29.6	22.4	30.0	25.2	45.7	29.8	22.3	13.5	29.9	17.6	58.3	33.6
1970	38.8	25.5	39.2	35.5	59.2	37.5	34.0	16.5	31.8	19.6	58.7	41.7
1980	82.4	86.0	86.8	81.0	90.9	83.1	74.9	87.7	75.8	65.7	77.7	86.0
1990	130.7	104.5	132.4	140.0	124.1	120.5	162.8	n.a.	n.a.	n.a.	n.a.	122.8
1992	140.3	108.1	137.9	151.2	131.9	126.5	190.1	n.a.	n.a.	n.a.	n.a.	129.1
1993	144.5	111.2	140.9	155.7	133.7	130.4	201.4	n.a.	n.a.	n.a.	n.a.	131.5
1994	148.2	111.7	144.3	160.5	133.4	134.3	211.0	n.a.	n.a.	n.a.	n.a.	133.4
1995	152.4	111.5	148.4	165.7	132.0	139.1	220.5	n.a.	n.a.	n.a.	n.a.	136.4

1. Includes upkeep. n.a. = not available. *Source: Monthly Labor Review, May 1996.*

Consumer Price Index for All Urban Consumers

(1982–84 = 100)

Group	March 1996	March 1995	Group	March 1996	March 1995
All items	155.7	151.4	Fuel oil, coal, bottled gas	99.3	89.0
Food	151.6	147.4	House operation[1]	124.6	122.6
Alcoholic beverages	157.4	153.1	House furnishings	111.7	111.2
Apparel and upkeep	134.8	134.4	Transportation	141.2	138.0
Men's and boys' apparel	129.1	127.2	Medical care	226.6	218.4
Women's and girls' apparel	129.9	131.5	Personal care	149.4	146.0
Footwear	128.1	125.9	Tobacco products	230.8	222.5
Housing, total	151.7	147.4	Entertainment	158.4	152.6
Rent	160.6	156.7	Personal and educational		
Gas and electricity	118.2	117.1	expenses	244.1	232.0

1. Combines house furnishings and operation. *Source: Monthly Labor Review, May 1996.*

Per Capita Personal Income

Year	Amount	Year	Amount	Year	Amount	Year	Amount	Year	Amount
1935	$474	1965	$2,773	1981	10,949	1986	14,597	1991	19,091
1945	1,223	1970	3,893	1982	11,480	1987	15,638	1992	20,105
1950	1,501	1975	5,851	1983	12,098	1988	16,615	1993	20,800
1955	1,881	1979	8,638	1984	13,114	1989	17,696	1994	21,809
1960	2,219	1980	$9,910	1985	$13,896	1990	$18,635	1995[1]	22,788

1. Preliminary. *Source:* Department of Commerce, Survey of Current Business.

Per Capita Income and Personal Consumption Expenditures

(In current dollars)

Year	Gross national product	Personal income	Disposable personal income	Durable goods	Nondurable goods	Services	Total
1950	$1,900	$1,504	$1,368	$203	$648	$416	$1,267
1955	2,456	1,901	1,687	235	755	570	1,560
1960	2,851	2,265	1,986	240	847	741	1,829
1965	3,268	2,840	2,505	327	987	954	2,268
1970	4,951	4,056	3,489	418	1,318	1,385	3,121
1975	7,401	6,081	5,291	627	1,927	2,135	4,689
1980	11,985	9,916	8,421	963	2,992	3,653	7,607
1985	16,776	13,895	11,861	1,555	3,807	5,622	10,985
1990	21,737	18,477	15,695	1,910	4,748	7,888	14,547
1991	22,500	19,100	16,700	1,800	5,000	8,700	15,400
1992	23,340	19,802	17,346	1,881	5,053	9,101	16,035
1993	24,576	20,810	18,153	2,083	5,185	9,683	16,951
1994	25,774	21,846	19,003	2,266	5,342	10,126	17,734
1995	27,510	23,193	20,174	2,305	5,649	10,764	18,718

Personal Consumption Expenditures columns: Durable goods, Nondurable goods, Services, Total

Source: U.S. Department of Commerce, *Survey of Current Business, May 1996.*

Total Family Income in 1992 CPI-U–XI Adjusted Dollars

(figures in percent)

Income range	White 1992	White 1990	White 1985	Black 1992	Black 1990	Black 1985	Hispanic[1] 1992	Hispanic[1] 1990	Hispanic[1] 1985
Families (thousands)[2]	57,858	56,803	54,991	7,888	7,471	6,921	5,318	4,981	4,206
Under $5,000	2.7	2.5	2.9	11.3	11.5	10.1	6.0	6.3	5.9
$5,000 to $9,999	4.5	4.7	5.6	15.0	14.1	15.7	11.7	12.3	13.6
$10,000 to $14,999	6.6	7.0	7.3	11.8	11.3	12.4	12.6	12.6	13.7
$15,000 to $24,999	15.2	16.0	17.0	18.8	19.5	21.2	21.7	21.7	20.9
$25,000 to $34,999	15.3	16.5	16.7	13.0	14.0	14.2	16.2	16.6	17.0
$35,000 to $49,999	20.0	20.8	21.1	14.0	15.0	14.2	15.1	15.7	15.1
$50,000 to $74,999	20.8	19.3	18.5	10.8	9.8	9.3	11.3	10.0	10.3
$75,000 to $99,999	8.2	7.3	6.3	3.4	3.4	2.1	3.4	2.9	2.4
$100,000 and over	6.7	5.9	4.5	1.8	1.3	0.9	2.0	1.9	1.2
Median income	$38,909	$36,915	$35,410	$21,161	$21,423	$20,390	$23,901	$23,431	$23,112

1. Persons of Hispanic origin may be of any race. 2. As of March 1993. *Source:* Department of Commerce, Bureau of the Census, *Current Population Reports, Consumer Income, Series P–60, No. 184.* NOTE: Data are latest available.

Median Weekly Earnings of Full-Time Workers by Occupation and Sex

Occupation	Men Number of workers (in thousands)	Men Median weekly earnings	Women Number of workers (in thousands)	Women Median weekly earnings	Total Number of workers (in thousands)	Total Median weekly earnings
Managerial and prof. specialty	13,684	$829	12,609	$605	26,292	$703
Executive, admin, and managerial	7,172	833	5,803	570	12,975	684
Professional specialty	6,512	827	6,806	632	13,317	718
Technical, sales, and admin. support	9,894	556	16,004	383	25,898	426
Technicians and related support	1,688	641	1,506	480	3,194	558
Sales occupations	5,000	579	3,862	330	8,862	454
Administrative support, incl. clerical	3,206	489	10,636	384	13,842	399
Service occupations	4,779	357	4,838	264	9,617	299
Private household	15	([1])	324	193	338	195
Protective service	1,691	552	266	438	1,957	528
Service, except private household and protective	3,073	300	4,249	264	7,322	277
Precision production, craft, and repair	10,046	534	957	371	11,003	519
Mechanics and repairers	3,658	538	150	550	3,808	539
Construction trades	3,541	507	66	400	3,607	506
Operators, fabricators, and laborers	11,529	413	3,462	297	14,991	380
Machine operators, assemblers, and inspectors	4,576	421	2,559	296	7,135	368
Transportation and material moving occupations	3,870	482	261	354	4,131	476
Handlers, equipment cleaners, helpers, and laborers	3,083	328	642	284	3,725	319
Farming, forestry, and fishing	1,290	294	190	249	1,480	287

1. Data not shown where base is less than 50,000. NOTE: Figures are for the year 1995. *Source:* U.S. Department of Labor, Bureau of Labor Statistics, "Employment and Earnings," January 1996.

Consumer Credit

(installment credit outstanding; in billions of dollars, not seasonally adjusted)

Holder	1996[4]	1995	1994	1993	1992	1991	1990	1985	1980	1975
Commercial banks	511.6	507.8	427.8	367.1	331.9	340.7	347.	245.1	147.0	82.9
Finance companies	156.3	152.6	134.8	117.0	117.1	121.9	133.3	111.7	62.3	32.7
Credit unions	136.9	131.9	119.5	114.4	97.6	92.7	93.1	72.7	44.0	25.7
Retailers[1]	71.2	85.1	38.4	47.4	42.1	39.8	43.5	43.0	28.7	18.2
Other[2]	40.3	40.1	60.9	37.5	47.8	50.3	57.0	53.8	20.1	9.2
Pools[3]	237.6	214.4	143.3	123.6	120.4	99.6	77.9	—	—	—
Total	1,154.0	1,131.9	925.0	807.1	756.9	745.0	751.9	526.3	302.1	168.7

1. Starting in 1994, source includes retailers and gasoline companies in nonfinancial business category. 2. Includes mutual savings banks, savings and loan associations, and gasoline companies (until 1994). 3. Beginning 1989, outstanding balances of pools upon which securities have been issued; these balances are no longer on the balance sheets for the loan originators. 4. Preliminary. *Source:* Federal Reserve Board.

The General Agreement on Tariffs and Trade (GATT)

GATT was formally signed on April 15, 1994, in Marrakesh, Morocco, by representatives from 124 member countries. GATT was known as the Uruguay Round of talks because the wide-ranging trade liberalization negotiations began in the Uruguayan resort of Punta del Este in 1986.

The sweeping trade pact opens global markets between member countries for goods and services and projects a worldwide reduction of tariffs of up to 40% and a $235-billion increase in annual global income.

The U.S. House of Representatives approved the legislation on November 29, 1994, and the Senate ratified the accord on December 1. President Clinton signed the bill on December 8.

The treaty established a successor to GATT, the World Trade Organization (WTO), and it replaced GATT on January 1, 1995. Because of U.S. concerns that some future decisions by the organization may be unacceptable under U.S. laws, a provision in the treaty allows any member to withdraw from the WTO six months after giving notice. ☐

North American Free Trade Agreement (NAFTA)

In three separate ceremonies in the three capitals on Dec. 17, 1992, President Bush, Mexican President Salinas, and Canadian Prime Minister Mulroney signed the historic North American Free Trade Agreement (NAFTA). The framework agreement proposed to eliminate restrictions on the flow of goods, services, and investment in North America. The House of Representatives approved NAFTA, by a vote of 234 to 200 on November 17, 1993, and the Senate voted 60 to 38 for approval on November 20. It was signed into law by President Clinton on December 8, 1993, and took effect on January 1, 1994.

Under NAFTA, the United States, Canada, and Mexico become a single, giant, integrated market of almost 400 million people with $6.5 trillion worth of goods and services annually. Mexico is the world's second largest importer of U.S. manufactured goods and the

third largest importer of U.S. agricultural products.

Prior to NAFTA, Mexican tariffs averaged about 250% as compared to U.S. duties. After the pact, about half of the tariffs on trade between Mexico and the United States were eliminated, and the remaining tariffs and restrictions on service and investment (as far as it is possible) will be phased out over a 15-year period. The United States and Canada have had a free-trade agreement since 1989.

The treaty provides full protection of intellectual property rights (patents, copyrights, and trademarks) and also includes provisions covering trade rules and dispute settlement and establishes trilateral commissions to administer them. NAFTA also marks the first time in the history of U.S. trade policy that environmental concerns have been directly addressed. ☐

Union Members in 1995

Source: U.S. Department of Labor, Bureau of Labor Statistics.

About 16.4 million wage and salary employees were union members in 1995, 14.9% of all such workers. These figures were down from 16.7 million and 15.5% in 1994. There were 9.4 million union members in private nonagricultural industries, where they constituted 10.4% of wage and salary employment, and 6.9 million in government (federal, state, and local), where they accounted for 37.8% of wage and salary employment.

Membership by Industry and Occupation

In private industry, transportation and public utilities had the highest proportion of workers who were union members (27%), followed by construction and manufacturing (each 18%) and mining (14%). The remaining private-industry groups had unionization rates ranging from 2%–6%.

Among major occupational groups, the precision production, craft, and repair group (including mechanics, electricians, and other skilled trades workers), and the operators, fabricators, and laborers group (including machine and vehicle operators, assemblers, cleaners, and helpers) had the highest proportions of union membership (each 23%). About 21% of workers in professional specialty occupations (including teachers, professional health occupations, engineers, and scientists) were unionized. In contrast, only 1 in 20 employees in sales or in farming, forestry, and fishing occupations were union members.

Although total union membership as a percent of employment has declined over the past decade, and most occupational groups have seen a concomitant decline, the proportion unionized has remained steady in a few occupational groups: technicians and related

support (12%); administrative support, including clerical (13%); and protective service (40%).

Demographic Characteristics of Union Members

Union membership was higher among men (17%) than women (12%), and higher among blacks (20%) than either whites (14%) or Hispanics (13%). Within these major groups, black men continued to have the highest union membership rate (23%), while white women had the lowest (11%). Workers aged 35 to 64 were more likely to be union members (19%) than were either younger or older workers. Seventeen percent of full-time workers were union workers, compared with 8% of part-timers.

Union Representation of Nonmembers

In 1995, 2.0 million wage and salary workers were represented at their workplace by a union, although they were not union members themselves. A little more than half (53%) of these worked in government.

Earnings

Among full-time wage and salary workers, union members had median usual weekly earnings of $602 in 1995, compared with a median of $447 for workers not represented by unions. This difference reflects a variety of influences in addition to coverage by a collective bargaining agreement, including variations in the distribution of union members and nonunion employees by gender, occupation, industry, firm size, or geographic region. The union–nonunion earnings ratio was greater for women than for men and for blacks and Hispanics than for whites. ☐

The Public Debt

Year	Gross debt Amount (in millions)	Per capita	Year	Gross debt Amount (in millions)	Per capita
1800 (Jan. 1)	$ 83	$ 15.87	1955	$272,807[1]	$1,650.63
1860 (June 30)	65	2.06	1960	284,093[1]	1,572.31
1865	2,678	75.01	1965	313,819[1]	1,612.70
1900	1,263	16.60	1970	370,094[1]	1,807.09
1920	24,299	228.23	1975	533,189	2,496.90
1925	20,516	177.12	1980	907,701	3,969.55
1930	16,185	131.51	1985	1,823,103	7,598.51
1935	28,701	225.55	1990	3,233,313	12,823,28
1940	42,968	325.23	1994	4,643,711	17,805.64
1945	258,682	1,848.60	1995	4,973,983	18,928.53
1950	256,087[1]	1,688.30	1996	5,217,305	19,681.26

1. Adjusted to exclude issues to the International Monetary Fund and other international lending institutions to conform to the budget presentation. *Source:* Department of the Treasury, Financial Management Service.

Gross Domestic Product or Expenditure[1]

(in billions)

Item	1995	1994	1993	1992	1990	1989	1987	1980	1970
Gross domestic product	7,245.8	6,931.4	6,343.3	6,038.5	5,513.8	5,244.0	4,539.9	2,708.0	1,010.7
GDP in chained (1992) dollars	6,739.0	6,604.2	6,383.8	6,244.4	6,138.7	6,060.4	5,648.4	4,611.9	3,388.2
Personal consumption expenditures	4,924.3	4,698.7	4,378.2	4,139.9	3,742.6	3,517.9	3,052.2	1,748.1	646.5
Durable goods	606.4	580.9	538.0	497.	465.9	459.8	403.0	212.5	85.3
Nondurable goods	1,486.1	1,429.7	1,339.2	1,300.9	1,217.7	1,146.9	1,011.1	682.9	270.4
Services	2,831.8	2,688.1	2,501.0	2,341.6	2,059.0	1,911.2	1,637.4	852.7	290.8
Gross private domestic investment	1,065.3	1,014.4	882.0	796.5	802.6	837.6	749.3	467.6	150.3
Residential	289.8	287.7	250.6	223.6	215.7	230.9	225.2	123.3	41.4
Nonresidential	738.5	667.2	616.1	565.5	587.0	570.7	497.8	353.8	106.7
Change in business inventories	37.0	59.5	15.4	7.3	0	36.0	26.3	−9.5	2.3
Net export of goods and services	−102.3	−96.4	−65.3	−29.6	−74.4	−82.9	−143.1	−14.7	1.2
Government purchases	1,358.5	1,314.7	1,148.4	1,131.8	1,042.9	971.4	881.5	507.1	212.7
Federal	516.7	516.3	443.6	448.8	424.9	401.4	384.9	209.1	100.1
State and local	841.7	798.4	704.7	683.0	618.0	570.0	496.6	298.0	112.6

1. Current dollars except as noted. *Source:* Department of Commerce, Bureau of Economic Analysis, *Survey of Current Business,* Vol. 76, No. 2, February 1996.

Producer Price Indexes by Major Commodity Groups

(1982 = 100)

Commodity	1995	1990	1985	1980	1975	1970
All commodities	124.7	116.3	103.2	89.8	58.4	38.1
Farm products	107.4	112.2	95.1	102.9	77.0	45.8
Processed foods and feeds	127.0	121.9	103.5	95.9	72.6	44.6
Textile products and apparel	120.8	114.9	102.9	89.7	67.4	52.4
Hides, skins, and leather products	153.7	141.7	108.9	94.7	56.5	42.0
Fuels and related products and power	78.0	82.2	91.4	82.8	35.4	15.3
Chemicals and allied products	142.5	123.6	103.7	89.0	62.0	35.0
Rubber and plastic products	124.3	113.6	101.9	90.1	62.2	44.9
Lumber and wood products	178.1	129.7	106.6	101.5	62.1	39.9
Pulp, paper, and allied products	172.2	141.3	113.3	86.3	59.0	37.5
Metals and metal products	134.5	123.0	104.4	95.0	61.5	38.7
Machinery and equipment	126.6	120.7	107.2	86.0	57.9	40.0
Furniture and household durables	128.2	119.1	107.1	90.7	67.5	51.9
Nonmetallic mineral products	129.0	114.7	108.6	88.4	54.4	35.3
Transportation equipment	139.7	121.5	107.9	82.9	56.7	41.9

Source: U.S. Department of Labor, Bureau of Labor Statistics, Division of Industrial Prices and Price Indexes.

Weekly Earnings[1] of Full-Time Women Workers

Major occupation group	1995 weekly earnings	% Men's weekly earnings
Managerial and professional specialty	$605	73.0
Executive, administrative, and managerial	570	68.4
Professional specialty	632	76.4
Technical, sales, and administrative support	383	68.9
Technicians and related support	480	74.9
Sales occupations	330	57.0
Administrative support, including clerical	384	78.5
Service occupations	264	73.9
Precision production, craft, and repair	371	69.5
Operators, fabricators, and laborers	297	71.9
Machine operators, assemblers, and inspectors	296	70.3
Transportation and material moving	354	73.4
Handlers, equipment cleaners, helpers, and laborers	284	86.6
Farming, forestry, and fishing	249	84.7

1. Median usual weekly earnings. Half the workers earn more and half the workers usually earn less each week. *Source:* U.S. Department of Labor, Bureau of Labor Statistics.

Median Four-Person Family Income[1]

Year	Income	Percent change	Year	Income	Percent change
1994	$47,012	4.1	1984	$31,097	6.6
1993	45,161	2.1	1983	29,184	5.7
1992	44,251	2.8	1982	27,619	5.1
1991	43,056	3.9	1981	26,274	8.0
1990	41,151	1.7	1980	24,332	8.6
1989	40,763	4.4	1979	22,395	9.6
1988	39,051	6.1	1978	20,428	9.1
1987	36,812	6.0	1977	18,723	8.1
1986	34,716	5.9	1976	17,315	9.3
1985	32,777	5.4	1975	15,848	7.5

Source: Income Statistics Branch/HHES Division, Department of Commerce, U.S. Bureau of the Census.

Expenditures for New Plant and Equipment[1]
(in billions of dollars)

Year	Manufacturing	Transportation[2]	Total nonmanufacturing	Total
1950	$7.73	$2.87	$18.08	$25.81
1955	12.50	3.10	24.58	37.08
1960	16.36	3.54	32.63	48.99
1965	25.41	5.66	45.39	70.79
1970	36.99	7.17	69.16	106.15
1975	53.66	9.95	108.95	162.60
1980	112.60	13.56	205.48	318.08
1985	152.88	14.57	302.05	454.93
1988	163.45	16.63	344.77	508.22
1989	183.80	18.84	380.13	563.93
1990	192.61	21.47	399.34	591.96
1991	182.81	22.66	405.12	587.93
1992	174.02	22.64	433.69	607.71
1993	179.47	21.77	470.95	650.41
1994	144.14[3]	32.32	412.14	556.29
1995[3]	173.21	34.23	419.69	592.90

1. Data exclude agriculture. 2. Transportation included in total nonmanufacturing. 3. Planned. *Source:* Department of Commerce, Bureau of the Census, February 1995.

Life Insurance in Force
(in millions of dollars)

As of Dec. 31	Ordinary	Group	Industrial	Credit	Total
1915	$16,650	$100	$4,279	—	$21,029
1930	78,576	9,801	17,963	$73	106,413
1945	101,550	22,172	27,675	365	151,762
1950	149,116	47,793	33,415	3,844	234,168
1955	216,812	101,345	39,682	14,493	372,332
1960	341,881	175,903	39,563	29,101	586,448
1965	499,638	308,078	39,818	53,020	900,554
1970	734,730	551,357	38,644	77,392	1,402,123
1980	1,760,474	1,579,355	35,994	165,215	3,541,038
1985	3,247,289	2,561,595	28,250	215,973	6,053,107
1990	5,366,982	3,753,506	24,071	248,038	9,392,597
1994	6,835,239	4,608,746	20,145	209,491	11,673,621

Source: American Council of Life Insurance.

New Housing Starts[1] and Mobile Homes Shipped
(in thousands)

Year	No. of units started	Year	No. of units started	Year	Mobile homes shipped
1900	189	1970	1,469	1965	216
1910	387	1975	1,171	1970	401
1920	247	1980	1,313	1975	213
1925	937	1985	1,745	1980	222
1930	330	1987	1,623	1985	284
1935	221	1988[2]	1,488	1988	218
1940	603	1990	1,193	1990	188
1945	326	1991	1,014	1991	171
1950	1,952	1992	1,200	1992	211
1955	1,646	1993	1,288	1993	254
1960[1]	1,296	1994	1,457	1994	304
1965	1,510	1995	1,354	1995	340

1. Prior to 1960, starts limited to nonfarm housing; from 1960 on, figures include farm housing. 2. As of 1988 data for housing starts no longer include public housing starts and only include private housing starts. *Sources:* Department of Commerce, Housing Construction Statistics, 1900–1965, and Construction Reports, Housing Starts, 1970–to present, Manufactured Housing Institute, 1965–to present.

Farm Indexes
(1990–92 = 100)

Year	Prices paid by famers[1]	Prices rec'd by farmers[2]	Ratio
1975	47	73	155
1980	75	98	137
1985	86	91	106
1990	99	104	105
1991	100	100	99
1992	101	98	98
1993	103	101	99
1994	106	100	94
1995	110	102	92

1. Commodities, interest, and taxes and wage rates. 2. All crops and livestock. *Source:* Department of Agriculture, National Agricultural Statistics Service.

Estimated Annual Retail and Wholesale Sales by Kind of Business

(in millions of dollars)

Kind of business	1994	1995	Kind of business	1994	1995
Retail trade, total	$2,231,233	$2,340,817	Electrical goods	$150,246	$172,901
Building materials, hardware, garden supplies, and mobile home dealers	122,692	124,626	Hardware, plumbing, heating, and supplies	63,732	69,089
Automotive dealers	519,722	560,624	Machinery, equipment, supplies	169,790	179,982
Furniture, home furnishings, and equipment stores	119,385	129,923	Professional and commercial equipment and supplies	165,724	191,227
General merchandise group stores	283,209	296,904	Metals and minerals except petroleum	92,426	99,944
Food stores	399,252	410,512	Miscellaneous durable goods	128,308	144,586
Gasoline service stations	142,412	148,192	Nondurable goods, total	993,366	1,078,066
Apparel and accessory stores	109,881	109,962	Paper and paper products	67,636	81,881
Eating and drinking places	223,360	233,606	Drugs, drug proprietaries, and druggists' sundries	83,222	93,284
Drug and proprietary stores	81,377	84,240	Apparel, piece goods, & notions	72,523	71,855
Liquor stores	22,148	22,463	Groceries and related products	288,563	300,808
Merchant wholesale trade, total	2,075,678	2,248,649	Beer, wine, distilled alcoholic beverages	53,044	53,633
Durable goods, total	1,082,312	1,170,583	Farm-product raw materials	95,363	111,492
Motor vehicles and automotive parts and supplies	197,230	198,387	Chemical and allied products	41,757	46,460
Furniture and home furnishings	36,724	39,280	Petroleum and petroleum products	143,015	154,096
Lumber and other construction materials	78,132	75,187	Miscellaneous nondurable goods	148,243	164,557

Source: Department of Commerce, Bureau of the Census.

Shareholders in Public Corporations

Characteristic	1992	1990	1985	1983	1980	1975	1970
Individual shareholders (thousands)	51,300	51,440	47,040	42,360	30,200	25,270	30,850
Adult shareowner incidence in population	1 in 3	1 in 4	1 in 4	1 in 4	1 in 5	1 in 6	1 in 4
Median household income	52,000	$43,800	$36,800	$33,200	$27,750	$19,000	$13,500
Adult shareowners with household income: under $10,000 (thousands)	n.a.	n.a.	2,151	1,460	1,742	3,420	8,170
$10,000 and over (thousands)	n.a.	n.a.	40,999	36,261	25,715	19,970	20,130
$15,000 and over (thousands)	48,600	42,920	39,806	33,665	22,535	15,420	12,709
$25,000 and over (thousands)	43,700	38,230	32,690	25,086	15,605	6,642	4,114
$50,000 and over (thousands)	28,500	17,910	11,321	7,918	3,982	1,216	n.a.
Adult female shareowners (thousands)	n.a.	17,750	17,547[1]	20,385	13,696	11,750	14,290
Adult male shareowners (thousands)	n.a.	30,220	27,446[1]	19,226	14,196	11,630	14,340
Median age	45	43	44	45	46	53	48

NOTE: 1990 results are not strictly comparable with previous studies because of differences in methodologies. 1. Revised to correspond to 1990 methodology. n.a. = not available. *Source:* New York Stock Exchange. Data are latest available as of May 1996 publication.

50 Most Active Stocks on NYSE, 1995

Stock	Share volume	Stock	Share volume	Stock	Share volume
Telefonos de Mexico (1)	1,006,441,600	PepsiCo, Inc. (17)	371,808,300	Disney (Walt) Company (25)	280,102,800
Micron Technology (19)	849,512,900	Home Depot Inc. (37)	342,490,600	Grupo Televisa, S.A.	278,328,900
Ford Motor (7)	679,125,100	Archer, Daniels, Midland Co.	335,004,800	Limited, Inc. (The) (38)	276,144,800
Motorola Inc. (14)	669,568,800	Hewlett-Packard Co.	331,388,600	Sears, Roebuck & Co. (45)	274,959,400
Int'l Business Machines (6)	659,178,000	National Semiconductor Corp. (33)	325,593,200	Abbott Laboratories (35)	272,203,400
Compaq Computer (12)	632,556,500	Coca-Cola Company (18)	321,818,400	WMX Technologies Inc. (23)	272,082,900
Wal-Mart Stores (5)	624,558,600	Advanced Micro Devices (42)	312,771,900	American Barrick (24)	269,109,500
AT&T Corp. (11)	572,086,700	YPF Sociedad Anonima (34)	310,214,900	Exxon Corp. (26)	263,808,100
K-Mart Corp. (20)	540,690,700	United Healthcare Corp.	308,323,000	LSI Logic Corporation	257,724,200
Merck & Co., Inc. (4)	517,858,600	American Express (16)	306,406,350	Vodafone Group PLC	256,999,900
General Motors (2)	477,870,400	du Pont de Nemours (32)	296,143,000	Chase Manhattan Corp	256,475,100
Chrysler Corporation (9)	472,278,800	McDonald's Corp. (30)	295,231,900	Humana Inc.	251,188,200
Hanson PLC (10)	457,887,300	Toys R Us Inc.	289,897,500	Chemical Banking Corp. (43)	246,689,600
Citicorp (15)	446,978,000	Digital Equipment Corp. (40)	289,310,000	GTE Corp. (27)	242,713,400
EMC Corporation (22)	445,072,200	Westinghouse Electric (47)	283,391,500	Columbia/HCA Healthcare Corp. (29)	242,172,700
RJR Nabisco Holdings (3)	444,839,400	BankAmerica Corporation (31)	280,313,100		
General Electric (13)	418,990,200				
Philip Morris (8)	403,279,300				
Texas Instruments	373,350,500				

NOTE: 1994 rankings in parentheses, if among top 50. In case of stock splits, volume in old and new issues was combined. *Source:* NYSE Fact Book.

Largest Businesses, 1995

Source: 1996 FORTUNE 500, copyright 1996 Time, Inc. All rights reserved.
Fortune is a registered mark of Time, Inc

Revenue Rank 1995	1994	Company	Revenues ($ millions)	Assets ($ millions)
1	1	General Motors	$168,828.6	$217,123.4
2	2	Ford Motor	137,137.0	243,283.0
3	3	Exxon	110,009.0[E]	91,296.0
4	4	Wal-Mart Stores[1]	93,627.0	37,871.0
5	5	AT&T	79,609.0	88,884.0
6	7	Intl. Business Machines	71,940.0	80,292.0
7	6	General Electric	70,028.0	228,035.0
8	8	Mobil	66,724.0[E]	42,138.0
9	11	Chrysler	53,195.0	53,756.0
10	10	Philip Morris	53,139.0[E]	53,811.0
11	13	Prudential Ins. Co. of America	41,330.0	219,380.0
12	12	State Farm Group	40,809.9	85,293.4
13	14	E.I. du Pont de Nemours	37,607.0[E]	37,312.0
14	16	Texaco	36,787.0	24,937.0
15	9	Sears Roebuck	35,181.0	33,130.0
16	15	Kmart[1]	34,654.0	15,397.0
17	19	Procter & Gamble[2]	33,434.0	28,125.0
18	18	Chevron	32,094.0[E]	34,330.0
19	17	Citicorp	31,690.0	256,853.0
20	22	Hewlett-Packard[3]	31,519.0	24,427.0
21	20	PepsiCo	30,421.0	25,432.0
22	27	Metropolitan Life Insurance	27,977.0	158,800.0
23	21	Amoco	27,665.0[E]	29,845.0
24	28	Motorola	27,037.0	22,801.0
25	26	American International Group	25,874.0	134,136.4
26	24	ConAgra[4]	24,108.9	10,801.0
27	25	Kroger	23,937.8	5,044.7
28	30	Dayton Hudson[1]	23,516.0	12,570.0
29	70	Lockheed Martin	22,853.0	17,648.0
30	31	United Technologies	22,802.0	15,958.0
31		Allstate	22,793.0	70,029.0
32	36	Fed. Natl. Mortgage Assn.	22,246.0	316,550.0
33	40	Merrill Lynch	21,513.0	176,857.0
34	32	J.C. Penney	21,419.0	17,102.0
35	35	United Parcel Service	21,045.0	12,645.0
36	33	Dow Chemical	20,957.0	23,582.0
37	46	BankAmerica Corp.	20,386.0	232,446.0
38	34	GTE	19,957.0	37,019.0
39	60	International Paper	19,797.0	23,977.0
40	29	Boeing	19,515.0	22,098.0
41	41	Xerox	18,963.0[A]	25,969.0
42	38	Cigna	18,955.0	95,903.0
43	52	Johnson & Johnson	18,842.0	17,873.0
44	64	Loews	18,770.0	65,058.0
45	39	American Stores[1]	18,308.0	7,363.0
46	47	PriceCostco[5]	18,247.3	4,437.4
47	45	USX	18,214.0[E]	16,743.0
48	48	Coca-Cola	18,018.0	15,041.0
49	44	BellSouth	17,886.0	31,880.0
50	56	Sara Lee[2]	17,719.0	12,431.0
51	97	Columbia/HCA Healthcare	17,695.0	19,892.0
52	51	Fleming	17,501.6	4,296.7
53	49	AMR	16,910.0	19,556.0
54	53	Atlantic Richfield	16,739.0[E]	23,999.0
55	59	Merck	16,681.1	23,831.8
56	37	Travelers Group	16,583.0	114,500.0
57	50	Supervalu[6]	16,563.8	4,305.1
58	54	Safeway	16,397.5	5,194.3
59	71	NationsBank Corp.	16,298.0	187,298.0
60	90	Intel	16,202.0	17,504.0
61	84	New York Life Insurance	16,201.7	74,280.6
62	58	Minnesota Mining & Mfg.	16,105.0	14,183.0
63	61	Caterpillar	16,072.0	16,830.0
64	57	RJR Nabisco Holdings	16,008.0	31,518.0
65	55	American Express	15,841.0	107,405.0
66	77	Home Depot[1]	15,470.4	7,354.0
67	43	Eastman Kodak	15,269.0	14,477.0
68	66	MCI Communications	15,265.0	19,301.0
69	141	Federated Department Stores[1]	15,048.5	14,295.1
70	62	UAL	14,943.0	11,641.0
71	74	Chemical Banking Corp.	14,884.0	182,926.0
72	100	Compaq Computer	14,755.0	7,818.0
73	72	AlliedSignal	14,346.0	12,465.0
74	69	McDonnell Douglas	14,332.0	10,466.0
75	73	Georgia-Pacific	14,292.0	12,335.0
76	87	J.P. Morgan & Co.	13,838.0	184,879.0
77	65	Digital Equipment[2]	13,813.1	9,947.2
78	160	Kimberly-Clark	13,788.6	11,439.2
79	86	Bristol-Myers-Squibb	13,767.0	13,929.0
80	75	Sprint	13,599.5	15,195.9
81	79	Phillips Petroleum	13,521.0[E]	11,978.0
82	122	Lehman Brothers Holdings[7]	13,476.0	115,303.0
83	63	Bell Atlantic	13,429.5	24,156.8
84	76	Ameritech	13,427.8	22,011.2
85	67	NYNEX	13,406.9	26,220.0
86	130	American Home Products	13,376.1	21,362.9
87	78	McKesson[8]	13,325.5	3,479.2
88	81	Goodyear Tire & Rubber	13,165.9	9,789.6
89	106	Texas Instruments	13,128.0	9,215.0
90	94	Rockwell International[9]	13,009.0	12,505.0
91	42	Aetna Life & Casualty	12,978.0	84,323.7
92	92	Archer Daniels Midland[2]	12,671.9	9,756.9
93	89	SBC Communications	12,669.7	22,002.5
94	83	IBP	12,667.6	2,027.6
95	104	Alcoa	12,654.9	13,643.4
96	88	Albertson's[1]	12,585.0	4,135.9
97	85	Anheuser-Busch	12,325.5[A,E]	10,590.9
98	80	Delta Air Lines[2]	12,194.0	12,143.0
99	82	May Department Stores[1]	12,187.0[A,E]	10,122.0
100		ITT Hartford Group[10]	12,150.0	93,855.0

A. Includes sales of discontinued operations of at least 10%. E. Excise taxes have been deducted. 1. Figures are for fiscal year ended Jan. 31, 1996. 2. Figures are for fiscal year ended June 30, 1995. 3. Figures are for fiscal year ended Oct. 31, 1995. 4. Figures are for fiscal year ended May 31, 1995. 5. Figures are for fiscal year ended August 31, 1995. 6. Figures are for fiscal year ended Feb. 28, 1995. 7. Figures are for fiscal year ended Nov. 30, 1995. 8. Figures are for fiscal year ended March 31, 1995. 9. Figures are for fiscal year ended Sept. 30, 1995. 10. One of three companies resulting from the breakup of ITT (1994 rank: 23), Dec. 19, 1995.

Black-Owned Businesses: Strongest in Services

Black-owned firms grew 46 percent between 1987 and 1992.

The number of black-owned businesses increased from 424,165 to 620,912—growing more than U.S. businesses as a whole. The number of all businesses increased by 26 percent, from 13.7 million to 17.3 million.

Receipts for black-owned firms grew at about the same rate as for all businesses. Black-owned business receipts increased from $19.8 billion to $32.2 billion (63%). Receipts for all businesses increased from $1,995 billion to $3,324 billion (67%). Receipts reported by black-owned businesses were about 1 percent of the total receipts for all firms in 1992, unchanged from 1987.

Lower Receipts for Black-Owned Businesses

Receipts for black-owned firms averaged $52,000 per firm, compared with $193,000 for all U.S. firms. Fifty-six percent of black-owned firms had receipts under $10,000. Less than 1% had receipts of $1 million or more. These firms sell less partly because they are in the service industries where average receipts are generally less. In contrast, 45% of all U.S. firms had receipts under $10,000 and 2% had receipts of a million or more.

Service Industries Dominate

In 1992, 54% of black-owned firms were in industries that provide services to individuals, businesses, and others. These firms accounted for 34% of all black-owned business receipts.

Business services (such as advertising firms and employment agencies) and personal services (such as dry cleaners and beauty shops) accounted for 47% of the total number of black-owned service industry firms and 35% of their receipts.

Source: U.S. Department of Commerce, Economics and Statistics Administration, Bureau of the Census.

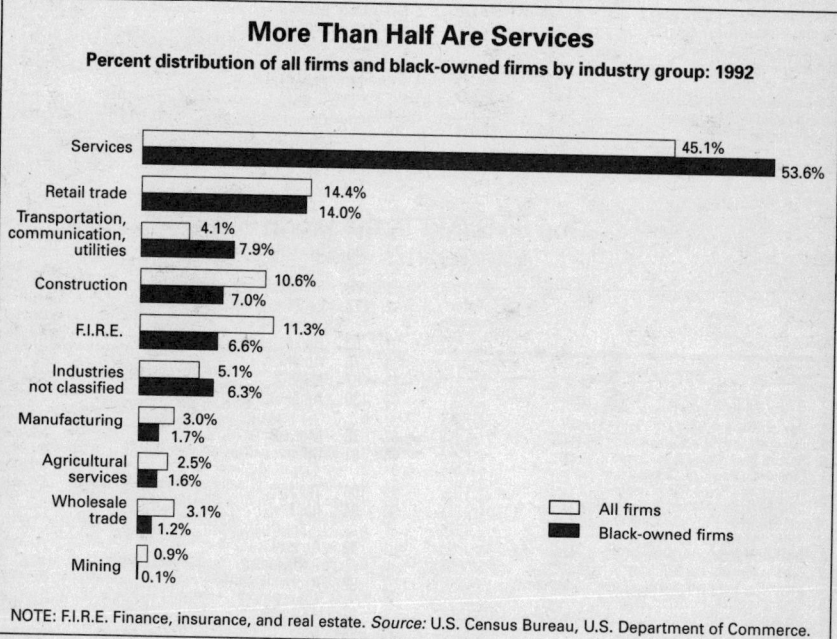

More Than Half Are Services

Percent distribution of all firms and black-owned firms by industry group: 1992

Services — 45.1% / 53.6%
Retail trade — 14.4% / 14.0%
Transportation, communication, utilities — 4.1% / 7.9%
Construction — 10.6% / 7.0%
F.I.R.E. — 11.3% / 6.6%
Industries not classified — 5.1% / 6.3%
Manufacturing — 3.0% / 1.7%
Agricultural services — 2.5% / 1.6%
Wholesale trade — 3.1% / 1.2%
Mining — 0.9% / 0.1%

☐ All firms
■ Black-owned firms

NOTE: F.I.R.E. Finance, insurance, and real estate. *Source:* U.S. Census Bureau, U.S. Department of Commerce.

New Business Concerns and Business Failures

Formations and failures	1994[1]	1993	1992	1991	1990	1989	1985	1980
Business formations								
Index, net formations (1967 = 100)	126.2	121.1	116.3	115.3	120.7	124.7	120.	129.9
New incorporations (1,000)	n.a.	70	667	629	647	677	663	534
Failures, number (1,000)	71.5	86.1	97.0	88.1	60.0	50.4	57.1	11.7
Rate per 10,000 concerns	79	96	109	107	75	65	115	42

1. Preliminary. n.a. = not available. *Sources:* U.S. Bureau of Economic Analysis and Dun & Bradstreet Corporation. From *Statistical Abstract of the United States 1995.* NOTE: Data are most recent available.

50 Leading NYSE Stocks in Market Value, December 29, 1995

Company (Symbol)	Listed shares (millions)	Market value (millions)	Company (Symbol)	Listed shares (millions)	Market value (millions)
Exxon Corp. (XON)	1,813	$145,252	Ameritech Corp. (AIT)	588	34,669
General Electric Co. (GE)	1,857	133,699	American Home Products (AHP)	355	34,477
Coca-Cola Co. (KO)	1,710	127,001	Disney (Walt) Company (DIS)	575	33,934
AT&T Corp. (T)	1,591	103,049	Motorola, Inc. (MOT)	591	33,686
Merck & Co. (MRK)	1,484	97,557	Abbott Laboratories (ABT)	803	33,530
Morris (Philip) Co. (MO)	935	84,646	Lilly (Eli) (LLY)	569	31,982
Johnson & Johnson (JNJ)	767	65,7610	Minnesota Mining & Manufacturing (MMM)	472	31,271
Procter & Gamble (PG)	730	60,605	Royal Dutch Petroleum (RD)	210	29,616
International Business Machines (IBM)	569	52,246	Ford Motor (F)	1,020	29,585
Wal-Mart Stores (WMT)	2,300	51,463	Bell Atlantic (BEL)	437	29,222
du Pont de Nemours (DD)	735	51,361	Gillette Company (G)	559	29,141
Mobil Corp. (MOB)	444	49,675	Schering-Plough (SGP)	503	27,537
PepsiCo, Inc. (PEP)	863	48,198	Boeing Company (BA)	349	27,375
American International Group (AIG)	506	46,811	Citicorp (CCI)	379	25,455
Bristol-Myers Squibb (BMY)	540	46,372	Eastman Kodak (EK)	374	25,035
Berkshire Hathaway (BRK)	1.4	44,340	General Motors, Class E (GME)	479	24,928
Bellsouth Corporation (BLS)	1,007	43,801	BankAmerica (BAC)	383	24,780
Hewlett-Packard Co. (HWP)	512	42,885	Kellogg Co. (K)	311	24,019
GTE Corp. (GTE)	972	42,767	NYNEX Corp. (NYN)	444	24,001
Pfizer Inc. (PFE)	676	42,576	Travelers Group (TRV)	372	23,416
General Motors (GM)	757	40,007	Kimberly-Clark Corporation (KMB)	282	23,311
McDonald's Corp. (MCD)	830	37,468	Anheuser-Busch (BUD)	346	23,144
Chevron Corp. (CHV)	712	37,406	Dow Chemical (DOW)	327	23,021
Amoco Corp. (AN)	506	36,345	Home Depot (HD)	476	22,805
SBC Communications (SBC)	620	35,677	**Total**	**34,923**	**$2,271,886**
Federal National Mortgage Association (FNM)	282	35,029			

Source: New York Stock Exchange.

Top 50 Banks in the World

(in millions of U.S. dollars)

Rank		Total assets 12/31/95	Rank		Total assets 12/31/95
1.	Deutsche Bank, AG, Frankfurt, Germany	502,279	27.	National Westminster Bank Plc, London, U.K.	257,838
2.	Sanwa Bank Ltd., Osaka, Japan	500,026	28.	Citicorp, New York, United States	255,311
3.	Sumitomo Bank Ltd., Osaka, Japan	498,917	29.	Barclays Bank Plc, London, United Kingdom	254,485
4.	Dai-Ichi Kangyo Bank Ltd., Tokyo, Japan	497,612	30.	Swiss Bank Corp., Basel, Switzerland	249,906
5.	Fuji Bank, Ltd., Tokyo, Japan	486,351	31.	Daiwa Bank, Ltd., Osaka, Japan	248,274
6.	Sakura Bank, Ltd., Tokyo, Japan	477,079	32.	Bayerische Vereinsbank, Munich, Germany	247,082
7.	Mitsubishi Bank Ltd., Tokyo Japan (a)	474,045	33.	Bank of Tokyo, Ltd., Japan (a)	237,255
8.	Norinchukin Bank, Tokyo, Japan	428,644	34.	BankAmerica Corp., San Francisco, United States	230,151
9.	Credit Agricole Mutuel, Paris, France	384,340	35.	Yasuda Trust & Banking Co. Ltd., Tokyo, Japan	224,186
10.	Industrial Bank of Japan, Ltd., Tokyo, Japan	360,638	36.	Credit Suisse, Zurich, Switzerland	212,022
11.	HSBC Holdings, Plc., London, United Kingdom	351,568	37.	Bayerische Landesbank Girozentrale, Munich, Germany	211,192
12.	ABN-AMRO Bank, N.V., Amsterdam, Netherlands	339,393	38.	Bayerische Hypotheken und Wechsel Bank, Munich, Germany	207,458
13.	Credit Lyonnais, Paris, France	337,595			
14.	Union Bank of Switzerland, Zurich, Switzerland	335,303	39.	Lloyds TSB Group, Inc., London, United Kingdom (b)	204,213
15.	Dresdner Bank, Frankfurt, Germany	332,148			
16.	Mitsubishi Trust & Banking Corp., Tokyo, Japan	330,076	40.	Deutsche Genossenschaftsbank, Frankfurt, Germany	199,681
17.	Societe Generale, Paris, France	324,776	41.	Bankgesellschaft Berlin, AG, Berlin, Germany	194,450
18.	Banque Nationale de Paris, France	323,526	42.	Toyo Trust & Banking Co. Ltd., Tokyo, Japan	189,723
19.	Sumitomo Trust & Banking Co., Ltd., Osaka, Japan	299,209	43.	NationsBank Corp., Charlotte, N.C., United States	186,380
20.	Tokai Bank Ltd., Nagoya, Japan	297,705	44.	J.P. Morgan & Co., Inc., New York, United States	184,642
21.	Long-Term Credit Bank of Japan Ltd., Tokyo, Japan	297,430	45.	Rabobank Nederland, Utrecht, Netherlands	182,273
22.	Westdeutsche Landesbank Girozentrale, Duesseldorf, Germany	290,648	46.	Chemical Banking Corp., New York, United States	181,747
23.	Mitsui Trust & Banking Co., Ltd., Tokyo, Japan	283,711	47.	Generale Bank, Brussels, Belgium	161,131
24.	Commerzbank, Frankfurt, Germany	280,743	48.	Sanpaolo Bank Holding, Turin, Italy	160,389
25.	Compagnie Financiere de Paribas, Paris, France	270,771	49.	ING Bank, Amsterdam, Netherlands (c)	153,484
26.	Asahi Bank, Ltd., Tokyo, Japan	265,969	50.	Abbey National Plc, London, United Kingdom	151,302

(a)–*Mitsubishi Bank Ltd.* merged with *Bank of Tokyo Ltd.* on April 1 to form the world's largest bank, the $711 billion-asset *Bank of Tokyo/Mitsubishi Ltd.* (b)–Formerly known as Lloyds Bank Plc. Changed title after merger with *TSB Group.* (c)–The bank is a member of the $246.1 billion-asset *ING Group.* Source: *American Banker, August 5, 1996.* Reprinted with permission. Copyright © American Banker/Bond Buyer.

National Labor Organizations With Membership Over 100,000

Members[1]	Union
747,936	Automobile, Aerospace and Agricultural Implement Workers of America; International Union, United[2]
110,000	Bakery, Confectionery, and Tobacco Workers International Union
123,041	Bridge, Structural and Ornamental Iron Workers, International Association of
510,000	Carpenters and Joiners of America, United Brotherhood of
650,000	Communications Workers of America
2,238,435	Education Association, National (Ind.)
750,000	Electrical Workers, International Brotherhood of
150,000	Electronic, Electrical, Salaried, Machine and Furniture Workers, International Union of
210,000	Fire Fighters, International Association of
1,400,000	Food and Commercial Workers International Union, United
210,000	Government Employees, American Federation of
175,000	Graphic Communications International Union
300,000	Hotel Employees and Restaurant Employees International Union
750,000	Laborers' International Union of North America
318,000	Letter Carriers, National Association of
600,000	* Machinists and Aerospace Workers, International Association of[2]
200,000	Mine Workers of America, United
355,000	* Needletrades, Industrial and Textile Employees, Union of[3]
182,000	Nurses Association, American (Ind.)
110,614	* Office and Professional Employees International Union
375,000	Operating Engineers, International Union of
135,000	Painters and Allied Trades, International Brotherhood of
290,000	Paperworkers International Union, United
292,000	Plumbing and Pipe Fitting Industry of the United States and Canada, United Association of Journeymen and Apprentices of the
365,000	* Postal Workers Union, American
100,000	Retail, Wholesale, and Department Store Union
100,000	Rubber, Cork, Linoleum, and Plastic Workers of America, United[4]
1,100,000	* Service Employees International Union
140,000	Sheet Metal Workers' International Association
1,300,000	State, County and Municipal Employees, American Federation of
700,000	Steelworkers of America, United[2]
900,000	* Teachers, American Federation of
1,500,000	* Teamsters, International Brotherhood of
160,000	* Transit Union, Amalgamated
125,000	Transportation • Communications International Union
135,000	Transportation Union, United

1. Data are for 1996, except *, which are 1995. Unless otherwise noted, unions are ALF-CIO affiliated. 2. These three unions announced on July 27, 1995, they will merge over a five year period. 3. Merger of the International Ladies Garment Workers' Union and the Amalgamated Clothing and Textile Workers Union. 4. Merged with the United Steelworkers of America.

Persons in the Labor Force

Year	Labor force[1]		Percent in labor force in[2]		Year	Labor force[1]		Percent in labor force in[2]	
	Number (thousands)	% Working-age population	Farm occupation	Nonfarm occupation		Number (thousands)	% Working-age population	Farm occupation	Nonfarm occupation
1840	5,420	46.6	68.6	31.4	1920	42,434	51.3	27.0	73.0
1850	7,697	46.8	63.7	36.3	1930	48,830	49.5	21.4	78.6
1860	10,533	47.0	58.9	41.1	1940	52,789	52.2	17.4	82.6
1870	12,925	45.8	53.0	47.0	1950	60,054	53.5	11.6	88.4
1880	17,392	47.3	49.4	50.6	1960	69,877	55.3	6.0	94.0
1890	23,318	49.2	42.6	57.4	1970	82,049	58.2	3.1	96.9
1900	29,073	50.2	37.5	62.5	1980	106,085	62.0	2.2	97.8
1910	37,371	52.2	31.0	69.0	1990	125,182	65.3	1.6	98.4

1. For 1830 to 1930, the data relate to the population and gainful workers at ages 10 and over. For 1940 to 1960, the data relate to the population and labor force at ages 14 and over; for 1970 and 1980, the data relate to the population and labor force at age 16 and over. For 1940 to 1980, the data include the Armed Forces. 2. The farm and nonfarm percentages relate only to the experienced civilian labor force. *Source:* Department of Commerce, Bureau of the Census.

Corporate Profits[1]

(in billions of dollars)

Item	1996[2]	1995	1994	1990	1985	1980	1975	1970
Domestic industries	541.6	494.1	453.7	236.4	190.8	161.9	107.6	62.4
Financial	134.9	119.1	94.4	18.7	21.0	26.9	11.8	12.1
Nonfinancial	406.7	375.0	359.3	217.7	169.7	134.9	95.8	50.2
Manufacturing	161.3	145.7	142.7	88.8	73.0	72.9	52.6	26.6
Wholesale and retail trade	79.2	68.3	76.7	41.5	49.7	23.6	21.3	9.5
Other	70.6	66.2	58.6	87.5	47.0	38.4	21.9	14.1
Rest of world	90.0	78.6	61.3	56.9	31.8	29.9	13.0	6.5
Total	**631.6**	**572.7**	**514.90**	**293.3**	**222.6**	**191.7**	**120.6**	**68.9**

1. Corporate profits before tax with inventory valuation adjustment. 2. First quarter (seasonally adjusted at annual rates). *Source:* U.S. Bureau of Economic Analysis, *Survey of Current Business,* June 1996.

National Income by Type

(in billions of dollars)

Type of share	1995	1994	1990	1985	1980	1975	1970	1965	1960
National income	5,799.2	5,495.1	4,611.9	3,351.5	2,216.1	1,295.5	836.6	587.8	426.2
Compensation of employees	4,209.1	4,008.3	3,352.8	2,425.7	1,653.9	951.3	618.1	399.8	296.7
Wages and salaries	3,419.7	3,255.9	2,757.5	1,995.7	1,377.6	814.7	551.5	363.7	272.8
Supplements to wages and salaries	799.5	752.4	595.2	430.0	276.3	136.6	66.6	36.1	23.8
Proprietors' income[1,2]	478.3	450.9	361.0	257.4	167.9	116.5	78.0	63.5	50.5
Farm	29.0	35.0	36.3	24.5	13.8	24.2	14.8	13.0	11.5
Business and professional	449.3	415.0	324.6	232.5	154.1	92.3	63.2	50.4	39.1
Rental income of persons[1]	122.2	116.6	61.4	49.1	35.3	26.6	24.7	22.5	19.1
Corporate profits[1,2]	588.6	526.5	369.5	282.2	167.1	121.1	75.7	80.9	48.8
Net interest	401.0	392.8	467.3	337.2	191.9	80.0	40.0	21.1	11.2

1. Includes capital consumption adjustment. 2. Includes inventory valuation adjustment. *Source:* Department of Commerce, Bureau of Economic Analysis.

Per Capita Personal Income by States

State	1995[1]	1993	1990	1980	State	1995[1]	1993	1990	1980
Alabama	$18,781	$17,129	$14,899	$7,465	Montana	$18,482	$17,316	$14,743	$8,342
Alaska	24,182	23,070	20,887	13,007	Nebraska	21,703	19,672	17,379	8,895
Arizona	20,421	18,085	16,262	8,854	Nevada	25,013	22,894	20,248	10,848
Arkansas	17,429	15,995	13,779	7,113	New Hampshire	25,151	22,357	20,231	9,150
California	23,699	21,895	20,656	11,021	New Jersey	28,858	26,876	24,182	10,966
Colorado	23,449	21,498	18,818	10,143	New Mexico	18,055	16,346	14,213	7,940
Connecticut	30,303	28,151	25,426	11,532	New York	26,782	24,824	22,322	10,179
Delaware	24,124	21,852	19,719	10,059	North Carolina	20,604	18,670	16,284	7,780
D.C.	32,274	29,500	24,643	12,251	North Dakota	18,663	17,072	15,320	8,642
Florida	22,916	20,650	18,785	9,246	Ohio	22,021	19,696	17,547	9,399
Georgia	21,278	19,249	17,121	8,021	Oklahoma	18,152	17,026	15,117	9,018
Hawaii	24,738	23,504	20,905	10,129	Oregon	21,736	19,437	17,201	9,309
Idaho	19,264	17,512	15,304	8,105	Pennsylvania	23,279	21,281	18,884	9,353
Illinois	24,763	22,560	20,159	10,454	Rhode Island	23,310	21,244	19,035	9,227
Indiana	21,273	19,213	16,815	8,914	South Carolina	18,788	16,861	15,101	7,392
Iowa	21,012	18,275	16,683	9,226	South Dakota	19,506	17,879	15,628	7,800
Kansas	21,825	19,849	17,639	9,880	Tennessee	20,376	18,439	15,903	7,711
Kentucky	18,612	16,889	14,751	7,679	Texas	20,654	19,145	16,747	9,439
Louisiana	18,827	16,612	14,279	8,412	Utah	18,223	16,136	14,063	7,671
Maine	20,527	18,780	17,041	7,760	Vermont	20,927	19,437	17,444	7,957
Maryland	25,927	23,908	22,088	10,394	Virginia	23,597	21,653	19,543	9,413
Massachusetts	26,994	24,410	22,248	10,103	Washington	23,639	21,774	19,268	10,256
Michigan	23,551	20,584	18,239	9,801	West Virginia	17,915	16,169	13,964	7,764
Minnesota	23,118	29,979	18,784	9,673	Wisconsin	21,839	19,806	17,399	9,364
Mississippi	16,531	14,745	12,578	6,573	Wyoming	21,321	19,719	16,905	11,018
Missouri	21,627	19,557	17,407	8,812	**United States**	**22,788**	**20,800**	**18,667**	**9,494**

1. Preliminary. *Source:* U.S. Department of Commerce, Bureau of Economic Analysis, *Survey of Current Business.*

The Federal Budget—Receipts and Outlays

(in billions of dollars)

Description	1997[1]	1996[1]	1995	Description	1997[1]	1996[1]	1995
RECEIPTS BY SOURCE				Commerce & housing credit	12.1	9.3	11.8
Individual income taxes	645.1	639.9	590.2	Transportation	42.5	37.1	39.3
Corporate income taxes	185.0	167.1	157.0	Community development	9.1	11.9	13.0
Social insurance taxes				Education	55.3	53.9	55.6
and contributions	536.2	507.5	484.5	Health	134.7	110.9	117.0
Excise taxes	59.6	53.9	57.5	Medicare	189.9	178.0	156.5
Estate and gift taxes	17.1	15.9	14.8	Income security	228.8	220.9	215.3
Customs duties	20.5	19.3	19.3	Social security	369.4	351.6	333.3
Miscellaneous receipts	31.8	32.1	31.9	Veterans benefits	39.5	38.8	38.2
Total budget receipts	**1,495.2**	**1,426.8**	**1,355.2**	Administration of justice	23.9	21.3	18.8
OUTLAYS BY FUNCTION				General government	14.8	13.3	13.2
National defense	254.4	263.3	266.3	Net interest	238.5	241.1	232.2
International affairs	16.6	16.3	25.9	Allowances			
Gen. science	17.9	16.7	16.7	Undistributed receipts	−41.0	−42.3	−44.5
Energy	1.4	2.0	5.0	**Total outlays**	**1,638.4**	**1,571.6**	**1,543.3**
Natural resources	21.9	20.7	21.0	**Total deficit**	**−143.2**	**−144.8**	**−188.1**
Agriculture	8.5	6.9	8.6				

1. Estimated. NOTE: The fiscal year is from Oct. 1 to Sept. 30. *Source:* Budget of the United States Government, Fiscal Year 1997.

Foreign Assistance

(in millions of dollars)

	Non-military programs			Military programs		
Calendar years	Net new grants	Net new credits	Net other assistance	Net grants	Net credits	Total net assistance[1]
1945–1950[2]	$18,413	$8,086	—	$ 1,525	—	$28,023
1951–60	18,750	2,012	2,767	26,555	49	50,132
1961–70	18,192	14,776	12	21,591	176	54,747
1971–80	27,216	16,519	−1,144	22,601	9,004	74,196
1981–90[3]	69,012	5,467	−120	30,596	1,605	106,561
1991[3]	−32,764	−3,842	23	4,622	−1,556	−33,517
1992[3]	8,824	205	(4)	7,017	−23	15,623
1993[3]	10,498	−817	−3	6,085	−257	15,506
1994	10,680	−1,293	−13	5,133	41	14,548
Total postwar period	**148,421**	**41,112**	**1,522**	**125,725**	**9,039**	**325,819**

1. Excludes investment in international nonmonetary financial institutions of $23,840 million. 2. Includes transactions after V-J Day (Sept. 2, 1945). 3. Includes contributions received from coalition partners for Persian Gulf operations. 4. Less than $500,000. NOTE: Detail may not add to total due to rounding. *Source:* Department of Commerce, Bureau of Economic Analysis.

Women in the Civilian Labor Force

(16 years of age and over; in thousands)

Labor force status	1995	1994[2]	1993	1992	1991	1990[1]	1989
In the labor force:	60,944	60,239	58,795	58,141	57,178	56,829	56,030
16 to 19 years of age	3,729	3,585	3,408	3,345	3,470	3,698	3,818
20 years and over	57,215	56,655	55,388	54,796	53,708	53,131	52,212
Employed	57,523	56,610	54,910	54,052	53,496	53,689	53,027
16 to 19 years of age	3,127	3,005	2,811	2,724	2,862	3,154	3,282
20 years and over	54,396	53,606	52,099	51,328	50,634	50,535	49,745
Unemployed	3,421	3,629	3,885	4,090	3,683	3,140	3,003
16 to 19 years of age	602	580	597	621	608	544	536
20 years and over	2,819	3,049	3,288	3,469	3,074	2,596	2,467
Not in the labor force:	42,462	42,221	42,711	42,394	42,468	41,957	41,601
Women as percent of labor force	46.1	46.0	45.5	45.4	45.3	45.2	45.2
Total civilian noninstitutional population	103,406	102,460	101,506	100,535	99,646	98,787	97,630

1. Data for 1990–93 have been revised. Data beginning in 1990 are not directly comparable with data for 1989 and earlier years due to the introduction of 1990 census-based population controls, adjusted for the estimated undercount. 2. Data beginning in 1994 are not directly comparable with data for 1993 and earlier years due to the introduction of a major redesign of the Current Population Survey. *Source:* Department of Labor, Bureau of Labor Statistics.

Employed Persons 16 Years and Over, by Race and Major Occupational Groups

(number in thousands)

Race and occupational group	1995 Number	1995 Percent distribution	1994 Number	1994 Percent distribution
WHITE				
Managerial and professional specialty	31,323	29.4	30,045	28.6
Executive, administrative, & managerial	15,398	14.5	14,605	13.9
Professional specialty	15,924	15.0	15,439	14.7
Technical, sales, & administrative support	32,184	30.2	32,232	30.6
Technicians & related support	3,361	3.2	3,301	3.1
Sales occupations	13,366	12.6	13,235	12.6
Administrative support, including clerical	15,457	14.5	15,696	14.9
Service occupations	13,208	12.4	13,207	12.6
Precision production, craft, and repair	11,949	11.2	11,974	11.4
Operators, fabricators, and laborers	14,496	13.6	14,416	13.7
Farming, forestry, fishing	3,330	3.1	3,315	3.2
Total	**106,490**	**100.0**	**105,190**	**100.0**
BLACK				
Managerial and professional specialty	2,651	20.0	2,405	18.7
Executive, administrative, & managerial	1,233	9.3	1,103	8.6
Professional specialty	1,418	10.7	1,302	10.1
Technical, sales, & administrative support	3,808	28.7	3,637	28.3
Technicians & related support	378	2.8	376	2.9
Sales occupations	1,183	8.9	1,056	8.2
Administrative support, including clerical	2,248	16.9	2,205	17.2
Service occupations	2,880	21.7	2,890	22.5
Precision production, craft, and repair	1,073	8.1	1,040	8.1
Operators, fabricators, and laborers	2,712	20.4	2,677	20.9
Farming, forestry, and fishing	154	1.2	187	1.5
Total	**13,279**	**100.0**	**12,835**	**100.0**

Source: Department of Labor, Bureau of Labor Statistics.

Mothers Participating in Labor Force

(figures in percentage)

Year	Mother with children Under 18 years	6 to 17 years	Under 6 years[1]
1955	27.0	38.4	18.2
1965	35.0	45.7	25.3
1975	47.4	54.8	38.9
1980	56.6	64.4	46.6
1985	62.1	69.9	53.5
1986	62.8	70.4	54.4
1987	64.7	72.0	56.7
1988	65.0	73.3	56.1
1989	n.a.	n.a.	n.a
1990	66.7	74.7	58.2
1991	66.6	74.4	58.4
1992	67.2	75.9	58.0
1993	66.9	75.4	57.9
1994	68.4	76.0	60.3
1995	69.7	76.4	62.3

1. May also have older children. NOTE: For 1955 data are for April; for 1965 and 1975–95, data are for March. *Source:* Department of Labor, Bureau of Labor Statistics. NOTE: Data are most recent available.

Women in the Civilian Labor Force

Year	Number[1] (thousands)	% Female population aged 16 and over[1]	% of Labor force population aged 16 and over[1]
1900	5,319	18.8	18.3
1910	7,445	21.5	19.9
1920	8,637	21.4	20.4
1930	10,752	22.0	22.0
1940	12,845	25.4	24.3
1950	18,389	33.9	29.6
1960[2]	23,240	37.7	33.4
1970	31,543	43.3	38.1
1980	45,487	51.5	42.5
1990[3]	56,829	57.5	45.2
1993	58,795	57.9	45.5
1994[4]	60,239	58.8	46.0
1995	60,944	58.9	46.1

1. For 1900–1930, data relate to population and labor force aged 10 and over; for 1940, to population and labor force aged 14 and over; beginning 1950, to civilian population and labor force aged 16 and over. 2. Beginning in 1960, figures include Alaska and Hawaii. 3. Data beginning in 1990 are not strictly comparable with data for prior years because of the introduction of 1990 census-based population controls, adjusted for the estimated undercount. 4. Data beginning 1994 are not strictly comparable with data for prior years because of the introduction of a major redesign of the Current Population Survey (household survey) questionnaire and collection methodology. *Sources:* Department of Commerce, Bureau of the Census, and Department of Labor, Bureau of Labor Statistics.

Manufacturing Industries—Gross Average Weekly Earnings and Hours Worked

Industry	1995 Earnings	1995 Hours worked	1990 Earnings	1990 Hours worked	1985 Earnings	1985 Hours worked	1980 Earnings	1980 Hours worked	1975 Earnings	1975 Hours worked	1970 Earnings	1970 Hours worked
All manufacturing	$512.53	41.5	$442.27	40.8	$385.56	40.5	$288.62	39.7	$189.51	39.4	$133.73	39.8
Durable goods	545.67	42.3	468.76	41.3	415.71	41.2	310.78	40.1	205.09	39.9	143.07	40.3
Lumber and wood products	410.87	40.6	365.82	40.2	326.36	39.8	252.18	38.5	167.35	39.1	117.51	39.7
Furniture and fixtures	388.48	39.6	333.52	39.1	283.29	39.4	209.17	38.1	142.13	37.9	108.58	39.2
Primary metal industries	641.96	44.0	550.83	42.7	484.72	41.5	391.78	40.1	246.80	40.0	159.17	40.5
Iron and steel foundries	590.52	44.4	484.99	42.1	429.62	40.8	328.00	40.0	220.99	40.4	151.03	40.6
Nonferrous foundries	479.34	41.9	413.48	40.3	388.74	41.8	291.27	39.9	190.03	39.1	138.16	39.7
Fabricated metal products	512.68	42.3	447.28	41.3	398.96	41.3	300.98	40.4	201.60	40.0	143.67	40.7
Hardware, cutlery, hand tools	512.40	42.0	440.08	40.9	396.42	40.7	275.89	39.3	187.07	39.3	132.33	40.1
Structural metal products	476.28	42.0	416.56	41.0	369.00	41.0	291.85	40.2	202.61	40.2	142.61	40.4
Electric and electronic equipment	485.47	41.6	420.65	40.8	384.48	40.6	276.21	39.8	180.91	39.5	130.54	39.8
Machinery, except electrical	572.86	43.3	494.34	42.0	427.04	41.5	328.00	41.0	219.22	40.9	154.95	41.1
Transportation equipment	728.04	43.7	592.20	42.0	542.72	42.7	379.61	40.6	242.61	40.3	163.22	40.3
Motor vehicles and equipment	772.80	44.8	619.46	42.4	584.64	43.5	394.00	40.0	262.68	40.6	170.07	40.3
Nondurable goods	469.80	40.5	405.60	40.0	342.86	39.5	255.45	39.0	168.78	38.8	120.43	39.1
Textile mill products	384.34	40.8	320.40	40.0	266.39	39.7	203.31	40.1	133.28	39.2	97.76	39.9
Apparel and other textile products	281.55	36.9	239.88	36.4	208.00	36.3	161.42	35.4	111.97	35.1	84.37	35.3
Leather and leather products	311.60	38.0	258.43	37.4	217.09	37.3	169.09	36.7	120.80	37.4	92.63	37.2
Food and kindred products	449.63	41.1	392.90	40.8	341.60	40.0	271.95	39.7	184.17	40.3	127.98	40.5
Tobacco manufactures	780.50	39.7	645.23	39.2	448.26	37.2	294.89	38.1	171.38	38.0	110.00	37.8
Paper and allied products	613.74	43.1	532.59	43.3	466.34	43.1	330.85	42.2	207.58	41.6	144.14	41.9
Printing and publishing	470.62	38.2	426.38	37.9	365.31	37.7	279.36	37.1	198.32	37.0	147.78	37.7
Chemicals and allied products	678.51	43.3	576.80	42.6	484.78	41.9	344.45	41.5	219.63	40.9	153.50	41.6
Petroleum and allied products	846.47	43.7	723.86	44.6	603.72	43.0	422.18	41.8	267.07	41.6	182.76	42.7

Source: Department of Labor, Bureau of Labor Statistics *Employment & Earnings, March 1996.*

Employee Benefits in Small Businesses

Most full-time employees of small, private businesses (fewer than 100 workers) are covered by diverse employee benefits, as shown by 1994 data issued by the Department of Labor's Bureau of Labor Statistics. For example:

- 66% participated in a health benefits plan provided by their employers;
- 88% had paid vacation plans, and 82% had paid holidays;
- 50% had paid sick leave, and 26% had employer-provided sickness and accident insurance plans;
- 61% participated in life insurance programs provided by their small-establishment employers; and
- 42% participated in retirement plans.

Health benefits: Employee participation in employer-provided health plans was lower in 1994 (66%) than two years earlier (71%). The trend away from traditional fee-for-service plans was significant in the small establishments surveyed, as had been observed in larger private sector firms. Three-quarters contributed to the cost of their family coverage, about the same proportion as in 1992. From 1992 to 1994, average monthly employee contributions increased from $37 to $41 for individual coverage and from $151 to $160 for family coverage.

Retirement benefits: About 42% of full-time employees in small establishments participated in employer-provided retirement plans—a slightly lower proportion than 2 years earlier (45%). This decline reflected reduced participation in defined benefit plans (22% versus 15%) over the period, coupled with stable participation in defined contribution plans (34% in 1994).

Family leave benefits: In 1992, prior to passage of the Family and Medical Leave Act, almost one out of five (18%) full-time employees in small establishments had unpaid maternity or paternity benefits available to them. In 1994, almost one out of two (47%) had an unpaid family leave benefit. In both years, paid benefits were rare.

Nonmanufacturing Industries—Gross Average Weekly Earnings and Hours Worked

Industry	1995 Earnings	1995 Hours worked	1990 Earnings	1990 Hours worked	1985 Earnings	1985 Hours worked	1975 Earnings	1975 Hours worked	1970 Earnings	1970 Hours worked
Bituminous coal and lignite mining	$842.02	45.1	$740.52	44.0	$630.77	41.4	$284.53	39.2	$186.41	40.8
Metal mining	735.40	43.8	602.07	42.7	547.24	40.9	250.72	42.3	165.68	42.7
Nonmetallic minerals	625.84	46.6	524.12	45.3	451.68	44.5	213.09	43.4	155.11	44.7
Telephone communications	672.34	41.4	578.74	40.9	512.52	41.1	221.18	38.4	131.60	39.4
Radio and TV broadcasting	532.92	34.9	438.61	34.7	381.39	37.1	214.50	39.0	147.45	38.2
Electric, gas, and sanitary services	753.02	42.4	636.76	41.7	534.59	41.7	246.79	41.2	172.64	41.5
Local and suburban transportation	428.99	38.2	376.65	38.2	309.85	38.3	196.89	40.1	142.30	42.1
Wholesale trade	474.92	38.3	411.48	38.1	358.36	38.7	188.75	38.6	137.60	40.0
Retail trade	221.76	28.8	195.26	28.8	177.31	29.7	108.22	32.4	82.47	33.8
Hotels and motels	244.42	30.9	214.68	30.8	176.90	30.5	89.64	31.9	68.16	34.6
Laundries and dry-cleaning plants	254.51	33.8	232.22	34.0	198.70	34.2	106.05	35.0	77.47	35.7
General building contracting	544.73	38.2	487.08	37.7	414.78	37.1	254.88	36.0	184.40	36.3

Source: Department of Labor, Bureau of Labor Statistics, *Employment & Earnings, March 1996.*

Mean Income Comparisons of Year-Round Workers, 1994

Years of school completed	Mean income Women[1]	Mean income Men[1]	Income gap in dollars	Women's income as a percent of men's	Men's income as a percent of women's
Less than 9th grade	$13,468	$19,724	$ 6,256	68%	146%
9th to 12th grade	$15,558	$23,316	$ 7,758	67%	150%
High school graduate	$20,807	$29,624	$ 8,817	70%	142%
Some college	$23,757	$33,744	$ 9,987	70%	142%
Bachelor's degree	$33,725	$52,193	$18,468	65%	155%
Master's degree	$43,601	$62,368	$18,767	70%	143%

1. Persons aged 18 and over as of March 1995. *Source:* Department of Commerce, Bureau of the Census.

Median Income of Households with Selected Characteristics, 1994

Characteristics	White as a % of all white households	White Median income	Black as a % of all black households	Black Median income	Hispanic Origin[1] as a % of all Hispanic households	Hispanic Origin[1] Median income	All Races as a % of all households	All Races Median income
Overall		34,028		21,027		23,421		32,264
Region								
Northeast	20%	36,477	17%	23,257	17%	19,021	20%	34,926
Midwest	25%	34,103	20%	17,963	6%	29,482	24%	32,505
South	33%	32,095	54%	20,603	33%	22,620	35%	30,021
West	22%	35,063	9%	25,716	43%	24,389	21%	34,452
Type of household								
Family households	70%	41,334	69%	25,475	80%	25,210	70%	39,390
Married-couple families	57%	45,555	33%	40,432	55%	29,915	54%	45,041
Single father household	3%	32,227	5%	23,073	6%	25,596	3%	30,472
Single mother household	10%	22,605	32%	14,650	19%	13,200	12%	19,872
Nonfamily households	30%	19,783	31%	13,320	20%	15,789	30%	18,947
Male living alone	10%	22,153	12%	15,223	7%	17,474	10%	21,216
Female living alone	15%	13,912	15%	9,621	8%	8,382	15%	13,431
Size of household								
One person	25%	16,818	27%	11,700	15%	11,598	25%	16,222
Two persons	33%	35,279	26%	22,637	22%	21,821	32%	33,955
Three persons	17%	43,541	19%	25,789	19%	25,150	17%	41,043
Four persons	15%	49,293	15%	29,055	20%	26,720	15%	46,757
Five persons	6%	47,990	8%	26,990	12%	26,801	7%	44,135
Six persons	2%	45,786	3%	30,185	6%	31,554	2%	42,683
Seven persons or more	1%	39,018	3%	27,761	5%	29,688	1%	36,622
Number of earners								
No earners	22%	13,412	24%	6,949	17%	7,427	22%	12,175
One	32%	27,775	41%	18,609	36%	17,722	33%	26,210
Two	36%	48,934	28%	39,752	34%	34,678	35%	47,734
Three	7%	61,697	6%	49,717	9%	42,013	7%	60,421
Four or more	2%	74,832	1%	71,191	3%	54,179	2%	74,276

1. Persons of Hispanic origin may be of any race.

Unemployment by Marital Status, Sex, and Race[1]

Marital status and race	Men Number	Men Unemployment rate	Women Number	Women Unemployment rate
White, 16 years and over	2,999,000	4.9	2,460,000	4.8
Married, spouse present	1,165,000	3.0	1,070,000	3.6
Widowed, divorced, or separated	428,000	6.4	526,000	5.5
Single (never married)	1,406,000	8.7	864,000	7.3
Black, 16 years and over	762,000	10.6	777,000	10.2
Married, spouse present	166,000	5.0	143,000	5.5
Widowed, divorced, or separated	100,000	9.3	155,000	7.5
Single (never married)	496,000	17.6	479,000	16.2
Total, 16 years and over	3,983,000	5.6	3,421,000	5.6
Married, spouse present	1,424,000	3.3	1,296,000	3.9
Widowed, divorced, or separated	551,000	6.9	712,000	5.9
Single (never married)	2,007,000	10.1	1,413,000	9.1

1. 1995 Annual Averages. *Source: Employment and Earnings,* January 1996, U.S. Department of Labor, Bureau of Labor Statistics.

Earnings Distribution of Year-Round, Full-Time Workers, by Sex, 1994

(persons 15 years old and over as of March 1995)

Earnings group	Number (in thousands) Women	Number (in thousands) Men	Distribution (%) Women	Distribution (%) Men	Women as a % of each earning level
$7,500 or less	6,233	6,038	14.0%	9.5%	50.8%
$7,501–$12,499	6,552	5,958	14.7%	9.4%	52.4%
$12,500–$19,999	9,729	9,703	21.9	15.2%	50.1%
$20,000–$29,999	10,580	13,013	23.8%	20.4%	44.8%
$30,000–$39,999	5,854	10,143	13.2%	15.9%	36.6%
$40,000–$49,999	2,849	6,739	6.4%	10.6%	29.7%
$50,000–$74,999	2,014	7,562	4.5%	11.9%	21.0%
$75,000–$99,999	342	2,251	0.8%	3.5%	13.2%
$100,000 and over	347	2,248	0.8%	3.5%	13.4%
Total	**44,500**	**63,655**	**100%**	**100%**	—

Source: Department of Commerce, Bureau of the Census.

Comparison of Median Earnings of Year-Round, Full-Time Workers 15 Years and Over, by Sex, 1960 to 1994

Year	Median earnings Men	Median earnings Women	Earnings gap in current dollars	Women's earnings as a percent of men's	Percent men's earnings exceeded women's
1994[a]	$30,854	$22,205	8,649	72.0%	39.0%
1993[b]	31,186	22,304	8,882	71.5%	39.8%
1992[c]	31,897	22,579	9,318	70.8%	41.3%
1991	32,013	22,364	9,649	69.9%	43.1%
1990	31,384	22,476	8,908	71.6%	39.6%
1989	32,665	22,432	10,233	68.7%	45.6%
1988	33,393	22,056	11,337	66.0%	51.4%
1987[d]	33,849	22,062	11,787	65.2%	53.4%
1986	34,151	21,949	12,202	64.3%	55.6%
1985[e]	33,324	21,519	11,805	64.6%	54.9%
1980	33,515	20,163	13,352	60.2%	66.2%
1970	32,173	19,101	13,072	59.4%	68.4%
1960	24,706	14,990	9,716	60.7%	64.8%

Numbers in thousands, in 1994 dollars; prior to 1989 are for civilian workers only. a. Introduction of new 1990 census sample design. b. Reflects revised data collection methods; increased earnings to $999,999; Social Security increased to $49,999; Supplemental Security Income and Public Assistance increased to $24,999; Child Support and Alimony decreased to $49,999. c. Implementation of 1990 census population controls. d. Implementation of new March CPS processing system. e. Recording of amounts for earnings from longest job increased to $299,999. *Source:* Department of Commerce, Bureau of the Census.

Occupations of Employed Women[1]
(16 years of age and over. Figures are percentage)

Occupations	1995	1994	1993	1992	1990	1988	1986
Managerial and professional	29.4	28.7	28.3	27.4	26.2	25.2	23.7
Technical, sales, administrative support	41.9	42.4	43.0	43.8	44.4	44.6	45.6
Service occupations	17.7	17.8	18.0	17.9	17.7	17.9	18.3
Precision production, craft and repair	2.1	2.2	2.1	2.1	2.2	2.3	2.4
Operators, fabricators, laborers	7.6	7.7	7.6	7.9	8.5	8.9	8.9
Farming, forestry, fishing	1.3	1.2	0.9	1.0	1.0	1.1	1.1

1. Annual averages. NOTE: Details may not add up to totals because of rounding. *Source:* Department of Labor.

Employed and Unemployed Workers by Full- and Part-Time Status, Sex, and Age: 1970 to 1995
(In thousands)

	1995	1994[2]	1993	1992	1990[1]	1985	1980	1970
Total 16 yr and over								
Employed	124,900	123,060	120,259	118,492	118,793	107,150	99,303	78,678
Full time	101,679	99,772	99,114	97,664	98,666	88,535	82,564	66,752
Part time	23,220	23,288	21,145	20,828	20,128	18,615	16,742	11,924
Unemployed	7,404	7,996	8,940	9,613	7,047	8,312	7,637	4,093
Full time	5,909	6,513	7,305	7,923	5,677	6,793	6,269	3,206
Part time	1,495	1,483	1,635	1,690	1,369	1,519	1,369	889
Men, 20 yr and over								
Employed	64,085	63,294	62,355	61,496	61,678	56,562	53,101	45,581
Full time	58,707	57,707	57,010	56,274	57,055	52,425	49,699	43,138
Part time	5,377	5,587	5,345	5,223	4,623	4,137	3,403	2,444
Unemployed	3,239	3,627	4,287	4,717	3,239	3,715	3,353	1,638
Full time	2,988	3,359	4,011	4,430	3,000	3,479	3,167	1,502
Part time	251	269	276	287	239	236	186	137
Women, 20 yr. and over								
Employed	54,396	53,606	52,099	51,328	50,535	44,154	38,492	26,952
Full time	40,943	40,183	40,209	39,544	39,138	33,604	29,391	20,654
Part time	13,453	13,423	11,890	11,783	11,397	10,550	9,102	6,297
Unemployed	2,819	3,049	3,288	3,469	2,596	3,129	2,615	1,349
Full time	2,265	2,506	2,670	2,840	2,079	2,536	2,135	1,077
Part time	554	543	619	628	517	593	480	271
Both sexes 16–19 yr.								
Employed	6,419	6,161	5,805	5,669	6,581	6,434	7,710	6,144
Full time	2,029	1,883	1,895	1,846	2,473	2,507	3,474	2,960
Part time	4,390	4,278	3,910	3,822	4,107	3,927	4,237	3,183
Unemployed	1,346	1,320	1,365	1,427	1,212	1,468	1,669	1,106
Full time	657	648	625	653	598	777	966	626
Part time	689	672	740	775	614	690	701	480

1. Data for 1990–93 have been revised. Data beginning in 1990 are not directly comparable with data for 1989 and earlier years due to the introduction of 1990 census-based population controls, adjusted for the estimated undercount. 2. Data beginning in 1994 are not directly comparable with data for 1993 and earlier years due to the introduction of a major redesign of the Current Population Survey. *Source:* U.S. Department of Labor, Bureau of Labor Statistics.

Work Stoppages Involving 1,000 Workers or More[1]

Year	Work stoppages	Workers involved (thousands)	Days idle (thousands)	Year	Work stoppages	Workers involved (thousands)	Days idle (thousands)
1950	424	1,698	30,390	1987	46	174	4,456
1960	222	896	13,260	1988	40	118	4,381
1970	381	2,468	52,761	1989	51	452	16,996
1975	235	965	17,563	1990	44	185	5,926
1980	187	795	20,844	1991	40	392	4,584
1983	81	909	17,461	1992	35	364	3,989
1984	68	391	8,499	1993	35	184	3,981
1985	61	584	7,079	1994	45	322	5,020
1986	72	900	11,861	1995	28	176	5,736

1. The number of stoppages and workers relate to stoppages that began in the year. Days of idleness include all stoppages in effect. Workers are counted more than once if they were involved in more than one stoppage during the year. *Source:* U.S. Department of Labor. Bureau of Labor Statistics, *Monthly Labor Review.* March 1996.

Leading Advertising Agencies in Revenues

(in thousands of dollars)

Agency	1995 revenues	1995 billings
McCann-Erickson	$1,236,321	$8,246,259
BBDO Worldwide	1,144,193	8,833,772
J. Walter Thompson	1,054,542	7,069,496
DDB Needham Worldwide	1,051,463	8,158,227
Ogilvy & Mather Worldwide	893,200	7,632,800
Young & Rubicam	817,577	7,112,061
Leo Burnett Worldwide	805,865	5,386,735
Grey Advertising	799,000	5,335,900
Ammirati Puris Lintas Worldwide	786,290	5,653,409
Saatchi & Saatchi Advertising	700,000[1]	7,000,000

1. Estimated. *Source: Adweek,* Top 20 U.S.-Based Agency Networks, April 15, 1996, edition. © 1996 Adweek. Used with permission of *Adweek.*

Unemployment Rate, 1995

Race and age	Women[1]	Men[1]
All races:	5.6	5.6
16 to 19 years	16.1	18.4
20 years and over	4.9	4.8
White	4.8	4.9
16 to 19 years	13.4	15.6
20 years and over	4.3	4.3
Minority races:	10.1	9.9
16 to 19 years	29.1	30.8
20 years and over	8.8	8.2

1. Annual averages. *Source:* Bureau of Labor Statistics, Department of Labor.

Unemployment Rate in the Civilian Labor Force

Year	Unemployment rate	Year	Unemployment rate
1920	5.2	1984	7.5
1928	4.2	1986	7.0
1930	8.7	1987	6.2
1932	23.6	1988	5.4
1934	21.7	1989	5.3
1936	16.9	1990	5.5
1938	19.0	1991	6.7
1940	14.6	1992	7.4
1942	4.7	1993	6.8
1944	1.2	1994	6.1
1946	3.9	1995	5.6
1948	3.8	Jan.	5.7
1950	5.3	Feb.	5.4
1952	3.0	March	5.5
1954	5.5	April	5.7
1956	4.1	May	5.6
1958	6.8	June	5.6
1960	5.5	July	5.7
1962	5.5	Aug.	5.6
1964	5.2	Sept.	5.6
1966	3.8	Oct.	5.5
1968	3.6	Nov.	5.6
1970	4.9	Dec.	5.6
1972	5.6	1996	
1974	5.6	Jan.	5.8
1976	7.7	Feb.	5.5
1978	6.0	March	5.6
1980	7.1	April	5.4
1982	9.7	May	5.6

NOTE: Estimates prior to 1940 are based on sources other than direct enumeration. *Source:* Department of Labor, Bureau of Labor Statistics.

Employment and Unemployment
(in millions of persons)

Category	1995	1994	1993	1990	1985	1980	1970	1950	1945	1932	1929
EMPLOYMENT STATUS[1]											
Civilian noninstitutional population	198.6	196.8	194.8	189.2	178.2	167.7	137.1	105.0	94.1	—	—
Civilian labor force	132.3	131.1	129.2	125.8	115.5	106.9	82.8	62.2	53.9	—	—
Civilian labor force participation rate	66.6	66.6	66.3	66.5	64.8	63.8	60.4	59.2	57.2	—	—
Employed	124.9	123.1	120.3	118.8	107.2	99.3	78.7	58.9	52.8	38.9	47.6
Employment-population ratio	62.9	62.5	61.7	62.8	60.1	59.2	57.4	56.1	56.1	—	—
Agriculture	3.4	3.4	3.1	3.2	3.2	3.4	3.5	7.2	8.6	10.2	10.5
Nonagricultural industries	121.5	119.7	117.1	115.6	104.0	95.9	75.2	51.8	44.2	28.8	37.2
Unemployed	7.4	8.0	8.9	7.1	8.3	7.6	4.1	3.3	1.0	12.1	1.6
Unemployment rate	5.6	6.1	6.9	5.6	7.2	7.1	4.9	5.3	1.9	23.6	3.2
Not in labor force	66.3	65.8	65.6	63.3	62.7	60.8	54.3	42.8	40.2	—	—
INDUSTRY											
Total nonfarm employment	117.2	114.2	110.7	109.4	97.4	90.4	70.9	45.2	40.4	23.6	31.3
Goods-producing industries	24.2	23.9	23.4	24.9	24.8	25.7	23.6	18.5	17.5	8.6	13.3
Mining	0.6	0.6	0.6	0.7	0.9	1.0	0.6	0.9	0.8	0.7	1.1
Construction	5.2	5.0	4.7	5.1	4.7	4.3	3.6	2.4	1.1	1.0	1.5
Manufacturing: Durable goods	11.1	10.2	10.4	10.7	11.5	12.2	11.2	8.1	9.1	—	—
Nondurable goods	8.0	7.9	7.9	7.8	7.8	8.1	8.2	7.2	6.4	—	—
Service-producing industries	93.0	90.3	87.4	84.5	72.5	64.7	47.3	26.7	22.9	15.0	18.0
Transportation and public utilities	6.2	6.0	5.8	5.8	5.2	5.1	4.5	4.0	3.9	2.8	3.9
Trade, Wholesale	6.4	6.2	6.0	6.2	5.7	5.3	4.0	2.6	2.0		
Retail	21.2	20.5	19.8	19.6	17.3	15.0	11.0	6.7	5.4	—	—
Finance, insurance, and real estate	6.8	6.9	6.8	6.7	5.9	5.2	3.6	1.9	1.5	—	—
Services	33.1	31.6	30.2	27.9	21.9	17.9	11.5	5.4	4.2	—	—
Federal government	3.1	2.9	2.9	2.8	2.9	2.9	2.7	1.9	2.8	—	—
State and local government	16.5	16.3	15.9	15.2	13.5	13.4	9.8	4.1	3.1	2.7	2.5

. For 1929–45, figures on employment status relate to persons 14 years and over; beginning in 1950, 16 years and over. Data for 1990–93 have been revised. Data beginning in 1990 are not directly comparable with the data for 1989 and earlier years due to the introduction of 1990 census-based population controls, adjusted for the estimated undercount. Data beginning in 1994 are not directly comparable with the data for 1993 and earlier years because of the introduction of major redesign of the Current Population Survey. *Source:* U.S. Department of Labor, Bureau of Labor Statistics.

Livestock on Farms (in thousands)

Type	1996	1995	1994	1993	1990	1985	1980	1975	1970	1965
Cattle[1]	103,819	102,755	100,988	99,176	95,816	109,582	111,242	132,028	112,369	109,000
Dairy cows[1]	9,412	9,487	9,528	9,658	10,015	10,311	10,758	13,303	13,303	16,981
Sheep[1]	8,457	8,886	9,714	10,201	11,358	10,716	12,699	14,515	20,423	25,127
Swine[2]	58,700	59,990	57,904	58,202	53,788	54,073	67,318	54,693	57,046	56,106
Chickens[3]	384,241	383,829	379,640	371,483	357,241	374,443	400,585	384,101	422,096	401,813
Turkeys[4]	n.a.	292,626	286,605	287,650	282,445	185,427	165,243	124,165	116,139	105,914

Except as noted, these figures represent the number of animals on a given day, rather than the number produced over the year. 1. As of January 1. 2. As of December 1 of the previous year. 3. As of December 1 of previous year; excludes commercial broilers. 4. Inventory data on turkeys is not available; represents the number produced. *Source:* Department of Agriculture, Statistical Reporting Service, Economic Research Service.

Agricultural Output by States, 1996 Crops

State	Corn (1,000 bu)	Wheat (1,000 bu)	Cotton[2] (1,000 ba)[3]	Potatoes[4] (1,000 cwt)	Tobacco (1,000 lb)	Cattle[5] (1,000 head)	Swine[6] (1,000 head)
Alabama	21,600	3,600*	740	1,539	—	1,750	—
Alaska	—	—	—	—	—	10.2	—
Arizona	6,125*	16,689*	878	1,755	—	840	—
Arkansas	18,050*	64,480*	1,530	—	—	1,910	790
California	38,500	53,700*	2,765	14,620	—	4,600	—
Colorado	131,600	76,060*	—	26,404	—	3,100	—
Connecticut[1]	—	—	—	—	3,466*	70	—
Delaware	18,750	4,446*	—	1,475	—	31	—
Florida	8,000*	380*	140*	9,003	18,469	1,990	—
Georgia	48,600	16,450*	2,000	—	103,500	1,500	900
Hawaii	—	—	—	—	—	171	—
Idaho	5,000*	117,000	—	131,274	—	1,770	—
Illinois	1,393,200	42,900*	—	1,485	—	1,770	4,800
Indiana	643,100	25,920*	—	1,196	15,200	1,130	3,900
Iowa	1,624,400	2,200*	—	232	—	3,950	13,000
Kansas	340,750	255,200*	1.1*	—	—	6,500	1,200
Kentucky	146,400	28,090*	—	—	448,630	2,700	730
Louisiana	58,850*	5,590*	1,380	—	—	1,020	—
Maine[1]	—	12,474	—	17,160	—	117	—
Maryland	55,800	—*	—	360	12,000	290	—
Massachusetts[1]	—	—	—	858	1,155*	68	—
Michigan	220,900	26,000*	—	16,500	—	1,170	1,000
Minnesota	805,000	104,750	—	20,790	—	2,900	4,900
Mississippi	56,730*	10,560*	1,640	—	—	1,390	—
Missouri	317,200	52,000*	590	1,587	6,380*	4,650	3,450
Montana	2,600*	190,125	—	2,940	—	2,750	—
Nebraska	1,146,750	73,100*	—	4,934	—	6,350	3,750
Nevada	—	1,645*	—	2,774	—	500	—
New Hampshire[1]	—	—	—	—	—	46	—
New Jersey	10,058*	1,900*	—	702	—	68	—
New Mexico	13,200*	4,125*	99	3,759	—	1,520	—
New York	77,700*	7,800*	—	7,695	—	1,510	—
North Carolina	89,280	26,550*	1,040	3,177	600,700	1,200	8,400
North Dakota	56,000	393,395	—	25,410	—	1,920	—
Ohio	297,000	55,350*	—	1,404	14,940	1,540	1,650
Oklahoma	18,900*	93,100*	170	—	—	5,600	1,050
Oregon	5,040*	69,950*	—	23,760	—	1,470	—
Pennsylvania	129,150	10,450*	—	4,080	15,680	1,790	1,040
Rhode Island[1]	—	—	—	239	—	8	—
South Carolina	28,500	12,960*	410	—	115,000	520	—
South Dakota	306,600	130,520	—	988	—	3,900	1,320
Tennessee	74,800	18,920*	650	2,570	116,500	2,700	—
Texas	171,000	69,600*	3,717	2,940	—	15,000	—
Utah	2,970*	7,620*	—	1,224	—	910	—
Vermont[1]	—	—	—	—	—	300	—
Virginia	36,000	15,400*	150*	2,040	100,099	1,800	—
Washington	20,700*	182,670	—	80,850	—	1,290	—
West Virginia	4,000*	572*	—	—	3,700*	470	—
Wisconsin	348,800	6,600*	—	27,135	5,130	3,800	860
Wyoming	6,325*	6,849*	—	390	—	1,410	—
U.S.	**8,803,928**	**2,295,690**	**17,900.1**	**442,309**	**1,580,549**	**103,819.2**	**52,740**

1. Individual state estimates not always available. 2. Production ginned and to be ginned. 3. 480-lb net weight bales. 4. Production for 1995; includes production formerly listed separately as summer or winter potatoes. 5. As of Jan. 1 1996. 6. Individual state estimates not available for the 33 other states, which contain another 4,400 head. *Estimate for current year carried forward from earlier forecast. *Source:* Department of Agriculture, Statistical Reporting Service.

Farm Income
(in millions of dollars)

Year	Crops	Cash receipts from marketings		Government payments	Total cash income[1]
		Livestock, livestock products			
1930	$3,868	$5,187		—	$9,055
1935	2,977	4,143		$573	7,693
1940	3,469	4,913		723	9,105
1945	9,655	12,008		742	22,405
1950	12,356	16,105		283	28,764
1955	13,523	15,967		229	29,842
1960	15,023	18,989		703	34,958
1965	17,479	21,886		2,463	42,215
1970	20,977	29,532		3,717	54,768
1975	45,813	43,089		807	90,707
1980	71,746	67,991		1,285	143,295
1985	74,293	69,822		7,705	157,854
1990	80,131	89,843		9,298	186,824
1991	82,060	86,735		8,214	184,858
1992	84,853	86,350		9,169	188,160
1993	84,497	90,555		13,402	197,215
1994	91,600	88,100		7,900	196,700
1995[2]	98,900	87,200		7,300	202,600

1. Includes items not listed. 2. Forecast. *Source:* Department of Agriculture, Economic Research Service. NOTE: Data are latest available.

Per Capita Consumption of Principal Foods[1]

Food	1994	1993	1992
Red meat[2]	114.8	112.1	114.1
Poultry[2]	63.7	62.6	60.9
Fish and shellfish[2]	15.1	14.9	14.7
Eggs	30.6	30.3	30.3
Fluid milk and cream[3]	225.7	226.8	230.9
Ice cream	16.1	16.1	16.3
Cheese (excluding cottage)	26.8	26.3	26.0
Butter (actual weight)	4.8	4.7	4.4
Margarine (actual weight)	9.9	11.1	11.0
Total fats and oils[4]	66.9	68.4	65.7
Fruits (farm weight)[5]	279.5	278.4	262.4
Peanuts (shelled)	5.8	6.0	6.2
Vegetables (farm weight)	398.3	402.0	394.3
Sugar (refined)	65.0	64.3	64.6
Corn sweeteners (dry weight)	81.3	78.7	75.3
Flour and cereal products	198.7	195.8	190.7
Soft drinks (gal)	52.2	50.2	48.5
Coffee (bean equivalent)	8.2	9.1	10.0
Cocoa (chocolate liquor equivalent)	4.1	4.4	4.6

1. As of December 1995. Except where noted, consumption is from commercial sources and is in pounds retail weight. 2. Boneless, trimmed equivalent. 3. Includes milk and cream produced and consumed on farms. 4. Fat-content basis. 5. Excludes wine grapes. NOTE: Data are latest available.

Government Employment and Payrolls

Year and function	Employees (in thousands)				October payrolls (in millions)			
	Total	Federal[1]	State	Local	Total	Federal[1]	State	Local
1940	4,474	1,128		3,346	$566	177		$389
1945	6,556	3,375		3,181	1,110	642		468
1950	6,402	2,117	1,057	3,228	1,528	613	218	696
1955	7,432	2,378	1,199	3,855	2,265	846	326	1,093
1960	8,808	2,421	1,527	4,860	3,333	1,118	524	1,691
1965	10,589	2,588	2,028	5,973	4,884	1,484	849	2,551
1970	13,028	2,881	2,755	7,392	8,334	2,428	1,612	4,294
1975	14,973	2,890	3,271	8,813	13,224	3,584	2,653	6,987
1980	16,213	2,898	3,753	9,562	19,935	5,205	4,285	10,445
1982	15,841	2,848	3,744	9,249	23,173	5,959	5,022	12,192
1983	16,034	2,875	3,816	9,344	24,525	6,302	5,346	12,878
1984	16,436	2,942	3,898	9,595	26,904	7,137	5,815	13,952
1985	16,690	3,021	3,984	9,685	28,945	7,580	6,329	15,036
1986	16,933	3,019	4,068	9,846	30,670	7,561	6,810	16,298
1987	17,212	3,091	4,116	10,005	32,669	7,924	7,263	17,482
1988	17,588	3,112	4,236	10,240	34,203	7,976	7,842	18,385
1990	18,369	3,105	4,503	10,760	39,228	8,999	9,083	21,146
1994, total	7,649	2,952	4,697	n.a.	10,533	n.a.	10,533	n.a.
National defense and international relations	882	882	(2)	(2)	0	n.a.	(2)	(2)
Postal service	827	827	(2)	(2)	0	n.a.	(2)	(2)
Education	2,125	13	2,112	n.a.	4,055	n.a.	4,055	n.a.
Instructional employees	657	n.a.	657	n.a.	1,869	n.a.	1,869	n.a.
Highways	266	4	262	n.a.	660	n.a.	660	n.a.
Health and hospitals	1,013	317	695	n.a.	1,643	n.a.	1,643	n.a.
Police protection	171	84	87	n.a.	269	n.a.	269	n.a.
Fire protection	0	(2)	(2)	n.a.	n.a.	n.a.	(2)	n.a.
Sewerage and solid waste management	2	(2)	2	n.a.	8	(2)	8	n.a.
Parks and recreation	73	27	46	n.a.	80	n.a.	80	n.a.
Natural resources	386	218	168	n.a.	390	n.a.	390	n.a.
Financial administration	303	134	169	n.a.	431	n.a.	431	n.a.
All other	1,600	447	1,153	n.a.	2,997	n.a.	2,997	n.a.

1. Civilians only. 2. Not applicable. NOTE: n.a. = not available. Detail may not add to totals because of rounding. Data are most recent available. *Source:* Department of Commerce, Bureau of the Census. NOTE: Data are latest available.

Receipts and Outlays of the Federal Government
(in millions of dollars)

From 1789 to 1842, the federal fiscal year ended Dec. 31; from 1844 to 1976, on June 30; and beginning 1977, on Sept. 30.

Receipts

Year	Customs (including tonnage tax)[1]	Internal revenue — Income and profits tax	Internal revenue — Other	Miscellaneous taxes and receipts	Total receipts	Net receipts[2]
1789–1791	$ 4	—	—	—	$ 4	$ 4
1800	9	—	$ −1	$ 1	11	11
1810	9	—	—	1	9	9
1820	15	—	—	3	18	18
1830	22	—	—	3	25	25
1840	14	—	—	6	20	20
1850	40	—	—	4	44	44
1860	53	—	—	3	56	56
1870	195	—	185	32	411	411
1880	187	—	124	23	334	334
1890	230	—	143	31	403	403
1900	233	—	295	39	567	567
1910	334	—	290	52	675	675
1915	210	$ 80	335	72	698	683
1929	602	2,331	607	493	4,033	3,862
1939	319	2,189	2,972	188	5,668	4,979
1944	431	34,655	7,030	3,325	45,441	43,563
1945	355	35,173	8,729	3,494	47,750	44,362
1950	423	28,263	11,186	1,439	41,311	36,422
1956	705	56,639	20,564	389	78,297	74,547
1960	1,123	67,151	28,266	1,190	97,730	92,492
1965	1,478	79,792	39,996	1,598	122,863	116,833
1970	2,494	138,689	65,276	3,424	209,883	193,743
1975	3,782	202,146	108,371	6,711	321,010	280,997
1980	7,482	359,927	192,436	12,797	572,641	520,050
1985	12,079	474,074	311,092	18,576	815,821	733,996
1988	16,198	495,376	377,469	19,909	(4)	908,953
1989	16,334	549,273	402,200	22,800	(4)	990,691
1990	16,707	560,391	426,893	27,470	(4)	1,031,462
1991	15,949	565,913	449,577	22,846	(4)	1,054,265
1992	17,359	576,234	470,401	26,459	(4)	1,090,453
1993	18,802	627,200	488,934	18,290	(4)	1,153,226
1994	20,099	683,439	531,924	21,988	(4)	1,257,451
1995	19,300	747,247	556,721	27,309	(4)	1,350,578

Outlays

Year	Department of Defense (Army, 1789–1950)	Department of the Navy	Interest on public debt	All other	Net outlays[3]	Surplus (+) or deficit (−)
1789–1791	$ 1	—	$ 2	$ 1	$ 4	—
1800	3	$ 3	3	1	11	—
1810	2	2	3	1	8	$ +1
1820	3	4	5	6	18	—
1830	5	3	2	5	15	+10
1840	7	6	—	11	24	−4
1850	9	8	4	18	40	+4
1860	16	12	3	32	63	−7
1870	58	22	129	101	310	+101
1880	38	14	96	120	268	+66
1890	45	22	36	215	318	+85
1900	135	56	40	290	521	+46
1910	190	123	21	359	694	−19
1915	202	142	23	379	746	−63
1929	426	365	678	1,658	3,127	+734
1939	695	673	941	6,533	8,841	−3,862
1944	49,438	26,538	2,609	16,401	94,986	−51,423
1945	50,490	30,047	3,617	14,149	98,303	−53,941
1950	5,789	4,130	5,750	23,875	39,544	−3,122
1956	35,693	—	6,787	27,981	70,460	+4,087

Year	Department of Defense (Army, 1789–1950)	Department of the Navy	Interest on public debt	All other	Net outlays[3]	Surplus (+) or deficit (–)
			Outlays			
1960	43,969	—	9,180	39,075	92,223	+269
1965	47,179	—	11,346	59,904	118,430	−1,596
1970	78,360	—	19,304	98,924	196,588	−2,845
1975	87,471	—	32,665	205,969	326,105	−45,108
1980	136,138	—	74,860	368,013	579,011	−58,961
1985	244,054	—	178,945	513,810	936,809	−202,813
1988	290,349	—	151,711	621,995	1,064,055	−155,102
1989	303,600	—	169,100	649,943	1,142,643	−123,785
1990	299,355	—	183,790	768,725	1,251,850	−220,388
1991	273,292	—	194,541	855,924	1,323,757	−269,492
1992	298,350	—	199,439	883,005	1,380,794	−290,340
1993	291,086	—	198,811	918,635	1,408,532	−255,306
1994	281,563	—	202,957	976,033	1,460,553	−203,102
1995	271,895	—	232,175	1,010,364	1,514,434	−163,856

1. Beginning 1933, tonnage tax is included in "Other receipts." 2. Net receipts equal total receipts less (a) appropriations to federal old-age and survivors' insurance trust fund beginning fiscal year 1939 and (b) refunds of receipts beginning fiscal year 1933. 3. Includes Air Force 1950–65 (in millions): 1950—$3,521; 1956—$16,750; 1960—$19,065; 1965—$18,471. 4. Net receipts are now the total receipts. Public Law 99–177 moved two social security trust funds off-budget. *Source:* Department of the Treasury, Financial Management Service.

Contributions to International Organizations
(for fiscal year 1995)

Organization	Amount
United Nations and Specialized Agencies	
Food and Agriculture Organization	$79,000,000
International Atomic Energy Agency	58,000,000
International Civic Aviation Organization	14,000,000
International Labor Organization	62,000,000
International Maritime Organization	1,000,000
International Telecommunications Union	8,000,000
United Nations	259,000,000
United Nations Industrial Development Organization	29,000,000
Universal Postal Union	1,000,000
World Health Organization	104,000,000
World Intellectual Property Organization	1,000,000
World Meteorological Organization	11,000,000
Peacekeeping Forces	
U.N. Disengagement Observer Force	7,000,000
U.N. Interim Force in Lebanon	40,000,000
U.N. Angola Verification Mission II/III	69,000,000
U.N. Iran–Kuwait Observer Mission	—
U.N. Observer Mission in El Salvador	5,000,000
U.N. Operations in the former Yugoslavia	26,000,000
War Crimes Tribunal—Yugoslavia	—
U.N. Observer Mission in Mozambique	11,000,000
U.N. Observer Mission in Georgia	7,000,000
U.N. Mission in Haiti	52,000,000
U.N. Observer Mission in Liberia	4,000,000
U.N. Assistance Mission for Rwanda	76,000,000

Organization	Amount
U.N. Force in Cyprus	6,000,000
U.N. Mission in Tajikistan	3,000,000
Inter-American Organizations	
Inter-American Institute for Cooperation on Agriculture	16,000,000
Organization of American States	52,000,000
Pan American Health Organization	49,000,000
Regional Organizations	
Asia-Pacific Economic Cooperation	—
North Atlantic Assembly	1,000,000
North Atlantic Treaty Organization	43,000,000
Organization for Economic Cooperation and Development	62,000,000
South Pacific Commission	1,000,000
Other International Organizations	
World Trade Organization/General Agreement on Tariffs and Trade	10,000,000
International Agency for Research on Cancer	2,000,000
International Bureau of Weights and Measures	1,000,000
International Wheat Council	—
Interparliamentary Union	1,000,000
Organization for Prohibition of Chemical Weapons	—
Other International Organizations	2,000,000
Total U.S. Contributions	**1,173,000,000**

Source: Budget of the United States Government Fiscal Year 1995.

U.S. Owes the U.N. $1.6 Billion in Overdue Dues

The United States is overdue in its payment of more than $1.6 billion to U.N. assessments for its share in the regular budget and in peacekeeping operations. The U.N.'s annual operating budget for 1996 is $2.6 billion, held to 1995 levels at U.S. insistence. Assessments to the G-7 nations account for 69% of this budget, with fully 25% of the total budget assessed to the U.S. alone. The next highest assessment, Japan's, is 60% of the U.S. assessment, and the remaining five G-7 countries combined contribute 29% of the total budget.

Faced with renewed military action in the Middle East and domestic political pressures in an election year, the U.S. is unlikely to give priority to resolution of the U.N. budget shortfalls. At the U.N., however, the nonpayment is causing a budgetary crisis. Without the promised payments by the U.S., the U.N. will need to borrow from its own peacekeeping budget to meet its day-to-day operational needs. Borrowing from the peacekeeping fund leaves the U.N. with insufficient funds to repay those countries who have deployed troops for U.N. peacekeeping initiatives, which may make it harder to rally support for future initiatives.

Social Welfare Expenditures Under Public Programs

(in millions of dollars)

Year and source of funds	Social insurance	Public aid	Health and medical programs[1]	Veterans' programs	Education	Housing	Other social welfare	All health and medical care[2]	Total social welfare	Percent of gross domestic product	Percent of total gov't outlays
FEDERAL											
1982	250,551	52,485	14,598	24,463	11,917	7,176	6,500	90,776	367,691	11.8	52.5
1983	274,212	55,895	15,594	25,561	12,397	8,087	7,046	100,274	398,792	12.1	51.9
1984	288,743	58,480	16,622	25,970	13,010	10,226	7,349	103,927	420,399	11.4	50.2
1985	313,108	61,985	18,630	26,704	13,796	11,088	7,548	118,955	452,860	11.4	47.8
1986	326,588	65,615	19,926	27,072	15,022	10,164	7,977	125,730	472,364	11.2	47.6
1987	345,082	69,233	22,219	27,641	16,054	11,110	8,504	143,020	499,844	11.2	50.4
1988	358,412	74,137	22,681	28,845	16,952	14,006	8,112	149,102	523,144	11.0	49.1
1989	387,291	81,731	21,148	29,638	18,660	15,184	8,492	166,056	565,143	10.9	49.5
1990	422,257	92,858	27,204	30,428	18,374	16,612	8,905	190,616	616,639	11.2	51.4
1991	453,534	113,235	29,668	32,331	19,084	18,696	9,831	213,811	676,380	11.9	52.8
1992	495,710	138,704	31,872	34,212	20,188	17,950	10,677	249,528	749,312	12.6	57.1
STATE AND LOCAL											
1982	52,481	28,367	19,195	245	121,957	778	5,154	40,738	228,178	7.4	62.6
1983	56,846	29,935	20,382	265	129,416	1,003	5,438	42,854	243,285	7.4	60.1
1984	52,378	32,206	20,383	301	139,046	1,306	5,946	44,540	251,569	7.0	58.9
1985	59,420	34,792	22,430	338	152,622	1,540	6,398	48,587	277,540	7.1	59.0
1986	63,816	37,464	24,408	373	163,495	1,872	6,728	53,884	298,158	7.3	58.2
1987	69,941	41,462	25,400	410	188,486	2,129	6,773	60,566	344,601	7.5	59.6
1988	73,783	46,237	29,859	409	202,416	2,550	7,368	70,511	362,622	7.5	60.1
1989	80,765	47,352	32,468	466	220,111	2,943	8,117	75,224	392,222	7.6	68.0
1990	91,565	53,953	36,263	488	240,011	2,856	9,012	85,775	434,148	7.9	68.0
1991	107,641	68,104	38,504	526	258,063	2,826	9,949	102,715	485,613	8.6	70.4
1992	121,266	69,241	39,163	555	272,011	2,668	10,855	104,559	515,758	8.7	70.6
TOTAL											
1982	303,033	80,852	33,793	24,708	133,874	7,954	11,654	131,514	595,869	19.2	55.7
1983	331,058	85,830	35,976	25,826	141,813	9,090	12,484	143,128	642,077	19.6	54.5
1984	341,120	90,685	37,006	26,275	152,056	11,532	13,295	148,467	671,969	18.3	52.8
1985	372,529	96,777	41,060	27,042	166,418	12,627	13,946	167,542	730,399	18.4	51.2
1986	390,404	103,079	44,334	27,445	178,518	12,036	14,705	179,614	770,522	18.5	47.9
1987	415,023	110,695	47,619	28,051	204,540	13,240	15,278	203,586	834,446	18.7	53.5
1988	432,195	120,375	52,540	29,254	219,368	16,556	15,480	219,613	885,766	18.5	52.8
1989	468,056	129,083	56,616	30,104	238,771	18,127	16,609	241,280	957,365	18.5	55.2
1990	513,823	146,811	63,467	30,916	258,385	19,468	17,918	276,391	1,050,788	19.2	56.7
1991	561,175	181,339	68,172	32,857	277,147	21,523	19,780	316,526	1,161,993	20.5	58.6
1992	616,975	207,945	71,035	34,767	292,198	20,617	21,532	354,058	1,265,070	21.3	61.6
PERCENT OF TOTAL, BY TYPE											
1985	51.0	13.2	5.6	3.7	22.8	1.7	1.9	22.9	100.0	(3)	(3)
1986	50.7	13.4	5.8	3.6	23.2	1.6	1.9	23.3	100.0	(3)	(3)
1987	49.7	13.3	5.7	3.4	24.5	1.6	1.8	24.4	100.0	(3)	(3)
1988	48.8	13.6	5.9	3.3	24.8	1.9	1.7	24.8	100.0	(3)	(3)
1989	49.0	14.0	6.0	3.0	25.0	2.0	1.0	25.0	100.0	(3)	(3)
1990	49.0	14.0	6.0	3.0	25.0	2.0	1.0	26.0	100.0	(3)	(3)
1991	48.0	16.0	6.0	3.0	24.0	2.0	1.0	27.0	100.0	(3)	(3)
1992	48.8	16.4	5.6	2.7	23.1	1.6	1.7	28.0	100.0	(3)	(3)
FEDERAL PERCENT OF TOTAL											
1985	84.0	64.0	45.4	98.8	8.3	87.8	54.1	71.0	62.0	(3)	(3)
1986	83.6	63.7	44.9	98.6	8.4	84.4	54.2	70.0	61.3	(3)	(3)
1987	83.1	62.5	46.7	98.5	7.8	83.9	55.7	70.3	59.9	(3)	(3)
1988	82.9	61.6	43.2	98.6	7.7	84.6	52.4	67.9	59.1	(3)	(3)
1989	83.0	63.0	43.0	98.0	8.0	84.0	51.0	69.0	59.0	(3)	(3)
1990	82.0	63.0	43.0	98.0	7.0	85.0	50.0	69.0	59.0	(3)	(3)
1991	81.0	62.0	44.0	98.0	7.0	87.0	50.0	68.0	58.0	(3)	(3)
1992	80.3	66.7	44.9	98.4	6.9	87.1	49.6	70.5	59.2	(3)	(3)

1. Excludes program parts of social insurance, public aid, veterans, and other social welfare. 2. Combines health and medical programs with medical services provided in connection with social insurance, public aid, veterans, and other social welfare programs. 3. Not applicable. NOTE: Figures are latest available. *Source:* Department of Health and Human Services, Social Security Administration.

Distribution of Federal Funds by State and Territory: FY 1995

(thousands of dollars)

State/Territory	Total	Grants to state and local governments	Salaries and wages	Direct payments to individuals	Procurement	Other programs
Alabama	22,796,055	3,704,320	2,960,077	12,803,782	3,059,430	268,446
Alaska	4,230,203	1,192,264	1,286,672	1,027,925	708,461	14,881
Arizona	20,906,317	3,544,322	2,412,841	11,696,779	3,097,967	154,407
Arkansas	11,768,073	2,117,653	1,005,271	7,740,431	420,563	484,155
California	153,835,179	29,805,680	18,375,680	77,196,657	26,537,278	1,919,884
Colorado	19,192,628	2,616,060	3,390,008	8,582,434	4,160,224	443,901
Connecticut	17,505,997	3,293,687	1,412,601	9,459,994	3,158,931	180,785
Delaware	3,310,073	639,083	482,639	1,968,236	189,849	30,267
District of Columbia	21,912,504	3,045,993	11,393,771	2,685,702	4,092,937	694,101
Florida	75,005,214	9,062,784	7,206,268	49,336,808	8,697,586	701,767
Georgia	33,414,551	5,897,573	5,800,507	16,991,041	4,314,721	410,709
Hawaii	7,449,969	1,083,473	2,310,213	3,221,662	777,265	57,356
Idaho	5,300,836	858,219	604,434	2,711,950	975,795	150,439
Illinois	50,889,161	9,489,548	5,436,234	31,792,813	3,255,409	915,157
Indiana	23,027,798	3,650,682	2,031,158	14,688,716	1,678,352	978,890
Iowa	13,007,865	2,182,869	929,021	7,869,110	809,231	1,767,262
Kansas	12,471,283	1,748,962	1,740,703	7,135,984	1,204,032	641,602
Kentucky	19,535,767	3,422,281	2,379,837	11,030,890	2,329,726	373,033
Louisiana	22,526,319	5,509,687	2,058,603	11,920,612	2,098,108	939,309
Maine	6,650,158	1,413,533	728,341	3,635,804	807,509	64,971
Maryland	37,090,137	4,484,748	7,191,838	14,058,915	9,108,881	2,245,755
Massachusetts	35,823,062	7,605,866	2,952,993	18,689,717	6,193,046	381,440
Michigan	39,568,460	8,126,869	2,867,464	26,150,405	2,014,285	409,436
Minnesota	19,015,559	4,062,321	1,648,683	10,798,172	1,594,573	911,809
Mississippi	14,251,493	2,766,449	1,553,668	7,769,581	1,935,998	225,797
Missouri	31,541,693	4,402,873	3,166,805	15,550,999	7,239,749	1,231,267
Montana	4,828,909	996,472	627,871	2,373,212	335,560	495,794
Nebraska	7,461,384	1,212,334	968,780	4,191,048	517,300	571,920
Nevada	6,665,118	1,007,095	816,246	3,878,828	917,315	45,633
New Hampshire	4,890,469	942,514	453,587	2,770,425	667,530	56,413
New Jersey	37,921,187	6,794,346	3,549,227	23,053,282	4,263,074	261,259
New Mexico	11,825,830	2,043,426	1,621,827	4,318,739	3,689,872	151,966
New York	94,664,977	25,261,028	7,159,627	55,250,502	6,083,109	910,711
North Carolina	30,694,683	5,896,622	4,532,473	18,028,693	2,009,164	227,731
North Dakota	3,778,877	817,077	598,991	1,681,300	231,318	450,190
Ohio	50,516,356	9,101,028	4,615,392	31,819,538	4,475,318	505,080
Oklahoma	16,132,320	2,516,383	2,613,914	9,448,933	1,151,774	401,316
Oregon	13,641,396	2,807,519	1,405,429	8,600,975	629,542	197,930
Pennsylvania	64,609,866	11,220,501	5,921,858	41,313,591	5,360,408	793,507
Rhode Island	5,788,697	1,285,002	637,874	3,348,081	464,034	53,705
South Carolina	17,839,258	3,112,701	2,289,129	9,511,895	2,779,417	146,115
South Dakota	3,865,063	859,025	539,428	1,937,745	261,835	267,030
Tennessee	26,610,888	4,638,329	2,691,464	14,571,539	4,471,481	238,076
Texas	83,865,061	14,483,849	10,593,647	43,331,628	13,769,174	1,686,762
Utah	8,582,760	1,502,148	1,518,500	3,764,353	1,625,394	172,365
Vermont	2,663,766	642,751	274,922	1,466,285	259,499	20,308
Virginia	51,490,236	3,923,265	12,016,238	17,960,698	16,598,065	991,969
Washington	28,834,151	4,695,737	4,395,797	14,511,345	4,760,423	470,848
West Virginia	10,208,450	2,337,838	797,004	6,311,822	707,507	54,478
Wisconsin	19,839,346	3,921,366	1,376,889	12,988,400	1,109,696	442,994
Wyoming	2,491,914	755,760	380,754	1,142,513	164,348	48,540
American Samoa	106,006	62,135	2,741	23,456	17,626	48
Guam	809,748	133,176	370,473	167,352	124,753	13,993
Northern Mariana Islands	62,410	54,521	1,787	4,506	1,567	28
Puerto Rico	10,002,829	3,453,740	704,025	5,400,221	365,553	79,289
Virgin Islands	471,843	237,044	45,463	154,232	33,616	1,488
Undistributed	25,380,874	155,413	1,302,924	18,537	23,904,000	—
Total U.S.	**1,368,571,026**	**242,597,944**	**168,150,611**	**729,808,793**	**202,209,184**	**26,354,312**

Source: Consolidated Federal Funds Report, Fiscal Year 1995 (6/14/96).

Domestic Freight Traffic by Major Carriers
(in millions of ton-miles)[1]

Year	Railroads Ton-miles	Railroads % of total	Inland waterways[2] Ton-miles	Inland waterways[2] % of total	Trucks Ton-miles	Trucks % of total	Oil pipelines Ton-miles	Oil pipelines % of total	Air carriers Ton-miles	Air carriers % of total
1940	379,201	61.3	118,057	19.1	62,043	10.0	59,277	9.6	14	—
1945	690,809	67.3	142,737	13.9	66,948	6.5	126,530	12.3	91	—
1950	596,940	56.2	163,344	15.4	172,860	16.3	129,175	12.1	318	—
1955	631,385	49.5	216,508	17.0	223,254	17.5	203,244	16.0	481	—
1960	579,130	44.1	220,253	16.8	285,483	21.7	228,626	17.4	778	—
1965	708,700	43.3	262,421	16.0	359,218	21.9	306,393	18.7	1,910	0.1
1970	771,168	39.8	318,560	16.4	412,000	21.3	431,000	22.3	3,274	0.2
1975	759,000	36.7	342,210	16.5	454,000	22.0	507,300	24.6	3,732	0.2
1980	932,000	37.2	420,000	16.9	567,000	22.6	588,000	23.1	4,528	0.2
1985	895,000	36.4	382,000	15.6	610,000	24.9	564,000	22.9	6,080	0.2
1988	1,028,000	37.0	438,000	15.8	700,000	25.2	601,000	21.6	9,330	0.3
1989	1,048,000	37.3	449,000	16.0	716,000	25.5	584,000	20.8	10,210	0.4
1990	1,071,000	37.4	460,000	16.1	735,000	25.7	584,000	20.4	10,420	0.4
1991	1,077,000	37.6	443,000	15.5	758,000	26.4	579,000	20.2	9,980	0.3
1992	1,107,000	37.4	454,000	15.3	815,000	27.5	573,000	19.4	10,990	0.4
1993	1,146,000	37.8	457,448	14.9	879,836	28.7	574,719	18.7	11,540	0.4
1994[3]	1,275,000	38.9	442,000	13.5	908,000	27.7	608,000	18.6	12,700	0.39

1. Mail and express included, except railroads for 1970. 2. Rivers, canals, and domestic traffic on Great Lakes. 3. Preliminary. *Source:* ENO Foundation for Transportation NOTE: Data are latest available.

Tonnage Handled by Principal U.S. Ports
Top 50 Ports in Total Tons

Port	1994	Port	1994
Port of South Louisiana	184,855,712	Huntington, W. Va.	25,629,485
Houston, Tex.	143,662,625	Paulsboro, N.J.	24,667,782
New York, N.Y. & N.J.	126,100,614	Richmond, Calif.	24,093,993
Baton Rouge, La.	86,245,856	Seattle, Wash.	22,335,514
Valdez, Alaska	85,095,176	Beaumont, Tex.	21,200,684
Corpus Christi, Tex.	78,138,462	Jacksonville, Fla.	18,910,150
New Orleans, La.	73,332,939	Boston, Mass.	18,869,586
Port of Plaquemine, La.	64,758,624	Detroit, Mich.	18,718,014
Long Beach, Calif.	56,522,167	Port Everglades, Fla.	18,135,257
Tampa, Fla.	51,902,190	Tacoma, Wash.	17,615,819
Pittsburgh, Pa.	49,056,218	Freeport, Tex.	17,450,109
Lake Charles, La.	48,331,266	San Juan, P.R.	16,299,654
Norfolk Harbor, Va.	45,773,648	Indiana Harbor, Ind.	16,144,862
Port Arthur, Tex.	45,585,136	Savannah, Ga.	15,904,910
Mobile, Ala.	44,996,849	Memphis, Tenn.	15,679,999
Texas City, Tex.	44,350,803	Newport News, Va.	15,671,052
Los Angeles, Calif.	43,139,632	Cleveland, Ohio	15,284,407
Duluth-Superior, Minn./Wis.	41,819,417	Lorain, Ohio	14,748,165
Baltimore, Md.	41,450,422	New Castle, Del.	14,738,190
Philadelphia, Pa.	40,745,690	Portland, Maine	14,245,338
Marcus Hook, Pa.	30,420,459	Toledo, Ohio	13,203,884
Portland, Ore.	30,164,479	Cincinnati, Ohio	13,192,767
Pascagoula, Miss.	30,048,859	Anacortes, Wash.	12,950,108
Chicago, Ill.	29,421,566	Oakland, Calif.	12,914,088
St. Louis, Mo./Ill.	29,418,967	Honolulu, Hawaii	11,672,245

Source: Department of the Army, Corps of Engineers.

Annual Railroad Carloadings[1]

Year	Total	Year	Total	Year	Total	Year	Total
1940	36,358,000	1965	28,344,381	1985	19,501,242	1991	20,868,297
1945	41,918,000	1970	27,015,020	1986	19,588,666	1992	21,205,530
1950	38,903,000	1975	22,929,843	1988	21,599,993	1993	21,682,874
1955	32,761,707	1980	22,223,000	1989	21,226,015	1994	23,178,599
1960	27,886,950	1984	20,945,536	1990	21,401,246	1995[2]	23,726,015

1. Only Class 1 railroads after 1950. 2. Estimated. *Source:* Association of American Railroads.

Estimated Motor Vehicle Registration, 1995

(in thousands; excludes military vehicles)

State	Autos[1]	Trucks and buses[2]	Motor-cycles	Total	State	Autos[1]	Trucks and buses[2]	Motor-cycles	Total
Alabama	1,941	1,178	41	3,160	Montana	511	447	20	978
Alaska	307	249	13	569	Nebraska	858	613	21	1,492
Arizona	1,841	918	68	2,827	Nevada	551	463	20	1,034
Arkansas'	791	827	13	1,631	New Hampshire	639	359	33	1,031
California	14,629	7,750	537	22,916	New Jersey	4,620	1,261	86	5,967
Colorado	1,637	1,043	96	2,776	New Mexico	748	705	33	1,486
Connecticut	2,035	548	48	2,631	New York	7,886	2,310	175	10,371
Delaware	413	179	9	601	North Carolina	3,470	1,957	64	5,491
Dist. of Col.	206	36	1	243	North Dakota	370	321	17	708
Florida	7,770	2,787	177	10,734	Ohio	7,268	2,540	224	10,032
Georgia	4,293	1,887	57	6,237	Oklahoma	1,546	1,271	54	2,871
Hawaii	513	274	12	799	Oregon	1,583	1,300	60	2,943
Idaho	552	495	33	1,080	Pennsylvania	6,104	2,519	169	8,792
Illinois	6,302	2,622	188	9,112	Rhode Island	552	151	16	719
Indiana	3,291	1,738	97	5,126	South Carolina	1,788	950	35	2,773
Iowa	1,838	990	115	2,943	South Dakota	468	295	26	789
Kansas	1,112	1,030	45	2,187	Tennessee	3,802	1,308	58	5,168
Kentucky	1,727	948	34	2,709	Texas	8,722	5,058	131	13,911
Louisiana	1,972	1,504	36	3,512	Utah	821	634	22	1,477
Maine	605	328	28	961	Vermont	314	179	16	509
Maryland	2,714	912	38	3,664	Virginia	3,996	1,606	58	5,660
Massachusetts	3,123	971	66	4,160	Washington	2,991	1,622	97	4,710
Michigan	5,323	2,341	113	7,777	West Virginia	882	612	17	1,511
Minnesota	2,702	1,415	130	4,247	Wisconsin	2,454	1,516	151	4,121
Mississippi	1,362	738	29	2,129	Wyoming	263	233	16	512
Missouri	2,775	1,527	57	4,359	**Total**	**134,981**	**65,465**	**3,700**	**204,146**

1. Preliminary estimates for 1995; NOTE: Data are latest available. 2. Personal passenger vans, passenger minivans, and utility-type vehicles are no longer included in the automobiles in this table; trucks include pickups, panels, and delivery vans. *Source:* Federal Highway Administration.

Passenger Car Production by Make

Companies and models	1995	1990	1985	1980	1975	1970
American Motors Corporation	—	—	109,919	164,725	323,704	276,127
Chrysler Corporation						
Plymouth	129,571	212,354	369,487	293,342	443,550	699,031
Dodge	331,253	361,769	482,388	263,169	354,482	405,699
Chrysler	121,022	136,339	414,193	82,463	102,940	158,614
Imperial	—	16,280	—	—	1,930	10,111
Total	**576,846**	**726,742**	**1,266,068**	**638,974**	**902,902**	**1,273,455**
Ford Motor Company						
Ford	1,012,818	933,466	1,098,627	929,627	1,301,414	1,647,918
Mercury	225,308	221,436	374,446	324,528	405,104	310,463
Lincoln	157,584	222,449	163,077	52,793	101,520	58,771
Total	**1,395,710**	**1,377,351**	**1,636,150**	**1,306,948**	**1,808,038**	**2,017,152**
General Motors Corporation						
Chevrolet	665,955	1,025,379	1,691,254	1,737,336	1,687,091	1,504,614
Pontiac	574,455	649,255	702,617	556,429	523,469	422,212
Oldsmobile	391,216	418,742	1,168,982	783,225	654,342	439,632
Buick	393,879	405,123	1,001,461	783,575	535,820	459,931
Cadillac	186,113	252,540	322,765	203,991	278,404	152,859
Saturn	301,540	4,245	—	—	—	—
Toyota/Cavalier	1,978	—	—	—	—	—
Total	**2,515,136**	**2,755,284**	**4,887,079**	**4,064,556**	**3,679,126**	**2,979,248**
Volkswagen of America	—	—	96,458	197,106	—	—
Honda	552,995	435,437	238,159	145,337	—	—
Mazda	148,932	184,428	—	—	—	—
Nissan	333,234	95,844	—	—	—	—
Toyota	516,878	321,523	43,810	—	—	—
Diamond Star	218,161	148,379	—	—	—	—
Subaru Legacy	80,669	32,461	—	—	—	—
Industry total	**6,350,433**	**6,077,449**	**8,184,821**	**6,375,506**	**6,716,951**	**6,550,128**

Source: American Automobile Manufacturers Association.

Motor Vehicle Data

	1994	1990	1980	1970	1960
U.S. passenger cars and taxis registered (thousands)	138,930	143,550	121,724	89,280	61,671
Total mileage of U.S. passenger cars (millions)	1,585,618	1,513,184	1,111,596	916,700	588,083
Total fuel consumption of U.S. passenger cars (millions of gallons)	73,825	71,989	71,883	67,820	41,169
World registration of cars, trucks, and buses (thousands)	629,077	582,982	411,113	246,368	126,955
U.S. registration of cars, trucks, and buses (thousands)	198,045	188,655	155,796	108,418	73,858
U.S. share of world registration of cars, trucks, and buses	31.5%	32.4%	37.9%	44.0%	58.2%

Source: American Automobile Manufacturers Association.

Domestic Motor Vehicles Sales

(in thousands)

Type of Vehicle	1993	1992	1991	1990	1989	1988	1985	1980
Passenger Cars								
Passenger car factory sales	5,960	5,684	5,407	6,050	6,807	7,105	8,002	6,400
Passenger car (new) retail sales[1]	8,518	8,214	8,175	9,300	9,772	10,530	11,042	8,979
Domestic[2]	6,734	6,277	6,137	6,897	7,073	7,526	8,205	6,581
Imports[3]	1,783	1,938	2,038	2,403	2,699	3,004	2,838	2,398
Trucks								
Truck and bus factory sales	4,895	4,042	3,375	3,719	4,062	4,121	3,357	1,667
Truck and bus retail sales[4]	5,318	4,513	3,842	4,261	4,483	4,608	3,984	2,232
Light duty (up to 14,000 GVWW)[5]	5,015	4,264	3,621	3,984	4,171	4,273	3,700	1,964
Med. duty (14,000–26,000 GVW)[5]	64	57	50	71	73	83	53	92
Heavy duty (over 26,000 GVW)[5]	239	192	171	207	239	251	231	176
Under 6,000 pounds	3,756	3,217	2,724	2,866	2,854	2,926	2,408	985
Utility	721	666	549	490	447	445	429	51
Van	18	21	17	31	43	47	115	79
Mini van (cargo)	70	63	66	83	97	105	103	(X)
Station wagon (truck chassis)	321	201	110	112	138	138	86	(X)
Mini passenger carrier	1,002	840	706	750	688	692	301	(X)
6,000 to 10,000 pounds[6]	1,232	1,021	876	1,097	1,297	1,333	1,280	975
Utility	60	51	37	68	93	90	108	108
Van	279	241	203	254	289	302	261	172
Pickup conventional	647	524	476	568	663	666	628	546
Station wagon (truck chassis)	60	80	55	85	100	104	95	39
10,001 pounds and over	330	275	242	298	331	349	295	271

1. Based on data from U.S. Dept. of Commerce. 2. Includes domestic models produced in Canada and Mexico. 3. Excludes domestic models produced in Canada. 4. Excludes motorcoaches and light-duty imports from foreign manufacturers. Includes imports sold by franchised dealers of U.S. manufacturers. Starting in 1987 includes sales of trucks over 10,000 lbs. GVW by foreign manufacturers. 5. Gross vehicle weight (fully loaded vehicles). 6. Includes vehicles not shown separately. *Source: Statistical Abstract of the United States 1995.* NOTE: Data are most recent available.

Domestic and Export Factory Sales of Motor Vehicles

(in thousands)

	From plants in United States								
	Passenger cars			Motor trucks and buses			Total motor vehicles		
Year	Total	Domestic	Exports	Total	Domestic	Exports	Total	Domestic	Exports
1970	6,547	6,187	360	1,692	1,566	126	8,239	7,753	486
1975	6,713	6,073	640	2,272	2,003	269	8,985	8,076	909
1980	6,400	5,840	560	1,667	1,464	203	8,067	7,304	763
1985	8,002	7,337	665	3,464	3,234	231	11,467	10,571	896
1990	6,050	5,502	548	3,725	3,455	270	9,775	8,957	818
1991	5,407	4,874	533	3,388	3,050	338	8,795	7,924	871
1992	5,685	5,165	520	4,062	3,702	360	9,747	8,847	880
1993	5,962	5,473	489	4,895	4,471	424	10,857	9,944	913
1994	6,549	5,964	585	5,640	5,139	501	12,189	11,103	1,088
1995	6,310	5,788	522	5,713	5,211	502	12,023	10,999	1,024

Source: American Automobile Manufacturers Association.

U.S. Direct Investment in EU Countries, 1995

(in millions of dollars)

Countries	All industries	Petroleum	Manufacturing	Wholesale trade	Banking	Finance, insurance, real estate	Services	Other industries
Belgium	$17,785	$325	$8,508	$2,197	(1)	$3,615	$2,829	(1)
Denmark	2,251	(1)	524	228	(1)	464	(1)	20
France	32,645	1,161	16,555	4,407	383	6,805	2,324	1,010
Germany	43,001	2,219	23,671	3,322	2,325	8,344	955	2,165
Greece	437	(1)	140	82	(1)	51	(1)	(1)
Ireland	10,970	(1)	6,894	252	(1)	3,018	621	104
Italy	16,718	529	9,822	2,676	401	1,875	1,257	158
Luxembourg	7,661	33	(1)	(1)	224	5,699	(1)	(1)
Netherlands	37,421	1,950	10,451	4,453	139	17,976	1,040	1,411
Portugal	1,712	(1)	512	382	(1)	133	281	2
Spain	9,689	167	5,086	875	1,541	729	421	148
Sweden	12,226	(1)	10,377	423	(1)	852	488	−10
United Kingdom	119,938	14,035	27,865	6,630	5,192	55,206	5,764	5,245
Total	**312,454**	**20,419**	**121,125**	**25,927**	**10,205**	**104,767**	**15,980**	**10,253**

1. Suppressed to avoid disclosure of data of individual companies. *Source: Survey of Current Business,* July 1996.

Balance of International Payments

(in billions of dollars)

Item	1995	1994	1990	1985	1980	1975	1970	1965	1960
Exports of goods, services, and income	$965.0	$838.8	$652.9	$366.0	$343.2	$157.9	$68.4	$42.7	$30.5
Merchandise, adjusted, excluding military	574.9	502.5	389.5	214.4	224.0	107.1	42.5	26.5	19.7
Transfers under U.S. military agency sales contracts	12.7	12.4	9.8	9.0	8.2	3.9	1.5	0.8	0.3
Receipts of income on U.S. investments abroad	181.3	137.6	130.0	90.0	75.9	25.4	11.8	7.4	4.6
Other services	196.2	186.3	123.3	45.0	36.5	19.3	9.9	6.4	4.3
Imports of goods and services	−1,087.8	−954.3	−722.7	−461.2	−333.9	−132.6	−60.0	−32.8	−23.7
Merchandise, adjusted, excluding military	−749.3	−668.6	−497.6	−339.0	−249.3	−98.0	−39.9	−21.5	−14.8
Direct defense expenditures	−9.9	−10.3	−17.1	−12.0	−10.7	−4.8	4.9	−3.0	−3.1
Payments of income on foreign assets in U.S.	−192.7	−147.0	−118.1	−65.0	−43.2	−12.6	−5.5	−2.1	−1.2
Other services	−135.9	−129.0	−89.8	−46.0	−30.7	−17.2	−9.8	−6.2	−4.6
Unilateral transfers, excluding military grants, net	−30.1	−36.0	−22.3	−15.0	−7.0	−4.6	−3.3	−2.9	−2.3
U.S. Government assets abroad, net	−0.3	−0.3	2.9	−2.8	−5.2	−3.5	−1.6	−1.6	−1.1
U.S. private assets abroad, net	−270.0	−131.0	−58.5	−26.0	−71.5	−35.4	−10.2	−5.3	−5.1
U.S. assets abroad, net	−280.0	−126.0	−57.7	−27.7	−86.1	−39.7	−9.3	−5.7	−4.1
Foreign assets in U.S., net	426.3	291.3	86.3	127.1	50.3	15.6	6.4	0.7	2.3
Statistical discrepancy	6.7	−14.2	63.5	23.0	29.6	5.5	−0.2	−0.5	−1.0
Balance on goods, services, and income	−122.8	−115.4	−69.7	−106.8	9.5	25.2	8.5	10.0	6.9
Balance on current account	−152.9	−151.2	−92.1	−118.0	3.7	18.4	2.4	5.4	2.8

NOTE: — denotes debits. *Source:* Department of Commerce, Bureau of Economic Analysis.

Foreign Investors in U.S. Business Enterprises

	Number				Investment outlays (millions of dollars)			
	1995[1]	1994	1993	1991	1995[1]	1994	1993	1991
Investments, total	1,133	1,036	980	1,091	$54,368	$45,626	$26,229	$25,538
Acquisitions	650	605	554	561	46,452	38,753	21,761	17,806
Establishments	483	431	426	530	7,917	6,873	4,468	7,732
Investors, total	1,231	1,144	1,094	1,220	54,368	45,626	28,229	25,538
Foreign direct investors	347	345	368	438	11,313	13,628	6,720	8,885
U.S. affilates	884	799	726	782	43,055	31,999	19,509	16,653

1. Figures are preliminary. *Source:* U.S. Department of Commerce, *Survey of Current Business,* July 1996.

Imports of Leading Commodities
(value in millions of dollars)

Commodity	1995	1994
Food and agricultural commodities	**$25,266**	**$23,766**
Animal feeds	473	433
Cocoa	723	698
Coffee	2,985	2,270
Corn	66	85
Cotton, raw	29	21
Dairy products, eggs	620	583
Fish and preparations	6,741	6,590
Furskins, undressed	59	78
Hides and skins, undressed	140	126
Live animals	1,727	1,392
Meat and preparations	2,316	2,627
Oils and fats, animal	24	21
Oils and fats, vegetable	1,157	1,051
Rice	121	130
Soybeans	32	46
Sugar	679	552
Tobacco, unmanufactured	555	697
Vegetables and fruits	6,581	6,075
Wheat	238	291
Machinery and transport equipment	**214,950**	**193,333**
ADP equip.; office machinery	62,824	52,058
Airplanes	3,552	3,719
Airplane parts	2,615	2,727
Cars and trucks	75,196	69,532
Parts	20,070	19,609
Spacecraft	169	219
General industrial machinery	24,113	21,330
Metalworking machinery	5,925	4,596
Power generating machinery	20,486	19,543
Manufactured goods	**181,608**	**163,965**
Artwork and antiques	2,671	2,432
Chemicals—fertilizers	1,392	1,298
Chemicals—medicinal	5,544	4,674
Chemicals-organic and inorganic	17,980	14,892
Clothing and footwear	51,632	48,460
Gem diamonds	5,971	5,756
Glass	1,467	1,350
Iron and steel mill products	12,296	12,896
Metal manufactures	10,009	8,847
Paper and paperboard	12,472	9,066
Photographic equipment	5,146	4,676
Plastic articles	5,103	4,517
Pottery	1,666	1,555
Printed matter	2,588	2,234
Rubber articles	1,417	1,253
Scientific instruments	11,572	9,963
Textile yarns, fabric	9,985	9,207
Tires and tubes, automotive	3,144	3,034
Toys, games, sporting goods	13,081	11,824
Watches, clocks, and parts	2,785	2,641
Wood manufactures	3,687	3,390
Mineral fuels and related products	**55,895**	**53,332**
Coal	703	646
Natural gas	3,275	3,937
Petroleum and petroleum products	51,917	48,749
Crude materials excluding agricultural products	**13,980**	**12,257**
Cork, wood, and lumber	6,153	6,680
Pulp and waste paper	3,827	2,315
Metal ores, scrap	4,000	3,262
Tobacco excluding agricultural, beverages	**1,906**	**1,896**
Cigarettes	64	70
Distilled alcoholic beverages	1,842	1,826
All others	**249,825**	**214,707**
Total	**743,430**	**663,256**

Exports of Leading Commodities
(value in millions of dollars)

Commodity	1995	1994
Food and agricultural commodities	**$50,117**	**$40,349**
Animal feeds	3,674	3,353
Cocoa	39	34
Coffee	15	53
Corn	7,533	4,197
Cotton, raw	3,714	2,641
Dairy products, eggs	776	717
Fish and preparations	3,177	3,036
Furskins, undressed	127	131
Hides and skins, undressed	1,620	1,391
Live animals	519	587
Meat and preparations	6,456	5,195
Oils and fats, animal	790	566
Oils and fats, vegetable	1,294	963
Rice	996	1,009
Soybeans	5,425	4,355
Sugar	5	5
Tobacco, unmanufactured	1,400	1,304
Vegetables and fruits	7,100	6,757
Wheat	5,457	4,055
Machinery and transport equipment	**154,202**	**147,512**
ADP equip.; office machinery	36,405	30,867
Airplanes	13,599	18,803
Airplane parts	10,364	9,824
Cars and trucks	19,629	20,204
Parts	22,839	21,314
Spacecraft	656	444
General industrial machinery	24,322	21,813
Metalworking machinery	4,627	3,897
Power generating machinery	21,761	20,346
Manufactured goods	**108,802**	**93,561**
Artwork and antiques	1,071	1,184
Chemicals—fertilizers	3,222	2,703
Chemicals—medicinal	6,433	6,096
Chemicals-organic and inorganic	20,624	16,856
Clothing and footwear	7,152	6,107
Gem diamonds	171	184
Glass	1,632	1,503
Iron and steel milll products	5,337	3,554
Metal manufactures	8,034	7,034
Paper and paperboard	9,575	7,448
Photographic equipment	3,349	3,016
Plastic articles	3,845	3,574
Pottery	99	104
Printed matter	4,323	3,971
Rubber articles	887	795
Scientific instruments and parts	18,570	16,475
Textile yarns, fabric	7,183	6,445
Tires and tubes, automotive	1,857	1,614
Toys, games and sporting goods	3,558	3,079
Watches, clocks, and parts	247	276
Wood manufactures	1,633	1,543
Mineral fuels and related products	**7,225**	**6,436**
Coal	3,713	2,966
Natural gas	266	254
Petroleum and petroleum products	3,246	3,216
Crude materials excluding agricultural products	**17,389**	**13,079**
Cork, wood, lumber	5,625	5,572
Pulp and waste paper	6,208	3,794
Metal ores, scrap	5,556	3,713
Tobacco excluding agricultural, beverages	**5,160**	**5,320**
Cigarettes	4,770	4,965
Distilled alcoholic beverages	390	355
All other	**240,970**	**206,369**
Total	**583,865**	**512,626**

Source: Department of Commerce, Bureau of the Census, Foreign Trade Division.

Information Please Almanac is not responsible and assumes no responsibility for any action undertaken by anyone utilizing the first aid procedures which follow.

The Heimlich Maneuver[1]

Food-Choking

What to look for: Victim cannot speak or breathe; turns blue; collapses.

To perform the Heimlich Maneuver when the victim is standing or sitting:
1. Stand behind the victim and wrap your arms around the victim's waist.
2. Place the thumb side of your fist against the victim's abdomen, slightly above the navel and below the rib cage.
3. Grasp your fist with the other hand and press your fist into the victim's abdomen with a quick upward thrust. Repeat as often as necessary.
4. If the victim is sitting, stand behind the victim's chair and perform the maneuver in the same manner.
5. After the food is dislodged, have the victim seen by a doctor.

When the victim has collapsed and cannot be lifted:
1. Lay the victim on his/her back.
2. Face the victim and kneel astride his/her hips.
3. With one hand on top of the other, place the heel of your bottom hand on the abdomen slightly above the navel and below the rib cage.
4. Press into the victim's abdomen with a quick upward thrust. Repeat as often as necessary
5. Should the victim vomit, quickly place the victim on one side and wipe out his/her mouth to prevent aspiration (drawing of vomit into the throat).
6. After the food is dislodged, have the victim seen by a doctor.

NOTE: If you start to choke when alone and help is not available, an attempt should be made to self-administer this maneuver.

Burns[2]

First Degree: Signs/Symptoms—reddened skin. **Treatment**—Immerse quickly in cold water or apply ice until pain stops.

Second Degree: Signs/Symptoms—reddened skin, blisters. **Treatment**—(1) Cut away loose clothing. (2) Cover with several layers of cold moist dressings or, if limb is involved, immerse in cold water for relief of pain. (3) Treat for shock.

Third Degree: Signs/Symtoms—skin destroyed, tissues damaged, charring. **Treatment**—(1) Cut away loose clothing (do not remove clothing adhered to skin). (2) Cover with several layers of sterile, cold, moist dressings for relief of pain and to stop burning action. (3) Treat for shock.

Poisons[2]

Treatment—(1) Dilute by drinking large quantities of water. (2) Induce vomiting except when poison is corrosive or a petroleum product. (3) Call the poison control center or a doctor.

Shock[2]

Shock may accompany any serious injury: blood loss, breathing impairment, heart failure, burns. Shock can kill—treat as soon as possible and continue until medical aid is available.

Signs/Symptoms—(1) Shallow breathing. (2) Rapid and weak pulse. (3) Nausea, collapse, vomiting. (4) Shivering. (5) Pale, moist skin. (6) Mental confusion. (7) Drooping eyelids, dilated pupils.

The Heimlich Maneuver

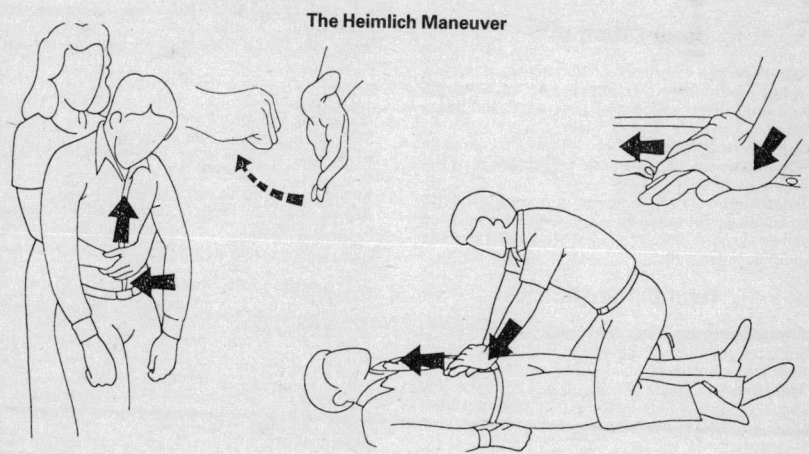

Courtesy of New York City Department of Health

Treatment—(1) Establish and maintain an open airway. (2) Control bleeding. (3) Keep victim lying down. Exception: Head and chest injuries, heart attack, stroke, sun stroke. If no spine injury, victim may be more comfortable and breathe better in a semi-reclining position. If in doubt, keep the victim flat. Elevate the feet unless injury would be aggravated. Maintain normal body temperature. Place blankets under and over victim.

Nosebleed[2]

Nosebleeds are more often annoying than life threatening. They are more common during cold weather, when heated air dries out nasal passages.
Treatment—(1) Keep the victim quietly seated, leaning forward if possible. (2) Gently pinch the nostrils closed. (3) Apply cold compresses to the victim's nose and face. (4) If the person is conscious, it may be helpful to apply pressure beneath the nostril above the lip. (5) Instruct victim not to blow his/her nose for several hours after the bleeding has stopped, or clots could be dislodged and start the bleeding again.

Frostbite[2]

Most frequently frostbitten: toes, fingers, nose, and ears. It is caused by exposure to cold.
Signs/Symptoms—(1) Skin becomes pale or a grayish-yellow color. (2) Parts feel cold and numb. (3) Frozen parts feel doughy.
Treatment—(1) Until victim can be brought inside, the victim should be wrapped in woolen cloth and kept dry. (2) Do not rub, chafe, or manipulate frostbitten parts. (3) Bring victim indoors. (4) Place in warm water (102° to 105°) and make sure it remains warm. Test water by pouring on inner surface of your forearm. Never thaw if the victim has to go back out into the cold, which may cause the affected area to be refrozen. (5) Do not use hot water bottles or a heat lamp, and do not place victim near a hot stove. (6) Do not allow victim to walk if feet are affected. (7) Once thawed, have victim gently exercise parts. (8) For serious frostbite, seek medical aid for thawing because pain will be intense and tissue damage extensive.

Heat Cramps[2]

Affects people who work or do strenuous exercises in a hot environment. To prevent it, such people should drink large amounts of cool water and add a pinch of salt to each glass of water
Signs/Symptoms—(1) Painful muscle cramps in legs and abdomen. (2) Faintness. (3) Profuse perspiration.
Treatment—(1) Move victim to a cool place. (2) Give victim sips of salted drinking water (one teaspoon of salt to one quart of water). (3) Apply manual pressure to the cramped muscle.

Heat Exhaustion[2]

Signs/Symptoms—(1) Pale and clammy skin. (2) Profuse perspiration. (3) Rapid and shallow breathing. (4) Weakness, dizziness, and headache.
Treatment—(1) Care for victim as if he or she were in shock. (2) Remove victim to a cool area, do not allow chilling. (3) If body gets too cold, cover victim.

Heat Stroke[2]

Signs/Symptoms—(1) Face is red and flushed. (2) Victim becomes rapidly unconscious. (3) Skin is hot and dry with no perspiration.

Treatment—(1) Lay victim down with head and shoulders raised. (2) Reduce the high body temperature as quickly as possible. (3) Apply cold applications to the body and head. (4) Use ice and fan if available. (5) Watch for signs of shock and treat accordingly. (6) Get medical aid as soon as possible.

Artificial Respiration[3]

(Mouth-to-Mouth Breathing—In Cases Like Drowning, Electric Shock, or Smoke Inhalation.)
There is need for help in breathing when breathing movements stop or lips, tongue, and fingernails become blue. When in doubt, apply artificial respiration until you get medical help. No harm can result from its use and delay may cost the victim his life. Start immediately. Seconds count. Clear mouth and throat of any obstructions with your fingers.
For Adults: Place victim on back with face up.
Lift the chin and tilt the head back. If air passage is still closed, pull chin up by placing fingers behind the angles of the lower jaw and pushing forward.
Take deep breath, place your mouth over victim's mouth, making leak-proof seal.
Pinch victim's nostrils closed.
Blow into victim's mouth until you see the chest rise.
—OR—
Take deep breath, place your mouth over victim's nose, making leak-proof seal.
Seal victim's mouth with your hand.
Blow into victim's nose until you see the chest rise.
Remove your mouth and let victim exhale.
Repeat about 12 times a minute. (If the victim's stomach rises markedly, exert moderate hand pressure on the stomach just below the rib cage to keep it from inflating.)
For Infants and Small Children: Place your mouth over victim's mouth and nose. Blow into mouth and nose until you see victim's chest rise normally.
Repeat 20 to 30 times per minute. (Don't exaggerate the tilted position of an infant's head.)
NOTE: For emergency treatment of heart attack, cardiopulmonary resuscitation (CPR) is recommended. Instruction in CPR can be obtained through local health organizations or schools.

Sources: 1. New York City Department of Health. NOTE: Heimlich Maneuver, T.M. Pending. 2. *First Aid*, Mining Enforcement and Safety Administration, U.S. Department of the Interior. 3. *Health Emergency Chart*, Council on Family Health.

NUTRITION & HEALTH

The Worldwide AIDS Situation

Source: World Health Organization (WHO), July 1996

Background

Acquired immunodeficiency syndrome (AIDS) was first recognized in 1981 among homosexual men in the United States. The human immunodeficiency virus (HIV) that causes AIDS was identified in 1983. According to the World Health Organization, extensive spread of HIV appears to have begun in the late 1970s and early 1980s among men and women with multiple sexual partners in East and Central Africa and among homosexual and bisexual men in certain urban areas of the Americas, Australasia, and Western Europe.

Two major types of HIV have been recognized, HIV-1 and HIV-2. HIV-1 is the dominant type worldwide. HIV-2 is found principally in West Africa but cases have been reported from East Africa, Europe, Asia, and Latin America. There are at least 10 different genetic subtypes of HIV-1, but their biological and epidemiological significance is unclear at present. Both HIV-1 and HIV-2 are transmitted in the same ways.

Global Estimates

According to the World Health Organization, 1,393,649 cases of AIDS in adults and children had been officially reported at the end of June 1996—an increase of approximately 19% over the same period in 1995. If one takes into account under-recognition, under-reporting, and reporting delays, it is estimated that more than 7.7 million AIDS cases have occurred since the beginning of the epidemic, and around 28 million people have been infected with HIV, some 25.5 million adults and 2.4 million children. Over 3.1 million new HIV infections are expected to occur during 1996, which translates to more than 8,500 infected each day (7,500 adults and 1,000 children).

Today, 21.8 million people are believed to be living with AIDS—21 million adults and 830,000 children. Of these, an estimated 4.5 million adults and 1.3 million children have died.

The majority of newly infected adults are between 15 and 24 years old. Approximately 42% of the adults living with HIV/AIDS are women and the proportion is growing.

Mode of Transmission

Worldwide, between 75 and 85 of every 100 adult HIV infections have been transmitted through unprotected sexual intercourse. Heterosexual (male-female) intercourse accounts for more than 70% of all infected adults to date and homosexual (male-male) intercourse for a further five to ten percent.

The sharing of HIV-infected needles by drug users accounts for 5–10% of all adult infections. This proportion is growing. In many parts of the world, injected drug use is the dominant mode of transmission.

Mother-to-child (vertical) transmission accounts for more than 90% of all infections in infants and children. Around 25–35% of all infants born to HIV–infected women themselves become infected with HIV before or during birth, or through breast-feeding.

Transfusion of HIV-infected blood or blood products accounts for 3–5% of all adult infections. In many parts of the world, HIV transmission through the transfusion of infected blood has been reduced by the use of voluntary blood donors, the routine screening of donated blood for HIV, and through a more rational use of blood aimed at reducing the number of transfusions.

Studies to date, primarily from industrialized countries, indicate that around 60% of adults will progress to AIDS within 12–13 years of becoming infected. Few data are available beyond 12 years but it is expected that the majority of HIV-infected people will probably develop AIDS.

Survival after the onset of AIDS has been increasing in industrialized countries from an average of less than a year to about three years at present. Survival time with AIDS in developing countries remains short and is estimated to be less than one year.

The majority of AIDS cases occur before age 35, and over 90% of all AIDS deaths occur in people under the age of 30. More than 90% of all adults with HIV infections or AIDS live in developing countries. □

Understanding AIDS

Acquired Immune Deficiency Syndrome, or AIDS, was first reported in the United States in mid-1981. The cumulative number of AIDS cases in the United States as of Dec. 31, 1995, that were reported to the Center for Disease Control and Prevention was 513,486. Adult and adolescent AIDS cases totaled 506,537 with 434,719 cases in males and 71,818 cases in females. There were 6,948 cases reported in children under age 13 at the time of diagnosis. Total AIDS deaths reported are 319,849, including 315,928 adults and adolescents, and 3,921 children.

AIDS is characterized by a defect in natural immunity against disease. People who have AIDS are vulnerable to serious illnesses which would not be a threat to anyone whose immune system was functioning normally. These illnesses are referred to as "opportunistic" infections or diseases: in AIDS patients the most common of these are Pneumocystis carinii pneumonia (PCP), a parasitic infection of the lungs; and a type of cancer known as Kaposi's sarcoma (KS). Other opportunistic infections include unusually severe infections with yeast, cytomegalovirus, herpes virus, and parasites such as Toxoplasma or Cryptosporidia. Milder infections with these organisms do not suggest immune deficiency.

AIDS is caused by a virus usually known as human immunodeficiency virus, or HIV. Symptoms of full-blown AIDS include a persistent cough, fever, and difficulty in breathing. Multiple purplish blotches and bumps on the skin may indicate Kaposi's sarcoma. The virus can also cause brain damage.

The credit for discovering the AIDS virus is jointly shared by Dr. Robert Gallo, a researcher at the National Cancer Institute, and Luc Montagnier of the Pasteur Institute, France.

Toll-Free AIDS Information

The government's HIV–AIDS Treatment Information Service toll-free phone line provides the latest research and treatment information in Spanish and English to people with AIDS, their families, and home care providers. The number is (800) HIV–0440, 9:00 a.m. to 7:00 p.m., EST, Monday through Friday. Access for the deaf is included and all calls are confidential.

There is also a National AIDS Hot Line: (800) 342-2437 for recorded information about AIDS, or (800) 433-0366 for specific questions. Information about where to go for confidential testing for the presence of the AIDS virus is provided by local and state health departments.

People infected with the virus can have a wide range of symptoms—from none to mild to severe. At least a fourth to a half of those infected will develop AIDS within four to ten years. Many experts think the percentage will be much higher.

AIDS is spread by sexual contact, needle sharing, or less commonly through transfused blood or its components. The risk of infection with the virus is increased by having multiple sexual partners, either homosexual or heterosexual, and sharing of needles among those using illicit drugs. The occurrence of the syndrome in hemophilia patients and persons receiving transfusions provides evidence for transmission through blood. It may be transmitted from infected mother to infant before, during, or shortly after birth (probably through breast milk).

The AIDS virus can be spread by sexual intercourse whether you are male or female, heterosexual, bisexual, or homosexual. This happens because a person infected with the AIDS virus may have the virus in semen or vaginal fluids. The virus can enter the body through the vagina, penis, rectum or mouth. Anal intercourse, with or without a condom, is risky. The rectum is easily injured during anal intercourse.

With no cure at present, prudence could save thousands of people in the U.S. who have yet to be exposed to the virus. Their fate will depend less on science than on the ability of large numbers of human beings to change their behavior in the face of growing danger. New drugs and tests have given researchers renewed optimism in treating AIDS. As of July 1996, three dozen preventative HIV vaccines were being tested in small-scale clinical trials around the world. They are poised to move into large-scale efficacy trials as soon as a suitable product is identified.

People who should be tested for HIV include gay men and intravenous drug users, their sex partners, and anyone who has had several sex partners, if their sexual history is unknown, during any one of the last five years. Anyone who tests positive should see a physician immediately for a medical evaluation. Persons testing positive should inform their sex partners and should use a condom during sex.

Other Sexually Transmitted Diseases (STD)

Other sexually transmitted diseases, such as gonorrhea, syphilis, herpes, and chlamydia, can be contracted through oral, anal, and vaginal intercourse.

Reliable data on the worldwide incidence of STD are not available. The World Health Organization's minimal estimates for the four major bacterial STD are: gonorrhea, 25 million cases; genital chlamydial infections, 50 million cases; infectious syphilis, 3.5 million cases; and chancroid, 2 million cases. Rough estimates of genital herpes, a viral STD, is 20 million cases.

Facts From the World Health Report 1996

Source: The World Health Organization (WHO)

Births

• About 139 million babies were born in 1995, a 12% increase over the last 15 years. However, mainly due to increasing contraceptive use, women are having fewer babies—an average of 3 today compared to 3.2 in 1990 and 3.7 in 1980.

• Between 1990–1995, about 15 million babies were born each year to teenagers or women over 35. Birth rates among young women aged 15–19 are twice as high in the developing world as in developed countries.

Life Expectancy

• Average life expectancy at birth globally in 1995 was more than 65 years, an increase of about 3 years since 1985. It was over 75 years in developed countries, 64 years in developing countries, and 52 years in least developed countries.

• The world's lowest life expectancy at birth, just 40 years, is in Sierra Leone—barely half of the world's highest, in Japan, where it is 79.7 years.

• At least 18 countries in Africa have a life expectancy at birth of 50 years or less.

• The number of countries with a life expectancy at birth of over 60 years has increased from at least 98 (with a total population of 2.7 billion) in 1980 to at least 120 (with a total population of 4.9 billion) in 1995.

• On average, women today can expect to live over 4 years longer than men—67.2 years versus 63 years. The female advantage is greatest in Europe—almost 8 more years—and smallest in Southeast Asia, where it is just one year.

Deaths

• About 52 million people died in 1995. The number is almost the same as it was 35 years ago, but the global population has almost doubled in that time.

• More than 17 million of the 52 million deaths in 1995 were due to infectious diseases.

• Of more than 11 million deaths among children under 5 in the developing world, about 9 million were attributed to infectious diseases, 25% of them preventable through vaccination.

• Cancer killed about 6.6 million people in 1995.

• About 8.4 million infants died last year before their first birthday. Developed market economies had only 6.9 infant deaths per 1,000 live births, compared to 106.2 infant deaths per 1,000 live births in the least developed countries.

Child Health

• The prevalence of underweight children under 5 years fell from 34% in 1985 to 31% in 1995 for developing countries as a whole; but it is 40% in the least developed countries.

• The number of countries with an infant mortality rate of below 50 per 1,000 live births has risen from at least 77 (with a total population of 1.3 billion) in 1980 to at least 103 (with a total population of 3.2 billion) in 1995.

Emerging and Re-emerging Infectious Diseases

• At least 30 new diseases have been scientifically recognized around the world in the last 20 years.

• Several new hepatitis viruses have been identified in recent years. Hepatitis B has infected 2 billion people, of whom 350 million are chronically infected and therefore at risk of death from liver disease. About 100 million are chronically and incurably infected with hepatitis C and are similarly at risk. Hepatitis E can cause major epidemics in countries with hot climates.

• A completely new strain of cholera, called *Vibrio cholerae* 0139, appeared in south-eastern India in 1992 and has since spread to other areas of India and parts of Southeast Asia.

• The Ebola virus was unknown 20 years ago. The Ebola haemorrhagic fever outbreak in Zaire in 1995 was fatal in about 80% of cases. The natural host of the virus remains a mystery.

• Recently recognized organisms such as cryptosporidium or new strains of bacteria such as *Escherichia coli* cause epidemics of foodborne and waterborne diseases in both industrialized and developing countries.

• Tuberculosis, once regarded as virtually under control, is making a deadly comeback, killing about 3.1 million people a year. Drug-resistant tuberculosis is spreading in many countries.

• Cholera, absent in South America for decades, struck Peru in 1991 and has since spread throughout the continent. Worldwide it is endemic in at least 80 countries and causes 120,000 deaths a year.

• Diphtheria epidemics that began in the Russian Federation in 1990 have since struck in 15 eastern European countries. WHO estimates there are 100,000 diphtheria cases and up to 8,000 deaths a year worldwide.

• The biggest epidemic of yellow fever in the Americas since 1950 struck Peru in 1995.

Disappearing Diseases

• Poliomyelitis is targeted for global eradication by the year 2000. There are now 145 countries completely free of the disease.

• Leprosy is steadily being defeated and should no longer represent a significant public health problem within the next few years.

• Guinea-worm disease (dracunculiasis) could be completely eradicated within the next few years. Cases worldwide have fallen from 3.5 million in 1986 to about 120,000 in 1995; only 1–4 cases remained in most endemic villages.

Infectious Diseases and Cancer

• Sexually transmitted human papilloma viruses are responsible for most of the 529,000 cases of cervical cancer a year—65% of the cases in industrialized countries, and 87% of those in developing countries.

• About 434,000 cases a year of liver cancer—82% of the world total—are due to hepatitis B or hepatitis C viruses. Hepatitis B causes 316,000 and hepatitis C causes 118,000 of the cases. The viruses are transmitted in several ways, including through contaminated blood and sexually.

• Some 550,000 new cases a year of stomach cancer are attributed to the bacterium *Helicobacter pylori*, transmitted in foods. The figure equals about 55% of all cases of this cancer worldwide.

Immunization

• May 1996 marked the 200th anniversary of the first successful immunization, by Dr. Edward Jenner in England, who protected a child against smallpox by innoculating him with cowpox virus.

• The global eradication of smallpox was officially declared at WHO's World Health Assembly in 1980. The last naturally acquired case of smallpox was reported in Somalia in 1977.

Cancer Risks You Can Avoid

Source: National Cancer Institute, National Institutes of Health.

What is Cancer?

Cancer is really a group of diseases. There are more than 100 different types of cancer, but they all are a disease of some of the body's cells.

Healthy cells that make up the body's tissues grow, divide, and replace themselves in an orderly way. This process keeps the body in good repair. Sometimes, however, normal cells lose their ability to limit and direct their growth. They divide too rapidly and grow without any order. Too much tissue is produced and *tumors* begin to form. Tumors can be either *benign* or *malignant*.

Benign tumors are not cancer. They do not spread to other parts of the body and they are seldom a threat to life. Often, benign tumors can be removed by surgery, and they are not likely to return. Malignant tumors are cancer. They can invade and destroy nearby tissue and organs. Cancer cells also can spread, or *metastasize*, to other parts of the body, and form new tumors.

Because cancer can spread, it is important for the doctor to find out as early as possible if a tumor is present and if it is cancer. As soon as a diagnosis is made, treatment can begin.

Signs and Symptoms of Cancer

Cancer and other illnesses often cause a number of problems you can watch for. The most common warning signs of cancer are:

Change in bowel or bladder habits;

A sore that does not heal;

Unusual bleeding or discharge;

Thickening or lump in the breast or elsewhere;

Indigestion or difficulty swallowing;

Obvious change in a wart or mole;

Nagging cough or hoarseness.

These signs and symptoms can be caused by cancer or by a number of other problems. They are *not* a sure sign of cancer. However, it is important to see a doctor if any problem lasts as long as 2 weeks. Don't wait for symptoms to become painful; pain is not an early sign of cancer.

Preventing Cancer

By choosing a lifestyle that avoids certain risks, you can help protect yourself from developing cancer. Many cancers are linked to factors that you can control.

Tobacco—Smoking and using tobacco in any form has been directly linked to cancer. Overall, smoking causes 30 percent of all cancer deaths. The risk of developing lung cancer is 10 times greater for smokers than for nonsmokers. The amount of risk from smoking depends on the number and type of cigarettes you smoke, how long you have been smoking, and how deeply you inhale. Smokers are also more likely to develop cancers of the mouth, throat, esophagus, pancreas, and bladder. And now there is emerging evidence that smoking can also cause cancer of the stomach and cervix.

The use of "smokeless" tobacco (chewing tobacco and oral snuff) increases the risk of cancer of the mouth and pharynx. Once you quit smoking or using smokeless tobacco, your risk of developing cancer begins to decrease right away.

Diet—What you eat may affect your chances of developing cancer. Scientists think there is a link between a high-fat diet and some cancers, particularly those of the breast, colon, endometrium, and prostate. Obesity is thought to be linked with increased death rates for cancers of the prostate, pancreas, breast, and ovary. Still other studies point to an increased risk of getting stomach cancer for those who frequently eat pickled, cured, and smoked foods. The National Cancer Institute believes that eating a well-balanced diet can reduce the risk of getting cancer. Americans should eat more high-fiber foods (such as whole-grain cereals and fruits and vegetables) and less fatty foods.

Sunlight—Repeated exposure to sunlight increases the risk of skin cancer, especially if you have fair skin or freckle easily. In fact, ultraviolet radiation from the sun is the main cause of skin cancer, which is the most common cancer in the United States. Ultraviolet rays are strongest from 11 a.m. to 2 p.m. during the summer, so that is when risk is greatest. Protective clothing, such as a hat and long sleeves, can help block out the sun's harmful rays. You can also use sunscreens to help protect yourself. Sunscreens with a number 15 on the label means most of the sun's harmful rays will be blocked out.

Alcohol—Drinking large amounts of alcohol (one or two drinks a day is considered moderate) is associated with cancers of the mouth, throat, esophagus,

and liver. People who smoke cigarettes and drink alcohol have an especially high risk of getting cancers of the mouth and esophagus.

X-rays—Large doses of radiation increase cancer risk. Although individual x-rays expose you to very little radiation, repeated exposure can be harmful. Therefore, it is a good idea to avoid unnecessary x-rays. It's best to talk about the need for each x-ray with your doctor or dentist. If you do need an x-ray, ask if shields can be used to protect other parts of your body.

Industrial Agents and Chemicals—Exposure to some industrial agents or chemicals increases cancer risk. Industrial agents cause damage by acting alone or together with another cancer-causing agent found in the workplace or with cigarette smoke. For example, inhaling asbestos fibers increases the risk of lung disease and cancer. This risk is especially high for workers who smoke. You should follow work and safety rules to avoid coming in contact with such dangerous materials.

Being exposed to large amounts of household solvent cleaners, cleaning fluids, and paint thinners should be avoided. Some chemicals are especially dangerous if inhaled in high concentrations, particularly in areas that are not well ventilated. In addition, inhaling or swallowing lawn and garden chemicals increases cancer risk. Follow label instructions carefully when using pesticides, fungicides, and other chemicals. Such chemicals should not come in contact with toys or other household items.

Hormones—Taking estrogen to relieve menopausal symptoms (such as hot flashes) has been associated with higher-than-average rates of cancer of the uterus. Numerous studies also have examined the relationship between oral contraceptives (the pill) and a variety of female cancers. Recent studies report that taking the

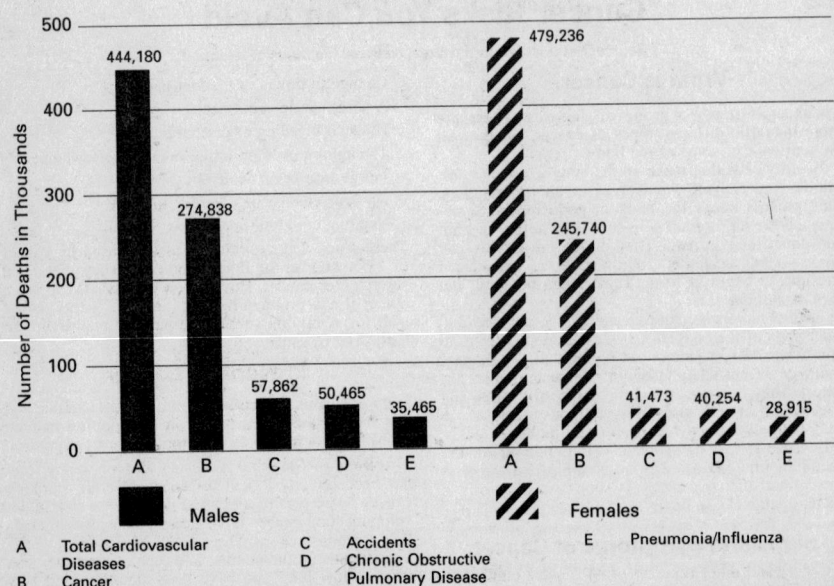

Leading Causes of Death for Males, Females
United States: 1992 Final Mortality

	Males					Females				
A Total Cardiovascular Diseases	444,180					479,236				
B Cancer		274,838					245,740			
C Accidents			57,862					41,473		
D Chronic Obstructive Pulmonary Disease				50,465					40,254	
E Pneumonia/Influenza					35,465					28,915

Number of Deaths in Thousands

Source: National Center for Health Statistics and the American Heart Association.

pill does not increase a woman's chance of getting breast cancer. Also, pill users appear to have a lower-than-average risk of cancers of the endometrium and ovary. However, some researchers believe that there may be a higher risk of cancer of the cervix among pill users. Women taking hormones (either estrogens or oral contraceptives) should discuss the benefits and risks with their doctor. □

The Nutritional Health of America

Source: "Third Report on Nutrition Monitoring in the United States," 1996

Although Americans are slowly adopting healthier diets, too many are still overweight and some report not having enough to eat, raising the risk of diet-related health problems. The latest government report found that:

- A considerable gap remains between public health recommendations and consumer practices;
- About one-third of adults and one-fifth of adolescents in the United States are overweight. These results represent increases in the prevalence of overweight persons since the 1970s;
- Twenty percent of Americans still have high serum cholesterol levels;
- Hypertension remains a major public health problem in middle-aged and elderly people;
- Many Americans are not getting the calcium they need to maintain optimal bone health and prevent age-related bone loss;
- Less than one-third of American adults meets the recommendation to consume five or more servings of fruits and vegetables per day;
- Approximately one in ten people living in low-income households or families experiences some degree of food insufficiency. □

Two Myths About Heart Disease

Source: "Heart and Stroke Facts: 1996 Statistical Supplement." 1995 © Copyright American Heart Association. Reproduced with permission.

Heart disease no longer represents a serious threat—Medical scientists have made tremendous progress in fighting cardiovascular diseases. Even so, every 33 seconds an American dies of CVD. That's more than 954,000 deaths annually, more than 42 percent of all deaths every year. In fact, since 1900 the number one killer in the United States has been CVD in every year but one (1918).

Deaths don't tell the whole story, either. Of the current U.S. population of about 258 million, more than 60 million people have some form of these diseases. And as the population ages, these diseases may have an even greater human and economic impact. Heart failure, for example, is becoming much more prevalent.

Cancer, AIDS, and other diseases deserve research and attention. But it's important to remember that CVD ranks far ahead of them as a cause of death. And total deaths from CVD, after years of decline, began rising in 1993.

Finally, according to the most recent computations done by the National Center for Health Statistics (NCHS), if all forms of major cardiovascular disease were eliminated, life expectancy would rise by 9.78 years. If all forms of cancer were eliminated, the gain would be three years.

If a heart attack doesn't kill you, you'll recover and be fine—People who survive the acute stage of a heart attack have a chance of illness and death that's two to nine times higher than the general population. The rates of another heart attack, sudden death, angina pectoris, heart failure and stroke—for both men and women—are all substantial. Within six years after a heart attack:

- 23 percent of men and 31 percent of women will have another heart attack;
- 41 percent of men and 34 percent of women will develop angina;
- About 20 percent will be disabled with heart failure;
- Nine percent of men and 18 percent of women will have a stroke; and
- 13 percent of men and six percent of women will experience sudden death.

About two-thirds of heart attack patients don't make a complete recovery, but 88 percent of those under age 65 are able to return to their usual work.

Prevalence—60,340,000 Americans—more than one in four—have one or more types of cardiovascular disease (CVD) according to current estimates.

- High blood pressure—50,000,000.
- Coronary heart disease—13,490,000.
- Stroke—3,820,000.
- Rheumatic heart disease—1,360,000.
- About one in five males and females have some form of major cardiovascular disease.

Mortality—Cardiovascular diseases claimed 954,138 lives in the United States in 1993. This is 42.1 percent of all deaths or 1 of every 2.4 deaths.

- More than 2,600 Americans die each day from cardiovascular diseases, an average of a death every 33 seconds.
- More than one-sixth of all people killed by CVD are under age 65.
- 1992 final CVD mortality: male deaths—444,180 (48.1 percent of deaths from CVD); female deaths—479,236 (51.9 percent of deaths from CVD).
- In 1992, 38 percent of deaths from cardiovascular diseases occurred prematurely (i.e., before age 75, the average life expectancy in that year).
- 1992 death rates from CVD were 230.2 for white males and 335.6 for black males (45.8 percent higher); 128.3 for white females and 217.1 (69.2 percent higher) for black females.
- From 1983 to 1993 death rates from CVD declined 23.1 percent. Despite this decline in the death rate, in the same 10-year period the actual number of deaths declined only 3.8 percent.
- Total deaths from CVD increased significantly in 1993. One reason given for this rise is that the total U.S. population, and particularly the population of middle-aged and older people, is increasing. Another reason is that recent advances in medical treatment have allowed more people to survive previously fatal cardiovascular events, but now these people are dying of subsequent cardiovascular illnesses (e.g., heart attack victims whose lives were saved by better emergency care may now be dying of congestive heart failure). □

New Dietary Guidelines for Americans

Source: U.S. Department of Agriculture, U.S. Department of Health and Human Services.

Eat a Variety of Foods

Foods contain combinations of nutrients and other healthful substances. No single food can supply all nutrients in the amounts you need. For example, oranges provide vitamin C but no vitamin B_{12}; cheese provides vitamin B_{12} but no vitamin C. To make sure you get all of the nutrients and other substances needed for health, choose the recommended number of daily servings from each of the five major food groups.

Grain, Vegetable, and Fruit Products Group

• Choose most of your foods from the grain products group (6–11 servings), the vegetable group (3–5 servings), and the fruit group (2–4 servings).

Milk, and Meat and Beans Group

• Eat moderate amounts of foods from the milk group (2–3 servings) and the meat and beans group (2–3 servings).

Fats and Sugars

• Choose sparingly foods that provide few nutrients and are high in fats and sugars.

NOTE: A range of servings is given for each food group. The smaller number is for people who consume about 1,600 calories a day, such as the sedentary or women. The larger number is for those who consume about 2,800 calories a day, for the very active or men.

What Counts as a Serving?*

Grain Products Group (bread, cereal, rice, and pasta):
• 1 slice of bread
• 1 ounce of ready-to-eat cereal
• 1/2 cup of cooked cereal, rice, or pasta

Vegetable Group:
• 1 cup of raw, leafy vegetables
• 1/2 cup of other vegetables—cooked or chopped raw
• 3/4 cup of vegetable juice

Fruit Group:
• 1 medium apple, banana, orange
• 1/2 cup of chopped, cooked, or canned fruit
• 3/4 cup of fruit juice

Milk Group (milk, yogurt, and cheese):
• 1 cup of milk or yogurt
• 1 1/2 ounces of natural cheese
• 2 ounces of processed cheese

Meat and Beans Group (meat, poultry, fish, dry beans, eggs, and nuts):
• 2–3 ounces of cooked lean meat, poultry, or fish
• 1/2 cup of cooked dry beans or 1 egg counts as 1 ounce of lean meat. Two tablespoons of peanut butter or 1/3 cup of nuts count as 1 ounce of meat.

*Some foods fit into more than one group. Dry Beans, peas, and lentils can be counted as servings in either the meat and beans group or vegetable group. These "crossover" foods can be counted as servings from either one or the other group, but not both.

What About Vegetarian Diets?

Some Americans eat vegetarian diets for reasons of culture, belief, or health. Most vegetarians eat milk products and eggs, and as a group, these lacto-ovo-vegetarians enjoy excellent health. Vegetarian diets are consistent with the *Dietary Guidelines for Americans* and can meet Recommended Dietary Allowances for nutrients. You can get enough protein from a vegetarian diet as long as the variety and amounts of foods consumed are adequate. Meat, fish, and poultry are major contributors of iron, zinc, and B vitamins in most American diets, and vegetarians should pay special attention to these nutrients.

Vegans eat only food of plant origin. Because animal products are the only sources of vitamin B_{12}, vegans must supplement their diets with a source of this vitamin. In addition, vegan diets, particularly those of children, require care to insure adequacy of vitamin D and calcium, which most Americans obtain from milk products.

Maintain a Healthy Weight

Many Americans gain weight in adulthood, increasing their risk for high blood pressure, heat disease, stroke, diabetes, certain types of cancer, arthritis, breathing problems, and other illness. Therefore, most adults should not gain weight.

In order to stay at the same body weight, people must balance the amount of calories in the foods and drinks they consume with the amount of calories the body uses. Physical activity is an important way to use food energy.

To burn calories, spend more time in activities like walking to the store or around the block. Use stairs rather than elevators. Less sedentary activity and more vigorous activity may help you reduce body fat and disease risk. Try to do 30 minutes or more of moderate physical activity on most—preferably all—days of the week.

Healthy Weight Ranges for Men and Women

Height*	Weight (in pounds)
4'10"	91–119
4'11"	94–124
5'0"	97–128
5'1"	101–132
5'2"	104–137
5'3"	107–141
5'4"	111–146
5'5"	114–150
5'6"	118–155
5'7"	121–160
5'8"	125–164
5'9"	129–169
5'10"	132–174
5'11"	136–170
6'0"	140–184
6'1"	144–189
6'2"	148–195
6'3"	152–200
6'4"	156–205
6'5"	160–211
6'6"	164–216

*Without shoes, without clothes. Weight *ranges* are given in the chart because people of the same height may have equal amounts of body fat but different amounts of muscle and bone. *Source:* Derived from National Research Council, 1989, for adults, p. 564.

Body Fat

Research suggests that the location of body fat also is an important factor in health risks for adults. Excess fat in the abdomen (stomach area) is a greater health risk than excess fat in the hips and thighs. Extra fat in the abdomen is linked to high blood pressure, diabetes, early heart disease, and certain types of cancer. Smoking and too much alcohol increase abdominal fat and the risk for diseases related to obesity. Vigorous exercise helps to reduce abdominal fat.

The easiest way to check your body fat distribution is to measure around your waistline with a tape measure and compare this with the measure around your hips or buttocks to see if your abdomen is larger. If you are in doubt, you may wish to seek advice from a health professional.

Although limiting fat intake may help to prevent excess weight gain in children, fat should not be restricted to children younger than two years of age. Helping overweight children to achieve a healthy weight along with normal growth requires more caution. Modest reductions in dietary fat, such as the use of lowfat milk are not hazardous. However, major efforts to change a child's diet should be accompanied by a monitoring of growth by a health professional at regular intervals.

Eat Plenty of Grains, Vegetables, and Fruits

Grain products, vegetables, and fruits are key parts of a varied diet. They are emphasized in this guideline because they provide vitamins, minerals, complex carbohydrates (starch and dietary fiber), and other substances that are important for good health. They are also generally low in fat, depending on how they are prepared and what is added to them at the table.

Fiber

Fiber is found only in plant foods like whole-grained breads and cereals, beans and peas, and other vegetables and fruits. Because there are different types of fiber in foods, choose a variety of foods daily. Eating a variety of fiber-containing plant foods is important for bowel function, can reduce symptoms of chronic constipation, diverticular disease, and hemorrhoids, and may lower the risk for heart disease and some cancers.

However, some of the health benefits associated with a high-fiber diet may come from other components present in these foods, not just the fiber itself. For this reason, fiber is best obtained from foods rather than supplements.

Diet With Plenty of Grain Products, Vegetables, and Fruits

6–11 servings of grain products (breads, cereals, pasta, and rice):

- Eat products made from a variety of whole grains, such as wheat, rice, oats, corn, and barley.
- Eat several servings of whole-grain breads and cereals daily.
- Prepare and serve grain products with little or no fats and sugars.

3–5 servings of various vegetables and vegetable juices:

- Choose dark-green leafy and deep-yellow vegetables often.
- Eat dry beans, peas, and lentils often.
- Eat starchy vegetables, such as potatoes and corn.
- Prepare and serve vegetables with little or no fats.

2–4 servings of various fruits and fruit juices:

- Choose citrus fruits or juices, melons, or berries regularly.
- Eat fruits as desserts or snacks.
- Drink fruit juices.
- Prepare and serve fruits with little or no added sugars.

Choose a Diet Low in Fat, Saturated Fat, and Cholesterol

Some dietary fat is needed for good health. Fats supply energy and essential fatty acids and promote absorption of the fat-soluble vitamins A, D, E, and K. More Americans are now eating less fat, saturated fat, and cholesterol-rich foods than in the recent past. Still, many people continue to eat high-fat diets. This guideline emphasizes the continued importance of choosing a diet with less total fat, saturated fat, and cholesterol.

Avoid High-Fat Foods

Some foods and food groups are higher in fat than others. Fats and oils, and some types of desserts and snack foods that contain fat provide calories but few nutrients. Many foods in the milk group and in the meat and beans group (which includes eggs and nuts, as well as meat, poultry, and fish) are also high in fat as are some processed foods in the grain group.

Fat, whether from plant or animal sources contains more than twice the number of calories of an equal amount of carbohydrate or protein. Choose a diet that provides no more than 30 percent of total calories from fat. The upper limit on the grams of fat in your diet will depend on the calories you need. Cutting back on fat can help you consume fewer calories. For example, at 2,000 calories per day, the suggested upper limit of calories from fat is about 600 calories (65 grams of fat × 9 calories per gram = about 600 calories).

Maximum Total Fat Intake at Different Calorie Levels			
Calories	1,600	2,200	2,800
Total fat (grams)	53	73	93

Saturated fat—Fats contain both saturated and unsaturated (monounsaturated and polyunsaturated) fatty acids. Saturated fats raises blood cholesterol more than other forms of fat. Reducing saturated fat to less than 10 percent of calories will help you lower your blood cholesterol level. The fats from meat, milk, and milk products are the main sources of saturated fats in most diets. Many bakery products are also sources of saturated fats. Vegetable oils supply smaller amounts of saturated fat.

Monounsaturated and polyunsaturated fat—Olive and canola oil are particularly high in monounsaturated fats; most other vegetable oils, nuts, and high-fat fish are good sources of polyunsaturated fats. Both kinds of unsaturated fats reduce blood cholesterol when they replace saturated fats in the diet. Remember that the total fat in the diet should be consumed at a moderate level—that is no more than 30 percent of calories. Mono- and polyunsaturated fat sources should replace saturated fats within this limit.

Partially hydrogenated vegetable oils, such as those used in many margarines and shortenings, contain a particular form of unsaturated fat known as trans-fatty acids that may raise blood cholesterol levels, although not as much as saturated fat.

Choose a Low Cholesterol Diet

The body makes the cholesterol it requires. In addition, cholesterol is obtained from food. Dietary cholesterol comes from animal sources such as egg yolks, meat (especially organ meats such as liver), poultry, fish, and higher fat milk products. Many of these foods are also high in saturated fats. Choosing foods with less cholesterol and saturated fat will help lower your blood pressure levels.

Avoid Too Much Sugar

Sugars are carbohydrates. Dietary carbohydrates also include the complex carbohydrates starch and fi-ber. During digestion all carbohydrates except fiber break down into sugars. Sugars and starches occur naturally in many foods that supply other nutrients. Examples of these foods include milk, fruits, some vegetables, breads, cereals, and grains. Some sugars are used as natural preservatives, thickeners, and baking aids in foods. The body cannot tell the difference between naturally occurring and added sugars because they are identical chemically.

Because maintaining a nutritious diet and a healthy weight is very important, sugars should be used in moderation by most healthy people and sparingly by people with low calorie needs.

Avoid Too Much Sodium

Sodium and sodium chloride—known commonly as salt—occur naturally in foods, usually in small amounts. In the body, sodium plays an essential role in regulation of fluids and blood pressure. Most evidence suggests that many people at risk for high blood pressure reduce their chances of developing this condition by consuming less salt or sodium. Some questions remain, partly because other factors may interact with sodium to affect blood pressure.

Drink Alcohol in Moderation

Alcoholic beverages have been used to enhance the enjoyment of meals by many societies throughout human history. If adults choose to drink alcoholic beverages, they should do so only in moderation.

Current evidence suggests that moderate drinking is associated with a lower risk for coronary heart disease in some individuals. However, higher levels of alcohol intake raise the risk for high blood pressure, stroke, heart disease, certain cancers, accidents, violence, suicides, birth defects, and overall mortality (deaths).

Too much alcohol may cause cirrhosis of the liver, inflammation of the pancreas, and damage to the brain and heart. Heavy drinkers also are at risk of malnutrition because alcohol contains calories that may substitute for those in more nutritious foods.

What is moderation?

Moderation is defined as no more than one drink per day for women and no more than two drinks per day for men.

Count as a drink:

12 ounces of regular beer (150 calories)
5 ounces of wine (100 calories)
1.5 ounces of 80-proof distilled spirits (100 calories)

Children Follow Parents' Smoking Example

Source: FACTS Science Service

The adult children of smoking parents are much more likely to smoke themselves, according to research from four academic centers across the United States—Northwestern University, the University of Alabama, the University of Minnesota, and Bowman Gray School of Medicine. The researchers studied 5,115 adults between 18 and 30 years of age on family tobacco use and education.

The less education parents had, the more likely their children eventually smoked cigarettes. However, the level of education of the offspring was more important. The greater the amount of formal education he or she had, the less likely the adult offspring smoked regardless of how little education the parents had.

When either parent smoked, their child was more likely to eventually smoke. Black men and women were about 1.7 times as likely to smoke if either parent smoked, all other circumstances being similar. White men had about 1.8 times the chance and white women 1.5 times the chance of smoking if either parent smoked. Interestingly, it did not increase the chance of their offspring smoking if both parents smoked.

Most adults are aware of the dangers of smoking. Therefore, it is unlikely that parents verbally encourage their children to smoke. This is another example (along with eating habits, exercise frequency, sexual habits, and others) where what example parents provide may be more important than what they say. □

Health Insurance Coverage: 1994

Source: U.S. Bureau of the Census

An estimated 39.7 million persons in the United States (15.2%) were without health insurance during the entire 1994 calendar year, the latest year for which data is available. Among the poor, 11.1 million persons were without coverage.

Despite the existence of programs such as Medicaid and Medicare, 29.1% of the poor had no health insurance of any kind during 1994. This percentage was about double the rate for all persons.

Several key factors influenced the chances of lacking coverage. They included:

• Age. Young adults aged 18 to 24 were more likely than other age groups to lack coverage (26.7 percent). The elderly were at the other extreme (0.9%).

• Race and Hispanic origin. Among poor and all persons alike, those of Hispanic origin had the highest chance of lacking coverage.

• Educational attainment. Among all adults, the likelihood of being uninsured declined as the level of education rose. Among the poor, however, there were no significant differences across the education groups.

• Work experience. Overall, part-time workers had the highest noncoverage rate. These workers were adults aged 15 or over who worked less than 35 hours per week in the majority of the weeks they worked in 1994. Thanks to Medicare coverage of the elderly and the Medicaid "safety net," nonworkers had the lowest rate (13.4%).

Firm Size Plays a Role

The Census study showed that employers are the leading providers and workers in large firms were most likely to have employer-provided insurance. Of the 139.1 million workers, 53.3% had employer-provided health insurance policies in their own name. The proportion varied by size of employer, with workers employed by small firms (less than 25 people) being less likely to have employer-provided health insurance policies in their own name. □

Percent Persons Not Covered by Health Insurance by State: 1994

State	Percent	State	Percent	State	Percent
Alabama	19.2	Kentucky	15.2	North Dakota	8.4
Alaska	13.3	Louisiana	19.2	Ohio	11.0
Arizona	20.2	Maine	13.1	Oklahoma	17.8
Arkansas	17.4	Maryland	12.6	Oregon	13.1
California	21.1	Massachusetts	12.5	Pennsylvania	10.6
Colorado	12.4	Michigan	10.8	Rhode Island	11.5
Connecticut	10.4	Minnesota	9.5	South Carolina	14.2
Delaware	13.5	Mississippi	17.8	South Dakota	10.0
D.C.	16.4	Missouri	12.2	Tennessee	10.2
Florida	17.2	Montana	13.6	Texas	24.2
Georgia	16.2	Nebraska	10.7	Utah	11.5
Hawaii	9.2	Nevada	15.7	Vermont	8.6
Idaho	14.0	New Hampshire	11.9	Virginia	12.0
Illinois	11.4	New Jersey	13.0	Washington	12.7
Indiana	10.5	New Mexico	23.1	West Virginia	16.2
Iowa	9.7	New York	16.0	Wisconsin	8.9
Kansas	12.9	North Carolina	13.3	Wyoming	15.4

Note: These estimates should not be used to rank the States. Results from different samplings could easily show different estimates and rankings because of small sampling sizes. For example, the high noncoverage for Texas is not statistically different from that of New Mexico. *Source:* U.S. Bureau of the Census.

Alzheimer's Disease is a Major Health Problem

Alzheimer's disease (AD) is the fourth leading cause of death in adults, after heart disease, cancer, and stroke. In Alzheimer's, nerve cells in areas of the brain responsible for speech, thought, memory, and reason die off and the victim eventually loses all ability to carry out normal daily activities. Although AD primarily affects the elderly it can strike some people in their 40s and 50s. Men and women are affected equally. The average person dies within eight years from the onset of symptoms.

Most Americans first became aware of the existence of Alzheimer's when screen actress Rita Hayworth (1918–1987) succumbed to it. Her daughter, Yasmin Aga Khan, became a leader in the fight against the disease.

Public awareness of the disease was again raised on November 3, 1994, when former President Reagan revealed that he was suffering from the early stages of Alzheimer's disease. Some other famous Alzheimer victims are artist Norman Rockwell, actor Edmond O'Brian, boxer Sugar Ray Robinson, and humorist E.B. White.

An estimated 4 million Americans are afflicted by AD and the National Center for Health Statistics (NHCH) reported that Alzheimer's disease accounted for 16,743 deaths in 1993 (the latest data available), 98 percent of which were Americans 65 years of age and older.

The disease is named after Alois Alzheimer, a German physician, who first described the disease in one of his patients in 1906. This patient, a 51-year old woman, suffered from memory loss, disorientation, depression, and hallucinations. She eventually suffered complete dementia and died five years later. Upon autopsy, her brain revealed extensive lesions of a type now considered characteristic of Alzheimer's disease.

Caring for an Alzheimer victim causes considerable emotional and economic hardship for the caregivers, who are usually relatives. Many AD victims become so difficult to care for that they are eventually sent to nursing homes.

The causes of AD are unknown and no known cure is available. Treatment consists mainly of alleviating the symptoms. Further information about AD can be obtained from the Alzheimer's Association by calling 800-272-3900. □

Toll–Free Numbers for Health Information • Dial 1–800

AL–ANON Family Group Headquarters, 356–9996
Alcohol and Drug Helpline, 821–4357
Allergy Information referral line, 822–2762
Alzheimer's Association, 272–3900
Alzheimer's Disease Education and Referral Center, 438–4380
American Association of Kidney Patients, 749–2257
American Cancer Society Response Line, 227–2345
American Council of the Blind, 424–8666
American Council on Alcoholism, 527–5344
American Diabetes Association, 232–3472
American Dietetic Association, 366–1655
American Foundation for Urologic Disease, 242–2383
American Heart Association Stroke Connection, 553–6321
American Institute for Cancer Research, 843–8114
American Kidney Fund, 638–8299
American Leprosy Missions (Hansen's Disease), 543–3131
American Liver Foundation, 223–0179
American Lupus Society, The, 331–1802
American Paralysis Association, 225–0292
American Parkinson Disease Association, 223–2732
American Speech–Language–Hearing Association, 638–8255
APA Spinal Cord Injury Hotline, 526–3456
Arthritis Foundation Information Hotline, 283–7800
ASPO/LAMAZE, 368–4404
Asthma and Allergy Foundation of America, 727–8462
Better Hearing Institute, 327–9355
Brain Injury Association, Family Helpline, 444–6443
Cancer Information Service, 4–CANCER; 422–6237
CDC National AIDS Clearinghouse, 428–5231; 243–7012 (TDD)
CDC National HIV and AIDS Hotline, 342–2437; 344–7432 (Spanish); 243–7889 (TDD)
CDC National STD Hotline, 227–8922
Child Abuse and Neglect Clearinghouse, 394–3366
Child Find of America, Inc., 426–5678; 292–9688
CHILDHELP USA/IOF Foresters National Child Abuse Hotline, 4–A–CHILD or 422–4453; 2–A–CHILD or 222–4453 (TDD)
Children's Hospice International, 242–4453
Cleft Palate Foundation, 24–CLEFT or 242–5338
Crohn's and Colitis Foundation of America, Inc., 932–2423
Cystic Fibrosis Foundation, 344–4823
Deafness Research Foundation, 535–3323
Depression Awareness, 421–4211
Endometriosis Association, 992–3636
Epilepsy Foundation of America, 332–1000
Facial Plastic Surgery Information Service, 332–3223
Food Labeling Hotline, Meat and Poultry Hotline, 535–4555
Grief Recovery Helpline, 445–4808
Guide Dog Foundation for the Blind, Inc. 548–4337
Huntington's Disease Society of America, 345–4372
Impotence Information Center, 843–4315; 543–9632
International Childbirth Education Association, 624–4934
"Just Say No" International, 258–2766
Juvenile Diabetes Foundation International Hotline, 223–1138
La Leche League International, LA–LECHE or 525–3243
Lighthouse National Center for Vision and Aging, The, 334–5497
Living Bank, The, 528–2971
Lung Line National Jewish Center for Immunology and Respiratory Medicine, 222–5864; 552–LUNG or 552–5864 (LUNG FACTS)
Lupus Foundation of America, 558–0121
Medic Alert Foundation, 432–5378; 344–3226
Medical Rehabilitation Education Foundation, GET–RE–HAB, 688–6167 (TDD)
Medicare Telephone Hotline, 638–6833
National Adoption Center, TO–ADOPT or 862–3678
National Center for the Blind, 638–7518

National Center for Sight, 331–2020
National Center for Stuttering, 221–2483
National Center for Youth with Disabilities, 333–6293
National Childwatch Campaign, 222–1464
National Clearinghouse for Alcohol and Drug Information, 729–6686; 487–4889 (TTY/TDD)
National Cocaine Hotline, 262–2463
National Council on Alcoholism and Drug Dependence Hopeline Inc., 622–2255
National Down Syndrome Society Hotline, 221–4602
National Eye Care Project Hotline, 222–EYES or 222–3937
National Eye Research Foundation, 621–2258
National Foundation for Depressive Illness, 248–4344
National Headache Foundation, 843–2256
National Health Information Center, 336–4797
National Center for Missing and Exploited Children, 843–5678
National Information Center for Children and Youth With Disabilities, 695–0285
National Information Clearinghouse for Infants With Disabilities and Life Threatening Conditions, 922–9234, ext. 201
National Information Center for Orphan Drugs and Rare Diseases, 300–7469
National Institute on Aging Information Center, 222–2225
National Institute on Deafness and Other Communication Disorders Information Clearinghouse, 241–1044; 241–1055 (TT)
National Kidney Foundation, 622–9010
National Lead Information Center, LEAD–FYI (Hotline) or 532–3394; 424–LEAD or 424–5323 (Clearinghouse); 526–5456 (TDD)
National Marrow Donor Program, MARROW–2 or 627–7692
National Mental Health Association Information Center, 969–6642
National Multiple Sclerosis Society, LEARN–MS or 532–7667
National Neurofibromatosis Foundation, 323–7938
National Organization for Rare Disorders, 999–6673
National Parkinson Foundation, Inc., 327–4545
National Pesticide Telecommunications Network, 858–7378
National Rehabilitation Information Center, 346–2742
National Resource Center on Child Abuse and Neglect, 227–5242
National Resource Center on Homelessness and Mental Illness, 444–7415
National Reye's Syndrome Foundation, 233–7393
National Runaway Switchboard, 621–4000
National Spinal Cord Injury Association, 962–9629
National Stroke Association, STROKES or 787–6537
National Tuberous Sclerosis Association, 225–6872
National Youth Crisis Hotline, 448–4663
NHTSA Auto Safety Hotline, 424–9393
Panic Disorder Information Line, 64–PANIC or 647–2642
Parkinson's Educational Program, 344–7872 (Leave recorded message)
Planned Parenthood, 230–PLAN or 230–7526
PMS Access, 222–4767
Project Inform HIV/AIDS Treatment Hotline, 822–7422
Runaway Hotline, 231–6946
Safe Drinking Water Hotline, 426–4791
Seafood Hotline, FDA–4010 or 332–4010
Sickle Cell Disease Association of America, 421–8453
Simon Foundation for Continence, The, 237–4666
Spina Bifida Association of America, 621–3141
Stuttering Foundation of America, 992–9392
Tourette Syndrome Association, 237–0717
United Cerebral Palsy Association, 872–5827
United Network for Organ Sharing, 243–6667
United Scleroderma Foundation, 722–HOPE or 722–4673
U.S. Coast Guard Customer Information Line, 368–5647
U.S. Consumer Product Safety Commission Hotline, 638–2772; 638–8270 (TDD)
Y–ME National Organization for Breast Cancer Information Support Program, 221–2141

HEADLINE HISTORY

In any broad overview of history, arbitrary compartmentalization of facts is self-defeating (and makes locating interrelated people, places, and things that much harder). Therefore, Headline History is designed as a "timeline"—a chronology that highlights both the march of time and interesting, sometimes surprising, juxtapositions.

Also see related sections of *Information Please,* particularly Inventions and Discoveries, Countries of the World, etc.

B.C.
Before Christ or Before Common Era (B.C.E.)

4.5 billion B.C.   Planet Earth formed.

3 billion B.C.   First signs of primeval life (bacteria and blue-green algae) appear in oceans.

600 million B.C.   Earliest date to which fossils can be traced.

4.4 million B.C.   Earliest known hominid fossils (*Ardipithecus ramidus*) found in Aramis, Ethiopia, 1994.

4.2 million B.C.   *Australopithecus anamensis* found in Lake Turkana, Kenya, 1995.

3.2 million B.C.   *Australopithecus afarenis* (nicknamed *"Lucy"*) found in Ethiopia, 1974.

2.5 million B.C.   *Homo Habilis* ("Handy Man"), first brain expansion and first chipped stones.

1.8 million B.C.   *Homo Erectus* ("Upright Man"). Brain size twice that of *Australopithecine* species.

1.7 million B.C.   *Homo Erectus* leaves Africa.

100,000 B.C.   First modern *Homo Sapiens* in South Africa.

70,000 B.C.   Neanderthal man (use of fire and advanced tools).

35,000 B.C.   Neanderthal man being replaced by later groups of *Homo sapiens* (i.e. Cro-Magnon man, etc.).

18,000 B.C.   Cro-Magnons being replaced by later cultures.

15,000 B.C.   Migrations across Bering Straits into the Americas.

10,000 B.C.   Semi-permanent agricultural settlements in Old World.

10,000–4,000 B.C.   Development of settlements into cities and development of skills such as the wheel, pottery and improved methods of cultivation in Mesopatamia and elsewhere.

NOTE: For further information on the geographic development in Earth's prehistory, see the Science section.

4500–3000 B.C.   Sumerians in the Tigris and Euphrates valleys develop a city-state civilization; first phonetic writing (**c.3500** B.C.). Egyptian agriculture develops. Western Europe is neolithic, without metals or written records. Earliest recorded date in Egyptian calendar (**4241** B.C.). First year of Jewish calendar (**3760** B.C.). Copper used by Egyptians and Sumerians.

3000–2000 B.C.   Pharaonic rule begins in Egypt. Cheops, 4th dynasty (**2700–2675** B.C.). The Great Sphinx of Giza. Earliest Egyptian mummies. Papyrus. Phoenician settlements on coast of what is now Syria and Lebanon. Semitic tribes settle in Assyria. Sargon, first Akkadian king, builds Mesopotamian empire. The Gilgamesh epic (**c.3000** B.C.). Abraham leaves Ur (**c.2000** B.C.). Systematic astronomy in Egypt, Babylon, India, China.

3000–1500 B.C.   The most ancient civilization on the Indian subcontinent, the sophisticated and extensive Indus Valley civilization, flourishes in what is today Pakistan.

2000–1500 B.C.   Hyksos invaders drive Egyptians from Lower Egypt (**17th century** B.C.). Amosis I frees Egypt from Hyksos (**c.1600** B.C.). Assyrians rise to power—cities of Ashur and Nineveh. Twenty-four-character alphabet in Egypt. Israelites enslaved in Egypt. Cuneiform inscriptions used by Hittites. Peak of Minoan culture on Isle of Crete—earliest form of written Greek. Hammurabi, king of Babylon, develops oldest existing code of laws (**18th century** B.C.). In Britain, Stonehenge erected on some unknown astronomical rationale.

1500–1000 B.C.   Ikhnaton develops monotheistic religion in Egypt (**c.1375** B.C.). His successor, Tutankhamen, returns to earlier gods. Moses leads Israelites out of Egypt into Canaan—Ten Commandments. Greeks destroy Troy (**c.1193** B.C.). End of Greek civilization in Mycenae with invasion of Dorians. Chinese civilization develops under Shang dynasty. Olmec civilization in Mexico—stone monuments; picture writing.

1000–900 B.C.   Solomon succeeds King David, builds Jerusalem temple. After Solomon's death, kingdom divided into Israel and Judah. Hebrew elders begin to write Old Testament books of Bible. Phoenicians colonize Spain with settlement at Cadiz.

Brontosaur

Moses

Egyptian chariots
(1500 B.C.)

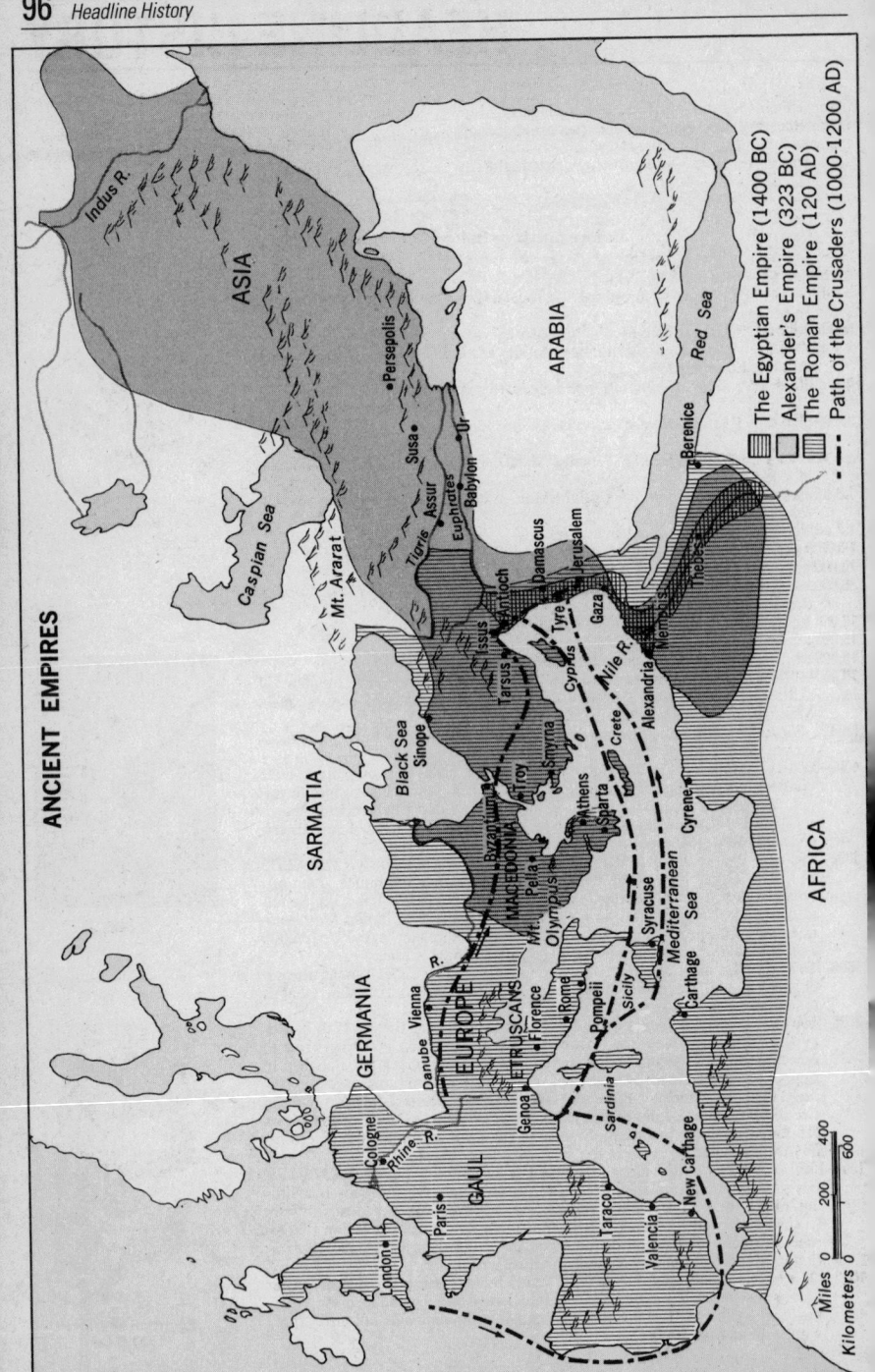

ANCIENT EMPIRES

The Egyptian Empire (1400 BC)
Alexander's Empire (323 BC)
The Roman Empire (120 AD)
Path of the Crusaders (1000–1200 AD)

ASIA

Indus R.

ARABIA

Red Sea

Caspian Sea

Mt. Ararat

Persepolis

Susa

Assur

Tigris

Euphrates

Babylon

Ur

Berenice

Damascus

Jerusalem

SARMATIA

Black Sea

Sinope

Antioch

Issus

Tarsus

Tyre

Gaza

Cyprus

Nile R.

Crete

Alexandria

Memphis

GERMANIA

Vienna

Danube R.

Byzantium

Troy

MACEDONIA

Pella

Mt. Olympus

Athens

Sparta

Cyrene

EUROPE

Rhine R.

Cologne

Paris

London

GAUL

ETRUSCANS

Florence

Genoa

Rome

Pompeii

Sicily

Syracuse

Mediterranean Sea

Carthage

Sardinia

Taraco

Valencia

New Carthage

AFRICA

Miles 0   200   400
Kilometers 0   600

Some Ancient Civilizations

Name	Approximate dates	Location	Major cities
Akkadian	2350–2230 B.C.	Mesopotamia, parts of Syria, Asia Minor, Iran	Akkad, Ur, Erich
Assyrian	1800–889 B.C.	Mesopotamia, Syria	Assur, Nineveh, Calah
Babylonian	1728–1686 B.C. (old) 625–539 B.C. (new)	Mesopotamia, Syria, Palestine	Babylon
Cimmerian	750–500 B.C.	Caucasus, northern Asia Minor	—
Egyptian	2850–715 B.C.	Nile valley	Thebes, Memphis, Tanis
Etruscan	900–396 B.C.	Northern Italy	—
Greek	900–200 B.C.	Greece	Athens, Sparta, Thebes, Mycenae, Corinth
Hittite	1640–1200 B.C.	Asia Minor, Syria	Hattusas, Nesa
Indus Valley	3000–1500 B.C.	Pakistan, Northwestern India	—
Lydian	700–547 B.C.	Western Asia Minor	Sardis, Miletus
Mede	835–550 B.C.	Iran	Media
Minoan	3000–1100 B.C.	Crete	Knossos
Persian	559–330 B.C.	Iran, Asia Minor, Syria	Persepolis, Pasargadae
Phoenician	1100–332 B.C.	Palestine (colonies: Gibraltar, Carthage Sardinia)	Tyre, Sidon, Byblos
Phrygian	1000–547 B.C.	Central Asia Minor	Gordion
Roman	500 B.C.–A.D. 300	Italy, Mediterranean region, Asia Minor, western Europe	Rome, Byzantium
Scythian	800–300 B.C.	Caucasus	—
Sumerian	3200–2360 B.C.	Mesopotamia	Ur, Nippur

900–800 B.C. Phoenicians establish Carthage (**c.810 B.C.**). The *Iliad* and the *Odyssey,* perhaps composed by Greek poet Homer.

800–700 B.C. Prophets Amos, Hosea, Isaiah. First recorded Olympic games (**776 B.C.**). Legendary founding of Rome by Romulus (**753 B.C.**). Assyrian king Sargon II conquers Hittites, Chaldeans, Samaria (end of Kingdom of Israel). Earliest written music. Chariots introduced into Italy by Etruscans.

700–600 B.C. End of Assyrian Empire (**616 B.C.**)—Nineveh destroyed by Chaldeans (Neo-Babylonians) and Medes (**612 B.C.**). Founding of Byzantium by Greeks (**c.660 B.C.**). Building of the Acropolis in Athens. Solon, Greek lawgiver (**640–560 B.C.**). Sappho of Lesbos, Greek poetess, Lao-Tse, Chinese philosopher and founder of Taoism (born **c.604 B.C.**).

600–500 B.C. Babylonian king Nebuchadnezzar builds empire, destroys Jerusalem (**586 B.C.**). Babylonian Captivity of the Jews (starting **587 B.C.**). Hanging Gardens of Babylon. Cyrus the Great of Persia creates great empire, conquers Babylon (**539 B.C.**), frees the Jews. Athenian democracy develops. Aeschylus, Greek dramatist (**525–465 B.C.**). Confucius (**551–479 B.C.**) develops philosophy-religion in China. Buddha (**563–483 B.C.**) founds Buddhism in India.

Confucius (551-479 B.C.)

500–400 B.C. Greeks defeat Persians: battles of Marathon (**490 B.C.**), Thermopylae (**480 B.C.**), Salamis (**480 B.C.**). Peloponnesian Wars between Athens and Sparta (**431–404 B.C.**)—Sparta victorious. Pericles comes to power in Athens (**462 B.C.**). Flowering of Greek culture during the Age of Pericles (**450–400 B.C.**). Sophocles, Greek dramatist (**496–c.406 B.C.**). Hippocrates, Greek "Father of Medicine" (born **460 B.C.**). Xerxes I, king of Persia (rules **485–465 B.C.**).

400–300 B.C. Pentateuch—first five books of the Old Testament evolve in final form. Philip of Macedon assassinated (**336 B.C.**) after conquering Greece; succeeded by son, Alexander the Great (**356–323 B.C.**), who destroys Thebes (**335 B.C.**), conquers Tyre and Jerusalem (**332 B.C.**), occupies Babylon (**330 B.C.**), invades India, and dies in Babylon. His empire is divided among his generals; one of them, Seleucis I, establishes Middle East empire with capitals at Antioch (Syria) and Seleucia (in Iraq). Trial and execution of Greek philosopher Socrates (**399 B.C.**). Dialogues recorded by his student, Plato. Euclid's work on geometry (**323 B.C.**). Aristotle, Greek philosopher (**384–322 B.C.**). Demosthenes, Greek orator (**384–322 B.C.**). Praxiteles, Greek sculptor (**400–330 B.C.**).

Plato (427?-347 B.C.)

400–251 B.C. First Punic War (**264–241 B.C.**): Rome defeats the Carthaginians and

**Archimedes
(287-212 B.C.)**

begins its domination of the Mediterranean. Temple of the Sun at Teotihua-can, Mexico (**c.300** B.C.). Invention of Mayan calendar in Yucatán—more exact than older calendars. First Roman gladiatorial games (**264** B.C.). Archimedes, Greek mathematician (**287–212** B.C.).

250–201 B.C. Second Punic War (**219–201** B.C.): Hannibal, Carthaginian general (**246–142** B.C.), crosses the Alps (**218** B.C.), reaches gates of Rome (**211** B.C.), retreats, and is defeated by Scipio Africanus at Zama (**202** B.C.). Great Wall of China built (**c.215** B.C.).

200–151 B.C. Romans defeat Seleucid King Antiochus III at Thermopylae (**191** B.C.)—beginning of Roman world domination. Maccabean revolt against Seleucids (**167** B.C.).

150–101 B.C. Third Punic War (**149–146** B.C.): Rome destroys Carthage, killing 450,000 and enslaving the remaining 50,000 inhabitants. Roman armies conquer Macedonia, Greece, Anatolia, Balearic Islands, and southern France. Venus de Milo (**c.140** B.C.). Cicero, Roman orator (**106–43** B.C.).

100–51 B.C. Julius Caesar (**100–44** B.C.) invades Britain (**55** B.C.) and conquers Gaul (France) (**c.50** B.C.). Spartacus leads slave revolt against Rome (**71** B.C.). Romans conquer Seleucid empire. Roman general Pompey conquers Jerusalem (**63** B.C.). Cleopatra on Egyptian throne (**51–31** B.C.). Chinese develop use of paper (**c.100** B.C.). Virgil, Roman poet (**70–19** B.C.). Horace, Roman poet (**65–8** B.C.).

50–1 B.C. Caesar crosses Rubicon to fight Pompey (**50** B.C.). Herod made Roman governor of Judea (**47** B.C.). Caesar murdered (**44** B.C.). Caesar's nephew Octavian, defeats Mark Antony and Cleopatra at Battle of Actium (**31** B.C.) and establishes Roman empire as Emperor Augustus—rules 27 B.C.—A.D. 14. Birth of Jesus Christ (variously given from **4** B.C. **to** A.D. **7**). Ovid, Roman poet (**43** B.C.—A.D. **18**).

A.D.

The Christian or Common Era (C.E.)

**Jesus Christ
(4? B.C.-29? A.D.)**

1–49 After Augustus, Tiberius becomes emperor (dies, **37**), succeeded by Caligula (assassinated, **41**), who is followed by Claudius. Crucifixion of Jesus (probably **30**). Han dynasty in China founded by Emperor Kuang Wu Ti. Buddhism introduced to China.

50–99 Claudius poisoned (**54**), succeeded by Nero (commits suicide, **68**). Missionary journeys of Paul the Apostle (**34–60**). Jews revolt against Rome. Jerusalem destroyed (**70**). Roman persecutions of Christians begin (**64**). Colosseum built in Rome (**71–80**). Trajan (rules **98–116**); Roman empire extends to Mesopotamia, Arabia, Balkans. First Gospels of St. Mark, St. John, St. Matthew.

100–149 Hadrian rules Rome (**117–138**); codifies Roman law, establishes postal system, builds wall between England and Scotland. Jews revolt under Bar Kokhba (**122–135**); final *Diaspora* (dispersion) of Jews begins.

150–199 Marcus Aurelius (rules Rome **161–180**). Oldest Mayan temples in Central America (**c.200**)., Mayan civilization develops writing, astronomy, mathematics.

200–249 Goths invade Asia Minor (**c.220**). Roman persecutions of Christians increase. Persian (Sassanid) empire re-established. End of Chinese Han dynasty.

250–299 Increasing invasions of the Roman empire by Franks and Goths. Buddhism spreads in China.

300–349 Constantine the Great (rules **312–337**) reunites eastern and western Roman empires, with new capital (Constantinople) on site of Byzantium (**330**); issues Edict of Milan legalizing Christianity (**313**); becomes a Christian on his deathbed (**337**). Council of Nicaea (**325**) defines orthodox Christian doctrine. First Gupta dynasty in India (**c.320**).

350–399 Huns (Mongols) invade Europe (**c.360**). Theodosius the Great (rules **392–395**)—last emperor of a united Roman empire. Roman empire permanently divided in **395**: western empire ruled from Rome; eastern empire ruled from Constantinople.

400–449 Western Roman empire disintegrates under weak emperors. Alaric, king of the Visigoths, sacks Rome (**410**). Attila, Hun chieftain, attacks Roman provinces (**433**). St. Patrick returns to Ireland (**432**). St. Augustine's *City of God* (**411**).

450–499 Vandals destroy Rome (**455**). Western Roman empire ends as Odoacer, German chieftain, overthrows last Roman emperor, Romulus Augustulus, and becomes king of Italy (**476**). Ostrogothic kingdom of Italy established by Theodoric the Great (**493**). Clovis, ruler of the Franks, is converted to Christianity (**496**). First schism between western and eastern churches (**484**). Peak of Mayan culture in Mexico (**c.460**).

500–549 Eastern and western churches reconciled (**519**). Justinian I, the Great,

(483–565), becomes Byzantine emperor **(527)**, issues his first code of civil laws **(529)**, conquers North Africa, Italy, and part of Spain. Plague spreads through Europe (from **542**). Arthur, semi-legendary king of the Britons (killed, **c.537**). Boëthius, Roman scholar (executed, **524**).

550–599 Beginnings of European silk industry after Justinian's missionaries smuggle silkworms out of China **(553)**. Mohammed, founder of Islam **(570–632)**. Buddhism in Japan **(c.560)**. St. Augustine of Canterbury brings Christianity to Britain **(597)**. After killing about half the population, plague in Europe subsides **(594)**.

600–649 Mohammed flees from Mecca to Medina (the *Hegira*); first year of the Muslim calendar **(622)**. Muslim empire grows **(634)**. Arabs conquer Jerusalem **(637)**, destroy Alexandrian library **(641)**, conquer Persians **(641)**. Fatima, Mohammed's daughter **(606–632)**.

650–699 Arabs attack North Africa **(670)**, destroy Carthage **(697)**. Venerable Bede, English monk **(672–735)**.

700–749 Arab empire extends from Lisbon to China (by **716**). Charles Martel, Frankish leader, defeats Arabs at Tours/Poitiers, halting Arab advance in Europe **(732)**. Charlemagne **(742–814)**.

750–799 Caliph Harun al-Rashid rules Arab empire **(786–809)**: the "golden age" of Arab culture. Vikings begin attacks on Britain **(790)**, land in Ireland **(795)**. Charlemagne becomes king of the Franks **(771)**. City of Machu Picchu flourishes in Peru.

800–849 Charlemagne (Charles the Great) crowned first Holy Roman Emperor in Rome **(800)**. Arabs conquer Crete, Sicily, and Sardinia **(826–827)**. Charlemagne dies **(814)**, succeeded by his son, Louis the Pious, who divides France among his sons **(817)**.

850–899 Norsemen attack as far south as the Mediterranean but are repulsed **(859)**, discover Iceland **(861)**. Alfred the Great becomes king of Britain **(871)**, defeats Danish invaders **(878)**. Russian nation founded by Vikings under Prince Rurik, establishing capital at Novgorod **(855–879)**.

900–949 Vikings discover Greenland **(c.900)**. Arab Spain under Abd ar-Rahman III becomes center of learning **(912–961)**.

950–999 Eric the Red establishes first Viking colony in Greenland **(982)**. Mieczyslaw I becomes first ruler of Poland **(960)**. Hugh Capet elected King of France in **987**; Capetian dynasty to rule until **1328**. Musical notation systematized **(c.990)**. Vikings and Danes attack Britain **(988–999)**. Holy Roman Empire founded by Otto I, King of Germany since **936**, crowned by Pope John XII in **962**.

11th century A.D.

c.1000 Hungary and Scandinavia converted to Christianity. Viking raider Leif Ericson discovers North America, calls it *Vinland.* Chinese invent gunpowder. *Beowulf,* Old English epic.

1009 Moslems destroy Holy Sepulchre in Jerusalem.

1013 Danes control England. Canute takes throne **(1016)**, conquers Norway **(1028)**, dies **(1035)**; kingdom divided among his sons: Harold Harefoot (England), Sweyn (Norway), Hardecanute (Denmark).

1040 Macbeth murders Duncan, king of Scotland.

1053 Robert Guiscard, Norman invader, establishes kingdom in Italy, conquers Sicily **(1072)**.

1054 Final separation between Eastern (Orthodox) and Western (Roman) churches.

1055 Seljuk Turks, Asian nomads, move west, capture Baghdad, Armenia **(1064)**, Syria, and Palestine **(1075)**.

1066 William of Normandy invades England, defeats last Saxon king, Harold II, at Battle of Hastings, crowned William I of England ("the Conqueror").

1073 Emergence of strong papacy when Gregory VII is elected. Conflict with English and French kings and German emperors will continue throughout medieval period.

1095 (*See* special material on "The Crusades.")

12th century A.D.

1150–67 Universities of Paris and Oxford founded in France and England.

1162 Thomas à Becket named Archbishop of Canterbury, murdered by Henry II's men **(1170)**. Troubadours (wandering minstrels) glorify romantic concepts of feudalism.

1189 Richard I ("the Lionhearted") succeeds Henry II in England, killed in France **(1199)**, succeeded by King John.

13th century A.D.

1211 Genghis Khan invades China, captures Peking **(1214)**, conquers Persia **(1218)**, invades Russia **(1223)**, dies **(1227)**.

**Viking Discovery
of Greenland (c.900)**

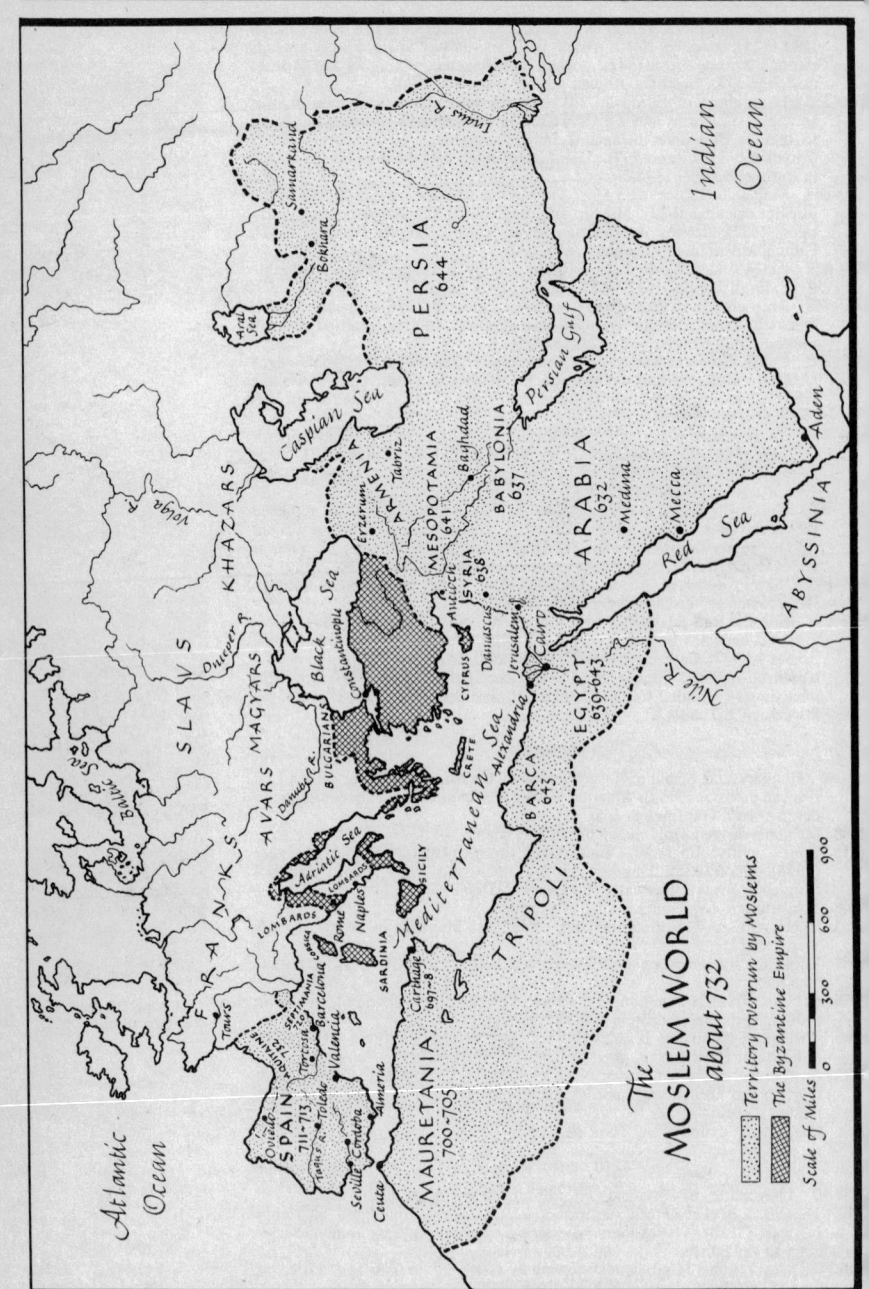

The **MOSLEM WORLD** about 732

Territory overrun by Moslems

The Byzantine Empire

Scale of Miles

0   300   600   900

Atlantic Ocean

FRANKS

SLAVS

AVARS   MAGYARS

KHAZARS

BULGARIANS

Constantinople

Black Sea

Caspian Sea

ARMENIA

Erzerum   Tabriz

PERSIA 644

Samarkand

Bokhara

Aral Sea

Indus R.

Indian Ocean

Danube R.

LOMBARDS

Rome

Naples

SARDINIA

SICILY

Adriatic Sea

CRETE

CYPRUS

Antioch

SYRIA 636

Damascus

Jerusalem

Alexandria

Cairo

EGYPT 639-643

BARCA 643

MESOPOTAMIA 641

Baghdad

BABYLONIA 637

Persian Gulf

ARABIA 632

Medina

Mecca

Red Sea

ABYSSINIA

Aden

Nile R.

TRIPOLI

Mediterranean Sea

Carthage 697-8

MAURETANIA 700-705

SPAIN 711-713

Tours R.   Toledo

Cordova

Seville   Cordova

Ceuta

Almeria

Valencia

Barcelona

Corsica

Volga R.

Dnieper R.

1215 King John forced by barons to sign Magna Carta at Runneymede, limiting royal power.

1233 The Inquisition begins as Pope Gregory IX assigns Dominicans responsibility for combatting heresy. Torture used **(1252)**. Ferdinand and Isabella establish Spanish Inquisition **(1478)**. Tourquemada, Grand Inquisitor, forces conversion or expulsion of Spanish Jews **(1492)**. Forced conversion of Moors **(1499)**. Inquisition in Portugal **(1531)**. First Protestants burned at the stake in Spain **(1543)**. Spanish Inquisition abolished **(1834)**.

1241 Mongols defeat Germans in Silesia, invade Poland and Hungary, withdraw from Europe after Ughetai, Mongol leader, dies.

1251 Kublai Khan governs China, becomes ruler of Mongols (1259), establishes Yuan dynasty in China (1280), invades Burma (1287), dies (1294).

1271 Marco Polo of Venice travels to China, in court of Kublai Khan (1275–1292), returns to Genoa (1295) and writes *Travels.*

1295 English King Edward I summons the Model Parliament.

14th century A.D.

John Wycliffe
(1320-1384)

1312–37 Mali Empire reaches its height in Africa under King Mansa Musa.

1337–1453 Hundred Years' War—English and French kings fight for control of France.

c.1325 The beginning of the Renaissance in Italy: writers Dante, Petrarch, Boccaccio; painter Giotto. Development of *No* drama in Japan. Aztecs establish capital on site of modern Mexico City. Peak of Moslem culture in Spain. Small cannon in use.

1347–1351 At least 25 million people die in Europe's "Black Death" (bubonic plague).

1368 Ming dynasty begins in China.

1376–82 John Wycliffe, pre-Reformation religious reformer and followers translate late Latin Bible into English.

1378 The Great Schism (to 1417)—rival popes in Rome and Avignon, France, fight for control of Roman Catholic Church.

c.1387 Chaucer's *Canterbury Tales.*

15th century A.D.

1415 Henry V defeats French at Agincourt. Jan Hus, Bohemian preacher and follower of Wycliffe, burned at stake in Constance as heretic.

1418–60 Portugal's Prince Henry the Navigator sponsors exploration of Africa's coast.

Joan of Arc
(1412-1431)

1428 Joan of Arc leads French against English, captured by Burgundians (1430) and turned over to the English, burned at the stake as a witch after ecclesiastical trial (1431).

1438 Inca rule in Peru.

1450 Florence becomes center of Renaissance arts and learning under the Medicis.

1453 Turks conquer Constantinople, end of the Byzantine empire. Hundred Years' War between France and England ends.

1455 The Wars of the Roses, civil wars between rival noble factions, begin in England (to 1485). Having invented printing with movable type at Mainz, Germany, Johann Gutenberg completes first Bible.

1462 Ivan the Great rules Russia until 1505 as first czar; ends payment of tribute to Mongols.

1492 Moors conquered in Spain by troops of Ferdinand and Isabella. Columbus discovers Caribbean islands, returns to Spain (1493). Second voyage to Dominica, Jamaica, Puerto Rico (1493–1496). Third voyage to Orinoco (1498). Fourth voyage to Honduras and Panama (1502–1504).

1497 Vasco da Gama sails around Africa and discovers sea route to India (1498). Establishes Portuguese colony in India (1502). John Cabot, employed by England, reaches and explores Canadian coast. Michelangelo's *Bacchus* sculpture.

Christopher Columbus
(1451-1506)

THE CRUSADES (1096–1291)

In 1095 at Council of Clermont, Pope Urban II calls for war to rescue Holy Land from Moslem infidels. *First Crusade* (1096)—about 500,000 peasants led by Peter the Hermit prove so troublesome that Byzantine Emperor Alexius ships them to Asia Minor; only 25,000 survive return after massacre by Seljuk Turks. Followed by organized army, led by nobility, which reaches Constantinople (1097), conquers Jerusalem (1099), Acre (1104), establishes Latin Kingdom protected by Knights of St. John the Hospitaller (1100), and Knights Templar (1123). Seljuk Turks start series of counterattacks (1144). *Second Crusade* (1146) led by King Louis VIII of France and Emperor Conrad III. Crusaders perish in Asia Minor (1147).

Saladin controls Egypt (1171), unites Islam in Holy War (*Jihad*) against Christians, recaptures Jerusalem (1187). *Third Crusade* (1189) under kings of France, England, and Germany fails to reduce Saladin's power. *Fourth Crusade* (1200–1204)—French knights sack Greek Christian Constantinople, establish Latin empire in Byzantium. Greeks re-establish Orthodox faith (1262).

Children's Crusade (1212)—Only 1 of 30,000 French children and about 200 of 20,000 German children survive to return home. Other Crusades—against Egypt (1217), *Sixth* (1228), *Seventh* (1248), *Eighth* (1270). Mamelukes conquer Acre; end of the Crusades (1291).

16th century A.D.

**Michelangelo Buonarroti
(1475-1564)**

**Martin Luther
(1483-1546)**

**Anthony Van Dyck
(1559-1641)**

1501 First black slaves in America brought to Spanish colony of Santo Domingo.

c.1503 Leonardo da Vinci paints the *Mona Lisa.*

1506 St. Peter's Church started in Rome; designed and decorated by such artists and architects as Bramante, Michelangelo, da Vinci, Raphael, and Bernini before its completion in **1626.**

1509 Henry VIII ascends English throne. Michelangelo paints the ceiling of the Sistine Chapel.

1517 Turks conquer Egypt, control Arabia. Martin Luther posts his 95 theses denouncing church abuses on church door in Wittenberg—start of the Reformation in Germany.

1519 Ulrich Zwingli begins Reformation in Switzerland. Hernando Cortes conquers Mexico for Spain. Charles I of Spain is chosen Holy Roman Emperor Charles V. Portuguese explorer Fernando Magellan sets out to circumnavigate the globe.

1520 Luther excommunicated by Pope Leo X. Suleiman I ("the Magnificent") becomes Sultan of Turkey, invades Hungary **(1521),** Rhodes **(1522),** attacks Austria **(1529),** annexes Hungary **(1541),** Tripoli **(1551),** makes peace with Persia **(1553),** destroys Spanish fleet **(1560),** dies **(1566).** Magellan reaches the Pacific, is killed by Philippine natives **(1521).** One of his ships under Juan Sebastián del Cano continues around the world, reaches Spain **(1522).**

1524 Verrazano, sailing under the French flag, explores the New England coast and New York Bay.

1527 Troops of the Holy Roman Empire attack Rome, imprison Pope Clement VII—the end of the Italian Renaissance. Castiglione writes *The Courtier.* The Medici expelled from Florence.

1532 Pizarro marches from Panama to Peru, kills the Inca chieftain, Atahualpa, of Peru **(1533).** Machiavelli's *Prince* published posthumously.

1535 Reformation begins as Henry VIII makes himself head of English Church after being excommunicated by Pope. Sir Thomas More executed as traitor for refusal to acknowledge king's religious authority. Jacques Cartier sails up the St. Lawrence River, basis of French claims to Canada.

1536 Henry VIII executes second wife, Anne Boleyn. John Calvin establishes Presbyterian form of Protestantism in Switzerland, writes *Institutes of the Christian Religion.* Danish and Norwegian Reformations. Michelangelo's *Last Judgment.*

1541 John Knox leads Reformation in Scotland, establishes Presbyterian church **(1560).**

1543 Publication of *On the Revolution of Heavenly Bodies* by Polish scholar Nicolaus Copernicus—giving his theory that the earth revolves around the sun.

1545 Council of Trent to meet intermittently until **1563** to define Catholic dogma and doctrine, reiterate papal authority.

1547 Ivan IV ("the Terrible") crowned as Czar of Russia, begins conquest of Astrakhan and Kazan **(1552),** battles nobles (boyars) for power **(1564),** kills his son **(1580),** dies, and is succeeded by a son who gives power to Boris Godunov **(1584).**

1553 Roman Catholicism restored in England by Queen Mary I, who rules until **1558.** Religious radical Michael Servetus burned as heretic in Geneva by order of John Calvin.

1554 Benvenuto Cellini completes the bronze *Perseus.*

1556 Akbar the Great becomes Mogul emperor of India, conquers Afghanistan **(1581),** continues wars of conquest (until **1605).**

1558 Queen Elizabeth I ascends the throne (rules to **1603).** Restores Protestantism, establishes state Church of England (Anglicanism). Renaissance will reach height in England—Shakespeare, Marlowe, Spenser.

1561 Persecution of Huguenots in France stopped by Edict of Orleans. French religious wars begin again with massacre of Huguenots at Vassy. St. Bartholomew's Day Massacre—thousands of Huguenots murdered **(1572).** Amnesty granted **(1573).** Persecution continues periodically until Edict of Nantes **(1598)** gives Huguenots religious freedom (until **1685).**

1568 Protestant Netherlands revolts against Catholic Spain; independence will be acknowledged by Spain in **1648.** High point of Dutch Renaissance—painters Rubens, Van Dyck, Hals, and Rembrandt.

1570 Japan permits visits of foreign ships. Queen Elizabeth I excommunicated by Pope. Turks attack Cyprus and war on Venice. Turkish fleet defeated at Battle of Lepanto by Spanish and Italian fleets **(1571).** Peace of Constantinople **(1572)** ends Turkish attacks on Europe.

1580 Francis Drake returns to England after circumnavigating the globe. Knighted by Queen Elizabeth I **(1581)**. Montaigne's *Essays* published.

1583 William of Orange rules The Netherlands; assassinated on orders of Philip II of Spain **(1584)**.

1587 Mary, Queen of Scots, executed for treason by order of Queen Elizabeth I. Monteverdi's *First Book of Madrigals*.

1588 Defeat of the Spanish Armada by English. Henry, King of Navarre and Protestant leader, recognized as Henry IV, first Bourbon king of France. Converts to Roman Catholicism in **1593** in attempt to end religious wars.

1590 Henry IV enters Paris, wars on Spain **(1595)**, marries Marie de Medici **(1600)**, assassinated **(1610)**. Spenser's *The Faerie Queen,* El Greco's *St. Jerome.* Galileo's experiments with falling objects.

1598 Boris Godunov becomes Russian Czar. Tycho Brahe describes his astronomical experiments.

**Francis Bacon
(1561-1626)**

17th century A.D.

1600 Giordano Bruno burned as a heretic. Ieyasu rules Japan, moves capital to Edo (Tokyo). Shakespeare's *Hamlet* begins his most productive decade. English East India Company established to develop overseas trade.

1607 Jamestown, Virginia, established—first permanent English colony on American mainland.

1609 Samuel de Champlain establishes French colony of Quebec.

1611 Gustavus Adolphus elected King of Sweden. King James Version of the Bible published in England. Rubens paints his *Descent from the Cross.*

1614 John Napier discovers logarithms.

1618 Start of the Thirty Years' War (to **1648**)—Protestant revolt against Catholic oppression; Denmark, Sweden, and France will invade Germany in later phases of war. Kepler proposes his Third Law of planetary motion.

1620 Pilgrims, after three-month voyage in *Mayflower,* land at Plymouth Rock. Francis Bacon's *Novum Organum.*

1633 Inquisition forces Galileo to recant his belief in Copernican theory.

1642 English Civil War. Cavaliers, supporters of Charles I, against Roundheads, parliamentary forces. Oliver Cromwell defeats Royalists **(1646)**. Parliament demands reforms. Charles I offers concessions, brought to trial **(1648)**, beheaded **(1649)**. Cromwell becomes Lord Protector **(1653)**. Rembrandt paints his *Night Watch.*

1644 End of Ming Dynasty in China—Manchus come to power. Descartes' *Principles of Philosophy.* John Milton's *Areopagitica* on the freedom of the press.

1648 End of the Thirty Years' War. German population about half of what it was in **1618** because of war and pestilence.

1658 Cromwell dies; his son, Richard, resigns and Puritan government collapses.

1660 English Parliament calls for the restoration of the monarchy; invites Charles II to return from France.

1661 Charles II is crowned King of England. Louis XIV begins personal rule as absolute monarch; starts to build Versailles.

**Giordano Bruno
(1548-1600)**

**George Washington
(1732-1799)**

THE FOUNDING OF THE AMERICAN NATION

Colonization of America begins: Jamestown, Va. **(1607)**; Pilgrims in Plymouth **(1620)**; Massachusetts Bay Colony **(1630)** New Netherland founded by Dutch West India Company **(1623)**, captured by English **(1664)**. Delaware established by Swedish trading company **(1638)**, absorbed later by Penn family. Proprietorships by royal grants to Lord Baltimore (Maryland, **1632**); Captain John Mason (New Hampshire, **1635**); Sir William Berkeley and Sir George Carteret (New Jersey, **1663**); friends of Charles II (the Carolinas, **1663**); William Penn (Pennsylvania, **1682**); James Oglethorpe and others (Georgia, **1732**).

Increasing conflict between colonists and Britain on western frontier because of royal edict limiting western expansion **(1763)**, and regulation of colonial trade and increased taxation of colonies (Writs of Assistance allow search for illegal shipments, **1761**; Sugar Act, **1764**; Currency Act, **1764**; Stamp Act, **1765**; Quartering Act, **1765**; Duty Act, **1767**.) Boston Massacre **(1770)**. Lord North attempts conciliation **(1770)**. Boston Tea Party **(1773)**, followed by punitive measures passed by Parliament—the "Intolerable Acts."

First Continental Congress **(1774)** sends "Declaration of Rights and Grievances" to king, urges colonies to form Continental Association. Paul Revere's Ride and Lexington and Concord battle between Massachusetts minutemen and British **(1775)**.

Second Continental Congress **(1775)**, while sending "olive branch" to the king, begins to raise army, appoints Washington commander-in-chief, and seeks alliance with France. Some colonial legislatures urge their delegates to vote for independence. Declaration of Independence **(July 4, 1776)**.

Major Battles of the Revolutionary War: *Long Island:* Howe defeats Putnam's division of Washington's Army in Brooklyn Heights, but Americans escape across East River **(1776)**. *Trenton and Princeton:* Washington defeats Hessians at Trenton. British at Princeton, winters at Morristown **(1776–77)**. Howe winters in Philadelphia; Washington at Valley Forge **(1777–78)**. Burgoyne surrenders British army to General Gates at *Saratoga* **(1777)**.

France recognizes American independence **(1778)**. The War moves south: Savannah captured by British **(1778)**; Charleston occupied **(1780)**; Americans fight successful guerrilla actions under Marion, Pickens, and Sumter. In the West, George Rogers Clark attacks Forts Kaskaskia and Vincennes **(1778–1779)**, defeating British in the region. Cornwallis surrenders at *Yorktown,* Virginia **(Oct. 19, 1781)**. By **1782**, Britain is eager for peace because of conflicts with European nations. *Peace of Paris* **(1783)**: Britain recognizes American independence.

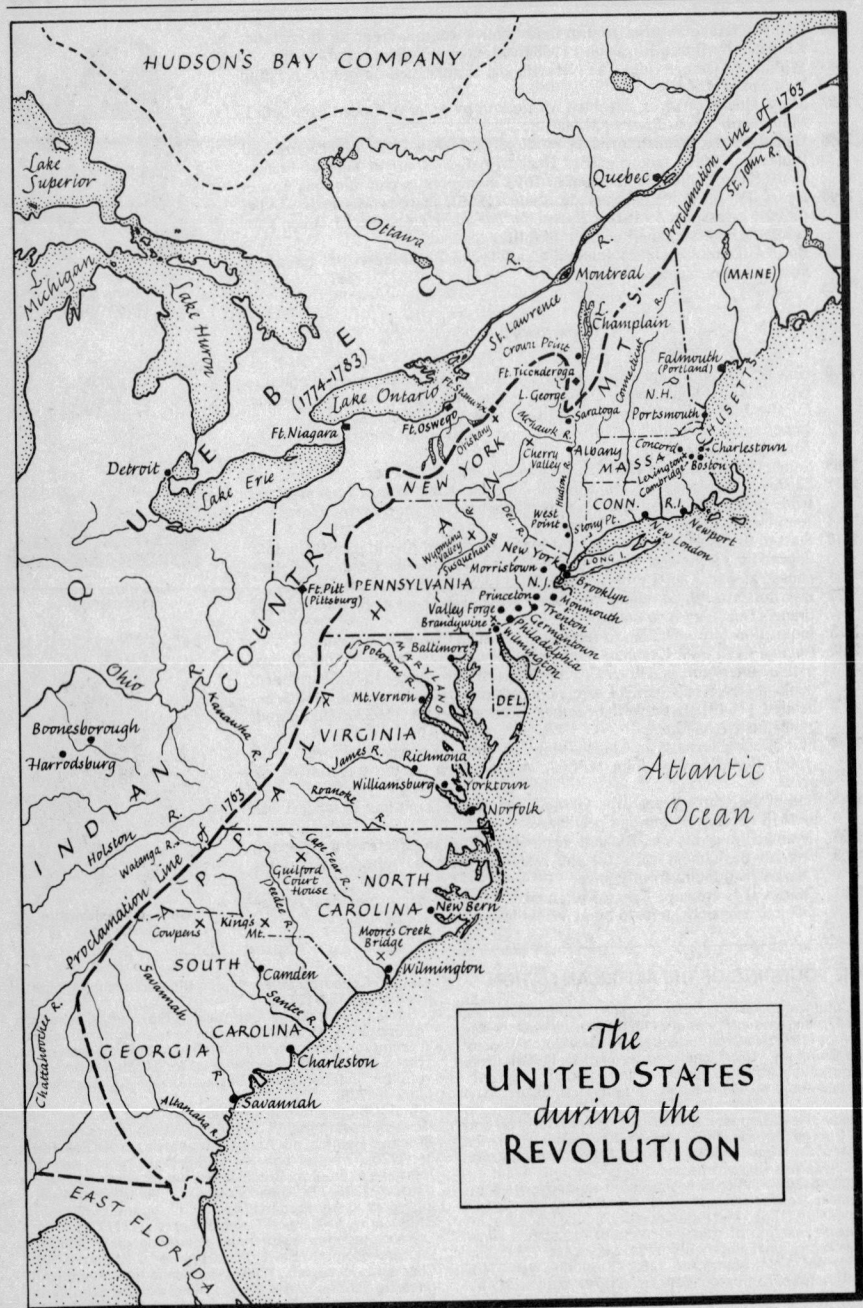

HUDSON'S BAY COMPANY

Lake Superior

Lake Michigan

Lake Huron

Ottawa R.

Quebec

Proclamation Line of 1763

St. John R.

Montreal

(MAINE)

St. Lawrence

Champlain

Crown Point

Ft. Ticonderoga

L. George

Saratoga

QUEBEC

(1774–1783)

Lake Ontario

Ft. Niagara

Ft. Oswego

Oswego R.

Mohawk R.

N.H.

Portsmouth

Falmouth (Portland)

Detroit

Lake Erie

Cherry Valley

Albany

Concord

Lexington

Charlestown

Boston

NEW YORK

MASS

CONN.

R.I.

Newport

West Point

Stony Pt.

LONG I.

New London

INDIAN COUNTRY

Ft. Pitt (Pittsburg)

Wyoming Valley

Susquehanna R.

Morristown

New York

N.J.

Monmouth

Brooklyn

PENNSYLVANIA

Princeton

Trenton

Valley Forge

Brandywine

Germantown

Philadelphia

Wilmington

Ohio R.

Kanawha R.

Mt. Vernon

Potomac R.

Baltimore

MARYLAND

DEL.

Boonesborough

Harrodsburg

Holston R.

Watauga R.

VIRGINIA

James R.

Richmond

Roanoke R.

Williamsburg

Yorktown

Norfolk

Proclamation Line of 1763

Cape Fear R.

Guilford Court House

NORTH CAROLINA

New Bern

Cowpens

King's Mt.

Pee Dee R.

Moore's Creek Bridge

Camden

Santee R.

Wilmington

SOUTH CAROLINA

Savannah R.

GEORGIA

Chattahoochee R.

Charleston

Altamaha R.

Savannah

Atlantic Ocean

EAST FLORIDA

The **UNITED STATES** *during the* **REVOLUTION**

1664 British take New Amsterdam from the Dutch. English limit "Nonconformity" with re-established Anglican Church. Isaac Newton's experiments with gravity.

1665 Great Plague in London kills 75,000.

1666 Great Fire of London. Molière's *Misanthrope*.

1683 War of European powers against the Turks (to **1699**). Vienna withstands three-month Turkish siege; high point of Turkish advance in Europe.

1685 James II succeeds Charles II in England, calls for freedom of conscience **(1687)**. Protestants fear restoration of Catholicism and demand "Glorious Revolution." William of Orange invited to England and James II escapes to France **(1688)**. William III and his wife, Mary, crowned. In France, Edict of Nantes of **1598**, granting freedom of worship to Huguenots (French Protestants), is revoked by Louis XIV; thousands of Protestants flee.

1689 Peter the Great becomes Czar of Russia—attempts to westernize nation and build Russia as a military power. Defeats Charles XII of Sweden at Poltava **(1709)**. Beginning of the French and Indian Wars (to **1763**), campaigns in America linked to a series of wars between France and England for domination of Europe.

1690 William III of England defeats former King James II and Irish rebels at Battle of the Boyne in Ireland. John Locke's *Human Understanding*.

**John Locke
(1632-1704)**

18th century A.D.

1701 War of the Spanish Succession begins—the last of Louis XIV's wars for domination of the continent. The Peace of Utrecht **(1714)** will end the conflict and mark the rise of the British Empire. Called Queen Anne's War in America, it ends with the British taking New Foundland, Acadia, and Hudson's Bay Territory from France, and Gibraltar and Minorca from Spain.

1704 Deerfield (Mass.) Massacre of English colonists by French and Indians. Bach's first cantata. Jonathan Swift's *Tale of a Tub*. *Boston News Letter*— first newspaper in America.

1707 United Kingdom of Great Britain formed—England, Wales, and Scotland joined by parliamentary Act of Union.

1729 J. S. Bach's *St. Matthew Passion*. Isaac Newton's *Principia* translated from Latin into English.

1735 John Peter Zenger, New York editor, acquitted of libel in New York, establishing press freedom.

1740 Capt. Vitus Bering, Dane employed by Russia, discovers Alaska.

1746 British defeat Scots under Stuart Pretender Prince Charles at Culloden Moor. Last battle fought on British soil.

1751 Publication of the *Encyclopédie* begins in France, the "bible" of the Enlightenment.

1755 Samuel Johnson's *Dictionary* first published. Great earthquake in Lisbon, Portugal—over 60,000 die. U.S. postal service established.

1756 Seven Years' War (French and Indian War in America) (to **1763**), in which Britain and Prussia defeat France, Spain, Austria, and Russia. France loses North American colonies; Spain cedes Florida to Britain in exchange for Cuba. In India, over 100 British prisoners die in "Black Hole of Calcutta."

1757 Beginning of British Empire in India as Robert Clive, British commander, defeats Nawab of Bengal at Plassey.

1759 British capture Quebec from French. Voltaire's *Candide*. Haydn's *Symphony No. 1*.

**Catherine II
(1729-1796)**

1762 Catherine II ("the Great") becomes Czarina of Russia. J. J. Rousseau's *Social Contract*. Mozart tours Europe as six-year-old prodigy.

1765 James Watt invents the steam engine.

1769 Sir William Arkwright patents a spinning machine—an early step in the Industrial Revolution.

1772 Joseph Priestley and Daniel Rutherford independently discover nitrogen. Partition of Poland—in **1772, 1793,** and **1795,** Austria, Prussia, and Russia divide land and people of Poland, end its independence.

1775 The American Revolution (*see* "The Founding of the American Nation"). Priestley discovers hydrochloric and sulfuric acids.

1776 Adam Smith's *Wealth of Nations*. Edward Gibbon's *Decline and Fall of the Roman Empire*. Thomas Paine's *Common Sense*. Fragonard's *Washerwoman*. Mozart's *Haffner Serenade*.

1778 Capt. James Cook discovers Hawaii. Franz Mesmer uses hypnotism.

1781 Immanuel Kant's *Critique of Pure Reason*. Herschel discovers Uranus.

1783 End of Revolutionary War (*see* special material on "The Founding of the

American Nation"). William Blake's poems. Beethoven's first printed works.

1784 Crimea annexed by Russia. John Wesley's *Deed of Declaration*, the basic work of Methodism.

1785 Russians settle Aleutian Islands.

1787 The Constitution of the United States signed. Lavoisier's work on chemical nomenclature. Mozart's *Don Giovanni*.

1788 French *Parlement* presents grievances to Louis XVI who agrees to convening of Estates-General in **1789**—not called since **1613.** Goethe's *Egmont.* Laplace's *Laws of the Planetary System.*

1789 French Revolution (*see* special material on the "French Revolution"). In U.S., George Washington elected President with all 69 votes of the Electoral College, takes oath of office in New York City. Vice President: John Adams. Secretary of State: Thomas Jefferson. Secretary of Treasury: Alexander Hamilton.

1790 H.M.S. *Bounty* mutineers settle on Pitcairn Island. Aloisio Galvani experiments on electrical stimulation of the muscles. Philadelphia temporary capital of U.S. as Congress votes to establish new capital on Potomac. U.S. population about 3,929,000, including 698,000 slaves. Lavoisier formulates *Table of 31 chemical elements.*

1791 U.S. Bill of Rights ratified. Boswell's *Life of Johnson.*

1794 Kosciusko's uprising in Poland quelled by the Russians. In U.S., Whiskey Rebellion in Pennsylvania as farmers object to liquor taxes.

1796 Napoleon Bonaparte, French general, defeats Austrians. In the U.S., Washington's Farewell Address (**Sept. 17**); John Adams elected President; Thomas Jefferson, Vice President. Edward Jenner introduces smallpox vaccination.

1798 Napoleon extends French conquests to Rome and Egypt. U.S. Navy Department established.

1799 Napoleon leads coup that overthrows Directory, becomes First Consul—one of three who rule France.

Napoleon Bonaparte (1769-1821)

19th century A.D.

1800 Napoleon conquers Italy, firmly establishes himself as First Consul in France. In the U.S., Federal Government moves to Washington. Robert Owen's social reforms in England. William Herschel discovers infrared rays. Alessandro Volta produces electricity.

1801 Austria makes temporary peace with France. United Kingdom of Great Britain and Ireland established with one monarch and one parliament; Catholics excluded from voting.

1803 U.S. negotiates Louisiana Purchase from France: For $15 million, U.S. doubles its domain, increasing its territory by 827,000 sq. mi. (2,144,500 sq km), from Mississippi River to Rockies and from Gulf of Mexico to British North America.

1804 Haiti declares independence from France; first black nation to gain freedom from European colonial rule. Napoleon proclaims himself emperor of France, systematizes French law under *Code Napoleon.* In the U.S., Alexander Hamilton is mortally wounded in duel with Aaron Burr. Lewis and Clark expedition begins exploration of what is now northwestern U.S.

1805 Lord Nelson defeats the French-Spanish fleets in the Battle of Trafalgar. Napoleon victorious over Austrian and Russian forces at the Battle of Austerlitz.

1807 Robert Fulton makes first successful steamboat trip on *Clermont* between New York City and Albany.

1808 French armies occupy Rome and Spain, extending Napoleon's empire. Britain begins aiding Spanish guerrillas against Napoleon in Peninsular War. In the U.S., Congress bars importation of slaves. Beethoven's *Fifth* and *Sixth Symphonies* performed.

1812 Napoleon's Grand Army invades Russia in June. Forced to retreat in winter, most of Napoleon's 600,000 men are lost. In the U.S., war with Britain

Thomas Jefferson (1743-1826)

Alexander Hamilton (1755-1804)

FRENCH REVOLUTION (1789–1799)

Revolution begins when Third Estate (Commons) delegates swear not to disband until France has a constitution. Paris mob storms Bastille, symbol of royal power (**July 14, 1789**). National Assembly votes for Constitution, Declaration of the Rights of Man, a limited monarchy, and other reforms (**1789–90**). Legislative Assembly elected, Revolutionary Commune formed, and French Republic proclaimed (**1792**). War of the First Coalition—Austria, Prussia, Britain, Netherlands, and Spain fight to restore French nobility (**1792–97**). Start of series of wars between France and European powers that will last, almost without interruption, for 23 years. Louis XVI and Marie Antoinette executed. Committee of Public Safety begins Reign of Terror as political control measure. Interfactional rivalry leads to mass killings. Danton and Robespierre executed. Third French Constitution sets up Directory government (**1795**).

declared over freedom of the seas for U.S. vessels. U.S.S. *Constitution* sinks British frigate. (*See* special material on the "War of 1812.")

1814 French defeated by allies (Britain, Austria, Russia, Prussia, Sweden, and Portugal) in War of Liberation. Napoleon exiled to Elba, off Italian coast. Bourbon King Louis XVIII takes French throne. George Stephenson builds first practical steam locomotive.

1815 Napoleon returns: "Hundred Days" begin. Napoleon defeated by Wellington at Waterloo, banished again to St. Helena in South Atlantic. Congress of Vienna: victorious allies change the map of Europe.

1817 Simón Bolívar establishes independent Venezuela, as Spain loses hold on South American countries. Bolívar named President of Colombia **(1819).** Peru, Guatemala, Panama, and Santo Domingo proclaim independence from Spain **(1821).**

1820 Missouri Compromise—Missouri admitted as slave state but slavery barred in rest of Louisiana Purchase north of 36°30′ N.

1822 Greeks proclaim a republic and independence from Turkey. Turks invade Greece. Russia declares war on Turkey **(1828).** Greece also aided by France and Britain. War ends and Turks recognize Greek independence **(1829).** Brazil becomes independent of Portugal. Schubert's *Eighth Symphony* ("The Unfinished").

1823 U.S. Monroe Doctrine warns European nations not to interfere in Western Hemisphere.

1824 Mexico becomes a republic, three years after declaring independence from Spain. Beethoven's *Ninth Symphony.*

1825 First passenger-carrying railroad in England.

1830 French invade Algeria. Louis Philippe becomes "Citizen King" as revolution forces Charles X to abdicate. Mormon church formed in U.S. by Joseph Smith.

1831 Polish revolt against Russia fails. Belgium separates from the Netherlands. In U.S., Nat Turner leads unsuccessful slave rebellion.

1833 Slavery abolished in British Empire.

1834 Charles Babbage invents "analytical engine," precursor of computer. McCormick patents reaper.

1836 Boer farmers start "Great Trek"—Natal, Transvaal, and Orange Free State founded in South Africa. Mexican army besieges Texans in Alamo. Entire garrison, including Davy Crockett and Jim Bowie, wiped out. Texans gain independence from Mexico after winning Battle of San Jacinto. Dickens's *Pickwick Papers.*

1837 Victoria becomes Queen of Great Britain. Mob kills Elijah P. Lovejoy, Illinois abolitionist publisher.

1839 First Opium War (to **1842**) between Britain and China, over importation of drug into China.

1840 Lower and Upper Canada united.

1841 U.S. President Harrison dies **(April 4)** one month after inauguration; John Tyler becomes first vice president to succeed to presidency.

1844 Democratic convention calls for annexation of Texas and acquisition of Oregon ("Fifty-four-forty-or-fight"). Five Chinese ports opened to U.S. ships. Samuel F. B. Morse patents telegraph.

1845 Congress adopts joint resolution for annexation of Texas.

1846 Failure of potato crop causes famine in Ireland. U.S. declares war on Mexico. California and New Mexico annexed by U.S. Brigham Young leads Mormons to Great Salt Lake. W.T. Morton uses ether as anesthetic. Sewing machine patented by Elias Howe.

1848 Revolt in Paris: Louis Philippe abdicates; Louis Napoleon elected President of French Republic. Revolutions in Vienna, Venice, Berlin, Milan, Rome, and Warsaw. Put down by royal troops in **1848–49.** U.S.-Mexico War ends; Mexico cedes claims to Texas, California, Arizona, New Mexico, Utah, Nevada. U.S. treaty with Britain sets Oregon Territory boundary at 49th parallel. Karl Marx and Friedrich Engels' *Communist Manifesto.*

1849 California gold rush begins.

1850 Henry Clay opens great debate on slavery, warns South against secession.

1851 Herman Melville's *Moby Dick.* Harriet Beecher Stowe's *Uncle Tom's Cabin.*

1852 South African Republic established. Louis Napoleon proclaims himself Napoleon III ("Second Empire").

Charles Dickens
(1812-1870)

Henry Clay
(1777-1852)

WAR OF 1812

British interference with American trade, impressment of American seamen, and "War Hawks" drive for western expansion lead to war. American attacks on Canada foiled; U.S. Commodore Perry wins battle of Lake Erie **(1813).** British capture and burn Washington **(1814)** but fail to take Fort McHenry at Baltimore. Andrew Jackson repulses assault on New Orleans after treaty of Ghent ends war **(1815).** War settles little but strengthens U.S. as independent nation.

**Dred Scott
(1795?-1858)**

**Abraham Lincoln
(1809-1865)**

**Ulysses S. Grant
(1822-1885)**

1853 Crimean War begins as Turkey declares war on Russia. Commodore Perry reaches Tokyo.

1854 Britain and France join Turkey in war on Russia. In U.S., Kansas-Nebraska Act permits local option on slavery; rioting and bloodshed. Japanese allow American trade. Antislavery men in Michigan form Republican Party. Tennyson's *Charge of the Light Brigade*. Thoreau's *Walden*.

1855 Armed clashes in Kansas between pro- and anti-slavery forces. Florence Nightingale nurses wounded in Crimea. Walt Whitman's *Leaves of Grass*.

1856 Flaubert's *Madame Bovary*.

1857 Supreme Court, in Dred Scott decision, rules that a slave is not a citizen. Financial crisis in Europe and U.S. Great Mutiny (Sepoy Rebellion) begins in India. India placed under crown rule as a result.

1858 Pro-slavery constitution rejected in Kansas. Abraham Lincoln makes strong antislavery speech in Springfield, Ill.: ". . . this Government cannot endure permanently half slave and half free." Lincoln-Douglas debates. First trans-Atlantic telegraph cable completed by Cyrus W. Field.

1859 John Brown raids Harpers Ferry; is captured and hanged. Work begins on Suez Canal. Unification of Italy starts under leadership of Count Cavour, Sardinian premier. Joined by France in war against Austria. Edward Fitzgerald's *Rubaiyat of Omar Khayyam*. Charles Darwin's *Origin of Species*. J. S. Mill's *On Liberty*

1861 U.S. Civil War begins as attempts at compromise fail (*see* special material on "The Civil War"). Congress creates Colorado, Dakota, and Nevada territories; adopts income tax; Lincoln inaugurated. Serfs emancipated in Russia. Pasteur's theory of germs. Independent Kingdom of Italy proclaimed under Sardinian King Victor Emmanuel II.

1863 French capture Mexico City; proclaim Archduke Maximilian of Austria emperor.

1865 Lincoln fatally shot at Ford's Theater by John Wilkes Booth. Vice President Johnson sworn as successor. Booth caught and dies of gunshot wounds; four conspirators are hanged. Joseph Lister begins antiseptic surgery. Gregor Mendel's *Law of Heredity*. Lewis Carroll's *Alice's Adventures in Wonderland*.

1866 Alfred Nobel invents dynamite (patented in Britain 1867). Seven Weeks' War: Austria defeated by Prussia and Italy.

1867 Austria-Hungary Dual Monarchy established. French leave Mexico; Maximilian executed. Dominion of Canada established. U.S. buys Alaska from Russia for $7,200,000. South African diamond field discovered. Volume I of Marx's *Das Kapital*. Strauss's *Blue Danube*.

1868 Revolution in Spain; Queen Isabella deposed, flees to France. In U.S., Fourteenth Amendment giving civil rights to blacks is ratified. Georgia under military government after legislature expels blacks.

1869 First U.S. transcontinental rail route completed. James Fisk and Jay Gould attempt to control gold market causes Black Friday panic. Suez Canal opened. Mendeleev's periodic table of elements.

1870 Franco-Prussian War (to **1871**): Napoleon III capitulates at Sedan. Revolt in Paris; Third Republic proclaimed.

THE CIVIL WAR

(The War Between the States or the War of the Rebellion)

Apart from the matter of slavery, the Civil War arose out of both the economic and political rivalry between an agrarian South and an industrial North and the issue of the right of states to secede from the Union.

1861 After South Carolina secedes **(Dec. 20, 1860)**, Mississippi, Florida, Alabama, Georgia, Louisiana, and Texas follow, forming the Confederate States of America, with Jefferson Davis as president **(Jan.–March)**. War begins as Confederates fire on Fort Sumter **(April 12)**. Lincoln calls for 75,000 volunteers. Southern ports blockaded by superior Union naval forces. Virginia, Arkansas, Tennessee, and North Carolina secede to complete 11-state Confederacy. Union army advancing on Richmond repulsed at first Battle of Bull Run **(July)**.

1862 Edwin M. Stanton named Secretary of War **(Jan.)**. Grant wins first important Union victory in West, at Fort Donelson; Nashville falls **(Feb.)**. Ironclads, Union's *Monitor* and Confederate's *Virginia (Merrimac)* duel at Hampton Roads **(March)**. New Orleans falls to Union fleet under Farragut; city occupied **(April)**. Grant's army escapes defeat at Shiloh. Memphis falls as Union gunboats control upper Mississippi **(June)**. Confederate general Robert E. Lee victorious at second Battle of Bull Run **(Aug.)**. Union army under McClellan halts Lee's attack on Washington in the Battle of Antietam **(Sept.)**. Lincoln removes McClellan for lack of aggressiveness. Burnside's drive on Richmond fails at Fredericksburg **(Dec.)**. Union forces under Rosecrans chase Bragg through Tennessee; battle of Murfreesboro **(Oct.–Jan. 1863)**.

1863 Lee defeats Hooker at Chancellorsville; "Stonewall" Jackson, Confederate general, dies **(May)**. Confederate invasion of Pennsylvania stopped at Gettysburg by George Meade—Lee loses 20,000 men—the greatest battle of the War **(July)**. It and the Union victory at Vicksburg mark the war's turning point. Union general George H. Thomas, the "Rock of Chickamauga," holds Bragg's forces on Georgia-Tennessee border **(Sept.)**. Sherman, Hooker, and Thomas drive Bragg back to Georgia. Tennessee restored to the Union **(Nov.)**.

1864 Ulysses S. Grant named commander-in-chief of Union forces **(March)**. In the Wilderness campaign, Grant forces Lee's Army of Northern Virginia back toward Richmond **(May–June)**. Sherman's Atlanta campaign and "march to the sea" **(May–Sept.)**. Farragut's victory at Mobile Bay **(Aug.)**. Hood's Confederate army defeated at Nashville. Sherman takes Savannah **(Dec.)**.

1865 Sheridan defeats Confederates at Five Forks; Confederates evacuate Richmond **(April)**. On April 9, Lee surrenders to Grant at Appomattox.

1871 France surrenders Alsace-Lorraine to Germany; war ends. German Empire proclaimed with Prussian King as Kaiser Wilhelm I. Fighting with Apaches begins in American West. Boss Tweed corruption exposed in New York. The Chicago Fire, with 250 deaths and $196-million damage. Stanley meets Livingston in Africa.

1872 Congress gives amnesty to most Confederates. Jules Verne's *Around the World in 80 Days.*

1873 Economic crisis in Europe. U.S. establishes gold standard.

1875 First Kentucky Derby.

1876 Sioux kill Gen. George A. Custer and 264 troopers at Little Big Horn River. Alexander Graham Bell patents the telephone.

1877 After Presidential election of **1876,** Electoral Commission gives disputed Electoral College votes to Rutherford B. Hayes despite Tilden's popular majority. Russo-Turkish war (ends in **1878** with power of Turkey in Europe broken). Reconstruction ends in the American South. Thomas Edison patents phonograph.

1878 Congress of Berlin revises Treaty of San Stefano ending Russo-Turkish War; makes extensive redivision of southeastern Europe. First commercial telephone exchange opened in New Haven, Conn.

1880 U.S.-China treaty allows U.S. to restrict immigration of Chinese labor.

1881 President Garfield fatally shot by assassin; Vice President Arthur succeeds him. Charles J. Guiteau convicted and executed (in **1882**).

Geronimo
(1829-1909)

1882 Terrorism in Ireland after land evictions. Britain invades and conquers Egypt. Germany, Austria, and Italy form Triple Alliance. In U.S., Congress adopts Chinese Exclusion Act. Rockefeller's Standard Oil Trust is first industrial monopoly. In Berlin, Robert Koch announces discovery of tuberculosis germ.

1883 Congress creates Civil Service Commission. Brooklyn Bridge and Metropolitan Opera House completed.

1885 British Gen. Charles G. "Chinese" Gordon killed at Khartoum in Egyptian Sudan.

1886 Bombing at Haymarket Square, Chicago, kills seven policemen and injures many others. Eight alleged anarchists accused—three imprisoned, one commits suicide, four hanged. (In **1893**, Illinois Governor Altgeld, critical of trial, pardons three survivors.) Statue of Liberty dedicated. Geronimo, Apache Indian chief, surrenders.

1887 Queen Victoria's Golden Jubilee. Sir Arthur Conan Doyle's first Sherlock Holmes story, "A Study in Scarlet."

1888 Historic March blizzard in Northeast U.S.—many perish, property damage exceeds $25 million. George Eastman's box camera (the Kodak). J.B. Dunlop invents pneumatic tire. Jack the Ripper murders in London.

Samuel Clemens
(Mark Twain)
(1835-1910)

1889 Second (Socialist) International founded in Paris. Indian Territory in Oklahoma opened to settlement. Thousands die in Johnstown, Pa., flood. Mark Twain's *A Connecticut Yankee in King Arthur's Court.*

1890 Congress votes Sherman Antitrust Act. Sitting Bull killed in Sioux uprising.

1892 Battle between steel strikers and Pinkerton guards at Homestead, Pa.; union defeated after militia intervenes. Silver mine strikers in Idaho fight non-union workers; U.S. troops dispatched. Diesel engine patented.

1894 Sino-Japanese War begins (ends in **1895** with China's defeat). In France, Capt. Alfred Dreyfus convicted on false treason charge (pardoned in **1906**). In U.S., Jacob S. Coxey of Ohio leads "Coxey's Army" of unemployed on Washington. Eugene V. Debs calls general strike of rail workers to support Pullman Company strikers; strike broken, Debs jailed for six months. Thomas A. Edison's kinetoscope given first public showing in New York City.

1895 X-rays discovered by German physicist, Wilhelm Roentgen.

1896 Supreme Court's *Plessy v. Ferguson* decision—"separate but equal" doctrine. Alfred Nobel's will establishes prizes for peace, science, and literature. Marconi receives first wireless patent in Britain. William Jennings Bryan delivers "Cross of Gold" speech at Democratic Convention in

Thomas A. Edison
(1847-1931)

SPANISH-AMERICAN WAR (1898–1899)

War fires stoked by "jingo journalism" as American people support Cuban rebels against Spain. American business sees economic gain in Cuban trade and resources and American power zones in Latin America. Outstanding events: Submarine mine explodes U.S. battleship *Maine* in Havana Harbor **(Feb. 15)**; 260 killed; responsibility never fixed. Congress declares independence of Cuba **(April 19)**. Spain declares war on U.S. **(Apr. 24)**; Congress **(Apr. 25)** formally declares nation has been at war with Spain since Apr. 21. Commodore George Dewey wins seven-hour battle of Manila Bay **(May 1)**. Spanish fleet destroyed off Santiago, Cuba **(July 3)**; city surrenders **(July 17)**. Treaty of Paris (ratified by Senate **1899**) ends war. U.S. given Guam and Puerto Rico and agrees to pay Spain $20 million for Philippines. Cuba independent of Spain; under U.S. military control for three years until **May 20, 1902**. Yellow fever is eradicated and political reforms achieved.

**Marie Curie
(1867-1934)**

**Theodore Roosevelt
(1858-1919)**

**Albert Einstein
(1879-1955)**

Chicago. First modern Olympic games held in Athens, Greece.

1898 Chinese "Boxers," anti-foreign organization, established. They stage uprisings against Europeans in **1900;** U.S. and other Western troops relieve Peking legations. Spanish-American War (*see* special material on the "Spanish-American War"). Pierre and Marie Curie discover radium and polonium.

1899 Boer War (or South African War). Conflict between British and Boers (descendants of Dutch settlers of South Africa). Causes rooted in longstanding territorial disputes and in friction over political rights for English and other "uitlanders" following 1886 discovery of vast gold deposits in Transvaal. (British victorious as war ends in **1902.**) Casualties: 5,774 British dead, about 4,000 Boers. Union of South Africa established in **1908** as confederation of colonies; becomes British dominion in **1910.**

20th century A.D.

1900 Hurricane ravages Galveston, Tex.; 6,000 drown. Sigmund Freud's *The Interpretation of Dreams.*

1901 Queen Victoria dies; succeeded by son, Edward VII. As President McKinley begins second term, he is shot fatally by anarchist Leon Czolgosz. Theodore Roosevelt sworn in as successor.

1902 Enrico Caruso's first gramophone recording.

1903 Wright brothers, Orville and Wilbur, fly first powered, controlled, heavier-than-air plane at Kitty Hawk, N.C. Henry Ford organizes Ford Motor Company.

1904 Russo-Japanese War—competition for Korea and Manchuria: In **1905,** Port Arthur surrenders to Japanese and Russia suffers other defeats; President Roosevelt mediates Treaty of Portsmouth, N.H., ending war with concessions for Japan. *Entente Cordiale:* Britain and France settle their international differences. General theory of radioactivity by Rutherford and Soddy. New York City subway opened.

1905 General strike in Russia; first workers' soviet set up in St. Petersburg. Sailors on battleship *Potemkin* mutiny; reforms including first Duma (parliament) established by Czar's "October Manifesto." Albert Einstein's special theory of relativity and other key theories in physics. Franz Lehar's *Merry Widow.*

1906 San Francisco earthquake and three-day fire; 500 dead. Roald Amundsen, Norwegian explorer, fixes magnetic North Pole.

1907 Second Hague Peace Conference, of 46 nations, adopts 10 conventions on rules of war. Financial panic of **1907** in U.S.

1908 Earthquake kills 150,000 in southern Italy and Sicily. U.S. Supreme Court, in Danbury Hatters' case, outlaws secondary union boycotts.

1909 North Pole reached by American explorers Robert E. Peary and Matthew Henson.

1910 Boy Scouts of America incorporated.

1911 First use of aircraft as offensive weapon in Turkish-Italian War. Italy defeats Turks and annexes Tripoli and Libya. Chinese Republic proclaimed after revolution overthrows Manchu dynasty. Sun Yat-sen named president. Mexican Revolution: Porfirio Diaz, president since 1877, replaced by Francisco Madero. Triangle Shirtwaist Company fire in New York; 145 killed. Richard Strauss's *Der Rosenkavalier.* Irving Berlin's *Alexander's Ragtime Band.* Amundsen reaches South Pole.

1912 Balkan Wars (**1912–13**) resulting from territorial disputes: Turkey defeated by alliance of Bulgaria, Serbia, Greece, and Montenegro; London peace treaty (**1913**) partitions most of European Turkey among the victors. In second war (**1913**), Bulgaria attacks Serbia and Greece and is defeated after Romania intervenes and Turks recapture Adrianople. *Titanic* sinks on maiden voyage; over 1,500 drown.

1913 Suffragettes demonstrate in London. Garment workers strike in New York and Boston; win pay raise and shorter hours. Sixteenth Amendment (income tax) and 17th (popular election of U.S. senators) adopted. Bill creating U.S. Federal Reserve System becomes law. Stravinsky's *The Rite of Spring.*

1914 World War I begins (*see* special material on "World War I"). Panama Canal officially opened. Congress sets up Federal Trade Commission, passes Clayton Antitrust Act. U.S. Marines occupy Veracruz, Mexico, intervening in civil war to protect American interests.

1915 U.S. protests German submarine actions and British blockade of Germany. U.S. banks lend $500 million to France and Britain. D. W. Griffith's film *Birth of a Nation.* Albert Einstein's *General Theory of Relativity.*

1916 Congress expands armed forces. Tom Mooney arrested for San Francisco bombing (pardoned in **1939**). Pershing fails in raid into Mexico in quest of

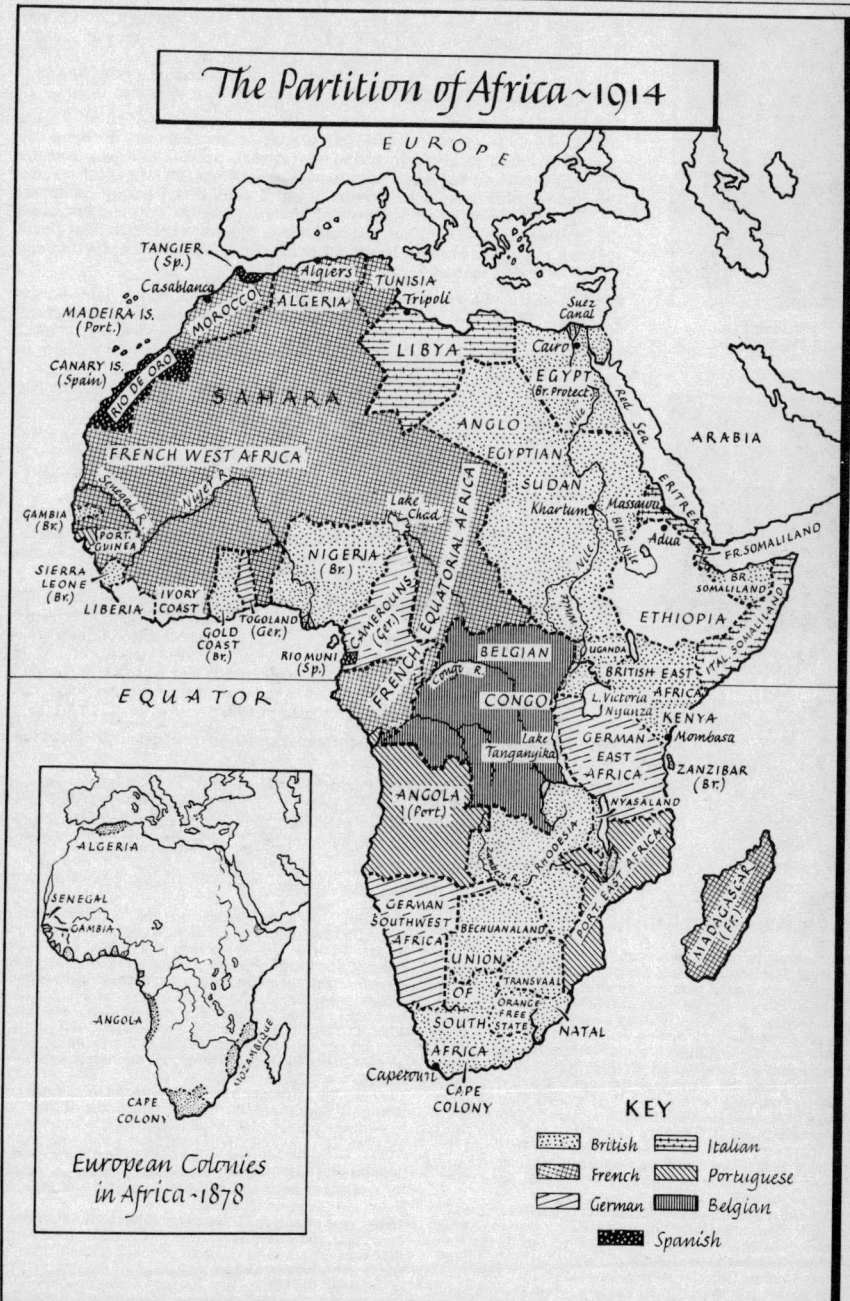

The Partition of Africa ~ 1914

EUROPE

TANGIER (Sp.)
Casablanca
MADEIRA IS. (Port.)
CANARY IS. (Spain)
Algiers
MOROCCO
ALGERIA
TUNISIA
Tripoli
LIBYA
Suez Canal
Cairo
EGYPT (Br. Protect.)
ARABIA
RIO DE ORO
SAHARA
ANGLO EGYPTIAN SUDAN
Khartum
Massawa
ERITREA
FRENCH WEST AFRICA
Lake Chad
FR.SOMALILAND
GAMBIA (Br.)
PORT. GUINEA
NIGERIA (Br.)
FRENCH EQUATORIAL AFRICA
Adua
BR. SOMALILAND
SIERRA LEONE (Br.)
LIBERIA
IVORY COAST
GOLD COAST (Br.)
TOGOLAND (Ger.)
RIO MUNI (Sp.)
CAMEROUNS (Ger.)
ETHIOPIA
ITAL. SOMALILAND
BELGIAN CONGO
UGANDA
BRITISH EAST AFRICA
L.Victoria Nyanza
KENYA
Mombasa
EQUATOR
Congo R.
Lake Tanganyika
GERMAN EAST AFRICA
ZANZIBAR (Br.)
ANGOLA (Port.)
NYASALAND
RHODESIA
PORT. EAST AFRICA
MADAGASCAR (Fr.)
GERMAN SOUTHWEST AFRICA
BECHUANALAND
UNION OF SOUTH AFRICA
TRANSVAAL
ORANGE FREE STATE
NATAL
Capetown
CAPE COLONY

European Colonies in Africa · 1878

ALGERIA
SENEGAL
GAMBIA
ANGOLA
MOZAMBIQUE
CAPE COLONY

KEY

British	Italian
French	Portuguese
German	Belgian
Spanish	

rebel Pancho Villa. U.S. buys Virgin Islands from Denmark for $25 million. President Wilson re-elected with "he kept us out of war" slogan. "Black Tom" explosion at munitions dock in Jersey City, N.J., $40,000,000 damages; traced to German saboteurs. Margaret Sanger opens first birth control clinic. Easter Rebellion in Ireland put down by British troops.

1917 First U.S. combat troops in France as U.S. declares war **(April 6)**. Russian Revolution—climax of long unrest under czars. February Revolution—Czar forced to abdicate, liberal government created. Kerensky becomes prime minister and forms provisional government **(July)**. In October Revolution, Bolsheviks seize power in armed coup d'état led by Lenin and Trotsky. Kerensky flees. Revolutionaries execute the czar and his family **(1918)**. Reds set up Third International in Moscow **(1919)**. Balfour Declaration promises Jewish homeland in Palestine. Sigmund Freud's *Introduction to Psychoanalysis.*

1918 Russian Civil War between Reds (Bolsheviks) and Whites (anti-Bolsheviks); Reds win in **1920**. Allied troops (U.S., British, French) intervene **(March)**; leave in **1919**. Japanese hold Vladivostok until **1922**. World-wide influenza epidemic strikes; by **1920**, nearly 20 million are dead. In U.S. alone, 500,000 perish.

1919 Third International (Comintern) establishes Soviet control over international Communist movements. Paris peace conference. Versailles Treaty, incorporating Wilson's draft Covenant of League of Nations, signed by Allies and Germany; rejected by U.S. Senate. Congress formally ends war in **1921**. Eighteenth (Prohibition) Amendment adopted. Alcock and Brown make first trans-Atlantic non-stop flight.

1920 League of Nations holds first meeting at Geneva, Switzerland. U.S. Dept. of Justice "red hunt" nets thousands of radicals; aliens deported. Women's suffrage (19th) amendment ratified. First Agatha Christie mystery. Sinclair Lewis's *Main Street.*

1921 Reparations Commission fixes German liability at 132 billion gold marks. German inflation begins. Major treaties signed at Washington Disarmament Conference limit naval tonnage and pledge to respect territorial integrity of China. Irish Free State formed in southern Ireland as self-governing dominion of British Empire. In U.S., Nicola Sacco and Bartolomeo Vanzetti, Italian-born anarchists, convicted of armed robbery murder; case stirs world-wide protests; they are executed in **1927**.

1922 Mussolini marches on Rome; forms Fascist government. Irish Free State officially proclaimed.

1923 Adolf Hitler's "Beer Hall Putsch" in Munich fails; in **1924** he is sentenced to five years in prison where he writes *Mein Kampf;* released after eight months. Occupation of Ruhr by French and Belgian troops to enforce reparations payments. Widespread Ku Klux Klan violence in U.S. George Gershwin's *Rhapsody in Blue.*

**Vladimir Lenin
(1870-1924)**

**Woodrow Wilson
(1856-1924)**

WORLD WAR I (1914–1918)

Imperial, territorial, and economic rivalries lead to the "Great War" between the Central Powers (Austria-Hungary, Germany, Bulgaria, and Turkey) and the Allies (U.S., Britain, France, Russia, Belgium, Serbia, Greece, Romania, Montenegro, Portugal, Italy, Japan). About 10 million combatants killed, 20 million wounded.

1914 Austrian Archduke Francis Ferdinand and wife assassinated in Sarajevo by Serbian nationalist, Gavrilo Princip **(June 28)**. Austria declares war on Serbia **(July 28)**. Germany declares war on Russia **(Aug. 1)**, on France **(Aug. 3)**, invades Belgium **(Aug. 4)**. Britain declares war on Germany **(Aug. 4)**. Germans defeat Russians in Battle of Tannenberg on Eastern Front **(Aug.)**. First Battle of the Marne **(Sept.)**. German drive stopped 25 miles from Paris. By end of year, war on the Western Front is "positional" in the trenches.

1915 German submarine blockade of Great Britain begins **(Feb.)**. Dardanelles Campaign—British land in Turkey **(April)**, withdraw from Gallipoli **(Dec. to Jan. 1916)**. Germans use gas at second Battle of Ypres **(April–May)**. *Lusitania* sunk by German submarine—1,198 lost, including 128 Americans **(May 7)**. On Eastern Front, German and Austrian "great offensive" conquers all of Poland and Lithuania; Russians lose 1 million men (by **Sept. 5)**. "Great Fall Offensive" by Allies results in little change from 1914 **(Sept.–Oct.)**. Britain and France declare war on Bulgaria **(Oct. 14)**.

1916 Battle of Verdun—Germans and French each lose about 350,000 men **(Feb.)**. Extended submarine warfare begins **(March)**. British-German sea battle of Jutland **(May)**; British lose more ships, but German fleet never ventures forth again. On Eastern front, the Brusilov offensive demoralizes Russians, costs them 1 million men **(June–Sept.)**. Battle of the Somme—British lose over 400,000; French, 200,000; Germans, about 450,000; all with no strategic results **(July–Nov.)**. Romania declares war on Austria-Hungary **(Aug. 27)**. Bucharest captured **(Dec.)**.

1917 U.S. declares war on Germany **(April 6)**. Submarine warfare at peak **(April)**. On Italian Front, Battle of Caporetto—Italians retreat, losing 600,000 prisoners and deserters **(Oct.–Dec.)**. On Western Front, Battles of Arras, Champagne, Ypres (third battle), etc. First large British tank attack **(Nov.)**. U.S. declares war on Austria-Hungary **(Dec. 7)**. Armistice between new Russian Bolshevik government and Germans **(Dec. 15)**.

1918 Great offensive by Germans **(March–June)**. Americans' first important battle role at Château-Thierry—as they and French stop German advance **(June)**. Second Battle of the Marne **(July–Aug.)**—start of Allied offensive at Amiens, St. Mihiel, etc. Battles of the Argonne and Ypres panic German leadership **(Sept.–Oct.)**. British offensive in Palestine **(Sept.)**. Germans ask for armistice **(Oct. 4)**. British armistice with Turkey **(Oct.)**. German Kaiser abdicates **(Nov.)**. Hostilities cease on Western Front **(Nov. 11)**.

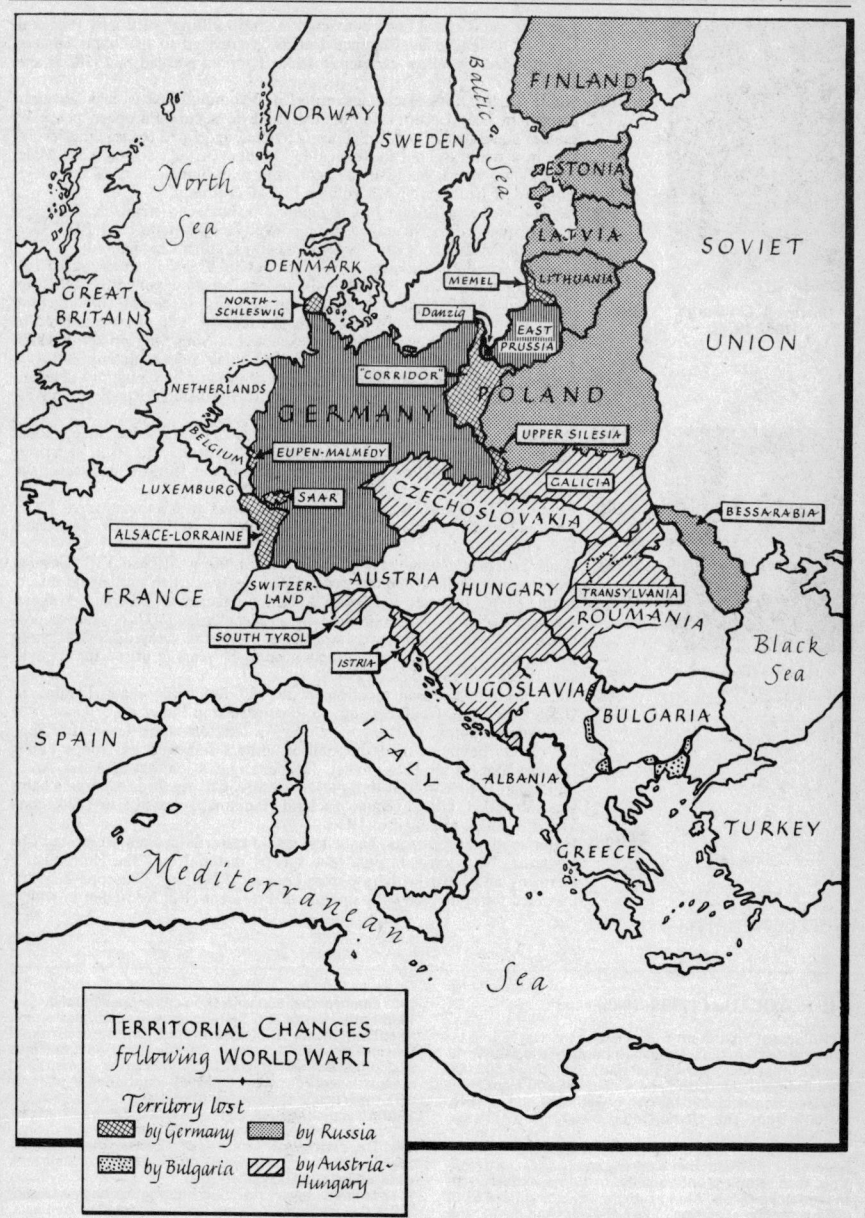

TERRITORIAL CHANGES
following WORLD WAR I

Territory lost
by Germany   by Russia
by Bulgaria   by Austria-Hungary

1924 Death of Lenin; Stalin wins power struggle, rules as Soviet dictator until death in **1953.** Italian Fascists murder Socialist leader Giacomo Matteotti. Interior Secretary Albert B. Fall and oilmen Harry Sinclair and Edward L. Doheny are charged with conspiracy and bribery in the Teapot Dome scandal, involving fraudulent leases of naval oil reserves. In **1931,** Fall is sentenced to year in prison; Doheny and Sinclair acquitted of bribery. Nathan

**Charles A. Lindbergh
(1902-1974)**

**Herbert Hoover
(1874-1964)**

Leopold and Richard Loeb convicted in "thrill killing" of Bobby Franks in Chicago; defended by Clarence Darrow; sentenced to life imprisonment. (Loeb killed by fellow convict in **1936**; Leopold paroled in **1958**, dies in **1971.**)

1925 Nellie Tayloe Ross elected governor of Wyoming; first woman governor elected in U.S. Locarno conferences seek to secure European peace by mutual guarantees. John T. Scopes convicted and fined for teaching evolution in a public school in Tennessee "Monkey Trial"; sentence set aside. John Logie Baird, Scottish inventor, transmits human features by television. Adolf Hitler publishes Volume I of *Mein Kampf.*

1926 General strike in Britain brings nation's activities to standstill. U.S. marines dispatched to Nicaragua during revolt; they remain until **1933**. Gertrude Ederle of U.S. is first woman to swim English Channel.

1927 German economy collapses. Socialists riot in Vienna; general strike follows acquittal of Nazis for political murder. Trotsky expelled from Russian Communist Party. Charles A. Lindbergh flies first successful solo non-stop flight from New York to Paris. Ruth Snyder and Judd Gray convicted of murder of Albert Snyder; they are executed at Sing Sing prison in **1928**. *The Jazz Singer,* with Al Jolson, first part-talking motion picture.

1928 Kellogg-Briand Pact, outlawing war, signed in Paris by 65 nations. Alexander Fleming discovers penicillin. Richard E. Byrd starts expedition to Antarctic; returns in **1930**.

1929 Trotsky expelled from U.S.S.R. Lateran Treaty establishes independent Vatican City. In U.S., stock market prices collapse, with U.S. securities losing $26 billion—first phase of Depression and world economic crisis. St. Valentine's Day gangland massacre in Chicago.

1930 Britain, U.S., Japan, France, and Italy sign naval disarmament treaty. Nazis gain in German elections. Cyclotron developed by Ernest O. Lawrence, U.S. physicist.

1931 Spain becomes a republic with overthrow of King Alfonso XIII. German industrialists finance 800,000-strong Nazi party. British parliament enacts statute of Westminster, legalizing dominion equality with Britain. Mukden Incident begins Japanese occupation of Manchuria. In U.S., Hoover proposes one-year moratorium of war debts. Harold C. Urey discovers heavy hydrogen. Gangster Al Capone sentenced to 11 years in prison for tax evasion (freed in **1939**; dies in **1947**).

1932 Nazis lead in German elections with 230 Reichstag seats. Famine in U.S.S.R. In U.S., Congress sets up Reconstruction Finance Corporation to stimulate economy. Veterans march on Washington—most leave after Senate rejects payment of cash bonuses; others removed by troops under Douglas MacArthur. U.S. protests Japanese aggression in Manchuria. Amelia Earhart is first woman to fly Atlantic solo. Charles A. Lindbergh's baby son kidnapped, killed. (Bruno Richard Hauptmann arrested in **1934**, convicted in **1935**, executed in **1936**.)

1933 Hitler appointed German chancellor, gets dictatorial powers. Reichstag fire in Berlin; Nazi terror begins. (*See* special material on "The Holocaust.") Germany and Japan withdraw from League of Nations. Giuseppe Zangara executed for attempted assassination of President-elect Roosevelt in which

---

THE HOLOCAUST (1933–1945)

"Holocaust" is the term describing the Nazi annihilation of about 6 million Jews (two thirds of the pre-World War II European Jewish population), including 4,500,000 from Russia, Poland, and the Baltic; 750,000 from Hungary and Romania; 290,000 from Germany and Austria; 105,000 from The Netherlands; 90,000 from France; 54,000 from Greece; etc.

The Holocaust was unique in its being *genocide*—the systematic destruction of a people solely because of religion, race, ethnicity, nationality, or homosexuality—on an unmatched scale. Along with the Jews, another 9 to 10 million people—Gypsies, Slavs (Poles, Ukrainians, and Belorussians)—were exterminated.

The only comparable act of genocide in modern times was launched in April 1915, when an estimated 600,000 Armenians were massacred by the Turks.

1933 Hitler named German Chancellor **(Jan.)**. Dachau, first concentration camp, established **(March)**. Boycotts against Jews begin **(April)**.
1935 Anti-Semitic Nuremberg Laws passed by Reichstag **(Sept.)**.

1937 Buchenwald concentration camp opens **(July)**.
1938 Extension of anti-Semitic laws to Austria after annexation **(March)**. *Kristallnacht* (Night of Broken Glass)—anti-Semitic riots in Germany and Austria **(Nov. 9)**. 26,000 Jews sent to concentration camps; Jewish children expelled from schools **(Nov.)**. Expropriation of Jewish property and businesses **(Dec.)**.
1940 As war continues, Nazi acts against Jews extended to German-conquered areas.
1941 Deportation of German Jews begins; massacres of Jews in Odessa and Kiev—68,000 killed **(Nov.)**; in Riga and Vilna—almost 60,000 killed **(Dec.)**.
1942 Unified Jewish resistance in ghettos begins **(Jan.)**. 300,000 Jews from Warsaw Ghetto deported to Treblinka death camp **(July)**.
1943 Warsaw Ghetto uprisings **(Jan. and April)**; Ghetto exterminated **(May)**.
1944 476,000 Hungarian Jews sent to Auschwitz **(May-June)**. D-day **(June 6)**. Soviet Army liberates Maidanek death camp **(July)**. Nazis try to hide evidence of death camps **(Nov.)**.
1945 Americans liberate Buchenwald and British liberate Bergen-Belsen camps **(April)**. Nuremberg War Crimes Trial **(Nov. 1945 to Oct. 1946)**.

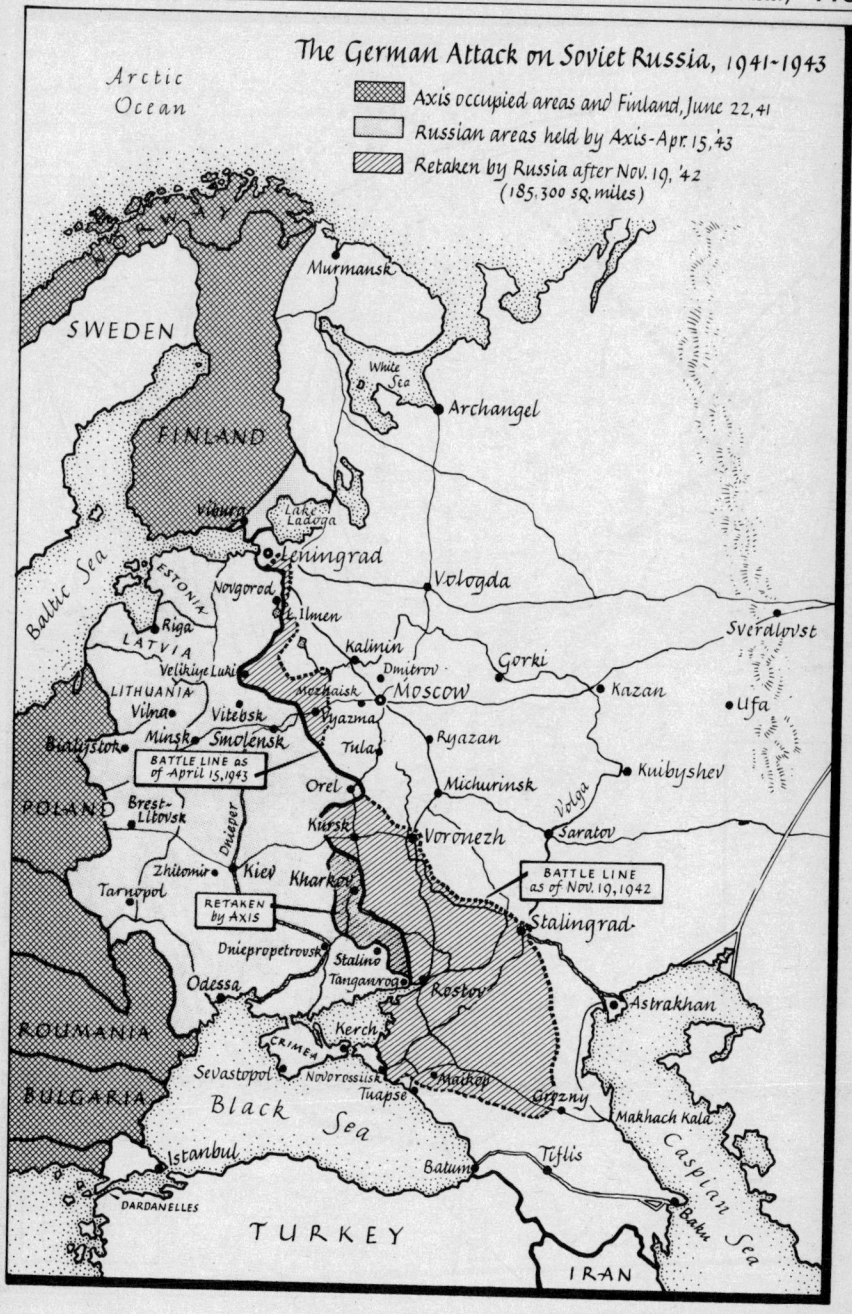

The German Attack on Soviet Russia, 1941–1943

Axis occupied areas and Finland, June 22, 41
Russian areas held by Axis–Apr. 15, '43
Retaken by Russia after Nov. 19, '42
(185,300 sq. miles)

Arctic Ocean

Murmansk

SWEDEN

FINLAND

White Sea

Archangel

Viborg

Lake Ladoga

Leningrad

Vologda

Baltic Sea

ESTONIA

Novgorod

L. Ilmen

Sverdlovst

Riga

LATVIA

Kalinin

Dmitrov

Gorki

Velikiye Luki

LITHUANIA

Mozhaisk

MOSCOW

Kazan

Ufa

Vilna

Vitebsk

Vyazma

Minsk

Smolensk

Tula

Ryazan

Bialystok

BATTLE LINE as of April 15, 1943

Orel

Michurinsk

Kuibyshev

POLAND

Brest-Litovsk

Dnieper

Kursk

Voronezh

Volga

Saratov

Zhitomir

Kiev

Tarnopol

Kharkov

BATTLE LINE as of Nov. 19, 1942

RETAKEN by AXIS

Dniepropetrovsk

Stalino

Stalingrad

Odessa

Tanganrog

Rostov

Astrakhan

ROUMANIA

Kerch

CRIMEA

Maikop

BULGARIA

Sevastopol

Novorossiisk

Tuapse

Grozny

Makhach Kala

Black Sea

Caspian Sea

Baku

Istanbul

Batum

Tiflis

DARDANELLES

TURKEY

IRAN

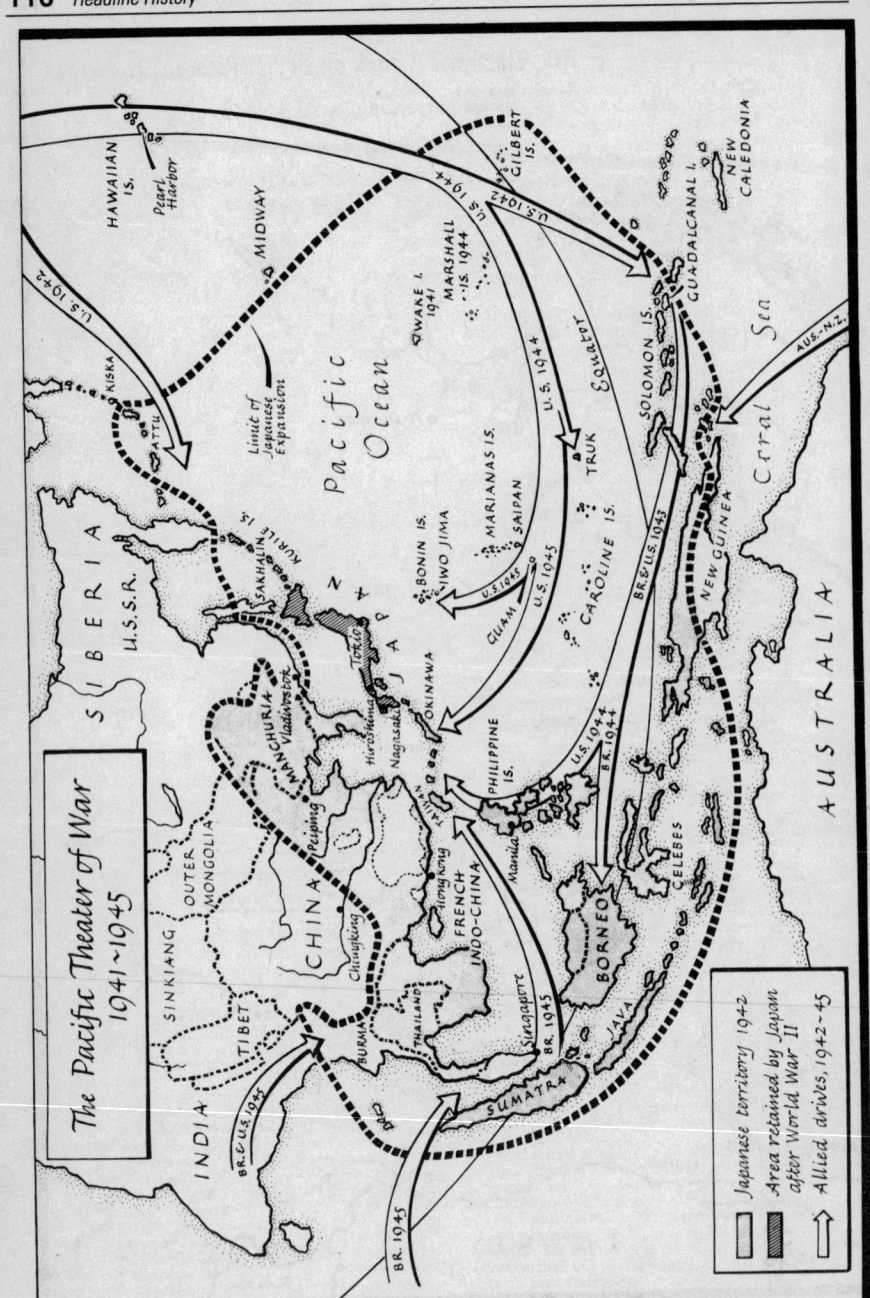

The Pacific Theater of War 1941~1945

Japanese territory 1942

Area retained by Japan after World War II

Allied drives, 1942-45

Chicago Mayor Cermak is fatally shot. Roosevelt inaugurated ("the only thing we have to fear is fear itself"); launches New Deal. Prohibition repealed. U.S.S.R. recognized by U.S.

1934 Chancellor Dollfuss of Austria assassinated by Nazis. Hitler becomes Führer. U.S.S.R. admitted to League of Nations. Dionne sisters, first quintuplets to survive beyond infancy, born in Canada.

1935 Saar incorporated into Germany after plebiscite. Nazis repudiate Versailles Treaty, introduce compulsory military service. Mussolini invades Ethiopia; League of Nations invokes sanctions. Roosevelt opens second phase of New Deal in U.S., calling for social security, better housing, equitable taxation, and farm assistance. Huey Long assassinated in Louisiana

1936 Germans occupy Rhineland. Italy annexes Ethiopia. Rome-Berlin Axis proclaimed (Japan to join in **1940**). Trotsky exiled to Mexico. King George V dies; succeeded by son, Edward VIII, who soon abdicated to marry American-born divorcée, and is succeeded by brother, George VI. Spanish civil war begins. (Franco's fascist forces defeat Loyalist forces by **1939**, when Madrid falls.) War between China and Japan begins, to continue through World War II. Japan and Germany sign anti-Comintern pact; joined by Italy in **1937**.

1937 Hitler repudiates war guilt clause of Versailles Treaty; continues to build German power. Italy withdraws from League of Nations. U.S. gunboat *Panay* sunk by Japanese in Yangtze River. Japan invades China, conquers most of coastal area. Amelia Earhart lost somewhere in Pacific on round-the-world flight.

1938 Hitler marches into Austria; political and geographical union of Germany and Austria proclaimed. Munich Pact—Britain, France, and Italy agree to let Germany partition Czechoslovakia. Douglas "Wrong-Way" Corrigan flies from New York to Dublin.

1939 Germany occupies Bohemia and Moravia; renounces pacts with Poland and England and concludes 10-year non-aggression pact with U.S.S.R. Russo-Finnish War begins; Finns to lose one-tenth of territory in **1940** peace treaty. World War II begins (*see* special material on "World War II"). In U.S., Roosevelt submits $1,319-million defense budget, proclaims U.S. neutrality, and declares limited emergency. Einstein writes FDR about feasibility of atomic bomb. New York World's Fair opens.

1940 Trotsky assassinated in Mexico. Estonia, Latvia, and Lithuania annexed by U.S.S.R. U.S. trades 50 destroyers for leases on British bases in Western Hemisphere. Selective Service Act signed.

**Amelia Earhart
(1898-1937)**

WORLD WAR II (1939–1945)

Axis powers (Germany, Italy, Japan, Hungary, Romania, Bulgaria) *vs.* Allies (U.S., Britain, France, U.S.S.R., Australia, Belgium, Brazil, Canada, China, Denmark, Greece, Netherlands, New Zealand, Norway, Poland, South Africa, Yugoslavia).

1939 Germany invades Poland and annexes Danzig; Britain and France give Hitler ultimatum (**Sept. 1**), declare war (**Sept. 3**). Disabled German pocket battleship *Admiral Graf Spee* blown up off Montevideo, Uruguay, on Hitler's orders (**Dec. 17**). Limited activity ("Sitzkrieg") on Western Front.

1940 Nazis invade Netherlands, Belgium, and Luxembourg (**May 10**). Chamberlain resigns as Prime Minister; Churchill takes over (**May 10**). Germans cross French frontier (**May 12**) using air/tank/infantry "Blitzkrieg" tactics. Dunkerque evacuation—about 335,000 out of 400,000 Allied soldiers rescued from Belgium by British civilian and naval craft (**May 26–June 3**). Italy declares war on France and Britain; invades France (**June 10**). Germans enter Paris; city undefended (**June 14**). France and Germany sign armistice at Compiègne (**June 22**). Nazis bomb Coventry, England (**Nov. 14**).

1941 Germans launch attacks in Balkans. Yugoslavia surrenders—General Mihajlovic continues guerrilla warfare; Tito leads left-wing guerrillas (**April 17**). Nazi tanks enter Athens; remnants of British Army quit Greece (**April 27**). Hitler attacks Russia (**June 22**). Atlantic Charter—FDR and Churchill agree on war aims (**Aug. 14**). Japanese attacks on Pearl Harbor, Philippines, Guam force U.S. into war; U.S. Pacific fleet crippled (**Dec. 7**). U.S. and Britain declare war on Japan. Germany and Italy declare war on U.S.; Congress declares war on those countries (**Dec. 11**).

1942 British surrender Singapore to Japanese (**Feb. 15**). U.S. forces on Bataan peninsula in Philippines surrender (**April 9**). U.S. and Filipino troops on Corregidor island in Manila Bay surrender to Japanese (**May 6**). Village of Lidice in Czechoslovakia razed by Nazis (**June 10**). U.S. and

Britain land in French North Africa (**Nov. 8**).

1943 Casablanca Conference—Churchill and FDR agree on unconditional surrender goal (**Jan. 14–24**). German 6th Army surrenders at Stalingrad—turning point of war in Russia (**Feb. 1–2**). Remnants of Nazis trapped on Cape Bon, ending war in Africa (**May 12**). Mussolini deposed; Badoglio named premier (**July 25**). Allied troops land on Italian mainland after conquest of Sicily (**Sept. 3**). Italy surrenders (**Sept. 8**). Nazis seize Rome (**Sept. 10**). Cairo Conference: FDR, Churchill, Chiang Kai-shek pledge defeat of Japan, free Korea (**Nov. 22–26**). Teheran Conference: FDR, Churchill, Stalin agree on invasion plans (**Nov. 28–Dec. 1**).

1944 U.S. and British troops land at Anzio on west Italian coast and hold beachhead (**Jan. 22**). U.S. and British troops enter Rome (**June 4**). D-Day—Allies launch Normandy invasion (**June 6**). Hitler wounded in bomb plot (**July 20**). Paris liberated (**Aug. 25**). Athens freed by Allies (**Oct. 13**). Americans invade Philippines (**Oct. 20**). Germans launch counteroffensive in Belgium—Battle of Bulge (**Dec. 16**).

1945 Yalta Agreement signed by FDR, Churchill, Stalin—establishes basis for occupation of Germany, returns to Soviet Union lands taken by Germany and Japan; U.S.S.R. agrees to friendship pact with China (**Feb. 11**). Mussolini killed at Lake Como (**April 28**). Admiral Doenitz takes command of Germany; suicide of Hitler announced (**May 1**). Berlin falls (**May 2**). V-E Day—Germany signs unconditional surrender terms at Rheims (**May 7**). Potsdam Conference—Truman, Churchill, Atlee (after **July 28**), Stalin establish council of foreign ministers to prepare peace treaties; plan German postwar government and reparations (**July 17–Aug. 2**). A-bomb blasts Hiroshima (**Aug. 6**). U.S.S.R. declares war on Japan (**Aug. 8**). Nagasaki hit by A-bomb (**Aug. 9**). Japan surrenders (**Aug. 14**). V-J Day—Japanese sign surrender terms aboard battleship *Missouri* (**Sept. 2**).

D-Day, June 6, 1944

**Winston Churchill,
Franklin D. Roosevelt,
and Joseph V. Stalin
at Yalta**

**Harry S. Truman
(1884-1972)**

1941 Japanese surprise attack on U.S. fleet at Pearl Harbor brings U.S. into World War II. Manhattan Project (atomic bomb research) begins. Roosevelt enunciates "four freedoms," signs lend-lease act, declares national emergency, promises aid to U.S.S.R.

1942 Declaration of United Nations signed in Washington. Women's military services established. Enrico Fermi achieves nuclear chain reaction. Japanese and persons of Japanese ancestry moved inland from Pacific Coast. Coconut Grove nightclub fire in Boston kills 491.

1943 President freezes prices, salaries, and wages to prevent inflation. Income tax withholding introduced.

1944 G.I. Bill of Rights enacted. Bretton Woods Conference creates International Monetary Fund and World Bank. Dumbarton Oaks Conference—U.S., British Commonwealth, and U.S.S.R. propose establishment of United Nations.

1945 Yalta Conference (Roosevelt, Churchill, Stalin) plans final defeat of Germany (**Feb.**). Germany surrenders (**May 7**). San Francisco Conference establishes U.N. (**April–June**). FDR dies (April 12). Potsdam Conference (Truman, Churchill, Stalin) establishes basis of German reconstruction (**July–Aug**). Japan signs surrender (**Sept. 2**).

1946 First meeting of U.N. General Assembly opens in London (**Jan. 10**). League of Nations dissolved (**April**). Italy abolishes monarchy (**June**). Verdict in Nuremberg war trial: 12 Nazi leaders (including 1 tried in absentia) sentenced to hang; 7 imprisoned; 3 acquitted (**Oct. 1**). Goering commits suicide a few hours before 10 other Nazis are executed (**Oct. 15**). Winston Churchill's "Iron Curtain" speech warns of Soviet expansion.

1947 Britain nationalizes coal mines (**Jan. 1**). Peace treaties for Italy, Romania, Bulgaria, Hungary, Finland signed in Paris (**Feb. 10**). Soviet Union rejects U.S. plan for U.N. atomic-energy control (**March 4**). Truman Doctrine proposed—the first significant U.S. attempt to "contain" communist expansion (**March 12**). Marshall Plan for European recovery proposed—a coordinated program to help European nations recover from ravages of war (**June**). (By **1951**, this "European Recovery Program" had cost $11 billion.) India and Pakistan gain independence from Britain (**Aug. 15**). Cominform (Communist Information Bureau) founded under Soviet auspices to rebuild contacts among European Communist parties, missing since dissolution of Comintern in **1943** (**Sept.**). (Yugoslav party expelled in **1948** and Cominform disbanded in **1956**.)

1948 Gandhi assassinated in New Delhi by Hindu fanatic (**Jan. 30**). Communists seize power in Czechoslovakia (**Feb. 23–25**). Burma and Ceylon granted independence by Britain. Organization of American States (OAS) Charter signed at Bogotá, Colombia (**April 30**). Nation of Israel proclaimed; British end Mandate at midnight; Arab armies attack (**May 14**). Berlin airlift begins (**June 21**); ends May 12, 1949. Stalin and Tito break (**June 28**). Independent Republic of Korea is proclaimed, following election supervised by U.N. (**Aug. 15**). Verdict in Japanese war trial: Tojo and six others sentenced to hang (hanged Dec. 23); 18 imprisoned (**Nov. 12**). United States of Indonesia established as Dutch and Indonesians settled conflict (**Dec. 27**). Alger Hiss, former U.S. State Department official, indicted on perjury charges after denying passing secret documents to communist spy ring. Convicted in second trial (**1950**) and sentenced to five-year prison term.

1949 Cease-fire in Palestine (**Jan. 7**). Truman proposes Point Four Program to help world's backward areas (**Jan. 20**). Israel signs armistice with Egypt (**Feb. 24**). Start of North Atlantic Treaty Organization (NATO)—treaty signed by 12 nations (**April 4**). German Federal Republic (West Germany) established (**Sept. 21**). Truman discloses Soviet Union has set off atomic explosion (**Sept. 23**). Communist People's Republic of China formally proclaimed by Chairman Mao Zedong. (**Oct. 1**).

1950 Truman orders development of hydrogen bomb (**Jan. 31**). Korean War (*see* special material on the "Korean War"). Assassination attempt on President Truman by Puerto Rican nationalists (**Nov. 1**). Brink's robbery in Boston; almost $3 million stolen (**Jan. 17**).

KOREAN WAR (1950–1953)

1950 North Korean Communist forces invade South Korea (June 25). U.N. calls for cease-fire and asks U.N. members to assist South Korea (June 27). Truman orders U.S. forces into Korea (June 27). North Koreans capture Seoul (June 28). Gen. Douglas MacArthur designated commander of unified U.N. forces (July 8). Pusan Beachhead—U.N. forces counterattack and capture Seoul (Aug.–Sept.), capture Pyongyang, North Korean capital (Oct.). Chinese Communists enter war (Oct. 26), force U.N. retreat toward 39th parallel (Dec.).

1951 Gen. Matthew B. Ridgeway replaces MacArthur after he threatens Chinese with massive retaliation (April 11). Armistice negotiations (July) continue with interruptions until June 1953.

1953 Armistice signed (June 26). Chinese troops withdraw from North Korea (Oct. 26, 1958), but over 200 violations of armistice noted in 1959.

1951 Six nations agree to Schuman Plan to pool European coal and steel (**March 19**)—in effect **Feb. 10, 1953**. Julius and Ethel Rosenberg sentenced to death for passing atomic secrets to Russians (**March**). Japanese peace treaty signed in San Francisco by 49 nations (**Sept. 8**). Color television introduced in U.S.

1952 George VI dies; his daughter becomes Elizabeth II (**Feb. 6**). NATO conference approves European army (**Feb.**). AEC announces "satisfactory" experiments in hydrogen-weapons research; eyewitnesses tell of blasts near Enewetak (**Nov.**).

1953 Gen. Dwight D. Eisenhower inaugurated President of United States (**Jan. 20**). Stalin dies (**March 5**). Malenkov becomes Soviet Premier; Beria, Minister of Interior; Molotov, Foreign Minister (**March 6**). Dag Hammarskjold begins term as U.N. Secretary-General (**April 10**). Edmund Hillary, of New Zealand, and Tenzing Norkay, of Nepal, reach top of Mt. Everest (**May 29**). East Berliners rise against Communist rule; quelled by tanks (**June 17**). Egypt becomes republic ruled by military junta (**June 18**). Julius and Ethel Rosenberg executed in Sing Sing prison (**June 19**). Korean armistice signed (**July 27**). Moscow announces explosion of hydrogen bomb (**Aug. 20**).

Dwight D. Eisenhower
(1890-1969)

1954 First atomic submarine *Nautilus*, launched (**Jan. 21**). Five U.S. Congressmen shot on floor of House as Puerto Rican nationalists fire from spectators' gallery; all five recover (**March 1**). Army *vs.* McCarthy inquiry—Senate subcommittee report blames both sides (**Apr. 22–June 17**). Dien Bien Phu, French military outpost in Vietnam, falls to Vietminh army (**May 7**). (*see* special material on the "Vietnam War.") U.S. Supreme Court (in *Brown* v. *Board of Education of Topeka*) unanimously bans racial segregation in public schools (**May 17**). Eisenhower launches world atomic pool without Soviet Union (**Sept. 6**). Eight-nation Southeast Asia defense treaty (SEATO) signed at Manila (**Sept. 8**). West Germany is granted sovereignty, admitted to NATO and Western European Union (**Oct. 23**). Dr. Jonas Salk starts innoculating children against polio. Algerian War of Independence against France begins (**Nov.**); France struggles to maintain colonial rule until 1962 when it agrees to Algeria's independence.

Joseph Stalin
(1879-1953)

1955 Nikolai A. Bulganin becomes Soviet Premier, replacing Malenkov (**Feb. 8**). Churchill resigns; Anthony Eden succeeds him (**April 6**). Federal Republic of West Germany becomes a sovereign state (**May 5**). Warsaw Pact,

---

VIETNAM WAR (1950–1975)

U.S., South Vietnam, and Allies versus North Vietnam and National Liberation Front (Viet Cong). Outstanding events:

1950 President Truman sends 35-man military advisory group to aid French fighting to maintain colonial power in Vietnam.

1954 After defeat of French at Dienbienphu, Geneva Agreements (July) provide for withdrawal of French and Vietminh to either side of demarcation zone (DMZ) pending reunification elections, which are never held. Presidents Eisenhower and Kennedy (from 1954 onward) send civilian advisors and, later, military personnel to train South Vietnamese.

1960 Communists from National Liberation Front in South.

1963 Ngo Dinh Diem, South Vietnam's premier, slain in coup (Nov. 1).

1961–1963 U.S. military advisors rise from 2,000 to 15,000.

1964 North Vietnamese torpedo boats reportedly attack U.S. destroyers in Gulf of Tonkin (Aug. 2). President Johnson orders retaliatory air strikes. Congress approves Gulf of Tonkin resolution (Aug. 7) authorizing President to take necessary steps to "maintain peace."

1965 U.S. planes begin combat missions over South Vietnam. In June, 23,000 American advisors committed to combat. By end of year over 184,000 U.S. troops in area.

1966 B-52s bomb DMZ, reportedly used by North Vietnam for entry into South (July 31).

1967 South Vietnam National Assembly approves election of Nguyen Van Thieu as President (Oct. 21).

1968 U.S. has almost 525,000 men in Vietnam. In Tet offensive (Jan.–Feb.), Viet Cong guerrillas attack Saigon, Hue, and some provincial capitals. President Johnson orders halt to U.S. bombardment of North Vietnam (Oct. 31). Saigon and N.L.F. join U.S. and North Vietnam in Paris peace talks.

1969 President Nixon announces Vietnam peace offer

(May 14)—begins troop withdrawals (June). Viet Cong forms Provisional Revolutionary Government. U.S. Senate calls for curb on commitments (June 25). Ho Chi Minh, 79, North Vietnam president, dies (Sept. 3); collective leadership chosen. Some 6,000 U.S. troops pulled back from Thailand and 1,000 marines from Vietnam (announced Sept. 30). Massive demonstrations in U.S. protest or support war policies (Oct. 15).

1970 Nixon announces sending of troops to Cambodia (April 30). Last U.S. troops removed from Cambodia (June 29).

1971 Congress bars use of combat troops, but not air power, in Laos and Cambodia (Jan. 1). South Vietnamese troops, with U.S. air cover, fail in Laos thrust. Many American ground forces withdrawn from Vietnam combat. *New York Times* publishes Pentagon papers, classified material on expansion of war (June).

1972 Nixon responds to North Vietnamese drive across DMZ by ordering mining of North Vietnam ports and heavy bombing of Hanoi-Haiphong area (April 1). Nixon orders "Christmas bombing" of north to get North Vietnamese back to conference table (Dec.).

1973 President orders halt to offensive operations in North Vietnam (Jan. 15). Representatives of North and South Vietnam, U.S., and N.L.F. sign peace pacts in Paris, ending longest war in U.S. history (Jan. 27). Last American troops departed in their entirety (March 29).

1974 Both sides accuse each other of frequent violations of cease-fire agreement.

1975 Full-scale warfare resumes. Communists victorious (April 30). South Vietnam Premier Nguyen Van Thieu resigns (April 21). U.S. Marine Embassy guards and U.S. civilians and dependents evacuated (April 30). More than 140,000 Vietnamese refugees leave by air and sea, many to settle in U.S. Provisional Revolutionary Government takes control (June 6).

1976 Election of National Assembly paves way for reunification of North and South.

**Yuri A. Gagarin
(1934-1968)**

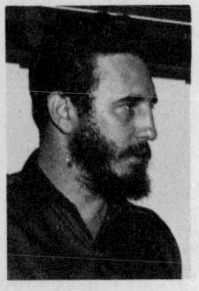

**Fidel Castro
(Aug. 13, 1926)**

east European mutual defense agreement, signed (**May 14**). Argentina ousts Perón (**Sept. 19**). President Eisenhower suffers coronary thrombosis in Denver (**Sept. 24**). Martin Luther King, Jr., leads black boycott of Montgomery, Ala., bus system (**Dec. 1**); desegregated service begun (**Dec. 21**). AFL and CIO become one organization—AFL-CIO (**Dec. 5**).

1956 Nikita Khrushchev, First Secretary of U.S.S.R. Communist Party, denounces Stalin's excesses (**Feb. 24**). First aerial H-bomb tested over Namu islet, Bikini Atoll—10 million tons TNT equivalent (**May 21**). Worker's uprising against Communist rule in Poznan, Poland, is crushed (**June 28–30**). Egypt takes control of Suez Canal (**July 26**). Israel launches attack on Egypt's Sinai peninsula and drives toward Suez Canal (**Oct. 29**). British and French invade Egypt at Port Said (**Nov. 5**). Cease-fire forced by U.S. pressure stops British, French, and Israeli advance (**Nov. 6**). Revolt starts in Hungary—Soviet troops and tanks crush anti-Communist rebellion (**Nov.**).

1957 Eisenhower Doctrine calls for aid to Mideast countries which resist armed aggression from Communist-controlled nations (**Jan. 5**). Eisenhower sends troops to Little Rock, Ark., to quell mob and protect school integration (**Sept. 24**). Russians launch *Sputnik I*, first earth-orbiting satellite—the Space Age begins (**Oct. 4**).

1958 Army's Jupiter-C rocket fires first U.S. earth satellite, *Explorer I*, into orbit (**Jan. 31**). Egypt and Syria merge into United Arab Republic (**Feb. 1**). European Economic Community (Common Market) established by Rome Treaty becomes effective **Jan. 1, 1958**. Khrushchev becomes Premier of Soviet Union as Bulganin resigns (**Mar. 27**). Gen. Charles de Gaulle becomes French premier (**June 1**), remaining in power until **1969**. New French constitution adopted (**Sept. 28**), de Gaulle elected president of 5th Republic (**Dec. 21**). Eisenhower orders U.S. Marines into Lebanon at request of President Chamoun, who fears overthrow (**July 15**).

1959 Cuban President Batista resigns and flees—Castro takes over (**Jan. 1**). Tibet's Dalai Lama escapes to India (**Mar. 31**). St. Lawrence Seaway opens, allowing ocean ships to reach Midwest (**April 25**).

1960 American U-2 spy plane, piloted by Francis Gary Powers, shot down over Russia (**May 1**). Khrushchev kills Paris summit conference because of U-2 (**May 16**). Powers sentenced to prison for 10 years (**Aug. 19**)—freed in **February 1962** in exchange for Soviet spy. Top Nazi murderer of Jews, Adolf Eichmann, captured by Israelis in Argentina (**May 23**)—executed in Israel in **1962**. Communist China and Soviet Union split in conflict over Communist ideology. Belgium starts to break up its African colonial empire, gives independence to Belgian Congo (Zaire) on **June 30**. Cuba begins confiscation of $770 million of U.S. property (**Aug. 7**).

1961 U.S. breaks diplomatic relations with Cuba (**Jan. 3**). John F. Kennedy inaugurated President of U.S. (**Jan. 20**). Kennedy proposes Alliance for Progress—10-year plan to raise Latin American living standards (**Mar. 13**). Moscow announces putting first man in orbit around earth, Maj. Yuri A. Gagarin (**April 12**). Cuba invaded at Bay of Pigs by an estimated 1,200 anti-Castro exiles aided by U.S.; invasion crushed (**April 17**). First U.S. spaceman, Navy Cmdr. Alan B. Shepard, Jr., rockets 116.5 miles up in 302-mile trip (**May 5**). Virgil Grissom becomes second American astronaut, making 118-mile-high, 303-mile-long rocket flight over Atlantic (**July 21**). Gherman Stepanovich Titov is launched in Soviet spaceship *Vostok II:* makes 17 1/2 orbits in 25 hours, covering 434,960 miles before landing safely (**Aug. 6**). East Germans erect Berlin Wall between East and West Berlin to halt flood of refugees (**Aug. 13**). U.S.S.R. fires 50-megaton hydrogen bomb, biggest explosion in history (**Oct. 29**).

1962 Lt. Col. John H. Glenn, Jr., is first American to orbit earth—three times in 4 hr 55 min (**Feb. 20**). Adolf Eichmann hanged in Israel for his part in Nazi extermination of six million Jews (**May 31**). France transfers sovereignty to new republic of Algeria (**July 3**). Cuban missile crisis—U.S.S.R. to build missile bases in Cuba; Kennedy orders Cuban blockade, lifts blockade after Russians back down (**Aug.-Nov.**). James H. Meredith, escorted by Federal marshals, registers in University of Mississippi (**Oct. 1**). Pope John XXIII opens Second Vatican Council (Oct. 11)—Council holds four sessions, finally closing Dec. 8, 1965. Cuba releases 1,113 prisoners of 1961 invasion attempt (**Dec. 24**).

1963 France and West Germany sign treaty of cooperation ending four centuries of conflict (**Jan. 22**). Pope John XXIII dies (**June 3**)—succeeded June 21 by Cardinal Montini, who becomes Paul VI. U.S. Supreme Court rules no locality may require recitation of Lord's Prayer or Bible verses in public schools (**June 17**). Civil rights rally held by 200,000 blacks and whites in Washington, D.C. (**Aug. 28**). Washington-to-Moscow "hot line" communications link opens, designed to reduce risk of accidental war (**Aug. 30**). President Kennedy shot and killed by sniper in Dallas, Tex. Lyndon B.

Johnson becomes President same day (**Nov. 22**). Lee Harvey Oswald, accused assassin of President Kennedy, is shot and killed by Jack Ruby, Dallas nightclub owner (**Nov. 24**).

1964 U.S. Supreme Court rules that Congressional districts should be roughly equal in population (**Feb. 17**). Jack Ruby convicted of murder in slaying of Lee Harvey Oswald; sentenced to death by Dallas jury (**March 14**)—conviction reversed **Oct. 5, 1966; Ruby dies Jan. 3, 1967**, before second trial can be held. Three civil rights workers—Schwerner, Goodman, and Cheney—murdered in Mississippi (**June**). Twenty-one arrests result in trial and conviction of seven by Federal jury. President's Commission on the Assassination of President Kennedy issues Warren Report concluding that Lee Harvey Oswald acted alone.

1965 Rev. Dr. Martin Luther King, Jr., and more than 2,600 other blacks arrested in Selma, Ala., during three-day demonstrations against voter-registration rules (**Feb. 1**). Malcolm X, black-nationalist leader, shot to death at Harlem rally in New York City (**Feb. 21**). U.S. Marines land in Dominican Republic as fighting persists between rebels and Dominican army (**April 28**). Medicare, senior citizens' government medical assistance program, begins (**July 1**). Blacks riot for six days in Watts section of Los Angeles: 34 dead, over 1,000 injured, nearly 4,000 arrested, fire damage put at $175 million (**Aug. 11-16**). Power failure in Ontario plant blacks out parts of eight northeastern states of U.S. and two provinces of southeastern Canada (**Nov. 9**).

John F. Kennedy (1917-1963)

1966 Black teen-agers riot in Watts, Los Angeles; two men killed and at least 25 injured (**March 15**). Michael E. De Bakey implants artificial heart in human for first time at Houston hospital; plastic device functions and patient lives (**April 21**).

1967 Three Apollo astronauts—Col. Virgil I. Grissom, Col. Edward White II, and Lt. Cmdr. Roger B. Chaffee—killed in spacecraft fire during simulated launch (**Jan. 27**). Israeli and Arab forces battle; six-day war ends with Israel occupying Sinai Peninsula, Golan Heights, Gaza Strip, and east bank of Suez Canal (**June 5**). Red China announces explosion of its first hydrogen bomb (**June 17**). Racial violence in Detroit; 7,000 National Guardsmen aid police after night of rioting. Similar outbreaks occur in New York City's Spanish Harlem, Rochester, N.Y., Birmingham, Ala., and New Britain, Conn. (**July 23**). Thurgood Marshall sworn in as first black U.S. Supreme Court justice (**Oct. 2**). Dr. Christiaan N. Barnard and team of South African surgeons perform world's first successful human heart transplant (**Dec. 3**)—patient dies 18 days later.

1968 North Korea seizes U.S. Navy ship *Pueblo;* holds 83 on board as spies (**Jan. 23**). President Johnson announces he will not seek or accept presidential renomination (**March 31**). Martin Luther King, Jr., civil rights leader, is slain in Memphis (**April 4**)—James Earl Ray, indicted in murder, captured in London on **June 8. In 1969** Ray pleads guilty and is sentenced to 99 years. Sen. Robert F. Kennedy is shot and critically wounded in Los Angeles hotel after winning California primary (**June 5**)—dies **June 6.** Sirhan B. Sirhan convicted **1969.** Czechoslovakia is invaded by Russians and Warsaw Pact forces to crush liberal regime (**Aug. 20**).

Lyndon B. Johnson (1908-1973)

1969 Richard M. Nixon is inaugurated 37th President of the U.S. (**Jan. 20**). Apollo 11 astronauts—Neil A. Armstrong, Edwin E. Aldrin, Jr., and Michael Collins—take man's first walk on moon (**July 20**). Sen. Edward M. Kennedy pleads guilty to leaving scene of fatal accident at Chappaquiddick, Mass. (**July 18**) in which Mary Jo Kopechne was drowned—gets two-month suspended sentence (**July 25**).

1970 Biafra surrenders after 32-month fight for independence from Nigeria (**Jan. 12**). Rhodesia severs last tie with British Crown and declares itself a racially segregated republic (**March 1**). Four students at Kent State University in Ohio slain by National Guardsmen at demonstration protesting April 30 incursion into Cambodia (**May 4**). Senate repeals Gulf of Tonkin resolution (**June 24**).

1971 Supreme Court rules unanimously that busing of students may be ordered to achieve racial desegregation (**April 20**). Anti-war militants attempt to disrupt government business in Washington (**May 3**)—police and military units arrest as many as 12,000; most are later released. Twenty-sixth Amendment to U.S. Constitution lowers voting age to 18. U.N. seats Communist China and expels Nationalist China (**Oct. 25**).

1972 President Nixon makes unprecedented eight-day visit to Communist China (**Feb.**). Britain takes over direct rule of Northern Ireland in bid for peace (**March 24**). Gov. George C. Wallace of Alabama is shot by Arthur H. Bremer at Laurel, Md., political rally (**May 15**). Five men are apprehended by police in attempt to bug Democratic National Committee headquarters in Washington D.C.'s Watergate complex—start of the Watergate scandal (**June 17**). Supreme Court rules that death penalty is **unconstitutional**

**Richard M. Nixon
(1913–1994)**

**Viking I and II
(Launched 1975)**

**Voyager I and II
(Launched 1977)**

(June 29). Eleven Israeli athletes at Olympic Games in Munich are killed after eight members of an Arab terrorist group invade Olympic Village; five guerrillas and one policeman are also killed **(Sept. 5).**

1973 Great Britain, Ireland, and Denmark enter European Common Market **(Jan. 1).** Nixon, on national TV, accepts responsibility, but not blame, for Watergate; accepts resignations of advisers H. R. Haldeman and John D. Ehrlichman, fires John W. Dean III as counsel. **(April 30).** Greek military junta abolishes monarchy and proclaims republic **(June 1).** U.S. bombing of Cambodia ends, marking official halt to 12 years of combat activity in Southeast Asia **(Aug. 15).** Fourth and biggest Arab-Israeli War begins as Egyptian and Syrian forces attack Israel as Jews mark Yom Kippur, holiest day in their calendar. **(Oct. 6).** Spiro T. Agnew resigns as Vice President and then, in Federal Court in Baltimore, pleads no contest to charges of evasion of income taxes on $29,500 he received in 1967, while Governor of Maryland. He is fined $10,000 and put on three years' probation **(Oct. 10).** In the "Saturday Night Massacre," Nixon fires special Watergate prosecutor Archibald Cox and Deputy Attorney General William D. Ruckelshaus; Attorney General Elliot L. Richardson resigns **(Oct. 20).** Egypt and Israel sign U.S.-sponsored cease-fire accord **(Nov. 11).**

1974 Patricia Hearst, 19-year-old daughter of publisher Randolph Hearst, kidnapped by Symbionese Liberation Army. **(Feb. 5).** House Judiciary Committee adopts three articles of impeachment charging President Nixon with obstruction of justice, failure to uphold laws, and refusal to produce material subpoenaed by the committee **(July 30).** Richard M. Nixon announces he will resign the next day, the first President to do so **(Aug. 8).** Vice President Gerald R. Ford of Michigan is sworn in as 38th President of the U.S. **(Aug. 9).** Ford grants "full, free, and absolute pardon" to ex-President Nixon **(Sept. 8).**

1975 John N. Mitchell, H. R. Haldeman, John D. Ehrlichman, and Robert C. Mardian found guilty of Watergate cover-up. Mitchell, Haldeman, and Ehrlichman are sentenced on Feb. 21 to 30 months-8 years in jail and Mardian to 10 months-3 years **(Jan. 1).** American merchant ship *Mayaguez*, seized by Cambodian forces, is rescued in operation by U.S. Navy and Marines, 38 of whom are killed **(May 15).** *Apollo* and *Soyuz* spacecraft take off for U.S.-Soviet link-up in space **(July 15).** President Ford escapes assassination attempt in Sacramento, Calif., **(Sept. 5).** President Ford escapes second assassination attempt in 17 days. **(Sept. 22).**

1976 Supreme Court rules that blacks and other minorities are entitled to retroactive job seniority **(March 24).** Ford signs Federal Election Campaign Act **(May 11).** Supreme Court rules that death penalty is not inherently cruel or unusual and is a constitutionally acceptable form of punishment **(July 3).** Nation celebrates Bicentennial **(July 4).** Israeli airborne commandos attack Uganda's Entebbe Airport and free 103 hostages held by pro-Palestinian hijackers of Air France plane; one Israeli and several Ugandan soldiers killed in raid **(July 4).** Mysterious disease that eventually claims 29 lives strikes American Legion convention in Philadelphia **(Aug. 4).** Jimmy Carter elected U.S. President **(Nov. 2).**

1977 First woman Episcopal priest ordained **(Jan. 1).** Scientists identify previously unknown bacterium as cause of mysterious "legionnaire's disease" **(Jan. 18).** Carter pardons Vietnam draft evaders **(Jan. 21).** Scientists report using bacteria in lab to make insulin **(May 23).** Supreme Court rules that states are not required to spend Medicaid funds on elective abortions **(June 20).** Deng Xiaoping, purged Chinese leader, restored to power as "Gang of Four" is expelled from Communist Party **(July 22).** Nuclear-proliferation pact, curbing spread of nuclear weapons, signed by 15 countries, including U.S. and U.S.S.R. **(Sept. 21).**

1978 President chooses Federal Appeals Court Judge William H. Webster as F.B.I. Director **(Jan. 19).** Rhodesia's Prime Minister Ian D. Smith and three black leaders agree on transfer to black majority rule **(Feb. 15).** Former Italian Premier Aldo Moro kidnapped by leftwing terrorists, who kill five bodyguards **(March 16);** he is found slain **(May 9).** U.S. Senate approves Panama Canal neutrality treaty **(March 16);** votes treaty to turn canal over to Panama by year 2000 **(April 18).** Californians in referendum approve Proposition 13 for nearly 60% slash in property tax revenues **(June 6).** Supreme Court, in Bakke case, bars quota systems in college admissions but affirms constitutionality of programs giving advantage to minorities **(June 28).** Pope Paul VI, dead at 80, mourned **(Aug. 6);** new Pope, John Paul I, 65, dies unexpectedly after 34 days in office **(Sept. 28);** succeeded by Karol Cardinal Wojtyla of Poland as John Paul II **(Oct. 16).** "Framework for Peace" in Middle East signed by Egypt's President Anwar el-Sadat and Israel Premier Menachem Begin after 13-day conference at Camp David led by President Carter **(Sept. 17).**

1979 Oil spills pollute ocean waters in Atlantic and Gulf of Mexico **(Jan. 1,**

June 8, July 21). Ohio agrees to pay $675,000 to families of dead and injured in Kent State University shootings (**Jan. 4**). Vietnam and Cambodian insurgents it backs announce fall of Phnom Penh, Cambodian capital, and collapse of Pol Pot regime (**Jan. 7**). Shah leaves Iran after year of turmoil (**Jan. 16**); revolutionary forces under Moslem leader, Ayatollah Ruhollah Khomeini, take over (**Feb. 1** et seq.). Conservatives win British election; Margaret Thatcher new Prime Minister (**March 28**). Nuclear power plant accident at Three Mile Island, Pa., releases radioactivity (**March 28**). Carter and Brezhnev sign SALT II agreement (**June 14**). Nicaraguan President Gen. Anastasio Somoza Debayle resigns and flees to Miami (**July 17**); Sandinistas form government (**July 19**). Earl Mountbatten of Burma, 79, British World War II hero, and three others killed by blast on fishing boat off Irish coast (**Aug. 27**); two I.R.A. members accused (**Aug. 30**). Iranian militants seize U.S. Embassy in Teheran and hold hostages (**Nov. 4**). Soviet invasion of Afghanistan stirs world protests (**Dec. 27**).

Margaret Thatcher
(Oct. 13, 1925)

1980 Six U.S. Embassy aides escape from Iran with Canadian help (**Jan. 29**). F.B.I.'s undercover operation "Abscam" (for Arab scam) implicates public officials (**Feb. 2**). U.S. breaks diplomatic ties with Iran (**April 7**). Eight U.S. servicemen are killed and five are injured as helicopter and cargo plane collide in abortive desert raid to rescue American hostages in Teheran (**April 25**). Supreme Court upholds limits on Federal aid for abortions (**June 30**). Shah of Iran dies at 60 (**July 27**). Anastasio Somoza Debayle, ousted Nicaragua ruler, and two aides assassinated in Asunción, Paraguay capital (**Sept. 17**). Iraq troops hold 90 square miles of Iran after invasion (**Sept. 19**). Ronald Reagan elected President in Republican sweep (**Nov. 4**). Three U.S. nuns and lay worker found shot in El Salvador (**Dec. 4**). John Lennon of Beatles shot dead in New York City (**Dec. 8**).

1981 U.S.-Iran agreement frees 52 hostages held in Teheran since Nov. 4, 1979 (**Jan. 18**); hostages welcomed back in U.S. (**Jan. 25**). Ronald Reagan takes oath as 40th President (**Jan. 20**). President Reagan wounded by gunman, with press secretary and two law-enforcement officers (**March 30**). Pope John Paul II wounded by gunman (**May 14**). Supreme Court rules, 4-4, that former President Nixon and three top aides may be required to pay monetary damages for unconstitutional wiretap of home telephone of former national security aide (**June 22**). Reagan nominates Judge Sandra Day O'Connor, 51, of Arizona, as first woman on Supreme Court (**July 7**). More than 110 die in collapse of aerial walkways in lobby of Hyatt Regency Hotel in Kansas City; 188 injured (**July 18**). Air controllers strike, disrupting flights (**Aug. 3**); Government dismisses strikers (**Aug. 11**).

Sally K. Ride
(May 26, 1951)

1982 British overcome Argentina in Falklands war (**April 2-June 15**). Israel invades Lebanon in attack on P.L.O. (**June 4**). John W. Hinckley, Jr. found not guilty because of insanity in shooting of President Reagan (**June 21**). Alexander M. Haig, Jr. resigns as Secretary of State (**June 25**). Equal rights amendment fails ratification (**June 30**). Lebanese Christian Phalangists kill hundreds of people in two Palestinian refugee camps in West Beirut (**Sept. 15**). Princess Grace, 52, dies of injuries when car plunges off mountain road; daughter, Stephanie, 17, suffers serious injuries (**Sept. 14**). Leonid I. Brezhnev, Soviet leader, dies at 75 (**Nov. 10**). Yuri V. Andropov, 68, chosen as successor (**Nov. 15**). Artificial heart implanted for first time in Dr. Barney B. Clark, 61, at University of Utah Medical Center in Salt Lake City (**Dec. 2**); Barney Clark dies (**March 23, 1983**).

1983 Pope John Paul II signs new Roman Catholic code incorporating changes brought about by Second Vatican Council (**Jan. 25**). Second space shuttle, *Challenger,* makes successful maiden voyage, which includes the first U.S. space walk in nine years (**April 4**). U.S. Supreme Court declares many local abortion restrictions unconstitutional (**June 15**). Sally K. Ride, 32, first U.S. woman astronaut in space as a crew member aboard space shuttle *Challenger* (**June 18**). U.S. admits shielding former Nazi Gestapo chief, Klaus Barbie, 69, the "butcher of Lyons," wanted in France for war crimes (**Aug. 15**). Benigno S. Aquino, Jr., 50, political rival of Philippines President Marcos, slain in Manila (**Aug. 21**). South Korean Boeing 747 jetliner bound for Seoul apparently strays into Soviet airspace and is shot down by a Soviet SU-15 fighter after it had tracked the airliner for two hours; all 269 aboard are killed, including 61 Americans (**Aug. 30**). Terrorist explosion kills 237 U.S. Marines in Beirut (**Oct. 23**). U.S. and Caribbean allies invade Grenada (**Oct. 25**).

Space Shuttle Columbia
(Launched April 12, 1981)

1984 Bell System broken up (**Jan. 1**). France gets first deliveries of Soviet natural gas (**Jan. 1**). Syria frees captured U.S. Navy pilot, Lieut. Robert O. Goodman, Jr. (**Jan. 3**). U.S. and Vatican exchange diplomats after 116-year hiatus (**Jan. 10**). Reagan orders U.S. Marines withdrawn from Beirut international peacekeeping force (**Feb. 7**). Yuri V. Andropov dies at 69; Konstantin U. Chernenko, 72, named Soviet Union leader (**Feb. 9**). Italy and Vatican agree to end Roman Catholicism as state religion (**Feb. 18**). Reagan ends U.S. role in Beirut by relieving Sixth Fleet from peacekeeping force (**March 30**). Congress rebukes President Reagan on use of federal funds for mining Nicaraguan harbors (**April 10**). Soviet Union withdraws from summer Olympic games in U.S., and other bloc nations follow (**May 7** et seq.). José Napoleón Duarte, moderate, elected president of El Salvador (**May 11**). Three hundred slain as Indian Army occupies Sikh Golden Temple in Amritsar (**June 6**). Thirty-ninth Democratic National Convention, in San Francisco, nominates Walter F. Mondale and Geraldine A. Ferraro (**July 16-19**). Thirty-third Republican National Convention, at Dallas, renominates President Reagan and Vice President Bush (**Aug. 20-25**). Brian Mulroney and Conservative party win Canadian election in landslide (**Sept. 4**). Indian Prime Minister Indira Gandhi assassinated by two Sikh bodyguards; 1,000 killed in anti-Sikh riots; son Rajiv succeeds her (**Oct. 31**). President Reagan re-elected in landslide with 59% of vote (**Nov. 7**). Toxic gas leaks from Union Carbide plant in Bhopal, India, killing 2,000 and injuring 150,000 (**Dec. 3**).

1985 Ronald Reagan, 73, takes oath for second term as 40th President (**Jan. 20**). General Westmoreland settles libel action against CBS (**Feb. 18**). Prime Minister Margaret Thatcher addresses Congress, endorsing Reagan's policies (**Feb. 20**). U.S.S.R. leader Chernenko dies at 73 and is replaced by Mikhail Gorbachev, 54 (**March 11**). Two Shiite Moslem gunmen capture TWA airliner with 133 aboard, 104 of them Americans (**June 14**); 39 remaining hostages freed in Beirut (**June 30**). Supreme Court, 5-4, bars public school teachers from parochial schools (**July 1**). Arthur James Walker, 50, retired naval officer, convicted by federal judge of participating in Soviet spy ring (**Aug. 9**). P.L.O. terrorists hijack *Achille Lauro*, Italian cruise ship, with 80 passengers, plus crew (**Oct. 7**); American, Leon Klinghoffer, killed (**Oct. 8**). Italian government toppled by political crisis over hijacking of *Achille Lauro* (**Oct. 16**). John A. Walker and son, Michael I. Walker, 22, sentenced in Navy espionage case (**Oct. 28**). Reagan and Gorbachev meet at summit (**Nov. 19**); agree to step up arms control talks and renew cultural contacts (**Nov. 21**). Terrorists seize Egyptian Boeing 737 airliner after takeoff from Athens (**Nov. 23**); 59 dead as Egyptian forces storm plane on Malta (**Nov. 24**). U.S. budget-balancing bill enacted (**Dec. 12**).

1986 Spain and Portugal join Common Market (**Jan. 1**). President freezes Libyan assets in U.S. (**Jan. 8**). Supreme Court bars racial bias in trial jury selection (**Jan. 14**). *Voyager 2* spacecraft reports secrets of Uranus (**Jan. 26**). Space shuttle *Challenger* explodes after launch at Cape Canaveral, Fla., killing all seven aboard (**Jan. 28**). Haiti President Jean-Claude Duvalier flees to France (**Feb. 7**). President Marcos flees Philippines after ruling 20 years, as newly elected Corazon Aquino succeeds him (**Feb. 26**). Prime Minister Olaf Palme of Sweden shot dead (**Feb. 28**). Kurt Waldheim service as Nazi army officer revealed (**March 3**). Union Carbide agrees to settlement with victims of Bhopal gas leak in India (**March 22**). Halley's Comet yields information on return visit (**April 10**). U.S. planes attack Libyan "terrorist centers" (**April 14**). Desmond Tutu elected Archbishop in South Africa (**April 14**). Major nuclear accident at Soviet Union's Chernobyl power station alarms world (**April 26** et seq.). Ex-Navy analyst, Jonathan Jay Pollard, 31, guilty as spy for Israel (**June 4**). Supreme Court reaffirms abortion right (**June 11**). World Court rules U.S. broke international law in mining Nicaraguan waters (**June 27**). Supreme Court voids automatic provisions of budget-balancing law (**July 7**). Jerry A. Whitworth, ex-Navy radioman, convicted as spy (**July 24**). Moslem captors release Rev. Lawrence Martin Jenco (**July 26**). Senate Judiciary Committee approves William H. Rehnquist to be Chief Justice of U.S. (**Aug. 14**). House votes arms appropriations bill rejecting Administration's "star wars" policy (**Aug. 15**). Three Lutheran church groups in U.S. set to merge (**Aug. 29**). Congress overrides Reagan veto of stiff sanctions against South Africa (**Sept. 29** and **Oct. 2**). Congress approves immigration bill barring hiring of illegal aliens, with amnesty provision (**Oct. 17**). Reagan signs $11.7-billion budget reduction measure (**Oct. 21**). He approves sweeping revision of U.S. tax code (**Oct. 22**). Democrats triumph in elections, gaining eight seats to win Senate majority (**Nov. 4**). Secret initiative to send arms to Iran revealed (**Nov. 6** et seq.); Reagan denies exchanging arms for hostages and halts arms sales (**Nov. 19**); diversion of funds from arms sales to Nicaraguan contras revealed (**Nov. 25**). Walkers, father and son, sentenced in naval spy ring (**Nov. 6**). Soviet lifts ban on Andrei D. Sakharov, rights activist (**Dec. 19**).

1987 William Buckley, U.S. hostage in Lebanon, reported slain (**Jan. 20**). U.S. puts Austrian President Kurt Waldheim on list of those banned from country (**April 27**). Quebec accepts Canadian Constitution as "distinct society" (**May 1**). Supreme Court rules Rotary Clubs must admit women (**May 4**). Iraqi missiles kill 37 in attack on U.S. frigate *Stark* in Persian Gulf (**May 17**); Iraqi president apologizes (**May 18**). Prime Minister Thatcher wins rare third term in Britain (**June 11**). Supreme Court Justice Lewis F. Powell, Jr., retires (**June 26**). Klaus Barbie, 73, Gestapo wartime chief in

Indira Gandhi
(1917-1984)

Ronald W. Reagan
(Feb. 6, 1911)

Mikhail S. Gorbachev
(March 2, 1931)

Lyons, sentenced to life by French court for war crimes **(July 4)**. Marine Lieut. Col. Oliver North, Jr., tells Congressional inquiry higher officials approved his secret Iran-Contra operations **(July 7–10)**. Admiral John M. Poindexter, former National Security Adviser, testifies he authorized use of Iran arms sale profits to aid Contras **(July 15–22)**. George P. Shultz testifies he was deceived repeatedly on Iran-Contra affair **(July 23–24)**. Defense Secretary Caspar W. Weinberger tells inquiry of official deception and intrigue **(July 31, Aug. 3)**. Reagan says Iran arms-Contra policy went astray and accepts responsibility **(Aug 12)**. Severe earthquake strikes Los Angeles, leaving 100 injured and six dead **(Oct. 1)**. Senate, 58–42, rejects Robert H. Bork as Supreme Court Justice **(Oct. 23)**

1988 U.S. and Canada reach free trade agreement **(Jan. 2)**. Supreme Court, 5–3, backs public school officials' power to censor student activities **(Jan. 13)**. Robert C. McFarlane, former National Security Adviser, pleads guilty in Iran–Contra case **(March 11)**. Supreme Court rules against private-club membership restrictions **(June 20)**. U.S. Navy ship shoots down Iranian airliner in Persian Gulf, mistaking it for jet fighter; 290 killed **(July 3)**. Terrorists kill nine tourists on Aegean cruise **(July 11)**. Democratic convention nominates Gov. Michael Dukakis of Massachusetts for President and Texas Senator Lloyd Bentsen for Vice President **(July 17 et seq.)**. Republicans nominate George Bush for President and Indiana Senator Dan Quayle for Vice President **(Aug. 15 et seq.)**. Plane blast kills Pakistani President Mohammad Zia ul-Haq **(Aug. 17)**. Republicans sweep 40 states in election. Vice President Bush beats Gov. Dukakis **(Nov. 8)**. Soviet legislature approves political restructuring and new national legislature **(Dec. 1)**. Benazir Bhutto, first Islamic woman prime minister, chosen to lead Pakistan's government **(Dec. 1)**. Pan-Am 747 explodes from terrorist bomb and crashes in Lockerbie, Scotland, killing all 259 aboard and 11 on ground **(Dec. 21)**.

Corazon C. Aquino
(Jan. 25, 1933)

1989 U.S. planes shoot down two Libyan fighters over international waters in Mediterranean **(Jan. 4)**. Emperor Hirohito of Japan dead at 87 **(Jan. 7)**. George Herbert Walker Bush inaugurated as 41st U.S. President **(Jan. 20)**. Iran's Ayatollah Khomeini declares author Salman Rushdie's book "The Satanic Verses" offensive and sentences him and his publishers to death **(Feb. 14)**. Ruptured tanker *Exxon Valdez* sends 11 million gallons of crude oil into Alaska's Prince William Sound **(March 24)**. Tens of thousands of Chinese students take over Beijing's central square in rally for democracy **(April 19 et seq.)**. More than one million in Beijing demonstrate for democracy; chaos spreads across nation **(mid-May et seq.)**. Mikhail S. Gorbachev named Soviet President **(May 25)**. U.S. jury convicts Oliver L. North in Iran-Contra affair **(May 4)**. Thousands killed as Chinese leaders take hard line toward demonstrators **(June 4 et seq.)**. Army Gen. Colin R. Powell is first black to become Chairman of Joint Chiefs of Staff **(Aug. 9)**. P.W. Botha quits as South Africa's President **(Aug. 14)**. *Voyager 2* spacecraft speeds by Neptune after making startling discoveries about the planet and its moons **(Aug. 29)**. L. Douglas Wilder, Democrat, is elected as first black governor of Virginia **(Nov. 7)**. Deng Xiaoping resigns from China's leadership **(Nov. 9)**. After 28 years, Berlin Wall is open to West **(Nov. 11)**. Czech Parliament ends Communists' dominant role **(Nov. 30)**. Romanian uprising overthrows Communist government **(Dec. 15 et seq.)**; President Ceausescu and wife executed **(Dec. 25)**. U.S. troops invade Panama, seeking capture of Gen. Manuel Noriega **(Dec. 20)**; resistance to U.S. collapses **(Dec. 24)**.

Kurt Waldheim
(Dec. 21, 1918)

1990 Gen. Manuel Noriega surrenders in Panama **(Jan. 3)**. Yugoslav Communists end 45-year monopoly of power **(Jan. 22)**. Soviet Communists relinquish sole power **(Feb. 7)**. South Africa frees Nelson Mandela, imprisoned 27 1/2 years **(Feb. 11)**. Violeta Barrios de Chamorro inaugurated as Nicaraguan President **(April 25)**. U.S.–Soviet summit reaches accord on armaments **(June 1)**. Supreme Court upsets law banning flag burning **(June 11)**. Western Alliance ends cold war and proposes joint action with Soviet Union and Eastern Europe **(July 6)**. U.S. Appeals Court overturns Oliver North's Iran–Contra conviction **(July 20)**. Iraqi troops invade Kuwait and seize petroleum reserves, setting off Persian Gulf War **(Aug. 2 et seq.)** East and West Germany reunited **(Aug. 31 et seq.)**. Republicans set back in midterm elections **(Nov. 8)**. Gorbachev assumes emergency powers **(Nov. 17)**. Leaders of 34 nations in Europe and North America proclaim a united Europe **(Nov. 21)**. Margaret Thatcher resigns as British Prime Minister **(Nov. 22)**; John Major succeeds her **(Nov. 28)**. Lech Walesa wins Poland's runoff Presidential election **(Dec. 9)**. Haiti elects leftist priest as President in first democratic election **(Dec. 17)**.

1991 Lithuania Government resigns **(Jan. 8)**. U.S. and Allies at war with Iraq **(Jan. 15)**. U.N. forces win Persian Gulf war **(Feb. 4 et seq.)**. Liberal priest becomes Haiti president **(Feb. 7)**. Warsaw Pact dissolves military alliance **(Feb 25)** Supreme Court limits race in trial jury selection **(April 1)**. Cease-fire ends Persian Gulf war **(April 3)**. Europeans end sanctions on

George H. Bush
(June 12, 1924)

L. Douglas Wilder
(Jan. 17, 1931)

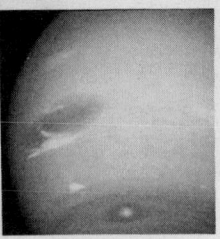

Neptune seen from
Voyager 2

South Africa **(April 15)**. Supreme Court limits death row appeals **(April 16)**. Winnie Mandela sentenced in kidnapping **(May 13)**. William H. Webster retires as Director of Central Intelligence; Robert H. Gates succeeds him **(May 14)**. France agrees to sign 1968 treaty banning spread of atomic weapons **(June 3)**. Communist Government of Albania resigns **(June 4)**. Jiang Qing, widow of Mao, commits suicide **(June 4)**. South African Parliament repeals apartheid laws **(June 5)**. Warsaw Pact dissolved **(July 1)**. Boris N. Yeltsin inaugurated as first freely elected president of Russian Republic **(July 10)**. Bush-Gorbachev summit negotiates strategic arms reduction treaty **(July 31)**. China accepts nuclear nonproliferation treaty **(Aug. 10)**. Coup fails to unseat Gorbachev after Soviet hardliners seize him; he credits Yeltsin for rescue **(Aug. 18 et seq.)**. Gorbachev seals Communist Party doom, resigns as secretary-general **(Aug. 24)**.Three Baltic republics win independence **(Aug. 25)**; Bush recognizes them **(Sept. 2)**. New Soviet ruling council recognizes independence of Lithuania, Estonia, and Latvia **(Sept. 6)**. Charges against Oliver North dropped **(Sept. 15)**. Haitian troops seize president in uprising **(Sept. 30)**. U.S. suspends assistance to Haiti **(Oct. 1)**. Professor Anita Hill accuses Judge Clarence Thomas of sexual harassment **(Oct. 6)**; Senate, 52–48, confirms Thomas for Supreme Court after stormy hearings **(Oct. 15)**. Israel and Soviet resume relations after 24 years **(Oct. 18)**. First photo ever taken of an asteroid in space, *Gaspara* **(Oct. 29)**. U.S. indicts two Libyans in 1988 bombing of Pan Am Flight 103 over Lockerbie, Scotland **(Nov. 15)**. Anglican envoy Terry Waite and U.S. Prof. Thomas M. Sutherland freed by Lebanese **(Nov. 18)**. Last three U.S. hostages freed in Lebanon **(Dec. 2–4)**. Soviet Union breaks up after President Gorbachev's resignation; constituent republics form Commonwealth of Independent States, which U.S. and other nations move to recognize **(Dec. 25)**.

1992 Yugoslav Federation broken up **(Jan. 15)**. Bush and Yeltsin proclaim formal end to Cold War **(Feb. 1)**. U.S. lifts trade sanctions against China **(Feb. 21)**. U.S. recognizes three former Yugoslav republics **(April 7)**. Gen. Noriega, former Panama leader, convicted in U.S. court **(April 9)**. Small new Yugoslavia proclaimed **(April 27)**. Four officers acquitted in Los Angeles beating; violence erupts in Los Angeles **(April 29 et seq.)**. Caspar W. Weinberger indicted in Iran-Contra affair **(June 16)**. Last Western hostages freed in Lebanon **(June 17)**. Supreme Court reaffirms right to abortion **(June 29)**. Gen. Noriega sentenced to 40 years on drug charges **(July 10)**. Court clears *Exxon Valdez* skipper **(July 10)**. Democrats nominate Bill Clinton and Al Gore **(July 1)**. Israeli Parliament approves Yitzhak Rabin's coalition government, dominated by Labor Party **(July 13)**. Supreme Court upholds return of Haitians **(Aug. 1)**. U.S. indicts four police officers in Los Angeles beating **(Aug. 5)**. North American trade compact announced **(Aug. 12)**. Republicans renominate Bush and Quayle **(Aug. 20)**. U.N. expels Serbian-dominated Yugoslavia **(Sept. 22)**. Senate ratifies second Strategic Arms Limitation Treaty **(Oct. 1)**. U.N. council creates Bosnian "no-fly" zone **(Oct. 9)**. Top Japanese leader, Shin Kanemaru, resigns in scandal **(Oct. 14)**. Bill Clinton elected President, Al Gore Vice President; Democrats keep control of Congress **(Nov. 3)**. Russian Parliament approves START treaty **(Nov. 4)**. U.S. forces leave Philippines, ending nearly a cen-

---

THE PERSIAN GULF WAR (Aug. 2, 1990–April 6, 1991)

1990: Iraq invades its tiny neighbor, Kuwait, after talks break down over oil production and debt repayment. Iraqi Pres. Saddam Hussein later annexes Kuwait and declares it a 19th province of Iraq **(Aug. 2)**. President Bush believes that Iraq intends to invade Saudi Arabia and take control of the region's oil supplies. He begins organizing a multinational coalition to seek Kuwait's freedom and restoration of its legitimate government. The U.N. Security Council authorizes economic sanctions against Iraq. Pres. Bush orders U.S. troops to protect Saudi Arabia at the Saudis' request and "Operation Desert Shield" begins **(Aug. 6)**. 230,000 American troops arrive in Saudi Arabia to take defensive action, but when Iraq continues a huge military buildup in Kuwait, the President orders an additional 200,000 troops deployed to prepare for a possible offensive action by the U.S.-led coalition forces. He subsequently obtains a U.N. Security Council resolution setting a Jan. 15, 1991, deadline for Iraq to withdraw unconditionally from Kuwait **(Nov. 8)**.

1991: Pres. Bush wins Congressional approval for his position with the most devastating air assault in history against military targets in Iraq and Kuwait **(Jan. 16)**. He rejects a Soviet-Iraq peace plan for a gradual withdrawal that does not comply with all the U.N. resolutions and

gives Iraq an ultimatum to withdraw from Kuwait by noon February 23 **(Feb. 22)**. The President orders the ground war to begin **(Feb. 24)**. In a brilliant and lightning-fast campaign, U.S. and coalition forces smash through Iraq's defenses and defeat Saddam Hussein's troops in only four days of combat. Allies enter Kuwait City **(Feb. 26)**. Iraqi army sets fire to over 500 of Kuwait's oil wells as final act of destruction to Kuwait's infrastructure. Pres. Bush orders a unilateral cease-fire 100 hours after the ground offensive started **(Feb. 27)**. Allied and Iraq military leaders meet on battlefield to discuss terms for a formal cease-fire to end the Gulf War. Iraq agrees to abide by all of the U.N. resolutions **(Mar. 3)**. The first Allied prisoners of war are released **(Mar. 4)**. Official cease-fire accepted and signed **(April 6)**. 532,000 U.S. forces served in Operation Desert Storm. There were a total of 148 battle deaths during the Gulf War, 145 nonbattle deaths, and 467 wounded in action. Battle deaths by branch of service were: Army, 98; Navy, 6; Marines, 24; Air Force, 20. Nonbattle deaths: Army, 105; Navy, 8; Marines, 26; and Air Force, 6. The United States estimated that Iraqi military casualties werre 100,000 killed, 300,000 wounded, and over 88,000 captured.

tury of American military presence **(Nov. 24)**. Czechoslovak Parliament approves separation into two nations **(Nov. 25)**. U.N. approves U.S.-led force to guard food for Somalia **(Dec. 3)**. Prince and Princess of Wales agree to separate **(Dec. 9)**. Bush pardons former Reagan Administration officials involved in Iran-Contra affair **(Dec. 24)**.

1993 Clinton withdraws Zoe Baird nomination as Attorney General **(Jan. 22)**. Vaclav Havel elected Czech President **(Jan. 26)**. Clinton agrees to compromise on military's ban on homosexuals **(Jan. 29)**. Judge Kimba M. Wood withdraws as Clinton's second choice for Attorney General **(Feb. 5)**; President names Janet Reno to post **(Feb. 11)**. U.S. begins airdrop of supplies to besieged Bosnian towns **(Feb. 28)**. Law agents besiege Texas Davidian religious cult after six are killed in raid **(March 1** et seq.**)**. Senate, 98–0, confirms Janet Reno as Attorney General **(March 11)**. Five arrested, sixth sought in bombing of World Trade Center in New York **(March 29)**. Russian Congress accepts Yeltsin call for national referendum **(March 29)**. Two police officers convicted in Los Angeles on rights charges in Rodney King beating **(April 17)**. Fire kills 72 as cult standoff in Texas ends with Federal assault **(April 19)**. President of Sri Lanka assassinated **(May 1)**. British Commons approves European unity pact **(May 20)**. Twenty-two U.N. troops killed in Somalia **(June 5)**. Ruth Bader Ginsburg, rights advocate, appointed to Supreme Court **(June 14)**. Iraq accepts U.N. weapons monitoring **(July 19)**. President dismisses F.B.I. Director William S. Sessions **(July 19)**; names Judge Louis J. Freeh as successor **(July 20)**. Vincent W. Foster, Jr., senior White House lawyer, is apparent suicide **(July 22)**. Midwest flood damage expected to exceed $10 billion **(July 24)**. Two Los Angeles police officers sentenced in Rodney King beating **(Aug. 4)**. Israeli-Palestinian accord reached **(Aug. 28)**. South Africa agrees to share transition powers **(Sept. 7)**. Yeltsin dissolves Russian Parliament **(Sept. 21)**. U.S. agents blamed in Waco, Tex., siege **(Oct. 1)**. Yeltsin's forces crush revolt in Russian Parliament **(Oct. 4** et seq.**)**. China breaks nuclear test moratorium **(Oct. 5)**. NATO offers "peace partnership" to Eastern European nations **(Oct. 20–21)**. Canada's opposition Liberal Party regains power in landslide **(Oct. 25)**. Europe's Maastricht Treaty takes effect, creating European Union **(Nov. 1)**. Jean Chretien sworn in as Canada's 20th Prime Minister **(Nov. 4)**. Yeltsin approves new draft constitution for Russia **(Nov. 8)**. House of Representatives approves North American Free Trade Agreement **(Nov. 17)**; Senate follows **(Nov. 21)**. South Africa adopts majority rule constitution **(Nov. 18)**. Clinton signs Brady bill regulating firearms purchases **(Nov. 30)**.

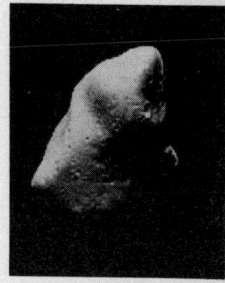

Asteroid *Gaspra*
(Oct. 29, 1991)

1994 Serbs heavy weapons pound Sarajevo **(Jan. 5–6)**. Olympic figure skater Nancy Kerrigan attacked **(Jan. 6)**; three arrested in attack **(Jan. 13)**. Major earthquake jolts Los Angeles; 51 dead **(Jan. 17** et seq.**)**. Clinton ends trade embargo on Vietnam **(Feb. 9)**. Aldrich Ames, high C.I.A. official, charged with spying for Soviet **(Feb. 22)**. Four convicted in World Trade Center bombing **(March 4)**. Mexican Presidential candidate assassinated **(March 23)**. Thousands dead in Rwanda tribal warfare **(April 6)**. Strike halts major trucking companies **(April 6)**; accord reached to end tie-up **(April 29)**. South Africa holds first interracial election **(April 29)**. V.M.I. upheld on exclusion of women **(May 1)**. Israel and Palestinians sign accord **(May 4)**. Clinton accused of sexual harassment while Governor **(May 6)**. Congress votes protection for abortion clinics **(May 12)**. Jacqueline Kennedy Onassis dies of cancer **(May 20)**. O.J. Simpson arrested in two killings **(June 18)**. Russia and NATO agree on close military ties **(June 22)**. Supreme Court approves limit on abortion protests **(June 30)**. Senate confirms Stephen G. Breyer for Supreme Court **(July 29)**. Abortion doctor shot dead outside Florida clinic **(July 29)**; U.S. indicts accused killer **(Aug. 12)**. Major league baseball players strike **(Aug. 13)**. Carlos, international terrorist, captured **(Aug. 15)**. I.R.A. declares cease-fire in Northern Ireland **(Aug. 31)**. Small plane crashes against White House **(Sept. 12)**. Baseball owners end season and cancel World Series **(Sept. 14)**. U.S. and Russia agree on arms reduction **(Sept. 29)**. Powerful earthquake strikes Japan **(Oct. 4)**. Aristide returns to joyous Haiti **(Oct. 4)**. Abortion protester guilty in clinic killings **(Oct. 5)**. U.S. sends forces to Persian Gulf **(Oct. 7)**. Ulster Protestants declare cease-fire **(Oct. 13)**. Israel and Jordan sign peace treaty **(Oct. 17)**. Gunman fires at White House **(Oct. 29)**. Abortion foe guilty of killing two at clinic **(Nov. 2)**; Florida jury recommends death penalty **(Nov. 3)**. Reagan, 83, reveals Alzheimer's disease **(Nov. 6)**. G.O.P. wins control of House and Senate **(Nov. 8)**. Aristide forms Haitian Government with Prime Minister and full Cabinet **(Nov. 9)**. Clinton orders Bosnian arms embargo ended **(Nov. 10)**. Killer of abortion doctor sentenced twice **(Dec. 2)**. Newt Gingrich named House Speaker **(Dec. 5)**. Bentsen resigns as Treasury Secretary **(Dec. 6)**. Russians attack secessionist Republic of Chechnya **(Dec. 11** et seq.**)**. James Woolsey, Jr., resigns as Director of Central Intelligence **(Dec. 28)**. Gunman kills two at Massachusetts abortion clinic **(Dec. 30)**.

William J. Clinton
(Aug. 19, 1946)

1995 Republicans take control of Congress (**Jan. 4**). Heavy rains inundate California (**Jan. 9** et seq.). More than 5,000 dead in Japanese earthquake (**Jan. 17** et seq.). Trial of O.J. Simpson opens in California (**Jan. 24**). Clinton offers $20 billion aid to Mexico (**Jan. 31**). Congress votes curbs on U.S. mandates to states (**Feb. 1**). U.S. shuttle rendezvous with Russian space station (**Feb. 3**). Clinton appoints retired Air Force general as intelligence chief (**Feb. 7**). U.S. rescues Mexico's economy with $20-billion aid program (**Feb. 21**). Senate rejects balanced-budget amendment (**March 2**). Russian space station greets first Americans (**March 14**). Nerve gas attack in Tokyo subway kills eight and injures thousands (**March 20**). Selena, 23, popular Spanish-language singer, slain in Texas (**March 31**). Major league baseball strike ends (**April 2**). Appeals Court upholds woman's plea to enter Citadel military academy (**April 13**). U.N. Council votes easier sanctions for Iraq (**April 14**). Scores killed as terrorist's car bomb blows up block-long Oklahoma City Federal building (**April 19**); Timothy McVeigh, 27, Army veteran, arrested as suspect (**April 21**); authorities seek second suspect, link right-wing paramilitary groups to bombing (**April 22**). Death toll 2,000 in Rwanda massacre (**April 22**). Fighting escalates in Bosnia and Croatia (**May 1**). Fiftieth anniversary of V.E. Day celebrated (**May 8**). White House imposes harsh trade sanctions on Japan (**May 16**). Japanese police seize cult leader in subway nerve gas attack (**May 18**). Supreme Court rejects term-limit laws (**May 22**). Clinton vetoes G.O.P. budget-cutting bill (**June 1**). Bosnian Serbs hold U.S. troops as hostages (**June 2**). Colombia seizes a top drug-ring leader (**June 9**). Supreme Court raises doubts on affirmative action (**June 12**). U.S. shuttle docks with Russian space station (**June 27**). U.S. indicts two in Oklahoma City bombing (**Aug. 10**). F.B.I. suspends four in Idaho siege inquiry (**Aug. 11**). NATO planes bomb Bosnian Serb targets (**Aug. 28** et seq.). Simpson jurors allowed to hear two taped epithets (**Aug. 31**). France explodes nuclear device in Pacific; wide protests ensue (**Sept. 5**). Senator Bob Packwood of Oregon resigns under pressure for sexual and official misconduct (**Sept. 6**). Israelis and Palestinians agree on transferring West Bank to Arabs (**Sept. 24**). Los Angeles jury finds O.J. Simpson not guilty of murder charges (**Oct. 3**). A.M.A. criticizes G.O.P.'s Medicare proposals (**Oct. 3**). Pope John Paul II visits U.S. on whirlwind tour (**Oct. 4–8**). Action on term limits falters in Congress (**Oct. 4**). Warring parties agree on cease-fire in Bosnia (**Oct. 5**). Million Man March draws hundreds of thousands of black men to capital (**Oct. 16**). World leaders gather in New York for 50th anniversary of founding of United Nations (**Oct. 22–24**). Fan club founder convicted of killing Selena, popular Mexican-American singer (**Oct. 23**). Russian President Yeltsin in hospital with heart attack (**Oct. 26**). Quebec narrowly rejects independence from Canada (**Oct. 30**). Israel Prime Minister Yitzhak Rabin slain by Jewish extremist at peace rally (**Nov. 4**). U.S. servicemen admit rape of Japanese schoolgirl in Okinawa (**Nov. 7**). Nigeria hangs writer and eight other minority rights advocates (**Nov. 10**). Clinton vetoes stopgap spending and debt-ceiling bills (**Nov. 13**). Irish voters approve end to constitutional ban on divorce (**Nov. 24**). White House defies subpoena in Senate Whitewater inquiry (**Dec. 12**). Combatants sign Bosnia peace treaty (**Dec. 14**). French rail workers end strike (**Dec. 15**). Russian voters rebuff reformers as Communists make biggest gains (**Dec. 17**). U.S. and Mexico delay trading-access provision in NAFTA (**Dec. 18**). House move stalls Congress–White House negotiations to avert Government shutdown (**Dec. 20**).

PICTURE CREDITS. The following credits list the names of organizations and individuals who have contributed illustrations to **HEADLINE HISTORY.** The editors wish to thank all of them for their assistance. The credits are arranged alphabetically by picture source, then picture title and page number in **HEADLINE HISTORY. Credits:** AIP Niels Bohr Library, **Marie Curie** and **Albert Einstein,** p. 108; British Information Services, **Margaret Thatcher,** p. 121; Embassy of The Philippines, **Corazon C. Aquino,** p. 123; Harry S. Truman Library, **Harry S. Truman,** p. 116; John Fitzgerald Kennedy Library, Boston, **John F. Kennedy,** p. 119; Matthew Kalmenoff, **Brontosaur,** p. 93; NASA Photos, **Charles A. Lindbergh,** p. 112, **Voyager and Viking,** p. 120, **Space Shuttle Columbia,** p. 121; **Sally K. Ride,** p. 121 and **Asteroid *Gaspra*,** p. 125; National Portrait Gallery, Smithsonian Institution, **Theodore Roosevelt,** p. 108; Novosti Photos, **Vladimir Lenin,** p. 110, **Yuri A. Gagarin,** p. 118; **Mikhail S. Gorbachev,** p. 122; The Library of Congress Picture Collection, **Christopher Columbus,** p. 99, **Dred Scott,** p. 106, **Geronimo,** p. 107, **Woodrow Wilson,** p. 110, **Herbert C. Hoover,** p. 112, **Amelia Earhart,** p. 115, **Dwight D. Eisenhower,** p. 117, **Lyndon B. Johnson,** p. 119, **Richard M. Nixon,** p. 120; The Permanent Mission of India to the U.N., **Indira Gandhi,** p. 122; Republican National Committee, **Ronald W. Reagan,** p. 122, **George H. Bush,** p. 123; U.S. Army Photos, **D-Day, Yalta Conference,** p. 116, **Joseph Stalin,** p. 117; U.N. Photo, **Fidel Castro,** p. 118, U.N. Photo by D. Burnett, **Kurt Waldheim,** p. 123; Bob McNeely, The White House,**William J. Clinton,** p. 126. **MAP CREDITS:** Maps on pp. 94, 98, 102, 109, 111, 113, and 114 from *An Encyclopedia of World History,* by William L. Langer, The Fifth Edition, Copyright 1940, 1948, 1952, and © 1967, 1972 by Houghton Mifflin Company. Reprinted by permission of Houghton Mifflin Company.

WORLD STATISTICS

A PROFILE OF THE WORLD

Source: The World Factbook, 1995.

GEOGRAPHY

Total area: 510.072 million sq km (196.93 million sq mi.). **Land area:** 148.94 million sq km (57.50 million sq mi.). **Water area:** 361.132 million sq km (139.43 million sq mi.). **Comparative area:** land area about 16 times the size of the United States. **Note:** 70.8% of the world is water, 29.2% is land.

Land boundaries: The land boundaries in the world total 250,883.64 km (155,891.81 mi.) (not counting shared boundaries twice)

Maritime claims:
Contiguous zone: 24 nm (nautical miles) claimed by most but can vary. *Continental shelf:* 200-m (656 ft) depth claimed by most or to the depth of exploitation, others claim 200 nm or to the edge of the continental margin. *Exclusive fishing zone:* 200 nm claimed by most but can vary. *Exclusive economic zone:* 200 nm claimed by most but can vary. *Territorial sea:* 12 nm claimed by most but can vary

Climate: Two large areas of polar climates are separated by two rather narrow temperate zones from a wide equatorial band of tropical to subtropical climates.

Terrain: Highest elevation is Mt. Everest at 8,848 meters (29,028 ft) and lowest depression is the Dead Sea at 392 meters (1,286 ft) below sea level; greatest ocean depth is the Marianas Trench at 10,924 meters (35,840 ft)

Natural resources: The rapid using up of nonrenewable mineral resources, the depletion of forest areas and wetlands, the extinction of animal and plant species, and the deterioration in air and water quality (especially in Eastern Europe and the former USSR) pose serious long-term problems that governments and people are only beginning to address.

Land use:
Arable land: 10%. Permanent crops: 1%. Meadows and pastures: 24%. Forest and woodland: 31%. Other: 34%.

Environment: Large areas are subject to severe weather (tropical cyclones), natural disasters (earthquakes, landslides, tsunamis, volcanic eruptions), overpopulation, industrial disasters, pollution (air, water, acid rain, toxic substances), loss of vegetation (overgrazing, deforestation, desertification), loss of wildlife resources, soil degradation, soil depletion, erosion.

PEOPLE

Population: 5,789,662,862 (Sept. 1996 est.)
Growth rate: 1.5% (1995 est.)
Birth rate: 24 births/1,000 population (1995 est.)
Death rate: 9 deaths/1,000 live births (1995 est.)
Infant mortality rate: 64 deaths/1,000 live births (1995 est.)
Life expectancy at birth:
Total population: 62 years. *Male:* 61 years. *Female:* 64 years (1995 est.)
Total fertility rate: 3.1 children born/woman (1995 est.)
Literacy: age 15 and over can read and write (1994 est.) *Combined:* 82%. *Male:* 68%. *Female:* 75%.
Labor force: 2.24 billion (1992)

GOVERNMENT

Administrative divisions: 265 sovereign nations, dependent areas, other, and miscellaneous entries
Legal system: Varies by individual country; 186 (not including Yugoslavia) are parties to the United Nations International Court of Justice (ICJ or World Court)

ECONOMY

Overview: Led by recovery in Western Europe and strong performances by the U.S., Canada, and key developing countries, real global output—gross world product (GWP)—rose 3% in 1994 compared with 2% in 1993. Results varied widely among regions and countries. Average growth of 3% in the GDP of industrialized countries (60% of GWP in 1994) and average growth of 6% in the GDP of less developed countries (34% of GWP) were partly offset by a further 11% drop in the GDP of the former USSR/Eastern Europe area (now only 6% of GWP). With the notable exception of Japan at 2.9%, unemployment was typically 5%–12% in the industrial world. The U.S. accounted for 22% of GWP in 1994; Western Europe accounted for another 22%; and Japan accounted for 8%. These are the three "economic superpowers" which are presumably destined to compete for mastery in international markets on into the 21st century. As for the less developed countries, China, India, and the Four Dragons—South Korea, Taiwan, Hong Kong, and Singapore—once again posted records of 5% growth or better; however, many other countries, especially in Africa, continued to suffer from drought, rapid population growth, inflation, and civil strife. Central Europe made considerable progress in moving toward "market-friendly" economies, whereas the 15 ex-Soviet countries (with the notable exceptions of the three Baltic states) typically experienced further declines in output, sometimes as high as 30%. Externally, the nation-state, as a bedrock economic-political institution, is steadily losing control over international flows of people, goods, funds, and technology. Internally, the central government in a number of cases is losing control over resources as separatist regional movements—typically based on ethnicity—gain momentum, for example, in the successor states of the former Soviet Union, in the former Yugoslavia, and in India. In Western Europe, governments face the difficult political problem of channeling resources away from welfare programs in order to increase investment and strengthen incentives to seek employment. The addition of nearly 100 million people each year to an already overcrowded globe is exacerbating the problems of pollution, desertification, underemployment, epidemics, and famine. Because of their own internal problems, the industrialized countries have inadequate resources to deal effectively with the poorer areas of the world, which, at least from the economic point of view, are becoming further marginalized.

National product: GWP (gross world product)—purchasing power equivalent—$30.7 trillion (1994 est.)
National product real growth rate: 3.2% (1994 est.)
National product per capita: $5,400 (1994 est.)
Inflation rate (consumer prices):
Developed countries: 5% (1994 est.). *Developing countries:* 50% (1994 est.).
Note: these figures vary widely in individual cases
Unemployment rate: developed countries typically 5%–12%; developing countries, 30% combined unemployment and underemployment (1994)
Exports: $4 trillion (f.o.b. 1994 est.) *Commodities:* the whole range of industrial and agricultural goods and services. *Partners:* in value, about 75% of exports from the developed countries.
Imports: $4.1 trillion (c.i.f., 1994 est.) *Commodities:* the whole range of industrial and agricultural goods and services. *Partners:* in value, about 75% of imports by the developed countries
External debt: $1 trillion for less developed countries (1993 est.)
Industrial production: growth rate —5% (1994 est.)
Electricity: 2,773,000,000 kW capacity; 11,601 trillion kWh produced, 1,937 kWh per capita (1993)
Industries: industry worldwide is dominated by the onrush of technology, especially in computers, robotics, telecommunications, and medicines and medical equipment; most of these advances take place in Organization for Economic Cooperation and Development[2] (OECD) nations; only a small portion of non-OECD countries have succeeded in rapidly adjusting to these technological forces, and the technological gap between the industrial nations and the less-developed countries continues to widen; the rapid development of new industrial (and agricultural) technology is complicating already grim environmental problems.

---

1. 24 full members: Australia, Austria, Belgium, Canada, Denmark, Finland, France, Germany, Greece, Iceland, Ireland, Italy, Japan, Luxembourg, Netherlands, New Zealand, Norway, Portugal, Spain, Sweden, Switzerland, Turkey, U.K., U.S.

Agriculture: The production of major food crops has increased substantially in the last 20 years; the annual production of cereals, for instance, has risen by 50%, from about 1.2 billion metric tons to about 1.8 billion metric tons; production increases have resulted mainly from increased yields rather than increases in planted areas; while global production is sufficient for aggregate demand, about one-fifth of the world's population remains malnourished, primarily because local production cannot adequately provide for large and rapidly growing populations, which are too poor to pay for food imports; conditions are especially bad in Africa where drought in recent years has intensified the consequences of overpopulation.

TRANSPORTATION

Railroads: 148,775 mi. (239,430 km) of narrow gauge track; 441,642 mi. (710,754 km) of standard gauge track; 156,059 mi. (251,153 km) of broad gauge track; includes about 118,060 to 121,167 mi. (190,000 to 195,000 km) of electrified routes of which 91,814 mi. (147,760 km) are in Europe, 15,229 mi. (24,509 km) in the Far East, 6,866 mi. (11,050 km) in Africa, 2,624 mi. (4,223 km) in South America, and only 2,585 mi. (4,160 km) in North America; fastest speed in daily service is 186 mph (300 km/hr) attained by France's SNCF TGV-Atlantique line
Ports: Mina al Ahmadi (Kuwait), Chiba, Houston, Kawasaki, Kobe, Marseille, New Orleans, New York, Rotterdam, Yokohama
Merchant marine: 25,364 ships (1,000 GRT [gross register ton] or over) totaling 435,458,296 GRT/697,171,651 DWT (dead weight ton) (April 1995)

DEFENSE FORCES

Branches: ground, maritime, and air forces at all levels of technology
Defense expenditures: A further decline in 1994, by perhaps 5%–10%, to roughly three-quarters of a trillion dollars, or 2.5% of gross world product (1994 est.)

Area and Population by Country
Mid-1996 Estimates

Country	Area[1]	Population	Country	Area[1]	Population
Afghanistan	250,000	22,664,136	Brunei	2,226	299,939
Albania	11,100	3,249,136	Bulgaria	42,823	8,612,757
Algeria	919,595	29,183,032	Burkina Faso	105,870	10,623,323
Andorra	175	67,509	Burundi	10,747	5,943,057
Angola	481,350	10,342,899	Cambodia	69,884	10,861,218
Antigua and Barbuda	171	65,647	Cameroon	183,569	14,261,557
Argentina	1,072,067	34,672,997	Canada	3,851,809	28,820,671
Armenia	11,500	3,463,574	Cape Verde	1,557	449,066
Australia	2,966,150	18,260,863	Central African Republic	241,313	3,274,426
Austria	32,375	8,013,614	Chad	495,752	6,976,845
Azerbaijan	33,400	7,676,953	Chile	292,132	14,333,258
Bahamas	5,380	259,367	China, People's Republic of	3,691,521	1,210,004,956
Bahrain	240	590,042	Colombia	439,735	36,813,161
Bangladesh	55,598	123,062,800	Comoros	690	569,237
Barbados	166	257,030	Congo	132,046	2,527,841
Belarus	80,200	10,415,973	Costa Rica	19,652	3,463,083
Belgium	11,781	10,098,264	Côte d'Ivoire	124,502	14,762,445
Belize	8,867	219,296	Croatia	21,829	5,004,112
Benin	43,483	5,709,529	Cuba	44,218	11,007,446
Bhutan	18,000	1,822,625	Cyprus	3,572	744,609
Bolivia	424,162	7,165,257	Czech Republic	30,464	10,321,120
Bosnia–Herzegovina	19,741	2,656,240	Denmark	16,631	5,210,833
Botswana	231,800	1,477,630	Djibouti	8,490	427,642
Brazil	3,286,470	162,661,214	Dominica	290	82,926

Country	Area[1]	Population	Country	Area[1]	Population
Dominican Republic	18,704	8,088,881	Namibia	318,261	1,677,243
Ecuador	106,927	11,466,291	Nepal	54,463	22.094,033
Egypt	386,900	63,575,107	Netherlands	16,041	15,531,940
El Salvador	8,260	5,828,987	New Zealand	103,884	3,547,983
Equatorial Guinea	10,830	431,282	Nicaragua	50,180	4,272,352
Eritrea	45,754	3,909,628	Niger	489,206	9,113,001
Estonia	18,370	1,459,428	Nigeria	356,700	103,912,489
Ethiopia	446,952	57,171,662	Norway	125,049	4,345,941
Fiji	7,078	782,381	Oman	82,030	2,186,548
Finland	130,119	5,100,213	Pakistan	310,400	129,275,660
France	212,918	58,317,450	Panama	29,761	2,655,094
Gabon	103,346	1,172,798	Papua New Guinea	178,704	4,394,537
Gambia	4,093	1,020,178	Paraguay	157,047	5,504,146
Georgia	26,900	5,219,810	Peru	496,222	24,523,408
Germany	137,838	83,536,115	Philippines	115,830	74,480,848
Ghana	92,100	17,698,271	Poland	120,727	38,642,565
Greece	50,961	10,718,518	Portugal	35,550	9,865,114
Grenada	133	94,961	Qatar	4,000	547,761
Guatemala	42,042	11,277,614	Romania	91,700	21,657,162
Guinea	94,925	7,411,981	Russia	6,592,800	148,190,419
Guinea–Bissau	13,948	1,151,330	Rwanda	10,169	6,853,359
Guyana	83,000	712,091	St. Kitts and Nevis	100	41,369
Haiti	10,714	6,731,539	St. Lucia	238	157,862
Honduras	43,277	5,605,193	St. Vincent and the Grenadines	150	118,344
Hungary	35,919	10,002,541	São Tomé and Príncipe	370	144,128
Iceland	39,709	268,369	Saudi Arabia	865,000	19,409,058
India	1,229,737	952,107,694	Senegal	75,954	9,092,749
Indonesia	735,268	206,611,600	Seychelles	175	77,575
Iran	636,293	66,094,264	Sierra Leone	27,700	4,793,121
Iraq	167,920	21,422,292	Singapore	246	3,396,924
Ireland	27,136	3,562,902	Slovakia	18,917	5,374,362
Israel	8,020	5,215,022	Slovenia	7,819	1,951,443
Italy	116,500	57,460,274	Solomon Islands	11,500	412,902
Jamaica	4,411	2,593,918	Somalia	246,199	9,639,715
Japan	145,874	125,449,703	South Africa	471,440	41,743,459
Jordan	34,573	4,212,152	Spain	194,884	38,853,397
Kazakhstan	1,049,000	16,916,463	Sri Lanka	25,332	18,553,074
Kenya	244,960	28,176,686	Sudan	967,491	31,065,229
Kiribati	280	80,919	Suriname	63,251	436,418
Korea, North	46,768	23,904,124	Swaziland	6,704	998,730
Korea, South	38,031	45,482,291	Sweden	173,800	8,861,270
Kuwait	6,880	1,950,047	Switzerland	15,941	7,124,745
Kyrgyzstan	76,000	4,529,648	Syria	71,498	15,608,648
Laos	91,429	4,975,772	Taiwan	13,895	21,465,881
Latvia	25,400	2,468,982	Tajikistan	55,300	5,916,373
Lebanon	4,015	3,776,317	Tanzania	364,879	29,058,470
Lesotho	11,720	1,970,781	Thailand	198,455	58,851,357
Liberia	43,000	2,109,789	Togo	21,925	4,570,530
Libya	679,536	5,445,436	Tonga	290	106,466
Liechtenstein	61	31,011	Trinidad and Tobago	1,980	1,272,385
Lithuania	25,174	3,646,041	Tunisia	63,379	9,019,687
Luxembourg	999	406,901	Turkey	300,947	62,484,478
Macedonia	9,928	2,104,035	Turkmenistan	188,500	4,149,283
Madagascar	226,660	13,670,507	Uganda	91,459	20,158,176
Malawi	45,747	9,452,844	Ukraine	233,000	50,864,009
Malaysia	128,328	19,962,893	United Arab Emirates	32,000	3,057,337
Maldives	115	270,758	United Kingdom	94,247	58,489,975
Mali	478,819	9,653,261	United States	3,536,341	266,476,278
Malta	122	372,314	Uruguay	68,040	3,238,952
Marshall Islands	70	58,363	Uzbekistan	172,700	23,418,381
Mauritania	397,953	2,336,048	Vanuatu	5,700	177,504
Mauritius	787	1,139,047	Venezuela	352,143	21,983,188
Mexico	761,600	95,772,462	Vietnam	127,246	73,976,973
Micronesia	271	125,377	Western Samoa	1,093	214,384
Moldova	13,000	4,463,847	Yemen	203,850	13,483,178
Mongolia	604,250	2,496,617	Yugoslavia[2]	39,449	10,614,558
Morocco	172,413	29,779,156	Zaire	905,365	46,498,539
Mozambique	303,073	17,877,927	Zambia	290,586	9,159,072
Myanmar	261,220	45,975,625	Zimbabwe	150,698	11,271,314

1. Square miles. 2. On April 27, 1992, Serbia and Montenegro formed a new state, the Federal Republic of Yugoslavia.
Source: U.S. Bureau of the Census, International Data Base.

World's Largest Cities by Rank
(Estimated Mid-Year Population in Thousands)

Rank in 1992	City	1992	1995	2000	Average Annual Growth Rate (%) 1992–95	Area (square miles)
1.	Tokyo–Yokohama, Japan	27,540	28,447	29,971	1.1	1,089
2.	Mexico City, Mexico	21,615	23,913	27,872	3.4	522
3.	Sao Paulo, Brazil	19,373	21,539	25,354	3.5	451
4.	Seoul, South Korea	17,334	19,065	21,976	3.2	342
5.	New York, United States	14,628	14,638	14,648	(Z)	1,274
6.	Osaka–Kobe–Kyoto, Japan	13,919	14,060	14,287	0.3	495
7.	Bombay, India	12,450	13,532	15,357	2.8	95
8.	Calcutta, India	12,137	12,885	14,088	2.0	209
9.	Rio de Janeiro, Brazil	12,009	12,788	14,169	2.1	260
10.	Buenos Aires, Argentina	11,743	12,232	12,911	1.4	535
11.	Manila, Philippines	10,554	11,342	12,846	2.4	188
12.	Moscow, Russia	10,526	10,769	11,121	0.8	379
13.	Cairo, Egypt	10,372	11,155	12,512	2.4	104
14.	Jakarta, Indonesia	10,185	11,151	12,804	3.0	76
15.	Tehran, Iran	10,102	11,681	14,251	4.8	112
16.	Los Angeles, United States	10,072	10,414	10,714	1.1	1,110
17.	Delhi, India	9,243	10,105	11,849	3.0	138
18.	London, United Kingdom	9,168	8,897	8,574	−1.0	874
19.	Paris, France	8,589	8,764	8,803	0.7	432
20.	Lagos, Nigeria	8,487	9,799	12,528	4.8	56
21.	Karachi, Pakistan	8,174	9,350	11,299	4.5	190
22.	Essen, Germany	7,506	7,364	7,239	−0.6	704
23.	Lima, Peru	7,028	7,853	9,241	3.7	120
24.	Shanghai, China	7,000	7,194	7,540	0.9	78
25.	Istanbul, Turkey	6,937	7,624	8,875	3.2	165
26.	Taipei, Taiwan	6,924	7,477	8,516	2.6	138
27.	Chicago, United States	6,493	6,541	6,568	0.2	762
28.	Bogota, Colombia	6,176	6,801	7,935	3.2	79
29.	Bangkok, Thailand	6,088	6,657	7,587	3.0	102
30.	Madras, India	5,998	6,550	7,384	2.9	115
31.	Beijing, China	5,791	5,865	5,993	0.4	151
32.	Hong Kong, Hong Kong	5,762	5,841	5,956	0.5	23
33.	Santiago, Chile	5,484	5,812	6,294	1.9	128
34.	Pusan, South Korea	5,161	5,748	6,700	3.6	54
35.	Bangalore, India	5,080	5,644	6,764	3.5	50
36.	Nagoya, Japan	4,909	5,017	5,303	0.7	307
37.	Tianjin, China	4,857	5,041	5,298	1.2	49
38.	Milan, Italy	4,718	4,795	4,839	0.5	344
39.	St. Petersburg, Russia	4,645	4,694	4,738	0.4	139
40.	Dhaka, Bangladesh	4,640	5,296	6,492	4.4	32
41.	Madrid, Spain	4,577	4,772	5,104	1.4	66
42.	Lahore, Pakistan	4,475	4,986	5,864	3.6	57
43.	Baghdad, Iraq	4,358	4,566	5,239	1.6	97
44.	Shenyang, China	4,323	4,457	4,684	1.0	39
45.	Barcelona, Spain	4,221	4,492	4,834	2.1	87
46.	San Francisco, United States	4,005	4,104	4,214	0.8	428
47.	Kinshasa, Zaire	3,997	4,520	5,646	4.1	57
48.	Manchester, United Kingdom	3,984	3,949	3,827	−0.3	357
49.	Philadelphia, United States	3,970	3,988	3,979	0.2	471
50.	Belo Horizonte, Brazil	3,920	4,373	5,125	3.6	79
51.	Ahmadabad, India	3,826	4,200	4,837	3.1	32
52.	Hyderabad, India	3,787	4,149	4,765	3.0	88
53.	Ho Chi Minh City, Vietnam	3,725	4,064	4,481	2.9	31
54.	Athens, Greece	3,613	3,670	3,866	0.5	116
55.	Sydney, Australia	3,528	3,619	3,708	0.9	338
56.	Guadalajara, Mexico	3,525	3,839	4,451	2.8	78
57.	Miami, United States	3,522	3,679	3,894	1.5	448
58.	Surabaya, Indonesia	3,327	3,428	3,632	1.0	43
59.	Guangzhou, China	3,314	3,485	3,652	1.7	79
60.	Caracas, Venezuela	3,247	3,338	3,435	0.9	54
61.	Wuhan, China	3,231	3,325	3,495	1.0	65
62.	Porto Alegre, Brazil	3,220	3,541	4,109	3.2	231
63.	Toronto, Canada	3,182	3,296	3,296	1.2	154
64.	Casablanca, Morocco	3,136	3,327	3,795	2.0	35

Rank in 1992	City	1992	1995	2000	Average Annual Growth Rate (%) 1992–95	Area (square miles)
65.	Monterrey, Mexico	3,084	3,385	3,974	3.1	77
66.	Rome, Italy	3,028	3,079	3,129	0.6	69
67.	Greater Berlin, Germany	3,020	3,018	3,006	(Z)	274
68.	Ankara, Turkey	3,000	3,263	3,777	2.8	55
69.	Naples, Italy	2,996	3,051	3,134	0.6	62
70.	Alexandria, Egypt	2,981	3,114	3,304	1.5	35
71.	Montreal, Canada	2,933	2,996	3,071	0.7	164
72.	Detroit, United States	2,890	2,865	2,735	−0.3	468
73.	Rangoon, Burma	2,876	3,075	3,332	2.2	47
74.	Melbourne, Australia	2,865	2,946	2,968	0.9	327
75.	Dallas, United States	2,856	2,972	3,257	1.3	419
76.	Taegu, South Korea	2,837	3,201	4,051	4.0	(n.a.)
77.	Kiev, Ukraine	2,837	2,983	3,237	1.7	62
78.	Singapore, Singapore	2,743	2,816	2,913	0.9	78
79.	Harbin, China	2,625	2,747	2,887	1.5	30
80.	Poona, India	2,617	2,987	3,647	4.4	(n.a.)
81.	Washington, D.C., United States	2,572	2,637	2,707	0.8	357
82.	Lisbon, Portugal	2,505	2,551	2,717	0.6	(n.a.)
83.	Chongqing, China	2,468	2,632	2,961	2.1	(n.a.)
84.	Tashkent, Uzbekistan	2,461	2,640	2,947	2.3	(n.a.)
85.	Boston, United States	2,460	2,480	2,485	0.3	303
86.	Vienna, Austria	2,392	2,474	2,647	1.1	(n.a.)
87.	Houston, United States	2,369	2,456	2,651	1.2	310
88.	Salvador, Brazil	2,366	2,694	3,286	4.3	(n.a.)
89.	Chengdu, China	2,365	2,465	2,591	1.4	25
90.	Budapest, Hungary	2,304	2,313	2,335	0.1	138
91.	Kanpur, India	2,184	2,356	2,673	2.5	(n.a.)
92.	Birmingham, United Kingdom	2,177	2,130	2,078	−0.7	223
93.	Bucharest, Romania	2,175	2,214	2,271	0.6	52
94.	Havana, Cuba	2,152	2,218	2,333	1.0	(n.a.)

Source: U.S. Bureau of the Census International Data Base. NOTE: For this table cities are defined as population clusters of continuous built-up area with a population density of at least 5,000 persons per square mile. The boundary of the city was determined by examining detailed maps of each city in conjunction with the most recent official population statistics. Exclaves of areas exceeding the minimum population density were added to the city if the intervening gap was less than one mile. To the extent practical, nonresidential areas such as parks, airports, industrial complexes, and water were excluded from the area reported for each city, thus making the population density reflective of the concentrations in the residential portions of the city. By using a consistent definition for the city, it is possible to make comparisons of the cities on the basis of total population, area, and population density.

Political and administrative boundaries were disregarded in determining the population of a city. Detroit includes Windsor, Canada.

The population of each city was projected based on the proportion each city was of its country total at the time of the last two censuses and projected country populations.

Population figures for the nine cities with (n.a.) in the area column were derived by a less precise method, not involving the use of detailed maps. Thirty-four other cities are projected to have at least 2,000,000 inhabitants by midyear 2000. These population figures may not agree with those in the Countries of the World section as the source is different, and the basis for these figures is spelled out above. Z less than .05.

Crude Marriage Rates for Selected Countries
(per 1,000 population)

Country	1995	1994	1993	1992	1991	1990	Country	1995	1994	1993	1992	1991	1990
Australia	n.a.	6.2	6.4	6.6	6.6	6.9	Japan	n.a.	6.3	6.4	6.1	6.0	5.8
Austria	5.4	5.4	5.6	5.8	5.6	5.8	Luxembourg	5.1	5.9	6.0	6.4	6.7	6.2
Belgium	5.1	5.2	5.4	5.8	6.2	6.6	Netherlands	5.2	5.4	5.8	6.4	6.3	6.4
Bulgaria	4.0	4.5	4.9	5.0	5.4	6.7	New Zealand	6.2	6.3	6.4	6.5	6.8	7.0
Czech Republic[1]	5.3	5.6	6.4	n.a.	6.7	8.4	Norway	n.a.	4.6	n.a.	4.5	4.7	5.2
Denmark	6.7	6.8	6.1	6.2	6.0	6.1	Poland	5.4	5.4	5.4	5.7	6.0	6.7
Finland	4.5	4.7	4.9	4.6	4.7	4.8	Portugal	n.a.	n.a.	6.9	7.1	6.8	7.3
France	n.a.	4.4	4.4	4.7	4.9	5.1	Romania	6.8	6.7	7.1	7.7	7.9	8.3
Germany[2]	5.3	5.4	5.4	5.7	6.3	6.5	Russia	7.3	7.3	n.a.	7.1	8.5	8.9
Greece	n.a.	5.4	5.9	4.7	6.0	5.8	Sweden	3.8	3.9	3.9	4.3	4.6	4.7
Hungary	5.3	5.3	5.3	5.5	5.9	6.4	Switzerland	5.6	6.1	6.2	6.6	7.0	6.9
Ireland	n.a.	4.6	4.5	4.5	4.8	5.0	United Kingdom	n.a.	n.a.	n.a.	6.1	6.1	6.8
Israel	n.a.	n.a.	6.2	6.5	6.5	7.0	United States	n.a.	9.1	9.0	9.2	9.4	9.8
Italy	n.a.	5.0	4.8	5.4	5.5	5.4	Yugoslavia[3]	5.7	5.7	5.8	6.0	n.a.	6.2

1. Data prior to 1993 pertain to the former Czechoslovakia. 2. All data pertaining to Germany prior to 1990 are for West Germany. 3. Beginning January 1992, data refer to the Federal Republic of Yugoslavia. Prior to that data, data refer to the Socialist Federal Republic of Yugoslavia. NOTE: n.a. = not available. *Source:* United Nations, *Monthly Bulletin of Statistics,* June 1996.

World Population by Country, 1996–2020

(In thousands. Covers countries with 10 million or more population in 1996)

Country	1996	2000	2010	2020
Afghanistan	22,664	26,668	34,098	43,050
Algeria	29,183	31,788	38,479	44,783
Angola	10,343	11,513	14,982	19,272
Argentina	34,673	36,202	39,947	43,190
Australia	18,261	18,950	20,434	21,696
Bangladesh	123,063	132,081	153,195	172,041
Belarus	10,416	10,545	10,924	11,059
Belgium	10,170	10,286	10,358	10,271
Brazil	162,661	169,545	183,747	194,246
Burkina Faso	10,623	11,684	14,150	16,569
Cambodia	10,861	12,098	15,679	20,208
Cameroon	14,262	15,966	20,630	25,896
Canada	28,821	29,989	32,534	34,753
Chile	14,333	14,996	16,382	17,535
China	1,210,005	1,253,438	1,340,357	1,413,251
Colombia	36,813	39,172	44,504	49,266
Côte d'Ivoire	14,762	16,172	20,261	24,634
Cuba	10,951	11,131	11,481	11,699
Czech Republic	10,321	10,358	10,445	10,271
Ecuador	11,466	12,360	14,534	16,546
Egypt	63,575	68,437	80,689	92,350
Ethiopia	57,172	63,514	81,169	100,813
France	58,041	58,816	60,562	61,087
Germany	83,536	85,684	88,975	88,870
Ghana	17,698	19,272	22,929	26,516
Greece	10,539	10,735	11,135	11,076
Guatemala	11,278	12,408	15,284	18,131
Hungary	10,003	9,795	9,456	9,103
India	952,108	1,012,909	1,155,830	1,289,473
Indonesia	206,612	219,267	249,679	276,017
Iran	66,094	71,879	88,231	104,282
Iraq	21,422	24,731	34,545	46,260
Italy	57,460	57,807	57,660	55,665
Japan	125,450	126,582	127,548	123,620
Kazakhstan	16,916	16,943	17,564	18,408
Kenya	28,177	30,490	33,920	35,236
Libya	5,445	6,294	8,913	12,391
Madagascar	13,671	15,295	20,096	25,988
Malaysia	19,963	21,610	25,691	29,830
Mexico	95,772	102,912	120,115	136,096
Morocco	29,779	32,229	38,442	44,519
Mozambique	17,878	19,829	25,116	30,810
Nepal	22,094	24,364	30,783	37,767
Netherlands	15,568	15,893	16,382	16,490
Nigeria	103,912	117,328	157,375	205,160
North Korea	23,904	25,491	28,491	30,969
Pakistan	129,276	141,145	170,750	198,722
Peru	24,523	26,198	29,988	33,226
Philippines	74,481	80,961	97,119	112,963
Poland	38,643	39,010	40,342	40,833
Romania	21,657	20,996	20,741	20,135
Russia	148,178	147,938	149,978	149,632
Saudi Arabia	19,409	22,246	31,198	43,255
Serbia and Montenegro	10,614	10,787	11,062	11,017
South Africa	41,743	44,462	49,200	52,264
South Korea	45,482	47,351	51,235	53,451
Spain	39,181	39,545	40,398	39,758
Sri Lanka	18,553	19,377	21,331	22,877
Sudan	31,065	35,454	46,512	58,545
Syria	15,609	17,759	23,329	28,926
Taiwan	21,466	22,214	23,966	25,155
Tanzania	29,058	31,045	36,076	40,102
Thailand	58,851	61,164	66,092	69,298
Turkey	62,484	66,618	76,570	85,643

Country	1996	2000	2010	2020
Uganda	20,158	21,891	26,355	30,872
Ukraine	50,864	50,380	49,915	49,038
United Kingdom	58,490	58,894	59,159	59,289
United States	265,563	274,943	298,026	323,052
Uzbekistan	23,418	25,245	30,536	36,628
Venezuela	21,983	23,596	27,345	30,876
Vietnam	73,977	78,350	88,602	99,153
Yemen	13,483	15,547	21,841	29,469
Zaire	46,499	51,374	69,293	91,548
Zimbabwe	11,271	11,777	11,905	11,344

Source: U.S. Department of Commerce, Bureau of the Census.

Estimates of World Population by Regions

Year	Estimated population in millions							
	North America[1]	Latin America[2]	Europe[3]	Former U.S.S.R.	Asia[4]	Africa	Oceania	World total
1650	1	7	103	(5)	257	100	2	470
1750	1	10	144	(5)	437	100	2	694
1850	26	33	274	(5)	656	100	2	1,091
1900	81	63	423	(5)	857	141	6	1,571
1950	166	164	392	180	1,380	219	13	2,513
1960	199	215	425	214	1,683	275	16	3,027
1970	226	283	460	244	2,091	354	19	3,678
1980	252	365	484	266	2,618	472	23	4,478
1990	276	442	501	289	3,130	625	26	5,292
1995	292	481	509	297	3,403	721	28	5,734
1996	295	488	507	293	3,428	731	29	5,772

1. U.S. (including Alaska and Hawaii), Bermuda, Canada, Greenland, and St. Pierre and Miquelon. 2. Mexico, Central and South America, and Caribbean Islands. 3. Includes Russia 1650-1900. 4. Excludes Russia (U.S.S.R.). 5. Included in Europe. NOTE: From 1930 on European Turkey included in Asia not Europe. *Sources:* W.F. Willcox, 1650-1900; United Nations, 1930-70. United States Department of Commerce, Bureau of the Census, 1980–96.

World's 20 Most Populous Countries: 1996 and 2020

	1996			2020	
Rank	Country	Population	Rank	Country	Population
1.	China	1,210,004,956	1.	China	1,413,251,000
2.	India	952,107,694	2.	India	1,289,473,000
3.	United States	266,476,278	3.	United States	323,052,000
4.	Indonesia	206,611,600	4.	Indonesia	276,017,000
5.	Brazil	162,661,214	5.	Nigeria	205,160,000
6.	Russia	148,190,419	6.	Brazil	194,246,000
7.	Pakistan	129,275,660	7.	Bangladesh	172,041,000
8.	Japan	125,449,703	8.	Pakistan	170,750,000
9.	Bangladesh	123,062,800	9.	Russia	149,632,000
10.	Nigeria	103,912,489	10.	Mexico	136,096,000
11.	Mexico	95,772,462	11.	Japan	123,620,000
12.	Germany	83,536,115	12.	Iran	104,282,000
13.	Philippines	74,480,848	13.	Ethiopia	100,813,000
14.	Vietnam	73,976,973	14.	Vietnam	99,153,000
15.	Iran	66,094,264	15.	Philippines	97,119,000
16.	Egypt	63,575,107	16.	Egypt	92,350,000
17.	Turkey	62,484,478	17.	Zaire	91,548,000
18.	Thailand	58,851,357	18.	Germany	88,870,000
19.	United Kingdom	58,489,975	19.	Turkey	85,643,000
20.	France	58,317,450	20.	Thailand	69,298,000

Source: U.S. Department of Commerce, Bureau of the Ceusus.

Infant Mortality Rates and Life Expectancy at Birth by Sex for Selected Countries, 1996

Country	Infant deaths per 1,000 live births			Life expectancy at birth (years)		
	Both sexes	Male	Female	Both sexes	Male	Female
NORTH AMERICA						
Canada	6.1	6.8	5.4	79.1	75.7	82.7
United States	6.7	7.7	5.6	76.0	72.7	79.4
Mexico	25.0	30.1	19.6	73.7	70.1	77.5
CENTRAL AND SOUTH AMERICA						
Brazil	55.3	58.8	51.6	61.6	56.7	66.8
Chile	13.6	14.8	12.4	74.5	71.3	77.7
Costa Rica	13.5	14.2	12.8	75.7	73.3	78.2
Ecuador	34.8	39.7	29.7	71.1	68.5	73.8
Guatemala	50.7	54.6	46.6	65.2	62.6	68.0
Panama	29.7	31.4	27.9	73.9	71.2	76.8
Peru	52.2	54.2	50.0	69.1	67.0	71.4
Trinidad and Tobago	18.2	20.5	15.8	70.3	67.9	72.8
Uruguay	15.4	16.9	13.7	74.9	71.8	78.3
Venezuela	29.5	33.3	25.5	72.1	69.1	75.3
EUROPE						
Austria	6.2	7.0	5.4	76.5	73.4	79.8
Belgium	6.4	7.0	5.7	77.1	73.9	80.5
Cyprus	8.4	10.6	6.2	76.3	74.1	78.5
Czech Republic	8.4	9.4	7.3	78.3	70.1	77.7
Denmark	4.8	5.6	4.1	77.3	73.8	81.0
Finland	4.9	4.7	5.1	75.5	73.8	77.2
France	6.2	7.1	5.2	78.4	74.5	82.5
Germany	6.0	6.6	5.3	76.0	72.8	79.3
Greece	7.4	7.9	6.9	78.1	75.6	80.8
Hungary	12.3	13.8	10.8	69.0	64.2	74.0
Ireland	6.4	7.1	5.7	75.6	72.9	78.5
Italy	6.9	7.6	6.2	78.1	74.9	81.5
Netherlands	4.9	5.4	4.3	77.7	74.9	80.7
Norway	4.9	5.6	4.2	77.5	74.6	80.6
Poland	12.4	13.8	11.0	72.1	68.0	76.4
Portugal	7.6	8.4	6.9	75.3	71.5	79.3
Russia	24.7	27.2	22.1	63.2	56.5	70.3
Slovakia	10.7	12.3	9.0	73.0	69.0	77.2
Spain	6.3	6.9	5.6	78.3	74.9	81.8
Sweden	4.5	4.9	4.1	78.1	75.6	80.6
Switzerland	5.4	6.0	4.8	77.6	74.6	80.8
United Kingdom	6.4	7.2	5.7	76.4	73.8	79.2
ASIA						
Bangladesh	102.3	110.1	94.2	55.9	56.0	55.7
China	39.6	31.5	48.6	69.6	68.3	71.1
India	71.0	71.0	71.2	59.7	59.1	60.3
Iran	52.7	53.4	52.1	67.4	66.1	68.7
Israel	8.5	9.2	7.8	78.0	76.2	80.0
Japan	4.4	4.8	4.0	79.6	76.6	82.7
Pakistan	96.8	98.3	95.3	58.5	57.7	59.3
South Korea	8.2	8.5	7.9	73.3	69.7	77.4
Sri Lanka	20..8	22.6	18.9	72.4	69.8	75.1
Syria	40.0	40.9	38.9	67.1	65.9	68.4
AFRICA						
Egypt	72.8	74.6	70.8	61.4	59.5	63.5
Kenya	55.3	58.3	52.2	55.6	55.5	55.7
South Africa	48.8	51.0	46.5	59.5	57.2	61.8
OCEANIA						
Australia	5.5	6.1	4.9	79.4	76.4	82.5
New Zealand	6.7	7.7	5.6	77.0	74.0	80.2

Source: U.S. Bureau of the Census, International Data Base.

Crude Birth and Death Rates for Selected Countries
(per 1,000 population)

Country	Birth rates						Death rates					
	1995	1994	1990	1985	1980	1995	1995	1994	1990	1985	1980	1975
Australia	n.a.	14.5	15.4	15.7	15.3	16.9	n.a.	7.1	7.0	7.5	7.4	7.9
Austria	11.0	11.5	11.6	11.6	12.0	12.5	10.0	10.0	10.6	11.9	12.2	12.8
Belgium	11.4	11.6	12.6	11.5	12.7	12.2	10.5	10.4	10.6	11.2	11.6	12.2
Czech Republic[1]	9.3	10.3	13.4	14.5	16.4	19.6	11.4	11.3	11.7	11.8	12.1	11.5
Denmark	13.4	13.4	12.4	10.6	11.2	14.2	12.1	11.8	11.9	11.4	10.9	10.1
Finland	12.4	12.9	13.2	12.8	13.1	13.9	9.7	9.4	10.0	9.8	9.3	9.3
France	12.5	12.3	13.5	13.9	14.8	14.1	9.1	9.0	9.3	10.1	10.2	10.6
Germany[2]	9.3	9.5	11.4	9.6	10.0	9.7	10.7	10.9	11.2	11.5	11.6	12.1
Greece	n.a.	9.9	10.2	11.7	15.4	15.7	n.a.	9.4	9.3	9.4	9.1	8.9
Hong Kong	n.a.	11.8	11.7	14.0	16.9	n.a.	n.a.	4.9	4.9	4.6	5.1	n.a.
Hungary	11.0	11.3	12.1	12.2	13.9	18.4	14.1	14.3	14.1	13.9	13.6	12.4
Ireland	n.a.	13.4	15.1	17.6	21.9	21.5	n.a.	8.6	9.1	9.4	9.7	10.6
Israel	21.0	21.2	22.2	23.5	24.1	28.2	6.3	6.3	6.2	6.6	6.7	7.1
Italy	n.a.	9.2	9.8	10.1	11.2	14.8	n.a.	9.6	9.4	9.5	9.7	9.9
Japan	n.a.	9.9	9.9	11.9	13.7	17.2	n.a.	7.0	6.7	6.2	6.2	6.4
Luxembourg	13.2	13.6	13.3	11.2	11.5	11.2	9.3	9.5	10.1	11.0	11.5	12.2
Mauritius	18.3	19.6	21.0	18.8	27.0	25.1	6.7	6.7	6.5	6.8	7.2	8.1
Netherlands	12.3	12.7	13.3	12.3	12.8	13.0	8.8	8.7	8.6	8.5	8.1	8.3
New Zealand	16.3	16.3	18.0	15.6	n.a.	18.4	7.9	7.8	7.9	8.4	n.a.	8.1
Norway	13.8	13.6	14.3	12.3	12.5	14.1	10.3	10.1	10.7	10.7	10.1	9.9
Panama	n.a.	21.7	23.9	26.6	26.8	32.3	n.a.	n.a.	n.a.	n.a.	n.a.	n.a.
Poland	11.5	12.5	14.3	18.2	19.5	18.9	10.0	10.1	10.2	10.3	9.8	8.7
Portugal	10.7	10.7	11.8	12.8	16.4	19.1	n.a.	9.9	10.4	9.6	9.9	10.4
Romania	10.4	11.0	13.6	15.8	n.a.	n.a.	12.0	11.6	10.6	10.9	n.a.	n.a.
Singapore	16.3	16.9	17.0	16.6	17.3	17.8	5.2	5.1	n.a.	5.2	5.2	5.1
Sweden	11.7	12.8	14.5	11.8	11.7	12.6	11.0	10.3	11.	11.3	11.0	10.8
Switzerland	11.6	11.9	12.5	11.6	11.3	12.3	8.6	8.9	9.5	9.2	9.2	8.7
Tunisia	n.a.	22.7	25.8	31.3	35.2	36.6	n.a.	n.a.	n.a.	n.a.	n.a.	n.a.
United Kingdom	n.a.	12.9	13.9	13.3	13.5	12.5	n.a.	10.7	11.2	11.8	11.8	11.9
United States	n.a.	15.2	16.7	15.7	16.2	14.0	n.a.	8.8	8.6	8.7	8.9	8.9
Yugoslavia[3]	13.2	13.2	14.0	15.9	17.0	18.2	10.2	10.1	9.0	9.1	9.0	8.7

1. Data prior to 1994 pertain to the former Czechoslovakia 2. All data pertaining to Germany prior to 1990 are for West Germany. 3. Beginning January 1992, data refer to the Federal Republic of Yugoslavia. Prior to that date, data refer to the Socialist Federal Republic of Yugoslavia. NOTE: n.a. = not available. *Source:* United Nations, *Monthly Bulletin of Statistics*, June 1996.

Legal Abortions in Selected Countries, 1985–1993

Country	1985	1986	1987	1988	1989	1990	1991	1992	1993
Bulgaria	132,041	134,686	133,815	—	132,021	144,644	—	132,891	—
Canada	60,956	62,406	63,585	—	70,705	71,092	—	—	—
Cuba	138,671	160,926	152,704	155,325	151,146	147,530	124,059	—	—
Denmark	19,919	20,067	20,830	21,199	21,456	20,589	19,729	18,833	—
Finland	13,832	13,310	13,000	12,995	12,658	12,232	—	—	—
France	173,335	166,797	161,036	163,000	165,199	161,646	—	—	—
Germany[1]							124,377	118,609	111,236
Greece	180	—	—	—	—	—	11,109	11,977	—
Hungary	81,970	83,586	84,547	87,106	90,508	90,394	89,931	87,065	75,258
Iceland	705	684	691	673	670	714	658	743	—
India	583,704	—	—	534,870	582,161	596,345	581,215	—	—
Israel	18,406	17,469	15,290	16,181	15,216	18,000	15,767	18,444	—
Italy	210,192	196,969	187,618	175,541	166,290	161,285	157,173	146,639	—
Japan	550,127	527,900	497,756	486,146	466,876	456,797	436,299	413,032	386,807
Netherlands	17,300	—	17,760	18,014	17,996	18,384	—	—	19,804
New Zealand	7,130	8,056	8,789	10,000	10,200	—	11,594	11,460	—
Norway	14,599	15,474	15,422	15,852	16,208	15,551	15,528	15,164	14,909
Poland	135,564	129,720	122,536	105,333	80,127	59,417	30,878	11,640	—
Russian Federation	—	—	4,385,627	4,608,953	4,427,713	4,103,425	3,608,412	3,436,695	3,243,957
Singapore	23,512	21,374	21,226	20,135	20,619	18,654	17,798	17,073	16,476
Sweden	30,838	33,090	34,707	37,585	37,920	37,489	35,788	34,849	34,169
United Kingdom	180,983	157,168	165,542	178,426	180,622	184,092	178,416	171,260	—
United States	1,588,600	1,574,000	1,559,000	1,590,800	—	—	1,388,937	—	—

1. Figures for Germany represent those available after the unification of the Federal Republic of Germany and the German Democratic Republic in October 1990. NOTE: Data latest available. *Source:* United Nations, *Demographic Yearbook, 1994.*

Cost of Living of United Nations Personnel in Selected Cities as Reflected by Index of Retail Prices, 1995

(New York City, December 1995 = 100)

City	Index	City	Index	City	Index
Abu Dhabi, United Arab Emirates	98	Guatemala City, Guatemala	85	Nassau, Bahamas	114
Addis Ababa, Ethiopia	95[1]	The Hague, Netherlands	113	New Delhi, India	86
Algiers, Algeria	97	Helsinki, Finland	112	Panama City, Panama	94
Amman, Jordan	82	Islamabad, Pakistan	81	Paris, France	119
Ankara, Turkey	93	Jakarta, Indonesia	97	Port-au-Prince, Haiti	89
Athens, Greece	92	Kabul, Afghanistan	72	Quito, Ecuador	85
Bangkok, Thailand	95	Kathmandu, Nepal	82	Rabat, Morocco	93
Beirut, Lebanon	111	Kiev, Ukraine	92	Rome, Italy	104
Bogota, Colombia	102	Kingston, Jamaica	94	Roseau, Dominica	104
Bonn, Germany	123[1]	La Paz, Bolivia	87	San Salvador, El Salvador	84
Bratislava, Czech Republic	95	Lagos, Nigeria	106[1]	Santiago, Chile	97
Brazzaville, Congo	108[1]	Lima, Peru	101	Seoul, South Korea	122
Brussels, Belgium	121	London, United Kingdom	101	Sofia, Bulgaria	104
Bucharest, Romania	89[1]	Madrid, Spain	106	Sydney, Australia	88
Budapest, Hungary	105	Managua, Nicaragua	88	Tallinn, Estonia	105
Buenos Aires, Argentina	112	Manila, Philippines	103	Tokyo, Japan	176
Cairo, Egypt	98	Mexico City, Mexico	89	Tripoli, Libya	140[1]
Caracas, Venezuela	90	Minsk, Belarus	92	Tunis, Tunisia	94
Copenhagen, Denmark	118	Montevideo, Uruguay	118	Valetta, Malta	90
Dhaka, Bangladesh	89	Montreal, Canada	80	Vienna, Austria	127
Dakar, Senegal	95	Moscow, Russia	110	Warsaw, Poland	95
Geneva, Switzerland	148	Nairobi, Kenya	84	Washington, D.C.	92

1. Calculated on the basis of cost of government or subsidized housing which is normally lower than prevailing rentals.
Source: United Nations, *Monthly Bulletin of Statistics, March 1996.*

Consumer Price Indexes for All Items for Selected Countries, 1995

(1990 = 100)

Country	Index	Country	Index	Country	Index
Australia	113.2	Hong Kong	155.7	Russian Federation[1]	194,236.0
Austria	117.3	Indonesia	153.7	Singapore	113.5
Canada	111.7	Italy	127.7	Slovakia[2]	168.9
Chile	191.1	Japan	107.0	South Africa	170.5
Czech Republic[1]	161.7	Jordan	123.2	Spain	128.6
Denmark	110.3	Korea, South	135.1	Sri Lanka	163.1
Egypt	178.7	Mexico[2]	166.3	Sweden	122.7
Finland	112.0	Morocco[1]	134.0	Turkey	1,872.3
France	111.6	Netherlands	114.4	United Kingdom	118.2
Germany[1]	114.8	Norway	112.5	United States	116.6
Greece	192.0	Philippines	163.9	Uruguay	1,079.5

1. Base: 1991 = 100. 2. Base: May 1995 = 100. *Source:* International Labour Office from *Monthly Bulletin of Statistics, July 1996.*

Labor Force Participation Rates by Sex[1]

Country	Females				Males				Females as percent of total labor force			
	1993	1990	1985	1980	1993	1990	1985	1980	1993	1990	1985	1980
Australia	47.75	49.3	42.9	41.9	66.0	71.3	70.4	75.1	42.3	41.3	38.4	36.4
Canada	51.4	53.7	48.8	46.2	64.7	69.8	68.7	73.0	45.5	44.7	42.7	39.7
France	40.6[2]	41.5	39.6	40.1	58.3[2]	61.3	62.3	68.5	43.6[2]	43.0	41.4	39.5
Germany[3]	41.4[2]	40.9[4]	37.1	37.7	62.2[2]	65.6	66.4	70.9	42.3[2]	41.0[2]	39.0	38.0
Italy	29.5[2,4]	29.2	27.8	27.9	59.3[2,4]	60.1[4]	62.5	66.0	35.4	34.7[2]	32.8	31.7
Japan	48.3	48.0	46.3	45.7	75.9	75.4	75.9	77.9	40.3	40.3	39.4	38.4
Netherlands	n.a.	n.a.	33.4	31.0	n.a.	n.a.	67.6	74.1	n.a.	n.a.	34.0	30.2
Sweden	55.3[2]	61.5	59.7	58.0	61.3[2]	70.2	70.5	73.6	48.7	47.8	47.2	45.2
United Kingdom	48.8[2]	45.7	44.3	44.8	64.1[2]	70.1	67.1	72.8	45.2[2]	43.5[2]	42.0	40.4

1. Civilian employment as a percent of the civilian working age population. 2. Preliminary. 3. Former West Germany. 4. Break in series. *Source:* U.S. Bureau of Labor Statistics, *Comparative Labor Force Statistics for Ten Countries, 1959–1993, August 1994.* From *Statistical Abstract of the United States 1995.* NOTE: n.a. = not available. Data are most recent available.

Unemployment Figures for Selected Countries: 1990–1995

(In thousands except for percentages)

Country	1995 No.	1995 %	1994 No.	1994 %	1993 No.	1993 %	1992 No.	1992 %	1991 No.	1991 %	1990 No.	1990 %
Australia	766.3	8.5	855.5	9.7	939.2	10.9	933.1	10.8	821.0	9.6	587.1	6.9
Austria[1]	215.7	6.6	214.9	6.5	222.3	6.8	193.1	5.9	185.0	5.8	165.8	5.4
Barbados	26.9	19.7	29.4	21.7	31.0	24.7	28.8	23.0	20.9	17.2	18.6	15.0
Belgium[1]	596.9	14.1	588.7	13.9	549.7	13.1	472.9	11.2	429.5	10.4	402.8	9.8
Canada	1,422.0	9.6	1,458.0	10.3	1,562.0	11.2	1,556.0	11.3	1,417.0	10.3	1,109.0	8.1
Chile[2]	248.1	4.7	311.3	5.9	223.6	4.5	n.a.	n.a.	253.7	5.3	281.3	5.6
Denmark[1]	284.7	10.1	340.4	12.1	348.8	12.4	314.7	11.3	293.9	10.5	269.1	9.6
Finland	429.6	17.2	456.0	18.4	444.0	17.9	328.0	13.1	193.0	7.6	88.0	3.4
Germany[1,3]	3,611.9	10.4	2,556.0	9.2	2,270.9	8.2	1,820.6	6.7	1,689.4	6.3	1,872.0	7.2
Hong-Kong	n.a.	n.a.	57.2	1.9	56.9	2.0	54.7	2.0	50.3	1.8	37.0	1.3
Ireland[4]	276.9	14.1	282.4	n.a.	294.0	n.a.	283.1	n.a.	253.9	19.1	224.7	17.4
Israel	132.3	6.3	158.5	7.8	2,360.0	10.4	207.5	11.2	187.4	10.6	157.9	9.6
Italy	n.a.	n.a.	2,561.0	11.3	2,360.0	10.4	2,799.0	11.5	2,653.0	10.9	2,621.0	11.0
Japan	2,098.3	3.1	1,920.0	2.9	1,655.8	2.5	1,420.8	2.1	1,370.0	2.1	1,340.0	2.1
Korea, South	419.0	2.0	488.8	2.4	551.1	2.8	463.4	2.4	436.0	2.3	451.0	2.5
Netherlands[1]	462.0	n.a.	486.0	7.6	415.0	6.5	303.0	4.2	319.0	4.5	346.0	4.9
New Zealand[1]	109.5	6.3	138.4	8.2	212.7	n.a.	216.9	n.a.	195.1	n.a.	164.0	7.7
Norway	107.0	4.9	116.5	5.4	127.0	6.0	126.0	5.9	116.0	5.5	112.0	4.3
Portugal	325.4	7.2	312.2	6.8	248.3	5.6	186.9	4.1	198.6	4.1	220.1	4.7
Sweden	332.4	7.7	340.0	8.0	326.1	8.7	214.0	4.8	122.0	2.7	69.0	1.6
Switzerland[1]	153.3	4.2	171.0	4.7	163.1	4.5	92.3	n.a.	39.2	1.3	18.1	0.6
Turkey[1]	n.a.	n.a.	n.a.	n.a.	682.6	n.a.	840.1	n.a.	859.0	n.a.	979.5	n.a.
United Kingdom[1,5]	2,325.6	8.3	2,636.5	9.4	2,919.2	10.4	2,778.6	9.8	2,291.9	8.1	1,664.5	5.9
United States	7,404.0	5.6	7,996.0	6.1	8,734.0	6.8	9,384.0	7.4	8,426.0	6.7	6,874.0	5.5

1. Employment office statistics. All others labor force sample surveys unless otherwise indicated. 2. Average of less than 12 months. 3. Data prior to October 3, 1990, are for West Germany. 4. Excluding agriculture, fishing, and private domestic services. 5. Excluding persons temporarily laid off. Excluding adult students registered for vacation employment. NOTE: n.a.= not available. *Source:* United Nations, *Monthly Bulletin of Statistics, July 1996.*

Employment for Selected Countries (Non-Agricultural), 1988–1995

(in thousands)

Country	1995	1994	1993	1992	1991	1990	1989	1988
Australia[1,2,3]	7,806.0	7,483.2	7,238.5	7,201.1	7,248.2	7,399.8	7,290.1	6,907.3
Canada[3,4]	12,951.6	12,746.0	12,457.0	12,299.0	12,344.0	12,614.0	12,534.0	11,804.0
Chile[3]	4,236.6	4,179.4	4,160.4	3,913.2	3,674.2	3,574.6	3,568.0	3,401.2
Finland[3]	1,910.0	1,857.0	1,867.0	1,987.0	2,154.0	2,260.0	2,252.0	2,193.0
Germany[4,6]	—	27,113.0	27,409.0	27,785.0	27,557.0	26,998.0	26,212.0	25,740.0
Hungary[5]	2,567.7	2,704.8	2,614.0	1,585.7	1,916.1	2,249.9	2,483.3	2,614.9
Israel	1,968.6	1,890.4	1,754.5	1,661.5	1,551.8	1,415.5	1,263.3	1,259.3
Italy[3]	—	18,546.0	18,919.0	19,710.0	19,769.0	19,409.0	19,058.0	19,045.0
Japan[3,4]	60,893.3	60,797.5	60,663.3	60,250.0	59,410.0	57,990.0	56,650.0	55,360.0
Korea, South[4]	17,836.4	17,138.0	16,425.0	15,970.0	15,548.0	14,848.0	14,122.0	13,386.0
New Caledonia	48.8	48.3	47.2	46.4	45.9	44.4	42.2	38.0
New Zealand[7]	1,474.3	1,397.8	1,338.1	1,307.5	1,294.6	1,315.9	1,310.8	1,346.7
Norway[3,8]	1,973.0	1,928.0	1,893.0	1,894.0	1,894.0	1,901.0	1,917.0	1,980.0
Poland	8,387.0	8,290.0	8,272.5	8,465.0	9,064.0	9,669.0	10,565.0	10,715.0
Portugal[3]	3,747.6	3,761.3	3,772.9	3,850.6	3,831.8	3,700.7	3,566.0	3,413.8
Spain[3]	10,935.8	10,579.2	—	10,933.5	11,264.3	11,093.3	10,660.4	10,078.4
Sweden[3,4]	3,862.5	3,791.0	3,827.3	4,113.0	4,226.0	4,296.0	4,245.0	4,231.0
Switzerland[4]	3,452.0	3,465.0	3,525.0	3,636.8	104.7	106.4	105.1	103.7
United States[3,4,9]	121,460.0	119,651.0[8]	116,232.0	114,391.0	113,644.0	114,728.0	114,142.0	111,800.0
U.S. Virgin Islands	—	—	48.6	44.8	43.8	43.1	42.0	41.5

1. Annual averages: one month of each year. 2. Excluding armed forces. 3. Persons aged 15 years and over (Finland: 15–74; Italy: 14; Norway and Sweden: 16–74, Spain, and U.S.A.: 16 years; Portugal: 12 years). 4. Civilian labor force. 5. Socialized sector. 6. All data shown for Germany prior to October 3 are based on its territories as West Germany at the time indicated. 7. Annual averages: average of less than 12 months. 8. Revised scope. 9. Including forestry and fishing. *Source:* United Nations, *Monthly Bulletin of Statistics, July 1996.*

Energy, Petroleum, and Coal, by Country

Country	Energy consumed[1] (coal equiv.) Total (mil. metric tons)		Per capita (kilograms)		Electric energy production[2] (bil. kwh)		Crude petroleum production[3] (mil. metric tons)		Coal production[4] (mil. metric tons)	
	1992	1990	1992	1990	1992	1990	1992	1990	1992	1990
Algeria	42	40	1,594	1,586	18	16	36	37	(Z)	(Z)[6]
Argentina	66	61	1,994	1,895	56	51	29	25	(Z)	(Z)
Australia	130	127	7,376	7,442	159	155	25	25	175	159
Austria	32	32	4,171	4,128	51	50	1	1	—	—
Bahrain	8	8	14,780	16,231	4	3	2	2	n.a.	n.a.
Bangladesh[7]	10	8	84	75	10	8	(Z)	(Z)[6]	n.a.	n.a.
Belgium	69	67	6,872	6,686	72	71	(X)	(X)	(Z)	1[8]
Brazil	125	117	810	785	241	223	31	32	5	5
Bulgaria	28	37	3,139	4,170	36	42	(Z)	(Z)	(Z)	(Z)[6]
Canada	300	292	10,965	10,957	521	482	79	76	32	38
Chile	18	17	1,305	1,328	22	18	1	1	2	2
China	973	893	833	788	754	621	142	138	1,116	1,080[10]
Colombia	29	27	854	821	36	35	22	22	24	20
Cuba	12	15	1,152	1,391	12	15	1	1[6]	(X)	(X)
Czechoslovakia	n.a.	96	n.a.	6,149	(X)	87	(Z)	(Z)	(X)	22[6,8]
Denmark	24	24	4,655	4,642	31	26	8	6	(X)	(X)
Ecuador	9	8	770	728	7	6	17	15	(X)	(X)
Egypt	39	37	704	697	45	39	46	44	n.a.	n.a.
Ethiopia	2	1	29	30	1	1	(X)	(X)	n.a.	n.a.
Finland	33	34	6,566	6,877	57[5]	54[5]	3	4	(X)	(X)
France[4]	311	295	5,434	5,191	462[5]	420[5]	(X)	(Z)	9	10[8]
Germany[12]	473	383	5,890	6,241	537	452	(X)	4[13]	72	77[6]
Greece	33	31	3,241	3,085	37	35	1	1[13]	(X)	(X)
Hong Kong	13	10	2,285	1,769	35	29	n.a.	n.a.	(X)	(X)
Hungary[9]	35	39	3,339	3,670	32	28	2	2	1	2[8]
India[9]	308	269	350	318	328	289	27	33	238	202
Indonesia	73	58	383	312	46	44	74	72	21	7
Iran[14]	102	93	1,661	1,596	53	51	172	159	2	1[6]
Iraq	24	16	1,247	887	25	29	26	101	n.a.	n.a.
Ireland	14	13	3,997	3,755	16	15	(X)	(X)	(Z)	(Z)
Israel	17	15	3,268	3,149	24	21	(Z)	(Z)	(X)	(X)
Italy[15]	232	224	4,019	3,878	226	217	4	5	(Z)	(Z)
Japan	589	564	4,735	4,567	895	857	1	1	8	8
Korea, North	96	94	4,256	4,322	38	54	(X)	(X)	70	68[8]
Korea, South	141	119	3,188	2,743	148	119	(X)	(X)	12	17
Kuwait[16]	8	15	4,038	6,895	11	19	54	60	n.a.	n.a.
Libya	17	16	3,458	3,508	17	17	69	67	(X)	(X)
Malaysia	34	27	1,801	1,490	32	23	31	30	(Z)	(Z)
Mexico	167	157	1,891	1,863	122[5]	122[5]	139	132	7	7[6]
Morocco	11	9	405	378	10	10	(Z)	(Z)	1	1
Myanmar[9]	2	2	53	59	3	3	1	1[6]	(Z)	(Z)[6]
Netherlands	108	109	7,122	7,286	1	1	(X)	(X)	—	—
New Zealand[17]	21	18	5,935	5,411	31	30	2	2	3	2
Nigeria	24	23	207	212	12	12	92	86	(Z)	(Z)[6]
Norway[18]	29	29	6,713	6,803	118	122	104	80	(Z)	(Z)
Pakistan[7]	37	34	299	292	52	44	4	3	3	3
Peru	11	11	484	495	13	14	6	7	2	1[6]
Philippines	26	25	404	398	22	26	(Z)	(Z)	2	1
Poland	134	137	3,484	3,590	133	136	(Z)	(Z)	132	148[6]
Portugal	21	19	2,111	1,947	30	29	(X)	(X)	(Z)	(Z)
Romania	63	80	2,702	3,445	54	64	7	8	4	4[6]
Saudi Arabia[16]	97	87	6,097	5,859	49	47	416	320	n.a.	n.a.
South Africa[19]	113	112	2,488	2,608	169	167	(X)	(X)	175	176
Soviet Union (former)	(X)	1,919	(X)	6,631	(X)	1,764	(X)	553	(X)	474
Spain	122	115	3,109	2,961	159	152	1	1	15	15[8]
Sudan	2	2	61	64	1	1	(X)	(X)	n.a.	n.a.
Sweden	60	57	6,937	6,707	146	146	(Z)	(Z)	(Z)	(Z)
Switzerland[20]	33	32	4,877	4,765	59	56	(X)	(X)	(X)	(X)
Syria	17	15	1,291	1,227	13	11	26	23	n.a.	n.a.
Taiwan[21]	n.a.	67	3,644	3,285	n.a.	90	(Z)	(Z)	n.a.	(Z)
Tanzania	1	1	35	39	1	1	(X)	(X)	(Z)	(Z)[6]
Thailand	50	42	888	765	60	46	1	1	(Z)	—
Trinidad and Tobago	11	10	8,422	7,946	4	4	7	8	n.a.	n.a.
Tunisia	6	6	733	791	6	6	5	5	(X)	(X)
Turkey	61	59	1,045	1,052	67	58	4	4	3	3

| Country | Energy consumed[1] (coal equiv.) | | | | Electric energy production[2] (bil. kwh) | | Crude petroleum production[3] (mil. metric tons) | | Coal production[4] (mil. metric tons) | |
| | Total (mil. metric tons) | | Per capita (kilograms) | | | | | | | |
	1992	1990	1992	1990	1992	1990	1992	1990	1992	1990
United Arab Emirates	44	35	26,072	21,980	17	17	104	102	n.a.	n.a.
United Kingdom	313	307	5,400	5,335	327	319	89	88	85	94[8]
United States	2,740	2,687	10,737	10,749	3,075[5]	3,012[5]	363	371	823	854
Venezuela	65	65	3,214	3,352	69	60	124	112	2	2
Vietnam	8	9	120	137	10	9	5	3	5	5
Zaire	3	2	64	66	6	6	1	1[6]	(Z)	(Z)[6]
Zambia	2	2	201	209	8	8	(X)	(X)	(Z)	(Z)
World, total	**10,948**	**10,826**	**1,993**	**2,004**	**12,027**	**11,774**	**2,992**	**3,003**	**3,527**	**3,517**

— Represents or rounds to zero. n.a. = not available. X = Not applicable. Z = Less than 50,000 metric tons. 1. Based on apparent consumption of coal, lignite, petroleum products, natural gas, and hydro, nuclear, and geothermal electricity. 2. Comprises production by utilities generating primarily for public use, and production by industrial establishments generating primarily for own use. Relates to production at generating centers, including station use and transmission losses. 3. Includes shale oil, but excludes natural gasoline. 4. Excludes lignite and brown coal, except as noted. 5. Net production, i.e., excluding station use. 6. Provisional. 7. For year ending June of year shown. 8. Includes recovered slurries. 9. For year ending April of year shown. 10. Includes lignite. 11. Includes Monaco. 12. Prior to 1991, data for former West Germany. 13. Includes inputs other than crude petroleum and natural gas liquids. 14. For year ending March 20 of year shown. 15. Includes San Marino. 16. Includes share of production and consumption in the Neutral Zone. 17. For the year ending March 31 for year shown. 18. Includes Svalbard and Jan Mayen Islands. 19. Includes Botswana, Lesotho, Namibia, and Swaziland. 20. Includes Liechtenstein. 21. Source: U.S. Bureau of the Census. Data from Republic of China publications. *Source:* Except as noted, Statistical Office of the United Nations, New York, N.Y. *Energy Statistics Yearbook* annual (copyright). From: *Statistical Abstract of the United States, 1995.* NOTE: Data are most recent available.

Wheat, Rice, and Corn—Production for Selected Countries

(in thousands of metric tons)

| Country | Wheat | | | Rice | | | Corn | | |
	1993	1992	1991	1993	1992	1991	1993	1992	1991
Argentina	10,000	9,685	9,000	502	695	347	11,300	10,699	7,768
Australia	15,328	16,184	9,633	961	1,128	726	250	210	159
Belgium[1]	1,526	1,428	1,620	(X)	(X)	(X)	77	86	62
Brazil	2,340	2,796	3,077	10,376	9,962	9,503	29,422	30,557	22,604
Canada	28,151	29,871	32,822	(X)	(X)	(X)	6,852	4,883	7,319
China: Mainland	103,005	101,594	95,003	181,600	188,290	187,450	93,380	95,760	93,350
Egypt	4,786	4,618	4,483	3,800	3,910	3,152	5,300	5,069	5,270
France	29,613	32,508	34,483	120	122	109	14,318	14,886	12,787
Germany[2]	15,520	15,542	11,948	(X)	(X)	(X)	2,730	2,139	1,809
Greece	2,350	2,385	2,750	110	101	127	1,600	2,048	1,700
Hungary	3,032	3,444	5,954	15	15	38	6,000	4,417	7,509
India	56,855	55,087	54,522	112,511	108,011	110,945	9,920	10,400	8,200
Indonesia	(X)	(X)	(X)	47,690	47,700	44,321	6,513	7,996	6,409
Iran	10,900	10,350	8,900	2,646	2,500	2,100	210	200	7
Iraq	1,187	1,006	525	180	180	125	280	260	74
Italy	8,400	8,943	9,289	1,300	1,284	1,236	7,000	7,679	6,208
Japan	770	759	860	10,540	13,216	12,005	1	1	1
Korea, South	—	1	1	6,466	7,835	7,478	6,466	1,835	75
Mexico	3,600	3,626	4,115	350	361	354	16,500	17,003	13,527
Myanmar	144	143	123	16,943	14,915	13,201	282	206	190
Pakistan	16,273	15,684	14,505	4,780	4,674	4,903	1,279	1,178	1,190
Soviet Union (former)	87,000	90,037	80,000	2,054	1,969	2,200	10,281	7,319	8,500
Sweden	1,770	1,411	1,524	(X)	(X)	(X)	(X)	(X)	(X)
Thailand	1	1	0	17,375	19,935	20,040	3,724	3,672	3,990
United Kingdom	12,400	14,092	14,300	(X)	(X)	(X)	—	—	—
United States	65,904	66,920	53,915	7,496	8,123	7,006	176,839	240,774	189,867
Yugoslavia	3,100	4,100	6,530	43	43	32	5,500	7,025	8,800
World, total	**564,349**	**566,282**	**550,993**	**518,808**	**526,360**	**519,869**	**477,538**	**530,067**	**478,775**

1. Includes Luxembourg. 2. Former West Germany (prior to unification). NOTES: Rice data cover paddy. Data for each country pertain to the calendar year in which all or most of the crop was harvested. X = Not applicable. — Represents or rounds to zero. *Source:* Food and Agriculture Organization of the United Nations, Rome, Italy, FAO AGRISTAT database. From: *Statistical Abstract of the United States, 1995.* NOTE: Data are most recent available.

Wheat, Rice and Corn Exports and Imports, 1980–1992

(In millions of dollars. Countries listed are the 10 leading exporters or importers in 1992)

Exporters	1992	1990	1980	Importers	1992	1990	1980
WHEAT				**WHEAT**			
United States	4,499	3,887	6,376	USSR (former)	3,420	2,490	2,891
Canada	3,871	2,863	3,302	China	1,663	2,157	2,582
France	3,302	3,296	2,110	Italy	1,651	1,217	773
Australia	1,161	1,971	2,425	Japan	1,177	1,019	1,236
Germany	883	504	198	Brazil	750	331	1,051
United Kingdom	776	760	260	Egypt	725	853	839
Argentina	716	871	816	India	600	n.a.	108
Turkey	341	4	52	South Korea	544	419	367
Greece	262	156	27	Belgium-Luxembourg	535	384	360
Saudi Arabia	210	211	—	Indonesia	402	282	162
RICE				**RICE**			
Thailand	1,426	1,086	953	Iran	375	225	209
United States	735	804	1,285	Saudi Arabia	320	153	230
Italy	452	357	289	USSR (former)	275	119	265
Pakistan	412	242	422	France	258	216	154
India	370	258	173	United Kingdom	232	209	98
Vietnam	285	305	10	Iraq	220	124	217
China	233	84	510	Germany	207	n.a.	n.a.
Australia	188	143	145	Indonesia	172	n.a.	n.a.
Spain	162	108	22	Hong Kong	169	150	158
Belgium-Luxembourg	159	168	91	Brazil	158	144	99
CORN				**CORN**			
United States	4,951	6,206	8,571	Japan	2,251	2,295	2,011
France	1,911	1,854	869	USSR (former)	980	1,690	1,508
China	1,220	404	17	South Korea	847	837	376
Argentina	637	329	513	China	717	750	716
Hungary	220	51	27	Netherlands	517	538	626
Greece	157	32	—	United Kingdom	417	396	547
South Africa	92	176	541	South Africa	413	n.a.	4
Germany	79	71	n.a.	Germany	402	4.86	n.a.
Yugoslavia	60	n.a.	86	Spain	289	307	668
Canada	51	28	113	Italy	287	363	450

— Represents or rounds to zero. *Source:* Food and Agriculture Organization of the United Nations, Rome, Italy, FOA AGRISTAT database. From *Statistical Abstract of the United States 1994.* NOTE: n.a. = not available. Data are most recent available.

Meat—Production by Country

(in thousands of metric tons)

Country	1993	1990	1980	Country	1993	1990	1980
Argentina	3,617	3,383	3,622	Mexico	3,628	3,478	2,540
Brazil	7,545	6,439	4,550	USSR (former)	15,566	19,996	15,072
France	6,085	5,765	5,455	Spain	3,701	3,466	2,648
Germany	5,947	7,292	6,972	United Kingdom	2,340	3,357	3,070
India	3,992	3,723	2,675	United States	31,350	28,632	24,599
Italy	3,936	3,950	3,564	**World**	**185,917**	**178,169**	**135,940**
Japan	3,378	3,503	3,046				

NOTE: Covers beef and veal (incl. buffalo meat), pork (incl. bacon and ham), and mutton and lamb (incl. goat meat), horsemeat and poultry. Refers to meat from animals slaughtered within the national boundaries irrespective of origin of animals, and relates to commercial and farm slaughter. Excludes lard, tallow, and edible offals. NOTE: Data are most recent available. *Source:* U.S. Department of Agriculture, Economic Research Service, *World Agriculture—Trends and Indicators* and Food and Agriculture Organization of the United Nations, Rome, Italy. *FAO Production Yearbook, 1992.* From: *Statistical Abstract of the United States 1995.* NOTE: Data are latest available

Major sources: Information Please Almanac questionnaires to the individual countries,
C.I.A. *World Factbook,* and Center for International Research, Bureau of the Census.
(As of August 1, 1996. For later reports, *see* Current Events of 1996.)

Definitions: Gross domestic product (GDP): The value of all goods and services produced domestically; Gross national product (GNP): the value of all goods and services produced domestically plus income earned abroad, minus income earned by foreigners from domestic production; c.i.f.: cost, insurance, and freight; f.o.b.: free on board; inflation: based on consumer prices; literacy: There are no universal definitions and standards of literacy. Literacy rates are those supplied by the individual countries or else taken from the World Fact Book. The standards that each country uses to assess the ability to read and write is beyond the scope of this almanac.

AFGHANISTAN

Islamic State of Afghanistan
President: Burhanuddin Rabbani (1992)
Prime Minister: Gulbuddin Hekmatyar (May 1996)
Area: 250,000 sq mi. (647,500 sq km).
Population (est. 1996): 22,664,136 (Average annual rate of natural increase: 2.49%); birth rate: 43/1000; infant mortality rate: 149.7/1000; density per square mile: 90.7
Capital: Kabul; **Largest cities (est. 1993):** Kabul, 1,424,400; Kandahar, 225,500; Herat, 177,300; Mazare–Sharif, 131,000.**Monetary unit:** Afghani.**Languages:** Pushtu, Dari Persian, other Turkic and minor languages. **Religion:** Islam (Sunni, 84%; Shiite, 15%; other 1%). **National name:** Dawlat Islami Afghanistan. **Literacy rate:** 29%
Economic summary: Gross domestic product (1989): $3 billion, $200 per capita. Average annual growth rate (1989 est.): .0%. Inflation (est. 1991): over 90%. Arable land: 12%; labor force: 4,980,000. Principal products: wheat, corn, barley, rice, cotton, fruit, nuts, karakul pelts, wool. Labor force in industry: 10.2%. Major industrial products: carpets, rugs, textiles, furniture, shoes, fertilizer, cement. Natural resources: natural gas, oil, coal, copper, sulfur, lead, zinc, iron, salt, precious and semi-precious stones. Exports: $1 billion (1992 est.): fresh and dried fruits, nuts, natural gas, carpets, karakul. Imports: $1.7 billion (est. 1992): petroleum products, sugar, manufactured goods, tea. Major trading partners: Europe, Central Asian republics, Japan, Singapore, Malaysia, India, and Pakistan.

Geography. Afghanistan, approximately the size of Texas, is bordered on the north by Turkmenistan, Uzbekistan, and Tajikistan, on the extreme northeast by China, on the east and south by Pakistan, and Iran in the west. The country is split east to west by the Hindu Kush mountain range, rising in the east to heights of 24,000 feet (7,315 m). With the exception of the southwest, most of the country is covered by high snow-capped mountains and is traversed by deep valleys.

Government. With the fall of the Marxist Najibullah regime in April 1992 the victorious insurgents established a 50-member ruling council of guerrillas, religious leaders, and intellectuals, who announced the creation of an Islamic republic and promised free elections. Mr. Rabbani signed peace accord May 27, 1996, with rival Hezb-i-Islami members and formed an interim administration.

History. Darius I and Alexander the Great were the first conquerors to use Afghanistan as the gateway to India. Islamic conquerors arrived in the 7th century and Genghis Khan and Tamerlane followed in the 13th and 14th centuries.

In the 19th century, Afghanistan became a battleground in the rivalry of imperial Britain and Czarist Russia for the control of Central Asia. The Afghan Wars (1838–42 and 1878–81) fought against the British by Dost Mohammed and his son and grandson ended in defeat.

Afghanistan regained autonomy by the Anglo-Russian agreement of 1907 and full independence by the Treaty of Rawalpindi in 1919. Emir Amanullah founded the kingdom in 1926.

After a coup in 1978, Noor Taraki's attempts to create a Marxist state with Soviet aid brought armed resistance from conservative Muslim opposition. Taraki was eventually succeeded by Babrak Karmal, who called for Soviet troops under a mutual defense treaty.

The Soviet invasion was met with unanticipated fierce resistance from the Afghan population, resulting in a bloody war. Soviet troops had to fight Afghan tribesmen who called themselves "mujahedeen," or "holy warriors." In the early fighting, many of the guerrillas were armed only with flintlock rifles, but later they acquired more modern weapons, including rockets that they used to attack Soviet installations.

In April 1988, the U.S.S.R., U.S.A., Afghanistan, and Pakistan signed accords calling for an end to outside aid to the warring factions, in return for Soviet withdrawal by 1989. This took place in February of that year.

An agreement signed in September 1991 between the U.S.S.R. and the U.S.A. called for an end to all outside military assistance to the warring factions. By mid-April 1992 then-President Najibullah was ousted as Islamic rebels advanced on the capital. Almost immediately the various rebel groups began fighting each other for control.

In late May 1996 a peace accord was reached between the government and an opposing Islamic faction led by former prime minister Hekmatyar, whereby he again assumed that office. Despite the government's concessions, it was not clear whether all rebel factions would accept the agreement as Kabul continued to be shelled by rocket fire.

ALBANIA

The Republic of Albania
President: Sali Berisha (1992)
Prime Minister: Alesander Meksi (1992)
Area: 11,100 sq mi. (28,748 sq km)
Population (est. 1996): 3,249,136 (average annual rate of natural increase: 1.46%); birth rate: 22.2/1000; infant mortality rate: 49.2/1000; density per square mile: 292.7
Capital and largest city (1991 est.): Tiranë, 300,000. **Monetary unit:** Lek. **Language:** Albanian, Greek. **Religions:** Muslim, 70%; Greek Orthodox, 20%; Roman Catholic, 10% **National name:** Rupublika e Shqiperise. **Literacy rate** 75%

Economic summary: Gross domestic product (1994 est.): $3.8 billion; per capita, $1,110; real growth rate, 11%; inflation, 16%; unemployment, 18%. Arable land: 21%; labor force: 1,500,000 (1987). Principal agricultural products: wheat, corn, potatoes, sugar beets, cotton, tobacco. Labor force in industry and commerce: 40%. Major products: textiles, timber, construction materials, fuels, semi-processed minerals. Exports: $112 million (f.o.b., 1993): asphalt, petroleum products, metals and metallic ores, electricity, crude oil, vegetables, fruits, and tobacco. Imports: $621 million (f.o.b., 1993): machinery, consumer goods, grains. Major trading partners: Italy, Macedonia, Germany, Czechoslovakia, Romania, Poland, Hungary, Bulgaria, Greece.

Geography. Albania is situated on the eastern shore of the Adriatic Sea, with the former Yugoslavia to the north and east and Greece to the south. Slightly larger than Maryland, it is a mountainous country, mostly over 3,000 feet (914 m) above sea level, with a narrow, marshy coastal plain crossed by several rivers. The centers of population are contained in the interior mountain plateaus and basins.

Government. A multi-party system was installed in March 1991. Elections in March 1992 gave the Democratic Party 92 of the 140 parliamentary seats, thus assuring it the two-thirds majority for enacting constitutional reform. Election of the president is by parliamentary majority.

History. A part of Illyria in ancient times, and later, of the Roman Empire, Albania was ruled by the Byzantine Empire from A.D. 535 to 1204. An alliance (1444–1466) of Albanian chiefs failed to halt the advance of the Turks and the country remained under at least nominal Turkish rule for more than four centuries, until it proclaimed its independence on Nov. 28, 1912.

Largely agricultural, Albania is one of the poorest countries in Europe. A battlefield in World War I, after the war it became a republic in which a conservative Moslem landlord, Ahmed Zogu, proclaimed himself President in 1925, and then proclaimed himself King Zog I in a monarchy in 1928. He ruled until Italy annexed Albania in 1939. Communist guerrillas under Enver Hoxha seized power in 1944, near the end of World War II. Hoxha was succeeded by Ramiz Alia, 59, who had been President since 1982.

The elections in March 1991 gave the Communists a decisive majority. But a general strike and street demonstrations soon forced the all-Communist cabinet to resign. In June 1991 the Communist Party of Labor renamed itself the Socialist Party and renounced its past ideology. The opposition Democratic Party won a landslide victory in 1992 elections.

The ruling Democratic Party overwhelmingly won the general election of May 1996, garnishing 101 of the 140 seats in parliament. The opposition Socialists and other groups, however, had boycotted the vote and refused to recognize the government's victory. Western observers reported electoral irregularities.

ALGERIA

Democratic and Popular Republic of Algeria
President: Liamine Zeroual (1995)
Prime Minister: Ahmed Ouyahia
Area: 919,595 sq mi. (2,381,751 sq km)

Population (est. 1996): 29,183,032 (average annual rate of natural increase: 2.26%); birth rate: 28.5/1000; infant mortality rate: 48.7/1000; density per square mile: 31.7
Capital: Algiers; **Largest cities (1987):** Algiers, 1,507,241; Oran, 628,558; Constantine, 440,842; Annaba, 305,526.
Monetary unit: Dinar. **Languages:** Arabic (official), French, Berber dialects. **Religion:** 99% Islam (Sunni).
National name: République Algérienne Democratique et Populaire—El Djemhouria El Djazaïria Demokratia Echaabia. **Literacy rate** (1990): 57%
Economic summary: Gross domestic product (1994 est.): $97.1 billion; $3,480 per capita; real growth rate, 0.2%; inflation, 30%; unemployment, 30%. Arable land: 3%; labor force: 6.2 million (1992 est.). Principal agricultural products: wheat, barley, oats, wine, citrus fruits, olives, livestock. Labor force in industry: 40%. Major industrial products: petroleum, gas, petrochemicals, fertilizers, iron and steel, textiles, transport equipment. Natural resources: petroleum, natural gas, iron ore, phosphates, lead, zinc, mercury, uranium. Exports: $9.1 billion (f.o.b., 1994): petroleum and natural gas, 97%. Imports: $9.2 billion (f.o.b., 1994 est.): capital goods, 39.7%; food and beverages, 2.7%; consumer goods, 11.8% (1990). Major trading partners: France, Germany, Italy, Spain, U.S., Japan.

Geography. Nearly four times the size of Texas, Algeria is bordered on the west by Morocco and Western Sahara, and on the east by Tunisia and Libya. To the south are Mauritania, Mali, and Niger. Low plains cover small areas near the Mediterranean coast, with 68% of the country a plateau between 2,625 and 5,250 feet (800 and 1,600 m) above sea level. The highest point is Mount Tahat in the Sahara, which rises 9,850 feet (3,000 m).

Government. Headed by a Chief of Government (official title) appointed in January 1996 after the presidential elections won by President Liamine Zeroual.

History. As ancient Numidia, Algeria became a Roman colony at the close of the Punic Wars (145 B.C.). Conquered by the Vandals about A.D. 440, it fell from a high state of civilization to virtual barbarism, from which it partly recovered after invasion by the Moslems about 650.

In 1492 the Moors and Jews, who had been expelled from Spain, settled in Algeria. Falling under Turkish control in 1518, Algiers served for three centuries as the headquarters of the Barbary pirates. The French took Algeria in 1830 and made it a part of France in 1848.

On July 5, 1962, Algeria was proclaimed independent. In October 1963, Ahmed Ben Bella was elected President. He began to nationalize foreign holdings and aroused opposition. He was overthrown in a military coup on June 19, 1965, by Col. Houari Boumediène, who suspended the Constitution and sought to restore financial stability.

Boumediène died in December 1978 after a long illness. Chadli Bendjedid, Secretary-General of the National Liberation Front, took the presidency in a smooth transition of power.

In December 1991 in the first parliamentary elections ever held in Algeria a militant Islamic fundamentalist party won. In an apparent effort to thwart the electoral results senior army commanders arranged the resignation of President Benjedid. The government then canceled the continuation of the electoral process. In late June President Boudiaf was assassinated.

Since January 1992 the country has been torn between Islamic militants and the security forces that appears increasingly like a civil war.

Zeroual proposed constitutional reforms in May 1996 that called among other things for the separation of religion from the state. Internal strife continued, however, with Islamic militants beheading seven French monks in May.

ANDORRA

Principality of Andorra
Head of Government: Marc Forné Molné (1995)
Area: 175 sq mi. (453 sq km)
Population (est. 1996): 67,509 (average annual growth rate: 0.51%); birth rate: 12.5/1000; infant mortality rate: 7.5/1000; density per square mile: 385.8
Capital and largest city (1993 est.): Andorra la Vella, 22,390. **Monetary units:** French franc and Spanish peseta. **Languages:** Catalán (official); French, Spanish. **Religion:** Roman Catholic. **National name:** Valls d'Andorra. **Literacy rate** 100%
Economic summary: Gross domestic product (1992 est): $760 million; per capita, $14,000. Arable land: 2%; labor force: NA. Principal agricultural products: oats, barley, cattle, sheep. Major industrial products: tobacco products and electric power; tourism. Natural resources: water power, mineral water. Exports: $30 million (f.o.b., 1993 est.): electricity, tobacco products, furniture. Imports: $ NA. (1993): consumer goods, food. Major trading partners: Spain and France, and E.U.

Geography. Andorra lies high in the Pyrenees Mountains on the French-Spanish border. The country is drained by the Valira River.

Government. A parliamentary democracy (since March 1993). A new constitution, their first, was approved on March 14, 1993, which redefined Andorra as a parliamentary co-principality and sharply differentiated the three branches of government.

History. An autonomous and semi-independent co-principality, Andorra has been under the joint suzerainty of the French state and the Spanish bishops of Urgel since 1278.

In 1990 Andorra approved a customs union treaty with the E.C. permitting free movement of industrial goods between the two, but Andorra would apply the E.C.'s external tariffs to third countries. This treaty went into effect on July 1, 1991.

Andorra became a member of the U.N. in 1993 and a member of the Council of Europe in 1994.

After losing a vote of confidence in parliament in November 1994 the government resigned. A new minority government, led by the Liberal Union Party, was sworn in the following month.

ANGOLA

People's Republic of Angola
President: José Eduardo dos Santos (1979)
Area: 481,350 sq mi. (1,246,700 sq km)
Population (est. 1996): 10,342,899 (average annual rate of natural increase: 2.69); birth rate: 44.6/1000; infant mortality rate: 138.9/1000; density per square mile: 21.5

Capital and largest city (1993): Luanda, 2,000,000. **Other large cities (est. 1993):** Huambo, 400,000; Lubango, 105,000. **Monetary unit:** Kwanza. **Languages:** Bantu, Portuguese (official). **Religions:** Roman Catholic, 47%; Protestant, 38%; indigenous, 15%. **Literacy rate:** 42%
Economic summary: Gross domestic product (1994 est.): $6.1 billion, $620 per capita; real growth rate –1%; inflation 20% per month; unemployment (1993 est.), 15%. Arable land: 2%. Labor force: 2,783,000; Labor force in agriculture: 85%. Principal agricultural products: coffee, sisal, corn, cotton, sugar, tobacco, bananas, cassava. Major industrial products: oil, diamonds, processed fish, tobacco, textiles, cement, processed food and sugar, brewing. Natural resources: diamonds, gold, iron, oil. Exports: $3 billion (f.o.b., 1993 est.): oil, coffee, diamonds, fish and fish products, iron ore, timber, corn. Imports: $1.6 billion (f.o.b., 1992 est.): machinery and electrical equipment, bulk iron, steel and metals, textiles, clothing, food, substantial military deliveries. Major trading partners: U.S., France, Germany, Netherlands, Brazil, Portugal, Spain.

Geography. Angola, more than three times the size of California, extends for more than 1,000 miles (1,609 km) along the South Atlantic in southwestern Africa. Zaire is to the north and east, Zambia to the east, and South-West Africa (Namibia) to the south. A plateau averaging 6,000 feet (1,829 m) above sea level rises abruptly from the coastal lowlands. Nearly all the land is desert or savanna, with hardwood forests in the northeast.

Government. President José Eduardo dos Santos, head of the Popular Movement for the Liberation of Angola–Workers Party, won a U.N.-certified election in September 1992 against the guerilla organization UNITA led by Jonas Savimbi. The U.S. recognized the new democratic Angolan administration on May 8, 1993.

History. Discovered by the Portuguese navigator Diego Cao in 1482, Angola became a link in trade with India and the Far East. Later it was a major source of slaves for Portugal's New World colony of Brazil. Development of the interior began after the Treaty of Berlin in 1885 fixed the colony's borders, and British and Portuguese investment pushed mining, railways, and agriculture.

Following World War II, independence movements began but were sternly suppressed by military force. The April revolution of 1974 brought about a reversal of Portugal's policy, and the next year President Francisco da Costa Gomes signed an agreement to grant independence to Angola. The plan called for election of a constituent assembly and a settlement of differences by the MPLA and the National Front for the Liberation of Angola (FNLA) and the National Union for the Total Independence of Angola (UNITA).

The Organization of African Unity recognized the MPLA government led by Agostinho Neto on Feb. 11, 1976, and the People's Republic of Angola became the 47th member of the organization.

In March 1977 and May 1978, Zairean refugees in Angola invaded Zaire's Shaba Province, bringing charges by Zairean President Mobutu Sese Seko that the unsuccessful invasions were Soviet-backed with Angolan help. Angola, the U.S.S.R., and Cuba denied complicity.

Neto died in Moscow of cancer on Sept. 10, 1979. The Planning Minister, José Eduardo dos Santos, was named President.

The South-West Africa People's Organization, or SWAPO, the guerrillas fighting for the independence of the disputed territory south of Angola also known as Namibia, fought from bases in Angola, and the South African armed forces also maintained troops there both to fight the SWAPO guerrillas and to assist the UNITA guerrillas against Angolan and Cuban troops.

In December 1988, Angola, Cuba, and South Africa signed agreements calling for Cuban withdrawal from Angola and South African withdrawal from Namibia by July 1991 and independence for Namibia.

Elections in late September 1992 gave the MPLA the most votes with UNITA second. A runoff was set when UNITA's Savimbi withdrew charging the election was unfair. Fighting resumed between the government and UNITA in October. Fighting between the government and UNITA continued throughout 1993 punctuated with on-and-off-again peace talks at various locales throughout the year.

The UN-negotiated accord between the government and UNITA, signed in Zambia in November 1994, provided an uneasy peace. In July 1995, the National Assembly voted to amend the constitution to allow for two vice presidents.

ANTIGUA AND BARBUDA

Sovereign: Queen Elizabeth II (1952)
Governor-General: Sir James Beethoven Carlisle (1993)
Prime Minister: Hon. Lester Bryant Bird
Land area: 171 sq mi. (442 sq km)
Population (est. 1996): 65,647 (average annual growth rate: 1.15%); birth rate: 16.8/1000; infant mortality rate: 17.2/1000; density per square mile: 383.9
Capital and largest city (1991): St. John's, 21,514. Capital of Barbuda is the village of Cordrington, est. pop. 1,000. **Monetary unit:** East Caribbean dollar.
Language: English. **Religions:** Anglican and Roman Catholic. **Literacy rate:** 90%
Member of Commonwealth of Nations
Economic summary: Gross domestic product (1993 est.): $400 million, per capita $6,000; real growth rate 3.4%; inflation rate 7%; unemployment rate (est. 1992) 6%. Arable land: 18%; Labor force: 30,000; Labor force in industry (1990): 19.7%; principal products: cotton, bananas, coconuts, cucumbers, mangoes. Major industry: tourism, which accounts for 60% of economic activity and over half of the GNP. Exports: $54.7 million (f.o.b., 1992): petroleum products, manufactures, machinery and transport equipment. Imports: $260.9 million (f.o.b., 1992): fuel, food, machinery. Major trading partners: U.K., U.S., Canada, Caribbean community and Common Market members.

Geography. Antigua, the larger of the two main islands, located 295 miles (420 km) south-southeast of San Juan, P.R., is low-lying except for a range of hills in the south that rise to their highest point at Boggy Peak (1,330 ft; 405 m). As a result of its relative flatness, Antigua suffers from cyclical drought, despite a mean annual rainfall of 44 inches. Barbuda (formally known as Dulcina) is a coral island, well-wooded.

Antigua is 108 sq. miles (280 sq km), and the island dependences of Redonda (an uninhabited rocky islet) and Barbuda are 0.5 sq miles (1.30 sq km) and 62 sq miles (161 sq km), respectively.

Government. Executive power is held by the Cabinet, presided over by Prime Minister Lester B. Bird. A 17-member Parliament is elected by universal suffrage. The Antigua Labour Party, led by Prime Minister Bird, holds 11 seats.

History. Antigua was discovered by Christopher Columbus in 1493 and named for the Church of Santa Maria la Antigua in Seville. Colonized by Britain in 1632, it joined the West Indies Federation in 1958. With the breakup of the Federation, it became one of the West Indies Associated States in 1967, self-governing in internal affairs. Full independence was granted Nov. 1, 1981.

Protests in early 1995 against new taxes yielded a government concession not to add any in the 1995 budget, but recent impositions were to remain.

Scandal continued to plague the Bird family that year, and a September hurricane caused major damage to the infrastructure. Rising crime against tourists led to increased police and military surveillance.

ARGENTINA

Argentine Republic
President: Carlos S. Menem (1989)
Area: 1,072,067 sq mi. (2,776,654 sq km)
Population (est. 1996): 34,672,997 (average annual rate of natural increase: 1.08%); birth rate: 19.4/1000; infant mortality rate: 28.3/1000; density per square mile: 32.3
Capital: Buenos Aires (plans to move to Viedma by 1990 indefinitely postponed). **Largest cities (est. 1991):** Buenos Aires, 2,961,000; Córdoba, 1,180,000; La Matanza, 1,121,164; General Sarmiento, 646,900; Morón, 641,540 (1983); Rosario, 950,000 (1983). **Monetary unit:** Peso. **Languages:** Spanish, English, Italian, German, French. **Religion:** Predominantly Roman Catholic (nominally). **National name:** República Argentina. **Literacy rate** 95%
Economic summary: Gross domestic product (1994 est.) $270.8 billion; $7,990 per capita; real growth rate 6%; inflation 3.9%; unemployment 12%. Arable land: 9%; labor force: est. 10,900,000. Principal products: grains, oilseeds, livestock products. Labor force (1985 est.): 10.9 million; industry: 31%, agriculture 12%, services 57%. Major products: processed foods, motor vehicles, consumer durables, textiles, chemicals. Natural resources: minerals, lead, zinc, tin, copper, iron, manganese, oil, uranium. Exports: $15.7 billion (f.o.b., 1994 est.): meat, wheat, corn, oilseed, hides, wool. Imports: $21.4 billion (c.i.f., 1994 est.): machinery and equipment, chemicals, fuels and lubricants, agricultural products. Major trading partners: U.S., Brazil, Bolivia, Germany, Japan, Italy, Netherlands.

Geography. With an area slightly less than one third of the United States and second in South America only to its eastern neighbor, Brazil, in size and population, Argentina is a plain, rising from the Atlantic to the Chilean border and the towering Andes peaks. Aconcagua (23,034 ft.; 7,021 m) is the highest peak in the world outside Asia. It is bordered also by Bolivia and Paraguay on the north, and by Uruguay on the east.

The northern area is the swampy and partly wooded Gran Chaco, bordering on Bolivia and Paraguay. South of that are the rolling, fertile pampas, rich for agriculture and grazing and supporting most of the population. Next southward is Patagonia, a region of cool, arid steppes with some wooded and fertile sections.

Government. Argentina is a federal union of 23 provinces, and the Federal District. Under the Constitution of 1853 the President and Vice President are elected every six years by popular vote through an electoral college. The President appoints his Cabinet. The Vice President presides over the Senate but has no other powers. The Congress consists of two houses: a 46-member Senate and a 254-member Chamber of Deputies.

History. Discovered in 1516 by Juan Díaz de Solis, Argentina developed slowly under Spanish colonial rule. Buenos Aires was settled in 1580; the cattle industry was thriving as early as 1600.

Invading British forces were expelled in 1806–07, and when Napoleon conquered Spain, the Argentinians set up their own government in the name of the Spanish King in 1810. On July 9, 1816, independence was formally declared.

As in World War I, Argentina proclaimed neutrality at the outbreak of World War II, but in the closing phase declared war on the Axis on March 27, 1945, and became a founding member of the United Nations. Juan D. Perón, an army colonel, emerged as the strongman of the postwar era, winning the Presidential elections of 1946 and 1951.

Opposition to Perón's increasing authoritarianism, led to a coup by the armed forces that sent Perón into exile in 1955. Argentina entered a long period of military dictatorships with brief intervals of constitutional government.

The former dictator returned to power in 1973 and his wife was elected Vice-President.

After Peron's death in 1974, his widow became the hemisphere's first woman chief of state, but was deposed in 1976 by a military junta.

In December 1981, Lt. Gen. Leopoldo Galtieri, commander of the army, was named president.

On April 2, 1982, Galtieri landed thousands of troops on the Falkland Islands and reclaimed the Malvinas, their Spanish name, as national territory. By May 21, 5,000 British marines and paratroops landed from the British armada and regained control of the islands.

Galtieri resigned three days after the surrender of the island garrison on June 14. Maj. Gen. Reynaldo Bignone took office as President on July 1.

In the presidential election of October 1983, Raúl Alfonsín, leader of the middle-class Radical Civic Union, handed the Peronist Party its first defeat since its founding.

Twin economic problems of growing unemployment and quadruple-digit inflation led to a Peronist victory in the elections of May 1989. Inflation of food prices led to riots that induced Alfonsín to step down in June 1989, six months early, in favor of the Peronist, Carlos Menem.

A group of army leaders and their followers attempted an uprising on December 3, 1990. Most commanders, however, stood by the legitimate government, and the insurrection was suppressed in less than 24 hours.

In 1991 President Menem hammered out a vast deregulation of the economy designed to reverse decades of state intervention and protectionism. The May 1995 presidential election saw the re-election of Menem.

The Radical Party's victory in the capital's first-ever mayoralty election in June 1996 reestablished it as a major opposition party and demonstrated dissatisfaction with Menem in Buenos Aires.

ARMENIA

President: Levon A. Ter-Petrossian (1990)
Prime Minister: Hrant Bagratyan (1993)
Vice President: Gaguik G. Haroutunian
Area: 11,500 sq mi. (29,800 sq km)
Population (est. 1996): 3,463,574 (average annual rate of increase: 1.08%) (Armenian, 93%; others, Kurds, Ukrainians, and Russians); birth rate: 16.3/1000; infant mortaility rate: 38.9/1000, density per square mile: 301.2
Capital and largest city (1994 est.): Yerevan, 1,226,000; other large cities (est. 1994): Gyumri (Leninakan), 120,000. **Money:** Dram. **Language:** Armenian. **Religion:** Armenian Orthodox, 94%. **Literacy rate:** 100% (1970)
Economic summary: Gross domestic product (1994 est.): $8.1 billion; $2,290 per capita; −2% growth rate; inflation: 27% per month; unemployment: 6.5%. Labor force (1992): 1,578,000. Agriculture: 49% of GDP; arable land, 29%; dairy farming, vineyards. Exports: $43 million (f.o.b., 1994): to countries outside the successor states of the former USSR: machinery and transport equipment, light industrial products, processed food. Imports: $120 million (c.i.f., 19944): from countries outside the successor states of the former USSR: machinery, energy, consumer goods. Major trading partners: Iran, Russia, Turkmenistan, Georgia, U.S., E.U.

Geography. Armenia is located in the southern Caucasus and is the smallest of the former Soviet republics. It is bounded by Georgia on the north, Azerbaijan on the east, Iran on the south, and Turkey on the west. It is a land of rugged mountains and extinct volcanoes. Mt. Aragats, 13,435 ft (4,095 m) is the highest point. Although the terrain is rugged and dry with few trees, it has excellent pastures. The largest lake, Sevan, 541 sq mi, is the main source of the republic's vast irrigation system and hydroelectric power.

Government: A presidential republic.

History: Armenia has been the scene of struggle throughout its long history with the Greeks, Romans, Persians, Mongols, and Turks. Russia acquired the present day Armenia S.S.R. from Persia in 1828. Armenia joined Azerbaijan and Georgia in 1917 to form the anti-Bolshevik Transcaucasian Federation, but it was dissolved in 1918. Armenia's independence was short-lived and she was annexed by the Red Army in 1920. On March 12, 1922, the Soviets joined Georgia, Armenia, and Azerbaijan to form the Transcaucasian Soviet Socialist Republic which became part of the U.S.S.R. In 1936, after a reorganization, Armenia became a separate constituent republic of the U.S.S.R.

Since 1983, Armenia has been involved in a territorial dispute with Azerbaijan over the enclave of Nagorno-Karabakh which both republics lay claim to. The autonomous region of Nagorno-Karabakh lies entirely within Azerbaijan. The majority population of the enclave are Armenian Christians who want to secede from Azerbaijan and join with Armenia.

The political disruption in Azerbaijan in June 1993 led to significant military advances for the Armenian forces, leaving them in control of much of the disputed region as well as a corridor to Armenia proper.

Although the economy showed signs of improvement in 1994, living standards remained quite low. In October the country joined the NATO Partnership in Peace program.

In March 1995 a treaty was signed with Russia permitting the latter to maintain two military bases in the country for 25 years. The ruling Armenian National Movement handily won July parliamentary elections after most opposition groups were banned from participating. A referendum on a new constitution was also approved bestowing additional powers on the president.

AUSTRALIA

Commonwealth of Australia
Sovereign: Queen Elizabeth II (1952)
Governor-General: Sir. William Deane (1996)
Prime Minister: John Howard (1996)
Area: 2,966,150 sq mi. (7,682,300 sq km)
Population (est. mid-1996): 18,260,863 (average annual rate of natural increase: 0.7%); birth rate: 14/1000; infant mortality rate: 5.5/1000; density per square mile: 6.2
Capital (est. 1994): Canberra, 278,904. **Largest cities (est. 1994):** Sydney, 3,738,500;   Melbourne, 3,198,200; Adelaide, 1,076,400; Perth, 1,239,400 Brisbane, 786,442
Monetary unit: Australian dollar. **Language:** English. **Religions:** 26.1% Anglican, 26.0% Roman Catholic, 24.3% other Christian. **Literacy rate:** 100%
Member of Commonwealth of Nations
Economic summary: Gross domestic product (1994 est.): $374.6 billion; per capita $20,720; real growth rate 6.4%; inflation 2.5%; unemployment: 8.9%. Arable land: 6%. Principal products: wool, meat, cereals, sugar, sheep, cattle, dairy products. Labor force (1992–93): 8,646,500; finance and services, 33.8%; public and community services, 22.3%; wholesale and retail trade, 20.1%; manufacturing, 16.2%. Natural resources: iron ore, bauxite, zinc, lead, tin, coal, oil, gas, copper, nickel, uranium. Exports: $50.4 billion (1994 est.): coal, gold, meat, wool, alumina, wheat, machinery and transport equipment. Imports: $51.1 billion (1994 est.): machinery and transport equipment, computers and office machines, crude oil and petroleum products. Major trading partners: Japan, U.S., U.K., New Zealand, Germany, South Korea, Singapore, Germany.

Geography. The continent of Australia, with the island state of Tasmania, is approximately equal in area to the United States (excluding Alaska and Hawaii), and is nearly 50% larger than Europe (excluding the U.S.S.R.).

Mountain ranges run from north to south along the east coast, reaching their highest point in Mount Kosciusko (7,308 ft; 2,228 m). The western half of the continent is occupied by a desert plateau that rises into barren, rolling hills near the west coast. It includes the Great Victoria Desert to the south and the Great Sandy Desert to the north. The Great Barrier Reef, extending about 1,245 miles (2,000 km), lies along the northeast coast.

The island of Tasmania (26,178 sq mi.; 67,800 sq km) is off the southeastern coast.

Government. The Federal Parliament consists of a bicameral legislature. The House of Representatives has 146 members elected for three years by popular vote. The Senate has 76 members elected by popular vote for six years. One half of the Senate is elected every three years. Voting is compulsory at 18. Supreme federal judicial power is vested in the High Court of Australia in the federal courts, and in the state courts invested by Parliament with federal jurisdiction. The High Court consists of seven justices, appointed by the Governor-General in Council. Each of the states has its own judicial system.

History. Dutch, Portuguese, and Spanish ships sighted Australia in the 17th century; the Dutch landed at the Gulf of Carpentaria in 1606. Australia was called New Holland, Botany Bay, and New South Wales until about 1820.

Captain James Cook, in 1770, claimed possession for Great Britain. A British penal colony was set up at what is now Sydney, then Port Jackson, in 1788, and about 161,000 transported English convicts were settled there until the system was suspended in 1839.

Free settlers established six colonies: New South Wales (1786), Tasmania (then Van Diemen's Land) (1825), Western Australia (1829), South Australia (1834), Victoria (1851), and Queensland (1859).

The six colonies became states and in 1901 federated into the Commonwealth of Australia with a Constitution that incorporated British parliamentary tradition and U.S. federal experience. Australia became known for liberal legislation: free compulsory education, protected trade unionism with industrial conciliation and arbitration, the "Australian" ballot facilitating selection, the secret ballot, women's suffrage, maternity allowances, and sickness and old age pensions.

In the election of 1983, Robert Hawke, head of the Labour Party, became Prime Minister. The Labour government was reelected in a Federal election in December 1984.

Amid a deep recession Hawke was ousted by Paul Keating in 1991—the first time an Australian prime minister was removed from office by his own party.

March 1993 general elections returned Prime Minister Keating and his Labour Party to power. Keating successfully campaigned for the 2000 Olympics to be held in Sydney, but his efforts to transform the country into a republic continued to arouse controversy.

In March 1996 the opposition Liberal Party–National Party coalition easily won the national elections, removing the Labour Party after 13 years.

Australian External Territories

Norfolk Island (13 sq mi.; 36.3 sq km) was placed under Australian administration in 1914. Population, 2,756 (July 1995); growth rate, 1.69%.

The Ashmore and Cartier Islands (.8 sq mi.), situated in the Indian Ocean off the northwest coast of Australia, came under Australian administration in 1934. In 1938 the islands were annexed to the Northern Territory. On the attainment of self-government by the Northern Territory in 1978, the islands, which are uninhabited, were retained as Commonwealth territory.

The Australian Antarctic Territory (2,360,000 sq mi.; 6,112,400 sq km), comprises all the islands and territories, other than Adélie Land, situated south of lat. 60°S and lying between long. 160° and 45°E. It came under Australian administration in 1936.

Heard Island and the McDonald Islands (158 sq mi.; 409.2 sq km), lying in the sub-Antarctic, were placed under Australian administration in 1947. The islands are uninhabited.

Christmas Island (52 sq mi.; 134.7 sq km) is situated in the Indian Ocean. It came under Australian administration in 1958. Population 889 (July 1995).

Coral Sea Islands (400,000 sq mi.; 1,036,000 sq km, but only a few sq mi. of land) became a territory of Australia in 1969. There is no permanent population on the islands.

Cocos (Keeling) Islands. The territory of the Cocos comprises a group of 27 small coral islands in two separate atolls in the Indian Ocean, 1,721 miles (2,768 kilometers) northwest of Perth. West Island is the largest, about 6.2 miles (10 kilometers) long. The islands became an Australian territory in 1955. Population 604 (July 1995); growth rate –0.5%.

AUSTRIA

Republic of Austria
President: Thomas Klestil (1992)
Chancellor: Franz Vranitzky (1986)
Area: 32,375 sq mi. (83,851 sq km)
Population (est. 1996): 8,013,614 (average annual rate of natural increase: 0.08%); birth rate: 11/1000; infant mortality rate: 6.8/1000; density per square mile: 247.5
Capital and largest city (1991): Vienna, 1,700,000; **Other large cities (est. 1991):** Graz, 232,150; Linz, 203,000; Salzburg, 144,000; Innsbruck, 115,000; **Monetary unit:** Schilling; **Languages:** German. Slovene, Croatian, Hungarian; **Religion:** Roman Catholic, 89%; **Literacy rate:** 98%
National name: Republik Österreich
Economic summary: Gross domestic product (1995): $152.91 billion; per capita $19,400; real growth rate: 2.1%; inflation rate: 3.9%; unemployment: 4.0%. Arable land: 17%. Labor force (1995): 2.2 million, 56.4% in services; principal agricultural products: livestock, forest products, grains, sugar beets, potatoes. Principal products: iron and steel, chemicals, machinery, paper and pulp. Natural resources: iron ore, petroleum, timber, magnesite, aluminum, coal, lignite, cement, copper, hydropower. Exports: $50.5 billion (1995): iron and steel products, timber, paper, textiles, chemical products. Imports: $61.5 billion (1995): machinery, chemicals, foodstuffs, textiles and clothing, petroleum. Major trading partners: Germany and European Community (EC), Eastern Europe, U.S., Japan, EU countries.

Geography. Slightly smaller than Maine, Austria includes much of the mountainous territory of the eastern Alps (about 75% of the area). The country contains many snowfields, glaciers, and snowcapped peaks, the highest being the Grossglockner (12,530 ft; 3,819 m). The Danube is the principal river. Forests and woodlands cover about 40% of the land area.

Almost at the heart of Europe, Austria has as its neighbors Italy, Switzerland, Germany, Czech Republic, Hungary, Slovenia, and Liechtenstein.

Government. Austria is a federal republic composed of nine provinces (Bundesländer), including Vienna. The President is elected by the people for a term of six years. The bicameral legislature consists of the Bundesrat, with 58 members chosen by the provincial assemblies, and the Nationalrat, with 183 members popularly elected for four years. Presidency of the Bundesrat revolves every six months, going to the provinces in alphabetical order.

History. Settled in prehistoric times, the Central European land that is now Austria was overrun in pre-Roman times by various tribes, including the Celts. Charlemagne conquered the area in 788 and encouraged colonization and Christianity. In 1252, Ottokar, King of Bohemia, gained possession, only to lose the territories to Rudolf of Hapsburg in 1278. Thereafter, until World War I, Austria's history was largely that of its ruling house, the Hapsburgs.

Austria emerged from the Congress of Vienna in 1815 as the continent's dominant power. The *Ausgleich* of 1867 provided for a dual sovereignty, the empire of Austria and the kingdom of Hungary, under Francis Joseph I, who ruled until his death on Nov. 21, 1916. His grandnephew, Charles I, succeeded him.

During World War I, Austria-Hungary was one of the Central Powers with Germany, Bulgaria, and Turkey, and the conflict left the country in political chaos and economic ruin. Austria, shorn of Hungary, was proclaimed a republic in 1918, and the monarchy was dissolved in 1919.

A parliamentary democracy was set up by the Constitution of Nov. 10, 1920. To check the power of Nazis advocating union with Germany, Chancellor Engelbert Dolfuss in 1933 established a dictatorship, but was assassinated by the Nazis on July 25, 1934. Kurt von Schuschnigg, his successor, struggled to keep Austria independent, but on March 12, 1938, German troops occupied the country, and Hitler proclaimed its *Anschluss* (union) with Germany, annexing it to the Third Reich.

After World War II, the U.S. and Britain declared the Austrians a "liberated" people. But the Russians prolonged the occupation. Finally Austria concluded a state treaty with the U.S.S.R. and the other occupying powers and regained its independence on May 15, 1955. The second Austrian republic, established Dec. 19, 1945, on the basis of the 1920 Constitution (amended in 1929), was declared by the federal parliament to be permanently neutral.

On June 8, 1986, former UN Secretary-General Kurt Waldheim was elected to the ceremonial office of President in a campaign marked by controversy over his alleged links to Nazi war-crimes in Yugoslavia.

The chief of Austria's diplomatic corps. Thomas Klestil, handily won election to the Presidency, paving the way for a normalization of relations strained during Waldheim's term.

Voters in June 1994 emphatically endorsed membership in the European Union, which took effect on January 1, 1995. Despite the membership Austria retained its strict constitutional neutrality and forbade the stationing of foreign troops on its soil.

Sudden elections in December 1995 reaffirmed the strength of the country's two largest parties, but subsequent negotiations on forming a coalition government took 83 days.

AZERBAIJAN

Republic of Azerbaijan
President: Heydar Aliyev (1993)
Prime Minister: Fuad Guliyev (1994)
Area: 33,400 sq mi. (86,600 sq km)
Population (est. 1996): 7,676,953 (average annual rate of natural increase: 1.4%); (Azerbaijanis, 83%; Russians and Armenians). The republic is noted for the longevity of its population. Forty-eight out of every 100,000 residents are over 100 years old. Birth rate: 22.3/1000; infant mortality rate: 74.5/1000; density per square mile: 229.8
Capital and largest city (1991): Baku, 1,713,300, a port on the Caspian Sea. Other large cities: Ganja (1989), 278,000; Sumgait, 231,000. **Monetary unit:** Manat. **Languages:** Azerbaijani Turkic, 82%; Russian, 7%; Armenian, 2%. **Religion:** Moslem, 87%; Russian Orthodox, 5.6%; Armenian Orthodox, 2%
Economic summary: Gross domestic product (1994 est.): $13.8 billion; $1,790 per capita; –22% real growth rate;

inflation: 28% per month; unemployment: 0.9%. Azerbaijan's Apsheron peninsula is an oil-rich area and is now being developed under a $7.4 billion contract with Western oil companies. Industries: petroleum and natural gas, petroleum products, oilfield equipment, steel, iron ore, cement, chemicals and petrochemicals, and textiles. Agricultural production includes cotton, wheat, tobacco, fruit, wine grapes, potatoes, sheep and other livestock. Labor force: 2,789,000 (1990): agriculture and forestry, 32%; industry and construction, 26%. Exports: $366 million (f.o.b., 1994) to outside the successor states of the former U.S.S.R: oil and gas, chemicals, textiles, cotton (1991). Imports: $296 million (c.i.f., 1994) from outside the successor states of the former USSR: machinery and parts, consumer durables, foodstuffs, textiles (1991). Major trading partners: Mostly CIS and European countries.

Geography: Azerbaijan is located on the western shore of the Caspian Sea at the southeastern extremity of the Caucasus. The region is mountainous country. About 7% of it is arable land. The Kura River Valley is the area's major agricultural zone. The republic is bounded on the north by Russia, by the Caspian Sea in the east, by Iran in the south, and by Georgia and Armenia in the west. Azerbaijan has about a 10-mile border with Turkey.

Government: A constitutional republic with a 125-seat parliament.

History: Azerbaijan was known in ancient times as Albania. The area was the site of many conflicts involving Arabs, Kazars, and the Turks. After the 11th century, the territory became dominated by the Turks and eventually became a stronghold of the Shi'ite Muslim religion and Islamic culture.

The territory of Soviet Azerbaijan was acquired by Russia from Persia through the Treaty of Gulistan in 1813 and the Treaty of Turkamanchai in 1828.

After the Bolshevik Revolution, Azerbaijan declared its independence from Russia in May 1918. The republic was reconquered by the Red Army in 1920, and was annexed into the Transcaucasian Soviet Federated Socialist Republic in 1922. It was later reestablished as a separate Soviet republic on Dec. 5, 1936.

Since 1983, the rival republics of Azerbaijan and Armenia have been feuding over the enclave of Nagorno-Karabakh located within Azerbaijan. Both nations claim this autonomous region. The majority of the enclave's residents are both Armenians and Christians and they are agitating to secede from the predominantly Muslim Azerbaijan and join with Armenia.

Campaigning on a platform calling for the country to break from the CIS and retain Nagorno-Karabakh, Popular Front leader Elchibey won the 1992 vote.

A power struggle in June 1993 sent Elchibey fleeing when rebel forces advanced on the capital. These events were set against a worsening of the economy and major reverses in the war with Armenia.

In November 1993 Aliyev received almost 99% of the vote in a presidential election. Forces loyal to then-prime minister Husseynov seized several cities but were overwhelmed by those loyal to the president. Although claiming innocence Husseynov was fired and charged with treason, whereupon he fled to Russia.

The ruling New Azerbaijan Party easily won a November election for a new parliament. Most opposition groups were barred from participating. A referendum on a new constitution was also approved.

BAHAMAS

Commonwealth of the Bahamas
Sovereign: Queen Elizabeth II (1952)
Governor-General: Sir Orville Alton Turnquest (1995)
Prime Minister: Hubert Ingraham (1992)
Area: 5,380 sq mi. (13,939 sq km)
Population (est. 1996): 259,367 (average annual rate of natural increase: 1.3%); birth rate: 18.7/1000; infant mortality rate: 23.3/1000; density per square mile: 48.2
Capital and largest city (1991 census): Nassau, 171,542;
  Monetary unit: Bahamian dollar; **Language:** English;
  Religions: Baptist, 29%; Anglican, 23%; Roman Catholic, 22%, others; **Literacy rate:** 95%
Member of Commonwealth of Nations
Economic summary: Gross domestic product (1994): $4.4 billion; $15,900 per capita; real growth rate 3.5%; inflation rate: 2.7%; unemployment: 13.1% (1993). Labor force: 127,400; Principal agricultural products: fruits, vegetables. Major industrial products: fish, refined petroleum, pharmaceutical products, banking, rum, cement, salt production, spiral welded steel pipe; tourism. Natural resources: salt, aragonite, timber. Exports: $257 million (f.o.b., 1993 est.) rum, crawfish, pharmaceuticals, cement, rum. Imports: $1.15 billion (f.o.b., 1993 est.): foodstuffs, manufactured goods, fuels. Major trading partners: U.S., U.K., Nigeria, Canada, Iran, Japan, Norway, France, Denmark.

Geography. The Bahamas are an archipelago of about 700 islands and 2,400 uninhabited islets and cays lying 50 miles off the east coast of Florida. They extend from northwest to southeast for about 760 miles (1,223 km). Only 22 of the islands are inhabited; the most important is New Providence (80 sq mi.; 207 sq km), on which Nassau is situated. Other islands include Grand Bahama, Abaco, Eleuthera, Andros, Cat Island, San Salvador (or Watling's Island), Exuma, Long Island, Crooked Island, Acklins Island, Mayaguana, and Inagua.

The islands are mainly flat, few rising above 200 feet (61 m). There are no fresh water streams. There are several large brackish lakes on several islands including Inagua and New Providence.

Government. The Bahamas moved toward greater autonomy in 1968 after the overwhelming victory in general elections of the Progressive Liberal Party, led by Prime Minister Lynden O. Pindling. The black leader's party won 29 seats in the House of Assembly to only 7 for the predominantly white United Bahamians, who had controlled the islands for decades before Pindling became Premier in 1967.

With its new mandate from the 85%-black population, Pindling's government negotiated a new constitution with Britain under which the colony became the Commonwealth of the Bahama Islands in 1969. On July 10, 1973, the Bahamas became an independent nation as the Commonwealth of the Bahamas. The islands established diplomatic relations with Cuba in 1974.

In the 1992 election, the Free National Movement won 32 of 49 seats in Parliament; the Progressive Liberal Party, 17. Hubert A. Ingraham was sworn in as Prime Minister on Aug. 20, 1992, ending 25 years of rule by the Progressive Liberal Party.

History. The islands were reached by Columbus in October 1492, and were a favorite pirate area in the early 18th century. The Bahamas were a crown colony from 1717 until they were granted internal self-government in 1964.

Immigrants from Cuba and Haiti posed a major problem in 1995. An agreement for repatriation was reached with the latter, though not the former.

BAHRAIN

State of Bahrain

Emir: Sheik Isa bin-Sulman al-Khalifa (1961)
Prime Minister: Sheik Khalifa bin Sulman al-Khalifa (1970)
Area: 240 sq mi. (620 sq km)
Population (est. 1996): 590,042 (average annual rate of natural increase: 2.03%); birth rate: 23.6/1000; infant mortality rate: 17.1/1000; density per square mile: 2,459
Capital (1992 est.): Al-Manámah, 140,401. **Monetary unit:** Bahrain dina.; **Languages:** Arabic (official), English, Farsi, Urdu. **Religions:** Shi'a Muslim, 70%; Sunni Muslim, 30%. **Literacy rate:** 80%
Economic summary: Gross domestic product (1994 est.): $7.1 billion, $12,100 per capita; real growth rate: 2.2%; inflation: 2%; unemployment: 15%. Labor force (1982): 140,000; labor force in industry and commerce: 85%. Principal agricultural products: eggs, vegetables, fruits. Major industries: petroleum processing and refining, aluminum smelting, offshore banking, ship repairing. Natural resources: oil, fish. Exports: $3.5 billion (f.o.b., 1993 est.): petroleum and petroleum products, 80%; aluminum, 7%. Imports: $3.7 billion (f.o.b., 1993 est.): machinery, oil-industry equipment, motor vehicles, foodstuffs. Major trading partners: Saudi Arabia, U.S., U.K., Japan, India, Pakistan, Singapore, Germany.

Geography. Bahrain is an archipelago in the Persian Gulf off the coast of Saudi Arabia. The islands for the most part are level expanses of sand and rock.

Government. Traditional monarchy. Political parties prohibited.

History. A sheikdom that passed from the Persians to the al-Khalifa family from Arabia in 1782, Bahrain became, by treaty, a British protectorate in 1820. It has become a major Middle Eastern oil center and, through use of oil revenues, is one of the most developed of the Persian Gulf sheikdoms. The Emir, Sheik Isa bin-Sulman al-Khalifa, who succeeded to the post in 1961, is a member of the original ruling family. Bahrain announced its independence on Aug. 14, 1971.

Protests by groups opposed to the monarchy occurred in December 1994 leading to violent clashes with government forces. Nine died and hundreds were arrested as a result of the protests.

In June 1996 the government arrested 29 on charges of plotting to overthrow the ruling family and establish an Iranian-style Muslim regime.

BANGLADESH

People's Republic of Bangladesh

President: Abdur Rahman Biswas
Prime Minister: Sheik Hasina Wazed (1996)
Area: 55,598 sq mi. (143,998 sq km)
Population (est. 1996): 123,062,800 (average annual rate of natural increase: 2.4%); birth rate: 36/1000; infant mortality rate: 102.3/1000; density per square mile: 2,213.4
Capital and largest city (mid-1994 est.): Dhaka, 7,000,000+; other large cities (est. mid-1994): Chittagong, 3,000,000; Khulna, 2,000,000; **Monetary unit:** Taka; **Principal languages:** Bangla (official), English; **Religions:** Islam, (official) 88.30%; Hindu, 10.51%; **Literacy rate:** 36%

Member of Commonwealth of Nations
Economic summary: Gross domestic product (1994 est.): $130.1 billion, per capita $1,040; real growth rate: 4.5%; inflation: 4.3% (1992 est.); unemployment rate: NA. Arable land: 67%. Agriculture accounts for 40% of GDP and 70% of employment. Principal agricultural products: rice, jute, tea, sugar, potatoes, beef. Labor force: 50.7 million est., 11% in industry and commerce. Major industrial products: jute goods, textiles, sugar, fertilizer, paper, processed foods. Natural resources: natural gas, uranium, timber. Exports: $2.534 billion (FY93/94): garments, jute and jute goods, leather and leather goods, seafood, tea, paper, fertilizer. Imports: $4.191 billion (FY93/94): capital goods, petroleum, food, textiles. Major trading partners: U.S., EU, Japan, China, India, Hong Kong, Singapore.

Geography. Bangladesh, on the northern coast of the Bay of Bengal, is surrounded by India, with a small common border with Burma in the southeast. It is approximately the size of Wisconsin. The country is low-lying riverine land traversed by the many branches and tributaries of the Ganges and Brahmaputra rivers. Elevations average less than 600 feet (183 m) above sea level. Tropical monsoons and frequent floods and cyclones inflict heavy damage in the delta region.

Government. Khaleda Zia, widow of assassinated President Ziaur Rahman, and her Bangladesh Nationalist Party won the election of late-February 1991. P.M. Zia returned Bangladesh to the parliamentary system. In a referendum in September 1991 the electorate voted to reduce the president to a figurehead.

History. The former East Pakistan was part of imperial British India until Britain withdrew in 1947. The two Pakistans were united by religion (Islam), but their peoples were separated by culture, physical features, and 1,000 miles of Indian territory. Bangladesh consists primarily of East Bengal (West Bengal is part of India and its people are primarily Hindu) plus the Sylhet district of the Indian state of Assam. For almost 25 years after independence from Britain, its history was as part of Pakistan (*see* Pakistan).

The East Pakistanis unsuccessfully sought greater autonomy from West Pakistan. The first general elections in Pakistani history, in December 1970, saw virtually all 171 seats of the region (out of 300 for both East and West Pakistan) go to Sheik Mujibur Rahman's Awami League.

Attempts to write an all-Pakistan Constitution to replace the military regime of Gen. Yahya Khan failed. Yahya put down a revolt in March 1971. An estimated one million Bengalis were killed in the fighting or later slaughtered. Ten million more took refuge in India.

In December 1971, India invaded East Pakistan, routed the West Pakistani occupation forces, and created Bangladesh. In February 1974, Pakistan agreed to recognize the independence of Bangladesh.

On March 24, 1982, Gen. Hossain Mohammad Ershad, army chief of staff, took control in a bloodless coup. Ershad assumed the office of President in 1983. Gen. Ershad resigned on December 6, 1990 amidst protests and numerous allegations of corruption.

After years of frequently violent protests Prime Minister Khaleda Zia resigned on March 30, 1996. Parliamentary elections in June provided a win for the liberal Awami League, whose leader, the daughter of the country's founding father, became prime minister later that month.

BARBADOS

Sovereign: Queen Elizabeth II
Governor-General: Sir Clifford Husbands (June 1996)
Prime Minister: Owen Arthur (1994)
Area: 166 sq. mi. (431 sq km)
Population (est. 1996): 257,030; growth rate: 0.71%.; birth rate: 15.3/1000; infant mortality rate: 18.7/1000; density per square mile: 1,548.4
Capital and largest city (1990): Bridgetown, 6,700; **Monetary unit:** Barbados dollar; **Language:** English; **Religions:** Anglican, 40%; Methodist, 7%; Pentecostal, 8%; Roman Catholic, 4%; **Literacy rate:** 99%
Member of Commonwealth of Nations
Economic summary: Gross domestic product (1994 est.): $2.4 billion; per capita $9,200; real growth rate 3%; inflation, 2%; unemployment, 20.5%. Arable land: 77%. Principal products: sugar cane, subsistence foods. Labor force (1991): 120,900; 37% services and government. Major industrial products: light manufactures, sugar milling, tourism. Tourism industry is major employer of labor force. Exports: $161 million (f.o.b., 1993 est.): sugar and molasses, chemicals, electrical components, clothing, rum, machinery and transport equipment. Imports: $703 million (c.i.f., 1993 est.): foodstuffs, consumer durables, raw materials, machinery, crude oil, construction materials, chemicals. Major trading partners: U.S., Caribbean nations, U.K., Canada.

Geography. An island in the Atlantic about 300 miles (483 km) north of Venezuela, Barbados is only 21 miles long (34 km) and 14 miles across (23 km) at its widest point. It is circled by fine beaches and narrow coastal plains. The highest point is Mount Hillaby (1,105 ft; 337 m) in the north central area.

Government. The Barbados legislature dates from 1627. It is bicameral, with a Senate of 21 appointed members and an Assembly of 28 elected members. The major political parties are the Barbados Labour Party (19 seats in Assembly), led by Prime Minister Owen Arthur; Democratic Labour Party (8 seats), led by David Thompson; and the National Democratic Party (1 seat).

History. Barbados, with a population 90% black, was settled by the British in 1627. It became a crown colony in 1885. It was a member of the Federation of the West Indies from 1958 to 1962. Britain granted the colony independence on Nov. 30, 1966, and it became a parliamentary democracy.

Prime Minister Sandiford handily won a second five-year term as a result of parliamentary elections in January 1991. With the support of several members of the governing party, the House of Representatives passed a no-confidence motion, forcing the government to call new elections ahead of time. Elections in September 1994 led to a return to power of the Labour Party.

Rejecting the advice of the IMF, the prime minister presented a deficit budget in April 1995, saying it was necessary to reduce unemployment.

BELARUS

Republic of Belarus
President: Aleksandr Lukashenko (1994)
Prime Minister: Mikhail Chyhir (1994)
Area: 80,200 sq mi. (207,600 sq km)
Population (est. 1996): 10,415,973 (average annual rate of natural increase: –0.15%) (In 1989: Belarusian, 77.9%; Russian, 13.2%; Polish, 4.1%; Ukrainian, 2.9%; Jewish, 1.1%); birth rate: 12.15/1000; infant mortality rate: 13.4/1000; density per square mile: 129.9
Capital (1992 est.): Mensk (Minsk), 1,666,000. **Other large cities (est. 1992):** Gomel, 517,000; Vitebsk, 373,000; Mogilyov, 364,000; Grodno, 291,800; Brest, 284,000; Bobruysk, 224,000. **Monetary unit:** Belarusian ruble. **Language:** Belarusian (White Russian). **Religion:** Orthodoxy is predominant. **Literacy rate:** 100%
Economic summary: Gross domestic product (1994 est.): $53.4 billion; per capita $5,130; –20% real growth rate; inflation 29% per month; unemployment 1.4%. Labor force (1992): 4..887 million. Industry and construction, 40%; agriculture and forestry, 21%. Industry accounts for about two-thirds of the country's income. Major industries include tractors, trucks, agricultural machinery, textiles, timber, chemical products including fertilizers, light manufacturing including TV sets, refrigerators, and computers, and food processing. Belarus's land is not well suited for farming. One-quarter of the republic's work force is employed in agriculture. High-yield agricultural crops are potatoes and vegetables, flax, rye, oats, other grains, sugar beets, fruit, and considerable quantities of meat, milk, and eggs. Exports: $968 million (f.o.b., 1994): to outside the successor states of the former USSR. Imports: $534 million (f.o.b., 1994): from outside of the successor states of the former USSR. Major trading partners: Russia, Ukraine, Poland.

Geography: Much of Belarus (formerly Byelorussia) is a hilly lowland with forests, swamps, and numerous rivers and lakes. There are wide rivers emptying into the Baltic and the Black Seas. Its forests cover over one-third of the land and its peat marshes are a valuable natural resource. The largest lake is Narach, 31 sq mi. (79.6 sq km). The republic borders Latvia and Lithuania on the north, Ukraine on the south, Russia on the east, and Poland on the west.

Government: A constitutional republic. The parliament (Supreme Soviet) has 260 deputies.

History: In the 5th century, Belarus (also known as White Russia) was colonized by east Slavic tribes and was dominated by Kiev from the 9th to 12th centuries. After the destruction of Kiev by the Mongols in the 13th century, the territory was conquered by the dukes of Lithuania. Belarus became part of the Grand Duchy of Lithuania, which merged with Poland in 1569.

Following the partitions of Poland in 1772, 1793, and the final partition which divided Poland between Russia, Prussia, and Austria, Belarus became part of the Russian empire.

The peace Treaty of Riga in March 1921 ending the Polish-Soviet War ceded west Belarus to Poland. The eastern part of the country was joined to the U.S.S.R. in 1922. In 1939, the Soviet Union took back West Belarus under the secret protocol of the Nazi-Soviet Nonaggression Pact and incorporated it into the Byelorussian Soviet Socialist Republic.

Following the end of World War II, Belarus was given membership in the United Nations in 1945.

Belarus declared its sovereignty in July 1990 and its independence in August 1991.

The Belarus president, Nikolai Dementei, a communist hard-liner, was forced to resign under pressure following the August 1991 attempted coup, and Stanislav S. Shushkevich, First Deputy Chairman of the Parliament, assumed leadership of the country. Belarus became a co-founder of the Commonwealth of Independent States (CIS) on Dec. 8, 1991.

In January 1994 the country's parliament ousted its reform-minded leader in protest against his support for market economics. In March parliament adopted a new constitution, creating a presidency, and reconstructed the 260-seat parliament. In the first-round, May 15 election Lukashenka received a plurality, and in the run-off June 23 balloting over 80% of the vote.

The prime ministers of Russia and Belarus signed a treaty in April to unify their monetary systems and lift customs barriers. The chairman of the Belarussian national bank opposed the monetary union, leaving its implementation in doubt.

In March 1996 Belarus and Russia announced approval of a draft accord leading to a union of the two states. The details and the extent of the planned merger, however, were yet to be determined.

BELGIUM

Kingdom of Belgium

Sovereign: King Albert II (1993)
Prime Minister: Jean-Luc Dehaene (1992)
Area: 11,781 sq mi. (30,518 sq km)
Population (1995): 10,131,863 (average annual rate of natural increase: 0.1%); birth rate: 11.6/1000; infant mortality rate: 7/1000; density per square mile: 857
Capital and largest city (1994): Brussels, 949,070 (metro area); **other large cities (1994):** Antwerp, 462,880; Ghent, 228,490; Charleroi, 206,898; Liege, 195,389; Bruges, 116,724; Namur, 104,610. **Monetary Unit:** Belgian franc. **Languages:** Dutch (Flemish), 57%, French, 32%; bilingual (Brussels), 10%; German, 0.7%. **Religion:** Roman Catholic, 75%. **Literacy rate:** 99%
National name: Royaume de Belgique—Koningrijk van België
Economic summary: Gross domestic product (1995): $264.7 billion; per capita $26,740; real growth rate 1.9%; inflation rate 1.5%; unemployment rate: 10.2%. Arable land: 46%. Agricultural products: pork, beef, milk, fruits and vegetables, ornamental plants, meats, sugar beets, eggs, dairy products. Labor force (1992): services, 70%; industry, 27%; agriculture, 2.5%. Major products: chemicals, mechanical, electrical and plastic equipment, textiles, nonferrous metals, iron and steel, glass. Exports: $117 billion (f.o.b., 1992): machinery, transportation equipment (cars), pharmaceutical and chemical products, mineral products, non-precious metals, precious metals. Imports: $120 billion (c.i.f., 1992): road vehicles and tractors, pharmaceuticals and chemicals, non-precious metals, plastics, precious metals and stones. Major trading partners: Germany, France, Netherlands, U.S.

Geography. A neighbor of France, Germany, the Netherlands, and Luxembourg, Belgium has about 40 miles of seacoast on the North Sea at the Strait of Dover. In area, it is approximately the size of Maryland. The northern third of the country is a plain extending eastward from the seacoast. North of the Sambre and Meuse Rivers is a low plateau; to the south lies the heavily wooded Ardennes plateau, attaining an elevation of about 2,300 feet (700 m).

The Schelde River, which rises in France and flows through Belgium, emptying into the Schelde estuaries, enables Antwerp to be an ocean port.

Government. Belgium, a parliamentary democracy under a constitutional monarch, consists of ten provinces. Its bicameral legislature has a Senate, with its 71 members elected for four years. The 150-member Chamber of Representatives is directly elected for four years by proportional representation. There is universal suffrage, and those who do not vote are fined.

Belgium joined the North Atlantic Alliance in 1949 and is a member of the European Community. NATO and the European Community have their headquarters in Brussels.

The late sovereign, Baudouin I, was born Sept. 7, 1930, the son of King Leopold III and Queen Astrid. He became King on July 17, 1951, after the abdication of his father. He married Doña Fabiola de Mora y Aragón on Dec. 15, 1960. Since he had no children, his brother, Prince Albert, became king upon his death in 1993.

History. Belgium occupies part of the Roman province of Belgica, named after the Belgae, a people of ancient Gaul. The area was conquered by Julius Caesar in 57–50 B.C., then was overrun by the Franks in the 5th century. It was part of Charlemagne's empire in the 8th century, then in the next century was absorbed into Lotharingia and later into the Duchy of Lower Lorraine. In the 12th century it was partitioned into the Duchies of Brabant and Luxembourg, the Bishopric of Liège, and the domain of the Count of Hainaut, which included Flanders.

In the 16th century, Belgium, with most of the area of the Low Countries, passed to the Duchy of Burgundy and was the marriage portion of Archduke Maximilian of Hapsburg and the inheritance of his grandson, Charles V, who incorporated it into his empire. Then, in 1555, they were united with Spain.

By the treaty of Utrecht in 1713, the country's sovereignty passed to Austria. During the wars that followed the French Revolution, Belgium was occupied and later annexed to France. But with the downfall of Napoleon, the Congress of Vienna in 1815 gave the country to the Netherlands. The Belgians revolted in 1830 and declared their independence.

Germany's invasion of Belgium in 1914 set off World War I. The Treaty of Versailles (1919) gave the areas of Eupen, Malmédy, and Moresnet to Belgium. Leopold III succeeded Albert, king during World War I, in 1934. In World War II, Belgium was overwhelmed by Nazi Germany, and Leopold III was made prisoner. When he attempted to return in 1950, Socialists and Liberals revolted. He abdicated July 16, 1951, and his son, Baudouin, became King the next day.

Despite the increasingly strong divisions between the French- and Flemish-speaking communities, a Christian Democrat-Liberal coalition that took office in December 1981 came close to setting a record for longevity among the 32 governments that had ruled Belgium since World War II. Political instability in Zaire (formerly the Belgian Congo) following riots there led to Belgian troops supervising an exodus of foreigners in September 1991.

In 1993 the constitution was changed, turning the country into a federal state. Compulsory military service was also eliminated.

National elections on May 21, 1995, gave the governing coalition a parliamentary majority. Despite protests from workers, the government continued to work on means to reduce the budget deficit to 3% in order to qualify for the introduction of a single European currency in 1999.

BELIZE

Sovereign: Queen Elizabeth II (1952)
Governor-General: Colville Young (1993)
Prime Minister: Manuel Esquivel (1993)

Area: 8,867 sq mi. (22,965 sq km)
Population (est. 1996): 219,296 (average annual rate of natural increase: 2.7%); birth rate: 32.8/1000; infant mortality rate: 33.9/1000.; density per sq mi.: 24.7
Capital (est. 1993): Belmopan, 3,852; **Largest city (1993):** Belize City, 447,724. **Monetary unit:** Belize dollar. **Languages:** English (official) and Spanish, Maya, Carib. **Religions:** Roman Catholic, 62%; Protestant, 30%. **Literacy rate:** 91% (est.)
Member of Commonwealth of Nations
Economic summary: Gross domestic product (1994 est.): $575 million, per capita $2,750; real growth rate 2%; inflation 5.5%; unemployment 10% (1993 est.). Principal products: sugar cane, citrus concentrate, corn, molasses, rice, bananas, livestock. Labor force: 51,500; 10.3% in manufacturing. Major products: timber, processed foods, furniture, rum, soap. Natural resources: timber, fish. Exports: $115 million (f.o.b., 1993): sugar, molasses, clothing, lumber, citrus concentrates, fish. Imports: $281 million (c.i.f., 1993): fuels, transportation equipment, foodstuffs, machinery, chemicals, pharmaceuticals, manufactured goods. Major trading partners: European Union, Mexico, CARICOM, U.S.

Geography. Belize (formerly British Honduras) is situated on the Caribbean Sea south of Mexico and east and north of Guatemala. In area, it is about the size of New Hampshire. Most of the country is heavily forested with various hardwoods. Mangrove swamps and cays along the coast give way to hills and mountains in the interior. The highest point is Victoria Peak, 3,681 feet (1,122 m).

Government. Formerly the colony of British Honduras, Belize became a fully independent commonwealth on Sept. 21, 1981, after having been self-governing since 1964. Executive power is nominally wielded by Queen Elizabeth II through an appointed Governor-General but effective power is held by the Prime Minister, who is responsible to a 29-member parliament elected by universal suffrage.

History. Once a part of the Mayan empire, the area was deserted until British timber cutters began exploiting valuable hardwoods in the 17th century. Efforts by Spain to dislodge British settlers, including a major naval attack in 1798, were defeated. The territory was formally named a British colony in 1862 but administered by the Governor of Jamaica until 1884.

Guatemala has long made claims to the territory. A tentative agreement was reached between Britain, Belize, and Guatemala in March 1981 that would offer access to the Caribbean through Belizean territory for Guatemala. The agreement broke down, however.

Guatemala recognized Belize's sovereignty in September 1991 and abandoned its territorial claim, although unease remains.

The general election of June 1993 saw a victory for the United Democratic Party, which won 16 of the 29 seats in the House of Representatives.

Local council elections in March 1994 provided victories to the UDP, putting the party in control of all seven councils, whereas previously it had but two.

BENIN

Republic of Benin
President: Mathieu Kerekou (1996)
Area: 43,483 sq mi. (112,622 sq km)

Population (est. 1996): 5,709,529 (average annual rate of natural increase: 3.3%); birth rate: 46.8/1000; infant mortality rate: 105/1000; density per square mile: 131
Capital and largest city (1996): Porto-Novo (official), 177,660; Cotonou (de facto capital), 33,212. **Other large city (1992): Djougou, 132,192. Monetary unit:** Franc CFA; **Ethnic groups:** Fons and Adjas, Baribas, Yorubas, Mahis; **Languages:** French, African languages; **Religions:** indigenous, 70%; Christian, 15%; Islam, 15%; **National name:** Republique du Benin; **Literacy rate (1990 est.):** 23%
Economic summary: Gross domestic product (1994 est.): $6.7 billion; $1,260 per capita; real growth rate: 4%; inflation rate 35%; unemployment n.a.. Arable land: 12%. Principal agricultural products: palm oils, peanuts, cotton, coffee, tobacco, corn, rice, livestock, fish. Labor force: 1,900,000; 60% in agriculture. Major industrial products: processed palm oil, palm kernel oil, textiles, beverages. Natural resources: limestone, some offshore oil, marble, timber. Exports: $332 million (f.o.b., 1993 est.): crude oil, cotton, palm products, cocoa. Imports: $571 million (f.o.b., 1993 est.): foodstuffs, beverages, tobacco, petroleum products, intermediate goods, capital goods, light consumer goods. Major trading partners: France and other Western European countries, Japan, U.S.

Geography. This West African nation on the Gulf of Guinea, between Togo on the west and Nigeria on the east, is about the size of Tennessee. It is bounded also by Burkina Faso and Niger on the north. The land consists of a narrow coastal strip that rises to a swampy, forested plateau and then to highlands in the north. A hot and humid climate blankets the entire country.

Government. The change in name from Dahomey to Benin was announced by President Mathieu Kerekou on November 30, 1975. Benin commemorates an African kingdom that flourished in the 17th century. Benin is a republic under a multiparty democratic rule with a unicameral legislature, the National Assembly. At the National Conference held at Cotonou, Feb. 19–28, 1990, Marxism–Leninism was abolished as the state philosophy, a multiparty system was established, and political detainees and prisoners were released.

History. One of the smallest and most densely populated states in Africa, Benin was annexed by the French in 1893. The area was incorporated into French West Africa in 1904. It became an autonomous republic within the French Community in 1958, and on Aug. 1, 1960, was granted its independence within the Community.

Gen. Christophe Soglo deposed the first president, Hubert Maga, in an army coup in 1963. He dismissed the civilian government in 1965, proclaiming himself chief of state. A group of young army officers seized power in December 1967, deposing Soglo. They promulgated a new constitution in 1968.

In December 1969, Benin had its fifth coup of the decade, with the army again taking power. In May 1970, a three-man presidential commission was created to take over the government. The commission had a six-year term. In May 1972, yet another army coup ousted the triumvirate and installed Lt. Col. Mathieu Kerekou as President.

Student protests and widespread strikes in 1989 and 1990 moved Benin toward multiparty democracy. In March 1991 Prime Minister Soglo won the first free presidential election.

Nominally above partisan politics the president in mid-1993 said he would join the Renaissance Party.

Presidential elections in March 1996 resulted in a victory for former-President and Marxist military ruler Kerekou, with 52.49%, over the incumbent Soglo. In the first round of voting over a fifth of the ballots were annulled due to irregularities.

BHUTAN

Kingdom of Bhutan
Ruler: King Jigme Singye Wangchuck (1972)
Area: 18,000 sq mi. (46,620 sq km)
Population (est. 1996): 1,822,625 (average annual rate of natural increase: 2.3%; birth rate: 38.5/1000; infant mortality rate: 116.3/1000; density per square mile: 101
Capital and largest city (1993): Thimphu (official), 30,340. **Monetary unit:** Ngultrum. **Language:** Dzongkha (official). **Religions:** Buddhist, 75%; Hindu, 25%. **National name:** Druk-yul. **Literacy rate:** not available
Economic summary: Gross domestic product (1994 est.): $1.2 billion; per capita $700; real growth rate 5%; inflation (Oct. '94) 10%; unemployment n.a. Arable land: 3%. Labor force in agriculture: 95%. Principal products: rice, barley, wheat, potatoes, fruit. Major industrial product: cement. Natural resources: timber, hydroelectric power. Exports: $66.8 million (f.o.b., FY93/94 est.): cardamom, gypsum, timber, handicrafts, cement, fruit, electricity (to India), precious stones, spices. Imports: $97.6 million (c.i.f., FY93/94 est.): fuels, machinery, vehicles, grain, fabrics. Major trading partner: India.

Geography. Mountainous Bhutan, half the size of Indiana, is situated on the southeast slope of the Himalayas, bordered on the north and east by Tibet and on the south and west and east by India. The landscape consists of a succession of lofty and rugged mountains running generally from north to south and separated by deep valleys. In the north, towering peaks reach a height of 24,000 feet (7,315 m).

Government. Bhutan is a constitutional monarchy. The King rules with a Council of Ministers and a Royal Advisory Council. There is a National Assembly (parliament), which meets semiannually, but no political parties.

History. British troops invaded the country in 1865 and negotiated an agreement under which Britain undertook to pay an annual allowance to Bhutan on condition of good behavior. A treaty with India in 1949 increased this subsidy and placed Bhutan's foreign affairs under Indian control.

In the 1960s, Bhutan undertook modernization, abolishing slavery and the caste system, emancipating women, and enacting land reform. In 1985, Bhutan made its first diplomatic links with non-Asian countries.

A pro-democracy campaign emerged in 1991 that the government claimed was composed largely of Nepalese immigrants.

Nepalese activism and a refugee problem continue to plague the country. The International Red Cross investigated charges of human rights violations in 1993. In 1994 as many as 100,000 remained in refugee camps. During 1995, discussions with Nepal over the problem bore little fruit, and immigration laws were tightened.

BOLIVIA

Republic of Bolivia
President: Gonzalo Sanchez de Lozada (1993)
Area: 424,162 sq mi. (1,098,581 sq km)
Population (est. 1996): 7,165,257 (average annual rate of natural increase: 2.16%; birth rate: 32.4/1000; infant mortality rate: 67.5/1000; density per sq mile: 16.9
Historic and Judicial capital (1992): Sucre, 130,952; **Administrative capital (1992):** La Paz, 711,036 **Largest cities (est. 1992):** Santa Cruz, 694,616; El Alto, 404,367; Cochabamba, 404,102; Oruro, 183,194. **Monetary unit:** Boliviano. **Languages:** Spanish, Quechua, Aymara. **Religion:** Roman Catholic, 85%. **National name:** República de Bolivia. **Literacy rate:** 78%
Economic summary: Gross national product (1994 est.): $18.3 billion; per capita, $2,370; real growth rate, 4.2%; inflation rate 8.5%; unemployment rate, 6.2%. Arable land: 3%. Principal agricultural products (1994): soybeans, timber, sugar, cotton, brazil nuts, coffee. Major industrial products: refined petroleum, processed foods, tires, textiles, clothing. Labor force (1993): 3.54 million; agriculture, n.a.; services and utilities, 20%; manufacturing, mining, and construction, 7%. Natural resources: petroleum, natural gas, tin, lead, zinc, copper, tungsten, bismuth, antimony, gold, sulfur, silver, iron ore. Exports: $1.035 billion (f.o.b., 1994): metals, 44.9%; hydrocarbons, 10.6%; nontraditional, 44.5% (soybeans, timber, sugar, cotton). Imports: $1.207 billion (c.i.f., 1994): food, petroleum, consumer goods, capital goods. Major trading partners: U.S., Argentina, U.K., Peru, Chile, Brazil, Japan, Germany.

Geography. Landlocked Bolivia, equal in size to California and Texas combined, lies to the west of Brazil. Its other neighbors are Peru and Chile on the west and Argentina and Paraguay on the south.

The country is a low alluvial plain throughout 60% of its area toward the east, drained by the Amazon and Plata river systems. The western part, enclosed by two chains of the Andes, is a great plateau—the Altiplano, with an average altitude of 12,000 feet (3,658 m). More than 43.7% of the population lives on the plateau, which also contains Oruro, Potosi, and La Paz. At an altitude of 11,910 feet (3,630 m), La Paz is the highest administrative capital city in the world.

Lake Titicaca, half the size of Lake Ontario, is one of the highest large lakes in the world, at an altitude of 12,507 feet (3,812 m). Islands in the lake hold ruins of the ancient Incas.

Government. The Bolivian Constitution provides for a democratic, representative, unitary republic, with a government made up of three branches: legislative, executive, and judicial. Executive power is exercised by the president, elected by a direct vote for a five-year term. Legislative power is vested in the National Congress, consisting of the Chamber of Deputies and the Senate. Judicial power is in the hands of the Supreme Court of Justice, made up of twelve members.

History. Famous since Spanish colonial days for its mineral wealth, modern Bolivia was once a part of the ancient Incan Empire. After the Spaniards defeated the Incas in the 16th century, Bolivia's predominantly Indian population was reduced to slavery. The country won its independence in 1825 and was named after Simón Bolívar, the famed liberator.

Harassed by internal strife, Bolivia lost great slices of territory to three neighbor nations. Several thousand square miles and its outlet to the Pacific were taken by Chile after the War of the Pacific (1879–84). In 1903 a piece of Bolivia's Acre province, rich in rubber, was ceded to Brazil. And in 1938, after a war with Paraguay, Bolivia gave up claim to nearly 100,000 square miles of the Gran Chaco.

In 1965 a guerrilla movement mounted from Cuba and headed by Maj. Ernesto (Ché) Guevara began a revolutionary war. With the aid of U.S. military advisers, the Bolivian army, helped by the peasants, smashed the guerrilla movement, wounding and capturing Guevara on Oct. 8, 1967, and shooting him to death the next day.

Faltering steps toward restoration of civilian government were halted abruptly on July 17, 1980, when Gen. Luis Garcia Meza Tejada seized power. A series of military leaders followed before the military moved, in 1982, to return the government to civilian rule. Hernán Siles Zuazo was inaugurated President on Oct. 10, 1982.

Under Siles' left-of-center government, the country was regularly shut down by work stoppages, the bulk of Bolivia's natural resources—natural gas, gold, lithium, potassium, and tungsten—were either sold on the black market or left in the ground, the country had the lowest per-capita income in South America, and inflation approached 3,000 percent.

As in 1985 the inconclusive presidential election of 1989 was decided in Congress, where the second-place finisher Bánzer threw his support to Paz Zamora, who finished third, in exchange for naming a majority of the new cabinet.

The presidential elections of June 1993 gave the post to a millionaire mining entrepreneur who ran on a platform calling for free market policies and privatization. A presidential proposal to privatize six state companies was passed by Congress in March 1994 but aroused disruptive protests.

The government in 1995 pursued its privatization program, but despite being lauded the program proved unpopular with the workers, who feared for their jobs.

BOSNIA AND HERZEGOVINA

Republic of Bosnia and Herzegovina
President: Alija Izetbegovic (1990)
Prime Minister: Hasan Muratovic (1996)
Area: 19,741 sq mi. (51,129 sq km)
Population (est. 1996) 2,656,240 (official figures not available due to ethnic cleansing); (average annual rate of natural increase: 0.7%); Muslims 44%; Serbs, 31%; Croats, 17%; other, 8%. Birth rate: 14/1000; infant mortality rate: 15.3/1000; density per square mile: 134.6
Capital and largest city (1994 est.): Sarajevo (Bosnia) 300,000 (unofficial); (1991 prewar est.): Banja Luka (Bosnia), 195,139. Mostar is capital of Herzegovina.
Monetary unit: Dinar. **Language:** Bosnian, written in Latin and Cyrillic. **Religions:** Slavic Muslim, 40%; Orthodox, 31%; Catholic, 15%; Protestant, 4%
Economic summary: (Reliable economic statistics not available.) Gross domestic product (1991): $14 billion, real growth rate –37%; inflation 80%; unemployment (Feb. 1992 est.): 28%. Labor force: 1,026,254 (1991 est.): 2% agriculture; 45% industry. Industries: steel production, mining (coal, iron ore, lead, zinc, manganese, and bauxite); vehicle assembly, textiles, tobacco products, wooden furniture, domestic appliances, oil refining. Agriculture: orchards, vineyards, livestock, some wheat and corn. Exports: $2,054 million. Imports: $1,891 million (1990). Major trading partners: principally the other former Yugoslav republics.

Geography: Bosnia and Herzegovina is a roughly triangular-shaped republic about one-half the size of

the state of Kentucky. The Bosnian region in the north is mountainous and covered with thick forests. The Herzegovina region in the south is largely rugged and flat farm land. The republic is bordered on the east by Serbia, the southeast by Montenegro, and in the north and west by the Republic of Croatia. It has a narrow coastline without natural harbors stretching 13 miles (20 km) along the Adriatic Sea. The Sava and Drina Rivers form much of the country's northern and eastern boundaries with Croatia and Serbia, respectively. The Sava and its tributaries are the nation's chief rivers.

Government: Democratic republic with bicameral legislature.

History: Bosnia and Herzegovina were once part of the Roman provinces of Illyricum and Pannonia. Serbs first settled in the land during the 7th century A.D., and by the end of the 10th century, Bosnia became an independent state. Later Bosnia came under Hungarian rule in the middle of the 12th century.

Medieval Bosnia reached the height of its power and prestige during the 14th century when it controlled many of the surrounding territories including Herzegovina. During this period, religious strife arose among the Roman Catholic, Orthodox, and Muslim populations which weakened the country, and in 1463, Ottoman Turks conquered the disunited nation.

At the Congress of Berlin in 1878 following the end of the Russo-Turkish War (1877–78), Austria was given a mandate to occupy and govern Bosnia and Herzegovina. Although the provinces were still officially part of the Ottoman Empire, they were annexed into the Austro-Hungarian empire on Oct. 7, 1908. As a result, relations with Serbia, which had claims on Bosnia and Herzegovina, became embittered. The hostile tension between the two countries climaxed in the assassination of Austrian archduke Francis Ferdinand at Sarajevo on June 28, 1914 by a Serbian nationalist. This event precipitated the start of World War I (1914–1918).

Bosnia and Herzegovina were annexed to Serbia as part of the newly formed Kingdom of Serbs, Croats, and Slovenes on Oct. 26, 1918. The name was later changed to Yugoslavia in 1929.

When Germany invaded Yugoslavia in 1941, Bosnia and Herzegovina were made part of a Croatian state that was controlled by a Fascist dictatorship. During the German and Italian occupation of their land Bosnian and Herzegovinan resistance fighters fought a fierce guerrilla warfare against the Fascist troops.

After the defeat of Germany in 1945, Bosnia and Herzegovina were reunited into a single state as one of the six republics of the newly reestablished Yugoslavia.

In December 1991, Bosnia and Herzegovina declared their independence from Yugoslavia and asked for recognition by the 12 member nations of the European Community (E.C.). The E.C. said that before it could recommend recognition, Bosnia and Herzegovina should hold a referendum on independence.

Most Bosnian voters chose independence during a referendum held in March 1992 and President Izetbegovic again declared the nation an independent state.

Attempting to carve out enclaves for themselves, the Serbian minority, with the help of the largely Serbian Yugoslav army, took the offensive and laid siege, particularly on Sarajevo, resulting in countless deaths. By the end of August, rebel Bosnian Serbs had conquered over 60% of Bosnia and Herzegovina.

The Serbs halted their siege of Sarajevo in February 1994 formally at the request of Russia. In March the government signed an agreement with Bosnian Croats linking their territories into a single federation.

U.S.-sponsored peace talks in Dayton, Ohio, led to an agreement, signed in Paris in December 1995, and called for a Muslim–Croat federation and a Serb entity. 60,000 NATO troops were to supervise its implementation for one year.

Fighting abated and orderly elections were held in September 1996. The Bosnian Muslim leader, President Alija Izetbegovic, won the majority of votes to become the leader of the three-member presidency called for under the Bosnian peace accords negotiated in Dayton, Ohio, in 1995.

BOTSWANA

Republic of Botswana

President: Quett K.J. Masire (1980)
Area: 231,800 sq mi. (600,360 sq km)
Population (est. 1996): 1,477,630 (average annual rate of natural increase: 1.63%); birth rate: 33.3/1000; infant mortality rate: 54.2/1000; density per square mile: 6.4
Capital and largest city (est. 1992): Gaborone, 138,000.
Monetary unit: Pula. **Languages:** English, Setswana. **Religions:** indigenous beliefs, 50%; Christian, 50%. **Member of Commonwealth of Nations. Literacy rate:** 80%
Economic summary: Gross domestic product (1994 est.): $4.3 billion, per capita $3,130; real growth rate 1%; inflation 10%; unemployment 25%. Arable land: 2%. Principal agricultural products: livestock, sorghum, corn, millet, cowpeas, beans. Labor force (1992): 428,000; 220,000 formal sector employees, most others involved in cattle raising and subsistence agriculture. 14,300 employed in South African mines. Major industrial products: diamonds, copper, nickel, salt, soda ash, potash, coal, frozen beef; tourism. Natural resources: diamonds, copper, nickel, salt, soda ash, potash, coal, natural gas. Exports: $1.8 billion (f.o.b., 1994): diamonds. 78%; copper and nickel, 6%; meat, 5%. Imports: $1.8 billion (c.i.f., 1992): foodstuffs, vehicles, textiles, petroleum products. Major trading partners: Switzerland, U.K., Southern African Customs Union (SACU), U.S.

Geography. Twice the size of Arizona, Botswana is in south central Africa, bounded by Namibia, Zambia, Zimbabwe, and South Africa. Most of the country is near-desert, with the Kalahari occupying the western part of the country. The eastern part is hilly, with salt lakes in the north.

Government. A parliamentary republic. The Botswana Constitution provides, in addition to the unicameral National Assembly, for a House of Chiefs, which has a voice on bills affecting tribal affairs. There is universal suffrage.

History. Botswana is the land of the Batawana tribes, which, when threatened by the Boers in Transvaal, asked Britain in 1885 to establish a protectorate over the country, then known as Bechuanaland. In 1961, Britain granted a constitution to the country. Self-government began in 1965, and on Sept. 30, 1966, the country became independent.

Owing to a land scandal the vice president and the minister of agriculture were forced to resign in March 1992. The minister of finance was selected to be the new vice president.

October 1994 elections for the Assembly gave 26 of the 40 contested seats to the Botswana Democratic Party. The Botswana National Front, however, picked up 13 seats, 10 more than previously. The president reduced the voting age to 18 in April 1995.

BRAZIL

Federative Republic of Brazil

President: Fernando Henrique Cardoso (1994)
Area: 3,286,470 sq mi. (8,511,957 sq km)
Population (est. 1996): 162,661,214 (average annual rate of natural increase: 1.16%); birth rate: 20.8/1000; infant mortality rate: 55.3/1000; density per square mile: 49.5
Capital (est. 1995): Brasília, 2,500,000. **Largest cities (est. 1995):** São Paulo, 15,800,000; Rio de Janeiro, 10,000,000; Porto Alegre, 3,000,000; Recife, 2,900,000; Salvador, 2,600,000; Belo Horizonte, 2,600,000. **Monetary unit:** Real. **Language:** Portuguese. **Religion:** Roman Catholic, 90% (nominal). **National name:** República Federativa do Brasil. **Literacy rate:** 81%
Economic summary: Gross domestic product (1995): $677 billion; per capita $4,345; 4.2% real growth rate; inflation 1.7% per month; unemployment 4.7%. Arable land: 7%. Principal products: world's largest producer of coffee. Sugar cane, oranges, cocoa, soybeans, tobacco, cattle. Labor force (1990 est.): 57,409,975; 27% in industry. Major industrial products: steel, chemicals, petrochemicals, machinery, motor vehicles, cement, lumber. Natural resources: iron ore, manganese, bauxite, nickel, other industrial metals, hydropower, timber. Exports: $43.6 billion (f.o.b., 1994 est.): coffee, iron ore, soybeans, sugar, beef, transport equipment, footwear, orange juice. Imports: $33.2 billion (f.o.b., 1994 est.): crude oil, capital goods, chemical products, foodstuffs, coal. Major trading partners: U.S., European Union, Japan, Latin America, Middle East.

Geography. Brazil covers nearly half of South America, extends 2,965 miles (4,772 km) north-south, 2,691 miles (4,331 km), east-west, and borders every nation on the continent except Chile and Ecuador.

More than a third of Brazil is drained by the Amazon and its more than 200 tributaries. The Amazon is navigable for ocean steamers to Iquitos, Peru, 2,300 miles (3,700 km) upstream. Southern Brazil is drained by the Plata system—the Paraguay, Uruguay, and Paraná Rivers. The most important stream entirely within Brazil is the São Francisco, navigable for 1,000 miles (1,903 km), but broken near its mouth by the 275-foot (84 m) Paulo Afonso Falls.

Government. A federal republic. The president and vice president are each elected for a 4-year term. They cannot be re-elected for a consecutive term. The National Congress maintains a bicameral structure—a Senate, whose members serve eight-year terms, and a Chamber of Deputies, elected for four-year terms.

History. Brazil is the only Latin American nation deriving its language and culture from Portugal. Adm. Pedro Alvares Cabral claimed the territory for the Portuguese in 1500. He brought to Portugal a cargo of wood, pau-brasil, from which the land received its name. Portugal began colonization in 1532 and made the area a royal colony in 1549.

During the Napoleonic wars, King João VI, then Prince Regent, fled the country in 1807 in advance of the French armies and in 1808 set up his court in Rio de Janeiro. João was drawn home in 1820 by a revolution, leaving his son as Regent. When Portugal sought to reduce Brazil again to colonial status, the prince declared Brazil's independence on Sept. 7, 1822, and became Pedro I, Emperor of Brazil.

Harassed by his parliament, Pedro I abdicated in 1831 in favor of his five-year-old son, who became Emperor in 1840 as Pedro II. The son was a popular monarch, but discontent built up and, in 1889, following a military revolt, he had to abdicate. Although a republic was proclaimed, Brazil was under two military dictatorships during the next four years. A revolt permitted a gradual return to stability under civilian Presidents.

The President during World War I, Wenceslau Braz, cooperated with the Allies and declared war on Germany.

In World War II, Brazil cooperated with the Western Allies, welcoming Allied air bases, patrolling the South Atlantic, and joining the invasion of Italy after declaring war on the Axis.

Gen. João Baptista de Oliveira Figueiredo, became President in 1979 and pledged a return to democracy in 1985.

The electoral college's choice of Tancredo Neves on Jan. 15, 1985, as the first civilian President since 1964 brought a nationwide wave of optimism, but the 75-year-old President-elect was hospitalized and underwent a series of intestinal operations. When Neves died on April 21, Vice President Sarney became President. He, however, was widely distrusted because he had previously been a member of the military regime's political party.

Collor de Mello won the election of late 1989 and took office in March 1990 despite his lack of support from a major party. In the campaign he pledged to lower the chronic hyperinflation following the path of free-market economics. Yet an economic recession still saw the inflation rate running at about 400% during the president's first year in office.

On the basis of a corruption scandal Collor in 1992 faced impeachment by Congress. Just minutes after the trial began on December 29 the president resigned, and the vice president assumed the presidency.

A former finance minister, Fernando Cordoso won the presidency in the October 1994 election with 54% of the vote. However, his party and its coalition allies failed to win a majority in either of the congressional houses.

President Cordoso in January 1996 revoked a previous decree that barred non-indigenous peoples from appealing land allocations by a government agency.

BRUNEI DARUSSALAM

State of Brunei Darussalam
Sultan: Haji Hassanal Bolkiah
Area: 2,226 sq mi. (5,765 sq km)
Population (est. 1996): 299,939 (annual rate of natural increase: 2.04%; birth rate: 25.5/1000; infant mortality rate: 24.2/1000; density per square mile: 134.7
Capital and largest city (est. 1991): Bandar Seri Begawan, 21,484. **Monetary unit:** Brunei dollar. **Ethnic groups:** 64% Malay, 20% Chinese, 16% other. **Languages:** Malay (official), Chinese, English. **Religions:** Islam (official religion), 63%; Christian, 8%; Buddhist, 14%; indigenous beliefs and other, 15%. **Literacy rate:** 85%
Economic summary: Gross domestic product (1993 est.): $4.43 billion, per capita $16,000; real growth rate –4%; inflation 2.5% (1993 est.); unemployment 5% (1993 est.) Arable land: 1%; principle agricultural products: fruit, rice, pepper, buffaloes. Labor force (1992): 90,000; Commerce and services, 26.4; government and public authorities, 40%; construction, 33%. Major industrial products: crude petroleum, liquified natural gas. Natural resources: petroleum, natural gas, timber. Exports: $2.2 billion (f.o.b., 1993 est.): crude petroleum, liquified natural gas. Imports: $1.2 billion (c.i.f., 1993 est.): machinery, transport equipment, manufactured goods,

foodstuffs, chemicals. Major trading partners: Japan, Thailand, U.S., U.K., Singapore, South Korea.

Geography. About the size of Delaware, Brunei is an independent sultanate on the northwest coast of the island of Borneo in the South China Sea, wedged between the Malaysian states of Sabah and Sarawak. Three quarters of the thinly populated country is covered with tropical rain forest; there are rich oil and gas deposits.

Government. Sultan Hassanal Bolkiah is ruler of the state, a former British protectorate which became fully sovereign and independent on New Year's Day, 1984, presiding over a Privy Council and Council of Ministers appointed by himself.

History. Brunei (pronounced broon-eye) was a powerful state from the 16th to the 19th century, ruling over the northern part of Borneo and adjacent island chains. But it fell into decay and lost Sarawak in 1841, becoming a British protectorate in 1888 and a British dependency in 1905.

The Sultan regained control over internal affairs in 1959, but Britain retained responsibility for the state's defense and foreign affairs until the end of 1983, when the sultanate became fully independent.

Sultain Bolkiah was crowned in 1968 at the age of 22, succeeding his father, Sir Omar Ali Saifuddin, who had abdicated. During his reign, exploitation of the rich Seria oilfield had made the sultanate wealthy.

Warning against opposition to his government, the Islamic religion, and himself, the sultan in 1990 said that the laws of the sultanate would be restructured into conformity with Islamic law.

Along with three other Pacific-rim countries, Brunei created in March 1994 the East Asian Growth Area. In October 1995 the country joined the IMF and the World Bank.

BULGARIA

Republic of Bulgaria
Prime Minister: Jan Videnov (1994)
President: Zhelyu Zhelev (1992)
Area: 42,823 sq mi. (110,912 sq km)
Population (est. 1996): 8,612,757 (average annual rate of natural increase: –0.52%); birth rate: 8.33/1000; infant mortality rate: 15.7/1000; density per square mile: 201.1
Capital and largest city (1994 est.): Sofia, 1,113,674; **Largest cities (est. 1994):** Plovdiv, 345,205; Varna, 307,200; Burgas, 198,439; Ruse, 170,209. **Monetary unit:** Lev. **Language:** Bulgarian. **Religions:** Eastern Orthodox, 90%; Muslim, Catholic, Protestant, Judaic, Armeno-Gregorian. **National name:** Narodna Republika Bulgariya. **Literacy rate:** 95%
Economic summary: Gross domestic product (1994 est.): $33.7 billion, per capita $3,830; real growth rate 0.2%; inflation 122%; unemployment 16%. Arable land: 34%. Principal products: grains, tobacco, fruits, vegetables. Labor force: 4,300,000, 33% in industry; 33% in agriculture. Major products: processed agricultural products, machinery, electronics, chemicals. Natural resources: metals, minerals, timber. Exports: $4.15 billion (f.o.b., 1994): machinery and transport equipment, fuels, minerals, raw materials, agricultural products. Imports: $3.98 billion (f.o.b., 1994): machinery and transportation equipment, fuels, raw materials, metals, agricultural raw materials. Major trading partners: C.I.S., U.S., Eastern European countries, EU.

Geography. Two mountain ranges and two great valleys mark the topography of Bulgaria, a country the size of Tennessee. Situated on the Black Sea in the eastern part of the Balkan peninsula, it shares borders with Serbia, Macedonia, Romania, Greece, and Turkey. The Balkan belt crosses the center of the country, almost due east-west, rising to a height of 6,888 feet (2,100 m). The Rhodope, Rila, and Pirin mountains straighten out along the western and southern border. Between the two ranges is the valley of the Maritsa, Bulgaria's principal river. Between the Balkan range and the Danube, which forms most of the northern boundary with Romania, is the Danubian tableland.

Southern Dobruja, a fertile region of 2,900 square miles (7,511 sq km), below the Danube delta, is an area of low hills, fens, and sandy steppes.

Government. An emerging democracy. The National Assembly, consisting of 240 members, is the legislative body. Direct elections for President and Vice President were held in January 1992.

History. The first Bulgarians, a tribe of wild horsemen akin to the Huns, crossed the Danube from the north in A.D. 679 and subjugated the Slavic population of Moesia. They adopted a Slav dialect and Slavic customs and twice conquered most of the Balkan peninsula between 893 and 1280. After the Serbs subjected their kingdom in 1330, the Bulgars gradually fell prey to the Turks, and from 1396 to 1878 Bulgaria was a Turkish province. In 1878, Russia forced Turkey to give the country its independence; but the European powers, fearing that Bulgaria might become a Russian dependency, intervened. By the Treaty of Berlin in 1878, Bulgaria became autonomous under Turkish sovereignty.

In 1887, Prince Ferdinand of Saxe-Coburg-Gotha was elected ruler of Bulgaria; on Oct. 5, 1908, he declared the country independent and took the title of Tsar.

Bulgaria joined Germany in World War I and lost. On Oct. 3, 1918, Tsar Ferdinand abdicated in favor of his son, Tsar Boris III. Boris assumed dictatorial powers in 1934–35. When Hitler awarded Bulgaria southern Dobruja, taken from Romania in 1940, Boris joined the Nazis in war the next year and occupied parts of Yugoslavia and Greece. Later the Germans tried to force Boris to send his troops against the Russians. Boris resisted and died under mysterious circumstances on Aug. 28, 1943. Simeon II, infant son of Boris, became nominal ruler under a regency. Russia declared war on Bulgaria on Sept. 5, 1944. An armistice was agreed to three days later, after Bulgaria had declared war on Germany. Russian troops streamed in the next day and under an informal armistice a coalition "Fatherland Front" cabinet was set up under Kimon Georgiev.

A Soviet-style people's republic was established in 1947 and Bulgaria acquired the reputation of being the most slavishly loyal to Moscow of all the East European Communist countries.

The General Secretary of the Bulgarian Communist Party, Todor Zhikov, resigned in 1989 after 35 years in power. His successor, Peter Mladenov, purged the Politburo, ended the Communist monopoly on power, and held free elections in May 1990 that led to a surprising victory for the Communists, renamed the Bulgarian Socialist Party. Mladenov was forced to resign in July 1990.

Parliamentary elections in October 1991 resulted in a victory for the opposition Union of Democratic Forces. In the presidential election of January 1992 UDF leader Zhelev won 53.5% of the vote.

December 1994 parliamentary elections gave an absolute majority in the Assembly to the Socialists. The economy, however, had deteriorated in recent years amid growing concern over the spread of organized crime.

The government's austerity measures led to demonstrations in May 1996. In June the president lost the presidential primary election to determine the candidate of the anti-Socialist Union of Democratic Forces. The turnout was only 12%.

BURKINA FASO

President: Blaise Compaore (1991)
Prime Minister: Kadre Desire Ouedraogo (1996)
Area: 105,870 sq mi. (274,200 sq km)
Population (est. 1996): 10,623,323 (average annual rate of natural increase: 2.7%); birth rate: 47/1000; infant mortality rate: 117.8/1000; density per sq mile: 100.3
Capital and largest city (est. 1994): Ouagadougou, 500,000. **Monetary unit:** Franc CFA. **Ethnic groups:** Mosse, Gourounsi, Lobi, Fulani, Gourmantche, Senofo, Boussance, Mande. **Languages:** French, tribal languages. **Religions:** Muslim, 50%; Christian (mainly Roman Catholic), 10%; indigenous beliefs, 40%. **National name:** Burkina Faso; **Literacy rate:** 18%
Economic summary: Gross domestic product (1993 est.): $6.5 billion, per capita $660; real growth rate 0.4%; inflation –0.6%; unemployment n.a. Arable land: 10%. Labor force: 3,300,000; in agriculture, 82%. Principal products: millet, sorghum, corn, rice, livestock, peanuts, sugar cane, cotton. Major industrial products: processed agricultural products, light industrial items, brick, brewed products. Natural resources: manganese, limestone, marble, gold, uranium, bauxite, copper. Exports: $273 million (f.o.b., 1993): oilseeds, cotton, live animals, gold. Imports: $636 million (f.o.b., 1993): grain, dairy products, petroleum, machinery. Major trading partners: E.U., Côte d'Ivoire, Africa, Taiwan, Japan.

Geography. Slightly larger than Colorado, Burkina Faso, formerly known as Upper Volta, is a landlocked country in West Africa. Its neighbors are the Ivory Coast, Mali, Niger, Benin, Togo, and Ghana. The country consists of extensive plains, low hills, high savannas, and a desert area in the north.

Government. In June 1991 voters approved a draft constitution providing for three branches of government and presidential elections every seven years. Seventeen political parties are represented in the National Assembly.

History. The country, called Upper Volta by the French, consists chiefly of the lands of the Mossi Empire, where France established a protectorate over the Kingdom of Ouagadougou in 1897. Upper Volta became a separate colony in 1919, was partitioned among Niger, the Sudan, and the Ivory Coast in 1932, and was reconstituted in 1947. An autonomous republic within the French Community, it became independent on Aug. 5, 1960.

President Maurice Yameogo was deposed on Jan. 3, 1966, by a military coup led by Col. Sangoulé Lamizana, who dissolved the National Assembly and suspended the Constitution. Constitutional rule returned in 1978 with the election of an Assembly and a presidential vote in June in which Gen. Lamizana won by a narrow margin over three other candidates.

On Nov. 25, 1980, there was a bloodless coup which placed Gen. Lamizana under house arrest. Col. Sayé Zerbo took charge as the President of the Military Committee of Reform for National Progress. Maj. Jean-Baptiste Ouedraogo toppled Zerbo in another coup on Nov. 7, 1982. Captain Thomas Sankara, in turn, deposed Ouedraogo a year later. His government changed the country's name on Aug. 3, 1984, to Burkina Faso (the "land of upright men") to sever ties with its colonial past. He was overthrown and killed by Blaise Compaore in 1987.

A devaluation of the local currency resulted in the resignation of the then prime minister in early 1994. The National Assembly in July approved legislation furthering the privatization program begun in 1991.

For unstated reasons, Prime Minister Kabore resigned in February 1996, being replaced by a little-known economist, Kadre Desire Ouedraogo.

BURMA

See Myanmar

BURUNDI

Republic of Burundi
President: Major Pierre Buyoya (July 1996)
Prime Minister: Pascal Firmin Ndmira (July 1996)
Area: 10,747 sq mi. (27,834 sq km)
Population (est. 1996): 5,943,057 (average annual rate of natural increase: 2.79%); birth rate: 43/1000; infant mortality rate: 102.2/1000; density per square mile: 553
Capital and largest city (est. 1994): Bujumbura, 300,000; **other large city:** Gitega, 101,827. **Monetary unit:** Burundi franc. **Languages:** Kirundi and French (official), Swahili. **Religions:** Roman Catholic, 62%; Protestant, 5%; indigenous, 32%. **National name:** Republika Y'Uburundi. **Literacy rate:** 50%
Economic summary: Gross domestic product (1994 est.): $3.7 billion, per capita $600; real growth rate –13.5%; inflation 10% (1993 est.). Arable land: 43%; Principal agricultural products: coffee, tea, cotton, bananas, sorghum. Labor force: 1,900,000 (1983 est.); 93% in agriculture. Major industrial products: light consumer goods. Natural resources: nickel, uranium, rare earth oxide, peat, cobalt, copper, unexploited platinum, vanadium. Exports: $40.8 million (f.o.b., 1992 est'): coffee, tea, cotton, hides and skins. Imports: $188 million (c.i.f., 1992 est.): food, petroleum products, capital goods, consumer goods. Major trading partners: U.S., Western Europe, Asia.

Geography. Wedged between Tanzania, Zaire, and Rwanda in east central Africa, Burundi occupies a high plateau divided by several deep valleys. It is equal in size to Maryland.

Government. A republic. Legislative and executive power is vested in the president. A new Constitution adopted by referendum on March 9, 1992, established a multi-party system.

History. Burundi was once part of German East Africa. An integrated society developed among the Watusi, a tall, warlike people and nomad cattle raisers, and the Bahutu, a Bantu people, who were subject farmers. Belgium won a League of Nations mandate in 1923, and subsequently Burundi, with Rwanda, was transferred to the status of a United Nations trust territory.

In 1962, Burundi gained independence and became a kingdom under Mwami Mwambutsa IV. His son deposed him in 1966 to rule as Ntare V. He was overthrown by Premier Micombero.

One of Africa's worst tribal wars, which became genocide, occurred in Burundi in April 1972, following the return of Ntare V. He was given a safe-conduct promise in writing by President Micombero but was "judged and immediately executed" by the Burundi leader. His return was apparently attended by an invasion of exiles of Burundi's Hutu tribe. Whether Hutus living in Burundi joined the invasion is unclear, but after it failed, the victorious Tutsis proceeded to massacre some 100,000 persons in six weeks, with possibly 100,000 more slain by summer.

On Nov. 1, 1976, Lt. Col. Jean-Baptiste Bagaza led a coup and assumed the presidency. He suspended the Constitution and announced that a 30-member Supreme Revolutionary Council would be the governing body.

Bagaza was elected head of the only legal political party in 1979 and was overthrown as party chieftain in 1987.

The Burundi Democracy Front's candidate Melchior Ndadaye won the first democratic presidential elections, held on June 2, 1993.

The presidents of Burundi and Rwanda were killed in a plane crash on April 6, 1994, after their plane had been hit by gunfire or a rocket.

The frequency of ethnic clashes increased, developing into a low-intensity civil war. A six-nation regional proposal to send troops into Burundi to maintain peace and order was devised in July 1996. Distrustful of the scheme, the Tutsi-dominated army led a coup deposing the Hutu President and installed Major Pierre Buyoya, a Tutsi, that month.

CAMBODIA

King: Prince Norodom Sihanouk (1991)
First Prime Minister: Norodom Ranariddh (1994)
Second Prime Minister: Hun Sen (1994)
Area: 69,884 sq mi. (181,035 sq km)
Population (est. mid-1995): 10,600,000 (average annual rate of natural increase: 2.8%); birth rate: 44/1000; infant mortality rate: 108/1000; density per square mile: 151.7
Capital and largest city (est. 1991): Phnom Penh, 900,000. **Monetary unit:** Riel. **Ethnic groups:** Khmer, 90%; Chinese, 5%; other minorities 5%. **Languages:** Khmer (official), French, English. **Religion:** Theravada Buddhist, 5% others. **Literacy rate:** 38%
Economic summary: Gross domestic product (1995 est.): $12 billion, per capita $1,266; real growth rate 4.9%; inflation 18%. Arable land: 16%. Principal agricultural products: rice, rubber, corn. Labor force: 2.5–3.0 million; 80% in agriculture. Major industrial products: fish, wood and wood products, milled rice, rubber, cement. Natural resources: timber, gemstones, iron ore, manganese, phosphate. Exports: $300 million (f.o.b., 1995): natural rubber, rice, pepper, wood. Imports: $560 million (c.i.f., 1995): foodstuffs, fuel, consumer goods. Major trading partners: Vietnam, Japan, India, Singapore, Malaysia, China, Thailand.

Geography. Situated on the Indochinese peninsula, Cambodia is bordered by Thailand and Laos on the north and Vietnam on the east and south. The Gulf of Siam is off the western coast. The country, the size of Missouri, consists chiefly of a large alluvial plain ringed in by mountains and on the east by the Mekong River. The plain is centered on Lake Tonle Sap, which is a natural storage basin of the Mekong.

Government. Constitutional monarchy.

History. Cambodia came under Khmer rule about A.D. 600. Under the Khmers, magnificent temples were built at Angkor. The Khmer kingdom once ruled over most of Southeast Asia, but attacks by the Thai and the Vietnamese almost annihilated the empire until the French joined Cambodia, Laos, and Vietnam into French Indochina.

Under Norodom Sihanouk, enthroned in 1941, and particularly under Japanese occupation during World War II, nationalism revived. After the ouster of the Japanese, the Cambodians sought independence, but the French returned in 1946, granting the country a constitution in 1947 and independence within the French Union in 1949. Sihanouk won full military control during the French-Indochinese War in 1953. He abdicated in 1955 in favor of his parents, remaining head of the government, and when his father died in 1960, became chief of state without returning to the throne. In 1963, he sought a guarantee of Cambodia's neutrality from all parties to the Vietnam War.

On March 18, 1970, while Sihanouk was abroad trying to get North Vietnamese and the Vietcong out of border sanctuaries near Vietnam, anti-Vietnamese riots occurred, and Sihanouk was overthrown.

The Vietnam peace agreement of 1973 stipulated withdrawal of foreign forces from Cambodia, but fighting continued between Hanoi-backed insurgents and U.S.-supplied government troops.

Fighting climaxed in April 1975 when the Lon Nol regime was overthrown by Pol Pot, leader of the communist Khmer Rouge forces.

Between 1975 and 1979, from several hundred to 2 million people were executed by the Khmer Rouge or died under the brutal conditions of forced labor. Border clashes with Vietnam developed into a Vietnamese invasion and Pol Pot was ousted by Vietnamese forces on Jan. 8, 1979, and a new government led by Heng Samrin was installed.

While Sihanouk remained in exile, about 9,000 noncommunist troops loyal to him and another 15,000 under Son Sann joined about 35,000 communist Pol Pot forces fighting the 170,000 Vietnamese troops supporting the Heng Samrin government.

The Vietnamese plan originally called for them to withdraw by early 1990 and negotiate a political settlement. The talks, however, stalled through 1990 on into 1991. In 1992 a UN agreement was signed in Paris under which Prince Sihanouk was to be the leader of a Supreme National Council that was to run the country until free elections in 1993.

Free elections in May 1993 saw the defeat of the ruling party. In June the victors, the royalist opposition, completed a power sharing deal with the ruling party. In September the constitution was changed, restoring the monarchy. Later that month Sihanouk was formally installed.

Stepped-up attacks by the Khmer Rouge in western Cambodia sent 55,000 people fleeing their homes in May 1994. Despite the king's plea for a coalition government that would include the Khmer Rouge, legislation was passed in July outlawing the group.

In 1995 with King Sihanouk ailing, the government pressed ahead with legislation reducing press freedom.

CAMEROON

Republic of Cameroon
President: Paul Biya (1988)
Prime Minister: Simon Achidi Achu (1992)
Area: 183,569 sq mi. (475,442 sq km)
Population (est. 1996): 14,261,557 (average annual rate of natural increase: 2.89%); birth rate: 42.5/1000; infant mortality rate: 78.7/1000; density per sq mile: 77.7
Capital: Yaoundé; **Largest cities (est. 1991):** Douala, 908,000; Yaoundé, 730,000. **Monetary unit:** Franc CFA.
Languages: French and English (both official); 24 major African language groups. **Religions:** 51% indigenous beliefs, 33% Christian, 16% Muslim. **National name:** République du Cameroun. **Literacy rate:** 56.2%

Economic summary: Gross domestic product (1994 est.): $15.7 billion, per capita $1,200; real growth rate –2.9%; inflation, –0.8% (FY91/92)); unemployment, 25% (1990 est.). Arable land: 13%. Agriculture: coffee, cocoa, timber, corn, peanuts, cotton, rubber, bananas, oilseed, grains, livestock, root starches. Labor force in agriculture: 74.4%. Industries: crude oil products, food processing, light consumer goods, textiles, sawmills. Natural resources: timber, some oil, bauxite, hydropower potential. Exports: $1.6 billion (f.o.b., 1993): cocoa, coffee, timber, petroleum, aluminum products. Imports: $1.96 billion (c.i.f., 1993): machines and electrical equipment, transport equipment, consumer goods. Major trading partners: France, U.S., Western European nations, African countries.

Geography. Cameroon is a central African nation on the Gulf of Guinea, bordered by Nigeria, Chad, the Central African Republic, the Congo, Equatorial Guinea, and Gabon. It is nearly twice the size of Oregon.

The interior consists of a high plateau, rising to 4,500 feet (1,372 m), with the land descending to a lower, densely wooded plateau and then to swamps and plains along the coast. Mount Cameroon (13,350 ft.; 4,069 m), near the coast, is the highest elevation in the country. The main rivers are the Benue, Nyong, and Sanaga.

Government. After a 1972 plebiscite, a unitary nation was formed out of East and West Cameroon to replace the former Federal Republic. At present the country is a multiparty democracy with a one-house legislative body, the National Assembly, holding 180 seats.

History. The Republic of Cameroon is inhabited by Hamitic and Semitic peoples in the north, where Islam is the principal religion, and by Bantu peoples in the central and southern regions, where native animism prevails. The tribes were conquered by many invaders.

The land escaped colonial rule until 1884, when treaties with tribal chiefs brought the area under German domination. After World War I, the League of Nations gave the French a mandate over 80% of the area, and the British 20% adjacent to Nigeria. After World War II, when the country came under a U.N. trusteeship in 1946, self-government was granted, and the Cameroun People's Union emerged as the dominant party by campaigning for reunification of French and British Cameroon and for independence. Accused of being under Communist control, it waged a campaign of revolutionary terror from 1955 to 1958, when it was crushed. In British Cameroon, unification was pressed also by the leading party, the Kamerun National Democratic Party, led by John Foncha.

France set up Cameroon as an autonomous state in 1957, and the next year its legislative assembly voted for independence by 1960. In 1959 a fully autonomous government of Cameroon was formed under Ahmadou Ahidjo. Cameroon became an independent republic on Jan. 1, 1960.

Biya won the presidential election in October 1992 but by a narrow margin.

The government convened in mid-1993 a Grand National Debate on Constitutional Reform, which the main opposition party, the Social Democratic Front, declined to attend. Political reform was suspended by the president.

The quarrelling opposition remained split and fragmented in 1995. In November the country was accepted into the Commonwealth of Nations.

CANADA

Sovereign: Queen Elizabeth II (1952)
Governor General: Roméo LeBlanc (1995)
Prime Minister: Jean Chrétien (1993)
Area: 3,851,809 sq mi. (9,976,186 sq km)
Population (est. 1996): 29,857,369. Average annual rate of natural increase: 0.62%; birth rate: 13.3/1000; infant mortality rate: 6.1/1000; density per square mile: 7.5
Capital: Ottawa, Ont.; **Largest cities (1991 census; metropolitan areas):** Toronto, 3,893,046; Montreal, 3,127,242; Vancouver: 1,602,502; Ottawa/Hull, 920,857; Edmonton, 839,924; Calgary, 754,033; Winnipeg, 652,354; Quebec, 645,550; Hamilton, 599,760; London, 381,522; St. Catherines-Niagara, 364,552; **Monetary Unit:** Canadian dollar; **Languages:** English, French; **Religions:** 46% Roman Catholic, 16% United Church, 10% Anglican; **Literacy rate:** 99%
Economic Summary: Gross domestic product (1995): $573.9 billion, per capita $19,215; real growth rate 3%; inflation 0.2% (1994); unemployment 9.5%. Arable land: 7.47%. Principal products: wheat, barley, oats, livestock. Labor force (1995): 14.93 million; 75% in manufacturing. Major industrial products; transportation equipment, petroleum, chemicals, wood products. Exports: $180.3 billion (1995): newsprint, wood pulp, timber, crude petroleum, machinery, natural gas, aluminum, motor vehicles and parts, telecommunications equipment. Imports: $164.6 billion (1995): crude petroleum, chemicals, motor vehicles and parts, durable consumer goods, computers, telecommunications equipment and parts. Major trading partners: U.S., Japan, U.K., C.I.S. nations, Germany, Mexico, South Korea, Taiwan.

Geography. Covering most of the northern part of the North American continent and with an area larger than that of the United States, Canada has an extremely varied topography. In the east the mountainous maritime provinces have an irregular coastline on the Gulf of St. Lawrence and the Atlantic. The St. Lawrence plain, covering most of southern Quebec and Ontario, and the interior continental plain, covering southern Manitoba and Saskatchewan and most of Alberta, are the principal cultivable areas. They are separated by a forested plateau rising from Lakes Superior and Huron.

Population by Provinces and Territories

Province	1996 (April 1)	1991 (Census)
Alberta	2,774,512	2,545,553
British Columbia	3,835,748	3,282,061
Manitoba	1,141,727	1,091,942
New Brunswick	761,873	723,900
Newfoundland	571,192	568,474
Nova Scotia	941,235	899,942
Ontario	11,209,474	10,084,885
Prince Edward Island	137,316	129,765
Quebec	7,366,883	6,895,963
Saskatchewan	1,020,138	988,928
Northwest Territories	66,164	57,649
Yukon Territory	31,107	27,797
Total	**29,857,369.**	**27,296,859**

Source: Statistics Canada.

Westward toward the Pacific, most of British Columbia, Yukon, and part of western Alberta are covered by parallel mountain ranges including the Rockies. The Pacific border of the coast range is ragged with fiords and channels. The highest point in Canada is Mount Logan (19,850 ft; 6,050 m), which is in the Yukon.

Canada has an abundance of large and small lakes. In addition to the Great Lakes on the U.S. border, there are 9 others that are more than 100 miles long (161 km) and 35 that are more than 50 miles long (80 km). The two principal river systems are the Mackenzie and the St. Lawrence. The St. Lawrence, with its tributaries, is navigable for over 1,900 miles (3,058 km).

Government. Canada, a self-governing member of the Commonwealth of Nations, is a federation of 10 provinces (Alberta, British Columbia, Manitoba, New Brunswick, Newfoundland, Nova Scotia, Ontario, Prince Edward Island, Quebec, and Saskatchewan) and two territories (Northwest Territories and Yukon) whose powers were spelled out in the British North America Act of 1867. With the passing of the Constitution Act of 1981, the act and the constitutional amending power were transferred from the British Parliament to Canada so that the Canadian Constitution is now entirely in the hands of the Canadians.

Actually the Governor General acts only with the advice of the Canadian Prime Minister and the Cabinet, who also sit in the federal Parliament. The Parliament has two houses: a Senate of 104 members appointed for life, and a House of Commons of 295 members apportioned according to provincial population. Elections are held at least every five years or whenever the party in power is voted down in the House of Commons or considers it expedient to appeal to the people. The Prime Minister is the leader of the majority party in the House of Commons—or, if no single party holds a majority, the leader of the party able to command the support of a majority of members of the House. Laws must be passed by both houses of Parliament and signed by the Governor General in the Queen's name.

The 10 provincial governments are nominally headed by Lieutenant Governors appointed by the federal government, but the executive power in each actually is vested in a Cabinet headed by a Premier, who is leader of the majority party. The provincial legislatures are composed of one-house assemblies whose members are elected for four-year terms. They are known as Legislative Assemblies, except in Newfoundland, where it is the House of Assembly, and in Quebec, where it is the National Assembly.

The judicial system consists of a Supreme Court in Ottawa (established in 1875), with appellate jurisdiction, and a Supreme Court in each province, as well as county courts with limited jurisdiction in most of the provinces. The Governor General in Council appoints these judges.

History. The Norse explorer Leif Ericson probably reached the shores of Canada (Labrador or Nova Scotia) in A.D. 1000, but the history of the white man in the country actually began in 1497, when John Cabot, an Italian in the service of Henry VII of England, reached Newfoundland or Nova Scotia. Canada was taken for France in 1534 by Jacques Cartier. The actual settlement of New France, as it was then called, began in 1604 at Port Royal in what is now Nova Scotia; in 1608, Quebec was founded. France's colonization efforts were not very successful, but French explorers by the end of the 17th century had pene-

Canadian Governors General and Prime Ministers Since 1867

Term of Office	Governor General	Term	Prime Minister	Party
1867–1868	Viscount Monck[1]	1867–1873	Sir John A. Macdonald	Conservative
1869–1872	Baron Lisgar	1873–1878	Alexander Mackenzie	Liberal
1872–1878	Earl of Dufferin	1878–1891	Sir John A. Macdonald	Conservative
1878–1883	Marquess of Lorne	1891–1892	Sir John J. C. Abbott	Conservative
1883–1888	Marquess of Lansdowne	1892–1894	Sir John S. D. Thompson	Conservative
1888–1893	Baron Stanley of Preston	1894–1896	Sir Mackenzie Bowell	Conservative
1893–1898	Earl of Aberdeen	1896	Sir Charles Tupper	Conservative
1898–1904	Earl of Minto	1896–1911	Sir Wilfrid Laurier	Liberal
1904–1911	Earl Grey	1911–1917	Sir Robert L. Borden	Conservative
1911–1916	Duke of Connaught	1917–1920	Sir Robert L. Borden	Unionist
1916–1921	Duke of Devonshire	1920–1921	Arthur Meighen	Unionist
1921–1926	Baron Byng of Vimy	1921–1926	W. L. Mackenzie King	Liberal
1926–1931	Viscount Willingdon	1926	Arthur Meighen	Conservative
1931–1935	Earl of Bessborough	1926–1930	W. L. Mackenzie King	Liberal
1935–1940	Baron Tweedsmuir	1930–1935	Richard B. Bennett	Conservative
1940–1946	Earl of Athlone	1935–1948	W. L. Mackenzie King	Liberal
1946–1952	Viscount Alexander	1948–1957	Louis S. St. Laurent	Liberal
1952–1959	Vincent Massey	1957–1963	John G. Diefenbaker	Conservative
1959–1967	George P. Vanier	1963–1968	Lester B. Pearson	Liberal
1967–1973	Roland Michener	1968–1979	Pierre Elliott Trudeau	Liberal
1974–1979	Jules Léger	1979–1980	Charles Joseph Clark	Conservative
1979–1984	Edward R. Schreyer	1980–1984	Pierre Elliott Trudeau	Liberal
1984–1990	Jeanne Sauvé	1984–1984	John Turner	Liberal
1990–1995	Raymond John Hnatyshyn	1984–1993	Brian Mulroney	Conservative
1995–	Roméo LeBlanc	1993–1993	Kim Campbell	Conservative
		1993–	Jean Chrétien	Liberal

1. Became Governor General of British North America in 1861.

rated beyond the Great Lakes to the western prairies and south along the Mississippi to the Gulf of Mexico. Meanwhile, the English Hudson's Bay Company had been established in 1670. Because of the valuable fisheries and fur trade, a conflict developed between the French and English; in 1713, Newfoundland, Hudson Bay, and Nova Scotia (Acadia) were lost to England.

During the Seven Years' War (1756–63), England extended its conquest, and the British Maj. Gen. James Wolfe won his famous victory over Gen. Louis Montcalm outside Quebec on Sept. 13, 1759. The Treaty of Paris in 1763 gave England control.

At that time the population of Canada was almost entirely French, but in the next few decades, thousands of British colonists emigrated to Canada from the British Isles and from the American colonies. In 1849, the right of Canada to self-government was recognized. By the British North America Act of 1867, the Dominion of Canada was created through the confederation of Upper and Lower Canada, Nova Scotia, and New Brunswick. Prince Edward Island joined the Dominion in 1873.

In 1869 Canada purchased from the Hudson's Bay Company the vast middle west (Rupert's Land) from which the provinces of Manitoba (1870), Alberta, and Saskatchewan (1905) were later formed. In 1871, British Columbia joined the Dominion. The country was linked from coast to coast in 1885 by the Canadian Pacific Railway.

During the formative years between 1866 and 1896, the Conservative Party, led by Sir John A. Macdonald, governed the country, except during the years 1873–78. In 1896, the Liberal Party took over and, under Sir Wilfrid Laurier, an eminent French Canadian, ruled until 1911.

By the Statute of Westminster in 1931 the British Dominions, including Canada, were formally declared to be partner nations with Britain, "equal in status, in no way subordinate to each other," and bound together only by allegiance to a common Crown.

Newfoundland became Canada's 10th province on March 31, 1949, following a plebiscite. Canada includes two territories—the Yukon Territory, the area north of British Columbia and east of Alaska, and the Northwest Territories, including all of Canada north of 60° north latitude except Yukon and the northernmost sections of Quebec and Newfoundland. This area includes all of the Arctic north of the mainland, Norway having recognized Canadian sovereignty over the Svendrup Islands in the Arctic in 1931.

The Liberal Party, led by William Lyon Mackenzie King, dominated Canadian politics from 1921 until 1957, when it was succeeded by the Progressive Conservatives. The Liberals, under the leadership of Lester B. Pearson, returned to power in 1963. Pearson remained Prime Minister until 1968, when he retired and was replaced by a former law professor, Pierre Elliott Trudeau. Trudeau maintained Canada's defensive alliance with the United States, but began moving toward a more independent policy in world affairs.

Trudeau's election was considered in part a response to the most serious problem confronting the country, the division between French- and English-speaking Canadians, which had led to a separatist movement in the predominantly French province of Quebec. In 1974, the provincial government voted to make French the official language of Quebec.

Despite Trudeau's removal of price and wage controls in 1978, continuing inflation and a high rate of unemployment caused him to delay elections until May 22, 1979. The delay gave Trudeau no advantage—the Progressive Conservatives under Charles Joseph Clark defeated the Liberals everywhere except in Quebec, New Brunswick, and Newfoundland.

His government collapsed after only six months when a motion to defeat the Tory budget carried by 139–133 on Dec. 13, 1979. On the same day, the Quebec law making French the exclusive official language of the province—an issue which had been expected to provide Clark's first major internal test—was voided by the Canadian Supreme Court. In national elections on Feb. 18, 1980, the resurgent Liberals under Trudeau scored an unexpectedly big victory.

Resolving a dispute that had occupied Trudeau since the beginning of his tenure, Queen Elizabeth II, in Ottawa on April 17, 1982, signed the Constitution Act, cutting the last legal tie between Canada and Britain. The Constitution retains Queen Elizabeth as Queen of Canada and keeps Canada's membership in the Commonwealth.

In the national election on Sept. 4, 1984, the Progressive Conservative Party scored an overwhelming victory, fundamentally changing the country's political landscape. The Conservatives, led by Brian Mulroney, a 45-year-old corporate lawyer, won the highest political majority in Canadian history. Mulroney was sworn in as Canada's 18th Prime Minister on Sept. 17.

The dominant foreign issue was a free trade pact with the U.S., a treaty bitterly opposed by the Liberal and New Democratic parties. The conflict led to elections in Nov. 1988 that solidly re-elected Mulroney and gave him a mandate to proceed with the agreement.

The issue of separatist sentiments in French-speaking Quebec flared up again in 1990 with the failure of the Meech Lake accord. The accord was designed to ease the Quebecers' fear of losing their identity within the English-speaking majority by giving Quebec constitutional status as a "distinct society."

In an attempt to keep Canada united, the three major political parties came to an agreement in February 1992 on constitutional reforms. Voters in the Northwest Territories authorized the division of their region in two, creating a homeland for Canadian Eskimos, the Inuits.

Also in 1992 Canada announced its decision to withdraw its combat units from NATO command. The economy continued to be mired in a long recession many blamed on the free trade agreement.

A national referendum was held in October 1992 on the proposal to change the constitution to insure greater representation in parliament for the more populous regions and thereby the French-speaking Quebecers. The referendum, however was defeated.

Brian Mulroney's popularity continued to slump in 1992 and early 1993, leading to his decision to retire prior to the required November election. The governing Progressive Conservative Party chose Defense Minister Kim Campbell as its leader in June, making her the first female prime minister in Canadian history.

The national election in October 1993 resulted in the reemergence of the Liberal Party, which won 177 seats in the House of Commons. The Progressive Conservatives captured but 2 seats, while the Bloc Québécois became the official opposition party.

The Quebec referendum on secession in October 1995 yielded a narrow rejection of the proposal. But the separatists vowed to try again. A controversial gun-control bill successfully passed through the two legislative houses.

CAPE VERDE

Republic of Cape Verde
President: Antonio Mascarenhas Monteiro (1991)
Prime Minister: Carlos Wahnon Veiga (1991)
Area: 1,557 sq mi. (4,033 sq km)

Population: (est. 1996): 449,066 (average annual rate of natural increase: 3.6%); birth rate: 44.3/1000; infant mortality rate: 54.3/1000; density per square mile: 288.4
Capital (1990): Praia 61,797; **Other large city (est. 1982):** Mindelo, 50,000. **Monetary unit:** Cape Verdean escudo. **Language:** Portuguese, Criuolo. **Religion:** Roman Catholic fused with indigenous beliefs. **National name:** República de Cabo Verde. **Literacy rate:** 66%
Economic summary: Gross domestic product (1993 est.): $410 million, per capita $1,000; real growth rate 3.5% (1992); inflation 7% (1992); unemployment 26% (1990). Arable land: 9%. Labor force in agriculture: 57%. Principal agricultural products: bananas, corn, sugar cane, beans. Major industry: fishing, salt mining. Natural resources: salt, siliceous rock. Exports: $4.4 million (f.o.b., 1992 est.): fish, bananas, salt. Imports: $173 million (c.i.f., 1992 est.): petroleum, foodstuffs, consumer goods, industrial products. Major trading partners: Portugal, Angola, Algeria, Italy, Netherlands, Spain, France, U.S., Germany, Sweden.

Geography: Cape Verde, only slightly larger than Rhode Island, is an archipelago in the Atlantic 385 miles (500 km) west of Senegal.

The islands are divided into two groups: Barlavento in the north, comprising Santo Antão (291 sq mi.; 754 sq km), Boa Vista (240 sq mi.; 622 sq km), São Nicolau (132 sq mi.; 342 sq km), São Vicente (88 sq mi.; 246 sq km), Sal (83 sq mi.; 298 sq km), and Santa Luzia (13 sq mi.; 34 sq km); and Sotavento in the south, consisting of São Tiago (383 sq mi.; 992 sq km), Fogo (184 sq mi.; 477 sq km), Maio (103 sq mi.; 267 sq km), and Brava (25 sq mi.; 65 sq km). The islands are mostly mountainous, with the land deeply scarred by erosion. There is an active volcano on Fogo.

Government. The islands became independent on July 5, 1975, under an agreement negotiated with Portugal in 1974. Elections of January 13, 1991, resulted in the ruling African Party for the Independence of Cape Verde losing its majority in the 79-seat parliament. The big winner was the Movement for Democracy, whose candidate, Antonio Monteiro, won the subsequent presidential election on February 17. These were the first free elections since independence in 1975.

History. Uninhabited upon their discovery in 1456, the Cape Verde islands became part of the Portuguese empire in 1495. A majority of their modern inhabitants are of mixed Portuguese and African ancestry.

The former opposition MPD that had won the parliamentary and the presidential elections early in 1991 also won 10 out of 14 councils in the country's first local elections.

The prime minister executed a cabinet reshuffle in January 1995 on the pretext of furthering a shift toward a free-market economy.

CENTRAL AFRICAN REPUBLIC

Head of Government: Gen. André Kolingba (1986)
President: Ange-Félix Patassé (1993)
Prime Minister: Jean-Paul Ngoupande (1996)
Area: 241,313 sq mi. (625,000 sq km)
Population (est. 1996): 3,274,426 (average annual rate of natural increase: 2.23%); birth rate: 39.9/1000; infant mortality rate: 111.7/1000; density per square mile: 13.6

Capital and largest city (1990 est.): Bangui, 706,000.
Monetary unit: Franc CFA. **Ethnic groups:** Baya, Banda, Sara, Mandjia, Mboum, M'Baka, 6,500 Europeans.
Languages: French (official), Sangho, Arabic, Hansa, Swahili. **Religions:** 24% indigenous beliefs, 50% Protestant and Roman Catholic with animist influence, 15% Muslim, 11% other. **National name:** République Centrafricaine. **Literacy rate:** 33%
Economic summary: Gross domestic product (1994 est.): $2.2 billion, per capita $700; real growth rate 5.5%; inflation 40%; unemployment n.a. Arable land: 3%. Principal products: cotton, coffee, peanuts, food crops, livestock. Labor force (1986 est.): 775,413; 85% in agriculture. Major industrial products: timber, textiles, soap, cigarettes, diamonds, processed food, brewed beverages. Natural resources: diamonds, uranium, timber. Exports: $123.5 million (f.o.b., 1992): diamonds, cotton, timber, coffee, tobacco. Imports: $165.1 million (f.o.b., 1992): machinery and electrical equipment, petroleum products, textiles, food, motor vehicles, chemicals, pharmaceuticals, consumer goods, industrial products. Major trading partners: France, Belgium, Italy, Japan, U.S., Western Europe, Algeria.

Geography. Situated about 500 miles north (805 km) of the equator, the Central African Republic is a landlocked nation bordered by Cameroon, Chad, the Sudan, Zaire, and the Congo. Twice the size of New Mexico, it is covered by tropical forests in the south and semidesert land in the east. The Ubangi and Shari are the largest of many rivers.

Government. The Central African Republic has been ruled since 1981 by General André Kolingba who came to power in a bloodless coup and was elected to a six-year term as President in 1986. A constitution was adopted on November 21, 1987, establishing a unicameral National Assembly. The following year the Central African Democracy Party (R.D.C.) was formed as the only political party. Since April 1991 other political parties legally registered by the Ministry of the Interior are allowed to compete for legislative and presidential elections, and presidential and legislative elections were held in September 1993.

History. As the colony of Ubangi-Shari, what is now the Central African Republic was united with Chad in 1905 and joined with Gabon and the Middle Congo in French Equatorial Africa in 1910. After World War II a rebellion in 1946 forced the French to grant self-government. In 1958 the territory voted to become an autonomous republic within the French Community, but on Aug. 13, 1960, President David Dacko proclaimed the republic's independence from France.

Dacko undertook to move the country into Peking's orbit, but was overthrown in a coup on Dec. 31, 1965, by the then Col. Jean-Bédel Bokassa, Army Chief of Staff.

On Dec. 4, 1976, the Central African Republic became the Central African Empire. Marshal Jean-Bédel Bokassa, who had ruled the republic since he took power in 1965, was declared Emperor Bokassa I. He was overthrown in a coup on Sept. 20, 1979. Former President David Dacko returned to power and changed the country's name back to the Central African Republic. An army coup on Sept. 1, 1981, deposed President Dacko again.

Although President Kolingba in 1991, under pressure, announced a move toward multi-party democracy no specifics were given, leading to further civil unrest.

Elections in August 1993 saw the defeat of Kolingba. Former prime minister Patassé won the presiden-

cy in the second round. Kolingba attempted to thwart the process but protests and opposition from France obstructed his maneuvers.

Although voters approved a referendum on a new constitution in December 1994, the turnout was relatively low. Rather than face a vote of no-confidence, the prime minister resigned in April 1995. His replacement promised an offensive against corruption.

CHAD

Republic of Chad
President: Gen. Idriss Deby (1991)
Prime Minister: Mr. Koibla Djimasta (1995)
Area: 495,752 sq mi. (1,284,000 sq km)
Population (est. 1996): 6,976,845 (average annual rate of natural increase, 2.7%); birth rate: 44.3/1000; infant mortality rate: 120.4/1000; density per square mile: 14
Capital and largest city (1993): N'Djamena, 529,555.
Monetary unit: Franc CFA. **Ethnic groups:** Baguirmiens, Kanembous, Saras, Massas, Arabs, Toubous, others. **Languages:** French and Arabic (official), many tribal languages. **Religions:** Islam, 44%; Christian, 33%; traditional, 23%. **National name:** République du Tchad; **Literacy rate:** 17%
Economic summary: Gross domestic product (1993): $2.8 billion, per capita $530; real growth rate 3.5%; inflation –4.1% (1992). Arable land: 2%; principal agricultural products: cotton, cattle, sugar, subsistence crops. Labor force in agriculture: 85%. Major products: livestock and livestock products, beer, food processing, textiles, cigarettes. Natural resources: petroleum, unexploited uranium, kaolin. Exports: $190 million (f.o.b.; 1992): cotton, livestock and animal products, fish, textiles. Imports: $261 million (f.o.b., 1992): machinery and transportation equipment, industrial goods, petroleum products, foodstuffs. Major trading partners: France, Nigeria, U.S., Cameroon.

Geography. A landlocked country in north central Africa, Chad is about 85% the size of Alaska. Its neighbors are Niger, Libya, the Sudan, the Central African Republic, Cameroon, and Nigeria. Lake Chad, from which the country gets its name, lies on the western border with Niger and Nigeria. In the north is a desert that runs into the Sahara.

Government. Hissen Habré was overthrown by Col. Idriss Deby in December 1990. A transitional government mandate expired April 1996.

History. Chad was absorbed into the colony of French Equatorial Africa, as part of Ubangi-Shari, in 1910. France began the country's development after 1920, when it became a separate colony. In 1946, French Equatorial Africa was admitted to the French Union. By referendum in 1958 the Chad territory became an autonomous republic within the French Union.

A movement led by the first Premier and President, François (later Ngarta) Tombalbaye, achieved complete independence on Aug. 11, 1960.

Tombalbaye was killed in the 1975 coup and was succeeded by Gen. Félix Malloum, who faced a Libyan-financed rebel movement throughout his tenure in office. A ceasefire backed by Libya, Niger, and the Sudan early in 1978 failed to end the fighting.

Nine rival groups meeting in Lagos, Nigeria, in March 1979 agreed to form a provisional government headed by Goukouni Oueddei, a former rebel leader. Fighting broke out again in Chad in March 1980, when Defense Minister Hissen Habré challenged Goukouni and seized the capital. By the year's end, Libyan troops supporting Goukouni recaptured N'djamena, and Libyan President Muammar el-Qaddafi, in January 1981, proposed a merger of Chad with Libya.

The Libyan proposal was rejected and Libyan troops withdrew from Chad but in 1983 poured back into the northern part of the country in support of Goukouni. France, in turn, sent troops into southern Chad in support of Habré.

Government troops then launched an offensive in early 1987 that drove the Libyans out of most of the country.

After the overthrow of Habré's government, Deby, a former defense minister, declared himself president, dissolved the legislature (elected the previous July), and suspended the constitution.

A national conference, convened in January 1993, was suspended after only 4 days. The reconvened conference in October elected Koumakoye prime minister.

A national legislature postponed the return to complete democracy in March 1995. In April it removed the prime minister and elected a replacement.

CHILE

Republic of Chile
President: Eduardo Frei Ruiz-Tagle (1994)
Area: 292,132 sq mi. (756,622 sq km)
Population (est. 1996): 14,333,258 (average annual rate of natural increase: 1.24%); birth rate: 18/1000; infant mortality rate: 13.6/1000; density per square mile: 49
Capital and largest city (1993 est.): Santiago, 4,628,320.
Other large cities (1993 est.): Valparaiso, 301,677; Concepción, 318,140; Viña del Mar, 319,440; Temuco, 262,624; Talcahuano, 257,767. **Monetary unit:** Peso.
Language: Spanish. **Religion:** Roman Catholic, 89%; Protestant, 11%; small Jewish and Muslim populations.. **National name:** República de Chile. **Literacy rate:** 94%
Economic summary: Gross domestic product (1995): $57 billion; $4,000 per capita; 8.5% real growth rate; inflation 8.2%; unemployment 5.4. Arable land: 7%. Principal agricultural products: wheat, corn, sugar beets, vegetables, wine, livestock. Labor force: 5,273,900, 31.3% in industry. Major industrial products: processed fish, iron and steel, pulp, paper, furniture, apparel, processed food. Natural resources: copper, gold, timber, fruits and vegetables, nitrates, iron. Exports: $16.03 billion (f.o.b., 1995): copper, bleached pulp, fishmeal, fresh fruit and timber, seafood, frozen and canned fruits, wine. Imports: $14.63 billion (c.i.f., 1995): oil, vehicles, computers, industrial machinery, electric and electronic equipment, chemicals. Major trading partners: U.S., Japan, European Union, Brazil, Argentina, Germany, South Korea, U.K.

Geography. Situated south of Peru and west of Bolivia and Argentina, Chile fills a narrow 1,800-mile (2,897 km) strip between the Andes and the Pacific. Its area is nearly twice that of Montana.

One third of Chile is covered by the towering ranges of the Andes. In the north is the mineral-rich Atacama Desert, between the coastal mountains and the Andes. In the center is a 700-mile-long (1,127 km) valley, thickly populated, between the Andes and the coastal plateau. In the south, the Andes border on the ocean.

At the southern tip of Chile's mainland is Punta Arenas, the southernmost city in the world, and beyond that lies the Strait of Magellan and Tierra del Fuego, an island divided between Chile and Argentina. The southernmost point of South America is Cape Horn, a 1,390-foot (424-m) rock on Horn Island in the Wollaston group, which belongs to Chile. Chile also claims sovereignty over 482,628 sq mi (1,250,000 sq km) of Antarctic territory.

The Juan Fernández Islands, in the South Pacific about 400 miles (644 km) west of the mainland, and Easter Island, about 2,000 miles (3,219 km) west, are Chilean possessions.

Government. The President serves a six-year term (with the exception of the 1990–1994 term). There is a bicameral legislature, the National Congress.

History. Chile was originally under the control of the Incas in the north and the fierce Araucanian people in the south. In 1541, a Spaniard, Pedro de Valdivia, founded Santiago. Chile won its independence from Spain in 1818 under Bernardo O'Higgins and an Argentinian, José de San Martin. O'Higgins, dictator until 1823, laid the foundations of the modern state with a two-party system and a centralized government.

The dictator from 1830 to 1837, Diego Portales, fought a war with Peru in 1836–39 that expanded Chilean territory. The Conservatives were in power from 1831 to 1861. Then the Liberals, winning a share of power for the next 30 years, disestablished the church and limited presidential power. Chile fought the War of the Pacific with Peru and Bolivia from 1879 to 1883, winning Antofagasta, Bolivia's only outlet to the sea, and extensive areas from Peru. A revolt in 1890 led by Jorge Montt overthrew, in 1891, José Balmaceda and established a parliamentary dictatorship that existed until a new constitution was adopted in 1925. Industrialization began before World War I and led to the formation of Marxist groups.

Juan Antonio Ríos, President during World War II, was originally pro-Nazi but in 1944 led his country into the war on the side of the U.S.

A small abortive army uprising in 1969 raised fear of military intervention to prevent a Marxist, Salvador Allende Gossens, from taking office after his election to the presidency on Sept. 4, 1970. Dr. Allende was the first president in a non-Communist country freely elected on a Marxist-Leninist program.

Allende quickly established relations with Cuba and the People's Republic of China and nationalized several American companies.

Allende's overthrow and death in an army assault on the presidential palace in September 1973 ended a 46-year era of constitutional government in Chile.

The takeover was led by a four-man junta headed by Army Chief of Staff Augusto Pinochet Ugarte, who assumed the office of President.

Committed to "exterminate Marxism," the junta embarked on a right-wing dictatorship. It suspended parliament, banned political activity, and broke relations with Cuba.

In 1977, Pinochet, in a speech marking his fourth year in power, promised elections by 1985 if conditions warranted. Earlier, he had abolished DINA, the secret police, and decreed an amnesty for political prisoners.

Pinochet was inaugurated on March 11, 1981, for an eight-year term as President, at the end of which, according to the constitution adopted six months earlier, the junta would nominate a civilian as successor. He stepped down in January 1990 in favor of Patricio Aylwin who was elected Dec. 1989 as the head of a 17-party coalition.

The presidential election of December 1993 saw the reemergence of a member of the Frei family. Eduardo Frei, the candidate of a center-left coalition, won. His father had been president from 1964–70.

The Supreme Court in May 1995 upheld the convictions of a former head of the secret police and a deputy during the Pinochet years. Also that month the minimum wage was raised by almost 13%.

CHINA

People's Republic of China
President: Jiang Zemin (1993)
Premier: Li Peng (1987)
Area: 3,691,521 sq mi. (9,561,000 sq km)[1]
Population (est. 1996): 1,210,004,956 (average rate of natural increase: 1.01%); birth rate: 17/1000; infant mortality rate: 39.6/1000; density per square mile: 327.8 China has 56 ethnic groups. In 1991, the Han people accounted for 92% of the population.
Capital: Beijing; **Largest cities (est. 1991):** Shanghai, 7,500,000; Beijing (Peking) 5,700,000; Tianjin (Tientsin) 4,575,000; Canton, 2,914,000; Wuhan, 3,284,200; Shenyang (Mukden), 3,604,000; Nanjing (Nanking), 2,100,000; Chongqing (Chongking), 2,267,000; Harbin, 2,443,400.
Monetary unit: Yuan. **Languages:** Chinese, Mandarin, also local dialects. **Religions:** Officially atheist but traditional religion contains elements of Confucianism, Taoism, Buddhism. **National name:** Zhonghua Renmin Gongheguo. **Literacy rate:** 78%
Economic summary: Gross domestic product (1994, extrapolated from U.N., World Bank 1992 est.): $2.9788 trillion; $2,500 per capita; 11.8% real growth rate; inflation rate (Dec. 1994 over Dec. 1993): 25.5%; unemployment rate in urban areas: 2.7%. Arable land: 10%. Principal agricultural products: rice, wheat, grains, cotton. Labor force: 567,400,000; 60% in agriculture and forestry, 25% in industry and commerce. Major industrial products: iron and steel, textiles, armaments, petroleum. Natural resources: coal, natural gas, limestone, marble, metals, hydropower potential. Exports: $121 billion (f.o.b., 1994): textiles, garments, footwear, toys, machinery and equipment, weapon systems. Imports: $115.7 billion (c.i.f., 1994): rolled steel, motor vehicles, textile machinery, oil products, aircraft. Major trading partners: Japan, Hong Kong, U.S., Germany, Taiwan and Macao, Russia.

1. Including Manchuria and Tibet.

Geography. China, which occupies the eastern part of Asia, is slightly larger in area than the U.S. Its coastline is roughly a semicircle. The greater part of the country is mountainous, and only in the lower reaches of the Yellow and Yangtze Rivers are there extensive low plains.

The principal mountain ranges are the Tien Shan, to the northwest; the Kunlun chain, running south of the Taklimakan and Gobi Deserts; and the Trans-Himalaya, connecting the Kunlun with the borders of China and Tibet. Manchuria is largely an undulating plain connected with the north China plain by a narrow lowland corridor. Inner Mongolia contains the relatively fertile southern and eastern portions of the Gobi. The large island of Hainan (13,200 sq mi.; 34,300 sq km) lies off the southern coast.

Hydrographically, China proper consists of three great river systems. The northern part of the country is drained by the Yellow River (Huang Ho), 2,109 miles long (5,464 km) and mostly unnavigable. The central part is drained by the Chang Jiang (Yangtze

Kiang), the third longest river in the world 2,432 miles (6,300 km). The Zhujiang (Si Kiang) in the south is 848 miles long (2,197 km) and navigable for a considerable distance. In addition, the Amur (1,144 sq mi.; 2,965 km) forms part of the northeastern boundary.

Government. With 2,978 deputies, elected for four-year terms by universal suffrage, the National People's Congress is the chief legislative organ. A State Council has the executive authority. The Congress elects the Premier and Deputy Premiers. All ministries are under the State Council, headed by the Premier. The Communist Party controls the government.

History. By 2000 B.C. the Chinese were living in the Huang Ho basin, and they had achieved an advanced stage of civilization by 1200 B.C. The great philosophers Lao-tse, Confucius Mo Ti, and Mencius lived during the Chou dynasty (1122–249 B.C.). The warring feudal states were first united under Emperor Ch'in Shih Huang Ti, during whose reign (246–210 B.C.) work was begun on the Great Wall. Under the Han dynasty (206 B.C.–A.D. 220), China prospered and traded with the West.

In the T'ang dynasty (618–907), often called the golden age of Chinese history, painting, sculpture, and poetry flourished, and printing made its earliest known appearance.

The Mings, last of the native rulers (1368–1644), overthrew the Mongol, or Yuan, dynasty (1280–1368) established by Kublai Khan. The Mings in turn were overthrown in 1644 by invaders from the north, the Manchus.

China closely restricted foreign activities, and by the end of the 18th century only Canton and the Portuguese port of Macao were open to European merchants. Following the Anglo-Chinese War of 1839–42, however, several treaty ports were opened, and Hong Kong was ceded to Britain. Treaties signed after further hostilities (1856–60) weakened Chinese sovereignty and removed foreigners from Chinese jurisdiction. The disastrous Chinese-Japanese War of 1894–95 was followed by a scramble for Chinese concessions by European powers, leading to the Boxer Rebellion (1900), suppressed by an international force.

The death of the Empress Dowager Tzu Hsi in 1908 and the accession of the infant Emperor Hsüan T'ung (Pu-Yi) were followed by a nation-wide rebellion led by Dr. Sun Yat-sen, who became first President of the Provisional Chinese Republic in 1911. The Manchus abdicated on Feb. 12, 1912. Dr. Sun resigned in favor of Yuan Shih-k'ai, who suppressed the republicans but was forced by a serious rising in 1915–16 to abandon his intention of declaring himself Emperor. Yuan's death in June 1916 was followed by years of civil war between rival militarists and Dr. Sun's republicans.

Nationalist forces, led by Gen. Chiang Kai-shek and with the advice of Communist experts, soon occupied most of China, setting up a Kuomintang regime in 1928. Internal strife continued, however, and Chiang broke with the Communists.

An alleged explosion on the South Manchurian Railway on Sept. 18, 1931, brought invasion of Manchuria by Japanese forces, who installed the last Manchu Emperor, Henry Pu-Yi, as nominal ruler of the puppet state of "Manchukuo." Japanese efforts to take China's northern provinces in July 1937 were resisted by Chiang, who meanwhile had succeeded in uniting most of China behind him. Within two years, however, Japan seized most of the ports and railways. The Kuomintang government retreated first to Han-

Provinces and Regions of China

Name	Area (sq mi.)	Area (sq km)	Capital
Provinces			
Anhui (Anhwei)	54,015	139,900	Hefei (Hofei)
Fujian (Fukien)	47,529	123,100	Fuzhou (Fukien)
Gansu (Kansu)	137,104	355,100	Lanzhou (Lanchow)
Guangdong (Kwangtung)	76,100	197,100	Canton
Guizhou (Kweichow)	67,181	174,000	Guiyang (Kweiyang)
Hainan	13,200	34,300	Haikou
Hebei (Hopei)	81,479	211,030	Shijiazhuang (Shitikiachwang)
Heilongjiang (Heilungkiang)[1]	178,996	463,600	Harbin
Henan (Honan)	64,479	167,000	Zhengzhou (Chengchow)
Hubei (Hupeh)	72,394	187,500	Wuhan
Hunan	81,274	210,500	Changsha
Jiangsu (Kiangsu)	40,927	106,000	Nanjing (Nanking)
Jiangxi (Kiangsi)	63,629	164,800	Nanchang
Jilin (Kirin)[1]	72,201	187,000	Changchun
Liaoning[1]	53,301	138,050	Shenyang
Quinghai (Chinghai)	278,378	721,000	Xining (Sining)
Shaanxi (Shensi)	75,598	195,800	Xian (Sian)
Shandong (Shantung)	59,189	153,300	Jinan (Tsinan)
Shanxi (Shansi)	60,656	157,100	Taiyuan
Sichuan (Szechwan)	219,691	569,000	Chengdu (Chengtu)
Yunnan	168,417	436,200	Kunming
Zhejiang (Chekiang)	39,305	101,800	Hangzhou (Hangchow)
Autonomous Regions			
Guangxi Zhuang (Kwangsi Chuang)	85,096	220,400	Nanning
Nei Monggol (Inner Mongolia)[1]	454,633	1,177,500	Hohhot (Huhehot)
Ningxia Hui	30,039	77,800	Yinchuan (Yinchwan)
Xinjiang Uygur (Sinkiang Uighur)[1]	635,829	1,646,800	Urumqi (Urumchi)
Xizang (Tibet)	471,660	1,221,600	Lhasa

1. Together constitute (with Taiwan) what has been traditionally known as Outer China, the remaining territory forming the historical China Proper. NOTE: Names are in Pinyin, with conventional spelling in parentheses.

kow and then to Chungking, while the Japanese set up a puppet government at Nanking headed by Wang Jingwei.

Japan's surrender in 1945 touched off civil war between Nationalist forces under Chiang and Communist forces led by Mao Zedong, the party chairman. Despite U.S. aid, the Chiang forces were overcome by the Maoists, backed by the Soviet bloc, and were expelled from the mainland. The Mao regime, established in Peking as the new capital, proclaimed the People's Republic of China on Oct. 1, 1949, with Zhou Enlai as Premier.

After the Korean War began in June 1950, China led the Communist bloc in supporting North Korea, and on Nov. 26, 1950, the Mao regime intervened openly.

In 1958, Mao undertook the "Great Leap Forward" campaign, which combined the establishment of rural communes with a crash program of village industrialization, but it failed and was abandoned.

China exploded its first atomic (fission) bomb in 1964 and produced a fusion bomb in 1967.

Mao moved to Shanghai, and from that base he and his supporters waged what they called a Cultural Revolution. In the spring of 1966 the Mao group formed Red Guard units dominated by youths and students, closing the schools to free the students for agitation.

The Red Guards campaigned against "old ideas, old culture, old habits, and old customs." Often they were no more than uncontrolled mobs, and brutality was frequent. Early in 1967 efforts were made to restore control. The Red Guards were urged to return home. Schools started opening.

Persistent overtures by the Nixon Administration resulted in the dramatic announcement in July that Henry Kissinger, President Richard M. Nixon's national security adviser, had secretly visited Peking and reached agreement on a visit by the President to China.

The movement toward reconciliation, which signaled the end of the U.S. containment policy toward China, provided irresistible momentum for Chinese admission to the U.N. Despite U.S. opposition to expelling Taiwan (Nationalist China), the world body overwhelmingly ousted Chiang in seating Peking.

President Nixon went to Peking for a week early in 1972, meeting Mao as well as Zhou. The summit ended with a historic communiqué on February 28, in which both nations promised to work toward improved relations. Full diplomatic relations were barred by China as long as the U.S. continued to recognize Nationalist China.

On Jan. 8, 1976, Zhou died. His successor, Vice Premier Deng Xiaoping was supplanted within a month by Hua Guofeng, former Minister of Public Security. Hua became permanent Premier in April. In October he was named successor to Mao as Chairman of the Communist Party.

After Mao died on Sept. 10, a campaign against his widow, Jiang Qing, and three of her "radical" colleagues began. The "Gang of Four" was denounced for having undermined the party, the government, and the economy. They were tried and convicted in 1981.

At the Central Committee meeting of 1977, Deng was reinstated as Deputy Premier, Chief of Staff of the Army, and member of the Central Committee of the Politburo.

At the same time, Jiang Qing, Wang Hongwen, Zhang Chunqiao, and Yao Wenyuan—the notorious "Gang of Four"—were removed from all official posts and banished from the party.

In May 1978, expulsion of ethnic Chinese by Vietnam produced an open rupture. Peking sided with Cambodia in the border fighting that flared between Vietnam and Cambodia, charging Hanoi with aggression.

Peking and Washington announced that they would open full diplomatic relations on Jan. 1, 1979, and the Carter Administration abrogated the Taiwan defense treaty. Deputy Premier Deng sealed the agreement with a visit to the U.S. that coincided with the opening of embassies in both capitals on March 1.

On Deng's return from the U.S. Chinese troops invaded Vietnam to avenge alleged violations of Chinese territory. The action was seen as a reaction to Vietnam's invasion of Cambodia.

After the Central Committee meeting of June 27–29, 1981, Hu Yaobang, a Deng protégé, was elevated to the party chairmanship, replacing Hua Guofeng. Deng became chairman of the military commission of the central committee, giving him control over the army. The committee's 215 members concluded the session with a statement holding Mao Zedong responsible for the "grave blunder" of the Cultural Revolution.

Under Deng Xiaoping's leadership, meanwhile, China's Communist idealogy was almost totally reinterpreted and sweeping economic changes were set in motion in the early 1980s. The Chinese scrapped the personality cult that idolized Mao Zedong, muted Mao's old call for class struggle and exportation of the Communist revolution, and imported Western technology and management techniques to replace the Marxist tenets that retarded modernization.

Also under Deng's leadership, the Chinese Communists worked out an arrangement with Britain for the future of Hong Kong after 1997. The flag of China will be raised but the territory will retain its present social, economic and legal system.

The removal of Hu Yaobang as party chairman in January 1987 was a sign of a hard-line resurgence. He was replaced by former Premier Zhao Ziyang. Conflict between hard-liners and moderates continued and reached a violent climax in 1989. Student demonstrations calling for accelerated liberalization were crushed by military force in June, resulting in several hundred deaths.

The rubber-stamp National People's Congress concluded its April 1992 session with a call to guard against "leftism," widely interpreted as a sign of consolidation and a call for accelerating the drive for economic reform. Nevertheless, several hard-liners remained in their conspicuous positions.

China settled its long-running feud with Vietnam and normalized its relations with Japan during 1991.

The annual session of the National People's Congress in March 1993 was widely seen as an effort by Deng Xiaoping, the paramount leader, to maintain China's moves toward a market economy while retaining political authoritarianism. Communist Party leader Jiang Zemin was elected president, while hard-liner Li Peng was reelected to another five-year term as prime minister despite, or perhaps because of, his politics.

The economy continued to grow rapidly in 1993. In November the Central Committee adopted a resolution envisaging the conversion of state-owned enterprises into joint-stock companies, the creation of a central bank and modern tax system.

Despite its intense efforts to intimidate Taiwan's voters in the island's first free presidential election in 1996, China was rebuked, while the U.S. Navy took a studied approach to Chinese actions.

COLOMBIA

Republic of Colombia

President: Ernesto Samper Pizano (1994)
Area: 439,735 sq mi. (1,138,910 sq km)
Population (est. 1996): 36,813,161 (average annual rate of natural increase, 1.67%); birth rate: 21.3/1000; infant mortality rate: 25.8/1000; density per square mile: 83.7
Capital and largest city (1995 est.): Santafé de Bogotá, 5,025,989. **Largest cities (1995 est.):** Cali, 1,718,871; Medellín, 1,621,356; Barranquilla, 1,064,255; Cartagena, 745,689. **Monetary unit:** Peso. **Language:** Spanish. **Religion:** 95% Roman Catholic. **National name:** República de Colombia. **Literacy rate:** 91.3
Economic summary: Gross domestic product (1994 est.): $172.4 billion, per capita $4,850; est. real growth rate 5.7%; inflation 22.6%; unemployment 7.9%. Arable land: 4%. Principal agricultural products: coffee, bananas, rice, corn, sugar cane, cotton, tobacco, oilseeds, fresh cut flowers. Labor force (1990): 12,000,000; 46% in services, 30% agriculture, 24% industry. Major industrial products: textiles, processed food, beverages, chemicals, cement. Natural resources: petroleum, natural gas, coal, iron ore, nickel, gold, copper, emeralds. Exports: $8.5 billion (f.o.b., 1994 est.): coffee, fuel oil, coal, bananas, fresh cut flowers, nickel, chemicals, emeralds. Imports: $10.9 billion (f.o.b., 1994 est.): machinery, paper products, aircraft, telecommunications equipment, vehicles, gasoline, wheat. Major trading partners: U.S., E.U., Japan, Venezuela, Brazil.

Geography. Colombia, in the northwestern part of South America, is the only country on that continent that borders on both the Atlantic and Pacific Oceans. It is nearly equal to the combined areas of California and Texas.

Through the western half of the country, three Andean ranges run north and south, merging into one at the Ecuadorean border. The eastern half is a low, jungle-covered plain, drained by spurs of the Amazon and Orinoco, inhabited mostly by isolated, tropical-forest Indian tribes. The fertile plateau and valley of the eastern range are the most densely populated parts of the country.

Government. Colombia's President, who appoints his own Cabinet, serves for a four-year term. The Senate, the upper house of Congress, has 102 members elected for four years by direct vote. The House of Representatives of 165 members is directly elected for four years. Mayors and state governors are also elected by direct vote for three-year terms.

History. Spaniards in 1510 founded Darien, the first permanent European settlement on the American mainland. In 1538 the Spaniards established the colony of New Granada, the area's name until 1861. After a 14-year struggle, in which Simón Bolívar's Venezuelan troops won the battle of Boyacá in Colombia on Aug. 7, 1819, independence was attained in 1824. Bolívar united Colombia, Venezuela, Panama, and Ecuador in the Republic of Greater Colombia (1819–30), but lost Venezuela and Ecuador to separatists. Bolívar's Vice President, Francisco de Paula Santander, founded the Liberal Party as the Federalists while Bolívar established the Conservatives as the Centralists.

Santander's presidency (1832–36) re-established order, but later periods of Liberal dominance (1849–57 and 1861–80), when the Liberals sought to disestablish the Roman Catholic Church, were marked by insurrection and even civil war. Rafael Nuñez, in a 15-year-presidency, restored the power of the central government and the church, which led in 1899 to a bloody civil war and the loss in 1903 of Panama over ratification of a lease to the U.S. of the Canal Zone. For 21 years, until 1930, the Conservatives held power as revolutionary pressures built up.

The Liberal administrations of Enrique Olaya Herrera and Alfonso López (1930–38) were marked by social reforms that failed to solve the country's problems, and in 1946, insurrection and banditry broke out, claiming hundreds of thousands of lives by 1958. Laureano Gómez (1950–53), the Army Chief of Staff, Gen. Gustavo Rojas Pinilla (1953–56), and a military junta (1956–57) sought to curb disorder by repression.

The Liberals won a solid majority in 1982, but a party split enabled Belisario Betancur Cuartas, the Conservative candidate, to win the presidency on May 31. After his inauguration, he ended the state of siege that had existed almost continuously for 34 years and renewed the general amnesty of 1981.

In an official war against drug trafficking Colombia became a public battleground with bombs, killings, and kidnapping. In 1989 a leading presidential candidate, Luis Carlos Galán, was murdered. In an effort to quell the terror President Gaviria proposed lenient punishment in exchange for surrender by the leading drug dealers. In addition in 1991 the constitutional convention voted to ban extradition.

A new constitution adopted in July 1991 provided for direct election of the state governors.

In the country's closest presidential contest in 24 years Mr. Samper, the candidate of the Liberal Party, won 50% of the vote in June 1994.

Amid allegations of having accepted campaign contributions from drug traffickers, Samper in May 1996 ordered emergency security measures in southern Colombia to fight leftist rebels. In June the House of Representatives absolved him of the charges by a 111–to–43 vote. A number of members of Congress remain under investigation.

COMOROS

Federal Islamic Republic of the Comoros
President: Mohamed Taki Abdoulkarim (1996)
Prime Minister: Tajiddine Ben Said Massonde (1996)
Area: 690 sq mi. (1,787 sq km)
Population (est. 1996): 569,237 (average annual rate of natural increase: 3.5%); birth rate: 45.8/1000; infant mortality rate: 75.3/1000; density per square mile: 825
Capital and largest city (est. 1990): Moroni (on Grande Comoro), 23,432 **Monetary unit:** Franc CFA. **Languages:** Shaafi Islam (Swahili dialect), Malagasu, French, Arabic. **Religions:** Sunni Muslim, 86%; Roman Catholic, 14%. **National name:** République Fédéral Islamique des Comores. **Literacy rate:** 48%
Economic summary: Gross domestic product (1994 est.): $370 million; $700 per capita; real growth rate 0.9%; inflation 15% (1993 est.); unemployment (1989): over 15.9%. Arable land: 35%. Labor force: 140,000 (1982); 80% in agriculture. Principal agricultural products: perfume essences, copra, coconuts, cloves, vanilla, cassava, bananas. Major industrial products: perfume distillations. Exports: $13.7 million (f.o.b., 1993 est.): perfume essences, vanilla, copra, cloves. Imports: $40.9 million (f.o.b., 1993 est.): foodstuffs, cement, petroleum products, consumer goods. Major trading partners: France, Germany, U.S., Africa, Pakistan, China.

Geography. The Comoros Islands—Grande Comoro, Anjouan, Mohéli, and Mayotte (which retains ties to France)—are an archipelago of volcanic origin in the Indian Ocean between Mozambique and Madagascar.

Government. Democratic elections were held in March 1990. The interim president Said Djohar, won from among a field of eight candidates. The constitution dates from October 1, 1978, and the country is an Islamic republic with a 42-member unicameral legislature.

History. Under French rule since 1886, the Comoros declared themselves independent July 6, 1975. However, Mayotte, with a Christian majority, voted against joining the other, mainly Islamic, islands in the move to independence and remains French.

A month after independence, Justice Minister Ali Soilih staged a coup with the help of mercenaries, overthrowing the new nation's first president, Ahmed Abdallah. He was overthrown on May 13, 1978.

Voters approved a new constitution in a referendum of June 1992.

In June 1993 the president dissolved the Federal Assembly, appointing an interim prime minister. Amid widespread irregularities the president's supporters won 50% of the seats in the Assembly.

An attempted coup in September 1995 was suppressed with the aid of French forces. When the ailing president left for medical treatment the prime minister declared himself president. The ailing president, however, sent word he intended to return and drew up his own list of ministers. Despite assistance from the OAU the situation remained fluid.

CONGO

Republic of the Congo
President: Prof. Pascal Lissouba (1992)
Prime Minister: Jacques Joachin Yhombi-Opango (1993)
Area: 132,046 sq mi. (342,000 sq km)
Population (est. 1996): 2,527,841 (average annual rate of natural increase: 2.18%); birth rate: 39/1000; infant mortality rate: 108/1000. Density per sq mile: 19
Capital and largest city (est. 1992): Brazzaville, 937,580.
Other large city (est. 1992): Pointe-Noire, 576,206.
Monetary unit: Franc CFA. **Ethnic groups:** About 15 Bantu groups, Europeans. **Languages:** French, Lingala, Kikongo, others. **Religions:** 50% Christian, 48% animist, 2% Muslim. **National name:** République Populaire du Congo. **Literacy rate:** 57%
Economic summary: Gross domestic product (1993): $6.7 billion, per capita $2,820 (1994 est.); real growth rate –2.1%; inflation 2.2%. Arable land: 2%. Principal agricultural products: cassava, rice, corn, peanuts, coffee, cocoa. Labor force: 79,100; 75% in agriculture. Major industrial products: crude oil, cigarettes, cement, beverages, milled sugar. Natural resources: wood, potash, petroleum, natural gas. Exports: $1.1 billion (f.o.b., 1993): oil, lumber, coffee, cocoa, sugar, diamonds. Imports: $472 million (c.i.f., 1991): foodstuffs, consumer goods, intermediate manufactures, capital equipment. Major trading partners: France, Italy, Spain, Germany, other E.C. countries, Brazil, Japan, U.S.

Geography. The Congo is situated in west Central Africa astride the Equator. It borders on Gabon, Cameroon, the Central African Republic, Zaire, and the Angola exclave of Cabinda, with a short stretch of coast on the South Atlantic. Its area is nearly three times that of Pennsylvania.

Most of the inland is tropical rain forest, drained by tributaries of the Zaire (Congo) River, which flows south along the eastern border with Zaire to Stanley Pool. The narrow coastal plain rises to highlands separated from the inland plateaus by the 200-mile-wide Niari River Valley, which gives passage to the coast.

History. The inhabitants of the former French Congo, mainly Bantu peoples with Pygmies in the north, were subjects of several kingdoms in earlier times.

The Frenchman Pierre Savorgnan de Brazza signed a treaty with Makoko, ruler of the Bateke people, in 1880, which established French control. The area, with Gabon and Ubangi-Shari, was constituted the colony of French Equatorial Africa in 1910. It joined Chad in supporting the Free French cause in World War II. The Congo proclaimed its independence without leaving the French Community in 1960.

Maj. Marien Ngouabi, head of the National Council of the Revolution, took power as president on Jan. 1, 1969. He was sworn in for a second five-year term in 1975.

A four-man commando squad assassinated Ngouabi in Brazzaville on March 18, 1977.

Col. Joachim Yhombi-Opango, Army Chief of Staff, assumed the presidency on April 4. Yombhi-Opango resigned on Feb. 4, 1979, and was replaced by Col. Denis Sassou-Neguessou.

In July 1990 the leaders of the ruling party voted to end the one-party system. A national political conference, hailed as a model for sub-Saharan Africa, in 1991 renounced Marxism, and scheduled the country's first free elections for 1992. The national conference ending in June 1991 rewrote the constitution.

Political and ethnic tensions remained high in 1993 particularly after legislative elections in May and runoffs in June. Soon afterward a state of emergency was declared.

The opposition's rejection of the results developed into violence. A peace agreement was achieved between the government and the opposition in August 1994.

Labor unrest erupted periodically in 1995 as a result of the government's attempted compliance with IMF guidelines.

COSTA RICA

Republic of Costa Rica
President: José María Figueres Olsen (1994)
Area: 19,652 sq mi. (50,898 sq km)
Population (est. 1996): 3,463,083 (average annual rate of natural increase: 1.9%); birth rate: 23.8/1000; infant mortality rate: 13.5/1000; density per square mile: 176.2
Capital and largest city (est. 1994): San José, 315,909.
   Monetary unit: Colón. **Language:** Spanish. **Religion:** 95% Roman Catholic. **National name:** República de Costa Rica. **Literacy rate (1984):** 93%
Economic summary: Gross domestic product (1994 est.): $16.9 billion; per capita $5,050; real growth rate 4.3%; inflation 9% (1993); unemployment 4% (1993). Arable land: 6%. Principal products: bananas, coffee, sugar cane, rice, corn, livestock. Labor force: 868,300; 35.1% in industry and commerce. Major products: processed foods, textiles and clothing, construction materials, fertilizer. Natural resource: hydropower potential. Exports: $2.1 billion (f.o.b., 1993): coffee, bananas, textiles, sugar. Imports: $2.9 billion (c.i.f., 1993): raw materials, consumer goods, capital equipment, petro-

leum. Major trading partners: U.S., Central American countries, Germany, Japan, United Kingdom, France, Netherlands.

Geography. This Central American country lies between Nicaragua to the north and Panama to the south. Its area slightly exceeds that of Vermont and New Hampshire combined.

Most of Costa Rica is tableland, from 3,000 to 6,000 feet (914 to 1,829 m) above sea level. Cocos Island (10 sq mi.; 26 sq km), about 300 miles (483 km) off the Pacific Coast, is under Costa Rican sovereignty.

Government. Under the 1949 Constitution, the president and the one-house Legislative Assembly of 57 members are elected for terms of four years.

The army was abolished in 1949. There is a civil guard and a rural guard.

History. Costa Rica was inhabited by 25,000 Indians when Columbus discovered it and probably named it in 1502. Few of the Indians survived the Spanish conquest, which began in 1563. The region was administered as a Spanish province. Costa Rica achieved independence in 1821 but was absorbed for two years by Agustín de Iturbide in his Mexican Empire. It was established as a republic in 1848.

Except for the military dictatorship of Tomás Guardia from 1870 to 1882, Costa Rica has enjoyed one of the most democratic governments in Latin America.

Rodrigo Carazo Odio, leader of a four-party coalition called the Unity Party, won the presidency in February 1978. His tenure was marked by a disastrous decline in the economy.

On Feb. 2, 1986, Oscar Arias Sanchez won the national elections on a neutralist platform. Arias initiated a policy of preventing contra usage of Costa Rican territory. Rafael Calderón won the presidential election of February 4, 1990 with 51% of the vote.

The presidential election in February 1994 was won by María Figueres Olsen, although the tone of the campaign shocked many Costa Ricans. Mr. Figueres proposed more government intervention in the economy.

As a result of IMF displeasure with the government's economic programs the World Bank withheld $100 million of financing.

CÔTE D'IVOIRE

Republic of Côte d'Ivoire
President: Henri Konan Bédié (1993)
Area: 124,502 sq mi. (322,462 sq km)
Population (est. 1996): 14,762,445 (average annual rate of natural increase: 3.5%); birth rate: 50/1000; infant mortality rate: 92/1000; density per square mile: 118.6
Capital (1988): Yamoussoukro[1] (since March 1983), 106,786. **Largest city (est. 1988):** Abidjan, 2,797,000.
   Monetary unit: Franc CFA. **Ethnic groups:** 60 different groups: principals are Baoule, Bete, Senoufou, Malinke, Agni. **Languages:** French and African languages (Diaula esp.). **Religions:** 60% indigenous, 17% Christian, 23% Islam. **National name:** République de la Côte d'Ivoire. **Literacy rate:** 54%
Economic summary: Gross domestic product (1994 est.): $20.5 billion; per capita $1,430; real growth rate 1.5%; inflation n.a. Arable land: 9%; Labor force: 5,718,000; over 85% in agriculture. Principal products: coffee, cocoa, corn, beans, timber. Major industrial products: food, wood, refined oil, textiles, fertilizer. Natural resources: diamonds, iron ore, crude oil, manganese, cobalt, bauxite, copper. Exports: $2.7 billion (f.o.b.,

1993): cocoa 30%, coffee 20%, tropical woods 11%, petroleum, cotton, bananas, pineapples, palm oil. Imports: $1.6 billion (f.o.b., 1993): food, capital goods, consumer goods, fuel. Major trading partners: France, Germany, Netherlands, Belgium, Spain, other E.C. countries, U.S., Nigeria, Guinea.

1. Not recognized by U.S., which recognizes Abidjan.

Geography. Côte d'Ivoire (also known as the Ivory Coast), in western Africa on the Gulf of Guinea, is a little larger than New Mexico. Its neighbors are Liberia, Guinea, Mali, Burkina Faso, and Ghana.

The country consists of a coastal strip in the south, dense forests in the interior, and savannas in the north. Rainfall is heavy, especially along the coast.

Government. The government is headed by a President who is elected every five years by popular vote, together with a National Assembly of 175 members.

History. Côte d'Ivoire attracted both French and Portuguese merchants in the 15th century. French traders set up establishments early in the 19th century, and in 1842, the French obtained territorial concessions from local tribes, gradually extending their influence along the coast and inland. The area was organized as a territory in 1893, became an autonomous republic in the French Union after World War II, and achieved independence on Aug. 7, 1960.

The Côte d'Ivoire formed a customs union in 1959 with Dahomey (Benin), Niger, and Burkina Faso.

Roman Catholic Pres. Houphouët-Boigny ordered the building of the largest Christian church in the world, Notre Dame de la Paix, in the capital city, which he periodically paid for.

Falling cocoa and coffee prices made this nation the largest per capita debtor in Africa. Massive protests by students, farmers and professionals forced the president to legalize opposition parties and hold the first contested presidential election. In October 1990 Houphouët-Boigny won 81% of the vote and is currently serving his seventh consecutive five-year term. In the first multiparty legislative elections in November the president's Democratic Party won 163 of the 175 seats.

The country's long-time president Houphouët-Boigny died in December 1993, but a smooth transition ensued to Bédié.

The presidential election of October 1995, marred by violence and a boycott by the opposition, was won by the incumbent. Legislative elections in November gave the ruling party 147 seats.

CROATIA

Republic of Croatia
President: Franjo Tudjman
Area: 21,829 sq mi. (56,537 sq km)
Population (est. 1996): 5,004,112 (average annual rate of natural increase: –0.15%), predominantly Croats, about 12% Serbs. Birth rate: 9.8/1000; infant mortality rate: 10.2/1000; density per square mile: 229
Capital (1991): Zagreb, 930,753. **Other large cities (1991):** Split, 189,444; Rijeka, 167,757; Osijek, 104,553. **Monetary unit:** Kuna (May 1994). **Languages:** Croatian; **Literacy rate:** est. 90%; **Religion:** predominantly Roman Catholic
Economic summary: Gross domestic product (1994 est.): $12.4 billion; $2,640 per capita; real growth rate 3.4%; inflation: 3%; unemployment: 17% (Dec. '94). Industries: chemicals, plastics, machine tools, fabricated metals, electronics, rolled steel products, aluminum proc-

essing, wood products, building materials, petroleum and petroleum refining, food processing, beverages, pharmaceuticals, shipbuilding. Agriculture: wheat, corn, oats, sugar beets, potatoes, livestock breeding and dairy farming, vineyards, fishing. Exports: $4.3 billion (1994). Imports: $5.2 billion (1994).

Geography: Croatia is about half the size of the state of Louisiana (or the size of West Virginia). It is bounded in the north by the Republic of Slovenia, in the northeast by Hungary, in the east and south by the Federal Republic of Yugoslavia (Serbia and Montenegro), in the south by the Republic of Bosnia and Herzegovina, and in the west by the Adriatic Sea. Part of Croatia is mountainous, rocky region lying in the Dinaric Alps. The Zagorje region north of the capital, Zagreb, is a land of rolling hills, and the fertile agricultural region of the Pannonian Plain is bordered by the Drava, Danube, and Sava Rivers in the east. Over one-third of Croatia is forested.

Government: A parliamentary democracy with two legislative houses.

History: The original home of the Slavic Croats was in an area that was part of the Republic of Ukraine. Other tribes that arrived in the region during the 6th century A.D., which was then part of the Roman province of Pannonia. The Croats converted to Christianity between the 7th and 9th centuries and adopted the Roman alphabet.

In A.D. 925, the Croats defeated Byzantine and Frankish invaders and established their own independent kingdom, which reached its peak during the 11th century.

A civil war ensued in 1089 which later led to the country being conquered by the Hungarians in 1091. The signing of the *Pacta Conventa* by Croatian tribal chiefs and the Hungarian king in 1102 united the two nations politically under the Hungarian monarch.

When the Hungarians were defeated by the Turks in 1526, most of Croatia fell under Ottoman rule until the end of the 17th century. The rest of Croatia elected Ferdinand of Austria as their king and became associated with the Hapsburgs of Austria.

After the establishment of the Austro-Hungarian kingdom in 1867, Croatia and Slovenia became part of Hungary until the collapse of Austria-Hungary in 1918 following their defeat in World War I.

On Oct. 29, 1918, Croatia proclaimed its independence and joined in union with Montenegro, Serbia, and Slovenia to form the Kingdom of Serbs, Croats, and Slovenes. The name was changed to Yugoslavia in 1929.

When Germany invaded Yugoslavia in 1941, an independent Croatian state was created that was controlled by a Fascist dictatorship. After Germany was defeated in 1945, Croatia was made into a republic of the newly reestablished nation of Yugoslavia.

In May 1991, Croatian voters supported a referendum calling for their republic's independence, and when the Croatian parliament passed a declaration of independence from Yugoslavia in June, a six-month civil war followed with the Serbian-dominated Yugoslavian army. The war claimed thousands of lives and wrought mass destruction on the land.

A UN cease-fire was arranged on Jan. 2, 1992. The Security Council in February approved sending a 14,000-member peacekeeping force to monitor the cease-fire and protect the minority Serbs in Croatia.

By the end of August, rebel Serbs in Croatia still controlled a third of that republic.

In a 1993 referendum the Serb-occupied portion of Croatia (Krajina) resoundingly voted for integration with Serbs in Bosnia and Serbia proper. Although the Zagreb government and representatives of Krajina signed a ceasefire in March 1994 further negotiations broke down shortly afterward over the political status of the latter region.

In a lightning operation the Croatian army retook western Slavonia in May 1995. Similarly, in August the central Croatian region of Krajina, held by Serbs, was returned to Zagreb's control.

Elections for the lower house of parliament in October gave the ruling party 75 of the 127 seats.

CUBA

Republic of Cuba

President: Fidel Castro Ruz (1976)

Area: 44,218 sq mi. (114,524 sq km)

Population (est. 1996): 11,007,446 (average annual rate of natural increase: 0.78%; birth rate: 14.4/1000; infant mortality rate: 8/1000; density per square mile: 248.9

Capital and largest city (1994 est.): Havana, 2,241,000. **Other large cities (est. 1994):** Santiago de Cuba, 440,084; Camagüey, 293,961; Holguin, 242,085; Guantánamo, 207,796; Santa Clara, 205,400. **Monetary unit:** Peso. **Language:** Spanish. **Religion:** at least 85% nominally Roman Catholic before Castro assumed power. **National name:** República de Cuba. **Literacy rate:** 94%

Economic summary: Gross domestic product (1994 est.): $14 billion, per capita $1,260; real growth rate 0.4%; inflation rate n.a.; unemployment rate n.a. Arable land: 23%. Principal agricultural products: sugar, tobacco, coffee, rice, fruits, sugar and sugar byproducts. Labor force (1988): 4,620,800; 30% in services and government, industry 22%, agriculture 20%. Major industrial products: processed sugar and tobacco, refined oil products, textiles, chemicals, paper and wood products, metals, consumer products. Natural resources: metals, primarily nickel, timber. Exports: $1.6 billion (f.o.b., 1994 est.): coffee, sugar (world's largest sugar exporter), nickel, shellfish, tobacco, medical products, citrus. Imports: $1.7 billion (c.i.f., 1994 est.): petroleum, food, machinery, chemicals. Trading partners: China, Canada, Japan, Italy, Spain, Russia, Morocco, Venezuela, France, Egypt.

Geography. The largest island of the West Indies group (equal in area to Pennsylvania), Cuba is also the westernmost—just west of Hispaniola (Haiti and the Dominican Republic), and 90 miles (145 km) south of Key West, Fla., at the entrance to the Gulf of Mexico. The island is mountainous in the southeast and south central area (Sierra Maestra). Elsewhere it is flat or rolling.

Government. Since 1976, elections have been held every five years to elect the National Assembly, which in turn elects the 31-member Council of States, its President, First Vice-President, five Vice-Presidents, and Secretary. Fidel Castro is President of the Council of State and of the government and First Secretary of the Communist Party of Cuba, the only political party.

History. Arawak Indians inhabiting Cuba when Columbus discovered the island in 1492 died off from diseases brought by sailors and settlers. By 1511, Spaniards under Diego Velásquez were founding settlements that served as bases for Spanish exploration. Cuba soon after served as an assembly point for treasure looted by the conquistadores, attracting

French and English pirates.

Black slaves and free laborers were imported to work sugar and tobacco plantations, and waves of chiefly Spanish immigrants maintained a European character in the island's culture. Early slave rebellions and conflicts between colonials and Spanish rulers laid the foundation for an independence movement that turned into open warfare from 1867 to 1878. The poet, José Marti, in 1895 led the struggle that finally ended Spanish rule, thanks largely to U.S. intervention in 1898 after the sinking of the battleship *Maine* in Havana harbor.

A treaty in 1899 made Cuba an independent republic under U.S. protection. The U.S. occupation, which ended in 1902, suppressed yellow fever and brought large American investment. From 1906 to 1909, Washington invoked the Platt Amendment to the treaty, which gave it the right to intervene in order to suppress any revolt. U.S. troops came back in 1912 and again in 1917 to restore order. The Platt Amendment was abrogated in 1934.

Fulgencio Batista, an army sergeant, led a revolt in 1933 that overthrew the regime of President Gerado Machado.

Batista's Cuba was a police state. Corrupt officials took payoffs from American gamblers who operated casinos, demanded bribes from Cubans for various public services, and enriched themselves with raids on the public treasury. Dissenters were murdered and their bodies dumped in gutters.

Fidel Castro Ruz, a tall, bearded attorney in his 30s, landed in Cuba on Christmas Day 1956 with a band of 12 fellow revolutionaries, evaded Batista's soldiers, and set up headquarters in the jungled hills of the Sierra Maestra range. By 1958 his force had grown to about 2,000 guerrillas, for the most part young and middle class. Castro's brother, Raul, and Ernesto (Ché) Guevara, an Argentine physician, were his top lieutenants. Businessmen and landowners who opposed the Batista regime gave financial support to the rebels. The United States, meanwhile, cut off arms shipments to Batista's army.

The beginning of the end for Batista came when the rebels routed 3,000 government troops and captured Santa Clara, capital of Las Villas province 150 miles from Havana, and a trainload of Batista reinforcements refused to get out of their railroad cars. On New Year's Day 1959, Batista flew to exile in the Dominican Republic and Castro took over the government. Crowds cheered the revolutionaries on their seven-day march to the capital.

The United States initially welcomed what looked like the prospect for a democratic Cuba, but a rude awakening came within a few months when Castro established military tribunals for political opponents, jailed hundreds, and began to veer leftward. Castro disavowed Cuba's 1952 military pact with the United States. He confiscated U.S. investments in banks and industries and seized large U.S. landholdings, turning them first into collective farms and then into Soviet-type state farms. The United States broke relations with Cuba on Jan. 3, 1961. Castro thereupon forged an alliance with the Soviet Union.

From the ranks of the Cuban exiles who had fled to the United States, the Central Intelligence Agency recruited and trained an expeditionary force, numbering less than 2,000 men, to invade Cuba, with the expectation that the invasion would spark an uprising of the Cuban populace against Castro. The invasion was planned under the Eisenhower administration and President John F. Kennedy gave the go-ahead for it in the first months of his administration, but rejected a

CIA proposal for U.S. planes to provide air support. The landing at the Bay of Pigs on April 17, 1961, was a fiasco. Not only did the invaders fail to receive any support from the populace, but Castro's tanks and artillery made short work of the small force.

A Soviet attempt to change the global power balance by installing in Cuba medium-range missiles—capable of striking targets in the United States with nuclear warheads—provoked a crisis between the superpowers in 1962 that had the potential of touching off World War III. After a visit to Moscow by Cuba's war minister, Raul Castro, work began secretly on the missile launching sites.

Denouncing the Soviets for "deliberate deception," President Kennedy on Oct. 22 announced that the U.S. navy would enforce a "quarantine" of shipping to Cuba and search Soviet bloc ships to prevent the missiles themselves from reaching the island. After six days of tough public statements on both sides and secret diplomacy, Soviet Premier Nikita Khrushchev on Oct. 28 ordered the missile sites dismantled, crated, and shipped back to the Soviet Union, in return for a U.S. pledge not to attack Cuba. Limited diplomatic ties were re-established on Sept. 1, 1977.

Emigration increased dramatically after April 1, 1980, when Castro, irritated by the granting of asylum to would-be refugees by the Peruvian embassy in Havana, removed guards and allowed 10,000 Cubans to swarm into the embassy grounds.

As an airlift began taking the refugees to Costa Rica, Castro opened the port of Mariel to a "freedom flotilla" of ships and yachts from the United States, many of them owned or chartered by Cuban-Americans to bring out relatives. It wasn't until after they had reached the United States that it was discovered that the regime had opened prisons and mental hospitals to permit criminals, homosexuals, and others unwanted in Cuba to join the refugees.

For most of President Ronald Reagan's first term, U.S.-Cuban relations were frozen. But late in 1984, an agreement was reached between the two countries. Cuba would take back more than 2,700 Cubans who had come to the United States in the Mariel exodus but were not eligible to stay in the country under U.S. immigration law because of criminal or psychiatric disqualification. Castro cancelled it when the U.S. began the Radio Marti broadcasts in May 1985 to bring a non-Communist view to the Cuban people.

In the face of sweeping changes in Eastern Europe and the Soviet Union itself, Cuba has reaffirmed its adherence to Marxism-Leninism.

With the collapse of Communism in Eastern Europe Cuba's foreign trade plummeted, as did aid from Russia, producing the worst economic crisis in the island's history.

The government moved slightly toward a mixed economy in 1993 by permitting limited private enterprise in a number of trades and services and allowing Cubans to possess convertible currencies.

Reports from a seldom-convened meeting of the Communist Party's Central Committee in March 1996 indicated that the state was moving to suppress opposition and step up economic reforms.

CYPRUS

Republic of Cyprus
President: Glafcos Clerides (1993)
Area: 3,572 sq mi (9,251 sq km)
Population (est. 1995): 736,636: Greek Cypriots, 78%; Turkish Cypriots, 18%.; Maronites, Armenians, Latins, 4%; (average annual rate of natural increase: 0.77%[1]); birth rate:

15.4/1000[1]; infant mortality rate: 8.4/1000[1]; density per square mile: 208.5
Capital and largest city (1993): Lefkosia (Nicosia) (in government-controlled area), 186,400 (in controlled area). **Monetary unit:** Cyprus pound. **Languages:** Greek, Turkish (official), English is widely spoken. **Religions (1993 est.):** Greek Orthodox, 78%; Sunni Muslim, 18%; Maronite, Armenian, Apostolic, Latin, and other, 4%. **National name:** Kypriaki Dimokratia—Kibris Cumhuriyeti. **Member of Commonwealth of Nations; Literacy rate (1993):** 94%
Economic summary: Gross domestic product (1994[1]): $7.5 billion, per capita $11,500; real growth rate 5%; inflation rate 4.7%; unemployment rate: 2.7%. Arable land: 40%. Principal agricultural products: potatoes, vegetables, citrus, vine products, olives, barley. Labor force: 288,000; 87% in industry. Major industrial products: food, beverages, metal products, pharmaceuticals, clothing, footwear, furniture. Tourism contributed 10.2% to GDP in 1992 (est. 8.2% in 1993). Natural resources: copper, asbestos, gypsum, timber, marble, clay, umber, ochre. Exports: $1.0 billion (f.o.b., 1994): citrus, potatoes, grapes, wine, cement, clothing, footwear, chemical products, paper products. Imports: $3.2 billion (c.i.f., 1994): consumer goods, petroleum and lubricants, food and feed grains, machinery. Major trading partners: U.K., Greece, Lebanon, Germany, Saudi Arabia.

1. Government-controlled area only.

Geography. The third largest island in the Mediterranean (one and one-half times the size of Delaware), Cyprus lies off the southern coast of Turkey and the western shore of Syria. Most of the country consists of a wide plain lying between two mountain ranges that cross the island. The highest peak is Mount Olympus at 6,406 feet (1,953 m).

Government. The president is elected for a five-year term and exercises executive power through an appointed Council of Ministers.

Legislative power lies with the House of Representatives, which comprises 80 members elected for five years. 56 members are Greek-Cypriots elected by the Greek-Cypriot community; 24 are Turkish-Cypriots elected by the Turkish-Cypriot community. Since the Turkish-Cypriot ministers and other officials withdrew from their posts in 1963, the 24 seats allotted to the Turkish Cypriots remain vacant. The Cypriot House assembly has been functioning with only its 56 Greek Cypriot members. Representatives from the Maronite, Armenian, and Latin minorities are also elected as observers. Mediation efforts by the U.N. seek to achieve reunification of the island under one federated system of government.

History. Cyprus was the site of early Phoenician and Greek colonies. For centuries its rule passed through many hands. It fell to the Turks in 1571, and a large Turkish colony settled on the island.

In World War I, on the outbreak of hostilities with Turkey, Britain annexed the island. It was declared a crown colony in 1925.

For centuries the Greek population, regarding Greece as its mother country, has sought self-determination and reunion with it *(enosis)*. The resulting quarrel with Turkey threatened NATO. Cyprus became an independent nation on Aug. 16, 1960, with Britain, Greece, and Turkey as guarantor powers.

Archbishop Makarios, president since 1959, was overthrown July 15, 1974, by a military coup led by the Cypriot National Guard. The new regime named Nikos Giorgiades Sampson as president and Bishop

Gennadios as head of the Cypriot Church to replace Makarios. Diplomacy failed to resolve the crisis. Turkey invaded Cyprus by sea and air July 20, 1974, asserting its right to protect the Turkish Cypriot minority.

Geneva talks involving Greece, Turkey, Britain, and the two Cypriot factions failed in mid-August, and the Turks subsequently gained control of 40% of the island. Greece made no armed response to the superior Turkish force, but bitterly suspended military participation in the NATO alliance.

The tension continued after Makarios returned to become President on Dec. 7, 1974. He offered self-government to the Turkish minority, but rejected any solution "involving transfer of populations and amounting to partition of Cyprus."

Turkish Cypriots proclaimed a separate state under Rauf Denktas in the northern part of the island in Nov. 1983, and proposed a "biregional federation."

Makarios died on Aug. 3, 1977, and Spyros Kyprianou was elected to serve the remainder of his term. Kyprianou was subsequently re-elected in 1978, 1983, and 1985. In 1988, George Vassiliou defeated Kyprianou.

Despite several attempts in 1991 by the UN to resolve the dispute, little if any progress was made.

Then-President Vassiliou won a plurality in the presidential election of February 1993 but fell short of a majority. A 73-year-old conservative and critic of UN proposals to reunify Cyprus narrowly won the second round of elections to become president

Parliamentary elections in May 1996 resulted in the ruling conservative-center coalition retaining a seat majority ahead of the Communists. The junior coalition partner, the Democratic Party, lost one seat.

Northern Cyprus—In 1974, Turkey invaded Cyprus and has since occupied 37% of the island in the north. Some 180,000 Greek Cypriots (about 40% of the Greek Cypriot population) were forced by the Turkish troops to flee to the government-controlled area in the south and are still prevented by the occupying forces from returning to their homes and properties.

On Nov. 15, 1993, Turkish Cypriot leader Rauf Denktas unilaterally declared the occupied area independent, naming it the "Turkish Republic of Northern Cyprus." The UN Security Council, in its Resolution 541 of Nov. 18, 1983, declared this action legally invalid and called for withdrawal. No country except Turkey has recognized this illegal entity. The government of the Republic of Cyprus is the only internationally recognized government on the island.

NORTHERN CYPRUS

Turkish Republic of Northern Cyprus
President: Rauf Denktas (1990)
Area: 1,295 sq mi. (3,355 sq km)
Population (est. 1994): 175,494: Turkish Cypriots, 174,818; Greek Cypriots, 488; Maronites, 188; (average annual rate of natural increase: 1.14%); birth rate: 18/1,000; infant mortality rate: 12/1000; density per square mile: 135

Capital and largest city (1983): Nicosia North (Lefkosa), 41,815.. **Monetary unit:** Turkish lira. **Official language:** Turkish. **Religions:** Moslem, 99%; others, 1%. **National name:** Kuzey Kibris Türk Cumhuriyeti (Turkish Republic of Northern Cyprus). **Literacy rate (1993):** 99%
Economic summary: Gross national product (1994): $554.3 million; per capita $3,092. Average rate of growth (1977–1994): 3.9%. Arable land (1994): 56.71%. Principal agricultural products: citrus, potatoes, tobacco, vegetables. Labor force (1993): 75,378; 24% in agriculture; 10.8% in industry. Major industrial products: concentrated citrus, hides, leathers, P.V.C. covered electric cables, footwear, clothing, consumables. Natural resources: pyrite mine. Exports: dairy products, citrus, live animals, potatoes, ready-made clothing, tobacco, carobs, hides and leathers. Imports: consumer goods, petroleum and lubricants, food, machinery and transport equipment, chemicals. Major trading partners: EU countries (mainly U.K. and Germany) and Turkey are the largest trading partners.

Geography. The Turkish Republic of Northern Cyprus covers the northern part of the island of Cyprus. North Cyprus consists of the coastal plains, the Besparmak (Five-Finger) Mountains (the highest peak is Mount Selvili at 3,360 feet), and the interior plains.

Government. The constitution envisages a parliamentary democracy. The legislative power is exercised by an Assembly composed of 50 deputies elected for five years. The President is head of state and represents the unity of the state. He appoints the Prime Minister from among the deputies.

Denktas dissolved parliament in October 1993 with a call for new elections in December, whose results led to the formation of a coalition government.

The European Court of Justice in July 1994 ordered an embargo on exports, consisting chiefly of fruits and clothing. Although this led to some deprivations, financial assistance from Turkey helped ameliorate the situation.

Negotiations were set to begin in 1996 on a move to integrate Cyprus into the European Union, providing incentives to Turkey, as a convoluted means of resolving the political impasse in the division of the island.

CZECH REPUBLIC

President: Vaclav Havel (1993)
Premier: Vaclav Klaus (1992)
Area: 30,464 sq mi. (78,902 sq km)
Population (est. 1996): 10,321,120 (average annual rate of natural increase: –0.5%); birth rate: 10.3/1000; infant mortality rate: 8.4/1000; density per square mile: 338.8
Capital and largest city (Jan. 1, 1994): Prague, 1,215,771. **Other large cities:** Brno, 389,727; Ostrava, 326,396; Plzen, 172,402; Olomouc, 106,003. **Monetary unit:** Koruna. **Language:** Czech. **Religions:** Roman Catholic major; other: Protestant, Orthodox. **Literacy rate:** 99%
Economic summary: Gross domestic product (1994): $76.5 billion; per capita $7,350; real growth rate, 2.2%; inflation 10%; unemployment, 2.9%. The Czech Republic has a developed but deteriorating industrialized economy—much of its plant equipment is among the oldest in Europe. Natural resources: hard coal, kaolin, clay, graphite. Industries: fuels, ferrous metallurgy, machinery and equipment, coal, motor vehicles, glass, armaments. Agriculture: diversified crops including grains, potatoes, sugar beets, hops, fruit, hogs, cattle

and poultry; exporter of forest products. Labor force (1994): 4,885,000; industry, 33.1%; agriculture, 6.9%; construction, 9.1%; communications and other, 50.8%. Exports: $12.4 billion (f.o.b., 1994 est.): manufactured goods, machinery and transport equipment, chemicals, fuels, minerals and metals. Imports: $13.1 billion (f.o.b., 1994 est.): machinery and transport equipment, fuels and lubricants, manufactured goods, raw materials, chemicals, agricultural products. Major trading partners: C.I.S., Slovakia, Germany, Hungary, Poland, Austria, Switzerland.

Geography. The Czech Republic lies in central Europe. It is bordered on the north by Poland, on the east by Slovakia, on the south by Austria, and on the west and northwest by Germany. The two principal regions are Bohemia and Moravia. The Bohemian landscape consists of rolling hills and plateaus surrounded by low mountains to the north, west, and south. Moravia is bordered on the north by mountains and generally has more hills than Bohemia. The principal rivers are the Elbe and the Vltava which are vital to the nation's waterborne and agricultural commerce. The Czech Republic is about the size of the state of South Carolina.

Government. A parliamentary democracy headed by the president. The parliament consists of two chambers—the 200-member House, elected for four-year terms, and the 81-member Senate, elected for six-year terms. The president is elected for a five-year term by both chambers of parliament.

History. Probably about the 5th century A.D., Slavic tribes from the Vistula basin settled in the region of the traditional Czech lands of Bohemia, Moravia, and Silesia. The Czechs founded the kingdom of Bohemia, the Premyslide dynasty, which ruled Bohemia and Moravia from the 10th to the 16th century.

One of the Bohemian kings, Charles IV, Holy Roman Emperor, made Prague an imperial capital and a center of Latin scholarship. The Hussite movement founded by Jan Hus (1369?–1415) linked the Slavs to the Reformation and revived Czech nationalism, previously under German domination. A Hapsburg, Ferdinand I, ascended the throne in 1526. The Czechs rebelled in 1618. Defeated in 1620, they were ruled for the next 300 years as part of the Austrian Empire. Full independence from the Hapsburgs was not achieved until the end of World War I following the collapse of the Austrian-Hungarian Empire.

A union of the Czech lands and Slovakia was proclaimed in Prague on Nov. 14, 1918, and the Czech nation became one of the two component parts of the newly formed Czechoslovakian state.

In March 1939, German troops occupied Czechoslovakia and Czech Bohemia and Moravia became German protectorates for the duration of World War II. The former government returned in April 1945 when the war ended and the country's pre-1938 boundaries were restored.

When elections were held in 1946, the Communists became the dominant political party and gained control of the Czechoslovakian government in 1948. Thereafter, the former democracy was turned into a Soviet-style state.

Nearly 42 years of Communist rule ended when Vaclav Havel was elected president of Czechoslovakia in 1989. The return of democratic political reform saw a strong Slovak nationalist movement emerge by the end of 1991 which sought independence for Slovakia as a sovereign nation and the breakup of the two Czechoslovakian republics.

When the general elections of June 1992 failed to resolve the continuing coexistence of the two republics within the federation, Czech and Slovak political leaders agreed to separate their states into two fully independent nations. On Aug. 26, 1992, they announced their intentions to disolve the Czechoslovakian federation on Jan. 1, 1993.

Havel was elected for a 5-year term as president in January 1993 by the 200-member parliament.

While the country enjoyed low unemployment and inflation, fundamental economic restructuring has not yet begun.

Unexpectedly inconclusive elections in May–June 1996 stripped the ruling center–right coalition of its majority in parliament. The prime minister formed a minority government under an agreement with the second-place Social Democrats.

DENMARK

Kingdom of Denmark
Sovereign: Queen Margrethe II (1972)
Prime Minister: Poul Nyrup Rasmussen
Area: 16,631 sq mi. (43,075 sq km[1]
Population (est. 1996): 5,210,833 (average annual rate of natural increase: 0.12%); birth rate: 12.3/1000; infant mortality rate: 6.6/1000; density per square mile: 313.3
Capital and largest city (1994 est.): Copenhagen, 1,339,395. **Other large cities (est. 1994):** Aarhus, 274,535; Odense, 181,824; Alborg, 158,141. **Monetary unit:** Krone. **Language:** Danish, Faroese, Greenlandic (an Inuit dialect), small German-speaking minority. **Religion (1992):** 88% Evangelical Lutheran. **National name:** Kongeriget Danmark. **Literacy rate:** 99%
Economic summary: Gross domestic product (1994 est.): $103 billion; $19,860 per capita; real growth rate, 4.5%; inflation rate 2%; unemployment rate: 12.3%. Arable land: 61%. Principal agricultural products: meat, dairy products, fish, grains. Labor force: 2,553,900: Private services, 37.1%; government services, 30.4%; manufacturing and mining, 20%. Major industrial products: processed foods, machinery and equipment, textiles. Natural resources: crude oil, natural gas, fish, salt, limestone. Exports: $42.9 billion (f.o.b., 1994): meat and dairy products, fish, industrial machinery, chemical products, transportation equipment. Imports: $37.1 billion (c.i.f., 1994 est.): machinery and equipment, transport equipment, petroleum, chemicals, grains and foodstuffs, textiles, paper. Major trading partners: Germany, Sweden, France, U.K., U.S., Norway, Japan.

1. Excluding Faeroe Islands and Greenland.

Geography. Smallest of the Scandinavian countries (half the size of Maine), Denmark occupies the Jutland peninsula, which extends north from Germany between the tips of Norway and Sweden. To the west is the North Sea and to the east the Baltic.

The country also consists of several Baltic islands; the two largest are Sjaelland, the site of Copenhagen, and Fyn. The narrow waters off the north coast are called the Skagerrak and those off the east, the Kattegat.

Government. Denmark has been a constitutional monarchy since 1849. Legislative power is held jointly by the Sovereign and parliament. The Constitution of 1953 provides for a unicameral parliament called the Folketing, consisting of 179 popularly elected members who serve for four years. The Cabinet is presided over by the Sovereign, who appoints the Prime Minister.

The Sovereign, Queen Margrethe II, was born April 16, 1940, and became Queen—the second in Denmark's history—Jan. 15, 1972, the day after her father, King Frederik IX, died at 72 in the 25th year of his reign. Margrethe was the eldest of his three daughters (by Princess Ingrid of Sweden). The nation's constitution was amended in 1953 to permit her to succeed her father in the absence of a male heir to the throne. (Denmark was ruled six centuries ago by Margrethe I, but she was never crowned Queen since there was no female right of succession.)

History. Denmark emerged with establishment of the Norwegian dynasty of the Ynglinger in Jutland at the end of the 8th century. Danish mariners played a major role in the raids of the Vikings, or Norsemen, on Western Europe and particularly England. The country was Christianized by St. Ansgar and Harald Blaatand (Bluetooth)—the first Christian king—in the 10th century. Harald's son, Sweyn, conquered England in 1013. His son, Canute the Great, who reigned from 1014 to 1035, united Denmark, England, and Norway under his rule; the southern tip of Sweden was part of Denmark until the 17th century. On Canute's death, civil war tore the country until Waldemar I (1157–82) re-established Danish hegemony over the north.

In 1282, the nobles won the Great Charter, and Eric V was forced to share power with parliament and a Council of Nobles. Waldemar IV (1340–75) restored Danish power, checked only by the Hanseatic League of north German cities allied with ports from Holland to Poland. His daughter, Margrethe, in 1397 united under her rule Denmark, Norway, and Sweden. But Sweden later achieved autonomy and in 1523, under Gustavus I, independence.

Denmark supported Napoleon, for which it was punished at the Congress of Vienna in 1815 by the loss of Norway to Sweden. In 1864, Bismarck, together with the Austrians, made war on the little country as an initial step in the unification of Germany. Denmark was neutral in World War I.

In 1940, Denmark was invaded by the Nazis. King Christian X reluctantly cautioned his countrymen to accept the occupation, but there was widespread resistance against the Nazis. In 1944, Iceland declared its independence from Denmark, ending a union that had existed since 1380.

Liberated by British troops in May 1945, the country staged a fast recovery in both agriculture and manufacturing and was a leader in liberalizing trade. It joined the United Nations in 1945 and NATO in 1949.

Disputes over economic policy led to elections in 1981 that led to Poul Schlüter coming to power in early 1982. Further disputes over his pro-NATO posture led to elections in May 1988 that marginally confirmed his position.

A second referendum on the Maastricht accord in May 1993 passed with 56.8 percent of the vote, but confidence in European monetary and political unity was waning in other European Community countries.

The Social Democratic Party took over the reins of government at the head of a four-party slightly left-leaning coalition in 1993.

The focus of political attention in 1995 remained the economy and the means to balance the budget while preserving the extensive welfare system already in place.

Outlying Territories of Denmark

FAEROE ISLANDS

Status: Autonomous part of Denmark
Chief of State: Queen Margrethe II (1972)
High Commissioner: Bent Klinte
Prime Minister: Edmund Joensen (1994)
Lagmand (President): Jogran Sundstein (1989)
Area: 540 sq mi. (1,399 sq km)
Population (est. 1996): 49,349 (average annual growth rate: 0.95%); birth rate: 17/1000; infant mortality rate: 7.7/1000; density per square mile: 91.4
Capital and largest city (est. 1993): Thorshavn, 16,100.
Monetary unit: Faeroese krone. **Literacy rate:** 99%
Economic summary: Gross domestic product (1989 est.): $662 million, per capita $14,000; real growth rate −10.8%; inflation (1993 est.) 6.8%; unemployment (1993) 23%. Arable land: 2%; principal agricultural products: sheep, vegetables. Labor force: 17,585, largely engaged in fishing manufacturing, transportation, commerce. Major industrial products: fish, ships, handicrafts. Exports: $345.3 million (f.o.b., 1993 est.): fish and fish products. Imports: $234.4 million (c.i.f., 1993 est.): machinery and transport equipment, foodstuffs, petroleum and petroleum products. Major trading partners: Denmark, U.S., U.K., Germany, Canada, France, Japan.

This group of 18 islands, lying in the North Atlantic about 200 miles (322 km) northwest of the Shetland Islands, joined Denmark in 1386 and has since been part of the Danish kingdom. The islands were occupied by British troops during World War II, after the German occupation of Denmark.

The Faeroes have home rule under a bill enacted in 1948; they also have two representatives in the Danish Folketing.

GREENLAND

Status: Autonomous part of Denmark
Chief of State: Queen Margrethe II (1972)
High Commissioner: Torben Hede Pedersen (1993)
Premier: Lars Emil Johansen (1991)
Area: 840,000 sq mi. (incl. 708,069 sq mi. covered by ice-cap) (2,175,600 sq km)
Population (est. 1996): 58,203 (growth rate: 1.0%); birth rate: 17/1000; infant mortality rate: 23.8/1000; density per square mile: 14.4. Ethnic divisions: Greenlander (Inuit and Greenland-born Caucasians), 86%; Danish, 14%
Capital and largest city (1995 est.): Godthaab, 12,723.
Monetary unit: Krone. **Literacy rate:** 99%
Economic summary: Gross national product (1988): $500 million, per capita $9,000; real growth rate 5%; inflation (1993 est.) 1.3%; unemployment (1993 est.) 6.6%. Arable land: 0%; principal agricultural products: hay, sheep, garden produce. Labor force: 22,800, largely engaged in fishing, hunting, sheep breeding. Major industries: fish processing, lead and zinc processing, handicrafts. Natural resources: metals, cryolite, iron ore, coal, uranium, fish. Exports: $330.5 million (f.o.b., 1993 est.): fish and fish products, metallic ores and concentrates. Imports: $369.6 million (c.i.f., 1993 est.): petroleum and petroleum products, machinery and transport equipment, foodstuffs, manufactured goods. Major trading partners: Denmark, U.S., Germany, Sweden, Japan, Norway.

Greenland, the world's largest island, was colonized in 985–86 by Eric the Red. Danish sovereignty, which covered only the west coast, was extended over the whole island in 1917. In 1941 the U.S. signed an agreement with the Danish minister in Washington, placing it under U.S. protection during World War II but maintaining Danish sovereignty. A definitive agreement for the joint defense of Greenland within the framework of NATO was signed in 1951. A large U.S. air base at Thule in the far north was completed in 1953.

Under 1953 amendments to the Danish Constitution, Greenland became part of Denmark, with two representatives in the Danish Folketing. On May 1, 1979, Greenland gained home rule, with its own local parliament (Landsting) replacing the Greenland Provincial Council.

In February 1982, Greenlanders voted to withdraw from the European Community, which they had joined as part of Denmark in 1973. Danish Premier Anker Jørgensen said he would support the request, but with reluctance.

An election in early March 1991 gave the Siumut Party 11 of the 27 available seats. The early election was called after a scandal allegedly involving overspending on entertainment by government officials.

DJIBOUTI

Republic of Djibouti
President: Hassan Gouled Aptidon (1977)
Prime Minister: Barkat Gourad Hamadou (1978)
Area: 8,490 sq mi. (22,000 sq km)
Population (est. 1996): 427,642 (average annual rate of natural increase: 2.72%); birth rate: 42.5/1000; infant mortality rate: 106.7/1000; density per square mile: 50.4
Capital (1992 est.): Djibouti, 395,000; **Monetary unit:** Djibouti franc; **Languages:** Arabic, French, Afar, Somali; **Religions:** Muslim, 94%; Christian, 6%; **National name:** Jumhouriyya Djibouti; **Literacy rate:** 48%
Economic summary: Gross domestic product (1994 est.): $500 million, $1,200 per capita; real growth rate –3%; inflation 6% (1993); unemployment over 30% (1994 est.). Arable land: 2%; principal agricultural products: goats, sheep, camels. Labor force: NA. Industries: small-scale enterprises such as dairy products and mineral- water bottling. Djibouti is a free port. Natural resources: salt, limestone, gypsum, perlite, diatoms. geothermal energy. Exports: $184 million (f.o.b., est. 1994): hides, skins, livestock. Imports: $384 million (f.o.b., 1994 est.): foodstuffs, machinery, transport equipment, consumer goods. Major trading partners: Ethiopia, Somalia, the Republic of Yemen, Saudi Arabia.

Geography. Djibouti lies in northeastern Africa on the Gulf of Aden at the southern entrance to the Red Sea. It borders on Ethiopia and Somalia. The country, the size of Massachusetts, is mainly a stony desert, with scattered plateaus and highlands.

Government. A republic with a unicameral legislature. On June 27, 1977, France tansferred sovereignty to the new nation of Djibouti. On Sept. 4, 1992, voters approved in referendum a new multiparty constitution. The last presidential election took place May 7, 1993, and President Aptidon was re-elected for another six-year term.

History. The territory that is now Djibouti was acquired by France between 1843 and 1886 by treaties with the Somali sultans. Small, arid, and sparsely populated, Djibouti is important chiefly because of the capital city's port, the terminal of the Djibouti-Addis Ababa railway that carries 60% of Ethiopia's foreign trade.

Originally known as French Somaliland, the colony voted in 1958 and 1967 to remain under French rule. It was renamed the Territory of the Afars and Issas in 1967 and took the name of its capital city on attaining independence.

The two principal opposition groups in exile banded to form a common front in early 1990.

A referendum in 1992 approved a new constitution permitting a multiparty system.

The President won the May 1993 election against four opponents in an election criticized for irregularities.

Feuding within the major rebel opposition led to the naming of a new leader in 1994. Two members of the major faction in the opposition and others joined the government in June 1995.

DOMINICA

Commonwealth of Dominica
President: Crispin Sorhaindo (1993)
Prime Minister: Edison James (1995)
Area: 290 sq mi. (751 sq km)
Population: (est. 1996): 82,926 (average annual rate of natural increase: 1.31%); birth rate: 18.3/1000; infant mortality rate: 9.6/1000; density per square mile: 286
Capital and largest city (1991): Roseau, 15,853; **Monetary unit:** East Caribbean dollar; **Languages:** English and French patois; **Religions:** Roman Catholic, 77%; Protestant, 15%; **Member of Commonwealth of Nations; Literacy rate:** 94%
Economic summary: Gross domestic product (1994 est.): $200 million, per capita $2,260; real growth rate 1.6%; inflation 1.6% (1993 est.); unemployment 15% (1992). Arable land: 9%. Principal products: bananas, citrus fruits, coconuts, plantains. Labor force: 30,600 (1989); 32% in industry and commerce. Major industries: agricultural processing; tourism. Exports: $48.3 million (f.o.b., 1993): bananas, coconuts, soap, vegetables, grapefruit, oranges. Imports: $98.8 million (f.o.b., 1993): manufactured goods, machinery and equipment, food, chemicals. Major trading partners: U.K., Caribbean countries, U.S., Italy, Canada.

Geography. Dominica is an island of the Lesser Antilles in the Caribbean south of Guadeloupe and north of Martinique.

Government. Dominica is a republic, with a president elected by the House of Assembly as head of state and a prime minister appointed by the president on the advice of the Assembly. The United Workers Party (11 of 21 seats in the Assembly) is led by Prime Minister Edison James. The Freedom Party holds five seats and the United Dominican Labor Party holds five seats.

History. Visited by Columbus in 1493, Dominica was claimed by Britain and France until 1815, when Britain asserted sovereignty. Dominica, along with other Windward Isles, became a self-governing member of the West Indies Associated States in free association with Britain in 1967.

Dissatisfaction over the slow pace of reconstruction after Hurricane David struck the island in September 1979 brought a landslide victory for the Freedom Party in July 1980. The vote gave the prime ministership to Mary Eugenia Charles, a strong advocate of free enterprise. The Freedom Party won again in 1985 elections, giving Miss Charles a second five-year term as prime minister. She and her party won a third term in elections on May 28, 1990, though with a greatly reduced mandate.

The government in 1993 pursued its policy of divesting itself of state enterprises.

The opposition United Workers' Party captured the general election of June 1995. The new government planned to privatize numerous enterprises, but severe autumn storms resulted in much damage.

DOMINICAN REPUBLIC

President: Leonel Fernández Reyna (1996)
Area: 18,704 sq mi. (48,442 sq km)
Population (est. 1996): 8,088,881 (average annual rate of natural increase: 1.79%); birth rate: 23.5/1000; infant mortality rate: 47.7/1000; density per square mile: 432.5
Capital and largest city (1993): Santo Domingo, 2,100,000. **Other large city (1993):** Santiago de los Caballeros, 690,000. **Monetary unit:** Peso. **Language:** Spanish, English widely spoken. **Religion:** 90% Roman Catholic. **National name:** República Dominicana. **Literacy rate:** 74%
Economic summary: Gross domestic product (est. 1994): $24 billion, $3,070 per capita, 2.9% real growth rate; inflation rate 14%; unemployment rate: 30%. Arable land: 23%. Principal agricultural products: sugar cane, coffee, cocoa, tobacco, beef, fruit and vegetables. Agriculture accounts for 15% of GDP and 49% of labor force. Labor force (1986): 2,300,000–2,600,000; 18% in industry. Major industries: tourism, sugar processing, ferronickel and gold mining, textiles, cement, tobacco. Natural resources: nickel, bauxite, gold, silver. Exports: $585 million (f.o.b., 1994): sugar, coffee, cocoa, gold, ferronickel, silver, meats, fruits and vegetables. Imports: $2.5 billion (c.i.f., 1994 est.): foodstuffs, petroleum, cotton and fabrics, chemicals, pharmaceuticals. Major trading partners: U.S., including Puerto Rico, E.U.

Geography. The Dominican Republic, in the West Indies, occupies the eastern two-thirds of the island of Hispaniola, which it shares with Haiti. Its area equals that of Vermont and New Hampshire combined.

Crossed from northwest to southeast by a mountain range with elevations exceeding 10,000 feet (3,048 m), the country has fertile, well-watered land in the north and east, where nearly two-thirds of the population lives. The southwest part is arid and has poor soil, except around Santo Domingo.

Government. The president is elected by direct vote every four years. Legislative powers rest with a Senate and a Chamber of Deputies, both elected by direct vote, also for four years. All citizens must vote when they reach 18 years of age, or even earlier if they are married.

History. The Dominican Republic was discovered by Columbus in 1492. He named it La Española, and his son, Diego, was its first viceroy. The capital, Santo Domingo, founded in 1496, is the oldest European settlement in the Western Hemisphere. Spain ceded the colony to France in 1795, and Haitian blacks under Toussaint L'Ouverture conquered it in 1801.

In 1808 the people revolted and the next year captured Santo Domingo, setting up the first republic. Spain regained title to the colony in 1814. In 1821 the people overthrew Spanish rule, but in 1822 they were reconquered by the Haitians. They revolted again in 1844, threw out the Haitians; and established the Dominican Republic, headed by Pedro Santana. Uprisings and Haitian attacks led Santana to make the country a province of Spain from 1861 to 1865. The U.S. Senate refused to ratify a treaty of annexation. Disorder continued until the dictatorship of Ulíses Heureaux; in 1916, when disorder broke out again, the U.S. sent in a contingent of marines, who remained until 1934.

A sergeant in the Dominican army trained by the marines, Rafaél Leonides Trujillo Molina, overthrew Horacio Vásquez in 1930 and established a dictatorship that lasted until his assassination 31 years later.

Leftists rebelled April 24, 1965, and President Lyndon Johnson sent in marines and troops. After an OAS ceasefire request May 6, a compromise installed Hector Garcia-Godoy as provisional president. Joaquin Balaguer won in free elections in 1966 against Bosch, and a peacekeeping force of 9,000 U.S. troops and 2,000 from other countries withdrew. Balaguer restored political and economic stability.

In 1978, the army suspended the counting of ballots when Balaguer trailed in a fourth-term bid. After a warning from President Jimmy Carter, however, Balaguer accepted the victory of Antonio Guzmán of the opposition Dominican Revolutionary Party.

Salvador Jorge Blanco of the Dominican Revolutionary Party was elected President on May 16, 1982, defeating Balaguer and Bosch. Austerity measures imposed by the International Monetary Fund, including sharply higher prices for food and gasoline, provoked rioting in the spring of 1984 that left more than 50 dead.

Balaguer was elected President in May 1986 and aimed economic policy at diversifying the economy.

In a bitter presidential contest Balaguer maintained a slim lead over his opponent in the May 1994 election before election officials stopped releasing tallies. The opposition charged widespread fraud. Eventually the crisis eased when a constitutional amendment gave the current president a two-year term with new elections scheduled for May 1996.

Opposition leader Pena Gomez obtained the most votes in the first round of that presidential election but fell short of a majority. In the runoff of June 30 U.S.-raised Leonel Fernandez secured more than 51% of the vote through an alliance with Balaguer.

ECUADOR

Republic of Ecuador
President: Abdala Bucaram Ortiz (1996)
Area: 106,822[1] sq mi. (276,670 sq km)
Population (est. 1996): 11,466,291 (average annual rate of natural increase: 1.96%); birth rate: 25/1000; infant mortality rate: 34.8/1000; density per square mile: 107
Capital: Quito. **Largest cities (1992):** Guayaquil, 1,475,118; Quito, 1,094,318; Cuenca, 195,738. **Monetary unit:** Sucre. **Languages:** Spanish (by 90% of population), Quéchua. **Religion:** Roman Catholic, 95%. **National name:** República del Ecuador. **Literacy rate:** 92%
Economic summary: Gross domestic product (1994, est.). $41.1 billion, per capita $3,840; real growth rate 3.9%; inflation 25%; unemployment 7.1%. Arable land: 6%; principal agricultural products: bananas, cocoa, coffee, sugar cane, manioc, plantains, potatoes, rice. Labor force (1995 est.): 3,751,247; 21% in manufactur-

ing; major industries: food processing, textiles, chemicals, fishing, timber, petroleum. Exports: $3.31 billion (f.o.b., 1994): petroleum, coffee, bananas, cocoa products, shrimp, fish products. Imports: $3.27 billion (f.o.b., 1994): transport equipment, vehicles, machinery, chemicals. Major trading partners: U.S., Latin America, EC, Caribbean, Japan.

1. Does not include area under dispute with Peru.

Geography. Ecuador, about equal in area to Nevada, is in the northwest part of South America fronting on the Pacific. To the north is Colombia and to the east and south is Peru. Two high and parallel ranges of the Andes, traversing the country from north to south, are topped by tall volcanic peaks. The highest is Chimborazo at 20,577 feet (6,272 m).

The Galápagos Islands (or Colón Archipelago) (3,029 sq mi.; 7,845 sq km), in the Pacific Ocean about 600 miles (966 km) west of the South American mainland, became part of Ecuador in 1832.

Government. A 1978 Constitution returned Ecuador to civilian government after eight years of military rule. The President is elected to a term of four years and a House of Representatives of 71 members is popularly elected for the same period.

History. The tribes in the northern highlands of Ecuador formed the Kingdom of Quito around A.D. 1000. It was absorbed, by conquest and marriage, into the Inca Empire. Pizarro conquered the land in 1532, and through the 17th century a thriving colony was built by exploitation of the Indians. The first revolt against Spain occurred in 1809. Ecuador then joined Venezuela, Colombia, and Panama in a confederacy known as Greater Colombia.

On the collapse of this union in 1830, Ecuador became independent. Subsequent history was one of revolts and dictatorships; it had 48 presidents during the first 131 years of the republic. Conservatives ruled until the Revolution of 1895 ushered in nearly a half century of Radical Liberal rule, during which the church was disestablished and freedom of worship, speech, and press was introduced.

In 1988, Rodrigo Borja was elected President. He was also able to form a coalition in the House, confirming a leftward shift in the government and promising smoother executive-legislative relations.

Blamed for econommic conditions the governing Social Democrats were defeated in elections of May 1992 by right-wing parties promising free-market reforms.

In the runoff presidential election of July 5, 1992 Sixto Duran Ballen captured 58% of the vote. A devaluation of the currency and the elimination of energy price subsidies led to a national strike in September.

The candidate of the center-left Roldosista Party defeated the Christian Democratic candidate in the July presidential election run-off. The incumbent is constitutionally banned from seeking a second term.

EGYPT

Arab Republic of Egypt
President: Hosni Mubarak (1981)
Prime Minister: Dr. Kamal Al-Ganzoury (1996)
Area: 386,900 sq. mi. (1,002,000 sq km)
Population (est. 1996): 63,575,107 (average annual rate of natural increase: 1.9%); birth rate: 28.1/1000; infant mortality rate: 72.8/1000; density per square mile: 164.3

Capital and largest city (1992 est.): Cairo, 6,849,000. **Other large cities (1992 est.):** Alexandria, 3,382,000; Giza, 2,144,000; Shubra el Khema, 834,000; El Mahalla el Kubra, 408,000. **Monetary unit:** Egyptian pound. **Language:** Arabic. **Religions:** Islam, 94%; Christian (mostly Coptic), 6%. **Literacy rate:** 50.2%

Economic summary: Gross domestic product (1994 est.): $151.5 billion; $2,490 per capita; 1.5% real growth rate; inflation rate 8%; unemployment rate: 20%. Arable land: 3%. Principal agricultural products: cotton, wheat, rice, corn, beans. Labor force: 15,000,000; 20% in privately owned services and manufacturing. Major industries: textiles, food processing, tourism, chemicals, petroleum, construction, cement, metals. Natural resources: crude oil, natural gas, iron ore, phosphates, manganese, limestone, gypsum, talc, asbestos, lead, zinc. Exports: $3.1 billion (f.o.b., FY 93/94 est.): cotton, petroleum, yarn, textiles, metal products, chemicals. Imports: $11.2 billion (c.i.f., FY 93/94 est.): foodstuffs, machinery, fertilizers, woods, durable consumer goods, capital goods. Major trading partners: U.S., Western Europe, Japan, Eastern Europe.

Geography. Egypt, at the northeast corner of Africa on the Mediterranean Sea, is bordered on the west by Libya, on the south by the Sudan, and on the east by the Red Sea and Israel. It is nearly one and one-half times the size of Texas.

The historic Nile flows through the eastern third of the country. On either side of the Nile valley are desert plateaus, spotted with oases. In the north, toward the Mediterranean, plateaus are low, while south of Cairo they rise to a maximum of 1,015 feet (309 m) above sea level. At the head of the Red Sea is the Sinai Peninsula, between the Suez Canal and Israel.

Navigable throughout its course in Egypt, the Nile is used largely as a means of cheap transport for heavy goods. The irrigation of the land depends mainly on water from the Nile. The Nile is one of the famous tourist spots in the country. The principal ports are Alexandria, Port Said, and Damietta.

The Nile delta starts 100 miles (161 km) south of the Mediterranean and fans out to a sea front of 155 miles between the cities of Alexandria and Port Said. From Cairo north, the Nile branches into many streams, the principal ones being the Damietta and the Rosetta.

Except for a narrow belt along the Mediterranean, Egypt lies in an almost rainless area, in which high daytime temperatures fall quickly at night.

Government. Executive power is held by the President, who is elected every six years and can appoint one or more Vice Presidents.

The National Democratic Party, led by President Hosni Mubarak, is the dominant political party. Elections on Nov. 1990 confirmed its huge majority. There are also 14 opposition parties and some independents in the parliament.

History. Egyptian history dates back to about 4000 B.C., when the kingdoms of upper and lower Egypt, already highly civilized, were united. Egypt's "Golden Age" coincided with the 18th and 19th dynasties (16th to 13th centuries B.C.), during which the empire was established. Persia conquered Egypt in 525 B.C.; Alexander the Great subdued it in 332 B.C.; and then the dynasty of the Ptolemies ruled the land until 30 B.C., when Cleopatra, last of the line, committed suicide and Egypt became a Roman province. From 641 to 1517 the Arab caliphs ruled Egypt, and then the Turks took it for their Ottoman Empire.

Napoleon's armies occupied the country from 1798 to 1801. In 1805, Mohammed Ali, leader of a band of Albanian soldiers, became Pasha of Egypt. After completion of the Suez Canal in 1869, the French and British took increasing interest in Egypt.

British troops occupied Egypt in 1882, and British resident agents became its actual administrators, though it remained under nominal Turkish sovereignty. In 1914, this fiction was ended, and Egypt became a protectorate of Britain.

Egyptian nationalism forced Britain to declare Egypt an independent, sovereign state on Feb. 28, 1922, although the British reserved rights for the protection of the Suez Canal and the defense of Egypt. In 1936, by an Anglo-Egyptian treaty of alliance, all British troops and officials were to be withdrawn, except from the Suez Canal Zone. When World War II started, Egypt remained neutral. British imperial troops finally ended the Nazi threat to Suez in 1942 in the battle of El Alamein, west of Alexandria.

In 1951, Egypt abrogated the 1936 treaty and the 1899 Anglo-Egyptian condominium of the Sudan (*See* Sudan). Rioting and attacks on British troops in the Suez Canal Zone followed, reaching a climax in January 1952. The army, led by Gen. Mohammed Naguib, seized power on July 23, 1952. Three days later, King Farouk abdicated in favor of his infant son. The monarchy was abolished and a republic proclaimed on June 18, 1953, with Naguib holding the posts of Provisional President and Premier. He relinquished the latter in 1954 to Gamal Abdel Nasser, leader of the ruling military junta. Naguib was deposed seven months later and Nasser confirmed as President in a referendum on June 23, 1956.

Nasser's policies embroiled his country in continual conflict. In 1956, the U.S. and Britain withdrew their pledges of financial aid for the building of the Aswan High Dam. In reply, Nasser nationalized the Suez Canal and expelled British oil and embassy officials. Israel, barred from the Canal and exasperated by terrorist raids, invaded the Gaza Strip and the Sinai Peninsula. Britain and France, after demanding Egyptian evacuation of the Canal Zone, attacked Egypt on Oct. 31, 1956. Worldwide pressure forced Britain, France, and Israel to halt the hostilities. A U.N. emergency force occupied the Canal Zone, and all troops were evacuated in the spring of 1957.

On June 5, 1967, Israel invaded the Sinai Peninsula, the East Bank of the Jordan River, and the zone around the Gulf of Aqaba. A U.N. ceasefire on June 10 saved the Arabs from complete rout.

Nasser declared the 1967 cease-fire void along the Canal in April 1969 and began a war of attrition. The U.S. peace plan of June 19, 1970, resulted in Egypt's agreement to reinstate the cease-fire for at least three months, (from August) and to accept Israel's existence within "recognized and secure" frontiers that might emerge from U.N.-mediated talks. In return, Israel accepted the principle of withdrawing from occupied territories.

Then, on Sept. 28, 1970, Nasser died, at 52, of a heart attack. The new President was Anwar el-Sadat, an associate of Nasser and a former newspaper editor.

In July 1972, Sadat ordered the expulsion of Soviet "advisors and experts" from Egypt because the Russians had not provided the sophisticated weapons he felt were needed to retake territory lost to Israel in 1967.

The fourth Arab-Israeli war broke out Oct. 6, 1973, while Israelis were commemorating Yom Kippur, the Jewish high holy day. Egypt swept deep into the Sinai, while Syria strove to throw Israel off the Golan Heights.

A U.N.-sponsored truce was accepted on October 22. In January 1974, both sides agreed to a settlement negotiated by U.S. Secretary of State Henry A. Kissinger that gave Egypt a narrow strip along the entire Sinai bank of the Suez Canal. In June, President Nixon made the first visit by a U.S. President to Egypt and full diplomatic relations were established. The Suez Canal was cleared and reopened on June 5, 1975.

In the most audacious act of his career, Sadat flew to Jerusalem at the invitation of Prime Minister Menachem Begin and pleaded before Israel's Knesset on Nov. 20, 1977, for a permanent peace settlement. The Arab world reacted with fury—only Morocco, Tunisia, Sudan, and Oman approved.

Egypt and Israel signed a formal peace treaty on March 26, 1979. The pact ended 30 years of war and established diplomatic and commercial relations.

Egyptian and Israeli officials met in the Sinai desert on April 26, 1979, to implement the peace treaty calling for the phased withdrawal of occupation forces from the peninsula. By mid-1980, two thirds of the Sinai was transferred, but progress here was not matched elsewhere—the negotiation of Arab autonomy in the Gaza Strip and the West Bank remained stymied.

Sadat halted further talks in August 1980 because of continued Israeli settlement of the West Bank. On October 6 1981, Sadat was assassinated by extremist Muslim soldiers at a parade in Cairo. Vice President Hosni Mubarak, a former Air Force chief of staff, was confirmed by the parliament as president the next day.

Although feared unrest in Egypt did not occur in the wake of the assassination, and Israel completed the return of the Sinai to Egyptian control on April 25, 1982, Mubarak was unable to revive the autonomy talks. Israel's invasion of Lebanon in June imposed a new strain on them, and brought a marked cooling in Egyptian-Israeli relations, but not a disavowal of the peace treaty.

While President Mubarak's stand during the Persian Gulf war won wide praise in the West, domestically this position proved far less popular. Nevertheless Egypt emerged with new clout and respect in the international community.

A presidential referendum in October 1993 supported Mubarak's bid for a third term although only a third of the population registered to vote.

The government has concentrated much of its time and attention in recent years combating Islamic extremism. In November 1995 elections took place for the People's Assembly. The ruling National Democratic Party won 416 seats and the opposition 13, with independents taking the remaining seats.

Suez Canal. The Suez Canal, in Egyptian territory between the Arabian Desert and the Sinai Peninsula, is an artificial waterway about 100 miles (161 km) long between Port Said on the Mediterranean and Suez on the Red Sea. Construction work, directed by the French engineer Ferdinand de Lesseps, was begun April 25, 1859, and the Canal was opened Nov. 17, 1869. The cost was 432,807,882 francs. The concession was held by an Egyptian joint stock company, Compagnie Universelle du Canal Maritime de Suez, in which the British government held 353,504 out of a total of 800,000 shares. The concession was to expire Nov. 17, 1968, but the company was nationalized July 26, 1956, by unilateral action of the Egyptian government.

The Canal was closed in June 1967 after the Arab-Israeli conflict. With the help of the U.S. Navy, work was begun on clearing the Canal in 1974, after the cease-fire ending the Arab-Israeli war. It was reopened to traffic June 5, 1975.

EL SALVADOR

Republic of El Salvador
President: Armando Calderón Sol (1994)
Area: 8,260 sq mi. (21,393 sq km)
Population (est. 1996): 5,828,987 (average annual rate of natural increase: 2.25%); birth rate: 28.3/1000; infant mortality rate: 31.9/1000; density per square mile: 705.7
Capital and largest city (1993 est.): San Salvador, 972,810; **Other large cities (est. 1993):** Santa Ana, 208,322; San Miguel, 161,156; Zacatecoluca, 81,035.
Monetary unit: Colón; **Language:** Spanish; **Religion:** Roman Catholic; **National name:** República de El Salvador; **Literacy rate:** 73%
Economic summary: Gross domestic product (1994 est..): $9.8 billion; $1,710 per capita; real growth rate 5%; inflation 10%; unemployment 6.7% (1993). Arable land: 27%. Principal agricultural products: coffee, cotton, corn, sugar, rice, sorghum. Labor force: 1.7 million (1992 est.); 40% in agriculture. Major industrial products: processed foods, clothing and textiles, petroleum products. Natural resources: hydro- and geothermal power, crude oil. Exports: $823 million (f.o.b., 1994 est.): coffee, cotton, sugar, shrimp. Imports: $2.1 billion (c.i.f., 1994 est.): raw materials, consumer goods, capital goods. Major trading partners: U.S., Guatemala, Germany, Mexico, Venezuela, Costa Rica.

Geography. Situated on the Pacific coast of Central America, El Salvador has Guatemala to the west and Honduras to the north and east. It is the smallest of the Central American countries, its area equal to that of Massachusetts, and the only one without an Atlantic coastline.

Most of the country is a fertile volcanic plateau about 2,000 feet (607 m) high. There are some active volcanoes and many scenic crater lakes.

Government. The President is elected for a nonrenewable, five-year term, and legislative power is in a unicameral 84-member National Assembly elected by universal suffrage and proportional representation.

History. Pedro de Alvarado, a lieutenant of Cortés, conquered El Salvador in 1525. El Salvador, with the other countries of Central America, declared its independence from Spain on Sept. 15, 1821, and was part of a federation of Central American states until that union was dissolved in 1838. Its independent career for decades thereafter was marked by numerous revolutions and wars against other Central American republics.

On Oct. 15, 1979, a junta deposed the President, Gen. Carlos Humberto Romero, seeking to halt increasingly violent clashes between leftist and rightist forces.

On Dec. 4, 1980, three American nuns and an American lay worker were killed in an ambush near San Salvador, causing the Carter Administration to suspend all aid pending an investigation. The naming of José Napoleón Duarte, a moderate civilian, as head of the governing junta brought a resumption of U.S. aid.

In an election closely monitored by U.S. and other foreign observers, Duarte was elected President in May 1984.

Duarte's Christian Democratic Party scored an unexpected electoral triumph in national legislative and municipal elections held in March 1985, a winning majority in the new National Assembly. The rightist parties that had been dominant in the previous Constituent Assembly demanded that the vote be nullified, but the army high command rejected their assertion that the voting had been fraudulent.

At the same time, U.S. officials said that while the rebels still were far from being defeated, there had been marked improvement in the effectiveness of government troops in the civil war against anti-government guerrillas that was being waged mainly in the countryside. Talks with the rebels broke down in September 1986. Duarte's inability to find solutions led to the rightwing ARENA party controlling half the seats in the National Assembly, in the elections of March, 1988. The decisive victory of Alfredo Cristiani, the ARENA candidate for President, gave the right-wing party effective control of the country, given its political control of most of the municipalities.

On January 16, 1992, the government signed a peace treaty with the guerrilla forces formally ending a 12-year civil war that had claimed 75,000 lives.

The candidate of the right-wing ARENA party, Calderón Sol won the presidential election of March 1994 on a pledge to continue the peace process.

A crime wave swept the country in 1995, and in May of that year the value-added tax was raised to 13% to pay for reforms and infrastructure repair.

EQUATORIAL GUINEA

Republic of Equatorial Guinea
President: Col. Teodoro Obiang Nguema Mbasogo (1979)
Prime Minister: Angel Serafin Seriche Dougan (1996)
Area: 10,830 sq mi. (28,051 sq km)
Population (est. 1996): 431,282 (average annual rate of natural increase: 2.6%); birth rate: 39.7/1000; infant mortality rate: 98/1000; density per square mile: 39.8
Capital and largest city (1983): Malabo, 30,418; **Monetary unit:** CFA Franc; **Languages:** Spanish (official), pidgin English, Fang, Bubi, Creole; **Religions:** Roman Catholic, Protestant, traditional; **National name:** República de Guinea Ecuatorial; **Literacy rate:** 50%
Economic summary: Gross domestic product (1993 est.): $280 million; $700 per capita; real growth rate n.a.; inflation: 1.6% (1992 est.); unemployment: n.a. Arable land: 8%. Principal products: cocoa, wood, coffee, rice, yams. Natural resources: wood, crude oil. Exports: $56 million (f.o.b., 1993): cocoa, wood, coffee. Imports: $62 million (c.i.f., 1993): petroleum, foodstuffs, textiles, machinery. Major trading partners: Spain, France, Nigeria, Cameroon, U.S.

Geography. Equatorial Guinea, formerly Spanish Guinea, consists of Rio Muni (10,045 sq mi.; 26,117 sq km), on the western coast of Africa, and several islands in the Gulf of Guinea, the largest of which is Bioko (formerly Fernando Po) (785 sq mi.; 2,033 sq km). The other islands are Annobón, Corisco, Elobey Grande, and Elobey Chico. The total area is twice that of Connecticut.

Government. A president with an 80-member House of Representatives exercises power.

History. Fernando Po and Annobón came under Spanish control in 1778. From 1827 to 1844, with Spanish consent, Britain administered Fernando Po, but in the latter year Spain reclaimed the island. Río Muni was given to Spain in 1885 by the Treaty of Berlin.

Negotiations with Spain led to independence on Oct. 12, 1968.

In 1969, anti-Spanish incidents in Río Muni, including the tearing down of a Spanish flag by national troops, caused 5,000 Spanish residents to flee for their safety, and diplomatic relations between the two nations became strained. A month later, President

Masie Nguema Biyogo Negue Ndong charged that a coup had been attempted against him. He seized dictatorial powers and arrested 80 opposition politicians and even several of his cabinet ministers and the secretary of the National Assembly.

A coup on Aug. 3, 1979, deposed Masie, and a junta led by Lieut. Col. Teodoro Obiang Nguema Mbasogo took over the government.

After delays the legislative elections of November 1993 resulted in an easy win for the governing party although turnout was low and opposition parties boycotted the process.

President Obiang handily won the presidential election of February 1996 with 99% of the vote. Outside observers and opposition members denounced the balloting as riddled with irregularities.

ERITREA

President: Isaias Afwerki (1993)
Area: 45,754 sq mi. (123,300 sq km)
Population (est. 1996): 3,909,628 (of which 0.5 million are refugees awaiting repatriation). Average annual rate of natural increase: 2.6%; birth rate: 45.5/1000; infant mortality rate: 118.9/1000; density per square mile: 85.4.
Capital and largest city (1993): Asmara, 400,000. Other major cities: the ports of Massawa and Assab; **Monetary unit:** Birr. **Languages:** Afar, Bilen, Kunama, Nara, Arabic, Tobedawi, Saho, Tigre, Tigrinya. **Religions:** Islam and Eritrean Orthodox Christianity. **Literacy rate:** 20%.
Economic summary: Gross domestic product (1994 est.): $1.8 billion; $500 per capita; 2% growth rate. The economy and infrastructure were severely damaged by the long war for independence and natural disasters. Eritrea has inherited the entire coastline of Ethiopia and has long-term prospects for revenues from the development of offshore oil, offshore fishing, and tourism. Major manufacturing industries are textiles, leather, food products, beverages. Most Eritreans are employed in agriculture; important crops are cotton, wheat, coffee. Major mineral resources are salt and copper. Major trading partners: Ethiopia, Saudi Arabia, Yemen, Italy, Germany, U.K.

Geography. Eritrea was formerly the northernmost province of Ethiopia and is about the size of Indiana. Much of the country is mountainous. Its narrow Red Sea coastal plain is one of the hottest and driest places in Africa. The cooler central highlands have fertile valleys that support agriculture. Eritrea is bordered by the Sudan on the north and west, the Red Sea on the north and east, and Ethiopia and Djibouti on the south.

Government. A transitional government committed to a democratic system.

History. Eritrea was part of the first Ethiopian kingdom of Askum until its decline in the 8th century A.D. It came under control of the Ottoman Empire in the 16th century, and later the Egyptians. The Italians captured the coastal areas in 1885, and the Treaty of Uccialli (May 2, 1889) gave Italy sovereignty over part of Eritrea. The Italians named their colony after the Roman name for the Red Sea—*Mare Erythraeum*—and ruled it up until World War II.

The British captured Eritrea in 1941 and later administered it as a U.N. Trust Territory until it became federated with Ethiopia on Sept. 15, 1952. It was made an Ethiopian province on Nov. 14, 1962.

A civil war broke out against the Ethiopian government led by rebel groups who opposed the union and wanted independence for Eritrea. The bitter conflict raged on for 17 years against the hard-line communist regime of the Ethiopian dictator, Mengistu Haile Mariam until he was overthrown in May 1991.

The Eritrean People's Liberation Front (EPLF) took control of Eritrea and shared power in a multi-party government in Addis Ababa with the Ethiopian People's Revolutionary Democratic Front (EPRDF). They agreed to hold a referendum on Eritrean independence within two years and on April 23–25, 1993, Eritrean voters almost unanimously opted for an independent republic. Ethiopia recognized Eritrea's sovereignty on May 3, 1993, and sought a new era of cooperation between the two countries.

While relations with Ethiopia remained good in 1995, those with the Sudan deteriorated, and the size of the civil service was cut.

ESTONIA

Republic of Estonia
President: Lennart Meri (1992)
Prime Minister: Tiit Vahi (1995)
Area: 18,370 sq mi. (47,549 sq km)
Population: (est. 1996): 1,459,428 (average annual rate of natural increase: –0.34%); (Estonians, 61.5%; Russians, 30.3%; Ukrainians, 3.17%; Byelorussians, 1.8%; Finns, 1.1%; other, 2.13%); birth rate: 10.7/1000; infant mortality rate: 17.4/1000; density per square mile: 79.4
Capital and largest city (1992 est.): Tallinn, 471,608. Other large city (1992 est.): Tartu, 113,400. **Monetary unit:** Kroon; **Languages:** Estonian (official), Russian, Finnish, English. **Religions (1937):** Lutheran, 78%; Orthodox, 19%. **National name:** Eesti; **Literacy rate:** 100%.
Economic summary: Gross national product (1995): $3.5 billion; $2,350 per capita; real growth rate: 4%; Inflation: 2.6% avg. Unemployment (March 93): 3%. Labor force (1993): 681,000, manufacturing, 154,000; agriculture, 76,000; trade and catering, 59,000; construction, 36,000; finance and business services, 28,900. The Estonian government has pursued a program of market reforms and rough stabilization measures which is rapidly transforming the economy. There is low inflation, living standards are rising, and the private sector is growing rapidly. Exports: $1.8 billion (1995): animals, animal products, food, beverages, tobacco, textiles and textile products, machinery and electrical equipment, vehicles, base metals. Imports $2.4 billion (1995): food, beverages, tobacco, mineral products, textiles, textile products, machinery, electrical equipment, vehicles. Major trading partners: Finland, Russia, Sweden, Germany, Holland, Latvia.

Geography. Estonia borders on the Baltic Sea in the west, the Gulfs of Riga and Finland in the southwest and north, respectively, Latvia in the south, and Russia in the east. It is mainly a lowland country with numerous lakes. Lake Peipus is the largest and is important to the fishing and shipping industries.

Government. Parliamentary democracy.

History. Born out of World War I, this small Baltic state enjoyed a mere two short decades of independence before it was absorbed again by its powerful neighbor, Russia. In the 13th century, the Estonians had been conquered by the Teutonic Knights of Germany, who reduced them to serfdom. In 1526, the Swedes took over, and the power of the German

(Balt) landowning class was curbed somewhat. But after 1721, when Russia succeeded Sweden as the ruling power, the Estonians were subjected to a double bondage—the Balts and the tsarist officials. The oppression lasted until the closing months of World War I, when Estonia finally achieved independence after a victorious War of Independence (1918–20).

Shortly after the start of World War II, the nation was occupied by Russian troops and was incorporated as the 16th republic of the U.S.S.R. in 1940. Germany occupied the nation from 1941 to 1944, when it was retaken by the Russians.

Soon after Lithuania's declaration of independence from the Soviet Union in March 1990, the Estonian congress renamed its country on May 8 and omitted the words "Soviet Socialist" and adopted the former (1918) coat of arms of the Republic of Estonia. Thereafter, the government cautiously promoted national autonomy.

After the attempted Soviet coup to remove President Gorbachev failed, Estonia formally declared its independence from the U.S.S.R. on August 20, 1991. Recognition by European and other countries followed. The Soviet Union recognized Estonia's independence on September 6 and it received UN membership on Sept. 17, 1991.

March 1995 elections gave 41 of the 101 seats in parliament to two left-leaning parties. The leader of the winning alliance, however, ran on a program embracing free-market reforms. His government collapsed in October, although a realignment allowed him to stay on as prime minister.

ETHIOPIA

Transitional Government of Ethiopia
President: Negasso Gidada (1995)
Prime Minister: Meles Zenawi (1995)
Area: 446,952 sq mi. (1,157,585 sq km)
Population (est. 1996): 57,171,662 (average annual rate of natural increase: 2.9%); birth rate: 46/1000; infant mortality rate: 122.8/1000; density per square mile: 127.9
Capital and largest city (1993 est.): Addis Ababa, 2,200,186. **Monetary unit:** Birr. **Languages:** Amharic (official), English, Orominga, Tigrigna, over 70 languages spoken. **Religions:** Ethiopian Orthodox, 35–40%; Islam, 40–45%; animist, 15-20%; other, 5%. **Literacy rate:** 33%
Economic summary: Gross domestic product (1993 est.): $20.3 billion; $380 per capita (1993 est.); real growth rate 6.4%; inflation (1995): 8%. Arable land: 12%. Principal agricultural products: coffee, barley, wheat, corn, sugar cane, cotton, oilseeds, livestock. Major industrial products: cement, textiles, processed foods, refined oil, beverages, footwear, furniture. Natural resources: potash, gold, platinum, copper. Exports: $219.8 million (f.o.b., 1993 est.): coffee, leather products, gold, petroleum products. Imports: $1.04 billion (c.i.f., 1993 est.): machinery and equipment, industrial inputs, pharmaceuticals, chemicals. Major trading partners: Japan, U.S., Djibouti, Saudi Arabia, Germany, Italy, France, Eritrea.

Geography. Ethiopia is in east central Africa, bordered on the west by the Sudan, the east by Somalia and Djibouti, the south by Kenya, and northeast by Eritrea. It is nearly three times the size of California.

Over its main plateau land, Ethiopia has several high mountains, the highest of which is Ras Dashan at 15,158 feet (4,620 m). The Blue Nile, or Abbai, rises in the northwest and flows in a great semicircle east, south, and northwest before entering the Sudan. Its chief reservoir, Lake Tana, lies in the northwestern part of the plateau.

Government. A constitution was ratified by a constituent assembly elected in June 1994. The bicameral parliament has 548 seats (House of People's Representatives, and the Federal Council has one seat for each nationality plus one seat for each additional one million of that nationality.)

History. Black Africa's oldest state, Ethiopia can trace 2,000 years of recorded history. Its now deposed royal line claimed descent from King Menelik I, traditionally believed to have been the son of the Queen of Sheba and King Solomon. The present nation is a consolidation of smaller kingdoms that owed feudal allegiance to the Ethiopian Emperor.

Hamitic peoples migrated to Ethiopia from Asia Minor in prehistoric times. Semitic traders from Arabia penetrated the region in the 7th century B.C. Its Red Sea ports were important to the Roman and Byzantine Empires. Coptic Christianity came to the country in A.D. 341, and a variant of that communion became Ethiopia's state religion.

Ancient Ethiopia reached its peak in the 5th century, then was isolated by the rise of Islam and weakened by feudal wars. Modern Ethiopia emerged under Emperor Menelik II, who established its independence by routing an Italian invasion in 1896. He expanded Ethiopia by conquest.

Disorders that followed Menelik's death brought his daughter to the throne in 1917, with his cousin, Tafari Makonnen, as Regent, heir presumptive, and strongman. When the Empress died in 1930, Tafari was crowned Emperor Haile Selassie I.

As Regent, Haile Selassie outlawed slavery. As Emperor, he worked for centralization of his diffuse realm, in which 70 languages are spoken, and for moderate reform. In 1931, he granted a Constitution, revised in 1955, that created a parliament, with an appointed Senate and an elected Chamber of Deputies, and a system of courts. But basic power remained with the Emperor.

Bent on colonial empire, fascist Italy invaded Ethiopia on Oct. 3, 1935, forcing Haile Selassie into exile in May 1936. Ethiopia was annexed to Eritrea, then an Italian colony, and Italian Somaliland to form Italian East Africa, losing its independence for the first time in recorded history. In 1941, British troops routed the Italians, and Haile Selassie returned to Addis Ababa.

In August 1974, the Armed Forces Committee nationalized Haile Selassie's palace and estates and directed him not to leave Addis Ababa. On Sept. 12, 1974, he was deposed after nearly 58 years as Regent and Emperor. The 82-year-old "Lion of Judah" was placed under guard. Parliament was dissolved, the Constitution suspended, and Ethiopia was proclaimed a socialist state.

Lt. Col. Mengistu Haile Mariam was named head of state, Feb. 2, 1977, and when a communist regime was established on Sept. 10, 1984, Mengistu became party leader.

A cut-off of Soviet aid led to mass animosity, and a rebel offensive began in February 1991. Mengistu resigned and fled the country in May. A group called the Ethiopian People's Revolutionary Democratic Front seized the capital. Also in May a separatist guerrilla organization, the Eritrean People's Liberation Front, took control of the province of Eritrea. The two groups agreed in early July that Eritrea would have an internationally supervised referendum on independence. This election took place in April 1993 with an almost unanimous support for Eritrean independence. Ethiopia accepted and recognized Eritrea as an independent state within a few days.

General elections in May 1995 gave the ruling coalition a landslide victory after a boycott by most opposition groups. A new government was established in August with a 17-member Council of Ministers chosen to reflect the ethnic makeup of the country.

FIJI

Republic of Fiji
President: Ratu Sir Kamisese Mara (1994)
Prime Minister: Maj. Gen. Sitiveni Rabuka (1992)
Area: 7,078 sq mi. (18,333 sq km)
Population (est. 1996): 782,381 (average annual rate of natural increase: 1.7%); birth rate: 23.4/1000; infant mortality rate: 17.4/1000; density per square mile: 110.5
Capital (1990 est.): Suva (on Viti Levu), 200,000; **Monetary unit:** Fiji dollar. **Languages:** Fijian, Hindustani, English (official). **Religions:** Christian, 52%; Hindu, 38%; Islam, 8%; other, 2%. **Literacy rate:** 86%
Economic summary: Gross domestic product (1994 est.): $4.3 billion; $5,650 per capita; real growth rate 5%; inflation rate 2.2% (1995); unemployment rate (est. 1991): 5.9%. Arable land: 8%. Principal products: sugar, copra, rice, ginger. Labor force (1996 est.): 287,000; 67% subsistence agriculture; 18% wage earners; salary earners, 15%. Major industrial products: refined sugar, gold, lumber. Natural resources: timber, fish, gold, copper. Exports: $405 million (f.o.b., 1993): sugar, copra, processed fish, lumber, gold, clothing. Imports: $634 million (c.i.f., 1993): machinery and transport equipment, food, petroleum products, consumer goods, chemicals. Major trading partners: EU, Australia, Japan, U.S., New Zealand, Pacific islands.

Geography. Fiji consists of more than 330 islands in the southwestern Pacific Ocean about 1,960 miles (3,152 km) from Sydney, Australia. The two largest islands are Viti Levu (4,109 sq mi.; 10,642 sq km) and Vanua Levu (2,242 sq mi.; 5,807 sq km). The island of Rotuma (18 sq mi.; 47 sq km), about 400 miles (644 km) to the north, is a province of Fiji. Overall, Fiji is nearly as large as New Jersey.

The largest islands in the group are mountainous and volcanic, with the tallest peak being Mount Victoria (4,341 ft; 1,323 m) on Viti Levu. The southeastern windward sides of the main islands have dense forests, while the west and northwestern leeward sides have grasslands and scattered light forests.

Government. Military coup leader Major General Sitiveni Rabuka formally declared Fiji a republic on Oct. 5, 1987. The Sept. 23, 1988, constitution provided for a bicameral parliament consisting of a 342-member Senate and a 70-member House of Representatives.

The new constitution of July 1990 ensured ethnic Fijians a majority of seats in the parliament, as well as the presidency, prime ministership and other central positions.

History. In 1874, an offer of cession by the Fijian chiefs was accepted, and Fiji was proclaimed a possession and dependency of the British Crown.

During World War II, the archipelago was an important air and naval station on the route from the U.S. and Hawaii to Australia and New Zealand.

Fiji became independent on Oct. 10, 1970. The next year it joined the five-island South Pacific Forum, which intended to become a permanent regional group to promote collective diplomacy of the newly independent members.

In Oct., 1987, then Brig. Gen. Sitiveni Rabuka, the coup leader, declared Fiji a republic and removed it from the British Commonwealth.

In elections of May 1992 Rabuka, as leader of the Fijian Politial Party, became prime minister.

Rabuka began his second term in February 1994 after his party's victory in a general election that month. The government strongly protested France's resumption of nuclear testing in 1995.

FINLAND

Republic of Finland
President: Martti Ahtisaari (1994)
Premier: Paavo Lipponen (1995)
Area: 130,558 sq mi. (338,145 sq km)
Population (est. 1996): 5,100,213 (average annual rate of natural increase: 0.23%); birth rate: 12/1000; infant mortality rate: 5.2/1000; density per square mile: 39
Capital and largest city (1995 est.): Helsinki, 515,765. **Other large cities (est. 1995):** Espoo, 186,507; Tampere, 179,251; Vantaa, 164,376; Turku, 162,370. **Monetary unit:** Markka; **Languages:** Finnish, Swedish. **Religions:** Evangelical Lutheran, 90%; Greek Orthodox, 1.2%. **National name:** Suomen Tasavalta—Republiken Finland. **Literacy rate:** 100%
Economic summary: Gross domestic product (1994 est.): $81.8 billion; $16,140 per capita; 3.5% real growth rate; inflation rate: 2.1% (1992); unemployment rate: 22% (1993). Arable land: 8.3%. Principal products: dairy and meat products, cereals, sugar beets, potatoes. Labor force: 2,470,000; 21% manufacturing. Major products: metal manufactures, forestry and wood products, refined copper, ships, machinery, chemicals, clothing, footwear. Natural resource: timber. Exports: $23.4 billion (f.o.b., 1993): timber, paper and pulp, ships, machinery, clothing, footwear, chemicals. Imports: $18 billion (c.i.f., 1993 est.): petroleum and petroleum products, chemicals, transportation equipment, machinery, textile yarns, foodstuffs, fodder grain, iron and steel. Major trading partners: Germany, Sweden, U.K., U.S., France, Russia, Denmark, Norway, Netherlands.

Geography. Finland stretches 721 miles (1,160 km) south to north. Russia extends along the entire eastern frontier while Norway is on her northern border and Sweden lies on her western border. In area, Finland is three times the size of Ohio.

Off the southwest coast are the Aland Islands, controlling the entrance to the Gulf of Bothnia. Finland has more than 200,000 lakes.

The Swedish-populated Aland Islands (581 sq mi.; 1,505 sq km) have an autonomous status under a law passed in 1921.

Government. The President, chosen for six years by popular vote, appoints the Cabinet. The one-chamber Diet, the Eduskunta, consists of 200 members elected for four-year terms by proportional representation.

History. At the end of the 7th century, the Finns came to Finland from their Volga settlements, taking the country from the Lapps, who retreated northward. The Finns' repeated raids on the Scandinavian coast impelled Eric IX, the Swedish King, to conquer the country in 1157 and bring it into contact with Western Christendom. By 1809 the whole of Finland was conquered by Alexander I of Russia, who set up Finland as a Grand Duchy.

The first period of Russification (1809–1905) resulted in a lessening of the powers of the Finnish Diet. The Russian language was made official, and the Finnish military system was superseded by the Russian. The pace of Russification was intensified from 1908 to 1914. When Russian control was weakened as a consequence of the March Revolution of 1917, the Diet on July 20, 1917, proclaimed Finland's independence, which became complete on Dec. 6, 1917.

Finland rejected Soviet territorial demands, and the U.S.S.R. attacked on Nov. 30, 1939. The Finns made an amazing stand of three months and finally capitulated, ceding 16,000 square miles (41,440 sq km) to the U.S.S.R. Under German pressure, the Finns joined the Nazis against Russia in 1941, but were defeated again and ceded the Petsamo area to the U.S.S.R. In 1948, a 20-year treaty of friendship and mutual assistance was signed by the two nations and renewed for another 20 years in 1970.

Premier Mauno Koivisto, leader of the Social Democratic Party, was elected President on Jan. 26, 1982, winning decisively over a conservative rival with support from Finnish Communists.

Running on a platform calling to invigorate the economy Ahtisaari, a Social Democrat, won the country's first direct presidential election in a runoff in February 1994. Previously the President had been chosen by electors.

Finland became a member of the European Union in January 1995 but made clear it would not become a full member of the Western European Union. In March elections the Social Democrats replaced the Centre Party as the largest group in parliament.

FRANCE

French Republic
President: Jacques Chirac (1995)
Premier: Alain Juppé (1995)
Area: 211,208 sq mi. (547,030 sq km)
Population (est. 1996): 58,317,450 (average annual rate of natural increase: 0.16%); birth rate: 10.8/1000; infant mortality rate: 5.3/1000; density per square mile: 276
Capital: Paris; **Largest cities (1990):** Paris, 2,152,000 (10,650,600, Paris region); Marseilles, 801,000; Lyons, 415,000; Toulouse, 359,000; Nice, 342,000; Strasbourg, 252,000; Nantes, 245,000; Bordeaux, 201,000. **Monetary unit:** French Franc. **Language:** French, declining regional dialects. **Religion:** Roman Catholic, 81%; Protestant, 1.7%; Muslim, 6.9%; Jewish, 1.3%. **National name:** République Française. **Literacy rate:** 99%
Economic summary: Gross domestic product (1995): $1.52 trillion; $26,200 per capita; –0.7% real growth rate; inflation 2.1%; unemployment 11.6%. Arable land: 32%. Principal products: cereals, feed grains, livestock and dairy products, wine, fruits, vegetables, potatoes. Labor force (1994): 22,127,000: services 69.2%, industry 27%. Major products: chemicals, automobiles, processed foods, iron and steel, aircraft, textiles, clothing. Natural resources: coal, iron ore, bauxite, fish, forests. Exports: $285.4 billion (1995): textiles and clothing, chemicals, machinery and transport equipment, agricultural products, foodstuffs. Imports: $264.4 billion (1995): machinery, crude petroleum, chemicals, agricultural products, iron and steel products. Major trading partners: Germany, Italy, U.S., Belgium-Luxembourg, U.K., Netherlands, Spain, Japan.

Geography. France is about 80% the size of Texas. In the Alps near the Italian and Swiss borders is Europe's highest point—Mont Blanc (15,781 ft; 4,810 m). The forest-covered Vosges Mountains are in the northeast, and the Pyrenees are along the Spanish border.

Except for extreme northern France, which is part of the Flanders plain, the country may be described as four river basins and a plateau. Three of the streams flow west—the Seine into the English Channel, the Loire into the Atlantic, and the Garonne into the Bay of Biscay. The Rhône flows south into the Mediterranean. For about 100 miles (161 km), the Rhine is France's eastern border.

West of the Rhône and northeast of the Garonne lies the central plateau, covering about 15% of France's area and rising to a maximum elevation of 6,188 feet (1,886 m). In the Mediterranean, about 115 miles (185 km) east-southeast of Nice, is Corsica (3,367 sq mi.; 8,721 sq km).

Government. The President is elected for seven years by universal suffrage. He appoints the Premier, and the Cabinet is responsible to Parliament. The President has the right to dissolve the National Assembly or to ask Parliament for reconsideration of a law. The Parliament consists of two houses: the National Assembly and the Senate.

History. The history of France, as distinct from ancient Gaul, begins with the Treaty of Verdun (843), dividing the territories corresponding roughly to France, Germany, and Italy among the three grandsons of Charlemagne. Julius Caesar had conquered part of Gaul in 57–52 B.C., and it remained Roman until Franks invaded it in the 5th century.

Charles the Bald, inheritor of *Francia Occidentalis,* founded the Carolingian dynasty, which ruled over a kingdom increasingly feudalized. By 987, the crown passed to Hugh Capet, a princeling who controlled only the Ile-de-France, the region surrounding Paris. For 350 years, an unbroken Capetian line added to its domain and consolidated royal authority until the accession in 1328 of Philip VI, first of the Valois line. France was then the most powerful nation in Europe, with a population of 15 million.

The missing pieces in Philip's domain were the French provinces still held by the Plantagenet kings of England, who also claimed the French crown. Beginning in 1338, the Hundred Years' War eventually settled the contest. English longbows defeated French armored knights at Crécy (1346) and the English also won the second landmark battle at Agincourt (1415), but the final victory went to the French at Castillon (1453).

Absolute monarchy reached its apogee in the reign of Louis XIV (1643–1715), the Sun King, whose brilliant court was the center of the Western world.

Revolution plunged France into a blood bath beginning in 1789 and ending with a new authoritarianism under Napoleon Bonaparte, who had successfully defended the infant republic from foreign attack and then made himself First Consul in 1799 and Emperor in 1804.

The Congress of Vienna (1815) sought to restore the pre-Napoleonic order in the person of Louis XVIII, but industrialization and the middle class, both fostered under Napoleon, built pressure for change, and a revolution in 1848 drove Louis Phillipe, last of the Bourbons, into exile.

A second republic elected as its president Prince Louis Napoleon, a nephew of Napoleon I, who declared the Second Empire in 1852 and took the throne as Napoleon III. His opposition to the rising power of Prussia ignited the Franco-Prussian War (1870–71), ending in his defeat and abdication.

Rulers of France

Name	Born	Ruled[1]		Name	Born	Ruled[1]
CAROLINGIAN DYNASTY				**FIRST REPUBLIC**		
Pepin the Short	c. 714	751–768		National Convention	—	1792–1795
Charlemagne[2]	742	768–814		Directory (Directoire)	—	1795–1799
Louis I the Debonair[3]	778	814–840				
Charles I the Bald[4]	823	840–877		**CONSULATE**		
Louis II the Stammerer	846	877–879		Napoleon Bonaparte[15]	1769	1799–1804
Louis III[5]	c. 863	879–882				
Carloman[5]	?	879–884		**FIRST EMPIRE**		
Charles II the Fat[6]	839	884–887 [7]		Napoleon I	1769	1804–1815 [16]
Eudes (Odo), Count						
of Paris	?	888–898		**RESTORATION OF**		
Charles III the Simple[8]	879	893–923 [9]		**HOUSE OF BOURBON**		
Robert I[10]	c. 865	922–923		Louis XVIII le Désiré	1755	1814–1824
Rudolf (Raoul), Duke				Charles X	1757	1824–1830 [17]
of Burgundy	?	923–936				
Louis IV d'Outremer	c. 921	936–954		**BOURBON-ORLEANS LINE**		
Lothair	941	954–986		Louis Philippe		
Louis V the Sluggard	c. 967	986–987		("Citizen King")	1773	1830–1848 [18]
CAPETIAN DYNASTY				**SECOND REPUBLIC**		
Hugh Capet	c. 940	987–996		Louis Napoleon[19]	1808	1848–1852
Robert II the Pious[11]	c. 970	996–1031				
Henry I	1008	1031–1060		**SECOND EMPIRE**		
Philip I	1052	1060–1108		Napoleon III		
Louis VI the Fat	1081	1108–1137		(Louis Napoleon)	1808	1852–1870 [20]
Louis VII the Young	c.1121	1137–1180				
Philip II (Philip Augustus)	1165	1180–1223		**THIRD REPUBLIC (PRESIDENTS)**		
Louis VIII the Lion	1187	1223–1226		Louis Adolphe Thiers	1797	1871–1873
Louis IX (St. Louis)	1214	1226–1270		Marie E. P. M.		
Philip III the Bold	1245	1270–1285		de MacMahon	1808	1873–1879
Philip IV the Fair	1268	1285–1314		François P. J. Grévy	1807	1879–1887
Louis X the Quarreler	1289	1314–1316		Sadi Carnot	1837	1887–1894
John I[12]	1316	1316		Jean Casimir–Périer	1847	1894–1895
Philip V the Tall	1294	1316–1322		François Félix Faure	1841	1895–1899
Charles IV the Fair	1294	1322–1328		Émile Loubet	1838	1899–1906
				Clement Armand Fallières	1841	1906–1913
HOUSE OF VALOIS				Raymond Poincaré	1860	1913–1920
Philip VI	1293	1328–1350		Paul E. L. Deschanel	1856	1920–1920
John II the Good	1319	1350–1364		Alexandre Millerand	1859	1920–1924
Charles V the Wise	1337	1364–1380		Gaston Doumergue	1863	1924–1931
Charles VI				Paul Doumer	1857	1931–1932
the Well–Beloved	1368	1380–1422		Albert Lebrun	1871	1932–1940
Charles VII	1403	1422–1461				
Louis XI	1423	1461–1483		**VICHY GOVERNMENT**		
Charles VIII	1470	1483–1498		**(CHIEF OF STATE)**		
Louis XII the Father				Henri Philippe Pétain	1856	1940–1944
of the People	1462	1498–1515				
Francis I	1494	1515–1547		**PROVISIONAL GOVERNMENT**		
Henry II	1519	1547–1559		**(PRESIDENTS)**		
Francis II	1544	1559–1560		Charles de Gaulle	1890	1944–1946
Charles IX	1550	1560–1574		Félix Gouin	1884	1946–1946
Henry III	1551	1574–1589		Georges Bidault	1899	1946–1947
HOUSE OF BOURBON				**FOURTH REPUBLIC (PRESIDENTS)**		
Henry IV of Navarre	1553	1589–1610		Vincent Auriol	1884	1947–1954
Louis XIII	1601	1610–1643		René Coty	1882	1954–1959
Louis XIV the Great	1638	1643–1715				
Louis XV the Well–Beloved	1710	1715–1774		**FIFTH REPUBLIC (PRESIDENTS)**		
Louis XVI	1754	1774–1792 [13]		Charles de Gaulle	1890	1959–1969
Louis XVII (Louis Charles				Georges Pompidou	1911	1969–1974
de France)[14]	1785	1793–1795		Valéry Giscard d'Estaing	1926	1974–1981
				François Mitterrand	1916	1981–1995
				Jacques Chirac		1995–

1. For Kings and Emperors through the Second Empire, year of end of rule is also that of death, unless otherwise indicated. 2. Crowned Emperor of the West in 800. His brother, Carloman, ruled as King of the Eastern Franks from 768 until his death in 771. 3. Holy Roman Emperor 814–840. 4. Holy Roman Emperor 875–877 as Charles II. 5. Ruled jointly 879–882. 6. Holy Roman Emperor 881–887 as Charles III. 7. Died 888. 8. King 893–898 in opposition to Eudes. 9. Died 929. 10. Not counted in regular line of Kings of France by some authorities. Elected by nobles but killed in Battle of Soissons. 11. Sometimes called Robert I. 12. Posthumous son of Louis X; lived for only five days. 13. Executed 1793. 14. Titular King only. He died in prison according to official reports, but many pretenders appeared during the Bourbon restoration. 15. As First Consul, Napoleon held the power of government. In 1804, he became Emperor. 16. Abdicated first time June 1814. Re–entered Paris March 1815, after escape from Elba; Louis XVIII fled to Ghent. Abdicated second time June 1815. He named as his successor his son, Napoleon II, who was not acceptable to the Allies. He died 1821. 17. Died 1836. 18. Died 1850. 19. President; became Emperor in 1852. 20. Died 1873.

A new France emerged from World War I as the continent's dominant power. But four years of hostile occupation had reduced northeast France to ruins. The postwar Third Republic was plagued by political instability and economic chaos.

From 1919, French foreign policy aimed at keeping Germany weak through a system of alliances, but it failed to halt the rise of Adolf Hitler and the Nazi war machine. On May 10, 1940, mechanized Nazi troops attacked, and, as they approached Paris, Italy joined with Germany. The Germans marched into an undefended Paris and Marshal Henri Philippe Pétain signed an armistice June 22. France was split into an occupied north and an unoccupied south, the latter becoming a totalitarian state with Pétain as its chief.

Allied armies liberated France in August 1944. The French Committee of National Liberation, formed in Algiers in 1943, established a provisional government in Paris headed by Gen. Charles de Gaulle. The Fourth Republic was born Dec. 24, 1946.

The Empire became the French Union; the National Assembly was strengthened and the presidency weakened; and France joined the North Atlantic Treaty Organization. A war against communist insurgents in Indochina was abandoned after the defeat at Dien Bien Phu. A new rebellion in Algeria threatened a military coup, and on June 1, 1958, the Assembly invited de Gaulle to return as Premier with extraordinary powers. He drafted a new Constitution for a Fifth Republic, adopted Sept. 28, which strengthened the presidency and reduced legislative power. He was elected President Dec. 21.

De Gaulle took France out of the NATO military command in 1967 and expelled all foreign-controlled troops from the country. He later went on to attempt to achieve a long-cherished plan of regional reform. This, however, aroused wide opposition. He decided to stake his fate on a referendum. At the voting in April 1969, the electorate defeated the plan.

His successor Georges Pompidou continued the de Gaulle policies of seeking to expand France's influence in the Mideast and Africa.

Socialist François Mitterrand attained a stunning victory in the May 10, 1981, presidential election over the Gaullist alliance that had held power since 1958.

The victors immediately moved to carry out campaign pledges to nationalize major industries, halt nuclear testing, suspend nuclear power plant construction, and impose new taxes on the rich. On Feb. 11, 1982, the nationalization bills became law.

The Socialists' policies during Mitterrand's first two years created a 12% inflation rate, a huge trade deficit, and devaluations of the franc. In early 1983, Mitterrand embarked on an austerity program to control inflation and reduce the trade deficit. He increased taxes and slashed government spending. A halt in economic growth, declining purchasing power for the average Frenchman, and an increase in unemployment to 10% followed. Mitterrand sank lower and lower in the opinion polls.

In March 1986, a center-right coalition led by Jacques Chirac won a slim majority in legislative elections. Chirac became Premier initiating a period of "cohabitation" between him and the Socialist President, Mitterrand.

Mitterrand's decisive reelection in May 1987 led to Chirac being replaced as Premier by Michel Rocard, a Socialist.

Relations, however, cooled with Rocard, and in May 1991 he was replaced with Edith Cresson, France's first female Prime Minister and like Mitterrand a Socialist.

In foreign policy France continued its active engagement in the Bosnian conflict and intervened in Rwanda to help halt the widespread slaughter there.

On his third try Chirac won the presidency in May 1995, gaining more than 52% of the vote. He campaigned vigorously on a platform to reduce unemployment, but moved quickly to cement ties with Germany.

Breaking a three-year international moratorium, France began a series of nuclear weapons tests in September 1995. International outcries were swift and vocal, leading to an early cessation of the tests in January 1996.

Overseas Departments

Overseas Departments elect representatives to the National Assembly, and the same administrative organization as that of mainland France applies to them.

FRENCH GUIANA (including ININI)

Status: Overseas Department
Prefect: Pierre Dartout (1995)
Area: 32,253 sq mi. (83,534 sq km)
Population (est. 1996): 151,187; growth rate: 2.01%; birth rate 24.7/1000; infant mortality rate 14.6/1000; density per square mile: 4.7
Capital and largest city (1995 est.): Cayenne, 41,659.
Monetary unit: Franc. **Language:** French. **Religion:** Roman Catholic. **Literacy rate:** 73%
Economic summary: Gross domestic product (1993 est.): $800 million; $6,000 per capita; inflation (1992): 2.5%; unemployment (1990): 13%. Arable land: negligible; principal agricultural products: rice, cassava, bananas, sugar cane. Labor force (1993): 46,300; 21.2% in industry. Major industrial products: timber, rum, rosewood essence, gold mining, processed shrimp. Natural resources: bauxite, timber, cinnabar, kaolin. Exports: $59 million (f.o.b., 1992): shrimp, timber, rum, rosewood essence. Imports: $1.5 billion (c.i.f., 1992): food, consumer and producer goods, petroleum. Major trading partners: U.S., France, Japan.

French Guiana, lying north of Brazil and east of Suriname on the northeast coast of South America, was first settled in 1637. Penal settlements, embracing the area around the mouth of the Maroni River and the Iles du Salut (including Devil's Island), were founded in 1852; they have since been abolished.

During World War II, French Guiana at first adhered to the Vichy government, but the Free French took over in 1943. French Guiana accepted in 1958 the new Constitution of the French Fifth Republic and remained an Overseas Department of the French Republic.

GUADELOUPE

Status: Overseas Department
Prefect: Michel Diefenbacher
Area: 327 sq mi. (848 sq km)
Population (est. 1996): 407,768 (average annual growth rate: 1.22%); birth rate: 17.8/1000; infant mortality rate: 8.3/1000; density per square mile: 1,247
Capital (1990): Basse-Terre, 14,000; **Largest city (1990):** Pointe-à-Pitre, over 26,029. **Monetary unit:** Franc. **Language:** French, Creole patois. **Religions:** Roman Catholic. **Literacy rate:** over 70%

Economic summary: Gross domestic product (1993 est.): $3.8 billion; $9,000 per capita; real growth rate n.a.; inflation (1990): 3.7%; unemployment (1990): 33.1%. Arable land: 18%; principal agricultural products: sugar cane, bananas, eggplant, flowers. Labor force (1993): 129,700; 25.8% industry. Major industries: construction, public works, sugar, rum, tourism. Exports: $130 million (f.o.b., 1992): sugar, rum, bananas. Imports: $1.5 billion (c.i.f., 1992): foodstuffs, clothing, consumer goods, construction materials, petroleum products, vehicles. Major trading partners: France, Martinique, Italy, Germany, U.S.

Guadeloupe, in the West Indies about 300 miles (483 km) southeast of Puerto Rico, was discovered by Columbus in 1493. It consists of the twin islands of Basse-Terre and Grande-Terre and five dependencies—Marie-Galante, Les Saintes, La Désirade, St. Barthélemy, and the northern half of St. Martin. The volcano Soufrière (4,813 ft; 1,467 m), also called La Grande Soufrière, is the highest point on Guadeloupe. Violent activity in 1976 and 1977 caused thousands to flee their homes.

French colonization began in 1635. In 1958, Guadeloupe voted in favor of the new Constitution of the French Fifth Republic and remained an Overseas Department of the French Republic.

MARTINIQUE

Status: Overseas Department
Prefect: Jean-François Cordet
Area: 436 sq mi. (1,128 sq km)
Population (est. 1996): 399,151 (average annual growth rate: 1.1%); birth rate: 16.9/1000; infant mortality rate: 7.1/1000; density per square mile: 915.5
Capital and largest city (1990): Fort-de-France, 100,072; Other large cities (1990): Le Lamentin, 30,026; Schoelcher, 19,683; Sainte-Marie, 19,683. **Monetary unit:** Franc. **Languages:** French, Creole patois. **Religion:** Roman Catholic. **Literacy rate:** over 70%
Economic summary: Gross domestic product (1993 est.): $3.9 billion; $10,000 per capita; inflation (1990): 3.9%; unemployment (1994): 23.5%. Average annual growth rate n.a. Arable land: 10%; principal agricultural products: sugar cane, bananas, rum, pineapples. Labor force (1994): 164,877; 31.7% in service industry. Major industries: sugar, rum, refined oil, cement, tourism. Natural resources: coastal scenery and beaches. Exports: $247 million (f.o.b., 1992): bananas, refined petroleum products, rum, sugar, pineapples. Imports: $1.75 billion (c.i.f., 1992): foodstuffs, clothing and other consumer goods, petroleum products, construction materials. Major trading partners: France, U.S., Guadeloupe, Germany, U.K., Italy, Japan.

Martinique, lying in the Lesser Antilles about 300 miles (483 km) northeast of Venezuela, was probably discovered by Columbus in 1502 and was taken for France in 1635. Following the Franco-German armistice of 1940, it had a semiautonomous status until 1943, when authority was relinquished to the Free French. The area, administered by a Prefect assisted by an elected council, is represented in the French Parliament. In 1958, Martinique voted in favor of the new Constitution of the French Fifth Republic and remained an Overseas Department of the French Republic.

RÉUNION

Status: Overseas Department
Prefect: Pierre Steinmetz (1995)
Area: 970 sq mi. (2,512 sq km)
Population (est. 1996): 679,198 (average annual growth rate, 1.93%); birth rate: 24/1000; infant mortality rate: 7.5/1000; density per square mile: 700.2
Capital and largest city (1993): Saint-Denis, 121,999. Other cities (est. 1993): Saint-Paul, 71,667; Saint-Pierre, 58,846; Le Tampon, 47,598; Saint-Louis, 37,420. **Monetary unit:** Franc. **Languages:** French, Creole. **Religion:** Roman Catholic
Economic summary: Gross domestic product (1993 est.): $2.5 billion; $3,900 per capita; inflation (1988) 1.3%; unemployment (Feb. 91) 35%. Arable land: 20%; principal agricultural products: rum, vanilla, bananas, perfume plants. Major industrial products: rum, cigarettes, processed sugar. Exports: $166 million (f.o.b., 1988): sugar, perfume essences, rum, molasses. Imports: $1.7 billion (c.i.f., 1988): manufactured goods, foodstuffs, beverages, machinery and transportation equipment, petroleum products. Major trading partners: France, Mauritius, Bahrain, South Africa, Italy.

Discovered by Portuguese navigators in the 16th century, the island of Réunion, then uninhabited, was taken as a French possession in 1642. It is located about 450 miles (724 km) east of Madagascar, in the Indian Ocean. In 1958, Réunion approved the Constitution of the Fifth French Republic and remained an Overseas Department of the French Republic.

Overseas Territories

Overseas Territories are comparable to Departments, except that their administrative organization includes a locally-elected government.

ST. PIERRE AND MIQUELON

Status: Overseas Territory
Prefect: René Maurice
Area: 93 sq mi. (242 sq km)
Population (est. 1996): 6,809; growth rate 0.71%; birth rate 12.8/1000; infant mortality rate 9.95/1000; density per square mile: 73.2
Capital (1990): Saint Pierre, 5,683
Economic summary: Gross domestic product (1993 est.): $66 million; $10,000 per capita; unemployment (1990) 9.6%. Major industries: fishing, canneries. Exports: $30 million (f.o.b., 1991 est.): fish, pelts. Imports: $82 million (c.i.f., 1991 est.): meat, clothing, fuel, electrical equipment, machinery, building materials. Major trading partners: Canada, France, U.S., U.K., the Netherlands.

The sole remnant of the French colonial empire in North America, these islands were first occupied by the French in 1604. Their only importance arises from proximity to the Grand Banks, located 10 miles south of Newfoundland, making them the center of the French Atlantic cod fisheries. On July 19, 1976, the islands became an Overseas Department of the French Republic.

FRENCH POLYNESIA

Status: Overseas Territory
High Commissioner: Paul Ronciere
Area: 1,609 sq mi. (4,167 sq km)
Population (est. 1996): 224,911 (average annual growth rate: 2.19%); birth rate: 27.2/1000; infant mortality rate: 14.4/1000; density per square mile: 139.8

Capital (1988): Papeete (on Tahiti), 23,555; **Monetary unit:** Pacific financial community franc. **Language:** French. **Religions:** Protestant, 55%; Roman Catholic, 32%

Economic summary: Gross domestic product (1993 est.): $1.5 billion; $7,000 per capita; inflation (1994) 1.5%; unemployment (1990 est.) 10%. Principal agricultural product: copra. Major industries: tourism, maintenance of French nuclear test base. Exports: $88.9 million (f.o.b., 1989): coconut products, mother of pearl, vanilla. Imports: $765 million (c.i.f., 1989): fuels, foodstuffs, equipment. Major trading partners: France, U.S.

The term French Polynesia is applied to the scattered French possessions in the South Pacific—Mangareva (Gambier), Makatea, the Marquesas Islands, Rapa, Rurutu, Rimatara, the Society Islands, the Tuamotu Archipelago, Tubuai, Raivavae, and the island of Clipperton—which were organized into a single colony in 1903. There are 120 islands, of which 25 are uninhabited.

The President of the Territorial Government is assisted by a Council of Government and a popularly elected Territorial Assembly. The principal and most populous island—Tahiti, in the Society group—was claimed as French in 1768. In 1958, French Polynesia voted in favor of the new Constitution of the French Fifth Republic and remained an Overseas Territory of the French Republic. The natives are mostly Maoris.

The Pacific Nuclear Test Center on the atoll of Mururoa, 744 miles (1,200 km) from Tahiti, was completed in 1966.

To compensate the residents for the nuclear weapons tests in 1995–96 France offered a 10-year $194 million annual compensation package.

MAYOTTE

Status: Territorial collectivity
Prefect: Alain Weil
Area: 146 sq mi. (378 sq km)
Population (est. 1996): 100,838; average annual rate of natural increase 3.78%; birth rate 47.9/1000; infant mortality rate 75.3/1000; density per square mile: 690.7
Capital and largest city (1991): Dzaoudzi (Mamoudzou), 20,450
Economic summary: Gross domestic product (1993 est.): $54 million, $600 per capita. Exports (1984): $4 million (f.o.b.). Imports $21.8 million (f.o.b., 1984). Principal products: vanilla, ylang-ylang, coffee, copra. Exports: Ylang-ylang, vanilla. Imports: building materials, transportation equipment, rice, clothing, flour. Major trading partners: France, Comoros, Reunion, Kenya, South Africa, Pakistan.

The most populous of the Comoro Islands in the Indian Ocean, with a Christian majority, Mayotte voted in 1974 and 1976 against joining the other, predominantly Moslem islands, in declaring themselves independent. It continues to retain its ties to France.

NEW CALEDONIA AND DEPENDENCIES

Status: Overseas Territory
High Commissioner: Didier Cultiaux
Area: 7,374 sq mi. (19,103 sq km)[1]
Population (est. 1996): 187,784 (average annual growth rate: 1.69%); birth rate: 21.8/1000; infant mortality rate: 13.8/1000; density per square mile: 25.5
Capital (1989): Nouméa, 65,110; **Monetary unit:** Pacific financial community franc. **Languages:** French, Mela-

nesian, and Polynesian dialects. **Religion:** Roman Catholic, 60%; Protestant, 30%. **Literacy rate:** 91%
Economic summary: Gross domestic product (1991 est): $1 billion; real growth rate (1988) 2.4%; per capita income $7,650 (1990); inflation (1990) 1.4%, unemployment (1989) 16%. Principal agricultural products: coffee, copra, beef, wheat, vegetables. Major industrial product: nickel. Natural resources: nickel, chromite, iron ore. Exports: $671 million (f.o.b., 1989): nickel, chrome. Imports: $764 million (c.i.f., 1989): mineral fuels, machinery, electrical equipment, foodstuffs. Major trading partners: France, Japan, U.S., Australia.

1. Including dependencies.

New Caledonia (6,466 sq mi.; 16,747 sq km), about 1,070 miles (1,722 km) northeast of Sydney, Australia, was discovered by Capt. James Cook in 1774 and annexed by France in 1853. The government also administers the Isle of Pines, the Loyalty Islands (Uvéa, Lifu, and Maré), the Belep Islands, the Huon Island group, and Chesterfield Islands.

The natives are Melanesians; about one third of the population is white and one fifth Indochinese and Javanese. The French National Assembly on July 31, 1984, voted a bill into law that granted internal autonomy to New Caledonia and opened the way to possible eventual independence. This touched off ethnic tensions and violence between the natives and the European settlers, with the natives demanding full independence and sovereignty while the settlers wanted to remain part of France. In June 1988, France resumed direct administration of the territory and promised a referendum on self-determination in 1998. This was agreed to by organizations representing the natives and the French settlers.

SOUTHERN AND ANTARCTIC LANDS

Status: Overseas Territory
Administrator: Christian Dors
Area: 3,004 sq mi. (7,781 sq km, excluding Adélie Land)
Capital: Port-au-Français

This territory is uninhabited except for the personnel of scientific bases. It consists of Adélie Land (166,752 sq mi.; 431,888 sq km) on the Antarctic mainland and the following islands in the southern Indian Ocean: the Kerguelen and Crozet archipelagos and the islands of Saint-Paul and New Amsterdam.

WALLIS AND FUTUNA ISLANDS

Status: Overseas Territory
Administrator: Léon-Alexandre Legrand
Area: 106 sq mi. (274 sq km)
Population (est. 1996): 14,659; growth rate 1.94%; birth rate 24.4/1000; infant mortality rate 23.6/1000; density per square mile: 138.3
Capital (1983): Mata-Utu. **Languages:** French, Wallisian. **Religion:** Roman Catholic. **Literacy rate:** 50%.
Economic summary: Gross domestic product (1994 est.): $28.7 million; $2,000 per capita. Exports: $6.6 million (f.o.b., 1986). Imports: $13.3 million (c.i.f., 1984): foodstuffs, manufactured goods, transport equipment, fuel.

The two island groups in the South Pacific between Fiji and Samoa were settled by French missionaries at the beginning of the 19th century. A protectorate was established in the 1880s. Following a referendum by the Polynesian inhabitants, the status was changed to that of an Overseas Territory in 1961.

GABON

Gabonese Republic
President: Omar Bongo (1967)
Premier: Paulin Obame-Nguema (1994)
Area: 103,346 sq mi. (267,667 sq km)
Population (est. 1996): 1,172,798 (average annual rate of natural increase: 1.47%); birth rate: 28.2/1000; infant mortality rate: 90.1/1000; density per square mile: 11.3
Capital and largest city (1994): Libreville, 419,596. **Other cities (1994):** Port-Gentil, 80,000; Franceville, 42,000.
Monetary unit: Franc CFA. **Main ethnic groups:** Fang 25%, Punu 23.8%, Nzeiby 11.26%, Mbedé 8%, Kota 7%, Myené 4.8%. **Languages:** French (official). **Religions:** Christian 65%, animist 34.5%, Muslim 0.5%. **National name:** République Gabonaise. **Member of French Community; Literacy rate:** 95%
Economic summary: Gross domestic product (1994 est.): $5.6 billion; $3,600 per capita (!995); real growth rate (1995 est.): 3%; inflation 32% (1995); unemployment 20% (1995). Arable land: more than 65%. Principal agricultural products: cocoa, coffee, wood, palm oil. Labor force: Industry 45%, services 47%, agriculture 8%. Major industrial products: petroleum, natural gas, processed wood, manganese, uranium. Natural resources: wood, petroleum, iron ore, manganese, uranium. Exports: $2.1 billion (f.o.b., 1993 est.): crude oil, manganese, wood, uranium. Imports: $832 million (c.i.f., 1993 est.): foodstuffs, chemical products, petroleum products, construction materials, manufactures, machinery. Major trading partners: France, U.S., Germany, Japan, Cameroon.

Geography. This West African country with the Atlantic as its western border is also bounded by Equatorial Guinea, Cameroon, and the Congo. Its area is slightly less than Colorado's.

From mangrove swamps on the coast, the land becomes divided plateaus in the north and east and mountains in the north. Most of the country is covered by a dense tropical forest.

Government. A republic, with a multiparty presidential regime (opposition parties legalized 1990). The president is elected for a five-year term. Legislative powers are exercised by a 120-seat National Assembly, which is elected for a five-year term. After his conversion to Islam in 1973, President Bongo changed his given name, Albert Bernard, to Omar. The Rassemblement Social Démocrate Gabonais is led by President Bongo. He was re-elected without opposition in 1973, 1980, and in 1993.

History. Little is known of Gabon's history, even in oral tradition, but Pygmies are believed to be the original inhabitants. Now there are many tribal groups in the country, the largest being the Fang people, who constitute a third of the population.

Gabon was first visited by the Portuguese navigator Diego Cam in the 15th century. In 1839, the French founded their first settlement on the left bank of the Gabon Estuary and gradually occupied the hinterland during the second half of the 19th century. It was organized as a French territory in 1888 and became an autonomous republic within the French Union after World War II and an independent republic on Aug. 17, 1960.

Following strikes and riots the president called a national conference in March 1990. In May it adopted a transitional constitution legalizing political parties and calling for free elections.

In its first multiparty election in December 1993 the incumbent president received just over 51% of the vote while the opposition candidate refused to accept defeat, charging fraud, and tried to establish a rival government.

Rioting in the capital caused the issuance of a state of siege in February 1994. Growing dissension within the army also led the president to call for a peace conference in September. As a result a coalition government was formed in November.

A referendum on a new constitution, supported by all political parties, took place in July 1995 and won approval.

GAMBIA, THE

Republic of the Gambia
Head of state: Capt. Yahya Ajj Jammeh
Area: 4,093 sq mi. (10,600 sq km)
Population (est. 1996): 1,020,178 (average annual rate of natural increase: 3.08%); birth rate: 45.5/1000; infant mortality rate: 118.1/1000; density per square mile: 249.2
Capital (1986): Banjul, 44,188. **Monetary unit:** Dalasi. **Languages:** Native tongues, English (official). **Religions:** Islam, 90%; Christian, 9%; traditional, 1%. **Literacy rate:** 27%. **Member of Commonwealth of Nations**
Economic summary: Gross domestic product (1993 est.): $1 billion; per capita $1,050; real growth rate n.a.; inflation 6.5%. Arable land: 16%. Principal products: peanuts, rice, palm kernels. Labor force: 400,000; 18.9% in industry, commerce, services. Major industrial products: processed peanuts, fish, hides. Natural resources: fish. Exports: $81 million (f.o.b., FY92/93 est.): peanuts and peanut products, fish, cotton, lint, palm kernels. Imports: $154 million (f.o.b., FY92/93 est.): foodstuffs, fuel, machinery, transport equipment, manufactures, raw materials. Major trading partners: U.S., E.C., Asia.

Geography. Situated on the Atlantic coast in westernmost Africa and surrounded on three sides by Senegal, Gambia is twice the size of Delaware. The Gambia River flows for 200 miles (322 km) through Gambia on its way to the Atlantic. The country, the smallest on the continent, averages only 20 miles (32 km) in width.

Government. A military regime following a coup on July 22, 1994. The constitution was suspended and political parties were banned.

History. During the 17th century, Gambia was settled by various companies of English merchants. Slavery was the chief source of revenue until it was abolished in 1807. Gambia became a crown colony in 1843 and an independent nation within the Commonwealth of Nations on Feb. 18, 1965.

Full independence was approved in a 1970 referendum, and on April 24 of that year Gambia proclaimed itself a republic.

Elections of April 29, 1992, returned Jawara for a fifth term. His People's Progressive Party won 25 of the 36 seats in the House of Representatives.

A military coup in July 1994 deposed the president, suspended the constitution, and banned political parties.

The government in 1995 continued to maintain it intended to restore civilian rule, and an attempted coup was suppressed in January.

GEORGIA

Republic of Georgia
President: Eduard Shevardnadze (1995)
Secretary of State: Niko Lekishvili (1995)
Area: 26,900 sq mi. (169,000 sq km)
Population (est. 1996): 5,219,810 (Georgians, 70%; largest minorities: Armenians; other: Russians and Azerbaijanis); average annual rate of natural increase: 0.06%; birth rate: 12.8/1000; infant mortality rate: 22.5/1000; density per square mile: 194
Capital and largest city (1991): Tbilisi, 1,279,000. Other cities (1989): Kutaisi, 235,000; Batumi, 136,000; and Sukhumi, 121,000. **Monetary unit:** coupon (temporary). **Language:** Georgian (official), 71%; Russian, 9%; Armenian, 7%; Azerbaijani, 6%. **Religion:** Georgian Orthodox, 65%; Russian Orthodox, 10%; Armenian Orthodox, 8%; Muslim, 11%
Economic summary: Gross domestic product (1994 est.) $6 billion, $1,060 per capita; –30% real growth rate; inflation 40.5% (per mo.); unemployment 5%. Labor force (1990): 2,763,000: industry and construction, 31%; agriculture and forestry, 25%. Industries: heavy industrial products include raw steel, rolled steel, cement, lumber, machine tools, foundry equipment, electric locomotives, tower cranes, welding equipment, meat packing, dairy and fishing, farm machinery. Agriculture: citrus fruits, grapes, sugar, vegetables, grains, cattle, sheep, goats, pigs, and poultry. Exports: $176 million (f.o.b., 1990): citrus fruits, tea, other agricultural products, diverse types of machinery, ferrous and non-ferrous metals, textiles. Imports: $1.5 billion (c.i.f., 1990): machinery and parts, fuel, transport equipment, textiles. Major trading partners: Russia, Turkey, Azerbaijan, Ukraine, Germany, U.S.

Geography. Georgia is a land of snow-capped mountains, turbulent rivers, dense forests, and fertile valleys. Mt. Kazbet, 16,541 ft (5,042 m) is the country's tallest peak. Georgia's principal rivers, Kura Mtkvari and the Rioni, and their tributaries are harnessed to provide an abundance of hydroelectric power for the country. Georgia is bordered by the Black Sea in the west, by Turkey and Armenia in the south, by Azerbaijan in the east, and Russia in the north. The republic also includes the Abkhaz and Adzhar autonomous republics and the Yugo-Ossetian Autonomous Oblast.

Government. A republic with a unicameral parliament. The president and 246-member parliament were elected on Nov. 5, 1995.

History. Georgia became a kingdom about 4 B.C. and reached its greatest period of expansion in the 12th century when its territory included the whole of Transcaucasia. The country was the scene of a struggle between Persia and Turkey from the 16th century on, and in the 18th century became a vassal to Russia in exchange for protection from the Turks.

Georgia joined Azerbaijan and Armenia in 1917 to establish the anti-Bolshevik Transcaucasian Federation, and upon its dissolution proclaimed its independence in 1918. In 1922, the Red Army invaded Georgia and replaced the republic with a Soviet government. In 1922, Georgia, Armenia, and Azerbaijan were annexed and formed into the Transcaucasian Soviet Socialist Republic affiliated with the U.S.S.R. In 1936, it became a separate Soviet republic.

Zviad Gamsakhurdia won the first directly elected Soviet presidency in 1990 with 86.5% of the vote, pledging to lead Georgia toward independence. Georgia proclaimed its independence on April 9, 1990.

Gamsakhurdia was later accused of dictatorial policies, the jailing of opposition leaders, human rights abuses, and clamping down on the media. A two-week civil war centered in the capital of Tbilisi ensued and Gamsakhurdia was forced to flee to Azerbaijan and later to Armenia.

During 1993 the government continued to fight separatists in Abkhazia.

In February 1994 Russia and Georgia signed a cooperation treaty that authorized Russia to keep three military bases in Georgia and allow Russians to train and equip the Georgian army. In March the country joined NATO's Partnership for Peace program.

The economy continued in free-fall, and the parliament failed to act on market reforms.

Parliament ratified the cooperation treaty with Russia in January 1996. In May Georgia and its breakaway region of South Ossetia agreed to a cessation of hostilities in their 6-year conflict.

GERMANY

Federal Republic of Germany
President: Roman Herzog (1994)
Chancellor: Helmut Kohl (1982)
Area: 137,826 sq mi. (356,970 sq km): Western Germany: 96,095 sq mi, the size of Wyoming; Eastern Germany: 41,731 sq mi, the size of Virginia.
Population (est. 1996): 83,536,115 (average annual growth rate: –0.15%; birth rate: 9.7/1000; infant mortality rate: 6/1000; density per square mile: 606
Capital and largest city (May 1995): Berlin (capital since Oct. 3, 1990), 3,057,895; Bonn (seat of government), 297,900. **Largest cities (1995):** Hamburg, 1,701,600; Munich, 1,256,300; Cologne, 961,600; Frankfurt, 663,600; Essen, 624,600; Dortmund, 602,400; Stuttgart, 598,000; Dusseldorf, 577,600; Hannover, 525,300; Bremen, 552,700; Duisburg, 538,100. **Monetary unit:** Deutsche Mark. **Language:** German. **Religions (1993):** Protestant, 34%; Roman Catholic, 34%; other or none, 31%. **National name:** Bundesrepublik Deutschland. **Literacy rate:** 98%
Economic summary: Gross domestic product (1995): $2,306 billion; **per capita:** $28,250; **Western Germany:** $2,005 billion; per capita $31,066; **Eastern Germany:** $250 billion; per capita $16,200; **real growth rate:** 1.9%; West 1.6%; East 5.7%; **Inflation (1994):** 1.7%; **Unemployment (Apr. 1994):** West 9%, East 16%. Labor force: 36.75 million, 45% in industry, agriculture 6%. Exports: $485.0 billion (1995): manufactures 86.6% (including machines and precision tools, chemicals, motor vehicles, iron and steel products), agricultural products 4.9%, raw materials 2.3%, fuels 1.3%. Imports: $422.8 billion (1995): manufactures 68.5%, agricultural products 12%, fuels 9.7%, raw materials 1.3%. **Industries:** West: among the world's largest producers of iron, steel, coal, cement, chemicals, machinery, vehicles, machine tools, electronics, food and beverages. East: metal fabrication, chemicals, brown coal, shipbuilding, machine building, food and beverages, textiles, petroleum refining. **Agriculture:** West: fishing and forestry, diversified crop and livestock farming; principal crops include potatoes, wheat, rye, barley, sugar beets, fruit, cabbage, cattle, pigs, poultry. East: fishing and forestry, principal crops include wheat, rye, barley, potatoes, sugar beets, fruit, pork, beef, chicken, milk, hides and skins. Natural resources: iron ore, coal, potash, timber, lignite, uranium, copper, natural gas, salt, nickel. Major trading partners: France, Netherlands, Italy, Belgium-Luxembourg, U.S., U.K.

Rulers of Germany and Prussia

Name	Born	Ruled[1]	Name	Born	Ruled[1]
KINGS OF PRUSSIA			**GERMAN FEDERAL REPUBLIC (WEST) (CHANCELLORS)**		
Frederick I[2]	1657	1701–1713	Konrad Adenauer	1876	1949–1963
Frederick William I	1688	1713–1740	Ludwig Erhard	1897	1963–1966
Frederick II the Great	1712	1740–1786	Kurt Georg Kiesinger	1904	1966–1969
Frederick William II	1744	1786–1797	Willy Brandt	1913	1969–1974
Frederick William III	1770	1797–1840	Helmut Schmidt	1918	1974–1984
Frederick William IV	1795	1840–1861	Helmut Kohl	1930	1984–1990
William I	1797	1861–1871 [3]			
EMPERORS OF GERMANY			**GERMAN DEMOCRATIC REPUBLIC (EAST)**		
William I	1797	1871–1888	Wilhelm Pieck[5]	1876	1949–1960
Frederick III	1831	1888–1888	Walter Ulbricht[8]	1893	1960–1973
William II	1859	1888–1918 [4]	Willi Stoph[9]	1914	1973–1976
			Erich Honecker[9]	1912	1976–1989
WEIMAR REPUBLIC			Egon Krenz[9]	1937	1989–1989
Friedrich Ebert[5]	1871	1919–1925	Manfred Gerlach[9]		1989–1990
Paul von Hindenburg[5]	1847	1925–1934	Sabine Bergman-Pohl[9]		1990–1990
THIRD REICH					
Adolf Hitler[6, 7]	1889	1934–1945	**GERMAN FEDERAL REPUBLIC CHANCELLORS**		
Karl Doenitz[6]	1891	1945–1945	Helmut Kohl	1930	1991–

1. Year of end of rule is also that of death, unless otherwise indicated. 2. Was Elector of Brandenburg (1688–1701) as Frederick III. 3. Became Emperor of Germany in 1871. 4. Died 1941. 5. President. 6. Führer. 7. Named Chancellor by President Hindenburg in 1933. 8. Chairman of Council of State. Died 1973. 9. Chairman of Council of State.

Geography. The Federal Republic of Germany was occupied by the United States, Britain, and France after World War II, when the eastern half of prewar Germany was split roughly between a Soviet-occupied zone, which became the German Democratic Republic, and an area annexed by Poland. After being divided for more than four decades, the two Germanys were reunited on Oct. 3, 1990. The united Federal Republic is about the size of Montana.

Located in central Europe, Germany's neighbors are Denmark to the north; Netherlands, Belgium, Luxembourg, France to the west; Switzerland, Austria to the south; and Czech Republic, Poland to the east.

The northern plain, the central hill country, and the southern mountain district constitute the main physical divisions of West Germany, which is slightly smaller than Oregon. The Bavarian plateau in the southwest averages 1,600 feet (488 m) above sea level, but it reaches 9,721 feet (2,962 m) in the Zugspitze Mountains, the highest point in the country.

Important navigable rivers are the Danube, rising in the Black Forest and flowing east across Bavaria into Austria, and the Rhine, which rises in Switzerland and flows across the Netherlands in two channels to the North Sea and is navigable by ocean-going and coastal vessels as far as Cologne. The Elbe, which also empties into the North Sea, is navigable within Germany for smaller vessels. The Weser, flowing into the North Sea, and the Main and Mosel (Moselle), both tributaries of the Rhine, are also important. In addition, the Oder and Neisse Rivers form the border with Poland. The rivers Danube and Rhine in the Black Sea and the North Sea were connected in 1992 with the completion of the Rhine Main-Danube Canal.

Government. Under the Constitution of May 23, 1949, the Federal Republic was established as a parliamentary democracy. The Parliament consists of the Bundesrat, an upper chamber representing and appointed by the Länder, or states, and the Bundestag, a lower house elected for four years by universal suffrage. A federal assembly composed of Bundestag deputies as well as deputies from the state parliaments elects the President of the Republic for a five-year term; the Bundestag alone chooses the Chancellor, or Prime Minister. Each of the 16 Länder have a legislature popularly elected for a four-year or five-year term.

The major political parties are the Christian Democratic Union–Christian Social Union, with 244 seats (CDU) and 50 seats (CSU), led by Chancellor Helmut Kohl; the Social Democratic Party (SPD) with 252 seats, led by Rudolf Scharping; the Free Democratic Party (FDP) with 47 seats, led by Klaus Kinkel; the Alliance '90/Greens with 49 seats, led by Krista Sager and Jürgen Trittin; the Party of Democratic Socialism (PDS) with 30 seats, led by Lothar Bisky. Kohl's government is a coalition with the Free Democrats.

History. Immediately before the Christian era, when the Roman Empire had pushed its frontier to the Rhine, what is now Germany was inhabited by several tribes believed to have migrated from Central Asia between the 6th and 4th centuries B.C. One of these tribes, the Franks, attained supremacy in western Europe under Charlemagne, who was crowned Holy Roman Emperor A.D. 800. By the Treaty of Verdun (843), Charlemagne's lands east of the Rhine were ceded to the German Prince Louis. Additional territory acquired by the Treaty of Mersen (870) gave Germany approximately the area it maintained throughout the Middle Ages. For several centuries after Otto the Great was crowned King in 936, the German rulers were also usually heads of the Holy Roman Empire.

Relations between state and church were changed by the Reformation, which began with Martin Luther's 95 theses, and came to a head in 1547, when Charles V scattered the forces of the Protestant League at Mühlberg. Freedom of worship was guaranteed by the Peace of Augsburg (1555), but a Counter Reformation took place later, and a dispute over the succession to the Bohemian throne brought on the Thirty Years' War (1618–48), which devastated Germany and left the empire divided into hundreds of small principalities virtually independent of the Emperor.

Meanwhile, Prussia was developing into a state of considerable strength. Frederick the Great (1740–86) reorganized the Prussian army and defeated Maria Theresa of Austria in a struggle over Silesia. After the defeat of Napoleon at Waterloo (1815), the struggle between Austria and Prussia for supremacy in Germany continued, reaching its climax in the defeat of Austria in the Seven Weeks' War (1866) and the formation of the Prussian-dominated North German Confederation (1867).

The architect of German unity was Otto von Bismarck, a conservative, monarchist, and militaristic Prussian Junker who had no use for "empty phrase-making and constitutions." From 1862 until his retirement in 1890 he dominated not only the German but also the entire European scene. He unified all Germany in a series of three wars against Denmark (1864), Austria (1866), and France (1870–71), which many historians believe were instigated and promoted by Bismarck in his zeal to build a nation through "blood and iron."

On Jan. 18, 1871, King Wilhelm I of Prussia was proclaimed German Emperor in the Hall of Mirrors at Versailles. The North German Confederation, created in 1867, was abolished, and the Second German Reich, consisting of the North and South German states, was born. With a powerful army, an efficient bureaucracy, and a loyal bourgeoisie, Chancellor Bismarck consolidated a powerful centralized state.

Wilhelm II dismissed Bismarck in 1890 and embarked upon a "New Course," stressing an intensified colonialism and a powerful navy. His chaotic foreign policy culminated in the diplomatic isolation of Germany and the disastrous defeat in World War I (1914–18).

The Second German Empire collapsed following the defeat of the German armies in 1918, the naval mutiny at Kiel, and the flight of the Kaiser to the Netherlands on November 10. The Social Democrats, led by Friedrich Ebert and Philipp Scheidemann, crushed the Communists and established a moderate republic with Ebert as President.

The Weimar Constitution of 1919 provided for a President to be elected for seven years by universal suffrage and a bicameral legislature, consisting of the Reichsrat, representing the states, and the Reichstag, representing the people. It contained a model Bill of Rights. It was weakened, however, by a provision that enabled the President to rule by decree.

President Ebert died Feb. 28, 1925, and on April 26, Field Marshal Paul von Hindenburg was elected president.

The mass of Germans regarded the Weimar Republic as a child of defeat, imposed upon a Germany whose legitimate aspirations to world leadership had been thwarted by a world conspiracy. Added to this were a crippling currency debacle, a tremendous burden of reparations, and acute economic distress.

Adolf Hitler, an Austrian war veteran and a fanatical nationalist, fanned discontent by promising a Greater Germany, abrogation of the Treaty of Versailles, restoration of Germany's lost colonies, and destruction of the Jews. When the Social Democrats and the Communists refused to combine against the Nazi threat, President Hindenburg made Hitler chancellor on Jan. 30, 1933.

With the death of Hindenburg on Aug. 2, 1934, Hitler repudiated the Treaty of Versailles and began full-scale rearmament. In 1935 he withdrew Germany from the League of Nations, and the next year he reoccupied the Rhineland and signed the anti-Comintern pact with Japan, at the same time strengthening relations with Italy. Austria was annexed in March 1938. By the Munich agreement in September 1938 he gained the Czech Sudetenland, and in violation of this agreement he completed the dismemberment of Czechoslovakia in March 1939. But his invasion of Poland on Sept. 1, 1939, precipitated World War II.

On May 8, 1945, Germany surrendered unconditionally to Allied and Soviet military commanders, and on June 5 the four-nation Allied Control Council became the *de facto* government of Germany.

(For details of World War II, *see* Headline History.)

At the Berlin (or Potsdam) Conference (July 17–Aug. 2, 1945) President Truman, Premier Stalin, and Prime Minister Clement Attlee of Britain set forth the guiding principles of the Allied Control Council. They were Germany's complete disarmament and demilitarization, destruction of its war potential, rigid control of industry, and decentralization of the political and economic structure. Pending final determination of territorial questions at a peace conference, the three victors agreed in principle to the ultimate transfer of the city of Königsberg (now Kaliningrad) and its adjacent area to the U.S.S.R. and to the administration by Poland of former German territories lying generally east of the Oder-Neisse Line.

For purposes of control Germany was divided in 1945 into four national occupation zones, each headed by a Military Governor.

The Western powers were unable to agree with the U.S.S.R. on any fundamental issue. Work of the Allied Control Council was hamstrung by repeated Soviet vetoes; and finally, on March 20, 1948, Russia walked out of the Council. Meanwhile, the U.S. and Britain had taken steps to merge their zones economically (Bizone); and on May 31, 1948, the U.S., Britain, France, and the Benelux countries agreed to set up a German state comprising the three Western Zones.

The U.S.S.R. reacted by clamping a blockade on all ground communications between the Western Zones and Berlin, an enclave in the Soviet Zone. The Western Allies countered by organizing a gigantic airlift to fly supplies into the beleaguered city, assigning 60,000 men to it. The U.S.S.R. was finally forced to lift the blockade on May 12, 1949.

The Federal Republic of Germany was proclaimed on May 23, 1949, with its capital at Bonn. In free elections, West German voters gave a majority in the Constituent Assembly to the Christian Democrats, with the Social Democrats largely making up the opposition. Konrad Adenauer became Chancellor, and Theodor Heuss of the Free Democrats was elected first President.

When the Federal Republic of Germany was established in West Germany, the East German states adopted a more centralized constitution for the Democratic Republic of Germany, and it was put into effect on Oct. 7, 1949. The U.S.S.R. thereupon dissolved its occupation zone but Soviet troops remained. The Western Allies declared that the East German Republic was a Soviet creation undertaken without self-determination and refused to recognize it. It was recognized only within the Soviet bloc.

The area that was occupied by East Germany, as well as adjacent areas in Eastern Europe, consisted of Mecklenburg, Brandenburg, Lusatia, Saxony, and Thuringia. Soviet armies conquered the five territories by 1945. In the division of 1945 they were allotted to the U.S.S.R. Soviet forces created a state controlled by the secret police with a single party, the Socialist Unity (Communist) Party. The Russians appropriated East German plants to restore their war-ravaged industry.

THE BERLIN WALL (1961–1990)

Major anti-Communist riots broke out in East Berlin in June 1953 and, on Aug. 13, 1961, the Soviet Sector was sealed off by a Communist-built wall, 26 1/2 miles (43 km) long, running through the city. It was built to stem the flood of refugees seeking freedom in the West, 200,000 having fled in 1961 before the wall was erected.

On Nov. 9, 1989, several weeks after the resignation of East Germany's long-time Communist leader, Erich Honecker, the wall's designer and chief proponent, the East German government opened its borders to the West and allowed thousands of its citizens to pass freely through the Berlin Wall. They were cheered and greeted by thousands of West Berliners, and many of

the jubilant newcomers celebrated their new freedom by climbing on top of the hated wall.

The following day, East German troops began dismantling parts of the wall. It was ironic that this wall was built to keep the citizens from leaving and, 28 years later, it was being dismantled for the same reason.

On Nov. 22, new passages were opened at the north and south of the Brandenburg Gate in an emotional ceremony attended by Chancellor Helmut Kohl of West Germany and Chancellor Hans Modrow of East Germany. The opening of the Brandenburg Gate climaxed the ending of the barriers that had divided the German people since the end of World War II. By the end of 1990, the entire wall had been removed.

The 25-year diplomatic hiatus between East Germany and the U.S. ended Sept. 4, 1974, with the establishment of formal relations.

Agreements in Paris in 1954 giving the Federal Republic full independence and complete sovereignty came into force on May 5, 1955. Under it, West Germany and Italy became members of the Brussels Treaty Organization created in 1948 and renamed the Western European Union. West Germany also became a member of NATO. In 1955 the U.S.S.R. recognized the Federal Republic. The Saar territory, under an agreement between France and West Germany, held a plebiscite and despite economic links to France voted to rejoin West Germany. It became a state of West Germany on Jan. 1, 1957.

In 1963, Chancellor Adenauer concluded a treaty of mutual cooperation and friendship with France and then retired. He was succeeded by his chief inner-party critic, Ludwig Erhard, who was followed in 1966 by Kurt Georg Kiesinger. He, in turn, was succeeded in 1969 by Willy Brandt, former Mayor of West Berlin.

The division between West Germany and East Germany was intensified when the Communists erected the Berlin Wall in 1961. In 1968, the East German Communist leader, Walter Ulbricht, imposed restrictions on West German movements into West Berlin. The Soviet-bloc invasion of Czechoslovakia in August 1968 added to the tension.

West Germany in 1970 signed a treaty with Poland, renouncing force and setting Poland's western border as the Oder-Neisse Line. It subsequently resumed formal relations with Czechoslovakia in a pact that "voided" the Munich treaty that gave Nazi Germany the Sudetenland.

By 1973, normal relations were established between East and West Germany and the two states entered the United Nations.

Brandt, winner of a Nobel Peace Prize for his foreign policies, was forced to resign in 1974 when an East German spy was discovered to be one of his top staff members.

Helmut Schmidt, Brandt's successor as Chancellor, staunchly backed U.S. military strategy in Europe nevertheless, staking his political fate on the strategy of placing U.S. nuclear missiles in Germany unless

the Soviet Union reduced its arsenal of intermediate missiles.

The Chancellor also strongly opposed nuclear freeze proposals and won 2–1 support for his stand at the convention of Social Democrats in April. The Free Democrats then deserted the Socialists after losing ground in local elections and joined with the Christian Democrats to unseat Schmidt and install Helmut Kohl as Chancellor in 1982. An economic upswing in 1986 led to Kohl's re-election.

The fall of the Communist government in East Germany left only Soviet objections to German reunification to be dealt with. This was resolved in July 1990. Soviet objections to a reunified Germany belonging to NATO were dropped in return for German promises to reduce their military and engage in wide-ranging economic cooperation with the Soviet Union.

In ceremonies beginning on the evening of Tuesday, Oct. 2, 1990, and continuing throughout the next day, the German Democratic Republic acceded to the Federal Republic and Germany became a united and sovereign state for the first time since 1945. Some one million people gathered at midnight Oct. 2 at the Reichstag in Berlin. At midnight, a replica of the Liberty Bell, a gift from the United States, rang, and unity was officially proclaimed.

Following unification, the Federal Republic became the second largest country in Europe, after the Soviet Union. A reunited Berlin serves as the official capital, although the government will initially remain in Bonn.

During the national election campaign of late 1990 the central issue remained the cost of unification, including the modernization of the former East German economy. The ruling Christian Democrats promised no tax increases would be needed, while the opposition Social Democrats argued that this was mere wishful thinking.

In the December 2 election the Christian Democrats emerged as the strongest group, taking 43.8% of the vote. Analysts generally considered the vote to be an expression of thanks and support to the Chancellor for his forceful drive for political unity. The Party of Democratic Socialism, formerly the Communist Party, won 17 seats in Parliament.

The new Parliament convened in January 1991 re-electing Helmut Kohl Chancellor. Nevertheless it soon became clear that previous official estimates of the cost and time required to absorb eastern Germany were considerably understated. The number of failed enterprises in the east continued to grow, and the exodus of personnel to western Germany ceased to abate.

On June 20, 1991 the German Parliament officially voted in favor of moving the seat of the federal government to Berlin, although given the huge expense of such a move it would be done slowly and require 12 years before Berlin would be a fully functional federal capital.

Germany ratified the Maastricht Treaty in October 1993, being the last of the 12 EC members to do so.

The Federal Constitutional Court in July 1994 ruled in favor of the use of German military forces outside the country if parliamentary approval is received first.

General elections in October 1994 gave the ruling coalition a majority in the Bundestag. In November Kohl received formal re-election in that body.

Voters in the relatively new state of Brandenburg in the east rejected in May 1996 a proposal to merge with Berlin, dramatizing a lingering psychological division between eastern and western Germany.

GHANA

Republic of Ghana
President: Jerry John Rawlings
Area: 92,100 sq mi. (238,537 sq km)
Population (est. 1996): 17,698,271 (average annual rate of natural increase: 2.39%); birth rate: 35/1000; infant mortality rate: 80.3/1000; density per square mile: 192
Capital: Accra; **Largest cities (est. 1988):** Accra, 949,100; Kumasi, 385,200 Tamale, 151,100. **Monetary unit:** Cedi.
Languages: English (official), Native tongues (Brong Ahafo, Twi, Fanti, Ga, Ewe, Dagbani). **Religions:** indigenous belief, 38%; Islam, 30%; Christian, 24%. **Literacy rate:** 60%
Member of Commonwealth of Nations
Economic summary: Gross domestic product (1994 est.): $22.6 billion; per capita $1,310; real growth rate 5%; inflation 25% (1993 est); unemployment (1991) 10%. Arable land: 5%. Principal products: cocoa, coconuts, coffee, cassava, yams, rice, rubber. Labor force (1983): 3,700,000; 18.7% in industry. Major products: mining products, cocoa products, aluminum. Natural resources: gold, industrial diamonds, bauxite, manganese, timber, fish. Exports: $1 billion (f.o.b., 1993 est.): cocoa beans and products, gold, timber, tuna, bauxite, and aluminum. Imports: $1.7 billion (c.i.f., 1993 est.): petroleum, consumer goods, foods, intermediate goods, capital equipment. Major trading partners: U.K., U.S., Germany, France, Japan, South Korea.

Geography. A West African country bordering on the Gulf of Guinea, Ghana is bounded by Côte d'Ivoire to the west, Burkina Faso to the north, Togo to the east, and the Atlantic Ocean to the south. It compares in size to Oregon.

The coastal belt, extending about 270 miles (435 km), is sandy, marshy, and generally exposed. Behind it is a gradually widening grass strip. The forested plateau region to the north is broken by ridges and hills. The largest river is the Volta.

Government. A republic. Presidential and parliamentary elections were held Nov. 3, 1992, and ushered in the Fourth Republic on Jan. 7, 1993.

History. Created an independent country on March 6, 1957, Ghana is the former British colony of the Gold Coast. The area was first seen by Portuguese traders in 1470. They were followed by the English (1553), the Dutch (1595), and the Swedes (1640). British rule over the Gold Coast began in 1820, but it was not until after quelling the severe resistance of the Ashanti in 1901 that it was firmly established. British Togoland, formerly a colony of Germany, was incorporated into Ghana by referendum in 1956. As the result of a plebiscite, Ghana became a republic on July 1, 1960.

Premier Kwame Nkrumah attempted to take leadership of the Pan-African Movement, holding the All-African People's Congress in his capital, Accra, in 1958 and organizing the Union of African States with Guinea and Mali in 1961. But he oriented his country toward the Soviet Union and China and built an autocratic rule over all aspects of Ghanaian life.

In February 1966, while Nkrumah was visiting Peking and Hanoi, he was deposed by a military coup led by Gen. Emmanuel K. Kotoka.

A series of military coups followed and on June 4, 1979, Flight Lieutenant Jerry Rawlings overthrew Lt. Gen. Frederick Akuffo's military rule. Rawlings permitted the election of a civilian president to go ahead as scheduled the following month, and Hilla Limann, candidate of the People's National Party, took office. Charging the civilian government with corruption and repression, Rawlings staged another coup on Dec. 31, 1981.

In a referendum of May 1992 over 92% of the voters approved a new constitution, which provided for a multi-party system.

In the elections of late 1992 Rawlings won a majority of the votes for president. The governing National Democratic Congress held 189 of the 200 seats in parliament. The country's favorable standing with the World Bank enabled it to receive a $2.1 billion aid grant.

Despite consistent economic growth, almost daily demonstrations occurred largely in protest against the introduction of a 17.5% value-added tax in March 1995. In June it was removed, and the finance minister resigned in July.

GREECE

Hellenic Republic
President: Costis Stephanopoulos (1995)
Prime Minister: Costas Simitis (1996)
Area: 50,961 sq mi. (131,990 sq km)
Population (est. 1996): 10,718,518 (average annual rate of natural increase: 0.13%); birth rate: 10.6/1000; infant mortality rate: 8.1/1000; density per square mile: 210
Capital: Athens; **Largest cities (1991 est.):** Athens, 3,000,000; Salonika, 720,000; Piraeus, 170,000; Patras, 155,000; Heraklion, 117,000; Larissa, 113,500; **Monetary unit:** Drachma. **Language:** Greek. **Religion:** Greek Orthodox, 98%; Muslim, 1.3%. **National name:** Elliniki Dimokratia. **Literacy rate:** 93%
Economic summary: Gross domestic product (1994 est.): $93.7 billion; $8,870 per capita; 0.4% real growth rate; inflation 10.9%; unemployment 10.1%. Arable land: 23%. Principal agricultural products: grains, fruits, vegetables, olives, olive oil, tobacco, cotton, livestock, dairy products. Labor force (1994): 4.077 million; 52% services, 23% agriculture, 25% industry. Major industrial products: textiles, chemicals, food processing. Natural resources: bauxite, lignite, magnesite, crude oil, marble. Exports: $9 billion (f.o.b., 1993): manufactured goods, food and live animals, fuels and lubricants, raw materials. Imports: $19.2 billion (f.o.b.,

1993): machinery and automotive equipment, petroleum, consumer goods, chemicals, foodstuffs. Major trading partners: Germany, Italy, France, U.S.A., U.K., Netherlands.

Geography. Greece, on the Mediterranean Sea, is the southernmost country on the Balkan Peninsula in southern Europe. It is bordered on the north by Albania, Yugoslavia, and Bulgaria; on the west by the Ionian Sea; and on the east by the Aegean Sea and Turkey. It is slightly smaller than Alabama.

North central Greece, Epirus, and western Macedonia all are mountainous. The main chain of the Pindus Mountains rises to 10,256 feet (3,126 m) in places, separating Epirus from the plains of Thessaly. Mt. Olympus, rising to 9,570 feet (2,909 m) in the north near the Aegean Sea, is the highest point in the country. Greek Thrace is mostly a lowland region separated from European Turkey by the lower Evros River.

Among the many islands are the Ionian group off the west coast; the Cyclades group to the southeast; other islands in the eastern Aegean, including the Dodecanese Islands, Euboea, Lesbos, Samos, and Chios; and Crete, the fourth largest Mediterranean island.

Government. A referendum in December 1974, five months after the collapse of a military dictatorship, ended the Greek monarchy and established a republic. Ceremonial executive power is held by the president; the prime minister heads the government and is responsible to a 300-member unicameral Parliament.

History. Greece, with a recorded history going back to 766 B.C., reached the peak of its glory in the 5th century B.C., and by the middle of the 2nd century B.C., it had declined to the status of a Roman province. It remained within the Eastern Roman Empire until Constantinople fell to the Crusaders in 1204.

In 1453, the Turks took Constantinople, and by 1460 Greece was a Turkish province. The insurrection made famous by the poet Lord Byron broke out in 1821, and in 1827 Greece won independence with sovereignty guaranteed by Britain, France, and Russia.

The protecting powers chose Prince Otto of Bavaria as the first king of modern Greece in 1832 to reign over an area only slightly larger than the Peloponnese Peninsula. Chiefly under the next king, George I, chosen by the protecting powers in 1863, Greece acquired much of its present territory. During his 57-year reign, a period in which he encouraged parliamentary democracy, Thessaly, Epirus, Macedonia, Crete, and most of the Aegean islands were added from the disintegrating Turkish empire. An unsuccessful war against Turkey after World War I brought down the monarchy, to be replaced by a republic in 1923.

Two military dictatorships and a financial crisis brought George II back from exile, but only until 1941, when Italian and German invaders defeated tough Greek resistance. After British and Greek troops liberated the country in October 1944, Communist guerrillas staged a long campaign during which the government received U.S. aid under the Truman Doctrine, the predecessor of the Marshall Plan.

A military junta seized power in April 1967, sending young King Constantine II into exile December 14. Col. George Papadopoulos, as Prime Minister, converted the government to republican form in 1973 and as President ended martial law. He was moving to restore democracy when he was ousted in November of that year by his military colleagues. The regime of the "colonels," which had tortured its opponents and scoffed at human rights, resigned July 23, 1974, after having bungled an attempt to seize Cyprus.

Former Premier Karamanlis returned from exile to become Prime Minister of Greece's first civilian government since 1967.

On Jan. 1, 1981, Greece became the 10th member of the European Community.

Double-digit inflation and scandals in the Socialist government led to them losing their majority in the elections of June 1989. Elections in April 1990 finally gave the conservative New Democracy Party a one-seat majority in parliament. Soon afterwards Karamanlis, the founder of that party, was elected President by parliament.

An election in October 1993 saw the return to power of Mr. Papandreou, who two years earlier had been acquitted of criminal charges.

In April 1994 the European Union started legal action against Greece for its refusal to remove a trade blockade against the Republic of Macedonia.

A January 1996 vote among socialist lawmakers to replace Papandreou as prime minister gave a victory to his rival Costas Simitis. Later that month tensions rose with Turkey over a disputed unpopulated 10-acre island.

GRENADA

State of Grenada

Sovereign: Queen Elizabeth II
Governor General: Sir Reginald Palmer (1992)
Prime Minister: Hon. Dr. Keith C. Mitchell (June 1995)
Area: 133 sq mi. (344 sq km)
Population (est. 1996): 94,961 (average annual growth rate, 2.34%); birth rate: 29.1/1000; infant mortality rate: 11.9/1000; density per square mile: 714
Capital and largest city (1991): St. George's, 4,439. **Monetary unit:** East Caribbean dollar. **Ethnic groups (1991):** Black African descent 85%, Mixed 11%, .1% white, other .3%. **Language:** English. **Religions:** Roman Catholic, 64%; Anglican, 21%. **Literacy rate:** 98%. **Member of Commonwealth of Nations**
Economic summary: Gross domestic product (1995): $193.14 million; $6,426 per capita; 2.8% real growth rate; inflation rate 2.1%; unemployment rate 25% (1994 est.). Arable land: 15%. Principal products: spices, cocoa, bananas. Tourism is the leading foreign exchange earner followed by agricultural exports. Exports: $63.4 million (f.o.b., 1993 est.): nutmeg, cocoa beans, bananas, mace, textiles. Imports: $349.7 million (c.i.f., 1993 est.): foodstuffs, machinery, manufactured goods, petroleum, chemicals, fuel. Labor force: 36,000; 31% in services, 24% agriculture. Major trading partners: U.K., Trinidad and Tobago, U.S., Japan, Canada.

Geography. Grenada (the first "a" is pronounced as in "gray") is the most southerly of the Windward Islands, about 100 miles (161 km) from the South American coast. It is a volcanic island traversed by a mountain range, the highest peak of which is Mount St. Catherine (2,756 ft.; 840 m).

Government. A Governor-General represents the sovereign, Elizabeth II. The Prime Minister is the head of government, chosen by a 15-member House of Representatives elected by universal suffrage every five years.

History. Grenada was discovered by Columbus in 1498. After more than 200 years of British rule, most recently as part of the West Indies Associated States, it became independent Feb. 7, 1974, with Eric M. Gairy as Prime Minister.

Prime Minister Maurice Bishop, a protégé of Cuba's President Castro, was killed in a military coup on Oct. 19, 1983. At the request of five members of the Organization of Eastern Caribbean States, President Reagan ordered an invasion of Grenada on Oct. 25 involving over 1,900 U.S. troops and a small military force from Barbados, Dominica, Jamaica, St. Lucia, and St. Vincent. The troops met strong resistance from Cuban military personnel on the island.

A centrist coalition led by Herbert A. Blaize, a 66-year-old lawyer, won 14 of the 15 seats in Parliament in an election in December 1984.

None of the four main parties won a clear victory in the election of March 1990. Negotiations led to the National Democratic Congress forming a government with the support of several members from other parties.

Parliamentary elections in June 1995 gave the opposition New National Party a majority of seats and allowed its leader to form a new government. The NNP had promised to eliminate the income tax that had been reintroduced by the NDC in 1994.

GUATEMALA

Republic of Guatemala
President: Alvaro Arzú Irigoyen (1996)
Area: 42,042 sq mi. (108,889 sq km)
Population (est. 1996): 11,277,614 (average annual rate of natural increase: 2.68%); birth rate: 33.9/1000; infant mortality rate: 50.7/1000; density per sq mile: 268
Capital and largest city (est. 1994): Guatemala City, 1,150,452. **Other large cities (est. 1994):** Mixco, 413,002; Villa Nueva, 154,508. **Monetary unit:** Quetzal.
Languages: Spanish, Indian languages. **Religion:** Roman Catholic, Protestant, Mayan.. **National name:** República de Guatemala. **Literacy rate:** 55%
Economic summary: Gross domestic product (1994 est.): $33 billion; per capita $3,080; real growth rate 4%; inflation 12%; unemployment 4.9%. Arable land: 12%. Principal products: corn, beans, coffee, cotton, cattle, sugar, bananas, fruits and vegetables. Labor force: 2,500,000; 14% in manufacturing. Principal products: sugar, textiles and clothing, furniture, chemicals, petroleum, metals, rubber. Natural resources: nickel, crude oil, rare woods, fish, chicle. Exports: $1.38 billion (f.o.b., 1994 est.): coffee, sugar, bananas, beef. Imports: $2.6 billion (c.i.f., 1994 est.): fuel and petroleum products, machinery, grain, fertilizers, motor vehicles. Major trading partners: U.S., Central American nations, Caribbean, Mexico, Germany.

Geography. The northernmost of the Central American nations, Guatemala is the size of Tennessee. Its neighbors are Mexico on the north and west, and Belize, Honduras, and El Salvador on the east. The country consists of three main regions—the cool highlands with the heaviest population, the tropical area along the Pacific and Caribbean coasts, and the tropical jungle in the northern lowlands. The principal mountain range rises to the highest elevation in Central America and contains many volcanic peaks. Volcanic eruptions are frequent.

The Petén region in the north contains important resources and archaeological sites of the Mayan civilization.

Government. A republic with a unicameral legislative branch, the Congress of the Republic.

History. Once the site of the ancient Mayan civiliza-

tion, Guatemala, conquered by Spain in 1524, set itself up as a republic in 1839. From 1898 to 1920, the dictator Manuel Estrada Cabrera ran the country, and from 1931 to 1944, Gen. Jorge Ubico Castaneda was the strongman.

Jacobo Arbenz Guzmán won the 1950 election. He expropriated the large estates, including plantations of the United Fruit Company. With covert U.S. backing, a revolt was led by Col. Carlos Castillo Armas, and Arbenz took refuge in Mexico. Castillo Armas became president but was assassinated in 1957. Gen. Miguel Ydigoras Fuentes was elected president in 1957.

A wave of terrorism, by left and right, began in 1967. Fear of anarchy led to the election in 1970 of Army Chief of Staff Carlos Araña Osorio. Araña, surprisingly, pledged social reforms when he took office. Another military candidate, Gen. Kjell Laugerud, won the presidency in 1974 amid renewed political violence.

The administration of Gen. Romeo Lucas Garcia, elected president in 1978, ended in a coup by a three-man military junta on March 23, 1982. Lucas Garcia was charged by Amnesty International with responsibility for at least 5,000 political murders in a reign of brutality and corruption that brought a cutoff of U.S. military aid in 1978. Hopes for improvement under the junta faded when Gen. José Efraín Ríos Montt took sole power in June.

President Oscar Mejía Victores, another general, seized power from Rios Montt in an August 1983 coup.

Jorge Serrano Elias presided over seven years of democratic rule until, in May 1993, he moved to dissolve congress and suspend the supreme court and suspend constitutional rights. Under strong foreign and domestic pressure the military deposed Serrano on June 1 and allowed the inauguration of de Leon Carpio, the former Attorney General of Human Rights and no particular friend of the military.

The basis for new negotiations to end a long-standing leftist rebellion was reached in January 1994. Yet rebel activity continued throughout the year with no end in sight.

In the January 1996 runoff presidential election Alvaro Arzú Irigoyen of the National Advancement Party defeated the far-right candidate.

GUINEA

Republic of Guinea
President: Brig. Gen. Lansana Conté (1984)
Area: 94,925 sq mi. (245,857 sq km)
Population (est. 1996): 7,411,981 (average annual rate of natural increase: 2.39%); birth rate: 42.5/1000; infant mortality rate: 134/1000; density per square mile: 78
Capital and largest city (1995 est.): Conakry, 1,508,000.
Monetary unit: Guinean franc. **Languages:** French (official), native tongues (Malinké, Susu, Fulani). **Religions:** Islam, 85%; 7% indigenous, 8% Christian. **National name:** République de Guinée. **Literacy rate:** 24% in French; 48% in local languages
Economic summary: Gross domestic product (1994 est.): $6.3 billion; per capita $980; real growth rate 0.8%; inflation 16.6%. (1992 est.). Arable land: 6%. Principal agricultural products: rice, cassava, millet, corn, coffee, bananas, pineapples. Labor force: 2,400,000 (1983); 11% in industry and commerce. Major industrial products: bauxite, alumina, light manufactured and processed goods, diamonds. Natural resources: bauxite, iron ore, diamonds, gold, water power. Exports: $622 million (f.o.b., 1992 est.): bauxite,

alumina, diamonds, pineapples, bananas, coffee. Imports: $768 million (c.i.f., 1992 est): petroleum, machinery, transport equipment, foodstuffs, textiles. Major trading partners: U.S., France, Brazil, Germany, Belgium, Ireland, Spain, Côte d'Ivoire, Hong Kong.

Geography. Guinea, in West Africa on the Atlantic, is also bordered by Guinea-Bissau, Senegal, Mali, the Ivory Coast, Liberia, and Sierra Leone. Slightly smaller than Oregon, the country consists of a coastal plain, a mountainous region, a savanna interior, and a forest area in the Guinea Highlands. The highest peak is Mount Nimba at 5,748 ft (1,752 m).

Government. Military government headed by President Lansana Conté, who promoted himself from colonel to brigadier general after a 1984 coup. In 1989, President Conté announced that Guinea would move to a multi-party democracy.

A new constitution approved in a nationwide referendum, December 1990, provided for the establishment of a directly elected multi-party parliament (five-year terms) and a popularly elected president for a maximum of two five-year terms, and a judiciary to be independent of either the presidency or the legislature. A transitional Committee for National Recovery (CTRN) replaced the military committee to guide implementation of the new constitution.

History. Previously part of French West Africa, Guinea achieved independence by rejecting the new French Constitution and, on Oct. 2, 1958, became an independent state with Sékou Touré as president. Touré led the country into being the first avowedly Marxist state in Africa. Diplomatic relations with France were suspended in 1965, with the Soviet Union replacing France as the country's chief source of economic and technical assistance.

Prosperity came in 1960 after the start of exploitation of bauxite deposits. Touré was re-elected to a seven-year term in 1974 and again in 1981.

After 26 years as President, Touré died in the United States in March 1984, following surgery. A week later, a military regime headed by Col. Lansana Conté took power with a promise not to shed any more blood after Touré's harsh rule. Conté became president and his co-conspirator in the coup, Col. Diara Traoré, became prime minister, but Conté later demoted Traoré to education minister. Traoré tried to seize power on July 4, 1985, while Conté was out of the country, but his attempted coup was crushed by troops loyal to Conté.

In 1991 voters approved a new constitution that would lead the country to democracy. Under mounting popular pressure Conté declared in April 1992 that constitutional rule would begin.

In December 1993 elections the president's Unity and Progress Party took almost 51% of the vote cast.

In February 1996 rebellious soldiers demanding pay in arrears besieged the presidential palace. Loyal troops repulsed the attacks.

GUINEA-BISSAU

Republic of Guinea-Bissau
President: João Bernardo Vieira (1980)
Area: 13,948 sq mi. (36,125 sq km)
Population (est. 1996): 1,151,330 (average annual rate of natural increase: 2.35%); birth rate: 39.7/1000; infant

mortality rate: 115.8/1000; density per square mile: 82.5

Capital and largest city (est. 1991): Bissau, 200,000.
Monetary unit: Guinea-Bissau peso. **Language:** Portugese Criolo, African languages. **Religions:** traditional, 65%; Islam, 30%; Christian, 5%. **National name:** República da Guiné-Bissau. **Literacy rate:** 36% (1991 est.)
Economic summary: Gross domestic product (1993 est.): $900 million; $840 per capita (1994 est.); real growth rate 2.9% (1993 est.); inflation: 55% (1991 est.). Arable land: 9%. Principal products: palm kernels, cotton, cashew nuts, peanuts. Labor force: 403,000 (est.): Agriculture, 90%; industry, services, and commerce, 5%; government, 5%. Major industries: food processing, beer, soft drinks. Natural resources: unexploited deposits of bauxite, petroleum, phosphates; fish and timber. Exports: $19 million (f.o.b., 1993): peanuts, cashews, fish, palm kernels. Imports: $56 million (f.o.b., 1993): capital equipment, consumer goods, semiprocessed goods, foods, petroleum. Major trading partners: Portugal, Spain, and other European countries, Senegal, U.S., China, India, Nigeria.

Geography. A neighbor of Senegal and Guinea in West Africa, on the Atlantic coast, Guinea-Bissau is about half the size of South Carolina.

The country is a low-lying coastal region of swamps, rain forests, and mangrove-covered wetlands, with about 25 islands off the coast. The Bijagos archipelago extends 30 miles (48 km) out to sea. Internal communications depend mainly on deep estuaries and meandering rivers, since there are no railroads. Bissau, the capital, is the main port.

Government. After the overthrow of Louis Cabral in November 1980, the nine-member Council of the Revolution formed an interm government. At present the government consists of a president and a single 100-member legislative body.

History. Guinea-Bissau was discovered in 1446 by the Portuguese Nuno Tristao, and colonists in the Cape Verde Islands obtained trading rights in the territory. In 1879 the connection with the Cape Verde Islands was broken. Early in the 1900s the Portuguese managed to pacify some tribesmen, although resistance to colonial rule remained.

The African Party for the Independence of Guinea-Bissau and Cape Verde was founded in 1956 and several years later began guerrilla warfare that grew increasingly effective. By 1974 the rebels controlled most of the countryside, where they formed a government that was soon recognized by scores of countries. The military coup in Portugal in April 1974 brightened the prospects for freedom, and in August the Lisbon government signed an agreement granting independence to the province as of Sept. 10. The new republic took the name Guinea-Bissau.

In November 1980, Prémier João Bernardo Vieira headed a coup that deposed Luis Cabral, president since 1974. A Revolutionary Council assumed the powers of government, with Vieira as its head. An extraordinary congress of the ruling party in January 1991 approved a multiparty system. In June the constitution was amended to allow for opposition parties.

July 1994 multiparty presidential and legislative elections gave the president's party 64 seats in the Assembly although Vieira himself less than a majority. In the runoff election Vieira officially received 52% of the vote.

Previously strained relations with Senegal were smoothed during 1995 with accord reached on several agreements.

GUYANA

Cooperative Republic of Guyana
President: Dr. Cheddi Jagan (1992)
Area: 83,000 sq mi. (214,969 sq km)
Population (est. 1996): 712,091 (average annual rate of natural increase: 0.95%); birth rate: 19/1000; infant mortality rate: 51.4/1000; density per square mile: 8
Capital and largest city (est. 1992): Georgetown, 248,500. **Monetary unit:** Guyana dollar. **Languages:** English (official), Amerindian dialects. **Religions:** Hindu, 34%; Protestant, 18%; Islam, 9%; Roman Catholic, 18%; Anglican, 16%. **Member of Commonwealth of Nations. Literacy rate:** 95%
Economic summary: Gross national product (1995 est.): $2 billion; $2,400 per capita; real growth rate 6.5%; inflation: 10%; unemployment (1994 est.): 8–10%. Arable land: 3%. Principal products: sugar, rice. Labor force (1995): 300,000; 44.5% industry and commerce. Major products: bauxite, alumina. Natural resources: bauxite, gold, diamonds, hardwood timber, shrimp. Exports: $550 million (f.o.b., 1995 est.): sugar, bauxite, rice, timber, shrimp, gold, molasses, rum. Imports: $620 million (c.i.f., 1995 est.): petroleum, food, machinery, manufactures. Major trading partners: U.K., U.S., Canada, Japan, Trinidad and Tobago, Germany.

Geography. Guyana is situated on the northern coast of South America east of Venezuela, west of Suriname, and north of Brazil. The country consists of a low coastal area and the Guiana Highlands in the south. There is an extensive north-south network of rivers. Guyana is the size of Idaho.

Government. Guyana, formerly British Guiana, proclaimed itself a republic on Feb. 23, 1970, ending its ties with Britain while remaining in the Commonwealth.

Guyana has a unicameral legislature, the National Assembly, with 53 members directly elected for five-year terms and 12 elected by local councils. A 13-member Cabinet is headed by the President.

History. British Guiana won internal self-government in 1952. The next year the People's Progressive Party, headed by Cheddi B. Jagan, an East Indian dentist, won the elections and Jagan became Prime Minister. British authorities deposed him for alleged Communist connections. A coalition ousted Jagan in 1964, installing a moderate Socialist, Forbes Burnham, a black, as Prime Minister. On May 26, 1966, the country became an independent member of the Commonwealth and resumed its traditional name, Guyana.

After ruling Guyana for 21 years, Burnham died on Aug. 6, 1985, in a Guyana hospital after a throat operation.

Jagan's People's Progressive Party won a majority in the general election of October 1992.

Local elections in 1994 gave a surprisingly strong showing for the governing alliance. The IMF also promised substantial financial aid. Major privatization plans were introduced in 1995.

HAITI

Republic of Haiti
President: René García Préval (1996)
Prime Minister: Rosny Smarth (1996)
Area: 10,714 sq mi. (27,750 sq km)
Population (est. 1996): 6,731,539 (average annual rate of natural increase: 2.22%); birth rate: 38.1/1000; infant mortality rate: 103.8/1000; density per square mile: 628.
Capital and largest city (est. 1993): Port-au-Prince, 1.5 million. **Monetary unit:** Gourde. **Languages:** Creole, French. **Religion:** Roman Catholic, 80%; Protestant, 16%; Vaudou, 95%. **National name:** République d'Haïti. **Literacy rate:** 25%
Economic summary: Gross domestic product (1994 est.): $5.6 billion; $870 per capita; –15% real growth rate; inflation 52% (FY93/94 est.); unemployment 50%. Arable land: 50%. Principal agricultural products: coffee, sugar cane, rice, corn, sorghum. Labor force: 2,300,000; 66% in agriculture. Major industrial products: refined sugar, textiles, flour, cement, light assembly products. Natural resource: bauxite. Exports: $173.3 million (f.o.b., 1993 est.): coffee, light industrial products, agricultural products. Imports: $476.8 million (f.o.b., 1993 est.): machines and manufactures, food and beverages, petroleum products, fats and oils, chemicals. Major trading partners: U.S., Italy, France, Japan.

Geography. Haiti, in the West Indies, occupies the western third of the island of Hispaniola, which it shares with the Dominican Republic. About the size of Maryland, Haiti is two-thirds mountainous, with the rest of the country marked by great valleys, extensive plateaus, and small plains. The most densely populated region is the Cul-de-Sac plain near Port-au-Prince.

Government. A republic with a bicameral assembly consisting of an upper house, or Senate, and a lower house, the House of Deputies. The National Assembly consists of 27 senate seats and 83 deputies.

Democratically elected Pres. Aristide was replaced by a de facto regime in October 1991 following a military coup on Sept. 30, 1991. He was reinstated in October 1993 by a U.S.-led multinational force appointed by U.N. Resolution 940. A U.S. peace mission in September 1994 reached a compromise with the military leaders, avoiding a U.S. invasion. Acting as peacekeepers, U.S. troops landed in Haiti, allowing Aristide to return in mid-October. President René Préval was elected Dec. 17, 1995, and was inaugurated on Feb. 7, 1996.

History. Discovered by Columbus, who landed at Môle Saint Nicolas on Dec. 6, 1492, Haiti in 1697 became a French possession known as Saint Domingue. An insurrection among a slave population of 500,000 in 1791 ended with a declaration of independence by Pierre-Dominique Toussaint l'Ouverture in 1801. Napoleon Bonaparte suppressed the independence movement, but it eventually triumphed in 1804 under Jean-Jacques Dessalines, who gave the new nation the aboriginal name Haiti.

Its prosperity dissipated by internal strife as well as disputes with neighboring Santo Domingo during a succession of 19th-century dictatorships, a bankrupt Haiti accepted a U.S. customs receivership from 1905 to 1941. Direct U.S. rule from 1915 to 1934 brought a measure of stability and a population growth that made Haiti the most densely populated nation in the hemisphere.

In 1949, after four years of democratic rule by President Dumarsais Estimé, dictatorship returned under Gen. Paul Magloire, who was succeeded by François Duvalier in 1957.

Duvalier established a dictatorship based on secret police, known as the "Ton-ton Macoutes," who gunned down opponents of the regime. Duvalier's son, Jean-Claude, or "Baby Doc," succeeded his father in 1971 as ruler of the poorest nation in the Western Hemisphere. Duvalier fled the country in 1986 after strong unrest.

Following the election of December 6, 1990 which he won, Jean-Bertrand Aristide, a Roman Catholic priest, was sworn in as president on February 7, 1991—the country's first freely elected chief executive.

In September 1991 elements of the military seized the president and took control of the government. Although the OAS attempted to have Aristide reinstated, the army forced the Assembly officially to depose him. The OAS call for economic blockade led to a sharp downturn in an already poor economy.

The population largely ignored parliamentary elections the following January. In July Aristide and the army signed an accord to return the exiled president to power. When the military leaders failed to resign the UN reimposed an embargo.

After Aristide's return to Haiti in October 1994 he moved quickly to replace the police force, downsize the military, and purge the officer corps.

The winner of the second free election in the country's history was René Preval, who was sworn into office in February 1996. In June the UN Security Council agreed to extend its peacekeeping mission for at least five additional months.

HONDURAS

Republic of Honduras
President: Carlos Roberto Reina Idiáquez (1994)
Area: 43,872 sq mi. (112,492 sq km)
Population (est. 1996): 5,605,193 (average annual rate of natural increase: 2.76%); birth rate: 33.4/1000; infant mortality rate: 41.8/1000; density per sq mi.: 127
Capital and largest city (1995): Tegucigalpa, 1,500,000; **Monetary unit:** Lempira. **Languages:** Spanish (official), English widely spoken in business. **Religion:** Roman Catholic, 94%; Protestant minority. **National name:** República de Honduras. **Literacy rate:** 73%
Economic summary: Gross domestic product (1994 est.): $9.7 billion; $1,820 per capita; real growth rate −1.9%; inflation 30%; unemployment 10%. Arable land: 14%. Principal products: bananas, coffee, timber, beef, shrimp, citrus. Labor force (1985): 1,300,000; agriculture 62%; services 20%. Major industrial products: processed agricultural products, textiles and clothing, wood products. Natural resources: timber, gold, silver, copper, lead, zinc, iron ore, antimony. Exports: $850 million (f.o.b., 1993 est.): bananas, coffee, lumber, shrimp and lobster, minerals. Imports: $1.1 billion (c.i.f., 1993 est.): manufactured goods, machinery, transportation equipment, chemicals, petroleum. Major trading partners: U.S., Caribbean countries, Western Europe, Japan, Latin America.

Geography. Honduras, in the north central part of Central America, has a 400-mile (644-km) Caribbean coastline and a 40-mile (64-km) Pacific frontage. Its neighbors are Guatemala to the west, El Salvador to the south, and Nicaragua to the east. Honduras is slightly larger than Tennessee. Generally mountainous, the country is marked by fertile plateaus, river valleys, and narrow coastal plains.

Government. The President serves a four-year term. There is a 128-member National Congress.

History. Columbus discovered Honduras on his last voyage in 1502. Honduras, with four other countries of Central America, declared its independence from Spain in 1821 and was part of a federation of Central American states until 1838. In that year it seceded

from the federation and became a completely independent country.

In July 1969, El Salvador invaded Honduras after Honduran landowners had deported several thousand Salvadorans. The fighting left 1,000 dead and tens of thousands homeless. By threatening economic sanctions and military intervention, the OAS induced El Salvador to withdraw.

Although parliamentary democracy returned with the election of Roberto Suazo Córdova as President in 1982 after a decade of military rule, Honduras faced severe economic problems and tensions along its border with Nicaragua. "Contra" rebels, waging a guerrilla war against the Sandinista regime in Nicaragua, used Honduras as a training and staging area. At the same time, the United States used Honduras as a site for military exercises and built bases to train both Honduran and Salvadoran troops.

In the first democratic transition of power since 1932 Rafael Callejas became President in January 1990. The immediate task was to deal with a deficit caused in part by reduced U.S. aid and the previous government's fiscal policies.

Running on a platform attacking governmental corruption and military influence the candidate of the Liberal Party, Carlos Reina, won the general election of November 1993 against the ruling National Party.

The Supreme Court in January 1996 supported the legality of a civilian trial for certain military personnel charged with a 1982 kidnapping and torture.

HUNGARY

Republic of Hungary
President: Arpad Goncz (1990)
Premier: Gyula Horn (1994)
Area: 35,919 sq mi. (93,030 sq km)
Population (est. 1996): 10,002,541 (average annual rate of natural increase: −0.43%); birth rate: 10.7/1000; infant mortality rate: 12.3/1000; density per square mile: 278
Capital and largest city (1994 est.): Budapest, 1,996,000; **Other large cities (1994 est.):** Debrecen, 218,000; Miskolc, 190,000; Szeged, 180,000; Péces, 173,000. **Monetary unit:** Forint. **Language:** Magyar. **Religions:** Roman Catholic, 67.5%; Protestant, 25%; atheist and others, 7.5%. **National name:** Magyar Köztársaság. **Literacy rate:** 99%
Economic summary: Gross domestic product (1994 est.): $58.8 billion; $5,700 per capita; 3% real growth rate; inflation rate 21%; unemployment rate 10.4% (year-end). Arable land: 54%. Principal agricultural products: corn, wheat, potatoes, sugar beets, sun flowers, livestock, dairy products. Labor force (1991): 5,400,000; 43.2% in services, trade, and government. Major industrial products: steel, chemicals, pharmaceuticals, textiles, transport equipment. Natural resources: bauxite, coal, natural gas. Exports: $10.3 billion (f.o.b., 1994 est.): raw materials, semi-finished goods, chemicals, machinery, light industry, food and agricultural, fuels and energy. Imports: $14.2 billion (f.o.b., 1994 est.): fuels and energy, raw materials, semi-finished goods, chemicals, machinery, light industry, food and agricultural. Major trading partners: C.I.S. countries, Eastern Europe.

Geography. This central European country the size of Indiana is bordered by Austria to the west, Slovakia to the north, Ukraine and Romania to the east, and Yugoslavia to the south.

Most of Hungary is a fertile, rolling plain lying east of the Danube River and drained by the Danube and Tisza rivers. In the extreme northwest is the Little Hungarian Plain. South of that area is Lake Balaton (250 sq mi.; 648 sq km).

Government. Hungary is a Republic with legislative power vested in the unicameral National Assembly, whose 386 members are elected directly for four-year terms. The National Assembly elects the President.

The major political parties are the Socialist Party, the Hungarian Democratic Forum, the Alliance of Free Democrats, the Independent Socialist Party, and the Independent Smallholder's Party and the Young Democrats (FIDESZ).

History. About 2,000 years ago, Hungary was part of the Roman provinces of Pannonia and Dacia. In A.D. 896 it was invaded by the Magyars, who founded a kingdom. Christianity was accepted during the reign of Stephen I (St. Stephen) (997–1038).

The peak of Hungary's great period of medieval power came during the reign of Louis I the Great (1342–82), whose dominions touched the Baltic, Black, and Mediterranean seas.

War with the Turks broke out in 1389, and for more than 100 years the Turks advanced through the Balkans. When the Turks smashed a Hungarian army in 1526, western and northern Hungary accepted Hapsburg rule to escape Turkish occupation. Transylvania became independent under Hungarian princes. Intermittent war with the Turks was waged until a peace treaty was signed in 1699.

After the suppression of the 1848 revolt against Hapsburg rule, led by Louis Kossuth, the dual monarchy of Austria-Hungary was set up in 1867.

The dual monarchy was defeated with the other Central Powers in World War I. After a short-lived republic in 1918, the chaotic Communist rule of 1919 under Béla Kun ended with the Romanians occupying Budapest on Aug. 4, 1919. When the Romanians left, Adm. Nicholas Horthy entered the capital with a national army. The Treaty of Trianon of June 4, 1920, cost Hungary 68% of its land and 58% of its population. Meanwhile, the National Assembly had restored the legal continuity of the old monarchy; and, on March 1, 1920, Horthy was elected Regent.

Following the German invasion of Russia on June 22, 1941, Hungary joined the attack against the Soviet Union, but the war was not popular and Hungarian troops were almost entirely withdrawn from the eastern front by May 1943. German occupation troops set up a puppet government after Horthy's appeal for an armistice with advancing Soviet troops on Oct. 15, 1944, had resulted in his overthrow. The German regime soon fled the capital, however, and on December 23 a provisional government was formed in Soviet-occupied eastern Hungary. On Jan. 20, 1945, it signed an armistice in Moscow. Early the next year, the National Assembly approved a constitutional law abolishing the thousand-year-old monarchy and establishing a republic.

By the Treaty of Paris (1947), Hungary had to give up all territory it had acquired since 1937 and to pay $300 million reparations to the U.S.S.R., Czechoslovakia, and Yugoslavia. In 1948 the Communist Party, with the support of Soviet troops seized control. Hungary was proclaimed a People's Republic and one-party state in 1949. Industry was nationalized, the land collectivized into state farms, and the opposition terrorized by the secret police.

The terror, modeled after that of the U.S.S.R., reached its height with the trial of József Cardinal Mindszenty, Roman Catholic primate. He confessed to fantastic charges under duress of drugs or brainwashing and was sentenced to life imprisonment in 1949. Protests were voiced in all parts of the world.

On Oct. 23, 1956, anti-Communist revolution broke out in Budapest. To cope with it, the Communists set up a coalition government and called former Premier Imre Nagy back to head it. But he and most of his ministers were swept by the logic of events into the anti-Communist opposition, and he declared Hungary a neutral power, withdrawing from the Warsaw Treaty and appealing to the United Nations for help.

One of his ministers, János Kádár, established a counter-regime and asked the U.S.S.R. to send in military power. Soviet troops and tanks suppressed the revolution in bloody fighting after 190,000 people had fled the country and Mindszenty, freed from jail, had taken refuge in the U.S. Embassy.

Kádár was succeeded as Premier, but not party secretary, by Gyula Kallai in 1965. Continuing his program of national reconciliation, Kádár emptied prisons, reformed the secret police, and eased travel restrictions.

Following local and parliamentary elections in October 1990, József Antall's Hungarian Democratic Forum and its conservative coalition parties held 60% of the parliamentary seats. The last Soviet troops left Hungary in June 1991, thereby ending almost 47 years of military presence.

The transition to a market economy proved difficult. Hungary strengthened its ties with Poland and Czechoslovakia but grew concerned about the fate of ethnic Hungarians in neighboring countries. Hungary cautiously watched the birth of Slovakia and its treatment of a large ethnic Hungarian minority.

Parliamentary elections in May 1994 gave the Socialists, formerly the Communists, a 15-seat majority. A coalition government with the Free Democrats was formed in July.

Despite political bungling the government introduced an austerity package in 1995 that made substantial cuts in welfare benefits.

The government made little progress in dealing with the explosive issue of the Hungarian diaspora.

ICELAND

Republic of Iceland
President: Mrs. Vigdis Finnbogadottir (1980)
Prime Minister: David Oddsson (1991)
Area: 39,709 sq mi. (102,846 sq km)[1]
Population (est. 1996): 268,369 (average annual rate of natural increase: 0.86%); birth rate: 15.3/1000; infant mortality rate: 4/1000; density per square mile: 6
Capital and largest city (est. 1994): Reykjavik, 103,036.
  Monetary unit: M.N. króna; **Language:** Icelandic; **Religion:** Evangelical Lutheran; **National name:** Lydveldid Island; **Literacy rate:** 100%
Economic summary: Gross domestic product (1994 est.): $4.5 billion; $17,250 per capita; real growth rate 2.4%; inflation 1.3%; unemployment 7%. Arable land: 1%; principal agricultural products: livestock, potatoes and turnips. Labor force: 127,900; 60% in commerce, transportation, and services. Major products: processed aluminum, fish. Natural resources: fish, diatomite, hydroelectric and geothermal power. Exports: $1.4 billion (f.o.b., 1993): fish, animal products, aluminum, diatomite, ferrosilicon. Imports: $1.3 billion (c.i.f., 1993): petroleum products, machinery and

transportation equipment, food, textiles. Major trading partners: European Communities (EC) countries, European Free Trade Association (EFTA) countries, U.S., Japan, and Denmark,.

1. Including some offshore islands.

Geography. Iceland, an island about the size of Kentucky, lies in the north Atlantic Ocean east of Greenland and just touches the Arctic Circle. It is one of the most volcanic regions in the world.

Small fresh-water lakes are to be found throughout the island, and there are many natural phenomena, including hot springs, geysers, sulfur beds, canyons, waterfalls, and swift rivers. More than 13% of the area is covered by snowfields and glaciers, and most of the people live in the 7% of the island comprising fertile coastlands.

Government. The President is elected for four years by popular vote. Executive power resides in the Prime Minister and his Cabinet. The Althing (Parliament) is composed of 63 members.

History. Iceland was first settled shortly before 900, mainly by Norse. A constitution drawn up about 930 created a form of democracy and provided for an Althing, or General Assembly.

In 1262–64, Iceland came under Norwegian rule and passed to ultimate Danish control through the formation of the Union of Kalmar in 1483. In 1874, Icelanders obtained their own constitution. In 1918, Denmark recognized Iceland as a separate state with unlimited sovereignty but still nominally under the Danish king.

On June 17, 1944, after a popular referendum, the Althing proclaimed Iceland an independent republic.

The British occupied Iceland in 1940, immediately after the German invasion of Denmark. In 1942, the U.S. took over the burden of protection. Iceland refused to abandon its neutrality in World War II and thus forfeited charter membership in the United Nations, but it cooperated with the Allies throughout the conflict. Iceland joined the North Atlantic Treaty Organization in 1949.

Iceland unilaterally extended its territorial waters from 12 to 50 nautical miles in 1972, precipitating a running dispute with Britain known as the "cod war."

Elections to the Althing in April 1991 gave the opposition Independence Party 26 of the 63 seats, up from 18. Prime Minister Hermannson resigned, allowing David Oddsson of the Independence Party to enter into talks with the Social Democrats about a coalition government.

General election results in April 1995 gave the former coalition Independence Party and Social Democrats what would have been only a one-seat majority. A new coalition was formed between the Independence Party and the centrist Progressives, who also oppose Iceland seeking membership in the European Union.

A dispute concerning fishing rights with Norway and Russia continued during 1995.

INDIA

Republic of India
President: Dr. Shankar Dayal Sharma (1992)
Prime Minister: H.D. Deve Gowda (1996)
Area: 1,229,737 sq mi. (3,185,019 sq km)
Population (est. 1996): 952,107,694 (average annual rate of natural increase: 1.53%); birth rate: 25.9/1000; infant mortality rate: 71.1/1000; density per square mile: 774

Capital (1991): New Delhi, 294,149; **Largest cities (1992):** Greater Bombay, 12,916,272; Calcutta, 10,916,272; Delhi, 8,375,188; Madras, 5,361,468; Ahmedabad, 4,775,670; Bangalore, 4,807,019; Kanpur, 2,284,000. **Monetary unit:** Rupee. **Principal languages;** Hindi (official), English (official), Bengali, Gujarati, Kashmiri, Malayalam, Marathi, Oriya, Punjabi, Tamil, Telugu, Urdu, Kannada, Assamese, Sanskrit, Sindhi (all recognized by the Constitution). Dialects, 1,652. **Religions:** Hindu, 82.6%; Islam, 11.3%; Christian, 2.4%; Sikh, 2%; Buddhists, 0.71%; Jains, 0.48%. **National name:** Bharat. **Literacy rate:** 52.11%. **Member of Commonwealth of Nations**
Economic summary: Gross domestic product (1994 est.): $1.17 trillion; $1,300 per capita; real growth rate 3.8%; inflation 8%; unemployment n.a. Arable land: 55%. Principal products: rice, wheat, oilseeds, cotton, tea, opium poppy (for pharmaceuticals). Labor force (1990): 314,751 million; 67% in agriculture. Major industrial products: jute, processed food, steel, machinery, transport machinery, cement. Natural resources: iron ore, coal, manganese, mica, bauxite, limestone, textiles. Exports: $24.4 billion (f.o.b., 1994 est.): gems and jewelry, clothing, engineering goods, leather manufactures, cotton yarn and fabric. Imports: $25.5 billion (c.i.f., 1994 est.): crude oil and petroleum products, gems, fertilizer, chemicals, machinery. Major trading partners: U.S., C.I.S. nations, Germany, Italy, Belgium.

Geography. One third the area of the United States, the Republic of India occupies most of the subcontinent of India in south Asia. It borders on China in the northeast. Other neighbors are Pakistan on the west, Nepal and Bhutan on the north, and Burma and Bangladesh on the east.

The country contains a large part of the great Indo-Gangetic plain, which extends from the Bay of Bengal on the east to the Afghan frontier and the Arabian Sea on the west. This plain is the richest and most densely settled part of the subcontinent. Another distinct natural region is the Deccan, a plateau of 2,000 to 3,000 feet (610 to 914 m) in elevation, occupying the southern portion of the subcontinent.

Forming a part of the republic are several groups of islands—the Laccadives (14 islands) in the Arabian Sea and the Andamans (204 islands) and the Nicobars (19 islands) in the Bay of Bengal.

India's three great river systems, all rising in the Himalayas, have extensive deltas. The Ganges flows south and then east for 1,540 miles (2,478 km) across the northern plain to the Bay of Bengal; part of its delta, which begins 220 miles (354 km) from the sea, is within the republic. The Indus, starting in Tibet, flows northwest for several hundred miles in the Kashmir before turning southwest toward the Arabian Sea; it is important for irrigation in Pakistan. The Brahmaputra, also rising in Tibet, flows eastward, first through India and then south into Bangladesh and the Bay of Bengal.

Government. India is a federal republic. It is also a member of the Commonwealth of Nations, a status defined at the 1949 London Conference of Prime Ministers, by which India recognizes the Queen as head of the Commonwealth. Under the Constitution effective Jan. 26, 1950, India has a parliamentary type of government.

The constitutional head of the state is the President, who is elected every five years. He is advised by the Prime Minister and a Cabinet based on a majority of the bicameral Parliament, which consists of a Council of States (Rajya Sabha) representing the constituent units of the republic and a House of the People (Lok Sabha) elected every five years by universal suffrage.

History. The Aryans who invaded India between 2400 and 1500 B.C. from the northwest found a land already well civilized. Buddhism was founded in the 6th century B.C. and spread through northern India, most notably by one of the greatest ancient kings, Asoka (c. 269–232 B.C.), who also unified most of the Indian subcontinent.

In 1526, Muslim invaders founded the great Mogul empire, centered on Delhi, which lasted, at least in name, until 1857. Akbar the Great (1542–1605) strengthened and consolidated this empire. The long reign of his great-grandson, Aurangzeb (1658–1707), represents both the greatest extent of the Mogul empire and the beginning of its decay.

Vasco da Gama, the Portuguese explorer, visited India first in 1498, and for the next 100 years the Portuguese had a virtual monopoly on trade with the subcontinent. Meanwhile, the English founded the East India Company, which set up its first factory at Surat in 1612 and began expanding its influence, fighting the Indian rulers and the French, Dutch, and Portuguese traders simultaneously.

Bombay, taken from the Portuguese, became the seat of English rule in 1687. The defeat of French and Islamic armies by Lord Clive in the decade ending in 1760 laid the foundation of the British Empire in India. From then until 1858, when the administration of India was formally transferred to the British Crown following the Sepoy Mutiny of native troops in 1857, the East India Company suppressed native uprisings and extended British rule.

After World War I, in which the Indian states sent more than 6 million troops to fight beside the Allies, Indian nationalist unrest rose to new heights under the leadership of a Hindu lawyer, Mohandas K. Gandhi, called Mahatma Gandhi. His tactics called for nonviolent revolts against British authority. He soon became the leading spirit of the All-India Congress Party, which was the spearhead of revolt. In 1919 the British gave added responsibility to Indian officials, and in 1935 India was given a federal form of government and a measure of self-rule.

In 1942, with the Japanese pressing hard on the eastern borders of India, the British War Cabinet tried and failed to reach a political settlement with nationalist leaders. The Congress Party took the position that the British must quit India. In 1942, fearing mass civil disobedience, the government of India carried out widespread arrests of Congress leaders, including Gandhi.

Gandhi was released in 1944 and negotiations for a settlement were resumed. Finally, in February 1947, the Labor government announced its determination to transfer power to "responsible Indian hands" by June 1948 even if a constitution had not been worked out.

Lord Mountbatten, as Viceroy, by June 1947 achieved agreement on the partitioning of India along religious lines and on the splitting of the provinces of Bengal and the Punjab, which the Muslims had claimed.

The Indian Independence Act, passed quickly by the British Parliament, received royal assent on July 18, 1947, and on August 15 the Indian Empire passed into history.

Jawaharlal Nehru, leader of the Congress Party, was made Prime Minister. Before an exchange of populations could be arranged, bloody riots occurred among the communal groups, and armed conflict broke out over rival claims to the princely state of Jammu and Kashmir. Peace was restored only with the greatest difficulty. In 1949 a Constitution, along the lines of the U.S. Constitution, was approved making India a sovereign republic. Under a federal structure the states were organized on linguistic lines.

The dominance of the Congress Party contributed to stability. In 1956 the republic absorbed the former French settlements. Five years later, it forcibly annexed the Portuguese enclaves of Goa, Damao, and Diu.

Nehru died in 1964. His successor, Lal Bahadur Shastri, died on Jan. 10, 1966. Nehru's daughter, Indira Gandhi, became Prime Minister, and she continued his policy of nonalignment.

In 1971 the Pakistani Army moved in to quash the independence movement in East Pakistan that was supported by clandestine aid from India, and some 10 million Bengali refugees poured across the border into India, creating social, economic, and health problems. After numerous border incidents, India invaded East Pakistan and in two weeks forced the surrender of the Pakistani army. East Pakistan was established as an independent state and renamed Bangladesh.

In the summer of 1975, the world's largest democracy veered suddenly toward authoritarianism when a judge in Allahabad, Mrs. Gandhi's home constituency, found her landslide victory in the 1971 elections invalid because civil servants had illegally aided her campaign. Amid demands for her resignation, Mrs. Gandhi decreed a state of emergency on June 26 and ordered mass arrests of her critics, including all opposition party leaders except the Communists.

In 1976, India and Pakistan formally renewed diplomatic relations.

Despite strong opposition to her repressive measures and particularly the resentment against compulsory birth control programs, Mrs. Gandhi in 1977 announced parliamentary elections for March. At the same time, she freed most political prisoners. The landslide victory of Morarji R. Desai unseated Mrs. Gandhi.

Mrs. Gandhi staged a spectacular comeback in the elections of January 1980.

In 1984, Mrs. Gandhi ordered the Indian army to root out a band of Sikh holy men and gunmen who were using the holiest shrine of the Sikh religion, the Golden Temple in Amritsar, as a base for terrorist raids in a violent campaign for greater political autonomy in the strategic Punjab border state. The perceived sacrilege to the Golden Temple kindled outrage among many of India's 14 million Sikhs and brought a spasm of mutinies and desertions by Sikh officers and soldiers in the army.

On Oct. 31, 1984, Mrs. Gandhi was assassinated by two men identified by police as Sikh members of her bodyguard. The ruling Congress I Party chose her older son, Rajiv Gandhi, to succeed her as Prime Minister.

One week after the resignation of Prime Minister Shekhar, India's President in March 1991 called for national elections. While at an election rally on May 22 former Prime Minister Rajiv Gandhi was assassinated. Final phases of the election were postponed a month. When they were resumed the Congress Party and its allies won 236 seats in the lower house, 20 short of a majority. P.V. Narasimha Rao was chosen to form a new government.

The ruling Congress Party lost the parliamentary elections of May 1996. The Hindu nationalist Bharatiya Janata Party's leader, Atal Bihari Vajpayee, became Prime Minister a week later. His government, however, lasted only 13 days. Deve Gowda of the United Front coalition, consisting of 13 parties with a variety of stances, next was sworn in as Prime Minister and won a vote of confidence in June. His is the country's first coalition government.

Native States. Most of the 560-odd native states and subdivisions of pre-1947 India acceded to the new nation, and the central government pursued a vigorous policy of integration. This took three forms: merger into adjacent provinces, conversion into centrally administered areas, and grouping into unions of states. Finally, under a controversial reorganization plan effective Nov. 1, 1956, the unions of states were abolished and merged into adjacent states, and India became a union of 15 states and 8 centrally administered areas. A 16th state was added in 1962, and in 1966 the Punjab was partitioned into two states. Today India consists of 25 states and 7 Union Territories.

Resolution of the territorial dispute over Kashmir grew out of peace negotiations following the two-week India-Pakistan war of 1971. After sporadic skirmishing, an accord reached July 3, 1972, committed both powers to withdraw troops from a temporary cease-fire line after the border was fixed. Agreement on the border was reached Dec. 7, 1972.

In April 1975, the Indian Parliament voted to make the 300-year-old kingdom of Sikkim a full-fledged Indian state, and the annexation took effect May 16. Situated in the Himalayas, Sikkim was a virtual dependency of Tibet until the early 19th century. Under an 1890 treaty between China and Great Britain, it became a British protectorate, and was made an Indian protectorate after Britain quit the subcontinent.

INDONESIA

Republic of Indonesia
President: Suharto (1993)[1]
Area: 735,268 sq mi. (1,904,344 sq km)[2]
Population (est. 1996): 206,611,600 (average annual rate of natural increase: 1.53%); birth rate: 23.7/1000; infant mortality rate: 63.1/1000; density per square mile: 281
Capital and largest city (1990):: Jakarta, 8,259,266.
 Other large cities (1990): Surabaya, 2,421,000; Medan, 1,685,972; Bandung, 2,026,893; Semarang, 1,005,316.
 Monetary unit: Rupiah. **Languages:** Bahasa Indonesia (official), Dutch, English, and more than 583 languages, and dialects. **Religions:** Islam, 87%; Christian, 9%; Hindu, 2%; other, 2%. **National name:** Republik Indonesia. **Literacy rate:** 86.3%
Economic summary: Gross domestic product (1994 est.): $619.4 billion; $3,090 per capita; real growth rate 6.7%; inflation 9.3%; unemployment 3%. Arable land: 8%. Principal agricultural products: rice, cassava, peanuts, rubber, coffee. Labor force: 67,000,000; 10% in manufacturing. Major industrial products: petroleum, timber, textiles, cement, fertilizer, rubber. Natural resources: oil, timber, nickel, natural gas, tin, bauxite, copper. Exports: $41.3 billion (f.o.b., 1994 est.): petroleum and liquid natural gas, timber, rubber, coffee, textiles. Imports: $31.4 billion (f.o.b., 1994 est.): chemicals, machinery, manufactured goods. Major trading partners: Japan, U.S., Singapore, E.U.

1. Reelected President for the 6th five-year term in office.
2. Includes West Irian (former Netherlands New Guinea), renamed Irian Jaya in March 1973 (159,355 sq mi.; 421,981 sq km), and former Portuguese Timor (5,763 sq mi.; 14,874 sq km), annexed in 1976.

Geography. Indonesia is part of the Malay archipelago in Southeast Asia with an area nearly three times that of Texas. It consists of the islands of Sumatra, Java, Bali, Madura, Kalimantan (Indonesia's part of Borneo, except Malaysia's Sarawak and Brunei Da-

russalam in the north), the Sulawesi (Celebes), the Maluku Islands, Irian Jaya (eastern part of New Guinea), and about 30 smaller archipelagos, totaling 17,508 islands, of which about 6,000 are inhabited. Its neighbor to the north is Malaysia and to the east Papua New Guinea.

A backbone of mountain ranges extends throughout the main islands of the archipelago. Earthquakes are frequent, and there are many active volcanoes.

Government. The President is elected by the People's Consultative Assembly, whose 1,000 members include the functioning legislative arm, the 500-member House of Representatives. Meeting at least once every five years, the Assembly has broad policy functions. The House, 100 of whose members are appointed from the armed forces, meets at least once annually. General Suharto was elected unopposed to a sixth five-year term in 1993.

History. Indonesia is inhabited by Javanese (45%), Sudanese (14%), Madurese (7.5%), and Malays (7.5%), as well as a host of other ethnic groups.

During the first few centuries of the Christian era, most of the islands came under the influence of Hindu priests and traders, who spread their culture and religion. Muslim invasions began in the 13th century, and most of the area was Muslim by the 15th. Portuguese traders arrived early in the 16th century but were ousted by the Dutch about 1595. After Napoleon subjugated the Netherlands homeland in 1811, the British seized the islands but returned them to the Dutch in 1816. In 1922 the islands were made an integral part of the Netherlands kingdom.

During World War II, Indonesia was under Japanese military occupation with nominal native self-government. When the Japanese surrendered to the Allies, President Sukarno and Mohammed Hatta, his Vice President, proclaimed Indonesian independence from the Dutch on Aug. 17, 1945. Allied troops—mostly British Indian troops—fought the nationalists until the arrival of Dutch troops. In November 1946, the Dutch and the Indonesians reached a draft agreement contemplating formation of a Netherlands-Indonesian Union, but differences in interpretation resulted in more fighting between Dutch and Indonesian forces.

On Nov. 2, 1949, Dutch and Indonesian leaders agreed upon the terms of union. The transfer of sovereignty took place at Amsterdam on Dec. 27, 1949. In February 1956 Indonesia abrogated the union with the Netherlands and in August 1956 repudiated its debt to the Netherlands. In 1963, Netherlands New Guinea was transferred to Indonesia and renamed West Irian. In 1973 it became Irian Jaya.

Hatta and Sukarno, the co-fathers of Indonesian independence, split after it was achieved over Sukarno's concept of "guided democracy." Under Sukarno, the country's leading political figure for almost a half century, the Indonesian Communist Party gradually gained increasing influence.

After an attempted coup was put down by General Suharto, the army chief of staff, and officers loyal to him, thousands of Communist suspects were sought out and killed all over the country. Suharto took over the reins of government, gradually eased Sukarno out of office, and took full power in 1967.

Suharto permitted national elections, which moved the nation back to representative government. He also ended hostilities with Malaysia. Under President Suharto, Indonesia has been strongly anticommunist. It also has been politically stable and has made progress in economic development.

Indonesia invaded the former Portuguese half of the island of Timor in 1975, and annexed the territory in 1976. More than 100,000 Timorese, a sixth of the mostly Catholic population, were reported to have died from famine, disease, and fighting since the annexation.

In March 1993 the 1,000-member People's Consultative Assembly, a body which meets every five years for the express purpose of choosing a president, reelected Suharto, who ran unopposed.

In early 1995 the government began a crackdown on magazine and newspaper reporters who were critical of the government.

Concern grew about Suharto's health in July 1996 and the lack of a clear political succession when the President left for Germany to undergo medical tests. In the weeks prior to his departure dissident groups voiced alarm at the mounting crackdown on opposition organizations.

IRAN

Islamic Republic of Iran

President: Hashemi Rafsanjani (1989)
Area: 636,293 sq mi. (1,648,000 sq km)
Population (est. 1996): 66,094,264 (average annual rate of natural increase: 2.71%); birth rate: 33.7/1000; infant mortality rate: 52.7/1000; density per square mile: 103
Capital: Teheran; **Largest cities (1991 est.):** Teheran, 6,450,500; Mashad, 1,500,000; Isfahan, 1,000,000; Tabriz, 1,090,000. **Monetary unit:** Rial. **Languages:** Farsi (Persian), Azari, Kurdish, Arabic. **Religions:** Shi'ite Muslim, 95%; Sunni Muslim, 4%. **Literacy rate:** 74% (1992)
Economic summary: Gross domestic product (1994 est.): $310 billion; $4,720 per capita; real growth rate −2%; inflation 35%; unemployment over 30%. Arable land: 8%. Principal agricultural products: wheat, barley, rice, sugar beets, cotton, dates, raisins, sheep, goats. Labor force: 15,400,000; 33% in agriculture. Major industrial products: crude and refined oil, textiles, petrochemicals, cement, processed foods, steel and copper fabrication. Natural resources: oil, gas, iron, copper. Exports: $16 billion (f.o.b., FY92/93 est.): petroleum, carpets, fruits, nuts, hides. Imports: $18 billion (c.i.f., FY92/93 est.): machinery, military supplies, foodstuffs, pharmaceuticals, metal works, technical services. Major trading partners: Japan, Germany, Netherlands, U.K., Italy, Spain, Turkey, France

Geography. Iran, a Middle Eastern country south of the Caspian Sea and north of the Persian Gulf, is three times the size of Arizona. It shares borders with Iraq, Turkey, Azerbaijan, Turkmenistan, Armenia, Afghanistan, and Pakistan.

In general, the country is a plateau averaging 4,000 feet (1,219 m) in elevation. There are also maritime lowlands along the Persian Gulf and the Caspian Sea. The Elburz Mountains in the north rise to 18,603 feet (5,670 m) at Mt. Damavend. From northwest to southeast, the country is crossed by a desert 800 miles (1,287 km) long.

Government. The Pahlavi monarchy regime was overthrown on Feb. 11, 1979. The Islamic Republic of Iran was established and endorsed by a universal referendum on March 30, the same year. A new constitution was drafted by the Assembly of Experts and was approved in a national referendum in Dec. 1979.

The Constitution recognizes the executive, legislative, and judiciary as independent branches. The President is elected by direct vote for a four-year term. He runs the government and is accountable for the implementation of the Constitution before the Parliament (*Majles*), which consists of 270 representatives popularly elected for a period of four years.

In the course of the Islamic Revolution, Ayatollah Khomeini emerged as the leader of Iran. After his death on July 3, 1989, the Assembly of Experts elected Ayatollah Ali Khameneie as his successor. The Assembly itself consists of experts elected directly by the nation.

History. Oil-rich Iran was called Persia before 1935. Its key location blocks the lower land gate to Asia and also stands in the way of traditional Russian ambitions for access to the Indian Ocean. After periods of Assyrian, Median, and Achaemenidian rule, Persia became a powerful empire under Cyrus the Great, reaching from the Indus to the Nile at its zenith in 525 B.C. It fell to Alexander in 331–30 B.C. and to the Seleucids in 312–02 B.C., and a native Persian regime arose about 130 B.C. Another Persian regime arose about A.D. 224, but it fell to the Arabs in 637. In the 12th century, the Mongols took their turn ruling Persia, and in the early part of the 18th century, the Turks occupied the country.

An Anglo-Russian convention of 1907 divided Persia into two spheres of influence. British attempts to impose a protectorate over the entire country were defeated in 1919. Two years later, Gen. Reza Pahlavi seized the government and was elected hereditary Shah in 1925. Subsequently he did much to modernize the country and abolished all foreign extraterritorial rights.

Increased pro-Axis activity led to Anglo-Russian occupation of Iran in 1941 and deposition of the Shah in favor of his son, Mohammed Reza Pahlavi.

Ali Razmara became Premier in 1950 and pledged to restore efficient and honest government, but he was assassinated after less than nine months in office and Mohammed Mossadegh took over. Mossadegh was ousted in August 1953, by Fazollah Zahedi, whom the Shah had named Premier.

Opposition to the Shah spread, despite the imposition of martial law in September 1978, and massive demonstrations demanded the return of the exiled Ayatollah Ruhollah Khomeini. Riots and strikes continued despite the appointment of a opposition leader, Shahpur Bakhtiar, as Premier on Dec. 29. The Shah and his family left Iran on Jan. 16, 1979, for a "vacation," leaving power in the hands of a regency council.

Khomeini returned on Feb. 1 to a nation in turmoil as military units loyal to the Shah continued to support Bakhtiar and clashed with revolutionaries. Khomeini appointed Mehdi Bazargan as Premier of the provisional government, and in two days of fighting, revolutionaries forced the military to capitulate on Feb. 11.

The new government began a program of nationalization of insurance companies, banks, and industries both locally and foreign-owned. Oil production fell amid the political confusion.

Khomeini, ignoring opposition, proceeded with his plans for revitalizing Islamic traditions. He urged women to return to the veil, or chador; banned alcohol and mixed bathing; and prohibited music from radio and television broadcasting, declaring it to be "no different from opium."

Revolutionary militants invaded the U.S. Embassy in Teheran on Nov. 4, 1979, seized staff members as hostages, and precipitated an international crisis.

Khomeini refused all appeals, even a unanimous vote by the U.N. Security Council demanding immediate release of the hostages.

Iranian hostility toward Washington was reinforced by the Carter administration's economic boycott and deportation order against Iranian students in the U.S., the break in diplomatic relations, and ultimately an aborted U.S. raid in April aimed at rescuing the hostages.

As the first anniversary of the embassy seizure neared, Khomeini and his followers insisted on their original conditions: guarantee by the U.S. not to interfere in Iran's affairs, cancellation of U.S. damage claims against Iran, release of $8 billion in frozen Iranian assets, an apology, and the return of the assets held by the former imperial family.

These conditions were largely met and the 52 American hostages were released on Jan. 20, ending 444 days in captivity.

From the release of the hostages onward, President Bani-Sadr and the conservative clerics of the dominant Islamic Republican Party clashed with growing frequency. He was stripped of his command of the armed forces by Khomeini on June 6 and ousted as President on June 22. On July 24, Prime Minister Mohammed Ali Rajai was elected overwhelmingly to the presidency.

Rajai and Prime Minister Mohammed Javad Bahonar were killed on Aug. 30 by a bomb in Bahonar's office. Hojatolislam Mohammed Ali Khamenei, a clergyman, leader of the Islamic Republican Party and spokesman for Khomeini, was elected President on Oct. 2, 1981.

The sporadic war with Iraq regained momentum in 1982, as Iran launched an offensive in March and regained much of the border area occupied by Iraq in late 1980.

Iran continued to be at war with Iraq well into 1988. Although Iraq expressed its willingness to cease fighting, Iran stated that it would not stop the war until Iraq agreed to make payment for war damages to Iran, and punish the Iraqi government leaders involved in the conflict.

On July 20, 1988, Khomeini, after a series of Iranian military reverses, agreed to cease-fire negotiations with Iraq. A cease-fire went into effect Aug. 20, 1988. Khomeini died in June 1989.

By early 1991 the Islamic Revolution appeared to have lost much of its militancy. Attempting to revive a stagnant economy President Rafsanjani took measures to decentralize the command system and introduce free-market mechanisms.

In 1995 Russia remained steadfast in the face of U.S. protests concerning the former's agreement with Iran to help build a nuclear power plant.

In June 1996 Ali Akbar Nateq-Nouri, a hard-liner, was reelected for one year as speaker of parliament.

IRAQ

Republic of Iraq

President: Saddam Hussein (1979)
Area: 167,920 sq mi. (434,913 sq km)
Population (est. 1996): 21,422,292 (average annual rate of natural increase: 3.65%); birth rate: 43/1000; infant mortality rate: 60/1000; density per square mile: 127
Capital: Baghdad; **Largest cities (est. 1985):** Baghdad, 4,648,609; Basra, 616,700; Mosul, 570,926. **Monetary**

unit: Iraqi dinar. **Languages:** Arabic (official) and Kurdish. **Religions:** Islam, 95%; Christian or other, 5%. **National name:** Jumhouriyat Al Iraq. **Literacy rate:** 55–65% (est.).

Economic summary: Gross domestic product (1989): $38 billion, $2,000 per capita; real growth rate n.a.; inflation: 200% (est.). Arable land: 12%. Principal products: dates, livestock, wheat, barley, cotton, rice. Labor force: 4,400,000 (1989); services, 48%; agriculture, 30%; industry, 22%. Major products: petroleum, chemicals, textiles,, construction materials. Natural resources: oil, natural gas, phosphates, sulfur. Exports: $10.4 billion (f.o.b., 1990): petroleum and refined products, machinery, chemicals, dates. Imports: $6.6 billion (c.i.f., 1990): manufactured goods, food. Major trading partners: France, Italy, Japan, Germany, Brazil, U.K., U.S., Turkey, C.I.S. countries.

Geography. Iraq, a triangle of mountains, desert, and fertile river valley, is bounded on the east by Iran, on the north by Turkey, the west by Syria and Jordan, and the south by Saudi Arabia and Kuwait. It is twice the size of Idaho.

The country has arid desertland west of the Euphrates, a broad central valley between the Euphrates and Tigris, and mountains in the northeast. The fertile lower valley is formed by the delta of the two rivers, which join about 120 miles (193 km) from the head of the Persian Gulf. The gulf coastline is 26 miles (42 km) long. The only port for seagoing vessels is Basra, which is on the Shatt-al-Arab River near the head of the Persian Gulf.

Government. Since the coup d'etat of July 1968, Iraq has been governed by the Arab Ba'ath Socialist Party through a Council of Command of the Revolution headed by the President. There is also a Council of Ministers headed by the President and a National Council (Parliament).

History. From earliest times Iraq was known as Mesopotamia—the land between the rivers—for it embraces a large part of the alluvial plains of the Tigris and Euphrates.

An advanced civilization existed by 4000 B.C. Sometime after 2000 B.C. the land became the center of the ancient Babylonian and Assyrian empires. It was conquered by Cyrus the Great of Persia in 538 B.C., and by Alexander in 331 B.C. After an Arab conquest in A.D. 637–40, Baghdad became capital of the ruling caliphate. The country was cruelly pillaged by the Mongols in 1258, and during the 16th, 17th, and 18th centuries was the object of repeated Turkish-Persian competition.

Nominal Turkish suzerainty imposed in 1638 was replaced by direct Turkish rule in 1831. In World War I, an Anglo-Indian force occupied most of the country, and Britain was given a mandate over the area in 1920. The British recognized Iraq as a kingdom in 1922 and terminated the mandate in 1932 when Iraq was admitted to the League of Nations. In World War II, Iraq generally adhered to its 1930 treaty of alliance with Britain, but in 1941, British troops were compelled to put down a pro-Axis revolt led by Premier Rashid Ali.

Iraq became a charter member of the Arab League in 1945, and Iraqi troops took part in the Arab invasion of Palestine in 1948.

Faisal II, born on May 2, 1935, succeeded his father, Ghazi I, who was killed in an automobile accident on April 4, 1939. Faisal and his uncle, Crown Prince Abdul-Illah, were assassinated in July 1958 in a swift revolutionary coup that brought to power a military junta headed by Abdul Karem Kassim. Kassim, in turn, was overthrown and killed in a coup staged March 8, 1963, by the Ba'ath Socialist Party.

Abdel Salam Arif, a leader in the 1958 coup, staged another coup in November 1963, driving the Ba'ath members of the revolutionary council from power. He adopted a new constitution in 1964. In 1966, he, two cabinet members, and other supporters died in a helicopter crash. His brother, Gen. Abdel Rahman Arif, assumed the presidency, crushed the opposition, and won an indefinite extension of his term in 1967. His regime was ousted in July 1968 by a junta led by Maj. Gen. Ahmed Hassan al-Bakr.

A long-standing dispute over control of the Shatt al-Arab waterway between Iraq and Iran broke into full-scale war on Sept. 20, 1980. Iraqi planes attacked Iranian airfields and the Abadan refinery, and Iraqi ground forces moved into Iran.

Despite the smaller size of its armed forces, Iraq took and held the initiative by seizing Abadan and Khurramshahr together with substantial Iranian territory by December and beating back Iranian counterattacks in January. Peace efforts by the Islamic nations, the nonaligned, and the United Nations failed as 1981 wore on and the war stagnated.

In 1982, the Iraqis fell back to their own country and dug themselves in behind sandbagged defensive fortifications. From the beginning of the war in September 1980 to September 1984, foreign military analysts estimated that more than 100,000 Iranians and perhaps 50,000 Iraqis had been killed. The Iraqis clearly wanted to end the war, but the Iranians refused.

In February 1986, Iranian forces gained on two fronts; but Iraq retook most of the lost ground in 1988 and the war continued a stalemate. In August, Iraq and Iran agreed they would hold direct talks after a ceasefire took effect.

In July 1990, President Hussein claimed that Kuwait was flooding world markets with oil and forcing down prices. A mediation attempt by Arab leaders failed, and on Aug. 2, 1990, over this and territorial claims, Iraqi troops invaded Kuwait and set up a puppet government. On January 18, 1991, U.N. forces, under the leadership of U.S. General Norman Schwarzkopf, launched Operation Desert Storm, liberating Kuwait in less than a week.

After the Gulf War, Saddam Hussein was still in power. The U.N. Security Council affirmed an embargo against military supplies to that country, and a trade embargo was still in place.

In May 1996 the country was permitted to sell $2 billion of oil over an initial six-month period so as to buy much-needed food and medicine. The government interpreted this as the first crack in international economic sanctions.

IRELAND

President: Mary Robinson (1990)
Taoiseach (Prime Minister): John Bruton (1994)
Area: 27,136 sq mi. (70,282 sq km)
Population (est. 1996): 3,562,902 (average annual rate of natural increase: 0.54%); birth rate: 13.4/1000; infant mortality rate: 7.0/1000; density per square mile: 131
Capital: Dublin; **Largest cities (1991):** Dublin, 1,024,429; Cork, 282,790; Limerick, 109,816. **Monetary unit:** Irish pound (punt). **Languages:** Irish, English. **Religions:** Roman Catholic, 92%; others, 8%. **National name:** Ireland, or Eire in the Irish language. **Literacy rate:** 99%

Economic summary: Gross national product (1995): $53.5 billion; $14,888 per capita; real growth rate 7%; inflation 2.5%; unemployment 12.9%. Arable land: 14%. Principal products: cattle and dairy products, pigs, poultry and eggs, sheep and wool, horses, barley, sugar beets. Labor force (1995): 1,397,000; 27.9% in manufacturing and construction. Major products: processed foods, brews, textiles, clothing, chemicals, pharmaceuticals, machinery, transportation equipment, glass and crystal. Natural resources: zinc, lead, natural gas, crude oil, barite, copper, gypsum, limestone, dolomite, peat, silver. Exports: $45 billion (1995 est.): livestock, dairy products, machinery, chemicals, data processing equipment. Imports: $37 billion (1995 est.): food, animal feed, chemicals, petroleum products, machinery, textile clothing. Major trading partners: U.K., Western European countries, U.S.

Geography. Ireland is situated in the Atlantic Ocean and separated from Britain by the Irish Sea. Half the size of Arkansas, it occupies the entire island except for the six counties which make up Northern Ireland.

Ireland resembles a basin—a central plain rimmed with mountains, except in the Dublin region. The mountains are low, with the highest peak, Carrantuohill in County Kerry, rising to 3,415 feet (1,041 m).

The principal river is the Shannon, which begins in the north central area, flows south and southwest for about 240 miles (386 km), and empties into the Atlantic.

Government. Ireland is a parliamentary democracy. The National Parliament (Oireachtas) consists of the president and two Houses, the House of Representatives (Dáil éireann) and the Senate (Seanad éireann), whose members serve for a maximum term of five years. The House of Representatives has 166 members elected by proportional representation; the Senate has 60 members, 11 of whom are nominated by the prime minister, 6 by the universities, and the remaining 43 from five vocational panels. The prime minister (Taoiseach), who is the head of government, is appointed by the president on the nomination of the House of Representatives, to which he is responsible.

History. In the Stone and Bronze Ages, Ireland was inhabited by Picts in the north and a people called the Erainn in the south, the same stock, apparently, as in all the isles before the Anglo-Saxon invasion of Britain. About the fourth century B.C., tall, red-haired Celts arrived from Gaul or Galicia. They subdued and assimilated the inhabitants and established a Gaelic civilization.

By the beginning of the Christian Era, Ireland was divided into five kingdoms—Ulster, Connacht, Leinster, Meath, and Munster. St. Patrick introduced Christianity in 432 and the country developed into a center of Gaelic and Latin learning. Irish monasteries, the equivalent of universities, attracted intellectuals as well as the pious and sent out missionaries to many parts of Europe and, some believe, to North America.

Norse depredations along the coasts, starting in 795, ended in 1014 with Norse defeat at the Battle of Clontarf by forces under Brian Boru. In the 12th century, the Pope gave all Ireland to the English Crown as a papal fief. In 1171, Henry II of England was acknowledged "Lord of Ireland," but local sectional rule continued for centuries, and English control over the whole island was not reasonably absolute until the 17th century. By the Act of Union (1801), England and Ireland became the "United Kingdom of Great Britain and Ireland."

A steady decline in the Irish economy followed in the next decades. The population had reached 8.25 million when the great potato famine of 1846–48 took many lives and drove millions to emigrate to America. By 1921 it was down to 4.3 million.

In the meantime, anti-British agitation continued along with demands for Irish home rule. The advent of World War I delayed the institution of home rule and resulted in the Easter Rebellion in Dublin (April 24–29, 1916), in which Irish nationalists unsuccessfully attempted to throw off British rule. Guerrilla warfare against British forces followed proclamation of a republic by the rebels in 1919.

The Irish Free State was established as a dominion on Dec. 6, 1922, with the six northern counties as part of the United Kingdom. Ireland was neutral in World War II.

In 1948, Eamon de Valera, American-born leader of the Sinn Fein, who had won establishment of the Free State in 1921 in negotiations with Britain's David Lloyd George, was defeated by John A. Costello, who demanded final independence from Britain. The Republic of Ireland was proclaimed on April 18, 1949. It withdrew from the Commonwealth but in 1955 entered the United Nations.

Through the 1960s, two antagonistic currents dominated Irish politics. One sought to bind the wounds of the rebellion and civil war. The other was the effort of the outlawed extremist Irish Republican Army to bring Northern Ireland into the republic.

In the elections of June 11, 1981, Garret M. D. FitzGerald, leader of the Fine Gael, was elected prime minister. FitzGerald resigned Jan. 27, 1982, after his presentation of an austerity budget aroused the opposition of independents who had backed him previously. Former Prime Minister Haughey was sworn in on March 9 and presented a budget with nearly a $1 billion deficit.

Three candidates vied in the November 1990 presidential election. Although Brian Lenihan of Fianna Fail led in the first round, Mary Robinson, supported by the Labour Party and the Workers Party, won the second round with 52.8% of the vote, becoming the first non-Fianna Fail president since 1945.

Amid allegations of scandal Prime Minister Haughey resigned in early 1992. Albert Reynolds was chosen by a majority of his Fianna Fail party to become the next prime minister. The general election of November 1992 saw Reynolds's Fianna Fail receive a plurality.

Reynolds's government fell in January 1995 over a scandal involving the handling of the extradition of a priest convicted of child molestation in the North.

A referendum on divorce, which hitherto had been constitutionally forbidden, under certain conditions was held in November 1995 and narrowly passed.

ISRAEL

State of Israel
President: Ezer Weizman (1993)
Prime Minister: Benjamin Netanyahu (1996)
Area: 8,020 sq mi. (20,772 sq km)
Population (est. 1996): 5,215,022[1] (average annual rate of natural increase: 1.39%); birth rate: 20.2/1000; infant mortality rate: 8.2/1000; density per square mile: 650
Capital and largest city (1993 est.): Jerusalem[2], 550,500. **Other large cities (est. 1993):** Tel Aviv, 355,900; Haifa, 250,000. **Monetary unit:** Shekel. **Languages:** Hebrew, Arabic, English. **Religions:** Judaism, 82%; Islam, 14%;

Christian, 2%; others, 2%. **National name:** Medinat Yisra'el. **Literacy rate:** 92%
Economic summary: Gross domestic product (1994 est.): $70.1 billion; $13,880 per capita; real growth rate 6.8%; inflation 14.5%; unemployment 7.5%. Arable land: 17%. Principal agricultural products: citrus and other fruits, vegetables, beef, dairy and poultry products. Labor force: (1992): 1,900,000; 29.3% in public services, industry 22.1%, commerce 13.9%. Major industrial products: processed foods, cut diamonds, clothing and textiles, chemicals, metal products, transport and electrical equipment, high-technology electronics. Natural resources: sulfur, copper, phosphates, potash, bromine. Exports: $16.2 billion (f.o.b., 1994 est.): polished diamonds, citrus and other fruits, clothing and textiles, processed foods, electronics, military hardware, fertilizer and chemical products. Imports: $22.5 billion (c.i.f., 1994 est.): rough diamonds, chemicals, oil, machinery, iron and steel, cereals, textiles, vehicles, ships, aircraft. Major trading partners: U.S., E.U., Switzerland, Japan, Hong Kong, Canada, South Africa.

---

1. Includes West Bank, Gaza Strip, East Jerusalem. 2. Not recognized by U.S. which recognizes Tel Aviv.

Geography. Israel, slightly smaller than Massachusetts, lies at the eastern end of the Mediterranean Sea. It is bordered by Egypt on the west, Syria and Jordan on the east, and Lebanon on the north. Northern Israel is largely a plateau traversed from north to south by mountains and broken by great depressions, also running from north to south.

The maritime plain of Israel is remarkably fertile. The southern Negev region, which comprises almost half the total area, is largely a wide desert steppe area. The National Water Project irrigation scheme is now transforming it into fertile land. The Jordan, the only important river, flows from the north through Lake Hule (Waters of Merom) and Lake Kinneret (Sea of Galilee or Sea of Tiberias), finally entering the Dead Sea, 1,290 feet (393 m) below sea level. This "sea," which is actually a salt lake (394 sq mi.; 1,020 sq km), has no outlet, its water balance being maintained by evaporation.

Government. Israel, which does not have a written constitution, has a republican form of government headed by a president elected for a five-year term by the Knesset. The president may serve no more than two terms. The Knesset has 120 members elected by universal suffrage under proportional representation for four years. The government is administered by the Cabinet, which is headed by the prime minister.

The Knesset decided in June 1950 that Israel would acquire a constitution gradually through the years by the enactment of fundamental laws. Israel grants automatic citizenship to every Jew who desires to settle within its borders, subject to control of the Knesset.

History. Palestine, cradle of two great religions and homeland of the modern state of Israel, was known to the ancient Hebrews as the "Land of Canaan." Palestine's name derives from the Philistines, a people who occupied the southern coastal part of the country in the 12th century B.C.

A Hebrew kingdom established in 1000 B.C. was later split into the kingdoms of Judah and Israel; they were subsequently invaded by Assyrians, Babylonians, Egyptians, Persians, Macedonians, Romans, and Byzantines. The Arabs took Palestine from the Byzantine Empire A.D. 634–40. With the exception of a Frankish Crusader kingdom from 1099 to 1187, Palestine remained under Muslim rule until the 20th century (Turkish rule from 1516), when British forces under Gen. Sir Edmund Allenby defeated the Turks and captured Jerusalem Dec. 9, 1917. The League of Nations granted Britain a mandate to govern Palestine, effective in 1923.

Jewish colonies—Jews from Russia established one as early as 1882—multiplied after Theodor Herzl's 1897 call for a Jewish state. The Zionist movement received official approval with the publication of a letter Nov. 2, 1917, from Arthur Balfour, British foreign secretary, to Lord Rothschild, a British Jewish leader. Balfour promised support for the establishment of a Jewish homeland in Palestine on the understanding that the civil and religious rights of non-Jewish Palestinians would be safeguarded.

A 1937 British proposal called for an Arab and a Jewish state separated by a mandated area incorporating Jerusalem and Nazareth. Arabs opposed this, demanding a single state with minority rights for Jews, and a 1939 British White Paper retreated, offering instead a single state with further Jewish immigration to be limited to 75,000. Although the White Paper satisfied neither side, further discussion ended on the outbreak of World War II, when the Jewish population stood at nearly 500,000. Illegal and legal immigration during the war brought the Jewish population to 678,000 in 1946, compared with 1,269,000 Arabs. Unable to reach a compromise, Britain turned the problem over to the United Nations in 1947, which on November 29 voted for partition—despite strong Arab opposition.

Britain did not help implement the U.N. decision and withdrew on expiration of its mandate May 14, 1948. Zionists had already seized control of areas designated as Jewish, and, on the day of British departure, the Jewish National Council proclaimed the State of Israel.

U.S. recognition came within hours. The next day, Jordanian and Egyptian forces invaded the new nation. At the cease-fire Jan. 7, 1949, Israel increased its original territory by 50%, taking western Galilee, a broad corridor through central Palestine to Jerusalem, and part of modern Jerusalem. (In April 1950, Jordan annexed areas of eastern and central Palestine that had been designated for an Arab state, together with the old city of Jerusalem.)

Chaim Weizmann and David Ben-Gurion became Israel's first president and prime minister. The new government was admitted to the U.N. May 11, 1949.

The next clash with Arab neighbors came when Egypt nationalized the Suez Canal in 1956 and barred Israeli shipping. Coordinating with an Anglo-French force, Israeli troops seized the Gaza Strip and drove through the Sinai to the east bank of the Suez Canal, but withdrew under U.S. and U.N. pressure. In 1967, Israel threatened retaliation against Syrian border raids, and Syria asked Egyptian aid. Egypt demanded the removal of U.N. peace-keeping forces from Suez, staged a national mobilization, closed the Gulf of Aqaba, and moved troops into the Sinai. Starting with simultaneous air attacks against Syrian, Jordanian, and Egyptian air bases on June 5, Israel during a six-day war totally defeated its Arab enemies. Expanding its territory by 200%, Israel at the cease-fire held the Golan Heights, the West Bank of the Jordan River, the Old City, and all of the Sinai and the east bank of the Suez Canal.

Israel insisted that Jerusalem remain a unified city and that peace negotiations be conducted directly, something the Arab states had refused to do because it would constitute a recognition of their Jewish neighbor.

Egypt's President Gamal Abdel Nasser renounced the 1967 cease-fire in 1969 and began a "war of attri-

tion" against Israel, firing Soviet artillery at Israeli forces on the east bank of the canal. Nasser died of a heart attack on Sept. 28, 1970, and was succeeded by Anwar el-Sadat.

In the face of Israeli reluctance even to discuss the return of occupied territories, the fourth Mideast war erupted Oct. 6, 1973, with a surprise Egyptian and Syrian assault on the Jewish high holy day of Yom Kippur. Initial Arab gains were reversed when a cease-fire took effect two weeks later, but Israel suffered heavy losses in manpower.

U.S. Secretary of State Henry A. Kissinger arranged a disengagement of forces on both the Egyptian and Syrian fronts. Geneva talks, aimed at a lasting peace, foundered, however, when Israel balked at inclusion of the Palestine Liberation Organization.

A second-stage Sinai withdrawal signed by Israel and Egypt in September 1975 required Israel to give up the strategic Mitla and Gidi passes and to return the captured Abu Rudeis oil fields. Egypt guaranteed passage of Israeli cargoes through the reopened Suez Canal, and both sides renounced force in the settlement of disputes. Two hundred U.S. civilian technicians were stationed in a widened U.N. buffer zone to monitor and warn either side of truce violations.

A dramatic breakthrough in the tortuous history of Mideast peace efforts occurred Nov. 9, 1977, when Egypt's President Sadat declared his willingness to go anywhere to talk peace. Prime Minister Menachem Begin on Nov. 15 extended an invitation to the Egyptian leader to address the Knesset. Sadat's arrival in Israel four days later raised worldwide hopes. But optimism ebbed even before Begin was invited to Ismailia by Sadat, December 25–26.

An Israeli peace plan unveiled by Begin on his return, and approved by the Knesset, offered to end military administration in the West Bank and the Gaza Strip, with a degree of Arab self-rule but no relinquishment of sovereignty by Israel. Sadat severed talks on Jan. 18 and, despite U.S. condemnation, Begin approved new West Bank settlements by Israelis.

On March 14, 1979, after a visit by President Carter, the Knesset approved a final peace treaty, and 12 days later Begin and Sadat signed the document, together with Carter, in a White House ceremony. Israel began its withdrawal from the Sinai on May 25 by handing over the coastal town of El Arish, and the two countries opened their border on May 29.

One of the most difficult periods in Israel's history began with a confrontation with Syria over the placing by Syria of Soviet surface-to-air missiles in the Bekaa Valley of Lebanon in April 1981. President Reagan dispatched Philip C. Habib to prevent a clash. While Habib was seeking a settlement, Begin ordered a bombing raid against an Iraqi nuclear reactor on June 7, invoking the theory of preemptive self-defense because he said Iraq was planning to make nuclear weapons to attack Israel.

Although Israel withdrew its last settlers from the Sinai in April 1982 and agreed to a Sinai "peace patrol" composed of troops from four West European nations, the fragile peace engineered by Habib in Lebanon was shattered on June 9 by a massive Israeli assault on southern Lebanon. The attack was in retaliation for what Israel charged was a PLO attack that had critically wounded the Israeli ambassador to London six days earlier.

Israeli armor swept through UNIFIL lines in southern Lebanon, destroyed PLO strongholds in Tyre and Sidon, and reached the suburbs of Beirut on June 10. As Israeli troops ringed Muslim East Beirut, where 5,000 PLO guerrillas were believed trapped, Habib sought to negotiate a safe exit for them.

A U.S.-mediated accord between Lebanon and Israel, signed on May 17, 1983, provided for Israeli withdrawal from Lebanon. Israeli withdrawal was conditioned on withdrawal of Syrian troops from the Bekaa Valley, however, and the Syrians refused to leave. Israel eventually withdrew its troops from the Beirut area, but kept them in southern Lebanon. Lebanon, under pressure from Syria, canceled the accord in March 1984.

Prime Minister Begin resigned on Sept. 15, 1983. On Oct. 10, Likud Party stalwart Yitzhak Shamir was elected prime minister.

After a close election, the two major parties worked out a carefully balanced power-sharing agreement and the Knesset, on Sept. 14, 1984 approved a national unity government including both the Labor Alignment and the Likud bloc.

In one hopeful development, the coalition government declared an economic emergency on July 1 and imposed sweeping austerity measures intended to break the country's 260% inflation. Key elements were an 18.8% devaluation of the shekel, price increases in such government-subsidized products as gasoline, dismissal of 9,000 government employees, government spending cuts, and a wage and price freeze. By the end of Peres' term in October 1986, the shekel had been revalued and stabilized and inflation was down to less than 20%.

In Dec. 1987, riots by Gazan Palestinians led to the current general uprising throughout the occupied territories, which consists of low-level violence and civil disobedience. As a consequence, in 1988 the PLO formally declared an independent state. Also, in response to the PLO's ostensible recognition of Israel in that year, the U.S. established low-level diplomatic contacts with the PLO.

A deadlock in the elections of Dec. 1988 led to a continuation of the Likud-Labor national unity government. This collapsed in 1990, leading to Shamir forming a right-wing coalition that included the religious parties.

The relaxation of Soviet emigration rules resulted in a massive wave of Jews entering Israel. Citing for one the severe housing shortage, but probably owing as much to political considerations, Israel embarked on constructing new settlements in the West Bank.

Elections in late June 1992 scored a major victory for Rabin's Labor Party but without a parliamentary majority, forcing the new prime minister to search for coalition partners.

In highly secretive Norwegian-sponsored talks Israel and the PLO hammered out an agreement for limited Palestinian self-rule and measured Israeli withdrawal from the West Bank. The accord itself was signed in Cairo in May 1994.

On November 4, 1995, Prime Minister Rabin was slain by a Jewish extremist, jeopardizing the tenuous progress toward peace. Shimon Peres succeeded him, until May 1996 elections for the Knesset gave Israel a new hard-line prime minister by a razor-thin margin.

Elections for seats on the Palestinian Council and for its president took place in January 1996. A number of independent candidates won a position, but Yasser Arafat obtained an easy victory as president.

ITALY

Italian Republic
President: Oscar Luigi Scalfaro (1992)
Prime Minister: Romano Prodi (1996)
Area: 116,500 sq mi. (301,278 sq km)

Population (est. 1996): 57,460,274 (average annual rate of natural increase: 0.1%); birth rate: 9.9/1000; infant mortality rate: 6.9/1000; density per square mile: 493
Capital and largest city (1994 est): Rome, 2,687,881.
Other large cities: Milan, 1,334,171; Naples, 1,061,583; Turin, 945,551; Palermo, 694,749; Genoa, 659,754, Bologna, 394,969; Florence, 392,800; Bari, 338,949; Catania, 327,163; Venice, 306,439. **Monetary unit:** Lira. **Language:** Italian. **Religion:** Roman Catholic, almost 100%. **National name:** Repubblica Italiana. **Literacy rate:** 97%
Economic summary: Gross domestic product (1994 est.): $998.9 billion, $17,180 per capita; 2.2% real growth rate; inflation rate 3.9%; unemployment rate 12.2% (Jan. 95). Arable land: 32%. Principal agricultural products: grapes, olives, citrus fruits, vegetables, wheat, corn. Labor force (1993): 23,697,000; 58.7% in services. Major industrial products: machinery, iron and steel, autos, textiles, shoes, chemicals. Natural resources: mercury, potash, sulfur, fish, gas, marble. Exports: $190.8 billion (f.o.b., 1994): textiles, wearing apparel, metals, transport equipment, chemicals. Imports: $168.7 billion (c.i.f., 1994): petroleum, industrial machinery, chemicals, food, metals. Major trading partners: United States, E.U., OPEC

Geography. Italy is a long peninsula shaped like a boot bounded on the west by the Tyrrhenian Sea and on the east by the Adriatic. Slightly larger than Arizona, it has for neighbors France, Switzerland, Austria, and Yugoslavia.

Approximately 600 of Italy's 708 miles (1,139 km) of length are in the long peninsula that projects into the Mediterranean from the fertile basin of the Po River. The Apennine Mountains, branching off from the Alps between Nice and Genoa, form the peninsula's backbone, and rise to a maximum height of 9,560 feet (2,912 m) at the Gran Sasso d'Italia (Corno). The Alps form Italy's northern boundary.

Several islands form part of Italy. Sicily (9,926 sq mi.; 25,708 sq km) lies off the toe of the boot, across the Strait of Messina, with a steep and rockbound northern coast and gentler slopes to the sea in the west and south. Mount Etna, an active volcano, rises to 10,741 feet (3,274 m), and most of Sicily is more than 500 feet (3,274 m) in elevation. Sixty-two miles (100 km) southwest of Sicily lies Pantelleria (45 sq mi.; 117 sq km), and south of that are Lampedusa and Linosa. Sardinia (9,301 sq mi.; 24,090 sq km), which is just south of Corsica and about 125 miles (200 km) west of the mainland, is mountainous, stony, and unproductive.

Italy has many northern lakes, lying below the snow-covered peaks of the Alps. The largest are Garda (143 sq mi.; 370 sq km), Maggiore (83 sq mi.; 215 sq km), and Como (55 sq mi.; 142 sq km).

The Po, the principal river, flows from the Alps on Italy's western border and crosses the Lombard plain to the Adriatic.

Government. The president is elected for a term of seven years by Parliament in joint session with regional representatives. The president nominates the premier and, upon the premier's recommendations, the members of the Cabinet. Parliament is composed of two houses: a Senate with 315 elective members and a Chamber of Deputies of 630 members elected by the people for a five-year term.

History. Until A.D. 476, when the German Odoacer became head of the Roman Empire in the west, the history of Italy was largely the history of Rome. From A.D. 800 on, the Holy Roman Emperors, Popes, Normans, and Saracens all vied for control over various segments of the Italian peninsula. Numerous city states, such as Venice and Genoa, and many small principalities flourished in the late Middle Ages.

In 1713, after the War of the Spanish Succession, Milan, Naples, and Sardinia were handed over to Austria, which lost some of its Italian territories in 1735. After 1800, Italy was unified by Napoleon, who crowned himself King of Italy in 1805; but with the Congress of Vienna in 1815, Austria once again became the dominant power in Italy.

Austrian armies crushed Italian uprisings in 1820–1821 and 1831. In the 1830s Giuseppe Mazzini, brilliant liberal nationalist, organized the Risorgimento (Resurrection), which laid the foundation for Italian unity.

Disappointed Italian patriots looked to the House of Savoy for leadership. Count Camille di Cavour (1810–61), premier of Sardinia in 1852 and the architect of a united Italy, joined England and France in the Crimean War (1853–56), and in 1859 helped France in a war against Austria, thereby obtaining Lombardy. By plebiscite in 1860, Modena, Parma, Tuscany, and the Romagna voted to join Sardinia. In 1860, Giuseppe Garibaldi conquered Sicily and Naples and turned them over to Sardinia. Victor Emmanuel II, king of Sardinia, was proclaimed King of Italy in 1861.

Allied with Germany and Austria-Hungary in the Triple Alliance of 1882, Italy declared its neutrality upon the outbreak of World War I on the ground that Germany had embarked upon an offensive war. In 1915, Italy entered the war on the side of the Allies.

Benito (Il Duce) Mussolini, a former Socialist, organized discontented Italians in 1919 into the Fascist Party to "rescue Italy from Bolshevism." He led his Black Shirts in a march on Rome and, on Oct. 28, 1922, became premier. He transformed Italy into a dictatorship, embarking on an expansionist foreign policy with the invasion and annexation of Ethiopia in 1935 and allying himself with Adolf Hitler in the Rome-Berlin Axis in 1936. He was executed by partisans on April 28, 1945, at Dongo on Lake Como.

Following the overthrow of Mussolini's dictatorship and the armistice with the Allies (Sept. 3, 1943), Italy joined the war against Germany as a co-belligerent. King Victor Emmanuel III abdicated May 9, 1946, and left the country after having installed his son as King Humbert II. A plebiscite rejected monarchy, however, and on June 13, King Humbert followed his father into exile.

The peace treaty of Sept. 15, 1947, required Italian renunciation of all claims in Ethiopia and Greece and the cession of the Dodecanese to Greece and of five small Alpine areas to France. Much of the Istrian Peninsula, including Fiume and Pola, went to Yugoslavia.

The Trieste area west of the new Yugoslav territory was made a free territory (until 1954, when the city and a 90-square-mile zone were transferred to Italy and the rest to Yugoslavia).

Scandal brought the long reign of the Christian Democrats to an end when Italy's 40th premier since World War II, Arnaldo Forlani, was forced to resign in the wake of disclosure that many high-ranking Christian Democrats and civil servants belonged to a secret Masonic lodge known as "P-2."

When the Socialists deserted the coalition, Forlani was forced to resign on May 26, 1981, leaving to Giovanni Spadolini of the small Republican Party the task of forming a new government.

In elections of April 1992 the Christian Democrats obtained less than one-third of the vote, their lowest

ever but still making them the largest party. Andreotti routinely handed in his resignation, but to compound matters President Cossiga also did so shortly afterwards.

During the early months of 1993 the nation was riveted by a political scandal of a seemingly ever-growing size involving the Mafia and many government leaders. In a referendum in mid-April voters approved changing the current proportional system of representation in the Senate for one utilizing majority voting.

As a result of March 1994 elections an alliance between the Forza Italia party and two other parties dislodged the Christian Democrats.

In the face of a gradual erosion of support during the year, Prime Minister Berlusconi was forced to resign in December. The Dini government nominated in January 1995 was seen as a reprieve from the ongoing corruption inquiries.

Just as Prime Minister Dini was to start as president of the European Union, he failed to win support in Parliament for his government. He submitted his resignation in January 1996.

JAMAICA

Sovereign: Queen Elizabeth II
Governor-General: H.E. The Most Hon. Sir Howard F.H. Cooke (1991)
Prime Minister: The Rt. Hon. Percival J. Patterson (1992)
Area: 4,411 sq mi. (11,424 sq km)
Population (est. 1996): 2,593,918 (average annual rate of natural increase: 1.6%); birth rate: 21.6/1000; infant mortality rate: 15.6/1000; density per square mile: 588
Capital and largest city (est. 1991): Kingston, 104,000.
Monetary unit: Jamaican dollar. **Language:** English, Jamaican Creole. **Religions:** Protestant, 55.9%; Roman Catholic, 5%; other, 39.1%. **Member of Commonwealth of Nations. Literacy rate:** 98%
Economic summary: Gross domestic product (1994 est.): $7.8 billion; $3,050 per capita; real growth rate 2%; inflation 26.7%; unemployment 15.7% (1992). Arable land: 19%. Principal products: sugar cane, citrus fruits, bananas, coffee, potatoes, livestock. Labor force (1991): 1,072,500; services, 41%; agriculture, 22.5%; industry, 19%. Industries: Tourism, bauxite mining, textiles, processed foods, light manufactures. Natural resources: bauxite, gypsum. Exports: $1.2 billion (f.o.b., 1994 est.): alumina, bauxite, sugar, bananas. Imports: $2.2 billion (f.o.b., 1994 est.): fuels, machinery, consumer goods, construction goods, food. Major trading partners: U.S., U.K., Canada, Norway, Trinidad and Tobago, Venezuela, Japan.

Geography. Jamaica is an island in the West Indies, 90 miles (145 km) south of Cuba and 100 miles (161 km) west of Haiti. It is a little smaller than Connecticut.

The island is made up of a plateau and the Blue Mountains, a group of volcanic hills, in the east. Blue Mountain (7,402 ft.; 2,256 m) is the tallest peak.

Government. The legislature is a 60-member House of Representatives elected by universal suffrage and an appointed Senate of 21 members. The Prime Minister is appointed by the Governor-General and must, in the Governor-General's opinion, be the person best able to command the confidence of a majority of the members of the House of Representatives.

History. Jamaica was inhabited by Arawak Indians when Columbus visited it in 1494 and named it St. Iago. It remained under Spanish rule until 1655, then became a British possession. The island prospered from wealth brought by buccaneers to their base, Port Royal, the capital, until the city disappeared in the sea in 1692 after an earthquake. The Arawaks died off from disease and exploitation, and slaves, mostly black, were imported to work sugar plantations. Abolition of the slave trade (1807), emancipation of the slaves (1833), and a gradual drop in sugar prices led to depressed economic conditions that resulted in an uprising in 1865.

The following year Jamaica's status was changed to that of a colony, and conditions improved considerably. Introduction of banana cultivation made the island less dependent on the sugar crop for its well-being.

On May 5, 1953, Jamaica attained internal autonomy, and in 1958 it led in organizing the West Indies Federation. This effort at Caribbean unification failed. A nationalist labor leader, Sir Alexander Bustamente, led a campaign for withdrawal from the Federation. As the result of a popular referendum in 1961, Jamaica became independent on Aug. 6, 1962.

Michael Manley became Prime Minister in 1972 and initiated a socialist program.

The Labour Party defeated Manley's People's National Party in 1980 and its capitalist-oriented leader, Edward P.G. Seaga, became Prime Minister. He instituted measures to encourage private investment.

Like other Caribbean countries, Jamaica was hard-hit by the 1981–82 recession. By 1984, austerity measures that Seaga instituted in the hope of bringing the economy back into balance included elimination of government subsidies. Devaluation of the Jamaican dollar made Jamaican products more competitive on the world market and Jamaica achieved record growth in tourism and agriculture. Manufacturing also grew. But at the same time, the cost of many foods went up 50% to 75% and thousands of Jamaicans fell deeper into poverty.

The PNP decisively won local elections in mid-July, 1987, signaling a weakening in Seaga's position. In 1989, Manley swept back into power with a clear-cut victory. He indicated that he would pursue more centrist policies than he did in his previous administration.

Manley stepped down in 1992 for reasons of health, being replaced by P.J. Patterson.

Parliamentary elections in March 1993 were marred by violence in which 11 died. The PNP received 53 of the 60 seats in parliament.

In October 1995, a third political party, the National Democratic Movement, was created by Bruce Golding, a disgruntled Labourite.

JAPAN

Emperor: Akihito (1989)
Prime Minister: Ryutaro Hashimoto
Area: 145,874 sq mi. (377,815 sq km)
Population (1995): 125,568,504; average annual rate of natural increase: 1.6% (1990 census); birth rate: 9.6/1000; infant mortality rate: 4.4/1000 (1991); density per square mile: 86
Capital: Tokyo; **Largest cities (Jan. 1993):** Tokyo, 8,112,000; Yokohama, 3,276,000; Osaka 2,601,000; Nagoya, 2,162,000; Sapporo, 1,719,000; Kobe, 1,501,000; Kyoto, 1,456,000; Fukuoka, 1,263,000; Kawasaki, 1,196,000; Hiroshima, 1,099,000. **Monetary unit:** Yen.
Language: Japanese. **Religions:** Shintoist, 111.8 million; Buddhist, 93.1 million; Christian, 1.4 million; other, 11.4 million. **National name:** Nippon. **Literacy rate:** 99.9%
Economic summary: Gross national product (1995): $5,150.8 billion; $41,019.7 per capita; real growth rate 0.9%; inflation −0.1%; unemployment 3.2%. Arable land: 14%. Principal agricultural products: rice, vegetables, fruits, meat and dairy products. Labor force (1995): 66,660,000; 54% in trade and services. Major industrial products: machinery and equipment, metals and metal products, autos, consumer electronics, chemicals, electrical and electronic equipment. Natural resource: fish. Exports: $442.9 billion (1995, customs clearance): machinery and equipment, automobiles, metals and metal products, consumer electronics, semiconductors. Imports: $336.1 billion (1995, customs clearance): fossil fuels, raw materials, foodstuffs, machinery and equipment. Major trading partners: U.S., Southeast Asia, European Union.

Geography. An archipelago extending in an arc more than 1,744 miles (2,790 km) from northeast to southwest in the Pacific, Japan is separated from the east coast of Asia by the Sea of Japan. It is approximately the size of Montana.

Japan's four main islands are Honshu, Hokkaido, Kyushu, and Shikoku. The Ryukyu chain to the southwest are U.S.-occupied and the Kuriles to the northeast are Russian-occupied. The surface of the main islands consists largely of mountains separated by narrow valleys. There are about 60 more- or less-active volcanoes, of which the best-known is Mount Aso. Mount Fuji, seen on postcards, is not active.

Government. Japan's Constitution, promulgated on Nov. 3, 1946, replaced the Meiji Constitution of 1889. The 1946 Constitution, sponsored by the U.S. during its occupation of Japan, brought fundamental changes to the Japanese political system, including the abandonment of the Emperor's divine rights. The Diet (parliament) consists of a House of Representatives of 500 members, elected for four years, and a House of Councilors of 252 members, half of whom are elected every three years for four-year terms. Executive power is vested in the Cabinet, which is headed by a Prime Minister, nominated by the Diet from its members.

On Jan. 7, 1989, Emperor Hirohito, Japan's longest-reigning monarch died and was succeeded by his son, Akihito (born 1933). He was married in 1959 to Michiko Shoda (the first time a Crown Prince married a commoner).

History. A series of legends attributes creation of Japan to the sun goddess, from whom the later emperors were allegedly descended. The first of them was Jimmu Tenno, supposed to have ascended the throne in 660 B.C.

Recorded Japanese history begins with the first contact with China in the 5th century A.D. Japan was then divided into strong feudal states, all nominally under the Emperor, but with real power often held by a court minister or clan. In 1185, Yoritomo, chief of the Minamoto clan, was designated Shogun (Generalissimo), with the administration of the islands under his control. A dual government system—Shogun and Emperor—continued until 1867.

First contact with the West came about 1542, when a Portuguese ship off course arrived in Japanese waters. Portuguese traders, Jesuit missionaries, and Spanish, Dutch, and English traders followed. Suspicious of Christianity and of Portuguese support of a local Japanese revolt, the shoguns prohibited all trade with foreign countries; only a Dutch trading post at Nagasaki was permitted. Western attempts to renew trading relations failed until 1853, when Commodore Matthew Perry sailed an American fleet into Tokyo Bay.

Japan now quickly made the transition from a medieval to a modern power. Feudalism was abolished and industrialization was speeded. An imperial army was established with conscription. The shogun system was abolished in 1868 by Emperor Meiji, and parliamentary government was established in 1889. After a brief war with China in 1894–95, Japan acquired Formosa (Taiwan), the Pescadores Islands, and part of southern Manchuria. China also recognized the independence of Korea (Chosen), which Japan later annexed (1910).

In 1904–05, Japan defeated Russia in the Russo-Japanese War, gaining the territory of southern Sakhalin (Karafuto) and Russia's port and rail rights in Manchuria. In World War I Japan seized Germany's Pacific islands and leased areas in China. The Treaty of Versailles then awarded it a mandate over the islands.

At the Washington Conference of 1921–22, Japan agreed to respect Chinese national integrity. The series of Japanese aggressions that was to lead to the nation's downfall began in 1931 with the invasion of Manchuria. The following year, Japan set up this area as a puppet state, "Manchukuo," under Emperor Henry Pu-Yi, last of China's Manchu dynasty. On Nov. 25, 1936, Japan joined the Axis by signing the anti-Comintern pact. The invasion of China came the next year and the Pearl Harbor attack on the U.S. on Dec. 7, 1941.

(For details of World War II (1939–45), *see* Headline History.)

Japan surrendered formally on Sept. 2, 1945, aboard the battleship *Missouri* in Tokyo Bay after atomic bombs had devastated Hiroshima and Nagasaki. Southern Sakhalin and the Kurile Islands reverted to the U.S.S.R., and Formosa (Taiwan) and Manchuria to China. The Pacific islands remained under U.S. occupation. General of the Army Douglas MacArthur was appointed Supreme Commander for the Allied Powers on Aug. 14, 1945.

A new Japanese Constitution went into effect in 1947. In 1949, many of the responsibilities of government were returned to the Japanese. Full sovereignty was granted to Japan by the Japanese Peace Treaty in 1951.

. Following the visit of Prime Minister Eisaku Sato to Washington in 1969, the U.S. agreed to return Okinawa and other Ryukyu Islands to Japan in 1972, and both nations renewed the security treaty in 1970.

The general election of July 1989 for the upper house of parliament scored a loss for the ruling Liberal Democratic Party, the first in 35 years. The following month, however, the party's president, Toshiki Kaifu, was elected prime minister.

Kaifu pledged to provide $9 billion to the U.S. to help defray the expense of the latter's operations in the Persian Gulf. The government attempted to push legislation that would have permitted Japan to send a military contingent to the Gulf in noncombat roles. This was defeated amid public outcry against it.

During Soviet President Gorbachev's visit to Tokyo in April 1991 he and Prime Minister Kaifu attempted to resolve a territorial dispute arising out of the last days of World War II. No breakthrough resulted, and the issue still remained at an impasse.

Rebellious legislators in June 1993 joined with the opposition to force a vote of no confidence in the government. In its wake Prime Minister Miyazawa dissolved parliament. Many of the rebels quit the ruling Liberal Democrats to form three new parties.

The elections of July saw the largest loss for the Liberal Democrats since the party's creation. Yet it managed to retain 223 of the 511 seats, making it the largest single party.

An odd partnership was formed in June 1994 when the Liberal Democrats were instrumental in electing the Socialist Party head as prime minister. Fears were immediately raised that all progress toward deregulating the economy and reforming the political system would grind to a halt.

A devastating earthquake shook on October 4, 1994. Particularly hard hit was the city of Hokkaido.

July 1995 elections for half the seats in the upper congressional house saw the Socialist tally diminish to just 38 in total. Although the coalition remained secure, the prime minister shuffled the Cabinet.

JORDAN

The Hashemite Kingdom of Jordan
Ruler: King Hussein I (1952)
Prime Minister: Abdul Karim Al-Kabariti
Area: 34,573 sq mi (89,544 sq km) excludes West Bank
Population (est. 1996): 4,212,152 (average annual rate of natural increase: 3.27%); birth rate: 36.7/1000; infant mortality rate: 31.5/1000; density per square mile: 121
Capital and largest city (1994 est.): Amman, 963,490.
Largest cities (est. 1994): Zarka, 420,900 (1990); Irbid, 208,201; As-Salt, 187,014. **Monetary unit:** Jordanian dinar. **Languages:** Arabic (official), English. **Religions:** Islam, 96%; Christian, 4%. **National name:** Al Mamlaka al Urduniya al Hashemiyah. **Literacy rate:** 82%
Economic summary: Gross domestic product (1994 est.): $17 billion; $4,280 per capita; 5.5% real growth rate; inflation: 6%; unemployment: 16%. Arable land: 4%. Principal products: wheat, fruits, vegetables, olive oil. Labor force (1992): 600,000: industry 11.4%; commerce, restaurants, and hotels 10.5%; construction 10%; transport and communications 8.7%; agriculture 7.4%. Major products: phosphate, refined petroleum products, cement. Natural resources: phosphate, potash. Exports: $1.4 billion (f.o.b., 1994 est.): phosphates, fruits and vegetables, shale oil, fertilizer, manufactures. Imports: $3.5 billion (c.i.f., 1994 est.): petroleum products, textiles, capital goods, motor vehicles, foodstuffs. Major trading partners: U.S., Japan, Saudi Arabia, Iraq, E.U., China, India, Iraq.

Geography. The Middle East kingdom of Jordan is bordered on the west by Israel and the Dead Sea, the north by Syria, the east by Iraq, and the south by Saudi Arabia. It is comparable in size to Indiana.

Arid hills and mountains make up most of the country. The southern section of the Jordan River flows through the country.

Government. Jordan is a constitutional monarchy with a bicameral parliament. The upper house consists of 40 members appointed by the king, and the lower house is composed of 80 members elected by popular vote. The Constitution guarantees freedom of religion, speech, press, association, and private property. Political parties were legalized in 1991.

History. In biblical times, the country that is now Jordan contained the lands of Edom, Moab, Ammon, and Bashan. In A.D. 106 it became part of the Roman province of Arabia and in 633–36 was conquered by the Arabs.

Taken from the Turks by the British in World War I, Jordan (formerly known as Transjordan) was separated from the Palestine mandate in 1920, and in 1921 placed under the rule of Abdullah ibn Hussein.

In 1923, Britain recognized Jordan's independence, subject to the mandate. In 1946, grateful for Jordan's loyalty in World War II, Britain abolished the mandate. That part of Palestine occupied by Jordanian troops was formally incorporated by action of the Jordanian Parliament in 1950.

King Abdullah was assassinated in 1951. His son Talal was deposed as mentally ill the next year. Talal's son Hussein, born Nov. 14, 1935, succeeded him.

From the beginning of his reign, Hussein had to steer a careful course between his powerful neighbor to the west, Israel, and rising Arab nationalism, frequently a direct threat to his throne. Riots erupted when he joined the Central Treaty Organization (the Baghdad Pact) in 1955, and he incurred further unpopularity when Britain, France, and Israel attacked the Suez Canal in 1956, forcing him to place his army under nominal command of the United Arab Republic of Egypt and Syria.

The 1961 breakup of the UAR eased Arab national pressure on Hussein, who was the first to recognize Syria after it reclaimed its independence. Jordan was swept into the 1967 Arab-Israeli war, however, and lost the old city of Jerusalem and all of its territory west of the Jordan river, the West Bank. Embittered Palestinian guerrilla forces virtually took over sections of Jordan in the aftermath of defeat, and open warfare broke out between the Palestinians and government forces in 1970.

Despite intervention of Syrian tanks, Hussein's Bedouin army defeated the Palestinians, suffering heavy casualties. A U.S. military alert and Israeli armor massed on the Golan Heights contributed psychological weight, but the Jordanians alone drove out the Syrians and invited the departure of 12,000 Iraqui troops who had been in the country since the 1967 war. Ignoring protests from other Arab states, Hussein by mid-1971 crushed Palestinian strength in Jordan and shifted the problem to Lebanon, where many of the guerrillas had fled.

In October 1974, Hussein concurred in an Arab summit resolution calling for an independent Palestinian state and endorsing the Palestine Liberation Organization as the "sole legitimate representative of the Palestinian people."

As Egypt and Israel neared final agreement on a peace treaty early in 1979, Hussein met with Yassir Arafat, the PLO leader, on March 17 and issued a joint statement of opposition. Although the U.S. pressed Jordan to break Arab ranks on the issue, Hussein elected to side with the great majority, cutting ties with Cairo and joining the boycott against Egypt.

In September 1980, Jordan declared itself with Iraq in its conflict with Iran and, despite threats from Syria, opened ports to war shipments for Iraq.

Jordan's stance during the Persian Gulf war strained relations with the U.S. and led to the termination of U.S. aid. The signing of a national charter by King Hussein and leaders of the main political groups in June 1991 meant political parties were permitted in exchange for acceptance of the constitution and the monarchy.

King Hussein's decision to join the Middle East peace talks in mid-1991 helped his country's relations with the U.S.

In July 1994 Hussein and the Israeli prime minister signed a declaration ending the state of belligerency between the two countries. A peace between the two

countries was signed on October 26, 1994, although a clause in it calling the King the "custodian" of Islamic holy shrines in Jerusalem angered the PLO. In the wake of the agreement Jordan's relations with the U.S. and with the moderate Arab states warmed. Normal relations with Saudi Arabia resumed.

KAZAKHSTAN

Republic of Kazakhstan
President: Nursultan A. Nazarbaev (1990)
Prime Minister: Arkezhan Kazhgeldin (1994)
Area: 1,049,000 sq mi. (2,717,300 sq km)
Population (est. 1996): 16,916,463 (Kazaks, 50%; Russians, 30%); average annual rate of natural increase: 0.94%; birth rate: 19/1000; infant mortality rate, 63.2/1000; density per square mile: 16
Capital and largest city (1991 est.): Almaty, 1,200,000. **Other large cities (1991):** Karaganda, 608,600;: Shymkent, 438,000; Ust'Kamenogorsk, 332,900; Aktyubinsk (Aktobe), 266,600; Dzhambul (Auliye-Ata), 312,300.
Monetary unit: Tenge. **Language:** Kazakh (Qazaq) official language, Russian. **Religion:** Muslim, 47%; Russian Orthodox; Lutheran. **Literacy rate:** 100%
Economic summary: Gross national product (1994 est.): $55.2 billion, $3,200 per capita; real growth rate –25%; inflation 24%; unemployment 1.1%. Labor force: 7,356,000 (1992); industry and construction 31%; agriculture and forestry 26%. Industries: extractive industries (oil, coal, iron ore, manganese, bauxite, gold, silver, phosphates, sulfur), iron and steel, nonferrous metals, tractors and other agricultural machinery, electric motors, construction materials. Agriculture: grains, meat, cotton, and wool. Exports: $3.1 billion (1994): to outside the former USSR: oil, ferrous and non-ferrous metals, chemicals, wool, grain, meat. Imports: $3.5 billion (1994): from outside the successor states of the former USSR: machinery and parts, industrial materials. Trading partners: Russia, Ukraine, Uzbekistan, and other former Soviet republics, China.

Geography: Kazakhstan lies in the north of the central Asian republics and is bounded by Russia in the north, China in the east, the Kyrgyzstan and Uzbekistan in the south, and the Caspian Sea and part of Turkmenistan in the west. It has almost 15,000 miles of coastline on the Caspian Sea. Kazakhstan is the second largest republic of the Commonwealth of Independent States in area and is slightly more than twice the size of Texas. The territory is mostly steppe land with hilly plains and plateaus.

Government: A constitutional republic.

History: The indigenous Kazakhs were a nomadic Turkic people who belonged to several divisions of Kazakh hordes. They grouped together in settlements and lived in dome-shaped tents made of felt called "yurts." Their tribes migrated seasonally to find pastures for their herds of sheep, horses, and goats. Although they had chiefs, the Kazakhs were rarely united as a single nation under one great leader. Their tribes fell under Mongol rule in the 13th century and they were dominated by Tartar Khanates until the area was conquered by Russia in the 18th century.

Kazakhstan became a constituent republic of the Soviet Union in 1936 and collective farming and modern industrial production methods were instituted.

The world's first fast-breeder nuclear reactor was built in the republic and the main space center for the Commonwealth of Independent States is located in Baikonur.

Kazakhstan sought greater political autonomy but delayed seeking independence from the former Soviet Union. Kazakhstan proclaimed its membership in the Commonwealth of Independent States on Dec. 21, 1991, along with ten other former Soviet republics.

In 1993 the country overwhelmingly approved the Nuclear Non-Proliferation Treaty.

In a referendum held on April 29, 1995, the electorate voted in support of extending the president's term to December 2000. Nazarbaev introduced a draft constitution in the summer that gave the president expanded powers. Although attacked from various quarters, it won the approval of 89% in a referendum held in August.

KENYA

Republic of Kenya
President: H.E. Daniel Toroitch arap Moi (1978)
Area: 224,960 sq mi. (582,646 sq km)
Population (est. 1996): 28,176,686 (average annual rate of natural increase: 2.31%); birth rate: 33.4/1000; infant mortality rate: 55.3/1000; density per square mile: 125
Capital and largest city (1991 est.): Nairobi, 2,000,000.
Other large city: Mombasa, 600,000. **Monetary unit:** Kenyan shilling. **Languages:** English (official), Swahili (national), and several other languages spoken by 25 ethnic groups. **Religions:** Protestant, 40%; Roman Catholic, 36%; traditional, 6%; Islam, 16%, others, 2%.
Literacy rate: 69%. **Member of Commonwealth of Nations. National name:** Jamhuri ya Kenya
Economic summary: Gross domestic product (1994 est.): $33.1 billion; $1,170 per capita; real growth rate: 3.3%; inflation 30%; unemployment: 35% (urban est.). Arable land: 3%. Principal agricultural products: coffee, sisal, tea, pineapples, livestock. Labor force: 9.2 million: services, 54.8%; industry, 26.2%; agriculture, 19%. Major industrial products: textiles, processed foods, consumer goods, refined oil. Natural resources: gold, limestone, minerals, wildlife. Exports: $1.45 billion (f.o.b., 1994 est.): tourism, tea, coffee, horticulture, petroleum products, cement, soda ash, and pyrethrum extracts. Imports: $1.85 billion (f.o.b., 1994 est.): crude oil, pharmaceuticals, industrial supplies, machinery, other capital equipment. Major trading partners: Uganda, U.K., Tanzania, Germany, Netherlands, France, Italy, Saudi Arabia, United Arab Emirates, U.S., Japan, India.

Geography. Kenya lies across the equator in east central Africa on the coast of the Indian Ocean. It is twice the size of Nevada. Kenya borders Somalia to the east, Ethiopia to the north, Tanzania to the south, Uganda to the west, and Sudan to the northwest.

In the north, the land is arid; the southwestern corner is in the fertile Lake Victoria Basin; and a length of the eastern depression of Great Rift Valley separates western highlands from those that rise from the lowland coastal strip. Large game reserves have been developed.

Government. Under its constitution Kenya has a one-house National Assembly of 188 members elected for five years by universal suffrage, and 12 nominated and 2 ex-officio, for a total of 202. Since 1992, the president has been elected in a presidential and parliamentary election.

History. Kenya, formerly a British colony and pro-

tectorate, was made a crown colony in 1920. The whites' domination of the rich plateau area, the White Highlands, long regarded by indigenous Kenyans as their territory, was a factor leading to native terrorism, called the Mau Mau movement, in 1952. In 1954 the British began preparing the territory for African rule and independence. In 1961 Jomo Kenyatta was freed from banishment to become leader of the Kenya African National Union (KANU).

Internal self-government was granted in 1963; Kenya became independent on Dec. 12, 1963, with Kenyatta the first president.

Moi's tenure has been marked by a consolidation of power which has included the harassment of political opponents and the banning of secret ballots. In December 1992 Moi won reelection, although the opposition disputed the results.

The government reimposed price controls and broke with the IMF and World Bank in March 1993, risking a break in Western aid. The opposition boycotted the opening of parliament in protest.

President Moi in early 1995 moved against the opposition, ordering the arrest of anyone who insulted him. In June the renowned paleontologist Richard Leakey registered a new political party.

Despite foreign approval of economic reforms in 1995, those countries rebuked Moi's authoritarianism.

KIRIBATI

Republic of Kiribati
President: Teburoro Tito (1994)
Area: 280 sq mi. (726 sq km)
Population (est. 1996): 80,919 (average annual growth rate: 1.86%); birth rate: 30.9/1000; infant mortality rate: 98.4/1000; density per square mile: 288
Capital (1990): Tarawa, 25,154. **Monetary unit:** Australian dollar. **Language:** English. **Religions:** Roman Catholic, 52.6%; Protestant, 40.9%. **Member of Commonwealth of Nations. Literacy rate:** 90%
Economic summary: Gross domestic product (1993 est.): $62 million; $800 per capita; 2.9% real growth rate; inflation 6.5%; unemployment 2% (1992 est.). Arable land: negligible. Principal agricultural products: copra, vegetables. Exports: $4.2 million (f.o.b., 1992): fish, copra. Imports: $33.1 million (c.i.f., 1992 est.): foodstuffs, fuel, transportation equipment. Major trading partners: New Zealand, Australia, Japan, American Samoa, U.K., U.S., Fiji.

Geography. Kiribati, formerly the Gilbert Islands, consists of three widely separated main groups of Southwest Pacific islands: the Gilberts on the equator, the Phoenix Islands to the east, and the Line Islands further east. Ocean Island, producer of phosphates until it was mined out in 1981, is also included in the two million square miles of ocean which give Kiribati an important fishery resource.

Government. The president holds executive power. The legislature consists of a House Assembly with 39 members.

History. A British protectorate since 1892, the Gilbert and Ellice Islands became a colony in 1915–16. The two island groups were separated in 1975 and given internal self-government.

Tarawa and others of the Gilbert group were occupied by Japan during World War II. Tarawa was the site of one of the bloodiest battles in U.S. Marine Corps history when Marines landed in November 1943 to dislodge the Japanese defenders.

Princess Anne, representing Queen Elizabeth II, presented the independence documents to the new government on July 12, 1979.

President Tabai resigned in July 1991 after the maximum 12 years in office, being succeeded by his vice president.

The government continued its moves in 1993–94 to privatize the public sector with its plans to sell off several major enterprises.

A no-confidence vote in the Assembly in May 1994 led to general elections in July. A coalition of opposition parties won a majority.

The government severed diplomatic ties with France when the latter resumed nuclear tests in 1995.

KOREA, NORTH

Democratic People's Republic of Korea
Head of State: Kim Jong Il (1994)
Premier: Kang Song San (1992)
Area: 46,768 sq mi. (121,129 sq km)
Population (est. 1996): 23,904,124 (average annual rate of natural increase: 1.74%); birth rate: 22.9/1000; infant mortality rate: 25.9/1000; density per sq mi.: 511
Capital and largest city (est. 1987): Pyongyang, 2,355,000. **Monetary unit:** Won. **Language:** Korean.
Religions: Buddhism and Confucianism, religious activities almost nonexistent. **National name:** Choson Minjujuui Inmin Konghwaguk. **Literacy rate:** 99%
Economic summary: Gross national product (1994 est.): $21.3 billion; $920 per capita; real growth rate 0%. Arable land: 18%. Principal agricultural products: corn, rice, vegetables. Labor force: 9,615,000; 64% nonagricultural. Major industrial products: machines, electric power, chemicals, textiles, processed food, metallurgical products. Natural resources: coal, iron ore, hydroelectric power. Exports: $1.02 billion (f.o.b., 1993 est.): minerals, metallurgical products, agricultural products, manufactures (including armaments). Imports: $1.64 billion (f.o.b., 1993 est.): machinery and equipment, petroleum, grain, coal. Major trading partners: C.I.S. countries, China, Japan, Hong Kong, Germany, Singapore.

Geography. Korea is a 600-mile (966 km) peninsula jutting from Manchuria and China (and a small portion of the U.S.S.R.) into the Sea of Japan and the Yellow Sea off eastern Asia. North Korea occupies an area slightly smaller than Pennsylvania north of the 38th parallel.

The country is almost completely covered by a series of north-south mountain ranges separated by narrow valleys. The Yalu River forms part of the northern border with Manchuria.

Government. The elected Supreme People's Assembly, as the chief organ of government, chooses a Presidium and a Cabinet. The Cabinet, which exercises executive authority, is subject to approval by the Assembly and the Presidium.

The Korean Workers (Communist) Party is the only political party.

History. According to myth, Korea was founded in 2333 B.C. by Tangun. In the 17th century, it became a vassal of China and was isolated from all but Chinese influence and contact until 1876, when Japan forced Korea to negotiate a commercial treaty, opening the land to the U. S. and Europe. Japan achieved control as the result of its wars with China (1894–95) and with Russia (1904–05) and annexed Korea in 1910.

Japan developed the country but never won over the Korean nationalists.

After the Japanese surrender in 1945, the country was divided into two occupation zones, the U.S.S.R. north of and the U.S. south of the 38th parallel. When the cold war developed between the U.S. and U.S.S.R., trade between the zones was cut off. In 1948, the division between the zones was made permanent with the establishment of separate regimes in the north and south. By mid-1949, the U.S. and U.S.S.R. withdrew all troops. The Democratic People's Republic of Korea (North Korea) was established on May 1, 1948. The Communist Party, headed by Kim Il Sung, was established in power.

On June 25, 1950, the North Korean army launched a surprise attack on South Korea. On June 26, the U.N. Security Council condemned the invasion as aggression and ordered withdrawal of the invading forces. On June 27, President Harry S. Truman ordered air and naval units into action to enforce the U.N. order. The British government did the same, and soon a multinational U.N. command was set up to aid the South Koreans. The North Korean invaders took Seoul and pushed the South Koreans into the southeast corner of their country.

Gen. Douglas MacArthur, U.N. commander, made an amphibious landing at Inchon on September 15 behind the North Korean lines, which resulted in the complete rout of the North Korean army. The U.N. forces drove north across the 38th parallel, approaching the Yalu River. Then Communist China entered the war, forcing the U.N. forces into headlong retreat. Seoul was lost again, then regained; ultimately the war stabilized near the 38th parallel but dragged on for two years while the belligerents negotiated. An armistice was agreed to on July 27, 1953.

Tensions continued to build in early 1994 over international inspection of North Korea's nuclear sites.

Kim Il Sung's death on July 8, 1994, introduced a period of uncertainty. Negotiations over the country's suspected atomic weapons program proved lengthy and thorny, but an agreement was reached in June 1995 which included providing the North with a South Korean nuclear reactor.

Ominous signs of a dire economic situation in the country continued to mount in 1996, and widespread famine was believed to be imminent. Repeated troop violations of the DMZ puzzled observers in April.

KOREA, SOUTH

Republic of Korea
President: Kim Young Sam (1993)
Prime Minister: Lee Soo Song (1995)
Area: 38,031 sq mi. (99,392 sq km)
Population (est. 1996): 45,482,291 (average annual rate of natural increase: 1.06%); birth rate: 16.2/1000; infant mortality rate: 8.2/1000; density per square mile: 1,195
Capital and largest city: Seoul, 10,229,000; **Other cities:** Pusan, 3,814,000; Taegu, 2,449,000; Inchon, 2,308,000.
Monetary unit: Won. **Language:** Korean. **Religions (est. mid-1996):** Christian, 48.2%; Buddhist, 48.8%; Confucianist, 8%; Chondogyo (religion of the Heavenly Way), 2%; Other, 2%. **National name:** Taehan Min'guk.
Literacy rate: 96%
Economic summary: Gross national product (1994 est.): $376.9 billion; $8,483 per capita; 8.4% real growth rate; inflation 4.5% (mid-'96 est.); unemployment 2% (mid-'96 est.). Arable land: 21%. Principal agricultural products: rice, soybeans, corn, barley. Labor force (April '96 est.): 21,168,000; 23% in mining and manufacturing. Major products: clothing, textiles, automobiles, steel, electronics equipment. Natural resources: coal,

iron, zinc, lead, tungsten, hydropower. Exports: $11.3 billion (May 1996 est.): agricultural products, electronics, machinery, textiles, steel and metal products, chemicals. Imports: $12.8 billion (May 1996 est.): machinery, mineral fuels, electronic parts, agricultural products, iron and steel products, raw materials. Major trading partners: U.S., Japan.

Geography. Slightly larger than Indiana, South Korea lies below the 38th parallel on the Korean peninsula. It is mountainous in the east; in the west and south are many harbors on the mainland and offshore islands.

Government. Constitutional amendments enacted in Sept. 1987 called for direct election of a President, who would be limited to a single five-year term, and increased the powers of the National Assembly vis-à-vis the President.

The National Assembly was expanded from 276 to 299 seats, filled by proportional representation.

History. South Korea came into being in the aftermath of World War II as the result of a 1945 agreement making the 38th parallel the boundary between a northern zone occupied by the U.S.S.R. and a southern zone occupied by U.S. forces. (For details, *see* North Korea.)

Elections were held in the U.S. zone in 1948 for a National Assembly, which adopted a republican Constitution and elected Syngman Rhee as President. The new republic was proclaimed on August 15 and was recognized as the legal government of Korea by the U.N. on Dec. 12, 1948.

On June 25, 1950, South Korea was attacked by North Korean Communist forces. U.S. armed intervention was ordered on June 27 by President Harry S. Truman, and on the same day the U.N. invoked military sanctions against North Korea. Gen. Douglas MacArthur was named commander of the U.N. forces. U.S. and South Korean troops fought a heroic holding action, but by the first week of August, they had been forced back to a 4,000-square-mile beachhead in southeast Korea.

There they stood off superior North Korean forces until September 15, when a major U.N. amphibious attack was launched far behind the Communist lines at Inchon, port of Seoul. By September 30, U.N. forces were in complete control of South Korea. They then invaded North Korea and were nearing the Manchurian and Siberian borders when several hundred thousand Chinese Communist troops entered the conflict in late October. U.N. forces were then forced to retreat below the 38th parallel.

On May 24, 1951, U.N. forces recrossed the parallel and had made important new inroads into North Korea when truce negotiations began on July 10. An armistice was finally signed at Panmunjom on July 27, 1953, leaving a devastated Korea in need of large-scale rehabilitation.

The U.S. and South Korea signed a mutual-defense treaty on Oct. 1, 1953.

Rhee, President since 1948, resigned in 1960 in the face of rising disorders. PoSun Yun was elected to succeed him, but political instability continued. In 1961, Gen. Park Chung Hee took power and subsequently built up the country. The U.S. stepped up military aid, building up South Korea's armed forces to 600,000 men. The South Koreans sent 50,000 troops to Vietnam, at U.S. expense.

Park's assassination on Oct. 26, 1979, by Kim Jae Kyu, head of the Korean Central Intelligence Agency, brought a liberalizing trend as Choi Kyu Hah, the new President, freed imprisoned dissidents. The release of opposition leader Kim Dae Jung in February 1980 generated anti-government demonstrations that turned into riots by May. Choi resigned on Aug. 16. Chun Doo Wha, head of a military Special Committee for National Security Measures, was the sole candidate as the electoral college confirmed him as President on Aug. 27.

Debate over the presidential succession in 1988 was the main dispute in 1986–87 with Chun wanting election by the electoral college and the opposition demanding a direct popular vote, charging that Chun could manipulate the college. On April 13, 1987, Chun declared a close on the debate but when, in June, he appointed Roh Tae Woo, the DJP chairman, as his successor, violent protests broke out. Roh, and later Chun, agreed that direct elections should be held. A split in the opposition led to Roh's election on Dec. 16, 1987, with 36.6% of the vote.

Weeks of anti-government protests in May 1991 led to the resignation of then-Prime Minister Ro Ja Bong.

In early 1991 the Soviet Union announced it would not oppose South Korea's application for U.N. membership.

In his first year in office President Kim began a massive anticorruption campaign, purging thousands of military men with links to previous regimes, bureaucrats and businessmen.

As part of the GATT, South Korea in December 1993 announced it would allow foreign rice imports, a move that led to a major Cabinet reshuffle.

During 1995 two past presidents were indicted for their role in a 1979 coup. Later one of them was also accused of accepting substantial bribes.

The ruling Democratic Liberal Party suffered badly in the June 1995 local and provincial elections.

KUWAIT

State of Kuwait

Emir: Sheik Jaber al-Ahmad al-Sabah (1977)
Prime Minister: Sheik Sa'ad Abdullah al-Salim (1978)
Area: 6,880 sq mi. (17,820 sq km)
Population (est. 1996): 1,950,047 (average annual rate of natural increase: 1.81%); birth rate: 20.3/1000; infant mortality rate: 11.1/1000; density per square mile: 283
Capital (est. 1990): Kuwait, 151,060; **Other large city (est. 1993):** as-Salimiyah, 116,104. **Monetary unit:** Kuwaiti dinar. **Languages:** Arabic and English. **Religions:** Islam. **National name:** Dawlat al Kuwayt. **Literacy rate:** 74%
Economic summary: Gross domestic product (1994 est.): $30.7 billion; $16,900 per capita; real growth rate 9.3%; inflation 3% (1993). Labor force: 566,000 (1986); 45% in services. Major products: crude and refined oil, petrochemicals, building materials, salt. Natural resources: petroleum, fish, shrimp. Exports: $10.5 billion (f.o.b., 1993 est.): oil 90%. Imports: $6 billion (f.o.b., 1993 est.): foodstuffs, automobiles, building materials, machinery, textiles. Major trading partners: U.S., Japan, Italy, U.K., Canada, France.

Geography. Kuwait is situated northeast of Saudi Arabia at the northern end of the Persian Gulf, south of Iraq. It is slightly larger than Hawaii. The low-lying land is mainly sandy and barren.

Government. Sheik Jaber al-Ahmad al-Sabah rules as Emir of Kuwait and appoints the Prime Minister, who appoints his cabinet (Council of Ministers). National elections were held in 1992 and the National

Assembly (legislative branch), dissolved in 1986, was reinstated. There are no political parties in Kuwait.

History. Kuwait obtained British protection in 1897 when the Sheik feared that the Turks would take over the area. In 1961, Britain ended the protectorate, giving Kuwait independence, but agreed to give military aid on request. Iraq immediately threatened to occupy the area and Sheik Sabah al-Salem al-Sabah called in British troops in 1961. Soon afterward the Arab League sent in troops, replacing the British. The prize was oil.

Oil was discovered in the 1930s. Kuwait proved to have 20% of the world's known oil resources. It has been a major producer since 1946, the world's second largest oil exporter. The Sheik, who gets half the profits, devotes most of them to the education, welfare, and modernization of his kingdom. In 1966, Sheik Sabah designated a relative, Jaber al-Ahmad al-Sabah, as his successor.

By 1968, the sheikdom had established a model welfare state, and it sought to establish dominance among the sheikdoms and emirates of the Persian Gulf.

In July 1990, Iraq President Hussein blamed Kuwait for falling oil prices. After a failed Arab mediation attempt to solve the dispute peacefully, Iraq invaded Kuwait on Aug. 2, 1990, and set up a pro-Iraqi provisional government.

A coalition of Arab and Western military forces drove Iraqi troops from Kuwait in February 1991. The Emir returned to his country from Saudi Arabia in mid-March. Martial law, in effect since the end of the Gulf war, ended in late June.

The U.S. sent 2,400 troops to the country in August 1992 as part of a training exercise, but this was widely interpreted as a show of strength to Saddam Hussein.

The general election of October 1992 was widely interpreted as a success for supporters of a return to Islamic law. A political independent was named speaker of the parliament, and the opposition held 31 of the 50 seats.

Iraqi "training" maneuvers near the Kuwaiti border in October 1994 renewed fears of aggression in the country. A Kuwaiti appeal brought the quick deployment of U.S. and British troops and equipment.

The oil industry continued to recover in 1995, and no new taxes were introduced.

KYRGYZSTAN

The Kyrgyz Republic
President: Askar Akaev (1990)
Prime Minister: Apas Jumagulov
Area: 76,000 sq mi. (198,500 sq km)
Population (est. 1996): 4,529,648; (Kyrgyz, 52%; Russian, 21%; Uzbek, 13%; other, 14%); average annual rate of natural increase: 1.72%; birth rate: 26/1000; infant mortality rate: 77.8/1000; density per square mile: 59
Capital and largest city (1994): Bishkek (Frunze), 631,000. Other (1994): Osh, 213,000. **Monetary unit:** The Som. **Language:** Kyrgyz (official), Russian is de facto second language of communication. **Religion:** Muslim, 70%; Russian Orthodox, n.a. **Literacy rate:** 100%
Economic summary: Gross domestic product (1994 est.): $8.4 billion, $1,790 per capita; −24% real growth rate; inflation 5.4%; unemployment 0.7%. Important natural resources are rare earth metals and gold, coal. Industrial production includes electrical engineering, hydroelectric power, agricultural machine building, washing machines, furniture, cement, paper, and brick. Agricul-

tural products are food crops: vegetables, grains, fruit. Also cotton, hemp, tobacco, livestock: cattle, sheep, goats. Labor force: 1,900,000 (1994): agriculture, 33%; industry, 28%. Exports: $116 million (outside former Soviet Union) (1994): wool, chemicals, cotton, ferrous and nonferrous metals, shoes, machinery, tobacco. Imports: $92.4 million (outside former Soviet Union) (1994): grain, lumber, industrial products, ferrous metals, fuel, machinery, textiles, footwear. Trading partners: Russia, 70%; others Ukraine, Uzbekistan, Kazakhstan.

Geography: Kyrgyzstan (formerly Kirghizia) is a rugged country with the Tien Shan mountain range covering approximately 95 percent of the whole territory. The mountain tops are covered with perennial snow and glaciers. Kyrgyzstan borders Kazakhstan on the north and northwest, Uzbekistan in the southwest, Tajikistan in the south, and China in the southeast. The republic is the same size in area as the state of Nebraska.

Government: A constitutional republic.

History: The native Kyrgyz are a Turkic people who in ancient times first settled in the Tien Shan mountains. They were traditionally pastoral nomads. There was extensive Russian colonization in the 1900s and Russian settlers were given much of the best agricultural land. This led to an unsuccessful and disastrous revolt by the Kyrgyz people in 1916. Kyrgyzstan became part of the Soviet Federated Socialist Republic in 1924, and was made an autonomous republic in 1926. Kyrgyzstan became a constituent republic of the U.S.S.R. in 1936. The Soviets forced the Kyrgyz to abandon their nomadic culture and brought modern farming and industrial production techniques into their society. It has greatly changed their traditional way of life.

President Askar Akaev supported Soviet President Gorbachev's reform programs and promoted them in his country.

Kyrgyzstan proclaimed its independence from the Soviet Union on Aug. 31, 1991. On Dec. 21, 1991, Kyrgyzstan joined the Commonwealth of Independent States.

The country joined the UN and the IMF in 1992 and adopted a shock-therapy economic program.

Voters formally and overwhelmingly endorsed market reforms in a referendum held in January 1994.

Incumbent President Akaev won the contested election of December 1995 with about 60% of the vote. In February 1996 referendum voters overwhelmingly endorsed proposed constitutional changes that enhanced the power of the president. The government resigned later that month, although it remained in place in a caretaker role.

LAOS

Lao People's Democratic Republic
President: Nouhak Phoumsavanh (1992)
Premier: Khamtai Siphandone (1991)
Area: 91,429 sq mi. (236,800 sq km)
Population (est. 1996): 4,9075,772 (average annual rate of natural increase: 2.81%); birth rate: 41.9/1000; infant mortality rate: 96.8/1000; density per square mile: 54.4
Capital and largest city (1990): Vientiane, 442,000. **Monetary unit:** Kip. **Languages:** Lao (official), French, English. **Religions:** Buddhist, 85%; animist and other, 15%. **Literacy rate:** 50%

Economic summary: Gross domestic product: (1994 est.): $4 billion; $850 per capita; 8.4% real growth rate; inflation rate: 6.5%; unemployment rate (1992 est.): 21%. Arable land: 4%. Principal agricultural products: rice, corn, vegetables. Labor force: 1–1.5 million; 85–90% in agriculture. Major industrial products: tin, timber, electric power, gypsum. Natural resources: tin, timber, hydroelectric power. Exports: $277 million (f.o.b., 1994 est.): electric power, forest products, tin concentrates, coffee, gypsum, cardamom, rattan, clothing and textiles. Imports: $528 million (c.i.f., 1994 est.): rice, foodstuffs, petroleum products, machinery, transport equipment. Major trading partners: Thailand, Malaysia, Vietnam, C.I.S. countries, Japan, France, U.S., Hong Kong, Singapore.

Geography. A landlocked nation in Southeast Asia occupying the northwestern portion of the Indochinese peninsula, Laos is surrounded by China, Vietnam, Cambodia, Thailand, and Myanmar. It is twice the size of Pennsylvania.

Laos is a mountainous country, especially in the north, where peaks rise above 9,000 feet (2,800 m). Dense forests cover the northern and eastern areas. The Mekong River, which forms the boundary with Myanmar and Thailand, flows entirely through the country for 932 miles (1,500 km) of its course.

Government. Laos is a people's democratic republic with executive power in the hands of the Premier. The monarchy was abolished Dec. 2, 1975, when the Pathet Lao ousted a coalition government and King Sisavang Vatthana abdicated. The King was appointed "Supreme Adviser" to the President, the former Prince Souphanouvong. Former Prince Souvanna Phouma, Premier since 1962, was made an "adviser" to the government. The Lao People's Revolutionary Party (Pathet Lao) is the only political party.

History. Laos became a French protectorate in 1893, and the territory was incorporated into the union of Indochina. A strong nationalist movement developed during World War II, but France reestablished control in 1946 and made the King of Luang Prabang constitutional monarch of all Laos. France granted semiautonomy in 1949 and then, spurred by the Viet Minh rebellion in Vietnam, full independence within the French Union in 1950. In 1951, Prince Souphanouvong organized the Pathet Lao, a Communist independence movement, in North Vietnam. The Viet Minh in 1953 established the Pathet Lao in power at Samneua. Viet Minh and Pathet Lao forces invaded central Laos, and civil war resulted.

By the Geneva agreements of 1954 and an armistice of 1955, two northern provinces were given the Pathet Lao, the royal regime the rest. Full sovereignty was given the kingdom by the Paris agreements of Dec. 29, 1954. In 1957, Prince Souvanna Phouma, the royal Premier, and the Pathet Lao leader, Prince Souphanouvong, the Premier's half-brother, agreed to reestablishment of a unified government, with Pathet Lao participation and integration of Pathet Lao forces into the royal army. The agreement broke down in 1959, and armed conflict broke out again.

In 1960, the struggle became three-way as Gen. Phoumi Nosavan, controlling the bulk of the royal army, set up in the south a pro-Western revolutionary government headed by Prince Boun Gum. General Phoumi took Vientiane in December, driving Souvanna Phouma into exile in Cambodia. The Soviet bloc supported Souvanna Phouma. In 1961, a cease-fire was arranged and the three princes agreed to a coalition government headed by Souvanna Phouma.

But North Vietnam, the U.S. (in the form of Central Intelligence Agency personnel), and China remained active in Laos after the settlement. North Vietnam used a supply line (Ho Chi Minh Trail) running down the mountain valleys of eastern Laos into Cambodia and South Vietnam, particularly after the U.S.-South Vietnamese incursion into Cambodia in 1970 stopped supplies via Cambodian seaports.

An agreement, reached in 1973, revived coalition government. The Communist Pathet Lao seized complete power in 1975, installing Souphanouvong as President and Kaysone Phomvihane as Premier. Since then other parties and political groups have been moribund and most of their leaders have fled the country.

The Supreme People's Assembly in August 1991 adopted a new constitution that dropped all references to socialism but retained the one-party state. In addition to implementing market-oriented policies, the country has passed laws governing property, inheritance, and contracts. Laos agreed to trade with Moscow and Hanoi in hard currency.

While the Pathet Lao's political control in 1993 remained firm, they proceeded apace in the creation of a market economy. Despite the rush to a free market, the Communists retained tight political control.

During 1995 the country continued to relax tensions with its neighbors. Laos announced it wished to join ASEAN, and economic agreements were reached with Myanmar. The U.S. announced a lifting of its ban on aid.

LATVIA

The Republic of Latvia

President: Guntis Ulmanis (1993)
Prime Minister: Andris Skele (1995)
Area: 25,400 sq mi. (65,786 sq km)
Population (est. 1996): 2,468,982 (Latvian, 53%; Russian, 33%; Ukrainians, Byelorussians, other 14%); average annual rate of natural increase: –0.43%; birth rate: 10.9/1000; infant mortality rate: 21.2/1000; density per square mile: 97
Capital and largest city (est. 1993): Riga, 874,000. **Other large cities:** Daugavpils, 125,000; Liepaja 108,000.
Monetary unit: Lats. **Language:** Latvian. **Religions:** Lutheran, Catholic, and Baptist. **National name:** Latvija. **Literacy rate:** 100%
Economic survey: Most industrialized of the Baltic states. Gross domestic product (1994 est.): $12.3 billion; per capita: $4,480; real growth rate: 2%; unemployment (1995): 6.6%. Labor force: 1,407,000: industry and construction 41%, agriculture and forestry 16% (1990). Latvia's major industries are: forestry, wood products, building materials, and metals. Agriculture is principally dairy farming and livestock raising. Natural resources: peat, sapropel, timber, limestone, dolomite, and clay. Exports: $1.272 billion (1995): timber and wood products, ferrous metals and products, electrical machinery and equipment, fish, furniture, apparel, pharmaceuticals, appliances, buses. Imports: $1.706 billion (1995): machinery and appliances, electrical equipment, natural gas, fuels, pharmaceuticals, electricity, cars, apparel. Major trading partners: European Union, CIS countries, Lithuania, Poland, Estonia, U.S., Czech Republic, Australia, Hungary, Japan.

Geography: Latvia borders Estonia on the north, Lithuania in the south, the Baltic Sea with the Gulf of Riga in the west, Russia in the east and Belarus in the southeast. Latvia is largely a fertile lowland with numerous lakes and hills to the east.

Government: Latvia is a parliamentary democracy.

History: Descended from Aryan stock, the Latvians were early tribesmen who settled along the Baltic Sea and, lacking a central government, fell an easy prey to more powerful peoples. The German Teutonic knights first conquered them in the 13th century and ruled the area, consisting of Livonia and Courland, until 1562.

Poland conquered the territory in 1562 and ruled until 1795 in Courland; control of Livonia was disputed between Sweden and Poland from 1562 to 1629. Sweden controlled Livonia from 1629 to 1721. Russia took over Livonia in the latter year and Courland after the third partition of Poland in 1795.

From that time until 1918, the Latvians remained Russian subjects, although they preserved their language, customs, and folklore. The Russian Revolution of 1917 gave them their opportunity for freedom, and the Latvian republic was proclaimed on Nov. 18, 1918.

The republic lasted little more than 20 years. It was occupied by Russian troops in 1939 and incorporated into the Soviet Union in 1940. German armies occupied the nation from 1941 to 1943–44, when they were driven out by the Russians. Most countries, including the United States, refused to recognize the Soviet annexation of Latvia.

When the coup against Soviet President Mikhail Gorbachev failed, the Baltic nations saw a historic opportunity to free themselves from Soviet domination, and following the actions of Lithuania and Estonia, Latvia declared its independence on Aug. 21, 1991.

European and most other nations quickly recognized their independence, and on Sept. 2, 1991, President Bush announced full diplomatic recognition for Latvia, Estonia, and Lithuania. The Soviet Union recognized Latvia's independence on September 6, and UN membership followed on Sept. 17, 1991.

In addition to severe economic problems the issue of citizenship loomed explosively, as almost half the population is non-Latvian.

In the first post-Soviet parliamentary elections in June 1993 an alliance of former Communists and emigres made a strong showing. The franchise, however, was by and large not extended to the non-ethnic-Latvian minority.

One of the coalition parties withdrew its support over the issue of food-import duties in July 1994, forcing the formation of a new grouping.

In August Latvia celebrated the official withdrawal of Russian troops from the country, although Russia was allowed to retain control of its radar station in Skrunda until mid-1998.

The citizenship law was amended in August in accordance with the wishes of the Council of Europe.

Latvia's parliament, the Saeima, reelected Ulmanis president in June 1996 over several other candidates.

LEBANON

Republic of Lebanon
President: Elias Hrawi (1989)
Premier: Rafik al-Hariri (1992)
Area: 4,015 sq mi. (10,400 sq km)
Population (est. 1996): 3,776,317 (average annual rate of natural increase: 2.16%); birth rate: 27.9/1000; infant mortality rate: 36.7/1000; density per square mile: 940
Capital and largest city (1991 est.): Beirut, 1,100,000;
Other large cities: Tripoli, 240,000; Sidon, 100,000.
Monetary unit: Lebanese pound. **Languages:** Arabic (official), French, English. **Religions:** Islam, 60%; Christian, 40% (17 recognized sects); Judaism, negl. % (1 sect). **National name:** Al-Joumhouriya al-Lubnaniya.
Literacy rate: 80%
Economic summary: Gross domestic product (1994 est.): $15.8 billion; $4,360 per capita; real growth rate: 8.5%; inflation: 12%; unemployment: 35% (1993 est.). Arable land: 21%; principal agricultural products: citrus fruits, vegetables, potatoes, tobacco, olives, shrimp. Labor force (1985): 650,000; 79% in industry, commerce and services. Major industrial products: processed foods, textiles, cement, chemicals, refined oil. Exports: $925 million (f.o.b., 1993 est.): fruits, vegetables, textiles, chemicals, semiprecious metals and jewelry, metals and metal products. Imports: $4.1 billion (c.i.f., 1993 est.): consumer goods, machinery and transport equipment, petroleum products. Major trading partners: U.S., Western European, and Arab countries.

Geography. Lebanon lies at the eastern end of the Mediterranean Sea north of Israel and west of Syria. It is four-fifths the size of Connecticut.

The Lebanon Mountains, which parallel the coast on the west, cover most of the country, while on the eastern border is the Anti-Lebanon range. Between the two lies the Bekaa Valley, the principal agricultural area.

Government. Lebanon is governed by a President, elected by Parliament for a six-year term, and a Cabinet of Ministers appointed by the President but responsible to Parliament.

The unicameral Parliament has 108 members elected for a four-year term by universal suffrage and chosen by proportional division of religious groups.

History. After World War I, France was given a League of Nations mandate over Lebanon and its neighbor Syria, which together had previously been a single political unit in the Ottoman Empire. France divided them in 1920 into separate colonial administrations, drawing a border that separated predominantly Muslim Syria from the kaleidoscope of religious communities in Lebanon in which Maronite Christians were then dominant. After 20 years of the French mandate regime, Lebanon's independence was proclaimed on Nov. 26, 1941, but full independence came in stages. Under an agreement between representatives of Lebanon and the French National Committee of Liberation, most of the powers exercised by France were transferred to the Lebanese government on Jan. 1, 1944. The evacuation of French troops was completed in 1946.

Civil war broke out in 1958, with Muslim factions led by Kamal Jumblat and Saeb Salam rising in insurrection against the Lebanese government headed by President Camille Chamoun, a Maronite Christian. At Chamoun's request, President Eisenhower on July 15 sent U.S. troops to reestablish the government's authority.

Clan warfare between various factions in Lebanon goes back centuries. The hodgepodge includes Maronite Christians, who since independence have dominated the government; Sunni Muslims, who have prospered in business and shared political power; the Druse, a secretive Islamic splinter group; and at the bottom of the heap until recently, Shiite Muslims.

A new—and bloodier—Lebanese civil war that broke out in 1975 resulted in the addition of still another ingredient in the brew—the Syrians. In the fighting between Lebanese factions, 40,000 Lebanese were estimated to have been killed and 100,000 wounded between March 1975 and November 1976. At that point, a Syrian-dominated Arab Deterrent Force intervened and brought large-scale fighting to a halt.

Palestinian guerrillas staging raids on Israel from Lebanese territory drew punitive Israeli raids on Lebanon, and two large-scale Israeli invasions. The Israelis withdrew in June after the U.N. Security Council created a 6,000-man peacekeeping force for the area, called UNIFIL. As they departed, the Israelis turned their strongpoints over to a Christian militia that they had organized, instead of to the U.N. force.

The second Israeli invasion came on June 6, 1982, and this time it was a total one. It was in response to an assassination attempt by Palestinian terrorists on the Israeli ambassador in London.

A U.S. special envoy, Philip C. Habib, negotiated the dispersal of most of the PLO to other Arab nations and Israel pulled back some of its forces. The violence seemed to have come to an end when, on Sept. 14, Bashir Gemayel, the 34-year-old President-elect, was killed by a bomb that destroyed the headquarters of his Christian Phalangist Party.

The day after Gemayel's assassination, Israeli troops moved into west Beirut in force. On Sept. 17 it was revealed that Christian militiamen had massacred hundreds of Palestinians in two refugee camps but Israel denied responsibility.

On Sept. 20, Amin Gemayel, older brother of Bashir Gemayel, was elected President by the parliament.

The massacre in the refugee camps prompted the return of a multinational peacekeeping force composed of U.S. Marines and British, French, and Italian soldiers. Their mandate was to support the central Lebanese government, but they soon found themselves drawn into the struggle for power between different Lebanese factions. During their stay in Lebanon, 260 U.S. Marines and about 60 French soldiers were killed, most of them in suicide bombings of the Marine and French Army compounds on Oct. 23, 1983. The multinational force left in the spring of 1984.

During 1984, Israeli troops remained in southern Lebanon and Syrian troops remained in the Bekaa Valley. By the third anniversary of the invasion, June 6, 1985, all Israeli "troops" had withdrawn except for several hundred "advisers" to a Christian militia trained and armed by the Israelis.

In July 1986, Syrian observers took position in Beirut to monitor a peacekeeping agreement. The agreement broke down and fighting between Shiite and Druze militia in West Beirut became so intense that Syrian troops moved in force in February 1987, suppressing militia resistance.

Amin Gemayel's Presidency expired on Sept. 23, 1988. The impossibility of setting up elections led Gemayel to designate a government under army chief Gen. Michael Aoun. Aoun's government was rejected by Prime Minister Selim al-Hoss who established a rival government in Muslim West Beirut.

In October 1989, Lebanese Christian and Muslim deputies approved a tentative peace accord and the new National Assembly selected a President.

In early 1991 the Lebanese government, backed by Syria, attempted to regain control over the south and disband all private militias, thereby ending the 16-year civil war.

In the general elections of August 1992 most Christians abstained from voting, demanding that Syrian forces first leave the country. The new legislature consisted of mostly pro-Syrian members. The largest Christian party was further weakened when in January 1993 it appeared to split into two factions.

In May 1995 the prime minister asked for a constitutional amendment to allow the presidential term to be extended by three years in the interests of stability. Despite some opposition, the amendment was passed in October.

LESOTHO

Kingdom of Lesotho
Sovereign: King Letsie III (1990)
Prime Minister: Dr. Ntsu Mokhehle
Area: 11,720 sq mi. (30,355 sq km)
Population (est. 1996): 1,970,781 (average annual rate of natural increase: 1.9%); birth rate: 32.7/1000; infant mortality rate: 81.6/1000; density per square mile: 168
Capital and largest city (1992): Maseru (1992), 170,000; **Monetary unit:** Loti; **Languages:** English and Sesotho (official); also Zulu and Xhosa; **Religions:** Christian, 80%; indigenous beliefs; Muslim; and Bahai; **Member of Commonwealth of Nations; Literacy rate:** 59% (1989)
Economic summary: Gross domestic product (1994 est.): $2.6 billion; $1,340 per capita; 6% real growth rate; inflation 13.9% (1993). Arable land: 10%. Principal products: corn, wheat, sorghum, barley. Labor force: 689,000; 86.2% in subsistence agriculture. Natural resources: diamonds. Exports: $109 million (f.o.b., 1992): wool, mohair, wheat, cattle, hides and skins, peas, beans, corn, baskets. Imports: $964 million (c.i.f., 1992): foodstuffs, building materials, clothing, vehicles, machinery, corn, medicines. Major trading partners: South Africa, E.U., North and South America, Asia.

Geography. Mountainous Lesotho, the size of Maryland, is surrounded by the Republic of South Africa in the east central part of that country except for short borders on the east and south with two discontinuous units of the Republic of Transkei. The Drakensberg Mountains in the east are Lesotho's principal chain. Elsewhere the region consists of rocky tableland.

Government. A constitutional monarchy. The executive power is with the prime minister and the cabinet (Council of Ministers).

History. Lesotho (formerly Basutoland) was constituted a native state under British protection by a treaty signed with the native chief Moshesh in 1843. It was annexed to Cape Colony in 1871, but in 1884 it was restored to direct control by the Crown.

The colony of Basutoland became the independent nation of Lesotho on Oct. 4, 1966, with King Moshoeshoe II as sovereign.

In the 1970 elections, Ntsu Mokhehle, head of the Basutoland Congress Party, claimed a victory, but Prime Minister Leabua Jonathan declared a state of emergency, suspended the constitution, and arrested Mokhehle.

King Moshoeshoe returned after a compromise with Jonathan in which the new constitution would name him head of state but forbid his participation in politics. After the king refused to approve the replacements in February 1990 of individuals dismissed by Justin Metsino Lekhanya, the chairman of the Military Council, the latter stripped the king of his executive power. Then in early March Lekhanya sent the king into exile. In November the king was dethroned, and his son was sworn in as King Letsie III.

Lekhanya was himself forced to resign in April 1991. Col. Ramaema became the new chairman in May.

In August 1994 the king attempted to dissolve the government and the legislature. The government, however, refused to step down. Mounting internal and international pressure led the king in September to restore the government officially.

In January 1995 the crown reverted to the father of Letsie III, Moshoeshoe II. Letsie again became crown prince. In 1996, however, King Moshoeshoe died in an automobile accident and Letsie again assumed the throne.

LIBERIA

Republic of Liberia
Interim President: Wilton Sankawaulo (Aug. 1995)
Area: 43,000 sq mi. (111,370 sq km)
Population (est. 1996): 2,109,789 (average annual rate of natural increase: 3.08%); birth rate: 42.7/1000; infant mortality rate: 108.1/1000; density per square mile: 49
Capital and largest city (est. 1993): Monrovia, 1,000,000.
Monetary unit: Liberian dollar. **Languages:** English (official) and tribal dialects. **Religions:** traditional, 70%; Christian, 10%; Islam, 20%. **Literacy rate:** 50%
Economic summary: Civil war since 1990 has destroyed much of Liberia's economy. Gross domestic product (1994 est.): $2.3 billion; $770 per capita; 1.5% real growth rate (1988); inflation (1989): 12%; unemployment (1988): 43% urban. Arable land: 1%. Principal agricultural products: rubber, rice, palm oil, cassava, coffee, cocoa. Labor force: 510,000; 70.5% in agriculture. Major industrial products: iron ore, diamonds, processed rubber, processed food, construction materials. Natural resources: iron ore, gold, timber, diamonds. Exports: $505 million (f.o.b., 1989 est.): iron ore, rubber, timber, coffee. Imports: $394 million (c.i.f., 1989 est.): machinery, petroleum products, transport equipment, foodstuffs. Major trading partners: U.S., E.U., Netherlands, Japan, China.

Geography. Lying on the Atlantic in the southern part of West Africa, Liberia is bordered by Sierra Leone, Guinea, and the Ivory Coast. It is comparable in size to Tennessee.

Most of the country is a plateau covered by dense tropical forests, which thrive under an annual rainfall of about 160 inches a year.

Government. An interim government headed by Mr. Wilton Sankawaulo as chairman, with five other members, Oscar Quiah, Tamba Tailor, George Boley, Alhaji G.V. Kromah, and Charles Taylor, as vice-presidents.

History. Liberia was founded in 1822 as a result of the efforts of the American Colonization Society to settle freed American slaves in West Africa. In 1847, it became the Free and Independent Republic of Liberia.

The government of Africa's first republic was modeled after that of the United States, and Joseph J. Roberts of Virginia was elected the first president. He laid the foundations of a modern state. The English-speaking descendants of U.S. blacks, known as Americo-Liberians, were the intellectual and ruling class. The indigenous inhabitants, divided, constitute 99% of the population.

After 1920, considerable progress was made toward opening up the interior, a process that was spurred in 1951 by the establishment of a 43-mile (69-km) railroad to the Bomi Hills from Monrovia.

In July 1971, while serving his sixth term as president, William V. S. Tubman died following surgery and was succeeded by his long-time associate, Vice President William R. Tolbert, Jr.

Tolbert was ousted in a military coup carried out April 12, 1980, by army enlisted men led by Master Sgt. Samuel K. Doe.

A rebellion led by Charles Taylor, a former Doe aide, started in December 1989 and, by mid-July 1990, had taken most of Liberia's key population and

economic centers and surrounded the capital.

A West African peacekeeping force intervened in Liberia and effectively partitioned the country into two zones. A national conference in March 1991 failed to reach an agreement but reelected Amos Sawyer as interim president.

Despite a 1991 peace, factional fighting continued at times in the country's civil war. In July 1993 the disputants reached a peace agreement that included a cease-fire, the establishment of an interim government, and democratic elections. The agreement fell apart, however, in November.

The various feuding parties met in May 1994 to form a government. Fighting, however, continued at various levels both then and in subsequent months. In late December another ceasefire was proclaimed. This, in turn, broke down in March 1995.

A peace agreement among six warlords took effect in 1995. After a few months, however, it began unraveling first in the rural areas, then in the capital. By mid-April 1996 the civil war destroyed any last vestige of normality and civil society.

LIBYA

Socialist People's Libyan Arab Jamahiriya
Head of State: Col. Muammar el-Qaddafi (1969)
Secretary of the General People's Committee: Abdulmajid Almabruk Alqaod (1994)
Area: 679,536 sq mi. (1,759,998 sq km)
Population (est. 1996): 5,445,436 (average annual rate of natural increase: 3.67%); birth rate: 44.4/1000; infant mortality rate: 59.5/1000; density per sq mile: 8
Capital: Tripoli; **Largest cities (est. 1988):** Tripoli, 591,062; Benghazi, 446,250; **Monetary unit:** Libyan dinar; **Language:** Arabic; Italian and English widely understood in major cities; **Religion:** Islam; **National name:** Socialist People's Libyan Arab Jamahiriya; **Literacy rate:** 64%
Economic summary: Gross domestic product (1994 est.): $32.9 billion; $6,510 per capita; real growth rate −0.9%; inflation 25% (1993 est.); unemployment (1988 est.) 2%. Arable land: 1%. Principal products: wheat, barley, olives, dates, citrus fruits, peanuts. Labor force: 1,000,000 (includes about 280,000 resident foreigners); 31% industry, services 27%, government 24%, agriculture 18%. Major products: petroleum, processed foods, textiles, handicrafts, cement. Natural resources: petroleum, natural gas. Exports: $7.2 billion (f.o.b., 1994 est.): petroleum, peanuts, hides, natural gas. Imports: $6.9 billion (f.o.b., 1994 est.): machinery, foodstuffs, manufactured goods. Major trading partners: Italy, Germany, U.K., France, Spain, Japan, Turkey, former USSR, Korea, Belgium/Luxembourg.

Geography. Libya stretches along the northeastern coast of Africa between Tunisia and Algeria on the west and Egypt on the east; to the south are the Sudan, Chad, and Niger. It is one sixth larger than Alaska. A greater part of the country lies within the Sahara. Along the Mediterranean coast and farther inland is arable plateau land.

Government. In a bloodless coup d'etat on Sept. 1, 1969, the military seized power in Libya. King Idris I, who had ruled since 1951, was deposed and the Libyan Arab Republic proclaimed. The official name was changed in 1977 to the Socialist People's Libyan Arab Jamahiriya—Jamahiriya (a state of the masses) in theory, governed by the populace through local councils; in fact, a military dictatorship. The Revolutionary Council that had governed since the coup was renamed the General Secretariat of the General People's Congress. The Arab Socialist Union Organization is the only political party.

History. Libya was a part of the Turkish dominions from the 16th century until 1911. Following the outbreak of hostilities between Italy and Turkey in that year, Italian troops occupied Tripoli; Italian sovereignty was recognized in 1912.

Libya was the scene of much desert fighting during World War II. After the fall of Tripoli on Jan. 23, 1943, it came under Allied administration. In 1949, the U.N. voted that Libya should become independent by 1952.

Discovery of oil in the Libyan Desert promised financial stability and funds for economic development.

On Aug. 19, 1981, two U.S. Navy F-14's shot down two Soviet-made SU-22's of the Libyan air force that had attacked them in air space above the Gulf of Sidra, claimed by Libya but held to be international by the U.S. In December, Washington asserted that Libyan "hit squads" had been dispatched to the U.S. and security was drastically tightened around President Reagan and other officials. When the Mobil Oil Company abandoned its operations in April 1982, only four U.S. firms were still in Libya, using Libyan or third-country personnel.

On March 24, 1986, U.S. and Libyan forces skirmished in the Gulf of Sidra, with two Libyan patrol boats being sunk. Qaddafi's troops also supported rebels in Chad but suffered major military reverses in 1987.

A two-year-old U.S. covert policy to destabilize the Libyan government with U.S.-trained Libyan ex-P.O.W.s ended in failure in December 1990 when a Libyan-supplied guerrilla force assumed power in Chad, where the commandos were based, and asked the band to leave.

For its refusal to extradite two Libyans accused of involvement in an airline bombing back in 1988, the UN approved trade and air traffic embargoes in April 1992, seriously affecting the Libyan economy.

The U.S. attempted in March 1995 to get a total international embargo of Libyan oil.

Distrustful of the loyalty of foreign workers in Libya, Qaddafi in 1995 sought to reduce their numbers. He also moved to reduce the size of the public sector.

LIECHTENSTEIN

Principality of Liechtenstein
Ruler: Prince Hans Adam (1989)
Prime Minister: Dr. Mario Frick (1994)
Area: 61 sq mi. (157 sq km)
Population (est. 1996): 31,011 (average annual growth rate: 0.62; birth rate: 12.7/1000; infant mortality rate: 5.3/1000; density per square mile: 508
Capital and largest city (1994): Vaduz, 5,067. **Monetary unit:** Swiss franc. **Language:** German. **Religions:** Roman Catholic, 80.36%; Protestant, 7.1%; other 12.5%. **Literacy rate:** 100%
Economic summary: Gross domestic product (1990 est.): $630 million; $22,300 per capita; inflation (1994) 0.9%; unemployment 1.03% (1994). Arable land: 25%. Principal agricultural products: livestock, vegetables, corn, wheat, potatoes, grapes. Labor force (1994): 21,109 (including 12,971 foreigners); industry, 47.6%; services, 50.7%. Major industrial products: electronics, metal products, textiles, ceramics, pharmaceuticals, food products, precision instruments. Natural resource: hydroelectric power. Exports: $2.6 billion (c.i.f., 1994): small specialty machinery, dental products, stamps, hardware, pottery. Imports: n.a.: machinery, processed foods, metal goods, textiles, motor vehicles. Major trading partners: Switzerland and other Western European countries.

Geography. Tiny Liechtenstein, not quite as large as Washington, D.C., lies on the east bank of the Rhine River south of Lake Constance between Austria and Switzerland. It consists of low valley land and Alpine peaks. Falknis (8,401 ft; 2,561 m) and Naafkopf (8,432 ft; 2,570 m) are the tallest.

Government. The Constitution of 1921 provides for a legislature, the Landtag, of 25 members elected by direct suffrage.

History. Founded in 1719, Liechtenstein was a member of the German Confederation from 1815 to 1866, when it became an independent principality. It abolished its army in 1868 and has managed to stay neutral and undamaged in all European wars since then. In a referendum on July 1, 1984, male voters granted women the right to vote, a victory for Prince Hans Adam.

Parliamentary elections in October 1993 gave a plurality to the centrist Fatherland Union (VU) party.

A treaty negotiated between EFTA and the then-European Community was ratified in a December 1993 vote, but in Switzerland it was rejected. The treaty was under revision during 1994 so as to maintain the country's traditional link with Switzerland. After renegotiation the treaty was again subjected to a referendum in April 1995 and approved.

LITHUANIA

Republic of Lithuania
President: Algirdas Mykolas Brazauskas (1993)
Prime Minister: I. Mindaugas Stankevicius (1996)
Area: 25,212 sq mi. (65,300 sq km)
Population (est. 1996): 3,718,000 (Lithuanian, 81%; Russian, 8.4%; Polish, 7%); (average annual rate of natural increase: 0.1%); birth rate: 13/1000; infant mortality rate: 14/1000; density per sq mi.: 147.5
Capital and largest city (1993 est.): Vilnius, 590,100. **Other large cities:** Kaunas, 429,000; Klaipéda, 206,400. **Monetary unit:** Litas. **Language:** Lithuanian. **Religion (1989):** Catholic, 85%. **National name:** Lietuva. **Literacy:** very high
Economic survey: Gross national product (1994 est.): $4.1 billion; $1,095 per capita; real growth rate 2.7% (1995); inflation 35.7% (1995). Labor force (1995): 1,640,000. Natural resources: peat, sand and gravel, quartz, gypsum, dolomite, clay, limestone, mineral water. Amber found on Baltic Sea coast. Industries: metal cutting, electric motors, TV sets, refrigerators and freezers, petroleum refining, shipbuilding, furniture, textiles, food processing, electronic components, computers. Agriculture (36% of labor force): Most

developed are the livestock and dairy branches. Lithuania is a net exporter of meat, milk, and eggs. Exports: $2.2 billion (1994): textiles, chemical products and related industries, mineral products, mechanical goods and electrical equipment. Imports: $2.7 billion (1994): mineral products (incl. oil and gas), machinery, electrical equipment, metals, transport equipment. Major trading parters: CIS nations , E.U. including Germany, the Netherlands, and Italy.

Geography: Lithuania is situated on the eastern shore of the Baltic Sea and borders Latvia on the north, Belarus on the east and south, Poland and the Kaliningrad region of Russia on the southwest. It is a country of gently rolling hills, many forests, and rivers, streams, and lakes. Its principal natural resource is agricultural land.

Government: Lithuania is a parliamentary democracy. The head of state is the directly-elected president. The president nominates the prime minister, who is then approved by the parliament (Seimas).

History: Southernmost of the three Baltic states, Lithuania in the Middle Ages was a grand duchy joined to Poland through royal marriage. Poles and Lithuanians merged forces to defeat the Teutonic knights of Germany at Tannenberg in 1410 and extended their power far into Russian territory. In 1795, however, following the third partition of Poland, Lithuania fell into Russian hands and did not regain its independence until 1918, toward the end of the first World War.

The republic was occupied by the Soviet Union in June 1940 and annexed in August. From June 1941 to 1944 it was occupied by German troops and then was retaken by Russia. Western countries, including the United States, never recognized the Russian annexation of Lithuania.

Nineteen eighty-eight saw a reemergence of the Lithuanian independence movement. Elections were held on Feb. 24, 1990, and Vytautas Landsbergis, the non-Communist head of the largest Lithuanian popular movement (Sajudis) was elected to parliament that day, and on March 11, 1990, the parliament elected him as its president. On the same day, the Supreme Council rejected Soviet rule and declared the restoration of Lithuania's independence, the first Baltic republic to take this action.

Confrontation with the Soviet Union ensued along with economic sanctions, but they were lifted after both sides agreed to a face-saving compromise.

Lithuania's independence was quickly recognized by major European and other nations. The Soviet Union finally recognized the independence of the Baltic states on September 6. UN admittance followed on Sept. 17, 1991.

Elections in February 1993 made Algirdas Brazauskas, a former Communist Party leader, president.

An expected improved relationship with Russia did not occur. The latter's parliament refused to grant Lithuania most-favored-nation trade status until the two countries reached an agreement on military transit to and from Kaliningrad.

As a result of a banking scandal and his handling of it, Adolfas Slezevicius was fired from the post of prime minister. The Seimas approved Mindaugas Stankevicius, a prominent figure in the Democratic Labor Party, as a replacement.

LUXEMBOURG

Grand Duchy of Luxembourg
Ruler: Grand Duke Jean (1964)
Premier: Jean-Claude Juncker (1994)
Area: 999 sq mi. (2,586 sq km)
Population (est. 1996): 406,901 (average annual rate of natural increase: 0.29%); birth rate: 12.3/1000; infant mortality rate: 6.5/1000; density per square mile: 407
Capital and largest city (1991): Luxembourg, 75,622;
Monetary unit: Luxembourg franc; **Languages:** Luxermbourgish, French, German; **Religion:** Mainly Roman Catholic; **National name:** Grand-Duché de Luxembourg; **Literacy rate:** 100%
Economic summary: Gross domestic product (1994): $9 billion; $22,000 per capita; real growth rate 1% (1993); inflation: 3.6% (1992); unemployment: 5.1% (March 1994). Arable land: 24%. Principal agricultural products: livestock, dairy products, wine. Labor force (1994): 203,200; one-third are foreign workers. Services, 65%; industry, 31.6%; agriculture, 3.4%. Major industrial products: banking, steel, processed food, chemicals, metal products, tires, glass. Natural resource: Iron ore. Exports: $6.3 billion (f.o.b., 1992): steel, chemicals, rubber products, glass, aluminum. Imports: $7.8 billion (c.i.f., 1992): minerals, metals, foodstuffs, consumer goods. Major trading partners: European Community countries.

Geography. Luxembourg is a neighbor of Belgium on the west, Germany on the east, and France on the south. The Ardennes Mountains extend from Belgium into the northern section of Luxembourg.

Government. Luxembourg's unicameral legislature, the Chamber of Deputies, consists of 60 members elected for five years.

History. Sigefroi, Count of Ardennes, an offspring of Charlemagne, was Luxembourg's first sovereign ruler. In 1060, the country came under the rule of the House of Luxembourg. From the 15th to the 18th century, Spain, France, and Austria held it in turn. The Congress of Vienna in 1815 made it a Grand Duchy and gave it to William I, King of the Netherlands. In 1839 the Treaty of London ceded the western part of Luxembourg to Belgium.

The eastern part, continuing in personal union with the Netherlands, and a member of the German Confederation, became autonomous in 1848 and a neutral territory by decision of the London Conference of 1867, governed by its Grand Duke. Germany occupied the duchy in World Wars I and II. Allied troops liberated the enclave in 1944.

In 1961, Prince Jean, son and heir of Grand Duchess Charlotte, was made head of state, acting for his mother. She abdicated in 1964, and Prince Jean became Grand Duke. Grand Duchess Charlotte died in 1985.

By a customs union between Belgium and Luxembourg, which came into force on May 1, 1922, to last for 50 years, customs frontiers between the two countries were abolished. On Jan. 1, 1948, a customs union with Belgium and the Netherlands (Benelux) came into existence. On Feb. 3, 1958, it became an economic union.

Luxembourg's parliament approved the "Maastricht Accord" in July 1992, with the proviso that the country negotiate an exemption to the clause granting foreigners the vote.

In 1995 former prime minister Jacques Santer began his tenure as president of the European Commission.

MACEDONIA[1]

Republic of Macedonia
President: Kiro Gilgorov
Prime Minister: Branko Crvenkovski (1992)
Area: 9,928 sq mi. (25,713 sq km)
Population (est. 1996): 2,104,035; (1994): Macedonians, 65%; Albanians, 22%; Turkish, 4%; Serb, 2%; Gypsies, 3%. (Average annual rate of natural increase: 0.48%); birth rate: 13.3/1000; infant mortality rate: 29.7/1000; density per square mile: 211
Capital and largest city (1991 est.): Skopje, 448,229. Other large cities: Bitola, 84,002; Kumanovo, 69,231; Prelep, 70,152; Tetovo, 51,472; Titov Veles, 47,326; Ohrid, 42,903; Sitip, 42,826. **Monetary unit:** Dinar. **Languages:** Macedonian, 70%; Albanian, 21%; Turkish, 3%; other, 6%. **Religions (1994):** Eastern Orthodox, 67%; Muslim, 30%. **National name:** Republica Makedonija
Economic summary: Gross domestic product (1994 est.): $1.9 billion; $900 per capita; real growth rate, –15%; inflation: 54%; unemployment: 30% (1993). Labor force: 507,324 (1990): manufacturing and mining, 40%; agriculture, 8%. Industries: low level technology (basic fuels) mining, basic textiles, wood products, and tobacco. Agriculture: rice, tobacco, wheat, corn, millet, cotton, citrus fruits, and vegetables. Exports (1993): $1.06 billion: manufactured goods, 40%; machinery and transport equipment, 14%; misc. mfg. articles, 23%; raw materials, 7.6%; food (rice) and live animals, 5.7%; beverages and tobacco, 4.5%; chemicals, 4.7% (1990). Imports (1993): $1.2 billion: fuel and lubricants, 19%; manufactured goods, 18%; machinery and transport euqipment, 15%; food and live animals, 14%; chemicals, 11.4%; raw materials, 10%. Major trading partners: Germany, Albania, Bulgaria, former Yugoslav republics, Greece

1. The U.N. recognized the Republic of Macedonia on April 8, 1993, under the temporary name the Former Yugoslav Republic of Macedonia. The U.S. recognized Macedonia as a state in February 1994.

Geography: Macedonia is a landlocked state in the heart of the Balkans and is slightly smaller than the state of Vermont. It is a mountainous country with small basins of agricultural land linked by rivers. It borders the Yugoslavian republic of Serbia in the north, Bulgaria in the east, Greece in the south, and Albania in the west. The three major rivers are the Aliakmon, the Vardar, and the Strymon. The Vardar is the largest and most important river.

Government: A democratic republic with a legislative house consisting of 120 deputies, each elected for a four-year term. The Assembly's president and vice presidents are elected from among its members.

History: The Republic of Macedonia occupies the western half of the ancient Kingdom of Macedonia. Historic Macedonia was defeated by Rome and became a Roman province in 148 B.C.

After the Roman Empire was divided in A.D. 395, Macedonia was intermittently ruled by the Byzantine Empire until Turkey took possession of the land in 1389. The Ottoman Turks dominated Macedonia for the next five centuries, up until 1913.

During the 19th and 20th centuries, there was a constant struggle by the Balkan powers to possess Macedonia for its economic and strategic military corridors.

The Treaty of San Stefano in 1878 ending the Russo-Turkish War gave the largest part of Macedonia to Bulgaria. Bulgaria lost much of its Macedonian territory when it was defeated by the Greeks and Serbs in the Second Balkan War of 1913. Most of Macedonia went to Serbia and the remainder was divided among Greece and Bulgaria.

In 1914, Serbia, which included Macedonia, joined in union with Croatia, Slovenia, and Montenegro to form the Kingdom of Serbs, Croats, and Slovenes, which was renamed Yugoslavia in 1929.

Bulgaria joined the Axis powers in World War II and occupied parts of Yugoslavia including Macedonia in 1941. During the occupation of their country, Macedonian resistance fighters fought a guerrilla warfare against the invading troops.

The Yugoslavian Republic was re-established after the defeat of Germany in 1945, and in 1946, the government removed Macedonia from Serbian control and made it an autonomous Yugoslavian republic. Later, when President Tito recognized the Macedonian people as a separate nation, the Macedonians strove to develop their own culture and language separate from Bulgaria and Serbia.

In January 1992, Macedonia declared its independence from Yugoslavia and asked for recognition from the European Community nations. In December 1993 six European nations recognized Macedonia.

The president won re-election in October 1994. As a result of that voting a coalition government was created from the Social Democratic Alliance, the Liberals, the Socialists, and a mainly ethnic-Albanian party.

In October 1995 Greece lifted its trade embargo as a result of an agreement reached in New York the previous month. In September the country was admitted into the Council of Europe. And in October the president was the target of an assassination attempt. He survived, but day-to-day affairs were taken over by the speaker of the parliament.

MADAGASCAR

Republic of Madagascar
President and Head of State: Albert Zafy (1993)
Prime Minister: Norbert Ratsirahonana (May 1996)
Area: 226,660 sq mi. (587,050 sq km)
Population (est. 1996): 13,670,507 (average annual rate of natural increase: 2.83%); birth rate: 42.6/1000; infant mortality rate: 93.5/1000; density per square mile: 60
Capital and largest city (est. 1993): Antananarivo, 1,000,000; **Monetary unit:** Malagasy franc; **Languages:** Malagasy, French. **Ethnic groups:** Merina (or Hova), Betsimisaraka, Betsileo, Tsimihety, Antaisaka, Sakalava, Antandroy. **Religions:** traditional, 52%; Christian, 41%; Islam, 7%. **National name:** Repoblikan'i Madagasikara. **Literacy rate:** 80%
Economic summary: Gross domestic product (1994 est.): $10.6 billion; $790 per capita; 2.8% real growth rate; inflation 35%. Arable land: 4%. Principal agricultural products: rice, livestock, coffee, vanilla, sugar, cloves, cardamom, beans, bananas. Labor force: 4,900,000; 90% in subsistence agriculture. Major industrial products: processed food, textiles, assembled automobiles, soap, cement. Natural resources: graphite, chromium, bauxite, semiprecious stones. Exports: $240 million (f.o.b., 1993 est.): coffee, cloves, vanilla, sugar, petroleum products. Imports: $510 million (f.o.b., 1993 est.): consumer goods, foodstuffs, crude petroleum. Major trading partners: France, U.S., Japan, Italy, Germany, U.K., and other E.U.

Geography. Madagascar lies in the Indian Ocean off the southeast coast of Africa opposite Mozambique. The world's fourth-largest island, it is twice the size of Arizona. The country's low-lying coastal area gives way to a central plateau. The once densely wooded interior has largely been cut down.

Government. A republic. Under the new constitution of the Third Republic, August 19, 1992, Albert Zafy was elected president, February 1993, for a 5-year term. The prime minister, Francisque Ravony, was elected by the unicameral National Assembly, composed of 19 political parties, which voted in August 1993.

History. The present population is of black and Malay stock, with perhaps some Polynesian, called Malagasy. The French took over a protectorate in 1885, and then in 1894–95 ended the monarchy, exiling Queen Rànavàlona III to Algiers. A colonial administration was set up, to which the Comoro Islands were attached in 1908, and other territories later. In World War II, the British occupied Madagascar, which retained ties to Vichy France.

An autonomous republic within the French Community since 1958, Madagascar became an independent member of the Community in 1960. In May 1973, an army coup led by Maj. Gen. Gabriel Ramanantsoa ousted Philibert Tsiranana, president since 1959.

On June 15, 1975, Comdr. Didier Ratsiraka was named president. He announced that he would follow a socialist course and, after nationalizing banks and insurance companies, declared all mineral resources nationalized.

In July 1991 opposition leaders named an alternative government. After a 15-day strike the president offered a referendum on a multiparty constitution and named a new prime minister. An interim government was formed in May that included the opposition and would prepare constitutional changes.

Albert Zafy decidedly won the second round of the presidential election in February 1993.

As a result of a referendum held in September 1995, the president was given the power to appoint and fire the prime minister. The then prime minister, who was frequently at odds with the president, resigned in October, being replaced by the agriculture minister.

MALAWI

Republic of Malawi
President: Bakili Muluzi (1994)
Area: 45,747 sq mi. (118,484 sq km)
Population (est. 1996): 9,452,844 (average annual rate of natural increase: 1.71%); birth rate: 41.6/1000; infant mortality rate: 139.9/1000; density per square mile: 206
Capital (1993 est.): Lilongwe, 260,000; **Largest city (1993 est.):** Blantyre, 399,000. **Monetary unit:** Kwacha. **Languages:** English and Chichewa (National). **Religions:** Christian, 75%; Islam, 20%. **Member of Commonwealth of Nations. Literacy rate:** 41.2%
Economic summary: Gross domestic product (1994 est.): $7.3 billion; $750 per capita; growth rate 9.3%; inflation rate 30%. Arable land: 25%. Agriculture accounts for 40% of GDP and 90% of export revenues. Principal agricultural products: tobacco, tea, sugar, corn, cotton. Labor force: 428,000 wage earners; 43% in agriculture. Major industrial products: food, tobacco, cement, processed wood, consumer goods. Natural

resources: limestone, uranium, coal, bauxite. Exports: $311 million (f.o.b., 1993): tobacco, sugar, tea, coffee, peanuts. Imports: $308 million (c.i.f., 1993, est.): transport equipment, food, petroleum, consumer goods. Major trading partners: U.K., U.S., Japan, Germany, South Africa, Zambia, Zimbabwe.

Geography. Malawi is a landlocked country the size of Pennsylvania in southeastern Africa, surrounded by Mozambique, Zambia, and Tanzania. Lake Malawi, formerly Lake Nyasa, occupies most of the country's eastern border. The north-south Rift Valley is flanked by mountain ranges and high plateau areas.

Government. Under a Provisional Constitution which came into effect on May 17, 1994, the president is the Head of State and Government. There is a vice president. The National Assembly (parliament) is composed of 177 members. There are eight registered parties, and the ruling party since May 17, 1994, is the United Democratic Front (UDF) of President Bakili Muluzi.

History. The first European to make extensive explorations in the area was David Livingstone in the 1850s and 1860s. In 1884, Cecil Rhodes's British South African Company received a charter to develop the country. The company came into conflict with the Arab slavers in 1887–89. After Britain annexed the Nyasaland territory in 1891, making it a protectorate in 1892, Sir Harry Johnstone, the first high commissioner, using Royal Navy gunboats, wiped out the slavers.

Nyasaland became the independent nation of Malawi on July 6, 1964. Two years later, it became a republic within the Commonwealth of Nations.

Dr. Hastings K. Banda, Malawi's first prime minister, became its first president. He pledged to follow a policy of "discretionary nonalignment." Banda alienated much of black Africa by maintaining good relations with South Africa.

The results of a referendum in June 1993 on Banda's one-party rule gave 63% in favor of a multiparty democracy.

Bakili Muluzi won the country's first free election in May 1994. He was sworn in a few days later and quickly released the remaining political prisoners. Budget trimming was the order of the day in 1995, which received commendation from the IMF.

MALAYSIA

Paramount Ruler: His Majesty Tuanku Ja'afar ibni Al-Marhum Tuanku Abdul Rahman (1994)
Prime Minister: Dato' Seri Dr. Mahathir bin Mohamad (1981)
Area: 128,328 sq mi. (332,370 sq km)
Population (est. 1996): 19,962,893 (average annual rate of natural increase: 2.07%); birth rate: 26.2/1000; infant mortality rate: 24/1000; density per square mile: 155
Capital: Kuala Lumpur; **Largest cities (1991 est.):** Kuala Lumpur, 1,145,000; Georgetown (Pinang), 220,000; Ipoh, 382,600. **Monetary unit:** Ringgit. **Languages:** Malay (official), Chinese, Tamil, English. **Ethnic divisions:** 59% Malay and other indigenous; 32% Chinese; 9% Indian. **Religions:** Malays all Muslims, Chinese predominantly Buddhists, Indians predominantly Hindus. **Member of Commonwealth of Nations. Literacy rate:** 78%

Economic summary: Gross domestic product (1995): $48.195 billion; $4,027 per capita; real growth rate 8% (1993 est.); inflation 3.7% (1994); unemployment 2.9% (1994). Arable land: 3%. Principal agricultural products: rice, rubber, palm products. Labor force (1995): 8 million. Major industrial products: processed rubber, timber, palm oil, tin, petroleum, light manufactures, electronics equipment. Natural resources: tin, oil, copper, timber. Exports: $48.55 billion (1995): natural rubber, palm oil, tin, timber, petroleum, electronics, textiles. Imports: $46.97 billion (1995): food, crude oil, capital equipment, chemicals, consumer goods. Major trading partners: Japan, Singapore, U.S., Western European countries, Taiwan.

Geography. Malaysia is on the Malay Peninsula in southeast Asia. The nation also includes Sabah and Sarawak on the island of Borneo to the east. Its area slightly exceeds that of New Mexico.

Most of Malaysia is covered by forest, with a mountain range running the length of the peninsula. Extensive forests provide ebony, sandalwood, teak, and other woods.

Government. Malaysia is a sovereign constitutional monarchy practicing parliamentary democracy based on universal suffrage. Malaysia is a member of the Commonwealth of Nations. The Paramount Ruler is elected for a five-year term by the hereditary rulers of the states from among themselves. He is advised by the prime minister and his cabinet. There is a bicameral legislature. The Senate, whose role is comparable more to that of the British House of Lords than to the U.S. Senate, has 68 members, partly appointed by the Paramount Ruler to represent minority and special interests, and partly elected by the legislative assemblies of the various states.

The House of Representatives, is made up of 192 members, who are elected for five-year terms.

History. Malaysia came into existence on Sept. 16, 1963, as a federation of Malaya, Singapore, Sabah (North Borneo), and Sarawak. In 1965, Singapore withdrew from the federation. Since 1966, the 11 states of former Malaya have been known as West Malaysia, and Sabah and Sarawak have been known as East Malaysia.

The Union of Malaya was established April 1, 1946, being formed from the Federated Malay States of Negri Sembilan, Pahang, Perak, and Selangor; the Unfederated Malay States of Johore, Kedah, Kelantan, Perlis, and Trengganu; and two of the Straits Settlements—Malacca and Penang. The Malay states had been brought under British administration during the late 19th and early 20th centuries.

It became the Federation of Malaya on Feb. 1, 1948, and the Federation attained full independence within the Commonwealth of Nations in 1957.

Sabah, constituting the extreme northern portion of the island of Borneo, was a British protectorate administered under charter by the British North Borneo Company from 1881 to 1946, when it assumed the status of a colony. It was occupied by Japanese troops from 1942 to 1945.

Sarawak extends along the northwestern coast of Borneo for about 500 miles (805 km). In 1841, part of the present territory was granted by the Sultan of Brunei to Sir James Brooke. Sarawak continued to be ruled by members of the Brooke family until the Japanese occupation.

From 1963, it was the target of guerrilla infiltration from Indonesia, but beat off invasion attempts. In 1966, when Sukarno fell and the Communist Party was liquidated in Indonesia, hostilities ended.

In the late 1960s, the country was torn by communal rioting directed against Chinese and Indians, who controlled a disproportionate share of the country's wealth. Beginning in 1968, the government moved to achieve greater economic balance through a national economic policy.

Malaysia felt the impact of the "boat people" fleeing Vietnam early in 1978. Because the refugees were mostly ethnic Chinese, the government was apprehensive about any increase of a minority that previously had been the source of internal conflict in the country. In April 1988, it announced that starting in April 1989 it would accept no more refugees.

General elections were held in October 1990 producing another victory for Prime Minister Mahathir and his Barisan National Coalition, which won 127 of the 180 parliamentary seats.

In 1994 the constitution was amended to state that any bill not signed by the monarch within 30 days became law automatically.

The prime minister's party scored a massive victory in parliamentary elections in 1995.

In January 1996 an international agreement was reached to repatriate all Vietnamese asylum seekers. This led to a riot at a refugee camp, with police using various means to restore order.

MALDIVES

Republic of Maldives
President: Maumoon Abdul Gayoom (1978)
Area: 115 sq mi. (298 sq km)
Population (est. 1996): 270,758 (average annual rate of natural increase: 3.52%); birth rate: 41.8/1000; infant mortality rate: 47/1000 (1994 est.); density per square mile: 2,354
Capital and largest city (1995 census): Malé, 62,973.
Monetary unit: Maldivian rufiyaa. **Language:** Dhivehi.
Religion: Islam (Sunni Muslim). **Literacy rate:** 98%
Economic summary: Gross domestic product (1993 est.): $360 million; $1,500 per capita; inflation, 20%; unemployment, negl. Arable land: 10%. Principal agricultural products: maize, sorghum, finger millet, alocasia, cassava, sweet potato, onion, coconut. Labor force: 66,000; 80% in fishing. Major products: fish, processed coconuts, handicraft. Natural resource: fish. Tourism is also an important sector of the economy. Exports: $38.5 million (f.o.b., 1993 est.): fish, clothing. Imports: $177.8 million (c.i.f., 1993 est.): intermediate and capital goods, consumer goods, petroleum products. Major trading partners: Thailand, U.S., Singapore, U.K., Germany, India.

Geography. The Republic of Maldives is a group of atolls in the Indian Ocean about 417 miles (671 km) southwest of Sri Lanka. Its 1,190 coral islets stretch over an area of 35,200 square miles (90,000 sq km). With concerns over global warming and the shrinking of the polar ice caps, Maldives feels directly threatened, as none of its islands rises more than six feet above sea level.

Government. The 15-member Cabinet is headed by the president. The Majlis (parliament) is a unicameral legislature consisting of 48 members. Eight of these are appointed by the president. The others are elected for five-year terms, 2 from the capital island of Malé and 2 from each of the 19 administrative atolls. There are no political parties in the Maldives.

History. The Maldives (formerly called the Maldive Islands) are inhabited by an Islamic seafaring people. Originally the islands were under the suzerainty of Ceylon. They came under British protection in 1887 and were a dependency of the then colony of Ceylon until 1948. The independence agreement with Britain was signed July 26, 1965.

For centuries a sultanate, the islands adopted a republican form of government in 1952, but the sultanate was restored in 1954. In 1968, however, as the result of a referendum, a republic was again established in the islands.

Ibrahim Nasir, president since 1968, was removed from office by the Majlis in November 1978 and replaced by Maumoon Abdul Gayoom. The president was elected to a fourth five-year term in October 1993.

There are no political parties and no political opposition groups.

MALI

Republic of Mali
President of the Republic: Alpha Oumar Konaré (1992)
Prime Minister: Ibrahima Boubacar Keita
Area: 478,819 sq mi. (1,240,142 sq km)
Population (est. 1996): 9,653,261 (average annual rate of natural increase: 3.19%); birth rate: 51.4/1000; infant mortality rate: 102.7/1000; density per square mile: 20.2
Capital and largest city (1992 est.): Bamako, 746,000.
Monetary unit: Franc CFA. **Ethnic groups:** Bambara, Peul, Soninke, Malinke, Songhai, Dogon, Senoufo, Minianka, Berbers, and Moors. **Languages:** French (official), African languages. **Religions:** Islam, 90%; traditional, 9%; Christian, 1%. **National name:** République de Mali. **Literacy rate:** 32%
Economic summary: Gross domestic product (1994 est.): $5.4 billion; $600 per capita; real growth rate 2.4%; inflation 35%. Arable land: 2%; Principal agricultural products: millet, corn, rice, cotton, peanuts, livestock. Labor force: 2,666,000; 80% in agriculture. Major industrial products: consumer goods, phosphates, gold, fish. Natural resources: bauxite, iron ore, manganese, phosphate, salt, limestone, gold. Exports: $415 million (f.o.b., 1993): cotton, livestock, gold. Imports: $842 million (f.o.b., 1993): machinery and equipment, foodstuffs, construction materials, petroleum, textiles. Major trading partners: Western Europe.

Geography. Most of Mali, in West Africa, lies in the Sahara. A landlocked country four fifths the size of Alaska, it is bordered by Guinea, Senegal, Mauritania, Algeria, Niger, Burkina Faso, and the Ivory Coast.

The only fertile area is in the south, where the Niger and Senegal Rivers provide irrigation.

Government. The army overthrew the government on Nov. 19, 1968, and formed a provisional government. The Military Committee of National Liberation consists of 14 members and forms the decision-making body.

Soldiers promising a multiparty democracy overthrew the dictatorship of General Traoré in March 1991.

The present government is a multiparty democracy with one parliamentary house of 129 seats, 13 of which are designated for Malians abroad.

History. Subjugated by France by the end of the 19th century, this area became a colony in 1904 (named French Sudan in 1920) and in 1946 became part of the French Union. On June 20, 1960, it became independent and, under the name of Sudanese Republic, was federated with the Republic of Senegal in the Mali Federation. However, Senegal seceded from the Federation on Aug. 20, 1960, and the Sudanese Republic then changed its name to the Republic of Mali on September 22.

In the 1960s, Mali concentrated on economic development, continuing to accept aid from both Soviet bloc and Western nations, as well as international agencies. In the late 1960s, it began retreating from close ties with China. But a purge of conservative opponents brought greater power to President Modibo Keita, and in 1968 the influence of the Chinese and their Malian sympathizers increased.

Mali, with Mauritania, the Ivory Coast, Senegal, Dahomey (Benin), Niger, and Burkina Faso signed a treaty establishing the Economic Community for West Africa.

Mali and Burkina Faso fought a brief border war from December 25 to 29, 1985.

The leader of the March 1991 coup, Lieut. Col. Amadou Toumani Touré, promised the army would return to the barracks. There were at least 59 casualties after the overnight coup, which France welcomed.

Multiparty elections in 1992 gave the Alliance for Democracy in Mali 76 of the 116 parliamentary seats, and the presidency went to that party's candidate, Alpha Oumar Konaré, with 70% of the vote.

Following large demonstrations and riots in early 1993 the prime minister resigned, being replaced by the minister of defense, Abdoulaye Sekou Sow.

Prime Minister Sow in turn resigned in February 1994 claiming political differences with the governing party. He was replaced with the foreign minister, Ibrahima Boubacar Keita. The two chief opposition parties withdrew from the coalition government citing failure to be brought into the negotiations concerning the new cabinet.

Groups in the north agreed to end their fighting in January 1995.

MALTA

Malta
President: Dr. Ugo Mifsud Bonnicí (1994)
Prime Minister: Dr. Edward Fenech Adami (1987)
Area: 122 sq mi. (316 sq km)
Population (est. 1996): 372,314 (average annual rate of natural increase: 0.55%); birth rate: 12.9/1000; infant mortality rate: 7.5/1000; density per square mile: 3,051
Capital (est. 1994): Valletta, 9,144.. **Monetary unit:** Maltese lira. **Languages:** Maltese and English. **Religion:** Roman Catholic. **National name:** Malta. **Member of Commonwealth of Nations. Literacy rate:** 84%
Economic summary: Gross domestic product (1994 est.): $3.9 billion; $10,760 per capita; real growth rate 4.4%; inflation 5%; unemployment 4.5% (Mar. 94). Arable land: 38%. Principal agricultural products: potatoes, wheat, barley, citrus, vegetables, hogs, poultry. Labor force: 125,674; 27% in manufacturing. Major manufacturing products are high-tech semiconductors, electrical switchgear, gold and silver items, rubber products, and textiles. The same products are exported. Tourism is also important to the economy. Exports: $1.3 billion (f.o.b., 1993): clothing, textiles, footwear, ships. Imports: $2.1 billion (c.i.f., 1993): food, petroleum, machinery, and semimanufactured goods. Major trading partners: Germany, Italy, U.K., U.S.

Geography. The five Maltese islands—with a combined land area smaller than Philadelphia—are in the Mediterranean about 60 miles (97 km) south of the southeastern tip of Sicily.

Government. The government is headed by a prime minister, responsible to a 65-member House of Representatives elected by universal suffrage.

The major political parties are the Nationalists (34 of 65 seats in the House), led by Prime Minister Dr. Edward Fenech-Adami, and the Malta Labor Party (31 seats), led by Dr. Alfred Sant.

History. The strategic importance of Malta was recognized by the Phoenicians, who occupied it, as did in their turn the Greeks, Carthaginians, and Romans. The apostle Paul was shipwrecked there in A.D. 58.

The Knights of St. John (Malta), who obtained the three habitable Maltese islands of Malta, Gozo, and Comino from Charles V in 1530, reached their highest fame when they withstood an attack by superior Turkish forces in 1565.

Napoleon seized Malta in 1798, but the French forces were ousted by British troops the next year, and British rule was confirmed by the Treaty of Paris in 1814.

Malta was heavily attacked by German and Italian aircraft during World War II, but was never invaded by the Axis.

Malta became an independent nation on Sept. 21, 1964, and a republic Dec. 13, 1974, but remained in the British Commonwealth. The Governor-General, Sir Anthony Mamo, was sworn in as the first president, and Dom Mintoff became prime minister.

Fenech Adami won reelection as prime minister in February 1992 when his party won an absolute majority of three seats in the parliament.

The European Council indicated in 1994 that Malta's application for membership in the European Union would be accepted in the next expansion phase.

The House of Representatives in 1995 approved pursuing membership in NATO's Partnership for Peace.

MARSHALL ISLANDS

Republic of the Marshall Islands
President: Amata Kabua (1979)
Total land area: 70 sq mi (181.3 sq km), includes the atolls of Bikini, Eniwetok, and Kwajalein
Population (est. 1996): 58,363; growth rate 3.85%; birth rate 45.7/1000; infant mortality rate 46.9/1000; density per square mile: 833
Capital and largest city (1990 est.): Majuro, 20,000. **Ethnic divisions:** almost entirely Micronesian. **Religion:** predominantly Christian, mostly Protestant. **Literacy rate:** 93%. **Language:** Both Marshallese and English are official languages. Marshallese is a dialect of the Malayo-Polynesian family
Net migration rate (1992): 0 migrant/1000 population
Comparative land area: slightly larger than Washington, D.C.
Economic summary: Gross domestic product (1992 est.): $75 million; per capita, $1,500; real growth rate, 6%; inflation, 7%; unemployment, 16% (1991 est.) Exports: $3.9 million (f.o.b., 1992 est.): coconut oil, fish, live animals, trichus shells. Imports: $62.9 million (c.i.f., 1992 est.): foodstuffs, machinery and equipment, beverages and tobacco, fuels. Agriculture, marine resources, and tourism are the top development priorities for the Republic of the Marshall Islands (RMI). The government of the RMI is the largest employer,

with some 2,000 workers. Direct U.S. aid under the Compact of Free Association; the U.S. is to provide approximately $40 million annually in aid. Major trading partners: U.S., Japan, Australia.

Geography. The Marshall Islands, east of the Carolines, are divided into two chains: the western, or Ralik, group, including the atolls Jaluit, Kwajalein, Wotho, Bikini, and Eniwetok; and the eastern, or Ratak, group, including the atolls Mili, Majuro, Maloelap, Wotje, and Likiep. The islands are of the coral-reef type and rise only a few feet above sea level.

Government. Constitutional government in free association with the United States.

History. The United States and the RMI signed a Compact of Free Association on October 15, 1986, which became effective as of October 21, 1986. The termination of the Trusteeship Agreement became effective on November 3, 1986. The Marshall Islands were admitted to the U.N. on Sept. 17, 1991.

The government in 1994 again considered allowing the dumping of nuclear waste on such islands as Bikini and Enewetak, which are already uninhabitable owing to nuclear tests decades ago.

Although parliament approved a 10% wage cut for public sector employees in 1995, it was not put into effect due to public opposition.

MAURITANIA

Islamic Republic of Mauritania
Chief of State and Head of Government: Pres. Maaouye Ould Sidi Ahmed Taya (1984)
Area: 397,953 sq mi. (1,030,700 sq km)
Population (est. 1996): 2,336,048 (average annual rate of natural increase: 3.17%); birth rate: 46.9/1000; infant mortality rate: 81.7/1000; density per square mile: 5
Capital and largest city (est. 1992): Nouakchott, 480,000.
Monetary unit: Ouguiya. **Ethnic groups:** Arabs, 80%; Africans, 20%. **Languages:** Arabic (official) and French. **Religion:** Islam. **National name:** République Islamique de Mauritanie. **Literacy rate:** 34%
Economic summary: Gross domestic product (1993 est.): $2.4 billion; $1,110 per capita; real growth rate 5%; inflation (1993) 10%; unemployment (1991 est.) 20%. Arable land: 1%; Principal agricultural products: livestock, millet, maize, wheat, dates, rice. Labor force: 465,000 (1981 est.); 45,000 wage earners; 14% in industry and commerce. Major industrial products: iron ore, processed fish. Natural resources: copper, iron ore, gypsum, fish. Exports: $410 million (f.o.b., 1993 est.): iron ore, fish, gum arabic, gypsum. Imports: $378 million (c.i.f., 1993 est.): foodstuffs, petroleum, capital goods. Major trading partners: E.U., Japan, Côte d'Ivoire, Algeria, China, U.S.

Geography. Mauritania, three times the size of Arizona, is situated in northwest Africa with about 350 miles (592 km) of coastline on the Atlantic Ocean. It is bordered by Morocco on the north, Algeria and Mali on the east, and Senegal on the south.

The country is mostly desert, with the exception of the fertile Senegal River valley in the south and grazing land in the north.

Government. An army coup on July 10, 1978, deposed Moktar Ould Daddah, who had been president since Mauritania's independence in 1960. President

Mohammed Khouna Ould Haldala, who seized power in the 1978 coup, was in turn deposed in a Dec. 12, 1984, coup by army chief of staff Maaouye Ould Sidi Ahmed Taya, who assumed the title of President.

In the January 1992 elections President Taya won 62% of the electorate vote.

The constitution guarantees freedom of press, opinion, and assembly, among others, to all Mauritanian citizens. There are about 20 political parties. There is a bicameral legislature Senate (Majlis al-Shuyukh) and a National Assembly (Majlis al-Watani).

History. Mauritania was first explored by the Portuguese. The French organized the area as a territory in 1904.

Mauritania became an independent nation on Nov. 28, 1960, and was admitted to the United Nations in 1961 over the strenuous opposition of Morocco, which claimed the territory. With Moors, Arabs, Berbers, and blacks frequently in conflict, the government in the late 1960s sought to make Arab culture dominant to unify the country.

Mauritania acquired administrative control of the southern part of the former Spanish Sahara when the colonial administration withdrew in 1975, under an agreement with Morocco and Spain.

Increased military spending and rising casualties in Western Sahara helped bring down the civilian government of Ould Daddah in 1978. A succession of military rulers followed.

In 1989 Mauritania fought a border war with Senegal. Although the country voted in the U.N. to support the embargo against Iraq, the government actually leaned the other way.

The government in April 1991 announced a transition to a multiparty system. A constitutional reform embodying these changes won approval in a referendum in July.

The opposition's call for a boycott of the March parliamentary elections reduced turnout to no more than 40%. Yet Taya's party won 67 of the 79 available seats.

Six opposition parties in July 1995 banded together in a new coalition to fight for democracy. However, the following month some disgruntled figures broke from the coalition to form yet another party.

MAURITIUS

President: Cassam Uteem (1992)
Prime Minister: Navinchandra Ramgoolam (1995)
Area: 787 sq mi. (2,040 sq km)
Population (est. 1996): 1,139,047 (average annual rate of natural increase: 1.22%); birth rate: 18.6/1000; infant mortality rate: 17.3/1000; density per square mile: 1,447
Capital and largest city (est. 1993): Port Louis, 134,516.
  Monetary unit: Mauritian rupee. **Languages:** English (official), French, Creole, Hindi, Urdu, Hakka, Bojpoori.
  Religions: Hindu, 52%, Christian, 28.3%. Islam, 16.6%; other, 3.1%. **Member of Commonwealth of Nations.**
  Literacy rate: 82.8%
Economic summary: Gross domestic product (1993 est.): $9.3 billion; $8,600 per capita (1994 est.); real growth rate, 4.7%; inflation 9.4%; unemployment 2.4% (1991 est.). Arable land: 54%. Principal products: sugar cane, tea. Labor force: 335,000; 22% in manufacturing; 29% in government services; 27% in agriculture and fishing. Major products: processed sugar, wearing apparel, chemical products, textiles. Natural re-

sources: fish. Exports: $1.32 billion (f.o.b., 1993 est.): sugar, light manufactures, textiles. Imports: $1.7 billion (f.o.b., 1993 est.): foodstuffs, manufactured goods. Major trading partners: E.U., South Africa, U.S.

Geography. Mauritius is a mountainous island in the Indian Ocean east of Madagascar.

Government. Mauritius is a republic within the British Commonwealth. The unicameral Legislative Assembly has 70 members, 62 of whom are elected by direct suffrage. The remaining 8 are chosen from among the unsuccessful candidates.

History. After a brief Dutch settlement, French immigrants who came in 1715 gave the name of Isle de France to the island and established the first road and harbor infrastructure, as well as the sugar industry, under the leadership of Gov. Mahe de Labourdonnais. Negroes from Africa and Madagascar came as slaves to work in the cane fields. In 1810, the British captured the island and in 1814, by the Treaty of Paris, it was ceded to Great Britain along with its dependencies.

Indian immigration, which followed the abolition of slavery in 1835, rapidly changed the fabric of Mauritian society, and the country flourished with the increased cultivation of sugar cane.

Mauritius became independent on March 12, 1968. The Labor Party government of Sir Seewoosagur Ramgoolam, who had ruled Mauritius since independence, was toppled in a 1982 election by the Movement Militant Mauricien, which had campaigned for recovery of Diego Garcia island, separated from Mauritius during the colonial period and leased by Britain to the United States for a naval base. But an Alliance Party coalition, including the Labor Party, regained power at the end of 1983 and brought back Ramgoolam as prime minister. He was succeeded by Aneerood Jugnauth of his party in 1982.

A transformation of the nation from a constitutional monarchy into a republic was attempted in mid-1990. Public dissent, however, arose, and the required parliamentary vote was never taken.

The country formally broke ties with the British crown in March 1992, becoming a republic. The president was elected by the Legislative Assembly on June 30.

The government in 1993 offered interest-free loans to its citizens to invest on the local stock exchange. The loans could be repaid over a 10-month period.

An allliance of opposition parties emerged victorious in December 1995 elections to the Assembly, capturing all the seats.

MEXICO

United Mexican States
President: Ernesto Zedillo Ponce de Léon (1994)
Area: 761,600 sq mi. (1,972,547 sq km)
Population (est. 1996): 95,772,462 (average annual rate of natural increase: 2.17%); birth rate: 26.2/1000; infant mortality rate: 25/1000; density per square mile: 125
Capital and largest city (1990): Mexico City, 9,815,795.
  Largest cities (1990): Guadalajara, 1,650,042; Nezahualcoyotl, 1,255,456; Monterey, 1,068,996; Puebla, 1,007,170. **Monetary unit:** Peso. **Languages:** Spanish, Indian languages. **Religion:** nominally Roman Catholic, 97%; Protestant, 3%. **Official name:** Estados Unidos Mexicanos. **Literacy rate:** 88%

Economic summary: Gross domestic product (1994 est.): $728.7 billion; $7,900 per capita; real growth rate 3.5%; inflation 7.1%; unemployment 9.8%. Arable land: 12%;principal products: corn, cotton, fruits, wheat, beans, coffee, tomatoes, rice. Labor force: 24,063,283 (1990); 27.9% in manufacturing; 22.6% in agriculture; 46.1% in services. Major products: processed foods, chemicals, basic metals and metal products, petroleum. Natural resources: petroleum, silver, copper, gold, lead, zinc, natural gas, timber. Exports: $60.8 billion (f.o.b., 1994 est.): motor vehicles, consumer electronics, cotton, shrimp, coffee, petroleum, petroleum products, engines. Imports: $79.4 billion (f.o.b., 1994 est.): grain, metal manufactures, agricultural machinery, electrical equipment, car parts for assembly, motor vehicle repair parts, aircraft and aircraft parts. Major trading partners: U.S., Japan, Western European countries.

Geography. The United States' neighbor to the south, Mexico is about one-fifth its size. Baja California in the west, an 800-mile (1,287-km) peninsula, forms the Gulf of California. In the east are the Gulf of Mexico and the Bay of Campeche, which is formed by Mexico's other peninsula, the Yucatán.

The center of Mexico is a great, high plateau, open to the north, with mountain chains on east and west and with ocean-front lowlands lying outside of them.

Government. The president, who is popularly elected for six years and is ineligible to succeed himself, governs with a cabinet of secretaries. Congress has two houses—a 500-member Chamber of Deputies, elected for three years, and a 64-member Senate, elected for six years, half of which is renewed every three years. Popularly elected officials (president, members of Congress, mayors, etc.) cannot seek reelection.

Each of the 31 states has considerable autonomy, with a popularly elected governor, a legislature, and a local judiciary. The president of Mexico appoints the mayor of the federal district (Mexico City).

History. At least two civilized races—the Mayas and later the Toltecs—preceded the wealthy Aztec empire, conquered in 1519–21 by the Spanish under Hernando Cortés. Spain ruled for the next 300 years until 1810 (the date was Sept. 16 and is now celebrated as Independence Day), when the Mexicans first revolted. They continued the struggle and finally won independence in 1821.

From 1821 to 1877, there were two emperors, several dictators, and enough presidents and provisional executives to make a new government on the average of every nine months. Mexico lost Texas (1836), and after defeat in the war with the U.S. (1846–48) it lost the area comprising the present states of California, Nevada, and Utah, most of Arizona and New Mexico, and parts of Wyoming and Colorado.

In 1855, the Indian patriot Benito Juárez began a series of liberal reforms, including the disestablishment of the Catholic Church, which had acquired vast property. A subsequent civil war was interrupted by the French invasion of Mexico (1861), the crowning of Maximilian of Austria as emperor (1864), and then his overthrow and execution by forces under Juárez, who again became president in 1867.

The years after the fall of the dictator Porfirio Diaz (1877–80 and 1884–1911) were marked by bloody political-military strife and trouble with the U.S., culminating in the punitive U.S. expedition into northern Mexico (1916–17) in unsuccessful pursuit of the revolutionary Pancho Villa. Since a brief period of civil war in 1920, Mexico has enjoyed a period of gradual agricultural, political, and social reforms. Relations with the U.S. were again disturbed in 1938 when all foreign oil wells were expropriated. Agreement on compensation was finally reached in 1941.

During 1983 and 1984, Mexico suffered its worst financial crisis in 50 years, leading to critically high unemployment and an inability to pay its foreign debt. The collapse of oil prices in 1986 cut into Mexico's export earnings and worsened the situation.

Although the ruling Institutional Revolutionary Party's candidate, Carlos Salinas de Gortari, won the presidential election of 1988, the opposition parties on the left and the right showed unprecedented strength.

At the start of 1994 peasant rebels seized a colonial city and declared war on the state. Negotiations and a cease-fire began in mid-January. In March the leading presidential candidate was shot and killed in Tijuana. The campaign manager was then selected to be the party's presidential candidate. Zedillo won the election by more than 20%, and the governing party retained its majority in both legislative houses.

In February 1995 agreement was reached with the U.S. to prevent the collapse of Mexico's private banks. The strict provisions, however, gave the U.S. virtual veto power over key elements in Mexico's economic policy.

As a consequence of the terms for receiving international support, the Mexican economy suffered a severe recession in 1995, and the value of the peso fell drastically.

MICRONESIA

Federated States of Micronesia
President: Bailey Olter (1991)
Total area: 271 sq mi (703 sq km). Land area, same (includes islands of Pohnpei, Truk, Yap, and Kosrae.
Population (est. 1996): 125,377 (average annual rate of natural increase: 2.17%); birth rate: 27.9/1000; infant mortality rate: 35.8/1000; density per square mile: 462
Capital: Palikir. **Ethnic divisions:** Nine ethnic Micronesian and Polynesian groups.. **Language:** English is the official and common language; major indigenous languages are Trukese, Pohnpeian, Yapase, and Kosrean.
Literacy rate: 90%
Economic summary: Gross national product (1990 est.): $160 million, per capita, $1,500; 4% growth rate. Exports: $3.2 million (f.o.b., 1990): copra. Imports: $91.2 million (c.i.f., 1990). Financial assistance from the U.S. is the primary source of revenue. Micronesia also earns about $4 million a year in fees from foreign fishing concerns. Economic activity consists primarily of subsistence farming and fishing. Unemployment rate: 80% **Aid:** Under the terms of the Compact of Free Association, the U.S. will provide $1.3 billion in grant aid during the period 1986–2001.

Geography. The Micronesian islands vary geologically from high mountainous islands to low, coral atolls, with volcanic outcroppings on Pohnpei, Kosrae, and Truk. The climate is tropical, with heavy, year-round rainfall. The islands are located 3,200 miles (5,150 km) west-southwest of Honolulu in the North Pacific Ocean, about three-quarters of the way between Hawaii and Indonesia.

Government. A constitutional government in free association with the United States since November 1986.

History. On April 2, 1947, the United Nations Security Council created the Trust Territory of the Pacific Islands under which the Northern Mariana, Caroline, and Marshall Islands were placed under the administration of the United States. These islands comprised what is now called the Federated States of Micronesia, and only the Republic of Palau is still administered as a Trust Territory. Micronesia was admitted to the United Nations on September 17, 1991. In July 1993 the country became a member of the International Monetary Fund. Elections for Congress took place in March 1995. The president, elected by Congress, retained his incumbency.

MOLDOVA

Republic of Moldova
President: Mircea Snegur (1990)
Prime Minister: Andrei Sangheli (1992)
Area: 13,000 sq mi. (33,700 sq km)
Population (est. 1996): 4,463,847 (Moldovans, 65.5%; Ukrainians, 13.9%; Russians, 13.0%; Gagauz, 3.5%; Bulgarians, 2.0%; Jews, 1.5%); (average annual rate of natural increase: 0.46%; birth rate: 16.3/1000; infant mortality rate: 47.6/1000, density per square mile: 343
Capital and largest city (1991): Chisinau, 676,700. Other large cities (est. 1991): Tiraspol, 186,000; Beltsy, 165,000; Bendery (Tighina), 141,500. **Monetary unit:** Moldovan lem. **Language:** Romanian official language since 1989
Economic summary: Gross domestic product (1994): $11.9 billion, $2,670 per capita; real growth rate −30%; inflation: 7.6% (per mo.); unemployment: 1%. Agriculture and food processing are the main industries. Others include power engineering, textiles, metalworking, building materials, machine building, TV sets, washing machines and other consumer goods, and manufacturing of electrical equipment. Agricultural products are wheat, corn, barley, sugar beets, fruits and wine grapes, soybeans, tobacco, and animal husbandry. Eighty-five percent of all the land is cultivated. Exports: $144 million to outside former Soviet Union countries (1994): foodstuffs, wine, tobacco, textiles and footwear, machinery, chemicals (1991). Imports: $174 million from outside former Soviet Union countries (1994): oil, gas, coal, steel machinery, foodstuffs, automobiles, and other consumer durables. Major trading partners: Russia, Kazakhstan, Ukraine, Uzbekistan, Romania, Germany.

Geography: Moldova (formerly Moldavia) is a landlocked republic of hilly plains lying in the southwestern part of the former Soviet Union between the Prut and Dnestr (Dneister) Rivers. The Prut River separates it from Romania in the west, and Ukraine borders it in the north, east, and south. The area is a very fertile region, with rich black soil (chernozem) covering three-quarters of the territory.

Government: A democratic republic in transition with a parliament made up of 101 deputies. The working body of the parliament is the Presidium.

History: Most of Moldova was an independent principality in the 14th century. In the 16th century it came under Ottoman Turkish rule. Russia acquired Moldovan territory in 1791, and in 1812 (the Treaty of Bucharest), when Turkey gave up the province of Bessarabia[1] to Russia. Turkey held the rest of Moldova but it was passed to Romania in 1918. Russia did

not recognize the cession of this territory.

In 1924, the U.S.S.R. established Moldova as an Autonomous Soviet Socialist Republic of the Ukraine. As a result of the Nazi-Soviet Nonaggression Pact of 1939, Romania was forced to cede all of Bessarabia to the Soviet Union in 1940, and the Moldovan A.S.S.R. was merged with the Romanian-speaking districts of Bessarabia to form the Moldovan Soviet Socialist Republic.

During World War II, Romania joined Germany in the attack on the Soviet Union and reconquered Bessarabia. Soviet troops retook the territory in 1944 and reestablished the Moldovan S.S.R.

For many years, a controversy existed between Romania and the U.S.S.R. over Bessarabia. Following the aborted coup against Soviet President Mikhail Gorbachev, Moldova proclaimed its independence in September 1991.

Following the demise of the Soviet Union, Moldova joined the C.I.S. along with ten other former Soviet republics on Dec. 21, 1991.

Conflict between ethnic Romanians and Slavs in Trans-Dniester has erupted since independence. The prime minister and most of his cabinet resigned in early June 1992 because of the continued strife. Russia and Moldova agreed in July 1992 to send a joint peace-keeping force to the region and outlined guarantees for its future.

The first parliamentary elections in February 1994 saw a victory for the former Communist establishment.

In April 1995 Russia agreed to withdraw its 14th Army in stages from the separatist-minded Trans-Dniester region. A referendum in December there gave approval to a separatist constitution.

1. The area between the Prut and Dnestr Rivers.

MONACO

Principality of Monaco
Ruler: Prince Rainier III (1949)
Minister of State: Paul Dijoud (1994)
Area: 0.73 sq mi. (465 acres)
Population (est. 1996): 31,719 (average annual growth rate: −0.15%); birth rate 10.7/1000; infant mortality rate: 6.9/1000; density per square mile: 43,450
Capital and largest city (1995 est.): Monaco, 30,400. **Monetary unit:** French franc. **Languages:** French, Monégasque, Italian. **Religion:** Roman Catholic, 95%. **National name:** Principauté de Monaco. **Literacy rate:** 99%
Economic summary: Gross domestic product: (1993 est.): $558 million; $18,000 per capita; real growth rate, n.a. About 50% of Monaco's revenues come from value-added taxes on hotels, banks, and industrial sector. About 25% of revenues comes from tourism.

Geography. Monaco is a tiny, hilly wedge driven into the French Mediterranean coast nine miles east of Nice.

Government. Prince Albert of Monaco gave the principality a constitution in 1911, creating a National Council of 18 members popularly elected for five years. The head of government is the Minister of State.

Prince Rainier III, born May 31, 1923, succeeded his grandfather, Louis II, on the latter's death, May 9, 1949. Rainier was married April 18, 1956, to Grace Kelly, U.S. actress. A daughter, Princess Caroline

Louise Margueritte, was born on Jan. 23, 1957 (married to Philippe Junot June 28, 1978, and divorced in 1980; married to Stefano Casiraghi Dec. 29, 1983, and gave birth to a son, Andrea Albert, June 9, 1984, a daughter, Charlotte, Aug. 3, 1986, a son, Pierre, Sept. 5, 1987. Stefano Casiraghi died Oct. 3, 1990); a son, Prince Albert Louis Pierre, on March 14, 1958; and Princess Stéphanie Marie Elisabeth, on Feb. 1, 1965. Princess Grace died Sept. 14, 1982, of injuries received the day before when the car she was driving went off the road near Monte Carlo. She was 52.

The special significance attached to the birth of descendants to Prince Rainier stems from a clause in the Treaty of July 17, 1919, between France and Monaco stipulating that in the event of vacancy of the crown, the Monégasque territory would become an autonomous state under a French protectorate.

The National and Democratic Union (all 18 seats in National Council), led by Jean Louis Campora, is the only political party.

History. The Phoenicians, and after them the Greeks, had a temple on the Monacan headland honoring Hercules. From *Monoikos,* the Greek surname for this mythological strong man, the principality took its name. After being independent for 800 years, Monaco was annexed to France in 1793 and was placed under Sardinia's protection in 1815. In 1861, it went under French guardianship but continued to be independent.

By a treaty in 1918, France stipulated that the French government be given a veto over the succession to the throne.

Monaco is a little land of pleasure with a tourist business that runs as high as 1.5 million visitors a year. It had popular gaming tables as early as 1856. Five years later, a 50-year concession to operate the games was granted to François Blanc, of Bad Homburg. This concession passed into the hands of a private company in 1898.

Monaco's practice of providing a tax shelter for French businessmen resulted in a dispute between the countries. When Rainier refused to end the practice, France retaliated with a customs tax. In 1967, Rainier took control of the Société des Bains de Mer, operator of the famous Monte Carlo gambling casino, in a program to increase hotel and convention space.

The country was admitted to the UN in May 1993, making it the smallest country represented there.

Amid speculation on Prince Rainier's successor, the country continued to diversify its economy away from absolute reliance on gambling proceeds.

MONGOLIA

Mongolia
President: Punsalmaagiin Ochirbat (1993)
Prime Minister: M. Enkhsaikhan (1996)
Area: 604,250 sq mi. (1,565,000 sq km)
Population (est. 1996): 2,496,617 (average annual rate of natural increase: 1.69%); birth rate: 25.5/1000; infant mortality rate: 69.7/1000; density per square mile: 4
Capital and largest city (est. 1993): Ulan Bator, 619,000.
Monetary unit: Tugrik. **Language:** Mongolian, 90%; also Turkic, Russian, and Chinese. **Religion:** predominantly Tibetan Buddhist; Islam about 4%. **Literacy rate:** 90% (est.)
Economic summary: Gross national product (1994 est.): $4.4 billion; $1,800 per capita; real growth rate 6.3% (1993); inflation 70%; unemployment 15% (1991 est.). Arable land: 1%. Principal agricultural products: livestock, wheat, potatoes, forage, barley. Mongolia has the highest number of livestock per person in the world. Major industrial products: coal, copper, and molybdenum concentrate. Natural resources: coal, copper, molybdenum, iron, oil, lead, gold, and tungsten. Exports: $511.6 million (1995): copper, cashmere, livestock, animal products, wool, nonferrous metals. Imports: $388.7 million (1995): fuels, food products, industrial consumer goods, chemicals, building materials, machinery and equipment. Major trading partners: C.I.S. nations, China, Japan, Austria.

Geography. Mongolia lies in central Asia between Siberia on the north and China on the south. It is slightly larger than Alaska.

The productive regions of Mongolia—a tableland ranging from 3,000 to 5,000 feet (914 to 1,524 m) in elevation—are in the north, which is well drained by numerous rivers, including the Hovd, Onon, Selenga, and Tula. Much of the Gobi Desert falls within Mongolia.

Government. In January 1992, the Great People's Hural (parliament) approved a new constitution which entered into force Feb. 12, 1992, and changed the name of the former Communist state to Mongolia. Mongolia became an independent sovereign republic now in transition from Communism. The highest organ of state power is the State Great Hural (SGH). The SGH has one chamber consisting of 76 members. Its chairman and vice-chairman are elected for a term of four years.

History. The State of Mongolia was formerly known as Outer Mongolia. It contains the original homeland of the historic Mongols, whose power reached its zenith during the 13th century under Kublai Khan. The area accepted Manchu rule in 1689, but after the Chinese Revolution of 1911 and the fall of the Manchus in 1912, the northern Mongol princes expelled the Chinese officials and declared independence under the Khutukhtu, or "Living Buddha."

In 1921, Soviet troops entered the country and facilitated the establishment of a republic by Mongolian revolutionaries in 1924 after the death of the last Living Buddha. China, meanwhile, continued to claim Outer Mongolia but was unable to back the claim with any strength. Under the 1945 Chinese-Russian Treaty, China agreed to give up Outer Mongolia, which, after a plebiscite, became a nominally independent country.

Allied with the U.S.S.R. in its dispute with China, Mongolia has mobilized troops along its borders since 1968 when the two powers became involved in border clashes on the Kazakh-Sinkiang frontier to the west and on the Amur and Ussuri Rivers. A 20-year treaty of friendship and cooperation, signed in 1966, entitled Mongolia to call upon the U.S.S.R. for military aid in the event of invasion.

Free elections were held in August 1990 that produced a multiparty government, though still largely Communist. As a result Mongolia has decided to move toward a market economy.

The former Communist Party won a landslide victory in parliamentary elections of June 1992, causing considerable consternation in the democratic forces.

As a result of a dispute between the president and the reformed Communist party, the latter supported a hard-line candidate in the first presidential election of June 1993. The incumbent won as the nominee of the National Democrats and Social Democrats.

During the spring of 1996 immense grass fires blazed across the country. Parliamentary elections were held in June and gave 50 of the 76 seats to the non-Communist opposition coalition.

MOROCCO

Kingdom of Morocco
Ruler: King Hassan II (1961)
Prime Minister: Abd al-Latif Filali (1995)
Area: 172,413 sq mi. (446,550 sq km)
Population (est. 1996): 29,779,156 (average annual rate of natural increase: 2.16%); birth rate: 27.4/1000; infant mortality rate: 43.2/1000; density per square mile: 172
Capital (1993 est.): Rabat, 1,220,000; **Largest cities:** Casablanca, 2,943,000; Marrakech, 602,000; Fez, 564,000; Salé, 521,000. **Monetary unit:** Dirham. **Languages:** Arabic, French, Berber dialects, Spanish; **Religions:** Islam, 98.7%, Christian, 1.1%; Jewish, 0.2%. **National name:** al-Mamlaka al-Maghrebia. **Literacy rate:** 50%
Economic summary: Gross domestic product (1994 est.): $87.5 billion; $3,060 per capita; real growth rate 8%; inflation 5.4%; unemployment 16%. Arable land: 20%. Products: barley, wheat, citrus fruits, vegetables. Labor force (1985): 7,400,000: agriculture 50%; services 26%. Major products: textiles, processed food, phosphates, leather goods. Natural resources: phosphates, lead, manganese, fisheries. Exports: $4.1 billion (f.o.b., 1994 est.): food and beverages, semiprocessed goods, consumer goods, phosphates. Imports: $7.5 billion (c.i.f., 1994 est.): capital goods, fuels, foodstuffs, raw materials, consumer goods. Major trading partners: E.U., C.I.S. nations, Japan, U.S., India, Iraq.

Geography. Morocco, about one-tenth larger than California, is just south of Spain across the Strait of Gibraltar and looks out on the Atlantic from the northwest shoulder of Africa. Algeria is to the east and Mauritania to the south.

On the Atlantic coast there is a fertile plain. The Mediterranean coast is mountainous. The Atlas Mountains, running northeastward from the south to the Algerian frontier, average 11,000 feet (3,353 m) in elevation.

Government. A constitutional monarchy. The king, after suspending the 1962 constitution and dissolving parliament in 1965, promulgated a new constitution in 1972. He continued to rule by decree until June 3, 1977, when the first free elections since 1962 took place. The constitution was revised and approved by referendum in 1992. The National Assembly has 306 seats. Morocco has 14 political parties, 8 of whom are represented in the House of Representatives.

History. Morocco was once the home of the Berbers, who helped the Arabs invade Spain in A.D. 711 and then revolted against them and gradually won control of large areas of Spain for a time after 739.

The country was ruled successively by various native dynasties and maintained regular commercial relations with Europe, even through the 17th and 18th centuries when it was the headquarters of the famous Salé pirates. In the 19th century, there were frequent clashes with the French and Spanish. Finally, in 1904, France and Spain divided Morocco into zones of French and Spanish influence, and these were established as protectorates in 1912.

Meanwhile, Morocco had become the object of big-power rivalry, which almost led to a European war in 1905 when Germany attempted to gain a foothold in the rich mineral country. By terms of the Algeciras Conference (1906), Morocco was internationalized economically, and France's privileges were limited.

The Tangier Statute, concluded by Britain, France, and Spain in 1923, created an international zone at the port of Tangier, permanently neutralized and demilitarized. In World War II, Spain occupied the zone, ostensibly to ensure order, but was forced to withdraw in 1945.

Sultan Mohammed V was deposed by the French in 1953 and replaced by his uncle, but nationalist agitation forced his return in 1955. On his death on Feb. 26, 1961, his son, Hassan, became king.

France and Spain recognized the independence and sovereignty of Morocco in 1956.

In 1975, tens of thousands of Moroccans crossed the border into Spanish Sahara to back their government's contention that the northern part of the territory was historically part of Morocco. At the same time, Mauritania occupied the southern half of the territory in defiance of Spanish threats to resist such a takeover. Abandoning its commitment to self-determination for the territory, Spain withdrew, and only Algeria protested.

When Mauritania signed a peace treaty with the Algerian-backed Polisario Front in August 1979, Morocco occupied and assumed administrative control of the southern part of the Western Sahara, in addition to the northern part it already occupied. Under pressure from other African leaders, Hassan agreed in mid-1981 to a cease-fire with a referendum under international supervision to decide the fate of the Sahara territory, but the referendum was never carried out.

King Hassan became the second Arab leader to meet with an Israeli leader when, on July 21, 1986, Israeli Prime Minister Shimon Peres came to Morocco.

Morocco became the first Arab state to condemn the 1990 Iraqi invasion of Kuwait and promised to send an 1,100-men contingent to Saudi Arabia. Public opinion, however, as evidenced by sanctioned marches in Rabat, mounted against Moroccan involvement and demanded withdrawal from the U.S.-led alliance.

The opposition was victorious in June 1993 parliamentary elections, although observers believed King Hassam's rule was secure owing to the need for a coalition and the limited powers of the Assembly.

In May 1995 the U.N. Security Council extended the mandate for U.N. forces in the Western Sahara by one month. In late June the Polisario rebels pulled out of a U.N.-sponsored voter registration program.

A new non-retroactive law required Arabic or Moroccan names on birth certificates with the stated aim of preventing children from bearing Western names obtained from the entertainment media.

MOZAMBIQUE

Republic of Mozambique
President: Joaquim Chissano (1986)
Prime Minister: Dr. Pascoal Mocumbi (1994)
Area: 303,073 sq mi. (799,380 sq km)
Population (est. 1996): 17,877,927 (average annual rate of natural increase: 2.65%); birth rate: 45.5/1000; infant mortality rate: 125.6/1000; density per square mile: 59
Capital and largest city (1991 est.): Maputo, 931,591.
Monetary unit: Metical. **Languages:** Portuguese (official), Bantu languages. **Religions:** traditional, 60%; Christian, 30%; Islam, 10%. **National name:** República de Moçambique. **Literacy rate:** 33%
Economic summary: Gross domestic product (1994 est.): $10.6 billion; $610 per capita; real growth rate 5.8%; inflation 50%; unemployment (1989 est.) 50%. Arable land: 4%. Principal agricultural products: cotton, cashew nuts, sugar, tea, shrimp. Labor force: 90% in agriculture. Major industrial products: processed

foods, petroleum products, beverages, textiles, tobacco. Natural resources: coal, titanium. Exports: $150 million (f.o.b., 1994 est.): cashew nuts, sugar, shrimp, copra, citrus. Imports: $1.14 billion (c.i.f., 1994 est.) incl. aid: food, clothing, farm equipment, petroleum. Major trading partners: Spain, South Africa, Portugal, U.S., France, U.K., Japan.

Geography. Mozambique stretches for 1,535 miles (2,470 km) along Africa's southeast coast. It is nearly twice the size of California. Tanzania is to the north; Malawi, Zambia, and Zimbabwe to the west; and South Africa and Swaziland to the south.

The country is generally a low-lying plateau broken up by 25 sizable rivers that flow into the Indian Ocean. The largest is the Zambezi, which provides access to central Africa. The principal ports are Maputo, Beira, and Nacala.

Government. After having been under Portuguese colonial rule for 470 years, Mozambique became independent on June 25, 1975. The first president, Samora Moises Machel, headed the National Front for the Liberation of Mozambique (FRELIMO) in its 10-year guerrilla war for independence. He died in a plane crash on Oct. 19, 1986, and was succeeded by his foreign minister, Joaquim Chissano.

History. Mozambique was discovered by Vasco da Gama in 1498, although the Arabs had penetrated into the area as early as the 10th century. It was first colonized in 1505, and by 1510 the Portuguese had control of all the former Arab sultanates on the east African coast.

FRELIMO was organized in 1963. Guerrilla activity had become so extensive by 1973 that Portugal was forced to dispatch 40,000 troops to fight the rebels. A cease-fire was signed in September 1974, when Portugal agreed to grant Mozambique independence.

On Jan. 25, 1985, after a decade of independence, the government was locked in a five-year-old, stalemated, paralyzing war with anti-government guerrillas, known as the MNR, backed by the white minority government in South Africa.

President Chissano decided to abandon Marxism-Leninism in 1989. A new constitution was drafted calling for three branches of government and granting civil liberties.

A cease-fire agreement was signed in October 1992 between the government and the MNR to end 16 years of civil war.

In April 1994 the president announced that a multiparty general election would be held in late October. On the first day of balloting the opposition leader declared that he and his party would boycott the process, but he changed his mind the next day. Although it lost the presidency to the incumbent, the main opposition party made a very respectable showing.

In November 1995 the country became the first non-former British colony to become a member of the British Commonwealth.

MYANMAR

Union of Myanmar
Head of State (Chairman): Senior Gen. Than Shwe (1992)
Area: 261,220 sq mi. (676,560 sq km)
Population (est. 1996): 49,975,625 (average annual rate of natural increase: 1.84%); birth rate: 30/1000; infant mortality rate: 80.7/1000; density per square mile: 191

Capital: Yangon; **Largest cities (est. 1983):** Yangon, 2,458,712; Mandalay, 532,895; **Monetary unit:** Kyat; **Language:** Myanmar, minority languages; **Religions:** Buddhist, 89.5%; Christian, 4.9%; Muslim, 3.8%; Hindu, 0.05%; Animist, 1.3%. **National name:** Pyidaungsu Myanmar Naingngandau; **Literacy rate:** 81%
Economic summary: Gross domestic product (1994 est.): $41.4 billion; $930 per capita; real growth rate 6.4%; inflation 38%. Arable land: 15%. Principal products: oilseed, sugar cane, corn, rice. Labor force (FY89 est.): 16,036,000: 65.2% agriculture, 14.3% industry. Major products: textiles, footwear, processed agricultural products, wood and wood products, refined petroleum. Natural resources: timber, tin, antimony, zinc, copper, precious stones, crude oil and natural gas. Exports (FY93/94 est.): $674 million: rice, teak, oilseeds, metals, rubber, gems. Imports (FY93/94 est.): $1.2 billion: machinery, transportation equipment, chemicals, food products. Major trading partners: Japan, E.U., China, Singapore, Thailand, India, Hong Kong, Malaysia.

Geography. Myanmar occupies the northwest portion of the Indochinese peninsula. India lies to the northwest and China to the northeast. Bangladesh, Laos, and Thailand are also neighbors. The Bay of Bengal touches the southwestern coast.

Slightly smaller than Texas, the country is divided into three natural regions: the Arakan Yoma, a long, narrow mountain range forming the barrier between Myanmar and India; the Shan Plateau in the east, extending southward into Tenasserim; and the Central Basin, running down to the flat fertile delta of the Irrawaddy in the south. This delta contains a network of intercommunicating canals and nine principal river mouths.

Government. A military regime. On March 2, 1962, the government of U Nu was overthrown and replaced by a Revolutionary Council, which assumed all power in the state. Gen. U Ne Win, as chairman of the Revolutionary Council, became the chief executive. In 1972, Ne Win and his colleagues resigned their military titles. In 1974, Ne Win dissolved the Revolutionary Council and became president under the new constitution. He voluntarily relinquished the presidency on Nov. 9, 1981. A military coup led by Gen. Saw Maung overthrew the civilian government in 1988.

In 1989, the military government changed the name of Burma to Myanmar.

On April 23, 1992, Senior Gen. Saw Maung handed over the power to Senior General Than Shwe, who continued to take the responsibility of the chairman of the State Law and Order Restoration Council. The State Law and Order Restoration Council (SLORC) is a military government and is made up of the chairman and 20 other members.

History. In 1612, the British East India Company sent agents to Burma, but the Burmese long resisted efforts of British traders, and Dutch and Portuguese as well, to establish posts on the Bay of Bengal. Through the Anglo-Burmese War in 1824–26 and two following wars, the British East India Company expanded to the whole of Burma by 1886. Burma was annexed to India. It became a separate colony in 1937.

During World War II, Burma was a key battleground: the 800-mile Burma Road was the Allies' vital supply line to China. The Japanese invaded the country in December 1941, and by May 1942 had occupied most of it, cutting off the Burma Road. After one of the most difficult campaigns of the war, Allied forces liberated most of Burma prior to the Japanese surrender in August 1945.

Burma became independent on Jan. 4, 1948. In 1951 and 1952 the Socialists achieved power.

In 1968, after the government had made headway against the Communist and separatist rebels, the military regime adopted a policy of strict nonalignment and followed "the Burmese Way" to socialism. But the insurgents continued to be active.

The civilian government was overthrown in Sept. 1988 by a military junta led by General Saw Maung, an associate of U Ne Win.

The new government held elections in May 1990 and the opposition National League for Democracy won in a landslide despite its leaders being in jail or under house arrest.

Under increasing international pressure and economic failure Saw Maung resigned in April 1992. In September martial law was lifted.

The ruling junta in July 1993 extended the house arrest of Nobel Peace Prize winner Aung San Suu Kyi. She was released on July 10, 1995, after being confined for almost six years.

A new constitution was drafted in 1994 that called for an elected executive branch but appeared designed specifically to forbid Aung San Suu Kyi from becoming president. In May 1996 she opened an opposition congress. Attempting to prevent it, the government arrested hundreds.

NAMIBIA

President: Sam Nujoma (1990)
Status: Independent Country
Area: 318,261 sq mi. (824,296 sq km)
Population (est. 1996): 1,677,243 (average annual growth rate: 2.93%); birth rate: 37.3/1000; infant mortality rate: 47.2/1000; density per square mile: 5
Capital and largest city (est. 1992): Windhoek, 161,000.
Summer capital (est. 1980): Swakopmund, 17,500.
Monetary unit: Namibian dollars. **Languages:** Afrikaans, German, English (official), several indigenous.
Religion: Predominantly Christian. **National name:** Republic of Namibia. **Literacy rate:** 58%
Economic summary: Gross domestic product (1994 est.): $5.8 billion; $3,600 per capita; real growth rate 5.8%; inflation 11%; unemployment (urban areas) 35%. Arable land: 1%. Principal products: corn, millet, sorghum, livestock. Labor force: 500,000; 60% in agriculture, 19% in industry and commerce. Major products: canned meat, dairy products, tanned leather, textiles, clothing. Natural resources: diamonds, copper, lead, zinc, uranium, fish. Exports: $1.3 billion (f.o.b., 1993 est.): diamonds, copper, lead, zinc, beef cattle, karakul pelts, marble, semi-precious stones, uranium, beef, gold. Imports: $1.1 billion (f.o.b., 1993 est.): construction materials, fertilizer, grain, foodstuffs, petroleum products and fuel. Major trading partners: South Africa, France, Germany, Switzerland, U.S., Japan.

Geography. Namibia is bounded on the north by Angola and Zambia, on the east by Botswana, and by South Africa in the south. The Portuguese explorer Bartholomius Diaz was the first European to visit Namibia in the late 15th century. It is for the most part a portion of the high plateau of southern Africa with a general elevation of 3,000 to 4,000 feet.

Government. Namibia became independent in 1990

after its new constitution was ratified. A multi-party democracy with an independent judiciary was established. There is a bicameral legislature consisting of a 26-seat National Council and a 72-seat National Assembly.

History. Formerly called South West Africa, the territory became a German colony in 1884 but was taken by South African forces in 1915, becoming a South African mandate by the terms of the Treaty of Versailles in 1920.

South Africa's application for incorporation of the territory was rejected by the U.N. General Assembly in 1946, and South Africa was invited to prepare a trusteeship agreement instead. By a law passed in 1949, however, the territory was brought into much closer association with South Africa—including representation in its Parliament.

In 1969, South Africa extended its laws to the mandate over the objection of the U.N., particularly its black African members. When South Africa refused to withdraw them, the Security Council condemned it.

Under a 1974 Security Council resolution, South Africa was required to begin the transfer of power to the Namibians by May 30, 1975, or face U.N. action, but 10 days before the deadline Prime Minister Balthazar J. Vorster rejected U.N. supervision. He said, however, that his government was prepared to negotiate Namibian independence, but not with the South West African People's Organization, the principal black separatist group. Meanwhile, the all-white legislature of South West Africa eased several laws on apartheid in public places.

Despite international opposition, the Turnhalle Conference in Windhoek drafted a constitution to organize an interim government based on racial divisions, a proposal overwhelmingly endorsed by white voters in the territory in 1977. At the urging of ambassadors of the five Western members of the Security Council—the U.S., Britain, France, West Germany, and Canada— South Africa on June 11 announced rejection of the Turnhalle constitution and acceptance of the Western proposal to include the South-West Africa People's Organization (SWAPO) in negotiations.

Although negotiations continued between South Africa, the Western powers, neighboring black African states, and internal political groups, there was still no agreement on a final independence plan. A new round of talks aimed at resolving the 18-year-old conflict ended in a stalemate on July 25, 1984.

As policemen wielding riot sticks charged demonstrators in a black, South-West Africa township, South Africa handed over limited powers to a new, multiracial administration in the former German colony on June 17, 1985. Installation of the new government ended South Africa's direct rule, but South Africa retained an effective veto over the new government's decisions along with responsibility for the territory's defense and foreign policy, and South Africa's efforts to quell the insurgents seeking independence continued.

An agreement between South Africa, Angola, and Cuba arranged for elections for a Constituent Assembly in Nov. 1989 to establish a new government. SWAPO won 57% of the vote, a majority but not enough to take a constitution unilaterally. In February 1990, SWAPO leader Sam Nujoma was elected president and took office when Namibia became independent on March 21, 1990.

SWAPO received a commanding vote in the December 1992 regional and local elections. The Namibian dollar was introduced in September 1993.

In December 1994 elections SWAPO obtained an overwhelming mandate, winning not only the presidency again for the incumbent but also absolute control of the parliament. Dissidents within SWAPO in May 1995 broke away to found a new party.

NAURU

Republic of Nauru
President: Lagumot Harris
Area: 8.2 sq mi. (21 sq km)
Population (est. 1996): 10,273; average annual growth rate: 1.29%; birth rate 18/1000; infant mortality rate 40.6/1000 (1995 est.); density per square mile: 1,252
Capital (1983): Yaren, 559; **Monetary unit:** Australian dollar. **Languages:** Nauruan and English. **Religions:** Protestant, 58%; Roman Catholic, 24%; Confucian and Taoist, 8%. **Special relationship within the Commonwealth of Nations. Literacy rate:** 99%
Economic summary: Gross national product (1993 est.): $100 million; $10,000 per capita. Major industrial products: phosphates. Natural resources: phosphates. Exports: $93 million (f.o.b., 1984): phosphates. Imports: $73 million (c.i.f., 1984): foodstuffs, fuel, machinery. Major trading partners: Australia, New Zealand, U.K., Japan.

Geography. Nauru (pronounced NAH oo roo) is an island in the Pacific just south of the equator, about 2,500 miles (4,023 km) southwest of Honolulu.

Government. Legislative power is invested in a popularly elected 18-member parliament, which elects the president from among its members. Executive power rests with the president, who is assisted by a five-member cabinet.

History. Nauru was annexed by Germany in 1888. It was placed under joint Australian, New Zealand, and British mandate after World War I, and in 1947 it became a U.N. trusteeship administered by the same three powers. On Jan. 31, 1968, Nauru became an independent republic.

In elections on December 9, 1989, Bernard Dowiyogo was elected and took office three days later.

In 1993 Australia offered an out-of-court settlement for damages Nauru presented to the International Court of Justice because of phosphate mining. Australia agreed to pay $2.5 million Australian dollars for 20 years, and New Zealand and the U.K. additionally agreed to pay a one-time settlement of $12 million each. The incumbent president Bernard Dowiyogo lost his bid for reelection in November 1995.

NEPAL

Kingdom of Nepal
Ruler: King Birendra Bir Bikram Shah Dev (1972)
Prime Minister: Sher Bahadur Deuba (1995)
Area: 54,463 sq mi. (141,059 sq km)
Population (est. 1996): 22,094,033 (average annual rate of natural growth: 2.44%); birth rate: 37/1000; infant mortality rate: 79/1000; density per square mile: 405
Capital and largest city (1993): Kathmandu, 535,000; Other large cities: Lalitpur, 190,000; Biratnagar, 132,000. **Monetary unit:** Nepalese rupee. **Languages:** Nepali (official), Newari, Bhutia, Maithali. **Religions:** Hindu, 90%; Buddhist, 5%; Islam, 3%. **Literacy rate:** 36%
Economic summary: Gross domestic product (1994 est.): $22.4 billion; $1,060 per capita; real growth rate 5%; inflation (June 94) 9.6%; unemployment n.a.. Arable land: 17%. Labor force: 4,100,000. Principal products: rice, maize, wheat, millet, jute, sugar cane, oilseed, potatoes. Agriculture is the mainstay of the economy, accounting for 60% of the GDP and 90% of the work force. Major products: sugar, textiles, jute, cigarettes, cement. Natural resources: water, timber, hydroelectric potential. Exports: $593 million (f.o.b., 1993, does not include unrecorded border trade with India): clothing, carpets, leather goods, grain. Imports: $899 million (c.i.f., 1993): petroleum products, fertilizer, machinery. Major trading partners: India, U.S., Germany, Singapore, U.K., Japan.

Geography. A landlocked country the size of Arkansas, lying between India and the Tibetan Autonomous Region of China, Nepal contains Mount Everest (29,108 ft; 8,872 m), the tallest mountain in the world. Along its southern border, Nepal has a strip of level land that is partly forested, partly cultivated. North of that is the slope of the main section of the Himalayan range, including Everest and many other peaks higher than 20,000 feet (6,096 m).

Government. In November, 1990, King Birendra promulgated a new constitution and introduced a multiparty democracy in Nepal. In the general elections held in November 1994, the Nepal Communist Party (NML) emerged as the single largest party, with 88 seats, and formed a minority government headed by Prime Minister Man Mohan Adhikari on Nov. 30, 1994. Parliament consists of two houses: the higher with 60 members and a lower house with 205.

History. The Kingdom of Nepal was unified in 1768 by King Prithwi Narayan Shah. A commercial treaty was signed with Britain in 1792, and in 1816, after more than a year's hostilities, the Nepalese agreed to allow British residents to live in Katmandu, the capital. In 1923, Britain recognized the absolute independence of Nepal. Between 1846 and 1951, the country was ruled by the Rana family, which always held the office of prime minister. In 1951, however, the king took over all power and proclaimed a constitutional monarchy.

Mahendra Bir Bikram Shah became king in 1955. After Mahendra, who had ruled since 1955, died of a heart attack in 1972, Prince Birendra, at 26, succeeded to the throne.

In the first election in 22 years, on May 2, 1980, voters approved the continued autocratic rule by the king with the advice of a partyless Parliament.

In 1990, a pro-democracy movement forced King Birendra to lift the ban on political parties and appoint an opposition leader to head an interim government as prime minister.

The first free election in three decades provided a victory for the liberal Nepali Congress Party in 1991, although the Communists made a strong showing.

Parliamentary elections held in November 1994 placed the Communists in control of 88 seats in the House of Representatives. The Communist leader became prime minister later that month.

In June 1995 the king dissolved parliament and ordered new elections. Two opposition parties contested that decision, and the Supreme Court agreed. The leader of the Congress Party became prime minister, forming a coalition government with the National Democratic Party.

THE NETHERLANDS

Kingdom of the Netherlands
Sovereign: Queen Beatrix (1980)
Premier: Win Kok (1994)
Area: 16,033 sq mi. (41,526 sq km)
Population (est. 1996): 15,531,940 (average annual rate of natural increase: 0.37%); birth rate: 12.2/1000; infant mortality rate: 5.9/1000; density per square mile: 968
Capital and largest city (1994 est.): Amsterdam, 724,096; **Other large cities (est. 1994):** Rotterdam, 598,521; The Hague (seat of government), 445,279; Utrecht, 234,106; Eindhoven, 196,130. **Monetary unit:** Guilder. **Language:** Dutch. **Religions:** Roman Catholic, 36%; Protestant, 27%; other, 4%; unaffiliated, 33%. **National name:** Koninkrijk der Nederlanden. **Literacy rate:** 99%
Economic summary: Gross domestic product (1994 est.): $275.8 billion; $17,940 per capita; real growth rate 2%; inflation 2.5% (Dec. 94); unemployment 8.8% (Dec. 94). Arable land; 25%. Principal products: wheat, barley, sugar beets, potatoes, meat and dairy products. Labor force: 6,955,000; 50.1% in services, 28.2% in manufacturing and construction. Major products: metal fabrication, electrical machinery and equipment, chemicals, electronic equipment, petroleum, fishing. Exports: $153 billion (f.o.b., 1994 est.): foodstuffs, natural gas, chemicals, metal products, textiles, tobacco, agricultural products. Imports: $137 billion (f.o.b., 1994 est.): raw materials, consumer goods, transportation equipment, food products, crude petroleum. Major trading partners: Germany, Belgium–Luxembourg, France, U.K., U.S.

Geography. The Netherlands, on the coast of the North Sea, has Germany to the east and Belgium to the south. It is twice the size of New Jersey.

Part of the great plain of north and west Europe, the Netherlands has maximum dimensions of 190 by 160 miles (360 by 257 km) and is low and flat except in Limburg in the southeast, where some hills rise to 300 feet (92 m). About half the country's area is below sea level, making the famous Dutch dikes a requisite to the use of much land. Reclamation of land from the sea through dikes has continued through recent times.

All drainage reaches the North Sea, and the principal rivers—Rhine, Maas (Meuse), and Schelde—have their sources outside the country. The Rhine is the most heavily used waterway in Europe.

Government. The Netherlands and its former colony, the Netherlands Antilles form the Kingdom of the Netherlands.

The Netherlands is a constitutional monarchy with a bicameral parliament. The Upper Chamber has 75 members elected for six years by representative bodies of the provinces, half of the members retiring every three years. The Lower Chamber has 150 members elected by universal suffrage for four years. The two chambers have the right of investigation and interpellation; the Lower Chamber can initiate legislation and amend bills.

The Sovereign, Queen Beatrix Wilhelmina Armgard, born Jan. 31, 1938, was married on March 10, 1966, to Claus von Amsberg, a former West German diplomat. The marriage drew public criticism because of the bridegroom's service in the German army during World War II. In 1967, Beatrix gave birth to a son, Willem-Alexander Claus George Ferdinand, the first male heir to the throne since 1884. She also has two other sons, Johan Friso Bernhard Christian David, born in 1968, and Constantijn Christof Frederik Aschwin, born the next year.

History. Julius Caesar found the low-lying Netherlands inhabited by Germanic tribes—the Nervii, Frisii, and Batavi. The Batavi on the Roman frontier did not submit to Rome's rule until 13 B.C., and then only as allies.

A part of Charlemagne's empire in the 8th and 9th centuries A.D., the area later passed into the hands of Burgundy and the Austrian Hapsburgs, and finally in the 16th century came under Spanish rule.

When Philip II of Spain suppressed political liberties and the growing Protestant movement in the Netherlands, a revolt led by William of Orange broke out in 1568. Under the Union of Utrecht (1579), the seven northern provinces became the Republic of the United Netherlands.

The Dutch East India Company was established in 1602, and by the end of the 17th century Holland was one of the great sea and colonial powers of Europe.

The nation's independence was not completely established until after the Thirty Years' War (1618–48), after which the country's rise as a commercial and maritime power began. In 1814, all the provinces of Holland and Belgium were merged into one kingdom, but in 1830 the southern provinces broke away to form the Kingdom of Belgium. A liberal constitution was adopted by the Netherlands in 1848.

In spite of its neutrality in World War II, the Netherlands was invaded by the Nazis in May 1940, and the East Indies were later taken by the Japanese. The nation was liberated in May 1945. In 1948, after a reign of 50 years, Queen Wilhelmina resigned and was succeeded by her daughter Juliana.

In 1949, after a four-year war, the Netherlands granted independence to the East Indies, which became the Republic of Indonesia. In 1963, it turned over the western half of New Guinea to the new nation, ending 300 years of Dutch presence in Asia. Attainment of independence by Suriname on Nov. 25, 1975, left the Dutch Antilles as the Netherlands' only overseas territory.

Prime Minister Van Agt lost his narrow majority in elections on May 26, 1981, in which the major issue was the deployment of U.S. cruise missiles on Dutch soil. Van Agt lost his centrist coalition in May 1982 in a dispute over economic policy, and was succeeded by Ruud Lubbers as premier.

A general election in May 1994 resulted in the ruling coalition of the Christian Democratic and Labor Parties losing a third of its legislative seats. Nevertheless Labor became the largest party in Parliament. The Christian Democratic Party leader attempted in vain to form a government. In August the Laborite leader succeeded in forming a cabinet without a single Christian Democratic member.

Severe flooding occurred in January–February 1995 along the banks of several rivers, and large areas had to be evacuated due to burst dikes. Provincial legislative elections in May saw a further decline in the fortunes of the Christian Democrats.

Netherlands Autonomous Countries

NETHERLANDS ANTILLES

Status: Part of the Kingdom of the Netherlands
Governor: Mr. J. M. Saleh (1990)
Premier: Mingull A. Pourier
Area: 313 sq mi. (800 sq km)
Population (est. 1996): 208,968 (average annual growth rate: 1.07%); birth rate: 16/1000; infant mortality rate: 8.9/1000; density per square mile: 667
Capital and largest city (est. 1993): Willemstad, 197,019.
Literacy rate: 95%

Economic summary: Gross domestic product (1993 est.): $1.85 billion; $10,000 per capita; real growth rate 1.8%; inflation 1.5% (1994 est.); unemployment 13.4%. Arable land: 8%. Principal agricultural products: aloes, sorghum, peanuts. Labor force: 89,000; 28% industry and commerce (1983). Major industries: oil refining, tourism. Natural resource: phosphate. Export: $240 million (f.o.b. 1993): petroleum products. Imports: $1.2 billion (f.o.b. 1993): crude petroleum, food. Major trading partners: U.S., Venezuela, Netherlands, U.K., Guadeloupe.

Geography. The Netherlands Antilles comprise two groups of Caribbean islands 500 miles (805 km) apart: one, about 40 miles (64 km) off the Venezuelan coast, consists of Curaçao (173 sq mi.; 448 sq km); Bonaire (95 sq mi.; 246 sq km), the other, lying to the northeast, consists of three small islands with a total area of 34 square miles (88 sq km).

Government. There is a constitutional government formed by the governor and cabinet and an elected Legislative Council. The area has complete autonomy in domestic affairs.

ARUBA

Status: Part of the Kingdom of the Netherlands
Governor: Olindo Koolman (1992)
Prime Minister: Henny Eman (1994)
Area: 75 sq mi. (193 sq km)
Population: (est. 1996): 66,404; growth rate 0.8%; birth rate: 14.2/1000; infant mortality rate 8..2/1000; density per square mile: 885
Capital and largest city: (1991 est.): Oranjestad, 20,050; **Literacy rate:** 95%
Economic summary: Gross domestic product (1993 est.): $1.2 billion; $17,400 per capita; real growth rate 5%; inflation 6.5%; unemployment 0.6% (1992). Little agriculture. Major industries: tourism, light manufacturing (tobacco, beverages, consumer goods). Exports: $1.3 billion (f.o.b., 1993): mostly petroleum products. Imports: $1.6 billion (f.o.b., 1993): food, consumer goods, manufactures. Major trading partners: U.S., E.C.

Geography. Aruba, an island slightly larger than Washington D.C., lies 18 miles (28.9 km) off the coast of Venezuela in the southern Caribbean.

Government. The governmental structure comprises the Governor, appointed by the Queen for a term of six years; the Legislature, consisting of 21 members elected by universal suffrage for terms not exceeding four years; and the Council of Ministers, presided over by the Prime Minister, which holds executive power.

NEW ZEALAND

Sovereign: Queen Elizabeth II
Governor-General: Sir Michael Hardie Boyes (1996)
Prime Minister: Rt. Hon. James Brendan Bolger
Area: 103,884 sq mi. (270,534 sq km) (excluding dependencies)
Population (est. 1996): 3,547,983 (average annual growth rate: 0.81%); birth rate: 15.8/1000; infant mortality rate: 6.7/1000; density per square mile: 34

Capital: Wellington; **Largest cities (est. 1995):** Auckland, 952,600; Wellington, 331,100; Christchurch, 324,400.
Monetary unit: New Zealand dollar. **Languages:** English, Maori. **Religions:** Christian, 81%; none or unspecified, 18%; Hindu, Confucian, and other, 1%. **Member of Commonwealth of Nations. Literacy rate:** 99%
Economic summary: Gross domestic product (1995): $52 billion; $14,400 per capita; real growth rate 2.5%; inflation 4.6%; unemployment 6.3%. Arable land: 2%. Principal products: wool, meat, dairy products, livestock. Labor force (1995): 1,730,000; services 67.4%; manufacturing 19.8%. Major products: processed foods, textiles, machinery, transport equipment, wood and paper products, financial services. Natural resources: forests, natural gas, iron ore, coal, gold. Exports: $16 billion (1995): meat, dairy products, wool. Imports: $16 billion (1995): consumer goods, petroleum, motor vehicles, industrial equipment. Major trading partners: Japan, Australia, E.U., U.S., China, South Korea, Taiwan.

Geography. New Zealand, about 1,250 miles (2,012 km) southeast of Australia, consists of two main islands and a number of smaller, outlying islands so scattered that they range from the tropical to the antarctic. The country is the size of Colorado.

New Zealand's two main components are North Island and South Island, separated by Cook Strait, which varies from 16 to 190 miles (26 to 396 km) in width. North Island (44,281 sq mi.; 115,777 sq km) is 515 miles (829 km) long and volcanic in its south-central part. This area contains many hot springs and beautiful geysers. South Island (58,093 sq mi.; 151,215 sq km) has the Southern Alps along its west coast, with Mount Cook (12,283.3 ft; 3,754 m) the highest point.

The largest of the outlying islands are the Auckland Islands (234 sq mi.; 606 sq km), Campbell Island (44 sq mi.; 114 sq km), the Antipodes Islands (24 sq mi.; 62 sq km), and the Kermadec Islands (13 sq mi.; 34 sq km).

Government. New Zealand was granted self-government in 1852, a full parliamentary system and ministries in 1856, and dominion status in 1907. The Queen is represented by the Governor-General, and the Cabinet is responsible to a unicameral Parliament of 99 members who are elected by popular vote for three years.

New Zealand voted in a referendum (1993) for the mixed member system of proportional representation which will replace the present system in the 1996 general election.

History. New Zealand was discovered and named in 1642 by Abel Tasman, a Dutch navigator. Captain James Cook explored the islands in 1769. In 1840, Britain formally annexed them.

From the first, the country has been in the forefront in instituting social welfare legislation. It adopted old age pensions (1898); a national child welfare program (1907); social security for the aged, widows, and orphans, along with family benefit payments; minimum wages; a 40-hour week and unemployment and health insurance (1938); and socialized medicine (1941).

The outcome of the November 1993 general election resulted in the governing National Party winning a bare majority of 50 seats to Labour's 45. Political maneuvering in 1994 kept the National Party with a majority despite anxious by-elections.

In February 1996 the National Party, now with a minority in Parliament, formed a coalition government with the United Party.

Cook Islands and Overseas Territories

The Cook Islands (93 sq mi.; 241 sq km) were placed under New Zealand administration in 1901. They achieved self-governing status in association with New Zealand in 1965. **Population (1996 est.):** 19,561; growth rate 1.77%; birth rate: 22.9/1000; infant mortality rate: 24.7/1000; density per square mile: 210. The seat of government is on Rarotonga Island.

Economic summary: Gross domestic product (1993 est.): $57 million; $3,000 per capita. Exports: $3.4 million (f.o.b., 1990): citrus juice, clothing, canned fruit, and pineapple juice. Imports: $50 million (c.i.f., 1990): foodstuffs, textiles, fuels, timber. Nearly all of the trade is with New Zealand, some with Japan, Australia, and U.S.

Niue (100 sq mi.; 259 sq km) was formerly administered as part of the Cook Islands. It was placed under separate New Zealand administration in 1901 and achieved self-governing status in association with New Zealand in 1974. The capital is Alofi. **Population (July 1995 est.):** 1,837; growth rate: –3.66%.

Economic summary: Gross national product (1993 est.): $2.4 million; per capita, $1,200. Exports: $117,500 (f.o.b., 1989): canned coconut cream, copra, honey, passion fruit products, pawpaw, root crops, limes, footballs, stamps, handicrafts. Imports: $4.1 million (c.i.f., 1989): food, live animals, manufactured goods, machinery, fuels, chemicals, lubricants, drugs. Major trading partners: New Zealand, 59%; Fiji, 20%; Japan, 13%.

The Ross Dependency (160,000 sq mi.; 414,400 sq km), an Antarctic region, was placed under New Zealand administration in 1923.

Tokelau (4 sq mi.; 10 sq km) was formerly administered as part of the Gilbert and Ellice Islands colony. It was placed under New Zealand administration in 1925. Its population is 1,503 (July 1995 est.).

NICARAGUA

Republic of Nicaragua
President: Violeta Barrios de Chamorro (1990)
Area: 50,180 sq mi. (130,000 sq km)
Population (est. 1996): 4,272,352 (average annual rate of natural increase: 2.8%); birth rate: 33.8/1000; infant mortality rate: 45.8/1000; density per sq mi.: 85
Capital and largest city (est. 1992): Managua, 974,000.
Monetary unit: Cordoba. **Language:** Spanish. **Religion:** Roman Catholic, 95%; Protestant, 5%. **National name:** República de Nicaragua. **Literacy rate:** 57%
Economic summary: Gross domestic product (1995): $6.4 billion (1993); $1,570 per capita (1994); real growth rate 4%; inflation 10%; unemployment 20.2%. Arable land: 9%. Principal products: coffee, sugar cane, corn, beans, cattle. Labor force: 1,459,000 (1995); 13% in industry (1986). Major products: processed foods, chemicals, metal products, clothing and textiles, beverages, footwear. Natural resources: timber, fisheries, gold, silver, copper, tungsten, lead, zinc. Exports: $470 million (1995): coffee, cotton, seafood, bananas, sugar, meat, chemicals. Imports: $861 million (1995): machinery, chemicals, food, clothing, petroleum. Major trading partners: E.U., U.S., Japan, Costa Rica, El Salvador, Mexico, Venezuela, Guatemala.

Geography. Largest but most sparsely populated of the Central American nations, Nicaragua borders on Honduras to the north and Costa Rica to the south. It is slightly larger than New York State.

Nicaragua is mountainous in the west, with fertile valleys. A plateau slopes eastward toward the Caribbean. Two big lakes—Nicaragua, about 100 miles long (161 km), and Managua, about 38 miles long (61 km)—are connected by the Tipitapa River. The Pacific coast is volcanic and very fertile. The Caribbean coast, swampy and indented, is aptly called the "Mosquito Coast."

Government. A republic. The president is chief of state and head of government. The National Assembly is the legislative branch.

History. Nicaragua, which established independence in 1838, was first visited by the Spaniards in 1522. The chief of the country's leading Indian tribe at that time was called Nicaragua, from whom the nation derived its name. A U.S. naval force intervened in 1909 after two American citizens had been executed, and a few U.S. Marines were kept in the country from 1912 to 1925. The Bryan-Chamorro Treaty of 1916 (terminated in 1970) gave the U.S. an option on a canal route through Nicaragua, and naval bases. Disorder after the 1924 elections brought in the Marines again.

A guerrilla leader, Gen. César Augusto Sandino, began fighting the occupation force in 1927. He fought the U.S. troops until their withdrawal in 1933. Gen. Anastasio Somoza García emerged and ruled as dictator from 1936 until his assassination in 1956. He was succeeded by his son Luis, who alternated with trusted family friends in the presidency until his death in 1967. Another son, Maj. Gen. Anastasio Somoza Debayle, became president in 1967.

Sandinista guerrillas, leftists who took their name from Gen. Sandino, launched an offensive in May 1979. After seven weeks of fighting, Somoza fled the country on July 17, 1979. The Sandinistas assumed power on July 19, promising to maintain a mixed economy, a non-aligned foreign policy, and a pluralist political system.

On Jan. 23, 1981, the Reagan Administration suspended U.S. aid, charging that Nicaragua, with the aid of Cuba and the Soviet Union, was supplying arms to rebels in El Salvador. The Sandinistas denied the charges. Later that year, Nicaraguan guerrillas, known as "contras," began a war to overthrow the Sandinistas.

The elections were finally held on Nov. 4, 1984, with Daniel Ortega Saavedra, the Sandinista junta coordinator, winning 63% of the votes cast for President. He began a six-year term on Jan. 10, 1985.

The war intensified in 1986–87, with the re-supplied contras establishing themselves inside the country. Negotiations sponsored by the Contadora (neutral Latin American) nations foundered, but a peace plan sponsored by Arias, the Costa Rican president, led to a treaty, signed by the Central American leaders in August 1987, that called for an end to outside aid to guerrillas and negotiations between hostile parties.

In 1989, an accord established a one-year advance in general elections to Feb. 1990.

Violetta Chamorro, owner of the opposition paper *La Prensa*, led a broad anti-Sandinista coalition to victory in the presidential and legislative elections, ending 11 years of Sandinista rule.

After a year in office Pres. Chamorro found herself besieged. Business groups were dissatisfied with the pace of reforms; Sandinistas, upset with what they regarded as the dismantling of their earlier achievements, threatened to take up arms again. In Feb. 1991 the president brought the military under her direct command.

In February 1995 the Sandinista military leader Humberto Ortego stepped down, marking the first peaceful transfer of that position in the country's history. Nevertheless, the president and the Assembly continued their bitter quarrel, this time over rival constitutions. Finally in June the president agreed to a new package that would bolster the legislative branch at the expense of the executive.

The presidential candidacy of Chamorro's son-in-law, Antonio Lacayo, aroused legal debates in early 1996, since the constitution forbids close relatives of a current president from seeking the office.

NIGER

Republic of Niger
Head of State: Col. Ibrahim Mainassara Bare (1996)
Prime Minister: Boukary Adfi (1996)
Area: 489,206 sq mi. (1,267,044 sq km)
Population (est. 1996): 9,113,001 (average annual rate of natural increase: 2.9%); birth rate: 54.5/1000; infant mortality rate: 117.6/1000; density per square mile: 18
Capital and largest city (1988): Niamey, 398,265; **Other large cities:** Zinder, 120,900; Maradi, 112,970; **Monetary unit:** Franc CFA; **Ethnic groups:** Hausa, 54%; Djerma and Songhai, 24%; Peul, 11%; **Languages:** French (official); Hausa, Songhai; Arabic; **Religions:** Islam, 80%; Animist and Christian, 20%; **National name:** République du Niger; **Literacy rate:** 28%
Economic summary: Gross domestic product (1993 est.): $4.6 billion; $550 per capita (1994); real growth rate 1.4%; inflation: n.a. Arable land: 3%. Principal products: peanuts, cotton, livestock, millet, sorghum, cassava, rice. Labor force: 2,500,000 (1982); 90% in agriculture. Major industrial products: uranium, cement, bricks, light industrial products. Natural resources: uranium, coal, iron ore, tin, phosphates. Exports: $246 million (f.o.b., 1993 est.): uranium, cowpeas, livestock, hides, skins. Imports: $286 million (c.i.f., 1993 est.): fuels, machinery, transport equipment, foodstuffs, consumer goods, pharmaceuticals, chemical products. Major trading partners: France, Nigeria, Algeria, U.S., Italy, Côte d'Ivoire, Germany.

Geography. Niger, in West Africa's Sahara region, is four-fifths the size of Alaska. It is surrounded by Mali, Algeria, Libya, Chad, Nigeria, Benin, and Burkina Faso.

The Niger River in the southwest flows through the country's only fertile area. Elsewhere the land is semiarid.

Government. Niger held its first democratic elections in April 1993 and formed a new coalition government on April 23, 1993. Political parties and the constitution were suspended after a coup on Jan. 27, 1996, led by Col. Mainassara. He promised new elections in July and a return to democratic rule. However, when he was declared winner of the new elections on July 10, he banned opposition parties.

History. Niger was incorporated into French West Africa in 1896. There were frequent rebellions, but when order was restored in 1922, the French made the area a colony. In 1958, the voters approved the French constitution and voted to make the territory an autonomous republic within the French Community. The republic adopted a constitution in 1959 and the next year withdrew from the Community, proclaiming its independence.

The 1974 army coup ousted President Hamani Diori, who had held office since 1960. An estimated 2 million people were starving in Niger, but 200,000 tons of imported food, half U.S.-supplied, substantially ended famine conditions by the year's end. The new president, Lt. Col. Seyni Kountché, chief of staff of the army, installed a 12-man military government. A predominantly civilian government was formed by Kountché in 1976.

The country's first multiparty election in February 1993 resulted in the need for a runoff for the presidency in March. Ousmane Mahamane, the candidate of the biggest opposition party, won.

In January 1996 a coup deposed the country's first democratically elected president. The constitution was suspended and the president arrested. In July the military leader of the coup was declared the winner of a presidential election by a commission he established after removing the independent commission during the balloting.

NIGERIA

Federal Republic of Nigeria
Head of State: Gen. Sani Abacha (1993)
Area: 356,700 sq mi. (923,853 sq km)
Population (est. 1996): 103,912,489; average annual rate of natural increase: 3.0%; birth rate: 42.9/1000; infant mortality rate: 72.4/1000; density per square mile: 291
Capital (1995 est.): Abuja, 339,100; **Other large cities:** Lagos, 1,484,000; Ibadan, 1,365,000; Ogbomosho, 711,900; Kano, 657,300. **Monetary unit:** Naira. **Languages:** English (official) Hausa, Yoruba, Ibo. **Religions:** Islam, 50%; Christian, 40%; indigenous, 10%. **Member of Commonwealth of Nations. Literacy rate:** 51%
Economic summary: Gross domestic product (1994 est.): $122.6 billion; $1,250 per capita; real growth rate –0.8%; inflation 53% (1993 est.); unemployment 28%. (1992 est.) Arable land: 31%. Principal products: peanuts, rubber, cocoa, grains, fish, yams, cassava, livestock. Labor force (1985): 42,844,000, 54% in agriculture; 15% in government; 19% in industry, commerce, and services. Major products: crude oil, natural gas, coal, tin, processed rubber, cotton, petroleum, hides, textiles, cement, chemicals. Natural resources: petroleum, tin, columbite, iron ore, coal, limestone, lead. Exports: $11.9 billion (f.o.b., 1992): oil, cocoa, palm products, rubber. Imports: $8.3 billion (c.i.f., 1992): consumer goods, capital equipment, raw materials, chemicals. Major trading partners: Western European countries, U.S., Japan

Geography. Nigeria, one-third larger than Texas and black Africa's most populous nation, is situated on the Gulf of Guinea in West Africa. Its neighbors are Benin, Niger, Cameroon, and Chad.

The lower course of the Niger River flows south through the western part of the country into the Gulf of Guinea. Swamps and mangrove forests border the southern coast; inland are hardwood forests.

Government. A military government since Dec. 31, 1983. The government annulled the results of the June 12, 1993, presidential election and suspended the return to civilian rule. Gen. Sani Abacha declared himself ruler in November 1993.

History. Between 1879 and 1914, private colonial developments by the British, with reorganizations of the Crown's interest in the region, resulted in the formation of Nigeria as it exists today. During World War I, native troops of the West African frontier force joined with French forces to defeat the German garrison in the Cameroons.

Nigeria became independent on Oct. 1, 1960. Organized as a loose federation of self-governing states, the independent nation faced an overwhelming task of unifying a country with 250 ethnic and linguistic groups.

Rioting broke out in 1966, the military commander was seized, and Col. Yakubu Gowon took power. Also in that year, the Moslem Hausas in the north massacred the predominantly Christian Ibos in the east, many of whom had been driven from the north. Thousands of Ibos took refuge in the Eastern Region, which declared its independence as the Republic of Biafra on May 30, 1967. Civil war broke out.

In January 1970, after 31 months of civil war, Biafra surrendered to the federal government.

Gowon's nine-year rule was ended in 1975 by a bloodless coup that made Army Brigadier Muritala Rufai Mohammed the new chief of state. The return of civilian leadership was established with the election of Alhaji Shehu Shagari, as president in 1979.

A coup on December 31, 1983, restored military rule. The military regime headed by Maj. Gen. Mohammed Buhari was overthrown in a bloodless coup on Aug. 27, 1985, led by Maj. Gen. Ibrahim Babangida, who proclaimed himself president.

The presidential election of June 1993 was almost immediately voided by the government. Nevertheless, Babangida resigned as president in August. In November the military, headed by defense minister Sani Abacha, seized power again. A constitutional conference, called in 1994 after violent political protests against the military government, set January 1, 1995, as the deadline for a return to civilian rule. The government, however, did not step aside. In June 1995 a two-year ban on political parties was lifted. In an October speech Gen. Abacha said that democracy would have to wait three years.

NORWAY

Kingdom of Norway

Sovereign: King Harald V (1991)
Prime Minister: Gro Harlem Brundtland (1991)
Area: 125,049 sq mi. (323,877 sq km)
Population (est. 1996): 4,345,941 (average annual growth rate: 0.21%); birth rate: 12.4/1000; infant mortality rate: 6/1000; density per square mile: 34
Capital and largest city (1995): Oslo, 483,401; Other large cities: Bergen, 221,717; Trondheim, 142,927; Stavanger, 103,496. **Monetary unit:** Krone. **Language:** Norwegian. **Religion:** Evangelical Lutheran (state), 94%; other Protestant and Roman Catholic, 4%. **National name:** Kongeriket Norge. **Literacy rate:** 100%
Economic summary: Gross domestic product (1994 est.): $95.7 billion; $22,170 per capita; real growth rate 5.5%; inflation 1.3%; unemployment 8.4%. Labor force (1994): 2,151,000: services, 34.7%; commerce, 18%; mining and manufacturing, 16.6%:. Arable land: 3%. Principal products: dairy products, livestock, grain, potatoes, furs, wool. Major products: oil and gas, fish, pulp and paper, ships, aluminum, iron, steel, nickel, fertilizers, transportation equipment, hydroelectric power, petrochemicals. Natural resources: fish, timber, hydroelectric power, ores, oil, gas. Exports: $36.6 billion (f.o.b., 1994): oil, natural gas, fish products, ships, pulp and paper, aluminum. Imports: $29.3 billion (c.i.f., 1994): machinery, fuels and lubricants, transportation equipment, chemicals, foodstuffs, and clothing. Major trading partners: U.K., Sweden, Germany, U.S., Denmark, Netherlands, Japan.

Geography. Norway is situated in the western part of the Scandinavian peninsula. It extends about 1,100 miles (1,770 km) from the North Sea along the Norwegian Sea to more than 300 miles (483 km) above the Arctic Circle, the farthest north of any European country. It is slightly larger than New Mexico. Sweden borders on most of the eastern frontier, with Finland and the U.S.S.R. in the northeast.

Nearly 70% of Norway is uninhabitable and covered by mountains, glaciers, moors, and rivers. The hundreds of deep fiords that cut into the coastline give Norway an overall oceanfront of more than 12,000 miles (19,312 km). Nearly 50,000 islands off the coast form a breakwater and make a safe coastal shipping channel.

Government. Norway is a constitutional hereditary monarchy. Executive power is vested in the king together with a cabinet, or Council of State, consisting of a prime minister and at least seven other members. The Storting, or parliament, is composed of 165 members elected by the people under proportional representation. The Storting discusses and votes on political and financial questions, but divides itself into two sections (Lagting and Odelsting) to discuss and pass on legislative matters. The king cannot dissolve the Storting before the expiration of its term.

The sovereign is Harald V, born in 1937, son of Olav V and Princess Martha of Sweden. He succeeded to the throne upon the death of his father in January 1991. He married Sonja Haraldsen, a daughter of a merchant, in 1968.

History. Norwegians, like the Danes and Swedes, are of Teutonic origin. The Norsemen, also known as Vikings, ravaged the coasts of northwestern Europe from the 8th to the 11th century.

In 1815, Norway fell under the control of Sweden. The union of Norway, inhabited by fishermen, sailors, merchants, and peasants, and Sweden, an aristocratic country of large estates and tenant farmers, was not a happy one, but it lasted for nearly a century. In 1905, the Norwegian parliament arranged a peaceful separation and invited a Danish prince to the Norwegian throne—King Haakon VII. A treaty with Sweden provided that all disputes be settled by arbitration and that no fortifications be erected on the common frontier.

When World War I broke out, Norway joined with Sweden and Denmark in a decision to remain neutral and to cooperate in the joint interest of the three countries. In World War II, Norway was invaded by the Germans on April 9, 1940. It resisted for two months before the Nazis took over complete control. King Haakon and his government fled to London, where they established a government-in-exile. Maj. Vidkun Quisling, whose name is now synonymous with traitor or fifth columnist, was the most notorious Norwegian collaborator with the Nazis. He was executed by the Norwegians on Oct. 24, 1945.

Despite severe losses in the war, Norway recovered quickly. The country led the world in social experimentation. It entered the North Atlantic Treaty Organization in 1949.

The Conservative government of Jan Syse resigned in October 1990 over the issue of Norway's future relationship to the E.C. A minority Labor government headed by Gro Brundtland was installed a few days later.

In an advisory referendum held in November 1994 voters rejected seeking membership for their nation in the European Union.

The political arena remained quiet in 1995, but the economy continued in robust condition. The country became the second largest net oil exporter after Saudi Arabia that year.

Dependencies of Norway

Svalbard (24,208 sq mi.; 62,700 sq km), in the Arctic Ocean about 360 miles north of Norway, consists of the Spitsbergen group and several smaller islands, including Bear Island, Hope Island, King Charles Land, and White Island (or Gillis Land). The capital is Longyearbyen. It came under Norwegian administration in 1925. Population (July 1995 est.): 2,914; growth rate –3.5%. Coal mining is major economic activity. There is also some trapping of seal, polar bear, fox, and walrus.

Bouvet Island (23 sq mi.; 60 sq km), in the South Atlantic about 1,600 miles south-southwest of the Cape of Good Hope, came under Norwegian administration in 1928. It is uninhabited.

Jan Mayen Island (147 sq mi.; 380 sq km), in the Arctic Ocean between Norway and Greenland, came under Norwegian administration in 1929. There are no permanent inhabitants.

Peter I Island (96 sq mi.; 249 sq km), lying off Antarctica in the Bellinghausen Sea, came under Norwegian administration in 1931.

Queen Maud Land, a section of Antarctica, came under Norwegian administration in 1939.

OMAN

Sultanate of Oman
Sultan: Qabus Bin Said (1970)
Area: 82,030 sq mi. (212,458 sq km)[1]
Population (est. 1996): 2,186,548 (average annual rate of natural increase: 3.34%); birth rate: 37.9/1000; infant mortality rate: 27.3/1000; density per square mile: 26
Capital and largest city (est. 1991): Muscat, 350,000;
Monetary unit: Omani Rial; **Language:** Arabic (official); also English and Indian languages; **Religion:** Islam, 95%; **National name:** Saltonat Uman; **Literacy rate:** 65.8%

Economic summary: Gross domestic product (1994 est.): $17 billion; $10,020 per capita; real growth rate 0.5%; inflation 1.2%, unemployment n.a. Principal agricultural products: dates, fruit, cereal, livestock. Labor force: 430,000; 40% in agriculture. Major industries: petroleum drilling, fishing, construction. Natural resources: oil, marble, copper, limestone. Exports: $4.8 billion (f.o.b., 1994 est.): oil, 87%; reexports: fish, processed copper, textiles. Imports: $4.1 billion (c.i.f., 1994 est.): machinery and transport equipment, food, manufactured goods, livestock, lubricants. Major trading partners: U.K., U.S., Japan, UAE, South Korea, France.

1. Excluding the Kuria Muria Islands.

Geography. Oman is a 1,000-mile-long (1,700-km) coastal plain at the southeastern tip of the Arabian peninsula lying on the Arabian Sea and the Gulf of Oman. The interior is a plateau. The country is the size of Kansas.

Government. The Sultan of Oman (formerly called Muscat and Oman), an absolute monarch, is assisted by a council of ministers, seven specialized councils, a Majllis Ashura, and personal advisers.

There are no political parties.

History. Although Oman is an independent state under the rule of the sultan, it has been under British protection since the early 19th century.

Muscat, the capital of the geographical area known as Oman, was occupied by the Portuguese from 1508 to 1648. Then it fell to Persian princes and later was regained by the sultan.

In a palace coup on July 23, 1970, the sultan, Sa'id bin Taimur, who had ruled since 1932, was overthrown by his son, who promised to establish a modern government and use new-found wealth to aid the people of this very isolated state.

A long border dispute with Yemen ended in late October 1992 when the sultan signed an agreement with the Yemeni president.

In the first round of voting for an expanded consultative assembly called by the sultan in November 1994, four women were elected.

The country continued to be the strongest supporter of the Palestinian-Israeli peace process in the Persian Gulf in 1995.

PAKISTAN

Islamic Republic of Pakistan
President: Farooq Ahmad Khan Leghari (1993)
Prime Minister: Benazir Bhutto (1993)
Area: 310,400 sq mi. (803,936 sq km)[1]
Population (est. 1996): 129,275,660 (average annual growth rate: 2.49%); birth rate: 36.1/1000; infant mortality rate: 96.8/1000; density per square mile: 416
Capital (1981 census): Islamabad, 201,000; **Largest cities (1981 census for metropolitan area):** Karachi, 5,208,100; Lahore, 2,952,700; Faisalabad, (Lyallpur) 1,920,000; Rawalpindi, 920,000; Hyderabad, 795,000;
Monetary unit: Pakistan rupee; **Principal languages:** Urdu (national), English (official), Punjabi, Sindhi, Pashtu, and Baluchi; **Religions:** Islam, 97%; Hindu, Christian, Buddhist, Parsi; **Literacy rate:** 35%
Economic summary: Gross national product (1994 est.): $248.5 billion; $1,930 per capita; real growth rate 4%; inflation (FY93/94) 12%; unemployment (FY90/91 est.) 10%. Arable land: 26%. Principal products: wheat, rice, cotton, sugarcane. Labor force (1987): 28,900,000; agriculture, 54%; services, 33%. Major products: cotton textiles, processed foods, petroleum products, construction materials. Natural resources: natural gas, limited petroleum, iron ore. Exports: $6.7 billion (1993): cotton, rice, textiles, clothing. Imports: $9.5 billion (1993): edible oil, crude oil, machinery, chemicals, transport equipment. Major trading partners: U.S., E.U., Japan, Hong Kong.

1. Excluding Kashmir and Jammu.

Geography. Pakistan is situated in the western part of the Indian subcontinent, with Afghanistan and Iran on the west, India on the east, and the Arabian Sea on the south. The name "Pakistan" is derived from two Persian words "Pak" (meaning pure) and "stan" (meaning country).

Nearly twice the size of California, Pakistan consists of towering mountains, including the Hindu Kush in the west, a desert area in the east, the Punjab plains in the north, and an expanse of alluvial plains. The 1,000-mile-long (1,609 km) Indus River flows through the country from the Kashmir to the Arabian Sea.

Government. Pakistan is a federal republic with a bicameral legislature—a 217-member National Assembly and an 87-member Senate.

History. Pakistan was one of the two original successor states to British India. For almost 25 years following independence in 1947, it consisted of two separate regions, East and West Pakistan, but now comprises only the western sector. It consists of Sind, Baluchistan, the former North-West Frontier Province, western Punjab, the princely state of Bahawalpur, and several other smaller native states.

The British became the dominant power in the region in 1757 following Lord Clive's military victory, but rebellious tribes kept the northwest in turmoil. In the northeast, the formation of the Moslem League in 1906 estranged the Moslems from the Hindus. In 1930, the League, led by Mohammed Ali Jinnah, demanded creation of a Moslem state wherever Moslems were in the majority. He supported Britain during the war. Afterward, the League received an almost unanimous Moslem vote in 1946, and Britain agreed to the formation of Pakistan as a separate dominion.

Pakistan was proclaimed a republic March 23, 1956. The election of 1970 set the stage for civil war when Sheik Muuibur told East Pakistanis to stop paying taxes to the central government. West Pakistan troops moved in and fighting began. The independent state of Bangladesh, or Bengali nation, was proclaimed March 26, 1971. The intervention of Indian troops protected the new state and brought President Yahya Kahn down. Zulfikar Ali Bhutto took over and accepted Bangladesh as an independent entity.

Diplomatically, 1976 saw the resumption of formal relations between India and Pakistan.

Pakistan's first elections under civilian rule took place in March 1977 and provoked bitter opposition protest when Bhutto's party was declared to have won 155 of the 200 elected seats in the 216-member National Assembly. A rising tide of violent protest and political deadlock led to a military takeover on July 5. Gen. Mohammed Zia ul-Haq became Chief Martial Law Administrator.

Bhutto was tried and convicted for the 1974 murder of a political opponent, and despite worldwide protests was executed on April 4, 1979, touching off riots by his supporters. Zia declared himself president on Sept. 16, 1978, a month after Fazel Elahi Chaudhry left office upon the completion of his 5-year term.

A measure of representative government was restored with the election of a new National Assembly in February 1985, although leaders of opposition parties were banned from the election.

On December 30, 1985, Zia ended martial law.

On August 19, 1988, President Zia was killed in a mid-air explosion of a Pakistani Air Force plane. Elections at the end of 1988 brought longtime Zia opponent Benazir Bhutto, daughter of Zulfikar Bhutto, into office as prime minister.

In August 1990, Pakistan's president dismissed Prime Minister Bhutto on charges of corruption and incompetence and dissolved parliament. Sharif's coalition, the Islamic Democratic Alliance, won the elections of October 1990.

In April 1993 the president dismissed the prime

minister on charges of corruption and dissolved the parliament. A month later, however, the country's supreme court overturned the order. The next day parliament gave the prime minister a vote of confidence. In July, however, the army demanded a resolution of the standoff.

October 1993 elections gave a plurality of parliamentary seats to Ms. Bhutto's Pakistan People's Party, ensuring her the prime ministry.

Ethnic violence flared during 1995, particularly in Karachi. The economy, however, showed signs of improving, and a deal was struck with the IMF in September.

REPUBLIC OF PALAU

President: Kuniwo Nakamura (1993)
Total area: 177 sq mi. (458 sq km)
Population (est. 1996): 16,952 (average rate of natural increase: 1.50%); birth rate: 21.6/1000; infant mortality rate: 25/1000; density per square mile: 95
Capital and largest city (1990): Koror, 10,501. **Monetary unit:** U.S. dollar used. **Language:** Palauan is the official language, though English is commonplace. **Ethnic divisions:** Palauans are a composite of Polynesian, Malayan, and Melanesian races. **Religion:** Christian. About one-third of the islanders observe Modekngei religion, indigenous to Palau. **Literacy rate:** 92%.
Economic summary: Gross domestic product (1994 est.): $81.8 million. Note: GDP numbers reflect U.S. spending. $5,000 per capita. Industries: Tourism, craft items (shell, wood, pearl), some commercial fishing, and agriculture (subsistence level production of coconut, copra, cassava, sweet potatoes. Exports: $600,000 (f.o.b., 1989) trochus (a shellfish), tuna, copra, handicrafts. Imports: $24.6 million (c.i.f., 1989). Major trading partners: U.S., Japan.

Geography. The Palau island chain consists of about 200 islands located in the North Pacific Ocean 528 mi. (650 km) southeast of the Philippines. The islands vary geologically from the high mountainous main island of Babelthuap to low coral islands usually fringed by large barrier reefs.

Government. A republic with a bicameral parliament. There is a 14-member Senate and a 16-member House of Delegates. Palau became a sovereign nation on October 1, 1994.

History. Spain held the islands for 300 years before selling them to Germany in 1899. Japan occupied Palau during WWI and received a mandate over them from the League of Nations in 1920. It remained in Japanese control and served as an important naval base until the U.S. seized it during WWII. After the war it became a U.N. trusteeship (1947) and was administered by the U.S. until 1994.

The first order of business in 1995 was to enter into diplomatic talks with the U.S., Japan, and Taiwan.

PANAMA

Republic of Panama
President: Ernesto Perez Balladares (1994)
Area: 29,761 sq mi. (77,082 sq km)
Population (est. 1996): 2,655,094 (average annual rate of natural increase: 1.78%); birth rate: 23.2/1000; infant mortality rate: 29.7/1000; density per square mile: 89

Capital and largest city (1993 est.): Panama City, 450,668; **Other large cities:** San Miguelito, 293,564; Colón, 137,825. **Monetary unit:** Balboa. **Language:** Spanish (official); many bilingual in English. **Religions:** Roman Catholic, over 93%; Protestant, 6%. **National name:** República de Panamá. **Literacy rate:** 88%
Economic summary: Gross domestic product (1994 est.): $12.3 billion; $4,670 per capita; real growth rate 3.6%; inflation 1.8%; unemployment 12.9%. Arable land: 6%. Principal agricultural products: bananas, corn, sugar, rice, coffee. Labor force: 979,000 (1994 est.): government and community services 31.8%; agriculture, hunting, fishing 26.8%; commerce, restaurants, hotels 16.4%. Major industrial products: refined petroleum, sugar, cement, paper products. Natural resources: copper, mahogany, shrimp. Exports: $520 million (f.o.b., 1994 est.): bananas, sugar, shrimp, coffee, clothing. Imports: $2.205 billion (c.i.f., 1994 est.): petroleum, manufactured goods, machinery and transportation equipment, food, chemicals. Major trading partners: U.S., E.U., Central America and Caribbean, Japan.

Geography. The southernmost of the Central American nations, Panama is south of Costa Rica and north of Colombia. The Panama Canal bisects the isthmus at its narrowest and lowest point, allowing passage from the Caribbean Sea to the Pacific Ocean.

Panama is slightly smaller than South Carolina. It is marked by a chain of mountains in the west, moderate hills in the interior, and a low range on the east coast. There are extensive forests in the fertile Caribbean area.

Government. Panama is a centralized republic. The executive power is vested in the president and two vice presidents who exercise power jointly with a cabinet of 12 ministers of state appointed by the president. Presidents and vice presidents are elected for five-year terms and may not succeed themselves. The legislative function is exercised through the National Assembly. The legislators are elected for five-year terms by direct vote and can be reelected.

History. Visited by Columbus in 1502 on his fourth voyage and explored by Balboa in 1513, Panama was the principal transshipment point for Spanish treasure and supplies to and from South and Central America in colonial days. In 1821, when Central America revolted against Spain, Panama joined Colombia, which already had declared its independence. For the next 82 years, Panama attempted unsuccessfully to break away from Colombia. After U.S. proposals for canal rights over the narrow isthmus had been rejected by Colombia, Panama proclaimed its independence with U.S. backing in 1903.

For canal rights in perpetuity, the U.S. paid Panama $10 million and agreed to pay $250,000 each year, increased to $430,000 after devaluation of the U.S. dollar in 1933 and was further increased under a revised treaty signed in 1955. In exchange, the U.S. got the Canal Zone—a 10-mile-wide strip across the isthmus—and a considerable degree of influence in Panama's affairs.

Panama and the U.S. agreed in 1974 to negotiate the eventual reversion of the canal to Panama, despite strongly expressed opposition in the U.S. Congress. The texts of two treaties—one governing the transfer of the canal and the other guaranteeing its neutrality after transfer—were negotiated by August 1977 and were signed by Pres. Omar Torrijos Herara and President Carter in Washington on September 7. A Panamanian referendum approved the treaties by more than two-thirds on October 23, but further changes were insisted upon by the U.S. Senate.

The principal change was a reservation specifying that despite the neutrality treaty's specification that only Panama shall maintain forces in its territory after transfer of the canal Dec. 31, 1999, the U.S. should have the right to use military force to keep the canal operating if it should become obstructed. The Senate approved the treaties in March–April 1978.

Nicolas Ardito Barletta, Panama's first directly elected president in 16 years, was inaugurated on Oct. 11, 1984, for a five-year term. He lacked the necessary support to solve the country's economic crisis and resigned September 28, 1985. He was replaced by Vice President Eric Arturo Delvalle.

In June 1986, reports surfaced that the behind-the-scenes strongman, Gen. Manuel Noriega, was involved in drug trafficking and the murder of an opposition leader. In 1987, Noriega was accused by his ex-chief of staff of assassinating Torrijos in 1981. He was indicted in the U.S. for drug trafficking, but when Delvalle attempted to fire him, he forced the National Assembly to replace Delvalle with Manuel Solis Palma.

The crisis continued when Noriega called presidential elections for when the current term expired. Despite massive fraud by Noriega, the opposition seemed headed to a landslide. Noriega annulled the elections and suppressed protests by the opposition.

In December 1989, the Assembly named Noriega the "maximum leader" and declared the U.S. and Panama to be in a state of war. A further series of incidents led to a U.S. invasion overthrowing Noriega, who was brought to the U.S. to stand trial for drug trafficking. Guillermo Endara, who probably would have won the election suppressed by Noriega, was instated as president.

In elections of May 1994 a left-of-center businessman won the country's presidential election.

A proposed labor-code reform served as the cause for clashes between striking workers and police in August 1995, but the reforms became law.

In July 1996 a widening drugs scandal enveloped a vice president and the ambassador to Costa Rica.

Panama Canal. First conceived by the Spaniards in 1524, when King Charles V of Spain ordered a survey of a waterway across the isthmus, a construction concession was granted by the Colombian government in 1878 to St. Lucien N. B. Wyse, representing a French company. Two years later, the French Canal Company, inspired by Ferdinand de Lesseps, began construction of what was to have been a sea-level canal. The effort ended in bankruptcy nine years later and the United States ultimately paid the French $40 million for their rights and assets.

The U.S. project, built on territory controlled by the United States, and calling for the creation of an interior lake connected to both oceans by locks, got under way in 1904. Completed in 1914, the canal is 50.7 miles long and lifts ships 85 feet above sea level through a series of three locks on the Pacific and Atlantic sides. Enlarged in later years, each lock now measures 1,000 feet in length, 110 feet in width, and 40 feet in depth of water.

PAPUA NEW GUINEA

Sovereign: Queen Elizabeth II
Governor General: Wiwa Korowi
Prime Minister: Sir Julius Chan (1994)

Area: 178,704 sq mi. (462,840 sq km)
Population (est. 1996): 4,394,537 (average annual rate of natural increase: 2.29%); birth rate: 32.9/1000; infant mortality rate: 60.1/1000; density per square mile: 24
Capital and largest city (1994): Port Moresby, 250,000.
Monetary unit: Kina. **Languages:** English, Melanesian pidgin, Hiri Motu, and 717 distinct native languages.
Religions: over half Christian, remainder indigenous.
Member of Commonwealth of Nations. Literacy rate: 52%
Economic summary: Gross domestic product (1994 est.): $5.8 billion; $2,000 per capita; 6.1% real growth rate; inflation 1.6%; unemployment n.a. Principal products: coffee, copra, palm oil, cocoa, tea, coconuts. Major industrial products: coconut oil, plywood, wood chips, gold, silver. Natural resources: copper, gold, silver, timber, natural gas. Exports: $2 billion (f.o.b., 1994): gold, copper, coffee, palm oil, copra, timber, lobster. Imports: $1.2 billion (c.i.f., 1993): food, machinery, transport equipment, fuels, chemicals, consumer goods. Major trading partners: Australia, U.K., Japan, Singapore, New Zealand, U.S., South Korea, Germany

Geography. Papua New Guinea occupies the eastern half of the island of New Guinea, just north of Australia, and many outlying islands. The Indonesian province of Irian Jaya is to the west. To the north and east are the islands of Manus, New Britain, New Ireland, and Bougainville, all part of Papua New Guinea.

Papua New Guinea is about one-tenth larger than California. Its mountainous interior has only recently been explored. The high-plateau climate is temperate, in contrast to the tropical climate of the coastal plains. Two major rivers, the Sepik and the Fly, are navigable for shallow-draft vessels.

Government. Papua New Guinea attained independence Sept. 16, 1975, ending a United Nations trusteeship under the administration of Australia. Parliamentary democracy was established by a constitution that invests power in a 109-member national legislature.

History. The eastern half of New Guinea was first visited by Spanish and Portuguese explorers in the 16th century, but a permanent European presence was not established until 1884, when Germany declared a protectorate over the northern coast and Britain took similar action in the south. Both nations formally annexed their protectorates, and in 1901 Britain transferred its rights to a newly independent Australia. Australian troops invaded German New Guinea in World War I and retained control under a League of Nations mandate that eventually became a United Nations trusteeship, incorporating a territorial government in the southern region, known as Papua.

Australia granted limited home rule in 1951. Autonomy in internal affairs came nine years later.

In February 1990 guerrillas of the Bougainville Revolutionary Army (BRA) attacked plantations, forcing the evacuation of numerous workers. In May the BRA declared Bougainville's independence, whereupon the government blockaded the island until January 1991, when a peace treaty was signed.

Rebel guerrillas who had occupied the Bougainville copper mine withdrew to the surrounding hills in September 1994 allowing government forces to reclaim it.

Talks leading to a ceasefire began in 1995 in Australia, but in November the prime minister announced their termination.

PARAGUAY

Republic of Paraguay
President: Juan Carlos Wasmosy (1993)
Area: 157,047 sq mi. (406,752 sq km)
Population (est. 1996): 5,504,146 (average annual rate of natural increase: 2.67%); birth rate: 40/1000; infant mortality rate: 23.2/1000; density per square mile: 35
Capital and largest city (1992): Asunción, 502,426. **Other large cities (1992):** Ciudad del Este, 133,893; San Lorenzo, 133,311. **Monetary unit:** Guarani. **Languages:** Spanish (official), Guaraní; **Religion:** Roman Catholic, 90%. **National name:** República del Paraguay. **Literacy rate:** 90%
Economic summary: Gross domestic product (1994 est.): $15.4 billion; $2,950 per capita; real growth rate 3.5%; inflation 18%; unemployment 11.2%. Arable land: 20%. Principal agricultural products: soybeans, cotton, timber, cassava, tobacco, corn, rice, sugar cane. Labor force (1993): 1,692,000; By occupation (1992 est.): 44% agriculture. Major industrial products: packed meats, crushed oilseeds, beverages, textiles, light consumer goods, cement. Natural resources: iron ore, timber, manganese, limestone, hydropower. Exports: $728 million (f.o.b., 1993 est.): cotton, soybeans, meat products, timber, coffee, tung oil, vegetable oils. Imports: $1.38 billion (c.i.f., 1993 est.): fuels and lubricants, beverages, tobacco, foodstuffs, capital goods, consumer goods, fuels and lubricants. Major trading partners: Argentina, Brazil, U.S., E.U., Japan.

Geography. California-size Paraguay is surrounded by Brazil, Bolivia, and Argentina in south central South America. Eastern Paraguay, between the Paraná and Paraguay Rivers, is upland country, with the thickest population settled on the grassy slope that inclines toward the Paraguay River. The greater part of the Chaco region to the west is covered with marshes, lagoons, dense forests, and jungles.

Government. The president is elected by popular vote for five years. The legislature is bicameral, consisting of a Senate of 45 members and a Chamber of Representatives of 80 members. There is also a Council of State, whose members are nominated by the government.

History. In 1526 and again in 1529, Sebastian Cabot explored Paraguay when he sailed up the Paraná and Paraguay Rivers. From 1608 until their expulsion from the Spanish dominions in 1767, the Jesuits maintained an extensive establishment in the south and east of Paraguay. In 1811, Paraguay revolted against Spanish rule and became a nominal republic under two consuls.

Actually, Paraguay was governed by three dictators during the first 60 years of independence. The third, Francisco López, waged war against Brazil and Argentina in 1865–70, a conflict in which the male population was almost wiped out. A new constitution in 1870, designed to prevent dictatorships and internal strife, failed to do so, and not until 1912 did a period of comparative economic and political stability begin.

After World War II, politics became particularly unstable.

Alfredo Stroessner ruled under a state of siege until 1965, when the dictatorship was relaxed and exiles returned. The constitution was revised in 1967 to permit Stroessner to be re-elected.

The Stroessner regime was criticized by the U.S. State Department during the Carter administration as a violator of human rights, but unlike Argentina and

Uruguay, Paraguay did not suffer cuts in U.S. military aid.

Stroessner was overthrown by an army leader, Gen. Andres Rodriguez, in 1989. Rodriguez won in Paraguay's first multi-candidate election in decades. The National Assembly in June 1991 approved a reform of the constitution.

The country's first democratic presidential election took place in May 1993. Juan Carlos Wasmosy, a wealthy businessman and the candidate of the governing Colorado Party, won a five-year term in an election that despite irregularities was regarded as reliable.

In April 1996 the president ordered the resignation of the country's army commander, who refused. Although tensions mounted, a deal was proclaimed that gave the general the defense ministry. Two days later, after nunmerous demonstrations, the president announced the general would not become defense minister.

PERU

Republic of Peru
President: Alberto Fujimori (1990)
Premier: Alberto Pandolf (1996)
Area: 496,222 sq mi. (1,285,216 sq km)
Population (est. 1996): 24,523,408 (average annual rate of natural increase: 1.82%); birth rate: 24.3/1000; infant mortality rate: 52.2/1000; density per sq mi.: 49
Capital and largest city (1993): Lima, 6,479,000; Other large cities: Arequipa, 939,800; Callao, 648,000; Trujillo, 1,287,000; Chiclayo, 951,000. **Monetary unit:** Nuevo Sol (1991). **Languages:** Spanish, Quéchua, Aymara, and other native languages. **Religion:** Roman Catholic. **National name:** República del Perú. **Literacy rate:** 85%
Economic summary: Gross domestic product (1994 est.): $44.11 billion; $3,110 (est.) per capita; real growth rate 7% (1995); inflation 10% (1995); unemployment 15% (1992 est.). Arable land: 3%. Principal products: wheat, potatoes, beans, rice, sugar, cotton, coffee. Labor force: 8,000,000 (1992); by occupation (1988): government and other services, 44%; agriculture, 37%, industry, 19%. Major products: processed minerals, fish meal, refined petroleum, textiles. Natural resources: silver, gold, iron, copper, fish, petroleum, timber. Exports: $5.57 billion (1995): copper, fish products, cotton, sugar, coffee, lead, silver, zinc, oil. Imports: $7.68 billion (1995): machinery, foodstuffs, chemicals, pharmaceuticals, transport equipment. Major trading partners: U.S., Japan, Western European and Latin American countries.

Geography. Peru, in western South America, extends for nearly 1,500 miles (2,414 km) along the Pacific Ocean. Colombia and Ecuador are to the north, Brazil and Bolivia to the east, and Chile to the south.

Five-sixths the size of Alaska, Peru is divided by the Andes Mountains into three sharply differentiated zones. To the west is the coastline, much of it arid, extending 50 to 100 miles (80 to 160 km) inland. The mountain area, with peaks over 20,000 feet (6,096 m), lofty plateaus, and deep valleys, lies centrally. Beyond the mountains to the east is the heavily forested slope leading to the Amazonian plains.

Government. A republic. The president, Alberto Fujimori, was elected in 1990 by universal suffrage for a five-year term and holds executive power. He was reelected in April 1995 by an absolute majority for five more years. A new 120-member Congress

was also elected by universal suffrage.

History. Peru was once part of the great Incan empire and later the major vice-royalty of Spanish South America. It was conquered in 1531–33 by Francisco Pizarro. On July 28, 1821, Peru proclaimed its independence, but the Spanish were not finally defeated until 1824. For a hundred years thereafter, revolutions were frequent, and a new war was fought with Spain in 1864–66.

Peru emerged from 20 years of dictatorship in 1945 with the inauguration of President José Luis Bustamente y Rivero after the first free election in many decades. But he served for only three years and was succeeded in turn by Gen. Manual A. Odria, Manuel Prado y Ugarteche, and Fernando Belaúnde Terry. On Oct. 3, 1968, Belaúnde was overthrown by Gen. Juan Velasco Alvarado.

Velasco nationalized the nation's second biggest bank and turned two large newspapers over to Marxists in 1970, but he also allowed a new agreement with a copper-mining consortium of four American firms.

In 1975, Velasco was replaced in a bloodless coup by his premier, Gen. Francisco Morales Bermudez, who promised to restore civilian government. In elections held on May 18, 1980, Belaunde Terry, the last previous civilian president and the candidate of the conservative parties that have traditionally ruled Peru, was elected president again.

Peru's fragile democracy survived this period of stress, and when he left office in 1985 Belaunde Terry was the first elected president to turn over power to a constitutionally elected successor since 1945.

In the June runoff to the April 1990 elections Alberto Fujimori won 56.5% of the vote. Citing continuing terrorism, drug trafficking, and corruption, Fujimori in April 1992 dissolved Congress, suspended the constitution, and imposed censorship. A new constitution received approval in a referendum held in October 1993.

In January 1995 fighting flared once again along part of the poorly-defined border with Ecuador, claiming nine lives. Peru declared a unilateral ceasefire in mid-February.

In the April elections, President Fujimori was reelected, and his party obtained a majority in the legislature.

As a result of an internal government squabble over economic policy Premier Cordova resigned in April 1996.

THE PHILIPPINES

Republic of the Philippines
President: Fidel V. Ramos (1992)
Vice President: Joseph Estrada (1992)
Area: 115,830 sq mi. (300,000 sq km)
Population (est. 1996): 74,480,848 (average annual rate of natural increase: 2.29%); birth rate: 29.5/1000; infant mortality rate: 35.9/1000; density per square mile: 643
Capital and largest city (1990): Manila, 1,601,234; Other large cities: Quezon City, 1,669,776; Cebu, 610,415.
Monetary unit: Peso. **Languages:** Filipino (based on Tagalog), English; regional languages: Tagalog, Ilocano, Cebuano, others. **Religions:** Roman Catholic, 84%; Protestant, 10%. Islam, 5%; Buddhist and other, 3%. **National name:** Republika ng Pilipinas. **Literacy rate:** 93.5%
Economic summary: Gross domestic product (1994 est.): $161.4 billion; $2,310 per capita; real growth rate 4.3%; inflation 7.1%; unemployment 9%. Arable land: 9.8%. Principal products: rice, corn, coconuts, sugar cane,

bananas, pineapple. Labor force (1989): 24,120,000; agriculture, 46%; services, 18.5%; industry and commerce, 16%. Major products: textiles, pharmaceuticals, chemicals, food processing, electronics assembly. Natural resources: forests, crude oil, metallic and non-metallic minerals. Exports: $13.4 billion (f.o.b., 1994): electrical equipment, coconut products, chemicals, logs and lumber, copper concentrates, nickel. Imports: $21.3 billion (f.o.b., 1994): petroleum, industrial equipment, raw materials. Major trading partners: U.S., Japan, E.C., Taiwan, Saudi Arabia.

Geography. The Philippine Islands are an archipelago of over 7,000 islands lying about 500 miles (805 km) off the southeast coast of Asia. The overall land area is comparable to that of Arizona. The northernmost island, Y'Ami, is 65 miles (105 km) from Taiwan, while the southernmost, Saluag, is 40 miles (64 km) east of Borneo.

Only about 7% of the islands are larger than one square mile, and only one-third have names. The largest are Luzon in the north (40,420 sq mi.; 104,687 sq km), Mindanao in the south (36,537 sq mi.; 94,631 sq km), Samar (5,124 sq mi.; 13,271 sq km).

The islands are of volcanic origin, with the larger ones crossed by mountain ranges. The highest peak is Mount Apo (9,690 ft; 2,954 m) on Mindanao.

Government. On February 2, 1987, the Filipino people voted for a new constitution that established a 24-seat Senate and a 250-seat House of Representatives and gave the president a six-year term. It limits the powers of the president, who can't be re-elected.

History. Fernando Magellan, the Portuguese navigator in the service of Spain, discovered the Philippines in 1521. Twenty-one years later, a Spanish exploration party named the group of islands in honor of Prince Philip, later Philip II of Spain. Spain retained possession of the islands for the next 350 years.

The Philippines were ceded to the U.S. in 1899 by the Treaty of Paris after the Spanish-American War. Meanwhile, the Filipinos, led by Emilio Aguinaldo, had declared their independence. They continued guerrilla warfare against U.S. troops until the capture of Aguinaldo in 1901. By 1902, peace was established except among the Moros.

The first U.S. civilian governor-general was William Howard Taft (1901–04). The Jones Law (1916) provided for the establishment of a Philippine legislature composed of an elective Senate and House of Representatives. The Tydings-McDuffie Act (1934) provided for a transitional period until 1946, at which time the Philippines would become completely independent.

Under a constitution approved by the people of the Philippines in 1935, the Commonwealth of the Philippines came into being, with Manuel Quezon y Molina as president.

On Dec. 8, 1941, the Philippines were invaded by Japanese troops. Following the fall of Bataan and Corregidor, Quezon established a government-in-exile, which he headed until his death in 1944. He was succeeded by Vice President Sergio Osmeña.

U.S. forces led by Gen. Douglas MacArthur reinvaded the Philippines in October 1944, and after the liberation of Manila in February 1945, Osmeña re-established the government.

The Philippines achieved full independence on July 4, 1946. Manual A. Roxas y Acuña was elected first president. Subsequent presidents have been Elpidio Quirino (1948–53), Ramón Magsaysay (1953–57), Carlos P. García (1957–61), Diosdado Macapagal (1961–65), Ferdinand E. Marcos (1965–86).

Marcos, who had freed the last of the national leaders still in detention, former Senator Benigno S. Aquino, Jr., in 1980 and permitted him to go to the United States, ended eight years of martial law on January 17, 1981.

Despite having been warned by First Lady Imelda Marcos that he risked being killed if he came back, opposition leader Aquino returned to the Philippines from self-exile on Aug. 21, 1983. He was shot to death as he was being escorted from his plane by military police at Manila International Airport. There was widespread suspicion that the Marcos government was involved in the murder.

In an attempt to re-secure American support, Marcos set presidential elections for Feb. 7, 1986. With the support of the Catholic church, Corazon Aquino, widow of Benigno Aquino, declared her candidacy. Marcos was declared the winner, but the vote was widely considered to be rigged and anti-Marcos protests continued. The defection of Defense Minister Juan Enrile and Lt. Gen. Fidel Ramos signaled an end of military support for Marcos, who fled into exile in the U.S. on Feb. 25, 1986.

The Aquino government survived coup attempts by Marcos supporters and other right-wing elements including one, in November, by Enrile. Legislative elections on May 11, 1987, gave pro-Aquino candidates a large majority.

Negotiations on renewal of leases for U.S. military bases threatened to sour relations between the two countries. The volcanic eruptions from Mount Pinatubo, however, severely damaged Clark Air Base. In July 1991 the U.S. decided simply to abandon the base.

In elections of May 1992 Gen. Fidel Ramos, who had the support of outgoing Corazon Aquino, won the presidency in a seven-way race. The opposition gained control of Congress.

The U.S. Navy turned over the Subic Bay naval base to the Philippines in September, ending a long U.S. military presence.

Elections for both houses of Congress in May 1995 gave a resounding victory to candidates backed by the president, and were widely hailed as providing him with a fresh mandate to proceed with economic reforms.

After protracted negotiations the Moro National Liberation Front agreed in 1996 to a government plan leading to more political autonomy in the south.

POLAND

Republic of Poland
President: Aleksander Kwasniewski (1995)
Prime Minister: Wlodzimierz Cimoszewics (1996)
Area: 120,727 sq mi. (312,683 sq km)
Population (est. 1996): 38,642,565 (average annual rate of natural increase: 0.18%); birth rate: 11.9/1000; infant mortality rate: 12.4/1000; density per square mile: 320
Capital and largest city (1994 est.): Warsaw, 1,642,700; **Other large cities:** Lodz, 833,700; Krakow, 745,100; Wroclaw, 642,300; Poznan, 582,.800; Gdansk, 463,100; Szczecin, 417,700. **Monetary unit:** Zloty. **Language:** Polish. **Religions:** Roman Catholic, 95%; Russian Orthodox, Protestant, and other, 5%. **National name:** Rzeczpospolita Polska. **Literacy rate:** 98%
Economic summary: Gross domestic product (1994 est.): $191.1 billion; $4,920 per capita; real growth rate 5.5%; inflation 30%; unemployment 16.1% (Nov. 94). Arable

land: 59%. Principal products: rye, rapeseed, potatoes, hogs and other livestock. Labor force: 17,400,000 (1994): industry and construction 37%, agriculture and food products 23%. Major products: iron and steel, chemicals, textiles, processed foods, machine building. Natural resources: coal, sulfur, copper, natural gas. Exports: $16.3 billion (f.o.b., 1994 est.): coal, machinery and equipment, industrial products, chemicals, metals. Imports: $18.1 billion (f.o.b., 1994 est.): machinery and equipment, fuels, agricultural and food products, chemicals. Major trading partners: Germany, former U.S.S.R., Italy, U.K., The Netherlands, U.S.

Geography. Poland, a country the size of New Mexico in north central Europe, borders on Germany to the west, Czech and Slovak Republics to the south, and Ukraine, Balarus, Lithuania, and Russia to the east. In the north is the Baltic Sea.

Most of the country is a plain with no natural boundaries except the Carpathian Mountains in the south and the Oder and Neisse Rivers in the west. Other major rivers, which are important to commerce, are the Vistula, Warta, and Bug.

Government. Parliament adopted a new temporary constitution on Oct. 17, 1992, which describes Poland as the Republic of Poland. Work on a permanent constitution continues. The supreme organ of state authority is the Sejm (parliament), which is composed of 460 members elected for four years, and a 100-member senate (Senat).

History. Little is known about Polish history before the 11th century, when King Boleslaus I (the Brave) ruled over Bohemia, Saxony, and Moravia. Meanwhile, the Teutonic knights of Prussia conquered part of Poland and barred the latter's access to the Baltic. The knights were defeated by Wladislaus II at Tannenberg in 1410 and became Polish vassals, and Poland regained a Baltic shoreline. Poland reached the peak of power between the 14th and 16th centuries, scoring military successes against the Russians and Turks. In 1683, John III (John Sobieski) turned back the Turkish tide at Vienna.

An elective monarchy failed to produce strong central authority, and Prussia and Austria were able to carry out a first partition of the country in 1772, a second in 1792, and a third in 1795. For more than a century thereafter, there was no Polish state, but the Poles never ceased their efforts to regain their independence.

Poland was formally reconstituted in November 1918, with Marshal Josef Pilsudski as chief of state. In 1919, Ignace Paderewski, the famous pianist and patriot, became the first premier. In 1926, Pilsudski seized complete power in a coup and ruled dictatorially until his death on May 12, 1935, when he was succeeded by Marshal Edward Smigly-Rydz.

Despite a 10-year nonaggression pact signed in 1934, Hitler attacked Poland on Sept. 1, 1939. Russian troops invaded from the east on September 17, and on September 28 a German-Russian agreement divided Poland between Russia and Germany. Wladyslaw Raczkiewicz formed a government-in-exile in France, which moved to London after France's defeat in 1940.

All of Poland was occupied by Germany after the Nazi attack on the U.S.S.R. in June 1941.

The legal Polish government soon fell out with the Russians, and, in 1944, a Communist-dominated Polish Committee of National Liberation received Soviet recognition. Moving to Lublin after that city's liberation, it proclaimed itself the Provisional Government of Poland. Some former members of the Polish government in London joined with the Lublin government to form the Polish Government of National Unity, which Britain and the U.S. recognized.

On Aug. 2, 1945, in Berlin, President Harry S. Truman, Joseph Stalin, and Prime Minister Clement Attlee of Britain established a new *de facto* western frontier for Poland along the Oder and Neisse Rivers. (The border was finally agreed to by West Germany in a nonaggression pact signed Dec. 7, 1970.) On Aug. 16, 1945, the U.S.S.R. and Poland signed a treaty delimiting the Soviet-Polish frontier. Under these agreements, Poland was shifted westward. In the east it lost 69,860 square miles (180,934 sq km) with 10,772,000 inhabitants; in the west it gained (subject to final peace-conference approval) 38,986 square miles (100,973 sq km) with a prewar population of 8,621,000.

A new constitution in 1952 made Poland a "people's democracy" of the Soviet type. In 1955, Poland became a member of the Warsaw Treaty Organization, and its foreign policy became identical with that of the U.S.S.R. The government undertook persecution of the Roman Catholic Church as a remaining source of opposition.

Wladyslaw Gomulka was elected leader of the United Workers (Communist) Party in 1956. He denounced the Stalinist terror, ousted many Stalinists, and improved relations with the church. Most collective farms were dissolved, and the press became freer.

A strike that began in shipyards and spread to other industries in August 1980 produced a stunning victory for workers when the economically hard-pressed government accepted for the first time in a Marxist state the right of workers to organize in independent unions.

Led by Solidarity, a free union founded by Lech Walesa, workers launched a drive for liberty and improved conditions. A national strike for a five-day week in January 1981 led to the dismissal of Premier Pinkowski and the naming of the fourth premier in less than a year, Gen. Wojciech Jaruzelski.

Martial law was declared on Dec. 13, when Walesa and other Solidarity leaders were arrested. It was formally ended in 1984 but the government retained emergency powers.

Increasing opposition to the government because of the failing economy led to a new wave of strikes in 1988. Unable to totally quell the dissent, the government relegalized Solidarity and allowed it to compete in elections.

Solidarity members won a stunning victory in 1989, taking almost all the seats in the Senate and all of the 169 seats they were allowed to contest in the Sejm. This gave them substantial influence in the new government. Taduesz Mazowiecki was appointed prime minister.

The presidential election of 1990 was essentially a three-way contest between Mazowiecki, Solidarity-leader Lech Walesa, and an almost unknown businessman, Stanislaw Tyminski. In the second round Walesa received 74% of the vote.

In 1991, the first fully free parliamentary election since WW II resulted in representation for 29 political parties.

In the second democratic parliamentary election of September 1993 voters returned power to ex-Communists and their allies.

The second round of the presidential election in November 1995 pitted Walesa against Aleksander Kwasniewski, leader of the successor to the Communist Party. The latter won despite strong support for Walesa from the Church. In February 1996 an insufficient number of voters turned out for a referendum on privatization of state assets for it to be legally binding.

PORTUGAL

Republic of Portugal
President: Jorge Sampaio (1996)
Prime Minister: Antonio Guterres (1995)
Area: 35,550 sq mi. (92,075 sq km)
Population (est. 1996): 9,865,114 (average annual rate of natural increase: 0.03%); birth rate: 10.5/1000; infant mortality rate: 7.6/1000; density per square mile: 277
Capital and largest city (1991): Lisbon, 677,790. **Other large city (1991)):** Oporto, 350,000. **Monetary unit:** Escudo. **Language:** Portuguese. **Religion:** Roman Catholic 97%, 1% Protestant, 2% other. **National name:** República Portuguesa. **Literacy rate:** 85%
Economic summary: Gross domestic product (1994 est.): $107.3 billion; $10,190 per capita; real growth rate 2.3% (1995); inflation 3.4% (1996); unemployment 7.5% (1996). Arable land: 32%. Principal products: grains, potatoes, olives, wine grapes. Labor force (1994 est.): 4.24 million: services 49%, industry 34%, agriculture 17%. Major products: textiles, footwear, wood pulp, paper, cork, metal products, refined oil, chemicals, canned fish, wine. Natural resources: fish, cork, tungsten, iron ore. Exports: $16 billion (f.o.b., 1994): cotton, textiles, cork and cork products, canned fish, wine, timber and timber products, resin, machinery, appliances. Imports: $24 billion (c.i.f., 1994): machinery and transport equipment, agricultural products, chemicals, petroleum, textiles. Major trading partners: Western European countries, U.S.

Geography. Portugal occupies the western part of the Iberian Peninsula, bordering on the Atlantic Ocean to the west and Spain to the north and east. It is slightly smaller than Indiana.

The country is crossed by many small rivers, and also by three large ones that rise in Spain, flow into the Atlantic, and divide the country into three geographic areas. The Minho River, part of the northern boundary, cuts through a mountainous area that extends south to the vicinity of the Douro River. South of the Douro, the mountains slope to the plains about the Tejo River. The remaining division is the southern one of Alentejo.

The Azores, stretching over 340 miles (547 km) in the Atlantic, consist of nine islands divided into three groups, with a total area of 902 square miles (2,335 sq km). The nearest continental land is Cape da Roca, Portugal, about 900 miles (1,448 km) to the east. The Azores are an important station on Atlantic air routes, and Britain and the U.S. established air bases there during World War II. Madeira, consisting of two inhabited islands, Madeira and Porto Santo, and two groups of uninhabited islands, lie in the Atlantic about 535 miles (861 km) southwest of Lisbon. The Madeiras are 307 square miles (796 sq km) in area.

Government. A republic. The president is elected for a five-year term, the unicameral legislature (the Assembly of the Republic), for four years.

History. Portugal was a part of Spain until it won its independence in the middle of the 12th century. King John I (1385–1433) unified his country at the expense of the Castilians and the Moors of Morocco. The expansion of Portugal was brilliantly coordinated by John's son, Prince Henry the Navigator. In 1488, Bartholomew Diaz reached the Cape of Good Hope, proving that the Far East was accessible by sea. In 1498, Vasco da Gama reached the west coast of India. By the middle of the 16th century, the Portuguese Empire extended to West and East Africa, Bra-

zil, Persia, Indochina, and Malaya.

In 1581, Philip II of Spain invaded Portugal and held it for 60 years, precipitating a catastrophic decline of Portuguese commerce. Courageous and shrewd explorers, the Portuguese proved to be inefficient and corrupt colonizers. By the time the Portuguese dynasty was restored in 1640, Dutch, English, and French competitors began to seize the lion's share of the world's colonies and commerce. Portugal retained Angola and Mozambique in Africa, and Brazil (until 1822).

The corrupt King Carlos, who ascended the throne in 1889, made Joao Franco the premier with dictatorial power in 1906. In 1908, Carlos and his heir were shot dead on the streets of Lisbon. The new king, Manoel II, was driven from the throne in the Revolution of 1910 and Portugal became a French-style republic.

Traditionally friendly to Britain, Portugal fought in World War I on the Allied side in Africa as well as on the Western Front. Weak postwar governments and a revolution in 1926 brought Antonio Oliveira Salazar to power. He kept Portugal neutral in World War II but gave the Allies naval and air bases after 1943.

Portugal lost the tiny remnants of its Indian empire—Goa, Daman, and Diu—to Indian military occupation in 1961, the year an insurrection broke out in Angola. For the next 13 years, Salazar, who died in 1970, and his successor, Marcello Caetano, fought independence movements amid growing world criticism. Leftists in the armed forces, weary of a losing battle, launched a successful revolution on April 25, 1974.

In late 1985, a PSP-PSD split ended Mario Soares's coalition government. Cavaco Silva, an advocate of free-market economics and the Social Democratic candidate, was elected as prime minister.

In July 1987, the governing Social Democratic Party was swept back into office with 50.22% of the popular vote, giving Portugal its first majority government since democracy was restored in 1974.

Mario Soares easily won a second five-year term as president in January 1991 elections.

General elections in October 1995 went to the Socialist Party, which fell just short of an absolute majority in the Assembly. Lisbon mayor Jorge Sampaio, a Socialist, won the race for president in January 1996.

Portuguese Overseas Territory

After the April 1974 revolution, the military junta moved to grant independence to the territories, beginning with Portuguese Guinea in September 1974, which became the Republic of Guinea-Bissau.

Mozambique and Angola followed, leaving only Portuguese Timor and Macao of the former empire. Despite Lisbon's objections, Indonesia annexed Timor.

MACAO

Status: Territory
Governor: Vasco Rocha Vieira (1991)
Area: 6 sq mi. (15.5 sq km)
Population (est. 1996): 496,837 (average annual growth rate: 0.9%); birth rate: 14/1000; infant mortality rate: 5.3/1000; density per square mile: 82,806
Capital (1991): Macao, 326,460. **Monetary unit:** Patacá.
Languages: Portuguese and Chinese are both official languages since December 31, 1991. Cantonese is most common, English is also spoken in business.
Religions: Buddhist 17%, Roman Catholic 7%, Protestant 7%. **Literacy rate (1981):** almost 100% among Portuguese and Macanese, no data on Chinese

Economic summary: Gross domestic product (1993 est.): $4.8 billion; $10,000 per capita; real growth rate 5%; inflation 6.3%. Major industrial products: clothing, textiles, plastics, furniture. Exports: $1.8 billion (1992 est.): textiles, clothing, toys. Imports: $2 billion (1992 est.). raw materials, foodstuffs, capital goods. Major trading partners: Hong Kong, China, U.S., Germany, France, Japan.

Macao comprises the peninsula of Macao and the two small islands of Taipa and Colôane on the South China coast, about 35 miles (53 km) from Hong Kong. Established by the Portuguese in 1557, it is the oldest European outpost in the China trade, but Portugal's sovereign rights to the port were not recognized by China until 1887. The port has been eclipsed in importance by Hong Kong, but it is still a busy distribution center and also has an important fishing industry. Portugal will return Macao to China in 1999.

QATAR

State of Qatar
Emir: Sheikh Hamad Bin Khalifa al-Thani (1995)
Area: 4,000 sq mi. (11,437 sq km)
Population (est. 1996): 547,761 (average annual rate of natural increase: 1.74%); birth rate: 21/1000; infant mortality rate: 19.6/1000; density per square mile: 136
Capital (est. 1990): Doha, 300,000. **Monetary unit:** Qatari riyal. **Language:** Arabic; English is also widely spoken. **Religion:** Islam, 95%. **Literacy rate:** 76%
Economic summary: Gross domestic product (1994 est.): $10.7 billion; $20,820 per capita; –1% real growth rate; inflation: 3% (1993). Labor force: 104,000. Major industrial product: oil. While Qatar depends on oil for much of its revenue, the government is increasing the development of its natural gas production. Qatar is one of the five leading gas producers in the world. Natural resources: oil, gas. Exports: $3.4 billion (f.o.b., 1993 est.): petroleum products 85%, steel, fertilizers. Imports: $1.8 billion (f.o.b., 1993 est.): machinery and equipment, consumer goods, food, chemicals. Major trading partners: France, U.K., U.S., Germany, Japan, Brazil, South Korea, UAE.

Geography. Qatar occupies a small peninsula that extends into the Persian Gulf from the east side of the Arabian Peninsula. Saudi Arabia is to the west and the United Arab Emirates to the south. The country is mainly barren.

Government. For a long time, Qatar was under Turkish protection, but in 1916, the Emir accepted British protection. After the discovery of oil in the 1940s and its exploitation in the 1950s and 1960s, political unrest spread to the sheikhdoms. Qatar declared its independence in 1971.

History. The Emir agreed to the deployment of Arab and Western forces in Qatar following the Iraqi invasion of Kuwait in 1991.

A border dispute erupted with Saudi Arabia that was settled in December 1992. A territorial dispute with Bahrain over the Hawar Islands remains unresolved, however.

In June Qatar signed a defense pact with the U.S., becoming the third Gulf state to do so.

In June 1995 Crown Prince Hamad bin Khalifa al-Thani asked his father, the Emir, to leave the country.

The Emir was not stripped or his title, and much of the power was already in the son's hands. In December Qatar announced it was reviewing its membership in the Gulf Cooperation Council.

ROMANIA

Republic of Romania
President: Ion Iliescu (1990)
Prime Minister: Nicolae Vacaroiu (1992)
Area: 91,700 sq mi. (237,500 sq km)
Population (est. 1996): 21,657,162: Romanian, 89.4%; Hungarian, 7.1%; Gypsies, 1.8% (average annual rate of natural increase: –0.25%); birth rate: 9.77/1000; infant mortality rate: 23.2/1000; density per square mile: 236
Capital: Bucharest; **Largest cities (1992):** Bucharest, 2,351,000; Constanta, 350,476; Iasi, 342,994; Timisoara, 334,278; Cluj-Napoca, 328,008; Galati, 325,788; Brasov, 323,835. **Monetary unit:** Leu. **Languages:** Romanian (official). **Religions:** Christian Orthodox, 86.8%; Roman Catholic, 5%; Protestant, 3.5%. **National name:** Romania. **Literacy rate:** 98%
Economic summary: Gross national product (1994 est.): $64.7 billion; $2,790 per capita; real growth rate 3.4%; inflation 62%; unemployment 10.9% (Dec. 94). Arable land: 43%. Principal products: corn, wheat, livestock, sunflowers, potatoes. Labor force 11.3 million (1992): industry 38%, agriculture 28%, other 34% (1989). Major products: timber, metal production and processing, chemicals, food processing, petroleum. Natural resources: oil, timber, natural gas, coal, iron ore. Exports: $6 billion (f.o.b., 1994): machinery, metals, chemicals, timber, furniture, textiles, foodstuffs. Imports: $6.3 billion (f.o.b., 1994): minerals, fuel, machinery, consumer goods. Major trading partners: Germany, Italy, Russia, France, U.K., U.S.

Geography. A country in southeastern Europe slightly smaller than Oregon, Romania is bordered on the west by Hungary and Yugoslavia, on the north and east by Moldova and Ukraine, on the east by the Black Sea, and on the south by Bulgaria.

The Carpathian Mountains divide Romania's upper half from north to south and connect near the center of the country with the Transylvanian Alps, running east and west.

North and west of these ranges lies the Transylvanian plateau, and to the south and east are the plains of Moldavia and Walachia. In its last 190 miles (306 km), the Danube River flows through Romania only. It enters the Black Sea in northern Dobruja, just south of the border with Ukraine.

Government. A multiparty republic with a bicameral Parliament consisting of an upper house, or Senate, and a lower house, the Chamber of Deputies.

History. Most of Romania was the Roman province of Dacia from about A.D. 100 to 271. From the 6th to the 12th century, wave after wave of barbarian conquerors overran the native Daco-Roman population. By the 16th century, the main Romanian principalities of Moldavia and Walachia had become satellites within the Ottoman Empire, although they retained much independence. After the Russo-Turkish War of 1828–29, they became Russian protectorates. The nation became a kingdom in 1881 after the Congress of Berlin.

King Ferdinand ascended the throne in 1914. At the start of World War I, Romania proclaimed its neutrality, but later joined the Allied side and in 1916 declared war on the Central Powers. The armistice of Nov. 11, 1918, gave Romania vast territories from Russia and the Austro-Hungarian Empire.

The gains of World War I, making Romania the largest Balkan state, included Bessarabia, Transylvania, and Bukovina. The Banat, a Hungarian area, was divided with Yugoslavia.

In 1925, Crown Prince Carol renounced his rights to the throne, and when King Ferdinand died in 1927, Carol's son, Michael (Mihai), became king under a regency. However, Carol returned from exile in 1930, was crowned King Carol II, and gradually became a powerful political force in the country. In 1938, he abolished the democratic constitution of 1923.

In 1940, the country was reorganized along Fascist lines, and the Fascist Iron Guard became the nucleus of the new totalitarian party. On June 27, the Soviet Union occupied Bessarabia and northern Bukovina. By the Axis-dictated Vienna Award of 1940, two-fifths of Transylvania went to Hungary, after which Carol dissolved Parliament and granted the new premier, Ion Antonescu, full power. He abdicated and again went into exile.

Romania subsequently signed the Axis Pact on Nov. 23, 1940, and the following June joined in Germany's attack on the Soviet Union, reoccupying Bessarabia. Following the invasion of Romania by the Red Army in August 1944, King Michael led a coup that ousted the Antonescu government. An armistice with the Soviet Union was signed in Moscow on Sept. 12, 1944.

A Communist-dominated government bloc won elections in 1946, Michael abdicated on Dec. 30, 1947, and Romania became a "people's republic." In 1955, Romania joined the Warsaw Treaty Organization and the United Nations.

Nikolae Ceausescu ruled from 1965 to 1989, when he was overthrown by a coup rising from opposition to his repressive domestic policies.

An army-assisted rebellion in Dec. 1989 led to Ceausescu's overthrow. He was tried and executed. Elections in May 1990 led to the head of the interim government, Ion Iliescu, being elected president.

The government remained torn between introducing free-market reforms and its pledges to hold down unemployment and reduce shortages. While some, though few, measures were implemented, price reforms in November 1990 led to strikes and demonstrations. The opposition remained weak and fragmented.

General elections in September 1992 saw the president returned for a second term, and his party became the largest single party in Parliament.

The country applied for membership in the EU in June 1995 and much legislation that year was crafted in hopes of meeting that objective. Nevertheless, the reform process proceeded slowly.

Local elections took place in June 1996 but were marked by very low voter turnout.

RUSSIA

Russian Federation
President: Boris N. Yeltsin (1991)
Vice President: Aleksandr V. Rutskoi
Area: 6,592,800 sq mi. (17,075,400 sq km)
Population (est. 1996): 148,190,419 (Russian, 82%. Minorities: Tartars, Ukrainians, and Chuvashes); (average annual rate of natural increase: −0.62%); birth rate: 10.2/1000; infant mortality rate: 24.7/1000; density per square mile: 22

Capital and largest city (1994 est.): Moscow, 8,792,000; **Other large cities:** St. Petersburg, 4,882,600; Novosibirsk, 1,418,200; Samara, 1,222,500; Chelyabinsk, 1,124,500; Yekaterinburg, 1,347,000; Nizhny Novgorod, 1,424,600; Kazau, 1,092,300; Perm, 1,086,100; Ufa, 1,091,800; Volgograd, 1,000,400. **Monetary unit:** Ruble. **Religion:** Mainly Eastern Orthodoxy. **Language:** Russian. **Literacy rate:** 100%

Economic summary: Russia is a highly industrialized-agrarian republic. Its vast mineral resources include oil and natural gas, coal, iron, zinc, lead, nickel, aluminum, molybdenum, gold, platinum, and other nonferrous metals. Russia has the world's largest oil and natural gas reserves. Three-quarters of the republic's mineral wealth is concentrated in Siberia and the Far East. Approximately ten million people are engaged in agriculture and they produce half of the region's grain, meat, milk, and other dairy products. The largest granaries are located in the North Caucasus and the Volga and Amur regions. Gross national product (UN, World Bank 1994 est.): $721.2 billion, $4,820 per capita; −15% real growth rate; inflation 10% (per mo. avg.); unemployment: 7.1% (Dec. 94). Labor force (1993 est.): 75 million. Exports: $48 billion (f.o.b., 1994): petroleum and petroleum products, natural gas, wood and wood products, coal, nonferrous metals, chemicals, civilian and military manufactures. Imports: $35.7 billion (f.o.b., 1994): machinery and equipment, chemicals, consumer goods, grain, meat, semifinished metal products. Foreign investment in Russia (1993 est.): $500 million. Major trading partners: Europe, N. America, Japan, Cuba.

Geography: The Russian Federation is the largest republic of the Commonwealth of Independent States. It occupies an area about one and four-fifths the size of the United States, and occupies most of eastern Europe and north Asia. Russia stretches from the Baltic Sea in the west to the Pacific Ocean in the east, and from the Arctic Ocean in the north to the Black Sea and the Caucasus, the Altai, and Sayan Mountains, and the Amur and Ussuri Rivers in the south. It is bordered by Norway and Finland in the northwest, Estonia, Latvia, Belarus, and Ukraine in the west, Georgia and Azerbaijan in the southwest, and Kazakhstan, Mongolia, and China along the southern border. The federation is composed of 21 republics.

Government: A constitutional republic. A new constitution adopted Dec. 12, 1993, gave the President considerable power to rule independently of Parliament. The upper house, or Federation Council, has 176 elected members, two from each of Russia's 88 constituent regions. The State Duma, or lower house, has 450 elected members. The President and Parliament are elected for four-year terms. The President is limited to two terms. President Yeltsin completed his first five-year term in June 1996, and won reelection to a second term.

History: Tradition says the Viking Rurik came to Russia in A.D. 862 and founded the first Russian dynasty in Novgorod. The various tribes were united by the spread of Christianity in the 10th and 11th centuries; Vladimir "the Saint" was converted in 988. During the 11th century, the grand dukes of Kiev held such centralizing power as existed. In 1240, Kiev was destroyed by the Mongols, and the Russian territory was split into numerous smaller dukedoms. Early dukes of Moscow extended their dominions through their office of tribute collector for the Mongols.

In the late 15th century, Duke Ivan III acquired Novgorod and Tver and threw off the Mongol yoke.

Ivan IV, the Terrible (1533–84), first Muscovite Tsar, is considered to have founded the Russian state. He crushed the power of rival princes and boyars (great landowners), but Russia remained largely medieval until the reign of Peter the Great (1689–1725), grandson of the first Romanov Tsar, Michael (1613–45). Peter made extensive reforms aimed at westernization, and through his defeat of Charles XII of Sweden at the Battle of Poltava in 1709, he extended Russia's boundaries to the west.

Catherine the Great (1762–96) continued Peter's westernization program and also expanded Russian territory, acquiring the Crimea and part of Poland. During the reign of Alexander I (1801–25), Napoleon's attempt to subdue Russia was defeated (1812–13) and new territory was gained, including Finland (1809) and Bessarabia (1812). Alexander originated the Holy Alliance, which for a time crushed Europe's rising liberal movement.

Alexander II (1855–81) pushed Russia's borders to the Pacific and into central Asia. Serfdom was abolished in 1861, but heavy restrictions were imposed on the emancipated class. Revolutionary strikes following Russia's defeat in the war with Japan forced Nicholas II (1894–1917) to grant a representative national body (Duma), elected by narrowly limited suffrage. It met for the first time in 1906, little influencing Nicholas in his reactionary course.

World War I demonstrated tsarist corruption and inefficiency, and only patriotism held the poorly equipped army together for a time. Disorders broke out in Petrograd (renamed Leningrad, now St. Petersburg) in March 1917, and defection of the Petrograd garrison launched the revolution. Nicholas II was forced to abdicate on March 15, 1917, and he and his family were killed by revolutionists on July 16, 1918.

A provisional government under the successive premierships of Prince Lvov and a moderate, Alexander Kerensky, lost ground to the radical, or Bolshevik, wing of the Socialist Democratic Labor Party. On Nov. 7, 1917, the Bolshevik revolution, engineered by N. Lenin[1] and Leon Trotsky, overthrew the Kerensky government, and authority was vested in a Council of People's Commissars, with Lenin as Premier.

The humiliating Treaty of Brest-Litovsk (March 3, 1918) concluded the war with Germany, but civil war and foreign intervention delayed Communist control of all Russia until 1920. A brief war with Poland in 1920 resulted in Russian defeat.

Emergence of the U.S.S.R.

The Union of Soviet Socialist Republics was established as a federation on Dec. 30, 1922.

The death of Lenin on Jan. 21, 1924, precipitated an intraparty struggle between Joseph Stalin, General Secretary of the party, and Trotsky, who favored swifter socialization at home and fomentation of revolution abroad. Trotsky was dismissed as Commissar of War in 1925 and banished from the Soviet Union in 1929. He was murdered in Mexico City on Aug. 21, 1940, by a political agent.

Stalin further consolidated his power by a series of purges in the late 1930s, liquidating prominent party leaders and military officers. Stalin assumed the premiership May 6, 1941.

Soviet foreign policy, at first friendly toward Germany and antagonistic toward Britain and France and then, after Hitler's rise to power in 1933, becoming anti-Fascist and pro-League of Nations, took an abrupt turn on Aug. 24, 1939, with the signing of a nonaggression pact with Nazi Germany. The next month, Moscow joined in the German attack on Poland, seizing territory later incorporated into the Ukrainian and Byelorussian S.S.R.'s. The war with Finland, 1939–40, added territory to the Karelian S.S.R. set up March 31, 1940; the annexation of Bessarabia and Bukovina from Romania became part of the new Moldavian S.S.R. on Aug. 2, 1940; and the annexation of the Baltic republics of Estonia, Latvia, and Lithuania in June 1940 created the 14th, 15th, and 16th Soviet Republics. The illegal annexation of the Baltic republics was never recognized by the U.S. for the 51 years leading up to Soviet recognition of Estonia, Latvia, and Lithuania's independence on September 6, 1991.

The Soviet-German collaboration ended abruptly with a lightning attack by Hitler on June 22, 1941, which seized 500,000 square miles of Russian territory before Soviet defenses, aided by U.S. and British arms, could halt it. The Soviet resurgence at Stalingrad from November 1942 to February 1943 marked the turning point in a long battle, ending in the final offensive of January 1945.

Then, after denouncing a 1941 nonaggression pact with Japan in April 1945, when Allied forces were nearing victory in the Pacific, the Soviet Union declared war on Japan on Aug. 8, 1945, and quickly occupied Manchuria, Karafuto, and the Kurile islands.

The U.S.S.R. built a cordon of Communist states running from Poland in the north to Albania and Bulgaria in the south, including East Germany, Czechoslovakia, Hungary, and Romania, composed of the territories Soviet troops occupied at the war's end. With its eastern front solidified, the Soviet Union launched a political offensive against the non-Communist West, moving first to block the Western access to Berlin. The Western powers countered with an airlift, completed unification of West Germany, and organized the defense of Western Europe in the North Atlantic Treaty Organization.

Stalin died on March 6, 1953, and was succeeded the next day by G. M. Malenkov as Premier.

The new power in the Kremlin was Nikita S. Khrushchev, First Secretary of the Party. Khrushchev formalized the Eastern European system into a Council for Mutual Economic Assistance (Comecon) and a Warsaw Pact Treaty Organization as a counterweight to NATO.

The Soviet Union exploded a hydrogen bomb in 1953, developed an intercontinental ballistic missile by 1957, sent the first satellite into space (Sputnik I) in 1957, and put Yuri Gagarin in the first orbital flight around the earth in 1961.

Khrushchev's downfall stemmed from his decision to place Soviet nuclear missiles in Cuba and then, when challenged by the U.S., backing down and removing the weapons. He was also blamed for the ideological break with China after 1963.

Khrushchev was forced into retirement on Oct. 15, 1964, and was replaced by Leonid I. Brezhnev as First Secretary of the Party and Aleksei N. Kosygin as Premier.

Carter and the ailing Brezhnev signed the SALT II treaty in Vienna on June 18, 1979, setting ceilings on each nation's arsenal of intercontinental ballistic missiles. Doubts about U.S. Senate ratification grew, and became a certainty on Dec. 27, when Soviet troops invaded Afghanistan.

Despite the tension between Moscow and Washington, Strategic Arms Reduction Talks (START) began in Geneva between U.S. and Soviet delegations in mid-1982. Negotiations on intermediate missile reduction also continued in Geneva.

---

1. N. Lenin was the pseudonym taken by Vladimir Ilich Ulyanov. It is sometimes given as Nikolai Lenin or V. Lenin.

Rulers of Russia Since 1533

Name	Born	Ruled[1]	Name	Born	Ruled[1]
Ivan IV the Terrible	1530	1533–1584	Alexander III	1845	1881–1894
Theodore I	1557	1584–1598	Nicholas II	1868	1894–1917 [7]
Boris Godunov	c.1551	1598–1605			
Theodore II	1589	1605–1605	**PROVISIONAL GOVERNMENT**		
Demetrius I[2]	?	1605–1606	**(PREMIERS)**		
Basil IV Shuiski	?	1606–1610 [3]	Prince Georgi Lvov	1861	1917–1917
"Time of Troubles"	—	1610–1613	Alexander Kerensky	1881	1917–1917
Michael Romanov	1596	1613–1645			
Alexis I	1629	1645–1676	**POLITICAL LEADERS OF U.S.S.R.**		
Theodore III	1656	1676–1682	N. Lenin	1870	1917–1924
Ivan V[4]	1666	1682–1689 [5]	Aleksei Rykov	1881	1924–1930
Peter I the Great[4]	1672	1682–1725	Vyacheslav Molotov	1890	1930–1941
Catherine I	c.1684	1725–1727	Joseph Stalin[8]	1879	1941–1953
Peter II	1715	1727–1730	Georgi M. Malenkov	1902	1953–1955
Anna	1693	1730–1740	Nikolai A. Bulganin	1895	1955–1958
Ivan VI	1740	1740–1741 [6]	Nikita S. Khrushchev	1894	1958–1964
Elizabeth	1709	1741–1762	Leonid I. Brezhnev	1906	1964–1982
Peter III	1728	1762–1762	Yuri V. Andropov	1914	1982–1984
Catherine II the Great	1729	1762–1796	Konstantin U. Chernenko	1912	1984–1985
Paul I	1754	1796–1801	Mikhail S. Gorbachev	1931	1985–1991
Alexander I	1777	1801–1825			
Nicholas I	1796	1825–1855	**PRESIDENT OF RUSSIA**		
Alexander II	1818	1855–1881	Boris Yeltsin	1931	1991–

1. For Tsars through Nicholas II, year of end of rule is also that of death, unless otherwise indicated. 2. Also known as Pseudo–Demetrius. 3. Died 1612. 4. Ruled jointly until 1689, when Ivan was deposed. 5. Died 1696. 6. Died 1764. 7. Killed 1918. 8. General Secretary of Communist Party, 1924–53.

On November 10, 1982, Soviet radio and television announced the death of Leonid Brezhnev. Yuri V. Andropov, who had formerly headed the K.G.B., was chosen to succeed Brezhnev as General Secretary. By mid-June 1983, Andropov had assumed all of Brezhnev's three titles.

The Soviet Union broke off both the START talks and the parallel negotiations on European-based missiles in November 1983 in protest against the deployment of medium-range U.S. missiles in Western Europe.

After months of illness, Andropov died in February 1984. Konstantin U. Chernenko, a 72-year-old party stalwart who had been close to Brezhnev, succeeded him as General Secretary and, by mid-April, had also assumed the title of President. In the months following Chernenko's assumption of power, the Kremlin took on a hostile mood toward the West of a kind rarely seen since the height of the cold war 30 years before. Led by Moscow, all the Soviet bloc countries except Romania boycotted the 1984 Summer Olympic Games in Los Angeles—tit-for-tat for the U.S.-led boycott of the 1980 Moscow Games, in the view of most observers.

After 13 months in office, Chernenko died on March 10, 1985. He had been ill much of the time and left only a minor imprint on Soviet history.

Chosen to succeed him as Soviet leader was Mikhail S. Gorbachev, at 54 the youngest man to take charge of the Soviet Union since Stalin. Under Gorbachev, the Soviet Union began its long-awaited shift to a new generation of leadership. Unlike his immediate predecessors, Gorbachev did not also assume the title of President but wielded power from the post of party General Secretary. In a surprise move, Gorbachev elevated Andrei Gromyko, 75, for 28 years the Soviet Union's stony-faced Foreign Minister, to the largely ceremonial post of President. He installed a younger man with no experience in foreign affairs, Eduard Shevardnadze, 57, as Foreign Minister.

The Soviet Union took much criticism in early 1986 over the April 24 meltdown at the Chernobyl nuclear plant and its reluctance to give out any information on the accident.

In June 1987, Gorbachev obtained the support of the Central Committee for proposals that would loosen some government controls over the economy, and in June 1988, an unusually open party conference approved several resolutions for changes in the structure of the Soviet system. These included a shift of some power from the Party to local soviets, and a ten-year limit on the terms of elected government and party officials. Gorbachev was elected President in 1989. The elections to the Congress were the first competitive elections in the Soviet Union since 1917. Dissident candidates won a surprisingly large minority although pro-government deputies maintained a strong lock on the Supreme Soviet.

The possible beginning of the fragmentation of the Communist party took place when Boris Yeltsin, leader of the Russian S.S.R., who urged faster reform, left the Communist Party along with other radicals.

In March 1991 the Soviet people were asked to vote on a referendum on national unity engineered by President Gorbachev. The resultant victory for the federal government was tempered by the separate approval in Russia of the creation of a popularly elected republic presidency. In addition, six republics boycotted the vote.

The bitter election contest for the Russian presidency, principally between Yeltsin and a Communist loyalist, resulted in a major victory for Yeltsin. He took the oath of office for the new position on July 10.

Reversing his relative hard-line position adopted in the autumn of 1990, Gorbachev together with leaders of nine Soviet republics signed an accord, called the Union Treaty, which was meant to preserve the unity of the nation. In exchange the federal government would turn over control of industrial and natural resources to the individual republics.

An attempted coup d'état took place on August 19 orchestrated by a group of eight senior officials calling itself the State Committee on the State of Emergency. Boris Yeltsin, barricaded in the Russian Parliament building, defiantly called for a general strike.

The next day huge crowds demonstrated in Leningrad, and Yeltsin supporters fortified barricades surrounding the Parliament building. On August 21 the coup committee disbanded, and at least some of its members attempted to flee Moscow. The Soviet Parliament formally reinstated Gorbachev as President. Two days later he resigned from his position as General Secretary of the Communist Party and recommended that its Central Committee be disbanded. On August 29 Parliament approved the suspension of all Communist Party activities pending an investigation of its role in the failed coup.

At the time of the attempted coup, the republic's President Boris Yeltsin was the most popular political figure in the lands comprising the former Soviet Union. A leading reformer, he became the first directly elected leader in Russian history and received 60% of the vote for President of the Russian Republic.

During the attempted coup in August 1991 by hard-line Communists to dislodge Mikhail Gorbachev, Yeltsin risked his life and rallied the opposition against the coup leaders. His heroism won him worldwide acclaim when the coup failed, and he gained new stature and influence.

Yeltsin championed the cause for national reconstruction and the adoption of a Union Treaty with the other republics to create a free-market economic association.

Dissolution of the U.S.S.R.

On Dec. 12, 1991, the Russian parliament ratified Yeltsin's plea to establish a new commonwealth of independent nations to all former members of the Soviet Union. The new union was created with the governments of Ukraine and Belarus, who along with Russia were the three original cofounders of the Soviet Union in 1922.

After the end of the Soviet Union, Russia and ten other Soviet republics joined in a Commonwealth of Independent States on Dec. 21, 1991.

At the start of 1992, Russia embarked on a series of dramatic economic reforms, including the freeing of prices on most goods, which led to an immediate downturn.

A national referendum on confidence in Yeltsin and his economic program took place in April 1993. To the surprise of many the President and his shock-therapy program won by a resounding margin. Yeltsin convened a constitutional conference in June which adopted a draft document in July. In September Yeltsin dissolved the legislative bodies left over from the Soviet era. The impasse between the executive and the legislature resulted in an armed conflict on October 3. Yeltsin prevailed largely through the support of the military and other forces.

The constitutional referendum on December 12 was a victory for Yeltsin, but the parliamentary election on the same day saw the rise of the extreme nationalist Vladimir Zhirinovsky, with Western-oriented parties performing relatively poorly.

The southern republic of Chechnya's President accelerated his region's drive for independence in 1994. In December Russian troops closed the borders and sought to squelch the independence drive. The Russian military forces met firm and costly resistance.

Shortly before the scheduled presidential election of June 1996 a ceasefire was arranged in Chechnya, with details of a political settlement to be decided later. Yeltsin started the year with slim chances for reelection. But bolstered by favorable media attention, fear of a Communist resurgence, and vigorous campaigning he won the second round of voting in July against a Communist opponent.

RWANDA

Rwandese Republic
President: Pasteur Bizimungu (1994)
Prime Minister: Pierre-Célestin Rwigema (1995)
Area: 10,169 sq mi. (26,338 sq km)
Population (est. 1996): 6,853,359 (average annual rate of natural increase: 1.85%); birth rate: 38.8/1000; infant mortality rate: 118.8/1000; density per square mile: 673
Capital and largest city (1991): Kigali, 232,733. **Monetary unit:** Rwanda franc. **Languages:** Kinyarwanda, French, Swahili, English. **Religions:** Roman Catholic, 56%; Protestant, 18%; Islam, 1%; animist, 25%. **National name:** Repubulika y'u Rwanda. **Literacy rate:** 5%
Economic summary: Gross domestic product (1993 est.): $7.9 billion; $950 per capita; real growth rate –8%; inflation 9.5% (1992 est.); unemployment n.a. Arable land: 29%. Principal products: coffee, tea, bananas, yams, beans. Labor force 3,600,000; in agriculture, 93%; in industry: 2%. Major products: processed foods, light consumer goods, minerals. Natural resources: gold, cassiterite, wolfram. Exports: $44 million (f.o.b., 1993 est.): coffee, tea, tungsten, tin, pyrethrum. Imports: $250 million (f.o.b., 1993 est.): textiles, foodstuffs, machinery and equipment, capital goods, steel. Major trading partners: Belgium, Germany, Kenya, Japan, France, U.S., Italy, U.K.

Geography. Rwanda, in east central Africa, is surrounded by Zaire, Uganda, Tanzania, and Burundi. It is slightly smaller than Maryland.

Steep mountains and deep valleys cover most of the country. Lake Kivu in the northwest, at an altitude of 4,829 feet (1,472 m), is the highest lake in Africa. Extending north of it are the Virunga Mountains, which include Volcan Karisimbi (14,187 ft; 4,324 m), Rwanda's highest point.

Government. A republic. A National Unity government was installed by the Rwandan Patriotic Front on July 19, 1994. Former president Gen. Juvénal Habyarimana was killed on April 6, 1994, in a mysterious plane crash over the capital Kigali. The new cabinet is composed of 22 members. Maj. Gen. Paul Kagame, the victorious Tutsi rebel leader, is both vice president and defense minister.

History. Rwanda, which was part of German East Africa, was first visited by European explorers in 1854. During World War I, it was occupied in 1916 by Belgian troops. After the war, it became a Belgian League of Nations mandate, along with Burundi, under the name of Ruanda-Urundi. The mandate was made a U.N. trust territory in 1946. Until the Belgian Congo achieved independence in 1960, Ruanda-Urundi was administered as part of that colony.

Ruanda became the independent nation of Rwanda on July 1, 1962.

In August 1992 a formal agreement was signed ending the civil war between the government and the Rwandan Patriotic Front.

After the downing of an aircraft in April 1994 carrying the presidents of Rwanda and Burundi, both of whom died in the crash, Tutsi rebels swept across the country in a 14-week civil war, routing the largely Hutu government. In the immediate aftermath an estimated 1.7 million Hutus fled across the border into neighboring Zaire, creating an international humanitarian problem.

The tragic ethnic war continued into and through 1995. A new government was appointed in August to include a number of Hutu, but to little avail.

ST. KITTS AND NEVIS

Federation of St. Kitts and Nevis
Sovereign: Queen Elizabeth II
Governor General: Sir Clement Athelston Arrindell (1985)
Prime Minister: Dr. Denzil Douglas (1995)
Area: St. Kitts 65 sq mi. (169 sq km); Nevis 35 sq mi. (93 sq km)
Population (est. 1996): 41,369 (average annual rate of natural increase: 1.41%); birth rate: 23.3/1000; infant mortality rate: 18.9/1000; density per square mile: 413
Capital: Basseterre (on St. Kitts), 19,000; **Largest town on Nevis:** Charlestown, 1,771. **Monetary unit:** East Caribbean dollar. **Literacy rate:** 98%.
Economic summary: Gross domestic product (1994 est.): $210 million; per capita $5,300; real growth rate 4.5%; inflation 1.6% (1993); unemployment (1990) 12.2%. Arable land: 22%. Principal agricultural products: sugar, rice, yams. Labor force: 20,000 (1981). Major industries: tourism, sugar processing, salt extraction. Exports: $32.4 million (f.o.b., 1992): sugar, manufactures, postage stamps. Imports: $100 million (f.o.b., 1992): foodstuffs, manufactured goods, machinery, fuels. Major trading partners: U.S., U.K., Japan, Trinidad and Tobago, Canada.

St. Christopher-Nevis, preferably St. Kitts and Nevis, was formerly part of the West Indies Associated States, which were established in 1967 and consisted of Antigua and St. Kitts-Nevis-Anguilla of the Leeward Islands, and Dominica, Grenada, St. Lucia, and St. Vincent of the Windward Islands. Statehood for St. Vincent was held up until 1969 because of local political uncertainties. Anguilla's association with St. Christopher-Nevis ended in 1980.

St. Christopher-Nevis, now St. Kitts and Nevis, became independent on September 19, 1983.

The premier of Nevis in 1990 announced that he intended to seek an end to the federation with St. Kitts by the end of 1992, but a local election in June 1992 removed the threat of secession for the time being.

Parliamentary elections held on July 3, 1995, for the 11 seats resulted in a victory for the opposition Labour Party. Hurricanes in September caused extensive structural damage on the islands.

ST. LUCIA

Sovereign: Queen Elizabeth II
Governor-General: H.E. William George Mallet (1996)
Prime Minister: Hon. Dr. Vaughan Lewis (1996)
Area: 238 sq mi. (616 sq km)
Population (est. mid-1994): 157,862 (average annual rate of natural increase: 1.60%); birth rate: 22/1000; infant mortality rate: 20/1000; density per square mile: 663
Capital and largest city (1992 est.): Castries, 13,600. **Monetary unit:** East Caribbean dollar. **Languages:** English and patois. **Religions:** Roman Catholic, 90%; Protestant, 7%; Anglican, 3%. **Member of Commonwealth of Nations. Literacy rate:** 90%
Economic summary: Gross domestic product (1994 est.): $610 million; $4,200 per capita; real growth rate 2%; inflation 0.8% (1993); unemployment (1993 est.) 25%. Arable land: 8%. Principal products: bananas, coconuts, cocoa, citrus fruit. Major industrial products: clothing, assembled electronics, beverages. Exports: $122.8 million (f.o.b., 1992): bananas, cocoa, clothing, vegetables, fruits, coconut oil. Imports: $276 million

(f.o.b., 1992): foodstuffs, machinery and equipment, fertilizers, petroleum products. Major trading partners: U.K., U.S., Caribbean countries, Japan, Canada.

Geography. One of the Windward Isles of the eastern Caribbean, St. Lucia lies just south of Martinique. It is of volcanic origin. A chain of wooded mountains runs from north to south, and from them flow many streams into fertile valleys.

Government. A governor-general represents the sovereign, Queen Elizabeth II. A prime minister is head of government, chosen by a 17-member House of Assembly elected by universal suffrage for a maximum term of five years.

History. Discovered by Spain in 1503 and ruled by Spain and then France, St. Lucia became a British territory in 1803. With other Windward Isles, St. Lucia was granted home rule in 1967 as one of the West Indies Associated States. On Feb. 22, 1979, St. Lucia achieved full independence in ceremonies boycotted by the opposition St. Lucia Labor Party, which had advocated a referendum before cutting ties with Britain.

Unrest and a strike by civil servants forced Prime Minister John Compton to hold elections in July 1979, in which his United Workers Party lost its majority for the first time in 15 years.

A Labor Party government was ousted in turn by Compton and his followers, in elections in May 1982.

Formerly dependent on a single crop, bananas, St. Lucia has sought to lower its chronic unemployment and payments deficit.

Elections of April 1982 returned the prime minister and his party once again to office.

Industrial action hampered the economy in 1995. Also, public-sector workers staged a strike disrupting the economy in the summer. The strike ended without a resolution of the underlying issues.

ST. VINCENT AND THE GRENADINES

Sovereign: Queen Elizabeth II
Governor-General: David Jack (1989)
Prime Minister: James Mitchell (1984)
Area: 150 sq mi. (389 sq km)
Population (est. 1996): 118,344 (average annual rate of natural increase: 1.4%); birth rate: 19.4/1000; infant mortality rate: 16.8/1000; density per square mile: 788
Capital and largest city (1992 est.): Kingstown, 15,466. **Monetary unit:** East Caribbean dollar. **Language:** English, some French patois. **Religions:** Anglican, 47%; Methodist, 28%; Roman Catholic, 13%. **Member of Commonwealth of Nations. Literacy rate:** 96%
Economic summary: Gross domestic product (1994 est.): $235 million; $2,000 per capita; 2% real growth rate; inflation (1993) 4%; unemployment: 35–40%. Arable land: 38%. Principal products: bananas, arrowroot, coconuts. Labor force: 67,000 (1984 est.). Major industry: food processing. Exports: $57.1 million (f.o.b., 1993): bananas, arrowroot, eddos and dasheen (taro), tennis racquets. Imports: $134.6 million (f.o.b., 1993): foodstuffs, machinery and equipment, chemicals, fuels, minerals. Major trading partners: U.K., U.S., Caribbean nations.

Geography. St. Vincent, chief island of the chain, is 18 miles (29 km) long and 11 miles (18 km) wide. One of the Windward Islands in the Lesser Antilles, it is 100 miles (161 km) west of Barbados. The island is mountainous and well forested. The Grenadines, a chain of nearly 600 islets with a total area of only 17 square miles (27 sq km), extend for 60 miles (96 km) from northeast to southwest between St. Vincent and Grenada, southernmost of the Windwards.

St. Vincent is dominated by the volcano La Soufrière, part of a volcanic range running north and south, which rises to 4,048 feet (1,234 m). The volcano erupted over a 10-day period in April 1979, causing the evacuation of the northern two-thirds of the island. (There is also a volcano of the same name on Basse-Terre, Guadeloupe, which became violently active in 1976 and 1977.)

Government. A governor-general represents the sovereign, Queen Elizabeth II. A prime minister, elected by a 15-member unicameral legislature, holds executive power.

History. Discovered by Columbus in 1498, and alternately claimed by Britain and France, St. Vincent became a British colony by the Treaty of Paris in 1783. The islands won home rule in 1969 as part of the West Indies Associated States and achieved full independence Oct. 26, 1979. Prime Minister Milton Cato's government quelled a brief rebellion Dec. 8, 1979, attributed to economic problems following the eruption of La Soufrière in April 1979. Unlike a 1902 eruption which killed 2,000, there was no loss of life but widespread losses to agriculture.

The election of February 1994 provided a victory for the prime minister and his party albeit with a reduced majority in parliament. The deputy prime minister resigned in September 1995 due to a "financial impropriety."

SAN MARINO

Most Serene Republic of San Marino
Co-Regents: Two selected every six months by Grand and General Council
Area: 23.6 sq mi. (62 sq km)
Population (est. 1996): 24,521 (average annual growth rate: 0.3%); birth rate: 10.8/1000; infant mortality rate: 5.5/1000; density per square mile: 1,039
Capital and largest city (est. 1995): San Marino, 2,315.
Monetary unit: Italian lira. **Language:** Italian. **Religion:** Roman Catholic. **National name:** Repubblica di San Marino. **Literacy rate:** 96%
Economic summary: Gross domestic product (1993 est.): $380 million; $15,800 per capita; 2.4% growth rate; inflation: 5.5%; unemployment: 4.9% (Dec. 93). Arable land: 17%. Principal products: wheat and other grains, grapes, olives, cheese. Labor force: approx. 4,300. The tourish sector contributes over 50% of GDP. Key industries are wearing apparel, electronics, and ceramics. Other industrial products: textiles, leather, cement, wine, olive oil. Exports: building stone, lime, chestnuts, wheat, hides, baked goods. Imports: manufactured consumer goods. Major trading partner: Italy.

Geography. One-tenth the size of New York City, San Marino is surrounded by Italy. It is situated in the Apennines, a little inland from the Adriatic Sea near Rimini.

Government. The country is governed by two co-regents. Executive power is exercised by ten ministers. In 1959, the Grand Council granted women the vote. San Marino is a member of the Conference on Security and Cooperation in Europe.

History. According to tradition, San Marino was founded about A.D. 350 and had good luck for centuries in staying out of the many wars and feuds on the Italian peninsula. It is the oldest republic in the world.

Those born in San Marino remain citizens and can vote no matter where they live.

Spring 1993 elections for the Great and General Council gave a majority to the Christian Democrats and Socialists.

Italian financial officials came to the country in 1995 to investigate whether bribes in the scandal rocking Italy had gone through local institutions.

SÃO TOMÉ AND PRÍNCIPE

Democratic Republic of São Tomé and Príncipe
President: Miguel Trovoada (1991)
Prime Minister: Armindo Vaz d'Almeida (1995)
Area: 370 sq mi. (958 sq km)
Population (est. 1996): 144,128 (average annual growth rate: 2.58%); birth rate: 34.4/1000; infant mortality rate: 61.1/1000; density per square mile: 389
Capital and largest city (est. 1990): São Tomé, 43,420.
Monetary unit: Dobra. **Language:** Portuguese. **Religions:** Roman Catholic, Evangelical Protestant, Seventh-Day Adventist. **Literacy rate:** 57% (est.)
Economic summary: Gross domestic product (1993 est.): $133 million; $1,000 per capita; inflation: 27% (1992); unemployment: n.a. Arable land: 1%. Principal agricultural products: cocoa, copra, coconuts, palm oil, coffee, bananas. Labor force: 21,096 (1981): mostly in subsistence agriculture. Major industrial products: shirts, soap, beer, processed fish and shrimp. Exports: $5.5 million (f.o.b., 1993 est.): cocoa, coffee, copra, palm oil. Imports: $31.5 million (f.o.b., 1992 est.): textiles, machinery, electrical equipment, fuels, food products. Major trading partners: Netherlands, Portugal, Germany, China, Angola.

Geography. The tiny volcanic islands of São Tomé and Príncipe lie in the Gulf of Guinea about 150 miles (240 km) off West Africa. São Tomé (about 330 sq mi.; 859 sq km) is covered by a dense mountainous jungle, out of which have been carved large plantations. Príncipe (about 40 sq mi.; 142 sq km) consists of jagged mountains. Other islands in the republic are Pedras Tinhosas and Rolas.

Government. The constitution grants supreme power to a 55-seat People's Assembly composed of members elected for four years. In 1990 a referendum approved a new constitution paving the way for a multi-party democracy.

History. São Tomé and Príncipe were discovered by Portuguese navigators in 1471 and settled by the end of the century. Intensive cultivation by slave labor made the islands a major producer of sugar during the 17th century, but output declined until the introduction of coffee and cacao in the 19th century brought new prosperity. The island of São Tomé was the world's largest producer of cacao in 1908, and the crop is still the most important. An exile liberation movement was formed in 1953 after Portuguese landowners quelled labor riots by killing several hundred African workers.

The Portuguese revolution of 1974 brought the end of the overseas empire and the new Lisbon government transferred power to the liberation movement on July 12, 1975.

A former prime minister and dissident Miguel Trovoada was elected president in March 1991 after the withdrawal of the two other candidates.

In April 1995 Príncipe became autonomous. In August a bloodless military coup was reversed through Angolan mediation. In December an agreement was struck on forming a coalition government.

SAUDI ARABIA

Kingdom of Saudi Arabia
King and Prime Minister: King Fahd bin 'Abdulaziz (1982)
Area: 865,000 sq mi. (2,250,070 sq km)
Population (est. 1996): 19,409,058 (average annual rate of natural increase: 3.3%); birth rate: 38.3/1000; infant mortality rate: 46.4/1000; density per square mile: 22
Capital: Riyadh; **Largest cities (1993):** Riyadh, 3,000,000; Jeddah, 2,500,000; Makkah (Mecca) (est. 1994) 550,000. **Monetary unit:** Riyal. **Language:** Arabic, English widely spoken. **Religion:** Islam, 100%. **National name:** Al-Mamlaka al-'Arabiya as-Sa'udiya. **Literacy rate:** 65%
Economic summary: Gross domestic product (1994 est.): $173.1 billion; $9,510 per capita; real growth rate –3%; inflation 1%. (1993 est.); unemployment 6.5% (1992 est.). Arable land: 5%. Principal agricultural products: dates, grains, livestock, wheat, fish, flowers. Labor force: 5,000,000; about 25% are foreign workers; in government, 34%; industry and oil, 28%. Major industrial products: petroleum, cement, plastic products, steel, packaged goods. Natural resources: oil, natural gas, iron ore. Exports: $39.4 billion (f.o.b, 1993 est.): petroleum and petroleum products. Imports: $28.9 billion (f.o.b, 1993 est.): manufactured goods, transport equipment, construction materials, processed food. Major trading partners: U.S., Germany, Great Britain and other Western European countries, South Korea, Taiwan, Japan.

Geography. Saudi Arabia occupies most of the Arabian Peninsula, with the Red Sea and the Gulf of Aqaba to the west, the Arabian Gulf to the east. Neighboring countries are Jordan, Iraq, Kuwait, Qatar, the United Arab Emirates, the Sultanate of Oman, Yemen, and Bahrain, connected to the Saudi mainland by a causeway.

A narrow coastal plain on the Red Sea rims a mountain range that spans the length of the western coastline. These mountains gradually rise in elevation from north to south. East of these mountains is a massive plateau which slopes gently downward toward the Arabian Gulf. Part of this plateau is covered by the world's largest continuous sand desert, the Rub Al-Khali, or Empty Quarter. Saudi Arabia's oil region lies primarily in the eastern province along the Arabian Gulf, but significant recent discoveries have also been made in the interior south of Riyadh.

Government. Saudi Arabia is a monarchy based on the Sharia (Islamic law), as revealed in the Koran (the holy book) and the Hadith (teachings and sayings of the prophet Mohammed). A Council of Ministers is formed in 1953, which acts as a cabinet under the leadership of the king. There are 21 ministries.

Royal and ministerial decrees account for most of the promulgated legislation, treaties, and conventions.

There are no political parties.

In March 1992 King Fahd announced new bylaws for the Consultative Council to propose and review laws. The cabinet, composed of 21 members (four are members of the Saudi royal family) passes laws.

History. Mohammed united the Arabs in the 7th century, and his followers, led by the caliphs, founded a great empire, with its capital at Medina. Later, the caliphate capital was transferred to Damascus and then Baghdad, but Arabia retained its importance because of the holy cities of Mecca and Medina. In the 16th and 17th centuries, the Turks established at least nominal rule over much of Arabia, and in the middle of the 18th century, it was divided into separate principalities.

The Kingdom of Saudi Arabia is almost entirely the creation of King Ibn Saud (1882–1953). A descendant of earlier Wahabi rulers, he seized Riyadh, the capital of Nejd, in 1901 and set himself up as leader of the Arab nationalist movement. By 1906 he had established Wahabi dominance in Nejd. He conquered Hejaz in 1924–25, consolidating it and Nejd into a dual kingdom in 1926. In 1932, Hejaz and Nejd became a single kingdom, which was officially named Saudi Arabia. A year later the region of Asir was incorporated into the kingdom.

Oil was discovered in 1936, and commercial production began during World War II. Saudi Arabia was neutral until nearly the end of the war, but it was permitted to be a charter member of the United Nations. The country joined the Arab League in 1945 and took part in the 1948–49 war against Israel.

On Ibn Saud's death in 1953, his eldest son, Saud, began an 11-year reign marked by an increasing hostility toward the radical Arabism of Egypt's Gamal Abdel Nasser. In 1964, the ailing Saud was deposed and replaced by the premier, Crown Prince Faisal, who gave vocal support but no military help to Egypt in the 1967 Mideast war.

Faisal's assassination by a deranged kinsman in 1975 shook the Middle East but failed to alter his kingdom's course. His successor was his brother, Prince Khalid. Khalid gave influential support to Egypt during negotiations on Israeli withdrawal from the Sinai desert.

King Khalid died of a heart attack June 13, 1982, and was succeeded by his half-brother, Prince Fahd bin 'Abdulaziz, 60, who had exercised the real power throughout Khalid's reign. King Fahd, a pro-Western modernist, chose his 58-year-old half-brother, Abdullah, as Crown Prince.

Saudi Arabia and the smaller, oil-rich Arab states on the Persian Gulf, fearful that they might become Ayatollah Ruhollah Khomeini's next targets if Iran conquered Iraq, made large financial contributions to the Iraqi war effort. They began being dragged into the conflict themselves in the spring of 1984, when Iraq and Iran extended their ground war to attacks on Gulf shipping. First, Iraq attacked tankers loading at Iran's Kharg Island terminal with air-to-ground missiles, then Iran struck back at tankers calling at Saudi Arabia and other Arab countries.

At the same time, cheating by some members of the Organization of Petroleum Exporting Countries, competition from nonmember oil producers, and conservation efforts by consuming nations combined to drive down the world price of oil. Saudi Arabia has one-third of all known oil reserves, but falling demand and rising production outside OPEC combined to reduce its oil revenues from $120 billion in 1980 to $43 billion in 1984 to less $25 billion in 1985, threatening the country with domestic unrest and undermining its influence in the Gulf area.

At the start of 1996 King Faud passed authority to his half-brother Abdullah, saying he needed rest. Although not an abdication, it was unclear how long the King would be absent.

In the wake of bombing in June that killed 19 Americans, the highest Saudi religious authority concluded that the act was a sin against Islam.

SENEGAL

Republic of Senegal
President: Abdou Diouf (1981)
Area: 75,954 sq mi. (196,722 sq km)
Population (est. 1996): 9,092,749 (average annual rate of natural increase: 3.37%); birth rate: 45.5/1000; infant mortality rate: 64/1000; density per square mile: 119
Capital and largest city (1994 est.): Dakar, 1,729,823.
Monetary unit: Franc CFA. **Ethnic groups:** Wolofs, Sereres, Peuls, Tukulers, and others. **Languages:** French (official); Wolof, Serer, other ethnic dialects. **Religions:** Islam, 92%; indigenous, 6%; Christian, 2%. **National name:** République du Sénégal. **Literacy rate:** 38%
Economic summary: Gross domestic product (1993 est.): $12.3 billion; $1,450 per capita; real growth rate –2%; inflation (1991 est.) –1.8%; unemployment n.a. Arable land: 27%. Principal agricultural products: peanuts, millet, corn, rice, sorghum. Labor force: 2,509,000; 77% subsistence agriculture workers. Major industrial products: processed food, phosphates, refined petroleum, cement, and fish. Natural resources: fish, phosphate, iron ore. Exports: $904 million (f.o.b., 1991 est.): peanuts, phosphate rock, canned fish, petroleum products. Imports: $1.2 billion (c.i.f., 1991 est.): foodstuffs, consumer goods, machinery, transport equipment, petroleum. Major trading partners: U.S., Western European countries, African neighbors, Japan, China, India.

Geography. The capital of Senegal, Dakar, is the westernmost point in Africa. The country, slightly smaller than South Dakota, surrounds Gambia on three sides and is bordered on the north by Mauritania, on the east by Mali, and on the south by Guinea and Guinea-Bissau.

Senegal is mainly a low-lying country, with a semi-desert area in the north and northeast and forests in the southwest. The largest rivers include the Senegal in the north and the Casamance in the south tropical climate region.

Government. There is a National Assembly of 120 members, elected every five years. There is universal suffrage and a constitutional guarantee of equality before the law.

History. The Portuguese had some stations on the banks of the Senegal River in the 15th century, and the first French settlement was made at Saint-Louis about 1650. The British took parts of Senegal at various times, but the French gained possession in 1840 and organized the Sudan as a territory in 1904. In 1946, together with other parts of French West Africa, Senegal became part of the French Union. On June 20, 1960, it became an independent republic federated with the Sudanese Republic in the Mali Federation, from which it withdrew two months later.

In 1973, Senegal joined with six other states to create the West African Economic Community.

In elections of February 21, 1993 President Diouf was reelected. In May legislative elections the president's Socialist Party captured 84 of the 120 seats.

A political demonstration in February 1994 organized by the opposition coalition resulted in the death of six policemen and injury to dozens more.

An opposition leader became a member of a new coalition government in March 1995.

SEYCHELLES

Republic of Seychelles
President: France-Albert René (1977)
Area: 175 sq mi. (453 sq km)
Population (est. 1996): 77,575 (average annual rate of natural increase: 1.37%); birth rate: 21/1000; infant mortality rate: 12.5/1000; density per square mile: 443
Capital and largest city (1993 est.): Victoria, 25,000.
Monetary unit: Seychelles rupee. **Languages:** English and French (official); Creole. **Religions:** Roman Catholic, 90%; Anglican, 8%. **Member of Commonwealth of Nations.** Literacy rate: 58%
Economic summary: Gross domestic product (1993 est.): $430 million; $6,000 per capita; real growth rate –2%; inflation 3.9%; unemployment n.a.. Arable land: 4%. Principal agricultural products: vanilla, coconuts, cinnamon. Labor force: 27,700; 31% in industry and commerce. Major industrial products: processed coconut and vanilla, coir rope. Exports: $50 million (f.o.b., 1993 est.): fish, canned tuna, copra, cinnamon bark. Imports: $261 million (f.o.b., 1993 est.): food, tobacco, manufactured goods, machinery, petroleum products, transport equipment. Major trading partners: U.K., France, Japan, Pakistan, Réunion, South Africa.

Geography. Seychelles consists of an archipelago of about 100 islands in the Indian Ocean northeast of Madagascar. The principal islands are Mahé (55 sq mi.; 142 sq km), Praslin (15 sq mi.; 38 sq km), and La Digue (4 sq mi.; 10 sq km). The Aldabra, Farquhar, and Desroches groups are included in the territory of the republic.

Government. A multiparty republic with one legislative house, the National Assembly.

History. Seized from France by Britain in 1810, the Seychelles Islands remained a colony until June 29, 1976. The state is an independent republic within the Commonwealth.

On June 5, 1977, Prime Minister Albert René ousted the islands' first president, James Mancham, suspending the constitution and the 25-member National Assembly. Mancham, whose "lavish spending" and flamboyance were cited by René in seizing power, charged that Soviet influence was at work. The new president denied this and, while more left than his predecessor, pledged to keep the Seychelles in the nonaligned group of countries.

An unsuccessful attempted coup against René attracted international attention when a group of 50 South African mercenaries posing as rugby players attacked the Victoria airport on Nov. 25, 1981.

An election was held in July 1992 for members of a commission to write a new constitution. Fourteen of the 23 seats went to the president's Seychelles People's Progressive Party. The draft constitution that emerged, however, was defeated in a referendum in November, failing to get the 60% of the vote needed for adoption.

The commission reconvened in January 1993 with the participation of the opposition Democratic Party. In May a draft constitution, institutionalizing a multiparty system and a 33-member National Assembly, was ready. In the June referendum more than 73% of the votes approved it. The presidential election in July under the new terms affirmed René's position and that of his party.

A new law in 1995 granted immunity from criminal prosecution to anyone investing $10 million in the country.

SIERRA LEONE

Republic of Sierra Leone
President: Alhaji Ahmad Tejan Kabba
Area: 27,925 sq mi. (73,326 sq km)
Population (est. 1996): 4,793,121 (average annual rate of natural increase: 2.89%); birth rate: 47.1/1000; infant mortality rate: 135.6/1000; density per square mile: 171
Capital and largest city (1994 est.): Freetown, 1,300,000.
Monetary unit: Leone. **Languages:** English (official), Mende, Temne, Krio. **Religions:** Islam, 40%; Christian, 35%; Indigenous, 20%. **Member of Commonwealth of Nations. Literacy rate:** 21%
Economic summary: Gross domestic product (FY 1993 est.): $4.5 billion; $1,000 per capita; real growth rate n.a.; inflation 22% (1993); unemployment n.a. Arable land: 25%; principal agricultural products: coffee, cocoa, palm kernels, rice. Labor force: 1,369,000 (est.); 65% in agriculture. Major industrial products: diamonds, bauxite, rutile, beverages, cigarettes, textiles, footwear. Natural resources: diamonds, bauxite, iron ore. Exports: $149 million (f.o.b., 1993): diamonds, rutile, bauxite, cocoa, coffee. Imports: $149 million (c.i.f., 1993): food, petroleum, products, capital goods. Major trading partners: U.K., U.S., Western European countries, Japan, China, Nigeria.

Geography. Sierra Leone, on the Atlantic Ocean in West Africa, is half the size of Illinois. Guinea, in the north and east, and Liberia, in the south, are its neighbors.

Mangrove swamps lie along the coast, with wooded hills and a plateau in the interior. The eastern region is mountainous.

Government. Sierra Leone became an independent nation on April 27, 1961, and declared itself a republic on April 19, 1971.

Sierra Leone became a one party state under the aegis of the All People's Congress Party in April 1978.

A military government came into power in April 1992.

History. The coastal area of Sierra Leone was ceded to English settlers in 1788 by the English as a home for blacks discharged from the British armed forces and also for runaway slaves who had found asylum in London. The British protectorate over the hinterland was proclaimed in 1896.

After elections in 1967, the British governor-general replaced Sir Albert Margai, head of the Sierra Leone People's Party (SLPP), which had held power since independence, with Siaka Stevens, head of All People's Congress (APC), as prime minister. The army took over the government; then another coup in April 1968 restored civilian rule and put the military leaders in jail.

A coup attempt early in 1971 by the army commander was apparently foiled by loyal army officers, but Prime Minister Stevens called in troops of neighboring Guinea's army, under a 1970 mutual defense pact, to guard his residence. After perfunctorily blaming the U.S. for the coup attempt, Stevens switched governors-general, changed the constitution, and ended up with a republic, of which he was first president. Dr. Stevens' picked successor, Major-General Joseph Saidu Momoh, was elected unopposed on Oct. 1, 1985.

Rebel soldiers in April 1992 toppled the government, voicing support for democracy. A few days later the ruling junta arrested their leader, placing in charge their second-in-command.

The government in December 1993 announced a timetable for a return to civilian rule and a multiparty democracy. Nevertheless, rebels continued to reject a government they considered corrupt.

A military coup ousted the country's military leader and president in January 1996. Nevertheless, a multi-party presidential election proceeded in February, despite being marred by violence. As no one reeived a majority, a runoff was necessary. As the second-round votes were counted in March a ceasefire with the rebels was announced. People's Party candidate Ahmed Tejan Kebbah won with 59.4% of the votes.

SINGAPORE

Republic of Singapore
President: Ong Teng Cheong (1993)
Prime Minister: Goh Chok Tong (1990)
Area: 246.7 sq mi. (639 sq km)
Population (est. 1996): 3,396,924 (average annual rate of natural increase: 1.17%); birth rate: 16.3/1000; infant mortality rate: 4.7/1000; density per square mile: 13,769
Capital (1995 est.): Singapore, 2,989,300. **Monetary unit:** Singapore dollar. **Languages:** Malay, Chinese (Mandarin), Tamil, English. **Religions:** Islam, Christian, Buddhist, Hindu, Taoist. **Member of Commonwealth of Nations. Literacy rate:** 91.3%
Economic summary: Gross domestic product (1994 est.): $57 billion; $19,940 per capita; real growth rate 10.1%; inflation 2.0%; unemployment 2.6%. Arable land: 4%. Principal agricultural products: poultry, rubber, copra, vegetables, fruits. Labor force (1994): 1,693,100; manufacturing 429,500; commerce 363,600; community, social, and personal services 344,100; financial and business services 173,400. Major industries: petroleum refining, ship repair, electronics, financial and business services, biotechnology. Exports: $96.4 billion (1994 est.): petroleum products, rubber, manufactured goods, electrical and electronics, computers and computer peripherals. Imports: $102.4 billion (c.i.f., 1994): aircraft, petroleum, chemicals, foodstuffs. Major trading partners: U.S., E.U., Hong Kong, Japan, Malaysia.

Geography. The Republic of Singapore consists of the main island of Singapore, off the southern tip of the Malay Peninsula between the South China Sea and the Indian Ocean, and 58 nearby islands.

There are extensive mangrove swamps extending inland from the coast, which is broken by many inlets.

Government. There is a cabinet, headed by the prime minister, and a parliament of 81 members elected by universal suffrage.

History. Singapore, founded in 1819 by Sir Stamford Raffles, became a separate crown colony of Britain in 1946, when the former colony of the Straits Settlements was dissolved. The other two settlements—Penang and Malacca—were transferred to the Union of Malaya, and the small island of Labuan was transferred to North Borneo. The Cocos (or Keeling) Islands and Christmas Island were transferred to Australia in 1955 and in 1958, respectively.

Singapore attained full internal self-government in 1959. On Sept. 16, 1963, it joined Malaya, Sabah (North Borneo), and Sarawak in the Federation of Malaysia. It withdrew from the Federation on Aug. 9, 1965, and proclaimed itself a republic the next month.

A law of January 1991 expanded the powers of the presidency. In August the ruling People's Action Party won 36 of the 40 contested parliamentary seats.

The first direct presidential election took place in August 1993. Ong Teng Cheong faced what initially appeared to be only token opposition but which took 40% of the vote.

The government announced in August 1994 that unwed mothers could no longer receive subsidized housing.

The country became the first to repatriate all Vietnamese boat people in 1996.

SLOVAKIA

Republic of Slovakia
President: Michal Kovac (1993)
Prime Minister: Vladimir Meciar (1994)
Area: 18,917 sq mi. (48,995 sq km)
Population (est. 1996): 5,374,362; 90% Slovaks, other: Hungarians, Czechs. (Average annual rate of natural increase: 0.33%); birth rate: 12.6/1000; infant mortality rate: 10.7/1000; density per square mile: 284
Capital and largest city (1993 est.): Bratislava, 446,600. Other large city (est. 1993): Kosice, 237,300. **Monetary unit:** Koruna. **Language:** Slovak (official), Hungarian. **Religions:** Protestant, Greek Catholic, Orthodox, Jewish. **Literacy rate:** 99%
Economic summary: Gross domestic product (1994 est.): $32.8 billion, $6,070 per capita; real growth rate: 4.3%; inflation: 12%; unemployment: 14.6%. Important industries are iron and nonferrous mining, metal processing, and shipbuilding. Other industries are construction materials, consumer appliances, and leather goods. Labor force: 2.484 million. Major agricultural products: grains, potatoes, sugar beets, fruit, vegetables, forestry. Livestock: pigs, cattle, poultry, sheep. Land use: 37% forest and woodland, 13% meadows and pastures, 1% permanent crops, 9% other. Exports: $6.3 billion (f.o.b., Jan.–Nov. 94): machinery and transport equipment, chemicals, fuels, minerals, metals, agricultural products. Imports: $61 billion (f.o.b., Jan.–Nov. 94): machinery, transport equipment, fuels and lubricants, manufactured goods, raw materials, chemicals, agricultural products. Major trading partners: Czech Republic, CIS republics, Germany, Poland, Austria, Hungary, Italy, U.K., U.S., Switzerland.

Geography. Slovakia is bordered by Poland in the north, Ukraine in the east, Hungary in the south, Austria in the southwest, and the Czech Republic in the west. The land has rugged mountains, rich in mineral resources, with vast forests and pastures. Southern Slovakia is a river island called "Zitny Ostrov," with fertile soil. Slovakia is about twice the size of the state of Maryland.

Government. A parliamentary democracy. The president is elected to a five-year term by the unicameral National Council (legislative branch). The 150 members of the National Council are elected for a four-year term.

History. Present day Slovakia was settled by Slavic Slovaks about the 5th century A.D. They were politically united in the Moravian empire in the 9th century. In 907, the Germans and the Magyars conquered the Moravian state and the Slovaks fell under Hungarian control from the 10th century up until 1918.

When the Hapsburg state collapsed in 1918 following World War I, the Slovaks joined the Czech lands of Bohemia, Moravia, and part of Silesia to form the new joint state of Czechoslovakia.

In March 1939, Germany occupied Czechoslovakia, established a German "protectorate," and created a puppet state out of Slovakia with Monsignor Josef Tiso as premier. The country was liberated from the Germans by the Soviet army in the spring of 1945, and Slovakia was restored to its pre-war status and rejoined to a new Czechoslovakian state.

After the Communist party took power in February 1948, Slovakia was again subjected to a centralized Czech-dominated government, and antagonism between the two republics developed. On January 1969, the nation became the Slovak Socialist Republic of Czechoslovakia.

Nearly 42 years of Communist rule for Slovakia ended when Vaclav Havel became president of Czechoslovakia in 1989 and democratic political reform began. However, with the demise of Communist power, a strong Slovak nationalist movement resurfaced and the rival relationship between the two states increased.

By the end of 1991, tensions heightened between Slovak and Czech political leaders following a debate over a Declaration of Slovak Sovereignty proclaimed by the Slovak parliament. Various attempts to resolve the issue by both parties failed. A crisis developed over whether the Czech and Slovak republics should continue to coexist within the federal structure or divide into two independent states.

The results of the general election in June 1992 failed to affirm the continuing coexistence of the Czech and Slovak Republics within a federal state and resulted in the Czech and Slovak political leaders agreeing to separate their nations into two fully independent republics. The Republic of Slovakia came into existence on January 1, 1993. The parliament in February elected Michael Kovac president.

Nationalist prime minister Vladimir Meciar lost a vote of confidence in March 1994. A coalition of 5 parties chose the more moderate Jozef Moravcik to form a new government.

General elections later that year produced an unexpectedly strong showing for Meciar's party, thrusting him again into the premiership.

Meciar signed a bilateral treaty with Hungary in March 1995, but it failed to end concern for ethnic minorities and at the end of the year was still not ratified by the legislature. The growing repression of a free press and other restrictions were viewed with alarm in the West, particularly in Germany.

SLOVENIA

Republic of Slovenia
President: Milan Kucan
Prime Minister: Janez Drnovsek
Area: 7,819 sq mi. (20,251 sq km)
Population (est. 1996): 1,951,433. Major ethnic groups: 87.6% Slovenes, 2.7% Croats, 2.4% Serbs, 1.4% Muslims; (average annual rate of natural increase: –.11%); birth rate: 8.27/1000; infant mortality rate: 7.3/1000; density per square mile: 249

Capital and largest city (est. 1994): Ljubljana, 270,759
Other large city: Maribor, 103,512. **Monetary unit:**
Slovenian Tolar. **Languages:** Slovenian; most can also
speak Serbo-Croatian. **Religions:** predominantly Roman Catholic. **Literacy rate:** est. 96%
Economic summary: (1994) Gross domestic product:
$14.2 billion; $7,180 per capita; real growth rate 4%;
inflation 20%; unemployment (est.): 9%. Principal
products are corn, rye, oats, potatoes, fruit, livestock
raising, and forestry. Mineral resources include coal,
iron, and mercury. Major manufactured products are
automobiles, iron and steel, cement, chemicals, textiles, furniture, shoes, electrical machinery, pharmaceuticals. Exports: $8.3 billion (f.o.b.; 1995): machinery
and transport equipment, 38%; other manufactured
goods, 44%; chemicals, 9%; food and live animals,
4.6%; raw materials, 3%. Imports: $9.5 billion (c.i.f.,
1995): machinery and transport equipment, 35%; other
manufactured goods, 26.7%; chemicals, 14.5%; raw
materials, 9.4%; fuels and lubricants, 7%. Trading
partners: Germany, Italy, France, Croatia, Austria,
Russia, Macedonia, U.S.

Geography: Slovenia occupies an area about the
size of the state of Massachusetts. It borders Austria
on the north, Hungary in the northeast, the Republic
of Croatia in the south, and Italy and the Adriatic Sea
in the west. It is largely a mountainous republic and
almost half of the land is forested, with hilly plains
spread across the central and eastern regions. Mount
Triglav, the highest peak, rises to 9,393 ft (2,864 m).

Government: A parliamentary democracy with two
legislative houses consisting of a 90-member National Assembly and 40-member State Council.

History: The Slovenes were a south-Slavic group
that settled in the region during the 6th century A.D.
During the 7th century, they established the Slavic
state of Samu which owed its allegiance to the Avars,
who dominated the Hungarian plain until Charlemagne defeated them in the late 8th century.
   In the 11th century, Slovenia was a separate province of the Kingdom of Hungary. When the Hungarians were defeated by the Turks in 1526, Hungary accepted Austrian Hapsburg rule in order to escape
Turkish domination. Thus, Slovenia and Croatia became part of the Austro-Hungarian kingdom when
the dual monarchy was established in 1857.
   After 1848, nationalism was revived in Slovenia,
and following the defeat and collapse of Austria-Hungary in World War I, Slovenia declared its independence. It formally joined with Montenegro, Serbia, and
Croatia on Dec. 4, 1918, to form the new nation called
the Kingdom of the Serbs, Croats, and Slovenes. The
name was later changed to Yugoslavia in 1929.
   During World War II, Germany occupied Yugoslavia
and Slovenia was divided among Germany, Italy, and
Hungary. For the duration of the war many Slovenes
fought a guerrilla warfare against the Nazis under the
leadership of the Croatian-born communist resistance
leader Marshal Tito. After the final defeat of the Axis
powers in 1945, Slovenia was again made into a republic of the newly established nation of Yugoslavia.
   Slovenia declared its independence from Yugoslavia on June 25, 1991. The Serbian-dominated Yugoslavian army tried to keep Slovenia in line and some
brief fighting took place, but the Yugoslavian army
withdrew its forces and, unlike neighboring Croatia,

Slovenia was able to maintain a peaceful status.
   A coalition government of the Liberal Democrats
and the Christian Democrats was formed in January
1993 in the wake of the December 1992 election.
   The coalition dissolved in May 1996 after the foreign minister received a no-confidence vote in parliament, which accused him of incompetence and for
failing to improve relations with Italy.

SOLOMON ISLANDS

Sovereign: Queen Elizabeth II
Governor-General: Sir Moses Pitakaka (1994)
Prime Minister: Hon. Solomon Mamaloni (1994)
Area: 11,500 sq mi. (29,785 sq km)
Population (est. 1996): 412,902 (average annual rate of
natural increase: 3.35%); birth rate: 37.9/1000; infant
mortality rate: 25.8/1000; density per square mile: 35
Capital and largest city (1990 est.): Honiara (on Guadal-
canal), 35,288. **Monetary unit:** Solomon Islands dollar.
Languages: English, Pidgin, 80 other languages and
dialects. **Religions:** Anglican; Roman Catholic; South
Seas Evangelical; Seventh-Day Adventist, United
(Methodist) Church, other Protestant. **Member of British Commonwealth. Literacy rate:** 30%
Economic summary: Gross domestic product (1992 est.):
$1 billion; $2,590 per capita; real growth rate 8%; inflation 13%. Arable land: 1%. Principal agricultural products: coconuts, palm oil, rice, cocoa, yams, pigs. Labor
force (1984): 23,448; agriculture, forestry, fishing
32.4%; services 25%. Major industrial products: processed fish, copra. Natural resources: fish, timber,
gold, bauxite. Exports: $84 million (f.o.b., 1991): fish,
timber, copra, palm oil. Imports: $110 million (c.i.f.,
1991): machinery and transport equipment, foodstuffs,
fuel. Major trading partners: Japan, E.U., Australia,
Thailand, Singapore, Hong Kong, China.

Geography. Lying east of New Guinea, this island
nation consists of the southern islands of the Solomon group: Guadalcanal, Malaita, Santa Isabel, San
Cristóbal, Choiseul, New Georgia, Santa Cruz group,
and numerous smaller islands.

Government. After 85 years of British rule, the Solomons achieved independence July 7, 1978. The
crown is represented by a governor-general and legislative power is vested in a unicameral legislature of
47 members, led by the prime minister.

History. Discovered in 1567 by Alvaro de Mendana,
the Solomons were not visited again for about 200
years. In 1886, Great Britain and Germany divided the
islands between them. In 1914, Australian forces took
over the German islands and the Solomons became an
Australian mandate in 1920. In World War II, most of
the islands were occupied by the Japanese. American
forces landed on Guadalcanal on Aug. 7, 1942.
   The general election in May 1993 resulted in a loss
of a parliamentary majority for Prime Minister Mamaloni. The National Coalition Partners, an alliance
of 7 groups, formed a new government.
   Francis Billy Hilly served as prime minister in
1993–94, but in early November Mamalonie assumed
the post for the third time. The new government
promised to urge the privatization of the public sector.

SOMALIA

Somali Democratic Republic
President: Vacant, no functioning government in place.
Prime Minister: Vacant.
Area: 246,199 sq mi. (637,655 sq km)
Population (est. 1996): 9,639,151 (average annual rate of natural increase: 3.10%); birth rate: 44.2/1000; infant mortality rate: 121.1/1000; density per sq mi.: 40
Capital and largest city (est. 1990): Mogadishu, 900,000.
Monetary unit: Somali shilling. **Language:** Somali (official), Arabic, English, Italian. **Religion:** Islam (Sunni).
National name: Al Jumhouriya As-Somalya al-Dimocradia. **Literacy rate:** 24%
Economic summary: Political turmoil in 1991–92 resulted in widespread famine and a substantial drop in economic output. Much of the economy has been devastated by the civil war. Agriculture is the most important sector with livestock accounting for about 40% of GDP and about 65% of export earnings. Gross domestic product (1994 est.): $3.3 billion; $500 per capita; real growth rate: n.a.. Arable land: 2%. Principal agricultural products: livestock, bananas, sorghum, cereals, sugar cane, maize. Labor force: 2,200,000; very few are skilled laborers. A few small industries: sugar refining, textiles, petroleum refining. Natural resources: uranium. Exports: $58 million (1990 est.): livestock, skins and hides, bananas. Imports: $249 million (1990 est.): textiles, foodstuffs, construction materials and equipment, petroleum products. Major trading partners: Saudi Arabia, Italy, U.S., U.K., Germany, Italy.

Geography. Somalia, situated in the Horn of Africa, lies along the Gulf of Aden and the Indian Ocean. It is bounded by Djibouti in the northwest, Ethiopia in the west, and Kenya in the southwest. In area it is slightly smaller than Texas. Generally arid and barren, Somalia has two chief rivers, the Shebelle and the Juba.

Government. None. Last president was overthrown in January 1991 and Somalia was plunged into anarchy.

History. From the 7th to the 10th century, Arab and Persian trading posts were established along the coast of present-day Somalia. Nomadic tribes occupied the interior, occasionally pushing into Ethiopian territory. In the 16th century, Turkish rule extended to the northern coast, and the Sultans of Zanzibar gained control in the south.

After British occupation of Aden in 1839, the Somali coast became its source of food. The French established a coaling station in 1862 at the site of Djibouti, and the Italians planted a settlement in Eritrea. Egypt, which for a time claimed Turkish rights in the area, was succeeded by Britain. By 1920, a British protectorate and an Italian protectorate occupied what is now Somalia. The British ruled the entire area after 1941, with Italy returning in 1950 to serve as United Nations trustee for its former territory.

In mid-1960, Britain and Italy granted independence to their respective sectors, enabling the two to join as the Republic of Somalia on July 1. Somalia broke diplomatic relations with Britain in 1963 when the British granted the Somali-populated Northern Frontier District of Kenya to the Republic of Kenya.

On Oct. 15, 1969, President Abdi Rashid Ali Shermarke was assassinated and the army seized power, dissolving the legislature and arresting all government leaders. Maj. Gen. Mohamed Siad Barre, as president of a renamed Somali Democratic Republic, leaned heavily toward the U.S.S.R.

In 1977, Somalia openly backed rebels in the easternmost area of Ethiopia, the Ogaden desert, which had been seized by Ethiopia at the turn of the century.

Somalia acknowledged defeat in an eight-month war against the Ethiopians that year, having lost much of its 32,000-man army and most of its tanks and planes.

President Siad Barre fled the country in late January 1991. His departure left Somalia in the hands of a number of clan-based guerrilla groups, none of which trusted each other.

U.S. troops were sent in to protect the delivery of food in December 1992. In May the U.N. took control of the relief efforts from the U.S. Peace talks in Kenya appeared to be moving slowly but steadily toward an agreement on an interim government, at least in principle, when on March 23, 1994, they collapsed. The last of the U.S. troops left in late March, leaving 19,000 UN troops behind.

U.S. marines arrived again in February 1995 to evacuate the last 2,500 U.N. troops from the country. The last of the marines left on March 3.

Although a renewal of intense civil war was feared, the country remained splintered among various regional warlords.

SOUTH AFRICA

Republic of South Africa
President: Nelson Mandela (1994)
Deputy President: Thabo Mbeki
Area: 471,440 sq mi. (1,221,030 sq km)
Population (est. 1996): 41,743,459 (average annual rate of natural increase: 1.76%); birth rate: 27.9/1000; infant mortality rate: 48.8/1000; density per sq mi.: 88
Administrative capital: Pretoria; **Legislative capital:** Capetown; **Judicial capital:** Bloemfontein. No decision has been made to relocate the seat of government. South Africa is demarcated into nine provinces, consisting of the Gauteng, Northern Province, Mpumalanga, North West, Kwa Zulu/Natal, Eastern Cape, Western Cape, Northern Cape, and Free State. Each province has its own capital. **Largest metropolitan areas (1995):** Cape Peninsula, 2,350,157; Johannesburg, 1,916,063; East Rand, 1,378,792; Durban/Pinetown, 1,137,378; Pretoria, 1,080,187. **Monetary unit:** Rand. **Languages:** English, Afrikaans, isiNdebele, Sesotho sa Leboa, Sesotho, siSwati, Xitsonga, Setswana, Tshivenda, isiXhosa, and isiZulu are the official languages of the interim period. **Religions:** Christian; Hindu; Islam. **National name:** Republic of South Africa. **Literacy rate:** 76%
Economic summary: Gross domestic product (1995): $133 billion; $3,066 est. per capita; 3.3% real growth rate; inflation 8.6%. Arable land: 11.59%. Principal agricultural products: corn, wool, wheat, sugar cane, fruits, vegetables. Labor force: 13.4 million economically active (1990); by occupation: services 35%, agriculture 30%, industry 20%, mining 9%, other 6%. Major industrial products: gold, chromium, diamonds, assembled automobiles, machinery, textiles, iron and steel, chemicals, fertilizer. Natural resources: gold, diamonds, platinum, uranium, coal, iron ore, phosphates, manganese. Exports: $25.4 billion (1995): gold, diamonds, minerals and metals, food, chemicals. Imports: $27.2 billion (1995): motor vehicle parts, machinery, metals, chemicals, textiles, scientific instruments. Major trading partners: Germany, U.S., other E.U., Japan, U.K., Hong Kong, Italy, Taiwan

Geography. South Africa, on the continent's southern tip, is washed by the Atlantic Ocean on the west and by the Indian Ocean on the south and east. Its neighbors are Namibia in the northwest, Zimbabwe and Botswana in the north, and Mozambique and Swaziland in the northeast. The kingdom of Lesotho forms an enclave within the southeastern part of South Africa. Bophuthatswana, Transkei, Ciskei, and Venda are independent states within South Africa, which occupies an area nearly three times that of California.

The country has a high interior plateau, or veld, nearly half of which averages 4,000 feet (1,219 m) in elevation.

There are no important mountain ranges, although the Great Escarpment, separating the veld from the coastal plain, rises to over 11,000 feet (3,350 m) in the Drakensberg Mountains in the east. The principal river is the Orange, rising in Lesotho and flowing westward for 1,300 miles (2,092 km) to the Atlantic.

The southernmost point of Africa is Cape Agulhas, located in the Western Cape Province about 100 miles (161 km) southeast of the Cape of Good Hope.

Government. The constitution provides for a government of national unity, three tiers of government, and a chapter for fundamental human rights. A schedule in the bill sets out binding and justiciable constitutional principles.

Parliament consists of a 400-member National Assembly and a 90-person Council of Provinces. The National Assembly consists of 200 members from the provincial ballot. Election to these bodies takes place on the basis of proportional representation.

Each of the nine provinces has its own constitution that is in accordance with the national constitution. A constitutional court has final jurisdiction on matters pertaining to the interpretation, protection, and enforcement of the constitution.

A new constitution was adopted in May 1996 guaranteeing equal rights for everyone. The constitution is to come into effect slowly over a three-year period.

History. The San people were the first settlers. The Dutch East India Company landed the first European settlers on the Cape of Good Hope in 1652, launching a colony that by the end of the 18th century numbered only about 15,000. Known as Boers or Afrikaners, speaking a Dutch dialect known as Afrikaans, the settlers as early as 1795 tried to establish an independent republic.

After occupying the Cape Colony in that year, Britain took permanent possession in 1814 at the end of the Napoleonic wars, bringing in 5,000 settlers. Anglicization of government and the freeing of slaves in 1833 drove about 12,000 Afrikaners to make the "great trek" north and east into African tribal territory, where they established the republics of the Transvaal and the Orange Free State.

The discovery of diamonds in 1867 and gold nine years later brought an influx of "outlanders" into the republics and spurred Cecil Rhodes to plot annexation. Rhodes's scheme of sparking an "outlander" rebellion to which an armed party under Leander Starr Jameson would ride to the rescue misfired in 1895, forcing Rhodes to resign as prime minister of the Cape colony. What British expansionists called the "inevitable" war with the Boers eventually broke out on Oct. 11, 1899.

The defeat of the Boers in 1902 led in 1910 to the Union of South Africa, composed of four provinces,

the two former republics and the old Cape and Natal colonies. Louis Botha, a Boer, became the first prime minister. Organized political activity among Africans started with the establishment of the African National Congress in 1912.

Jan Christiaan Smuts brought the nation into World War II on the Allied side against Nationalist opposition, and South Africa became a charter member of the United Nations in 1945 but refused to sign the Universal Declaration of Human Rights. Apartheid—racial separation—dominated domestic politics as the Nationalists gained power and imposed greater restrictions on Bantus, Coloreds, and Asians. African voters were removed from the voter rolls in 1936.

Afrikaner hostility to Britain triumphed in 1961 with the declaration on May 31 of the Republic of South Africa and the severing of ties with the Commonwealth. Nationalist Prime Minister H. F. Verwoerd's government in 1963 asserted the power to restrict freedom of those who opposed rigid racial laws. Three years later, amid increasing racial tension and criticism from the outside world, Verwoerd was assassinated. His Nationalist successor, Balthazar J. Vorster, launched a campaign of conciliation toward conservative black African states, offering development loans and trade concessions.

Elections on May 7, 1987, increased the power of President Botha's Nationalist party while enabling the far-right Conservative Party to replace the liberal Progressives as the official opposition. The results of the whites-only vote indicated a strong conservative reaction against Botha's policy of limited reform.

A stroke led Botha to step down as leader of his party in 1989 in favor of F. W. de Klerk. De Klerk accelerated the pace of reform. He unbanned the African National Congress, the principal anti-apartheid organization, and released Nelson Mandela, the ANC deputy president and all other anti-apartheid movements/organizations after 27 1/2 years imprisonment. Negotiations between the government and the ANC commenced.

On June 5, 1991, Parliament scrapped the country's apartheid laws concerning property ownership. On June 17 Parliament did the same for the Population Registration Act of 1950, which classified all South Africans at birth by race.

In February 1993 the ANC approved a plan that would allow minority parties to participate in the government for five years after the end of white rule. Also in February the first nonwhites entered the cabinet in an apparent bid to broaden the base of the ruling National Party.

The 1994 election, as expected, resulted in a massive victory for Mandela and his ANC. The new president was sworn in on May 10. The new government included six ministers from the National Party and three from the Inkatha Freedom Party.

Local elections in November 1995 were by and large a victory for the ANC.

SPAIN

Kingdom of Spain
Ruler: King Juan Carlos I (1975)
Prime Minister: José María Aznar (1996)
Area: 195,364.5 sq mi. (505,992 km)[1]
Population (est. 1996): 38,853,397 (average annual growth rate: –0.14%; birth rate: 8/1000; infant mortality rate: 6.9/100; density per square mile: 198

Capital and largest city (1994 est.): Madrid, 3,041,101.
Largest cities: Barcelona, 1,630,867; Valencia, 764,293;
Seville, 714,148. **Monetary unit:** Peseta. **Languages:**
Spanish, Basque, Catalan, Galician. **Religion:** Roman
Catholic, 99%. **National name:** Reino de España. **Literacy rate:** 97%
Economic summary: Gross domestic product (1994 est.):
$515.8 billion; $13,120 per capita; real growth rate
1.8%; inflation 4.9%; unemployment (year-end 94)
24.5%. Arable land: 31%. Principal agricultural products: cereals, vegetables, citrus fruits, wine, olives
and olive oil, livestock. Labor force (1988): 14,621,000:
services 53%; 24% in industry. Major industrial products: processed foods, textiles, footwear, petrochemicals, steel, automobiles, ships. Natural resources:
coal, lignite, water power, uranium, mercury, pyrites,
fluorspar, gypsum, iron ore, zinc, lead, tungsten, copper. Exports: $72.8 billion (f.o.b., 1993): cars and
trucks, semifinished manufactured goods, foodstuffs,
machinery and electrical equipment. Imports: $92.5
billion (c.i.f., 1993): machinery and transportation
equipment, chemicals, petroleum, semifinished goods,
consumer goods, machines and electrical equipment.
Major trading partners: Germany, France, Italy, U.S.,
U.K.

1. Including the Balearic and Canary Islands.

Geography. Spain occupies 85% of the Iberian Pen-
insula in southwestern Europe, which it shares with
Portugal; France is to the northeast, separated by the
Pyrenees. The Bay of Biscay lies to the north, the
Atlantic Ocean to the west, and the Mediterranean
Sea to the south and east: Africa is less than 10 miles
(16 km) south at the Strait of Gibraltar.

A broad central plateau slopes to the south and east,
crossed by a series of mountain ranges and river valleys.

Principal rivers are the Ebro in the northeast, the Tajo
in the central region, and the Guadalquivir in the south.

Off Spain's east coast in the Mediterranean are the
Balearic Islands (1,936 sq mi.; 5,014 sq km), the largest
of which is Majorca. Sixty miles (97 km) west of Africa
are the Canary Islands (2,808 sq mi.; 7,273 sq km).

Government. A parliamentary monarchy. The
Cortes, or parliament, consists of a Chamber of Deputies of 350 members and a Senate of 208, all
elected by universal suffrage.

History. Spain, originally inhabited by Celts, Iberi-
ans, and Basques, became a part of the Roman Empire in 206 B.C., when it was conquered by Scipio
Africanus. In A.D. 412, the barbarian Visigothic leader
Ataulf crossed the Pyrenees and ruled Spain, first in
the name of the Roman emperor and then independently. In 711, the Moslems under Tariq entered Spain
from Africa and within a few years completed the
subjugation of the country. In 732, the Franks, led by
Charles Martel, defeated the Moslems near Poitiers,
thus preventing the further expansion of Islam in
southern Europe. Internal dissension of Spanish Islam
invited a steady Christian conquest from the north.

Aragon and Castile were the most important Spanish states from the 12th to the 15th century, consolidated by the marriage of Ferdinand II and Isabella I
in 1469. The last Moslem stronghold, Granada, was
captured in 1492. Roman Catholicism was established
as the official state religion and the Jews (1492) and
the Moslems (1502) expelled.

In the era of exploration, discovery, and colonization, Spain amassed tremendous wealth and a vast colonial empire through the conquest of Peru by Pizarro
(1532–33) and of Mexico by Cortés (1519–21). The
Spanish Hapsburg monarchy became for a time the
most powerful in the world.

In 1588, Philip II sent his Invincible Armada to
invade England, but its destruction cost Spain its supremacy on the seas and paved the way for England's
colonization of America. Spain then sank rapidly to
the status of a second-rate power and never again
played a major role in European politics. Its colonial
empire in the Americas and the Philippines vanished
in wars and revolutions during the 18th and 19th centuries.

In World War I, Spain maintained a position of
neutrality. In 1923, Gen. Miguel Primo de Rivera became dictator. In 1930, King Alfonso XIII revoked
the dictatorship, but a strong antimonarchist and republican movement led to his leaving Spain in 1931.
The new constitution declared Spain a workers' republic, broke up the large estates, separated church
and state, and secularized the schools. The elections
held in 1936 returned a strong Popular Front majority, with Manuel Azaña as president.

On July 18, 1936, a conservative army officer in
Morocco, Francisco Franco Bahamonde, led a mutiny
against the government. The civil war that followed
lasted three years and cost the lives of nearly a million people. Franco was aided by Fascist Italy and
Nazi Germany, while Soviet Russia helped the Loyalist side. Several hundred leftist Americans served in
the Abraham Lincoln Brigade on the side of the republic. The war ended when Franco took Madrid on
March 28, 1939.

Franco became head of the state, national chief of
the Falange Party (the governing party), and premier
and caudillo (leader). In a referendum in 1947, the
Spanish people approved a Franco-drafted succession
law declaring Spain a monarchy again. Franco, however, continued as chief of state.

In 1969, Franco and the Cortes designated Prince
Juan Carlos Alfonso Victor María de Borbón (who
married Princess Sophia of Greece on May 14, 1962)
to become King of Spain when the provisional government headed by Franco came to an end.

Franco died of a heart attack on Nov. 20, 1975,
after more than a year of ill health, and Juan Carlos
was proclaimed king seven days later.

Under pressure from Catalonian and Basque nationalists, Premier Adolfo Suárez granted home rule
to these regions in 1979.

With the overwhelming election of Prime Minister
Felipe González Márquez and his Spanish Socialist
Workers Party in the Oct. 20, 1982, parliamentary
elections, the Franco past was finally buried. The
thrust of González, a pragmatic moderate, was to
modernize rather than radicalize Spain.

A treaty admitting Spain, along with Portugal, to
the European Economic Community took effect on
Jan. 1, 1986. Later that year, in June, Spain voted to
remain in NATO, but outside of its military command.

General elections of June 1993 returned the Socialist Party to power through the assistance of Catalo-
nia's main nationalist party, which increasingly
pressed in 1994 for greater self-government for the
region as the price for that support.

General elections in March 1996 produced a victory for the conservative Popular Party, which, although
lacking an absolute majority in the Cortes, received
the backing of regional parties for a coalition government with Aznar as prime minister. Aznar promised
greater fiscal responsibility and a battle with terrorism.

SRI LANKA

Democratic Socialist Republic of Sri Lanka
President: Chandrika B. Kumaratunga (1994)
Prime Minister: Sirimao R.D. Bandaranayake
Area: 25,332 sq mi. (65,610 sq km)
Population (est. 1996): 18,553,074 (average annual rate of natural increase: 1.21%); birth rate: 17.9/1000; infant mortality rate: 20.8/1000; density per sq mi.: 732
Capital and largest city (1992 est.): Sri Jayewardenepura Kotte (Colombo), 1,994,000. **Other large cities (est. 1992):** Gampaha, 1,543,000; Kurunegala, 1,445,000; Kandy, 1,257,000. **Monetary unit:** Sri Lanka rupee. **Languages:** Sinhala, Tamil, English. **Religions:** Buddhist, 69%; Hindu, 15%; Islam, 8%; Christian, 8%. **Member of Commonwealth of Nations. Literacy rate:** 89%
Economic summary: Gross domestic product (1994 est.): $57.6 billion; $3,190 per capita; real growth rate 5%; inflation 12%; unemployment (1993 est.) 13.6%. Arable land: 16%. Principal products: tea, coconuts, rubber, rice, spices. Labor force: 6,600,000; 13.3% in mining and manufacturing. Major products: processed rubber, tea, coconuts, textiles, cement, refined petroleum. Natural resources: limestone, graphite, gems. Exports: $2.9 billion (f.o.b., 1993): textiles, tea, rubber, petroleum products, gems and jewelry. Imports: $4 billion (c.i.f., 1993): petroleum, machinery, transport equipment, sugar. Major trading partners: U.S., U.K., Germany, Japan, Singapore, India, Iran, Taiwan, Belgium, Hong Kong, China.

Geography. An island in the Indian Ocean off the southeast tip of India, Sri Lanka is about half the size of Alabama. Most of the land is flat and rolling; mountains in the south central region rise to over 8,000 feet (2,438 m).

Government. Ceylon became an independent country in 1948 after British rule and reverted to the traditional name ("resplendent island") on May 22, 1972. A new constitution adopted in 1978 set up the National State Assembly, a 225-member unicameral legislature that serves for six years unless dissolved earlier.

History. Following Portuguese and Dutch rule, Ceylon became an English crown colony in 1798. The British developed coffee, tea, and rubber plantations and granted six constitutions between 1798 and 1924. The Constitution of 1931 gave a large measure of self-government. Ceylon became a self-governing dominion of the Commonwealth of Nations in 1948.

Presidential elections were held in December 1982, and won by J.R. Jayewardene.

Tension between the Tamil minority and the Sinhalese majority continued to build and erupted in bloody violence in 1983 that has grown worse since. There are about 2.6 million Tamils in Sri Lanka, while the Sinhalese make up about three-quarters of the 17-million population. Tamil extremists are fighting for a separate nation.

The civil war continued during 1990 after a 13-month cease-fire collapsed. The president ruled month to month. The Tamil guerrillas announced a unilateral cease-fire to take effect on January 1, 1991, and the government, too, suspended operations.

India had sent soldiers in July 1987 to help enforce an accord granting the Tamil minority limited autonomy. The agreement failed, and Indian troops withdrew at the end of 1989.

President Ranasinghe Premadasa was assassinated at a May Day political rally in 1993 when a Tamil rebel detonated explosives strapped to himself.

A general election in August 1994 gave a coalition of left-of-center opposition parties 105 seats in the state assembly. A November presidential election was won by the coalition's head running on a peace platform and support for a free-market economy.

The war with Tamil rebels continued unabated through mid-1996. In April the president extended the state of emergency to the entire country. In May the military claimed a major victory in Jaffna peninsula. However, rebel bombing occurred in July.

SUDAN

Republic of the Sudan
President: Lt. Gen. Omar Hassam Ahmed Bashir
Area: 967,491 sq mi. (2,505,802 sq km)
Population (est. 1996): 31,065,229 (average annual rate of natural increase: 2.94%); birth rate: 40.8/1000; infant mortality rate: 76/1000; density per sq mi.: 32
Capital (1993 est.): Khartoum, 924,505; **Largest cities:** Omdurman, 1,267,077; Port Sudan, 305,385. **Monetary unit:** Sudanese pound. **Languages:** Arabic, English, tribal dialects. **Religions:** Islam, 70% (Sunni); indigenous, 20%; Christian, 5%. **National name:** Jamhuryat es-Sudan. **Literacy rate:** 32%
Economic summary: Gross domestic product (1994 est.): $23.7 billion; $870 per capita; real growth rate 7%; inflation 112% (FY93/94 est.); unemployment 30% (FY92/93 est.). Arable land: 5%. Principal agricultural products: cotton, oil seeds, gum arabic, sorghum, wheat, millet, sheep. Labor force: 6,500,000; 80% in agriculture. Major industrial products: cement, textiles, pharmaceuticals, shoes, soap, refined petroleum, gold. Natural resources: crude oil, some iron ore, copper, chrome, industrial metals. Exports: $419 million (f.o.b., FY93/94): cotton, peanuts, gum arabic, sesame. Imports: $1.7 billion (c.i.f., FY93/94): petroleum products, machinery and equipment, medicines and chemicals. Major trading partners: Western Europe, Saudi Arabia, Eastern Europe, Japan.

Geography. The Sudan, in northeast Africa, is the largest country on the continent, measuring about one fourth the size of the United States. Its neighbors are Chad and the Central African Republic on the west, Egypt and Libya on the north, Ethiopia and Eritrea on the east, and Kenya, Uganda, and Zaire on the south. The Red Sea washes about 500 miles of the eastern coast.

The country extends from north to south about 1,200 miles (1,931 km) and west to east about 1,000 miles (1,609 km). The northern region is a continuation of the Libyan Desert. The southern region is fertile, abundantly watered, and, in places, heavily forested. It is traversed from north to south by the Nile, all of whose great tributaries are partly or entirely within its borders.

Government. On January 31, 1991, a criminal code became law that applied Islamic law in the predominantly Moslem north. The ruling military council passed a decree in 1993 dividing the country into 26 states, each administered by a governor and a cabinet of ministers.

History. The early history of the Sudan (known as the Anglo-Egyptian Sudan between 1898 and 1955) is linked with that of Nubia, where a powerful local kingdom was formed in Roman times with its capital at Dongola. After conversion to Christianity in the

6th century, the Sudan joined with Ethiopia and resisted Mohammedanization until the 14th century. Thereafter the area was broken up into many small states until 1820–22, when it was conquered by Mohammed Ali, Pasha of Egypt. Egyptian forces were evacuated during the Mahdist revolt (1881–98), but the Sudan was reconquered by the Anglo-Egyptian expeditions of 1896–98 and in 1899 became an Anglo-Egyptian condominium, which was reaffirmed by the Anglo-Egyptian treaty of 1936.

Egypt and Britain agreed in 1953 to grant self-government to the Sudan under an appointed governor-general. An all-Sudanese Parliament was elected in November–December 1953, and an all-Sudanese government was formed. In December 1955, Parliament declared the independence of the Sudan, which, with the approval of Britain and Egypt, was proclaimed on Jan. 1, 1956.

In October 1969, Maj. Gen. Gaafar Mohamed Nimeiri, the president of the Council for the Revolution, took over as prime minister. He was elected the nation's first president in 1971.

In 1976, a third coup was attempted against Nimeiri. Nimeiri accused President Muammar el Qaddafi of Libya of having instigated the attempt and broke relations with Libya.

On April 6, 1985, while out of the country on visits to the United States and Egypt, Nimeiri lost power by a military coup headed by his defense minister, Gen. Abdel Rahman Siwar el-Dahab.

Among the problems that the new government faced were a debilitating civil war with rebels in the south of the country, other sectarian and tribal conflicts, and a famine.

During 1992 the government attempted to impose militant Islam throughout the nation as well as initiate capitalistic economic reforms, including the lifting of subsidies on basic commodities.

March 1996 elections gave an easy victory to the incumbent president, who faced largely unknown opponents. His supporters also did well in the parliamentary voting.

SURIMANE

Republic of Suriname
President: Ronald Venetiaan (1991)
Vice President: Jules Adjodhia (1991)
Area: 63,251 sq mi. (163,820 sq km)
Population (est. 1996): 436,418 (average annual rate of natural increase: 1.83%); birth rate: 24.2/1000; infant mortality rate: 29.3/1000; density per square mile: 6
Capital and largest city (1993 est.): Paramaribo, 200,970.
  Monetary unit: Suriname guilder. **Languages:** Dutch, Surinamese (lingua franca), English widely spoken.
  Religions: Protestant, 25.2%; Roman Catholic, 22.8%; Hindu, 27.4%; Islam, 19.6%; indigenous, about 5%. Literacy rate: 95%
Economic summary: Gross domestic product (1994 est.): $1.2 billion; $2,800 per capita; real growth rate –0.8%; inflation 225%; unemployment (1990) 16.5%. Arable land: negl. %. Principal products: rice. Work force: 104,000. Major products: aluminum, alumina, processed foods, lumber. Natural resources: bauxite, iron ore, timber, fish, shrimp. Exports: $443.3 million (f.o.b, 1993 est.): bauxite, alumina, aluminum, rice, shrimp and fish, bananas. Imports: $520.5 million (f.o.b., 1993 est.): capital equipment, petroleum, cotton, foodstuffs, consumer goods.Major trading partners: U.S., Trinidad, Netherlands, Norway, Germany, Brazil, U.K., Japan, Netherlands Antilles.

Geography. Suriname lies on the northeast coast of South America, with Guyana to the west, French Guiana to the east, and Brazil to the south. It is about one-tenth larger than Michigan. The principal rivers are the Corantijn on the Guyana border, the Marowijne in the east, and the Suriname, on which the capital city of Paramaribo is situated. The Tumuc-Humac Mountains are on the border with Brazil.

Government. Suriname, formerly known as Dutch Guiana, became an independent republic on Nov. 25, 1975. The executive branch consists of the president and prime minister, Cabinet of Ministers, and Council of State. The legislative branch consists of a unicameral National Assembly with 51 members.

History. England established the first European settlement on the Suriname River in 1650 but transferred sovereignty to the Dutch in 1667 in the Treaty of Breda, by which the British acquired New York. Colonization was confined to a narrow coastal strip, and until the abolition of slavery in 1863, African slaves furnished the labor for the plantation economy. After 1870, laborers were imported from British India and the Dutch East Indies.

In 1948, the colony was integrated into the Kingdom of the Netherlands and two years later was granted full home rule in other than foreign affairs and defense. After race rioting over unemployment and inflation, the Netherlands offered complete independence in 1973.

During much of the 1980s Suriname was under the control of Lieut. Col. Dési Bouterse, who in late December 1990 resigned as commander of the armed forces. The following night President Ramsewak Shankar was ousted in a bloodless coup. A few days later interim president Johan Krug acted to reinstate Bouterse.

A deadlocked Parliament in 1991 gave way to an assembly, consisting of members of Parliament and elected representatives of local councils, convened to select Venetiaan as president.

In 1992 a draft peace treaty was signed between the government and several guerrilla groups.

President Venetiaan won the election of May 1996 against challenger Dési Bouterse, a former dictator. The incumbent's coalition, however, failed to gain the needed two-thirds majority for an outright win.

SWAZILAND

Kingdom of Swaziland
Ruler: King Mswati III (1986)
Prime Minister: Barnabas Sibusiso Dlamini (July 1996)
Area: 6,704 sq mi. (17,363 sq km)
Population (est. 1996): 998,730 (average annual rate of natural increase: 3.24%); birth rate: 42.9/1000; infant mortality rate: 88.4/1000; density per sq mi.: 148
Capital and largest city (1990 est.): Mbabane, 47,020;
  Monetary unit: Lilangeni; **Languages:** English and Swazi (official); **Religions:** Christian, 60%; indigenous, 40%; **Member of Commonwealth of Nations; Literacy rate:** 55%
Economic summary: Gross domestic product (1994 est.): $3.3 billion; $3,490 per capita; 4.5% real growth rate; inflation 11.3 (1993 est.)%; unemployment 15% (1992 est.) Arable land: 8%. The economy is based on subsistence agriculture, which occupies more than 60% of the population and contributes nearly 25% to GDP. Manufacturing, which includes a number of agro-processing factories, accounts for another quarter of

GDP. Principal agricultural products: corn, livestock, sugar cane, citrus fruits, cotton, sorghum, peanuts. Labor force: 195,000; about 92,000 wage earners with 14% in manufacturing. Major industrial products: milled sugar, ginned cotton, processed meat and wood. Natural resources: asbestos, diamonds. Exports: $632 million (f.o.b., 1993 est.): sugar, wood pulp, asbestos, citrus fruits. Imports: $734 million (f.o.b., 1993 est.): motor vehicles, transport equipment, petroleum products, foodstuffs, chemicals. Major trading partners: South Africa, U.K., U.S.

Geography. Swaziland, 85% the size of New Jersey, is surrounded by South Africa and Mozambique. The country consists of a high veld in the west and a series of plateaus descending from 6,000 feet (1,829 m) to a low veld of 1,500 feet (457 m).

Government. In 1967, a new constitution established King Sobhuza II as head of state and provided for an Assembly of 24 members elected by universal suffrage, together with a Senate of 12 members—half appointed by the Assembly and half by the king. In 1973, the king renounced the constitution, suspended political parties, and took total power for himself. In 1977, he replaced the Parliament with an assembly of tribal leaders. The Parliament reconvened in 1979.

History. Bantu peoples migrated southwest to the area of Mozambique in the 16th century. A number of clans broke away from the main body in the 18th century and settled in Swaziland. In the 19th century they organized as a tribe, partly because they were in constant conflict with the Zulu. Their ruler, Mswazi, applied to the British in the 1840s for help against the Zulu. The British and the Transvaal governments guaranteed the independence of Swaziland in 1881.

South Africa held Swaziland as a protectorate from 1894 to 1899, but after the Boer War, in 1902, Swaziland was transferred to British administration. The Paramount Chief was recognized as the native authority in 1941.

In 1963, the territory was constituted a protectorate, and on Sept. 6, 1968, it became the independent nation of Swaziland.

The king in October 1992 dissolved Parliament and announced plans for a new constitution allowing a multiparty democracy. The first democratic elections took place in September 1993.

Labor unrest from March through July 1995 disrupted the country until the government instituted new measures against unions.

SWEDEN

Kingdom of Sweden
Sovereign: King Carl XVI Gustaf (1973)
Prime Minister: Göran Persson (1996)
Area: 173,800 sq mi. (449,964 sq km)
Population (est. 1996): 8,861,270 (average annual rate of natural increase: 0.21%); birth rate: 12.9/1000; infant mortality rate: 5.5/1000; density per sq mi.: 50
Capital and largest city (1994): Stockholm, 703,627.
Largest cities: Göteborg, 444,553; Malmö, 242,706; Uppsala, 181,191. **Monetary unit:** Krona. **Language:** Swedish. **Religions:** Evangelical Lutheran, 93.5%; Roman Catholic, 1%; other, 5.5%. **National name:** Konungariket Sverige. **Literacy rate:** 99%
Economic summary: Gross domestic product (1994 est.): $163.1 billion; $18,580 per capita; real growth rate 2.4%; inflation 2.5% (est.); unemployment 7.5% (May 1995). Arable land: 7%. Principal agricultural products:

dairy products, grains, sugar beets, potatoes. Labor force: 4.3 million (almost 50% are women); 37.4% in government services; 23.1% in mining, manufacturing, electricity, and water service; 22.2% in private services. Major products: iron and steel, precision equipment, wood pulp and paper products, automobiles. Natural resources: forests, iron ore, hydroelectric power, zinc, uranium. Exports: $59.9 billion (f.o.b., 1994): machinery, motor vehicles, wood pulp, paper products, chemicals, petroleum and petroleum products, iron and steel products. Imports: $49.6 billion (c.i.f., 1994): machinery, clothing, petroleum and petroleum products, foodstuffs, iron and steel, chemicals. Major trading partners: Norway, Germany, U.K., Denmark, U.S., France, Finland, Netherlands.

Geography. Sweden occupies the eastern part of the Scandinavian peninsula, with Norway to the west, Finland and the Gulf of Bothnia to the east, and Denmark and the Baltic Sea in the south. Sweden is the fourth largest country in Europe and is one-tenth larger than California.

The country slopes eastward and southward from the Kjölen Mountains along the Norwegian border, where the peak elevation is Kebnekaise at 6,965 feet (2,123 m) in Lapland. In the north are mountains and many lakes. To the south and east are central lowlands, and south of them are fertile areas of forest, valley, and plain.

Along Sweden's rocky coast, chopped up by bays and inlets, are many islands, the largest of which are Gotland and Öland.

Government. Sweden is a constitutional monarchy. Under the 1975 Constitution, the Riksdag is the sole governing body. The prime minister is the political chief executive.

In 1967, agreement was reached on part of a new constitution after 13 years of work. It provided for a single-house Riksdag of 350 members (later amended to 349 seats) to replace the 104-year old bicameral Riksdag. The members are popularly elected for three years. One hundred fifteen present members of the Riksdag are women.

The king, Carl XVI Gustaf, was born April 30, 1946, and succeeded to the throne Sept. 19, 1973, on the death at 90 of his grandfather, Gustaf VI Adolf. Carl Gustaf was married on June 19, 1976, to Silvia Sommerlath, a West German commoner. They have three children: Princess Victoria, born July 14, 1977; Prince Carl Philip, born May 13, 1979; and Princess Madeleine, born June 10, 1982. Under the new Act of Succession, effective Jan. 1, 1980, the first child of the reigning monarch, regardless of sex, is heir to the throne.

History. The earliest historical mention of Sweden is found in Tacitus' *Germania*, where reference is made to the powerful king and strong fleet of the Suiones. Toward the end of the 10th century, Olaf Sköttkonung established a Christian stronghold in Sweden. Around 1400, an attempt was made to unite the northern nations into one kingdom, but this led to bitter strife between the Danes and the Swedes.

In 1520, the Danish king, Christian II, conquered Sweden and in the "Stockholm Bloodbath" put leading Swedish personages to death. Gustavus Vasa (1523–60) broke away from Denmark and fashioned the modern Swedish state.

Sweden played a leading role in the second phase (1630–35) of the Thirty Years' War (1618–48). By the Treaty of Westphalia (1648), Sweden obtained western Pomerania and some neighboring territory on the Baltic. In 1700, a coalition of Russia, Poland, and

Denmark united against Sweden and by the Peace of Nystad (1721) forced it to relinquish Livonia, Ingria, Estonia, and parts of Finland.

Sweden emerged from the Napoleonic Wars with the acquisition of Norway from Denmark and with a new royal dynasty stemming from Marshal Jean Bernadotte of France, who became King Charles XIV (1818–44). The artificial union between Sweden and Norway led to an uneasy relationship, and the union was finally dissolved in 1905.

Sweden maintained a position of neutrality in both World Wars.

An elaborate structure of welfare legislation, imitated by many larger nations, began with the establishment of old-age pensions in 1911. Economic prosperity based on its neutralist policy enabled Sweden, together with Norway, to pioneer in public health, housing, and job security programs.

Forty-four years of Socialist government were ended in 1976 with the election of a conservative coalition headed by Thorbjörn Fälldin, a 50-year-old sheep farmer.

Fälldin resigned on Oct. 5, 1978, when his conservative coalition partners demanded fewer restrictions on nuclear power, and his successor, Ola Ullsten, resigned a year later after failing to achieve a consensus on the issue. Returned to office by his coalition partners, Fälldin said he would follow the course directed by a national referendum.

Olaf Palme and the Socialists were returned to power in the election of 1982. In February 1986, Palme was killed by an unknown assailant.

Elections in September 1991 ousted the Social Democrats from power. The new coalition of four conservative parties pledged to cut taxes and cut back on the welfare state but not alter Sweden's traditional neutrality.

General elections in September 1994 saw the emergence again of the Social Democrats after three years of being in opposition. Short of a majority by 13 seats in the Riksdag they decided to establish a minority government.

In a referendum held in November 1994 voters approved joining the European Union.

Ingvar Carlsson retired as prime minister in March 1996, as promised. The Social Democrats chose Finance Minister Persson, a technocrat, to succeed him.

SWITZERLAND

Swiss Confederation
President: Jean-Pascal Delamuraz (1996)
Area: 15,941 sq mi. (41,288 sq km)
Population (est. 1996): 7,124,745 (average annual rate of natural increase: 0.27%); birth rate: 11.8/1000; infant mortality rate: 6.2/1000; density per sq mi.: 446
Capital (1994 est): Bern, 129,423. **Largest cities:** Zurich, 343,045; Basel, 176,220; Geneva, 171,744; Lausanne, 117,153. **Monetary unit:** Swiss franc. **Languages:** German, 65%; French, 18%; Italian, 10%; Romansch, 1%. **Religions:** Roman Catholic, 49%; Protestant, 48%. **National name:** Schweiz/Suisse/Svizzera/Svizra. **Literacy rate:** 99%
Economic summary: Gross domestic product (1994 est.): $148.4 billion; $22,080 per capita; real growth rate 1.8%; inflation 0.9%; unemployment 4.7%. Arable land: 10%. Principal products: cheese and other dairy products, livestock. Labor force: 3.48 million (900,000 foreign workers). Major products: watches and clocks, precision instruments, machinery, chemicals, pharmaceuticals, textiles. Natural resources: water power, timber, salt. Exports: $69.6 billion (f.o.b., 1994 est.):

machinery and equipment, precision instruments, textiles, foodstuffs, metal products. Imports: $68.2 billion (c.i.f., 1994 est.): transport equipment, foodstuffs, chemicals, textiles, construction material. Major trading partners: U.S., Japan, Western Europe.

Geography. Switzerland, in central Europe, is the land of the Alps. Its tallest peak is the Dufourspitze at 15,203 feet (4,634 m) on the Swiss side of the Italian border, one of 10 summits of the Monte Rose massif in the Apennines. The tallest peak in all of the Alps, Mont Blanc (15,771 ft; 4,807 m), is actually in France.

Most of Switzerland comprises a mountainous plateau bordered by the great bulk of the Alps on the south and by the Jura Mountains on the northwest. About one-fourth of the total area is covered by mountains and glaciers.

The country's largest lakes—Geneva, Constance (Bodensee), and Maggiore—straddle the French, German-Austrian, and Italian borders, respectively.

The Rhine, navigable from Basel to the North Sea, is the principal inland waterway. Other rivers are the Aare and the Rhône.

Switzerland, twice the size of New Jersey, is surrounded by France, West Germany, Austria, Liechtenstein, and Italy.

Government. The Swiss Confederation consists of 23 sovereign cantons, of which three are divided into six half-cantons. Federal authority is vested in a bicameral legislature. The Ständerat, or State Council, consists of 46 members, two from each canton. The lower house, the Nationalrat, or National Council, has 200 deputies, elected for four-year terms.

Executive authority rests with the Bundesrat, or Federal Council, consisting of seven members chosen by Parliament. Parliament elects the president, who serves for one year and is succeeded by the vice president. The federal government regulates foreign policy, railroads, postal service, and the national mint. Each canton reserves for itself important local powers.

History. Called Helvetia in ancient times, Switzerland in the Middle Ages was a league of cantons of the Holy Roman Empire. Fashioned around the nucleus of three German forest districts of Schwyz, Uri, and Unterwalden, the Swiss Confederation slowly added new cantons. In 1648 the Treaty of Westphalia gave Switzerland its independence from the Holy Roman Empire.

French revolutionary troops occupied the country in 1798 and named it the Helvetic Republic, but Napoleon in 1803 restored its federal government. By 1815, the French- and Italian-speaking peoples of Switzerland had been granted political equality.

In 1815, the Congress of Vienna guaranteed the neutrality and recognized the independence of Switzerland. In the revolutionary period of 1847, the Catholic cantons seceded and organized a separate union called the *Sonderbund*. In 1848 the new Swiss Constitution established a union modeled upon that of the U.S. The Federal Constitution of 1874 established a strong central government while maintaining large powers of control in each canton.

National unity and political conservatism grew as the country prospered from its neutrality. Its banking system became the world's leading repository for international accounts. Strict neutrality was its policy in World Wars I and II. Geneva was the seat of the League of Nations (later the European headquarters of the United Nations) and of a number of international organizations.

A referendum in December on merging the European Community with the 7-nation European Free Trade Association was narrowly defeated.

Voters in a national referendum in June 1994 rejected the creation of a volunteer military force for deployment as part of U.N. peacekeeping operations.

General elections in October 1995 resulted in the Social Democrats winning twelve parliamentary seats more than previously. The Christian Democrats and the Greens lost seats.

SYRIA

Syrian Arab Republic
President: Hafez al-Assad (1971)
Premier: Mahmoud al-Zubi (1987)
Area: 71,498 sq mi. (185,180 sq km)
Population (est. 1996): 15,608,648 (average annual rate of natural increase: 3.37%); birth rate: 39.5/1000; infant mortality rate: 40/1000; density per sq mi.: 218
Capital (1994 est.): Damascus, 1,549,932. **Largest cities:** Aleppo, 1,591,400; Homs, 644,204; Latakia, 306,535; Hama, 229,000. **Monetary unit:** Syrian pound. **Languages:** Arabic (official), French and English widely understood. **Religions:** Islam, 90%; Christian, 10%. **National name:** Al-Jamhouriya al Arabiya As-Souriya. **Literacy rate:** 64%
Economic summary: Gross domestic product (1994 est.): $74.4 billion; $5,000 per capita; real growth rate 4%; inflation 16.3% (1993 est.); unemployment: 7.5% (1993 est.). Arable land: 28%. Principal agricultural products: Cotton, wheat, barley, lentils, sheep, goats. Labor force: 4.3 million (1994 est.): miscellanous and government services 36%, agriculture 32%, industry and construction 32%. Major industrial products: textiles, phosphate, petroleum, processed food. Natural resources: chrome, manganese, asphalt, iron ore, rock salt, phosphate, oil, gypsum. Exports: $3.6 billion (f.o.b., 1994 est.): petroleum, textiles, cotton, fruits and vegetables, phosphates. Imports: $4 billion (c.i.f., 1994 est.): petroleum, machinery, base metals, foodstuffs and beverages. Major trading partners: E.U. countries, U.S., Canada, Arab countries, former U.S.S.R. nations.

Geography. Slightly larger than North Dakota, Syria lies at the eastern end of the Mediterranean Sea. It is bordered by Lebanon and Israel on the west, Turkey on the north, Iraq on the east, and Jordan on the south.

Coastal Syria is a narrow plain, in back of which is a range of coastal mountains, and still farther inland a steppe area. In the east is the Syrian Desert, and in the south is the Jebel Druze Range. The highest point in Syria is Mount Hermon (9,232 ft; 2,814 m) on the Lebanese border.

Government. A republic under a military regime since March 1963 with a unicameral legislature, the People's Council. The ruling party is the Arab Socialist Resurrectionist (Ba'th) Party.

History. Ancient Syria was conquered by Egypt about 1500 B.C., and after that by Hebrews, Assyrians, Chaldeans, Persians, and Greeks. From 64 B.C. until the Arab conquest in A.D. 636, it was part of the Roman Empire except during brief periods. The Arabs made it a trade center for their extensive empire, but it suffered severely from the Mongol invasion in 1260 and fell to the Ottoman Turks in 1516. Syria remained a Turkish province until World War I.

A secret Anglo-French pact of 1916 put Syria in the French zone of influence. The League of Nations gave France a mandate over Syria after World War I, but the French were forced to put down several nationalist uprisings. In 1930, France recognized Syria as an independent republic but still subject to the mandate. After nationalist demonstrations in 1939, the French High Commissioner suspended the Syrian constitution. In 1941, British and Free French forces invaded Syria to eliminate Vichy control. During the rest of World War II, Syria was an Allied base.

Again in 1945, nationalist demonstrations broke into actual fighting, and British troops had to restore order. Syrian forces met a series of reverses while participating in the Arab invasion of Palestine in 1948. In 1958, Egypt and Syria formed the United Arab Republic, with Gamal Abdel Nasser of Egypt as president. However, Syria became independent again on Sept. 29, 1961, following a revolution.

In the war of 1967, Israel quickly vanquished the Syrian army. Before acceding to the U.N. cease-fire, the Israeli forces took over control of the fortified Golan Heights commanding the Sea of Galilee.

Syria joined Egypt in attacking Israel in October 1973 in the fourth Arab-Israeli war, but was pushed back from initial successes on the Golan Heights to end up losing more land. However, in the settlement worked out by U.S. Secretary of State Henry A. Kissinger in 1974, the Syrians recovered all the territory lost in 1973 and a token amount of territory, including the deserted town of Quneitra, lost in 1967.

Syrian troops, in Lebanon since 1976 as part of an Arab peacekeeping force whose other members subsequently departed, intervened increasingly during 1980 and 1981 on the side of Moslem Lebanese in their clashes with Christian militants supported by Israel. When Israeli jets shot down Syrian helicopters operating in Lebanon in April 1981, Syria moved Soviet-built surface-to-air (SAM 6) missiles into Lebanon's Bekaa Valley. Israel demanded that the missiles be removed because they violated a 1976 understanding between the governments. The demand, backed up by bombing raids, prompted the Reagan administration to send veteran diplomat Philip C. Habib as a special envoy to avert a new conflict between the nations.

Habib's carefully engineered cease-fire was shattered by a new Israeli invasion in June 1982, when Israeli aircraft bombed Bekaa Valley missile sites.

Nevertheless, while the Israelis overran most of the rest of Lebanon, the Syrians retained their positions in the Bekaa Valley. As the various Lebanese factions fought each other, the Syrians became the dominant force in the country, both militarily and politically.

The first Arab country to condemn Iraq's invasion of Kuwait, Syria sent troops to help defend Saudi Arabia from possible Iraqi attack. After the Gulf war hope for peace negotiations between Israel and Arab states, particularly Syria, rose then foundered.

In 1990 President Assad ruled out any possibility of legalizing opposition political parties. According to official sources, voters in December 1991 approved Assad staying on for a fourth term in office, giving him 99.98% of the vote.

An August general election saw another victory for the ruling party and its allies, albeit with a relatively low voter turnout.

With Israel's peace with Jordan and the peace process with the Palestinians proceeding, diplomatic eyes turned toward Syria during 1994 and 1995. Nevertheless, no major breakthroughs emerged. In fact relations deteriorated after October 1995, and the Likud electoral victory in Israel in 1996 made peace between the two seem ever more distant.

TAIWAN

Republic of China

President: Lee Teng-hui (1988)
Premier: Lien Chan (1993)
Area: 13,895 sq mi. (35,988 sq km)
Population (1995): 21,304,000 (average annual rate of natural increase: 0.96%); birth rate: 15.5/1000; infant mortality rate: 5.6/1000; density per square mile: 1,533
Capital and largest city (1995): Taipei, 2,643,439; **Largest cities:** Kaohsiung, 1,423,163; Tai Chung, 848,320; Tainan, 705,565; Keelung, 367,668. **Monetary unit:** New Taiwan dollar. **Languages:** Chinese (Mandarin). **Religions:** Buddhist, 4.86 million; Taoist, 3.3 million; Protestant, 422,000; Catholic, 304,000. **Literacy rate:** 93.4%
Economic summary: Gross national product (1995): $263.4 billion; per capita income $12,439; real growth rate 6.10%; inflation 3.68%; unemployment 2.03%. Arable land: 25%; principal products: rice, yams, sugar cane, bananas, pineapples, citrus fruits. Labor force (1995): 9,272,000; 39.1% in industry; 11.5% in agriculture; 49.4% in services. Major products: textiles, clothing, chemicals, processed foods, electronic equipment, cement, ships, plywood. Natural resources: coal, natural gas, limestone, marble. Exports: $111.6 billion (1995): textiles, electronic products, information and commercial products, plywood. Imports: $103.5 billion (1995): machinery, basic metals, crude oil, chemicals. Major trading partners: U.S., Hong Kong, Japan, Germany.

Geography. The Republic of China today consists of the island of Taiwan, an island 100 miles (161 km) off the Asian mainland in the Pacific; two off-shore islands, Kinmen (Quemoy) and Matsu; and the nearby islets of the Pescadores chain. It is slightly larger than the combined areas of Massachusetts and Connecticut.

Taiwan is divided by a central mountain range that runs from north to south, rising sharply on the east coast and descending gradually to a broad western plain, where cultivation is concentrated.

Government. The central government consists of five major branches called Yuans: Executive, Legislative, Judicial, Control, and Examination. The President and Vice President are popularly elected for a term of four years. The role of parliament is jointly filled by the National Assembly, the members of which are elected for four-year terms, and the Legislative Yuan, to which members are elected for three-year terms. Taiwan's internal affairs are administered by the Taiwan Provincial Government, led by the Provincial Governor under the supervision of the Provincial Assembly, both popularly elected.

The majority and ruling party is the Kuomintang (KMT; Nationalist Party) led by President Lee Teng-hui. The main opposition parties are the Democratic Progressive Party (DPP) and the New Party.

History. Taiwan was inhabited by aborigines of Malayan descent when Chinese from the areas now designated as Fukien and Kwangtung began settling it beginning in the 7th century, becoming the majority.

The Portuguese explored the area in 1590, naming it The Beautiful (Formosa). In 1624 the Dutch set up forts in the south, the Spanish in the north. The Dutch threw out the Spanish in 1641 and controlled the island until 1661, when the Chinese general Koxinga took it over, established an independent kingdom, and expelled the Dutch. The Manchus seized the island in 1683 and held it until 1895, when it passed to Japan after the first Sino-Japanese War. Japan developed and exploited it, and it was heavily bombed by American planes during World War II, af-

ter which it was restored to China.

After the defeat of its armies on the mainland, the Nationalist Government of Generalissimo Chiang Kai-shek retreated to Taiwan in December 1949. With only 15% of the population consisting of the 1949 immigrants, Chiang dominated the island, maintaining a 600,000-man army in the hope of eventually recovering the mainland. Japan renounced its claim to the island by the San Francisco Peace Treaty of 1951.

By stationing a fleet in the Strait of Formosa the U.S. prevented a mainland invasion in 1953.

The "China seat" in the U.N., which the Nationalists held with U.S. help for over two decades, was lost in October 1971, when the People's Republic of China was admitted and Taiwan ousted by the world body.

Chiang died at 87 of a heart attack on April 5, 1975. His son, Chiang Ching-kuo, continued as premier and dominant power in the Taipei regime.

Martial law was lifted in 1987. In April 1991 President Lee Teng-Hui formally declared an end to emergency rule, yet without abandoning his government's claim to be the sole legitimate government of China.

In the first full election in many decades the governing Kuomintang in December 1991 won 71% of the vote, affirming the party's opposition to independence in principle from China.

In February 1993 the president, himself a native Taiwanese, nominated Lien Chan, another native, to be prime minister, marking a further generational shift away from mainland exiles.

December 1994 regional and local elections gave a victory to the opposition Democratic Progressive Party's candidate in his bid for the mayoralty of Taipei, and the Nationalist Party candidate won in the second largest city.

In the island's first free presidential election voters defied mainland intimidation and gave 54% of the vote to incumbent president Lee Teng-hui. The second-place finisher, with 21%, advocated complete independence from China.

TAJIKISTAN

Republic of Tajikistan

Chairman, Supreme Council: Imomali Rakhmonov (1993)
Prime Minister: Yakhyo Azimov (1996)
Area: 55,300 sq mi. (143,100 sq km)
Population (est. 1996): 5,916,373 (1989: Tajiks, 62.3%; Uzbeks, 23.5%; Russians, 7.6%; Tatars, 1.4%; Kyrgyz, 1.3%); (average annual rate of natural increase: 2.54%); birth rate, 33.8/1000; infant mortality rate: 113.1/1000; density per square mile: 106
Capital and largest city (1994 est.): Dushanbe, 524,000; **Other large city:** Khodzhent (Leninabad), 164,500. **Monetary unit:** Tajik ruble. **Religion:** Sunni Moslem, 80%. **Language:** Tajik. **Literacy rate:** 98% (1989)
Economic summary: Gross national product (1994 est): $8.5 billion, per capita $1,415; real growth rate −12%; inflation n.a.; unemployment 1.5% (Sept. 94). Arable land: 6%. Labor force: 1,950,000 (1992): agriculture and forestry 43%, government and services 24%, industry 14%, trade and communications 11%, construction (1990) 8%. Industries: Aluminum, zinc, lead, cement, vegetable oil, metal cutting machine tools, refrigerators and freezers. Agriculture: cotton, grain, fruits, and grapes. Exports: $320 million (1994 to outside the former USSR countries): aluminum, cotton, fruits, vegetable oil, textiles. Imports: $318 million from outside the former USSR countries (1994): chemicals, machinery and transport equipment, textiles, foodstuffs. Major trading partners: Russia, Kazakhstan, Ukraine, Uzbekistan, Turkmenistan.

Geography: Ninety-three percent of Tajikistan's territory is mountainous, and the mountain glaciers are the source of its rivers. Tajikistan is an earthquake-prone area. The republic is bounded by China in the east, Afghanistan to the south, Uzbekistan and Kirghizia to the west and north. The central Asian republic also includes the Gorno-Badakh Shan autonomous region. Tajikistan is slightly larger than the state of Illinois in area.

Government: A parliamentary democracy. The Assembly (parliament) is the Majlis.

History: The name Tadzhikstan (now Tajikistan) dates from the 1920s when the territory became an official Russian administrative area. The Tajiks had an ancient nomadic culture and were ruled at different times by Afghanistan and Persia.

Tajikistan declared its sovereignty in August 1990. In 1991, the republic's Communist leadership supported the attempted coup against Soviet president Mikhail Gorbachev. Shortly afterward pro-Communist president Makhkamov was forced to resign by mounting pressure from pro-democracy groups, and the Tajikistan parliament restored an earlier ban on the Communist Party. The ban was rescinded in late September but again restored. The election of November 24 went to Rakhmon Nabiyev, former head of the local Communist Party.

Tajikistan joined with ten other former Soviet republics in the Commonwealth of Independent States on Dec. 21, 1991. A parliamentary republic was proclaimed and presidential rule abolished on November 1992. Former Communists dominated the government.

The new government immediately set out to destroy the anti-Communist coalition, consisting principally of Western-oriented intellectuals and Muslims.

Despite international efforts to end a three-year civil war, periodic fighting continued into 1996. In January a pro-Moscow Muslim leader was assassinated. In early February, bowing to rebel demands, the senior deputy prime minister agreed to resign. A few days later the prime minister also resigned. He was replaced by a carpet factory manager commited to market reforms.

TANZANIA

United Republic of Tanzania
President: Benjamin William Mkapa (1995)
Prime Minister: Frederick Tluway Sumaye (1995)
Area: 364,879 sq mi. (945,037 sq km)[1]
Population (est. 1996): 29,058,470 (average annual rate of natural increase: 2.18%); birth rate: 41.3/1000; infant mortality rate: 105.9/1000; density per sq mi.: 79
Capital and largest city (1988): Dar es Salaam,[2] 1,360,850; **Monetary unit:** Tanzanian shilling; **Languages:** Swahili, English, local languages; **Religions:** Christian, 40%; Muslim, 33%. **Member of Commonwealth of Nations; Literacy rate:** 46%
Economic summary: Gross domestic product (1994 est.): $21 billion; $750 per capita; 3% real growth rate; inflation 25%; unemployment n.a. Arable land: 5%. Principal agricultural products: tobacco, corn, cassava, wheat, cotton, coffee, sisal, cashew nuts, pyrethrum, cloves. Labor force: 732,200; 90% in agriculture. Major industrial products: textiles, wood products, refined oil, processed agricultural products, diamonds, cement, fertilizer. Natural resources: hydroelectric potential, phosphates, iron and coal. Exports: $462 million (f.o.b., 1994): coffee, cotton, sisal, cloves, cashew nuts, coffee, tobacco, tea. Imports: $1.4 billion (c.i.f., 1994): manufactured goods, machinery and transport equipment, crude oil, foodstuffs, cotton piece goods. Major trading partners: Germany, U.K., U.S., Japan, Italy, Denmark, Kenya, Netherlands, Hong Kong.

1. Including Zanzibar. 2. Some government offices have been transferred to Dodoma, which is planned as the new national capital by the end of the 1990s.

Geography. Tanzania is in East Africa on the Indian Ocean. To the north are Uganda and Kenya; to the west, Burundi, Rwanda, and Zaire; and to the south, Mozambique, Zambia, and Malawi. Its area is three times that of New Mexico.

Tanzania contains three of Africa's best-known lakes—Victoria in the north, Tanganyika in the west, and Nyasa in the south. Mount Kilimanjaro in the north, 19,340 feet (5,895 m), is the highest point on the continent.

Government. Under the republican form of government, Tanzania has a president elected by universal suffrage who appoints the cabinet ministers. The 275 members of the National Assembly are composed of 252 elected members from the mainland, 50 elected from Zanzibar, 10 members appointed by the president (from both Tanganyika and Zanzibar), 5 national members (elected by the National Assembly after nomination by various national institutions), 20 members elected by Zanzibar's House of Representatives, 25 Regional Commissioners sitting as *ex officio* members, and 15 seats reserved for women (elected by the National Assembly).

The Tanganyika African National Union, the only authorized party on the mainland, and the Afro-Shirazi Party, the only party in Zanzibar and Pemba, merged in 1977 as the Revolutionary Party (Chama Cha Mapinduzi) and elected Julius K. Nyerere as its head. There are now 13 registered political parties (including the CCM, the ruling party). Tanzania will hold general elections on Oct. 29, 1995, under a multiparty system.

History. Arab traders first began to colonize the area in A.D. 700. Portuguese explorers reached the coastal regions in 1500 and held some control until the 17th century, when the Sultan of Oman took power. With what are now Burundi and Rwanda, Tanganyika became the colony of German East Africa in 1885. After World War I, it was administered by Britain under a League of Nations mandate and later as a U.N. trust territory.

Although not mentioned in old histories until the 12th century, Zanzibar was believed always to have had connections with southern Arabia. The Portuguese made it one of their tributaries in 1503 and later established a trading post, but they were driven out by Arabs from Oman in 1698. Zanzibar was declared independent of Oman in 1861, and in 1890 it became a British protectorate.

Tanganyika became independent on Dec. 9, 1961; Zanzibar, on Dec. 10, 1963. On April 26, 1964, the two nations merged into the United Republic of Tanganyika and Zanzibar. The name was changed to Tanzania six months later.

An invasion by Ugandan troops in November 1978 was followed by a counterattack in January 1979, in which 5,000 Tanzanian troops were joined by 3,000 Ugandan exiles opposed to President Idi Amin. Within a month, full-scale war developed.

Tanzanian president Julius Nyerere kept troops in Uganda in open support of former Ugandan president Milton Obote, despite protests from opposition groups, until the national elections in December 1980.

In November 1985, Nyerere stepped down as president. Ali Hassan Mwinyi, his vice-president, succeeded him. Running unopposed Mwinyi was elected president in October. Shortly thereafter plans were announced to study the benefits of instituting a multiparty democracy.

The crisis in Rwanda in 1994 sent hundreds of thousands of refugees fleeing into Tanzania, taxing the already meager resources of the country. The government immediately appealed for international aid.

In October 1995 the country's first multiparty elections since independence took place. Although the opposition claimed irregularities had occurred, it came just short of victory in both the presidential voting and that for the legislature.

THAILAND

Kingdom of Thailand
Ruler: King Bhumibol Adulyadej (1946)
Prime Minister: Banharn Silpa-archa (1995)
Area: 198,455 sq mi. (514,000 sq km)
Population (est. 1996): 58,851,357 (average annual rate of natural increase: 1.03%); birth rate: 17.3/1000; infant mortality rate: 33.4/1000; density per square mile: 296
Capital and largest city (est. 1993): Bangkok, 5,572,712; **Other large cities:** Nonthanburi, 261,335; Chiang Mai, 170,397. **Monetary unit:** Baht. **Languages:** Thai (Siamese), Chinese, English. **Religions:** Buddhist, 94.4%; Islam, 4%; Hinduism, 1.1%; Christian, 0.5%. **National name:** Thailand. **Literacy rate:** 93%
Economic summary: Gross national product (1994 est.): $355.2 billion; $5,970 per capita; real growth rate 8%; inflation 5%; unemployment 3.2% (1993 est.). Arable land: 34%. Principal agricultural products: rice, rubber, corn, tapioca, sugar, coconuts. Labor force (1989 est.): 30,870,000; 62% in agriculture; 13% in commerce; 11% in services, including government. Major industries: Tourism largest source of foreign exchange, textiles and garments, agricultural processing, beverages, tobacco, cement, light manufacturing, electric appliances and components, integrated circuits, furniture, plastics, tungsten and tin. Natural resources: fish, natural gas, forests, fluorite, tin, tungsten. Exports: $46 billion (f.o.b., 1994 est.): machinery and manufactures, 76.9%; agricultural products, 14.9%; fisheries products, 5.9%. Imports: $52.6 billion (c.i.f., 1994 est.): capital goods, 41.4%; intermediate goods and raw materials, 32.8%; consumer goods, 10.4%; oil, 8.2%. Major trading partners: Japan, U.S., Singapore, Germany, Taiwan, Malaysia, Hong Kong, South Korea, U.K., France.

Geography. Thailand occupies the western half of the Indochinese peninsula and the northern two-thirds of the Malay peninsula in southeast Asia. Its neighbors are Myanmar on the north and west, Laos on the north and northeast, Cambodia on the east, and Malaysia on the south. Thailand is about the size of France.

Most of the population is supported in the fertile central alluvial plain, which is drained by the Chao Phraya River and its tributaries.

Government. A constitutional monarchy. The government is run by an elected civilian coalition of political parties. King Bhumibol Adulyadej, who was born Dec. 5, 1927, second son of Prince Mahidol of Songkhla, succeeded to the throne on June 9, 1946. He was married on April 28, 1950, to Queen Sirikit; their son, Vajiralongkorn, born July 28, 1952, is the crown prince.

History. The Thais first began moving down into their present homeland from the Asian continent in the 6th century A.D. and by the end of the 13th century ruled most of the western portion. During the next 400 years, the Thais fought sporadically with the Cambodians and the Burmese. The British obtained recognition of paramount interest in Thailand in 1824, and in 1896 an Anglo-French accord guaranteed the independence of Thailand.

A coup in 1932 changed the absolute monarchy into a representative government with universal suffrage. After five hours of token resistance on Dec. 8, 1941, Thailand yielded to Japanese occupation and became one of the springboards in World War II for the Japanese campaign against Malaya.

After the fall of its pro-Japanese puppet government in July 1944, Thailand pursued a policy of passive resistance against the Japanese, and after the Japanese surrender, Thailand repudiated the declaration of war it had been forced to make against Britain and the U.S. in 1942.

Thailand's major problem in the late 1960s was suppressing guerrilla action by Communist invaders in the north.

Although Thailand had received $2 billion in U.S. economic and military aid since 1950 and had sent troops (paid by the U.S.) to Vietnam while permitting U.S. bomber bases on its territory, the collapse of South Vietnam and Cambodia in the spring of 1975 brought rapid changes in the country's diplomatic posture.

At the Thai government's insistence, the U.S. agreed to withdraw all 23,000 U.S. military personnel remaining in Thailand by March 1976. Diplomatic relations with China were established in 1975.

After three years of civilian government ended with a military coup on Oct. 6, 1976, Thailand reverted to military rule. Political parties, banned after the coup, gained limited freedom in 1980. The same year, the National Assembly elected Gen. Prem Tinsulanonda as prime minister. General elections on April 18, 1983, and July 27, 1986, resulted in Prem continuing as prime minister over a coalition government.

Refugees from Laos, Cambodia, and Vietnam flooded into Thailand in 1978 and 1979, and despite efforts by the United States and other Western countries to resettle them, a total of 130,000 Laotian and Vietnamese refugees were living in camps along the Cambodian border in mid-1980. A drive by Vietnamese occupation forces on western Cambodian areas loyal to the Pol Pot government, culminating in invasions of Thai territory in late June, drove an estimated 100,000 Cambodians across the line as refugees, adding to the 200,000 of their countrymen already in Thailand.

On April 3, 1981, a military coup against the Prem government failed. Another coup attempt on Sept. 9, 1985, was crushed by loyal troops after 10 hours of fighting in Bangkok. Four persons were killed and about 60 wounded.

In February 1991 a nonviolent military coup led by Gen. Suchinda Kraprayoon overthrew the democratic government, charging corruption. The junta leaders, declaring a state of emergency and martial law, dismissed the houses of Parliament and abolished the constitution.

Parliamentary elections in March 1992 gave more than half the seats at stake to pro-military parties. In April the top military commander was appointed prime minister.

A scandal over a land-reform program caused the fall of the government in May 1995. The prime minister dissolved parliament and set a date for new elections. The results of the early July voting gave the largest number of seats in parliament to the Thai Nation Party, whose leader moved quickly to form a coalition government. The resulting cabinet quickly won universal disapproval, containing as it did ministers with questionable pasts.

TOGO

Republic of Togo

President: Gen. Gnassingbé Eyadema (1967)
Prime Minister: Kwassi Klutse (Aug. 1996)
Area: 21,925 sq mi. (56,785 sq km)
Population (est. 1996): 4,570,530 (average annual rate of natural increase: 3.56%); birth rate: 46.2/1000; infant mortality rate: 84.3/1000; density per sq mi.: 208
Capital and largest city (1990 est.): Lomé, 513,000. **Monetary unit:** Franc CFA. **Languages:** Ewé, Mina (south), Kabyé, Cotocoli (north), French (official), and many dialects. **Religions:** Indigenous beliefs, 70%; Christian, 20%; Islam, 10%. **National name:** République Togolaise. **Literacy rate:** 43%
Economic summary: Gross domestic product (1994 est.): $3.3 billion; $800 per capita; real growth rate 0%; inflation 0.5% (1991 est.); unemployment (1987 est.) 2%. Arable land: 25%. Principal agricultural products: yams, cotton, millet, sorghum, cocoa, coffee, rice. Labor force: 78% in agriculture. Major industrial products: phosphate, textiles, processed food. Natural resources: marble, phosphate, limestone. Exports: $221 million (f.o.b., 1993): phosphate, cocoa, coffee, cotton. Imports: $292 million (c.i.f., 1993): consumer goods, fuels, machinery, foodstuffs, chemical products. Major trading partners: E.U., Japan, U.S., Africa

Geography. Togo, twice the size of Maryland, is on the south coast of West Africa, bordering on Ghana to the west, Burkina Faso to the north, and Benin to the east. The Gulf of Guinea coastline, only 32 miles long (51 km), is low and sandy. The only port is at Lomé. The Togo hills traverse the central section.

Government. The government of Nicolas Grunitzky was overthrown in a bloodless coup, on Jan. 13, 1967, led by Lt. Col. Etienne Eyadema (now Gen. Gnassingbé Eyadema). A National Reconciliation Committee was set up to rule the country. In April, however, Eyadema dissolved the Committee and took over as president. In December 1979, a 67-member National Assembly was voted in by national referendum. The Assembly of the Togolese People is the only political party.

History. Freed slaves from Brazil were the first traders to settle in Togo. Established as a German colony (Togoland) in 1884, the area was split between the British and the French as League of Nations mandates after World War I and subsequently administered as U.N. trusteeships. The British portion voted for incorporation with Ghana. Togo became independent on April 27, 1960.

The presidential election held in August 1993 gave Eyadema more than 96% of the vote, but only 36% of the electorate went to the polls. Many of the major opposition candidates withdrew prior to the election.

Elections to the National Assembly in February 1994 gave opposition parties a majority of seats. A coalition government was formed in June, although the president's party was allotted a disproportionately large number of ministries. As a result the principal opposition party boycotted the Assembly. The impasse ended in August when the government announced that an independent electoral commission would oversee future balloting.

TONGA

Kingdom of Tonga

Sovereign: King Taufa'ahau Tupou IV (1965)
Prime Minister: Baron Vaea (1991)
Area: 290 sq mi. (751 sq km)
Population (est. 1996): 106,466 (average annual growth rate: 1.72%); birth rate: 24.0/1000; infant mortality rate: 20.2/1000 (1995 est.); density per square mile: 367
Capital and largest city (1990 est.): Nuku'alofa, 34,000. **Monetary unit:** Pa'anga. **Languages:** Tongan, English. **Religions:** Christian; Free Wesleyan Church claims over 30,000 adherents. **Member of Commonwealth of Nations. Literacy rate:** 57%
Economic summary: Gross domestic product (1994 est.): $214 million; $2,050 per capita; real growth rate 5%; inflation 3% (1993). Arable land: 25%. Principal agricultural products: vanilla, coffee, ginger, black pepper, coconuts, bananas, copra. Labor force: 70% in agriculture. Natural resources: fish, copra. Exports: $11.3 million (f.o.b., FY92/93): copra, coconut products, bananas, fruits, vegetables, fish, vanilla. Imports: $56 million (c.i.f., FY92/93): foodstuffs, machinery and transport equipment, fuels, chemicals, building materials. Major trading partners: New Zealand, Australia, Fiji, U.S., Japan, E.U.

Geography. Situated east of the Fiji Islands in the South Pacific, Tonga (also called the Friendly Islands) consists of some 150 islands, of which 36 are inhabited. Most of the islands contain active volcanic craters; others are coral atolls.

Government. Tonga is a constitutional monarchy. Executive authority is vested in the sovereign, a privy council, and a cabinet headed by the prime minister. Legislative authority is vested in the Legislative Assembly. Nine seats are reserved for commoners; the others are filled by appointees of the king.

History. The present dynasty of Tonga was founded in 1831 by Taufa'ahau Tupou, who took the name George I. He consolidated the kingdom by conquest and in 1875 granted a constitution.

In 1900, his great-grandson, George II, signed a treaty of friendship with Britain, and the country became a British-protected state. The treaty was revised in 1959. Tonga became independent on June 4, 1970.

Moves were made in 1992 to form a political party independent of the hereditary nobility that dominates the parliament.

A general election in February 1993 gave six of the nine contested parliamentary seats to pro-democracy candidates. The king, however, refused major changes in the system of government. Discussions concerning the king's power and the role of democracy dominated politics during 1995.

TRINIDAD AND TOBAGO

Republic of Trinidad and Tobago

President: Noor Hassanali (1987)
Prime Minister: Basdeo Panday (1995)
Area: 1,980 sq mi. (5,128 sq km)
Population (est. 1996): 1,272,385 (East Indian descent 40.3%; African descent 39.6%) (average annual rate of natural increase: 0.94%); birth rate: 16.25/1000; infant mortality rate: 18.2/1000; density per square mile: 642
Capital and largest city (1992 est.): Port-of-Spain, 52,451. **Monetary unit:** Trinidad and Tobago dollar. **Languages:** English (official); Hindi, French, Spanish. **Religions:** Roman Catholic, 33%; Hindu, 25%; Anglican, 15%; other Christian, 14%; Muslim, 6%. **Member of Commonwealth of Nations. Literacy rate:** 98%

Economic summary: Gross domestic product (1994 est.): $15 billion; $11,280 per capita; real growth rate 3%; inflation 10.1%; unemployment 18.1%. Arable land: 14%. Principal products: sugar cane, cocoa, coffee, citrus. Labor force: 463,900; 14.8% in manufacturing, mining, and quarrying. Major industrial products: petroleum, processed food, cement. Natural resources: petroleum, natural gas, asphalt. Exports: $1.9 billion (f.o.b., 1994): including reexports—petroleum and petroleum products, steel products, fertilizer, sugar, cocoa, coffee, citrus fruits (1988). Imports: $996 million (c.i.f., 1994): raw materials, capital goods, consumer goods. Major trading partners: U.S., Caribbean, Latin America, Western Europe, U.K., Canada.

Geography. Trinidad and Tobago lies in the Caribbean Sea off the northeast coast of Venezuela. The area of the two islands is slightly less than that of Delaware. Trinidad, the larger, is mainly flat and rolling, with mountains in the north that reach a height of 3,085 feet (940 m) at Mount Aripo. Tobago is heavily forested with hardwood trees.

Government. A parliamentary democracy. The legislature consists of a 24-member Senate and a 36-member House of Representatives. The political parties are the People's National Movement led by Prime Minister Mr. Patrick Manning (21 seats in the House of Representatives); the United National Congress led by Mr. Basdeo Panday (19 seats); and the National Alliance for Reconstruction led by Mr. Selby Wilson (2 seats).

History. Trinidad was discovered by Columbus in 1498 and remained in Spanish possession, despite raids by other European nations, until it capitulated to the British in 1797 during a war between Britain and Spain.

Trinidad was ceded to Britain in 1802, and in 1899 it was united with Tobago as a colony. From 1958 to 1962, Trinidad and Tobago was a part of the West Indies Federation, and on Aug, 31, 1962, it became independent.

On Aug. 1, 1976, Trinidad and Tobago cut its ties with Britain and became a republic, remaining within the Commonwealth and recognizing Queen Elizabeth II as head of that organization.

The People's National Movement won a landslide victory in elections of December 1991, making Manning prime minister.

Manning called an early election in November 1995. His party lost seats and he would not enter into a coalition, which the opposition was willing to do with the National Alliance for Reconstruction.

TUNISIA

Republic of Tunisia

President: Mr. Zine El Abidine Ben Ali (1987)
Prime Minister: Hamed Karoui (1989)
Area: 63,170 sq mi. (163,610 sq km)
Population (est. 1996): 9,019,687 (average annual rate of natural increase: 1.89%; birth rate: 24/1000; infant mortality rate: 35.1/1000; density per sq mi.: 143
Capital and largest city (1994): Tunis, 887,800. **Monetary unit:** Tunisian dinar. **Languages:** Arabic, French. **Religion:** Islam (Sunni), 98%; Christian, 1%; Jewish, less than 1%. **National name:** Al-Joumhouria Attunisia. **Literacy rate:** 65%
Economic summary: Gross domestic product (1994): $15.904 billion; $1,800 per capita; real growth rate 3.3%; inflation 4.5% (1993); unemployment 16.2% (!993). Arable land: 20%. Principal agricultural products: wheat, olives, oranges, grapes, dates. Labor force: 2,250,000. Manufacturing 21% of GDP, agriculture 15%, Tourism 7%. Major industrial products: textiles, and leather, chemical fertilizers, petroleum, phosphate, iron ore. Tourism is an important industry. Natural resources: oil, phosphates, iron ore, lead, zinc. Exports: $4.7 billion (f.o.b., 1994): textiles, crude oil, olive oil, phosphoric acid, chemical fertilizers, triple superphosphate, fish, dates. Imports: $6.6 billion (c.i.f., 1994): raw materials, consumer goods, machinery and equipment, foodstuffs. Major trading partners: France, Italy, Germany, U.S., Belgium and Luxembourg, Spain, the Netherlands.

Geography. Tunisia, at the northernmost bulge of Africa, thrusts out toward Sicily to mark the division between the eastern and western Mediterranean Sea. Twice the size of South Carolina, it is bordered on the west by Algeria and by Libya on the south.

Coastal plains on the east rise to a north-south escarpment which slopes gently to the west. Saharan in the south, Tunisia is more mountainous in the north, where the Atlas range continues from Algeria.

Government. Executive power is vested by the constitution in the president, elected for five years and eligible for re-election to two additional terms. Legislative power is vested in a Chamber of Deputies elected by universal suffrage.

In 1975, the Chamber of Deputies amended the constitution to make Habib Bourguiba president for life. At 71, Bourguiba was re-elected to a fourth five-year term when he ran unopposed in 1974. He was deposed by Gen. Zine Ben Ali in 1987. Ben Ali was reelected in 1989, and again for another five-year term in 1994. Opposition parties entered Chamber of Deputies for the first time (19 seats out of 163).

History. Tunisia was settled by the Phoenicians and Carthaginians in ancient times. Except for an interval of Vandal conquest in A.D. 439–533, it was part of the Roman Empire until the Arab conquest of 648–69. It was ruled by various Arab and Berber dynasties until the Turks took it in 1570–74. French troops occupied the country in 1881, and the bey signed a treaty acknowledging a French protectorate.

Nationalist agitation forced France to grant internal autonomy to Tunisia in 1955 and to recognize Tunisian independence and sovereignty in 1956. The Constituent Assembly deposed the bey on July 25, 1957, declared Tunisia a republic, and elected Habib Bourguiba as president. Bourguiba maintained a pro-Western foreign policy that earned him enemies. Tunisia refused to break relations with the U.S. during the Israeli-Arab war in June 1967.

Developments in 1986–87 were characterized by a consolidation of power by the 84-year-old Bourguiba and his failure to arrange for a successor. This issue was settled when the prime minister, Gen. Ben Ali, deposed Bourguiba.

Concerned with Islamic fundamentalist plots against the state, the government stepped up efforts to eradicate the movement, including censorship and frequent detention of suspects.

Elections in March 1994 gave a vast majority of seats to the ruling party. The president ran unopposed as no other candidate was able to qualify.

An Association Agreement was signed in July 1995 with the EU that after 12 years would make the country a part of a free-trade area around the Mediterranean, called the European Economic Area.

TURKEY

Republic of Turkey
President: Suleyman Demirel (1993)
Prime Minister: Necmettin Erbakan (1996)
Area: 300,947 sq mi. (incl. 9,121 in Europe) (779,452 sq km)
Population (est. 1996): 62,484,478; average annual rate of natural increase 1.67%; birth rate: 22.3/1000; infant mortality rate: 43.2/1000; density per square mile: 207
Capital: Ankara (2,719,981); **Largest cities (1993):** Istanbul, 7,331,927; Izmir, 1,920,807; Adana, 1,010,363; Bursa, 949,810; Gaziantep, 683,557. **Monetary unit:** Turkish Lira. **Language:** Turkish. **Religion:** Islam (mostly Sunni), 98%. **National name:** Türkiye Cumhuriyeti. **Literacy rate:** 90.7%
Economic summary: Gross domestic product (1994): $305.2 billion; $4,910 per capita; real growth rate –5%; inflation: 106%; unemployment: 12.6%. Arable land: 20%. Principal agricultural products: cotton, tobacco, cereals, sugar beets, fruits, olives. Labor force: 21,586,032; industry, 16.9%; agriculture, 47%; transportation, 4%. Major industrial products: textiles, coal, minerals, processed foods, steel, petroleum. Natural resources: coal, chromite, copper, borate, sulfur, petroleum. Exports: $18.1 billion (1994): agricultural products, textiles, leather, glass. Imports: $23.2 billion (1994): crude oil, machinery, motor vehicles, metals, mineral fuels, fertilizer, chemicals. Major trading partners: Germany, France, Italy, U.S., U.K., Iran, Japan, Russia.

Geography. Turkey is at the northeastern end of the Mediterranean Sea in southeast Europe and southwest Asia. To the north is the Black Sea and to the west the Aegean Sea. Its neighbors are Greece and Bulgaria to the west, Russia and Ukraine to the north (through the Black Sea), Georgia, Armenia, Azerbaijain, and Iran to the east, and Syria and Iraq to the south. The Dardanelles, the Sea of Marmara, and the Bosporus divide the country.

Turkey in Europe comprises an area about equal to the state of Massachusetts. It is hilly country drained by the Maritsa River and its tributaries.

Turkey in Asia, or Anatolia, about the size of Texas, is roughly a rectangle in shape with its short sides on the east and west. Its center is a treeless plateau rimmed by mountains.

Government. The president is elected by the Grand National Assembly for a seven-year term and is not eligible for re-election. The prime minister and the Council of Ministers hold the executive power, although the president has the right to veto legislation.

History. The Ottoman Turks first appeared in the early 13th century in Anatolia, subjugating Turkish and Mongol bands pressing against the eastern borders of Byzantium. They gradually spread through the Near East and Balkans, capturing Constantinople in 1453 and storming the gates of Vienna two centuries later. At its height, the Ottoman Empire stretched from the Persian Gulf to western Algeria.

Defeat of the Turkish navy at Lepanto by the Holy League in 1571 and failure of the siege of Vienna heralded the decline of Turkish power. By the 18th century, Russia was seeking to establish itself as the protector of Christians in Turkey's Balkan territories. Russian ambitions were checked by Britain and France in the Crimean War (1854–56), but the Russo-Turkish War (1877–78) gave Bulgaria virtual independence and Romania and Serbia liberation from their nominal allegiance to the sultan.

Turkish weakness stimulated a revolt of young liberals known as the Young Turks in 1909. They forced Sultan Abdul Hamid to grant a constitution and install a liberal government. Reforms were no barrier to further defeats, however, in a war with Italy (1911–12) and the Balkan Wars (1912–13). Under the influence of German military advisors, Turkey signed a secret alliance with Germany on Aug. 2, 1914, that led to a declaration of war by the Allied powers and the ultimate humiliation of the occupation of Turkish territory by Greek and other Allied troops.

In 1919, the new Nationalist movement, headed by Mustafa Kemal, was organized to resist the Allied occupation, and in 1920, a National Assembly elected him president of both the Assembly and the government. Under his leadership, the Greeks were driven out of Smyrna and other Allied forces were withdrawn.

The present Turkish boundaries (with the exception of Alexandretta, ceded to Turkey by France in 1939) were fixed by the Treaty of Lausanne (1923) and later negotiations. The caliphate and sultanate were separated, and the sultanate was abolished in 1922. On Oct. 29, 1923, Turkey formally became a republic, with Mustafa Kemal, who took the name Kemal Atatürk, as its first president. The caliphate was abolished in 1924, and Atatürk proceeded to carry out an extensive program of reform, modernization, and industrialization.

Gen. Ismet Inönü was elected to succeed Atatürk in 1938 and was re-elected in 1939, 1943, and 1946. Defeated in 1950, he was succeeded by Celâl Bayar. In 1939, a mutual assistance pact was concluded with Britain and France. Neutral during most of World War II Turkey, on Feb. 23, 1945, declared war on Germany and Japan but took no active part in the conflict.

Turkey became a full member of NATO in 1952.

Turkey invaded Cyprus by sea and air July 20, 1974, following the failure of diplomatic efforts to resolve the crisis caused by the ouster of Archbishop Makarios.

Talks in Geneva involving Greece, Turkey, Britain, and Greek Cypriot and Turkish Cypriot leaders broke down in mid-August. Turkey unilaterally announced a cease-fire August 16, after having gained control of 40% of the island. Turkish Cypriots established their own state in the north on Feb. 13, 1975.

In July 1975, after a 30-day warning, Turkey took over control of all the U.S. installations except the big joint defense base at Incirlik, which it reserved for "NATO tasks alone."

The establishment of military government in September 1980 stopped the slide toward anarchy and brought some improvement in the economy.

A Constituent Assembly, consisting of the six-member National Security Council and members appointed by them, drafted a new constitution that was approved by an overwhelming (91.5%) majority of the voters in a Nov. 6, 1982, referendum. Prime Minister Turgut Özal's Motherland Party came to power in parliamentary elections held in late 1983. Özal was re-elected in November 1987.

The sudden death of Turgut Özal in April 1993 led to Suleyman Demirel assuming the presidency in May. In June the True Path Party chose Tansu Ciller as its new leader, leading to her appointment as Turkey's first female prime minister.

In March 1995 as many as 35,000 Turkish troops moved into northern Iraq seeking to root out Kurdish rebels, who had used Iraq as a base. That operation lasted six weeks, but another followed in July.

Inconclusive elections in December 1995 resulted in a six-month power struggle. In June 1996 an agreement was reached with the Welfare Party (RP). The resulting government committed itself to secularism, capitalism, and the Western alliances.

TURKMENISTAN

Republic of Turkmenistan
President: Saparmurad A. Niyazov (1990)
Prime Minister: Khan Akhmedov (1992)
Area: 188,500 sq mi. (488,100 sq km)
Population (est. 1996): 4,149,283 (Turkmen, 72%; Russian, 10%; other minorities, Uzbeks, Kazakhs, Ukrainians); (average annual rate of natural increase: 2.02%); birth rate: 29.1/100; infant mortality rate: 81.6/100; density per square mile: 22
Capital and largest city (1994 est.): Ashkhabad, 518,000; **Largest cities:** Chardzhou, 166,400; Tashauz, 117,000. **Monetary unit:** Manat. **Languages:** Turkmen, 72%; Russian, 12%; Uzbek, 9%. **Religions:** Islam, 85%; Eastern Orthodox, 10%. **Literacy rate:** 98%.
Economic summary: Gross national product (UN, World Bank 1994 est.): $13.1 billion, $3,280 per capita; real growth rate –24%; inflation 25% (per mo.); unemployment (1992 est.) 2.9%. Labor force: 1.642 million (Jan. 1994): agriculture and forestry, 44%; industry and construction, 20%. Industries: oil and gas, petrochemicals, fertilizers, food processing, textiles. Agriculture: cotton, fruits, vegetables. Exports: $382 million to outside former USSR countries (1994): natural gas, oil, chemicals, cotton, textiles, carpets. Imports: $304 million from outside the former USSR countries (1994): machinery and parts, plastics and rubber, consumer durables, textiles, grain, foodstuffs. Major trading partners: Ukraine, Russia, Kazakhstan, Uzbekistan, Georgia, Azerbaijan, Eastern Europe, Turkey, Argentina.

Geography. Turkmenistan (formerly Turkmenia) is bounded by the Caspian Sea in the west, Kazakhstan in the north, Uzbekistan in the east, and Iran and Afghanistan in the south. Eighty percent of the republic's territory is desert. The largest desert is the Kara-Kum (Black Sand), approximately 138,966 sq mi. (360,000 sq km) in area. A 684-mile-long (1,100 km) canal runs across the Kara-Kum Desert and it supplies water from the Amu Darya River for irrigation and hydroelectric power.

Government. A republic. The constitution allows for a strong presidential rule. The president heads the Cabinet of Ministers, whose members he appoints with the consent of the Meglis (parliament). There are two parliamentary bodies, the unicameral People's Council (Halk Maslahaty) with over 100 members and the 50-member unicameral Assembly (Majlis).

History. Turkmenistan was once part of the ancient Persian empire. The Turkmen people were originally pastoral nomads and some of them continued their unsettled way of life up into the 20th century, living in transportable dome-shaped felt tents. The territory was ruled by the Seljuk Turks in the 11th century. The Mongols of Ghenghis Khan conquered the land in the 13th century and dominated the area for the next two centuries until they were deposed in the late 15th century by invading Uzbeks.

Prior to the 19th century, Turkmenia was divided into two lands, one belonging to the Khanate of Khiva and the other belonging to the Khanate of Bukhara. In 1868, the Khanate of Khiva was made part of the Russian empire and Turkmenia became known as the Transcaspia Region of Russian Turkistan. Turkmenistan was later formed out of the Turkistan Autonomous Soviet Socialist Republic, founded in 1922, and was made an independent Soviet Socialist Republic on May 13, 1925.

Turkmenistan declared its sovereignty in August 1990 and became a member of the Commonwealth of Independent States on Dec. 21, 1991, together with ten other former Soviet republics.

In the presidential election of June 1992 voters reelected President Niyazov in a one-candidate race. A new constitution was adopted in May 1992 making Turkmenistan the first Central Asian state to do so.

The country left the ruble zone in November 1993, introducing its own currency emblazoned with the president's image. Protests both domestic and foreign against his authoritarian rule and practices notwithstanding, the president extended his term into the next century.

TUVALU

Sovereign: Queen Elizabeth II
Governor-General: Tulaga Manuella (1994)
Prime Minister: Kamuta Laatasi (1993)
Area: 10 sq mi. (26 sq km)
Population (est. 1996): 10,146; growth rate 1.51%; birth rate, 24/1000; infant mortality rate, 27.6/1000; density per square mile: 1,014
Capital and largest city (1991): Funafuti, 3,839. **Monetary unit:** Tuvaluan dollar, Australian dollar. **Languages:** Tuvaluan, English. **Religion:** Church of Tuvalu (Congregationalist), 97%. **Member of the Commonwealth of Nations. Literacy rate:** less than 50%
Economic summary: Gross national product (1993 est.): $7.8 million., per capita income: $800; 4% real growth rate; inflation n.a. Principal agricultural products: copra and coconuts. Exports: $165,000 (f.o.b., 1989): copra. Imports: $4.4 million (c.i.f., 1989): food, fuels, machinery, animals, manufactured goods. Major trading partners: Australia, Fiji, New Zealand

Geography. Formerly the Ellice Islands, Tuvalu consists of nine small islands scattered over 500,000 square miles of the western Pacific, just south of the equator.

Government. Official executive power is vested in a governor-general, representing the queen, who is appointed by her on the recommendation of the Tuvalu government. Actual executive power lies with a prime minister, who is responsible to a House of Assembly composed of eight elected members.

History. The Ellice Islands became a British protectorate in 1892 and were annexed by Britain in 1915–16 as part of the Gilbert and Ellice Islands Colony. The Ellice Islands were separated in 1975, given home rule, and renamed Tuvalu. Full independence was granted on Sept. 30, 1978.

Unable to select a prime minister after a mid-1993 election the governor-general dissolved parliament in September. A new election in November led ultimately to a new prime minister in December.

A new flag that did not bear the British Union Jack was unfurled publicly in October 1995.

UGANDA

Republic of Uganda
President: Yoweri Museveni (1986)
Prime Minister: Kintu Musoke
Area: 91,459 sq mi. (236,880 sq km)
Population (est. 1996): 20,158,176 (average annual rate of natural increase: 2.52%); birth rate: 45.9/1000; infant mortality rate: 99.4/1000; density per sq mi.: 220
Capital and largest city (est. 1991): Kampala, 773,463. **Monetary unit:** Ugandan shilling. **Languages:** English

(official), Swahili, Luganda, Ateso, Luo. **Religions:** Christian, 66%; Islam, 16%. **Member of Commonwealth of Nations. Literacy rate:** 48%

Economic summary: Gross domestic product (1994 est.): $16.2 billion; $850 per capita; real growth rate 6%; inflation 41.5% (1992 est.). Arable land: 23%. Principal agricultural products: coffee, tea, cotton, sugar. Labor force: 4,500,000 (est.); 94% in subsistence activities. Major industrial products: refined sugar, beer, tobacco, cotton textiles, cement. Natural resources: copper, cobalt, limestone, salt. Exports: $237 million (f.o.b., 1993 est.): coffee 97%, cotton, tea. Imports: $696 million (c.i.f., 1993 est.): petroleum products, machinery, transport equipment, metals, food. Major trading partners: U.S., U.K., Kenya, Italy, France, Spain, South Africa.

Geography. Uganda, twice the size of Pennsylvania, is in East Africa. It is bordered on the west by Zaire, on the north by the Sudan, on the east by Kenya, and on the south by Tanzania and Rwanda. The country, which lies across the equator, is divided into three main areas—swampy lowlands, a fertile plateau with wooded hills, and a desert region. Lake Victoria forms part of the southern border.

Government. The country has been run by the National Resistance Movement (NRM) since January 1986.

History. Uganda was first visited by European explorers as well as Arab traders in 1844. An Anglo-German agreement of 1890 declared it to be in the British sphere of influence in Africa, and the Imperial British East Africa Company was chartered to develop the area. The company did not prosper financially, and in 1894 a British protectorate was proclaimed.

Uganda became independent on Oct. 9, 1962.

Sir Edward Mutesa was elected the first president and Milton Obote the first prime minister of the newly independent country. With the help of a young army officer, Col. Idi Amin, Prime Minister Obote seized control of the government from President Mutesa four years later.

On Jan. 25, 1971, Col. Amin deposed President Obote. Obote went into exile in Tanzania. Amin expelled Asian residents and launched a reign of terror against Ugandan opponents, torturing and killing tens of thousands. In 1976, he had himself proclaimed President for Life. In 1977, Amnesty International estimated that 300,000 may have died under his rule, including church leaders and recalcitrant cabinet ministers.

After Amin held military exercises on the Tanzanian border, angering Tanzania's President Julius Nyerere, a combined force of Tanzanian troops and Ugandan exiles loyal to former president Obote invaded Uganda and chased Amin into exile.

After a series of interim administrations, President Obote led his People's Congress Party to victory in 1980 elections that opponents charged were rigged.

On July, 27, 1985, army troops staged a coup, taking over the government. Obote fled into exile. The military regime installed Gen. Tito Okello as chief of state.

The National Resistance Army (NRA), an anti-Obote group led by Yoweri Musevni, kept fighting after being excluded from the new regime. They seized Kampala on January 29, 1986, and Musevni was declared president.

In October 1995 a constituent assembly produced a constitution that provided for a ban on political parties but that still called for elections in 1996.

In the presidential ballotting of May 1996 the incumbent won 72% of the vote, reflecting his popularity due to the country's economic recovery.

UKRAINE

Ukraine
President: Leonid D. Kuchma (1994)
Prime Minister: Pavlo Lazarenko (1996)
Area: 233,000 sq mi. (603,700 sq km)
Population (est. 1996): 50,864,009 (Ukrainians, 73%; Russians, 22%; Jews, Poles, Moldovians, Bulgarians); (average annual rate of natural increase: −0.4%): birth rate: 11.2/1000; infant mortality rate: 22.5/1000; density per square mile: 218
Capital: Kyiv (Kiev); **Largest cities:** Kyiv, 2,637,000; Kharkiv, 1,622,000; Donetske, 1,121,000; Odessa, 1,104,000; Lviv, 803,000; **Monetary unit:** Karbovanets. **Language:** Ukrainian; **Religion:** Orthodox, 76%; Ukrainian Catholic, 13.5%; Jewish, 2.3%; Baptist, Mennonite, Protestant, and Moslem, 8.2%; **Literacy rate (1992):** 99%
Economic summary: Gross domestic product (UN, World Bank 1994 est.): $189.2 billion; per capita: $3,650; real growth rate: −19%; inflation (per mo.): 14%; unemployment: 0.4%. Labor force (Jan. 94): 23.55 million; industry and construction, 33%; agriculture and forestry, 21%; health, education, and culture, 16%; trade and distribution, 7%; transport and communication, 7%. Mineral resources are iron ore, coal, manganese, natural gas, oil, salt, sulfur, graphite, titanium, magnesium, kaolin, nickel, mercury, and timber. Important agricultural crops are grain, vegetables, meat, and milk. Exports: $11.8 billion (1994): coal, electric power, ferrous and nonferrous metals, chemicals, machinery and transportation equipment, grain and meat. Imports: $14.2 billion (1994): machinery and parts, transportation equipment, chemicals, and textiles. Major trading partners: FSU countries, Germany, Poland, Czech Republic, China, Italy, Switzerland.

Geography. Located in southeastern Europe, the country consists largely of fertile black soil steppes. Mountainous areas include the Carpathians in the southwest and the Crimean chain in the south. There are forest lakes in the north. It is bordered by Belarus on the north and the Russian Federation on the northeast and east, by Poland on the west, by Romania, and Moldova in the southwest, by Hungary, Slovakia, and Poland on the west, and the Baltic Sea and the Sea of Azov in the south.

Government. A constitutional republic. The unicameral parliament, or Supreme Council, has 450 members.

History. Ukraine was known as "Rus" (from which Russia is a derivative) up until the 16th century. In the 9th century, Kiev was the major political and cultural center in eastern Europe. Kievian Rus reached the height of its power in the 10th century and adopted Byzantine Christianity and the Cyrillic alphabet during that period.

The Mongol conquest in 1240 ended Kievian power. From the 13th to the 16th century, Kiev was under the influence of Poland and western Europe. In 1654, Ukraine asked the czar of Moscovy for protection against Poland, and the Treaty of Pereyasav signed that year recognized the suzerainty of Moscow. The agreement was interpreted by Moscow as an invitation to take over Kiev, and the Ukrainian state was eventually absorbed into the Russian empire.

After the Russian revolution, Ukraine declared its independence from Russia on Jan. 28, 1918, and several years of warfare ensued with several groups. The Red Army finally was victorious over Kiev, and in

1920, Ukraine became a Soviet republic. In 1922, Ukraine became one of the founders of the United Soviet Socialist Republics.

Ukraine was one of the most devastated Soviet republics during World War II.

On April 15, 1986, the nation's nuclear power plant at Chernobyl was the site of the world's worst nuclear accident. On Oct. 29, 1991, the Ukrainian parliament voted to shut down the reactor within two years' time and asked for international assistance in dismantling it.

When President Leonid Kravchuk was elected by the Ukrainian parliament in 1990, he vowed to seek Ukrainian sovereignty. Ukraine declared its independence on Aug. 24, 1991.

New elections were held Dec. 1, 1991 and Mr. Kravchuk was elected president with 61.5% of the vote. Voters also overwhelmingly approved a referendum to establish full independence from the Soviet Union.

On December 8, 1991, Ukrainian, Russian, and Belarus leaders cofounded a new Commonwealth of Independent States, with the new capital to be situated in Minsk, Belarus. The Commonwealth was formally established on Dec. 21, 1991, with ten other former Soviet republics.

After independence Ukraine sought to affirm and exercise its territorial claim on the Crimea, which had been legally transferred from Russian jurisdiction in 1954.

The U.S. announced in January 1994 that an agreement had been reached with Russia and Ukraine for the destruction of Ukraine's entire nuclear arsenal. Later that month a candidate favoring the separation of Crimea from Ukraine and integration with Russia won that region's presidency. A presidential election in July saw the surprise ascent of Leonid Kuchma to the presidency of Ukraine. His campaign called for closer ties to Moscow.

His promises notwithstanding, Kuchma in October 1994 began a program of economic liberalization and moved to re-establish central authority over Crimea. In March 1995 the region's separatist leader was removed and the Crimean constitution revoked. In June parliament approved legislation that expanded presidential powers.

In June 1996 the last strategic nuclear warhead was removed to Russia. Also that month parliament approved a new constitution that allows for private ownershp of land.

UNITED ARAB EMIRATES

President: Sheikh Zayed Bin Sultan Al-Nahyan (1971)
Prime Minister: Sheikh Maktoum Bin Rashid Al-Maktoum (1990)
Area: 32,000 sq mi. (82,880 sq km)
Population (est. 1996): 3,057,337 (average annual rate of natural increase: 2.34%); birth rate: 26.4/1000; infant mortality rate: 20.4/1000; density per square mile: 95
Capital and largest city (est. 1989): Abu Dhabi, 363,432.
Monetary unit: U.A.E. Dirham. **Language:** Arabic. English as a second language. **Religions:** Islam (Sunni 80%, Shiite 16%), others 4%. **Literacy rate:** 83.3% (1993)

Economic summary: Gross domestic product (1994 est.): $36.8 billion; $22,470 per capita; real growth rate 2.9%; inflation 3%. Arable land: 0%, irrigated land, 19.3 sq mi. Principal agricultural products: vegetables, dates, poultry, fish. Labor force: 856,000 (1993 est.): 80% is foreign; 85% in industry and commerce. Major industrial products: light manufactures, petroleum, construction materials. Natural resource: oil. Exports:

$25.8 billion (f.o.b., 1994 est.): oil and gas exports: $12.3 billion; non-oil exports and re-exports: $13.5 billion. Imports: $21 billion (f.o.b, 1994 est.): consumer goods, food, capital goods. Major trading partners: Japan, Western Europe, U.S., Singapore, Korea, India, Iran, China, Taiwan.

Geography. The United Arab Emirates, in the eastern part of the Arabian Peninsula, extends along part of the Gulf of Oman and the southern coast of the Persian Gulf. The nation is the size of Maine. Its neighbors are Saudi Arabia in the west and south, Qatar in the north, and Oman in the east. Most of the land is barren and sandy.

Government. The United Arab Emirates was formed in 1971 by seven emirates known as the Trucial States—Abu Dhabi (the largest), Dubai, Sharjah, Ajman, Fujairah, Ras al Khaimah and Umm al-Qaiwain.

The loose federation allows joint policies in foreign relations, defense, and development, with each member state keeping its internal local system of government headed by its own ruler. A 40-member legislature consists of eight seats each for Abu Dhabi and Dubai, six seats each for Ras al Khaimah and Sharjah, and four each for the others. It is a member of the Arab League.

History. Originally the area was inhabited by a seafaring people who were converted to Islam in the seventh century. Later, a dissident sect, the Carmathians, established a powerful sheikdom, and its army conquered Mecca. After the sheikdom disintegrated, its people became pirates.

Threatening the sultanate of Muscat and Oman early in the 19th century, the pirates provoked the intervention of the British, who in 1820 enforced a partial truce and in 1853 a permanent truce. Thus what had been called the Pirate Coast was renamed the Trucial Coast.

A crisis with Iran over sovereignty of three islands near the Strait of Hormuz arose in 1992. Despite efforts to settle the issue little progress has been made.

The country signed a military defense agreement with the U.S. in 1994 and one with France in 1995.

UNITED KINGDOM

United Kingdom of Great Britain and Northern Ireland

Sovereign: Queen Elizabeth II (1952)
Prime Minister: John Major (1990)
Area: 94,247 sq mi. (244,100 sq km)
Population (est. 1996): 58,489,975 (average annual rate of natural increase: 0.19%); birth rate: 13.1/1000; infant mortality rate: 6.4/1000; density per square mile: 621
Capital and largest city (1992 est.): London, 6,679,699;
Other large cities: Birmingham, 1,009,100; Leeds, 721,800; Glasgow, 681,470; Liverpool, 479,000; Bradford, 477,500; Edinburgh, 439,800; Manchester, 434,600; Bristol, 396,600. **Monetary unit:** Pound sterling (£).
Languages: English, Welsh, Scots, Gaelic. **Religions:** Church of England (established church); Church of Wales (disestablished); Church of Scotland (established church—Presbyterian); Church of Ireland (disestablished); Roman Catholic; Methodist; Congregational; Baptist; Jewish. **Literacy rate:** 99%

Economic summary: Gross domestic product (1994 est.): $1.0452 trillion; $17,980 per capita; real growth rate 4.2%; inflation 2.4%; unemployment 9.3%. Arable land: 29%. Principal agricultural products: wheat, barley, potatoes, sugar beets, livestock, dairy products.

Labor force (June 1992): 28,048,000: services, 60.6%; mfg. and construction, 27.2%. Major industrial products: machinery and transport equipment, metals, processed food, paper, textiles, chemicals, clothing, aircraft, shipbuilding, electronics and communications. Natural resources: coal, oil, gas. Exports: $200 billion (f.o.b., 1994 est.): machinery, transport equipment, chemicals, petroleum, manufactured goods, semifinished goods. Imports: $215 billion (c.i.f., 1994 est.): foodstuffs, machinery, manufactured goods, semifinished goods, consumer goods. Major trading partners: Western European nations, U.S.

Geography. The United Kingdom, consisting of England, Wales, Scotland, and Northern Ireland, is twice the size of New York State. England, in the southeast part of the British Isles, is separated from Scotland on the north by the granite Cheviot Hills; from them the Pennine chain of uplands extends south through the center of England, reaching its highest point in the Lake District in the northwest. To the west along the border of Wales—a land of steep hills and valleys—are the Cambrian Mountains, while the Cotswolds, a range of hills in Gloucestershire, extend into the surrounding shires.

The remainder of England is plain land, though not necessarily flat, with the rocky sand-topped moors in the southwest, the rolling downs in the south and southeast, and the reclaimed marshes of the low-lying fens in the east central districts.

Scotland is divided into three physical regions—the Highlands, the Central Lowlands, containing two-thirds of the population, and the Southern Uplands. The western Highland coast is intersected throughout by long, narrow sea-lochs, or fiords. Scotland also includes the Outer and Inner Hebrides and other islands off the west coast and the Orkney and Shetland Islands off the north coast.

Wales is generally hilly; the Snowdon range in the northern part culminates in Mount Snowdon (3,560 ft, 1,085 m), highest in both England and Wales.

Important rivers flowing into the North Sea are the Thames, Humber, Tees, and Tyne. In the west are the Severn and Wye, which empty into the Bristol Channel and are navigable, as are the Mersey and Ribble.

Government. The United Kingdom is a constitutional monarchy, with a Queen and a Parliament that has two houses: the House of Lords with about 830 hereditary peers, 26 spiritual peers, about 270 life peers and peeresses, and 9 law-lords, who are hereditary, or life, peers; and the House of Commons, which has 650 popularly elected members. Supreme legislative power is vested in Parliament, which sits for five years unless sooner dissolved.

The executive power of the Crown is exercised by the Cabinet, headed by the Prime Minister. The latter, normally the head of the party commanding a majority in the House of Commons, is appointed by the Sovereign, with whose consent he or she in turn appoints the rest of the Cabinet. All ministers must be members of one or the other house of Parliament; they are individually and collectively responsible to the Crown and Parliament. The Cabinet proposes bills and arranges the business of Parliament, but it depends entirely on the votes in the House of Commons. The Lords cannot hold up "money" bills, but they can delay other bills for a maximum of one year.

By the Act of Union (1707), the Scottish Parliament was assimilated with that of England, and Scotland is now represented in Commons by 71 members. The Secretary of State for Scotland, a member of the Cabinet, is responsible for the administration of Scottish affairs.

Ruler. Queen Elizabeth II, born April 21, 1926, elder daughter of King George VI and Queen Elizabeth, succeeded to the throne on the death of her father on Feb. 6, 1952; married Nov. 20, 1947, to Prince Philip, Duke of Edinburgh, born June 10, 1921; their children are Prince Charles[1] (heir presumptive), born Nov. 14, 1948; Princess Anne, born Aug. 15, 1950; Prince Andrew, born Feb. 19, 1960; and Prince Edward, born March 10, 1964. The Queen's sister is Princess Margaret, born Aug. 21, 1930. Prince William Arthur Philip Louis, son of the Prince and Princess of Wales and second in line to the throne, was born June 21, 1982. A second son, Prince Henry Charles Albert David, was born Sept. 15, 1984, and is third in line.

History. Roman invasions of the 1st century B.C. brought Britain into contact with the Continent. When the Roman legions withdrew in the 5th century A.D., Britain fell easy prey to the invading hordes of Angles, Saxons, and Jutes from Scandinavia and the Low Countries. Seven large kingdoms were established, and the original Britons were forced into Wales and Scotland. It was not until the 10th century that the country finally became united under the kings of Wessex. Following the death of Edward the Confessor (1066), a dispute about the succession arose, and William, Duke of Normandy, invaded England, defeating the Saxon King, Harold II, at the Battle of Hastings (1066). The Norman conquest introduced Norman law and feudalism.

The reign of Henry II (1154–89), first of the Plantagenets, saw an increasing centralization of royal power at the expense of the nobles, but in 1215 John (1199–1216) was forced to sign the Magna Carta, which awarded the people, especially the nobles, certain basic rights. Edward I (1272–1307) continued the conquest of Ireland, reduced Wales to subjection, and made some gains in Scotland. In 1314, however, English forces led by Edward II were ousted from Scotland after the Battle of Bannockburn. The late 13th and early 14th centuries saw the development of a separate House of Commons with tax-raising powers.

Edward III's claim to the throne of France led to the Hundred Years' War (1338–1453) and the loss of almost all the large English territory in France. In England, the great poverty and discontent caused by the war were intensified by the Black Death, a plague that reduced the population by about one-third. The Wars of the Roses (1455–85), a struggle for the throne between the House of York and the House of Lancaster, ended in the victory of Henry Tudor (Henry VII) at Bosworth Field (1485).

During the reign of Henry VIII (1509–47), the Church in England asserted its independence from the Roman Catholic Church. Under Edward VI and Mary, the two extremes of religious fanaticism were reached, and it remained for Henry's daughter, Elizabeth I (1558–1603), to set up the Church of England on a moderate basis. In 1588, the Spanish Armada, a fleet sent out by Catholic King Philip II of Spain, was defeated by the English and destroyed during a storm. During Elizabeth's reign, England became a world power.

Elizabeth's heir was a Stuart—James VI of Scotland—who joined the two crowns as James I (1603–25). The Stuart kings incurred large debts and were forced either to depend on Parliament for taxes

---

1. The title Prince of Wales, which is not inherited, was conferred on Prince Charles by his mother on July 26, 1958. The investiture ceremony took place on July 1, 1969. The previous Prince of Wales was Prince Edward Albert, who held the title from 1911 to 1936 before he became Edward VIII.

Rulers of England and Great Britain

Name	Born	Ruled[1]
SAXONS[2]		
Egbert[3]	c.775	828–839
Ethelwulf	?	839–858
Ethelbald	?	858–860
Ethelbert	?	860–866
Ethelred I	?	866–871
Alfred the Great	849	871–899
Edward the Elder	c.870	899–924
Athelstan	895	924–939
Edmund I the Deed-doer	921	939–946
Edred	c.925	946–955
Edwy the Fair	c.943	955–959
Edgar the Peaceful	943	959–975
Edward the Martyr	c.962	975–979
Ethelred II the Unready	968	979–1016
Edmund II Ironside	c.993	1016–1016
DANES		
Canute	995	1016–1035
Harold I Harefoot	c.1016	1035–1040
Hardecanute	c.1018	1040–1042
SAXONS		
Edward the Confessor	c.1004	1042–1066
Harold II	c.1020	1066–1066
HOUSE OF NORMANDY		
William I the Conqueror	1027	1066–1087
William II Rufus	c.1056	1087–1100
Henry I Beauclerc	1068	1100–1135
Stephen of Boulogne	c.1100	1135–1154
HOUSE OF PLANTAGENET		
Henry II	1133	1154–1189
Richard I Coeur de Lion	1157	1189–1199
John Lackland	1167	1199–1216
Henry III	1207	1216–1272
Edward I Longshanks	1239	1272–1307
Edward II	1284	1307–1327
Edward III	1312	1327–1377
Richard II	1367	1377–1399 [4]
HOUSE OF LANCASTER		
Henry IV Bolingbroke	1367	1399–1413
Henry V	1387	1413–1422
Henry VI	1421	1422–1461 [5]

Name	Born	Ruled[1]
HOUSE OF YORK		
Edward IV	1442	1461–1483 [5]
Edward V	1470	1483–1483
Richard III	1452	1483–1485
HOUSE OF TUDOR		
Henry VII	1457	1485–1509
Henry VIII	1491	1509–1547
Edward VI	1537	1547–1553
Jane (Lady Jane Grey)[6]	1537	1553–1553
Mary I ("Bloody Mary")	1516	1553–1558
Elizabeth I	1533	1558–1603
HOUSE OF STUART		
James I[7]	1566	1603–1625
Charles I	1600	1625–1649
COMMONWEALTH		
Council of State	—	1649–1653
Oliver Cromwell[8]	1599	1653–1658
Richard Cromwell[8]	1626	1658–1659 [9]
RESTORATION OF HOUSE OF STUART		
Charles II	1630	1660–1685
James II	1633	1685–1688 [10]
William III[11]	1650	1689–1702
Mary II[11]	1662	1689–1694
Anne	1665	1702–1714
HOUSE OF HANOVER		
George I	1660	1714–1727
George II	1683	1727–1760
George III	1738	1760–1820
George IV	1762	1820–1830
William IV	1765	1830–1837
Victoria	1819	1837–1901
HOUSE OF SAXE-COBURG[12]		
Edward VII	1841	1901–1910
HOUSE OF WINDSOR[12]		
George V	1865	1910–1936
Edward VIII	1894	1936–1936 [13]
George VI	1895	1936–1952
Elizabeth II	1926	1952–

1. Year of end of rule is also that of death, unless otherwise indicated. 2. Dates for Saxon kings are still subject of controversy. 3. Became King of West Saxons in 802; considered (from 828) first King of all England. 4. Died 1400. 5. Henry VI reigned again briefly 1470–71. 6. Nominal Queen for 9 days; not counted as Queen by some authorities. She was beheaded in 1554. 7. Ruled in Scotland as James VI (1567–1625). 8. Lord Protector. 9. Died 1712. 10. Died 1701. 11. Joint rulers (1689–1694). 12. Name changed from Saxe–Coburg to Windsor in 1917. 13. Was known after his abdication as the Duke of Windsor, died 1972.

or to raise money by illegal means. In 1642, war broke out between Charles I and a large segment of the Parliament; Charles was defeated and executed in 1649, and the monarchy was then abolished. After the death in 1658 of Oliver Cromwell, the Lord Protector, the Puritan Commonwealth fell to pieces and Charles II was placed on the throne in 1660. The struggle between the King and Parliament continued, but Charles II knew when to compromise. His brother, James II (1685–88), possessed none of his ability and was ousted by the Revolution of 1688, which confirmed the primacy of Parliament. James's daughter, Mary, and her husband, William of Orange, were now the rulers.

Queen Anne's reign (1702–14) was marked by the Duke of Marlborough's victories over France at Blenheim, Oudenarde, and Malplaquet in the War of the Spanish Succession. England and Scotland meanwhile were joined by the Act of Union (1707). Upon the death of Anne, the distant claims of the elector of Hanover were recognized, and he became King of Great Britain and Ireland as George I.

The unwillingness of the Hanoverian kings to rule resulted in the formation by the royal ministers of a Cabinet, headed by a Prime Minister, which directed all public business. Abroad, the constant wars with France expanded the British Empire all over the globe, particularly in North America and India. This imperial growth was checked by the revolt of the American colonies (1775–81).

British Prime Ministers Since 1770

Name	Term	Name	Term
Lord North (Tory)	1770–1782	William E. Gladstone (Liberal)	1886–1886
Marquis of Rockingham (Whig)	1782–1782	Marquis of Salisbury (Conservative)	1886–1892
Earl of Shelburne (Whig)	1782–1783	William E. Gladstone (Liberal)	1892–1894
Duke of Portland (Coalition)	1783–1783	Earl of Rosebery (Liberal)	1894–1895
William Pitt, the Younger (Tory)	1783–1801	Marquis of Salisbury (Conservative)	1895–1902
Henry Addington (Tory)	1801–1804	Arthur James Balfour (Conservative)	1902–1905
William Pitt, the Younger (Tory)	1804–1806	Sir H. Campbell-Bannerman (Liberal)	1905–1908
Baron Grenville (Whig)	1806–1807	Herbert H. Asquith (Liberal)	1908–1915
Duke of Portland (Tory)	1807–1809	Herbert H. Asquith (Coalition)	1915–1916
Spencer Perceval (Tory)	1809–1812	David Lloyd George (Coalition)	1916–1922
Earl of Liverpool (Tory)	1812–1827	Andrew Bonar Law (Conservative)	1922–1923
George Canning (Tory)	1827–1827	Stanley Baldwin (Conservative)	1923–1924
Viscount Goderich (Tory)	1827–1828	James Ramsay MacDonald (Labor)	1924–1924
Duke of Wellington (Tory)	1828–1830	Stanley Baldwin (Conservative)	1924–1929
Earl Grey (Whig)	1830–1834	James Ramsay MacDonald (Labor)	1929–1931
Viscount Melbourne (Whig)	1834–1834	James Ramsay MacDonald (Coalition)	1931–1935
Sir Robert Peel (Tory)	1834–1835	Stanley Baldwin (Coalition)	1935–1937
Viscount Melbourne (Whig)	1835–1841	Neville Chamberlain (Coalition)	1937–1940
Sir Robert Peel (Tory)	1841–1846	Winston Churchill (Coalition)	1940–1945
Earl Russell (Whig)	1846–1852	Clement R. Attlee (Labor)	1945–1951
Earl of Derby (Tory)	1852–1852	Sir Winston Churchill (Conservative)	1951–1955
Earl of Aberdeen (Coalition)	1852–1855	Sir Anthony Eden (Conservative)	1955–1957
Viscount Palmerston (Liberal)	1855–1858	Harold Macmillan (Conservative)	1957–1963
Earl of Derby (Conservative)	1858–1859	Sir Alec Frederick Douglas–Home	
Viscount Palmerston (Liberal)	1859–1865	(Conservative)	1963–1964
Earl Russell (Liberal)	1865–1866	Harold Wilson (Labor)	1964–1970
Earl of Derby (Conservative)	1866–1868	Edward Heath (Conservative)	1970–1974
Benjamin Disraeli (Conservative)	1868–1868	Harold Wilson (Labor)	1974–1976
William E. Gladstone (Liberal)	1868–1874	James Callaghan (Labor)	1976–1979
Benjamin Disraeli (Conservative)	1874–1880	Margaret Thatcher (Conservative)	1979–1990
William E. Gladstone (Liberal)	1880–1885	John Major (Conservative)	1990–
Marquis of Salisbury (Conservative)	1885–1886		

Struggles with France broke out again in 1793 and during the Napoleonic Wars, which ended at Waterloo in 1815.

The Victorian era, named after Queen Victoria (1837–1901), saw the growth of a democratic system of government that had begun with the Reform Bill of 1832. The two important wars in Victoria's reign were the Crimean War against Russia (1853–56) and the Boer War (1899–1902), the latter enormously extending Britain's influence in Africa.

Increasing uneasiness at home and abroad marked the reign of Edward VII (1901–10). Within four years after the accession of George V in 1910, Britain entered World War I when Germany invaded Belgium. The nation was led by coalition cabinets, headed first by Herbert Asquith and then, starting in 1916, by the Welsh statesman David Lloyd George. Postwar labor unrest culminated in the general strike of 1926.

King Edward VIII succeeded to the throne on Jan. 20, 1936, at his father's death, but abdicated on Dec. 11, 1936 (in order to marry an American divorcee, Wallis Warfield Simpson) in favor of his brother, who became George VI.

The efforts of Prime Minister Neville Chamberlain to stem the rising threat of Nazism in Germany failed with the German invasion of Poland on Sept. 1, 1939, which was followed by Britain's entry into World War II on September 3. Allied reverses in the spring of 1940 led to Chamberlain's resignation and the formation of another coalition war cabinet by the Conservative leader, Winston Churchill, who led Britain through most of World War II. Churchill resigned shortly after V-E Day,

May 7, 1945, but then formed a "caretaker" government that remained in office until after the parliamentary elections in July, which the Labor Party won overwhelmingly. The government formed by Clement R. Attlee began a moderate socialist program.

For details of World War II (1939–45), see Headline History.

In 1951, Churchill again became Prime Minister at the head of a Conservative government. George VI died Feb. 6, 1952, and was succeeded by his daughter Elizabeth II.

Churchill stepped down in 1955 in favor of Sir Anthony Eden, who resigned on grounds of ill health in 1957 and was succeeded by Harold Macmillan and Sir Alec Douglas-Home. In 1964, Harold Wilson led the Labor Party to victory.

A lagging economy brought the Conservatives back to power in 1970. Prime Minister Edward Heath won Britain's admission to the European Community.

Margaret Thatcher became Britain's first woman Prime Minister as the Conservatives won 339 seats on May 3, 1979.

An Argentine invasion of the Falkland Islands on April 2, 1982, involved Britain in a war 8,000 miles from the home islands. Although Argentina had long claimed the Falklands, known as the Malvinas in Spanish, negotiations were in progress until a month before the invasion.

When more than 11,000 Argentine troops on the Falklands surrendered on June 14, 1982, Mrs. Thatcher declared her intention to garrison the islands indefinitely, together with a naval presence.

Although there were continuing economic problems and foreign policy disputes, an upswing in the economy in 1986–87 led Thatcher to call elections for June 11 in which she won a near-unprecedented third consecutive term.

Through much, if not all, of 1990 the Conservatives were losing the confidence of the electorate. The unpopularity of her poll tax together with an uncompromising position toward further European integration eroded support within her own party. When John Major won the Conservative Party leadership in November, Mrs. Thatcher resigned, paving the way for the Queen to ask Mr. Major to form a government.

In the middle of a long recession John Major called a national election for April 1992. Confounding many political observers the Conservatives won, but by a far narrower margin than previously.

After months of political maneuvering the U.K. ratified the Maastricht treaty in August 1993.

Waning public enthusiasm for the Conservatives was evident in municipal elections in May 1996.

The marital problems of Prince Charles continued to be aired in public, leading the Queen in December 1995 to call for a final resolution of the matter.

NORTHERN IRELAND

Status: Part of United Kingdom
Secretary of State: Sir Patrick Mayhew (1992)
Area: 5,452 sq mi. (14,121 sq km)
Population (1993 est.): 1,631,800; **Density per square mile:** 300
Capital and largest city (June 30, 1992): Belfast, 287,500
Monetary unit: British pound sterling; **Languages:** English, Gaelic; **Religions:** Roman Catholic, Presbyterian, Church of Ireland, Methodist.

Geography. Northern Ireland comprises the counties of Antrim, Armagh, Down, Fermanagh, Londonderry, and Tyrone, which make up predominantly Protestant Ulster and form the northern part of the island of Ireland, westernmost of the British Isles. It is slightly larger than Connecticut.

Government. Northern Ireland is an integral part of the United Kingdom (it has 12 representatives in the British House of Commons), but under the terms of the government of Ireland Act in 1920, it had a semi-autonomous government. But in 1972, after three years of internal strife which resulted in more than 400 dead and thousands injured, Britain suspended the Ulster parliament. The Ulster counties became governed directly from London after an attempt to return certain powers to an elected Assembly in Belfast.

The Northern Ireland Assembly was dissolved in 1975 and a Constitutional Convention was elected to write a Constitution acceptable to Protestants and Catholics. The convention failed to reach agreement and closed down the next year.

History. Ulster was part of Catholic Ireland until the reign of Elizabeth I (1558–1603) when, after crushing three Irish rebellions, the crown confiscated lands in Ireland and settled in Ulster the Scot Presbyterians who became rooted there. Another rebellion in 1641–51, crushed as brutally by Oliver Cromwell, resulted in the settlement of Anglican Englishmen in Ulster. Subsequent political policy favoring Protestants and disadvantaging Catholics encouraged further settlement in Northern Ireland.

But the North did not separate from the South until William Gladstone presented in 1886 his proposal for home rule in Ireland as a means of settling the Irish Question. The Protestants in the North, although they had grievances like the Catholics in the South, feared domination by the Catholic majority. Industry, moreover, was concentrated in the north and dependent on the British market.

When World War I began, civil war threatened between the regions. Northern Ireland, however, did not become a political entity until the six counties accepted the Home Rule Bill of 1920. This set up a semi-autonomous Parliament in Belfast and a Crown-appointed Governor advised by a Cabinet of the Prime Minister and eight ministers, as well as a 12-member representation in the House of Commons in London.

As the Republic of Ireland gained its sovereignty, relations improved between North and South, although the Irish Republican Army, outlawed in recent years, continued the struggle to end the partition of Ireland. In 1966–69, communal rioting and street fighting between Protestants and Catholics occurred in Londonderry, fomented by extremist nationalist Protestants, who feared the Catholics might attain a local majority, and by Catholics demonstrating for civil rights.

Rioting, terrorism, and sniping killed more than 2,200 people from 1969 through 1984 and the religious communities, Catholic and Protestant, became hostile armed camps. British troops were brought in to separate them but themselves became a target of Catholics.

In 1973, a new British charter created a 78-member Assembly elected by proportional representation that gave more weight to Catholic strength. It created a Province Executive with committee chairmen of the Assembly heading all government departments except law enforcement, which remained under London's control. Assembly elections in 1973 produced a majority for the new Constitution that included Catholic assemblymen.

Ulster's leaders agreed in 1973 to create an 11-member Executive Body with six seats assigned to Unionists (Protestants) and four to members of Catholic parties. Unionist leader Brian Faulkner headed the Executive. Also agreed to was a Council of Ireland, with 14 seats evenly divided between Dublin and Belfast, which could act only by unanimous vote.

Although the Council lacked real authority, its creation sparked a general strike by Protestant extremists in 1974. The two-week strike caused Faulkner's resignation from the Executive and resumption of direct rule from London.

In April 1974, London instituted a new program that responded to some Catholic grievances, but assigned more British troops to cut off movement of arms and munitions to Ulster's violence-racked cities.

Violence continued unabated, with new heights reached early in 1976 when the British government announced the end of special privileges for political prisoners in Northern Ireland. British Prime Minister James Callaghan visited Belfast in July and pledged that Ulster would remain part of the United Kingdom unless a clear majority wished to separate.

In October 1977, the 1976 Nobel Prize for Peace was awarded to Mairead Corrigan and Betty Williams for their campaign for peace in Northern Ireland. Intermittent violence continued, however, and on Aug. 27, 1979, an I.R.A. bomb killed Earl Mountbatten as he was sailing off southern Ireland.

New talks aimed at a restoration of home rule in Northern Ireland began and quickly ended in 1980.

On November 15, 1985, Mrs. Thatcher signed an agreement with Irish Prime Minister Garrett Fitzgerald giving Ireland a consultative role in the affairs of Northern Ireland. It was met with intense disapproval by the Ulster Unionists.

In November 1995, a new agreement was reached that established a 3-member international commission. The British and Irish governments in February 1995 announced an approved framework within which a settlement of the status of Northern Ireland could eventually be reached.

Dependencies of the United Kingdom

ANGUILLA

Status: Dependency
Governor: Alan Hoole (1995)
Area: 35 sq mi. (91 sq km)
Population (est. 1996): 7,147; average annual rate of natural increase: 1.64%; birth rate: 24/1000; infant mortality rate: 17.1/1000; density per sq mi.: 205
Capital (1992): The Valley, 1,400. **Monetary unit:** East Caribbean dollar. **Literacy:** 95%
Economy summary: Gross domestic product (1993 est.): $49 million, $7,000 per capita; 7.5% (1992) real growth rate. Major industries: Tourism, boat building, salt, lobster fishing. Exports: $556,000 (f.o.b., 1992). Imports: $33.5 million (f.o.b., 1992)

Anguilla was originally part of the West Indies Associated States as a component of St. Kitts-Nevis-Anguilla.

In 1967, Anguilla declared its independence from the St. Kitts-Nevis-Anguilla federation. Britain however, did not recognize this action. In February 1969, Anguilla voted to cut all ties with Britain and become an independent republic. In March, Britain landed troops on the island and, on March 30, a truce was signed. In July 1971, Anguilla became a dependency of Britain and two months later Britain ordered the withdrawal of all its troops.

A new constitution for Anguilla, effective in February 1976, provides for separate administration and a government of elected representatives. The Associated State of St. Kitts-Nevis-Anguilla ended Dec. 19, 1980.

BERMUDA

Status: Self-governing dependency
Governor: Lord Waddington (1992)
Premier: David Saul (1995)
Area: 20 sq mi. (52 sq km)
Population (est. 1996): 62,099; average annual rate of natural increase: 0.77%; birth rate: 15.5/1000; infant mortality rate: 13.2/1000; density per sq mi.: 3,105
Capital (1994 est.): Hamilton, 1,100. **Monetary unit:** Bermuda dollar. **Literacy rate:** 98%
Economic summary: Gross domestic product (1994 est.): $1.7 billion; $28,000 per capita; 2.5% real growth rate; unemployment: 6% (1991). Arable land: 0%. Principal agricultural products: bananas, vegetables, citrus fruits, dairy products. Labor force: 32,000; 47% clerical and in services. Major industrial products: structural concrete, paints, pharmaceuticals. Natural resource: limestone. Exports: $60 million (f.o.b., 1991) semitropical produce, light manufactures. Imports: $519 million (f.o.b., 1993) foodstuffs, fuel, machinery. Major trading partners: U.S., U.K., Canada, Venezuela, Japan.

Bermuda is an archipelago of about 360 small islands, 580 miles (934 km) east of North Carolina. The largest is (Great) Bermuda, or Long Island. Discovered by Juan de Bermúdez, a shipwrecked Spaniard, early in the 16th century, the islands were settled in 1612 by an offshoot of the Virginia Company and became a crown colony in 1684.

In 1940, sites on the islands were leased for 99 years to the U.S. for air and navy bases. Bermuda is also the headquarters of the West Indies and Atlantic squadron of the Royal Navy.

In 1968, Bermuda was granted a new constitution, its first prime minister, and autonomy, except for foreign relations, defense, and internal security. The predominantly white United Bermuda Party has retained power in four elections against the opposition—the black-led Progressive Laborites—although Bermuda's population is 60% black.

The 1991 budget called for tax increases, and control of the island's offshore banking sector was tightened.

BRITISH ANTARCTIC TERRITORY

Status: Dependency
Commissioner: Peter M. Newton (1992)
Area: 500,000 sq mi. (1,395,000 sq km)
Population (1992): no permanent residents

The British Antarctic Territory consists of the South Shetland Islands, South Orkney Islands, and nearby Graham Land on the Antarctic continent, largely uninhabited. They are dependencies of the British crown colony of the Falkland Islands but received a separate administration in 1962, being governed by a British-appointed High Commissioner who is governor of the Falklands.

BRITISH INDIAN OCEAN TERRITORY

Status: Dependency
Commissioner: David Ross MacLennan (1994)
Administrative headquarters: Victoria, Seychelles
Area: 85 sq mi. (220 sq km)

This dependency, consisting of the Chagos Archipelago and other small island groups, was formed in 1965 by agreement with Mauritius and the Seychelles. There is no permanent civilian population in the territory.

BRITISH VIRGIN ISLANDS

Status: Dependency
Governor: Peter Alfred Penfold (1992)
Area: 59 sq mi. (153 sq km)
Population (est. 1996): 13,195; average annual rate of natural increase: 1.41%; birth rate: 20.2/1000; infant mortality rate: 19.5/1000; density per square mile: 224
Capital (1991 census): Road Town (on Tortola): 3,983. **Monetary unit:** U.S. dollar
Economic summary: Gross domestic product (1991): $133 million; $10,600 per capita; 2% real growth rate.

Some 36 islands in the Caribbean Sea northeast of Puerto Rico and west of the Leeward Islands, the British Virgin Islands are economically interdependent with the U.S. Virgin Islands to the south. They were formerly part of the administration of the Leeward Islands. They received a separate administration in 1956 as a crown colony. In 1967 a new constitution was promulgated that provided for a ministerial system of government headed by the governor. The principal islands are Tortola, Virgin Gorda, Anegada, and Jost Van Dyke.

CAYMAN ISLANDS

Status: Dependency
Governor: John Waynne Owen (1995)
Area: 100 sq mi. (259 sq km)
Population (est. 1996): 34,646; density per sq mi.: 347
Capital (est. 1992): George Town (on Grand Cayman), 15,000; **Monetary unit:** Cayman Islands dollar
Economic summary: Gross domestic product (1993 est.): $700 million, $23,000 per capita; inflation: 2.5% (1993 est.); unemployment: 7% (1992). Exports: $10 million (f.o.b., 1993, est.): turtle products, manufactured goods. Imports: $312 million (c.i.f., 1993 est.): foodstuffs, manufactured goods. Major trading partners: U.S., Trinidad and Tobago, U.K., Netherland Antilles, Japan.

This dependency consists of three islands—Grand Cayman (76 sq mi.; 197 sq km), Cayman Brac (22 sq mi.; 57 sq km), and Little Cayman (20 sq mi.; 52 sq km)—situated about 180 miles (290 km) northwest of Jamaica. They were dependencies of Jamaica until 1959, when they became a unit territory within the Federation of the West Indies. In 1962, upon the dissolution of the Federation, the Cayman Islands became a British dependency.

The islands' chief export is turtle products.

CHANNEL ISLANDS

Status: Crown dependencies
Lieutenant Governor of Jersey: Air Marshall Sir John Sutton (1990)
Lieutenant Governor of Guernsey: Vice Adm. Sir John Coward (1994)
Area: 120 sq mi. (311 sq km)
Populations (1996 est.): Jersey, 87,250; Guernsey, 64,975
Capital of Jersey (1986): St. Helier, 27,083. **Capital of Guernsey (1986):** St. Peter Port, 16,085. **Monetary units:** Guernsey pound; Jersey pound

This group of islands, lying in the English Channel off the northwest coast of France, is the only portion of the Duchy of Normandy belonging to the English Crown, to which it has been attached since the conquest of 1066. It was the only British possession occupied by Germany during World War II.

For purposes of government, the islands are divided into the Bailiwick of Jersey (45 sq mi.; 117 sq km) and the Bailiwick of Guernsey (30 sq mi.; 78 sq km), including Alderney (3 sq mi.; 7.8 sq km), Sark (2 sq mi.; 5.2 sq km), Herm, Jethou, etc. The islands are administered according to their own laws and customs by local governments. Acts of Parliament in London are not binding on the islands unless they are specifically mentioned. The queen is represented in each Bailiwick by a lieutenant governor.

FALKLAND ISLANDS AND DEPENDENCIES

Status: Dependency
Governor: Richard Ralph (1996)
Chief Executive: R. Sampson
Area: 4,700 sq mi. (12,173 sq km)
Population (est. July 1995): 2,317; density per sq mi.: .5
Capital (1991): Stanley (on East Falkland), 1,643
Monetary unit: Falkland Island pound

This sparsely inhabited dependency consists of a group of islands in the South Atlantic, about 250 miles (402 km) east of the South American mainland. The largest islands are East Falkland and West Falkland. Dependencies are South Georgia Island (1,450 sq mi.; 3,756 sq km), the South Sandwich Islands, and other islets. Three former dependencies—Graham Land, the South Shetland Islands, and the South Orkney Islands—were established as a new British dependency, the British Antarctic Territory, in 1962.

The chief industry is sheep raising and, apart from the production of wool, hides and skins, and tallow, there are no known resources. The whaling industry is carried on from South Georgia Island.

The chief export is wool.

GIBRALTAR

Status: Self-governing dependency
Governor: Sir Hugo White (1995)
Chief Minister: Peter Caruana (1996)
Area: 2.25 sq mi. (5.8 sq km)
Population (est. 1996): 32,067 average annual rate of natural increase: 0.59%; birth rate: 14.8/1000; infant mortality rate: 7.7/1000; density per sq mi.: 14,252.
Monetary unit: Gibraltar pound. **Literacy rate:** 99% (est.)
Economic summary: Gross national product (1993 est.): $205 million; $6,600 per capita. Exports: $57 million (f.o.b., 1992): re-exports of tobacco, petroleum, wine. Imports: $420 million (c.i.f., 1992): manufactured goods, fuels, foodstuffs. Major trading partners: U.K., Morocco, Portugal, Netherlands, Spain, U.S.

Gibraltar, at the south end of the Iberian Peninsula, is a rocky promontory commanding the western entrance to the Mediterranean. Aside from its strategic importance, it is also a free port, naval base, and coaling station. It was captured by the Arabs crossing from Africa into Spain in A.D. 711. In the 15th century, it passed to the Moorish ruler of Granada and later became Spanish. It was captured by an Anglo-Dutch force in 1704 during the War of the Spanish Succession and passed to Great Britain by the Treaty of Utrecht in 1713. Most of the inhabitants of Gibraltar are of Spanish, Italian, and Maltese descent.

Spanish efforts to recover Gibraltar culminated in a referendum in 1967 in which the residents voted overwhelmingly to retain their link with Britain. Spain sealed Gibraltar's land border in 1969 and did not open communications until April 1980, after the two governments had agreed to resolve their dispute in keeping with a United Nations resolution calling for restoration of the "Rock" to Spain.

The last British military battalion on the "Rock" was withdrawn in March 1991. Spain suggested a form of joint control, but the U.K. refused.

HONG KONG

Status: Dependency
Governor: Christopher Patten (1992)
Area: 416 sq mi. (1,077 sq km)
Population (est. 1996): 6,305,413 (average annual rate of natural increase: 0.53%); birth rate: 10.5/1000; infant mortality rate: 5.1/1000; density per square mile: 15,158
Capital (1995 est.): Victoria (Hong Kong Island), 6,205,300. **Monetary unit:** Hong Kong dollar. **Literacy rate:** 77%
Economic summary: Gross domestic product (1994 est.): $136.1 billion; $24,530 per capita; real growth rate 5.5%; inflation 8.5%; unemployment 1.9%. Arable land: 7%. Principal agricultural products: vegetables, rice,

dairy products. Labor force (1990): 2,800,000: 28.5% manufacturing; 27.9%, wholesale, retail, hotels, restaurants. Major industrial products: textiles, clothing, toys, transistor radios, watches, electronic components. Exports: $168.7 billion (including re-exports of $121 billion) (f.o.b., 1994 est.): clothing, textiles, toys, watches, electrical appliances, footwear. Imports: $160 billion (c.i.f., 1994 est.): raw materials, transport equipment, food. Major trading partners: U.S., U.K., Japan, Germany, China, Taiwan.

The crown colony of Hong Kong comprises the island of Hong Kong (32 sq mi.; 83 sq km), Stonecutters' Island, Kowloon Peninsula, and the New Territories on the adjoining mainland. The island of Hong Kong, located at the mouth of the Pearl River about 90 miles (145 km) southeast of Canton, was ceded to Britain in 1841.

Stonecutters' Island and Kowloon were annexed in 1860, and the New Territories, which are mainly agricultural lands, were leased from China in 1898 for 99 years. Hong Kong was attacked by Japanese troops Dec. 7, 1941, and surrendered the following Christmas. It remained under Japanese occupation until August 1945.

After two years of painstaking negotiation, authorities of Britain and the People's Republic of China agreed in 1984 that Hong Kong would return to Chinese sovereignty on June 30, 1997, when Britain's lease on the New Territories expires. They also agreed that the vibrant capitalist enclave on China's coast would retain its status as a free port and its social, economic, and legal system as a special administrative region of China. Current laws will remain basically unchanged.

Under a unique "One Country, Two Systems" arrangement, the Chinese government promised that Hong Kong's lifestyle would remain unchanged for 50 years, and that freedoms of speech, press, assembly, association, travel, right to strike, and religious belief would be guaranteed by law. However, the chief executive and some of the legislature will be appointed by Beijing.

Hong Kong will continue to have its own finances and issue its own travel documents, and Peking will not levy taxes.

Despite threats from China the legislature voted in June 1994 to transform that body into a much more democratic institution. Legislative elections in September 1995, the first under the reforms, saw low voter turnout. China vowed to disband the legislature after it takes control.

ISLE OF MAN

Status: Self-governing crown dependency
Lieutenant Governor: Air Marshall Sir Laurence Jones
Area: 221 sq mi. (572 sq km)
Population (1996 est.): 73,459; growth rate 0.1%; density per square mile: 333
Capital (1991): Douglas, 22,214; **Monetary unit:** Isle of Man pound

Situated in the Irish Sea, equidistant from Scotland, Ireland, and England, the Isle of Man is administered according to its own laws by a government composed of the Lieutenant Governor, a Legislative Council, and a House of Keys, one of the most ancient legislative assemblies in the world.

The chief exports are beef and lamb, fish, and livestock.

LEEWARD ISLANDS

See British Virgin Islands; Montserrat

MONTSERRAT

Status: Dependency
Governor: Frank Savage (1993)
Chief Minister: Reuben Meade (1991)
Area: 38 sq mi. (98 sq km)
Population (est. 1996): 12,771; average annual rate of natural increase: 0.53%; birth rate: 15.1/1000; infant mortality rate: 11.7/1000; density per square mile: 336
Capital (est. 1991): Plymouth, 2,500. **Monetary unit:** East Caribbean dollar
Economic summary: Gross domestic product (1993 est.): $55.6 million, $4,380 per capita; inflation: 2.8% (1992). Exports: $2.8 million (f.o.b., 1992): electric parts, plastic bags, apparel, hot peppers, live plants, cattle. Imports: $80.6 million (f.o.b., 1992): machinery and transportation equipment, foodstuffs, manufactured goods, fuels, lubricants and related materials.

The island of Montserrat is in the Lesser Antilles of the West Indies. Until 1956, it was a division of the Leeward Islands. It did not join the West Indies Associated States established in 1967.

The chief exports are cattle, potatoes, cotton, lint, recapped tires, mangoes, and tomatoes.

PITCAIRN ISLAND

Status: Dependency
Governor: Robert John Alston (nonresident)
Island Magistrate: Jay Warren
Area: 1.75 sq mi. (4.5 sq km)
Population (July 1995 est.): 73; density per square mile: 42
Capital: Adamstown

Pitcairn Island, in the South Pacific about midway between Australia and South America, consists of the island of Pitcairn and the three uninhabited islands of Henderson, Duicie, and Oeno. The island of Pitcairn was settled in 1790 by British mutineers from the ship *Bounty,* commanded by Capt. William Bligh. It was annexed as a British colony in 1838. Overpopulation forced removal of the settlement to Norfolk Island in 1856, but about 40 persons soon returned.

The colony is governed by a 10-member Council presided over by the Island Magistrate, who is elected for a three-year term.

ST. HELENA

Status: Dependency
Governor: A.N. Hoole (1991–95)
Area: 120 sq mi. (310 sq km)
Population (est. 1996): 6,782; density per sq mi.: 57
Capital (1987): Jamestown, 1,332
Monetary unit: Pound sterling

St. Helena is a volcanic island in the South Atlantic about 1,100 miles (1,770 km) from the west coast of Africa. It is famous as the place of exile of Napoleon (1815–21).

It was taken for England in 1659 by the East India Company and was brought under the direct government of the crown in 1834.

St. Helena has two dependencies: Ascension (34 sq mi.; 88 sq km), an island about 700 miles (1,127 km) northwest of St. Helena; and Tristan da Cunha (40 sq mi.; 104 sq km), a group of six islands about 1,500 miles (2,414 km) south-southwest of St. Helena.

TURKS AND CAICOS ISLANDS

Status: Dependency
Governor: Martin Bourk (1993)
Area: 193 sq mi. (500 sq km)
Population (est. 1996): 14,302; average annual rate of natural increase: 0.77%; birth rate: 12.9/1000; infant mortality rate: 12.6/1000; density per square mile: 75
Capital (1990): Cockburn Town, 3,720
Monetary unit: U.S. dollar.
Economic summary: Gross domestic product (1992 est.): $80.8 million, $6,000 per capita. Exports: $6.8 million (f.o.b., 1993): lobster, dried and fresh conch, conch shells. Imports: $42.8 million (1993): food and beverages, tobacco, clothing, manufactures, construction materials. Major trading partners: U.S., U.K.

These two groups of islands are situated at the southeast end of the Bahamas. The principal islands in the Turks group are Grand Turk and Salt Cay; the principal ones in the Caicos group are South Caicos, East Caicos, Middle (or Grand) Caicos, North Caicos, Providenciales, and West Caicos.

The Turks and Caicos Islands were dependencies of Jamaica until 1959, when they became a unit territory within the Federation of the West Indies. In 1962, when Jamaica became independent, the Turks and Caicos became a British crown colony. The present constitution has been in force since 1969.

VIRGIN ISLANDS

See British Virgin Islands

UNITED STATES

The United States of America
President: William J. Clinton (1993)
Vice President: Albert A. Gore, Jr. (1993)
Land area: 3,536,341 sq mi. (9,159,123 sq km)
Resident population (est. June 17, 1996): 265,089,998; (1990 census): 248,709,873 (% change 1980–1990: +9.80). White: 199,686,070 (80.3%); Black: 29,986,060 (12.1%); American Indian, Eskimo, or Aleut: 1,959,234 (0.8%); Asian or Pacific Islander: 7,273,662 (2.9%); Other Race: 9,804,847 (3.9%); Hispanic Origin[1]: 22,354,059 (9.0%); (average annual rate of natural increase: 0.7%); birth rate: 16/1000; infant mortality rate: 8.3/1000; density per square mile: 74.9
Capital (1990 census.): Washington, D.C., 606,900; **Largest cities (1990 census):** New York, 7,322,564; Los Angeles, 3,485,398; Chicago, 2,783,726; Houston, 1,630,553; Philadelphia, 1,585,577; San Diego, 1,110,549; Detroit, 1,027,974; Dallas, 1,006,877; Phoenix, 983,403; San Antonio, 935,933; **Monetary unit:** Dollar; **Languages:** predominantly English, sizable Spanish-speaking minority; **Religions:** Protestant, 61%; Roman Catholic, 25%; Jewish, 2%; other, 5%; none, 7%; **Literacy rate:** Age 15 and over having completed 5 or more years of schooling (1991) 97.9%
Economic summary: Gross domestic product (1995): $7,245.8 billion; per capita personal income (1995 est.): $22,788. Civilian labor force (July 1996): 126.9 million. Arable land: 20%. Principal products: corn, wheat, barley, oats, sugar, potatoes, soybeans, fruits, beef, veal, pork. Major industrial products: petroleum products, fertilizers, cement, pig iron and steel, plastics

and resins, newsprint, motor vehicles, machinery, natural gas, electricity. Natural resources: coal, oil, copper, gold, silver, minerals, timber. Exports: machinery, chemicals, aircrafts, military equipment, cereals, motor vehicles, grains. Illicit drugs: illicit producer of cannabis for domestic consumption. Ongoing eradication program aimed at small plots and greenhouses unsuccessful. Imports: crude and partly refined petroleum, machinery, automobiles. Major trading partners: Canada, Japan, Western Europe.

1. Persons of Hispanic origin can be of any race.

Government. The president is elected for a four-year term and may be re-elected only once. The bicameral Congress consists of the 100-member Senate, elected to a six-year term with one-third of the seats becoming vacant every two years, and the 435-member House of Representatives, elected every two years. The minimum voting age is 18.

(**See also** Profile of the United States, U.S. States, U.S. Cities, and U.S. Statistics.)

URUGUAY

Oriental Republic of Uruguay
President: Julio Sanguinetti Cairolo
Area: 68,040 sq mi. (176,224 sq km)
Population (est. 1996): 3,238,952 (average annual rate of natural increase: 0.8%); birth rate: 17/1000; infant mortality rate: 15.4/1000; density per sq mi.: 48
Capital and largest city (est. 1992): Montevideo, 1,500,000. **Monetary unit:** Peso. **Language:** Spanish.
Religion: Roman Catholic, 66%; Protestant, 2%; Jewish, 2%. **National name:** Republica Oriental del Uruguay. **Literacy rate:** 94%
Economic summary: Gross domestic product (1994 est.): $23 billion; $7,200 per capita; real growth rate 4%; inflation 36% (1995); unemployment 9%. Arable land: 8%. Principal products: livestock, grains, Labor force (1991 est.): 1,355,000: government, 25%; manufacturing, 19%; commerce, 12%; agriculture, 11%. Major products: processed meats, wool and hides, textiles, shoes, handbags and leather wearing apparel, cement, refined petroleum. Natural resources: hydroelectric power potential. Exports: $1.78 billion (f.o.b., 1994 est.): meat, hides, wool, fish. Imports: $2.461 billion (c.i.f., 1994 est.): transportation equipment, chemicals, machinery, plastics, minerals. Major trading partners: U.S., Brazil, Argentina, Germany, China, Italy, Nigeria.

Geography. Uruguay, on the east coast of South America south of Brazil and east of Argentina, is comparable in size to Oklahoma.

The country consists of a low, rolling plain in the south and a low plateau in the north. It has a 120-mile (193 km) Atlantic shore line, a 235-mile (378 km) frontage on the Rio de la Plata, and 270 miles (435 km) on the Uruguay River, its western boundary.

Government. A republic. Presidents serve a single five-year term. The bicameral congress, the General Assembly, consists of the Chamber of Senators and the Chamber of Representatives.

History. Juan Díaz de Solis, a Spaniard, discovered Uruguay in 1516, but the Portuguese were first to settle it when they founded Colonia in 1680. After a long struggle, Spain wrested the country from Portugal in 1778. Uruguay revolted against Spain in 1811, only to be conquered in 1817 by the Portuguese from Brazil. Independence was reasserted with Argentine help in 1825, and the republic was set up in 1828.

Independence, however, did not restore order, and a revolt in 1836 touched off nearly 50 years of factional strife, with occasional armed intervention from Argentina and Brazil.

Uruguay, made prosperous by meat and wool exports, founded a welfare state early in the 20th century. A decline began in the 1950s as successive governments struggled to maintain a large bureaucracy and costly social benefits. Economic stagnation and political frustration followed.

A military coup ousted the civilian government in 1973. The military dictatorship that followed used fear and terror to demoralize the population, taking thousands of political prisoners.

After ruling for 12 years, the military regime permitted election of a civilian government in November 1984 and relinquished rule in March 1985.

Luis Lacalle became president in March 1990, becoming the first Blanco Party member to assume that office in 23 years.

The president's continuing attempts in 1993 at economic reform met much resistance.

Presidential and legislative elections in November 1994 resulted in a narrow victory for the Colorado Party and its presidential candidate, Julio Sanguinetti Cairolo, who assumed office in March 1995.

The new president pushed for constitutional and economic reforms aimed at reducing inflation and the size of the public sector, partially through tax increases and privatization.

UZBEKISTAN

Republic of Uzbekistan
President: Islam A. Karimov (1990)
Prime Minister: Otkir Sultonov (1995)
Area: 172,700 sq mi. (447,400 sq km)
Population (est. 1996): 23,418,381 (Uzbeks, 71%; Russians, 8%; other minorities: Tajiks, Kazakhs, and Tartars); (average annual rate of natural increase: 2.18%); birth rate: 29.9/1000; infant mortality rate: 79.6/1000; density per square mile: 136
Capital and largest city (1992 est.): Tashkent, 2,106,000. **Other large cities:** Samarkand, 372,000; Andijon, 302,000. **Language:** Uzbek, 85%; Russian, 5%. **Religion:** Muslim (mostly Sunnis) 75–80%. **Literacy rate:** 100%
Economic summary: Gross domestic product (UN, World Bank 1993 est.): $53.7 billion, $2,430 per capita; –3.5% real growth rate; inflation: 18% (per mo.); unemployment: 0.2% (officially registered). Labor force (1992): 8.324 million: agriculture and forestry, 43%; industry and construction, 22%. Natural resources: natural gas, petroleum, coal, gold, uranium, silver, copper, lead and zinc, tungsten, molybdenum. Agriculture: major crop is cotton. Exports (1994): $943.7 million to outside the former USSR countries: cotton, gold, textiles, chemicals, mineral fertilizers, vegetable oil. Imports (1994): $1.15 billion from outside the former USSR countries: machinery and parts, consumer durables, grain and other food. Trading partners: Russia, Ukraine, Eastern Europe, U.S., Czech Republic.

Geography. Uzbekistan is situated in the former Soviet Central Asia between the Amu Darya and Syr Darya Rivers, the Aral Sea, and the slopes of the Tien Shan Mountains. It is bounded by Kazakhstan in the north and northwest, Kyrgyzstan and Tajikistan in the east and southeast, and Turkmenistan in the southwest. The republic also includes the Kara-Kalpak Autonomous S.S.R. (since 1936) with its capital, Nukus, 1987 population, 152,000. The land is made up of deserts, oases, and mountains with valleys. Two-thirds of the territory is occupied by deserts and semi-deserts. The country is about one-tenth larger in area than the state of California.

Government. A constitutional republic.

History. The Uzbekistan land was once part of the ancient Persian empire and was later conquered by Alexander the Great in 4 B.C. During the 8th century, the nomadic Turkic tribes living there were converted to Islam by invading Arab forces who dominated the area. The Mongols under Ghengis Khan took over the region from the Seljuk Turks in the 13th century and it later became part of Tamerlane the Great's empire and his successors' until the 16th century.

The Uzbeks invaded the territory in the early 16th century and merged with the other inhabitants in the area. Their empire broke up into separate Uzbek principalities, the khanates of Khiva, Bukhara, and Kokand. These city-states resisted Russian expansion into the area, but were conquered by the Russian forces in the mid-19th century.

The territory was made into the Uzbek Republic in 1924 and became the independent Uzbekistan Soviet Socialist Republic in 1925.

Uzbekistan joined with ten other former Soviet republics on Dec. 21, 1991, in the Commonwealth of Independent States.

In February 1992, President Karimov, a former Communist Party boss, affirmed his commitment to democracy and human rights. An election in December 1991 had given him 85% of the vote, but the main opposition parties were not allowed to field candidates.

Opposition forces in mid-1993 formed a coalition. However, the government closed their headquarters and arrested the leaders. The criminal code was amended to impose stricter penalties for antigovernment activity.

Parliamentary elections in December 1994 produced a huge victory for the ruling party and an allied party. Opposition groups were largely excluded.

To counter the increasing ties between its neighbors and Iran, the country improved its relations with the West during 1995. In March a referendum produced a big win for extending the president's term until 2000 in the name of political stability.

VANUATU

Republic of Vanuatu
President: Jean-Marie Leye (1994)
Prime Minister: Maxime Carlot (1991)
Area: 5,700 sq mi. (14,763 sq km)
Population (est. 1996): 177,504 (average annual rate of natural increase: 2.17%); birth rate: 30.5/1000; infant mortality rate: 64.6/1000; density per square mile: 32
Capital and largest city (est. 1993): Port Vila, 26,100. **Monetary unit:** Vatu. **Religions:** Presbyterian, 36.7%; Roman Catholic, 15%; Anglican, 15%; other Christian, 10%; indigenous beliefs, 7.6%, other, 15.7%. **Literacy rate:** 53%
Economic Summary: Gross national product (1993 est.): $200 million, $1,200 per capita; real growth rate: n.a.; inflation (1992 est.) 2.3%. Arable land: 1%. Principal agricultural products: copra, cocoa, coffee. Agri-

culture accounts for 40% of GDP. Exports: $14.9 million (f.o.b., 1991): copra, cocoa, coffee, frozen fish, timber, beef Imports: $74 million (f.o.b., 1991): machines and vehicles, food, raw materials, fuel, chemicals. Major trading partners: France, New Zealand, Japan, Australia, Netherlands, Belgium, New Caledonia.

Geography. Formerly known as the New Hebrides, Vanuatu is an archipelago of some 80 islands lying between New Caledonia and Fiji in the South Pacific. Largest of the islands is Espiritu Santo (875 sq mi.; 2,266 sq km); others are Efate, Malekula, Malo, Pentecost, and Tanna. The population is largely Melanesian of mixed blood.

Government. The constitution by which Vanuatu achieved independence on July 30, 1980, vests executive authority in a president, elected by an electoral college for a five-year term. A unicameral legislature of 46 members exercises legislative power.

History. The islands were discovered by Pedro Fernandes de Queiros of Portugal in 1606 and were charted and named by the British navigator James Cook in 1774. Conflicting British and French interests were resolved by a joint naval commission that administered the islands from 1887. A condominium government was established in 1906.

The islands' plantation economy, based on imported Vietnamese labor, was prosperous until the 1920s, when markets for its products declined. The New Hebrides escaped Japanese occupation in World War II and the French population was among the first to support the Gaullist Free French movement.

A brief rebellion by French settlers and plantation workers on Espiritu Santo in May 1980 threatened the scheduled independence of the islands. Britain sent a company of Royal Marines and France a contingent of 50 policemen to quell the revolt, which the new government said was financed by the Phoenix Foundation, a right-wing U.S. group. With the British and French forces replaced by soldiers from Papua New Guinea, independence ceremonies took place on July 30. The next month it was reported that the revolt had been quelled.

Disaffection with Prime Minister Lini in August 1991 led to his dismissal as head of his party. Lini formed another to contest the November general elections. The Union of Moderate Parties won and formed an alliance with Lini's. Lini's party, however, withdrew from the coalition in August 1993. While the prime minister's party retained a parliamentary majority, its position became precarious.

Unlike other nations in the region, Vanuatu refused to condemn France's resumption of nuclear testing in 1995, saying it was a French internal matter.

VATICAN CITY (HOLY SEE)

Ruler: Pope John Paul II (1978)
Area: 0.17 sq mi. (0.44 sq km)
Population (July 95 est.): 830; population growth rate: 1.15%: density per square mile: 4,883
Monetary unit: Lira. **Languages:** Latin, Italian, and various other languages. **Religion:** Roman Catholic
Labor force: High dignataries, priests, nuns, guards, and 3,000 lay workers who live outside the Vatican
National name: Stato della Città del Vaticano
Budget (1993): Revenues: $169 million; Expenditures: $167.5 million, including capital expenditures.

Geography. The Vatican City State is situated on the Vatican hill, on the right bank of the Tiber River, within the commune of Rome.

Government. The Pope has full legal, executive, and judicial powers. Executive power over the area is in the hands of a Commission of Cardinals appointed by the Pope. The College of Cardinals is the Pope's chief advisory body, and upon his death the cardinals elect his successor for life. The cardinals themselves are created for life by the Pope.

In the Vatican the central administration of the Roman Catholic Church throughout the world (Holy See) is carried on by the Secretariat of State, nine congregations, six commissions, three tribunals, eleven councils, and five offices. In its diplomatic relations, the Holy See is represented by the Papal Secretary of State.

History. The Vatican City State, sovereign and independent, is the survivor of the papal states that in 1859 comprised an area of some 17,000 square miles (44,030 sq km). During the struggle for Italian unification, from 1860 to 1870, most of this area became part of Italy.

By an Italian law of May 13, 1871, the temporal power of the Pope was abrogated, and the territory of the papacy was confined to the Vatican and Lateran palaces and the villa of Castel Gandolfo. The popes consistently refused to recognize this arrangement and, by the Lateran Treaty of Feb. 11, 1929, between the Vatican and the Kingdom of Italy, the exclusive dominion and sovereign jurisdiction of the Holy See over the city of the Vatican was again recognized, thus restoring the Pope's temporal authority over the area.

The first session of Ecumenical Council Vatican II was opened by John XXIII on Oct. 11, 1962, to plan and set policies for the modernization of the Roman Catholic Church. Pope Paul VI continued the Council, opening the second session on Sept. 29, 1963.

On Aug. 26, 1978, Cardinal Albino Luciani was chosen by the College of Cardinals to succeed Paul VI, who had died of a heart attack on Aug. 6. The new Pope, who took the name John Paul I, was born on Oct. 17, 1912, at Forno di Canale in Italy.

(For a listing of all the popes, *see* the Index.)

Only 34 days after his election, John Paul I died of a heart attack, ending the shortest reign in 373 years. On Oct. 16, Cardinal Karol Wojtyla, 58, was chosen Pope and took the name John Paul II.

On May 13, 1981, a Turkish terrorist shot the Pope in St. Peter's Square, the first assassination attempt against the Pontiff in modern times.

On June 3, 1985, the Vatican and Italy ratified a new church-state treaty, known as a concordat, replacing the Lateran Pact of 1929. The new accord affirmed the independence of Vatican City but ended a number of privileges the Catholic Church had in Italy, including its status as the state religion. The treaty ended Rome's status as a "sacred city."

Relations, diplomatic and ecclesiastical, with Eastern Europe have improved dramatically with the fall of Communism. Relations with the Soviet Union, while improving, have not yet reached the ambassadorial level.

Diplomatic relations were established in 1992 with a host of new countries.

Diplomatic ties were established in March 1994 with Jordan and full relations established with Israel in June. Six months earlier the two nations had accorded each other mutual recognition.

On October 5, 1995, Pope John Paul II addressed the United Nations General Assembly on the occasion of the Organization's 50th anniversary.

VENEZUELA

Republic of Venezuela
President: Rafael Caldera (1994)
Area: 352,143 sq mi. (912,050 sq km)
Population (est. 1996): 21,983,188 (average annual rate of natural increase: 1.93%); birth rate: 24.4/1000; infant mortality rate: 29.5/1000; density per sq mi.: 63
Capital: Caracas; **Largest cities (est. 1990):** Caracas, 1,290,087; Maracaibo, 1,206,726; Valencia, 616,000; Barquisimento, 723,587. **Monetary unit:** Bolivar. **Language:** Spanish, Indian dialects in interior. **Religion:** Roman Catholic. **National name:** Republica de Venezuela. **Literacy rate:** 90%
Economic summary: Gross domestic product (1994 est.): $178.3 billion, $8,760 per capita; real growth rate –3.3%; inflation 71%; unemployment 9%. Arable land: 3%. Principal agricultural products: rice, coffee, corn, cacao, sugar, bananas, dairy and meat products. Labor force: 7.6 million (1993): 63% in services, 25% in industry. Principal industrial products: refined petroleum products, aluminum, iron and steel, cement, textiles, transport equipment. Natural resources: petroleum, natural gas, iron ore, hydroelectric power. Exports: $15.2 billion (f.o.b., 1994 est.): petroleum, iron ore, bauxite. Imports: $7.6 billion (f.o.b., 1994 est.): industrial machinery and equipment, manufactures, chemicals, foodstuffs. Major trading partners: U.S., Japan, Germany, Italy, Netherlands, Canada.

Geography. Venezuela, a third larger than Texas, occupies most of the northern coast of South America on the Caribbean Sea. It is bordered by Colombia to the west, Guyana to the east, and Brazil to the south.

Mountain systems break Venezuela into four distinct areas: (1) the Maracaibo lowlands; (2) the mountainous region in the north and northwest; (3) the Orinoco basin, with the llanos (vast grass-covered plains) on its northern border and great forest areas in the south and southeast; (4) the Guiana Highlands, south of the Orinoco, accounting for nearly half the national territory. About 80% of Venezuela is drained by the Orinoco and its tributaries.

Government. Venezuela is a federal republic consisting of 22 states, the Federal District, and 72 islands in the Caribbean. There is a bicameral Congress, the 50 members of the Senate and the 199 members of the Chamber of Deputies being elected by popular vote to five-year terms. The President is also elected for five years. He must be a Venezuelan by birth and over 30 years old. He is not eligible for re-election until 10 years after the end of his term.

History. Columbus discovered Venezuela on his third voyage in 1498. A subsequent Spanish explorer gave the country its name, meaning "Little Venice." There were no important settlements until Caracas was founded in 1567. Simón Bolívar, who led the liberation of much of the continent from Spain, was born in Caracas in 1783. With Bolívar taking part, Venezuela was one of the first South American colonies to revolt against Spain, in 1810, but it was not until 1821 that independence was won. Federated at first with Colombia and Ecuador, the country set up a republic in 1830 and then sank for many decades into a condition of revolt, dictatorship, and corruption.

From 1908 to 1935, Gen. Juan Vicente Gómez was an absolute dictator. A military junta ruled after his death in 1935. Dr. Rómulo Betancourt and the liberal Acción Democrática Party won a majority of seats in a constituent assembly to draft a new constitution in 1946. A well-known writer, Rómulo Gallegos, candidate of Betancourt's party, easily won the presidential election of 1947. But the army ousted Gallegos the next year and instituted a military junta.

The country overthrew the dictatorship in 1958 and thereafter enjoyed democratic government. Rafael Caldera Rodríguez, president from 1969 to 1974, legalized the Communist Party and established diplomatic relations with Moscow.

In 1974, President Carlos Andrés Pérez took office. In 1976, Venezuela nationalized 21 oil companies, mostly subsidiaries of U.S. firms, offering compensation of $1.28 billion.

Despite difficulties at home, Pérez continued to play an active foreign role in extending economic aid to Latin neighbors, in backing the human-rights policy of President Carter, and in supporting Carter's return of the Panama Canal to Panama.

Opposition Christian Democrats capitalized on Pérez's domestic problems to elect Luis Herrera Campíns president in Venezuela's fifth consecutive free election, on Dec. 3, 1978.

When the Falklands war broke out, Venezuela became one of the most vigorous advocates of the Argentine cause and one of the sharpest critics of the U.S. decision to back Britain.

In the presidential election of December 1988 former president Carlos Andrés Pérez of the Democratic Action party easily won.

President Pérez surrendered his powers in May 1993 in order to defend himself in impeachment proceedings arising out of corruption charges. Ramon Velasquez was elected by Congress to serve as acting president pending the outcome of the impeachment proceedings.

In the presidential election of December 1993 Mr. Velasquez came in fourth. After a partial recount Rafael Caldera, a former president, was declared the winner with 30 percent of the vote in January 1994.

In June 1994 approximately half of the country's banking sector collapsed. Price increases of 20 percent were announced in February 1995, and the president's popularity fell during the year.

On the other hand, the government's efforts to create a market-oriented economy won the approval of the IMF, which granted Venezuela a large credit in July 1996.

VIETNAM

Socialist Republic of Vietnam
President: Le Duc Anh (1992)
Premier: Vo Van Kiet (1991)
Area: 127,246 sq mi. (329,566 sq km)
Population (est. 1996): 73,976,973 (average annual rate of natural increase: 1.61%); birth rate: 23/1000; infant mortality rate: 38.4/1000; Density per square mile: 582
Capital: Hanoi; **Largest cities (1992):** Ho Chi Minh City (Saigon),[1] 4,000,000; Hanoi, 2,000,000. Other large cities (1989): Haiphong, 456,049; Da Nang, 370,670; Nha Trang, 213,687; Qui Nho'n, 160,091; Hué 211,085. **Monetary unit:** Dong. **Languages:** Vietnamese (official), French, English, Khmer, Chinese. **Religions:** Buddhist, Roman Catholic, Islam, Taoist, Confucian, animist. **National name:** Công Hòa Xa Hôi Chú Nghia Viêt Nam. **Literacy rate:** 88%
Economic summary: Gross national product (1994 est.): $83.5 billion; $1,140 per capita; 8.8% real growth rate; inflation 14.4%; unemployment 20%. Arable land: 22%. Principal agricultural products: rice, rubber, fruits and vegetables, corn, sugar cane, fish. Labor force: 32,700,000; 65% in agriculture. Major industrial

products: processed foods, textiles, cement, chemical fertilizers, glass, tires. **Natural resources:** phosphates, forests, coal. **Exports:** $3.6 billion (f.o.b., 1994 est.): agricultural products, minerals, marine products, coffee, petroleum, rice. **Imports:** $4.2 billion (f.o.b., 1994 est.): petroleum, steel products, railroad equipment, chemicals, medicines, raw cotton, fertilizer, grain. **Major trading partners:** Singapore, Japan, Hong Kong, Thailand, Germany, Indonesia, South Korea, Taiwan.

1. Includes suburb of Cholon.

Geography. Vietnam occupies the eastern and southern part of the Indochinese peninsula in Southeast Asia, with the South China Sea along its entire coast. China is to the north and Laos and Cambodia to the west. Long and narrow on a north-south axis, Vietnam is about twice the size of Arizona.

The Mekong River delta lies in the south and the Red River delta in the north. Heavily forested mountain and plateau regions make up most of the country.

Government. On April 30, 1975, a joint National Assembly convened with 249 deputies representing the North and 243 representing the South. The Assembly set July 2, 1976, as the official reunification date. Hanoi became the capital.

A new constitution was adopted in April 1992 which called for the creation of a presidency and a prime ministry. The document affirmed the free-market economy, and the role of the Communist Party is limited to that of guidance. Foreign assets are guaranteed against nationalization. The Assembly has 395 members.

History. The Vietnamese are descendants of Mongoloid nomads from China and migrants from Indonesia. They recognized Chinese suzerainty until the 15th century, an era of nationalistic expansion, when Cambodians were pushed out of the southern area of what is now Vietnam.

A century later, the Portuguese were the first Europeans to enter the area. France established its influence early in the 19th century and within 80 years conquered the three regions into which the country was then divided—Cochin-China in the south, Annam in the center, and Tonkin in the north.

France first unified Vietnam in 1887, when a single governor-generalship was created, followed by the first physical links between north and south—a rail and road system. Even at the beginning of World War II, however, there were internal differences among the three regions.

Japan took over military bases in Vietnam in 1940 and a pro-Vichy French administration remained until 1945. A veteran Communist leader, Ho Chi Minh, organized an independence movement known as the Vietminh to exploit a confused situation. At the end of the war, Ho's followers seized Hanoi and declared a short-lived republic, which ended with the arrival of French forces in 1946.

Paris proposed a unified government within the French Union under the former Annamite emperor, Bao Dai. Cochin-China and Annam accepted the proposal, and Bao Dai was proclaimed emperor of all Vietnam in 1949. Ho and the Vietminh withheld support, and the revolution in China gave them the outside help needed for a war of resistance against French and Vietnamese troops armed largely by the U.S.

A bitter defeat at Dien Bien Phu in northwest Vietnam on May 5, 1954, broke the French military campaign and brought the division of Vietnam at the conference of Geneva that year.

In the new South, Ngo Dinh Diem, premier under Bao Dai, deposed the monarch in 1955 and established a republic with himself as president. Diem used strong U.S. backing to create an authoritarian regime that suppressed all opposition but could not eradicate the Northern-supplied Communist Viet Cong.

Skirmishing grew into a full-scale war, with escalating U.S. involvement. A military coup, U.S.-inspired in the view of many, ousted Diem Nov. 1, 1963, and a kaleidoscope of military governments followed. The most savage fighting of the war occurred in early 1968, during the Tet holidays.

Although the Viet Cong failed to overthrow the Saigon government, U.S. public reaction to the apparently endless war forced a limitation of U.S. troops to 550,000 and a new emphasis on shifting the burden of further combat to the South Vietnamese. Ho Chi Minh's death on Sept. 3, 1969, brought a quadrumvirate to replace him but no flagging in Northern will to fight.

U.S. bombing and invasion of Cambodia in the summer of 1970—an effort to destroy Viet Cong bases in the neighboring state—marked the end of major U.S. participation in the fighting. Most American ground troops were withdrawn from combat by mid-1971 as heavy bombing of the Ho Chi Minh trail from North Vietnam appeared to cut the supply of men and matériel to the South.

Secret negotiations for peace by Secretary of State Henry A. Kissinger with North Vietnamese officials during 1972 after heavy bombing of Hanoi and Haiphong brought the two sides near agreement in October. When the Northerners demanded the removal of the South's President Nguyen Van Thieu as their price, President Nixon ordered the "Christmas bombing" of the North. The conference resumed and a peace settlement was signed in Paris on Jan. 27, 1973. It called for release of all U.S. prisoners, withdrawal of U.S. forces, limitation of both sides' forces inside South Vietnam, and a commitment to peaceful reunification.

An armored attack across the 17th parallel in January 1975 panicked the South Vietnamese army and brought the invasion within 40 miles of Saigon by April 9. Thieu resigned on April 21 and fled, to be replaced by Vice President Tran Van Huong, who quit a week later, turning over the office to Gen. Duong Van Minh. "Big Minh" surrendered Saigon on April 30, ending a war that took 1.3 million Vietnamese and 58,000 American lives, at the cost of $141 billion in U.S. aid.

On May 3, 1977, the U.S. and Vietnam opened negotiations in Paris to normalize relations. One of the first results was the withdrawal of U.S. opposition to Vietnamese membership in the United Nations, formalized in the Security Council on July 20. Two major issues remained to be settled, however: the return of the bodies of some 2,500 U.S. servicemen missing in the war, and the claim by Hanoi that former President Nixon had promised reconstruction aid under the 1973 agreement. Negotiations failed to resolve these issues.

The new year also brought an intensification of border clashes between Vietnam and Cambodia and accusations by China that Chinese residents of Vietnam were being subjected to persecution. Peking cut off all aid and withdrew 800 technicians.

Hanoi was undoubtedly preoccupied with a continuing war in Cambodia, where 60,000 Vietnamese troops were aiding the Heng Samrin regime in suppressing the last forces of the pro-Chinese Pol Pot regime. In early 1979, Vietnam was conducting a two-front war, defending its northern border against a Chinese invasion and at the same time supporting its army in Cambodia.

Economic troubles continued, with the government seeking to reschedule its $1.4-billion foreign hard-currency debt, owed mainly to Japan and the International Monetary Fund. In late 1987, a shuffle of the Vietnamese Politburo brought in new leaders who were expected to slightly relax the government grip on the economy and crack down on corruption within the party.

In 1988, Vietnam also began limited troop withdrawals from Laos and Cambodia. Vietnam supported the Cambodian peace agreement signed in October 1991.

General elections in July 1992 saw 601 candidates competing for the 395 seats in the assembly.

The economy grew remarkably during 1993. The currency stabilized and the rate of inflation fell to a relatively low level.

The U.S. trade embargo was lifted in February 1994, although the Party reiterated its opposition to political reform throughout the year despite its continued pursuit of major economic reforms. Full diplomatic relations were announced between the U.S. and Vietnam in July 1995.

Reform-minded officials were named in May 1996 to head the Hanoi and Ho Chi Minh City Community Party organizations.

(For a Vietnam War chronology, see Headline History.)

WESTERN SAMOA

Independent State of Western Samoa
Head of State: Malietoa Tanumafili II (1962)
Prime Minister: Tofilau Eti Alesana (1988)
Area: 1,093 sq mi. (2,831 sq km)
Population (est. 1996): 214,384 (average annual growth rate: 2.54%); birth rate: 31.1/1000; infant mortality rate: 34.3/1000; density per square mile: 197
Capital and largest city (1991): Apia, 32,859. **Monetary unit:** Tala. **Languages:** Samoan and English. **Religions:** Christian, 99.7%. **National name:** Western Samoa. **Member of Commonwealth of Nations. Literacy rate:** 97%
Economic summary: Gross domestic product (1992 est.): $400 million; $2,000 per capita; –4.3% real growth rate; inflation 7%. Arable land: 19%. Principal agricultural products: copra, coconuts, cocoa, bananas, taro, yams. Labor force (1987): 38,000; 22,000 employed in agriculture. Agriculture accounts for 50% of GDP. Major industrial products: timber, processed food, fish. Natural resource: timber. Exports: $6.4 million (f.o.b., 1993): copra, cocoa, coconut oil and cream, timber. Imports: $11.5 million (c.i.f., 1992 est.): food, manufactured goods, machinery. Major trading partners: New Zealand, E.C., Australia, U.S., Fiji, Japan

Geography. Western Samoa, the size of Rhode Island, is in the South Pacific Ocean about 2,200 miles (3,540 km) south of Hawaii midway to Sydney, Australia, and about 800 miles (1,287 km) northeast of Fiji. The larger islands in the Samoan chain are mountainous and of volcanic origin. There is little level land except in the coastal areas, where most cultivation takes place.

Government. Western Samoa has a 49-member Legislature, consisting mainly of the titleholders (chiefs) of family groups, with two non-title members. All members are elected by universal suffrage. When the present head of state dies, successors will be elected by the Legislature for five-year terms.

History. The Samoan islands were discovered in the 18th century and visited by Dutch and French traders. Toward the end of the 19th century, conflicting interests of the U.S., Britain, and Germany resulted in a treaty signed in 1899. It recognized the paramount interests of the U.S. in those islands east of 171° west longitude (American Samoa) and Germany's interests in the other islands (Western Samoa).

New Zealand occupied Western Samoa in 1914, and was granted a League of Nations mandate. In 1947, the islands became a U.N. trust territory administered by New Zealand. Western Samoa became independent on Jan. 1, 1962.

A referendum of 1990 gave most women the right to vote for the first time. The April 1991 election gave the ruling Human Rights Protection Party a narrow victory.

A value-added tax was introduced at the start of 1994 that produced widespread dissatisfaction and resistance. Government attempts to ameliorate the impact of the tax failed to soothe public opposition.

The government in 1995 attempted to put Polynesian Airlines on a financially sound course while shoring it up with needed cash.

REPUBLIC OF YEMEN

President: Ali Abdullah Saleh
Prime Minister: Abd al-Aziz al-Ghani (1994)
Area: 203,850 sq mi. (527,970 sq km)
Population (est. 1996): 13,483,178 (average annual rate of natural increase: 3.56%); birth rate: 45.2/1000; infant mortality rate: 71.5/1000; density per square mile: 67
Capital 1995: Sanaá, 972,011; **Largest cities (1995):** Taiz, 2,205,947; Hodiedah, 1,749,944; Aden, 562,162. **Monetary unit:** Rial. **Language:** Arabic. **Religion:** Islam (Sunni and Shiite). **Literacy rate:** 38%
Economic summary: Gross domestic product (1994 est.): $23.4 billion; $1,995 per capita; real growth rate –1.4%; inflation: 145%; unemployment: 30% (Dec. 94). Principal agricultural products: wheat, sorghum, cattle, sheep, cotton, fruits, coffee, dates. Principal industrial products: crude and refined oil, textiles, leather goods, handicrafts, fish. Exports: $1.75 billion (f.o.b., 1994 est.): cotton, coffee, hides, vegetables, dried fish; Imports: $2.65 billion (f.o.b., 1994 est.): textiles, manufactured consumer goods, foodstuffs, sugar, grain, flour. Major trading partners: U.K., Japan, Saudi Arabia, Australia, U.S.

Geography. Formerly known as the states of Peoples Democratic Republic of Yemen and the Yemen Arab Republic, the Republic of Yemen occupies the southwestern tip of the Arabian Peninsula on the Red Sea opposite Ethiopia, and extends along the southern part of the Arabian Peninsula on the Gulf of Aden and the Indian Ocean. Saudi Arabia is to the north and Oman is to the east. The country is about the size of France. A 700-mile (1,130-km) narrow coastal plain in the south gives way to a mountainous region and then a plateau area. Some of the interior highlands in the west attain a height of 12,000 feet (3,660 m).

Government. Parliamentary. The Presidential Council was abolished by a new constitution approved in September 1994.

History. The history of Yemen dates back to the Minaean kingdom (1200–650 B.C.). It accepted Islam in A.D. 628, and in the 10th century came under the control of the Rassite dynasty of the Zaidi sect. The Turks occupied the area from 1538 to 1630 and from 1849 to 1918. The sovereign status of Yemen was confirmed by treaties signed with Saudi Arabia and Britain in 1934.

In 1962, a military revolt of elements favoring President Gamal Abdel Nasser of Egypt broke out. A ruling junta proclaimed a republic, and Yemen became an international battleground, with Egypt and the U.S.S.R. supporting the revolutionaries, and King Saud of Saudi Arabia and King Hussein of Jordan the royalists. The civil war continued until the war between the Arab states and Israel broke out in June 1967. Nasser had to pull out many of his troops and agree to a cease-fire and withdrawal of foreign forces. The war finally ended with the defeat of the royalists in mid-1969.

The People's Republic of Southern Yemen was established Nov. 30, 1967, when Britain granted independence to the Federation of South Arabia. This Federation consisted of the state (once the colony) of Aden and 16 of the 20 states of the Protectorate of South Arabia (once the Aden Protectorate). The four states of the Protectorate that did not join the Federation later became part of Southern Yemen.

The Republic of Yemen was established on May 23, 1990, when pro-Western Yemen and Marxist Yemen Arab Republic merged after 300 years of separation to form the new nation. The union had been approved by both governments in November 1989.

The new president, Ali Abdullah Saleh of Yemen, was elected by the parliaments of both countries. The parliaments also chose South Yemen's Ali Salem al-Baidh, secretary general of the ruling socialist party, to be the new vice-president.

In the Gulf War, Yemen favored Iraq. Consequently, many expatriates in Saudi Arabia were forced to return. A referendum in May 1992 on a constitution resulted in a landslide in favor of it.

Differences over power-sharing and the pace of integration between the north and south came to a head in 1994, resulting in a civil war. The north's superior forces quickly overwhelmed the south in May and early June despite the south's brief declaration of secession. The victorious north presented a reconciliation plan providing for a general amnesty and pledges to protect political democracy.

Border clashes occurred periodically with Saudi Arabia during 1995 despite ongoing talks.

YUGOSLAVIA

Federal Republic of Yugoslavia
President: Zoan Lilic (1993)
Prime Minister: Radoje Kontic (1993)
Area: 39,449 sq mi. (102,169 sq km)
Population (est. 1996): 10,611,558; (average annual rate of natural increase: 1.0%); birth rate: 13/1000; infant mortality rate: 26/1000; density per square mile: 269
Capital and largest city (1994 est.): Belgrade, 1,168,454; **Other large cities:** Novi Sad, 179,626; Nis 175,391; Pristina, 155,499. **Monetary unit:** Yugoslav new Dinar. **Languages:** Serbo-Croatian 100%. **Religions:** Orthodox, 65%; Muslim, 19%; Christian religions, 5%. **National name:** Federativna Republika Jugoslavijá. **Literacy rate:** 90.5%
Economic summary: Gross domestic product (1994 est.): $10 billion; per capita $1,000; growth rate n.a.; inflation 20% (Jan.–Nov. 94): unemployment more than 40%. Labor force (1990): 2,640,909; industry and mining, 40%; agriculture, 5%. Industries: machine building (incl. aircraft, trucks, automobiles), nonferrous metallurgy, consumer goods, electronics, chemicals, petroleum products, pharmaceuticals. Exports: $4.4 billion

(f.o.b., 1990): machinery and transportation equipment, manufactured goods and articles, chemicals, food, and live animals. Imports: $6.4 billion (c.i.f., 1990): machinery and transport equipment, fuels and lubricants, other manufactures, chemicals, raw materials, food, and animals. Trading partners: C.I.S. countries, E.U., U.S., Eastern European countries.

Geography. Yugoslavia consists of the two states of Serbia and Montenegro. The nation is bordered by Hungary in the north, Romania and Bulgaria in the east, Macedonia in the south, Albania and the Adriatic Sea in the west, and the former Yugoslavian republics of Bosnia-Herzegovina and Croatia in the west. Yugoslavia is about the size of the state of Kentucky.

Yugoslavia is largely a mountainous country. The northeastern section of Serbia is part of the rich, fertile Danubian Plain drained by the Danube, Tisa, Sava, and Morava River systems. Montenegro is a jumbled mass of mountains, containing also some grassy slopes and fertile river valleys.

Government. Yugoslavia (Serbia and Montenegro) is a federal republic. The bicameral Federal Assembly consists of an upper house, or Chamber of Republics, and a lower house, or Chamber of Deputies.

History. Yugoslavia was formed Dec. 4, 1918, from the patchwork of Balkan states and territories where World War I began with the assassination of Archduke Ferdinand of Austria at Sarajevo on June 28, 1914. The new Kingdom of Serbs, Croats, and Slovenes included the former kingdoms of Serbia and Montenegro; Bosnia-Herzegovina, previously administered jointly by Austria and Hungary; Croatia-Slavonia, a semi-autonomous region of Hungary; and Dalmatia, formerly administered by Austria. King Peter I of Serbia became the first monarch, his son acting as regent until his accession as Alexander I on Aug. 16, 1921.

Croatian demands for a federal state forced Alexander to assume dictatorial powers in 1929 and to change the country's name to Yugoslavia. Serbian dominance continued despite his efforts, amid the resentment of other regions. A Macedonian associated with Croatian dissidents assassinated Alexander in Marseilles, France, on Oct. 9, 1934, and his cousin, Prince Paul, became regent for the king's son, Prince Peter.

Paul's pro-Axis policy brought Yugoslavia to sign the Axis Pact on March 25, 1941, and opponents overthrew the government two days later. On April 6 the Nazis occupied the country, and the young king and his government fled. Two guerrilla armies —the Chetniks under Draza Mihajlovic supporting the monarchy and the Partisans under Tito (Josip Broz) leaning toward the U.S.S.R.—fought the Nazis for the duration of the war. In 1943, Tito established an Executive National Committee of Liberation to function as a provisional government.

Tito won the election held in the fall of 1945, as monarchists boycotted the vote. A new Assembly abolished the monarchy and proclaimed the Federal People's Republic of Yugoslavia, with Tito as prime minister. Ruthlessly eliminating opposition, the Tito government executed Mihajlovic in 1946.

Tito broke with the Soviet bloc in 1948 and Yugoslavia followed a middle road, combining orthodox Communist control of politics and general overall economic policy with a varying degree of freedom in the arts, travel, and individual enterprise. Tito became president in 1953 and president for life under a revised constitution adopted in 1963.

After Tito's death on May 4, 1980, a rotating presidency designed to avoid internal dissension was put into effect immediately, and the feared clash of Yugoslavia's multiple nationalities and regions appeared to have been averted.

In May 1991 Croatian voters supported a referendum calling for their republic to become an independent nation. A similar referendum passed in December in Slovenia. In June the respective parliaments in both republics passed declarations of independence. Ethnic violence flared almost immediately. The largely Serbian-led Yugoslav military pounded breakaway Bosnia and Herzegovina, leading the U.N. Security Council in May 1992 to impose economic sanctions on the Belgrade government.

Despite rampant inflation reaching approximately 3000% per month in December 1993 the Serbian government of Slobodan Milosevic maintained its effective control over the rump Yugoslavia. Final results of the late year parliamentary elections gave the Socialist Party the largest number of seats, just three short of a majority.

Trade sanctions were lifted in December 1995 following the signing of the Dayton Accords. In June 1996 the UN Security Council lifted its heavy weapons embargo.

The economy continued to be very depressed in 1995 and 1996, with industrial production almost half that of 1991.

ZAIRE

Republic of Zaire
President: Mobutu Sese Seko (1965)
Area: 905,365 sq mi. (2,344,885 sq km)
Population (est. 1996): 46,498,539 (average annual rate of natural increase: 3.12%); birth rate: 48.1/1000; infant mortality rate: 108/1000; density per sq mi.: 52
Capital and largest city (1994 est.): Kinshasa, 4,655,313; **Other large cities:** Lubumbashi, 851,381; Mbuji-Mayi, 806,475; Kisangani, 417,517; Kolwezi, 417,810. **Monetary unit:** Zaire. **Languages:** French (official), English, Bantu dialects, mainly Swahili, Lingala, Ishiluba, and Kikongo. **Religions:** Roman Catholic 50%, Protestant 20%, Kimbanguist 10%, Islam 10%; syncretic and traditional, 10%. **Ethnic groups:** Bantu, Sudanese, Nilotics, Pygmies, Hamites. **National name:** République du Zaïre.
Literacy rate: 72%
Economic summary: Gross domestic product (1994 est.): $18.8 billion; $440 per capita; 4% real growth rate; inflation 40% per mo. (1993 est.); unemployment: n.a. Arable land: 3%. Principal agricultural products: coffee, palm oil, rubber, quinine, cassava, bananas, plantains, vegetables, fruits. Labor force: 15,000,000; 13% in industry. Major industrial products: processed and unprocessed minerals, consumer goods. Natural resources: copper, cobalt, zinc, industrial diamonds, manganese, tin, gold, silver, bauxite, iron, coal, crude oil, hydroelectric potential. Exports: $362 million (f.o.b., 1993 est.): copper, cobalt, diamonds, petroleum, coffee. Imports: $356 million (f.o.b., 1993 est.): consumer goods, foodstuffs, mining and other machinery, transport equipment, and fuels. Major trading partners: Belgium, France, U.S., Germany, South Africa, Italy, Japan, U.K.

Geography. Zaire is situated in west central Africa and is bordered by the Congo, the Central African Republic, the Sudan, Uganda, Rwanda, Burundi, Tanzania, Zambia, Angola, and the Atlantic Ocean. It is one quarter the size of the U.S.

The principal rivers are the Ubangi and Bomu in the north and the Zaire (Congo) in the west, which flows into the Atlantic. The entire length of Lake Tanganyika lies along the eastern border with Tanzania and Burundi.

Government. A republic with a multiparty unicameral legislature. The president and the legislature are elected by universal suffrage for five-year terms.

History. Formerly the Belgian Congo, this territory was inhabited by ancient Negrito peoples (Pygmies), who were pushed into the mountains by Bantu and Nilotic invaders. The American correspondent Henry M. Stanley navigated the Congo River in 1877 and opened the interior to exploration. Commissioned by King Leopold II of the Belgians, Stanley made treaties with native chiefs that enabled the king to obtain personal title to the territory at the Berlin Conference of 1885.

Criticism of forced labor under royal exploitation prompted Belgium to take over administration of the Congo, which remained a colony until agitation for independence forced Brussels to grant freedom on June 30, 1960. Moise Tshombe, premier of the then Katanga Province, seceded from the new republic on July 11, and another mining province, South Kasai, followed. Belgium sent paratroopers to quell the civil war, and with President Joseph Kasavubu and Premier Patrice Lumumba of the national government in conflict, the United Nations flew in a peacekeeping force.

Kasavubu staged an army coup in 1960 and handed Lumumba over to the Katangan forces. A U.N. investigating commission found that Lumumba had been killed by a Belgian mercenary in the presence of Tshombe. Dag Hammarskjold, U.N. secretary-general, died in a plane crash en route to a peace conference with Tshombe on Sept. 17, 1961.

U.N. Secretary-General U Thant submitted a national reconciliation plan in 1962 that Tshombe rejected. Tshombe's troops fired on the U.N. force in December, and in the ensuing conflict Tshombe capitulated on Jan. 14, 1963. The peacekeeping force withdrew, and, in a complete about-face, Kasavubu named Tshombe premier to fight a spreading rebellion. Tshombe used foreign mercenaries and, with the help of Belgian paratroops airlifted by U.S. planes, defeated the most serious opposition, a Communist-backed regime in the northeast.

Kasavubu abruptly dismissed Tshombe in 1965 and was himself ousted by Gen. Joseph-Desiré Mobutu, army chief of staff. The new president nationalized the Union Minière, the Belgian copper mining enterprise that had been a dominant force in the Congo since colonial days. The plane carrying the exiled Tshombe was hijacked in 1967 and he was held prisoner in Algeria until his death from a heart attack was announced June 29, 1969.

Mobutu eliminated opposition to win election in 1970 to a term of seven years, which was renewed in a 1977 election. In 1975, he nationalized much of the economy, barred religious instruction in schools, and decreed the adoption of African names.

On March 8, 1977, invaders from Angola calling themselves the Congolese National Liberation Front pushed into Shaba and threatened the important mining center of Kolwezi. France and Belgium responded to Mobutu's pleas for help with weapons, but the U.S. gave only nonmilitary supplies.

In April, France flew 1,500 Moroccan troops to Shaba to defeat the invaders, who were, Mobutu charged, Soviet-inspired and Cuban-led. U.S. intelligence sources, however, confirmed Soviet and Cuban denials of any participation and identified the rebels as former Katanga gendarmes who had fled to Angola after their 1963 defeat.

In April 1990 Mobutu announced he intended to introduce multiparty democracy, but that elections in January 1991 would reduce the number of political parties to two besides his own. Opposition leaders denounced the scheme as giving Mobutu's party an unfair advantage.

A national conference was scheduled for July 1991, but in June three opposition groups announced a boycott. The conference was postponed. The conference finally convened in August, but, boycotted by the main opposition parties, it was adjourned without achieving anything. Mobutu offered the prime ministerial post to an opposition leader. The ensuing power struggle led to his dismissal in October.

In early 1993 Mobutu rejected Western demands that he yield power and announced plans to regroup his one-party parliament, dismissing the main opposition leader, Prime Minister Tshisekedi. In January 1994 Mobutu dissolved parliament and dismissed his prime minister, which led to a general strike in the capital.

Although 1995 started with Mobutu's call for an end to the continuing political crisis, it soon became clear that little progress would be made soon. Battles broke out in July shortly after the transitional government stated it would continue in power for two more years. Later in the year the problem of refugees from Rwanda and Burundi took center stage.

ZAMBIA

Republic of Zambia
President: Frederick T.J. Chiluba (1991)
Vice President: Levy Mwanawasa (1991)
Area: 290,586 sq mi. (752,618 sq km)
Population (est. 1996): 9,159,072 (average annual rate of natural increase: 2.11%); birth rate: 44.7/1000; infant mortality rate: 96.1/1000; density per sq mi.: 32
Capital: Lusaka; **Largest cities (1990):** Lusaka, 982,362; Kitwe, 338,207; Ndola, 376,311; Chingola, 167,954.
Monetary unit: Kwacha. **Languages:** English and local dialects. **Religions:** Christian, 50–75%; Islam and Hindu, 1%; remainder indigenous beliefs. **Member of Commonwealth of Nations.** Literacy rate: 75.7%
Economic summary: Gross domestic product (1994 est.): $7.9 billion; $860 per capita; real growth rate 4%; inflation 89%; unemployment n.a. Arable land: 7%. Principal agricultural products: corn, tobacco, rice, sugar cane. Labor force: 3.4 million: agriculture 85%. Major industrial products: copper, textiles, chemicals, zinc, fertilizers. Natural resources: copper, zinc, lead, cobalt, coal. Exports: $1.01 billion (f.o.b., 1993 est.): copper, zinc, lead, cobalt, tobacco. Imports: $1.13 billion (c.i.f., 1993 est.): manufactured goods, machinery and transport equipment, foodstuffs, fuels. Major trading partners: Western Europe, Japan, South Africa, U.S., Saudi Arabia, India.

Geography. Zambia, a landlocked country in south central Africa, is about one-tenth larger than Texas. It is surrounded by Angola, Zaire, Tanzania, Malawi, Mozambique, Zimbabwe, Botswana, and Namibia (formerly South-West Africa). The country is mostly a plateau that rises to 8,000 feet (2,434 m) in the east.

Government. A multiparty system. Zambia (formerly Northern Rhodesia) is governed by a president, elected by universal suffrage, and a unicameral Legislative Assembly, consisting of 150 members elected by universal suffrage.

History. Empire builder Cecil Rhodes obtained mining concessions in 1889 from King Lewanika of the Barotse and sent settlers to the area soon thereafter. It was ruled by the British South Africa Company, which he established, until 1924, when the British government took over the administration.

From 1953 to 1964, Northern Rhodesia was federated with Southern Rhodesia and Nyasaland in the Federation of Rhodesia and Nyasaland. On Oct. 24, 1964, Northern Rhodesia became the independent nation of Zambia.

Kenneth Kaunda, the first president, kept Zambia within the Commonwealth of Nations. The country's economy, dependent on copper exports, was threatened when Rhodesia declared its independence from British rule in 1965 and defied U.N. sanctions, which Zambia supported, an action that deprived Zambia of its trade route through Rhodesia. The U.S., Britain, and Canada organized an airlift in 1966 to ship gasoline into Zambia. In 1967, Britain agreed to finance new trade routes for Zambia.

Kaunda visited China in 1967, and China later agreed to finance a 1,000-mile railroad from the copper fields to Dar es Salaam in Tanzania. A pipeline was opened in 1968 from Ndola in Zambia's copper belt to the Indian Ocean at Dar es Salaam, ending the three-year oil drought.

In 1969, Kaunda announced the nationalization of the foreign copper-mining industry, with Zambia to take 51% (over $1 billion, estimated), and an agreement was reached with the companies on payment. He then announced a similar takeover of foreign oil producers.

With a soaring debt and inflation rate the government in 1990 turned to the International Monetary Fund and the World Bank, with whom an agreement was reached in exchange for economic reforms. Soaring prices in June 1990 led to riots in Lusaka, resulting in a number of killings. Mounting domestic pressure forced Kaunda to move Zambia toward multiparty democracy.

National elections on October 31, 1991 brought a stunning defeat to the long-serving President Kaunda and a repudiation of his long belief in a one-party state. The newly-elected chief executive, Frederick Chiluba, called for sweeping economic reforms including privatization and the establishing of a stock market.

The president declared a state of emergency in March 1993 after the uncovering of a plot to overthrow the government. The state of emergency was lifted in May. In November by-elections the president's party won only three of the eight contested seats.

Parliament passed a bill in May 1996 that stated a president may serve only two terms, thus preventing any possible political return of Kenneth Kaunda.

ZIMBABWE

Republic of Zimbabwe
Executive President: Robert Mugabe (1987)
Area: 150,698 sq mi. (390,308 sq km)
Population (est. 1996): 11,271,314 (average annual rate of natural increase: 1.41%); birth rate: 32.3/1000; infant mortality rate: 72.8/1000; density per square mile: 75
Capital and largest city (1992): Harare, 1,184,169; **Other large cities:** Bulawayo, 620,936; Chitungwiza, 274,035.
Monetary unit: Zimbabwean dollar. **Languages:** English (official), Ndebele, Shona. **Religions:** Christian, 25%; animist, 24%; syncretic, 50%. **Literacy rate:** 74%
Economic summary: Gross domestic product (1994 est.): $17.4 billion; $1,580 per capita; real growth rate 3.5%; inflation 22% (Dec. 94); unemployment: at least 45%. Arable land: 7%. Principal agricultural products: tobacco, corn, sugar, cotton, livestock. Labor force:

3,100,000; 74% in agriculture; 16%, transport and services. Major industrial products: steel, textiles, chemicals, vehicles, gold, copper. Natural resources: gold, copper, chrome, nickel, tin, asbestos. Exports: $1.8 billion (f.o.b., 1994 est.): gold, tobacco, asbestos, copper, meat, chrome, nickel, corn, sugar. Imports: $1.8 billion (c.i.f., 1992 est.): machinery, petroleum products, transport equipment. Major trading partners: U.K., South Africa, Germany, Japan, U.S.

Geography. Zimbabwe, a landlocked country in south central Africa, is slightly smaller than California. It is bordered by Botswana on the west, Zambia on the north, Mozambique on the east, and South Africa on the south.

A high veld up to 6,000 feet (1,829 m) crosses the country from northeast to southwest. This is flanked by a somewhat lower veld that contains ranching country. Tropical forests that yield hardwoods lie in the southeast.

In the north, on the border with Zambia, is the 175-mile-long (128-m) Kariba Lake, formed by the Kariba Dam across the Zambezi River. It is the site of one of the world's largest hydroelectric projects.

Government. A parliamentary democracy with a 150-seat unicameral legislature, the House of Assembly. The Executive President is chief of state and head of government. There are two co-vice presidents.

History. Zimbabwe was colonized by Cecil Rhodes's British South Africa Company at the end of the 19th century. In 1923, European settlers voted to become the self-governing British colony of Southern Rhodesia rather than merge with the Union of South Africa. After a brief federation with Northern Rhodesia and Nyasaland in the post-World War II period, Southern Rhodesia (also known as Rhodesia) chose to remain a colony when its two partners voted for independence in 1963.

On Nov. 11, 1965, the white-minority government of Rhodesia unilaterally declared its independence from Britain.

In 1967, the U.N. imposed mandatory sanctions against Rhodesia. The country moved slowly toward meeting the demands of black Africans. The white-minority regime of Prime Minister Ian Smith withstood British pressure, economic sanctions, guerrilla attacks, and a right-wing assault.

On March 1, 1970, Rhodesia formally proclaimed itself a republic, and within the month nine nations, including the U.S., closed their consulates there.

Heightened guerrilla war and a withdrawal of South African military aid—particularly helicopters—marked the beginning of the collapse of Smith's 11 years of resistance in the spring of 1976. Under pressure from South Africa, Smith agreed with the U.S. that majority rule should come within two years.

In the fall, Smith met with black nationalist leaders in Geneva. The meeting broke up six weeks later when the Rhodesian premier insisted that whites must retain control of the police and armed forces during the transition to majority rule. A British proposal called for Britons to take over these powers.

Divisions between Rhodesian blacks—Bishop Abel Muzorewa of the African National Congress and Ndabaningi Sithole as moderates versus Robert Mugabe and Joshua Nkomo of the Patriotic Front as advocates of guerrilla force—sharpened in 1977 and no agreement was reached. In July, with white residents leaving in increasing numbers and the economy showing the strain of war, Smith rejected outside mediation and called for general elections in order to work out an "internal solution" of the transfer of power.

On March 3, 1978, Smith, Muzorewa, Sithole, and Chief Jeremiah Chirau signed an agreement to transfer power to the black majority by Dec. 31, 1978. They constituted themselves an Executive Council, with chairmanship rotating but Smith retaining the title of Prime Minister. Blacks were named to each cabinet ministry, serving as co-ministers with the whites already holding these posts. African nations and the Patriotic Front leaders immediately denounced the action, but Western governments were more reserved, although none granted recognition to the new regime.

White voters ratified a new constitution on Jan. 30, 1979, enfranchising all blacks, establishing a black majority Senate and Assembly, and changing the country's name to Zimbabwe Rhodesia.

Muzorewa agreed to negotiate with Mugabe and Nkomo in British-sponsored talks beginning Sept. 9. By December, all parties accepted a new draft constitution, a cease-fire, and a period of British administration pending a general election.

In voting completed on Feb. 29, 1980, Mugabe's ZANU-Patriotic Front party won 57 of the 80 Assembly seats reserved for blacks. In an earlier vote on Feb. 14, the Rhodesian Front won all 20 seats reserved for whites in the Assembly.

On April 18, 1980, Britain formally recognized the independence of Zimbabwe.

In January 1981, Mugabe dismissed Nkomo as Home Minister and his onetime rival left the government in protest.

The 1985 harvest was good in Zimbabwe and the country could feed itself. But political turmoil and civil strife continued. In what Western analysts viewed as a free and fair election, President Mugabe's African National Union increased its sizeable majority in the House of Assembly but Mugabe was frustrated because it did not win the 70 seats he sought to cement one-party rule. After the election, Mugabe cracked down on Nkomo's ZANU-Patriotic Front party.

In April 1990, Mugabe was re-elected and his ZANU(PF) party given virtual unanimity in the Assembly.

In December 1990 the parliament voted by 113 to 3 to amend the original 1980 constitution to allow the compulsory acquisition of white-owned farmland at government-set prices. Indeed, white farmers would have no judiciary recourse. Britain and the U.S. warned that forceful land acquisitions would deter foreign investments and further depress the country.

A split in the opposition Zimbabwe Unity Movement in June 1991 reduced pressure on the ruling ZANU(PF). At that time the latter deleted all references to Marxism-Leninism and scientific socialism from its constitution.

The Land Acquisition Act was amended in 1992 to permit compensation for compulsorily acquired land.

Parliamentary elections in April 1995 gave Mugabe's party a stunning victory with 63 of the 65 contested seats. Mugabe won another six-year term as president in a March 1996 election. He ran unopposed as the only other candidate withdrew just prior to the voting.

(For late reports, see Current Events of 1996)

UNITED NATIONS

The 185 Members of the United Nations

Country	Joined U.N.[1]	Country	Joined U.N.[1]	Country	Joined U.N.[1]
Afghanistan	1946	Germany	1973	Norway	1945
Albania	1955	Ghana	1957	Oman	1971
Algeria	1962	Greece	1945	Pakistan	1947
Andorra	1993	Grenada	1974	Palau	1994
Angola	1976	Guatemala	1945	Panama	1945
Antigua and Barbuda	1981	Guinea	1958	Papua New Guinea	1975
Argentina	1945	Guinea-Bissau	1974	Paraguay	1945
Armenia	1992	Guyana	1966	Peru	1945
Australia	1945	Haiti	1945	Philippines	1945
Austria	1955	Honduras	1945	Poland	1945
Azerbaijan	1992	Hungary	1955	Portugal	1955
Bahamas	1973	Iceland	1946	Qatar	1971
Bahrain	1971	India	1945	Romania	1955
Bangladesh	1974	Indonesia	1950	Russian Federation	1945
Barbados	1966	Iran, Islamic Republic of	1945	Rwanda	1962
Belarus	1945	Iraq	1945	St. Kitts and Nevis	1983
Belgium	1945	Ireland	1955	St. Lucia	1979
Belize	1981	Israel	1949	St. Vincent and the Grenadines	1980
Benin	1960	Italy	1955	Samoa, Western	1976
Bhutan	1971	Jamaica	1962	San Marino	1992
Bolivia	1945	Japan	1956	São Tomé and Príncipe	1975
Bosnia and Herzegovina	1992	Jordan	1955	Saudi Arabia	1945
Botswana	1966	Kazakhstan	1992	Senegal	1960
Brazil	1945	Kenya	1963	Seychelles	1976
Brunei Darussalam	1984	Korea, Democratic People's Republic of	1991	Sierra Leone	1961
Bulgaria	1955			Singapore	1965
Burkina Faso	1960	Korea, Republic of	1991	Slovakia[3]	1993
Burundi	1962	Kuwait	1963	Slovenia	1992
Cambodia	1955	Kyrgyzstan	1992	Solomon Islands	1978
Cameroon	1960	Lao People's Democratic Republic	1955	Somalia	1960
Canada	1945			South Africa	1945
Cape Verde	1975	Latvia	1991	Spain	1955
Central African Republic	1960	Lebanon	1945	Sri Lanka	1955
Chad	1960	Lesotho	1966	Sudan	1956
Chile	1945	Liberia	1945	Suriname	1975
China[2]	1945	Libyan Arab Jamahiriya	1955	Swaziland	1968
Colombia	1945	Liechtenstein	1990	Sweden	1946
Comoros	1975	Lithuania	1991	Syrian Arab Republic	1945
Congo	1960	Luxembourg	1945	Tajikistan	1992
Costa Rica	1945	Madagascar	1960	Tanzania	1961
Côte d'Ivoire	1960	Malawi	1964	Thailand	1946
Croatia	1992	Malaysia	1957	The former Yugoslav Republic of Macedonia[4]	1993
Cuba	1945	Maldives	1965		
Cyprus	1960	Mali	1960	Togo	1960
Czech Republic[3]	1993	Malta	1964	Trinidad and Tobago	1962
Denmark	1945	Marshall Islands	1991	Tunisia	1956
Djibouti	1977	Mauritania	1961	Turkey	1945
Dominica	1978	Mauritius	1968	Turkmenistan	1992
Dominican Republic	1945	Mexico	1945	Uganda	1962
Ecuador	1945	Micronesia, Federated States of	1991	Ukraine	1945
Egypt	1945	Moldova, Republic of	1992	United Arab Emirates	1971
El Salvador	1945	Monaco	1993	United Kingdom	1945
Equatorial Guinea	1968	Mongolia	1961	United States	1945
Eritrea	1993	Morocco	1956	Uruguay	1945
Estonia	1991	Mozambique	1975	Uzbekistan	1992
Ethiopia	1945	Myanmar	1948	Vanuatu	1981
Fiji	1970	Namibia	1990	Venezuela	1945
Finland	1955	Nepal	1955	Vietnam	1977
France	1945	Netherlands	1945	Yemen, Republic of	1947
Gabon	1960	New Zealand	1945	Yugoslavia	1945
Gambia	1965	Nicaragua	1945	Zaire	1960
Georgia	1992	Niger	1960	Zambia	1964
		Nigeria	1960	Zimbabwe	1980

1. The U.N. officially came into existence on Oct. 24, 1945. 2. On Oct. 25, 1971, the U.N. voted membership to the People's Republic of China, which replaced the Republic of China (Taiwan) in the world body. 3. Czechoslovakia was an original member of the United Nations from Oct. 24, 1945. As of December 31, 1992 it ceased to exist and the Czech Republic and Slovakia as successor states were admitted January 19, 1993. 4. The General Assembly on April 8, 1993 decided to admit the State provisionally being referred to as "The Former Yugoslav Republic of Macedonia" pending settlement of the difference that has arisen over its name.

Member Countries' Assessments to U.N. Budget, 1996

Country	Total	Country	Total	Country	Total
Afghanistan	$128,557	Greece	4,885,159	Oman	514,227
Albania	128,557	Grenada	128,557	Pakistan	771,341
Algeria	2,056,909	Guatemala	257,113	Palau	128,557
Andorra	128,557	Guinea	128,557	Panama	128,557
Angola	128,557	Guinea-Bissau	128,557	Papua New Guinea	128,557
Antigua and Barbuda	128,557	Guyana	128,557	Paraguay	128,557
Argentina	6,170,728	Haiti	128,557	Peru	771,341
Armenia	707,062	Honduras	128,557	Philippines	771,341
Australia	19,026,411	Hungary	1,799,795	Poland	4,338,793
Austria	11,120,166	Iceland	385,670	Portugal	3,535,313
Azerbaijan	1,510,543	India	3,985,262	Qatar	514,227
Bahamas	257,113	Indonesia	1,799,795	Romania	1,928,352
Bahrain	257,113	Iran, Islamic Republic of	6,010,032	Russian Federation	57,207,789
Bangladesh	128,557	Iraq	1,799,795	Rwanda	128,557
Barbados	128,557	Ireland	2,699,693	St. Kitts and Nevis	128,557
Belarus	3,760,287	Israel	3,438,895	St. Lucia	128,557
Belgium	12,952,100	Italy	66,817,412	St. Vincent & the Grenadines	128,557
Belize	128,557	Jamaica	128,557	Samoa, Western	128,557
Benin	128,557	Japan	198,427,466	San Marino	128,557
Bhutan	128,557	Jordan	128,557	São Tomé and Príncipe	128,557
Bolivia	128,557	Kazakhstan	2,571,136	Saudi Arabia	9,256,092
Bosnia and Herzegovina	160,696	Kenya	128,557	Senegal	128,557
Botswana	128,557	Korea, Democratic People's		Seychelles	128,557
Brazil	20,826,206	Republic of	642,784	Sierra Leone	128,557
Brunei Darussalam	257,113	Korea, Republic of	10,509,521	Singapore	1,799,795
Bulgaria	1,060,594	Kuwait	2,442,580	Slovakia	1,060,594
Burkina Faso	128,557	Kyrgyzstan	417,810	Slovenia	899,898
Burundi	128,557	Lao People's Democratic		Solomon Islands	128,557
Cambodia	128,557	Republic	128,557	Somalia	128,557
Cameroon	128,557	Latvia	1,060,594	South Africa	4,145,958
Canada	39,884,756	Lebanon	128,557	Spain	30,371,551
Cape Verde	128,557	Lesotho	128,557	Sri Lanka	128,557
Central African Republic	128,557	Liberia	128,557	Sudan	128,557
Chad	128,557	Libyan Arab Jamahiriya	2,603,276	Suriname	128,557
Chile	1,028,454	Liechtenstein	128,557	Swaziland	128,557
China	9,448,927	Lithuania	1,092,733	Sweden	15,780,351
Colombia	1,285,568	Luxembourg	899,898	Syrian Arab Republic	642,784
Comoros	128,557	Madagascar	128,557	Tajikistan	257,113
Congo	128,557	Malawi	128,557	Tanzania	128,557
Costa Rica	128,557	Malaysia	1,799,795	Thailand	1,671,239
Côte d'Ivoire	128,557	Maldives	128,557	The Former Yugoslav	
Croatia	1,157,011	Mali	128,557	Republic of Macedonia	128,557
Cuba	674,923	Malta	128,557	Togo	128,557
Cyprus	385,670	Marshall Islands	128,557	Trinidad and Tobago	417,810
Czech Republic	3,342,477	Mauritania	128,557	Tunisia	385,670
Denmark	9,223,952	Mauritius	128,557	Turkey	4,820,881
Djibouti	128,557	Mexico	10,123,850	Turkmenistan	417,810
Dominica	128,557	Micronesia, Federated		Uganda	128,557
Dominican Republic	128,557	States of	128,557	Ukraine	14,655,478
Ecuador	257,113	Moldova, Republic of	1,092,733	United Arab Emirates	2,442,580
Egypt	899,898	Monaco	128,557	United Kingdom	68,327,955
El Salvador	128,557	Mongolia	128,557	United States	321,392,073
Equatorial Guinea	128,557	Morocco	385,670	Uruguay	514,227
Eritrea	128,557	Mozambique	128,557	Uzbekistan	1,767,656
Estonia	546,366	Myanmar	128,557	Vanuatu	128,557
Ethiopia	128,557	Namibia	128,557	Venezuela	4,338,793
Fiji	128,557	Nepal	128,557	Vietnam	128,557
Finland	7,938,384	Netherlands	20,408,396	Yemen	128,557
France	82,372,788	New Zealand	3,085,364	Yugoslavia	1,317,707
Gabon	128,557	Nicaragua	128,557	Zaire	128,557
Gambia	128,557	Niger	128,557	Zambia	128,557
Georgia	1,510,543	Nigeria	1,478,403	Zimbabwe	128,557
Germany	116,247,513	Norway	7,199,182	**TOTAL**	**1,285,696,850**
Ghana	128,557				

Preamble of the United Nations Charter

The Charter of the United Nations was adopted at the San Francisco Conference of 1945. The complete text may be obtained by writing to the United Nations Sales Section, United Nations, New York, N.Y. 10017, and enclosing $1.

We the peoples of the United Nations determined to save succeeding generations from the scourge of war, which twice in our lifetime has brought untold sorrow to mankind, and

To reaffirm faith in fundamental human rights, in the dignity and worth of the human person, in the equal rights of men and women and of nations large and small, and

To establish conditions under which justice and respect for the obligations arising from treaties and other sources of international law can be maintained, and

To promote social progress and better standards of life in larger freedom, and for these ends

To practice tolerance and live together in peace with one another as good neighbors, and

To unite our strength to maintain international peace and security, and

To insure, by the acceptance of principles and the institution of methods, that armed force shall not be used, save in the common interest, and

To employ international machinery for the promotion of the economic and social advancement of all peoples, have resolved to combine our efforts to accomplish these aims.

Accordingly, our respective Governments, through representatives assembled in the city of San Francisco, who have exhibited their full powers found to be in good and due form, have agreed to the present Charter of the United Nations and do hereby establish an international organization to be known as the United Nations.

Principal Organs of the United Nations

Secretariat

This is the directorate on U.N. operations, apart from political decisions. All members contribute to its upkeep. Its headquarters staff of about 4,800 specialists is recruited from member nations on the basis of as wide a geographical distribution as possible. The staff works under the Secretary-General, whom it assists and advises.

Secretaries-General

Boutros Boutros-Ghali, Egypt, Jan. 1, 1992.
Javier Pérez de Cuéllar, Peru, Jan. 1, 1982, to Dec. 31, 1991.
Kurt Waldheim, Austria, Jan. 1, 1972, to Dec. 31, 1981.
U Thant, Burma (Myanmar), Nov. 3, 1961, to Dec. 31, 1971.
Dag Hammarskjöld, Sweden, April 11, 1953, to Sept. 17, 1961.
Trygve Lie, Norway, Feb. 1, 1946, to April 10, 1953.

General Assembly

The General Assembly is the world's forum for discussing matters affecting world peace and security, and for making recommendations concerning them. It has no power of its own to enforce decisions.

The Assembly is composed of the 51 original member nations and those admitted since, a total of 185. Each nation has one vote. On important questions including international peace and security, a two-thirds majority of those present and voting is required. Decisions on other questions are made by a simple majority.

The Assembly's agenda can be as broad as the Charter. It can make recommendations to member nations, the Security Council, or both. Emphasis is given on questions relating to international peace and security brought before it by any member, the Security Council, or nonmembers.

The Assembly also maintains a broad program of international cooperation in economic, social, cultural, educational, and health fields, and for assisting in human rights and freedoms.

Among other duties, the Assembly has functions relating to the trusteeship system, and considers and approves the U.N. Budget. Every member contributes to operating expenses according to its means.

Security Council

The Security Council is the primary instrument for establishing and maintaining international peace. Its main purpose is to prevent war by settling disputes between nations.

Under the Charter, the Council is permitted to dispatch a U.N. force to stop aggression. All member nations undertake to make available armed forces, assistance, and facilities to maintain international peace and security.

Any member may bring a dispute before the Security Council or the General Assembly. Any nonmember may do so if it accepts the charter obligations of pacific settlement.

The Security Council has 15 members. There are five permanent members: the United States, the Russian Federation, Britain, France, and China; and 10 temporary members elected by the General Assembly for two-year terms, from five different regions of the world.

Voting on procedural matters requires a nine-vote majority to carry. However, on questions of substance, the vote of each of the five permanent members is required.

The ten non-permanent members of the Council in 1996 are Botswana (1996), Chile (1997), Egypt (1997), Germany (1996), Guinea-Bissau (1997), Honduras (1996), Indonesia (1996), Italy (1996), Poland (1997), and Republic of Korea (1997).

Economic and Social Council

This council is composed of 54 members elected by the General Assembly to 3-year terms. It works closely with the General Assembly as a link with groups formed within the U.N. to help peoples in such fields as education, health, and human rights. It insures that there is no overlapping and sets up commissions to deal with economic conditions and collect facts and figures on conditions over the world. It issues studies and reports and may make recommendations to the Assembly and specialized agencies.

Functional Commissions

Commission on Population and Development; Commission for Social Development; Commission on Human Rights; Commission on the Status of Women; Statistical Commission; Commission on Narcotic Drugs; Commission on Sustainable Development; Commission on Crime Prevention and Criminal Justice; Commission on Science and Technology for Development.

Regional Commissions

Economic Commission for Europe (ECE); Economic and Social Commission for Asia and the Pacific (ESCAP); Economic Commission for Latin America and the Caribbean (ECLAC); Economic Commission for Africa (ECA); Economic and Social Commission for Western Asia (ESCWA).

Trusteeship Council

The Trusteeship Council has five members: China, France, Russian Federation, United Kingdom, and the United States. With the independence of Palau, the last remaining United Nations trust territory, the Council formally suspended operation on November 1, 1994. By a resolution adopted on that day, the Council amended its rules of procedure to drop the obligation to meet annually and agreed to meet as occasion required—by its decision or the decision of its President, or at the request of a majority of its members or the General Assembly or the Security Council.

International Court of Justice

The International Court of Justice sits at The Hague, the Netherlands. Its 15-judge bench was established to hear disputes among states, which must agree to accept its verdicts. Its judges, charged with administering justice under international law, deal with cases ranging from disputes over territory to those concerning rights of passage.

Following are the members of the Court and the years in which their terms expire on Feb. 5:

President: Mohammed Bedjaoui, Algeria (1997 as president; 2000 term)
Vice President: Stephen M. Schwebel (1997)
Luigi Ferrari Bravo, Italy (1997)
Mohamed Shahabuddeen, Guyana (1997)
Stephen Schwebel, United States (1997)
Mohammed Bedjaoui, Algeria (2000)
Vladlen Vereshchetin, Russian Federation (1997)
Gilbert Guillaume, France (2000)
Gonzalo Parra-Aranguren, Venezuela (2000)
Raymond Ranjeva, Madagascar (2000)
Christopher Gregory Weeramantry, Sri Lanka (2000)
Roslyn Higgins, United Kingdom (2000)
Carl-August Fleischauer, Germany (2003)
Géza Herczegh, Hungary (2003)
Abdul G. Koroma, Sierra Leone (2003)
Shigeru Oda, Japan (2003)
Jiuyong Shi, China (2003)

Agencies of the United Nations

INTL. ATOMIC ENERGY AGENCY (IAEA)

Established: Statute for IAEA, approved on Oct. 26, 1956, at a conference held at U.N. Headquarters, New York, came into force on July 29, 1957. The Agency is under the aegis of the U.N., but unlike the following, it is not a specialized agency.

Purpose: To promote the peaceful uses of atomic energy; to ensure that assistance provided by it or at its request or under its supervision or control is not used in such a way as to further any military purpose.

Headquarters: Vienna International Center, P.O. Box 100, Wagramer Strasse 5, A-1400 Vienna, Austria

FOOD AND AGRICULTURE ORGANIZATION OF THE UNITED NATIONS (FAO)

Established: October 16, 1945, when constitution became effective.

Purpose: To raise nutrition levels and living standards; to secure improvements in production and distribution of food and agricultural products.

Headquarters: Via delle Terme di Caracalla, 00100, Rome, Italy.

WORLD TRADE ORGANIZATION (WTO)

Established: Jan. 1, 1995.

Purpose: The World Trade Organization (WTO) replaced the General Agreement on Tariffs and Trade (GATT) as the major entity overseeing international trade. Unlike GATT, which was a treaty serviced by an ad hoc Secretariat, the WTO is a full-fledged organization in its own right.

Headquarters: Geneva, Switzerland.

INTERNATIONAL BANK FOR RECONSTRUCTION AND DEVELOPMENT (IBRD) (WORLD BANK)

Established: December 27, 1945, when Articles of Agreement drawn up at Bretton Woods Conference in July 1944 came into force. Began operations on June 25, 1946.

Purpose: To assist in reconstruction and development of economies of members by facilitating capital investment and by making loans to governments and furnishing technical advice.

Headquarters: 1818 H St., N.W., Washington, D.C. 20433.

INTL. CIVIL AVIATION ORGANIZATION (ICAO)

Established: April 4, 1947, after working as a provisional organization since June 1945.

Purpose: To study problems of international civil aviation; to establish international standards and regulations; to promote safety measures, uniform regulations for operation, simpler procedures at international borders, and the use of new technical methods and equipment. It has evolved standards for meteorological services, traffic control, communications, radio beacons and ranges, search and rescue organization, and other facilities. It has brought about much simplification of customs, immigration, and public health regulations as they apply to international air transport. It drafts international air law conventions, and is concerned with economic aspects of air travel.

Headquarters: 1000 Sherbrooke St. West, Montreal, Quebec, H3A 2R2, Canada.

INTL. DEVELOPMENT ASSOCIATION (IDA)

Established: Sept. 24, 1960. An affiliate of the World Bank, IDA has the same officers and staff as the Bank.

Purpose: To further economic development of its members by providing finance on terms which bear less heavily on balance of payments of members than those of conventional loans.

Headquarters: 1818 H St., N.W., Washington, D.C. 20433.

INTERNATIONAL FINANCE CORPORATION (IFC)

Established: Charter of IFC came into force on July 20, 1956. Although IFC is affiliated with the World Bank, it is a separate legal entity, and its funds are entirely separate from those of the Bank. However, membership in the Corporation is open only to Bank members.

Purpose: To further economic development by encouraging the growth of productive private enterprise in its member countries, particularly in the less developed areas; to invest in productive private enterprises in association with private investors, without government guarantee of repayment where sufficient private capital is not available on reasonable terms; to serve as a clearing house to bring together investment opportunities, private capital (both foreign and domestic), and experienced management.

Headquarters: 1818 H St., N.W., Washington, D.C. 20433.

INTERNATIONAL FUND FOR AGRICULTURAL DEVELOPMENT (IFAD)

Established: June 18, 1976. Began operations in December 1977.

Purpose: To mobilize additional funds for agricultural and rural development in developing countries through projects and programs directly benefiting the poorest rural populations.

Headquarters: 107 Via del Serafico, 00142, Rome, Italy.

INTERNATIONAL LABOR ORGANIZATION (ILO)

Established: April 11, 1919, when constitution was adopted as Part XIII of Treaty of Versailles. Became specialized agency of U.N. in 1946.

Purpose: To contribute to establishment of lasting peace by promoting social justice; to improve labor conditions and living standards through international action; to promote economic and social stability. The U.S. withdrew from the ILO in 1977 and resumed membership in 1980.

Headquarters: 4, Route des Morillons, CH-1211 Geneva 22, Switzerland.

INTERNATIONAL MARITIME ORGANIZATION (IMO)

Established: March 17, 1958.

Purpose: To give advisory and consultative help to promote international cooperation in maritime navigation and to encourage the highest standards of safety and navigation. Its aim is to bring about a uniform system of measuring ship tonnage; systems now vary widely in different parts of the world. Other activities include cooperation with other U.N. agencies on matters affecting the maritime field.

Headquarters: 4 Albert Embankment, London SE 1 7SR England.

INTERNATIONAL MONETARY FUND (IMF)

Established: Dec. 27, 1945, when Articles of Agreement drawn up at Bretton Woods Conference in July 1944 came into force. Fund began operations on March 1, 1947.

Purpose: To promote international monetary cooperation and expansion of international trade; to promote exchange stability; to assist in establishment of multilateral system of payments in respect of currency transactions between members.

Headquarters: 700 19th St., N.W., Washington, D.C. 20431.

INTERNATIONAL TELECOMMUNICATION UNION (ITU)

Established: 1865. Became specialized agency of U.N. in 1947.

Purpose: To extend technical assistance to help members keep up with present day telecommunication needs; to standardize communications equipment and procedures; to lower costs. It also works for orderly sharing of radio frequencies and makes studies and recommendations to benefit its members.

Headquarters: Place des Nations, 1211 Geneva 20, Switzerland.

UNITED NATIONS EDUCATIONAL, SCIENTIFIC, AND CULTURAL ORGANIZATION (UNESCO)

Established: Nov. 4, 1946, when twentieth signatory to constitution deposited instrument of acceptance with government of U.K.

Purpose: To promote collaboration among nations through education, science, and culture in order to further justice, rule of law, and human rights and freedoms without distinction of race, sex, language, or religion.

Headquarters: UNESCO House. 7, Place de Fontenoy, 75007 Paris, France.

UNITED NATIONS INDUSTRIAL DEVELOPMENT ORGANIZATION (UNIDO)

Established: Nov. 17, 1966. Became specialized agency of the U.N. in 1986.

Purpose: To promote and accelerate the industrialization of the developing countries.

Headquarters: UNIDO, Vienna International Centre, P.O. Box 300, A-1400 Vienna, Austria.

UNIVERSAL POSTAL UNION (UPU)

Established: Oct. 9, 1874. Became specialized agency of U.N. in 1947.

Purpose: To facilitate reciprocal exchange of correspondence by uniform procedures by all UPU members; to help governments modernize and speed up mailing procedures.

Headquarters: Weltpoststrasse 4, Berne, Switzerland.

WORLD HEALTH ORGANIZATION (WHO)

Established: April 7, 1948, when 26 members of the U.N. had accepted its constitution, adopted July 22, 1946, by the International Health Conference in New York City.

Purpose: To aid attainment by all people of highest possible level of health.

Headquarters: 20 Avenue Appia, 1211 Geneva 27, Switzerland.

WORLD INTELLECTUAL PROPERTY ORGANIZATION (WIPO)

Established: April 26, 1970, when its Convention came into force. Originated as International Bureau of Paris Union (1883) and Berne Union (1886), later succeeded by United International Bureau for the Protection of Intellectual Property (BIRPI). Became a specialized agency of the U.N. in December 1974.

Purpose: To promote legal protection of intellectual property, including artistic and scientific works, artistic performances, sound recordings, broadcasts, inventions, trademarks, industrial designs, and commercial names.

Headquarters: 34 Chemin des Colombettes, CH-1211 Geneva 20, Switzerland.

WORLD METEOROLOGICAL ORGANIZATION (WMO)

Established: March 23, 1950, succeeding the International Meteorological Organization, a non-governmental organization founded in 1873.

Purpose: To promote international exchange of weather reports and maximum standardization of observations; to help developing countries establish weather services for their own economic needs; to fill gaps in observation stations; to promote meterological investigations affecting jet aircraft, satellites, energy resources, etc.

Headquarters: 41, Avenue Giuseppe-Motta, CH-1211 Geneva 2, Switzerland.

The Seven Wonders of the World

(Not all classical writers list the same items as the Seven Wonders, but most of them agree on the following.)

The Pyramids of Egypt. A group of three pyramids, *Khufu, Khafra,* and *Menkaura* at Giza, outside modern Cairo, is often called the first wonder of the world. The largest pyramid, built by Khufu (Cheops), a king of the fourth Dynasty, had an original estimated height of 482 ft (now approximately 450 ft). The base has sides 755 ft long. It contains 2,300,000 blocks; the average weight of each is 2.5 tons. Estimated date of construction is 2800 B.C. Of all the Seven Wonders, the pyramids alone survive.

Hanging Gardens of Babylon. Often listed as the second wonder, these gardens were supposedly built by Nebuchadnezzar about 600 B.C. to please his queen, Amuhia. They are also associated with the mythical Assyrian Queen, Semiramis. Archeologists surmise that the gardens were laid out atop a vaulted building, with provisions for raising water. The terraces were said to rise from 75 to 300 ft.

The Walls of Babylon, also built by Nebuchadnezzar, are sometimes referred to as the second (or the seventh) wonder instead of the Hanging Gardens.

Statue of Zeus (Jupiter) at Olympia. The work of Phidias (5th century B.C.), this colossal figure in gold and ivory was reputedly 40 ft high. All trace of it is lost, except for reproductions on coins.

Temple of Artemis (Diana) at Ephesus. A beautiful structure, begun about 350 B.C. in honor of a non-Hellenic goddess who later became identified with the Greek goddess of the same name. The temple, with Ionic columns 60 ft high, was destroyed by invading Goths in A.D. 262.

Mausoleum at Halicarnassus. This famous monument was erected by Queen Artemisia in memory of her husband, King Mausolus of Caria in Asia Minor, who died in 353 B.C. Some remains of the structure are in the British Museum. This shrine is the source of the modern word "mausoleum."

Colossus at Rhodes. This bronze statue of Helios (Apollo), about 105 ft high, was the work of the sculptor Chares, who reputedly labored for 12 years before completing it in 280 B.C. It was destroyed during an earthquake in 224 B.C.

Pharos of Alexandria. The seventh wonder was the Pharos (lighthouse) of Alexandria, built by Sostratus of Cnidus during the 3rd century B.C. on the island of Pharos off the coast of Egypt. It was destroyed by an earthquake in the 13th century.

Famous Structures

Ancient

The *Great Sphinx of Egypt,* one of the wonders of ancient Egyptian architecture, adjoins the pyramids of Giza and has a length of 240 ft. It was built in the 4th dynasty.

Other Egyptian buildings of note include the *Temples of Karnak* and *Edfu* and the *Tombs at Beni Hassan.*

The *Parthenon of Greece,* built on the Acropolis in Athens, was the chief temple to the goddess Athena. It was believed to have been completed by 438 B.C. The present temple remained intact until the 5th century A.D. Today, though the Parthenon is in ruins, its majestic proportions are still discernible.

Other great structures of ancient Greece were the *Temples at Paestum* (about 540 and 420 B.C.); the *Temple of Poseidon* (about 460 B.C.); the *Temple of Apollo* at Corinth (about 540 B.C.); the *Temple of Apollo* at Bassae (about 450–420 B.C.); the famous *Erechtheum* atop the Acropolis (about 421–405 B.C.); the *Temple of Athena Niké* at Athens (about 426 B.C.); the *Olympieum* at Athens (174 B.C.–A.D. 131); the *Athenian Treasury* at Delphi (about 515 B.C.); the *Propylaea* of the Acropolis at Athens (437–432 B.C.); the *Theater of Dionysus* at Athens (about 350–325 B.C.); the *House of Cleopatra* at Delos (138 B.C.) and the *Theater* at Epidaurus (about 325 B.C.).

The *Colosseum (Flavian Amphitheater) of Rome,* the largest and most famous of the Roman amphitheaters, was opened for use A.D. 80. Elliptical in shape, it consisted of three stories and an upper gallery, rebuilt in stone in its present form in the third century A.D. Its seats rise in tiers, which in turn are buttressed by concrete vaults and stone piers. It could seat between 40,000 and 50,000 spectators. It was principally used for gladiatorial combat.

The *Pantheon* at Rome, begun by Agrippa in 27 B.C. as a temple, was rebuilt in its present circular form by Hadrian (A.D. 110–25). Literally the Pantheon was intended as a temple of "all the gods." It is remarkable for its perfect preservation today, and it has served continuously for 20 centuries as a place of worship.

Famous Roman arches include the *Arch of Constantine* (about A.D. 315) and the *Arch of Titus* (about A.D. 80).

Later European

St. Mark's Cathedral in Venice (1063–67), one of the great examples of Byzantine architecture, was begun in the 9th century. Partly destroyed by fire in 976, it was later rebuilt as a Byzantine edifice.

Other famous Byzantine examples of architecture are *St. Sophia* in Istanbul (A.D. 532–37); *San Vitale* in Ravenna (542); *St. Paul's Outside the Walls,* Rome (5th century); *Assumption Cathedral* in the Kremlin, Moscow (begun in 1475); and *St. Lorenzo Outside the Walls,* Rome, begun in 588.

The *Cathedral Group* at Pisa (1067–1173), one of the most celebrated groups of structures built in Romanesque-style, consists of the cathedral, the cathedral's baptistery, and the *Leaning Tower.* This trio forms a group by itself in the northwest corner of the city. The cathedral and baptistery are built in varicolored marble. The campanile *(Leaning Tower)* is 179 ft. high and leans more than 16 ft out of the perpendicular. There is little reason to believe that the architects intended to have the tower lean.

Other examples of Romanesque architecture include the *Vézelay Abbey* in France (1130); the *Church of Notre-Dame-du-Port* at Clermont-Ferrand in France (1100); the *Church of San Zeno* (begun in 1138) at Verona, and *Durham Cathedral* in England.

The *Alhambra* (1248–1354), located in Granada, Spain, is universally esteemed as one of the greatest masterpieces of Moslem architecture. Designed as a palace and fortress for the Moorish monarchs of Granada, it is surrounded by a heavily fortified wall more than a mile in perimeter. The location of the Alhambra in the Sierra Nevada provides a magnificent setting for this jewel of Moorish Spain.

The *Tower of London* is a group of buildings and towers covering 13 acres along the north bank of the Thames. The central *White Tower*, begun in 1078 during the reign of William the Conqueror, was originally a fortress and royal residence, but was later used as a prison. The *Bloody Tower* is associated with Anne Boleyn and other notables.

Westminster Abbey, in London, was begun in 1045 and completed in 1065. It was rebuilt and enlarged in 1245–50.

Notre-Dame de Paris (begun in 1163), one of the great examples of Gothic architecture, is a twin-towered church with a steeple over the crossing and immense flying buttresses supporting the masonry at the rear of the church.

Other famous Gothic structures are *Chartres Cathedral* (12th century); *Sainte Chapelle*, Paris (1246–48); *Laon Cathedral*, France (1160–1205); *Reims Cathedral* (about 1210–50; rebuilt after its almost complete destruction in World War I); *Rouen Cathedral* (13th–16th centuries); *Amiens Cathedral* (1218–69); *Beauvais Cathedral* (begun 1247); *Salisbury Cathedral* (1220–60); *York Minster* or the *Cathedral of St. Peter* (begun in the 7th century); *Milan Cathedral* (begun 1386); and *Cologne Cathedral* (13th–19th centuries; badly damaged in World War II).

The Duomo (cathedral) in Florence was founded in 1298, completed by Brunelleschi and consecrated in 1436. The oval-shaped dome dominates the entire structure.

The *Vatican* is a group of buildings in Rome comprising the official residence of the Pope. The *Basilica of St. Peter*, the largest church in the Christian world, was begun in 1450. The *Sistine Chapel*, begun in 1473, is noted for the art masterpieces of Michelangelo, Botticelli, and others. The *Basilica of the Savior* (known as *St. John Lateran*) is the first-ranking Catholic Church in the world, for it is the cathedral of the Pope.

Other examples of Renaissance architecture are the *Palazzo Riccardi*, the *Palazzo Pitti* and the *Palazzo Strozzi* in Florence; the *Farnese Palace* in Rome; *Palazzo Grimani* (completed about 1550) in Venice; the *Escorial* (1563–93) near Madrid; the *Town Hall* of Seville (1527–32); the *Louvre*, Paris; the *Château* at Blois, France; *St. Paul's Cathedral*, London (1675–1710); badly damaged in World War II); the *École Militaire*, Paris (1752); the *Pazzi Chapel*, Florence, designed by Brunelleschi (1429); the Palace of *Fontainebleau* and the *Château de Chambord* in France.

The *Palace of Versailles*, containing the famous Hall of Mirrors, was built during the reign of Louis XIV and served as the royal palace until 1793.

Outstanding European buildings of the 18th and 19th centuries are the *Superga* at Turin, the *Hôtel-Dieu* in Lyons, the *Belvedere Palace* at Vienna, the *Royal Palace* of Stockholm, the *Opera House* of Paris (1863–75); the *Bank of England*, the *British Museum*, the *University of London*, and the *Houses of Parliament*, all in London; the *Panthéon*, the *Church*

of the *Madeleine*, the *Bourse*, and the *Palais de Justice* in Paris.

The *Eiffel Tower*, in Paris, was built for the Exposition of 1889 by Alexandre Eiffel. It is 984 ft high (1,056 ft, including the television tower).

Asiatic and African

The *Taj Mahal* (1632–50), at Agra, India, built by Shah Jahan as a tomb for his wife, is considered by some as the most perfect example of the Mogul style and by others as the most beautiful building in the world. Four slim white minarets flank the building, which is topped by a white dome; the entire structure is of marble.

Other examples of Indian architecture are the temples at Benares and Tanjore.

Among famed Moslem edifices are the *Dome of the Rock* or *Mosque of Omar*, Jerusalem (A.D. 691); the *Citadel* (1166), and the *Tombs of the Mamelukes* (15th century), in Cairo; the *Tomb of Humayun* in Delhi; the *Blue Mosque* (1468) at Tabriz, and the *Tamerlane Mausoleum* at Samarkand.

Angkor Wat, outside the city of Angkor Thom, Cambodia, is one of the most beautiful examples of Cambodian or Khmer architecture. The sanctuary was built during the 12th century.

Great Wall of China (228 B.C.?), designed specifically as a defense against nomadic tribes, has large watch towers that could be called buildings. It was erected by Emperor Ch'in Shih Huang Ti and is 1,400 miles long. Built mainly of earth and stone, it varies in height between 18 and 30 ft.

Typical of Chinese architecture are the pagodas or temple towers. Among some of the better-known pagodas are the *Great Pagoda of the Wild Geese* at Sian (founded in 652); *Nan t'a* (11th century) at Fang Shan; the *Pagoda of Sung Yueh Ssu* (A.D. 523) at Sung Shan, Honan.

Other well-known Chinese buildings are the *Drum Tower* (1273), the *Three Great Halls* in the Purple Forbidden City (1627), *Buddha's Perfume Tower* (19th century), the *Porcelain Pagoda*, and the *Summer Palace*, all at Beijing.

United States

Rockefeller Center, in New York City, extends from 5th Ave. to the Avenue of the Americas between 48th and 52nd Sts. (and halfway to 7th Ave. between 47th and 51st Sts.). It occupies more than 22 acres and has 19 buildings.

The Cathedral of St. John the Divine, at 112th St. and Amsterdam Ave. in New York City, was begun in 1892 and is now in the final stages of completion. When completed, it will be the largest cathedral in the world: 601 ft long, 146 ft wide at the nave, 320 ft wide at the transept. The east end is designed in Romanesque-Byzantine style, and the nave and west end are Gothic.

St. Patrick's Cathedral, at Fifth Ave. and 50th St. in New York City, has a seating capacity of 2,500. The nave was opened in 1877, and the cathedral was dedicated in 1879.

Louisiana Superdome, in New Orleans, is the largest arena in the history of mankind. The main area can accommodate up to 95,000 people. It is the world's largest steel-constructed room. Unobstructed by posts, it covers 13 acres and reaches 27 stories at its peak.

World Trade Center, in New York City, was dedicated in 1973. Its twin towers are 110 stories high (1,350 ft), and the complex contains over 9 million sq ft of office space. A restaurant is on the 107th floor of the North Tower.

Notable Modern Bridges

Name	Location	Length of main span		Year completed
		ft	m	
Suspension	**United States**			
Verrazano-Narrows	Lower New York Bay	4,260	1,298	1964
Golden Gate	San Francisco Bay	4,200	1,280	1937
Mackinac Straits	Michigan	3,800	1,158	1957
George Washington	Hudson River at New York City	3,500	1,067	1931
Tacoma Narrows II	Puget Sound at Tacoma, Wash.	2,800	853	1950
San Francisco-Oakland Bay[1]	San Francisco Bay	2,310	704	1936
Bronx-Whitestone	East River, New York City	2,300	701	1939
Delaware Memorial (twin)	Delaware River near Wilmington, Del.	2,150	655	1951, 1968
Seaway Skyway	St. Lawrence River at Ogdensburg, N.Y.	2,150	655	1960
Walt Whitman	Delaware River at Philadelphia	2,000	610	1957
Ambassador International	Detroit River at Detroit	1,850	564	1929
Throgs Neck	East River, New York City	1,800	549	1961
Benjamin Franklin	Delaware River at Philadelphia	1,750	533	1926
Bear Mountain	Hudson River at Peekskill, N.Y.	1,632	497	1924
Wm. Preston Lane, Jr., Memorial (twin)	Near Annapolis, Md.	1,600	488	1952, 1973
Williamsburg	East River, New York City	1,600	488	1903
Newport	Narragansett Bay at Newport, R.I.	1,600	488	1969
Chesapeake Bay	Sandy Point, Md.	1,600	488	1952
Brooklyn	East River, New York City	1,595	486	1883
	International			
Akashi Kaikyo	Japan	6,529	1,990	1998
Storebelt	Denmark	5,328	1,624	1997
Humber	Hull, Britain	4,626	1,410	1981
Tsing Ma Bridge	Hong Kong	4,518	1.377	1997
Minami Bisan–Seto	Japan	3,609	1,100	1988
Second Bosporus	Istanbul, Turkey	3,576	1,090	1988
First Bosporus	Istanbul	3,524	1,074	1973
Ponte 25 de Abril	Tagus River at Lisbon	3,323	1,013	1966
Forth Road	Queensferry, Scotland	3,300	1,006	1964
Kita Bisan–Seto	Japan	3,248	990	1988
Severn	Severn River at Beachley, England	3,240	988	1966
Shimotsui Straits	Japan	3,084	940	1988
Ohnaruto	Japan	2,874	876	1988
Cantilever	**United States**			
Commodore John Barry	Chester, Pa.	1,644	501	1974
Greater New Orleans[1]	Mississippi River, Louisiana	1,576	480	1958
Transbay Bridge	San Francisco Bay	1,400	427	1936
Baton Rouge	Mississippi River, Louisiana	1,235	376	1968
Tappan Zee	Hudson River at Tarrytown, N.Y.	1,212	369	1955
Longview	Columbia River at Longview, Wash.	1,200	366	1930
Patapsco River	Baltimore Outer Harbor Crossing	1,200	366	1976
Queensboro	East River, New York City	1,182	360	1909
	International			
Quebec Railway	St. Lawrence River at Quebec, Canada	1,800	549	1917
Forth Railway[1]	Queensferry, Scotland	1,710	521	1890
Minato Ohashi	Osaka, Japan	1,673	510	1974
Howrah	Hooghly River at Calcutta	1,500	457	1943
Steel Arch	**United States**			
New River Gorge	Fayetteville, W. Va.	1,700	518	1977
Bayonne	Kill Van Kull at Bayonne, N.J.	1,675	510	1931
Fremont	Portland, Ore.	1,255	383	1973
	International			
Sydney Harbor	Sydney, Australia	1,670	509	1932
Zdákov	Vltava River, Czech Republic	1,244	380	1967
Port Mann	Fraser River at Vancouver, British Columbia	1,200	366	1964
Thatcher Ferry	Panama Canal, Panama	1,128	344	1962
Laviolette	St. Lawrence River, Trois Rivieres, Quebec	1,100	335	1967
Runcorn-Widnes	Mersey River, England	1,082	330	1961
Birchenough	Sabi River at Fort Victoria, Zimbabwe	1,080	329	1935

Name	Location	Length of main span ft	Length of main span m	Year completed
Cable-Stayed	**United States**			
Dame Point	Jacksonville, Florida	1,300	396	1988
Houston Ship Channel	Baytown, Texas	1,250	381	1995
Hale Boggs Memorial	Luling, Louisiana	1,222	373	1983
Sunshine Skyway	Tampa, Florida	1,200	366	1987
	International			
Tatara	Ehime, Japan	2,920	890	1999
Ponte de Normandie	Le Havre, France	2,808	856	1994
Yang Pu	Shanghai, China	1,975	602	1993
Skarnsundet Bridge	near Trondheim, Norway	1,739	530	1991
Ikuchi	Honshu-Shikoku, Japan	1,608	490	1991
Alex Fraser	Vancouver, B.C., Canada	1,525	465	1986
Yokohama-ko-odan	Kanagawa, Japan	1,509	460	1989
Second Hooghly	Calcutta, India	1,500	457	1992
Second Severn Crossing	Severn River, England	1,496	456	1994
Dartford	Thames River, Dartford, England	1,476	450	1992
Dao Kanong	Chao Phraya River, Bangkok, Thailand	1,476	450	1987
Barrio de Luna	Cordillera, Spain	1,444	440	1983
Helgeland	Sandnessjoen, Nordland, Norway	1,394	425	1991
Continuous Truss	**United States**			
Central Bridge	Ohio River, Newport, Ky.	1,849	564	1995
Mark Clark Expressway I-526	Cooper River, at Charleston, S.C.	1,600	487	1992
Astoria	Columbia River at Astoria, Oregon	1,232	376	1966
Croton Reservoir	Croton, N.Y.	1,052	321	1970
Ravenswood	Ohio River, Ravenswood, W. Va.	902	275	1981
Dubuque	Mississippi River at Dubuque, Iowa	845	258	1943
Braga Memorial	Taunton River at Somerset, Mass.	840	256	1966
	International			
Oshima	Oshima Island, Japan	1,066	325	1976
Tenmon	Kumamoto, Japan	984	300	1966
Kuronoseto	Nagashima-Kyushu, Japan	984	300	1974
Graf Spee	Germany	839	256	1936
Concrete Arch	**United States**			
Natchez Trace Pkwy.	Franklin, Tenn.	582	177	1994
Westinghouse	Pittsburgh, Pa.	460	140	1931
Jack's Run	Pittsburgh, Pa.	400	120	1930
Cappelen	Minneapolis, Minn.	400	120	1923
	International			
Krk	Krk, Croatia	1,280	390	1979
Gladesville	Parramatta River at Sydney, Australia	1,000	305	1964
Amizade	Paraná River at Foz do Iguassu, Brazil	951	290	1964
Arrábida	Porto, Portugal	886	270	1963
Sandö	Angerman River at Kramfors, Sweden	866	264	1943
Fiumarella	Catanzaro, Italy	758	231	1961
Zaporozhe	Old Dnepr River, Ukraine	748	228	1952
Segmental Construction	**United States**			
Jesse H. Jones Memorial	Houston Ship Channel, Texas	750	228	1982

1. Twin span.

World's Highest Dams

Name	River, Country or State	Structural height feet	Structural height meters	Gross reservoir capacity thousands of acre feet	Gross reservoir capacity millions of cubic meters	Year completed
Rogun	Vakhsh, Tajikistan	1099	335	9,404	11,600	1985
Nurek	Vakhsh, Tajikistan	984	300	8,512	10,500	1980
Grande Dixence	Dixence, Switzerland	935	285	324	400	1962
Inguri	Inguri, Georgia	892	272	801	1,100	1984
Chicoasén	Grijalva, Mexico	869	265	1,346	1,660	1981
Vaiont	Vaiont, Italy	869	265	137	169	1961
Tehri	Bhagirathi, India	856	261	2,869	3,540	UC
Kinshau	Tons, India	830	253	1,946	2,400	1985

Name	River, Country or State	Structural height feet	Structural height meters	Gross reservoir capacity thousands of acre feet	Gross reservoir capacity millions of cubic meters	Year completed
Guavio	Orinoco, Colombia	820	250	811	1,000	1989
Mica	Columbia, Canada	794	242	20,000	24,670	1972
Sayano-Shushensk	Yenisei, Russia	794	242	25,353	31,300	1980
Mihoesti	Aries, Romania	794	242	5	6	1983
Chivor	Batá, Colombia	778	237	661	815	1975
Mauvoisin	Drance de Bagnes, Switzerland	777	237	146	180	1957
Oroville	Feather, California	770	235	3,538	4,299	1968
Chirkey	Sulak, Ukraine	764	233	2,252	2,780	1977
Bhakra	Sutlej, India	741	226	8,002	9,870	1963
El Cajón	Humuya, Honduras	741	226	4,580	5,650	1984
Hoover	Colorado, Arizona/Nevada	726	221	28,500	35,154	1936
Contra	Verzasca, Switzerland	722	220	70	86	1965
Dabaklamm	Dorferbach, Austria	722	220	191	235	UC
Mratinje	Piva, Herzegovina	722	220	713	880	1973
Dworshak	N. Fk. Clearwater, Idaho	717	219	3,453	4,259	1974
Glen Canyon	Colorado, Arizona	710	216	27,000	33,304	1964
Toktogul	Naryn, Kyrgyzstan	705	215	15,800	19,500	1978
Daniel Johnson	Manicouagan, Canada	703	214	115,000	141,852	1968
San Roque	Agno, Philippines	689	210	803	990	UC
Luzzone	Brenno di Luzzone, Switzerland	682	208	71	87	1963
Keban	Firat, Turkey	679	207	25,110	31,000	1974
Dez	Dez, Abi, Iran	666	203	2,707	3,340	1963
Almendra	Tormes, Spain	662	202	2,148	2,649	1970
Kölnbrein	Malta, Austria	656	200	166	205	1977
Kärün	Karun, Iran	656	200	2,351	2,900	1976
Altinkaya	Kizil Irmak, Turkey	640	195	4,672	5,763	1986
New Bullards Bar	No. Yuba, California	637	194	960	1,184	1968
Lakhwar	Yamuna, India	630	192	470	580	1985
New Melones	Stanislaus, California	625	191	2,400	2,960	1979
Itaipu	Paraná, Brazil/Paraguay	623	190	23,510	29,000	1982
Kurobe 4	Kurobe, Japan	610	186	162	199	1964
Swift	Lewis, Washington	610	186	756	932	1958
Mossyrock	Cowlitz, Washington	607	185	1,300	1,603	1968
Oymopinar	Manavgat, Turkey	607	185	251	310	1983
Atatürk	Firat, Turkey	604	184	39,482	48,700	1990
Shasta	Sacramento, California	602	183	4,550	5,612	1945
Bennett WAC	Peace, Canada	600	183	57,006	70,309	1967
Karakaya	Firat, Turkey	591	180	7,767	9,580	1986
Tignes	Isère, France	591	180	186	230	1952
Amir Kabir (Karad)	Karadj, Iran	591	180	166	205	1962
Tachien	Tachia, Taiwan	591	180	188	232	1974
Dartmouth	Mitta-Mitta, Australia	591	180	3,243	4,000	1978
Özköy	Gediz, Turkey	591	180	762	940	1983
Emosson	Barberine, Switzerland	590	180	184	225	1974
Zillergründl	Ziller, Austria	590	180	73	90	1986
Los Leones	Los Leones, Chile	587	179	86	106	1986
New Don Pedro	Tuolumne, California	585	178	2,030	2,504	1971
Alpa-Gera	Cormor, Italy	584	178	53	65	1965
Kopperston Tailings 3	Jones Branch, West Virginia	580	177	—	—	1963
Takase	Takase, Japan	577	176	62	76	1979
Nader Shah	Marun, Iran	574	175	1,313	1,620	1978
Hasan Ugurlu	Yesil Irmak, Turkey	574	175	874	1,078	1980
Pauti-Mazar	Mazar, Ecuador	540	165	405	500	1984
Hungry Horse	S.Fk., Flathead, Montana	564	172	3,470	4,280	1953
Longyangxia	Huanghe, China	564	172	20,025	24,700	1983
Cabora Bassa	Zambezi, Mozambique	561	171	51,075	63,000	1974
Maqarin	Yarmuk, Jordan	561	171	259	320	1987
Amaluza	Paute, Ecuador	558	170	81	100	1982
Idikki	Periyar, India	554	169	1,618	1,996	1974
Charvak	Chirchik, Uzbekistan	552	168	1,620	2,000	1970
Gura Apelor Retezat	Riul Mare, Romania	552	168	182	225	1980
Grand Coulee	Columbia, Washington	550	168	9,390	11,582	1942
Boruca	Terraba, Costa Rica	548	167	12,128	14,960	UC
Vidraru	Arges, Romania	545	166	380	465	1965
Kremasta (King Paul)	Achelöus, Greece	541	165	3,850	4,750	1965

NOTE: UC = under construction. *Source:* Department of the Interior, Bureau of Reclamation and *International Water Power and Dam Construction.*

World's Largest Dams

| Dam | Location | Volume (thousands) | | Year completed |
		Cubic meters	Cubic yards	
Pati (Chapetón)	Argentina	200,000	261,590	UC
Tarbela	Pakistan	121,720	159,203	1976
Fort Peck	Montana	96,049	125,628	1940
Atatürk	Turkey	84,500	110,522	1990
Yacyretá-Apipe	Paraguay/Argentina	81,000	105,944	UC
Guri (Raul Leoni)	Venezuela	78,000	102,014	1986
Rogun	Tajikistan	75,500	98,750	1985
Oahe	South Dakota	70,339	92,000	1963
Mangĺa	Pakistan	65,651	85,872	1967
Gardiner	Canada	65,440	85,592	1968
Afsluitdijk	Netherlands	63,400	82,927	1932
Oroville	California	59,639	78,008	1968
San Luis	California	59,405	77,700	1967
Nurek	Tajikistan	58,000	75,861	1980
Garrison	North Dakota	50,843	66,500	1956
Cochiti	New Mexico	48,052	62,850	1975
Tabka (Thawra)	Syria	46,000	60,168	1976
Bennett W.A.C.	Canada	43,733	57,201	1967
Tucuruí	Brazil	43,000	56,242	1984
Boruca	Costa Rica	43,000	56,242	UC
High Aswan (Sadd-el-Aali)	Egypt	43,000	56,242	1970
San Roque	Philippines	43,000	56,242	UC
Kiev	Russia	42,841	56,034	1964
Dantiwada Left Embankment	India	41,040	53,680	1965
Saratov	Russia	40,400	52,843	1967
Mission Tailings 2	Arizona	40,088	52,435	1973
Fort Randall	South Dakota	38,227	50,000	1953
Kanev	Ukraine	37,860	49,520	1976
Mosul	Iraq	36,000	47,086	1982
Kakhovka	Ukraine	35,640	46,617	1955
Itumbiara	Brazil	35,600	46,563	1980
Lauwerszee	Netherlands	35,575	46,532	1969
Beas	India	35,418	46,325	1974
Oosterschelde	Netherlands	35,000	45,778	1986

NOTE: UC = under construction. *Source:* Department of the Interior, Bureau of Reclamation and *International Water Power and Dam Construction.*

World's Largest Hydroelectric Plants

| Name of Dam | Location | Rated capacity (MW) | | Year of initial operation |
		Present	Ultimate	
Itaipu	Brazil/Paraguay	1,400	12,600	1984
Grand Coulee	Washington	6,480	10,080	1942
Guri (Raul Leoni)	Venezuela	2,800	10,060	1968
Tucuruí	Brazil	—	7,500	1985
Sayano-Shushensk	Former U.S.S.R.	—	6,400	1980
Krasnoyarsk	Russia	6,096	6,096	1968
Corpus-Posadas	Argentina/Paraguay	—	6,000	UC
LaGrande 2	Canada	5,328	5,328	1982
Churchill Falls	Canada	5,225	5,225	1971
Bratsk	Siberia	4,100	4,600	1964
Ust-Ilimsk	Russia	3,675	4,500	1974
Cabora Bassa	Mozambique	2,075	4,150	1974
Yacyretá-Apipe	Argentina/Paraguay	—	4,050	UC
Rogun	Tajikistan	—	3,600	1985
Paulo Afonso	Brazil	3,409	3,409	1954
Salto Santiago	Brazil	1,332	3,333	1980
Pati (Chapetón)	Argentina	—	3,300	UC
Iha Solteira	Brazil	3,200	3,200	1973
Inga I	Zaire	360	2,820	1974
Gezhouba	China	965	2,715	1981
John Day	Oregon/Washington	2,160	2,700	1969
Nurek	Tajikistan	900	2,700	1976
Revelstoke	Canada	900	2,700	1984
Sáo Simao	Brazil	2,680	2,680	1979

Name of Dam	Location	Rated capacity (MW) Present	Rated capacity (MW) Ultimate	Year of initial operation
LaGrande 4	Canada	2,637	2,637	1984
Mica	Canada	1,736	2,610	1976
Volgograd—22nd Congress	Russia	2,560	2,560	1958
Fos do Areia	Brazil	2,511	2,511	1983
Itaparica	Brazil	—	2,500	1985
Bennett W.A.C.	Canada	2,116	2,416	1969
Chicoasén	Mexico	—	2,400	1980
Atatürk	Turkey	—	2,400	1990
LaGrande 3	Canada	2,310	2,310	1982
Volga—V.I. Lenin	Russia	2,300	2,300	1955
Iron Gates I	Romania/Yugoslavia	2,300	2,300	1970
Iron Gates II	Romania/Yugoslavia	270	2,160	1983
Bath County	Virginia	—	2,100	1985
High Aswan (Saad-el-Aali)	Egypt	2,100	2,100	1967
Tarbela	Pakistan	1,400	2,100	1977
Piedra del Aquila	Argentina	—	2,100	1993
Itumbiara	Brazil	2,080	2,080	1980
Chief Joseph	Washington	2,069	2,069	1956
McNary	Oregon	980	2,030	1954
Green River	North Carolina	—	2,000	1980
Tehri	India	—	2,000	UC
Cornwall	New York	—	2,000	1978
Ludington	Michigan	1,979	1,979	1973
Robert Moses—Niagara	New York	1,950	1,950	1961
Salto Grande	Argentina/Uruguay	—	1,890	1979

Note: MW = Megawatts, UC = under construction. *Source:* Department of the Interior, Bureau of Reclamation and *International Water Power and Dam Construction.*

Notable U.S. Skyscrapers

City	Building	Stories	Height ft	Height m
Chicago	Sears Tower	110	1,454	443
New York	World Trade Center	110	1,377	419
New York	Empire State	102	1,250	381
Chicago	AMOCO	80	1,136	346
Chicago	John Hancock Center	100	1,127	343
New York	Chrysler	77	1,046	319
Los Angeles	First Interstate World Center	73	1,017	310
Atlanta	Nations Bank Plaza	55	1,025	312
Houston	Texas Commerce Tower	75	1,002	305
Houston	First Interstate Plaza	71	985	300
Chicago	311 South Wacker Drive	65	969	295
New York	American International	66	952	290
Cleveland	Society Tower	57	948	289
Philadelphia	One Liberty Place	62	945	288
Seattle	Columbia Seafirst Center	76	943	287
New York	Citicorp Center	59	915	279
Atlanta	One Peachtree Center	60	902	275
New York	40 Wall Tower	71	900	274
Chicago	Two Prudential Center	64	900	274
Seattle	Two Union Square	56	886	270
Philadelphia	Mellon Bank Center	56	880	268
Charlotte	NationsBank Corporate Center	60	875	267
Chicago	Water Tower Place	74	859	262
Los Angeles	First Interstate Bank	62	858	261
San Francisco	Transamerica Pyramid	61	853	260
Chicago	First National Bank	60	851	259
New York	RCA	70	850	259
Seattle	Washington Mutual Tower	56	849	259
Philadelphia	Two Liberty Place	52	845	257
Pittsburgh	USX Tower	64	841	256
Atlanta	One Atlantic Center	50	825	251
New York	Chase Manhattan	60	813	248
New York	Met Life	59	808	246
New York	Woolworth	55	792	241
Boston	John Hancock Tower	60	790	241
San Francisco	Bank of America	52	779	237
Minneapolis	IDS Tower	57	775	236
New York	One Liberty Plaza	54	775	236
Chicago	Three First National Plaza	57	775	236
New York	One Penn Plaza	57	774	236
Minneapolis	Norwest Center	57	772	235
Minneapolis	First Bank Place	56	770	235
Miami	First Union Financial Ctr.	55	765	233
Atlanta	Westin Peachtree Plaza	73	754	230
New York	Exxon	54	750	229
Boston	Prudential Tower	52	750	229
Dallas	First Interst. Bank Tower	60	744	227
Los Angeles	Security Pacific Plaza	55	743	226
Los Angeles	Wells Fargo Center	54	743	227
Atlanta	Georgia-Pacific Center	52	741	226
Atlanta	191 Peachtree Tower	50	740	225
New York	One Astor Plaza	54	730	222
Chicago	Olympia Centre	63	727	222
Houston	Chevron Tower	52	725	221
New York	Marine Midland	52	724	221
Los Angeles	Mitsui (North Tower) Fudosan Tower	52	716	218
Pittsburgh	One Mellon Bank Center	54	715	218
Houston	One Shell Plaza	50	714	218
Detroit	Detroit Westin Hotel	73	712	220
Indianapolis	Banc One Center Tower	51	711	216
Dallas	Renaissance Tower	56	710	216
Cleveland	Terminal Tower	52	708	216
New York	Union Carbide	52	707	215
New York	General Motors	50	705	215
Seattle	Key Tower	62	702	214
New York	Metropolitan Life	50	700	213
Philadelphia	Blue Cross Tower	50	700	213
Chicago	Leo Burnett Building	46	700	213

NOTE: Height does not include TV towers and antennas. *Source: Information Please* questionnaires.

Notable Tunnels

Name	Location	Length		Year completed
		mi.	km	
Railroad, excluding subways				
Seikan	Tsugara Strait, Japan	33.1	53.3	1983
Channel[1]	English Channel, England, France	31.0	49.9	1994
Simplon (I and II)	Alps, Switzerland-Italy	12.3	19.8	1906 & 1922
Apennine	Bologna-Florence, Italy	11.5	18.5	1934
St. Gotthard	Swiss Alps	9.3	14.9	1881
Lötschberg	Swiss Alps	9.1	14.6	1911
Mont Cénis	French Alps	8.5[2]	13.7	1871
New Cascade	Cascade Mountains, Washington	7.8	12.6	1929
Vosges	Vosges, France	7.0	11.3	1940
Flathead	Rocky Mountains, Montana	7.0	11.3	1970
Arlberg	Austrian Alps	6.3	10.1	1884
Moffat	Rocky Mountains, Colorado	6.2	9.9	1928
Shimuzu	Shimuzu, Japan	6.1	9.8	1931
Rimutaka	Wairarapa, New Zealand	5.5	8.9	1955
Vehicular				
St. Gotthard	Alps, Switzerland	10.2	16.4	1980
Mt. Blanc	Alps, France-Italy	7.5	12.1	1965
Mt. Ena	Japan Alps, Japan	5.3	8.5	1976[3]
Great St. Bernard	Alps, Switzerland-Italy	3.4	5.5	1964
Mount Royal	Montreal, Canada	3.2	5.1	1918
Lincoln	Hudson River, New York-New Jersey	1.6	2.6	1937
Queensway Road	Mersey River, Liverpool, England	2.2	3.5	1934
Brooklyn-Battery	East River, New York City	1.7	2.7	1950
Holland	Hudson River, New York-New Jersey	1.6	2.6	1927
Fort McHenry	Baltimore, Maryland	1.6	2.6	1985
Hampton Roads	Norfolk, Virginia	1.4	2.3	1957
Queens-Midtown	East River, New York City	1.3	2.1	1940
Liberty Tubes	Pittsburgh, Pennsylvania	1.2	1.9	1923
Baltimore Harbor	Baltimore, Maryland	1.2	1.9	1957
Allegheny Tunnels	Pennsylvania Turnpike	1.2	1.9	1940[4]

1. Twin-rail. One tunnel for passenger trains, the other for shuttle trains carrying vehicles plus a central service tunnel. 2. Lengthened to its present 8.5 miles in 1881. 3. Parallel tunnel begun in 1976. 4. Parallel tunnel built in 1965, twin tunnel in 1966. *Source:* American Society of Civil Engineers and International Bridge, Tunnel & Turnpike Association, Wittiker's.

Famous Ship Canals

Name	Location	Length (miles)[1]	Width (feet)	Depth (feet)	Locks	Year opened
Albert	Belgium	80.0	53.0	16.5	6	1939
Amsterdam-Rhine	Netherlands	45.0	164.0	41.0	3	1952
Beaumont-Port Arthur	United States	40.0	200.0	34.0	—	1916
Chesapeake and Delaware	United States	19.0	250.0	27.0	—	1927
Houston	United States	50.0	[2]	40.0	—	1914
Kiel (Nord-Ostsee Kanal)	Germany	61.3	144.0	36.0	4	1895
Panama	Panama	50.7	110.0	41.0	12	1914
St. Lawrence Seaway	U.S. and Canada	2,400.0[3]	[4]	—	—	1959
Montreal to Prescott	U.S. and Canada	11.5	80.0	30.0	7	1959
Welland	Canada	27.5	80.0	27.0	8	1931
Sault Ste. Marie	Canada	1.2	60.0	16.8	1	1895
Sault Ste. Marie	United States	1.6	80.0	25.0	4	1915
Suez	Egypt	100.6[5]	197.0	36.0	—	1869

1. Statute miles. 2. 300–400 feet. 3. From Montreal to Duluth. 4. 442–550 feet; there are 11.5 miles of locks, 80 feet wide and 30 feet deep. 5. From Port Said lighthouse to entrance channel in Suez roads. *Source:* American Society of Civil Engineers.

MEDIA

Leading Magazines: United States and Canada

Magazine	Circulation[1]	Magazine	Circulation[1]
American Health—Fitness of Body and Mind	816,241	National Geographic Magazine	8,988,444
Architectural Digest	834,964	Nation's Business	863,156
Better Homes and Gardens	7,603,207	New Woman	1,262,003
Bon Appetit	1,128,932	Newsweek	3,155,155
Business Week (North America)	882,583	The New Yorker	847,201
Car and Driver	1,108,975	Organic Gardening	809,356
Chatelaine	808,922	Outdoor Life	1,358,647
Conde Nast Traveler	850,007	Parenting Magazine	979,849
Consumers Digest	1,254,879	Parents	1,848,008
Cooking Light	1,213,158	PC Magazine	1,107,187
Cosmopolitan	2,569,186	PC World	1,016,889
Country America	961,106	PC/Computing	964,507
Country Home	1,030,694	Penthouse	1,100,679
Country Living	1,838,808	People Weekly	3,321,198
Discover	1,320,701	Playboy	3,283,272
Ebony	1,927,675	Popular Mechanics	1,586,137
Elle	922,048	Popular Science	1,805,525
Entertainment Weekly	1,195,926	Prevention	3,252,115
Essence	1,000,184	Reader's Digest	15,103,830
Family Circle	6,007,542	Reader's Digest (Canadian English Edition)	1,190,698
The Family Handyman	1,046,398	Redbook	3,173,313
Field & Stream	2,001,875	Rolling Stone	1,180,217
First for Women	1,237,449	Self	1,211,024
Food & Wine	788,128	Sesame Street Magazine	1,021,807
Forbes	779,901	Seventeen	2,172,923
Fortune (North America)	758,171	Shape	865,257
Glamour	2,141,752	Smithsonian	2,151,172
Globe	981,889	Soap Opera Digest	1,372,316
Golf Digest	1,501,525	Southern Living	2,471,170
Golf Magazine	1,263,925	Sport	786,714
Good Housekeeping	5,372,786	Sports Illustrated	3,157,303
Gourmet	896,352	Star	2,406,150
Harper's Bazaar	779,015	Sunset, The Magazine of Western Living	1,451,846
Health	974,728	'Teen	1,360,411
Home	1,005,916	Tennis	806,607
Home Mechanix	1,012,411	Time	4,083,105
Hot Rod	818,295	Traditional Home	800,025
House Beautiful	980,423	Travel & Leisure	988,053
Jet	965,870	True Story Plus	1,028,637
Kiplinger's Personal Finance Magazine	1,020,931	TV Guide	13,175,549
Ladies Home Journal	5,045,644	TV Guide (Canada)	790,129
Life	1,556,189	U.S. News & World Report	2,220,327
Mademoiselle	1,280,169	US	1,201,377
Martha Stewart Living	1,449,744	Vanity Fair	1,173,077
McCall's	4,520,186	Victoria	963,277
Men's Health	1,314,802	Vogue	1,146,037
Midwest Living	838,969	Weight Watchers Magazine	1,001,148
Money	1,922,737	Woman's Day	4,707,330
Motor Trend	968,719	Working Woman	764,206
National Enquirer	2,613,647	YM	2,165,079

1. Average total paid circulation for the six-month period ending December 31, 1995. The table lists magazines with combined newsstand and subscription circulation of over 750,000. n.a. = not available. *Source:* Audit Bureau of Circulations. Publishers' Statements for six-month period ending December 31, 1995.

Major U.S. Daily Newspapers[1]

City and Newspaper	Net paid circulation			
	Morning[2]	All-Day[2]	Evening[2]	Sunday
Akron, Ohio: *Beacon Journal*	152,760		—	218,760
Albany, N.Y.: *Times Union* (M & S)	100,831		—	156,644
Albuquerque, N.M.: *Journal* (M & S); *Tribune* (E)	109,929		29,248	158,728
Allentown, Pa.: *Call* (M & S)	133,735		—	186,557

City and Newspaper	Net paid circulation			
	Morning[2]	All-Day[2]	Evening[2]	Sunday
Anchorage, Alaska: *News*	71,239[3]		—	91,863
Ann Arbor, Mich.: *News*	—		58,409	78,508
Appleton, Wis.: *Post-Crescent*	—		60,480	76,548
Asbury Park, N.J.: *Press*	156,617			226,112
Asheville, N.C.: *Citizen-Times*	63,154		—	73,569
Atlanta: *Constitution* (M); *Journal* (E);				
Journal-Constitution (S)	317,273[4]		123,536[4]	715,397
Atlantic City, N.J.: *Press*	74,194		—	95,745
Augusta, Ga.: *Chronicle* (M & S)	74,820[5]		—	98,993
Austin, Tex.: *American-Statesman*	182,925		—	242,236
Bakersfield, Calif.: *Californian*	73,747		—	88,446
Baltimore: *Sun*	337,292			488,562
Bangor, Me.: *News*	69,779		—	85,648[6]
Baton Rouge, La.: *Advocate* (M & S)	99,960		—	137,368
Bergen County (Hackensack), N.J.: *Record*	153,661		—	210,061
Beaumont, Tex.: *Enterprise*	62,091		—	75,974
Binghamton, N.Y.: *Press & Sun-Bulletin* (M & S)	66,674		—	87,105
Birmingham, Ala.: *Post-Herald* (M); *News* (E & S)	57,030		158,880	201,023
Boise, Idaho: *Statesman*	66,325		—	88,308
Boston: *Globe*	486,403		—	777,902
Herald	294,507		—	203,977
Christian Science Monitor	87,259		—	—
Buffalo, N.Y.: *News*	272,995		—	361,344
Camden, N.J.: *Courier-Post*	91,260		—	101,325
Canton, Ohio: *Repository*	—		61,998	79,111
Cedar Rapids, Iowa: *Gazette*	68,645		—	84,720
Charleston, S.C.: *Post and Courier*	109,244		—	122,713
Charleston, W. Va.: *Gazette* (M); *Mail* (E);				
Gazette-Mail (S)	53,346		43,898	104,647
Charlotte, N.C.: *Observer*	240,170		—	303,106
Chattanooga, Tenn.: *Times* (M); *Free Press* (E & S)	41,538		41,696	111,549
Chicago: *Tribune*	667,908			1,066,393
Sun-Times	501,115		—	469,161
Cincinnati: *Enquirer* (M & S); *Post* (E)	205,591		79,652[5]	352,893
Cleveland: *Plain Dealer*	398,398		—	528,818
Colorado Springs, Colo.: *Gazette Telegraph*	105,939		—	126,503
Columbia, S.C.: *State*	126,274		—	163,832
Columbus, Ohio: *Dispatch*	268,670		—	401,612
Corpus Christi, Tex.: *Caller-Times*	66,461		—	90,519
Dallas: *News*	494,266[4]		—	803,610
Wall Street Journal (Southwest edition)	166,585[5]		—	—
Davenport, Iowa: *Quad-City Times*	51,942		—	80,700
Dayton, Ohio: *News*	161,016		—	217,976
Daytona Beach, Fla.: *News-Journal*	103,932		—	122,133
Denver: *Post*	316,027		—	456,057
Rocky Mountain News	333,471		—	439,295
Des Moines, Iowa: *Register*	174,842		—	294,510
Detroit: *Free Press* (M); *News* (E);				
News and Free Press (S)	531,825[5,7]		354,403[5,7]	1,107,645[7]
Duluth, Minn.: *News-Tribune*	52,377		—	80,107
El Paso, Tex.: *Times* (M & S); *Herald-Post* (E)	67,182[5]		21,662[5]	99,364
Erie, Pa.: *News* (M); *Times* (E); *Times-News* (S)	32,914[5]		37,390[5]	99,157
Eugene, Ore.: *Register-Guard*	75,881[5]		—	79,428
Evansville, Ind.: *Courier* (M); *Press* (E); *Courier* (S)	61,246		23,822	112,789
Fayetteville, N.C.: *Observer-Times*	71,165[5]		—	83,862
Flint, Mich.: *Journal*	97,007		—	118,968
Fort Lauderdale, Fla.: *Sun-Sentinel*	272,258		—	391,063
Fort Myers, Fla.: *News-Press*	101,782		—	113,315
Fort Wayne, Ind.: *Journal Gazette* (M & S); *News-Sentinel* (E)	61,628		51,023	138,979
Fort Worth: *Star-Telegram*	225,462[4]		—	342,221
Fresno, Calif.: *Bee*	156,309		—	189,855
Gary, Ind.: *Post-Tribune*	67,355		—	76,026
Grand Rapids, Mich.: *Press*	—		139,359	191,226
Green Bay, Wis.: *Press-Gazette*	57,126		—	87,697
Greensboro, N.C.: *News & Record*	94,722[5]		—	122,449
Greensburg, Pa.: *Tribune-Review*	82,610		—	141,031
Greenville, S.C.: *News* (M & S); *Piedmont* (E)	101,635[5]		117,118[5]	139,931
Harrisburg, Pa.: *Patriot* (M); *News* (E);				
Patriot-News (S)	64,283[5]		37,740[5]	174,106

City and newspaper	Net paid circulation			
	Morning[2]	All-Day[2]	Evening[2]	Sunday
Hartford, Conn.: *Courant*	207,816		—	306,058
Honolulu: *Advertiser* (M); *Star-Bulletin* (E);				
Advertiser (S)	109,624		74,886	194,728
Houston: *Chronicle*	551,553		—	764,443
Huntsville, Ala.: *Times*	—		59,795[5]	79,082
Indianapolis: *Star* (M & S); *News* (E)	231,299		62,726	404,614
Jackson, Miss.: *Clarion-Ledger*	107,876		—	127,393
Jacksonville, Fla.: *Times-Union*	197,706		—	251,216
Kalamazoo, Mich.: *Gazette*	—		61,293[5]	78,438
Kansas City, Mo.: *Star* (M & S)	285,086[5]		—	425,337
Knoxville, Tenn.: *News-Sentinel* (M & S)	119,529[4]		—	174,375
Lakeland, Fla.: *Ledger*	80,459		—	100,162
Lancaster, Pa.: *Intelligencer-Journal* (M); *New Era* (E);				
News (S)	43,283		48,437	105,306
Lansing, Mich.: *State Journal*	71,636		—	95,637
Las Vegas, Nev.: *Review-Journal* (M); *Sun* (E);				
Review-Journal/Sun (S)	148,854		41,464	216,932
Levittown–Bristol–Langhorne, Pa.:				
Bucks County Courier Times (M & S)	70,835[5]		—	77,115
Lexington, Ky.: *Herald-Leader*	115,362[4]		—	165,795
Lincoln, Neb.: *Journal-Star*	78,098		—	84,382
Little Rock, Ark: *Democrat-Gazette*	179,609		—	292,057
Long Beach, Calif.: *Press-Telegram*	109,255[5]		—	125,577
Long Island (Melville), N.Y.: *Newsday*	555,203[5]		—	643,421
Los Angeles: *Times*	1,021,121[5]		—	1,391,076
Daily News	204,220[5]		—	217,652
La Opinion	101,890[5]		—	61,967
Louisville, Ky.: *Courier-Journal*	236,864		—	323,697
Lubbock, Tex.: *Avalanche-Journal*	66,661		—	78,061
Macon, Ga.: *Telegraph*	74,555		—	102,408
Madison, Wis.: *State Journal* (M & S); *Capital Times* (E)	86,289[5]		21,488[5]	162,607
Melbourne, Fla.: *Today*	88,471		—	117,261
Memphis, Tenn.: *Commercial Appeal*	178,181[8]		—	267,935
Miami, Fla.: *Herald*	378,195		—	500,654
Middletown, N.Y.: *Times Herald-Record* (M); *Record* (S)	86,017		—	101,267
Milwaukee: *Sentinel* (M); *Journal* (E & S)	286,741[5]		269,984[5]	462,168
Minneapolis: *Star Tribune*	388,120[9]		—	682,318
Mobile, Ala.: *Register* (M); *Press* (E); *Press Register* (S)	74,333[5]		26,893[5]	118,862
Modesto, Calif.: *Bee*	83,441		—	90,825
Montgomery, Ala. *Advertiser*	60,073		—	74,063
Munster, Ind.: *Times*	88,349		—	94,902
Naperville, Ill.: *Wall Street Journal* (Midwest edition)	490,604[5]		—	—
Nashville, Tenn.: *Tennessean* (M & S); *Banner* (E)	149,292[5]		49,978[5]	284,571
New Haven, Conn.: *Register*	100,261		—	120,251
New Orleans: *Times-Picayune*	262,462		—	311,264
New York: *News*	758,509[5]		—	1,010,504
Times	1,157.656		—	1,746,707
Post	418,255[5]		—	
Wall Street Journal (Eastern edition)	792,091[5]		—	—
Newark, N.J.: *Star-Ledger*	433,317[5]		—	641,393
Newport News-Hampton-Williamsburg, Va.: *Press*	102,037		—	124,903
Norfolk-Portsmouth-Virginia Beach-Chesapeake, Va.:				
Virginian-Pilot	201,981[5]			239,754
Oklahoma City: *Oklahoman*	219,158[5]		—	312,732
Omaha, Neb.: *World-Herald*	—	232,336[5]	—	292,682
Orange County (Santa Ana), Calif.: *Register*	358,173		—	419,401
Orlando, Fla.: *Sentinel*	273,689		—	396,244
Palo Alto, Calif.: *Wall Street Journal* (Western edition)	391,908[5]		—	—
Pensacola, Fla.: *News Journal*	61,178		—	84,673
Peoria, Ill.: *Journal Star*	—	75,244[5]	—	104,610
Philadelphia: *Inquirer*	446,842[5]		—	901,891
News	184,906[5]		—	—
Phoenix, Ariz.: *Republic* (M & S); *Gazette* (E)	399,830		62,929	597,255
Pittsburgh: *Post-Gazette, Sun-Telegraph*	240,043		—	440,504
Pontiac, Mich.: *Oakland Press*	84,365		—	98,936

City and newspaper	Morning[2]	All-Day[2]	Evening[2]	Sunday
		Net paid circulation		
Portland, Me.: *Press Herald* (M); *Telegram* (S)	71,861		—	128,442
Portland, Or.: *Oregonian*	—	349,193[5]	—	445,293
Providence, R.I.: *Journal-Bulletin* (M); *Journal* (S)	171,733		—	254,012
Quincy, Mass.: *Patriot Ledger*	—	83,742[5]	—	—
Raleigh, N.C.: *News & Observer*	151,159[5]		—	201,357
Reading, Pa.: *Times* (M); *Eagle* (E & S)	49,062[5]		22,031[5]	106,027
Reno, Nev.: *Gazette-Journal*	67,179		—	84,884
Richmond, Va.: *Times-Dispatch* (M & S)	211,992		—	249,902
Riverside, Calif.: *Press-Enterprise*	169,231		—	175,367
Roanoke, Va.: *Times & World-News*	109,346		—	122,217
Rochester, N.Y.: *Democrat & Chronicle* (M & S); *Times-Union* (E)	143,451		50,002	251,923
Rockford, Ill.: *Register Star*	75,228		—	87,916
Sacramento, Calif.: *Bee*	282,594		—	352,712
St. Louis: *Post-Dispatch*	323,374		—	541,991
St. Paul: *Pioneer Press*	206,488[5]		—	272,330
St. Petersburg, Fla.: *Times*	364,810		—	462,103
Salt Lake City, Utah: *Tribune* (M & S); *Deseret News* (E & S)	127,805		63,108	161,802
San Antonio: *Express-News*	222,413[4]		—	285,413
San Bernardino, Calif.: *Sun*	80,384		—	93,321
San Diego, Calif.: *Union–Tribune*	376,511		—	453,891
Transcript	7,961[5, 7]		—	—
San Francisco: *Chronicle* (M); *Examiner* (E); *Examiner & Chronicle* (S)	493,942[5]		115,184	646,171
San Jose, Calif.: *Mercury News*	—	288,792[5]	—	350,199
Santa Rosa, Calif.: *Press Democrat*	93,354		—	102,766
Sarasota, Fla.: *Herald-Tribune* (M & S)	122,198		—	151,255
Savannah, Ga.: *News* (M); *Press* (E); *News, Press* (S)	55,039[5]		12,466[5]	77,176
Scranton, Pa.: *Tribune* (M); *Times* (E & S)	30,922[5]		38,816[5]	61,691
Seattle: *Post-Intelligencer* (M); *Times* (E); combined (S)	202,156[5]		235,963[5]	506,216
Shreveport, La.: *Times* (M & S)	79,605		—	99,035
Sioux Falls, S.D.: *Argus Leader*	49,847		—	73,167
South Bend-Mishawaka, Ind.: *Tribune*	—		82,711	114,967
Spokane, Wash.: *Spokesman-Review* (M & S)	118,770[5]		—	147,328
Springfield, Ill.: *State Journal-Register*	65,631		—	75,319
Springfield, Mass.: *Union-News; Republican* (S)	101,145		—	151,370
Springfield, Mo.: *News-Leader*	63,709		—	100,894
Staten Island, N.Y.: *Advance* (E&S)			70,889	90,907
Syracuse, N.Y.: *Post-Standard* (M); *Herald-Journal* (E); *Herald-American/Post-Standard* (S)	86,175		73,119	204,628
Tacoma, Wash.: *News Tribune*	129,382		—	148,396
Tallahassee, Fla.: *Democrat*	56,086		—	78,097
Tampa, Fla.: *Tribune* (M); *Tribune & Times* (S)	269,349		—	371,086
Toledo, Ohio: *Blade*	145,899		—	201,155
Trenton, N.J.: *Times* (M&S)	85,893		—	95,036
Trentonian (M & S)	64,631[5]		—	51,276
Tucson, Ariz.: *Star* (M & S); *Citizen* (E)	100,429		48,215	186,257
Tulsa, Okla.: *World* (M & S)	162,111		—	227,884
Walnut Creek, Calif.: *Contra Costa Times*	97,500		—	107,221
Washington, D.C.: *Post*	834,641[5]		—	1,140,564
Times	100,932[5]		—	61,856
USA Today	1,617,743[4]		—	—
Waterbury, Conn.: *Republican–American* (M); *Republican* (S)	59,876		—	74,673
West Palm Beach, Fla.: *Post*	188,996		—	239,531
Wichita, Kan.: *Eagle*	100,932		—	177,402
Wilmington, Del.: *News Journal*	124,669		—	149,517
Winston-Salem, N.C.: *Journal*	92,998		—	104,334
Worcester, Mass.: *Telegram & Gazette* (M); *Telegram* (S)	112,398		—	143,323
York, Pa.: *Record* (M); *Dispatch* (E); *News* (S)	42,975		40,303	93,233
Youngstown, Ohio: *Vindicator*	—		83,117	124,275

1. Listing is of cities in which any one edition of a newspaper exceeds an average net paid circulation of 75,000; newspapers of smaller circulation in those cities are also included. 2. Unless otherwise indicated, figures are average Monday-through-Saturday circulation for six-month period ending March 31, 1996. 3. Average Monday through Thursday and Saturday. 4. Monday through Thursday. 5. Monday through Friday. 6. Week-end edition. 7. 1995 figures; 1996 figures not available at press time. 8. Monday, Tuesday, and Thursday. 9. Wednesday through Saturday. *Source:* Audit Bureau of Circulations.

U.S. English-Language Daily and Sunday Newspapers
(number of newspapers as of Feb. 1, 1996; circulation as reported for Sept. 30, 1995)

State	Morning papers and circulation		Evening papers and circulation		Total M and E and circulation		Sunday papers and circulation	
Alabama	19	416,617	7	326,340	26	742,957	18	754,182
Alaska	4	99,499	3	13,313	7	112,812	4	128,873
Arizona	9	548,873	13	231,771	22	780,644	16	916,870
Arkansas	13	374,257	18	103,674	31	477,931	16	529,664
California[1]	67	5,594,429	31	499,120	98	6,093,549	62	6,415,736
Colorado	17	924,108	13	132,565	30	1,056,673	11	1,253,990
Connecticut[2]	13	648,729	8	145,423	18	794,151	11	830,894
Delaware[2]	3	87,639	1	62,839	3	150,477	2	183,903
District of Columbia	2	895,041	0	0	2	895,041	2	1,193,396
Florida[2]	34	2,934,716	7	187,942	40	3,122,658	35	3,972,247
Georgia	17	741,385	18	327,127	35	1,068,512	19	1,293,776
Hawaii	3	135,510	3	103,292	6	238,802	5	260,795
Idaho	7	144,817	5	80,517	12	225,334	8	240,646
Illinois[2]	21	1,897,970	48	589,198	68	2,487,168	31	2,665,412
Indiana	16	738,774	55	712,890	71	1,451,664	21	1,344,117
Iowa	13	441,474	25	235,871	38	677,345	12	710,746
Kansas	8	285,574	39	205,536	47	491,110	15	448,609
Kentucky	8	454,781	15	188,158	23	642,939	12	679,245
Louisiana[2]	13	502,468	14	247,587	26	750,054	21	848,956
Maine	5	233,095	2	25,071	7	258,166	4	222,874
Maryland	10	562,651	4	83,898	14	646,549	7	682,495
Massachusetts[1]	10	1,272,240	26	552,958	36	1,825,198	14	1,450,158
Michigan	11	746,438	39	1,319,562	50	2,066,000	27	2,366,220
Minnesota	14	784,190	11	137,596	25	921,786	14	1,184,613
Mississippi	6	217,087	16	185,794	22	402,881	16	395,564
Missouri	12	802,150	32	205,925	44	1,008,075	23	1,329,618
Montana	6	155,120	5	40,706	11	195,826	7	201,691
Nebraska[2]	5	252,014	13	217,524	17	469,538	6	443,178
Nevada	4	227,541	5	58,013	9	285,554	4	317,138
New Hampshire[2]	8	143,609	5	93,197	12	236,805	6	200,180
New Jersey	13	1,199,608	7	281,579	20	1,481,187	16	1,775,966
New Mexico	7	200,801	11	99,607	18	300,408	13	299,916
New York[1, 2]	26	5,415,574	45	1,160,348	69	6,575,921	44	5,440,435
North Carolina	20	1,020,959	30	374,154	50	1,395,113	38	1,518,453
North Dakota	7	167,773	3	13,655	10	181,428	7	185,400
Ohio	18	1,649,567	66	971,675	84	2,621,242	37	2,877,932
Oklahoma	11	480,874	35	215,059	46	695,933	39	857,537
Oregon[2]	6	345,814	14	336,907	19	682,721	10	715,767
Pennsylvania	42	2,144,505	45	833,088	87	2,977,593	40	3,331,416
Rhode Island	3	228,581	3	33,737	6	262,318	3	294,709
South Carolina	11	581,841	4	56,846	15	638,687	14	758,144
South Dakota	6	133,998	5	334,429	11	167,427	4	139,054
Tennessee	12	661,190	15	244,974	27	906,164	16	1,107,138
Texas	36	2,613,206	53	374,347	89	2,987,553	85	4,039,961
Utah	1	126,076	5	190,961	6	317,037	6	361,052
Vermont	4	95,460	4	33,090	8	128,550	3	106,103
Virginia[1, 2]	18	2,389,071	12	214,616	28	2,603,686	15	1,010,317
Washington	11	732,817	13	470,837	24	1,203,654	16	1,285,816
West Virginia	10	250,648	12	145,275	22	395,923	11	402,010
Wisconsin	10	539,706	25	466,084	35	1,005,790	18	1,189,928
Wyoming	6	69,387	3	19,470	9	88,857	4	66,456
Totals	**656**	**44,310,252**	**891**	**13,883,145**	**1,533**	**58,193,391**	**888**	**61,229,296**
Total U.S., Sept. 30, 1994	635	43,381,578	935	15,923,865	1,548	59,305,436	886	62,294,799
Total U.S., Sept. 30, 1993	623	43,093,866	954	16,717,737	1,556	59,811,584	884	62,565,574
Total U.S., Sept. 30, 1992	596	42,387,813	996	17,776,686	1,570	60,164,499	891	62,159,971
Total U.S., Sept. 30, 1991	571	41,469,756	1,042	19,217,369	1,586	60,687,125	875	62,067,820
Total U.S., Sept. 30, 1990	559	41,311,167	1,084	21,016,795	1,611	62,327,962	863	62,634,512
Total U.S., Sept. 30, 1989	530	40,759,016	1,125	21,890,202	1,626	62,649,218	847	62,008,154
Total U.S., Sept. 30, 1988	520	40,452,815	1,141	22,242,001	1,642	62,694,816	840	61,474,189
Total U.S., Sept. 30, 1987	511	39,123,807	1,166	23,702,466	1,645	62,826,273	820	60,111,863
Total U.S., Sept. 30, 1986	499	37,441,125	1,188	25,060,911	1,657	62,502,036	802	58,924,518

1. Includes nationally circulated daily. Circulation counted only in the state indicated. 2. "All-day" newspapers are listed in morning and evening columns but only once in the total, and their circulations are divided between morning and evening figures. Adjustments have been made in state and U.S. total figures. *Source: Editor and Publisher International Yearbook, 1996.*

***See** the Entertainment and Culture section for additional Media information.*

SPACE

NASA Approves Experimental Spacecraft Tests

On July 2, 1996, Vice President Al Gore announced that the Lockheed Martin Corporation had been selected to build and test fly a one-half scale prototype of their X–33 experimental reusable launch rocket ship. The X–33 is scheduled to complete its first flight by March of 1999 and will be launched from Edwards Air Force Base in California. NASA's decision to build a demonstration model of a new type of spacecraft will pave the way towards replacing the aging space shuttle fleet.

NASA issued a cooperative agreement with Lockheed Martin worth approximately $1 billion over 42 months to build and fly the X–33. The cooperative agreement is a partnership mechanism between the government and industry that allows both parties to contribute resources towards the common goal of achieving low-cost space access. No profit is being made by industry, and Lockheed Martin is cost sharing over $200 million on the X–33 program.

Lockheed Martin's revolutionary design is a pilotless, wingless, flat-bottomed, wedge-shaped aircraft called *VentureStar,* that would take off vertically and land horizontally on a runway like the space shuttle. Unlike the shuttles there are no costly external fuel tanks and boosters. The X–33 will use a radically new type of engine called the aerospike, which lacks the traditional cone-shaped nozzles used on conventional rockets. It will be fueled by liquid oxygen and liquid hydrogen to propel the spacecraft to over Mach 15. □

Space Station Alpha

Construction of the international space station nicknamed *Alpha* is scheduled to begin in November 1997 with Russia as a partner. The former space station name *Freedom* was officially dropped by NASA.

The multinational space station design will utilize a modular build-up approach that will use existing flight-proven hardware as well as cost-effective designs from the former space station *Freedom* systems. The Johnson Space Center in Houston is the host center for *Alpha* and the Boeing Defense and Space Group is the prime contractor. Some of the components will come from parts originally intended for Russia's planned second generation *Mir-2* space station.

The crew-occupied modules are being rearranged to accommodate Russian hardware and the space station's orbit was also changed to accommodate Russian high-altitude launch sites.

The first phase of the joint program started on February 3, 1995, when the space shuttle *Discovery* made a close approach rendezvous with the *Mir.* On June 29, 1995, the shuttle *Atlantis* docked with the *Mir* for the first time. Additional docking missions are planned over a three-year period to test procedures and equipment for the new space station. (*See* Notable Manned Space Flights table and Current Events for other dockings.) The Space Shuttle will also assist with crew exchange, resupply, and payload activities for *Mir.*

During the second phase, Russia will launch a core module in May 1997, and nine American and Russian launches will bring additional hardware. Finally, the U.S. will develop a human-tended facility connected to the *Mir* module by December 1997.

During the third and last expansion phase, European and Japanese modules will be added along with supporting hardware. The space station will be completed and permanently manned with six crew members in June 2002.

A Russian *Soyuz* capsule will be docked at the station to serve as an emergency crew escape vehicle. NASA would like to build an alternative to the Russian rescue capsule in case Russia has problems with regularly sending their rescue *Soyuz* to the station. The *Soyuz* was not designed for long exposure in space and must be replaced every six months.

The United States agreed to pay Russia $100 million each year through 1997 for access to *Mir.* It is believed that the Russian involvement will save the United States two to four billion dollars. □

Mars Pathfinder Mission

NASA's Mars Pathfinder Project will place a lander and a small six-wheeled robotic rover on the surface of Mars on July 4, 1997. The spacecraft is being built at the Jet Propulsion Laboratory (JPL) in Pasadena, California.

The Pathfinder will be launched on a Delta–2 rocket in December 1996 and fly directly to Mars, enter its atmosphere, and land without first going into orbit around the planet. During its descent to the surface with the aid of parachutes, rockets, and airbags, the spacecraft will study the planet's atmospheric gases. After landing, the Pathfinder will deploy the rover to explore the ancient sediment-covered *Ares Vallis* floodplain.

The small rover weighs 22 lb (10 kg), is 10.9 inches (280 mm) high with a ground clearance of 5 inches (130 mm). It is 24.5 inches (630 mm) long and 18.7 inches (480 mm) wide. Three solar panels will provide the necessary power; however it will also have batteries. The rover will carry an X-ray spectrometer to determine soil composition.

Although the rover is technically named the Microrover Flight Experiment or MFEX, the vehicle has been named *Sojourner Truth,* after the African-American abolitionist and champion of women's rights. Although the information gained from the rover's technology experiments such as soil mechanics are of scientific interest, the rover's main science objectives are to deploy an alpha-proton-X-ray spectrometer (APXS) and take close-up images of Martian features. The APXS is provided by the Max Planck Institute of Mains, Germany, and the University of Chicago.

The APXS will be placed against a rock, collect a spectrum of the rock to determine its composition, and then transmit the spectrum to the lander for return to earth. A full APXS measurement of a rock requires ten hours. The microrover will also take black and white pictures of any rock on which the APXS is used.

The rover is controlled by an Earth-based operator, but because of the time delay between Earth and Mars (variously from six to 41 minutes), some autonomy is needed in the rover. The operator on Earth will view the work station with a stereo display of the lander's image of the terrain through three-dimensional glasses. □

ULYSSES

Ulysses is an international project to study the poles of the Sun and interstellar space above and below the poles. The 814-lb (370-kg) spacecraft was put into an orbit at right angles to the solar system's ecliptic plane. (The ecliptic is the plane in which the Earth and most of the planets orbit the Sun.) This special orbit allows the spacecraft to examine for the first time the regions of the Sun's north and south poles. Besides examining the Sun's energy fields, instruments on *Ulysses* are studying other phenomena from the Milky Way and beyond.

While scientists have studied the Sun for centuries, they know very little about matter reaching the solar system from other nearby stars. This is because particles reaching the Sun's magnetic field from beyond the solar system are greatly changed by the Sun's magnetic field and by collision with particles flowing outward from the Sun. No spacecraft has ever left the solar system to make actual measurements of the interstellar medium.

The *Ulysses* spacecraft was launched from the space shuttle *Discovery* on Oct. 6, 1990, reached the Sun's south pole in Septemebr 1994, and completed its pass in November. The spacecraft found that the Sun appears to have a south magnetic pole. A second encounter took place when it passed over the Sun's north pole in October 1995. *Ulysses* will continue to orbit the Sun and will pass over the north and south poles again in 2000 and 2001.

On Feb. 8, 1992, *Ulysses* flew past Jupiter at 61,249 mph, using the planet's gravity as a slingshot to send it toward the Sun. During the flyby (Jan. 31–Feb. 16, 1992), the spacecraft studied unexplored portions of Jupiter's huge magnetic field.

THE CASSINI MISSION

The ringed planet Saturn, its major moon Titan, and a complex system of at least 19 other satellites will be the destinations for NASA's and the European Space Agency's Cassini Mission. Cassini is named for the Italian-French astronomer, Gian Domenico Cassini (1625–1712), who discovered four of Saturn's major moons and a dark, narrow gap ("Cassini's Division") splitting the planet's rings.

The mission to Saturn is scheduled for launch on Oct. 6, 1997. Cassini is to arrive at Saturn in June 2004. The cost of the mission is approximately $1.9 billion.

Early during the spacecraft's four-year tour orbiting Saturn, it will launch a parachuted probe descending through Titan's dense atmosphere to the surface of the satellite, which has unique organic-like chemistry that could provide clues to the origin of life on Earth.

In order to reach Saturn, Cassini will first execute flybys of the Earth and Jupiter to gain "gravity assist" boosts in velocity before sending it on its way. The first flyby of Earth will take place 26 months after launch, followed by the Jupiter flyby some 19 months later. During the first leg of its trip, before its first Earth flyby, Cassini will navigate through part of the asteroid belt

and could perform an encounter with the asteroid Maja. Maja is a carbonaceous, or "C" type asteroid about 50 miles (78 kilometers) in diameter. Two small asteroids are being considered as possible additional targets, but only one of them can be visited.

The spacecraft's final encounter before proceeding to Saturn will be with Jupiter, which it will pass at a distance of about 2.2 million miles (3.6 million kilometers). Its flight path will take it for 130 days down through a region that no spacecraft has explored more than briefly—the giant planet's magnetotail. Cassini will fly down the magnetotail[1] of Jupiter, performing studies complementing the Galileo mission to Jupiter.

Upon reaching Saturn, the spacecraft will begin the first of some three dozen highly elliptical orbits during the remainder of its mission. Eighty-five days later, it will release its probe to Titan. Eleven days later, the probe will enter Titan's dense atmosphere and descend to the surface by parachute.

The $260-million probe is called *Huygens* after the famous Dutch astronomer Christiaan Huygens (1629–1695) who was the first to correctly interpret the rings of Saturn. He was also the discoverer of Saturn's largest satellite, *Titan*.

Because of the dense atmosphere shrouding the moon Titan, little is known of its surface. Scientists hope to gain a better understanding of the abundances of elements and compounds in its atmosphere, winds, and temperatures, and its surface state and composition.

After relaying to Earth data from the Titan probe's experiments, Cassini will continue with orbits of Saturn and flybys of most of the planet's 16 or more moons. In addition to 36 close encounters with Titan, the spacecraft's orbits will allow it to study Saturn's polar regions after examining the planet's equatorial zone. □

GALILEO

The Galileo mission allows scientists to study—at close range and for almost two years—the largest planet in the solar system, its satellites and massive energy field.

The spacecraft is studying the chemical composition and physical state of Jupiter's atmosphere and the four moons, as well as the structure and dynamics of the Jovian magnetosphere.

The spacecraft was carried aloft by the space shuttle *Atlantis* and launched toward Jupiter on Oct. 18, 1989. After a six-year journey, it achieved orbit around the planet on Dec. 7, 1995 and released a probe into the planet's atmosphere.

During its 57-minute descent before it was destroyed by the planet's extreme temperature and pressure, the probe determined some of the physical and chemical properties of Jupiter's cloudy upper atmosphere. Early results indicated a lower than expected abundance of water vapor and an apparent excess of krypton and xenon. Very little lightning was detected near the entry site and the probe found stronger winds and atmospheric turbulence than predicted.

On Oct. 29, 1991, Galileo took a historic photograph of asteroid 951 *Gaspera* from a distance of 10,000 miles (16,200 kilometers). It was the first close-up photo ever taken of an asteroid in space.

Galileo encountered Asteroid 243 *Ida* on Aug. 28, 1993 and took first close up photos which revealed that *Ida* had a tiny moon.

---

1. A tube of Jupiter's energy field, which trails away from the sun for several million miles.

The Dawning of the Space Age

On Oct. 4, 1957, the Soviet Union put the world's first artificial satellite, *Sputnik I,* into Earth orbit and ushered in the modern space age. *Sputnik* ("traveling companion") was spherical in shape with four antennas about 8 to 9 feet in length, 23 inches in diameter, and weighed 183.4 pounds. It circled the globe every 96 minutes at a speed of 18,000 miles per hour for 92 days until Jan. 4, 1958, when it re-entered the atmosphere and burned up.

Sputnik I orbited the Earth between 156 miles at its perigee (low point) and 560 miles at its apogee (high point). Its two radio transmitters marked the first time in history that man-made radio signals were sent from space to the Earth.

A month later on Nov. 3, 1957, the Soviet Union launched *Sputnik II,* the world's first satellite put into orbit with an animal housed aboard, an 11 lb mongrel dog named *Laika* ("barker"). She died a week later after the oxygen supply ran out. The satellite carried more sophisticated instrumentation, weighed 1,120 lbs and circled the Earth every 103.7 minutes. Its orbit was approximately 145 miles at its perigee and 1,056 miles at its apogee. The satellite burned up after being in orbit for 162 days.

During its first flyby of Ganymede on June 25, 1996, the spacecraft discovered that the face of the satellite has been heavily bombarded by comets and asteroids and wrinkled and torn by similar tectonic forces that have shaped the Earth.

Images taken by Galileo on its June 27, 1996, flyby of Io revealed that continuous volcanic activity had transformed much of Io's surface since the *Voyager* spacecraft observed the moon 17 years ago.

Galileo will make repeated close flybys of Io, Ganymede, Callisto, and Europa during the remainder of its mission in orbit around Jupiter.

Near-Earth Asteroid Rendezvous Mission (NEAR)

The NEAR spacecraft was launched on February 17, 1996; its main mission is to rendezvous with the near-Earth asteroid *Eros* in February 1999. The NEAR is the first of NASA's Discovery series of low-cost spacecraft, costing $122 million. It will fly past asteroid 253 *Mathilde* in June 1997 and swing back to Earth for a gravity assist and then on to asteroid 433 *Eros* in February 1999 where it will orbit the asteroid for 11 months. The NEAR spacecraft will ultimately orbit *Eros* at a distance of 62 miles (100 km) and make comprehensive measurements of its surface, size, volume, mass, spin, and magnetic field.

Is There Ice on the Moon?

Unlike the rest of the Moon's surface, the temperature of its polar regions remains permanently about –390° to –315° F and some of its craters remain perpetually in the dark. Some scientists have speculated that ice may have accumulated in the dark craters over long eons of time.

Data transmitted from the 1994 survey of the lunar surface by the *Clementine* spacecraft strongly suggests the presence of ice in the permanently shaded craters at the south pole.

The Lunar Prospector

NASA is planning on sending a small spacecraft to fly in a low-altitude orbit around the Moon. The mission, known as *Lunar Prospector,* is scheduled for launch in June 1997 and will last for at least one year. The $55-million *Prospector* will map the chemical composition of the lunar surface and the Moon's global magnetic and gravity fields at a level of detail greater than that achieved by previous missions. It will also detect traces of gases escaping from the lunar surface. The mission also should locate any significant quantities of frozen water in shadowed craters near the lunar poles. The presence of ice would be of great importance for any future human habitation on the Moon.

The *Lunar Prospector* is being built and will be launched on a Lockheed Launch Vehicle by Lockheed Missiles and Space Company of Sunnyvale, California.

The Mars Balloon

The original Mars program called for two launches, one in October 1994 for arrival in September 1995 and the other in 1996. During the first mission, the spacecraft will drop one or two balloons which will carry several scientific packages for analyzing Martian meteorological and surface conditions over a wide range of the planet.

The Mars mission program has encountered many delays, and one launch is scheduled for late 1996 and the other for late 1998. Russian financial problems have hampered the project.

Russia's *Mars '96* spacecraft is scheduled to launch in November 1996 to study the planet's surface, atmosphere, and climate. It will carry an orbiter and four landers for arrival at Mars in October 1997. The orbiter will carry stereo cameras for viewing the planet's surface and will investigate the composition and structure of the planet's upper atmosphere. Two of the landers will study the chemical and physical properties of the Martian soil. The orbiter is designed to operate for one year.

The balloon segment of the mission is a joint undertaking by Russia, France, and the United States, which has greatly benefitted from the successful balloon deployed at Venus in 1985 under the Soviet VEGA program.

The balloon will carry both a suspended payload (gondola) and a distributed payload (SNAKE) which will come into contact with the planet's surface as the balloon descends during the Martian night. The SNAKE will carry its own instruments to investigate the Martian surface. The sun's light will heat the gases within the lightweight balloon during the daytime, causing the balloon to rise and drift with the winds above the planet's surface. At night, the gases will cool, causing the balloon to descend and rest on the Martian soil.

The French Space Agency, The Centre National d'Etudes Spatials (CENES) is building the balloon that will carry the SNAKE.

Total mass of the balloon system is targeted for 60 to 65 kilograms (130 to 134 pounds). The gondola will weigh about 15 kilograms (33 pounds).

First U.S. Satellite

The first successful U.S. satellite, *Explorer I*, was launched into Earth orbit by the Army on January 31, 1958, at Cape Canaveral, Florida, four months after Russia orbited *Sputnik*. The 18-pound satellite had a cylindrical shape and was 80 inches long and six inches in diameter.

Explorer I's small package of instruments produced the first major discovery of the Space Age—The Van Allen radiation belts surrounding the Earth. *Explorer I* burned up in the atmosphere on March 30, 1970.

Mars Global Surveyor

There has been a need to follow up in greater detail on what was learned from the Viking mission to Mars in 1976. The *Mars Global Surveyor* will be a polar-orbiting spacecraft at Mars designed to provide global maps of the planet's surface topography, distribution of minerals, and monitoring of the Martian weather.

The spacecraft will be launched with a Delta II expendable vehicle from Cape Canaveral, Florida, in November 1996, and will cruise 10 months to Mars, where it initially will be inserted into an elliptical capture orbit. During the following four months, thruster firings and aerobraking techniques will be used to reach the nearly circular mapping orbit over the Martian polar caps. Mapping operations are expected to begin in late January 1998.

The spacecraft will circle Mars once every two hours, maintaining a "sun synchronous" orbit that will put the sun at a standard angle above the horizon in each image and allow the mid-afternoon lighting to cast shadows in such a way that surface features will stand out.

The *Mars Global Surveyor* will carry a portion of the *Mars Observer* instrument payload and will use these instruments to acquire data of Mars for a full Martian year, the equivalent of about two Earth years. The spacecraft will then be used as a data relay station for signals from U.S. and international landers and low-altitude probes for an additional three years.

The *Mars Global Surveyor* is the first mission of a new decade-long program of robotic exploration of Mars, called the *Mars Surveyor Program*. This will be an aggressive series of orbiters and landers to be launched every 26 months, as Mars moves into alignment with Earth. International participation, collaboration, and coordination will enhance all missions of the program.

NASA plans to launch the *Mars Surveyor '98* orbiter and lander in 1998 and 1999, respectively. The *Mars Surveyor '98* orbiter will study the planet's weather-related changes in the atmosphere and on the surface. The *Mars Surveyor '98* lander will be the first probe to land in the polar region of Mars. It will photograph the surface of the south polar region as it descends. After landing, it will deploy a package of stereo cameras, study weather conditions, and analyze soil samples dug up with a robotic arm.

Landers in future years—2001, 2003, and 2005—will capitalize on the experience of the *Mars Pathfinder* lander mission to be launched in December 1996. Small orbiters launched in the 1998 and 2003 opportunities will carry other instruments from the *Mars Observer* payload and will serve as data relay stations for international missions of the future.

X-ray Explorer

NASA launched the X-ray Timing Explorer (XTE) into orbit on Dec. 30, 1995 from Cape Canaveral by a Delta-2 rocket. The XTE is monitoring space for invisible X-ray emissions from black holes and other collapsed stars.

A device aboard the satellite called the All-Sky Monitor is scanning the heavens for X-ray sources. Once a target is identified, the satellite will be locked on to it and its other high-tech instruments will take measurements.

The two-year mission is expected to provide scientists with a great deal of new knowledge about black holes, neutron stars, and white dwarf stars which represent the final stages of stellar evolution.

U.S. Unmanned Planetary and Lunar Programs

Lunar Orbiter. Series of spacecraft designed to orbit the Moon, taking pictures and obtaining data in support of the subsequent manned Apollo landings. The U.S. launched five *Lunar Orbiters* between Aug. 10, 1966 and Aug. 2, 1967.

Mariner. Designation for a series of spacecraft designed to fly past or orbit the planets, particularly Mercury, Venus, and Mars. *Mariners* provided the early information on Venus and Mars. *Mariner 9*, orbiting Mars in 1971, returned the most startling photographs of that planet and helped pave the way for a *Viking* landing in 1976. *Mariner 10* explored Venus and Mercury in 1973 and was the first probe to use a planet's gravity to whip it toward another.

Pioneer. Designation for the United States' first series of sophisticated interplanetary spacecraft. *Pioneers 10* and *11* reached Jupiter in 1973 and 1974 and continued on to explore Saturn and the other outer planets. *Pioneer 11*, renamed *Pioneer Saturn*, examined the Saturn system in September 1979. Significant discoveries were the finding of a small new moon and a narrow new ring. In 1986, *Pioneer 10* was the first man-made object to escape the solar system. *Pioneer Venus 1* and *2* reached Venus in 1978 and provided detailed information about that planet's surface and atmosphere.

Ranger. NASA's earliest Moon exploration program. Spacecraft were designed for a crash landing on the Moon, taking pictures and returning scientific data up to the moment of impact. Provided the first closeup views of the lunar surface. The *Rangers* provided more than 17,000 closeup pictures, giving us more information about the Moon in a few years than in all the time that had gone before.

Surveyor. Series of unmanned spacecraft designed to land gently on the Moon and provide information on the surface in preparation for the manned lunar landings. Their legs were instrumented to return data on the surface hardness of the Moon. *Surveyor* dispelled the fear that Apollo spacecraft might sink several feet or more into the lunar dust.

Viking. Designation for two spacecraft designed to conduct detailed scientific examination of the planet Mars, including a search for life. *Viking 1* landed on July 20, 1976; *Viking 2*, Sept. 3, 1976. More was learned about the Red Planet in a few short months than in all the time that had gone before. But the question of life on Mars remains unresolved.

Voyager. Designation for two spacecraft designed to explore Jupiter and the other outer planets. *Voyager 1* and *Voyager 2* passed Jupiter in 1979 and sent back startling color TV images of that planet and its moons. They took a total of about 33,000 pictures. *Voyager 1* passed Saturn November 1980. *Voyager 2* passed Saturn August 1981 and Uranus in January 1986.

It encountered Neptune on August 29, 1989 and made many startling discoveries. Found four rings around the planet, six new moons, a Giant Spot, and evidence of volcanic-like activity on its largest moon, Triton. The spacecraft sent back over 9,000 pictures of the planet and its system.

On February 13, 1990, at a distance of 3.7 billion miles, *Voyager 1* took its final pictures—the Sun and six of its planets as seen from deep space. NASA released the extraordinary images to the public on June 6, 1990. Only Mercury, Mars, and Pluto were not seen.

Notable Unmanned Lunar and Interplanetary Probes

Spacecraft	Launch date	Destination	Remarks
Pioneer 3 (U.S.)	Dec. 6, 1958	Moon	Max. alt.: 66,654 mi. Discovered outer Van Allen layer.
Luna 2 (U.S.S.R.)	Sept. 12, 1959	Moon	Impacted on Sept. 14. First space vehicle to reach moon.
Luna 3 (U.S.S.R.)	Oct. 4, 1959	Moon	Flew around Moon and transmitted first pictures of lunar far side, Oct. 7.
Mariner 2 (U.S.)	Aug. 27, 1962	Venus	Venus probe. Successful mid-course correction. Passed 21,648 mi. from Venus Dec. 14, 1962. Reported 800°F. surface temp. Contact lost Jan. 3, 1963 at 54 million mi.
Mariner 4 (U.S.)	Nov. 28, 1964	Mars	Transmitted first close-up pictures on June 14, 1965, from altitude of 6,000 mi.
Ranger 7 (U.S.)	July 28, 1964	Moon	Impacted near Crater Guericke 68.5 h after launch. Sent 4,316 pictures during last 15 min of flight as close as 1,000 ft above lunar surface.
Luna 9 (U.S.S.R.)	Jan. 31, 1966	Moon	3,428 lb. Instrument capsule of 220 lb soft-landed Feb. 3, 1966. Sent back about 30 pictures.
Surveyor 1 (U.S.)	May 30, 1966	Moon	Landed June 2, 1966. Sent almost 10,400 pictures, a number after surviving the 14-day lunar night.
Lunar Orbiter 1 (U.S.)	Aug. 10, 1966	Moon	Orbited Moon Aug. 14. 21 pictures sent.
Surveyor 3 (U.S.)	April 17, 1967	Moon	Soft-landed 65 h after launch on Oceanus Procellarum. Scooped and tested lunar soil.
Venera 4 (U.S.S.R.)	June 12, 1967	Venus	Arrived Oct. 17. Instrument capsule sent temperature and chemical data.
Surveyor 5 (U.S.)	Sept. 8, 1967	Moon	Landed near lunar equator Sept. 10. Radiological analysis of lunar soil. Mechanical claw for digging soil.
Surveyor 7 (U.S.)	Jan. 6, 1968	Moon	Landed near Crater Tycho Jan. 10. Soil analysis. Sent 3,343 pictures.
Pioneer 9 (U.S.)	Nov. 8, 1968	Sun Orbit	Achieved orbit. Six experiments returned solar radiation data.
Venera 5 (U.S.S.R.)	Jan. 5, 1969	Venus	Landed May 16, 1969. Returned atmospheric data.
Mariner 6 (U.S.)	Feb. 24, 1969	Mars	Came within 2000 mi. of Mars July 31, 1969. Sent back data & TV pictures.
Luna 16 (U.S.S.R.)	Sept. 12, 1970	Moon	Soft-landed Sept. 20, scooped up rock, returned to Earth Sept. 24.
Luna 17 (U.S.S.R.)	Nov. 10, 1970	Moon	Soft-landed on Sea of Rains Nov. 17. Lunokhod 1, self-propelled vehicle, used for first time. Sent TV photos, made soil analysis, etc.
Mariner 9 (U.S.)	May 30, 1971	Mars	First craft to orbit Mars, Nov. 13. 7,300 pictures, 1st close-ups of Mars' moon. Transmission ended Oct. 27, 1972.
Luna 20 (U.S.S.R.)	Feb. 14, 1972	Moon	Soft-landed Feb. 21 in Sea of Fertility. Returned Feb. 25 with rock samples.
Pioneer 10 (U.S.)	March 3, 1972	Jupiter	620-million-mile flight path through asteroid belt passed Jupiter Dec. 3, 1973, to give man first closeup of planet. In 1986, it became first man-made object to escape solar system.
Luna 21 (U.S.S.R.)	Jan. 8, 1973	Moon	Soft-landed Jan. 16. Lunokhod 2 (moon-car) scooped up soil samples, returned them to Earth Jan. 27.
Mariner 10 (U.S.)	Nov. 3, 1973	Venus, Mercury	Passed Venus Feb. 5, 1974. Arrived Mercury March 29, 1974, for man's first closeup look at planet. First time gravity of one planet (Venus) used to whip spacecraft toward another (Mercury).
Viking 1 (U.S.)	Aug. 20, 1975	Mars	Carrying life-detection labs. Landed July 20, 1976, for detailed scientific research, including pictures. Designed to work for only 90 days, it operated for almost 6 1/2 years before it went silent in November 1982.

Spacecraft	Launch date	Destination	Remarks
Viking 2 (U.S.)	Sept. 9, 1975	Mars	Like Viking 1. Landed Sept. 3, 1976. Functioned 3 1/2 years.
Luna 24 (U.S.S.R.)	Aug. 9, 1976	Moon	Soft-landed Aug. 18, 1976. Returned soil samples Aug. 22, 1976.
Voyager 1 (U.S.)	Sept. 5, 1977	Jupiter, Saturn	Fly-by mission. Reached Jupiter in March 1979; passed Saturn Nov. 1980; passed Uranus 1986.
Voyager 2 (U.S.)	Aug. 20, 1977	Jupiter, Saturn, Uranus	Launched before *Voyager 1*. Encountered Jupiter in July 1979; flew by Saturn Aug. 1981; passed Uranus January 1986; and passed Neptune in August 1989.
Pioneer Venus 1 (U.S.)	May 20, 1978	Venus	Arrived Dec. 4 and orbited Venus, photographing surface and atmosphere. Crashed into planet's surface mid-October 1992 after circling Venus for 14 years.
Pioneer Venus 2 (U.S.)	Aug. 8, 1978	Venus	Four-part multi-probe, landed Dec. 9.
Venera 13 (U.S.S.R.)	Oct. 30, 1981	Venus	Landed March 1, 1982. Took first X-ray fluorescence analysis of the planet's surface. Transmitted data 2 hours 7 minutes.
VEGA 1 (U.S.S.R.)	Deployed on Venus, June 10, 1985	Encounter with Halley's Comet	In flyby over Venus while enroute to encounter with Halley's Comet, VEGA 1 and 2 dropped scientific capsules onto Venus to study atmosphere and surface material. Encountered Halley's Comet on March 6 and March 9, 1986.
VEGA 2 (U.S.S.R.)	Deployed on Venus, June 14, 1985		
Suisei (Japan)	Encountered Halley's Comet March 8, 1986	Halley's Comet	Spacecraft made fly-by of comet and studied atmosphere with ultraviolet camera. Observed rotation nucleus.
Sakigake (Japan)	Encountered Halley's Comet March 10, 1986	Halley's Comet	Spacecraft made fly-by to study solar wind and magnetic fields. Detected plasma waves.
Giotto (ESA)	Encountered Halley's Comet March 13, 1986	Halley's Comet	European Space Agency spacecraft made closest approach to comet. Studied atmosphere and magnetic fields. Sent back best pictures of nucleus. Flew by comet Grigg-Skjellerup, July 10, 1992. Unable to send pictures.
Phobos Mission (U.S.S.R.)	July 7 and July 12, 1988	Mars and Phobos	Two spacecraft to probe Martian moon Phobos starting April 1989. Were to study orbit, soil chemistry, send TV pictures and data of planet. Contact was lost with Phobos 1 in August 1988 and later with Phobos 2 in March 1989 after it reached the Martian moon.
Magellan (U.S.)	May 4, 1989	Venus	Arrived at Venus on Aug. 10, 1990 and made a geologic map of planet with a powerful radar. Crashed into Venus Oct. 12, 1994.
Galileo (U.S.)	Oct. 18, 1989	Jupiter	To study Jupiter's atmosphere and its moons during 22-month mission. It will reach the planet in 1995.
Hubble Space Telescope (U.S., E.S.A.)[1]	April 25, 1990	Earth Orbit	Studies distant stars and galaxies and searches for evidence of planets in other solar systems. Crew of Endeavour STS-61 repaired telescope Dec. 2–13, 1993.
Ulysses (U.S., ESA)	Oct. 6, 1990	The Sun	To study the poles of the Sun and interstellar space above and below the poles. First solar encounter to be in 1994. Second encounter to be in 1995.
Gamma-Ray Observatory (U.S.)	April 7, 1991	Earth Orbit	To make first survey of gamma ray sources across the whole sky, studying explosive energic sources such as supernovae, quasars, neutron stars, pulsars, and black holes.
Mars Observer (U.S.)	Sept. 25, 1992	Mars	Spacecraft to arrive at Mars Aug. 1993 and orbit the planet for one full Martian year to study atmosphere and surface change during the planet's seasons. Mission failed after communications with *Observer* lost August 21, 1993.
Clementine (U.S.)	Jan. 25, 1994	Moon and asteroid Geographos 1620	Entered lunar orbit February 21 and took close-up photos of lunar surface for two months. Computer malfunction prevented planned rendezvous with *Geographos*.
Mars '96/'98 (Russia)	1996[1]	Mars	Two spacecraft to study Mars over an 18-month period. Will investigate Martian surface and deploy a balloon-borne package during second mission to study the planet's atmosphere.

1. European Space Agency (E.S.A.), responsible for furnishing the solar arrays, the Faint Object Camera, and participation in flight operations aspects of the mission.

U.S. Manned Space Flights

Mercury. *Project Mercury,* initiated in 1958 and completed in 1963, was the United States' first man-in-space program. It was designed to further knowledge about man's capabilities in space.

In April 1959, seven military jet test pilots were introduced to the public as America's first astronauts. They were: Lt. M. Scott Carpenter, USN; Capt. L. Gordon Cooper, Jr., USAF; Lt. Col. John H. Glenn, Jr., USMC; Cap. Virgil I. Grissom, USAF; Lt. Comdr. Walter M. Shirra, Jr., USN; Lt. Comdr. Alan B. Shepard, Jr., USN; and Capt. Donald K. Slayton, USAF. Six of the original seven would make a Mercury flight. Slayton was grounded for medical reasons, but remained a director of the astronaut office. He returned to flight status in 1975 as Docking Module Pilot on the Apollo-Soyuz flight.

Flight Summary

Each astronaut named his capsule and added the numeral 7 to denote the teamwork of the original astronauts.

May 5, 1961. Alan B. Shepard, Jr., makes a suborbital flight in *Freedom 7* and becomes the first American in space. Time: 15 minutes, 22 seconds.

July 21, 1961. Virgil I. Grissom makes the second successful suborbital flight in *Liberty Bell 7,* but spacecraft sank shortly after splashdown. Time: 15 minutes, 37 seconds. Grissom was later killed in *Apollo 1* fire, Jan. 27, 1967.

February 20, 1962. John H. Glenn, Jr., makes a three-orbit flight and becomes the first American in orbit. Time: 4 hours, 55 minutes.

May 24, 1962. M. Scott Carpenter duplicates Glenn's flight in *Aurora 7.* Time: 4 hours, 56 minutes.

October 3, 1962. Walter M. Schirra, Jr., makes a six-orbit engineering test flight in *Sigma 7.* Time: 9 hours, 13 minutes.

May 15–16, 1963. L. Gordon Cooper, Jr., performs the last *Mercury* mission and completes 22 orbits in *Faith 7* to evaluate effects of one day in space. Time: 34 hours, 19 minutes.

Gemini. *Gemini* was an extension of *Project Mercury,* to determine the effects of prolonged space flight on man—two weeks or longer—the time it takes to reach the Moon and return. "Walks in space" provided invaluable information for astronauts' later walks on the Moon. The *Gemini* spacecraft, twice as large as the *Mercury* capsule, accommodated two astronauts. Its crew named the project *Gemini* for the third constellation of the Zodiac and its twin stars, Castor and Pollux. The capsule differed from the *Mercury* spacecrafts in that it had hatches above the capsules so that the astronauts could leave the spacecraft and perform spacewalks or extra vehicular activities (EVAs).

There were ten manned flights in the *Gemini* program, starting with *Gemini 3* on March 23, 1965, and ending with the *Gemini 12* mission on Nov. 15, 1966. *Gemini 1* and 2 were unmanned test flights of the equipment.

When the *Gemini* program ended, U.S. astronauts had perfected rendezvous and docking maneuvers with other orbiting vehicles.

Apollo. *Apollo* was the designation for the United States' effort to land a man on the Moon and return him safely to Earth. The goal was successfully accomplished with *Apollo 11* on July 20, 1969, culminating eight years of rehearsal and centuries of dreaming. Astronauts Neil A. Armstrong and Col. Edwin E. Aldrin, Jr., scooped up and brought back the first lunar rocks ever seen on Earth—about 47 pounds.

Tragedy struck Jan. 27, 1967, on the launch pad during a preflight test of what would have become *Apollo 1,* the first manned mission. Astronauts Lt. Col. Virgil "Gus" Grissom, Lt. Col. Edward H. White, and Lt. Cdr. Roger Chafee lost their lives when a fire swept through the command module.

Six *Apollo* flights followed, ending with *Apollo 17* in December, 1972. The last three *Apollos* carried mechanized vehicles called lunar rovers for wide-ranging surface exploration of the Moon by astronauts. The rendezvous and docking of an *Apollo* spacecraft with a Russian *Soyuz* craft in Earth orbit on July 18, 1975, closed out the *Apollo* program.

During the Apollo project, the following 12 astronauts explored the lunar terrain:

Col. Edwin E. "Buzz" Aldrin, Jr., and Neil A. Armstrong, *Apollo 11;* Cdr. Alan L. Bean and Cdr. Charles Conrad, Jr., *Apollo 12;* Edgar D. Mitchell and Alan B. Shepard, *Apollo 14;* Lt. Col. James B. Irwin (1930–1991) and Col. David R. Scott, *Apollo 15;* Col. Charles M. Duke, Jr., and Capt. John W. Young, *Apollo 16;* and Capt. Eugene A. Cernan and Dr. Harrison H. Schmitt, *Apollo 17.*

Apollo was a three-part spacecraft: the command module (CM), the crew's quarters and flight control section; the service modules (SM) for the propulsion and spacecraft support systems (when together, the two modules were called CSM); and the lunar module (LM) to take two of the crew to the lunar surface, support them on the Moon, and return them to the CSM in orbit. The crews that made the lunar flights where both command modules and lunar modules were involved selected call names for the vehicles. The call names for the spacecraft in the six lunar landing missions with the command module and lunar module designations respectively were:

Apollo 11, Columbia and *Eagle; Apollo 12, Yankee Clipper* and *Intrepid;* (NOTE: The third lunar attempt, *Apollo 13,* April 11–17, 1970, 5 days, 22.9 hours, was aborted after the service module oxygen tank ruptured. The *Apollo 13* crew members were James A. Lovell, Jr., John L. Swigert, Jr., and Fred W. Haise, Jr. The mission was classified as a "Successful failure," because the crew was rescued. The call names for their spacecraft were *Odyssey* (CM) and *Aquarius* (LM).) *Apollo 14, Kitty Hawk* and *Antares; Apollo 15, Endeavor* and *Falcon; Apollo 16, Casper* and *Orion;* and *Apollo 17, America* and *Challenger.*

Skylab. America's first Earth-orbiting space station. *Project Skylab* was designed to demonstrate that men can work and live in space for prolonged periods without ill effects. Originally the spent third stage of a Saturn 5 moon rocket, *Skylab* measured 118 feet from stem to stern, and carried the most varied assortment of experimental equipment ever assembled in a single spacecraft. Three three-man crews visited the space stations, spending more than 740 hours observing the Sun and bringing home more than

175,000 solar pictures. These were the first recordings of solar activity above Earth's obscuring atmosphere. *Skylab* also evaluated systems designed to gather information on Earth's resources and environmental conditions. *Skylab*'s biomedical findings indicated that man adapts well to space for at least a period of three months, provided he has a proper diet and adequately programmed exercise, sleep, work, and recreation periods. *Skylab* orbited Earth at a distance of about 300 miles. Five years after the last *Skylab* mission, the 77-ton space station's orbit began to deteriorate faster than expected, owing to unexpectedly high sunspot activity. On July 11, 1979, the parts of *Skylab* that did not burn up in the atmosphere came crashing down on parts of Australia and the Indian Ocean. No one was hurt.

Space Shuttle. The NASA orbiter is 122.2 feet long and has a wingspan of 78.6 feet.

The *Space Shuttle Columbia* was successfully launched on April 12, 1981. It made five flights (the first four were test runs), the last completed on November 16, 1982. The second shuttle, *Challenger*, made its maiden flight on April 4, 1983. In April 1984, crew members of the *Challenger* captured, repaired, and returned the Solar Max satellite to orbit, making it the first time a disabled satellite had been repaired in space. The third shuttle, *Discovery*, made its first flight on August 30, 1984. The fourth space shuttle, *Atlantis*, made its maiden flight on Oct. 3, 1985.

A tragedy occurred on Jan. 28, 1986, when the shuttle *Challenger* exploded, killing the crew of seven 73 seconds after takeoff. It was the world's worst space flight disaster.

NASA has estimated that the risk of a catastrophic failure is about 1 in 145 for each shuttle flight. Eventually, another disaster could occur.

The first U.S. space mission since the *Challenger* disaster was launched 32 months later on Sept. 29, 1988, with the flight of *Discovery*. It had a crew of five and deployed a communications satellite.

The fifth and last orbiter, *Endeavour*, was built as a replacement for *Challenger*. It was named after the British explorer James Cook's first ship. *Endeavour* was launched on its maiden voyage on May 7, 1992 with a crew of seven astronauts. They made four spacewalks and retrieved a disabled Intelsat-6 communications satellite. During the mission, Dr. Kathryn Thornton became the second American woman to walk in space.

The shuttle *Endeavour* set a record 16 days, 15 hours in space, March 2–18, 1995.

The crew of the 50th mission aboard the *Endeavour*, launched Sept. 12, 1992, included the first black woman astronaut, Dr. Mae C. Jemison, and the first married couple to fly together in space, Air Force Lt. Col. Mark C. Lee and Dr. N. Jan Davis.

Lt. Col. Eileen M. Collins became the first woman to pilot a shuttle, *Discovery*, during the spacecraft's historic rendezvous with the Russian space station *Mir* on February 6, 1995. The shuttle *Atlantis* made the first linkup with the *Mir* on June 29, 1995.

Soviet Manned Space Flight Programs

Vostok. The Soviets' first manned capsule, roughly spherical, used to place the first six cosmonauts in Earth orbit (1961–65).

Voskhod. Adaptation of the *Vostok* capsule to accommodate two and three cosmonauts. *Voskhod 1* orbited three persons, and *Voskhod 2* orbited two persons performing the world's first manned extra-vehicular activity.

Soyuz. Late-model manned spacecraft with provisions for three cosmonauts and a "working compartment" accessible through a hatch. Soyuz is the Russian word for "union". The *Soyuz* spacecraft can carry three cosmonauts, and routinely brings cosmonauts and their foreign "guests" to the *Mir* space station. *Soyuz 19*, launched July 15, 1975, docked with the American *Apollo* spacecraft.

Salyut. Earth-orbiting space station intended for prolonged occupancy and re-visitation by cosmonauts. They are usually launched by Soviet Proton rockets. *Salyut 1* was launched April 19, 1971. *Salyut 2*, launched April 3, 1973, malfunctioned in orbit and was never occupied. *Salyut 3* was launched June 25, 1974. *Salyut 4* was launched Dec. 26, 1974. *Salyut 5* was launched June 22, 1976. *Salyut 6* was launched on Sept. 29, 1977. *Salyut 7* was launched on April 19, 1982. A record breaking Russian endurance flight was set (Feb. 8, 1984–Oct. 2, 1985) when Soviet astronauts spent 237 days in orbit aboard *Salyut 7*. *Salyut 7* re-entered the atmosphere and crashed into the Atlantic Ocean on Feb. 6, 1991.

Mir. The former Soviet Union's space station was launched into orbit on Feb. 20, 1986. Since that time, several space endurance records have been set in the *Mir*. On Dec. 29, 1987, Col. Yuri Romanenko set a single-mission record of 326.5 days in space. On Dec. 21, 1989, Col. Vladimir Titov and Musa Manarov returned to Earth after spending 366 days aboard the orbiting space station. On March 22, 1995, Russian cosmonaut Valeriy Polyakov set a new record for the longest human flight in space—439 days. U.S. astronaut Dr. Norman E. Thagard set a U.S. record of 112 days in space aboard the *Mir* on July 4, 1995.

The *Mir* will be abandoned when the international space station *Alpha* is constructed in 1997. However, the unpiloted *Mir* will be operated by remote control for a year or longer to test a solar power system to be used in *Alpha*.

The Russian Space Shuttle *Buran*

The successful test flight of the former Soviet Union's first reusable space shuttle *Buran* (Russian for "snowstorm") was made on Nov. 15, 1988. The unmanned flight circled the Earth for two orbits and lasted 3 hr 25 min.

The Russian and American space shuttles closely resemble each other in size and appearance and have similar delta wings and vertical tail structures. Some major differences between the two shuttles are that the Russian craft has no large rocket engines of its own. It uses the giant disposable *Energiya* rocket for most of its propulsion, and has only small rockets for maneuvering.

Unlike the American version, the *Buran* was designed for fully automatic flight, from takeoff to landing, a difficult engineering feat.

The crew cabin of *Buran* can accommodate two to four astronauts and has seats for six passengers or other crew members.

The Russian craft is 19 ft (5.6 m) in diameter compared with NASA's shuttle, 17 ft (5.2 m). The wingspan is 79.2 ft (24 m). NASA's orbiter is 78.6 ft (23.79 m). *Buran's* length is 119 ft (36 m), the U.S. shuttle is 122.2 ft long (37.24 m).

Additional flights in the *Buran* were never made.

Notable Manned Space Flights

Designation and country	Date	Astronauts	Flight time (h/min)	Remarks
Vostok 1(U.S.S.R.)	April 12, 1961	Yuri A. Gagarin	1/48	First manned orbital flight
MR III (U.S.)	May 5, 1961	Alan B. Shepard, Jr.	0/15	Range 486 km (302 mi.), peak 187 km (116.5 mi); capsule recovered. First American in space.
Vostok 2 (U.S.S.R.)	Aug. 6–7, 1961	Gherman S. Titov	25/18	First long-duration flight
MA VI (U.S.)	Feb. 20, 1962	John H. Glenn, Jr.	4/55	First American in orbit
MA IX (U.S.)	May 15–16, 1963	L. Gordon Cooper, Jr.	34/20	Longest Mercury flight
Vostok 6 (U.S.S.R.)	June 16–19, 1963	Valentina V. Tereshkova	70/50	First orbital flight by female cosmonaut
Voskhod 1 (U.S.S.R.)	Oct. 12, 1964	Vladimir M. Komarov; Konstantin P. Feoktistov; Boris G. Yegorov	24/17	First 3-man orbital flight; also first flight without space suits
Voskhod 2 (U.S.S.R.)	March 18, 1965	Alexei A. Leonov; Pavel I. Belyayev	26/2	First "space walk" (by Leonov), 10 min
GT III (U.S.)	March 23, 1965	Virgil I. Grissom; John W. Young	4/53	First manned test of Gemini spacecraft
GT IV (U.S.)	June 3–7, 1965	James A. McDivitt; Edward H. White, 2d	97/48	First American "space walk" (by White), lasting slightly over 20 min
GT VIII (U.S.)	March 16–17, 1966	Neil A. Armstrong; David R. Scott	10/42	First docking between manned space-craft and an unmanned space vehicle (an orbiting Agena rocket).
Apollo 7 (U.S.)	Oct. 11–22, 1968	Walter M. Schirra, Jr.; Donn F. Eisele; R. Walter Cunningham	260/9	First manned test of Apollo command module; first live TV transmissions from orbit
Soyuz 3 (U.S.S.R.)	Oct. 26–30, 1968	Georgi T. Bergeovoi	94/51	First manned rendezvous and possible docking by Soviet cosmonaut
Apollo 8 (U.S.)	Dec. 21–27, 1968	Frank Borman; James A. Lovell, Jr.; William A. Anders	147/00	First spacecraft in circumlunar orbit; TV trans-missions from this orbit. The three astro-nauts were also the first men to view the Earth whole.
Apollo 9 (U.S.)	Mar. 3–13, 1969	James A. McDivitt; David R. Scott; Russell L. Schweikart	241/1	First manned flight of Lunar Module
Apollo 10 (U.S.)	May 18–26, 1969	Thomas P. Stafford; Eugene A. Cernan; John W. Young	192/3	First descent to within 9 miles of moon's surface by manned craft
Apollo 11 (U.S.)	July 16–24, 1969	Neil A. Armstrong; Edwin E. Aldrin, Jr.; Michael Collins	195/18	First manned landing and EVA on Moon; soil and rock samples collected; ex-periments left on lunar surface
Soyuz 6 (U.S.S.R.)	Oct. 11–16, 1969	Gorgiy Shonin; Valriy Kabasov	118/42	Three spacecraft and seven men put into earth orbit simultaneously for first time
Apollo 12 (U.S.)	Nov. 14–24, 1969	Charles Conrad, Jr.; Richard F. Gordon, Jr.; Alan Bean	244/36	Manned lunar landing mission; investi-gated Surveyor 3 spacecraft; collected lunar samples. EVA time: 15 h 30 min
Apollo 13 (U.S.)	April 11–17, 1970	James A. Lovell, Jr.; Fred W. Haise, Jr.; John L. Swigert, Jr.	142/54	Third manned lunar landing attempt; aborted due to pressure loss in liquid oxygen in service module and failure of fuel cells
Apollo 14 (U.S.)	Jan. 31–Feb. 9, 1971	Alan B. Shepard; Stuart A. Roosa; Edgar D. Mitchell	216/42	Third manned lunar landing: returned largest amount of lunar material
Soyuz 11 (U.S.S.R.)	June 6–30, 1971	Georgiy Tomofeyevich Dobrovolskiy; Vladislav Nikolayevich Volkov; Viktor Ivanovich Patsyev	569/40	Linked up with first space station, Salyut 1. Astronauts died just before re-en-try due to loss of pressurization in spacecraft
Apollo 15 (U.S.)	July 26–Aug. 7, 1971	David R. Scott; James B. Irwin; Alfred M. Worden	295/12	Fourth manned lunar landing; first use of Lunar Rover propelled by Scott and Irving; first live pictures of LM lift-off from Moon; exploration time: 18 hours
Apollo 16 (U.S.)	April 16–27, 1972	John W. Young; Thomas K. Mattingly; Charles M. Duke, Jr.	265/51	Fifth manned lunar landing; second use of Lunar Rover Vehicle, propelled by Young and Duke Total exploration time on the Moon was 20 h 14 min, setting new record. Mattingly's in-flight "walk in space" was 1 h 23 min. Approximately 213 lb of lunar rock returned
Apollo 17 (U.S.)	Dec. 7–19, 1972	Eugene A. Cernan; Ronald E. Evans; Harrison H. Schmitt	301/51	Sixth and last manned lunar landing; third to carry lunar rover. Cernan and Schmitt, during three EVA's, completed total of 22 h 05 min 3 sec. USS Ticonderoga recovered crew and about 250 lb of lunar samples
Skylab SL-2 (U.S.)	May 25–June 22, 1973	Charles Conrad, Jr.; Joseph P. Kerwin; Paul J. Weitz	672/50	First manned Skylab launch. Established Skylab Orbital Assembly and conducted scientific and medical experiments
Skylab SL-3 (U.S.)	July 28–Sept. 25, 1973	Alan L. Bean, Jr.; Jack R. Lousma; Owen K. Garriott	1427/9	Second manned Skylab launch. New crew remained in space for 59 days, continuing scientific and medical experiments and earth observations from orbit

Designation and country	Date	Astronauts	Flight time (h/min)	Remarks
Skylab SL-4 (U.S.)	Nov. 16, 1973–Feb. 8, 1974	Gerald Carr; Edward Gibson; William Pogue	2017/16	Third manned Skylab launch; obtained medical data on crew for use in extending the duration of manned space flight; crews "walked in space" 4 times, totaling 44 h 40 min. Longest space mission yet—84 d 1 h 16 min. Splashdown in Pacific, Feb. 9, 1974
Apollo/Soyuz Test Project (U.S. and U.S.S.R.)	July 15–24, 1975 (U.S.)	U.S.: Brig. Gen. Thomas P. Stafford; Vance D. Brand; Donald K. Slayton	216/05	World's first international manned rendezvous and docking in space; aimed at developing a space rescue capability
	July 15–21, 1975 (U.S.S.R.)	U.S.S.R.: Col. A. A. Leonov; V. N. Kubasov	223/35	Apollo and Soyuz docked and crewmen exchanged visits on July 17, 1975. Mission duration for Soyuz: 142 h 31 min. For Apollo: 217 h, 28 min.
Columbia (U.S.)	April 12–14, 1981	Capt. Robert L. Crippen; John W. Young	54/20	Maiden voyage of *Space Shuttle,* the first spacecraft designed specifically for re-use up to 100 times
Salyut 7 (U.S.S.R.)	Feb. 8, 1984–Oct. 2, 1985	Leonid Kizim; Vladimir Solovyov; Oleg Atkov	237 days	Record Soviet team endurance flight in orbiting space station
Mir (U.S.S.R.)	Feb. 8, 1987–Dec. 29, 1987	Yuri V. Romanenko[1]	326.5 days	Record Soviet single endurance flight in orbiting space station.
Mir (U.S.S.R.)	Dec. 1, 1987–Dec. 21, 1988	Col. Vladimir Titov and Musa Manarov	366 days	Record Soviet team endurance flight in orbiting space station.
Endeavour (U.S.)	May 7–13, 1992	Richard J. Hieb; Maj. Thomas D. Akers; Comdr. Pierre J. Thugt	—	The three mission specialists remained free of the *Endeavour* for 8 hours and 20 minutes on May 13 during the repair of communications satellite, setting an absolute record for extravehicular duration in space. First capture of a satellite using hands only.
Endeavour (U.S.)	Dec. 2–13, 1993	Col. Richard O. Covey; Comdr. Kenneth D. Bowersox; Lt. Col. Tom Akers*; Dr. Jeffrey A. Hoffman**; Dr. Story Musgrave**; Claude Nicollier; Dr. Kathryn C. Thornton* (*two space walks, **three space walks)	10 days, 19 hr., 59 min.	Repaired Hubble Space Telescope. Replaced gyroscopes, solar arrays, camera, electronics and hardware. Installed COSTAR corrective optics to compensate for flaw in Hubble's primary mirror. Record five space walks in a single mission.
Discovery (U.S.)	Feb. 3–11, 1994	Col. Charles F. Bolden; Capt. Kenneth S. Reightier, Jr.; Dr. N. Jan Davis; Dr. Frankling R. Chang-Diaz; Dr. Ronald M. Sega; Russian cosmonaut, Sergei K. Krikalev	8 days, 7 hr., 22 sec.	Test flight of Wake Shield Facility, an experimental, retrievable, free-flying satellite for use in developing exotic materials. Cargo bay carried a private, commercial pressurized-laboratory, Spacelab, for experimental use, leased by NASA. Crew member Sergei K. Krikalev, was first Russian cosmonaut to be launched in an American spacecraft
Columbia (U.S.)	July 8–23, 1994	Col. Robert D. Cabana; Lieut. Col. James D. Halsell, Jr.; Richard J. Hieb; Lieut. Col. Carl E. Walz; Dr. Leroy Chiao; Dr. Donald A. Thomas; and Dr. Chiaki Naito-Mukai, the first Japanese woman astronaut.	14 days, 17 hr., 55 min.	Studied the effects of limited gravity of orbital flight on materials and living things including goldfish, killifish, jellyfish, sea urchins, and Japanesered-bellied newts.
Mir–17 (Russia)	Jan. 8, 1994–Mar. 22, 1995	Dr. Valery Polyakov	439[2] days	Record single endurance flight in orbiting space station. Returned to earth with crewmates cosmonaut Helena Kondakova and commander Alexander Viktorenko who spent 169 days each in the *Mir.*
Discovery (U.S.)	Feb. 3–11, 1995	Comdr. James D. Wetherbee; Lt. Col. Eileen M. Collins; Dr. Janice Voss; Dr. Bernard A. Harris, Jr.*; Dr. C. Michael Foale*; Russian cosmonaut Co. Vladimir G. Titov. (*performed spacewalks.)	8 days, 6 hr., 29 min.	First rendezvous of U.S. spacecraft with a Russian space station (*Mir*), Feb. 6. Lt. Col. Collins was first female shuttle pilot. Deployed and retrieved solar observatory satellite. Extra-vehicular activity to test new space suit modifications and practice space station assembly techniques. EVA time: 4 h, 35 min.
Endeavour (U.S.)	March 2–18, 1995	Comdr. Stephen Oswald; Lt. Col. William Gregory; Lt. Comdr. Wendy Lawrence; Dr. John Grunsfeld; Dr. Tamara Jernigan; Samuel Durrance; Ronald Parise	16 days, 15 hr., 8 min.	Old record aerospace mission in duration and in orbit with more than two astronauts. Performed astrophysics research with three ultraviolet telescopes. Studied ultraviolet light streaming from stars, galaxies, quasars, the Moon, and the Earth.

Designation and country	Date	Astronauts	Flight time (h/min)	Remarks
Soyuz TM–21 (Russia)	March 14–16, 1995	Russian cosmonauts: Lt. Col. Vladimir N. Dezhurov; Gennady M. Strekalov; and U.S. astronaut Dr. Norman E. Thagard	—	Dr. Thagard became the first American astronaut to fly aboard a Soyuz spacecraft with a Russian crew launched from Baikonur Space Center in Kazakhstan. He also became the first American to enter the *Mir* space station on March 16. Also see *Atlantis*, June 27–July 7, 1995.
Atlantis (U.S.)	June 27–July 7, 1995	Lt. Col. Charles J. Prescourt; Capt. Robert L. (Hoot) Gibson; Dr. Ellen S. Baker; Gregory J. Harbaugh; Dr. Bonnie Dunbar; Russian cosmonauts: *Mir–19* commander, Anatoly Y. Solovyev; Nikolai M. Budarin	10 days	Marked 100th human mission in U.S. space program and first shuttle linkup with the *Mir*: docked June 29, undocked July 4. Joined spacecraft held a record 10 people: 6 Americans and 4 Russians. Three *Mir* crew: cosmonauts: *Mir–18* commander, Lieut. Col. Vladimir N. Dezhurov, Gennady M. Strekalov, and U.S. astronaut Dr. Norman E. Thagard returned to earth aboard the *Atlantis*. Dr. Thagard set U.S. space record of 112 days in space aboard *Mir*. Cosmonauts Solovyez and Budarin remained aboard the *Mir*.
Atlantis (U.S.)	Nov. 12–20, 1995	Col. Kenneth D. Cameron; Lieut. Col. James D. Halsell, Jr.; Col. Jerry L. Ross; Lieut. Col. William S. McArthur, Jr.; Canadian Major Chris A. Hadfield who operated the robot arm.	8 days, 4 hr., 31 min.	Second docking with *Mir*. Carried 15-foot-long Russian-made docking module and attached it to the *Mir*. Brought two new solar-powered panels for *Mir* and also supplies and scientific equipment. U.S. and Russian astronauts spent 3 days together on *Mir* conducting experiments.
Endeavour (U.S.)	Jan. 11–20, 1996	Col. Brian Duffy, Brent Jett; Dr. Leroy Chiao**; Capt. Winston E. Scott;* Dr. Daniel T. Berry;* and Japanese astronaut Koichi Wakata, who operated robot arm. (*one spacewalk. ** two spacewalks)	8 days, 22 hr., 01 min.	Deployed and retrieved NASA satellite, retrieved Japanese satellite. Two spacewalks performed to test spacesuit components and practice space station construction, tools, and techniques. Total EVA time: 13 hours.
Columbia (U.S.)	Feb. 22–March 9, 1996	Lieut. Col. Andrew M. Allen; Lt. Col. Scott J. Horowitz; Dr. Franklin R. Chang–Diaz; Dr. Jeffrey A. Hoffman; Italian astronauts Maurizio Cheli and Dr. Umberto Guidoni; and Swiss astronaut Nicollier Claude.	15 days, 17 hr., 40 min.	Microgravity research flight. Second attempt to deploy Italian-built electricity-conducting satellite failed when metallic debris punctured insulation and broke tether after it was unreeled to almost its 12.5 mile length.
Atlantis (U.S.)	March 22–31, 1996	Col. Kevin P. Chilton; Lieut. Col. Richard A. Searfoss; Dr. Ronald M. Sega; Dr. Linda M. Goodwin; Lieut. Col. Michael R. Clifford; and Dr. Shannon W. Lucid.	9 days, 5 hr., 15 min.	Third linkup with *Mir* (March 22–27). Clifford and Goodwin conducted 6-hour spacewalk in shuttle cargo bay while docked with *Mir*. Dr. Lucid remained on board *Mir* for scheduled 140-day tour to conduct biomedical and material science experiments. Booster problems delayed her return until mid-September. (*See* Current Events.) Lucid is first American woman to live on *Mir*. On July 15, 1996, she broke the previous record for the longest U.S. manned space flight.
Endeavour (U.S.)	May 19–29, 1996	Col. John H. Casper; Lieut. Col. Curtis L. Brown, Jr.; Comdr. Daniel W. Bursch; Mario Runco, Jr.; Dr. Andrew S.W. Thomas; and Canadian astronaut Dr. Marc Garneau.	10 days, 0 hr., 40 min.	Made record four satellite rendezvous, including three with small PAMS satellite to test the concept of a self-stabilizing satellite in orbit. Deployed and retrieved a Spartan satellite that carried an experimental inflatable antenna.
Columbia (U.S.)	June 20–July 7, 1996	Col. Terence T. Henricks; Kevin R. Kregel; Lieut. Col. Susan J. Helms; Richard M. Linnehan; Comdr. Charles E. Brady, Jr.; French astronaut Dr. Jean-Jacques Favier; and Canadian astronaut Dr. Robert Brent Thirsk.	16 days, 21 hr., 48 min.	Longest mission to date. Studied the effects of weightlessness on people, plants, and animals, and material manufacturing in near-zero gravity.

NOTE: The letters MR stand for Mercury (capsule) and Redstone (rocket); MA, for Mercury and Atlas (rocket); GT, for Gemini (capsule) and Titan-II (rocket). The first astronaut listed in the Gemini and Apollo flights is the command pilot. The Mercury capsules had names: MR-III was *Freedom 7*, MR-IV was *Liberty Bell 7*, MA-VI was *Friendship 7*, MA-VII was *Aurora 7*, MA-VIII was *Sigma 7*, and MA-IX was *Faith 7*. The figure 7 referred to the fact that the first group of U.S. astronauts numbered seven men. Only one Gemini capsule had a name: GT-III was called *Molly Brown* (after the Broadway musical *The Unsinkable Molly Brown*); thereafter the practice of naming the capsules was discontinued. 1. Returned to earth with two fellow cosmonauts, Aleksandr P. Aleksandrov and Anatoly Levchenko, who had spent a shorter stay aboard the *Mir*. 2. From launch to landing.

ASTRONOMY

Astronomical Terms

Planet is the term used for a body in orbit around the sun. Its origin is Greek; even in antiquity it was known that a number of "stars" did not stay in the same relative positions to the others. There were five such restless "stars" known—Mercury, Venus, Mars, Jupiter, and Saturn—and the Greeks referred to them as *planetes*, a word which means "wanderers." That the earth is one of the planets was realized later. The additional planets were discovered after the invention of the telescope.

In 1994, Dr. Alexander Wolszcan, an astronomer at Pennsylvania State University, presented convincing evidence of the first known planets to exist outside our solar system. They circle a pulsar or exploded star in the constellation *Virgo.* Two of the planets are two to three times the size of the Earth and a third is about the size of our moon.

In 1995, several of these *extrasolar planets* were discovered orbiting ordinary stars similar to our sun as a result of observing gravitational variations of the stars. Swiss astronomers found a planet orbiting star 57 in the constellation Pegasus, about 40 light-years away. It is the first planet ever discovered to circle a normal sunlike star. The new planet's mass is about half that of Jupiter. It orbits 51 Pegasi every 4.2 days and is closer to the parent star than Mercury is to the sun. Because its surface temperature is about 1,300° C (2,756° F), it is too hot to support life.

California astronomers discovered two huge planets 35 light-years away—the second and third found outside the solar system.

A planet was found orbiting Ursae Majoris in the Big Dipper (Ursa Major). It has a mass about three and one-half times the size of Jupiter and it circles the planet every 1,100 days. Although its surface temperature is estimated at –90° C (–134° F) its atmosphere is warm enough to contain liquid water.

Another planet was detected circling the star 70 Virginis in the constellation Virgo. Its mass is estimated to be about eight times that of Jupiter, making it the most massive planet known. It orbits the star once every 116 days. The surface temperature of the new planet is about 83° C (184° F) and it is temperate enough to have liquid water.

The discovery that the two new planets appear warm enough for water to exist in liquid form raises the intriguing possibility that the planets could harbor life.

In June 1996, it was reported that astronomers had detected what appears to be two large objects that may be planets orbiting the star 21185 Lalande, 8.1 light-years away from Earth. Researchers have also found evidence of planets orbiting the stars tau Boötes, 55 rho¹ Cancri, and upsilon Andromedae.

Satellite (or *moon*) is the term for a body in orbit around a planet. As long as our own moon was the only moon known, there was no need for a general term for the moons of planets. But when Galileo Galilei discovered the four main moons of the planet Jupiter, Johannes Kepler (in a letter to Galileo) suggested "satellite" (from the Latin *satelles*, which means attendant) as a general term for such bodies. The word is used interchangeably with "moons": astronomers speak and write about the moons of Neptune, Saturn, etc. A satellite may be any size.

Orbit is the term for the path traveled by a body in space. It comes from the Latin *orbis,* which means circle, circuit, etc., and *orbita,* which means a rut or a wheel track. Theoretically, four mathematical figures are possible orbits: two are open (hyperbola and parabola) and two are closed (ellipse and circle), but in reality all closed orbits are ellipses. These ellipses can be nearly circular, as are the orbits of most planets, or very elongated, as are the orbits of most comets. In these orbits, the sun is in one focal point of the ellipse, and the other focal point is empty. In the orbits of satellites, the planet stands in one focal point of the orbit. The *primary* of an orbit is the body in the focal point. For planets, the point of the orbit closest to the sun is the *perihelion,* and the point farthest from the sun is the *aphelion.* For orbits around the Earth, the corresponding terms are *perigee* and *apogee;* for orbits around other planets, corresponding terms are coined when necessary.

Two heavenly bodies are in *inferior* or *superior conjunction* when they have the same Right Ascension, or are in the same meridian; that is, when one is due north or south of the other. If the bodies appear near each other as seen from the Earth, they will rise and set at the same time. They are in *opposition* when they are opposite each other in the heavens: when one rises as the other is setting. *Greatest elongation* is the greatest apparent angular distance from the sun, when a planet is most favorably suited for observation. Mercury can be seen with the naked eye only at about this time. An *occultation* of a planet or star is an eclipse of it by some other body, usually the moon.

Stars are the basic units of population in the universe. Our sun is the nearest star. Stars are very large (our sun has a diameter of 865,400 miles—a comparatively small star). Stars are composed of intensely hot gasses, deriving their energy from nuclear reactions going on in their interiors.

Galaxies are immense systems containing billions of stars. All that you can see in the sky (with a very few exceptions) belongs to our galaxy—a system of roughly 200 billion stars. The few exceptions are other galaxies. Our own galaxy, the rim of which we see as the "Milky Way," is about 100,000 light-years in diameter and about 10,000 light-years in thickness. Its shape is roughly that of a thick lens; more precisely it is a "spiral nebula," a term first used for other galaxies when they were discovered and before it was realized that these were separate and distant galaxies. The spiral galaxy nearest to ours is in the constellation Andromeda. It is somewhat larger than our own galaxy and is visible to the naked eye. Astronomers have estimated that the universe could contain 40 to 50 billion galaxies.

In 1994, English astronomers reported compelling evidence that a dwarf galaxy in the constellation *Sagittarius* lies 50,000 light-years from the Milky Way's center. Until then, the Large Magellanic Cloud, 169,000 light-years away from us, was considered the Milky Way's nearest neighbor.

In 1996, astronomers at the Keck Observatory in Hawaii detected a galaxy about 14 billion light-years away in the constellation Virgo. Its red shift is 4.38, making it the most distant galaxy observed so far.

Quasars ("quasi-stellar" objects), originally thought to be peculiar stars in our own galaxy, are now believed to be the most remote objects in the Universe. Spectral studies of quasars indicate that some are 9 billion light-years away and moving away from us at the incredible rate of 150,000 miles per second. Quasars emit tremendous amounts of light and microwave radiation. Although they appear to be far smaller than ordinary galaxies, some quasars emit as much as 100 times more energy. Some astronomers believe that quasars are the cores of violently exploding galaxies.

Pulsars are believed to be rapidly spinning neutron stars, so crushed by their own gravity that a million tons of their matter would hardly fill a thimble. Pulsars are so named because they emit bursts of radio energy at regular intervals.

Pulsar *Geminga*, estimated to be within 300 light-years from Earth, is the closest known pulsar to the solar system. In 1993, astronomers reported the discovery of a pulsar about 400 light-years from Earth.

Evidence of two Earth-sized planets circling a pulsar in *Virgo* was confirmed in 1994. A third is believed to be moon-sized.

A *black hole* is the theoretical end-product of the total gravitational collapse of a massive star or group of stars. Crushed even smaller than an incredibly dense neutron star, such a body may become so dense that not even light can escape its gravitational field. It has been suggested that black holes may be detectable in proximity to normal stars when they draw matter away from their visible neighbors. Strong sources of X-rays in our galaxy and beyond may also indicate the presence of black holes. The first possible black hole to be studied is the invisible companion to a supergiant star in the constellation Cygnus.

In May 1994, astronomers using the Hubble Space Telescope found conclusive evidence of a massive black hole in the center of Galaxy M87 located 50 million light-years away in the constellation *Virgo*.

The existence of brown dwarfs, also called failed stars, was confirmed in November 1995 when astronomers at Palomar Observatory in California took the first photograph of this mysterious object. Brown dwarfs lack the mass to generate nuclear fission like true stars but are also too massive and hot to be a planet.

The newly discovered brown dwarf is orbiting the small star Gliese 229, 19 light-years from Earth, and has been designated GL229B. Its mass has been estimated to be between 20 to 50 times that of Jupiter and it is one-250,000th as bright as the sun.

Gliese 229B's spectra indicates methane which is a sign of it having a temperature too low to be that of a true star.

Origin of the Universe

Evidence tends to confirm that the universe began its existence about 15 billion years ago as a dense, hot globule of gas expanding rapidly outward. At that time, the universe contained nothing but hydrogen and a small amount of helium. There were no stars and no planets. The first stars probably began to condense out of the primordial hydrogen when the universe was about 100 million years old and continued to form as the universe aged. The sun arose in this way 4.6 billion years ago. Many stars came into being before the sun was formed; many others formed after the sun appeared. This process continues, and through telescopes we can now see stars forming out of compressed pockets of hydrogen in outer space.

In 1992, instruments aboard the Cosmic Background Explorer (COBE) satellite, launched in 1989, showed that 99.97% of the radiant energy of the universe was released within the first year of the primeval explosion. This evidence seems to confirm the Big Bang theory which holds that the universe originated from a single violent explosion (a *big bang*) of a very small agglomeration of matter of extremely high density and temperatures. Astronomers also theorize that 99% of the matter in the universe is invisible or *dark matter* composed of some kind of matter that they cannot yet detect.

In March 1995, astronomers found supporting evidence for the Big Bang when they concluded data obtained from the space shuttle's *Astro 2* observatory showed that helium was widespread in the early universe. The theory holds that hydrogen and helium were the first elements created when the universe was formed.

Birth and Death of a Star

When a star begins to form as a dense cloud of gas, the individual hydrogen atoms fall toward the center of the cloud under the force of the star's gravity. As they fall, they pick up speed, and their energy increases. The increase in energy heats the gas. When this process has continued for some millions of years, the temperature reaches about 20 million degrees Fahrenheit. At this temperature, the hydrogen within the star ignites and burns in a continuing series of nuclear reactions in which all the elements in the universe are manufactured from hydrogen and helium. The onset of these reactions marks the birth of a star. When a star begins to exhaust its hydrogen supply, its life nears an end. The first sign of old age is a swelling and reddening of its outer regions. Such an aging, swollen star is called a red giant. The sun, a middle-aged star, will probably swell to a red giant in 5 billion years, vaporizing the earth and any creatures that may be left on its surface. When all its fuel has been exhausted, a star cannot generate sufficient pressure at its center to balance the crushing force of gravity. The star collapses under the force of its own weight; if it is a small star, it collapses gently and remains collapsed. Such a collapsed star, at its life's end, is called a white dwarf. The sun will probably end its life in this way. A different fate awaits a large star. Its final collapse generates a violent explosion, blowing the innards of the star out into space. There, the materials of the exploded star mix with the primeval hydrogen of the universe. Later in the history of the galaxy, other stars are formed out of this mixture. The sun is one of these stars. It contains the debris of countless other stars that exploded before the sun was born.

Supernovas

On Feb. 24, 1987, Canadian astronomer Ian Shelter at the Las Campas Observatory in Chile discovered a supernova—an exploding star—from a photograph taken on Feb. 23 of the Large Magellanic Cloud, a galaxy some 160,000 light-years away from Earth. Astronomers believe that the dying star was Sanduleak −69°202, a 10-million-year-old blue supergiant.

Supernova 1987A was the closest and best studied supernova in almost 400 years. One was previously observed by Johannes Kepler in 1604, four years before the telescope was invented.

In April 1992, researchers observed the most distant supernova explosion, 5 billion light-years away from Earth.

Astronomical Constants

Light–year (distance traveled by light in one year)	5,880,000,000,000 mi.
Parsec (parallax of one second, for stellar distances)	3.259 light-yrs.
Velocity of light	186,281.7 mi./sec.
Astronomical unit (A.U.), or mean distance earth-to-sun	ca. 93,000,000 mi.[1]
Mean distance, earth to moon	238,860 mi.
General precession	50".26
Obliquity of the ecliptic	23° 27'8".26–0".4684(t–1900)[2]
Equatorial radius of the earth	3963.34 statute mi.
Polar radius of the earth	3949.99 statute mi.
Earth's mean radius	3958.89 statute mi.
Oblateness of the earth	1/297
Equatorial horizontal parallax of the moon	57' 2".70
Earth's mean velocity in orbit	18.5 mi./sec.
Sidereal year	365d.2564
Tropical year	365d.2422
Sidereal month	27d.3217
Synodic month	29d.5306
Mean sidereal day	23h56m4s.091 of mean solar time
Mean solar day	24h3m56s.555 of sidereal time

1. Actual mean distance derived from radar bounces: 92,935,700 mi. The value of 92,897,400 mi. (based on parallax of 8,.80) is used in calculations. 2. *t* refers to the year in question, for example, 1997.

Two mysterious giant rings around 1987A were discovered by the Hubble Space Telescope in 1994.

Formation of the Solar System

The sun's age was calculated in 1989 to be 4.49 billion years old, less than the 4.7 billion years previously believed. It was formed from a cloud of hydrogen mixed with small amounts of other substances that had been manufactured in the bodies of other stars before the sun was born. This was the parent cloud of the solar system. The dense hot gas at the center of the cloud gave rise to the sun; the outer regions of the cloud—cooler and less dense—gave birth to the planets.

Our solar system consists of one star (the sun), nine planets and all their moons, several thousand minor planets called asteroids or planetoids, and an equally large number of comets.

The Sun

All the stars, including our sun, are gigantic balls of superheated gas, kept hot by atomic reactions in their centers. In our sun, this atomic reaction is hydrogen fusion: four hydrogen atoms are combined to form one helium atom. The temperature at the core of our sun must be 20 million degrees centigrade, the surface temperature averages 6,000 degrees centigrade, or about 11,000 degrees Fahrenheit. The diameter of the sun is 865,400 miles, and its surface area is approximately 12,000 times that of the Earth. Compared with other stars, our sun is just a bit below average in size and temperature, and is a yellow dwarf star. Its fuel supply (hydrogen) is estimated to last for another 5 billion years.

Our sun is not motionless in space; in fact it has two proper motions. One is a seemingly straight-line motion in the direction of the constellation Hercules at the rate of about 12 miles per second. But since the sun is a part of the Milky Way system and since the whole system rotates slowly around its own center, the sun also moves at the rate of 175 miles per second as part of the rotating Milky Way system.

In addition to this motion, the sun rotates on its axis. Observing the motion of sun spots (darkish areas which look like enormous whirling storms) and solar flares, which are usually associated with sun spots, has shown that the rotational period of our sun is just short of 25 days. But this figure is valid for the sun's equator only; the sections near the sun's poles seem to have a rotational period of 34 days. Naturally, since the sun generates its own heat and light, there is no temperature difference between poles and equator.

What we call the sun's "surface" is technically known as the photosphere. Since the whole sun is a ball of very hot gas, there is really no such thing as a surface; it is a question of visual impression. The next layer outside the photosphere is known as the chromosphere, which extends several thousand miles beyond the photosphere. It is in steady motion, and often enormous prominences can be seen to burst from it, extending as much as 100,000 miles into space. Outside the chromosphere is the corona. The corona consists of very tenuous gases (essentially hydrogen) and makes a magnificent sight when the sun is eclipsed.

As the sun ages, it gradually expands and heats. In 1994, American astrophysicists studying the eventual fate of the sun estimated that its brilliancy will increase by 10% over the next 1.1 billion years or more and, in about 6.5 billion years hence, our aging star will have doubled its present luminosity. The extreme heat generated will cause a catastrophic greenhouse effect on Earth and our oceans will boil away, and life on Earth as we know it will end.

The sun will eventually expand enormously to 166 times its present size and become over 2,000 times as bright. Eight billion years from now, the sun's radius will engulf the planet Mercury and extend beyond the present orbit of Venus.

However, as the sun expands, it will also lose considerable mass (as much as one-half) and weaken its gravitational pull on Venus and the other lifeless planets, causing them to orbit further away from the sun and escape total destruction.

The Moon

Mercury and Venus do not have any moons. Therefore, the Earth is the planet nearest the sun to be orbited by a moon.

THE MILKY WAY GALAXY. Our sun is one of 200-billion stars banded together by gravity in an enormous spiral disk called the Milky Way Galaxy. The arrow indicates our position three-fifths of the way out from the center. It takes light 100,000 years to traverse our Galaxy, one of billions of galaxies in the universe. Copyright 1990 Hansen Planetarium, Salt Lake City, Utah. Reproduced with Permission.

OUR PLACE IN THE GALAXY

The next planet farther out, Mars, has two very small moons. Jupiter has four major moons and twelve minor ones. Saturn, the ringed planet, has 19 known moons (and possibly more), of which one (Titan) is larger than the planet Mercury. Uranus has fifteen moons, (four of them large) as well as rings, while Neptune has one large and seven small moons. Pluto has one moon, discovered in 1978. Some astronomers still consider Pluto to be a "runaway moon" of Neptune.

Our own moon, with a diameter of 2,160 miles, is one of the larger moons in our solar system and is especially large when compared with the planet that it orbits. In fact, the common center of gravity of the Earth-Moon system is only about 1,000 miles below the Earth's surface. The closest our moon can come to us (its perigee) is 221,463 miles; the farthest it can go away (its apogee) is 252,710 miles. The period of rotation of our moon is equal to its period of revolution around the Earth. Hence from Earth we can see only one hemisphere of the moon. Both periods are 27 days, 7 hours, 43 minutes and 11.47 seconds. But while the rotation of the moon is constant, its velocity in its orbit is not, since it moves more slowly in apogee than in perigee. Consequently, some portions near the rim which are not normally visible will appear briefly. This phenomenon is called "libration," and by taking advantage of the librations, astronomers have succeeded in mapping approximately 59% of the lunar surface. The other 41% can never be seen from the earth but has been mapped by American and Russian moon-orbiting spacecraft.

Though the moon goes around the Earth in the time mentioned, the interval from new moon to new moon is 29 days, 12 hours, 44 minutes and 2.78 seconds. This delay of nearly two days is due to the fact that the Earth is moving around the sun, so that the moon needs two extra days to reach a spot in its orbit where no part is illuminated by the sun, as seen from Earth.

If the plane of the Earth's orbit around the sun (the ecliptic) and the plane of the moon's orbit around the Earth were the same, the moon would be eclipsed by the Earth every time it is full, and the sun would be eclipsed by the moon every time the moon is "new" (it would be better to call it the "black moon" when it is in this position). But because the two orbits do not coincide, the moon's shadow normally misses the Earth and the Earth's shadow misses the moon. The inclination of the two orbital planes to each other is 5 degrees. The tides are, of course, caused by the moon with the help of the sun, but in the open ocean they are surprisingly low, amounting to about one yard. The very high tides which can be observed near the shore in some places are due to funnelling effects of the shorelines. At new moon and at full moon the tides raised by the moon are reinforced by the sun; these are the "spring tides." If the sun's tidal power acts at right angles to that of the moon (quarter moons) we get the low "neap tides."

Data from the Defense Department's *Clementine* space probe has given support to the theory that the moon was formed after a cosmic collision between the Earth and another celestial body. *Clementine* data show that the moon is poor in iron while the Earth is relatively rich in iron under its crust. The data also show that the surface of the moon was melted early in its history.

Our Planet Earth

The Earth, circling the sun at an average distance of 93 million miles, is the fifth largest planet and the third from the sun. It orbits the sun at a speed of 67,000 miles per hour, making one revolution in 365 days, 5 hours, 48 minutes, and 45.51 seconds. The Earth completes one rotation on its axis every 23 hours, 56 minutes, and 4.09 seconds. Actually a bit pear-shaped rather than a true sphere, the Earth has a

The Brightest Stars

Star	Constellation	Mag.	Dist. (l.-y.)	Star	Constellation	Mag.	Dist. (l.-y.)
Sirius	Canis Major	−1.6	8	Antares	Scorpius	1.2	170
Canopus	Carina	−0.9	650	Fomalhaut	Piscis Austrinus	1.3	27
Alpha Centauri	Centaurus	+0.1	4	Deneb	Cygnus	1.3	465
Vega	Lyra	0.1	23	Regulus	Leo	1.3	70
Capella	Auriga	0.2	42	Beta Crucis	Crux	1.5	465
Arcturus	Boötes	0.2	32	Eta Carinae	Carina	1–7	—
Rigel	Orion	0.3	545	Alpha-one Crucis	Crux	1.6	150
Procyon	Canis Minor	0.5	10	Castor	Gemini	1.6	44
Achernar	Eridanus	0.6	70	Gamma Crucis	Crux	1.6	—
Beta Centauri	Centaurus	0.9	130	Epsilon Canis Majoris	Canis Major	1.6	325
Altair	Aquila	0.9	18	Epsilon Ursae Majoris	Ursa Major	1.7	50
Betelgeuse	Orion	0.9	600	Bellatrix	Orion	1.7	215
Aldebaran	Taurus	1.1	54	Lambda Scorpii	Scorpius	1.7	205
Spica	Virgo	1.2	190	Epsilon Carinae	Carina	1.7	325
Pollux	Gemini	1.2	31	Mira	Cetus	2–10	250

diameter of 7,927 miles at the Equator and a few miles less at the poles. It has an estimated mass of about 6.6 sextillion tons, with an average density of 5.52 grams per cubic centimeter. The Earth's surface area encompasses 196,949,970 square miles of which about three-fourths is water.

Origin of the Earth. The Earth, along with the other planets, is believed to have been born 4.5 billion years ago as a solidified cloud of dust and gases left over from the creation of the sun. For perhaps 500 million years, the interior of the Earth stayed solid and relatively cool, perhaps 2000° F. The main ingredients, according to the best available evidence, were iron and silicates, with small amounts of other elements, some of them radioactive. As millions of years passed, energy released by radioactive decay—mostly of uranium, thorium, and potassium—gradually heated the Earth, melting some of its constituents. The iron melted before the silicates, and, being heavier, sank toward the center. This forced upward the silicates that it found there. After many years, the iron reached the center, almost 4,000 miles deep, and began to accumulate. No eyes were around at that time to view the turmoil which must have taken place on the face of the surface—gigantic heaves and bubbling of the surface, exploding volcanoes, and flowing lava covering everything in sight. Finally, the iron in the center accumulated as the core. Around it, a thin but fairly stable crust of solid rock formed as the Earth cooled. Depressions in the crust were natural basins in which water, rising from the interior of the planet through volcanoes and fissures, collected to form the oceans. Slowly the Earth acquired its present appearance.

The Earth Today. As a result of radioactive heating over millions of years, the Earth's molten *core* is probably fairly hot today, around 11,000° F. By comparison, lead melts at around 800° F. Most of the Earth's 2,100-mile-thick core is liquid, but there is evidence that the center of the core is solid. The liquid outer portion, about 95% of the core, is constantly in motion, causing the Earth to have a magnetic field that makes compass needles point north and south. The details are not known, but the latest evidence suggests that planets which have a magnetic field probably have a solid core or a partially liquid one.

Outside the core is the Earth's *mantle*, 1,800 miles

thick, and extending nearly to the surface. The mantle is composed of heavy silicate rock, similar to that brought up by volcanic eruptions. It is somewhere between liquid and solid, slightly yielding, and therefore contributing to an active, moving Earth. Most of the Earth's radioactive material is in the thin *crust* which covers the mantle, but some is in the mantle and continues to give off heat. The crust's thickness ranges from 5 to 25 miles.

Scientists recently discovered that the Earth's core is not a perfect sphere. X-ray like images of inside the Earth show that there are vast mountains six to seven miles high and deep valleys on the core. These features are in an upside down relationship to the Earth's surface.

Continental Drift. A great deal of recent evidence confirms the theory that the continents of the Earth, made mostly of relatively light granite, float in the slightly yielding mantle, like logs in a pond. For many years it had been noticed that if North and South America could be pushed toward western and southern Europe and western Africa, they would fit like pieces in a jigsaw puzzle. Today, there is little question—the continents have drifted widely and continue to do so.

In 10 million years, the world as we know it may be unrecognizable, with California drifting out to sea, Florida joining South America, and Africa moving farther away from Europe and Asia.

The Earth's Atmosphere. The thin blanket of atmosphere that envelops the Earth extends several hundred miles into space. From sea level—the very bottom of the ocean of air—to a height of about 60 miles, the air in the atmosphere is made up of the same gases in the same ratio: about 78% nitrogen, 21% oxygen, and the remaining 1% being a mixture of argon, carbon dioxide, and tiny amounts of neon, helium, krypton, xenon, and other gases. The atmosphere becomes less dense with increasing altitude: more than three-fourths of the Earth's huge envelope is concentrated in the first 5 to 10 miles above the surface. At sea level, a cubic foot of the atmosphere weighs about an ounce and a quarter. The entire atmosphere weighs 5,700,000,000,000,000 tons, and the force with which gravity holds it in place causes it to exert a pressure of nearly 15 pounds per square

(Continued on page 333)

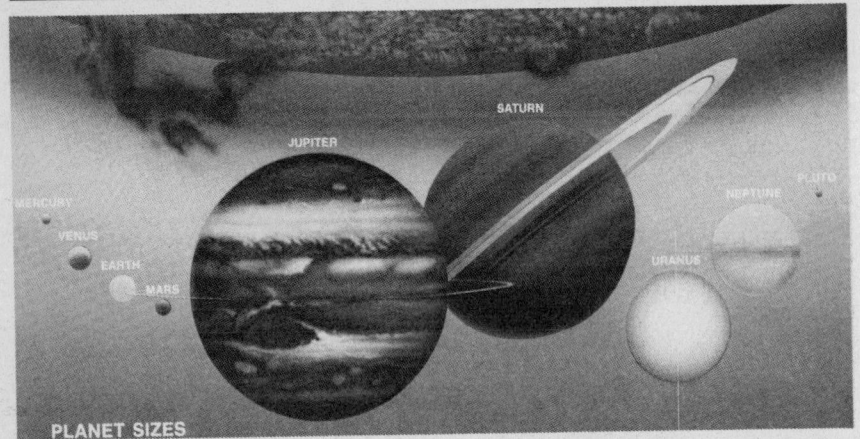

PLANET SIZES PLANET SIZES. Shown from left to right: Mercury, Venus, Earth, Mars, Jupiter, Saturn, Uranus, Neptune, and Pluto.

Copyright 1990 Hansen Planetarium, Salt Lake City, Utah. Reproduced with Permission.

Basic Planetary Data

	Mercury	Venus	Earth	Mars	Jupiter
Mean distance from sun (Millions of kilometers)	57.9	108.2	149.6	227.9	778.3
(Millions of miles)	36.0	67.24	92.9	141.71	483.88
Period of revolution	88 days	224.7 days	365.2 days	687 days	11.86 yrs
Rotation period	59 days	243 days retrograde	23 hr 56 min 4 sec	24 hr 37 min	9 hr 55 min 30 sec
Inclination of axis	Near 0°	3°	23°27′	25°12′	3°5′
Inclination of orbit to ecliptic	7°	3.4°	0°	1.9°	1.3°
Eccentricity of orbit	.206	.007	.017	.093	.048
Equatorial diameter (Kilometers)	4,880	12,100	12,756	6,794	142,800
(Miles)	3,032.4	7,519	7,926.2	4,194	88,736
Atmosphere (Main components)	Virtually none	Carbon dioxide	Nitrogen oxygen	Carbon dioxide	Hydrogen helium
Satellites	0	0	1	2	16
Rings	0	0	0	0	1

	Saturn	Uranus	Neptune	Pluto
Mean distance from sun (Millions of kilometers)	1,427	2,870	4,497	5,900
(Millions of miles)	887.14	1,783.98	2,796.46	3,666
Period of revolution	29.46 yrs	84 yrs	165 yrs	248 yrs
Rotation period	10 hr 40 min 24 sec	16.8 hr(?) retrograde	16 hr 11 min(?)	6 days 9 hr 18 mins retrograde
Inclination of axis	26°44′	97°55′	28°48′	60° (?)
Inclination of orbit to ecliptic	2.5°	0.8°	1.8°	17.2°
Eccentricity of orbit	.056	.047	.009	.254
Equatorial diameter (Kilometers)	120,660	51,810	49,528	2,290 (?)
(Miles)	74,978	32,193	30,775	1,423 (?)
Atmosphere (Main components)	Hydrogen helium	Helium hydrogen methane	Hydrogen helium methane	None detected
Satellites	19	15	8	1
Rings	1,000 (?)	11	4	?

Source: Basic NASA data and other sources.

(Continued from page 331)

inch. Going out from the Earth's surface, the atmosphere is divided into five regions. The regions, and the heights to which they extend, are: *Troposphere,* 0 to 7 miles (at middle latitudes); *stratosphere,* 7 to 30 miles; *mesosphere,* 30 to 50 miles; *thermosphere,* 50 to 400 miles; and *exosphere,* above 400 miles. The boundaries between each of the regions are known respectively as the *tropopause, stratopause, mesopause,* and *thermopause.* Alternate terms often used for the layers above the troposphere are *ozonosphere* (for stratosphere) and *ionosphere* for the remaining upper layers.

The Seasons. Seasons are caused by the 23.4 degree tilt of the Earth's axis, which alternately turns the North and South Poles toward the sun. Times when the sun's apparent path crosses the Equator are known as *equinoxes.* Times when the sun's apparent path is at the greatest distance from the Equator are known as *solstices.* The lengths of the days are most extreme at each solstice. If the Earth's axis were perpendicular to the plane of the Earth's orbit around the sun, there would be no seasons, and the days always would be equal in length. Since the Earth's axis is at an angle, the sun strikes the Earth directly at the Equator only twice a year: in March (vernal equinox) and September (autumnal equinox). In the Northern Hemisphere, spring begins at the vernal equinox, summer at the summer solstice, fall at the autumnal equinox, and winter at the winter solstice. The situation is reversed in the Southern Hemisphere.

Mercury

Mercury is the planet nearest the sun. Appropriately named for the wing-footed Roman messenger of the gods, Mercury whizzes around the sun at a speed of 30 miles per second completing one circuit in 88 days. The days and nights are long on Mercury. It takes 59 Earth days for Mercury to make a single rotation. It spins at a rate of about 10 kilometers (about 6 miles) per hour, measured at the equator, as compared to the Earth's spin of about 1,600 kilometers (about 1,000 miles) per hour at the equator.

The photographs *Mariner 10* (1974–75) radioed back to Earth revealed an ancient, heavily cratered surface on Mercury, closely resembling our own moon. The pictures showed huge cliffs, or scarps, crisscrossing the planet. These apparently were created when Mercury's interior cooled and shrank, compressing the planet's crust. The cliffs are as high as two kilometers (1.2 miles) and as long as 1,500 kilometers (932 miles). Another unique feature is the Caloris Basin, a large impact crater about 1,300 kilometers (808 miles) in diameter.

Mercury, like the Earth, appears to have a crust of light silicate rock. Scientists believe it has a heavy iron-rich core that makes up about half of its volume.

Instruments onboard *Mariner 10* discovered that the planet has a weak magnetic field and a trace of atmosphere—a trillionth the density of the Earth's and composed chiefly of argon, neon, and helium. The spacecraft reported temperatures ranging from 510° C (950° F) on Mercury's sunlit side to –210° C (–346° F) on the dark side. Mercury literally bakes in daylight and freezes at night.

Until the *Mariner 10* probe, little was known about the planet. Even the best telescopic views from Earth showed Mercury as an indistinct object lacking any surface detail. The planet is so close to the sun that it is usually lost in the sun's glare.

Radar images taken by astronomers at Jet Propulsion Laboratories and California Institute of Technology during the summer of 1991 suggest that the polar regions of Mercury may be covered with patches of water ice. Although this seems impossible due to the planet's sizzling heat, the polar regions receive very little sunlight and may get as cold as –235° F. The radar images showed bright patterns at the poles which are characteristic of ice reflecting the radar signals. Other explanations may be offered for this unexpected discovery.

• Mercury is a naked eye object at morning or evening twilight when it is at greatest elongation.

Venus

Although Venus is Earth's closest neighbor, very little is known about the planet because it is permanently covered by thick clouds. In 1962, Soviet and American space probes, coupled with Earth-based radar and infrared spectroscopy, began slowly unraveling some of the mystery surrounding Venus. Twenty-eight years later, the *Magellan* spacecraft sent by the United States arrived at Venus in August 1990 and began radar-mapping the planet's surface in greater detail.

According to the latest results, Venus' atmosphere exerts a pressure at the surface 94.5 times greater than Earth's. Walking on Venus would be as difficult as walking a half-mile beneath the ocean. Because of a thick blanket of carbon dioxide, a "greenhouse effect" exists on Venus. Venus intercepts twice as much of the sun's light as does the Earth. The light enters freely through the carbon dioxide gas and is changed to heat radiation in molecular collisions. But carbon dioxide prevents the heat from escaping. Consequently, the temperature of the surface of Venus is over 800° F, hot enough to melt lead.

The atmospheric composition of Venus is about 96% carbon dioxide, 4% nitrogen, and minor amounts of water, oxygen, and sulfur compounds. There are at least four distinct cloud and haze layers that exist at different altitudes above the planet's surface. The haze layers contain small aerosol particles, possibly droplets of sulfuric acid. A concentration of sulfur dioxide above the cloud tops has been observed to be decreasing since 1978. The source of sulfur dioxide at this altitude is unknown; it may be injected by volcanic explosions or atmospheric overturning.

Measurements of the Venusian atmosphere and its cloud patterns reveal nearly constant high-speed zonal winds, about 100 meters per second (220 miles per hour) at the equator. The winds decrease toward the poles so that the atmosphere at cloud-top level rotates almost like a solid body. The wind speeds at the equator correspond to Venus' rotation period of four to five days at most latitudes. The circulation is always in the same direction—east to west—as Venus' slow retrograde motion. Earth's winds blow from west to east, the same direction as its rotation.

Venus is quite round, very different from the other planets and from the moon. Venus has neither polar flattening nor an equatorial bulge. The diameter of Venus is 12,100 kilometers (7,519 miles). Venus has a retrograde axial rotation period of 243.1 Earth days. The surface atmospheric pressure is 1,396 pounds per square inch (95 Earth atmospheres). The planet's mean distance from the sun is 108.2 million kilometers (67.2 million miles). The period of its revolution around the sun is 224.7 days.

The highest point on Venus is the summit of Maxwell Montes, 10.8 kilometers (6.71 miles) above the

(Continued on page 335)

THE SOLAR SYSTEM

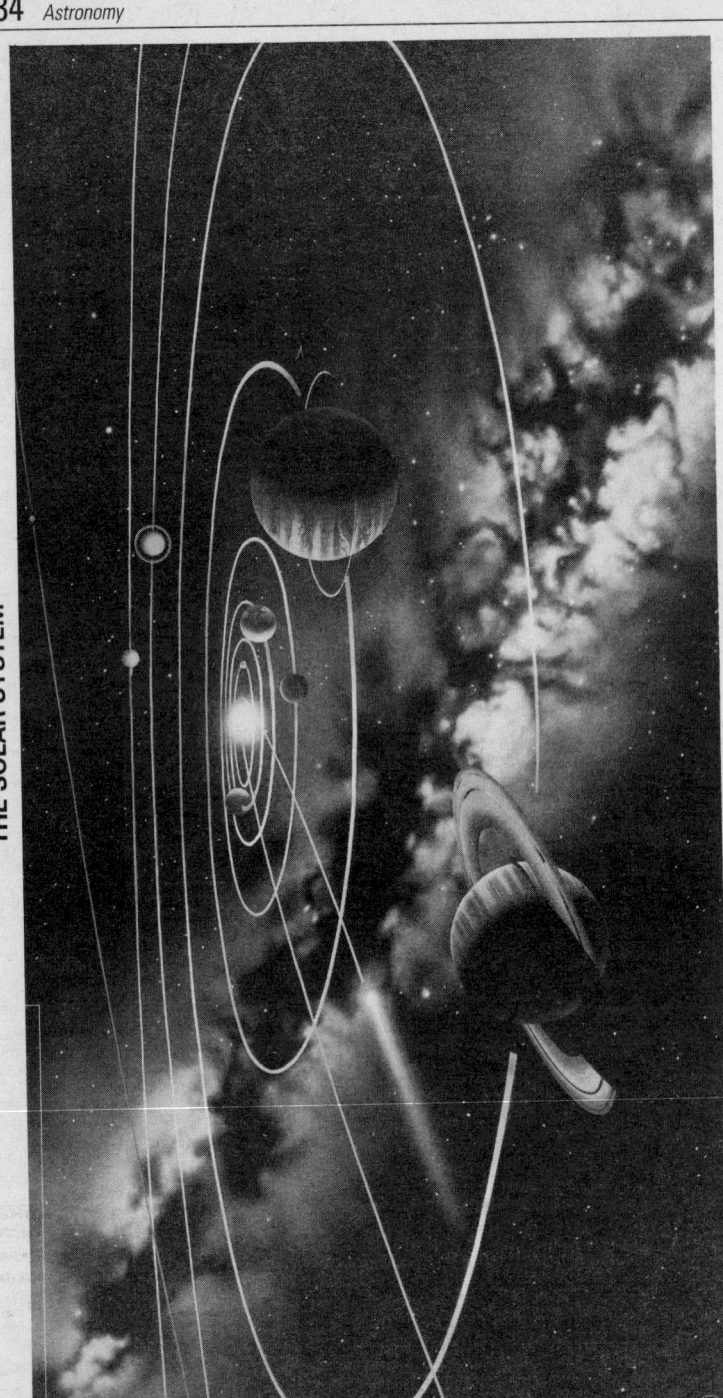

THE SOLAR SYSTEM. Orbiting around the sun are Mercury, Venus, Earth, Mars, Jupiter, Saturn, Uranus, Neptune, and Pluto. Our solar system was born nearly five billion years ago out of a cloud of interstellar gas and dust. Gravity caused this nebula to contract and flatten into a spinning disk. Near the center, where the density was greatest, a body formed which was so massive that its internal pressures ignited and sustained a nuclear reaction, creating a star we call the sun. Elsewhere in the cloud, smaller bodies coalesced and cooled—nine planets, perhaps fifty moons, millions of asteroids, and billions of comets. Within our Milky Way Galaxy, there may be billions of other solar systems. Copyright 1990 Hansen Planetarium, Salt Lake City, Utah. Reproduced with permission.

(Continued from page 333)

mean level, more than a mile taller than Mount Everest. There is some evidence that this huge mountain is an active volcano. The lowest point is in the rift valley, Diana Chasma, 2.9 kilometers (1.8 miles) below the mean level. This point is about one-fifth the greatest depth on Earth in the Marianas Trench.

Venus has an extreme lowland basin, Atalanta Planitia, which is about the size of Earth's North Atlantic Ocean basin. The smooth surface of the Atalanta Planitia resembles the mare basins of the moon.

There are only two highland or continental masses on Venus: Ishtar Terra and Aphrodite Terra. Ishtar Terra is 11 kilometers (6.8 miles) at its highest points (the highest peaks on Venus) and those of Aphrodite Terra rise to about 5 kilometers (3.10 miles) above the planet. Ishtar Terra is about the size of the continental United States and Aphrodite Terra is about the size of Africa.

The unmanned NASA spacecraft *Magellan* was launched on May 4, 1989, from the shuttle *Atlantis* and arrived at Venus Aug. 10, 1990, to map most of the planet. Despite some problems with its radio transmissions, the results of the radar mapping delighted scientists and provided them with the sharpest images ever taken of the planet's surface. Images taken from *Magellan* show ten times more detail than ever seen before.

The radar images provided scientists with compelling evidence that the planet has been dominated by volcanism on a global scale. The photos also showed that the planet's second highest mountain, Maat Mons, rising five miles (eight kilometers) above the Venusian plains, appears to be covered with fresh lava and is possibly an active volcano.

Magellan discovered the longest known channel in the solar system on Venus. It is 4,200 miles (6,800 kilometers) long and averages slightly over a mile (1.8 kilometers) wide. Its origin is puzzling to scientists because high temperature lava is unlikely to have caused such a long distance flow on the surface and there are no known substances that could remain liquid long enough under the planet's atmospheric pressure and temperature to have carved out this snake-like feature. The channel is slightly longer than the Nile River, the longest river on Earth. *Magellan* ended its radar and emissions mapping in September 1992 after covering 98% of the planet's surface.

• Venus is the brightest of all the planets and is often visible in the morning or evening, when it is frequently referred to as the Morning Star or Evening Star. At its brightest, it can sometimes be seen with the naked eye in full daylight, if one knows where to look.

Mars

Mars, on the other side of the Earth from Venus, is Venus' direct opposite in terms of physical properties. Its atmosphere is cold, thin, and transparent, and readily permits observation of the planet's features. We know more about Mars than any other planet except Earth. Mars is a forbidding, rugged planet with huge volcanoes and deep chasms. The largest volcano, Olympus Mons (Olympic Mountain) rises 78,000 feet above the surface, higher than Mount Everest. The plains of Mars are pockmarked with the hits of thousands of meteors over the years.

Most of our information about Mars comes from the Mariner 9 spacecraft, which orbited the planet in 1971. Mariner 9, photographing 100% of the planet, uncovered spectacular geological formations, including a Martian Grand Canyon that dwarfs the one on Earth. Called Valles Marineris (Mariner Valley) it

stretches more than 3,000 miles along the equatorial region of Mars and is over 4 kilometers (2.5 miles) deep in places and 80 to 100 kilometers (50 to 62 miles) wide. The spacecraft's cameras also recorded what appeared to be dried riverbeds, suggesting the onetime presence of water on the planet. The latter idea gives encouragement to scientists looking for life on Mars, for where there is water, there may be life. However, to date, no evidence of life has been found. Temperatures near the equator range from –17 degrees F. in the daytime to –130 degrees F. at night.

The landing of two robot Viking spacecraft on the surface of Mars in 1976 provided more information about Mars in a few months than in all the time that had gone before.

None of these probes have clearly shown whether Mars has its own magnetic field. Scientists hoped that the failed *Mars Observer*, launched Sept. 25, 1992, would provide a conclusive answer. (See *Mars Observer* in Space Section.)

Mars rotates upon its axis in nearly the same period as Earth—24 hours, 37 minutes—so that a Mars day is almost identical to an Earth day. Mars takes 687 days to make one trip around the sun. Because of its eccentric orbit Mars' distance from the sun can vary by about 36 million miles. Its distance from Earth can vary by as much as 200 million miles. The atmosphere of Mars is much thinner than Earth's; atmospheric pressure is about 1% that of our planet. Its gravity is one-third of Earth's. Major constituents are carbon dioxide and nitrogen. Water vapor and oxygen are minor constituents. Mars' polar caps, composed mostly of frozen carbon dioxide (dry ice), recede and advance according to the Martian seasons.

Scientists have not yet determined if the Martian snow (as water ice or carbon dioxide particles) actually crystallizes on the polar caps or whether it falls from the clouds over them.

Mars has four seasons like Earth, but they are much longer. For example, in the northern hemisphere, the Martian spring is 198 days, and the winter season lasts 158 days.

Images taken by the Hubble space telescope in 1995 showed that the Martian climate has become cooler and drier since the *Viking* spacecraft visited the planet in the 1970s. NASA researchers believe that the planet's cooling may be due to diminished dust storms.

Mars was named for the Roman god of war, because when seen from Earth its distinct red color reminded the ancient people of blood. We know now that the reddish hue reflects the oxidized (rusted) iron in the surface material.

The Martian moons

Mars has two very small elliptical-shaped moons, Deimos and Phobos—the Greek names for the companions of the God Mars: Deimos (Terror) and Phobos (Fear). They were discovered in August 1877 by the American astronomer Asaph Hall (1829–1907) of the U.S. Naval Observatory in Washington, D.C.

The inner satellite Phobos is 27 kilometers (16.78 miles) long and it revolves around the planet in 7.6 hours. The outer moon, Deimos, is 15 kilometers (9.32 miles) long and it circles the planet in 30.35 hours. The short orbital period of Phobos means that the satellite travels around Mars twice in a Martian day. If an observer were suitably situated on the planet, he would see Phobos rise and set twice in a day.

Recent studies of Phobos indicate that its orbit is

(Continued on page 337)

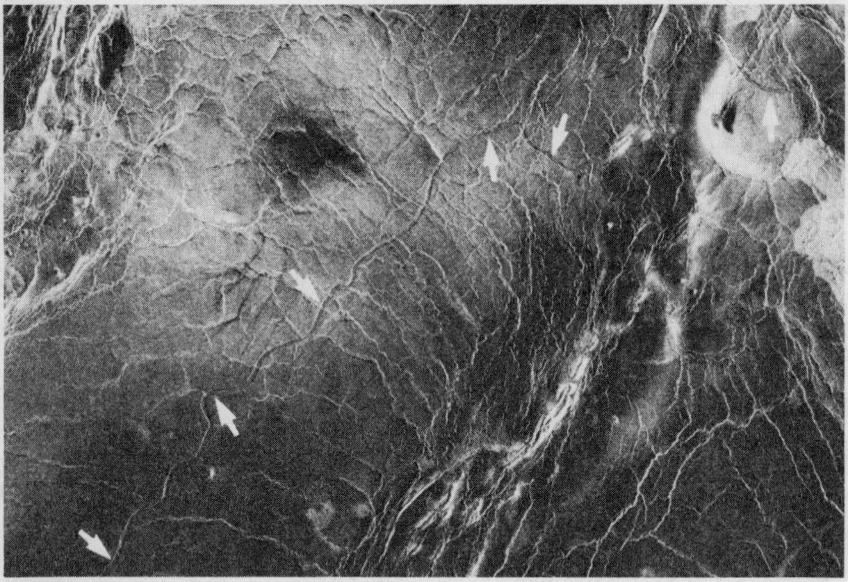

LARGEST CHANNEL IN SOLAR SYSTEM. *Magellan* took the above image of the largest known channel on Venus. At 4,200 miles (6,800 kilometers) long and an average of 1.1 miles (1.8 kilometers) in width, it is longer than the Nile River, Earth's longest river, making it the longest known channel in the solar system. The channel was originally discovered by the Soviet *Venera 15* and *16* spacecraft orbiters. NASA.

Magellan radar image of Golubkina Crater on Venus. The impact crater is 20.4 miles (34 kilometers) in diameter. NASA.

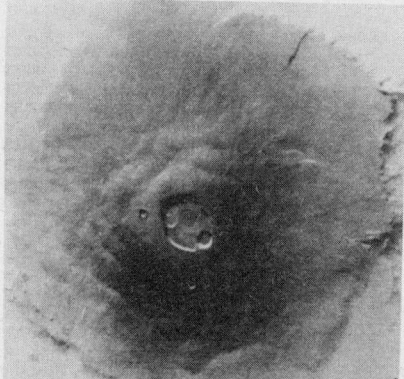

Giant Olympus Mons, the tallest volcano on Mars, is also the highest mountain in the solar system. It is 540 kilometers (336 miles) across and rises 10 miles higher than Mount Everest. NASA photo.

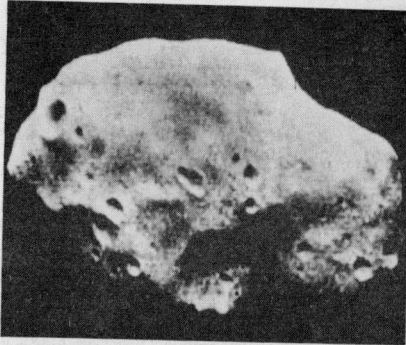

Phobos, Mars' tiny inner moon, is covered with a large number of craters.

(Continued from page 335)

slowly decreasing downward and that in approximately 40 million years, it will crash into the planet's surface.

In 1988, the Soviet Union launched two spacecraft to study the geology, climate, and atmosphere of Mars, and explore its moon, Phobos. The attempt was unsuccessful as contact was lost with both spacecraft.

Meteorites From Mars

Our knowledge of the origin and history of Mars has been greatly enhanced by recent research showing that a group of eight meteorites, labeled SNC[1] (named for towns where they were found: Shergotty, India, in 1865; Nakhla, Egypt, in 1911; and Chassigny, France, in 1815), are probably samples of Mars. This hypothesis is based largely on the composition of noble gases (particularly argon and xenon) trapped in the meteorites, and the Shergottites in particular, which resemble measurements of the Martian atmosphere made by the *Viking* spacecraft. Major element compositions of the SNCs are also similar to Martian soil analyses made by *Viking*.

These meteorites suggest that the Martian mantle is two to four times richer than Earth in moderately volatile elements such as potassium, rubidium, chlorine, bromine, sodium, zinc, and lead. In contrast, nitrogen, carbon dioxide, and the noble gases are more depleted than expected in the Martian atmosphere, suggesting an episode of severe atmospheric loss at some time in its history.

The relatively young isotopic ages of the SNC meteorites (1.3 billion years or less) suggest that Mars has been volcanically active during its recent past.

In 1991, a ninth meteorite, LEW 88516, was identified as having reached Earth from Mars some 180 million years ago. It was discovered in December 1988 near Lewis Cliff in Antarctica. The meteorite is very small with a dark pitted surface and weighs 13.2 grams (less than half an ounce).

A 4-pound, 7-ounce (1.9 kilograms) meteorite, ALH84001, found in the Allen Hills of Antarctica

in 1984 was reclassified in 1993 as coming from the Red Planet, making it the tenth known to have originated from Mars. Its high carbonate content may have resulted when water rich in carbon dioxide crystallized within the meteorite, thus supporting the theory that Mars once had water.

A 40-pound meteorite that crashed to Earth in Nigeria in 1962 has been classified as coming from Mars. It was named Zagami for the region it was found in.

A 0.38-ounce (12-gram) meteorite (QUE94201) found in Antarctica in 1995 became the 12th meteorite identified as having a Martian origin.

Scientists do not know how the meteorites were thrown off the Martian surface.

Jupiter

Jupiter is the largest planet in the solar system—a gaseous world as large as 1,300 Earths. Its equatorial diameter is 142,800 kilometers (88,736 miles), while from pole to pole, Jupiter measures only 133,500 kilometers (84,201 miles). For comparison, the diameter of the Earth is 12,756 kilometers (7,926.2 miles). The massive planet rotates at a dizzying speed—once every 9 hours and 55 minutes. It takes Jupiter almost 12 Earth years to complete a journey around the sun.

The giant planet appears as a banded disk of turbulent clouds with all of its stripes running parallel to its bulging equator. Large dusky gray regions surround each pole. Darker gray or brown stripes called

Jupiter's ring. A line has been drawn around a photograph of Jupiter to show the position of the extremely thin faint ring. NASA photo.

1. Pronounced "snick."

belts intermingle with lighter, yellow-white stripes called zones. The belts are regions of descending air masses and the zones are rising cloudy air masses. The strongest winds—up to 400 kilometers (250 miles) per hour—are found at boundaries between the belts and zones.

This uniquely colorful atmosphere is mainly hydrogen and helium. It contains small amounts of methane, ammonia, ethane, acetylene, phosphine, germanium tetrahydride, and possibly hydrogen cyanide.

Cloud-type lightning bolts similar to those on Earth have been found in the Jovian atmosphere. At the polar regions, auroras have been observed. A very thin ring of material less than one kilometer (0.6 mile) in thickness and about 6,000 kilometers (4,000 miles) in radial extent has been observed circling the planet about 55,000 kilometers (35,000 miles) above the cloud tops.

The most prominent feature on Jupiter is its Great Red Spot, an oval larger than the planet Earth. It is a tremendous atmospheric storm that rotates counter-clockwise with one revolution every six days at the outer edge, while at the center almost no motion can be seen. The Spot is about 25,000 kilometers (16,000 miles) on its long axis, and would cover three Earths. The outer rim shows streamline shapes of 360-kilometer (225-mile) winds.

Jupiter emits 67% more heat than it absorbs from the sun. This heat is thought to be accumulated during the planet's formation several billion years ago.

Twenty-one fragments of Comet Shoemaker-Levy 9 bombarded the cloud-covered surface of Jupiter, July 16–22, 1994. It was the most violent event in the recorded history of our solar system. The cometary explosions caused towering plumes of debris and hot gas to rise from the darkened impact sites.

On Dec. 7, 1995, the *Galileo* spacecraft released a probe into Jupiter's atmosphere to study the planet's physical and chemical properties. The probe lasted 57 minutes and early results indicated a lower abundance of water than was expected.

Jovian moons

The four great moons of Jupiter were discovered by Galileo Galilei (1564–1642) in January 1610, and are called the Galilean satellites after their discoverer. Their names are Io, Europa, Ganymede, and Callisto. Like our moon, the satellites always keep the same face turned toward the Earth. Jupiter has 16 known satellites.

Ganymede

Ganymede, 5,270 kilometers (3,275 miles) in diameter, is Jupiter's largest moon, and also it is the largest satellite in the solar system. Ganymede is about one and one-half times the size of our moon. It is heavily cratered and probably has the greatest variety of geologic process recorded on its surface. Ganymede is half water and half rock, resulting in a density about two-thirds that of Europa, an ice-coated satellite. No atmosphere has been detected on it.

The first close-up photos of Ganymede taken by the *Galileo* spacecraft during its June 27, 1996, flyby revealed a surface pockmarked with ancient craters and a landscape wrinkled and torn by the same forces that make mountains and move continents on Earth. *Galileo*'s findings also indicated that Ganymede is enveloped in its own magnetic field, possibly created by a molten iron core or even a thin layer of conducting salty water underneath its icy crust.

Ganymede is the first known moon with its own magnetosphere. Additional data about the satellite will be obtained when *Galileo* revisits it three more times during its mission.

Europa

Europa, 3,130 kilometers (1,945 miles) in diameter, the brightest of Jupiter's Galilean satellites, may have a surface of thin ice crust overlying water or softer ice, with large-scale fracture and ridge systems appearing in the crust. Europa has a density about three times that of water, suggesting that it is a mixture of silicate rock and some water. Very few impact craters are visible on the surface.

Hubble space telescope observations of Europa in 1994 revealed that it has a tenuous oxygen-bearing atmosphere.

Callisto

Callisto, 4,840 kilometers (3,008 miles) in diameter, is the least active geologically of the Galilean satellites. Its icy, dirt-laden surface appears to be very ancient and heavily cratered. Callisto's density (less than twice that of water) is very close to that of Ganymede, yet there is little or no evidence of the crustal motion and internal activity that is visible on Ganymede.

Io

Io, 3,640 kilometers (2,262 miles) in diameter, is the most spectacular of the Galilean moons. Its brilliant colors of red, orange, and yellow set it apart from any other planet. Eight active volcanoes have been detected on Io, with some plumes extending up to 320 kilometers (200 miles) above the surface. The relative smoothness of Io's surface and its volcanic activity suggest that it has the youngest surface of Jupiter's moons. Its surface is composed of large amounts of sulfur and sulfur-dioxide frost, which account for the primarily yellow-orange surface color.

The volcanoes seem to eject a sufficient amount of sulfur dioxide to form a doughnut-shaped ring (torus) of ionized sulfur and oxygen atoms around Jupiter near Io's orbit. *Galileo* images taken in June 1996 revealed that Io's landscape undergoes constant change due to the numerous sulfur volcanoes that continuously erupt on its surface.

In 1996, the *Galileo* spacecraft detected a huge iron core within Io that occupies half the moon's diameter. *Galileo* also discovered evidence that Io has its own magnetic field.

Amalthea

Amalthea, Jupiter's most innermost satellite, was discovered in 1892. It is so small—265 kilometers (165 miles) long and 150 kilometers (90 miles) wide—that it is extremely difficult to observe from Earth. Amalthea is an elongated, irregularly shaped satellite of reddish color. It orbits the planet every 12 hours and is in synchronous rotation, with its long axis always oriented toward Jupiter.

Jupiter's other moons are named Adrasta, Metis, Thebe, Leda, Himalia, Lysithea, Elara, Ananke, Carne, Pasiphae, and Sinope.

The Magnetosphere

Perhaps the largest structure in the solar system is the magnetosphere of Jupiter. This is the region of space which is filled with Jupiter's magnetic field and is bounded by the interaction of that magnetic field with the solar wind, which is the sun's outward flow of charged particles. The plasma of electrically charged particles that exists in the magnetosphere is flattened into a large disk more than 4.8 million kilometers (3 million miles) in diameter, is coupled to the magnetic field, and rotates around Jupiter. The Galilean satellites are located in the inner regions of the magnetosphere and are subjected to intense radiation bombardment.

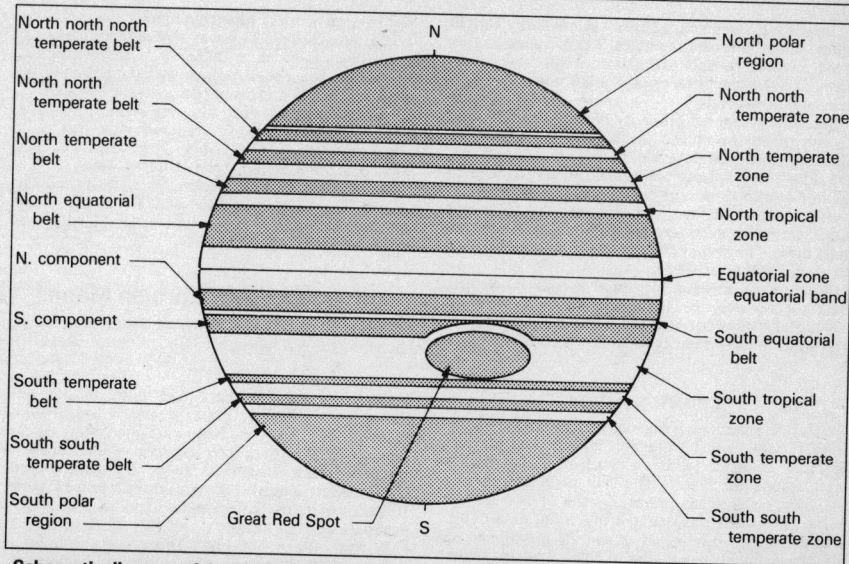

North north north temperate belt

North north temperate belt

North temperate belt

North equatorial belt

N. component

S. component

South temperate belt

South south temperate belt

South polar region

Great Red Spot

N

S

North polar region

North north temperate zone

North temperate zone

North tropical zone

Equatorial zone equatorial band

South equatorial belt

South tropical zone

South temperate zone

South south temperate zone

Schematic diagram of Jupiter's major features. NASA illustration.

Ganymede, Jupiter's largest satellite and also the largest known moon in the solar system. Its diverse surface indicates several periods of geologic activity.

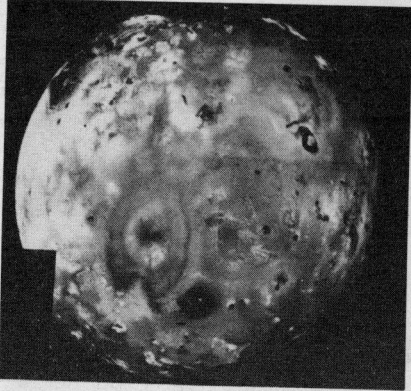

A computer-generated image of Io, the most volcanically active planetary body known in the solar system. Io's volcanoes and lava lakes cover the landscape and continually reface it, so that many impact craters have disappeared. NASA photo.

The intense radiation field that surrounds Jupiter is fatal to humans. If astronauts were one day able to approach the planet as close as the *Voyager 1* spacecraft did, they would receive a dose of 400,000 rads or roughly 1,000 times the lethal dose for humans.

In 1989, evidence from ground-based infrared spectra of Io indicated that the Jovian moon has hydrogen sulfide (H_2S) on its surface and in its atmosphere. It is the first time that the presence of H_2S has been detected outside the Earth.

• Even when nearest the Earth, Jupiter is still almost 400 million miles away. But because of its size, it may rival Venus in brilliance when near. Jupiter's four large moons may be seen through field glasses, moving rapidly around Jupiter and changing their position from night to night.

Saturn

Saturn, the second largest planet in the solar system, is the least dense. Its mass is 95 times the mass of the Earth and its density is 0.70 gram per cubic centimeter, so that it would float in an ocean if there were one big enough to hold it.

Saturn radiates more energy than it receives from the sun, about 80% more. However, the excess thermal energy cannot be primarily attributed to Saturn's primordial heat loss, as is speculated for Jupiter.

Saturn's diameter is 120,660 kilometers (74,978 miles) but 10% less at the poles, a consequence of its rapid rotation. Its axis of rotation is tilted by 27 degrees and the length of its day is 10 hours, 39 minutes, and 24 seconds.

Saturn is composed primarily of liquid metallic hydrogen (about 80%) and the second most common element is believed to be helium.

Saturn's atmospheric appearance is very similar to Jupiter's with dark and light cloud markings and swirls, eddies, and curling ribbons; the belts and zones are more numerous and a thick haze mutes the markings. The temperature ranges from 80° K to 90° K (176° F to –203° F).

Winds blow at extremely high speeds on Saturn. Near the equator, the *Voyagers* measured winds of about 500 meters per second (1,100 miles per hour). The winds blow primarily in an eastward direction.

Saturn's Rings

Saturn's spectacular ring system is unique in the solar system, with uncountable billions of tiny particles of water ice (with traces of other material) in orbit around the planet. The ring particles range in size from smaller than grains of sugar to as large as a house. The main rings stretch out from about 7,000 kilometers (4,350 miles) to above the atmosphere of the planet out to the F ring, a total span of 74,000 kilometers (45,984 miles). Saturn's rings can be likened to a phonograph, rings within rings numbering in the hundreds, and spokes in the B rings, and shepherding satellites controlling the F ring.

The main rings are called the A, B, and C rings moving from outside to inside. The gap between the A and B rings is called the Cassini Division and is named for the Italian-French astronomer, Gian Domenico Cassini, who discovered four of Saturn's major moons and the dark, narrow gap, "Cassini's Division," splitting the planet's rings.

Saturn's magnetic field has well-defined north and south magnetic poles, and is aligned with Saturn's axis of rotation to within one degree.

Saturn's Moons

Saturn has 19 known moons. In May 1995, American astronomers using the Hubble Space Telescope, reported discovering several new satellites of Saturn bringing the total to 20 or more. However, it was later determined that only one of them is a moon. The five largest moons, Tethys, Dione, Rhea, Titan, and Iapetus, range from 1060 to 5150 kilometers (650 to 3,200 miles) in diameter. The planet's outstanding satellite is Titan, first discovered by the Dutch astronomer Christiaan Huygens in 1656.

Titan

Titan is remarkable because it is the only known moon in the solar system that has a substantial atmosphere—largely nitrogen with a minor amount of methane and a rich variety of other hydrocarbons. Its surface is completely hidden from view (except at infrared and radio wavelengths) by a dense, hazy atmosphere.

The diameter of Titan is 5,150 kilometers (3,200 miles) and it is the second largest satellite in the solar system after Jupiter's Ganymede. Titan is larger than the planet Mercury.

Titan's surface temperature is about –175° C (–280° F) and its surface pressure is about 50% greater than the surface pressure of the Earth. After the Voyager I flyby in 1980, scientists hypothesized that Titan

may have an ocean of liquid hydrogen covering its surface. However, in 1990 it was shown that Titan's surface reflects and scatters radio waves, suggesting that the satellite has a solid surface with the possibility of small hydrocarbon lakes or ponds on the surface.

The data were obtained by using NASA's 70-meter antenna in California to transmit powerful radio waves to Titan, and the Very Large Array in New Mexico as the receiver of the reflected waves.

NASA plans to send a scientific probe to the surface of Titan in the summer of 2004 as part of its Cassini Mission. The probe will be provided by the European Space Agency (ESA).

Other Notable Saturnian Moons

The other four largest moons of Saturn are: Tethys, Dione, Rhea, and Iapetus.

Tethys is 1,060 kilometers (650 miles) in diameter. Its surface is heavily cratered and it has a huge, globe-girdling canyon, Ithaca Chasma. Part of the canyon stretches over three-quarters of the satellite's surface. Ithaca Chasma is about 2,500 kilometers (1,550 miles) long. It has an average width of about 100 kilometers (62 miles) and a depth of 3 to 5 kilometers (1.8 to 3.1 miles).

Tethys also has a huge impact crater named Odysseus, 400 kilometers (244 miles) in diameter, or more than one-third its diameter.

Dione is slightly larger than Tethys, 1,120 kilometers (696 miles) and is more than half composed of water ice. It has bright, wispy markings resembling thin veils covering its features.

Rhea, the largest of the inner satellites, is 1,530 kilometers (951 miles) in diameter. It is composed mainly of water ice, causing its reflective surface to present an almost uniform white appearance.

Iapetus is the outermost of Saturn's icy satellites. Its appearance is unique because it has one dark and one bright hemisphere. The origin of the black coating of its dark face is unknown. Iapetus has a diameter of 1,460 kilometers (907 miles).

Other notable moons of Saturn are Mimas, Enceladus, Hyperion, and Phoebe.

Mimas is small, only 329 kilometers (244 miles) in diameter. It has a huge impact crater, Herschel, nearly one-third of its diameter. The crater is about 130 kilometers (81 miles) wide and its icy peak rises almost 10 kilometers (6.2 miles) above the floor.

Mimas is believed to be composed mainly of water ice and to contain between 20 to 50% rock.

Enceladus is remarkable in that its surface shows signs of extensive and recent geological activity. There may be active water volcanism. The surface is extremely bright, reflecting more than 90% of incident sunlight. This suggests that its surface is composed of extremely pure ice without dust or rocks to contaminate it. Enceladus has a diameter of 500 kilometers (310 miles).

Hyperion orbits between Iapetus and Titan. It is irregular in shape, measuring about 400 by 250 by 200 kilometers (248 by 155 by 124 miles). It may be a remnant of a much larger object which was shattered by impact with another space body. It appears that Hyperion is composed primarily of water ice.

Hyperion orbits Saturn in a random-like motion ("chaotic tumbling").

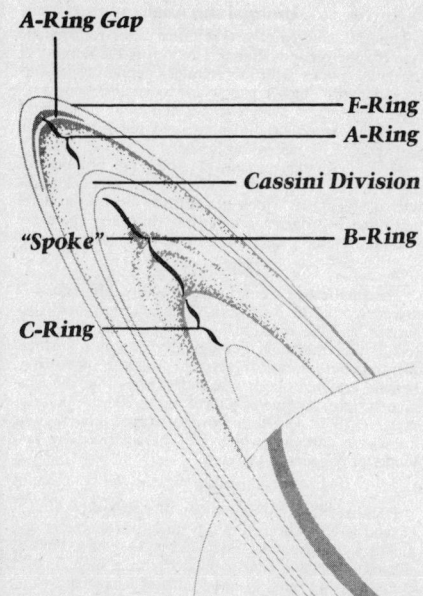

A-Ring Gap

F-Ring

A-Ring

Cassini Division

"Spoke"

B-Ring

C-Ring

Photo of icy Mimas shows the largest meteorite crater which is about one-quarter the diameter of the entire moon. A huge mountain can be seen rising up almost 20,000 feet from the center of the crater. The crater's walls average 16,000 feet in height. NASA photo.

NASA illustration of the divisions in Saturn's ring system.

Phoebe is Saturn's outermost satellite. It travels in a retrograde orbit at a distance of over 10 million kilometers (6.2 million miles) away from the planet. It is the darkest moon of Saturn and is the planet's only known satellite that does not keep the same face always turned to Saturn. It has been speculated that it is an asteroid that was captured by the planet. Phoebe rotates in about nine hours and orbits Saturn in 406 days. It has a diameter of 200 kilometers (124 miles).

Pan was discovered in 1990 from *Voyager 2* photos taken in 1981. An official name, Pan, is to be approved by the International Astronomical Union. The satellite is estimated to be about 20 kilometers (12.43 miles) in diameter, which makes it the planet's smallest known moon. It orbits within the Encke Gap, a 325-kilometer (202 mile) division in Saturn's A ring. It was identified by Johann Franz Encke (1791–1865) in 1837.

The remaining eight moons range from 25 to 190 kilometers (15 to 120 miles) in diameter. They are all non-spherical in shape. Their names are Atlas, Prometheus, Pandora, Epimetheus, Janus, Telesto, Calypso, and Helene.

NASA's planned Cassini Mission to Saturn in October 1997 will shed more light on the planet's mysteries. (*See* Cassini Mission in the Space Section.)

• Saturn is the last of the planets visible to the naked eye. Saturn is never an object of overwhelming brilliance, but it looks like a bright star. The rings can be seen with a small telescope.

Uranus

Uranus, the first planet discovered in modern times by Sir William Herschel in 1781, is the seventh planet from the sun, twice as far out as Saturn. Its mean distance from the sun is 2,869 million kilometers (1,783 million miles). Uranus's equatorial diameter is 51,810 kilometers (32,200 miles). The axis of Uranus is tilted at 97 degrees, so it goes around the sun nearly lying on its side.

Due to Uranus' unusual inclination, the polar regions receive more sunlight during a Uranus year of 84 Earth years. Scientists had thought that the temperature of its poles would be warmer than that at its equator, but *Voyager 2* discovered that the equatorial temperatures were similar to the temperatures at the poles, −209° C (−344° F), implying that some redistribution of heat toward the equatorial region must occur within the atmosphere. The wind patterns are much like Saturn's, flowing parallel to the equator in the direction of the planet's rotation.

Ninety-eight percent of the upper atmosphere is composed of hydrogen and helium; the remaining two percent is methane. Scientists speculate that the bulk of the atmosphere is composed of water (perhaps as much as 50%), methane, and ammonia. Methane is responsible for Uranus' blue-green color because it selectively absorbs red sunlight and condenses to form clouds of ice crystals in the cooler, higher regions of Uranus' atmosphere.

It was also discovered that the planet's magnetic field was 60 degrees tilted from the planet's axis of rotation and offset from the planet's center by one-third of Uranus' radius. It may be generated at a depth where water is under sufficient pressure to be electrically conductive.

The Uranian Rings

Voyager 2 also expanded the body of information pertaining to the rings and moons of Uranus. *Voyager*'s cameras obtained the first images of nine previously known narrow rings and discovered at least two new rings, one narrow and one broadly diffused, bringing the total known rings to eleven. It was found

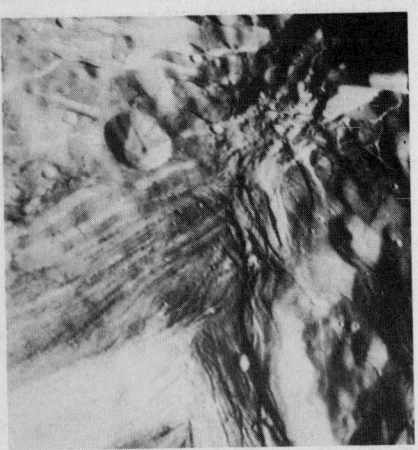

The Uranian moon Miranda is one of the strangest objects in the solar system. Photo shows some of its complex surface terrain. NASA photo.

that a highly structured distribution of fine dust exists throughout the ring system.

The outermost (epsilon) ring contains nothing smaller than fist-sized particles. It is flanked by two small moons discovered interior to the orbit of the Uranian moon Miranda. The moons exert a shepherding influence on the epsilon ring and on the outer edges of the gamma and delta rings.

All of the rings lie within one planetary radius[1] of Uranus' cloud tops. Most of Uranus' rings are narrow, ranging in width from 1 to 93 kilometers (0.6 to 58 miles) and are only a few kilometers thick. The Uranian rings are colorless and extremely dark. The dark material may be either irradiated methane ice or organic-rich minerals mixed with water-impregnated, silicon-based compounds. There is evidence that incomplete rings, or "ring arcs," exist at Uranus.

The Uranian Moons

There are 15 known moons of Uranus. In order of decreasing distance from the planet, the moons are Oberon, Titania, Umbriel, Ariel, Miranda, Puck, Belinda, Cressida, Portia, Rosalind, Desdemona, Juliet, Bianca, Ophelia, and Cordelia. Nine of the new moons range in size from 26 to 108 kilometers (16 to 67 miles) in diameter and, being closer to the planet, have faster periods of revolution (8 to 15 hours) than their more distant relatives.

Oberon and Titania

The two largest moons, Oberon, 1,516 kilometers (942 miles) in diameter, and Titania (1,580 kilometers (982 miles) in diameter, are less than half the diameter of Earth's moon. Titania, the reddest of Uranus' moons, may have endured global tectonics as evidenced by complex valleys and fault lines etched into its surface. Smooth sections indicate that volcanic resurfacing has taken place.

1. The equatorial radius of Uranus is 25,560 kilometers (15,880 miles) at a pressure of 1 bar.

Umbriel and Ariel

Umbriel and Ariel are roughly three-fourths the size of Oberon and Titania. Umbriel is the darkest of the large moons with huge craters peppering its surface. Umbriel has a paucity of what are known as bright ray craters, which are formed on an older darker surface when bright submerged ice is excavated and sprayed by meteoroid impacts.

In contrast, the surface of Ariel, the brightest of the Uranian moons, is relatively free of pockmarks due to volcanism which periodically erases the damage done by foreign projectiles. However, there are several extremely deep cuts on Ariel's surface.

Miranda

The smallest of Uranus' large moons, Miranda, 472 kilometers (293 miles) in diameter, has been described as "the most bizarre body in the solar system," with the most geologically complex surface. Miranda's remarkable terrain consists of rolling, heavily cratered plains (the oldest known in the Uranian system) adjoined by three huge, 200 to 300 kilometer (120 to 180 mile) oval-to-trapezoidal regions known as coronae, which are characterized by networks of concentric canyons.

Puck

Puck was the first new moon discovered by *Voyager*, and is 154 kilometers (96 miles) in diameter and makes a trip around Uranus every 18 hours. Puck is shaped somewhat like a potato with a huge impact crater marring roughly one-fourth of its surface.

• Uranus can—on rare occasions—become bright enough to be seen with the naked eye, if one knows exactly where to look; normally, a good set of field glasses or a small portable telescope is required.

Neptune

Little was known about Neptune until August 1989, when NASA's *Voyager 2* became the first spacecraft to observe the planet. Passing about 4,950 kilometers (3,000 miles) above Neptune's north pole, *Voyager 2* made its closest approach to any planet since leaving Earth twelve years prior. The spacecraft passed about 40,000 kilometers (25,000 miles) from Neptune's largest moon, Triton, the last solid body that *Voyager 2* will have studied.

Nearly 4.5 billion kilometers (3 billion miles) from the sun, Neptune orbits the sun once in 165 years, and therefore has made not quite a full circle around the sun since it was discovered.[1]

With an equatorial diameter of 49,528 kilometers (30,775 miles), Neptune is the smallest of our solar system's four gas giants.[2] Even so, its volume could hold nearly 60 Earths. Neptune is also denser than the other gas giants—Jupiter, Saturn, and Uranus, about 64% heavier than if it were composed entirely of water.

1. Astronomers have studied Neptune since Sept. 23, 1846, when Johann Gottfried Galle, of the Berlin Observatory, and Louis d'Arrest, an astronomy student, discovered the eighth planet on the basis of mathematical predictions by Urbain Jean Joseph Le Verrier. Similar predictions were made independently by John Couch Adams. Galileo Galilei had seen Neptune during several nights of observing Jupiter, in January 1613, but didn't realize he was seeing a new planet.
2. These four planets are about 4 to 12 times greater in diameter than Earth. They have no solid surfaces, but possess massive atmospheres that contain substantial amounts of hydrogen and helium with traces of other gases.

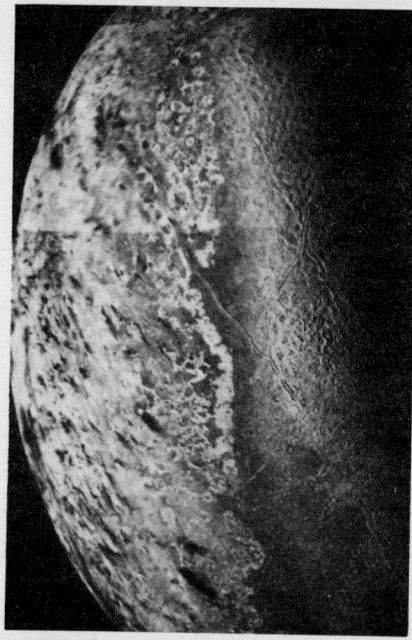

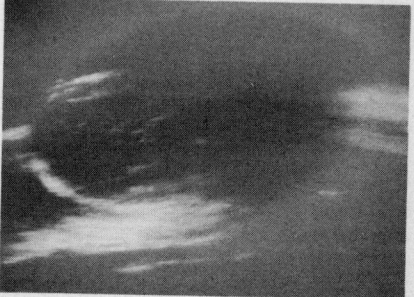

ABOVE LEFT: The rugged terrain of Triton, Neptune's largest moon. *Voyager 2* **photographed geyser-like eruptions of nitrogen gas on Triton. ABOVE RIGHT: High-altitude clouds in Neptune's atmosphere. BELOW RIGHT: The Great Dark Spot is the most prominent feature in the planet's atmosphere. It is a counter-clockwise storm about the size of the Earth.**

Neptune has a blue color as a result of methane in its atmosphere. Methane preferentially absorbs the longer wavelengths of sunlight (those near the red end of the spectrum). What are left to be reflected are colors at the blue end of the spectrum.

The atmosphere of Neptune is mainly composed of hydrogen, with helium and traces of methane and ammonia.

Neptune is a dynamic planet even though it receives only three percent as much sunlight as Jupiter does. *Voyager 2* discovered several large, dark spots that were prominent features on the planet. The largest spot was about the size of the Earth and was designated the "Great Dark Spot" by its discoverers. It appeared to be an anticyclone similar to Jupiter's Great Red Spot. While Neptune's Great Dark Spot is comparable in size, relative to the planet, and at the same latitude (22° south latitude) as Jupiter's Great Red Spot, it was far more variable in size and shape than its Jovian counterpart. Bright, wispy "cirrus-type" clouds overlaid the Great Dark Spot at its southern and northeastern boundaries.

At about 42° south, a bright, irregularly shaped, eastward-moving cloud circles much faster than did the Great Dark Spot, "scooting" around Neptune in about 16 hours. This "scooter" may have been a cloud plume rising between cloud decks.

Another spot, designated "D2," was located far to the south of the Great Dark Spot at 55° S latitude. It is almond-shaped, with a bright central core, and moves eastward around the planet in about 16 hours.

In 1995, images taken by the Hubble space telescope showed that the Great Dark Sport has vanished.

The great storm center has either dissipated or is obscured by other atmospheric conditions.

The atmosphere above Neptune's clouds is hotter near the equator, cooler in the mid-latitudes, and warm again at the south pole. Temperatures in the stratosphere were measured to be 750 kelvins (900° F), while at the 100 millibar pressure level, they were measured to be 55° K (−360° F).

Long, bright clouds, reminiscent of cirrus clouds on Earth, were seen high in Neptune's atmosphere. They appear to form above most of the methane, and consequently are not blue.

At northern low latitudes (27° N), *Voyager* captured images of cloud streaks casting their shadows on cloud decks estimated to be about 50 to 100 kilometers (30 to 60 miles) below. The widths of these cloud streaks range from 50 to 200 kilometers (30 to 125 miles). Cloud streaks were also seen in the southern polar regions (71° S) where the cloud heights were about 50 kilometers (30 miles).

Most of the winds on Neptune blow in a westward direction, which is retrograde, or opposite to the rotation of the planet. Near the Great Dark Spot, there are retrograde winds blowing up to 1,500 miles an hour—the strongest winds measured on any planet.

The Magnetic Field

Neptune's magnetic field is tilted 47 degrees from the planet's rotation axis, and is offset at least 0.55 radii (about 13,500 kilometers or 8,500 miles) from the physical center. The dynamo electric currents produced within the planet, therefore, must be relatively closer to the surface than for Earth, Jupiter, or Saturn. Because of its unusual orientation, and the tilt of the planet's rotation axis, Neptune's magnetic field goes through dramatic changes as the planet rotates in the solar wind.

Voyager's planetary radio astronomy instrument measured the periodic radio waves generated by the magnetic field and determined that the rotation rate of the interior of Neptune is 16 hours 7 minutes.

Voyager also detected auroras, similar to the northern and southern lights on Earth, in Neptune's atmosphere. Unlike those on Earth, due to Neptune's complex magnetic field, the auroras are extremely complicated processes that occur over wide regions of the planet, not just near the planet's magnetic poles.

Neptune's moons

Triton

The largest of Neptune's eight known satellites, Triton is different from all other icy moons that *Voyager* has studied. Triton circles Neptune in a tilted, circular, retrograde orbit, completing an orbit in 5.875 days at an average distance of 330,000 kilometers (205,000 miles) above the planet's cloud tops.

Triton shows evidence of a remarkable geologic history, and *Voyager 2* images show active geyser-like eruptions spewing invisible nitrogen gas and dark dust particles 2 to eight kilometers (1 to 5 miles) into space.

Triton is about three-quarters the size of Earth's moon and has a diameter of about 2,705 kilometers (1,680 miles), and a mean density of about 2.066 grams per cubic centimeter. (The density of water is 1.0 gram per cubic centimeter.) This means that Triton contains more rock in its interior than the icy satellites of Saturn and Uranus do.

The relatively high density and the retrograde orbit offer strong evidence that Triton did not originate near Neptune, but is a captured object.

An extremely thin atmosphere extends as much as 800 kilometers (500 miles) above the satellite's surface. Tiny nitrogen ice particles may form thin clouds a few kilometers above the surface. Triton is very bright, reflecting 60 to 95% of the sunlight that strikes it. (By comparison, Earth's moon reflects only 11 percent.)

The atmospheric pressure at Triton's surface is about 14 microbars, a mere 1/70,000th the surface pressure on Earth. Temperature at the surface is about 38 kelvins (−391° F), making it the coldest surface of any body yet visited in the solar system.

The Smaller Satellites

In addition to the previously known moons Triton and Nereid, *Voyager 2* found six more satellites, making the total eight.

Nereid

Nereid was discovered in 1948 through Earth-based telescopes. Little is known about Nereid, which is slightly smaller than Proteus, having a diameter of 340 kilometers (211 miles). The satellite's surface reflects about 14% of the sunlight that strikes it. Nereid's orbit is the most eccentric in the solar system, ranging from about 1,353,600 km (841,100 miles) to 9,623,700 (5,980,200 mi.).

Proteus

Like all six of Neptune's recently discovered small satellites, it is one of the darkest objects in the solar system—"as dark as soot" is a good description. It reflects only 6% of the sunlight that strikes it. Proteus is an ellipsoid about 258 kilometers (415 miles) in diameter, larger than Nereid. It circles Neptune at a distance of about 92,800 kilometers (57,700 miles) above the cloud tops, and completes one orbit in 26 hours 54 minutes. Scientists say that it is about as large as a satellite can be without being pulled into a spherical shape by its own gravity.

Larissa

This object is only about 48,800 kilometers (30,300 miles) from Neptune and circles the planet in 13 hours 18 minutes. Its diameter is 190 kilometers (120 miles).

Despina

The satellite is 27,700 kilometers (17,200 miles) from Neptune's clouds and makes one orbit every 8 hours. Its diameter is about 150 kilometers (90 miles).

Galatea

It lies 37,200 kilometers (23,100 miles) from Neptune. Its diameter is 180 kilometers (110 miles) and it completes an orbit in 10 hours 18 minutes.

Thalassa

The satellite appears to be about 80 kilometers (50 miles) in diameter. It orbits Neptune in 7 hours 30 minutes some 25,200 kilometers (15,700 miles) above the cloud tops.

Naiad

The last satellite discovered, it is about 60 kilometers (37 miles) in diameter and orbits Neptune about 23,200 kilometers (14,400 miles) above the clouds in 7 hours 6 minutes.

Proteus and its tiny companions are cratered and irregularly shaped—they are not round—and show no signs of any geologic modifications. All circle the planet in the same direction as Neptune rotates, and remain close to Neptune's equatorial plane.

Neptune's Rings

Voyager found four rings and evidence of ring *arcs* or incomplete rings. The "Main Ring" orbits Neptune at about 38,100 kilometers (23,700 miles) above the cloud tops. The "Inner Ring" is about 28,400 kilometers (17,700 miles) from Neptune's cloud tops. An "Inside Diffuse Ring"—a complete ring—is located about 17,100 kilometers (10,600 miles) from the planet's cloud tops. Some scientists suspect that this ring may extend all the way down to Neptune's cloud tops. An area called "the Plateau" is a broad, diffuse sheet of fine material just outside the so-called "Inner Ring." The fine material is approximately the size of smoke particles. All other rings contain a greater proportion of larger material.

Pluto

Pluto, the outermost and smallest planet in the solar system, is the only planet not visited by an exploring spacecraft. So little is known about it, that it is difficult to classify. Its distance is so great that the Hubble Space Telescope cannot reveal its surface features. Appropriately named for the Roman god of the underworld, it must be frozen, dark, and dead. Pluto's mean distance from the sun is 5,900 million kilometers (3,666 million miles).

In 1978, light curve studies gave evidence of a moon revolving around Pluto with the same period as Pluto's rotation. Therefore, it stays over the same point on Pluto's surface. In addition, it keeps the same face toward the planet. The satellite was later named Charon and is estimated to be about 789 miles (1,270 kilometers) in diameter. Recent estimates indi-

The First Ten Minor Planets (Asteroids)

Name	Year of discovery	Mean Distance from sun (millions of miles)	Orbital period (years)	Diameter (miles)	Magnitude
1. Ceres	1801	257.0	4.60	485	7.4
2. Pallas	1802	257.4	4.61	304	8.0
3. Juno	1804	247.8	4.36	118	8.7
4. Vesta	1807	219.3	3.63	243	6.5
5. Astraea	1845	239.3	4.14	50	9.9
6. Hebe	1847	225.2	3.78	121	8.5
7. Iris	1847	221.4	3.68	121	8.4
8. Flora	1847	204.4	3.27	56	8.9
9. Metis	1848	221.7	3.69	78	8.9
10. Hygeia	1849	222.6	5.59	40 (?)	9.5

cate Pluto's diameter is about about 1,441.6 miles (2,220 kilometers), making the pair more like a double planet than any other in the solar system. Previously, the Earth-Moon system held this distinction. The density of Pluto is slightly greater than that of water.

There is evidence that Pluto has an atmosphere containing methane and polar ice caps that increase and decrease in size with the planet's seasons. It is not known to have water. The Hubble space telescope's faint object camera revealed light and dark regions on Pluto indicating an ice cap at the planet's north pole. It is not known if there is an ice cap at Pluto's south pole.

Pluto was predicted by calculation when Percival Lowell (1855–1916) noticed irregularities in the orbits of Uranus and Neptune. Clyde Tombaugh (1906–   ) discovered the planet in 1930, precisely where Lowell predicted it would be. The name Pluto was chosen because the first two letters represent the initials of Percival Lowell.

• Pluto has the most eccentric orbit in the solar system, bringing it at times closer to the sun than Neptune. Pluto approached the perihelion of its orbit on Sept. 5, 1989, and for the rest of this century will be closer to the sun than Neptune. Even then, it can be seen only with a large telescope.

The Asteroids

Between the orbits of Mars and Jupiter are an estimated 30,000 pieces of rocky debris, known collectively as the asteroids, or planetoids. The first and, incidentally, the largest (Ceres) was discovered during the New Year's night of 1801 by the Italian astronomer Father Piazzi (1746–1826), and its orbit was calculated by the German mathematician Karl Friedrich Gauss (1777–1855). Gauss invented a new method of calculating orbits on that occasion. A German amateur astronomer, the physician Olbers (1748–1840), discovered the second asteroid, Pallas. The number now known, catalogued, and named is over 6,000 and could reach 10,000 by the end of the 20th century. A few asteroids do not move in orbits beyond the orbit of Mars, but in orbits which cross the orbit of Mars. The first of them was named Eros because of this peculiar orbit. It had become the rule to bestow female names on the asteroids, but when it was found that Eros crossed the orbit of a major planet, it received a male name. Since then around two dozen orbit-crossers have been discovered, and they are often referred to as the "male asteroids." A few of them—Albert, Adonis, Apollo, Amor, and Icarus—cross the orbit of the Earth, and two of them may come closer than our moon; but the crossing is like a bridge crossing a highway, not

like two highways intersecting. Hence there is very little danger of collision from these bodies. They are all small; three to five miles in diameter, and therefore very difficult objects to identify, even when quite close. Some scientists believe the asteroids represent the remains of an exploded planet. Asteroid 1992 AD, discovered January 1992, is the outermost asteroid known. It takes 93 years to orbit the sun. This minor planet's orbit crosses the paths of Saturn, Uranus, and Neptune.

On Oct. 29, 1991, the Galileo spacecraft took a historic photograph of asteroid 951 Gaspra from a distance of 10,000 miles (16,200 kilometers) away. It was the first close-up photo ever taken of an asteroid in space.

Gaspra was discovered to be an irregular, potato-shaped object about 12.5 mi (20 km) by 7.5 mi (12 km) by 7 mi (11 km) in size. Its surface is covered with a layer of loose rubble and its terrain is covered with several dozen small craters.

Scientists believe that Gaspra is a fragment of a larger body which was shattered from collisions with other asteroids.

The asteroid was named after a Black Sea retreat favored by Russian astronomer Grigoriy N. Neujmin who discovered it in 1916.

Closeup photos of Asteroid 243 Ida taken by the Galileo spacecraft on Aug. 28, 1993, revealed that Ida had a tiny egg-shaped moon measuring 0.9 miles by 0.7 miles (1.6 by 1.2 kilometers). The moon has been named Dactyl.

NASA's Near-Earth Asteroid Rendezvous spacecraft was launched on Feb. 17, 1996. It will fly past minor planet Mathilde 253 in June 1997 and will swing back and enter an orbit around the 25-mile wide asteroid 433 Eros in February 1999.

Comets

Comets, according to the noted astronomer, Fred L. Whipple (1906–   ), are enormous "snowballs" of frozen gases (mostly carbon dioxide, methane, and water vapor) and contain very little solid material. The whole behavior of comets can then be explained as the behavior of frozen gas being heated by the sun. When the comet Kohoutek made its first appearance to man in 1973, its behavior seemed to confirm this theory and later, the international study by five spacecraft that encountered Comet Halley in March 1986 confirmed Whipple's idea of the make-up of comets.

Since comets appear in the sky without any warning, people in classical times and especially during the Middle Ages believed that they had a special meaning, which, of course, was bad. Since a natural catastrophe of some sort of a military conflict occurs every year, it was quite simple to blame the comet that happened to be visible. But even in the past, there were some people who used logical reasoning. When, in Roman times, a comet was blamed for the loss of a battle and hence was called a "bad omen," a Roman writer observed that the victors in the battle probably did not think so.

Up until the middle of the sixteenth century, comets were believed to be phenomena of the upper atmosphere; they were usually "explained" as "burning vapors" which had risen from "distant swamps." That nobody had ever actually seen burning vapors rise from a swamp did not matter.

But a large comet which appeared in 1577 was carefully observed by Tycho Brahe (1546–1601), a Danish astronomer who is often, and with the best of reasons, called "eccentric" but who insisted on precise measurements for everything. It was Tycho Brahe's accumulation of literally thousands of precise measurements which later enable his younger collaborator, Johannes Kepler (1571–1630), to discover the laws of planetary motion. Measuring the motion of the comet of 1577, Tycho Brahe could show that it had been far beyond the atmosphere, even though he could not give figures for the distance. Tycho Brahe's work proved that comets were astronomical and not meteorological phenomena.

In 1682, the second Astronomer Royal of Great Britain, Dr. Edmond Halley (1656–1742), checked the orbit of a bright comet that was in the sky then and compared it with earlier comet orbits which were known in part. Halley found that the comet of 1682 was the third to move through what appeared to be the same orbit. And the three appearances were roughly 76 years apart. Halley concluded that this was the same comet, moving around the sun in a closed orbit, like the planets. He predicted that it would reappear in 1758 or 1759. Halley himself died in 1742, but a large comet appeared sixteen years after his death as predicted and was immediately referred to as "Halley's comet."

Halley's Comet appeared again in 1986, sparking a worldwide effort to study it up close. Five satellites in all took readings from the comet at various distances. Two Soviet craft, *Vega 1* and *Vega 2*, went in close to provide detailed pictures of the comet, including the first of the comet's core. The European Space Agency's craft, *Giotto*, entered the comet itself, coming to within 450 miles of the comet's center and successfully passing through its tail. In addition, two Japanese craft, the *Suisei* and the *Sakigake*, passed at a longer distance and analyzed the cloud and tail of the comet and the effect of solar radiation upon it.

Astronomers refer to comets as "periodic" or as "non-periodic" comets, but the latter term does not mean that these comets have no period; it merely means that their period is not known. The actual periods of comets run from 3.3 years (the shortest known) to many thousands of years. Their orbits are elliptical, like those of the planets, but they are very eccentric, long and narrow ellipses. Only comet Schwassmann–Wachmann has an orbit which has such a low eccentricity (for a cometary orbit) that it could be the orbit of a minor planet.

When a comet, coming from deep space, approaches the sun, it is at first indistinguishable from a minor planet. Somewhere between the orbits of Mars and Jupiter its outline becomes fuzzy; it is said to develop a "coma" (the word used here is the Latin word *coma*, which means "hair," not the phonetically identical Greek word which means "deep sleep").

Then, near the orbit of Mars, the comet develops its tail, which at first trails behind. This grows steadily as the comet comes closer and closer to the sun. As it rounds the sun (as first noticed by Girolamo Fracastoro, 1483–1553) the tail always points away from the sun so that the comet, when moving away from the sun, points its tail ahead like the landing lights of an airplane.

The reason for this behavior is that the tail is pushed in these directions by the radiation pressure of the sun. It sometimes happens that a comet loses its tail at perihelion; it then grows another one. Although the tail is clearly visible against the black of the sky, it is very tenuous. It has been said that if the tail of Halley's comet could be compressed to the density of iron, it would fit into a small suitcase.

Although very low in mass, comets are among the largest members of the solar system. The nucleus of a comet may be up to 10,000 miles in diameter; its coma between 10,000 and 50,000 miles in diameter; and its tail as long as 28 million miles.

Comet Shoemaker–Levy 9 broke up into 21 fragments in July 1992 and crashed into the surface of Jupiter July 16–22, 1994, in the worst violent event in the recorded history of the solar system.

In 1951, Dutch astronomer Gerard Kuiper first suggested the existence of a disk-shaped swarm of short-period comets that begin beyond the orbit of Neptune and extend past Pluto. In 1995, the Hubble Telescope detected the long-sought Kuiper Belt and an estimated 200 million comets were discovered orbiting in it.

Meteors and Meteorites

The term "meteor" for what is usually called a "shooting star" bears an unfortunate resemblance to the term "meteorology," the science of weather and weather forecasting. This resemblance is due to an ancient misunderstanding which wrongly considered meteors an atmospheric phenomenon. Actually, the streak of light in the sky that scientists call a meteor is essentially an astronomical phenomenon: the entry of a small piece of cosmic matter into our atmosphere.

The distinction between "meteors" and "fireballs" (formerly also called "bolides") is merely one of convenience; a fireball is an unusually bright meteor. Incidentally, it also means that a fireball is larger than a faint meteor.

Bodies which enter our atmosphere become visible when they are about 60 miles above the ground. The fact that they grow hot enough to emit light is not due to the "friction" of the atmosphere, as one can often read. The phenomenon responsible for the heating is one of compression. Unconfined air cannot move faster than the speed of sound. Since the entering meteorite moves with 30 to 60 times the speed of sound, the air simply cannot get out of the way. Therefore, it is compressed like the air in the cylinder of a Diesel engine and is heated by compression. This heat—or part of it—is transferred to the moving body. The details of this process are now fairly well understood as a result of re-entry tests with ballistic-missile nose cones.

The average weight of a body producing a faint "shooting star" is only a small fraction of an ounce. Even a bright fireball may not weigh more than 2 or 3 pounds. Naturally, the smaller bodies are worn to dust by the passage through the atmosphere; only rather large ones reach the ground. Those that are found are called meteorites. (The "meteor," to repeat, is the term for the light streak in the sky.) About 1,000 meteorites fall to the Earth each year.

The 88 Recognized Constellations

In astronomical works, the Latin names of the constellations are used. The letter N or S following the Latin name indicates whether the constellation is located to the north or south of the Zodiac. The letter Z indicates that the constellation is within the Zodiac.

Latin name	Letter	English version	Latin name	Letter	English version	Latin name	Letter	English version
Andromeda	N	Andromeda	Delphinus	N	Dolphin	Pavo	S	Peacock
Antlia	S	Airpump	Dorado	S	Swordfish	Pegasus	N	Pegasus
Apus	S	Bird of Paradise			(Goldfish)	Perseus	N	Perseus
Aquarius	Z	Water Bearer	Draco	N	Dragon	Phoenix	S	Phoenix
Aquila	N	Eagle	Equuleus	N	Filly	Pictor	S	Painter (or his
Ara	S	Altar	Eridanus	S	Eridanus (river)			Easel)
Aries	Z	Ram	Fornax	S	Furnace	Pisces	Z	Fishes
Auriga	N	Charioteer	Gemini	Z	Twins	Piscis		
Boötes	N	Herdsmen	Grus	S	Crane	Austrinus	S	Southern Fish
Caelum	S	Sculptor's Tool	Hercules	N	Hercules	Puppis	S	Poop (of Argo)[1]
Camelopardalis	N	Giraffe	Horologium	S	Clock	Pyxis	S	Mariner's
Cancer	Z	Crab	Hydra	N	Sea Serpent			Compass
Canes Venatici	N	Hunting Dogs	Hydrus	S	Water Snake	Reticulum	S	Net
Canis Major	S	Great Dog	Indus	S	Indian	Sagitta	N	Arrow
Canis Minor	S	Little Dog	Lacerta	N	Lizard	Sagittarius	Z	Archer
Capricornus	Z	Goat (or Sea-	Leo	Z	Lion	Scorpius	S	Scorpion
		Goat)	Leo Minor	N	Little Lion	Sculptor	S	Sculptor
Carina	S	Keel (of Argo)[1]	Lepus	S	Hare	Scutum	N	Shield
Cassiopeia	N	Cassiopeia	Libra	Z	Scales	Serpens	N	Serpent
Centaurus	S	Centaur	Lupus	S	Wolf	Sextans	S	Sextant
Cepheus	N	Cepheus	Lynx	N	Lynx	Taurus	Z	Bull
Cetus	S	Whale	Lyra	N	Lyre (Harp)	Telescopium	S	Telescope
Chameleon	S	Chameleon	Mensa	S	Table	Triangulum	N	Triangle
Circinus	S	Compasses			(mountain)	Triangulum	S	Southern
Columba	S	Dove	Microscopium	S	Microscope	Australe		Triangle
Coma Berenices	N	Berenice's Hair	Monoceros	S	Unicorn	Tucana	S	Toucan
Corona Australis	S	Southern Crown	Musca	S	Southern Fly	Ursa Major	N	Big Dipper
Corona Borealis	N	Northern Crown	Norma	S	Rule	Ursa Minor	N	Little Dipper
Corvus	S	Crow (Raven)			(straightedge)	Vela	S	Sail (of Argo)[1]
Crater	S	Cup	Octans	S	Octant	Virgo	Z	Virgin
Crux	S	Southern Cross	Ophiuchus	N	Serpent-Bearer	Volans	S	Flying Fish
Cygnus	N	Swan	Orion	S	Orion	Vulpecula	N	Fox

1. The original constellation Argo Navis (the Ship Argo) has been divided into Carina, Puppis, and Vela. Normally the brightest star in each constellation is designated by alpha, the first letter of the Greek alphabet, the second brightest by beta, the second letter of the Greek alphabet, and so forth. But the Greek letters run through Carina, Puppis, and Vela as if it were still one constellation.

The largest meteorite known is still imbedded in the ground near Grootfontein in SW Africa and is estimated to weigh 70 tons. The second largest known is the 34-ton Anighito (on exhibit in the Hayden Planetarium, New York), which was found by Admiral Peary in 1892 at Cape York in Greenland. The largest meteorite found in the United States is the Willamette meteorite (found in Oregon, weight ca. 15 tons), but large portions of this meteorite weathered away before it was found. Its weight as it struck the ground may have been 20 tons.

All these are iron meteorites (an iron meteorite normally contains about 7% nickel), which form one class of meteorites. The other class consists of the stony meteorites, and between them there are the so-called "stony irons." The so-called "tektites" consist of glass similar to our volcanic glass obsidian, and because of the similarity, there is doubt in a number of cases whether the glass is of terrestrial or of extra-terrestrial origin.

Though no meteorite larger than the Grootfontein is actually known, we do know that the Earth has, on occasion, been struck by much larger bodies. Evidence for such hits are the meteorite craters, of which an especially good example is located near the Cañon Diablo in Arizona. Another meteor crater in the United States is a rather old crater near Odessa, Texas. A large

number of others are known, especially in eastern Canada; and for many "probables," meteoric origin has now been proved.

The 13th known lunar meteorite was found in December 1993 by a team from the Antarctic Search for Meteorites project. It is approximately two inches long and weighs 0.75 of an ounce.

Some scientists theorize that the mass extermination of dinosaurs from the face of the Earth 65 million years ago was due to a large meteor that struck out planet at that time.

The meteor showers are caused by multitudes of very small bodies travelling in swarms. The Earth travels in its orbit through these swarms like a car driving through falling snow. The point from which the meteors seem to emanate is called the *radiant* and is named for the constellation in that area. The Perseid meteor shower in August is the most spectacular of the year, boasting at peak roughly 60 meteors per hour under good atmospheric conditions. The presence of a bright moon diminishes the number of visible meteors.

The Constellations

Constellations are groupings of stars which form patterns that can be easily recognized and remembered, for example, Orion and the Big Dipper. The Big

Dipper is actually an asterism, not a constellation, because it is only part of the constellation Ursa Major (the Big Bear). Actually, the stars of the majority of all constellations do not "belong together." Usually they are at greatly varying distances from the Earth and just happen to lie more or less in the same line of sight as seen from our solar system. But in a few cases the stars of a constellation are actually associated; most of the bright stars of the Big Dipper travel together and form what astronomers call an open cluster.

If you observe a planet, say Mars, for one complete revolution, you will see that it passes successively through twelve constellations. All planets (except Pluto at certain times) can be observed only in these twelve constellations, which form the so-called Zodiac, and the sun also moves through the Zodiacal signs, though the sun's apparent movement is actually caused by the movement of the Earth.

Although the constellations are due mainly to the optical accident of line of sight and have no real significance, astronomers have retained them as reference areas. It is much easier to speak of a star in Orion than to give its geometrical position in the sky. During the Astronomical Congress of 1928, it was decided to recognize 88 constellations. A description of their agreed-upon boundaries was published at Cambridge, England, in 1930, under the title *Atlas Céleste.*

The Auroras

The "northern lights" *(Aurora borealis)* as well as the "southern lights" *(Aurora australis)* are upper-atmosphere phenomena of astronomical origin. The auroras center around the magnetic (not the geographical) poles of the Earth, which explains why, in the Western Hemisphere, they have been seen as far to the south as New Orleans and Florida while the equivalent latitude in the Eastern Hemisphere never sees an aurora. The northern magnetic pole happens to be in the Western Hemisphere.

The lower limit of an aurora is at about 50 miles. Upper limits have been estimated to be as high as 400 miles. Since about 1880, a connection between the auroras on Earth and the sun spots has been suspected and has gradually come to be accepted. It was said that the sun spots probably eject "particles" (later the word *electrons* was substituted) which on striking the Earth's atmosphere, cause the auroras. But this explanation suffered from certain difficulties. Sometimes a very large sun spot group on the sun, with individual spots bigger than the Earth itself, would not cause an aurora. Moreover, even if a sun spot caused an aurora, the time that passed between the appearance of the one and the occurrence of the other was highly unpredictable.

This problem of the time lag is, in all probability, solved by the discovery of the Van Allen layer by artificial satellite *Explorer I.* The Van Allen layer[1] is a double layer of charged sub-atomic particles around the Earth. The inner layer, with its center some 1,500 miles from the ground, reaches from about 40° N. to about 40° S. and does not touch the atmosphere. The outer layer, much larger and with its center several thousand miles from the ground, does touch the atmosphere in the vicinity of the magnetic poles.

It seems probable that the "leakage" of electrons from the outer Van Allen layer causes the auroras. A new burst of electrons from the sun seems to be caught in the outer layer first. Under the assumption that all electrons are first caught in the outer layer, the time lag can be understood. There has to be an "overflow" from the outer layer to produce an aurora.

The Atmosphere

Astronomically speaking, the presence of our atmosphere is deplorable. Though reasonably transparent to visible light, the atmosphere may absorb as much as 60% of the visible and near-visible light. It is opaque to most other wave-lengths, except certain fairly short radio waves. In addition to absorbing much light, our atmosphere bends light rays entering at a slant (for a given observer) so that the true position of a star close to the horizon is not what it seems to be. One effect is that we see the sun above the horizon before it actually is. And the unsteady movement of the atmosphere causes the "twinkling" of the stars, which may be romantic but is a nuisance when it comes to observing.

The composition of our atmosphere near the ground is 78% nitrogen and 21% oxygen, the remaining 1% consisting of other gases, most of it argon. The composition stays the same to an altitude of at least 70 miles (except that higher up two impurities, carbon dioxide and water vapor, are missing), but the pressure drops very fast. At 18,000 feet, half of the total mass of the atmosphere is below, and at 100,000 feet, 99% of the mass of the atmosphere is below. The upper limit of the atmosphere is usually given as 120 miles; no definitive figure is possible, since there is no boundary line between the incredibly attenuated gases 120 miles up and space.

Astronomical Telescopes

Optical telescopes used in astronomy are of two basic kinds: refracting and reflecting. In the *refractor telescope,* a lens is used to collect light from a distant object and bring it to a focus. A second lens, the eyepiece, then magnifies the image which may be examined visually or photographed directly. The *reflector telescope* uses a concave mirror instead of a lens, which reflects the light rays back toward the upper end of the telescope where they are magnified and observed or photographed. Most large optical telescopes now being built are reflectors.

Radio telescopes are used to study radio waves coming from outside the Earth's atmosphere. The waves are gathered by an antenna or "dish," which is a parabolic reflecting surface made of metal or finely meshed wire. Radio signals have been received from the sun, moon, and planets, and from the center of our galaxy and other galaxies. Radio signals are the means by which the distant and mysterious quasars and pulsars were discovered.

Some Giant Telescopes

- The world's largest fixed-dish radio telescope (1963) is located near Arecibo, Puerto Rico. It is 1,000 ft (35 m) in diameter and spans some 25 acres.
- The Very Large Array (VLA) telescope (1980) near Socorro, N.M. is the world's most powerful radio telescope. It is Y-shaped and has 27 separate mobile antennas (each 82 ft in diameter) and is spread out over about a 25-mile area.
- The world's largest fully-steerable radio telescope (1972) located at Effelsberg, Germany, has a 100-meter (328 ft) antenna.
- The Very Long Baseline Array (VLBA) radio telescope was scheduled for operation in August

---

1. Named after the American physicist, James Alfred Van Allen (1914–   ) who discovered the broad bands of intense radiation surrounding the Earth in 1958.

1993. The VLBA is a system linking ten widely scattered radio dishes—across the continental U.S., Hawaii, and the U.S. Virgin Islands—that will act as a single telescope. Each of the ten dish-shaped antenna is 82 feet (25.29 meters) in diameter. The VLBA is controlled by a "correlator" computer system located at Socorro, New Mexico.

The Very Long Baseline Array will study the most far out violent phenomena and exotic objects in the universe such as quasars, pulsars, and colliding galaxies with unprecedented accuracy. It should have a "seeing" ability that is 500 times better than the Hubble space telescope after it is repaired to operate in perfect condition.

• The Very Large Telescope of the European Southern Observatory (ESO) located at La Silla, Chile, will be the world's largest ground-based reflector when it is completed around the year 2000. It will consist of four 8-meter (26.24 ft) telescopes whose mirrors will combine their images to simulate a single 16 meter (52.49 ft) diameter telescope thereby giving it the power of a 630-inch primary mirror.

• The W.M. Keck Telescope (1991) at Mauna Kea, Hawaii, is the world's most powerful reflector telescope. It has a primary mirror composed of 36 hexagonal segments, each 1.8 meters in size. The Keck Telescope has a light gathering power four times greater than the 200-inch Hale.

• The 200-inch (5 meter) Hale telescope at Mount Palomar, Calif. (1948) is the second largest reflector in use.

• The 236-inch Special Astrophysical Observatory (1976) at Zelenchukskaya on the northern slopes of the Caucasus Mountains in the Russian Federation is the world's largest reflector telescope in use. However, problems with it make it less useful than the 200-inch Hale.

• The 40-inch (1.01 meter) telescope at Yerkes Observatory (1897) at Williams Bay, Wisc. is the world's largest refracting telescope.

• The Edwin P. Hubble Space Telescope was released by the space shuttle *Discovery* on April 25, 1990. It is able to peer far out in space and back in time, producing imagery of unprecedented clarity, of galaxies, star systems, and some of the universe's more intriguing objects: quasars, pulsars, and exploding galaxies. It can distinguish fine details—in planetary atmospheres or nearby star fields—with ten times the clarity of the best ground observatories. When pointed at Jupiter, for example, the telescope provides images comparable to those from Voyager flybys.

The $1.6-billion Space Telescope has a primary mirror 2.4 m (94 inches) in diameter. The mirror is almost half the diameter of the 5-m (200 inch) telescope at Mt. Palomar, the most powerful ground-based telescope in the western world.

After it was placed in orbit at 380 miles (611.5 km) altitude, the Hubble Telescope became the principal tool for exploring the universe through this decade and the next.

The Space telescope can view galaxies and quasars over distances up to 14 billion light years. Seeing that far will show us the universe as it was early in its lifetime and will reveal how matter has evolved over the eons. It will also teach us more about the large structure of the universe, providing clues as to whether the universe will continue to expand.

It was discovered in June 1990 that there was a spherical aberration in one of the telescope's mirrors. In 1991, two of the craft's six gyroscopes failed, and a third failed on Nov. 18, 1992, causing additional problems. NASA successfully repaired the Space Telescope during the Dec. 2–13, 1993, mission of the *Endeavour.*

Although the telescope's planned 15-year mission is scheduled to end in 2005, some NASA officials would like to extend its life for several more years until it can be replaced. Astronomers are debating what instrument will be needed to replace the Hubble space telescope when it is deactivated. NASA is planning a mission to service the telescope in February 1997.

The Gamma Ray Observatory

The Gamma Ray Observatory (GRO) launched from the space shuttle *Atlantis* April 7, 1991, was the second of the four "Great Observatories" NASA had planned for studying the Universe in this decade. The first of the "Great Observatories" was the Hubble Space Telescope, launched April 24, 1990. The others are the Advanced X-ray Astrophysics Facility (AXAF) expected to launch in 1997 but budget cuts delayed the project. It is now expected to lift off in 1998. The Space Infrared Telescope Facility (SIRTF) is being replaced and rescheduled for possible launching around the year 2000. The mission will last two and one half years and it will study substellar objects in a wide range of infrared light.

Unlike visible radiation and radio waves, gamma rays cannot be focused with telescopes. Instead, gamma rays are detected when they interact with matter. Their passage through the detectors on the GRO convert the rays to flashes of visible light which are counted and measured. From those flashes, scientists can determine their energy level and source. Gamma rays cannot be detected on Earth because they do not penetrate the atmosphere.

The $617-million spacecraft was built by TRW and measures 70 feet (21 meters) between the tips of its solar arrays. The solar arrays provide 1800 watts of electrical power required for the operation of the observatory. The spacecraft was designed to have a minimum life of two years, but it is expected to operate for at least six years.

Gamma rays are the highest energy radiations in the electromagnetic spectrum, ranging from tens of thousands to tens of billions of electron volts (eV). An eV is a measure of the amount of energy impacted to an electron when subjected to an electrical potential of 1 volt. In contrast, visible light corresponds to only a few electron volts. These gamma rays provide a means of studying some of the primary forces of change in the astrophysical processes.

Gamma rays are thought to originate with the "Big Bang" and subsequent expansion of the universe we witness today. Through these gamma-ray observations, we may witness the birth of elements and deaths of stars, gain clues into the mysteries of quasars, pulsars, neutron stars, and get a glimpse into the spacetime precipice of a black hole. In all these cases, large amounts of energy are released and gamma rays produced.

Gamma rays are generated by **supernovas** and by their very dense remains, **neutron stars.** These stars spin very rapidly, some—perhaps all—emit radiation in pulses and are known as pulsars. Pulsars are thought to be remnants of supernova explosions. One of the fastest known **pulsars** makes 643 complete rotations in one second. How these stars convert their rotational energy to gamma rays is not known. Since the first pulsar was discovered in 1968, we now have located more than 500 of them.

Phenomena, 1997

Configurations of Sun, Moon, and Planets

NOTE: The hour listings are in Universal Time. For conversion to United States time zones, see conversion table on next page.

JANUARY

d	h	
1	04	Mars 3° N of moon
2	00	Earth at perihelion
2	01	Mercury in inferior conjunction
2	02	LAST QUARTER
7	17	Venus 5° S of moon
9	04	NEW MOON
10	09	moon at perigee
12	14	Mercury 3° N of Venus
12	21	Mercury stationary
14	05	Saturn 2° S of moon
14	07	Ceres in conjunction with sun
15	20	FIRST QUARTER
17	13	Neptune in conjunction with sun
19	06	Aldebaran 0°.7 S of moon (Occn.)
19	13	Jupiter in conjunction with sun
23	15	FULL MOON
24	05	Mercury greatest elong. W (25°)
24	14	Uranus in conjunction with sun
25	17	moon at apogee
28	23	Mars 3° N of moon
31	20	LAST QUARTER

FEBRUARY

d	h	
1	11	Venus 1°0 S of Neptune
3	06	Vesta in conjunction with sun
6	00	Venus 0°.3 S of Jupiter
6	04	Mercury 5° S of moon
6	08	Neptune 4° S of moon
6	18	Mars stationary
7	12	Venus 0°.2 S of Uranus
7	15	NEW MOON
7	20	Mercury 1°4 S of Neptune
7	21	moon at perigee
10	17	Saturn 1°.8 S of moon
12	14	Mercury 1°.0 S of Jupiter
13	00	Mercury 0°.9 S of Uranus
14	09	FIRST QUARTER
15	11	Aldebaran 0°.6 S of moon (Occn.)
16	08	Jupiter 0°.2 N of Uranus
21	17	moon at apogee
22	10	FULL MOON
25	01	Mars 3° N of moon

MARCH

d	h	
2	10	LAST QUARTER
5	20	Neptune 4° S of moon
6	09	Uranus 5° S of moon
6	14	Jupiter 5° S of moon
8	09	moon at perigee
9	01	NEW MOON (eclipse)
10	06	Pluto stationary
10	09	Saturn 1°.4 S of moon
11	16	Mercury in superior conjunction
14	19	Aldebaran 0°.5 S of moon (Occn.)
16	00	FIRST QUARTER
17	08	Mars at opposition
20	14	Equinox

APRIL

d	h	
2	05	Neptune 4° S of moon
2	14	Venus in superior conjunction
2	19	Uranus 5° S of moon
3	08	Jupiter 4° S of moon
6	00	moon at perigee
6	01	Mercury greatest elong. E (19°)
7	11	NEW MOON
8	16	Mercury 6° N of moon
11	04	Aldebaran 0°.5 S of moon (Occn.)
14	17	FIRST QUARTER
15	05	Mercury stationary
17	15	moon at apogee
19	06	Mars 4° N of moon
22	21	FULL MOON
25	11	Mercury in inferior conjunction
29	06	Mars stationary
29	11	Neptune 4° S of moon
30	03	LAST QUARTER
30	03	Uranus 5° S of moon
30	21	Jupiter 4° S of moon

MAY

d	h	
1	23	Neptune stationary
3	11	moon at perigee
4	16	Saturn 0°.8 S of moon (Occn.)
5	16	Mercury 1°.2 N of moon (Occn.)
6	21	NEW MOON
7	18	Mercury stationary
8	14	Aldebaran 0°.6 S of moon (Occn.)
13	09	Uranus stationary
14	11	FIRST QUARTER
15	10	moon at apogee
16	12	Pallas stationary
16	16	Mars 2° N of moon
19	08	Venus 6° N of Aldebaran
22	09	FULL MOON
22	23	Mercury greatest elong. W (25°)
25	10	Pluto at opposition
26	16	Neptune 4° S of moon
27	08	Uranus 4° S of moon
28	06	Jupiter 4° S of moon
29	07	moon at perigee
29	08	LAST QUARTER

JUNE

d	h	
1	03	Saturn 0°.5 S of moon (Occn.)
3	13	Mercury 1°.6 N of moon
5	07	NEW MOON
7	00	Venus 6° N of moon
10	11	Jupiter stationary
12	05	moon at apogee
13	05	FIRST QUARTER
13	16	Mars 0°.3 N of moon (Occn.)
14	14	Mercury 5° N of Aldebaran

d	h	
20	17	Mars closest approach
21	00	moon at apogee
23	14	Mars 4° N of moon
24	05	FULL MOON (Eclipse)
30	22	Saturn in conjunction with sun
31	20	LAST QUARTER

JULY

d	h	
2	05	Aldebaran 0°.6 S of moon (Occn.)
4	19	Earth at aphelion
4	19	NEW MOON
5	04	Mercury 5° S of Pollux
7	02	Venus 5° N of moon
9	23	moon at apogee
12	01	Mars 1°.8 S of moon
12	22	FIRST QUARTER
14	17	Ceres stationary
19	10	Pallas at opposition
20	03	FULL MOON
20	06	Neptune 4° S of moon
20	21	Uranus 4° S of moon
21	07	Neptune at opposition
21	17	Jupiter 4° S of moon
21	23	moon at perigee
23	01	Venus 1°.2 N of Regulus
24	16	Juno in conjunction with sun
25	19	Saturn 0°.02 N of moon (Occn.)
26	18	LAST QUARTER
27	00	Mercury 0°.5 S of Regulus
29	11	Aldebaran 0°.4 S of moon (Occn.)
29	19	Uranus at opposition

AUGUST

d	h	
2	19	Saturn stationary
2	23	Mars 1°.7 N of Spica
3	08	NEW MOON
4	00	Mercury greatest elong. E (27°)
5	19	Mercury 1°.0 S of moon (Occn.)
6	09	Venus 1°.6 N of moon
6	14	moon at apogee
9	14	Jupiter at opposition
9	15	Mars 4° S of moon
11	13	FIRST QUARTER
16	05	Pluto stationary
16	16	Neptune 4° S of moon
17	03	Mercury stationary
17	05	Uranus 4° S of moon
17	22	Jupiter 4° S of moon
18	11	FULL MOON
19	05	moon at perigee
22	02	Saturn 0°.008 N of moon (Occn.)
25	02	LAST QUARTER
25	17	Aldebaran 0°.3 S of moon (Occn.)
30	03	Ceres at opposition
31	14	Mercury in inferior conjunction

SEPTEMBER

1	07	Vesta stationary
2	00	NEW MOON (Eclipse)
2	21	moon at apogee
5	12	Venus 3° S of moon
6	05	Venus 1°.9 N of Spica
7	09	Mars 5° S of moon
8	01	Pallas stationary
9	06	Mercury stationary
10	02	FIRST QUARTER
13	01	Neptune 4° S of moon
13	14	Uranus 4° S of moon
14	04	Jupiter 4° S of moon
16	15	moon at apogee
16	19	FULL MOON (Eclipse)
16	22	Mercury greatest elong. W (18°)
18	10	Saturn 0°.2 S of moon (Occn.)
22	00	Aldebaran 0°.3 S of Moon (Occn.)
23	00	Equinox
23	14	LAST QUARTER
29	23	moon at apogee

OCTOBER

1	17	NEW MOON
5	13	Venus 7° S of moon
6	06	Mars 6° S of moon
8	07	Jupiter stationary
8	22	Neptune stationary
9	12	FIRST QUARTER
10	04	Saturn at opposition
10	09	Neptune 4° S of moon
10	22	Uranus 4° S of moon
11	11	Jupiter 4° S of moon

11	22	Mars 3° N of Antares
13	21	Mercury in superior conjunction
14	14	Uranus stationary
15	02	moon at perigee
15	18	Saturn 0°.4 S of moon (Occn.)
16	04	FULL MOON
16	22	Venus 1°.7 N of Antares
17	05	Vesta at opposition
19	09	Aldebaran 0°.3 S of moon (Occn.)
23	05	LAST QUARTER
24	21	Ceres stationary
26	23	Venus 2° S of Mars
27	09	Moon at apogee
31	10	NEW MOON

NOVEMBER

4	05	Mars 6° S of moon
4	11	Venus 9° S of moon
6	07	Venus greatest elong. E (47°)
6	15	Neptune 4° S of moon
7	05	Uranus 4° S of moon
7	20	Jupiter 4° S of moon
7	22	FIRST QUARTER
12	01	Saturn 0°.4 S of moon (Occn.)
12	08	moon at perigee
14	04	Mercury 2° N of Antares
14	14	FULL MOON
15	20	Aldebaran 0°.5 S of moon (Occn.)
22	00	LAST QUARTER
24	02	moon at apogee
27	17	Pluto in conjunction with sun

28	16	Mercury in greatest elong. E (22°)
30	02	NEW MOON

DECEMBER

1	20	Mercury 7° S of moon
3	05	Mars 5° S of moon
3	17	Venus 7° S of moon
3	22	Neptune 3° S of moon
4	12	Uranus 4° S of moon
5	08	Jupiter 3° S of moon
6	18	Vesta stationary
7	06	FIRST QUARTER
7	16	Mercury stationary
7	20	Venus 3° S of Neptune
9	07	Saturn 0°.2 S of moon (Occn.)
9	17	moon at perigee
11	23	Venus greatest brilliancy
13	05	Aldebaran 0°.5 S of moon (Occn.)
14	03	FULL MOON
15	19	Mars 1°.6 S of Neptune
17	08	Mercury in inferior conjunction
17	11	Saturn stationary
21	20	Solstice
21	22	LAST QUARTER
21	23	moon at apogee
22	11	Venus 1°.1 N of Mars
25	14	Venus stationary
26	20	Mars 0°.6 S of Uranus
27	13	Mercury stationary
28	03	Mercury 2° S of moon
29	17	NEW MOON
31	06	Neptune 3° S of moon
31	13	Venus 1°.3 S of moon
31	21	Uranus 4° S of moon

Conversion of Universal Time (U. T.) to Civil Time

U.T.	E.D.T.[1]	E.S.T.[2]	C.S.T.[3]	M.S.T.[4]	P.S.T.[5]	U.T.	E.D.T.[1]	E.S.T.[2]	C.S.T.[3]	M.S.T.[4]	P.S.T.[5]
00	*8P	*7P	*6P	*5P	*4P	12	8A	7A	6A	5A	4A
01	*9P	*8P	*7P	*6P	*5P	13	9A	8A	7A	6A	5A
02	*10P	*9P	*8P	*7P	*6P	14	10A	9A	8A	7A	6A
03	*11P	*10P	*9P	*8P	*7P	15	11A	10A	9A	8A	7A
04	M	*11P	*10P	*9P	*8P	16	N	11A	10A	9A	8A
05	1A	M	*11P	*10P	*9P	17	1P	N	11A	10A	9A
06	2A	1A	M	*11P	*10P	18	2P	1P	N	11A	10A
07	3A	2A	1A	M	*11P	19	3P	2P	1P	N	11A
08	4A	3A	2A	1A	M	20	4P	3P	2P	1P	N
09	5A	4A	3A	2A	1A	21	5P	4P	3P	2P	1P
10	6A	5A	4A	3A	2A	22	6P	5P	4P	3P	2P
11	7A	6A	5A	4A	3A	23	7P	6P	5P	4P	3P

1. Eastern Daylight Time. 2. Eastern Standard Time, same as Central Daylight Time. 3. Central Standard Time, same as Mountain Daylight Time. 4. Mountain Standard Time, same as Pacific Daylight Time. 5. Pacific Standard Time. NOTES: *denotes previous day. N = noon. M = midnight.

When Is The moon a "Blue moon"?

Source: The U.S. Naval Observatory.

The second time the moon is full within a particular month, it is called a "blue moon." This condition occurs once every few years when the date of the first full moon is at or near the beginning of the month so that the following full moon comes before the end of the month. The expression "once in a blue moon," meaning "very seldom," stems from this phenomenon. Over the years a "blue moon" appears to have meant any rarely occurring kind of moon. A "blue moon" can also refer to a moon that appears to be blue in color, which is caused by unusual atmospheric conditions.

Full moons occur about every 29.53 days, or 12.3683 times a year. Therefore, months containing two full moons occur on the average every 2.72 years. Approximately once every 19 years, one year will have two months with two full moons because February will have no full moon at all. February can never have two new or full moons because the shortest time between them is 29.27 days.

DECLINATION OF SUN AND PLANETS, 1997

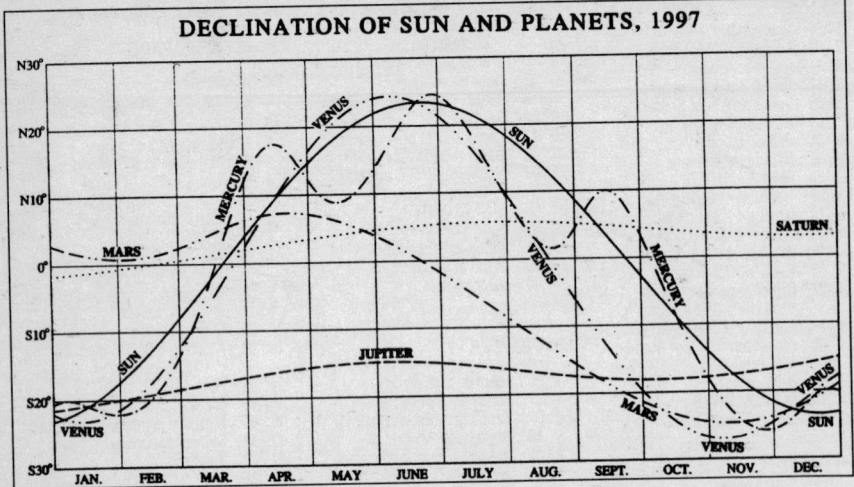

Visibility of Planets, 1997

The planet diagram on page 354 shows, in graphical form for any date during the year, the local mean times of meridian passage of the sun, of the five planets, Mercury, Venus, Mars, Jupiter, and Saturn, and of every 2ʰ of right ascension. Intermediate lines, corresponding to particular stars, may be drawn in by the user if desired. The diagram is intended to provide a general picture of the availability of planets and stars for observation during the year.

On each side of the line marking the time of meridian passage of the sun, a band 45ᵐ wide is shaded to indicate that planets and most stars crossing the meridian within 45ᵐ of the sun are generally too close to the sun for observation.

For any date the diagram provides immediately the local mean time of meridian passage of the sun, planets and stars, and thus the following information:

(a) whether a planet or star is too close to the sun for observation;
(b) visibility of a planet or star in the morning or evening;
(c) location of a planet or star during twilight;
(d) proximity of planets to stars or other planets.

When the meridian passage of a body occurs at midnight, it is close to opposition to the sun and is visible all night, and may be observed in both morning and evening twilights. As the time of meridian passage decreases, the body ceases to be observable in the morning, but its altitude above the eastern horizon during evening twilight gradually increases until it is on the meridian at evening twilight. From then onwards the body is observable above the western horizon, its altitude at evening twilight gradually decreasing, until it becomes too close to the sun for observation. When it again becomes visible, it is seen in the morning twilight, low in the east. Its altitude at morning twilight gradually increases until meridian passage occurs at the time of morning twilight, then as the time of meridian passage decreases to 0ʰ, the body is observable in the west in the morning twilight with a gradually decreasing altitude, until it once again reaches opposition.

Notes on the visibility of the principal planets, except Pluto, are given on page 353. Further information on the visibility of planets may be obtained from the diagram above which shows, in graphical form for any date during the year, the declinations of the bodies plotted on the planet diagram on page 354.

Mercury can only be seen low in the east before sunrise, or low in the west after sunset (about the time of the beginning or end of civil twilight). It is visible in the mornings between the following approximate dates: January 8 to March 1, May 4 to June 18, September 8 to October 2, and December 23 to December 31. The planet is brighter at the end of each period, (the best conditions in northern latitudes occur during the third week of September, and in southern latitudes from mid-May to the first few days of June). It is visible in the evenings between the following approximate dates: March 21 to April 17, July 3 to August 25, and October 29 to December 11. The planet is brighter at the beginning of each period, (the best conditions in northern latitudes occur from the end of March to the beginning of the second week of April, and in southern latitudes from mid-July to mid-August).

Venus is a brilliant object in the morning sky from the beginning of the year until the end of the third week of February when it becomes too close to the sun for observation. During the second week of May it reappears in the evening sky where it stays until the end of the year. Venus is in conjunction with Mercury on January 12, with Jupiter on February 6, and with Mars on October 26 and December 22.

Mars can be seen in the morning sky in Virgo until a few days after mid-March. It is at opposition on March 17 when it is visible throughout the night. Its eastward elongation gradually decreases, moving into Leo in late March and into Virgo in early

(Continued on page 353)

Visibility of Planets in Morning and Evening Twilight

Morning

Venus	January 1 — February 21
Mars	January 1 — March 17
Jupiter	February 2 — August 9
Saturn	April 18 — October 10

Evening

Venus	May 12 — December 31
Mars	March 17 — December 31
Jupiter	January 1 — January 6
	August 9 — December 31
Saturn	January 1 — March 13
	October 10 — December 31

(Continued from page 352)

June (passing 1.°7 N of *Spica* on August 2). It can only be seen in the evening sky after mid-June moving into Libra in late August, Scorpius in late September, and Ophiuchus in the second week of October (passing 3° N of *Antares* on October 11). It then continues into Sagittarius in early November and into Capricornus after mid-December. Mars is in conjunction with Venus on October 26 and December 22.

Jupiter can be seen in the evening sky in Sagittarius for the first week of January after which it becomes too close to the sun for observation. It reappears in the morning sky from the beginning of February in Capricornus, in which constellation it remains throughout the year. Its westward elongation gradually increases and after mid-May it can be seen for more than half the night. It is at opposition on August 9 when it is visible throughout the night. Its eastward elongation then decreases and after the first week of November until the end of the year it can only be seen in the evening sky. Jupiter is in conjunction with Venus on February 6 and with Mercury on February 12.

Saturn can be seen in the evening sky in Pisces until mid-March when it becomes too close to the sun for observation. It reappears in the morning sky from mid-April in Cetus. Its westward elongation gradually increases passing into Pisces again during the second week of April in which constellation it remains for the rest of the year. It is at opposition on October 10 when it is visible throughout the night. Its eastward elongation then gradually decreases and for the rest of the year can be seen for more than half the night.

Uranus is visible as an evening star at the beginning of the year in Capricornus and remains in this constellation throughout the year. It then becomes too close to the sun for observation until mid-February, when it reappears in the morning sky. It is at opposition on July 29 when it can be seen throughout the night, after which its eastward elongation gradually decreases until from the end of October it can only be seen in the evening sky.

Neptune is too close to the sun for observation until after the first week of February when it appears in the morning sky in Sagittarius. It passes into Capricornus after the first week of April and into Sagittarius again at the end of May, remaining in this constellation throughout the year. It is at opposition on July 21 when it can be seen throughout the night. Its eastward elongation gradually decreases from mid-October until late December when it can be seen in the evening sky, after which it again becomes too close to the sun for observation.

Do not confuse (1) Venus with Mercury around mid-January, at the beginning of the third week in February and late July to early August and with Jupiter during the first half of February; on all occasions Venus is the brighter object. (2) Mars with Venus from mid-October to mid-November and around mid-December when Venus is the brighter object. (3) Jupiter with Mercury around mid-February when Jupiter is the brighter object.

Eclipses of the Sun and Moon, 1997

NOTE: The day of an eclipse is given in Universal Time (U.T.) and may start a day earlier or later depending on your time zone. See Phenomena, 1996 table to find time of eclipse in your area.

March 8–9. Total eclipse of the sun. Visible in East Asia except in the south, and northern Pacific Ocean including Japan, Arctic regions, Alaska, and western Canada.

March 24. Partial eclipse of the moon. The beginning of the umbral phase visible in North America except Alaska and northwestern Canada, Central America, South America, Europe, extreme western Asia, Africa except the eastern extremity, Greenland, parts of Antarctica (including Marie Byrd Land, the Palmer Peninsula, and Queen Maud Land), the eastern South Pacific Ocean, the southeastern North Pacific Ocean, and the Atlantic Ocean; the end visible in North America except the western Aleutian Islands, Hawaii, the South Island of New Zealand, Central America, South America, most of Greenland, extreme western Europe, the western extremity of Africa, parts of Antarctica (including Victoria Land, Marie Byrd Land, the Palmer Peninsula, and part of Queen Maud Land), the eastern half of the Pacific Ocean, the North Atlantic Ocean, and the western South Atlantic Ocean.

September 1–2. Partial eclipse of the sun. Visible in the southeastern Indian Ocean, part of Antarctica, Australia, New Zealand, and the southwestern Pacific Ocean.

September 16. Total eclipse of the moon. The beginning of the umbral phase visible in eastern Europe, Asia, the eastern half of Africa, Australia, New Zealand, the western Aleutian Islands, parts of Antarctica (including Queen Maud Land, Wilkes Land, and Victoria Land), the Indian Ocean, and the western half of the Pacific Ocean; the end visible in extreme eastern South America, Europe, extreme Greenland, Asia except the extreme east, Africa, Australia except the east coast, parts of Antarctica (including Queen Maud Land, Wilkes Land, and part of Victoria Land), the eastern North Atlantic Ocean, most of the South Atlantic Ocean, and the Indian Ocean.

LOCAL MEAN TIME OF MERIDIAN PASSAGE

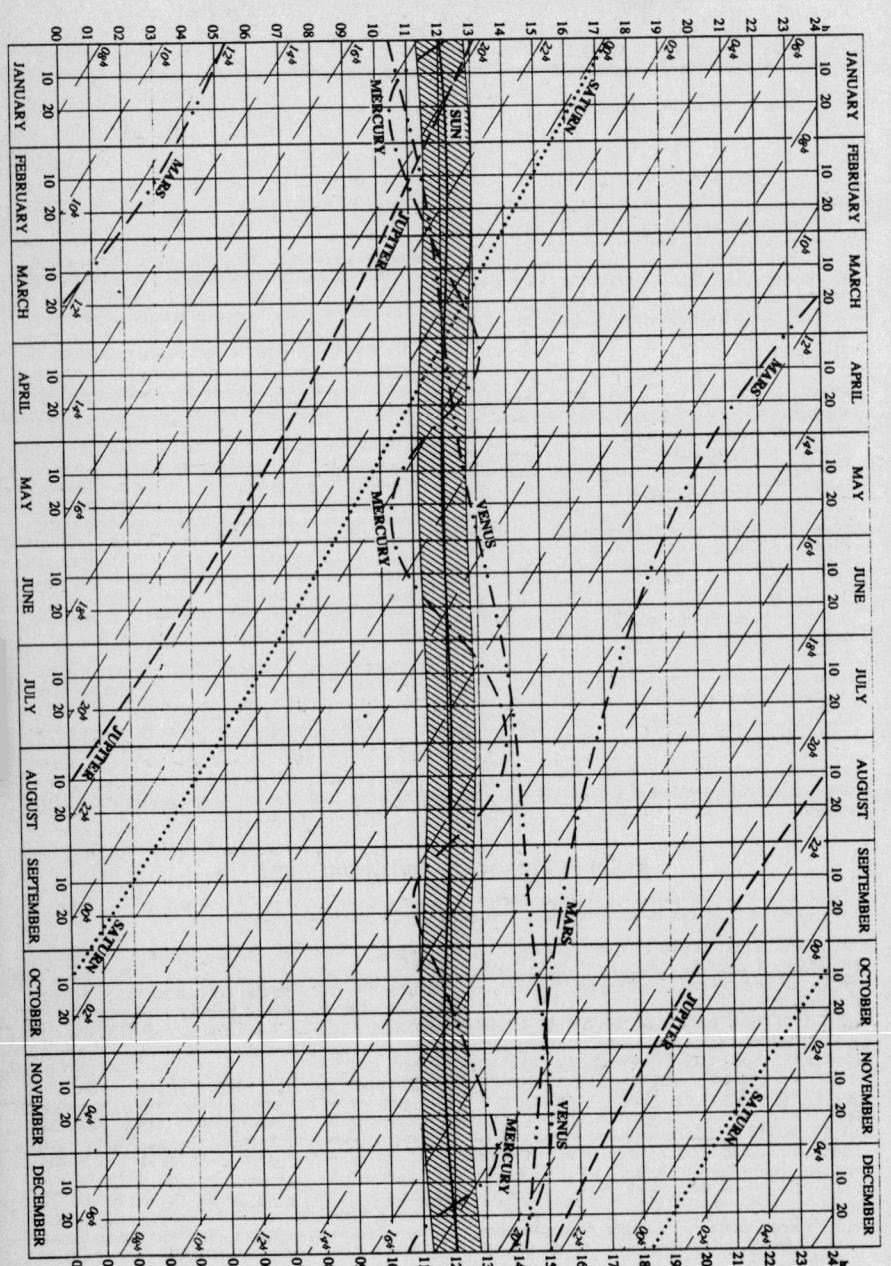

AVIATION

Famous Firsts in Aviation

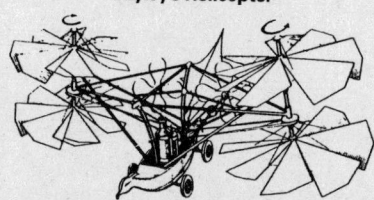

Cayley's Helicopter

Sir George Cayley's Helicopter design

Sir George Cayley of England (1773-1857) designed the first practical helicopter in 1842-43. He designed and built the first successful man-carrying glider in 1853 and sent his coachman aloft in it on its first flight. He also formulated the basic principles of modern aerodynamics and is the father of British aeronautics.

1782 First balloon flight. Jacques and Joseph Montgolfier of Annonay, France, sent up a small smoke-filled balloon about mid-November.

1783 First hydrogen-filled balloon flight. Jacques A. C. Charles, Paris physicist, supervised construction by A. J. and M. N. Robert of a 13-ft diameter balloon that was filled with hydrogen. It got up to about 3,000 ft and traveled about 16 mi. in a 45-min flight (Aug. 27).

First human balloon flights. A Frenchman, Jean Pilâtre de Rozier made the first captive-balloon ascension (Oct. 15). With the Marquis d'Arlandes, Pilâtre de Rozier made the first free flight, reaching a peak altitude of about 500 ft, and traveling about 5 1/2 mi. in 20 min (Nov. 21).

1784 First powered balloon. Gen. Jean Baptiste Marie Meusnier developed the first propeller-driven and elliptically-shaped balloon—the crew cranking three propellers on a common shaft to give the craft a speed of about 3 mph.

First woman to fly. Mme. Thible, a French opera singer (June 4).

1793 First balloon flight in America. Jean Pierre Blanchard, a French pilot, made it from Philadelphia to near Woodbury, Gloucester County, N.J., in a little over 45 min (Jan. 9).

1794 First military use of the balloon. Jean Marie Coutelle, using a balloon built for the French Army, made two 4-hr observation ascents. The military purpose of the ascents seems to have been to damage the enemy's morale.

1797 First parachute jump. André-Jacques Garnerin dropped from about 6,500 ft over Monceau Park in Paris in a 23-ft diameter parachute made of white canvas with a basket attached (Oct. 22).

1843 First air transport company. In London, William S. Henson and John Stringfellow filed articles of incorporation for the Aerial Transit Company (March 24). It failed.

1852 First dirigible. Henri Giffard, a French engineer, flew in a controllable (more or less) steam-engine powered balloon, 144 ft long and 39 ft in diameter, inflated with 88,000 cu ft of coal gas. It reached 6.7 mph on a flight from Paris to Trappe (Sept. 24).

1860 First aerial photographers. Samuel Archer King and William Black made two photos of Boston, still in existence.

1872 First gas-engine powered dirigible. Paul Haenlein, a German engineer, flew in a semi-rigid-frame dirigible, powered by a 4-cylinder internal-combustion engine running on coal gas drawn from the supporting bag.

1873 First transatlantic attempt. *The New York Daily Graphic* sponsored the attempt with a 400,000 cu ft balloon carrying a lifeboat. A rip in the bag during inflation brought collapse of the balloon and the project.

1897 First successful metal dirigible. An all-metal dirigible, designed by David Schwarz, a Hungarian, took off from Berlin's Tempelhof Field and, powered by a 16-hp Daimler engine, got several miles before leaking gas caused it to crash (Nov. 13).

1900 First Zeppelin flight. Germany's Count Ferdinand von Zeppelin flew the first of his long series of rigid-frame airships. It attained a speed of 18 mi. per h and got 3 1/2 mi. before its steering gear failed (July 2).

1903 First successful heavier-than-air machine flight. Aviation was really born on the sand dunes at Kitty Hawk, N.C., when Orville Wright crawled to his prone position between the wings of the biplane he and his brother Wilbur had built, opened the throttle of their homemade 12-hp engine and took to the air. He covered 120 ft in 12 sec. Later that day, in one of four flights, Wilbur stayed up 59 sec and covered 852 ft (Dec. 17).

1904 First airplane maneuvers. Orville Wright made the first turn with an airplane (Sept. 15); 5 days later his brother Wilbur made the first complete circle.

Did the Wrights Fly First?

Supporters of Gustave A. Whitehead are seeking to prove that the German-born inventor flew a powered-batwing aircraft on Aug. 14, 1901, in Bridgeport, Conn., two years before the Wright Brothers made their first powered flight.

While photographs of Whitehead's plane exist, none of them show it flying, nor is there much useful evidence to prove or disprove this claim.

Although Whitehead supporters have built what they claim is a replica of his plane and have flown it on several short hops in 1986, it should be noted that blueprints of Whitehead's actual craft do not exist.

The current opinion of the Smithsonian is that none of Gustave Whitehead's planes actually flew and the controversy remains.

Dec. 17, 1903. Orville Wright at the controls, Wilbur runs alongside him. National Air and Space Museum, Smithsonian Institution. (SI Neg. No. A 26767B).

1905 First airplane flight over half an hour. Orville Wright kept his craft up 33 min 17 sec (Oct. 4).

1906 First European airplane flight. Alberto Santos-Dumont, a Brazilian, flew a heavier-than-air machine at Bagatelle Field, Paris (Sept. 13).

1908 First airplane fatality. Lt. Thomas E. Selfridge, U.S. Army Signal Corps, was in a group of officers evaluating the Wright plane at Fort Myer, Va. He was up about 75 ft with Orville Wright when the propeller hit a bracing wire and was broken, throwing the plane out of control, killing Selfridge and seriously injuring Wright (Sept. 17).

1909 First cross-Channel flight. Louis Blériot flew in a 25-hp Blériot VI monoplane from Les Baraques near Calais, France, and landed near Dover Castle, England, in a 26.61-mi. (38-km) 37-min flight across the English Channel (July 25).

First International Aviation Competition Meeting. American Glenn Curtis narrowly beats France's Louis Blériot in main event and wins the Gordon Bennett Cup. Meet held at Rheims, France (Aug. 22–28).

1910 First licensed woman pilot. Baroness Raymonde de la Roche of France, who learned to fly in 1909, received ticket No. 36 on March 8.

First flight from shipboard. Lt. Eugene Ely, USN, took a Curtiss plane off from the deck of cruiser *Birmingham* at Hampton Roads, Va., and flew to Norfolk (Nov. 14). The following January, he reversed the process, flying from Camp Selfridge to the deck of the armored cruiser *Pennsylvania* in San Francisco Bay (Jan. 18).

First aircraft to take off from water. Henri Fabrer in Gnome-powered floatplane, at Martigues, France (March 28).

1911 First U.S. woman pilot. Harriet Quimby, a magazine writer, got ticket No. 37, making her the second licensed female pilot in the world.

1912 First woman's cross-Channel flight. Harriet Quimby flew from Dover, England, across the English Channel, and landed at Hardelot, France (25 mi. south of Calais) in a Blériot monoplane loaned to her by Louis Blériot

Harriet Quimby was the leading woman aviator of her day. (Leslie's Weekly Illustrated Newspaper)

(April 16). She was later killed in a flying accident over Dorchester Bay during a Harvard-Boston aviation meet on July 1, 1912.

First parachute jump from a powered airplane. Albert Berry jumps in a test over Jefferson Barracks military post, St. Louis (March 1). Some sources credit Grant Morton as making first jump in 1911.

1913 First multi-engined aircraft. Built and flown by Igor Ivan Sikorsky while still in his native Russia.

1914 First aerial combat. In August, Allied and German pilots and observers started shooting at each other with pistols and rifles—with negligible results.

1915 First air raids on England. German Zeppelins started dropping bombs on four English communities (Jan. 19).

1918 First U.S. air squadron. The U.S. Army Air Corps made its first independent raids over enemy lines, in DH-4 planes (British-designed) powered with 400-hp American-designed Liberty engines (April 8).

First regular airmail service. Operated for the Post Office Department by the Army, the first regular service was inaugurated with one round trip a day (except Sunday) between Washington, D.C., and New York City (May 15).

1919 First transatlantic flight. The NC-4, one of four Curtiss flying boats commanded by Lt. Comdr. Albert C. Read, reached Lisbon, Portugal, (May

27) after hops from Trepassy Bay, Newfoundland, to Horta, Azores (May 16–17), to Ponta Delgada (May 20). The Liberty-powered craft was piloted by Walter Hinton.

First nonstop transatlantic flight. Capt. John Alcock and Lt. Arthur Whitten Brown, British World War I flyers, made the 1,900 mi. from St. John's, Newfoundland, to Clifden, Ireland, in 16 h 12 min in a Vickers-Vimy bomber with two 350-hp Rolls-Royce engines (June 15–16).

First lighter-than-air transatlantic flight. The British dirigible R-34, commanded by Maj. George H. Scott, left Firth of Forth, Scotland, (July 2) and touched down at Mineola, L.I., 108 h later. The eastbound trip was made in 75 h (completed July 13).

First scheduled London-Paris passenger service (using airplanes). Aircraft Travel and Transport inaugurated London-Paris service (Aug. 25). Later the company started the first trans-channel mail service on the same route (Nov. 10).

First free-fall parachute jump. Leslie Irvin jumps over McCook Field, Dayton, Ohio, to prove that you won't lose consciousness during a delayed free-fall using a manually-operated parachute (April 28).

1921 First U.S. black female pilot. Bessie Coleman received license June 15. Was killed April 30, 1926, in flying accident.

First naval vessel sunk by aircraft. Two battleships being scrapped by treaty were sunk by bombs dropped from Army planes in demonstration put on by Brig. Gen. William S. Mitchell (July 21).

First helium balloon. The C-7, non-rigid Navy dirigible was first to use non-inflammable helium as lifting gas, making a flight from Hampton Roads, Va., to Washington, D.C. (Dec. 1).

1922 First member of Caterpillar Club. Lt. (later Maj. Gen.) Harold Harris bailed out of a crippled plane he was testing at McCook Field, Dayton, Ohio (Oct. 20), and became the first man to join the Caterpillar Club—those whose lives have been saved by parachute.

1923 First nonstop transcontinental flight. Lts. John A. Macready and Oakley Kelly flew a single-engine Fokker T-2 nonstop from New York to San Diego, a distance of just over 2,500 mi. in 26 h 50 min (May 2–3).

First autogyro flight. Juan de la Cierva, a brilliant Spanish mathematician, made the first successful flight in a rotary wing aircraft in Madrid (June 9).

1924 First round-the-world flight. Four Douglas Cruiser biplanes of the U.S. Army Air Corps took off from Seattle under command of Maj. Frederick Martin (April 6). 175 days later, two of the planes (Lt. Lowell Smith's and Lt. Erik Nelson's) landed in Seattle after a circuitous route—one source saying 26,345 mi., another saying 27,553 mi.

1926 First polar flight. Then-Lt. Cmdr. Richard E. Byrd, acting as navigator, and Floyd Bennett as pilot, flew a trimotor Fokker from Kings Bay, Spitsbergen, over the North Pole and back in 15 1/2 h (May 8–9).

1927 First solo, nonstop transatlantic flight. Charles Augustus Lindbergh lifted his Wright-powered Ryan monoplane, *Spirit of St. Louis,* from Roosevelt Field, L.I., to stay aloft 33 h 39 min and traveled 3,600 mi. to Le Bourget Field outside Paris (May 20–21). Although 91 persons in

Charles A. Lindbergh and *The Spirit of St. Louis.* National Air and Space Museum, Smithsonian Institution. (SI Neg. No. 87-8992).

13 separate flights crossed the Atlantic before him, he flew directly between two great world cities and did it alone.

First transatlantic passenger. Charles A. Levine was piloted by Clarence D. Chamberlin from Roosevelt Field, L.I., to Eisleben, Germany, in a Wright-powered Bellanca (June 4–5).

1928 First east-west transatlantic crossing. Baron Guenther von Huenefeld, piloted by German Capt. Hermann Koehl and Irish Capt. James Fitzmaurice, left Dublin for New York City (April 12) in a single-engine all-metal Junkers-monoplane. Some 37 h later, they crashed on Greely Island, Labrador. Rescued.

First U.S.-Australia flight. Sir Charles Kingsford-Smith and Capt. Charles T. P. Ulm, Australians, and two American navigators, Harry W. Lyon and James Warner, crossed the Pacific from Oakland to Brisbane. They went via Hawaii and the Fiji Islands in a trimotor Fokker (May 31–June 8).

First transarctic flight. Sir Hubert Wilkins, an Australian explorer and Carl Ben Eielson, who served as pilot, flew from Point Barrow, Alaska, to Spitsbergen (mid-April).

1929 First of the endurance records. With Air Corps Maj. Carl Spaatz in command and Capt. Ira Eaker as chief pilot, an Army Fokker, aided by refueling in the air, remained aloft 150 h 40 min at Los Angeles (Jan. 1–7).

First round-the-world airship flight. The LZ-127, known as the *Graf Zeppelin,* flew 21,300 miles in 20 days and 4 hours. Also set distance record (August).

First blind flight. James H. Doolittle proved the feasibility of instrument-guided flying when he took off and landed entirely on instruments (Sept. 24).

First rocket-engine flight. Fritz von Opel, a German auto maker, stayed aloft in his small rocket-powered craft for 75 sec, covering nearly 2 mi. (Sept. 30).

First South Pole flight. Comdr. Richard E. Byrd, with Bernt Balchen as pilot, Harold I. June, radio operator, and Capt. A. C. McKinley, photographer, flew a trimotor Fokker from the Bay of Whales, Little America, over the South Pole and back (Nov. 28–29).

1930 First Paris-New York nonstop flight. Dieudonné Coste and Maurice Bellonte, French pilots, flew a Hispano-powered Breguet biplane from Le Bourget Field to Valley Stream, L.I., in 37 h 18 min. (Sept. 2–3).

Chuck Yeager alongside the Bell X-1 named *Glamorous Glennis* after his wife. National Air and Space Museum, Smithsonian Institution. (SI Neg. No. 86-4483).

1931 First flight into the stratosphere. Auguste Piccard, a Swiss physicist, and Charles Knipfer ascended in a balloon from Augsburg, Germany, and reached a height of 51,793 ft in a 17-h flight that terminated on a glacier near Innsbruck, Austria (May 27).

First nonstop transpacific flight. Hugh Herndon and Clyde Pangborn took off from Sabishiro Beach, Japan, dropped their landing gear, and flew 4,860 mi. to near Wenatchee, Wash., in 41 h 13 min. (Oct. 4–5).

1932 First woman's transatlantic solo. Amelia Earhart, flying a Pratt & Whitney Wasp-powered Lockheed Vega, flew alone from Harbor Grace, Newfoundland, to Ireland in approximately 15 h (May 20–21).

First westbound transatlantic solo. James A. Mollison, a British pilot, took a de Havilland Puss Moth from Portmarnock, Ireland, to Pennfield, N.B. (Aug. 18).

First woman airline pilot. Ruth Rowland Nichols, first woman to hold three international records at the same time—speed, distance, altitude—was employed by N.Y.-New England Airways.

1933 First round-the-world solo. Wiley Post took a Lockheed Vega, *Winnie Mae*, 15,596 mi. around the world in 7 d 18 h 49 1/2 min (July 15–22).

1937 First successful helicopter. Hanna Reitsch, a German pilot, flew Dr. Heinrich Focke's FW-61 in free, fully controlled flight at Bremen (July 4).

1939 First turbojet flight. Just before their invasion of Poland, the Germans flew a Heinkel He-178 plane powered by a Heinkel S3B turbojet (Aug. 27).

1940 First wartime use of military gliders. German commandos make successful glider assault on Belgium's Fort Eben-Emael during WW II (May 10).

1941–1945 Most combat missions flown by a pilot in any war. Captain Hans-Ulrich Rudel of Germany flew 2,530 combat missions during WW II while flying a JU-87 Stuka dive bomber. He survived the war.

1942–1945 Top scoring fighter pilot of any war. German Luftwaffe ace Maj. Erich Hartmann scored 352 victories all while flying a Messerschmitt BF 109 during WW II. He was involved in 800 dogfights, and flew 1,425 missions. Maj. Hartmann survived the war.

1942 First and only enemy bombing of U.S. mainland. During World War II, a floatplane launched from a Japanese submarine off Cape Blanco, Oregon, dropped incendiary bombs on the Oregon forest in two attempts to start forest fires and terrorize American civilians, but the bombs did little damage (Sept. 9 and 29).

First American jet plane flight. Robert Stanley, chief pilot for Bell Aircraft Corp., flew the Bell XP-59 *Airacomet* at Muroc Army Base, Calif. (Oct. 1).

First woman fighter pilot to shoot down an enemy aircraft. Soviet Lieutenant Lilya Litvyak, flying a Yak-1 fighter of the women's 586th Fighter Aviation Regiment, shoots down two German planes over Stalingrad on Sept. 13, 1942.

1944 The first production stage rocket-engine fighter plane, the German Messerschmitt Me 163B *Komet* (test flown 1941) becomes operational in June 1944. Some 350 of these delta-wing fighters were built before WW II in Europe ended.

1947 First piloted supersonic flight in an airplane. Capt. Charles E. Yeager, U.S. Air Force, flew the X-1 rocket-powered research plane built by Bell Aircraft Corp., faster than the speed of sound at Muroc Air Force Base, California (Oct. 14).

1949 First round-the-world nonstop flight. Capt. James Gallagher and USAF crew of 13 flew a Boeing B-50A Superfortress around the world nonstop from Ft. Worth, returning to same point: 23,452 mi. in 94 h 1 min, with 4 aerial refuelings enroute (Feb. 27–March 2).

1950 First nonstop transatlantic jet flight. Col. David C. Schilling (USAF) flew 3,300 mi. from England to Limestone, Maine, in 10 h 1 min (Sept. 22).

1951 First solo across North Pole. Charles F. Blair, Jr., flew a converted P-51 (May 29).

1952 First jetliner service. De Havilland Comet flight inaugurated by BOAC between London and Johannesburg, South Africa (May 2). Flight, including stops, took 23 h 38 min.

First transatlantic helicopter flight. Capt. Vincent H. McGovern and 1st Lt. Harold W. Moore piloted 2 Sikorsky H-19s from Westover, Mass., to Prestwick, Scotland (3,410 mi.). Trip was made in 5 steps, with flying time of 42 h 25 min (July 15–31).

First transatlantic round trip in same day. British Canberra twin-jet bomber flew from Aldergrove, Northern Ireland, to Gander, Newfoundland, and back in 7 h 59 min flying time (Aug. 26).

1955 First transcontinental round trip in same day. Lt. John M. Conroy piloted F-86 Sabrejet across U.S. (Los Angeles-New York) and back—5,085 mi.—in 11 h 33 min 27 sec (May 21).

1957 First round-the-world, nonstop jet plane flight. Maj. Gen. Archie J. Old, Jr., USAF, led a flight of 3 Boeing B-52 bombers, powered with 8 10,000-lb. thrust Pratt & Whitney Aircraft J57 engines around the world in 45 h 19 min; distance 24,325 mi.; average speed 525 mph. (Completed Jan. 18.)

1958 First transatlantic jet passenger service. BOAC, New York to London (Oct. 4). Pan American started daily service, N.Y. to Paris (Oct. 26).

First domestic jet passenger service. National Airlines inaugurated service between New York and Miami (Dec. 10).

1968 Prototype of world's first supersonic airliner, the Soviet-designed Tupolev Tu-144 made first flight, Dec. 31. It first achieved supersonic speed on June 5, 1969.

World's 25 Busiest Airports in 1995

	City/Code	Total passengers	% Chg	Total freight	% Chg	Total movements	% Chg
1.	Chicago, O'Hare (ORD)	67,253,358	1.2	1,235,618	−1.6	900,279	1.9
2.	Atlanta, Hartsfield (ATL)	57,734,755	6.7	771,390	−4.2	754,108	5.3
3.	Dallas/Ft. Worth Airport (DFW)	56,493,851	7.3	777,696	7.2	879,371	4.6
4.	London, Heathrow (LHR)	54,452,634	5.3	1,125,610	7.4	434,524	2.3
5.	Los Angeles Intl. (LAX)	53,909,223	5.6	1,597,222	3.4	732,639	6.2
6.	Tokyo, Haneda (HND)	45,822,503	8.5	655,224	8.6	210,994	3.9
7.	Frankfurt/Main (FRA)	38,179,543	8.7	1,461,284	−18.9	378,388	3.7
8.	San Francisco (SFO)	36,232,745	4.6	696,233	2.6	423,907	0.4
9.	Miami (MIA)	33,235,658	10.0	1,584,683	18.9	576,936	3.5
10.	Denver, Stapleton (DEN)	31,036,622	−6.3	376,179	−1.3	465,903	−12.0
11.	Seoul (SEL)	30,919,462	14.2	1,215,962	18.2	197,596	10.2
12.	New York, Kennedy (JFK)	30,379,781	5.4	1,584,332	8.4	340,025	−1.0
13.	Paris, Charles de Gaulle (CDG)	28,355,470	−1.1	929,031	5.3	508,037	4.7
14.	Detroit (DTW)	28,200,358	5.2	325,398	−0.9	331,365	2.0
15.	Hong Kong (HKG)	28,043,338	8.1	1,484,742	12.5	164,672	1.7
16.	Las Vegas (LAS)	28,027,239	4.4	50,769	8.5	503,698	1.6
17.	Phoenix, Sky Harbor (PHX)	27,856,195	8.7	260,006	11.4	514,079	4.9
18.	Minneapolis/St. Paul (MSP)	26,787,287	9.5	364,946	2.0	465,454	2.4
19.	Paris, Orly (ORY)	26,653,878	0.1	291,224	−7.1	239,529	10.7
20.	Newark, N.J. (EWR)	26,626,231	−5.0	942,666	9.4	420,390	−3.7
21.	St. Louis (STL)	25,719,351	10.1	127,566	0.0	519,156	8.2
22.	Amsterdam, Schiphol (AMS)	25,355,007	7.6	1,019,315	−16.5	314,812	5.0
23.	Houston (IAH)	24,726,592	9.8	296,483	4.6	378,084	6.3
24.	Boston, Logan (BOS)	24,358,540	−2.4	394,474	−5.8	466,327	1.7
25.	Tokyo, Narita (NRT)	24,210,286	2.0	1,667,913	3.9	124,392	−0.9

Airports participating in the ACI Annual Traffic Statistics Collection. Total passengers: enplaned + deplaned passengers; passengers in transit counted once. Total cargo: loaded + unloaded freight + mail in metric tons. Total movements: landing and takeoff of an aircraft. *Source:* Airport Council International, Geneva, Switzerland.

1973 **First female pilot of a U.S. major scheduled airline.** Emily H. Warner became employed by Frontier Airlines on January 29 as second officer on a Boeing 737.

1976 **First regularly-scheduled commercial supersonic transport (SST) flights begin.** Air France and British Airways inaugurate service (January 21). Air France flies the Paris-Rio de Janeiro route; B.A., the London-Bahrain. Both airlines begin SST service to Washington, D.C. (May 24).

1977 **First successful man-powered aircraft.** Paul MacCready, an aeronautical engineer from Pasadena, Calif., was awarded the Kremer Prize for creating the world 's first successful man-powered aircraft. The *Gossamer Condor* was flown by Bryan Allen over the required 3-mile course on Aug. 23.

1978 **First successful transatlantic balloon flight.** Three Albuquerque, N.M., men, Ben Abruzzo, Larry Newman, and Maxie Anderson, completed the crossing (Aug. 16. Landed, Aug. 17) in their helium-filled balloon, *Double Eagle II.*

1979 **First man-powered aircraft to fly across the English Channel.** The Kremer Prize for the Channel crossing was won by Bryan Allen who flew the *Gossamer Albatross* from Folkestone, England to Cap Gris-Nez, France, in 2 h 55 min (June 12).

1980 **First successful balloon flight over the North Pole.** Sidney Conn and his wife Eleanor, in hot-air balloon *Joy of Sound* (April 11).

First nonstop transcontinental balloon flight, and also record for longest overland voyage in a balloon. Maxie Anderson and his son, Kris, completed four-day flight from Fort Baker, Calif., to successful landing outside Matane, Quebec, on May 12 in their helium-filled balloon, *Kitty Hawk.*

First long-distance solar-powered flight. Janice Brown, 98-lb former teacher, flew tiny experimental solar-powered aircraft, *Solar Challenger* six miles in 22-min near Marana, Ariz. (Dec. 3). The craft was powered by a 2.75-hp engine.

First solar-powered aircraft to fly across the English Channel. Stephen R. Ptacek flew the 210-lb *Solar Challenger* at the average speed of 30 mph from Cormeilles-en-Vexin near Paris to the Royal Manston Air Force Base on England's southeastern coast in 5 h 30 min (July 7).

1984 **First solo transatlantic balloon flight.** Joe W. Kittinger landed Sept. 18 near Savona, Italy, in his helium-filled balloon *Rosie O'Grady's Balloon of Peace* after a flight of 3,535 miles from Caribou, Me.

1986 **First nonstop flight around the world without refueling.** From Edwards AFB, Calif., Dick Rutan and Jeana Yeager flew in *Voyager* around the world (24,986.727 mi.), returning to Edwards in 216 h 3 min 44 s (Dec. 14–23).

1987 **First transatlantic hot-air balloon flight.** Richard Branson and Per Lindstrand flew 2,789.6 miles from Sugarloaf Mt., Maine, to Ireland in the hot-air balloon *Virgin Atlantic Flyer* (July 2–4).

1991 **First transpacific hot-air balloon flight.** Richard Branson and Per Lindstrand flew about 6,700 miles from Miyakonyo, Japan, to 150 miles west of Yellowknift, Northwest Territories, Canada (Jan. 15–17). Record pending verification.

1992 **World's longest balloon flight.** Americans Richard Abruzzo and Troy Bradley made a flight of 3,318.23 miles from Bangor, Maine to Sidi Amar El Kadmiri, Ben Slimane, Morocco in 144 hours and 16 minutes in Cameron R-77 (Sept. 16–22).

1993 **First woman to co-pilot a commercial supersonic plane.** Barbara Harmer, British Airways, flew as first officer on the Concorde from London to New York City (March 25).

1995 First solo transpacific balloon flight. Steve Fossett made a flight of more than 5,430 miles from Seoul, South Korea, to Leader, Saskatchewan, Canada, in a helium-filled balloon. Also set record for distance (Feb. 18–21, 1995). Record pending verification.

Active Pilot Certificates Held

Year	Total	Airline transport	Commercial	Private
1970	720,028	31,442	176,585	299,491
1980	814,667	63,652	182,097	343,276
1985	722,376	79,192	155,929	320,086
1990	702,659	107,732	149,666	299,111
1992	682,959	115,855	146,385	288,078
1993	665,069	117,070	143,014	283,700
1994	654,088	117,434	138,728	284,236
1995	639,184	123,877	133,980	261,399

NOTE: Includes other pilot categories—student 101,279, helicopter 7,183, glider 11,234, and recreational 232. Also nonpilot, i.e., mechanic, parachute rigger, etc. (Nonpilot total, 651,341). Data as of Dec. 31, 1995. *Source:* Department of Transportation, Federal Aviation Administration.

World Class Helicopter Records

Selected records. *Source:* National Aeronautic Association.

Great Circle Distance Without Landing
International: 2,213.04 mi.; 3,561.55 km.
Robert G. Ferry (U.S.) in Hughes YOH-6A helicopter powered by Allison T-63-A-5 engine; from Culver City, Calif., to Ormond Beach, Fla., April 6–7, 1966.

Distance, Closed Circuit
International: 1,739.96 mi.; 2,800.20 km.
Jack Schweibold (U.S.) in Hughes YOH-6A helicopter powered by Allison T-62-A-5 engine; Edwards Air Force Base, Calif., March 26, 1966.

Altitude Without Payload
International: 40,820 ft; 12,442 m.
Jean Boulet (France) in Alouette SA 315-001 "Lama" powered by Artouste IIIB 735 KW engine; Istres, France, June 21, 1972.

Altitude in Horizontal Flight
International: 36,122 ft; 11,010 m.
CWO James K. Church, (U.S.) in Sikorsky CH-54B helicopter powered by 2 P&W JFTD-12 engines; Stratford, CT., Nov. 4, 1971.

Speed Around the World
35.40 mph; 56.97 kph.
H. Ross Perot, Jr., pilot; J.W. Coburn, co-pilot (U.S.) in Bell 206 L-II Long Ranger, powered by one Allison 250-C28B of 435 hp. Elapsed time: 29 days 3 h 8 min 13 sec, Sept. 10–30, 1982.

Speed Around the World, Eastbound
40.99 mph; 65.97 kph.
Joe Ronald Bower (U.S.) pilot, in Bell JetRanger III, powered by one Allison 250-C20J of 317 shp., covered 23,800 miles in 24 days, 4 hours, 36 minutes. June 28–July 22, 1994 (pending FAI approval).

Absolute World Records, Balloons

Selected records. *Source:* National Aeronautic Association.

Altitude (USA)
113,739.9 ft; 34,668 km.
Cmdr. M.D. Ross (USNR) and Lt. Cmdr. V.A. Prather, *Lee Lewis Memorial,* Gulf of Mexico, May 4, 1961.

Distance (USA)
5,435.82 mi; 8,748.11 km.

J. Stephen Fossett, *Cameron R-150.* Seoul, Korea, to Mendham, SK, Canada, February 17–22,1995.

Duration (USA)
144 hours, 16 minutes
Richard Abruzzo and Troy Bradley, *Cameron R–77,* Bangor, Maine, USA, to Ben Slimane, Morocco, Sept. 16–22, 1992.

World Class Records, Single-Seater Gliders

Selected records. *Source:* National Aeronautic Association.

Straight Distance (W. Germany)
907.70 mi; 1,460.80 km
Hans Werner Grosse, ASK 12, Luebeck to Biarritz, April 25, 1972.

Distance to a Goal and Return (USA)
1,023.25 mi; 1,646.68 km
Thomas L. Knauff, Nimbus III, Ridge Soaring Gliderport–Williamsport Airport, Pa., April 25, 1983.

Absolute Altitude (USA)
49,009 ft; 14,938 m
Robert Harris, Burkhart Grob, G–102, California City, Calif., February 17, 1986.

Speed Over a Commerical Air Route (U.S.)

Selected records. *Source:* National Aeronautic Association.

These records are for speed between two U.S. cities made by a commercial airliner on a regularly scheduled commercial route, and are timed from takeoff to landing.

West to East Transcontinental
680.90 mph
Capt. Wylie H. Drummond, American Airlines Boeing 707–123, powered by four P&W JT3D engines, from Los Angeles International to Idlewild International, 2,474 miles in 3 hr 38 min 00 sec. April 10, 1963.

East to West Transcontinental
575.52 mph
Capt. Gene Kruse, American Airlines, Boeing 707–720B, powered by four P&W JT3D engines, from Idlewild International to Los Angeles International, 2,474 miles in 4 hr 19 min 15 sec. Aug. 15, 1962.

Parachutes

Selected records. *Source:* National Aeronautic Association.

Largest Freefall Formations

General Category (International)
200 persons, Myrtle Beach, S.C., Oct. 23, 1992.

Feminine Category (International)
101 persons, Le Canet des Maures, France, Aug. 14, 1992.

Largest Canopy Formation

General Category (International)
46 persons, Davis, CA, October 12, 1994.

Feminine Category (International)
16 persons, Madera, Calif., Oct. 7, 1990.

Individual Altitude (Freefall Distance)

General Category
E. Andreev (U.S.S.R.), 80,360 ft, 24,500 m, Nov. 1, 1962.

Feminine Category
E. Fomitcheva (U.S.S.R.), 48,556 ft, 14,800 m, Oct. 26, 1977.

Absolute World Records

(Maximum Performance in Any Class)
Source: National Aeronautic Association

These official Absolute World Records are the supreme achievements of all the hundreds of records open to flying machines. They are the most outstanding of all the major types, and thus warrant the highest respect.

All types of airplanes are eligible for these few very special records. Airplanes may be powered by piston, turboprop, turbojet, rocket engines or a combination. They may be landplanes, seaplanes or amphibians; they may be lightplanes, business planes, military or commercial airplanes.

Over the years, many different categories of aircraft have held these records. In the past, the cost of developing high-performance aircraft has been so great that only airplanes created for military purposes

have held these records. There have been two exceptions to this situation.

Most recently and most dramatically, the Rutan designed "Voyager" shattered the theory that only a complicated military behemoth could hold an Absolute World Record. The Voyager team and its non-stop, non-refueled flight around the world proved that the dreams of dedicated individuals, combined with creative engineering, new technology, and hard work, could conquer the world.

The other exception was the X-15 rocket-powered research airplane. Holder of one record, it was used for both civilian and military research during its highly productive lifetime.

Speed Around the World, Nonstop, Nonrefueled

Speed (mph)	Date	Type Plane	Pilots	Place
115.65	Dec. 14-23, 1986	*Voyager*	Dick Rutan & Jeana Yeager (U.S.)	Edwards AFB, Calif.—Edwards AFB, Calif.

Distance, Great Circle Without Landing, also Distance, Closed Circuit Without Landing

Distance (mi.)	Date	Pilots	Place
24,986.727	Dec. 14-23, 1986	Dick Rutan & Jeana Yeager (U.S.)	Edwards AFB, Calif.—Edwards AFB, Calif.

Speed Over a Straight Course

Speed (mph)	Date	Type Plane	Pilot	Place
2,193.16	July 28, 1976	Lockheed SR-71A	Capt. Eldon W. Joersz (USAF)	Beale AFB, Calif.

Speed Over A Closed Circuit

Speed (mph)	Date	Type Plane	Pilot	Place
2,092.294	July 27, 1976	Lockheed SR-71A	Maj. Adolphus H. Bledsoe, Jr. (USAF)	Beale, AFB, Calif.

Altitude

Height (ft)	Date	Type Plane	Pilot	Place
123,523.58	Aug. 31, 1977	MIG-25, E-266M	Alexander Fedotov (U.S.S.R.)	U.S.S.R.

Altitude in Horizontal Flight

Height (ft)	Date	Pilot	Place
85,068.997	July 28, 1976	Capt. Robert C. Helt (USAF)	Beale AFB, Calif.

Altitude, Aircraft Launched From A Carrier Airplane

Height (ft)	Date	Type Plane	Pilot	Place
314,750.00	July 17, 1962	N. American X-15-1	Maj. Robert White (USAF)	Edwards AFB, Calif.

The Speed of Sound

Source: Air & Space/Smithsonian.

The speed of sound varies with temperature. At sea level Mach 1 is around 742 mph. It decreases with altitude until it reaches about 661 mph at 36,000 feet, then remains at that speed in a band of steady temperature up to 60,000 feet. Because of the variation, it is possible for an airplane flying supersonic at high

altitude to be slower than a subsonic flight at sea level. The transsonic band extends from around Mach .8—when the first supersonic shock waves form on the wing—to Mach 1.2, when the entire wing has gone supersonic.

The National Aviation Hall of Fame

Dedicated to honoring and preserving the history of outstanding air and space pioneers, the Aviation Hall of Fame was established in Dayton, Ohio, on October 5, 1962, with five Daytonians as its founding fathers: James W. Jacobs, Gregory C. Karas, John A. Lombard, Larry E. O'Neil, and Gerald E. Weller. The first annual enshrinement ceremonies were held in December that same year. The United States Congress passed Public Law 88–372 in July 1964 granting the NAHF a national charter.

For additional information, contact the National Aviation Hall of Fame, Dayton Convention Center, Dayton, Ohio 45402, (513) 226-0800.

(With Year of Enshrinement)

Allen, William McPherson (1971)
Andrews, Frank M. (1986)
Armstrong, Neil Alden (1979)
Arnold, Henry Harley (1967)
Atwood, J. Leland (1984)
Balchen, Bernt (1973)
Baldwin, Thomas Scott (1964)
Beachey, Lincoln (1966)
Beech, Olive Ann (1981)
Beech, Walter Herschel (1977)
Bell, Alexander Graham (1965)
Bell, Lawrence Dale (1977)
Bellanca, Giuseppe Mario (1993)
Bendix, Vincent Hugo (1991)
Boeing, William Edward (1966)
Bong, Richard L. (1986)
Borman, Frank (1982)
Boyd, Albert (1984)
Bradley, Mark E. (1992)
Brown, George Scratchley (1985)
Byrd, Richard Evelyn (1968)
Cessna, Clyde Vernon (1978)
Chamberlin, Clarence Duncan (1976)
Chanute, Octave (1963)
Chennault, Claire Lee (1972)
Cochran, Jacqueline (1972)
Collins, Michael (1985)
Combs, Harry B. (1996)
Conrad, Charles, Jr. (1980)
Crawford, Frederick C. (1993)
Crossfield, A. Scott (1983)
Cunningham, Alfred Austell (1965)
Curtiss, Glenn Hammond (1964)
Davis, Jr. Benjamin O. (1994)
deSeversky, Alexander P. (1970)
Doolittle, James Harold (1967)
Douglas, Donald Wills (1969)
Draper, Charles Stark (1981)
Eaker, Ira Clarence (1970)
Eielson, Carl Benjamin (1985)
Ellyson, Theodore Gordon (1964)
Ely, Eugene Burton (1965)
Everest, Frank K. (1989)
Fairchild, Sherman Mills (1979)
Fleet, Rueben Hollis (1975)
Fokker, Anthony Herman Gerard (1980)
Ford, Henry (1984)
Foss, Joseph Jacob (1984)
Foulois, Benjamin Delahauf (1963)
Frye, William John (1992)
Gabreski, Francis Stanley (1978)
Gentile, Dominic S. (1995)
Gilruth, Robert R. (1994)
Glenn, John Herschel, Jr. (1976)
Goddard, George William (1976)

Goddard, Robert Hutchings (1966)
Godfrey, Arthur (1987)
Goldwater, Barry Morris (1982)
Grissom, Virgil I. (1987)
Gross, Robert Ellsworth (1970)
Grumman, Leroy Randle (1972)
Guggenheim, Harry Frank (1971)
Haughton, Daniel J. (1987)
Hegenberger, Albert Francis (1976)
Heinemann, Edward Henry (1981)
Hoover, Robert A. (1988)
Ingalls, David Sinton (1983)
James, Daniel, Jr. (1993)
Jeppesen, Elrey B. (1990)
Johnson, Clarence Leonard (1974)
Johnston, Alvin M. (1993)
Jones, Thomas V. (1992)
Kenney, George Churchill (1971)
Kettering, Charles Franklin (1979)
Kindelberger, James Howard (1972)
Knabenshue, A. Roy (1965)
Knight, William J. (1988)
Lahm, Frank Purdy (1963)
Langley, Samuel Pierpont (1963)
Lear, William Powerll, Sr. (1978)
LeMay, Curtis Emerson (1972)
LeVier, Anthony William (1978)
Lindbergh, Anne Morrow (1979)
Lindbergh, Charles Augustus (1967)
Link, Edwin Albert (1976)
Lockheed, Allan H. (1986)
Loening, Grover (1969)
Luke, Frank, Jr. (1975)
Macready, John Arthur (1968)
Macready, Paul B. (1991)
Martin, Glenn Luther (1966)
McCampbell, David (1996)
McDonnell, James Smith (1977)
Meyer, John C. (1988)
Mitchell, William (1966)
Mitscher, Marc A. (1988)
Montgomery, John Joseph (1964)
Moorer, Thomas H. (1987)
Moss, Sanford Alexander (1976)
Neumann, Gerhard (1986)
Nichols, Ruth Rowland (1992)
Norden, Carl L. (1994)
Northrop, John Knudsen (1974)
Pangborn, Clyde Edward (1995)
Patterson, William Allan (1976)
Piper, William Thomas, Sr.

(1980)
Pitcairn, Harold Frederick (1995)
Post, Wiley Hardeman (1969)
Putnam, Amelia Earhart (1968)
Read, Albert Cushing (1965)
Reeve, Robert Campbell (1965)
Rentschler, Frederick Brant (1982)
Richardson, Holden Chester (1978)
Rickenbacker, Edward Vernon (1965)
Rodgers, Calbraith Perry (1964)
Rogers, Will (1977)
Rushworth, Robert A. (1990)
Rutan, Elbert L. (1995)
Ryan, T. Claude (1974)
Schirra, Walter M., Jr. (1986)
Schriever, Bernard Adolf (1980)
Selfridge, Thomas Etholen (1965)
Shepard, Alan Bartlett, Jr. (1977)
Sikorsky, Igor Ivan (1968)
Six, Robert Forman (1980)
Slayton, Donald K. "Deke" (1996)
Smith, C.R. (1974)
Spaatz, Carl Andrew (1967)
Sperry, Elmer Ambrose, Sr. (1973)
Sperry, Lawrence Burst, Sr. (1981)
Stanley, Robert M. (1990)
Stapp, John Paul (1985)
Stearman, Lloyd C. (1989)
Taylor, Charles Edward (1965)
Thomas, Lowell (1992)
Tibbets, Paul W., Jr. (1996)
Towers, John Henry (1966)
Trippe, Juan Terry (1970)
Turner, Roscoe (1975)
Twining, Nathan Farragut (1976)
Vandenberg, Hoyt S. (1991)
von Braun, Wernher (1982)
von Karman, Theodore (1983)
von Ohain, Hans P. (1990)
Vought, Chance M. (1989)
Wade, Leigh (1974)
Walden, Henry W. (1964)
Wells, Edward Curtis (1991)
Wilson, Thornton Arnold (1983)
Woolman, Collett Everman (1994)
Wright, Orville (1962)
Wright, Wilbur (1962)
Yeager, Charles Elwood (1973)
Young, John W. (1988)

Travel Help from Uncle Sam

Source: U.S. State Depatment, Bureau of Public Affairs.

The U.S. Department of State's Consular Information Program provides Travel Warnings and Consular Information Sheets. Travel Warnings are issued when the Department of State recommends that Americans avoid travel to a certain country. Consular Information Sheets exist for all countries and include information on immigration practices, currency regulations, health conditions, areas of instability, crime and security information, political disturbances, and the address of the U.S. embassies and consulates in the subject country.

They can be obtained by telephone at (202) 647–5225, by fax at (202) 647–3000, or on the Internet at http://travel.state.gov.

Bureau of Consular Affairs' publications on obtaining passports and planning a safe trip abroad are available from the Superintendent of Documents, U.S. Government Printing Office, Washington, D.C. 20402, (202) 783–3238.

Emergency information concerning Americans traveling abroad may be obtained from the Office of Overseas Citizens Services at (202) 647–5225.

While planning a trip, travelers can check on the latest health requirements and conditions with the U.S. Centers for Disease Control and Prevention in Atlanta, Georgia. A hotline at (404) 332–4559 provides telephonic or fax information on the most recent health advisories, immunization recommendations or requirements, and advice on food and drinking water safety for regions and countries.

A booklet entitled *Health Information for International Travel* (HHS publication number CDC–94–8280, price $7.00, subject to change) is available from the Superintendent of Documents, U.S. Government Printing Office, Washington, D.C. 20402, phone (202) 512–1800. The same information is available on the Internet at http://www.cdc.gov.

Information on current travel conditions, visa requirements, currency and customs regulations, legal holidays, and other items of interest to travelers also may be obtained before your departure from a country's embassy and/or consulate in the U.S.

Current Travel Warnings

Source: U.S. Department of State (http://travel.state.gov)

Country	Date Warning Issued	Country	Date Warning Issued
Burundi	8/9/96	Iran	10/4/95
Lebanon	7/15/96	Angola	9/20/95
Afghanistan	7/2/96	Rwanda	9/12/95
Somalia	6/28/96	Nigeria	6/5/95
Bosnia and Herzegovina	6/5/96	Algeria	5/22/95
Colombia	5/23/96	Sierra Leone	2/1/95
Central African Republic	5/21/96	Libya	12/22/94
Liberia	4/16/96	Iraq	9/15/94
Sudan	1/31/96		

Vaccine Recommendations for International Travelers
(Two Years of Age and Older)

Source: Centers for Disease Control, Jan. 19, 1996 (http://www.cdc.gov)

The following vaccines should be reviewed with a physician at least ten weeks before departure to ensure the proper scheduling of the various appropriate vaccines and dosages.

Primary Vaccine Series. For travelers over two years of age the following immunizations normally given during childhood should be up to date:

- Measles, Mumps, and Rubella (MMR) Vaccine
- Diphtheria, Tetanus, and Pertussis (DTP or DTaP) Vaccine until age 7, then Td Vaccine
- Polio (OPV) Vaccine
- Haemophilus Influenza B (HbCV) Vaccine
- Hepatitis B (HBV) Vaccine

Children over two should be "on schedule" with each vaccine's primary-series schedule, while adults should have completed the primary series. If you are unsure about your vaccine history, consult with your physician. In addition, adult travelers may want to consider:

- Influenza (Flu) Vaccine—(Recommended for adults 65 years or older, or other high risk individuals)
- Pneumococcal Vaccine—(Recommended for adults 65 years or older, or other high risk individuals)

- Booster or Additional Doses:
  - Tetanus and diphtheria: A booster dose of adult Tetanus-diphtheria (Td) is recommended every ten years.
  - Polio: An additional single dose of vaccine should be received by adult travelers going to the developing countries of Africa, Asia, Latin America, the Middle East, and the Indian Subcontinent, and the majority of the newly independent states of the former Soviet Union. This additional dose of polio vaccine should be received only once during the adult years. Enhanced Inactivated Polio Vaccine (eIPV) is recommended for this dose.
  - Measles: Persons born in or after 1957 should consider a second dose of measles vaccine before traveling abroad.

Additional Vaccines. Yellow Fever vaccine is recommended if traveling to certain parts of Africa and South America. Hepatitis B vaccine should be considered for those who will live six months or more in areas of developing countries where Hepatitis B is prevalent (Southeast Asia, Africa, the Middle East, the islands of the South and Western Pacific, and the

Amazon region of South America), and who will have frequent close contact with the local population. Hepatitis A Vaccine and/or Immune Globulin (IG) is recommended for travelers to all areas *except* Japan, Australia, New Zealand, Northern and Western Europe and North America (except Mexico). Typhoid vaccine is recommended for travelers spending four weeks or more in areas where food and water precautions are recommended—many parts of the world, especially developing countries. Meningococcal vaccine is recommended for travelers to sub-Saharan Africa, especially if close contact with the locals is anticipated, or if travel occurs during the dry season from December through June. Japanese Encephalitis or Tick-borne Encephalitis vaccines should be considered for long-term travelers to geographic areas of risk. Cholera vaccine is of questionable benefit to travelers of any age.

U.S. Passport and Customs Information

Source: Department of State, Bureau of Consular Affairs and Department of the Treasury, Customs Service.

Passports

With a few exceptions, a passport is required for all U.S. citizens to depart and enter the United States and to enter most foreign countries. A valid U.S. passport is the best documentation of U.S. citizenship available. Persons who travel to a country where a U.S. passport is not required should be in possession of documentary evidence of their U.S. citizenship and identity to facilitate reentry into the United States. Travelers should check passport and visa requirements with consular officials of the countries to be visited well in advance of their departure date.

Application for a passport may be made at a passport agency; to a clerk of any Federal court or State court of record; or a judge or clerk of any probate court accepting applications; or at a post office selected to accept passport applications. Passport agencies are located in Boston, Chicago, Honolulu, Houston, Los Angeles, Miami, New Orleans, New York, Philadelphia, San Francisco, Seattle, Stamford, Conn., and Washington, D.C.

All persons are required to obtain individual passports in their own names. Neither spouses nor children may be included in each others' passports. Applicants age 13 years and older must appear in person before the clerk or agent executing the application. For children under the age of 13, a parent or legal guardian may execute an application for them.

First time passport applicants must apply in person. Applicants must present evidence of citizenship (e.g., a certified copy of birth certificate), personal identification (e.g., a valid driver's license), two identical black and white or color photographs taken within six months (2 × 2 inches, with the image size measured from the bottom of the chin to the top of the head [including hair] not less than 1 inch nor more than 1 3/8 inches on a plain white or off–white background, vending machine photographs not acceptable), plus a completed passport application (DSP–11). If you were born abroad, you may also use as proof of citizenship: a Certificate of Naturalization, a Certificate of Citizenship, a Report of Birth Abroad of a Citizen of the United States of America or a Certification of Birth. A fee of $55 plus a $10 execution fee is charged for adults 18 years and older for a passport valid for ten years from the date of issue. The fee for minor children under 18 years of age is $30 for a five–year passport plus $10 for the execution of the application.

You may apply for a passport by mail if you have been the bearer of a passport issued within 12 years prior to the date of a new application, are able to submit your most recent U.S. passport with your new application, and your previous passport was not issued before your 18th birthday. If you are eligible to apply by mail, include your previous passport, a completed, signed, and dated DSP–82 "Application for Passport by Mail," new photographs, and the passport fee of $55. The $10 execution fee is not required when renewing your passport. Mail the application and attachments in accordance with the instructions on the form.

Passports may be presented for amendment to show a married name or legal change of name or to correct descriptive data. Any alterations to the passport by the bearer other than in the spaces provided for change of address and next of kin data are forbidden.

If you **must** have your passport within 10 days, you will need to pay an additional $30 expedite fee and provide proof of the need for this service.

Loss, theft or destruction of a passport should be reported to Passport Services, 1111 19th Street, N.W., Washington, D.C. 20522-1705 immediately, or to the nearest passport agency. If you are overseas, report loss to the nearest U.S. Embassy or consulate and to local police authorities. Your passport is a valuable citizenship and identity document. It should be carefully safeguarded. Its loss could cause you unnecessary travel complications as well as significant expense. It is advisable to photocopy the data page of your passport and keep it in a place separate from your passport to facilitate the issuance of a replacement passport should one be necessary.

Portsmouth National Passport Center

The Department of State has the largest passport processing center in the United States at Portsmouth, New Hampshire. Known as the National Passport Center, the facility is capable of issuing 6,000 passports per day but can be expanded to issue 9,000 passports per day.

The Center is processing passport mail renewal applications from around the United States. Passport fees are deposited in Pittsburgh, with the applications subsequently express mailed to Portsmouth for processing. The other passport agencies will process first-time applications and any other requests for passport services presented in person.

To renew a passport by mail, applicants must:

1. Obtain an "Application for Passport by Mail" (Form DSP-82) from a passport acceptance facility (post office, court house or passport agency);

2. Complete and sign the application and attach the most recent passport issued not more than 12 years ago but after the applicant's 18th birthday, two identical 2″ × 2″ passport photographs, and a check or money order for $55 payable to Passport Services.

3. Mail the above items to the National Passport Center, Post Office Box 371971, Pittsburgh, Pennsylvania 15250-7971.

Customs

United States residents must declare all articles acquired abroad and in their possession at the time of their return. In addition, articles acquired in the U.S. Virgin Islands, American Samoa, or Guam and not accompanying you must be declared at the time of your return. The wearing or use of an article acquired abroad does *not* exempt it from duty. Customs declaration forms are distributed on vessels and planes, and should be prepared in advance of arrival for presentation to the customs inspectors.

If you have not exceeded the duty–free exemption allowed, you may make an oral declaration to the customs inspector. However, the inspector can request a written declaration and may do so. A written declaration is necessary when (1) the total fair retail value of articles exceeds the personal exemption of $400; (2) over 1 liter of liquor, 200 cigarettes, or 100 cigars are included; (3) items are not intended for your personal or household use, or articles brought home for another person; (4) when a customs duty or internal revenue tax is collectible on any article in your possession; and (5) if your personal exemption was used in the last 30 days.

An exception to the above are regulations applicable to articles purchased in the U.S. Virgin Islands, American Samoa, or Guam where you may receive a customs exemption of $1,200. Not more than $400 of this exemption may be applied to merchandise obtained elsewhere than in these islands or $600 if acquired in a Caribbean Basin beneficiary country. Five liters of alcoholic beverages and 1000 cigarettes may be included provided not more than one liter and 200 cigarettes were acquired elsewhere than in these islands. Articles acquired in and sent from these islands to the United States may be claimed under your duty–free personal exemption if properly declared at the time of your return. For information on rules applying to beneficiary countries and a list of them check with your local Customs office or write for the pamphlet "GSP and the Traveler" from the U.S. Customs Services, P.O. Box 7407, Washington, D.C. 20044. Since rules change it is always wise to check with customs before leaving, to get information pertinent to the areas you will be visiting.

Articles accompanying you, in excess of your personal exemption, up to $1000 will be assessed at a flat rate of duty of 10% based on fair retail value in country of acquisition. (If articles were acquired in the insular possessions, the flat rate of duty is 5% and these goods may accompany you or be shipped home.) These articles must be for your personal use or for use as gifts and not for sale. This provision may be used every 30 days, excluding the day of your last arrival. Any items which have a "free" duty rate will be excluded before duty is calculated.

You may mail articles bought for your personal use back to the U.S. at a duty free rate of $200 per day (excluding restricted items such as liquor).

Other exemptions include in part: automobiles, boats, planes, or other vehicles taken abroad for non-commercial use. Foreign–made personal articles (e.g., watches, cameras, etc.) taken abroad should be registered with Customs before departure. Customs will register anything with a serial number or identifying marks. Sales receipt or insurance document are sufficient Customs identification. Registration of articles for which you have documented proof of purchase is redundant and is not necessary. Gifts of not more than $100 can be shipped back to the United States tax and duty free ($200 if mailed from the Virgin Islands, American Samoa, or Guam). Household effects and tools of trade which you take out of the United States are duty free at time of return.

Prohibited and restricted articles include in part: absinthe, narcotics and dangerous drugs, obscene articles and publications, seditious and treasonable materials, hazardous articles (e.g., fireworks, dangerous toys, toxic and poisonous substances, and switchblade knives), biological materials of public health or veterinary importance, fruit, vegetables and plants, meats, poultry and products thereof, birds, monkeys, and turtles. You can get additional information on this subject from the publication *Pets, Wildlife, U.S. Customs*. For a free copy write to the U.S. Customs Service, P.O. Box 7407, Washington, D.C. 20044.

If you understate the value of an article you declare, or if you otherwise misrepresent an article in your declaration, you may have to pay a penalty in addition to payment of duty. Under certain circumstances, the article could be seized and forfeited if the penalty is not paid.

If you fail to declare an article acquired abroad, not only is the article subject to seizure and forfeiture, but you will be liable for a personal penalty in an amount equal to the value of the article in the United States. In addition, you may also be liable to criminal prosecution.

If you carry more than $10,000 into or out of the United States in currency (either United States or foreign money), negotiable instruments in bearer form, or travelers checks, a report must be filed with United States Customs at the time you arrive or depart with such amounts.

For more information about Customs regulations for travelers, write the above address for a copy of "Know Before You Go."

Foreign Embassies in the United States

Source: U.S. Department of State.

Embassy of the Republic of Afghanistan, 2341 Wyoming Ave., N.W., Washington, D.C. 20008. Phone: (202) 234–3770, 3771.

Embassy of the Republic of Albania, 1511 K St., N.W., Suite 1010, Washington, D.C. 20005. Phone: (202) 223-4942, 8187.

Embassy of the Democratic & Popular Republic of Algeria, 2118 Kalorama Rd., N.W., Washington, D.C. 20008. Phone: (202) 265–2800.

Embassy of the Republic of Angola, 1819 L St., N.W., Suite 400, Washington, D.C. 20036. Phone: (202) 785-1156.

Embassy of Antigua & Barbuda, 3216 New Mexico Ave., N.W., Washington, D.C. 20016. Phone: (202) 362–5211, 5166, 5122.

Embassy of the Argentine Republic, 1600 New Hampshire Ave., N.W., Washington, D.C. 20009. Phone: (202) 939–6400 to 6403, inclusive.

Embassy of the Republic of Armenia, 1660 L St., N.W., 11th Fl., Washington, D.C. 20036. Phone: (202) 628-5766.

Embassy of Australia, 1601 Massachusetts Ave., N.W., Washington, D.C. 20036. Phone: (202) 797–3000.

Embassy of Austria, 3524 International Court, N.W., Washington, D.C. 20008. Phone: (202) 895-6700.

Embassy of the Republic of Azerbaijan, 927 15th St., N.W., Suite 700, Washington, D.C. 20005. Phone: (202) 842-0001.

Embassy of The Commonwealth of The Bahamas, 2220 Massachusetts Ave., N.W., Washington, D.C. 20008. Phone: (202) 319-2660.

Embassy of the State of Bahrain, 3502 International Dr., N.W., Washington, D.C. 20008. Phone: (202) 342-0741, 0742.

Embassy of the People's Republic of Bangladesh, 2201 Wisconsin Ave., N.W., Washington, D.C. 20007. Phone: (202) 342–8372 to 8376.

Embassy of Barbados, 2144 Wyoming Ave., N.W., Washington, D.C. 20008. Phone: (202) 939–9200 to 9202.

Embassy of the Republic of Belarus, 1619 New Hampshire Ave., N.W., Washington, D.C. 20009. Phone: (202) 986-1640.

Embassy of Belgium, 3330 Garfield St., N.W., Washington, D.C. 20008. Phone: (202) 333–6900.

Embassy of Belize, 2535 Massachusetts Ave., N.W., Washington, D.C. 20008. Phone: (202) 332-9636.

Embassy of the Republic of Benin, 2737 Cathedral Ave., N.W., Washington, D.C. 20008. Phone: (202) 232–6656 to 6658.

Embassy of Bolivia, 3014 Massachusetts Ave., N.W., Washington, D.C. 20008. Phone: (202) 483–4410 to 4412.

Embassy of the Republic of Bosnia and Herzegovina, 1707 L St., N.W., Suite 760, Wshington, D.C. 20036. Phone: (202) 833-3612, 3613, and 3615.

Embassy of the Republic of Botswana, 3400 International Dr., N.W., Suite 7M, Washington, D.C. 20008. Phone: (202) 244–4990, 4991.

Brazilian Embassy, 3006 Massachusetts Ave., N.W., Washington, D.C. 20008. Phone: (202) 745–2700.

Embassy of the State of Brunei Darussalam, Watergate, 2600 Virginia Ave., N.W., Suite 300, Washington, D.C. 20037. Phone: (202) 342–0159.

Embassy of the Republic of Bulgaria, 1621 22nd St., N.W., Washington, D.C. 20008. Phone: (202) 387–7969.

Embassy of Burkina Faso, 2340 Massachusetts Ave., N.W., Washington, D.C. 20008. Phone: (202) 332–5577, 6895.

Embassy of the Republic of Burundi, 2233 Wisconsin Ave., N.W., Suite 212, Washington, D.C. 20007. Phone: (202) 342–2574.

Royal Embassy of Cambodia, 4500 16th St., N.W., Washington, D.C. 20011. Phone: (202) 726–7742.

Embassy of the Republic of Cameroon, 2349 Massachusetts Ave., N.W., Washington, D.C. 20008. Phone: (202) 265–8790 to 8794.

Embassy of Canada, 501 Pennsylvania Ave., N.W., Washington, D.C. 20001. Phone: (202) 682–1740.

Embassy of the Republic of Cape Verde, 3415 Massachusetts Ave., N.W., Washington, D.C. 20007. Phone: (202) 965–6820.

Embassy of Central African Republic, 1618 22nd St. N.W., Washington, D.C. 20008. Phone: (202) 483–7800, 7801.

Embassy of the Republic of Chad, 2002 R St., N.W., Washington, D.C. 20009. Phone: (202) 462–4009.

Embassy of Chile, 1732 Massachusetts Ave., N.W., Washington, D.C. 20036. Phone: (202) 785–1746.

Embassy of the People's Republic of China, 2300 Connecticut Ave., N.W., Washington, D.C. 20008. Phone: (202) 328–2500 to 2502.

Embassy of Colombia, 2118 Leroy Pl., N.W., Washington, D.C. 20008. Phone: (202) 387–8338.

Embassy of the Federal and Islamic Republic of Comoros, c/o Permanent Mission of the Federal and Islamic Republic of Comoros to the United Nations, 336 E. 45th St., 2nd floor, New York, N.Y. 10017. Phone: (212) 972–8010.

Embassy of the Republic of Congo, 4891 Colorado Ave., N.W., Washington, D.C. 20011. Phone: (202) 726–0825.

Embassy of Costa Rica, 2114 S St., N.W., Washington, D.C. 20008. Phone: (202) 234–2945.

Embassy of the Republic of Cote d'Ivoire, 2424 Massachusetts Ave., N.W., Washington, D.C. 20008. Phone: (202) 797–0300.

Embassy of the Republic of Croatia, 2343 Massachusetts Ave., N.W., Washington, D.C. 20008. Phone: (202) 588-5899.

Cuban Interests Section, 2630 16th St., N.W., Washington, D.C. 20009. Phone: (202) 797–8518 to 8520.

Embassy of the Republic of Cyprus, 2211 R St. N.W., Washington, D.C. 20008. Phone: (202) 462–5772.

Embassy of the Czech Republic, 3900 Spring of Freedom St., N.W., Washington, D.C. 20008. Phone: (202) 363–6315, 6316.

Royal Danish Embassy, 3200 Whitehaven St., N.W., Washington, D.C. 20008. Phone: (202) 234–4300.

Embassy of the Republic of Djibouti, 1156 15th St., N.W., Suite 515, Washington, D.C. 20005. Phone: (202) 331-0270.

Embassy of the Commonwealth of Dominica, 3216 New Mexico Ave., N.W., Washington, D.C. 20016. Phone: (202) 364-6781.

Embassy of the Dominican Republic, 1715 22nd St., N.W., Washington, D.C. 20008. Phone: (202) 332–6280.

Embassy of Ecuador, 2535 15th St., N.W., Washington, D.C. 20009. Phone: (202) 234–7200.

Embassy of the Arab Republic of Egypt, 3521 International Court, N.W., Washington, D.C. 20008. Phone: (202) 895-5400.

Embassy of El Salvador, 2308 California St., N.W., Washington, D.C. 20008. Phone: (202) 265–9671, 9672.

Embassy of Equatorial Guinea, 57 Magnolia Ave., Mount Vernon, N.Y. 10553. Phone: (914) 738-9584 and 667-6913.

Embassy of the State of Eritrea, 910 17th St., N.W., Suite 400, Washington, D.C. 20006. Phone: (202) 429-1991.

Embassy of Estonia, 1030 15th St., N.W., Suite 1000, Washington, D.C. 20005. Phone: (202) 789-0320.

Embassy of Ethiopia, 2134 Kalorama Rd., N.W., Washington, D.C. 20008. Phone: (202) 234–2281, 2282.

Embassy of The Republic of Fiji, 2233 Wisconsin Ave., N.W., Suite 240, Washington, D.C. 20007. Phone: (202) 337–8320.

Embassy of Finland, 3301 Massachusetts Ave., N.W., Washington, D.C. 20008. Phone: (202) 298-5800.

Embassy of France, 4101 Reservoir Rd., N.W., Washington, D.C. 20007. Phone: (202) 944–6000.

Embassy of the Gabonese Republic, 2034 20th St., N.W., Suite 200, Washington, D.C. 20009. Phone: (202) 797–1000.

Embassy of The Gambia, 1155 15th St., N.W., Suite 1000, Washington, D.C. 20005. Phone: (202) 785-1399, 1379, 1425.

Embassy of the Republic of Georgia, 1511 K St., N.W., Suite 424, Washington, D.C. 20005. Phone: (202) 393-6060, 393-5959.

Embassy of the Federal Republic of Germany, 4645 Reservoir Rd., N.W., Washington, D.C. 20007. Phone: (202) 298–4000.

Embassy of Ghana, 3512 International Dr., N.W., Washington, D.C. 20008 (202) 686–4520.

Embassy of Greece, 2221 Massachusetts Ave., N.W., Washington, D.C. 20008. Phone (202) 939–5800.

Embassy of Grenada, 1701 New Hampshire Ave., N.W., Washington, D.C. 20009. Phone: (202) 265–2561.

Embassy of Guatemala, 2220 R St., N.W., Washington, D.C. 20008. Phone: (202) 745–4952 to 4954.

Embassy of the Republic of Guinea, 2112 Leroy Pl., N.W., Washington, D.C. 20008. Phone: (202) 483–9420.

Embassy of the Republic of Guinea–Bissau, 918 16th St., N.W., Mezzanine Suite, Washington, D.C. 20006. Phone: (202) 872-4222.

Embassy of Guyana, 2490 Tracy Pl., N.W. Washington, D.C. 20008. Phone: (202) 265–6900 to 6901.

Embassy of the Republic of Haiti, 2311 Massachusetts Ave., N.W., Washington, D.C. 20008. Phone: (202) 332–4090 to 4092.

Apostolic Nunciature of the Holy See, 3339 Massachusetts Ave., N.W., Washington, D.C. 20008. Phone: (202) 333–7121.

Embassy of Honduras, 3007 Tilden St., N.W., P004-M, Washington, D .C. 20008. Phone: (202) 966–7702, 2604, 5008, 4596.

Embassy of the Republic of Hungary, 3910 Shoemaker St., N.W., Washington, D.C. 20008. Phone: (202) 362–6730.

Embassy of Iceland,1156 15th St., N.W., Suite 1200, Washington, D.C. 20005. Phone: (202) 265–6653 to 6655.

Embassy of India, 2107 Massachusetts Ave., N.W., Washington, D.C. 20008. Phone: (202) 939–7000.

Embassy of the Republic of Indonesia, 2020 Massachusetts Ave., N.W., Washington, D.C. 20036. Phone: (202) 775–5200.

Iranian Interests Section, 2209 Wisconsin Ave., N.W., Washington, D.C. 20007. Phone: (202) 965-4990.

Iraqi Interests Section, 1801 P St., N.W., Washington, D.C. 20036. Phone: (202) 483–7500.

Embassy of Ireland, 2234 Massachusetts Ave., N.W., Washington, D.C. 20008. Phone: (202) 462–3939.

Embassy of Israel, 3514 International Dr., N.W., Washington, D.C. 20008. Phone: (202) 364–5500.

Embassy of Italy, 1601 Fuller St., N.W., Washington, D.C. 20009. Phone: (202) 328–5500.

Embassy of Jamaica, 1520 New Hampshire Ave., N.W., Washington, D.C. 20036. Phone: (202) 452–0660.

Embassy of Japan, 2520 Massachusetts Ave., N.W., Washington, D.C. 20008. Phone: (202) 939–6700.

Embassy of the Hashemite Kingdom of Jordan, 3504 International Dr., N.W., Washington, D.C. 20008. Phone: (202) 966–2664.

Embassy of the Republic of Kazakhstan, 3421 Massachusetts Ave., N.W., Wshington, D.C. 20008. Phone: (202) 333-4504–7.

Embassy of the Republic of Kenya, 2249 R St., N.W., Washington, D.C. 20008. Phone: (202) 387–6101.

Embassy of Korea, 2450 Massachusetts Ave., N.W., Washington, D.C. 20008. Phone: (202) 939–5600.

Embassy of the State of Kuwait, 2940 Tilden St., N.W., Washington, D.C. 20008. Phone: (202) 966–0702.

Embassy of the Republic of Kyrgystan, 1511 K St., N.W., Suite 705, Washington, D.C. 20005. Phone: (202) 347-3732, 3733, and 3718.

Embassy of the Lao People's Democratic Republic, 2222 S St., N.W., Washington, D.C. 20008. Phone: (202) 332–6416, 6417.

Embassy of Latvia, 4325 17th St., N.W., Washington, D.C. 20011. Phone: (202) 726–8213, 8214.

Embassy of Lebanon, 2560 28th St., N.W., Washington, D.C. 20008. Phone: (202) 939–6300.

Embassy of the Kingdom of Lesotho, 2511 Massachusetts Ave., N.W., Washington, D.C. 20008. Phone: (202) 797–5533 to 5536.

Embassy of the Republic of Liberia, 5201 16th St., N.W., Washington, D.C. 20011.

Embassy of the Republic of Lithuania, 2622 16th St., N.W., Washington, D.C. 20009. Phone: (202) 234–5860, 2639.

Embassy of Luxembourg, 2200 Massachusetts Ave., N.W., Washington, D.C. 20008. Phone: (202) 265–4171.

Embassy of the Democratic Republic of Madagascar, 2374 Massachusetts Ave., N. W., Washington, D.C. 20008. Phone: (202) 265–5525, 5526.

Malawi Embassy, 2408 Massachusetts Ave., N.W., Washington, D.C. 20008. Phone: (202) 797–1007.

Embassy of Malaysia, 2401 Massachusetts Ave., N.W., Washington, D.C. 20008. Phone: (202) 328–2700.

Embassy of the Republic of Mali, 2130 R St., N.W., Washington, D.C. 20008. Phone: (202) 332–2249; (202) 939–8950.

Embassy of Malta, 2017 Connecticut Ave., N.W., Washington, D.C. 20008. Phone: (202) 462–3611, 3612.

Embassy of the Republic of the Marshall Islands, 2433 Massachusetts Ave., N.W., Washington, D.C. 20008. Phone: (202) 234-5414.

Embassy of the Islamic Republic of Mauritania, 2129 Leroy Pl., N.W., Washington, D.C. 20008. Phone: (202) 232–5700.

Embassy of Mauritius, 4301 Connecticut Ave., N.W., Suite 441, Washington, D.C. 20008. Phone: (202) 244–1491, 1492.

Embassy of Mexico, 1911 Pennsylvania Ave., N.W., 20006, Washington, D.C. Phone: (202) 728–1600.

Embassy of the Federated States of Micronesia, 1725 N St., N.W., Washington, D.C. 20036. Phone: (202) 223-4383.

Embassy of the Republic of Moldova, 1511 K St., N.W., Suites 329, 333, Washington, D.C. 20005. Phone: (202) 783-3012.

Embassy of Mongolia, 2833 M St., N.W., Washington, D.C. 20007. Phone: (202) 333-7117.

Embassy of the Kingdom of Morocco, 1601 21st St., N.W., Washington, D.C. 20008. Phone: (202) 462–7979 to 7982, inclusive.

Embassy of the Republic of Mozambique, 1990 M St., N.W., Suite 570, Washington, D.C. 20036. Phone: (202) 293–7146.

Embassy of the Union of Myanmar, 2300 S St., N.W., Washington, D.C. 20008. Phone: (202) 332–9044, 9045.

Embassy of the Republic of Namibia, 1605 New Hampshire Ave., N.W., Washington, D.C. 20009. Phone: (202) 986-0540.

Royal Nepalese Embassy, 2131 Leroy Pl., N.W., Washington, D.C. 20008. Phone: (202) 667–4550.

Embassy of the Netherlands, 4200 Wisconsin Ave., N.W., Washington, D.C. 20016. Phone: (202) 244–5300; after 6 p.m. (202) 494-8594..

Embassy of New Zealand, 37 Observatory Circle, N.W., Washington, D.C. 20008. Phone: (202) 328–4800.

Embassy of Nicaragua, 1627 New Hampshire Ave., N.W., Washington, D.C. 20009. Phone: (202) 939–6570.

Embassy of the Republic of Niger, 2204 R St., N.W., Washington, D.C. 20008. Phone: (202) 483–4224 to 4227, inclusive.

Embassy of the Federal Republic of Nigeria, 1333 16th St., N.W., Washington, D.C. 20036. Phone: (202) 986-8400.

Royal Norwegian Embassy, 2720 34th St., N.W., Washington, D.C. 20008. Phone: (202) 333–6000.

Embassy of the Sultanate of Oman, 2535 Belmont Rd., N.W., Washington, D.C. 20008. Phone: (202) 387–1980 to 1982.

Embassy of Pakistan, 2315 Massachusetts Ave., N.W., Washington, D.C. 20008. Phone: (202) 939–6200.

Embassy of the Republic of Palau, 2000 L. St., N.W., Suite 407, Washington, D.C. 20036. Phone: (202) 452-6814.

Embassy of the Republic of Panama, 2862 McGill Terrace, N.W., Washington, D.C. 20008. Phone: (202) 483–1407.

Embassy of Papua New Guinea, 1615 New Hampshire Ave., N.W., 3rd floor, Washington, D.C. 20009. Phone: (202) 745-3680.

Embassy of Paraguay, 2400 Massachusetts Ave., N.W., Washington, D.C. 20008. Phone: (202) 483–6960 to 6962.

Embassy of Peru, 1700 Massachusetts Ave., N.W., Washington, D.C. 20036. Phone: (202) 833–9860 to 9869.

Embassy of the Philippines, 1600 Massachusetts Ave., N.W., Washington, D.C. 20036. Phone: (202) 467–9300..

Embassy of the Republic of Poland, 2640 16th St., N.W., Washington, D.C. 20009. Phone: (202) 234–3800 to 3802.

Embassy of Portugal, 2125 Kalorama Rd., N.W., Washington, D.C. 20008. Phone: (202) 328–8610.

Embassy of the State of Qatar, 4200 Wisconsin Ave., N.W., Washington, D.C. 20016. Phone: (202) 274-1600.

Embassy of Romania, 1607 23rd St., N.W., Washington, D.C. 20008. Phone: (202) 332-4846, 4848, 4851; after hours 332-4846.

Embassy of the Russian Federation, 2650 Wisconsin Ave., N.W. Washington, D.C. 20007. Phone: (202) 298-5700 to 5704 inclusive.

Embassy of the Republic of Rwanda, 1714 New Hampshire Ave., N.W., Washington, D.C. 20009. Phone: (202) 232–2882.

Embassy of Saint Kitts and Nevis, 3216 New Mexico Ave., N.W. Washington, D.C. 20016. Phone: (202) 686-2636..

Embassy of Saint Lucia, 3216 New Mexico Ave., N.W., Washington, D.C. 20016. Phone: (202) 364-6792 to 6795.

Embassy of Saint Vincent and the Grenadines, 1717 Massachusetts Ave., N.W., Suite 102, Washington, D.C. 20036. Phone: (202) 462-7806, 7846.

Embassy of Saudi Arabia, 601 New Hampshire Ave., N.W., Washington, D.C. 20037. Phone: (202) 342–3800.

Embassy of the Republic of Senegal, 2112 Wyoming Ave., N.W., Washington, D.C. 20008. Phone: (202) 234–0540, 0541.

Embassy of the Republic of Seychelles, c/o Permanent Mission of Seychelles to the United Nations, 820 Second Ave., Suite 900F, New York, N.Y. 10017. Phone: (212) 687–9766/9767.

Embassy of Sierra Leone, 1701 19th St., N.W., Washington, D.C. 20009. Phone: (202) 939–9261.

Embassy of the Republic of Singapore, 1824-25 R St., N.W., Washington, D.C. 20009. Phone: (202) 537-3100.

Embassy of the Slovak Republic, 2201 Wisconsin Ave., N.W., Suite 380, Washington, D.C. 20007. Phone: (202) 965-5166.

Embassy of the Republic of Slovenia, 1525 New Hampshire Ave., N.W., Washington, D.C. 20036. Phone: (202) 667–5363.

Embassy of South Africa, 3051 Massachusetts Ave., N.W., Washington, D.C. 20008. Phone: (202) 232–4400.

Embassy of Spain, 2375 Pennsylvania Ave. N.W., Washington, D.C. 20037. Phone: (202) 452–0100 and 728–2340.

Embassy of the Democratic Socialist Republic of Sri Lanka, 2148 Wyoming Ave., N.W., Washington, D.C. 20008. Phone: (202) 483–4025 to 4028.

Embassy of the Republic of the Sudan, 2210 Massachusetts Ave., N.W., Washington, D.C. 20008. Phone: (202) 338–8565 to 8570.

Embassy of the Republic of Suriname, 4301 Connecticut Ave., N.W., Suite 108, Washington, D.C. 20008. Phone: (202) 244–7488, 7490 to 7492.

Embassy of the Kingdom of Swaziland, 3400 International Drive, N.W., Washington, D.C. 20008. Phone: (202) 362–6683, 6685.

Embassy of Sweden, 1501 M St., N.W., Washington, D.C. 20005. Phone: (202) 467-2600.

Embassy of Switzerland, 2900 Cathedral Ave. N.W., Washington, D.C. 20008. Phone: (202) 745–7900.

Embassy of the Syrian Arab Republic, 2215 Wyoming Ave., N.W., Washington, D.C. 20008. Phone: (202) 232–6313.

Embassy of the United Republic of Tanzania, 2139 R St., N.W., Washington, D.C. 20008. Phone: (202) 939–6125.

Embassy of Thailand, 1024 Wisconsin Ave., N.W., Washington, D.C. 20007. Phone: (202) 944-3600.

Embassy of the Republic of Togo, 2208 Massachusetts Ave., N.W., Washington, D.C. 20008. Phone: (202) 234–4212.

Embassy of Trinidad and Tobago, 1708 Massachusetts Ave., N.W., Washington, D.C. 20036. Phone: (202) 467–6490.

Embassy of Tunisia, 1515 Massachusetts Ave., N.W., Washington, D.C. 20005. Phone: (202) 862-1850.

Embassy of the Republic of Turkey, 1714 Massachusetts Ave., N.W., Washington, D.C. 20036. Phone: (202) 659–8200.

Embassy of the Republic of Turkmenistan, 1511 K St., N.W., Suite 412, Washington, D.C. 20005. Phone: (202) 737-4800.

Embassy of the Republic of Uganda, 5911 16th St., N.W., Washington, D.C. 20011. Phone: (202) 726–7100 to 7102, 0416.

Embassy of Ukraine, 3350 M St., N.W., Washington, D.C. 20007. Phone: (202) 333-0606.

Embassy of the United Arab Emirates, 3000 K St., N.W., Suite 600, Washington, D.C. 20007. Phone: (202) 338–6500.

United Kingdom of Great Britain & Northern Ireland—British Embassy, 3100 Massachusetts Ave., N.W., Washington, D.C. 20008. Phone: (202) 462–1340.

Embassy of Uruguay, 1918 F St., N.W., Washington D.C. 20006. Phone: (202) 331–1313 to 1316, inclusive.

Embassy of the Republic of Uzbekistan, 1511 K St., N.W., Suites 619 and 623, Washington, D.C. 20005. Phone: (202) 638–4266, 4267.

Embassy of the Republic of Venezuela, 1099 30th St., N.W., Washington D.C. 20007. Phone: (202) 342-2214.

Embassy of Vietnam, 1233 20th St., N.W., Suite 501, Washington, D.C. 20036. Phone: (202) 861-0737.

Embassy of Western Samoa, 820 Second Ave., Suite 800D, New York, N.Y. 10017. Phone: (212) 599-6196, 6197.

Embassy of the Republic of Yemen, 2600 Virginia Ave., N.W. Suite 705, Washington, D.C. 20037. Phone: (202) 965–4760, 4761.

Embassy of the former Socialist Federal Republic of Yugoslavia, 2410 California St., N.W., Washington, D.C. 20008. Phone: (202) 462–6566.

Embassy of the Republic of Zaire, 1800 New Hampshire Ave., N.W., Washington, D.C. 20009. Phone: (202) 234–7690, 7691.

Embassy of the Republic of Zambia, 2419 Massachusetts Ave., N.W., Washington, D.C. 20008. Phone: (202) 265–9717 to 9719.

Embassy of the Republic of Zimbabwe, 1608 New Hampshire Ave., N.W., Washington, D.C. 20009. Phone: (202) 332–7100.

Diplomatic Personnel To and From the U.S.

Country	U.S. Representative to[1]	Rank	Representative from[2]	Rank
Afghanistan	—	—	Yar Mohammad Mohabbat	Cd'A.
Albania	Joseph E. Lake	Amb.	Lublin Dilja	Amb.
Algeria	Ronald E. Neumann	Amb.	Hadj Osmane Bencherif	Amb.
Angola	Edmund T. DeJarnette	Dir.	Jose Goncalves Martins Patricio	Amb.
Antigua and Barbuda	(Post closed)		Dr. Patrick Albert Lewis	Amb.
Argentina	James R. Cheek	Amb.	Raul Enrique Granillo Ocampo	Amb.

Country	U.S. Representative to[1]	Rank	Representative from[2]	Rank
Armenia	Harry J. Gilmore	Amb.	Rouben Robert Shugarian	Amb.
Australia	Edward Perkins	Amb.	Dr. Donald Eric Russell	Amb.
Austria	Swanee G. Hunt	Amb.	Helmut Tuerk	Amb.
Azerbaijan	Richard D. Kauzlarich	Cd'A.	Hafiz Mir Jalal Pashayev	Amb.
Bahamas	Sidney Williams	Amb.	Timothy Baswell Donaldson	Amb.
Bahrain	David M. Ransom	Amb.	Muhammad Abdul Ghaffar Abdulla	Amb.
Bangladesh	David N. Merrill	Amb.	Humayun Kabir	Amb.
Barbados	Jeanette W. Hyde	Amb.	Courtney N. Blackman	Amb.
Belarus	Kenneth Spenser Yalowitz	Amb.	Serguei Nikolaevich Martynov	Amb.
Belgium	Alan J. Blinken	Amb.	Andre Adam	Amb.
Belize	George Charles Bruno	Amb.	Dean R. Lindo	Amb.
Benin	Ruth A. Davis	Amb.	Lucien Edgar Tonoukouin	Amb.
Bermuda	Robert A. Farmer	Cons. Gen.	—	
Bolivia	Curt Warren Kamman	Amb.	Andres Petricevic R	Amb.
Bosnia-Herzegovina	Victor Jackovich	Amb.	Sven Alkalaj	Amb.
Botswana	Howard F. Jeter	Amb.	Mustaq Ahmed Moorqd	Cd'A
Brazil	Melvyn Levitsky	Amb.	Paulo-Tarso Flecha de Lima	Amb.
Brunei	Theresa A. Tull	Amb.	Haji Jaya bin Abdul Latif	Amb.
Bulgaria	William D. Montgomery	Amb.	Snejana Damianova Botoucharova	Amb.
Burkina Faso	Donald J. McConnell	Amb.	Gaetan R. Ouedraogo	Amb.
Burundi	Robert C. Krueger	Amb.	Severin Ntahomvukiye	Amb.
Cambodia	Charles H. Twining	Dir.	Var Huoth	Amb.
Cameroon	Harriet W. Isom	Amb.	Jerome Mendouga	Amb.
Canada	James Johnston Blanchard	Amb.	Raymond A.J. Chretien	Amb.
Cape Verde	Joseph M. Segars	Amb.	Corentino Virgilio Santos	Amb.
Central African Republic	Robert E. Gribbin III	Amb.	Henry Koba	Amb.
Chad	Laurence E. Pope II	Amb.	Ahmat Mahamat-Saleh	Amb.
Chile	Curtis W. Kamman	Amb.	John Biehl	Amb.
China	J. Stapleton Roy	Amb.	Li Daoyu	Amb.
Colombia	Myles R.R. Frechette	Amb.	Carlos Lleras	Amb.
Comoros	(Post closed)			
Congo, Republic of	William C. Ramsay	Amb.	Pierre Damien Boussouko-Boumba	Amb.
Costa Rica	(Vacancy)		Sonia Picado	Min.
Côte d'Ivoire	Hume A. Horan	Amb.	Koffi Moise Koumoue	Amb.
Croatia	Peter W. Galbraith	Amb.	Peter A. Sarcevic	Amb.
Cyprus	Richard A. Boucher	Amb.	Andrew J. Jacovides	Amb.
Czech Republic	Adrian A. Basora	Amb.	Michael Zantovsky	Amb.
Denmark	Edward E. Elson	Amb.	K. Erik Tygesen	Amb.
Djibouti	Martin L. Cheshes	Amb.	Roble Olhaye	Amb.
Dominica	—		Edward I. Watty	Amb.
Dominican Republic	Donna Jean Hrinak	Amb.	Jose del Carmen Ariza	Amb.
Ecuador	Peter F. Romero	Amb.	Edgar Teran-Teran	Amb.
Egypt	Edward S. Walker, Jr.	Amb.	Ahmed Maher El Sayed	Amb.
El Salvador	Alan H. Flanigan	Amb.	Ana Cristina Sol	Amb.
Equatorial Guinea	John E. Bennett	Amb.	Pastor Micha Ondo Bile	Amb.
Eritrea	Robert G. Houdek	Amb.	Amdemicael Kahsai	Amb.
Estonia	(Vacancy)	Amb.	Toomas Hendrik Ilves	Amb.
Ethiopia	Irvin Hicks	Cd'A.	Berhane Gebre-Christos	Amb.
Fiji	(Vacancy)	Amb.	Pita Kewa Nacuva	Amb.
Finland	Derek N. Shearer	Amb.	Jukka Valtasaari	Amb.
France	Pamela C. Harriman	Amb.	Jacques Andreani	Amb.
Gabon	Joseph C. Wilson IV	Amb.	Paul Boundoukou-Latha	Amb.
Gambia	Andrew J. Winter	Amb.	Tombong Saidy	Cd'A.
Georgia	Kent N. Brown	Cd'A.	Tedo Djaparidze	Amb.
Germany	Charles E. Redman	Amb.	Juergen Chrobog	Amb.
Ghana	Kenneth L. Brown	Amb.	Ekwow Spio-Garbrah	Amb.
Greece	Thomas M.T. Niles	Amb.	Loucas Tsilas	Amb.
Grenada	(Vacancy)	Amb.	Denneth Modeste	Amb.
Guatemala	Marilyn McAfee	Amb.	Edmond Mulet	Amb.
Guinea	Joseph A. Saloom III	Amb.	Elhadj Boubacar Barry	Amb.
Guinea–Bissau	Roger A. McGuire	Amb.	Alfredo Lopes Cabral	Amb.
Guyana	George F. Jones	Amb.	Mohammed Ali Odeen Ishmael	Amb.
Haiti	William Lacy Swing	Amb.	Jean Casimir	Amb.
Holy See	Raymond L. Flynn	Amb.	Most Rev. Agostino Cacciavillan	Pro–Nuncio
Honduras	William T. Pryce	Amb.	Roberto Flores Bermudez	Amb.
Hong Kong	Richard W. Mueller	Cons. Gen.	—	
Hungary	Donald M. Blinken	Amb.	Gyorgy Banlaki	Amb.
Iceland	Parker W. Borg	Amb.	Einar Benediktsson	Amb.
India	Frank G. Wisner	Amb.	Siddhartha S. Ray	Amb.
Indonesia	Robert L. Barry	Amb.	Arifin Mohamad Siregar	Amb.
Ireland	Jean Kennedy Smith	Amb.	Dermot A. Gallagher	Amb.
Israel	(Vacancy)	Amb.	Itamar Rabinovich	Amb.

Country	U.S. Representative to[1]	Rank	Representative from[2]	Rank
Italy	Reginald Bartholomew	Amb.	Boris Biancheri	Amb.
Jamaica	(Vacancy)	Amb.	Richard Leighton Bernal	Amb.
Japan	Walter F. Mondale	Amb.	Takakazu Kuriyama	Amb.
Jordan	Wesley E. Egan, Jr.	Amb.	Fayez A. Tarawneh	Amb.
Kazakhstan	William H. Courtney	Amb.	Touleoutai S. Souleimenov	Amb.
Kenya	Aurelia Brazeal	Amb.	Benjamin Edgar Kipkorir	Amb.
Korea, South	James T. Laney	Amb.	Kun Woo Park	Amb.
Kuwait	Ryan C. Crocker	Amb.	Mohammed Sabah Al-Salim Al-Sabah	Amb.
Kyrgyzstan	Eileen A. Malloy	Amb.	Almas Chukin	Consl.
Laos	Victor L. Tomseth	Amb.	Hiem Phommachanh	Amb.
Latvia	Ints M. Silins	Amb.	Ojars Eriks Kalnins	Amb.
Lebanon	Mark G. Hambley	Amb.	Riad Tabbarah	Amb.
Lesotho	(Vacancy)	Amb.	Eunice M. Bulane	Amb.
Liberia	William P. Twaddell	Cd'A.	Konah K. Blackett	Cd'A.
Lithuania	James W. Swihart, Jr.	Amb.	Alfonsas Eidintas	Amb.
Luxembourg	Clay Constantinou	Amb.	Alphonse Berns	Amb.
Macedonia (the former Yugoslav Republic of)	Victor R. Conras	P.O.	—	—
Madagascar	Dennis P. Barrett	Amb.	Pierrot J. Rajaonarivelo	Amb.
Malawi	Peter R. Chaveas	Amb.	W. Chokani	Amb.
Malaysia	John S. Wolf	Amb.	Dato Mohamed Abdul Majid	Amb.
Mali	William H. Dameron III	Amb.	Siragatou Ibrahim Cisse	Amb.
Malta	Joseph R. Paolino, Jr.	Amb.	Albert Borg Olivier De Puget	Amb.
Marshall Islands	David C. Fields	Amb.	Wilfred I. Kendall	Amb.
Mauritania	Dorothy Myers Sanpas	Amb.	Ismail Ould Iyahi	Amb.
Mauritius	Leslie M. Alexander	Amb.	Anund Priyay Neewoor	Amb.
Mexico	James R. Jones	Amb.	Jesus Silva Herzog	Amb.
Micronesia	March Fong Eu	Amb.	Jesse B. Marehalau	Amb
Moldova	Mary C. Pendleton	Amb.	Nicolae Tau	Amb.
Mongolia	Donald C. Johnson	Amb.	Knalzkhuu Narankuu	Cd'A.
Morocco	Marc C. Ginsberg	Amb.	Mohamed Benaissa	Amb.
Mozambique	Dennis Coleman Jett	Amb.	Hipolito Pereira Zozimo Patricio	Amb.
Myanmar (Burma)	(Vacancy)	Amb.	U Thaung	Amb.
Namibia	Marshall F. McCallie	Amb.	Tuliameni Kalomoh	Amb.
Nepal	Sandra L. Vogelgesang	Amb.	Basudev Prasad Dhungna	Amb.
Netherlands	K. Terry Dornbush	Amb.	Adriaan Pieter Roetert Jacobovits de Szeged	Amb.
New Zealand	Josiah Horton Beeman	Amb.	L. John Wood	Amb.
Nicaragua	John F. Maisto	Amb.	Roberto Genaro Mayorga-Cortes	Amb.
Niger	John S. Davison	Amb.	Adamou Seydou	Amb.
Nigeria	Walter C. Carrington	Amb.	Zubair Mahmud Kazaure	Amb.
Norway	Thomas A. Loftus	Amb.	Kjeld Vibe	Amb.
Oman	David J. Dunford	Amb.	Abdulla Moh'd Aqeel Al-Dhahab	Amb.
Pakistan	John C. Monjo	Amb.	Dr. Maleeha Lodhi	Amb.
Palau	Ihjod W. Moss	USLO	Isaac Ngewakl Soaladaob	Cd'A.
Panama	(Vacancy)	Amb.	Ricardo Alberto Arias	Amb.
Papua New Guinea	Richard W. Teare	Amb.	Kepas Isimel Watamgia	Amb.
Paraguay	(Vacancy)	Amb.	Jorge G. Prieto	Amb.
Peru	Alvin P. Adams, Jr.	Amb.	Ricardo V. Luna	Amb.
Philippines	John D. Negroponte	Amb.	Raul Ch. Rabe	Amb.
Poland	Nicholas Andrew Rey	Amb.	Jerzy Kozminski	Amb.
Portugal	Elizabeth Frawley Bagley	Amb.	Fernando Antonio Andresen Guimaraes	Amb.
Qatar	Kenton W. Keith	Amb.	Abdulrahman bin Saud Al-Thani	Amb.
Romania	Alfred H. Moses	Amb.	Ion Gorita	Cd'A.
Russia	Thomas R. Pickering	Amb.	Yuli M. Vorontsov	Amb.
Rwanda	David P. Rawson	Amb.	Joseph W. Mutaboba	Consl.
Saint Kitts and Nevis	—		John P. Irish	Min.-Consl.
Saint Lucia	—		Dr. Joseph Edsel Edmunds	Amb.
Saint Vincent and the Grenadines	—	—	Kingsley C.A. Layne	Amb.
Saudi Arabia	Raymond E. Mabus, Jr.	Amb.	Prince Bandar Bin Sultan	Amb.
Senegal	Mark Johnson	Amb.	Mamadou Mansour Seck	Amb.
Serbia-Montenegro[3]	(Vacancy)	Amb.	Zoran Popovic	Consl.
Seychelles	Carl Burton Stokes	Amb.	Marc Michael Rogers Marengo	Amb.
Sierra Leone	Lauralee M. Peters	Amb.	Thomas Kahota Kargbo	Amb.
Singapore	Timothy A. Chorba	Amb.	S.R. Nathan	Amb.
Slovak Republic	Theodore E. Russell	Amb.	Branislav Lichardus	Amb.
Slovenia	E. Allan Wendt	Amb.	Dr. Ernest Petric	Amb.
Somalia	Richard W. Bogosian	Amb.	(Closed operations)	
South Africa	Princeton N. Lyman	Amb.	Franklin Sonn	Amb.
Spain	Richard N. Gardner	Amb.	Jaime de Ojeda	Amb.
Sri Lanka	Teresita C. Schaffer	Amb.	Janantha Dhanapala	Amb.

Country	U.S. Representative to[1]	Rank	Representative from[2]	Rank
Sudan	Donald K. Petterson	Amb.	Mirghani Mohamed Salih	Min.
Suriname	Roger R. Gamble	Amb.	Willem A. Udenhout	Amb.
Swaziland	John T. Sprott	Amb.	Mary M. Kanya	Amb.
Sweden	Thomas L. Siebert	Amb.	Carl Henrik Sihver Liljegren	Amb.
Switzerland	M. Larry Lawrence	Amb.	Carlo Jagmetti	Amb.
Syria	Christopher W.S. Ross	Amb.	Walid Al-Moualem	Amb.
Tajikistan	Stanley T. Escudero	Amb.	—	—
Tanzania	Steven A. Browning	Amb.	Mustafa Salim Nyang'anyi	Amb.
Thailand	David F. Lambertson	Amb.	Manaspas Xuto	Amb.
Togo	Johnny Young	Amb.	Kossivi Osseyi	Amb.
Trinidad and Tobago	Sally G. Cowal	Amb.	Corinne Averille McKnight	Amb.
Tunisia	Mary Ann Casey	Amb.	Azouz Ennifar	Amb.
Turkey	Marc Grossman	Amb.	Nuzhet Kandemir	Amb.
Turkmenistan	Joseph S. Hulings III	Amb.	Halil Ugur	Amb.
Uganda	E. Michael Southwick	Amb.	Stephen Kapimpina Katenta–Apuli	Amb.
Ukraine	William Green Miller	Amb.	Yuriy Mikolayevych Shcherbak	Amb.
United Arab Emirates	William A. Rugh	Amb.	Mohammad bin Hussein Al-Shaali	Amb.
United Kingdom	William J. Crowe	Amb.	John Olav Kerr	Amb.
Uruguay	Thomas J. Dodd	Amb.	Alvaro Diez de Medina	Amb.
Uzbekistan	Henry L. Clarke	Amb.	Fatikh Teshabaev	Amb.
Venezuela	Jeffery Davidow	Amb.	Pedro Luis Echeverria	Amb.
Vietnam	James H. Hall	USLO	Bang Van Le	Cd'A.
Western Samoa	Josiah Horton Beeman	Amb.	Tuiloma Neroni Slade	Amb.
Yemen	Arthur H. Hughes	Amb.	Mohsin A. Alaini	Amb.
Yugoslavia (former)			Zoran Popovic	Cd'A.
Zaire	(Vacancy)	Amb.	Mukendi Tambo a Kabila	Min.-Consl.
Zambia	Roland K. Kuchel	Amb.	Dunstan Weston Kamana	Amb.
Zimbabwe	E. Gibson Lanpher	Amb.	Amos Bernard Muvengwa Midzi	Amb.

1. As of Fall 1995. 2. As of May 1996. 3. Formerly Yugoslavia. NOTE: Amb.=Ambassador; Cd'A.=Charge d'Affaires; Secy.=Secretary; Cons. Gen.= Consul General. Consl.=Counselor; Min.=Minister; P.O.=Principal Officer; Dir.=Director; USLO=U.S. Liaison Office. *Source:* U.S. Department of State.

State and City Tourism Offices

The following is a selected list of state tourism offices. Where a toll-free 800 number is available, it is given. However, the numbers are subject to change.

ALABAMA
Bureau of Tourism & Travel
P.O. Box 4927
Montgomery, AL
36103-4927
334–242–4169 or
1–800–ALABAMA

ALASKA
Alaska Division of Tourism
P.O. Box 110801
Juneau, AK 99811-0801
907–465–2010

ARIZONA
Arizona Office of Tourism
2702 N. 3rd St., Ste. 4015
Phoenix, AZ 85004
602–230–7733 or
1–800–842–8257

ARKANSAS
Arkansas Department of
Parks and Tourism
1 Capitol Mall
Little Rock, AR 72201
501–682–7777 or
1–800–NATURAL
(to receive literature both
in and out of state)

CALIFORNIA
California Division
of Tourism
P.O. Box 1499
Sacramento, CA
95812-1499
1–800–862–2543 U.S. only

COLORADO
No longer has a tourism
board. Tourists need to contact individual cities.

CONNECTICUT
Tourism Promotion Service
CT Dept. of Economic
Development
865 Brook Street
Rocky Hill, CT 06067–3405
203–258–4355 or 800–CT
BOUND (nationwide)

DELAWARE
Delaware Tourism Office
Delaware Economic
Development Office
99 Kings Highway
P.O. Box 1401
Dover, DE 19903
302–739–4271 or
1–800–441–8846
(both in and out of state)

DISTRICT OF COLUMBIA
DC Office of Tourism &
Promotion
1212 New York Ave. NW
#200
Washington, DC 20005
202–727–4511

FLORIDA
Department of Commerce
Visitors Inquiry
126 Van Buren St.

Tallahassee, FL 32399–2000
904–487–1462

GEORGIA
Tourist Division
P.O. Box 1776
Atlanta, GA 30301-1776
404–656–3590
1-800-VISIT GA
(1-800-847-4842)

HAWAII
Hawaii Visitors Bureau
2270 Kalakaua Ave.,
Suite 801
Honolulu, HI 96815
808–923–1811

IDAHO
Department of Commerce,
Tourism Development
700 W. State St.
P.O. Box 83720
Boise, ID 83720-0093
208–334–2470 or
1–800–635–7820

ILLINOIS
Illinois Bureau of Tourism
100 W. Randolph,
Suite 3–400
Chicago, IL 60601
312–814–4732
800–2CONNECT
http:\\www.
enjoyillinois.com

Average Daily Temperatures (°F) in Tourist Cities

Location	January		April		July		October	
	High	Low	High	Low	High	Low	High	Low
U.S. CITIES (See Weather and Climate Section)								
CANADA								
Ottawa	21	3	51	31	81	58	54	37
Quebec	18	2	45	29	76	57	51	37
Toronto	30	16	50	34	79	59	56	40
Vancouver	41	32	58	40	74	54	57	44
MEXICO								
Acapulco	85	70	87	71	89	75	88	74
Mexico City	66	42	78	52	74	54	70	50
OVERSEAS								
Australia (Sydney)	78	65	71	58	60	46	71	56
Austria (Vienna)	34	26	57	41	75	59	55	44
Bahamas (Nassau)	77	65	81	69	88	75	85	73
Bermuda (Hamilton)	68	58	71	59	85	73	79	69
Brazil (Rio de Janeiro)	84	73	80	69	75	63	77	66
Denmark (Copenhagen)	36	29	50	37	72	55	53	42
Egypt (Cairo)	65	47	83	57	96	70	86	65
France (Paris)	42	32	60	41	76	55	59	44
Germany (Berlin)	35	26	55	38	74	55	55	41
Greece (Athens)	54	42	67	52	90	72	74	60
Hong Kong	64	56	75	67	87	78	81	73
India (Calcutta)	80	55	97	76	90	79	89	74
Italy (Rome)	54	39	68	46	88	64	73	53
Israel (Jerusalem)	55	41	73	50	87	63	81	59
Japan (Tokyo)	47	29	63	46	83	70	69	55
Nigeria (Lagos)	88	74	89	77	83	74	85	74
Netherlands (Amsterdam)	40	34	52	43	69	59	56	48
Puerto Rico (San Juan)	81	67	84	69	87	74	87	73
South Africa (Cape Town)	78	60	72	53	63	45	70	52
Spain (Madrid)	47	33	64	44	87	62	66	48
United Kingdom (London)	44	35	56	40	73	55	58	44
United Kingdom (Edinburgh)	43	35	50	39	65	52	53	44
Russia (Moscow)	21	9	47	31	76	55	46	34
Venezuela (Caracas)	75	56	81	60	78	61	79	61
Yugoslavia (Belgrade)	37	27	64	45	84	61	65	47

INDIANA
Indiana Dept. of Commerce
Tourism & Film Develop-
ment Division
One North Capitol
Suite 700
Indianapolis, IN
46204–2288
1–800–289–6646

IOWA
Iowa Department of
Economic Development
Division of Tourism
200 East Grand Avenue
Des Moines, IA 50309
515–242–4705
1-800-345-IOWA

KANSAS
Kansas Department of
Commerce & Housing
Travel & Tourism
Development Division
700 SW Harrison St.,
Suite 1300
Topeka, KS 66603–3712
913–296–2009
1–800–2KANSAS

KENTUCKY
Department of Travel
Development
Dept. MR
P.O. Box 2011
Frankfort, KY 40602
1–800–225–TRIP Ext. 67
(From the United States
and Canada)

LOUISIANA
Office of Tourism
P.O. Box 94291
Baton Rouge, LA
70804–9291
504–342–8119 or
1–800–33GUMBO

MAINE
Maine Publicity Bureau
P.O. Box 2300
Hallowell, ME 04347–2300
207–623–0363

MARYLAND
Office of Tourism
Development
217 E. Redwood St.,
9th Floor
Baltimore, MD 21202
410–767–3400 Business
Office only

1–800–543–1036—
Maryland Travel Kit

MASSACHUSETTS
Office of Travel and
Tourism
100 Cambridge St., 13th
Floor
Boston, MA 02202
617–727–3201
800–447–MASS (6277)—
Mass Getaway Guide

MICHIGAN
Michigan Jobs
Commission
Travel Bureau
P.O. Box 3393
Livonia, MI 48151
1–800–5432–YES
http://www.travel-michigan.
state.mi.us

MINNESOTA
Minnesota Office of
Tourism
100 Metro Square
121 Seventh Place E
St. Paul, MN 55101-2112
612–296–5029 or
1–800–657–3700

MISSISSIPPI
Department of Economic
and Community
Development
Tourism Development
P.O. Box 1705
Ocean Springs, MS
39566-1705
601-359-3297 or
1-800-927-6378

MISSOURI
Missouri Division of
Tourism
Truman State Office Bldg.
301 W. High St.
P.O. Box 1055
Jefferson City, MO 65102
573-751-4133
1-800-877-1234

MONTANA
Department of Commerce
Travel Montana
P.O. Box 200533
Helena, MT 59620-0533
406-444-2654 or
1-800-VISIT MT

NEBRASKA
Dept. of Economic
Development
Division of Travel and
Tourism
P.O. Box 98913
Lincoln, NE 68509
402-471-3796 or
1-800-228-4307
(In-state or out of state)

NEVADA
Commission on Tourism
Capitol Complex
Carson City, NV 89710
1-800-Nevada-8

NEW HAMPSHIRE
Office of Travel
and Tourism
P.O. Box 1856
Concord, NH 03302-1856
603-271-2666
or for recorded weekly
events, ski conditions,
foliage reports
1-800-258-3608

NEW JERSEY
Division of Travel and
Tourism
CN 826
Trenton, NJ 08625
1-800-JERSEY-7

NEW MEXICO
New Mexico Department
of Tourism
Room 751 Lamy Bldg.
491 Old Santa Fe Trail
Santa Fe, NM 87503
505-827-7400 or
1-800-545-2040 Ext. 751

NEW YORK
Division of Tourism
1 Commerce Plaza
Albany, NY 12245
Toll free from anywhere in
the U.S. and its territorial
possessions

1-800-225-5697. From
Canada, call 518-474-4116

NORTH CAROLINA
Travel and Tourism Division
Department of Commerce
430 North Salisbury St.
Raleigh, NC 27603
919-733-4171 or
1-800-VISIT NC

NORTH DAKOTA
North Dakota Tourism
604 E. Boulevard
Bismarck, ND 58505
701-328-2525 or
1-800-435-5663

OHIO
Ohio Division of Travel and
Tourism
P.O. Box 1001
Columbus, OH 43266-1010
614-466-8844 (Business
Office)
1-800-BUCKEYE
(U.S. and Canada
Toll-Free Travel Hotline)

OKLAHOMA
Oklahoma Tourism and
Recreation Dept.
Literature Distribution
Center
P.O. Box 60789
Oklahoma City, OK
73146-9910
405-521-2409 (In
Oklahoma City area) or
nationwide at
1-800-652-6552

OREGON
Tourism Commission
775 Summer St. NE
Salem, OR 97310
503-986-0000 (Business
Office)
1-800-547-7842 (Travel
Information)

PENNSYLVANIA
Office of Travel & Tourism
Room 453 Forum Building
Harrisburg, PA 17120
717-787-5453 (Business
Office)
1-800-VISIT PA, ext. 257
(To order single free copy
of PA Travel Guide)

RHODE ISLAND
Rhode Island Tourism
Division
1 West Exchange Street
Providence, RI 02903
401-277-2601 or
1-800-556-2484 (in
U.S. and Canada)

SOUTH CAROLINA
South Carolina Division of
Tourism
Box 71
Columbia, SC 29202
803-734-0122

SOUTH DAKOTA
Department of Tourism
711 E. Wells Ave.

Pierre, South Dakota 57501
605-773-3301 or
1-800-S-DAKOTA

TENNESSEE
Department of Tourist
Development
P.O. Box 23170
Nashville, TN 37202
615-741-2158
1-800-TENN-200

TEXAS
Travel Information Services
Texas Department of
Transportation
P.O. Box 5064
Austin, TX 78763-5064
1-800-452-9292

UTAH
Utah Travel Council
Council Hall, Capitol Hill
Salt Lake City, UT 84114
801-538-1030
Fax 801-538-1399
http://www.netpub.
com.utah!

VERMONT
Department of Travel
and Tourism
134 State St.
P.O. Box 1471
Montpelier, VT 05601-1471
1-800-VERMONT

VIRGINIA
Virginia Division
of Tourism
901 East Byrd St.
Richmond, VA 23219
804-786-4484
1-800-932-5827

WASHINGTON
Washington State Dept. of
Community, Trade and
Economic Development
906 Columbia St. SW
P.O. Box 48300
Olympia, WA 98504-8300
360-753-2200

WASHINGTON, D.C.
See District of Columbia

WEST VIRGINIA
Division of Tourism
2101 Washington St. E.
Charleston, WV 25305
304-558-2286 or
1-800-CALL-WVA

WISCONSIN
Travel Information
Department of Tourism
Box 7976
Madison, WI 53707
Toll free in WI and neigh-
bor states 1-800-372-2737
others: 608-266-2161
Nationally 1-800-432-TRIP

WYOMING
Wyoming Division of
Tourism
I-25 at College Drive
Cheyenne, WY 82002
307-777-7777 or
1-800-225-5996

Travel Warning on Drugs Abroad

The U.S. Department of State, Bureau of Consular Affairs, warns that many Americans are finding out the hard way that drug possession or trafficking equals jail in foreign countries. If you are caught with drugs abroad, there is very little that anyone can do to help you. Once arrested, the American consular officer cannot get you out of jail.

What the U.S. Consular Officer Can Do:

- Visit you in jail after being notified of your arrest.
- Give you a list of local attorneys (the U.S. Government cannot assume responsibility for the professional ability or integrity of these individuals).
- Notify your family and/or friends and relay requests for money and other aid—but only with your authorization.
- Intercede with local authorities to make sure that your rights under local law are fully observed and that you are being treated humanely, according to internationally accepted standards.
- Protest mistreatment or abuse to the appropriate authorities.

What the U.S. Consular Officer Cannot Do:

- Demand your immediate release or get you out of jail or the country!
- Represent you at trial or give legal counsel.
- Pay legal fees and/or fines with U.S. Government funds.

Facts About Drug Arrests Abroad

- If you are caught buying, selling, carrying or using any type of drug—from hashish to heroin, marijuana to mescaline, cocaine to quaaludes—**IT CAN MEAN:**
- Interrogation and delays before trial including mistreatment and solitary confinement for up to one year under very primitive conditions.
- Lengthy trials conducted in a foreign language, with delays and postponements.
- Two years to life in jail. Some places include hard labor and heavy fines if found guilty.
- The death penalty in a growing number of countries (e.g., Saudi Arabia, Malaysia, Pakistan, Turkey, Thailand).
- A number of countries, including Mexico, Jamaica, the Bahamas, and the Dominican Republic, have enacted more stringent drug laws which impose mandatory jail sentences for individuals convicted of possessing even small amounts of marijuana or cocaine for personal use.
- Once you leave the United States, you are not covered by U.S. laws and constitutional rights.
- Bail is not granted in many countries when drugs are involved.
- The burden of proof in many countries is on the accused to prove his/her innocence.
- In some countries, evidence obtained illegally by local authorities may be admissible in court.
- Few countries offer drug offenders jury trials or even require the prisoner's presence at his/her trial.
- Many countries have mandatory prison sentences for seven years or more without parole for drug violations. □

Travel Scams: You Don't Get Something for Nothing

Source: U.S. Department of Consumer Affairs

Beware of travel companies that misrepresent information about the bookings and transportation costs. For example, a company that offers an unbelievably low airfare may make up the loss in another way such as overpriced hotel accommodations. In most cases, one should assume that "If it sounds too good to be true, it probably is." The following tips from the U.S. Department of Consumer Affairs can save you from a disappointing vacation.

Don't be taken by solicitations by postcard, letter, or phone claiming you've won a free trip or can get discounts on hotels and airfares. These offers usually don't disclose the hidden fees involved, for example, deposits, surcharges, excessive handling fees or taxes.

Some travel scams require you to purchase a product to get a trip that is "free" or "two-for-one." You'll end up paying for the "free trip" or more for the product than the trip is worth, and the two-for-one deal might be more expensive than if you had arranged a trip yourself by watching airfare deals.

Be wary of travel offers which ask you to redeem vouchers or certificates from out-of-state companies. Their offers are usually valid only for a limited time and on a space-available basis. The hotels are often budget rooms and very uncomfortable. The company charges you for the trip in advance, but will the company still be in business when you're ready to take the trip?

Check the reputation of any travel service you use, especially travel clubs offering discounts on their services in exchange for an annual fee. Contact your state or local consumer protection agency or the Better Business Bureau.

Request copies of a travel club's or agent's brochures and contracts before purchasing your ticket. Don't rely on oral promises. Find out about cancellation policies and never sign contracts that have blank or incomplete spaces.

Never give out your credit card number to a club or company with which you're unfamiliar or which requires you to call 900 numbers for information.

Don't feel pressured by requests for an immediate decision or a statement that the offer is only good "if you act now." Don't deal with companies that request payment in advance or that don't have escrow accounts where your deposit is held.

Research cut-rate offers, especially when dealing with travel consolidators who might not be able to provide your tickets until close to your departure date.

You can protect yourself by using a credit card to purchase travel services. If you don't get what you paid for, contact the credit card issuer and you might be able to get the charges reversed. Be aware that you have 60 days to dispute a charge. □

Road Mileages Between U.S. Cities[1]

Cities	Birming-ham	Boston	Buffalo	Chicago	Cleveland	Dallas	Denver
Birmingham, Ala.	—	1,194	947	657	734	653	1,318
Boston, Mass.	1,194	—	457	983	639	1,815	1,991
Buffalo, N.Y.	947	457	—	536	192	1,387	1,561
Chicago, Ill.	657	983	536	—	344	931	1,050
Cleveland, Ohio	734	639	192	344	—	1,205	1,369
Dallas, Tex.	653	1,815	1,387	931	1,205	—	801
Denver, Colo	1,318	1,991	1,561	1,050	1,369	801	—
Detroit, Mich.	754	702	252	279	175	1,167	1,301
El Paso, Tex.	1,278	2,358	1,928	1,439	1,746	625	652
Houston, Tex.	692	1,886	1,532	1,092	1,358	242	1,032
Indianapolis, Ind.	492	940	510	189	318	877	1,051
Kansas City, Mo.	703	1,427	997	503	815	508	616
Los Angeles, Calif.	2,078	3,036	2,606	2,112	2,424	1,425	1,174
Louisville, Ky.	378	996	571	305	379	865	1,135
Memphis, Tenn.	249	1,345	965	546	773	470	1,069
Miami, Fla.	777	1,539	1,445	1,390	1,325	1,332	2,094
Minneapolis, Minn.	1,067	1,402	955	411	763	969	867
New Orleans, La.	347	1,541	1,294	947	1,102	504	1,305
New York, N.Y.	983	213	436	840	514	1,604	1,780
Omaha, Neb.	907	1,458	1,011	493	819	661	559
Philadelphia, Pa.	894	304	383	758	432	1,515	1,698
Phoenix, Ariz.	1,680	2,664	2,234	1,729	2,052	1,027	836
Pittsburgh, Pa.	792	597	219	457	131	1,237	1,411
St. Louis, Mo.	508	1,179	749	293	567	638	871
Salt Lake City, Utah	1,805	2,425	1,978	1,458	1,786	1,239	512
San Francisco, Calif.	2,385	3,179	2,732	2,212	2,540	1,765	1,266
Seattle, Wash.	2,612	3,043	2,596	2,052	2,404	2,122	1,373
Washington, D.C.	751	440	386	695	369	1,372	1,635

Cities	Detroit	El Paso	Houston	Indian-apolis	Kansas City	Los Angeles	Louisville
Birmingham, Ala.	754	1,278	692	492	703	2,078	378
Boston, Mass.	702	2,358	1,886	940	1,427	3,036	996
Buffalo, N.Y.	252	1,928	1,532	510	997	2,606	571
Chicago, Ill.	279	1,439	1,092	189	503	2,112	305
Cleveland, Ohio	175	1,746	1,358	318	815	2,424	379
Dallas, Tex.	1,167	625	242	877	508	1,425	865
Denver, Colo.	1,310	652	1,032	1,051	616	1,174	1,135
Detroit, Mich.	—	1,696	1,312	290	760	2,369	378
El Paso, Tex.	1,696	—	756	1,418	936	800	1,443
Houston, Tex.	1,312	756	—	1,022	750	1,556	981
Indianapolis, Ind.	290	1,418	1,022	—	487	2,096	114
Kansas City, Mo.	760	936	750	487	—	1,609	519
Los Angeles, Calif.	2,369	800	1,556	2,096	1,609	—	2,128
Louisville, Ky.	378	1,443	981	114	519	2,128	—
Memphis, Tenn.	756	1,095	586	466	454	1,847	396
Miami, Fla.	1,409	1,957	1,237	1,225	1,479	2,757	1,111
Minneapolis, Minn.	698	1,353	1,211	600	466	2,041	716
New Orleans, La.	1,101	1,121	365	839	839	1,921	725
New York, N.Y.	671	2,147	1,675	729	1,216	2,825	785
Omaha, Neb.	754	1,015	903	590	204	1,733	704
Philadelphia, Pa.	589	2,065	1,586	647	1,134	2,743	703
Phoenix, Ariz.	1,986	402	1,158	1,713	1,226	398	1,749
Pittsburgh, Pa.	288	1,778	1,395	360	847	2,456	416
St. Louis, Mo.	529	1,179	799	239	255	1,864	264
Salt Lake City, Utah	1,721	877	1,465	1,545	1,128	728	1,647
San Francisco, Calif.	2,475	1,202	1,958	2,299	1,882	403	2,401
Seattle, Wash.	2,339	1,760	2,348	2,241	1,909	1,150	2,355
Washington, D.C.	526	1,997	1,443	565	1,071	2,680	601

1. These figures represent estimates and are subject to change.

Road Mileages Between U.S. Cities

Cities	Memphis	Miami	Minne—apolis	New Orleans	New York	Omaha	Phila-delphia
Birmingham, Ala.	249	777	1,067	347	983	907	894
Boston, Mass.	1,345	1,539	1,402	1,541	213	1,458	304
Buffalo, N.Y.	965	1,445	955	1,294	436	1,011	383
Chicago, Ill.	546	1,390	411	947	840	493	758
Cleveland, Ohio	773	1,325	763	1,102	514	819	432
Dallas, Tex.	470	1,332	969	504	1,604	661	1,515
Denver, Colo.	1,069	2,094	867	1,305	1,780	559	1,698
Detroit, Mich.	756	1,409	698	1,101	671	754	589
El Paso, Tex.	1,095	1,957	1,353	1,121	2,147	1,015	2,065
Houston, Tex.	586	1,237	1,211	365	1,675	903	1,586
Indianapolis, Ind.	466	1,225	600	839	729	590	647
Kansas City, Mo.	454	1,479	466	839	1,216	204	1,134
Los Angeles, Calif.	1,847	2,757	2,041	1,921	2,825	1,733	2,74 3
Louisville, Ky.	396	1,111	716	725	785	704	703
Memphis, Tenn.	—	1,025	854	401	1,134	658	1,045
Miami, Fla.	1,025	—	1,801	892	1,328	1,683	1,239
Minneapolis, Minn.	854	1,801	—	1,255	1,259	373	1,177
New Orleans, La.	401	892	1,255	—	1,330	1,043	1,241
New York, N.Y.	1,134	1,328	1,259	1,330	—	1,315	93
Omaha, Neb.	658	1,683	373	1,043	1,315	—	1,233
Philadelphia, Pa.	1,045	1,239	1,177	1,241	93	1,233	—
Phoenix, Ariz.	1,464	2,359	1,644	1,523	2,442	1,305	2,360
Pittsburgh, Pa.	810	1,250	876	1,118	386	932	304
St. Louis, Mo.	295	1,241	559	696	968	459	886
Salt Lake City, Utah	1,556	2,571	1,243	1,743	2,282	967	2,200
San Francisco, Calif.	2,151	3,097	1,997	2,269	3,036	1,721	2,954
Seattle, Wash.	2,363	3,389	1,641	2,606	2,900	1,705	2,818
Washington, D.C.	902	1,101	1,114	1,098	229	1,170	140

Cities	Phoenix	Pitts—burgh	St. Louis	Salt Lake City	San Francisco	Seattle	Wash—ington
Birmingham, Ala.	1,680	792	508	1,805	2,385	2,612	751
Boston, Mass.	2,664	597	1,179	2,425	3,179	3,043	440
Buffalo, N.Y.	2,234	219	749	1,978	2,732	2,596	386
Chicago, Ill.	1,729	457	293	1,458	2,212	2,052	695
Cleveland, Ohio	2,052	131	567	1,786	2,540	2,404	369
Dallas, Tex.	1,027	1,237	638	1,239	1,765	2,122	1,372
Denver, Colo.	836	1,411	871	512	1,266	1,373	1,635
Detroit, Mich.	1,986	288	529	1,721	2,475	2,339	526
El Paso, Tex.	402	1,778	1,179	877	1,202	1,760	1,997
Houston, Tex.	1,158	1,395	799	1,465	1,958	2,348	1,443
Indianapolis, Ind.	1,713	360	239	1,545	2,299	2,241	565
Kansas City, Mo.	1,226	847	255	1,128	1,882	1,909	1,071
Los Angeles, Calif.	398	2,456	1,864	728	403	1,150	2,680
Louisville, Ky.	1,749	416	264	1,647	2,401	2,355	601
Memphis, Tenn.	1,464	810	295	1,556	2,151	2,363	902
Miami, Fla.	2,359	1,250	1,241	2,571	3,097	3,389	1,101
Minneapolis, Minn.	1,644	876	559	1,243	1,997	1,641	1,114
New Orleans, La.	1,523	1,118	696	1,743	2,269	2,626	1,098
New York, N.Y.	2,442	386	968	2,282	3,036	2,900	229
Omaha, Neb.	1,305	932	459	967	1,721	1,705	1,178
Philadelphia, Pa.	2,360	304	886	2,200	2,954	2,818	140
Phoenix, Ariz.	—	2,073	1,485	651	800	1,482	2,278
Pittsburgh, Pa.	2,073	—	599	1,899	2,653	2,517	241
St. Louis, Mo.	1,485	599	—	1,383	2,137	2,164	836
Salt Lake City, Utah	651	1,899	1,383	—	754	883	2,110
San Francisco, Calif.	800	2,653	2,137	754	—	817	2,864
Seattle, Wash.	1,482	2,517	2,164	883	817	—	2,755
Washington, D.C.	2,278	241	836	2,110	2,864	2,755	—

Air Distances Between U.S. Cities in Statute Miles

Cities	Birming-ham	Boston	Buffalo	Chicago	Cleveland	Dallas	Denver
Birmingham, Ala.	—	1,052	776	578	618	581	1,095
Boston, Mass.	1,052	—	400	851	551	1,551	1,769
Buffalo, N. Y.	776	400	—	454	173	1,198	1,370
Chicago, Ill.	578	851	454	—	308	803	920
Cleveland, Ohio	618	551	173	308	—	1,025	1,227
Dallas, Tex.	581	1,551	1,198	803	1,025	—	663
Denver, Colo.	1,095	1,769	1,370	920	1,227	663	—
Detroit, Mich.	641	613	216	238	90	999	1,156
El Paso, Tex.	1,15 2	2,072	1,692	1,252	1,525	572	557
Houston, Tex.	567	1,605	1,286	940	1,114	225	879
Indianapolis, Ind.	433	807	435	165	263	763	1,000
Kansas City, Mo.	579	1,251	861	414	700	451	558
Los Angeles, Calif.	1,802	2,596	2,198	1,745	2,049	1,240	831
Louisville, Ky.	331	826	483	269	311	726	1,038
Memphis, Tenn.	217	1,137	803	482	630	420	879
Miami, Fla.	665	1,255	1,181	1,188	1,087	1,111	1,726
Minneapolis, Minn.	862	1,123	731	355	630	862	700
New Orleans, La.	312	1,359	1,086	833	924	443	1,082
New York, N. Y.	864	188	292	713	405	1,374	1,631
Omaha, Neb.	732	1,282	883	432	739	586	488
Philadelphia, Pa.	783	271	279	666	360	1,299	1,579
Phoenix, Ariz.	1,456	2,300	1,906	1,453	1,749	887	586
Pittsburgh, Pa.	608	483	178	410	115	1,070	1,320
St. Louis, Mo.	400	1,038	662	262	492	547	796
Salt Lake City, Utah	1,466	2,099	1,699	1,260	1,568	999	371
San Francisco, Calif.	2,013	2,699	2,300	1,858	2,166	1,483	949
Seattle, Wash.	2,082	2,493	2,117	1,737	2,026	1,681	1,021
Washington, D.C.	661	393	292	597	306	1,185	1,494

Cities	Detroit	El Paso	Houston	Indian-apolis	Kansas City	Los Angeles	Louisville
Birmingham, Ala.	641	1,152	567	433	579	1,802	331
Boston, Mass.	613	2,072	1,605	807	1,251	2,596	826
Buffalo, N. Y.	216	1,692	1,286	435	861	2,198	483
Chicago, Ill.	238	1,252	940	165	414	1,745	269
Cleveland, Ohio	90	1,525	1,114	263	700	2,049	311
Dallas, Tex.	999	572	225	763	451	1,240	726
Denver, Colo.	1,156	557	879	1,000	558	831	1,038
Detr oit, Mich.	—	1,479	1,105	240	645	1,983	316
El Paso, Tex.	1,479	—	676	1,264	839	701	1,254
Houston, Tex.	1,105	676	—	865	644	1,374	803
Indianapolis, Ind.	240	1,264	865	—	453	1,809	107
Kansas City, Mo.	645	839	644	453	—	1,356	480
Los Angeles, Calif.	1,983	701	1,374	1,809	1,356	—	1,829
Louisville, Ky.	316	1,254	803	107	480	1,829	—
Memphis, Tenn.	623	976	484	384	369	1,603	320
Miami, Fla.	1,152	1,643	968	1,024	1,241	2,339	919
Minneapolis, Minn.	543	1,157	1,056	511	413	1,524	605
New Orleans, La.	939	983	318	712	680	1,673	623
New York, N. Y.	482	1,905	1,420	646	1,097	2,451	652
Omaha, Neb.	669	878	794	525	166	1,315	580
Philadelphia, Pa.	443	1,836	1,341	585	1,038	2,394	582
Phoenix, Ariz.	1,690	346	1,017	1,499	1,049	357	1,508
Pittsburgh, Pa.	205	1,590	1,137	330	781	2,136	344
St. Louis, Mo.	455	1,034	679	231	238	1,589	242
Salt Lake City, Utah	1,492	689	1,200	1,356	925	579	1,402
San Francisco, Calif.	2,091	995	1,645	1,949	1,506	347	1,986
Seattle, Wash.	1,938	1,376	1,891	1,872	1,506	959	1,943
Washington, D.C.	396	1,728	1,220	494	945	2,300	476

Source: National Geodetic Survey.

Air Distances Between U.S. Cities in Statute Miles

Cities	Memphis	Miami	Minneapolis	New Orleans	New York	Omaha	Philadelphiae
Birmingham, Ala.	217	665	862	312	864	732	783
Boston, Mass.	1,137	1,255	1,123	1,359	188	1,282	271
Buffalo, N.Y.	803	1,181	731	1,086	292	883	279
Chicago, Ill.	482	1,188	355	833	713	432	666
Cleveland, Ohio	630	1,087	630	924	405	739	360
Dallas, Tex.	420	1,111	862	443	1,374	586	1,299
Denver, Colo.	879	1,726	700	1,082	1,631	488	1,579
Detroit, Mich.	623	1,152	543	939	482	669	443
El Paso, Tex.	976	1,643	1,157	983	1,905	878	1,836
Houston, Tex.	484	968	1,056	318	1,420	794	1,341
Indianapolis, Ind.	384	1,024	511	712	646	525	585
Kansas City, Mo.	369	1,241	413	680	1,097	166	1,038
Los Angeles, Calif.	1,603	2,339	1,524	1,673	2,451	1,315	2,394
Louisville, Ky.	320	919	605	623	652	580	582
Memphis, Tenn.	—	872	699	358	957	529	881
Miami, Fla.	872	—	1,511	669	1,092	1,397	1,019
Minneapolis, Minn.	699	1,511	—	1,051	1,018	290	985
New Orleans, La.	358	669	1,051	—	1,171	847	1,089
New York, N.Y.	957	1,092	1,018	1,171	—	1,144	83
Omaha, Neb.	529	1,397	290	847	1,144	—	1,094
Philadelphia, Pa.	881	1,019	985	1,089	83	1,094	—
Phoenix, Ariz.	1,263	1,982	1,280	1,316	2,145	1,036	2,083
Pittsburgh, Pa.	660	1,010	743	919	317	836	259
St. Louis, Mo.	240	1,061	466	598	875	354	811
Salt Lake City, Utah	1,250	2,089	987	1,434	1,972	833	1,925
San Francisco, Calif.	1,802	2,594	1,584	1,926	2,571	1,429	2,523
Seattle, Wash.	1,867	2,734	1,395	2,101	2,408	1,369	2,380
Washington, D.C.	765	923	934	966	205	1,014	123

Cities	Phoenix	Pittsburgh	St. Louis	Salt Lake City	San Francisco	Seattle	Washington
Birmingham, Ala.	1,456	608	400	1,466	2,013	2,082	661
Boston, Mass.	2,300	483	1,038	2,099	2,699	2,493	393
Buffalo, N.Y.	1,906	178	662	1,699	2,300	2,117	292
Chicago, Ill.	1,453	410	262	1,260	1,858	1,737	597
Cleveland, Ohio	1,749	115	492	1,568	2,166	2,026	306
Dallas, Tex.	887	1,070	547	999	1,483	1,681	1,185
Denver, Colo.	586	1,320	796	371	949	1,021	1,494
Detroit, Mich.	1,690	205	455	1,492	2,091	1,938	396
El Paso, Tex.	346	1,590	1,034	689	995	1,376	1,728
Houston, Tex.	1,017	1,137	679	1,200	1,645	1,891	1,220
Indianapolis, Ind.	1,499	330	231	1,356	1,949	1,872	494
Kansas City, Mo.	1,049	781	238	925	1,506	1,506	945
Los Angeles, Calif.	357	2,136	1,589	579	347	959	2,300
Louisville, Ky.	1,508	344	242	1,402	1,986	1,943	476
Memphis, Tenn.	1,263	660	240	1,250	1,802	1,867	765
Miami, Fla.	1,982	1,010	1,061	2,089	2,594	2,734	923
Minneapolis, Minn.	1,280	743	466	987	1,584	1,395	934
New Orleans, La.	1,316	919	598	1,434	1,926	2,101	966
New York, N.Y.	2,145	317	875	1,972	2,571	2,408	205
Omaha, Neb.	1,036	836	354	833	1,429	1,369	1,014
Philadelphia, Pa.	2,083	259	811	1,925	2,523	2,380	123
Phoenix, Ariz.	—	1,828	1,272	504	653	1,114	1,983
Pittsburgh, Pa.	1,828	—	559	1,668	2,264	2,138	192
St. Louis, Mo.	1,272	559	—	1,162	1,744	1,724	712
Salt Lake City, Utah	504	1,668	1,162	—	600	701	1,848
San Francisco, Calif.	653	2,264	1,744	600	—	678	2,442
Seattle, Wash.	1,114	2,138	1,724	701	678	—	2,329
Washington, D.C.	1,983	192	712	1,848	2,442	2,329	—

Source: National Geodetic Survey.

Air Distances Between World Cities in Statute Miles

Cities	Berlin	Buenos Aires	Cairo	Calcutta	Cape Town	Caracas	Chicago
Berlin	—	7,402	1,795	4,368	5,981	5,247	4,405
Buenos Aires	7,402	—	7,345	10,265	4,269	3,168	5,598
Cairo	1,795	7,345	—	3,539	4,500	6,338	6,129
Calcutta	4,368	10,265	3,539	—	6,024	9,605	7,980
Cape Town, South Africa	5,981	4,269	4,500	6,024	—	6,365	8,494
Caracas, Venezuela	5,247	3,168	6,338	9,605	6,365	—	2,501
Chicago	4,405	5,598	6,129	7,980	8,494	2,501	—
Hong Kong	5,440	11,472	5,061	1,648	7,375	10,167	7,793
Honolulu, Hawaii	7,309	7,561	8,838	7,047	11,534	6,013	4,250
Istanbul	1,078	7,611	768	3,638	5,154	6,048	5,477
Lisbon	1,436	5,956	2,363	5,638	5,325	4,041	3,990
London	579	6,916	2,181	4,947	6,012	4,660	3,950
Los Angeles	5,724	6,170	7,520	8,090	9,992	3,632	1,745
Manila	6,132	11,051	5,704	2,203	7,486	10,620	8,143
Mexico City	6,047	4,592	7,688	9,492	8,517	2,232	1,691
Montreal	3,729	5,615	5,414	7,607	7,931	2,449	744
Moscow	1,004	8,376	1,803	3,321	6,300	6,173	4,974
New York	3,965	5,297	5,602	7,918	7,764	2,132	713
Paris	545	6,870	1,995	4,883	5,807	4,736	4,134
Rio de Janeiro	6,220	1,200	6,146	9,377	3,773	2,810	5,296
Rome	734	6,929	1,320	4,482	5,249	5,196	4,808
San Francisco	5,661	6,467	7,364	7,814	10,247	3,904	1,858
Shanghai, China	5,218	12,201	5,183	2,117	8,061	9,501	7,061
Stockholm	504	7,808	2,111	4,195	6,444	5,420	4,278
Sydney, Australia	10,006	7,330	8,952	5,685	6,843	9,513	9,272
Tokyo	5,540	11,408	5,935	3,194	9,156	8,799	6,299
Warsaw	320	7,662	1,630	4,048	5,958	5,517	4,667
Washington, D.C.	4,169	5,218	5,800	8,084	7,901	2,059	597

Cities	Hong Kong	Honolulu	Istanbul	Lisbon	London	Los Angeles	Manila
Berlin	5,440	7,309	1,078	1,436	579	5,724	6,132
Buenos Aires	11,472	7,561	7,611	5,956	6,916	6,170	11,051
Cairo	5,061	8,838	768	2,363	2,181	7,520	5,704
Calcutta	1,648	7,047	3,638	5,638	4,947	8,090	2,203
Cape Town, South Africa	7,375	11,534	5,154	5,325	6,012	9,992	7,486
Caracas, Venezuela	10,167	6,013	6,048	4,041	4,660	3,632	10,620
Chicago	7,793	4,250	5,477	3,990	3,950	1,745	8,143
Hong Kong	—	5,549	4,984	6,853	5,982	7,195	693
Honolulu, Hawaii	5,549	—	8,109	7,820	7,228	2,574	5,299
Istanbul	4,984	8,109	—	2,012	1,552	6,783	5,664
Lisbon	6,853	7,820	2,012	—	985	5,621	7,546
London	5,982	7,228	1,552	985	—	5,382	6,672
Los Angeles, Calif.	7,195	2,574	6,783	5,621	5,382	—	7,261
Manila	693	5,299	5,664	7,546	6,672	7,261	—
Mexico City	8,782	3,779	7,110	5,390	5,550	1,589	8,835
Montreal	7,729	4,910	4,789	3,246	3,282	2,427	8,186
Moscow	4,439	7,037	1,091	2,427	1,555	6,003	5,131
New York	8,054	4,964	4,975	3,364	3,458	2,451	8,498
Paris	5,985	7,438	1,400	904	213	5,588	6,677
Rio de Janeiro	11,021	8,285	6,389	4,796	5,766	6,331	11,259
Rome	5,768	8,022	843	1,161	887	6,732	6,457
San Francisco	6,897	2,393	6,703	5,666	5,357	347	6,967
Shanghai, China	764	4,941	4,962	6,654	5,715	6,438	1,150
Stockholm	5,113	6,862	1,348	1,856	890	5,454	5,797
Sydney, Australia	4,584	4,943	9,294	11,302	10,564	7,530	3,944
Tokyo	1,794	3,853	5,560	6,915	5,940	5,433	1,866
Warsaw	5,144	7,355	863	1,715	899	5,922	5,837
Washington, D.C.	8,147	4,519	5,215	3,562	3,663	2,300	8,562

Source: Encyclopaedia Britannica.

Air Distances Between World Cities in Statute Miles

Cities	Mexico City	Montreal	Moscow	New York	Paris	Rio de Janeiro	Rome
Berlin	6,047	3,729	1,004	3,965	545	6,220	734
Buenos Aires	4,592	5,615	8,376	5,297	6,870	1,200	6,929
Cairo	7,688	5,414	1,803	5,602	1,995	6,146	1,320
Calcutta	9,492	7,607	3,321	7,918	4,883	9,377	4,482
Cape Town, South Africa	8,517	7,931	6,300	7,764	5,807	3,773	5,249
Caracas, Venezuela	2,232	2,449	6,173	2,132	4,736	2,810	5,196
Chicago	1,691	744	4,974	713	4,134	5,296	4,808
Hong Kong	8,782	7,729	4,439	8,054	5,985	11,021	5,768
Honolulu	3,779	4,910	7,037	4,964	7,438	8,285	8,022
Istanbul	7,110	4,789	1,091	4,975	1,400	6,389	843
Lisbon	5,390	3,246	2,427	3,364	904	4,796	1,161
London	5,550	3,282	1,555	3,458	213	5,766	887
Los Angeles	1,589	2,427	6,003	2,451	5,588	6,331	6,732
Manila	8,835	8,186	5,131	8,498	6,677	11,259	6,457
Mexico City	—	2,318	6,663	2,094	5,716	4,771	6,366
Montreal	2,318	—	4,386	320	3,422	5,097	4,080
Moscow	6,663	4,386	—	4,665	1,544	7,175	1,474
New York	2,094	320	4,665	—	3,624	4,817	4,281
Paris	5,716	3,422	1,544	3,624	—	5,699	697
Rio de Janeiro	4,771	5,097	7,175	4,817	5,699	—	5,684
Rome	6,366	4,080	1,474	4,281	697	5,684	—
San Francisco	1,887	2,539	5,871	2,571	5,558	6,621	6,240
Shanghai, China	8,022	7,053	4,235	7,371	5,754	11,336	5,677
Stockholm	5,959	3,667	762	3,924	958	6,651	1,234
Sydney, Australia	8,052	9,954	9,012	9,933	10,544	8,306	10,136
Tokyo	7,021	6,383	4,647	6,740	6,034	11,533	6,135
Warsaw	6,365	4,009	715	4,344	849	6,467	817
Washington, D.C.	1,887	488	4,858	205	3,829	4,796	4,434

Cities	San Francisco	Shanghai	Stockholm	Sydney	Tokyo	Moscow	Washington
Berlin	5,661	5,218	504	10,006	5,540	320	4,169
Buenos Aires	6,467	12,201	7,808	7,330	11,408	7,662	5,218
Cairo	7,364	5,183	2,111	8,952	5,935	1,630	5,800
Calcutta	7,814	2,117	4,195	5,685	3,194	4,048	8,084
Cape Town, South Africa	10,247	8,061	6,444	6,843	9,156	5,958	7,901
Caracas, Venezuela	3,904	9,501	5,420	9,513	8,799	5,517	2,059
Chicago	1,858	7,061	4,278	9,272	6,299	4,667	597
Hong Kong	6,897	764	5,113	4,584	1,794	5,144	8,147
Honolulu	2,393	4,941	6,862	4,943	3,853	7,355	4,519
Istanbul	6,703	4,962	1,348	9,294	5,560	863	5,215
Lisbon	5,666	6,654	1,856	11,302	6,915	1,715	3,562
London	5,357	5,715	890	10,564	5,940	899	3,663
Los Angeles	347	6,438	5,454	7,530	5,433	5,922	2,300
Manila	6,967	1,150	5,797	3,944	1,866	5,837	8,562
Mexico City	1,887	8,022	5,959	8,052	7,021	6,365	1,887
Montreal	2,539	7,053	3,667	9,954	6,383	4,009	488
Moscow	5,871	4,235	762	9,012	4,647	715	4,858
New York	2,571	7,371	3,924	9,933	6,740	849	205
Paris	5,558	5,754	958	10,544	6,034	849	3,829
Rio de Janeiro	6,621	11,336	6,651	8,306	11,533	6,467	4,796
Rome	6,240	5,677	1,234	10,136	6,135	817	4,434
San Francisco	—	6,140	5,361	7,416	5,135	5,841	2,442
Shanghai, China	6,140	—	4,825	4,899	1,097	4,951	7,448
Stockholm	5,361	4,825	—	9,696	5,051	501	4,123
Sydney, Australia	7,416	4,899	9,696	—	4,866	9,696	9,758
Tokyo	5,135	1,097	5,051	4,866	—	5,249	6,772
Warsaw	5,841	4,951	501	9,696	5,249	—	4,457
Washington, D.C.	2,442	7,448	4,123	9,758	6,772	4,457	—

Source: Encyclopaedia Britannica.

MILITARY & VETERAN'S AFFAIRS

Active Military Duty Personnel, 1940–1995[1]

As of September 30, 1995, there were 1,518,224 active duty military personnel. This is a decrease of 92,226 (7,781 officers; 84,311 enlisted; and 174 cadets and midshipmen) from the FY 1994 figure. The "U.S., Territories, and Special Locations" region accounted for 43,736 of the total force reduction. For the last five years, the officer/enlisted ratio has been between 5.3 and 6.0. The largest decrease of officer personnel was in the Captain-Lieutenant category, while the largest decrease among enlisted personnel was in pay grade E-5. The number of female officers, cadets, and enlisted personnel showed a decrease of 3,572 from the FY 1994 figure, but the percentage of female active duty military personnel actually rose from 12.4 to 12.9 percent.

Year	Army[2]	Air Force[2, 3]	Navy	Marine Corps	Total
1940	269,023		160,997	28,345	458,365
1945	8,266,373		3,319,586	469,925	12,055,884
1950	593,167	411,277	380,739	74,279	1,459,462
1955	1,109,296	959,946	660,695	205,170	2,935,107
1960	873,078	814,752	616,987	170,621	2,475,438
1965	969,066	824,662	669,985	190,213	2,653,926
1970	1,322,548	791,349	691,126	259,737	3,064,760
1975	784,333	612,751	535,085	195,951	2,128,120
1980	777,036	557,969	527,153	188,469	2,050,627
1985	780,787	601,515	570,705	198,025	2,151,032
1990	732,403	535,233	579,417	196,652	2,043,705
1991	710,821	510,432	570,262	194,040	1,985,555
1992	610,450	470,315	541,883	184,529	1,807,177
1993	572,423	444,351	509,950	178,379	1,705,103
1994	541,343	426,327	468,662	174,158	1,610,490
1995	508,559	400,409	434,617	174,639	1,518,224

1. Military personnel on extended or continuous active duty. Excludes reserves on active duty for training. Prior year totals have been corrected. 2. Represents "Command Strength" prior to June 30, 1956. 3. Army Air Forces and its predecessors for period prior to September 18, 1947. *Source:* Department of Defense.

Female Military Personnel on Active Duty

Year	Army	% of all personnel	Air Force	% of all personnel	Navy	% of all personnel	Marine Corps	% of all personnel	Total	% of all personnel
1970	16,724	1.3	13,654	1.7	8,683	1.3	2,418	0.9	41,479	1.4
1980	69,338	8.9	60,394	10.8	34,980	6.6	6,706	3.6	171,418	8.4
1985	79,247	3.7	70,061	11.6	52,603	9.2	9,695	4.9	211,606	9.8
1989	86,494	n/a	77,103	n/a	59,518	n/a	9,708	n/a	232,823	n/a
1990	83,621	11.4	74,134	13.9	59,907	10.3	9,356	4.8	227,018	11.1
1991	80,306	11.3	72,436	14.2	59,391	10.4	9,005	4.6	221,138	11.1
1992	73,430	12.0	68,789	14.6	59,305	10.9	8,524	4.6	210,048	11.6
1993	71,328	12.5	66,732	15.0	57,601	11.3	7,845	4.4	203,506	11.9
1994	69,878	12.9	66,314	15.6	55,825	11.9	7,671	4.4	199,688	12.4
1995	68,046	13.4	64,147	16.0	55,830	12.8	8,093	4.6	196,116	12.9

Data as of September 30th.

Female Military Personnel on Active Duty by Grade

Rank/Grade	Army	Air Force	Navy	Marine Corps	Total DoD
Total officers	10,786	12,068	7,899	690	31,443
Total enlisted	56,776	51,478	47,347	7,403	163,004
Cadets & midshipmen	484	601	584[1]	—	1,669
Grand total	68,046	64,147	55,830	8,093	196,116

1. Excludes other naval officer candidates. Date as of September 30, 1995.

U.S. Military Pay Grades

Source: U.S. Department of Defense

Pay Grade	Army	Navy	Marines	Air Force
COMMISSIONED OFFICERS				
O–1	Second Lieutenant	Ensign	Second Lieutenant	Second Lieutenant
O–2	First Lieutenant	Lieutenant Junior Grade	First Lieutenant	First Lieutenant
O–3	Captain	Lieutenant	Captain	Captain
O–4	Major	Lieutenant Commander	Major	Major
O–5	Lieutenant Colonel	Commander	Lieutenant Colonel	Lieutenant Colonel
O–6	Colonel	Captain	Colonel	Colonel
O–7	Brigadier General	Commodore	Brigadier General	Brigadier General
O–8	Major General	Rear Admiral	Major General	Major General
O–9	Lieutenant General	Vice Admiral	Lieutenant General	Lieutenant General
O–10	General	Admiral	General	General
Special grades[1] (5 stars)	General of The Army	Fleet Admiral	(none)	General of The Air Force

WARRANT OFFICERS (ALL SERVICES)

W–1   Warrant Officer. Grades W–2 to W–5 Chief Warrant Officer

Pay Grade	Army	Navy	Marines	Air Force
ENLISTED PERSONNEL				
E–1	Private	Seaman Recruit	Private	Airman Basic
E–2	Private	Seaman Apprentice	Private First Class	Airman
E–3	Private First Class	Seaman	Lance Corporal	Airman First Class
E–4	Corporal Specialist 4	Petty Officer, Third Class	Corporal	Sergeant Senior Airman
E–5	Sergeant Specialist 5	Petty Officer, Second Class	Sergeant	Staff Sergeant
E–6	Staff Sergeant Specialist 6	Petty Officer, First Class	Staff Sergeant	Technical Sergeant
E–7	Sergeant First Class Specialist 7	Chief Petty Officer	Gunnery Sergeant	Master Sergeant
E–8	First Sergeant Master Sergeant	Senior Chief Petty Officer	First Sergeant Master Sergeant	Senior Master Sergeant
E–9	Command Sergeant Major Sergeant Major	Master Chief Petty Officer	Sergeant Major Master Gunnery Sergeant	Chief Master Sergeant
Special grades[2]	Sergeant Major of the Army	Master Chief Petty Officer of the Navy	Sergeant Major of the Marine Corps	Chief Master Sergeant of the Air Force

1. There are no living 5-star commissioned officers. 2. Senior enlisted advisors. There is only one for each branch of service.

Monthly Basic Pay Rates by Grade Effective 1996

Grade	< 2	2	4	6	10	14	16	18	20	26
					Years of Service					
COMMISSIONED OFFICERS										
O–10	7,145.70	7,397.10	7,397.10	7,397.10	7,681.20	8,106.60	8,686.50	8,686.50	9,268.20	9,845.40
O–9	6,333.00	6,498.90	6,637.50	6,637.50	6,806.10	7,089.30	7,681.20	7,681.20	8,106.60	8,686.50
O–8	5,736.00	5,908.20	6,048.30	6,048.30	6,498.90	6,806.10	7,089.30	7,397.10	7,681.20	7,870.50
O–7	4,766.10	5,090.40	5,090.40	5,318.70	5,626.80	5,908.20	6,498.90	6,945.90	6,945.90	6,945.90
O–6	3,532.50	3,881.10	4,135.50	4,135.50	4,135.50	4,276.20	4,952.40	5,205.00	5,318.70	6,102.60
O–5	2,825.40	3,317.40	3,546.90	3,546.90	3,654.00	4,109.10	4,416.60	4,669.50	4,811.40	4,979.40
O–4	2,381.40	2,900.10	3,093.60	3,150.90	3,514.50	3,881.10	4,051.80	4,163.10	4,163.10	4,163.10
O–3	2,213.10	2,474.40	2,926.80	3,066.90	3,348.90	3,600.60	3,600.60	3,600.60	3,600.60	3,600.60
O–2	1,929.90	2,107.50	2,617.20	2,671.50	2,671.50	2,671.50	2,671.50	2,671.50	2,671.50	2,671.50
O–1	1,675.50	1,743.90	2,107.50	2,107.50	2,107.50	2,107.50	2,107.50	2,107.50	2,107.50	2,107.50
WARRANT OFFICERS										
W–5	0.00	0.00	0.00	0.00	0.00	0.00	0.00	0.00	3,848.10	4,282.50
W–4	2,254.80	2,419.20	2,474.40	2,586.90	2,814.30	3,150.90	3,261.60	3,348.90	3,456.90	3,851.10
W–3	2,049.30	2,223.00	2,251.80	2,277.90	2,586.90	2,756.10	3,838.60	2,926.80	3,041.10	3,261.60
W–2	1,794.90	1,941.90	1,998.30	2,107.50	2,307.30	2,474.40	2,561.40	2,645.40	2,728.50	2,838.60
W–1	1,495.20	1,714.50	1,857.60	1,941.90	2,107.50	2,277.90	2,362.80	2,444.70	2,532.30	2,532.30

Grade	< 2	2	4	6	10	14	16	18	20	26
					Years of Service					

ENLISTED MEMBERS

Grade	< 2	2	4	6	10	14	16	18	20	26
E–9	0.00	0.00	0.00	0.00	2,623.20	2,742.60	2,805.60	2,868.60	2,924.10	3,377.10
E–8	0.00	0.00	0.00	0.00	2,262.90	2,382.60	2,445.60	2,501.40	2,562.90	3,015.90
E–7	1,535.70	1,658.10	1,779.60	1,840.20	1,959.60	2,112.00	2,172.00	2,232.00	2,261.40	2,713.50
E–6	1,321.20	1,440.30	1,563.90	1,622.70	1,742.70	1,890.00	1,950.90	1,980.60	1,980.60	1,980.60
E–5	1,159.50	1,262.10	1,380.90	1,471.80	1,592.10	1,680.90	1,680.90	1,680.90	1,680.90	1,680.90
E–4	1,081.20	1,142.10	1,302.60	1,354.20	1,354.20	1,354.20	1,354.20	1,354.20	1,354.20	1,354.20
E–3	1,019.10	1,074.90	1,161.90	1,161.90	1,161.90	1,161.90	1,161.90	1,161.90	1,161.90	1,161.90
E–2	980.70	980.70	980.70	980.70	980.70	980.70	980.70	980.70	980.70	980.70
E–1>4	874.80	874.80	874.80	874.80	874.80	874.80	874.80	874.80	874.80	874.80

NOTE: E–1 with less than 4 months: $809.10. Basic allowance for quarters ranges from $193.50 per month for an enlisted E–1 with no dependents and less than 4 months service and up to $970.50 per month for an officer with dependents in grade O–10.

Service Academies

U.S. Military Academy

Source: U.S. Military Academy.

Established in 1802 by an act of Congress, the U.S. Military Academy is located on the west bank of the Hudson River some 50 miles north of New York City. To gain admission a candidate must first secure a nomination from an authorized source. These sources are:

Congressional Sources

Representatives
Senators
Other: Vice Presidential
District of Columbia
Puerto Rico
Am. Samoa, Guam, Virgin Is.

Military-Service-Connected Sources

Presidential—Sons or daughters of active duty or retired service members
Enlisted members of Army
Enlisted members of Army Reserve/
  National Guard
Sons and daughters of deceased and disabled veterans
Honor military, naval schools
  and ROTC
Sons and daughters of persons awarded the
  Medal of Honor

Any number of applicants can meet the requirements for a *nomination* in these categories. *Appointments* (offers of admission), however, can only be made to a much smaller number, about 1,200 each year.

Candidates may be nominated for vacancies during the year preceding the day of admission, which occurs in late June or early July. The best time to apply is during the junior year in high school.

Candidates must be citizens of the U.S., be unmarried, be at least 17 but not yet 22 years old on July 1 of the year admitted, have a secondary-school education or its equivalent, and be able to meet the academic, medical, and physical aptitude requirements. Academic qualification is determined by an analysis of entire scholastic record, and performance on either the American College Testing (ACT) Assessment Program Test or the College Entrance Examination Board Scholastic Assessment Tests (SAT). Entrance requirements and procedures for appointment are described in the Admissions Bulletin and the Admissions Prospectus, available without charge from Admissions, U.S. Military Academy, West Point, N.Y. 10996-1797. Telephone: (914) 938-4041.

Cadets are members of the U.S. Army. As such they receive annual salaries from which they pay for their uniforms, textbooks, and incidental expenses. There is no tuition and room and board are provided. Upon successful completion of the four-year course, the graduate receives the degree of Bachelor of Science and is commissioned a second lieutenant in the U.S. Army with a requirement to serve as an officer for a minimum of five years.

U.S. Naval Academy

Source: U.S. Naval Academy.

The Naval School, established in 1845 at Fort Severn, Annapolis, Md., was renamed the U.S. Naval Academy in 1850. A four-year course was adopted a year later. The "Yard" as the campus is referred to, blends French Renaissance and modern architecture with many new academic, athletics, and laboratory facilities.

The Superintendent is a Navy admiral. A civilian academic dean heads the academic program. A captain heads the 4,000 members of the Brigade of Midshipmen and military, professional, and physical training. The faculty is half military and half civilian, with 650 members; 95% of the civilian faculty hold PhD's. The faculty-student ratio at 1:7 is one of the lowest in the nation and provides for classes that rarely exceed seventeen.

Eighteen majors are offered, including chemistry, math, computer science, economics, general engineering, history, English, ocean engineering, aerospace engineering, electrical engineering, oceanography, political science, mechanical engineering, marine engineering, physics, and naval architecture. Graduates are awarded the Bachelor of Science or Bachelor of Science in Engineering and are commissioned as officers in the U.S. Navy or Marine Corps.

To have basic eligibility for admission, candidates must be citizens of the U.S., of good moral character, at least 17 and not more than 22 years of age on July 1 of their entering year, unmarried, not pregnant, and without legal obligation for dependents.

The Admissions Board at the Naval Academy examines each candidate's school record, College Board or ACT scores, recommendations from school officials, extracurricular activities, and evidence from other sources concerning his or her character, leadership potential, academic preparation, and physical fitness. Qualification for admission is based on all of the above factors.

Tuition, board, lodging, and medical and dental care are provided. Midshipmen receive over $540 a month for books, uniforms, and personal needs.

For general information or answers to specific questions, write: Director of Candidate Guidance, U.S. Naval Academy, Annapolis, Md. 21402-5018, or call 1-800-638-9156.

U.S. Air Force Academy

Source: U.S. Air Force Academy.

The bill establishing the Air Force Academy was signed by President Eisenhower on April 1, 1954. The first class of 306 cadets was sworn in on July 11, 1955, at Lowry Air Force Base, Denver, the Academy's temporary location. The Cadet Wing moved into the Academy's permanent home north of Colorado Springs, Colorado, in 1958.

Cadets receive four years of academic, military, and physical education to prepare them for leadership as officers in the Air Force. The Academy is authorized a total of 4,000 cadets. Each new class averages 1,000. The candidates for the Academy must be at least 17 and not have passed their 22nd birthday on July 1 of the year for which they enter the Academy, must be a United States citizen, never married, and be able to meet the mental and physical requirements. International students authorized admission are exempt from the U.S. citizenship requirement. A candidate is required to take the following examinations and tests: (1) the Service Academies' Qualifying Medical Examination; (2) either the American College Testing (ACT) Assessment Program test or the College Entrance Examination Board Scholastic Aptitude Test (SAT); and (3) a Candidate Fitness Test.

Cadets receive their entire education at government expense and, in addition, are paid more than $540 per month base pay. From this sum, they pay for their uniforms, textbooks, tailoring, laundry, entertainment tickets, etc. Upon completion of the four-year program, leading to a Bachelor of Science degree, a cadet who meets the qualifications is commissioned a second lieutenant in the U.S. Air Force. For details on admissions, write: HQ USAFA/RRS, 2304 Cadet Drive, Suite 200, USAF Academy, CO 80840-5025.

U.S. Coast Guard Academy

Source: U.S. Coast Guard Academy.

The U.S. Coast Guard Academy is the only one of the four Armed Forces service academies that offers appointments based solely on the basis of an annual nationwide competition, with no congressional appointments or geographical quotas. Competition is open to all American citizens who have reached their seventeenth but not their twenty-second birthday by July 1 of the entering year.

In selecting students for admission, the Academy prohibits discrimination based on gender, race, color, national origin, or religion. Factors considered in the competition include SAT I or ACT scores, high school standing, and leadership potential as demonstrated by participation in high school extracurricular activities, community affairs, or part-time employment. All candidates must pass a rigid medical and physical fitness examination.

A viewbook or video can be obtained by writing to: Director of Admission, U.S. Coast Guard Academy, 15 Mohegan Avenue, New London, CT 06320, or by calling 1-800-883-8724.

U.S. Merchant Marine Academy

Source: U.S. Merchant Marine Academy.

The U.S. Merchant Marine Academy, situated at Kings Point, N.Y., on the north shore of Long Island, was dedicated Sept. 30, 1943. It is maintained by the Department of Transportation under direction of the Maritime Administration.

The Academy has a complement of approximately 950 men and women representing every state, D.C., the Canal Zone, Puerto Rico, Guam, American Samoa, and the Virgin Islands. It is also authorized to admit up to 12 candidates from the Western Hemisphere and 30 other foreign students at any one time.

Candidates are nominated by Senators and members of the House of Representatives. Nominations to the Academy are governed by a state and territory quota system based on population and the results of the College Entrance Examination Board tests.

A candidate must be a citizen not less than 17 and not yet 22 years of age by July 1 of the year in which admission is sought. Fifteen high school credits, including 3 units in mathematics (from algebra, geometry and/or trigonometry), 1 unit in science (physics or chemistry) and 3 in English are required.

The course is four years and includes one year of practical training aboard a merchant ship. Study includes marine engineering, navigation, satellite navigation and communications, electricity, ship construction, naval science and tactics, economics, business, languages, history, etc.

Upon completion of the course of study, a graduate receives a Bachelor of Science degree, a license as a merchant marine deck or engineering officer, and a commission as an Ensign in the Naval Reserve. □

Gays in the Military

Pentagon policy allows gay men and lesbians to serve in the armed forces as long as they do not engage in homosexual acts. They can privately acknowledge their homosexual feelings to another person provided they are not engaging in homosexual behavior. Under these somewhat ambiguous rules, holding hands, even off duty, could constitute evidence that such behavior was occurring. However, reading gay publications, displaying same-sex pictures, visiting a gay bar, and marching in a gay-rights parade are permissible.

Hostile treatment of or violence to gay or lesbian service personnel will not be tolerated. □

U.S. Casualties in Major Wars

War	Branch of service	Numbers engaged	Battle deaths	Other deaths	Total deaths	Wounds not mortal	Total casualties[1]
Revolutionary War	Army	n.a.	4,044	n.a.	n.a.	6,004	n.a.
1775 to 1783	Navy	n.a.	342	n.a.	n.a.	114	n.a.
	Marines	n.a.	49	n.a.	n.a.	70	n.a.
	Total	**n.a.**	**4,435**	**n.a.**	**n.a.**	**6,188**	**n.a.**
War of 1812	Army	n.a.	1,950	n.a.	n.a.	4,000	n.a.
1812 to 1815	Navy	n.a.	265	n.a.	n.a.	439	n.a.
	Marines	n.a.	45	n.a.	n.a.	66	n.a.
	Total	**286,730**	**2,260**	**n.a.**	**n.a.**	**4,505**	**n.a.**
Mexican War	Army	n.a.	1,721	11,550	13,271	4,102	17,373
1846 to 1848	Navy	n.a.	1	n.a.	n.a.	3	n.a.
	Marines	n.a.	11	n.a.	n.a.	47	n.a.
	Total	**78,718**	**1,733**	**n.a.**	**n.a.**	**4,152**	**n.a.**
Civil War[2]	Army	2,128,948	138,154	221,374	359,528	280,040	639,568
1861 to 1865	Navy	84,415	2,112	2,411	4,523	1,710	6,233
	Marines		148	312	460	131	591
	Total	**2,213,363**	**140,414**	**224,097**	**364,511**	**281,881**	**646,392**
Spanish-American War	Army	280,564	369	2,061	2,430	1,594	4,024
1898	Navy	22,875	10	0	10	47	57
	Marines	3,321	6	0	6	21	27
	Total	**306,760**	**385**	**2,061**	**2,446**	**1,662**	**4,108**
World War I	Army	4,057,101	50,510	55,868	106,378	193,663	300,041
1917 to 1918	Navy	599,051	431	6,856	7,287	819	8,106
	Marines	78,839	2,461	390	2,851	9,520	12,371
	Total	**4,734,991**	**53,402**	**63,114**	**116,516**	**204,002**	**320,518**
World War II	Army[3]	11,260,000	234,874	83,400	318,274	565,861	884,135
1941 to 1946	Navy	4,183,466	36,950	25,664	62,614	37,778	100,392
	Marines	669,100	19,733	4,778	24,511	67,207	91,718
	Total	**16,112,566**	**291,557**	**113,842**	**405,399**	**670,846**	**1,076,245**
Korean War	Army	2,834,000	27,704	9,429	37,133	77,596	114,729
1950 to 1953	Navy	1,177,000	458	4,043	4,501	1,576	6,077
	Marine	424,000	4,267	1,261	5,528	23,744	29,272
	Air Force	1,285,000	1,200	5,884	7,084	368	7,452
	Total	**5,720,000**	**33,629**	**20,617**	**54,246**	**103,284**	**157,530**
War in Southeast Asia[4]	Army	4,368,000	30,914	7,275	38,189	96,802	134,991
	Navy	1,842,000	1,631	928	2,559	4,178	6,737
	Marines	794,000	13,082	1,754	14,836	51,392	66,228
	Air Force	1,740,000	1,739	844	2,583	931	3,514
	Total	**8,744,000**	**47,366**	**10,801**	**58,167**	**153,303**	**211,470**

1. Excludes captured or interned and missing in action who were subsequently returned to military control. 2. Union forces only. Totals should probably be somewhat larger as data or disposition of prisoners are far from complete. Final Confederate deaths, based on incomplete returns, were 133,821, to which should be added 26,000–31,000 personnel who died in Union prisons. 178,975 blacks served in the Union Army. 2,894 were killed in battle or mortally wounded, 33,953 died from other causes including 29,658 deaths from disease. 3. Army data include Air Force. 4. Vietnam figures provided by the U.S. Center of Military History, Reference Division, Washington, D.C., February 1994. Navy figures exclude Coast Guard of which there were 5 battle deaths. NOTE: All data are subject to revision. For wars before World War I, information represents best data from available records. However, due to incomplete records and possible difference in usage of terminology, reporting systems, etc., figures should be considered estimates. n.a. = not available. *Source:* Department of Defense.

Friendly Fire: The Curse of Battles

During the Gulf War, 35 Americans were killed and 72 wounded by their own forces. It is hard for those without military experience to understand how these accidents, termed "friendly fire," can occur. Combat is not a normal experience for those involved in it and it induces a heightened sense of danger that can play tricks on one's mind. Today's use of high-tech weapons in battle with their awesome destructiveness compounds the tragedies.

During Operation Desert Storm, the troops were fighting in a sweeping, fast-moving battle, much of it at night, in inclement weather, and with poor visibili-ty, which gave rise to misidentification of friend and foe.

One military historian believes that thousands of U.S. casualties in WWII were the result of Americans firing on their own troops. The same accidental deaths occurred during the fighting in Korea, Vietnam, and even Grenada.

Military service is a hazardous occupation and hundreds of accidental deaths occur each year in peacetime. Other people who work in life-threatening occupations such as police work also fall victim to friendly fire. □

The National Guard

Source: Departments of the Army and the Air Force, National Guard Bureau.

The National Guard is unique among the United States reserve military forces, filling both federal and state missions. In peacetime, the National Guard is commanded by the governors of the states and territories and may be called to state active duty by the governor in response to natural disasters, civil disturbances, or other state emergencies. During a war or national emergency, the National Guard may be called to active duty by the President or Congress, and serves as the primary source of augmentation for the active Army and active Air Force.

The men and women of the National Guard are described as citizen soldiers and airmen. They have full-time civilian careers, but, each month they meet with their unit for military training. National Guard members receive the same training, use the same equipment, and wear the same uniform as their active duty counterparts.

The foundation for the National Guard's dual state and federal mission can be traced to the earliest militias of the 13 original colonies. The oldest units were organized in the Massachusetts Bay Colony in 1636, and have been in continuous existence ever since. Framers of the U.S. Constitution provided for the continuation of the militia, a principle that has been further developed through subsequent legislation.

From its colonial beginnings, the militia system has evolved into today's Army National Guard and Air National Guard, our nation's community-based defense force of modern military units that serve their respective states and are part of the nation's overall military forces. In addition to countless call-ups for state duty, the National Guard has fought in every American war, from the Pequot War in 1637 to Operation DESERT STORM in which 75,000 members of the National Guard volunteered or were called to active duty.

As a reserve component of the U.S. military, the National Guard makes up a significant part of what is called the Total Force—active duty service members, the reserve components, and the civilians who are employed by the Department of Defense. The other federal reserve components include the Army Reserve, Naval Reserve, Marine Corps Reserve, Air Force Reserve, and Coast Guard Reserve. Members in all of these organizations are trained and equipped in units which are available for full-time duty in case of war or national emergency. However, the other federal reserve components of the military services, unlike the National Guard, are legally and operationally linked only to the active duty services, not the states. This distinction of having both federal and state missions makes the National Guard unique.

The Army National Guard is made up of more than 3,360 units located in 2,200 communities throughout the 50 states, Puerto Rico, Guam, the Virgin Islands, and the District of Columbia. The U.S. Army's largest reserve force, the Army National Guard provides roughly 55 percent of the Army's total combat capability, and approximately 35% of its combat support and 35% of its combat service support units. Units are provided modern military equipment including M-1 tanks, Bradley Fighting Vehicles, and Blackhawk helicopters.

The Air National Guard has 88 flying units and 1,500 support units at 200 locations. This represents approximately one-third of the U.S. Air Force's fighter and air transport assets. Air National Guard units fly F-16 fighters, KC-135 tankers, B–1B bombers, and C-130 transports, among other aircraft.

As part of the nation's total military force, Army and Air National Guard units are trained and equipped to mesh with active duty and other federal reserve component forces. Typically, members of the National Guard report for training duty one weekend per month, along with a minimum of 15 days of continuous unit training each year. Weekend training usually is performed at the unit's community armory or nearby military training facility. The annual training usually is performed at a large military training base or overseas location, frequently in cooperation with active duty and other reserve units. In recent years, Army National Guard units have trained in more than 30 nations, including locations in Central America, Europe, Asia, and Africa. Air National Guard units train with active Air Force and Air Force Reserve units on a regular basis at worldwide locations.

Approximately one-half of the National Guard's members join their units with no previous military experience. They complete basic military training and a technical school at an active duty training base and then return to their unit. The balance of the National Guard's membership consists of personnel who have had prior active duty in any U.S. military service.

National Guard members receive a full day's pay at their military rank for each unit training assembly they attend, for the 15 days of annual training, and for any military school or special assignment they may complete. All such training counts toward retirement. A member who has 20 or more years of qualifying military service begins to collect retired pay at age 60.

The National Guard offers its members a broad range of educational opportunities beyond the training and on-the-job experiences they receive for their military specialties. These benefits include participation in the Montgomery GI Bill and additional enlistment incentives for select military career fields. Members of the National Guard have access to active duty military shopping centers in addition to participation in many other active duty military benefit programs. Many states offer additional benefits and civilian educational incentives.

For 1996, the mission strength of the Army National Guard was 373,000, and the Air National Guard 112,400. The 1996 federal budget for the Army National Guard was $5.8 billion, the Air National Guard $4.0 billion. States and territories provide additional funds to support state missions, recruiting and training administration, armory construction, and funding for state-salaried employees.

Additional information about the National Guard may be obtained from local units or from the National Guard Bureau, 2500 Army Pentagon, Washington, D.C. 20310-2500.

Veterans' Benefits

Veterans have been provided for by the individual states and the federal government since Colonial days. In 1944, Federal benefits for veterans were broadened in scope and value under the G.I. Bill. On March 15, 1989, the Veterans Administration, the federal agency that administers benefits for veterans, became the Department of Veterans Affairs.

The following benefits available to veterans generally require certain minimum periods of active duty during qualifying periods of service. Certain types of discharges are subject to special adjudication to determine eligibility.

For information or assistance in applying for veterans benefits, write, call, or visit a VA Regional Office. Consult your local telephone directory under United States Government, Department of Veterans Affairs (VA) for the address and telephone number. Toll-free telephone service is available in all 50 States: 1-800-827-1000.

Unemployment allowances. Veterans are provided special job referral assistance through state employment agencies. Disabled veterans are provided a full range of assistance, including training, education, and placement by VA.

Loan Guaranty. VA will guarantee loans to buy or build a home; to purchase a manufactured home with or without a lot; and to refinance a home presently owned and occupied by the veteran. VA will guarantee the lender against loss of between 40% and 50% on loans of $22,500 to $144,000, and 25% on loans of more than $144,000. On manufactured home loans, the amount of the guarantee is 40% of the loan to a maximum of $20,000.

Disability compensation. Veterans with permanent service-connected disabilities are provided from $91 to $1,823 per month, depending upon the extent of disability. For special conditions, additional payments may be paid, plus allowances for dependents, up to $240 per month, when the disability is 30 percent or more.

Vocational Rehabilitation. VA provides professional counseling, training, and other assistance to help service-disabled veterans, rated 10 percent or more who have an employment handicap, to achieve maximum independence in daily living and, to the extent possible, to obtain and maintain suitable employment. Generally, a veteran may receive up to 48 months of this assistance within 12 years from the date he or she is notified of entitlement to VA compensation. All the expenses of a veteran's rehabilitation program are paid by VA. In addition, the veteran receives a subsistence allowance which varies based on the rate of training and number of dependents. For example, a single veteran training full time would receive $385.80 monthly.

Vocational Training for VA Pension Recipients. Veterans who are awarded pension before December 31, 1995, may participate in a program of vocational training similar to that provided in VA's vocational rehabilitation program. A veteran continues to receive pension while receiving training.

Medical and dental care. Free medical care may be provided in VA and, in certain instances, in non-VA, or other federal hospitals to disabled and low-income veterans. This includes outpatient treatment at a VA field facility or, in some cases, by an approved private physician or dentist. Full domiciliary care also may be provided to veterans with low incomes. Nursing home care may be provided at certain VA medical facilities or in approved private nursing homes. Hospital and other medical care may also be provided for the spouse and child dependents of a veteran who is permanently and totally disabled due to a service-connected disability; or for survivors of a veteran who dies from a service-connected disability; or for survivors of a veteran who at the time of death had a total disability, permanent in nature, resulting from a service-connected disability. Dependent treatment is usually provided in nonfederal facilities. Veterans must agree to make a copayment for the care they receive from VA if their incomes exceed levels that vary with number of dependents and they do not have a service-connected disability or service in certain early war periods. Veterans and/or their dependents or survivors should apply in advance. Contact the nearest VA medical facility for eligibility.

Readjustment Counseling. VA provides readjustment counseling to veterans of the Vietnam Era or the war or conflict zones of Lebanon, Grenada, Panama, or the Somalia or Persian Gulf theaters in need of assistance in resolving post-war readjustment problems in the areas of family, education, and personal readjustment including post-traumatic stress disorder. Services are provided at community-based Vet Centers and at VA Medical Centers. Services include individual, family and group counseling, employment and educational counseling, and assistance in obtaining referrals to various governmental and nongovernmental agencies. Contact the nearest Vet Center or VA facility.

Dependents compensation. Payments are made to surviving dependents of veterans who died while on active duty or, after discharge, of a service-connected injury or disease. Beginning January 1, 1993, all surviving spouses of veterans who died on or after that date will receive at least $810 a month. An additional $177 per month is added if the deceased veteran was 100 percent disabled for eight years before death Parents and children may be eligible for additional payments.

Dependents' educational assistance. VA pays a maximum of $404 per month for up to 45 months of schooling to spouses and children of veterans who died of service-connected causes or who were permanently and totally disabled from service-connected causes or died while permanently and totally disabled or who are currently missing in action, captured in the line of duty, or forcibly detained or interned in line of duty by a foreign power for more than 90 days.

Montgomery GI Bill. This Act provides education benefits for individuals entering the military after June 30, 1985. Servicepersons entering active duty after that date will have their basic pay reduced by $100 per month for the first 12 months of their service, unless they specifically elect not to participate in the program.

Active duty for three years (two years, if the initial obligated period of active duty is less than three years), or two years active duty plus four years in the Selected Reserve or National Guard will entitle an individual to $416.62 per month basic benefits for 36 months. Those who enlist for less than three years will receive $338.51 per month for 36 months. VA pays an additional amount, commonly called a "kicker," if directed by the Defense Department.

An educational entitlement program is also available for members of the Selected Reserve. Eligibility applies to individuals who, after June 30, 1985 enlist, re-enlist, or extend an enlistment for a six-year period. Benefits may be paid to eligible members of the Selected Reserve who complete their initial period of active duty training. Full-time payments are $197.90 per month for 36 months.

Pensions. Pension benefits ranging from $8,246 per year for a single veteran may be payable to wartime veterans permanently and totally disabled from non-service-connected causes. These benefits are based on need. Surviving spouses and children of wartime veterans are eligible for Nonservice-Connected Death Pensions that range from $5,527 per year, based on the veteran's honorable wartime service and level of need.

Insurance. The VA life insurance programs have approximately 5.5 million policyholders with total coverage of about $490.1 billion. Detailed information on veterans insurance may be obtained by calling 1-800-669-8477.

Burial benefits. Burial is provided in any VA national cemetery with available grave space to deceased veterans who were discharged under conditions other than dishonorable. Also eligible for burial in a national cemetery are the veteran's spouse, widow, widower, minor children, and, under certain conditions, unmarried adult children. Arlington Cemetery is administered by the Army and has different eligibility requirements.

Headstone or marker. A government headstone or marker is furnished for the grave of a veteran anywhere in the world who was discharged under conditions other than dishonorable and is interred in a national, state veterans', military, or private cemetery. VA also will furnish markers to veterans' eligible dependents interred in a national, military, or state veterans' cemetery. To apply, write to NCS, Department of Veterans Affairs, Washington, D.C. 20420.

Military Personnel on Active Duty in Selected Foreign Countries, 1995

(as of end of fiscal year)

Country	1995	Country	1995	Country	1995
In foreign countries	238,064	Egypt	1,123	Nicaragua	16
Ashore	208,836	El Salvador	25	Nigeria	15
Afloat	29,288	Ethiopia	8	Norway	57
Albania	4	Finland	14	Oman	27
Antarctica	24	France	67	Pakistan	28
Antigua	41	Germany	73,280	Panama	7,727
Argentina	26	Greece	489	Paraguay	12
Australia	314	Greenland	131	Peru	26
Austria	35	Guatemala	18	Philippines	126
Bahamas, The	36	Haiti	1,616	Poland	16
Bahrain	618	Honduras	193	Portugal	1,066
Bangladesh	9	Hong Kong	28	Romania	12
Barbados	12	Hungary	16	Russia	60
Belgium	1,689	Iceland	1,982	Saudi Arabia	1,077
Bolivia	29	India	27	Senegal	13
Brazil	50	Indonesia	46	Singapore	166
Bulgaria	11	Israel	46	Somalia	419
Burma	9	Italy	12,007	South Africa	24
Cameroon	9	Jamaica	13	Spain	2,799
Canada	214	Japan	39,134	Sri Lanka	8
Chile	28	Jordan	24	Sudan	7
China	30	Kenya	40	Sweden	14
Colombia	44	Korea, South	36,016	Switzerland	26
Costa Rica	12	Kuwait	771	Syria	8
Cote D'Ivoire	33	Liberia	10	Thailand	99
Croatia	10	Macedonia[1]	591	Tunisia	20
Cuba (Guantanamo)	5,129	Malaysia	35	Turkey	3,111
Cyprus	24	Mexico	36	United arab Emirates	30
Czech Republic	8	Morocco	22	United Kingdom	12,131
Denmark	37	Nepal	7	Uruguay	14
Diego Garcia	897	Netherlands	687	Venezuela	35
Dominican Republic	13	New Zealand	51	Zimbabwe	8
Ecuador	86				

1. Macedonia, Former Republic of Yugoslavia. *Source:* Department of Defense, *Selected Manpower Statistics,* Fiscal Year 1995.

Highest Ranking Officers in U.S. History

GENERAL AND COMMANDER-IN-CHIEF[1]

George Washington (1739–1799), b. Westmoreland County, Va., unanimously voted by Congress on June 15, 1775, to the rank of General and Commander-in-Chief (of the Continental Army).

GENERAL OF THE ARMIES[2]

John Joseph Pershing (1860–1948), b. Linn County, Mo., made permanent general of the armies, 1919.

GENERAL OF THE ARMY, GENERAL OF THE AIR FORCE (5-STARS)

George Catlett Marshall (1880–1959), b. Uniontown, Pa., promoted December 1944.

Douglas MacArthur (1880–1964), b. Little Rock, Ark., promoted December 1944.

Dwight David Eisenhower (1890–1969), b. Denison, Texas, promoted December 1944.

Henry Harley Arnold (1866–1950), b. Gladwyne, Pa. General Arnold had the unique distinction of being a five-star general twice—first conferred on him in 1944 as general of the army, and later in June 1949 as general of the air force. He is the only air force general to have held the five-star rank.

Omar Nelson Bradley (1893–1981), b. Clark, Mo., promoted September 1950.

FLEET ADMIRAL (5-STAR)

William Daniel Leahy (1875–1959), b. Hampton, Iowa, promoted December 1944.

Ernest Joseph King (1878–1956), b. Lorain, Ohio, promoted December 1944.

Chester William Nimitz (1885–1966), b. Fredericksburg, Texas, promoted December 1944.

William Frederick Halsey (1882–1959), b. Elizabeth, N.J., promoted December 1945.

---

1. On March 15, 1978, George Washington was promoted posthumously to the newly-created rank of General of the Armies of the United States. Congress authorized this title to make it clear that Washington is the Army's senior general. *Source:* Department of Defense. 2. General Pershing was given the option of 5 stars but he declined. *Source:* U.S. Army Historian, Research and Analysis Center.

The Joint Chiefs of Staff (JCS)

The Joint Chiefs of Staff consist of the Chairman, the Vice Chairman, the Chief of Staff of the Army, the Chief of Naval Operations, the Chief of Staff of the Air Force, and the Commandant of the Marine Corps.

The collective body of the JCS is headed by the Chairman (or Vice Chairman in the Chairman's absence), who sets the agenda and presides over JCS meetings. Their responsibilities take precedence over their duties as the Chiefs of Military Services. The Chairman is the principal military advisor to the President, Secretary of Defense, and the National Security Council (NSC); however, all JCS members are by law military advisors, and they may respond to a request or voluntarily submit, through the Chairman, advice or opinions to the President, the Secretary of State, or the NSC. The Joint Chiefs of Staff have no executive authority to command combatant forces.

The Department of Defense Reorganization Act of 1986 created the position of Vice Chairman of the Joint Chiefs of Staff, who performs duties as the Chief of the JCS may prescribe. By law, the Vice Chairman is the second highest ranking member of the Armed Forces and replaces the Chairman in his absence or disability. He or she is a full voting member of the JCS.

In addition to their responsibilities on the JCS, the military Service Chiefs are responsible to the Secretaries of their Military Departments for management of the services. The Service Chiefs serve for four years. By custom the Vice Chiefs of the Services act for their chiefs in most matters having to do with day-to-day operation of the services.

Joint Chiefs of Staff, mid-1996

Chairman of the Joint Chiefs of Staff, General John M. Shalikashvili, U.S. Army; Vice Chairman of the Joint Chiefs of Staff, General Joseph W. Ralston, U.S. Air Force, (the fourth officer to hold the position); General Dennis J. Reimer, Chief of Staff of the Army; Admiral Jay L. Johnson, Chief of Naval Operations; General Ronald R. Fogleman, Chief of Staff of the U.S. Air Force; and Gen. Charles C. Krulak, Commandant of the Marine Corps.

Origin of the Joint Chiefs of Staff

At the beginning of WWII, President Roosevelt created a committee of U.S. staff commanders to coordinate operational strategy for the armed services. It was established as the American component of the Combined Chiefs of Staff of Great Britain and the United States, which prepared and implemented Allied strategy. The group became known as the U.S. Joint Chiefs of Staff. The members of the new JCS were the counterparts of the British Chiefs of the Army, Navy, and Royal Air Force.

The first members of the JCS were Adm. William D. Leahy, President Roosevelt's special military advisor, with the title of Chief of Staff to the Commander in Chief of the Army and Navy, who presided over the JCS; Gen. George C. Marshall, Chief of Staff of the Army; Adm. Ernest J. King, Chief of Naval Operations and Commander in Chief of the U.S. Fleet; and Gen. Henry H. Arnold, Deputy Army Chief of Staff for Air and Chief of the Army Air Corps. Each member was promoted to five-star rank in December 1944, when the new grades were established.

The National Security Act of 1947 formally established the Joint Chiefs of Staff and laid the foundation for a series of legislative and executive changes that produced today's defense organization.

Past Chairmen of the Joint Chiefs of Staff

General of the Army, Omar N. Bradley, 1949–1953; Adm. Arthur W. Radford, U.S. Navy, 1953–1957; Gen. Nathan F. Twining, U.S. Air Force, 1957–1960; Gen. Lyman L. Lemnitzer, U.S. Army, 1960–1962; Gen. Maxwell D. Taylor, U.S. Army, 1962–1964; Gen. Earle G. Wheeler, U.S. Air Force, 1964–1970; Adm. Thomas H. Moorer, U.S. Navy, 1970–1974; Gen. George S. Brown, U.S. Air Force, 1974–1978; Gen. David C. Jones, U.S. Air Force, 1978–1982; Gen. John W. Vessey, Jr., U.S. Army, 1982–1985; Adm. William J. Crowe, U.S. Navy, 1985–1989; Gen. Colin L. Powell, U.S. Army, 1989–1993.

Casualties in World War I

Country	Total mobilized forces	Killed or died[1]	Wounded	Prisoners or missing	Total Casualties
Austria-Hungary	7,800,000	1,200,000	3,620,000	2,200,000	7,020,000
Belgium	267,000	13,716	44,686	34,659	93,061
British Empire[2]	8,904,467	908,371	2,090,212	191,652	3,190,235
Bulgaria	1,200,000	87,500	152,390	27,029	266,919
France[2]	8,410,000	1,357,800	4,266,000	537,000	6,160,800
Germany	11,000,000	1,773,700	4,216,058	1,152,800	7,142,558
Greece	230,000	5,000	21,000	1,000	27,000
Italy	5,615,000	650,000	947,000	600,000	2,197,000
Japan	800,000	300	907	3	1,210
Montenegro	50,000	3,000	10,000	7,000	20,000
Portugal	100,000	7,222	13,751	12,318	33,291
Romania	750,000	335,706	120,000	80,000	535,706
Russia	12,000,000	1,700,000	4,950,000	2,500,000	9,150,000
Serbia	707,343	45,000	133,148	152,958	331,106
Turkey	2,850,000	325,000	400,000	250,000	975,000
United States	4,734,991	116,516	204,002	—	320,518

1. Includes deaths from all causes. 2. Official figures. NOTE: For additional U.S. figures, *see* the table on U.S. Casualties in Major Wars in this section.

Casualties in World War II

Country	Men in war	Battle deaths	Wounded
Australia	1,000,000	26,976	180,864
Austria	800,000	280,000	350,117
Belgium	625,000	8,460	55,513[1]
Brazil[2]	40,334	943	4,222
Bulgaria	339,760	6,671	21,878
Canada	1,086,343[7]	42,042[7]	53,145
China[3]	17,250,521	1,324,516	1,762,006
Czechoslovakia	—	6,683[4]	8,017
Denmark	—	4,339	
Finland	500,000	79,047	50,000
France	—	201,568	400,000
Germany	20,000,000	3,250,000[4]	7,250,000
Greece	—	17,024	47,290
Hungary	—	147,435	89,313
India	2,393,891	32,121	64,354
Italy	3,100,000	149,496[4]	66,716
Japan	9,700,000	1,270,000	140,000
Netherlands	280,000	6,500	2,860
New Zealand	194,000	11,625[4]	17,000
Norway	75,000	2,000	
Poland	—	664,000	530,000
Romania	650,000[5]	350,000[6]	—
South Africa	410,056	2,473	
U.S.S.R.	—	6,115,000[4]	14,012,000
United Kingdom	5,896,000	357,116[4]	369,267
United States	16,112,566	291,557	670,846
Yugoslavia	3,741,000	305,000	425,000

1. Civilians only. 2. Army and Navy figures. 3. Figures cover period July 7, 1937–Sept. 2, 1945, and concern only Chinese regular troops. They do not include casualties suffered by guerrillas and local military corps. 4. Deaths from all causes. 5. Against Soviet Russia; 385,847 against Nazi Germany. 6. Against Soviet Russia; 169,822 against Nazi Germany. 7. National Defense Ctr., Canadian Forces Hq., Director of History. NOTE: The figures in this table are unofficial estimates obtained from various sources.

Merchant Marine Casualties in World War II

In 1988, the U.S. Government conferred official veterans status on those who served aboard oceangoing merchant ships in World War II. The officers and crews played a key role in transporting the troops and war material that enabled the United States and its allies to defeat the Axis powers.

During the war, merchant seamen died as a result of enemy attacks at a rate that proportionately exceeded all branches of the armed services, with the exception of the U.S. Marine Corps.

Enemy action sank more than 700 U.S.-flag merchant ships and claimed the lives of over 6,000 civilian seafarers. Untold thousands of additional seamen were wounded or injured during these attacks, and nearly 600 were made prisoners of war.

The Medal of Honor

Often called the Congressional Medal of Honor, it is the Nation's highest military award for "uncommon valor" by men and women in the armed forces. It is given for actions that are above and beyond the call of duty in combat against an armed enemy. The medal was first awarded by the Army on March 25, 1863. In April 1991, President Bush awarded posthumously the Medal of Honor to World War I veteran, Army Cpl. Freddie Stowers. He was the first black soldier to receive the nation's highest honor for valor in either World Wars.

The only conscientious objector to be awarded the medal was Pfc. Desmond Doss, a Seventh-Day Adventist who served as a medic in the Pacific Theater during WWII.

Recipients of the medal receive $400 per month for life, a right to burial at Arlington National Cemetery, admission for themselves or their children to a service academy (if they qualify and quotas permit), and free travel on government aircraft to almost anywhere in the world, on a space-available basis.

In 1989, medals were restored to William F. Cody (Buffalo Bill) and four other scouts who had them revoked in 1917 due to a new ruling.

President Clinton awarded the last medals to date. They were awarded posthumously on May 23, 1994, to two members of the ill-fated Delta Forces operation to capture warlord Gen. Aidid in Mogadishu on Oct. 3, 1993. The recipients were Master Sgt. Gary Gordon and Sgt. 1st Class Randall Shughart who were killed trying to protect and rescue wounded crew members under enemy fire.

Medal of Honor Recipients[1]

	Total	Army	Navy	Marines	Air Force	Coast Guard
Civil War	1,520	1,195	308	17	—	—
Indian Wars (1861-1898)	428	428	—	—	—	—
Korea (1871)	15	—	9	6	—	—
Spanish-American War	109	30	64	15	—	—
Philippines/Samoa	91	70	12	9	—	—
Boxer Rebellion	59	4	22	33	—	—
Veracruz (1914)	55	—	46	9	—	—
Haiti (1915)	6	—	—	6	—	—
Dominican Republic	3	—	—	3	—	—
Haiti (1919–1920)	2	—	—	2	—	—
Nicaragua (1927–1933)	2	—	—	2	—	—
Peacetime (1865–1870)	12	—	12	—	—	—
Peacetime (1871–1898)	103	—	101	2	—	—
Peacetime (1899–1911)	51	1	48	2	—	—
Peacetime (1915–1916)	8	—	8	—	—	—
Peacetime (1920-1940)	18	2	15	1	—	—
World War I	124	96	21	7	—	—
World War II	433	294	57	81	—	1
Korean War	131	78	7	42	4	—
Vietnam War	239	155	15	57	12	—
Somalia (1993)	2	2	—	—	—	—
Unknown Soldiers	9	—	—	—	—	—
Total	**3,420**	**2,355**	**745**	**294**	**16**	**1**

1. These totals reflect the total number of Medals of Honor awarded. Nineteen (19) men received a second award. The total number of Medal of Honor receipients is 3,401. *Source:* The Congressional Medal of Honor Society, Mt. Pleasant, S.C.

Estimated Educational Level of Active Duty Military Personnel, 1995

(Cumulative Percent—End of Fiscal Year)

Personnel/Educational Level	1995	1994	Personnel/Educational Level	1995	1994
Total Officers			**Warrant Officers**		
Graduated from college	93.5	94.0	Graduated from college	30.6	29.4
Completed 2 or more years college	97.0	97.6	Completed 2 or more years college	66.9	70.1
Completed some college	98.9	98.9	Completed some college	88.0	87.3
Graduated from high school	100.0	100.0	Graduated from high school	100.0	100.0
			Enlisted		
			Graduated from college	3.3	3.1
Commissioned Officers			Completed 2 or more years college	12.6	12.1
Graduated from college	97.2	97.7	Completed some college	33.4	22.5
Completed 2 or more years college	98.8	99.2	Graduated from high school	99.1	99.0
Completed some college	96.6	99.6	Completed some high school	100.0	100.0
Graduated from high school	100.0	100.0	Graduated from grade school	100.0	100.0

NOTE: The percentage distributions should be considered as approximate. *Source:* Department of Defense, Washington Headquarters Services, Directorate for Information Operations and Reports.

WEATHER & CLIMATE

Climate of 100 Selected U.S. Cities

| City | Average Monthly Temperature (°F)[1] | | | | Precipitation | | Snowfall | |
	Jan.	April	July	Oct	Average (in.)[1]	annual (days)[2]	Average annual (in.)[2]	Years[2]
Albany, N.Y.	21.1	46.6	71.4	50.5	35.74	134	65.5	38
Albuquerque, N.M.	34.8	55.1	78.8	57.4	8.12	59	10.6	45
Anchorage, Alaska	13.0	35.4	58.1	34.6	15.20	115	69.2	41[3]
Asheville, N.C.	36.8	55.7	73.2	56.0	47.71	124	17.5	20
Atlanta, Ga.	41.9	61.8	78.6	62.2	48.61	115	1.9	50
Atlantic City, N.J.	31.8	51.0	74.4	55.5	41.93	112	16.4	40[3]
Austin, Texas	49.1	68.7	84.7	69.8	31.50	83	0.9	43
Baltimore, Md.	32.7	54.0	76.8	56.9	41.84	113	21.8	34
Baton Rouge, La.	50.8	68.4	82.1	68.2	55.77	108	0.1	34[3]
Billings, Mont.	20.9	44.6	72.3	49.3	15.09	96	57.2	50
Birmingham, Ala.	42.9	62.8	80.1	62.6	54.52	117	1.3	41
Bismarck, N.D.	6.7	42.5	70.4	46.1	15.36	96	40.3	45
Boise, Idaho	29.9	48.6	74.6	51.9	11.71	92	21.4	45
Boston, Mass.	29.6	48.7	73.5	54.8	43.81	127	41.8	49[3]
Bridgeport, Conn.	29.5	48.6	74.0	56.0	41.56	117	26.0	36
Buffalo, N.Y.	23.5	45.4	70.7	51.5	37.52	169	92.2	41
Burlington, Vt.	16.6	42.7	69.6	47.9	33.69	153	78.2	41
Caribou, Maine	10.7	37.3	65.1	43.1	36.59	160	113.3	45
Casper, Wyom.	22.2	42.1	70.9	47.1	11.43	95	80.5	34
Charleston, S.C.	47.9	64.3	80.5	65.8	51.59	113	0.6	42
Charleston, W.Va.	32.9	55.3	74.5	55.9	42.43	151	31.5	37
Charlotte, N.C.	40.5	60.3	78.5	60.7	43.16	111	6.1	45
Cheyenne, Wyom.	26.1	41.8	68.9	47.5	13.31	98	54.1	49
Chicago, Ill.	21.4	48.8	73.0	53.5	33.34	127	40.3	26
Cleveland, Ohio	25.5	48.1	71.6	53.2	35.40	156	53.6	43
Columbia, S.C.	44.7	63.8	81.0	63.4	49.12	109	1.9	37
Columbus, Ohio	27.1	51.4	73.8	53.9	36.97	137	28.3	37[3]
Concord, N.H.	19.9	44.1	69.5	48.3	36.53	125	64.5	43
Dallas–Ft. Worth, Texas	44.0	65.9	86.3	67.9	29.46	78	3.1	31
Denver, Colo.	29.5	47.4	73.4	51.9	15.31	88	59.8	50
Des Moines, Iowa	18.6	50.5	76.3	54.2	30.83	107	34.7	45
Detroit, Mich.	23.4	47.3	71.9	51.9	30.97	133	40.4	26
Dodge City, Kan.	29.5	54.3	80.0	57.7	20.66	78	19.5	42
Duluth, Minn.	6.3	38.3	65.4	44.2	29.68	135	77.4	41[3]
El Paso, Texas	44.2	63.6	82.5	63.6	7.82	47	5.2	45
Fairbanks, Alaska	-12.7	30.2	61.5	25.1	10.37	106	67.5	33
Fargo, N.D.	4.3	42.1	70.6	46.3	19.59	100	35.9	42
Grand Junction, Colo.	25.5	51.7	78.9	54.9	8.00	72	26.1	38
Grand Rapids, Mich.	22.0	46.3	71.4	50.9	34.35	143	72.4	21
Hartford, Conn.	25.2	48.8	73.4	52.4	44.39	127	50.0	30
Helena, Mont.	18.1	42.3	67.9	45.1	11.37	96	47.9	44
Honolulu, Hawaii	72.6	75.7	80.1	79.5	23.47	100	0.0	38[3]
Houston, Texas	51.4	68.7	83.1	69.7	44.76	105	0.4	50
Indianapolis, Ind.	26.0	52.4	75.1	54.8	39.12	125	23.1	53[3]
Jackson, Miss.	45.7	65.1	81.9	65.0	52.82	109	1.2	21
Jacksonville, Fla.	53.2	67.7	81.3	69.5	52.76	116	T	43
Juneau, Alaska	21.8	39.1	55.7	41.8	53.15	220	102.8	41
Kansas City, Mo.	28.4	56.9	80.9	59.6	29.27	98	20.0	43
Knoxville, Tenn.	38.2	59.6	77.6	59.5	47.29	127	12.3	42
Las Vegas, Nev.	44.5	63.5	90.2	67.5	4.19	26	1.4	36
Lexington, Ky.	31.5	55.1	75.9	56.8	45.68	131	16.3	40
Little Rock, Ark.	39.9	62.4	82.1	63.1	49.20	104	5.4	42
Long Beach, Calif.	55.2	60.9	72.8	67.5	11.54	32	T	41[3]
Los Angeles, Calif.	56.0	59.5	69.0	66.3	12.08	36	T	49
Louisville, Ky.	32.5	56.6	77.6	57.7	43.56	125	17.5	37
Madison, Wisc.	15.6	45.8	70.6	49.5	30.84	118	40.8	36
Memphis, Tenn.	39.6	62.6	82.1	62.9	51.57	107	5.5	34
Miami, Fla.	67.1	75.3	82.5	77.9	57.55	129	0.0	42
Milwaukee, Wisc.	18.7	44.6	70.5	50.9	30.94	125	47.0	44

City	Average Monthly Temperature (°F)[1]				Precipitation		Snowfall	
	Jan.	April	July	Oct	Average (in.)[1]	annual (days)[2]	Average annual (in.)[2]	Years[2]
Minneapolis–St. Paul, Minn.	11.2	46.0	73.1	49.6	26.36	115	48.9	46
Mobile, Ala.	50.8	68.0	82.2	68.5	64.64	123	0.3	43
Montgomery, Ala.	46.7	65.2	81.7	65.3	49.16	108	0.3	40
Mt. Washington, N.H.	5.1	22.4	48.7	30.5	89.92	209	246.8	52
Nashville, Tenn.	37.1	59.7	79.4	60.2	48.49	119	11.1	43
Newark, N.J.	31.2	52.1	76.8	57.2	42.34	122	28.2	43
New Orleans, La.	52.4	68.7	82.1	69.2	59.74	114	0.2	38[3]
New York, N.Y.	31.8	51.9	76.4	57.5	42.82	119	26.1	40[3]
Norfolk, Va.	39.9	58.2	78.4	61.3	45.22	115	7.9	36
Oklahoma City, Okla.	35.9	60.2	82.1	62.3	30.89	82	9.0	45
Olympia, Wash.	37.2	47.3	63.0	50.1	50.96	164	18.0	43
Omaha, Neb.	20.2	52.2	77.7	54.5	30.34	98	31.1	49[3]
Philadelphia, Pa.	31.2	52.9	76.5	56.5	41.42	117	21.9	42[3]
Phoenix, Ariz.	52.3	68.1	92.3	73.4	7.11	36	T	47[3]
Pittsburgh, Pa.	26.7	50.1	72.0	52.5	36.30	154	44.6	32
Portland, Maine	21.5	42.8	68.1	48.5	43.52	128	72.4	44
Portland, Ore.	38.9	50.4	67.7	54.3	37.39	154	6.8	44
Providence, R.I.	28.2	47.9	72.5	53.2	45.32	124	37.1	31
Raleigh, N.C.	39.6	59.4	77.7	59.7	41.76	112	7.7	40
Reno, Nev.	32.2	46.4	69.5	50.3	7.49	51	25.3	42
Richmond, Va.	36.6	57.9	77.8	58.6	44.07	113	14.6	47
Roswell, N.M.	41.4	61.9	81.4	61.7	9.70	52	11.4	37[3]
Sacramento, Calif.	45.3	58.2	75.6	63.9	17.10	58	0.1	36[3]
Salt Lake City, Utah	28.6	49.2	77.5	53.0	15.31	90	59.1	56
San Antonio, Texas	50.4	69.6	84.6	70.2	29.13	81	0.4	42
San Diego, Calif.	56.8	61.2	70.3	67.5	9.32	43	T	44
San Francisco, Calif.	48.5	54.8	62.2	60.6	19.71	63	T	57
Savannah, Ga.	49.1	66.0	81.2	66.9	49.70	111	0.3	34
Seattle–Tacoma, Wash.	39.1	48.7	64.8	52.4	38.60	158	12.8	40
Sioux Falls, S.D.	12.4	46.4	74.0	49.4	24.12	96	39.9	39
Spokane, Wash.	25.7	45.8	69.7	47.5	16.71	114	51.5	37
Springfield, Ill.	24.6	53.3	76.5	56.0	33.78	114	24.5	37
St. Louis, Mo.	28.8	56.1	78.9	57.9	33.91	111	19.8	48[3]
Tampa, Fla.	59.8	71.5	82.1	74.4	46.73	107	T	38
Toledo, Ohio	23.1	47.8	71.8	51.7	31.78	137	38.3	29
Tucson, Ariz.	51.1	64.9	86.2	70.4	11.14	52	1.2	44
Tulsa, Okla.	35.2	61.0	83.2	62.6	38.77	89	9.0	46
Vero Beach, Fla.	61.9	71.7	81.1	75.2	51.41	n.a.	n.a.	0
Washington, D.C.	35.2	56.7	78.9	59.3	39.00	112	17.0	41[3]
Wilmington, Del.	31.2	52.4	76.0	56.3	41.38	117	20.9	37
Wichita, Kan.	29.6	56.3	81.4	59.1	28.61	85	16.4	31

1. Based on 30 year period 1951–80. Data latest available. 2. Data through 1984 based on number of years as indicated in Years column. 3. For snowfall data where number of years differ from that for precipitation data. T = trace. n.a. = not available. *Source:* National Oceanic and Atmospheric Administration.

Wind Chill Factors

Wind speed (mph)	Thermometer reading (degrees Fahrenheit)																
	35	30	25	20	15	10	5	0	–5	–10	–15	–20	–25	–30	–35	–40	–45
5	33	27	21	19	12	7	0	–5	–10	–15	–21	–26	–31	–36	–42	–47	–52
10	22	16	10	3	–3	–9	–15	–22	–27	–34	–40	–46	–52	–58	–64	–71	–77
15	16	9	2	–5	–11	–18	–25	–31	–38	–45	–51	–58	–65	–72	–78	–85	–92
20	12	4	–3	–10	–17	–24	–31	–39	–46	–53	–60	–67	–74	–81	–88	–95	–103
25	8	1	–7	–15	–22	–29	–36	–44	–51	–59	–66	–74	–81	–88	–96	–103	–110
30	6	–2	–10	–18	–25	–33	–41	–49	–56	–64	–71	–79	–86	–93	–101	–109	–116
35	4	–4	–12	–20	–27	–35	–43	–52	–58	–67	–74	–82	–89	–97	–105	–113	–120
40	3	–5	–13	–21	–29	–37	–45	–53	–60	–69	–76	–84	–92	–100	–107	–115	–123
45	2	–6	–14	–22	–30	–38	–46	–54	–62	–70	–78	–85	–93	–102	–109	–117	–125

NOTES: This chart gives equivalent temperatures for combinations of wind speed and temperatures. For example, the combination of a temperature of 10° Fahrenheit and a wind blowing at 10 mph has a cooling power equal to –9° F. Wind speeds of higher than 45 mph have little additional cooling effect.

World and U.S. Extremes of Climate

Highest recorded temperature

	Place	Date	Degree Fahrenheit	Degree Centigrade
World (Africa)	El Azizia, Libya	Sept. 13, 1922	136	58
North America (U.S.)	Death Valley, Calif.	July 10, 1913	134	57
Asia	Tirat Tsvi, Israel	June 21, 1942	129	54
Australia	Cloncurry, Queensland	Jan. 16, 1889	128	53
Europe	Seville, Spain	Aug. 4, 1881	122	50
South America	Rivadavia, Argentina	Dec. 11, 1905	120	49
Canada	Midale and Yellow Grass, Saskatchewan	July 5, 1937	113	45
Persian Gulf (sea–surface)		August 5, 1924	96	36
South Pole		Dec. 27, 1978	7.5	−14
Antarctica	Vanda Station	Jan. 5, 1974	59	15

Lowest recorded temperature

	Place	Date	Degree Fahrenheit	Degree Centigrade
World (Antarctica)	Vostok	July 21, 1983	−129	−89
Asia	Verkhoyansk/Oimekon	Feb. 6, 1933	−90	−68
Greenland	Northice	Jan. 9, 1954	−87	−66
North America (excl. Greenland)	Snag, Yukon, Canada	Feb. 3, 1947	−81	−63
Alaska	Prospect Creek, Endicott Mts.	Jan. 23, 1971	−80	−62
U.S., excluding Alaska	Rogers Pass, Mont.	Jan. 20, 1954	−70	−56.5
Europe	Ust 'Shchugor, U.S.S.R.	n.a.	−67	−55
South America	Sarmiento, Argentina	Jan. 1, 1907	−27	−33
Africa	Ifrane, Morocco	Feb. 11, 1935	−11	−24
Australia	Charlotte Pass, N.S.W.	July 22, 1947	−8	−22
United States	Prospect Creek, Alaska	Jan. 23, 1971	−80	−62

Greatest rainfalls

	Place	Date	Inches	Centimeters
1 minute (World)	Unionville, Md.	July 4, 1956	1.23	3.1
20 minutes (World)	Curtea–de–Arges, Romania	July 7, 1889	8.1	20.5
42 minutes (World)	Holt, Mo.	June 22, 1947	12	30.5
12 hours (World)	Foc–Foc, La Réunion	Jan. 7–8, 1966	45	114
24 hours (World)	Foc–Foc, La Réunion	Jan. 7–8, 1966	72	182.5
24 hours (N. Hemisphere)	Paishih, Taiwan	Sept. 10–11, 1963	49	125
24 hours (Australia)	Bellenden Ker, Queensland	Jan. 4, 1979	44	114
24 hours (U.S.)	Alvin, Texas	July 25–26, 1979	43	109
24 hours (Canada)	Ucluelet Brynnor Mines, British Columbia	Oct. 6, 1967	19	49
5 days (World)	Commerson, La Réunion	Jan. 23–28, 1980	156	395
1 month (World)	Cherrapunji, India	July 1861	366	930
12 months (World)	Cherrapunji, India	Aug. 1860–Aug. 1861	1,042	2,647
12 months (U.S.)	Kukui, Maui, Hawaii	Dec. 1981–Dec. 1982	739	1878

Greatest snowfalls

	Place	Date	Inches	Centimeters
1 month (U.S.)	Tamarack, Calif.	Jan. 1911	390	991
24 hours (N. America)	Silver Lake, Colo.	April 14–15, 1921	76	192.5
24 hours (Alaska)	Thompson Pass	Dec. 29, 1955	62	157.5
19 hours (France)	Bessans	April 5–6, 1969	68	173
1 storm (N. America)	Mt. Shasta Ski Bowl, Calif.	Feb. 13–19, 1959	189	480
1 storm (Alaska)	Thompson Pass	Dec. 26–31, 1955	175	445.5
1 season (N. America)	Paradise Ranger Sta., Wash.	1971–1972	1,122	2,850
1 season (Alaska)	Thompson Pass	1952–1953	974.5	2,475
1 season (Canada)	Revelstoke Mt. Copeland, British Columbia	1971–1972	964	2,446.5

Source: U.S. Army Corps of Engineers, Engineer Topographic Laboratories.

Tropical Storms and Hurricanes, 1886–1995

	Jan.–April	May	June	July	Aug.	Sept.	Oct.	Nov.	Dec.	Total
Number of tropical storms (incl. hurricanes)	4	14	58	73	230	316	193	46	6	940
Number of tropical storms that reached hurricane intensity	1	3	24	36	157	199	99	23	3	545

Other Recorded Extremes

Highest average annual mean temperature (World): Dallol, Ethiopia (Oct. 1960–Dec. 1966), 94° F (35° C). **(U.S.):** Key West, Fla. (30–year normal), 78.2° F (25.7° C).

Lowest average annual mean temperature (Antarctica): Plateau Station –70° F (–57° C). **(U.S.):** Barrow, Alaska (30–year normal), 9.3° F (–13° C).

Greatest average yearly rainfall (U.S.): Mt. Waialeale, Kauai, Hawaii (32–year avg), 460 in. (1,168 cm). **(India):** Cherrapunji (74–year avg), 450 in. (1,143 cm).

Minimum average yearly rainfall (Chile): Arica (59–year avg), 0.03 in. (0.08 cm) (no rainfall for 14 consecutive years). **(U.S.):** Death Valley, Calif. (42–year avg), 1.63 in. (4.14 cm). Bagdad, Calif., holds the U.S. record for the longest period with no measurable rain, 767 days, from Oct. 3, 1912 to Nov. 8, 1914).

Hottest summer avg in Western Hemisphere (U.S.): Death Valley, Calif., 98° F (36.7° C).

Longest hot spell (W. Australia): Marble Bar, 100° F (38° C) (or above) for 162 consecutive days, Oct. 30, 1923–Apr. 7, 1924.

Largest hailstone (U.S.): Coffeyville, KS, 17.5 in. (44.5 cm), Sept. 3, 1979.

Weather Glossary

blizzard: storm characterized by strong winds, low temperatures, and large amounts of snow.

cold wave warning: indicates that a change to abnormally cold weather is expected; greater than normal protective measures will be required.

cyclone: circulation of winds rotating counterclockwise in the northern hemisphere and clockwise in the southern hemisphere. Hurricanes and tornadoes are both examples of cyclones.

drifting snow: strong winds will blow loose or falling snow into significant drifts.

drizzle: uniform close precipitation of tiny drops with diameter of less than .02 inch.

flash flood: dangerous rapid rise of water levels in streams, rivers, or over land area.

freezing rain or drizzle: rain or drizzle that freezes on contact with the ground or other objects forming a coating of ice on exposed surfaces.

gale warning: winds in the 33–48 knot (38–55 mph) range forecast.

hail: small balls of ice falling separately or in lumps; usually associated with thunderstorms and temperatures that may be well above freezing.

heavy snow warnings: issued when 4 inches or more of snow are expected to fall in a 12–hour period or when 6 inches or more are anticipated in a 24–hour period.

hurricane: devastating cyclonic storm; winds over 74 mph near storm center; usually tropical in origin; called cyclone in Indian Ocean, typhoon in the Pacific.

hurricane warning: winds in excess of 64 knots (74 mph) in connection with hurricane.

rain: precipitation of liquid particles with diameters larger than .02 inch.

sleet: translucent or transparent ice pellets; frozen rain; generally a winter phenomenon.

small craft warning: indicates winds as high as 33 knots (38 mph) and sea conditions dangerous to small boats.

snow flurries: snow falling for a short time at intermittent periods; accumulations are usually small.

snow squall: brief, intense falls of snow, usually accompanied by gusty winds.

storm warnings: winds greater than 48 knots (55 mph) are forecast.

temperature–humidity index (THI): measure of personal discomfort based on the combined effects of temperature and humidity. Most people are uncomfortable when the THI is 75. A THI of 80 produces acute discomfort for almost everyone.

tidal waves: series of ocean waves caused by earthquakes; can reach speeds of 600 mph; they grow in height as they reach shore and can crest as high as 100 feet.

thunder: the sound produced by the rapid expansion of air heated by lightning.

tornado: dangerous whirlwind associated with the cumulonimbus clouds of severe thunderstorms; winds up to 300 mph.

tornado warning: tornado has actually been detected by radar or sighted in designated area.

tornado watch: potential exists in the watch area for storms that could contain tornadoes.

tsunami: *see* tidal waves.

wind–chill factor: combined effect of temperature and wind speed as compared to equivalent temperature in calm air .

The World's Hottest Year

The world's average global surface temperature rose to a record seven-tenths of a degree above the average in 1995, causing the United Nations' World Meteorological Organization to declare it the world's hottest year. The UN panel concluded that it is "unlikely natural in origin" and "suggests a discernible human influence on climate" (primarily due to fossil fuel burning). However, it is unclear how much of the climatic change humans are responsible for and what part the result of natural climate variability plays.

The panel predicted that the average global temperature would rise by an additional 1.8 to 6.3 degrees Fahrenheit by the year 2100.

During July 1995, a heatwave struck the U.S. Midwest and Northeast killing a total of more than 800 persons. In Illinois, where the temperature-humidity index reached 125°F (52°C), over 560 people in Chicago died, most of them elderly persons who lived alone.

Record Highest Temperatures by State

State	Temp. °F	Temp °C	Date	Station	Elevation, feet
Alabama	112	44	Sept. 5, 1925	Centerville	345
Alaska	100	38	June 27, 1915	Fort Yukon	est. 420
Arizona	128	53	June 29, 1994	Lake Havasu	785
Arkansas	120	49	Aug. 10, 1936	Ozark	396
California	134	57	July 10, 1913	Greenland Ranch	-178
Colorado	118	48	July 11, 1888	Bennett	5,484
Connecticut	106	41	July 15, 1995	Danbury	457
Delaware	110	43	July 21, 1930	Millsboro	20
D.C.	106	41	July 20, 1930	Washington	410
Florida	109	43	June 29, 1931	Monticello	207
Georgia	113	45	May 27, 1978	Greenville	860
Hawaii	100	38	Apr. 27, 1931	Pahala	850
Idaho	118	48	July 28, 1934	Orofino	1,027
Illinois	117	47	July 14, 1954	E. St. Louis	410
Indiana	116	47	July 14, 1936	Collegeville	672
Iowa	118	48	July 20, 1934	Keokuk	614
Kansas	121	49	July 24, 1936*	Alton (near)	1,651
Kentucky	114	46	July 28, 1930	Greensburg	581
Louisiana	114	46	Aug. 10, 1936	Plain Dealing	268
Maine	105	41	July 10, 1911*	North Bridgton	450
Maryland	109	43	July 10, 1936*	Cumberland & Frederick	623;325
Massachusetts	107	42	Aug. 2, 1975	New Bedford & Chester	120;640
Michigan	112	44	July 13, 1936	Mio	963
Minnesota	114	46	July 6, 1936*	Moorhead	904
Mississippi	115	46	July 29, 1930	Holly Springs	600
Missouri	118	48	July 14, 1954*	Warsaw & Union	687;560
Montana	117	47	July 5, 1937	Medicine Lake	1,950
Nebraska	118	48	July 24, 1936*	Minden	2,169
Nevada	125	52	June 29, 1994	Laughlin	680
New Hampshire	106	41	July 4, 1911	Nashua	125
New Jersey	110	43	July 10, 1936	Runyon	18
New Mexico	122	50	June 27, 1994	Lakewood	3,418
New York	108	42	July 22, 1926	Troy	35
North Carolina	110	43	Aug. 21, 1983	Fayetteville	81
North Dakota	121	49	July 6, 1936	Steele	1,857
Ohio	113	45	July 21, 1934*	Gallipolis (near)	673
Oklahoma	120	49	June 29, 1994*	Tipton	1,251
Oregon	119	48	Aug. 10, 1898	Pendleton	1,074
Pennsylvania	111	44	July 10, 1936*	Phoenixville	100
Rhode Island	104	40	Aug. 2, 1975	Providence	51
South Carolina	111	44	June 28, 1954*	Camden	170
South Dakota	120	49	July 5, 1936	Gannvalley	1,750
Tennessee	113	45	Aug. 9, 1930*	Perryville	377
Texas	120	49	Aug. 12, 1936	Seymour	1,291
Utah	117	47	July 5, 1895	Saint George	2,880
Vermont	105	41	July 4, 1911	Vernon	310
Virginia	110	43	July 15, 1954	Balcony Falls	725
Washington	118	48	Aug. 5, 1961*	Ice Harbor Dam	475
West Virginia	112	44	July 10, 1936*	Martinsburg	435
Wisconsin	114	46	July 13, 1936	Wisconsin Dells	900
Wyoming	114	46	July 12, 1900	Basin	3,500

*Also on earlier dates at the same or other places. *Source:* National Climatic Data Center, Asheville, N.C., and Storm Phillips, STORMFAX, INC.

Record Lowest Temperatures by State

State	Temp. °F	Temp °C	Date	Station	Elevation, feet
Alabama	−27	−33	Jan. 30, 1966	New Market	760
Alaska	−80	−62	Jan. 23, 1971	Prospect Creek	1,100
Arizona	−40	−40	Jan. 7, 1971	Hawley Lake	8,180
Arkansas	−29	−34	Feb. 13, 1905	Pond	1,250
California	−45	−43	Jan. 20, 1937	Boca	5,532
Colorado	−61	−52	Feb. 1, 1985	Maybell	5,920
Connecticut	−32	−36	Feb. 16, 1943	Falls Village	585
Delaware	−17	−27	Jan. 17, 1893	Millsboro	20
D.C.	−15	−26	Feb. 11, 1899	Washington	410
Florida	−2	−19	Feb. 13, 1899	Tallahassee	193
Georgia	−17	−27	Jan. 27, 1940	CCC Camp F−16	est. 1,000
Hawaii	12	−11	May 17, 1979	Mauna Kea	13,770
Idaho	−60	−51	Jan. 18, 1943	Island Park Dam	6,285
Illinois	−35	−37	Jan. 22, 1930	Mount Carroll	817
Indiana	−36	−38	Jan. 19, 1994	New Whiteland	785
Iowa	−47	−44	Jan. 12, 1912	Washta	1,157
Kansas	−40	−40	Feb. 13, 1905	Lebanon	1,812
Kentucky	−34	−37	Jan. 28, 1963	Cynthiana	684
Louisiana	−16	−27	Feb. 13, 1899	Minden	194
Maine	−48	−44	Jan. 19, 1925	Van Buren	510
Maryland	−40	−40	Jan. 13, 1912	Oakland	2,461
Massachusetts	−35	−37	Jan. 12, 1981	Chester	640
Michigan	−51	−46	Feb. 9, 1934	Vanderbilt	785
Minnesota	−59	−51	Feb. 16, 1903*	Pokegama Dam	1,280
Mississippi	−19	−28	Jan. 30, 1966	Corinth	420
Missouri	−40	−40	Feb. 13, 1905	Warsaw	700
Montana	−70	−57	Jan. 20, 1954	Rogers Pass	5,470
Nebraska	−47	−44	Feb. 12, 1899	Camp Clarke	3,700
Nevada	−50	−46	Jan. 8, 1937	San Jacinto	5,200
New Hampshire	−46	−43	Jan. 28, 1925	Pittsburg	1,575
New Jersey	−34	−37	Jan. 5, 1904	River Vale	70
New Mexico	−50	−46	Feb. 1, 1951	Gavilan	7,350
New York	−52	−47	Feb. 18, 1979*	Old Forge	1,720
North Carolina	−34	−37	Jan. 21, 1985	Mt. Mitchell	6,525
North Dakota	−60	−51	Feb. 15, 1936	Parshall	1,929
Ohio	−39	−39	Feb. 10, 1899	Milligan	800
Oklahoma	−27	−33	Jan. 18, 1930	Watts	958
Oregon	−54	−48	Feb. 10, 1933*	Seneca	4,700
Pennsylvania	−42	−41	Jan. 5, 1904	Smethport	est. 1,500
Rhode Island	−23	−31	Jan. 11, 1942	Kingston	100
South Carolina	−20	−28	Jan. 18, 1977	Caesars Head	3,100
South Dakota	−58	−50	Feb. 17, 1936	McIntosh	2,277
Tennessee	−32	−36	Dec. 30, 1917	Mountain City	2,471
Texas	−23	−31	Feb. 8, 1933*	Seminole	3,275
Utah	−69	−56	Feb. 1, 1985	Peters Sink	8,095
Vermont	−50	−46	Dec. 30, 1933	Bloomfield	915
Virginia	−30	−34	Jan. 22, 1985	Mountain Lake	3,870
Washington	−48	−44	Dec. 30, 1968	Mazama & Winthrop	2,120;1,765
West Virginia	−37	−38	Dec. 30, 1917	Lewisburg	2,200
Wisconsin	−54	−48	Jan. 24, 1922	Danbury	908
Wyoming	−63	−53	Feb. 9, 1933	Moran	6,770

*Also on earlier dates at the same or other places. *Source:* National Climatic Data Center, Asheville, N.C., and Storm Phillips, STORMFAX, INC.

Record High and Low Temperature in U.S. for Each Month

Source: National Climatic Data Center, Asheville, N.C., and Storm Phillips, STORMFAX, Inc.
NOTE: for the contiguous states only.

January

The highest temperature ever recorded for the month of January occurred on January 17, 1936, again in 1954, in Laredo, Tex. (elevation 421 ft) where the temperature reached 98° F.

The lowest temperature ever recorded for the month of January occurred on January 20, 1954, in Rogers Pass, Mont. (elevation 5,470 ft) where the temperature fell to –70° F.

February

The highest temperature ever recorded for the month of February occurred on February 3, 1963, in Montezuma, Ariz. (elevation 735 ft) where the temperature reached 105° F.

The lowest temperature ever recorded for the month of February occurred on February 1, 1985, at the Peters Sink station in Utah (elevation 8,095 ft) where the temperature fell to –69° F.

March

The highest temperature ever recorded for the month of March occurred on March 31, 1954, in Rio Grande City, Tex. (elevation 168 ft) where the temperature reached 108° F.

The lowest temperature ever recorded for the month of March occurred on March 17, 1906, in Snake River, Wyo. (elevation 6,862 ft) where the temperature dropped to –50° F.

April

The highest temperature ever recorded for the month of April occurred on April 25, 1898, at Volcano Springs, Calif. (elevation –220 ft) where the temperature reached 118° F.

The lowest temperature ever recorded for the month of April occurred on April 5, 1945, in Eagle Nest, N. Mex. (elevation 8,250 ft) where the temperature dropped to –36° F.

May

The highest temperature ever recorded for the month of May occurred on May 27, 1896, in Salton, Calif. (elevation –263 ft) where the temperature reached 124° F.

The lowest temperature ever recorded for the month of May occurred on May 7, 1964, in White Mountain 2, Calif. (elevation 12,470 ft) where the temperature dropped to –15° F.

June

The highest temperature ever recorded for the month of June occurred on June 23, 1902, at Volcano Springs, Calif. (elevation –220 ft) where the temperature reached 129° F.

The lowest temperature ever recorded for the month of June occurred on June 13, 1907, in Tamarack, Calif. (elevation 8,000 ft) where the temperature dropped to 2° F.

July

The highest temperature ever recorded for the month of July occurred on July 10, 1913, at Greenland Ranch, Calif. (elevation –178 ft) where the temperature reached 134° F.

The lowest temperature ever recorded for the month of July occurred on July 21, 1911, at Painter, Wyo. (elevation 6,800 ft) where the temperature fell to 10° F.

August

The highest temperature ever recorded for the month of August occurred on August 12, 1933, at Greenland Ranch, Calif. (elevation –178 ft) where the temperature reached 127° F.

The lowest temperature ever recorded for the month of August occurred on August 25, 1910, in Bowen, Mont. (elevation 6,080 ft) where the temperature fell to 5° F.

September

The highest temperature ever recorded for the month of September occurred on September 2, 1950, in Mecca, Calif. (elevation –175 ft) where the temperature reached 126° F.

The lowest temperature ever recorded for the month of September occurred on September 24, 1926, at Riverside Ranger Station, Mont. (elevation 6,700 ft) where the temperature fell to –9 F.

October

The highest temperature ever recorded for the month of October occurred on October 5, 1917, in Sentinel, Ariz. (elevation 685 ft) where the temperature reached 116° F.

The lowest temperature ever recorded for the month of October occurred on October 29, 1917, in Soda Butte, Wyo. (elevation 6,600 ft) where the temperature fell to –33° F.

November

The highest temperature ever recorded for the month of November occurred on November 12, 1906, in Craftonville, Calif. (elevation 1,759 ft) where the temperature reached 105° F.

The lowest temperature ever recorded for the month of November occurred on November 16, 1959, at Lincoln, Mont. (elevation 5,130 ft) where the temperature fell to –53° F.

December

The highest temperature ever recorded for the month of December occurred on December 8, 1938, in La Mesa, Calif. (elevation 539 ft) where the temperature reached 100° F.

The lowest temperature ever recorded for the month of December occurred on December 19, 1924, at Riverside Ranger Station, Mont. (elevation 6,700 ft) where the temperature fell to –59° F.

Temperature Extremes in The United States

Source: National Oceanic and Atmospheric Administration, Environmental Data and Information Service, and National Climatic Center

The Highest Temperature Extremes

Greenland Ranch, California, with 134° F on July 10, 1913, holds the record for the highest temperature ever officially observed in the United States. This station was located in barren Death Valley, 178 feet below sea level. Death Valley is about 140 miles long, four to six miles wide, and oriented north to south in southwestern California. Much of the valley is below sea level and is flanked by towering mountain ranges with Mt. Whitney, the highest landmark in the 48 conterminous states, rising to 14,495 feet above sea level, less than 100 miles to the west. Death Valley has the hottest summers in the Western Hemisphere, and is the only known place in the United States where nighttime temperatures sometimes remain above 100° F.

The highest annual normal (1941–70 mean) temperature in the United States, 78.2° F, and the highest summer (June–August) normal temperature, 92.8° F, are for Death Valley, California. The highest winter (December–February) normal temperature is 72.8° F for Honolulu, Hawaii.

Amazing temperature rises of 40° to 50° F in a few minutes occasionally may be brought about by Chinook winds.[1]

Some Outstanding Temperature Rises

In 12 hours: 83° F, Granville, N.D., Feb. 21, 1918, from −33° F to 50° F from early morning to late afternoon.

In 15 minutes: 42° F, Fort Assiniboine, Mont., Jan. 19, 1892, from −5° F to 37° F.

In seven minutes: 34° F, Kipp, Mont., Dec. 1, 1896. The observer also reported that a total rise of 80° F occurred in a few hours and that 30 inches of snow disappeared in one–half day.

In two minutes: 49° F, Spearfish, S.D., Jan. 22, 1943 from −4° F at 7:30 a.m. to 45° F at 7:32 a.m.

The Lowest Temperature Extremes

The lowest temperature on record in the United States, −79.8° F, was observed at Prospect Creek Camp in the Endicott Mountains of northern Alaska (latitude 66° 48′N, longitude 150° 40′W) on Jan. 23, 1971. The lowest ever recorded in the conterminous 48 states, −69.7° F, occurred at Rogers Pass, in Lewis and Clark County, Mont., on Jan. 20, 1954. Rogers Pass is in mountainous and heavily forested terrain about one–half mile east of and 140 feet below the summit of the Continental Divide.

The lowest annual normal (1941–70 mean) temperature in the United States is 9.3° F for Barrow, Alaska, which lies on the Arctic coast. Barrow also has the coolest summers (June–August) with a normal temperature of 36.4° F. The lowest winter (December–February) normal temperature, is −15.7° F for Barter Island on the arctic coast of northeast Alaska.

In the 48 conterminous states, Mt. Washington, N.H. (elevation 6,262 feet) has the lowest annual normal temperature 26.9° F and the lowest normal summer temperature, 46.8° F. A few stations in the northeastern United States and in the upper Rocky Mountains have normal annual temperatures in the 30s; summer normal temperatures at these stations are in the low 50s. Winter normal temperatures are lowest in northeastern North Dakota, 5.6° F for Langdon Experiment Farm, and in northwestern Minnesota, 5.3° F for Hallock.

Some Outstanding Temperature Falls

In 24 hours: 100° F, Browing, Mont., Jan. 23–24, 1916, from 44° to −56° F.

In 12 hours: 84° F, Fairfield, Mont., Dec. 24, 1924, from 63° at noon to −21° F at midnight.

In 2 hours: 62° F, Rapid City, S.D., Jan. 12, 1911, from 49° F at 6:00 a.m. to −13° F at 8:00 a.m.

In 27 minutes: 58° F, Spearfish, S.D., Jan. 22, 1943, from 54° F at 9:00 a.m. to −4° F at 9:27 a.m.

In 15 minutes: 47° F, Rapid City, S.D., Jan. 10, 1911, from 55° F at 7:00 a.m. to 8° F. at 7:15 a.m.

1. A warm, dry wind that descends from the eastern slopes of the Rocky Mountains, causing a rapid rise in temperature.

Winter Indoor Comfort and Relative Humidity

Compared to summer when the moisture content of the air (relative humidity) is an important factor of body discomfort, air moisture has a lesser effect on the human body during outdoor winter activities. But it is a big factor for winter indoor comfort because it has a direct bearing on health and energy consumption.

The colder the outdoor temperature, the more heat must be added indoors for body comfort. However, the heat that is added will cause a drying effect and lower the indoor relative humidity, unless an indoor moisture source is present.

While a room temperature between 71° and 77° F may be comfortable for short periods of time under very dry conditions, prolonged exposure to dry air has varying effects on the human body and usually causes discomfort. The moisture content of the air is important, and by increasing the relative humidity to

above 50% within the above temperature range, 80% or more of all average dressed persons would feel comfortable.

Effects of Dry Air on the Body

Studies have shown that dry air has four main effects on the human body:

1. Breathing dry air is a potential health hazard which can cause such respiratory ailments as asthma, bronchitis, sinusitis, and nosebleeds, or general dehydration since body fluids are depleted during respiration.

2. Skin moisture evaporation can cause skin irritations and eye itching.

3. Irritative effects, such as static electricity which causes mild shocks when metal is touched, are common when the air moisture is low.

Average Indoor Relative Humidity, %, for January

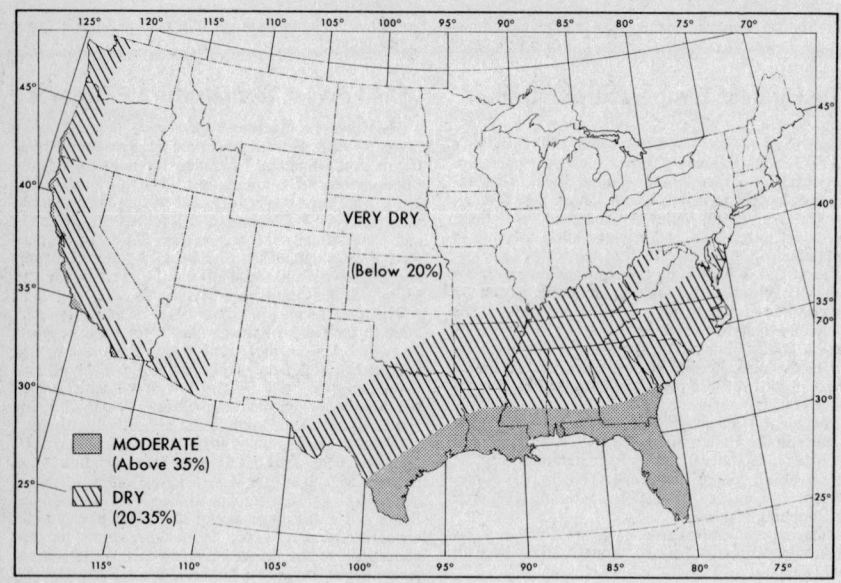

Source: National Oceanic and Atmospheric Administration, Environmental Data and Information Service, National Climatic Center.

4. The "apparent temperature" of the air is lower than what the thermometer indicates, and the body "feels" colder.

These problems can be reduced by simply increasing the indoor relative humidity. This can be done through use of humidifiers, vaporizers, steam generators, sources such as large pans, or water containers made of porous ceramics. Even wet towels or water in a bathtub will be of some help. The lower the room temperature the easier the relative humidity can be brought to its desired level. A relative humidity indicator (hygrometer) may be of assistance in determining the humidity in the house.

Referring to item 4, a more detailed discussion is necessary. While the indoor temperature as read from a thermometer may be 75° F, the apparent temperature (what it feels like) may be warmer or colder depending on the moisture content of the air. Apparent temperature can vary as much as 8° F within a relative humidity range of 10 to 80 percent (these limits are generally possible in a closed room). Because of evaporation the human body cools when exposed to dry air, and the sense of coldness increases as the humidity decreases. With a room temperature of 70° F, for example, a person will feel colder in a dry room than in a moist room; this is especially noticeable when entering a dry room after bathing.

The table on the following page gives apparent temperatures for various combinations of room temperature and relative humidity. As an example of how to read the table, a room temperature of 70° F combined with a relative humidity of 10% feels like 64° F, but at 80% it feels like 71° F.

Although degrees of comfort vary with age, health, activity, clothing, and body characteristics, the table can be used as a general guideline when raising the apparent temperature and the level of comfort through an increase in room moisture, rather than by an addition of heat to the room. This method of changing the apparent temperature can give the direct benefit of reducing heating costs because comfort can be maintained with a lower thermostat setting if moisture is added. For example, an apparent comfortable temperature can be maintained with a thermostat setting of 75° F with 20% relative humidity or with a 70° F setting with 80 percent humidity. A relative humidity of 20 percent is common for homes without a humidifier during winter in the northern United States. □

Hurricane Advisories and Warnings

Source: Federal Emergency Management Agency and NOAA.

Thanks to modern detection and tracking devices, the National Weather Service can usually provide 12 to 24 hours of advance warning. Advisories are issued by the Weather Service if NOAA hurricanes approach land.

A "hurricane watch" is issued whenever a hurricane becomes a threat to coastal areas. Everyone in the area covered by the "watch" should listen for further advisories and be prepared to act promptly if a hurricane warning is issued.

A "hurricane warning" is issued when hurricane winds of 74 miles an hour or higher, or a combination of dangerously high water and very rough seas, are expected in a specific coastal area within 24 hours. Precautionary actions should begin immediately. □

Apparent Temperature for Values of Room Temperature and Relative Humidity

RELATIVE HUMIDITY (%)

ROOM TEMPERATURE (F)	0	10	20	30	40	50	60	70	80	90	100
75	68	69	71	72	74	75	76	76	77	78	79
74	66	68	69	71	72	73	74	75	76	77	78
73	65	67	68	70	71	72	73	74	75	76	77
72	64	65	67	68	70	71	72	73	74	75	76
71	63	64	66	67	68	70	71	72	73	74	75
70	63	64	65	66	67	68	69	70	71	72	73
69	62	63	64	65	66	67	68	69	70	71	72
68	61	62	63	64	65	66	67	68	69	70	71
67	60	61	62	63	64	65	66	67	68	68	69
66	59	60	61	62	63	64	65	66	67	67	68
65	59	60	61	61	62	63	64	65	65	66	67
64	58	59	60	60	61	62	63	64	64	65	66
63	57	58	59	59	60	61	62	62	63	64	64
62	56	57	58	58	59	60	61	61	62	63	63
61	56	57	57	58	59	59	60	60	61	61	62
60	55	56	56	57	58	58	59	59	60	60	61

Source: National Oceanic and Atmospheric Administration, Environmental Data and Information Service and National Climatic Center.

GREAT DISASTERS

The following lists are not all-inclusive due to space limitations. Only disasters involving great loss of life and/or property, historical interest, or unusual circumstances are listed. Data as of Aug. 1, 1996. For later disasters see *Current Events.*

WORST UNITED STATES DISASTERS

Aircraft

1979 May 25, Chicago: American Airlines DC-10 lost left engine upon take-off and crashed seconds later, killing all 272 persons aboard and three on the ground in worst U.S. air disaster.

Dam

1928 March 12, Santa Paula, Calif.: collapse of St. Francis Dam left 450 dead.

Drought

1930s Many states: longest drought of the 20th century. Peak periods were 1930, 1934, 1936, 1939, and 1940. During 1934, dry regions stretched solidly from New York and Pennsylvania across the Great Plains to the California coast. A great "dust bowl" covered some 50 million acres in the south central plains during the winter of 1935–1936.

Earthquake

1906 April 18, San Francisco: earthquake accompanied by fire razed more than 4 sq mi.; more than 500 dead or missing.

Epidemic

1918 Nationwide: Spanish influenza killed over 500,000 Americans.

Explosion

1947 April 16–18, Texas City, Texas: Most of the city destroyed by a fire and subsequent explosion on the French freighter *Grandcamp* carrying a cargo of ammonium nitrate. At least 516 were killed and over 3,000 injured.

Fire

1871 Oct. 8, Peshtigo, Wis.: over 1,200 lives lost and 2 billion trees burned in forest fire.

Flood

1889 May 31, Johnstown, Pa.: more than 2,200 died in flood.

Hurricane

1900 Aug. 27–Sept. 15, Galveston, Tex.: over 6,000 died from devastation due to both winds and tidal wave.

Marine

1865 April 27, *Sultana*: boiler explosion on Mississippi River steamboat near Memphis, 1,547 killed.

Mine

1907 Dec. 6, Monongha, W. Va.: coal mine explosion killed 361.

Oil Spill

1989 Mar. 24, Prince William Sound, Alaska: Tanker, *Exxon Valdez*, hit an undersea reef and released 10 million plus gallons of oil into the waters, causing the worst oil spill in U.S. history.

Railroad

1918 July 9, Nashville, Tenn.: 101 killed in a two-train collision near Nashville.

Submarine

1963 April 10, *Thresher*: atomic-powered submarine sank in North Atlantic: 129 dead.

Terrorist Attack

1995 April 19, Oklahoma City: Terrorist car bomb exploded outside Federal office building, collapsing wall and floors. 168 persons were killed, including 19 children and one person who died in rescue effort. Over 220 buildings sustained damage. Bombing motive believed to be in revenge for the deaths of Branch Davidians in the Waco, Texas, compound, April 19, 1993, resulting from a botched assault by government agents. It is worst terrorist bombing on U.S. soil. *See also,* Miscellaneous, 1993, April 19, Waco, Texas.

Tornado

1925 March 18, Great Tri-State Tornado: Missouri, Illinois, and Indiana; 695 deaths. Eight additional tornadoes in Kentucky, Tennessee, and Alabama raised day's toll to 792 dead.

Winter Storm

1888 March 11–14, East Coast: The Blizzard of 1888. 400 people died, as much as 5 feet of snow. Damage was estimated at $20 million.

Earthquakes and Volcanic Eruptions

A.D. 79 Aug. 24, Italy: eruption of Mt. Vesuvius buried cities of Pompeii and Herculaneum, killing thousands.

1556 Jan. 24, Shaanxi (Shensi) Province, China: most deadly earthquake in history; 830,000 killed.

1755 Nov. 1, Portugal: one of the most severe of recorded earthquakes leveled Lisbon and was felt as far away as southern France and North Africa; 10,000–20,000 killed in Lisbon.

1811 Dec. 16, Mississippi Valley near New Madrid, Missouri: The quake reversed the course of the Mississippi River. Fatalities unknown due to the sparse population in the area. Aftershocks and tremors continued into 1812. It has been estimated that three of the series of earthquakes had surface-wave magnitudes of 8.6, 8.4, and 8.8 on the Richter Scale. It is the largest series of earthquakes known to have occurred in North America.

1883 Aug. 26–28, Netherlands Indies: eruption of Krakatau; violent explosions destroyed two thirds of island. Sea waves occurred as far away as Cape Horn, and possibly England. Estimated 36,000 dead.

1886 Aug. 31, Charleston, S.C.: Sixty persons killed and damage to city extensive. The magnitude was 7.7 on the Richter Scale.

1902 May 8, Martinique, West Indies: Mt. Pelée erupted and wiped out city of St. Pierre; 40,000 dead.

1908 Dec. 28, Messina, Sicily: about 85,000 killed and city totally destroyed.

1915 Jan. 13, Avezzano, Italy: earthquake left 29,980 dead.

1920 Dec. 16, Gansu (Kansu) Province, China: earthquake killed 200,000.

1923 Sept. 1, Japan: earthquake destroyed third of Tokyo and most of Yokohama; more than 140,000 killed.

1933 March 10, Long Beach, Calif.: 117 left dead by earthquake.

1935 May 31, India: earthquake at Quetta killed an estimated 50,000.

1939 Jan. 24, Chile: earthquake razed 50,000 sq mi.; about 30,000 killed.
Dec. 27, Northern Turkey: severe quakes destroyed city of Erzingan; about 100,000 casualties.

1950 Aug. 15, India: earthquake affected 30,000 sq mi. in Assam; 20,000–30,000 believed killed.

1964 March 27, Alaska: strongest earthquake ever to strike North America hit 80 miles east of Anchorage; followed by seismic wave 50 feet high that traveled 8,445 miles at 450 miles per hour; 117 killed.

1970 May 31, Peru: earthquake left 50,000 dead, 17,000 missing.

1972 Dec. 22, Managua, Nicaragua: earthquake devastated city, leaving up to 6,000 dead.

1976 Feb. 4, Guatemala: earthquake left over 23,000 dead.
July 28, Tangshan, China: earthquake devastated 20-sq-mi. area of city leaving estimated 242,000 dead.
Aug. 17, Mindanao, Philippines: earthquake and tidal wave left up to 8,000 dead or missing.

1978 Sept. 16, Tabas, Iran: earthquake destroyed city in eastern Iran, leaving 25,000 dead.

1985 Sept. 19–20, Mexico: earthquake registering 8.1 on Richter scale struck central and southwestern regions, devastating part of Mexico City and three coastal states. An estimated 25,000 killed.
Nov. 14–16, Colombia: eruption of Nevada del Ruiz, 85 miles northwest of Bogotá, caused mud slides which buried most of the town of Armero and devastated Chinchiná. An estimated 25,000 were killed.

1988 Dec. 7, Armenia: an earthquake measuring 6.9 on the Richter scale killed nearly 25,000, injured 15,000, and left at least 400,000 homeless.

1989 Oct. 17, San Francisco Bay Area: an earthquake measuring 7.1 on the Richter Scale killed 67 and injured over 3,000. The quake damaged or destroyed over 100,000 buildings and caused billions of dollars of damage.

1990 June 21, Northwestern Iran: an earthquake measuring 7.7 on the Richter scale destroyed cities, towns, and villages in Caspian Sea area. At least 50,000 killed, over 60,000 injured, and 400,000 homeless.

1994 Jan. 17, San Fernando Valley, Calif.: Earthquake measuring 6.6 on the Richter Scale killed 61 persons and injured over 8,000. Damage estimated at $13–20 billion.

1995 Jan. 17, Osaka, Kyoto, Kobe, Japan: 5,100 killed and 26,800 injured, estimated damage $100 billion. Epicenter 12 miles under Awaji Island in the Inland Sea. Magnitude: 7.2

Major U.S. Epidemics

1793 Philadelphia. More than 4,000 residents died from yellow fever.

1832 July–August, New York City. Over 3,000 people killed in a cholera epidemic. **October, New Orleans.** Cholera took the lives of 4,340 persons.

1848 New York City. More than 5,000 deaths caused by cholera.

1853 New Orleans. Yellow fever killed 7,790 residents.

1867 New Orleans. 3,093 persons perished from yellow fever.

1878 Southern States. Over 13,000 people died from yellow fever in lower Mississippi Valley.

1916 Nationwide. Over 7,000 deaths occurred and 27,363 cases were reported of polio (infantile paralysis) in America's worst polio epidemic.

1918 March–November, Nationwide. Outbreak of influenza killed over 500,000 people in the worst single U.S. epidemic.

1949 Nationwide. 2,720 deaths occurred from polio and 42,173 cases were reported.

1952 Nationwide. Polio killed 3,300; 57,628 cases reported; worst epidemic since 1916.

1981 To present. 78,180 AIDS cases were reported to the Center for Disease Control in 1995. A total of 513,486 AIDS cases have been reported to the CDC since the outbreak through 1995. The CDC estimates that approximately one in 250 Americans are infected with HIV.

Floods, Avalanches, and Tidal Waves

1228 Holland: 100,000 persons reputedly drowned by sea flood in Friesland.

1642 China: rebels destroyed Kaifeng seawall; 300,000 drowned.

1896 June 15, Sanriku, Japan: earthquake and tidal wave killed 27,000.

1953 Northwest Europe: storm followed by floods devastated North Sea coastal areas. Netherlands was hardest hit with 1,794 dead.

1959 Dec. 2, Frejus, France: flood caused by collapse of Malpasset Dam left 412 dead.

1960 Agadir, Morocco: 10, 000–12,000 dead as earthquake set off tidal wave and fire, destroying most of city.

1962 Jan. 10, Peru: avalanche down Huascaran, extinct Andean volcano, killed more than 3,000 persons.

1963 Oct. 9, Italy: landslide into the Vaiont Dam; flood killed about 2,000.

1966 Oct. 21, Aberfan, Wales: avalanche of coal, waste, mud, and rocks killed 144 persons, including 116 children in school.

1969 Jan. 18–26, Southern California: floods and mudslides from heavy rains caused widespread property damage; at least 100 dead. Another downpour (Feb. 23–26) caused further floods and mudslides; at least 18 dead.

1970 Nov. 13, East Pakistan: 200,000 killed by cyclone-driven tidal wave from Bay of Bengal. Over 100,000 missing.

1972 Feb. 26, Man, W. Va.: more than 118 died when slag-pile dam collapsed under pressure of torrential rains and flooded 17-mile valley.
June 9–10, Rapid City, S.D.: flash flood caused 237 deaths and $160 million in damage.
June 20, Eastern Seaboard: tropical storm Agnes, in 10-day rampage, caused widespread flash floods. Death toll was 129, 115,000 were left homeless, and damage estimated at $3.5 billion.
1976 Aug. 1, Loveland, Colo.: Flash flood along Route 34 in Big Thompson Canyon left 139 dead.
1988 August-September, Bangladesh: Heaviest monsoon in 70 years innundates three-fourths of country, killing more than 1,300 people and leaving 30 million homeless. Damage is estimated at over $1 billion.
1993 June–August, Ill., Iowa, Kan., Ky., Minn., Mo., Neb., N.D., S.D., Wis.: Two months of heavy rain caused Mississippi River and its tributaries to flood in ten states, causing almost 50 deaths and an estimated $12 billion in damage to property and agriculture in the Midwest. Almost 70,000 people left homeless.

Tropical Storms

Cyclones, typhoons, and hurricanes are the same kind of tropical storms but are called by different names in different areas of the world. For example: a typhoon is a severe tropical hurricane that occurs in the western Pacific and China Sea.

Cyclones

1864 Oct. 5, India: most of Calcutta denuded by cyclone; 70,000 killed.
1942 Oct. 16, India: cyclone devastated Bengal; about 40,000 lives lost.
1960 Oct. 10, East Pakistan: cyclone and tidal wave killed about 6,000.
1963 May 28–29, East Pakistan: cyclone killed about 22,000 along coast.
1965 May 11–12 and June 1–2, East Pakistan: cyclones killed about 47,000.
Dec. 15, Karachi, Pakistan: cyclone killed about 10,000.
1970 Nov. 12–13, East Pakistan: cyclone and tidal waves killed 200,000 and another 100,000 were reported missing.
1971 Sept. 29, Orissa State, India: cyclone and tidal wave off Bay of Bengal killed as many as 10,000.
1974 Dec. 25, Darwin, Australia: cyclone destroyed nearly the entire city, causing mass evacuation; 50 reported dead.
1977 Nov. 19, Andhra Pradesh, India: cyclone and tidal wave claimed lives of 20,000.
1991 April 30, southeastern Bangladesh: cyclone killed over 131,000 and left as many as 9 million homeless. Thousands of survivors died from hunger and water borne disease.

U.S. Hurricanes

(U.S. deaths only, except where noted)

1775 Sept. 2–Sept. 9, North Carolina to Nova Scotia: called the "Hurricane of Independence," it is believed that 4,170 in the U.S. and Canada died in the storm.
1856 Aug. 11, Last Island, La.: 400 died.

1893 Aug. 28, Savannah, Ga., Charleston, S.C., Sea Islands, S.C.: at least 1,000 died.
1900 Aug. 27–Sept. 15, Galveston, Tex. and Texas Gulf Coast: more than 6,000 died in hurricane and tidal wave.
1909 Sept. 10–21, Louisiana and Mississippi: 350 deaths.
1915 Aug. 5–23, East Texas and Louisiana: 275 killed.
1919 Sept. 2–15, Florida, Louisiana and Texas: 287 deaths, and 488 deaths at sea.
1926 Sept. 11–22, Florida and Alabama: 243 deaths.
1928 Sept. 6–20, Southern Florida: 1,836 died and 1,870 injured.
1935 Sept. 29–Sept. 10, Southern Florida: 408 killed.
1938 Sept. 10–22, Long Island and Southern New England: 600 deaths; 1,764 injured.
1944 Sept. 9–16, North Carolina to New England: 46 deaths, and 344 deaths at sea.
1947 Sept. 4–21, Florida and Mid-Gulf Coast: 51 killed.
1954 Aug. 25–31, North Carolina to New England: "Carol" killed 60 and injured 1,000 in Long Island–New England area.
Oct. 5–18, South Carolina to New York: "Hazel" killed 95 in U.S.; about 400-1000 in Haiti; 78 in Canada.
1955 Aug. 7–21, North Carolina to New England: "Diane" took 184 lives.
1957 June 25–28. Texas to Alabama: "Audrey" wiped out Cameron, La., causing 390 deaths.
1960 Aug. 29–Sept. 13, Florida to New England: "Donna" killed 50 in the United States. 115 deaths in Antilles—mostly from flash floods in Puerto Rico.
1961 Sept. 3–15, Texas coast: "Carla" devastated Texas gulf cities, taking 46 lives.
1965 Aug. 27–Sept. 12, Southern Florida and Louisiana: "Betsy" killed 75 people.
1969 Aug. 14–22, Mississippi, Louisiana, Alabama, Virginia, W. Virginia: 256 killed and 68 persons missing as a result of "Camille."
1972 June 14–23, Florida to New York: "Agnes" caused 117 deaths (50 in Pennsylvania).
1979 Aug. 25–Sept. 7, Caribbean Islands to New England: "David" caused 5 U.S. deaths; 1,200 in the Dominican Republic.
1980 Aug. 3–10, Caribbean Islands to Texas Gulf: "Allen" killed 28 in the U.S.; over 200 killed in Caribbean.
1989 Sept. 10–22, Caribbean Sea and South and North Carolina: "Hugo" claimed 49 U.S. lives (71 killed overall) and $4.2 billion were paid in insurance claims.
1992 Aug. 22–26, South Florida, Louisiana, and Bahamas: Gulf Coast Hurricane "Andrew" with damage in South Florida alone estimated at $20.6 billion (est. $7.3 billion in private insurance claims) is most costly U.S. hurricane.

Other Hurricanes

1926 Oct. 20, Cuba: worst hurricane in 80 years, 650 reported dead.
1930 Sept. 3 Santo Domingo: hurricane killed about 2,000 and injured 6,000.
1934 Sept. 21, Japan: hurricane killed more than 4,000 on Honshu.
1955 Sept. 19, Mexico: Hurricane "Hilda" took 200 lives.
Sept. 22–28, Caribbean: Hurricane "Janet" killed 200 in Honduras and 300 in Mexico.
1961 Oct. 31, British Honduras: Hurricane "Hattie" devastated capital Belize, killed at least 400.

Nuclear Power Plant Accidents

1952 Dec. 12, Chalk River, near Ottawa, Canada: A partial meltdown of the reactor's uranium fuel core resulted after the accidental removal of four control rods. Although millions of gallons of radioactive water accumulated inside the reactor, there were no injuries.

1957 Oct. 7, Windscale Pile No. 1, north of Liverpool, England: Fire in a graphite-cooled reactor spewed radiation over the countryside, contaminating a 200 sq mi area.

South Ural Mountains: Explosion of radioactive wastes at Soviet nuclear weapons factory 12 miles from city of Kyshtym forces the evacuation of over 10,000 people from a contaminated area. No casualties were reported by Soviet officials.

1976 near Greifswald, East Germany. Radioactive core of reactor in the Lubmin nuclear power plant nearly melted down due to the failure of safety systems during a fire.

1979 March 28, Three Mile Island, near Harrisburg, Pa.: One of two reactors lost its coolant, which caused the radioactive fuel to overheat and caused a partial meltdown. Some radioactive material was released.

1986 April 26, Chernobyl, near Kiev, U.S.S.R.: Explosion and fire in the graphite core of one of four reactors released radioactive material which spread over part of the Soviet Union, Eastern Europe, Scandinavia, and later Western Europe. 31 claimed dead. Total casualties are unknown and estimates run into the thousands. Is the worst such accident to date.

1963 Oct. 2–7, Caribbean: Hurricane "Flora" killed up to 7,000 in Haiti and Cuba.

1966 Sept. 24–30, Caribbean area: Hurricane "Inez" killed 293.

1974 Sept. 20, Honduras: Hurricane "Fifi" struck northern section of country, leaving 8,000 dead, 100,000 homeless.

1988 Sept. 12–17, Caribbean Sea and Gulf of Mexico: Hurricane "Gilbert," worst Atlantic storm ever recorded, took at least 260 lives and caused some 39 tornadoes in Texas.

Tornadoes

1884 Feb. 19: tornadoes in Mississippi, Alabama, North and South Carolina, Tennessee, Kentucky and Indiana caused estimated 800 deaths.

1925 Mar. 18: tornadoes in Missouri, Illinois, Indiana, Kentucky, Tennessee, and Alabama killed 792.

1932 March 21: outbreak of tornadoes in Alabama, Mississippi, Georgia, and Tennessee killed 268.

1936 April 5–6: series of tornadoes in Arkansas, Alabama, Tennessee, Georgia, and South Carolina killed 498.

1952 March 21–22: tornadoes in Arkansas, Tennessee, Missouri, Mississippi, Alabama, and Kentucky caused 343 deaths.

1953 May 11: a single tornado struck Wako, Texas, killing 114.

June 8: another tornado killed 116 in Flint, Michigan.

1965 April 11: Tornadoes in Iowa, Illinois, Indiana, Ohio, Michigan, and Wisconsin caused 256 deaths.

1974 April 3–4: a series of tornadoes in East, South, and Midwest killed approximately 315.

Typhoons

1906 Sept. 18, Hong Kong: typhoon with tsunami killed an estimated 10,000 persons.

1949 Dec. 5, Off Korea: typhoon struck fishing fleet; several thousand men reported dead.

1959 Aug. 20, Fukien Province, China: Typhoon "Iris" killed 2,334.

Sept. 27, Honshu, Japan: Typhoon "Vera" killed an estimated 4,464.

1960 June 9, Fukien Province, China: Typhoon "Mary" caused at least 1,600 deaths.

1984 Sept. 2–3, Philippines: Typhoon "Ike" hit seven major islands leaving 1,300 dead.

1991 Nov. 5, Central Philippines: Flash floods triggered by tropical storm "Thelma" killed about 3,000 people. Leyte city of Ormoc was worst hit.

Fires and Explosions

1666 Sept. 2, England: "Great Fire of London" destroyed St. Paul's Church, etc. Damage £10 million.

1835 Dec. 16, New York City: 530 buildings destroyed by fire.

1871 Oct. 8, Chicago: the "Chicago Fire" burned 17,450 buildings, killed 250 persons; $196 million damage.

1872 Nov. 9, Boston: fire destroyed 800 buildings; $75-million damage.

1876 Dec. 5, New York City: fire in Brooklyn Theater killed more than 300.

1881 Dec. 8, Vienna: at least 620 died in fire at Ring Theatre.

1894 Sept. 1, Minnesota: forest fire over 480-square-mile area destroyed six towns and killed 480 people.

1900 May 1, Scofield, Utah: explosion of blasting powder in coal mine killed 200.

June 30, Hoboken, N.J.: piers of North German Lloyd Steamship line burned; 326 dead.

1903 Dec. 30, Chicago: Iroquois Theatre fire killed 602.

1906 March 10, France: explosion in coal mine in Courrières killed 1,060.

1907 Dec. 19, Jacobs Creek, Pa.: explosion in coal mine left 239 dead.

1909 Nov. 13, Cherry, Ill.: explosion in coal mine killed 259.

1911 March 25, New York City: fire in Triangle Shirtwaist Factory fatal to 145.

1913 Oct. 22, Dawson, N.M.: coal mine explosion left 263 dead.

1917 April 10, Eddystone, Pa.: explosion in munitions plant killed 133.

Dec. 6, Canada: 1,600 people died when French ammunition ship *Mont Blanc* collided with Belgium steamer in Halifax Harbor.

1930 April 21, Columbus, Ohio: fire in Ohio State Penitentiary killed 320 convicts.

1937 March 18, New London, Tex.: explosion destroyed schoolhouse; 294 killed.

1942 April 26, Manchuria: explosion in Honkeiko Colliery killed 1,549.

Nov. 28, Boston: Cocoanut Grove nightclub fire killed 491.

1944 July 6, Hartford, Conn.: fire and ensuing stampede in main tent of Ringling Brothers Circus killed 168, injured 487.

July 17, Port Chicago, Calif.: 322 killed as ammunition ships explode.

Oct. 20, Cleveland: liquid-gas tanks exploded, killing 130.

1946 Dec. 7, Atlanta: fire in Winecoff Hotel killed 119.

1948 Dec. 3, Shanghai: Chinese passenger ship *Kiangya*, carrying refugees fleeing Communist troops during civil war, struck an old mine, exploded, and sank off Shanghai. Over 3,000 people are believed killed.

1949 Sept. 2, China: fire on Chongqing (Chungking) waterfront killed 1,700.

1954 May 26, off Quonset Point, R.I.: explosion and fire aboard aircraft carrier *Bennington* killed 103 crewmen.

1956 Aug. 7, Colombia: about 1,100 reported killed when seven army ammunition trucks exploded at Cali.

Aug. 8, Belgium: 262 died in coal mine fire at Marcinelle.

1960 Jan. 21, Coalbrook, South Africa: coal mine explosion killed 437.

Nov. 13, Syria: 152 children killed in moviehouse fire.

1961 Dec. 17, Niteroi, Brazil: circus fire fatal to 323.

1962 Feb. 7, Saarland, West Germany: coal mine gas explosion killed 298.

1963 Nov. 9, Japan: explosion in coal mine at Omuta killed 447.

1965 May 28, India: coal mine fire in state of Bihar killed 375.

June 1, near Fukuoka, Japan: coal mine explosion killed 236.

1967 May 22, Brussels: fire in L'Innovation, major department store killed 322 dead.

July 29, off North Vietnam: fire on U.S. carrier *Forrestal* killed 134.

1969 Jan. 14, Pearl Harbor, Hawaii: nuclear aircraft carrier *Enterprise* ripped by explosions; 27 dead, 82 injured.

1970 Nov. 1, Saint-Laurent-du-Pont, France: fire in dance hall killed 146 young people.

1972 May 13, Osaka, Japan: 118 people died in fire in nightclub on top floor of Sennichi department store.

June 6, Wankie, Rhodesia: explosion in coal mine killed 427.

1973 Nov. 29, Kumamoto, Japan: fire in Taiyo department store killed 101.

1974 Feb. 1, Sao Paulo, Brazil: fire in upper stories of bank building killed 189 persons, many of whom leaped to death.

1975 Dec. 27, Dhanbad, India: explosion in coal mine followed by flooding from nearby reservoir left 372 dead.

1977 May 28, Southgate, Ky.: fire in Beverly Hills Supper Club; 167 dead.

1978 July 11, Tarragona, Spain: 140 killed at coastal campsite when tank truck carrying liquid gas overturned and exploded.

Aug. 20, Abadan, Iran: nearly 400 killed when arsonists set fire to crowded theater.

1982 Dec. 18–21, Caracas, Venezuela: power-plant fire leaves 128 dead.

1986 Dec. 31, San Juan, P. R.: arson fire in Dupont Plaza Hotel set by three hotel employees kills 96.

1989 June 3, Ural Mountains: Liquified petroleum gas leaking from a pipeline running alongside the Trans-Siberian railway near Uta, 720 miles east of Moscow, exploded and destroyed two passing passenger trains. About 500 travelers were killed and 723 injured of an estimated 1,200 passengers on both trains.

Oct. 23, Pasadena, Texas. A huge explosion followed by a series of others and a raging fire at a plastics manufacturing plant owned by Phillips Petroleum Co. killed 22 and injured more than 80 persons. A large leak of ethylene was presumed to be the cause.

1990 March 25, New York City. Arson fire in illegal *Happy Land Social Club*, Bronx, killed 87.

1991 Oct. 20–23, Oakland–Berkeley, Calif.: Brush fire in drought-stricken area destroyed over 3,000 homes and apartments. At least 24 persons died, damage estimated at $1.5 billion.

1993 May 10, near Bangkok, Thailand: Fire in doll factory killed at least 187 persons and injured 500 others. Is world's deadliest factory fire.

Shipwrecks

1833 May 11, *Lady of the Lake:* bound from England to Quebec, struck iceberg; 215 perished.

1853 Sept. 29 *Annie Jane:* emigrant vessel off coast of Scotland; 348 died.

1898 Nov. 26, *City of Portland:* Loss of 157 off Cape Cod.

1904 June 15, *General Slocum:* excursion steamer burned in East River, New York; 1,021 perished.

1912 March 5, *Principe de Asturias:* Spanish steamer struck rock off Sebastien Point; 500 drowned.

April 15, *Titanic:* sank after colliding with iceberg; 1,513 died.

1914 May 29, *Empress of Ireland:* sank after collision in St. Lawrence River; 1,024 perished.

1915 July 24, *Eastland:* Great Lakes excursion steamer overturned in Chicago River; 812 died.

1928 Nov. 12, *Vestris:* British steamer sank in gale off Virginia; 110 died.

1934 Sept. 8, *Morro Castle:* 134 killed in fire off Asbury Park, N.J.

1939 May 23, *Squalus:* submarine with 59 men sank off Hampton Beach, N.H.; 33 saved.

June 1, Submarine *Thetis:* sank in Liverpool Bay, England; 99 perished.

1942 Oct. 2, *Queen Mary:* rammed and sank a British cruiser; 338 aboard the cruiser died.

1945 April 9: U.S. ship, loaded with aerial bombs, exploded at Bari, Italy; at least 360 killed.

1947 November, Yingkow: Unidentified Chinese troopship evacuating Nationalist troops from Manchuria sank, killing an estimated 6,000 persons.

1949 Sept. 17, *Noronic:* Canadian Great Lakes cruise ship burned at Toronto dock; about 130 died.

1952 April 26, *Hobson:* minesweeper collided with aircraft carrier *Wasp* and sank during night maneuvers in mid-Atlantic; 176 persons lost.

1953 Jan. 9, *Chang Tyong-Ho:* South Korean ferry foundered off Pusan; 249 reported dead.

Jan. 31, *Princess Victoria:* British ferry sank in Irish Sea; 133 lost.

1956 July 25, *Andrea Doria:* Italian liner collided with Swedish liner *Stockholm* off Nantucket Island, Mass., sinking next day; 52, mostly passengers on Italian ship, dead or unaccounted for; over 1,600 rescued.

1962 April 8, *Dara,* British liner, exploded and sank in Persian Gulf; 236 persons dead. Caused by time bomb.

1963 May 4: U.A.R. ferry capsized and sank in upper Nile; over 200 died.

1968 Late May, *Scorpion:* nuclear submarine sank in Atlantic 400 miles S.W. of Azores; 99 dead. (Located Oct. 31.)

1970 Dec. 15: ferry in Korean Strait capsized; 261 lost.

1976 Oct. 20, Luling, La.: *George Prince,* Mississippi River ferry, rammed by Norwegian tanker *Frosta;* 77 dead.

1983 May 25, *10th of Ramadan,* Nile steamer, caught fire and sank in Lake Nasser, near Aswan, Egypt; 272 dead and 75 missing.

1987 March 9, Belgium: British ferry capsizes after leaving Belgian port of Zeebrugge with 500 abroad; 134 drowned. Water rushing through open bow is believed to be probable cause.

1987 Dec. 20. Manila: Over 1,500 people killed when passenger ferry *Dona Paz* collided with oil tanker *Victor* off Mindoro Is., 110 miles south of Manila.

1990 April 7, Skagerrak Strait off Norway. Suspected arson fire aboard Danish-owned North Sea ferry, *Scandinavian Star,* kills at least 110 passengers.

April 7, Myanmar (Burma). Double-decker ferry sinks in Gyaing River during a storm and 215 persons are believed drowned.

1991 Dec. 14, off coast of Safaga, Egypt: Ferry carrying 569 passengers sank in Red Sea after hitting a coral reef. Over 460 people believed drowned.

1993 Feb. 17, off southern peninsula, Haiti: Triple-deck ferry *Neptune* capsized during a squall. Over 1,000 passengers believed drowned. About 300 survived the sinking.

1994 Sept. 28, off coast of southwest Finland: Passenger ferry *Estonia* capsized and sank in a stormy Baltic Sea. Only about 140 of the estimated 1,040 passengers aboard survived.

Mysterious Disappearances

1872 The brigantine *Mary Celeste* set sail from New York harbor for Genoa, Italy, on November 5. A British brigantine, the *DeGratia,* discovered the ship derelict on December 5 and boarded her. Everyone aboard the *Mary Celeste* had vanished—her captain, his family, and its 14-man crew. The ship was in perfect order with ample supplies and there was no sign of violence or trouble. The fate of the crew remains unknown today.

1928 Dec. 22: The five-masted Danish steel barque *Köbenhavn,* a sail-training ship with a crew of 75 including 45 boy cadets, sailed from the River Plate for Melbourne, Australia, on December 14. The last radio contact with the ship was made on December 22 and all was well. The *Köbenhavn* and its crew disappeared without a trace and no one knows what happened to it.

Aircraft Accidents

(150 deaths or more, with exceptions)

1921 Aug. 24, England: *AR-2* British dirigible, broke in two on trial trip near Hull; 62 died.

1925 Sept. 3, Caldwell, Ohio: U.S. dirigible *Shenandoah* broke apart; 14 dead.

1930 Oct. 5, Beauvais, France: British dirigible R 101 crashed, killing 47.

1933 April 4, New Jersey Coast: U.S. dirigible *Akron* crashed; 73 died.

1937 May 6, Lakehurst, N.J.: German zeppelin *Hindenburg* destroyed by fire at tower mooring; 36 killed.

1945 July 28, New York City: U.S. Army bomber crashed into Empire State Building; 13 dead.

1960 Dec. 16, New York City: United and Trans World planes collided in fog, crashed in two boroughs, killing 134 in air and on ground.

1961 Feb. 15, near Brussels: 72 on board and farmer on ground killed in crash of Sabena plane; U.S. figure skating team wiped out.

1966 Dec. 24, Binh Thai, South Vietnam: crash of military-chartered plane into village killed 129.

1971 July 30, Morioka, Japan: Japanese Boeing 727 and F-86 fighter collided in mid-air; toll was 162.

1972 Aug. 14, East Berlin, East Germany: Soviet-built East German Ilyushin plane crashed, killing 156.
Dec. 3, Santa Cruz de Tenerife, Canary Islands: Spanish charter jet carrying West German tourists crashed on take-off; all 155 aboard killed.

1973 Jan. 22, Kano, Nigeria: 171 Nigerian Moslems returning from Mecca and five crewmen died in crash.

1973 Feb. 21: Civilian Libyan Arab Airlines Boeing 727 shot down by Israeli fighters over Sinai after it had strayed off course; 108 died, five survived. Officials claimed that the pilot had ignored fighters' warnings to land.

1974 March 3, Paris: Turkish DC-10 jumbo jet crashed in forest shortly after take-off; all 346 passengers and crew killed.
Dec. 4, Colombo, Sri Lanka: Dutch DC-8 carrying Moslems to Mecca crashed on landing approach, killing all 191 persons aboard.

1975 April 4, near Saigon, Vietnam: Air Force Galaxy C-5A crashed after take-off, killing 172, mostly Vietnamese children.
Aug. 3, Agadir, Morocco: Chartered Boeing 707, returning Moroccan workers home after vacation in France, plunged into mountainside; all 188 aboard killed.

1976 Sept. 10, Zagreb, Yugoslavia: midair collision between British Airways Trident and Yugoslav charter DC-9 fatal to all 176 persons aboard; worst mid-air collision on record.

1977 March 27, Santa Cruz de Tenerife, Canary Islands: Pan American and KLM Boeing 747s collided on runway. All 249 on KLM plane and 333 of 394 aboard Pan Am jet killed. Total of 582 is highest for any type of aviation disaster.

1978 Jan. 1, Bombay: Air India 747 with 213 aboard exploded and plunged into sea minutes after takeoff.
Sept. 25, San Diego, Calif.: Pacific Southwest plane collided in midair with Cessna. All 135 on airliner, 2 in Cessna, and 7 on ground killed for total of 144.
Nov. 15, Colombo, Sri Lanka: Chartered Icelandic Airlines DC-8, carrying 249 Moslem pilgrims from Mecca, crashed in thunderstorm during landing approach; 183 killed.

Space Accidents

1967 Jan. 27, Apollo 1: A fire aboard the space capsule on the ground at Cape Kennedy, Fla. killed astronauts Virgil I. Grissom, Edward H. White, and Roger Chaffee.

April 23–24, Soyuz 1: Vladimir M. Komarov was killed when his craft crashed after its parachute lines, released at 23,000 feet for re-entry, became snarled.

1971 June 6–30, Soyuz 11: Three cosmonauts, Georgi T. Dolrovolsky, Vladislav N. Volkov, and Viktor I. Patsayev, found dead in the craft after its automatic landing. Apparently the cause of death was loss of pressurization in the space craft during re-entry into the earth's atmosphere.

1980 March 18, U.S.S.R. A Vostok rocket exploded on its launch pad while being refueled, killing 50 at the Plesetsk Space Center.

1986 Jan 28, Challenger Space Shuttle: Exploded 73 seconds after lift off, killing all seven crew members. They were: Christa McAuliffe, Francis R. Scobee, Michael J. Smith, Judith A. Resnick, Ronald E. McNair, Ellison S. Onizuka, and Gregory B. Jarvis. A booster leak ignited the fuel, causing the explosion.

1979 Nov. 26, Jidda, Saudi Arabia: Pakistan International Airlines 707 carrying pilgrims returning from Mecca crashed on take-off; all 156 aboard killed.

Nov. 28, Mt. Erebus, Antarctica: Air New Zealand DC-10 crashed on sightseeing flight; 257 killed.

1980 Aug. 19, Riyadh, Saudi Arabia: all 301 aboard Saudi Arabian jet killed when burning plane made safe landing but passengers were unable to escape.

1981 Dec. 1, Ajaccio, Corsica: Yugoslav DC-9 Super 80 carrying tourists crashed into mountain on landing approach, killing all 178 aboard.

1983 Aug. 30, near island of Sakhalin off Siberia, South Korean civilian jetliner Boeing 747, flight KAL-007 shot down by Soviet fighter after it strayed off course into Soviet airspace. All 269 people aboard killed.

Secret Soviet documents released in October 1992, revealed that the plane was flying a straight course for two hours with its navigational lights on, it did not take evasive action, its crew members were unaware of its location, they never saw the Soviet fighter that shot them down and the Soviet fighter did not give a warning by firing tracer bullets as originally claimed. Recorded conversations indicated that the crew did not know what hit them.

Nov. 26, Madrid: A Columbian Avianca Boeing 747 crashed near Mejorada del Campó Airport killing 183 persons aboard. Eleven people survived the accident.

1985 June 23: Air-India Boeing 747 exploded over the Atlantic off the coast of Ireland, all 329 aboard killed.

Aug. 12, Japan Air Lines Boeing 747 crashed into a mountain, killing 520 of the 524 aboard.

Dec. 12, A chartered Arrow Air DC-8, bringing American soldiers home for Christmas, crashed on takeoff from Gander, Newfoundland. All 256 aboard died.

1987 May 9, Poland: Polish airliner, Ilyushin 62M on charter flight to New York, crashes after takeoff from Warsaw killing 183.

Aug. 16, Detroit: Northwest Airlines McDonnell Douglas MD-30 plunges to heavily traveled boulevard, killing 156. Girl 4, only survivor.

Nov. 26: South African Airways Boeing 747 goes down south of Mauritius in rough seas; 160 die.

Nov. 29: Korean Air Boeing 747 jetliner explodes from bomb planted by North Korean agents and crashes into sea off Burma, killing all 115 aboard.

1988 July 3, Persian Gulf: U.S. Navy cruiser *Vincennes* shot down Iran Air A300 Airbus, killing 290 persons, after mistaking it for an attacking jet fighter.

Aug. 28, Ramstein Air Force Base, West Germany: Three jets from Italian Air Force acrobatic team collided in mid-air during air show and crashed, killing 70 persons, including the pilots and spectators on the ground. It is worst air-show disaster in history.

Dec. 21, Lockerbie, Scotland: A New-York-bound Pan-Am Boeing 747 exploded in flight from a terrorist bomb and crashed into Scottish village, killing all 259 aboard and 11 persons on the ground. Passengers included 38 Syracuse University students and many U.S. military personnel.

1989 June 7, Paramaribo, Suriname: A Surinam Airways DC-8 carrying 174 passengers and nine crew members crashed into the jungle while making a third attempt to land in a thick fog, killing 168 aboard.

1991 July 11, Jedda, Saudi Arabia: Canadian-chartered DC-8 carrying pilgrims returning to Nigeria crashes after takeoff, killing 261 persons.

1994 April 14, northern Iraq: Two American F-15C fighter aircraft mistake two U.S. Army Blackhawk helicopters for Russian-made Iraqi MI-24 helicopters and shot them down over no-fly zone, killing all 26 on board them.

April 26, Nagoya, Japan: A China Airlines A–300 Airbus from Taiwan crash-landed and exploded on the tarmac. Only 7 of the 271 passengers aboard survived.

June 6, Xian, China: A Russian-built Tupolev-154 airliner of China Northwest Airlines crashed 10 minutes after takeoff, killing all 160 aboard.

1995 Dec. 20, near Cali, Colombia: 160 people killed when American Airlines Boeing 757 crashed in Andean Mountains.

1996 Jan. 8, Kinshasa, Zaire: A Russian-built Antonov-32 cargo plane crashed after takeoff from Kinshasa into the center of the city, killing over 350 people and injuring at least 470.

Feb. 5, off coast of Puerto Plata, Dominican Republic: A Boeing 737 crashed into Atlantic Ocean after takeoff, killing 189.

July 18, off coast of Long Island, N.Y.: A TWA Boeing 747-100 bound for Paris from New York explodes over waters of eastern L.I. and crashes into Atlantic Ocean, killing all 230 aboard.

Railroad Accidents

NOTE: Very few passengers were killed in a single U.S. train wreck up until 1853. These early trains ran slowly, made short trips, night travel was rare, and there were not many of them in operation.

1831 June 17: The boiler exploded on America's first passenger locomotive, *The Best Friend of Charleston*, killing the fireman. He was the first person in America to be killed in a railroad accident.

1833 Nov. 8, near Heightstown, N.J.: the world's first train wreck and the first passenger fatalities recorded. A 24-passenger Camden & Amboy train was derailed due to a broken axle, killing two passengers and injuring all others. Former president, John Quincy Adams and Cornelius Vanderbilt, who later made a fortune in railroads, were aboard the train.

1853 May 6, Norwalk, Conn: a New Haven Railroad train ran through an open drawbridge and plunged into the Norwalk River. Forty-six passengers were crushed to death or drowned. This was the first major drawbridge accident.

1856 July 17, Camp Hill, Pa.: two Northern Penn trains crashed head-on. Sixty-six church school children bound for a picnic died in the flaming wreckage.

1876 Dec. 29, Ashtabula, Ohio: a Lake Shore train fell into the Ashtabula River when a bridge it was crossing collapsed during a snowstorm. Ninety-two were killed.

1887 Aug. 10, near Chatsworth, Ill.: a burning railroad trestle collapsed while a Toledo, Peoria & Western train was crossing, killing 81 and injuring 372.

1904 Aug. 7, Eden, Colo.: Train derailed on bridge during flash flood; 96 killed.

1910 March 1, Wellington, Wash.: two trains swept into canyon by avalanche; 96 dead.

1915 May 22, Gretna, Scotland: two passenger trains and troop train collided; 227 killed.

1917 Dec. 12, Modane, France: nearly 550 killed in derailment of troop train near mouth of Mt. Cenis tunnel.

1918 Nov. 1, New York City: derailment of subway train in Malbone St. tunnel in Brooklyn left 92 dead.

1926 March 14, Virilla River Canyon, Costa Rica: An over-crowded train carrying pilgrims was derailed while crossing the Colima Bridge, killing over 300 people and injuring hundreds more.

1939 Dec. 22, near Magdeburg, Germany: more than 125 killed in collision; 99 killed in another wreck near Friedrichshafen.

1943 Dec. 16, near Rennert, N.C.: 72 killed in derailment and collision of two Atlantic Coast Line trains.

1944 March 2, near Salerno, Italy: 521 suffocated when Italian train stalled in tunnel.

1949 Oct. 22, near Nowy Dwor, Poland: more than 200 reported killed in derailment of Danzig-Warsaw express.

1950 Nov. 22, Richmond Hill, N.Y.: 79 died when one Long Island Rail Road commuter train crashed into rear of another.

1951 Feb. 6, Woodbridge, N.J.: 85 died when Pennsylvania Railroad commuter train plunged through temporary overpass.

Oct. 8, Harrow-Wealdstone, England: two express trains crashed into commuter train; 112 dead.

1957 Sept. 1, near Kendal, Jamaica: about 175 killed when train plunged into ravine.

Sept. 29, near Montgomery, West Pakistan: express train crashed into standing oil train; nearly 300 killed.

Dec. 4, St. John's, England: 92 killed, 187 injured as one commuter train crashed into another in fog.

1960 Nov. 14, Pardubice, Czechoslovakia: two trains collided; 110 dead, 106 injured.

1962 May 3, near Tokyo: 163 killed and 400 injured when train crashed into wreckage of collision between inbound freight train and outbound commuter train.

1963 Nov. 9, near Yokohama, Japan: two passenger trains crashed into derailed freight, killing 162.

1964 July 26, Custoias, Portugal: passenger train derailed; 94 dead.

1970 Feb. 4, near Buenos Aires: 236 killed when express train crashed into standing commuter train.

1972 July 21, Seville, Spain: head-on crash of two passenger trains killed 76.

Oct. 6, near Saltillo, Mexico: train carrying religious pilgrims derailed and caught fire, killing 204 and injuring over 1,000.

Oct. 30, Chicago: two Illinois Central commuter trains collided during morning rush hour; 45 dead and over 200 injured.

1974 Aug. 30, Zagreb, Yugoslavia: train entering station derailed, killing 153 and injuring over 60.

1981 June 6, Near Mansi, India: Driver of train carrying over 500 passengers, braked to avoid hitting cow, causing train to plunge off a bridge into Baghmati River; 268 passengers were reported killed, but at least 300 more were missing.

1982 July 11, Tepic, Mexico: Nogales-Guadalajara train plunges down mountain gorge killing 120.

1989 Jan. 15, Maizdi Khan, Bangladesh: A train carrying Muslim pilgrims crashed head-on with a mail train killing at least 110 persons and injuring as many as 1,000. Many people were riding on the roof of the trains and between the cars.

1989 Aug. 10, near Los Mochis, Mexico: A second-class passenger train traveling from Mazatlán to Mexicali, plunged off a bridge at Puente del Rio Bamoa into the river and killed an estimated 85 people and injured 107.

1990 Jan. 4, Sangi village, Sindh province, Pakistan: An overcrowded sixteen-car passenger train was switched to the wrong track and rammed into a standing freight train. At least 210 persons were killed and 700 were believed injured in what is said to be Pakistan's worst train disaster.

1993 Sept. 22, near Mobile, Ala.: Amtrak's Sunset Limited, en route to Miami, jumps rails on weakened bridge that had been damaged by a barge, and plunges into Big Bayou Canot, killing 47 persons.

1995 Aug. 20, Firozabad, northern India: A speeding passenger train rammed another train that had stalled after hitting a cow. About 300 persons were killed and over 400 injured.

Oil Spills

1978 March 16, off Portsall, France: Wrecked supertanker *Amoco Cadiz* spilled 68 million gallons causing widespread environmental damage over 100 miles of coast of Brittany. Is world's largest tanker disaster.

1979 June 8, Gulf of Mexico: Exploratory oil well, Ixtoc 1, blew out, spilling an estimated 140 million gallons of crude into the open sea. Although it is the largest known oil spill, it had a low environmental impact.

1989 Dec. 19. Off Las Palmas, the Canary Islands. An explosion in Iranian supertanker, the *Kharg-5*, tore through its hull and caused 19 million gallons of crude oil to spill out into the Atlantic Ocean about 400 miles north of Las Palmas, forming a 100-square-mile oil slick.

1994 Aug. 12, near Ursinsk, Russia: Huge oil spill from ruptured pipeline. September 8: a dam built to contain oil bursts spilled oil into tributary of Kolva River. U.S. Energy Department estimates spill at 2 million barrels. Russian state-owned oil company claims spill was only 102,000 barrels.

1996 Feb. 15, off Welsh coast: Supertanker, *Sea Empress*, ran aground at port of Milford Haven, Wales, and spewed out 70,000 tons of crude and created a 25-mile slick.

Wartime Spills

1991 Jan. 25, Southern Kuwait: during the Persian Gulf War, Iraq deliberately released an estimated 460 million gallons of crude oil into the Persian Gulf from tankers at Mina al-Ahmadi and Sea Island Terminal 10 miles off Kuwait. Spill had little military significance. On Jan. 27, U.S. warplanes bombed pipe systems to stop the flow of oil.

Sports

1955 June 11, Le Mans, France: Racing car in Grand Prix hurtled into grandstand, killing 82 spectators.

1964 May 24, Lima, Peru: More than 300 soccer fans killed and over 500 injured during riot and panic following unpopular ruling by referee in Peru vs. Argentina soccer game. It is worst soccer disaster on record.

1971 Jan. 2, Glasgow, Scotland: Sixty-six persons killed in a crush at the Glasgow Rangers home stadium when fans trying to leave encountered fans trying to return to the stadium after hearing that a late goal had been scored.

1982 Oct. 20, Moscow: According to *Sovietsky Sport*, as many as 340 persons were killed at Lenin Stadium when exiting soccer fans collided with returning fans after final goal was scored. All the fans had been crowded into one section of stadium by police.

1985 May 11, Bradford, England: 56 persons burned to death and over 200 injured when fire engulfed the main grandstand at Bradford's soccer stadium.

May 29, Brussels, Belgium: Drunken group of British soccer fans supporting Liverpool club stormed stand filled with Italian supporters of Juventus team before European Champion's Cup final. While British fans attacked rival spectators at the Heysel Stadium, concrete retaining wall collapsed and 39 persons were crushed or trampled to death, 32 of them Italians. More than 400 persons were injured.

1988 March 12, Katmandu, Nepal: Some 80 soccer fans seeking cover during a violent hail storm at the national stadium were trampled to death in a stampede because the stadium doors were locked.

1989 April 15, Sheffield, England: Ninety-four people were killed and 170 injured at Hillsborough stadium when throngs of Liverpool soccer fans, many without tickets, collapsed a stadium barrier in a mad rush to see the game between Liverpool and Nottingham Forest. It was Britain's worst soccer disaster.

Terrorist Attacks in U.S.

1920 Sept. 16, New York City: TNT bomb planted in unattended horse-drawn wagon exploded on Wall Street opposite House of Morgan, killing 35 persons and injuring hundreds more. Bolshevist or anarchist terrorists believed responsible but crime never solved.

1975 Jan. 24, New York City: Bomb set off in historical Fraunces Tavern killed four and injured more than 50 persons. Puerto Rican nationalist group (FALN) claimed responsibility and police tied 13 other bombings to them.

Dec. 29, New York City: Bomb exploded in locker area of main terminal at La Guardia Airport, killing 11 persons and injuring 75 others. Puerto Rican nationalist group (FALN) was the prime suspect.

1993 Feb. 26, New York City: Bomb exploded in basement garage of World Trade Center; killed 6 persons and injured at least 1,040 others.

Miscellaneous

1958 January–October, Austria, France, Germany, Italy, and Switzerland: 283 people were killed in mountain climbing accidents in Alps Mountains.

1980 Jan. 20, Sincelejo, Colombia: Bleachers at a bullring collapsed, leaving 222 dead.

March 30, Stavanger, Norway: Floating hotel in North Sea collapsed, killing 123 oil workers.

1981 July 18, Kansas City, Mo.: suspended walkway in Hyatt Regency Hotel collapses; 113 dead, 186 injured.

1984 Dec. 3, Bhopal, India: Toxic gas, methyl isocyanate, seeped from Union Carbide insecticide plant, killing more than 2,000; injuring about 150,000.

1987 Sept. 18. Goiânia, Brazil: 244 people contaminated with cesium-137 removed from steel cylinder taken from cancer-therapy machine in abandoned clinic and sold as scrap. Four people died in worst radiation disaster in Western Hemisphere.

1988 July 6, North Sea off Scotland: 166 workers killed in explosion and fire on Occidental Petroleum's Piper Alpha rig in North Sea off Scottish coast; 64 survivors rescued. It is the world's worst offshore oil disaster.

1990 July 2, Mecca, Saudi Arabia: a stampede in a 1,800 foot-long pedestrian tunnel leading from Mecca to a tent city for pilgrims, killed 1,426 pilgrims who were trampled to death.

1991 Nov. 29, near Coalinga, Calif.: A massive traffic accident occurred during a severe dust storm involving 104 vehicles in a pileup on Interstate 5; 17 persons killed.

1993 April 19, Waco, Texas: A 51-day stalemate between B.A.T.F. and F.B.I. agents seeking to investigate child abuse charges and members of the Christian Branch Davidian cult ended in a fiery tragedy after Federal agents botched their assault on the sect's compound. Earlier, on February 28, four Federal agents were shot to death in a failed attack on the heavily armed compound. About 80 Branch Davidians, including at least 17 children, died when the compound burned to the ground in a suspicious blaze.

1995 June 29, Seoul, Korea: Five-story wing of Sampoong Department Store collapsed, killing at least 206 people, injuring 910 others.

July 12–17, U.S. Midwest and Northeast: Over 800 persons, including 560 in Chicago, die in record heat wave.

1996 May 10–11, Mt. Everest, Nepal: Eight climbers die at summit during storm on mountain. Is worst single loss of life to occur on Mt. Everest.

Wartime Disasters

1915 May 6: Despite German warnings in newspapers, the Cunard Liner *Lusitania* sailed from New York for Liverpool, England, on May 1st and was sunk off the coast of Ireland by a German submarine. 1,198 passengers and crew, 128 of them Americans, died. Unknown to the passengers, the ship was carrying a cargo of small arms. The disaster contributed to the entry of the United States into World War I.

1916 Feb. 26: 3,100 people died when the French cruiser *Provence* was sunk by a German submarine in the Mediterranean.

1940 Sept. 13. The luxury liner *S.S. City of Benares* sailed from Liverpool with over 90 British children who were being evacuated to Canada to escape harm during World War II. About 600 miles out to sea, the ship was torpedoed by a German submarine during the night and only 13 of the children survived the disaster.[1]

1941 Dec. 7, Pearl Harbor, Hawaii: 1,177 crewmen were killed when U.S. Battleship *Arizona* was sunk during a surprise attack on the American naval base by Japanese warplanes. The devastating air strike, which damaged or destroyed the ships of the entire battleship force of the U.S. Pacific fleet, was the worst naval catastrophe in U.S. history.

1943 Nov. 26, Mediterranean Sea: 1,015 U.S. soldiers died when the British troopship *HMT Rohna*, was sunk by a German air-to-surface guided missile. It is the worst U.S. troopship disaster.

Dec., Bari Harbor, Italy: U.S. ship, damaged during German bombing attack, leaked mustard gas into harbor, killing 83 U.S. servicemen and nearly 1,000 civilians.

1944 Sept. 12, South China Sea: U.S. submarines torpedoed and sank two Japanese troop ships[2], the *Kachidoki Maru* and the *Rakuyo Maru*. Unknown to the submarines, the Japanese, in disregard for the rules of treatment of prisoners of war, had forced 2,000 British, Australian, and American POWs into the holds of the ships which were designed to hold only 300 troops. Later, when the subs discovered the tragedy, they sought to rescue as many survivors as possible. Japanese vessels picked up most of *Kachidoki Maru*'s prisoners but abandoned those

from the *Rakuyo Maru*, taking only the Japanese survivors. Of the 1,300 POWs aboard the *Rakuyo Maru*, 159 were rescued, but only seven lived.

Oct. 24, South China Sea: The *Arisan Maru*[2] carrying 1,800 American prisoners was torpedoed by a U.S. submarine and sunk. The Japanese destroyer escort rescued Japanese military and civilian personnel and left the POWs to their fate. It is estimated that only ten prisoners survived the disaster.

Dec. 17–18, Philippine Sea: A typhoon struck U.S. Third Fleet's Task Force 38, sank three destroyers, damaged seven other ships, destroyed 186 aircraft, and killed 800 officers and men.

1945 Jan. 30: 7,700 persons died in world's largest marine disaster when the Nazi passenger ship *Wilhelm Gustoff* car rying Germans fleeing Poland was torpedoed in the Baltic by a Soviet submarine.

May 3, Cap Arcona: Several days before World War II ended in Europe, the German passenger ship carrying about 6,000, of which an estimated 5,000 were concentration camp prisoners, was sunk by British aircraft. An estimated 5,000 persons were killed, most of them prisoners who were about to gain their freedom.

May 4, Gearhart Mountain, south-central Oregon: Six picnicking persons, including a mother and her unborn child, were the only persons ever killed by an exploding balloon-carried bomb launched from Japan. During war, Japan launched some six thousand FUGO ("windship weapons") balloons to drift across the Pacific to the U.S. and Canada, each carrying bombs and incendiaries for starting forest fires and creating death and havoc among the American people. Although over 200 of the deadly balloons floated to the U.S. before the war ended, the government kept it a secret from the American people.

July 29, near Leyte Gulf: The heavy cruiser *Indianapolis* was torpedoed and sunk by a Japanese submarine before the ship could send an SOS for help. Of the crew of 1,199 men, only 316 survived. Due to Navy blundering, the warship was not reported missing when it did not arrive at Leyte on July 31 as scheduled and therefore no search was made for its crew. The survivors were discovered by a Navy patrol plane 82 hours after the ship had gone down.

1991 February, Kuwait: during the Persian Gulf War, Iraqi troops systematically dynamited and set fire to 650 of Kuwait's 950 oil wells, causing the world's worst man-made environmental disaster. A total of 749 wells were damaged including those set ablaze. The last of the oil fires was extinguished on Nov. 6, 1991.

---

1. During the war (1939-1945), some 10,000 children were evacuated to stay with foster parents in the United States and Canada. The sinking of the *City of Benares* ended the British government's evacuation program.
2. The ships had no identification that they were transporting prisioners of war.

RELIGION

Major Religions of the World

Judaism

The determining factors of Judaism are: descendance from Israel, the *Torah*, and Tradition.

The name Israel (Jacob, a patriarch) also signifies his descendants as a people. During the 15th–13th centuries B.C., Israelite tribes, coming from South and East, gradually settled in Palestine, then inhabited by Canaanites. They were held together by Moses, who gave them religious unity in the worship of *Jahweh*, the God who had chosen Israel to be his people.

Under Judges, the 12 tribes at first formed an amphictyonic covenant. Saul established kingship (circa 1050 B.C.), and under David, his successor (1000–960 B.C.), the State of Israel comprised all of Palestine with Jerusalem as religio-political center. A golden era followed under Solomon (965–926 B.C.), who built *Jahweh* a temple.

After Solomon's death, the kingdom separated into Israel in the North and Judah in the South. A period of conflicts ensued, which ended with the conquest of Israel by Assyria in 722 B.C. The Babylonians defeated Judah in 586 B.C., destroying Jerusalem and its temple, and deporting many to Babylon.

The era of the kings is significant also in that the great prophets worked in that time, emphasizing faith in *Jahweh* as both God of Israel and God of the universe, and stressing social justice.

When the Persians permitted the Jews to return from exile (539 B.C.), temple and cult were restored in Jerusalem. The Persian rulers were succeeded by the Seleucides. The Maccabaean revolt against these Hellenistic kings gave independence to the Jews in 128 B.C., which lasted till the Romans occupied the country.

Important groups that exerted influence during these times were the Sadducees, priests in the temple in Jerusalem; the Pharisees, teachers of the Law in

Worldwide Adherents of All Religions, Mid–1995

Statistics of the world's religions are only very rough approximations. Aside from Christianity, few religions, if any, attempt to keep statistical records; and even Protestants and Catholics employ different methods of counting members. All persons of whatever age who have received baptism in the Catholic Church are counted as members, while in most Protestant Churches only those who "join" the church are numbered. The compiling of statistics is further complicated by the fact that in China one may be at the same time a Confucian, a Taoist, and a Buddhist. In Japan, one may be both a Buddhist and a Shintoist.

Religion	Africa	Asia[1]	Europe[2]	Latin America	Northern America	Oceania	World
Baha'is	1,851,000	3,010,000	93,000	719,000	356,000	75,000	6,104,000
Buddhists[3]	36,000	320,691,000	1,478,000	569,000	920,000	200,000	323,894,000
Chinese folk religionists[4]	12,000	224,828,000	116,000	66,000	98,000	17,000	225,137,000
Christians	348,176,000	306,762,000	551,892,000	448,006,000	249,277,000	23,840,000	1,927,953,000
Roman Catholics	122,108,000	90,041,000	270,677,000	402,691,000	74,243,000	8,265,000	968,025,000
Protestants	135,088,000	435,430,000	110,625,000	328,370,000	130,076,000	14,228,000	466,397,000
Orthodox	29,645,000	14,881,000	165,795,000	481,000	6,480,000	666,000	217,948,000
Other Christians	61,335,000	158,297,000	4,795,000	11,997,000	38,478,000	681,000	275,583,000
Confucians	1,000	5,220,000	4,000	2,000	26,000	1,000	5,254,000
Ethnic religionists	72,777,000	36,579,000	1,200,000	1,061,000	47,000	113,000	111,777,000
Hindus[5]	1,535,000	775,252,000	1,522,000	748,000	1,185,000	305,000	780,547,000
Jains	58,000	4,804,000	15,000	4,000	4,000	1,000	4,886,000
Jews	163,000	4,294,000	2,529,000	1,098,000	5,942,000	91,000	14,117,000
Muslims[6]	300,317,000	760,181,000	31,975,000	1,329,000	5,450,000	382,000	1,099,634,000
New-Religionists[7]	19,000	118,591,000	808,000	913,000	956,000	10,000	121,297,000
Shintoists	0	2,840,000	1,000	1,000	1,000	1,000	2,844,000
Sikhs	36,000	18,130,000	490,000	8,000	490,000	7,000	19,161,000
Spiritists	4,000	1,100,000	17,000	8,768,000	300,000	1,000	10,190,000
Other religionists[8]	89,000	296,000	444,000	185,000	1,069,000	43,000	2,156,000
Nonreligious[9]	2,573,000	701,175,000	94,330,000	15,551,000	25,050,000	2,870,000	841,549,000
Atheists[10]	427,000	174,174,000	40,085,000	2,977,000	1,670,000	592,000	219,925,000
Total population[11]	**728,074,000**	**3,457,957,000**	**728,999,000**	**482,005,000**	**292,841,000**	**28,549,000**	**5,716,425,000**

1. Asia includes the former U.S.S.R. central Asian republics. 2. Europe includes the Russian Federation, extending to its easternmost boundaries. 3. Buddhists: 56% Mahayana, 38% Theravada (Hinayana), and 6% Tantrayana (Lamaism). 4. Followers of the traditional Chinese religion (local deities, ancestor veneration, Confucian ethics, Taoism, universism, divination, some Buddhist elements). 5. Hindus: including 70% Vaishnavites, 25% Shaivites, 2% neo-Hindus and reform Hindus. 6. Muslims: 83% Sunnites, 16% Shi'ites, 1% other. 7. Followers of Asian 20th-century New Religions, New Religious movements, radical new crisis religions, and non-Christian syncretistic mass religions, all founded since 1800 and most since 1945. 8. Including 70 minor world religions and a large number of spiritist religions, New Age religions, quasi religions, and religious or mystic belief systems. 9. Persons professing no religion, nonbelievers, agnostics, freethinkers, and formerly religious secularists. 10. Persons professing atheism, skepticism, disbelief, or antireligion (opposed to all religion). 11. Total population figures are the U.N. medium variant figures for mid-1995 as given in *World Population Prospects: The 1994 Revision* (1995). Reprinted with permission from *1996 Britannica Book of the Year.* © 1996 Encyclopaedia Britannica, Inc.

the synagogues; Essenes, a religious order (from whom Dead Sea Scrolls, discovered in 1947, came); Apocalyptists, who were expecting the heavenly Messiah; and Zealots, who were prepared to fight for national independence.

When the latter turned against Rome in A.D. 66, Roman armies under Titus suppressed the revolt, destroying Jerusalem and its temple in A.D. 70. The Jews were scattered in the *diaspora* (Dispersion), subject to oppressions until the Age of the Enlightenment (18th century) brought their emancipation, although persecutions did not end entirely.

The fall of the Jerusalem temple was an important event in the religious life of the Jews, which now developed around *Torah* (Law) and synagogue. Around A.D. 100 the Sacred Scriptures were codified. Synagogue worship became central, with readings from *Torah* and prophets. Most important prayers are the *Shema* (Hear) and the Prayer of the 18 Benedictions.

Religious life is guided by the commandments contained in the *Torah:* circumcision and *Sabbath,* as well as other ethical and ceremonial commandments.

The *Talmud,* based on the *Mishnah* and its interpretations, took shape over many centuries in the Babylonian and Palestinian Schools. It was a strong binding force of Judaism in the Dispersion.

In the 12th century, Maimonides formulated his "13 Articles of Faith," which carried great authority. Fundamental in this creed are: belief in God and his oneness (*Sherma*), belief in the changeless *Torah,* in the words of Moses and the prophets, belief in reward and punishment, the coming of the Messiah, and the resurrection of the dead.

Judaism is divided into theological schools, the main divisions of which are Orthodox, Conservative, and Reform.

Christianity

Christianity is founded upon Jesus Christ, to whose life the New Testament writings testify. Jesus, a Jew, was born in about 7 B.C. and assumed his public life, after his 30th year, in Galilee. The Gospels tell of many extraordinary deeds that accompanied his ministry. He proclaimed the Kingdom of God, a future reality that is at the same time already present. Nationalistic-Jewish expectations of the Messiah he rejected. Rather, he referred to himself as the "Son of Man," the Christ, who has power to forgive sins now and who shall also come as Judge at the end of time. Jesus set forth the religio-ethical demands for participation in the Kingdom of God as change of heart and love of God and neighbor.

At the Last Supper he signified his death as a sacrifice, which would inaugurate the New Covenant, by which many would be saved. Circa A.D. 30 he died on a cross in Jerusalem. The early Church carried on Jesus' proclamation, the apostle Paul emphasizing his death and resurrection.

The person of Jesus is fundamental to the Christian faith since it is believed that in his life, death, and resurrection, God's revelation became historically tangible. He is seen as the turning point in history, and man's relationship to God as determined by his attitude to Jesus.

Historically Christianity thus arose out of Judaism, claiming fulfillment of the promises of the Old Testament in Jesus. The early Church designated itself as "the true Israel," which expected the speedy return of Jesus. The mother church was at Jerusalem, but churches were soon founded in many other places. The apostle Paul was instrumental in founding and

extending a Gentile Christianity that was free from Jewish legalism.

The new religion spread rapidly throughout the eastern and western parts of the Roman Empire. In coming to terms with other religious movements within the Empire, Christianity began to take definite shape as an organization in its doctrine, liturgy, and ministry circa A.D. 200. In the 4th century the Catholic Church had taken root in countries stretching from Spain in the West to Persia and India in the East. Christians had been repeatedly subject to persecution by the Roman state, but finally gained tolerance under Constantine the Great (A.D. 313). Since that time, the Church became favored under his successors and in 380 the Emperor Theodosius proclaimed Christianity the State religion. Paganism was suppressed and public life was gradually molded in accordance with Christian ethical demands.

It was in these years also that the Church was able to achieve a certain unity of doctrine. Due to differences of interpretation of basic doctrines concerning Christ, which threatened to divide the Catholic Church, a standard Christian Creed was formulated by bishops at successive Ecumenical Councils, the first of which was held in A.D. 325 (Nicaea). The chief doctrines formulated concerned the doctrine of the Trinity, i.e., that there is one God in three persons: Father, Son, and Holy Spirit (Constantinople, A.D. 381); and the nature of Christ as both divine and human (Chalcedon, A.D. 541).

Through differences and rivalry between East and West the unity of the Church was broken by schism in 1054. In 1517 a separation occurred in the Western Church with the Reformation. From the major Protestant denominations [Lutheran, Presbyterian, Anglican (Episcopalian)], many Free Churches separated themselves in an age of individualism.

In the 20th century, however, the direction is toward unity. The Ecumenical Movement led to the formation of the World Council of Churches in 1948 (Amsterdam), which has since been joined by many Protestant and Orthodox Churches.

Through its missionary activity Christianity has spread to most parts of the globe.

U.S. Religious Bodies with Members Over 2,000,000

Religious body	Members
Roman Catholic Church	60,190,605
Southern Baptist Convention	15,614,060
United Methodist Church	8,584,125
National Baptist Convention, U.S.A.	8,200,000
Church of God in Christ	5,499,875
Evangelical Lutheran Church in America	5,199,048
Church of Jesus Christ of Latter-day Saints	4,613,000
Presbyterian Church (U.S.A.)	3,698,136
African Methodist Episcopal Church	3,500,000
National Baptist Convention of America (DAARB)	3,500,000
Lutheran Church–Missouri Synod	2,596,927
Episcopal Church	2,504,682
National Missionary Baptist Convention of America	2,500,000
Progressive National Baptist Convention	2,500,000
Assemblies of God	2,324,615

Source: Yearbook of American & Canadian Churches, 1996.

Eastern Orthodoxy

Eastern Orthodoxy comprises the faith and practice of Churches stemming from ancient Churches in the Eastern part of the Roman Empire. The term covers Orthodox Churches in communion with the See of Constantinople and Nestorian and Monophysite Churches.

The Orthodox, Catholic, Apostolic Church is the direct descendant of the Byzantine State Church and consists of a series of independent national churches that are united by Doctrine, Liturgy, and Hierarchical organization (deacons and priests, who may either be married or be monks before ordination, and bishops, who must be celibates). The heads of these Churches are patriarchs or metropolitans; the Patriarch of Constantinople is only "first among equals." Rivalry between the Pope of Rome and the Patriarch of Constantinople, aided by differences and misunderstandings that existed for centuries between the Eastern and Western parts of the Empire, led to a schism in 1054. Repeated attempts at reunion have failed in past centuries. The mutual excommunication pronounced in that year was lifted in 1965, however, and because of greater interaction in theology between Orthodox Churches and those in the West, a climate of better understanding has been created in the 20th century. First contacts were with Anglicans and Old Catholics. Orthodox Churches belong to the World Council of Churches.

The Eastern Orthodox Churches recognize only the canons of the seven Ecumenical Councils (325–787) as binding for faith and they reject doctrines that have been added in the West.

The central worship service is called the Liturgy, which is understood as representation of God's acts of salvation. Its center is the celebration of the Eucharist, or Lord's Supper.

In their worship icons (sacred pictures) are used that have a sacramental meaning as representation. The Mother of Christ, angels, and saints are highly venerated.

The number of sacraments in the Orthodox Church is the same as in the Western Catholic Church.

Orthodox Churches are found in the Balkans and the Soviet Union also, since the 20th century, in Western Europe and other parts of the world, particularly in America.

Eastern Rite Churches

These include the Uniate Churches that recognize the authority of the Pope but keep their own traditional liturgies and those Churches dating back to the 5th century that emanicipated themselves from the Byzantine State Church: the Nestorian Church in the Near East and India and the Monophysite Churches (Coptic, Ethiopian, Syrian, Armenian, and the Mar Thoma Church in India).

Roman Catholicism

Roman Catholicism comprises the belief and practice of the Roman Catholic Church. The Church stands under the authority of the Bishop of Rome, the Pope, and is ruled by him and bishops who are held to be, through ordination, successors of Peter and the Apostles, respectively. Fundamental to the structure of the Church is the juridical aspect: doctrine and sacraments are bound to the power of jurisdiction and consecration of the hierarchy. The Pope, as the head of the hierarchy of archbishops, bishops, priests, and deacons, has full ecclesiastical power, granted him by Christ, through Peter. As successor to Peter, he is the Vicar of Christ. The powers that others in the hierarchy possess are delegated.

Roman Catholics believe their Church to be the one, holy, catholic, and apostolic Church, possessing all the properties of the one, true Church of Christ.

The faith of the Church is understood to be identical with that taught by Christ and his Apostles and contained in Bible and Tradition, i.e. the original deposit of faith, to which nothing new may be added. New definitions of doctrines, such as the Immaculate Conception of Mary (1854) and the bodily Assumption of Mary (1950), have been declared by Popes, however, in accordance with the principle of development (implicit-explicit doctrine).

At Vatican Council I (1870) the Pope was proclaimed "endowed with infallibility, *ex cathedra,* i.e., when exercising the office of Pastor and Teacher of all Christians."

The center of Roman Catholic worship is the celebration of the Mass, the Eucharist, which is the commemoration of Christ's sacrificial death and of his resurrection. Other sacraments are Baptism, Confirmation, Confession, Matrimony, Ordination, and Extreme Unction, seven in all. The Virgin Mary and saints, and their relics, are highly venerated and prayers are made to them to intercede with God, in whose presence they are believed to dwell.

The Roman Catholic Church is the largest Christian organization in the world, found in most countries.

Since Vatican Council II (1962–65), and the effort to "update" the Church, many interesting changes and developments have been taking place.

Protestantism

Protestantism comprises the Christian churches that separated from Rome during the Reformation in the 16th century, initiated by an Augustinian monk, Martin Luther. "Protestant" was originally applied to followers of Luther, who protested at the Diet of Spires (1529) against the decree which prohibited all further ecclesiastical reforms. Subsequently, Protestantism came to mean rejection of attempts to tie God's revelation to earthly institutions, and a return to the Gospel and the Word of God as sole authority in matters of faith and practice. Central in the biblical message is the justification of the sinner by faith alone. The Church is understood as a fellowship and the priesthood of all believers stressed.

The Augsburg Confession (1530) was the principal statement of Lutheran faith and practice. It became a model for other Confessions of Faith, which in their turn had decisive influence on Church policy. Major Protestant denominations are the Lutheran, Reformed (Calvinist), Presbyterian, and Anglican (Episcopal). Smaller ones are the Mennonite, Schwenkfeldians, and Unitarians. In Great Britain and America there are the Congregationalists, Baptists, Quakers, Methodists, and other free church types of communities. (In regarding themselves as being faithful to original biblical Christianity, these Churches differ from such religious bodies as Unitarians, Mormons, Jehovah's Witnesses, and Christian Scientists, who either teach new doctrines or reject old ones.)

Since the latter part of the 19th century, national councils of churches have been established in many countries, e.g. the Federal Council of Churches of Christ in America in 1908. Denominations across countries joined in federations and world alliances, beginning with the Anglican Lambeth Conference in 1867.

Protestant missionary activity, particularly strong in the last century, resulted in the founding of many younger churches in Asia and Africa. The Ecumenical Movement, which originated with Protestant missions, aims at unity among Christians and churches.

Islam

Islam is the religion founded in Arabia by Mohammed between 610 and 632. There are an estimated 5.4 million Muslims in Northern America and more than 1 billion Muslims worldwide.

Mohammed was born in A.D. 570 at Mecca and belonged to the Quraysh tribe, which was active in caravan trade. At the age of 25 he joined the caravan trade from Mecca to Syria in the employment of a rich widow, Khadiji, whom he married. Critical of the idolatry of the inhabitants of Mecca, he began to lead a contemplative life in the deserts. There he received a series of revelations. Encouraged by Khadiji, he gradually became convinced that he was given a God-appointed task to devote himself to the reform of religion and society. Idolatry was to be abandoned.

The *Hegira (Hijra)* (migration) of Mohammed from Mecca, where he was not honored, to Medina, where he was well received, occurred in 622 and marks the beginning of the Muslim era. In 630 he marched on Mecca and conquered it. He died at Medina in 632. His grave there has since been a place of pilgrimage.

Mohammed's followers, called Muslims, revered him as the prophet of *Allah* (God), beside whom there is no other God. Although he had no close knowledge of Judaism and Christianity, he considered himself succeeding and completing them as the seal of the Prophets. Sources of the Islamic faith are the *Qur'an*, regarded as the uncreated, eternal Word of God, and Tradition *(hadith)* regarding sayings and deeds of the prophet.

Islam means surrender to the will of *Allah*. He is the all-powerful, whose will is supreme and determines man's fate. Good deeds will be rewarded at the Last Judgment in paradise and evil deeds will be punished in hell.

The Five Pillars, primary duties, of Islam are: witness; confessing the oneness of God and of Mohammed, his prophet; prayer, to be performed five times a day; almsgiving to the poor and the mosque (house of worship); fasting during daylight hours in the month of Ramadan; and pilgrimage to Mecca at least once in the Muslim's lifetime.

Islam, upholding the law of brotherhood, succeeded in uniting an Arab world that had disintegrated into tribes and castes. Disagreements concerning the succession of the prophet caused a great division in Islam between *Sunnis* and *Shias*. Among these, other sects arose *(Wahhabi)*. Doctrinal issues also led to the rise of different schools of thought in theology. Nevertheless, since Arab armies turned against Syria and Palestine in 635, Islam has expanded successfully under Mohammed's successors. Its rapid conquests in Asia and Africa are unsurpassed in history. Turning against Europe, Muslims conquered Spain in 713. In 1453 Constantinople fell into their hands and in 1529 Muslim armies besieged Vienna. Since then, Islam has lost its foothold in Europe.

In modern times it has made great gains in Africa.

Hinduism

Hinduism is the major religion of India where there are more than 7.6 million adherents. In contrast to other religions, it has no founder. Considered the oldest religion in the world, it dates back, perhaps, to prehistoric times.

Hinduism is hard to define, there being no common creed, no one doctrine to bind Hindus together. Intellectually there is complete freedom of belief, and one can be monotheist, polytheist, or atheist.

The most important sacred texts of the Hindu religion are written in Sanskrit and called the *Vedas*

(Veda-knowledge). There are four Vedic books, of which the *Rig-Veda* is the oldest. It speaks of many gods and also deals with questions concerning the universe and creation. The dates of these works are unknown (1000 B.C.?).

The *Upanishads* (dated 1000–300 B.C.), commentaries on the Vedic texts, have philosophical speculations on the origin of the universe, the nature of deity, of *atman* (the human soul), and its relationship to *Brahman* (the universal soul).

Brahman is the principle and source of the universe who can be indicated only by negatives. As the divine intelligence, he is the ground of the visible world, a presence that pervades all beings. Thus the many Hindu deities came to be understood as manifestations of the one *Brahman* from whom everything proceeds and to whom everything ultimately returns. The religio-social system of Hinduism is based on the concept of reincarnation and transmigration in which all living beings, from plants below to gods above, are caught in a cosmic system that is an everlasting cycle of becoming and perishing.

Life is determined by the law of *karma*, according to which rebirth is dependent on moral behavior in a previous phase of existence. In this view, life on earth is regarded as transient *(maya)* and a burden. The goal of existence is liberation from the cycle of rebirth and redeath and entrance into the indescribable state of what in Buddhism is called *nirvana* (extinction of passion).

Further important sacred writings are the Epics *(ithasas)*, which contain legendary stories about gods and men. They are the *Mahabharata* (composed between 200 B.C. and A.D. 200) and the *Ramayana*. The former includes the poem *Bhagavad-Gita* (Song of the Lord).

The practice of Hinduism consists of rites and ceremonies centering on the main socio-religious occasions of birth, marriage, and death. There are many Hindu temples, which are dwelling places of the deities and to which people bring offerings. There are also places of pilgrimages, the chief one being Benares on the Ganges, most sacred among the rivers in India.

Orthodox Hindu society in India was divided into four major hereditary casts: 1) Brahmans (priestly and learned class); 2) Kshatriyas (military, professional, rulers and governing occupations); 3) Vaisyas (landowners, merchants, and business occupations); and 4) Sudras (artisans, laborers, and peasants). Below the Sudras was a fifth group, the untouchables (lowest menial occupations and no social standing). The Indian government banned discrimination against the untouchables in 1949.

In modern times work has been done to reform and revive Hinduism. One of the outstanding reformers was Ramakrishna (1836–86), who inspired many followers, one of whom founded the Ramakrishna mission. The mission is active both in India and in other countries and is known for its scholarly and humanitarian works.

Buddhism

Founded in the 6th century B.C. in northern India by Gautama Buddha, who was born in southern Nepal as son to a king. His birth is surrounded by many legends, but Western scholars agree that he lived from 563 to 483 B.C. Warned by a sage that his son would become an ascetic or a universal monarch, the king confined him to his home. He was able to escape and began the life of a homeless wanderer in search of peace, passing through many disappointments until he finally came to the Tree of Enlightenment, under which he lived in meditation till enlightenment came to him and he became a Buddha (enlightened one).

Now he understood the origin of suffering, summarized in the *Four Noble Truths*, which constitutes the foundation of Buddhism. The Four are the truth of suffering, which all living beings must endure; of the origin of suffering, which is craving and which leads to rebirth; that it can be destroyed; and of the way that leads to cessation of pain, i.e., the *Noble Eightfold Way*, which is the rule of practical Buddhism: right views, right intention, right speech, right action, right livelihood, right effort, right concentration, and right ecstasy.

Nirvana is the goal of all existence, the state of complete redemption, into which the redeemed enters. Buddha's insight can free every man from the law of reincarnation through complete emptying of the self.

The nucleus of Buddha's church or association was originally formed by monks and lay-brothers, whose houses gradually became monasteries used as places for religious instruction. The worship service consisted of a sermon, expounding of Scripture, meditation, and confession. At a later stage pilgrimages to the holy places associated with the Buddha came into being, as well as veneration of relics.

In the 3rd century B.C., King Ashoka made Buddhism the State religion of India but, as centuries passed, it gradually fell into decay through splits, persecutions, and the hostile Brahmans. Buddhism spread to countries outside India, however.

At the beginning of the Christian era, there occurred a split that gave rise to two main types: *Hinayana* (Little Vehicle), or southern Buddhism, and *Mahayana* (Great Vehicle), or northern Buddhism. The former type, more individualistic, survived in Ceylon and southern Asia. *Hinayana* retained more closely the original teachings of the Buddha, which did not know of a personal god or soul. *Mahayana*, more social, polytheistic, and developing a pluralistic pompous cult, was strong in the Himalayas, Tibet, Mongolia, China, Korea, and Japan.

In the present century, Buddhism has found believers also in the West and there are an estimated 920,000 Buddhists in Northern America.

Confucianism

Confucius (K'ung Fu-tzu), born in the state of Lu (northern China), lived from 551 to 479 B.C. Tradition, exaggerating the importance of Confucius in life, has depicted him as a great statesman but, in fact, he seems to have been a private teacher. Anthologies of ancient Chinese classics, along with his own Analects *(Lun Yu)*, became the basis of Confucianism. These Analects were transmitted as a collection of his sayings as recorded by his students, with whom he discussed ethical and social problems. They developed into men of high moral standing, who served the State as administrators.

In his teachings, Confucius emphasized the importance of an old Chinese concept *(li)*, which has the connotation of proper conduct. There is some disagreement as to the religious ideas of Confucius, but he held high the concepts handed down from centuries before him. Thus he believed in Heaven *(T'ien)* and sacrificed to his ancestors. Ancestor worship he indeed encouraged as an expression of filial piety, which he considered the loftiest of virtues.

Piety to Confucius was the foundation of the family as well as the State. The family is the nucleus of the State, and the "five relations," between king and subject, father and son, man and wife, older and younger brother, and friend and friend, are determined by the virtues of love of fellow men, righteousness, and respect.

An extension of ancestor worship may be seen in the worship of Confucius, which became official in the 2nd century B.C. when the emperor, in recognition of Confucius' teachings as supporting the imperial rule, offered sacrifices at his tomb.

Mencius (Meng Tse), who lived around 400 B.C., did much to propagate and elaborate Confucianism in its concern with ordering society. Thus, for two millennia, Confucius' doctrine of State, with its emphasis on ethics and social morality, rooted in ancient Chinese tradition and developed and continued by his disciples, has been standard in China and the Far East.

With the revolution of 1911 in China, however, students, burning Confucius in effigy, called for the removal of "the old curiosity shop."

Shintoism

Shinto, the Chinese term for the Japanese *Kami no Michi*, i.e., the Way of the Gods, comprises the religious ideas and cult indigenous to Japan. *Kami*, or gods, considered divine forces of nature that are worshipped, may reside in rivers, trees, rocks, mountains, certain animals, or, particularly, in the sun and moon. The worship of ancestors, heroes, and deceased emperors was incorporated later.

After Buddhism had come from Korea, Japan's native religion at first resisted it. Then there followed a period of compromise and amalgamation with Buddhist beliefs and ceremonies, resulting, since the 9th century A.D., in a syncretistic religion, a Twofold Shinto. Buddhist deities came to be regarded as manifestations of Japanese deities and Buddhist priests took over most of the Shinto shrines.

In modern times Shinto regained independence from Buddhism. Under the reign of the Emperor Meiji (1868–1912) it became the official State religion, in which loyalty to the emperor was emphasized. The line of succession of emperors is traced back to the first Emperor Jimmu (660 B.C.) and beyond him to the Sun-goddess *Amaterasuomikami*.

The centers of worship are the shrines and temples in which the deities are believed to dwell and believers approach them through *torii* (gateways). Most important among the shrines is the imperial shrine of the Sun-goddess at Ise, where state ceremonies were once held in June and December. The *Yasukuni* shrine of the war dead in Tokyo is also well known.

Acts of worship consist of prayers, clapping of hands, acts of purification, and offerings. On feast days processions and performances of music and dancing take place in the shrines, and priests read prayers before the gods for good harvest, the well-being of people and emperor, etc. In Japanese homes there is a god-shelf, a small wooden shrine that contains the tablets bearing the names of ancestors. Offerings are made and candles lit before it.

After World War II the Allied Command ordered the disestablishment of State Shinto. To be distinguished from State Shinto is Sect Shinto, consisting of 13 recognized sects. These have arisen in modern times. Most important among them is *Tenrikyo* in Tenri City (Nara), in which healing by faith plays a central role.

Taoism

Taoism, a religion of China, was, according to tradition, founded by Lao Tse, a Chinese philosopher, long considered one of the prominent religious leaders from the 6th century B.C.

Data about him are for the most part legendary, however, and the *Tao Te Ching* (the classic of the Way and of its Power), traditionally ascribed to him, is now believed by many scholars to have originated in the 3rd century B.C. The book is composed in short chapters, written in aphoristic rhymes. Central are the word *Tao*, which means way or path and, in a deeper sense, signifies the principle that underlies the reality of this world and manifests itself in nature and in the lives of men, and the word *Te* (power).

The virtuous man draws power from being absorbed in *Tao*, the ultimate reality within an ever-changing world. By non-action and keeping away from human striving it is possible for man to live in harmony with the principles that underlie and govern the universe. *Tao* cannot be comprehended by reason and knowledge, but only by inward quiet.

Besides the *Tao Te Ching*, dating from approximately the same period, there are two Taoist works, written by Chuang Tse and Lieh Tse.

Theoretical Taoism of this classical philosophical movement of the 4th and 3rd centuries B.C. in China differed from popular Taoism, into which it gradually degenerated. The standard of theoretical Taoism was maintained in the classics, of course, and among the upper classes it continued to be alive until modern times.

Religious Taoism is a form of religion dealing with deities and spirits, magic and soothsaying. In the 2nd century A.D. it was organized with temples, cult, priests, and monasteries and was able to hold its own in the competition with Buddhism that came up at the same time.

After the 7th century A.D., however, Taoist religion further declined. Split into numerous sects, which often operate like secret societies, it has become a syncretistic folk religion in which some of the old deities and saints live on.

Roman Catholic Pontiffs

St. Peter, of Bethsaida in Galilee, Prince of the Apostles, was the first Pope. He lived first in Antioch and then in Rome for 25 years. In AD 64 or 67, he was martyred. St. Linus became the second Pope.

Name	Birthplace	Reigned From	Reigned To	Name	Birthplace	Reigned From	Reigned To
St. Linus	Tuscia	67	76	St. Leo I (the Great)	Tuscany	440	461
St. Anacletus (Cletus)	Rome	76	88	St. Hilary	Sardinia	461	468
St. Clement	Rome	88	97	St. Simplicius	Tivoli	468	483
St. Evaristus	Greece	97	105	St. Felix III (II)[2]	Rome	483	492
St. Alexander I	Rome	105	115	St. Gelasius I	Africa	492	496
St. Sixtus I	Rome	115	125	Anastasius II	Rome	496	498
St. Telesphorus	Greece	125	136	St. Symmachus	Sardinia	498	514
St. Hyginus	Greece	136	140	St. Hormisdas	Frosinone	514	523
St. Pius I	Aquileia	140	155	St. John I	Tuscany	523	526
St. Anicetus	Syria	155	166	St. Felix IV (III)	Samnium	526	530
St. Soter	Campania	166	175	Boniface II	Rome	530	532
St. Eleutherius	Epirus	175	189	John II	Rome	533	535
St. Victor I	Africa	189	199	St. Agapitus I	Rome	535	536
St. Zephyrinus	Rome	199	217	St. Silverius	Campania	536	537
St. Callistus I	Rome	217	222	Vigilius	Rome	537	555
St. Urban I	Rome	222	230	Pelagius I	Rome	556	561
St. Pontian	Rome	230	235	John III	Rome	561	574
St. Anterus	Greece	235	236	Benedict I	Rome	575	579
St. Fabian	Rome	236	250	Pelagius II	Rome	579	590
St. Cornelius	Rome	251	253	St. Gregory I (the Great)	Rome	590	604
St. Lucius I	Rome	253	254	Sabinianus	Tuscany	604	606
St. Stephen I	Rome	254	257	Boniface III	Rome	607	607
St. Sixtus II	Greece	257	258	St. Boniface IV	Marsi	608	615
St. Dionysius	Unknown	259	268	St. Deusdedit (Adeodatus I)	Rome	615	618
St. Felix I	Rome	269	274				
St. Eutychian	Luni	275	283	Boniface V	Naples	619	625
St. Caius	Dalmatia	283	296	Honorius I	Campania	625	638
St. Marcellinus	Rome	296	304	Severinus	Rome	640	640
St. Marcellus I	Rome	308	309	John IV	Dalmatia	640	642
St. Eusebius	Greece	309[1]	309[1]	Theodore I	Greece	642	649
St. Meltiades	Africa	311	314	St. Martin I	Todi	649	655
St. Sylvester I	Rome	314	335	St. Eugene I[3]	Rome	654	657
St. Marcus	Rome	336	336	St. Vitalian	Segni	657	672
St. Julius I	Rome	337	352	Adeodatus II	Rome	672	676
Liberius	Rome	352	366	Donus	Rome	676	678
St. Damasus I	Spain	366	384	St. Agatho	Sicily	678	681
St. Siricius	Rome	384	399	St. Leo II	Sicily	682	683
St. Anastasius I	Rome	399	401	St. Benedict II	Rome	684	685
St. Innocent I	Albano	401	417	John V	Syria	685	686
St. Zozimus	Greece	417	418	Conon	Unknown	686	687
St. Boniface I	Rome	418	422	St. Sergius I	Syria	687	701
St. Celestine I	Campania	422	432	John VI	Greece	701	705
St. Sixtus III	Rome	432	440				

Name	Birthplace	Reigned From	To	Name	Birthplace	Reigned From	To
John VII	Greece	705	707	Victor II	Germany	1055	1057
Sisinnius	Syria	708	708	Stephen IX (X)	Lorraine	1057	1058
Constantine	Syria	708	715	Nicholas II	Burgundy	1059	1061
St. Gregory II	Rome	715	731	Alexander II	Milan	1061	1073
St. Gregory III	Syria	731	741	St. Gregory VII	Tuscany	1073	1085
St. Zachary	Greece	741	752	Bl. Victor III	Benevento	1086	1087
Stephen II (III)[4]	Rome	752	757	Bl. Urban II	France	1088	1099
St. Paul I	Rome	757	767	Paschal II	Ravenna	1099	1118
Stephen III (IV)	Sicily	768	772	Gelasius II	Gaeta	1118	1119
Adrian I	Rome	772	795	Callistus II	Burgundy	1119	1124
St. Leo III	Rome	795	816	Honorius II	Flagnano	1124	1130
Stephen IV (V)	Rome	816	817	Innocent II	Rome	1130	1143
St. Paschal I	Rome	817	824	Celestine II	Città di Castello	1143	1144
Eugene II	Rome	824	827				
Valentine	Rome	827	827	Lucius II	Bologna	1144	1145
Gregory IV	Rome	827	844	Bl. Eugene III	Pisa	1145	1153
Sergius II	Rome	844	847	Anastasius IV	Rome	1153	1154
St. Leo IV	Rome	847	855	Adrian IV	England	1154	1159
Benedict III	Rome	855	858	Alexander III	Siena	1159	1181
St. Nicholas I (the Great)	Rome	858	867	Lucius III	Lucca	1181	1185
				Urban III	Milan	1185	1187
Adrian II	Rome	867	872	Gregory VIII	Benevento	1187	1187
John VIII	Rome	872	882	Clement III	Rome	1187	1191
Marinus I	Gallese	882	884	Celestine III	Rome	1191	1198
St. Adrian III	Rome	884	885	Innocent III	Anagni	1198	1216
Stephen V (VI)	Rome	885	891	Honorius III	Rome	1216	1227
Formosus	Portus	891	896	Gregory IX	Anagni	1227	1241
Boniface VI	Rome	896	896	Celestine IV	Milan	1241	1241
Stephen VI (VII)	Rome	896	897	Innocent IV	Genoa	1243	1254
Romanus	Gallese	897	897	Alexander IV	Anagni	1254	1261
Theodore II	Rome	897	897	Urban IV	Troyes	1261	1264
John IX	Tivoli	898	900	Clement IV	France	1265	1268
Benedict IV	Rome	900	903	Bl. Gregory X	Piacenza	1271	1276
Leo V	Ardea	903	903	Bl. Innocent V	Savoy	1276	1276
Sergius III	Rome	904	911	Adrian V	Genoa	1276	1276
Anastasius III	Rome	911	913	John XXI[7]	Portugal	1276	1277
Landus	Sabina	913	914	Nicholas III	Rome	1277	1280
John X	Tossignano	914	928	Martin IV[8]	France	1281	1285
Leo VI	Rome	928	928	Honorius IV	Rome	1285	1287
Stephen VII (VIII)	Rome	928	931	Nicholas IV	Ascoli	1288	1292
John XI	Rome	931	935	St. Celestine V	Isernia	1294	1294
Leo VII	Rome	936	939	Boniface VIII	Anagni	1294	1303
Stephen VIII (IX)	Rome	939	942	Bl. Benedict XI	Treviso	1303	1304
Marinus II	Rome	942	946	Clement V	France	1305	1314
Agapitus II	Rome	946	955	John XXII	Cahors	1316	1334
John XII	Tusculum	955	964	Benedict XII	France	1334	1342
Leo VIII[5]	Rome	963	965	Clement VI	France	1342	1352
Benedict V[5]	Rome	964	966	Innocent VI	France	1352	1362
John XIII	Rome	965	972	Bl. Urban V	France	1362	1370
Benedict VI	Rome	973	974	Gregory XI	France	1370	1378
Benedict VII	Rome	974	983	Urban VI	Naples	1378	1389
John XIV	Pavia	983	984	Boniface IX	Naples	1389	1404
John XV	Rome	985	996	Innocent VII	Sul mona	1404	1406
Gregory V	Saxony	996	999	Gregory XII	Venice	1406	1415
Sylvester II	Auvergne	999	1003	Martin V	Rome	1417	1431
John XVII	Rome	1003	1003	Eugene IV	Venice	1431	1447
John XVIII	Rome	1004	1009	Nicholas V	Sarzana	1447	1455
Sergius IV	Rome	1009	1012	Callistus III	Jativa	1455	1458
Benedict VIII	Tusculum	1012	1024	Pius II	Siena	1458	1464
John XIX	Tusculum	1024	1032	Paul II	Venice	1464	1471
Benedict IX[6]	Tusculum	1032	1044	Sixtus IV	Savona	1471	1484
Sylvester III	Rome	1045	1045	Innocent VIII	Genoa	1484	1492
Benedict IX (2nd time)	—	1045	1045	Alexander VI	Jativa	1492	1503
Gregory VI	Rome	1045	1046	Pius III	Siena	1503	1503
Clement II	Saxony	1046	1047	Julius II	Savona	1503	1513
Benedict IX (3rd time)	—	1047	1048	Leo X	Florence	1513	1521
				Adrian VI	Utrecht	1522	1523
				Clement VII	Florence	1523	1534
Damasus II	Bavaria	1048	1048	Paul III	Rome	1534	1549
St. Leo IX	Alsace	1049	1054	Julius III	Rome	1550	1555

Name	Birthplace	Reigned From	Reigned To	Name	Birthplace	Reigned From	Reigned To
Marcellus II	Montepulciano	1555	1555	Innocent XIII	Rome	1721	1724
Paul IV	Naples	1555	1559	Benedict XIII	Gravina	1724	1730
Pius IV	Milan	1559	1565	Clement XII	Florence	1730	1740
St. Pius V	Bosco	1566	1572	Benedict XIV	Bologna	1740	1758
Gregory XIII	Bologna	1572	1585	Clement XIII	Venice	1758	1769
Sixtus V	Grottammare	1585	1590	Clement XIV	Rimini	1769	1774
Urban VII	Rome	1590	1590	Pius VI	Cesena	1775	1799
Gregory XIV	Cremona	1590	1591	Pius VII	Cesena	1800	1823
Innocent IX	Bologna	1591	1591	Leo XII	Genga	1823	1829
Clement VIII	Florence	1592	1605	Pius VIII	Cingoli	1829	1830
Leo XI	Florence	1605	1605	Gregory XVI	Belluno	1831	1846
Paul V	Rome	1605	1621	Pius IX	Senegallia	1846	1878
Gregory XV	Bologna	1621	1623	Leo XIII	Carpineto	1878	1903
Urban VIII	Florence	1623	1644	St. Pius X	Riese	1903	1914
Innocent X	Rome	1644	1655	Benedict XV	Genoa	1914	1922
Alexander VII	Siena	1655	1667	Pius XI	Desio	1922	1939
Clement IX	Pistoia	1667	1669	Pius XII	Rome	1939	1958
Clement X	Rome	1670	1676	John XXIII	Sotto il Monte	1958	1963
Bl. Innocent XI	Como	1676	1689	Paul VI	Concesio	1963	1978
Alexander VIII	Venice	1689	1691	John Paul I	Forno di Canale	1978	1978
Innocent XII	Spinazzola	1691	1700	John Paul II	Wadowice, Poland	1978	
Clement XI	Urbino	1700	1721				

1. Or 310. 2. He should be called Felix II, and his successors of the same name should be numbered accordingly. The discrepancy was caused by the erroneous insertion in some lists of the name of St. Felix of Rome, Martyr. 3. He was elected during the exile of St. Martin I, who endorsed him as Pope. 4. After St. Zachary died, a Roman priest named Stephen was elected but died before his consecration as Bishop of Rome. His name is not included in all lists for this reason. In view of this historical confusion, the *National Catholic Almanac* lists the true Stephen II as Stephen II (III), the true Stephen III as Stephen III (IV), etc. 5. Confusion exists concerning the legitimacy of claims. If the deposition of John was invalid, Leo was an antipope until after the end of Benedict's reign. If the deposition of John was valid, Leo was the legitimate Pope and Benedict an antipope. 6. If the triple removal of Benedict IX was not valid, Sylvester III, Gregory VI, and Clement II were antipopes. 7. Elimination was made of the name of John XX in an effort to rectify the numerical designation of Popes named John. The error dates back to the time of John XV. 8. The names of Marinus I and Marinus II were construed as Martin. In view of these two pontificates and the earlier reign of St. Martin I, this pontiff was called Martin IV. *Source: National Catholic Almanac, from Annuarto Pontificio.*

The Books of the Bible
New Revised Standard Version

**The Old Testament
with the Apocryphal/
Deuterocanonical
Books**

The Hebrew Scriptures

Genesis
Exodus
Leviticus
Numbers
Deuteronomy
Joshua
Judges
Ruth
1 Samuel
2 Samuel
1 Kings
2 Kings
1 Chronicles
2 Chronicles
Ezra
Nehemiah
Esther
Job
Psalms
Proverbs

Ecclesiastes
Song of Solomon
Isaiah
Jeremiah
Lamentations
Ezekiel
Daniel
Hosea
Joel
Amos
Obadiah
Jonah
Micah
Nahum
Habakkuk
Zephaniah
Haggai
Zechariah
Malachi

*The Apocryphal/
Deuterocanonical Books*

Tobit
Judith
Additions to the Book
    of Esther

Wisdom of Solomon
Ecclesiasticus, or the
    Wisdom of Jesus
    Son of Sirach
Baruch
The Letter of Jeremiah
The Prayer of Azariah
    and the Song of the
    Three Jews
Susanna
Bel and the Dragon
1 Maccabees
2 Maccabees
1 Esdras
Prayer of Manasseh
Psalm 151
3 Maccabees
2 Esdras
4 Maccabees

The New Testament

Matthew
Mark
Luke

John
Acts of the Apostles
Romans
1 Corinthians
2 Corinthians
Galatians
Ephesians
Philippians
Colossians
1 Thessalonians
2 Thessalonians
1 Timothy
2 Timothy
Titus
Philemon
Hebrews
James
1 Peter
2 Peter
1 John
2 John
3 John
Jude
Revelation

(See the Calendar and Holidays section for listings of religious holidays.)

PERSONAL FINANCE

How Bank Mergers May Affect You

Source: Federal Deposit Insurance Corporation.

New legislation will allow banks in 1997 to go where they couldn't go before—across state lines, for example (except individual states can decide not to permit it).

Banking is a business like any other, and profits are the name of the game. Bank earnings are being eroded by competition from other financial institutions and credit card-issuing companies like AT&T and General Motors. "Two can live as cheaply as one" really works in a bank merger, as combined institutions can cut costs by using one processing facility, fewer buildings, and of course, fewer personnel.

Automated teller machines have sprung up like mushrooms. You can conduct just about all common financial transactions without setting foot in a traditional banking office. A recent study predicts that half of all U.S. bank branches—and 450,000 bank jobs—will disappear over the next 10 years as customers increasingly turn to electronic transactions.

What does a merger mean for customers? For one thing, you should pay careful attention to any mail you receive from your bank or savings association. Written notice is usually provided about any changes affecting the terms of your accounts or loans, so don't throw away what may look like junk mail without looking at it first. Those notices may contain important information about changes in services, interest rates, checks, loans, credit and ATM cards and deposit insurance. Here are some of the possibilities.

Services and Branches

One immediate effect of two institutions combining could be changes in the services offered and the fees for those services. Also, business hours may be changed, minimum balance requirements may vary, free checking may be offered (or not), new electronic banking services may be offered, etc. Again, you'll probably receive a notice explaining the details.

One of the more obvious results of a merger is the closing of branches. If banks that merge have branches near each other, it's often good business sense to close one or more of them. It's also possible that the overall number of branches available to you may increase after the merger. Before a branch is closed, though, a notice usually must be mailed to customers of the affected office at least 90 days in advance. In addition, notices must be posted in the lobby of the branch to be closed at least 30 days before the doors actually shut for good.

Interest Rates

A "new" institution typically will honor the original interest rate and other account terms for certificates of deposit (CDs) purchased at an institution that is acquired before the CDs mature. But rates paid on savings, checking and Negotiable Order of Withdraw-

al (NOW) accounts may be changed at any time (your "old" bank could do that, too).

Checks

Checks written on your old bank should clear as usual. In most cases, you can continue using checks from your old checkbook until you use them up. The "new" institution will send you instructions about obtaining new ones. If your bank acquires another institution, you can probably continue as before; it's the customers of the acquired bank who will need new checks with the name of their "new" bank. Unless, of course, the name of the combined institution is something entirely different; then everyone will need new checks!

Certification

After some mergers, depositors must "certify" their accounts of the new institution. In most cases, you can do this simply by making a deposit or withdrawal or filling out a new signature card. The purpose of this requirement is simply to make sure you are still alive and at the address on record. Contact your new bank to see what procedures may be in place. If certification is necessary and you don't do it, your funds could be turned over to the state after a certain length of time.

Loan Accounts

If you were in the process of applying for a loan at the old bank when the merger took place but had not yet "signed on the dotted line," you should contact a loan officer or another official at the new bank to see if the loan would be approved, and if so, whether the same terms are available.

If you have an existing loan at an institution that has been bought by another, you should continue to make your loan payments as before until the new institution tells you to do otherwise. Business loans are more complex, so commercial customers may experience more changes to their loan accounts. All loan customers will be notified of any changes affecting their accounts.

The terms and conditions of the existing loan contract cannot be altered, but you should know what's in your contract. For instance, if a loan is "callable," an institution can request payment in full at any time. Check with your new institution. Loans are not generally called unless a poor payment history is reflected in the bank's records.

You may have a loan with a variable interest rate tied to a certain index. Just be aware that certain indices are more vulnerable to interest rate swings, with the result that your loan payment may be less predictable. (This is true whether your bank is merging or not.)

"Plastic"

Institutions involved in a merger most likely issued their own ATM and credit cards before they joined forces. These operations will probably be combined and new cards issued. Merging institutions (and acquirers of failed banks, too) usually go to great pains to make sure there is as little disruption to electronic banking as possible during any changeover. Thus, you should be able to use your ATM card as before or until a new one is provided. The same is true for credit cards such as MasterCard and Visa.

If you are issued a new credit card, you can expect the interest rate to fluctuate just as it did on the old one. And don't forget to check those fees—they could change. And if they do, you'll have to decide whether it's worth the effort—and the risk that other institutions will make similar changes—to switch to another card.

Deposit Insurance

If you end up with more than $100,000 in the resulting institution after a merger, you're in no immediate risk of having uninsured funds. As a general rule most deposit accounts you had at one institution would continue to be insured separately from those at the "new" institution for six months. If you have CDs, this separate insurance coverage could last even longer, depending on each CD's maturity date. Consult your bank to determine the exact amount of insurance provided for your accounts.

Final Thoughts

In the unlikely event that a bank of savings association fails, these same rules apply, with a couple of exceptions. If a healthy institution takes over a failed one, the 90-day notice of branch closing is not required. Also, an acquiring bank or savings association is not always required to honor the original interest rate or other account terms on CDs. If the rate or terms are altered, however, customers can either withdraw their money without paying an early withdrawal penalty or accept the new rate. The new institution may only alter the rates and terms on existing CDs within a certain number of days after the closing (often 14 days). If your CD rate is lowered, it is no longer considered a CD; it is considered a savings account and receives separate insurance for six months.

The important thing to remember about a bank (or savings association) merger is that the acquiring institution wants your business, so it will be trying to keep you as a satisfied customer. Even if a merger has no immediate effect on you, it's a good idea to contact your new bank to see what additional or different services may be available and the locations of branches you can use, if you haven't already received that information. ☐

What's New in Reverse Mortgages?

Source: Fannie Mae.

A reverse mortgage is a loan on your home. It differs from conventional mortgages in that it reverses the direction of the payments by paying the homeowner in regular installments instead of the lender. Unlike the loan balance of a conventional mortgage, which becomes smaller with each monthly payment, the loan balance of a reverse mortgage grows larger over time. The loan principal increases with each payment that you receive, and the interest and other charges accrue each month on the total funds advanced to you to date.

Fannie Mae, the nation's largest source of home mortgage funds, has created a new type of reverse mortgage program called the Home Keeper Mortgage. It is designed to help senior homeowners tap the equity that they have in their homes and offers them the flexibility to choose among several plans that can best fit their financial needs.

Unlike traditional mortgages or home equity loans, no repayment of the Home Keeper Mortgage is required until the owner no longer occupies the home as his or her principal residence. Another difference between the Home Keeper loan and the typical home equity loan is that your income is not considered when qualifying you for the loan.

Interest Rates

The Home Keeper is an adjustable-rate mortgage (also called a "variable interest rate"). Interest rates for the Home Keeper are tied to the one-month CD index that is published weekly by the Federal Reserve. This monthly adjusting rate cannot change by more than 12 percent over the life of the loan. There is no limit to the amount the rate can change at each monthly adjustment, as long as it does not exceed the 12 percent lifetime cap.

A change in the adjustable rate has no effect on the amount or number of loan advances you receive. Interest rate changes will cause the loan balance to grow faster with a higher rate or slower with a lower rate.

Credit Limits

The maximum amount that you can borrow—the principal limit—is based on three factors: the number of borrowers, the ages of those borrowers, and the adjusted property value. The adjusted property value is the lesser of the appraised value of your home or the Fannie Mae loan limit. Currently, this limit is $203,150.

Payment options

When you receive your loan, you will select one of the following payment plans.

• *Tenure Option.* You receive equal monthly payments for as long as you occupy the home as your principal residence.

• *Line of Credit Option.* You draw upon the principal limit of cash available at times and in amounts of your choosing.

• *Modified Tenure Option.* You may set aside a portion of loan proceeds as a line of credit and receive the rest in the form of equal monthly payments.

Borrowers are permitted to change payment plans at any time and as many times as they wish.

Repayment is deferred until the borrower no longer occupies the property as his or her principal residence. A borrower cannot be forced to sell or vacate the property to pay off the loan, even if the total of the

Typical Line of Credit Plan

Adjusted property value

Age	$100,000	$150,000	$207,000
75	33,964	53,330	76,010
80	42,463	66,229	93,490
85	51,681	79,912	112,270
90	57,597	88,741	124,420

Typical Line of Credit Plan With Equity Share Option

Adjusted property value

Age	$100,000	$150,000	$207,000
75	50,337	78,037	109,790
80	59,336	91,386	128,098
85	67,814	103,864	145,136
90	68,369	104,419	145,691

NOTE: These figures are approximate and assume financing of $4,200, $5,450, or $6,700 in closing costs and points for the three different home values and deduction for a $30 monthly servicing fee.

mortgage payments plus interest exceeds the value of the home. A Home Keeper Mortgage becomes due and payable when the borrower dies, moves, sells the property, or transfers title to another individual.

The example table shows the line of credit that could be available to the borrower for different ages and property values.

Repaying the Loan

When you no longer occupy your home or the lender declares the loan due and payable due to your failure to meet your loan obligations (default), your loan balance is immediately due and payable. At that point, the loan must be repaid in one payment rather than periodic payments.

The loan funds do not affect your Social Security or Medicare benefits because they are not based on the assets of the recipient. However, in the federal Supplemental Security Income program, beneficiaries must keep their liquid resources under certain limits ($2,000 for individuals and $3,000 for couples). If you do not spend Home Keeper advances in the month received, then such funds are considered part of your liquid resources and may adversely affect your eligibility for SSI.

Who's Eligible?

Borrowers must be 62 years of age or older;
• Either own their home free and clear, or be able to pay off existing liens at the time the loan is closed using reverse mortgage proceeds or other funds. Your home must be a single-family home. Condominiums and cooperatives are not currently eligible for Home Keeper loans.
• You must also agree to attend a consumer education session on reverse mortgages. Family members are strongly encouraged to attend these sessions.

Benefits to Borrowers

• Help seniors become independent.
• Surveys show that 84% of seniors would like to stay in their current home and never move (AARP study).
• Provide needed funds to offset unexpected costs such as home repair, property taxes, or in-home medical care.

Usually, the loan balance of a reverse mortgage is paid off from the proceeds of the sale of the borrower's home, but the sale of the property is not required. For example, you might choose to pay off the loan by cashing in assets other than your home. Or you might be able to refinance your home to pay off the loan if you still have sufficient home equity to do so (this situation may be unlikely, but it is not prohibited). Or your heirs might choose to pay off the loan with their own funds rather than sell the property; or they might take out a mortgage on the property and pay off the loan with those funds.

It is important to keep in mind that you or your heirs will never owe the lender more than the loan balance plus any equity share or the market value of the property—whichever is less—at the time the loan is declared due and payable. If, for some reason, your loan balance is more than your home is worth when the loan falls due, you pay only the market value of the home.

How to Apply

You can obtain the Home Keeper Mortgage from any lender authorized by Fannie Mae to offer it. To identify Home Keeper lenders in your area, call your local mortgage lenders to see if they offer the Home Keeper Mortgage, or contact Fannie Mae's Office of Public Information by calling 1-800-7FANNIE (1-800-732-6643) and ask for a list of participating lenders. You can also write to:

Fannie Mae
Public Information Office
3900 Wisconsin Avenue, NW
Washington, D.C. 20016-2899

You may also request *Money From Home,* Fannie Mae's guide to Home Keeper and Home Equity Conversion Mortgages. ☐

Choosing a Credit Card

Source: U.S. Office of Consumer Affairs.

Check the following terms before selecting a credit card.

• Annual Percentage Rate (APR)—the cost of credit as a yearly rate.

• Free or Grace Period—allows you to avoid any finance charge by paying your balance in full before the due date. If there is no free period, you will pay a finance charge from the date of the transaction, even if you pay your entire balance when you receive your bill.

• Fees and Charges—most issuers charge an annual fee; some might also charge a fee for a cash advance or if you fail to make a payment on time or go over your credit limit.

• For a small fee, you can purchase a list of the most competitive interest rates and credit cards in the country and find out how to qualify for the lowest rate possible by contacting Bankcard Holders of America, 524 Branch Drive, Salem, VA 24153, (540) 389-5445.

Mortgage Qualifications for Buying a Home

Source: Federal National Mortgage Association (Fannie Mae).

Your Job History

Your job history is important and it will be a major factor in whether you qualify for a loan. If you have been working continuously for two years or more, you are considered to have steady employment. However, you do not have to have held the same job for two years in order to be approved for a loan. Job moves that result in equal or more pay and continue to use proven skills are a plus for you. If there are good reasons why you haven't worked continuously for the last two years, you can explain them to the mortgage lender.

Your Credit History

How you paid your bills in the past gives a lender some indication of how you can be expected to pay them in the future. You will be asked to list all your debts, the amount of your monthly payments, and the number of months or years left to pay on the debts. Your lender will order a credit report to verify the information that you give.

The Down Payment

When you buy a home, you need money for a down payment and "closing costs." The amount of the down payment may vary, but generally you must make a down payment that equals at least five percent of the purchase price. You will also need money for closing costs. These costs can be expensive, depending upon where you live.

The mortgage lender will want proof that you have saved the funds that you will use for a down payment and part or all of the closing costs. If the funds are in a savings account, the lender will ask the financial institution to verify the amount and the length of time that the funds have been in your account. The lender wants to make sure that you are not borrowing all the money you will use for the down payment and closing costs.

The Mortgage Payment

The amount of your monthly payment depends upon the amount you borrow, the interest rate, and the repayment period or "term." The shorter the term, the higher your monthly payment. For that reason, most home buyers repay their mortgage over the longest term possible, usually 30 years.

Housing Expense Guideline

When you first approach a lender about financing a mortgage for you, they will use the following two commonly accepted guidelines to help determine your ability to make mortgage payments:

1. Your monthly housing costs (including mortgage payments, property taxes, homeowner and mortgage insurance, and homeowner's fees) should total no more than 28 percent of your monthly gross (before taxes) income. In addition to your regular pay, your income can include funds you receive from overtime work, a part-time job or second job; retirement, VA, and Social Security benefits; disability; welfare and unemployment benefits; alimony; and child support.

2. Your monthly housing costs plus other long-term debts such as payments on car loans, student loans, or other installment debt (debts with more than ten months left to repay) should total no more than 36 percent of your monthly gross income. Depending upon your household income, you may be eligible for special assistance programs. These programs may make it easier for you to get a larger mortgage loan than you normally would be able to using the above qualifying rules. ☐

How Large a Mortgage Do You Qualify For?

Source: Fannie Mae (Federal National Mortgage Association) 1995.

Interest Rates	Annual Income					
	$15,000	**$20,000**	**$25,000**	**$30,000**	**$35,000**	**$40,000**
6.5%	$49,400	$65,900	$82,400	$98,800	$115,300	$131,800
7.0%	47,000	62,600	78,300	93,900	109,600	125,300
7.5%	44,600	59,600	74,500	89,400	104,300	119,200
8.0%	45,000	56,700	70,900	85,100	99,300	113,500
8.5%	40,600	54,100	67,700	81,200	94,800	108,300
9.0%	38,800	51,700	64,700	77,700	90,600	103,500
9.5%	37,200	49,500	61,900	74,300	86,700	99,100
10.0%	35,600	47,400	59,300	71,200	83,000	94,900
10.5%	34,200	45,500	56,900	68,300	79,700	91,100
	$45,000	**$50,000**	**$55,000**	**$60,000**	**$65,000**	**$70,000**
6.5%	$148,300	$164,800	$181,300	$197,700	$214,200	$230,000
7.0%	140,900	156,600	172,300	187,900	203,600	219,200
7.5%	134,100	149,000	163,900	178,800	193,700	208,600
8.0%	127,700	141,900	156,100	170,300	184,500	198,700
8.5%	121,900	135,400	149,000	162,500	176,100	189,600
9.0%	116,500	129,400	142,400	155,300	168,200	181,200
9.5%	111,400	123,800	136,200	148,600	161,000	173,400
10.0%	106,800	118,600	130,500	142,400	154,300	166,100
10.5%	102,400	113,800	125,200	136,600	148,000	159,400

The above chart can help you find out how large a mortgage you might qualify for based on your annual income and the interest rate currently being quoted for 30-year fixed-rate mortgages. Rather than using the normal 28 percent ratio, this chart uses a 25 percent ratio and assumes that the amount you need to set aside to pay for taxes and insurance would amount to approximately the 3 percent difference. This simplified approach should give you a fairly accurate answer.

Calculate Your Mortgage Payment

Source: Fannie Mae (Federal National Mortgage Association).

Loan Amount	Interest Rates								
	6.5%	7%	7.5%	8%	8.5%	9%	9.5%	10%	10.5%
$20,000	$126	$133	$140	$147	$154	$161	$168	$176	$183
25,000	158	166	175	183	192	201	210	219	229
30,000	190	200	210	220	231	241	252	263	274
35,000	221	233	245	257	269	282	294	307	320
40,000	253	266	280	294	308	322	336	351	366
45,000	284	299	315	330	346	362	378	395	412
50,000	316	333	350	367	384	402	420	439	457
55,000	348	366	385	404	423	443	462	483	503
60,000	380	399	420	440	461	483	505	527	549
65,000	411	432	454	477	500	523	547	570	595
70,000	442	466	489	514	538	563	589	614	640
75,000	474	499	524	550	577	603	631	658	686
80,000	506	532	559	587	615	644	673	702	732
85,000	537	566	594	624	654	684	715	746	778
90,000	569	599	629	660	692	724	757	790	823
95,000	600	632	664	697	730	764	799	834	869
100,000	632	665	699	734	769	805	841	878	915

Use the chart above to calculate how much your monthly mortgage payment might be. Let's suppose that you want to purchase a house that costs $50,000. If you make a $5,000 down payment, you would need a $45,000 mortgage. As you can see on the chart, the monthly payment on a $45,000 mortgage at 8 percent interest is $330. The $330 monthly payment only covers the principal, or a portion of the amount you borrowed, and interest on the mortgage loan. There are other expenses that will be added to your monthly payment. These include taxes and homeowner's insurance. If your down payment is less than 20 percent, you may need to pay private mortgage insurance. These costs vary depending upon where you live and the cost of your home, but they can add a hundred dollars or more to your monthly payment. In addition, if you are thinking about buying a unit in a condo or cooperative building, or a house in a planned unit development, you may also need to pay monthly homeowner's fees to cover maintenance expenses or special assessments related to the common areas. ☐

How to Measure the Shrinking Value of the Dollar

Source: Martin Lefkowitz, economist, U.S. Chamber of Commerce.

How to use this table. The value of a dollar is given for any year relative to the 1996 dollar. For example: What weekly salary would you need to earn in 1996 to equal the purchasing power of a weekly salary of $100 in 1960? Take the 1960 multiplier, 5.30, times $100 and you would need to earn $530 a week in 1996 to achieve the same salary.

Again, what income would you need in 1996 to equal the purchasing power of $1000 in 1985? The 1985 multiplier, 1.46, times $1000, equals $1,460 needed to stay even with inflation during those past ten years.

Year	Value of dollar in 1996 dollars	Year	Value of dollar in 1996 dollars	Year	Value of dollar in 1996 dollars
1946	8.05	1963	5.13	1980	1.91
1947	6.74	1964	5.06	1981	1.73
1948	6.51	1965	4.98	1982	1.63
1949	6.60	1966	4.85	1983	1.58
1950	6.51	1967	4.70	1984	1.51
1951	6.04	1968	4.51	1985	1.46
1952	5.92	1969	4.28	1986	1.43
1953	5.88	1970	4.05	1987	1.38
1954	5.84	1971	3.88	1988	1.33
1955	5.86	1972	3.76	1989	1.27
1956	5.77	1973	3.54	1990	1.20
1957	5.59	1974	3.18	1991	1.15
1958	5.43	1975	2.92	1992	1.12
1959	5.40	1976	2.76	1993	1.09
1960	5.30	1977	2.59	1994	1.06
1961	5.25	1978	2.41	1995	1.03
1962	5.20	1979	2.16	1996	1.00

NOTE: These figures are based on projected consumer price increases of 3.0% in 1996.

How to Stop Thieves From Using Your Checks

Source: Federal Deposit Insurance Corporation.

Don't have your Social Security or driver's license number imprinted on your checks. These numbers, combined with other information on your checks (your name, address, account number, telephone number) could supply a thief with enough details to apply for a loan, credit card, or a phony bank account in your name.

Notify your bank if you ordered checks and haven't received them in a reasonable time period, or if some checks are missing. These could be signs the checks have been stolen.

When writing checks, don't leave blank spaces on the lines designating who the check is payable to and the amount. Better to write details as close together as possible, avoid abbreviations and draw lines to fill any gaps. Otherwise, a criminal can easily change what you've written—such as, a check payable to I.B.M. could be doctored to read I.B. Mooney.

Use dark ink, never light colors (green, pink) or pencil that can easily be erased or covered over. And if you change your mind after writing all or part of a check, first mark "void" across the front and then shred it to pieces.

Most experts advise against writing your credit card number on a check to a merchant, even if the merchant asks for this information. If possible, don't make a check payable to "cash" (it's too easily cashed by just anyone). And never endorse a check until you're ready to cash or deposit it. Preferably, deposited checks should be endorsed "For Deposit Only" and your account number should be included. That way, if the check is stolen it can't be cashed.

Try to use your own pre-printed deposit slips. If that isn't possible, make sure the deposit slips stacked in the bank lobby don't have someone else's account number already written or printed on them. Believe it or not, many depositors don't pay attention to what's on deposit slips—a mistake some thieves have used to enrich their own accounts.

Keep checks in a safe place. In fact, treat them as if they were cash. You may not ultimately be responsible for checks stolen and forged against your account, but it can take a long time to clear up the problems. Contact your bank immediately if your checkbook or individual checks are lost or stolen. And if you use signature stamps, check imprinters or personal computers to make your check-writing easier, keep them secure so you know who has access to them.

Don't just throw out cancelled checks, unused deposit slips, old bank statements, or credit card and automated teller machine (ATM) receipts. Shred and destroy them as best you can. These items could be used by a thief to make new checks or order them from a mail-order check printing firm.

When balancing your checkbook, be alert to paid checks that are out of sequence or any other unusual items. For example, if your newly cancelled checks include one numbered in the 400s when the rest are in the 200s, that could be a sign that a thief got to your supply.

Also notify your bank if you don't receive your statement within a reasonable time. A bank statement contains account numbers, balance information and other details that could be useful in a fraud. Many depository institutions (and their customers) also prefer not to have cancelled checks sent in bank statements as one way to prevent thieves from stealing the actual checks or getting examples or signatures. (Institutions that don't return checks generally microfilm them and can supply a copy of a check, for a nominal fee, if requested to do so.)

Don't give out any personal information, like account numbers and Social Security numbers, to anyone over the telephone unless you initiate the call and you know you're dealing with a reputable organization or firm. A common telemarketing scheme is to get you on the phone, supposedly to discuss a gift you've "won," but really to obtain your checking account information. If successful, this person can use the information to issue a bank draft that deducts funds from your account. □

A Brief History of Checking

No one is quite sure when the first checks appeared. Some experts think the Romans may have invented the check about 352 B.C. But even if that were true, the idea apparently didn't catch on. According to most history texts, it probably wasn't until the early 1500s, in Holland, that the check first got widespread usage. Amsterdam in the sixteenth century was a major international shipping and trading center. People who had accumulated cash began depositing it with Dutch "cashiers," for a fee, as a safer alternative to keeping the money at home. Eventually the cashiers agreed to pay their depositors' debts out of the money in each account, based on the depositor's written order or "note" to do so.

The concept of writing and depositing checks as a method of arranging payments soon spread to England and elsewhere, but not without resistance. Many people in the sixteenth and seventeenth centuries still had doubts about trusting their hard-earned money to strangers and little pieces of paper. In the United States, checks are said to have first been used in 1681 when cash-strapped businessmen in Boston mortgaged their land to a "fund," against which they could write checks.

The first printed checks are traced to 1762 and British banker Lawrence Childs. The world "check" also may have originated in England in the 1700s when serial numbers were placed on these pieces of paper as a way to keep track of, or "check" on, them.

As checks became more widely accepted, bankers discovered they had a big problem: how to collect the money due from so many other banks. At first, each bank sent messengers to the other banks to present checks for collection, but that meant a lot of traveling and a lot of cash being hauled around. The solution to this problem was found in the 1700s, according to banking lore, at a British coffee shop. The story goes that a London bank messenger stopped for coffee and noticed another bank messenger. They got to talking, realized that they each had checks drawn on the other's bank, and decided to exchange them and save each other the extra trip. The practice evolved into a system of check "clearinghouses"—networks of banks that exchange checks with each other—that still is in use. Today banks in the U.S. can present checks to the Federal Reserve System or private clearinghouses for regional and national check collection. □

GENDER ISSUES

Is Gender Still an Issue?

By Frieda Reitman, Ph.D., Professor of Management Emerita, Lubin School of Business, Pace University. Reprinted with permission from Pace Magazine, Spring/Summer 1996, copyright © 1996 by Pace University.

Even as more and more women obtain M.B.A.s, gender discrimination persists in the workplace of the 90s.

Are the managerial careers of men and women developing at a similar rate and in a similar fashion? Or are women still faced with the "glass ceiling"—the denial of high level executive positions because of gender?

Until recently, the term "managerial careers" referred only to men, and descriptions and theories of career development focused solely on them. However, as more women entered management, questions were raised as to whether women's careers would become more like those of men or if they would develop differently.

To determine whether women with master's degrees in business administration (considered an important credential for a managerial career) are keeping up with their male counterparts in reaching the top rungs of management, Joy A. Schneer, Ph.D., associate professor of management at Rider University's College of Business, and I tracked the career paths of 676 men and women who received M.B.A.s between 1975 and 1980 from two northeastern universities and compared their progress.

The results of our study, "The Impact of Gender as Managerial Careers Unfold," published in the December 1995 issue of the *Journal of Vocational Behavior,* suggest that male and female managerial paths are not parallel: women with the same background, training, and experience as men continued to lag behind them in both salary and career advancement (see table below). Also, fewer M.B.A. women than men remain in the full-time work force through midcareer.

The data for this study, collected in 1987 and 1993, found that for those M.B.A.s who were employed full-time through midcareer, women earned less income, worked fewer hours, and achieved lower levels of management. Female executives employed full-time through midcareer earned 19 percent less than the males: an average of $102,540 a year for men, as compared to $83,370 for women.

The gender penalty is apparent even when factors that impact income and affect men and women differently have been controlled. This divergence between the incomes of men and women after controlling relevant work-related variables implies that discrimination against women still exists in the workplace. Twenty-three percent of the men had reached the executive suite, as compared to less than 10 percent of the women when we examine those men and women who are not self-employed. Women do move into upper-middle management by midcareer, but they seem to go no further (see table). This barrier to advancement, or "glass ceiling," may explain why more than 20 percent of the women we surveyed had left full-time employment by midcareer and why another nine percent opted for self-employment.

Despite the negative outcome on both income and management levels for women, the study found that both sexes are equally satisfied with their careers. This satisfaction exists despite the fact that more than a quarter of the women felt they had been denied a position or promotion because of sex discrimination as compared to five percent of the men. Perhaps this reflects a lower level of expectation on the part of women as compared to men.

Although organizations would probably agree that only competence should determine compensation, many previous studies have also concluded that gender discrimination exists; the evidence has been so strong that legislation to counter discrimination has been enacted at both the national and state levels. Discrimination may reflect many issues, including the difficulties in evaluating managerial performance, the bias of supervisors who have been socialized to expect males to be more competent than females in management, and the desire to adequately compensate men who are the "breadwinners" of the family.

This partiality to men who are the traditional "breadwinners" is underscored by an examination of the importance of family structure to the career paths of managers. Dr. Schneer and I found that "traditional" family men with children and non-working wives earned 20 percent more than men with children and working wives. In 1993, that was equal to over $23,000 a year.

This study, based on 925 men and women with M.B.A.s, was first reported in "Effects of Alternate Family Structures on Managerial Career Paths," *Academy of Management Journal,* August 1993. An update, based on 676 M.B.A.s, was presented at the annual meeting of the Academy of Management in

Income and Management Level of Men and Women Managers*

Income	Men	Women
Income in early career	$ 68,480	$ 57,210
Income in mid-career	102,540	83,370
Management level		
Top level management	23%	9%
Upper-middle management	33	43
Lower-middle management	21	22
Supervisory management	8	10
Non-management	15	16

Source: "The Impact of Gender as Managerial Careers Unfold," by Joy A. Schneer, Rider University, and Frieda Reitman, Pace University, *Journal of Vocational Behavior.*
*Excludes self-employed.

August 1995. Our work indicates that despite the prevalence of the "post-traditional family," where both parents are employed, organizations are still likely to think in terms of their fast-track managers as "traditional" family men whose wives will manage the household, allowing them to focus their full attention on the job. Thus, we conclude there may be an element of discrimination against post-traditional men as well as against women.

This study also noted that nonemployed professional mothers tended to be at home not because their husbands earned high salaries, but because they could not find an appropriate job, could not afford adequate child care, found work environments unsupportive, or thought they should be at home with their children. However, working women in post-traditional families earned about as much as other married women and actually earned more than single women, long considered the model for the woman manager. These findings challenge prior research on women that suggested a negative relationship between parental status and income and no relationship between marital status and income.

The results of both studies indicate that gender continues to have an impact as managerial careers unfold. Some may remain optimistic that societal values are changing and that all employed women will be viewed as valuable resources regardless of marital or parental status. Workforce 2000, a report issued by the Hudson Institute, suggests that organizations will need to utilize all talents, and that women will comprise an increasing percentage of the workforce by the year 2000. If organizations are to get the most from employees, they must encourage, support, and reward all workers. To accomplish this, they can offer "family friendly" programs such as extended leave, child care assistance, care for the sick and elderly, and flexible benefits to ease family demands. More importantly, organizations can revise the model of the successful manager to one that addresses the dynamics of the post-traditional family structure. This would include fewer hours, less travel and relocation, and more flexible work routines than have typified managerial work in the past.

However, 30 years after Title VII of the Civil Rights Act, equality has not occurred. How much longer will it take? There was hope that with stronger legislation—the Civil Rights Act of 1991—there would be greater numbers of women in management.

With the time to prove their ability, women in mid-career would receive rewards comparable to men and reach the upper echelons of corporate America. This has not yet happened. The "glass ceiling" is still in place and still quite glaring. Today, even with some progress, less than five percent of the top executive positions in the Fortune 500 companies are held by women.

Dr. Frieda Reitman received a Ph.D. in economics from the New School for Social Research and has been a professor of management at Pace since 1982, serving as chair of the Management Department and associate dean of the Lubin School of Business. Her current research interests include managerial careers, gender issues, and work ethic. She received the 1994 Academy of Management Addison–Wesley Careers Division Best Paper Award for "Effects of Early and Mid-Career Employment Gaps on Career Outcomes," with Dr. Joy A. Schneer.

Facts on Women Workers

Women make up nearly half of our nation's workforce and a staggering 99% of women will work for pay sometime in their lives.

Source: U.S. Department of Labor, Women's Bureau

According to the latest data from the Census Bureau, released May 1995, there were 102 million women age 16 and over in the United States in 1994. Of that total, a record 60 million were in the civilian labor force. Their share of the total labor force was 46% and continues to rise. It is projected that they will comprise 48% by the year 2005. The Census report noted the following facts:

• Nearly six out of every ten women—58%—age 16 and over were working or looking for work in 1994.

• Divorced and separated women have higher participation rates mainly because they are the primary or the only wage earners.

• Women between 20 and 54 years old comprised at least 70% of the workforce.

• Their unemployment rate in 1994 was only 6.4%. For white women it was 5.2%, 11.0% for black women, and 10.7% for Hispanic women.

• Unemployed women are more inclined to contact the prospective employer directly (67%); and less likely to send out resumes or fill out applications (42%); place or answer ads (22%); contact friends or relatives (16%); use public employment agencies (19%); and use private employment agencies (7%).

• Of the 57 million women employed in 1994, most still work in technical, sales, and clerical occupations. However, in the past ten years, women have also made substantial progress in obtaining jobs in the managerial and professional specialties. In 1984,

they held one third (33.6%) of managerial and executive and nearly half (48.5%) of the professional occupations. By 1994, they held 48.1% of managerial/executive positions and accounted for over half (52.8%) of workers employed in professional occupations.

• Two-thirds of all part-time workers are women.

• Many women who work part-time are multiple job holders. The highest rate of multiple job holding was among women 20 to 24 years old (7.6%). More women are employed at more than one job primarily for economic reasons—to meet regular household expenses, to pay off debts, and to save for the future.

• The ratio of women's 1994 median earnings to men's is 76.4%. Even in traditionally female occupations where women outnumber men, women still earn less than men.

• With women still concentrated in lower paying occupations and having overall earnings about three-fourths that of men, it is no wonder that more adult women are below the poverty level.

• Of all labor force participants, women were more likely to have completed high school than were men. Ninety-one percent of female workers held a minimum of a high school diploma compared to 88% for men. A somewhat lower percentage of women than men were college graduates. Regardless of race, women with college degrees were more apt to have bachelor's degrees in professional and technical disciplines than in other areas of study.

The Earnings Gap Between Men and Women

Source: U.S. Department of Labor, Women's Bureau

What's the Earnings Gap?

No matter how we measure them, women's earnings are below those received by men. Very often men's earnings are used as the "yardstick" to measure women's and we say women's earnings are a percentage of men's. The earnings gap is the difference between this percentage ratio and 100 percent.

How Large Is the Gap?

In 1992 (the most recent year for which data are available), for those receiving hourly rates, women's median hourly earnings were 79.4% of men's; for full-time wage and salary workers, women's median weekly earnings were 75.4% of men's; and the median annual earnings for women were 70.6% of men's.

The measures that compare earnings differ for several reasons. Median weekly and annual earnings relate to full-time wage and salary earners, while hourly earnings relate to wage and salary workers whether or not they are full-time or year-round employees. Furthermore, women tend to work fewer hours and have higher turnover rates than men, which may also contribute to the difference.

Relationship Between Education and Earnings

Another study using 1984 data provided statistics on working women and men with no employment interruptions (defined as 6 months or more without a job or business) by age and education. For young women (those 21 through 29 in 1984), the earnings ratio of women to men was 80% or more, no matter how many years of school had been completed. However, for young women who had completed four or more years of college, hourly earnings were 86% of their male coworkers.

Sex Discrimination

Although sex discrimination still exists in the American workplace, the magnitude of its effect on the earnings gap is hard to measure. Statistical studies have successfully measured the effects on the male-female earnings differential of several factors such as occupation, education, and experience. Most often the effects of discrimination in these studies are included in an "all other" category and are not measured separately. However, federal agencies and individuals continue to win sex discrimination cases, thus proving that this problem persists.

Is the Gap Closing?

Bureau of Labor statistics have shown that a gradual closing of the wage gap has taken place since 1973. There has been a steady climb in women's real earnings while men's earnings peaked in 1973 and have drifted downward since. Recessionary dips appear in both men and women's earnings in the early 1980s, while the recessionary period in 1990–1991 shows an increase in men's earnings compared with women's earnings. This unexpected change occurred because more low-wage earning men lost their jobs in the recession, leaving a larger proportion of men with higher earnings in the work force. With fewer low-wage earners, the estimate of earnings for men rose as employment of men declined. Women did not experience similar employment losses, and their annual earnings held steady during the recessionary period.

The earnings gap should continue to narrow as women work more hours in the week, spend more years at paid work in their lifetimes, continue to increase their educational investment, widen their occupational choices, and equal opportunity becomes a reality. □

Gender in the Workplace

Source: U.S. Census Bureau Survey

According to the U.S. Census Bureau survey, the gender and education of business owners directly affects the gender composition of the firm's employees.

• Female small business owners hire more female employees than do male owners. While about 39 percent of employees hired by men are women, 52 percent of employees hired by women are women.

• The higher the educational attainment of the male small business owner, the larger the percentage of female employee he hires. The percentage of women rises from 31.8 in firms owned by men with 8 or fewer years of education to 49.7 in firms owned by men with 16 or more years of education.

One possible explanation for this finding is that men with more education are often doctors, dentists, or lawyers who are hiring support staff in female-dominated occupations (nurses, paralegals, receptionists). Men with less education may own firms characterized by occupations dominated by males, such as electrical appliance repairs or shoe repairs.

The most popular explanation for the differences in pay between men and women—and for the preponderance of women in some workplaces and men in others—is that there is discrimination by employers against women in the labor market.

However, some occupations and industries tend to have more of one gender in the first place, and thus, the owner and the employees may more likely be of the same gender. For example, auto repair shops tend to be male-dominated; hair-styling salons tend to be female-dominated.

Also, some industries, or segments within industries, that employ mostly women—such as health, educational, personal or social services—also tend to use more part-time workers. □

Women's Earnings Decline After a Career Break

Women who leave and later return to the workforce tend to earn less than their counterparts who never left.

Source: Family Economics and Nutrition Review, 1996, U.S. Department of Agriculture

What happens to a woman's long-term earnings after she returns to the work force following a gap in employment as compared to the earnings of her counterparts who remained in the work force during her absence? Previous studies have shown that these gaps in employment do affect earnings.

The latest study to date has focused on the rebound effect—whether a woman's wages will eventually catch up with those women of comparable experience who never left the labor market.

The data, published in the *Monthly Labor Review 118(9): 14–19*, 1995, were taken from the 1984 panel of the Survey of Income and Program Participation which examined data collected on each individual in the sample for 32 consecutive months (June 1983–April 1986).

The study found that women who interrupt their careers and leave the labor market for family responsibilities often return to find that their wages lag behind those of women at comparable stages in their careers who did not leave the labor force. Many reasons account for this lag. First, women who leave the labor force and later re-enter do not build up seniority, with associated higher wages. Second, women who return to the labor force are less likely to receive on-the-job training to increase their productivity and thereby raise their pay. Third, when women are not in the work force, their job skills may decline. Finally, employers may view gaps in work history as an indication that women may leave again. Some employers would, therefore, hire them for less important, lower paying jobs to limit the impact of a future leave.

To illustrate the cost of taking an employment gap for a particular case, assume a woman with the following characteristics: graduates college at age 21, immediately begins full-time work (40 hours a week, 50 weeks a year) in a pink-collar occupation in a city outside the South. She leaves work at age 25 for 7 years and re-enters full-time work in 1984 at age 32. The difference between her earnings and what they would have been had she remained constantly employed is $52,000. Part of this is caused by her fewer years of experience; part is due to her decision to leave the labor force. This amount is equal to 15 percent of her prospective earnings had she worked constantly—or about 3 years of wages. Thus, the cost of taking a 7-year gap is 10 years of earnings.

Although there is strong evidence for a partial rebound effect, the wages of women who have taken a leave from the labor market never catch up to the wages of women who never left. Even women whose labor force gap occurred more than 20 years ago still earn between 5 and 7 percent less than women who never left the labor force and have comparable levels of experience. □

Women Own One-Third of American Businesses

The growth of women-owned businesses exceeds the national average in every state.

Source: U.S. Bureau of the Census

According to the Census Bureau's latest report, "1992 Women-Owned Businesses," published in 1996, the number of women-owned businesses in the United States reached 6.4 million in 1992, representing one-third of all domestic firms and 40% of all retail and service firms. Businesses owned by women generated $1.6 trillion in annual revenues and employed 13.2 million people. About 19% of these were businesses with paid employees, averaging 10.6 workers and $1.2 million in receipts per firm. The new data indicated that the growth of women-owned businesses exceeds the national average in every state and in nearly every industry sector.

The report marks the first time the Census Bureau has included regular C corporations, which tend to be the fastest growing and largest companies. A C corporation is any incorporated business other than a subchapter S corporation. About 518,000 of these firms were C corporations, nearly 26% of the total C corporations in the United States. They had receipts of $932 billion, about 9% of the total receipts of all C corporations.

Eighty percent of these businesses were employers with 7 million employees and $154 billion in payroll.

The proportion of C corporations owned by women was relatively evenly distributed by type of business, ranging from 22% each in mining and manufacturing to 31% in retail trade.

Previously, the Census Bureau only surveyed sole proprietorships, partnerships, and subchapter S corporations. A subchapter S corporation is an incorporated business with 35 or fewer shareholders who elect to be taxed as individuals. Only those with $500 or more in receipts were included. A partnership is an unincorporated business owned by two or more persons.

In addition to C corporations, women owned 5.9 million sole proprietorships, partnerships, and subchapter S corporations. In 1992, these women-owned "non-C" businesses generated nearly $643 billion in revenues, over 40% of the total for all women-owned firms. They were predominantly in the retail and services industries.

Another report compiled by the National Foundation of Women Business Owners in 1996, estimated that the number of women-owned businesses in 1992 was 6.5 million, differing only slightly from the Census Bureau's analysis. □

Sexual Assault: The Silent, Violent Epidemic

Source: The American Medical Association (AMA).

According to the AMA, sexual assault continues to represent the most rapidly growing violent crime in America, claiming a victim every 45 seconds. Because many of these attacks occurring daily go unreported and unrecognized, sexual assault can be considered a "silent-violent epidemic" in the United States today.

The National Victim Center reports that over 700,000 women are raped or sexually assaulted annually. Of these victims, 61% are under age 18. Less is known about the frequency of rapes perpetrated against men. The American Academy of Pediatrics estimates that male victims represent about five percent of reported sexual assaults.

The legal term "rape" has traditionally referred to forced vaginal penetration of a woman by a male assailant. Many states have now abandoned this concept in favor of the gender neutral concept of sexual assault. Among the acts classified as sexual assault is acquaintance or date rape, generally defined as an assault in which the assailant is known to the victim. Approximately 20% of sexual assaults against women are perpetrated by assailants unknown to the victim. The remainder are committed by friends, acquaintances, intimates, and family members. Acquaintance rape is particularly common among adolescent victims.

The majority of sexual assault victims are young. A 1991 report stated that 32% of sexual assaults by acquaintances occur when the victim is between the ages of 11 and 17.

Women with a history of rape or attempted rape during adolescence are almost twice as likely to experience a sexual assault during college, and were three times as likely to be victimized by a husband.

As is true of other violent crimes, it is difficult to get accurate estimates of the incidence of sexual assault. It is generally accepted that less than half of rapes are reported to authorities; some estimates are as low as 10%. Many factors contribute to underreporting, including embarrassment, fear of further injury, and fear of court procedures that, too often, scrutinize and judge the victim's behavior and history.

Sexual assaults can and do occur within marital relationships. Most often, these assaults occur within a context of ongoing domestic violence. While reports and prosecutions of spousal rape are fairly infrequent, some convictions have occurred. Sexual assault is reported by 33% to 46% of women who are being physically assaulted by their husbands.

Several sociocultural influences contribute to the incidence and prevalence of sexual assault. These include increased acceptance of interpersonal violence, adversarial stereotypes of male-female relationships, prevalent myths about rape, and sex-role stereotyping. Some victims of attacks meeting the legal definition of rape do not label their experience as sexual assault.

Common myths surrounding rape include: only women can be sexually assaulted; victims who truly resist cannot be raped; no really doesn't mean no; nice girls don't get raped; and "she asked for it." Male rape victims may feel that others will question their sexuality if they report the incident or that they, in fact, subconsciously desired and complied with their assault.

The use of alcohol and drugs also contributes to the risk of sexual assault. A study of sexual assaults among college students found that 73% of the assailants and 55% of the victims had used drugs, alcohol, or both immediately before the assault.

"Sexual assault is a 'silent-violent epidemic' growing at an alarming rate and traumatizing the women and children of our nation," said Lonnie Bristow, M.D., AMA president. "This crime is shrouded in silence, caused by unfair social myths and biases that incriminate victims rather than offenders." These myths push victims into the shadows, afraid to step forward and seek help from their physicians."

Societal Attitudes About Rape

Teenagers

In a survey of high school students, 56% of girls and 76% of the boys believed forced sex was acceptable under some circumstances.

A survey of 11-to-14 year-olds found:

51% of the boys and 41% of the girls said forced sex as acceptable if the boy, "spent a lot of money" on the girl;

31% of the boys and 32% of the girls said it was acceptable for a man to rape a women with past sexual experience;

87% of the boys and 79% of the girls said sexual assault was acceptable if the man and the woman were married;

65% of the boys and 47% of the girls said it was acceptable for a boy to rape a girl if they had been dating for more than six months.

College Students

A survey of 6,159 college students enrolled at 32 institutions in the U.S. found:

54% of the women surveyed had been victims of some form of sexual abuse;

More than one in four college-aged women had been the victim of rape or attempted rape;

57% of the assaults occurred on dates;

42% of the victims told no one.

In a survey of male college students, 35% anonymously admitted that, under certain circumstances, they would commit rape if they believed they could get away with it.

One in 12 admitted to committing acts that met the legal definitions of rape, and 84% of men who committed rape did not label it as rape.

In another survey of college males, 43% admitted to using coercive behavior to have sex, including ignoring a woman's protest, using physical aggression, and forcing intercourse.

15% acknowledged that they had committed acquaintance rape, and 11% acknowledged using physical restraints to force a woman to have sex.

The National Women's Hall of Fame

The National Women's Hall of Fame is the only national membership organization that honors and celebrates the achievements of American women. Founded in 1969 in Seneca Falls, New York, where in 1848 the first Women's Rights Convention was held, the Hall inducts distinguished women and offers programs and exhibits in Seneca Falls, the Finger Lakes area, Washington, D.C. and elsewhere.

Women are chosen for inclusion in the Hall of Fame on the basis of:

- The value of their contribution to society, to significant groups within society, or to the progress and freedom of women.
- Their contributions to art, athletics, business, government, philanthropy, humanities, science, and education.
- The enduring value of their achievements.

For further information, contact The National Women's Hall of Fame, 76 Fall Street, Seneca Falls, N.Y. 13148. Phone: (315) 568–8060.

1996 Honorees

Louisa May Alcott (1832–1888) Author who produced the first literature for the mass market of juvenile girls in the 19th century. Her best-known work, *Little Women,* has appeared continuously in print since its first publication in 1868–69.

Charlotte Anne Bunch (1944–) As founder and director of the Center for Women's Global Leadership at Rutgers University, Bunch helped shape the global feminist movement and created consciousness about gender-based human rights.

St. Frances Xavier Cabrini (1850–1917) Established orphanages, day care centers, schools, clinics and hospitals for immigrants in the United States and around the world. She established a missionary order of women and was the first American citizen to be canonized a saint.

Dr. Maria Goeppert Mayer (1906–1972) First U.S. woman and second woman ever to win the Nobel Prize in Physics. Prize was awarded for developing the shell model of the nucleus of the atom, the basic model for the description of nuclear properties.

Mary A. Hallaren (1907–) A leader who championed permanent status for women in the military after World War II as director of the Women's Army Corps.

Oveta Culp Hobby (1905–1995) Shaped the development of two major government institutions as first director of the Women's Army Corps and first Secretary of the Department of Health, Education and Welfare. First female to attain the rank of United States Colonel and the only woman to serve in President Dwight D. Eisenhower's cabinet.

Wilhelmina Cole Holladay (1922–) Founder of the National Museum of Women in the Arts in Washington, D.C., which brings attention to the vast contributions of women to the history of art nationally and internationally.

Anne Morrow Lindbergh (1906–) Notable author of numerous elegant essays, journals, and books. Also excelled as co-pilot and navigator with her husband, Charles, on their historic flights to promote the development of international aviation.

Ernestine Louise Potowski Rose (1810–1892) Early advocate for women's rights who traveled for more than three decades giving eloquent speeches and seeking petition signatures. She sought women's rights, the abolition of slavery, and many other reforms before others took up the causes.

Maria Tallchief (1925–) Prima ballerina with the New York City Ballet and artistic director for the Lyric Opera Ballet in Chicago. She created a distinctive style and interpretation that continues to influence contemporary ballet. Tallchief used her international acclaim to bring about greater understanding and appreciation of Native American cultures.

Edith Wharton (1862–1937) One of the major American novelists and short story writers of the 20th century. The first woman to receive the Pulitzer Prize for fiction and a prolific writer who average more than a book a year after age 40 until her death.

Past Honorees

Bella Abzug	Carrie Chapman Catt	Martha Griffiths	Mary Mahoney
Abigail Adams	Shirley Chisholm	Fannie Lou Hamer	Wilma Mankiller
Jane Addams	Jacqueline Cochran	Alice Hamilton	Barbara McClintock
Ethel Percy Andrus	Eileen Collins	Helen Hayes	Louise McManus
Marian Anderson	Ruth Colvin	Mary Harris "Mother	Margaret Mead
Susan B. Anthony	Jane Cunningham Croly	Jones"	Maria Mitchell
Virginia Apgar	Emily Dickinson	Dorothy Height	Constance Baker Motley
Ella Baker	Dorothea Dix	Grace Hopper	Lucretia Mott
Ann Bancroft	Elizabeth Hanford Dole	Dolores Huerta	Antonio Novello
Clara Barton	Anne Dallas Dudley	Helen Hunt	Annie Oakley
Mary McLeod Bethune	Amelia Earhart	Zora Neale Hurston	Sandra Day O'Connor
Antoinette Blackwell	Catherine East	Anne Hutchinson	Georgia O'Keeffe
Elizabeth Blackwell	Mary Baker Eddy	Mary Jacobi	Rosa Parks
Emily Blackwell	Marian Wright Edelman	Frances Wisebart Jacobs	Alice Paul
Amelia Bloomer	Gertrude Belle Elion	Mae Jemison	Frances Perkins
Margaret Bourke-White	Alie Evans	Barbara Jordan	Esther Peterson
Myra Bradwell	Geraldine Ferraro	Helen Keller	Jeannette Rankin
Mary Breckinridge	Ella Fitzgerald	Nannerl O. Keohane	Ellen Swallow Richards
Gwendolyn Brooks	Betty Friedan	Billie Jean King	Linda Richards
Pearl S. Buck	Margaret Fuller	Maggie Kuhn	Sally Ride
Annie Jump Cannon	Matilda Joslyn Gage	Suzette La Flesche	Eleanor Roosevelt
Rachel Carson	Lillian Moller Gilbreth	Belva Lockwood	Sister Elaine Roulet
Mary Cassatt	Charlotte Perkins Gilman	Juliette Gordon Low	Wilma Rudolph
Willa Cather	Ella Grasso	Mary Lyon	Josephine St. Pierre Ruffin

Florence Sabin	Bessie Smith	Harriet Beecher Stowe	Ida B. Wells-Barnett
Margaret Sanger	Margaret Chase Smith	Helen Brook Taussig	Oprah Winfrey
Katherine Siva Saubel	Hannah Greenebaum	Sojourner Truth	Sarah Winnemucca
Betty Bone Schiess	Solomon	Harriet Tubman	Fanny Wright
Patricia Schroeder	Elizabeth Cady Stanton	Lillian D. Wald	Rosalyn Yalow
Mother Elizabeth Seton	Gloria Steinem	Madam C.J. Walker	Gloria Yerkovich
Florence Seibert	Nettie Stevens	(Sarah Breedlove)	Mildred "Babe" Didrickson
Muriel Siebert	Lucy Stone	Faye Wattleton	Zaharias

Domestic Violence: A Leading Cause of Injuries to Women

Sources: National Coalition Against Domestic Violence, *Public Health Reports,* and *Health Words for Women*

According to findings by the Surgeon General, domestic violence is the leading cause of injury to women between ages 15 to 24, more common than automobile accidents, muggings, and cancer deaths combined. Every 15 seconds, a woman is battered in the United States by her husband, boyfriend, or live-in partner.

One-fifth to one-third of all women are physically abused during their lifetime. Ten percent of the time the injury is serious enough to require hospitalization or emergency room treatment. The combination of physical and psychological symptoms that occur in women who suffer chronic abuse is known medically as the battered woman syndrome.

Physicians can't always recognize the physical symptoms of abuse without help from the victims themselves. Many abused women have difficulty in admitting it because of the fear, guilt, or shame that they may feel, or because of a deep-seated denial that they are abused.

In the home, women are just about as violent as men—they hit, bite, and kick just as often as men—but they don't do as much damage. Men inflict more harm because of their generally greater size and strength. In addition, violence by women is often in retaliation or self-defense. Women commit only about eight percent of all homicides in the United States, but 51% of them are against partners with a history of abuse.

Abuse occurs in all relationships, including gay and lesbian, which suggests that domestic violence is an issue of power, not necessarily one of gender. ☐

The National Domestic Violence Hotline

The Violence Against Women Act (VAWA) was passed as part of the Crime Act of 1994 and combines tough new penalties with programs to prosecute offenders and help women victims of violence.

Among the initiatives undertaken by the VAWA was the establishment of a 24-hour, toll-free, national domestic violence hotline in February 1996 to provide crisis assistance and local shelter referrals to women across the country. Hotline counselors are also available for non-English speakers and for people who are hearing impaired. The vast majority of callers are first time help-seekers.

The voice number is 1-800-799-SAFE. The TDD number for the hearing impaired is 1-800-787-3224.

The hotline is operated by the Texas Council on Family Violence, through a Health and Human Services (HHS) grant authorized under the Violence Against Women Act. HHS's Administration for Children and Families, Centers for Disease Control and Prevention, and Substance Abuse and Mental Health Services Administration contribute funding for the hotline. ☐

Signs of Abuse

Keep in mind there are many forms of abuse directed toward women. Experts say that a woman's "Yes" answers to any of the following questions may suggest an abusive relationship:

1. Is she frightened at times by her partner's temper?
2. Is she afraid to disagree with him?
3. Is she constantly apologizing for her partner's behavior, especially when he has treated her badly?
4. Does she have to justify everything she does, every place she goes, or every person she sees to avoid her partner's anger?
5. Does her partner put her down, but then tell her that he loves her?
6. Has her partner ever hit, kicked, shoved, or thrown things at her?
7. Does she not see friends or family because of her partner's jealousy?
8. Has her partner ever forced her to have sex?
9. Is she afraid to break up with her partner or leave him because he has threatened to hurt her, her children or himself?

Recognizing the Potential Batterer

Experts have found that male batterers tend to fit a profile. The characteristics listed below aren't definitive signs that a man is a batterer—only that he may have the potential to become one:

- The man reports having been physically or psychologically abused as a child.
- His mother was battered by his father.
- He plays with guns and uses them to protect himself against other people.
- He commits random acts of violence against objects and things.
- He drinks alcohol to excess.
- He becomes enraged when his partner doesn't listen to his advice.
- He appears to have a dual personality.
- There's a sense of "overdoing it" in his cruelty—or in his kindness.
- He has rigid ideas of what other people should or shouldn't do that are determined by male or female sex-role stereotypes.

To receive the best care possible, a victim of abuse must be honest with her doctor about her home life. Admitting to abuse can be scary, to say the least, but it's the first step on the road to recovery. ☐

FAMILY TRENDS

Beneficial Aspects of Marriage

Marriage has several benefits over cohabiting or divorce, according to recent research.

Dr. Linda Waite, in a review of recent research from the University of Chicago, stated that married persons tend to have healthier behavior than nonmarried persons. For example, married men have only half the rate of problem drinking that divorced men have. Widowers fall somewhere in between married and divorced persons. Divorced women had the highest rate of problem drinking of the women, but theirs was much lower than any of the groups of men.

Other studies have shown that the married men and women had about 60% of the tendency for risk-taking behavior (such as drug use, driving while drinking and fighting) as single people. The researcher also noted that marital disruption increases stress and decreases sense of well-being.

Married men and women tend to live longer than persons who have never married or whose previous marriage ended in divorce. Dr. Waite suggested that married persons are better off because of (1) reduction of risky behavior, (2) increased material well-being which allows better medical care, diet, and safer surroundings, (3) a stronger support network, and (4) a readily available sex partner, making high-risk sexual behavior less likely.

Married persons also have sex at twice the rate of single adults. Cohabiting men and women have sex at about the same rate as married persons. However, married men and women have a statistically higher rate of emotional satisfaction with the sex in their lives. Cohabitation tends to have decreased satisfaction according to Dr. Waite, because cohabiting partners have a lower rate of faithfulness and the partners often bring a different level of commitment to the relationship.

Probably the greatest advantage married people have over the unmarried is that their household wealth is much higher. Married persons have 3.1 times the wealth of widowed, 3.8 times the wealth of the never married, and 3.9 times the wealth of divorced persons in the 51–61 age group. Dr. Waite suggests that the reason for the disparity is that two people live together cheaper, specialization by each partner allows for better efficiency in the marriage, and the married have a greater tendency to save for the future.

Children from married families tend to thrive better than children from single-parent families. Children drop out of school at about twice the rate as children from two-parent families. They are more likely to give birth as teenagers and to be unemployed as adults. Children from two-parent families have more access to adult attention, more help with homework, and more time with both father and mother than with one-parent families. They also have poorer relationships with their parents than children from two-parent families.

Source: FACTS Science Service, a publication of the Foundation for Acquisition of Community and Therapeutic Sciences (FACTS), Austin, Texas.

Gay Marriage May Be Near

In a case brought up by three homosexual couples, the Hawaiian State Supreme Court ruled three to one on May 5, 1993, that a ban on marriages between couples of the same sex may violate the State Constitution's prohibition against sex discrimination. However, the court did not overturn the ban. The Supreme Court sent the case back to the Trial Court to determine whether preserving the marriage ban was a "compelling state interest."

No state currently permits same sex couples to marry. If Hawaii eventually permitted same sex couples to marry, the union would have to be recognized nationwide because marriages in one state are legally recognized in all states. However, there may be legal problems with the states where sodomy is a criminal act.

In April 1996, Hawaii's state senators voted 15 to 10 against a House bill to ban legalizing same-sex marriages. In anticipation that Hawaii will eventually sanction gay and lesbian unions and thereby require other states to recognize their marriages under law, opponents have made strong efforts to prevent this recognition by enacting state laws to ban their licensing.

Opinion polls show that the majority of Americans oppose the idea and even President Clinton, a staunch supporter of gay rights, is opposed to homosexual marriages. On July 12, 1996, the House of Representatives overwhelmingly passed the "Defense of Marriage Act," that withholds federal recognition of same-sex marriages, and President Clinton has promised to sign the bill when it reaches his desk. (*See also* Current Events.)

Lesbian and gay couples want to have the same rights—in other words, joint tax returns, welfare, insurance, and health benefits, pension benefits, inheritance rights—that male–female couples enjoy.

Homosexuals argue that marriage is a basic human right and should not be denied to anyone. They believe that the decision to marry belongs to individuals and religious values should not dictate who can get married. Their supporters also say that their marriages would promote stable relationships and long-term commitments between homosexual couples. ☐

Unmarried Childbearing

Of the nation's 22.7 million never-married women aged 15–44, one out of every five had given birth to at least one child by 1994, according to the Census Bureau. Approximately seven percent of never-married teens and about 40% of never-married women in their thirties had a child out-of-wedlock.

Foreign-born women in this country had a birth rate about one and one-half times higher than that of native-born women, 93 and 62 births per 1,000 women, respectively. Mexican-American women had a birth rate of 111 births per 1,000 women, nearly double that of non-Hispanic women (61 per 1,000).

American Families: Traditional and Otherwise

Source: U.S. Department of Commerce, Bureau of the Census.

Since 1960, the American family has undergone many changes in the traditional family pattern of two biological or adoptive parents and a working bread-winner father and a full-time at-home mother. Among the forces of change were a massive influx of women into the workforce, an emphasis on self-fulfillment, and the destigmatization of divorce and cohabitation. The women's movement also contributed to the liberation of women from their former predetermined roles as homemakers and workers.

Since 1986, the United States has had the highest divorce rate in the world, and is now the world's leader in fatherless families.

Over the past three decades, the divorce rate doubled and gender roles changed with the growing number of working mothers (which may reach 70% by the year 2000), the burgeoning number of single-parent households, and the rise of couples living together and out of wedlock.

These changes have resulted in new family groups such as dual-career couples, single parents, at-home fathers, gay and lesbian families, domestic partnerships, and even child-bearing families created by post-menopausal mothers.

In 1994, the latest year for which Census data is available, there were 11.4 million single parents. About 9.9 million were single mothers and 1.6 million were single fathers. Single parents accounted for almost two-thirds or 65% of all black family groups with children present versus 25% for whites. About 38% of the single parents had never married and about roughly the same percentage were divorced.

Married couple families accounted for 55% of all households in 1994, a decline of 16% since 1970. Families maintained by women alone increased to 13% of households and those maintained by men alone represented only 3% of households. Only about half of American families had one or more children present in the home.

Delaying Marriage

Although the number of currently married persons has grown 21% since 1970, Americans are postponing marriage longer than ever before—the proportion of all adults they represent dropped from 72 to 61 percent, and the number of unmarried adults doubled since 1970.

The estimated median age at first marriage was 24.5 years for women and 26.7 years for men in 1994. Between 1970 and 1994, the number of men and women age 30 to 34 years who have never married more than tripled from 9% to 30% for men and from 6% to 20% for women. In 1890, the first year for which data is available, men first married around 26.1 years of age and women at 22 years old.

The Never-Married

Never-married adults are now the fastest growing segment of the adult population and they represent 23% of all adults in the United States. Two-thirds of women in the 20 to 24 year age group had never married and the number of never-married women in their late twenties and thirties tripled between 1970 and 1974.

Historically, men tend to marry at a later age than women. In 1994, 81% of men between the ages of 20 to 24 had never married (up from 55% in 1970) and one-half of men ages 25 to 29 had never married.

The proportion of never married men in their thirties more than tripled between 1970 and 1974 for 30 to 34 year olds and more than doubled for the 35 to 39 year age group.

Interracial Couples

According to the Census Bureau, there were 1.3 million interracial married couples in the reported period, 296,000 of whom were black/white, 909,000 were white/other (other than black) and 78,000 were black/other (other than white). Between 1970 and 1994, the number of interracial couples has increased from 310,000 to 1.3 million.

Living With Grandparents

Grandparents have also felt the impact of the new family structures. In 1994, there were 3.7 million children under 18 living in the home of their grandparent(s). This represented 5% of all children under age 18, up only slightly from 3% in 1970. Twelve percent of the children also had both parents living with them in the grandparent's home, 47% had only their mother present, 5% had only their father present, and 36% had neither parent present. Thirteen percent of black children lived in their grandparents' home compared with 4% for whites and 6% for Hispanics. High levels of divorce and the rise of out-of-wedlock childbearing have had a substantial role in these situations.

Cohabiting Couples

The number of unmarried-couple households (cohabiting couples) was 3.7 million in 1994, up from 523,000 in 1970. Of these, 1.3 million or 35% had children under fifteen. Today there are seven unmarried couples for every 100 married couples, compared with only one for every 100 in 1970.

The Elderly

In 1994, there were 30.8 million elderly persons who were 65 or older (excluding institutional population). Fifty-five percent lived with their spouse, 30% lived alone, 13% lived with other relatives, and 2% with nonrelatives.

The majority of elderly are women (18 million women versus 12.7 million men). Women on the average live longer than men and longevity is a major factor affecting gender difference in elderly living arrangements. The "older elderly" (age 75 and over) are more likely than the "young elderly" (age 65 to 74) to live with other relatives.

Although the American family structure is in transition, recent statistics still give high marks to married couples. Studies presented at the Population Conference of America in April 1995 indicated that married life was more beneficial to the health, financial, and emotional well-being of couples than either cohabitation or single life.

Researchers also found that those who live together before marriage have higher divorce rates than couples who didn't cohabit and they are generally less happy together than married couples are.

Two disturbing trends that have emerged in recent decades are the rise in family violence and the growing problem of child abuse and neglect. The disintegration of traditional family values has been blamed for many of today's societal problems and has become a controversial political issue.   □

Teen Pregnancy Costs Taxpayers $7 Billion Annually

Groundbreaking study warns that adolescent childbearing should be regarded as a national calamity

Source: The Robin Hood Foundation

In June 1996, The Robin Hood Foundation released "Kids Having Kids," the most comprehensive study to date on teenage childbearing. According to the report, adolescent parenthood has devastating effects on families, increasing poverty and significantly increasing the likelihood that the children of these young parents will face a life of poor health, physical abuse, neglect, prison, and early childbearing.

"Kids Having Kids" is the most comprehensive report done on the costs and consequences of teenage childbearing to parents, children, and society. According to the study, adolescent childbearing costs U.S. taxpayers $6.9 billion per year, and the cost to the nation in lost productivity rises to as much as $29 billion annually.

Working in teams on eight coordinated studies, a collection of some of the nation's leading scholars focused their research on the roughly 175,000 American girls who bear their first baby at the age of 17 or younger and compared the associated economic and social costs to those mothers who delay childbirth until the age of 20 or 21, which is still two or three years younger than the national average.

"Adolescent childbearing is not only a significant personal tragedy, it should be regarded as a national calamity in that it commits young parents to a life of hardship, increases the likelihood that their children will suffer the same fate and has staggering economic and social costs for our nation as a whole," said David Saltzman, executive director of Robin Hood Foundation.

"Early parenting wreaks havoc socially—from the completion of education of the mother and father to their higher poverty rates," said Rebecca Maynard, "Kids Having Kids" editor and professor of education and social policy, Graduate School of Education, University of Pennsylvania. "But the devastation to the lives of their children is prevalent and wide-ranging."

A few of the hundreds of findings about children born to teenage mothers:

Reproducing the Cycle of Poverty. The girls born to adolescent moms are up to 83 percent more likely to become teenage moms themselves, thus reproducing the cycle of poverty and disadvantage for yet another generation.

Trouble in School. They are 50 percent more likely to repeat a grade and perform significantly worse on cognitive development tests. They are also far more likely to drop out of high school than are the children born to women from the same socio-economic background who wait until the age of 20 or 21 to have children.

More Childhood Health Problems. They are more likely to be born prematurely and 50 percent more likely to be born low birthweight than if their mothers had waited four years to bear them.

Increased Child Abuse and Neglect. They are twice as likely to be abused or neglected.

Behind Bars. The teen sons of adolescent mothers are up to 2.7 times more likely to land in prison than their counterparts in the comparison group. By extension, adolescent childbearing in and of itself costs taxpayers roughly $1 billion each year to build and maintain prisons for the sons of young mothers.

Foster Children. Of the estimated 427,000 foster children in the United States, over 23,000 are the children of adolescent mothers, which in turn results in a taxpayer burden of approximately $900 million.

The study also examined the consequences of early parenting on teen mothers and the fathers:

• 70 percent of the mothers drop out of school.
• They are twice as likely to be dependent on welfare.

Unlike past studies, the report is the first to examine the costs and consequences of teen pregnancy on society. It found that teen childbearing costs U.S. taxpayers almost $7 billion every year. The cost to society in lost national productivity and avoidable expenditure of social service resources is as much as $29 billion each year.

The Robin Hood Foundation was created as a public charity in 1988 to find, fund, and provide management help to the best and most innovative programs serving poor people in New York City. Since then, the foundation has provided ore than $35 million in money, volunteer resources and material goods to these programs.

Adults Father Most Teens' Babies

The latest studies on teen pregnancies indicate that most children born to teenage mothers are fathered by adults. This discovery is changing the prevailing perception of teenage mothers. Too often teenage girls are the victims of sexual abuse, not promiscuous or irresponsible behavior.

The studies found that men 20 years or older are the fathers of two out of three teenage births. Other surveys have confirmed this. A reported published in August 1995 by the Alan Guttmacher Institute found that 63% of unwed mothers 15 to 19 years old had children by men 20 or older. These revelations have caused some state legislatures to enforce rarely used statutory rape laws which prohibit sex between adults and minors in an effort to deter these relationships.

The Alan Guttmacher report, "How Old Are U.S. Fathers?" by David J. Landry and Jacqueline Darroch Forreset, stated that "age information for men makes clear that some assumptions underlying many of the programs and policies aimed at reducing teenage pregnancy are not correct. Policies that equate teenage pregnancy with males under 20 miss many of the partners of adolescent women."

It further noted that "while a certain degree of age disparity between mothers and fathers is common in the United States, wide gaps between young teenage mothers and older fathers merits some concern. One in five mothers aged 15–17 has a partner six or more years older. This type of age difference suggests, at the least, very different levels of pressure and abuse. Data from the National Survey of Children indicate that about 18% of women 17 and younger who have had intercourse were forced at least once to do so."

A pilot program in sixteen California counties has begun to prosecute men who have sex with underage girls. California has the highest teenage pregnancy rate in the nation and spends billions annually in state and federal aid to teenage families. The state's controversial crackdown is intended to send a strong message to would-be statutory rapists that they can't get away with it.

Even if "jail-bait" laws are enacted, however, it can be difficult to prosecute a sexual predator if the teenage victim is unwilling to testify against him for reasons of fear, shame, or emotional attachment to her abuser. □

One-Parent Families in Metro Areas Remain High

According to the January 1995 census data on the nation's 46 metropolitan areas with one million or more people, New York led the list in 1990 with the highest percentage of single-parent families (36%), New Orleans, La., was second at 34%, followed by Miami–Hialeah, Fla. (31%), Detroit, Mich. (29%) and Sacramento, Calif., and Baltimore, Md., with 28% each.

The census report also showed that four in ten single-parent renters living in metro areas were either unemployed or not in the labor force. The rate for single-parent owners was less than half that, at 16 percent.

According to the latest Census data, the declining trend of two-parent families reversed itself slightly in 1994 when married-couple families increased by 600,000. However, the slight growth is still far outpaced by single-parent households. □

Metro Areas With 25% or More Single-Parent Families, 1990

(Metro areas with 1 million or more persons)

	Number of family households with own children under 18	Percent of all family households with own children	Single-Parent Families		
			Number maintained by mothers	Number maintained by fathers	Mother-to-father ratio
New York, NY PMSA	925,042	35.9	286,976	44,839	6.4
New Orleans, LA MSA	160,702	33.6	46,801	7,134	6.6
Miami–Hialeah, FL PMSA	219,409	30.8	53,692	13,913	3.9
Detroit, MI PMSA	551,789	29.2	138,398	22,608	6.1
Sacramento, CA MSA	186,950	28.2	41,923	10,767	3.9
Baltimore, MD MSA	285,017	28.2	67,173	13,070	5.1
Milwaukee, WI PMSA	179,714	27.6	43,073	6,599	6.5
Cleveland, OH PMSA	217,724	27.4	51,270	8,489	6.0
Los Angeles–Long Beach, CA PMSA	1,015,965	27.2	208,090	68,140	3.1
Chicago, IL PMSA	709,586	27.2	162,982	30,131	5.4
Oakland, CA PMSA	251,284	26.7	53,609	13,447	4.0
Fort Lauderdale–Hollywood–Pompano Beach, FL PMSA	130,400	26.6	27.240	7,410	3.7
Tampa–St. Petersburg–Clearwater, FL MSA	215,622	26.5	46,280	10,821	4.3
San Antonio, TX MSA	173,352	25.6	37,408	6,997	5.3
Denver, CO PMSA	213,599	25.3	43,399	10,714	4.1
Rochester, NY MSA	125,191	25.2	26,415	5,163	5.1
St. Louis, MO–IL MSA	312,148	25.1	65,981	12,426	5.3
Cincinnati, OH–KY–IN PMSA	190,856	25.1	40,897	7,060	5.8
Phoenix, AZ MSA	259,911	25.1	50,044	15,255	3.3
Philadelphia, PA–NJ PMSA	560,904	25.0	116,248	23,977	4.8
San Diego, CA MSA	291,335	25.0	57,149	15,588	3.7

NOTE: Counts reflect 100-percent response rates and are not subject to sampling variability. Metro areas correspond to the definitions that were in place in 1990. MSA—Metropolitan Statistical Area. PMSA—Primary Metropolitan Statistical Area. *Source:* U.S. Bureau of the Census.

Unmarried-Couple Households, With Children: 1970 to 1994

(Numbers in thousands)

Year	Total married couples	Unmarried couples			Ratio of unmarried couples per 100 married couples
		Total	Without children under 15 years	With children under 15 years	
1994	54,261	3,661	2,391	1,270	7
1990	53,256	2,856	1,966	891	5
1985	51,114	1,983	1,380	603	4
1980	49,714	1,589	1,159	431	3
1970 Census	44,593	523	327	196	1

Source: Marital Status and Living Arrangements: March 1994 Current Populatrion Reports: Population Characteristics P20–484. Source of 1970 data: "U.S. Bureau of the Census, 1970 Census of Population, PC(2)–4B, Persons by Family Characteristics, table 11.

Who's Minding Our Preschoolers?

Source: Current Population Reports, P70–53, March 1996, Census Bureau

The fall of 1993 is the most recent year for which the Census Bureau has data on preschool child care arrangements. The results of this information were not released until April 1996.

In the fall of 1993, there were 9.9 million children under five years old who needed child care while their mothers were working. Relatives took care of almost half (49%) of the preschool-age children. Seventeen percent of the preschoolers were cared for by their grandparents and almost as many were cared for by their fathers. The majority were watched by relatives, either their grandparents or their dads, each accounting for a third of the care provided by relatives. A smaller role was played by aunts, uncles, and cousins amounting to about 9% of all preschool arrangements and about 6% of the children were cared for by their mothers, most of these by moms who worked at home.

A little more than half (52%) of the children of working mothers were cared for by someone other than their relatives. In 1993, more preschoolers received care in organized child care facilities than in any other single arrangement; one third were cared for in day care or preschool centers. One in five children were cared for by nonrelatives, including baby-sitters and day care providers.

The Census Bureau found in 1993 that about one in three preschoolers received care in each of the three major child care environments: the child's home, the provider's home, and in organized child care facilities.

Noteworthy changes in child care have occurred in the past few years. Between 1988 and 1991, the proportion of preschoolers who were cared for in organized centers declined from 26% to 23 percent. However, between 1991 and 1993, this trend reversed itself and the use of organized facilities jumped from 23% to 30%, representing a 30% increase over the two year period.

During the same time frame these shifts were occurring, there were offsetting changes in the number of preschoolers being watched by their fathers and day care providers. Care by fathers, while remaining at about the 15% level between 1977 and 1988, sharply increased to 20% by 1991. However, between 1991 and 1993, that number fell to 16%.

Family day care had also been a consistent source of child care arrangements, providing 23% of all arrangements for preschoolers in 1987 and 1988. However, the proportion of children cared for by family day care providers sharply fell from 24% in 1988 to 18% in 1991 and remained at this historically low level in 1993.

The Census Bureau concluded that the decreases in the use of organized care centers and the increase of care by fathers may have resulted from the economic recession which occurred at that time. Increases in the number of unemployed fathers and those working at part-time jobs meant that more dads were available to watch their children. The Census Bureau also noted that the decline in care by fathers and the increased use in organized facilities occurred at the same time as the recession was ending.

These shifts also may have reflected the desire of parents to cut down on child care costs by switching to more parental supervision of their children whenever possible. Note that between 1991 and 1993, not only did father care decline, but mother care declined as well, from 9% in 1991 to 6% in 1993. The continued unpopularity of family day care may in part reflect a growing uneasiness of parents to use a minimally regulated arrangement where there is a single provider, as opposed to a heavily regulated arrangement—an organized child care facility—where there are a number of providers. Recent media reports of child neglect and abuse at the hands of baby-sitters and family day care providers may also be a factor in the decline of day care and preschool centers.

Other Findings

In 1993, preschoolers in married-couple families were fourteen times more likely to be cared for by their fathers than preschoolers whose parents were divorced, widowed, or separated, and four times more likely to be cared for by their fathers than children who lived with a never-married parent.

In contrast, children in one-parent families were much more likely to be cared for by grandparents and other relatives than those in married-couple families.

Child care costs constitute an especially large share of a poor family's budget, so it comes as no surprise that poor families rely more heavily on relatives to help them out with child care than non-poor families do. In 1993, relatives provided 60% of all child care for poor families, compared with 46% for non-poor families.

Families in the South were more likely to use organized child care facilities and depend less on relatives as their primary providers. In contrast, families in the Northeast were most likely to call on relatives to supply care for the preschoolers. The greater use of relatives in the Northeast can be attributed to the greater use of fathers in the region, where one in four children were watched by their dads, compared to one in six in the Midwest and West, only one in ten in the South. □

Mother-Child Bonding Unaffected by Day Care

The latest study on day care followed infants to age 15 months. The findings show that regular child care provided outside the home has no direct adverse effect on mother–child relations.

However, the report found that mothers who were insensitive and unresponsive to their children were likely to have insecurely attached infants. A secure child will establish a positive contact with its mother after a brief separation and for example, will hug its mother, whereas an insecure infant will either ignore or avoid its mother when she returns.

The findings, released in April 1996, are the result of the most comprehensive child-care study to date. It was initiated and coordinated by the National Institute on Child Health and Human Development (NICHD). The study is tracking over 1,300 children from birth to seven years old to learn the effects of child care on child development. Psychologists caution that the data on attachment is only one of the many developmental traits that is being studied in their research.

Child Abuse and Neglect

Source: U.S. Department of Health and Human Services, National Center on Child Abuse and Neglect.

Although child abuse occurs in all racial, ethnic, cultural, and socioeconomic groups, physical abuse and neglect are more likely among people in poverty. There is also a link between substance abuse and child abuse. Parental abuse of alcohol and use of other drugs has been identified as a major factor contributing to child maltreatment and death.

This is the fifth consecutive year that child maltreatment data submitted annually by the states to the National Center on Child Abuse and Neglect (NCCAN) have been published. Highlights of the findings from *Child Maltreatment 1994: Reports from the States to the National Center on Child Abuse and Neglect* are given below.

In 1994, 48 states reported that 1,011,628 children were determined to have been victims of abuse and neglect. State child protective service agencies received reports of alleged maltreatment involving more than 2.9 million children. Professional reporting sources, such as educators, social workers, medical professionals, and law enforcement and justice officials, reported more than half of all reports of alleged maltreatment.

About 53% of the victims suffered from neglect, and almost 26% of them were physically abused. About 14% of the victims experienced sexual abuse and 5% suffered from emotional maltreatment. Nearly 80% of perpetrators of child maltreatment were parents, and an additional 10% were other relatives of the victims. States reported that 1,111 children were known to have died as a result of abuse or neglect.

The number of children who were the subjects of reports of alleged maltreatment increased from 2.6 million in 1990 to 2.9 million in 1994. The number of "substantiated" or "indicated" victims of maltreatment increased from 798,318 in 1990 to 1,011,628 in 1994, an increase of almost 27 percent.

The majority of victims, almost 56%, were white. African American victims represented the second largest group at about 26%. Hispanic victims made up about 9 percent. Native American victims were about 2% and Asian/Pacific Islander victims accounted for less than 1 percent.

Characteristics of victims were consistent across the years. In each of the five years, neglect was the predominant type of maltreatment. The number of neglect victims was consistently more than two times the number of victims of physical abuse, the next most common type of maltreatment. About 13% of the victims had been sexually abused, and 5% suffered emotional maltreatment. Almost half of the victims were eight years of age or younger. Fifty-two percent of all victims were female children, and 46% were male children.

Child protective services agencies identified almost 5,400 children who died as a result of abuse or neglect from 1990 through 1994. ☐

Need Help in Collecting Child Support?

Sources: Organization for the Enforcement of Child Support, Inc. (OECS), and U.S. Department of Health and Human Services, Office of Child Support Enforcement.

It is essential to your child's future that you legally establish paternity and obtain a court order for support. Some mothers may feel that it is easier to raise a child alone than to hassle with the problems of child support enforcement. But remember, 18 years is a long time. Who knows what one's financial and emotional circumstances may be in the future.

If paternity is not determined, the child loses all inheritance rights and survivor's benefits such as medical and insurance benefits, social security, and veteran's benefits. New laws directly affecting child support enforcement were enacted in fiscal year 1994. Among other things, these new laws facilitate enforcement, close bankruptcy loopholes, and utilize credit reporting to strengthen the child support system.

As a result, a record 590,819 children had their paternity established by the child support program in 1994. This represented an increase of almost 7% over the previous year and a cumulative 50% increase over the last five years. During the year, states collected nearly $10 billion in child support and established over one million new support orders. They also located over four million non-custodial parents.

While these numbers are impressive, millions of children still receive little or no support from their non-custodial parents. When these parents evade their responsibilities and fail to pay support, the result is often more poverty, welfare dependency, and tougher lives for the children.

Do You Have a Court Order? A separation agreement is NOT a court order. It is simply a contract between two parties. It must be reduced to a court order as soon as possible. Separation agreements are only enforceable by law suits. Without a court order you cannot proceed with other enforcement mechanisms. Do not delay! If you have no court order for support (which may be in your divorce decree) then file a petition for one immediately. Such a petition can, and should, be filed the day the non-custodial parent leaves.

Provide the Obligor's Address. Enforcement agencies, courts, and lawyers request that you furnish the absent parent's current address before any action can be taken. According to the OECS, this is bad advice, because any delay in filing will result in a delay in receipt of the child's support. But, most importantly, statutes of limitations must be considered, and the child may lose claim to arrearages. Some laws allow child support to be ordered retroactively to the date a petition was filed in court. If you don't know the obligor's address, use his/her last-known address.

Using the Federal Court. In interstate cases, if the responding state (the state in which the obligor resides) fails to cooperate, ask to have the case taken into Federal Court. This court has jurisdiction over *all* states.

Need Help? You can contact the Organization for the Enforcement of Child Support, Inc., (OECS) at 1712 Deer Park Road, Finksburg, MD 21048. Phone: (410) 876-1826. When writing, please enclose a stamped, self-addressed envelope. The OECS is a nonprofit group of volunteers established in July 1979 to address the numerous problems of child support enforcement. ☐

SOCIAL SECURITY & AGING

Ending Social Security As We Know It

Will Congress approve investing the program's taxes in the stock market?

Our Social Security system is what economists call an intergenerational income transfer program through which active workers help support former workers who are now retired. When today's retirees were still employed, they paid into the system to assist those who had gone before. Thus, Social Security is a direct means of one generation taking care of another.

This arrangement worked well for over half a century when the available pool of workers paying into the system was much larger than the number of retirees taking benefits out of the system. For example, in 1950, there were 16 workers for every Social Security beneficiary. This has all changed primarily because more people are living longer and collecting Social Security benefits for a longer duration, and our declining birthrate is reducing the number of workers available to pay into the system.

Today, the pool of workers has shrunk to just over three workers for every beneficiary and it is expected to decrease to less than two by 2030. The system will be paying more money than it takes in, resulting in a projected insolvency by the year 2030 as millions of Baby Boomers enter retirement.

The 13-member Advisory Council on Social Security, appointed by the President, meets regularly every four years to review the status of the Social Security trust funds. At this year's spring 1996 meeting, the group unveiled several new proposals to insure the long-term solvency of the program. Two of the main reforms suggested by the Council involve the partial privatization of Social Security and are briefly outlined here.

One proposal, led by Robert M. Ball, a former Social Security Commissioner, and five other colleagues suggested a plan in which a higher return on the program's surplus funds would be obtained by investing up to 37 percent of Social Security trust funds in private stocks instead of low-yielding Treasury securities. Historically, stocks have returned a higher average of 10 percent over the long-term compared to the low interest rates paid on the government bonds held by Social Security.

Under Ball's plan, the Government, not individuals, would do the investing in a broad range of stocks, relieving workers of the need to make their own investment decisions.

In addition, some benefits would be reduced, the annual Social Security payroll tax would be raised from its current rate of 12.4 to 14 percent in 2045, and more retirees would have to pay tax on their benefits. The plan also assumes that cost of living increases will be lower than they are now.

Chile is a prime example of a government that privatized Social Security. In 1981, Chile let wage earners have the option of investing their retirement income in tax-free investment accounts instead of Social Security. The reform is highly popular in the country and is considered such an economic success that other Latin American countries are considering a similar private-sector pension option.

A second radical idea proposed by economist Sylvester Schieber and his four colleagues would also partially privatize Social Security. The Schieber scheme would lower workers' 6.2 percent payroll taxes to 1.2 percent and require employees to invest the remaining 5 percent in personal savings accounts (PSAs) resembling the familiar Individual Retirement Accounts (IRAs). As with IRAs, workers could open a PSA in a financial services company such as a bank or brokerage house and invest in the stocks and bonds of their choice.

On the downside, workers who earn low wages would have less money to invest in PSAs and those with no investing experience would face a greater risk of losing their nest egg from making bad investments.

The plan would contain a provision for basic protections and provide for disability and survivors benefits and a safety-net benefit of $360 to $410 a month for retirees. Like the Ball plan, it also assumes lower cost of living increases for retirees.

A third rescue plan proposed by two of the panelists would just tinker a bit with the Social Security system. They suggested scaling back some benefits for higher income earners and imposing an additional 1.6 percent payroll tax which would be used to create mandatory Personal Investment Plans that would be invested in private stocks. They would be converted into a fixed income annuity when a worker retires.

Legislation on the proposed fixes to save Social Security will probably not take place until the next president's term in office and any one of the items in the Council's suggested rescue plans could be changed as they pass through Congressional scrutiny. Only one thing is certain, we can't stay with our current 60-year-old, pay-as-you-go system.—*Ed.*

Benefits Are Major Source of Elderly Money Income

Source: 65+ in the United States, Bureau of the Census

Social Security, combined with pension benefits, accounted for 42 percent of the total household income of elderly retirement pension recipients in 1991. Since the 1940s, there has been a marked increase in reliance on Social Security and a decline in the importance of earnings even though earnings make a great difference in the economic position of older people. In 1940, less than one percent of the elderly received Social Security benefits and 22 percent received general welfare assistance. In 1992, 93 percent received Social security benefits (mean income was $6,634) and 6 percent received public assistance or Supplemental Security Income (SSI) (mean income from these sources was $2,276).

The Social Security program was the major source of income (provided at least 50 percent of total income) for 63 percent of beneficiaries in 1992. It contributed almost all of the income (90 percent or more) for 26 percent and was the only source of income for 14 percent of beneficiaries. □

Social Security

The original Social Security Act was passed in 1935 and amended in 1939, 1946, 1950, 1952, 1954, 1956, 1958, 1960, 1961, 1965, 1967, 1969, 1972, 1974, 1977, 1980-1984, 1986, 1988-1989, 1994, and 1996.

The act is administered by the Social Security Administration and the Health Care Financing Administration, and other agencies within the Department of Health and Human Services.

For purposes of clarity, the explanations given below will describe the provisions of the act as amended.

Old Age, Disability, and Survivors Insurance

Nine out of ten workers in the U.S. are in employment or self-employment covered by the retirement, survivors, disability, and hospital insurance programs. The major groups not covered are:

A. Federal civilian employees hired before 1984.

B. Employees of state and local governments who are members of their employer's retirement system and who have not been covered by a voluntary Federal/State Social Security Agreement.

C. Certain agricultural and domestic workers.

Cash tips count for Social Security if they amount to $20 or more in a month from employment with a single employer.

Social Security Contribution and Rate Schedule

(percent of covered earnings)

Year	Retirement survivors, and disability insurance	Hospital insurance	Year
EMPLOYERS AND EMPLOYEES			
1978	4.95%	1.10%	6.05%
1979-80	5.08	1.05	6.13
1981	5.35	1.30	6.65
1982-83	5.40	1.30	6.70
1984	5.70	1.30	7.00
1985	5.70	1.35	7.05
1986-87	5.70	1.45	7.15
1988-89	6.06	1.45	7.51
1990 & later	6.20	1.45	7.65
SELF-EMPLOYED			
1978	7.00%	1.10%	8.10%
1979-80	7.05	1.05	8.10
1981	8.00	1.30	9.30
1982	8.05	1.30	9.35
1983	8.05	1.30	9.35
1984	11.40	2.60	*14.00
1985	11.40	2.70	*14.10
1986-87	11.40	2.90	*14.30
1988-89	12.12	2.90	*15.02
1990 & later	12.40	2.90	*15.30

*The law provides credit against self-employment tax liability in the following manner: 2.7% in 1984; 2.3% in 1985; 2.09% 1986-1989 and, beginning with the 1990 taxable year, the credit is replaced with two special provisions. First self-employed persons will be allowed a 7.65% deduction from net profit before computing their SECA tax and an income tax deduction equal to one-half of the SECA tax.

To qualify for benefits or make payments possible for your survivors, you must be in work covered by the law for a certain number of "quarters of coverage," or credits. Before 1978, a credit was earned if a worker was paid $50 or more in wages in a 3-month calendar quarter. A self-employed person got 4 credits for a year in which his net earnings were $400 or more.

In 1978, a worker, whether employed or self-employed, received one credit for each $250 of covered annual earnings up to a maximum of four for a year. The credit measure was increased to $260 in 1979 and $290 in 1980, $310 in 1981, $340 in 1982, $370 in 1983, $390 in 1984, $410 in 1985, $440 in 1986, $460 in 1987, $470 in 1988, $500 in 1989, $520 in 1990, $540 in 1991, $570 in 1992, $590 in 1993, $620 in 1994, $630 in 1995, $640 in 1996, and will increase automatically in future years to keep pace with increases in average wages. The number of credits needed differs for different persons and depends on the date of your birth; in general, it is related to the number of years after 1950, or after the year you reach 21, if later, and up to the year you reach 62, become disabled, or die. One credit is required for each such year in order for you or your family to get benefits. Credits earned at any time are used to decide if you have the number needed to qualify. No one will need more than 40 credits. Your local Social Security office can tell you how long you need to work.

Who Pays for the Insurance?

Both workers and their employers pay for the workers' insurance. Self-employed persons pay their own social security contributions annually along with their income tax. The rates include the cost of Medicare hospital insurance. The contribution and benefit base is $57,600 for 1993 for retirement, survivor and disability coverage, and $135,000 for 1993 for Medicare coverage, and will increase automatically in future years as earnings levels rise. The contribution rate schedules under present law are shown in the table in this section.

The separate payroll contribution to finance hospital insurance is placed in a separate trust fund in the U.S. Treasury. In addition, the medical insurance premiums, currently $46.10 a month in 1995, and the government's shares go into another separate trust fund.

How to Apply for Benefits

You apply for benefits by filing a claim either in person, by mail, or by telephone at any social security office. You can get the address of your nearest office either from the post office, from the phone book under the listing, United States Government—Social Security Administration, or by calling Social Security's toll-free number 1–800–772–1213. You will need certain kinds of proof, depending upon the type of benefit you are claiming. If it is a retirement benefit, you should provide your social security number and a birth certificate or religious record (preferably recorded before age 5). If you are unable to get these documents, other old documents showing your age or date of birth—such as census records, school records, early naturalization certificate, etc.—may be acceptable. A widow, or widower, 60 or older who is claiming widow's benefits based on his/her spouse's earnings should have his/her own social security number, his/her spouse's social security number, proof of age and a copy of the marriage certificate. A child claiming child's benefits should provide a birth certificate, his/her own social security number, and the social security number of the parent on whose record benefits are being claimed. If formal proof is not available, the Social Security office will tell you what kinds of information will be acceptable. Do not delay applying even if you do not have the necessary information or proofs.

What Does Social Security Offer?

The Social Security contribution you pay gives you four different kinds of protection: (1) retirement benefits, (2) survivors' benefits, (3) disability benefits, and (4) Medicare hospital insurance benefits.

Retirement and Dependents' benefits. Currently, a worker becomes eligible for the full amount of his retirement benefits at age 65, if he has retired under the definition in the law. A worker may retire at 62 and get 80% of his full benefit. The closer he is to age 65 when he starts collecting his benefit, the larger is the fraction of his full benefit that he will get. Once the worker receives a reduced benefit, the reduction continues after age 65.

The amount of the retirement benefit you are entitled to at 65 is the key to all other benefits under the program. The retirement benefit is based on covered earnings, generally those after 1950.

Benefits to workers who attain age 62 after 1978 and their dependents are based, in part, on earnings that have been adjusted to take account of increases in average wages since they were earned. Your covered earnings will be updated (indexed) to the second year before you reach age 62, become disabled, or die, and will reflect the increases in average wages that have occurred since the earnings were paid. The largest 35 years of adjusted earnings are averaged together and a formula is applied to the adjusted average to figure the benefit rate.

A worker who delays his retirement past age 65, or who does not receive a benefit for some months after age 65 because of high earnings will get a special credit that can mean a larger benefit. The credit adds to a worker's benefits 1% (3% for workers age 62 from 1979–1986) for each year (1/12 of 1% for each month) from age 65 to age 70 for which he did not get benefits. (*See* table.)

If a worker receives a pension from work not covered by Social Security, a different formula, which yields a smaller benefit, applies. This modified formula is used to eliminate the weighting in the Social Security formula which applies to workers whose careers were spent in lower paying jobs.

The law provides a special minimum benefit at retirement for people who worked under Social Security for many years. The provision will help people who had low incomes, but above a specific level, during their working years. The amount of the special minimum depends on the number of years above a specific earnings level called "years of coverage." For a worker retiring at 65 in Jan. 1996 with 30 or more years of coverage, the special minimum benefit would be $532.90. These benefits are reduced if a worker is under 65 and are increased automatically for increases in the cost of living.

If you retired at age 65 in Jan. 1996 with average earnings, you would get a benefit of $885.00.

If your spouse is also 65, then he or she will get a spouse's benefit that is equal to half your benefit. So if your benefit is $885.00, your spouse gets $442.00.

Delayed Retirement Credit Rates

Age 65	Monthly percentage	Yearly percentage
Prior to 1982	1/12 of 1%	1%
1982–1989	1/4 of 1%	3%
1990–1991	7/24 of 1%	3.5%
1992–1993	1/3 of 1%	4%
1994–1995	3/8 of 1%	4.5%
1996–1997	5/12 of 1%	5%
1998–1999	11/24 of 1%	5.5%
2000–2001	1/2 of 1%	6%
2002–2003	13/24 of 1%	6.5%
2004–2005	7/12 of 1%	7%
2006–2007	5/8 of 1%	7.5%
2008 or later	2/3 of 1%	8%

If your spouse is between ages 62 and 65, he or she can draw a reduced benefit; the amount depends on the number of months before 65 that he or she starts getting checks. If he or she draws his or her benefit when he or she is 62, he or she will get about 3/8 of your basic benefit, or $331.00. (He or she will get this amount for the rest of his or her life, unless you should die first; then he or she can start getting widow's or widower's benefits, described below.)

If the spouse is entitled to a worker's retirement benefit on his or her own earnings, he or she can draw whichever amount is larger. If the spouse is entitled to a retirement benefit which is less than the spouse's benefit, he or she will receive his or her own retirement benefit plus the difference between the retirement benefit and the spouse's benefit.

If you have children under 18 or a child under age 19 and in full-time attendance at an elementary or secondary school or a son or daughter who became totally disabled prior to reaching age 22, when you retire they will get a benefit equal to half your full retirement benefits (subject to a maximum monthly payment that can be made to a family). Children who can qualify for benefits include your biological or legally adopted child, or dependent stepchild or grandchild. If your spouse is caring for your child who is under 16 or who became disabled before 22 (and getting benefits too), he or she is eligible for benefits, even if he or she is under 62.

In general, the highest retirement check that can be paid to a worker who retired at 65 in Jan. 1996 is about $1248.00 a month. Maximum payment to the family of this retired worker is about $3,251.40 in Jan. 1996. When your children reach age 18, their benefits will stop except for children age 19 and under attending an elementary or secondary school full time and except for a benefit that is going to a son or daughter who became totally disabled before attaining age 22. Such a person can continue to get his benefits as long as his disability meets the definition in the law.

If you are divorced, you can get Social Security benefits (the same as a spouse or widow, or widower), based on your ex-spouse's earnings record if you were married at least 10 years and if your ex-spouse has retired, or become disabled. If a divorced spouse has been divorced for at least 2 years, the spouse may be eligible for benefits even if the worker is not receiving benefits. However, both the worker and spouse must be age 62 or over and the worker must be fully insured. In either case, the divorced spouse must be unmarried.

Work Credits Required for Living Persons to Be Fully Insured at Age 62

Individual's date of birth	Number of credits Men	Women	Individual's date of birth	Number of credits (men & women)
1/1/1893 or earlier	6	6	1/2/13–1/1/14	24
1/2/93–1/1/94	7	6	1/2/14–1/1/15	25
1/2/94–1/1/95	8	6	1/2/15–1/1/16	26
1/2/95–1/1/96	9	6	1/2/16–1/1/17	27
1/2/96–1/2/97	10	7	1/2/17–1/1/18	28
1/2/97–1/1/98	11	8	1/2/18–1/1/19	29
1/2/98–1/1/99	12	9	1/2/19–1/1/20	30
1/2/1899– 1/1/1900	13	10	1/2/20–1/1/21	31
			1/2/21–1/1/22	32
			1/2/22–1/1/23	33
1/2/00–1/1/01	14	11	1/2/23–1/1/24	34
1/2/01–1/1/02	15	12	1/2/24–1/1/25	35
1/2/02–1/1/03	16	13	1/2/25–1/1/26	36
1/2/03–1/1/04	17	14	1/2/26–1/1/27	37
1/2/04–1/1/05	18	15	1/2/27–1/1/28	38
1/2/05–1/1/06	19	16	1/2/28–1/1/29	39
1/2/06–1/1/07	20	17	1/2/29 or later	40
1/2/07–1/1/08	21	18		
1/2/08–1/1/09	22	19		
1/2/09–1/1/10	23	20		
1/2/10–1/1/11	24	21		
1/2/11–1/1/12	24	22		
1/2/12–1/1/13	24	23		

Survivor benefits. This feature of the social security program gives your family valuable life insurance protection—in some cases benefits to a family could amount to $100,000 or more over a period of years. The amount of protection is again geared to what the worker would be entitled to if he had been age 65 when he died. Your survivors could get:

1. A one-time cash payment. [NOTE: There is no restriction on the use of the lump-sum death payment.] This "lump-sum death payment" is $255.

2. A benefit for each child until he reaches 18, or 19 if the child is in full-time attendance at an elementary or secondary school or at any age if disabled before 22. "Child" includes biological or legally adopted child, or dependent stepchild or grandchild. Each eligible child receives 75% of the basic benefit (subject to reduction for the family maximum). (A disabled child can continue to collect benefits after age 22.) If certain conditions are met, dependent grandchildren of insured workers can receive survivor or dependent benefits.

3. A benefit for your widow(er), including your surviving divorced spouse, at any age, if she/he has your entitled children under 16 or disabled in care. The are called mother/father benefits. "Your children" includes your biological or legally adopted children, dependent stepchildren or grandchildren. In the case of a surviving divorced spouse, the child must also be the divorced spouse's biological or legally adopted child. Her/his benefit is also 75% of the basic benefit. She/he can collect this as long as she/he has an entitled child under 16 or disabled now "in care." If payments terminate they will start again upon application when she/he is 60 at a slightly lower amount.

Total family survivor benefits are estimated to be as high as $2,534.00 a month if the worker dies in 1995.

4. Your spouse or divorced spouse can get a widow's, widower's, or surviving divorced spouse's benefit starting at age 60. This benefit equals 71 1/2% of the basic amount at age 60. A widow, or widower, who first becomes entitled at 65 or later will get 100% of his or her deceased spouse's basic amount (or the amount of the deceased spouse's reduced benefits). A widow(er) or surviving divorced spouse, including those who are disabled, must be unmarried. However, a marriage occurring after age 60, or after age 50 if disabled at the time of the remarriage, is disregarded.

5. Dependent parents can sometimes collect survivors' benefits. They are usually eligible if: (a) they were getting at least half their support from the deceased worker at (1) the time of the worker's death if the worker did not qualify for disability benefits before death, or (2) if the worker had been entitled to disability benefits which had not been terminated before death either at the beginning of the period of disability or at the time of death; (b) they have reached 62; and (c) they are not eligible for a greater retirement benefit based on their own earnings. One surviving parent can then get 82 1/2% of the basic benefit. If two parents are eligible, each would get 75%.

Here is an example of survivors' benefits in one family situation: John Jones died at age 29 in June 1996 leaving a wife and two children aged one and three. He had average covered earnings under Social Security. Family survivors' benefits would include: (1) a lump-sum death payment of $255, and (2) a total monthly benefit of $1,618 for the family. When the children reach 18, their benefits stop unless they are attending an elementary or secondary school full time, in which case payments continue up to age 19. When the older child no longer collects benefits, the widow and younger child continue to get benefits with the widow entitled until that child is age 16. The child will still get a benefit until age 18 (or age 19, if he or she attends elementary or secondary school full time). When Mrs. Jones becomes 60 (assuming she has not remarried), she will be able to get a reduced widow's benefit if she so chooses, or she can wait until age 65 to get a full benefit.

If in addition to your Social Security benefit as a wife, husband, divorced spouse, widow, widower, or surviving divorced spouse you receive a pension based on your work in employment not covered by Social Security, your benefit as a spouse or survivor will be reduced by 2/3rds of the amount of that pension. Under an exception in the law, your government pension will not affect your spouse's or survivor's benefit if you became eligible for that pension before December 1982 and if, at the time you apply or become entitled to your social security benefit as a spouse or survivor, you could have qualified for that benefit if the law in effect in January 1977 had remained in effect (e.g., at that time, men had to prove they were dependent upon their wives for 1/2 support to be eligible for benefits as a spouse or survivor.) There are also several other exceptions in the law. Your government pension may also affect Social Security benefits based on your own work covered by social security. (*See* discussion under *Retirement Benefits.*)

Disability benefits. Disability benefits can be paid to several groups of people:

Disabled workers under 65 and their families.

Persons disabled before 22 who continue to be disabled. These benefits are payable as early as 18 when a parent (or stepparent or grandparent under certain circumstances) receives social security retirement or disability benefits or when an insured parent dies.

Disabled widows and widowers and (under certain conditions) disabled surviving divorced spouses of workers who were insured at death. These benefits are payable as early as 50.

A disabled person is eligible for Medicare after being entitled to disability payments for 24 months.

If you are a worker and become severely disabled, you will be eligible for monthly benefits if you have worked under Social Security long enough and recently enough. The amount of work you will need depends on your age when you become disabled:

Before 24: You need credit for 1 1/2 years of work in the 3-year period ending when your disability begins.

24 through 30: You need credit for having worked half the time during the period between 21 and the time you become disabled.

To be considered disabled under the social security law you must be: (1) unable to engage in any substantial gainful activity because of any medically determinable physical or mental impairment which can be expected to result in death or has lasted or can be expected to last for 12 continuous months, or (2) blind. A person whose vision is no better than 20/200 even with glasses, or who has a limited visual field of 20 degrees or less, is considered "blind" under the social security law.

If you meet these conditions, you may be able to get payments even if your recovery from the disability is expected.

The medical evidence from your physician or other sources will show the existence and severity of your condition and the extent to which it prevents you from doing substantial gainful work. Your age, education, training, and work experience also may be considered in deciding whether you are able to work. If you can't do your regular work but can do other substantial gainful work, you will not be considered disabled.

While you are receiving benefits as a disabled worker, payments can also be made to certain members of your family. These family members include:

Your unmarried children under 18.

Your children [under 19] if they are unmarried and attending an elementary or secondary school full time.

Your unmarried children 18 or older who were disabled before reaching 22 and continue to be disabled.

Your spouse at any age if she/he has in-care a child who is under 16 or disabled and who is getting benefits based on your social security record.

Your spouse 62 or older even if there are no children entitled to benefits.

Children who can qualify for benefits include your biological or legally adopted child or dependent stepchild or grandchild.

Benefits generally (no-waiting-period cases are an exception) begin after a waiting period of 5 full calendar months. No benefits can be paid for these first 5 months of disability; therefore, the first payment is for the 6th full month. If you are disabled more than 6 full months before you apply, back benefits may be payable, but not before the 6th full month of disability. It is important to apply soon after the disability starts because back payments are limited to the 12 months preceding the month you apply.

After they have been entitled to disability checks for 2 years or more, certain disabled people under 65 are eligible for Medicare. They include disabled workers at any age, persons who became disabled before age 22, and disabled widows and widowers age 50 or over.

Medicare protection generally ends when monthly disability benefits end, and can continue an additional 3 years after benefits stop because an individual returns to gainful work. (Under certain circumstances, former disability beneficiaries may purchase continued Medicare coverage. *See* "Do You Qualify for Hospital Insurance?" in this section.)

If a person becomes entitled to disability benefits again, Medicare coverage starts at the same time if a worker becomes disabled again within 5 years after benefits end (or within 7 years for a disabled widow, widower, or person disabled before age 22).

Benefits to workers disabled after 1978 and their dependents are based, in part, on earnings that have been adjusted to take account of increases in average wages since they were earned. The adjusted earnings are averaged together and a formula is applied to the adjusted average to figure the benefit rate. If they are entitled to a pension based on work not covered by social security, a different formula, which yields a smaller benefit, applies.

Monthly benefits in Jan. 1996 or later can be as high as $1,482.00 for a worker and as high as $2,223.00 for a worker with a family. Once a person starts receiving benefits, the amount will increase automatically in future years to keep pace with the rising cost of living.

If you receive benefits as a disabled worker, an adult disabled since childhood, or a disabled widow or widower, you are not subject to the general rule under which some benefits are withheld if you have substantial earnings. There are special rules, which include medical considerations, for determining how any work you do might affect your disability payments.

If one of your dependents who is under 65 and who is not disabled works and earns more than $8,160 in 1995, some of the dependent's benefits may be withheld. In general, $1 in benefits is withheld for each $2 over $8,160. Different rules apply to your dependents who are 65 or over. A person 65 or over can earn $11,280 in 1995 without having benefits withheld. For persons 65 or over, $1 in benefits is withheld for $3 in earnings over $11,280.

The amount a person can earn without having any benefits withheld will increase in future years as the level of average wages rises.

If you are receiving disability benefits, you are required by law to let the Social Security Administration know if your condition improves or if you return to work no matter how little you earn.

If at any time medical evidence shows that you no longer meet the requirements for entitlement to disability benefits, you will still receive benefits for a 3-month period of adjustment. Benefits will then be stopped.

Whether or not you report a return to work or that your condition has improved, Social Security will review your claim periodically to see if you continue to meet the requirements for benefits.

If you are a disabled worker or a person disabled in childhood and you return to work in spite of a severe condition, your benefits may continue to be paid during a trial work period of up to 9 months—not necessarily consecutive months. This will give you a chance to test your ability to work. If after 9 service months it is decided that you are able to do substantial gainful work, your benefits will be paid for an adjustment period of 3 additional months.

Thus, if you go to work in spite of your disability, you may continue to receive disability benefits for up to 12 months, even though the work is substantial gainful work. If your benefits are stopped because you return to work and you become unable to continue working within the next 33 months, your benefits can be restarted automatically. You do not have to file a new disability application. If it is decided that the work you are able to do is not substantial and gainful, you may continue to receive benefits. Of course, should you no longer meet the requirements for entitlement to disability, your benefits would be stopped after a 3-month adjustment period even though your trial work period might not be over.

Disabled widows and widowers also can have a trial work period and extended eligibility for up to 33 months.

You Can Earn Income Without Losing Benefits

If you are 70 or over you can earn any amount and still get all your benefits. If you are under 70, you can receive all benefits if your earnings do not exceed the annual exempt amount. The annual amount for 1996 is $12,500 for people 65 or over and $8,280 for people under 65.

If your earnings go over the annual amount, $1 in benefits is withheld for each $2 ($3 if age 65-69) of earnings above the limit.

The monthly measure used for 1977 and earlier years to determine whether benefits could be paid for any month during which they earned 1/12 or less of the annual exempt amount and did not perform substantial work in their business has been eliminated. A person can now use the monthly test only in the first year that he or she has a month in which earnings do not exceed 1/12 of the annual exempt amount or does not perform substantial services in self-employment. If such a month occurs in 1996, a benefit can be paid for any month in which you earn $1,042 or less (if 65 or older) or $690 or less (if under 65) and don't perform substantial services in self-employment even though your total yearly earnings exceed the annual amount.

The annual exempt amount will increase automatically as the level of average wages rises.

If a worker's earnings exceed the exempt amount, social security benefits to his dependents may be reduced. However, a dependent's benefits will not be reduced if another dependent has excess earnings.

Anyone earning over the annual exempt amount a year while receiving benefits (and under age 70) must report their earnings to the Social Security Administration. If you continue to work after you have applied for social security, your additional earnings may increase the amount of your monthly payment. This will be done automatically by the Social Security Administration. You need not ask for it.

Medicare

The Medicare program is administered by the Health Care Financing Administration.

Most people 65 and over and many under 65 who have been entitled to disability checks for at least 2 years have Medicare protection. So do insured people and their dependents who need a kidney transplant or dialysis treatment because of permanent kidney failure.

The hospital insurance part of Medicare helps pay the cost of inpatient hospital care and certain kinds of follow-up care. The medical insurance part helps pay for the cost of doctors' services, outpatient hospital services, and for certain other medical items and services.

A person who is eligible for monthly benefits at 65 gets hospital insurance automatically and does not have to pay a premium. He does pay a monthly premium for medical insurance.

Supplemental Security Income

The supplemental security income (SSI) program is a federally funded program administered by the Social Security Administration. Its basic purpose is to assure a minimum level of income to people who are elderly (65 or over), blind or disabled, and who have limited income and resources.

In 1996, the maximum Federal SSI payment was $470 a month for an individual and $705 a month for a couple. But in many States, SSI payments are much higher because the State adds to the Federal payment.

Countable resources must be valued at $2,000 or less for an individual or $3,000 or less for a couple. But not all the things people own count for SSI. For instance, the house a person lives in and the land around it, and usually, one car does not count.

Generally, depending on the State, people who get SSI can also get Medicaid to pay for their health care costs as well as food stamps and other social services. And in many States an application for SSI is an application for Medicaid, so people do not have to make separate applications. Certain people can also apply for food stamps at the same Social Security office where they apply for SSI.

Social Security representatives will need information about the income and resources and the citizenship or alien status of people applying for benefits. If the person is living with a spouse, or the application is for a disabled child living with parents, the same information is needed about the spouse/parents.

People who are age 65 or over will need proof of their age such as a birth certificate, or religious record. And if a person who is filing is disabled or blind, Social Security will need information about the impairment and its treatment history.

It helps if people have this information and evidence with them when they talk to their Social Security representative. But they do not need to have **any** of these things to **start** their application. All they need to do is to call Social Security to find out if they are eligible for SSI payments and the other benefits that come with it. Benefits are not retroactive, so delay can cost money.

The Social Security representative will explain just what information/evidence is needed for the SSI claim, and will provide help in getting it if help is needed. Most Social Security offices will make an appointment for an office visit or for a telephone interview if that is more convenient. Or people can just walk in, and wait until someone is free to help them.

Over 6 million people receive SSI benefits now. Many receive both SSI and Social Security. Do not wait. Call 1-800-772-1213, and find out more about SSI. Even the call is free!

How to Protect Your Social Security Record

Always show your Social Security card when you start a new job. In that way you will be sure that your earnings will be credited to *your* Social Security record and not someone else's. If you lose your Social Security card, contact Social Security to find out how to apply for a new one. When a woman marries, she should apply for a new card showing her married name (and the same number).

Public Assistance

The Federal government makes grants to the states to help them provide financial assistance, medical care, and social services to certain persons in need, including children dependent because of the death, absence from home, incapacity, or (in some states) unemployment of a parent. In addition, some help is provided from only state and/or local funds to some other needy persons.

Federal sharing in state cash assistance expenditures made in accordance with the Social Security Act is based on formulas which are set forth in the Act. The Social Security Act gives the states the option of using one of two formulas, whichever is to its benefit. One formula limits the amount of assistance payment in which there is federal sharing. The other formula permits federal sharing without a limit on the amount of assistance payment. Administrative costs in all the programs are shared equally by the federal and state governments.

Within these and other general patterns set by the requirements of the Social Security Act and their administrative interpretations, each state initiates and administers its own public assistance programs, including the determination of who is eligible to receive assistance, and how much can be granted and under what conditions. Assistance is in the form of cash payments made to recipients, except that direct payments are used for medical care, and restricted payments may be used in cases of mismanagement. Other social services are provided, in some instances, to help assistance recipients increase their capacity for self-care and self-support or to strengthen family life.

In the medical assistance Medicaid program, federal funds pay 50% to 83% of the costs for medical care. If it is to a state's benefit, it may use the Medicaid formula for federal sharing for its money payment programs, ignoring the maximum on dollar amounts per recipient.

Medicare Program

The Medicare program is a federal health-insurance program for persons 65 and over, and certain disabled people under 65.

Enacted under the Social Security Amendments of 1965, Medicare's official name is Title XVIII of the Social Security Act. These amendments also carried Title XIX, providing federal assistance to state medical-aid programs, which has come to be known as Medicaid.

Medicare

It will be helpful to your understanding of the Medicare program if you keep the following points in mind:

- The federal health-insurance program does not of itself offer medical services. It helps pay hospital, doctor, and other medical bills. You should always make sure that health care facilities or persons who provide you with treatment or services are participating in Medicare. Usually, Medicare cannot pay for care from non-participating health care organizations.
- If you live in an area served by a managed care plan, you can get your Medicare benefits either through the fee-for-service system or through a managed care plan such as a health maintenance organization (HMO). Under fee-for-service, you can choose your doctor, hospital, or other health care provider. A fee is generally charged for each service and Medicare pays its share of the bill. Under managed care, you usually must get all of your care from the doctors, hospitals, and other health care providers that are part of the plan. Medicare pays the HMO for your care. Depending on the plan, you may have to pay a monthly premium and a copayment each time you go to the doctor or use other services.
- There are two parts of the program: (1) The hospital insurance part for the payment of most of the cost of covered care provided by participating hospitals, skilled nursing facilities, home health agencies, and hospices. (2) The medical insurance part which helps pay doctors' bills and certain other expenses.
- Another important point to remember: While Medicare pays the major share of the costs of many illnesses requiring hospitalization, it does not offer adequate protection for long-term illness or mental illness and Medicare does not pay for custodial care.
- Therefore, it may be advisable not to cancel any private health insurance you now carry. You may wish to cancel a policy whose benefits are duplicated by the federal program, and consider a new policy that will provide for the payment of costs not covered by the federal program. Private insurance companies offer policies supplementing the protection offered by the federal program.
- If you want help in deciding whether to buy private supplemental insurance, ask at any social security office for the pamphlet, *Guide to Health Insurance for People with Medicare.* This free pamphlet describes the various types of supplemental insurance available.

Do You Qualify for Hospital Insurance?

If you're entitled to monthly social security or railroad retirement checks (as a worker, dependent, or survivor), you have hospital insurance protection automatically when you're 65. People 65 or older who are not entitled to monthly benefits must have worked long enough under Social Security or the railroad retirement system or in covered Federal, state, and local employment to get hospital insurance without paying a monthly premium. If they do not have enough work, they can get hospital insurance by paying a monthly premium. Disabled people under 65 will have hospital insurance automatically after they have been entitled to social security disability benefits for 24 months. Effective July 1, 1990, former disability beneficiaries will be able to purchase hospital insurance if their premium-free coverage stops due to work activity. Federal, state, or local employees who are disabled before 65 may be eligible on the basis of their government employment. People are eligible at any age if they need maintenance dialysis or a kidney transplant for permanent kidney failure and are getting monthly Social Security or railroad retirement benefits or have worked long enough.

To be sure your protection will start the month you reach 65, apply for Medicare insurance 3 months before reaching 65, even if you don't plan to retire.

Do You Qualify for Medicare Medical Insurance?

The medical insurance plan is a vital supplement to the hospital plan. It helps pay for doctors' and other medical services. Many people have not been able to obtain such insurance from private companies because they could not afford it or because of their medical histories.

Any person who can get premium-free hospital insurance benefits based on work as described above can enroll in the medical insurance plan and get medical insurance benefits. In addition, most United States residents age 65 or over can enroll in the medical insurance plan.

People who get social security benefits or retirement benefits under the railroad retirement system will be enrolled automatically for medical insurance—unless they say they don't want it—when they become entitled to hospital insurance. Automatic enrollment does not apply to people who have not applied for Social Security or Railroad Retirement benefits, who have permanent kidney failure, who are eligible for Medicare on the basis of government employment, or people who have not worked long enough to be eligible for hospital insurance. These people have to apply for medical insurance if they want it. People who have medical insurance pay a monthly premium covering part of the cost of this protection. They should enroll for Part B as soon as they are eligible to avoid paying premium surcharges for delayed enrollment. The basic premium for enrollees is $42.50 a month in 1996.

Is Other Insurance Necessary?

As already indicated, Medicare provides only partial reimbursement. Therefore, you should know how much medical cost you can bear and perhaps arrange for other insurance.

In 1996, for the first 60 days of inpatient hospital care in each benefit period, hospital insurance pays for all covered services except for the first $736. For the 61st through 90th day of a covered inpatient hospital stay, hospital insurance pays for all covered services except for $184 a day. People who need to be in a hospital for more than 90 days in a benefit period can use some or all of their 60 lifetime reserve days. Hospital insurance pays for all covered services except for $368 a day for each reserve day used. Hospital insurance pays the full cost of the first 20 days of an inpatient stay in a skilled nursing facility per benefit period.

Under medical insurance, the patient must meet an annual deductible. In 1996, the annual deductible is $100. After the patient has met the deductible, each year, medical insurance generally pays 80% of the approved amounts for any additional covered services the patient receives during the rest of the year.

How You Obtain Coverage

If you are receiving Social Security or railroad retirement monthly benefits, you will receive from the government information concerning Medicare about 3 months before you become eligible for hospital insurance.

All other eligible people have to file an application for Medicare. They should contact a social security office to apply for Medicare.

New Medicare Benefits

Breast Cancer Screening (Mammography): Medicare medical insurance now helps pay for X-ray screenings to detect breast cancer. Women 65 or older can use the benefit every other year. Younger disabled women covered by Medicare can use it more frequently. Medicare will pay 80 percent of up to $62.10 for each screening in 1996.

Physician Payment Reforms: In 1996, physicians who do not accept assignment may not charge you for office and hospital visits more than 115 percent of the Medicare approved amount. Physicians who knowingly charge more than these amounts are subject to sanctions.

You no longer have to file claims to Medicare for covered medical insurance services. Doctors, suppliers, and other providers of services must submit the claims to Medicare within one year of providing the service to you or be subject to certain penalties. □

The Growth Rate of Our Aging Population

Source: 65+ in the United States, Current Population Reports, P23–190, issued April 1996.

Our nation's population continues to age. In 1860, half the population was under age 20; in 1994, half were age 34 or older; by 2030, at least half could be 39 years or older.

In July 1994, there were 33.2 million elderly (aged 65 or older), one-eighth of the total population. Among the elderly, 18.7 million were aged 65 to 74, 11.0 million were aged 75 to 84, and 3.5 million were aged 85 or older.

The elderly population increased eleven-fold from 1900 to 1994, compared with only a three-fold increase for those under age 65. Elderly population growth rates for the 1990–2010 period will be modest, but during the 2010–30 period, elderly growth rates will increase dramatically as the Baby Boom generation ages into the 65 and over group.

From 1960 to 1994, the oldest old population (persons aged 85 and over) increased by 274 percent, compared with 100 percent for the 65 and over, and 45 percent for the total population. The oldest old population in 1994 would more than double to 7 million in 2020 under middle series projections. The oldest old would reach 19 million by 2050, or as many as 27 million under the Census Bureau's "highest series" assumptions of future life expectancy and net immigration.

The number of centenarians, persons aged 100 years or older, has grown rapidly in recent years. This group has more than doubled since 1980. About 4 in 5 centenarians are women.

From 1995 to 2005, persons reaching age 65 will be those born during the 1930s Depression era. As a result, the growth rate of the population 65 and over will be relatively modest over the next decade. However, when the Baby Boom generation, born between 1946 and 1964, begins to turn 65 in 2011, we will start to witness a rapid growth rate of persons 65 and over. □

New Generation Cars: Hybrid Vehicles

Main source; U.S. Department of Energy.

In 1996, the German company Daimler-Benz AG displayed its electric car—the first in the world to be powered by electricity generated from an onboard fuel cell. The car is a mini-van capable of carrying six people for a range of 150 miles and at speeds of up to 60 miles per hour. The fuel cell utilizes hydrogen stored in a tank on the vehicle and oxygen from the atmosphere. The emissions from the cell are water vapor.

Most experts agree that the car of the future, that has the same versatility as a conventional vehicle, will be a hybrid electricity vehicle (HEV) of some kind. The energy density of electric batteries will never equal that of liquid or gaseous fuel cells, necessitating that these fuels remain a critical part of future vehicles to maintain the driving range and quick refueling found in today's conventional vehicles.

Even fuel cells, which are a promising long-term technology for personal transportation, will most likely still be put in an HEV configuration with a high-power energy storage/buffer device on board. Rather than having only one propulsion system choice when buying a future vehicle, it may be possible to select the propulsion system in the same way that one selects a 4-cylinder engine or a V8. In the future, you may be able to select a vehicle and then choose if you want a conventional engine, batteries only, or an energy storage device (batteries, flywheels, ultracapacitors, or some combustion) a Hybrid Power Unit (HPU) (fuel cell, turbine, diesel engine, Stirling engine, or conventional internal combustion engine).

Hybrid electric vehicles are currently under development in the United States. Each American auto manufacturer has its own schedule for completing the development of a production-feasible HEV. General Motors' (GM), Ford's, and Chrysler's programs are funded 50% by the Department of Energy (DOE).

General Motors and Ford each initiated their subcontracts with the DOE in 1994 and the program activities are scheduled for five years. Chrysler's subcontract was signed in March 1996 and the program will last four years.

What Is a Hybrid Electric Vehicle?

An HEV is a vehicles that has two sources of motive energy. There are many hybrid system concepts using fuel cells, gas turbines, diesels, and lean burn gasoline engines in combination with flywheels, batteries, and ultracapacitors. No matter which concept is used, there are two ways to build the electric and fuel system of an HEV: using a *Parallel* configuration or a *Series* configuration.

With two drive trains, an internal combustion engine (ICE) running on gasoline or alternative fuels and a battery-driven electric drive train, the HEV is able to operate approximately two times more efficiently than traditional internal combustion engines.

That is because the energy loss of an HEV is much less than that of a traditional ICE vehicle.

HEVs have several advantages over internal combustion engine cars:
- Regenerative braking capability helps minimize the energy lost when driving.
- Engine is sized to average load, not peak load, which reduces the weight of the engine.
- Fuel efficiency is greatly increased, while emissions are greatly decreased.
- HEVs can be operated using alternative fuels; therefore they need not be dependent on fossil fuels.

Performance

Hybrid vehicles are expected to meet or exceed current performance characteristics in all respects. The car companies know that a new vehicle that is not as good as or better than the previous year's vehicles will not sell, so when they begin selling hybrids, there will be equal or better performance. The electric drives possible in HEVs in the next few years also allow the potential for higher-power drive systems.

Emissions

According to the U.S. Environmental Protection Agency (EPA), vehicle emissions currently contribute between one-third and one-half of the total U.S. atmospheric burden of three major pollutants: carbon monoxide (CO), nitrogen oxides (NOx), and hydrocarbons (HC). Their impact is even greater in many U.S. urban areas.

The pollution from hybrid vehicles will depend on the type of hybrid power unit and fuel used. At a minimum, DOE has specified that the propulsion systems developed in the HV Propulsion Program will meet federal Tier II standards, which are 1.8, 0.16, and 0.13 g/mile for CO, NOx, and HC respectively (versus the current federal standards of 4.2, 0.60, and 0.31 g/mile). The ultimate HEV, from an emission standpoint, might be one that runs on hydrogen, which would emit only water vapor and perhaps very low levels of NOx.

Safety

All HEVs will be manufactured using the same stringent rules, standards, and restrictions as today's conventional vehicles. Of course, some modifications to the standards may have to be made because the propulsion system will consist of different components (batteries, smaller internal combustion engine, controller, etc.). All components will be thoroughly tested and approved by the National Highway Safety Administration before being sold to the public. □

Energy Overview

Source: Annual Energy Review, 1995.

Production

Historically, three fossil fuels have accounted for the bulk of domestic energy production, which by 1995 totaled 71 quadrillion Btu. Coal accounted for the largest share of domestic energy production in 1949–1951 and, after a long hiatus, again in 1982 and in 1984 through 1995. In the interim, first crude oil and then natural gas dominated domestic production. In 1995, coal production totaled 22 quadrillion Btu. Dry natural gas production totaled 19 quadrillion Btu and crude oil production totaled 14 quadrillion Btu. Natural gas plant liquids accounted for another 2.4 quadrillion Btu.

Net generation of electricity by electric utilities increased throughout the 1949–1995 period, registering only two year-to-year declines (during the 1982 recession and again in 1992). However, the rate of growth of electricity net generation slowed during the 47-year period. From 1949 through 1979, the annual growth rate averaged 7.1 percent, whereas from 1980 through 1995, the annual growth rate averaged 1.8 percent. After the mid-1970s, coal and nuclear fuels provided increasing shares of fuel input for electricity generation and, to a lesser extent, natural gas.

Hydroelectric generation (conventional and pumped storage) accounted for over 1.4 quadrillion Btu of electricity in 1949, and from the 1970s through 1995 usually provided about 3 quadrillion Btu per year. However, in 1988, the second year of drought, hydroelectric generation totaled only 2.3 quadrillion Btu. In 1995, it totaled 3.2 quadrillion Btu.

Indicators of Energy Intensity

The relationship between total energy consumption and real gross domestic product (GDP) is a traditional indicator of the energy intensity of the economy. In 1970, 20 thousand Btu of energy were consumed for each chained (1992) dollar of GDP. Higher energy prices in the early 1970s led to increases in energy efficiency and a significant restructuring of the energy-intensive activities of the manufacturing sector. In 1985, the energy intensity of the economy as a whole fell below 14 thousand Btu per chained (1992) dollar, where it remained through 1995.

A second indicator of energy intensity is per capita consumption. Throughout the 1960s and early 1970s, the growth of end-use energy consumption was greater than the growth of the population. Per capita consumption rose from 212 million Btu in 1960 to a peak of 285 million Btu in 1973. Thereafter, per capita consumption trended downward to as low as 226 million Btu in 1983. In the 1990s, low petroleum prices encouraged energy use, and end-use energy consumption rose to 264 million Btu per capita in 1995.[1]

1. The inclusion of non-electric consumption of renewable energy in the totals of U.S. energy consumption for 1990 through 1994 increased the per capita values.

Other renewable energy sources also contributed to the domestic energy supply. Biofuels, a category which includes wood and waste, contributed 2.9 quadrillion Btu to the 1995 total. Geothermal, solar, and wind energy combined contributed 0.5 quadrillion Btu. Renewable energy production (including conventional hydroelectric power and excluding hydroelectric pumped storage) totaled 6.6 quadrillion Btu, 9.3 percent of U.S. total energy production.

Consumption

Energy consumption more than doubled during the 1949 to 1995 period, increasing from 30 quadrillion Btu in 1949 to 74 quadrillion Btu in 1973, and the U.S. economy grew at about the same rate. The domestic energy market was dominated by rapid growth in petroleum and natural gas consumption, which more than tripled during the period. After the 1973 oil shock, energy consumption fluctuated, influenced by dramatic changes in oil prices, changes in the rate of growth of the domestic economy, and such factors as concerns about the effect of energy use on the environment. The post-1973 low point of energy consumption, 71 quadrillion Btu, occurred in 1983 following a period of very high oil prices. The highest level of energy consumption, 91 quadrillion Btu, occurred in 1995, following several years when oil prices were low.

The composition of demand after 1973 reflected an increasing emphasis on electricity generated by coal, nuclear, and renewable energy sources and on nonelectric utility use of renewable sources. In 1973, petroleum and natural gas accounted for 77 percent of total energy consumption; by 1995, their share had declined to 63 percent.

Changing Patterns of Trade

From 1958 forward, the United States consumed more energy than it produced, and the difference was met by energy imports. Net imports of energy (primarily petroleum) grew rapidly through 1973, as demand for cheap foreign oil eroded quotas on petroleum imports. The oil embargo of 1973–1974, coupled with the increase in the price of crude oil, interrupted growth in petroleum net imports; nevertheless, they climbed to a peak of 18 quadrillion Btu in 1977. That year, U.S. dependence on foreign sources of petroleum reached an all-time high of 47 percent. A second round of price increases in 1979 through 1981 suppressed demand for foreign oil. In 1985, petroleum net imports totaled 9.0 quadrillion Btu, and U.S. dependence fell to 27 percent of consumption. Subsequently, petroleum net imports increased every year through 1989, when U.S. dependence on foreign sources of petroleum reached 42 percent of consumption. In 1995, the fifth consecutive year of low crude oil prices, petroleum net imports rose to 17 quadrillion Btu and U.S. dependence on them equaled 45 percent—the second highest level in 18 years.

Natural gas trade was limited to border countries until the advent of shipping natural gas in liquefied form in the late 1960s. In 1995, natural gas net imports reached the record level of 2.6 quadrillion Btu.

Throughout the 1949–1995 period, the United States was a net exporter of coal. In 1995, coal net exports totaled 2.1 quadrillion Btu.

Energy Production by Source, 1995

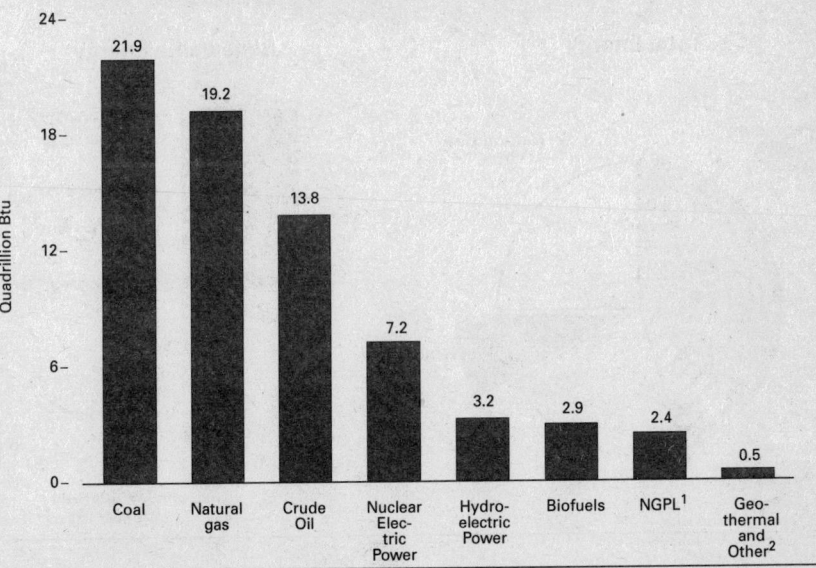

1. Natural gas plant liquids. 2. Conventional and pumped-storage hydroelectric power. *Source:* Energy Information Administration, *Annual Energy Review, 1995.*

Energy Consumption by Source, 1995

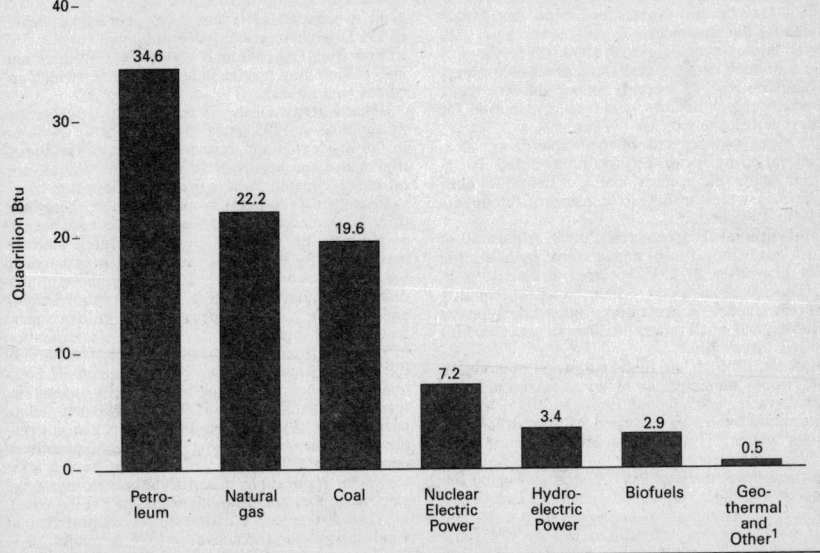

1. Conventional and pumped-storage hydroelectric power. *Source:* Energy Information Administration, *Annual Energy Review, 1995.*

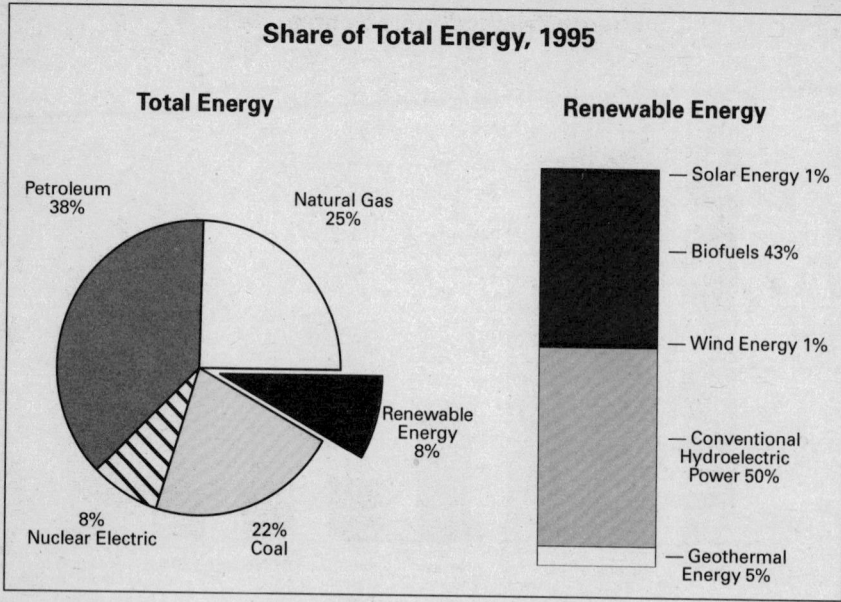

Share of Total Energy, 1995

Total Energy

Petroleum 38%

Natural Gas 25%

Renewable Energy 8%

8% Nuclear Electric

22% Coal

Renewable Energy

— Solar Energy 1%

— Biofuels 43%

— Wind Energy 1%

— Conventional Hydroelectric Power 50%

— Geothermal Energy 5%

Renewable Energy Consumption

Source: Annual Energy Review, 1995.

In 1995, the United States consumed an estimated 6.9 quadrillion Btu of renewable energy. Conventional hydroelectric power and biofuels accounted for the largest shares (50 percent and 43 percent, respectively). Geothermal, solar, and wind energy accounted for the remainder.

Over the six-year period of 1990–1995 (the only years for which data are available), renewable energy consumption rose 12 percent. Among the five major renewable energy sources, wind energy showed the greatest percentage increase (71 percent).

The types and amounts of renewable energy consumed varied by sector. Electric utilities and the industrial sector (the primary source of nonutility electric power) were the biggest consumers throughout the 1990–1995 period.

Conventional Hydroelectric Power. Almost all of the 3.5 quadrillion Btu of conventional hydroelectric power generation in 1995 occurred at electric utilities. The industrial sector, which includes nonutility power producers (cogenerators, independent power producers, and small power producers), accounted for only 153 trillion Btu.

Biofuels. Biofuels are fuelwood, wood byproducts, waste wood, municipal solid waste, manufacturing process waste, and alcohol fuels. In 1995, biofuel consumption totaled an estimated 2.9 quadrillion Btu, most of which (2.4 quadrillion Btu) was wood energy. Some industries, such as the paper and lumber industries, have ready access to wood and wood byproducts, and those rely heavily on wood as an energy source. Consumption of municipal solid waste and other wastes totaled 486 trillion Btu in 1995, and consumption of alcohol fuels (ethanol) totaled 105 trillion Btu.

Geothermal Energy. The third biggest source of renewable energy in 1995 was geothermal energy, which can be used directly, for purposes such as space heating, or converted to electricity. In 1960, the Geysers in California became the first U.S. power plant to generate electricity from geothermal steam. In 1995, geothermal energy consumption reached 362 trillion Btu, 118 trillion Btu at electric utilities and 244 trillion Btu by the industrial sector (which includes nonutilities).

Solar Energy. Of the 74 trillion Btu of solar energy supplied in 1995, most (64 trillion Btu) was used in the residential and commercial sector. The industrial sector accounted for 10 trillion Btu and electric utilities accounted for less than 0.5 trillion Btu.

Because it is difficult to measure solar energy use directly, producer shipments of equipment are used as an indicator. Shipments of low-temperature collectors, used primarily for heating swimming pools, totaled 6.8 million square feet in 1994. Shipments of medium-temperature collectors, used for pool heating and domestic hot water, peaked at 12 million square feet in 1983 and 1984 but, following the expiration of the federal energy tax credit in 1985, totaled only 0.8 million square feet in 1994. Shipments of high-temperature collectors, used for electricity generation, reached 5.2 million square feet in 1990 but fell to near zero in 1991 through 1994, when Luz International Ltd. ceased operating. In 1994, shipments of photovoltaic cells and modules, which have a wide variety of applications, rose for the tenth consecutive year, to 26 thousand peak kilowatts.

Wind Energy. An estimated 41 trillion Btu of wind energy was consumed in 1995, virtually all in the industrial sector (which includes nonutilities). Very small amounts (less than 0.5 trillion Btu) were consumed at electric utilities. □

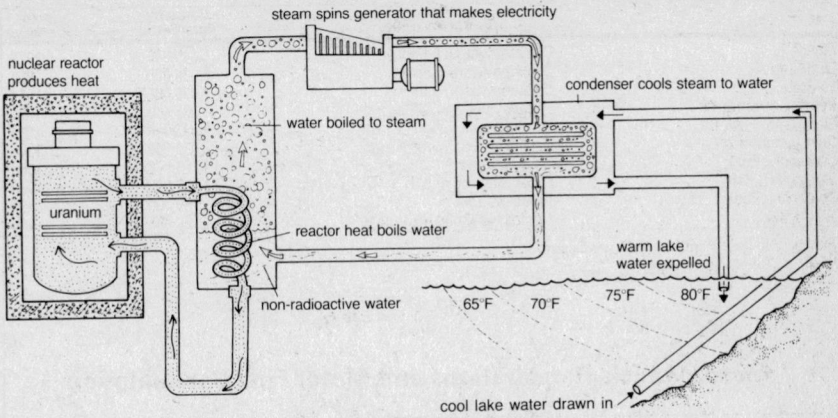

steam spins generator that makes electricity

nuclear reactor produces heat

condenser cools steam to water

water boiled to steam

uranium

reactor heat boils water

warm lake water expelled

non-radioactive water

65°F   70°F   75°F   80°F

cool lake water drawn in

Simplified diagram of a nuclear reactor. Laurel Cook, Boston, MA.

Largest Nuclear Power Plants in the United States
(over a million kilowatts)

Plant	Operating utility	Capacity (kilowatts)	Year operative
South Texas 1, TX	Houston Lighting & Power	1,250,000	1988
South Texas 2	Houston Lighting	1,250,000	1989
Palo Verde 1, AZ	Arizona Public Service	1,221,000	1986
Palo Verde 2, AZ	Arizona Public Service	1,221,000	1986
Palo Verde 3, AZ	Arizona Public Service	1,221,000	1988
Perry 1, OH	Cleveland Electric Illumination	1,205,000	1987
Sequoyah 1, TN	Tennessee Valley Authority	1,148,000	1981
Sequoyah 2, TN	Tennessee Valley Authority	1,148,000	1982
Callaway, MO	Union Electric	1,145,000	1984
Grand Gulf 1, MS	System Energy Resources	1,142,000	1985
Millstone 3, CT	Northeast Nuclear Energy	1,142,000	1986
Catawba 1, SC	Duke Power Co.	1,129,000	1985
Catawba 2, SC	Duke Power Co.	1,129,000	1986
McGuire 1, NC	Duke Power Co.	1,129,000	1981
McGuire 2, NC	Duke Power Co.	1,129,000	1984
Wolf Creek 1, KS	Wolf Creek Nuclear Operating	1,128,000	1985
Braidwood 1, IL	Commonwealth Edison	1,120,000	1988
Braidwood 2, IL	Commonwealth Edison	1,120,000	1988
Salem 1, DE	Public Service Electric & Gas	1,106,000	1977
Salem 2, DE	Public Service Electric & Gas	1,106,000	1981
Byron 1, IL	Commonwealth Edison	1,105,000	1985
Byron 2, IL	Commonwealth Edison	1,105,000	1987
Vogtle 2	Georgia Power	1,083,000	1989
Trojan, OR	Portland General Electric	1,095,000	1976
Fermi 2, OH	Detroit Edison	1,093,000	1988
Diablo Canyon 2	Pacific Gas & Electric	1,087,000	1986
Nine Mile Point 2, NY	Niagara Mohawk Power	1,080,000	1988
San Onofre 3, CA	Southern California Edison	1,080,000	1984
Vogtle 1, GA	Georgia Power	1,079,000	1987
Waterford 3, LA	Louisiana Power & Light	1,075,000	1985
Diablo Canyon 1, CA	Pacific Gas & Electric	1,073,000	1985
San Onofre 2, CA	Southern California Edison	1,070,000	1983
Hope Creek 1, DE	Public Service Electric & Gas	1,067,000	1986
Browns Ferry 1, AL	Tennessee Valley Authority	1,065,000	1974
Browns Ferry 2, AL	Tennessee Valley Authority	1,065,000	1975
Browns Ferry 3, AL	Tennessee Valley Authority	1,065,000	1977
Limerick 2	Philadelphia Elec	1,065,000	1990
Cook 2, MI	Indiana & Michigan Power	1,060,000	1978
Limerick 1, PA	Philadelphia Electric	1,055,000	1986
Peach Bottom 2, PA	Philadelphia Electric	1,051,000	1974
Zion 1, IL	Commonwealth Edison	1,040,000	1973

Plant	Operating utility	Capacity (kilowatts)	Year operative
Zion 2, IL	Commonwealth Edison	1,040,000	1974
La Salle 1, IL	Commonwealth Edison	1,036,000	1984
La Salle 2, IL	Commonwealth Edison	1,036,000	1984
Peach Bottom 3, PA	Philadelphia Gas & Electric	1,035,000	1974
Susquehanna 1, PA	Pennsylvania Power & Light	1,032,000	1983
Susquehanna 2, PA	Pennsylvania Power & Light	1,032,000	1985
Comanche Peak 1, TX	Texas Utilities	1,159,000	1990
Seabrook 1, NH	Public Service of N.H.	1,150,000	1990
Comanche Peak 2, TX	Texas Utilities	1,150,000	1993
Watts Bar I	Tennessee Valley Authority	1,160,000	1996

Source: Nuclear Regulatory Commission.

Motor Vehicle Registrations and Motor Fuel Consumption

Year	Motor vehicle registrations (millions)					Motor fuel consumption[1] (thousand barrels per day)		
	Passenger Cars	Motorcycles	Buses	Trucks	Total	Gasoline[2]	Other Fuels[3]	Total[4]
1980	121.7	5.7	0.5	33.6	161.6	6,820	896	7,716
1985	132.1	5.4	(5)	39.6	177.1	7,020	1,158	8,178
1989	143.1	4.4	(5)	44.2	191.7	7,437	1,385	8,822
1990	143.5	4.3	(5)	45.1	192.9	7,454	1,396	8,849
1991	143.0	4.2	(5)	45.4	192.5	7,323	1,349	8,672
1992	144.2	4.1	(5)	46.1	194.4	7,472	1,430	8,902
1993	146.3	4.0	(5)	47.7	198.0	7,607	1,534	9,141
1994	133.9 R, 6	3.7 R	(5)	64.1 R, 6	201.8 R	7,807 R	1,639 R	9,446 R
1995E	135.0	3.7	(5)	65.5	204.1	7,964	1,680	9,374

1. Includes only motor fuel taxed at the prevailing tax rates in each state. Excludes motor fuel exempt from tax payment, subject to tax refund, or taxed at rates other than the prevailing tax rate. Experience has shown that the total motor fuel consumption quantity cited here equals more than 99.0% of gross reported motor fuel consumption. 2. Motor gasoline, aviation gasoline, and gasohol. 3. Distillate fuel oil (diesel oil), liquefied gases, and kerosene when they are used to operate vehicles on highways. Excludes jet fuel begining in 1962. 4. Excludes losses allowed for evaporation, handling, etc. 5. Included in trucks. 6. Beginning with 1994, personal passenger vans, passenger minivans, and utility-type vehicles are included in "Trucks" instead of "Automobiles." R = Revised data. E = Estimate. NOTE: Sum of components may not equal total due to independent rounding. *Sources:* 1976–86—Federal Highway Administration, *Highway Statistics Annual,* Tables MV-1, MF-21, and MF-25; 1987 forward—Federal Highway Administration, *Selected Highway Statistics and Charts 1994.*

Motor Vehicle Efficiency

Year	Passenger cars			All motor vehicles[1]		
	Miles per car	Gallons per car	Miles per gallon	Miles per vehicle	Gallons per vehicle	Miles per gallon
1980	9,141	591	15.46	9,458	712	13.29
1985	9,560	525	18.20	10,018	685	14.62
1989	10,332	509	20.31	10,936	688	15.90
1990	10,548	502	21.02	11,107	677	16.40
1991	10,757	496	21.69	11,294	668	16.90
1992	11,100	512	21.68	11,558	683	16.91
1993	11,759 R	559 R	21.04 R	11,597 R	693	16.73 R
1994 P	11,838	551	21.48	11,695	695	16.83

1. Passenger cars, motorcycles, buses, and trucks. R = Revised data. P = Preliminary data. *Sources:* 1960–1985—Federal Highway Administration, *Highway Statistics Summary to 1985,* Table VM-201A; 1986 forward—Federal Highway Administration, *Highway Statistics,* annual, Table VM-1M.

International Energy

World Leaders

Worldwide energy production of 355 quadrillion Btu in 1994 was 51 quadrillion Btu greater than in 1985. The relative contributions of the four leading energy producers changed markedly over the ten-year period.

In 1985, the United States was the leading producer of energy, and U.S. production of 65 quadrillion Btu accounted for 21.3 percent of the world total. The former U.S.S.R., the second leading producer, accounted for 63 quadrillion Btu, a 20.7 percent share.

As of December 31, 1991, the U.S.S.R. ceased to exist as a political entity. Three of the U.S.S.R.'s constituent republics (Russia, Ukraine, and Kazakhstan) together produced 47 quadrillion Btu of energy in 1994. That year the United States produced 71 quadrillion Btu.

Energy production in China, the third largest producer of energy in 1985, produced 24 quadrillion Btu of energy, much of which was coal. By 1994, Chinese production had reached 34 quadrillion Btu.

At 8.6 quadrillion Btu, Saudi Arabia was the sixth largest producer of energy in 1985. During the remainder of the ten-year period, however, Saudi Arabian energy production exhibited the greatest growth, in absolute terms. By 1994, it had risen to 20 quadrillion Btu, making Saudi Arabia the fourth largest producer of energy.

Crude Oil Production in 1995

World production of crude oil totaled 62.23 million barrels per day in 1995, up 2.2 percent from the 1994 level. The most noticeable production increases occurred in Venezuela and the United Kingdom. Small production declines occurred in the United States, where production fell from 6.66 million barrels per day in 1994 to 6.53 million barrels per day in 1995, and in Mexico, where production declined from 2.69 million barrels per day to 2.62 million barrels per day. In Saudi Arabia, the largest producer of crude oil in 1995, production rose slightly to 8.23 million barrels per day. Crude oil production by all members of the Organization of Petroleum Exporting Countries combined rose to 26.48 million barrels per day and accounted for 43 percent of the world total in 1995.

Natural Gas Production in 1994

World production of dry natural gas totaled 77 trillion cubic feet and, on a Btu basis, equaled 22 percent of world energy production in 1994. Natural gas production in 1994 was 1.1 percent above the 1993 level. Russia was the major producer of natural gas in 1994 and accounted for 21 trillion cubic feet, a 28 percent share of the world total. The United States was the second largest producer and accounted for 19 trillion cubic feet, a 24 percent share.

Coal Production in 1994

World production of coal totaled 5.0 billion short tons and, on a Btu basis, equaled 25 percent of world energy production in 1994. China, the leading producer, accounted for 1.4 billion short tons in 1994. Coal production in the United States, the second leading producer, totaled 1.0 billion short tons, a record level. Germany and India each accounted for 295 million short tons, and Russia accounted for 294 million short tons.

Electricity Generation

As of January 1, 1994, world electricity installed capacity at all sites (including nonutility power producers) totaled 2.8 billion kilowatts. Most of the capacity (66 percent) was fossil fuel–fired. Hydroelectric generating capacity accounted for 21 percent and nuclear electric generating capacity accounted for 12 percent. Renewable sources, such as biofuels and geothermal, solar, and wind energy, accounted for less than 1 percent of the world total.

World fossil fuel–fired net generation totaled 7.6 trillion kilowatthours in 1993. The United States, with 2.4 trillion kilowatthours, was by far the largest producer of fossil fuel–fired net generation. China's net generation totaled 645 billion kilowatthours and Russia's totaled 623 billion kilowatthours. World hydroelectric power net generation in 1994 totaled 2.3 trillion kilowatthours, down slightly from the 1993 level. Canada, the United States, Brazil, Russia, and China were the world leaders in hydroelectric power net generation and together accounted for 50 percent of the world total. In 1995, nuclear-based electricity gross generation totaled 2.3 trillion kilowatthours. The U.S. share of the world total was 31 percent. France accounted for 17 percent and Japan for 13 percent of the world total.

Petroleum Prices and Demand

Following Iraq's invasion of Kuwait in August 1990, the average price of crude oil rose to $22.22 per barrel, the highest in five years, and year-to-year growth in world petroleum consumption of only 0.2 percent was the lowest in those years. In 1991, following the resolution of the war in the Persian Gulf, the average price of crude oil fell to $19.06 per barrel. World consumption of petroleum rose 0.8 percent to 67 million barrels per day. In 1992 through 1994, the average price of crude oil fell further, reaching $15.59 per barrel. In real terms, the 1994 price was the lowest in 21 years. Reflecting the price decline, world consumption of petroleum rose to 68 million barrels per day.

From 1960 through 1994, the United States consumed more petroleum by far than any other country. In 1994, U.S. consumption accounted for 42 percent of the 42 million barrels per day consumed by the Organization for Economic Cooperation and Development (OECD) countries. Japan consumed 5.7 million barrels per day. Of the non-OECD countries, Russia and China were the biggest consumers, accounting for 3.3 million barrels per day and 3.2 million barrels per day, respectively.

Dry Natural Gas Consumption in 1994

Although natural gas can be transported across borders in pipelines and some natural gas is shipped as liquefied natural gas, in general, natural gas tends to be consumed closer to its site of production than does petroleum. Not surprisingly, the two top producers of dry natural gas in 1994 were also the top consumers. U.S. consumption of dry natural gas totaled 21 trillion cubic feet, equal to 111 percent of its production. Russia consumed 15 trillion cubic feet, an amount equal to 70 percent of its production of dry natural gas. Ukraine, the third largest consumer of natural gas, consumed 3.1 trillion cubic feet and Germany consumed 3.0 trillion cubic feet.

Coal Consumption in 1994

World coal consumption in 1994 totaled 5.0 billion short tons, up slightly from the level of consumption in 1993. China, the United States, and Germany, three of the world's leading producers of coal, were the leading consumers. China consumed 1.4 billion short tons, the United States consumed 930 million short tons, and Germany consumed 316 million short tons of coal in 1994. □

DRUG USE AND ABUSE

Teenage Marijuana and Drug Use Continues to Rise

The drug crisis of the 1980s may be on the way back

A nationwide survey commissioned by the Partnership for a Drug-Free America, of 9,342 teenagers, pre-teens, and parents, confirmed that a profound reversal in adolescent drug trends—driven by changes in teen attitudes about marijuana—is continuing. According to the study, released in February 1996, anti-drug attitudes among youths eroded again in 1995, continuing a trend that began in 1990. Today's teens are less likely to consider drug use harmful and risky, more likely to believe that drug use is widespread and tolerated, and feel more pressure to try illegal drugs than teens did just two years ago.

Although more parents said that they were talking to their teenagers about drugs today than were two years ago, the drug-savvy Baby Boomer parents seriously underestimated drug experimentation among their own children. Only 14% of parents surveyed believed it was possible that their teenagers might have experimented with marijuana, while 38% of teens reported smoking pot.

The report also noted that parents and teenagers experience a communications gap when discussing drug use. Ninety-five percent of parents said that they talked to their children about drugs, but only 77% of teenagers said that their parents had done so.

After drug use declined steadily in the 1980s, anti-drug attitudes among youngsters began weakening in 1990, leading to an increase in drug use in 1991. Further erosions in anti-drug attitudes followed, fueling more use among young people. Since 1991, the proportion of eighth graders taking any illicit drugs in the past 12 months has almost doubled (from 11% to 21%). Since 1992, the proportion of 10th graders using drugs in the past 12 months has risen by nearly two-thirds (from 20% to 33%) and increased from 27% to 39% among 12th graders.

Researchers and drug experts point to a number of reasons for the significant erosions of drug attitudes among youth, including:

Teens are receiving fewer discouraging and more encouraging messages about drugs. Increasingly, drugs—and marijuana in particular—are directly or indirectly glamorized in music and mass media.

• Select music groups encourage legalization of marijuana, and some artists dedicate entire CDs to the drug.

• More examples of drug use, especially marijuana use, being portrayed lightly and/or as a non-consequential behavior are appearing on television and in movies.

• A marijuana fashion craze began in the early 90s, attracting widespread media attention.

And, interestingly enough, the continuing public debate on the legalization of drugs may be having a detrimental impact on teens' perceptions of drugs and drug use.

According to the Partnership's data, about 50% of teens believe musicians make marijuana and other drugs look tempting and cool. Also, teens seem to be picking up on the public discussion on legalization: In 1993, one in three older teens (16 to 17 years old)

agreed it should be okay for adults to get high in private, while half of the young adult population (18 to 24 year olds) agreed. By 1995, older teens had caught up with the young adult attitude, with one in two also agreeing pot-smoking in private is acceptable.

"Teenagers today receive fewer warnings and more positive messages about drugs, especially those coming from popular culture," Ginna Marston, director of research and strategic development for PDFA, said. "Music, media, and fashion have a profound influence on the way young people see the world around them. And what they're seeing is a world that increasingly tells them that smoking pot is fun, cool, inconsequential, and a normal part of growing up."

Other factors contributing to their increase in drug use may be due to the lack of attention to illicit drugs by elected and political leaders as compared to the late 1980s, less attention being paid to the drug problem by the news media. Cuts in drug education and shifts away from drug-education programs may also be a factor.

"Changes in attitudes drive changes in behavior," noted Ginna Marston. "These finding tell us one thing: Drug use will continue increasing among teenagers until these attitudes change."

The study—the 1995 Partnership Attitude Tracking Study (PATS)—is the largest, ongoing body of research on drug-related attitudes in America, funded, in part, by an organizational grant from the Robert Wood Johnson Foundation.

The Crisis in Perspective

Source: National Survey Results on Drug Use from The Monitoring The Future Study, 1975–1994, The University of Michigan Institute for Social Research and National Institute on Drug Abuse, published 1996.

This nation's secondary school students and young adults show a level of involvement with illicit drugs that is greater than has been documented in any other industrialized nation in the world. Heavy drinking also remains widespread and troublesome, and certainly the continuing initiation of a large and growing proportion of young people to cigarette smoking is a matter of the greatest public health concern.

Finally, we note the seemingly unending capacity of pharmacological experts and amateurs to discover new substances with abuse potential that can be used to alter mood and consciousness, as well as the potential for our young people to "discover" the abuse potential of existing products like Robitussin™, and to "rediscover" older drugs, such as LSD.

The problem of illegal drug use in the United States continues to rise and fall in waves corresponding to new generations of young adults. To best respond to and contain the problem, ongoing and consistent programs of drug education and awareness must be made available to each generation of American children.

Commonly Abused Drugs

NARCOTICS OF NATURAL ORIGIN

Opium

There were no legal restrictions on the importation or use of opium until the early 1900s. In those days, patent medicines often contained opium without any warning label. Today, there are state, federal, and international laws governing the production and distribution of narcotics substances, and there is little abuse of opium in the United States.

Although a small amount of opium is used to make antidiarrheal preparations, such as paregoric, virtually all the opium imported into this country is broken down into its alkaloid constituents, principally morphine and codeine.

Morphine

The principal constituent of opium, ranging in concentration from 4 to 21 percent, morphine is one of the most effective drugs known for the relief of pain. It is marketed in the form of white crystals, hypodermic tablets, and injectable preparations. Its licit use is restricted primarily to hospitals. Morphine is odorless, tastes bitter, and darkens with age. It may be administered subcutaneously, intramuscularly, or intravenously, the latter method being the one most frequently resorted to by addicts.

Codeine

This alkaloid is found in raw opium in concentrations ranging from 0.7 to 2.5 percent. It was first isolated in 1832 as an impurity in a batch of morphine. Although it occurs naturally, most codeine is produced from morphine.

SEMI-SYNTHETIC NARCOTICS

Heroin

First synthesized from morphine in 1874, heroin was not extensively used in medicine until the beginning of this century. While it received widespread acceptance, the medical profession for years remained unaware of its potential for addiction. The first comprehensive control of heroin in the United States was established with the Harrison Narcotic Act of 1914.

Pure heroin is a white powder with a bitter taste. Illicit heroin may vary in both form and color. Most illicit heroin is a powder which may vary in color from white to dark brown because of impurities left from the manufacturing process or the presence of additives, such as food coloring, cocoa, or brown sugar.

Pure heroin is rarely sold on the street. A "bag"—slang for a single dosage unit of heroin—may weigh about 100 mg, usually containing about five percent heroin. To increase the bulk of the material sold to the addict, diluents are mixed with the heroin in ratios ranging from 9 to 1 to as much as 99 to 1. Sugars, starch, powdered milk, and quinine are among the diluents used.

Hydromorphone

Most commonly sold as Dilaudid, hydromorphone is the second oldest semi-synthetic narcotic analgesic. Marketed both in tablet and injectable form, it is shorter acting and more sedating than morphine, but its potency is from two to eight times as great. It is, therefore, a highly abusable drug, much sought after by narcotic addicts, who usually obtain it through fraudulent prescription or theft.

Oxycodone

Oxycodone is synthesized from thebaine. It is similar to codeine, but more potent and with a higher dependence potential. It is effective orally and is marketed in combination with aspirin as Percodan for the relief of pain. Addicts take Percodan orally or dissolve tablets in water, filter out the insoluble material, and "mainline" the active drug.

SYNTHETIC NARCOTICS

In contrast to pharmaceutical products derived directly or indirectly from narcotics of natural origin, synthetic narcotics are produced entirely within the laboratory. A continuing search for a product that will retain the analgesic properties of morphine without the consequent dangers of tolerance and dependence has yet to yield a drug that is not susceptible to abuse. The two that are most widely available are meperidine and methadone.

Meperidine (Pethidine)

The first synthetic narcotic, meperidine, is chemically dissimilar to morphine but resembles it in its analgesic effect. It is probably the most widely used drug for the relief of moderate to severe pain. Available in pure form as well as in products containing other medicinal ingredients, it is administered either orally or by injection, the latter method being the most widely abused. Tolerance and dependence develop with chronic use, and large doses can result in convulsions or death.

Methadone

German scientists synthesized methadone during World War II because of a shortage of morphine. Although chemically unlike morphine or heroin, it produces many of the same effects. Introduced into the United States in 1947, it became widely used in the 1960s in the treatment of narcotic addicts. The effects of methadone differ from morphine-based drugs in that they have a longer duration of action, lasting up to 24 hours, thereby permitting administration only once a day in heroin detoxification and maintenance programs. Moreover, methadone is almost as effective when administered orally as it is by injection. But tolerance and dependence may develop, and withdrawal symptoms, though they develop more slowly and are less severe, are more prolonged. Ironically, methadone, designed to control narcotic addiction, has emerged in some metropolitan areas as a major cause of overdose deaths.

DEPRESSANTS

Depressants have a potential for abuse associated with both physical and psychological dependence. Taken as prescribed as a physician, depressants may be beneficial for the relief of anxiety, irritability, and tension, and for the symptomatic treatment of insomnia. In excessive amounts, however, they produce a state of intoxication that is remarkably similar to that of alcohol.

Tolerance to the intoxicating effects develops rapidly, leading to a progressive narrowing of the margin of safety between an intoxicating and lethal dose. The person who is unaware of the dangers of increasing dependence will often increase the daily dose up to 10 or 20 times the recommended therapeutic level. The source of supply may be no farther than the family medicine cabinet. Depressants are also frequently obtained by theft, illegal prescription, or purchase on the illicit market.

In the world of illicit drug use, depressants often are used as self-medication to soothe jangled nerves brought on by the use of stimulants, to quell the anxiety of "flashbacks" resulting from prior use of hallucinogens, or to ease withdrawal from heroin. The dangers, it should be stressed, are compounded when depressants are used in combination with alcohol or other drugs. Chronic intoxication, though it affects every age group, is not common in middle age. The problem often remains unrecognized until the user exhibits recurrent confusion or an obvious inability to function.

Barbiturates

Among the drugs most frequently prescribed to induce sedation and sleep by both physicians and veterinarians are the barbiturates. About 2,500 derivatives of barbituric acid have been synthesized, but of these only about 15 remain in medical use. Small therapeutic doses tend to calm nervous conditions, and larger doses cause sleep 20 to 60 minutes after oral administration. As in the case of alcohol, some individuals may experience a sense of excitement before sedation takes effect. If dosage is increased, however, the effects of the barbiturates may progress through successive stages of sedation, sleep, and coma to death from respiratory arrest and cardiovascular complications.

STIMULANTS

Cocaine

The most potent stimulant of natural origin, cocaine is extracted from the leaves of the coca plant (Erythroxylon coca), which has been grown in the Andean highlands of South America since prehistoric times. The leaves of the plant are chewed in the region for refreshment and relief from fatigue.

Pure cocaine, the principal psychoactive ingredient, was first isolated in the 1880s. It was used as an anesthetic in eye surgery for which no previously known drug had been suitable. It became particularly useful in surgery of the nose and throat because of its ability to anesthetize tissue while simultaneously constricting blood vessels and limiting bleeding. Many of its therapeutic applications are now obsolete because of the development of safer drugs as local anesthetics.

Illicit cocaine is usually distributed as a white crystalline powder, often diluted by a variety of other ingredients, the most common of which are sugars such as lactose, inositol, mannitol, and local anesthetics such as lidocaine. The frequent adulteration is to increase volume and thus to multiply profits.

The drug is most commonly administered by being "snorted" through the nasal passages. Symptoms of repeated use in this manner may resemble the congested nose of a common cold.

The intensity of the psychological effects of cocaine, as with many psychoactive drugs, depends on the rate of entry into the blood. Intravenous injection or smoking produces an almost immediate intense experience. Cocaine hydrochloride, the usual form in which cocaine is sold, while soluble in water and sometimes injected, is fairly insensitive to heat. Conversion of cocaine hydrochloride to cocaine base yields a substance that will become volatile when heated. "Crack," or cocaine base in the form of chips, chunks or "rocks," is usually vaporized in a pipe or smoked with plant material in a cigarette or a "joint."

Inhalation of the cocaine fumes produces effects that are very fast in onset, very intense, and are quickly over. These intense effects are often followed within minutes by a dysphoric "crash," leading to frequently repeated doses and rapid addiction.

Excessive doses of cocaine may cause seizures and death from, for example, respiratory failure, stroke, cerebral hemorrhage, or heart failure. There is no specific treatment for cocaine overdose. Nor does tolerance develop to the toxic effects of cocaine. In fact, there are studies which indicate that repeated use lowers the dose at which toxicity occurs. There is no "safe" dose of cocaine.

Amphetamines

Amphetamine, dextroamphetamine, and methamphetamine are so similar in the effects they induce that they can be differentiated from one another only by laboratory analysis. Amphetamine was first used clinically in the mid-1930s to treat narcolepsy, a rare disorder resulting in an uncontrollable tendency to sleep. After the introduction of the amphetamines into medical practice, the number of conditions for which they were prescribed multiplied, as did the quantities made available.

For a time, they were sold without prescription in inhalers and other over-the-counter preparations. Abuse became popular. Many segments of the population, especially those concerned with extensive or irregular hours, were among those who used amphetamines orally in excessive amounts. "Speed freaks," who injected amphetamines, became known for their bizarre and often violent behavior. Over-the-counter availability (except inhalers) was terminated and amphetamines now are available only by prescription. Inhalers still are available over-the-counter.

Their illicit use closely parallels that of cocaine in the range of its short-term and long-term effects. Despite broad recognition of the risks, clandestine laboratories produce vast quantities of amphetamines, particularly methamphetamine, for distribution on the illicit market.

Methamphetamine Abusers

Abuse patterns suggest an estimated two- to four-year latency period from first use to full addiction. Most treatment clients interviewed initiated use by intranasal snorting, but then turned to intravenous (IV) administration. Compulsive abuse accelerates with IV use because of the drug's rapid onset of action in a pattern similar to crack cocaine abuse. Although crack is not injected, inhalation of its vapors provides a rapid pulmonary delivery of the drug in concentrated dose to the brain promoting an intensified onset of action. This method, like IV methamphetamine use, triggers an initial, short-term jolt which compels the user to repeat drug use again and again in a futile attempt to re-experience the drug's exhilarating effects.

CANNABIS

Cannabis sativa L., the hemp plant, grows wild throughout most of the tropic and temperate regions of the world. It is a single species. This plant has long been cultivated for the tough fiber of the stem, the seed used in feed mixtures, and the oil as an ingredient of paint, as well as for its biologically active substances, most highly concentrated in the leaves and resinous flowering tops.

The plant material has been used as a drug for centuries. In 1839, it entered the annals of western medicine with the publication of an article surveying its therapeutic potential, including possible uses as an analgesic and anticonvulsant agent. It was alleged to be effective in treating a wide range of physical and mental ailments during the remainder of the 19th century. With the introduction of many new synthetic drugs in the 20th century, interest in it as a medication waned.

The controls imposed with the passage of the Marijuana Tax Act of 1937 further curtailed its use in treatment, and by 1941 it had been deleted from the *U.S. Pharmacopoeia* and the *National Formulary,* the official compendia of drugs.

Cannabis products are usually smoked in the form of loosely rolled cigarettes ("joints"). They may be used alone or in combination with other substances. They may also be administered orally, but are reported to be about three times more potent when smoked. The effects are felt within minutes, reach their peak in 10 to 30 minutes, and may linger for 2 or 3 hours.

A condensed description of these effects is apt to be inadequate or even misleading. So much depends upon the experience and expectations of the individual as well as the activity of the drug itself. Low doses tend to induce restlessness and an increasing sense of well-being, followed by a dreamy state of relaxation, and frequently hunger, especially a craving for sweets. Changes of sensory perception—a more vivid sense of sight, smell, touch, taste, and hearing—may be accompanied by subtle alterations in thought formation and expression. Stronger doses intensify reactions. The individual may experience shifting sensory imagery, rapidly fluctuating emotions, a flight of fragmentary thoughts with disturbed associations, an altered sense of self-identity, impaired memory, and a dulling of attention despite an illusion of heightened insight. This state of intoxication may not be noticeable to an observer. High doses may result in image distortion, a loss of personal identity, and fantasies and hallucination. Very high doses may result in a toxic psychosis.

Marijuana

The term marijuana is used in this country to refer to the cannabis plant and to any part or extract of it that produces somatic or psychic changes in humans. A tobacco-like substance produced by drying the leaves and flowering tops of the plant, marijuana varies significantly in its potency, depending on the source and selectivity of plant materials used.

Marijuana use by adolescents has continued to rise in recent years after years of decline. The resurgence is due in part to "inter-generational forgetting"—meaning that new generations fail to learn the same dangers about drugs that former generations knew.

HALLUCINOGENS

Hallucinogenic drugs, both natural and synthetic, are substances that distort the perception of objective reality. They induce a state of excitation of the central nervous system, manifested by alterations of mood, usually euphoric, but sometimes severely depressive. Under the influence of hallucinogens, the senses of direction, distance, and time becomes disoriented. A user may speak of "seeing" sounds and "hearing" colors. If taken in a large enough dose, the drug produces delusions and visual hallucinations. Occasionally, depersonalization and depression are so severe that suicide is possible, but the most common danger is impaired judgment, leading to rash decisions and accidents. Persons in hallucinogenic states should, therefore, be closely supervised and upset as little as possible to keep them from harming themselves and others. Acute anxiety, restlessness, and sleeplessness are common until the drug wears off.

Facts on Drugs and Violence

Source: National Institute of Justice.

Of all psychoactive substances, alcohol is the only one whose consumption has been shown to commonly increase aggression. After large doses of amphetamines, cocaine, LSD, and PCP, certain individuals may experience violent outbursts, probably because of preexisting psychosis.

For at least the last several decades, alcohol drinking—by the perpetrator of a crime, the victim, or both—has immediately preceded at least half of all violent events, including murders, in the samples studied by researchers. In addition, chronic drinkers are more likely than other people to have histories of violent behavior.

Marijuana and opiates temporarily inhibit violent behavior, but withdrawal from opiate addiction tends to exaggerate both aggressive and defensive responses to provocations.

Several common assumptions about drugs and violence are called into question by research findings:

There is no evidence to support the claim that snorting or injecting cocaine stimulates violent behavior. However, more research is needed on the behavioral effects of smoking cocaine in crack form, which affects the brain more directly.

Anecdotal reports notwithstanding, no research evidence supports the notion that becoming high on hallucinogens, amphetamines, or PCP stimulates violent behavior in any systematic manner. The anecdotes usually describe chronic users with histories of psychosis or antisocial behavior, which may or may not be related to their chronic use of drugs.

Long after hallucinogens are eliminated from the body, users may experience flashbacks—fragmentary recurrences of psychedelic effects—such as the intensification of a perceived color, the apparent motion of a fixed object, or the mistaking of one object for another. Recurrent use produces tolerance, which tends to encourage resorting to greater amounts. Although no evidence of physical dependence is detectable when the drugs are withdrawn, recurrent use tends to produce psychic dependence, varying according to the drug, the dose, and the individual user. It should be stressed that the hallucinogens are unpredictable in their effects each time they are used.

LSD (LSD-25, lysergide)

LSD is an abbreviation of the German expression for lysergic acid diethylamide. It is produced from lysergic acid, a substance derived from the ergot fungus which grows on rye or from lysergic acid amide, a chemical found in morning glory seeds.

LSD was first synthesized in 1938. Its psychotomimetic effects were discovered in 1943 when a chemist accidentally took some LSD. As he began to experience the effects now known as a "trip," he was aware of vertigo and an intensification of light. Closing his eyes, he saw a stream of fantastic images of extraordinary vividness accompanied by a kaleidoscopic play of colors. This condition lasted for about two hours.

Because of the extremely high potency of LSD, its structural relationship to a chemical which is present in the brain, and its similarity in effects to certain aspects of psychosis, LSD was used as a tool of research to study the mechanism of mental illness.

LSD is usually sold in the form of tablets, thin squares of gelatin ("window panes"), or impregnated paper ("blotter acid"). The average effective oral dose is from 30 to 50 micrograms, but the amount per dosage unit varies greatly. The effects of higher doses persist for 10 to 12 hours. Tolerance develops rapidly.

Phencyclidine (PCP)

PCP is sold under at least 50 other names, including Angel Dust, Crystal, Supergrass, Killer Weed, Embalming Fluid, and Rocket Fuel, that reflect the range of its bizarre and volatile effects. It is also frequently misrepresented as mescaline, LSD, or THC. In its pure form, it is a white crystalline powder that readily dissolves in water. Most PCP now contains contaminants resulting from its makeshift manufacture, causing the color to range from tan to brown and the consistency from a powder to a gummy mass. Although sold in tablets and capsules, as well as in powder and liquid form, it is commonly applied to a leafy material, such as parsley, mint, oregano, or marijuana, and smoked.

The drug is as variable in its effects as it is in its appearance. A moderate amount often produces in the user a sense of detachment, distance, and estrangement from the surroundings. Numbness, slurred or blocked speech, and a loss of coordination may be accompanied by a sense of strength and invulnerability. A blank stare, rapid and involuntary eye movements, and an exaggerated gait are among the more common observable effects. Auditory hallucinations, image distortion as in a fun-house mirror, and severe mood disorders may also occur, producing in some acute anxiety and a feeling of impending doom, in others paranoia and violent hostility. PCP is unique among popular drugs of abuse in its power to produce psychoses indistinguishable from schizophrenia.

ALCOHOL

Source: U.S. Department of Education.

Alcohol is the number one drug problem among youth. The easy availability, widespread acceptability, and extensive promotion of alcoholic beverages within our society make alcohol the most widely used and abused drug. Some 15 million Americans are alcoholics and alcohol is responsible for about 100,000 deaths each year.

Effects.—Alcohol consumption causes a number of marked changes in behavior. Even low doses significantly impair the judgment and coordination required to drive a car safely, increasing the likelihood that the driver will be involved in an accident. Low to moderate doses of alcohol also increase the incidence of a variety of aggressive acts, including spouse and child abuse. Moderate to high doses of alcohol cause marked impairments in higher mental functions, severely altering a person's ability to learn and remember information. Very high doses cause respiratory depression and death. If combined with other depressants of the central nervous system, much lower doses of alcohol will produce the effects just described.

Repeated use of alcohol can lead to dependence. Sudden cessation of alcohol intake is likely to produce withdrawal symptoms, including severe anxiety, tremors, hallucinations, and convulsions. Alcohol withdrawal can be life-threatening. Long-term consumption of large quantities of alcohol, particularly when combined with poor nutrition, can also lead to permanent damage to vital organs such as the brain and the liver.

Mothers who drink alcohol during pregnancy may give birth to infants with fetal alcohol syndrome. These infants have irreversible physical abnormalities and mental retardation. In addition, research indicates that children of alcoholic parents are at greater risk than other youngsters of becoming alcoholics.

TOBACCO

Major source: U.S. Department of Education.

According to the U.S. Surgeon General, the annual estimated number of smoking-related deaths is 400,000.

Effects.—The smoking of tobacco products is the chief avoidable cause of death in our society. Smokers are more likely than nonsmokers to contract heart disease. Lung, larynx, esophageal, bladder, pancreatic, and kidney cancers also strike smokers at increased rates. Some 30 percent of cancer deaths (130,000 per year) are linked to smoking. Chronic obstructive lung diseases such as emphysema and chronic bronchitis are 10 times more likely to occur among smokers than among nonsmokers.

Smoking during pregnancy also poses serious risks. Spontaneous abortion, preterm birth, low birth weights, and fetal and infant deaths are all more likely to occur when the pregnant woman/mother is a smoker.

A 1996 study found that pregnant women who smoke are 50% more likely to have mentally retarded children. In the study, children were considered retarded if their I.Q. was lower than 70 when they were ten years old.

Perhaps the most dangerous substance in tobacco smoke is nicotine. Although it is implicated in the onset of heart attacks and cancer, its most dangerous role is reinforcing and strengthening the desire to smoke. Because nicotine is highly addictive, addicts find it very difficult to stop smoking. Of 1,000 typical smokers, fewer than 20 percent succeed in stopping on the first try.

About 5 million U.S. adults use smokeless tobacco and a 1993 survey reported that 20% of male high school students used smokeless tobacco. An alarming trend is the increased use of "dipping snuff," which is highly addictive and exposes the body to levels of nicotine equal to those of cigarettes. According to the Surgeon General, users are at greater risk of oral cancer than non-tobacco users.

Although the harmful effects of smoking cannot be questioned, people who quit can make significant strides in repairing damage done by smoking. For pack-a-day smokers, the increased risk of heart attack dissipates after 10 years. The likelihood of contracting lung cancer as a result of smoking can also be greatly reduced by quitting.

Sources of Information

U.S. Clearinghouse—(A publication list is available on request, along with placement on a mailing list for new publications. Single copies are free.) National Clearinghouse for Alcohol and Drug Information (NCADI), P.O. Box 2345, Rockville, Md. 20852. Telephone (301) 468-2600

Adcare Hospital—Dedicated exclusively to the care of substance abuse problems, can offer 24-hour referrals, as well as in-patient and out-patient services. 109 Lincoln St., Worcester, Mass. 01605. (800) 252-6465.

Families Anonymous—This worldwide organization offers a 12-step, self-help program for families and friends of people with behavioral problems usually associated with drug abuse. The organization is similar in structure to Alcoholics Anonymous. P.O. Box 3475, Culver City, Calif. 90230. Telephone (310) 313-5800.

A Concise Guide to Style

From *Webster's II New Riverside University Dictionary.* © 1984 by Houghton Mifflin Company.

This section discusses and illustrates the basic conventions of American capitalization, punctuation, and italicization.

Capitalization

Capitalize the following:

1. The first word of a sentence: Some spiders are poisonous; others are not. Are you my new neighbor?

2. The first word of a direct quotation, except when the quotation is split: Joyce asked, "Do you think that the lecture was interesting?" "No," I responded, "it was very boring." Tom Paine said, "The sublime and the ridiculous are often so nearly related that it is difficult to class them separately."

3. The first word of each line in a poem in traditional verse: Half a league, half a league,/Half a league onward,/All in the valley of Death/Rode the six hundred.—Alfred, Lord Tennyson

4. The names of people, of organizations and their members, of councils and congresses, and of historical periods and events: Marie Curie, Benevolent and Protective Order of Elks, an Elk, Protestant Episcopal Church, an Episcopalian, the Democratic Party, a Democrat, the Nuclear Regulatory Commission, the U.S. Senate, the Middle Ages, World War I, the Battle of Britain.

5. The names of places and geographic divisions, districts, regions, and locales: Richmond, Vermont, Argentina, Seventh Avenue, London Bridge, Arctic Circle, Eastern Hemisphere, Continental Divide, Middle East, Far North, Gulf States, East Coast, the North, the South Shore.

Do not capitalize words indicating compass points unless a specific region is referred to: Turn north onto Interstate 91.

6. The names of rivers, lakes, mountains, and oceans: Ohio River, Lake Como, Rocky Mountains, Atlantic Ocean.

7. The names of ships, aircraft, satellites, and space vehicles: U.S.S. *Arizona, Spirit of St. Louis,* the spy satellite Ferret-D, Voyager II, the space shuttle Challenger.

8. The names of nationalities, races, tribes, and languages: Spanish, Maori, Bantu, Russian.

9. Words derived from proper names, except in their extended senses: the Byzantine Empire. *But:* byzantine office politics.

10. Words indicating family relationships when used with a person's name as a title: Aunt Toni and Uncle Jack. *But:* my aunt and uncle, Toni and Jack Walker.

11. A title (i.e., civil, judicial, military, royal and noble, religious, and honorary) when preceding a name: Justice Marshall, General Jackson, Mayor Daley, Queen Victoria, Lord Mountbatten, Pope John Paul II, Professor Jacobson, Senator Byrd.

12. All references to the President and Vice President of the United States: The President has entered the hall. The Vice President presides over the Senate.

13. All key words in titles of literary, dramatic, artistic, and musical works: the novel *The Old Man and the Sea,* the short story "Notes from Underground," an article entitled "On Passive Verbs," James

Dickey's poem "In the Tree House at Night," the play *Cat on a Hot Tin Roof,* Van Gogh's *Wheat Field and Cypress Trees,* Beethoven's *Emperor Concerto.*

14. *The* in the title of a newspaper if it is a part of the title: *The Wall Street Journal. But:* the New York *Daily News.*

15. The first word in the salutation and in the complimentary close of a letter: My dear Carol, Yours sincerely.

16. Epithets and substitutes for the names of people and places: Old Hickory, Old Blood and Guts, The Oval Office, the Windy City.

17. Words used in personifications: When is not Death at watch/Within those secret waters?/What wants he but to catch/Earth's heedless sons and daughters?—Edmund Blunden

18. The pronoun *I:* I told them that I had heard the news.

19. Names for the Deity and sacred works: God, the Almighty, Jesus, Allah, the Supreme Being, the Bible, the Koran, the Talmud.

20. Days of the week, months of the year, holidays, and holy days: Tuesday, May, Independence Day, Passover, Ramadan, Christmas.

21. The names of specific courts: The Supreme Court of the United States, the Massachusetts Appeals Court, the United States Court of Appeals for the First Circuit.

22. The names of treaties, accords, pacts, laws, and specific amendments: Panama Canal Treaty, Treaty of Paris, Geneva Accords, Warsaw Pact countries, Sherman Antitrust Law, Labor Management Relations Act, took the Fifth Amendment.

23. Registered trademarks and service marks: Day-Glo, Comsat.

24. The names of geologic eras, periods, epochs, and strata and the names of prehistoric divisions: Paleozoic Era, Precambrian, Pleistocene, Age of Reptiles, Bronze Age, Stone Age.

25. The names of constellations, planets, and stars: Milky Way, Southern Crown, Saturn, Jupiter, Uranus, Polaris.

26. Genus but not species names in binomial nomenclature: *Rana pipiens.*

27. New Latin names of classes, families, and all groups higher than genera in botanical and zoological nomenclature: Nematoda.

But do not capitalize derivatives from such names: nematodes.

28. Many abbreviations and acronyms: Dec., Tues., Lt. Gen., M.F.A., UNESCO, MIRV.

Italicization

Use italics to:

1. Indicate titles of books, plays, and epic poems: *War and Peace, The Importance of Being Earnest, Paradise Lost.*

2. Indicate titles of magazines and newspapers: *New York* magazine, *The Wall Street Journal,* the New York *Daily News.*

3. Set off the titles of motion pictures and radio and television programs: *Star Wars, All Things Con-*

sidered, Masterpiece Theater.

4. Indicate titles of major musical compositions: Handel's *Messiah*, Adam's *Giselle*.

5. Set off the names of paintings and sculpture: *Mona Lisa, Pietà*.

6. Indicate words, letters, or numbers that are referred to: The word *hiss* is onomatopoeic. *Can't* means *won't* in your lexicon. You form your *n*'s like *u*'s. A *6* looks like an inverted *9*.

7. Indicate foreign words and phrases not yet assimilated into English: *C'est la vie* was the response to my complaint.

8. Indicate the names of plaintiff and defendant in legal citations: *Roe* v. *Doe*.

9. Emphasize a word or phrase: When you appear on the national news, you are *somebody*. Use this device sparingly.

10. Distinguish New Latin names of genera, species, subspecies, and varieties in botanical and zoological nomenclature: *Homo sapiens*.

11. Set off the names of ships and aircraft but not space vehicles: U.S.S. *Arizona, Spirit of St. Louis,* Voyager II, the space shuttle Challenger, the spy satellite Ferret-D.

Punctuation

Apostrophe

1. Indicates the possessive case of singular and plural nouns, indefinite pronouns, and surnames combined with designations such as *Jr., Sr.,* and *II:* my sister's husband, my three sisters' husbands, anyone's guess, They answer each other's phones, John Smith, Jr.'s car.

2. Indicates joint possession when used with the last of two or more nouns in a series: Doe and Roe's report.

3. Indicates individual possession or authorship when used with each of two or more nouns in a series: Smith's, Roe's, and Doe's reports.

4. Indicates the plurals of words, letters, and figures used as such: 60's and 70's; *x*'s, *y*'s, and *z*'s.

5. Indicates omission of letters in contractions: aren't, that's, o'clock.

6. Indicates omission of figures in dates: the class of '63.

Brackets

1. Enclose words or passages in quoted matter to indicate insertion of material written by someone other than the author: A tough but nervous, tenacious but restless race [the Yankees]; materially ambitious, yet prone to introspection. . . .—Samuel Eliot Morison

2. Enclose material inserted within matter already in parentheses: (Vancouver [B.C.] January 1, 19—).

Colon

1. Introduces words, phrases, or clauses that explain, amplify, or summarize what has gone before: Suddenly I realized where we were: Rome. "There are two cardinal sins from which all the others spring: impatience and laziness."—Franz Kafka

2. Introduces a long quotation: In his original draft of the *Declaration of Independence,* Jefferson wrote: "We hold these truths to be sacred and undeniable; that all men are created equal and independent, that from that equal creation they derive rights inherent and inalienable. . . ."

3. Introduces a list: We need the following items: pens, paper, pencils, blotters, and erasers.

4. Separates chapter and verse numbers in Biblical references: James 1:4.

5. Separates city from publisher in footnotes and bibliographies: Chicago: Riverside Press, 1983.

6. Separates hour and minute(s) in time designa-

tions: 9:30 a.m., a 9:30 meeting.

7. Follows the salutation in a business letter: Gentlemen:

Comma

1. Separates the clauses of a compound sentence connected by a coordinating conjunction: A difference exists between the musical works of Handel and Haydn, and it is a difference worth noting. The comma may be omitted in short compound sentences: I heard what you said and I am furious. I got out of the car and I walked and walked.

2. Separates *and* or *or* from the final item in a series of three or more: Red, yellow, and blue may be mixed to produce all colors.

3. Separates two or more adjectives modifying the same noun if *and* could be used between them without altering the meaning: a solid, heavy gait. *But:* a polished mahogany dresser.

4. Sets off nonrestrictive clauses or phrases (i.e., those that if eliminated would not affect the meaning of the sentences): The burglar, who had entered through the patio, went straight to the silver chest. The comma should not be used when a clause is restrictive (i.e., essential to the meaning of the sentence): The burglar who had entered through the patio went straight to the silver chest; the other burglar searched for the wall safe.

5. Sets off words or phrases in apposition to a noun or noun phrase: Plato, the famous Greek philosopher, was a student of Socrates. The comma should not be used if such words or phrases precede the noun: The Greek philosopher Plato was a student of Socrates.

6. Sets off transitional words and short expressions that require a pause in reading or speaking: Unfortunately, my friend was not well traveled. Did you, after all, find what you were looking for? I live with my family, of course.

7. Sets off words used to introduce a sentence: No, I haven't been to Paris. Well, what do you think we should do now?

8. Sets off a subordinate clause or a long phrase that precedes a principal clause: By the time we found the restaurant, we were starved. Of all the illustrations in the book, the most striking are those of the tapestries.

9. Sets off short quotations and sayings: The candidate said, "Actions speak louder than words." "Talking of axes," said the Duchess, "chop off her head"—Lewis Carroll

10. Indicates omission of a word or words: To err is human; to forgive, divine.

11. Sets off the year from the month in full dates: Nicholas II of Russia was shot on July 16, 1918. But note that when only the month and the year are used. no comma appears: Nicholas II of Russia was shot in July 1918.

12. Sets off city and state in geographic names: Atlanta, Georgia, is the transportation center of the South. 34 Beach Drive, Bedford, VA 24523.

13. Separates series of four or more figures into thousands, millions, etc.: 67,000; 200,000.

14. Sets off words used in direct address: "I tell you, folks, all politics is applesauce."—Will Rogers Thank you for your expert assistance, Dolores.

15. Separates a tag question from the rest of a sentence: You forgot your keys again, didn't you?

16. Sets off sentence elements that could be misunderstood if the comma were not used: Some time after, the actual date for the project was set.

17. Follows the salutation in a personal letter and the complimentary close in a business or personal letter: Dear Jessica, Sincerely yours.

18. Sets off titles and degrees from surnames and from the rest of a sentence: Walter T. Prescott, Jr.; Gregory A. Rossi, S.J.; Susan P. Green, M.D., presented the case.

Dash

1. Indicates a sudden break or abrupt change in continuity: "If—if you'll just let me explain—" the student stammered. And the problem—if there really is one—can then be solved.

2. Sets apart an explanatory, a defining, or an emphatic phrase: Foods rich in protein—meat, fish, and eggs—should be eaten on a daily basis.

More important than winning the election, is governing the nation. That is the test of a political party—the acid, final test.—Adlai E. Stevenson

3. Sets apart parenthetical matter: Wolsey, for all his faults—and he had many—was a great statesman, a man of natural dignity with a generous temperament. . . .—Jasper Ridley

4. Marks an unfinished sentence: "But if my bus is late—" he began.

5. Sets off a summarizing phrase or clause: The vital measure of a newspaper is not its size but its spirit—that is its responsibility to report the news fully, accurately, and fairly.—Arthur H. Sulzberger

6. Sets off the name of an author or source, as at the end of a quotation: A poet can survive everything but a misprint.—Oscar Wilde

Ellipses

1. Indicate, by three spaced points, omission of words or sentences within quoted matter: Equipped by education to rule in the nineteenth century, . . . he lived and reigned in Russia in the twentieth century.—Robert K. Massie

2. Indicate, by four spaced points, omission of words at the end of a sentence: The timidity of bureaucrats when it comes to dealing with . . . abuses is easy to explain. . . .—*New York*

3. Indicate, when extended the length of a line, omission of one or more lines of poetry:

Roll on, thou deep and dark blue
    ocean—roll!

. . . .

Man marks the earth with ruin—his
    control
Stops with the shore.—Lord Byron

4. Are sometimes used as a device, as for example, in advertising copy:

To help you Move and Grow
    with the Rigors of
Business in the 1980's . . .
    and Beyond.—*Journal of Business Strategy*

Exclamation Point

1. Terminates an emphatic or exclamatory sentence: Go home at once! You've got to be kidding!

2. Terminates an emphatic interjection: Encore!

Hyphen

1. Indicates that part of a word of more than one syllable has been carried over from one line to the next:
During the revolution, the nation was
beset with problems—looting, fighting, and famine.

2. Joins the elements of some compounds: great-grandparent, attorney-at-law, ne'er-do-well.

3. Joins the elements of compound modifiers preceding nouns: high-school students, a fire-and-brimstone lecture, a two-hour meeting.

4. Indicates that two or more compounds share a single base: four- and six-volume sets, eight- and nine-year olds.

5. Separates the prefix and root in some combinations; check the Dictionary when in doubt about the

spelling: anti-Nazi, re-elect, co-author, re-form/reform, re-cover/recover, re-creation/recreation.

6. Substitutes for the word *to* between typewritten inclusive words or figures: pp. 145–155, the Boston-New York air shuttle.

7. Punctuates written-out compound numbers from 21 through 99: forty-six years of age, a person who is forty-six, two hundred fifty-nine dollars.

Parentheses

1. Enclose material that is not essential to a sentence and that if not included would not alter its meaning: After a few minutes (some say less) the blaze was extinguished.

2. Often enclose letters or figures to indicate subdivisions of a series: A movement in sonata form consists of the following elements: (1) the exposition, (2) the development, and (3) the recapitulation.

3. Enclose figures following and confirming written-out numbers, especially in legal and business documents: The fee for my services will be two thousand dollars ($2,000.00).

4. Enclose an abbreviation for a term following the written-out term, when used for the first time in a text: The patient is suffering from acquired immune deficiency syndrome (AIDS).

Period

1. Terminates a complete declarative or mild imperative sentence: There could be no turning back as war's dark shadow settled irrevocably across the continent of Europe.—W. Bruce Lincoln. Return all the books when you can. Would you kindly affix your signature here.

2. Terminates sentence fragments: Gray clouds—and what looks like a veil of rain falling behind the East German headland. A pair of ducks. A tired or dying swan, head buried in its back feathers, sits on the sand a few feet from the water's edge.—Anthony Bailey

3. Follows some abbreviations: Dec., Rev., St., Blvd., pp., Co.

Question Mark

1. Punctuates a direct question: Have you seen the new play yet? Who goes there? *But:* I wonder who said "Nothing is easy in war." I asked if they planned to leave.

2. Indicates uncertainty: Ferdinand Magellan (1480?–1521), Plato (427?–347 B.C.).

Quotation Marks

1. Double quotation marks enclose direct quotations: "What was Paris like in the Twenties?" our daughter asked. "Ladies and Gentlemen," the Chief Usher said, "the President of the United States." Robert Louis Stevenson said that "it is better to be a fool than to be dead." When advised not to become a lawyer because the profession was already overcrowded, Daniel Webster replied, "There is always room at the top."

2. Double quotation marks enclose words or phrases to clarify their meaning or use or to indicate that they are being used in a special way: This was the border of what we often call "the West" or "the Free World." "The Windy City" is a name for Chicago.

3. Double quotation marks set off the translation of a foreign word or phrase: *die Grenze,* "the border."

4. Double quotation marks set off the titles of series of books, of articles or chapters in publications, of essays, of short stories and poems, of individual radio and television programs, and of songs and short musical pieces: "The Horizon Concise History" series; an article entitled "On Reflexive Verbs in English"; Chapter Nine, "The Prince and the Peasant"; Pushkin's "The Queen of Spades"; Tennyson's "Ode on the Death of the Duke of Wellington"; "The Bob Hope Special"; Schubert's "Death and the Maiden."

5. Single quotation marks enclose quotations within quotations: The blurb for the piece proclaimed,

"Two years ago at Geneva, South Vietnam was virtually sold down the river to the Communists. Today the spunky little . . . country is back on its own feet, thanks to "a mandarin in a sharkskin suit who's upsetting the Red timetable.' "—Frances FitzGerald

Put commas and periods inside quotation marks; put semicolons and colons outside. Other punctuation, such as exclamation points and question marks, should be put inside the closing quotation marks only if part of the matter quoted.

Semicolon

1. Separates the clauses of a compound sentence having no coordinating conjunction: Do not let us speak of darker days; let us rather speak of sterner days.—Winston Churchill

2. Separates the clauses of a compound sentence in which the clauses contain internal punctuation, even when the clauses are joined by conjunctions: Skis in hand, we trudged to the lodge, stowed our lunches, and donned our boots; and the rest of our party waited for us at the lifts.

3. Separates elements of a series in which items already contain commas: Among those at the diplomatic reception were the Secretary of State; the daughter of the Ambassador to the Court of St. James's, formerly of London; and two United Nations delegates.

4. Separates clauses of a compound sentence joined by a conjunctive adverb, such as *however, nonetheless,* or *hence:* We insisted upon a hearing; however, the Grievance Committee refused.

5. May be used instead of a comma to signal longer pauses for dramatic effect: But I want you to know that when I cross the river my last conscious thought will be of the Corps; and the Corps; and the Corps.—General Douglas MacArthur

Virgule

1. Separates successive divisions in an extended date: fiscal year 1983/84.

2. Represents *per:* 35 km/hr, 1,800 ft/sec.

3. Means *or* between the words *and* and *or:* Take water skis and/or fishing equipment when you visit the beach this summer.

4. Separates two or more lines of poetry that are quoted and run in on successive lines of a text: The student actress had a memory lapse when she came to the lines "Double, double, toil and trouble/Fire burn and cauldron bubble/Eye of newt and toe of frog/Wool of bat and tongue of dog" and had to leave the stage in embarrassment.

Forms of Address

Source: *Webster's II New Riverside University Dictionary.* Copyright © 1984 by Houghton Mifflin Company.

Academics

Dean, college or university. *Address:* **Dean** _____ . *Salutation:* Dear Dean _____

President. *Address:* President _____ . *Salutation:* Dear President _____ .

Professor, college or university. *Address:* Professor _____ . *Salutation:* Dear Professor _____ .

Clerical and Religious Orders

Abbot. *Address:* The Right Reverend _____ O.S.B. Abbot of _____ . *Salutation:* Right Reverend Abbot or Dear Father Abbot.

Archbishop, Eastern Orthodox. *Address:* The Most Reverend Joseph, Archbishop of _____ . *Salutation:* Your Eminence.

Archbishop, Roman Catholic. The Most Reverend _____ , Archbishop of _____ . *Salutation:* Your Excellency.

Archdeacon, Episcopal. *Address:* The Venerable _____ , Archdeacon of _____ . *Salutation:* Venerable Sir or Dear Archdeacon _____ .

Bishop, Episcopal. *Address:* The Right Reverend _____ , Bishop of _____ . *Salutation:* Right Reverend Sir or Dear Bishop _____

Bishop, other Protestant. *Address:* The Reverend _____ . *Salutation:* Dear Bishop _____ .

Bishop, Roman Catholic. *Address:* The Most Reverend _____ , Bishop of _____ . *Salutation:* Your Excellency or Dear Bishop _____ .

Brotherhood, Roman Catholic. *Address:* Brother _____ , C.F.C. *Salutation:* Dear Brother or Dear Brother Joseph.

Brotherhood, superior of. *Address:* Brother Joseph C.F.C. Superior. *Salutation:* Dear Brother Joseph.

Cardinal. *Address:* His Eminence Joseph Cardinal Stone. *Salutation:* Your Eminence.

Clergyman/woman, Protestant. *Address:* The Reverend _____ or The Reverend _____ , D.D. *Salutation:* Dear Mr./Ms. _____ or Dear Dr. _____ .

Dean of a cathedral, Episcopal. *Address:* The Very Reverend _____ , Dean of _____ . *Salutation:* Dear Dean _____ .

Monsignor. *Address:* The Right Reverend Monsignor _____ . *Salutation:* Dear Monsignor.

Patriarch, Greek Orthodox. *Address:* His All Holiness Patriarch Joseph. *Salutation:* Your All Holiness.

Patriarch, Russian Orthodox. *Address:* His Holiness the Patriarch of _____ . *Salutation:* Your Holiness.

Pope. *Address:* His Holiness The Pope. *Salutation:* Your Holiness or Most Holy Father.

Priest, Roman Catholic. *Address:* The Reverend _____ , S.J. *Salutation:* Dear Reverend Father or Dear Father.

Rabbi, man or woman. *Address:* Rabbi _____ or _____ D.D.. *Salutation:* Dear Rabbi _____ or Dear Dr. _____ .

Sisterhood, Roman Catholic. *Address:* Sister _____ , C.S.J. *Salutation:* Dear Sister or Dear Sister _____ .

Sisterhood, superior of. *Address:* The Reverend Mother Superior, S.C. *Salutation:* Reverend Mother.

Diplomats

Ambassador, U.S. *Address:* The Honorable _____ The Ambassador of the United States. *Salutation:* Sir/Madam or Dear Mr./Madam Ambassador.

Ambassador to the U.S. *Address:* His/Her Excellency _____ , The Ambassador of _____ . *Salutation:* Excellency or Dear Mr./Madam Ambassador.

Chargé d'Affaires, U.S. *Address:* The Honorable _____ , United States Chargé d'Affaires. *Salutation:* Dear Mr./Ms. _____ .

Consul, U.S. *Address:* _____ , Esq., United States Consul. *Salutation:* Dear Mr./Ms. _____ .

Minister, U.S. or to U.S. *Address:* The Honorable _____ , The Minister of _____ . *Salutation:* Sir/Madam or Dear Mr./Madame Minister.

Secretary General, United Nations. *Address:* His/Her Excellency ____ ____ , Secretary General of the United Nations. *Salutation:* Dear Mr./Madam/Madame Secretary General.

United Nations Representative (Foreign). *Address:* His/Her Excellency ____ ____ Representative of ____ to the United Nations. *Salutation:* Excellency or My dear Mr./Madame ____ .

United Nations Representative (U.S.) *Address:* The Honorable ____ ____ , United States Representative to the United Nations. *Salutation:* Sir/Madam or Dear Mr./Ms. ____ .

Government Officials

Assemblyman. *Address:* The Honorable ____ . *Salutation:* Dear Mr./Ms. ____ .

Associate Justice, U.S. Supreme Court. *Address:* Mr./Madam Justice ____ . *Salutation:* Dear Mr./Madam Justice or Sir/Madam.

Attorney General, U.S. *Address:* The Honorable ____ ____ , Attorney General of the United States. *Salutation:* Dear Mr./Madam or Attorney General.

Cabinet member: *Address:* The Honorable ____ ____ , Secretary of ____ . *Salutation:* Sir/Madam or Dear Mr./Madam Secretary.

Chief Justice, U.S. Supreme Court. *Address:* The Chief Justice of the United States. *Salutation:* Dear Mr. Chief Justice.

Commissioner (federal, state, local). *Address:* The Honorable ____ ____ . *Salutation:* Dear Mr./Ms. ____ .

Governor. *Address:* The Honorable ____ ____ , Governor of ____ . *Salutation:* Dear Governor ____ .

Judge, Federal: *Address:* The Honorable ____ ____ , Judge of the United States District Court for the ____ , District of ____ . *Salutation:* Sir/Madam or Dear Judge ____ .

Judge, state or local. *Address:* The Honorable ___ ____ , Judge of the Court of ____ . *Salutation:* Dear Judge ____ .

Lieutenant Governor. *Address:* The Honorable ____ ____ , Lieutenant Governor of ____ . *Salutation:* Dear Mr./Ms. ____ .

Mayor. *Address:* The Honorable ____ ____ , Mayor of ____ . *Salutation:* Dear Mayor ____ .

President, U.S. *Address:* The President. *Salutation:* Dear Mr. President.

President, U.S., former. *Address:* The Honorable ____ ____ . *Salutation:* Dear Mr. ____ .

Representative, state. *Address:* The Honorable ____ ____ . *Salutation:* Dear Mr./Ms. ____ .

Representative, U.S. *Address:* The Honorable ____ ____ , United States House of Representatives. *Salutation:* Dear Mr./Ms. ____ .

Senator, state. *Address:* The Honorable ____ ____ , The State Senate, State Capitol. *Salutation:* Dear Senator ____ .

Senator, U.S. *Address:* The Honorable ____ ____ , United States Senate. *Salutation:* Dear Senator ____ .

Speaker, U.S. House of Representatives. *Address:* The Honorable ____ ____ , Speaker of the House of Representatives. *Salutation:* Dear Mr./Madam Speaker.

Vice President, U.S. *Address:* The Vice President of the United States. *Salutation:* Sir or Dear Mr. Vice President.

Military and Naval Officers

Rank. *Address:* Full rank, USN (or USCG, USAF, USA, USMC). *Salutation:* Dear (full rank) ____ .

Professions

Attorney. *Address:* Mr./Ms. ____ ____ , Attorney at law or ____ ____ , Esq. *Salutation:* Dear Mr./Ms. ____ .

Dentist. *Address:* ____ ____ , D.D.S. *Salutation:* Dear Dr. ____ .

Physician. *Address:* ____ ____ , M.D. *Salutation:* Dear Dr. ____ .

Veterinarian. *Address:* ____ ____ , D.V.M. *Salutation:* Dear Dr. ____ .

Foreign Words and Phrases

(The English meanings given are not necessarily literal translations.)

Source: Webster's II New Riverside University Dictionary. Copyright © 1984 Houghton Mifflin Company.

ad infinitum [Lat.]: to infinity

au courant [Fr.]: up-to-date

bête noire [Fr.]: one particularly disliked

bona fide [Lat.]: in good faith; genuine

bon mot [Fr.]: a clever saying

carpe diem [Lat.]: enjoy today

carte blanche [Fr.]: unrestricted power to act on one's own

caveat emptor [Lat.]: let the buyer beware

comme ci comme ça [Fr.]: so-so

coup de grâce [Fr.]: finishing blow

cri de coeur [Fr.]: heartfelt appeal

de facto [Lat.]: in reality or fact

de gustibus non est disputandum [Lat.]: there is no arguing in matters of taste

deus ex machina [Lat.]: a contrived device to resolve a situation

ecce homo [Lat.]: behold the man

éminence grise [Fr.]: gray eminence; power behind the throne

entre nous [Fr.]: between ourselves; confidentially

fait accompli [Fr.]: an accomplished fact, presumably irreversible

faux pas [Fr.]: a social blunder

flagrante delicto [Lat.]: in the act

hoi polloi [Gk.]: the common people

in vino veritas [Lat.]: in wine there is truth

ipso facto [Lat.]: by the fact itself

je ne sais quoi [Fr.]: I know not what; an elusive quality

Kinder, Kirche, Küche [G.]: children, church, kitchen

mea culpa [Lat.]: I am to blame

modus operandi [Lat.]: a method of operating

nom de plume [Fr.]: pen name

persona non grata [Lat.]: unacceptable or unwelcome person

pro bono publico [Lat.]: for the public good

quid pro quo [Lat.]: something for something; an equal exchange

repondez s'il vous plaît [Fr.]: please reply— Used on invitation cards (abbr. R.S.V.P.)

savoir faire [Fr.]: the ability to say and do the correct thing

sic transit gloria mundi [Lat.]: thus passes away the glory of the world

sine qua non [Lat.]: indispensable

terra incognita [Lat.]: unknown territory

tout le monde [Fr.]: everybody; everyone of importance

WEIGHTS & MEASURES

Measures and Weights

Source: Department of Commerce, National Bureau of Standards.

The International System (Metric)

The International System of Units is a modernized version of the metric system, established by international agreement, that i.e. provides a logical and interconnected framework for all measurements in science, industry, and commerce. The system is built on a foundation of seven basic units, and all other units are derived from them. (Use of metric weights and measures was legalized in the United States in 1866, and our customary units of weights and measures are defined in terms of the meter and kilogram.)

Length. Meter. Up until 1893, the meter was defined as 1,650,764.73 wavelengths in vacuum of the orange-red line of the spectrum of krypton-86. Since then, it is equal to the distance traveled by light in a vacuum in 1/299,792,458 of a second.

Time. Second. The second is defined as the duration of 9,192,631,770 cycles of the radiation associated with a specified transition of the cesium 133 atom.

Mass. Kilogram. The standard for the kilogram is a cylinder of platinum-iridium alloy kept by the International Bureau of Weights and Measures at Paris. A duplicate at the National Bureau of Standards serves as the mass standard for the United States. The kilogram is the only base unit still defined by a physical object.

Temperature. Kelvin. The kelvin is defined as the fraction 1/273.16 of the thermodynamic temperature of the triple point of water; that is, the point at which water forms an interface of solid, liquid and vapor. This is defined as 0.01°C on the Centigrade or Celsius scale and 32.02°F on the Fahrenheit scale. The temperature 0°K is called "absolute zero."

Electric Current. Electric current. The ampere is defined as that current that, if maintained in each of two long parallel wires separted by one meter in free space, would produce a force between the two wires (due to their magnetic fields) of 2×10^{-7} newton for each meter of length. (A newton is the unit of force which when applied to one kilogram mass would experience an acceleration of one meter per second per second.)

Luminous Intensity. Candela. The candela is defined as the luminous intensity of 1/600,000 of a square meter of a cavity at the temperature of freezing platinum (2,042K).

Amount of Substance. Mole. The mole is the amount of substance of a system that contains as many elementary entities as there are atoms in 0.012 kilogram of carbon-12.

Tables of Metric Weights and Measures

LINEAR MEASURE

10 millimeters (mm) =	1 centimeter (cm)
10 centimeters =	1 decimeter (dm) = 100 millimeters
10 decimeters =	1 meter (m) = 1,000 millimeters
10 meters =	1 dekameter (dam)
10 dekameters =	1 hectometer (hm) = 100 meters
10 hectometers =	1 kilometer (km) = 1,000 meters

AREA MEASURE

100 square millimeters (mm²) =	1 sq centimeter (cm²)
10,000 square centimeters =	1 sq meter (m²) = 1,000,000 sq millimeters
100 square meters =	1 are (a)
100 ares =	1 hectare (ha) = 10,000 sq meters
100 hectares =	1 sq kilometer (km²) = 1,000,000 sq meters

VOLUME MEASURE

10 milliliters (ml) =	1 centiliter (cl)
10 centiliters =	1 deciliter (dl) = 100 milliliters
10 deciliters =	1 liter (l) = 1,000 milliliters
10 liters =	1 dekaliter (dal)
10 dekaliters =	1 hectoliter (hl) = 100 liters
10 hectoliters =	1 kiloliter (kl) = 1,000 liters

CUBIC MEASURE

1,000 cubic millimeters (mm³) =	1 cu centimeter (cm³)
1,000 cubic centimeters =	1 cu decimeter (dm³) = 1,000,000 cu millimeters
1,000 cubic decimeters =	1 cu meter (m³) = 1 stere = 1,000,000 cu centimeters = 1,000,000,000 cu millimeters

WEIGHT

10 milligrams (mg) =	1 centigram (cg)
10 centigrams =	1 decigram (dg) = 100 milligrams
10 decigrams =	1 gram (g) = 1,000 milligrams
10 grams =	1 dekagram (dag)
10 dekagrams =	1 hectogram (hg) = 100 grams
10 hectograms =	1 kilogram (kg) = 1,000 grams
1,000 kilograms =	1 metric ton (t)

Tables of Customary U.S. Weights and Measures

LINEAR MEASURE

12 inches (in.) =	1 foot (ft)
3 feet =	1 yard (yd)
5 1/2 yards =	1 rod (rd), pole, or perch (16 1/2 ft)
40 rods =	1 furlong (fur) = 220 yds = 660 ft
8 furlongs =	1 statute mile (mi.) = 1,760 yds = 5,280 ft
3 land miles =	1 league
5,280 feet =	1 statute or land mile
6,076.11549 feet =	1 international nautical mile

AREA MEASURE

144 square inches =	1 sq ft
9 square feet =	1 sq yd = 1,296 sq in.
30 1/4 square yards =	1 sq rd = 272 1/4 sq ft
160 square rods =	1 acre = 4,840 sq yds = 43,560 sq ft
640 acres =	1 sq mi.
1 mile square =	1 section (of land)
6 miles square =	1 township = 36 sections = 36 sq mi.

CUBIC MEASURE

1,728 cubic inches =	1 cu ft
27 cubic feet =	1 cu yd

LIQUID MEASURE

When necessary to distinguish the liquid pint or quart from the dry pint or quart, the word "liquid" or the abbreviation "liq" should be used in combination with the name or abbreviation of the liquid unit.

4 gills (gi) =	1 pint (pt) (= 28.875 cu in.)
2 pints =	1 quart (qt) (= 57.75 cu in.)
4 quarts =	1 gallon (gal) (= 231 cu in.) = 8 pts = 32 gills

APOTHECARIES' FLUID MEASURE

60 minims (min.) =	1 fluid dram (fl dr) (= 0.2256 cu in.)
8 fluid drams =	1 fluid ounce (fl oz) (= 1.8047 cu in.)
16 fluid ounces =	1 pt (= 28.875 cu in.) = 128 fl drs
2 pints =	1 qt (= 57.75 cu in.) = 32 fl oz = 256 fl drs
4 quarts =	1 gal (= 231 cu in.) = 128 fl oz = 1,024 fl drs

DRY MEASURE

When necessary to distinguish the dry pint or quart from the liquid pint or quart; the word "dry" should be used in combination with the name or abbreviation of the dry unit.

2 pints =	1 qt (=67.2006 cu in.)
8 quarts =	1 peck (pk) (=537.605 cu in.) = 16 pts
4 pecks =	1 bushel (bu) (= 2,150.42 cu in.) = 32 qts

AVOIRDUPOIS WEIGHT

When necessary to distinguish the avoirdupois dram from the apothecaries dram, or to distinguish the avoirdupois dram or ounce from the fluid dram or ounce, or to distinguish the avoirdupois ounce or pound from the troy or apothecaries, ounce or pound, the word "avoirdupois" or the abbreviation "avdp" should be used in combination with the name or abbreviation of the avoirdupois unit. (The "grain" is the same in avoirdupois, troy, and apothecaries weights.)

27 11/32 grains =	1 dram (dr)
16 drams =	1 oz = 437 1/2 grains
16 ounces =	1 lb = 256 drams = 7,000 grains
100 pounds =	1 hundredweight (cwt)[1]
20 hundredweights =	1 ton (tn) = 2,000 lbs[1]

In "gross" or "long" measure, the following values are recognized:

112 pounds =	1 gross or long cwt[1]
20 gross or long hundredweights =	1 gross or long ton = 2,240 lbs[1]

1. When the terms "hundredweight" and "ton" are used unmodified, they are commonly understood to mean the 100–pound hundredweight and the 2,000–pound ton, respectively; these units may be designated "net" or "short" when necessary to distinguish them from the corresponding units in gross or long measure.

UNITS OF CIRCULAR MEASURE

Second (") =	—
Minute (') =	60 seconds
Degree (°) =	60 minutes
Right angle =	90 degrees
Straight angle =	180 degrees
Circle =	360 degrees

TROY WEIGHT

24 grains =	1 pennyweight (dwt)
20 pennyweights =	1 ounce troy (oz t) = 480 grains
12 ounces troy =	1 pound troy (lb t) = 240 pennyweights = 5,760 grains

APOTHECARIES' WEIGHT

20 grains =	1 scruple (s ap)
3 scruples =	1 dram apothecaries' (dr ap) = 60 grains
8 drams apothecaries =	1 ounce apothecaries' (oz ap) = 24 scruples = 480 grains
12 ounces apothecaries =	1 pound apothecaries' (lb ap) = 96 drams apothecaries' = 288 scruples = 5,760 grains

GUNTER'S OR SURVEYOR'S CHAIN MEASURE

7.92 inches =	1 link (li)
100 links =	1 chain (ch) = 4 rods = 66 ft
80 chains =	1 statute mile = 320 rods = 5,280 ft

Metric and U.S. Equivalents

1 angstrom[1] (light wave measurement)	0.1 millimicron 0.000 1 micron 0.000 000 1 millimeter 0.000 000 004 inch	1 decimeter	3.937 inches
		1 dekameter	32.808 feet
1 cable's length	120 fathoms 720 feet 219.456 meters	1 fathom	6 feet 1.8288 meters
		1 foot	0.3048 meter
1 centimeter	0.3937 inch	1 furlong	10 chains (surveyor's) 660 feet 220 yards 1/8 statute mile 201.168 meters
1 chain (Gunter's or surveyor's)	66 feet 20.1168 meters		

1 inch	2.54 centimeters
1 kilometer	0.621 mile
1 league (land)	3 statute miles 4.828 kilometers
1 link (Gunter's or surveyor's)	7.92 inches 0.201 168 meter
1 meter	39.37 inches 1.094 yards
1 micron	0.001 millimeter 0.000 039 37 inch
1 mil	0.001 inch 0.025 4 millimeter
1 mile (statute or land)	5,280 feet 1.609 kilometers
1 mile (nautical international)	1.852 kilometers 1.151 statute miles 0.999 U.S. nautical miles
1 millimeter	0.03937 inch
1 millimicron (m+GRKm)	0.001 micron 0.000 000 039 37 inch
1 nanometer	0.001 micrometer or 0.000 000 039 37 inch
1 point (typography)	0.013 837 inch 1/72 inch (approximately) 0.351 millimeter
1 rod, pole, or perch	16 1/2 feet 5.0292 meters
1 yard	0.9144 meter

AREAS OR SURFACES

1 acre	43,560 square feet 4,840 square yards 0.405 hectare
1 are	119.599 square yards 0.025 acre
1 hectare	2.471 acres
1 square centimeter	0.155 square inch
1 square decimeter	15.5 square inches
1 square foot	929.030 square centimeters
1 square inch	6.4516 square centimeters
1 square kilometer	0.386 square mile 247.105 acres
1 square meter	1.196 square yards 10.764 square feet
1 square mile	258.999 hectares
1 square millimeter	0.002 square inch
1 square rod, square pole or square perch	25.293 square meters
1 square yard	0.836 square meters

CAPACITIES OR VOLUMES

1 barrel, liquid	31 to 42 gallons[2]
1 barrel, standard for fruits, vegetables, and other dry commodities except cranberries	7,056 cubic inches 105 dry quarts 3.281 bushels, struck measure
1 barrel, standard, cranberry	5.286 cubic inches 86 45/64 dry quarts 2.709 bushels, struck measure
1 bushel (U.S.) struck measure	2,150.42 cubic inches 35.238 liters
1 bushel, heaped (U.S.)	2,747.715 cubic inches 1.278 bushels, struck measure[3]
1 cord (firewood)	128 cubic feet
1 cubic centimeter	0.061 cubic inch
1 cubic decimeter	61.024 cubic inches
1 cubic foot	7.481 gallons 28.316 cubic decimeters
1 cubic inch	0.554 fluid ounce 4.433 fluid drams 16.387 cubic centimeters
1 cubic meter	1.308 cubic yards
1 cubic yard	0.765 cubic meter
1 cup, measuring	8 fluid ounces 1/2 liquid pint
1 dram, fluid or liquid (U.S.)	1/8 fluid ounces 0.226 cubic inch 3.697 milliliters 1.041 British fluid drachms
1 dekaliter	2.642 gallons 1.135 pecks
1 gallon (U.S.)	231 cubic inches 3.785 liters 0.833 British gallon 128 U.S. fluid ounces
1 gallon (British Imperial)	277.42 cubic inches 1.201 U.S. gallons 4.546 liters 160 British fluid ounces
1 gill	7.219 cubic inches 4 fluid ounces 0.118 liter
1 hectoliter	26.418 gallons 2.838 bushels
1 liter	1.057 liquid quarts 0.908 dry quart 61.024 cubic inches
1 milliliter	0.271 fluid dram 16.231 minims 0.061 cubic inch
1 ounce, fluid or liquid (U.S.)	1.805 cubic inch 29.574 milliliters 1.041 British fluid ounces

Unit	Equivalent
1 peck	8.810 liters
1 pint, dry	33.600 cubic inches 0.551 liter
1 pint, liquid	28.875 cubic inches 0.473 liter
1 quart, dry (U.S.)	67.201 cubic inches 1.101 liters 0.969 British quart
1 quart, liquid (U.S.)	57.75 cubic inches 0.946 liter 0.833 British quart
1 quart (British)	69.354 cubic inches 1.032 U.S. dry quarts 1.201 U.S. liquid quarts
1 tablespoon, measuring	3 teaspoons 4 fluid drams 1/2 fluid ounce
1 teaspoon, measuring	1/3 tablespoon 1 1/3 fluid drams
1 assay ton[4]	29.167 grams
1 carat	200 milligrams 3.086 grains
1 dram, apothecaries'	60 grains 3.888 grams
1 dram, avoirdupois	27 11/32 (=27.344) grains 1.772 grams
1 grain	64.798 91 milligrams
1 gram	15.432 grains 0.035 ounce, avoirdupois
1 hundredweight, gross or long[5]	112 pounds 50.802 kilograms
1 hundredweight, net or short	100 pounds 45.359 kilograms
1 kilogram	2.205 pounds
1 microgram [μg (the Greek letter mu in combination with the letter g)]	0.000 001 gram
1 milligram	0.015 grain
1 ounce, avoirdupois	437.5 grains 0.911 troy or apothecaries, ounce 28.350 grams
1 ounce, troy or apothecaries	480 grains 1.097 avoirdupois ounces 31.103 grams
1 pennyweight	1.555 grams
1 point	0.01 carat 2 milligrams
1 pound, avoirdupois	7,000 grains 1.215 troy or apothecaries pounds 453.592 37 grams
1 pound, troy or apothecaries	5,760 grains 0.823 avoirdupois pound 373.242 grams
1 ton, gross or long[5]	2,240 pounds 1.12 net tons 1.016 metric tons
1 ton, metric	2,204.623 pounds 0 .984 gross ton 1.102 net tons
1 ton, net or short	2,000 pounds 0.893 gross ton 0.907 metric ton

1. The angstrom is basically defined as 10^{-10} meter. 2. There is a variety of "barrels" established by law or usage. For example, federal taxes on fermented liquors are based on a barrel of 31 gallons; many state laws fix the "barrel for liquids" at 31 1/2 gallons; one state fixes a 36–gallon barrel for cistern measurement; federal law recognizes a 40–gallon barrel for "proof spirits"; by custom, 42 gallons comprise a barrel of crude oil or petroleum products for statistical purposes, and this equivalent is recognized "for liquids" by four states. 3. Frequently recognized as 1 1/4 bushels, struck measure. 4. Used in assaying. The assay ton bears the same relation to the milligram that a ton of 2,000 pounds avoirdupois bears to the ounce troy; hence the weight in milligrams of precious metal obtained from one assay ton of ore gives directly the number of troy ounces to the net ton. 5. The gross or long ton and hundredweight are used commercially in the United States to only a limited extent, usually in restricted industrial fields. These units are the same as the British "ton" and "hundredweight."

Miscellaneous Units of Measure

Acre: An area of 43,560 square feet. Originally, the area a yoke of oxen could plow in one day.

Agate: Originally a measurement of type size (5 1/2 points). Now equal to 1/14 inch. Used in printing for measuring column length.

Ampere: Unit of electric current. A potential difference of one volt across a resistance of one ohm produces a current of one ampere.

Astronomical Unit (A.U.): 93,000,000 miles, the average distance of the earth from the sun. Used for astronomy.

Bale: A large bundle of goods. In the U.S., the approximate weight of a bale of cotton is 500 pounds. The weight varies in other countries.

Board Foot (fbm): 144 cubic inches (12 in. × 12 in. × 1 in.). Used for lumber.

Bolt: 40 yards. Used for measuring cloth.

Btu: British thermal unit. Amount of heat needed to increase the temperature of one pound of water by one degree Fahrenheit (252 calories).

Carat (c): 200 milligrams or 3.086 grains troy. Originally the weight of a seed of the carob tree in the Mediterranean region. Used for weighing precious stones. *See also* Karat.

Chain (ch): A chain 66 feet or one–tenth of a furlong in length, divided into 100 parts called links. One mile is equal to 80 chains. Used in surveying and sometimes called Gunter's or surveyor's chain.

Cubit: 18 inches or 45.72 cm. Derived from distance between elbow and tip of middle finger.

Decibel: Unit of relative loudness. One decibel is the smallest amount of change detectable by the human ear.

Ell, English: 1 1/4 yards or 1/32 bolt. Used for measuring cloth.

Freight, Ton (also called Measurement Ton): 40 cubic feet of merchandise. Used for cargo freight.

Great Gross: 12 gross or 1728.

Gross: 12 dozen or 144.

Hand: 4 inches or 10.16 cm. Derived from the width of the hand. Used for measuring the height of horses at withers.

Hertz: Modern unit for measurement of electromagnetic wave frequencies (equivalent to "cycles per second").

Hogshead (hhd): 2 liquid barrels or 14,653 cubic inches.

Horsepower: The power needed to lift 33,000 pounds a distance of one foot in one minute (about 1 1/2 times the power an average horse can exert). Used for measuring power of steam engines, etc.

Karat (kt): A measure of the purity of gold, indicating how many parts out of 24 are pure. For example: 18 karat gold is 3/4 pure. Sometimes spelled *carat*.

Knot: Not a distance, but the rate of speed of one nautical mile per hour. Used for measuring speed of ships.

League: Rather indefinite and varying measure, but usually estimated at 3 miles in English-speaking countries.

Light-Year: 5,880,000,000,000 miles, the distance light travels in a vacuum in a year at the rate of 186,281.7 miles (299,792 kilometers) per second. (If an astronomical unit were represented by one inch, a light-year would be represented by about one mile.) Used for measurements in interstellar space.

Magnum: Two-quart bottle. Used for measuring wine, etc.

Ohm: Unit of electrical resistance. A circuit in which a potential difference of one volt produces a current of one ampere has a resistance of one ohm.

Parsec: Approximately 3.26 light-years of 19.2 million miles. Term is combination of first syllables of *par*allax and *sec*ond, and distance is that of imaginary star when lines drawn from it to both earth and sun form a maximum angle or parallax of one second (1/3600 degree). Used for measuring interstellar distances.

Pi (π): 3.14159265+. The ratio of the circumference of a circle to its diameter. For practical purposes, the value is used to four decimal places: 3.1416.

Pica: 1/6 inch or 12 points. Used in printing for measuring column width, etc.

Pipe: 2 hogsheads. Used for measuring wine and other liquids.

Point: .013837 (approximately 1/72) inch or 1/12 pica. Used in printing for measuring type size.

Quintal: 100,000 grams or 220.46 pounds avoirdupois.

Quire: Used for measuring paper. Sometimes 24 sheets but more often 25. There are 20 quires to a ream.

Ream: Used for measuring paper. Sometimes 480 sheets, but more often 500 sheets.

Roentgen: International Unit of radiation exposure produced by X-rays.

Score: 20 units.

Sound, Speed of: Usually placed at 1,088 ft per second at 32°F at sea level. It varies at other temperatures and in different media.

Span: 9 inches or 22.86 cm. Derived from the distance between the end of the thumb and the end of the little finger when both are outstretched.

Square: 100 square feet. Used in building.

Stone: Legally 14 pounds avoirdupois in Great Britain.

Therm: 100,000 Btu's.

Township: U.S. land measurement of almost 36 square miles. The south border is 6 miles long. The east and west borders, also 6 miles long, follow the meridians, making the north border slightly less than 6 miles long. Used in surveying.

Tun: 252 gallons, but often larger. Used for measuring wine and other liquids.

Watt: Unit of power. The power used by a current of one ampere across a potential difference of one volt equals one watt.

Kelvin Scale

Absolute zero, –273.16° on the Celsius (Centigrade) scale, is 0° Kelvin. Thus, degrees Kelvin are equivalent to degrees Celsuis plus 273.16. The freezing point of water, 0°C. and 32°F., is 273.16°K. The conversion formula is K° = C° + 273.16.

Conversion of Miles to Kilometers and Kilometers to Miles

Miles	Kilometers	Miles	Kilometers	Miles	Kilometers	Kilometers	Miles	Kilometers	Miles	Kilometers	Miles
1	1.6	8	12.8	60	96.5	1	0.6	8	4.9	60	37.2
2	3.2	9	14.4	70	112.6	2	1.2	9	5.5	70	43.4
3	4.8	10	16.0	80	128.7	3	1.8	10	6.2	80	49.7
4	6.4	20	32.1	90	144.8	4	2.4	20	12.4	90	55.9
5	8.0	30	48.2	100	160.9	5	3.1	30	18.6	100	62.1
6	9.6	40	64.3	1,000	1609	6	3.7	40	24.8	1,000	621
7	11.2	50	80.4			7	4.3	50	31.0		

Bolts and Screws: Conversion from Fractions of an Inch to Millimeters

Inch	mm	Inch	mm	Inch	mm	Inch	mm
1/64	0.40	17/64	6.75	33/64	13.10	49/64	19.45
1/32	0.79	9/32	7.14	17/32	13.50	25/32	19.84
3/64	1.19	19/64	7.54	35/64	13.90	51/64	20.24
1/16	1.59	5/16	7.94	9/16	14.29	13/16	20.64
5/64	1.98	21/64	8.33	37/64	14.69	53/64	21.03
3/32	2.38	11/32	8.73	19/32	15.08	27/32	21.43
7/64	2.78	23/64	9.13	39/64	15.48	55/64	21.83
1/8	3.18	3/8	9.53	5/8	15.88	7/8	22.23
9/64	3.57	25/64	9.92	41/64	16.27	57/64	22.62
5/32	3.97	13/32	10.32	21/32	16.67	29/32	23.02
11/64	4.37	27/64	10.72	43/64	17.06	59/64	23.42
3/16	4.76	7/16	11.11	11/16	17.46	15/16	23.81
13/64	5.16	29/64	11.51	45/64	17.86	61/64	24.21
7/32	5.56	15/32	11.91	23/32	18.26	31/32	24.61
15/64	5.95	31/64	12.30	47/64	18.65	63/64	25.00
1/4	6.35	1/2	12.70	3/4	19.05	1	25.40

U.S.—Metric Cooking Conversions

U.S. customary system				Metric			
Capacity		**Weight**		**Capacity**		**Weight**	
1/5 teaspoon	1 milliliter	1 fluid oz	30 milliliters	1 milliliter	1/5 teaspoon	1 gram	.035 ounce
1 teaspoon	5 ml		28 grams	5 ml	1 teaspoon	100 grams	3.5 ounces
1 tablespoon	15 ml	1 pound	454 grams	15 ml	1 tablespoon	500 grams	1.10 pounds
1/5 cup	50 ml			34 ml	1 fluid oz	1 kilogram	2.205 pounds
1 cup	240 ml						35 oz
2 cups (1 pint)	470 ml			100 ml	3.4 fluid oz		
4 cups (1 quart)	.95 liter			240 ml	1 cup		
4 quarts (1 gal.)	3.8 liters			1 liter	34 fluid oz		
					4.2 cups		
					2.1 pints		
					1.06 quarts		
					0.26 gallon		

Cooking Measurement Equivalents

16 tablespoons =	1 cup	2 tablespoons =	1/8 cup
12 tablespoons =	3/4 cup	2 tablespoons + 2 teaspoons =	1/6 cup
10 tablespoons + 2 teaspoons =	2/3 cup	1 tablespoon =	1/16 cup
8 tablespoons =	1/2 cup	2 cups =	1 pint
6 tablespoons =	3/8 cup	2 pints =	1 quart
5 tablespoons + 1 teaspoon =	1/3 cup	3 teaspoons =	1 tablespoon
4 tablespoons =	1/4 cup	48 teaspoons =	1 cup

Prefixes and Multiples

Prefix	Suffix	Equivalent	Multiple/ submultiple	Prefix	Suffix	Equivalent	Multiple/ submultiple
atto	a	quintillionth part	10^{-18}	deci	d	tenth part	10^{-1}
femto	f	quadrillionth part	10^{-15}	deka	da	tenfold	10
pico	p	trillionth part	10^{-12}	hecto	h	hundredfold	10^{2}
nano	n	billionth part	10^{-9}	kilo	k	thousandfold	10^{3}
micro	μ	millionth part	10^{-6}	mega	M	millionfold	10^{6}
milli	m	thousandth part	10^{-3}	giga	G	billionfold	10^{9}
centi	c	hundredth part	10^{-2}	tera	T	trillionfold	10^{12}

Common Formulas

Circumference

Circle: $C = \pi d$, in which π is 3.1416 and d the diameter.

Area

Triangle: $A = \dfrac{ab}{2}$, in which a is the base and b the height.

Square: $A = a^2$, in which a is one of the sides.

Rectangle: $A = ab$, in which a is the base and b the height.

Trapezoid: $A = \dfrac{h(a+b)}{2}$, in which h is the height, a the longer parallel side, and b the shorter.

Regular pentagon: $A = 1.720a^2$, in which a is one of the sides.

Regular hexagon: $A = 2.598a^2$, in which a is one of the sides.

Regular octagon: $A = 4.828a^2$, in which a is one of the sides.

Circle: $A = \pi r^2$, in which π is 3.1416 and r the radius.

Volume

Cube: $V = a^3$, in which a is one of the edges.

Rectangular prism: $V = abc$, in which a is the length, b is the width, and c the depth.

Pyramid: $V = \dfrac{Ah}{3}$, in which A is the area of the base and h the height.

Cylinder: $V = \pi r^2 h$, in which π is 3.1416, r the radius of the base, and h the height.

Cone: $V = \dfrac{\pi r^2 h}{3}$, in which π is 3.1416, r the radius of the base, and h the height.

Sphere: $V = \dfrac{4 \pi r^3}{3}$, in which π is 3.1416 and the radius.

Miscellaneous

Distance in feet traveled by falling body: $d = 16t^2$, in which t is the time in seconds.

Speed in sound in feet per second through any given temperature of air:
$$V = \frac{1087\sqrt{273+t}}{16.52}$$
in which t is the temperature Centigrade.

Cost in cents of operration of electrical device: $C = \dfrac{Wtc}{1000}$, in which W is the number of watts, t the time in hours, and c the cost in cents per hilowatt-hour.

Conversion of matter into energy (Einstein's Theorem): $E = mc^2$, in which E is the energy in ergs, m the mass of the matter in grams, and c the speed of light in centimeters per second ($c^2 = 9 \times 10^{20}$).

Decimal Equivalents of Common Fractions

1/2	.5000	1/10	.1000	2/7	.2857	3/11	.2727	5/9	.5556	7/11	.6364
1/3	.3333	1/11	.0909	2/9	.2222	4/5	.8000	5/11	.4545	7/12	.5833
1/4	.2500	1/12	.0833	2/11	.1818	4/7	.5714	5/12	.4167	8/9	.8889
1/5	.2000	1/16	.0625	3/4	.7500	4/9	.4444	6/7	.8571	8/11	.7273
1/6	.1667	1/32	.0313	3/5	.6000	4/11	.3636	6/11	.5455	9/10	.9000
1/7	.1429	1/64	.0156	3/7	.4286	5/6	.8333	7/8	.8750	9/11	.8182
1/8	.1250	2/3	.6667	3/8	.3750	5/7	.7143	7/9	.7778	10/11	.9091
1/9	.1111	2/5	.4000	3/10	.3000	5/8	.6250	7/10	.7000	11/12	.9167

Conversion Factors

To change	To	Multiply by	To change	To	Multiply by
cres	hectares	.4047	liters	pints (dry)	1.8162
cres	square feet	43,560	liters	pints (liquid)	2.1134
cres	square miles	.001562	liters	quarts (dry)	.9081
tmospheres	cms. of mercury	76	liters	quarts (liquid)	1.0567
BTU	horsepower-hour	.0003931	meters	feet	3.2808
BTU	kilowatt-hour	.0002928	meters	miles	.0006214
BTU/hour	watts	.2931	meters	yards	1.0936
bushels	cubic inches	2150.4	metric tons	tons (long)	.9842
bushels (U.S.)	hectoliters	.3524	metric tons	tons (short)	1.1023
centimeters	inches	.3937	miles	kilometers	1.6093
centimeters	feet	.03281	miles	feet	5280
circumference	radians	6.283	miles (nautical)	miles (statute)	1.1516
cubic feet	cubic meters	.0283	miles (statute)	miles (nautical)	.8684
cubic meters	cubic feet	35.3145	miles/hour	feet/minute	88
cubic meters	cubic yards	1.3079	millimeters	inches	.0394
cubic yards	cubic meters	.7646	ounces avdp.	grams	28.3495
degrees	radians	.01745	ounces	pounds	.0625
dynes	grams	.00102	ounces (troy)	ounces (avdp)	1.09714
fathoms	feet	6.0	pecks	liters	8.8096
feet	meters	.3048	pints (dry)	liters	.5506
feet	miles (nautical)	.0001645	pints (liquid)	liters	.4732
feet	miles (statute)	.0001894	pounds ap or t	kilograms	.3782
feet/second	miles/hour	.6818	pounds avdp	kilograms	.4536
furlongs	feet	660.0	pounds	ounces	16
furlongs	miles	.125	quarts (dry)	liters	1.1012
gallons (U.S.)	liters	3.7853	quarts (liquid)	liters	.9463
grains	grams	.0648	radians	degrees	57.30
grams	grains	15.4324	rods	meters	5.029
grams	ounces avdp	.0353	rods	feet	16.5
grams	pounds	.002205	square feet	square meters	.0929
hectares	acres	2.4710	square kilometers	square miles	.3861
hectoliters	bushels (U.S.)	2.8378	square meters	square feet	10.7639
horsepower	watts	745.7	square meters	square yards	1.1960
hours	days	.04167	square miles	square kilometers	2.5900
inches	millimeters	25.4000	square yards	square meters	.8361
inches	centimeters	2.5400	tons (long)	metric tons	1.016
kilograms	pounds avdp or t	2.2046	tons (short)	metric tons	.9072
kilometers	miles	.6214	tons (long)	pounds	2240
kilowatts	horsepower	1.341	tons (short)	pounds	2000
knots	nautical miles/hour	1.0	watts	Btu/hour	3.4129
knots	statute miles/hour	1.151	watts	horsepower	.001341
liters	gallons (U.S.)	.2642	yards	meters	.9144
liters	pecks	.1135	yards	miles	.0005682

Fahrenheit and Celsius (Centigrade) Scales

Zero on the Fahrenheit scale represents the temperature produced by the mixing of equal weights of snow and common salt.

	F	C
Boiling point of water	212°	100°
Freezing point of water	32°	0°
Absolute zero	−459.6°	−273.1°

Absolute zero is theoretically the lowest possible temperature, the point at which all molecular motion would cease.

To convert Fahrenheit to Celsius (Centigrade), subtract 32 and multiply by 5/9.

To convert Celsius (Centigrade) to Fahrenheit, multiiply by 9/5 and add 32.

°Centigrade	°Fahrenheit	°Centigrade	°Fahrenheit
−273.1	−459.6	30	86
−250	−418	35	95
−200	−328	40	104
−150	−238	45	113
−100	−148	50	122
−50	−58	55	131
−40	−40	60	140
−30	−22	65	149
−20	−4	70	158
−10	14	75	167
0	32	80	176
5	41	85	185
10	50	90	194
15	59	95	203
20	68	100	212
25	77		

Roman Numerals

Roman numerals are expressed by letters of the alphabet and are rarely used today except for formality or variety.

There are three basic principles for reading Roman numerals:

1. A letter repeated once or twice repeats its value that many times (XXX = 30, CC = 200, etc.).

2. One or more letters placed after another letter of greater value increases the greater value by th[e] amount of the smaller. (VI = 6, LXX = 70, MCC = 1200, etc.).

3. A letter placed before another letter of greate[r] value decreases the greater value by the amount o[f] the smaller. (IV = 4, XC = 90, CM = 900, etc.).

Letter	Value	Letter	Value	Letter	Value	Letter	Value	Letter	Value
I	1	VII	7	XXX	30	LXXX	80	$\overline{\text{V}}$	5,000
II	2	VIII	8	XL	40	XC	90	$\overline{\text{X}}$	10,000
III	3	IX	9	L	50	C	100	$\overline{\text{L}}$	50,000
IV	4	X	10	LX	60	D	500	$\overline{\text{C}}$	100,000
V	5	XX	20	LXX	70	M	1,000	$\overline{\text{D}}$	500,000
VI	6							$\overline{\text{M}}$	1,000,000

Mean and Median

The mean, also called the average, of a series of quantities is obtained by finding the sum of the quantities and dividing it by the number of quantities. In the series 1, 3, 5, 18, 19, 20, 25, the mean or average is 13—i.e., 91 divided by 7.

The median of a series is that point which so divides it that half the quantities are on one side, half on the other. In the above series, the median is 18.

The median often better expresses the common-run, since it is not, as is the mean, affected by an excessively high or low figure. In the series 1, 3, 4, 7, 55, the median of 4 is a truer expression of the common-run than is the mean of 14.

Prime Numbers Between 1 and 1,000

	2	3	5	7	11	13	17	19	23
29	31	37	41	43	47	53	59	61	67
71	73	79	83	89	97	101	103	107	109
113	127	131	137	139	149	151	157	163	167
173	179	181	191	193	197	199	211	223	227
229	233	239	241	251	257	263	269	271	277
281	283	293	307	311	313	317	331	337	347
349	353	359	367	373	379	383	389	397	401
409	419	421	431	433	439	443	449	457	461
463	467	479	487	491	499	503	509	521	523
541	547	557	563	569	571	577	587	593	599
601	607	613	617	619	631	641	643	647	653
659	661	673	677	683	691	701	709	719	727
733	739	743	751	757	761	769	773	787	797
809	811	821	823	827	829	839	853	857	859
863	877	881	883	887	907	911	919	929	937
941	947	953	967	971	977	983	991	997	(1009)

Definitions of Gold Terminology

The term "fineness" defines a gold content in parts per thousand. For example, a gold nugget containing 885 parts of pure gold, 100 parts of silver, and 15 parts of copper would be considered 885-fine.

The word "karat" indicates the proportion of solid gold in an alloy based on a total of 24 parts. Thus, 14-karat (14K) gold indicates a composition of 14 parts of gold and 10 parts of other metals.

The term "gold-filled" is used to describe articles of jewelry made of base metal which are covered on one or more surfaces with a layer of gold alloy. No article having a gold alloy portion of less than one twentieth by weight may be marked "gold-filled." Articles may be marked "rolled gold plate" provided the proportional fraction and fineness designations are also shown.

Electroplated jewelry items carrying at least 7 mil-lionths of an inch of gold on significant surfaces may be labeled "electroplate." Plate thicknesses less than this may be marked "gold-flashed" or "gold-washed."

Portraits and Designs of U.S. Paper Currency[1]

Currency	Portrait	Design on back	Currency	Portrait	Design on back
$1	Washington	ONE between obverse and reverse of Great Seal of U.S.	$50	Grant	U.S. Capitol
			$100	Franklin	Independence Hall
$2[2]	Jefferson	Monticello	$500	McKinley	Ornate FIVE HUNDRED
$2[3]	Jefferson	"The Signing of the Declaration of Independence"	$1,000	Cleveland	Ornate ONE THOUSAND
			$5,000	Madison	Ornate FIVE THOUSAND
$5	Lincoln	Lincoln Memorial	$10,000	Chase	Ornate TEN THOUSAND
$10	Hamilton	U.S. Treasury Building	$100,000[4]	Wilson	Ornate ONE HUNDRED THOUSAND
$20	Jackson	White House			

1. Denominations of $500 and higher were discontinued in 1969. 2. Discontinued in 1966. 3. New issue, April 13, 1976. 4. For use only in transactions between Federal Reserve System and Treasury Department.

World Geography
Explorations
(All years are A.D. unless B.C. is specified.)

Country or place	Event	Explorer	Date
AFRICA			
Sierra Leone	Visited	Hanno, Carthaginian seaman	c. 520 B.C.
Zaire River (Congo)	Mouth visited[1]	Diogo Cão, Portuguese explorer	c. 1484
Cape of Good Hope	Rounded	Bartolomeu Diaz, Portuguese explorer	1488
Gambia River	Explored	Mungo Park, Scottish explorer	1795
Sahara	Crossed	Dixon Denham and Hugh Clapperton, English explorers	1822–23
Zambezi River	Visited[1]	David Livingstone, Scottish explorer	1851
Sudan	Explored	Heinrich Barth, German explorer	1852–55
Victoria Falls	Visited[1]	Livingstone	1855
Lake Tanganyika	Visited[1]	Richard Burton and John Speke, British explorers	1858
Zaire River (Congo)	Traced	Sir Henry M. Stanley, British explorer	1877
ASIA			
Punjab (India)	Visited	Alexander the Great	327 B.C.
China	Visited	Marco Polo, Italian traveler	c. 1272
Tibet	Visited	Odoric of Pordenone, Italian monk	c. 1325
Southern China	Explored	Niccolò dei Conti, Venetian traveler	c. 1440
India	Visited (Cape route)	Vasco da Gama, Portuguese navigator	1498
Japan	Visited	St. Francis Xavier of Spain	1549
Arabia	Explored	Carsten Niebuhr, German explorer	1762
China	Explored	Ferdinand Richthofen, German scientist	1868
Mongolia	Explored	Nikolai M. Przhevalsky, Russian explorer	1870–73
Central Asia	Explored	Sven Hedin, Swedish scientist	1890–1908
EUROPE			
Shetland Islands	Visited	Pytheas of Massilia (Marseille)	c. 325 B.C.
North Cape	Rounded	Ottar, Norwegian explorer	c. 870
Iceland	Colonized	Norwegian noblemen	c. 890–900
NORTH AMERICA			
Greenland	Colonized	Eric the Red, Norwegian	c. 985
Labrador; Nova Scotia(?)	Visited[1]	Leif Ericson, Norse explorer	1000
West Indies	Visited[1]	Christopher Columbus, Italian	1492
North America	Coast visited[1]	Giovanni Caboto (John Cabot), for British	1497
Pacific Ocean	Sighted[1]	Vasco Núñez de Balboa, Spanish explorer	1513
Florida	Explored	Ponce de León, Spanish explorer	1513
Mexico	Conquered	Hernando Cortés, Spanish adventurer	1519–21
St. Lawrence River	Visited[1]	Jacques Cartier, French navigator	1534
Southwest U. S.	Explored	Francisco Coronado, Spanish explorer	1540–42
Colorado River	Visited[1]	Hernando de Alarcón, Spanish explorer	1540
Mississippi River	Visited[1]	Hernando de Soto, Spanish explorer	1541
Frobisher Bay	Visited[1]	Martin Frobisher, English seaman	1576
Maine Coast	Explored	Samuel de Champlain, French explorer	1604
Jamestown, Va.	Settled	John Smith, English colonist	1607
Hudson River	Explored	Henry Hudson, English navigator	1609

Country or place	Event	Explorer	Date
Hudson Bay (Canada)	Visited[1]	Henry Hudson	1610
Baffin Bay	Visited[1]	William Baffin, English navigator	1616
Lake Michigan	Navigated	Jean Nicolet, French explorer	1634
Arkansas River	Visited[1]	Jacques Marquette and Louis Jolliet, French explorers	1673
Mississippi River	Explored	Sieur de La Salle, French explorer	1682
Bering Strait	Visited[1]	Vitus Bering, Danish explorer	1728
Alaska	Visited[1]	Vitus Bering	1741
Mackenzie River (Canada)	Visited[1]	Sir Alexander Mackenzie, Scottish–Canadian explorer	1789
Northwest U. S.	Explored	Meriwether Lewis and William Clark	1804–06
Northeast Passage (Arctic Ocean)	Navigated	Nils Nordenskjöld, Swedish explorer	1879
Greenland	Explored	Robert Peary, American explorer	1892
Northwest Passage	Navigated	Roald Amundsen, Norwegian explorer	1906
SOUTH AMERICA			
Continent	Visited	Columbus, Italian	1498
Brazil	Visited[1]	Pedro Alvarez Cabral, Portuguese	1500
Peru	Conquered	Francisco Pizarro, Spanish explorer	1532–33
Amazon River	Explored	Francisco Orellana, Spanish explorer	1541
Cape Horn	Visited[1]	Willem C. Schouten, Dutch navigator	1615
OCEANIA			
Papua New Guinea	Visited	Jorge de Menezes, Portuguese explorer	1526
Australia	Visited	Abel Janszoon Tasman, Dutch navigator	1642
Tasmania	Visited[1]		
Australia	Explored	John McDouall Stuart, English explorer	1828
Australia	Explored	Robert Burke and William Wills, Australian explorers	1861
New Zealand	Sighted (and named)	Abel Janszoon Tasman	1642
New Zealand	Visited	James Cook, English navigator	1769
ARCTIC, ANTARCTIC, AND MISCELLANEOUS			
Africa, Middle East, South and Southeast Asia, Europe	Visited	Ibn Batuta, greatest Arab traveler	1325–49
Ocean exploration	Expedition	Magellan's ships circled globe	1519–22
Galápagos Islands	Visited	Diego de Rivadeneira, Spanish captain	1535
Spitsbergen	Visited	Willem Barents, Dutch navigator	1596
Antarctic Circle	Crossed	James Cook, English navigator	1773
Antarctica	Visited[1]	Nathaniel Palmer, U. S. whaler (archipelago) and Fabian Gottlieb von Bellingshausen, Russian admiral (mainland)	1820–21
Antarctica	Explored	Charles Wilkes, American explorer	1840
North Pole	Reached	Robert E. Peary, American explorer	1909
South Pole	Reached	Roald Amundsen, Norwegian explorer	1911

1. First European to reach the area.

The Continents

A continent is defined as a large unbroken land mass completely surrounded by water, although in some cases continents are (or were in part) connected by land bridges.

The hypothesis first suggested late in the 19th century was that the continents consist of lighter rocks that rest on heavier crustal material in about the same manner that icebergs float on water. That the rocks forming the continents are lighter than the material below them and under the ocean bottoms is now established. As a consequence of this fact, Alfred Wegener (for the first time in 1912) suggested that the continents are slowly moving, at a rate of about one yard per century, so that their relative positions are not rigidly fixed. Many geologists that were originally skeptical have come to accept this theory of Continental Drift.

When describing a continent, it is important to remember that there is a fundamental difference between a deep ocean, like the Atlantic, and shallow seas, like the Baltic and most of the North Sea, which are merely flooded portions of a continent. Another and entirely different point to remember is that political considerations have often overridden geographical facts when it came to naming continents.

Geographically speaking, Europe, including the British Isles, is a large western peninsula of the continent of Asia; and many geographers, when referring to Europe and Asia, speak of the Eurasian Continent. But traditionally, Europe is counted as a separate continent, with the Ural and the Caucasus mountains forming the line of demarcation between Europe and Asia.

To the south of Europe, Asia has an odd-shaped peninsula jutting westward, which has a large number of political subdivisions. The northern section is taken up by Turkey; to the south of Turkey there are Syria, Iraq, Israel, Jordan, Saudi Arabia, and a number of smaller Arab countries. All this is part of Asia. Traditionally, the island of Cyprus in the Mediterranean is also considered to be part of Asia, while the island of Crete is counted as European.

The large islands of Java, Borneo, and Sumatra and the smaller islands near them are counted as part of "tropical Asia," while New Guinea is counted as related to Australia. In the case of the Americas, the problem arises as to whether they should be considered one or two continents. There are good arguments on both sides, but since there is now a land bridge between North and South America (in the past it was often flooded) and since no part of the sea east of the land bridge is deep ocean, it is more logical to consider the Americas as one continent.

Politically, based mainly on history, the Americas are divided into North America (from the Arctic to the Mexican border), Central America (from Mexico to Panama, with the Caribbean islands), and South America. Greenland is considered a section of North America, while Iceland is traditionally counted as a European island because of its political ties with the Scandinavian countries.

The island groups in the Pacific are often called "Oceania," but this name does *not* imply that scientists consider them the remains of a continent.

The seven continents are North America, South America, Europe, Asia, Africa, Australia, and Antarctica.

Volcanoes of the World

About 500 volcanoes have had recorded eruptions within historical times. Almost two thirds of these are in the Northern Hemisphere. Most volcanoes occur at the boundaries of the earth's crustal plates, such as the famous "Ring of Fire" that surrounds the Pacific Ocean plate. Of the world's active volcanoes, about 60% are along the perimeter of the Pacific, about 17% on mid-oceanic islands, about 14% in an arc along the south of the Indonesian islands, about 9% in the Mediterranean area, Africa, and Asia Minor. Many of the world's volcanoes are submarine and have unrecorded eruptions.

Pacific "Ring of Fire"

NORTHWEST
Japan: At least 33 active vents.

Aso (5,223 ft; 1,592 m), on Kyushu, has one of the largest craters in the world.

Asama (over 8,300 ft; 2,530 m), on Honshu, is continuously active; violent eruption in 1783.

Azuma (nearly 7,700 ft; 2,347 m), on Honshu, erupted in 1900.

Chokai (7,300 ft; 2,225 m), on Honshu, erupted in 1974 after having been quiescent since 1861.

Fujiyama (Fujisan) (12,385 ft; 3,775 m), on Honshu, southwest of Tokyo. Symmetrical in outline, snow-covered. Regarded as a sacred mountain.

On-take (3,668 ft; 1,118 m), on peninsula of Kyushu. Strong smoke emissions and explosions began November 1973 and continued through 1974.

Mt. Unzen (4,500 ft; 1,371 m), on Kyushu erupted on June 3, 1991. Last eruption was in 1792.

Russia: Kamchatka peninsula, 14–18 active volcanoes. Klyuchevskaya (Kluchev) (15,500 ft; 4,724 m) reported active in 1974.

Kurile Islands: At least 13 active volcanoes and several submarine outbreaks.

SOUTHWEST
New Zealand: Mt. Tarawera (3,645 ft; 1,112 m), on North Island, had a severe eruption in 1886 that destroyed the famous Pink and White sinter terraces of Rotomahana, a hot lake.

Ngauruhoe (7,515 ft; 2,291 m), on North Island, emits steam and vapor constantly. Erupted 1974.

Mt. Raupehu (9,176 ft; 2,796 m), the highest peak on North Island, erupted on June 17, 1996. It previously erupted in September 1995 after being dormant for almost 50 years.

Papua New Guinea: Karkar Island (4,920 ft; 1,500 m). Mild eruptions in 1974.

Philippine Islands: About 100 eruptive centers; Hibok Hibok, on Camiguin, erupted September 1950 and again in December 1951, when about 750 were reported killed or missing; eruptions continued during 1952–53.

Taal (4,752 ft; 1,448 m), on Luzon. Major eruption in 1965 killed 190; erupted again in 1968.

Mt. Pinatubo (4,795 ft; 1,462 m), on Luzon erupted on June 9, 1991, causing the third largest eruption this century.

Volcano Islands: Mt. Suribachi (546 ft; 166 m), on Iwo Jima. A sulfurous steaming volcano. Raising of U.S. flag over Mt. Suribachi was one of the dramatic episodes of World War II.

NORTHEAST
Alaska: Mt. Wrangell (14,163 ft; 4,317 m) and Mt. Katmai (about 6,700 ft; 2,042 m). On June 6, 1912, a violent eruption (Novarupta) of Mt. Katmai occurred, during which the "Valley of Ten Thousand Smokes" was formed. It was the second largest eruption this century.

Aleutian Islands: There are 32 active vents known and numerous inactive cones. Akutan Island (over 4,000 ft; 1,220 m) erupted in 1974, with ash and debris rising over 300 ft.

Great Sitkin (5,741 ft; 1,750 m). Explosive activity February-September 1974, accompanied by earthquake originating at volcano that registered 2.3 on the Richter scale.

Augustine Island: Augustine volcano (4,000 ft; 1,220 m) erupted March 27, 1986. It last erupted in 1976.

California, Oregon, Washington: Lassen Peak (10,453 ft; 3,186 m) in California is one of two observed active volcanoes in the U.S. outside Alaska and Hawaii. The last period of activity was 1914–17. Mt. St. Helens (9,677 ft; 2,950 m) in the Cascade Range of southwest Washington became active on March 27, 1980, and erupted on May 18 after being inactive since 1857. From April 15 through May 1, 1986, weak activity began for the first time in two years. Other mountains of volcanic origin include Mt. Shasta (California), Mt. Hood (Oregon), Mt. Mazama (Oregon)—the mountain containing Crater Lake—Mt. Rainier (Washington), and Mt. Baker (Washington), which has been steaming since October 1975, but gives no sign of an impending eruption.

Continued on page 478

The Pacific Ocean "Ring of Fire"

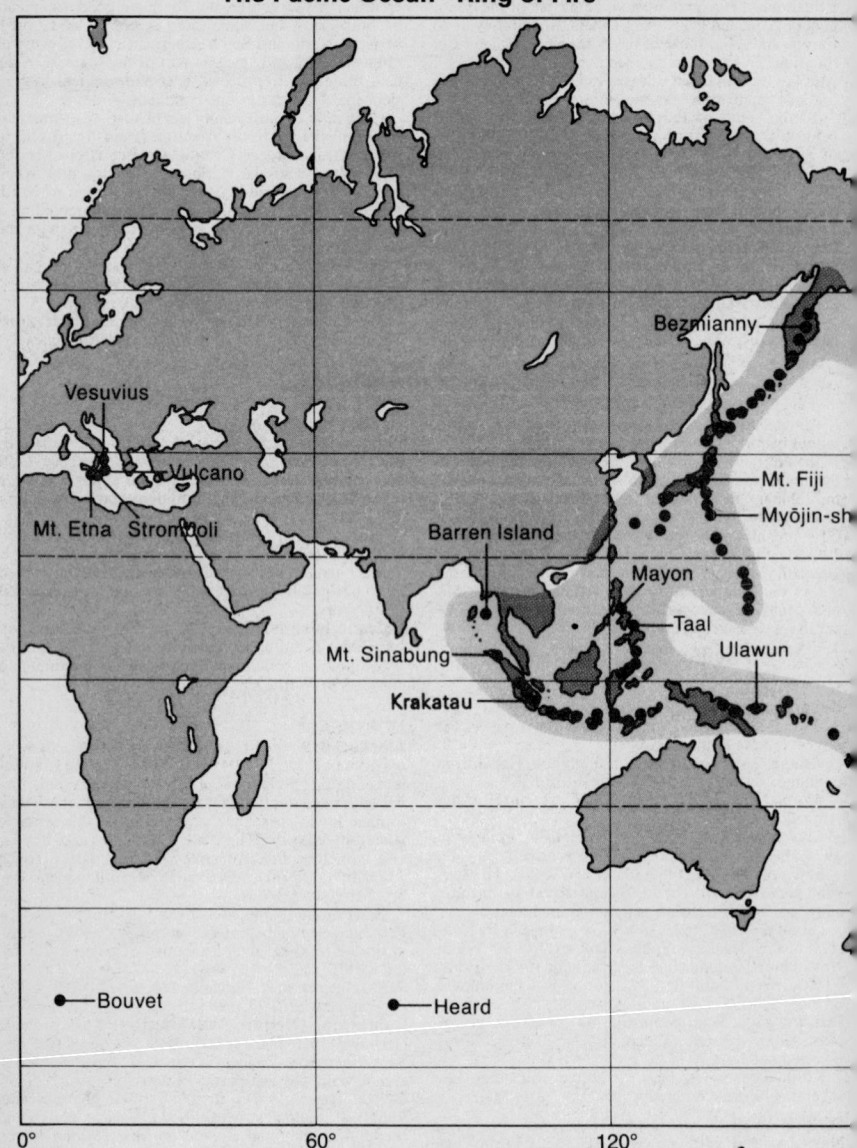

Vesuvius
Vulcano
Mt. Etna Stromboli
Bezmianny
Mt. Fiji
Myōjin-sh
Barren Island
Mayon
Taal
Ulawun
Mt. Sinabung
Krakatau

Bouvet Heard

0°   60°   120°

Giant West Coast Quake Forecast

Segments of the Washington–Oregon coastline are rising faster than normal—in millimeters per year—providing additional strong evidence that the area is due for a massive earthquake. In 1994, a team of scientists from the University of Oregon and the University of Washington found that many areas of the Western coastline are rising almost ten times faster than expected each year.

This indicates that pressure is building underground, a sign of an imminent earthquake. According to Oregon State University geologist, Robert Yeats, there is little doubt among other geologists that the

Source: U.S. Department of the Interior, U.S. Geological Survey.

Surtsey — Hekla

Mt. Katmai

haldin

Mt. St. Helens — Mt. Rainier
Mt. Shasta — Mt. Adams
Lassen Peak

Fayal

Mauna Loa

La Palma

auea

Parícutin

Fogo

Cerro Negro

Mt. Pelée

Irazú

Cotopaxi

El Misti

Tarawera

Azul

Burney

60°

40°

0°

40°

60°

120° 60° 0°

Northwest is due for a giant quake. The main question confronting scientists is whether the area known as the Cascadia subduction zone will buckle all at once or in smaller pieces.

The subduction zone is an area off the Northwestern coastline where two sections of the Earth's crust—the undersea Juan de Fuca plate and the North American plate—are pushing against each other. If the whole subduction zone goes at once, it may produce a massive quake stronger than the 1964 Alaska Good Friday earthquake, the strongest quake ever to strike North America. □

(Continued from p. 475)

SOUTHEAST

Chile and Argentina: About 25 active or potentially active vents.

Colombia: Huila (nearly 18,900 ft; 5,760 m), a vapor-emitting volcano, and Tolima (nearly 18,500 ft; 5,640 m). Eruption of Puracé (15,600 ft; 4,755 m) in 1949 killed 17 people. Nevado del Ruiz (16,200 ft; 4,938 m.), erupted November 13, 1985, sending torrential floods of mud and water engulfing the town of Armero and killing more than 22,000 people.

Ecuador: Cayambe (nearly 19,000 ft; 5,791 m). Almost on the equator.

Cotopaxi (19,344 ft; 5,896 m). Perhaps highest active volcano in the world. Possesses a beautifully formed cone.

Reventador (11,434 ft; 3,485 m). Observed in active state in late 1973.

El Salvador: Izalco ("beacon of Central America") (7,830 ft; 2,387 m) first appeared in 1770 and is still growing (erupted in 1950, 1956; last erupted in October-November 1966). San Salvador (6,187 ft; 1,886 m) had a violent eruption in 1923. Conchagua (about 4100 ft; 1,250 m) erupted with considerable damage early in 1947.

Guatemala: Santa Maria Quezaltenango (12,361 ft; 3,768 m). Frequent activity between 1902–08 and 1922–28 after centuries of quiescence. The 1902 eruption was this century's largest. Most dangerously active vent of Central America. Other volcanoes include Tajumulco (13,814 ft; 4,211 m) and Atitlán (11,633 ft; 3,546 m).

Mexico: Boquerón ("Big Mouth"), on San Benedicto, about 250 mi. south of Lower California. Newest volcano in Western Hemisphere, discovered September 1952.

Colima (about 14,000 ft; 4,270 m), in group that has had frequent eruptions.

Orizaba (Citlaltépetl) (18,701 ft; 5,700 m).

Parícutin (7,450 ft; 2,270 m). First appeared in February 1943. In less than a week, a cone over 140 ft high developed with a crater one quarter mile in circumference. Cone grew more than 1,500 ft (457 m) in 1943. Erupted in 1952.

Popocatépetl (17,887 ft; 5,452 m) last erupted on March 5, 1996, issuing a column of gas and ash 2,600 ft high.

El Chinchonal (7,300 ft; 1,005.6 m) about 15 miles from Pichucalco. Long inactive, it erupted in March 1982.

Nicaragua: Volcanoes include Telica, Coseguina, and Momotombo. Between Momotombo on the west shore of Lake Managua and Coseguina overlooking the Gulf of Fonseca, there is a string of more than 20 cones, many still active. One of these, Cerro Negro, erupted in July 1947, with considerable damage and loss of life, again in 1971, and most recently, in November–December 1995.

Concepción (5,100 ft; 1,555 m). Ash eruptions 1973–74.

Mid-oceanic Islands

Canary Islands: Pico de Teide (12,192 ft; 3,716 m), on Tenerife.

Cape Verde Islands: Fogo (nearly 9,300 ft; 2,835 m). Severe eruption in 1857, followed by eruptions in 1951 and 1995.

Caribbean: La Soufrière (4,813 ft; 1,467 m), on Basse-Terre, Guadeloupe. Also called La Grande Soufrière. Violent activity in July-August 1976 caused evacuation of 73,000 people; renewed activity in April 1977 again caused thousands to flee their homes.

La Soufrière (4,048 ft; 1,234 m), on St. Vincent. Major eruption in 1902 killed over 1,000 people.

Eruptions over 10-day period in April 1979 caused evacuation of northern two thirds of island.

Comoros: One volcano, Karthala (nearly 8,000 ft; 2,440 m), is visible for over 100 miles. Last erupted in 1904.

Hawaii: Mauna Loa ("Long Mountain") (13,680 ft; 4,170 m), on Hawaii, discharges from its high side vents more lava than any other volcano. Largest volcanic mountain in the world in cubic content. Area of crater is 3.7 sq mi. Violent eruption in June 1950, with lava pouring 25 miles into the ocean. Last major eruption in March 1984.

Mauna Kea (13,796 ft; 4,205 m), on Hawaii. Highest mountain in state.

Kilauea (4,090 ft; 1,247 m) is a vent in the side of Mauna Loa, but its eruptions are apparently independent. One of the most spectacular and active craters, with an area of 4.14 sq mi. An earthquake in July 1975 caused a major eruption. Eruptions began in September 1977 and reached a height of 980 ft (300 m). Activity ended October 1. Became active again in January 1983, exploding in earnest in March 1983 forming the volcanic cone Pu'u O, which has erupted periodically ever since. By May 1990, the lava flow had traveled 20 miles, obliterating the community of Kalapana on the southeast coast. By summer it had reached the Pacific Ocean. Lava flow continues in 1996.

Iceland: At least 25 volcanoes active in historical times. Very similar to Hawaiian volcanoes. Askja (over 4,700 ft; 1,433 m) is the largest. Hekla, one of the most active volcanoes in Iceland, erupted on January 17, 1990 after 10 years of repose.

Lesser Antilles (West Indian Islands): Mt. Pelée (over 4,500 ft; 1,370 m), northwestern Martinique. Eruption in 1902 destroyed town of St. Pierre and killed approximately 40,000 people.

Réunion Island (east of Madagascar): Piton de la Fournaise (Le Volcan) (8,610 ft; 2,624 m). Large lava flows. Last erupted in 1972.

Samoan Archipelago: Savai'i Island had an eruption in 1905 that caused considerable damage. Niuafoo (Tin Can), in the Tonga Islands, has a crater that extends 6,000 feet below and 600 feet above water.

Indonesia

Indonesia has 130 active volcanoes, more than any other country.

Mt. Merapi, Java (9,554 ft; 2,912 m), is the most active, and has had at least twelve eruptions causing fatalities. The last eruption began on November 22, 1994.

Mt. Bromo, Java (7,639 ft; 2,329 m), has erupted 53 times since 1804, most recently in 1984.

Mt. Semeru, Java (12,060 ft; 3,339 m), the highest mountain on the island, was active in 1996.

The most famous of Indonesian volcanoes is Krakatau, a small volcanic island in the Sunda Strait between Sumatra and Java. Its eruption in 1883 was one of the world's most violent. Giant forty-meter tidal waves hurled ashore blocks of coral weighing as much as 600 tons. More than 36,000 people were killed. Three months after the eruption a volcanic dust veil surrounded the Earth, acting as a solar filter that lowered the global temperature as much as 1.2°C in the year following the eruption. The most recent volcanic activity took place on the island of Anak Krakatau ("Child of Krakatau"—a remnant of the main island) in March 1995.

Mediterranean Area

Italy: Mt. Etna (10,902 ft; 3,323 m), eastern Sicily, the largest volcano in Europe. Two new craters formed in eruptions of February–March 1947. Worst eruption in 50 years occurred November 1950–January 1951. Forty-six eruptions have occurred in the last two decades, the last in 1995.

Stromboli (about 3,000 ft; 914 m), Lipari Islands (north of Sicily). Called "Lighthouse of the Mediterranean." Minor activity reported in 1996.

Mt. Vesuvius (4,200 ft; 1,280 m), southeast of Naples. Pompeii buried by an eruption, A.D. 79. Only active volcano on European mainland.

Antarctica

The discovery of two small active volcanoes in 1982 brings to five the total number known on Antarctica. The new ones, 30 miles apart, are on the Weddell Sea side of the Antarctic Peninsula. The largest, Mt. Erebus (13,000 ft; 3,962 m), rises from McMurdo Sound. Mt. Melbourne (9,000 ft; 2,743 m) is in Victoria Land. The fifth, off the northern tip of the Antarctic Peninsula, is a crater known as Deception Island.

Principal Types of Volcanoes

(*Source:* U.S. Dept. of Interior, Geological Survey.)

Geologists generally group volcanoes into four main kinds—cinder cones, composite volcanoes, shield volcanoes, and lava domes.

Cinder Cones

Cinder cones are the simplest type of volcano. They are built from particles and blobs of congealed lava ejected from a single vent. As the gas-charged lava is blown violently into the air, it breaks into small fragments that solidify and fall as cinders around the vent to form a circular or oval cone. Most cinder cones have a bowl-shaped crater at the summit and rarely rise more than a thousand feet or so above their surroundings. Cinder cones are numerous in western North America as well as throughout other volcanic terrains of the world.

Composite Volcanoes

Some of the Earth's grandest mountains are composite volcanoes—sometimes called *stratovolcanoes.* They are typically steep-sided, symmetrical cones of large dimension built of alternating layers of lava flows, volcanic ash, cinders, blocks, and bombs and may rise as much as 8,000 feet above their bases. Some of the most conspicuous and beautiful mountains in the world are composite volcanoes, including Mt. Fuji in Japan, Mt. Cotopaxi in Ecuador, Mt. Shasta in California, Mt. Hood in Oregon, and Mt. St. Helens and Mt. Rainier in Washington.

Most composite volcanoes have a crater at the summit which contains a central vent or a clustered group of vents. Lavas either flow through breaks in the crater wall or issue from fissures on the flanks of the cone. Lava, solidified within the fissures, forms *dikes* that act as ribs which greatly strengthen the cone.

The essential feature of a composite volcano is a conduit system through which magma from a reservoir deep in the Earth's crust rises to the surface. The volcano is built up by the accumulation of material erupted through the conduit and increases in size as lava, cinders, ash, etc., are added to its slopes.

Shield Volcanoes

Shield volcanoes, the third type of volcano, are built almost entirely of fluid lava flows. Flow after flow pours out in all directions from a central summit vent, or group of vents, building a broad, gently sloping cone of flat, domical shape, with a profile much like that of a warrior's shield. They are built up slowly by the accretion of thousands of flows of highly fluid basaltic (from *basalt,* a hard, dense dark volcanic rock) lava that spread widely over great distances, and then cool as thin, gently dipping sheets. Lavas also commonly erupt from vents along fractures (rift zones) that develop on the flanks of the cone. Some of the largest volcanoes in the world are shield volcanoes. In northern California and Oregon, many shield volcanoes have diameters of 3 or 4 miles and heights of 1,500 to 2,000 feet. The Hawaiian Islands are composed of linear chains of these volcanoes, including Kilauea and Mauna Loa on the island of Hawaii.

In some shield-volcano eruptions, basaltic lava pours out quietly from long fissures instead of central vents and floods the surrounding countryside with lava flow upon lava flow, forming broad plateaus. Lava plateaus of this type can be seen in Iceland, southeastern Washington, eastern Oregon, and southern Idaho.

Lava Domes

Volcanic or lava domes are formed by relatively small, bulbous masses of lava too viscous to flow any great distance; consequently, on extrusion, the lava piles over and around its vent. A dome grows largely by expansion from within. As it grows its outer surface cools and hardens, then shatters, spilling loose fragments down its sides. Some domes form craggy knobs or spines over the volcanic vent, whereas others form short, steep-sided lava flows known as "coulees." Volcanic domes commonly occur within the craters or on the flanks of large composite volcanoes. The nearly circular Novarupta Dome that formed during the 1912 eruption of Katmai Volcano, Alaska, measures 800 feet across and 200 feet high. The internal structure of this dome—defined by layering of lava fanning upward and outward from the center—indicates that it grew largely by expansion from within. Mt. Pelée in Martinique, West Indies, and Lassen Peak and Mono domes in California, are examples of lava domes.

Submarine Volcanoes

Submarine volcanoes and volcanic vents are common features on certain zones of the ocean floor. Some are active at the present time and, in shallow water, disclose their presence by blasting steam and rock-debris high above the surface of the sea. Many others lie at such great depths that the tremendous weight of the water above them results in high, confining pressure and prevents the formation and release of steam and gases. Even very large, deepwater eruptions may not disturb the ocean floor.

The famous black sand beaches of Hawaii were created virtually instantaneously by the violent interaction between hot lava and sea water.

Earth's Greatest Volcanic Field

The largest known concentration of active volcanoes on earth was discovered by scientists aboard the research vessel *Melville* during the period November 1992 to January 1993. The vast volcanic cluster is situated under the South Pacific Ocean, 600 miles northwest of Easter Island.

A total of 1,133 seamounts and volcanic cones were found in the area which is about the size of New York State. Some of them rise to a height of almost 7,000 feet and their peaks are 2,500 to 5,000 feet below the ocean's surface.

Plate-Tectonics Theory—The Lithosphere Plates of the Earth

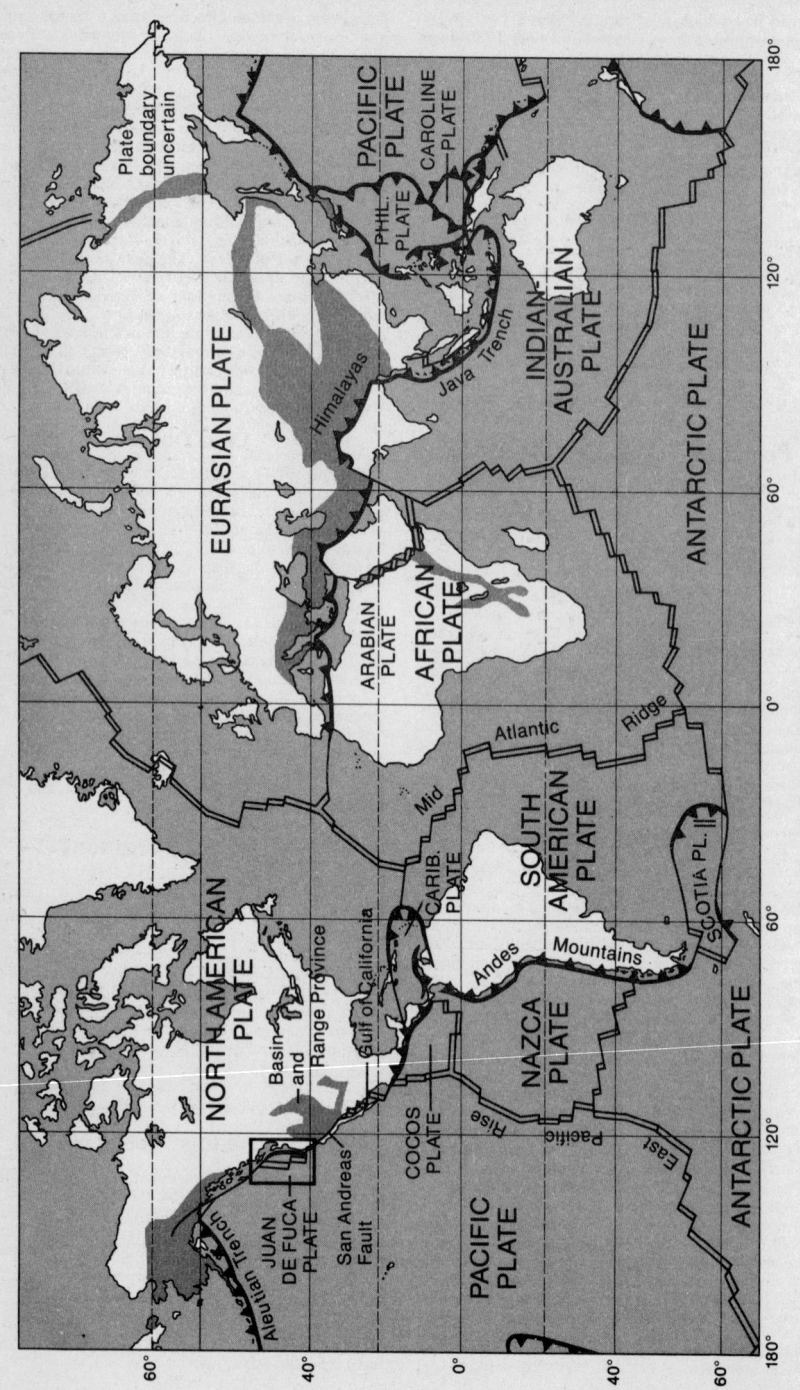

Source: U.S. Department of the Interior, U.S. Geological Survey.

World Population, Land Areas, and Elevations

Area	Estimated population, mid-1995	Approximate land area sq mi.	Percent of total land area	Population density per sq mi.	Elevation, feet	
					Highest	Lowest
WORLD	5,734,106,000	58,433,000	100.0	98.1 [1]	Mt. Everest, Asia, 29,028	Dead Sea, Asia, 1,290 below sea level
ASIA, incl. Philippines, Indonesia, and European and Asiatic Turkey; excl. Asiatic former U.S.S.R	3,403,451,000	10,644,000	18.2	319.7	Mt. Everest, Tibet-Nepal, 29,028	Dead Sea, Israel-Jordan, 1,290 below sea level
AFRICA	721,472,000	11,707,000	20.0	61.2	Mt. Kilimanjaro, Tanzania, 19,340	Lake Assal, Djibouti, 571 below sea level
NORTH AMERICA, including Hawaii, Central America, and Caribbean region	454,187,000	9,360,000	16.0	48.5	Mt. McKinley, Alaska, 20,320	Death Valley, Calif., 282 below sea level
SOUTH AMERICA	319,553,000	6,883,000	11.8	46.2	Mt. Aconcagua, Arg.-Chile, 23,034	Valdes Peninsula, 131 below sea level
ANTARCTICA	—	6,000,000	10.3	—	Vinson Massif, Sentinel Range, 16,863	Sea level
EUROPE, incl. Iceland; excl. European former U.S.S.R. and European Turkey	509,254,000	1,905,000	3.3	267.3	Mont Blanc, France, 15,781	Sea level
OCEANIA, incl. Australia, New Zealand, Melanesia, Micronesia, and Polynesia[2]	28,680,000	3,284,000	5.6	8.7	Wilhelm, Papua New Guinea, 14,793	Lake Eyre, Australia, 38 below sea level
Former U.S.S.R., both European and Asiatic	297,508,000	8,647,000	14.8	34.4	Communism Peak, Pamir, 24,590	Caspian Sea, 96 below sea level

1. In computing density per square mile, the area of Antarctica is omitted. 2. Although Hawaii is geographically part of Oceania, its population is included in the population figure for North America. *Source:* U.S. Bureau of the Census, International Data Base, for population figures. NOTE: The land area of Asia including the Asiatic portion of the former U.S.S.R. is 17,240,000 sq miles.

Plate-Tectonics Theory

(*Source:* U.S. Dept. of the Interior, Geological Survey.)

According to the generally accepted "plate-tectonics" theory, scientists believe that the Earth's surface is broken into a number of shifting slabs or plates, which average about 50 miles in thickness. These plates move relative to one another above a hotter, deeper, more mobile zone at average rates as great as a few inches per year. Most of the world's active volcanoes are located along or near the boundaries between shifting plates and are called "plate-boundary" volcanoes. However, some active volcanoes are not associated with plate boundaries, and many of these so-called "intra-plate" volcanoes form roughly linear chains in the interior of some oceanic plates. The Hawaiian Islands provide perhaps the best example of an "intra-plate" volcanic chain, developed by the northwest-moving Pacific plate passing over an inferred "hot spot" that initiates the magma-generation and volcano-formation process. The peripheral areas of the Pacific Ocean Basin, containing the boundaries of several plates, are dotted by many active volcanoes that form the so-called "Ring of Fire." The "Ring" provides excellent examples of "plate-boundary" volcanoes, including Mt. St. Helens.

The accompanying figure on page 480 shows the boundaries of lithosphere plates that are active at present. The double lines indicate zones of spreading from which plates are moving apart. The lines with barbs show zones of underthrusting (subduction), where one plate is sliding beneath another. The barbs on the lines indicate the overriding plate. The single line defines a strike-slip fault along which plates are sliding horizontally past one another. The stippled areas indicate a part of a continent, exclusive of that along a plate boundary, which is undergoing active extensional, compressional, or strike-slip faulting.

The Severity of an Earthquake

(*Source:* U.S. Dept. of the Interior, Geological Survey.)

The Richter Magnitude Scale

The Richter magnitude scale was developed in 1935 by Charles F. Richter of the California Institute of Technology as a mathematical device to compare the size of earthquakes. The magnitude of an earthquake is determined from the logarithm of the amplitude of waves recorded by seismographs. Adjustments are included in the magnitude formula to compensate for the variation in the distance between the various seismographs and the epicenter of the earthquakes. On the Richter Scale, magnitude is expressed in whole numbers and decimal fractions. For example, a magnitude of 5.3 might be computed for a moderate earthquake, and a strong earthquake might be rated as magnitude 6.3. Great earthquakes, such as the 1906 earthquake in San Francisco, have magnitudes of 8.0 or higher. Although the Richter Scale has no upper limit, the largest known shocks have had magnitudes in the 8.8 to 8.9 range.

The Richter Scale is not used to express damage. An earthquake in a densely populated area which results in many deaths and considerable damage may have the same magnitude as a shock in a remote area that does nothing more than frighten the wildlife. Large-magnitude earthquakes that occur beneath the oceans may not even be felt by humans.

The Richter scale has been largely abandoned by seismologists because it isn't very accurate for the biggest earthquakes, those in the range of 8 or 9. Because it is based on readings taken close to quakes, 100 miles or so, it is less precise in other parts of the world where the nearest seismograph may be many hundreds of miles away.

New ways have been developed to rate the magnitude of the quake in numbers similar to the familiar Richter scale. The U.S. Geological Survey's National Earthquake Information Center in Golden, Colorado, uses surface-wave magnitude which measures the seismic waves crackling around the Earth's surface. Other seismologists use a measure known as the moment magnitude which is based on the size of the fault on which an earthquake occurs and the amount the earth slips. So nowadays, when most seismologists announce a magnitude number, they no longer say "on the Richter scale."

The Modified Mercalli Intensity Scale

The effect of an earthquake on the Earth's surface is called the intensity. The intensity scale consists of a series of certain key responses such as people awakening, movement of furniture, damage to chimneys, and finally—total destruction. Although numerous *intensity scales* have been developed over the last several hundred years to evaluate the effects of earthquakes, the one currently used in the United States is the Modified Mercalli (MM) Intensity Scale. It was developed in 1931 by the American seismologists Harry Wood and Frank Neumann. This scale, composed of 12 increasing levels of intensity that range from imperceptible shaking to catastrophic destruction, is designated by Roman numerals. It does not have a mathematical basis; instead it is an arbitrary ranking based on observed effects.

The Modified Mercalli Intensity value assigned to a specific site after an earthquake has a more meaningful measure of severity to the nonscientist than the magnitude because intensity refers to the effects actually experienced at that place. After the occurrence of widely-felt earthquakes, the Geological Survey mails questionnaires to postmasters in the disturbed area requesting the information so that intensity values can be assigned. The results of this postal canvass and information furnished by other sources are used to assign an intensity value, and to compile isoseismal maps that show the extent of various levels of intensity within the felt area. The maximum observed intensity generally occurs near the epicenter.

The *lower* numbers of the intensity scale generally deal with the manner in which the earthquake is felt by people. The *higher* numbers of the scale are based on observed structural damage. Structural engineers usually contribute information for assigning intensity values of VIII or above.

The Mexico City earthquake on September 19, 1985, was assigned an intensity of IX on the Mercalli Scale.

The following is an abbreviated description of the 12 levels of Modified Mercalli intensity.

I. Not felt except by a very few under especially favorable conditions.

II. Felt only by a few persons at rest, especially on upper floors of buildings. Delicately suspended objects may swing.

III. Felt quite noticeably by persons indoors, especially on upper floors of buildings. Many people do not recognize it as an earthquake. Standing motor cars may rock slightly. Vibration similar to the passing of a truck. Duration estimated.

IV. Felt indoors by many, outdoors by few during the day. At night, some awakened. Dishes, windows, doors disturbed; walls make cracking sound. Sensation like heavy truck striking building. Standing motor cars rocked noticeably.

V. Felt by nearly everyone; many awakened. Some dishes, windows broken. Unstable objects overturned. Pendulum clocks may stop.

VI. Felt by all, many frightened. Some heavy furniture moved; a few instances of fallen plaster. Damage slight.

VII. Damage negligible in buildings of good design and construction; slight to moderate in well-built ordinary structures; considerable damage in poorly built or badly designed structures; some chimneys broken.

VIII. Damage slight in specially designed structures; considerable damage in ordinary substantial buildings with partial collapse. Damage great in poorly built structures. Fall of chimneys, factory stacks, columns, monuments, walls. Heavy furniture overturned.

IX. Damage considerable in specially designed structures; well-designed frame structures thrown out of plumb. Damage great in substantial buildings, with partial collapse. Buildings shifted off foundations.

X. Some well-built wooden structures destroyed; most masonry and frame structures destroyed with foundations. Rails bent.

XI. Few, if any (masonry) structures remain standing. Bridges destroyed. Rails bent greatly.

XII. Damage total. Lines of sight and level are distorted. Objects thrown into the air.

Latitude and Longitude of World Cities

(and time corresponding to 12:00 noon, eastern standard time)

City	Lat. °	′	Long. °	′	Time
Aberdeen, Scotland	57	9 n	2	9 w	5:00 p.m.
Adelaide, Australia	34	55 s	138	36 e	2:30 a.m. [1]
Algiers	36	50 n	3	0 e	6:00 p.m.
Amsterdam	52	22 n	4	53 e	6:00 p.m.
Ankara, Turkey	39	55 n	32	55 e	7:00 p.m.
Asunción, Paraguay	25	15 s	57	40 w	1:00 p.m.
Athens	37	58 n	23	43 e	7:00 p.m.
Auckland, New Zealand	36	52 s	174	45 e	5:00 a.m. [1]
Bangkok, Thailand	13	45 n	100	30 e	midnight
Barcelona	41	23 n	2	9 e	6:00 p.m.
Beijing	39	55 n	116	25 e	1:00 a.m. [1]
Belém, Brazil	1	28 s	48	29 w	2:00 p.m.
Belfast, Northern Ireland	54	37 n	5	56 w	5:00 p.m.
Belgrade, Yugoslavia	44	52 n	20	32 e	6:00 p.m.
Berlin	52	30 n	13	25 e	6:00 p.m.
Birmingham, England	52	25 n	1	55 w	5:00 p.m.
Bogotá, Colombia	4	32 n	74	15 w	12:00 noon
Bombay	19	0 n	72	48 e	10:30 p.m.
Bordeaux, France	44	50 n	0	31 w	6:00 p.m.
Bremen, Germany	53	5 n	8	49 e	6:00 p.m.
Brisbane, Australia	27	29 s	153	8 e	3:00 a.m. [1]
Bristol, England	51	28 n	2	35 w	5:00 p.m.
Brussels	50	52 n	4	22 e	6:00 p.m.
Bucharest	44	25 n	26	7 e	7:00 p.m.
Budapest	47	30 n	19	5 e	6:00 p.m.
Buenos Aires	34	35 s	58	22 w	2:00 p.m.
Cairo	30	2 n	31	21 e	7:00 p.m.
Calcutta	22	34 n	88	24 e	10:30 p.m.
Canton, China	23	7 n	113	15 e	1:00 a.m. [1]
Cape Town, South Africa	33	55 s	18	22 e	7:00 p.m.
Caracas, Venezuela	10	28 n	67	2 w	1:00 p.m.
Cayenne, French Guiana	4	49 n	52	18 w	1:00 p.m.
Chihuahua, Mexico	28	37 n	106	5 w	11:00 a.m.
Chongqing, China	29	46 n	106	34 e	1:00 a.m. [1]
Copenhagen	55	40 n	12	34 e	6:00 p.m.
Córdoba, Argentina	31	28 s	64	10 w	2:00 p.m.
Dakar, Senegal	14	40 n	17	28 w	5:00 p.m.
Darwin, Australia	12	28 s	130	51 e	2:30 a.m. [1]
Djibouti	11	30 n	43	3 e	8:00 p.m.
Dublin	53	20 n	6	15 w	5:00 p.m.
Durban, South Africa	29	53 s	30	53 e	7:00 p.m.
Edinburgh, Scotland	55	55 n	3	10 w	5:00 p.m.
Frankfurt	50	7 n	8	41 e	6:00 p.m.
Georgetown, Guyana	6	45 n	58	15 w	1:15 p.m.
Glasgow, Scotland	55	50 n	4	15 w	5:00 p.m.
Guatemala City, Guatemala	14	37 n	90	31 w	11:00 a.m.
Guayaquil, Ecuador	2	10 s	79	56 w	12:00 noon
Hamburg	53	33 n	10	2 e	6:00 p.m.
Hammerfest, Norway	70	38 n	23	38 e	6:00 p.m.
Havana	23	8 n	82	23 w	12:00 noon
Helsinki, Finland	60	10 n	25	0 e	7:00 p.m.
Hobart, Tasmania	42	52 s	147	19 e	3:00 a.m. [1]
Iquique, Chile	20	10 s	70	7 w	1:00 p.m.
Irkutsk, Russia	52	30 n	104	20 e	1:00 a.m. [1]
Jakarta, Indonesia	6	16 s	106	48 e	0:30 a.m. [1]
Johannesburg, South Africa	26	12 s	28	4 e	7:00 p.m.
Kingston, Jamaica	17	59 n	76	49 w	12:00 noon
Kinshasa, Zaire	4	18 s	15	17 e	6:00 p.m.

City	Lat. °	′	Long. °	′	Time
La Paz, Bolivia	16	27 s	68	22 w	1:00 p.m.
Leeds, England	53	45 n	1	30 w	5:00 p.m.
Lima, Peru	12	0 s	77	2 w	2:00 noon
Lisbon	38	44 n	9	9 w	5:00 p.m.
Liverpool, England	53	25 n	3	0 w	5:00 p.m.
London	51	32 n	0	5 w	5:00 p.m.
Lyons, France	45	45 n	4	50 e	6:00 p.m.
Madrid	40	26 n	3	42 w	6:00 p.m.
Manchester, England	53	30 n	2	15 w	5:00 p.m.
Manila	14	35 n	120	57 e	1:00 a.m. [1]
Marseilles, France	43	20 n	5	20 e	6:00 p.m.
Mazatlán, Mexico	23	12 n	106	25 w	10:00 a.m.
Mecca, Saudi Arabia	21	29 n	39	45 e	8:00 p.m.
Melbourne	37	47 s	144	58 e	3:00 a.m. [1]
Mexico City	19	26 n	99	7 w	11:00 a.m.
Milan, Italy	45	27 n	9	10 e	6:00 p.m.
Montevideo, Uruguay	34	53 s	56	10 w	2:00 p.m.
Moscow	55	45 n	37	36 e	8:00 p.m.
Munich, Germany	48	8 n	11	35 e	6:00 p.m.
Nagasaki, Japan	32	48 n	129	57 e	2:00 a.m. [1]
Nagoya, Japan	35	7 n	136	56 e	2:00 a.m. [1]
Nairobi, Kenya	1	25 s	36	55 e	8:00 p.m.
Nanjing (Nanking), China	32	3 n	118	53 e	1:00 a.m. [1]
Naples, Italy	40	50 n	14	15 e	6:00 p.m.
Newcastle-on-Tyne, England	54	58 n	1	37 w	5:00 p.m.
Odessa, Ukraine	46	27 n	30	48 e	8:00 p.m.
Osaka, Japan	34	32 n	135	30 e	2:00 a.m. [1]
Oslo	59	57 n	10	42 e	6:00 p.m.
Panama City, Panama	8	58 n	79	32 w	12:00 noon
Paramaribo, Surinam	5	45 n	55	15 w	1:30 p.m.
Paris	48	48 n	2	20 e	6:00 p.m.
Perth, Australia	31	57 s	115	52 e	1:00 a.m. [1]
Plymouth, England	50	25 n	4	5 w	5:00 p.m.
Port Moresby, Papua New Guinea	9	25 s	147	8 e	3:00 a.m. [1]
Prague	50	5 n	14	26 e	6:00 p.m.
Reykjavik, Iceland	64	4 n	21	58 w	4:00 p.m.
Rio de Janeiro	22	57 s	43	12 w	2:00 p.m.
Rome	41	54 n	12	27 e	6:00 p.m.
Salvador, Brazil	12	56 s	38	27 w	2:00 p.m.
Santiago, Chile	33	28 s	70	45 w	1:00 p.m.
St. Petersburg	59	56 n	30	18 e	8:00 p.m.
Sao Paulo, Brazil	23	31 s	46	31 w	2:00 p.m.
Shanghai, China	31	10 n	121	28 e	1:00 a.m. [1]
Singapore	1	14 n	103	55 e	0:30 a.m. [1]
Sofia, Bulgaria	42	40 n	23	20 e	7:00 p.m.
Stockholm	59	17 n	18	3 e	6:00 p.m.
Sydney, Australia	34	0 s	151	0 e	3:00 a.m. [1]
Tananarive, Madagascar	18	50 s	47	33 e	8:00 p.m.
Teheran, Iran	35	45 n	51	45 e	8:30 p.m.
Tokyo	35	40 n	139	45 e	2:00 a.m. [1]
Tripoli, Libya	32	57 n	13	12 e	7:00 p.m.
Venice	45	26 n	12	20 e	6:00 p.m.
Veracruz, Mexico	19	10 n	96	10 w	11:00 a.m.
Vienna	48	14 n	16	20 e	6:00 p.m.
Vladivostok, Russia	43	10 n	132	0 e	3:00 a.m. [1]
Warsaw	52	14 n	21	0 e	6:00 p.m.
Wellington, New Zealand	41	17 s	174	47 e	5:00 a.m. [1]
Yangon, Myanmar	16	50 n	96	0 e	11:30 p.m.
Zürich	47	21 n	8	31 e	6:00 p.m.

1. On the following day.

Highest Mountain Peaks of the World

(For U.S. peaks, see Index)

Mountain peak	Range	Location	Height feet	Height meters
Everest	Himalayas	Nepal-Tibet	29,028[1]	8,848
Godwin Austen (K-2)	Karakoram	Kashmir	28,250[1]	8,611
Kanchenjunga	Himalayas	Nepal-Sikkim	28,208	8,598
Lhotse	Himalayas	Nepal-Tibet	27,890	8,501
Makalu	Himalayas	Tibet-Nepal	27,790	8,470
Dhaulagiri I	Himalayas	Nepal	26,810	8,172
Manaslu	Himalayas	Nepal	26,760	8,156
Cho Oyu	Himalayas	Nepal	26,750	8,153
Nanga Parbat	Himalayas	Kashmir	26,660	8,126
Annapurna I	Himalayas	Nepal	26,504	8,078
Gasherbrum I	Karakoram	Kashmir	26,470	8,068
Broad Peak	Karakoram	Kashmir	26,400	8,047
Gasherbrum II	Karakoram	Kashmir	26,360	8,033
Gosainthan	Himalayas	Tibet	26,291	8,013
Gasherbrum III	Karakoram	Kashmir	26,090	7,952
Annapurna II	Himalayas	Nepal	26,041	7,937
Gasherbrum IV	Karakoram	India	26,000	7,925
Kangbachen	Himalayas	Nepal	25,925	7,902
Gyachung Kang	Himalayas	Nepal	25,910	7,897
Himal Chuli	Himalayas	Nepal	25,895	7,893
Disteghil Sar	Karakoram	Kashmir	25,868	7,885
Nuptse	Himalayas	Nepal	25,850	7,829
Kunyang Kish	Karakoram	Kashmir	25,760	7,852
Dakum (Peak 29)	Himalayas	Nepal	25,760	7,852
Masherbrum	Karakoram	Kashmir	25,660	7,821
Nanda Devi	Himalayas	India	25,645	7,817
Chomolonzo	Himalayas	Nepal-Tibet	25,640	7,815
Rakaposhi	Karakoram	Kashmir	25,550	7,788
Batura	Karakoram	Kashmir	25,540	7,785
Kanjut Sar	Karakoram	Kashmir	25,460	7,760
Kamet	Himalayas	India-Tibet	25,447	7,756
Namche Barwa	Himalayas	Tibet	25,445	7,756
Dhaulagiri II	Himalayas	Nepal	25,427	7,750
Saltoro Kangri	Karakoram	India	25,400	7,742
Gurla Mandhata	Himalayas	Tibet	25,355	7,728
Ulugh Muztagh	Kunlun	Tibet	25,341	7,724
Trivor	Karakoram	Kashmir	25,330	7,721
Jannu	Himalayas	Nepal	25,294	7,710
Tirich Mir	Hindu Kush	Pakistan	25,230	7,690
Saser Kangri	Karakoram	India	25,170	7,672
Makalu II	Himalayas	Nepal	25,130	7,660
Chogolisa	Karakoram	India	25,110	7,654
Dhaulagiri IV	Himalayas	Nepal	25,064	7,639
Fang	Himalayas	Nepal	25,013	7,624
Kula Kangri	Himalayas	Bhutan	24,783	7,554
Changtse	Himalayas	Tibet	24,780	7,553
Muztagh Ata	Muztagh Ata	China	24,757	7,546
Skyang Kangri	Himalayas	Kashmir	24,750	7,544
Communism Peak	Pamir	Tajikistan	24,590	7,495
Victory Peak	Pamir	Tajikistan	24,406	7,439
Sia Kangri	Himalayas	Kashmir	24,340	7,419
Chamlang	Himalayas	Nepal	24,012	7,319
Alung Gangri	Himalayas	Tibet	23,999	7,315
Chomo Lhari	Himalayas	Tibet-Bhutan	23,996	7,314
Muztagh (K-5)	Kunlun	China	23,891	7,282
Amne Machin	Kunlun	China	23,490	7,160
Gaurisankar	Himalayas	Nepal-Tibet	23,440	7,145
Lenin Peak	Tien-Shan	Tajikistan/Kyrgyzstan	23,405	7,134
Korzhenevski Peak	Pamir	Tajikistan	23,310	7,105
Kangto	Himalayas	Tibet	23,260	7,090
Dunagiri	Himalayas	India	23,184	7,066
Pauhunri	Himalayas	India-Tibet	23,180	7,065
Aconcagua	Andes	Argentina-Chile	23,034	7,021
Revolution Peak	Pamir	Tajikistan	22,880	6,974
Kangchenjhan	Himalayas	India	22,700	6,919
Siniolchu	Himalayas	India	22,620	6,895

Mountain peak	Range	Location	Height feet	Height meters
Ojos des Salado	Andes	Argentina-Chile	22,588	6,885
Bonete	Andes	Argentina-Chile	22,546	6,872
Simvuo	Himalayas	India	22,346	6,811
Tup	Andes	Argentina	22,309	6,800
Kungpu	Himalayas	Bhutan	22,300	6,797
Falso-Azufre	Andes	Argentina-Chile	22,277	6,790
Moscow Peak	Pamir	Tajikistan	22,260	6,785
Veladero	Andes	Argentina	22,244	6,780
Pissis	Andes	Argentina	22,241	6,779
Mercedario	Andes	Argentina-Chile	22,211	6,770
Huascarán	Andes	Peru	22,198	6,766
Tocorpuri	Andes	Bolivia-Chile	22,162	6,755
Karl Marx Peak	Pamir	Tajikistan	22,067	6,726
Llullaillaco	Andes	Argentina-Chile	22,057	6,723
Libertador	Andes	Argentina	22,047	6,720
Kailas	Himalayas	Tibet	22,027	6,714
Lingtren	Himalayas	Nepal-Tibet	21,972	6,697
Incahuasi	Andes	Argentina-Chile	21,719	6,620
Carnicero	Andes	Peru	21,689	6,611
Kurumda	Pamir	Tajikistan	21,686	6,610
Garmo Peak	Pamir	Tajikistan	21,637	6,595
Sajama	Andes	Bolivia	21,555	6,570
Ancohuma	Andes	Bolivia	21,490	6,550
El Muerto	Andes	Argentina-Chile	21,456	6,540
Nacimiento	Andes	Argentina	21,302	6,493
Illimani	Andes	Bolivia	21,184	6,457
Antofalla	Andes	Argentina-Chile	21,129	6,440
Coropuña	Andes	Peru	21,079	6,425
Cuzco (Ausangate)	Andes	Peru	20,995	6,399
Toro	Andes	Argentina-Chile	20,932	6,380
Parinacota	Andes	Bolivia-Chile	20,768	6,330
Chimboraso	Andes	Ecuador	20,702	6,31
Salcantay	Andes	Peru	20,575	6,271
General Manuel Belgrano	Andes	Argentina	20,505	6,250
Chañi	Andes	Argentina	20,341	6,200
Caca Aca	Andes	Bolivia	20,328	6,196
McKinley	Alaska	Alaska	20,320	6,194
Vudor Peak	Pamir	Tajikistan	20,118	6,132
Condoriri	Andes	Bolivia	20,095	6,125
Solimana	Andes	Peru	20,069	6,117
Nevada	Andes	Argentina	20,023	6,103

1. India gives the height as 29,028 feet (8,848 meters), however, in 1987, an Italian expedition recalculated its height to be 29,108 feet and K-2 to be 29,064 feet.

Oceans and Seas

Name	Area sq mi.	Area sq km	Average depth feet	Average depth meters	Greatest known depth feet	Greatest known depth meters	Place greatest known depth
Pacific Ocean	64,000,000	165,760,000	13,215	4,028	36,198	11,033	Mariana Trench
Atlantic Ocean	31,815,000	82,400,000	12,880	3,926	30,246	9,219	Puerto Rico Trough
Indian Ocean	25,300,000	65,526,700	13,002	3,963	24,460	7,455	Sunda Trench
Arctic Ocean	5,440,200	14,090,000	3,953	1,205	18,456	5,625	77° 45′ N; 175° W
Mediterranean Sea[1]	1,145,100	2,965,800	4,688	1,429	15,197	4,632	Off Cape Matapan, Greece
Caribbean Sea	1,049,500	2,718,200	8,685	2,647	22,788	6,946	Off Cayman Islands
South China Sea	895,400	2,319,000	5,419	1,652	16,456	5,016	West of Luzon
Bering Sea	884,900	2,291,900	5,075	1,547	15,659	4,773	Off Buldir Island
Gulf of Mexico	615,000	1,592,800	4,874	1,486	12,425	3,787	Sigsbee Deep
Okhotsk Sea	613,800	1,589,700	2,749	838	12,001	3,658	146° 10′ E; 46° 50′ N
East China Sea	482,300	1,249,200	617	188	9,126	2,782	25° 16′ N; 125° E
Hudson Bay	475,800	1,232,300	420	128	600	183	Near entrance
Japan Sea	389,100	1,007,800	4,429	1,350	12,276	3,742	Central Basin
Andaman Sea	308,100	797,700	2,854	870	12,392	3,777	Off Car Nicobar Island
North Sea	222,100	575,200	308	94	2,165	660	Skagerrak
Red Sea	169,100	438,000	1,611	491	7,254	2,211	Off Port Sudan
Baltic Sea	163,000	422,200	180	55	1,380	421	Off Gotland

1. Includes Black Sea and Sea of Azov. NOTE: For Caspian Sea, *see* Large Lakes of World elsewhere in this section.

World's Greatest Man-Made Lakes[1]

Name of dam	Location	Millions of cubic meters	Thousands of acre-feet	Year completed
Owen Falls	Uganda	204,800	166,000	1954
Kariba	Zimbabwe	181,592	147,218	1959
Bratsk	Siberia	169,270	137,220	1964
High Aswan (Sadd-el-Aali)	Egypt	168,000	136,200	1970
Akosombo	Ghana	148,000	120,000	1965
Daniel Johnson	Canada	141,852	115,000	1968
Guri (Raul Leoni)	Venezuela	136,000	110,256	1986
Krasnoyarsk	Siberia	73,300	59,425	1967
Bennett W.A.C.	Canada	70,309	57,006	1967
Zeya	Russia	68,400	55,452	1978
Cabora Bassa	Mozambique	63,000	51,075	1974
LaGrande 2	Canada	61,720	50,037	1982
LaGrande 3	Canada	60,020	48,659	1982
Ust'-Ilimsk	Russia	59,300	48,075	1980
Volga-V.I. Lenin	Russia	58,000	47,020	1955
Caniapiscau	Canada	53,790	43,608	1981
Pati (Chapetón)	Argentina	53,700	43,535	UC
Upper Wainganga	India	50,700	41,103	1987
São Felix	Brazil	50,600	41,022	1986
Bukhtarma	Former U.S.S.R.	49,740	40,325	1960
Atatürk (Karababa)	Turkey	48,700	39,482	1990
Cerros Colorados	Argentina	48,000	38,914	1973
Irkutsk	Russia	46,000	37,290	1956
Tucuruí	Brazil	36,375	29,489	1984
Vilyuy	Russia	35,900	29,104	1967
Sanmenxia	China	35,400	28,700	1960
Hoover	Nevada/Arizona	35,154	28,500	1936
Sobridinho	Brazil	34,200	27,726	1981
Glen Canyon	Arizona	33,304	27,000	1964
Jenpeg	Canada	31,790	25,772	1975

1. Formed by construction of dams. NOTE: UC = under construction, *Source:* Department of the Interior, Bureau of Reclamation and *International Water Power and Dam Construction.*

Large Lakes of the World
(Area more than 1,600 sq miles)

Name and location	Area sq mi.	Area km	Length mi.	Length km	Maximum depth feet	Maximum depth meters
Caspian Sea, Azerbaijan-Russia-Kazakhstan-Turkmenistan-Iran[1]	152,239	394,299	745	1,199	3,104	946
Superior, U.S.-Canada	31,820	82,414	383	616	1,333	406
Victoria, Tanzania-Uganda	26,828	69,485	200	322	270	82
Aral, Kazakhstan-Uzbekistan	25,659	66,457	266	428	223	68
Huron, U.S.-Canada	23,010	59,596	247	397	750	229
Michigan, U.S.	22,400	58,016	321	517	923	281
Tanganyika, Tanzania-Zaire	12,700	32,893	420	676	4,708	1,435
Baikal, Russia	12,162	31,500	395	636	5,712	1,741
Great Bear, Canada	12,000	31,080	232	373	270	82
Nyasa, Malawi-Mozambique-Tanzania	11,600	30,044	360	579	2,316	706
Great Slave, Canada	11,170	28,930	298	480	2,015	614
Chad,[2] Chad-Niger-Nigeria	9,946	25,760	—	—	23	7
Erie, U.S.-Canada	9,930	25,719	241	388	210	64
Winnipeg, Canada	9,094	23,553	264	425	204	62
Ontario, U.S.-Canada	7,520	19,477	193	311	778	237
Balkhash, Kazakhstan	7,115	18,428	376	605	87	27
Ladoga, Russia	7,000	18,130	124	200	738	225
Onega, Russia	3,819	9,891	154	248	361	110
Titicaca, Bolivia-Peru	3,141	8,135	110	177	1,214	370
Nicaragua, Nicaragua	3,089	8,001	110	177	230	70
Athabaska, Canada	3,058	7,920	208	335	407	124
Rudolf, Kenya	2,473	6,405	154	248	—	—
Reindeer, Canada	2,444	6,330	152	245	—	—
Eyre, South Australia	2,400[3]	6,216	130	209	varies	varies
Issyk-Kul, Kyrgyzstan	2,394	6,200	113	182	2,297	700
Urmia,[2] Iran	2,317	6,001	81	130	49	15
Torrens, South Australia	2,200	5,698	130	209	—	—

Name and location	Area		Length		Maximum depth	
	sq mi.	km	mi.	km	feet	meters
Vänern, Sweden	2,141	5,545	87	140	322	98
Winnipegosis, Canada	2,086	5,403	152	245	59	18
Mobutu Sese Seko, Uganda	2,046	5,299	100	161	180	55
Nettilling, Baffin Island, Canada	1,950	5,051	70	113	—	—
Nipigon, Canada	1,870	4,843	72	116	—	—
Manitoba, Canada	1,817	4,706	140	225	22	7
Great Salt, U.S.	1,800	4,662	75	121	15/25	5/8
Kioga, Uganda	1,700	4,403	50	80	about 30	9
Koko-Nor, China	1,630	4,222	66	106	—	—

1. The Caspian Sea is called "sea" because the Romans, finding it salty, named it *Mare Caspium*. Many geographers, however, consider it a lake because it is land-locked. 2. Figures represent high-water data. 3. Varies with the rainfall of the wet season. It has been reported to dry up almost completely on occasion.

Principal Rivers of the World

(For other U.S. rivers, see Index)

River	Source	Outflow	Approx. length	
			miles	km
Nile	Tributaries of Lake Victoria, Africa	Mediterranean Sea	4,180	6,690
Amazon	Glacier-fed lakes, Peru	Atlantic Ocean	3,912	6,296
Mississippi-Missouri-Red Rock	Source of Red Rock, Montana	Gulf of Mexico	3,710	5,970
Yangtze Kiang	Tibetan plateau, China	China Sea	3,602	5,797
Ob	Altai Mts., Russia	Gulf of Ob	3,459	5,567
Huang Ho (Yellow)	Eastern part of Kunlan Mts., west China	Gulf of Chihli	2,900	4,667
Yenisei	Tannu-Ola Mts., western Tuva, Russia	Arctic Ocean	2,800	4,506
Paraná	Confluence of Paranaiba and Grande rivers	Río de la Plata	2,795	4,498
Irtish	Altai Mts., Russia	Ob River	2,758	4,438
Zaire (Congo)	Confluence of Lualab and Luapula rivers, Zaire	Atlantic Ocean	2,716	4,371
Heilong (Amur)	Confluence of Shilka (Russia) and Argun (Manchuria) rivers	Tatar Strait	2,704	4,352
Lena	Baikal Mts., Russia	Arctic Ocean	2,652	4,268
Mackenzie	Head of Finlay River, British Columbia, Canada	Beaufort Sea (Arctic Ocean)	2,635	4,241
Niger	Guinea	Gulf of Guinea	2,600	4,184
Mekong	Tibetan highlands	South China Sea	2,500	4,023
Mississippi	Lake Itasca, Minnesota	Gulf of Mexico	2,348	3,779
Missouri	Confluence of Jefferson, Gallatin, and Madison rivers, Montana	Mississippi River	2,315	3,726
Volga	Valdai plateau, Russia	Caspian Sea	2,291	3,687
Madeira	Confluence of Beni and Maumoré rivers, Bolivia-Brazil boundary	Amazon River	2,012	3,238
Purus	Peruvian Andes	Amazon River	1,993	3,207
São Francisco	Southwest Minas Gerais, Brazil	Atlantic Ocean	1,987	3,198
Yukon	Junction of Lewes and Pelly rivers, Yukon Territory, Canada	Bering Sea	1,979	3,185
St. Lawrence	Lake Ontario	Gulf of St. Lawrence	1,900	3,058
Rio Grande	San Juan Mts., Colorado	Gulf of Mexico	1,885	3,034
Brahmaputra	Himalayas	Ganges River	1,800	2,897
Indus	Himalayas	Arabian Sea	1,800	2,897
Danube	Black Forest, Germany	Black Sea	1,766	2,842

River	Source	Outflow	Approx. length	
			miles	km
Euphrates	Confluence of Murat Nehri and Kara Su rivers, Turkey	Shatt-al-Arab	1,739	2,799
Darling	Central part of Eastern Highlands, Australia	Murray River	1,702	2,739
Zambezi	11°21'S, 24°22'E, Zambia	Mozambique Channel	1,700	2,736
Tocantins	Goiás, Brazil	Pará River	1,677	2,699
Murray	Australian Alps, New South Wales	Indian Ocean	1,609	2,589
Nelson	Head of Bow River, western Alberta, Canada	Hudson Bay	1,600	2,575
Paraguay	Mato Grosso, Brazil	Paraná River	1,584	2,549
Ural	Southern Ural Mts., Russia	Caspian Sea	1,574	2,533
Ganges	Himalayas	Bay of Bengal	1,557	2,506
Amu Darya (Oxus)	Nicholas Range, Pamir Mts., Turkmenistan	Aral Sea	1,500	2,414
Japurá	Andes, Colombia	Amazon River	1,500	2,414
Salween	Tibet, south of Kunlun Mts.	Gulf of Martaban	1,500	2,414
Arkansas	Central Colorado	Mississippi River	1,459	2,348
Colorado	Grand County, Colorado	Gulf of California	1,450	2,333
Dnieper	Valdai Hills, Russia	Black Sea	1,419	2,284
Ohio-Allegheny	Potter County, Pennsylvania	Mississippi River	1,306	2,102
Irrawaddy	Confluence of Nmai and Mali rivers, northeast Burma	Bay of Bengal	1,300	2,092
Orange	Lesotho	Atlantic Ocean	1,300	2,092
Orinoco	Serra Parima Mts., Venezuela	Atlantic Ocean	1,281	2,062
Pilcomayo	Andes Mts., Bolivia	Paraguay River	1,242	1,999
Xi Jiang (Si Kiang)	Eastern Yunnan Province, China	China Sea	1,236	1,989
Columbia	Columbia Lake, British Columbia, Canada	Pacific Ocean	1,232	1,983
Don	Tula, Russia	Sea of Azov	1,223	1,968
Sungari	China-North Korea boundary	Amur River	1,215	1,955
Saskatchewan	Canadian Rocky Mts.	Lake Winnipeg	1,205	1,939
Peace	Stikine Mts., British Columbia, Canada	Great Slave River	1,195	1,923
Tigris	Taurus Mts., Turkey	Shatt-al-Arab	1,180	1,899

Highest Waterfalls of the World

Waterfall	Location	River	Height	
			feet	m
Angel	Venezuela	Tributary of Caroni	3,281	1,000
Tugela	Natal, South Africa	Tugela	3,000	914
Cuquenán	Venezuela	Cuquenán	2,000	610
Sutherland	South Island, N.Z.	Arthur	1,904	580
Takkakaw	British Columbia	Tributary of Yoho	1,650	503
Ribbon (Yosemite)	California	Creek flowing into Yosemite	1,612	491
Upper Yosemite	California	Yosemite Creek, tributary of Merced	1,430	436
Gavarnie	Southwest France	Gave de Pau	1,384	422
Vettisfoss	Norway	Mörkedola	1,200	366
Widows' Tears (Yosemite)	California	Tributary of Merced	1,170	357
Staubbach	Switzerland	Staubbach (Lauterbrunnen Valley)	984	300

Waterfall	Location	River	Height	
			feet	m
Middle Cascade (Yosemite)	California	Yosemite Creek, tributary of Merced	909	277
King Edward VIII	Guyana	Courantyne	850	259
Gersoppa	India	Sharavati	829	253
Kaieteur	Guyana	Potaro	822	251
Skykje	Norway	In Skykjedal (valley of Inner Hardinger Fjord)	820	250
Kalambo	Tanzania-Zambia	—	720	219
Fairy (Mt. Rainier Park)	Washington	Stevens Creek	700	213
Trummelbach	Switzerland	Trummelbach (Lauterbrunnen Valley)	700	213
Aniene (Teverone)	Italy	Tiber	680	207
Cascata delle Marmore	Italy	Velino, tributary of Nera	650	198
Maradalsfos	Norway	Stream flowing into Ejkisdalsvand (lake)	643	196
Feather	California	Fall River	640	195
Maletsunyane	Lesotho	Maletsunyane	630	192
Bridalveil (Yosemite)	California	Yosemite Creek	620	189
Multnomah	Oregon	Multnomah Creek, tributary of Columbia	620	189
Vøringsfos	Norway	Bjoreia	597	182
Nevada (Yosemite)	California	Merced	594	181
Skjeggedal	Norway	Tysso	525	160
Marina	Guyana	Tributary of Kuribrong, tributary of Potaro	500	152
Tequendama	Colombia	Funza, tributary of Magdalena	425	130
King George's	Cape of Good Hope, South Africa	Orange	400	122
Illilouette (Yosemite)	California	Illilouette Creek, tributary of Merced	370	113
Victoria	Rhodesia-Zambia boundary	Zambezi	355	108
Handöl	Sweden	Handöl Creek	345	105
Lower Yosemite	California	Yosemite	320	98
Comet (Mt. Rainier Park)	Washington	Van Trump Creek	320	98
Vernal (Yosemite)	California	Merced	317	97
Virginia	Northwest Territories, Canada	South Nahanni, tributary of Mackenzie	315	96
Lower Yellowstone	Wyoming	Yellowstone	310	94

NOTE: Niagara Falls (New York-Ontario), though of great volume, has parallel drops of only 158 and 167 feet.

Large Islands of the World

Island	Location and status	Area	
		sq mi.	sq km
Greenland	North Atlantic (Danish)	839,999	2,175,597
New Guinea	Southwest Pacific (Irian Jaya, Indonesian, west part; Papua New Guinea, east part)	316,615	820,033
Borneo	West mid-Pacific (Indonesian, south part, Brunei and Malaysian, north part)	286,914	743,107
Madagascar	Indian Ocean (Malagasy Republic)	226,657	587,042
Baffin	North Atlantic (Canadian)	183,810	476,068
Sumatra	Northeast Indian Ocean (Indonesian)	182,859	473,605
Honshu	Sea of Japan-Pacific (Japanese)	88,925	230,316
Great Britain	Off coast of NW Europe (England, Scotland, and Wales)	88,758	229,883
Ellesmere	Arctic Ocean (Canadian)	82,119	212,688
Victoria	Arctic Ocean (Canadian)	81,930	212,199
Sulawesi (Celebes)	West mid-Pacific (Indonesian)	72,986	189,034
South Island	South Pacific (New Zealand)	58,093	150,461
Java	Indian Ocean (Indonesian)	48,990	126,884
North Island	South Pacific (New Zealand)	44,281	114,688

Island	Location and status	Area	
		sq mi.	sq km
Cuba	Caribbean Sea (republic)	44,218	114,525
Newfoundland	North Atlantic (Canadian)	42,734	110,681
Luzon	West mid-Pacific (Philippines)	40,420	104,688
Iceland	North Atlantic (republic)	39,768	102,999
Mindanao	West mid-Pacific (Philippines)	36,537	94,631
Ireland	West of Great Britain (republic, south part; United Kingdom, north part)	32,597	84,426
Hokkaido	Sea of Japan—Pacific (Japanese)	30,372	78,663
Hispaniola	Caribbean Sea (Dominican Republic, east part; Haiti, west part)	29,355	76,029
Tasmania	South of Australia (Australian)	26,215	67,897
Sri Lanka (Ceylon)	Indian Ocean (republic)	25,332	65,610
Sakhalin (Karafuto)	North of Japan (Russia)	24,560	63,610
Banks	Arctic Ocean (Canadian)	23,230	60,166
Devon	Arctic Ocean (Canadian)	20,861	54,030
Tierra del Fuego	Southern tip of South America (Argentinian, east part; Chilean, west part)	18,605	48,187
Kyushu	Sea of Japan—Pacific (Japanese)	16,223	42,018
Melville	Arctic Ocean (Canadian)	16,141	41,805
Axel Heiberg	Arctic Ocean (Canadian)	15,779	40,868
Southampton	Hudson Bay (Canadian)	15,700	40,663

Principal Deserts of the World

Desert	Location	Approximate size	Approx. elevation, ft
Atacama	North Chile	400 mi. long	7,000–13,500
Black Rock	Northwest Nevada	About 1,000 sq mi.	2,000–8,500
Colorado	Southeast California from San Gorgonio Pass to Gulf of California	200 mi. long and a maximum width of 50 mi.	Few feet above to 250 below sea level
Dasht-e-Kavir	Southeast of Caspian Sea, Iran	—	2,000
Dasht-e-Lut	Northeast of Kerman, Iran	—	1,000
Gobi (Shamo)	Covers most of Mongolia	500,000 sq mi.	3,000–5,000
Great Arabian	Most of Arabia	1,500 mi. long	—
An Nafud (Red Desert)	South of Jauf	400 mi. by avg of 140 mi.	3,000
Dahna	Northeast of Nejd	400 mi. by 30 mi.	—
Rub' al-Khali	South portion of Nejd	Over 200,000 sq mi.	—
Syrian (Al-Hamad)	North of lat. 30°N	—	1,850
Great Australian	Western portion of Australia	About one half the continent	600–1,000
Great Salt Lake	West of Great Salt Lake to Nevada—Utah boundary	About 110 mi. by 50 mi.	4,500
Kalahari	South Africa—South-West Africa	About 120,000 sq mi.	Over 3,000
Kara Kum (Desert of Kiva)	Southwest Turkmenistan	115,000 sq mi.	—
Kyzyl Kum	Uzbekistan and Kazakhstan	Over 100,000 sq mi.	160 near Lake Aral to 2,000 in southeast
Libyan	Libya, Egypt, Sudan	Over 500,000 sq mi.	—
Mojave	North of Colorado Desert and south of Death Valley, southeast California	15,000 sq mi.	2,000
Nubian	From Red Sea to great west bend of the Nile, Sudan	—	2,500
Painted Desert	Northeast Arizona	Over 7,000 sq mi.	High plateau, 5,000
Sahara	North Africa to about lat. 15°N and from Red Sea to Atlantic Ocean	3,200 mi. greatest length along lat. 20°N; area over 3,500,000 sq mi.	440 below sea level to 11,000 above; avg elevation, 1,400–1,600
Sonoran	Southwestern Arizona, southeastern California, and northwestern Mexico	120,000 sq mi.	—
Takla Makan	South central Sinkiang, China	Over 100,000 sq mi.	—
Thar (Indian)	Pakistan–India	Nearly 100,000 sq mi.	Over 1,000

Interesting Caves and Caverns of the World

Aggtelek. In village of same name, northern Hungary. Large stalactitic cavern about 5 miles long.

Altamira Cave. Near Santander, Spain. Contains animal paintings (Old Stone Age art) on roof and walls.

Antiparos. On island of same name in the Grecian Archipelago. Some stalactites are 20 ft long. Brilliant colors and fantastic shapes.

Blue Grotto. On island of Capri, Italy. Cavern hollowed out in limestone by constant wave action. Now half filled with water because of sinking coast. Name derived from unusual blue light permeating the cave. Source of light is a submerged opening, light passing through the water.

Carlsbad Caverns. Southeast New Mexico. Largest underground labyrinth yet discovered. Three levels: 754, 900, and 1,320 ft below the surface.

Fingal's Cave. On island of Staffa off coast of western Scotland. Penetrates about 200 ft inland. Contains basaltic columns almost 40 ft high.

Ice Cave. Near Dobsina, Czechoslovakia. Noted for its beautiful crystal effects.

Jenolan Caves. In Blue Mountain plateau, New South Wales, Australia. Beautiful stalactitic formations.

Kent's Cavern. Near Torquay, England. Source of much information on Paleolithic man.

Luray Cavern. Near Luray, Va. Has large stalactitic and stalagmitic columns of many colors.

Mammoth Cave. Limestone cavern in central Kentucky. Cave area is about 10 miles in diameter but has over 300 miles of irregular subterranean passageways at various levels. Temperature remains fairly constant at 54°F.

Peak Cavern or Devil's Hole. Derbyshire, England. About 2,250 ft into a mountain. Lowest part is about 600 ft below the surface.

Postojna (Postumia) Grotto. Near Postumia in Julian Alps, about 25 miles northeast of Trieste. Stalactitic cavern, largest in Europe. Piuca (Pivka) River flows through part of it. Caves have numerous beautiful stalactites.

Singing Cave. Iceland. A lava cave; name derived from echoes of people singing in it.

Wind Cave. In Black Hills of South Dakota. Limestone caverns with stalactites and stalagmites almost entirely missing. Variety of crystal formations called "boxwork."

Wyandotte Cave. In Crawford County, southern Indiana. A limestone cavern with five levels of passages; one of the largest in North America. "Monumental Mountain," approximately 135 ft high, is believed to be one of the world's largest underground "mountains."

U.S. Geography

Miscellaneous Data for the United States

Source: Department of the Interior, U.S. Geological Survey.

Highest point: Mt. McKinley, Alaska	20,320 ft (6,198 m)
Lowest point: Death Valley, Calif.	282 ft (86 m) below sea level
Approximate mean elevation	2,500 ft (763 m)
Points farthest apart (50 states):	5,859 mi. (9,429 km)
Log Point, Elliot Key, Fla., and Kure Island, Hawaii	
Geographic center (50 states):	44° 58′ N. lat.103° 46′ W. long.
In Butte County, S.D. (west of Castle Rock)	
Geographic center (48 conterminous states):	39° 50′ N. lat.98° 35′ W. long.
In Smith County, Kan. (near Lebanon)	
Boundaries:	
Between Alaska and Canada	1,538 mi. (2,475 km)
Between the 48 conterminous states and Canada (incl. Great Lakes)	3,987 mi. (6,416 km)
Between the United States and Mexico	1,933 mi. (3,111 km)

Extreme Points of the United States (50 States)

Extreme point	Latitude	Longitude	Distance[1] mi.	km
Northernmost point: Point Barrow, Alaska	71°23′ N	156°29′ W	2,507	4,034
Easternmost point: West Quoddy Head, Me.	44°49′ N	66°57′ W	1,788	2,997
Southernmost point: Ka Lae (South Cape), Hawaii	18°55′ N	155°41′ W	3,463	5,573
Westernmost point: Cape Wrangell, Alaska (Attu Island)	52°55′ N	172°27′ E	3,625	5,833

1. From geographic center of United States (incl. Alaska and Hawaii), west of Castle Rock, S.D., 44°58′ N. lat., 103°46′ W long.

Highest, Lowest, and Mean Elevations in the United States

State	Elevation ft[1]	Highest point	Elevation ft	Lowest point	Elevation ft
Alabama	500	Cheaha Mountain	2,405	Gulf of Mexico	Sea level
Alaska	1,900	Mt. McKinley	20,320	Pacific Ocean	Sea level
Arizona	4,100	Humphreys Peak	12,633	Colorado River	70
Arkansas	650	Magazine Mountain	2,753	Ouachita River	55
California	2,900	Mt. Whitney	14,494	Death Valley	−282 [2]
Colorado	6,800	Mt. Elbert	14,433	Arkansas River	3,350
Connecticut	500	Mt. Frissell, on south slope	2,380	Long Island Sound	Sea level
Delaware	60	Ebright Road, Del.–Pa. state line	448	Atlantic Ocean	Sea level
D.C.	150	Tenleytown, at Reno Reservoir	410	Potomac River	1
Florida	100	Sec. 30, T6N, R20W, Walton County	345	Atlantic Ocean	Sea level
Georgia	600	Brasstown Bald	4,784	Atlantic Ocean	Sea level
Hawaii	3,030	Puu Wekiu, Mauna Kea	13,796	Pacific Ocean	Sea level
Idaho	5,000	Borah Peak	12,662	Snake River	710
Illinois	600	Charles Mound	1,235	Mississippi River	279
Indiana	700	Franklin Township, Wayne County	1,257	Ohio River	320
Iowa	1,100	Sec. 29, T100N, R41W, Osceola County	1,670	Mississippi River	480
Kansas	2,000	Mt. Sunflower	4,039	Verdigris River	679
Kentucky	750	Black Mountain	4,139	Mississippi River	257
Louisiana	100	Driskill Mountain	535	New Orleans	−8 [2]
Maine	600	Mt. Katahdin	5,267	Atlantic Ocean	Sea level
Maryland	350	Backbone Mountain	3,360	Atlantic Ocean	Sea level
Massachusetts	500	Mt. Greylock	3,487	Atlantic Ocean	Sea level
Michigan	900	Mt. Arvon	1,979	Lake Erie	572
Minnesota	1,200	Eagle Mountain	2,301	Lake Superior	600
Mississippi	300	Woodall Mountain	806	Gulf of Mexico	Sea level
Missouri	800	Taum Sauk Mountain	1,772	St. Francis River	230
Montana	3,400	Granite Peak	12,799	Kootenai River	1,800
Nebraska	2,600	Johnson Township, Kimball County	5,424	Missouri River	840
Nevada	5,500	Boundary Peak	13,140	Colorado River	479
New Hampshire	1,000	Mt. Washington	6,288	Atlantic Ocean	Sea level
New Jersey	250	High Point	1,803	Atlantic Ocean	Sea level
New Mexico	5,700	Wheeler Peak	13,161	Red Bluff Reservoir	2,842
New York	1,000	Mt. Marcy	5,344	Atlantic Ocean	Sea level
North Carolina	700	Mt. Mitchell	6,684	Atlantic Ocean	Sea level
North Dakota	1,900	White Butte	3,506	Red River	750
Ohio	850	Campbell Hill	1,549	Ohio River	455
Oklahoma	1,300	Black Mesa	4,973	Little River	289
Oregon	3,300	Mt. Hood	11,239	Pacific Ocean	Sea level
Pennsylvania	1,100	Mt. Davis	3,213	Delaware River	Sea level
Rhode Island	200	Jerimoth Hill	812	Atlantic Ocean	Sea level
South Carolina	350	Sassafras Mountain	3,560	Atlantic Ocean	Sea level
South Dakota	2,200	Harney Peak	7,242	Big Stone Lake	966
Tennessee	900	Clingmans Dome	6,643	Mississippi River	178
Texas	1,700	Guadalupe Peak	8,749	Gulf of Mexico	Sea level
Utah	6,100	Kings Peak	13,528	Beaverdam Wash	2,000
Vermont	1,000	Mt. Mansfield	4,393	Lake Champlain	95
Virginia	950	Mt. Rogers	5,729	Atlantic Ocean	Sea level
Washington	1,700	Mt. Rainier	14,410	Pacific Ocean	Sea level
West Virginia	1,500	Spruce Knob	4,861	Potomac River	240
Wisconsin	1,050	Timms Hill	1,951	Lake Michigan	579
Wyoming	6,700	Gannett Peak	13,804	Belle Fourche River	3,099
United States	2,500	Mt. McKinley (Alaska)	20,320	Death Valley (California)	−282 [2]

1. Approximate mean elevation. 2. Below sea level. *Source:* Department of the Interior, U.S. Geological Survey.

The Continental Divide

The Continental Divide is a ridge of high ground which runs irregularly north and south through the Rocky Mountains and separates eastward-flowing from westward-flowing streams. The waters which flow eastward empty into the Atlantic Ocean, chiefly by way of the Gulf of Mexico; those which flow westward empty into the Pacific.

Mason and Dixon's Line

Mason and Dixon's Line (often called the Mason-Dixon Line) is the boundary between Pennsylvania and Maryland, running at a north latitude of 39°43′19.11″. The greater part of it was surveyed from 1763–67 by Charles Mason and Jeremiah Dixon, English astronomers who had been appointed to settle a dispute between the colonies. As the line was partly the boundary between the free and the slave states, it has come to signify the division between the North and the South.

Latitude and Longitude of U.S. and Canadian Cities

(and time corresponding to 12:00 noon, eastern standard time)

City	Lat. °	Lat. '	Long. °	Long. '	Time	City	Lat. °	Lat. '	Long. °	Long. '	Time
Albany, N.Y.	42	40	73	45	12:00 noon	Memphis, Tenn.	35	9	90	3	11:00 a.m.
Albuquerque, N.M.	35	05	106	39	10:00 a.m.	Miami, Fla.	25	46	80	12	12:00 noon
Amarillo, Tex.	35	11	101	50	11:00 a.m.	Milwaukee	43	2	87	55	11:00 a.m.
Anchorage, Alaska	61	13	149	54	8:00 a.m.	Minneapolis	44	59	93	14	11:00 a.m.
Atlanta	33	45	84	23	12:00 noon	Mobile, Ala.	30	42	88	3	11:00 a.m.
Austin, Tex.	30	16	97	44	11:00 a.m.	Montgomery, Ala.	32	21	86	18	11:00 a.m.
Baker, Ore.	44	47	117	50	9:00 a.m.	Montpelier, Vt.	44	15	72	32	12:00 noon
Baltimore	39	18	76	38	12:00 noon	Montreal, Que.	45	30	73	35	12:00 noon
Bangor, Me.	44	48	68	47	12:00 noon	Moose Jaw, Sask.	50	37	105	31	10:00 a.m.
Birmingham, Ala.	33	30	86	50	11:00 a.m.	Nashville, Tenn.	36	10	86	47	11:00 a.m.
Bismarck, N.D.	46	48	100	47	11:00 a.m.	Nelson, B.C.	49	30	117	17	9:00 a.m.
Boise, Idaho	43	36	116	13	10:00 a.m.	Newark, N.J.	40	44	74	10	12:00 noon
Boston	42	21	71	5	12:00 noon	New Haven, Conn.	41	19	72	55	12:00 noon
Buffalo, N.Y.	42	55	78	50	12:00 noon	New Orleans	29	57	90	4	11:00 a.m.
Calgary, Alberta	51	1	114	1	10:00 a.m.	New York	40	47	73	58	12:00 noon
Carlsbad, N.M.	32	26	104	15	10:00 a.m.	Nome, Alaska	64	25	165	30	8:00 a.m.
Charleston, S.C.	32	47	79	56	12:00 noon	Oakland, Calif.	37	48	122	16	9:00 a.m.
Charleston, W. Va.	38	21	81	38	12:00 noon	Oklahoma City	35	26	97	28	11:00 a.m.
Charlotte, N.C.	35	14	80	50	12:00 noon	Omaha, Neb.	41	15	95	56	11:00 a.m.
Cheyenne, Wyo.	41	9	104	52	10:00 a.m.	Ottawa, Ont.	45	24	75	43	12:00 noon
Chicago	41	50	87	37	11:00 a.m.	Philadelphia	39	57	75	10	12:00 noon
Cincinnati	39	8	84	30	12:00 noon	Phoenix, Ariz.	33	29	112	4	10:00 a.m.
Cleveland	41	28	81	37	12:00 noon	Pierre, S.D.	44	22	100	21	11:00 a.m.
Columbia, S.C.	34	0	81	2	12:00 noon	Pittsburgh	40	27	79	57	12:00 noon
Columbus, Ohio	40	0	83	1	12:00 noon	Port Arthur, Ont.	48	30	89	17	12:00 noon
Dallas	32	46	96	46	11:00 a.m.	Portland, Me.	43	40	70	15	12:00 noon
Denver	39	45	105	0	10:00 a.m.	Portland, Ore.	45	31	122	41	9:00 a.m.
Des Moines, Iowa	41	35	93	37	11:00 a.m.	Providence, R.I.	41	50	71	24	12:00 noon
Detroit	42	20	83	3	12:00 noon	Quebec, Que.	46	49	71	11	12:00 noon
Dubuque, Iowa	42	31	90	40	11:00 a.m.	Raleigh, N.C.	35	46	78	39	12:00 noon
Duluth, Minn.	46	49	92	5	11:00 a.m.	Reno, Nev.	39	30	119	49	9:00 a.m.
Eastport, Me.	44	54	67	0	12:00 noon	Richfield, Utah	38	46	112	5	10:00 a.m.
El Centro, Calif.	32	38	115	33	9:00 a.m.	Richmond, Va.	37	33	77	29	12:00 noon
El Paso	31	46	106	29	10:00 a.m.	Roanoke, Va.	37	17	79	57	12:00 noon
Eugene, Ore.	44	3	123	5	9:00 a.m.	Sacramento, Calif.	38	35	121	30	9:00 a.m.
Fargo, N.D.	46	52	96	48	11:00 a.m.	St. John, N.B.	45	18	66	10	1:00 p.m.
Flagstaff, Ariz.	35	13	111	41	10:00 a.m.	St. Louis	38	35	90	12	11:00 a.m.
Fort Worth, Tex.	32	43	97	19	11:00 a.m.	Salt Lake City, Utah	40	46	111	54	10:00 a.m.
Fresno, Calif.	36	44	119	48	9:00 a.m.	San Antonio	29	23	98	33	11:00 a.m.
Grand Junction, Colo.	39	5	108	33	10:00 a.m.	San Diego, Calif.	32	42	117	10	9:00 a.m.
Grand Rapids, Mich.	42	58	85	40	12:00 noon	San Francisco	37	47	122	26	9:00 a.m.
Havre, Mont.	48	33	109	43	10:00 a.m.	San Jose, Calif.	37	20	121	53	9:00 a.m.
Helena, Mont.	46	35	112	2	10:00 a.m.	San Juan, P.R.	18	30	66	10	1:00 p.m.
Honolulu	21	18	157	50	7:00 a.m.	Santa Fe, N.M.	35	41	105	57	10:00 a.m.
Hot Springs, Ark.	34	31	93	3	11:00 a.m.	Savannah, Ga.	32	5	81	5	12:00 noon
Houston, Tex.	29	45	95	21	11:00 a.m.	Seattle	47	37	122	20	9:00 a.m.
Idaho Falls, Idaho	43	30	112	1	10:00 a.m.	Shreveport, La.	32	28	93	42	11:00 a.m.
Indianapolis	39	46	86	10	12:00 noon	Sioux Falls, S.D.	43	33	96	44	11:00 a.m.
Jackson, Miss.	32	20	90	12	11:00 a.m.	Sitka, Alaska	57	10	135	15	9:00 a.m.
Jacksonville, Fla.	30	22	81	40	12:00 noon	Spokane, Wash.	47	40	117	26	9:00 a.m.
Juneau, Alaska	58	18	134	24	8:00 a.m.	Springfield, Ill.	39	48	89	38	11:00 a.m.
Kansas City, Mo.	39	6	94	35	11:00 a.m.	Springfield, Mass.	42	6	72	34	12:00 noon
Key West, Fla.	24	33	81	48	12:00 noon	Springfield, Mo.	37	13	93	17	11:00 a.m.
Kingston, Ont.	44	15	76	30	12:00 noon	Syracuse, N.Y.	43	2	76	8	12:00 noon
Klamath Falls, Ore.	42	10	121	44	9:00 a.m.	Tampa, Fla.	27	57	82	27	12:00 noon
Knoxville, Tenn.	35	57	83	56	12:00 noon	Toledo, Ohio	41	39	83	33	12:00 noon
Las Vegas, Nev.	36	10	115	12	9:00 a.m.	Toronto, Ont.	43	40	79	24	12:00 noon
Lewiston, Idaho	46	24	117	2	9:00 a.m.	Tulsa, Okla.	36	09	95	59	11:00 a.m.
Lincoln, Neb.	40	50	96	40	11:00 a.m.	Victoria, B.C.	48	25	123	21	9:00 a.m.
London, Ont.	43	2	81	34	12:00 noon	Virginia Beach, Va.	36	51	75	58	12:00 noon
Long Beach, Calif.	33	46	118	11	9:00 a.m.	Washington, D.C.	38	53	77	02	12:00 noon
Los Angeles	34	3	118	15	9:00 a.m.	Wichita, Kan.	37	43	97	17	11:00 a.m.
Louisville, Ky.	38	15	85	46	12:00 noon	Wilmington, N.C.	34	14	77	57	12:00 noon
Manchester, N.H.	43	0	71	30	12:00 noon	Winnipeg, Man.	49	54	97	7	11:00 a.m.

Named Summits in the U.S. Over 14,000 Feet Above Sea Level

Name	State	Height	Name	State	Height	Name	State	Height
Mt. McKinley	Alaska	20,320	Castle Peak	Colo.	14,265	Mt. Eolus	Colo.	14,083
Mt. St. Elias	Alaska	18,008	Quandary Peak	Colo.	14,265	Windom Peak	Colo.	14,082
Mt. Foraker	Alaska	17,400	Mt. Evans	Colo.	14,264	Mt. Columbia	Colo.	14,073
Mt. Bona	Alaska	16,500	Longs Peak	Colo.	14,255	Mt. Augusta	Alaska	14,070
Mt. Blackburn	Alaska	16,390	Mt. Wilson	Colo.	14,246	Missouri Mtn.	Colo.	14,067
Mt. Sanford	Alaska	16,237	White Mtn.	Calif.	14,246	Humboldt Peak	Colo.	14,064
Mt. Vancouver	Alaska	15,979	North Palisade	Calif.	14,242	Mt. Bierstadt	Colo.	14,060
South Buttress	Alaska	15,885	Mt. Cameron	Colo.	14,238	Sunlight Peak	Colo.	14,059
Mt. Churchill	Alaska	15,638	Mt. Shavano	Colo.	14,229	Split Mtn.	Calif.	14,058
Mt. Fairweather	Alaska	15,300	Crestone Needle	Colo.	14,197	Handies Peak	Colo.	14,048
Mt. Hubbard	Alaska	14,950	Mt. Belford	Colo.	14,197	Culebra Peak	Colo.	14,047
Mt. Bear	Alaska	14,831	Mt. Princeton	Colo.	14,197	Mt. Lindsey	Colo.	14,042
East Buttress	Alaska	14,730	Mt. Yale	Colo.	14,196	Ellingwood Point	Colo.	14,042
Mt. Hunter	Alaska	14,573	Mt. Bross	Colo.	14,172	Little Bear Peak	Colo.	14,037
Browne Tower	Alaska	14,530	Kit Carson Mtn.	Colo.	14,165	Mt. Sherman	Colo.	14,036
Mt. Alverstone	Alaska	14,500	Mt. Wrangell	Alaska	14,163	Redcloud Peak	Colo.	14,034
Mt. Whitney	Calif.	14,494 [1]	Mt. Shasta	Calif.	14,162	Mt. Langley	Calif.	14,027
University Peak	Alaska	14,470	El Diente Peak	Colo.	14,159	Conundrum Peak	Colo.	14,022
Mt. Elbert	Colo.	14,433	Point Success	Wash.	14,158	Mt. Tyndall	Calif.	14,019
Mt. Massive	Colo.	14,421	Maroon Peak	Colo.	14,156	Pyramid Peak	Colo.	14,018
Mt. Harvard	Colo.	14,420	Tabeguache Mtn.	Colo.	14,155	Wilson Peak	Colo.	14,017
Mt. Rainier	Wash.	14,410	Mt. Oxford	Colo.	14,153	Wetterhorn Peak	Colo.	14,015
Mt. Williamson	Calif.	14,370	Mt. Sill	Calif.	14,153	North Maroon Peak	Colo.	14,014
La Plata Peak	Colo.	14,361	Mt. Sneffels	Colo.	14,150	San Luis Peak	Colo.	14,014
Blanca Peak	Colo.	14,345	Mt. Democrat	Colo.	14,148	Middle Palisade	Calif.	14,012
Uncompahgre Peak	Colo.	14,309	Capitol Peak	Colo.	14,130	Mt. Muir	Calif.	14,012
Crestone Peak	Colo.	14,294	Liberty Cap	Wash.	14,112	Mt. of the Holy Cross	Colo.	14,005
Mt. Lincoln	Colo.	14,286	Pikes Peak	Colo.	14,110	Huron Peak	Colo.	14,003
Grays Peak	Colo.	14,270	Snowmass Mtn.	Colo.	14,092	Thunderbolt Peak	Calif.	14,003
Mt. Antero	Colo.	14,269	Mt. Russell	Calif.	14,088	Sunshine Peak	Colo.	14,001
Torreys Peak	Colo.	14,267						

1. National Geodetic Survey. *Source:* Department of the Interior, U.S. Geological Survey.

Rivers of the United States

(350 or more miles long)

Alabama-Coosa (600 mi.; 966 km): From junction of Oostanula and Etowah R. in Georgia to Mobile R.

Altamaha-Ocmulgee (392 mi.; 631 km): From junction of Yellow R. and South R., Newton Co. in Georgia to Atlantic Ocean.

Apalachicola-Chattahoochee (524 mi.; 843 km): From Towns Co. in Georgia to Gulf of Mexico in Florida.

Arkansas (1,459 mi.; 2,348 km): From Lake Co. in Colorado to Mississippi R. in Arkansas.

Brazos (923 mi.; 1,490 km): From junction of Salt Fork and Double Mountain Fork in Texas to Gulf of Mexico.

Canadian (906 mi.; 1,458 km): From Las Animas Co. in Colorado to Arkansas R. in Oklahoma.

Cimarron (600 mi.; 966 km): From Colfax Co. in New Mexico to Arkansas R. in Oklahoma.

Colorado (1,450 mi.; 2,333 km): From Rocky Mountain National Park in Colorado to Gulf of California in Mexico.

Colorado (862 mi.; 1,387 km): From Dawson Co. in Texas to Matagorda Bay.

Columbia (1,243 mi.; 2,000 km): From Columbia Lake in British Columbia to Pacific Ocean (entering between Oregon and Washington).

Colville (350 mi.; 563 km): From Brooks Range in Alaska to Beaufort Sea.

Connecticut (407 mi.; 655 km): From Third Connecticut Lake in New Hampshire to Long Island Sound in Connecticut.

Cumberland (720 mi.; 1,159 km): From junction of Poor and Clover Forks in Harlan Co. in Kentucky to Ohio R.

Delaware (390 mi.; 628 km): From Schoharie Co. in New York to Liston Point, Delaware Bay.

Gila (649 mi.; 1,044 km): From Catron Co. in New Mexico to Colorado R. in Arizona.

Green (360 mi.; 579 km): From Lincoln Co. in Kentucky to Ohio R. in Kentucky.

Green (730 mi.; 1,175 km): From Sublette Co. in Wyoming to Colorado R. in Utah.

Illinois (420 mi.; 676 km): From St. Joseph Co. in Indiana to Mississippi R. at Grafton in Illinois.

James (sometimes called *Dakota*) (710 mi.; 1,143 km): From Wells Co. in North Dakota to Missouri R. in South Dakota.

Kanawha-New (352 mi.; 566 km): From junction of North and South Forks of New R. in North Carolina, through Virginia and West Virginia (New River becoming Kanawha River), to Ohio River.

Kansas (743 mi.; 1,196 km) From source of Arikaree R. in Elbert Co., Colorado, to Missouri R. at Kansas City, Kansas.

Koyukuk (470 mi.; 756 km): From Brooks Range in Alaska to Yukon R.

Kuskokwim (724 mi.; 1,165 km): From Alaska Range in Alaska to Kuskokwim Bay.

Licking (350 mi.; 563 km): From Magoffin Co. in Kentucky to Ohio R. at Cincinnati in Ohio.

Little Missouri (560 mi.; 901 km): From Crook Co. in Wyoming to Missouri R. in North Dakota.

Milk (625 mi.; 1,006 km): From junction of forks in Alberta Province to Missouri R.

Mississippi (2,340 mi.; 3,766 km): From Lake Itasca in Minnesota to mouth of Southwest Pass in La.

Coastline of the United States

State	Lengths, statute miles		State	Lengths, statute miles	
	General coastline[1]	Tidal shoreline[2]		General coastline[1]	Tidal shoreline[2]
Atlantic Coast:			Gulf Coast:		
Maine	228	3,478	Florida (Gulf)	770	5,095
New Hampshire	13	131	Alabama	53	607
Massachusetts	192	1,519	Mississippi	44	359
Rhode Island	40	384	Louisiana	397	7,721
Connecticut	—	618	Texas	367	3,359
New York	127	1,850	Total Gulf coast	1,631	17,141
New Jersey	130	1,792	Pacific Coast:		
Pennsylvania	—	89	California	840	3,427
Delaware	28	381	Oregon	296	1,410
Maryland	31	3,190	Washington	157	3,026
Virginia	112	3,315	Hawaii	750	1,052
North Carolina	301	3,375	Alaska (Pacific)	5,580	31,383
South Carolina	187	2,876	Total Pacific coast	7,623	40,298
Georgia	100	2,344	Arctic Coast:		
Florida (Atlantic)	580	3,331	Alaska (Arctic)	1,060	2,521
Total Atlantic coast	2,069	28,673	Total Arctic coast	1,060	2,521
			States Total	**12,383**	**88,633**

1. Figures are lengths of general outline of seacoast. Measurements made with unit measure of 30 minutes of latitude on charts as near scale of 1:1,200,000 as possible. Coastline of bays and sounds is included to point where they narrow to width of unit measure, and distance across at such point is included. 2. Figures obtained in 1939–40 with recording instrument on largest–scale maps and charts then available. Shoreline of outer coast, offshore islands, sounds, bays, rivers, and creeks is included to head of tidewater, or to point where tidal waters narrow to width of 100 feet. *Source:* Department of Commerce, National Oceanic and Atmospheric Administration, National Ocean Service.

Mississippi-Missouri-Red Rock (3,710 mi.; 5,970 km): From source of Red Rock R. in Montana to mouth of Southwest Pass in Louisiana.

Missouri (2,315 mi.; 3,726 km): From junction of Jefferson R., Gallatin R., and Madison R. in Montana to Mississippi R. near St. Louis.

Missouri-Red Rock (2,540 mi.; 4,090 km): From source of Red Rock R. in Montana to Mississippi R. near St. Louis.

Mobile-Alabama-Coosa (645 mi.; 1,040 km): From junction of Etowah R. and Oostanula R. in Georgia to Mobile Bay.

Neosho (460 mi.; 740 km): From Morris Co. in Kansas to Arkansas R. in Oklahoma.

Niobrara (431 mi.; 694 km): From Niobrara Co. in Wyoming to Missouri R. in Nebraska.

Noatak (350 mi.; 563 km): From Brooks Range in Alaska to Kotzebue Sound.

North Canadian (800 mi.; 1,290 km): From Union Co. in New Mexico to Canadian R. in Oklahoma.

North Platte (618 mi.; 995 km): From Jackson Co. in Colorado to junction with So. Platte R. in Nebraska to form Platte R.

Ohio (981 mi.; 1,579 km): From junction of Allegheny R. and Monongahela R. at Pittsburgh to Mississippi R. between Illinois and Kentucky.

Ohio-Allegheny (1,306 mi.; 2,102 km): From Potter Co. in Pennsylvania to Mississippi R. at Cairo in Illinois.

Osage (500 mi.; 805 km): From east-central Kansas to Missouri R. near Jefferson City in Missouri.

Ouachita (605 mi.; 974 km): From Polk Co. in Arkansas to Red R. in Louisiana.

Pearl (411 mi.; 661 km): From Neshoba County in Mississippi to Gulf of Mexico (Mississippi-Louisiana).

Pecos (926 mi.; 1,490 km): From Mora Co. in New Mexico to Rio Grande in Texas.

Pee Dee-Yadkin (435 mi.; 700 km): From Watauga Co. in North Carolina to Winyah Bay in South Carolina.

Pend Oreille-Clark Fork (531 mi.; 855 km): Near Butte in Montana to Columbia R. on Washington-Canada border.

Platte (990 mi.; 1,593 km) From source of Grizzly Creek in Jackson Co., Colorado, to Missouri R. south of Omaha, Nebraska.

Porcupine (569 mi.; 916 km): From Yukon Territory, Canada, to Yukon R. in Alaska.

Potomac (383 mi.; 616 km): From Garrett Co. in Md. to Chesapeake Bay at Point Lookout in Md.

Powder (375 mi.; 603 km): From junction of forks in Johnson Co. in Wyoming to Yellowstone R. in Montana.

Red (1,290 mi.; 2,080 km): From source of Tierra Blanca Creek in Curry County, New Mexico to Mississippi R. in Louisiana.

Red (also called *Red River of the North*) (545 mi.; 877 km): From junction of Otter Tail R. and Bois de Sioux R. in Minnesota to Lake Winnipeg in Manitoba.

Republican (445 mi.; 716 km): From junction of North Fork and Arikaree R. in Nebraska to junction with Smoky Hill R. in Kansas to form the Kansas R.

Rio Grande (1,900 mi.; 3,060 km): From San Juan Co. in Colorado to Gulf of Mexico.

Roanoke (380 mi.; 612 km): From junction of forks in Montgomery Co. in Virginia to Albemarle Sound in North Carolina.

Sabine (380 mi.; 612 km): From junction of forks in Hunt Co. in Texas to Sabine Lake between Texas and Louisiana.

Sacramento (377 mi.; 607 km): From Siskiyou Co. in California to Suisun Bay.

Saint Francis (425 mi.; 684 km): From Iron Co. in Missouri to Mississippi R. in Arkansas.

Salmon (420 mi.; 676 km): From Custer Co. in Idaho to Snake R.

San Joaquin (350 mi.; 563 km): From junction of forks in Madera Co. in California to Suisun Bay.

San Juan (360 mi.; 579 km): From Archuleta Co. in Colorado to Colorado R. in Utah.

Santee-Wateree-Catawba (538 mi.; 866 km): From McDowell Co. in North Carolina to Atlantic Ocean in South Carolina.

Smoky Hill (540 mi.; 869 km): From Cheyenne Co. in Colorado to junction with Republican R. in Kansas to form Kansas R.

Snake (1,038 mi.; 1,670 km): From Ocean Plateau in Wyoming to Columbia R. in Washington.
South Platte (424 mi.; 682 km): From Park Co. in Colorado to junction with North Platte R. in Nebraska to form Platte R.
Stikine (379 mi.; 610 km) From British Columbia in Canada to Stikine Strait near Wrangell, Alaska.
Susquehanna (444 mi.; 715 km): From Otsego Lake in New York to Chesapeake Bay in Maryland.
Tanana (659 mi.; 1,060 km): From Wrangell Mts. in Yukon Territory, Canada, to Yukon R. in Alaska.
Tennessee (652 mi.; 1,049 km): From junction of Holston R. and French Broad R. in Tennessee to Ohio R. in Kentucky.
Tennessee-French Broad (886 mi.; 1,417 km): From Transylvania Co. in North Carolina to Ohio R. at Paducah in Kentucky.

Tombigbee (525 mil; 845 km): From junction of forks in Itawamba Co. in Mississippi to Mobile R. in Alabama.
Trinity (360 mi.; 579 km): From junction of forks in Dallas Co. in Texas to Galveston Bay.
Wabash (512 mi.; 824 km): From Darke Co. in Ohio to Ohio R. between Illinois and Indiana.
Washita (500 mi.; 805 km): From Hemphill Co. in Texas to Red R. in Oklahoma.
White (722 mi.; 1,160 km): From Madison Co. in Arkansas to Mississippi R.
Wisconsin (430 mi.; 692 km): From Vilas Co. in Wisconsin to Mississippi R.
Yellowstone (692 mi.; 1,110 km): From Park Co. in Wyoming to Missouri R. in North Dakota.
Yukon (1,979 mi.; 3,185 km): From source of McNeil R. in Yukon Territory, Canada, to Bering Sea in Alaska.

Geysers in The United States

Geysers are natural hot springs that intermittently eject a column of water and steam into the air. They exist in many parts of the volcanic regions of the world such as Japan and South America but their greatest development is in Iceland, New Zealand, and Yellowstone National Park.

There are 120 named geysers in Yellowstone National Park, Wyoming, and perhaps half that numebr unnamed. Most of the geysers and the 4,000 or more hot springs are located in the western portion of the park. The most important are the following:

Norris Geyser Basin has 24 or more active geysers; the number varies. There are scores of steam vents and hot springs. *Valentine* is highest, erupting 50–75 ft at intervals varying from 18 hr to 3 days or more. *Minuté* erupts 15–20 ft high, several hours aprt. Others include *Steamboat, Fearless, Veteran, Vixen, Corporal, Whirligig, Little Whirligig,* and *Pinwheel.*

Lower Geyser Basin has at least 18 active geysers. *Fountain* throws water 50–75 ft in all directions at unpredictable intervals. *Clepsydra* erupts violently from four vents up to 30 ft. *Great Fountain* plays every 8 to 15 hr in spurts from 30 to 90 ft high.

Midway Geyser Basin has vast steaming terraces of red, orange, pink and other colors; there are pools and springs, including the beautiful *Grand Prismatic Spring. Excelsior* crater discharges boiling water into Firehole River at the rate of 6 cu ft per second.

Giant erupts up to 200 ft at intervals of 2 1/2 days to 3 mo; eruptions last about 1 1/2 hr. *Daisy* sends water up to 75 ft but is irregular and frequently inactive.

Old Faithful sends up a column varying from 116 to 175 ft at intervals of about 65 min, varying from 33 to 90 min. Eruptions last about 4 min, during which time about 12,000 gal are discharged.

Giantess seldom erupts, but during its active period sends up streams 150–200 ft.

Lion Group: *Lion* plays up to 60 ft every 2–4 days when active; *Little Cub* up to 10 ft every 1–2 hr. *Big Cub* and *Lioness* seldom erupt.

Mammoth Hot Springs: There are no geysers in this area. The formation is travertine. Sides of a hill are steps and terraces over which flow the steaming waters of hot springs laden with minerals. Each step is tinted by algae to many shades of orange, pink, yellow, brown, green, and blue. Terraces are white where no water flows.

One Lake or Two?

It is a widely accepted fact that Lake Superior, with an area of 31,820 square miles is the world's largest freshwater lake. However this fact is based on an historical inaccuracy in the naming of Lake Huron and Lake Michigan. What should have been considered one body of water, Lake Michigan-Huron with an area of 45,410 square miles, was mistakenly given two names, one for each lobe. The explorers in colonial times incorrectly believed each lobe to be a separate lake because of its great size.

Why should the two lakes be considered one? The Huron Lobe and the Michigan Lobe are at the same elevation. There are connected by the 120-foot deep Mackinac Strait, also at the same elevation. Lakes are separated from each other by streams and rivers. The Strait of Mackinac is not a river. It is 3.6 to 5 miles wide, wider than most lakes are long. In essence, it is just a narrowing, not a separation of the two lobes of Lake Michigan-Huron.

The flow between the two lakes can reverse. Because of the large connecting channel, the two can equalize rapidly whenever a water level imbalance occurs. Gage records for the lakes clearly show them to have identical water level regimes and mean long-term behavior; that is, Lake Michigan and Lake Huron act as one lake for many purposes. Hydrologically they are considered one lake.

Historical names are not easily changed. The separate names for the lake are a part of history and are also legally institutionalized since Lake Michigan is treated as American and Lake Huron is bisected by the international boundary between the United States and Canada.

Of all the world's freshwater lakes, North America's Great Lakes are unique. Their five basins combine to form a single watershed with one common outlet to the ocean. The total volume of the lakes is about 5,475 cubic miles, more than 6,000 trillion gallons.

The Great Lakes are: Superior with an area of 31,820 square miles (82,414 km) shared by the United States and Canada; Huron with an area of 23,010 square miles (59,596 sq km) shared by the United States and Canada; Michigan with an area of 22,400 square miles (58,016 sq km) entirely in the United States; Erie with an area of 9,930 square miles (25,719 km) shared by the United States and Canada; and Ontario with an area of 7,520 square miles (19,477 km) shared by the United States and Canada.

The United States also has another large lake, Great Salt Lake in Utah with an area of 1,800 square miles (4,662 sq km). However it is not a freshwater lake.

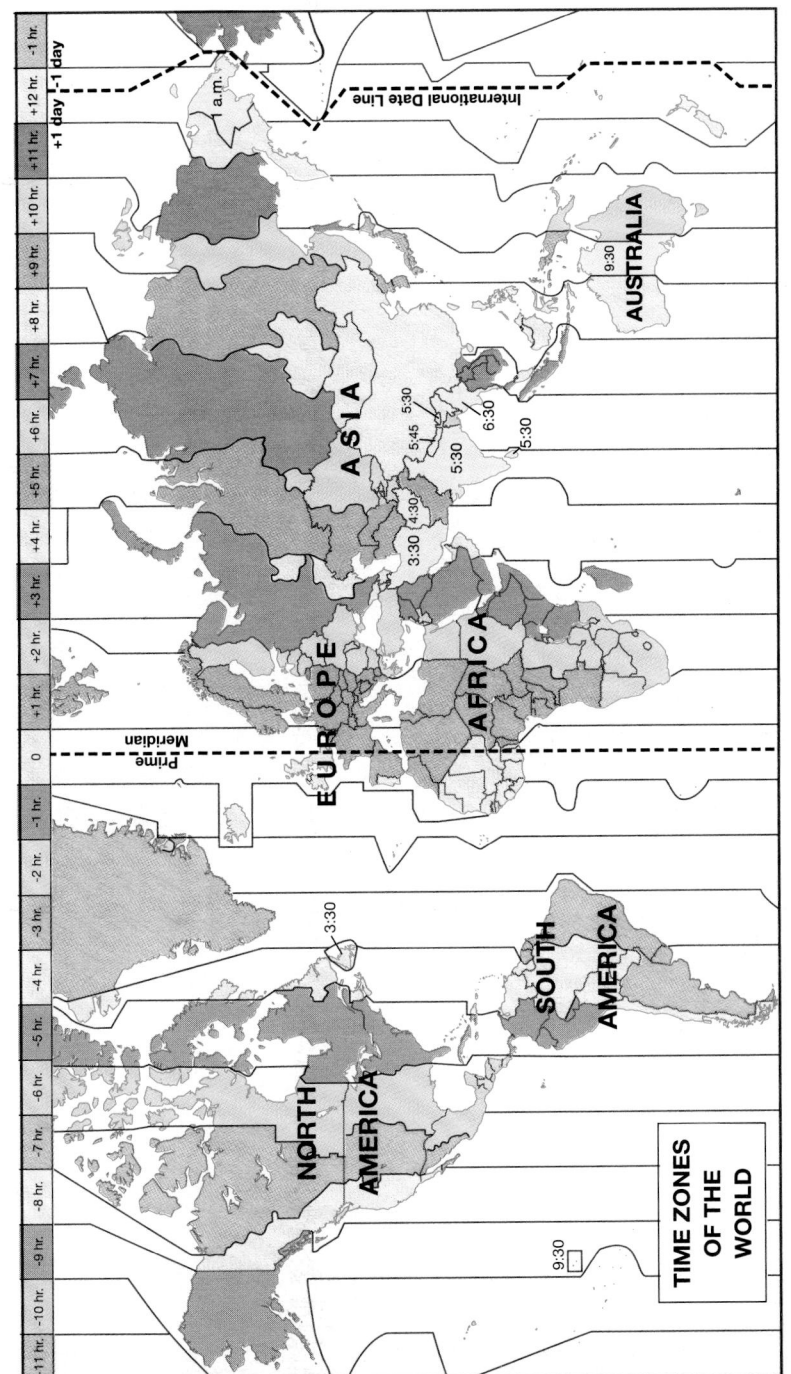

TIME ZONES OF THE WORLD

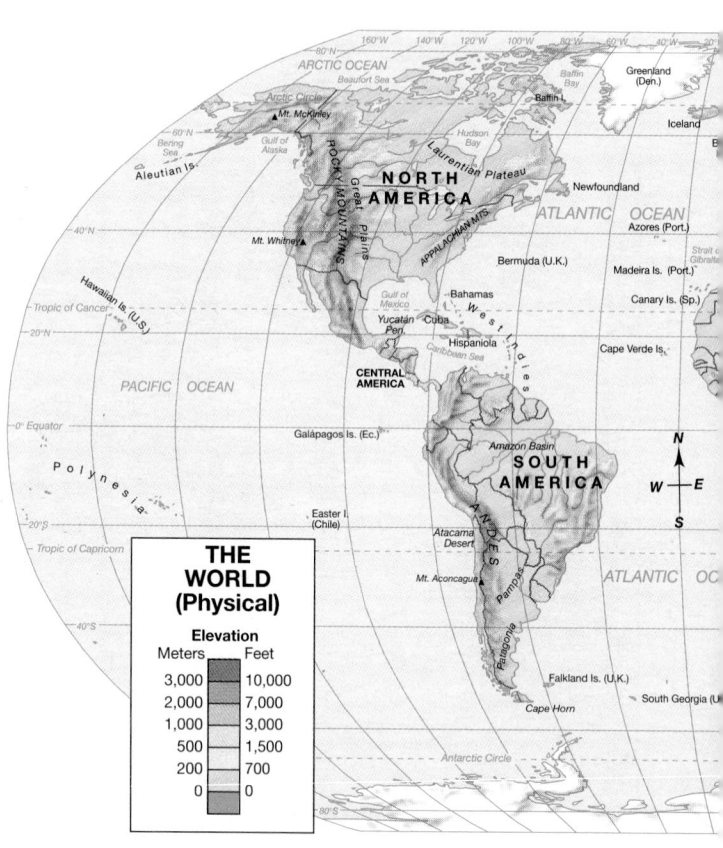

THE
WORLD
(Physical)

Elevation

Meters		Feet
3,000		10,000
2,000		7,000
1,000		3,000
500		1,500
200		700
0		0

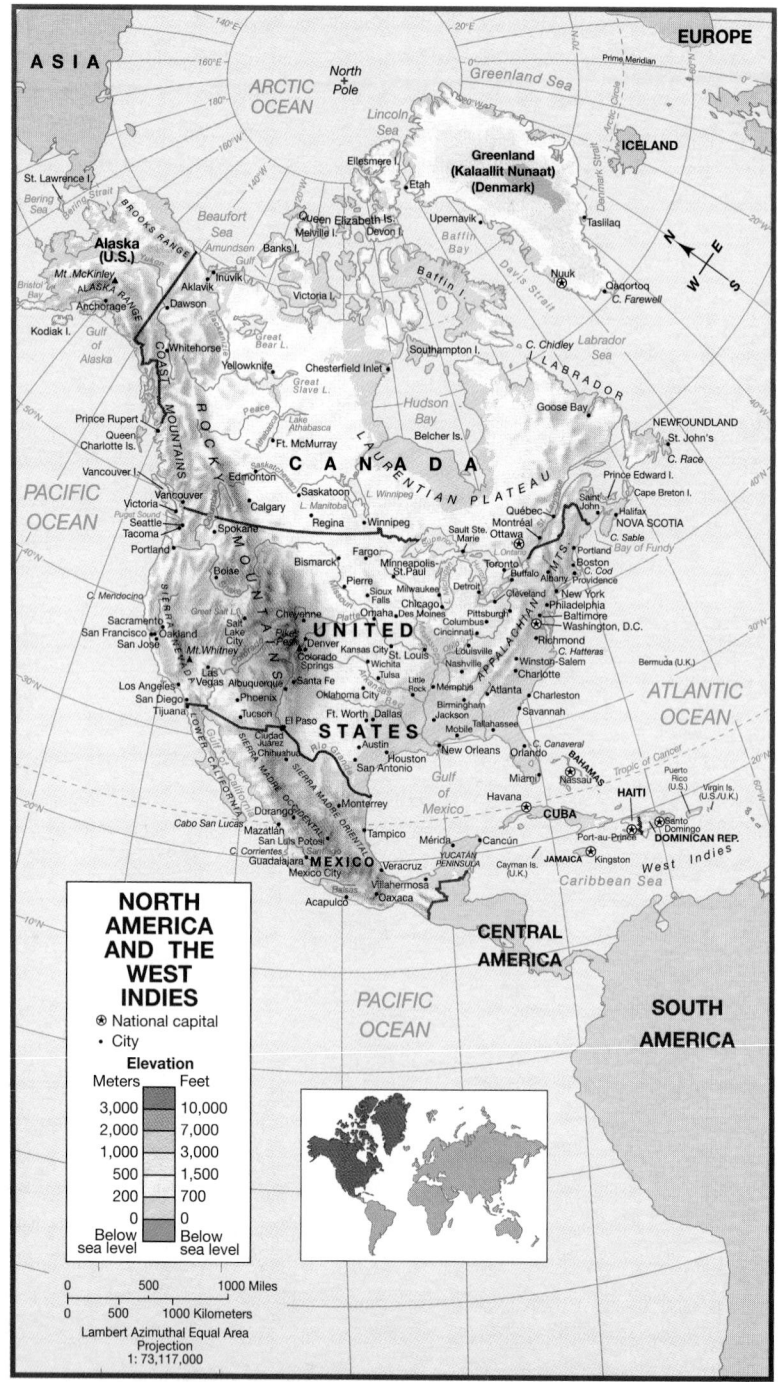

NORTH AMERICA AND THE WEST INDIES

⊛ National capital
• City

Elevation

Meters		Feet
3,000		10,000
2,000		7,000
1,000		3,000
500		1,500
200		700
0		0
Below sea level		Below sea level

0   500   1000 Miles
0   500   1000 Kilometers
Lambert Azimuthal Equal Area
Projection
1: 73,117,000

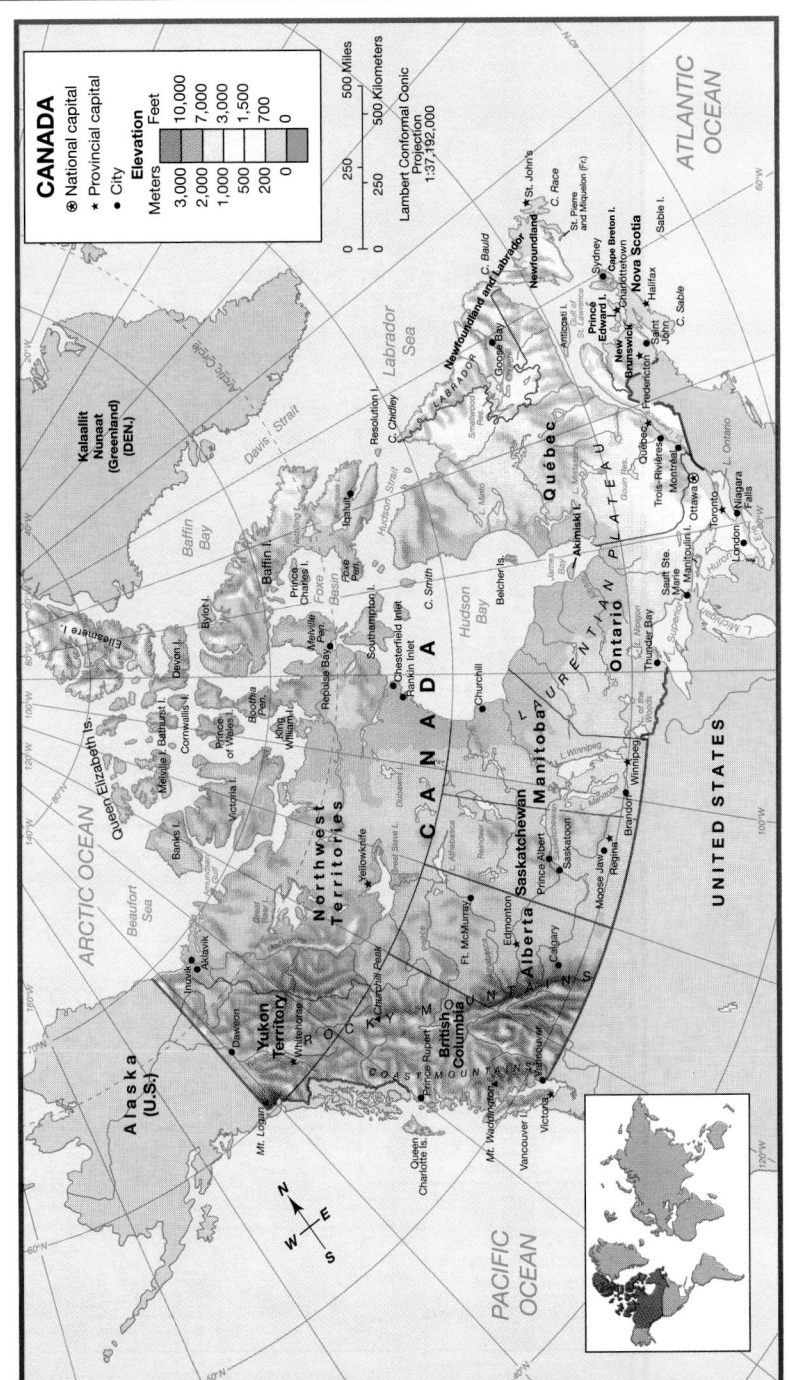

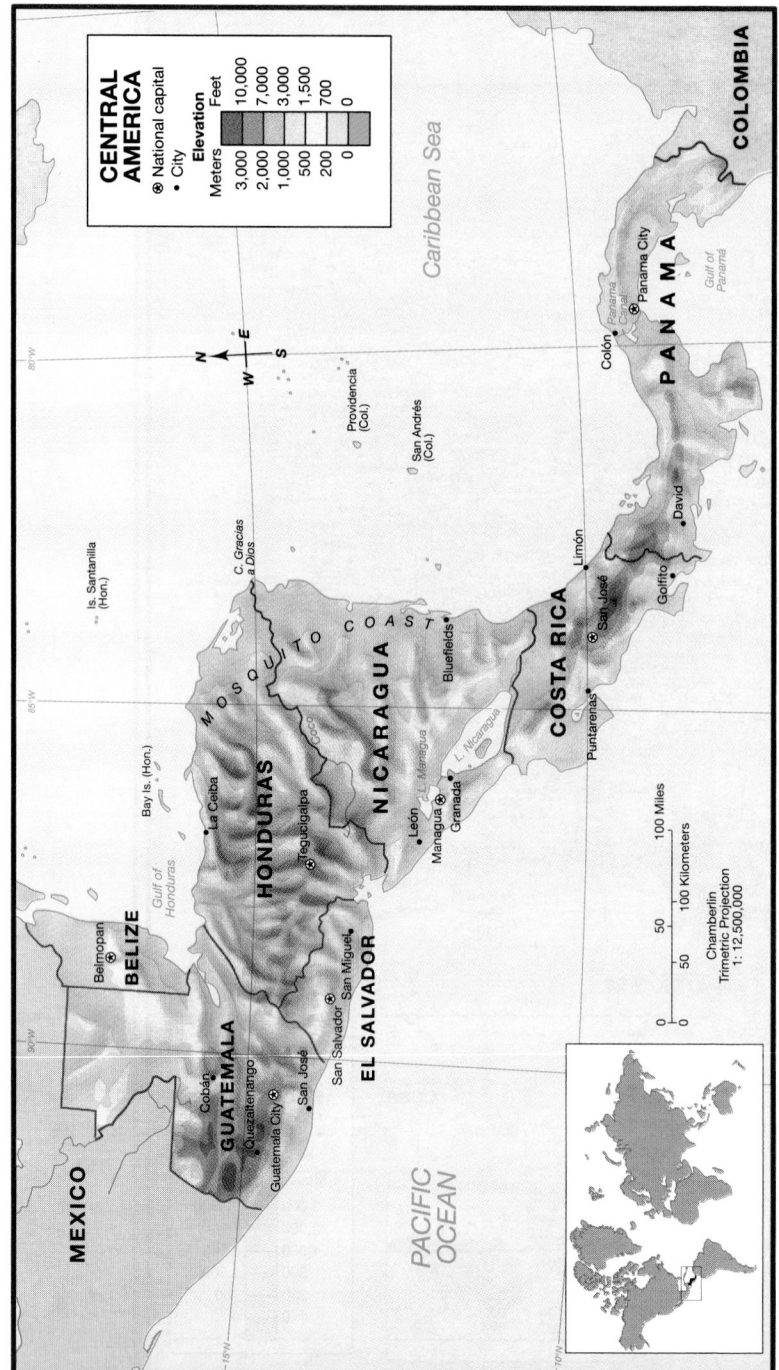

CENTRAL AMERICA

⊛ National capital
• City

Elevation

Meters	Feet
3,000	10,000
2,000	7,000
1,000	3,000
500	1,500
200	700
0	0

Caribbean Sea

COLOMBIA

Gulf of Panama

Panama City

PANAMA

Colón

David

Golfito

Limón

COSTA RICA

San José ⊛

Puntarenas

Bluefields

NICARAGUA

León
Managua ⊛
Granada

L. Managua

L. Nicaragua

MOSQUITO COAST

C. Gracias a Dios

Providencia (Col.)

San Andrés (Col.)

Is. Santanilla (Hon.)

Bay Is. (Hon.)

La Ceiba

HONDURAS

Tegucigalpa ⊛

Gulf of Honduras

Belmopan ⊛

BELIZE

MEXICO

GUATEMALA

Cobán

Quezaltenango ⊛
Guatemala City ⊛
San José

San Salvador ⊛
San Miguel

EL SALVADOR

PACIFIC OCEAN

N E S W

0	50	100 Miles
0	50	100 Kilometers

Chamberlin
Trimetric Projection
1:12,500,000

Galápagos Is. (Ecuador)

I. Marchena
I. San Salvador
I. Santa Cruz
I. San Cristóbal
I. Isabela
I. Fernandina
I. Sta.Maria
I. Española

WEST INDIES

Caribbean Sea

Neth. Antilles (Neth.)
Curaçao
I. de Margarita

CENTRAL AMERICA

Gulf of Venezuela
Barranquilla
Cartagena
Maracaibo
Caracas
VENEZUELA

Gulf of Urabá
Montería
Cúcuta
San Cristóbal
Medellín
Bucaramanga
Ciudad Bolívar
Alto Ritacuva

Gulf of Panamá
Manizales
Bogotá

I. Malpelo (Colombia)
C. Corrientes
Mt. Tolima
Buenaventura
Cali
Mt. Huila

Morawhanna
Georgetown
New Amsterdam
Paramaribo
GUYANA
SURINAME
Devil's I.
Cayenne
French Guiana (Fr.)

COLOMBIA

I. de Maracá
I. Caviana

ECUADOR
Mt. Cotopaxi
Mt. Chimborazo
Quito
Guayaquil
Gulf of Guayaquil
Cuenca

Equator

Manaus
Belém
I. São Luís

Iquitos

Fortaleza

Piura
PERU

C. São Roque

ANDES
Recife

Trujillo
Mt. Huascarán

BRAZIL

Callao
Cuzco

La Paz
Trinidad
BOLIVIA
Brasília

Arequipa
Cochabamba
Santa Cruz
Sucre

Salvador

Iquique

Belo Horizonte

Antofagasta

PARAGUAY

C. São Tomé
Rio de Janeiro

San Felix (Chile)
San Ambrosio (Chile)

Asunción
São Paulo
Santos

San Miguel de Tucumán

Mt. Ojos del Salado
CHILE

Curitiba
I. de Santa Catarina
Pôrto Alegre

Córdoba
Rivera
Salto
Paysandú
URUGUAY
Montevideo

Juan Fernández Is. (Chile)
I. Alejandro Selkirk
I. Robinson Crusoe

Viña del Mar
Mt. Aconcagua
Valparaíso
Mendoza
Santiago
Mt. Maipo
Rosario
Buenos Aires
La Plata
C. San Antonio
Mar del Plata

ARGENTINA

Concepción

Bahía Blanca

ANDES

I. de Chiloé
I. de Corcovado

Gulf of San Matías
Pen. Valdés

PACIFIC OCEAN

ATLANTIC OCEAN

Archipiélago de los Chonos
Pen. Taitao
C. Tres Montes

Gulf of San Jorge

ATLANTIC OCEAN

Gulf of Penas

Falkland Islands
(U.K.; claimed by Arg.)
Stanley

Strait of Magellan
Tierra del Fuego
I. Sta. Inés
Cape Horn
I. de los Estados

South Georgia (U.K.)

Antarctic Circle

SOUTH AMERICA

⊗ National capital
• City

Elevation

Meters	Feet
3,000	10,000
2,000	7,000
1,000	3,000
500	1,500
200	700
0	0

0   300   600 Miles
0   300   600 Kilometers

Lambert Azimuthal
Equal-Area Projection
1: 43,697,000

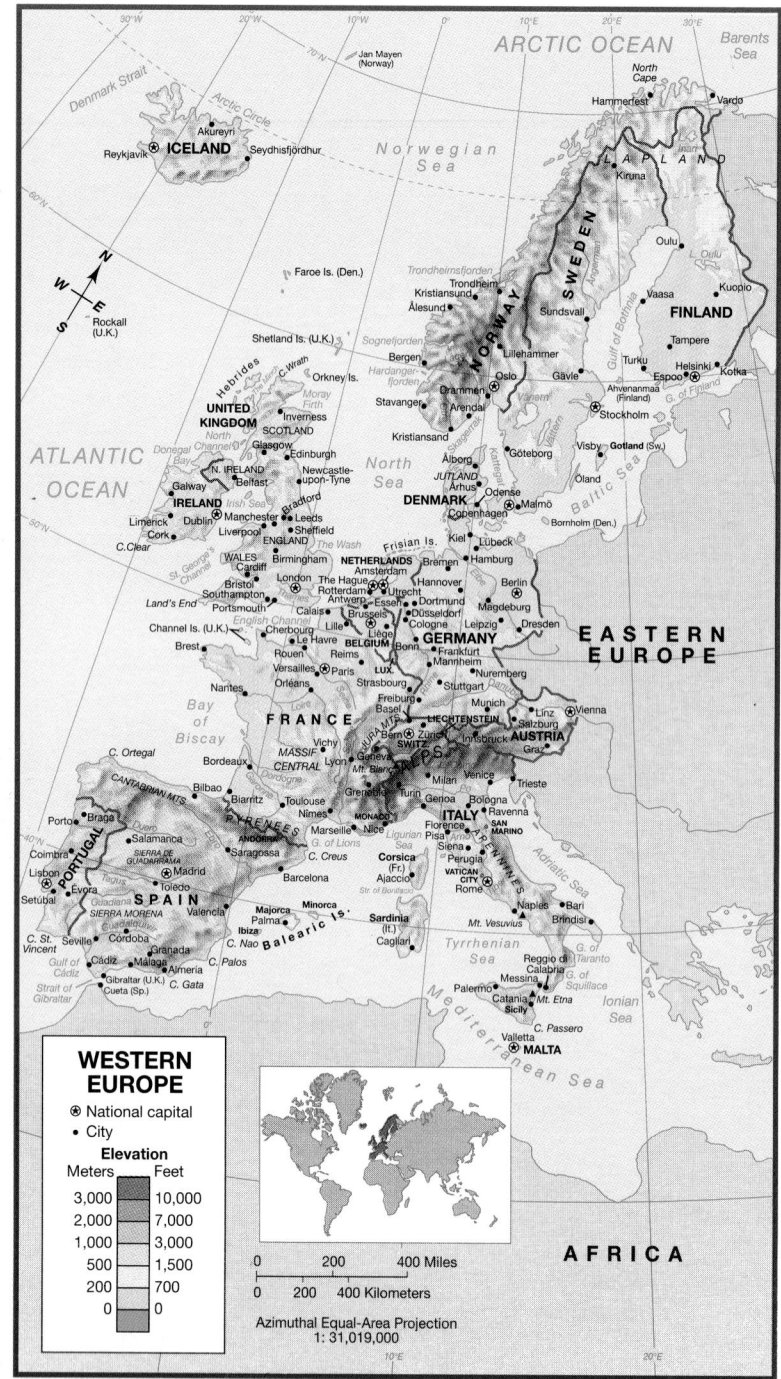

WESTERN EUROPE

⊛ National capital
• City

Elevation

Meters	Feet
3,000	10,000
2,000	7,000
1,000	3,000
500	1,500
200	700
0	0

0   200   400 Miles

0   200   400 Kilometers

Azimuthal Equal-Area Projection
1: 31,019,000

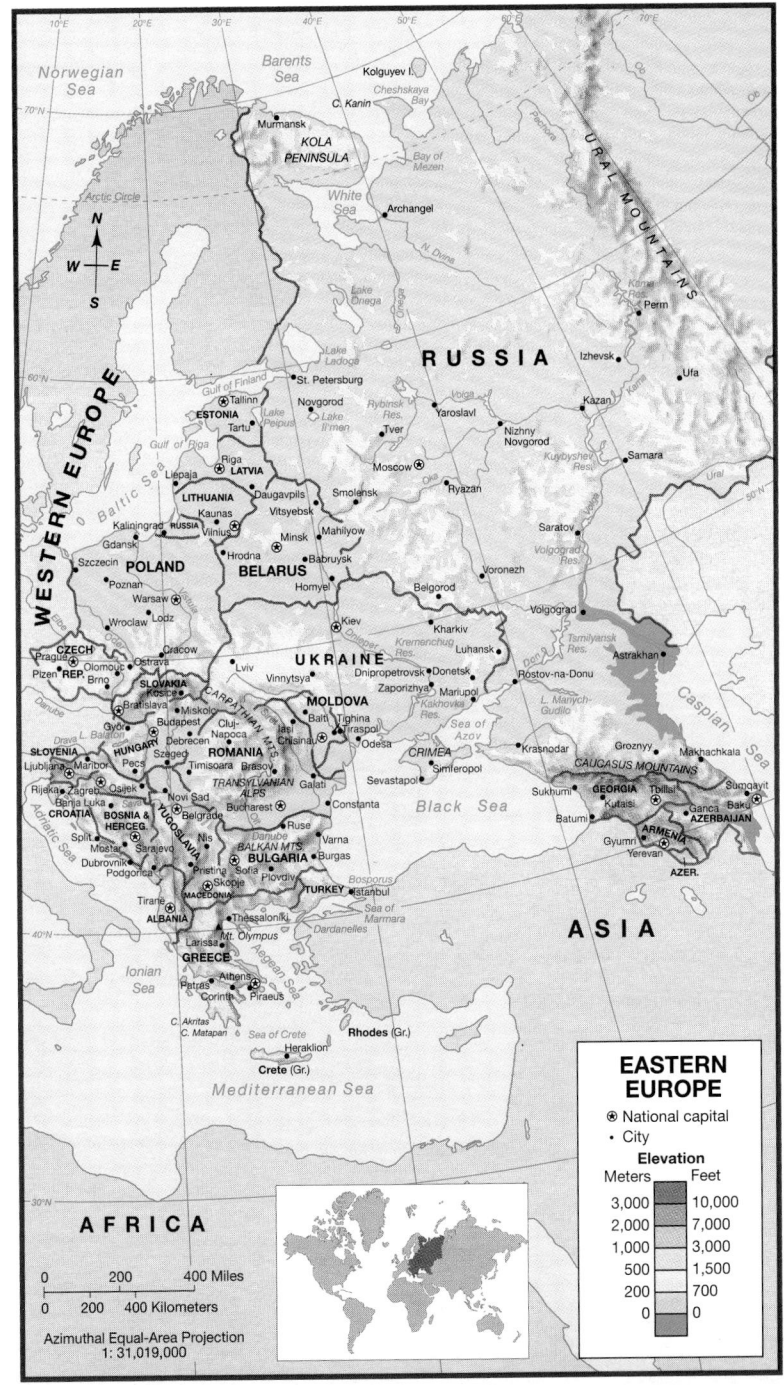

EASTERN EUROPE

⊛ National capital
· City

Elevation

Meters		Feet
3,000		10,000
2,000		7,000
1,000		3,000
500		1,500
200		700
0		0

AFRICA

0   200   400 Miles
0   200   400 Kilometers

Azimuthal Equal-Area Projection
1 : 31,019,000

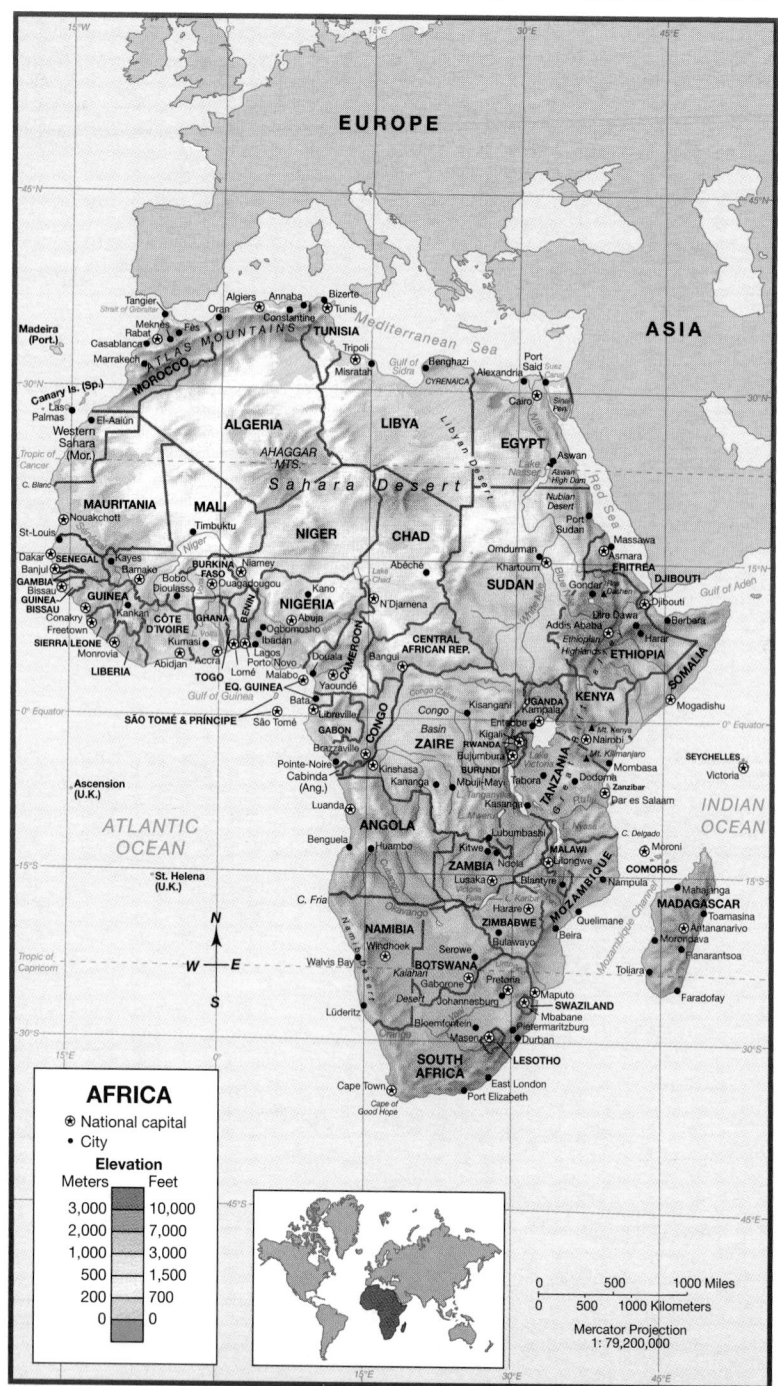

AFRICA

⊛ National capital
• City

Elevation

Meters	Feet
3,000	10,000
2,000	7,000
1,000	3,000
500	1,500
200	700
0	0

0   500   1000 Miles
0   500   1000 Kilometers

Mercator Projection
1: 79,200,000

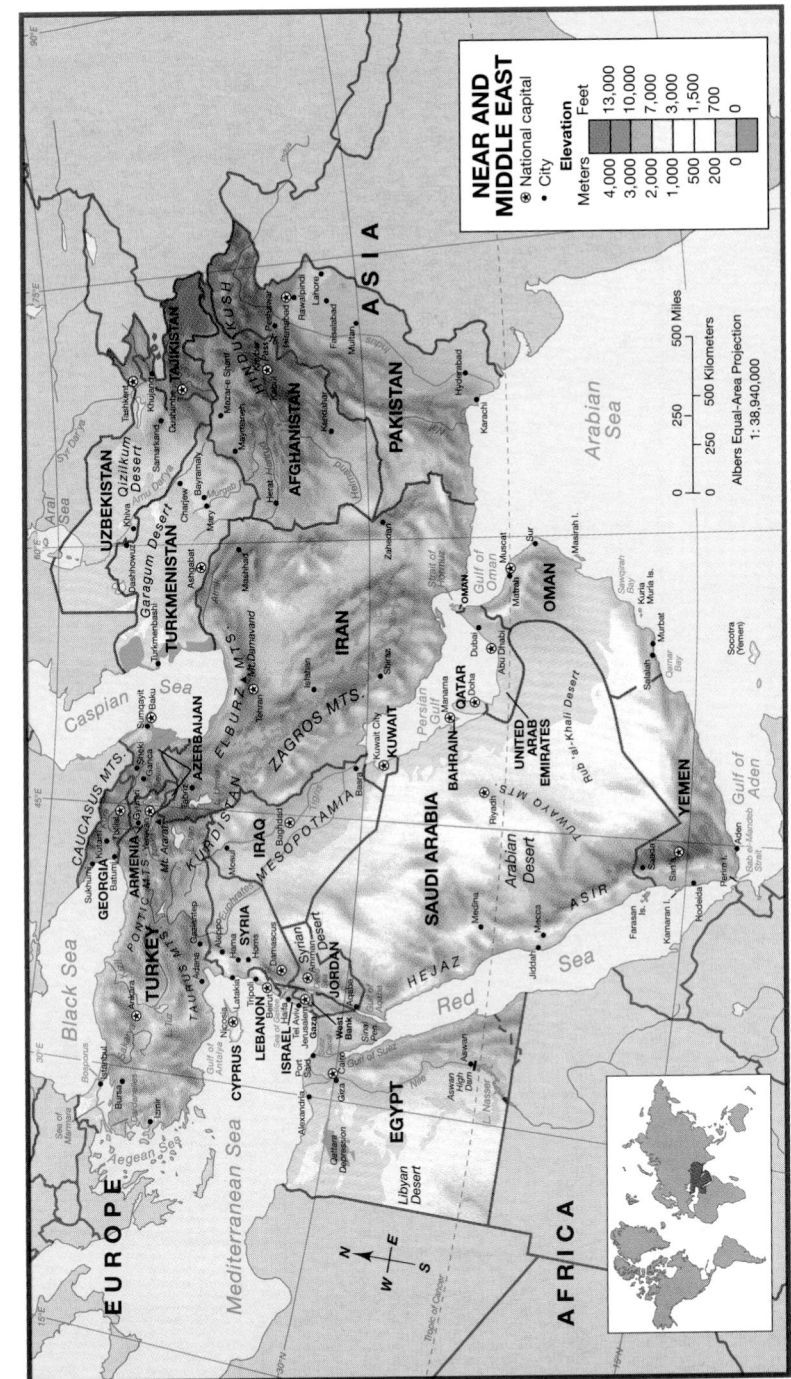

NEAR AND
MIDDLE EAST

⊛ National capital
• City

Elevation
Meters	Feet
4,000	13,000
3,000	10,000
2,000	7,000
1,000	3,000
500	1,500
200	700
0	0

Albers Equal-Area Projection
1: 38,940,000

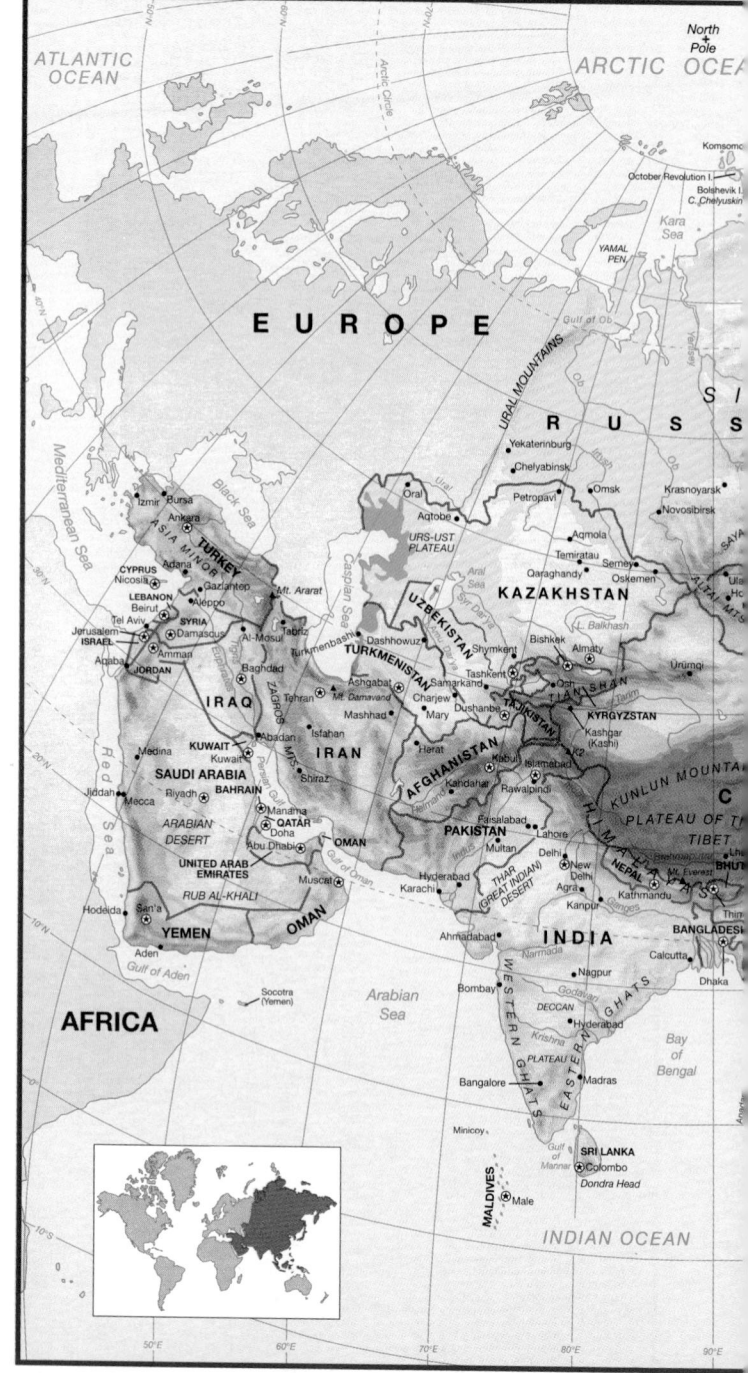

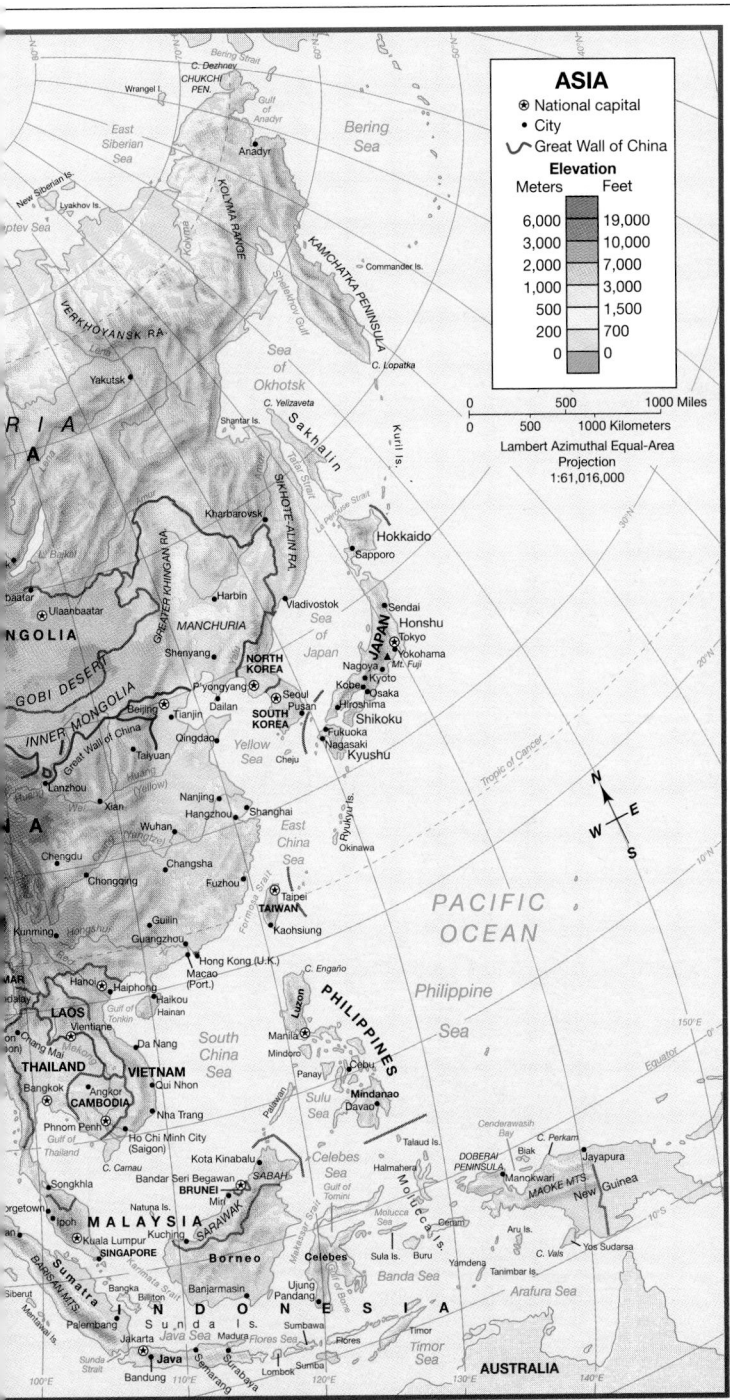

ASIA
⊗ National capital
• City
〰 Great Wall of China

Elevation

Meters	Feet
6,000	19,000
3,000	10,000
2,000	7,000
1,000	3,000
500	1,500
200	700
0	0

0   500   1000 Miles
0   500   1000 Kilometers
Lambert Azimuthal Equal-Area
Projection
1:61,016,000

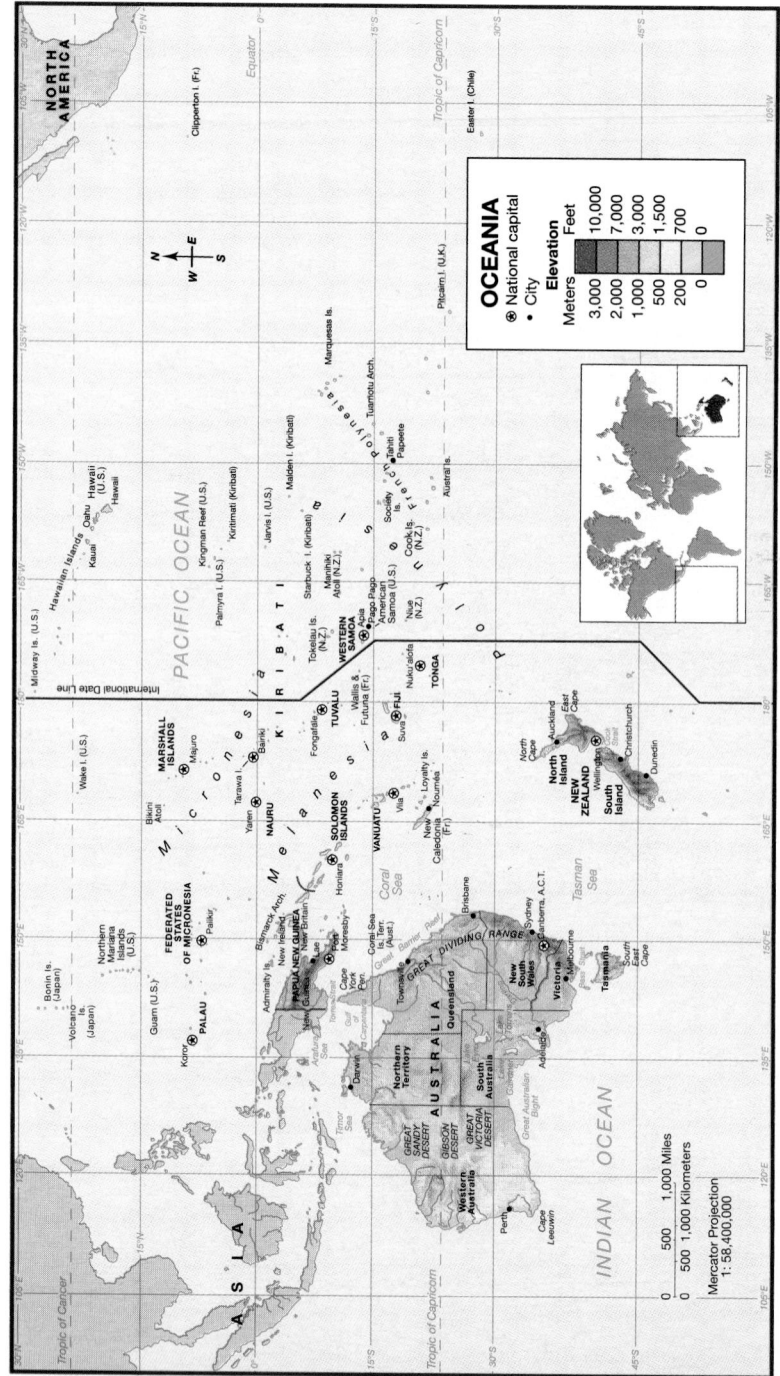

OCEANIA

⊛ National capital
• City

Elevation

Meters	Feet
3,000	10,000
2,000	7,000
1,000	3,000
500	1,500
200	700
0	0

Mercator Projection
1: 58,400,000

0   500   1,000 Miles
0   500 1,000 Kilometers

THE YEAR IN PICTURES

AT THE FRONT—President Clinton visits U.S. troops in war-torn Bosnia and praises their peacekeeping efforts. *Reuters/Win McNamee/Archive photos*

INAUGURATED—Former Haitian President Aristide congratulates President René Preval (right) after he was sworn in as Haiti's second elected president. *Reuters/Carole Devillers/Archive photos*

DEAD—Former Greek Prime Minister Andreas Papandreou (shown here in the 1960s) died at age 77 in Athens. He founded the Panhellenic Socialist Movement (Pasok) in 1974, which brought him to power in 1981. *Archive photos*

BLIZZARD OF '96—New Yorkers try to shovel out of their unplowed street in the wake of a record breaking storm that blanketed the Eastern seaboard. The storm left more than two feet of snow in the city. *Reuters/Jeff Christensen/Archive photos*

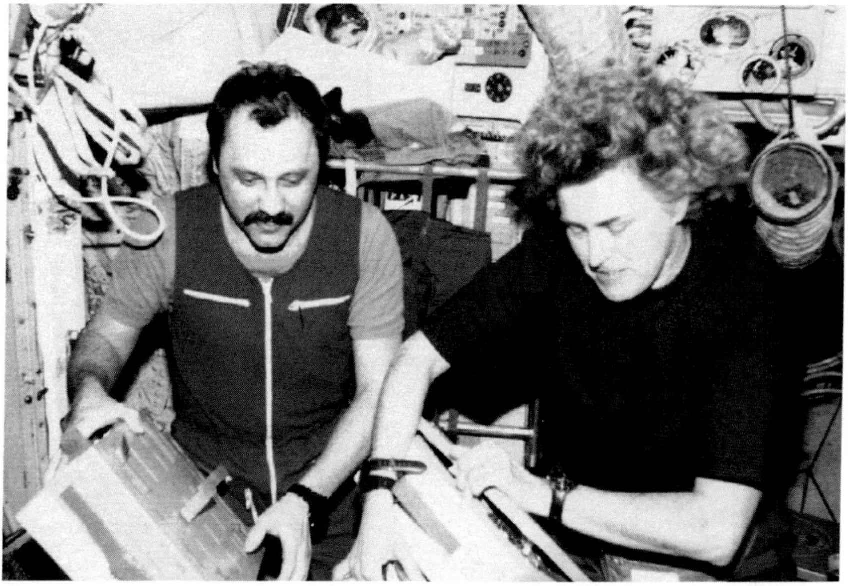

SPACE RECORD—Cosmonaut Yuri Usachev (left) and American astronaut Shannon Lucid prepare their meals aboard the Russian space station *Mir*. Lucid broke the spaceflight endurance records by an American and a woman with her 188-day mission. *Reuters/NASA/Archive photos*

TOURING—First Lady Hillary Clinton meets U.S. soldiers at an outpost in northern Bosnia as part of an eight-day European goodwill tour. *Reuters/Win McNamee/Archive photos*

KREMLIN SUMMIT—Leaders of the Group of Seven most industrialized nations (G7), Russia, and the E.U. pose during Moscow summit meeting on nuclear safety and security. (Left to Right) Japanese P.M. Ryutaro Hashimoto, Canadian P.M. Jean Chrétien, German Chancellor Helmut Kohl, French President Jacques Chirac, Russian President Boris Yeltsin, U.S. President Bill Clinton, British P.M. John Major, Italian P.M. Lamberto Dini, and President of the E.U. Commission Jacques Santer. *Reuters/Dima Sokolov/ Archive photos*

PEACEMAKERS—President Bill Clinton (center) holds hands with other leaders during a group picture taken at the end of the Summit of Peacemakers, held at Sharm El Sheikh, Egypt. At right is Russian President Boris Yeltsin and at left are Israeli P.M. Shimon Peres and Jordan's King Hussein (far left). *Reuters/ Gregg Newton/Archive photos*

APPREHENDED—Unabomber suspect Theodore Kaczynski is led into federal court. *Reuters/stringer/Archive photos*

VICTOR—Russian voters re-elected Boris Yeltsin, shown casting his ballot. *Reuters/Pool/Archive photos*

DISASTER—A large section of fuselage from TWA Flight 800 is lifted to shore from a Navy barge at the Shinnecock Coast Guard station on Long Island. The jumbo jet exploded and crashed into the Atlantic Ocean killing all 229 aboard. *Reuters/Jeff Christensen/Archive photos*

KILLED—U.S. Commerce Secretary Ron Brown (right) converses with a G.I. in Bosnia. His plane crashed following a visit to troops in the Balkans. *Reuters/Wade Goddard/Archive photos*

VISITING—During his state visit to Japan, President Bill Clinton chats with Emperor Akihito and Empress Michiko at a welcoming ceremony at Tokyo's Akasaka Guesthouse. *Reuters/Eriko Sugita/Archive photos*

ROYAL WELCOME—President Nelson Mandela of South Africa and Queen Elizabeth II pass cheering crowds on the way to Buckingham Palace during a state visit. *Express Syndication photo*

HISTORIC MEETING—Palestinian President Yasir Arafat (left) and President Clinton meet in the Oval Office at the White House. *Reuters/Rick Wilking/Archive photos*

MESSENGERS—Tens of thousands parade in Washington at the start of the "Stand for Children" rally to demand greater attention for the needs of children. *Reuters/Gregg Newton/Archive photos*

U.S. BASE BOMBING—A shattered building in Dhahran, Saudi Arabia, where 19 U.S. servicemen died and more than 250 were injured by a terrorist bomb. *Reuters/Greg Marinovich/Archive photos*

WINNER—Israeli Prime Minister–elect Benjamin Netanyahu greets followers in Tel Aviv. He won the election by the narrowest of margins. *Reuters/Havakuk Levison/Archive photos*

A New Beginning
Welfare to Work

NEW BEGINNING—Onlookers watch as President Clinton signs into law a bill reforming welfare, which ends 61 years of federal guarantees aiding the poor. *Reuters/Stephen Jaffe/Archive photos*

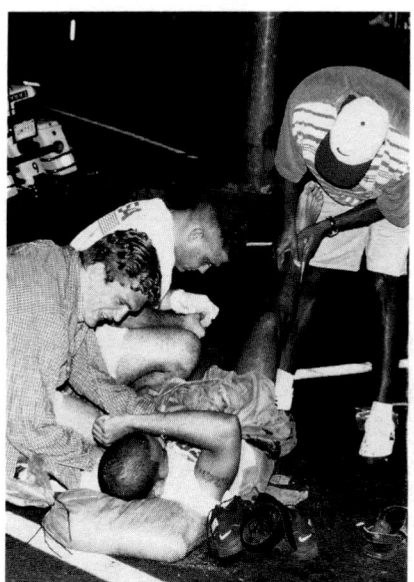

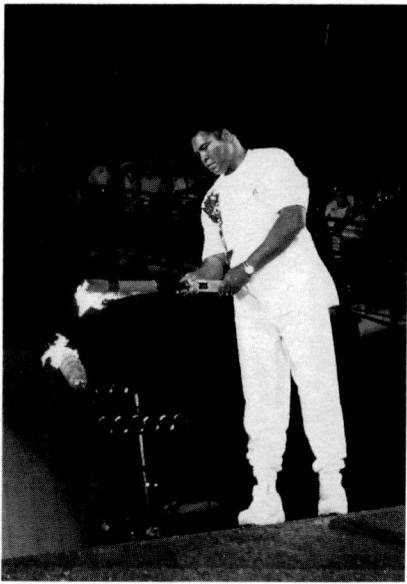

OLYMPIC BOMBING—A victim of terrorist bombing at Centennial Olympic Park in Atlanta, which injured more than 100. *Reuters/Grigory Dukor/Archive photos*

OLYMPIC TORCH—Former Olympic boxer Muhammad Ali lights the Olympic Cauldron during opening ceremonies. *Reuters/Andy Clark/Archive photos*

WAGE HIKE—President Clinton signs into law a bill to increase the minimum wage to $5.15 per hour in an elaborate ceremony on the White House lawn. He was joined by minimum wage earners and their children who represented the beneficiaries of the new law. *Reuters/Mike Theiler/Archive photos*

MAGNIFICENT—Members of U.S. women's gymnastics team wave to the crowd after capturing the first team gold medal in the nation's history. *Reuters/Mike Blake/Archive photo*

JUBILANT—Members of the U.S. women's softball team pile on their pitcher after winning the first Olympic gold medal in the sport. *Reuters/Jeff Vinnick/Archive photos*

BEAMING—Amy Van Dyken of Denver shows off her gold medal after becoming the first American woman to earn four gold medals at one Olympics with her 50-meter freestyle win over the world record-holder Le Jingyi of China. *Reuters/Mark Baker/Archive photos*

RARE GOLD—Michael Johnson celebrates his gold medal after becoming the first man to win both the 200- and 400-meter sprints in the same Olympics. *Reuters/Mike Blake/Archive photos*

SOUVENIR—Carl Lewis collects sand from the long jump pit after winning his ninth Olympic gold medal with his long jump victory. *Reuters/Jerry Lampen/Archive photos*

HURRAH—President Clinton (right) and Vice President Al Gore wave to crowds at the Democratic National Convention following Clinton's speech accepting the nomination for a second term. *Reuters/Luc Novovitch/Archive photos*

RALLYING—Republican Party presidential candidate Bob Dole (right) and his newly announced running mate Jack Kemp stand together at a campaign rally in Dole's hometown, Russell, Kansas. At left is Kemp's wife, Joanne. *Reuters/Luc Novovitch/Archive photos*

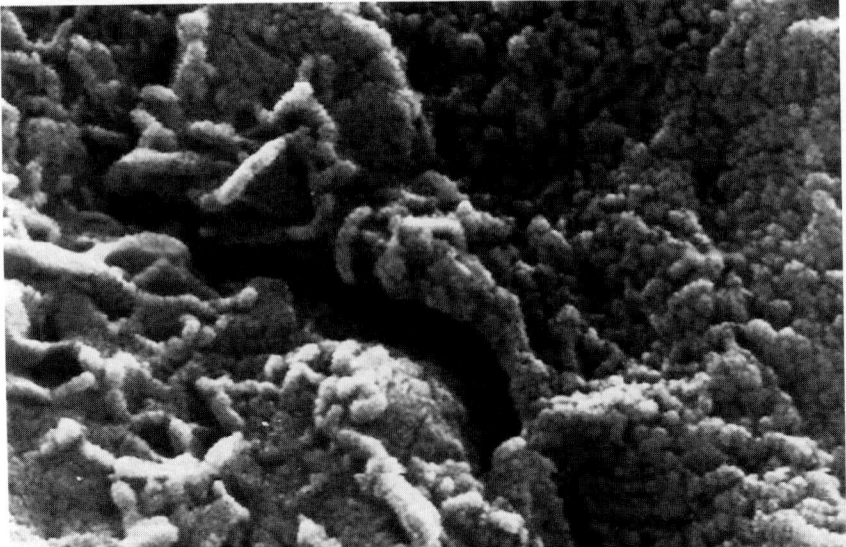

DIFFERENT DRUMMER—Reform Party presidential candidate Ross Perot addresses members of the VFW during their annual national convention in Louisville, Kentucky. Mr. Perot launched his campaign in Philadelphia several days earlier and vowed to end the two-party system. *Reuters/John Summers II/ Archive photos*

ALIEN LIFE—Electron microscope image from a Martian meteorite that NASA believes shows evidence of tiny tubular structures, possible fossils of bacteria-like organisms that may have lived on Mars more than 3.6 billion years ago. *Reuters/NASA/Archive photos*

CROSSWORD PUZZLE GUIDE

First Aid to Crossword Puzzlers

We cannot begin to list all the odd words you might encounter in your daily and Sunday crossword puzzles, for such words run into many thousands. But we have tried to include those that turn up most frequently, as well as many others that should be of help to you when you are unable to go any further.

Also, we do not guarantee that the definitions in your puzzle will be exactly the same as ours, although we have checked every word with a standard dictionary and have followed its definition.

In nearly every case, we have used as the key word the principal noun of the definition, rather than any adjective, adjective phrase, or noun used as an adjective. And, to simplify your searching, we have grouped the words according to the number of spaces you have to fill.

For a list of Foreign Phrases, *see* Index. For Rulers of England and Great Britain, France, Germany and Prussia, and Russia, *see* Countries of the World.

Words of Two Letters

Ambary, DA
And (French, Latin), ET
Article (Arabic), AL
   (French), LA, LE, UN
   (Spanish), EL, LA, UN
At the (French), AU
   (Spanish), AL
Behold, LO
Bird: Hawaiian, OO
Birthplace: Abraham's, UR
Bone, OS
Buddha, FO
Butterfly: Peacock, IO
Champagne, AY
Chaos, NU
Chief: Burmese, BO
Coin: Roman, AS
   Siamese, AT
Concerning, RE
Dialect: Chinese, WU
Double (Egy. relig.), KA
Drama: Japanese, NO
Egg (comb. form), OO
Esker, OS
Eye (Scotch), EE
Factor: Amplification, MU
Fifty (Greek), NU
Fish: Carplike, ID
Force, OD
Forty (Greek), MU
From (French, Latin, Spanish), DE

(Latin prefix), AB
From the (French), DU
God: Babylonian, EA, ZU
   Egyptian sun, RA
   Hindu unknown, KA
   Semitic, EL
Goddess: Babylonian, AI
   Greek earth, GE
Gold (heraldry), OR
Gulf: Arctic, OB
Heart (Egy. relig.), AB
Indian: South American, GE
King: Of Bashan, OG
Language: Artificial, RO
   Assamese, AO
Lava: Hawaiian, AA
Letter: Greek, MU, NU, PI, XI
   Hebrew, HE, PE
Lily: Palm, TI
Measure: Annamese, LY
   Chinese, HO, HU, KO, LI, MU, PU,
   TO, TU
   Japanese, GO, JO, MO, RI, SE, TO
   Metric land, AR
   Netherlands, EL
   Portuguese, PE
   Siamese, WA
   Swedish, AM
   Type, EM, EN
Monk: Buddhist, BO
Month: Jewish, AB

Mouth, OS
Mulberry: Indian, AL
Native: Burmese, WA
Note: Of Scale, DO, FA, MI, LA, RE, TI
Of (French, Latin, Spanish), DE
Of the (French), DU
One (Scotch), AE
Pagoda: Chinese, TA
Plant: East Indian fiber, DA
Ridge: Sandy, AS, OS
River: Russian, OB
Sloth: Three-toed, AI
Soul (Egy. relig.), BA
Sound: Hindu mystic, OM
Suffix: Comparative, ER
The. *See* Article
To the: French, AU
   Spanish, AL
Tree: Buddhist sacred, BO
Tribe: Assamese, AO
Type: Jumbled, PI
Weight: Annamese, TA
   Chinese, LI
   Danish, ES
   Japanese, MO
   Roman, AS
Whirlwind: Faeroe Is., OE
Yes (German), JA
   (Italian, Spanish), SI
   (Russian), DA

Words of Three Letters

Adherent: IST
Again, BIS
Age, ERA
Antelope: African, GNU, KOB
Apricot: Japanese, UME
Article (German): DAS, DEM, DEN,
   DER, DES, DIE, EIN
   (French), LES, UNE
   (Spanish), LAS, LOS, UNA
Banana: Polynesian, FEI
Barge, HOY
Bass: African, IYO
Beak, NEB, NIB
Beard: Grain, AWN
Beetle: June, DOR
Being, ENS
Berry: Hawthorn, HAW
Beverage: Hawaiian, AVA
Bird: Australian, EMU
   Crowlike, JAY
   Extinct, MOA

Fabulous, ROC
Frigate, IWA
Parson, POE, TUE, TUI
Sea, AUK
Blackbird, ANI, ANO
Born, NEE
Bronze: Roman, AES
Bugle: Yellow, IVA
By way of, VIA
Canton: Swiss, URI
Cap: Turkish, FEZ
Catnip, NEP
Character: In "Faerie Queene," UNA
Coin: Afghan, PUL
   Albanian, LEK
   British Guiana, BIT
   Bulgarian, LEV, LEW
   French, ECU, SOU
   Indian, PIE
   Japanese, SEN, YEN
   Korean, WON

   Lithuanian, LIT
   Macao, Timor, AVO
   Palestinian, MIL
   Persian, PUL
   Peruvian, SOL
   Rumanian, BAN, LEU, LEY
   Scandinavian, ORE
   Siamese, ATT
   See also Money of account
Collection: Facts, ANA
Commune: Belgian, ANS, ATH
   Netherlands, EDE, EPE
Community: Russian, MIR
Constellation: Southern, ARA
Contraction: Poetic, EEN, EER, OER
Covering: Apex of roof, EPI
Crab: Fiddler, UCA
Crag: Rocky, TOR
Cry: Crow, rook, raven, CAW
Cup: Wine, AMA
Cymbal, Oriental, TAL, ZEL

529

Disease: Silkworm, UJI
Division: Danish territorial, AMT
  Geologic, EON
Doctrine, ISM
Dowry, DOT
Dry (French), SEC
Dynasty: Chinese, CHI, HAN, SUI,
  WEI, YIN
Eagle: Sea, ERN
Earth (comb. form), GEO
Egg: Louse, NIT
Eggs: Fish, ROE
Emmet, ANT
Enzyme, ASE
Equal (comb. form), ISO
Extension: building, ELL
Far (comb. form), TEL
Farewell, AVE
Fiber: Palm, TAL
Finial, EPI
Fish: Carplike, IDE
  Pikelike, GAR
Flatfish, DAB
Fleur-de-lis, LIS, LYS
Food: Hawaiian, POI
Formerly, NEE
Friend (French), AMI
Game: Card, LOO
Garment: Camel-hair, ABA
Gateway, DAR
Gazelle: Tibetan, GOA
Genus: Ducks, AIX
  Grasses, POA
  Grasses (maize), ZEA
  Herbs or shrubs, IVA
  Lizards, UTA
  Rodents (incl. house mice), MUS
  Ruminants (incl. cattle), BOS
  Swine, SUS
Gibbon: Malay, LAR
God: Assyrian, SIN
  Babylonian, ABU, ANU, BEL, HEA,
    SIN, UTU
  Irish sea, LER
  Phrygian, MEN
  Polynesian, ORO
Goddess: Babylonian, AYA
  Etruscan, UNI
  Hindu, SRI, UMA, VAC
  Teutonic, RAN
Governor: Algerian, DEY
  Turkish, BEY
Grampus, ORC
Grape, UVA
Grass: Meadow, POA
Gypsy, ROM
Hail, AVE
Hare: Female, DOE
Hawthorn, HAW
Hay: Spread for drying, TED
Herb: Japanese, UDO
  Perennial, PIA
  Used for blue dye, WAD
Herd: Whales, GAM, POD
Hero: Spanish, CID
High (music), ALT
Honey (pharm.), MEL
Humorist: American, ADE
I (Latin), EGO
I love (Latin), AMO
Indian: Algonquian, FOX, SAC, WEA
  Chimakuan, HOH
  Keresan, SIA
  Mayan, MAM
  Shoshonean, UTE
  Siouan, KAW, OTO
  South American, ITE, ONA, URO,
    URU, YAO
  Tierra del Fuego, ONA
  Wakashan, AHT
Ingot, PIG
Inlet: Narrow, RIA
Island: Cyclades, IOS
  Dodecanese, COS, KOS
  (French), ILE
  River, AIT

Jackdaw, DAW
John (Gaelic), IAN
Keelbill, ANI, ANO
Kiln, OST
King: British legendary LUD
Kobold, NIS
Lace: To make, TAT
Lamprey, EEL
Language: Artificial, IDO
  Bantu, ILA
  Siamese, LAO, TAI
Leaf: Palm, OLA, OLE
Leaving, ORT
Left: Cause to turn, HAW
Letter: Greek, CHI, ETA, PHI, PSI,
  RHO, TAU
  Hebrew, MEM, NUN, SIN, TAV, VAU
Lettuce, COS
Life (comb. form), BIO
Lily: Palm, TOI
Lizard, EFT
Louse: Young, NIT
Love (Anglo-Irish), GRA
Lute: Oriental, TAR
Macaw: Bralizian, ARA
Marble, TAW
Match: Shooting (French), TIR
Meadow, LEA
Measure: Abyssinian, TAT
  Algerian, PIK
  Annamese, GON, MAU, NGU,
    VUO, SAO, TAO, TAT
  Arabian, DEN, SAA
  Belgian, VAT
  Bulgarian, OKA, OKE
  Chinese, FEN, TOU, YIN
  Cloth, ELL
  Cyprus, OKA, OKE, PIK
  Czech, LAN, SAH
  Danish, FOD, MIL, POT
  Dominican Republic, ONA
  Dutch, old, AAM
  East Indian, KIT
  Egyptian, APT, HEN, PIK, ROB
  Electric, MHO, OHM
  Energy, ERG
  English, PIN
  Estonian, TUN
  French, POT
  German, AAM
  Greek, PIK
  Hebrew, CAB, HIN, KOR, LOG
  Hungarian, AKO
  Icelandic, FET
  Indian, GAZ, GUZ, JOW, KOS
  Japanese, BOO, CHO, KEN, RIN,
    SHO, SUN, TAN
  Malabar, ADY
  Metric land, ARE
  Netherlands, KAN, KOP, MUD,
    VAT, ZAK
  Norwegian, FOT, POT
  Persian, GAZ, GUZ, MOU, ZAR, ZER
  Polish, CAL
  Rangoon, DHA, LAN
  Roman, PES, URN
  Russian, FUT, LOF
  Scotch, COP
  Siamese, KEN, NIU, RAI, SAT,
    SEN, SOK, WAH, YOT
  Somaliland, TOP
  Spanish, PIE
  Straits Settlements, PAU, TUN
  Swedish, ALN, FOT, MIL, REF, TUM
  Swiss, POT
  Tunisian, SAA
  Turkish, OKA, OKE, PIK
  Wire, MIL
  Württemberg, IMI
  Yarn, LEA
  Yugoslavian, OKA, RIF
Milk, LAC
Milkfish, AWA
Moccasin, PAC
Money: Yap stone, FEI
Money of Account: Anglo-Saxon, ORA,

ORE
  French, SOU
  Indian, LAC
  Japanese, RIN
  Oman, GAJ
  Virgin Islands, BIT
  See also Coin
Monkey: Capuchin, SAI
Morsel, ORT
Mother: Peer Gynt's, ASE
Mountain: Asia Minor, IDA
Mulberry: Indian, AAL, ACH, AWL
Muttonbird: New Zealand, OII
Nahoor, SNA
Native: Mindanao, ATA
Neckpiece, BOA
Newt, EFT
No (Scotch), NAE
Note: Guido's highest, ELA
  Of scale, SOL
Nursemaid: Oriental, AMA, IYA
Ocher: Yellow, SIL
One (Scotch), YIN
Ornament: Pagoda, TEE
Oven: Polynesian, UMU
Ox: Tibetan, YAK
Pagoda: Chinese, TAA
Parrot: Hawk, HIA
  New Zealand, KEA
Part: Footlike, PES
Particle: Electrified, ION
Pasha, DEY
Pass: Mountain, COL
Paste: Rice, AME
Pea: Indian split, DAL
Peasant: Philippine, TAO
Penpoint, NEB, NIB
Piece out, EKE
Pigeon, NUN
Pine: Textile screw, ARA
Pistol (slang), GAT
Pit: Baking, IMU
Plant: Pepper, AVA
Play: By Capek, RUR
Poem: Old French, DIT
Porgy: Japanese, TAI
Priest: Biblical high, ELI
Prince Ethiopian, RAS
Pseudonym: Dickens', BOZ
Queen: Fairy, MAB
Quince: Bengal, BEL
Record: Ship's, LOG
Refuse: Flax (Scotch), PAB, POB
Resin, LAC
Resort, SPA
Revolver (slang), GAT
Right: Cause to turn, GEE
River: Scotch or English, DEE
  (Spanish), RIO
  Swiss, AAR
Room: Harem, ODA
Rootstock: Fern, ROI
Rose (Persian), GUL
Ruff: Female, REE
Rule: Indian, RAJ
Sailor, GOB, TAR
Saint: Female (abbr.), STE
  Mohammedan, PIR
Salt, SAL
Sash: Japanese, OBI
Scrap, ORT
Seed: Poppy, MAW
  Small, PIP
Self, EGO
Serpent: Vedic sky, AHI
Sesame, TIL
Sheep: Female, EWE
  Indian, SHA
  Male, RAM
Sheepfold (Scotch), REE
Shelter, LEE
Shield, ECU
Shooting match (French), TIR
Shrew: European, ERD
Shrub: Evergreen, YEW
Silkworm, ERI

Snake, ASP, BOA
Soak, RET
Son-in-law: Mohammed's, ALI
Sorrel: Wood, OCA
Spade: Long, narrow, LOY
Spirit: Malignant, KER
Spot: Playing-card, PIP
Spread for drying, TED
Spring: Mineral, SPA
Sprite: Water, NIX
Statesman: Japanese, ITO
Stern: Toward, AFT
Stomach: Bird's, MAW
Street (French), RUE
Summer (French), ETE
Sun, SOL
Swamp, BOG, FEN
Swan: Male, COB
Tea: Chinese, CHA
Temple: Shinto, SHA
The. *See* Article
Thing (law), RES
Title: Etruscan, LAR
    Monk's, FRA
    Portuguese, DOM
    Spanish, DON
    Turkish, AGA, BEY
Tool: Cutting, ADZ, AXE
    Mining, GAD
    Piercing, AWL
Tree: Candlenut, AMA
    Central American, EBO
    East Indian, SAJ, SAL

Evergreen, YEW
Hawaiian, KOA, KOU
Indian, BEL, DAR
Linden, LIN
New Zealand, AKE
Philippine, DAO, TUA, TUI
Rubber, ULE
    South American, APA
Tribe: New Zealand, ATI
Turmeric, REA
Twice, BIS
Twin: Siamese, ENG
Uncle (dialect), EAM, EME
Veil: Chalice, AER, AIR
Vessel: Wine, AMA
Vestment: Ecclesiastical, ALB
Vetch: Bitter, ERS
Victorfish, AKU
Vine: New Zealand, AKA
    Philippine, IYO
Wallaba, APA
Wapiti, ELK
Water (French), EAU
Waterfall, LIN
Watering place: Prussian, EMS
Weave: Designating plain, UNI
Weight: Annamese, CAN
    Bulgarian, OKA, OKE
    Burmese, MOO, VIS
    Chinese, FEN, HAO, KIN, SSU,
    TAN, YIN
    Cyprus, OKA, OKE
    Danish, LOD, ORT, VOG

East Indian, TJI
Egyptian, KAT, OKA, OKE
English, for wool, TOD
German, LOT
Greek, MNA, OKA, OKE
Indian, SER
Japanese, FUN, KIN, RIN, SHI
Korean, KON
Malacca, KIP
Mongolian, LAN
Netherlands, ONS
Norwegian, LOD
Polish, LUT
Rangoon, PAI
Roman, BES
Russian, LOT
Siamese, BAT, HAP, PAI
Swedish, ASS, ORT
Turkish, OKA, OKE
Yugoslavian, OKA, OKE
Whales: Herd, GAM, POD
Wildebeest, GNU
Wing, ALA
Witticism, MOT
Wolframite, CAL
Worm: African, LOA
Wreath: Hawaiian, LEI
Yale, ELI
Yam: Hawaiian, HOI
Yes (French), OUI
Young: Bring forth, EAN
Z (letter), ZED

Words of Four Letters

Aborigine: Borneo, DYAK
Agave, ALOE
Animal: Footless, APOD
Ant: White, ANAI, ANAY
Antelope: African, ASSE, BISA,
    GUIB, KOBA, KUDU, ORYX, POKU,
    PUKU, TOPI, TORA
Apoplexy: Plant, ESCA
Apple, POME
Apricot, ANSU
Ardor, ELAN
Armadillo, APAR, PEBA, PEVA, TATU
Ascetic: Mohammedan, SUFI
Association: Chinese, TONG
Astronomer: Persian, OMAR
Avatar: Of Vishnu, RAMA
Axillary, ALAR
Band: Horizontal (heraldry), FESS
Barracuda, SPET
Bark: Mulberry, TAPA
Base: Column, DADO
Bearing (heraldry), ORLE
Beer: Russian, KVAS
Beige, ECRU
Being, ESSE
Beverage: Japanese rice, SAKE
Bird: Asian, MINA, MYNA
    Egyptian sacred, IBIS
    Extinct, DODO, MAMO
    Flightless, KIWI
    Gull-like, TERN
    Hawaiian, IIWI, MAMO
    Parson, KOKO
    Unfledged, EYAS
Birds: As class, AVES
Black, EBON
    (French), NOIR
Blackbird: European, MERL
Boat: Flat-bottomed, DORY
Bone: Forearm, ULNA
Bones, OSSA
Box, Japanese, INRO
Bravo (rare), EUGE
Buffalo: Indian wild, ARNA
Bull (Spanish), TORO
Burden, ONUS
Cabbage: Sliced, SLAW

Caliph: Mohammedan, OMAR
Canoe: Malay, PRAU, PROA
Cap: Military, KEPI
Cape, NESS
Capital: Ancient Irish, TARA
Case: Article, ETUI
Cat: Wild, BALU, EYRA
Chalcedony, SARD
Chamber: Indian ceremonial, KIVA
Channel: Brain, ITER
Cheese: Dutch, EDAM
Chest: Sepulchral stone, CIST
Chieftain: Arab, EMIR
Church: Part of, APSE, NAVE
    (Scotch), KIRK
Claim (law), LIEN
Cluster: Flower, CYME
Coin: Chinese, TAEL, YUAN
    German, MARK
    Indian, ANNA
    Iranian, RIAL
    Italian, LIRA
    Moroccan, OKIA
    Siamese, BAHT
    South American, PESO
    Spanish, DURO, PESO
    Turkish, PARA
Commune: Belgian, AATH
Composition: Musical, OPUS
Compound: Chemical, DIOL
Constellation: Southern, PAVO
Council: Russian, DUMA
Counsel, REDE
Covering: Seed, ARIL
Cross: Egyptian, ANKH
Cry: Bacchanalian, EVOE
Cup (Scotch), TASS
Cupbearer, SAKI
Dagger, DIRK
    Malay, KRIS
Dam: River, WEIR
Dash, ELAN
Date: Roman, IDES
Dawn: Pertaining to, EOAN
Dean: English, INGE
Decay: In fruit, BLET
Deer: Sambar, MAHA

Disease: Skin, ACNE
Disk: Solar, ATEN
Dog: Hunting, ALAN
Drink: Hindu intoxicating, SOMA
Duck, SMEE, SMEW, TEAL
Dynasty: Chinese, CHEN, CHIN,
    CHOU, CHOW, HSIA, MING, SUNG,
    TANG, TSIN
    Mongol, YUAN
Eagle: Biblical, GIER
    Sea, ERNE
Egyptian: Christian, COPT
Ear: Pertaining to, OTIC
Entrance: Mine, ADIT
Esau, EDOM
Escutcheon: Voided, ORLE
Eskers, OSAR
Evergreen: New Zealand, TAWA
Fairy: Persian, PERI
Family: Italian, ESTE
Far (comb. form), TELE
Farewell, VALE
Father (French), PERE
Fennel: Philippine, ANIS
Fever: Malarial, AGUE
Fiber: East Indian, JUTE
Firn, NEVE
Fish: Carplike, DACE
    Hawaiian, ULUA
    Herringlike, SHAD
    Mackerellike, CERO
    Marine, HAKE
    Sea, LING, MERO, OPAH
    Spiny-finned, GOBY
Food: Tropical, TARO
Foot: Metric, IAMB
Formerly, ERST
Founder: Of Carthage, DIDO
France: Southern, MIDI
Furze, ULEX
Gaelic, ERSE
Gaiter, SPAT
Game: Card, FARO, SKAT
Garlic: European wild, MOLY
Garment: Hindu, SARI
    Roman, TOGA
Gazelle, CORA

Gem, JADE, ONYX, OPAL, RUBY
Genus: Amphibians (incl. frogs), RANA
  Amphibians (incl. tree toads), HYLA
  Antelopes, ORYX
  Auks, ALCA, URIA
  Bees, APIS
  Birds (American ostriches), RHEA
  Birds (cranes), CRUS
  Birds (magpies), PICA
  Birds (peacocks), PAVO
  Cetaceans, INIA
  Ducks (incl. mallards), ANAS
  Fishes (burbots), LOTA
  Fishes (incl. bowfins), AMIA
  Geese (snow geese), CHEN
  Gulls, XEMA
  Herbs, ARUM, GEUM
  Insects (water scorpions), NEPA
  Lilies, ALOE
  Mammals (mankind), HOMO
  Orchids, DISA
  Owls, ASIO, BUBO, OTUS
  Palms, NIPA
  Sea birds, SULA
  Sheep, OVIS
  Shrubs, Eurasian, ULEX
  Shrubs (hollies), ILEX
  Shrubs (incl. Virginia Willow), ITEA
  Shrubs, tropical, EVEA
  Snakes (sand snakes), ERYX
  Swans, OLOR
  Trees, chocolate, COLA
  Trees (ebony family), MABA
  Trees (incl. maples), ACER
  Trees (olives), OLEA
  Trees, tropical, EVEA
  Turtles, EMYS
Goat: Wild, IBEX, KRAS, TAHR, TAIR, THAR
God: Assyrian, ASUR
  Babylonian, ADAD, ADDU, ENKI, ENZU, IRRA, NABU, NEBO, UTUG
  Celtic, LLEU, LLEW
  Hindu, AGNI, CIVA, DEVA, DEWA, KAMA, RAMA, SIVA, VAYU
  Phrygian, ATYS
  Semitic, BAAL
  Teutonic, HLER
Goddess: Babylonian, ERUA, GULA
  Hawaiian, PELE
  Hindu, DEVI, KALI, SHRI, VACH
Gooseberry: Hawaiian, POHA
Gourd, PEPO
Grafted (heraldry), ENTE
Grandfather (obsolete), AIEL
Grandparents: Pertaining to, AVAL
Grass: Hawaiian, HILO
Gray (French), GRIS
Green (heraldry), VERT
Groom: Indian, SYCE
Half (prefix), DEMI, HEMI, SEMI
Hamlet, DORP
Hammer-head: Part of, PEEN
Handle, ANSA
Harp: Japanese, KOTO
Hartebeest, ASSE, TORA
Hautboy, OBOE
Hawk: Taken from nest (falconry), EYAS
Hearing (law), OYER
Heater: For liquids, ETNA
Herb: Aromatic, ANET, DILL
  Fabulous, MOLY
  Perennial, GEUM, SEGO
  Pot, WORT
  Used for blue dye, WADE, WOAD
Hill: Flat-topped, MESA
  Sand, DENE, DUNE
Hoarfrost, RIME
Hog: Immature female, GILT
Holly, ILEX
House: Cow, BYRE
  (Spanish), CASA
Ice: Floating, FLOE
Image, ICON, IKON
Incarnation: Of Vishnu, RAMA

Indian: Algonquian, CREE, SAUK
  Central American, MAYA
  Iroquoian, ERIE
  Mexican, CORA
  Peruvian, CANA, INCA, MORO
  Shoshonean, HOPI
  Siouan, OTOE
  Southwestern, HOPI, PIMA, YUMA, ZUNI
Insect: Immature, PUPA
Instrument: Stringed, LUTE, LYRE
Ireland, EIRE, ERIN
Jacket: English, ETON
Jail (British), GAOL
Jar, OLLA
Judge: Mohammedan, CADI
Juniper: European, CADE
Kiln, OAST, OVEN
King: British legendary, LUDD, NUDD
Kiss, BUSS
Knife: Philippine, BOLO
Koran: Section of, SURA
Laborer: Spanish American, PEON
Lake: Mountain, TARN
  (Scotch), LOCH
Lamp: Miner's, DAVY
Landing place: Indian, GHAT
Language: Buddhist, PALI
  Japanese, AINU
Latvian, LETT
Layer: Of iris, UVEA
Leaf: Palm, OLAY, OLLA
Legislature: Ukrainian, RADA
Lemur, LORI
Leopard, PARD
Let it stand, STET
Letter: Greek, BETA, IOTA, ZETA
  Hebrew, AYIN, BETH, CAPH, KOPH, RESH, SHIN, TETH, YODH
  Papal, BULL
Lily, ALOE
Literature: Hindu sacred, VEDA
Lizard, GILA
  Monitor, URAN
Loquat, BIWA
Magistrate: Genoese or Venetian, DOGE
Man (Latin), HOMO
Mark: Omission, DELE
  armoset: South American, MICO
Meadow: Fertile, VEGA
Measure: Electric, VOLT, WATT
  Force, DYNE
  Hebrew, OMER
  Printing, PICA
  Spanish or Portuguese, VARA
  Swiss land, IMMI
Medley, OLIO
Merganser, SMEW
Milk (French), LAIT
Molding, GULA
  Curved, OGEE
Mongoose: Crab-eating, URVA
Monk: Tibetan, LAMA
Monkey: African, MONA, WAAG
  Ceylonese, MAHA
  Cochin-China, DOUC
  South American, SAKI, TITI
Monkshood, ATIS
Month: Jewish, ADAR, ELUL, IYAR
Mother (French), MERE
Mountain: Thessaly, OSSA
Mouse: Meadow, VOLE
Mythology: Norse, EDDA
Nail (French), CLOU
Native: Philippine, MORO
Nest: Of pheasants, NIDE
Network, RETE
No (German), NEIN
Noble: Mohammedan, AMIR
Notice: Death, OBIT
Novel: By Zola, NANA
Nursemaid: Oriental AMAH, AYAH, EYAH
Nut: Philippine, PILI

Oak: Holm, ILEX
Oil (comb. form), OLEO
Ostrich: American, RHEA
Oven, KILN, OAST
Owl: Barn, LULU
Ox: Celebes wild, ANOE
  Extinct wild, URUS
Palm, ATAP, NIPA, SAGO
Parliament, DIET
Parrot: New Zealand, KAKA
Pass: Indian mountain, GHAT
Passage: Closing (music), CODA
Peach: Clingstone, PAVY
Peasant: Indian, RYOT
  Old English, CARL
Pepper: Australasian, KAVA
Perfume, ATAR
Persia, IRAN
Person: Extraordinary, ONER
Pickerel or pike, ESOX
Pitcher, EWER
Plant: Aromatic, NARD
  Century, ALOE
  Indigo, ANIL
  Pepper, KAVA
Platform: Raised, DAIS
Plum: Wild, SLOE
Pods: Vegetable, OKRA, OKRO
Poem: Epic, EPOS
Poet: Persian, OMAR
  Roman, OVID
Poison, BANE
  Arrow, INEE
Porkfish, SISI
Portico: Greek, STOA
Premium, AGIO
Priest: Mohammedan, IMAM
Prima donna, DIVA
Prong: Fork, TINE
Pseudonym: Lamb's, ELIA
Queen: Carthaginian, DIDO
  Hindu, RANI
Rabbit, CONY
Race: Of Japan, AINU
Rail: Ducklike, COOT
  North American, SORA
Redshank, CLEE
Refuse: After pressing, MARC
Regiment: Turkish, ALAI
Reliquary, ARCA
Resort: Italian, LIDO
Ridges: Sandy, ASAR, OSAR
River: German, ELBE, ODER
  Italian, ADDA
  Siberian, LENA
Road: Roman, ITER
Rockfish: California, RENA
Rodent: Mouselike, VOLE
  South American, PACA
Rootstock, TARO
Salamander, NEWT
Salmon: Silver, COHO
  Young, PARR
Same (Greek), HOMO
  (Latin), IDEM
Sauce: Fish, ALEC
School: English, ETON
Seaweed, AGAR, ALGA, KELP
Secular, LAIC
Sediment, SILT
Seed: Dill, ANET
  Of vetch, TARE
Serf, ILOT
Sesame, TEEL
Settlement: Eskimo, ETAH
Shark: Atlantic, GATA
  European, TOPE
Sheep: Wild, UDAD
Sheltered, ALEE
Shield, EGIS
Ship: Jason's, ARGO
  Left side of, PORT
  Two-masted, BRIG
Shrine: Buddhist, TOPE
Shrub: New Zealand, TUTU

Sign: Magic, RUNE
Silkworm, ERIA
Skin: Beaver, PLEW
Skink: Egyptian, ADDA
Slave, ESNE
Sloth: Two-toed, UNAU
Smooth, LENE
Snow: Glacial, NEVE
Soapstone, TALC
Society: African secret, EGBO, PORO
Son: Of Seth, ENOS
Song (German), LIED
　Unaccompanied, GLEE
Sound: Lung, RALE
Sour, ACID
Sow: Young, GILT
Spike: Brad-shaped, BROB
Spirit: Buddhist evil, MARA
Stake: Poker, ANTE
Star: Temporary, NOVA
Starch: East Indian, SAGO
Stone: Precious, OPAL
Strap: Bridle, REIN
Strewn (heraldry), SEME
Sweetsop, ATES, ATTA
Sword: Fencing, EPEE, FOIL
Tambourine: African, TAAR
Tapir: Brazilian, ANTA
Tax, CESS
Tea: South American, MATE
Therefore (Latin), ERGO
Thing: Extraordinary, ONER
Three (dice, cards, etc.), TREY
Thrush: Hawaiian, OMAO

Tide, NEAP
Tipster: Racing, TOUT
Tissue, TELA
Title: Etruscan, LARS
　Hindu, BABU
　Indian, RAJA
　Mohammedan, EMIR, IMAM
　Persian, BABA
　Spanish, DONA
　Turkish, AGHA, BABA
Toad: Largest-known, AGUA
　Tree, HYLA
Tool: Cutting, ADZE
Track: Deer, SLOT
Tract: Sandy, DENE
Tree: Apple, SORB
　Central American, EBOE
　East Indian, TEAK
　Eucalyptus, YATE
　Guiana and Trinidad, MORA
　Javanese, UPAS
　Linden, LIME, LINN, TEIL, TILL
　Sandarac, ARAR
　Sassafras, AGUE
　Tamarisk salt, ATLE
Tribe: Moro, SULU
Trout, CHAR
Urchin: Street, ARAB
Vessel: Arab, DHOW
Vestment: Ecclesiastical, COPE
Vetch, TARE
Vine: East Indian, SOMA
Violinist: Famous, AUER

Vortex, EDDY
Wampum, PEAG
Wapiti, STAG
Waste: Allowance for, TRET
Watchman: Indian, MINA
Water (Spanish), AGUA
Waterfall, LINN
Wavy (heraldry), ONDE, UNDE
Wax, CERE
　Chinese, PELA
Weed: Biblical, TARE
Weight: Ancient, MINA
　Danish (pl.), ESER
　East Asian, TAEL
　Greek, MINA
　Siamese, BAHT
Well done (rare), EUGE
Whale, CETE
　Killer, ORCA
　White, HUSE, HUSO
Whirlpool, EDDY
Wife: Of Geraint, ENID
Willow: Virginia, ITEA
Wine, PORT
Winged, ALAR
　(Heraldry), AILE
Wings, ALAE
Withered, SERE
Without (French), SANS
Wool: To comb, CARD
Work, OPUS
Wrong: Civil, TORT
Young: Bring forth, YEAN

Words of Five Letters

Abode of dead: Babylonian, ARALU
Aborigine: Borneo DAYAK
Aftersong, EPODE
Aloe, AGAVE
Animal: Footless, APODE
Ant, EMMET
Antelope: African, ADDAX, BEISA, CAAMA, ELAND,
　GUIBA, ORIBI, TIANG
　Goat, GORAL, SEROW
　Indian, SASIN
　Siberian, SAIGA
Arch: Pointed, OGIVE
Armadillo, APARA, POYOU, TATOU
Arrowroot, ARARU
Artery: Trunk, AORTA
Association: Russian, ARTEL
　Secret, CABAL
Author: English, READE
Automaton, GOLEM, ROBOT
Award: Motion-picture, OSCAR
Basket: Fishing, CREEL
Beer: Russian, KVASS
Bible: Mohammedan, KORAN
Bird: Asian, MINAH, MYNAH
　Indian, SHAMA
　Larklike, PIPIT
　Loonlike, GREBE
　Oscine, VIREO
　South American, AGAMI
　Swimming, GREBE
Black: (French), NOIRE
　(Heraldry), SABLE
Blackbird: European, MERLE, OUSEL, OUZEL
Block: Glacial, SERAC
Blue (heraldry), AZURE
Boat: Eskimo, BIDAR, UMIAK
Bobwhite, COLIN, QUAIL
Bone (comb. form), OSTEO
　Leg, TIBIA
　Thigh, FEMUR
Broom: Twig, BESOM
Brother (French), FRERE
　Moses, AARON
Canoe: Eskimo, BIDAR, KAYAK
Cape: Papal, FANON, ORALE
Caravansary, SERAI

Card: Old playing, TAROT
Caterpillar: New Zealand, AWETO
Catkin, AMENT
Cavity: Stone, GEODE
Cephalopod, SQUID
Cetacean, WHALE
Chariot, ESSED
Cheek: Pertaining to, MALAR
Chieftain: Arab, EMEER
Child (Scotch), BAIRN
Cigar, CLARO
Coating: Seed, TESTA
Cockatoo: Palm, ARARA
Coin: Costa Rican, COLON
　Danish, KRONE
　Ecuadorian, SUCRE
　English, GROAT, PENCE
　French, FRANC
　German, KRONE, TALER
　Hungarian, PENGO
　Icelandic, KRONA
　Indian, RUPEE
　Iraqi, DINAR
　Norwegian, KRONE
　Polish, ZLOTY
　Russian, COPEC, KOPEK, RUBLE
　Swedish, KRONA
　Turkish, ASPER
　Yugoslav, DINAR
Collar: Papal, FANON, ORALE
　Roman, RABAT
Commune: Italian, TREIA
Composition: Choral, MOTET
Compound: Chemical, ESTER
Conceal (law), ELOIN
Council: Ecclesiastical, SYNOD
Court: Anglo-Saxon, GEMOT
　Inner, PATIO
Crest: Mountain, ARETE
Crown: Papal, TIARA
Cuttlefish, SEPIA
Date: Roman, NONES
Decree: Mohammedan, IRADE
　Russian, UKASE
Deposit: Loam, LOESS
Desert: Gobi, SHAMO

Devilfish, MANTA
Disease: Cereals, ERGOT
Disk, PATEN
Dog: Wild, DHOLE, DINGO
Dormouse, LEROT
Drum, TABOR
Duck: Sea, EIDER
Dynasty: Chinese, CHING, LIANG, SHANG
Earthquake, SEISM
Eel, ELVER, MORAY
Ermine: European, STOAT
Ether: Crystalline, APIOL
Fabric: Velvetlike, PANNE
Fabulist, AESOP
Family: Italian, CENCI
Fiber: West Indian, SISAL
Fig: Smyrna, ELEME, ELEMI
Figure: Of speech, TROPE
Finch: European, SERIN
Fish: American small, KILLY
Flower: Garden, ASTER
Friend (Spanish), AMIGO
Fruit: Tropical, MANGO
Fungus: Rye, ERGOT
Furze, GORSE
Gateway, TORAN, TORII
Gem, AGATE, BERYL, PEARL, TOPAZ
Genus: Barnacles, LEPAS
  Bears, URSUS
  Birds (loons), GAVIA
  Birds (nuthatches), SITTA
  Cats, FELIS
  Dogs, CANIS
  Fishes (chiros), ELOPS
  Fishes (perch), PERCA
  Geese, ANSER
  Grasses, STIPA
  Grasses (incl. oats), AVENA
  Gulls, LARUS
  Hares, rabbits, LEPUS
  Hawks, BUTEO
  Herbs, old world, INULA
  Herbs, trailing or climbing, APIOS
  Herbs, tropical, TACCA, URENA
  Horses, EQUUS
  Insects (olive flies), DACUS
  Lice, plant, APHIS
  Lichens, USNEA
  Lizards, AGAMA
  Moles, TALPA
  Mollusks, OLIVA
  Monkeys, CEBUS
  Palms, ARECA
  Pigeons, GOURA
  Plants (amaryllis family), AGAVE
  Ruminants (goats), CAPRA
  Shrubs, Asiatic, SABIA
  Shrubs (heath), ERICA
  Shrubs (incl. raspberry), RUBUS
  Shrubs, tropical, IXORA, TREMA, URENA
  Ticks, ARGAS
  Trees (of elm family), TREMA, ULMUS
  Trees, tropical, IXORA, TREMA
Goat: Bezoar, PASAN
God: Assyrian, ASHIR, ASHUR, ASSUR
  Babylonian, DAGAN, SIRIS
  Gaelic, DAGDA
  Hindu, BHAGA, INDRA, SHIVA
  Japanese, EBISU
  Philistine, DAGON
  Phrygian, ATTIS
  Teutonic, AEGIR, GYMIR
  Welsh, DYLAN
Goddess: Babylonian, ISTAR, NANAI
  Hindu, DURGA, GAURI, SHREE
Group: Of six, HEXAD
Grove: Sacred to Diana, NEMUS
Growing out, ENATE
Guitar: Hindu, SITAR
Gull: PEWEE, PEWIT
Hartebeest, CAAMA
Headdress: Jewish or Persian, TIARA
  Liturgical, MITER, MITRE
Heath, ERICA
Herb: Grasslike marsh, SEDGE

Heron, EGRET
Hog: Young, SHOAT, SHOTE
Image, EIKON
Indian: Cariban, ARARA
  Iroquoian, HURON
  Mexican, AZTEC, OPATA, OTOMI
  Muskhogean, CREEK
  Siouan, OSAGE, TETON
  Spanish American, ARARA, CARIB
Inflorescence: Racemose, AMENT
Insect: Immature, LARVA
Intrigue, CABAL
Iris: Yellow, SEDGE
Juniper, GORSE, RETEM
Kidneys: Pertaining to, RENAL
King: British legendary, LLUDD
Kite: European, GLEDE
Kobold, NISSE
Land: Cultivated, ARADA, ARADO
Landholder (Scotch), LAIRD, THANE
Language: Dravidian, TAMIL
Lariat, LASSO, REATA
Laughing, RIANT
Lawgiver: Athenian, DRACO, SOLON
Leaf: Calyx, SEPAL
  Fern, FROND
Lemur, LORIS
Letter: English, AITCH
  Greek, ALPHA, DELTA, GAMMA, KAPPA, OMEGA,
    SIGMA, THETA
  Hebrew, ALEPH, CHETH, GIMEL, SADHE, ZAYIN
Lichen, USNEA
Lighthouse, PHARE
Lizard: Old World, AGAMA
Loincloth, DHOTI
Louse: Plant, APHID
Macaw: Brazilian, ARARA
Mahogany: Philippine, ALMON·
Mammal: Badgerlike, RATEL
  Civetlike, GENET
  Giraffelike, OKAPI
  Raccoonlike, COATI
Man (French), HOMME
Marble, AGATE
Mark: Insertion, CARET
Market place: Greek, AGORA
Marsupial: Australian, KOALA
Measure: Electric, FARAD, HENRY
  Energy, JOULE
  Metric, LITER, STERE
  Printing, AGATE
  Russian, VERST
Mixture: Smelting, MATTE
Mohicans: Last of, UNCAS
Molding: Convex, OVOLO, TORUS
Mole, TALPA
Monkey: African, PATAS
  Capuchin, SAJOU
  Howling, ARABA
Monkshood, ATEES
Month: Jewish, NISAN, SIVAN, TEBET
Museum (French), MUSEE
Musketeer, ATHOS
Native: Aleutian, ALEUT
  New Zealand, MAORI
Neckpiece: Ecclesiastical, AMICE
Nerve (comb. form), NEURO
Nest: Eagle's or hawk's, AERIE
  Insect's, NIDUS
Net: Fishing, SEINE
Newsstand, KIOSK
Nitrogen, AZOTE
Noble: Mohammedan, AMEER
Nodule: Stone, GEODE
Nostrils, NARES
Notched irregularly, EROSE
Nymph: Mohammedan, HOURI
Official: Roman, EDILE
Oleoresin, ELEMI
Opening: Mouthlike, STOMA
Oration: Funeral, ELOGE
Ostiole, STOMA
Page: Left-hand, VERSO
  Right-hand, RECTO
Palm, ARECA, BETEL

Park: Colorado, ESTES
Perfume, ATTAR
Philosopher: Greek, PLATO
Pillar: Stone, STELA, STELE
Pinnacle: Glacial, SERAC
Plain, LLANO
Plant: Century, AGAVE
  Climbing, LIANA
  Dwarf, CUMIN
  East Asian perennial, RAMIE
  Medicinal, SENNA
  Mustard family, CRESS
Plate: Communion, PATEN
Poem: Lyric, EPODE
Point: Lowest, NADIR
Poplar, ABELE, ALAMO, ASPEN
Porridge: Spanish American, ATOLE
Post: Stair, NEWEL
Priest: Mohammedan, IMAUM
Protozoan, AMEBA
Queen: (French), REINE
  Hindu, RANEE
Rabbit, CONEY
Rail, CRAKE
Red (heraldry), GULES
Religion: Moslem, ISLAM
Resin, ELEMI
Revoke (law), ADEEM
Rich man, MIDAS, NABOB
Ridge: Sandy, ESKAR, ESKER
River: French, LOIRE, SEINE
Rockfish: California, REINA
Rootstock: Fragrant, ORRIS
Ruff: Female, REEVE
Sack: Pack, KYACK
Salt: Ethereal, ESTER
Saltpeter, NITER, NITRE
Salutation: Eastern, SALAM
Sandpiper: Old World, TEREK
Scented, OLENT
School: Fish, SHOAL
  French public, LYCEE
Scriptures: Mohammedan, KORAN
Seaweeds, ALGAE
Seed: Aromatic, ANISE
Seraglio, HAREM, SERAI
Serf, HELOT
Sheep: Wild, AUDAD
Sheeplike, OVINE
Shield, AEGIS
Shoe: Wooden, SABOT
Shoots: Pickled bamboo, ACHAR
Shot: Billiard, CAROM, MASSE
Shrine: Buddhist, STUPA
Shrub: Burning bush, WAHOO
  Ornamental evergreen, TOYON
  Used in tanning, SUMAC
Silk: Watered, MOIRE
Sister (French), SOEUR
  (Latin), SOROR
Six: Group of, HEXAD

Skeleton: Marine, CORAL
Slave, HELOT
Snake, ABOMA, ADDER, COBRA, RACER
Soldier: French, POILU
  Indian, SEPOY
Sour, ACERB
Spirit: Air, ARIEL
Staff: Shepherd's, CROOK
Starwort, ASTER
Steel (German), STAHL
Stockade: Russian, ETAPE
Stop (nautical), AVAST
Storehouse, ETAPE
Subway: Parisian, METRO
Tapestry, ARRAS
Tea: Paraguayan, YERBA
Temple: Hawaiian, HEIAU
Terminal: Positive, ANODE
Theater: Greek, ODEON, ODEUM
Then (French), ALORS
Thread: Surgical, SETON
Thrush: Wilson's, VEERY
Title: Hindu, BABOO
  Indian, RAJAH, SAHEB, SAHIB
  Mohammedan, EMEER, IMAUM
Tree: Buddhist sacred, PIPAL
  East Indian cotton, SIMAL
  Hickory, PECAN
  Light-wooded, BALSA
  Malayan, TERAP
  Mediterranean, CAROB
  Mexican, ABETO
  Mexican pine, OCOTE
  New Zealand, MAIRE
  Philippine, ALMON
  Rain, SAMAN
  South American, UMBRA
  Tamarack, LARCH
  Tamarisk salt, ATLEE
  West Indian, ACANA
Trout, CHARR
Troy, ILION, ILIUM
Twin: Siamese, CHANG
Vestment: Ecclesiastical, STOLE
Violin: Famous, AMATI, STRAD
Volcano: Mud, SALSE
Wampum, PEAGE
War cry: Greek, ALALA
Wavy (heraldry), UNDEE
Weight: Jewish, GERAH
Wen, TALPA
Wheat, SPELT
Wheel: Persian water, NORIA
Whitefish, CISCO
Willow, OSIER
Window: Bay, ORIEL
Wine, MEDOC, RHINE, TINTA, TOKAY
Winged, ALATE
Woman (French), FEMME
Year: Excess of solar over lunar, EPACT
Zoroastrian, PARSI

Words of Six or More Letters

Agave, MAGUEY
Alkaloid: Crystalline, ESERIN, ESERINE
Alligator, CAYMAN
Amphibole, EDENITE, URALITE
Ant: White, TERMITE
Antelope: African, DIKDIK, DUIKER, GEMSBOK, IMPALA, KOODOO
  European, CHAMOIS
  Indian, NILGAI, NILGAU, NILGHAI, NILGHAU
Ape: Asian or East Indian, GIBBON
Appendage: Leaf, STIPEL, STIPULE
Armadillo, PELUDO, TATOUAY
Arrowroot, ARARAO
Ascetic: Jewish, ESSENE
Ass: Asian wild, ONAGER
Avatar: Of Vishnu, KRISHNA
Babylonian, ELAMITE
Badge: Shoulder, EPAULET
Baldness, ALOPECIA

Barracuda, SENNET
Bark: Aromatic, SINTOC
Bearlike, URSINE
Beetle, ELATER
Bible: Zoroastrian, AVESTA
Bird: Sea, PETREL
  South American, SERIEMA
  Wading, AVOCET, AVOSET
Bone: Leg, FIBULA
Branched, RAMATE
Brother (Latin), FRATER
Bunting: European, ORTOLAN
Call: Trumpet, SENNET
Canoe: Eskimo, BAIDAR, OOMIAK
Caravansary, IMARET
Cat: Asian or African, CHEETAH
  Leopardlike, OCELOT
Cenobite: Jewish, ESSENE
Centerpiece: Table, EPERGNE

Cetacean, DOLPHIN, PORPOISE
Chariot, ESSEDA, ESSEDE
Chief: Seminole, OSCEOLA
Claim: Release as (law), REMISE
Clock: Water, CLEPSYDRA
Cloud, CUMULUS, NIMBUS
Coach: French hackney, FIACRE
Coin: Czech, KORUNA
  Ethiopian, TALARI
  Finnish, MARKKA
  German, THALER
  Greek, DRACHMA
  Haitian, GOURDE
  Honduran, LEMPIRA
  Hungarian, FORINT
  Indo-Chinese, PIASTER
  Netherlands, GUILDER
  Panamanian, BALBOA
  Paraguayan, GUARANI
  Portuguese, ESCUDO
  Russian, COPECK, KOPECK, ROUBLE
  Spanish, PESETA
  Venezuelan, BOLIVAR
Communion: Last holy, VIATICUM
Conceal (law), ELOIGN
Confection, PRALINE
Construction: Sentence, SYNTAX
Convexity: Shaft of column, ENTASIS
Court: Anglo-Saxon, GEMOTE
Cow: Sea, DUGONG, MANATEE
Cylindrical, TERETE
Dagger, STILETTO
  Malay, CREESE, KREESE
Date: Roman, CALENDS, KALENDS
Deer, CARIBOU, WAPITI
Disease: Plant, ERINOSE
Doorkeeper, OSTIARY
Dragonflies: Order of, ODANATA
Drink: Of gods, NECTAR
Drum: TABOUR
  Moorish, ATABAL, ATTABAL
Duck: Fish-eating, MERGANSER
  Sea, SCOTER
Dynasty: Chinese, MANCHU
Eel, CONGER
Edit, REDACT
Envelope: Flower, PERIANTH
Eskimo, AMERIND
Ether: Crystalline, APIOLE
Excuse (law), ESSOIN
Eyespots, OCELLI
Fabric, ESTAMENE, ESTAMIN, ETAMINE
Falcon: European, KESTREL
Figure: Used as column, CARYATID, TELAMON
Fine: For punishment, AMERCE
Fish: Asian fresh-water, GOURAMI
  Pikelike, BARRACUDA
Five: Group of, PENTAD
Fly: African, TSETSE
Foot: Metric, ANAPEST, IAMBUS
Foxlike, VULPINE
Frying pan, SPIDER
Fur, KARAKUL
Galley: Greek or Roman, BIREME, TRIREME
Game: Card, ECARTE
Garment: Greek, CHLAMYS
Gateway, GOPURA, TORANA
Genus: Birds (ravens, crows), CORVUS
  Eels, CONGER
  Fishes, ANABAS
  Foxes, VULPES
  Herbs, ANEMONE
  Insects, CICADA
  Lemurs, GALAGO
  Mints (incl. catnip), NEPETA
  Mollusks, ANOMIA, ASTARTE, TEREDO
  Mollusks (incl. oysters), OSTREA
  Monkeys (spider monkeys), ATELES
  Thrushes (incl. robins), TURDUS
  Trees (of elm family), CELTIS
  Trees (inc. dogwood), CORNUS
  Trees, tropical American, SAPOTA
  Wrens, NANNUS
Gibbon, SIAMANG, WOUWOU
Gland: Salivary, RACEMOSE

Goat: Bezoar, PASANG
Goatlike, CAPRINE
God: Assyrian, ASHSHUR, ASSHUR
  Babylonian, BABBAR, MARDUK, MERODACH,
    NANNAR, NERGAL, SHAMASH
  Hindu, BRAHMA, KRISHNA, VISHNU
  Tahitian, TAAROA
Goddess: Babylonian, ISHTAR
  Hindu, CHANDI, HAIMAVATI, LAKSHMI, PARVATI,
    SARASVATI, SARASWATI
Government, POLITY
Governor: Persian, SATRAP
Grandson (Scotch), NEPOTE
Group: Of five, PENTAD
  Of nine, ENNEAD
  Of seven, HEPTAD
Hare: in first year, LEVERET
Harpsichord, SPINET
Herb: Alpine, EDELWEISS
  Chinese, GINSENG
  South African, FREESIA
Hermit, EREMITE
Hero: Legendary, PALADIN
Heron, BITTERN
Horselike, EQUINE
Hound: Short-legged, BEAGLE
House (French), MAISON
Idiot, CRETIN
Implement: Stone, NEOLITH
Incarnation: Hindu, AVATAR
Indian, APACHE, COMANCHE, PAIUTE, SENECA
Inn: Turkish, IMARET
Insects: Order of, DIPTERA
Instrument: Japanese banjolike, SAMISEN
  Musical, CLAVIER, SPINET
Interstice, AREOLA
Ironwood, COLIMA
Juniper: Old Testament, RAETAM
Kettledrum, ATABAL
King: Fairy, OBERON
Kneecap, PATELLA
Knife, MACHETE
Langur: Sumatran, SIMPAI
Legislature: Spanish, CORTES
Lemur: African, GALAGO
  Madagascar, AYEAYE
Letter: Greek, EPSILON, LAMBDA, OMICRON, UPSILON
  Hebrew, DALETH, LAMEDH, SAMEKH
Lighthouse, PHAROS
Lizard, IGUANA
Llama, ALPACA
Lockjaw, TETANUS
Locust, CICADA, CICALA
Macaw: Brazilian, MARACAN
Maid: Of Astolat, ELAINE
Mammal: Madagascar, TENDRAC, TENREC
Man (Spanish), HOMBRE
Marmoset: South American, TAMARIN
Marsupial, BANDICOOT, WOMBAT
Massacre, POGROM
Mayor: Spanish, ALCALDE
Measure: Electric, AMPERE, COULOMB, KILOWATT
Medicine: Quack, NOSTRUM
Member: Religious order, CENOBITE
Molasses, TREACLE
Monkey: African, GRIVET, NISNAS
  Asian, LANGUR
  Philippine, MACHIN
  South American, PINCHE, SAIMIRI, SAMIRI, SAPAJOU
Monster, CHIMERA, GORGON
  (Comb. form), TERATO
  Cretan, MINOTAUR
Month: Jewish, HESHVAN, KISLEV, SHEBAT, TAMMUZ,
  TISHRI, VEADAR
Mountain: Asia Minor, ARARAT
Mulct, AMERCE
Musketeer, ARAMIS, PORTHOS
Nearsighted, MYOPIC
Net, TRAMMEL
New York City, GOTHAM
Nine: Group of, ENNEAD
Nobleman: Spanish, GRANDEE
Official: Roman, AEDILE
Onyx: Mexican, TECALI
Order: Dragonflies, ODANATA

Insects, DIPTERA
Organ: Plant, PISTIL
Ornament: Shoulder, EPAULET
Overcoat: Military, CAPOTE
Ox: Wild, BANTENG
Oxidation: Bronze or copper, PATINA
Paralysis: Incomplete, PARESIS
Pear: Alligator, AVOCADO
Persimmon: Mexican, CHAPOTE
Pipe: Peace, CALUMET
Plaid (Scotch), TARTAN
Plain, PAMPAS, STEPPE, TUNDRA
Plant: Buttercup family, ANEMONE
   Century, MAGUEY
   On rocks, LICHEN
Plowing: Fit for, ARABLE
Poem: Heroic, EPOPEE
   Six-lined, SESTET
Point: Highest, ZENITH
Potion: Love, PHILTER, PHILTRE
Protozoan, AMOEBA
Punish, AMERCE
Purple (heraldry), PURPURE
Queen: Fairy, TITANIA
Race: Skiing, SLALOM
Rat, BANDICOOT, LEMMING
Retort, RIPOST, RIPOSTE
Ring: Harness, TERRET
   Little, ANNULET
Rodent: Jumping, JERBOA
   Spanish American, AGOUTI, AGOUTY
Sailor: East Indian, LASCAR
Salmon: Young, GRILSE
Salutation: Eastern, SALAAM
Sandpiper, PLOVER
Sandy, ARENOSE
Sapodilla, SAPOTA, SAPOTE
Saw: Surgical, TREPAN
Seven: Group of, HEPTAD
Sexes: Common to both, EPICENE
Shawl: Mexican, SERAPE
Sheathing: Flower, SPATHE
Sheep: Wild, AOUDAD, ARGALI
Shipworm, TEREDO
Shoes: Mercury's winged, TALARIA
Shortening: Syllable, SYSTOLE
Shrub, SPIRAEA

Sickle-shaped, FALCATE
Silver (heraldry), ARGENT
Snake, ANACONDA
Speech: Loss of, APHASIA
Spiral, HELICAL
Staff: Bishop's, CROSIER, CROZIER
Stalk: Plant, PETIOLE
State: Swiss, CANTON
Studio, ATELIER
Swan: Young, CYGNET
Swimming, NATANT
Sword-shaped, ENSATE
Terminal: Negative, CATHODE
Third (music), TIERCE
Thrust: Fencing, RIPOST, RIPOSTE
Tile: Pertaining to, TEGULAR
Tomb: Empty, CENOTAPH
Tooth (comb. form), ODONTO
Tower: Mohammedan, MINARET
Tree: African timber, BAOBAB
   Black gum, TUPELO
   East Indian, MARGOSA
   Locust, ACACIA
   Malayan, SINTOC
   Marmalade, SAPOTE
Urn: Tea, SAMOVAR
Vehicle, LANDAU, TROIKA
Verbose, PROLIX
Viceroy: Egyptian, KHEDIVE
Vulture: American, CONDOR
Warehouse (French), ENTREPOT
Whale: White, BELUGA
Whirlpool, VORTEX
Will: Addition to, CODICIL
   Having left, TESTATE
Wind, CHINOOK, MONSOON, SIMOOM, SIMOON, SIROCCO
Window: In roof, DORMER
Wine, BARBERA, BURGUNDY, CABERNET, CHABLIS, CHIANTI, CLARET, MUSCATEL, RIESLING, SAUTERNE, SHERRY, ZINFANDEL
Wolfish, LUPINE
Woman: Boisterous, TERMAGANT
Woolly, LANATE
Workshop, ATELIER
Zoroastrian, PARSEE

Old-Testament Names

(We do not pretend that this list is all-inclusive. We include only those names that occur most often in crossword puzzles.)

Aaron: First high priest of Jews; son of Amram; brother of Miriam and Moses; father of Abihu, Eleazer, Ithamar, and Nadab.

Abel: Son of Adam; slain by Cain.

Abigail: Wife of Nabal; later, wife of David.

Abihu: Son of Aaron.

Abimelech: King of Gerar.

Abner: Commander of army of Saul and Ishbosheth; slain by Joab.

Abraham (or Abram): Patriarch; forefather of the Jews; son of Terah; husband of Sarah; father of Isaac and Ishmael.

Absalom: Son of David and Maacah; revolted against David; slain by Joab.

Achish: King of Gath; gave refuge to David.

Achsa (or Achsah): Daughter of Caleb; wife of Othniel.

Adah: Wife of Lamech.

Adam: First man; husband of Eve; father of Cain, Abel, and Seth.

Adonijah: Son of David and Haggith.

Agag: King of Amalek; spared by Saul; slain by Samuel.

Ahasuerus: King of Persia; husband of Vashti and, later, Esther; sometimes identified with Xerxes the Great.

Ahijah: Prophet; foretold accession of Jeroboam.

Ahinoam: Wife of David.

Amasa: Commander of army of David; slain by Joab.

Amnon: Son of David and Ahinoam; ravished Tamar; slain by Absalom.

Amram: Husband of Jochebed; father of Aaron, Miriam and Moses.

Asenath: Wife of Joseph.

Asher: Son of Jacob and Zilpah.

Balaam: Prophet; rebuked by his donkey for cursing God.

Barak: Jewish captain; associated with Deborah.

Baruch: Secretary to Jeremiah.

Bathsheba: Wife of Uriah; later, wife of David.

Belshazzar: Crown prince of Babylon.

Benaiah: Warrior of David; proclaimed Solomon King.

Ben-Hadad: Name of several kings of Damascus.

Benjamin: Son of Jacob and Rachel.

Bezaleel: Chief architect of tabernacle.

Bildad: Comforter of Job.

Bilhah: Servant of Rachel; mistress of Jacob.

Boaz: Husband of Ruth; father of Obed.

Cain: Son of Adam and Eve; slayer of Abel; father of Enoch.

Cainan: Son of Enos.

Caleb: Spy sent out by Moses to visit Canaan; father of Achsa.

Canaan: Son of Ham.

Chilion: Son of Elimelech; husband of Orpah.

Cush: Son of Ham; father of Nimrod.

Dan: Son of Jacob and Bilhah.

Daniel: Prophet; saved from lions by God.

Deborah: Hebrew prophetess; helped Israelites conquer Canaanites.

Delilah: Mistress and betrayer of Samson.

Elam: Son of Shem.

Eleazar: Son of Aaron; succeeded him as high priest.

Eli: High priest and judge; teacher of Samuel; father of Hophni and Phinehas.

Eliakim: Chief minister of Hezekiah.

Eliezer: Servant of Abraham.

Elihu: Comforter of Job.

Elijah (or Elias): Prophet; went to heaven in chariot of fire.

Elimelech: Husband of Naomi; father of Chilion and Mahlon.

Eliphaz: Comforter of Job.

Elisha (or Eliseus): Prophet; successor of Elijah.

Elkanah: Husband of Hannah; father of Samuel.

Enoch: Son of Cain.

Enoch: Father of Methuselah.

Enos: Son of Seth; father of Cainan.

Ephraim: Son of Joseph.

Esau: Son of Isaac and Rebecca; sold his birthright to his brother Jacob.

Esther: Jewish wife of Ahasuerus; saved Jews from Haman's plotting.

Eve: First woman; created from rib of Adam.

Ezra (or Esdras): Hebrew scribe and priest.

Gad: Son of Jacob and Zilpah.

Gehazi: Servant of Elisha.

Gideon: Israelite hero; defeated Midianites.

Goliath: Philistine giant; slain by David.

Hagar: Handmaid of Sarah; concubine of Abraham; mother of Ishmael.

Haggith: Mother of Adonijah.

Ham: Son of Noah; father of Cush, Mizraim, Phut, and Canaan.

Haman: Chief minister of Ahasuerus; hanged on gallows prepared for Mordecai.

Hannah: Wife of Elkanah; mother of Samuel.

Hanun: King of Ammonites.

Haran: Brother of Abraham; father of Lot.

Hazael: King of Damascus.

Hephzi-Bah: Wife of Hezekiah; mother of Mannaseh.

Hiram: King of Tyre.

Holofernes: General of Nebuchadnezzar; slain by Judith.

Hophni: Son of Eli.

Isaac: Hebrew patriarch; son of Abraham and Sarah; half brother of Ishmael; husband of Rebecca; father of Esau and Jacob.

Ishmael: Son of Abraham and Hagar; half brother of Isaac.

Issachar: Son of Jacob and Leah.

Ithamar: Son of Aaron.

Jabal: Son of Lamech and Adah.

Jabin: King of Hazor.

Jacob: Hebrew patriarch, founder of Israel; son of Isaac and Rebecca; husband of Leah and Rachel; father of Asher, Benjamin, Dan, Gad, Issachar, Joseph, Judah, Levi, Naphtali, Reuben, Simeon, and Zebulun.

Jael: Slayer of Sisera.

Japheth: Son of Noah.

Jehoiada: High priest; husband of Jehoshabeath; revolted against Athaliah and made Joash King of Judah.

Jehoshabeath (or Jehosheba): Daughter of Jehoram of Judah; wife of Jehoiada.

Jephthah: Judge in Israel; sacrificed his only daughter because of vow.

Jesse: Son of Obed; father of David.

Jethro: Midianite priest; father of Zipporah.

Jezebel: Phoenician princess; wife of Ahab; mother of Ahaziah, Athaliah, and Jehoram.

Joab: Commander in chief under David; slayer of Abner, Absalom, and Amasa.

Job: Patriarch; underwent many afflictions; comforted by Bildad, Elihu, Eliphaz and Zophar.

Jochebed: Wife of Amram.

Jonah: Prophet; cast into sea and swallowed by great fish.

Jonathan: Son of Saul; friend of David.

Joseph: Son of Jacob and Rachel; sold into slavery by his brothers; husband of Asenath; father of Ephraim and Manassah.

Joshua: Successor of Moses; son of Nun.

Jubal: Son of Lamech and Adah.

Judah: Son of Jacob and Leah.

Judith: Slayer of Holofernes.

Kish: Father of Saul.

Laban: Father of Leah and Rachel.

Lamech: Son of Methuselah; father of Noah.

Lamech: Husband of Adah and Zillah; father of Jabal, Jubal, and Tubal-Cain.

Leah: Daughter of Laban; wife of Jacob.

Levi: Son of Jacob and Leah.

Lot: Son of Haran; escaped destruction of Sodom.

Maacah: Mother of Absalom and Tamar.

Mahlon: Son of Elimelech; first husband of Ruth.

Manasseh: Son of Joseph.

Melchizedek: King of Salem.

Methuselah: Patriarch; son of Enoch; father of Lamech.

Michal: Daughter of Saul; wife of David.

Miriam: Prophetess; daughter of Amram; sister of Aaron and Moses.

Mizraim: Son of Ham.

Mordecai: Uncle of Esther; with her aid, saved Jews from Haman's plotting.

Moses: Prophet and lawgiver; son of Amram; brother of Aaron and Miriam; husband of Zipporah.

Naaman: Syrian captain; cured of leprosy by Elisha.

Nabal: Husband of Abigail.

Naboth: Owner of vineyard; stoned to death because he would not sell it to Ahab.

Nadab: Son of Aaron.

Nahor: Father of Terah.

Naomi: Wife of Elimelech; mother-in-law of Ruth.

Naphtali: Son of Jacob and Bilhah.

Nathan: Prophet; reproved David for causing Uriah's death.

Nebuchadnezzar (or Nebuchadrezzar): King of Babylon; destroyer of Jerusalem.

Nehemiah: Jewish leader; empowered by Artaxerxes to rebuild Jerusalem.

Nimrod: Mighty hunter; son of Cush.

Noah: Patriarch; Son of Lamech; escaped Deluge by building Ark; father of Ham, Japheth and Shem.

Nun (or Non): Father of Joshua.

Obed: Son of Boaz; father of Jesse.

Og: King of Bashan.

Orpah: Wife of Chilion.

Othniel: Kenezite; judge of Israel; husband of Achsa.

Phinehas: Son of Eleazer.

Phinehas: Son of Eli.

Phut (or Put): Son of Ham.

Potiphar: Egyptian official; bought Joseph.

Rachel: Wife of Jacob.

Rebecca (or Rebekah): Wife of Isaac.

Reuben: Son of Jacob and Leah.

Ruth: Wife of Mahlon, later of Boaz; daughter-in-law of Naomi.

Samson: Judge of Israel; famed for strength; betrayed by Delilah.

Samuel: Hebrew judge and prophet; son of Elkanah.

Sarah (or Sara, Sarai): Wife of Abraham.

Sennacherib: King of Assyria.

Seth: Son of Adam; father of Enos.

Shem: Son of Noah; father of Elam.

Simeon: Son of Jacob and Leah.

Sisera: Canaanite captain; slain by Jael.

Tamar: Daughter of David and Maachah; ravished by Amnon.

Terah: Son of Nahor; father of Abraham.

Tubal-Cain: Son of Lamech and Zillah.

Uriah: Husband of Bathsheba; sent to death in battle by David.

Vashti: Wife of Ahasuerus; set aside by him.

Zadok: High priest during David's reign.

Zebulun (or Zabulon): Son of Jacob and Leah.

Zillah: Wife of Lamech.

Zilpah: Servant of Leah; mistress of Jacob.

Zipporah: Daughter of Jethro; wife of Moses.

Zophar: Comforter of Job.

Kings of Judah and Israel

Kings Before Division of Kingdom

Saul: First King of Israel; son of Kish; father of sh-Bosheth, Jonathan and Michal.

Ish-Bosheth (or Eshbaal): King of Israel; son of Saul.

David: King of Judah; later of Israel; son of Jesse; husband of Abigail, Ahinoam, Bathsheba, Michal, etc.; father of Absalom, Adonijah, Amnon, Solomon, Tamar, etc.

Solomon: King of Israel and Judah; son of David; father of Rehoboam.

Rehoboam:
Son of Solomon; during his reign the kingdom was divided into Judah and Israel.

Kings of Judah (Southern Kingdom)

Rehoboam: First King.

Abijah (or Abijam or Abia): Son of Rehoboam.

Asa: Probably son of Abijah.

Jehoshaphat: Son of Asa.

Jehoram (or Joram): Son of Jehoshaphat; husband of Athaliah.

Ahaziah: Son of Jehoram and Athaliah.

Athaliah: Daughter of King Ahab of Israel and Jezebel; wife of Jehoram.

Joash (or Jehoash): Son of Ahaziah.

Amaziah: Son of Joash.

Uzziah (or Azariah): Son of Amaziah.

Jotham: Regent, later King; son of Uzziah.

Ahaz: Son of Jotham.

Hezekiah: Son of Ahaz; husband of Hephzi-Bah.

Manasseh: Son of Hezekiah and Hephzi-Bah.

Amon: Son of Manasseh.

Josiah (or Josias): Son of Amon.

Jehoahaz (or Joahaz): Son of Josiah.

Jehoiakim: Son of Josiah.

Jehoiachin: Son of Jehoiakim.

Zedekiah: Son of Josiah; kingdom overthrown by Babylonians under Nebuchadnezzar.

Kings of Israel (Northern Kingdom)

Jeroboam I: Led secession of Israel.

Nadab: Son of Jeroboam I.

Baasha: Overthrew Nadab.

Elah: Son of Baasha.

Zimri: Overthrew Elah.

Omri: Overthrew Zimri.

Ahab: Son of Omri; husband of Jezebel.

Ahaziah: Son of Ahab.

Jehoram (or Joram): Son of Ahab.

Jehu: Overthrew Jehoram.

Jehoahaz (or Joahaz): Son of Jehu.

Jehoash (or Joash): Son of Jehoahaz.

Jeroboam II: Son of Jehoash.

Zechariah: Son of Jeroboam II.

Shallum: Overthrew Zechariah.

Menahem: Overthrew Shallum.

Pekahiah: Son of Menahem.

Pekah: Overthrew Pekahiah.

Hoshea: Overthrew Pekah; kingdom overthrown by Assyrians under Sargon II.

Prophets

Major.—Isaiah, Jeremiah, Ezekiel, Daniel.
Minor.—Hosea, Obadiah, Nahum, Haggai, Joel, Jonah, Habakkuk, Zechariah, Amos, Micah, Zephaniah, Malachi.

Greek and Roman Mythology

(Most of the Greek deities were adopted by the Romans, although in many cases there was a change of name. In the list below, information is given under the Greek name; the name in parentheses is the Latin equivalent. However, all Latin names are listed with cross references to the Greek ones. In addition, there are several deities which were exclusively Roman.)

Acheron: *See* Rivers.

Achilles: Greek warrior; slew Hector at Troy; slain by Paris, who wounded him in his vulnerable heel.

Actaeon: Hunter; surprised Artemis bathing; changed by her to stag and killed by his dogs.

Admetus: King of Thessaly; his wife, Alcestis, offered to die in his place.

Adonis: Beautiful youth loved by Aphrodite.

Aeacus: One of three judges of dead in Hades; son of Zeus.

Aeëtes: King of Colchis; father of Medea; keeper of Golden Fleece.

Aegeus: Father of Theseus; believing Theseus killed in Crete, he drowned himself, Aegean Sea named for him.

Aegisthus: Son of Thyestes; slew Atreus; with Clytemnestra, his paramour, slew Agamemnon; slain by Orestes.

Aegyptus: Brother of Danaus; his sons, except Lynceus, slain by Danaides.

Aeneas: Trojan; son of Anchises and Aphrodite; after fall of Troy, led his followers eventually to Italy; loved and deserted Dido.

Aeolus: *See* Winds.

Aesculapius: *See* Asclepius.

Aeson: King of Ioclus; father of Jason; overthrown by his brother Pelias; restored to youth by Medea.

Aether: Personification of sky.

Aethra: Mother of Theseus.

Agamemnon: King of Mycenae; son of Atreus; brother of Menelaus; leader of Greeks against Troy; slain on his return home by Clytemnestra and Aegisthus.

Agiaia: *See* Graces.

Ajax: Greek warrior; killed himself at Troy because Achilles' armor was awarded to Odysseus.

Alcestis: Wife of Admetus; offered to die in his place but saved from death by Hercules.

Alcmene: Wife of Amphitryon; mother by Zeus of Hercules.

Alcyone: *See* Pleiades.

Alecto: *See* Furies.

Alectryon: Youth changed by Ares into cock.

Althaea: Wife of Oeneus; mother of Meleager.

Amazons: Female warriors in Asia Minor; supported Troy against Greeks.

Amor: *See* Eros.

Amphion: Musician; husband of Niobe; charmed stones to build fortifications for Thebes.

Amphitrite: Sea goddess; wife of Poseidon.

Amphitryon: Husband of Alcmene.

Anchises: Father of Aeneas.

Ancile: Sacred shield that fell from heavens; palladium of Rome.

Andraemon: Husband of Dryope.

Andromache: Wife of Hector.

Andromeda: Daughter of Cepheus; chained to cliff for monster to devour; rescued by Perseus.

Anteia: Wife of Proetus; tried to induce Bellerophon to elope with her.

Anteros: God who avenged unrequited love.

Antigone: Daughter of Oedipus; accompanied him to Colonus; performed burial rite for Polynices and hanged herself.

Antinoüs: Leader of suitors of Penelope; slain by Odysseus.

Aphrodite (Venus): Goddess of love and beauty; daughter of Zeus; mother of Eros.

Apollo: God of beauty, poetry, music; later identified with Helios as Phoebus Apollo; son of Zeus and Leto.

Aquilo: *See* Winds.

Arachne: Maiden who challenged Athena to weaving contest; changed to spider.

Ares (Mars): God of war; son of Zeus and Hera.

Argo: Ship in which Jason and followers sailed to Colchis for Golden Fleece.

Argus: Monster with hundred eyes; slain by Hermes; his eyes placed by Hera into peacock's tail.

Ariadne: Daughter of Minos; aided Theseus in slaying Minotaur; deserted by him on island of Naxos and married to Dionysus.

Arion: Musician; thrown overboard by pirates but saved by dolphin.

Artemis (Diana): Goddess of moon; huntress; twin sister of Apollo.

Asclepius (Aesculapius): Mortal son of Apollo; slain by Zeus for raising dead; later deified as god of medicine. Also known as Asklepios.

Astarte: Phoenician goddess of love; variously identified with Aphrodite, Selene, and Artemis.

Astraea: Goddess of Justice; daughter of Zeus and Themis.

Atalanta: Princess who challenged her suitors to a foot race; Hippomenes won race and married her.

Athena (Minerva): Goddess of wisdom; known poetically as Pallas Athene; sprang fully armed from head of Zeus.

Atlas: Titan; held world on his shoulders as punishment for warring against Zeus; son of Iapetus.

Atreus: King of Mycenae; father of Menelaus and Agamemnon; brother of Thyestes, three of whose sons he slew and served to him at banquet; slain by Aegisthus.

Atropos: *See* Fates.

Aurora: *See* Eos.

Auster: *See* Winds.

Avernus: Infernal regions; name derived from small vaporous lake near Vesuvius which was fabled to kill birds and vegetation.

Bacchus: *See* Dionysus.

Bellerophon: Corinthian hero; killed Chimera with aid of Pegasus; tried to reach Olympus on Pegasus and was thrown to his death.

Bellona: Roman goddess of war.

Boreas: *See* Winds.

Briareus: Monster of hundred hands; son of Uranus and Gaea.

Briseis: Captive maiden given to Achilles; taken by Agamemnon in exchange for loss of Chryseis, which caused Achilles to cease fighting, until death of Patroclus.

Cadmus: Brother of Europa; planter of dragon seeds from which first Thebans sprang.

Calliope: *See* Muses.

Calypso: Sea nymph; kept Odysseus on her island Ogygia for seven years.

Cassandra: Daughter of Priam; prophetess who was never believed; slain with Agamemnon.

Castor: *See* Dioscuri.

Celaeno: *See* Pleiades.

Centaurs: Beings half man and half horse; lived in mountains of Thessaly.

Cephalus: Hunter; accidentally killed his wife Procris with his spear.

Cepheus: King of Ethiopia; father of Andromeda.

Cerberus: Three-headed dog guarding entrance to Hades.

Ceres: *See* Demeter.

Chaos: Formless void; personified as first of gods.

Charon: Boatman on Styx who carried souls of dead to Hades; son of Erebus.

Charybdis: Female monster; personification of whirlpool.

Chimera: Female monster with head of lion, body of goat, tail of serpent; killed by Bellerophon.

Chiron: Most famous of centaurs.

Chronos: Personification of time.

Chryseis: Captive maiden given to Agamemnon; his refusal to accept ransom from her father Chryses caused Apollo to send plague on Greeks besieging Troy.

Circe: Sorceress; daughter of Helios; changed Odysseus' men into swine.

Clio: *See* Muses.

Clotho: *See* Fates.

Clytemnestra: Wife of Agamemnon, whom she slew with aid of her paramour, Aegisthus; slain by her son Orestes.

Cocytus: *See* Rivers.

Creon: Father of Jocasta; forbade burial of Polynices; ordered burial alive of Antigone.

Creüsa: Princess of Corinth, for whom Jason deserted Medea; slain by Medea, who sent her poisoned robe; also known as Glaüke.

Creusa: Wife of Aeneas; died fleeing Troy.

Cronus (Saturn): Titan; god of harvests; son of Uranus and Gaea; dethroned by his son Zeus.

Cupid: *See* Eros.

Cybele: Anatolian nature goddess; adopted by Greeks and identified with Rhea.

Cyclopes: Race of one-eyed giants (singular: Cyclops).

Daedalus: Athenian artificer; father of Icarus; builder of Labyrinth in Crete; devised wings attached with wax for him and Icarus to escape Crete.

Danae: Princess of Argos; mother of Perseus by Zeus, who appeared to her in form of golden shower.

Danaïdes: Daughters of Danaüs; at his command, all except Hypermnestra slew their husbands, the sons of Aegyptus.

Danaüs: Brother of Aegyptus; father of Danaïdes; slain by Lynceus.

Daphne: Nymph; pursued by Apollo; changed to laurel tree.

Decuma: *See* Fates.

Deino: *See* Graeae.

Demeter (Ceres): Goddess of agriculture; mother of Persephone.

Diana: *See* Artemis.

Dido: Founder and queen of Carthage; stabbed herself when deserted by Aeneas.

Diomedes: Greek hero; with Odysseus, entered Troy and carried off Palladium, sacred statue of Athena.

Diomedes: Owner of man-eating horses, which Hercules, as ninth labor, carried off.

Dione: Titan goddess; mother by Zeus of Aphrodite.

Dionysus (Bacchus): God of wine; son of Zeus and Semele.

Dioscuri: Twins Castor and Pollux; sons of Leda by Zeus.

Dis: *See* Hades.

Dryads: Wood nymphs.

Dryope: Maiden changed to Hamadryad.

Echo: Nymph who fell hopelessly in love with Narcissus; faded away except for her voice.

Electra: Daughter of Agamemnon and Clytemnestra; sister of Orestes; urged Orestes to slay Clytemnestra and Aegisthus.

Electra: *See* Pleiades.

Elysium: Abode of blessed dead.

Endymion: Mortal loved by Selene.

Enyo: *See* Graeae.

Eos (Aurora): Goddess of dawn.

Epimetheus: Brother of Prometheus; husband of Pandora.

Erato: *See* Muses.

Erebus: Spirit of darkness; son of Chaos.

Erinyes: *See* Furies.

Eris: Goddess of discord.

Eros (Amor or Cupid): God of love; son of Aphrodite.

Eteocles: Son of Oedipus, whom he succeeded to rule alternately with Polynices; refused to give up throne at end of year; he and Polynices slew each other.

Eumenides: *See* Furies.

Euphrosyne: *See* Graces.

Europa: Mortal loved by Zeus, who, in form of white bull, carried her off to Crete.

Eurus: *See* Winds.

Euryale: *See* Gorgons.

Eurydice: Nymph; wife of Orpheus.

Eurystheus: King of Argos; imposed twelve labors on Hercules.

Euterpe: *See* Muses.

Fates: Goddesses of destiny; Clotho (Spinner of thread of life), Lachesis (Determiner of length), and Atropos (Cutter of thread); also called Moirae. Identified by Romans with their goddesses of fate; Nona, Decuma, and Morta; called Parcae.

Fauns: Roman deities of woods and groves.

Faunus: *See* Pan.

Favonius: *See* Winds.

Flora: Roman goddess of flowers.

Fortuna: Roman goddess of fortune.

Furies: Avenging spirits; Alecto, Megaera, and Tisiphone; known also as Erinyes or Eumenides.

Gaea: Goddess of earth; daughter of Chaos; mother of Titans; known also as Ge, Gea, Gaia, etc.

Galatea: Statue of maiden carved from ivory by Pygmalion; given life by Aphrodite.

Galatea: Sea nymph; loved by Polyphemus.

Ganymede: Beautiful boy; successor to Hebe as cupbearer of gods.

Glaucus: Mortal who became sea divinity by eating magic grass.

Glauke: *See* Creüsa.

Golden Fleece: Fleece from ram that flew Phrixos to Colchis; Aeëtes placed it under guard of dragon; carried off by Jason.

Gorgons: Female monsters; Euryale, Medusa, and Stheno; had snakes for hair; their glances turned mortals to stone. *See* Medusa.

Graces: Beautiful goddesses; Aglaia (Brilliance), Euphrosyne (Joy), and Thalia (Bloom); daughters of Zeus.

Graeae: Sentinels for Gorgons; Deino, Enyo, and Pephredo; had one eye among them, which passed from one to another.

Hades (Dis): Name sometimes given Pluto; also, abode of dead, ruled by Pluto.

Haemon: Son of Creon; promised husband of Antigone; killed himself in her tomb.

Hamadryads: Tree nymphs.

Harpies: Monsters with heads of women and bodies of birds.

Hebe (Juventas): Goddess of youth; cupbearer of gods before Ganymede; daughter of Zeus and Hera.

Hecate: Goddess of sorcery and witchcraft.

Hector: Son of Priam; slayer of Patroclus; slain by Achilles.

Hecuba: Wife of Priam.

Helen: Fairest woman in world; daughter of Zeus and Leda; wife of Menelaus; carried to Troy by Paris, causing Trojan War.

Heliades: Daughters of Helios; mourned for Phaëthon and were changed to poplar trees.

Helios (Sol): God of sun; later identified with Apollo.

Helle: Sister of Phrixos; fell from ram of Golden Fleece; water where she fell named Hellespont.

Hephaestus (Vulcan): God of fire; celestial blacksmith; son of Zeus and Hera; husband of Aphrodite.

Hera (Juno): Queen of heaven; wife of Zeus.

Hercules: Hero and strong man; son of Zeus and Alcmene; performed twelve labors or deeds to be free from bondage under Eurystheus; after death, his mortal share was destroyed, and he became immortal. Also known as Herakles or Heracles. Labors: (1) killing Nemean lion; (2) killing Lernaean Hydra; (3) capturing Erymanthian boar; (4) capturing Cerynean hind; (5) killing man-eating Stymphalian birds; (6) procuring girdle of Hippolyte; (7) cleaning Augean stables; (8) capturing Cretan bull; (9) capturing man-eating horses of Diomedes; (10) capturing cattle of Geryon; (11) procuring golden apples of Hesperides; (12) bringing Cerberus up from Hades.

Hermes (Mercury): God of physicians and thieves; messenger of gods; son of Zeus and Maia.

Hero: Priestess of Aphrodite; Leander swam Hellespont nightly to see her; drowned herself at his death.

Hesperus: Evening star.

Hestia (Vesta): Goddess of hearth; sister of Zeus.

Hippolyte: Queen of Amazons; wife of Theseus.

Hippolytus: Son of Theseus and Hippolyte; falsely accused by Phaedra of trying to kidnap her; slain by Poseidon at request of Theseus.

Hippomenes: Husband of Atalanta, whom he beat in race by dropping golden apples, which she stopped to pick up.

Hyacinthus: Beautiful youth accidentally killed by Apollo, who caused flower to spring up from his blood.

Hydra: Nine-headed monster in marsh of Lerna; slain by Hercules.

Hygeia: Personification of health.

Hyman: God of marriage.

Hyperion: Titan; early sun god; father of Helios.

Hypermnestra: Daughter of Danaüs; refused to kill her husband Lynceus.

Hypnos (Somnus): God of sleep.

Iapetus: Titan; father of Atlas, Epimetheus, and Prometheus.

Icarus: Son of Daedalus; flew too near sun with wax-attached wings and fell into sea and was drowned.

Io: Mortal maiden loved by Zeus; changed by Hera into heifer.

Iobates: King of Lycia; sent Bellerophon to slay Chimera.

Iphigenia: Daughter of Agamemnon; offered as sacrifice to Artemis at Aulis; carried by Artemis to Tauris where she became priestess; escaped from there with Orestes.

Iris: Goddess of rainbow; messenger of Zeus and Hera.

Ismene: Daughter of Oedipus; sister of Antigone.

Iulus: Son of Aeneas.

Ixion: King of Lapithae; for making love to Hera he was bound to endlessly revolving wheel in Tartarus.

Janus: Roman god of gates and doors; represented with two opposite faces.

Jason: Son of Aeson; to gain throne of Ioclus from Pelias, went to Colchis and brought back Golden Fleece; married Medea; deserted her for Creüsa.

Jocasta: Wife of Laius; mother of Oedipus; unwittingly became wife of Oedipus; hanged herself when relationship was discovered.

Juno: *See* Hera.

Jupiter: *See* Zeus.

Juventas: *See* Hebe.

Lachesis: *See* Fates.

Laius: Father of Oedipus, by whom he was slain.

Laocoön: Priest of Apollo at Troy; warned against bringing wooden horse into Troy; destroyed with his two sons by serpents sent by Athena.

Lares: Roman ancestral spirits protecting descendants and homes.

Lavinia: Wife of Aeneas after defeat of Turnus.

Leander: Swam Hellespont nightly to see Hero; drowned in storm.

Leda: Mortal loved by Zeus in form of Swan; mother of Helen, Clytemnestra, Dioscuri.

Lethe: *See* Rivers.

Leto (Latona): Mother by Zeus of Artemis and Apollo.

Lucina: Roman goddess of childbirth; identified with Juno.

Lynceus: Son of Aegyptus; husband of Hypermnestra; slew Danaüs.

Maia: Daughter of Atlas; mother of Hermes.

Maia: *See* Pleiades.

Manes: Souls of dead Romans, particularly of ancestors.

Mars: *See* Ares.

Marsyas: Shepherd; challenged Apollo to music contest and lost; flayed alive by Apollo.

Medea: Sorceress; daughter of Aeëtes; helped Jason obtain Golden Fleece; when deserted by him for Creüsa, killed her children and Creüsa.

Medusa: Gorgon; slain by Perseus, who cut off her head.

Megaera: *See* Furies.

Meleager: Son of Althaea; his life would last as long as brand burning at his birth; Althaea quenched and saved it but destroyed it when Meleager slew his uncles.

Melpomene: *See* Muses.

Memnon: Ethiopian king; made immortal by Zeus; son of Tithonus and Eos.

Menelaus: King of Sparta; son of Atreus; brother of Agamemnon; husband of Helen.

Mercury: *See* Hermes.

Merope: *See* Pleiades.

Mezentius: Cruel Etruscan king; ally of Turnus against Aeneas; slain by Aeneas.

Midas: King of Phrygia; given gift of turning to gold all he touched.

Minerva: *See* Athena.

Minos: King of Crete; after death, one of three judges of dead in Hades; son of Zeus and Europa.

Minotaur: Monster, half man and half beast, kept in Labyrinth in Crete; slain by Theseus.

Mnemosyne: Goddess of memory; mother by Zeus of Muses.

Moirae: *See* Fates.

Momus: God of ridicule.

Morpheus: God of dreams.

Mors: *See* Thanatos.

Morta: *See* Fates.

Muses: Goddesses presiding over arts and sciences: Calliope (epic poetry), Clio (history), Erato (lyric and love poetry), Euterpe (music), Melpomene (tragedy), Polymnia or Polyhymnia (sacred poetry), Terpsichore (choral dance and song), Thalia (comedy and bucolic poetry), Urania (astronomy); daughters of Zeus and Mnemosyne.

Naiads: Nymphs of waters, streams, and fountains.

Napaeae: Wood nymphs.

Narcissus: Beautiful youth loved by Echo; in punishment for not returning her love, he was made to fall in love with his image reflected in pool; pined away and became flower.

Nemesis: Goddess of retribution.

Neoptolemus: Son of Achilles; slew Priam; also known as Pyrrhus.

Neptune: *See* Poseidon.

Nereids: Sea nymphs; attendants on Poseidon.

Nestor: King of Pylos; noted for wise counsel in expedition against Troy.

Nike: Goddess of victory.

Niobe: Daughter of Tantalus; wife of Amphion; her children slain by Apollo and Artemis; changed to stone but continued to weep her loss.

Nona: *See* Fates.

Notus: *See* Winds.

Nox: *See* Nyx.

Nymphs: Beautiful maidens; inferior deities of nature.

Nyx (Nox): Goddess of night.

Oceanids: Ocean nymphs; daughters of Oceanus.

Oceanus: Eldest of Titans; god of waters.

Odysseus (Ulysses): King of Ithaca; husband of Penelope; wandered ten years after fall of Troy before arriving home.

Oedipus: King of Thebes; son of Laius and Jocasta; unwittingly murdered Laius and married Jocasta; tore his eyes out when relationship was discovered.

Oenone: Nymph of Mount Ida; wife of Paris, who abandoned her; refused to cure him when he was poisoned by arrow of Philoctetes at Troy.

Ops: *See* Rhea.

Oreads: Mountain nymphs.

Orestes: Son of Agamemnon and Clytemnestra; brother of Electra; slew Clytemnestra and Aegisthus; pursued by Furies until his purification by Apollo.

Orion: Hunter; slain by Artemis and made heavenly constellation.

Orpheus: Famed musician; son of Apollo and Muse Calliope; husband of Eurydice.

Pales: Roman goddess of shepherds and herdsmen.

Palinurus: Aeneas' pilot; fell overboard in his sleep and was drowned.

Pan (Faunus): God of woods and fields; part goat; son of Hermes.

Pandora: Opener of box containing human ills; mortal wife of Epimetheus.

Parcae: *See* Fates.

Paris: Son of Priam; gave apple of discord to Aphrodite, for which she enabled him to carry off Helen; slew Achilles at Troy; slain by Philoctetes.

Patroclus: Great friend of Achilles; wore Achilles' armor and was slain by Hector.

Pegasus: Winged horse that sprang from Medusa's body at her death; ridden by Bellerophon when he slew Chimera.

Pelias: King of Ioclus; seized throne from his brother Aeson; sent Jason for Golden Fleece; slain unwittingly by his daughters at instigation of Medea.

Pelops: Son of Tantalus; his father cooked and served him to gods; restored to life; Peloponnesus named for him.

Penates: Roman household gods.

Penelope: Wife of Odysseus; waited faithfully for him for ten years while putting off numerous suitors.

Pephredo: *See* Graeae.

Periphetes: Giant; son of Hephaestus; slain by Theseus.

Persephone (Proserpine): Queen of infernal regions; daughter of Zeus and Demeter; wife of Pluto.

Perseus: Son of Zeus and Danaë; slew Medusa; rescued Andromeda from monster and married her.

Phaedra: Daughter of Minos; wife of Theseus; caused the death of her stepson, Hippolytus.

Phaethon: Son of Helios; drove his father's sun chariot and was struck down by Zeus before he set world on fire.

Philoctetes: Greek warrior who possessed Hercules' bow and arrows; slew Paris at Troy with poisoned arrow.

Phineus: Betrothed of Andromeda; tried to slay Perseus but turned to stone by Medusa's head.

Phlegethon: *See* Rivers.

Phosphor: Morning star.

Phrixos: Brother of Helle; carried by ram of Golden Fleece to Colchis.

Pirithous: Son of Ixion; friend of Theseus; tried to carry off Persephone from Hades; bound to enchanted rock by Pluto.

Pleiades: Alcyone, Celaeno, Electra, Maia, Merope, Sterope or Asterope, Taygeta; seven daughters of Atlas; transformed into heavenly constellation, of which six stars are visible (Merope is said to have hidden in shame for loving a mortal).

Pluto (Dis): God of Hades; brother of Zeus.

Plutus: God of wealth.

Pollux: *See* Dioscuri.

Polymnia: *See* Muses.

Polynices: Son of Oedipus; he and his brother Eteocles killed each other; burial rite, forbidden by Creon, performed by his sister Antigone.

Polyphemus: Cyclops; devoured six of Odysseus' men; blinded by Odysseus.

Polyxena: Daughter of Priam; betrothed to Achilles, whom Paris slew at their betrothal; sacrificed to shade of Achilles.

Pomona: Roman goddess of fruits.

Pontus: Sea god; son of Gaea.

Poseidon (Neptune): God of sea; brother of Zeus.

Priam: King of Troy; husband of Hecuba; ransomed Hector's body from Achilles; slain by Neoptolemus.

Priapus: God of regeneration.

Procris: Wife of Cephalus, who accidentally slew her.

Procrustes: Giant; stretched or cut off legs of victims to make them fit iron bed; slain by Theseus.

Proetus: Husband of Anteia; sent Bellerophon to lobates to be put to death.

Prometheus: Titan; stole fire from heaven for man. Zeus punished him by chaining him to rock in Caucasus where vultures devoured his liver daily.

Proteus: Sea god; assumed various shapes when called on to prophesy.

Psyche: Beloved of Eros; punished by jealous Aphrodite; made immortal and united with Eros.

Pygmalion: King of Cyprus; carved ivory statue of maiden which Aphrodite gave life as Galatea.

Pyramus: Babylonian youth; made love to Thisbe through hole in wall; thinking Thisbe slain by lion, killed himself.

Pyrrhus: *See* Neoptolemus.

Python: Serpent born from slime left by Deluge; slain by Apollo.

Quirinus: Roman war god.

Remus: Brother of Romulus; slain by him.

Rhadamanthus: One of three judges of dead in Hades; son of Zeus and Europa.

Rhea (Ops): Daughter of Uranus and Gaea; wife of Cronus; mother of Zeus; identified with Cybele.

Rivers of Underworld: Acheron (woe), Cocytus (wailing), Lethe (forgetfulness), Phlegethon (fire), Styx (across which souls of dead were ferried by Charon).

Romulus: Founder of Rome; he and Remus suckled in infancy by she-wolf; slew Remus; deified by Romans.

Sarpedon: King of Lycia; son of Zeus and Europa; slain by Patroclus at Troy.

Saturn: *See* Cronus.

Satyrs: Hoofed demigods of woods and fields; companions of Dionysus.

Sciron: Robber; forced strangers to wash his feet, then hurled them into sea where tortoise devoured them; slain by Theseus.

Scylla: Female monster inhabiting rock opposite Charybdis; menaced passing sailors.

Selene: Goddess of moon.

Semele: Daughter of Cadmus; mother by Zeus of Dionysus; demanded Zeus appear before her in all his splendor and was destroyed by his lightnings.

Sibyis: Various prophetesses; most famous, Cumaean sibyl, accompanied Aeneas into Hades.

Sileni: Minor woodland deities similar to satyrs (singular: silenus). Sometimes Silenus refers to eldest of satyrs, son of Hermes or of Pan.

Silvanus: Roman god of woods and fields.

Sinis: Giant; bent pines, by which he hurled victims against side of mountain; slain by Theseus.

Sirens: Minor deities who lured sailors to destruction with their singing.

Sisyphus: King of Corinth; condemned in Tartarus to roll huge stone to top of hill; it always rolled back down again.

Sol: *See* Helios.

Somnus: *See* Hypnos.

Sphinx: Monster of Thebes; killed those who could not answer her riddle; slain by Oedipus. Name also refers to other monsters having body of lion, wings, and head and bust of woman.

Sterope: *See* Pleiades.

Stheno: *See* Gorgons.

Styx: *See* Rivers.

Symplegades: Clashing rocks at entrance to Black Sea; Argo passed through, causing them to become forever fixed.

Syrinx: Nymph pursued by Pan; changed to reeds, from which he made his pipes.

Tantalus: Cruel king; father of Pelops and Niobe; condemned in Tartarus to stand chin-deep in lake surrounded by fruit branches; as he tried to eat or drink, water or fruit always receded.

Tartarus: Underworld below Hades; often refers to Hades.

Taygeta: *See* Pleiades.

Telemachus: Son of Odysseus; made unsuccessful journey to find his father.

Tellus: Roman goddess of earth.

Terminus: Roman god of boundaries and landmarks.

Terpsichore: *See* Muses.

Terra: Roman earth goddess.

Thalia: *See* Graces; Muses.

Thanatos (Mors): God of death.

Themis: Titan goddess of laws of physical phenomena; daughter of Uranus; mother of Prometheus.

Theseus: Son of Aegeus; slew Minotaur; married and deserted Ariadne; later married Phaedra.

Thisbe: Beloved of Pyramus; killed herself at his death.

Thyestes: Brother of Atreus; Atreus killed three of his sons and served them to him at banquet.

Tiresias: Blind soothsayer of Thebes.

Tisiphone: *See* Furies.

Titans: Early gods from which Olympian gods were derived; children of Uranus and Gaea.

Tithonus: Mortal loved by Eos; changed into grasshopper.

Triton: Demigod of sea; son of Poseidon.

Turnus: King of Rutuli in Italy; betrothed to Lavinia; slain by Aeneas.

Ulysses: *See* Odysseus.

Urania: *See* Muses.

Uranus: Personification of Heaven; husband of Gaea; father of Titans; dethroned by his son Cronus.

Venus: *See* Aphrodite.

Vertumnus: Roman god of fruits and vegetables; husband of Pomona.

Vesta: *See* Hestia.

Vulcan: *See* Hephaestus.

Winds: Aeolus (keeper of winds), Boreas (Aquilo) (north wind), Eurus (east wind), Notus (Auster) (south wind), Zephyrus (Favonius) (west wind).

Zephyrus: *See* Winds.

Zeus (Jupiter): Chief of Olympian gods; son of Cronus and Rhea; husband of Hera.

Norse Mythology

Aesir: Chief gods of Asgard.

Andvari: Dwarf; robbed of gold and magic ring by Loki.

Angerbotha (Angrbotha): Giantess; mother by Loki of Fenrir, Hel, and Midgard serpent.

Asgard (Asgarth): Abode of gods.

Ask (Aske, Askr): First man; created by Odin, Hoenir, and Lothur.

Asynjur: Goddesses of Asgard.

Atli: Second husband of Gudrun; invited Gunnar and Hogni to his court, where they were slain; slain by Gudrun.

Audhumia (Audhumbla): Cow that nourished Ymir, created Buri by licking ice cliff.

Balder (Baldr, Baldur): God of light, spring, peace, joy; son of Odin; slain by Hoth at instigation of Loki.

Bifrost: Rainbow bridge connecting Midgard and Asgard.

Bragi (Brage): God of poetry; husband of Ithunn.

Branstock: Great oak in hall of Volsungs; into it, Odin thrust Gram, which only Sigmund could draw forth.

Brynhild: Valkyrie; wakened from magic sleep by Sigurd; married Gunnar; instigated death of Sigurd; killed herself and was burned on pyre beside Sigurd.

Bur (Bor): Son of Buri; father of Odin, Hoenir, and Lothur.

Buri (Bori): Progenitor of gods; father of Bur; created by Audhumla.

Embla: First woman; created by Odin, Hoenir, and Lothur.

Fafnir: Son of Rodmar, whom he slew for gold in Otter's skin; in form of dragon, guarded gold; slain by Sigurd.

Fenrir: Wolf; offspring of Loki; swallows Odin at Ragnarok and is slain by Vitharr.

Forseti: Son of Balder.

Frey (Freyr): God of fertility and crops; son of Njorth; originally one of Vanir.

Freya (Freyja): Goddess of love and beauty; sister of Frey; originally one of Vanir.

Frigg (Frigga): Goddess of sky; wife of Odin.

Garm: Watchdog of Hel; slays, and is slain by, Tyr at Ragnarok.

Gimle: Home of blessed after Ragnarok.

Giuki: King of Nibelungs; father of Gunnar, Hogni, Guttorm, and Gudrun.

Glathsehim (Gladsheim): Hall of gods in Asgard.

Gram (meaning "Angry"): Sigmund's sword; re-welded by Regin; used by Sigurd to slay Fafnir.

Greyfell: Sigmund's horse; descended from Sleipnir.

Grimhild: Mother of Gudrun; administered magic potion to Sigurd which made him forget Brynhild.

Gudrun: Daughter of Giuki; wife of Sigurd; later wife of Atli and Jonakr.

Gunnar: Son of Giuki; in his semblance Sigurd won Brynhild for him; slain at hall of Atli.

Guttorm: Son of Giuki; slew Sigurd at Brynhild's request.

Heimdall (Heimdallr): Guardian of Asgard.

Hel: Goddess of dead and queen of underworld; daughter of Loki.

Hiordis: Wife of Sigmund; mother of Sigurd.

Hoenir: One of creators of Ask and Embla; son of Bur.

Hogni: Son of Giuki; slain at hall of Atli.

Hoth (Hoder, Hodur): Blind god of night and darkness; slayer of Balder at instigation of Loki.

Ithunn (Ithun, Iduna): Keeper of golden apples of youth; wife of Bragi.

Jonakr: Third husband of Gudrun.

Jormunrek: Slayer of Swanhild; slain by sons of Gudrun.

Jotunnheim (Jotunheim): Abode of giants.

Lif and Lifthrasir: First man and woman after Ragnarok.

Loki: God of evil and mischief; instigator of Balder's death.

Lothur (Lodur): One of creators of Ask and Embla.

Midgard (Midgarth): Abode of mankind; the earth.

Midgard Serpent: Sea monster; offspring of Loki; slays, and is slain by, Thor at Ragnarok.

Mimir: Giant; guardian of well in Jotunnheim at root of Yggdrasill; knower of past and future.

Mjollnir: Magic hammer of Thor.

Nagifar: Ship to be used by giants in attacking Asgard at Ragnarok; built from nails of dead men.

Nanna: Wife of Balder.

Nibelungs: Dwellers in northern kingdom ruled by Giuki.

Niflheim (Nifelheim): Outer region of cold and darkness; abode of Hel.

Njorth: Father of Frey and Freya; originally one of Vanir.

Norns: Demigoddesses of fate: Urth (Urdur) (Past), Verthandi (Verdandi) (Present), Skuld (Future).

Odin (Othin): Head of Aesir; creator of world with Vili and Ve; equivalent to Woden (Wodan, Wotan) in Teutonic mythology.

Otter: Son of Rodmar; slain by Loki; his skin filled with gold hoard of Andvari to appease Rodmar.

Ragnarok: Final destruction of present world in battle between gods and giants; some minor gods will survive, and Lif and Lifthrasir will repeople world.

Regin: Blacksmith; son of Rodmar; foster-father of Sigurd.

Rerir: King of Huns; son of Sigi.

Rodmar: Father of Regin, Otter, and Fafnir; demanded Otter's skin be filled with gold; slain by Fafnir, who stole gold.

Sif: Wife of Thor.

Siggeir: King of Goths; husband of Signy; he and his sons slew Volsung and his sons, except Sigmund; slain by Sigmund and Sinflotli.

Sigi: King of Huns; son of Odin.

Sigmund: Son of Volsung; brother of Signy, who bore him Sinflotli; husband of Hiordis, who bore him Sigurd.

Signy: Daughter of Volsung; sister of Sigmund; wife of Siggeir; mother by Sigmund of Sinflotli.

Sigurd: Son of Sigmund and Hiordis; wakened Brynhild from magic sleep; married Gudrun; slain by Guttorm at instigation of Brynhild.

Sigyn: Wife of Loki.

Sinflotli: Son of Sigmund and Signy.

Skuld: *See* Norns.

Sleipnir (Sleipner): Eight-legged horse of Odin.

Surt (Surtr): Fire demon; slays Frey at Ragnarok.

Svartalfaheim: Abode of dwarfs.

Swanhild: Daughter of Sigurd and Gudrun; slain by Jormunrek.

Thor: God of thunder; oldest son of Odin; equivalent to Germanic deity Donar.

Tyr: God of war; son of Odin; equivalent to Tiu in Teutonic mythology.

Ull (Ullr): Son of Sif; stepson of Thor.

Urth: *See* Norns.

Valhalla (Valhall): Great hall in Asgard where Odin received souls of heroes killed in battle.

Vali: Odin's son; Ragnarok survivor.

Valkyries: Virgins, messengers of Odin, who selected heroes to die in battle and took them to Valhalla; generally considered as nine in number.

Vanir: Early race of gods; three survivors, Njorth, Frey, and Freya, are associated with Aesir.

Ve: Brother of Odin; one of creators of world.

Verthandi: *See* Norns.

Vili: Brother of Odin; one of creators of world.

Vingolf: Abode of goddesses in Asgard.

Vitharr (Vithar): Son of Odin; survivor of Ragnarok.

Volsung: Descendant of Odin, and father of Signy, Sigmund; his descendants were called Volsungs.

Yggdrasill: Giant ash tree springing from body of Ymir and supporting universe; its roots extended to Asgard, Jotunnheim, and Niffheim.

Ymir (Ymer): Primeval frost giant killed by Odin, Vili, and Ve; world created from his body; also, from his body sprang Yggdrasill.

Egyptian Mythology

Aaru: Abode of the blessed dead.

Amen (Amon, Ammdn): One of chief Theban deities; united with sun god under form of Amen-Ra.

Amenti: Region of dead where souls were judged by Osiris.

Anubis: Guide of souls to Amenti; son of Osiris; jackal-headed.

Apis: Sacred bull, an embodiment of Ptah; identified with Osiris as Osiris-Apis or Serapis.

Geb (Keb, Seb): Earth god; father of Osiris; represented with goose on head.

Hathor (Athor): Goddess of love and mirth; cowheaded.

Horus: God of day; son of Osiris and Isis; hawk-headed.

Isis: Goddess of motherhood and fertility; sister and wife of Osiris.

Khepera: God of morning sun.

Khnemu (Khnum, Chnuphis, Chnemu, Chnum): Ramheaded god.

Khonsu (Khensu, Khuns): Son of Amen and Mut.

Mentu (Ment): Solar deity, sometimes considered god of war; falcon-headed.

Min (Khem, Chem): Principle of physical life.

Mut (Maut): Wife of Amen.

Nephthys: Goddess of the dead; sister and wife of Set.

Nu: Chaos from which world was created, personified as a god.

Nut: Goddess of heavens; consort of Geb.

Osiris: God of underworld and judge of dead; son of Geb and Nut.

Ptah (Phtha): Chief deity of Memphis.

Ra: God of the Sun, the supreme god; son of Nut; Pharaohs claimed descent from him; represented as lion, cat, or falcon.

Serapis: God uniting attributes of Osiris and Apis.

Set (Seth): God of darkness or evil; brother and enemy of Osiris.

Shu: Solar deity; son of Ra and Hathor.

Tem (Atmu, Atum, Tum): Solar deity.

Thoth (Dhouti): God of wisdom and magic; scribe of gods; ibis-headed

Modern Wedding Anniversary Gift List

Anniversay	Gift	Anniversary	Gift	Anniversary	Gift
1st	Gold jewelry	10th	Diamond jewelry	19th	Aquamarine
2nd	Garnet	11th	Turquoise	20th	Emerald
3rd	Pearls	12th	Jade	25th	Silver jubilee
4th	Blue topaz	13th	Citrine	30th	Pearl jubilee
5th	Sapphire	14th	Opal	35th	Emerald
6th	Amethyst	15th	Ruby	40th	Ruby
7th	Onyx	16th	Peridot	45th	Sapphire
8th	Tourmaline	17th	Watches	50th	Golden jubilee
9th	Lapis	18th	Cat's–eye	60th	Diamond jubilee

Source: Jewelry Industry Council

SCIENCE

Controversy Continues Over Names of Elements 104 to 109

By Michael Freemantle, European Science Editor, *Chemical & Engineering News*

Elements are the building blocks of nature. Water, for example, is a compound consisting of the elements hydrogen and oxygen. Each element is a pure substance which cannot be split up into any simpler pure substance.

The smallest particle of an element that can exist is an atom. An atom consists of sub-atomic particles. The most important of these are protons, which have positive electrical charges, electrons, which have negative electrical charges, and neutrons, which are electrically neutral.

The atomic number of an element is the number of protons in one atom of the element. Each element has a different atomic number. For example, the atomic numbers of hydrogen and oxygen are 1 and 8, respectively.

Elements with atomic numbers 1 (hydrogen) to 92 (uranium) occur naturally on Earth. Those with atomic numbers 93 (neptunium) onwards are artificial. They have to be synthesized from elements with lower atomic numbers. Element 100 is named fermium. Elements with atomic numbers 101 onwards are known as the transfermium elements. They are also known as heavy elements because their atoms have very large masses compared with atoms of hydrogen, the lightest of all elements.

The heaviest element synthesized to date is element 112. One atom of this element was synthesized by scientists at the Heavy–Ion Research Center (Gesellschaft für Schwerionenforschung [GSI]) in Darmstadt, Germany, in February 1996. They made it by bombarding the element lead (atomic number 82) with a high-energy beam of atoms of the element zinc (atomic number 30). The atom existed for a fraction of a second before splitting up. Elements 110 and 111 were discovered by the same group of scientists in 1994.

To date, no names have been proposed for elements 110 to 112. The names of transfermium elements 104 to 109, however, have been the subject of a long-running controversy rooted in disagreements about the discoveries of these elements.

In the late 1960s and early 1970s, groups of scientists at the Lawrence Berkeley Laboratory in California, and the Joint Institute for Nuclear Research in Dubna, Russia, both laid claim to discovering elements 104 and 105. The two discovery groups proposed different names for these elements. A joint Transfermium Working Group (TWG) was set up by the International Union of Pure and Applied Chemistry (IUPAC) and the International Union of Pure and Applied Physics to resolve the dispute. They concluded that the Russian and U.S. teams should share credit for the discovery of these elements.

In 1994, IUPAC, the body that makes recommendations on chemical names, chose two Russian-proposed names—*dubnium*, based on Dubna, and *joliotium*, after French physicist Frédéric Joliot-Curie—for elements 104 and 105 respectively.

The U.S. team was credited by TWG with the discovery of element 106. The team proposed the name *seaborgium* for the element after team member Glenn T. Seaborg. But IUPAC rejected *seaborgium* because it is based on the name of a living person. Instead, IUPAC chose *rutherfordium*, which the Americans had proposed for element 104. The name is based on British physicist Ernest Rutherford.

Elements 107 to 109 were discovered by scientists at GSI between 1981 and 1984. The German group proposed the names *nielsbohrium* (after Danish physicist Niels Bohr) for element 107, *hassium* (after Hassia, the Latin name for the German state where GSI is located) for element 108, and *meitnerium* (after Austrian physicist Lise Meitner) for element 109. IUPAC agreed that element 109 should be called *meitnerium* but chose *bohrium* for element 107 and *hahnium*, after German chemist Otto Hahn, for element 108.

The IUPAC recommendations caused a furor in the scientific community. The German team was unhappy that IUPAC rejected its proposed names for elements 107 and 108. The American Chemical Society, based in Washington, D.C., rejected some of the IUPAC names and independently adopted its own slate of names for elements 104 to 109. This forced IUPAC to think again. In 1995, IUPAC proposed a compromise slate of names which is currently being considered by the world's scientific community. IUPAC's final recommendations for these names, as yet unannounced, will be submitted for ratification at the 39th IUPAC General Assembly to be held in Geneva, Switzerland, in August 1997.

Proposed Slates of Names for Elements 104 to 109

Atomic number	American Chemical Society slate (1995)	International Union of Pure and Applied Chemistry slate (1994)	Compromise slate proposed by IUPAC (1995)
104	Rutherfordium	Dubnium	Dubnium
105	Hahnium	Joliotium	Joliotium
106	Seaborgium	Rutherfordium	Seaborgium
107	Nielsbohrium	Bohrium	Nielsbohrium
108	Hassium	Hahnium	Hahnium
109	Meitnerium	Meitnerium	Meitnerium

Major Discoveries of Human Ancestors

Living and extinct human beings and their near human ancestors are called "Hominids," and belong to the family *Hominidae* of primates. They are not to be confused with "Hominoids" which belong to the family *Hominoidea* of primates that include apes and humans. Scientists theorize that the human and ape lines branched off from a common ancestor 8 to 6 million years ago.

Years	Species	Discovered	Remarks
c. 4.4 million	Ardipithecus ramidus	1994 in Ethiopia	Oldest known human ancestor. Had chimpanzee-like skull.
c. 4.2 million	Australopithecus anamensis	1995, two sites at Lake Turkana, Kanapoi, and Allia Bay, Kenya	Possible ancestor of A. afarensis (Lucy). Walked upright.
c. 3.2 million	Australopithecus afarensis	1974 at Hadar in the Afar triangle of eastern Ethiopia	Nicknamed "Lucy." Her skeleton was 3.5 feet (100 cm) tall. Had ape-like skull. Walked fully upright. Lived in family groups throughout eastern Africa.
c. 2.5 million	Australopithecus africanus	1924 at Taung, northern Cape Province, South Africa	Descendant of "Lucy." Lived in social groups.
c. 2 million	Australopithecus Robustus	1938 in Kromdraai, South Africa	Was related to africanus
c. 2 million	Homo habilis ("skillful man")	1960 in Olduvai Gorge, Tanzania	First brain expansion; is believed to have used stone tools
c. 1.8 million	Homo erectus ("upright man")	1891 at Trinil, Java	Brain size twice that of Australopithecine species. Regarded as ancestor of Homo sapiens. Invented the hand ax. Could probably make fires. Was first to migrate out of Africa.
c. 100,000(?)	Homo sapien ("knowing or wise man"	1868, Cro-Magnon, France	Anatomically modern humans

Two Radically Different Types of Humans

The Neanderthals *(Homo sapiens neandertalensis)*, c. 150,000–35,000 years ago, are the best known of all extinct human sub-species. They first appeared in Europe and their fossil remains, the first anatomically human forms to be discovered, were found in 1856 in the Neander Valley, Germany. They spread throughout Europe and Western Asia. There is recent evidence that they coexisted with modern humans and no one knows why they suddenly vanished.

The Cro-Magnon *(Homo sapiens sapiens)*, c. 100,000(?) years ago, completely resembled modern humans. Although usage of the term Cro-Magnon strictly applies only to those who lived in southwestern France, it has been used by many to generally describe *Homo sapiens sapiens* that lived everywhere else. Their skeletons were discovered in a rock shelter in the Cro-Magnon valley, Les Eyzies, southwestern France, in 1868.

There is evidence obtained through thermoluminescent (TL) dating and electron-spin resonance (ESR) dating at sites of modern hominids in Mount Carmel, Israel, that modern humans existed in Israel c. 100,000 years ago, long before the Neanderthal peoples arrived there. If these dates are correct, they imply that these two distinct human ancestors coexisted together for many thousands of years.

More evidence emerged in 1996 when researchers announced that Neanderthals living about 34,000 years ago near Auxerre in central France may have had cultural contacts with Cro-Magnons. Their conclusion was based on stone and bone tools and jewelry-like ornaments discovered in rock shelters occupied by Neanderthals that were similar to those made by Cro-Magnons. The evidence implies that some Neanderthals may have traded with Cro-Magnons rather than learned how to make the more sophisticated artifacts themselves. The stone tools were discovered in the 1950s, but a positive identification of their origin could not be established until recently.

Table of Geological Periods

It is now generally assumed that planets are formed by the accretion of gas and dust in a cosmic cloud, but there is no way of estimating the length of this process. Our earth acquired its present size, more or less, between 4,000 and 5,000 million years ago. Life on earth originated about 2,000 million years ago, but there are no good fossil remains from periods earlier than the Cambrian, which began about 550 million years ago. The largely unknown past before the Cambrian Period is referred to as the Pre-Cambrian and is subdivided into the Lower (or older) and Upper (or younger) Pre-Cambrian—also called the Archaeozoic and Proterozoic Eras.

The known geological history of the earth since the beginning of the Cambrian Period is subdivided into three "eras," each of which comprises a number of "periods." They, in turn, are subdivided into "subperiods." In a subperiod, a certain section may be especially well known because of rich fossil finds. Such a section is called a "formation," and it is usually identified by a place name.

Paleozoic Era

This era began 550 million years ago and lasted for 355 million years. The name was compounded from Greek *palaios* (old) and zoön *(animal).*

Period	Duration[1]	Subperiods	Events
Cambrian (from *Cambria*, Latin name for Wales)	70	Lower Cambrian Middle Cambrian Upper Cambrian	Invertebrate sea life of many types, proliferating during this and the following period
Ordovician (from Latin *Ordo-vices*, people of early Britain)	85	Lower Ordovician Upper Ordovician	
Silurian (from Latin *Silures*, people of eary Wales)	40	Lower Silurian Upper Silurian	First known fishes; gigantic sea scorpions
Devonian (from Devonshire in England)	50	Lower Devonian Upper Devonian	Proliferation of fishes and other forms of sea life, land still largely lifeless
Carboniferous (from Latin *carbo* = coal + *fero* = to bear)	85	Lower or Mississippian Upper or Pennsylvanian	Period of maximum coal formation in swampy forests; early insects and first known amphibians
Permian (from district of Perm in Russia)	25	Lower Permian Upper Permian	Early reptiles and mammals; earliest form of turtles

Mesozoic Era

This era began 195 million years ago and lasted for 135 million years. The name was compounded form Greek *mesos* (middle) and *zoön* (animal). Popular name: Age of Reptiles.

Period	Duration[1]	Subperiods	Events
Triassic (from *trias* = triad)	35	Lower or Buntsandstein (from German *bunt* = colorful + *Sandstein* = sandstone) Middle of Muschelkalk (from German *Muschel* = clam + *Kalk* = limestone) Upper or Keuper (old miner's term)	Early saurians
Jurrassic (from Jura Mountains)	35	Lower of Black Jurassic, or Lias (from French *liais* = hard stone) Middle or Brown Jurassic, or Dogger (old provincial English for ironstone) Upper or White Jurasic, or Malm (Middle English for sand)	Many sea-going reptiles; early large dinosaurs; somewhat later, flying reptile (pterosaurs), earliest known birds
Cretaceous (from Latin *creta* = chalk)	65	Lower Cretaceous Upper Cretaceous	Maximum development of dinosaurs; birds proliferating; opossum-like mammals

Cenozoic Era

This era began 60 million years ago and includes the geological present. The name was compounded from Greek *kainos* (new) and *zoön* (animal). Popular name: Age of Mammals.

Period	Duration[1]	Subperiods	Events
Tertiary (originally thought to be the third of only three periods)	c. 60	Palecene (from Greek *palaios* = old + *kainos* = new)	First mammals other than marsupials
		Eocene (from Greek *eos* = dawn + *kainos* = new)	Formation of amber; rich insect fauna; early bats
		Oligocene (from Greek *oligos* = few + *kainos* = new)	Steady increase of large mammals
		Miocene (from Greek *meios* = less + *kainos* = new)	
		Pliocene (from Greek *pleios* = more + *kainos* = new)	Mammals closely resembling present types; protohumans
Pleistocene (from Greek *pleistos* = most + *kainos* = new) (popular name: Ice Age)	1	Four major glaciations, named Günz, Mindel, Riss, and Würm originally the name of rivers Last glaciation ended 10,000 to 15,000 years ago	Various forms of early man
Holocene (from Greek *holos* = entire + *kainos* = new)		The present	The last 3,000 years are called "history"

1. In millions of years.

Chemical Elements

Element	Symbol	Atomic no.	Atomic weight	Specific gravity	Melting point °C	Boiling point °C	Number of isotopes[1]	Discoverer	Year
Actinium	Ac	89	227[2]	10.07[2]	1050	3200±300	11	Debierne	1899
Aluminum	Al	13	26.9815	2.6989	660.37	2467	8	Wöhler	1827
Americum	Am	95	243[6]	13.67	994 +4	2607	13[3]	Seaborg et al.	1944
Antimony	Sb	51	121.75	6.61	630.74	1750	29	Early historic times	—
Argon	Ar	18	39.948	1.7837[4]	−189.2	−185.7	8	Rayleigh and Ramsay	1894
Arsenic (gray)	As	33	74.9216	5.73	817 (28 atm.)	613[5]	14	Albertus Magnus	1250?
Astatine	At	85	−210		302	337	21	Corson et al.	1940
Barium	Ba	56	137.34	3.5	725	1640	25	Davy	1808
Berkelium	Bk	97	247[6]	14.00[7]			8[3]	Seaborg et al.	1949
Beryllium	Be	4	9.01218	1.848	1278 +5	2970 (5 mm.)	6	Vauquelin	1798
Bismuth	Bi	83	208.9806	9.747	271.3	1560±5	19	Geoffroy	1753
Boron	B	5	10.81	2.37[8]	2300	2550[5]	6	Gay-Lussac and Thénard; Davy	1808
Bromine	Br	35	79.904	3.12[4]	−7.2	58.78	19	Balard	1826
Cadmium	Cd	48	112.40	8.65	320.9	765	22	Stromeyer	1817
Calcium	Ca	20	40.08	1.55	839 +2	1484	14	Davy	1808
Californium	Cf	98	251[6]				12[3]	Seaborg et al.	1950
Carbon	C	6	12.011	1.8–3.5[9]	−3550	4827	7	Prehistoric	—
Cerium	Ce	58	140.12	6.771	798 +3	3257	19	Berzelius and Hisinger; Klaproth	1803
Cesium	Cs	55	132.9055	1.873	28.40	678.4	22	Bunsen and Kirchoff	1860
Chlorine	Cl	17	35.453	1.56[4]	−100.98	−34.6	11	Scheele	1774
Chromium	Cr	24	51.996	7.18–7.20	1857 +20	2672	9	Vauquelin	1797
Cobalt	Co	27	58.9332	8.9	1495	2870	14	Brandt	c.1735
Copper	Cu	29	63.546	8.96	1083.4±0.2	2567	11	Prehistoric	—
Curium	Cm	96	247[6]	13.51[2]	1340 +40		13[3]	Seaborg et al.	1944
Dysprosium	Dy	66	162.50	8.540	1409	2335	21	Boisbaudran	1886
Einsteinium	Es	99	254[6]				12[3]	Ghiorso et al.	1952
Erbium	Er	68	167.26	9.045	1522	2510	16	Mosander	1843
Europium	Eu	63	151.96	5.283	822 +5	1597	21	Demarcay	1896
Fermium	Fm	100	257[6]				10[3]	Ghiorso et al.	1953
Fluorine	F	9	18.9984	1.108[4]	−219.62	−188.14	6	Moissan	1886
Francium	Fr	87	223[6]		27[2]	677[2]	21	Perey	1939
Gadolinium	Gd	64	157.25	7.898	1311 +1	3233	17	Marignac	1880
Gallium	Ga	31	69.72	5.904	29.78	2403	14	Boisbaudran	1875
Germanium	Ge	32	72.59	5.323	937.4	2830	17	Winkler	1886
Gold	Au	79	196.9665	19.32	1064.43	2807	21	Prehistoric	—
Hafnium	Hf	72	178.49	13.31	2227 +20	4602	17	Coster and von Hevesy	1923
Hahnium	Ha	105	262				—	Ghiorso et al.	1970
Helium	He	2	4.00260	0.1785[4]	−272.2 (26 atm.)	−268.934	5	Janssen	1868
Holmium	Ho	67	164.9303	8.781	1470	2720	29	Delafontaine and Soret	1878
Hydrogen	H	1	1.0080	0.070[4]	−259.14	−252.87	3	Cavendish	1766
Indium	In	49	114.82	7.31	156.61	2080	34	Reich and Richter	1863
Iodine	I	53	126.9045	4.93	113.5	184.35	24	Cortois	1811
Iridium	Ir	77	192.22	22.42	2410	4130	25	Tennant	1804
Iron	Fe	26	55.847	7.894	1535	2750	10	Prehistoric	—
Krypton	Kr	36	83.80	3.733[4]	−156.6	−152.30±0.10	23	Ramsay and Travers	1898

Element	Symbol	Atomic no.	Atomic weight	Specific gravity	Melting point °C	Boiling point °C	Number of isotopes[1]	Discoverer	Year
Lanthanum	La	57	138.9055	6.166	920 +5	3454	19	Mosander	1839
Lawrencium	Lr	103	257[6]	—	—	—	20[3]	Ghiorso et al.	1961
Lead	Pb	82	207.2	11.35	327.502	1740	29	Prehistoric	—
Lithium	Li	3	6.941	0.534	180.54	1347	5	Arfvedson	1817
Lutetium	Lu	71	174.97	9.835	1656 +5	3315	22	Urbain	1907
Magnesium	Mg	12	24.305	1.738	648.8+0.5	1090	8	Black	1755
Manganese	Mn	25	54.9380	7.21–7.44[10]	1244 +3	1962	11	Gahn, Scheele, and Bergman	1774
Mendelevium	Md	101	256[6]	—	—	—	3[3]	Ghiorso et al.	1955
Mercury	Hg	80	200.59	13.546	−38.87	356.58	26	Prehistoric	—
Molybdenum	Mo	42	95.94	10.22	2617	4612	20	Scheele	1778
Neodymium	Nd	60	144.24	6.80 & 7.004[10]	1010	3127	16	von Weisbach	1885
Neon	Ne	10	20.179	0.89990 (g/1 0°C/1 atm)	−248.67	−246.048	8	Ramsay and Travers	1898
Neptunium	Np	93	237.0482	20.25	640 +1	3902	15[3]	McMillan and Abelson	1940
Nickel	Ni	28	58.71	8.902	1453	2732	11	Cronstedt	1751
Niobium (Columbium)	Nb	41	92.9064	8.57	2468 +10	4742	24	Hatchett	1801
Nitrogen	N	7	14.0067	0.808[4]	−209.86	−195.8	8	Rutherford	1772
Nobelium	No	102	254[6]	—	—	—	7[3]	Ghiorso et al.	1957
Osmium	Os	76	190.2	22.57	3045 +30	5027+100	19	Tennant	1803
Oxygen	O	8	15.9994	1.14[4]	−218.4	−182.962	8	Priestley	1774
Palladium	Pd	46	106.4	12.02	1552	3140	21	Wollaston	1803
Phosphorous	P	15	30.9738	1.82 (White)	44.1	280	7	Brand	1669
Platinum	Pt	78	195.09	21.45	1772	3827+100	32	Ulloa	1735
Plutonium	Pu	94	244[6]	19.84	641	3232	16[3]	Seaborg et al.	1940
Poionium	Po	84	210[6]	9.32	254	962	34	Curie	1898
Potassium	K	19	39.102	0.862	63.65	774	10	Davy	1807
Praseodymium	Pr	59	140.9077	6.772	931 +4	3212	15	von Weisbach	1885
Promethium	Pm	61	145[6]	—	≈1080	2460?	14	Marinsky et al.	1945
Protactinium	Pa	91	231.0359	15.37[2]	<1600	—	14	Hahn and Meitner	1917
Radium	Ra	88	226.0254	5.0[?]	700	1140	15	P. and M. Curie	1898
Radon	Rn	86	222[6]	4.4[4]	−71	−61.8	20	Dorn	1900
Rhenium	Re	75	186.2	21.02	3180	5627	21	Noddack, Berg, and Tacke	1925
Rhodium	Rh	45	102.9055	12.41	1966 +3	3727+100	20	Wollaston	1803
Rubidium	Rb	37	85.4678	1.532	38.89	688	20	Bunsen and Kirchoff	1861
Rutherfordium	Rf	104	261	—	—	—	—	Ghiorso et al.	1969
Ruthenium	Ru	44	101.07	12.44	2310	3900	16	Klaus	1844
Samarium	Sm	62	150.4	7.536	1072 +5	1778	17	Boisbaudran	1879
Scandium	Sc	21	44.9559	2.989	1539	2832	15	Nilson	1879
Seaborgium	Sg	106	263	—	—	—	—	Ghiorso et al.	1974
Selenium	Se	34	78.96	4.79 (gray)	217	684.9+1	20	Berzelius	1817
Silicon	Si	14	28.086	2.33	1410	2355	8	Berzelius	1824
Silver	Ag	47	107.868	10.5	961.93	2212	27	Prehistoric	—
Sodium	Na	11	22.9898	0.971	97.81+0.03	882.9	7	Davy	1807
Strontium	Sr	38	87.62	2.54	769	1384	18	Davy	1808
Sulfur	S	16	32.06	2.07[11]	112.8	444.674	10	Prehistoric	—
Tantalum	Ta	73	180.9479	16.654	2996	5425+100	19	Ekeberg	1801
Technetium	Tc	43	98.062	11.50[2]	2172	4877	23	Perrier and Segré	1937
Tellurium	Te	52	127.60	6.24	449.5+0.3	989.8+3.8	29	von Reichenstein	1782
Terbium	Tb	65	158.9254	8.234	1360 +4	3041	24	Mosander	1843
Thallium	Tl	81	204.37	11.85	303.5	1457+10	28	Crookes	1861
Thorium	Th	90	232.0381	11.72	1750	4790	12	Berzelius	1828
Thulium	Tm	69	168.9342	9.314	1545 +15	1727	18	Cleve	1879
Tin	Sn	50	118.69	7.31 (white)	231.9681	2270	28	Prehistoric	—
Titanium	Ti	22	47.90	4.55	1660 +10	3287	9	Gregor	1791
Tungsten (Wolfram)	W	74	183.85	19.3	3410 +20	5660	22	J. and F. d'Elhuyar	1783
Uranium	U	92	238.029	≈18.95	1132.3+0.8	3818	15	Peligot	1841
Vanadium	V	23	50.9414	6.11	1890 +10	3380	9	del Rio	1801
Xenon	Xe	54	131.30	3.52[4]	−111.9	−107.1+3	31	Ramsay and Travers	1898
Ytterbium	Yb	70	173.04	6.972	824 +5	1193	16	Marignac	1878
Yttrium	Y	39	88.9059	4.457	1523 +8	3337	21	Gadolin	1794
Zinc	Zn	30	65.38	7.133	419.58	907	15	Prehistoric	—
Zirconium	Zr	40	91.22	6.506[2]	1852 +2	4377	20	Klaproth	1789

Elements No. 101–111—See NOTE at end of footnotes.

. Isotopes are different forms of the same element having the same atomic number but different atomic weights. 2. Calculated figure. 3. Artificially produced. 4. Liquid 5. Sublimation point. 6. Mass number of the isotope of longest known life. . Estimated. 8. Amorphous. 9. Depending on whether amorphous, graphite or diamond. 10. Depending on allotropic orm. 11. Rhombic. ≈ Is approximately. < Is less than. **NOTE:** In October 1994, the International Union of Pure and Applied Chemistry (IUPAC) recommended renaming the provisional names for elements 101 through 109. They rejected seaborgium for element 106 because of a newly adopted rule that no element may bear the name of a living person. *See* article on page 545. Elements 110 and 111: In November 1994, German physicists at the Heavy Ion Research Center (GSI), Darmstadt, reported creating element 110, atomic mass 269. In December 1994, they announced they had produced element 111. Creating new elements is becoming old hat at Darmstadt. On February 21, 1996, an international team at the physics research center announced that they had created element number 112. The new element, a "relative" of zinc, cadmium, and mercury that is 227 times heavier than hydrogen, was produced by bombarding lead foil with highly accelerated zinc atoms. The new atom has a nucleus of 112 protons and 165 neutrons, giving it an atomic mass of 227 and making it the heaviest nucleus created in a laboratory. At GIS, researchers are now seeking to create elements 113 and 114.

INVENTIONS & DISCOVERIES

See also Famous Firsts in Aviation, Nobel Prize Awards

Abacus: *See* Calculating machine

Adding machine: *See* Calculating machine; Computer

Adrenaline: (isolation of) John Jacob Abel, U.S., 1897

Aerosol can: Erik Rotheim, Norway, 1926

Air brake: George Westinghouse, U.S., 1868

Air conditioning: Willis Carrier, U.S., 1911

Airplane: (first powered, sustained, controlled flight) Orville and Wilbur Wright, U.S., 1903. *See also* Jet propulsion

Airship: (non-rigid) Henri Giffard, France, 1852; (rigid) Ferdinand von Zeppelin, Germany, 1900

Aluminum manufacture: (by electrolytic action) Charles M. Hall, U.S., 1866

Anatomy, human: (*De fabrica corporis humani,* an illustrated systematic study of the human body) Andreas Vesalius, 1543; (comparative: parts of an organism are correlated to the functioning whole) Georges Cuvier, 1799–1805

Anesthetic: (first use of anesthetic—ether—on man) Crawford W. Long, U.S., 1842

Antibiotics: (first demonstration of antibiotic effect) Louis Pasteur, Jules-François Joubert, France, 1887; (discovery of penicillin, first modern antibiotic) Alexander Fleming, England, 1928; (penicillin's infection-fighting properties) Howard Florey, Ernst Chain, England, 1940

Antiseptic: (surgery) Joseph Lister, England, 1867

Antitoxin, diphtheria: Emil von Behring, Germany, 1890

Appliances, electric: (fan) Schuyler Wheeler, U.S., 1882; (flatiron) Henry W. Seely, U.S., 1882; (stove) Hadaway, U.S., 1896; (washing machine) Alva Fisher, U.S., 1906

Aqualung: Jacques-Yves Cousteau, Emile Gagnan, France, 1943

Aspirin: Dr. Felix Hoffman,, Germany, 1899

Astronomical calculator: The Antikythera device, first century B.C., Greece. Found off island of Antikythera in 1900

Atom: (nuclear model of) Ernest Rutherford, 1911

Atomic theory: (ancient) Leucippus, Democritus, Greece, c.500 B.C.; Lucretius, Rome, c.100 B.C.; (modern) John Dalton, England, 1808

Automobile: (first with internal combustion engine, 250 rpm) Karl Benz, Germany, 1885; (first with practical high-speed internal combustion engine, 900 rpm) Gottlieb Daimler, Germany, 1885; (first true automobile, not carriage with motor) René Panhard, Emile Lavassor, France, 1891; (carburetor, spray) Charles E. Duryea, U.S., 1892

Autopilot: (for aircraft) Elmer A. Sperry, U.S., c.1910, first successful test, 1912, in a Curtiss flying boat

Avogadro's law: (equal volumes of all gases at the same temperature and pressure contain equal number of molecules) Amedeo Avogadro, 1811

Bacteria: Anton van Leeuwenhoek, The Netherlands, 1683

Bakelite: *See* Plastics

Balloon, hot-air: Joseph and Jacques Montgolfier, France, 1783

Ball-point pen: *See* Pen

Barbed wire: (most popular) Joseph E. Glidden, U.S., 1873

Bar codes: (computer-scanned binary signal code) (retail trade use) Monarch Marking, U.S. 1970; (industrial use) Plessey Telecommunications, England, 1970

Barometer: Evangelista Torricelli, Italy, 1643

Bicycle: Karl D. von Sauerbronn, Germany, 1816; (first modern model) James Starley, England, 1884

Bifocal lens: *See* Lens, bifocal

Big Bang theory: (the universe originated with a huge explosion) Edwin Hubble, U.S., 1929; (confirmed) Arno Penzias, Robert Wilson, 1965

Blood, circulation of: William Harvey, England, 1628

Boyle's law: (relation between pressure and volume in gases) Robert Boyle, Ireland, 1662

Braille: Louis Braille, France, 1829

Bridges: (suspension, iron chains) James Finley, Pa., 1800; (wire suspension) Marc Seguin, Lyons, 1825; (truss) Ithiel Town, U.S., 1820

Bullet: (conical) Claude Minié, France, 1849

Calculating machine: (Abacus) China, c.190; (logarithms: made multiplying easier and thus calculators practical) John Napier, Scotland, 1614; (slide rule) William Oughtred, England, 1632; (digital calculator) Blaise Pascal, 1642; (multiplication machine) Gottfried Leibniz, Germany, 1671; (important 19th-century contributors to modern machine) Frank S. Baldwin, Jay R. Monroe, Dorr E. Felt, W. T. Ohdner, William Burroughs, all U.S.; ("analytical engine" design, included concepts of programming, taping) Charles Babbage, England, 1835. *See also* Computer

Calculus: Isaac Newton, England, 1669; (differential calculus) Gottfried Leibniz, Germany, 1684

Camera: (hand-held) George Eastman, U.S., 1888; (Polaroid Land) Edwin Land, U.S., 1948. *See also* Photography

"Canals" of Mars: Giovanni Schiaparelli, 1877

Carburetor: *See* Automobile

Carpet sweeper: Melville R. Bissell, U.S., 1876

Car radio: William Lear, Elmer Wavering, U.S. 1929, manufactured by Galvin Manufacturing Co., "Motorola"

Celanese: *See* Fibers, man-made

Celluloid: *See* Plastics

Cells: (word used to describe microscopic examination of cork) Robert Hooke, 1665; (theory cells are common structural and functional unit of all living organisms) Theodor Schwann, Matthias Schleiden, 1838–39

Cement, Portland: Joseph Aspdin, England, 172?

Chewing gum: (spruce-based) John Curtis, U.S. 1848; (chicle-based) Thomas Adams, U.S., 1871

Cholera bacterium: Robert Koch, Germany, 188?

Circuit, integrated: (theoretical) G.W.A. Dummer England, 1952; (phase-shift oscillator) Jack S Kilby, Texas Instruments, U.S., 1959

Classification of plants: (first modern, based o comparative study of forms) Andrea Cesalpino 1583; (classification of plants and animals b genera and species) Carolus Linnaeus, Swede 1737–53

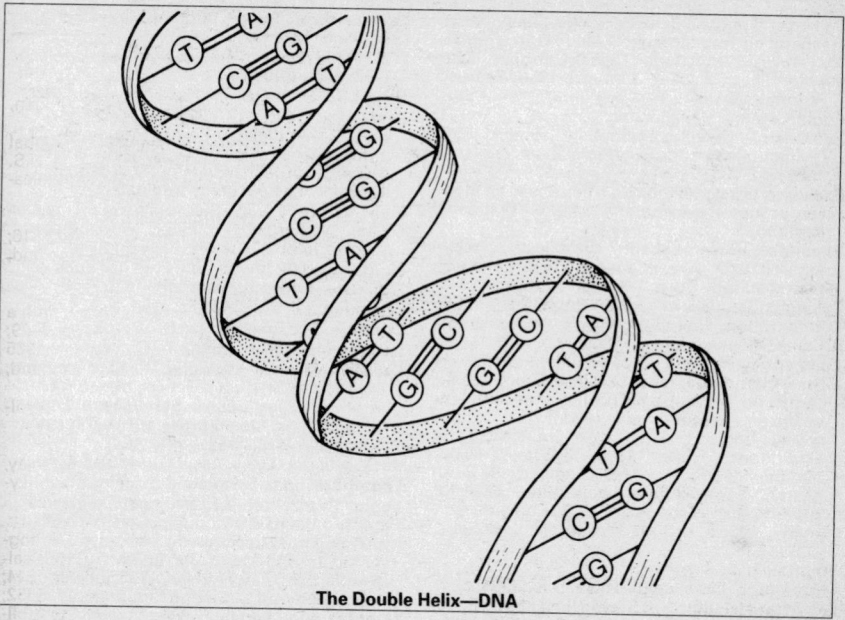

The Double Helix—DNA

Clock, pendulum: Christian Huygens, The Netherlands, 1656

Coca-Cola: John Pemberton, U.S., 1886

Combustion: (nature of) Antoine Lavoisier, France, 1777

Compact disk: RCA, U.S., 1972

Computer: (differential analyzer, mechanically operated) Vannevar Bush, U.S., 1928; (Mark I, first information-processing digital computer) Howard Aiken, U.S., 1944; (ENIAC, Electronic Numerical Integrator and Calculator, first all-electronic) J. Presper Eckert, John W. Mauchly, U.S., 1946; (stored-program concept) John von Neumann, U.S., 1947

Concrete: (reinforced) Joseph Monier, 1877

Condensed milk: Gail Borden, U.S., 1853

Conditioned reflex: Ivan Pavlov, Russia, c.1910

Conservation of electric charge: (the total electric charge of the universe or any closed system is constant) Benjamin Franklin, U.S., 1751–54

Contagion theory: (infectious diseases caused by living agent transmitted from person to person) Girolamo Fracastoro, 1546

Continental drift theory: Antonio Snider-Pellegrini, 1858

Contraceptive, oral: Gregory Pincus, Min Chuch Chang, John Rock, Carl Djerassi, U.S., 1951

Converter, Bessemer: William Kelly, U.S., 1851

Cosmetics: Egypt, c.4000 B.C.

Cotton gin: Eli Whitney, U.S., 1793

Crossbow: China, c.300 B.C.

Cyclotron: Ernest O. Lawrence, U.S., 1931

Deuterium: (heavy hydrogen) Harold Urey, U.S., 1931

Disease: (chemicals in treatment of) crusaded by Philippus Paracelsus, 1527–1541; (germ theory) Louis Pasteur, 1862–77

DNA: (deoxyribonucleic acid) Friedrich Meischer, Germany, 1869; (determination of double-heli-

cal structure) F. H. Crick, England, James D. Watson, U.S., 1953

Dyes: (aniline, start of synthetic dye industry) William H. Perkin, 1856

Dynamite: Alfred Nobel, Sweden, 1867

Electric cooking utensil: (first) patented by St. George Lane-Fox, England, 1874

Electric generator (dynamo): (laboratory model) Michael Faraday, England, 1832; Joseph Henry, U.S., 1832; (hand-driven model) Hippolyte Pixii, France, 1833; (alternating-current generator) Nikola Tesla, U.S., 1892

Electric lamp: (arc lamp) Sir Humphrey Davy, England, 1801; (fluorescent lamp) A.E. Becquerel, France, 1867; (incandescent lamp) Sir Joseph Swann, England, Thomas A. Edison, U.S., contemporaneously, 1870s; (carbon arc street lamp) Charles F. Brush, U.S., 1879; (first widely marketed incandescent lamp) Thomas A. Edison, U.S., 1879; (mercury vapor lamp) Peter Cooper Hewitt, U.S., 1903; (neon lamp) Georges Claude, France, 1911; (tungsten filament) Irving Langmuir, U.S., 1915

Electric motor: *See* Motor

Electrocardiography: demonstrated by Augustus Waller, 1887; (first practical device for recording activity of heart) Willem Einthoven, 1903, Dutch physiologist

Electromagnet: William Sturgeon, England, 1823

Electron: Sir Joseph J. Thompson, England, 1897

Elevator, passenger: (safety device permitting use by passengers) Elisha G. Otis, U.S., 1852; (elevator utilizing safety device) 1857

E = mc²: (equivalence of mass and energy) Albert Einstein, Switzerland, 1907

Engine, internal combustion: No single inventor. Fundamental theory established by Sadi Carnot, France, 1824; (two-stroke) Etienne Lenoir, France, 1860; (ideal operating cycle for four-stroke) Alphonse Beau de Roche, France, 1862; (operating four-stroke) Nikolaus Otto, Germany, 1876; (diesel) Rudolf Diesel, Germany, 1892; (rotary) Felix Wankel, Germany, 1956. *See also* Automobile

Engine, steam: *See* Steam engine

Evolution: (organic) Jean-Baptiste Lamarck, 1809; (by natural selection) Charles Darwin, England, 1859

Exclusion principle: (no two electrons in an atom can occupy the same energy level) Wolfgang Pauli, 1925

Expanding universe theory: (galaxies are receding from each other at speeds proportionate to their distance) George Lemaître, 1927

Falling bodies, law of: Galileo Galilei, Italy, 1590

Fermentation: (micro-organisms as cause of) Louis Pasteur, France, c.1860

Fiber optics: Narinder Kapany, England, 1955

Fibers, man-made: (nitrocellulose fibers treated to change flammable nitrocellulose to harmless cellulose, precursor of rayon) Sir Joseph Swann, England, 1883; (rayon) Count Hilaire de Chardonnet, France, 1889; (Celanese) Henry and Camille Dreyfuss, U.S., ,England, 1921; (research on polyesters and polyamides, basis for modern man-made fibers) U.S., England, Germany, 1930s; (nylon) Wallace H. Carothers, U.S., 1935

Fountain pen: *See* Pen

Frozen food: Clarence Birdseye, U.S. (1924)

Gene transfer: (human) Steven Rosenberg, R. Michael Blaese, W. French Anderson, U.S., 1989

Geometry, elements of: Euclid, Alexandria, Egypt, c.300 B.C.; (analytic) René Descartes, France; and Pierre de Fermat, Switzerland, 1637

Gravitation, law of: Sir Isaac Newton, England, c.1665 (published 1687)

Gunpowder: China, c.700

Gyrocompass: Elmer A. Sperry, U.S., 1905

Gyroscope: Léon Foucault, France, 1852

Halley's Comet: Edmund Halley, 1705

Heart, artificial: Dr. Robert Jarvik, U.S., 1982

Helicopter: (double rotor) Heinrich Focke, Germany, 1936; (single rotor) Igor Sikorsky, U.S., 1939

Helium first observed on sun: Sir Joseph Lockyer, England, 1868

Heredity, laws of: Gregor Mendel, Austria, 1865

Holograph: Dennis Gabor, England, 1947

Home videotape systems (VCR): (Betamax) Sony, Japan, 1975; (VHS) Matsushita, Japan, 1975

Ice age theory: Louis Agassiz, 1840

Induction, electric: Joseph Henry, U.S., 1828

Insulin: Sir Frederick G. Banting, J. J. R. MacLeod, Canada, 1922

Intelligence testing: Alfred Binet, Theodore Simon, France, 1905

Interferon: Alick Isaacs, Jean Lindemann, England, Switzerland, 1957

Isotopes: (concept of) Frederick Soddy, England, 1912; (stable isotopes) J. J. Thompson, England, 1913; (existence demonstrated by mass spectrography) Francis W. Ashton, 1919

Jet propulsion: (engine) Sir Frank Whittle, England, Hans von Ohain, Germany, 1936; (aircraft) *Heinkel He 178*, 1939

Kinetic theory of gases: (molecules of a gas are in a state of rapid motion) Daniel Bernoulli, 1738

Laser: (theoretical work on) Charles H. Townes, Arthur L. Schawlow, U.S., N. Basov, A. Prokhorov, U.S.S.R., 1958; (first working model) T. H. Maiman, U.S., 1960

Lawn mower: Edwin Budding, John Ferrabee, England, 1830 (31)

LCD (liquid crystal display): Hoffmann-La Roche, Switzerland, 1970

Lens, bifocal: Benjamin Franklin, U.S., c.1760

Leyden jar: (prototype electrical condenser) Canon E.G. von Kleist of Kamin, Pomerania, 1745; independently evolved by Cunaeus and P. van Musschenbroek, University of Leyden, Holland, 1746, from where name originated

Light, nature of: (wave theory) Christian Huygens, The Netherlands, 1678; (electromagnetic theory) James Clerk Maxwell, England, 1873

Light, speed of: (theory that light has finite velocity) Olaus Roemer, Denmark, 1675

Lightning rod: Benjamin Franklin, U.S., 1752

Linotype: *See* Printing

Lithography: *See* Printing

Locomotive: (steam powered) Richard Trevithick, England, 1804; (first practical, due to multiple-fire-tube boiler) George Stephenson, England, 1829; (largest steam-powered) Union Pacific's "Big Boy," U.S., 1941

Lock, cylinder: Linus Yale, U.S., 1851

Logarithms: *See* Calculating machine

Loom: (horizontal, two-beamed) Egypt, c.4400 B.C.; (Jacquard drawloom, pattern controlled by punch cards) Jacques de Vaucanson, France, 1745, Joseph-Marie Jacquard, 1801; (flying shuttle) John Kay, England, 1733; (power-driven loom) Edmund Cartwright, England, 1785

Machine gun: James Puckle, England, 1718; Richard J. Gatling, U.S., 1861

Magnet, Earth is: William Gilbert, 1600

Match: (phosphorus) François Derosne, France, 1816; (friction) Charles Sauria, France, 1831; (safety) J. E. Lundstrom, Sweden, 1855

Measles vaccine: John F. Enders, Thomas Peebles, U.S., 1953

Mendelian law: *See* Heredity

Metric system: revolutionary government of France, 1790–1801

Microphone: Charles Wheatstone, England, 1827

Microscope: (compound) Zacharias Janssen, The Netherlands, 1590; (electron) Vladimir Zworykin et al., U.S., Canada, Germany, 1932–1939

Microwave oven: Percy Spencer, U.S., 1947

Motion, laws of: Isaac Newton, England, 1687

Motion pictures: Thomas A. Edison, U.S., 1893

Motion pictures, sound: Product of various inventions. First picture with synchronized musical score: *Don Juan*, 1926; with spoken dialogue: *The Jazz Singer*, 1927; both Warner Bros.

Motor, electric: Michael Faraday, England, 1822; (alternating-current) Nikola Tesla, U.S., 1892

Motor, gasoline: *See* Engine, internal combustion

Motorcycle: (motor tricycle) Edward Butler, England, 1884; (gasoline-engine motorcycle) Gottlieb Daimler, Germany, 1885

National Science Foundation: established by U.S. Congress, 1950 based on report by Vannevar Bush, 1945

Neptune: (discovery of) Johann Galle, 1846

Neptunium: (first transuranic element, synthesized of) Edward M. McMillan, Philip H. Abelson, U.S., 1940

Neutron: James Chadwick, England, 1932

Neutron-induced radiation: Enrico Fermi et al., Italy, 1934

Nitroglycerin: Ascanio Sobrero, Italy, 1846

Bell demonstrating the long-distance capability of his invention at Salem, Mass., on March 15, 1877. A hook-up was made with Boston, 18 miles away, and an extended conversation took place between the two cities.

Nuclear fission: Otto Hahn, Fritz Strassmann, Germany, 1938

Nuclear reactor: Enrico Fermi, et al., 1942

Nylon: *See* Fibers, man-made

Ohm's law: (relationship between strength of electric current, electromotive force, and circuit resistance) Georg S. Ohm, Germany, 1827

Oil well: Edwin L. Drake, Titusville, Pa., 1859

Oxygen: (isolation of) Joseph Priestley, 1774; Carl Scheele, 1773

Ozone: Christian Schöonbein, Germany, 1839

Pacemaker: (internal) Clarence W. Lillehie, Earl Bakk, U.S., 1957

Paper: China, c.100 B.C.

Parachute: Louis S. Lenormand, France, 1783

Pen: (fountain) Lewis E. Waterman, U.S., 1884; (ball-point, for marking on rough surfaces) John H. Loud, U.S., 1888; (ball-point, for hand-writing) Lazlo Biro, Argentina, 1944

Penicillin: *See* Antibiotics

Periodic law: (that properties of elements are functions of their atomic weights) Dmitri Mendeleev, Russia, 1869

Periodic table: (arrangement of chemical elements based on periodic law) Dmitri Mendeleev, Russia, 1869

Phonograph: Thomas A. Edison, U.S., 1877

Photography: (first paper negative, first photograph, on metal) Joseph Nicéphore Niepce, France, 1816–1827; (discovery of fixative powers of hyposulfite of soda) Sir John Herschel, England, 1819; (first direct positive image on silver plate, the daguerreotype) Louis Daguerre, based on work with Niepce, France, 1839; (first paper negative from which a number of positive prints could be made) William Talbot, England, 1841. Work of these four men, taken together, forms basis for all modern photography. (First color images) Alexandre Becquerel, Claude Niepce de Saint-Victor, France, 1848–60; (commercial color film with three emulsion layers, Kodachrome) U.S., 1935. *See also* Camera

Photovoltaic effect: (light falling on certain materials can produce electricity) Edmund Becquerel, France, 1839

Piano: (Hammerklavier) Bartolommeo Cristofori, Italy, 1709; (pianoforte with sustaining and damper pedals) John Broadwood, England, 1873

Planetary motion, laws of: Johannes Kepler, Germany, 1609, 1619

Plant respiration and photosynthesis: Jan Ingenhousz, 1779

Plastics: (first material, nitrocellulose softened by vegetable oil, camphor, precursor to Celluloid) Alexander Parkes, England, 1855; (Celluloid, involving recognition of vital effect of camphor) John W. Hyatt, U.S., 1869; (Bakelite, first completely synthetic plastic) Leo H. Baekeland, U.S., 1910; (theoretical background of macromolecules and process of polymerization on which modern plastics industry rests) Hermann Staudinger, Germany, 1922. *See also* Fibers, man-made

Plate tectonics: Alfred Wegener, Germany, 1912–15

Plow, forked: Mesopotamia, before 3000 B.C.

Plutonium, synthesis of: Glenn T. Seaborg, Edwin M. McMillan, Arthur C. Wahl, Joseph W. Kennedy, U.S., 1941

Polaroid Land camera: *See* Camera

Polio, vaccine against: (vaccine made from dead virus strains) Jonas E. Salk, U.S., 1954; (vaccine made from live virus strains) Albert Sabin, U.S., 1960

Positron: Carl D. Anderson, U.S., 1932

Pressure cooker: (early version) Denis Papin, France, 1679

Printing: (block) Japan, c.700; (movable type) Korea, c.1400; Johann Gutenberg, Germany, c.1450 (lithography, offset) Aloys Senefelder, Germany, 1796; (rotary press) Richard Hoe, U.S., 1844; (linotype) Ottmar Mergenthaler, U.S., 1884

Probability theory: René Descartes, France; and Pierre de Fermat, Switzerland, 1654

Programming, information: *See* Calculating machine

Proton: Ernest Rutherford, England, 1919

Psychoanalysis: Sigmund Freud, Austria, c.1904

Pulsars: Jocelyn Bell Bunnell, England, 1968

Quantum theory: (general) Max Planck, Germany, 1900; (sub-atomic) Niels Bohr, Denmark, 1913; (quantum mechanics) Werner Heisenberg, Erwin Schrödinger, Germany, 1925

Quarks: Jerome Friedman, Henry Kendall, Richard Taylor, U.S. (1967)

Quasars: Marten Schmidt, U.S., 1963

Rabies immunization: Louis Pasteur, France, 1885

Radar: (limited to one-mile range) Christian Hulsmeyer, Germany, 1904; (pulse modulation, used for measuring height of ionosphere) Gregory Breit, Merle Tuve, U.S., 1925; (first practical radar—radio detection and ranging) Sir Robert Watson-Watt, England, 1934–35

Radio: (electromagnetism, theory of) James Clerk Maxwell, England, 1873; (spark coil, generator of electromagnetic waves) Henrich Hertz, Germany, 1886; (first practical system of wireless telegraphy) Guglielmo Marconi, Italy, 1895; (vacuum electron tube, basis for radio telephony) Sir John Fleming, England, 1904; (triode amplifying tube) Lee de Forest, U.S., 1906; (regenerative circuit, allowing long-distance sound reception) Edwin H. Armstrong, U.S., 1912; (frequency modulation—FM) Edwin H. Armstrong, U.S., 1933

Radioactivity: (X-rays) Wilhelm K. Roentgen, Germany, 1895; (radioactivity of uranium) Henri Becquerel, France, 1896; (radioactive elements, radium and polonium in uranium ore) Marie Sklodowska-Curie, Pierre Curie, France, 1898; (classification of alpha and beta particle radiation) Pierre Curie, France, 1900; (gamma radiation) Paul-Ulrich Villard, France, 1900; (carbon dating) Willard F. Libby et al., U.S., 1955

Radio signals, extraterrestrial: first known radio noise signals were received by U.S. engineer, Karl Jansky, originating from the Galactic Center, 1931.

Radio waves: (cosmic sources, led to radio astronomy) Karl Jansky, 1932

Rayon: *See* Fibers, man-made

Razor: (safety, successfully marketed) King Gillette, U.S., 1901; (electric) Jacob Schick, U.S., 1928(31)

Reaper: Cyrus McCormick, U.S., 1834

Refrigerator: Alexander Twining, U.S., James Harrison, Australia, 1850; (first with a compressor device) the Domelse, Chicago, U.S., 1913

Refrigerator ship: (first) the *Frigorifique,* 1877, cooling unit designed by Charles Teller, France

Relativity: (special and general theories of) Albert Einstein, Germany, U.S., 1905–53

Revolver: Samuel Colt, U.S., 1835

Richter scale: Charles F. Richter, U.S., 1935

Rifle: (muzzle-loaded) Italy, Germany, c1475; (breech-loaded) England, France, Germany, U.S., c.1866; (bolt-action) Paul von Mauser, Germany, 1889; (automatic) John Browning, U.S., 1918

Rocket: (liquid-fueled) Robert Goddard, U.S., 1926

Roller bearing: (wooden for cartwheel) Germany or France, c.100 B.C.

Rotation of earth: Jean Bernard Foucault, 1851

Royal Observatory, Greenwich: established by Charles II of England, John Flamsteed first Astronomer Royal

Rubber: (vulcanization process) Charles Goodyear, U.S., 1839

Saccharin: Constantine Fuhlberg, Ira Remsen, U.S., 1879

Safety match: *See* Match

Safety pin: Walter Hunt, U.S., 1849

Saturn, ring around: Christian Huygens, The Netherlands, 1659

"Scotch" tape: Richard Drew, U.S., 1929

Screw propeller: Sir Francis P. Smith, England 1836; John Ericsson, England, worked independently of and simultaneously with Smith 1837

Seismograph: (first accurate) John Milne, 1880

Sewing machine: Elias Howe, U.S., 1846; (continuous stitch) Isaac Singer, U.S., 1851

Solar energy: first realistic application of solar energy using parabolic solar reflector to drive caloric engine on steam boiler, Jon Ericsson 1860s

Solar system, universe: (sun-centered universe) Nicolaus Copernicus, Warsaw, 1543; (establishment of planetary orbits as elliptical) Johanne Kepler, Germany, 1609; (infinity of universe) Giordano Bruno, Italian monk, 1584

Spectrum: (heterogeneity of light) Sir Isaac Newton, England, 1665–66

Spectrum analysis: Gustav Kirchoff, Robert Bunsen, 1859

Spermatozoa: Anton van Leeuwenhoek, The Netherlands, 1683

Spinning: (spinning wheel) India, introduced t Europe in Middle Ages; (Saxony wheel, continuous spinning of wool or cotton yarn) England c.1500–1600; (spinning jenny) James Hargreaves, England, 1764; (spinning frame) Sir Richard Arkwright, England, 1769; (spinning mule, completed mechanization of spinning permitting production of yarn to keep up with demands of modern looms) Samuel Crompton England, 1779

Star catalog: (first modern) Tycho Brahe, 1572

Steam engine: (first commercial version based o principles of French physicist Denis Papin) Thomas Savery, England, 1639; (atmospher steam engine) Thomas Newcomen, England 1705; (steam engine for pumping water from collieries) Savery, Newcomen, 1725; (moder condensing, doubleacting) James Watt, England, 1782

Steam engine, railroad: *See* Locomotive

Steamship: Claude de Jouffroy d'Abbans, Franc 1783; James Rumsey, U.S., 1787; John Fitc

Johannes Gutenberg.

U.S., 1790. All preceded Robert Fulton, U.S., 1807, credited with launching first commercially successful steamship

Stethoscope: René Laënnec, 1819

Sulfa drugs: (parent compound, para-aminobenzenesulfanomide) Paul Gelmo, Austria, 1908; (antibacterial activity) Gerhard Domagk, Germany, 1935

Superconductivity: (theory) Bardeen, Cooper, Scheiffer, U.S., 1957

Symbolic logic: George Boule, 1854; (modern) Bertrand Russell, Alfred North Whitehead, 1910–13

Syphilis, test for: *See* Wassermann test

Tank, military: Sir Ernest Swinton, England, 1914

Tape recorder: (magnetic steel tape) Valdemar Poulsen, Denmark, 1899

Teflon: DuPont, U.S., 1943

Telegraph: Samuel F.B. Morse, U.S., 1837

Telephone: Alexander Graham Bell, U.S., 1876

Telescope: Hans Lippershey, The Netherlands, 1608; (astronomical) Galileo Galilei, Italy, 1609; (reflecting) Isaac Newton, England, 1668

Television: (mechanical disk-scanning method) successfully demonstrated by J.K. Baird, England, C.F. Jenkins, U.S., 1926; (electronic scanning method) Vladimir K. Zworykin, U.S., 1928; (color, all-electronic) Zworykin, 1926; (color, mechanical disk) Baird, 1928; (color, compatible with black and white) George Valensi, France, 1938; (color, sequential rotating filter) Peter Goldmark, U.S., first introduced, 1951; (color, compatible with black and white) commercially introduced in U.S., National Television Systems Committee, 1953

Thermodynamics: (first law: energy cannot be created or destroyed, only converted from one form to another) Julius von Mayer, Germany, 1842; James Joule, England, 1843; (second law: heat cannot of itself pass from a colder to a warmer body) Rudolph Clausius, Germany, 1850; (third law: the entropy of ordered solids reaches zero at the absolute zero of temperature) Walter Nernst, Germany, 1918

Thermometer: (open-column) Galileo Galilei, c.1593; (clinical) Santorio Santorio, Padua, c.1615; (mercury, also Fahrenheit scale) Gabriel D. Fahrenheit, Germany, 1714; (centigrade scale) Anders Celsius, Sweden, 1742; (absolute-temperature, or Kelvin, scale) William Thompson, Lord Kelvin, England, 1848

Tire, pneumatic: Robert W. Thompson, England, 1845; (bicycle tire) John B. Dunlop, Northern Ireland, 1888

Toilet, flush: Product of Minoan civilization, Crete, c.2000 B.C. Alleged invention by "Thomas Crapper" is untrue.

Tractor: Benjamin Holt, U.S., 1900

Transformer, electric: William Stanley, U.S., 1885

Transistor: John Bardeen, William Shockley, Walter Brattain, U.S., 1948

Tuberculosis bacterium: Robert Koch, Germany, 1882

Typewriter: Christopher Sholes, Carlos Glidden, U.S., 1867

Uncertainty principle: (that position and velocity of an object cannot both be measured exactly, at the same time) Werner Heisenberg, Germany, 1927

Uranus: (first planet discovered in recorded history) William Herschel, 1781

Vaccination: Edward Jenner, England, 1796

Vacuum cleaner: (manually operated) Ives W. McGaffey, 1869; (electric) Hubert C. Booth, England, 19091; (upright) J. Murray Spangler, U.S., 1907

Vacuum tube: *See* Radio

Van Allen (radiation) Belt: (around the earth) James Van Allen, U.S., 1958

Video disk: Philips Co., The Netherlands, 1972

Vitamins: (hypothesis of disease deficiency) Sir F. G. Hopkins, Casimir Funk, England, 1912; (vitamin A) Elmer V. McCollum, M. Davis, U.S., 1912–14; (vitamin B) Elmer V. McCollum, 1915–16; (thiamin, B_1) Casimir Funk, England, 1912; (riboflavin, B_2) D. T. Smith, E. G. Hendrick, U.S., 1926; (niacin) Conrad Elvehjem, U.S., 1937; (B_6) Paul Gyorgy, U.S., 1934; (vitamin C) A. Hoist, T. Froelich, Norway, 1912; (vitamin D) Elmer V. McCollum, U.S., 1922; (folic acid) Lucy Wills, England, 1933

Voltaic pile: (forerunner of modern battery, first source of continuous electric current) Alessandro Volta, 1800

Wallpaper: Europe, 16th and 17th century

Wassermann test: (for syphilis) August von Wassermann, Germany, 1906

Weaving, cloth: *See* Loom

Wheel: (cart, solid wood) Mesopotamia, c.3800–3600 B.C.

Windmill: Persia, c.600

X-ray: *See* Radioactivity

Xerography: Chester Carlson, U.S., 1938

Zero: India, c.600; (absolute zero temperature, cessation of all molecular energy) William Thompson, Lord Kelvin, England, 1848

Zipper: W.L. Judson, U.S., 1891

The National Inventors Hall of Fame

The Inventors Hall of Fame, located in Akron, Ohio, was established in 1973 by the National Council of Patent Law Associations, now the National Council of Intellectual Property Law Associations, and the Patent and Trademark Office of the U.S. Department of Commerce. The year of induction is in parentheses at the end of the entry.

Alexanderson, Ernst 1872–1975 (b. Sweden) HIGH FREQUENCY ALTERNATOR—Alexanderson built a high frequency machine that would operate at high speeds and produce a continuous wave transmission. His inventions included such fields as railway electrification, motors, telephone relays and radio and television. (1983)

Alford, Andrew 1904–1992 (b. Samara, Russia) LOCALIZER ANTENNA SYSTEM—Alford invented and developed antennas for radio navigation systems, including VOR and instrument landing systems, and the "Alford Loop" antenna. (1983)

Alvarez, Luis Walter 1911–1988 (b. San Francisco, Calif.) RADIO DISTANCE AND DIRECTION INDICATOR—Alvarez was awarded the Nobel Prize for Physics in 1968. He helped design a ground-controlled radar system for aircraft landings and with his son developed the meteorite theory of dinosaur extinction. (1978)

Armstrong, Edwin 1890–1954 (b. New York City) METHOD OF RECEIVING HIGH FREQUENCY OSCILLATIONS—Armstrong devised wide-band frequency modulation (FM radio) as a means of reducing background static. He also invented the regenerative circuit, the superheterodyne, and the super-regenerative circuit. (1980)

Baekeland, Leo Hendrik 1863–1944 (b. Ghent, Belgium) SYNTHETIC RESINS—Baekeland developed the thermosetting synthetic resin bakelite which helped found the modern plastics industry. He also invented Velox photographic paper. (1978)

Bardeen, John 1908–1991 (b. Madison, Wisconsin); **Shockley, William Bradford** 1910–1989 (b. London, England); **Brattain, Walter H.** 1902–1987 (b. Amoy, China) TRANSISTOR—Bardeen, Shockley and Brattain shared the 1956 Nobel Prize for Physics for the invention of the transistor. The transistor replaced the vacuum tube and paved the way for the integrated circuit. (1974)

Beckman, Arnold O. 1900– (b. Cullom, Ill.) APPARATUS FOR TESTING ACIDITY—Beckman founded Beckman Instruments, Inc. in 1935 with the development of a pH meter for measuring acidity and alkalinity. He also developed the helical potentiometer, a precision electronic component, and the quartz spectrophotometer, an instrument which pioneered automatic chemical analysis. (1987)

Bell, Alexander Graham 1847–1922 (b. Edinburgh, Scotland) TELEGRAPHY—In addition to the telephone, Bell held patents for the telegraph, photophone, phonograph, aerial vehicles, hydroairplanes, and a selenium cell. He was also noted for his medical research and work in teaching speech to the deaf. (1974)

Bennett, Willard Harrison 1903–1987 (b. Findlay, Ohio) RADIO FREQUENCY MASS SPECTROMETER—Bennett studies in gases ionized by high voltage electricity was used in controlled thermonuclear fusion research. His radio frequency mass spectrometer was the first launched into space to measure the masses of atoms. (1991)

Berliner, Emile 1851–1929 (b. Hanover, Germany) MICROPHONE AND GRAMOPHONE—The Berliner microphone enhanced Bell's telephone that had been limited to short transmissions. The gramophone introduced the flat disk which provided a method for inexpensive mass production. (1994)

Binnig, Gerd Karl 1947– (b. Frankfurt, Germany); **Rohrer, Heinrich** 1933– (b. Bucs, Switzerland) SCANNING TUNNELING MICROSCOPE—Binnig and Rohrer's microscope can trace details smaller than a single atom and has provided views of the atomic structure of atoms, the interaction of chemical catalysts, and views of microbe enviral interaction. (1994)

Bird, Forest M. 1921– (b. Stoughton, Mass.) MEDICAL RESPIRATORS—Bird developed the first highly reliable, low-cost mass-produced respirator in the world. His "Babybird" respirator reduced infant mortality from respiratory problems from 70% to 10% worldwide. (1995)

Black, Harold Stephen 1898–1983 (b. Leominster, Mass.) NEGATIVE FEEDBACK AMPLIFIER—Black's negative feedback concept involved feeding systems output back to the input as a method of system control thus helping to eliminate distortion in telecommunications and to extend the frequency range of the amplifier. (1981)

Blumberg, Baruch 1925– (b. New York City); **Millman, Irving** 1923– (b. New York City) TEST AND VACCINE FOR HEPATITIS B—The use of the test reduced the occurrence of hepatitis B after blood transfusions. The vaccine protects people exposed to the hepatitis B virus and has been administered to millions, particularly in Asia and Africa. With hepatitis B an unknown factor associated with the development of liver cancer, the vaccine was the first against a major form of cancer. (1993)

Brattain, Walter H. See under Bardeen, John.

Brown, Rachel Fuller See under Hazen, Elizabeth Lee.

Burbank, Luther 1849–1926 (b. Lancaster, Mass. PEACH—Burbank developed more than 800 new strains and varieties of plants including varieties of potato, plums, prunes, berries, flowers and trees. (1986)

Burckhalter, Joseph H. 1912– (b. Columbia, S.C.) **Seiwald, Robert J.** 1925– (b. Fort Morgan, Colo. DYES FOR DIAGNOSING INFECTIOUS DISEASES—Burckhalter and Seiwald synthesized fluorescein isothiocyanate (FITC), an antibody labeling agent FITC has become widely used for rapid, accurate, and economic diagnosis of infectious diseases, including AIDS and syphilis. FITC and another agent are used together to quickly diagnose leukemia and lymphoma. (1995)

Burroughs, William Seward 1857–1898 (b. Rochester, N.Y.) CALCULATING MACHINE—In 1885 Burroughs submitted his first patent for his "calculating machine." This first model needed a special knack to use and Burroughs was dissatisfied with its durability. His 1892 patent not only improved the machine but added a printer. (1987)

Burton, William Meriam 1865–1954 (b. Cleveland, Ohio) MANUFACTURE OF GASOLINE—Burton developed the high heat and high pressure cracking process of fuel oil which more than doubled the potential yield of gasoline from crude oil. (1984)

Camras, Marvin 1916–1995 (b. Chicago, Ill.) METHOD AND MEANS OF MAGNETIC RECORDING—Camras's inventions are used in modern magnetic tape and wire recorders, including high frequency bias, improved recording heads, wire and tape material, magnetic sound for motion pictures, multi-track tape machines, stereophonic sound reproduction and video tape recording. (1985)

Carlson, Chester F. 1906–1968 (b. Seattle, Wash. ELECTROPHOTOGRAPHY—Carlson invented xerographic dry-copy printing basing his process on electrostatics as opposed to chemical or photographic processes. (1981)

Carothers, Wallace Hume 1896–1937 (b. Burlington, Iowa) DIAMINE-DICARBOXYLIC ACID SALTS AND PROCESS OF PREPARING SAME AND SYNTHETIC FIBER—Carothers work involved the theory of linear polymerization which culminated in the production of the synthetic material nylon. Nylon was first commercially used in toothbrush bristles. Carothers's work also led others to develop the first successful synthetic rubber, neoprene. (1984)

Carrier, Willis Haviland 1876–1950 (b. Angola, N.Y.) APPARATUS FOR TREATING AIR—Carrier developed the first safe, low pressure centrifugal refrigeration machine using nontoxic, nonflammable refrigerant. By controlling humidity as well as temperature, he invented modern air conditioning. (1985)

Carver, George Washington 1864–1943 (b. Diamond Grove, Mo.) COSMETIC AND PROCESS OF PRODUCING SAME; PAINT AND STAIN AND PROCESS OF PRODUCING THE SAME—When Carver's method of crop rotation produced a surplus of peanuts, sweet potatoes and pecans he devised hundreds of uses for the extra crops, from cooking oil to highway paving material. He also synthesized organic dyes which proved superior to aniline dyes. (1990)

Colton, Frank B. 1923– (b. Poland) ORAL CONTRACEPTIVES—Colton has made many important contributions to medicinal organic chemistry, and particularly to steroid chemistry. His most important research resulted in the discovery of Enovid, the first oral contraceptive. (1988)

Conover, Lloyd H. 1923– (b. Orange, N.J.) TETRACYCLINE—Conover's invention of tetracycline in 1952 was the first creation of an antibiotic made by chemically modifying a naturally-produced drug. Tetracycline quickly became the most prescribed broad spectrum antibiotic in the U.S. 40 years later tetracycline is still being used to combat such serious infections as Rocky Mountain Spotted Fever and Lyme Disease. (1992)

Coolidge, William D. 1873–1974 (b. Hudson, Mass.) VACUUM TUBE—Coolidge invented ductile tungsten, the filament material still used in incandescent lamps. He also invented the "Coolidge tube", the model upon which all X-ray tubes for medical applications are patterned. (1975)

Cottrell, Frederick G. 1877–1948 (b. Oakland, Calif.) ELECTROSTATIC PRECIPITATOR—Cottrell's invention used high voltage electricity to remove from 90 to 98 percent of the ash, dust, and acid which industrial smokestacks spewed into the air. Besides eliminating this particulate pollution, this process also allowed some of the minerals and chemicals to be re-used. (1992)

Damadian, Raymond V. 1936– (b. Forest Hills, N.Y.) APPARATUS AND METHOD FOR DETECTING CANCER IN TISSUE—Damadian invented the magnetic resonance imaging (MRI) scanner that has revolutionized diagnostic medicine. The MRI yields radio signal outputs from the body's tissue that can be either transformed into images or analyzed to provide the chemical composition of the tissue. (1989)

Deere, John 1804–1886 (b. Rutland, Vt.) PLOW—Deere's plow had a cutting part made of steel and a moldboard made of polished wrought iron which proved more effective than implements then in use for cutting and turning prairie soils. (1989)

de Forest, Lee 1873–1961 (b. Council Bluffs, Iowa) AUDION AMPLIFIER—De Forest inserted a third electrode between the cathode and anode to make his audion tube. Radio signals are picked up by connecting an antenna to the tube's grid. (1977)

Diesel, Rudolf 1857–1913 (b. Paris, France) INTERNAL COMBUSTION ENGINE—Diesel is best known for his invention of the pressure-ignited heat engine that bears his name. The Diesel engine was able to supplant the large, expensive, and fuel-wasting steam engine. (1976)

Djerassi, Carl 1923– (b. Vienna, Austria) ORAL CONTRACEPTIVES—Along with developing the oral contraceptive Djerassi's research has included work with steroids, antibiotics, synthesis of antihistamines and anti-inflammatory agents. (1978)

Dow, Herbert Henry 1866–1930 (b. Belleville, Ontario) PROCESS OF EXTRACTING BROMINE—Dow invented an entirely new method of extracting bromine from underground brine. (1983)

Draper, Charles Stark 1901– (b. Windsor, Mo.) GYROSCOPIC APPARATUS—Draper developed a spinning gyroscope, stabilizing U.S. Navy antiaircraft gunsights which led to an inertial guidance system for launching long-range missiles at supersonic jet targets. His Instrumentation Lab at MIT contributed to Project Apollo and men on the moon. (1981)

Durant, Graham J. 1934– (b. Newport, England); **Emmett, John Colin** 1939– (b. Bradford, England); **Ganellin, C. Robin** 1934– (b. London, England) ANTIULCER COMPOUNDS AND COMPOSITIONS—Durant, Emmett and Ganellin discovered the drug cimetidine (trade name Tagamet) which inhibits the production of stomach acid. Cimetidine has the ability to heal stomach ulcers without surgery. (1990)

Eastman, George 1854–1932 (b. Waterville, N.Y.) METHOD AND APPARATUS FOR COATING PLATES FOR USE IN PHOTOGRAPHY—Before Eastman, photographers used glass plates with light-sensitive emulsions on them. Eastman put the emulsions first on paper, then on film rolls. He also developed a stronger motion picture film. (1977)

Edgerton, Harold E. 1903–1990 (b. Fremont, Neb.) STROBOSCOPE—Edgerton's research in the fields of stroboscopy and ultra-high speed photography led to the modern electronic speed flash. He was noted for his photographs revealing operations which move at speeds beyond the capacity of the human eye. (1986)

Edison, Thomas Alva 1847–1931 (b. Milan, Ohio) ELECTRIC LAMP—Edison held 1,093 patents, including those for the incandescent electric lamp, the phonograph, the carbon telephone transmitter, and the motion-picture projector. He also created the world's first industrial research laboratory. (1973)

Elion, Gertrude Belle 1918– (b. New York City) 6-MERCAPTOPURINE—Elion synthesized the leukemia-fighting drug 6-mercaptopurine. Her other developments were drugs used to block organ rejections in kidney transplant patients, for the treatment of gout and to battle herpes virus infections. (1991)

Emmett, John Colin *See under* Durant, Graham

Ericsson, John 1803–1889 (b. Vermland, Sweden) PROPELLER—Ericsson's propeller—still the main form of marine propulsion 150 years later—replaced the inefficient and vulnerable steam-driven oars and paddlewheels. He designed and built the Civil War ironclad *Monitor* which defeated the Confederate *Merrimac*. Ericsson also developed a calorific engine designed to use solar energy. (1993)

Faggin, Federico *See under* Hoff, Marcian Edward "Ted", Jr.

Farnsworth, Philo Taylor 1906–1971 (b. Beaver, Utah) TELEVISION SYSTEM—At the age of 20 Farnsworth produced the first all-electronic television image. In addition to his television system he invented the first cold cathode ray tubes and the first simple electronic microscope. He used radio waves to get direction (radar) and black light for seeing at night. (1984)

Fermi, Enrico 1901–1954 (b. Rome, Italy) NEU-TRONIC REACTOR—Fermi was awarded the 1938 Nobel Prize for Physics for his work in the field of atomic fission. In 1942 he accomplished the controlled release of nuclear energy via the atomic pile. (1976)

Ford, Henry 1863–1947 (b. Wayne County, Mich.) TRANSMISSION MECHANISM—Ford holds numerous patents on automotive mechanisms and helped devise the factory assembly line method of mass production. (1982)

Forrester, Jay W. 1918– (b. Climax, Nebraska) MULTICOORDINATED DIGITAL INFORMATION STORAGE DEVICE—While working on the Whirlwind, the largest computer project in the late 1940s and early 1950s, Forrester devised the magnetic core memory storage which replaced the unreliable and short-lived electrostatic tubes which had previously been used. (1979)

Ganellin, C. Robin *See under* Durant, Graham

Germer, Edmund 1901–1987 (b. Berlin, Germany) HIGH-PRESSURE MERCURY VAPOR LAMP; FUORESCENT LIGHT—The incandescent lamp is rather inefficient, converting only about 6% of its energy input into visible light while the remaining 94% is released as heat. His development of the fluorescent lamp and the high-pressure mercury-vapor lamp significantly increased the efficiency of lighting devices allowing for more economical operation while producing less heat. (1996)

Ginsburg, Charles P. 1920–1992 VIDEOTAPE RECORDER—After World War II audio tape recorders were run at very high speeds to record the very high frequency television signals. Ginsburg developed a new machine that ran much slower for television recording. It was first used by CBS TV in 1956. (1990)

Goddard, Robert Hutchings 1882–1945 (b. Worcester, Mass.) CONTROL MECHANISM FOR ROCKET APPARATUS—Goddard launched the first liquid-fuel rocket in 1926. Other rocket design developments led to the bazooka and rocket-assisted takeoff of carrier planes. (1979)

Goodyear, Charles 1800–1860 (b. New Haven, Conn.) IMPROVEMENT IN INDIA-RUBBER FABRICS—Goodyear discovered the vulcanizing process when some rubber mixed with sulfur accidently dropped on a hot stove. Prior to this, rubber's applications were limited because of its adhesiveness and its inability to withstand temperature extremes. (1976)

Gould, Gordon 1920– (b. New York City) OPTICALLY-PUMPED LASER AMPLIFIERS, GAS-DISCHARGE-EXCITED LIGHT AMPLIFIERS—Gould's lasers are used in 80% of industrial, commercial, and medical applications. He also holds patents on laser uses and fiber optic communications. (1991)

Greatbatch, Wilson 1919– (b. Buffalo, N.Y.) MEDICAL CARDIAC PACEMAKER—Greatbatch's was trained as an electrical engineer but his research combined engineering with medical electronics, agricultural genetics, and the electrochemistry of pacemaker batteries. The first implantable pacemaker was a result of his pacemaker patent. (1986)

Greene, Leonard Michael 1918– (b. New York City) AIRPLANE STALL WARNING DEVICE—Greene developed his airplane stall warning device at a time when more than half of all aviation deaths were called by the stall/spin. He also developed a wind shear warning device for pilots. (1991)

Hall, Charles Martin 1863–1914 (b. Thompson, Ohio) MANUFACTURE OF ALUMINUM—Hall discovered the modern electrolytic method of producing aluminum cheaply which enabled the metal to be put into wide commercial use. (1976)

Hall, Robert N. 1919– (b. New Haven, Conn.) HIGH-VOLTAGE, HIGH-POWER SEMICONDUCTOR PIN RECTIFIER—Hall's invention boosted efficiency and reduced wasted power and destructive heat build-up in large-scale power transmission. (1994)

Hanford, William Edward 1908– (b. Bristol, Pa.); **Holmes, Donald Fletcher** 1910–1980 (b. Woodbury, N.J.) POLYURETHANE—The Hanford and Holmes process is the basis today for the manufacture of all polyurethane. Polyurethane is used as an upholstery material, heat insulating material, in artificial hearts, safety padding in automobiles and in carpeting. (1991)

Hazen, Elizabeth Lee 1885–1975 (b. rural Mississippi); **Brown, Rachel Fuller** 1898–1980 (b. Springfield, Mass.) NYSTATIN—Nystatin was the world's first non-toxic anti-fungal antibiotic. It cured fungal infections of the skin, mouth, throat and intestinal tract and could be combined with antibacterial drugs to balance their effects. (1994)

Hewlett, William R. 1913– (b. Ann Arbor, Mich.) VARIABLE FREQUENCY OSCILLATION GENERATOR—Also known as the "audio oscillator," this was the first practical method of generating high-quality audio frequencies needed in communications, geophysics, medicine, and defense work. Walt Disney Studios ordered eight audio oscillators to use in producing the soundtrack of the film, "Fantasia." (1992)

Higgonnet, Rene Alphonse *See under* Moyroud, Louis Marius.

Hillier, James 1915– (b. Ontario, Canada) ELECTRON LENS CORRECTION DEVICE—Hillier is noted for his contributions to the development of the electron microscope. The electron lens is used to focus a beam of electrons just as an optical lens focuses light rays. In 1937 he helped build a model that magnified 7000 times. (1980)

Hoff, Marcian Edward "Ted", Jr. 1937– (b. Rochester, N.Y.); **Mazor, Stanley,** 1941– (b. Chicago, Ill.; **Faggin, Federico,** 1941– (b. Vicenza, Italy) MICROPROCESSOR CONCEPT AND ARCHITECTURE—Ted Hoff was the first to recognize that Intel's new silicon-gated MOS technology might make a single-chip CPU possible if a sufficiently simple architecture could be developed. He developed such an architecture with just over 2000 transistors. In 1969, Japanese calculator manufacturer, Busicom, accepted Hoff's (Intel's) proposal for an alternate architecture in which a single-chip general-purpose computer central processor (CPU) would be programmed to perform most calculator functions. Further refinements in architecture and logic design by Faggin and Mazor led to development of first working CPU in February 1971, which had as much computing power as the room-filling ENIAC (1946), and the introduction of the Intel 4004 microprocessor in November 1971. (1996)

Hollerith, Herman 1860–1929 (b. Buffalo, N.Y.) ART OF COMPILING STATISTICS—Hollerith invented a punch card tabulation machine system that revolutionized statistical computation. His system enabled the 1890 census to save $5 million and more than two years time. (1990)

Holmes, Donald Fletcher *See under* Hanford, William

Houdry, Eugene 1892–1962 (b. Domont, France) LIQUID FUELS— Up until World War I enough gasoline was produced from crude oil by distillation. Cracking fuel oil, another product of distillation, was necessary to meet increased gasoline demands. Early processes used high heat and pressure but Houdry discovered that a catalyst enabled the process to be done at a lower temperature, more quickly, and more cheaply. He also invented the catalytic muffler which reduces the amount of carbon dioxide and unburned carbons released into the atmosphere. (1990)

Julian, Percy Lavon 1899–1975 (b. Montgomery, Ala.) PREPARATION OF CORTISONE—Julian's notable discoveries were the synthesis of cortisone, used in the treatment of arthritis; Aerofoam, used to suffocate gasoline and oil fires, and the synthesis of physostigmine, a treatment for glaucoma. Physostigmine is also being explored in the treatment of Alzheimer's Disease. (1990)

Keck, Donald *See under* Maurer, Robert.

Kettering, Charles Franklin 1876–1958 (b. Ohio) ENGINE STARTING DEVICES AND IGNITION SYSTEM—Kettering invented the first electrical ignition system and the self-starter for automobiles and the first practical engine-driven generator (the "Delco"). His other scientific work includes research in higher octane gasoline, high compression automobile engines, improved Diesel engine, and a nontoxic and nonflammable refrigerant. (1980)

Kilby, Jack S. 1923– (b. Jefferson City, Mo.) MINIATURIZED ELECTRONIC CIRCUITS—Kilby is responsible for the design and development of thick film integrated circuits, integrated circuit development and applications, and also invented the monolithic integrated circuit widely used in electronic systems. (1982)

Kolff, Willem J. 1911– (b. Netherlands) SOFT SHELL MUSHROOM SHAPED HEART—Kolff invented the artificial kidney dialysis machine and headed a team which invented and tested an artificial heart. (1985)

Kwolek, Stephanie Louise 1923– (b. New Kensington, KEVLAR (AROMATIC POLYAMIDES AND FIBERS)—Kwolek's processes have resulted in hundreds of new polymers used in producing mooring ropes, fiber-optic cables, aircraft parts, and canoes. The most famous product was Kevlar, five times stronger than the same weight in steel, used in light-weight bullet-resistant vests. (1995)

Land, Edwin 1909–1991 (b. Connecticut) PHOTOGRAPHIC PRODUCT COMPRISING A RUPTURABLE CONTAINING CARRYING A PHOTOGRAPHIC PROCESSING LIQUID—Land developed the first modern light polarizers and also optical devices. His most famous invention, the Polaroid camera, combined positive and negative film with developing chemicals. (1977)

Langmuir, Irving 1881–1957 (b. Brooklyn, N.Y.) INCANDESCENT ELECTRIC LAMP—Langmuir's major inventions were the high-vacuum electron tube and the gas-filled incandescent lamp. He also contributed to the fields of electronics, plasma physics, atomic, and molecular structure. (1989)

Lawrence, Ernest Orlando 1901–1958 (b. Canton, So. Dakota) METHOD AND APPARATUS FOR THE ACCELERATION OF IONS—Lawrence's cyclotron enabled him to study the structure of the atom, transmute certain elements, and produce artificial radioactivity. His research included the use of radiation in biology and medicine and he helped isolate uranium 235 which was used in the first atomic bomb. Lawrence received the 1939 Nobel Prize for Physics. (1982)

Lear, William 1902–1978 (b. Hannibal, Mo.) RADIO APPARATUS–AUTOMOBILE—Lear's design of a practical car radio launched the Motorola Company. He then turned to navigational aids for aircraft and formed Lear, Inc., LearAvia Corp., and then Learjet, a leading supplier of corporate jets. He also designed the eight-track tape player. (1993)

Ledley, Robert S. 1926– (b. New York City) DIAGNOSTIC X-RAY SYSTEMS—Ledley developed the ACTA diagnostic x-ray scanner, the first whole-body computerized tomography (CT) machine. He was the first to do medical imaging, three-dimensional reconstructions and to use CT in radiation therapy planning for cancer patients and the diagnosis of bone disease. (1990)

Maiman, Theodore Harold 1927– (b. Los Angeles, Calif.) RUBY LASER SYSTEMS—In 1960 Maiman built and patented the prototype of the ruby laser. The amplified light of the laser has many uses in industry, surgery, military range finders, as well as bar code scanners and compact disk players. (1984)

Marconi, Guglielmo 1874–1937 (b. Bologna, Italy) TRANSMITTING ELECTRICAL SIGNALS—Marconi's experiments led to practical wireless telegraphy and radio. In 1901 he successfully received signals transmitted from England to Newfoundland. He was awarded the 1909 Nobel Prize for Physics. (1975)

Maurer, Robert 1924– (b. St. Louis, Mo.); **Keck, Donald** 1941– (b. Lansing, Mich.); **Schultz, Peter** 1942– (b. Brooklyn, N.Y.) FUSED SILICA OPTICAL WAVEGUIDE—The inventors designed and produced the first optical fiber with light loss during transmission low enough for wide use in telecommunications. This paved the way for the commercialization of optical fiber and created a revolution in telecommunications. (1993)

Mazor, Stanley *See under* Hoff, Marcian Edward "Ted", Jr.

McCormick, Cyrus 1809–1884 (b. Rockbridge County, Va.) REAPER—While others had also invented the mechanical grain reaper McCormick's constant improvements and astute business sense enabled him to turn his small family-run business into a worldwide corporation. (1976)

Mergenthaler, Ottmar 1854–1899 (b. Germany) MACHINE FOR PRODUCING PRINTING BARS—Mergenthaler's linotype composing machine allowed one operator to be machinist, typesetter, justifier, typefounder and type distributor by means of a board similar to a typewriter's keyboard. (1982)

Millman, Irving *See under* Blumberg, Baruch.

Morse, Samuel F.B. 1791–1872 (b. Charlestown, Mass.) TELEGRAPH SIGNALS—In 1844 Morse built the first telegraph line between Baltimore and Washington and relayed the first telegraphic message. He also devised the Morse code for his machine. (1975)

Moyer, Andrew J. 1899–1959 (b. Star City, Inc.) METHOD FOR PRODUCTION OF PENICILLIN—Moyer found that by culturing the *Penicillium* mold in a culture broth comprising corn steep liquor and lactose, penicillin yields could be increased many fold over the known methods. His discovery became the model for the development of all other antibiotic fermentations. (1987)

Moyroud, Louis Marius 1914– (b. Moirans, France); **Higonnet, Rene Alphonse** 1902–1983 (b. Valence, France) PHOTO COMPOSING MACHINE—Moyroud and Higonnet developed the first practical phototypesetting machine, the Lumitype—later known as the Photon—which was first demonstrated in 1946 and introduced in America in 1948. (1985)

Nieuwland, Rev. Julius A. 1878–1936 (b. Hansbeke, Belgium) SYNTHETIC RUBBER (NEOPRENE)—He invented the first synthetic rubber, Neoprene, manufactured by the Du Pont Company, whose outstanding properties—including resistance to abrasion, wear, cutting, chipping, tearing, and high and low temperatures—have made it popular in many industries. Rev. Nieuwland has the distinction of being the only Catholic priest in the National Inventors Hall of Fame. (1996)

Noyce, Robert N. 1927–1990 (b. Iowa) SEMICONDUCTOR DEVICE-AND-LEAD STRUCTURE—Noyce, as research director of Fairchild Semiconductor, was responsible for the initial development of silicon mesa and planar transistors, which led to a commercially applicable integrated circuit. He holds 16 patents for semiconductor devices, methods and structures. (1983)

Olsen, Kenneth H. 1926– (b. Stratford, Conn.) MAGNETIC CORE MEMORY—Olsen and his Digital Equipment Corporation developed the first successful minicomputer. Digital also developed the MicroVAX which placed a minicomputer structure on a single microchip. (1990)

Otis, Elisha Graves 1811–1861 (b. Halifax, Vt.) IMPROVEMENT IN HOISTING APPARATUS—Otis built the first modern passenger elevator which used his invention of a safety device which prevented the car from falling if the cables broke. (1988)

Otto, Nicolaus August 1832–1891 (b. Holzhausen, Germany) GAS MOTOR ENGINE—Otto introduced the four-stroke piston cycle on which most modern internal combustion engines are based. (1981)

Parker, Louis W. 1906–1993 (b. Budapest, Hungary) TELEVISION RECEIVER—Parker is best known for the "Intercarrier Sound System" used in all television receivers in the world. He also invented the first color television system using vertical color lines which made it possible to change from the original three color dot system to the simpler vertical color line system. (1988)

Parsons, John T. 1913– (b. Detroit, Mich.) NUMERICAL CONTROL OF MACHINE TOOLS—Parsons built a milling machine which was fed data to automatically activate servo-mechanisms to perform automatic contour cutting. First deveolped for making jet plane wings, the method is now widely used in the manufacture and assembly of many goods, from automobiles to computer chips. (1993)

Pasteur, Louis 1822–1895 (b. France) BREWING BEER AND ALE—Pasteur formulated the fundamental tenets of the germ theory of fermentation and of diseases which led to his pasteurization process of sterilization. He is also known for his pioneer work with vaccines, notably against anthrax and rabies. (1996)

Plank, Charles J. 1915–1989 (b. Calcutta, India); **Rosinski, Edward J.** 1921– (b. Gloucester County, N.J.) CATALYTIC CRACKING OF HYDROCARBONS WITH A CRYSTALLINE ZEOLITE CATALYST COMPOSITE—Plank and Rosinski developed the first commercially useful zeolite catalyst introduced in the petroleum industry for catalytic cracking. (1979)

Plunkett, Roy J. 1910–1994 (b. New Carlisle, Ohio) TETRAFLUOROETHYLENE POLYMERS—Plunkett discovered "Teflon" and also worked on the development of many other fluorochemical products and processes used in the refrigeration, aerosol, electronic and aerospace industries. (1985)

Rines, Robert H. 1922– (b. Boston, Mass.) HIGH RESOLUTION-IMAGE-SCANNING RADAR AND SONAR—Rines' radar and sonar inventions have been used by the military in the Persian Gulf War. In peacetime they have been used in locating the *Titanic* and *Bismarck* and also in a scientific sonar search for the Loch Ness Monster. (1994)

Rohrer, Heinrich *See under* Binnig, Gerd Karl.

Rosinski, Edward *See under* Plank, Charles J.

Rubin, Benjamin A. 1917– (b. New York City) BIFURCATED VACCINATION NEEDLE—Until 1967 smallpox killed at least 2 million people annually. In 1980 the World Health Organization declared that smallpox had been defeated. Rubin ground down the eyelet of a sewing machine needle to invent the bifurcated vaccination needle which could easily be used by natives under difficult conditions. (1992)

Sarett, Lewis Hastings 1917– (b. Champaign, Ill.) THE PROCESS OF TREATING PREGNENE COMPOUNDS—Sarett prepared the first synthetic cortisone. He and several collaborators developed synthesis from raw materials derived from coal, air, lime and water,

leading to the first route which was independent of naturally occurring starting materials. (1980)

Schawlow, Arthur L. 1921– (b. Mount Vernon, N.Y.) LASER—Co-inventor of the laser. Schawlow worked with Charles H. Townes who was inducted into the Inventors Hall of Fame in 1976. Today, the laser is prevalent in many areas, including the medical, defense, and communications fields. Schawlow is also a 1981 recipient of the Nobel Prize in physics for his work in laser spectroscopy. (1996)

Schultz, Peter *See under* Maurer, Robert.

Seiwald, Robert J. *See under* Burckhalter, Joseph H.

Semon, Waldo L. 1898– (b. Demopolis, Ala.) PVC PLASTISOLS—Semon's work turned polyvinyl chloride (PVC), first considered worthless, into the world's second-best selling plastic. He also provided the technical leadership that led to the discovery of thermoplastic polyurethane, synthetic "natural" rubber, and the first oil-resistant synthetic rubber. (1995)

Sheehan, John C. 1915–1992 (b. Battle Creek, Mich.) SEMI-SYNTHETIC PENICILLIN—For almost 30 years after Sir Alexander Fleming's discovery of penicillin, the process for harvesting the drug took months to generate a small amount. Sheehan succeeded in a general total synthesis of the antibiotic. (1995)

Shockley, William Bradford *See under* Bardeen, John.

Sikorsky, Igor I. 1889–1972 (b. Kiev, Russia) HELICOPTER CONTROLS—Sikorsky's patents covered control and stability improvements. The single rotor helicopter developed by Sikorsky represented a major breakthrough in helicopter technology. (1987)

Sperry, Elmer Ambrose 1860–1930 (b. Cortland, N.Y.) GYROSCOPIC COMPASS—The gyroscope was the basis of Sperry's inventions of an autopilot and an airplane turn indicator that allowed flying without visual reference to the ground. His ideas are used today to stabilize space vehicles. (1991)

Stanley, Jr., William 1858–1916 (b. Brooklyn, N.Y.) INDUCTION COIL—Stanley designed a practical induction coil system that varied alternating current (AC) voltage. His coil became the prototype for all future transformers and made practical the transmitting of electricity for consumer uses such as lighting. (1995)

Steinmetz, Charles Proteus 1865–1923 (b. Breslau, Germany) SYSTEM OF ELECTRICAL DISTRIBUTION—Steinmetz developed theories for alternating current making possible the expansion of the electric power industry in the United States. (1977)

Stibitz, George R. 1904–1995 (b. York, Pa.) COMPLEX COMPUTER—Stibitz is internationally recognized as the father of the modern digital computer. In 1939 Stibitz helped design the Model I complex number calculator which could add two eight-digit decimal numbers in a tenth of a second. (1983)

Szilard, Leo 1898–1964 (b. Budapest, Hungary) NUCLEAR REACTOR—Szilard was awarded a patent for the nuclear fission reactor along with Enrico Fermi. Throughout his life, Szilard made significant contributions to the field of statistical mechanics, nuclear physics, nuclear engineering, genetics, molecular biology, and political science. (1996)

Tabern, Donalee L. *See under* Volwiler, Ernest H.

Tesla, Nikola 1856–1943 (b. Smiljan Lika, Croatia) ELECTRO-MAGNETIC MOTOR—Tesla invented the induction motor which had a rotating magnetic field. The electro-magnetic motor was instrumental in converting electrical energy into mechanical energy, enabling electric motors to power machines. (1975)

Tishler, Max 1906–1989 (b. Boston, Mass.) SYNTHESIS OF RIBOFLAVIN AND SULFAQUINOXALINE—Tishler found a new process for the economical and large-scale synthesis of riboflavin (vitamin B_2). He also developed a production process for sulfaquinoxaline, the first effective antibiotic for the prevention and cure of the poultry disease coccidiosis. (1982)

Townes, Charles Hard 1915– (b. Greenville, South Carolina) MASERS—Townes constructed the maser (microwave amplification by stimulated emission of radiation) and also suggested the laser. Both are used in communications, medicine, industry, astronomy and navigation. (1976)

Volwiler, Ernest H. 1893–1992 (b. Hamilton, Ohio); **Tabern, Donalee` L.** 1900–1974 (b. Bowling Green, Ohio) THIO-BARBITURIC ACID DERIVATIVES—Volwiler and Tabern came up with Pentothal when they were seeking an anesthetic which could be injected directly into the bloodstream. (1986)

Wang, An 1920–1990 (b. Shanghai, China) MAGNETIC PULSE CONTROLLING DEVICE—Wang's contributions to computer technology included the magnetic pulse controlling device, the principle upon which magnetic core memory is based. He is noted for his innovations in the office automation and information processing field. (1988)

Westinghouse, George 1846–1914 (b. Central Bridge, N.Y.) STEAM-POWER BRAKE DEVICES—Westinghouse invented a system of railroad brakes that would centralize control in the hands of the engineer. Westinghouse, Tesla and other inventors developed alternating current motors and apparatus for the transmission of high tension current leading to large scale municipal lighting. (1989)

Whitney, Eli 1765–1825 (b. Westboro, Mass.) COTTON GIN—Whitney invented the cotton gin, a machine that greatly increased the speed for separating the cotton from its pod and seeds and to clean it. Whitney also adopted the concept of interchangeable parts in manufacturing. (1974)

Williams, Robert R., Jr. 1886–1965 (b. Nellore, India) SYNTHESIS OF VITAMIN B_1—Williams isolated thiamine in crystalline form and synthesized vitamin B_1. He was instrumental in achieving enrichment of flour, cornmeal and other cereal grains, helping to eliminate pellagra and riboflavin deficiency among poor people. He also invented processes for making submarine insulation. (1991)

Wright, Orville 1871–1948 (b. Dayton, Ohio); **Wright, Wilbur** 1867–1912 (b. Millville, Ind.) FLYING MACHINE—The Wright brothers achieved the first powered, sustained and controlled flight of a heavier than air machine at Kitty Hawk, North Carolina in 1903. (1975)

Zworykin, Vladimir Kosma 1889–1982 (b. Murom, Russia) CATHODE RAY TUBE—Zworykin invented the iconoscope, a television transmitting tube and the kinetoscope, a cathode ray tube that projects pictures it receives onto a screen. He also invented an infrared image tube and helped develop an electron microscope. (1977)

Record-Breaking Patents Filed

Source: U.S. Patent Office

As the table below shows, 236,679 patents were filed and 114,241 patents were granted in fiscal year 1995. Most of the patents are issued in the utility category, 101,895, which are given for inventions such as a new process or machine manufacture.

IBM headed the list of leading organizations receiving the most utility patents, Canon Kabushiki Kaisha, was second, and the U.S. government ranked third. The remaining organizations in the top ten, given in order of rank, were Motorola, NEC Corporation, Mitsubishi DKK, Toshiba, Hitachi, Matsushita, and Eastman Kodak.

Over half, 64,410 of the patents granted in fiscal 1995 went to U.S. resident inventors.

Summary of Patent Examining Activities

(As of September 30 of each fiscal year)

Patent examining activity	1991	1992	1993	1994	1995
Applications Filed					
Total	178,083	185,446	188,099	201,554	236,679
Utility[1]	166,765	171,623	173,619	185,087	220,141
Reissue	536	581	572	430	647
Plant	414	335	362	606	516
Design	10,368	12,907	13,546	15,431	15,375
First Actions					
Design	15,503	16,076	16,074	16,832	18,223
Utility, plant, and reissue	158,319	165,294	171,799	168,722	176,220
PCT/Chapter 1	5,680	7,247	7,459	8,363	9,454
Patents Issued[1]					
Total	101,860	109,728	107,332	113,268	114,241
Utility	91,822	99,405	96,676	101,270	101,895
Reissue	334	375	302	347	294
Plant	316	336	408	513	390
Design	9,380	9,612	9,946	11,138	11,662

1. Chemical, electrical, and mechanical applications. *Source:* U.S. Patent Office.

COMPUTER NOTES

The Software Industry: The Birth of a New Species

by Christopher Anderson, *The Economist*

About 570 million years ago, in the ancient oceans of the early earth, something odd happened. In the space of just a few million years, the seas, which had previously held only microscopic organisms, exploded with a huge variety of life, from a meter-long armored slab of a fish with a mouth like a rubbish disposal chute to a bizarre beast that walked on 14 stilts and had seven mouths on stalks. For the next few hundred million years, evolution progressed at its usual stately pace. Then, 225 million years ago, something else odd happened. Perhaps an asteroid hit the planet; scientists cannot agree. Whatever it was, it caused 96% of marine species to disappear and dinosaurs to appear. There followed another uneventful interval, until 65 million years ago it was suddenly out with the dinosaurs and in with the large mammals, including, eventually, humans.

This sort of progression, described beautifully in Stephen Jay Gould's *Wonderful Life,* is called "punctuated equilibrium." Over millions of years species adapt to fill every imaginable niche. Then along comes some external force—a volcano, an asteroid, an ice age—that changes all the niches and launches a mad scramble for survival. Evolution favors new forms of life that, through a sort of biological lateral thinking, can find a whole new way to thrive. Wings, legs, lungs: all were revolutionary mutations once. Life down the ages has tended to evolve in sudden great leaps, separated by long periods of slow change.

The same is true for technology, though the time scale is a little more compressed. In the past half-century, computer technology has evolved in three large jumps, each one followed by an explosion of new companies, a period of rapid change, and then the gradual emergence of a few dominant species that rule until the next digital disturbance. José Ortega y Gasset, a Spanish philosopher, once said that "a revolution lasts only 15 years, a period that coincides with the effectiveness of a generation." As it happens, computer revolutions have taken place at roughly the same intervals.

Start around 1950, with the IBM mainframe, when the term "data processing" entered the language. The next big upheaval came in the mid-1960s, when the minicomputer arrived to open the computing market to a host of upstarts such as Digital Equipment, and programmers—the spiritual fathers of today's code geeks—started to abandon their ties. Then, in 1981, IBM introduced the personal computer, causing a market explosion from which emerged some of today's strongest companies: Intel, Microsoft, Compaq.

Tomorrow's Dinosaurs

Now the time has come round for another shock, duly delivered in the shape of the Internet, which has emerged practically overnight from 25 years of boffin obscurity into the light of mass-media ubiquity. It was made possible by the serendipitous convergence of three technological developments: the spread of PCs and computer networks in offices; a rapid drop in communications costs; and the appearance of the World Wide Web, a brilliantly simple way of linking multimedia documents around the world over the Internet. But there was nothing planned about it: it grew, organically, simply because people used it, each adding to its reach and depth by virtue of the parts of their world they brought to it.

The Internet will shake up plenty of established industries, from telecoms to travel. It is everywhere, it is cheap, and it is, above all, open. For the price of a dinner for two a month, any company can now reach the world through a virtual shopfront on the Internet that will look just as impressive as the one used by General Motors. Cheap, global data communications will shape the 21st century as much as the telephone did the 20th.

John Doerr, one of Silicon Valley's leading venture capitalists, has calculated that the introduction of the PC caused the largest creation of wealth in the history of the planet; just Microsoft, Intel, and Compaq among them have a market valuation of $130 billion, more than all the film studios in Hollywood, or all of America's television and cable companies. Morgan Stanley's Mary Meeker, one of the computer industry's most respected analysts, reckons that the Internet has the potential to become even bigger.

The starting point for realizing that potential is the software industry. The Internet is mostly software. The big advantage of today's digital world is that machines—from PCs to telecoms networks—can assume radically different shapes when they are colonized by new code. The Internet consists largely of the existing telephone and office data networks linked up by Internet software, which runs over their lines and equipment. Just as the PC was little more than an exotic novelty before the appearance of Lotus 1-2-3, a spreadsheet that helped to change companies, so the Internet lay in the shadows until the arrival of software that could give it wings, from Web browsers to Internet telephones, payment schemes, and search services.

But just as software has transformed the Internet, so the Internet will transform software. This is not just because software is the ultimate information industry, tailor-made for distribution through the digital ether. Software has also reached its dinosaur age, ripe for transformation. The success of Microsoft, Oracle, IBM/Lotus, Computer Associates, and other giants marks out a relatively mature industry, as rooted in the past as in the future. For example, to maintain compatibility with older programs, Windows 95 must include millions of lines of code carrying the ghost of Windows past, and of the DOS operating system before it.

With revenues of more than $200 billion and a growth rate of some 13% a year, software is one of the world's largest and fastest-growing industries. Even so, it has recently been in danger of becoming a rather dull and closed club. In the early 1980s, when the PC was still new, the niches it opened up seemed innumerable. In 1983 Philippe Kahn, then a recent arrival in America from France, started Borland, a programming-tools company, by convincing a computer magazine to run his ad on credit. A month later, he had 100,000 orders and the beginnings of a company that would at its peak be worth $2.1 billion. Making software did not require a factory, just an idea and a computer. It was an exciting time when many software fortunes were started up. Today the tally includes half a dozen billionaires and several thousand millionaires.

But for most of the 1990s, software has increasingly been dominated by big companies making big, complicated programs. At a time when the operating system that comes with each PC already includes a word processor, e-mail, all the disk utilities you might ever need, and even a few games, it has become hard to imagine much of a role for a handful of enthusiasts in the proverbial garage.

Glamour Stock

Now, suddenly, the fun is back. In August 1995 Netscape Communications, a software firm then 14 months old, went public, triggering a stockmarket frenzy that at its height valued the firm at $6.7 billion—before it had made a single dime. Software firms that had not even existed two years earlier, such as CyberCash, Yahoo, Spyglass, Spry, and Ubique, commanded huge sums as they went public or were bought by established firms. Broadview Associates, a consultancy, in 1995 recorded mergers and acquisitions worth $28 billion in the software and related services industry, a rise of more than 60% on the year before. Venture capital investments in software firms hit $1.2 billion, up 57%. Nobody knows just how many software firms have been founded in the past year, but everybody is sure it must be more than 1,000.

Put it down to the Internet. It will change the soft-ware industry even more than the PC did a decade and a half ago. Just like the PC then, the Internet is a new "platform"—a fundamental technology on which a new market can be built. Platforms are not unique to the computer world: in the entertainment industry, for example, they include television and music CDs. All these are technological standards for products that will work everywhere the medium extends.

A new platform by itself will not necessarily cause a revolution. Attics are full of odd computers that did not take off, along with digital audio tape, laser discs, and other failures. New platforms are often troubled early on by a nasty chicken-and-egg problem: consumers will not buy them until lots of compatible products are available, and companies will not develop compatible products until they see a market. But the platforms that succeed can change the way most of us live. Once VHS had conquered Betamax in the videotape-standards war, sales skyrocketed. Within 15 years, more than three-quarters of American households had a video recorder. CD players took off even faster.

The PC won acceptance because it was backed by a then-mighty IBM. Mostly by accident, the Internet has taken a stealthier tack. It achieved near-ubiquity on the back of existing computer and communications networks in part because it offered a uniform way to connect otherwise incompatible computers. Just as a modem turns a regular telephone line into a data link, the Internet turned the world's telephone networks into an information highway, without much extra effort or expense. □

The article excerpted here appeared in the May 25, 1996, issue of *The Economist,* and is reprinted with permission. © 1996 The Economist Group, Inc. Further reproduction prohibited.

Connecting to the Internet: A Beginner's Guide

by Tasha Vincent, Inso Corporation

As if actually buying the computer and getting it out of the box weren't enough, now you have to sort through the myriad of disks and flyers offering to make your computer an onramp to the information superhighway. Most computers purchased today come with offers from Internet service providers, and have preinstalled software to connect you with online services such as America Online, CompuServe, Microsoft Network, and Prodigy. Which should you choose?

Though it is easy to get intimidated by all the decisions required to get online, it's really not all that difficult. Really. Once you get over your reservations you will find yourself keeping in touch with college roommates that were always "too busy to write letters"; finding out what's playing at the movies or what's happening in the news without checking the newspaper; researching airline flight schedules without the aid of a travel agent; or swapping opinions on the latest political issues with people across the country and around the world. (*See* the Internet Resource Guide section, pp. 603–604 for a selection of information to be found online.)

First you need to get connected, for which you will need a modem and an analog phone line. If you recently purchased your computer, it probably came standard with a modem; if not, you can purchase an external one that plugs into the back of your computer. When choosing a modem, keep in mind faster is better since it will take less time to download data or send faxes and, especially in the world of online services, time is money. Modem speeds are measured in bps ("bits per second") referring to the amount of data that can be transferred in a second. Speeds currently range from 14,400 bps to 33,600 bps. In most cases, the phone line you already have will be analog; if you have an ISDN or digital line, however, you will need an adapter to plug it into the analog modem.

Okay, so now the car has wheels; how do you get to the highway? You basically have two choices: a commercial online service, which includes forums (or discussion groups) with other members, as well as access to certain reference and information sources often not available elsewhere on the Internet; or an Internet service provider, which provides you with direct access to the Internet, but no services. Commercial services, such as America Online, CompuServe, Microsoft Network, or Prodigy offer "one-stop shopping" for a variety of features and services. Depending on the service, you may have access to online newspapers or magazines, shopping services, and chat groups (restricted to members of that service), which are devoted to particular hobbies or interests ranging from real estate to bull fighting. Each service provider chooses a set of services and features that will appeal to its users. By presenting users with only a few of the options in each category, online services simplify the process of finding what you need, but that can also limit your choices.

To meet the growing demand of more experienced users for more choices, all the commercial online services now offer access to the Internet—the infamous Information Superhighway whose number of sites doubles every 57 days. Here users can send e-mail anywhere in the world, and find an endless list of sites in every category imaginable, with the quality ranging from the truly spectacular to the merely useless. Internet service providers, unlike online services, provide only access to the Internet. In short, the online services provide a user-friendly way to get information online, sort of like swimming in the kiddie pool with a lifeguard nearby.

The truly adventurous will sign up for the direct Internet access through an Internet service provider. This is like heading straight out into the Pacific; lifeguards may or may not be present, depending on where you choose to swim. Many of the same newspapers and magazines offered via online services can also be found here, but users need to know where to look. You can still find out the weather in Moscow, or the current leader in Malawi, but it often takes a tenacious user to track down the site with the sought-after information.

The cost of connecting to the world at large ranges from about $5 to $30 per month, depending on the type of service you choose and the amount of time you spend logged in. Some people are perfectly content in the swimming pool, and prefer the ease of use of the online service. For those who wish to spend hours surfing the 'Net, however, the hourly charges can add up. Also, subscribers to online services pay for all the features provided, regardless of how rarely they are used. If you don't think you'll use all the features of an online service, or plan to swim more than 20 hours a month in the Pacific, the direct Internet connection may be more cost-effective since there is usually a flat monthly fee, regardless of amount of time spent logged in.

Whether you choose to swim in the pool or the ocean, it's the perfect time to get your feet wet and join the 30 million others who can connect to the Internet today. □

Computer Glossary

ASCII: American Standard Code for Information Interchange, an encoding system for converting keyboard characters and instructions into the binary number code that the computer understands.

Baud Rate: The speed at which data is transmitted over a modem, measured in bits per second.

Bit: (Stands for binary digit). It is the smallest piece of computer information and is either the number 0 or 1. All information is given to the computer in the binary number system. With proper coding, the computer can "understand" any number, letter, punctuation mark, or symbol through an appropriate combination of the numbers 0 and 1.

Boot: To start up a computer.

Browser: Software used to navigate the Internet. Netscape Navigator is today's most popular browser for accessing the World Wide Web. Other browsers include Microsoft Internet Explorer and Mosaic.

Bug: A malfunction due to an error in the program or a defect in the equipment.

Byte: Most computers use combinations of eight bits to represent one character of data. These eight-bit combinations are called bytes. Bytes can represent data or instructions. For example, the word "cat" has three characters, and it would be represented by three bytes.

CD-ROM: (Compact Disc Read-Only Memory.) Similar to a CD music disc, but designed for computers, a single disc can hold an entire library of books such as encyclopedias or other reference works, and multimedia programs for quick, convenient viewing.

Chip: A tiny wafer of silicon containing miniature electric circuits that can store millions of bits of information.

Client: A single user of a networked application run off a server. A client/server architecture allows many people to use the same data simultaneously; the program's main component (the data) resides on a centralized server, with smaller components (user interface) on each client.

CPU: Central Processing Unit. The "brains" or part of a computer where all the incoming information is controlled and executed by its electronic circuitry.

Cursor: A moving position-indicator displayed on the computer monitor that shows the computer operator where he is working.

Cyberspace: Slang for the Internet; the continuum of computer networks and bulletin board systems in which online communication takes place.

Database: A collection of similar information stored in a file, for example, a database of addresses. This information may be created and stored in a database management system (DBMS).

Debug: Computer slang for finding and correcting equipment defects or malfunctions in the program.

Desktop Publishing: Use of a personal computer in combination with text, graphics, and page layout programs to produce publication quality documents.

Directory: A list of files stored in the computer.

Disk: Two distinct types: the so-called "hard disk" that is inside the computer and stores vast amounts of data (new computers currently come standard with 1 gigabyte hard drives); and the "floppy" disk, which is portable, 3.5" square, and can store about 1.4 megabytes of data (the name is a vestige of early 5 1/4" disks, which were flexible).

Disk Drive: The equipment that a floppy disk is inserted into so that information may be stored or retrieved from the disk.

Documentation: The instruction manual for a piece of hardware or software.

Domain: The name of a network or computer linked to the Internet. It is found in an e-mail address after an @ sign. The e-mail address of this almanac, for example, is ipa@inso.com, "Inso.com" being its domain. A domain ends with an abbreviation indicating the type of organization involved (e.g., "com" stands for company, "gov" for government, "org" for organization, and "edu" for educational institution).

DOS: Disk Operating System. Operating system designed for early IBM-compatible PCs.

E-mail: Electronic mail; messages, including memos or letters, sent electronically between networked computers that may be sent across the office or around the world.

File: A set of data that is stored in the computer.

Flame: An inflammatory message sent electronically.

Fonts: Sets of typefaces (or characters) that come in different styles and sizes.

Forum: A discussion group offered by certain online services; allows users to post messages on a given topic and solicit responses from other users. Also referred to as a chat group or news group.

FTP (File Transfer Protocol): The format and rules for transferring files from a host to a remote computer.

Gigabyte (GB): One thousand megabytes.

Glitch: The cause of an unexpected malfunction.

Graphics: Pictorial matter such as charts, graphs, and diagrams that can be programmed into a computer's video display.

Gopher: An Internet search tool that allows users to access textual information through a series of menus.

GUI: Graphical User Interface. A system that simplifies selecting computer commands by enabling the user to point to symbols or illustrations (called "icons") on the computer screen with a mouse.

Groupware: Software that allows networking groups to collaborate on documents.

Hacker: A person with technical expertise who enjoys tinkering with computer systems in order to produce additional features. Also one who intentionally accesses all or part of a computer or a computer system without authorization to do so. (A crime in some states.)

Hard Copy: A paper printout of what you have prepared on the computer.

Hardware: The physical and mechanical components of a computer system. They include electronic circuitry, chips, screens, disk drives, keyboards, modems, and printers.

Home page: The main page of a Web site used to greet visitors, provide information about the site, or to direct the viewer to other pages on the site.

HTML (Hypertext Markup Language): A standard of text markup conventions used for documents on the World Wide Web. Browsers interpret the codes to give the text formatting (such as bold, blue, or italic).

HTTP (Hypertext Transfer Protocol): A common system used to request and send HTML documents on the World Wide Web. It is the first portion of all URL addresses on the World Wide Web (e.g., http://www.whitehouse.gov).

Hypermedia: Integrates audio, graphics, and/or video.

Hypertext: A system of organizing text through links, as opposed to a menu-driven hierarchy such as Gopher. Most Web pages include hypertext links to other pages at that site, or to other sites on the World Wide Web.

Icons: Symbols or illustrations appearing on the computer screen that indicate program files or other computer functions.

Input: Data that goes into a computer device.

Interface: The interconnections that allow a device, a program, or a person, to interact. Hardware interfaces are the cables that connect the device to its power source and to other devices. Software interfaces allow the program to communicate with other programs (such as the operating system), and user interfaces allow the user to communicate with the program (e.g., via mouse, menu commands, icons, voice commands, etc.).

Internet: The world's largest conglomeration of interconnected computer networks. Developed in the late 1970s, the Internet is a non-tangible entity not controlled by any single source. Its original focus was research and communications, but it continues to expand, offering a wide array of resources for business and home users.

Java: An object-oriented programming language that allows users to create small programs or applications ("applets") to enhance Web sites. Java was designed specifically for programs (particularly multimedia) to be used over the Internet.

Kilobyte (K or KB): Equal to 1,024 bytes.

Laptop and Notebook: Small, lightweight, portable battery-powered computers that can fit onto your lap. They have a thin, flat, liquid crystal display screen.

Machine Language: The CPU or "brains" of the computer can only understand instructions written in binary form (bits of 0's and 1's). The commands the operator or program gives the computer are translated into this machine language by the computer using the binary number system.

Megabyte (MB): Equal to 1,048,576 bytes, usually rounded off to one million bytes. Computer memories are measured in terms of the number of bytes they can store.

Memory: A computer device or series of devices that store information.

Menu: A list of options displayed on the computer terminal that you can choose from.

Merge: To combine two or more files into a single file arrangement.

Microprocessor: A complete central processing unit (CPU) contained on a single silicon chip.

Modem: A device that will connect two compatible computers together by a direct connection to the telephone line. Modems accomplish this by converting the computer's data into an audio signal.

Monitor: A video display terminal.

Mouse: A small hand-held device for controlling the cursor movement on the screen by moving the "mouse" back and forth on a desk.

Multimedia: Software programs that combine text and graphics with sound, video, and animation. A **multimedia PC** contains the hardware to support these capabilities.

MS-DOS: An early operating system developed by Microsoft Corporation.

Network: Computers that are connected to other computers.

OS/2: An operating system developed by IBM for IBM PCs and compatible computers with a graphical user interface.

Output: Data that come out of a computer device.

PC: Personal computer.

Pen Computer: A type of laptop PC tat uses a stylus (pen) to write directly on the screen rather than using a keyboard.

Pentium chip: Intel's fifth generation of sophisticated high-speed microprocessors. Pentium means "the fifth element."

Personal computer: A single-user computer containing a central processing unit (CPU) and one or more memory circuits.

Power PC: A competitor to the Pentium chip. It is a new generation of powerful sophisticated microprocessors produced from an Apple–IBM–Motorola alliance.

Printer: A mechanical device for printing your computer's output on paper. The three major types of printers are **Dot Matrix,** in which individual letters are made up of a series of tiny ink dots. The dots are formed by punching a ribbon with the ends of tiny wires; **Ink Jet,** which sprays tiny droplets of ink particles onto paper; and **Laser,** which uses a beam of light to reproduce the image of each page, then dry toner is applied to the image and transferred to paper.

Program: A precise series of instructions written in a computer language that tells the computer what to do and how to do it. Programs are also called "software" or "applications."

Programming Language: A series of instructions written by a programmer according to a given set of rules or conventions ("syntax"). High-level programming languages are independent of the device on which the application (or program) will eventually run; low-level languages are specific to each program or platform. Programming language instructions are converted into programs in language specific to a particular machine or operating system ("machine language") so that the computer can interpret and carry out the instructions. Some common programming languages are BASIC, C, C++, dBASE, FORTRAN, and PERL.

RAM: Random Access Memory. One of two basic types of memory. RAM is a memory that your computer can add to, retrieve from, or alter at will.

ROM: Read-Only Memory. One of the two basic types of memory. As its name implies, information in it cannot be altered by the computer operator. ROM contains only permanent information put there by the manufacturer.

Scanner: An electronic device that uses light-sensing equipment to scan paper images such as text, photos, and illustrations and translate the images into signals that the computer can understand and copy.

Search Engine: Software that makes it possible to look for and retrieve material on the Internet, particularly the Web. Some popular search engines are Alta Vista, Yahoo, and Lycos.

Server: A computer that shares its resources and information with other computers on a network.

Software: Computer programs.

Spreadsheets: Software that allows one to calculate numbers in a format that is similar to pages in a conventional ledger.

Surfing: Exploring the Internet.

Trackball: Input device that controls the position of the cursor on the screen; the unit is mounted near the keyboard, and movement is controlled by moving a ball.

URL (Uniform Resource Locator): The protocol for identifying a document on the Web; the Web address (e.g., http://www.census.gov).

USENET: A large unmoderated and unedited bulletin board on the Internet that offers thousands of forums, called newsgroups. These range from newsgroups exchanging information on scientific advances to celebrity fan clubs.

User Friendly: It means that the system and the instructions are supposed to be written in simple language and be easy to operate for people with a nontechnical background.

Virtual Reality (VR): A technology that allows you to experience and interact with the image on the computer screen in a simulated three-dimensional environment. For example, you could design a room in a house on your computer and actually feel that you are walking around in it even though it was never built. (The holodeck in the science fiction TV series "Star Trek: The Next Generation" would be the ultimate virtual reality.) Current technology requires the user to wear a special helmet, viewing goggles, gloves, and other equipment that is wired to the computer.

Virus: An unauthorized piece of computer code attached to a computer program or portions of a computer system that secretly spreads from one computer to another by shared disks and over telephone lines.

Windows: A graphical environment developed by Microsoft Corp. that enables users to select commands by pointing to illustrations or symbols with a mouse.

World Wide Web (WWW or The Web): A network of servers on the Internet that use hypertext-linked databases and files. It was developed in 1989 by Tim Berners-Lee, a British computer scientist, and is now the primary platform of the Internet. The feature that distinguishes the Web from other Internet applications is its ability to display graphics in addition to text.

Word Processor: A computer system or program for setting, editing, revising, correcting, storing, and the printing of text.

Worm: An unauthorized independent program that penetrates computers and replicates itself, thereby affecting computers and computer networks. In 1988, Robert T. Morris, a Cornell University graduate student shut down a nationwide computer network with the best-known computer worm in history.

Computers Per Capita

Rank	Computers/1000 People	1985	1988	1989	1991	1992	1993	1994	1995	2000[1]
1.	United States	90.1	166.0	191.7	245.4	266.9	296.6	329.2	364.7	580.0
2.	Australia	21.5	58.4	75.3	120.5	155.0	191.9	222.7	264.3	525.7
3.	Norway	28.4	61.2	77.7	120.7	148.2	180.5	218.5	259.5	515.4
4.	Canada	36.4	77.4	96.2	136.6	157.5	189.0	219.2	254.8	511.9
5.	Denmark	25.9	58.6	76.7	127.3	153.8	184.6	217.2	252.5	510.2
6.	Finland	25.4	56.2	76.0	119.3	146.2	178.8	211.0	245.5	505.0
7.	Sweden	24.5	58.5	77.0	114.2	139.6	169.9	204.0	244.1	508.9
8.	New Zealand	25.7	57.2	73.5	115.6	136.4	159.8	191.2	224.8	499.2
9.	United Kingdom	36.4	74.8	90.7	125.7	144.8	164.8	187.4	216.5	441.1
10.	Netherlands	22.4	51.9	69.2	109.7	131.1	156.9	184.3	214.8	450.3
11.	Switzerland	24.2	53.0	70.2	109.0	126.6	149.5	174.3	201.6	443.7
12.	Singapore	17.8	46.5	59.7	84.7	104.8	126.9	153.8	188.8	412.0
13.	Belgium	20.1	47.0	63.2	100.2	117.3	138.3	161.2	188.6	405.2
14.	Ireland	23.8	54.1	68.3	102.0	117.4	136.1	159.1	186.4	404.1
15.	Germany	24.0	54.2	67.6	91.5	108.6	129.2	151.3	174.6	361.8
	Europe	14.3	31.7	40.8	60.2	71.0	83.5	97.3	113.4	248.9
	Worldwide	7.8	15.4	18.5	25.2	29.1	33.6	38.8	44.9	90.3

1. Projected. *Source:* Karen Petska-Juliussen and Egil Juliussen, *8th Annual Computer Industry Almanac,* Copyright ©1996 by Computer Industry Almanac Inc., (702) 749-5053; (800) 377-6810 (U.S. only).

Countries With the Most Computers

(in millions)

Country[1]	Computers in use	1985	1988	1989	1991	1992	1993	1994	1995	2000[2]
United States	Total computers	21.5	40.8	47.6	62.0	68.2	76.5	85.8	96.2	160.5
	Total PCs	19.1	37.9	44.5	58.6	64.6	72.6	81.5	91.5	154.0
Japan	Total computers	2.1	5.1	6.4	9.2	10.8	12.6	14.9	18.3	46.8
	Total PCs	1.8	4.7	5.9	8.7	10.2	12.0	14.2	17.4	45.0
Germany	Total computers	1.9	4.2	5.2	7.3	8.7	10.4	12.3	14.2	29.8
	Total PCs	1.6	3.9	4.9	6.9	8.3	9.9	11.7	13.5	28.6
United Kingdom	Total computers	2.1	4.3	5.2	7.2	8.4	9.6	10.9	12.6	26.0
	Total PCs	1.8	3.9	4.8	6.8	7.9	9.1	10.4	12.0	25.0
France	Total computers	1.3	3.1	4.0	5.7	6.5	7.5	8.6	10.0	21.8
	Total PCs	1.1	2.9	3.7	5.4	6.2	7.1	8.2	9.5	21.0
Canada	Total computers	0.9	2.0	2.5	3.7	4.3	5.2	6.2	7.2	15.3
	Total PCs	0.8	1.9	2.4	3.5	4.1	5.0	5.9	6.9	14.7
Italy	Total computers	0.9	2.1	2.6	3.7	4.3	5.0	5.9	6.7	17.5
	Total PCs	0.8	1.9	2.4	3.5	4.1	4.8	5.6	6.4	16.8
Australia	Total computers	0.34	0.95	1.24	2.1	2.7	3.4	4.0	4.8	10.2
	Total PCs	0.28	0.87	1.15	1.96	2.6	3.2	3.8	4.6	9.8
South Korea	Total computers	0.13	0.28	0.43	1.0	1.4	1.9	2.6	3.5	10.6
	Total PCs	0.10	0.26	0.40	0.9	1.3	1.8	2.5	3.4	10.2
Spain	Total computers	0.20	0.50	0.79	1.44	1.8	2.3	2.9	3.5	8.1
	Total PCs	0.17	0.46	0.73	1.35	1.7	2.2	2.7	3.3	7.8
Netherlands	Total computers	0.32	0.76	1.02	1.65	2.0	2.4	2.8	3.3	7.1
	Total PCs	0.27	0.70	0.95	1.55	1.9	2.3	2.7	3.2	6.8
China	Total computers	0.12	0.28	0.40	0.67	0.92	1.34	2.0	2.9	13.3
	Total PCs	0.09	0.25	0.36	0.63	0.87	1.26	1.9	2.8	12.7
Russia	Total computers	0.10	0.23	0.34	0.65	0.93	1.37	1.9	2.7	9.2
	Total PCs	0.08	0.20	0.31	0.61	0.88	1.29	1.8	2.6	8.8
Mexico	Total computers	0.15	0.37	0.49	0.87	1.21	1.61	2.05	2.6	6.3
	Total PCs	0.12	0.34	0.46	0.82	1.14	1.52	1.94	2.4	6.0
Brazil	Total computers	0.10	0.24	0.31	0.62	0.91	1.27	1.76	2.4	7.8
	Total PCs	0.08	0.22	0.29	0.59	0.86	1.20	1.67	2.3	7.5
Worldwide Total	Total computers	38.1	79.4	97.0	136.9	159.2	186.9	218.8	257.2	556.9
	Total PCs	33.2	73.4	90.6	129.4	150.8	177.4	208.0	245.0	535.6

1. List represents the fifteen countries with the most computers. 2. Projected. *Source:* Karen Petska-Juliussen and Egil Juliussen, *8th Annual Computer Industry Almanac,* Copyright ©1996 by Computer Industry Almanac Inc., (702) 749-5053; (800) 377-6810 (U.S. only).

Access and Use of Computers in the United States

(Numbers in thousands)

Access, use and age	Number			Percent		
	1984	1989	1993	1984	1989	1993
Households with computer	6,980	13,683	22,605	8.2	15.0	22.8
ALL RACES						
3 to 17 years	51,482	52,667	55,827			
Access to a computer	7,697	12,082	17,829	15.3	24.2	31.9
Use home computer	5,679	8,547	12,527	74.2	71.1	74.7
Use computer at school	12,284	20,664	28,848	28.0	46.0	60.6
Use computer any place	15,542	24,216	32,659	30.2	46.0	58.5
18 years and over	169,786	180,123	187,405			
Access to a computer	14,999	29,615	47,988	9.1	17.3	25.6
Use home computer	7,757	16,758	30,165	53.3	58.4	65.6
Use computer at school	3,839	5,564	7,439	30.8	43.6	53.8
Use computer at work	24,172	40,245	51,106	24.6	36.8	45.8
Use computer any place	31,099	50,668	67,397	18.3	28.1	36.0
WHITE						
3 to 17 years	41,915	42,262	44,242			
Access to a computer	7,048	10,773	15,821	17.1	26.7	35.8
Use home computer	5,186	7,685	11,248	74.0	71.7	75.3
Use computer at school	10,827	17,463	23,799	30.3	48.2	62.7
Use computer any place	13,782	20,662	27,178	32.9	48.9	61.4
18 years and over	146,693	154,236	158,927			
Access to a computer	13,782	26,902	42,814	9.6	18.3	26.9
Use home computer	7,151	15,462	27,417	53.4	59.2	66.7
Use computer at school	3,269	4,709	5,980	31.0	43.6	53.1
Use computer at work	21,795	35,977	45,326	25.3	37.8	47.1
Use computer any place	27,940	45,264	59,532	19.0	29.4	37.5
BLACK						
3 to 17 years	7,721	8,212	8,836			
Access to a computer	461	806	1,152	6.1	10.6	13.0
Use home computer	350	518	721	75.9	65.0	67.3
Use computer at school	1,032	2,416	3,786	15.9	35.1	50.9
Use computer any place	1,254	2,622	4,031	16.2	31.9	45.6
18 years and over	18,403	20,007	21,361			
Access to a computer	780	1,573	2,949	4.4	8.4	13.8
Use home computer	406	733	1,582	54.0	50.6	56.8
Use computer at school	367	506	909	26.1	38.9	54.8
Use computer at work	1,724	2,990	4,072	18.3	27.6	36.1
Use computer any place	2,259	3,673	5,335	12.3	18.4	25.0
HISPANIC ORIGIN						
3 to 17 years	4,266	5,734	6,569			
Access to a computer	191	514	795	4.6	9.6	12.1
Use home computer	128	326	459	67.4	64.3	68.4
Use computer at school	634	1,724	2,829	18.2	37.5	52.7
Use computer any place	717	1,853	2,991	16.8	32.3	45.5
18 years and over	9,362	13,301	15,103			
Access to a computer	372	1,005	1,954	4.1	8.0	12.9
Use home computer	165	508	1,090	45.6	54.0	61.3
Use computer at school	177	323	534	28.0	37.7	50.0
Use computer at work	863	1,779	2,492	16.4	22.5	29.3
Use computer any place	1,091	2,246	3,322	11.7	16.9	22.0

NOTE: Percents based on the following: Use home computer based on persons with home computer. Use computer at school based on persons enrolled. Use computer at work based on persons with a job. Use computer any place (home, work, school combined) based on persons in age group. Persons of Hispanic origin may be of any race. *Source:* U.S. Bureau of the Census, "Computer Use in the United States: 1993." Data are from Current Population Survey (CPS), October 1993.

Global Warming: A Coming World Health Crisis?

One of the most feared consequences of global warming is the rise in sea level. Medical experts warn that it would also have a disastrous impact on world health.

According to an article in the January 1996 issue of *The Journal of the American Medical Association*, global warming could open a Pandora's box of infectious diseases. Dr. Jonathan A. Patz, M.D., M.P.H., Johns Hopkins School of Public Health, Baltimore, Md., and colleagues warned that changes in global temperatures could introduce new infectious diseases as well as expand the areas already at risk.

Dr. Patz based his warning on the latest information showing that global temperatures are expected to rise an unprecedented 2°C or 3.6°F by the year 2100. Sea level is expected to rise about 50 centimeters or 1.6 feet in the same period.

The danger would not be limited to third world countries but also to the United States. For example, the pulmonary Hantavirus epidemic in the southwest United States was blamed on an upsurge in rodent populations as a result of climate and ecological conditions, including six years of drought, followed by extremely heavy spring rains, and a tenfold increase in the population of deer mice, which are the largest known carriers of Hantavirus.

There is also a known relationship between temperature and dengue, or "breakbone fever," a severe viral illness occurring sporadically and in epidemics. There is no vaccine or antiviral medication available for dengue, which is spread by mosquitoes. During an unseasonably warm summer in 1988, dengue spread in an area of Mexico usually left undisturbed.

According to the Centers for Disease Control and Prevention, there are now over 2 billion persons at risk of infection and millions of cases occur each year. It is anticipated that there will be increased dengue transmission in all tropical areas of the world during the next several years.

In contrast, higher temperatures could lead to a reduction of some diseases. Dr. Patz referred to tick-borne diseases which favor cooler temperatures. One example would be Rocky Mountain spotted fever seen in the southern United States.

According to Dr. Patz, the incidence of mosquito-borne diseases, including malaria, dengue, and viral encephalitides, are among the most sensitive to climate. Climate change would directly increase disease transmission by increasing the vector's geographic range and reproductive and biting rates, and by shortening pathogen incubation period. Climate-related increases in sea surface temperature and sea level can lead to higher incidence of water-borne infections and toxin-related illnesses, such as cholera and shellfish poisoning.

Human migration and damage to health infrastructures would also be affected and could indirectly contribute to disease transmission. Human susceptibility to infections might be further compounded by malnutrition due to climate stress on agriculture and potential alterations in the immune system caused by increased flux of ultraviolet radiation.

Probability of Sea Level Rise

Many climatologists believe that increasing atmospheric concentrations of carbon dioxide and other gases released by human activities are warming the Earth by a mechanism commonly known as the "greenhouse effect." This warming effect appears to be partly offset by the cooling effect of sulfate aerosols, which reflect sunlight back into space. The Earth's average surface temperature has risen by approximately 0.6°C (1°F) in the last century, and the nine warmest years have all occurred since 1980.

Climate modeling studies generally estimate that global temperatures will rise a few degrees Celsius (Centigrade) in the next century. Such a warming is likely to raise sea level by expanding ocean water, and melting glaciers and portions of the Greenland Ice Sheet. Warmer polar ocean temperatures could also melt portions of the Ross and other Antarctic ice shelves, which might increase the rate which Antarctic ice streams convey ice into the oceans.

Warmer polar air temperatures, however, would probably increase annual snowfall, which would partly offset the rise in sea level caused by warmer temperatures. Along much of the United States coast, sea level is already rising 2.5–3.0 mm/yr (10 to 12 inches per century).

Coastal areas and their major cities, such as Shanghai, London, and New York, are most at risk from rising sea levels, along with other densely populated, low-lying regions of the world such as those in Asia.

In 1995, a report released by the Environmental Protection Agency (EPA) entitled "The Probability of Sea Level Rise," further confirmed the probability of sea level rise. It provided estimates of the impact of greenhouse gas emissions on coastline sea level elevations. The report projected that, along the U.S. Atlantic and Gulf of Mexico coasts, the sea level is most likely to rise 26 centimeters (10.24 inches) by the year 2050 and 55 centimeters (21.65 inches) by the year 2100. It also estimated that there is a one percent chance that the sea level will rise 30 centimeters (11.81 inches) in the next thirty years, 120 centimeters (47.24 inches) in the next century, and four meters (13.12 feet) over the next two centuries.

The EPA's projections are consistent with those of the Intergovernmental Panel on Climate Change (IPCC), a United Nations-sponsored organization made up of over 1,500 climate experts from 60 nations. The IPCC published a report in November 1995 which concluded that "The balance of evidence suggests that there is a discernible human influence on global climate." It also stated for the first time that the predicted warming could cause widespread climatic disruption. The U.N. agency's best estimate forecasts a global temperature rise of 2°C (3.6°F) by the year 2100. Their estimates call for a rise in sea level of 15 to 90 centimeters (6 inches to 3 feet) for the same period, with a best estimate of 48 centimeters (1 foot 7 inches).

The report also noted that, among the major disruptions of modern society that could be caused by the impact of climate change, human health with a significant loss of life would be threatened by the expanding range of animal-borne infectious diseases. □

Threatened and Endangered Species
(as of June 30, 1996)

Source: U.S. Fish and Wildlife Service, Dept. of the Interior

Group	Endangered[1] U.S.	Endangered[1] Foreign	Threatened[2] U.S.	Threatened[2] Foreign	Total listings[3]	Species with recovery plans[4]
Mammals	55	252	9	19	335	40
Birds	74	178	16	6	274	73
Reptiles	14	65	19	15	113	31
Amphibians	7	8	6	1	22	11
Fishes	65	11	40	0	116	72
Snails	15	1	7	0	23	18
Clams	51	2	6	0	59	42
Crustaceans	14	0	3	0	17	4
Insects	20	4	9	0	33	20
Arachnids	5	0	0	0	5	4
Flowering plants	403	1	92	0	496	270
Conifers	2	0	0	2	4	1
Ferns & others	26	0	2	0	28	15
Grand Total	**751**	**522**	**209**	**42**	**1,525**	**601**

1. *Endangered species* are those in danger of extinction. 2. *Threatened species* are those likely to become an endangered species within the foreseeable future. 3. Separate populations of a species listed both as endangered and threatened are tallied twice. Those species are the argali, leopard, gray wolf, piping plover, roseate tern, chimpanzee, green sea turtle, and olive ridley sea turtle. 4. There are 424 approved recovery plans sponsored by the endangered species program of the U.S. Fish and Wildlife Service. They are dedicated to restoring species to a secure status in the wild. Some recovery plans cover more than one species, and a few species have separate plans covering different parts of their ranges. Recovery plans are drawn up only for species in the United States.

Some Endangered Species of the World

Source: U.S. Fish and Wildlife Service, Dept. of the Interior

The following list comprises some of the more familiar endangered species. Due to space limitations, it represents only a portion of the mammals, birds, reptiles, amphibians, and fishes considered endangered, and none of the clams, crustaceans, snails, insects, or plants.

Common Name	Scientific Name	Range
MAMMALS		
Bat, gray	*Myotis grisescens*	U.S. (Central and Southeastern)
Bear, brown	*Ursus arctos pruinosus*	China (Tibet)
Cheetah	*Acinonyx jubatus*	Africa, Middle East, South Asia
Chimpanzee	*Pan troglodytes*	Africa (Western and Central)
Deer, Key	*Odocoileus virginianus*	U.S. (Florida Keys)
Dolphin, Chinese River	*Lipotes vexillifer*	China
Elephant, Asian	*Elephas maximus*	South and Southeast Asia
Ferret, black-footed	*Mustela nigripes*	U.S. and Canada
Gazelle, slender-horned	*Gazella leptoceros*	Saharan Africa
Gorilla	*Gorilla gorilla*	Africa (Western and Central)
Ibex, Walia	*Capra walie*	Ethiopia
Kangaroo, Tasmanian forester	*Macropus giganteus tasmaniensis*	Australia (Tasmania)
Leopard, snow	*Panthera uncia*	Central Asia
Lion, Asiatic	*Panthera leo persica*	Middle East, South Asia
Manatee, West Indian	*Trichechus manatus*	U.S., Mexico, Caribbean, South America
Monkey, spider	*Ateles geoffroyi frontatus*	Costa Rica, Nicaragua
Orangutan	*Pongo pygmaeus*	Sumatra, Borneo
Otter, marine	*Lutra felina*	South America
Panda, giant	*Ailuropoda melanoleuca*	China
Panther, Florida	*Felis concolor coryi*	U.S. (Southeast)
Pronghorn, Sonoran	*Antilocapra americana sonoriensis*	Mexico, U.S.
Puma, Costa Rican	*Felis concolor costaricensis*	Nicaragua, Panama, Costa Rica
Rhinoceros, black	*Diceros bicornis*	Africa
Tiger	*Panthera tigris*	Asia
Wallaby, brindled nail-tailed	*Onycholgalea fraenata*	Australia
Whale, blue	*Balaenoptera musculus*	All oceans
Whale, humpback	*Megaptera novaeangliae*	All oceans
Wolf, gray	*Canis lupus*	Holarctic
Yak, wild	*Bos grunniens mutus*	China (Tibet), India
Zebra, mountain	*Equus zebra zebra*	South Africa

Common Name	Scientific Name	Range
BIRDS		
Albatross, short-tailed	*Diomedea albatrus*	Japan, Russia, U.S., North Pacific
Condor, Andean	*Vultur gryphus*	South America
Crane, whooping	*Grus americana*	Canada, U.S., Mexico
Eagle, Philippine	*Pithecophaga jefferyi*	Philippines
Falcon, American peregrine	*Falco peregrinus anatum*	U.S., Canada, Mexico, South America
Ostrich, Arabian	*Struthio camelus syriacus*	Jordan, Saudi Arabia
Parrot, red-browed	*Amazona rhodocorytha*	Brazil
Pelican, brown	*Pelecanus occidentalis*	U.S., Central and South America, Caribbean
Plover, piping	*Charadrius melodus*	U.S., Canada, Mexico, Caribbean
Stork, Oriental white	*Ciconia ciconia boyciana*	China, Japan, Korea, Russia
Woodpecker, ivory-billed	*Campephilus principalis*	Cuba, U.S.
REPTILES		
Crocodile, American	*Crocodylus acutus*	U.S., Mexico, Caribbean, Central and South America
Gecko, Day	*Phelsuma edwardnewtoni*	Mauritius
Iguana, Allen's Cay	*Cyclura cychlura inornata*	Bahamas
Python, Indian	*Python molurus molurus*	India, Sri Lanka
Snake, San Francisco garter	*Thamnophis sirtalis tetrataenia*	U.S. (California)
Tortoise, Galapagos	*Geochelone elephantopus*	Ecuador (Galapagos Islands)
Turtle, aquatic box	*Terrapene coahuila*	Mexico
AMPHIBIANS		
Frog, Israel Painted	*Discoglossus nigriventer*	Israel
Salamander, Texas blind	*Typhlomolge rathbuni*	U.S. (Texas)
Toad, Puerto Rican crested	*Peltophryne lemur*	Puerto Rico, British Virgin Islands
FISHES		
Catfish, giant	*Pangasianodon gigas*	Thailand
Salmon, Sockeye	*Oncorhynchus nerka*	Pacific North Basin
Trout, Gila	*Oncorhynchus gilae*	U.S. (Arizona, New Mexico)

U.S. Zoos and Aquariums

Source: The facilities listed are members of, and accredited by, the American Zoo and Aquarium Association (AZA) to ensure that they are maintaining professional standards. It also accredits facilities outside of the United States.

Abilene Zoological Gardens, Texas
Akron Zoological Park, Ohio
Alameda Park Zoo, Alamogordo, N.M.
Albuquerque Biological Park, N.M.
Alexandria Zoological Park, La.
Aquarium for Wildlife Conservation, The, Brooklyn, N.Y.
Aquarium of the Americas, New Orleans, La.
Arizona-Sonora Desert Museum, Tucson
Audubon Park and Zoological Garden, New Orleans
John Ball Zoological Garden, Grand Rapids, Mich.
Baltimore Zoo, The, Md.
Beardsley Zoological Gardens, Bridgeport, Conn.
Belle Isle Zoo, Detroit
Bergen County Zoological Park, Paramus, N.J.
Binder Park Zoo, Battle Creek, Mich.
Birmingham Zoo, Ala.
Blank Park Zoo, Des Moines, Iowa
Bramble Park Zoo, Watertown, S.D.
Brandywine Zoo, Wilmington, Del.
Bronx Zoo/Wildlife Conservation Park, N.Y.
Brookfield Zoo, Ill.
Brookgreen Gardens, Murrells Inlet, S.C.
Buffalo Zoological Gardens, N.Y.
Burnet Park Zoo, Syracuse, N.Y.
Busch Gardens, Tampa, Fla.
Caldwell Zoo, Tyler, Texas
Cameron Park Zoo, Waco, Texas
Cape May County Park Zoo, Cape May Court House, N.J.
Central Florida Zoological Park, Lake Monroe, Fla.
Central Park Wildlife Center, New York, N.Y.
Chaffee Zoological Gardens of Fresno, Calif.

Chahinkapa Zoo, Wahpeton, N.D.
Cheyenne Mountain Zoological Park, Colorado Springs
Cincinnati Zoo and Botanical Garden, Ohio
Cleveland Metroparks Zoo, Ohio
Columbus Zoological Gardens, Ohio
Dakota Zoo, Bismarck, N.D.
Dallas Aquarium, Texas
Dallas Zoo, Texas
Denver Zoological Gardens, Colo.
Detroit Zoological Park, Mich.
Dickerson Park Zoo, Springfield, Mo.
Discovery Island Zoological Park, Lake Buena Vista, Fla.
Dreher Park Zoo, West Palm Beach, Fla.
El Paso Zoo, Texas
Emporia Zoo, Kan.
Erie Zoo, Pa.
Folsom Children's Zoo & Botanical Garden, Lincoln, Neb.
Fort Wayne Children's Zoo, Ind.
Fort Worth Zoological Park, Texas
Fossil Rim Wildlife Center, Glen Rose, Texas
Franklin Park Zoo, Boston, Mass.
Glen Oak Zoo, Peoria, Ill.
Grassmere Wildlife Park, Nashville, Tenn.
Great Plains Zoo & Musem, Sioux Falls, S.D.
Greater Baton Rouge Zoo, La.
Greenville Zoo, S.C.
Happy Hollow Zoo, San Jose, Calif.
Honolulu Zoo, Hawaii
Houston Zoological Gardens, Texas
Indianapolis Zoo, Ind.

International Crane Foundation, Baraboo, Wis.
Jackson Zoological Park, Miss.
Jacksonville Zoological Park, Fla.
Kansas City Zoological Gardens, Mo.
Knoxville Zoological Gardens, Tenn.
Lake Superior Zoological Gardens, Duluth, Minn.
Lincoln Park Zoological Gardens, Chicago
Little Rock Zoological Garden, Ark.
Living Desert, The, Palm Desert, Calif.
Living Seas, The, Lake Buena Vista, Fla.
Los Angeles Zoo, Calif.
Louisville Zoological Garden, Ky.
Lowry Park Zoological Garden, Tampa, Fla.
Marine World Africa USA, Vallejo, Calif.
Memphis Zoological Garden and Aquarium, Tenn.
Mesker Park Zoo, Evansville, Ind.
Metro Washington Park Zoo, Portland, Ore.
Miami Metrozoo, Fla.
Micke Grove Zoo, Lodi, Calif.
Miller Park Zoo, Bloomington, Ill.
Mill Mountain Zoo, Roanoke, Va.
Milwaukee County Zoological Gardens, Wis.
Minnesota Zoological Garden, Apple Valley, Minn.
Monterey Bay Aquarium, Calif.
Montgomery Zoo, Ala.
Mystic Marinelife Aquarium, Mystic, Conn.
National Aquarium in Baltimore, Md.
National Aviary in Pittsburgh, Pa.
National Zoological Park, Washington, D.C.
New England Aquarium, Boston
New Jersey State Aquarium at Camden
North Carolina Aquarium at Fort Fisher, Kure Beach
North Carolina Aquarium at Pine Knoll Shores, Atlantic Beach
North Carolina Aquarium on Roanoke Island, Manteo
North Carolina Zoological Park, Asheboro
North Eastern Wisconsin Zoo, Green Bay, Wis.
Northwest Trek Wildlife Park, Eatonville, Wash.
Oakland Zoo, The Calif.
Oglebay's Good Children's Zoo, Wheeling, W.Va.
Oklahoma City Zoological Park, Okla.
Omaha's Henry Doorly Zoo, Neb.
Charles Paddock Zoo, Atascadero, Calif.
Parrot Jungle and Gardens, Miami, Fla.
Clyde Peeling's Reptiland Ltd., Allenwood, Pa.
Philadelphia Zoological Garden, Pa.
Phoenix Zoo, The Ariz.
Pittsburgh Zoo, Pa.
Point Defiance Zoo and Aquarium, Tacoma, Wash.
Gladys Porter Zoo, Brownsville, Texas
Potawatomi Zoo, South Bend, Ind.
Potter Park Zoological Gardens, Lansing, Mich.
Prospect Park Wildlife Center, Brooklyn, N.Y.
Pueblo Zoo, Colo.
Queens Wildlife Center, Flushing, N.Y.

Racine Zoological Gardens, Wis.
Reid Park Zoo, Tucson, Ariz.
Lee Richardson Zoo, Garden City, Kan.
Riverbanks Zoological Park and Botanical Garden, Columbia, S.C.
Riverside Zoo, Scottsbluff, Neb.
Henson Robinson Zoo, Springfield, Ill.
Roosevelt Zoo, Minot, N.D.
Ross Park Zoo, Binghamton, N.Y.
Sacramento Zoo, Calif.
St. Augustine Alligator Farm, Fla.
St. Louis Zoological Park, Mo.
St. Paul's Como Zoo, Minn.
Salisbury Zoological Park, Md.
San Antonio Zoological Gardens and Aquarium, Texas
San Diego Wild Animal Park, Calif.
San Diego Zoo, Calif.
San Francisco Zoological Gardens, Calif.
Santa Ana Zoo, Calif.
Santa Barbara Zoological Gardens, Calif.
Sea Life Park Hawaii, Waimanalo
Sea World of California, San Diego
Sea World of Florida, Orlando
Sea World of Ohio, Aurora
Sea World of Texas, San Antonio
Seattle Aquarium, The Wash.
Sedgwick County Zoo, Wichita, Kan.
Seneca Park Zoo, Rochester, N.Y.
Sequoia Park Zoo, Eureka, Calif.
John G. Shedd Aquarium, Chicago
Staten Island Zoo, N.Y.
Steinhart Aquarium, San Francisco, Calif.
Sunset Zoological Park, Manhattan, Kan.
Tennessee Aquarium, Chattanooga, Tenn.
Texas State Aquarium, Corpus Christi
Texas Zoo, The Victoria, Texas
Toledo Zoological Gardens, Ohio
Topeka Zoological Park, Kan.
Tracy Aviary, Salt Lake City, Utah
Trevor Zoo, Millbrook, N.Y.
Ellen Trout Zoo, Lufkin, Texas
Tulsa Zoo and Living Museum, Okla.
Utah's Hogle Zoo, Salt Lake City
Utica Zoo, N.Y.
Henry Vilas Zoo, Madison, Wis.
Virginia Zoological Park, Norfolk, Va.
Waikiki Aquarium, Hawaii
Wildlife Safari, Winston, Ore.
Wildlife World Zoo, Litchfield Park, Ariz.
The Wilds, Cumberland, Ohio
Roger Williams Park Zoo, Providence, R.I.
Woodland Park Zoological Gardens, Seattle
The ZOO, Gulf Breeze, Fla.
Zoo Atlanta, Ga.
ZOOAMERICA North American Wildlife Park, Hershey, Pa.

Animal Names: Male, Female, and Young

Animal	Male	Female	Young	Animal	Male	Female	Young	Animal	Male	Female	Young
Ass	Jack	Jenny	Foal	Duck	Drake	Duck	Duckling	Sheep	Ram	Ewe	Lamb
Bear	Boar	Sow	Cub	Elephant	Bull	Cow	Calf	Swan	Cob	Pen	Cygnet
Cat	Tom	Queen	Kitten	Fox	Dog	Vixen	Cub	Swine	Boar	Sow	Piglet
Cattle	Bull	Cow	Calf	Goose	Gander	Goose	Gosling	Tiger	Tiger	Tigress	Cub
Chicken	Rooster	Hen	Chick	Horse	Stallion	Mare	Foal	Whale	Bull	Cow	Calf
Deer	Buck	Doe	Fawn	Lion	Lion	Lioness	Cub	Wolf	Dog	Bitch	Pup
Dog	Dog	Bitch	Pup	Rabbit	Buck	Doe	Bunny				

Source: James G. Doherty, General Curator, The Wildlife Conservation Society.

Gestation, Incubation, and Longevity of Certain Animals

Animal	Gestation or incubation, in days & (average)	Longevity, in years (& record exceptions)	Animal	Gestation or incubation, in days & (average)	Longevity, in years (& record exceptions)
Ass	365	18–20 (63)	Horse	329–345 (336)	20–25 (50+)
Bear	180–240[1]	15–30 (47)	Kangaroo	32–39[1]	4–6 (23)
Cat	52–69 (63)	10–12 (26+)	Lion	105–113 (108)	10 (29)
Chicken	22	7–8 (14)	Man	253–303	(2)
Cow	c. 280	9–12 (39)	Monkey	139–270[1]	12–15[1](29)
Deer	197–300[1]	10–15 (26)	Mouse	19–31[1]	1–3 (4)
Dog	53–71 (63)	10–12 (24)	Parakeet (Budgerigar)	17–20 (18)	8 (12+)
Duck	21–35[1](28)	10 (15)	Pig	101–130 (115)	10 (22)
Elephant	510–730 (624)[1]	30–40 (71)	Pigeon	11–19	10–12 (39)
Fox	51–63[1]	8–10 (14)	Rabbit	30–35 (31)	6–8 (15)
Goat	136–160 (151)	12 (17)	Rat	21	3 (5)
Groundhog	31–32	4–9	Sheep	144–152 (151)[1]	12 (16)
Guinea pig	58–75 (68)	3 (6)	Squirrel	44	8–9 (15)
Hamster, golden	15–17	2 (8)	Whale	365–547[1]	
Hippopotamus	220–255 (240)	30 (49+)	Wolf	60–63	10–12 (16)

1. Depending on kind. 2. For life expectancy charts, see Index. *Source:* James G. Doherty, General Curator, The Wildlife Conservation Society.

Animal Group Terminology

Source: James G. Doherty, General Curator, The Wildlife Conservation Society and *Information Please* data.

ants: colony
bears: sleuth, sloth
bees: grist, hive, swarm
birds: flight, volery
cattle: drove
cats: clutter, clowder
chicks: brood, clutch
clams: bed
cranes: sedge, seige
crows: murder
doves: dule
ducks: brace, team
elephants: herd
elks: gang
finches: charm
fish: school, shoal, draught
foxes: leash, skulk
geese: flock, gaggle, skein
gnats: cloud, horde
goats: trip

gorillas: band
hares: down, husk
hawks: cast
hens: brood
hogs: drift
horses: pair, team
hounds: cry, mute, pack
kangaroos: troop
kittens: kindle, litter
larks: exaltation
lions: pride
locusts: plague
magpies: tidings
mules: span
nightingales: watch
oxen: yoke
oysters: bed
parrots: company
partridges: covey

peacocks: muster, ostentation
pheasants: nest, bouquet
pigs: litter
ponies: string
quail: bevy, covey
rabbits: nest
seals: pod
sheep: drove, flock
sparrows: host
storks: mustering
swans: bevy, wedge
swine: sounder
toads: knot
turkeys: rafter
turtles: bale
vipers: nest
whales: gam, pod
wolves: pack, route
woodcocks: fall

Speed of Animals

Most of the following measurements are for maximum speeds over approximate quarter–mile distances. Exceptions—which are included to give a wide range of animals—are the lion and elephant, whose speeds were clocked in the act of charging; the whippet, which was timed over a 200–yard course; the cheetah over a 100–yard distance; man for a 15–yard segment of a 100–yard run; and the black mamba, six–lined race runner, spider, giant tortoise, three–toed sloth, and garden snail, which were measured over various small distances.

Animal	Speed mph	Animal	Speed mph	Animal	Speed mph
Cheetah	70	Zebra	40	Man	27.89
Pronghorn antelope	61	Mongolian wild ass	40	Elephant	25
Wildebeest	50	Greyhound	39.35	Black mamba snake	20
Lion	50	Rabbit (domestic)	35	Six–lined race runner	18
Thomson's gazelle	50	Mule deer	35	Squirrel	12
Quarter horse	47.5	Reindeer	32	Pig (domestic)	11
Elk	45	Giraffe	32	Chicken	9
Cape hunting dog	45	White–tailed deer	30	Spider (Tegenearia atrica)	1.17
Coyote	43	Wart hog	30	Giant Tortoise	0.17
Gray fox	42	Grizzly bear	30	Three–toed sloth	0.15
Hyena	40	Cat (domestic)	30	Garden snail	0.03

Source: Natural History Magazine, March 1974, copyright 1974. The American Museum of Natural History; and James G. Doherty, General Curator, The Wildlife Conservation Society.

Major Air Pollutants

Pollutant	Sources	Effects
Ozone. A colorless gas that is the major constituent of photochemical smog at the Earth's surface. In the upper atmosphere (stratosphere), however, ozone is beneficial, protecting us from the sun's harmful rays.	Ozone is formed in the lower atmosphere as a result of chemical reactions between oxygen, volatile organic compounds, and nitrogen oxides in the presence of sunlight, especially during hot weather. Sources of such harmful pollutants include vehicles, factories, landfills, industrial solvents, and numerous small sources such as gas stations, farm and lawn equipment.	Ozone causes significant health and environmental problems at the Earth's surface. It can irritate the respiratory tract, produce impaired lung function and cause throat irritation, chest pain, cough, and lung inflammation. It can also reduce yield of agricultural crops and injure forests and other vegetation. Ozone is the most injurious pollutant to plant life.
Carbon Monoxide. Odorless and colorless gas emitted in the exhaust of motor vehicles and other kinds of engines where there is incomplete fossil fuel combustion.	Automobiles, buses, trucks, small engines, and some industrial processes. High concentrations can be found in confined spaces like parking garages, poorly ventilated tunnels, or along roadsides during periods of heavy traffic.	Reduces the ability of blood to deliver oxygen to vital tissues, affecting primarily the cardiovascular and nervous systems. Lower concentrations have been shown to adversely affect individuals with heart disease; higher concentrations can cause dizziness, headaches, and fatigue.
Nitrogen Dioxide. Light brown gas at lower concentrations; in higher concentrations becomes an important component of unpleasant-looking brown, urban haze.	Result of burning fuels in utilities, industrial boilers, cars, and trucks.	One of the major pollutants that causes smog and acid rain. Can harm humans and vegetation when concentrations are sufficiently high.
Particulate Matter. Solid matter or liquid droplets from smoke, dust, fly ash and condensing vapors that can be suspended in the air for long periods of time.	Industrial processes, smelters, automobiles, burning industrial fuels, woodsmoke, dust from paved and unpaved roads, construction, and agricultural ground breaking.	These microscopic particles can affect breathing and respiratory symptoms, causing increased respiratory disease and lung damage, and possibly premature death.
Sulfur Dioxide. Colorless gas, odorless at low concentrations but pungent at very high concentrations.	Emitted largely from industrial, institutional, utility and apartment-house furnaces and boilers, as well as petroleum refineries, smelters, paper mills, and chemical plants.	One of the major pollutants that causes smog. Can also, at high concentrations, affect human health, especially among asthmatics, and acidify lakes and streams.
Lead. Lead and lead compounds can adversely affect human health through either ingestion of lead-contaminated soil, dust, paint, or direct inhalation.	Transportation sources using lead in their fuels, coal combustion, smelters, car battery plants, and combustion of garbage containing lead products.	Elevated lead levels can adversely affect mental development, kidney function, and blood chemistry. Young children are particularly at risk.
Toxic Air Pollutants. Includes pollutants such as arsenic, asbestos, and benzenes.	Chemical plants, industrial processes, motor vehicle emissions and fuels, and building materials.	Known or suspected to cause cancer, respiratory effects, birth defects, and reproductive and other serious health effects.
Stratospheric Ozone Depleters. Chemicals such as chlorofluorocarbons (CFCs), halons, carbon tetrachloride, and methyl chloroform. These chemicals rise to the upper atmosphere where they destroy the protective ozone layer.	Industrial household refrigeration, cooling and cleaning processes, car and home air conditioners, some fire extinguishers, and plastic foam products.	Increased exposure to UV radiation could potentially cause an increase in skin cancer, increased cataract cases, suppression of the human immune response system, and environmental damage.
Greenhouse gases. Gases that build up in the atmosphere that may induce global climate change or the "greenhouse effect." They include carbon dioxide, methane, and nitrous oxide.	The main man-made source of carbon dioxide emissions is fossil fuel combustion for energy-use and transportation. Methane comes from landfills, cud-chewing livestock, coal mines, and rice paddies. Nitrous oxide results from industrial processes, such as nylon fabrication.	The extent of the effects of climate change on human health and the environment is still uncertain, but could include increased global temperature, increased severity and frequency of storms and other "weather extremes," melting of the polar ice cap, and sea-level rise.

Source: Environmental Protection Agency, EPA 450-K-92-002, October 1992.

The National Park System

Source: Department of the Interior, National Park Service.

The National Park System of the United States is administered by the National Park Service, a bureau of the Department of the Interior. Started with the establishment of Yellowstone National Park in 1872, the system includes not only the most extraordinary and spectacular scenic exhibits in the United States but also a large number of sites distinguished either for their historic or prehistoric importance or scientific interest, or for their superior recreational assets. The number and extent of the various types of areas that make up the system follow.

Type of area	Number	Total acreage[1]	Type of area	Number	Total acreage[1]
International Historic Site	1	35.39	National Parkways	4	170,706.51
National Battlefields	11	13,098.41	National Preserves	15	23,689,219.85
National Battlefield Parks	3	8,727.27	National Recreation Areas	18	3,700,629.20
National Battlefield Site	1	1.00	National Reserves	2	33,407.19
National Historic Sites	72	23,111.03	National Rivers[2]	6	416,018.22
National Historical Parks	37	161,976.48	National Scenic Trails	3	184,234.65
National Lakeshores	4	228,847.52	National Seashores	10	592,627.65
National Memorials	26	8,049.24	National Wild and Scenic		
National Military Parks	9	38,016.36	Rivers and Parkways[3]	9	219,377.93
National Monuments	73	2,064,444.67	Without Designation[4]	18	38,945.07
National Parks	54	51,711,507.00	**Total**	**369**	**83,302,980.64**

1. Acreages as of December 31, 1994. 2. National Park System units only. 3. National Park System units and components of the Wild and Scenic Rivers system. 4. Includes White House, National Mall, and other areas.

National Parks

Name, location, and year authorized	Acreage	Outstanding characteristics
Acadia (Maine), 1919	41,951.06	Rugged seashore on Mt. Desert Island and adjacent mainland
Arches (Utah), 1971	73,373.98	Unusual stone arches, windows, pedestals caused by erosion
Badlands (S.D.), 1978	242,755.94	Arid land of fossils, prairie, bison, deer, bighorn, antelope
Big Bend (Tex.), 1935	801,163.02	Mountains and desert bordering the Rio Grande
Biscayne (Fla.), 1980	172,924.73	Aquatic, coral reef park south of Miami was a national monument, 1968–80
Bryce Canyon (Utah), 1924	35,835.08	Area of grotesque eroded rocks brilliantly colored
Canyonlands (Utah), 1964	337,570.43	Colorful wilderness with impressive red-rock canyons, spires, arches
Capitol Reef (Utah), 1971	241,904.26	Highly colored sedimentary rock formations in high, narrow gorges
Carlsbad Caverns (N.M.), 1930	46,766.45	The world's largest known caves
Channel Islands (Calif.) 1980	249,353.77	Area is rich in marine mammals, sea birds, endangered species and archeology
Crater Lake (Ore.), 1902	183,223.77	Deep blue lake in heart of inactive volcano
Death Valley (Calif.–Nev.), 1994	3,367,627.68	Large desert, surrounded by high mountains, containing the lowest point in the Western hemisphere.
Denali (Alaska), 1917	4,741,910.00	Mt. McKinley National Park was renamed and enlarged by Act of Dec. 2, 1980. Contains Mt. McKinley, N. America's highest mountain (20,320 ft)
Dry Tortugas (Fla.), 1992	64,700.00	Formerly Ft. Jefferson National Monument. Located 70 miles off Key West. Features an underwater nature trail.
Everglades (Fla.), 1934	1,506,499.40	Subtropical area with abundant bird and animal life
Gates of the Arctic (Alaska), 1980	7,523,888.00	Diverse north central wilderness contains part of Brooks Range
Glacier Bay (Alaska), 1980	3,225,284.00	Park was a national monument (1925–1980) popular for wildlife, whale-watching, glacier-calving, and scenery
Glacier (Mont.), 1910	1,013,572.42	Rocky Mountain scenery with many glaciers and lakes
Grand Canyon (Ariz.), 1919	1,217,159.32	Mile-deep gorge, 4 to 18 miles wide, 217 miles long
Grand Teton (Wyo.), 1929	309,974.28	Picturesque range of high mountain peaks
Great Basin (Nev.), 1986	77,180.00	Exceptional scenic, biologic, and geologic attractions
Great Smoky Mts. (N.C.-Tenn), 1926	520,269.44	Highest mountain range east of Black Hills; luxuriant plant life
Guadalupe Mountains (Tex.), 1966	86,415.97	Contains highest point in Texas: Guadalupe Peak (8,751 ft)
Haleakala (Hawaii), 1960	28,099.00	World-famous 10,023-ft. Haleakala volcano (dormant)
Hawaii Volcanoes (Hawaii), 1916	229,177.03	Spectacular volcanic area; luxuriant vegetation at lower levels
Hot Springs (Ark.), 1921	5,839.24	47 mineral hot springs said to have therapeutic value
Isle Royale (Mich.), 1931	571,790.11	Largest wilderness island in Lake Superior; moose, wolves, lakes
Joshua Tree (Calif.), 1936	794,000.00	Desert region featuring Joshua trees and a great variety of plants and animals.

Name, location, and year authorized	Acreage	Outstanding characteristics
Katmai (Alaska), 1980	3,586,000.00	Expansion may assure brown bear's preservation. Park was national monument 1918–80; is known for fishing, 1912 eruption, bears
Kenai Fjords (Alaska), 1980	689,541.00	Mountain goats, marine mammals, birdlife are features at this seacoast park near Seward
Kings Canyon (Calif.), 1940	461,901.20	Huge canyons; high mountains; giant sequoias
Kobuk Valley (Alaska), 1980	1,750,736.86	Native culture and anthropology center around the broad Kobuk River in northwest Alaska
Lake Clark (Alaska), 1980	2,636,839.00	Park provides scenic and wilderness recreation across Cook Inlet from Anchorage
Lassen Volcanic (Calif.), 1916	106,372.36	Exhibits of impressive volcanic phenomena
Mammoth Cave (Ky.), 1926	52,823.97	Vast limestone labyrinth with underground river
Mesa Verde (Colo.), 1906	52,121.93	Best-preserved prehistoric cliff dwellings in United States
Mount Rainier (Wash.), 1899	235,612.50	Single-peak glacial system; dense forests, flowered meadows
National Park of American Samoa	9,000.00	Samoa National Park, American Samoa: two rain forest preserves and a coral reef on the island of Ofu are home to unique tropical animals. The park also includes several thousand acres on the islands of Tutuila and Ta'u.
North Cascades (Wash.), 1968	504,780.94	Roadless Alpine landscape; jagged peaks; mountain lakes; glaciers
Olympic (Wash.), 1938	922,651.01	Finest Pacific Northwest rain forest; scenic mountain park
Petrified Forest (Ariz.), 1962	93,532.57	Extensive natural exhibit of petrified wood
Redwood (Calif.), 1968	110,232.40	Coastal redwood forests; contains world's tallest known tree (369.2 ft)
Rocky Mountain (Colo.), 1915	265,727.15	Section of the Rocky Mountains; 107 named peaks over 10,000 ft
Saguaro (Ariz.), 1994	91,116.04	Giant saguaro cacti, unique to the Sonoran Desert, sometimes reach a height of 50 ft in this cactus forest.
Sequoia (Calif.), 1890	402,482.38	Giant sequoias; magnificent High Sierra scenery, including Mt. Whitney
Shenandoah (Va.), 1926	196,466.19	Tree-covered mountains; scenic Skyline Drive
Theodore Roosevelt (N.D.), 1978	70,446.59	Scenic valley of Little Missouri River; T.R. Ranch; Wildlife
Virgin Islands (U.S. V.I.), 1956	14,688.87	Beaches; lush hills; prehistoric Carib Indian relics
Voyageurs (Minn.), 1971	218,035.33	Wildlife, canoeing, fishing, and hiking
Wind Cave (S.D.), 1903	28,295.03	Limestone caverns in Black Hills; buffalo herd
Wrangell-St. Elias (Alaska), 1980	7,730,645.18	Largest Park System area has abundant wildlife, second highest peak in U.S. (Mt. St. Elias); adjoins Canadian park
Yellowstone (Wyo.-Mont.-Idaho), 1872	2,219,790.71	World's greatest geyser area; abundant falls, wildlife, and canyons
Yosemite (Calif.), 1890	761,236.20	Mountains; inspiring gorges and waterfalls; giant sequoias
Zion (Utah), 1919	146,597.64	Multicolored gorge in heart of southern Utah desert

NATIONAL HISTORICAL PARKS

Name and location	Total acreage
Appomattox Court House (Va.)	1,325.08
Boston (Mass.)	41.03
Chaco Culture (N.M.)	33,974.29
Chesapeake and Ohio Canal (Md.-W.Va.-D.C.)	19,236.60
Colonial (Va.)	9,327.37
Cumberland Gap (Ky.-Tenn.-Va.)	20,445.81
Dayton Aviation Heritage, (Oh.)	.00
George Rogers Clark (Ind.)	26.17
Harpers Ferry (W.Va.-Md.)	2,287.48
Hopewell Culture (Oh.)	1,032.20
Independence (Pa.)	44.85
Jean Lafitte (La.)	20,020.00
Kalaupapa (Hawaii)	10,778.88
Kaloko-Honokohau (Hawaii)	1,160.91
Keewenaw (Mich.)	.00
Klondike Goldrush (Alaska, Wash.)	13,191.35
Lowell (Mass.)	136.86
Lyndon B. Johnson (Tex.)	1,571.93
Marsh–Billings (Vt.)	643.10
Minute Man (Mass.)	789.53
Morristown (N.J.)	1,683.61
Natchez (Miss.)	108.29
Nez Perce (Idaho)	2,109.61

Name and location	Total acreage
Pecos (N.M.)	6,570.54
Púuchonua o Honaunau (Hawaii)	181.80
Salt River Bay (U.S. V.I.)	912.00
San Antonio Missions (Tex.)	820.01
San Franisco Maritime (Calif.)	50.00
San Juan Island (Wash.)	1,751.99
Saratoga (N.Y.)	3,392.82
Sitka (Alaska)	106.83
Tumacacori (Ariz.)	46.52
Valley Forge (Pa.)	3,468.06
War in the Pacific (Guam)	1,960.07
Women's Rights (N.Y.)	5.73
Yorktown National Cemetery	2.91
Zuni-Cibola (N.M.)	800.00

NATIONAL MONUMENTS

Agate Fossil Beds (Neb.)	3,055.22
Alibates Flint Quarries (Tex.)	1,370.97
Aniakchak (Alaska)	137,176.00
Aztec Ruins (N.M.)	319.47
Bandelier (N.M.)	32,737.20
Black Canyon (Colo.)	20,766.14
Booker T. Washington (Va.)	223.92
Buck Island Reef (U.S. V.I.)	880.00

Name and location	Total acreage
Cabrillo (Calif.)	137.06
Canyon de Chelly (Ariz.)	83,840.00
Cape Krusenstern (Alaska)	659,807.00
Capulin Volcano (N.M.)	792.84
Casa Grande (Ariz.)	472.50
Castillo de San Marcos (Fla.)	20.51
Castle Clinton (N.Y.)	1.00
Cedar Breaks (Utah)	6,154.60
Chiricahua (Ariz.)	11,984.80
Colorado (Colo.)	20,453.93
Congaree Swamp (S.C.)	22,200.00
Craters of the Moon (Idaho)	53,545.05
Devils Postpile (Calif.)	798.46
Devils Tower (Wyo.)	1,346.91
Dinosaur (Utah-Colo.)	210,844.02
Effigy Mounds (Iowa)	1,481.39
El Malpais (N.M.)	114,272.09
El Morro (N.M.)	1,278.72
Florissant Fossil Beds (Colo.)	5,998.09
Fort Frederica (Ga.)	216.35
Fort Matanzas (Fla.)	227.76
Fort McHenry (Md.)	43.26
Fort Pulaski (Ga.)	5,623.10
Fort Stanwix (N.Y.)	15.52
Fort Sumter (S.C.)	194.60
Fort Union (N.M.)	720.60
Fossil Butte (Wyo.)	8,198.00
George Washington Birthplace (Va.)	550.23
George Washington Carver (Mo.)	210.00
Gila Cliff Dwellings (N.M.)	533.13
Grand Portage (Minn.)	709.97
Great Sand Dunes (Colo.)	38,662.18
Hagerman Fossil Beds (Idaho)	4,280.00
Hohokam Pima (Ariz.)	1,690.00
Homestead (Neb.)	195.11
Hovenweep (Utah-Colo.)	784.93
Jewel Cave (S.D.)	1,273.51
John Day Fossil Beds (Ore.)	14,014.10
Lava Beds (Calif.)	46,559.87
Little Big Horn Battlefield (Mont.)	765.34
Montezuma Castle (Ariz.)	857.69
Muir Woods (Calif.)	553.55
Natural Bridges (Utah)	7,636.49
Navajo (Ariz.)	360.00
Ocmulgee (Ga.)	701.54
Oregon Caves (Ore.)	487.98
Organ Pipe Cactus (Ariz.)	330,688.86
Petroglyph (N.M.)	5,195.34
Pinnacles (Calif.)	16,265.44
Pipe Spring (Ariz.)	40.00
Pipestone (Minn.)	281.78
Poverty Point (La.)	910.85
Rainbow Bridge (Utah)	160.00
Russell Cave (Ala.)	310.45
Salinas (N.M.)	1,100.64
Scotts Bluff (Neb.)	3,003.03
Statue of Liberty (N.Y.-N.J.)	58.38
Sunset Crater (Ariz.)	3,040.00
Timpanogos Cave (Utah)	250.00
Tonto (Ariz.)	1,120.00
Tuzigoot (Ariz.)	800.62
Walnut Canyon (Ariz.)	2,249.46
White Sands (N.M.)	143,732.92
Wupatki (Ariz.)	35,253.24
Yucca House (Colo.)	9.60

NATIONAL PRESERVES

Aniakchak (Alaska)	465,603.00
Bering Land Bridge (Alaska)	2,784,960.00
Big Cypress (Fla.)	716,000.00
Big Thicket (Tex.)	85,797.20
Denali (Alaska)	1,334,618.00

Name and location	Total acreage
Gates of the Arctic (Alaska)	948,629.00
Glacier Bay (Alaska)	57,884.00
Katmai (Alaska)	374,000.00
Lake Clark (Alaska)	1,407,293.00
Little River Canyon	.00
Mojave (Calif.)	1,450,000.00
Noatak (Alaska)	6,574,481.00
Timucuan Ecological and Historic Preserve (Fla.)	46,000.00
Wrangell-St. Elias (Alaska)	4,733,061.09
Yukon-Charley (Alaska)	2,523,509.00

NATIONAL RESERVE

City of Rocks (Idaho)	14.407.19
Ebey's Landing (Wash.)	17,400.00

NATIONAL MILITARY PARKS

Chickamauga and Chattanooga (Ga.-Tenn.)	8,106.04
Fredericksburg and Spotsylvania (Va.)	7,780.73
Fredericksburg National Cemetery	12.00
Gettysburg Nat. Mil. Park (Pa.)	5,875.27
Gettysburg Nat. Cemetery (Pa.)	20.58
Guilford Courthouse (N.C.)	220.25
Horseshoe Bend (Ala.)	2,040.00
Kings Mountain (S.C.)	3,945.29
Pea Ridge (Ark.)	4,300.35
Shiloh Nat. Cemetery (Tenn.)	10.05
Shiloh Nat. Mil. Park (Tenn.)	3,962.82
Vicksburg Nat. Cemetery (Miss.)	116.28
Vicksburg Nat. Mil. Park (Miss.)	1,625.27

NATIONAL BATTLEFIELDS

Antietam (Md.)	3,244.37
Big Hole (Mont.)	655.61
Cowpens (S.C.)	841.56
Fort Donelson (Tenn.)	536.35
Fort Necessity (Pa.)	902.80
Monocacy (Md.)	1,647.01
Moores Creek (N.C.)	86.52
Petersburg (Va.)	2,735.38
Stones River (Tenn.)	719.81
Tupelo (Miss.)	1.00
Wilson's Creek (Mo.)	1,749.00

NATIONAL BATTLEFIELD PARKS

Kennesaw Mountain (Ga.)	2,884.52
Manassas (Va.)	5,071.62
Richmond (Va.)	771.51

NATIONAL BATTLEFIELD SITE

Brices Cross Roads (Miss.)	1.00

NATIONAL HISTORIC SITES

Abraham Lincoln Birthplace (Ky.)	116.50
Adams (Mass.)	9.82
Allegheny Portage Railroad (Pa.)	1,246.97
Andersonville (Ga.)	494.61
Andrew Johnson (Tenn.)	16.68
Bent's Old Fort (Colo.)	799.80
Boston African American (Mass.)	0.00
Brown v. Board of Education (Kans.)	1.85
Carl Sandburg Home (N.C.)	263.52
Charles Pinckney (S.C.)	28.45
Christiansted (V.I.)	27.15
Clara Barton (Md.)	8.59
Edgar Allan Poe (Pa.)	0.52
Edison (N.J.)	21.25
Eisenhower (Pa.)	690.46
Eleanor Roosevelt (N.Y.)	180.50
Eugene O'Neill (Calif.)	13.19

Name and location	Total acreage
Ford's Theatre (Lincoln Museum) (D.C.)	0.29
Fort Bowie (Ariz.)	1,000.00
Fort Davis (Tex.)	40.00
Fort Laramie (Wyo.)	832.85
Fort Larned (Kan.)	718.39
Fort Point (Calif.)	29.00
Fort Raleigh (N.C.)	512.93
Fort Scott (Kan.)	16.69
Fort Smith (Ark.-Okla.)	75.00
Fort Union Trading Post (N.D.-Mont.)	442.45
Fort Vancouver (Wash.)	208.89
Frederick Douglass Home (D.C.)	8.53
Frederick Law Olmsted (Mass.)	1.75
Friendship Hill (Pa.)	674.56
Golden Spike (Utah)	2,735.28
Grant-Kohrs Ranch (Mont.)	1,498.38
Hampton (Md.)	62.04
Harry S. Truman (Mo.)	1.41
Herbert Hoover (Iowa)	186.80
Home of F. D. Roosevelt (N.Y.)	290.34
Hopewell Furnace (Pa.)	848.06
Hubbell Trading Post (Ariz.)	160.09
James A. Garfield (Ohio)	7.82
Jimmy Carter (Ga.)	70.54
John F. Kennedy (Mass.)	0.09
John Muir (Calif.)	340.04
Knife River Indian Villages (N.D.)	1,758.35
Lincoln Home (Ill.)	12.24
Longfellow (Mass.)	1.98
Maggie L. Walker (Va.)	1.29
Manzanar National Historic Site (Calif.)	500.00
Martin Luther King, Jr. (Ga.)	23.18
Martin Van Buren (N.Y.)	39.58
Mary McLeod Bethune Council House National Historic Site (D.C.)	—
Ninety Six (S.C.)	989.14
Palo Alto Battlefield (Tex.)	3,357.42
Pennsylvania Avenue (D.C.)	0.00
Puukohola Heiau (Hawaii)	80.47
Sagamore Hill (N.Y.)	83.02
Saint-Gaudens (N.H.)	148.23
Saint Paul's Church (N.Y.)	6.13
Salem Maritime (Mass.)	9.02
San Juan (P.R.)	75.13
Saugus Iron Works (Mass.)	8.51
Springfield Armory (Mass.)	54.93
Steamtown (Pa.)	62.48
Theodore Roosevelt Birthplace (N.Y.)	0.11
Theodore Roosevelt Inaugural (N.Y.)	1.03
Thomas Stone (Md.)	328.25
Tuskegee Institute (Ala.)	57.62
Ulysses S. Grant (Mo.)	9.60
Vanderbilt Mansion (N.Y.)	211.65
Weir Farm (Conn.)	58.77
Whitman Mission (Wash.)	98.15
William Howard Taft (Ohio)	3.07

NATIONAL MEMORIALS

Arkansas Post (Ark.)	389.18
Arlington House, the Robert E. Lee Memorial (Va.)	27.91
Chamizal (Tex.)	54.90
Coronado (Ariz.)	4,750.22
De Soto (Fla.)	26.84
Federal Hall (N.Y.)	0.45
Fort Caroline (Fla.)	138.39
Fort Clatsop (Ore.)	125.20
General Grant (N.Y.)	0.76
Hamilton Grange (N.Y.)	0.11
Jefferson National Expansion Memorial (Mo.)	90.96
Johnstown Flood (Pa.)	164.12
Korean War Veterans (D.C.)	2.2
Lincoln Boyhood (Ind.)	199.65

Name and location	Total acreage
Lincoln Memorial (D.C.)	109.63
Lyndon Baines Johnson Memorial Grove on the Potomac (D.C.)	17.00
Mount Rushmore (S.D.)	1,278.45
Perry's Victory and International Peace Memorial (Ohio)	25.38
Roger Williams (R.I.)	4.56
Thaddeus Kosciuszko (Pa.)	0.02
Theodore Roosevelt Island (D.C.)	88.50
Thomas Jefferson Memorial (D.C.)	18.36
USS Arizona Memorial (Hawaii)	0.00
Vietnam Veterans Memorial (D.C.)	2.00
Washington Monument (D.C.)	106.01
Wright Brothers (N.C.)	431.40

NATIONAL CEMETERIES[1]

Antietam (Md.)	11.36
Battleground (D.C.)	1.03
Fort Donelson (Tenn.)	15.30
Poplar Grove (Va.)	8.72
Stones River (Tenn.)	719.81
Yorktown (Va.)	

1. The National Cemeteries are not independent areas of the National Park System; each is part of a military park, battlefield, etc., except Battleground. Their acreage is kept separately. Arlington National Cemetery is under the Department of the Army. *See* Index.

NATIONAL SEASHORES

Assateague Island (Md.-Va.)	39,636.75
Canaveral (Fla.)	57,661.69
Cape Cod (Mass.)	43,569.21
Cape Hatteras (N.C.)	30,319.43
Cape Lookout (N.C.)	28,243.36
Cumberland Island (Ga.)	36,415.09
Fire Island (N.Y.)	19,578.55
Gulf Islands (Fla.-Miss.)	135,624.51
Padre Island (Tex.)	130,434.27
Point Reyes (Calif.)	71,048.78

NATIONAL PARKWAYS

Blue Ridge (Va.-N.C.)	87,782.01
George Washington Memorial (Va.-Md.)	7,247.63
John D. Rockefeller, Jr., Memorial (Wyo.)	23,777.22
Natchez Trace (Miss.-Tenn.-Ala.)	51,739.93

NATIONAL LAKESHORES

Apostle Islands (Wis.)	69,371.89
Indiana Dunes (Ind.)	14,981.31
Pictured Rocks (Mich)	73,174.12
Sleeping Bear Dunes (Mich.)	71,189.15

NATIONAL WILD AND SCENIC RIVERS

Alagnak Wild River (Alaska)	24,038.00
Bluestone National Scenic River (W. Va.)	4,268.00
Delaware (N.Y.-N.J.-Pa.)	1,973.33
Great Egg Harbor River (N.J.)	n.a.
Missouri National Recreational River (Neb., S.D.)	n.a.
Obed Wild & Scenic River (Tenn.)	5,066.94
Rio Grande Wild & Scenic (Tex.)	9,600.00
St. Croix (Minn.-Wis.)	92,735.85
Upper Delaware (N.Y., N.J.-Pa.)	75,000.00

NATIONAL RIVERS

Big South Fork National River & Recreation Area (Ky.-Tenn.)	125,000.00
Buffalo (Ark.)	94,218.55
Mississippi National River & Recreation Area (Minn.)	53,775.00
New River Gorge (W.Va.)	62,143.69

Name and location	Total acreage
Niobrara/Missouri National Scenic Riverways (Neb.–S.D.)	n.a.
Ozark (Mo.)	80,790.04

OTHER PARKS

Catoctin Mountain (Md.)	5,770.22
Constitution Gardens, (D.C.)	52.00
Fort Washington Park (Md.)	341.00
Greenbelt (Md.)	1,175.99
National Capital Parks (D.C.)	c. 1000.00
National Mall (D.C.)	146.35
Piscataway (Md.)	4,262.52
Prince William Forest (Va.)	18,571.55
Rock Creek Park (D.C.)	1,754.3
White House (D.C.)	18.07
Wolf Trap Farm Park for the Performing Arts (Va.)	130.28

NATIONAL RECREATION AREAS

Amistad (Tex.)	58,500.00
Bighorn Canyon (Wyo.-Mont.)	120,296.22
Chattahoochee River (Ga.)	9,259.91
Chickasaw (Okla.)	9,930.95
Coulee Dam (Wash.)	100,390.31
Curecanti (Colo.)	42,114.47
Cuyahoga Valley (Ohio)	32,524.76
Delaware Water Gap (Pa.-N.J.)	67,204.92
Gateway (N.Y.-N.J.)	26,310.93
Gauley River (W. Va.)	10,300.00
Glen Canyon (Ariz.-Utah)	1,236,880.00
Golden Gate (Calif.)	73,179.90
Lake Chelan (Wash.)	61,886.98
Lake Mead (Ariz.-Nev.)	1,495,665.52
Lake Meredith (Tex.)	44,977.63
Ross Lake (Wash.)	117,574.59
Santa Monica Mountains (Calif.)	150,050.00
Whiskeytown-Shasta-Trinity (Calif.)	42,503.46

NATIONAL SCENIC TRAIL

Appalachian (Maine, N.H., Vt., Mass., Conn., N.Y., N.J., Pa., Md., W.Va., Va., N.C., Tenn., Ga.)	165,504.63
Natchez Trace (Ga.-Ala.-Tenn.)	10,995.00
Potomac Heritage (D.C.-Md.-Va.-Pa.)	0.00

INTERNATIONAL HISTORIC SITE

Saint Croix Island (Maine)	35.39

AFFILIATED AREAS

(National Historic Sites unless otherwise noted.)

Name and location	Total acreage
American Memorial Park (N. Mariana Is.)	0.00
Benjamin Franklin (Pa.)[1]	0.00
Blackstone River Valley National Heritage Corridor (Mass., R.I.)	0.00
Chicago Portage (Ill.)	91.20
Chimney Rock (Neb.)	83.36
David Berger (Ohio)[1]	0.00
Delaware and Lehigh Navigation Canal National Heritage Corridor (Pa.)	0.00
Father Marquette (Mich.)[1]	52.00
Gloria Dei Church (Pa.)	3.71
Green Springs Historic District (Va.)	5,490.59
Historic Camden (S.C.)	0.00
Ice Age Scenic Trail (Wis.)	0.00
Ice Age (Wis.)[2]	32,500.00
Iditarod National Historic Trail (Alaska)	0.00
Illinois and Michigan Canal National Heritage Corridor	0.00
International Peace Garden (N.D.)	2,330.30
Jamestown (Va.)	20.63
Lewis & Clark Natl. Historic Trail (Ill., Mo., Kan., Neb., Iowa, Idaho, S.D., N.D., Mont., Ore., Wash.)	39.11
Mary McLeod Bethune Council House (D.C.)	0.00
McLoughlin House (Ore.)	0.63
Mormon Pioneer Natl. Historic Trail (Ill., Iowa, Neb., Wyo., Utah)	0.00
North Country Nat'l Scenic Trail (N.Y., Pa., Ohio, Mich., Wis., Minn., N.D.)	0.00
Oregon Natl. Historic Trail (Mo., Kan., Neb., Wyo., Idaho, Ore., Wash.)	0.00
Overmountain Victory Trail (Mo. to Ore.)	0.00
Pinelands Natl. Reserve (N.J.)	0.00
Red Hill Patrick Henry (Va.)[1]	0.00
Roosevelt-Campobello International Park (Canada)	2,721.50
Santa Fe National Historic Trail (Mo. to N.M.)	0.00
Sewell-Belmont House National Historic Site (D.C.)	0.35
Touro Synagogue (R.I.)	0.23
Trail of Tears National Historic Trail (N.C. to Okla.)	0.00

1. National Memorial. 2. National Scientific Reserve.

Water Supply of the World[1]

The Antarctic Icecap is the largest supply of fresh water, nearly 2 percent of the world's total of fresh and salt water. As can be seen from the table below, the amount of water in our atmosphere is over ten times as large as the water in all the rivers taken together. The fresh water actually available for human use in lakes and rivers and the accessible ground water amounts to only about one third of one percent of the world's total water supply.

	Surface area (square miles)	Volume (cubic miles)	Percentage of total
Salt Water			
The oceans	139,500,000	317,000,000	97.2
Inland seas and saline lakes	270,000	25,000	0.008
Fresh Water			
Freshwater lakes	330,000	30,000	0.009
All rivers (average level)	—	300	0.0001
Antarctic Icecap	6,000,000	6,300,000	1.9
Arctic Icecap and glaciers	900,000	680,000	0.21
Water in the atmosphere	197,000,000	3,100	0.001
Ground water within half a mile from surface	—	1,000,000	0.31
Deep-lying ground water	—	1,000,000	0.31
Total (rounded)	—	**326,000,000**	**100.00**

1. All figures are estimated. *Source:* Department of the Interior, Geological Survey.

CALENDAR & HOLIDAYS

1997

JANUARY

S	M	T	W	T	F	S
			1	2	3	4
5	6	7	8	9	10	11
12	13	14	15	16	17	18
19	20	21	22	23	24	25
26	27	28	29	30	31	

1—New Year's Day
6—Epiphany
10—1st Day of Ramadan
20—Martin Luther
     King Jr. Day
     Observed

FEBRUARY

S	M	T	W	T	F	S
						1
2	3	4	5	6	7	8
9	10	11	12	13	14	15
16	17	18	19	20	21	22
23	24	25	26	27	28	

2—Groundhog Day
12—Lincoln's Birthday
12—Ash Wednesday
14—Valentine's Day
17—Washington's Birthday
     Observed

MARCH

S	M	T	W	T	F	S
						1
2	3	4	5	6	7	8
9	10	11	12	13	14	15
16	17	18	19	20	21	22
23	24	25	26	27	28	29
30	31					

17—St. Patrick's Day
23—Purim
23—Palm Sunday
28—Good Friday
30—Easter

APRIL

S	M	T	W	T	F	S
		1	2	3	4	5
6	7	8	9	10	11	12
13	14	15	16	17	18	19
20	21	22	23	24	25	26
27	28	29	30			

6—Daylight Savings
     Time begins
22—1st Day of Passover

MAY

S	M	T	W	T	F	S
				1	2	3
4	5	6	7	8	9	10
11	12	13	14	15	16	17
18	19	20	21	22	23	24
25	26	27	28	29	30	31

8—Ascension Day
11—Mother's Day
18—Pentecost
26—Memorial Day
     Observed

JUNE

S	M	T	W	T	F	S
1	2	3	4	5	6	7
8	9	10	11	12	13	14
15	16	17	18	19	20	21
22	23	24	25	26	27	28
29	30					

11—1st Day of
     Shavuot
14—Flag Day
15—Father's Day

JULY

S	M	T	W	T	F	S
		1	2	3	4	5
6	7	8	9	10	11	12
13	14	15	16	17	18	19
20	21	22	23	24	25	26
27	28	29	30	31		

1—Canada Day
4—Independence Day

AUGUST

S	M	T	W	T	F	S
					1	2
3	4	5	6	7	8	9
10	11	12	13	14	15	16
17	18	19	20	21	22	23
24	25	26	27	28	29	30
31						

SEPTEMBER

S	M	T	W	T	F	S
	1	2	3	4	5	6
7	8	9	10	11	12	13
14	15	16	17	18	19	20
21	22	23	24	25	26	27
28	29	30				

1—Labor day

OCTOBER

S	M	T	W	T	F	S
			1	2	3	4
5	6	7	8	9	10	11
12	13	14	15	16	17	18
19	20	21	22	23	24	25
26	27	28	29	30	31	

2—1st Day of Rosh
     Hashana
11—Yom Kippur
13—Columbus Day
     Observed
13—Thanksgiving Day
     (Canada)
26—Daylight Savings
     Time ends
31—Halloween

NOVEMBER

S	M	T	W	T	F	S
						1
2	3	4	5	6	7	8
9	10	11	12	13	14	15
16	17	18	19	20	21	22
23	24	25	26	27	28	29
30						

1—All Saints' Day
4—Election Day
11—Veterans' Day
27—Thanksgiving
30—1st Sunday of
     Advent

DECEMBER

S	M	T	W	T	F	S
	1	2	3	4	5	6
7	8	9	10	11	12	13
14	15	16	17	18	19	20
21	22	23	24	25	26	27
28	29	30	31			

24—1st Day of
     Hanukkah
25—Christmas

Seasons for the Northern Hemisphere, 1997

Eastern Standard Time

March 20, 8:55 a.m., sun enters sign of Aries;
     spring begins

June 21, 3:20 a.m., sun enters sign of Cancer;
     summer begins

Sept. 22, 6:56 p.m., sun enters sign of Libra;
     fall begins

Dec. 21, 3:07 p.m., sun enters sign of Capricorn;
     winter begins

1996

JANUARY
S	M	T	W	T	F	S
	1	2	3	4	5	6
7	8	9	10	11	12	13
14	15	16	17	18	19	20
21	22	23	24	25	26	27
28	29	30	31			

FEBRUARY
S	M	T	W	T	F	S
				1	2	3
4	5	6	7	8	9	10
11	12	13	14	15	16	17
18	19	20	21	22	23	24
25	26	27	28	29		

MARCH
S	M	T	W	T	F	S
					1	2
3	4	5	6	7	8	9
10	11	12	13	14	15	16
17	18	19	20	21	22	23
24	25	26	27	28	29	30
31						

APRIL
S	M	T	W	T	F	S
	1	2	3	4	5	6
7	8	9	10	11	12	13
14	15	16	17	18	19	20
21	22	23	24	25	26	27
28	29	30				

MAY
S	M	T	W	T	F	S
			1	2	3	4
5	6	7	8	9	10	11
12	13	14	15	16	17	18
19	20	21	22	23	24	25
26	27	28	29	30	31	

JUNE
S	M	T	W	T	F	S
						1
2	3	4	5	6	7	8
9	10	11	12	13	14	15
16	17	18	19	20	21	22
23	24	25	26	27	28	29
30						

JULY
S	M	T	W	T	F	S
	1	2	3	4	5	6
7	8	9	10	11	12	13
14	15	16	17	18	19	20
21	22	23	24	25	26	27
28	29	30	31			

AUGUST
S	M	T	W	T	F	S
				1	2	3
4	5	6	7	8	9	10
11	12	13	14	15	16	17
18	19	20	21	22	23	24
25	26	27	28	29	30	31

SEPTEMBER
S	M	T	W	T	F	S
1	2	3	4	5	6	7
8	9	10	11	12	13	14
15	16	17	18	19	20	21
22	23	24	25	26	27	28
29	30					

OCTOBER
S	M	T	W	T	F	S
		1	2	3	4	5
6	7	8	9	10	11	12
13	14	15	16	17	18	19
20	21	22	23	24	25	26
27	28	29	30	31		

NOVEMBER
S	M	T	W	T	F	S
					1	2
3	4	5	6	7	8	9
10	11	12	13	14	15	16
17	18	19	20	21	22	23
24	25	26	27	28	29	30

DECEMBER
S	M	T	W	T	F	S
1	2	3	4	5	6	7
8	9	10	11	12	13	14
15	16	17	18	19	20	21
22	23	24	25	26	27	28
29	30	31				

1998

JANUARY
S	M	T	W	T	F	S
				1	2	3
4	5	6	7	8	9	10
11	12	13	14	15	16	17
18	19	20	21	22	23	24
25	26	27	28	29	30	31

FEBRUARY
S	M	T	W	T	F	S
1	2	3	4	5	6	7
8	9	10	11	12	13	14
15	16	17	18	19	20	21
22	23	24	25	26	27	28

MARCH
S	M	T	W	T	F	S
1	2	3	4	5	6	7
8	9	10	11	12	13	14
15	16	17	18	19	20	21
22	23	24	25	26	27	28
29	30	31				

APRIL
S	M	T	W	T	F	S
			1	2	3	4
5	6	7	8	9	10	11
12	13	14	15	16	17	18
19	20	21	22	23	24	25
26	27	28	29	30		

MAY
S	M	T	W	T	F	S
					1	2
3	4	5	6	7	8	9
10	11	12	13	14	15	16
17	18	19	20	21	22	23
24	25	26	27	28	29	30
31						

JUNE
S	M	T	W	T	F	S
	1	2	3	4	5	6
7	8	9	10	11	12	13
14	15	16	17	18	19	20
21	22	23	24	25	26	27
28	29	30				

JULY
S	M	T	W	T	F	S
			1	2	3	4
5	6	7	8	9	10	11
12	13	14	15	16	17	18
19	20	21	22	23	24	25
26	27	28	29	30	31	

AUGUST
S	M	T	W	T	F	S
						1
2	3	4	5	6	7	8
9	10	11	12	13	14	15
16	17	18	19	20	21	22
23	24	25	26	27	28	29
30	31					

SEPTEMBER
S	M	T	W	T	F	S
		1	2	3	4	5
6	7	8	9	10	11	12
13	14	15	16	17	18	19
20	21	22	23	24	25	26
27	28	29	30			

OCTOBER
S	M	T	W	T	F	S
				1	2	3
4	5	6	7	8	9	10
11	12	13	14	15	16	17
18	19	20	21	22	23	24
25	26	27	28	29	30	31

NOVEMBER
S	M	T	W	T	F	S
1	2	3	4	5	6	7
8	9	10	11	12	13	14
15	16	17	18	19	20	21
22	23	24	25	26	27	28
29	30					

DECEMBER
S	M	T	W	T	F	S
		1	2	3	4	5
6	7	8	9	10	11	12
13	14	15	16	17	18	19
20	21	22	23	24	25	26
27	28	29	30	31		

Hindu Festival Dates, 1997
Source: Jantri 500, by Pal Singh Purewal.

Jan. 13	Makar Sankranti
Feb. 11	Vasant Panchami
March 7	Maha Shivaratri (fast)
March 24	Holi (last day)
April 8	Bikarami 2054 begins
April 8	Chetra Navratras begin
April 13	Vaisakhi (solar new year)
April 16	Ram Navmi
Aug. 18	Raksha Bandhan
Aug. 24	Sri Krishna Jyanti
Sept. 6	Ganesh Chaturthi
Sept. 16	Saradhas begin
Oct. 2	Asuj Navratras begin
Oct. 11	Dassehra
Oct. 19	Karva Chauth Vrat (fast)
Oct. 30	Diwali (Festival of Lights)

(For Sikh Festivals see page 589)

PERPETUAL CALENDAR

1800 ... 4	1844 .. 9	1888 .. 8	1932 . 13	1976 . 12	2020 . 11
1801 ... 5	1845 .. 4	1889 .. 3	1933 ... 1	1977 ... 7	2021 ... 6
1802 ... 6	1846 .. 5	1890 .. 4	1934 ... 2	1978 ... 1	2022 ... 7
1803 ... 7	1847 .. 6	1891 .. 5	1935 ... 3	1979 ... 2	2023 ... 1
1804 .. 8	1848 .. 14	1892 . 13	1936 . 11	1980 . 10	2024 ... 9
1805 ... 3	1849 .. 2	1893 .. 1	1937 ... 6	1981 ... 5	2025 ... 4
1806 ... 4	1850 .. 3	1894 .. 2	1938 ... 7	1982 ... 6	2026 ... 5
1807 ... 5	1851 .. 4	1895 .. 3	1939 ... 1	1983 ... 7	2027 ... 6
1808 . 13	1852 .. 12	1896 . 11	1940 ... 9	1984 ... 8	2028 .. 14
1809 ... 1	1853 .. 7	1897 .. 6	1941 ... 4	1985 ... 3	2029 ... 2
1810 ... 2	1854 .. 1	1898 .. 7	1942 ... 5	1986 ... 4	2030 ... 3
1811 ... 3	1855 .. 2	1899 .. 1	1943 ... 6	1987 ... 5	2031 ... 4
1812 . 11	1856 .. 10	1900 .. 2	1944 . 14	1988 . 13	2032 . 12
1813 ... 6	1857 .. 5	1901 .. 3	1945 ... 2	1989 ... 1	2033 ... 7
1814 ... 7	1858 .. 6	1902 .. 4	1946 ... 3	1990 ... 2	2034 ... 1
1815 ... 1	1859 .. 7	1903 .. 5	1947 ... 4	1991 ... 3	2035 ... 2
1816 ... 9	1860 .. 8	1904 . 13	1948 . 12	1992 . 11	2036 . 10
1817 ... 4	1861 .. 3	1905 .. 1	1949 ... 7	1993 ... 6	2037 ... 5
1818 ... 5	1862 .. 4	1906 .. 2	1950 ... 1	1994 ... 7	2038 ... 6
1819 ... 6	1863 .. 5	1907 .. 3	1951 ... 2	1995 ... 1	2039 ... 7
1820 . 14	1864 .. 13	1908 . 11	1952 . 10	1996 ... 9	2040 ... 8
1821 ... 2	1865 .. 1	1909 .. 6	1953 ... 5	1997 ... 4	2041 ... 3
1822 ... 3	1866 .. 2	1910 .. 7	1954 ... 6	1998 ... 5	2042 ... 4
1823 ... 4	1867 .. 3	1911 .. 1	1955 ... 7	1999 ... 6	2043 ... 5
1824 . 12	1868 .. 11	1912 .. 9	1956 ... 8	2000 . 14	2044 . 13
1825 ... 7	1869 .. 6	1913 .. 4	1957 ... 3	2001 ... 2	2045 ... 1
1826 ... 1	1870 .. 7	1914 .. 5	1958 ... 4	2002 ... 3	2046 ... 2
1827 ... 2	1871 .. 1	1915 .. 6	1959 ... 5	2003 ... 4	2047 ... 3
1828 . 10	1872 .. 9	1916 . 14	1960 . 13	2004 . 12	2048 . 11
1829 ... 5	1873 .. 4	1917 .. 2	1961 ... 1	2005 ... 7	2049 ... 6
1830 ... 6	1874 .. 5	1918 .. 3	1962 ... 2	2006 ... 1	2050 ... 7
1831 ... 7	1875 .. 6	1919 .. 4	1963 ... 3	2007 ... 2	2051 ... 1
1832 .. 8	1876 . 14	1920 . 12	1964 . 11	2008 . 10	2052 ... 9
1833 ... 3	1877 .. 2	1921 .. 7	1965 ... 6	2009 ... 5	2053 ... 4
1834 ... 4	1878 .. 3	1922 .. 1	1966 ... 7	2010 ... 6	2054 ... 5
1835 ... 5	1879 .. 4	1923 .. 2	1967 ... 1	2011 ... 7	2055 ... 6
1836 . 13	1880 . 12	1924 . 10	1968 ... 9	2012 ... 8	2056 . 14
1837 ... 1	1881 .. 7	1925 .. 5	1969 ... 4	2013 ... 3	2057 ... 2
1838 ... 2	1882 .. 1	1926 .. 6	1970 ... 5	2014 ... 4	2058 ... 3
1839 ... 3	1883 .. 2	1927 .. 7	1971 ... 6	2015 ... 5	2059 ... 4
1840 . 11	1884 .. 10	1928 .. 8	1972 . 14	2016 . 13	2060 . 12
1841 ... 6	1885 .. 5	1929 .. 3	1973 ... 2	2017 ... 1	2061 ... 7
1842 ... 7	1886 .. 6	1930 .. 4	1974 ... 3	2018 ... 2	2062 ... 1
1843 ... 1	1887 .. 7	1931 .. 5	1975 ... 4	2019 ... 3	2063 ... 3

DIRECTIONS: The number given with each year in the key above is number of calendar to use for that year

1

```
     JANUARY               FEBRUARY                 MARCH                  APRIL
S  M  T  W  T  F  S    S  M  T  W  T  F  S    S  M  T  W  T  F  S    S  M  T  W  T  F  S
1  2  3  4  5  6  7                   1  2  3  4                   1  2  3  4                      1
8  9 10 11 12 13 14    5  6  7  8  9 10 11    5  6  7  8  9 10 11    2  3  4  5  6  7  8
15 16 17 18 19 20 21  12 13 14 15 16 17 18   12 13 14 15 16 17 18    9 10 11 12 13 14 15
22 23 24 25 26 27 28  19 20 21 22 23 24 25   19 20 21 22 23 24 25   16 17 18 19 20 21 22
29 30 31              26 27 28               26 27 28 29 30 31      23 24 25 26 27 28 29
                                                                    30

      MAY                    JUNE                   JULY                  AUGUST
S  M  T  W  T  F  S    S  M  T  W  T  F  S    S  M  T  W  T  F  S    S  M  T  W  T  F  S
      1  2  3  4  5                1  2  3                      1    1  2  3  4  5
6  7  8  9 10 11 12    4  5  6  7  8  9 10    2  3  4  5  6  7  8    6  7  8  9 10 11 12
13 14 15 16 17 18 19   11 12 13 14 15 16 17    9 10 11 12 13 14 15   13 14 15 16 17 18 19
20 21 22 23 24 25 26   18 19 20 21 22 23 24   16 17 18 19 20 21 22   20 21 22 23 24 25 26
27 28 29 30 31         25 26 27 28 29 30      23 24 25 26 27 28 29   27 28 29 30 31
                                              30 31

    SEPTEMBER               OCTOBER                NOVEMBER               DECEMBER
S  M  T  W  T  F  S    S  M  T  W  T  F  S    S  M  T  W  T  F  S    S  M  T  W  T  F  S
                1  2    1  2  3  4  5  6  7                1  2  3  4                   1  2
3  4  5  6  7  8  9    8  9 10 11 12 13 14    5  6  7  8  9 10 11    3  4  5  6  7  8  9
10 11 12 13 14 15 16   15 16 17 18 19 20 21   12 13 14 15 16 17 18   10 11 12 13 14 15 16
17 18 19 20 21 22 23   22 23 24 25 26 27 28   19 20 21 22 23 24 25   17 18 19 20 21 22 23
24 25 26 27 28 29 30   29 30 31               26 27 28 29 30         24 25 26 27 28 29 30
                                                                     31
```

2

```
     JANUARY               FEBRUARY                 MARCH                  APRIL
S  M  T  W  T  F  S    S  M  T  W  T  F  S    S  M  T  W  T  F  S    S  M  T  W  T  F  S
   1  2  3  4  5  6                1  2  3                1  2  3    1  2  3  4  5  6  7
7  8  9 10 11 12 13    4  5  6  7  8  9 10    4  5  6  7  8  9 10    8  9 10 11 12 13 14
14 15 16 17 18 19 20   11 12 13 14 15 16 17   11 12 13 14 15 16 17   15 16 17 18 19 20 21
21 22 23 24 25 26 27   18 19 20 21 22 23 24   18 19 20 21 22 23 24   22 23 24 25 26 27 28
28 29 30 31           25 26 27 28            25 26 27 28 29 30 31    29 30

      MAY                    JUNE                   JULY                  AUGUST
S  M  T  W  T  F  S    S  M  T  W  T  F  S    S  M  T  W  T  F  S    S  M  T  W  T  F  S
         1  2  3  4                      1    1  2  3  4  5  6  7                1  2  3  4
6  7  8  9 10 11 12    3  4  5  6  7  8  9    8  9 10 11 12 13 14    5  6  7  8  9 10 11
13 14 15 16 17 18 19   10 11 12 13 14 15 16   15 16 17 18 19 20 21   12 13 14 15 16 17 18
20 21 22 23 24 25 26   17 18 19 20 21 22 23   22 23 24 25 26 27 28   19 20 21 22 23 24 25
27 28 29 30 31         24 25 26 27 28 29 30   29 30 31               26 27 28 29 30 31

    SEPTEMBER               OCTOBER                NOVEMBER               DECEMBER
S  M  T  W  T  F  S    S  M  T  W  T  F  S    S  M  T  W  T  F  S    S  M  T  W  T  F  S
                   1          1  2  3  4  5                1  2  3                1  2  3  4
2  3  4  5  6  7  8    6  7  8  9 10 11 12    4  5  6  7  8  9 10    5  6  7  8  9 10 11
9 10 11 12 13 14 15    13 14 15 16 17 18 19   11 12 13 14 15 16 17   12 13 14 15 16 17 18
16 17 18 19 20 21 22   20 21 22 23 24 25 26   18 19 20 21 22 23 24   19 20 21 22 23 24 25
23 24 25 26 27 28 29   27 28 29 30 31         25 26 27 28 29 30      26 27 28 29 30 31
30
```

3

```
     JANUARY               FEBRUARY                 MARCH                  APRIL
S  M  T  W  T  F  S    S  M  T  W  T  F  S    S  M  T  W  T  F  S    S  M  T  W  T  F  S
      1  2  3  4  5                   1  2                   1  2                1  2  3
6  7  8  9 10 11 12    3  4  5  6  7  8  9    3  4  5  6  7  8  9    7  8  9 10 11 12 13
13 14 15 16 17 18 19   10 11 12 13 14 15 16   10 11 12 13 14 15 16   14 15 16 17 18 19 20
20 21 22 23 24 25 26   17 18 19 20 21 22 23   17 18 19 20 21 22 23   21 22 23 24 25 26 27
27 28 29 30 31        24 25 26 27 28         24 25 26 27 28 29 30    28 29 30
                                              31

      MAY                    JUNE                   JULY                  AUGUST
S  M  T  W  T  F  S    S  M  T  W  T  F  S    S  M  T  W  T  F  S    S  M  T  W  T  F  S
         1  2  3  4                      1       1  2  3  4  5  6                1  2  3
5  6  7  8  9 10 11    2  3  4  5  6  7  8    7  8  9 10 11 12 13    4  5  6  7  8  9 10
12 13 14 15 16 17 18    9 10 11 12 13 14 15   14 15 16 17 18 19 20   11 12 13 14 15 16 17
19 20 21 22 23 24 25   16 17 18 19 20 21 22   21 22 23 24 25 26 27   18 19 20 21 22 23 24
26 27 28 29 30 31      23 24 25 26 27 28 29   28 29 30 31            25 26 27 28 29 30 31
                       30

    SEPTEMBER               OCTOBER                NOVEMBER               DECEMBER
S  M  T  W  T  F  S    S  M  T  W  T  F  S    S  M  T  W  T  F  S    S  M  T  W  T  F  S
1  2  3  4  5  6  7          1  2  3  4  5                   1  2    1  2  3  4  5  6  7
8  9 10 11 12 13 14    6  7  8  9 10 11 12    3  4  5  6  7  8  9    8  9 10 11 12 13 14
15 16 17 18 19 20 21   13 14 15 16 17 18 19   10 11 12 13 14 15 16   15 16 17 18 19 20 21
22 23 24 25 26 27 28   20 21 22 23 24 25 26   17 18 19 20 21 22 23   22 23 24 25 26 27 28
29 30                  27 28 29 30 31         24 25 26 27 28 29 30   29 30 31
```

4

```
     JANUARY               FEBRUARY                 MARCH                  APRIL
S  M  T  W  T  F  S    S  M  T  W  T  F  S    S  M  T  W  T  F  S    S  M  T  W  T  F  S
         1  2  3  4                      1                      1       1  2  3  4  5
5  6  7  8  9 10 11    2  3  4  5  6  7  8    2  3  4  5  6  7  8    6  7  8  9 10 11 12
12 13 14 15 16 17 18    9 10 11 12 13 14 15    9 10 11 12 13 14 15   13 14 15 16 17 18 19
19 20 21 22 23 24 25   16 17 18 19 20 21 22   16 17 18 19 20 21 22   20 21 22 23 24 25 26
26 27 28 29 30 31      23 24 25 26 27 28      23 24 25 26 27 28 29   27 28 29 30
                                              30 31

      MAY                    JUNE                   JULY                  AUGUST
S  M  T  W  T  F  S    S  M  T  W  T  F  S    S  M  T  W  T  F  S    S  M  T  W  T  F  S
            1  2  3    1  2  3  4  5  6  7       1  2  3  4  5                   1  2
4  5  6  7  8  9 10    8  9 10 11 12 13 14    6  7  8  9 10 11 12    3  4  5  6  7  8  9
11 12 13 14 15 16 17   15 16 17 18 19 20 21   13 14 15 16 17 18 19   10 11 12 13 14 15 16
18 19 20 21 22 23 24   22 23 24 25 26 27 28   20 21 22 23 24 25 26   17 18 19 20 21 22 23
25 26 27 28 29 30 31   29 30                  27 28 29 30 31         24 25 26 27 28 29 30
                                                                     31

    SEPTEMBER               OCTOBER                NOVEMBER               DECEMBER
S  M  T  W  T  F  S    S  M  T  W  T  F  S    S  M  T  W  T  F  S    S  M  T  W  T  F  S
   1  2  3  4  5  6             1  2  3  4                      1       1  2  3  4  5  6
7  8  9 10 11 12 13    5  6  7  8  9 10 11    2  3  4  5  6  7  8    7  8  9 10 11 12 13
14 15 16 17 18 19 20   12 13 14 15 16 17 18    9 10 11 12 13 14 15   14 15 16 17 18 19 20
21 22 23 24 25 26 27   19 20 21 22 23 24 25   16 17 18 19 20 21 22   21 22 23 24 25 26 27
28 29 30              26 27 28 29 30 31       23 24 25 26 27 28 29   28 29 30 31
                                              30
```

5

```
     JANUARY               FEBRUARY                 MARCH                  APRIL
S  M  T  W  T  F  S    S  M  T  W  T  F  S    S  M  T  W  T  F  S    S  M  T  W  T  F  S
            1  2  3    1  2  3  4  5  6  7    1  2  3  4  5  6  7                1  2  3  4
4  5  6  7  8  9 10    8  9 10 11 12 13 14    8  9 10 11 12 13 14    5  6  7  8  9 10 11
11 12 13 14 15 16 17   15 16 17 18 19 20 21   15 16 17 18 19 20 21   12 13 14 15 16 17 18
18 19 20 21 22 23 24   22 23 24 25 26 27 28   22 23 24 25 26 27 28   19 20 21 22 23 24 25
25 26 27 28 29 30 31                          29 30 31               26 27 28 29 30

      MAY                    JUNE                   JULY                  AUGUST
S  M  T  W  T  F  S    S  M  T  W  T  F  S    S  M  T  W  T  F  S    S  M  T  W  T  F  S
               1  2       1  2  3  4  5  6             1  2  3  4                      1
3  4  5  6  7  8  9    7  8  9 10 11 12 13    5  6  7  8  9 10 11    2  3  4  5  6  7  8
10 11 12 13 14 15 16   14 15 16 17 18 19 20   12 13 14 15 16 17 18    9 10 11 12 13 14 15
17 18 19 20 21 22 23   21 22 23 24 25 26 27   19 20 21 22 23 24 25   16 17 18 19 20 21 22
24 25 26 27 28 29 30   28 29 30               26 27 28 29 30 31      23 24 25 26 27 28 29
31                                                                   30 31

    SEPTEMBER               OCTOBER                NOVEMBER               DECEMBER
S  M  T  W  T  F  S    S  M  T  W  T  F  S    S  M  T  W  T  F  S    S  M  T  W  T  F  S
      1  2  3  4  5                1  2  3    1  2  3  4  5  6  7                1  2  3  4
6  7  8  9 10 11 12    4  5  6  7  8  9 10    8  9 10 11 12 13 14    5  6  7  8  9 10 11
13 14 15 16 17 18 19   11 12 13 14 15 16 17   15 16 17 18 19 20 21   12 13 14 15 16 17 18
20 21 22 23 24 25 26   18 19 20 21 22 23 24   22 23 24 25 26 27 28   19 20 21 22 23 24 25
27 28 29 30           25 26 27 28 29 30 31    29 30                  26 27 28 29 30 31
```

6

```
     JANUARY               FEBRUARY                 MARCH                  APRIL
S  M  T  W  T  F  S    S  M  T  W  T  F  S    S  M  T  W  T  F  S    S  M  T  W  T  F  S
               1  2       1  2  3  4  5  6       1  2  3  4  5  6                1  2  3
3  4  5  6  7  8  9    7  8  9 10 11 12 13    7  8  9 10 11 12 13    4  5  6  7  8  9 10
10 11 12 13 14 15 16   14 15 16 17 18 19 20   14 15 16 17 18 19 20   11 12 13 14 15 16 17
17 18 19 20 21 22 23   21 22 23 24 25 26 27   21 22 23 24 25 26 27   18 19 20 21 22 23 24
24 25 26 27 28 29 30   28                     28 29 30 31            25 26 27 28 29 30
31

      MAY                    JUNE                   JULY                  AUGUST
S  M  T  W  T  F  S    S  M  T  W  T  F  S    S  M  T  W  T  F  S    S  M  T  W  T  F  S
                  1             1  2  3  4  5             1  2  3    1  2  3  4  5  6  7
2  3  4  5  6  7  8    6  7  8  9 10 11 12    4  5  6  7  8  9 10    8  9 10 11 12 13 14
9 10 11 12 13 14 15    13 14 15 16 17 18 19   11 12 13 14 15 16 17   15 16 17 18 19 20 21
16 17 18 19 20 21 22   20 21 22 23 24 25 26   18 19 20 21 22 23 24   22 23 24 25 26 27 28
23 24 25 26 27 28 29   27 28 29 30            25 26 27 28 29 30 31   29 30 31
30 31

    SEPTEMBER               OCTOBER                NOVEMBER               DECEMBER
S  M  T  W  T  F  S    S  M  T  W  T  F  S    S  M  T  W  T  F  S    S  M  T  W  T  F  S
         1  2  3  4                   1  2       1  2  3  4  5  6             1  2  3  4
5  6  7  8  9 10 11    3  4  5  6  7  8  9    7  8  9 10 11 12 13    5  6  7  8  9 10 11
12 13 14 15 16 17 18   10 11 12 13 14 15 16   14 15 16 17 18 19 20   12 13 14 15 16 17 18
19 20 21 22 23 24 25   17 18 19 20 21 22 23   21 22 23 24 25 26 27   19 20 21 22 23 24 25
26 27 28 29 30        24 25 26 27 28 29 30    28 29 30               26 27 28 29 30 31
                       31
```

7 (common year — January 1 falls on Saturday)

```
        JANUARY                 FEBRUARY                  MARCH                    APRIL
  S  M  T  W  T  F  S     S  M  T  W  T  F  S      S  M  T  W  T  F  S      S  M  T  W  T  F  S
                    1        1  2  3  4  5           1  2  3  4  5                       1  2
  2  3  4  5  6  7  8     6  7  8  9 10 11 12      6  7  8  9 10 11 12      3  4  5  6  7  8  9
  9 10 11 12 13 14 15    13 14 15 16 17 18 19     13 14 15 16 17 18 19     10 11 12 13 14 15 16
 16 17 18 19 20 21 22    20 21 22 23 24 25 26     20 21 22 23 24 25 26     17 18 19 20 21 22 23
 23 24 25 26 27 28 29    27 28                    27 28 29 30 31           24 25 26 27 28 29 30
 30 31

          MAY                     JUNE                     JULY                    AUGUST
  S  M  T  W  T  F  S     S  M  T  W  T  F  S      S  M  T  W  T  F  S      S  M  T  W  T  F  S
  1  2  3  4  5  6  7              1  2  3  4                       1  2        1  2  3  4  5  6
  8  9 10 11 12 13 14     5  6  7  8  9 10 11      3  4  5  6  7  8  9      7  8  9 10 11 12 13
 15 16 17 18 19 20 21    12 13 14 15 16 17 18     10 11 12 13 14 15 16     14 15 16 17 18 19 20
 22 23 24 25 26 27 28    19 20 21 22 23 24 25     17 18 19 20 21 22 23     21 22 23 24 25 26 27
 29 30 31                26 27 28 29 30           24 25 26 27 28 29 30     28 29 30 31
                                                  31

       SEPTEMBER                 OCTOBER                 NOVEMBER                 DECEMBER
  S  M  T  W  T  F  S     S  M  T  W  T  F  S      S  M  T  W  T  F  S      S  M  T  W  T  F  S
           1  2  3                          1        1  2  3  4  5              1  2  3
  4  5  6  7  8  9 10     2  3  4  5  6  7  8      6  7  8  9 10 11 12      4  5  6  7  8  9 10
 11 12 13 14 15 16 17     9 10 11 12 13 14 15     13 14 15 16 17 18 19     11 12 13 14 15 16 17
 18 19 20 21 22 23 24    16 17 18 19 20 21 22     20 21 22 23 24 25 26     18 19 20 21 22 23 24
 25 26 27 28 29 30       23 24 25 26 27 28 29     27 28 29 30              25 26 27 28 29 30 31
                         30 31
```

8 (leap year — January 1 falls on Sunday)

```
        JANUARY                 FEBRUARY                  MARCH                    APRIL
  S  M  T  W  T  F  S     S  M  T  W  T  F  S      S  M  T  W  T  F  S      S  M  T  W  T  F  S
  1  2  3  4  5  6  7              1  2  3  4              1  2  3                    1  2  3  4
  8  9 10 11 12 13 14     5  6  7  8  9 10 11      4  5  6  7  8  9 10      5  6  7  8  9 10 11
 15 16 17 18 19 20 21    12 13 14 15 16 17 18     11 12 13 14 15 16 17     12 13 14 15 16 17 18
 22 23 24 25 26 27 28    19 20 21 22 23 24 25     18 19 20 21 22 23 24     19 20 21 22 23 24 25
 29 30 31                26 27 28 29              25 26 27 28 29 30 31     26 27 28 29 30

          MAY                     JUNE                     JULY                    AUGUST
  S  M  T  W  T  F  S     S  M  T  W  T  F  S      S  M  T  W  T  F  S      S  M  T  W  T  F  S
        1  2  3  4  5                    1  2      1  2  3  4  5  6  7              1  2  3  4
  6  7  8  9 10 11 12     3  4  5  6  7  8  9      8  9 10 11 12 13 14      5  6  7  8  9 10 11
 13 14 15 16 17 18 19    10 11 12 13 14 15 16     15 16 17 18 19 20 21     12 13 14 15 16 17 18
 20 21 22 23 24 25 26    17 18 19 20 21 22 23     22 23 24 25 26 27 28     19 20 21 22 23 24 25
 27 28 29 30 31          24 25 26 27 28 29 30     29 30 31                 26 27 28 29 30 31

       SEPTEMBER                 OCTOBER                 NOVEMBER                 DECEMBER
  S  M  T  W  T  F  S     S  M  T  W  T  F  S      S  M  T  W  T  F  S      S  M  T  W  T  F  S
                    1        1  2  3  4  5  6              1  2  3                          1
  2  3  4  5  6  7  8     7  8  9 10 11 12 13      4  5  6  7  8  9 10      2  3  4  5  6  7  8
  9 10 11 12 13 14 15    14 15 16 17 18 19 20     11 12 13 14 15 16 17      9 10 11 12 13 14 15
 16 17 18 19 20 21 22    21 22 23 24 25 26 27     18 19 20 21 22 23 24     16 17 18 19 20 21 22
 23 24 25 26 27 28 29    28 29 30 31              25 26 27 28 29 30        23 24 25 26 27 28 29
 30                                                                        30 31
```

9 (leap year — January 1 falls on Monday)

```
        JANUARY                 FEBRUARY                  MARCH                    APRIL
  S  M  T  W  T  F  S     S  M  T  W  T  F  S      S  M  T  W  T  F  S      S  M  T  W  T  F  S
     1  2  3  4  5  6           1  2  3                 1  2                    1  2  3  4  5  6
  7  8  9 10 11 12 13     4  5  6  7  8  9 10      3  4  5  6  7  8  9      7  8  9 10 11 12 13
 14 15 16 17 18 19 20    11 12 13 14 15 16 17     10 11 12 13 14 15 16     14 15 16 17 18 19 20
 21 22 23 24 25 26 27    18 19 20 21 22 23 24     17 18 19 20 21 22 23     21 22 23 24 25 26 27
 28 29 30 31             25 26 27 28 29           24 25 26 27 28 29 30     28 29 30
                                                  31

          MAY                     JUNE                     JULY                    AUGUST
  S  M  T  W  T  F  S     S  M  T  W  T  F  S      S  M  T  W  T  F  S      S  M  T  W  T  F  S
           1  2  3  4                       1        1  2  3  4  5  6              1  2  3
  5  6  7  8  9 10 11     2  3  4  5  6  7  8      7  8  9 10 11 12 13      4  5  6  7  8  9 10
 12 13 14 15 16 17 18     9 10 11 12 13 14 15     14 15 16 17 18 19 20     11 12 13 14 15 16 17
 19 20 21 22 23 24 25    16 17 18 19 20 21 22     21 22 23 24 25 26 27     18 19 20 21 22 23 24
 26 27 28 29 30 31       23 24 25 26 27 28 29     28 29 30 31              25 26 27 28 29 30 31
                         30

       SEPTEMBER                 OCTOBER                 NOVEMBER                 DECEMBER
  S  M  T  W  T  F  S     S  M  T  W  T  F  S      S  M  T  W  T  F  S      S  M  T  W  T  F  S
  1  2  3  4  5  6  7           1  2  3  4  5                 1  2          1  2  3  4  5  6  7
  8  9 10 11 12 13 14     6  7  8  9 10 11 12      3  4  5  6  7  8  9      8  9 10 11 12 13 14
 15 16 17 18 19 20 21    13 14 15 16 17 18 19     10 11 12 13 14 15 16     15 16 17 18 19 20 21
 22 23 24 25 26 27 28    20 21 22 23 24 25 26     17 18 19 20 21 22 23     22 23 24 25 26 27 28
 29 30                   27 28 29 30 31           24 25 26 27 28 29 30     29 30 31
```

10 (leap year — January 1 falls on Tuesday)

```
        JANUARY                 FEBRUARY                  MARCH                    APRIL
  S  M  T  W  T  F  S     S  M  T  W  T  F  S      S  M  T  W  T  F  S      S  M  T  W  T  F  S
        1  2  3  4  5                 1  2                          1              1  2  3  4  5
  6  7  8  9 10 11 12     3  4  5  6  7  8  9      2  3  4  5  6  7  8      6  7  8  9 10 11 12
 13 14 15 16 17 18 19    10 11 12 13 14 15 16      9 10 11 12 13 14 15     13 14 15 16 17 18 19
 20 21 22 23 24 25 26    17 18 19 20 21 22 23     16 17 18 19 20 21 22     20 21 22 23 24 25 26
 27 28 29 30 31          24 25 26 27 28 29        23 24 25 26 27 28 29     27 28 29 30
                                                  30 31

          MAY                     JUNE                     JULY                    AUGUST
  S  M  T  W  T  F  S     S  M  T  W  T  F  S      S  M  T  W  T  F  S      S  M  T  W  T  F  S
           1  2  3        1  2  3  4  5  6  7              1  2  3  4  5                 1  2
  4  5  6  7  8  9 10     8  9 10 11 12 13 14      6  7  8  9 10 11 12      3  4  5  6  7  8  9
 11 12 13 14 15 16 17    15 16 17 18 19 20 21     13 14 15 16 17 18 19     10 11 12 13 14 15 16
 18 19 20 21 22 23 24    22 23 24 25 26 27 28     20 21 22 23 24 25 26     17 18 19 20 21 22 23
 25 26 27 28 29 30 31    29 30                    27 28 29 30 31           24 25 26 27 28 29 30
                                                                           31

       SEPTEMBER                 OCTOBER                 NOVEMBER                 DECEMBER
  S  M  T  W  T  F  S     S  M  T  W  T  F  S      S  M  T  W  T  F  S      S  M  T  W  T  F  S
     1  2  3  4  5  6           1  2  3  4                          1          1  2  3  4  5  6
  7  8  9 10 11 12 13     5  6  7  8  9 10 11      2  3  4  5  6  7  8      7  8  9 10 11 12 13
 14 15 16 17 18 19 20    12 13 14 15 16 17 18      9 10 11 12 13 14 15     14 15 16 17 18 19 20
 21 22 23 24 25 26 27    19 20 21 22 23 24 25     16 17 18 19 20 21 22     21 22 23 24 25 26 27
 28 29 30                26 27 28 29 30 31        23 24 25 26 27 28 29     28 29 30 31
                                                  30
```

11 (leap year — January 1 falls on Wednesday)

```
        JANUARY                 FEBRUARY                  MARCH                    APRIL
  S  M  T  W  T  F  S     S  M  T  W  T  F  S      S  M  T  W  T  F  S      S  M  T  W  T  F  S
           1  2  3  4                       1      1  2  3  4  5  6  7              1  2  3  4
  5  6  7  8  9 10 11     2  3  4  5  6  7  8      8  9 10 11 12 13 14      5  6  7  8  9 10 11
 12 13 14 15 16 17 18     9 10 11 12 13 14 15     15 16 17 18 19 20 21     12 13 14 15 16 17 18
 19 20 21 22 23 24 25    16 17 18 19 20 21 22     22 23 24 25 26 27 28     19 20 21 22 23 24 25
 26 27 28 29 30 31       23 24 25 26 27 28 29     29 30 31                 26 27 28 29 30

          MAY                     JUNE                     JULY                    AUGUST
  S  M  T  W  T  F  S     S  M  T  W  T  F  S      S  M  T  W  T  F  S      S  M  T  W  T  F  S
              1  2           1  2  3  4  5  6              1  2  3  4                          1
  3  4  5  6  7  8  9     7  8  9 10 11 12 13      5  6  7  8  9 10 11      2  3  4  5  6  7  8
 10 11 12 13 14 15 16    14 15 16 17 18 19 20     12 13 14 15 16 17 18      9 10 11 12 13 14 15
 17 18 19 20 21 22 23    21 22 23 24 25 26 27     19 20 21 22 23 24 25     16 17 18 19 20 21 22
 24 25 26 27 28 29 30    28 29 30                 26 27 28 29 30 31        23 24 25 26 27 28 29
 31                                                                        30 31

       SEPTEMBER                 OCTOBER                 NOVEMBER                 DECEMBER
  S  M  T  W  T  F  S     S  M  T  W  T  F  S      S  M  T  W  T  F  S      S  M  T  W  T  F  S
        1  2  3  4  5              1  2  3      1  2  3  4  5  6  7              1  2  3  4  5
  6  7  8  9 10 11 12     4  5  6  7  8  9 10      8  9 10 11 12 13 14      6  7  8  9 10 11 12
 13 14 15 16 17 18 19    11 12 13 14 15 16 17     15 16 17 18 19 20 21     13 14 15 16 17 18 19
 20 21 22 23 24 25 26    18 19 20 21 22 23 24     22 23 24 25 26 27 28     20 21 22 23 24 25 26
 27 28 29 30             25 26 27 28 29 30 31     29 30                    27 28 29 30 31
```

12 (leap year — January 1 falls on Thursday)

```
        JANUARY                 FEBRUARY                  MARCH                    APRIL
  S  M  T  W  T  F  S     S  M  T  W  T  F  S      S  M  T  W  T  F  S      S  M  T  W  T  F  S
              1  2  3     1  2  3  4  5  6  7        1  2  3  4  5  6                    1  2  3
  4  5  6  7  8  9 10     8  9 10 11 12 13 14      7  8  9 10 11 12 13      4  5  6  7  8  9 10
 11 12 13 14 15 16 17    15 16 17 18 19 20 21     14 15 16 17 18 19 20     11 12 13 14 15 16 17
 18 19 20 21 22 23 24    22 23 24 25 26 27 28     21 22 23 24 25 26 27     18 19 20 21 22 23 24
 25 26 27 28 29 30 31    29                       28 29 30 31              25 26 27 28 29 30

          MAY                     JUNE                     JULY                    AUGUST
  S  M  T  W  T  F  S     S  M  T  W  T  F  S      S  M  T  W  T  F  S      S  M  T  W  T  F  S
                    1        1  2  3  4  5                    1  2  3      1  2  3  4  5  6  7
  2  3  4  5  6  7  8     6  7  8  9 10 11 12      4  5  6  7  8  9 10      8  9 10 11 12 13 14
  9 10 11 12 13 14 15    13 14 15 16 17 18 19     11 12 13 14 15 16 17     15 16 17 18 19 20 21
 16 17 18 19 20 21 22    20 21 22 23 24 25 26     18 19 20 21 22 23 24     22 23 24 25 26 27 28
 23 24 25 26 27 28 29    27 28 29 30              25 26 27 28 29 30 31     29 30 31
 30 31

       SEPTEMBER                 OCTOBER                 NOVEMBER                 DECEMBER
  S  M  T  W  T  F  S     S  M  T  W  T  F  S      S  M  T  W  T  F  S      S  M  T  W  T  F  S
           1  2  3  4                 1  2        1  2  3  4  5  6              1  2  3  4
  5  6  7  8  9 10 11     3  4  5  6  7  8  9      7  8  9 10 11 12 13      5  6  7  8  9 10 11
 12 13 14 15 16 17 18    10 11 12 13 14 15 16     14 15 16 17 18 19 20     12 13 14 15 16 17 18
 19 20 21 22 23 24 25    17 18 19 20 21 22 23     21 22 23 24 25 26 27     19 20 21 22 23 24 25
 26 27 28 29 30          24 25 26 27 28 29 30     28 29 30                 26 27 28 29 30 31
                         31
```

13 (leap year — January 1 falls on Friday)

```
        JANUARY                 FEBRUARY                  MARCH                    APRIL
  S  M  T  W  T  F  S     S  M  T  W  T  F  S      S  M  T  W  T  F  S      S  M  T  W  T  F  S
                 1  2        1  2  3  4  5  6        1  2  3  4  5                       1  2
  3  4  5  6  7  8  9     7  8  9 10 11 12 13      6  7  8  9 10 11 12      3  4  5  6  7  8  9
 10 11 12 13 14 15 16    14 15 16 17 18 19 20     13 14 15 16 17 18 19     10 11 12 13 14 15 16
 17 18 19 20 21 22 23    21 22 23 24 25 26 27     20 21 22 23 24 25 26     17 18 19 20 21 22 23
 24 25 26 27 28 29 30    28 29                    27 28 29 30 31           24 25 26 27 28 29 30
 31

          MAY                     JUNE                     JULY                    AUGUST
  S  M  T  W  T  F  S     S  M  T  W  T  F  S      S  M  T  W  T  F  S      S  M  T  W  T  F  S
  1  2  3  4  5  6  7              1  2  3  4                       1  2        1  2  3  4  5  6
  8  9 10 11 12 13 14     5  6  7  8  9 10 11      3  4  5  6  7  8  9      7  8  9 10 11 12 13
 15 16 17 18 19 20 21    12 13 14 15 16 17 18     10 11 12 13 14 15 16     14 15 16 17 18 19 20
 22 23 24 25 26 27 28    19 20 21 22 23 24 25     17 18 19 20 21 22 23     21 22 23 24 25 26 27
 29 30 31                26 27 28 29 30           24 25 26 27 28 29 30     28 29 30 31
                                                  31

       SEPTEMBER                 OCTOBER                 NOVEMBER                 DECEMBER
  S  M  T  W  T  F  S     S  M  T  W  T  F  S      S  M  T  W  T  F  S      S  M  T  W  T  F  S
           1  2  3                          1        1  2  3  4  5              1  2  3
  4  5  6  7  8  9 10     2  3  4  5  6  7  8      6  7  8  9 10 11 12      4  5  6  7  8  9 10
 11 12 13 14 15 16 17     9 10 11 12 13 14 15     13 14 15 16 17 18 19     11 12 13 14 15 16 17
 18 19 20 21 22 23 24    16 17 18 19 20 21 22     20 21 22 23 24 25 26     18 19 20 21 22 23 24
 25 26 27 28 29 30       23 24 25 26 27 28 29     27 28 29 30              25 26 27 28 29 30 31
                         30 31
```

14 (leap year — January 1 falls on Saturday)

```
        JANUARY                 FEBRUARY                  MARCH                    APRIL
  S  M  T  W  T  F  S     S  M  T  W  T  F  S      S  M  T  W  T  F  S      S  M  T  W  T  F  S
                    1        1  2  3  4  5              1  2  3  4                          1
  2  3  4  5  6  7  8     6  7  8  9 10 11 12      5  6  7  8  9 10 11      2  3  4  5  6  7  8
  9 10 11 12 13 14 15    13 14 15 16 17 18 19     12 13 14 15 16 17 18      9 10 11 12 13 14 15
 16 17 18 19 20 21 22    20 21 22 23 24 25 26     19 20 21 22 23 24 25     16 17 18 19 20 21 22
 23 24 25 26 27 28 29    27 28 29                 26 27 28 29 30 31        23 24 25 26 27 28 29
 30 31                                                                     30

          MAY                     JUNE                     JULY                    AUGUST
  S  M  T  W  T  F  S     S  M  T  W  T  F  S      S  M  T  W  T  F  S      S  M  T  W  T  F  S
     1  2  3  4  5  6           1  2  3                    1  2  3                 1  2  3  4  5
  7  8  9 10 11 12 13     4  5  6  7  8  9 10      2  3  4  5  6  7  8      6  7  8  9 10 11 12
 14 15 16 17 18 19 20    11 12 13 14 15 16 17      9 10 11 12 13 14 15     13 14 15 16 17 18 19
 21 22 23 24 25 26 27    18 19 20 21 22 23 24     16 17 18 19 20 21 22     20 21 22 23 24 25 26
 28 29 30 31             25 26 27 28 29 30        23 24 25 26 27 28 29     27 28 29 30 31
                                                  30 31

       SEPTEMBER                 OCTOBER                 NOVEMBER                 DECEMBER
  S  M  T  W  T  F  S     S  M  T  W  T  F  S      S  M  T  W  T  F  S      S  M  T  W  T  F  S
              1  2        1  2  3  4  5  6  7              1  2  3  4                    1  2
  3  4  5  6  7  8  9     8  9 10 11 12 13 14      5  6  7  8  9 10 11      3  4  5  6  7  8  9
 10 11 12 13 14 15 16    15 16 17 18 19 20 21     12 13 14 15 16 17 18     10 11 12 13 14 15 16
 17 18 19 20 21 22 23    22 23 24 25 26 27 28     19 20 21 22 23 24 25     17 18 19 20 21 22 23
 24 25 26 27 28 29 30    29 30 31                 26 27 28 29 30           24 25 26 27 28 29 30
                                                                           31
```

The Calendar

History of the Calendar

The purpose of a calendar is to reckon time in advance, to show how many days have to elapse until a certain event takes place—the harvest or a religious festival, for example. The earliest calendars, naturally, were crude, and they must have been strongly influenced by the geographical location of the people who made them. In the Scandinavian countries, for example, where the seasons are pronounced, the concept of the year was determined by the seasons, specifically by the end of winter. The Norsemen, before becoming Christians, are said to have had a calendar consisting of ten months of 30 days each.

But in warmer countries, where the seasons are less pronounced, the moon became the basic unit for time reckoning; an old Jewish book actually makes the statement that "the moon was created for the counting of the days." All the oldest calendars of which we have reliable information were lunar calendars, based on the time interval from one new moon to the next—a so-called "lunation." But even in a warm climate there are annual events that pay no attention to the phases of the moon. In some areas it was a rainy season; in Egypt it was the annual flooding of the Nile. It was, therefore, necessary to regulate daily life and religious festivals by lunations, but to take care of the annual event in some other manner.

The calendar of the Assyrians was based on the phases of the moon. The month began with the first appearance of the lunar crescent, and since this can best be observed in the evening, the day began with sunset. They knew that a lunation was 29 1/2 days long, so their lunar year had a duration of 354 days, falling eleven days short of the solar year.[1] After three years a lunar calendar would be off by 33 days, or more than one lunation. We know that the Assyrians added an extra month from time to time, but we do not know whether they had developed a special rule for doing so or whether the priests proclaimed the necessity for an extra month from observation. If they made every third year a year of 13 lunations, their three-year period would cover 1,091 1/2 days (using their value of 29 1/2 days for one lunation), or just about four days too short. In one century this mistake would add up to 133 days by their reckoning (in reality closer to 134 days), requiring four extra lunations per century.

We now know that an eight-year period, consisting of five years with 12 months and three years with 13 months would lead to a difference of only 20 days per century, but we do not know whether such a calendar was actually used.

The best approximation that was possible in antiquity was a 19-year period, with seven of these 19 years having 13 months. This means that the period contained 235 months. This, still using the old value for a lunation, made a total of 6,932 1/2 days, while 19 solar years added up to 6,939.7 days, a difference of just one week per period and about five weeks per century. Even the 19-year period required constant adjustment, but it was the period that became the

basis of the religious calendar of the Jews. The Arabs used the same calendar at first, but Mohammed forbade shifting from 12 months to 13 months, so that the Islamic religious calendar, even today, has a lunar year of 354 days. As a result the Islamic religious festivals run through all the seasons of the year three times per century.

The Egyptians had a traditional calendar with 12 months of 30 days each. At one time they added five extra days at the end of every year. These turned into a five-day festival because it was thought to be unlucky to work during that time.

When Rome emerged as a world power, the difficulties of making a calendar were well known, but the Romans complicated their lives because of their superstition that even numbers were unlucky. Hence their months were 29 or 31 days long, with the exception of February, which had 28 days. However, four months of 31 days, seven months of 29 days, and one month of 28 days added up to only 355 days. Therefore, the Romans invented an extra month called Mercedonius of 22 or 23 days. It was added every second year.

Even with Mercedonius, the Roman calendar was so far off that Caesar, advised by the astronomer Sosigenes, ordered a sweeping reform in 45 B.C. One year, made 445 days long by imperial decree, brought the calendar back in step with the seasons. Then the solar year (with the value of 365 days and 6 hours) was made the basis of the calendar. The months were 30 or 31 days in length, and to take care of the six hours, every fourth year was made a 366-day year. Moreover, Caesar decreed, the year began with the first of January, not with the vernal equinox in late March.

This was the Julian calendar, named after Julius Caesar. It is still the calendar of the Eastern Orthodox churches.

However, the year is 11 1/2 minutes shorter than the figure written into Caesar's calendar by Sosigenes, and after a number of centuries, even 11 1/2 minutes add up. *See* table.

While Caesar could decree that the vernal equinox should not be used as the first day of the new year, the vernal equinox is still a fact of Nature that could not be disregarded. One of the first (as far as we know) to become alarmed about this was Roger Bacon. He sent a memorandum to Pope Clement IV, who apparently was not impressed. But Pope Sixtus IV (reigned 1471 to 1484) decided that another reform was needed and called the German astronomer Regiomontanus to Rome to advise him. Regiomontanus arrived in 1475, but one year later he died in an epidemic, one of the recurrent outbreaks of the plague. The Pope himself survived, but his reform plans died with Regiomontanus.

Less than a hundred years later, in 1545, the Council of Trent authorized the then Pope, Paul III, to reform the calendar once more. Most of the mathematical and astronomical work was done by Father Christopher Clavius, S.J. The immediate correction, advised by Father Clavius and ordered by Pope Gregory XIII, was that Thursday, Oct. 4, 1582, was to be the last day of the Julian calendar. The next day was Friday, with the date of October 15. For long-range accuracy, a formula suggested by the Vatican librarian Aloysius Giglio (latinized into Lilius) was adopted: every fourth year is a leap year *unless* it is a century year like 1700 or 1800. Century years can be

1. The correct figures are: lunation: 29 d, 12 h, 44 min, 2.8 sec (29.530585 d); solar year: 365 d, 5 h, 48 min, 46 sec (365.242216 d); 12 lunations: 354 d, 8 h, 48 min, 34 sec (354.3671 d).

Drift of the Vernal Equinox in the Julian Calendar

Date	Julian year	Date	Julian year	Date	Julian Year
March 21	325 A.D.	March 17	837 A.D.	March 13	1349 A.D.
March 20	453 A.D.	March 16	965 A.D.	March 12	1477 A.D.
March 19	581 A.D.	March 15	1093 A.D.	March 11	1605 A.D.
March 18	709 A.D.	March 14	1221 A.D.		

leap years *only* when they are divisible by 400 (e.g., 1600). This rule eliminates three leap years in four centuries, making the calendar sufficiently correct for all ordinary purposes.

Unfortunately, all the Protestant princes in 1582 chose to ignore the papal bull; they continued with the Julian calendar. It was not until 1698 that the German professor Erhard Weigel persuaded the Protestant rulers of Germany and of the Netherlands to change to the new calendar. In England the shift took place in 1752, and in Russia it needed the revolution to introduce the Gregorian calendar in 1918.

The average year of the Gregorian calendar, in spite of the leap year rule, is about 26 seconds longer than the earth's orbital period. But this discrepancy will need 3,323 years to build up to a single day.

Modern proposals for calendar reform do not aim at a "better" calendar, but at one that is more convenient to use, especially for commercial purposes. A 365-day year cannot be divided into equal halves or quarters; the number of days per month is haphazard; the months begin or end in the middle of a week; a holiday fixed by date (e.g., the Fourth of July) will wander through a week; a holiday fixed in another manner (e.g., Easter) can fall on thirty-five possible dates. The Gregorian calendar, admittedly, keeps the calendar dates in reasonable unison with astronomical events, but it still is full of minor annoyances. Moreover, you need a calendar every year to look up dates; an ideal calendar should be one that you can memorize for one year and that is valid for all other years, too.

In 1834 an Italian priest, Marco Mastrofini, suggested taking one day out of every year. It would be made a holiday and *not* be given the name of a weekday. That would make every year begin with January 1 as a Sunday. The leap-year day would be treated the same way, so that in leap years there would be two unnamed holidays at the end of the years.

About a decade later the philosopher Auguste Comte also suggested a 364-day calendar with an extra day, which he called Year Day.

Since then there have been other unsuccessful attempts at calendar reform.

Time and Calendar

The two natural cycles on which time measurements are based are the year and the day. The year is defined as the time required for the Earth to complete one revolution around the sun, while the day is the time required for the Earth to complete one turn upon its axis. Unfortunately the Earth needs 365 days plus about six hours to go around the sun once, so that the year does not consist of so and so many days; the fractional day has to be taken care of by an extra day every fourth year.

But because the Earth, while turning upon its axis, also moves around the sun there are two kinds of days. A day may be defined as the interval between the highest point of the sun in the sky on two succes-

sive days. This, averaged out over the year, produces the customary 24-hour day. But one might also define a day as the time interval between the moments when a certain point in the sky, say a conveniently located star, is directly overhead. This is called:

Sidereal time. Astronomers use a point which they call the "vernal equinox" for the actual determination. Such a sidereal day is somewhat shorter than the "solar day," namely by about 3 minutes and 56 seconds of so-called "mean solar time."

Apparent solar time is the time based directly on the sun's position in the sky. In ordinary life the day runs from midnight to midnight. It begins when the sun is invisible by being 12 hours from its zenith. Astronomers use the so-called "Julian Day," which runs from noon to noon; the concept was invented by the astronomer Joseph Scaliger, who named it after his father Julius. To avoid the problems caused by leap-year days and so forth, Scaliger picked a conveniently remote date in the past and suggested just counting days without regard to weeks, months, and years. The Julian Day for 0^h Jan. 31, 1996 is 245 0082.5. The reason for having the Julian Day run from noon to noon is the practical one that astronomical observations usually extend across the midnight hour, which would require a change in date (or in the Julian Day number) if the astronomical day, like the civil day, ran from midnight to midnight.

Mean solar time, rather than apparent solar time, is what is actually used most of the time. The mean solar time is based on the position of a fictitious "mean sun." The reason why this fictitious sun has to be introduced is the following: the Earth turns on its axis regularly; it needs the same number of seconds regardless of the season. But the movement of the Earth around the sun is not regular because the Earth's orbit is an ellipse. This has the result (as explained in the section The Seasons) that the Earth moves faster in January and slower in July. Though it is the Earth that changes velocity, it looks to us as if the sun did. In January, when the Earth moves faster, the *apparent* movement of the sun looks faster. The "mean sun" of time measurements, then, is a sun that moves regularly all year round; the real sun will be either ahead of or behind the "mean sun." The difference between the real sun and the fictitious mean sun is called the *equation of time.*

When the real sun is west of the mean sun we have the "sun fast" condition, with the real sun crossing the meridian ahead of the mean sun. The opposite is the "sun slow" situation when the real sun crosses the meridian after the mean sun. Of course, what is observed is the real sun. The equation of time is needed to establish mean solar time, kept by the reference clocks.

But if all clocks were actually set by mean solar time we would be plagued by a welter of time differences that would be "correct" but a major nuisance. A clock on Long Island, correctly showing mean solar time for its location (this would be *local civil time*), would be slightly ahead of a clock in Newark, N.J. The Newark clock would be slightly ahead of a

The Names of Days

Latin	Old English	English	German	French	Italian	Spanish
Dies Solis	Sun's Day	Sunday	Sonntag	dimanche	domenica	domingo
Dies Lunae	Moon's Day	Monday	Montag	lundi	lunedì	lunes
Dies Martis	Tiw's Day	Tuesday	Dienstag	mardi	martedì	martes
Dies Mercurii	Woden's Day	Wednesday	Mittwoch	mercredi	mercoledì	miércoles
Dies Jovis	Thor's Day	Thursday	Donnerstag	jeudi	giovedì	jueves
Dies Veneris	Frigg's Day	Friday	Freitag	vendredi	venerdì	viernes
Dies Saturni	Seterne's Day	Saturday	Samstag	samedi	sabato	sábado

NOTE: The seven-day week originated in ancient Mesopotamia and became part of the Roman calendar in A.D. 321. The names of the days are based on the seven celestial bodies (the sun, the moon, Mars, Mercury, Jupiter, Venus, and Saturn), believed at that time to revolve around the earth and influence its events. Most of Western Europe adopted the Roman nomenclature. The Germanic languages substituted the names of four of the Roman gods for their Germanic equivalents: Tiw, the god of war, replaced Mars; Woden, the god of wisdom, replaced Mercury; Thor, the god of thunder, replaced Jupiter; and Frigg, the goddess of love, replaced Venus.

clock in Trenton, N.J., which, in turn, would be ahead of a clock in Philadelphia. This condition prevailed until 1884, when a system of standard time was adopted by the International Meridian Conference. The earth's surface was divided into 24 zones. The standard time of each zone is the mean astronomical time of one of 24 meridians, 15 degrees apart, beginning at the Greenwich, England, meridian and extending east and west around the globe to the international dateline, (This system was actually put into use a year earlier by the railroad companies of the U.S. and Canada who, until then, had to contend with some 100 conflicting local sun times observed in terminals across the land.)

For practical purposes, this convention is sometimes altered. For example, Alaska, for a time, consisted of four of the eight U.S. time zones: the Pacific Standard Time zone (east of Juneau) and the 6th (Juneau), 7th (Anchorage), and 8th (Nome) zones, encompassing the 135°, 150°, and 165° meridians, respectively. In 1983, by Act of Congress, the entire state (except the westward-most Aleutians) was united into the 6th zone, Alaska Standard Time.

The eight U.S. Standard Time Zones are: Atlantic (includes Puerto Rico and the Virgin Islands), Eastern, Central, Mountain, Pacific, Alaska, Hawaii–Aleutian (includes all of Hawaii and those Aleutians west of the Fox Islands), and Samoa Standard Time.

The date line. While the time zones are based on the natural event of the sun crossing the meridian, the date must be an arbitrary decision. The meridians are traditionally counted from the meridian of the observatory of Greenwich in England, which is called the zero meridian. The logical place for changing the date is 12 hours, or 180° from Greenwich. Fortunately, the 180th meridian runs mostly through the open Pacific. The date line makes a zigzag in the north to incorporate the eastern tip of Siberia into the Siberian time system and then another one to incorporate a number of islands into the Hawaii-Aleutian time zone. In the south there is a similar zigzag for the purpose of tying a number of British-owned islands to the New Zealand time system. Otherwise the date line is the same as 180° from Greenwich. At points to the east of the date line the calendar is one day earlier than at points to the west of it. A traveller going eastward across the date line from one island to another would not have to re-set his watch because he would stay inside the time zone (provided he does so where the date line does *not* coincide with the 180° meridian), but it would be the same time of the previous day.

The Seasons

The seasons are caused by the tilt of the Earth's axis (23.4°) and not by the fact that the Earth's orbit around the sun is an ellipse. The average distance of the Earth from the sun is 93 million miles; the difference between aphelion (farthest away) and perihelion (closest to the sun) is 3 million miles, so that perihelion is about 91.4 million miles from the sun. The Earth goes through the perihelion point a few days after New Year, just when the northern hemisphere has winter. Aphelion is passed during the first days in July. This by itself shows that the distance from the sun is not important within these limits. What is important is that when the Earth passes through perihelion, the northern end of the Earth's axis happens to tilt away from the sun, so that the areas beyond the Tropic of Cancer receive only slanting rays from a sun low in the sky.

The Names of the Months

January: named after Janus, protector of the gateway to heaven

February: named after Februalia, a time period when sacrifices were made to atone for sins

March: named after Mars, the god of war, presumably signifying that the campaigns interrupted by the winter could be resumed

April: from *aperire*, Latin for "to open" (buds)

May: named after Maia, the goddess of growth of plants

June: from *juvenis*, Latin for "youth"

July: named after Julius Caesar

August: named after Augustus, the first Roman Emperor

September: from *septem*, Latin for "seven"

October: from *octo*, Latin for "eight"

November: from *novem*, Latin for "nine"

December: from *decem*, Latin for "ten"

NOTE: The earliest Latin calendar was a 10-month one; thus September was the seventh month, October, the eighth, etc. July was originally called Quintilis, as the fifth month; August was originally called Sextilis, as the sixth month.

The tilt of the Earth's axis is responsible for four lines you find on every globe. When, say, the North Pole is tilted away from the sun as much as possible, the farthest points in the North which can still be reached by the sun's rays are 23 1/2° from the pole. This is the Arctic Circle. The Antarctic Circle is the corresponding limit 23.4° from the South Pole; the sun's rays cannot reach beyond this point when we have mid-summer in the North.

When the sun is vertically above the equator, the day is of equal length all over the Earth. This happens twice a year, and these are the "equinoxes" in March and in September. After having been over the equator in March, the sun will seem to move northward. The northernmost point where the sun can be straight overhead is 23.4° north of the equator. This is the Tropic of Cancer; the sun can never be vertically overhead to the north of this line. Similarly the sun cannot be vertically overhead to the south of a line 23.4° south of the equator—the Tropic of Capricorn.

This explains the climatic zones. In the belt (the Greek word *zone* means "belt") between the Tropic of Cancer and the Tropic of Capricorn, the sun can be straight overhead; this is the tropical zone. The two zones where the sun cannot be overhead but will be above the horizon every day of the year are the two temperate zones; the two areas where the sun will not rise at all for varying lengths of time are the two polar areas, Arctic and Antarctic.

Holidays

Religious and Secular, 1997

Since 1971, by federal law, Washington's Birthday, Memorial Day, Columbus Day, and Veterans' Day have been celebrated on Mondays to create three-day weekends for federal employees. Many states now observe these holidays on the same Mondays. The dates given for the holidays listed below are the traditional ones.

New Year's Day, Wednesday, Jan. 1. A legal holiday in all states and the District of Columbia, New Year's Day has its origin in Roman Times, when sacrifices were offered to Janus, the two-faced Roman deity who looked back on the past and forward to the future.

Epiphany, Monday, Jan. 6. Falls the twelfth day after Christmas and commemorates the manifestation of Jesus as the Son of God, as represented by the adoration of the Magi, the baptism of Jesus, and the miracle of the wine at the marriage feast at Cana. Epiphany originally marked the beginning of the carnival season preceding Lent, and the evening (sometimes the eve) is known as Twelfth Night.

First Day of Ramadan. Friday, Jan. 10. This day marks the beginning of a month-long fast which all Moslems must keep during the daylight hours. Only a few are exempt: the sick, those on a journey. It commemorates the first revelation of the Koran.

Martin Luther King, Jr.'s Birthday, Wednesday, Jan. 15. Honors the late civil rights leader. Became a legal public holiday in 1986.

Ground-hog Day, Sunday, Feb. 2. Legend has it that if the ground-hog sees his shadow, he'll return to his hole, and winter will last another six weeks.

Lincoln's Birthday, Wednesday, Feb. 12. A legal holiday in many states, this day was first formally observed in Washington, D.C., in 1866, when both houses of Congress gathered for a memorial address in tribute to the assassinated President.

St. Valentine's Day, Friday, Feb. 14. This day is the festival of two third-century martyrs, both named St. Valentine. It is not known why this day is associated with lovers. It may derive from an old pagan festival about this time of year, or it may have been inspired by the belief that birds mate on this day.

Washington's Birthday, Saturday, Feb. 22. The birthday of George Washington is celebrated as a legal holiday in every state of the Union, the District of Columbia, and all territories. The observance began in 1796.

Shrove Tuesday, Feb. 11. Falls the day before Ash Wednesday and marks the end of the carnival season, which once began on Epiphany but is now usually celebrated the last three days before Lent. In France, the day is known as Mardi Gras (Fat Tuesday), and Mardi Gras celebrations are also held in several American cities, particularly in New Orleans. The day is sometimes called Pancake Tuesday by the English because fats, which were prohibited during Lent, had to be used up.

Ash Wednesday, Feb. 12. The first day of the Lenten season, which lasts 40 days. Having its origin sometime before A.D. 1000, it is a day of public penance and is marked in the Roman Catholic Church by the burning of the palms blessed on the previous year's Palm Sunday. With his thumb, the priest then marks a cross upon the forehead of each worshipper. The Anglican Church and a few Protestant groups in the United States also observe the day, but generally without the use of ashes.

St. Patrick's Day, Monday, March 17. St. Patrick, patron saint of Ireland, has been honored in America since the first days of the nation. There are many dinners and meetings but perhaps the most notable part of the observance is the annual St. Patrick's Day parade on Fifth Avenue in New York City.

Purim (Feast of Lots), Sunday, March 23. A day of joy and feasting celebrating deliverance of the Jews from a massacre planned by the Persian Minister Haman. The Jewish Queen Esther interceded with her husband, King Ahasuerus, to spare the life of her uncle, Mordecai, and Haman was hanged on the same gallows he had built for Mordecai. The holiday is marked by the reading of the Book of Esther (megillah), and by the exchange of gifts, donations to the poor, and the presentation of Purim plays.

Palm Sunday, March 23. Is observed the Sunday before Easter to commemorate the entry of Jesus into Jerusalem. The procession and the ceremonies introducing the benediction of palms probably had their origin in Jerusalem.

Good Friday, March 28. This day commemorates the Crucifixion, which is retold during services from the Gospel according to St. John. A feature in Roman Catholic churches is the Liturgy of the Passion; there is no Consecration, the Host having been consecrated the previous day. The eating of hot cross buns on this day is said to have started in England.

Easter Sunday, March 30. Observed in all Christian churches, Easter commemorates the Resurrection of Jesus. It is celebrated on the first Sunday after the full moon which occurs on or next after March 21 and is therefore celebrated between March 22 and April 25 inclusive. This date was fixed by the Council of Nicaea in A.D. 325. The Orthodox Church celebrates Easter on April 27, 1997.

First Day of Passover (Pesach), Tuesday, April 22. The Feast of the Passover, also called the Feast of Unleavened Bread, commemorates the escape of the Jews from Egypt. As the Jews fled they ate unleavened bread, and from that time the Jews have allowed no leavening in the houses during Passover, bread being replaced by matzoh.

Ascension Day, Thursday, May 8. Took place in the presence of His apostles 40 days after the Resurrection of Jesus. It is traditionally held to have occurred on Mount Olivet in Bethany.

Mother's Day, Sunday, May 11. Observed the second Sunday in May, as proposed by Anna Jarvis of Philadelphia in 1907.

Pentecost (Whitsunday), Sunday, May 18. This day commemorates the descent of the Holy Ghost upon the apostles 50 days after the Resurrection. The sermon by the Apostle Peter, which led to the baptism of 3,000 who professed belief, originated the ceremonies that have since been followed. "Whitsunday" is believed to have come from "white Sunday" when, among the English, white robes were worn by those baptized on the day.

Memorial Day, Friday, May 30. Also known as Decoration Day, Memorial Day is a legal holiday in most of the states and in the territories, and is also observed by the armed forces. In 1868, Gen. John A. Logan (Retired), Commander in Chief of the Grand Army of the Republic, issued an order designating the day as one in which the graves of soldiers would be decorated. The holiday was originally devoted to honoring the memory of those who fell in the Civil War, but is now also dedicated to the memory of all war dead.

First Day of Shavuot (Hebrew Pentecost), Wednesday, June 11. This festival, sometimes called the Feast of Weeks, or of Harvest, or of the First Fruits, falls 50 days after Passover and originally celebrated the end of the seven-week grain harvesting season. In later tradition, it also celebrated the giving of the Law to Moses on Mount Sinai.

Flag Day, Saturday, June 14. This day commemorates the adoption by the Continental Congress on June 14, 1777, of the Stars and Stripes as the U.S. flag. Although it is a legal holiday only in Pennsylvania, President Truman, on Aug. 3, 1949, signed a bill requesting the President to call for its observance each year by proclamation.

Father's Day, Sunday, June 15. Observed the third Sunday in June. First celebrated June 19, 1910.

Independence Day, Friday, July 4. The day of the adoption of the Declaration of Independence in 1776, celebrated in all states and territories. The observance began the next year in Philadelphia.

Labor Day, Monday, Sept. 1. Observed the first Monday in September in all states and territories. Labor Day was first celebrated in New York in 1882 under the sponsorship of the Central Labor Union, following the suggestion of Peter J. McGuire, of the

Knights of Labor, that the day be set aside in honor of labor.

First Day of Rosh Hashana (Jewish New Year), Thursday, Oct. 2. This day marks the beginning of the Jewish year 5758 and opens the Ten Days of Penitence closing with Yom Kippur.

Yom Kippur (Day of Atonement), Saturday, Oct. 11. This day marks the end of the Ten Days of Penitence that began with Rosh Hashana. It is described in *Leviticus* as a "Sabbath of rest," and synagogue services begin the preceding sundown, resume the following morning, and continue to sundown.

Columbus Day, Sunday, Oct. 12. A legal holiday in many states, commemorating the discovery of America by Columbus in 1492. Quite likely the first celebration of Columbus Day was that organized in 1792 by the Society of St. Tammany, or Columbian Order, widely known as Tammany Hall.

First Day of Sukkot (Feast of Tabernacles), Thursday, Oct. 16. This festival, also known as the Feast of the Ingathering, originally celebrated the fruit harvest, and the name comes from the booths or tabernacles in which the Jews lived during the harvest, although one tradition traces it to the shelters used by the Jews in their wandering through the wilderness. During the festival many Jews build small huts in their back yards or on the roofs of their houses.

Simhat Torah (Rejoicing of the Law), Friday, Oct. 24. This joyous holiday falls on the eighth day of Sukkot. It marks the end of the year's reading of the Torah (Five Books of Moses) in the synagogue every Saturday and the beginning of the new cycle of reading.

United Nations Day, Friday, Oct. 24. Marking the founding of the United Nations.

Halloween, Friday, Oct. 31. Eve of All Saints' Day, formerly called All Hallows and Hallowmass. Halloween is traditionally associated in some countries with old customs such as bonfires, masquerading, and the telling of ghost stories. These are old Celtic practices marking the beginning of winter.

All Saints' Day, Saturday, Nov. 1. A Roman Catholic and Anglican holiday celebrating all saints, known and unknown.

Election Day, (legal holiday in certain states), Tuesday, Nov. 4. Since 1845, by Act of Congress, the first Tuesday after the first Monday in November is the date for choosing Presidential electors. State elections are also generally held on this day.

Veterans' Day, Tuesday, Nov. 11. Armistice Day was established in 1926 to commemorate the signing in 1918 of the Armistice ending World War I. On June 1, 1954, the name was changed to Veterans Day to honor all men and women who have served America in its armed forces.

Thanksgiving, Thursday, Nov. 27. Observed nationally on the fourth Thursday in November by Act of Congress (1941), the first such national proclamation having been issued by President Lincoln in 1863, on the urging of Mrs. Sarah J. Hale, editor of *Godey's Lady's Book.* Most Americans believe that the holiday dates back to the day of thanks ordered by Governor Bradford of Plymouth Colony in New England in 1621, but scholars point out that days of thanks stem from ancient times.

First Sunday of Advent, Nov. 30. Advent is the season in which the faithful must prepare themselves for the advent of the Savior on Christmas. The four Sundays before Christmas are marked by special church services.

First Day of Hanukkah (Festival of Lights), Wednesday, Dec. 24. This festival was instituted by Judas Maccabaeus in 165 B.C. to celebrate the purification of the Temple of Jerusalem, which had been desecrated three years earlier by Antiochus Epiphanes, who set up a pagan altar and offered sacrifices to Zeus Olympius. In Jewish homes, a light is lighted on each night of the eight-day festival.

Christmas (Feast of the Nativity), Thursday, Dec. 25. The most widely celebrated holiday of the Christian year, Christmas is observed as the anniversary of the birth of Jesus. Christmas customs are centuries old. The mistletoe, for example, comes from the Druids, who, in hanging the mistletoe, hoped for peace and good fortune. Use of such plants as holly comes from the ancient belief that such plants blossomed at Christmas. Comparatively recent is the Christmas tree, first set up in Germany in the 17th century, and the use of candles on trees developed from the belief that candles appeared by miracle on the trees at Christmas. Colonial Manhattan Islanders introduced the name Santa Claus, a corruption of the Dutch name for the 4th-century Asia Minor St. Nicholas.

Sikh Festival Dates, 1997
Source: *Jantri 500*, by Pal Singh Purewal.

Jan. 13	Maghi
Jan. 15	Birthday Guru Gobind Singh Ji
March 25	Hola Mohalla
April 13	Vaisakhi KE 299 (Khalsa Era) begins
June 9	Martyrdom of Guru Arjan Dev Ji
Sept. 2	First Parkash Granth Sahib Ji
Oct. 30	Diwali
Nov. 2	Installation of Holy Scriptures as Guru Granth Sahib Ji
Nov. 14	Birthday of Guru Nanak Dev Ji
Dec. 4	Martyrdom of Guru Tegh Bahadur Ji

State Observances

January 6, Three Kings' Day: Puerto Rico.
January 8, Battle of New Orleans Day: Louisiana.
January 11, De Hostos' Birthday: Puerto Rico.
January 19, Robert E. Lee's Birthday: Arkansas, Florida, Kentucky, Louisiana, South Carolina, **(third Monday)** Alabama, Mississippi.
January 19, Confederate Heroes Day: Texas.
January (third Monday): Lee-Jackson-King Day: Virginia.
January 30, F.D. Roosevelt's Birthday: Kentucky.
February 15, Susan B. Anthony's Birthday: Florida, Minnesota.
March (first Tuesday), Town Meeting Day: Vermont.
March 2, Texas Independence Day: Texas.
March (first Monday), Casimir Pulaski's Birthday: Illinois.
March 17, Evacuation Day: Massachusetts (in Suffolk County).
March 20 (First Day of Spring), Youth Day: Oklahoma.
March 22, Abolition Day: Puerto Rico.
March 25, Maryland Day: Maryland.
March 26, Prince Jonah Kuhio Kalanianaole Day: Hawaii.
March (last Monday), Seward's Day: Alaska.
April 2, Pascua Florida Day: Florida
April 13, Thomas Jefferson's Birthday: Alabama, Oklahoma.
April 16, De Diego's Birthday: Puerto Rico.
April (third Monday), Patriots' Day: Maine, Massachusetts.
April 21, San Jacinto Day: Texas.
April 22, Arbor Day: Nebraska.
April 22, Oklahoma Day: Oklahoma.
April 26, Confederate Memorial Day: Florida, Georgia.
April (fourth Monday), Fast Day: New Hampshire.
April (last Monday), Confederate Memorial Day: Alabama, Mississippi.
May 1, Bird Day: Oklahoma.
May 8, Truman Day: Missouri.
May 11, Minnesota Day: Minnesota.

May 20, Mecklenburg Independence Day: North Carolina.
June (first Monday), Jefferson Davis's Birthday: Alabama, Mississippi.
June 3, Jefferson Davis's Birthday: Florida, South Carolina.
June 3, Confederate Memorial Day: Kentucky, Louisiana.
June 9, Senior Citizens Day: Oklahoma.
June 11, King Kamehameha I Day: Hawaii.
June 15, Separation Day: Delaware.
June 17, Bunker Hill Day: Massachusetts (in Suffolk County).
June 19, Emancipation Day: Texas.
June 20, West Virginia Day: West Virginia.
July 17, Muñoz Rivera's Birthday: Puerto Rico.
July 24, Pioneer Day: Utah.
July 25, Constitution Day: Puerto Rico.
July 27, Barbosa's Birthday: Puerto Rico.
August (first Sunday), American Family Day: Arizona.
August (first Monday), Colorado Day: Colorado.
August (second Monday), Victory Day: Rhode Island.
August 16, Bennington Battle Day: Vermont.
August (third Friday), Admission Day: Hawaii.
August 27, Lyndon B. Johnson's Birthday: Texas.
August 30, Huey P. Long Day: Louisiana.
September 9, Admission Day: California.
September 12, Defenders' Day: Maryland.
September 16, Cherokee Strip Day: Oklahoma.
September (first Saturday after full moon), Indian Day: Oklahoma.
October 10, Leif Erickson Day: Minnesota.
October 10, Oklahoma Historical Day: Oklahoma.
October 18, Alaska Day: Alaska.
October 31, Nevada Day: Nevada.
November 4, Will Rogers Day: Oklahoma.
November (week of the 16th), Oklahoma Heritage Week: Oklahoma.
November 19, Discovery Day: Puerto Rico.
December 7, Delaware Day: Delaware.

Movable Holidays, 1997–2001

CHRISTIAN AND SECULAR

Year	Ash Wednesday	Easter	Pentecost	Labor Day	Election Day	Thanksgiving	1st Sun. Advent
1997	Feb. 12	March 30	May 18	Sept. 1	Nov. 4	Nov. 27	Nov. 30
1998	Feb. 25	April 12	May 31	Sept. 7	Nov. 3	Nov. 26	Dec. 6
1999	Feb. 17	April 4	May 23	Sept. 6	Nov. 2	Nov. 25	Nov. 28
2000	March 8	April 23	June 11	Sept. 4	Nov. 7	Nov. 23	Dec. 3
2001	Feb. 28	April 15	June 3	Sept. 3	Nov. 6	Nov. 22	Dec. 2

Shrove Tuesday: 1 day before Ash Wednesday
Palm Sunday: 7 days before Easter
Maundy Thursday: 3 days before Easter
Good Friday: 2 days before Easter

Holy Saturday: 1 day before Easter
Ascension Day: 10 days before Pentecost
Trinity Sunday: 7 days after Pentecost
Corpus Christi: 11 days after Pentecost

NOTE: Easter is celebrated on April 27, 1997, by the Orthodox Church.

JEWISH

Year	Purim[1]	1st day Passover[2]	1st day Shavuot[3]	1st day Rosh Hashana[4]	Yom Kippur[5]	1st day Sukkot[6]	Simhat Torah[7]	1st day Hanukkah[8]
1997	March 23	April 22	June 11	Oct. 2	Oct. 11	Oct. 16	Oct. 24	Dec. 24
1998	March 12	April 11	May 31	Sept. 21	Sept. 30	Oct. 5	Oct. 13	Dec. 14
1999	March 2	April 1	May 21	Sept. 11	Sept. 20	Sept. 25	Oct. 3	Dec. 4
2000	March 21	April 20	June 9	Sept. 30	Oct. 9	Oct. 14	Oct. 22	Dec. 22

1. Feast of Lots. 2. Feast of Unleavened Bread. 3. Hebrew Pentecost; or Feast of Weeks, or of Harvest, or of First Fruits. 4. Jewish New Year. 5. Day of Atonement. 6. Feast of Tabernacles, or of the Ingathering. 7. Rejoicing of the Law. 8. Festival of Lights.

Length of Jewish holidays (O=Orthodox, C=Conservative, R=Reform):

Passover: O & C, 8 days (holy days: first 2 and last 2); R, 7 days (holy days: first and last)
Shavuot: O & C, 2 days; R, 1 day
Rosh Hashana: O & C, 2 days; R, 1 day.
Yom Kippur: All groups, 1 day

Sukkot: All groups, 7 days (holy days: O & C, first 2; R, first only) O & C observe two additional days: Shemini Atseret (Eighth Day of the Feast) and Simhat Torah. R observes Shemini Atseret but not Simhat Torah
Hanukkah: All groups, 8 days

NOTE: All holidays begin at sundown on the evening before the date given.

Islamic 1997

Jan. 10	First day of the month of Ramadan	May 8	First day of month of Muharram (Beginning of liturgical year)
Feb. 8	'Id al Fitr (Festival of end of Ramadan)		
April 17	'Id al-Adha (Festival of Sacrifice at time of annual pilgrimage to Mecca)	July 17	Mawlid al-Nabi (Anniversary of Prophet Mohammad's birthday)

NOTE: All holidays begin at sundown on the evening before the date given.

Chinese Calendar

The Chinese lunar year is divided into 12 months of 29 or 30 days. The calendar is adjusted to the length of the solar year by the addition of extra months at regular intervals.

The years are arranged in major cycles of 60 years.

Each successive year is named after one of 12 animals. These 12-year cycles are continuously repeated. The Chinese New Year is celebrated at the second new moon after the winter solstice and falls between January 21 and February 19 on the Gregorian calendar.

Rat	Ox	Tiger	Cat (Rabbit)	Dragon	Snake	Horse	Sheep (Goat)	Monkey	Rooster	Dog	Pig
1900	1901	1902	1903	1904	1905	1906	1907	1908	1909	1910	1911
1912	1913	1914	1915	1916	1917	1918	1919	1920	1921	1922	1923
1924	1925	1926	1927	1928	1929	1930	1931	1932	1933	1934	1935
1936	1937	1938	1939	1940	1941	1942	1943	1944	1945	1946	1947
1948	1949	1950	1951	1952	1953	1954	1955	1956	1957	1958	1959
1960	1961	1962	1963	1964	1965	1966	1967	1968	1969	1970	1971
1972	1973	1974	1975	1976	1977	1978	1979	1980	1981	1982	1983
1984	1985	1986	1987	1988	1989	1990	1991	1992	1993	1994	1995
1996	1997	1998	1999	2000	2001	2002	2003	2004	2005	2006	2007

National Holidays Around the World, 1997

Country	Date	Country	Date	Country	Date
Afghanistan	Aug. 19	Ghana	March 6	Oman	Nov. 18
Albania	Nov. 28	Greece	March 25	Pakistan	March 23
Algeria	Nov. 1	Grenada	Feb. 7	Panama	Nov. 3
Andorra	Sept. 8	Guatemala	Sept. 15	Papua New Guinea	Sept. 16
Angola	Nov. 11	Guinea	Oct. 2	Paraguay	May 15
Antigua and Barbuda	Nov. 1	Guinea-Bissau	Sept. 24	Peru	July 28
Argentina	May 25	Guyana	Feb. 23	Philippines	June 12
Armenia	Sept. 21	Haiti	Jan. 1	Poland	May 3
Australia	Jan. 26	Honduras	Sept. 15	Portugal	June 10
Austria	Oct. 26	Hungary	Aug. 20	Qatar	Sept. 3
Azerbaijan	May 28	Iceland	June 17	Romania	Dec. 1
Bahamas	July 10	India	Jan. 26	Rwanda	July 1
Bahrain	Dec. 16	Indonesia	Aug. 17	St. Kitts and Nevis	Sept. 19
Bangladesh	March 26	Iran	Feb. 11	St. Lucia	Feb. 22
Barbados	Nov. 30	Iraq	July 17	St. Vincent and	
Belarus	July 27	Ireland	March 17	the Grenadines	Oct. 27
Belgium	July 21	Israel	May 12[1]	Samoa	June 1
Belize	Sept. 21	Italy	June 2	San Marino	Sept. 3
Benin	Aug. 1	Jamaica	Aug. 4[2]	São Tomé and Príncipe	July 12
Bhutan	Dec. 17	Japan	Dec. 23	Saudi Arabia	Sept. 23
Bolivia	Aug. 6	Jordan	May 25	Senegal	April 4
Botswana	Sept. 30	Kazakhstan	Oct. 25	Seychelles	June 18
Brazil	Sept. 7	Kenya	Dec. 12	Sierra Leone	April 27
Brunei	Feb. 23	North Korea	Sept. 9	Singapore	Aug. 9
Bulgaria	March 3	South Korea	Aug. 15	Slovak Republic	Sept. 1
Burkina Faso	Aug. 4	Kuwait	Feb. 25	Slovenia	June 25
Burundi	July 1	Kyrgyzstan	Aug. 31	Solomon Islands	July 7
Cambodia	Nov. 9	Laos	Dec. 2	Somalia	Oct. 21
Cameroon	May 20	Latvia	Nov. 18	South Africa	May 31
Canada	July 1	Lebanon	Nov. 22	Spain	Oct. 12
Cape Verde	July 5	Lesotho	Oct. 4	Sri Lanka	Feb. 4
Central African Republic	Dec. 1	Liberia	July 26	Sudan	Jan. 1
Chad	Aug. 11	Libya	Sept. 1	Suriname	Nov. 25
Chile	Sept. 18	Liechtenstein	Aug. 15	Swaziland	Sept. 6
China	Oct. 1	Lithuania	Feb. 16	Sweden	June 6
Colombia	July 20	Luxembourg	June 23	Switzerland	Aug. 1
Comoros	July 6	Macedonia	Aug. 2	Syria	April 17
Congo	Aug. 15	Madagascar	June 26	Tajikistan	Sept. 9
Costa Rica	Sept. 15	Malawi	July 6	Tanzania	April 26
Côte d'Ivoire	Dec. 7	Malaysia	Aug. 31	Thailand	Dec. 5
Croatia	May 30	Maldives	July 26	Togo	Jan. 13
Cuba	Jan. 1	Mali	Sept. 22	Tonga	June 4
Cyprus	Oct. 1	Malta	Sept. 21	Trinidad and Tobago	Aug. 31
Czech Republic	Oct. 28	Marshall Islands	May 1	Tunisia	March 20
Denmark	April 16	Mauritania	Nov. 28	Turkey	Oct. 29
Djibouti	June 27	Mauritius	March 12	Turkmenistan	Oct. 27
Dominica	Nov. 3	Mexico	Sept. 16	Uganda	Oct. 9
Dominican Republic	Feb. 27	Micronesia	Nov. 3	Ukraine	Aug. 24
Ecuador	Aug. 10	Moldova	Aug. 27	United Arab Emirates	Dec. 2
Egypt	July 23	Monaco	Nov. 19	United Kingdom	June 14[3]
El Salvador	Sept. 15	Mongolia	July 11	United States	July 4
Equatorial Guinea	Oct. 12	Morocco	March 3	Uruguay	Aug. 25
Eritrea	May 24	Mozambique	June 25	Uzbekistan	Sept. 1
Estonia	Feb. 24	Myanmar	Jan. 4	Vanuatu	July 30
Ethiopia	Sept. 12	Namibia	March 21	Venezuela	July 5
Fiji	Oct. 10	Nepal	Dec. 28	Viet Nam	Sept. 2
Finland	Dec. 6	Netherlands	April 30	Western Samoa	June 1
France	July 14	New Zealand	Feb. 6	Yemen, Republic of	May 22
Gabon	Aug. 17	Nicaragua	Sept. 15	Yugoslavia	April 27
Gambia	Feb. 18	Niger	Dec. 18	Zaire	June 30
Georgia	May 26	Nigeria	Oct. 1	Zambia	Oct. 24
Germany	Oct. 3	Norway	May 17	Zimbabwe	April 18

1. Changes yearly according to Hebrew calendar. 2. Celebrated on first Monday in August. 3. Celebrated the second Saturday in June.

CONSUMER'S RESOURCE GUIDE

Watch Out! Scamsters Are Still Out There!

Source: Federal Deposit Insurance Corporation (FDC).

Although it can happen to anybody, law enforcement folks believe a growing number of older adults are being swindled through old-fashioned confidence crimes that require the victim to make large cash withdrawals from the bank or unexpectedly write a check.

People of any age can be a victim of these con schemes—we'll detail some of the most popular scams in a bit—but older citizens seem to be more vulnerable than any other age group.

Why? Scamsters deliberately target older people because they think many retired persons are lonely and willing to listen. These con artists are very persuasive. Law enforcers also say that con artists believe seniors tend to respect authority figures, which is important to making many con games work. Also, many older people make good targets because they may be affluent. Finally, older citizens are generally too embarrassed to admit having lost money through a confidence game.

Investigators believe that fraud involving older citizens will be with us well into the next century because the population is greying.

Con Games That Endure

Let's look at some of these perennial confidence crimes, some of which have been around for centuries:

The Phony Bank Examiner

A depositor is called by someone claiming to be a bank examiner (or a policeman). The victim is asked to help uncover a suspected crime at the bank. In some cases they are told to call 911 to verify the caller's identity, but the call is picked up by the scamster, not the police. This is done by the con man not disconnecting from the call or, investigators believe, by tapping into the phone service. The victim is asked to withdraw thousands of dollars and turn it over to the caller—and instructed not to discuss the transaction with bank employees. The victim is convinced to withdraw the money so that the "investigator" can mark the bills and catch the dishonest bank employee. Sometimes a second withdrawal is made, with the phony investigator perhaps promising a reward for helping with the investigation.

The Pigeon Drop

One of the oldest con games. This traditionally involves two con artists befriending the victim, then convincing the victim that a package of currency has been found and should be shared equally. The victim is then convinced to make a large bank withdrawal in order to put up "good-faith" money that will be returned along with a one-third share of the found money. The victim is then instructed to go to an office building to meet with an authority figure, like an attorney or a broker, only to discover the person doesn't exist and the suspects have fled with the victim's money.

Bogus Home Repairs

There are many variations on this scam. Essentially the homeowner is convinced of the need for some type of home repair or improvement. However, the workmanship and materials turn out to be inferior or even dangerous and the cost is far above the estimate. For example, a truck pulls up at your house and the driver tells you he just finished a big job nearby, but has enough sealant left over to do your driveway at a low price. The sealant may turn out to be, say, oil that will only mess up your shoes and wash off after a few rains. The victim, however, is then coerced into paying the bill, either in cash or by check, which is immediately cashed at the victim's bank.

The Recovery Game

After a victim has lost money in a scam, his or her name may be sold by one telemarketer to another. Or in another kind of scheme the con artist who talked the victim out of money may bring in another scamster who specializes in portraying a police officer or an investigator. The victim is then approached by the phony investigator who claims to want to help recover the victim's money. But first he will need some money . . .

The Embarrassed Victim

The sad part of all this is that only about 3 percent to 10 percent of the fraud against seniors, like the types described previously, is reported. This according to John Bordenet, a senior program specialist in the Criminal Justice Services section of the American Association of Retired Persons.

Retired Americans, say experts in the field, often won't report that they've been victims of such scams, because they're too embarrassed. Also, they may fear that if they tell family members, it will mean an end to independent living.

The key to making these con games work is controlling the victim. In some cases that means the con artist will go to the bank and speak on behalf of the victim. Some banks have adopted a program developed in Milwaukee. It provides instructions to tellers on how to handle a customer, especially a senior, who wants to make a substantial withdrawal. A bank officer talks with the customer about the withdrawal and asks the customer to read and sign a form. This form points out how the customer may be a potential victim of a con game such as you have just read about.

The Milwaukee program attempts to give the potential victim time to think about the situation, away from the control of the con artist. It is control over the victim that often leaves the person saying, "I don't know what I was thinking" after he or she has been taken for a chunk—or all—or his or her savings. □

Copyrights

Source: Copyright Office, Washington, D.C.

Copyright is a form of protection provided by the laws of the United States (title 17 U.S. Code) to the authors of "original works of authorship" including literary, dramatic, musical, artistic, and certain other intellectual works. This protection is available to both published and unpublished works. Section 106 of the Copyright Act generally gives the owner of copyright the exclusive right to do and to authorize others to do the following:

- **To reproduce** the copyrighted work in copies or phonorecords;
- To prepare **derivative works** based upon the copyrighted work;
- **To distribute copies or phonorecords** of the copyrighted work to the public by sale or other transfer of ownership, or by rental, lease, or lending;
- **To perform the copyrighted work publicly,** in the case of literary, musical, dramatic, and choreographic works, pantomimes, and motion pictures and other audiovisual works; and
- **To display the copyrighted work publicly,** in the case of literary, musical, dramatic, and choreographic works, including the individual images of a motion picture or other audiovisual work.

It is illegal for anyone to violate any of the rights provided by the Act to the owner of copyright. These rights, however, are not unlimited in scope. Sections 107 through 119 of the Copyrighted Act establish limitations on these rights. In some cases, these limitations are specified exemptions from copyright liability. One major limitation is the doctrine of "fair use," which is given a statutory basis in section 107 of the Act. In other instances, the limitation takes the form of a "compulsory license" under which certain limited uses of copyrighted works are permitted upon payment of specified royalties and compliance with statutory conditions. For further information about the limitations of any of these rights, consult the Copyright Act or write to the Copyright Office.

Who Can Claim Copyright

Copyright protection subsists from the time the work is created in fixed form; that is, it is an incident of the process of authorship. The copyright in the work of authorship **immediately** becomes the property of the author who created it. Only the author or those deriving their rights through the author can rightfully claim copyright.

In the case of works made for hire, the employer and not the employee is presumptively considered the author. Section 101 of the copyright statute defines a "work made for hire" as:

(1) a work prepared by an employee within the scope of his or her employment; or

(2) a work specially ordered or commissioned for use as a contribution to a collective work, as a part of a motion picture or other audiovisual work, as a translation, as a supplementary work, as a compilation, as an instructional text, as a test, as answer material for a test, or as an atlas, if the parties expressly agree in a written instrument signed by them that the work shall be considered a work made for hire. . . .

The authors of a joint work are co-owners of the copyright in the work, unless there is an agreement to the contrary.

Copyright in each separate contribution to a periodical or other collective work is distinct from copyright in the collective work as a whole and vests initially with the author of the contribution.

Two General Principles

- Mere ownership of a book, manuscript, painting, or any other copy or phonorecord does not give the possessor the copyright. The law provides that transfer of ownership of any material object that embodies a protected work does not of itself convey any rights in the copyright.
- Minors may claim copyright, but state laws may regulate the business dealings involving copyrights owned by minors. For information on relevant state laws, consult an attorney.

Copyright and National Origin of the Work

Copyright protection is available for all unpublished works, regardless of the nationality or domicile of the author.

Published works are eligible for copyright protection in the United States if **any** one of the following conditions is met:

- On the date of first publication, one or more of the authors is a national or domiciliary of the United States or is a national, domiciliary, or sovereign authority of a foreign nation that is a party to a copyright treaty to which the United States is also a party, or is a stateless person wherever that person may be domiciled; or
- The work is first published in the United States or in a foreign nation that, on the date of first publication, is a party to the Universal Copyright Convention; or the work comes within the scope of a Presidential proclamation; or
- The work is first published on or after March 1, 1989, in a foreign nation that on the date of first publication, is a party to the Berne Convention; or, if the work is **not** first published in a country party to the Berne Convention, it is published (on or after March 1, 1989) within 30 days of first publication in a country that is party to the Berne Convention; or the work, first published on or after March 1, 1989, is a pictorial, graphic, or sculptural work that is incorporated in a permanent structure located in the United States; or, if the work, first published on or after March 1, 1989, is a published audiovisual work, all the authors are legal entities with headquarters in the United States.

What Works Are Protected

Copyright protects "original works of authorship" that are fixed in a tangible form of expression. The fixation need not be directly perceptible, so long as it may be communicated with the aid of a machine or device. Copyrightable works include the following categories:

(1) literary works;

(2) musical works, including any accompanying words;

(3) dramatic works, including any accompanying music;

(4) pantomimes and choreographic works;

(5) pictorial, graphic, and sculptural works;

(6) motion pictures and other audiovisual works;

(7) sound recordings; and

(8) architectural works.

These categories should be viewed quite broadly; for example, computer programs and most "compilations" are registrable as "literary works;" maps and architectural plans are registrable as "pictorial, graphic, and sculptural works."

What Is Not Protected by Copyright

Several categories of material are generally not eligible for statutory copyright protection. These include among others:

• Works that have **not** been fixed in a tangible form of expression. For example: choreographic works that have not been notated or recorded, or improvisational speeches or performances that have not been written or recorded.

• Titles, names, short phrases, and slogans; familiar symbols or designs; mere variations of typographic ornamentation, lettering, or coloring; mere listings of ingredients or contents.

• Ideas, procedures, methods, systems, processes, concepts, principles, discoveries, or devices, as distinguished from a description, explanation, or illustration.

• Works consisting **entirely** of information that is common property and containing no original authorship. For example: standard calendars, height and weight charts, tape measures and rulers, and lists or tables taken from public documents or other common sources.

How to Secure a Copyright
Copyright Secured Automatically Upon Creation

The way in which copyright protection is secured under the present law is frequently misunderstood. No publication or registration or other action in the Copyright Office is required to secure copyright.

Copyright is secured **automatically** when the work is created, and a work is "created" when it is fixed in a copy or phonorecord for the first time. "Copies" are material objects from which a work can be read or visually perceived either directly or with the aid of a machine or device, such as books, manuscripts, sheet music, film, videotape, or microfilm. "Phonorecords" are material objects embodying fixations of sounds (excluding, by statutory definition, motion picture soundtracks), such as cassette tapes, CDs or LPs. Thus, for example, a song (the "work") can be fixed in sheet music ("copies") or in phonograph disks ("phonorecords"), or both.

If a work is prepared over a period of time, the part of the work that is fixed on a particular date constitutes the created work as of that date.

Notice of Copyright

When a work is published, it may bear a notice of copyright to identify the year of publication and the name of the copyright owner and to inform the public that the work is protected by copyright. Use of the notice was required under the 1976 Copyright Act; however, when the United States adhered to the Berne Convention, this requirement was eliminated effective March 1, 1989. For works published prior to that date without notice, copyright protection could have been lost, unless corrective steps were taken. However, certain foreign works that entered the public domain because they were originally published without notice have had their copyrights restored under the Uruguay Rounds Agreement Act, effective January 1, 1996. For more information on the restoration of foreign copyrights under the URAA, contact the Copyright Office and request Circular 38b.

Use of the notice is recommended because it informs the public that the work is protected by copyright, identifies the copyright owners, and shows the year of first publication. Furthermore, in the event that a work is infringed, if the work carries a proper notice, the court will not allow a defendant to claim "innocent infringement"—that is, that he or she did not realize that the work is protected. (A successful innocent infringement claim may result in a reduction in damages that the copyright owner would otherwise receive.)

The use of the copyright notice is the responsibility of the copyright owner and does not require advance permission from, or registration with, the Copyright Office.

Form of Notice for Visually Perceptible Copies

The notice for visually perceptible copies should contain all of the following three elements:

1. **The symbol** © (the letter C in a circle), or the word "Copyright," or the abbreviation "Copr."; and

2. **The year of publication** of the work. In the case of compilations or derivative works incorporating previously published material, the year date of first publication of the compilation or derivative work is sufficient. The year date may be omitted where a pictorial, graphic, or sculptural work, with accompanying textual matter, if any, is reproduced in or on greeting cards, postcards, stationery, jewelry, dolls, toys, or any useful article; and

3. **The name of the owner of copyright** in the work, or an abbreviation by which the name can be recognized, or a generally known alternative designation of the owner.

Example: © 1996 John Doe

The "C in a circle" notice is used only on "visually perceptible copies." Certain kinds of works—for example, musical, dramatic, and literary works—may be fixed not in "copies" but by means of sound in an audio recording. Since audio recordings such as audio tapes and phonograph disks are "phonorecords" and not "copies," the "C in a circle" notice is not used to indicate protection of the underlying musical, dramatic, or literary work that is recorded.

Form of Notice for Phonorecords of Sound Recordings

The copyright notice for phonorecords of sound recordings* has somewhat different requirements. The notice appearing on phonorecords should contain the following three elements:

1. **The symbol** ℗ (the letter P in a circle); and

2. **The year of first publication** of the sound recording; and

3. **The name of the owner of copyright** in the sound recording, or an abbreviation by which the name can be recognized, or a generally known alternative designation of the owner. If the producer of the sound recording is named on the phonorecord labels or containers, and if no other name appears in conjunction with the notice, the producer's name shall be considered a part of the notice.

Example: ℗ 1996 A.B.C., Inc.

> **NOTE:** Since questions may arise from the use of variant forms of the notice, any form of the notice other than those given here should not be used without first seeking legal advice.

Position of Notice

The notice should be affixed to copies or phonorecords of the work in such a manner and location as

---

*Sound recordings are defined as "works that result from the fixation of a series of musical, spoken, or other sounds, but not including the sounds accompanying a motion picture or other audiovisual work, regardless of the nature of the material objects, such as disks, tapes, or other phonorecords, in which they are embodied."

to "give reasonable notice of the claim of copyright." The notice on phonorecords may appear on the surface of the phonorecord or on the phonorecord label or container, provided the manner of placement and location give reasonable notice of the claim. The three elements of the notice should ordinarily appear together on the copies or phonorecords. The Copyright Office has issued regulations concerning the form and position of the copyright notice in the *Code of Federal Regulations* (37 CF Part 201). For more information, request circular 3.

Publications Incorporating United States Government Works

Works by the U.S. Government are not eligible for copyright protection. For works published on and after March 1, 1989, the previous notice requirement for works consisting primarily of one or more U.S. Government works has been eliminated. However, use of the copyright notice for these works is still strongly recommended. Use of a notice on such a work will defeat a claim of innocent infringement as previously described **provided** the notice also includes a statement that identifies one of the following: those portions of the work in which copyright is claimed or those portions that constitute U.S. Government material. An example is:

© 1996 Jane Brown. Copyright claimed in Chapters 7–10, exclusive of U.S. Government maps.

Works published before March 1, 1989, that consist primarily of one or more works of the U.S. Government **must** bear a notice and the identifying statement.

Unpublished Works

To avoid an inadvertent publication without notice, the author or other owner of copyright may wish to place a copyright notice on any copies or phonorecords that leave his or her control. An appropriate notice for an unpublished work is: Unpublished work © 1996 Jane Doe.

How Long Copyright Protection Endures

Works Originally Created On or After January 1, 1978

A work that is created (fixed in tangible form for the first time) on or after January 1, 1978, is automatically protected from the moment of its creation, and is ordinarily given a term enduring for the author's life, plus an additional 50 years after the author's death. In the case of "a joint work prepared by two or more authors who did not work for hire," the term lasts for 50 years after the last surviving author's death. For works made for hire, and for anonymous and pseudonymous works (unless the author's identity is revealed in Copyright Office records), the duration of copyright will be 75 years from publication or 100 years from creation, whichever is shorter.

Works Originally Created Before January 1, 1978, But Not Published or Registered by That Date

Works that were created but not published or registered for copyright before January 1, 1978, have been automatically brought under the statute and are now given Federal copyright protection. The duration of copyright in these works will generally be computed in the same way as for works created on or after January 1, 1978: the life-plus-50 or 75/100-year terms will apply to them as well. The law provides that in no case will the term of copyright for works in this category expire before December 31, 2002, and for works published on or before December 31, 2002, the term of copyright will not expire before December 31, 2027.

Works Originally Created and Published or Registered Before January 1, 1978

Under the law in effect before 1978, copyright was secured either on the date a work was published or on the date of registration if the work was registered in unpublished form. In either case, the copyright endured for a first term of 28 years from the date it was secured. During the last (28th) year of the first term, the copyright was eligible for renewal. The current copyright law has extended the renewal term from 28 to 47 years for copyrights that were subsisting on January 1, 1978, making these works eligible for a total term of protection of 75 years.

Public Law 102–307, enacted on June 26, 1992, amended the Copyright Act of 1976 to extend automatically the term of copyrights secured between January 1, 1964, and December 31, 1977, to the further term of 47 years and increased the filing fee from $12 to $20. This fee increase applies to all renewal applications filed on or after June 29, 1992.

P.L. 102–307 makes renewal registration optional. There is no need to make the renewal filing in order to extend the original 28-year copyright term to the full 75 years. However, some benefits accrue to making a renewal registration during the 28th year of the original term.

For more detailed information on the copyright term, write to the Copyright Office and request Circulars 15, 15a, and 15t. For information on how to search the Copyright Office records concerning the copyright status of a work, request Circular 22.

International Copyright Protection

There is no such thing as an "international copyright" that will automatically protect an author's work throughout the entire world. Protection against unauthorized use in a particular country depends basically on the national laws of that country. However, most countries do offer protection to foreign works under certain conditions, and these conditions have been greatly simplified by international copyright treaties and conventions. The United States belong to both global, multilateral copyright treaties—the Universal Copyright Convention (UCC) and the Berne Convention for the Protection of Literary and Artistic Works.

A U.S. author may obtain copyright protection in all countries that are members of the Berne Convention and the UCC. Some UCC countries may require formalities, which may be satisfied by the use of a UCC notice, which should consist of the symbol © accompanied by the name of the copyright proprietor and the year of the work. Example: © John Smith 1996.

An author who wishes protection for his or her work in a particular country should first find out the extent of protection of foreign works in that country. If possible, this should be done before the work is published anywhere, since protection may depend on the facts existing at the time of first publication.

For a list of countries that maintain copyright relations with the United States, request Circular 38a from the Copyright Office.

Copyright Registration

Copyright registration is a legal formality intended to make a public record of the basic facts of a particular copyright. Even though registration is not a requirement for protection, the copyright law provides several incentives to encourage copyright owners to register. They include the following:

• Registration establishes a public record of the copyright claim;

• Before an infringement suit may be filed in court, registration is necessary for works of U.S. origin and for foreign works not originating in a Berne Union country. (For more information on when a work is of U.S. origin, request Circular 93.);

• If made before or within 5 years of publication, registration will establish prima facie evidence in court of the validity of the copyright and of the facts stated in the certificate; and

• If registration is made within 3 months after publication of the work or prior to an infringement of the work, statutory damages and attorney's fees will be available to the copyright owner in court actions. Otherwise, only an award of actual damages and profits is available to the copyright owner.

• Copyright registration allows the owner of the copyright to record the registration with the U.S. Customs Service for protection against the importation of infringing copies. For additional information, request Publication No. 563 from: IPR Branch, Franklin Court, Suite 4000, U.S. Customs Service, 1301 Constitution Ave., N.W., Washington, D.C. 20229.

Registration may be made at any time within the life of the copyright. Unlike the law before 1978, when a work has been registered in unpublished form, it is not necessary to make another registration when the work becomes published (although the copyright owner may register the published edition, if desired).

To register a work, send the following three elements **in the same envelope or package** to the Registrar of Copyrights, Copyright Office, Library of Congress, Washington, D.C. 20559–6000:

1. A properly completed application form;

2. A nonrefundable filing fee of $20 for each application;

3. A nonreturnable deposit of the work that is being registered. Generally the deposit is two copies if the work is published and one copy if the work is unpublished. The application form details the specific deposit requirements.

A copyright registration is effective on the date the Copyright Office receives all of the required elements in acceptable form, regardless of how long it takes to process the application and mail the certificate of registration. Because of the large number of claims the Copyright Office receives, processing may take 120 days.

Mandatory Deposit For Works Published in the United States

Although a copyright registration is not required, the Copyright Act establishes a mandatory deposit re-

quirement for works published in the United States. In general, the owner of copyright or the owner of the exclusive right of publication in the work has a legal obligation to deposit in the Copyright Office, within 3 months of publication in the United States, 2 copies (or in the case of sound recordings, 2 phonorecords) for the use of the Library of Congress. Failure to make the deposit can result in fines and other penalties but does not affect copyright protection.

Certain categories of works are **exempt entirely** from the mandatory deposit requirements, and the obligation is reduced for certain other categories. For further information about mandatory deposit, request Circular 7d.

Use of Mandatory Deposit to Satisfy Registration Requirements

For works published in the United States the Copyright Act contains a provision under which a single deposit can be made to satisfy both the deposit and registration requirements for the Library and the registration requirements. In order to have this dual effect, the copies or phonorecords must be accompanied by the prescribed application and filing fee.

For More Information

Information on registration and application forms may be obtained free of charge by writing or calling the Copyright Office. Circular 1 contains general copyright information, including a list of application forms for copyright registration. Address inquiries to: Copyright Office, Publications Section, LM–455, Library of Congress, Washington, D.C. 20559–6000. To speak with an information specialist, call (202) 707–3000 (TTY: (202) 707–6737) between 8:30 a.m.–5:00 p.m., Eastern Time, Monday to Friday, except Federal holidays. Requests for information may also be left on a 24–hour basis by calling (202) 707–9100. To receive information via fax, call (202) 707–2600. Registration forms are not available via fax.

Copyright information, including the most frequently requested circulars, is available via the Internet. Internet site addresses are:

World Wide Web URL: http://lcweb.loc.gov/copyright
Gopher: marvel.loc.gov.port70

Copyright Office records of registrations and other related documents from 1978 forward are also available over the Internet via the above addresses or telnet directly to LOCIS (Library of Congress Information System) at:

Telnet: locis.loc.gov ☐

Unemployment Insurance

Unemployment insurance is managed jointly by the states and the federal government. Most states began paying benefits in 1938 and 1939.

Under What Conditions Can the Worker Collect?

The laws vary from state to state. In general, a waiting period of one week is required in most states after a claim is filed before collecting unemployment

insurance; the worker must be able to work, must not have quit without good cause or have been discharged for misconduct; he must not be involved in a labor dispute; above all, he must be ready and willing to work. He may be disqualified if he refuses, without good cause, to accept a job which is suitable for him in terms of his qualifications and experience, unless the wages, hours and working conditions offered are substantially less favorable than those prevailing for similar jobs in the community.

The unemployed worker must go to the local state employment security office and register for work. If that office has a suitable opening available, he must accept it or lose his unemployment payments, unless he has good cause for the refusal. If a worker moves out of his own state, he can still collect at his new residence; the state in which he is now located will act as agent for the other state, which will pay his benefits.

Benefits are paid only to unemployed workers who have had at least a certain amount of recent past employment or earnings in a job covered by the state law. The amount of employment or earnings, and the period used to measure them, vary from state to state, but the intent of the various laws is to limit benefits to workers whose recent records indicate that they are members of the labor force. The amount of benefits an unemployed worker may receive for any week is also determined by application to his past wages of a formula specified in the law. The general objective is to provide a weekly benefit which is about half the worker's customary weekly wages, up to a maximum set by the law (see table). In a majority of states, the total benefits a worker may receive in a 12-month period is limited to a fraction of his total wages in a prior 12-month period, as well as to a stated number of weeks. Thus, not all workers in a state are entitled to benefits for the number of weeks shown in the table.

Who Pays for the Insurance?

The total cost is borne by the employer in all but a few states. Each state has a sliding scale of rates. The standard rate is set at 6.2% of taxable payroll in most states. But employers with records of less unemployment (that is, with fewer unemployment benefits paid to their former workers) are rewarded with rates lower than the standard state rate.

During periods of high unemployment in a state, federal-state extended benefits are available to workers who have exhausted their regular benefits. An unemployed worker may receive benefits equal to the weekly benefit he received under the state program for one half the weeks of his basic entitlement to benefits up to a maximum (including regular benefits) of 39 weeks.

Federal Programs

Amendments to the Social Security Act provided unemployment insurance for Federal civilian employees (1954) and for ex-servicemen (1958). Benefits under these programs are paid by state employment security agencies as agents of the federal government under agreements with the Secretary of Labor. For federal civilian employees and ex-servicemembers, eligibility for benefits and the amount of benefits paid are determined according to the terms and conditions of the applicable state unemployment insurance law.

State Unemployment Compensation Maximums, 1996

State	Weekly benefit[1]	Maximum duration, weeks	State	Weekly benefit[1]	Maximum duration, weeks
Alabama	180	26	Nebraska	184	26
Alaska	212–284	26	Nevada	237	26
Arizona	185	26	New Hampshire	216	26
Arkansas	264	26	New Jersey	362	26
California	230	26	New Mexico	212	26
Colorado	272	26	New York	300	26
Connecticut	350–400	26	North Carolina	297	26
Delaware	300	26	North Dakota	243	26
D.C.	359	26	Ohio	253–339	26
Florida	250	26	Oklahoma	247	26
Georgia	205	26	Oregon	301	26
Hawaii	347	26	Pennsylvania	352–360	26
Idaho	248	26	Puerto Rico	133	26
Illinois	251–332	26	Rhode Island	324–404	26
Indiana	217	26	South Carolina	213	26
Iowa	224–274	26	South Dakota	180	26
Kansas	260	26	Tennessee	200	26
Kentucky	238	26	Texas	252	26
Louisiana	181	26	Utah	263	26
Maine	202–303	26	Vermont	212	26
Maryland	250	26	Virgin Islands	214	26
Massachusetts	347–521	30	Virginia	208	26
Michigan	293	26	Washington	350	30
Minnesota	303	26	West Virginia	290	26
Mississippi	180	26	Wisconsin	274	26
Missouri	175	26	Wyoming	233	26
Montana	228	26			

1. Maximum amounts. When two amounts are shown, higher includes dependents' allowances. *Source:* Department of Labor, Employment and Training Administration.

Trademarks

Source: Department of Commerce, Patent and Trademark Office.

A trademark may be defined as a word, letter, device, or symbol, as well as some combination of these, which is used in connection with merchandise and which points distinctly to the origin of the goods.

Certificates of registration of trademarks are issued under the seal of the Patent and Trademark Office and may be registered by the owner if he is engaged in interstate or foreign commerce which may lawfully be regulated by Congress since any Federal jurisdiction over trademarks arises under the commerce clause of the Constitution. Effective November 16, 1989, applications to register may also be based on a "bona fide intention to use the mark in commerce." Trademarks may be registered by foreign owners who comply with our law, as well as by citizens of foreign countries with which the U.S. has treaties relating to trademarks. American citizens may register trademarks in foreign countries by complying with the laws of those countries. The right to registration and protection of trademarks in many foreign countries is guaranteed by treaties.

General jurisdiction in trademark cases involving Federal Registrations is given to Federal courts. Adverse decisions of examiners on applications for registration are appealable to the Trademark Trial and Appeal Board, whose affirmances, and decisions in *inter partes* proceedings, are subject to court review. Before adopting a trademark, a person should make a search of prior marks to avoid infringing unwittingly upon them.

The duration of a trademark registration is 10 years, but it may be renewed indefinitely for 10-year periods, provided the trademark is still in use at the time of expiration.

The application fee is $245 per class.

Patents

Source: Department of Commerce, Patent and Trademark Office.

A patent, in the most general sense, is a document issued by a government, conferring some special right or privilege. The term is now restricted mainly to patents for inventions; occasionally, land patents.

The grant of a patent for an invention gives the inventor the privilege, for a limited period of time, of excluding others from making, using, or selling a certain article.

In the U.S., the law provides that a patent may be granted, for a term of 20* years, to any person who has invented or discovered any new and useful art, machine, manufacture, or composition of matter, as well as any new and useful improvements thereof. A patent may also be granted to a person who has invented or discovered and asexually reproduced a new and distinct variety of plant (other than a tuber-propagated one) or has invented a new, original and ornamental design for an article of manufacture for a term of 20 years and 14 years, respectively.

A patent is granted only upon a regularly filed application, complete in all respects; upon payment of the fees; and upon determination that the disclosure is complete and that the invention is new, useful, and, in view of the prior art, unobvious to one skilled in the art. The disclosure must be of such nature as to enable others to reproduce the invention.

A complete application, which must be addressed to the Commissioner of Patents and Trademarks, Washington, D.C. 20231, consists of a specification with one or more claims; oath or declaration; drawing (whenever the nature of the case admits of it); and a basic filing fee of $375.[1] The filing fee is not returned to the applicant if the patent is refused. If the patent is allowed, another fee of $625[1] is required before the patent is issued. The fee for design patent application is $155; the issue fee is $215[1]. The fee for a plant patent application is $255; the issue fee is $315. The basic utility fee is $375. The issue fee is $625. Maintenance fees are required on utility patents at stipulated intervals.

Applications are ordinarily considered in the order in which they are received. Patents are not granted for printed matter, for methods of doing business, or for devices for which claims contrary to natural laws are made. Applications for a perpetual-motion machine have been made from time to time, but until a working model is presented that actually fulfills the claim, no patent will be issued.

*As a result of the GATT Uruguay Round implementing legislation, the term of utility and plant patents is 20 years measured from the date of filing an application in the U.S. effective June 8, 1995.
1. Fees quoted are for small entities. Fees are double for corporations.

Birthstones

Month	Stone	Month	Stone
January	Garnet	August	Peridot or Sardonyx
February	Amethyst	September	Sapphire or Star Sapphire
March	Aquamarine or Bloodstone	October	Opal or Tourmaline
April	Diamond	November	Topaz or Citrine
May	Emerald	December	Turquoise, Lapis Lazuli, Blue
June	Pearl, Alexandrite or Moonstone		Zircon or Blue Topaz
July	Ruby or Star Ruby		

Source: Jewelry Industry Council.

National Consumer Organizations

Alliance Against Fraud in Telemarketing (AAFT), 1701 K St., N.W., Ste. 1200, Washington, DC 20006, (202) 835–3323, (202) 835–0747 (fax).

The Alliance, is an international coalition of public interest groups, trade associations, labor unions, businesses, law enforcement agencies, consumer reporters and consumer protection agencies. AAFT members promote cooperative educational efforts to alert potential victims to the threat of telemarketing fraud and steps consumers can take to protect themselves.

American Association of Retired Persons (AARP, Consumer Affairs Section, 601 E. St., N.W., Washington, DC 20049, (202) 434–6030, (202) 434–6466 (fax),.

AARP's Consumer Affairs Section advocates on behalf of mid-life and older consumers, develops and distributes consumer information, and educates the private sector about the specific needs of older consumers. Programs and materials on housing, insurance, funeral practices, eligibility for public benefits, financial security, transportation and consumer protection issues are developed, with special focus on the needs and problems of older consumers.

American Council on Consumer Interests (ACCI), 240 Stanley Hall, University of Missouri–Columbia, Columbia, MO 65211, (314) 882–3817, (314) 884–6571 (fax). Contact: Anita B. Metzen, Executive Director.

Serving the professional needs of consumer educators, researchers and policymakers, ACCI publications and educational programs foster the production, synthesis and dissemination of information in the consumer interest.

American Council on Science and Health (ACSH), 1995 Broadway, 2nd Fl., New York, NY 10023–5860, (212) 362–7044, (212) 362–4919 (fax).

A non-profit public education group, ACSH's goal is to provide up-to-date, sound information on the relationship between health and chemicals, foods, lifestyles and the environment. Booklets and special reports on a variety of topics are available, as is a quarterly magazine, *Priorities.*

Bankcard Holders of America (BHA), 524 Branch Dr., Salem, VA 24153, (540) 389–5445, (540) 389–3020 (fax).

A non-profit organization, BHA assists consumers in saving money on credit, getting out of debt and resolving credit problems. It offers lists of low-rate and secured credit cards, more than 20 guidebooks and educational brochures on credit topics, and a newsletter.

Call for Action, 3400 Idaho Ave., N.W., Ste. 101, Washington, DC 20016, Network Hotline (202) 362–3813, (202) 537–0585, (202) 244–4881 (fax).

Call for Action does assist consumers with marketplace problems. An international non-profit hotline, Call for Action is affiliated with radio and television stations and helps consumers and small businesses through mediation of marketplace disputes. A list of the affiliated radio and television stations is available by contacting the hotline.

Center for Auto Safety (CAS), 2001 S St., N.W., Ste. 410, Washington, DC 20009, (202) 328–7700

CAS does assist consumers with auto-related problems. CAS advocates on behalf of consumers in auto safety and quality, fuel efficiency, emissions and related issues. For advice on specific problems, CAS requests that consumers write, including a brief statement of the problem or question; year, make and model of the vehicle; and a stamped self-addressed envelope.

Center for Science in the Public Interest (CSPI), 1875 Connecticut Ave., N.W., Ste. 300, Washington, DC 20009, (202) 332–9110, (202) 265–4954 (fax).

A non-profit, membership organization, CSPI conducts research, education and advocacy on nutrition, health, food safety and related issues and publishes the monthly *Nutrition Action Healthletter,* as well as other consumer information materials.

Citizen Action, 1730 Rhode Island Ave., N.W., Ste. 403, Washington, DC 20036, (202) 775–1580, (202) 296–4054 (fax).

Citizen Action works on behalf of its 3 million members and 32 state organizations on health care reform, environment and energy issues.

COCO (Congress of Consumer Organizations), P.O. Box 158, Newton Center, MA 02159, (617) 552–8184.

COCO publishes a monthly newsletter, the *COCO IN-TERCOM,* on a broad range of consumer issues.

Community Nutrition Institute (CNI), 910 17th St., N.W., Ste. 413, Washington, DC 20006, (202) 776–0595, (202) 776–0599 (fax).

An advocate for programs and services to enable consumers to enjoy a diet that is adequate, safe and healthy, CNI works to increase citizen participation in the state and Federal policy and administrative processes to achieve these goals. CNI publishes *Nutrition Week,* a newsletter covering nutrition and food safety issues.

Congress Watch, 215 Pennsylvania Ave., S.E., Washington, DC 20003, (202) 546–4996, (202) 547–7392 (fax).

An arm of Public Citizen, Congress Watch works for consumer-related legislation, regulation and policies in such areas as trade, health and safety, and campaign financing, and has publications available on the issues with which it deals.

Consumer Action (CA), 116 New Montgomery, Ste. 233, San Francisco, CA 94105, (415) 777–9635 (consumer complaint hotline, 10 a.m.–2 p.m., PST), (415) 777–5267 (fax).

Consumer Action does assist consumers with marketplace problems. An education and advocacy organization specializing in credit, finance and telecommunications issues, Consumer Action offers a multi-lingual consumer complaint hotline, free information on its surveys of banks and long-distance telephone companies, and consumer education materials in as many as eight languages.

Consumer Alert, 1735 I St., N.W., Ste. 603, Washington, DC 20006, (202) 467–5809, (202) 467–5814 (fax).

Consumer Alert is a non-profit, membership organization whose mission is to inform the public about the consumer benefits of competitive enterprise, advancing competition as the best regulator of business. A bimonthly newsletter and other materials are available.

Consumer Federation of America (CFA), 1424 16th St., Ste. 604, Washington, DC 20036, (202) 387–6121, (202) 265–7989 (fax).

Made up of more than 240 organizations representing a membership exceeding 50 million consumers, CFA is a consumer advocacy and education organization. Issues on which it currently represents consumer interests before Congress and Federal regulatory agencies include telephone service, insurance and financial services, product safety, indoor air pollution, health care, product liability and utility rates. It develops and distributes studies of various consumer issues, as well as consumer guides in book and pamphlet form. In addition, CFA publishes several newsletters. The National Consumer Organization (NICO) has merged with CFA and is now known as CFA Insurance Group.

Consumers for World Trade (CWT), 2000 L St., N.W., Ste. 200, Washington, DC 20036, (202) 785–4835, (202) 416–1734 (fax).

A non-profit organization, CWT supports trade expansion and liberalization to promote economic growth and increase consumer choice and price competition in the marketplace. Various publications are available.

Consumers Union of U.S., Inc. (CU), 101 Truman Ave., Yonkers, NY 10703–1057, (914) 378–2000, (914) 378–2900 (fax).

A non-profit, independent organization, CU researches and tests consumer goods and services and disseminates the results in its monthly magazine, *Consumer Reports,* as well as other publications and media.

Council of Better Business Bureaus, Inc. (CBBB), 4200 Wilson Blvd., Arlington, VA 22203, (703) 276–1000, (703) 525–8277 (fax).

Sponsored by national companies and the nation's Better Business Bureaus, the Council of Better Business Bureaus provides coordination and leadership to the 163 Better Business Bureaus (BBBs) in the United States, offers a national advertising review program, dispute resolution services, an advisory service that reports on national charities, consumer information services, and voluntary industry guidelines for advertising and selling products and services.

Families USA Foundation, 1334 G St., N.W., Ste. 300, Washington, DC 20005, (202) 628–3030, (202) 347–2417 (fax).

A national, non-profit membership organization committed to access to affordable health and long–term care, Families USA works to educate and mobilize consumers on health care issues. In addition to its two grassroots advocacy networks, a.s.a.p., a network of health and long–term care reform activists, and HealthLink USA, a nationwide health reform computer network for public interest groups, Families USA develops and distributes reports and other materials on health and long–term care issues.

Health Research Group (HRG), 1600 20th St., N.W., Washington, DC 20009, (202) 588–1000.

A division of Public Citizen, HRG works for protection against unsafe foods, drugs, medical devices and workplaces, and advocates for greater consumer control over personal health decisions. A monthly *Health Letter* and other publications are available.

National Association of Consumer Agency Administrators (NACAA), 1010 Vermont Ave., N.W., Ste. 514, Washington, DC 20005, (202) 347–7395, (202) 347–2563 (fax).

An association of the administrators of local, state and Federal government consumer protection agencies, NACAA provides training programs, public policy studies and conferences, professional publications and other member services.

National Association of State Utility Consumer Advocates (NASUCA), 1133 15th St., N.W., Ste 50, Washington, DC 20005, (202) 727–3908, (202) 727–3911 (fax).

A national organization of 41 utility ratepayer advocate offices in 38 states and the District of Columbia, NASUCA members represent millions of consumers served by investor-owned gas, telephone, electric and water companies before Congress, state regulatory commissions, the courts, the Federal Energy Regulatory Commission and the Federal Communications Commission.

National Coalition for Consumer Education (NCCE), 295 Main St., Ste. 200, Madison, NJ 07940, (201) 377–8987, (201) 377–4828 (fax).

The coalition brings together people and resources from government, business, education, consumer organizations and the media to educate consumers about such important issues as financial management, health and safety, and the environment. The coalition develops and provides educational materials and resources to consumer educators, but does not handle requests from individuals.

National Consumers League (NCL), 1701 K St., N.W., Ste. 1200, Washington, DC 20006, (202) 835–3323, (202) 835–0747 (fax).

Founded in 1899, NCL is America's pioneer consumer advocacy organization. The league is a non-profit, membership organization working for consumer health and safety protection and fairness in the marketplace and workplace. Current principal issue areas include consumer fraud, food and drug safety, fair labor standards, child labor, health care, the environment, financial services and telecommunications. The league develops and distributes consumer education materials and newsletters.

National Foundation For Consumer Credit, Inc. (NFCC), 8611 2nd Ave., Ste. 100, Silver Spring, MD 20910, (301) 589–5600, **1 (800) 388–2227** (toll free), (301) 495–5623 (fax).

A membership organization for non-profit community organizations which are often called Consumer Credit Counseling Service agencies and are in more than 1,100 locations in the United States and Canada. The agencies educate and counsel individuals and families on credit issues. Consumers are taught to budget and use credit wisely and may be helped to resolve their credit problems. The 800 number provides the location of the nearest agency.

National Fraud Information Center (NFIC), P.O. Box 65868, Washington, DC 20035, **1 (800) 876–7060** (toll free—TDD available), (202) 835–0767 (fax).

NFIC does assist consumers with recognizing and filing complaints about fraud. A project of the National Consumers League, the center's toll-free hotline assists consumers with information to help them avoid becoming victims of fraud, referral to appropriate law enforcement agencies and professional associations, and assistance in filing complaints. The center also provides professionals involved in consumer fraud prevention and enforcement with telecommunications systems and data links to improve fraud regulation, prevention and law enforcement.

National Institute for Consumer Education (NICE), 207 Rackham Bldg, College of Education, Eastern Michigan University, Ypsilanti, MI 48197, (313) 487–2292, (313) 487–7153 (fax).

A consumer education resource and professional development center for K–12 classroom teachers, business, government, labor and community educators, NICE conducts training programs, develops teaching guides and resource lists, and manages a national clearinghouse of consumer education materials, including videos, software programs, textbooks and curriculum guides.

National Insurance Consumer Organization (NICO) *See* **Consumer Federation of America (CFA)**

Public Citizen, Inc., 1600 20th St., N.W., Washington, DC 20009, (202) 588–1000.

A national, non-profit membership organization representing consumer interests through lobbying, litigation, research and publications, Public Citizen represents consumer interests in Congress, the courts, government agencies and the media. Primary current areas of interest include product liability, health care delivery, safe medical devices and medications, open and ethical government, and safe and sustainable energy use.

Public Voice for Food and Health Policy, 1101 14th St., N.W., Washington, DC 20005, (202) 371–1840, (202) 371–1910 (fax).

A national research, education and advocacy organization, Public Voice works for food and agriculture policies and practices that improve the safety, health and affordability of the food supply and protect the environment. Public Voice develops and distributes consumer information materials on pesticide reduction, nutrition labeling and seafood safety.

Society of Consumer Affairs Professionals in Business (SOCAP), 801 N. Fairfax St., Ste. 404, Alexandria, VA 22314, (703) 519–3700, (703) 549–4886 (fax).

An international professional organization, SOCAP provides training, conferences and publications to encourage and maintain the integrity of business in transactions with consumers; to encourage and promote effective communication and understanding among business, government and consumers; and to define and advance the consumer affairs profession.

U.S. Public Interest Research Group (U.S. PIRG), 218 D St., S.E., Washington, DC 20003–1900, (202) 546–9707.

The group is the national lobbying office for state public interest research groups, consumer/environmental advocacy groups active in 33 states that lobby and publish reports on issues, including credit bureau errors; bank fees and services; toy, ATV and product safety; toxic chemicals in art supplies and other consumer products; and recycling, over-packaging and green consumerism. U.S. PIRG does not handle individual consumer complaints directly, but measures complaint levels to gauge the need for remedial legislation.

WHERE TO FIND OUT MORE

Reference Books and Other Sources

While it is impossible to construct a comprehensive list of reference works in just a few pages, the editors of the *Information Please Almanac* have compiled a list of suggested sources where readers can find more detail on the information presented in this book.

General References

To find out a little bit of information on virtually any topic, a good place to start is a dictionary or an encyclopedia. The most authoritative dictionaries are (for American English) *The American Heritage Dictionary, Third Edition; Webster's Collegiate Dictionary, Tenth Edition;* and *Webster's Third New International Dictionary of the English Language, Unabridged.* For British English or for those interested in the history of the language, the multi-volume *Oxford English Dictionary, Second Edition* is incomparable, providing definitions in historical order.

Encyclopedias generally present more substantive information on a variety of topics. Multi-volume sets, such as the *Encyclopedia Britannica* and the *Encyclopedia Americana*, provide greater depth and breadth but are more costly and less convenient than their single-volume counterparts. Among the best single-volume encyclopedias are *The Columbia Encyclopedia, Fifth Edition*, and *The Random House Encyclopedia*.

AIDS

The AIDS Directory: An Essential Guide to the 1500 Leaders in Research, Service, Policy, Advocacy and Funding/1995–96, Frank Baran
AIDS Sourcebook, Karen Bellenir, Peter D. Dresser

Art

Dictionary of Architecture & Construction, Cyril M. Harris
American Architecture Since 1780: A guide to the Styles, Marcus Whiffen
Architecture and the Sites of History: Interpretations of Buildings and Cities, Iain Borden, David Dunster
The History of Art, H.W. Janson
The Oxford Dictionary of Art, Ian Chilvers & others, editors
Illustrated Dictionary of Symbols in Eastern and Western Art, James Hall, Chris Puleston
Museums of the World (5th Ed), Elisabeth Richter, et al
The Power of Art: Highlights from World Art in American Museums, Richard Lewis, Susan I. Lewis

Associations

Encyclopedia of Associations, Gale Research Co.

Business

Information Please Business Almanac, Seth Godin
75 Best Business Practices for Socially Responsible Companies, Alan Reder
AMA Complete Guide to Marketing Research for Small Business, Holly Edmunds
Encyclopedia of Banking & Finance, Charles J. Woelfel
Occupational Outlook Handbook, U.S. Bureau of Labor Statistics
The Wall Street Journal Guide to Understanding Personal Finance, Kenneth M. Morris, Alan M. Siegel

Consumers

Consumer Reports Buying Guide Issue, 1996 (Annual),
Consumer Reports

Education

College Costs & Financial Aid Handbook 1997, College Board Staff
Peterson's Guide to Private Secondary Schools 1996–97

Environment

Beyond the Numbers: A Reader on Population, Consumption, and the Environment, Laurie Ann Mazur
Dictionary of the Environment, Michael Allaby
The Dictionary of Ecology and Environmental Science, Henry W. Art
The Almanac of Renewable Energy, Richard Golob, Eric Brus
Alternative Sources of Energy, Warren Brown, Russell E. Train
The Complete Guide to America's National Parks 1996–1997: The Official Visitor's Guide, Jane Bangley McQueen, National Park Foundation

Geography

Webster's New Geographical Dictionary
The Book of the States 1996–97
Pocket Data Book United States of America, U.S. Department of Commerce
Geography of Travel and Tourism, Lloyd E. Hudman, Richard H. Jackson
The World Factbook, Central Intelligence Agency
World Geographical Encyclopedia, Sybil P. Parker

Government

America Votes, Richard M. Scammon, Alice V. McGillivray
Congressional Quarterly's Washington Guidebook
Finding Government Information on the Internet: A How-To-Do-It Manual, John Maxymuk

Health

Alternative Health Care Resources: A Directory and Guide, Brett Jason Sinclair
Back to Reform: Values, Markets, and the Health Care System, Charles J. Dougherty
The Health Care Almanac: A Resource Guide to the Medical Field, Lorri A. Zipperer
The U.S.P. Guide to Vitamins & Minerals, U.S. Pharmacopeia

Hobbies

Antiques & Collectibles Price Guide 1996: An Illustrated Comprehensive Price Guide to the Entire Field of Antiques and Collectibles, Kyle Husfloen
Automobile Book: All New 1996, (Consumer Guide Automobile Book)
Ward's Automotive Yearbook 1996 (58th Ed)
Automobile Facts and Figures, Hindustan Motors Ltd.
A Field Guide to the Birds, Roger Tory Peterson, Virginia Marie Peterson
The Computer Glossary: The Complete Illustrated Desk Reference, Alan Freedman
The Encyclopedia of Computer Science, Ralston
_____ *for Dummies* (software application how-to series), various authors, published by IDG
The American Horticultural Society Encyclopedia of Gardening, Christopher Brickell, et al

The Essence of Herbs, An Environmental Guide to Herb Gardening, Ruth D. Wrensch

History

The Reader's Companion to American History, Eric Foner and John A. Garraty
The Americans, Daniel J. Boorstin
Album of American History, James T. Adams
Famous First Facts, Joseph Nathan Kane
Encyclopedia of North American Indians, Frederick E. Hoxie, Editor
The Native Americans: An Illustrated History, Betty Ballantine and Ian Ballantine
The Cambridge Illustrated History of the Islamic World, Francis Robinson
Chicano!: The History of the Mexican American Civil Rights Movement, Francisco A. Rosales, et al
A History of the African American People: The History, Traditions & Culture of African Americans, James Horton, Lois Horton
The Illustrated Encyclopedia of World History, Donker Van Heel

Homosexuality

Psychiatry, Psychology, and Homosexuality (Issues in Lesbian and Gay Life), Ellen Herman
Gay American History: Lesbians and Gay Men in the U.S.A.: A Documentary History, Jonathan Katz
A Road to Stonewall: Male Homosexuality and Homophobia in English and American Literature, 1750–1969, Byrne R.S. Fone

Literature

African-American Literature: An Anthology of Nonfiction, Fiction, Poetry, and Drama, Demetrice A. Worley, Jesse Perry
American Indian Literature: An Anthology, Alan R. Velie
The Norton Anthology of American Literature, Nina Baym
Women's Works: An Anthology of American Literature, Barbara Perkins, et al
A Writer's Eye: Collected Book Reviews, Eudora Welty, Pearl Amelia McHaney
Children's Books and Their Creators, Anita Silvey, Editor
The Oxford Companion to Classical Literature, M.C. Howatson
Theater in America: 250 Years of Plays, Players, and Productions, Mary C. Henderson
The Cambridge Guide to Theater, Martin Banham
The Oxford Companion to English Literature, Margaret Drabble, Paul Harvey
Columbia Dictionary of Modern European Literature, Jean-Albert Bede
Benet's Reader's Encyclopedia, George Perkins, et al
The Dictionary of Classical Mythology, Pierre Grimal, A.R. Maxwell-Hyslop
Mythology, Edith Hamilton
Tradition, Stephen Fredman
Brewer's Dictionary of Phrase & Fable, Ebenezer Cobham Brewer, et al

Medicine

Mosby Medical Encyclopedia, Walter D. Glanze, et al
Anatomy of the Human Body, Henry Gray, Carmine D. Clemente
Complete Guide to Prescription & Nonprescription Drugs, H. Winter Griffith

Music

Dictionary of Musical Terms, Theodore Baker
The Oxford Dictionary of Music, Michael Kennedy
Great Composers, Piero Ventura

All Music Guide to Jazz, Michael Erlewine, et al
The La Scala Encyclopedia of the Opera, Giorgio Bagnoli, Graham Fawcett
The New Rolling Stone Encyclopedia of Rock & Roll, Patricia Romanowski, et al

Performing Arts

For an Audience: A Philosophy of the Performing Arts, Paul Thom
The New York Public Library Performing Arts Desk Reference, Published by Macmillan
A Dictionary of Ballet Terms (A Da Capo Paperback), Leo Kersley
The Encyclopedia of Film, James Monaco, Editors of Baseline
The Film Encyclopedia, Ephraim Katz

Quotations

Bartlett's Familiar Quotations,
Oxford Dictionary of Quotations, Angela Partington

References

The Cambridge Biographical Dictionary, David Crystal
Who's Who in African-American History, Sande Smith
Who's Who in American Art 1995–96, Published by R.R. Bowker
Classic Mystery Writers (Writers of English: Lives and Works), Harold Bloom
Current Biography Yearbook, Published by H.W. Wilson
Contemporary Authors, Susan M. Trotsky
American Library Directory 1996–97, R.R. Bowker Database Publishing Group
World Guide to Libraries (12th Ed)
An Etymological Dictionary of Family and Christian Names, William Arthur

Religions

A Dictionary of All Religions and Religious Denominations: Jewish, Heathen, Mahometan, Christian, Ancient, and Modern, Hannah Adams
The Modern Catholic Encyclopedia, Michael Glazier, Monika K. Hellwig
The Oxford Dictionary of the Christian Church, F.L. Cross, Elizabeth A. Livingston
The New Standard Jewish Encyclopedia, Geoffrey Wigoder
Dictionary of Islam, Thomas Patrick Hughes

Science

CRC Handbook of Chemistry and Physics, David R. Lide
Van Nostrand's Scientific Encyclopedia, Douglas M. Considine, Glenn D. Considine
McGraw-Hill Concise Encyclopedia of Science and Technology, Sybil P. Parker
The Cambridge Astronomy Guide, William Liller, Ben Mayer
Lange's Handbook of Chemistry, John A. Dean
Fundamentals of Physics, David Halliday, et al

Senior Citizens

Encyclopedia of Senior Citizens Information Sources, Paul Wasserman, Barbara Koehler, Yvonne Lev (Editor)
Social Security Benefits Handbook, Stanley A. Tomkiel

Sports

Information Please Sports Almanac, John Hassan, Editor
Facts & Dates of American Sports, Gorton Carruth & Eugene Ehrlich

Women's Issues

Notable American Women, Edward T. James, Janet W. James

Internet Resource Guide

So you've just called AOL or CompuServe or MSN and signed yourself up for an Internet account. Now what? Where do you go? What do you see? What is all this hype about, anyway?

If you're like most 'Net neophytes, you're a bit overwhelmed by the possibilities of accessing a worldwide network of information, and probably also frustrated that it's not better organized and easier to find what you're looking for. Here are a few tips to finding your way around the Internet, as well as some addresses that should serve as a starting place for you to explore this brave new world.

Generally, you can determine the "genre" of a site based on a 3-digit extension in the address. If it ends in ".gov" it is a government site (e.g., http://www.whitehouse.gov); ".edu" is an educational institution (e.g., http://www.harvard.edu); ".com" is a company (e.g., http://www.cnn.com); and ".org" is an organization (e.g., http://www/un.org)—likely non-profit, or it would appear as a ".com." The default is for addresses in the U.S. so international addresses usually also include a 2-digit country code (e.g., "uk" for United Kingdom, "de" for Germany, "fr" for

France, "nl" for the Netherlands, etc.). Chances are, if you are looking for information on a company or a college, you could access a "home page" of data over the internet by typing "http://www.<name of company>.com" or "http://www.<name of institution>.edu."

Not all addresses are that simple, though. If you can't find what you need, go to the site of one of the search engines listed below. Search engines maintain an index of words that appear on Internet sites within their stated scope (some are worldwide, others are industry- or topic-specific). The engine will return you a list of sites containing your search terms. You may go to those sites by simply clicking on the address (all underlined terms on the Internet are "links" that provide direct access to other information simply by clicking on the term).

To get you started, here are a few topically arranged addresses. Many of these sites also offer links to other sites with more information. Though the Internet may at first appear to be a labyrinth full of dead ends and wrong turns, the journey itself is almost always interesting.

Search engines

Alta Vista	http://www.altavista.digital.com/
Infoseek	http://www2.infoseek.com/
Lycos	http://lycos.cs.cmu.edu/
Web Crawler	http://webcrawler.com/
Yahoo	http://www.yahoo.com
CINet: The Computer Network	http://search.com

Media

Information Service
Internet NewsService	http://www.cnet.com
BBC	http://www.bbcnc.org.uk/
Business Wire	http://www.hnt.com/bizwire
NewsLink	http://www.newslink.org
Reuters NewMedia	http://www.yahoo.com/headlines/current/news

Magazines
Discover	http://www.enews.com:80/magazines/discover
Entertainment Weekly	http://www.pathfinder.com/
People Magazine	http://www.pathfinder.com/
Popular Mechanics	http://www.popularmechanics.com
The Economist	http://www.economist.com
Time Magazine	http://www.pathfinder.com/time
Ziff-Davis	http://www.zdnet.com

Networks
C-SPAN	http://www.c-span.org
CNN Interactive	http://www.cnn.com
Discovery Channel Online	http://www.discovery.com
PBS	http://www.pbs.org
National Public Radio	http://www.npr.org
NBC	http://www.nbc.com
ABC	http://www.abc.com
CBS	http://www.cbs.com
Fox	http://www.fox.com
ESPNET	http://www.espnet.sportszone.com/

Newspapers
Chicago Tribune	http://www.chicago.tribune.com
Irish Times	http://www.irish-times.ie
New York Times	http://www.nytimes.com
San Jose Mercury News	http://www.sjmercury.com
USA Today	http://www.usatoday.com
Wall Street Journal	http://www.wsj.com

Online Magazines
HotWired	http://www.hotwired.com
The Biz	http://www.bizmag.com
Urban Desires	http://www.desires.com/issues.html
Salon	http://www.salon1999.com/
Playbill Online	http://piano.symgrp.com/playbill/
Slate	http://www.slate.com
Ecola's Newsstand	http://www.ecola.com/news/magazine/

Leisure

Art
Worldwide Art Resources	http://www.concourse.com/wwar/default.html
Artnetweb	http://artnetweb.com
Christie's	http://www.christies.com
Sotheby's	http://www.sothebys.com

Art Museums
Boston Museum of Fine Art	http://www.boston.com/mfa
Metropolitan Museum of Art	http://www.metmuseum.org
Sistine Chapel	http://www.christusrex.org
The Louvre	http://www.paris.org/Musees/Louvre
The National Museum of American Art	http://www.nmaa.si.edu:80

Diversions
Books That Work	Home Improvement Software http://www.btw.com
Interesting Places for Kids	http://www.crc.ricoh.com/people/steve/kids.html
S.P.Q.R.: The Virtual Rome	http://www.pathfinder.com/@@/PhaM2uHPFgAAOJ18/twep/ro
The Dilbert Zone	http://www.unitedmedia.com/comics/dilbert/
The Gigaplex	http://www.directnet.com/wow

Movies
Academy Awards	http://www.oscars.org.
Disney and Buena Vista Pictures	http://www.disney.com/BVPM/MooVPlex.html
Hollywood Online	http://www.hollywood.com
Internet Movie Database	http://us.imdb.com/
MCA/Universal Pictures	http://www.mca.com/universal_pictures/
MGM	http://www.mgmua.com/MGM
MovieWeb	http://www.movieweb.com/movie/movie.html
Paramount Pictures	http://www.paramount.com
Sony Pictures	http://www.spe.sony.com/

Photography

Center for Creative Photography
http://www.ccp.arizona.edu:80/ccp.html
Photo Perspectives http://www.i3tele.com/photo
perspectives/exhibitisions.html
Robert Atlman's Website http://www.cea.edu/robert
Sight Magazine http://www.sightphoto.com/photo.html
UC Riverside- California Museum of Photography
http://138.23.124.01/frames/

Shopping

Access Market Square http://www.icw.com/ams.html
Amazon.com Books http://www.amazon.com
Branch Mall http://www.branch.com
Cyberspace Malls International
http://www.cyspacemalls.com/
iMall http://www.imall.com/homepage.html
Interactive Super Mall http://www.supermall.com
Internet Shopping Network http://www.internet.net/
marketplaceMCI http://www.internetmci.com
CDNow http://www.cdnow.com
Hot! Hot! Hot! http://www.hot.presence.com/g/p/
H3/index.html
Product (Clothes catalog) http://www.ProductNet.com
Speak To Me! http://www.clickshop.com
Bookwire http://www.bookwire.com

Small Business Resources

General

Idea Cafe "The Small Business Gathering Place
http://www.IdeaCafe.com
Small Business Foundation of America
http://web.miep.org/sbfa/
Small & Home-Based Business Links
http://www.ro.com/small_business/homebased.html
Institute of Management and Administration
http://www.ioma.com/ioma/direct.html
All Business Network: Marketing
http://www.all-biz.com/mktg.html
Business Cycle Indicators
http://www.cris.com:80/~netlink/bci/bci.html
County and City Data Books
http://www.lib.virginia.edu/socsi/ccdb/

Organizations

The Better Business Bureau http://www.bbb.org
The Federal Trade Commission http://www.ftc.gov
U.S. Securities & Exchange Commission
http://www.sec.gov
Software Publishers' Association http://www.spa.org

Research

Business Researcher's Interests
http://www.pitt.edu/~malhotra/interest.html
Find/SVP http://www.findsvp.com
The Market Research Center
http://www.asiresearch.com
U.S. Demography Home Page
http://www.ciesin.org/datasets/us-demog/us-demog-
home.htm
Profound InfoSort http://www.profound.com

Job Search Sites

CareerMosiac http://www.careermosaic.com
CareerPath.com http://www.Careerpath.com
CareerWEB http://www.cweb.com
IntelliMatch http://www.intellimatch.com
The Internet's Online Career Center
http://www.occ.com
The Monster Board http://www.monster.com/home.html

Government & Politics

Agencies

Central Intelligence Agency http://www.odci.gov/cia
Federal Government Agencies
http://www.lib.lsu.edu/gov/fedgov.html

SEC, Patent, GSA, Federal Reserve
http://town.hall.org/govt/govt.html
U.S. Dept. of Justice http://www.usdoj.gov/
U.S. Department of Commerce http://www.doc.gov/
U.S.D.A. Center for Nutrition Policy and Promotion
http://www.usda.gov/fcs/cnpp.html
U.S. Geological Survey http://www.usgs.gov/

Government

Congressional Quarterly http://voter96.cqalert.com
Guide to Government databases
http://www.fedworld.gov/
The White House http://www.whitehouse.gov
Consumer Information Catalog http://www.gsa.org
Federal Register, U.S. Code, Congressional bills
http://www.lib.auburn.edu/gpo/index.html
U.S. Census Bureau http://www.census.gov
U.S. Patent Search Database
http://patents.cnidr.org:4242/
SEC EDGAR Database http://www.sec.gov/edgarhp.htm
Statesearch, state- level information
http://www.state.ky.us/nasire/NASIREhome.html
Statistical Abstract of the U.S.
http://www.census.gov/state_abstract
The Library of Congress http://www.loc.gov

International

United Nations http://www.un.org
The U.S. Dept. of State
http://www.state.gov/index.html

Health & Medicine

Organizations

HIVNet http://www.hivnet.org
MS Foundation http://www.nptn.org/cyber.serv/hwp/
support/ms/menu.html
Centers for Disease Control http://www.cdc.gov
World Health Net http://www.world-health.net/

Resources

Physicians Online http://www.po.com
New England Journal of Medicine http://www.nejm.org

Reference

Company Information

Hoover's Online http://www.hoovers.com/

Financial

Financial Sites of Interest http://www.secaok.org/
PODIUM/sites.html
Information and links on finance and investing
http://www.moneypages.com/syndicate/index.html
also http://www.investorama.com

General References

Bartlett's Familiar Quotations http://www.cc.
columbia.edu/acis/bartleby/bartlett
Fina A Business/Person http://www.switchboard.com
History of Science, Technology and Medicine
http://www.asap.unimelb.edu.au/hstm/hstm_ove.htm
Virtual Reference Desk http://www.refdesj.cin
A&E Biography http://www.biography.com
Current Biography http://www.hwwilson.com/

Stock Quotes

Data Broadcasting Corp. http://www.dbc.com
SEC Quote Server http://www.secapl.com
Silicon Investor http://www.techstocks.com
Stock Smart http://www.stocksmart.com

Travel

CIA World Factbook http://www.odci.gov/cia/
publications/95fact/
Travel Channel Online http://www.travelchannel.com
Business Traveler Resource Center
http://www.travelweb.com
Travelon http://www.travelon.com/

U.S. SOCIETIES & ASSOCIATIONS

Source: Information Please questionnaires to organizations. Names are listed alphabetically according to key word in title; figure in parentheses is year of founding; other figure is membership.

The following is a partial list selected for general readership interest. A comprehensive listing of approximately 23,000 national and international organizations can be found in the *Encyclopedia of Associations*, 31st ed., 1996, published by Gale Research Company, 835 Penobscot Building, 645 Griswold St., Detroit, Mich. 48226-4049, available in most public libraries.

AARP (American Association of Retired Persons) (1958): 601 E St. N.W., Washington, D.C. 20049. 32,000,000. Phone: (202) 434-2277.

Abortion Federation, National (1977): 1436 U St. N.W., Suite 103, Washington, D.C. 20009. Phone: (202) 667-5881 or (800) 772-9100.

Accountants, American Institute of Certified Public (1887): 1211 Avenue of the Americas, New York, N.Y. 10036-8775. 320,000. Phone: (212) 596-6200.

Acoustical Society of America (1929): 500 Sunnyside Blvd., Woodbury, N.Y. 11797. 7,000. Phone: (516) 576-2360.

ACSM: American Congress on Surveying and Mapping (1941): 5410 Grosvenor Lane, Suite 100, Bethesda, Md. 20814. 8,000. Phone: (301) 493-0200.

Actors' Equity Association (1913): 165 W. 46th St., New York, N.Y. 10036. Phone: (212) 869-8530.

Actuaries, Society of (1949): 475 N. Martingale Rd., Suite 800, Schaumburg, Ill. 60173-2226. 16,500. Phone: (708) 706-3500.

Adirondack Mountain Club (1922): 814 Goggins Rd., Lake George, N.Y. 12845-4117. 22,000. Phone: (518) 668-4447.

Aeronautic Association, National (1905): 1815 N. Fort Myer Dr., Suite 700, Arlington, Va. 22209. 300,000. Phone: (703) 527-0226.

Aerospace Industries Association of America, Inc. (1919): 1250 Eye St. N.W., Washington, D.C. 20005. 52 companies. Phone: (202) 371-8400.

Aerospace Medical Association (1929): 320 S. Henry St., Alexandria, Va. 22314-3579. 4,000. Phone: (703) 739-2240.

African-American Institute, The (1953): 380 Lexington Ave., New York, N.Y. 10168-4298. Phone: (212) 949-5666.

AFS–USA, Inc. (American Field Service) (1947): 220 E. 42nd St., 3rd Floor, New York, N.Y. 10017. 100,000. Phone: (212) 949-4242 or (800) AFS-INFO.

Aging Association, American (1970): 2129 Providence Ave., Chester, Pa. 19013. 500. Phone: (610) 874-7550.

Agricultural History Society (1919): 1301 New York Ave. N.W., Washington, D.C. 20005-4788. 1,400. Phone: (202) 219–0786.

Agronomy, American Society of (1907): 677 S. Segoe Rd., Madison, Wis. 53711-1086. 12,300. Phone: (608) 273-8080.

Air & Waste Management Association (1907): One Gateway Center, 3rd Floor, Pittsburgh, Pa. 15222. Phone: (412) 232-3444.

Aircraft Association, Experimental (1953): 3000 Poberezny Rd., Oshkosh, Wis. 54903-3086. 162,000. Phone: (414) 426-4800.

Aircraft Owners and Pilots Association (1939): 421 Aviation Way, Frederick, Md. 21701-4798. 340,000. Phone: (301) 695-2000.

Air Force Association (1946): 1501 Lee Highway, Arlington, Va. 22209-1198. 173,000. Phone: (703) 247-5800.

Air Line Pilots Association (1931): 1625 Massachusetts Ave. N.W., Washington, D.C. 20036 and 535 Herndon Pkwy., Herndon, Va. 22070. 43,000. Phone: (703) 689-2270.

Air Transport Association of America (1936): 1301 Pennsylvania Ave. N.W., Suite 1100, Washington, D.C. 20004-1707. 21 airlines. 3 airline associate members. Phone: (202) 626-4000.

Al-Anon Family Group Headquarters, Inc. For families and friends of alcoholics. (1951): 1600 Corporate Landing Pkwy., Virginia Beach, Va. 23456-5617. 31,000 groups worldwide. Phone: (804) 563-1600.

Alateen. For children of alcoholics: 1600 Corporate Landing Pkwy., Virginia Beach, Va. 23456-5617. 4,100 groups worldwide. Phone: (800) 356–9996, fax: (757) 563-1655.

Alcoholics Anonymous (1935): General Service Office, A.A. World Services, Inc., 475 Riverside Dr., 11th Floor, New York, N.Y. 10115. 1,800,000. Phone: (212) 870-3400.

Alcoholism and Drug Dependence, National Council on (1944): 12 W. 21st St., New York, N.Y. 10010. 130 affiliates. Phone: (212) 206-6770.

Alcohol Problems, American Council on (1895): 3426 Bridgeland Dr., Bridgeton, Mo. 63044. 3,500. Phone: (314) 739-5944.

Alexander Graham Bell Association for the Deaf (1890): 3417 Volta Place N.W., Washington, D.C. 20007. 6,200. Phone: (202) 337-5220 V, TTY; fax: (202) 337-5200; e-mail: agbell2@aol.com.

Allergy, Asthma, and Immunology, American Academy of (1943): 611 E. Wells St., Milwaukee, Wis. 53202. 5,000. Phone: (414) 272-6071.

Alzheimer's Disease and Related Disorders Association, Inc. (1980): 919 N. Michigan Ave., Suite 1000, Chicago, Ill. 60611-1676. More than 200 Chapters in all 50 states, over 2,000 Family Support Groups. Phone: (312) 335-8700; toll-free (800) 272-3900.

American Alliance for Health, Physical Education, Recreation and Dance (1885): 1900 Association Dr., Reston, Va. 22091. 35,000. Phone: (703) 476-3400.

American Antiquarian Society (1812): 185 Salisbury St., Worcester, Mass. 01609. 650. Phone: (508) 755-5221.

American Automobile Association (1902): 1000 AAA Dr., Heathrow, Fla. 32746-5063. Phone: (407) 444-7000.

American Civil Liberties Union (1920): 132 W. 43rd St., New York, N.Y. 10036. 275,000. Phone: (212) 944-9800.

American Contract Bridge League (1927): 2990 Airways Blvd., Memphis, Tenn. 38116-3847. Phone: (901) 332-5586, fax: (901) 398-7754; e-mail: 74431.3434@CompuServe.com.

American Correctional Association (1870): 4300 Forbes Boulevard, Lanham, Md. 20706-4322. 20,000. Phone: (301) 918-1800 or (800) 222-5646.

American Electroplaters and Surface Finishers Society (AESF) (1909): 12644 Research Pkwy., Orlando, Fla. 32826. 7,500. Phone: (407) 281-6441.

American Federation of Labor and Congress of Industrial Organizations (AFL-CIO) (1955): 815 16th St. N.W., Washington, D.C. 20006. 14,500,000. Phone: (202) 637-5000.

American Federation of Musicians of the United States and Canada (1896): 1501 Broadway, Suite 600 Paramount Bldg., New York, N.Y. 10036. Phone: (212) 869-1330.

American Forest Foundation (1932): 1111 19th St. N.W., Suite 780, Washington, D.C. 20036. 100. Phone: (202) 463-2462.

American Forests (1875): 1516 P St. N.W., Washington, D.C. 20005. 115,000. Phone: (202) 667-3300.

American Foundrymen's Society, Inc. (1896): 505 State St., Des Plaines, Ill. 60016-8399. 13,000. Phone: (847) 824-0181.

American Friends Service Committee (1917): 1501 Cherry St., Philadelphia, Pa. 19102-1479. Phone: (215) 241-7000.

American Geographical Society, The (1851): 156 Fifth Ave., Suite 600, New York, N.Y. 10010-7002. 1,500. Phone: (212) 242-0214; fax: (212) 989-1583; e-mail: amgeosoc@village.ios.com.

American Geriatrics Society (1942): 770 Lexington Ave., Suite 300, New York, N.Y. 10021. 6,500. Phone: (212) 308-1414.

American Heart Association (1924): 7272 Greenville Ave., Dallas, Tex. 75231-4596. 4,200,000 volunteers. Phone: (800) AHA-USA1

American Historical Association (1884): 400 A St. S.E., Washington, D.C. 20003. 19,000. Phone: (202) 544-2422.

American Hospital Association (1899): One North Franklin, Chicago, Ill. 60606. 5,000 institutions. Phone: (312) 422-3000.

American Indian Affairs, Association on (1923): Tekakwitha Complex, Agency Road #7, Box 268, Sisseton, S.D. 57262. 40,000. Phone: (605) 698-3998 or 3787.

American Jail Association (1981): 2053 Day Rd., Suite 100, Hagerstown, Md. 21740-9795. 5,000. Phone: (301) 790-3930; fax: (301) 790-2941; http://www.corrections.com/aja.

American Kennel Club (1884): 51 Madison Ave., New York, N.Y. 10010. 505 member clubs. Phone: (212) 696-8200 or (919) 233-9767 (customer service).

American Legion, The (1919): P.O. Box 1055, Indianapolis, Ind. 46206. 3,100,000. Phone: (317) 630-1200.

American Legion Auxiliary (1919): 777 N. Meridian St., Indianapolis, Ind. 46204. 1,000,000. Phone: (317) 635-6291.

American Mensa, Ltd. (1960): 201 Main St., Suite 1101, Fort Worth, Texas 76102. 50,000. Phone: (817) 332-2600.

American Montessori Society (1960): 150 Fifth Ave., Suite 203, New York, N.Y. 10011. 12,000. Phone: (212) 924-3209.

American Museum of Natural History (1869): Central Park West at 79th St., New York, N.Y. 10024-5192. 531,000. Phone: (212) 769-5100.

American Philosophical Society (1743): 105 S. 5th St., Philadelphia, Pa. 19106-3386. 584 (resident), 126 (foreign). Phone: (215) 440-3400.

American Planning Association (1909): 1776 Massachusetts Ave. N.W., Washington, D.C. 20036 (headquarters). 30,000. Phone: (202) 872-0611. Administrative Offices: 122 S.Michigan Ave., Chicago, Ill. 60603. Phone: (312) 431-9100.

Americans for Democratic Action, Inc. (1947): 1625 K St. N.W., Suite 210, Washington, D.C. 20006. 70,000. Phone: (202) 785-5980.

American Society for Public Administration (ASPA) (1939): 1120 G St. N.W., Suite 700, Washington, D.C. 20005. 14,000. Phone: (202) 393-7878.

American Society of CLU & ChFC (1928): 270 S. Bryn Mawr Ave., Bryn Mawr, Pa. 19010-2195. Phone: (610) 526-2500.

American Universities, Association of (1900): One Dupont Circle N.W., Suite 730, Washington, D.C. 20036. Phone: (202) 466-5030.

American Water Resources Association (1964): 950 Herndon Parkway, Ste. 300, Herndon, Va. 22070-5528. 4,000. Phone: (703) 904-1225; fax: (703) 904-1228; e-mail: awrahq@aol.com; http://www.uwin.siuedu/~awra.

America's Community Bankers (1992): 900 19th St. N.W., Suite 400, Washington, D.C. 20006. Phone: (202) 857-3100.

AMIDEAST (America-Mideast Educational and Training Services) (1951): 1730 M St. N.W., Suite 1100, Washington, D.C. 20036-4505. 192 institutional members. Phone: (202) 776-9600.

Amnesty International/USA (1961): 322 Eighth Ave., New York, N.Y. 10001-4808. 300,000. Phone: (212) 807-8400.

AMVETS (American Veterans of World War II, Korea, and Vietnam) (1944): 4647 Forbes Blvd., Lanham, Md. 20706-4380. 250,000. Phone: (301) 459-9600.

Animal Protection Institute (1968): 2831 Fruitridge Rd., P.O. Box 22505, Sacramento, Calif. 95822. Phone: (916) 731-5521.

Animals, The American Society for the Prevention of Cruelty to (ASPCA) (1866): 424 E. 92nd St., New York, N.Y. 10128. 400,000+. Phone: (212) 876-7700.

Animals, The Fund For, Inc. (1967): 200 W. 57th St., New York, N.Y. 10019. 175,000. Phone: (212) 246-2096.

Animal Welfare Institute (1951): P.O. Box 3650, Washington, D.C. 20007. 4,500. Phone: (202) 337-2332.

Anthropological Association, American (1902): 4350 N. Fairfax Dr., Suite 640, Arlington, Va. 22203-1620. 11,500. Phone: (703) 528-1902.

Anti-Defamation League of B'nai B'rith (1913): 823 United Nations Plaza, New York, N.Y. 10017-3560. Phone: (212) 885-7700.

Anti-Vivisection Society, The American (1883): 801 Old York Rd., #204, Jenkintown, Pa. 19046-1685. 15,000. Phone: (215) 887-0816; fax: (215) 887-2088.

APMI International (1958): 105 College Rd. East, Princeton, N.J. 08540. 2,800. Phone: (609) 452-7700.

Appraisers, American Society of (1936): P.O. Box 17265, Washington, D.C. 20041. 6,500. Phone: (800) ASA-VALU or (703) 478-2228.

Arboriculture, International Society of (1924): P.O. Box GG, Savoy, Ill. 61874-9902. 8,000. Phone: (217) 355-9411; fax: (217) 355-9516.

Archaeological Institute of America (1879): 656 Beacon St., Boston, Mass. 02215-2010. 11,000. Phone: (617) 353-9361.

Architects, The American Institute of (1857): 1735 New York Ave. N.W., Washington, D.C. 20006-5292. 58,000. Phone: (202) 626-7300.

Architectural Historians, Society of (1940): 1365 N. Astor St., Chicago, Ill. 60610-2144. 4,000. Phone: (312) 573-1365; fax: (312) 573-1141.

Army, Association of the United States (1950): 2425 Wilson Blvd., Arlington, Va. 22210-3385. 111,000. Phone: (703) 841-4300.

Arthritis Foundation (1948): 1330 West Peachtree St., Atlanta, Ga. 30309. 69 local chapters. Phone: (404) 872-7100 or (800) 283-7800.

Arts, National Endowment for the (1965): 1100 Pennsylvania Ave. N.W., Washington, D.C. 20506. Phone: (202) 682-5400.

Arts, The American Federation of (1909): 41 E. 65th St., New York, N.Y. 10021. 525+ institutional members (museums), 400+ individual members (patrons). Phone: (212) 988-7700.

Arts and Letters, American Academy of (1898): 633 W. 155th St., New York, N.Y. 10032. 250. Phone: (212) 368-5900.

ASAE—The Society for engineering in agricultural, food, and biological systems (1907): 2950 Niles Rd., St. Joseph, Mich. 49085. 10,000. Phone: (616) 429-0300.

ASM International® (1913): Materials Park, Ohio 44073-0002. 48,000. Phone: (216) 338-5151; fax: (216) 338-4634.

Association for Investment Management and Research (1990): 5 Boar's Head Lane, P.O. Box 3668, Charlottesville, Va. 22903. 26,000. Phone: (804) 980-3668.

Astronomical Society, American (1899): Office of Secretary, Dept. of Physics and Astronomy, Baton Rouge, La. 70803-4001. 6,300. Phone: (504) 388-1160.

Astronomical Society of the Pacific (1889): 390 Ashton Ave., San Francisco, Calif. 94112. 6,200. Phone: (415) 337-1100.

Atheists, American (1963):7215 Cameron Rd., Austin, Tex. 78752. 40,000 Families. Phone: (512) 458-1244.

Auctioneers Association, National (1949): 8880 Ballentine, Overland Park, Kan. 66214-1985. 5,591. ·Phone: (913) 541-8084; fax: (913) 894-5281; e-mail: naahq@aol.com.

Audubon Society, National (1905): 700 Broadway, New York, N.Y. 10003-9562. 600,000. Phone: (212) 979-3000.

Authors League of America (1912): 330 W. 42nd St., 29th Floor, New York, N.Y. 10036-6902. 14,000. Phone: (212) 564–8350.

Autism Society of America (1965): 7910 Woodmont Ave., Suite 650, Bethesda, Md. 20814. Phone: (301) 657-0881; or (800) 3AUTISM.

Automobile Club, National (1924): Bayside Plaza, 188 The Embarcadero, #300, San Francisco, Calif. 94105. 300,000. Phone: (415) 777-4000.

Automotive Hall of Fame (1939): P.O. Box 1727, Midland, Mich. 48641-1727. Phone: (517) 631-5760.

AZA (American Zoo and Aquarium Association) (1924): Exec. Office/Conservation Center, 7970-D Old Georgetown Rd., Bethesda, Md. 20814-2493. 6,000. Phone: (301) 907-7777.

Bar Association, American (1878): 750 N. Lake Shore Dr., Chicago, Ill. 60611-4497. 371,000. Phone: (312) 988-5000.

Barber Shop Quartet Singing in America, Society for the Preservation and Encouragement of (SPEBSQSA, Inc.) (1938): 6315 Third Ave., Kenosha, Wis., 53143-5199. 34,000. Phone: (414) 653-8440.

Better Business Bureaus, Council of (1970): 4200 Wilson Blvd., Suite 800, Arlington, Va. 22203-1804. Phone: (703) 276-0100; fax: (703) 525-8277.

Bible Society, American (1816): 1865 Broadway, New York, N.Y. 10023-9980. 300,000. Phone: (212) 408-1200.

Biblical Literature, Society of (1880): 1201 Clair-mont Ave., Suite 300, Decatur, Ga. 30030.. 6,500 members, 1,200 subscribers. Phone: (404) 636-4744.; fax: (404) 248-0815.

Bibliographical Society of America (1904): P.O. Box 397, Grand Central Station, New York, N.Y. 10163. 1,200. Phone/fax: (212) 647-9171.

Big Brothers Big Sisters of America (1977): 230 N. 13th St., Philadelphia, Pa. 19107. Phone: (215) 567-7000.

Biochemistry and Molecular Biology, American Society for (1906): 9650 Rockville Pike, Bethesda, Md. 20814. 9,000. Phone: (301) 530-7145.

Biological Sciences, American Institute of (1947): 1444 Eye St. N.W., Washington, D.C. 20005. 14,000. Phone: (202) 628-1500.

Blind, American Council of the (1961): 1155 15th St. N.W., Suite 720, Washington, D.C. 20005. 40,000. Phone: (202) 467–5081.

Blind, National Federation of the (1940): 1800 Johnson St., Baltimore, Md. 21230. 50,000. Phone: (410) 659-9314.

Blindness, Research to Prevent (1960): 645 Madison Ave., New York, N.Y. 10022-1010. 1,250. Phone: (212) 752-4333.

Blue Cross and Blue Shield Association (1948 and 1946): 676 N. St. Clair St., Chicago, Ill. 60611. 63 Plans. Phone: (312) 440-6000.

B'nai B'rith International (1843): 1640 Rhode Island Ave. N.W., Washington, D.C. 20036-3278. 500,000. Phone: (202) 857-6600.

Booksellers Association, American (1900): 828 So. Broadway, Tarrytown, N.Y. 10591. 7,500. Phone: (914) 591-2665, (800) 637-0037.

Boys & Girls Clubs of America (1906): 1230 West Peachtree St. N.W., Atlanta, Ga. 30309-3447. 2,420,834 youths served. Phone: (404) 815-5700; fax: (404) 815-5757.

Boy Scouts of America (1910): 1325 W. Walnut Hill Lane, P.O. Box 152079, Irving, Tex. 75015-2079. 5,456,641. Phone: (214) 580-2000.

Bridge, Tunnel, and Turnpike Association, International (1932): 2120 L St. N.W., Suite 305, Washington, D.C. 20037-1527. 250. Phone: (202) 659-4620.

Broadcasters, National Association of (1922): 1771 N St. N.W., Washington, D.C. 20036-2891. 6,500. Phone: (202) 429-5300.

Brookings Institution, The (1916): 1775 Massachusetts Ave. N.W., Washington, D.C. 20036-2188. Phone: (202) 797-6000.

Brooks Bird Club, Inc., The (1932): 707 Warwood Ave., Wheeling, W. Va. 26003. 1,000. Phone: (614) 635-9246.

Business Education Association, National (1946): 1914 Association Dr., Reston, Va. 22091-1596. 14,000. Phone: (703) 860-8300.

Business Women's Association, American (1949): 9100 Ward Parkway, P.O. Box 8728, Kansas City, Mo. 64114-0728. 90,000. Phone: (816) 361-6621.

Camp Fire Boys and Girls (1910): 4601 Madison Ave., Kansas City, Mo. 64112-1278. 700,000. Phone: (816) 756-1950.

Camping Association, The American (1910): 5000 State Rd. 67 N., Martinsville, Ind. 46151-7902. 5,500. Phone: (317) 342-8456.

Cancer Society, American (1913): 1599 Clifton Rd. N.E., Atlanta, Ga. 30329. 2,646,070 volunteers. Phone: (800) ACS-2345 or check local listings.

CARE, Inc. (1945): 151 Ellis St. NE, Atlanta, Ga. 30303-2349. Programs in 61 developing countries. Phone: (404) 681-2552.

Carnegie Endowment for International Peace (1910): 2400 N St. N.W., Washington, D.C. 20037. Phone: (202) 862-7900; fax: (202) 862-2610.

Catholic Charities USA (1910): 1731 King St., Alexandria, Va. 22314. 3,000 individuals, 1,200 agencies and institutions. Phone: (703) 549-1390.

Catholic Daughters of the Americas (1903): 10 W. 71st St., New York, N.Y. 10023. 125,000. Phone: (212) 877-3041.

Catholic Historical Society, American (1884): 263 S. Fourth St., Philadelphia, Pa. 19106. 950. Phone: (215) 925-5752.

Catholic War Veterans of the U.S.A. Inc. (1935): 441 N. Lee St., Alexandria, Va. 22314. 30,000. Phone: (703) 549-3622.

Ceramic Society, The American (1899): P.O. Box 6136, Westerville, Ohio 43081-6136.

Cerebral Palsy Associations, Inc., United (1949): 1660 L St. N.W., Suite 700, Washington, D.C. 20036. 160 affiliates. Phone: (202) 776-0406/TT (202) 842-1266.

Chamber of Commerce of the U.S. (1912): 1615 H St. N.W., Washington, D.C. 20062-2000. 220,000. Phone: (202) 659-6000.

Chemical Engineers, American Institute of (1908): 345 E. 47th St., New York, N.Y. 10017-2395. 59,000. Phone: (212) 705-7338 or (800) 242-4363.

Chemical Manufacturers Association, Inc. (1872): 1300 Wilson Blvd., Arlington, Va. 22209. 189 companies. Phone: (703) 741-5000.

Chemical Society, American (1876): 1155 16th St. N.W., Washington, D.C. 20036. 151,024. Phone: (202) 872-4600.

Chemists, The American Institute of (1923): 501 Wythe St., Alexandria, Va. 22314-1917. 5,000. Phone: (703) 836-2090; fax: (703) 836-2091; e-mail: 76744.2677@compuserve.com.

Chess Federation, United States (1939): 186 Rt. 9W, New Windsor, N.Y. 12553. 83,000. Phone: (914) 562-8350/(800) 388–KING.

Child Labor Committee, National (1904): 1501 Broadway, Rm. 1111, New York, N.Y. 10036. Phone: (212) 840-1801.

Children's Aid Society, The (1853): 105 E. 22nd St., New York, N.Y. 10010. Child welfare services, community centers, camps, health services, foster care/adoption, and community schools. Phone: (212) 949-4800.

Children's Book Council (1945): 568 Broadway, Suite 404, New York, N.Y. 10012. 77 imprints. Phone: (212) 966-1990; fax: (212) 966-2073; e-mail: staff@cbcbooks.org; http://www.cbcbooks.org.

Child Welfare League of America (1920): 440 First St. N.W., Suite 310, Washington, D.C. 20001-2085. Phone: (202) 638-2952.

Chiropractic Association, American (1963): 1701 Clarendon Blvd., Arlington, Va. 22209. 21,300. Phone: (703) 276-8800.

Cities, National League of (1924): 1301 Pennsylvania Ave. N.W., Washington, D.C. 20004. 17,000 cities and towns. Phone: (202) 626-3000.

Civil Air Patrol, National Headquarters (1941): 105 S. Hansell St., Bldg. 714, Maxwell AFB, Ala. 36116-6332. 52,048. Phone: (334) 953-4287.

Civil Engineers, American Society of (1852): 345 E. 47th St., New York, N.Y. 10017-2398. 120,000. Phone: (212) 705-7496.

Clinical Chemistry, Inc., American Association for (1948): 2101 L St. N.W., Suite 202, Washington, D.C. 20037. 11,000. Phone (202) 857-0717.

Clinical Pathologists, American Society of (1922): 2100 W. Harrison St., Chicago, Ill. 60612-3798. 62,821. Phone: (312) 738-1336; fax: (312) 738-9798

Collectors Association, American (1939): Box 39106, Minneapolis, Minn. 55439-0106. Over 3,600 debt collection agencies. Phone: (612) 926-6547.

College Board, The (1900): 45 Columbus Ave., New York, N.Y. 10023-6992. 2,900 institutions. Phone: (212) 713-8000.

The College Fund/UNCF (1944): 8260 Willow Oaks Corporate Dr., P.O. Box 10444, Fairfax, Va. 22031-4511. Phone: (703) 205-3400; fax: (703) 205-3577.

Colleges and Employers, National Association of (formerly College Placement Council) (1956): 62 E. Highland Ave., Bethlehem, Pa. 18017. 2,937. Phone: (610) 868-1421.

Common Cause (1970): 1250 Connecticut Ave. N.W., Washington, D.C. 20036. 250,000. Phone: (202) 833-1200.

Community Colleges, American Association of (1920): One Dupont Circle N.W., Suite 410, Washington, D.C. 20036-1176. 1,100 institutions. Phone: (202) 728-0200.

Community Cultural Center Association, American (1978): 149 Cannongate III, Nashua, N.H. 03063. Phone: (603) 886-2748.

Composers/USA, National Association of (1932): P.O. Box 49256, Barrington Station, Los Angeles, Calif. 90049. 550. Phone: (310) 541-8213.

Congress of Racial Equality (CORE) (1942): 30 Cooper Square, New York, N.Y. 10003. Phone: (212) 598-4000. Nationwide network of chapters.

Conscientious Objectors, Central Committee for (1948): 1515 Cherry St., Philadelphia, Pa. 19102. Phone: (215) 563-8787; 655 Sutter St., Suite 514, San Francisco, Calif. 94102. Phone: (415) 474-3002.

Conservation Engineers, Association of (1961): Alabama Dept. of Cons. & Natural Resources, Engineering Section, 64 N. Union St., Montgomery, Ala. 36130. Phone: (334) 242-3476.

Consulting Chemists & Chemical Engineers, Inc., Association of (1928): The Chemists Club, 40 W. 45th St., New York, N.Y. 10036. 130. Phone: (212) 983-3160; fax: (212) 983-3161; e-mail: ACC+CE104206,1620; http://www.wwwprovider.com/chem/

Consumer Federation of America (1968): 1424 16th St. N.W., Suit 604, Washington, D.C. 20036. 240 member organizations. Phone: (202) 387-6121.

Consumer Interests, American Council on (1953): 240 Stanley Hall, Univ. of Missouri, Columbia, Mo. 65211. 1,500. Phone: (573) 882-3817.

Consumers League, National (1899): 1701 K St. N.W., Suite 1200, Washington, D.C. 20006. Phone: (202) 835-3323.

Consumers Union (1936): 101 Truman Ave., Yonkers, N.Y. 10703-1057. 4.6 million subscribers to *Consumer Reports Magazine*. Phone: (914) 378-2000.

Counselors, American College of (1984): 100 Camellia Lane, Indianapolis, Ind. 46219. Phone: (317) 898-3211.

Country Music Association (1958): One Music Circle South, Nashville, Tenn. 37203. 7,000+. Phone: (615) 244-2840.

Credit Management, National Association of (1896): 8815 Centre Park Dr., Suite 200, Columbia, Md. 21045. Phone: (410) 740-5560.

Credit Union National Association (1934): P.O. Box 431, Madison, Wis. 53701. 51 state leagues representing 12,400 credit unions. Phone: (608) 231-4000.

Crime and Delinquency, National Council on (1907): 685 Market St., #620, San Francisco, Calif. 94105. Criminal justice research, nationwide membership. Phone: (415) 896-6223.

CSA/USA, Celiac Sprue Association/United States of America, Inc., P.O. Box 31700, Omaha,

Neb. 68131-0700. 6 regions in U.S., 74 chapters, 36 active resource units. Phone: (402) 558-0600; fax: (402) 558-1347.

Dairy Council, National (1915): 10255 W. Higgins Rd., Suite 900, Rosemont, Ill. 60018-5616. Phone: (847) 803-2000; fax: (847) 803-2077.

Daughters of the American Revolution, National Society (1890): 1776 D St. N.W., Washington, D.C. 20006. 200,000. Phone: (202) 628-1776.

Deaf, National Association of the (1880): 814 Thayer Ave., Silver Spring, Md. 20910. Phone: (301) 587-1788 V; (301) 587-1789 TTY.

Defenders of Wildlife (1947): 1101 14th St. N.W., #1400, Washington, D.C. 20005. 137,000 members and supporters. Phone: (202) 682-9400.

Defense Preparedness Association, American (1919): Two Colonial Place, Suite 400, 2101 Wilson Blvd., Arlington, Va. 22201-3061. 24,000 individual, 700 corporate. Phone: (703) 522-1820.

Dental Association, American (1859): 211 E. Chicago Ave., Chicago, Ill. 60611. 140,000. Phone: (312) 440-2500.

Diabetes Association, American (1940): 1660 Duke St., Alexandria, Va. 22314. Phone: (703) 549-1500.

Dignity (1969): 1500 Massachusetts Ave. N.W., Suite 11, Washington, D.C. 20005. 5,000. Phone: (202) 861-0017 and (800) 877-8797.

Disabled American Veterans (1920): 807 Maine Ave. S.W., Washington, D.C. 20024. 1.4 million. Phone: (202) 554-3501.

Dowsers, Inc., The American Society of (1961): P.O. Box 24, Danville, Vt. 05828-0024. 5,000. Phone: (802) 684-3417; fax: (802) 748-8565; e-mail: ASD@dowsers.org; http://www.new hampshire.com/dowser/asd.htm

Drug, Chemical & Allied Trades Association, Inc., The (1890): 2 Roosevelt Ave., 3301, Syosset, N.Y. 11791. 575. Phone (516) 496-3317.

Ducks Unlimited, Inc. (1937): One Waterfowl Way, Memphis, Tenn. 38120. 581,000. Phone: (901) 758-3825.

Earthwatch (1972): 680 Mt. Auburn St., Box 403N, Watertown, Mass. 02272. 75,000. Phone: (800) 776-0188.

Eastern Star, Order of, General Grand Chapter (1876): 1618 New Hampshire Ave. N.W., Washington, D.C. 20009. 1,207,301. Phone: (202) 667-4737.

Easter Seal Society, The National (1919): 230 W. Monroe, 18th Floor, Chicago, Ill. 60606-4802. 124 state and local affiliate societies operating 409 service sites. Phone: (800) 221-6827 and (312) 726-4258 TDD.

Economic Association, American (1885): 2014 Broadway, Suite 305, Nashville, Tenn. 37203-2418. 21,000. 6,000 inst. subscribers. Phone: (615) 322-2595.

Economic Development, Committee for (1942): 477 Madison Ave., New York, N.Y. 10022. 250 trustees. Phone: (212) 688-2063.

Edison Electric Institute (1933): 701 Pennsylvania Ave. N.W., Washington, D.C. 20004-2696.

Education, American Council on (1918): One Dupont Circle N.W., Washington, D.C. 20036-1193. 1,600 institutions; over 200 organizations. Phone: (202) 939-9300.

Education, Council for Advancement and Support of (CASE) (1974): 11 Dupont Circle N.W., Suite 400, Washington, D.C. 20036-1261. 2,928 institutions; 14,500 individuals. Phone: (202) 328-5900.

Educational Exchange, International, Council on (1947): 205 E. 42nd St., New York, N.Y. 10017. 265. Phone: (212) 822-2600.

Educational Research Association, American (1916): 1230 17th St. N.W., Washington, D.C. 20036. 22,000. Phone: (202) 223-9485.

Education Association, National (1857): 1201 16th St. N.W., Washington, D.C. 20036-3290. 2.2 million. Phone: (202) 833-4000.

Electrochemical Society, The (1902): 10 S. Main St., Pennington, N.J. 08534-2896. 6,400. Phone: (609) 737-1902; fax: (609) 737-2743; e-mail: ecs@electrochem.org; http://electrochem.org.

Electronic Industries Association (1924): 2500 Wilson Blvd., Arlington, Va. 22201. 1,000 member companies. Phone: (703) 907-7500.

Elks of the U.S.A., Benevolent and Protective Order of the (1868): 2750 N. Lakeview Ave., Chicago, Ill. 60614. 1,300,000. Phone: (312) 477-2750.

Energy Engineers, Association of (1977): 4025 Pleasantdale Rd., Suite 420, Atlanta, Ga. 30340. 8,500. Phone: (770) 447-5083; fax: (770) 446-3969; http://www.aeecenter.org.

Engineering Science & Mechanics, Dept. of, Virginia Polytechnic Institute & State Univ., Blacksburg, Va. 24061-0219. Phone: (540) 231-6651; fax: (540) 231-4574; http://www.esm.vt.edu/esm.html.

English-Speaking Union of the United States (1920): 16 E. 69th St., New York, N.Y. 10021. 18,000. Phone: (212) 879-6800.

Entomological Society of America (1889): 9301 Annapolis Rd., Lanham, Md. 20706-3115. 8,500. Phone: (301) 731-4535.

Esperanto League for North America, The (1952): P.O. Box 1129, El Cerrito, Calif. 94530. Over 1,000. Phone: (800) 828-5944.

Exceptional Children, The Council for (1922): 1920 Association Dr., Reston, Va. 22091. 54,000. Phone: (703) 620-3660.

Experimental Test Pilots, The Society of (1956): 44814 Elm St., Lancaster, Calif. 93534. 1,950. Phone: (805) 942-9574.

Exploration Geophysicists, Society of (1930): P.O. Box 702740, Tulsa, Okla. 74170-2740. 14,500. Phone: (918) 497-5500.

Family and Consumer Sciences, American Association of (1909): 1555 King St., Alexandria, Va. 22314. 20,000. Phone: (703) 706-4600.

Family Campers & RVers (1949): 4804 Transit Rd., Bldg. 2, Depew, N.Y. 14043-4906. 24,000 families. Phone: (716) 668-6242.

Family Physicians, American Academy of (1947): 8880 Ward Pkwy., Kansas City, Mo. 64114-2797. 80,000. Phone: (816) 333-9700.

Family Relations, National Council on (1938): 3989 Central Ave. N.E., #550, Minneapolis, Minn. 55421-3921. 3,800. Phone: (612) 781-9331.

Family Service America, Inc. (1911): 11700 W. Lake Park Dr., Park Place, Milwaukee, Wis. 53224. Approximately 280 member agencies. Phone: (414) 359-1040 or (800) 221-2681.

Farm Bureau Federation, American (1919): 225 Touhy Ave., Park Ridge, Ill. 60068. 4.4 million member families. Phone: (312) 399-5700.

Federal Bar Association (1920): 1815 H St. N.W., Suite 408, Washington, D.C. 20006-3697. 15,000. Phone: (202) 638-0252; fax: (202) 775-0295.

Federal Employees, National Federation of (1917): 1016 16th St. N.W., Washington, D.C. 20036. Rep. 150,000. Phone: (202) 862-4400.

Feline and Canine Friends, Inc. (1973): 505 N. Bush St., Anaheim, Calif. 92805. 500. Phone: (714) 635-7975.

Fellowship of Reconciliation (1915): Box 271, Nyack, N.Y. 10960. 20,000. Phone: (914) 358-4601.

Female Executives, National Association for (1972): 30 Irving Place, New York, N.Y. 10003. 200,000. Phone: (212) 477-2200.

FFA Organization, National (1928): 5632 Mt. Vernon Memorial Hwy., P.O. Box 15160, Alexandria, Va. 22309-0160. 401,574. Phone: (703) 360-3600.

Fire Protection Association, National (1896): One Batterymarch Park, P.O. Box 9101, Quincy, Mass. 02269-9101. 68,000. Phone: (617) 770-3000.

Flag Foundation, National (1968): Flag Plaza, Pittsburgh, Pa. 15219-3630. 3,000+. Phone: (412) 261-1776.

Fleet Reserve Association (1924): 125 N. West St., Alexandria, Va. 22314-2754. 156,000. Phone: (703) 683-1400.

Flight Test Engineers, Society of (1968): P.O. Box 4047, Lancaster, Calif. 93539-4047. 1,000. Phone: (805) 538-9715.

Foreign Policy Association (1918): 470 Park Ave. So., New York, N.Y. 10016. Phone: (212) 481-8100/(800) 628-5754.

Foreign Relations, Council on (1921): 58 E. 68th St., New York, N.Y. 10021. 2,600. Phone: (212) 734-0400.

Foreign Study, American Institute for (1965): 102 Greenwich Ave., Greenwich, Conn. 06830. Phone: (203) 869-9090/(800) 727-AIFS.

Foreign Trade Council, Inc., National (1914): 1270 Avenue of the Americas, New York, N.Y. 10020-1702. Over 550 companies. Phone: (212) 399-7128. Also, 1625 K St. N.W., Washington, D.C. 20006. Phone: (202) 887-0278.

Forensic Sciences, American Academy of (1948): 410 N. 21st St., Suite 203/80904, P.O. Box 669, Colorado Springs, Colo. 80901-0669. 4,315. Phone: (719) 636-1100; fax: (719) 636-1993; http://www.aafs.org.

Foresters, Society of American (1900): 5400 Grosvenor Lane, Bethesda, Md. 20814-2198. 19,000. Phone: (301) 897-8720.

4-H Program (early 1900s): Room 3441-S, U.S. Department of Agriculture, Washington, D.C. 20250. 5.6 million. Phone: (202) 720-2908.

Freedom of Information Center (1958): 127 Neff Annex, Univ. of Missouri, Columbia, Mo. 65211. Phone: (573) 882-4856.

French-American Chamber of Commerce (1896): 1350 Ave. of the Americas, New York, N.Y. 10019. 605. Membership Association. Phone: (212) 765-4460.

French Institute/Alliance Française (1898): 22 E. 60th St., New York, N.Y. 10022-1077. 9,000. Phone: (212) 355-6100.

Friendship and Good Will, International Society of (1978): 908 Hogan Way, Bakersfield, Calif. 93309. 4,236 members in 189 countries. Phone: (805) 836-0692.

Friends of Animals Inc. (1957): 777 Post Rd., Suite 205, Darien, Conn. 06820. 120,000. Phone: (203) 656-1522.

Friends of the Earth (1969): 1025 Vermont Ave. N.W., Suite 300, Washington, D.C. 20005. 35,000. Phone: (202) 783-7400.

Future Homemakers of America, Inc. (1945): 1910 Association Dr., Reston, Va. 20191. 250,000. Phone: (703) 476-4900.

Gamblers Anonymous: Box 17173, Los Angeles, Calif. 90017. Phone: (213) 386-8789.

Gay and Lesbian Task Force, National (1973): 2320 17th St. N.W., Washington, D.C. 20009-2702. 35,000 members. Phone: (202) 332-6483.

Genealogical Society, National (1903): 4527 17th St. N., Arlington, Va. 22207-2399. 15,000. Phone: (703) 525-0050; fax: (703) 525-0052; http://geneaology.org/ngs/

Genetic Association, American (1903): P.O. Box 257, Buckeystown, Md. 21717. 800. Phone/fax: (301) 695-9292.

Geographers, Association of American (1904): 1710 16th St. N.W., Washington, D.C. 20009-3198. 7,400. Phone: (202) 234-1450; fax: (202) 234-2744; e-mail: gaia@aag.org.

Geographic Education, National Council for (1915): 16A Leonard Hall, Indiana University of Pennsylvania, Indiana, Pa. 15705. 3,700. Phone: (412) 357-6290.

Geographic Society, National (1888): 1145 17th St. N.W., Washington, D.C. 20036. 9,200,000. Phone: (202) 857-7000.

Geological Institute, American (1948): 4220 King St., Alexandria, Va. 22302-1507. 29 geoscience societies representing 80,000 geoscientists. Phone: (703) 379-2480.

Geological Society of America, Inc. (1888): 3300 Penrose Pl., P.O. Box 9140, Boulder, Colo. 80301. 14,400. Phone: (303) 447-2020.

German American National Congress, The (Deutsch-Amerikanischer National Congress—D.A.N.K.) (1958): 4740 N. Western Ave., Executive Office, Chicago, Ill. 60625-2097. Phone: (312) 275-1100.

Gideons International, The (1889): 2900 Lebanon Rd., Nashville, Tenn. 37214-0800. 125,000. Phone: (615) 883-8533.

Gifted, The Association for the (1958): The Council for Exceptional Children, 1920 Association Dr., Reston, Va. 22091. 2,200. Phone: (703) 620-3660.

Girl Scouts of the U.S.A. (1912): 420 Fifth Ave., New York, N.Y. 10018. 3.5 million. Phone: (212) 852-8000.

Girls Incorporated (1945): 30 E. 33rd St., New York, N.Y. 10016. 350,000. Phone: (212) 689-3700.

Graphoanalysis Society, International (1929): 111 N. Canal St., Chicago, Ill. 60606. 10,000. Phone: (312) 930-9446.

Gray Panthers (1970): P.O. Box 21477, Washington, D.C. 20009-9477. Over 50 chapters (networks). Phone: (202) 466-3132.

Greenpeace (1971): 1436 U St. N.W., Washington, D.C. 20009. 1,600,000. Phone: (202) 462-1177.

Group Psychotherapy Association, American (1942): 25 E. 21st St., 6th Floor, New York, N.Y. 10010. 4,400 Phone: (212) 477-2677.

Guide Dog Foundation for the Blind, Inc.® (1946): 371 E. Jericho Turnpike, Smithtown, N.Y. 11787-2976. 80,000. Phone: (516) 265-2121; (800) 548-4337.

Hadassah, The Women's Zionist Organization of America (1912): 50 W. 58th St., New York, N.Y. 10019. 385,000. Phone: (212) 355-7900.

Handgun Control, Inc. (1974): 1225 Eye St. N.W., Washington, D.C. 20005. 400,000. Phone: (202) 898-0792.

Heating, Refrigerating and Air-Conditioning Engineers, Inc., American Society of (1894): 1791 Tullie Circle N.E., Atlanta, Ga. 30329. 50,000. Phone: (404) 636-8400.

Helicopter Association International (1948): 1635 Prince St., Alexandria, Va. 22314. Phone: (703) 683-4646.

Hemispheric Affairs, Council on (1975): 724 9th St. N.W., Rm. 401, Washington, D.C. 20001. Phone: (202) 393-3322.

Historians, The Organization of American (1907): Indiana Univ., 112 N. Bryan St., Bloomington, Ind. 47408. 12,000. Phone: (812) 855-7311.

Historic Preservation, National Trust for (1949): 1785 Massachusetts Ave. N.W., Washington, D.C. 20036. 260,000. Phone: (202) 588-6000.

Horse Council, Inc., American (1969): 1700 K St. N.W., #300, Washington, D.C. 20006. More than 190 organizations and 2,400 individuals. Phone: (202) 296-4031.

Horse Shows Association, Inc., American (1917): 220 E. 42nd St., New York, N.Y. 10017-5876. 65,000. Phone: (212) 972-2472.

Horticultural Association, National Junior (1935): 1424 N. 8th, Durant, Okla. 74701. Phone: (405) 924-0771.

Horticultural Society, American (1922): 7931 East Boulevard Dr., Alexandria, Va. 22308. 20,000. Phone: (703) 768-5700 or (800) 777-7931; fax: (703) 765-6032; e-maili: gardenahs@aol.com

Hostelling International—American Youth Hostels (1934): 733 15th St. N.W., Suite 840, Washington, D.C. 20005. 124,000. Phone: (202) 783-6161 for membership and reservations.

Housing Science, International Association for (1972): P.O. Box 340254, Coral Gables/Miami, Fla. 33114. 500 professionals. Phone: (305) 446-9462.

Humane Association, American (1877): 63 Inverness Drive East, Englewood, Colo. 80112-5117. Phone: (303) 792-9900.

Humane Association, The American—Children's Division (1877): 63 Inverness Dr. East, Englewood, Colo. 80112. Phone: (303) 792-9900; fax: (303) 792-5333.

Humane Society of the United States (1954): 2100 L St. N.W., Washington, D.C. 20037. 3,100,000. Phone: (202) 452-1100.

Humanities, National Endowment for the (1965): 1100 Pennsylvania Ave. N.W., Washington, D.C. 20506. Phone: (202) 606-8400.

Hydrogen Energy, International Association for (1975): P.O. Box 248266, Coral Gables, Fla. 33124. 2,500. Phone: (305) 284-4666.

Illustrators, Society of (1901): 128 E. 63rd St., New York, N.Y. 10021. 865. Phone: (212) 838-2560 .

Industrial Engineers, Institute of (1948): 25 Technology Park/Atlanta, Norcross, Ga. 30092. 30,000. Phone: (770) 449-0461.

Interfraternity Conference, National (1909): 3901 W. 86th St., Suite 390, Indianapolis, Ind. 46268-1791. 62. Phone: (317) 872-1112.

International Credit Association (ICA) (1912): P.O. Box 419057, St. Louis, Mo. 63141-1757. 7,500 members, 100 local associations. Phone: (314) 991-3030; fax: (314) 991-3029.

Iron and Steel Institute, American (1908): 1101 17th St. N.W., Washington, D.C. 20036-4700. 1,200. Phone: (202) 452-7100.

Izaak Walton League of America (1922): 707 Conservation Lane, Gaithersburg, Md. 20878-2983. 55,000. Phone: (301) 548-0150.

Jewish Community Centers, World Confederation of (1946): 12 Hess St., Jerusalem, Israel 94185. Phone: (02) 251 265.

Jewish Community Centers Association (JCC) of North America (1917): 15 E. 26th St., New York, N.Y. 10010-1579. 281 affiliated Jewish Community Centers, YM-YWHAs, and camps serving 1 million+ members. Phone: (212) 532-4949; fax: (212) 481-4179; e-mail: info@jcca.org.

Jewish Congress, American (1918): 15 E. 84th St., New York, N.Y. 10028. 50,000. Phone: (212) 879-4500.

Jewish Historical Society, American (1892): 2 Thornton Rd., Waltham, Mass. 02154. 3,500. Phone: (617) 891-8110; fax: (617) 899-9208.

Jewish War Veterans of the U.S.A. (1896): 1811 R St. N.W., Washington, D.C. 20009-1659. Phone: (202) 265-6280.

Jewish Women, National Council of (1893): 53 W. 23rd St., New York, N.Y. 10010. 90,000. Phone: (212) 645-4048; fax: (212) 645-7466.

John Birch Society (1958): P.O. Box 8040, Appleton, Wis. 54913. Under 100,000. Phone: (414) 749-3780.

Journalists, Society of Professional, (1909): 16 S. Jackson, Greencastle, Ind. 46135-0077. 14,000. Phone: (317) 653-3333.

Journalists and Authors, American Society of (1948): 1501 Broadway, Suite 302, New York, N.Y. 10036. 800. Phone: (212) 997-0947; fax: (212) 768-7414; e-mail: 75227.1650@compuserve.com.

Judaism, American Council for (1943): P.O. Box 9009, Alexandria, Va. 22304. 10,000. Phone: (703) 836-2546.

Junior Achievement Inc. (1919): One Education Way, Colorado Springs, Colo. 80906-4477. 2.7 million. Phone: (719) 540-8000.

Junior Chamber of Commerce, The United States, Jaycees (1920): P.O. Box 7, Tulsa, Okla. 74102-0007. 132,000. Phone: (918) 584-2481; fax: (918) 582-7736.

Junior Leagues International, Inc., Association of (1921): 660 First Ave., New York, N.Y. 10016-3241. 293 Leagues, 200,000 members. Phone: (212) 683-1515.

Junior Statesmen of America (1934): 60 E. Third Ave., Suite 320, San Mateo, Calif. 94401. 15,000. Phone: (415) 347-1600 or (800) 334-5353.

Kiwanis International (1915): 3636 Woodview Trace, Indianapolis, Ind. 46268-3196. 325,000. Phone: (317) 875-8755.

Knights of Columbus (1882): One Columbus Plaza, New Haven, Conn. 06510-3326. 1,556,310. Phone: (203) 772-2130.

Knights Templar, Grand Encampment of (1816): 5097 N. Elston, Suite 101, Chicago, Ill. 60630. 225,000. Phone: (312) 777-3300.

La Leche League International (1956): 1400 N. Meacham Rd., P.O. Box 4079, Schaumburg, Ill. 60168-4079. 50,000. Phone: (847) 519-7730.

Law, American Society of International (1906): 2223 Massachusetts Ave. N.W., Washington, D.C. 20008. 4,300. Phone: (202) 939-6000.

League of Women Voters of the U.S. (1920): 1730 M St. N.W., Washington, D.C. 20036. Phone: (202) 429-1965; fax: (202) 429-0854.

Legal Aid and Defender Association, National (1911): 1625 K St. N.W., Suite 800, Washington, D.C. 20006. 2,400. Phone: (202) 452-0620.

Legal Secretaries, National Association of (1950): 2448 E. 81st St., Ste. 3400, Tulsa, Okla. 74137. 12,000. Phone: (918) 493-3540.

Leukemia Society of America (1949): 600 Third Ave., 4th Floor, New York, N.Y. 10016. Phone: (212) 573-8484.

Library Association, American (1876): 50 E. Huron St., Chicago, Ill. 60611. 55,356. Phone: (312) 944-6780; (800) 545-2433.

Life Insurance, American Council of (1976): 1001 Pennsylvania Ave. N.W., Washington, D.C. 20004-2599. 606. Phone: (202) 624-2000.

Life Underwriters, National Association of (1890): 1922 F St. N.W., Washington, D.C. 20006-4387. Phone: (202) 331-6000.

Lions Clubs International (1917): 300 22nd St., Oak Brook, Ill. 60521-8842. 1,419,408. Phone: (708) 571-5466.

Lung Association, American (1904): 1740 Broadway, New York, N.Y. 10019-4374. 105 constituent and affiliate associations. Phone: (800) LUNG-USA/(800) 586-4872.

Magazine Editors, American Society of (1963): 919 Third Ave., 22nd Floor, New York, N.Y. 10022. 800. Phone: (212) 872-3700.

Magazine Publishers of America (1919): 919 Third Ave., New York, N.Y. 10022. 334 companies, 1,200+ publications. Phone: (212) 872-3700.

Management Accountants, Institute of (1919): 10 Paragon Dr., Montvale, N.J. 07645-1760. 84,000. Phone: (201) 573-9000.

Management Association, American (1923): 1601 Broadway, New York, N.Y. 10019-7406. 70,000. Phone: (212) 586-8100.

Management Consultants, Institute of (1968): 521 Fifth Ave., 35th Floor, New York, N.Y. 10175-3598. 2,600 individuals. Phone: (212) 697-8262,.

Management Consulting Firms, Association of—ACME (1929): 521 Fifth Ave., 35th Floor, New York, N.Y. 10175-3598. 50 firms international. Phone: (212) 697-9693.

Manufacturers, National Association of (1895): 1331 Pennsylvania Ave. N.W., Suite 1500-North, Washington, D.C. 20004-1790. Approx. 14,000. Phone: (202) 637-3065.

Manufacturers' Agents National Association (MANA) (1947): 23016 Mill Creek Rd., P.O. Box 3467, Laguna Hills, Calif. 92654-3467. 7,000. Phone: (714) 859-4040.

March of Dimes Birth Defects Foundation (1938): 1275 Mamaroneck Ave., White Plains, N.Y. 10605. 104 chapters. Phone: (914) 428-7100.

Marine Conservation, Center for (1972): 1725 De Sales St. N.W., Suite 600, Washington, D.C. 20036. 120,000. Phone: (202) 429-5609.

Marine Corps Association (1913): Bldg. #715, Marine Corps Base, Quantico, Va. 22134. 100,723. Phone: (703) 640-6161/(800) 336-0291.

Marine Corps League (1937): 8626 Lee Hwy., Suite 201, Fairfax, Va. 22031. Correspondence address: P.O. Box 3070, Merrifield, Va. 22116-3070. 44,000. Phone: (703) 207-9588 or (703) 207-9589; fax: (703) 207-0047.

Marine Technology Society (1963): 1828 L St. N.W., Suite 906, Washington, D.C. 20036-5104. 2,700. Phone: (202) 775-5966; fax: (202) 429-9417.

Masons, Ancient and Accepted Scottish Rite, Northern Masonic Jurisdiction, Supreme Council 33 (1813): 33 Marrett Rd., Lexington, Mass. 02173. 358,479. Phone: (617) 862-4410.

Masons, Ancient and Accepted Scottish Rite, Southern Jurisdiction, Supreme Council 33° (1801): 1733 16th St. N.W., Washington, D.C. 20009. 500,000. Phone: (202) 232-3579.

Masons, Royal Arch, General Grand Chapter International (1797): P.O. Box 489, Danville, Ky. 40423-0489. 230,000. Phone: (606) 236-0757.

Massachusetts Audubon Society (1896): South Great Rd., Lincoln, Mass. 01773. 55,000 member households, 19 staffed wildlife sanctuaries. Phone: (617) 259-9500.

Mathematical Association of America (1915): 1529 18th St. N.W., Washington, D.C. 20036. 29,000. Phone: (202) 387-5200.

Mathematical Society, American (1888): P.O. Box 6248, Providence, R.I. 02940-6248. 29,350.

Phone: (401) 455-4000; e-mail: ams@ams.org; http://www.ams.org/

Mathematical Statistics, Institute of (1935): 3401 Investment Blvd. #7, Hayward, Calif. 94545-3819. 4,000. Phone: (510) 783-8141; fax: (510) 783-4131; e-mail: ims@stat.berkeley.edu.

Mayflower Descendants, General Society of (1897): 4 Winslow St., P.O. Box 3297, Plymouth, Mass. 02361. 25,000. Phone: (508) 746-3188.

Mechanical Engineers, American Society of (1880): 345 E. 47th St., New York, N.Y. 10017. 125,000. Phone: (212) 705-7722.

Mechanics, American Academy of (1969): Dept. of Engineering Science & Mechanics, VPI & State University, Blacksburg, Va. 24061-0219. 1,600. Phone: (540) 231-6841.

Medical Association, American (1847): 515 N. State St., Chicago, Ill. 60610-4377. Phone: (312) 464-5000.

Medical Library Association (1898): Six N. Michigan Ave., Suite 300, Chicago, Ill. 60602. 5,000. Phone: (312) 419-9094.

Mental Health Association, National (1909): 1021 Prince St., Alexandria, Va., 22314-2971. 1,000,000. Phone: (703) 684-7722.

Meteorological Society, American (1919): 45 Beacon St., Boston, Mass. 02108-3693. 10,000. Phone: (617) 227-2425.

Military Chaplains Association of the U.S.A. (1925): P.O. Box 42660, Washington, D.C. 20015-0660. 1,500. Phone: (202) 574-2423.

Mining, Metallurgical, and Petroleum Engineers, The American Institute of (1871): 345 E. 47th St., New York, N.Y. 10017. 4 Member Societies: Society for Mining, Metallurgy and Exploration, The Minerals, Metals & Materials Society, Iron & Steel Society, Society of Petroleum Engineers. Phone: (212) 705-7695.

Mining and Metallurgical Society of America (1910): 9 Escalle Lane, Larkspur, Calif. 94939. 370. Phone: (415) 924-7441.

Model Aeronautics, Academy of (1936): 5151 East Memorial Dr., Muncie, Ind. 47302. 160,000. Phone: (317) 287-1256.

Modern Language Association of America (1883): 10 Astor Place, New York, N.Y. 10003. 32,000. Phone: (212) 475-9500.

Modern Woodmen of America (1883): 1701 1st Ave., Rock Island, Ill. 61201. 756,392. Phone: (309) 786-6481.

Moose International, Inc. (1888): Mooseheart, Ill. 60539. 1,750,000. Phone: (708) 859-2000.

Mothers Against Drunk Driving (MADD) (1980): 511 E. John Carpenter Frwy., Suite 700, Irving, Texas 75062-8187. 3.2 million. Phone: (214) 744-6233; victim hotline: (800) GET-MADD.

Motion Picture & Television Engineers, Society of (1916): 595 W. Hartsdale Ave., White Plains, N.Y. 10607. 9,500. Phone: (914) 761-1100.

Motion Picture Arts & Sciences, Academy of (1927): 8949 Wilshire Blvd., Beverly Hills, Calif. 90211-1972. Phone: (310) 247-3000.

Multiple Sclerosis Society, National (1946): 733 Third Ave., New York, N.Y. 10017-3288. 400,000. Phone: (212) 986-3240/(800) FIGHT-MS (344-4867).

Muscular Dystrophy Association (1950): 3300 East Sunrise Dr., Tucson, Ariz. 85718. 2,300,000 volunteers. Phone: (520) 529-2000.

Museums, American Association of (1906): 1225 Eye St. N.W., Suite 200, Washington, D.C. 20005. 14,400. Phone: (202) 289-1818; fax: (202) 289-6578; tty: (202) 289-8439.

Muzzle Loading Rifle Association, National (1933): P.O. Box 67, Friendship, Ind. 47021. 25,000. Phone: (812) 667-5131.

NAFSA: Association of International Educators (1948): 1875 Connecticut Ave. N.W., Suite 1000, Washington, D.C. 20009-5728. 8,100. Phone: (202) 462-4811.

National Abortion and Reproductive Rights Action League (NARAL) (1969): 1156 15th St. N.W., Washington, D.C. 20005. 250,000. Phone: (202) 973-3000.

National Association for the Advancement of Colored People (1909): 4805 Mt. Hope Dr., Baltimore, Md. 21215-3297. 500,000+. Phone: (410) 358-8900.

National Audubon Society (1905): 700 Broadway, New York, N.Y. 10003-9501. 550,000. Phone: (212) 979-3000.

National Conference, The (founded as The Natl. Conf. of Christians & Jews) (1927): 71 Fifth Ave., New York, N.Y. 10003. 200,000. Phone: (212) 206-0006.

National Cooperative Business Association (formerly Cooperative League of the U.S.A.) (1916): 1401 New York Ave. N.W., Suite 1100, Washington, D.C. 20005. Phone: (202) 638-6222.

National Council of the Churches of Christ in the USA (1950): 475 Riverside Drive, New York, N.Y. 10115. 33 Protestant and Orthodox communions. Phone: (212) 870-2227.

National Grange, The (1867): 1616 H St. N.W., Washington, D.C. 20006-4999. 300,000. Phone: (202) 628-3507.

National Press Club (1908): National Press Bldg., 529 14th St. N.W., Washington, D.C. 20045. 4,500. Phone: (202) 662-7500.

National PTA (National Congress of Parents and Teachers) (1897): 330 N. Wabash Ave., Suite 2100, Chicago, Ill. 60611-3690. 7.0 million. Phone: (312) 670-6782; http://www.pta.org.

National Rifle Association of America (1871): 11250 Waples Mill Rd., Fairfax, Va. 22030. 3,300,000. Phone: (703) 267-1000.

National Urban League, Inc. (1910): 500 E. 62nd St., New York, N.Y. 10021. 113 affiliates in 34 states and D.C. Phone: (212) 310-9000.

Nature Conservancy, The (1951): 1815 N. Lynn St., Arlington, Va. 22209. 825,000. Phone: (703) 841-5300.

Naturopathic Physicians, American Association of (1986): 2366 Eastlake Ave., E. Ste. 322; Seattle, Wash. 98102. 450 ND members, 200 student; 45 corporate, 50 other. Phone: (206) 328-8510; fax: (206) 323-7612; e-mail: 75602.3715@ Compuserve.com; http://Infinite.org/Naturopathic.Physician

Naval Architects and Marine Engineers, The Society of (1893): 601 Pavonia Ave., Jersey City, N.J. 07306. 10,000. Phone: (201) 798-4800.

Naval Engineers, American Society of (1888): 1452 Duke St., Alexandria, Va. 22314. 6,800. Phone: (703) 836-6727.

Naval Institute, United States (1873): 118 Maryland Ave., Annapolis, Md. 21402-5035. 90,000. Phone: (410) 268-6110.

Navigation, The Institute of (1945): 1800 Diagonal Rd., Suite 480, Alexandria, Va. 22314. 3,800. Phone: (703) 683-7101; fax: (703) 683-7105; e-mail: postmaster@ion.org.

Navy League of the United States (1902): 2300 Wilson Blvd., Arlington, Va. 22201-3308. 71,500; John R. Dalrymple, Rear Admiral, USN (Ret.), Executive Director.

Neurofibromatosis Foundation, Inc., The National (1978): 95 Pine St., 16th Floor, New York, N.Y. 10005. 33,000. Phone: (800) 323-7938; in N.Y. State (212) 344NNFF; fax: (212) 747-0004; e-mail: nnff@aol.com; http://www.nf.org.

Newspaper Association of America (1887): The Newspaper Center, 11600 Sunrise Valley Dr., Reston, Va. 20191. 1,050. Phone: (703) 648-1000.

Newspaper Editors, American Society of (1922): P.O. Box 4090, Reston, Va. 20195-1700. 870. Phone: (703) 648-1144.

Nondestructive Testing, Inc., The American Society for (1941): 1711 Arlingate Lane, P.O. Box 28518, Columbus, Ohio 43228-0518. 10,240. Phone: (800) 222-ASNT.

NOT SAFE (National Organization Taunting Safety and Fairness Everywhere) (1980): P.O. Box 5743, Montecito, Calif. 93150. 975. Phone: (805) 969-6217.

Nuclear Society, American (1954): 555 N. Kensington Ave., La Grange Park, Ill. 60526. 14,700. Phone: (708) 352-6611.

Numismatic Association, American (1891): 818 N. Cascade Ave., Colorado Springs, Colo. 80903-3279. 30,000. Phone: (719) 632-2646; e-mail: ana@money.org.

Nurses Association, American (1896): 600 Maryland Ave. S.W., Suite 100, Washington, D.C. 20024-2571. 209,000. Phone: (202) 651-7000.

Nutrition, American Institute of (1928): 9650 Rockville Pike, Bethesda, Md. 20814-3990. 3,600. Phone: (301) 530-7050.

Odd Fellows, Sovereign Grand Lodge, Independent Order of (1819): 422 Trade St., Winston-Salem, N.C. 27101-2830. 460,000. Phone: (910) 725-5955.

Olympic Committee, United States (1921): One Olympic Plaza, Colorado Springs, Colo. 80909-5760. Phone: (719) 632-5551.

Optimist International (1919): 4494 Lindell Blvd., St. Louis, Mo. 63108. 155,000. Phone: (314) 371-6000.

Optometric Association, American (1898): 243 N. Lindbergh Blvd., St. Louis, Mo. 63141. 31,000. Phone: (314) 991-4100.

Organization of American States, General Secretariat (1890): 1889 F St. N.W., Washington, D.C. 20006. 35 member nations. Phone: (202) 458-3000.

Ornithologists' Union, American (1883): c/o National Museum of Natural History, NHB E607, MRC-116, Smithsonian Institution, Washington, D.C. 20560. 5,000. Phone: (202) 357-2051.

Overeaters Anonymous, Inc. (1960): P.O. Box 44020, Rio Rancho, N. Mex. 87174-4020. 150,000. Phone: (505) 891-2664.

Parents, Families and Friends of Lesbians and Gays (1981): 1101 14th St. N.W., Suite 1030, Washington, D.C. 20005. 42,000+ members. 365 chapters in 12 countries. Phone: (202) 638-4200.

Parents Without Partners (1957): 401 N. Michigan Ave., Chicago, Ill. 60611-4267. Phone: (312) 644-6610.

Pathology, American Society for Investigative (1976): 9650 Rockville Pike, Bethesda, Md. 20814-3993. 2,300. Phone: (301) 530-7130.

Peace Action (a merger of SANE and the Nuclear Weapons Freeze Campaign) (1957): 1819 H St. N.W., Suite 420, Washington, D.C. 20006-3603. 50,000. Phone: (202) 862-9740.

People For the American Way (1980): 2000 M St. N.W., Suite 400, Washington, D.C. 20036. 300,000. Phone: (202) 467-4999.

Petroleum Geologists, American Association of (1917): P.O. Box 979, Tulsa, Okla. 74101-0979. 31,500. Phone: (918) 584-2555.

Pharmaceutical Association, American (1852): 2215 Constitution Ave. N.W., Washington, D.C. 20037. 48,000. Phone: (202) 628-4410.

Philatelic Society, American (1886): P.O. Box 8000, State College, Pa. 16803. 57,000. Phone: (814) 237-3803.

Photogrammetry and Remote Sensing, American Society for (1934): 5410 Grosvenor Lane, Suite 210, Bethesda, Md. 20814-2160. Phone: (301) 493-0290; fax: (301) 493-0208; e-mail: asprs@asprs.org.

Photographic Society of America (1934): 3000 United Founders Blvd., Suite 103, Oklahoma City, Okla. 73112. Phone: (405) 843-1437.

Photography, International Center of (1974): 1130 Fifth Ave., New York, N.Y. 10128. Midtown branch: 1133 Avenue of the Americas, New York, N.Y. 10036. Phone: (212) 860-1777.

Physical Society, The American (1899): One Physics Ellipse, College Park, Md. 20740-3844. 41,000. Phone: (301) 209-3269.

Physical Therapy Association, American (APTA) (1921): 1111 N. Fairfax St., Alexandria, Va. 22314. 70,000. Phone: (703) 684-2782.

Physics, American Institute of (1931): One Physics Ellipse, College Park, Md. 20740-3843. 125,000. Phone: (301) 209-3100.

Pilot International (1921): Pilot International Headquarters, 244 College St., P.O. Box 4844, Macon, Ga. 31213-0599. 17,000. Phone: (912) 743-7403.

Planetary Society, The (1979): 65 N. Catalina Ave., Pasadena, Calif. 91106. 120,000. Phone: (818) 793-5100.

PLAN International (1937): P.O. Box 7670, 155 PLAN Way, Warwick, R.I. 02887. Phone: (401) 294–3693; fax: (401) 295–7062

Planned Parenthood® Federation of America, Inc., (1916): 810 Seventh Ave., New York, N.Y. 10019. 150 affiliates. Phone: (212) 541-7800; fax: (212) 245-1845; www.http://www.ppfa.org/ppfa.

Plastics Engineers, Society of (1942): 14 Fairfield Dr., Brookfield, Conn. 06804-0403. 37,000. Phone: (203) 775-0471.

Police, American Federation of (1966): Records Center, 3801 Biscayne Blvd., Miami, Fla. 33137. 100,000. Phone: (305) 573-0070.

Police, International Association of Chiefs of (1893): 515 N. Washington St., Alexandria, Va. 22314-2357. 14,000. Phone: (703) 836-6767.

Police Hall of Fame, American (1960): 3801 Biscayne Blvd., Miami, Fla. 33137. 55,000. Phone: (305) 573-0070.

Political and Social Science, American Academy of (1889): 3937 Chestnut St., Philadelphia, Pa. 19104. Phone: (215) 386-4594.

Political Science, Academy of (1880): 475 Riverside Dr., Suite 1274, New York, N.Y. 10115-1274. 7,300. Phone: (212) 870-2500.

Prevent Blindness America (1908): 500 E. Remington Rd., Schaumburg, Ill. 60173-5611. 25 affiliates and divisions. Phone: (708) 843-2020/(800) 331-2020.

Professional Engineers, National Society of (1934): 1420 King St., Alexandria, Va. 22314. 69,000. Phone: (703) 684-2800.

Professional Photographers of America, Inc. (1880): 57 Forsyth St. N.W., Suite 1600, Atlanta, Ga. 30303. 14,000. Phone: (404) 522-8600.

Psychiatric Association, American (1844): 1400 K St. N.W., Washington, D.C. 20005. 40,537. Phone: (202) 682-6000.

Psychoanalytic Association, The American (1911): 309 E. 49th St., New York, N.Y. 10017. 3,116 psychoanalysts. Phone: (212) 752-0450; fax: (212) 593-0571; e-mail: 71644,2164@compuserve.com.

Psychological Association, American (1892): 750 First St. N.E., Washington, D.C. 20002-4242. 142,000. Phone: (202) 336-5500; TDD: (202) 336-5662.

Public Health Association, American (1872): 1015 15th St. N.W., Suite 300, Washington, D.C. 20005-2600. 50,000+. Phone: (202) 789-5600.

Puppeteers of America (1937): 5 Cricklewood Path, Pasadena, Calif. 91107-1002. Phone: (818) 797-5748.

Quality Control, The American Society for (1946): 611 E. Wisconsin Ave., P.O. Box 3005, Milwaukee, Wis. 53201-3005. 130,000+. Phone: (414) 272-8575.

Railroads, Association of American (1934): 50 F St. N.W., Washington, D.C. 20001-1564. Phone: (202) 639-2100.

Recording Arts & Sciences, Inc., National Academy of (1958): 3402 Pico Blvd., Santa Monica, Calif. 90405. 10,000. Phone: (310) 392-3777.

Red Cross, American (1881): 17th and D Sts. N.W., Washington, D.C. 20006. Approx. 1,650 chapters. Phone: (202) 737-8300.

Rehabilitation Association, National (1925): 633 S. Washington St., Alexandria, Va. 22314-4193. 14,000. Phone: (703) 836-0850.

Research and Enlightenment, Association for (Edgar Cayce Foundation) (1931): P.O. Box 595, Virginia Beach, Va. 23451. 55,000. Phone: (804) 428-3588.

Reserve Officers Association of the United States (1922): 1 Constitution Ave. N.E., Washington, D.C. 20002. 93,000. Phone: (202) 479-2200.

Retired Federal Employees, National Association: 1533 New Hampshire Ave. N.W., Washington, D.C. 20036-1279. 500,000. Phone: (202) 234-0832.

Reye's Syndrome Foundation, National (1974): P.O. Box 829, Bryan, Ohio 43506. Phone: (800) 233-7393; fax: (419) 636–3366; e-mail: reyes-syn@bright.net

RID-USA (Remove Intoxicated Drivers) (1978): Box 520, Schenectady, N.Y. 12301. Over 150/41 state chapters. Phone: (518) 372-0034/(518) 393-HELP.

Right to Life Committee, Inc., National (1973): 419 7th St. N.W., Suite 500, Washington, D.C. 20004. Phone: (202) 626-8800.

Rotary International (1905): One Rotary Center, 1560 Sherman Ave., Evanston, Ill. 60201. 1,171,599 in 154 countries and 34 geographical regions. Phone: (847) 866-3000.

SAE (Society of Automotive Engineers) (1905): 400 Commonwealtlh Dr., Warrendale, Pa. 15096-0001. 68,000. Phone: (412) 776-4841.

Safety Council, National (1913): 1121 Spring Lake Dr., Itasca, Ill. 60143-3201. Phone: (708) 285-1121.

Salvation Army, The (1865): National Headquarters, 615 Slaters Lane, P.O. Box 269, Alexandria, Va. 22313. 443,246. Phone: (703) 684-5500.

Save-the-Redwoods League (1918): 114 Sansome St., Suite 605, San Francisco, Calif. 94104. 45,000. Phone: (415) 362-2352.

Science, American Association for the Advancement of (1848): 1200 New York Ave. N.W., Washington, D.C. 20005. 143,000. Phone: (202) 326-6400.

Science and Health, American Council on (1978): 1995 Broadway, 2nd Floor, New York, N.Y. 10023-5860. Phone: (212) 362-7044; fax: (212) 362–4919; e-mail: acsh@acsh.org; http://www.acsh.org.

Science Fiction Society, World (1939): c/o Southern California Institute for Fan Interests, P.O. Box 8442, Van Nuys, Calif. 91409. 6,000. Phone: (818) 366-3827.

Science Writers, Inc., National Association of (1934): P.O. Box 294, Greenlawn, N.Y. 11740. 1,830. Phone: (516) 757-5664.

Scientists, Federation of American (FAS) (1945): 307 Massachusetts Ave. N.E., Washington, D.C. 20002. 4,000. Phone: (202) 546-3300.

SCRABBLE® Association, National (1972): P.O. Box 700, Front Street Garden, Greenport, N.Y. 11944. 15,000. Phone: (516) 477-0033.

Screen Actors Guild (1933): 5757 Wilshire Blvd., Los Angeles, Calif. 90036. 90,000. Phone: (213) 954-1600.

Sculpture Society, National (1893): 1177 Ave. of the Americas, New York, N.Y. 10036. 4,000. Phone: (212) 764-5645.

Seeing Eye Inc., The (1929): P.O. Box 375. Morristown, N.J. 07963-0375. Phone: (201) 539-4425.

Senior Citizens, National Alliance of (1974): 1700 18th St. N.W., Suite 401, Washington, D.C. 20009. 117,000. Phone: (202) 986-0117.

Shriners of North America and Shriners Hospitals for Crippled Children, The (1872): Box 31356, Tampa, Fla. 33631-3356. 637,000. Phone: (813) 281-0300.

Sierra Club (1892): 85 2nd Street, San Francisco, Calif. 94105–3441. 550,000. Phone: (415) 977–5500.

SIETAR INTERNATIONAL (The International Society for Intercultural Education, Training and Research) (1974): 808 17th St. N.W., Suite 200, Washington, D.C. 20006-3910. 2,000+. Phone: (202) 466-7883.

Simon Wiesenthal Center (1978): 9786 W. Pico Blvd., Los Angeles, Calif. 90035-4792. 375,000 member families. Phone: (310) 553-9036.

Small Business United, National (1937): 1156 15th St. N.W., Washington, D.C. 20005–1711. 65,000+. Phone: (202) 293-8830; fax: (202) 872–8543; e-mail: nsbu@nsbu.org; http://www.nsbu.org.

SMYAL, Sexual Minority Youth Assistance League (1984): 333 1/2 Pennsylvania Ave. SE, Washington, D.C. 20003-1148. 1,000 members. Phone: (202) 546-5940.

Social Work Education, Council on (1952): 1600 Duke St., Alexandria, Va. 22314-3421. Phone: (703) 683-8080.

Social Workers, National Association of (1955): 750 First St. N.E., Suite 700, Washington, D.C. 20002-4241. Phone: (202) 408-8600.

Society for Integrative and Comparative Biology (formerly the American Society of Zoologists) (1890): 401 N. Michigan Ave., Chicago, Ill. 60611. 2,200. Phone: (312) 527-6697; (800) 955-1236.

Soil and Water Conservation Society (1945): 7515 N.E. Ankeny Rd., Ankeny, Iowa 50021-9764. 11,000. Phone: (515) 289-2331 or (800) THE-SOIL; fax: (515) 289-1227; e-mail: swcs@ne-tins.net.

Songwriters Guild of America, The (1931): 1500 Harbor Blvd., Weehawken, N.J. 07087-6732. Phone: (201) 867-7603.

Sons of Italy in America, Order (1905): 219 E St. N.E., Washington, D.C. 20002. 475,000. Phone: (202) 547-2900.

Sons of the American Revolution, National Society of the (1889): 1000 S. 4th St., Louisville, Ky. 40203. 27,000. Phone: (502) 589-1776.

Soroptimist International of the Americas (1921): Two Penn Center Plaza, Suite 1000, Philadelphia, Pa. 19102-1883. 50,000. Phone: (215) 557-9300.

Southern Early Childhood Association (formerly SACUS) (1948): P.O. Box 56130, Little Rock, Ark. 72215-6130. 19,300. Phone: (501) 663-0353.

Space Education Association, U.S. (1973): Global Operations Center, 231 School Lane, P.O. Box 249, Rheems, Pa. 17570-0249. Voice/Fax: (717) 367-5196.

Space Society, National (1974): 922 Pennsylvania Ave. S.E., Washington, D.C. 20003. 24,000. Phone: (202) 543-1900; http://www.nss.org/

Special Olympics International, Inc. (1968): 1325 G St. N.W., Suite 500, Washington, D.C., 20005-3104. 1,000,000. Phone: (202) 628-3630.

Speech-Language-Hearing Association, American (1925): 10801 Rockville Pike, Rockville, Md. 20852. 82,000. Phone: (301) 897-5700.

Sports Car Club of America Inc. (1944): 9033 E. Easter Place, Englewood, Colo. 80112-2105. 54,000. Phone: (303) 694-7222.

State Governments, The Council of (1933): P.O. Box 11910, Lexington, Ky. 40578-1910. All state officials, all 50 states. Phone: (606) 244-8000; fax: (606) 244-8001.

Statistical Association, American (1839): 1429 Duke St., Alexandria, Va. 22314. 19,000.

Student Association, United States (1947): 1612 K Street, N.W. #510, Washington, D.C. 20006. 350 schools (3.5 million students). Phone: (202) 347-8772.

Surgeons, American College of (1913): 55 E. Erie St., Chicago, Ill. 60611-2797. 58,000+. Phone: (312) 664-4050.

Symphony Orchestra League, American (1942): 1156 Fifteenth St. N.W., Suite 800, Washington, D.C. 20005-1704. 5,500. Phone: (202) 776-0212.

TASH: The Association for Persons with Severe Handicaps (1976): 29 W. Susquehanna Ave., Suite 210, Baltimore, Md. 21204. 8,500. Phone: (410) 828-TASH.

Tax Foundation (1937): 1250 H St. N.W., Suite 750, Washington, D.C. 20005. Phone: (202) 783-2760; fax: (202) 942-7675; e-mail: taxfnd@intr.net; http://www.taxfoundation.org

Teachers, American Federation of (1916): 555 New Jersey Ave. N.W., Washington, D.C., 20001. 800,000+. Phone: (202) 879-4400.

Testing & Materials, American Society for (1898): 100 Barr Harbor Dr., W. Conshohocken, Pa. 19428-2959. 33,000. Phone: (610) 832-9500.

The Arc, a national organization on mental retardation (1950): 500 E. Border St., Suite 300, Arlington, Texas 76010. 140,000 members, 1,200 state and local chapters. Phone: (817) 261-6003.

Theatre Guild, Inc. (1919): 226 W. 47th St., New York, N.Y. 10036. 72,000. Phone: (212) 869-5470.

Theosophical Society in America, The (1875): P.O. Box 270, Wheaton, Ill. 60189-0270. 4,800. Phone: (630) 668-1571.

Tin Can Sailors, Inc. (1976): P.O. Box 100, Somerset, Mass. 02726-0100. 15,000+. Phone: (508) 677-0515.

Toastmasters International (1924): P.O. Box 9052, Mission Viejo, Calif. 92690-7052, and 23182 Arroyo Vista, Rancho Santa Margarita, Calif. 92688. 180,000. Phone: (714) 858-8255, club information voice mail: (800) 9WE-SPEAK; fax: (714) 858-1207; e-mail: tminfo@toast masters.org.

TOUGHLOVE International (1977): P.O. Box 1069, Doylestown, Pa. 18901. 750 registered groups. Phone: (215) 348-7090; (800) 333-1069.

TransAfrica Forum (1981): 1744 R St. N.W., Washington, D.C. 20009. Phone: (202) 797-2301; fax: (202) 797-2382

Travel Agents, American Society of (ASTA) (1931): 1101 King St., Alexandria, Va. 22314. 27,000. Phone: (703) 739-2782.

Travelers Aid Services (1905/1982); 2 Lafayette St., New York, N.Y. 10007. Lucy N. Friedman, Executive Director. (Result of merger of Travelers Aid Society of New York and Victim Services Agency in 1982). Phone: (212) 577-7700. **Client Services:** Times Square Office, 1451 Broadway, 2nd Floor, Manhattan (212) 944-0013; JFK Airport Office, International Arrivals Bldg. 50, Jamaica, Queens (718) 656-4870; 24-Hour Crime Victims Hotline (212) 577-7777; Immigration Hotline (718) 899-4000.

Tuberous Sclerosis Association, Inc., National (1975): 8181 Professional Place, Suite 110, Landover, Md. 20785. 5,000. Phone: (301) 459-9888 or (800) 225-6872; fax: (301) 459-0394; e-mail: ntsa@aol.com.

UFOs, National Investigations Committee on (1967): 14617 Victory Blvd., Suite 4, Van Nuys, Calif. 91411. Phone: (818) 989-5942; fax: (818) 989-2165.

UNICEF, U.S. Committee for (1947): 333 E. 38th St., New York, N.Y. 10016. 20,000 volunteers. Phone: (212) 686-5522.

Union of Concerned Scientists (1969): 2 Brattle Square, Cambridge, Mass. 02238-9105. 80,000. Phone: (617) 547-5552.

United Daughters of the Confederacy® (1894): 328 N. Boulevard, Richmond, Va. 23220-4057. 24,000. Phone: (804) 355-1636.

United Jewish Appeal (1939): 99 Park Ave., New York, N.Y. 10016. Phone: (212) 818-9100.

United Way of America (1918): 701 N. Fairfax St., Alexandria, Va. 22314-2045. 1,900 local United Ways. Phone: (703) 836-7100.

University Foundation, International (1973): 1301 S. Noland Rd., Independence, Mo. 64055. 67,000. Phone: (816) 461-3633.

University Women, American Association of (1881): 1111 16th St. N.W., Washington, D.C. 20036. 150,000. Phone: (202) 785-7700.

USO (United Service Organizations) (1941): World Headquarters, Washington Navy Yard, 901 M St., S.E., Bldg. 198, Washington, D.C. 20374-5096. Phone: (202) 610-5700.

Variety Clubs International (1927): 1560 Broadway, Suite 1209, New York, N.Y. 10036. 15,000. Phone: (212) 704-9872.

Veterans Committee, American (AVC) (1944): 6309 Bannockburn Dr., Bethesda, Md. 20817. 15,000. Phone & FAX: (301) 320-6490.

Veterans of Foreign Wars of the U.S. (1899): 406 W. 34th St., Kansas City, Mo. 64111. VFW and Auxiliary, 2,850,000. Phone: (816) 756-3390.

Veterinary Medical Association, American (1863): 1931 N. Meacham Rd., Suite 100, Schaumburg, Ill. 60173-4360. 57,700. Phone: (847) 925-8070.

Visual Impairments, Division on (1948): The Council for Exceptional Children, 1920 Association Dr., Reston, Va. 22091. 1,000. Phone: (703) 620-3660.

Volunteers of America (1896): 3939 N. Causeway Blvd., Metairie, La. 70002. Provides human services in more than 400 U.S. communities. Phone: 1-800-899-0089.

War Resisters League (1923): 339 Lafayette St., New York, N.Y. 10012. 12,000. Phone: (212) 228-0450; fax: (212) 228-6193; e-mail: wrl@igc.apc.org.

Washington Legal Foundation (1976): 2009 Massachusetts Ave. N.W., Washington, D.C. 20036. 100,000. Phone: (202) 588-0302.

Water Quality Association (1974): 4151 Naperville Rd., Lisle, Ill. 60532. 2,500. Phone: (708) 505-0160.

Welding Society, American (1919): 550 N.W. LeJeune Rd., Miami, Fla. 33126. 45,000. Phone: (305) 443-9353; toll free (800) 443-9353.

Wildlife Federation, National (1936): 8925 Leesburg Pike, Vienna, Va. 22184. 4,000,000+. Phone: (703) 790-4000.

Wildlife Fund, World (1961): 1250 24th St. N.W., Washington, D.C. 20037-1175. 1.2 million. Phone: (202) 293-4800.

Woman's Christian Temperance Union, National (1874): 1730 Chicago Ave., Evanston, Ill. 60201. Under 20,000. Phone: (847) 864-1396.

Women, National Organization for (NOW) (1966): 1000 16th St. N.W., Suite 700, Washington, D.C. 20036-5705. 270,000. Phone: (202) 331-0066.

Women Police, The International Association of (1915): RR1, Box 149, Deer Isle, Me. 04627. 3,000. Phone: (207) 348-6976; fax: (207) 348-6171.

Women's American ORT (1927): 315 Park Ave. South, New York, N.Y. 10010. Chapters throughout the U.S. Phone: (212) 505-7700.

Women's Educational and Industrial Union (1877): 356 Boylston St., Boston, Mass. 02116. 1,500. Phone: (617) 536-5651; fax: (617) 247-8826.

Women's International League for Peace and Freedom (1915): 1213 Race St., Philadelphia, Pa. 19107-1691. 10,000. Phone: (215) 563-7110.

World Future Society (1966): 7910 Woodmont Ave., Suite 450, Bethesda, Md. 20814. 30,000. Phone: (301) 656-8274; fax: (301) 951-0394.

World Health, American Association for (1953): 1825 K St. N.W., Washington, D.C. 20036. Phone: (202) 466-5883.

World Peace, International Association of Educators for (1969): P.O. Box 3282, Mastin Lake Station, Huntsville, Ala. 35810-0282. 25,000. Phone: (205) 534-5501.

World Peace Foundation (1910): One Eliot Square, Cambridge, Mass. 02138. Phone: (617) 491-5085.

Worldwatch Institute (1974): 1776 Massachusetts Ave. N.W., Washington, D.C. 20036. Global environmental research organization. Phone: (202) 452-1999.

Writers Union, National (1983): 113 University Place, 6th Floor, New York, N.Y. 10003. 4,500. Phone: (212) 254-0279.

YMCA of the USA (1844): 101 N. Wacker Dr., Chicago, Ill. 60606. 13,500,000. Phone: (312) 977-0031.

Young Women's Christian Association of the U.S.A. (1858 in U.S.A., 1855 in England): 726 Broadway, New York, N.Y. 10003. 1,800,000. Phone: (212) 614-2700.

Zero Population Growth (1968): 1400 Sixteenth St. N.W., Suite 320, Washington, D.C. 20036. 50,000. Phone: (202) 332-2200.

Zionist Organization of America (1897): ZOA House, 4 E. 34th St., New York, N.Y. 10016. 110,000. Phone: (212) 481-1500; fax: (212) 481-1515.

THE DECLARATION OF INDEPENDENCE

In Congress, July 4, 1776

The unanimous Declaration of the thirteen united States of America.

When in the Course of human events it becomes necessary for one people to dissolve the political bands which have connected them with another, and to assume among the powers of the earth, the separate and equal station to which the Laws of Nature and of Nature's God entitle them, a decent respect to the opinions of mankind requires that they should declare the causes which impel them to the separation.

We hold these truths to be self-evident, that all men are created equal, that they are endowed by their Creator with certain unalienable Rights, that among these are Life, Liberty and the pursuit of Happiness.—That to secure these rights, Governments are instituted among Men, deriving their just powers from the consent of the governed,—That whenever any Form of Government becomes destructive of these ends, it is the Right of the People to alter or to abolish it, and to institute new Government, laying its foundation on such principles and organizing its powers in such form, as to them shall seem most likely to effect their Safety and Happiness. Prudence, indeed, will dictate that Governments long established should not be changed for light and transient causes; and accordingly all experience hath shewn that mankind are more disposed to suffer, while evils are sufferable, than to right themselves by abolishing the forms to which they are accustomed. But when a long train of abuses and usurpations, pursuing invariably the same Object evinces a design to reduce them under absolute Despotism, it is their right, it is their duty, to throw off such Government, and to provide new Guards for their future security.—Such has been the patient sufferance of these Colonies; and such is now the necessity which constrains them to alter their former Systems of Government. The history of the present King of Great Britain is a history of repeated injuries and usurpations, all having in direct object the establishment of an absolute Tyranny over these States. To prove this, let Facts be submitted to a candid world.

He has refused his Assent to Laws, the most wholesome and necessary for the public good.

He has forbidden his Governors to pass Laws of immediate and pressing importance, unless suspended in their operation till his Assent should be obtained; and when so suspended, he has utterly neglected to attend to them.

He has refused to pass other Laws for the accommodation of large districts of people, unless those people would relinquish the right of Representation in the Legislature, a right inestimable to them and formidable to tyrants only.

He has called together legislative bodies at places unusual, uncomfortable, and distant from the depository of their Public Records, for the sole purpose of fatiguing them into compliance with his measures.

He has dissolved Representative Houses repeatedly, for opposing with manly firmness his invasions on the rights of the people.

He has refused for a long time, after such dissolutions, to cause others to be elected; whereby the Legislative Powers, incapable of Annihilation, have returned to the People at large for their exercise; the State remaining in the mean time exposed to all the dangers of invasion from without, and convulsions within.

He has endeavoured to prevent the population of these States; for that purpose obstructing the Laws for Naturalization of Foreigners; refusing to pass others to encourage their migrations hither, and raising the conditions of new Appropriations of Lands.

He has obstructed the Administration of Justice, by refusing his Assent to Laws for establishing Judiciary Powers.

He has made Judges dependent on his Will alone, for the tenure of their offices, and the amount and payment of their salaries.

He has erected a multitude of New Offices, and sent hither swarms of Officers to harass our people, and eat out their substance.

He has kept among us, in times of peace, Standing Armies without the Consent of our legislatures.

He has affected to render the Military independent of and superior to the Civil Power.

He has combined with others to subject us to a jurisdiction foreign to our constitution, and unacknowledged by our laws; giving his Assent to their Acts of pretended Legislation:

For quartering large bodies of armed troops among us:

For protecting them, by a mock Trial, from punishment for any Murders which they should commit on the Inhabitants of these States:

For cutting off our Trade with all parts of the

NOTE: On April 12, 1776, the legislature of North Carolina authorized its delegates to the Continental Congress to join with others in a declaration of separation from Great Britain; the first colony to instruct its delegates to take the actual initiative was Virginia on May 15. On June 7, 1776, Richard Henry Lee of Virginia offered a resolution to the Congress to the effect "that these United Colonies are, and of right ought to be, free and independent States. . . ." A committee, consisting of Thomas Jefferson, John Adams, Benjamin Franklin, Robert R. Livingston, and Roger Sherman was organized to "prepare a declaration to the effect of the said first resolution." The Declaration of Independence was adopted on July 4, 1776.

Most delegates signed the Declaration August 2, but George Wythe (Va.) signed August 27; Richard Henry Lee (Va.), Elbridge Gerry (Mass.), and Oliver Wolcott (Conn.) in September; Matthew Thornton (N.H.), not a delegate until September, in November; and Thomas McKean (Del.), although present on July 4, not until 1781 by special permission, having served in the army in the interim.

world:

For imposing Taxes on us without our Consent:

For depriving us in many cases, of the benefits of Trial by Jury:

For transporting us beyond Seas to be tried for pretended offences:

For abolishing the free System of English Laws in a neighbouring Province, establishing therein an Arbitrary government, and enlarging its Boundaries so as to render it at once an example and fit instrument for introducing the same absolute rule into these Colonies:

For taking away our Charters, abolishing our most valuable Laws and altering fundamentally the Forms of our Governments:

For suspending our own Legislatures, and declaring themselves invested with power to legislate for us in all cases whatsoever.

He has abdicated Government here, by declaring us out of his Protection and waging War against us.

He has plundered our seas, ravaged our Coasts, burnt our towns, and destroyed the lives of our people.

He is at this time transporting large Armies of foreign Mercenaries to compleat the works of death, desolation, and tyranny, already begun with circumstances of Cruelty & Perfidy scarcely paralleled in the most barbarous ages, and totally unworthy the Head of a civilized nation.

He has constrained our fellow Citizens taken Captive on the high Seas to bear Arms against their Country, to become the executioners of their friends and Brethren, or to fall themselves by their Hands.

He has excited domestic insurrections amongst us, and has endeavoured to bring on the inhabitants of our frontiers, the merciless Indian Savages, whose known rule of warfare, is an undistinguished destruction of all ages, sexes and conditions.

In every stage of these Oppressions We have Petitioned for Redress in the most humble terms: Our repeated Petitions have been answered only by repeated injury. A Prince, whose character is thus marked by every act which may define a Tyrant, is unfit to be the ruler of a free people.

Nor have We been wanting in attentions to our Brittish brethren. We have warned them from time to time of attempts by their legislature to extend an unwarrantable jurisdiction over us. We have reminded them of the circumstances of our emigration and settlement here. We have appealed to their native justice and magnanimity, and we have conjured them by the ties of our common kindred to disavow these usurpations, which would inevitably interrupt our connections and correspondence. They too have been deaf to the voice of justice and of consanguinity. We must, therefore, acquiesce in the necessity, which denounces our Separation, and hold them, as we hold the rest of mankind, Enemies in War, in Peace Friends.

We, therefore, the Representatives of the United States of America, in General Congress, Assembled, appealing to the Supreme Judge of the world for the rectitude of our intentions, do, in the Name, and by Authority of the good People of these Colonies, solemnly publish and declare, That these United Colonies are, and of Right ought to be Free and Independent States; that they are Absolved from all Allegiance to the British Crown, and that all political connection between them and the State of Great Britain, is and ought to be totally dissolved; and that as Free and Independent States, they have full Power to levy War, conclude Peace, contract Alliances, establish Commerce, and to do all other Acts and Things which Independent States may of right do.—And for the support of this Declaration, with a firm reliance on the protection of Divine Providence, we mutually pledge to each other our Lives, our Fortunes and our sacred Honor.

—John Hancock

New Hampshire	*Pennsylvania*	*Virginia*
Josiah Bartlett	Robt. Morris	George Wythe
Wm. Whipple	Benjamin Rush	Richard Henry Lee
Matthew Thornton	Benj. Franklin	Th. Jefferson
	John Morton	Benj. Harrison
	Geo. Clymer	Ths. Nelson, Jr.
Rhode Island	Jas. Smith	Francis Lightfoot Lee
Step. Hopkins	Geo. Taylor	Carter Braxton
William Ellery	James Wilson	
	Geo. Ross	
		North Carolina
Connecticut		Wm. Hooper
Roger Sherman	*Massachusetts-Bay*	Joseph Hewes
Sam'el Huntington	Saml. Adams	John Penn
Wm. Williams	John Adams	
Oliver Wolcott	Robt. Treat Paine	
	Elbridge Gerry	*South Carolina*
		Edward Rutledge
New York		Thos. Heyward, Junr.
Wm. Floyd	*Delaware*	Thomas Lynch, Junr.
Phil. Livingston	Caesar Rodney	Arthur Middleton
Frans. Lewis	Geo. Read	
Lewis Morris	Tho. M'Kean	
		Georgia
		Button Gwinnett
New Jersey	*Maryland*	Lyman Hall
Richd. Stockton	Samuel Chase	Geo. Walton
Jno. Witherspoon	Wm. Paca	
Fras. Hopkinson	Thos. Stone	
John Hart	Charles Carroll of Carrollton	
Abra. Clark		

Constitution of the
United States of America

(Historical text has been edited to conform to contemporary American usage.
The bracketed words are designations for your convenience; they are not part of the Constitution.)

The oldest federal constitution in existence was framed by a convention of delegates from twelve of the thirteen original states in Philadelphia in May, 1787, Rhode Island failing to send a delegate. George Washington presided over the session, which lasted until September 17, 1787. The draft (originally a preamble and seven Articles) was submitted to all thirteen states and was to become effective when ratified by nine states. It went into effect on the first Wednesday in March, 1789, having been ratified by New Hampshire, the ninth state to approve, on June 21, 1788. The states ratified the Constitution in the following order:

Delaware	December 7, 1787	South Carolina	May 23, 1788
Pennsylvania	December 12, 1787	New Hampshire	June 21, 1788
New Jersey	December 18, 1787	Virginia	June 25, 1788
Georgia	January 2, 1788	New York	July 26, 1788
Connecticut	January 9, 1788	North Carolina	November 21, 1789
Massachusetts	February 6, 1788	Rhode Island	May 29, 1790
Maryland	April 28, 1788		

[Preamble]

We the people of the United States, in order to form a more perfect Union, establish justice, insure domestic tranquility, provide for the common defence, promote the general welfare, and secure the blessings of liberty to ourselves and our posterity, do ordain and establish this Constitution for the United States of America.

Article I

Section 1

[Legislative powers vested in Congress.] All legislative powers herein granted shall be vested in a Congress of the United States, which shall consist of a Senate and House of Representatives.

Section 2

[Composition of the House of Representatives.—1.] The House of Representatives shall be composed of members chosen every second year by the people of the several States, and the electors in each State shall have the qualifications requisite for electors of the most numerous branch of the State Legislature.

[Qualifications of Representatives.—2.] No Person shall be a Representative who shall not have attained to the age of twenty-five years, and been seven years a citizen of the United States, and who shall not, when elected, be an inhabitant of that State in which he shall be chosen.

[Apportionment of Representatives and direct taxes—census.[1]—3.] (Representatives and direct taxes shall be apportioned among the several States which may be included within this Union, according to their respective numbers, which shall be determined by adding to the whole number of free persons, including those bound to service for a term of years, and excluding Indians not taxed, three fifths of all other persons.) The actual enumeration shall be made within three years after the first meeting of the Congress of the United States, and within every subsequent term of ten years, in such manner as they shall by law direct. The number of Representatives shall not exceed one for every thirty thousand, but each State shall have at least one Representative; and until such enumeration shall be made, the State of New Hampshire shall be entitled to choose three,

Massachusetts eight, Rhode-Island and Providence Plantations one, Connecticut five, New York six, New Jersey four, Pennsylvania eight, Delaware one, Maryland six, Virginia ten, North Carolina five, South Carolina five, and Georgia three.

[Filling of vacancies in representation.—4.] When vacancies happen in the representation from any State, the Executive Authority thereof shall issue writs of election to fill such vacancies.

[Selection of officers; power of impeachment.—5.] The House of Representatives shall choose their Speaker and other officers; and shall have the sole power of impeachment.

Section 3[2]

[The Senate.—1.] The Senate of the United States shall be composed of two Senators from each State, chosen by the Legislature thereof, for six years; and each Senator shall have one vote.

[Classification of Senators; filling of vacancies.—2.] Immediately after they shall be assembled in consequence of the first election, they shall be divided as equally as may be into three classes. The seats of the Senators of the first class shall be vacated at the expiration of the second year, of the second class at the expiration of the fourth year, and of the third class at the expiration of the sixth year, so that one-third may be chosen every second year; and if vacancies happen by resignation, or otherwise, during the recess of the Legislature of any State, the Executive thereof may make temporary appointments (until the next meeting of the Legislature, which shall then fill such vacancies).

[Qualification of Senators.—3.] No person shall be a Senator who shall not have attained to the age of thirty years, and been nine years a citizen of the United States, and who shall not, when elected, be an inhabitant of that State for which he shall be chosen.

[Vice President to be President of Senate.—4.] The Vice President of the United States shall be President of the Senate, but shall have no vote, unless they be equally divided.

[Selection of Senate officers; President pro tempore.—5.] The Senate shall choose their other officers, and also a President pro tempore, in the absence of the Vice President, or when he shall exercise the office of President of the United States.

[Senate to try impeachments.—6.] The Senate

shall have the sole power to try all impeachments. When sitting for that purpose, they shall be on oath or affirmation. When the President of the United States is tried, the Chief Justice shall preside: and no person shall be convicted without the concurrence of two thirds of the members present.

[**Judgment in cases of Impeachment.—7.**] Judgment in cases of impeachment shall not extend further than to removal from office, and disqualification to hold and enjoy any office of honor, trust, or profit under the United States: but the party convicted shall nevertheless be liable and subject to indictment, trial, judgment and punishment, according to Law.

Section 4

[**Control of congressional elections.—1.**] The times, places, and manner of holding elections for Senators and Representatives, shall be prescribed in each State by the Legislature thereof; but the Congress may at any time by law make or alter such regulations, except as to the places of choosing Senators.

[**Time for assembling of Congress**[3]**—2.**] The Congress shall assemble at least once in every year, and such meeting shall be on the first Monday in December, unless they shall by law appoint a different day.

Section 5

[**Each house to be the judge of the election and qualifications of its members; regulations as to quorum.—1.**] Each House shall be the judge of the elections, returns, and qualifications of its own members, and a majority of each shall constitute a quorum to do business; but a smaller number may adjourn from day to day, and may be authorized to compel the attendance of absent members, in such manner, and under such penalties as each House may provide.

[**Each house to determine its own rules.—2.**] Each House may determine the rules of its proceedings, punish its members for disorderly behavior, and, with the concurrence of two thirds, expel a member.

[**Journals and yeas and nays.—3.**] Each House shall keep a journal of its proceedings, and from time to time publish the same, excepting such parts as may in their judgment require secrecy; and the yeas and nays of the members of either House on any question shall, at the desire of one fifth of those present, be entered on the journal.

[**Adjournment.—4.**] Neither House, during the session of Congress, shall, without the consent of the other, adjourn for more than three days, nor to any other place than that in which the two Houses shall be sitting.

Section 6

[**Compensation and privileges of members of Congress.—1.**] The Senators and Representatives shall receive a compensation for their services, to be ascertained by law, and paid out of the Treasury of the United States. They shall in all cases, except treason, felony, and breach of the peace, be privileged from arrest during their attendance at the session of their respective Houses, and in going to and returning from the same; and for any speech or debate in either House, they shall not be questioned in any other place.

[**Incompatible offices; exclusions.—2.**] No Senator or Representative shall, during the time for which he was elected, be appointed to any civil office under the authority of the United States, which shall have been created, or the emoluments whereof shall have been increased during such time; and no person holding any office under the United States shall be a member of either House during his continuance in office.

Section 7

[**Revenue bills to originate in House.—1.**] All bills for raising revenue shall originate in the House of Representatives; but the Senate may propose or concur with amendments as on other bills.

[**Manner of passing bills; veto power of President.—2.**] Every bill which shall have passed the House of Representatives and the Senate, shall, before it becomes a law, be presented to the President of the United States; if he approve he shall sign it, but if not he shall return it, with his objections to that House in which it shall have originated, who shall enter the objections at large on their journal, and proceed to reconsider it. If after such reconsideration two thirds of that House shall agree to pass the bill, it shall be sent, together with the objections, to the other House, by which it shall likewise be reconsidered, and if approved by two thirds of that House, it shall become a law. But in all such cases the votes of both Houses shall be determined by yeas and nays, and the names of the persons voting for and against the bill shall be entered on the journal of each house, respectively. If any bill shall not be returned by the President within ten days (Sundays excepted) after it shall have been presented to him, the same shall be a law, in like manner as if he had signed it, unless the Congress by their adjournment prevent its return, in which case it shall not be a law.

[**Concurrent orders or resolutions, to be passed by President.—3.**] Every order, resolution, or vote to which the concurrence of the Senate and House of Representatives may be necessary (except on a question of adjournment) shall be presented to the President of the United States; and before the same shall take effect, shall be approved by him, or being disapproved by him, shall be repassed by two thirds of the Senate and House of Representatives, according to the rules and limitations prescribed in the case of a bill.

Section 8

[**General powers of Congress.**[4]]
[**Taxes, duties, imposts, and excises.—1.**] The Congress shall have power to lay and collect taxes, duties, imposts and excises, to pay the debts and provide for the common defense and general welfare of the United States; but all duties, imposts and excises shall be uniform throughout the United States;

[**Borrowing of money.—2.**] To borrow money on the credit of the United States;

[**Regulation of commerce.—3.**] To regulate commerce with foreign nations, and among the several States, and with the Indian tribes;

[**Naturalization and bankruptcy.—4.**] To establish a uniform rule of naturalization, and uniform laws on the subject of bankruptcies throughout the United States;

[**Money, weights and measures.—5.**] To coin money, regulate the value thereof, and of foreign coin, and fix the standard of weights and measures;

[**Counterfeiting.—6.**] To provide for the punishment of counterfeiting the securities and current coin of the United States;

[**Post offices.—7.**] To establish post offices and post roads;

[**Patents and copyrights.—8.**] To promote the

progress of science and useful arts, by securing for limited times to authors and inventors the exclusive right to their respective writings and discoveries;

[Inferior courts.—9.] To constitute tribunals inferior to the Supreme Court;

[Piracies and felonies.—10.] To define and punish piracies and felonies committed on the high seas, and offences against the law of nations;

[War; marque and reprisal.—11.] To declare war, grant letters of marque and reprisal, and make rules concerning captures on land and water;

[Armies.—12.] To raise and support armies, but no appropriation of money to that use shall be for a longer term than two years;

[Navy.—13.] To provide and maintain a navy;

[Land and naval forces.—14.] To make rules for the government and regulation of the land and naval forces;

[Calling out militia.—15.] To provide for calling forth the militia to execute the laws of the Union, suppress insurrections, and repel invasions;

[Organizing, arming, and disciplining militia.—16.] To provide for organizing, arming, and disciplining, the militia, and for governing such part of them as may be employed in the service of the United States, reserving to the States, respectively, the appointment of the officers, and the authority of training the militia according to the discipline prescribed by Congress;

[Exclusive legislation over District of Columbia.—17.] To exercise exclusive legislation in all cases whatsoever, over such district (not exceeding ten miles square) as may, by cession of particular States, and the acceptance of Congress, become the seat of the Government of the United States, and to exercise like authority over all places purchased by the consent of the Legislature of the State in which the same shall be, for the erection of forts, magazines, arsenals, dock-yards, and other needful buildings;—And

[To enact laws necessary to enforce Constitution.—18.] To make all laws which shall be necessary and proper for carrying into execution the foregoing powers, and all other powers vested by this Constitution in the Government of the United States, or in any department or officer thereof.

Section 9

[Migration or importation of certain persons not to be prohibited before 1808.—1.] The migration or importation of such persons as any of the States now existing shall think proper to admit, shall not be prohibited by the Congress prior to the year one thousand eight hundred and eight, but a tax or duty may be imposed on such importation, not exceeding ten dollars for each person.

[Writ of habeas corpus not to be suspended; exception.—2.] The privilege of the writ of habeas corpus shall not be suspended, unless when in cases of rebellion or invasion the public safety may require it.

[Bills of attainder and ex post facto laws prohibited.—3.] No bill of attainder or ex post facto law shall be passed.

[Capitation and other direct taxes.—4.] No capitation, or other direct, tax shall be laid, unless in proportion to the census or enumeration herein before directed to be taken.[5]

[Exports not to be taxed.—5.] No tax or duty shall be laid on articles exported from any State.

[No preference to be given to ports of any States; interstate shipping.—6.] No preference shall be given by any regulation of commerce or revenue to the ports of one State over those of another: nor shall vessels bound to, or from, one State, be obliged to enter, clear, or pay duties in another.

[Money, how drawn from treasury; financial statements to be published.—7.] No money shall be drawn from the Treasury, but in consequence of appropriations made by law; and a regular statement and account of the receipts and expenditures of all public money shall be published from time to time.

[Titles of nobility not to be granted; acceptance by government officers of favors from foreign powers.—8.] No title of nobility shall be granted by the United States: and no person holding any office of profit or trust under them, shall, without the consent of the Congress, accept of any present, emolument, office, or title, of any kind whatever, from any king, prince, or foreign state.

Section 10

[Limitations of the powers of the several States.—1.] No State shall enter into any treaty, alliance, or confederation; grant letters of marque and reprisal; coin money; emit bills of credit; make any thing but gold and silver coin a tender in payment of debts; pass any bill of attainder, ex post facto law, or law impairing the obligation of contracts, or grant any title of nobility.

[State imposts and duties.—2.] No State shall, without the consent of the Congress, lay any imposts or duties on imports or exports, except what may be absolutely necessary for executing its inspection laws; and the net produce of all duties and imposts, laid by any State on imports or exports, shall be for the use of the Treasury of the United States; and all such laws shall be subject to the revision and control of the Congress.

[Further restrictions on powers of States.—3.] No State shall, without the consent of Congress, lay any duty of tonnage, keep troops, or ships of war in time of peace, enter into any agreement or compact with another state, or with a foreign power, or engage in war, unless actually invaded, or in such imminent danger as will not admit of delay.

Article II

Section 1

[The President; the executive power.—1.] The executive power shall be vested in a President of the United States of America. He shall hold his office during the term of four years, and, together with the Vice President, chosen for the same term, be elected, as follows

[Appointment and qualifications of presidential electors.—2.] Each State shall appoint, in such manner as the Legislature thereof may direct, a number of electors, equal to the whole number of Senators and Representatives to which the State may be entitled in the Congress: but no Senator or Representative, or person holding an office of trust or profit under the United States, shall be appointed an elector.

[Original method of electing the President and Vice President.[6]] (The electors shall meet in their respective States, and vote by ballot for two persons, of whom one at least shall not be an inhabitant of the same State with themselves. And they shall make a list of all the persons voted for, and of the number of votes for each; which list they shall sign and certify, and transmit sealed to the seat of the Government of the United States, directed to the President of the

Senate. The President of the Senate shall, in the presence of the Senate and House of Representatives, open all the certificates, and the votes shall then be counted. The person having the greatest number of votes shall be the President, if such number be a majority of the whole number of electors appointed; and if there be more than one who have such majority, and have an equal number of votes, then the House of Representatives shall immediately choose by ballot one of them for President; and if no person have a majority, then from the five highest on the list the said House shall in like manner choose the President. But in choosing the President, the votes shall be taken by States, the representation from each State having one vote; A quorum for this purpose shall consist of a member or members from two thirds of the States, and a majority of all the states shall be necessary to a choice. In every case, after the choice of the President, the person having the greatest number of votes of the electors shall be the Vice President. But if there should remain two or more who have equal votes, the Senate should choose from them by ballot the Vice President.)

[Congress may determine time of choosing electors and day for casting their votes.—3.] The Congress may determine the time of choosing the electors, and the day on which they shall give their votes; which day shall be the same throughout the United States.

[Qualifications for the office of President.[7]—4.] No person except a natural born citizen, or a citizen of the United States, at the time of the adoption of this Constitution, shall be eligible to the office of President; neither shall any person be eligible to that office who shall not have attained to the age of thirty-five years, and been fourteen years a resident within the United States.

[Filling vacancy in the office of President.[8]—5.] In case of the removal of the President from office, or of his death, resignation, or inability to discharge the powers and duties of the said office, the same shall devolve on the Vice President, and the Congress may by law provide for the case of removal, death, resignation or inability, both of the President and Vice President, declaring what officer shall then act as President, and such officer shall act accordingly, until the disability be removed, or a President shall be elected.

[Compensation of the President.—6.] The President shall, at stated times, receive for his services, a compensation, which shall neither be increased nor diminished during the period for which he shall have been elected, and he shall not receive within that period any other emolument from the United States, or any of them.

[Oath to be taken by the President.—7.] Before he enter on the execution of his office, he shall take the following oath or affirmation:—"I do solemnly swear (or affirm) that I will faithfully execute the office of President of the United States, and will to the best of my ability, preserve, protect, and defend the Constitution of the United States."

Section 2

[The President to be commander in chief of army and navy and head of executive departments; may grant reprieves and pardons.—1.] The President shall be Commander in Chief of the Army and Navy of the United States, and of the militia of the several States, when called into the actual service of the United States; he may require the opinion, in writing, of the principal officer in each of the executive departments, upon any subject relating to the duties of their respective offices, and he shall have power to grant reprieves and pardons for offences against the United States, except in cases of impeachment.

[President may, with concurrence of Senate, make treaties, appoint ambassadors, etc.; appointment of inferior officers, authority of Congress over.—2.] He shall have power, by and with the advice and consent of the Senate, to make treaties, provided two thirds of the Senators present concur; and he shall nominate, and by and with the advice and consent of the Senate, shall appoint ambassadors, other public ministers and consuls, judges of the Supreme Court, and all other officers of the United States, whose appointments are not herein otherwise provided for, and which shall be established by law: but the Congress may by law vest the appointment of such inferior officers, as they think proper, in the President alone, in the courts of law, or in the heads of departments.

[President may fill vacancies in office during recess of Senate.—3.] The President shall have power to fill up all vacancies that may happen during the recess of the Senate, by granting commissions which shall expire at the end of their session.

Section 3

[President to give advice to Congress; may convene or adjourn it on certain occasions; to receive ambassadors, etc.; have laws executed and commission all officers.] He shall from time to time give to the Congress information of the state of the Union, and recommend to their consideration such measures as he shall judge necessary and expedient; he may, on extraordinary occasions, convene both Houses, or either of them, and in case of disagreement between them, with respect to the time of adjournment, he may adjourn them to such time as he shall think proper; he shall receive ambassadors and other public ministers: he shall take care that the laws be faithfully executed, and shall commission all the officers of the United States.

Section 4

[All civil officers removable by impeachment.] The President, Vice President, and all civil officers of the United States shall be removed from office on impeachment for, and conviction of, treason, bribery, or other high crimes and misdemeanors.

Article III

Section 1

[Judicial powers; how vested; term of office and compensation of judges.] The judicial Power of the United States, shall be vested in one Supreme Court, and in such inferior courts as the Congress may from time to time ordain and establish. The judges, both of the supreme and inferior courts, shall hold their offices during good behavior, and shall, at stated times, receive for their services, a compensation, which shall not be diminished during their continuance in office.

Section 2

[Jurisdiction of Federal courts[9]—1.] The judicial power shall extend to all cases, in law and equity, arising under this Constitution, the laws of the United States, and treaties made, or which shall be made, under their authority; to all cases affecting ambassadors, other public ministers and consuls; to all cases of admiralty and maritime jurisdiction; to controversies to which the United States, shall be a party; to controversies between two or more States; between a State and citizens of another State; between citizens of different States; between citizens of the same State claiming lands under grants of different states, and between a State, or the citizens thereof, and foreign states, citizens, or subjects.

[Original and appellate jurisdiction of Supreme Court.—2.] In all cases affecting ambassadors, other public ministers and consuls, and those in which a State shall be party, the Supreme Court shall have original jurisdiction. In all the other cases before mentioned, the Supreme Court shall have appellate jurisdiction, both as to law and fact, with such exceptions, and under such regulations, as the Congress shall make.

[Trial of all crimes, except impeachment, to be by jury.—3.] The trial of all crimes, except in cases of impeachment, shall be by jury; and such trial shall be held in the State where the said crimes shall have been committed; but when not committed within any State, the trial shall be at such place or places as the Congress may by law have directed.

Section 3

[Treason defined; conviction of.—1.] Treason against the United States, shall consist only in levying war against them, or, in adhering to their enemies, giving them aid and comfort. No person shall be convicted of treason unless on the testimony of two witnesses to the same overt act, or on confession in open court.

[Congress to declare punishment for treason; proviso.—2.] The Congress shall have power to declare the punishment of treason, but no attainder of treason shall work corruption of blood, or forfeiture except during the life of the person attained.

Article IV

Section 1

[Each State to give full faith and credit to the public acts and records of other States.] Full faith and credit shall be given in each State to the public acts, records, and judicial proceedings of every other State. And the Congress may by general laws prescribe the manner in which such acts, records, and proceedings shall be proved, and the effect thereof.

Section 2

[Privileges of citizens.—1.] The citizens of each State shall be entitled to all privileges and immunities of citizens in the several States.

[Extradition between the several States.—2.] A person charged in any State with treason, felony, or other crime, who shall flee from justice, and be found in another State, shall on demand of the Executive authority of the State from which he fled, be delivered up, to be removed to the State having jurisdiction of the crime.

[Persons held to labor or service in one State, fleeing to another, to be returned.—3.] No person held to service or labor in one State, under the laws thereof, escaping into another, shall, in consequence of any law or regulation therein, be discharged from

such service or labor, but shall be delivered up on claim of the party to whom such service or labor may be due.

Section 3

[New States.—1.] New States may be admitted by the Congress into this Union; but no new State shall be formed or erected within the jurisdiction of any other State; nor any State be formed by the junction of two or more States, or parts of States, without the consent of the Legislatures of the States concerned as well as of the Congress.

[Regulations concerning territory.—2.] The Congress shall have power to dispose of and make all needful rules and regulations respecting the territory or other property belonging to the United States; and nothing in this Constitution shall be so construed as to prejudice any claims of the United States, or of any particular State.

Section 4

[Republican form of government and protection guaranteed the several States.] The United States shall guarantee to every State in this Union a Republican form of government, and shall protect each of them against invasion; and on application of the Legislature, or of the Executive (when the Legislature cannot be convened) against domestic violence.

Article V

[Ways in which the Constitution can be amended.] The Congress, whenever two thirds of both Houses shall deem it necessary, shall propose amendments to this Constitution, or, on the application of the Legislatures of two thirds of the several States shall call a convention for proposing amendments, which, in either case, shall be valid to all intents and purposes, as part of this Constitution, when ratified by the Legislatures of three fourths of the several States, or by conventions in three fourths thereof, as the one or the other mode of ratification may be proposed by the Congress; provided that no amendment which may be made prior to the year one thousand eight hundred and eight shall in any manner affect the first and fourth clauses in the ninth Section of the first Article; and that no State, without its consent, shall be deprived of its equal suffrage in the Senate.

Article VI

[Debts contracted under the confederation secured.—1.] All debts contracted and engagements entered into, before the adoption of this Constitution, shall be as valid against the United States under this Constitution, as under the Confederation.

[Constitution, laws, and treaties of the United States to be supreme.—2.] This Constitution, and the laws of the United States which shall be made in pursuance thereof; and all treaties made, or which shall be made, under the authority of the United States, shall be the supreme law of the land; and the judges in every State shall be bound thereby, any thing in the Constitution or laws of any State to the

1. The clause included in parentheses is amended by the 14th Amendment, Section 2. 2. The first paragraph of this section and the part of the second paragraph included in parentheses are amended by the 17th Amendment. 3. Amended by the 20th Amendment, Section 2. 4. By the 16th Amendment, Congress is given the power to lay and collect taxes on income. 5. See the 16th Amendment. 6. This clause has been superseded by the 12th Amendment. 7. For qualifications of the Vice President, see 12th Amendment. 8. Amended by the 20th Amendment, Sections 3 and 4. 9. This section is abridged by the 11th Amendment. 10. See the 13th Amendment.

contrary notwithstanding.

[Who shall take constitutional oath; no religious test as to official qualification.—3.] The Senators and Representatives before mentioned, and the members of the several State Legislatures, and all executive and judicial officers, both of the United States and of the several States, shall be bound by oath or affirmation, to support this Constitution; but no religious test shall ever be required as a qualification to any office or public trust under the United States.

Article VII

[Constitution to be considered adopted when ratified by nine States.] The ratification of the conventions of nine States shall be sufficient for the establishment of this Constitution between the States so ratifying the same.

Done in convention by the unanimous consent of the States present the seventeenth day of September in the year of our Lord one thousand seven hundred and eighty seven and of the independence of the United States of America the Twelfth. In witness whereof we have hereunto subscribed our names.

GEORGE WASHINGTON
President and Deputy from Virginia

NEW HAMPSHIRE
John Langdon   Nicholas Gilman

MASSACHUSETTS
Nathaniel Gorham   Rufus King

CONNECTICUT
Wm. Saml. Johnson   Roger Sherman

NEW YORK
Alexander Hamilton

NEW JERSEY
Wil. Livingston   Wm. Paterson
David Brearley   Jona. Dayton

PENNSYLVANIA
B. Franklin   Thomas Mifflin
Robt. Morris   Geo. Clymer
Thos. FitzSimons   Jared Ingersoll
James Wilson   Gouv. Morris

DELAWARE
Geo. Read   Gunning Bedford Jun.
John Dickinson   Richard Bassett
Jaco. Broom

MARYLAND
James McHenry   Dan. of St. Thos. Jenifer
Danl. Carroll

VIRGINIA
John Blair   James Madison, Jr.

NORTH CAROLINA
Wm. Blount   Richd Dobbs Spaight
Hu. Williamson

SOUTH CAROLINA
J. Rutledge   Charles Cotesworth
Charles Pinckney   Pinckney
                            Pierce Butler

GEORGIA
William Few   Abr. Baldwin
Attest: William Jackson, Secretary

Amendments to the Constitution of the United States

(Amendments I to X inclusive, popularly known as the Bill of Rights, were proposed and sent to the states by the first session of the First Congress. They were ratified Dec. 15, 1791.)

Article I

[Freedom of religion, speech, of the press, and right of petition.] Congress shall make no law respecting an establishment of religion, or prohibiting the free exercise thereof; or abridging the freedom of speech, or of the press; or the right of the people peaceably to assemble, and to petition the Government for a redress of grievances.

Article II

[Right of people to bear arms not to be infringed.] A well regulated militia, being necessary to the security of a free State, the right of the people to keep and bear arms, shall not be infringed.

Article III

[Quartering of troops.] No soldier shall, in time of peace be quartered in any house, without the consent of the owner, nor in time of war, but in a manner to be prescribed by law.

Article IV

[Persons and houses to be secure from unreasonable searches and seizures.] The right of the people to be secure in their persons, houses, papers, and effects, against unreasonable searches and seizures, shall not be violated, and no warrants shall issue, but upon probable cause, supported by oath or affirmation, and particularly describing the place to be searched, and the persons or things to be seized.

Article V

[Trials for crimes; just compensation for private property taken for public use.] No person shall be held to answer for a capital, or otherwise infamous crime, unless on a presentment or indictment of a Grand Jury, except in cases arising in the land or naval forces, or in the militia, when in actual service in time of war or public danger; nor shall any person be subject for the same offence to be twice put in jeopardy of life or limb; nor shall be compelled in any criminal case to be a witness against himself, nor be deprived of life, liberty, or property, without due process of law; nor shall private property be taken for public use, without just compensation.

Article VI

[Civil rights in trials for crimes enumerated.] In all criminal prosecutions, the accused shall enjoy the right to a speedy and public trial, by an impartial jury of the State and district wherein the crime shall have been committed, which district shall have been previously ascertained by law, and to be informed of the nature and cause of the accusation; to be confronted with the witnesses against him; to have compulsory process for obtaining witnesses in his favor, and to have the assistance of counsel for his defense.

Article VII

[Civil rights in civil suits.] In suits at common law, where the value in controversy shall exceed twenty dollars, the right of trial by jury shall be preserved, and no fact tried by a jury, shall be otherwise re-examined in any court of the United States, than according to the rules of the common law.

Article VIII

[Excessive bail, fines, and punishments prohibited.] Excessive bail shall not be required, nor excessive fines imposed, nor cruel and unusual punishments inflicted.

Article IX

[Reserved rights of people.] The enumeration in the Constitution, of certain rights, shall not be construed to deny or disparage others retained by the people.

Article X

[Powers not delegated, reserved to states and people respectively.] The powers not delegated to the United States by the Constitution, nor prohibited by it to the States, are reserved to the States, respectively, or to the people.

Article XI

(The proposed amendment was sent to the states Mar. 5, 1794, by the Third Congress. It was ratified Feb. 7, 1795.)

[Judicial power of United States not to extend to suits against a State.] The judicial power of the United States shall not be construed to extend to any suit in law or equity, commenced or prosecuted against one of the United States by citizens of another State, or by citizens or subjects of any foreign state.

Article XII

(The proposed amendment was sent to the states Dec. 12, 1803, by the Eighth Congress. It was ratified July 27, 1804.)

[Present mode of electing President and Vice-President by electors.'] The electors shall meet in their respective states, and vote by ballot for President and Vice President, one of whom, at least, shall not be an inhabitant of the same state with themselves; they shall name in their ballots the person voted for as President, and in distinct ballots the person voted for as Vice President, and they shall make distinct lists of all persons voted for as President, and of all persons voted for as Vice President, and of the number of votes for each, which lists they shall sign and certify, and transmit sealed to the seat of the government of the United States, directed to the President of the Senate; the President of the Senate shall, in the presence of the Senate and House of Representatives, open all the certificates and the votes shall then be counted; the person having the greatest number of votes for President, shall be the President, if such number be a majority of the whole number of electors appointed; and if no person have such majority, then from the persons having the highest numbers not exceeding three on the list of those voted for as President, the House of Representatives shall choose immediately, by ballot, the President. But in choosing the President, the votes shall be taken by states, the representation from each State having one vote; a quorum for this purpose shall consist of a member or members from two thirds of the states, and a majority of all the states shall be necessary to a choice. And if the House of Representatives shall not choose a President whenever the right of choice shall devolve upon them, before the fourth day of March next following, then the Vice President shall act as President, as in the case of the death or other constitutional disability of the President. The person having the greatest number of votes as Vice President, shall be the Vice President, if such number be a majority of the whole number of electors appointed, and if no person have a majority, then from the two highest numbers on the list, the Senate shall choose the Vice President; a quorum for the purpose shall consist of two thirds of the whole number of Senators, and a majority of the whole number shall be necessary to a choice. But no person constitutionally ineligible to the office of President shall be eligible to that of Vice President of the United States.

Article XIII

(The proposed amendment was sent to the states Feb. 1, 1865, by the Thirty-eighth Congress. It was ratified Dec. 6, 1865.)

Section 1

[Slavery prohibited.] Neither slavery nor involuntary servitude, except as a punishment for crime whereof the party shall have been duly convicted, shall exist within the United States, or any place subject to their jurisdiction.

Section 2

[Congress given power to enforce this article.] Congress shall have power to enforce this article by appropriate legislation.

Article XIV

(The proposed amendment was sent to the states June 16, 1866, by the Thirty-ninth Congress. It was ratified July 9, 1868.)

Section 1

[Citizenship defined; privileges of citizens.] All persons born or naturalized in the United States, and subject to the jurisdiction thereof, are citizens of the United States and of the State wherein they reside. No State shall make or enforce any law which shall abridge the privileges or immunities of citizens of the United States; nor shall any State deprive any person of life, liberty, or property, without due process of law; nor deny to any person within its jurisdiction the equal protection of the laws.

Section 2

[**Apportionment of Representatives.**] Representatives shall be apportioned among the several States according to their respective numbers, counting the whole number of persons in each State, excluding Indians not taxed. But when the right to vote at any election for the choice of electors for President and Vice President of the United States, Representatives in Congress, the executive and judicial officers of a State, or the members of the Legislature thereof, is denied to any of the male inhabitants of such State, being twenty-one years of age, and citizens of the United States, or in any way abridged, except for participation in rebellion, or other crime, the basis of representation therein shall be reduced in the proportion which the number of such male citizens shall bear to the whole number of male citizens twenty-one years of age in such State.

Section 3

[**Disqualification for office; removal of disability.**] No person shall be a Senator or Representative in Congress, or elector of President and Vice President, or hold any office, civil or military, under the United States, or under any State, who, having previously taken an oath, as a member of Congress, or as an officer of the United States, or as a member of any State Legislature, or as an executive or judicial officer of any State, to support the Constitution of the United States, shall have engaged in insurrection or rebellion against the same, or given aid or comfort to the enemies thereof. But Congress may, by a vote of two thirds of each House, remove such disability.

Section 4

[**Public debt not to be questioned; payment of debts and claims incurred in aid of rebellion forbidden.**] The validity of the public debt of the United States, authorized by law, including debts incurred for payment of pensions and bounties for services in suppressing insurrection or rebellion, shall not be questioned. But neither the United States nor any State shall assume or pay any debt or obligation incurred in aid of insurrection or rebellion against the United States, or any claim for the loss or emancipation of any slave; but all such debts, obligations, and claims shall be held illegal and void.

Section 5

[**Congress given power to enforce this article.**] The Congress shall have power to enforce, by appropriate legislation, the provisions of this article.

Article XV

(The proposed amendment was sent to the states Feb. 27, 1869, by the Fortieth Congress. It was ratified Feb. 3, 1870.)

Section 1

[**Right of certain citizens to vote established.**] The right of citizens of the United States to vote shall not be denied or abridged by the United States or by any State on account of race, color, or previous condition of servitude.

Section 2

[**Congress given power to enforce this article.**] The Congress shall have power to enforce this article by appropriate legislation.

Article XVI

(The proposed amendment was sent to the states July 12, 1909, by the Sixty-first Congress. It was ratified Feb. 3, 1913.)

[**Taxes on income; Congress given power to lay and collect.**] The Congress shall have power to lay and collect taxes on incomes, from whatever source derived, without apportionment among the several States, and without regard to any census or enumeration.

Article XVII

(The proposed amendment was sent to the states May 16, 1912, by the Sixty-second Congress. It was ratified April 8, 1913.)

[**Election of United States Senators; filling of vacancies; qualifications of electors.**] The Senate of the United States shall be composed of two Senators from each State, elected by the people thereof, for six years; and each Senator shall have one vote. The electors in each State shall have the qualifications requisite for electors of the most numerous branch of the State Legislatures.

When vacancies happen in the representation of any State in the Senate, the executive authority of such State shall issue writs of election to fill such vacancies: Provided, that the legislature of any State may empower the executive thereof to make temporary appointment until the people fill the vacancies by election as the legislature may direct.

This amendment shall not be so construed as to affect the election or term of any Senator chosen before it becomes valid as part of the Constitution.

Article XVIII[2]

(The proposed amendment was sent to the states Dec. 18, 1917, by the Sixty-fifth Congress. It was ratified by three quarters of the states by Jan. 16, 1919, and became effective Jan. 16, 1920.)

Section 1

[**Manufacture, sale, or transportation of intoxicating liquors, for beverage purposes, prohibited.**] After one year from the ratification of this article the manufacture, sale, or transportation of intoxicating liquors within, the importation thereof into, or the exportation thereof from the United States and all territory subject to the jurisdiction thereof for beverage purposes is hereby prohibited.

Section 2

[**Congress and the several States given concurrent power to pass appropriate legislation to enforce this article.**] The Congress and the several States shall have concurrent power to enforce this article by appropriate legislation.

Section 3

[**Provisions of article to become operative, when adopted by three fourths of the States.**] This article shall be inoperative unless it shall have been ratified as an amendment to the Constitution by the legislatures of the several States, as provided in the Constitution, within seven years from the date of the submission hereof to the States by Congress.

Article XIX

(The proposed amendment was sent to the states June 4, 1919, by the Sixty-sixth Congress. It was ratified Aug. 18, 1920.)

[The right of citizens to vote shall not be denied because of sex.] The right of citizens of the United States to vote shall not be denied or abridged by the United States or by any State on account of sex.

[Congress given power to enforce this article.] Congress shall have power to enforce this article by appropriate legislation.

Article XX

(The proposed amendment, sometimes called the "Lame Duck Amendment," was sent to the states Mar. 3, 1932, by the Seventy-second Congress. It was ratified Jan. 23, 1933; but, in accordance with Section 5, Sections 1 and 2 did not go into effect until Oct. 15, 1933.)

Section 1

[Terms of President, Vice President, Senators, and Representatives.] The terms of the President and Vice President shall end at noon on the twentieth day of January, and the terms of Senators and Representatives at noon on the third day of January, of the years in which such terms would have ended if this article had not been ratified; and the terms of their successors shall then begin.

Section 2

[Time of assembling Congress.] The Congress shall assemble at least once in every year, and such meeting shall begin at noon on the third day of January, unless they shall by law appoint a different day.

Section 3

[Filling vacancy in office of President.] If, at the time fixed for the beginning of the term of the President, the President-elect shall have died, the Vice President-elect shall become President. If a President shall not have been chosen before the time fixed for the beginning of his term, or if the President-elect shall have failed to qualify, then the Vice President shall have qualified; and the Congress may by law provide for the case wherein neither a President-elect nor a Vice President-elect shall have qualified, declaring who shall then act as President, or the manner in which one who is to act shall be selected, and such person shall act accordingly until a President or Vice President shall have qualified.

Section 4

[Power of Congress in Presidential succession.] The Congress may by law provide for the case of the death of any of the persons from whom the House of Representatives may choose a President whenever the right of choice shall have devolved upon them, and for the case of the death of any of the persons from whom the Senate may choose a Vice President whenever the right of choice shall have devolved upon them.

Section 5

[Time of taking effect.] Sections 1 and 2 shall take effect on the 15th day of October following the ratification of this article.

Section 6

[Ratification.] This article shall be inoperative unless it shall have been ratified as an amendment to the Constitution by the legislatures of three fourths of the several States within seven years from the date of its submission.

Article XXI

(The proposed amendment was sent to the states Feb. 20, 1933, by the Seventy-second Congress. It was ratified Dec. 5, 1933.)

Section 1

[Repeal of Prohibition Amendment.] The eighteenth article of amendment to the Constitution of the United States is hereby repealed.

Section 2

[Transportation of intoxicating liquors.] The transportation or importation into any State, territory, or possession of the United States for delivery or use therein of intoxicating liquors, in violation of the laws thereof, is hereby prohibited.

Section 3

[Ratification.] This article shall be inoperative unless it shall have been ratified as an amendment to the Constitution by convention in the several States, as provided in the Constitution, within seven years from the date of the submission thereof to the States by the Congress.

Article XXII

(The proposed amendment was sent to the states Mar. 21, 1947, by the Eightieth Congress. It was ratified Feb. 27, 1951.)

Section 1

[Limit to number of terms a President may serve.] No person shall be elected to the office of the President more than twice, and no person who has held the office of President, or acted as President, for more than two years of a term to which some other person was elected President shall be elected to the office of the President more than once. But this article shall not apply to any person holding the office of President when this article was proposed by the Congress, and shall not prevent any person who may be holding the office of President, or acting as President, during the term within which this article becomes operative from holding the office of President or acting as President during the remainder of such term.

Section 2

[Ratification.] This article shall be inoperative unless it shall have been ratified as an amendment to the Constitution by the legislatures of three fourths of the several States within seven years from the date of its submission to the States by the Congress.

Article XXIII

(The proposed amendment was sent to the states June 16, 1960, by the Eighty-sixth Congress. It was ratified March 29, 1961.)

Section 1

[Electors for the District of Columbia.] The District constituting the seat of Government of the United States shall appoint in such manner as the Congress may direct: A number of electors of President and Vice President equal to the whole number of Senators and Representatives in Congress to which the District would be entitled if it were a State, but in no event more than the least populous State; they shall be in addition to those appointed by the States, but they shall be considered, for the purposes of the election of President and Vice President, to be electors appointed by a State; and they shall meet in the District and perform such duties as provided by the twelfth article of amendment.

628 *U.S. Constitution*

Section 2

[Congress given power to enforce this article.] The Congress shall have the power to enforce this article by appropriate legislation.

Article XXIV

(The proposed amendment was sent to the states Aug. 27, 1962, by the Eighty-seventh Congress. It was ratified Jan. 23, 1964.)

Section 1

[Payment of poll tax or other taxes not to be prerequisite for voting in federal elections.] The right of citizens of the United States to vote in any primary or other election for President or Vice President, for electors for President or Vice President, or for Senator or Representative in Congress, shall not be denied or abridged by the United States or any State by reasons of failure to pay any poll tax or other tax.

Section 2

[Congress given power to enforce this article.] The Congress shall have the power to enforce this article by appropriate legislation.

Article XXV

(The proposed amendment was sent to the states July 6, 1965, by the Eighty-ninth Congress. It was ratified Feb. 10, 1967.)

Section 1

[Succession of Vice President to Presidency.] In case of the removal of the President from office or of his death or resignation, the Vice President shall become President.

Section 2

[Vacancy in office of Vice President.] Whenever there is a vacancy in the office of the Vice President, the President shall nominate a Vice President who shall take office upon confirmation by a majority vote of both Houses of Congress.

Section 3

[Vice President as Acting President.] Whenever the President transmits to the President pro tempore of the Senate and the Speaker of the House of Representatives his written declaration that he is unable to discharge the powers and duties of his office, and until he transmits to them a written declaration to the contrary, such powers and duties shall be discharged by the Vice President as Acting President.

Section 4

[Vice President as Acting President.] Whenever the Vice President and a majority of either the principal officers of the executive departments or of such other body as Congress may by law provide, transmit to the President pro tempore of the Senate and the Speaker of the House of Representatives their written declaration that the President is unable to discharge the powers and duties of his office, the Vice President shall immediately assume the powers and duties of the office as Acting President.

Thereafter, when the President transmits to the President pro tempore of the Senate and the Speaker of the House of Representatives his written declaration that no inability exists, he shall resume the powers and duties of his office unless the Vice President and a majority of either the principal officers of the executive department or of such other body as Congress may by law provide, transmit within four days to the President pro tempore of the Senate and the Speaker of the House of Representatives their written declaration that the President is unable to discharge the powers and duties of his office. Thereupon Congress shall decide the issue, assembling within forty-eight hours for that purpose if not in session. If the Congress, within twenty-one days after receipt of the latter written declaration, or, if Congress is not in session, within twenty-one days after Congress is required to assemble, determines by two thirds vote of both Houses that the President is unable to discharge the powers and duties of his office, the Vice President shall continue to discharge the same as Acting President; otherwise, the President shall resume the powers and duties of his office.

Article XXVI

(The proposed amendment was sent to the states Mar. 23, 1971, by the Ninety-second Congress. It was ratified July 1. 1971.)

Section 1

[Voting for 18-year-olds.] The right of citizens of the United States, who are 18 years of age or older, to vote shall not be denied or abridged by the United States or by any state on account of age.

Section 2

[Congress given power to enforce this article.] The Congress shall have power to enforce this article by appropriate legislation.

Article XXVII

(Ratified May 7, 1992.)

[Congressional raises.] No law, varying the compensation for the services of the Senators and Representatives, shall take effect, until an election of Representativies shall have intervened.

1. Amended by the 20th Amendment, Sections 3 and 4. 2. Repealed by the 21st Amendment.

The White House

Source: Department of the Interior, U.S. National Park Service.

The White House, the official residence of the President, is at 1600 Pennsylvania Avenue in Washington, D.C. 20500. The site, covering about 18 acres, was selected by President Washington and Pierre Charles L'Enfant, and the architect was James Hoban. The design appears to have been influenced by Leinster House, Dublin, and James Gibb's *Book of Architecture*. The cornerstone was laid Oct. 13, 1792, and the first residents were President and Mrs. John Adams in November 1800. The building was fired by the British in 1814.

From December 1948 to March 1952, the interior of the White House was rebuilt, and the outer walls were strengthened.

The rooms for public functions are on the first floor; the second and third floors are used as the residence of the President and First Family. The most celebrated public room is the East Room, where formal receptions take place. Other public rooms are the Red Room, the Green Room, and the Blue Room. The State Dining Room is used for formal dinners. There are 132 rooms.

The Mayflower Compact

On Sept. 6, 1620, the *Mayflower,* a sailing vessel of about 180 tons, started her memorable voyage from Plymouth, England, with about 100[1] pilgrims aboard, bound for Virginia to establish a private permanent colony in North America. Arriving at what is now Provincetown, Mass., on Nov. 11 (Nov. 21, new style calendar), 41 of the passengers signed the famous "Mayflower Compact" as the boat lay at anchor in that Cape Cod harbor. A small detail of the pilgrims, led by William Bradford, assigned to select a place for permanent settlement landed at what is now Plymouth, Mass., on Dec. 21 (n.s.).

The text of the compact follows:

In the name of God, Amen. We, whose names are underwritten, the Loyal Subjects of our dread Sovereign Lord, King *James,* by the Grace of God, of *Great Britain, France and Ireland,* King, *Defender of the Faith, &*

Having undertaken for the Glory of God, and Advancement of the Christian Faith, and the Honour of our King and Country, a voyage to plant the first colony in the northern Parts of Virginia; do by these Presents, solemnly and mutually in the Presence of God and one of another, covenant and combine ourselves together into a civil Body Politick, for our better Ordering and Preservation, and Furtherance of the Ends aforesaid; And by Virtue hereof to enact, constitute, and frame, such just and equal Laws, Ordinances, Acts, Constitutions and Offices, from time to time, as shall be thought most meet and convenient for the General good of the Colony; unto which we promise all due Submission and Obedience.

In Witness whereof we have hereunto subscribed our names at *Cape Cod* the eleventh of *November,* in the Reign of our Sovereign Lord, King *James* of *England, France* and *Ireland,* the eighteenth, and of *Scotland* the fifty-fourth. *Anno Domini,* 1620

John Carver	William Mullins	John Billington	Peter Brown
Digery Priest	Thomas English	Thomas Tinker	John Turner
William Brewster	John Howland	Samuel Fuller	Edward Tilly
Edmund Margesson	Stephen Hopkins	Richard Clark	John Craxton
John Alden	Edward Winslow	John Allerton	Thomas Rogers
George Soule	Gilbert Winslow	Richard Warren	John Goodman
James Chilton	Miles Standish	Edward Liester	Edward Fuller
Francis Cooke	Richard Bitteridge	William Bradford	Richard Gardiner
Moses Fletcher	Francis Eaton	Thomas Williams	William White
John Ridgate	John Tilly	Isaac Allerton	Edward Doten
Christopher Martin			

1. Historians differ as to whether 100, 101, or 102 passengers were aboard.

The Monroe Doctrine

The Monroe Doctrine was announced in President James Monroe's message to Congress, during his second term on Dec. 2, 1823, in part as follows:

"In the discussions to which this interest has given rise, and in the arrangements by which they may terminate, the occasion has been deemed proper for asserting as a principle in which rights and interests of the United States are involved, that the American continents, by the free and independent condition which they have assumed and maintain, are henceforth not to be considered as subjects for future colonization by any European power. . . . We owe it, therefore, to candor and to the amicable relations existing between the United States and those powers to declare that we should consider any attempt on their part to extend their system to any portion of this hemisphere as dangerous to our peace and safety. With the existing colonies or dependencies of any European power we have not interfered and shall not interfere. But with the governments who have declared their independence and maintain it, and whose independence we have, on great consideration and on just principles, acknowledged, we could not view any interposition for the purpose of oppressing them or controlling in any other manner their destiny by any European power in any other light than as the manifestation of an unfriendly disposition toward the United States."

Order of Presidential Succession

1. The Vice President
2. Speaker of the House
3. President pro tempore of the Senate
4. Secretary of State
5. Secretary of the Treasury
6. Secretary of Defense
7. Attorney General
8. Secretary of the Interior
9. Secretary of Agriculture
10. Secretary of Commerce
11. Secretary of Labor
12. Secretary of Health and Human Services
13. Secretary of Housing and Urban Development
14. Secretary of Transportation
15. Secretary of Energy
16. Secretary of Education
17. Secretary of Veterans Affairs

NOTE: An official cannot succeed to the Presidency unless that person meets the Constitutional requirements.

The Star-Spangled Banner

Francis Scott Key, 1814

O say, can you see, by the dawn's early light,
What so proudly we hail'd at the twilight's last gleaming?
Whose broad stripes and bright stars, thro' the perilous fight,
O'er the ramparts we watch'd, were so gallantly streaming?
And the rockets' red glare, the bombs bursting in air,
Gave proof thro' the night that our flag was still there.
O say, does that star-spangled banner yet wave
O'er the land of the free and the home of the brave?

On the shore dimly seen thro' the mists of the deep,
Where the foe's haughty host in dread silence reposes,
What is that which the breeze, o'er the towering steep,
As it fitfully blows, half conceals, half discloses?
Now it catches the gleam of the morning's first beam,
In full glory reflected, now shines on the stream:
'T is the star-spangled banner: O, long may it wave
O'er the land of the free and the home of the brave!

And where is that band who so vauntingly swore
That the havoc of war and the battle's confusion,
A home and a country should leave us no more?
Their blood has wash'd out their foul footsteps' pollution.
No refuge could save the hireling and slave
From the terror of flight or the gloom of the grave:
And the star-spangled banner in triumph doth wave
O'er the land of the free and the home of the brave.

O thus be it ever when free-men shall stand
Between their lov'd home and the war's desolation;
Blest with vict'ry and peace, may the heav'n-rescued land
Praise the Pow'r that hath made and preserv'd us a nation!
Then conquer we must, when our cause it is just,
And this be our motto: "In God is our trust!"
And the star-spangled banner in triumph shall wave
O'er the land of the free and the home of the brave!

On Sept. 13, 1814, Francis Scott Key visited the British fleet in Chesapeake Bay to secure the release of Dr. William Beanes, who had been captured after the burning of Washington, D.C. The release was secured, but Key was detained on ship overnight during the shelling of Fort McHenry, one of the forts defending Baltimore. In the morning, he was so delighted to see the American flag still flying over the fort that he began a poem to commemorate the occasion. First published under the title "Defense of Fort M'Henry," and later as "The Star-Spangled Banner," the poem soon attained wide popularity as sung to the tune "To Anacreon in Heaven." The origin of this tune is obscure, but it may have been written by John Stafford Smith, a British composer born in 1750. "The Star-Spangled Banner" was officially made the National Anthem by Congress in 1931, although it had been already adopted as such by the Army and the Navy.

The Emancipation Proclamation

January 1, 1863

By the President of the United States of America:

A Proclamation.

Whereas on the 22d day of September, A.D. 1862, a proclamation was issued by the President of the United States, containing, among other things, the following, to wit:

"That on the 1st day of January, A.D. 1863, all persons held as slaves within any State or designated part of a State the people whereof shall then be in rebellion against the United States shall be then, thenceforward, and forever free; and the executive government of the United States, including the military and naval authority thereof, will recognize and maintain the freedom of such persons and will do not act or acts to repress such persons, or any of them, in any efforts they may make for their actual freedom.

"That the executive will on the 1st day of January aforesaid, by proclamation, designate the States and parts of States, if any, in which the people thereof, respectively, shall then be in rebellion against the United States; and the fact that any State or the people thereof shall on that day be in good faith represented in the Congress of the United States by members chosen thereto at elections wherein a majority of the qualified voters of such States shall have participated shall, in the absence of strong countervailing testimony, be deemed conclusive evidence that such State and the people thereof are not then in rebellion against the United States."

Now, therefore, I, Abraham Lincoln, President of

the United States, by virtue of the power in me vested as Commander-in-Chief of the Army and Navy of the United States in time of actual armed rebellion against the authority and government of the United States, and as a fit and necessary war measure for suppressing said rebellion, do, on this 1st day of January, A.D. 1863, and in accordance with my purpose so to do, publicly proclaimed for the full period of one hundred days from the first day above mentioned, order and designate as the States and parts of States wherein the people thereof, respectively, are this day in rebellion against the United States the following, to wit:

Arkansas, Texas, Louisiana (except the parishes of St. Bernard, Plaquemines, Jefferson, St. John, St. Charles, St. James, Ascension, Assumption, Terrebonne, Lafourche, St. Mary, St. Martin, and Orleans, including the city of New Orleans), Mississippi, Alabama, Florida, Georgia, South Carolina, North Carolina, and Virginia (except the forty-eight counties designated as West Virginia, and also the counties of Berkeley, Accomac, Northhampton, Elizabeth City, York, Princess Anne, and Norfolk, including the cities of Norfolk and Portsmouth), and which excepted parts are for the present left precisely as if this proclamation were not issued.

And by virtue of the power and for the purpose aforesaid, I do order and declare that all persons held as slaves within said designated States and parts of States are, and henceforward shall be, free; and that the Executive Government of the United States, including the military and naval authorities thereof, will recognize and maintain the freedom of said persons.

And I hereby enjoin upon the people so declared to be free to abstain from all violence, unless in necessary self-defense; and I recommend to them that, in all cases when allowed, they labor faithfully for reasonable wages.

And I further declare and make known that such persons of suitable condition will be received into the armed service of the United States to garrison forts, positions, stations, and other places, and to man vessels of all sorts in said service.

And upon this act, sincerely believed to be an act of justice, warranted by the Constitution upon military necessity, I invoke the considerate judgment of mankind and the gracious favor of Almighty God.

The Confederate States of America

State	Seceded from Union	Readmiited to Union[1]	State	Seceded from Union	Readmitted to Union[1]
1. South Carolina	Dec. 20, 1860	July 9, 1868	7. Texas	March 2, 1861	March 30, 1870
2. Mississippi	Jan. 9, 1861	Feb. 23, 1870	8. Virginia	April 17, 1861	Jan. 26, 1870
3. Florida	Jan. 10, 1861	June 25, 1868	9. Arkansas	May 6, 1861	June 22, 1868
4. Alabama	Jan. 11, 1861	July 13, 1868	10. North Carolina	May 20, 1861	July 4, 1868
5. Georgia	Jan. 19, 1861	July 15, 1870[2]	11. Tennessee	June 8, 1861	July 24, 1866
6. Louisiana	Jan. 26, 1861	July 9, 1868			

1. Date of readmission to representation in U.S. House of Representatives. 2. Second readmission date. First date was July 21, 1868, but the representatives were unseated March 5, 1869. NOTE: Four other slave states—Delaware, Kentucky, Maryland, and Missouri—remained in the Union.

Lincoln's Gettysburg Address

The Battle of Gettysburg, one of the most noted battles of the Civil War, was fought on July 1, 2, and 3, 1863. On Nov. 19, 1863, the field was dedicated as a national cemetery by President Lincoln in a two-minute speech that was to become immortal. At the time of its delivery the speech was relegated to the inside pages of the papers, while a two-hour address by Edward Everett, the leading orator of the time, caught the headlines.

The following is the text of the address revised by President Lincoln from his own notes:

Fourscore and seven years ago our fathers brought forth on this continent a new nation conceived in liberty and dedicated to the proposition that all men are created equal. Now we are engaged in a great civil war testing whether that nation, or any nation so conceived and so dedicated, can long endure. We are met on a great battlefield of that war. We have come to dedicate a portion of that field as a final resting-place for those who here gave their lives that that nation might live. It is altogether fitting and proper that we should do this. But, in a larger sense, we cannot dedicate, we cannot consecrate, we cannot hallow this ground. The brave men, living and dead, who struggled here have consecrated it far above our poor power to add or detract. The world will little note nor long remember what we say here, but it can never forget what they did here. It is for us the living rather to be dedicated here to the unfinished work which they who fought here have thus far so nobly advanced. It is rather for us to be here dedicated to the great task remaining before us—that from these honored dead we take increased devotion to that cause for which they gave the last full measure of devotion—that we here highly resolve that these dead shall not have died in vain, that this nation under God shall have a new birth of freedom, and that government of the people, by the people, for the people shall not perish from the earth.

The Early Congresses

At the urging of Massachusetts and Virginia, the First Continental Congress met in Philadelphia on Sept. 5, 1774, and was attended by representatives of all the colonies except Georgia. Patrick Henry of Virginia declared: "The distinctions between Pennsylvanians, New Yorkers and New Englanders are no more. I am not a Virginian but an American." This Congress, which adjourned Oct. 26, 1774, passed intercolonial resolutions calling for extensive boycott by the colonies against British trade.

The following year, most of the delegates from the colonies were chosen by popular election to attend the Second Continental Congress, which assembled in Philadelphia on May 10. As war had already begun between the colonies and England, the chief problems before the Congress were the procuring of military supplies, the establishment of an army and proper defenses, the issuing of continental bills of credit, etc. On June 15, 1775, George Washington was elected to command the Continental army. Congress adjourned Dec. 12, 1776.

Other Continental Congresses were held in Baltimore (1776–77), Philadelphia (1777), Lancaster, Pa. (1777), York, Pa. (1777–78), and Philadelphia (1778–81).

In 1781, the Articles of Confederation, although establishing a league of the thirteen states rather than a strong central government, provided for the continuance of Congress. Known thereafter as the Congress of the Confederation, it held sessions in Philadelphia (1781–83), Princeton, N.J. (1783), Annapolis, Md. (1783–84), and Trenton, N.J. (1784). Five sessions were held in New York City between the years 1785 and 1789.

The Congress of the United States, established by the ratification of the Constitution, held its first meeting on March 4, 1789, in New York City. Several sessions of Congress were held in Philadelphia, and the first meeting in Washington, D.C., was on Nov. 17, 1800.

Presidents of the Continental Congresses

Name	Elected	Birth and Death Dates	Name	Elected	Birth and Death Dates
Peyton Randolph, Va.	9/5/1774	c.1721–1775	John Hanson, Md.	11/5/1781	1715–1783
Henry Middleton, S.C.	10/22/1774	1717–1784	Elias Boudinot, N.J.	11/4/1782	1740–1821
Peyton Randolph, Va.	5/10/1775	c.1721–1775	Thomas Mifflin, Pa.	11/3/1783	1744–1800
John Hancock, Mass.	5/24/1775	1737–1793	Richard Henry Lee, Va.	11/30/1784	1732–1794
Henry Laurens, S.C.	11/1/1777	1724–1792	John Hancock, Mass.[1]	11/23/1785	1737–1793
John Jay, N.Y.	12/10/1778	1745–1829	Nathaniel Gorham, Mass.	6/6/1786	1738–1796
Samuel Huntington, Conn.	9/28/1779	1731–1796	Arthur St. Clair, Pa.	2/2/1787	1734–1818
Thomas McKean, Del.	7/10/1781	1734–1817	Cyrus Griffin, Va.	1/22/1788	1748–1810

1. Resigned May 29, 1786, never having served, because of continued illness.

The Great Seal of the U.S.

On July 4, 1776, the Continental Congress appointed a committee consisting of Benjamin Franklin, John Adams, and Thomas Jefferson "to bring in a device for a seal of the United States of America." After many delays, a verbal description of a design by William Barton was finally approved by Congress on June 20, 1782. The seal shows an American bald eagle with a ribbon in its mouth bearing the device *E pluribus unum* (One out of many). In its talons are the arrows of war and an olive branch of peace. On the reverse side it shows an unfinished pyramid with an eye (the eye of Providence) above it. Although this description was adopted in 1782, the first drawing was not made until four years later, and no die has ever been cut.

The American's Creed

William Tyler Page

"I believe in the United States of America as a government of the people, by the people, for the people; whose just powers are derived from the consent of the governed; a democracy in a republic; a sovereign Nation of many sovereign States; a perfect union, one and inseparable; established upon those principles of freedom, equality, justice, and humanity for which American patriots sacrificed their lives and fortunes.

"I therefore believe it is my duty to my country to love it, to support its Constitution, to obey its laws, to respect its flag, and to defend it against all enemies."

NOTE: William Tyler Page, Clerk of the U.S. House of Representatives, wrote "The American's Creed" in 1917. It was accepted by the House on behalf of the American people on April 3, 1918.

U.S. Capitol

When the French architect and engineer Maj. Pierre L'Enfant first began to lay out the plans for a new Federal city (now Washington, D.C.), he noted that Jenkins' Hill, overlooking the area, seemed to be "a pedestal waiting for a monument." It was here that the U.S. Capitol would be built. The basic structure as we know it today evolved over a period of more than 150 years. In 1792 a competition was held for the design of a capitol building. Dr. William Thornton, a physician and amateur architect, submitted the winning plan, a simple, low-lying structure of classical proportions with a shallow dome. Later, internal modifications were made by Benjamin Henry Latrobe. After the building was burned by the British in 1814, Latrobe and architect Charles Bulfinch were responsible for its reconstruction. Finally, under Thomas Walter, who was Architect of the Capitol from 1851 to 1865, the House and Senate wings and the imposing cast iron dome topped with the Statue of Freedom were added, and the Capitol assumed the form we see today. It was in the old Senate chamber that Daniel Webster cried out, "Liberty and Union, now and forever, one and inseparable!" In Statuary Hall, which used to be the old House chamber, a small disk on the floor marks the spot where John Quincy Adams was fatally stricken after more than 50 years of service to his country. A whisper from one side of this room can be heard across the vast space of the hall. Visitors can see the original Supreme Court chamber a floor below the Rotunda.

In addition to its historical association, the Capitol Building is also a vast artistic treasure house. The works of such famous artists as Gilbert Stuart, Rembrandt Peale, and John Trumbull are displayed on the walls. The Great Rotunda, with its 180-foot-(54.9-m-) high dome, is decorated with a massive fresco by Constantino Brumidi, which extends some 300 feet (90 m) in circumference. Throughout the building are many paintings of events in U.S. history and sculptures of outstanding Americans. The Capitol itself is situated on a 68-acre (27.5-ha) park designed by the 19th-century landscape architect Frederick Law Olmsted. There are free guided tours of the Capitol, which include admission to the House and Senate galleries. Those who wish to visit the visitors' gallery in either wing without taking the tour may obtain passes from their Senators or Congressmen. Visitors may ride on the monorail subway that joins the House and Senate wings of the Capitol with the Congressional office buildings.

Washington Monument

Construction of this magnificent Washington, D.C., monument, which draws some two million visitors a year, took nearly a century of planning, building, and controversy. Provision for a large equestrian statue of George Washington was made in the original city plan, but the project was soon dropped. After Washington's death it was taken up again, and a number of false starts and changes of design were made. Finally, in 1848, work was begun on the monument that stands today. The design, by architect Robert Mills, then featured an ornate base. In 1854, however, political squabbling and a lack of money brought construction to a halt. Work was resumed in 1880, and the monument was completed in 1884 and opened to the public in 1888. The tapered shaft, faced with white marble and rising from walls 15 feet thick (4.6 m) at the base was modeled after the obelisks of ancient Egypt. The monument, one of the tallest masonry constructions in the world, stands just over 555 feet (169 m). Memorial stones from the 50 States, foreign countries, and organizations line the interior walls. The top, reached only by elevator, commands a panoramic view of the city.

The Liberty Bell

The Liberty Bell was cast in England in 1752 for the Pennsylvania Statehouse (now named Independence Hall) in Philadelphia. It was recast in Philadelphia in 1753. It is inscribed with the words, "Proclaim liberty throughout all the land unto all the inhabitants thereof" (Lev. 25:10). The bell was rung on July 8, 1776, for the first public reading of the Declaration of Independence. Hidden in Allentown during the British occupation of Philadelphia, it was replaced in Independence Hall in 1778. The bell cracked on July 8, 1835, while tolling the death of Chief Justice John Marshall. In 1976 the Liberty Bell was moved to a special exhibition building near Independence Hall.

Arlington National Cemetery

Arlington National Cemetery occupies 612 acres in Virginia on the Potomac River, directly opposite Washington. This land was part of the estate of John Parke Custis, Martha Washington's son. His son, George Washington Parke Custis, built the mansion which later became the home of Robert E. Lee. In 1864, Arlington became a military cemetery. More than 240,000 servicemembers and their dependents are buried there. Expansion of the cemetery began in 1966, using a 180-acre tract of land directly east of the present site.

In 1921, an Unknown American Soldier of World War I was buried in the cemetery; the monument at the Tomb was opened to the public without ceremony in 1932. Two additional Unknowns, one from World War II and one from the Korean War, were buried May 30, 1958. The Unknown Serviceman of Vietnam was buried on May 28, 1984. The inscription carved on the Tomb of the Unknowns reads:

HERE RESTS IN
HONORED GLORY
AN AMERICAN
SOLDIER
KNOWN BUT TO GOD

History of the Flag

Source: Encyclopaedia Britannica.

The first official American flag, the Continental or Grand Union flag, was displayed on Prospect Hill, Jan. 1, 1776, in the American lines besieging Boston. It had 13 alternate red and white stripes, with the British Union Jack in the upper left corner.

On June 14, 1777, the Continental Congress adopted the design for a new flag, which actually was the Continental flag with the red cross of St. George and the white cross of St. Andrew replaced on the blue field by 13 stars, one for each state. No rule was made as to the arrangement of the stars, and while they were usually shown in a circle, there were various other designs. It is uncertain when the new flag was first flown, but its first official announcement is believed to have been on Sept. 3, 1777.

The first public assertion that Betsy Ross made the first Stars and Stripes appeared in a paper read before the Historical Society of Pennsylvania on March 14, 1870, by William J. Canby, a grandson. However, Mr. Canby on later investigation found no official documents of any action by Congress on the flag before June 14, 1777. Betsy Ross's own story, according to her daughter, was that Washington, Robert Morris, and George Ross, as representatives of Congress, visited her in Philadelphia in June 1776, showing her a rough draft of the flag and asking her if she could make one. However, the only actual record of the manufacture of flags by Betsy Ross is a voucher in Harrisburg, Pa., for 14 pounds and some shillings for flags for the Pennsylvania navy.

On Jan. 13, 1794, Congress voted to add two stars and two stripes to the flag in recognition of the admission of Vermont and Kentucky to the Union. By 1818, there were 20 states in the Union, and as it was obvious that the flag would soon become unwieldy, Congress voted April 18 to return to the original 13 stripes and to indicate the admission of a new state simply by the addition of a star the following July 4. The 49th star, for Alaska, was added July 4, 1959; and the 50th star, for Hawaii, was added July 4, 1960.

The first Confederate flag, adopted in 1861 by the Confederate convention in Montgomery, Ala., was called the Stars and Bars; but because of its similarity in colors to the American flag, there was much confusion in the Battle of Bull Run. To remedy this situation, Gen. G. T. Beauregard suggested a battle flag, which was used by the Southern armies throughout the war. The flag consisted of a red field on which was placed a blue cross of St. Andrew separated from the field by a white fillet and adorned with 13[1] white stars for the Confederate states. In May 1863, at Richmond, an official flag was adopted by the Confederate Congress. This flag was white and twice as long as wide; the union, two-thirds the width of the flag, contained the battle flag designed for Gen. Beauregard. A broad transverse stripe of red was added Feb. 4, 1865, so that the flag might not be mistaken for a signal of truce.

1. 11 states formally seceded, and unofficial groups in Kentucky and Missouri adopted ordinances of secession. On this basis, these two states were admitted to the Confederacy, although the official state governments remained in the Union.

The Pledge of Allegiance[1] to the Flag

"I pledge allegiance to the Flag of the United States of America, and to the Republic for which it stands, one Nation under God,[2] indivisible, with liberty and justice for all."

1. The original pledge was published in the Sept. 8, 1892, issue of *The Youth's Companion* in Boston. For years, the authorship was in dispute between James B. Upham and Francis Bellamy of the magazine's staff. In 1939, after a study of the controversy, the United States Flag Association decided that authorship be credited to Bellamy. 2. The phrase "under God" was added to the pledge on June 14, 1954.

The Statue of Liberty

The Statue of Liberty ("Liberty Enlightening the World") is a 225-ton, steel-reinforced copper female figure, 152 ft in height, facing the ocean from Liberty[1] Island in New York Harbor. The right hand holds aloft a torch, and the left hand carries a tablet upon which is inscribed: "July IV MDCCLXXVI."

The statue was designed by Frédéric Auguste Bartholdi of Alsace as a gift to the United States from the people of France to memorialize the alliance of the two countries in the American Revolution and their abiding friendship. The French people contributed the $250,000 cost.

The 150-foot pedestal was designed by Richard M. Hunt and built by Gen. Charles P. Stone, both Americans. It contains steel underpinnings designed by Alexander Eiffel of France to support the statue. The $270,000 cost was borne by popular subscription in this country. President Grover Cleveland accepted the statue for the United States on Oct. 28, 1886.

On Sept. 26, 1972, President Richard M. Nixon dedicated the American Museum of Immigration, housed in structural additions to the base of the stat-

1. Called Bedloe's Island prior to 1956.

ue. In 1984 scaffolding went up for a major restoration and the torch was extinguished on July 4. It was relit with much ceremony July 4, 1986 to mark its centennial.

On a tablet inside the pedestal is engraved the following sonnet, written by Emma Lazarus (1849–1887):

The New Colossus

Not like the brazen giant of Greek fame.
With conquering limbs astride from land to land;
Here at our sea-washed, sunset gates shall stand
A mighty woman with a torch, whose flame
Is the imprisoned lightning, and her name
Mother of Exiles. From her beacon-hand
Glows world-wide welcome; her mild eyes command
The air-bridged harbor that twin cities frame.
"Keep, ancient lands, your storied pomp!" cries she
With silent lips. "Give me your tired, your poor,
Your huddled masses yearning to breathe free,
The wretched refuse of your teeming shore.
Send these, the homeless, tempest-tost to me,
I lift my lamp beside the golden door!"

Presidents

Name and (party)[1][2]	Term	State of birth	Born	Died	Religion	Age at inaug.	Age at death
1. Washington (F)[2]	1789–1797	Va.	2/22/1732	12/14/1799	Episcopalian	57	67
2. J. Adams (F)	1797–1801	Mass.	10/30/1735	7/4/1826	Unitarian	61	90
3. Jefferson (DR)	1801–1809	Va.	4/13/1743	7/4/1826	Deist	57	83
4. Madison (DR)	1809–1817	Va.	3/16/1751	6/28/1836	Episcopalian	57	85
5. Monroe (DR)	1817–1825	Va.	4/28/1758	7/4/1831	Episcopalian	58	73
6. J. Q. Adams (DR)	1825–1829	Mass.	7/11/1767	2/23/1848	Unitarian	57	80
7. Jackson (D)	1829–1837	S.C.	3/15/1767	6/8/1845	Presbyterian	61	78
8. Van Buren (D)	1837–1841	N.Y.	12/5/1782	7/24/1862	Reformed Dutch	54	79
9. W. H. Harrison (W)[3]	1841	Va.	2/9/1773	4/4/1841	Episcopalian	68	68
10. Tyler (W)	1841–1845	Va.	3/29/1790	1/18/1862	Episcopalian	51	71
11. Polk (D)	1845–1849	N.C.	11/2/1795	6/15/1849	Methodist	49	53
12. Taylor (W)[3]	1849–1850	Va.	11/24/1784	7/9/1850	Episcopalian	64	65
13. Fillmore (W)	1850–1853	N.Y.	1/7/1800	3/8/1874	Unitarian	50	74
14. Pierce (D)	1853–1857	N.H.	11/23/1804	10/8/1869	Episcopalian	48	64
15. Buchanan (D)	1857–1861	Pa.	4/23/1791	6/1/1868	Presbyterian	65	77
16. Lincoln (R)[4]	1861–1865	Ky.	2/12/1809	4/15/1865	Liberal	52	56
17. A. Johnson (U)[5]	1865–1869	N.C.	12/29/1808	7/31/1875	[6]	56	66
18. Grant (R)	1869–1877	Ohio	4/27/1822	7/23/1885	Methodist	46	63
19. Hayes (R)	1877–1881	Ohio	10/4/1822	1/17/1893	Methodist	54	70
20. Garfield (R)[4]	1881	Ohio	11/19/1831	9/19/1881	Disciples of Christ	49	49
21. Arthur (R)	1881–1885	Vt.	10/5/1830	11/18/1886	Episcopalian	50	56
22. Cleveland (D)	1885–1889	N.J.	3/18/1837	6/24/1908	Presbyterian	47	71
23. B. Harrison (R)	1889–1893	Ohio	8/20/1833	3/13/1901	Presbyterian	55	67
24. Cleveland (D)[7]	1893–1897	—	—	—	—	55	—
25. McKinley (R)[4]	1897–1901	Ohio	1/29/1843	9/14/1901	Methodist	54	58
26. T. Roosevelt (R)	1901–1909	N.Y.	10/27/1858	1/6/1919	Reformed Dutch	42	60
27. Taft (R)	1909–1913	Ohio	9/15/1857	3/8/1930	Unitarian	51	72
28. Wilson (D)	1913–1921	Va.	12/28/1856	2/3/1924	Presbyterian	56	67
29. Harding (R)[3]	1921–1923	Ohio	11/2/1865	8/2/1923	Baptist	55	57
30. Coolidge (R)	1923–1929	Vt.	7/4/1872	1/5/1933	Congregationalist	51	60
31. Hoover (R)	1929–1933	Iowa	8/10/1874	10/20/1964	Quaker	54	90
32. F. D. Roosevelt (D)[3]	1933–1945	N.Y.	1/30/1882	4/12/1945	Episcopalian	51	63
33. Truman (D)	1945–1953	Mo.	5/8/1884	12/26/1972	Baptist	60	88
34. Eisenhower (R)	1953–1961	Tex.	10/14/1890	3/28/1969	Presbyterian	62	78
35. Kennedy (D)[4]	1961–1963	Mass.	5/29/1917	11/22/1963	Roman Catholic	43	46
36. L. B. Johnson (D)	1963–1969	Tex.	8/27/1908	1/22/1973	Disciples of Christ	55	64
37. Nixon (R)[8]	1969–1974	Calif.	1/9/1913	4/22/1994	Quaker	56	81
38. Ford (R)	1974–1977	Neb.	7/14/1913	—	Episcopalian	61	—
39. Carter (D)	1977–1981	Ga.	10/1/1924	—	Southern Baptist	52	—
40. Reagan (R)	1981–1989	Ill.	2/6/1911	—	Disciples of Christ	69	—
41. Bush (R)	1989–1993	Mass.	6/12/24	—	Episcopalian	64	—
42. Clinton (D)	1993–	Ark.	8/19/46	—	Baptist	46	—

1. F—Federalist; DR—Democratic-Republican; D—Democrat; W—Whig; R—Republican; U—Union. 2. No party for first election. The party system in the U.S. made its appearance during Washington's first term. 3. Died in office. 4. Assassinated in office. 5. The Republican National Convention of 1864 adopted the name Union Party. It renominated Lincoln for President; for Vice President it nominated Johnson, a War Democrat. Although frequently listed as a Republican Vice President and President, Johnson undoubtedly considered himself strictly a member of the Union Party. When that party broke apart after 1868, he returned to the Democratic Party. 6. Johnson was not a professed church member; however, he admired the Baptist principles of church government. 7. Second nonconsecutive term. 8. Resigned Aug. 9, 1974.

Vice Presidents

Name and (party)[1][2]	Term	State of birth	Birth and death dates	President served under
1. John Adams (F)[2]	1789–1797	Massachusetts	1735–1826	Washington
2. Thomas Jefferson (DR)	1797–1801	Virginia	1743–1826	J. Adams
3. Aaron Burr (DR)	1801–1805	New Jersey	1756–1836	Jefferson
4. George Clinton (DR)[3]	1805–1812	New York	1739–1812	Jefferson and Madison
5. Elbridge Gerry (DR)[3]	1813–1814	Massachusetts	1744–1814	Madison
6. Daniel D. Tompkins (DR)	1817–1825	New York	1774–1825	Monroe
7. John C. Calhoun[4]	1825–1832	South Carolina	1782–1850	J. Q. Adams and Jackson
8. Martin Van Buren (D)	1833–1837	New York	1782–1862	Jackson
9. Richard M. Johnson (D)	1837–1841	Kentucky	1780–1850	Van Buren
10. John Tyler (W)[5]	1841	Virginia	1790–1862	W. H. Harrison
11. George M. Dallas (D)	1845–1849	Pennsylvania	1792–1864	Polk
12. Millard Fillmore (W)[5]	1849–1850	New York	1800–1874	Taylor
13. William R. King (D)[3]	1853	North Carolina	1786–1853	Pierce
14. John C. Breckinridge (D)	1857–1861	Kentucky	1821–1875	Buchanan

Name and (party)[1]	Term	State of birth	Birth and death dates	President served under
15. Hannibal Hamlin (R)	1861–1865	Maine	1809–1891	Lincoln
16. Andrew Johnson (U)[5]	1865	North Carolina	1808–1875	Lincoln
17. Schuyler Colfax (R)	1869–1873	New York	1823–1885	Grant
18. Henry Wilson (R)[3]	1873–1875	New Hampshire	1812–1875	Grant
19. William A. Wheeler (R)	1877–1881	New York	1819–1887	Hayes
20. Chester A. Arthur (R)[5]	1881	Vermont	1830–1886	Garfield
21. Thomas A. Hendricks (D)[3]	1885	Ohio	1819–1885	Cleveland
22. Levi P. Morton (R)	1889–1893	Vermont	1824–1920	B. Harrison
23. Adlai E. Stevenson (D)	1893–1897	Kentucky	1835–1914	Cleveland
24. Garrett A. Hobart (R)[3]	1897–1899	New Jersey	1844–1899	McKinley
25. Theodore Roosevelt (R)[5]	1901	New York	1858–1919	McKinley
26. Charles W. Fairbanks (R)	1905–1909	Ohio	1852–1918	T. Roosevelt
27. James S. Sherman (R)[3]	1909–1912	New York	1855–1912	Taft
28. Thomas R. Marshall (D)	1913–1921	Indiana	1854–1925	Wilson
29. Calvin Coolidge (R)[5]	1921–1923	Vermont	1872–1933	Harding
30. Charles G. Dawes (R)	1925–1929	Ohio	1865–1951	Coolidge
31. Charles Curtis (R)	1929–1933	Kansas	1860–1936	Hoover
32. John N. Garner (D)	1933–1941	Texas	1868–1967	F. D. Roosevelt
33. Henry A. Wallace (D)	1941–1945	Iowa	1888–1965	F. D. Roosevelt
34. Harry S. Truman (D)[5]	1945	Missouri	1884–1972	F. D. Roosevelt
35. Alben W. Barkley (D)	1949–1953	Kentucky	1877–1956	Truman
36. Richard M. Nixon (R)	1953–1961	California	1913–1994	Eisenhower
37. Lyndon B. Johnson (D)[5]	1961–1963	Texas	1908–1973	Kennedy
38. Hubert H. Humphrey (D)	1965–1969	South Dakota	1911–1978	Johnson
39. Spiro T. Agnew (R)[6]	1969–1973	Maryland	1918–	Nixon
40. Gerald R. Ford (R)[7]	1973–1974	Nebraska	1913–	Nixon
41. Nelson A. Rockefeller (R)[8]	1974–1977	Maine	1908–1979	Ford
42. Walter F. Mondale (D)	1977–1981	Minnesota	1928–	Carter
43. George Bush (R)	1981–1989	Massachusetts	1924–	Reagan
44. J. Danforth Quayle (R)	1989–1993	Indiana	1947–	Bush
45. Albert A. Gore, Jr. (D)	1993–	Washington, D.C.	1948–	Clinton

1. F—Federalist; DR—Democratic-Republican; D—Democratic; W—Whig; R—Republican; U—Union. 2. No party for first election. The party system in the U.S. made its appearance during Washington's first term as President. 3. Died in office. 4. Democratic-Republican with J. Q. Adams; Democratic with Jackson. Calhoun resigned in 1832 to become a U.S. Senator. 5. Succeeded to presidency on death of President. 6. Resigned Oct. 10, 1973, after pleading no contest to Federal income tax evasion charges. 7. Nominated by Nixon on Oct. 12, 1973, under provisions of 25th Amendment. Confirmed by Congress on Dec. 6, 1973, and was sworn in same day. He became President Aug. 9, 1974, upon Nixon's resignation. 8. Nominated by Ford Aug. 20, 1974; confirmed by Congress on Dec. 19, 1974, and was sworn in same day.

Burial Places of the Presidents

President	Burial place	President	Burial place
Washington	Mt. Vernon, Va.	Hayes	Fremont, Ohio
J. Adams	Quincy, Mass.	Garfield	Cleveland, Ohio
Jefferson	Charlottesville, Va.	Arthur	Albany, N.Y.
Madison	Montpelier Station, Va.	Cleveland	Princeton, N.J.
Monroe	Richmond, Va.	B. Harrison	Indianapolis
J. Q. Adams	Quincy, Mass.	McKinley	Canton, Ohio
Jackson	The Hermitage, nr. Nashville, Tenn.	T. Roosevelt	Oyster Bay, N.Y.
		Taft	Arlington National Cemetery
Van Buren	Kinderhook, N.Y.	Wilson	Washington National Cathedral
W. H. Harrison	North Bend, Ohio	Harding	Marion, Ohio
Tyler	Richmond, Va.	Coolidge	Plymouth, Vt.
Polk	Nashville, Tenn.	Hoover	West Branch, Iowa
Taylor	Louisville, Ky.	F. D. Roosevelt	Hyde Park, N.Y.
Fillmore	Buffalo, N.Y.	Truman	Independence, Mo.
Pierce	Concord, N.H.	Eisenhower	Abilene, Kan.
Buchanan	Lancaster, Pa.	Kennedy	Arlington National Cemetery
Lincoln	Springfield, Ill.	L. B. Johnson	Stonewall, Tex.
A. Johnson	Greeneville, Tenn.	Nixon	Yorba Linda, Calif.
Grant	New York City		

"In God We Trust"

"In God We Trust" first appeared on U.S. coins after April 22, 1864, when Congress passed an act authorizing the coinage of a 2-cent piece bearing this motto. Thereafter, Congress extended its use to other coins. On July 30, 1956, it became the national motto.

Wives and Children of the Presidents

President	Wife's name	Year and place of wife's birth	Married	Wife died	Sons	Daughters
Washington	Martha Dandridge Custis	1732, Va.	1759	1802	—	—
John Adams	Abigail Smith	1744, Mass.	1764	1818	3	2
Jefferson	Martha Wayles Skelton	1748, Va.	1772	1782	1	5
Madison	Dorothy "Dolley" Payne Todd	1768, N.C.	1794	1849	—	—
Monroe	Elizabeth "Eliza" Kortright	1768, N.Y.	1786	1830	—	2
J. Q. Adams	Louisa Catherine Johnson	1775, England	1797	1852	3	1
Jackson	Mrs. Rachel Donelson Robards	1767, Va.	1791	1828	—	—
Van Buren	Hannah Hoes	1788, N.Y.	1807	1819	4	—
W. H. Harrison	Anna Symmes	1775, N.J.	1795	1864	6	4
Tyler	Letitia Christian	1790, Va.	1813	1842	3	4
	Julia Gardiner	1820, N.Y.	1844	1889	5	2
Polk	Sarah Childress	1803, Tenn.	1824	1891	—	—
Taylor	Margaret Smith	1788, Md.	1810	1852	1	5
Fillmore	Abigail Powers	1798, N.Y.	1826	1853	1	1
	Caroline Carmichael McIntosh	1813, N.J.	1858	1881	—	—
Pierce	Jane Means Appleton	1806, N.H.	1834	1863	3	—
Buchanan	(Unmarried)	—	—	—	—	—
Lincoln	Mary Todd	1818, Ky.	1842	1882	4	—
A. Johnson	Eliza McCardle	1810, Tenn.	1827	1876	3	2
Grant	Julia Dent	1826, Mo.	1848	1902	3	1
Hayes	Lucy Ware Webb	1831, Ohio	1852	1889	7	1
Garfield	Lucretia Rudolph	1832, Ohio	1858	1918	5	2
Arthur	Ellen Lewis Herndon	1837, Va.	1859	1880	2	1
Cleveland	Frances Folsom	1864, N.Y.	1886	1947	2	3
B. Harrison	Caroline Lavinia Scott	1832, Ohio	1853	1892	1	1
	Mary Scott Lord Dimmick	1858, Pa.	1896	1948	—	1
McKinley	Ida Saxton	1847, Ohio	1871	1907	—	2
T. Roosevelt	Alice Hathaway Lee	1861, Mass.	1880	1884	—	1
	Edith Kermit Carow	1861, Conn.	1886	1948	4	1
Taft	Helen Herron	1861, Ohio	1886	1943	2	1
Wilson	Ellen Louise Axson	1860, Ga.	1885	1914	—	3
	Edith Bolling Galt	1872, Va.	1915	1961	—	—
Harding	Florence Kling DeWolfe	1860, Ohio	1891	1924	—	—
Coolidge	Grace Anna Goodhue	1879, Vt.	1905	1957	2	—
Hoover	Lou Henry	1875, Iowa	1899	1944	2	—
F. D. Roosevelt	Anna Eleanor Roosevelt	1884, N.Y.	1905	1962	5	1
Truman	Bess Wallace	1885, Mo.	1919	1982	—	1
Eisenhower	Mamie Geneva Doud	1896, Iowa	1916	1979	2	—
Kennedy	Jacqueline Lee Bouvier	1929, N.Y.	1953	1994	2	1
L. B. Johnson	Claudia Alta "Lady Bird" Taylor	1912, Tex.	1934		—	2
Nixon	Thelma Catherine "Pat" Ryan	1912, Nev.	1940	1993	—	2
Ford	Elizabeth "Betty" Bloomer Warren	1918, Ill.	1948		3	1
Carter	Rosalynn Smith	1928, Ga.	1946		3	1
Reagan	Jane Wyman	1914, Mo.	1940[2]		1[3]	1
	Nancy Davis	1921 (?)[4], N.Y.	1952		1	1
Bush	Barbara Pierce	1925, N.Y.	1945		4	2
Clinton	Hillary Rodham	1946, Ill.	1975		—	1

1. Includes children who died in infancy. 2. Divorced in 1948. 3. Adopted. 4. Birthday officially given as 1923 but her high school and college records show 1921 for year of birth.

Figures and Legends in American Folklore

Appleseed, Johnny (John Chapman, 1774–1847): Massachusetts-born nurseryman; reputed to have spread seeds out of which grew the apple orchards of the Midwest.

Billy the Kid (William H. Bonney, 1859–1881): Desperado who killed his first man before he reached his teens; after short life of crime in Wild West was gunned down by Sheriff Pat Garrett; symbol of lawless West.

Boone, Daniel (1734–1820): Frontiersman and Indian fighter, about whom legends of early America have been built; figured in Byron's *Don Juan*.

Buffalo Bill (William F. Cody, 1846–1917): Buffalo hunter and Indian scout; many of the legends about him stem from his own Wild West show, which he operated in late 19th century.

Bunyan, Paul: Mythical lumberjack; subject of tall tales throughout timber country (that he dug the Grand Canyon, for example).

Crockett, David (1786–1836): Frontiersman, Congressman, and defender of the Alamo, his backwoods humor and larger-than-life adventures made him synonymous with the Wild West.

James, Jesse (1847–1882): Bank and train robber; often portrayed as the American Robin Hood.

Jones, Casey (John Luther Jones, 1863–1900): Example of heroic locomotive engineer given to feats of prowess; died in wreck when his Illinois Central "Cannonball" express hit freight train at Vaughan, Miss.

Ross, Betsy (1752–1836): Member of Philadelphia flag-making family; reported to have designed and sewn first American flag. (Report is without confirmation.)

Uncle Sam: Personification of U.S. and its people; origin uncertain; may be based on inspector of government supplies in Revolutionary War and War of 1812.

Elections

How a President Is Nominated and Elected

The Conventions

The National Conventions of both major parties are held during the summer of a presidential-election year. Earlier, each party selects delegates by primaries, conventions, committees, etc.

At each convention, a temporary chairman is chosen. After a credentials committee seats the delegates, a permanent chairman is elected. The convention then votes on a platform, drawn up by the platform committee.

By the third or fourth day, presidential nominations begin. The chairman calls the roll of states alphabetically. A state may place a candidate in nomination or yield to another state.

Voting, again alphabetically by roll call of states, begins after all nominations have been made and seconded. A simple majority is required in each party, although this may require many ballots.

Finally, the vice-presidential candidate is selected. Although there is no law saying that the candidates *must* come from different states, it is, practically, necessary for this to be the case. Otherwise, according to the Constitution (*see* Amendment XII), electors from that state could vote for only one of the candidates and would have to cast their other vote for some person of another state. This could result in a presidential candidate's receiving a majority electoral vote and his running mate's failing to.

The Electoral College

The next step in the process is the nomination of electors in each state, according to its laws. These electors must not be Federal office holders. In the November election, the voters cast their votes for electors, not for President. In some states, the ballots include only the names of the presidential and vice-presidential candidates; in others, they include

only names of the electors. Nowadays, it is rare for electors to be split between parties. The last such occurrence was in North Carolina in 1968[1]; the last before that, in Tennessee in 1948. On three occasions (1824, 1876, and 1888), the presidential candidate with the largest popular vote failed to obtain an electoral-vote majority.

Each state has as many electors as it has Senators and Representatives. For the 1992 election, the total electors were 538, based on 100 Senators, 435 Representatives, plus 3 electoral votes from the District of Columbia as a result of the 23rd Amendment to the Constitution.

On the first Monday after the second Wednesday in December, the electors cast their votes in their respective state capitols. Constitutionally they may vote for someone other than the party candidate but usually they do not since they are pledged to one party and its candidate on the ballot. Should the presidential or vice-presidential candidate die between the November election and the December meetings, the electors pledged to vote for him could vote for whomever they pleased. However, it seems certain that the national committee would attempt to get an agreement among the state party leaders for a replacement candidate.

The votes of the electors, certified by the states, are sent to Congress, where the president of the Senate opens the certificates and has them counted in the presence of both Houses on January 6. The new President is inaugurated at noon on January 20.

Should no candidate receive a majority of the electoral vote for President, the House of Representatives chooses a President from among the three highest candidates, voting, not as individuals, but as states, with a majority (now 26) needed to elect. Should no vice-presidential candidate obtain the majority, the Senate, voting as individuals, chooses from the highest two.

1. In 1956, 1 of Alabama's 11 electoral votes was cast for Walter B. Jones. In 1960, 6 of Alabama's 11 electoral votes and 1 of Oklahoma's 8 electoral votes were cast for Harry Flood Byrd. (Byrd also received all 8 of Mississippi's electoral votes.)

Electoral College
List of States and Votes, 1996 Presidential Election

Total: 538; Majority Needed to Elect: 270

State	Votes	State	Votes	State	Votes
Alabama	9	Kentucky	8	North Dakota	3
Alaska	3	Louisiana	9	Ohio	21
Arizona	8	Maine	4	Oklahoma	8
Arkansas	6	Maryland	10	Oregon	7
California	54	Massachusetts	12	Pennsylvania	23
Colorado	8	Michigan	18	Rhode Island	4
Connecticut	8	Minnesota	10	South Carolina	8
Delaware	3	Mississippi	7	South Dakota	3
District of Columbia	3	Missouri	11	Tennessee	11
Florida	25	Montana	3	Texas	32
Georgia	13	Nebraska	5	Utah	5
Hawaii	4	Nevada	4	Vermont	3
Idaho	4	New Hampshire	4	Virginia	13
Illinois	22	New Jersey	15	Washington	11
Indiana	12	New Mexico	5	West Virginia	5
Iowa	7	New York	33	Wisconsin	11
Kansas	6	North Carolina	14	Wyoming	3

National Political Conventions Since 1856

Opening date	Party	Where held	Opening date	Party	Where held
June 17, 1856	Republican	Philadelphia	June 26, 1928	Democratic	Houston
June 2, 1856	Democratic	Cincinnati	June 14, 1932	Republican	Chicago
May 16, 1860	Republican	Chicago	June 27, 1932	Democratic	Chicago
April 23, 1860	Democratic	Charleston and Baltimore	June 9, 1936	Republican	Cleveland
			June 23, 1936	Democratic	Philadelphia
June 7, 1864	Republican[1]	Baltimore	June 24, 1940	Republican	Philadelphia
Aug. 29, 1864	Democratic	Chicago	July 15, 1940	Democratic	Chicago
May 20, 1868	Republican	Chicago	June 26, 1944	Republican	Chicago
July 4, 1868	Democratic	New York City	July 19, 1944	Democratic	Chicago
June 5, 1872	Republican	Philadelphia	June 21, 1948	Republican	Philadelphia
June 9, 1872	Democratic	Baltimore	July 12, 1948	Democratic	Philadelphia
June 14, 1876	Republican	Cincinnati	July 17, 1948	[3]	Birmingham
June 28, 1876	Democratic	St. Louis	July 22, 1948	Progressive	Philadelphia
June 2, 1880	Republican	Chicago	July 7, 1952	Republican	Chicago
June 23, 1880	Democratic	Cincinnati	July 21, 1952	Democratic	Chicago
June 3, 1884	Republican	Chicago	Aug. 20, 1956	Republican	San Francisco
July 11, 1884	Democratic	Chicago	Aug. 13, 1956	Democratic	Chicago
June 19, 1888	Republican	Chicago	July 25, 1960	Republican	Chicago
June 6, 1888	Democratic	St. Louis	July 11, 1960	Democratic	Los Angeles
June 7, 1892	Republican	Minneapolis	July 13, 1964	Republican	San Francisco
June 21, 1892	Democratic	Chicago	Aug. 24, 1964	Democratic	Atlantic City
June 16, 1896	Republican	St. Louis	Aug. 5, 1968	Republican	Miami Beach
July 7, 1896	Democratic	Chicago	Aug. 26, 1968	Democratic	Chicago
June 19, 1900	Republican	Philadelphia	July 10, 1972	Democratic	Miami Beach
July 4, 1900	Democratic	Kansas City	Aug. 21, 1972	Republican	Miami Beach
June 21, 1904	Republican	Chicago	July 12, 1976	Democratic	New York City
July 6, 1904	Democratic	St. Louis	Aug. 16, 1976	Republican	Kansas City, Mo.
June 16, 1908	Republican	Chicago	Aug. 11, 1980	Democratic	New York City
July 7, 1908	Democratic	Denver	July 14, 1980	Republican	Detroit
June 18, 1912	Republican	Chicago	Aug. 20, 1984	Republican	Dallas
June 25, 1912	Democratic	Baltimore	July 16, 1984	Democratic	San Francisco
June 7, 1916	Republican	Chicago	July 18, 1988	Democratic	Atlanta
June 14, 1916	Democratic	St. Louis	Aug. 15, 1988	Republican	New Orleans
June 8, 1920	Republican	Chicago	July 13, 1992	Democratic	New York City
June 28, 1920	Democratic	San Francisco	Aug. 17, 1992	Republican	Houston
June 10, 1924	Republican	Cleveland	Aug. 10, 1996	Republican	San Diego
June 24, 1924[2]	Democratic	New York City	Aug. 26, 1996	Democratic	Chicago
June 12, 1928	Republican	Kansas City			

1. The Convention adopted name Union party to attract War Democrats and others favoring prosecution of the war. 2. In session until July 10, 1924. 3. States' Rights delegates from 13 Southern states.

National Committee Chairmen Since 1944

Chairman and (state)	Term	Chairman and (state)	Term
REPUBLICAN		Haley Barbour (Miss.)	1993–
Herbert Brownell, Jr. (N.Y.)	1944–46	**DEMOCRATIC**	
Carroll Reece (Tenn.)	1946–48	Robert E. Hannegan (Mo.)	1944–47
Hugh D. Scott, Jr. (Pa.)	1948–49	J. Howard McGrath (R.I.)	1947–49
Guy G. Gabrielson (N.J.)	1949–52	William M. Boyle, Jr. (Mo.)	1949–51
Arthur E. Summerfield (Mich.)	1952–53	Frank E. McKinney (Ind.)	1951–52
Wesley Roberts (Kan.)	1953–	Stephen A. Mitchell (Ill.)	1952–54
Leonard W. Hall (N.Y.)	1953–57	Paul M. Butler (Ind.)	1955–60
Meade Alcorn (Conn.)	1957–59	Henry M. Jackson (Wash.)	1960–61
Thruston B. Morton (Ky.)	1959–61	John M. Bailey (Conn.)	1961–68
William E. Miller (N.Y.)	1961–64	Lawrence F. O'Brien (Mass.)	1968–69
Dean Burch (Ariz.)	1964–65	Fred R. Harris (Okla.)	1969–70
Ray C. Bliss (Ohio)	1965–69	Lawrence F. O'Brien (Mass.)	1970–72
Rogers C. B. Morton (Md.)	1969–71	Jean Westwood (Utah)	1972
Robert Dole (Kan.)	1971–73	Robert S. Strauss (Tex.)	1972–77
George H. Bush (Tex.)	1973–74	Kenneth M. Curtis (Me.)	1977
Mary Louise Smith (Iowa)	1974–77	John C. White (Tex.)	1977–81
William E. Brock III (Tenn.)	1977–81	Charles T. Manatt (Calif.)	1981–85
Richard Richards (Utah)	1981–83	Paul G. Kirk, Jr. (Mass.)	1985–89
Frank J. Fahrenkopf, Jr. (Nevada)	1983–89	Ronald H. Brown (D.C.)	1989–93
Lee Atwater (S.C.)	1989–91	David Wilhelm (Ill.)	1993–94
Clayton K. Yeutter (Neb.)	1991–92	Christopher J. Dodd (Conn.)	1995–
Richard Bond (N.Y.)	1992–93		

Republican National Committee: 310 First St., S.E., Washington, D. C. 20003.
Democratic National Committee: 430 South Capitol St., S.E., Washington, D.C. 20003.

Presidential Elections, 1789 to 1992

For the original method of electing the President and the Vice President (elections of 1789, 1792, 1796, and 1800), see Article II, Section 1, of the Constitution. The election of 1804 was the first one in which the electors voted for President and Vice President on separate ballots. (See Amendment XII to the Constitution.)

Year	Presidential candidates	Party	Electoral vote	Year	Presidential candidates	Party	Electoral vote
1789[1]	George Washington	(no party)	69	1796	John Adams	Federalist	71
	John Adams	(no party)	34		Thomas Jefferson	Dem.-Rep.	68
	Scattering	(no party)	35		Thomas Pinckney	Federalist	59
	Votes not cast		8		Aaron Burr	Dem.-Rep.	30
					Scattering		48
1792	George Washington	Federalist	132				
	John Adams	Federalist	77	1800[2]	Thomas Jefferson	Dem.-Rep.	73
	George Clinton	Anti-Federalist	50		Aaron Burr	Dem.-Rep.	73
	Thomas Jefferson	Anti-Federalist	4		John Adams	Federalist	65
	Aaron Burr	Anti-Federalist	1		Charles C. Pinckney	Federalist	64
	Votes not cast		6		John Jay	Federalist	1

Year	Presidential candidates	Party	Electoral vote	Vice-presidential candidates	Party	Electoral vote
1804	Thomas Jefferson	Dem.-Rep.	162	George Clinton	Dem.-Rep.	162
	Charles C. Pinckney	Federalist	14	Rufus King	Federalist	14
1808	James Madison	Dem.-Rep.	122	George Clinton	Dem.-Rep.	113
	Charles C. Pinckney	Federalist	47	Rufus King	Federalist	47
	George Clinton	Dem.-Rep.	6	John Langdon	Ind. (no party)	9
	Votes not cast		1	James Madison	Dem.-Rep.	3
				James Monroe	Dem.-Rep.	3
				Votes not cast		1
1812	James Madison	Dem.-Rep.	128	Elbridge Gerry	Dem.-Rep.	131
	De Witt Clinton	Federalist	89	Jared Ingersoll	Federalist	86
	Votes not cast		1	Votes not cast		1
1816	James Monroe	Dem.-Rep.	183	Daniel D. Tompkins	Dem.-Rep.	183
	Rufus King	Federalist	34	John E. Howard	Federalist	22
	Votes not cast		4	James Ross	Ind. (no party)	5
				John Marshall	Federalist	4
				Robert G. Harper	Ind. (no party)	3
				Votes not cast		4
1820	James Monroe	Dem-Rep	231	Daniel D. Tompkins	Dem.-Rep.	218
	John Quincy Adams	Ind. (no party)	1	Richard Stockton	Ind. (no party)	8
	Votes not cast		3	Daniel Rodney	Ind. (no party)	4
				Richard Rush	Ind. (no party)	1
				Robert G. Harper	Ind. (no party)	1
				Votes not cast		3
1824[3]	John Quincy Adams	(no party)	84	John C. Calhoun	(no party)	182
	Andrew Jackson	(no party)	99	Nathan Sanford	(no party)	30
	William H. Crawford	(no party)	41	Nathaniel Macon	(no party)	24
	Henry Clay	(no party)	37	Andrew Jackson	(no party)	13
				Martin Van Buren	(no party)	9
				Henry Clay	(no party)	2
				Votes not cast		1
1828	Andrew Jackson	Democratic	178	John C. Calhoun	Democratic	171
	John Quincy Adams	Natl. Rep.	83	Richard Rush	Natl. Rep.	83
				William Smith	Democratic	7
1832	Andrew Jackson	Democratic	219	Martin Van Buren	Democratic	189
	Henry Clay	Natl. Rep.	49	John Sergeant	Natl. Rep.	49
	John Floyd	Ind. (no party)	11	Henry Lee	Ind. (no party)	11
	William Wirt	Antimasonic[4]	7	Amos Ellmaker	Antimasonic	7
	Votes not cast		2	William Wilkins	Ind. (no party)	30
				Votes not cast		2

Year	Presidential candidates	Party	Electoral vote	Vice-presidential candidates	Party	Electoral vote
1836	Martin Van Buren	Democratic	170	Richard M. Johnson[5]	Democratic	147
	William H. Harrison	Whig	73	Francis Granger	Whig	77
	Hugh L. White	Whig	26	John Tyler	Whig	47
	Daniel Webster	Whig	14	William Smith	Ind. (no party)	23
	W. P. Mangum	Ind. (no party)	11			
1840	William H. Harrison[6]	Whig	234	John Tyler	Whig	234
	Martin Van Buren	Democratic	60	Richard M. Johnson	Democratic	48
				L. W. Tazewell	Ind. (no party)	11
				James K. Polk	Democratic	1
1844	James K. Polk	Democratic	170	George M. Dallas	Democratic	170
	Henry Clay	Whig	105	Theo. Frelinghuysen	Whig	105
1848	Zachary Taylor[7]	Whig	163	Millard Fillmore	Whig	163
	Lewis Cass	Democratic	127	William O. Butler	Democratic	127
1852	Franklin Pierce	Democratic	254	William R. King	Democratic	254
	Winfield Scott	Whig	42	William A. Graham	Whig	42
1856	James Buchanan	Democratic	174	John C. Breckinridge	Democratic	174
	John C. Fremont	Republican	114	William L. Dayton	Republican	114
	Millard Fillmore	American[8]	8	A. J. Donelson	American[8]	8
1860	Abraham Lincoln	Republican	180	Hannibal Hamlin	Republican	180
	John C. Breckinridge	Democratic	72	Joseph Lane	Democratic	72
	John Bell	Const. Union	39	Edward Everett	Const. Union	39
	Stephen A. Douglas	Democratic	12	H. V. Johnson	Democratic	12
1864	Abraham Lincoln[9]	Union[10]	212	Andrew Johnson	Union[15]	212
	George B. McClellan	Democratic	21	G. H. Pendleton	Democratic	21
1868	Ulysses S. Grant	Republican	214	Schuyler Colfax	Republican	214
	Horatio Seymour	Democratic	80	Francis P. Blair, Jr.	Democratic	80
	Votes not counted[11]		23	Votes not counted[11]		23

Year	Presidential candidates	Party	Electoral vote	Popular vote	Vice-presidential candidates and party
1872	Ulysses S. Grant	Republican	286	3,597,132	Henry Wilson—R
	Horace Greeley	Dem., Liberal Rep.	([12])	2,834,125	B. Gratz Brown—D, LR—(47)
	Thomas A. Hendricks	Democratic	42		Scattering—(19)
	B. Gratz Brown	Dem., Liberal Rep.	18		Votes not counted—(14)
	Charles J. Jenkins	Democratic	2		
	David Davis	Democratic	1		
	Votes not counted		17		
1876[13]	Rutherford B. Hayes	Republican	185	4,033,768	William A. Wheeler—R
	Samuel J. Tilden	Democratic	184	4,285,992	Thomas A. Hendricks—D
	Peter Cooper	Greenback	0	81,737	Samuel F. Cary—G
1880	James A. Garfield[14]	Republican	214	4,449,053	Chester A. Arthur—R
	Winfield S. Hancock	Democratic	155	4,442,035	William H. English—D
	James B. Weaver	Greenback	0	308,578	B. J. Chambers—G
1884	Grover Cleveland	Democratic	219	4,911,017	Thomas A. Hendricks—D
	James G. Blaine	Republican	182	4,848,334	John A. Logan—R
	Benjamin F. Butler	Greenback	0	175,370	A. M. West—G
	John P. St. John	Prohibition	0	150,369	William Daniel—P
1888	Benjamin Harrison	Republican	233	5,440,216	Levi P. Morton—R
	Grover Cleveland	Democratic	168	5,538,233	A. G. Thurman—D
	Clinton B. Fisk	Prohibition	0	249,506	John A. Brooks—P
	Alson J. Streeter	Union Labor	0	146,935	Charles E. Cunningham—UL
1892	Grover Cleveland	Democratic	277	5,556,918	Adlai E. Stevenson—D
	Benjamin Harrison	Republican	145	5,176,108	Whitelaw Reid—R
	James B. Weaver	People's[15]	22	1,041,028	James G. Field—Peo
	John Bidwell	Prohibition	0	264,133	James B. Cranfill—P

Year	Presidential candidates	Party	Electoral vote	Popular vote	Vice-presidential candidates and party
1896	William McKinley	Republican	271	7,035,638	Garret A. Hobart—R
	William J. Bryan	Dem., People's[15]	176	6,467,946	Arthur Sewall—D—(149)
					Thomas E. Watson—Peo—(27)
	John M. Palmer	Natl. Dem.	0	133,148	Simon B. Buckner—ND
	Joshua Levering	Prohibition	0	132,007	Hale Johnson—P
1900	William McKinley[16]	Republican	292	7,219,530	Theodore Roosevelt—R
	William J. Bryan	Dem., People's[15]	155	6,358,071	Adlai E. Stevenson—D, Peo
	Eugene V. Debs	Social Democratic	0	94,768	Job Harriman—SD
1904	Theodore Roosevelt	Republican	336	7,628,834	Charles W. Fairbanks—R
	Alton B. Parker	Democratic	140	5,084,491	Henry G. Davis—D
	Eugene V. Debs	Socialist	0	402,400	Benjamin Hanford—S
1908	William H. Taft	Republican	321	7,679,006	James S. Sherman—R
	William J. Bryan	Democratic	162	6,409,106	John W. Kern—D
	Eugene V. Debs	Socialist	0	402,820	Benjamin Hanford—S
1912	Woodrow Wilson	Democratic	435	6,286,214	Thomas R. Marshall—D
	Theodore Roosevelt	Progressive	88	4,126,020	Hiram Johnson—Prog
	William H. Taft	Republican	8	3,483,922	Nicholas M. Butler—R[17]
	Eugene V. Debs	Socialist	0	897,011	Emil Seidel—S
1916	Woodrow Wilson	Democratic	277	9,129,606	Thomas R. Marshall—D
	Charles E. Hughes	Republican	254	8,538,221	Charles W. Fairbanks—R
	A. L. Benson	Socialist	0	585,113	G. R. Kirkpatrick—S
1920	Warren G. Harding[18]	Republican	404	16,152,200	Calvin Coolidge—R
	James M. Cox	Democratic	127	9,147,353	Franklin D. Roosevelt—D
	Eugene V. Debs	Socialist	0	917,799	Seymour Stedman—S
1924	Calvin Coolidge	Republican	382	15,725,016	Charles G. Dawes—R
	John W. Davis	Democratic	136	8,385,586	Charles W. Bryan—D
	Robert M. LaFollette	Progressive, Socialist	13	4,822,856	Burton K. Wheeler—Prog S
1928	Herbert Hoover	Republican	444	21,392,190	Charles Curtis—R
	Alfred E. Smith	Democratic	87	15,016,443	Joseph T. Robinson—D
	Norman Thomas	Socialist	0	267,420	James H. Maurer—S
1932	Franklin D. Roosevelt	Democratic	472	22,821,857	John N. Garner—D
	Herbert Hoover	Republican	59	15,761,841	Charles Curtis—R
	Norman Thomas	Socialist	0	884,781	James H. Maurer—S
1936	Franklin D. Roosevelt	Democratic	523	27,751,597	John N. Garner—D
	Alfred M. Landon	Republican	8	16,679,583	Frank Knox—R
	Norman Thomas	Socialist	0	187,720	George Nelson—S
1940	Franklin D. Roosevelt	Democratic	449	27,244,160	Henry A. Wallace—D
	Wendell L. Willkie	Republican	82	22,305,198	Charles L. McNary—R
	Norman Thomas	Socialist	0	99,557	Maynard C. Krueger—S
1944	Franklin D. Roosevelt[19]	Democratic	432	25,602,504	Harry S. Truman—D
	Thomas E. Dewey	Republican	99	22,006,285	John W. Bricker—R
	Norman Thomas	Socialist	0	80,518	Darlington Hoopes—S
1948	Harry S. Truman	Democratic	303	24,179,345	Alben W. Barkley—D
	Thomas E. Dewey	Republican	189	21,991,291	Earl Warren—R
	J. Strom Thurmond	States' Rights Dem.	39	1,176,125	Fielding L. Wright—SR
	Henry A. Wallace	Progressive	0	1,157,326	Glen Taylor—Prog
	Norman Thomas	Socialist	0	139,572	Tucker P. Smith—S
1952	Dwight D. Eisenhower	Republican	442	33,936,234	Richard M. Nixon—R
	Adlai E. Stevenson	Democratic	89	27,314,992	John J. Sparkman—D
1956	Dwight D. Eisenhower	Republican	457	35,590,472	Richard M. Nixon—R
	Adlai E. Stevenson	Democratic	73[20]	26,022,752	Estes Kefauver—D
1960	John F. Kennedy[22]	Democratic	303	34,226,731	Lyndon B. Johnson—D
	Richard M. Nixon	Republican	219[21]	34,108,157	Henry Cabot Lodge—R

Year	Presidential candidates	Party	Electoral vote	Popular vote	Vice-presidential candidates and party
1964	Lyndon B. Johnson	Democratic	486	43,129,484	Hubert H. Humphrey—D
	Barry M. Goldwater	Republican	52	27,178,188	William E. Miller—R
1968	Richard M. Nixon	Republican	301	31,785,480	Spiro T. Agnew—R
	Hubert H. Humphrey	Democratic	191	31,275,166	Edmund S. Muskie—D
	George C. Wallace	American Independent	46	9,906,473	Curtis E. LeMay—AI
1972	Richard M. Nixon[23]	Republican	520[24]	47,169,911	Spiro T. Agnew—R
	George McGovern	Democratic	17	29,170,383	Sargent Shriver—D
	John G. Schmitz	American	0	1,099,482	Thomas J. Anderson—A
1976	Jimmy Carter	Democratic	297	40,830,763	Walter F. Mondale—D
	Gerald R. Ford	Republican	240[25]	39,147,973	Robert J. Dole—R
	Eugene J. McCarthy	Independent	0	756,631	None
1980	Ronald Reagan	Republican	489	43,899,248	George Bush—R
	Jimmy Carter	Democratic	49	36,481,435	Walter F. Mondale—D
	John B. Anderson	Independent	0	5,719,437	Patrick J. Lucey—I
1984	Ronald Reagan	Republican	525	54,455,075	George Bush—R
	Walter F. Mondale	Democratic	13	37,577,185	Geraldine A. Ferraro—D
1988	George H. Bush	Republican	426	48,886,097	J. Danforth Quayle—R
	Michael S. Dukakis	Democratic	111[26]	41,809,074	Lloyd Bentsen—D
1992	William J. Clinton	Democratic	370	44,909,889	Albert A. Gore, Jr.—D
	George H. Bush	Republican	168	39,104,545	J. Danforth Quayle—R
	H. Ross Perot	Independent	0	19,742,267	James B. Stockdale—I

1. Only 10 states participated in the election. The New York legislature chose no electors, and North Carolina and Rhode Island had not yet ratified the Constitution. 2. As Jefferson and Burr were tied, the House of Representatives chose the President. In a vote by states, 10 votes were cast for Jefferson, 4 for Burr; 2 votes were not cast. 3. As no candidate had an electoral-vote majority, the House of Representatives chose the President from the first three. In a vote by states, 13 votes were cast for Adams, 7 for Jackson, and 4 for Crawford. 4. The Antimasonic Party on Sept. 26, 1831, was the first party to hold a nominating convention to choose candidates for President and Vice-President. 5. As Johnson did not have an electoral-vote majority, the Senate chose him 33–14 over Granger, the others being legally out of the race. 6. Harrison died April 4, 1841, and Tyler succeeded him April 6. 7. Taylor died July 9, 1850, and Fillmore succeeded him July 10. 8. Also known as the Know-Nothing Party. 9. Lincoln died April 15, 1865, and Johnson succeeded him the same day. 10. Name adopted by the Republican National Convention of 1864. Johnson was a War Democrat. 11. 23 Southern electoral votes were excluded. 12. See Election of 1872 in *Unusual Voting Results* under Elections, Presidential, in Index. 13. See Election of 1876 in *Unusual Voting Results* under Elections, Presidential, in Index. 14. Garfield died Sept. 19, 1881, and Arthur succeeded him Sept. 20. 15. Members of People's Party were called Populists. 16. McKinley died Sept. 14, 1901, and Roosevelt succeeded him the same day. 17. James S. Sherman, Republican candidate for Vice President, died Oct. 30, 1912, and the Republican electoral votes were cast for Butler. 18. Harding died Aug. 2, 1923, and Coolidge succeeded him Aug. 3. 19. Roosevelt died April 12, 1945, and Truman succeeded him the same day. 20. One electoral vote from Alabama was cast for Walter B. Jones. 21. Sen. Harry F. Byrd received 15 electoral votes. 22. Kennedy died Nov. 22, 1963, and Johnson succeeded him the same day. 23. Nixon resigned Aug. 9, 1974, and Gerald R. Ford succeeded him the same day. 24. One electoral vote from Virginia was cast for John Hospers, Libertarian Party. 25. One electoral vote from Washington was cast for Ronald Reagan. 26. One electoral vote from West Virginia was cast for Lloyd Bentsen.

Gerrymander

Source: "The Reader's Companion to American History," Houghton Mifflin Company.

Gerrymander refers to the drawing of boundaries of legislative districts to benefit one party or group and handicap another. Although the practice dates back to the colonial period, its name is derived from Elbridge Gerry, a signer of the Declaration of Independence, a nonsigning delegate to the Federal Convention of 1787, and a leader of the Jeffersonian Republican party.

In 1812, while Gerry was governor of Massachusetts, the Republican-dominated legislature redrew district lines to weigh representation in favor of Republicans and against Federalists. The Federalists attacked the redistricting, specifically blaming Gerry although he had nothing to do with the project and, in private, opposed it. A Federalist newspaper published a political cartoon depicting the oddly shaped district covering Essex County as a salamander; the cartoonist dubbed his creation a "Gerry-mander." The word quickly passed into common parlance.

Since the 1950s, the federal courts have been increasingly willing to examine states' defining of representative districts to determine their adherence to the principle of "one man, one vote," as enunciated in *Baker* v. *Carr* (1962). Ironically, in light of the term's New England origins, most gerrymanders examined by the Supreme Court have come from southern states, where local legislatures sought to dilute the representation of urban residents and African-Americans. □

Large Voter Turnout

Voter turnout for the presidential election of 1992 was the largest since 1972 with 61% of the voting-age population going to the polls. Furthermore, the 1992 turnout rate was four percentage points higher than in 1988 (57%). □

Qualifications for Voting

The Supreme Court decision of March 21, 1972, declared lengthy requirements for voting in state and local elections unconstitutional and suggested that 30 days was an ample period. Most of the states have changed or eliminated their durational residency requirements to comply with the ruling, as shown.

NO DURATIONAL RESIDENCY REQUIREMENT

Alabama,[6] Arkansas, Connecticut,[13] Delaware,[12] District of Columbia,[16] Florida,[5] Georgia,[2] Hawaii,[2] Iowa,[6] Louisiana,[8] Maine, Maryland, Massachusetts,[3] Missouri,[4] Nebraska,[9] New Hampshire,[17] New Mexico,[7] Oklahoma, South Carolina,[22] South Dakota,[10] Tennessee,[20] Texas,[2] Virginia, West Virginia,[2] Wyoming[2]

30-DAY RESIDENCY REQUIREMENT

Alaska,[18] Arizona,[11] Idaho,[23] Illinois, Indiana, Michigan, Mississippi,[21] Montana, Nevada, New Jersey, New York, North Carolina, North Dakota, Ohio, Pennsylvania,[2] Rhode Island, Utah, Washington[2]

OTHER

California,[19] Colorado,[1] Minnesota,[15] and Oregon,[24] 20 days; Kentucky, 28 days; Kansas, 14 days; Vermont, 10–12 days;[14] Wisconsin, 10 days

1. 25 days immediately preceding the election. 2. 30-day registration requirement. 3. No residency required to register to vote. 4. Must be registered by the fourth Wednesday prior to election. 5. 29-day registration requirement before national election; 29-day registration requirement before first state primary, if change of party before second primary have to re-register. 6. 10-day registration requirement. In-person registration by 5 PM, eleven days before election date. 7. Must register 28 days before election. 8. Register 24 days prior to any election. 9. Registration requirement, 2nd Friday prior to elections. 10. 15-day registration requirement. 11. Residency in the state 29 days next preceding the election. 12. Must reside in Delaware and register by the last day that the books are open for registration. 13. Registration deadline 14th day before election; registration and party enrollment deadline by 12 noon the day before primary. 14. Administrative cut-off date for processing applications 2nd Saturday before the election by 12 noon. 15. Permits registration and voting on election day with approved ID. 16. Registration stops 30 days before any election. Voters must inform Board of Elections of change of address within 30 days of moving. 17. Registration requirement, 10 days prior to elections. Same day registration for Federal and State elections. 18. If otherwise qualified but has not been a resident of the election district for at least 30 days preceding the date of a presidential election, is entitled to register and vote for presidential and vice-presidential candidates. 19. Must be a registered voter 29 days before an election. 20. Must register at least 30 days before an election. 21. 30 days registration required, 60 days if registration is by mail. 22. Registration certificate not valid for 30 days but if you move within the state you can vote in old precinct during the 30 days. 23. May register 25 days prior to any election with County Clerk. If eligible to vote, an individual may register in person at the polling place on election day at the resident precinct and complete a registration card, make an oath and provide proof of residence. 24. By close of business day registering agencies (which varies) 21st day before the election. *Source: Information Please* questionnaires to the states.

Facts About Elections

Candidate with highest populate vote: Reagan (1984), 54,455,075.
Candidate with highest electoral vote: Reagan (1984), 525.
Candidate carrying most states: Nixon (1972) and Reagan (1984), 49.
Candidate running most times: Norman Thomas, 6 (1928, 1932, 1936, 1940, 1944, 1948).
Candidate elected, defeated, then reelected: Cleveland (1884, 1888, 1892).

Plurality and Majority

In order to win a plurality, a candidate must receive a greater number of votes than anyone running against him. If he receives 50 votes, for example, and two other candidates receive 49 and 2, he will have a plurality of one vote over his closest opponent.

However, a candidate does not have a majority unless he receives more than 50% of the total votes cast. In the example above, the candidate does not have a majority, because his 50 votes are less than 50% of the 101 votes cast.

Unusual Voting Results

Election of 1872

The presidential and vice-presidential candidates of the Liberal Republicans and the northern Democrats in 1872 were Horace Greeley and B. Gratz Brown. Greeley died Nov. 29, 1872, before his 66 electors voted. In the electoral balloting for President, 63 of Greeley's votes were scattered among four other men, including Brown.

Election of 1876

In the election of 1876 Samuel J. Tilden, the Democratic candidate, received a popular majority but lacked one undisputed electoral vote to carry a clear majority of the electoral college. The crux of the problem was in the 22 electoral votes which were in dispute because Florida, Louisiana, South Carolina and Oregon each sent in two sets of election returns. In the three southern states, Republican election boards threw out enough Democratic votes to certify the Republican candidate, Hayes. In Oregon, the Democratic governor disqualified a Republican elector, replacing him with a Democrat. Since the Senate was Republican and the House of Representatives Democratic, it seemed useless to refer the disputed returns to the two houses for solution. Instead Congress appointed an Electoral Commission with five representatives each from the Senate, the House, and the Supreme Court. All but one Justice was named giving the Commission seven Republican and seven Democratic members. The naming of the fifth Justice was left to the other four. He was a Republican who first favored Tilden but, under pressure from his party, switched to Hayes, ensuring his election by the Commission voting 8 to 7 on party lines.

Minority Presidents

Sixteen candidates have become President of the United States with a popular vote less than 50% of the total cast. It should be noted, however, that in elections before 1872, presidential electors were not chosen by popular vote in all states. Adams' election in 1824 was by the House of Representatives, which chose him over Jackson, who had a plurality of both electoral and popular votes, but not a majority in the electoral college.

Besides Jackson in 1824, only two other candidates receiving the largest popular vote have failed to gain a majority in the electoral college—Samuel J. Tilden (D) in 1876 and Grover Cleveland (D) in 1888. The "minority" Presidents follow:

Vote Received by Minority Presidents

Year	President	Electoral Percent	Popular vote Percent
1824	John Q. Adams	31.8	29.8
1844	James K. Polk (D)	61.8	49.3
1848	Zachary Taylor (W)	56.2	47.3
1856	James Buchanan (D)	58.7	45.3
1860	Abraham Lincoln (R)	59.4	39.9
1876	Rutherford B. Hayes (R)	50.1	47.9
1880	James A. Garfield (R)	57.9	48.3
1884	Grover Cleveland (D)	54.6	48.8
1888	Benjamin Harrison (R)	58.1	47.8
1892	Grover Cleveland (D)	62.4	46.0
1912	Woodrow Wilson (D)	81.9	41.8
1916	Woodrow Wilson (D)	52.1	49.3
1948	Harry S. Truman (D)	57.1	49.5
1960	John F. Kennedy (D)	56.4	49.7
1968	Richard M. Nixon (R)	56.1	43.4
1992	William J. Clinton (D)	68.8	43.0

Percent of Persons Voting in Presidential Elections 1964–1992

(Numbers in thousands. Civilian noninstitutional population.)

United States	1992	1988	1984	1980	1976	1972	1968	1964
Total voting age	185,684	178,098	169,963	157,085	146,548	136,203	116,535	110,604
Percent voted	61.3	57.4	59.9	59.2	59.2	63.0	67.8	69.3
White	63.6	59.1	61.4	60.9	60.9	64.5	69.1	70.7
Black	54.0	51.5	55.8	50.5	48.7	52.1	57.6	58.5 [2]
Hispanic origin [1]	28.9	28.8	32.6	29.9	31.8	37.5	n.a.	n.a.
Male	60.2	56.4	59.0	59.1	59.6	64.1	69.8	71.9
Female	62.3	58.3	60.8	59.4	58.8	62.0	66.0	67.0
18 to 24 years	42.8	36.2	40.8	39.9	42.2	49.6	50.4 [3]	50.9 [3]
25 to 44 years	58.3	54.0	58.4	58.7	58.7	62.7	66.6	69.0
45 to 64 years	70.0	67.9	69.8	69.3	68.7	70.8	74.9	75.9
65 years and over	70.1	68.8	67.7	65.1	62.2	63.5	65.8	66.3

1. Persons of Hispanic origin may be of any race. 2. Black and other races in 1964. 3. Prior to 1972, includes persons 18 to 20 years old in Georgia and Kentucky, 19 and 20 in Alaska, and 20 years old in Hawaii. n.a. = not available. *Source:* Bureau of the Census, *Current Population Reports,* April 1993.

How a Bill Becomes a Law

When a Senator or a Representative introduces a bill, he sends it to the clerk of his house, who gives it a number and title. This is the *first reading,* and the bill is referred to the proper committee.

The committee may decide the bill is unwise or unnecessary and *table* it, thus killing it at once. Or it may decide the bill is worthwhile and hold hearings to listen to facts and opinions presented by experts and other interested persons. After members of the committee have debated the bill and perhaps offered amendments, a vote is taken; and if the vote is favorable, the bill is sent back to the floor of the house.

The clerk reads the bill sentence by sentence to the house, and this is known as the *second reading.* Members may then debate the bill and offer amendments. In the House of Representatives, the time for debate is limited by a *cloture rule,* but there is no such restriction in the Senate for cloture, where 60 votes are required. This makes possible a *filibuster,* in which one or more opponents hold the floor to defeat the bill.

The *third reading* is by title only, and the bill is put to a vote, which may be voice or roll call, depending on the circumstances and parliamentary rules. Members who must be absent at the time but who wish to record their vote may be paired if each negative vote has a balancing affirmative one.

The bill then goes to the other house of Congress, where it may be defeated, or passed with or without amendments. If the bill is defeated, it dies. If it is passed with amendments, a joint Congressional committee must be appointed by both houses to iron out the differences.

After its final passage by both houses, the bill is sent to the President. If he approves, he signs it, and the bill becomes a law. However, if he disapproves, he *vetoes* the bill by refusing to sign it and sending it back to the house of origin with his reasons for the veto. The objections are read and debated, and a roll-call vote is taken. If the bill receives less than a two-thirds vote, it is defeated and goes no farther. But if it receives a two-thirds vote or greater, it is sent to the other house for a vote. If that house also passes it by a two-thirds vote, the President's veto is *overridden,* and the bill becomes a law.

Should the President desire neither to sign nor to veto the bill, he may retain it for ten days, Sundays excepted, after which time it automatically becomes a law without signature. However, if Congress has adjourned within those ten days, the bill is automatically killed, that process of indirect rejection being known as a *pocket veto.*

Government Officials

Cabinet Members With Dates of Appointment

Although the Constitution made no provision for a President's advisory group, the heads of the three executive departments (State, Treasury, and War) and the Attorney General were organized by Washington into such a group; and by about 1793, the name "Cabinet" was applied to it. With the exception of the Attorney General up to 1870 and the Postmaster General from 1829 to 1872, Cabinet members have been heads of executive departments.

A Cabinet member is appointed by the President, subject to the confirmation of the Senate; and as his term is not fixed, he may be replaced at any time by the President. At a change in Administration, it is customary for him to tender his resignation, but he remains in office until a successor is appointed.

The table of Cabinet members lists only those members who actually served after being duly commissioned.

The dates shown are those of appointment. "Cont." indicates that the term continued from the previous Administration for a substantial amount of time.

With the creation of the Department of Transportation in 1966, the Cabinet consisted of 12 members. This figure was reduced to 11 when the Post Office Department became an independent agency in 1970 but, with the establishment in 1977 of a Department of Energy, became 12 again. Creation of the Department of Education in 1980 raised the number to 13. Creation of the Department of Veterans' Affairs in 1989 raised the number to 14.

WASHINGTON

Secretary of State	Thomas Jefferson 1789
	Edmund Randolph 1794
	Timothy Pickering 1795
Secretary of the Treasury	Alexander Hamilton 1789
	Oliver Wolcott, Jr. 1795
Secretary of War	Henry Knox 1789
	Timothy Pickering 1795
	James McHenry 1796
Attorney General	Edmund Randolph 1789
	William Bradford 1794
	Charles Lee 1795

J. ADAMS

Secretary of State	Timothy Pickering (Cont.)
	John Marshall 1800
Secretary of the Treasury	Oliver Wolcott, Jr. (Cont.)
	Samuel Dexter 1801
Secretary of War	James McHenry (Cont.)
	Samuel Dexter 1800
Attorney General	Charles Lee (Cont.)
Secretary of the Navy	Benjamin Stoddert 1798

JEFFERSON

Secretary of State	James Madison 1801
Secretary of the Treasury	Samuel Dexter (Cont.)
	Albert Gallatin 1801
Secretary of War	Henry Dearborn 1801
Attorney General	Levi Lincoln 1801
	Robert Smith 1805
	John Breckinridge 1805
	Caesar A. Rodney 1807
Secretary of the Navy	Benjamin Stoddert (Cont.)
	Robert Smith 1801

MADISON

Secretary of State	Robert Smith 1809
	James Monroe 1811
Secretary of the Treasury	Albert Gallatin (Cont.)
	George W. Campbell 1814
	Alexander J. Dallas 1814
	William H. Crawford 1816
Secretary of War	William Eustis 1809
	John Armstrong 1813
	James Monroe 1814
	William H. Crawford 1815

Attorney General	Caesar A. Rodney (Cont.)
	William Pinckney 1811
	Richard Rush 1814
Secretary of the Navy	Paul Hamilton 1809
	William Jones 1813
	B. W. Crowninshield 1814

MONROE

Secretary of State	John Quincy Adams 1817
Secretary of the Treasury	William H. Crawford (Cont.)
Secretary of War	John C. Calhoun 1817
Attorney General	Richard Rush (Cont.)
	William Wirt 1817
Secretary of the Navy	B. W. Crowninshield (Cont.)
	Smith Thompson 1818
	Samuel L. Southard 1823

J. Q. ADAMS

Secretary of State	Henry Clay 1825
Secretary of the Treasury	Richard Rush 1825
Secretary of War	James Barbour 1825
	Peter B. Porter 1828
Attorney General	William Wirt (Cont.)
Secretary of the Navy	Samuel L. Southard (Cont.)

JACKSON

Secretary of State	Martin Van Buren 1829
	Edward Livingston 1831
	Louis McLane 1833
	John Forsyth 1834
Secretary of the Treasury	Samuel D. Ingham 1829
	Louis McLane 1831
	William J. Duane 1833
	Roger B. Taney[3] 1833
	Levi Woodbury 1834
Secretary of War	John H. Eaton 1829
	Lewis Cass 1831
Attorney General	John M. Berrien 1829
	Roger B. Taney 1831
	Benjamin F. Butler 1833
Postmaster General[1]	William T. Barry 1829
	Amos Kendall 1835
Secretary of the Navy	John Branch 1829
	Levi Woodbury 1831
	Mahlon Dickerson 1834

VAN BUREN

Secretary of State	John Forsyth (Cont.)
Secretary of the Treasury	Levi Woodbury (Cont.)
Secretary of War	Joel R. Poinsett 1837
Attorney General	Benjamin F. Butler (Cont.)
	Felix Grundy 1838
	Henry D. Gilpin 1840
Postmaster General	Amos Kendall (Cont.)
	John M. Niles 1840
Secretary of the Navy	Mahlon Dickerson (Cont.)
	James K. Paulding 1838

W. H. HARRISON

Secretary of State	Daniel Webster 1841
Secretary of the Treasury	Thomas Ewing 1841
Secretary of War	John Bell 1841
Attorney General	John J. Crittenden 1841
Postmaster General	Francis Granger 1841
Secretary of the Navy	George E. Badger 1841

TYLER

Secretary of State	Daniel Webster (Cont.)
	Abel P. Upshur 1843
	John C. Calhoun 1844
Secretary of the Treasury	Thomas Ewing (Cont.)
	Walter Forward 1841
	John C. Spencer[3] 1843
	George M. Bibb 1844
Secretary of War	John Bell (Cont.)
	John C. Spencer 1841
	James M. Porter[3] 1843
	William Wilkins 1844
Attorney General	John J. Crittenden (Cont.)
	Hugh S. Legaré 1841
	John Nelson 1843
Postmaster General	Francis Granger (Cont.)
	Charles A. Wickliffe 1841
Secretary of the Navy	George E. Badger (Cont.)
	Abel P. Upshur 1841
	David Henshaw[3] 1843
	Thomas W. Gilmer 1844
	John Y. Mason 1844

POLK

Secretary of State	James Buchanan 1845
Secretary of the Treasury	Robert J. Walker 1845
Secretary of War	William L. Marcy 1845
Attorney General	John Y. Mason 1845
	Nathan Clifford 1846
	Isaac Toucey 1848
Postmaster General	Cave Johnson 1845
Secretary of the Navy	George Bancroft 1845
	John Y. Mason 1846

TAYLOR

Secretary of State	John M. Clayton 1849
Secretary of the Treasury	William M. Meredith 1849
Secretary of War	George W. Crawford 1849
Attorney General	Reverdy Johnson 1849
Postmaster General	Jacob Collamer 1849
Secretary of the Navy	William B. Preston 1849
Secretary of the Interior	Thomas Ewing 1849

FILLMORE

Secretary of State	Daniel Webster 1850
	Edward Everett 1852
Secretary of the Treasury	Thomas Corwin 1850
Secretary of War	Charles M. Conrad 1850
Attorney General	John J. Crittenden 1850
Postmaster General	Nathan K. Hall 1850
	Samuel D. Hubbard 1852
Secretary of the Navy	William A. Graham 1850
	John P. Kennedy 1852
Secretary of the Interior	Thos. M. T. McKennan 1850
	Alex. H. H. Stuart 1850

PIERCE

Secretary of State	William L. Marcy 1853
Secretary of the Treasury	James Guthrie 1853
Secretary of War	Jefferson Davis 1853

Attorney General	Caleb Cushing 1853
Postmaster General	James Campbell 1853
Secretary of the Navy	James C. Dobbin 1853
Secretary of the Interior	Robert McClelland 1853

BUCHANAN

Secretary of State	Lewis Cass 1857
	Jeremiah S. Black 1860
Secretary of the Treasury	Howell Cobb 1857
	Philip F. Thomas 1860
	John A. Dix 1861
Secretary of War	John B. Floyd 1857
	Joseph Holt 1861
Attorney General	Jeremiah S. Black 1857
	Edwin M. Stanton 1860
Postmaster General	Aaron V. Brown 1857
	Joseph Holt 1859
	Horatio King 1861
Secretary of the Navy	Isaac Toucey 1857
Secretary of the Interior	Jacob Thompson 1857

LINCOLN

Secretary of State	William H. Seward 1861
Secretary of the Treasury	Salmon P. Chase 1861
	William P. Fessenden 1864
	Hugh McCulloch 1865
Secretary of War	Simon Cameron 1861
	Edwin M. Stanton 1862
Attorney General	Edward Bates 1861
	James Speed 1864
Postmaster General	Montgomery Blair 1861
	William Dennison 1864
Secretary of the Navy	Gideon Welles 1861
Secretary of the Interior	Caleb B. Smith 1861
	John P. Usher 1863

A. JOHNSON

Secretary of State	William H. Seward (Cont.)
Secretary of the Treasury	Hugh McCulloch (Cont.)
Secretary of War	Edwin M. Stanton (Cont.)
	John M. Schofield 1868
Attorney General	James Speed (Cont.)
	Henry Stanbery 1866
	William M. Evarts 1868
Postmaster General	William Dennison (Cont.)
	Alexander W. Randall 1866
Secretary of the Navy	Gideon Welles (Cont.)
Secretary of the Interior	John P. Usher (Cont.)
	James Harlan 1865
	Orville H. Browning 1866

GRANT

Secretary of State	Elihu B. Washburne 1869
	Hamilton Fish 1869
Secretary of the Treasury	George S. Boutwell 1869
	William A. Richardson 1873
	Benjamin H. Bristow 1874
	Lot M. Morrill 1876
Secretary of War	John A. Rawlins 1869
	William W. Belknap 1869
	Alphonso Taft 1876
	James D. Cameron 1876
Attorney General	Ebenezer R. Hoar 1869
	Amos T. Akerman 1870
	George H. Williams 1871
	Edwards Pierrepont 1875
	Alphonso Taft 1876
Postmaster General	John A. J. Creswell 1869
	Marshall Jewell 1874
	James N. Tyner 1876
Secretary of the Navy	Adolph E. Borie 1869
	George M. Robeson 1869
Secretary of the Interior	Jacob D. Cox 1869
	Columbus Delano 1870
	Zachariah Chandler 1875

HAYES

Secretary of State	William M. Evarts 1877
Secretary of the Treasury	John Sherman 1877
Secretary of War	George W. McCrary 1877
	Alexander Ramsey 1879

Attorney General	Charles Devens 1877
Postmaster General	David M. Key 1877
	Horace Maynard 1880
	Richard W. Thompson 1877
	Nathan Goff, Jr. 1881
Secretary of the Interior	Carl Schurz 1877

GARFIELD

Secretary of State	James G. Blaine 1881
Secretary of the Treasury	William Windom 1881
Secretary of War	Robert T. Lincoln 1881
Attorney General	Wayne MacVeagh 1881
Postmaster General	Thomas L. James 1881
Secretary of the Navy	William H. Hunt 1881
Secretary of the Interior	Samuel J. Kirkwood 1881

ARTHUR

Secretary of State	James G. Blaine (Cont.)
	F. T. Frelinghuysen 1881
Secretary of the Treasury	William Windom (Cont.)
	Charles J. Folger 1881
	Walter Q. Gresham 1884
	Hugh McCulloch 1884
Secretary of War	Robert T. Lincoln (Cont.)
Attorney General	Wayne MacVeagh (Cont.)
	Benjamin H. Brewster 1881
Postmaster General	Thomas L. James (Cont.)
	Timothy O. Howe 1881
	Walter Q. Gresham 1883
	Frank Hatton 1884
Secretary of the Navy	William H. Hunt (Cont.)
	William E. Chandler 1882
Secretary of the Interior	Samuel J. Kirkwood (Cont.)
	Henry M. Teller 1882

CLEVELAND

Secretary of State	Thomas F. Bayard 1885
Secretary of the Treasury	Daniel Manning 1885
	Charles S. Fairchild 1887
Secretary of War	William C. Endicott 1885
Attorney General	Augustus H. Garland 1885
Postmaster General	William F. Vilas 1885
	Don M. Dickinson 1888
Secretary of the Navy	William C. Whitney 1885
Secretary of the Interior	Lucius Q. C. Lamar 1885
	William F. Vilas 1888
Secretary of Agriculture	Norman J. Colman 1889

B. HARRISON

Secretary of State	James G. Blaine 1889
	John W. Foster 1892
Secretary of the Treasury	William Windom 1889
	Charles Foster 1891
Secretary of War	Redfield Proctor 1889
	Stephen B. Elkins 1891
Attorney General	William H. H. Miller 1889
Postmaster General	John Wanamaker 1889
Secretary of the Navy	Benjamin F. Tracy 1889
Secretary of the Interior	John W. Noble 1889
Secretary of Agriculture	Jeremiah M. Rusk 1889

CLEVELAND

Secretary of State	Walter Q. Gresham 1893
	Richard Olney 1895
Secretary of the Treasury	John G. Carlisle 1893
Secretary of War	Daniel S. Lamont 1893
Attorney General	Richard Olney 1893
	Judson Harmon 1895
Postmaster General	Wilson S. Bissell 1893
	William L. Wilson 1895
Secretary of the Navy	Hilary A. Herbert 1893
Secretary of the Interior	Hoke Smith 1893
	David R. Francis 1896
Secretary of Agriculture	Julius Sterling Morton 1893

MCKINLEY

Secretary of State	John Sherman 1897
	William R. Day 1898
	John Hay 1898
Secretary of the Treasury	Lyman J. Gage 1897
Secretary of War	Russell A. Alger 1897
	Elihu Root 1899
Attorney General	Joseph McKenna 1897

	John W. Griggs 1898
	Philander C. Knox 1901
Postmaster General	James A. Gary 1897
	Charles E. Smith 1898
Secretary of the Navy	John D. Long 1897
Secretary of the Interior	Cornelius N. Bliss 1897
	Ethan A. Hitchcock 1898
Secretary of Agriculture	James Wilson 1897

T. ROOSEVELT

Secretary of State	John Hay (Cont.)
	Elihu Root 1905
	Robert Bacon 1909
Secretary of the Treasury	Lyman J. Gage (Cont.)
	Leslie M. Shaw 1902
	George B. Cortelyou 1907
Secretary of War	Elihu Root (Cont.)
	William H. Taft 1904
	Luke E. Wright 1908
Attorney General	Philander C. Knox (Cont.)
	William H. Moody 1904
	Charles J. Bonaparte 1906
Postmaster General	Charles E. Smith (Cont.)
	Henry C. Payne 1902
	Robert J. Wynne 1904
	George B. Cortelyou 1905
	George von L. Meyer 1907
Secretary of the Navy	John D. Long (Cont.)
	William H. Moody 1902
	Paul Morton 1904
	Charles J. Bonaparte 1905
	Victor H. Metcalf 1906
	Truman H. Newberry 1908
Secretary of the Interior	Ethan A. Hitchcock (Cont.)
	James R. Garfield 1907
Secretary of Agriculture	James Wilson (Cont.)
Secretary of Commerce and Labor	George B. Cortelyou 1903
	Victor H. Metcalf 1904
	Oscar S. Straus 1906

TAFT

Secretary of State	Philander C. Knox 1909
Secretary of the Treasury	Franklin MacVeagh 1909
Secretary of War	Jacob M. Dickinson 1909
	Henry L. Stimson 1911
Attorney General	George W. Wickersham 1909
Postmaster General	Frank H. Hitchcock 1909
Secretary of the Navy	George von L. Meyer 1909
Secretary of the Interior	Richard A. Ballinger 1909
	Walter L. Fisher 1911
Secretary of Agriculture	James Wilson (Cont.)
Secretary of Commerce and Labor	Charles Nagel 1909

WILSON

Secretary of State	William J. Bryan 1913
	Robert Lansing 1915
	Bainbridge Colby 1920
Secretary of the Treasury	William G. McAdoo 1913
	Carter Glass 1918
	David F. Houston 1920
Secretary of War	Lindley M. Garrison 1913
	Newton D. Baker 1916
Attorney General	James C. McReynolds 1913
	Thomas W. Gregory 1914
	A. Mitchell Palmer 1919
Postmaster General	Albert S. Burleson 1913
Secretary of the Navy	Josephus Daniels 1913
Secretary of the Interior	Franklin K. Lane 1913
	John B. Payne 1920
Secretary of Agriculture	David F. Houston 1913
	Edwin T. Meredith 1920
Secretary of Commerce	William C. Redfield 1913
	Joshua W. Alexander 1919
Secretary of Labor	William B. Wilson 1913

HARDING

Secretary of State	Charles E. Hughes 1921
Secretary of the Treasury	Andrew W. Mellon 1921
Secretary of War	John W. Weeks 1921
Attorney General	Harry M. Daugherty 1921
Postmaster General	Will H. Hays 1921
	Hubert Work 1922

Secretary of the Navy	Harry S. New 1923
Secretary of the Interior	Edwin Denby 1921
	Albert B. Fall 1921
	Hubert Work 1923
Secretary of Agriculture	Henry C. Wallace 1921
Secretary of Commerce	Herbert Hoover 1921
Secretary of Labor	James J. Davis 1921

COOLIDGE

Secretary of State	Charles E. Hughes (Cont.)
	Frank B. Kellogg 1925
Secretary of the Treasury	Andrew W. Mellon (Cont.)
Secretary of War	John W. Weeks (Cont.)
	Dwight F. Davis 1925
Attorney General	Harry M. Daugherty (Cont.)
	Harlan F. Stone 1924
	John G. Sargent 1925
Postmaster General	Harry S. New (Cont.)
Secretary of the Navy	Edwin Denby (Cont.)
	Curtis D. Wilbur 1924
Secretary of the Interior	Hubert Work (Cont.)
	Roy O. West 1928
Secretary of Agriculture	Henry C. Wallace (Cont.)
	Howard M. Gore 1924
	William M. Jardine 1925
Secretary of Commerce	Herbert Hoover (Cont.)
	William F. Whiting 1928
Secretary of Labor	James J. Davis (Cont.)

HOOVER

Secretary of State	Frank B. Kellogg (Cont.)
	Henry L. Stimson 1929
Secretary of the Treasury	Andrew W. Mellon (Cont.)
	Ogden L. Mills 1932
Secretary of War	James W. Good 1929
	Patrick J. Hurley 1929
Attorney General	William D. Mitchell 1929
Postmaster General	Walter F. Brown 1929
Secretary of the Navy	Charles F. Adams 1929
Secretary of the Interior	Ray Lyman Wilbur 1929
Secretary of Agriculture	Arthur M. Hyde 1929
Secretary of Commerce	Robert P. Lamont 1929
	Roy D. Chapin 1932
Secretary of Labor	James J. Davis (Cont.)
	William N. Doak 1930

F. D. ROOSEVELT

Secretary of State	Cordell Hull 1933
	E. R. Stettinius, Jr. 1944
Secretary of the Treasury	William H. Woodin 1933
	Henry Morgenthau, Jr. 1934
Secretary of War	George H. Dern 1933
	Harry H. Woodring 1936
	Henry L. Stimson 1940
Attorney General	Homer S. Cummings 1933
	Frank Murphy 1939
	Robert H. Jackson 1940
	Francis Biddle 1941
Postmaster General	James A. Farley 1933
	Frank C. Walker 1940
Secretary of the Navy	Claude A. Swanson 1933
	Charles Edison 1940
	Frank Knox 1940
	James Forrestal 1944
Secretary of the Interior	Harold L. Ickes 1933
Secretary of Agriculture	Henry A. Wallace 1933
	Claude R. Wickard 1940
Secretary of Commerce	Daniel C. Roper 1933
	Harry L. Hopkins 1938
	Jesse H. Jones 1940
	Henry A. Wallace 1945
Secretary of Labor	Frances Perkins 1933

TRUMAN

Secretary of State	E. R. Stettinius, Jr. (Cont.)
	James F. Byrnes 1945
	George C. Marshall 1947
	Dean Acheson 1949
Secretary of the Treasury	Henry Morgenthau, Jr. (Cont.)
	Frederick M. Vinson 1945
	John W. Snyder 1946
Secretary of Defense	James Forrestal 1947
	Louis A. Johnson 1949
	George C. Marshall 1950
	Robert A. Lovett 1951
Attorney General	Francis Biddle (Cont.)
	Tom C. Clark 1945
	J. Howard McGrath 1949
	James P. McGranery 1952
Postmaster General	Frank C. Walker (Cont.)
	Robert E. Hannegan 1945
	Jesse M. Donaldson 1947
Secretary of the Interior	Harold L. Ickes (Cont.)
	Julius A. Krug 1946
	Oscar L. Chapman 1949
Secretary of Agriculture	Claude R. Wickard (Cont.)
	Clinton P. Anderson 1945
	Charles F. Brannan 1948
Secretary of Commerce	Henry A. Wallace (Cont.)
	W. Averell Harriman 1946
	Charles Sawyer 1948
Secretary of Labor	Frances Perkins (Cont.)
	Lewis B. Schwellenbach 1945
	Maurice J. Tobin 1948
Secretary of War [2]	Henry L. Stimson (Cont.)
	Robert P. Patterson 1945
	Kenneth C. Royall 1947
Secretary of the Navy [2]	James Forrestal (Cont.)

EISENHOWER

Secretary of State	John Foster Dulles 1953
	Christian A. Herter 1959
Secretary of the Treasury	George M. Humphrey 1953
	Robert B. Anderson 1957
Secretary of Defense	Charles E. Wilson 1953
	Neil H. McElroy 1957
	Thomas S. Gates, Jr. 1959
Attorney General	Herbert Brownell, Jr. 1953
	William P. Rogers 1958
Postmaster General	Arthur E. Summerfield 1953
Secretary of the Interior	Douglas McKay 1953
	Frederick A. Seaton 1956
Secretary of Agriculture	Ezra Taft Benson 1953
Secretary of Commerce	Sinclair Weeks 1953
	Lewis L. Strauss[3] 1958
	Frederick H. Mueller 1959
Secretary of Labor	Martin P. Durkin 1953
	James P. Mitchell 1953
Secretary of Health, Education, and Welfare	Oveta Culp Hobby 1953
	Marion B. Folsom 1955
	Arthur S. Flemming 1958

KENNEDY

Secretary of State	Dean Rusk 1961
Secretary of the Treasury	C. Douglas Dillon 1961
Secretary of Defense	Robert S. McNamara 1961
Attorney General	Robert F. Kennedy 1961
Postmaster General	J. Edward Day 1961
	John A. Gronouski 1963
Secretary of the Interior	Stewart L. Udall 1961
Secretary of Agriculture	Orville L. Freeman 1961
Secretary of Commerce	Luther H. Hodges 1961
Secretary of Labor	Arthur J. Goldberg 1961
	W. Willard Wirtz 1962
Secretary of Health, Education, and Welfare	Abraham A. Ribicoff 1961
	Anthony J. Celebrezze 1962

L. B. JOHNSON

Secretary of State	Dean Rusk (Cont.)
Secretary of the Treasury	C. Douglas Dillon (Cont.)
	Henry H. Fowler 1965
	Joseph W. Barr[4] 1968
Secretary of Defense	Robert S. McNamara (Cont.)
	Clark M. Clifford 1968
Attorney General	Robert F. Kennedy (Cont.)
	N. de B. Katzenbach 1965
	Ramsey Clark 1967
Postmaster General	John A. Gronouski (Cont.)
	Lawrence F. O'Brien 1965
	W. Marvin Watson 1968
Secretary of the Interior	Stewart L. Udall (Cont.)
Secretary of Agriculture	Orville L. Freeman (Cont.)

Secretary of Commerce	Luther H. Hodges (Cont.)
	John T. Connor 1964
	A. B. Trowbridge 1967
	C. R. Smith 1968
Secretary of Labor	W. Willard Wirtz (Cont.)
Secretary of Health, Education, and Welfare	Anthony J. Celebrezze (Cont.)
	John W. Gardner 1965
	Wilbur J. Cohen 1968
Secretary of Housing and Urban Development	Robert C. Weaver 1966
	Robert C. Wood[4] 1969
Secretary of Transportation	Alan S. Boyd 1966

NIXON

Secretary of State	William P. Rogers 1969
	Henry A. Kissinger 1973
Secretary of the Treasury	David M. Kennedy 1969
	John B. Connally 1971
	George P. Shultz 1972
	William E. Simon 1974
Secretary of Defense	Melvin R. Laird 1969
	Elliot L. Richardson 1973
	James R. Schlesinger 1973
Attorney General	John N. Mitchell 1969
	Richard G. Kleindienst 1972
	Elliot L. Richardson 1973
	William B. Saxbe 1974
Postmaster General[5]	William M. Blount 1969
Secretary of the Interior	Walter J. Hickel 1969
	Rogers C. B. Morton 1971
Secretary of Agriculture	Clifford M. Hardin 1969
	Earl L. Butz 1971
Secretary of Commerce	Maurice H. Stans 1969
	Peter G. Peterson 1972
	Frederick B. Dent 1973
Secretary of Labor	George P. Shultz 1969
	James D. Hodgson 1970
	Peter J. Brennan 1973
Secretary of Health, Education, and Welfare	Robert H. Finch 1969
	Elliot L. Richardson 1970
	Caspar W. Weinberger 1973
Secretary of Housing and Urban Development	George Romney 1969
	James T. Lynn 1973
Secretary of Transportation	John A. Volpe 1969
	Claude S. Brinegar 1973

FORD

Secretary of State	Henry A. Kissinger (Cont.)
Secretary of the Treasury	William E. Simon (Cont.)
Secretary of Defense	James R. Schlesinger (Cont.)
	Donald H. Rumsfeld 1975
Attorney General	William B. Saxbe (Cont.)
	Edward H. Levi 1975
Secretary of the Interior	Rogers C. B. Morton (Cont.)
	Stanley K. Hathaway 1975
	Thomas S. Kleppe 1975
Secretary of Agriculture	Earl L. Butz (Cont.)
	John Knebel 1976
Secretary of Commerce	Frederick B. Dent (Cont.)
	Rogers C. B. Morton 1975
	Elliot L. Richardson 1976
Secretary of Labor	Peter J. Brennan (Cont.)
	John T. Dunlop 1975
	William J. Usery, Jr. 1976
Secretary of Health, Education, and Welfare	Caspar W. Weinberger (Cont.)
	F. David Mathews 1975
Secretary of Housing and Urban Development	James T. Lynn (Cont.)
	Carla A. Hills 1975
Secretary of Transportation	Claude S. Brinegar (Cont.)
	William T. Coleman, Jr. 1975

CARTER

Secretary of State	Cyrus R. Vance 1977
	Edmund S. Muskie 1980
Secretary of the Treasury	W. Michael Blumenthal 1977
	G. William Miller 1979

Secretary of Defense	Harold Brown 1977
Attorney General	Griffin B. Bell 1977
	Benjamin R. Civiletti 1979
Secretary of the Interior	Cecil D. Andrus 1977
Secretary of Agriculture	Bob S. Bergland 1977
Secretary of Commerce	Juanita M. Kreps 1977
	Philip M. Klutznick 1979
Secretary of Labor	F. Ray Marshall 1977
Secretary of Health and Human Services[6]	Joseph A. Califano, Jr. 1977
	Patricia Roberts Harris 1979
Secretary of Housing and Urban Development	Patricia Roberts Harris 1977
	Moon Landrieu 1979
Secretary of Transportation	Brock Adams 1977
	Neil E. Goldschmidt 1979
Secretary of Energy	James R. Schlesinger 1977
	Charles W. Duncan, Jr. 1979
Secretary of Education	Shirley Mount Hufstedler 1979

REAGAN

Secretary of State	Alexander M. Haig, Jr. 1981
	George P. Shultz 1982
Secretary of the Treasury	Donald T. Regan 1981
	James A. Baker 3rd 1985
	Nicholas F. Brady 1988
Secretary of Defense	Caspar W. Weinberger 1981
	Frank C. Carlucci 1987
Attorney General	William French Smith 1981
	Edwin Meese 3rd 1985
	Richard L. Thornburgh 1988
Secretary of the Interior	James G. Watt 1981
	William P. Clark 1983
	Donald P. Hodel 1985
Secretary of Agriculture	John R. Block 1981
	Richard E. Lyng 1986
Secretary of Commerce	Malcolm Baldrige 1981
	C. William Verity, Jr. 1987
Secretary of Labor	Raymond J. Donovan 1981
	William E. Brock 1985
	Ann Dore McLaughlin 1987
Secretary of Health and Human Services	Richard S. Schweiker 1981
	Margaret M. Heckler 1983
	Otis R. Bowen 1985
Secretary of Housing and Urban Development	Samuel R. Pierce, Jr. 1981
Secretary of Transportation	Andrew L. Lewis, Jr. 1981
	Elizabeth H. Dole 1983
	James H. Burnley 4th 1987
Secretary of Energy	James B. Edwards 1981
	Donald P. Hodel 1983
	John S. Herrington 1985
Secretary of Education	T. H. Bell 1981
	William J. Bennett 1985
	Lauro F. Cavazos 1988

BUSH

Secretary of State	James A. Baker 3d 1989
	Lawrence S. Eagleburger 1992
Secretary of the Treasury	Nicholas F. Brady (Cont.)
Secretary of Defense	Richard Cheney 1989
Attorney General	Richard L. Thornburgh (Cont.)
	William P. Barr 1992
Secretary of the Interior	Manuel Lujan Jr. 1989
Secretary of Agriculture	Clayton K. Yeutter 1989
	Edward Madigan 1991
Secretary of Commerce	Robert A. Mosbacher Sr. 1989
	Barbara H. Franklin 1992
Secretary of Labor	Elizabeth H. Dole 1989
	Lynn Martin 1991
Secretary of Health and Human Services	Louis W. Sullivan 1989
Secretary of Housing and Urban Development	Jack F. Kemp 1989
Secretary of Transportation	Samuel K. Skinner 1989
	Andrew Card 1992
Secretary of Energy	James D. Watkins 1989
Secretary of Education	Lauro F. Cavazos (Cont.)
	Lamar Alexander 1991
Secretary of Veterans Affairs	Edward J. Derwinski 1989

CLINTON

Secretary of State	Warren M. Christopher 1993
Secretary of the Treasury	Lloyd Bentsen 1993
	Robert E. Rubin 1995
Secretary of Defense	Les Aspin 1993
	William J. Perry 1994
Attorney General	Janet Reno 1993
Secretary of the Interior	Bruce Babbitt 1993
Secretary of Agriculture	Mike Espy 1993
	Dan Glickman 1995
Secretary of Commerce	Ronald H. Brown 1993
	Mickey Kantor 1996

Secretary of Labor	Robert B. Reich 1993
Secretary of Health and Human Services	Donna E. Shalala 1993
Secretary of Housing and Urban Development	Henry G. Cisneros 1993
Secretary of Transportation	Federico F. Pena 1993
Secretary of Energy	Hazel R. O'Leary 1993
Secretary of Education	Richard W. Riley 1993
Secretary of Veterans Affairs	Jesse Brown 1993

1. The Postmaster General did not become a Cabinet member until 1829. Earlier Postmasters General were: Samuel Osgood (1789), Timothy Pickering (1791), Joseph Habersham (1795), Gideon Granger (1801), Return J. Meigs, Jr. (1814), and John McLean (1823). 2. On July 26, 1947, the Departments of War and of the Navy were incorporated into the Department of Defense. 3. Not confirmed by the Senate. 4. Recess appointment. 5. The Postmaster General is no longer a Cabinet member. 6. Known as Department of Health, Education, and Welfare until May 1980.

Members of the Supreme Court of the United States

Name; apptd. from	Service		Birth		Died	Religion
	Term	Yrs	Place	Date		
CHIEF JUSTICES						
John Jay, N.Y.	1789–1795	5	N.Y.	1745	1829	Episcopal
John Rutledge, S.C.	1795	0	S.C.	1739	1800	Church of England
Oliver Ellsworth, Conn.	1796–1800	4	Conn.	1745	1807	Congregational
John Marshall, Va.	1801–1835	34	Va.	1755	1835	Episcopal
Roger B. Taney, Md.	1836–1864	28	Md.	1777	1864	Roman Catholic
Salmon P. Chase, Ohio	1864–1873	8	N.H.	1808	1873	Episcopal
Morrison R. Waite, Ohio	1874–1888	14	Conn.	1816	1888	Episcopal
Melville W. Fuller, Ill.	1888–1910	21	Me.	1833	1910	Episcopal
Edward D. White, La.	1910–1921	10	La.	1845	1921	Roman Catholic
William H. Taft, Conn.	1921–1930	8	Ohio	1857	1930	Unitarian
Charles E. Hughes, N.Y.	1930–1941	11	N.Y.	1862	1948	Baptist
Harlan F. Stone, N.Y.	1941–1946	4	N.H.	1872	1946	Episcopal
Frederick M. Vinson, Ky.	1946–1953	7	Ky.	1890	1953	Methodist
Earl Warren, Calif.	1953–1969	15	Calif.	1891	1974	Protestant
Warren E. Burger, Va.	1969–1986	17	Minn.	1907	1995	Presbyterian
William H. Rehnquist, Ariz.	1986–		Wis.	1924	—	Lutheran
ASSOCIATE JUSTICES						
James Wilson, Pa.	1789–1798	8	Scotland	1742	1798	Episcopal
John Rutledge, S.C.	1790–1791	1	S.C.	1739	1800	Church of England
William Cushing, Mass.	1790–1810	20	Mass.	1732	1810	Unitarian
John Blair, Va.	1790–1796	5	Va.	1732	1800	Presbyterian
James Iredell, N.C.	1790–1799	9	England	1751	1799	Episcopal
Thomas Johnson, Md.	1792–1793	0	Md.	1732	1819	Episcopal
William Paterson, N.J.	1793–1806	13	Ireland	1745	1806	Protestant
Samuel Chase, Md.	1796–1811	15	Md.	1741	1811	Episcopal
Bushrod Washington, Va.	1799–1829	30	Va.	1762	1829	Episcopal
Alfred Moore, N.C.	1800–1804	3	N.C.	1755	1810	Episcopal
William Johnson, S.C.	1804–1834	30	S.C.	1771	1834	Presbyterian
Brockholst Livingston, N.Y.	1807–1823	16	N.Y.	1757	1823	Presbyterian
Thomas Todd, Ky.	1807–1826	18	Va.	1765	1826	Presbyterian
Gabriel Duval, Md.	1811–1835	23	Md.	1752	1844	French Protestant
Joseph Story, Mass.	1812–1845	33	Mass.	1779	1845	Unitarian
Smith Thompson, N.Y.	1823–1843	20	N.Y.	1768	1843	Presbyterian
Robert Trimble, Ky.	1826–1828	2	Va.	1777	1828	Protestant
John McLean, Ohio	1830–1861	31	N.J.	1785	1861	Methodist-Epis.
Henry Baldwin, Pa.	1830–1844	14	Conn.	1780	1844	Trinity Church
James M. Wayne, Ga.	1835–1867	32	Ga.	1790	1867	Protestant
Philip P. Barbour, Va.	1836–1841	4	Va.	1783	1841	Episcopal
John Catron, Tenn.	1837–1865	28	Pa.	1786	1865	Presbyterian
John McKinley, Ala.	1837–1852	14	Va.	1780	1852	Protestant
Peter V. Daniel, Va.	1841–1860	18	Va.	1784	1860	Episcopal
Samuel Nelson, N.Y.	1845–1872	27	N.Y.	1792	1873	Protestant
Levi Woodbury, N.H.	1845–1851	5	N.H.	1789	1851	Protestant
Robert C. Grier, Pa.	1846–1870	23	Pa.	1794	1870	Presbyterian
Benjamin R. Curtis, Mass.	1851–1857	5	Mass.	1809	1874	(2)
John A. Campbell, Ala.	1853–1861	8	Ga.	1811	1889	Episcopal

Name; apptd. from	Service		Birth		Died	Religion
	Term	Yrs	Place	Date		
Nathan Clifford, Maine	1858–1881	23	N.H.	1803	1881	(¹)
Noah H. Swayne, Ohio	1862–1881	18	Va.	1804	1884	Quaker
Samuel F. Miller, Iowa	1862–1890	28	Ky.	1816	1890	Unitarian
David Davis, Ill.	1862–1877	14	Md.	1815	1886	(⁴)
Stephen J. Field, Calif.	1863–1897	34	Conn.	1816	1899	Episcopal
William Strong, Pa.	1870–1880	10	Conn.	1808	1895	Presbyterian
Joseph P. Bradley, N.J.	1870–1892	21	N.Y.	1813	1892	Presbyterian
Ward Hunt, N.Y.	1872–1882	9	N.Y.	1810	1886	Episcopal
John M. Harlan, Ky.	1877–1911	33	Ky.	1833	1911	Presbyterian
William B. Woods, Ga.	1880–1887	6	Ohio	1824	1887	Protestant
Stanley Matthews, Ohio	1881–1889	7	Ohio	1824	1889	Presbyterian
Horace Gray, Mass.	1882–1902	20	Mass.	1828	1902	(³)
Samuel Blatchford, N.Y.	1882–1893	11	N.Y.	1820	1893	Presbyterian
Lucius Q. C. Lamar, Miss.	1888–1893	5	Ga.	1825	1893	Methodist
David J. Brewer, Kan.	1889–1910	20	Asia Minor	1837	1910	Protestant
Henry B. Brown, Mich.	1890–1906	15	Mass.	1836	1913	Protestant
George Shiras, Jr., Pa.	1892–1903	10	Pa.	1832	1924	Presbyterian
Howell E. Jackson, Tenn.	1893–1895	2	Tenn.	1832	1895	Baptist
Edward D. White, La.	1894–1910	16	La.	1845	1921	Roman Catholic
Rufus W. Peckham, N.Y.	1895–1909	13	N.Y.	1838	1909	Episcopal
Joseph McKenna, Calif.	1898–1925	26	Pa.	1843	1926	Roman Catholic
Oliver W. Holmes, Mass.	1902–1932	29	Mass.	1841	1935	Unitarian
William R. Day, Ohio	1903–1922	19	Ohio	1849	1923	Protestant
William H. Moody, Mass.	1906–1910	3	Mass.	1853	1917	Episcopal
Horace H. Lurton, Tenn.	1909–1914	4	Ky.	1844	1914	Episcopal
Charles E. Hughes, N.Y.	1910–1916	5	N.Y.	1862	1948	Baptist
Willis Van Devanter, Wyo.	1910–1937	26	Ind.	1859	1941	Episcopal
Joseph R. Lamar, Ga.	1910–1916	4	Ga.	1857	1916	Ch. of Disciples
Mahlon Pitney, N.J.	1912–1922	10	N.J.	1858	1924	Presbyterian
James C. McReynolds, Tenn.	1914–1941	26	Ky.	1862	1946	Disciples of Chris
Louis D. Brandeis, Mass.	1916–1939	22	Ky.	1856	1941	Jewish
John H. Clarke, Ohio	1916–1922	5	Ohio	1857	1945	Protestant
George Sutherland, Utah	1922–1938	15	England	1862	1942	Episcopal
Pierce Butler, Minn.	1923–1939	16	Minn.	1866	1939	Roman Catholic
Edward T. Sanford, Tenn.	1923–1930	7	Tenn.	1865	1930	Episcopal
Harlan F. Stone, N.Y.	1925–1941	16	N.H.	1872	1946	Episcopal
Owen J. Roberts, Pa.	1930–1945	15	Pa.	1875	1955	Episcopal
Benjamin N. Cardozo, N.Y.	1932–1938	6	N.Y.	1870	1938	Jewish
Hugo L. Black, Ala.	1937–1971	34	Ala.	1886	1971	Baptist
Stanley F. Reed, Ky.	1938–1957	19	Ky.	1884	1980	Protestant
Felix Frankfurter, Mass.	1939–1962	23	Austria	1882	1965	Jewish
William O. Douglas, Conn.	1939–1975	36	Minn.	1898	1980	Presbyterian
Frank Murphy, Mich.	1940–1949	9	Mich.	1890	1949	Roman Catholic
James F. Byrnes, S.C.	1941–1942	1	S.C.	1879	1972	Episcopal
Robert H. Jackson, Pa.	1941–1954	13	N.Y.	1892	1954	Episcopal
Wiley B. Rutledge, Iowa	1943–1949	6	Ky.	1894	1949	Unitarian
Harold H. Burton, Ohio	1945–1958	13	Mass.	1888	1964	Unitarian
Tom C. Clark, Tex.	1949–1967	17	Tex.	1899	1977	Presbyterian
Sherman Minton, Ind.	1949–1956	7	Ind.	1890	1965	Roman Catholic
John M. Harlan, N.Y.	1955–1971	16	Ill.	1899	1971	Presbyterian
William J. Brennan, Jr., N.J.	1956–1990	33	N.J.	1906	—	Roman Catholic
Charles E. Whittaker, Mo.	1957–1962	5	Kan.	1901	1973	Methodist
Potter Stewart, Ohio	1958–1981	23	Mich.	1915	1985	Episcopal
Byron R. White, Colo.	1962–1993	31	Colo.	1917	—	Episcopal
Arthur J. Goldberg, Ill.	1962–1965	2	Ill.	1908	1990	Jewish
Abe Fortas, Tenn.	1965–1969	3	Tenn.	1910	1982	Jewish
Thurgood Marshall, N.Y.	1967–1991	24	Md.	1908	1993	Episcopal
Harry A. Blackmun, Minn.	1970–1994	24	Ill.	1908	—	Methodist
Lewis F. Powell, Jr., Va.	1972–1987	15	Va.	1907	—	Presbyterian
William H. Rehnquist, Ariz.	1972–1986	14	Wis.	1924	—	Lutheran
John Paul Stevens, Ill.	1975–	—	Ill.	1920	—	Protestant
Sandra Day O'Connor, Ariz.	1981–	—	Tex.	1930	—	Episcopal
Antonin Scalia, D.C.	1986–	—	N.J.	1936	—	Roman Catholic
Anthony M. Kennedy, Calif.	1988–	—	Calif.	1936	—	Roman Catholic
David H. Souter, N.H.	1990–	—	Mass.	1939	—	Episcopal
Clarence Thomas, D.C.	1991–	—	Ga.	1948	—	Roman Catholic
Ruth Bader Ginsburg, D.C.	1993–	—	N.Y.	1933	—	Jewish
Stephen G. Breyer, Mass.	1994–	—	Calif.	1938	—	n.a.

1. Congregational; later Unitarian. 2. Unitarian; then Episcopal. 3. Unitarian or Congregational. 4. Not a member of any church. NOTE: n.a. = not available.

Milestone Cases in Supreme Court History

1803 *Marbury* v. *Madison* was the first instance in which a law passed by Congress was declared unconstitutional. The decision greatly expanded the power of the Court by establishing its right to overturn acts of Congress, a power not explicitly granted by the Constitution.

1819 *McCulloch* v. *Maryland* upheld the right of Congress to create a Bank of the United States, ruling that it was a power implied but not enumerated in the Constitution. The case is significant because it advanced the doctrine of implied powers, or a loose construction of the Constitution. The Court, Chief Justice John Marshall wrote, would sanction laws reflecting "the letter and spirit" of the Constitution.

1857 *Dred Scott* v. *Sanford* was a highly controversial case that intensified the national debate over slavery. The case involved Dred Scott, a slave, who was taken from a slave state to a free territory. Scott filed a lawsuit claiming that because he had lived on free soil he was entitled to his freedom. Chief Justice Roger B. Taney disagreed, ruling that blacks were not citizens and therefore could not sue in Federal Court. Taney further inflamed antislavery forces by declaring that Congress had no right to ban slavery from U.S. territories.

1896 *Plessy* v. *Fergusson* was the infamous case that asserted that "equal but separate accommodations" for blacks on railroad cars did not violate the "equal protection under the laws" clause of the 14th Amendment. By defending the constitutionality of racial segregation, the Court paved the way for the repressive Jim Crow laws of the south. The lone dissenter on the Court, Justice John Marshall Harlan, protested, "The thin disguise of 'equal' accommodations . . . will not mislead anyone."

1954 *Brown* v. *Board of Education of Topeka* invalidated racial segregation in schools, and led to the unraveling of de jure segregation in all areas of public life. In a unanimous decision spearheaded by Chief Justice Earl Warren, the Court invalidated the Plessy ruling, declaring "in the field of public education, the doctrine of 'separate but equal' has no place," and contending that "separate educational facilities are inherently unequal." Future Supreme Court Justice Thurgood Marshall was one of the NAACP lawyers who successfully argued the case.

1973 *Roe* v. *Wade* legalized abortion and is at the center of the current controversy between "Pro-Life" and "Pro-Choice" advocates. The Court ruled that a woman has the right to an abortion without interference from the government in the first trimester of pregnancy, contending that it is part of her "right to privacy." The Court maintained that right to privacy is not absolute, however, and granted states the right to intervene in the second and third trimesters of pregnancy.

Major Decisions of the U.S. Supreme Court, 1996

Government Seizure of Property Upheld (March 4): Supreme Court rules, 5–4, that property used in a crime may be forfeited even when the owner was innocent of any wrongdoing

Court Upholds Employees' Rights on Benefits (March 19): Justices, 6–3, strengthen Federal law protecting pensions and benefits, ruling that workers can sue when employers trick them into giving up benefits.

Federal Ban on Age Discrimination Tightened (April 1): Justices rule unanimously that displaced worker's lawsuit can succeed even if worker is replaced by someone over 40, the age when protection begins.

Protections for Retarded Defendants Tightened (April 16): Justices rule unanimously that it would violate the basic right to a fair trial for a state to prosecute a person shown to be incompetent by "preponderance of the evidence."

Crucial Role in Patents Given to Judges (April 23): Justices rule unanimously that in infringement suits, judges rather than juries, must resolve the crucial issue of what a patent means.

Ban on Liquor Price Advertising Rejected (May 13): All nine Justices agree that Rhode Island statute violates First Amendment free speech guarantee.

Race Statistics in Drug Cases Overruled (May 13): By 8–1, high court says figures showing most Federal crack cocaine defendants are black are not by themselves sufficient to support defense claims.

New Standards for Punitive Damages Set (May 20): Court voids $2 million award to Alabama man over purchase of repainted car. Justices, 5–4, set new standards for determining "grossly excessive" verdicts.

A Victory for Homosexual Rights (May 20): Justices, 6–3, reject provision of Colorado constitution nullifying existing civil rights protection and barring passage of new antidiscrimination laws.

Late Fees for Credit Cards Approved (June 3): Banks with interstate card operations win major victory. Justices rule unanimously that they can charge any fee permitted by their home state regardless of law in state where the card holder lives.

Arrests After Valid Traffic Stop Upheld (June 10): Court rules unanimously that search for drugs in car is lawful even if minor traffic violation is pretext.

Officers Upheld in Rodney King Case (June 13): Court rules unanimously that Federal Court properly took prisoner's conduct into account in reducing sentences for two policemen guilty in Los Angeles beating.

Privacy Rights in Psychotherapy Upheld (June 13): Justices rule, 7–2, that confidentiality serves important public as well as private right. Verdict creates new privilege in civil and criminal cases.

Race Issue Invalidates Voting Districts (June 13): Two 5–4 rulings by Justices find one in North Carolina and three in Texas products of unconstitutional racial gerrymandering. Previous rulings cited.

Antitrust Decision Backs Employers (June 20): Ruling, 8–1, in football case states it is not violation for companies within an industry to join on new contract terms after negotiations with union have failed.

Military College Ordered to Admit Women (June 26): By 8–1, Court rules that under "skeptical scrutiny" policy State of Virginia cannot justify keeping state-supported Virginia Military Institute for men only. (June 28): The Citadel, state's only other state-supported military college, agrees to admit women.

Court Divided on Cable Indecency Law (June 28): Justices shift in decisions on Federal law intended to protect children. Court rules system operators may ban indecent programs from certain commercial channels but not from access channels used by local governments and community groups.

Free-Speech Protection Extended (June 28): Court rules in two cases that independent Government contractors have First Amendment right to speak out on public issues or back political candidates.

New Limit on Federal Appeals by Inmates Upheld (June 28): In unanimous ruling, Justices stipulate that Supreme Court itself retains jurisdiction in state cases.

Assassinations and Attempts in U. S. Since 1865

Cermak, Anton J. (Mayor of Chicago): Shot Feb. 15, 1933, in Miami by Giuseppe Zangara, who attempted to assassinate Franklin D. Roosevelt; Cermak died March 6.

Ford, Gerald R. (President of U.S.): Escaped assassination attempt Sept. 5, 1975, in Sacramento, Calif., by Lynette Alice (Squeaky) Fromm, who pointed but did not fire .45-caliber pistol. Escaped assassination attempt in San Francisco, Calif., Sept. 22, 1975, by Sara Jane Moore, who fired one shot from a .38-caliber pistol that was deflected.

Garfield, James A. (President of U.S.): Shot July 2, 1881, in Washington, D.C., by Charles J. Guiteau; died Sept. 19.

Jordan, Vernon E., Jr. (civil rights leader): Shot and critically wounded in assassination attempt May 29, 1980, in Fort Wayne, Ind.

Kennedy, John F. (President of U.S.): Shot Nov. 22, 1963, in Dallas, Tex., allegedly by Lee Harvey Oswald; died same day. Injured was Gov. John B. Connally of Texas. Oswald was shot and killed two days later by Jack Ruby.

Kennedy, Robert F. (U.S. Senator from New York): Shot June 5, 1968, in Los Angeles by Sirhan Bishara Sirhan; died June 6.

King, Martin Luther, Jr. (civil rights leader): Shot April 4, 1968, in Memphis by James Earl Ray; died same day.

Lincoln, Abraham (President of U.S.): Shot April 14, 1865, in Washington, D.C., by John Wilkes Booth; died April 15.

Long, Huey P. (U.S. Senator from Louisiana): Shot Sept. 8, 1935, in Baton Rouge by Dr. Carl A. Weiss; died Sept. 10.

McKinley, William (President of U.S.): Shot Sept. 6, 1901, in Buffalo by Leon Czolgosz; died Sept. 14.

Reagan, Ronald (President of U.S.): Shot in left lung in Washington by John W. Hinckley, Jr., on March 30, 1981; three others also wounded.

Roosevelt, Franklin D. (President-elect of U.S.): Escaped assassination unhurt Feb. 15, 1933, in Miami. *See* Cermak.

Roosevelt, Theodore (ex-President of U.S.): Escaped assassination (though shot) Oct. 14, 1912, in Milwaukee while campaigning for President.

Seward, William H. (Secretary of State): Escaped assassination (though injured) April 14, 1865, in Washington, D.C., by Lewis Powell (or Paine), accomplice of John Wilkes Booth.

Truman, Harry S. (President of U.S.): Escaped assassination unhurt Nov. 1, 1950, in Washington, D.C., as 2 Puerto Rican nationalists attempted to shoot their way into Blair House.

Wallace, George C. (Governor of Alabama): Shot and critically wounded in assassination attempt May 15, 1972, at Laurel, Md., by Arthur Herman Bremer. Wallace paralyzed from waist down.

Impeachments of Federal Officials

Source: Congressional Directory

The procedure for the impeachment of Federal officials is detailed in Article I, Section 3, of the Constitution. See Index

The Senate has sat as a court of impeachment in the following cases:

William Blount, Senator from Tennessee; charges dismissed for want of jurisdiction, January 14, 1799.

John Pickering, Judge of the U.S. District Court for New Hampshire; removed from office March 12, 1804.

Samuel Chase, Associate Justice of the Supreme Court; acquitted March 1, 1805.

James H. Peck, Judge of the U.S. District Court for Missouri; acquitted Jan. 31, 1831.

West H. Humphreys, Judge of the U.S. District Court for the middle, eastern, and western districts of Tennessee; removed from office June 26, 1862.

Andrew Johnson, President of the United States; acquitted May 26, 1868.

William W. Belknap, Secretary of War; acquitted Aug. 1, 1876.

Charles Swayne, Judge of the U.S. District Court for the northern district of Florida; acquitted Feb. 27, 1905.

Robert W. Archbald, Associate Judge, U.S. Commerce Court; removed Jan. 13, 1913.

George W. English, Judge of the U.S. District Court for eastern district of Illinois; resigned Nov. 4, 1926; proceedings dismissed.

Harold Louderback, Judge of the U.S. District Court for the northern district of California; acquitted May 24, 1933.

Halsted L. Ritter, Judge of the U.S. District Court for the southern district of Florida; removed from office April 17, 1936.

Harry E. Claiborne, Judge of the U.S. District Court for the district of Nevada; removed from office October 9, 1986.

Alcee L. Hastings, Judge of the U.S. District Court for the southern district of Florida; removed from office October 20, 1989.

Walter L. Nixon, Jr., Judge of the U.S. District Court for Mississippi; removed from office November 3, 1989.

Executive Departments and Agencies

Source: United States Government Manual 1995–96.
Unless otherwise indicated, addresses shown are in Washington, D.C.

CENTRAL INTELLIGENCE AGENCY (CIA)
Washington, D.C. (20505).
  Established: 1947.
  Director: John M. Deutch.
COUNCIL OF ECONOMIC ADVISERS (CEA)
Room 314, Old Executive Office Bldg. (20500).
  Members: 3.
  Established: Feb. 20, 1946.
  Chair: Laura D. Tyson.
COUNCIL ON ENVIRONMENTAL QUALITY
722 Jackson Pl., N.W. (20503).
  Members: 3.
  Established: 1969.
  Chair: Kathleen A. McGinty.
NATIONAL SECURITY COUNCIL (NSC)
Old Executive Office Bldg. (20506).
  Members: 4.
  Established: July 26, 1947.
  Chair: The President.
  Other members: Vice President; Secretary of State; Secretary of Defense.
OFFICE OF ADMINISTRATION
Old Executive Office Bldg. (20503).
  Established: Dec. 12, 1977.
  Director: Patsy L. Thomasson.
OFFICE OF MANAGEMENT AND BUDGET
Old Executive Office Bldg. (20503).
  Established: July 1, 1970.
  Director: Alice M. Rivlin.
OFFICE OF SCIENCE AND TECHNOLOGY POLICY
Old Executive Office Bldg. (20500).
  Established: May 11, 1976.
  Director: John H. Gibbons.
OFFICE OF THE UNITED STATES TRADE REPRESENTATIVE
600 17th St., N.W. (20506).
  Established: Jan. 15, 1963.
  Trade Representative: Charlene Barshefsky.
OFFICE OF NATIONAL DRUG CONTROL POLICY
Executive Office of the President (20500).
  Established: March 13, 1989.
  Director: Lee Patrick Brown.

Executive Departments

DEPARTMENT OF STATE
2201 C St., N.W. (20520).
  Established: 1781 as Department of Foreign Affairs; reconstituted, 1789, following adoption of Constitution; name changed to Department of State Sept. 15, 1789.
  Secretary: Warren Christopher.
  Deputy Secretary: Strobe Talbott.
  Chief Delegate to U.N.: Madelaine Konibel Albright.
DEPARTMENT OF THE TREASURY
15th St. & Pennsylvania Ave., N.W. (20220).
  Established: Sept. 2, 1789.
  Secretary: Robert E. Rubin.
  Deputy Secretary: Lawrence H. Summers.
  Treasurer of the U.S.: Mary Ellen Withrow.
  Comptroller of the Currency: Eugene Ludwig.
DEPARTMENT OF DEFENSE
The Pentagon (20301).
  Established: July 26, 1947, as National Department Establishment; name changed to Department of Defense on Aug. 10, 1949. Subordinate to Secretary

of Defense are Secretaries of Army, Navy, Air Force.
  Secretary: William J. Perry.
  Deputy Secretary: John M. Deutch.
  Secretary of Army: Togo G. West, Jr.
  Secretary of Navy: John H. Dalton.
  Secretary of Air Force: Sheila E. Widnall
  Commandant of Marine Corps: Gen. Charles C. Krulak.
  Joint Chiefs of Staff: Gen. John M. Shalikashvili, Chairman; Gen. Joseph W. Ralston, Vice Chairman; Gen. Dennis J. Reimer, Army; Adm. Jay L. Johnson, Navy (acting chief); Gen. Ronald R. Fogleman, Air Force; Gen. Richard D. Hearney, Marine Corps.
DEPARTMENT OF JUSTICE
Constitution Ave. between 9th & 10th Sts., N.W. (20530).
  Established: Office of Attorney General was created Sept. 24, 1789. Although he was one of original Cabinet members, he was not executive department head until June 22, 1870, when Department of Justice was established.
  Attorney General: Janet Reno.
  Deputy Attorney General: Jamie S. Gorelick.
  Solicitor General: Drew Days 3rd
  Director of FBI: Louis Joseph Freeh.
DEPARTMENT OF THE INTERIOR
C St. between 18th & 19th Sts., N.W. (20240).
  Established: March 3, 1849.
  Secretary: Bruce Babbitt.
  Deputy Secretary: John Garamendi.
DEPARTMENT OF AGRICULTURE
Independence Ave. between 12th & 14th Sts., S.W. (20250).
  Established: May 15, 1862. Administered by Commissioner of Agriculture until 1889, when it was made executive department.
  Secretary: Dan Glickman.
  Deputy Secretary: Richard Rominger.
DEPARTMENT OF COMMERCE
14th St. between Constitution Ave. & E St., N.W. (20230).
  Established: Department of Commerce and Labor was created Feb. 14, 1903. On March 4, 1913, all labor activities were transferred out of Department of Commerce and Labor and it was renamed Department of Commerce.
  Secretary: Mickey Kantor.
  Deputy Secretary: David L. Barram.
DEPARTMENT OF LABOR
200 Constitution Ave., N.W. (20210).
  Established: Bureau of Labor was created in 1884 under Department of the Interior; later became independent department without executive rank. Returned to bureau status in Department of Commerce and Labor, but on March 4, 1913, became independent executive department under its present name.
  Secretary: Robert Reich.
  Deputy Secretary: Thomas P. Glynn.
DEPARTMENT OF HEALTH AND HUMAN SERVICES[1]
200 Independence Ave., S.W. (20201).
  Established: April 11, 1953, replacing Federal Security Agency created in 1939.
  Secretary: Donna Shalala.
  Surgeon General: (Vacancy)

1. Originally Department of Health, Education and Welfare. Name changed in May 1980 when Department of Education was activated.

DEPARTMENT OF HOUSING AND URBAN DE-VELOPMENT
451 7th St., S.W. (20410).
Established: 1965, replacing Housing and Home Finance Agency created in 1947.
Secretary: Henry Cisneros.
Deputy Secretary: Dwight P. Robinson.

DEPARTMENT OF TRANSPORTATION
400 7th St., S.W. (20590).
Established: Oct. 15, 1966, as result of Department of Transportation Act, which became effective April 1, 1967.
Secretary: Frederico Pena.
Deputy Secretary: Mort Downey.

DEPARTMENT OF ENERGY
1000 Independence Ave., S.W. (20585).
Established: Aug. 1977.
Secretary: Hazel R. O'Leary.
Deputy Secretary: William White.

DEPARTMENT OF EDUCATION
400 Maryland Avenue, S.W. (20202).
Established: Oct. 17, 1979.
Secretary: Richard Riley.
Deputy Secretary: Madeline Kunin.

DEPARTMENT OF VETERANS' AFFAIRS
810 Vermont Avenue, N.W. (20420).
Established: March 15, 1989, replacing Veterans Administration created in 1930.
Secretary: Jesse Brown.
Deputy Secretary: Hershel Gober.

Major Independent Agencies

CONSUMER PRODUCT SAFETY COMMISSION
4330 East West Towers, Bethesda, Md. (20814).
Members: 5.
Established: Oct. 27, 1972.
Chair: Ann Brown.

CORPORATION FOR NATIONAL SERVICE (Incorporating ACTION)
1201 New York Ave. N.W. (20525)
Established: April 9, 1994
CEO and President: Harris Wofford.

ENVIRONMENTAL PROTECTION AGENCY (EPA)
401 M St., S.W. (20460).
Established: Dec. 2, 1970.
Administrator: Carol M. Browner.

EQUAL EMPLOYMENT OPPORTUNITY COMMISSION (EEOC)
1801 L St., N.W. (20507).
Members: 5.
Established: July 2, 1965.
Chair: Gilbert Casellas.

FARM CREDIT ADMINISTRATION (FCA)
1501 Farm Credit Dr., McLean, Va. (22102).
Members: 13.
Established: July 17, 1916.
Chair: Marsha Pyle Martin.

FEDERAL COMMUNICATIONS COMMISSION (FCC)
1919 M St., N.W. (20554).
Members: 7.
Established: 1934.
Chair: Reed E. Hundt.

FEDERAL DEPOSIT INSURANCE CORPORATION (FDIC)
550 17th St., N.W. (20429).
Members: 3.
Established: June 16, 1933.
Chair: Ricki Tigert Helfer.

FEDERAL ELECTION COMMISSION (FEC)
999 E St., N.W. (20463).
Members: 6.
Established: 1974.
Chair: Lee Ann Elliott.

FEDERAL MARITIME COMMISSION
800 North Capitol St., N.W. (20573–0001).
Members: 5.
Established: Aug. 12, 1961.
Chair: William D. Hathaway.

FEDERAL MEDIATION AND CONCILIATION SERVICE (FMCS)
2100 K St., N.W. (20427).
Established: 1947.
Director: John Calhoun Wells.

FEDERAL RESERVE SYSTEM (FRS), BOARD OF GOVERNORS OF
20th St. & Constitution Ave., N.W. (20551).
Members: 7.
Established: Dec. 23, 1913.
Chair: Alan Greenspan.

FEDERAL TRADE COMMISSION (FTC)
Pennsylvania Ave. at 6th St., N.W. (20580).
Members: 5.
Established: Sept. 26, 1914.
Chair: Robert Pitofsky.

GENERAL SERVICES ADMINISTRATION (GSA)
18th and F Sts., N.W. (20405).
Established: July 1, 1949.
Acting Administrator: David J. Barram.

NATIONAL AERONAUTICS AND SPACE ADMINISTRATION (NASA)
300 E St., S.W. (20546).
Established: 1958.
Administrator: Daniel S. Goldin.

NATIONAL FOUNDATION ON THE ARTS AND THE HUMANITIES
1100 Pennsylvania Ave., N.W., (20506).
Established: 1965.
Chairs: National Endowment for the Arts, Chair, Jane Alexander; National Endowment for the Humanities, Chair, Sheldon Hackney.

NATIONAL LABOR RELATIONS BOARD (NLRB)
1099 14th St. N.W. (20570).
Members: 5.
Established: July 5, 1935.
Chair: William Gould IV.

NATIONAL MEDIATION BOARD
Suite 250 East, 1301 K St., N.W. (20572).
Members: 3.
Established: June 21, 1934.
Chair: Magdalena G. Jacobsen

NATIONAL SCIENCE FOUNDATION (NSF)
4201 Wilson Blvd., Arlington, Va. (22230)
Established: 1950.
Director: Dr. Neal F. Lane.

NATIONAL TRANSPORTATION SAFETY BOARD
490 L'Enfant Plaza, S.W. (20594).
Members: 5.
Established: April 1, 1975.
Chair: James Hall.

NUCLEAR REGULATORY COMMISSION (NRC)
Washington, D.C. (20555).
Members: 5.
Established: Jan. 19, 1975.
Chair: Shirley Jackson.

OFFICE OF PERSONNEL MANAGEMENT (OPM)
1900 E St., N.W. (20415).
Members: 3.
Established: Jan. 1, 1979.
Director: James B. King.

SECURITIES AND EXCHANGE COMMISSION (SEC)
450 5th St., N.W. (20549).
Members: 5.
Established: July 2, 1934.
Chair: Arthur Levitt.

SELECTIVE SERVICE SYSTEM (SSS)
National Headquarters 1515 Wilson Blvd., Arlington, Va. 22209
Established: Sept. 16, 1940.
Director: Gil Coronado.

SMALL BUSINESS ADMINISTRATION (SBA)
409 3rd St., N.W. (20416).
Established: July 30, 1953.
Administrator: Philip Lader.

TENNESSEE VALLEY AUTHORITY (TVA)
400 West Summit Hill Drive, Knoxville, Tenn. (37902).
Washington office: One Massachusetts Ave., N.W. (20444–0001).
Members of Board of Directors: 3.
Established: May 18, 1933.
Directors: William Kennoy and Johnny H. Hayes.

U.S. AGENCY FOR INTERNATIONAL DEVELOPMENT
320 21st St., N.W. (20523).
Established: Oct. 1, 1979.
Administrator: J. Brian Atwood.

U.S. ARMS CONTROL AND DISARMAMENT AGENCY
320 21st St., N.W., (20451).
Established: Sept. 26, 1961.
Director: John Holum.

U.S. COMMISSION ON CIVIL RIGHTS
624 9th St., N.W. (20425).
Members: 8.
Established: 1957.
Chair: Mary Frances Berry.

U.S. INFORMATION AGENCY
301 Fourth St., S.W. (20547).
Established: Aug. 1, 1953. Reorganized April 1, 1978.
Director: Dr. Joseph Duffey.

U.S. INTERNATIONAL TRADE COMMISSION
500 E St., N.W. (20436).
Members: 6.
Established: Sept. 8, 1916.
Chair: Peter S. Watson.

U.S. POSTAL SERVICE
475 L'Enfant Plaza West, S.W. (20260).
Postmaster General: Marvin T. Runyon.
Deputy Postmaster General: Michael S. Coughlin.
Established: In 1775 with the appointment of Benjamin Franklin as the first Postmaster General under the Continental Congress. In 1970 became independent agency headed by 11-member board of governors.

Other Independent Agencies

Administrative Conference of the United States—Suite 500, 2120 L St., N.W. (20037).
American Battle Monuments Commission—Room 5127 Pulaski Bldg. 20 Massachusetts Ave., N.W. (20314).

Appalachian Regional Commission—1666 Connecticut Ave., N.W. (20235).
Board for International Broadcasting—Suite 400, 1201 Connecticut Ave., N.W. (20036).
Commission of Fine Arts—Pension Bldg. 441 F St., N.W. (20001).
Commodity Futures Trading Commission—2033 K St., N.W. (20581).
Export-Import Bank of the United States—811 Vermont Ave., N.W. (20571).
Federal Emergency Management Agency—500 C St., S.W. (20472).
Federal Housing Finance Board—1777 F St. N.W. (20006).
Federal Labor Relations Authority—607 14th St. N.W. (20424).
Inter-American Foundation—901 N. Stuart St., Arlington, Va. (22203).
Merit Systems Protection Board—1120 Vermont Ave., N.W. (20419).
National Commission on Libraries and Information Science—Suite 820, 1110 Vermont Ave., N.W. (20005).
National Credit Union Administration—1775 Duke St., Alexandria, Va. (22314–3428).
Occupational Safety and Health Review Commission—1120 20th St., N.W. (20036-3419).
Panama Canal Commission—Suite 1050, 1825 I St., N.W. (20006).
Peace Corps—1990 K St., N.W. (20526).
Pension Benefit Guaranty Corporation—1200 K St., N.W. (20006).
Postal Rate Commission—Suite 300, 1333 H St., N.W. (20268-0001).
President's Committee on Employment of People With Disabilities—Suite 300, 1331 F St., N.W. (20004)
President's Council on Physical Fitness and Sports—701 Pennsylvania Ave., N.W., Suite 250 (20004).
Railroad Retirement Board (RRB)—844 Rush St., Chicago, Ill. (60611); Office of Legislative Affairs: Suite 500, 1310 G St., N.W. (20005–3004).
U.S. Parole Commission— 5550 Friendship Blvd., Chevy Chase, Md. (20815).

Legislative Department

Architect of the Capitol—Room SB-15 U.S. Capitol Building (20515).
General Accounting Office (GAO)—441 G St., N.W. (20548).
Government Printing Office (GPO)—North Capitol & H Sts., N.W. (20401).
Library of Congress—10 First St. S.E. (20540).
Office of Technology Assessment—600 Pennsylvania Ave., S.E. (20510).
United States Botanic Garden—Office of Director, 245 First St., S.W. (20024).

Quasi-Official Agencies

American National Red Cross—17th & D Sts., N.W. (20006).
Legal Services Corporation—750 First St., N.E. (20002-4250).
National Academy of Sciences, National Academy of Engineering, National Research Council, Institute of Medicine—2101 Constitution Ave., N.W. (20418).
National Railroad Passenger Corporation (Amtrak)—60 Massachusetts Ave., N.E. (20002).
Smithsonian Institution—1000 Jefferson Dr., S.W. (20560).

Biographies of the Presidents

GEORGE WASHINGTON was born on Feb. 22, 1732 (Feb. 11, 1731/2, old style) in Westmoreland County, Va. While in his teens, he trained as a surveyor, and at the age of 20 he was appointed adjutant in the Virginia militia. For the next three years, he fought in the wars against the French and Indians, serving as Gen. Edward Braddock's aide in the disastrous campaign against Fort Duquesne. In 1759, he resigned from the militia, married Martha Dandridge Custis, a widow, and settled down as a gentleman farmer at Mount Vernon, Va.

As a militiaman, Washington had been exposed to the arrogance of the British officers, and his experience as a planter with British commercial restrictions increased his anti-British sentiment. He opposed the Stamp Act of 1765 and after 1770 became increasingly prominent in organizing resistance. A delegate to the Continental Congress, Washington was selected as commander in chief of the Continental Army and took command at Cambridge, Mass., on July 3, 1775.

Inadequately supported and sometimes covertly sabotaged by the Congress, in charge of troops who were inexperienced, badly equipped, and impatient of discipline, Washington conducted the war on the policy of avoiding major engagements with the British and wearing them down by harrassing tactics. His able generalship, along with the French alliance and the growing weariness within Britain, brought the war to a conclusion with the surrender of Cornwallis at Yorktown, Va., on Oct. 19, 1781.

The chaotic years under the Articles of Confederation led Washington to return to public life in the hope of promoting the formation of a strong central government. He presided over the Constitutional Convention and yielded to the universal demand that he serve as first President. He was inaugurated on April 30, 1789, in New York, the first national capital. In office, he sought to unite the nation and establish the authority of the new government at home and abroad. Greatly distressed by the emergence of the Hamilton-Jefferson rivalry, Washington worked to maintain neutrality but actually sympathized more with Hamilton. Following his unanimous re-election in 1792, his second term was dominated by the Federalists. His Farewell Address on Sept. 17, 1796 (published but never delivered) rebuked party spirit and warned against "permanent alliances" with foreign powers.

He died at Mount Vernon on Dec. 14, 1799.

JOHN ADAMS was born on Oct. 30 (Oct. 19, old style), 1735, at Braintree (now Quincy), Mass. A Harvard graduate, he considered teaching and the ministry but finally turned to law and was admitted to the bar in 1758. Six years later, he married Abigail Smith. He opposed the Stamp Act, served as lawyer for patriots indicted by the British, and by the time of the Continental Congresses, was in the vanguard of the movement for independence. In 1778, he went to France as commissioner. Subsequently he helped negotiate the peace treaty with Britain, and in 1785 became envoy to London. Resigning in 1788, he was elected Vice President under Washington and was re-elected in 1792.

Though a Federalist, Adams did not get along with Hamilton, who sought to prevent his election to the presidency in 1796 and thereafter intrigued against his administration. In 1798, Adam's independent policy averted a war with France but completed the break with Hamilton and the right-wing Federalists; at the same time, the enactment of the Alien and Sedition Acts, directed against foreigners and against critics of the government, exasperated the Jeffersonian opposition. The split between Adams and Hamilton resulted in Jefferson's becoming the next President. Adams retired to his home in Quincy. He and Jefferson died on the same day, July 4, 1826, the 50th anniversary of the signing of the Declaration of Independence.

His *Defence of the Constitutions of Government of the United States* (1787) contains original and striking, if conservative, political ideas.

THOMAS JEFFERSON was born on April 13 (April 2, old style), 1743, at Shadwell in Goochland (now Albemarle) County, Va. A William and Mary graduate, he studied law, but from the start showed an interest in science and philosophy. His literary skill and political clarity brought him to the forefront of the revolutionary movement in Virginia. As delegate to the Continental Congress, he drafted the Declaration of Independence. In 1776, he entered the Virginia House of Delegates and initiated a comprehensive reform program for the abolition of feudal survivals in land tenure and the separation of church and state.

In 1779, he became governor, but constitutional limitations on his power, combined with his own lack of executive energy, caused an unsatisfactory administration, culminating in Jefferson's virtual abdication when the British invaded Virginia in 1781. He retired to his beautiful home at Monticello, Va., to his family. His wife, Martha Wayles Skelton, whom he married in 1772, died in 1782.

Jefferson's *Notes on Virginia* (1784–85) illustrate his many-faceted interests, his limitless intellectual curiosity, his deep faith in agrarian democracy. Sent to Congress in 1783, he helped lay down the decimal system and drafted basic reports on the organization of the western lands. In 1785 he was appointed minister to France, where the Anglo-Saxon liberalism he had drawn from John Locke, the British philosopher, was stimulated by contact with the thought that would soon ferment in the French Revolution. In 1789, Washington appointed him Secretary of State. While favoring the Constitution and a strengthened central government, Jefferson came to believe that Hamilton contemplated the establishment of a monarchy. Growing differences resulted in Jefferson's resignation on Dec. 31, 1793.

Elected vice president in 1796, Jefferson continued to serve as spiritual leader of the opposition to Federalism, particularly to the repressive Alien and Sedition Acts. He was elected President in 1801 by the House of Representatives as a result of Hamilton's decision to throw the Federalist votes to him rather than to Aaron Burr, who had tied him in electoral votes. He was the first President to be inaugurated in Washington, which he had helped to design.

The purchase of Louisiana from France in 1803, though in violation of Jefferson's earlier constitutional scruples, was the most notable act of his administration. Re-elected in 1804, with the Federalist Charles C. Pinckney opposing him, Jefferson tried desperately to keep the United States out of the Napoleonic Wars in Europe, employing to this end the unpopular embargo policy.

After his retirement to Monticello in 1809, he developed his interest in education, founding the University of Virginia and watching its development with never-flagging interest. He died at Monticello on July 4, 1826. Jefferson had an enormous variety of interests and skills, ranging from education and science to architecture and music.

JAMES MADISON was born in Port Conway, Va., on March 16, 1751 (March 5, 1750/1, old style). A Princeton graduate, he joined the struggle for independence on his return to Virginia in 1771. In the 1770s and 1780s he was active in state politics, where he championed the Jefferson reform program, and in the Continental Congress. Madison was influential in the Constitutional Convention as leader of the group favoring a strong central government and as recorder of the debates; and he subsequently wrote, in collaboration with Alexander Hamilton and John Jay, the *Federalist* papers to aid the campaign for the adoption of the Constitution.

Serving in the new Congress, Madison soon emerged as the leader in the House of the men who opposed Hamilton's financial program and his pro-British leanings in foreign policy. Retiring from Congress in 1797, he continued to be active in Virginia and drafted the Virginia Resolution protesting the Alien and Sedition Acts. His intimacy with Jefferson made him the natural choice for Secretary of State in 1801.

In 1809, Madison succeeded Jefferson as President, defeating Charles C. Pinckney. His attractive wife, Dolley Payne Todd, whom he married in 1794, brought a new social sparkle to the executive mansion. In the meantime, increasing tension with Britain culminated in the War of 1812—a war for which the United States was unprepared and for which Madison lacked the executive talent to clear out incompetence and mobilize the nation's energies. Madison was re-elected in 1812, running against the Federalist De Witt Clinton. In 1814, the British actually captured Washington and forced Madison to flee to Virginia.

Madison's domestic program capitulated to the Hamiltonian policies that he had resisted 20 years before and he now signed bills to establish a United States Bank and a higher tariff.

After his presidency, he remained in retirement in Virginia until his death on June 28, 1836.

JAMES MONROE was born on April 28, 1758, in Westmoreland County, Va. A William and Mary graduate, he served in the army during the first years of the Revolution and was wounded at Trenton. He then entered Virginia politics and later national politics under the sponsorship of Jefferson. In 1786, he married Elizabeth (Eliza) Kortright.

Fearing centralization, Monroe opposed the adoption of the Constitution and, as senator from Virginia, was highly critical of the Hamiltonian program. In 1794, he was appointed minister to France, where his ardent sympathies with the Revolution exceeded the wishes of the State Department. His troubled diplomatic career ended with his recall in 1796. From 1799 to 1802, he was governor of Virginia. In 1803, Jefferson sent him to France to help negotiate the Louisiana Purchase and for the next few years he was active in various negotiations on the Continent.

In 1808, Monroe flirted with the radical wing of the Republican Party, which opposed Madison's candidacy; but the presidential boom came to naught and, after a brief term as governor of Virginia in 1811, Monroe accepted Madison's offer to become Secretary of State. During the War of 1812, he vainly sought a field command and instead served as Secretary of War from September 1814 to March 1815.

Elected President in 1816 over the Federalist Rufus King, and re-elected without opposition in 1820, Monroe, the last of the Virginia dynasty, pursued the course of systematic tranquilization that won for his administrations the name "the era of good feeling." He continued Madison's surrender to the Hamiltonian domestic program, signed the Missouri Compromise, acquired Florida, and with the able assistance of his Secretary of State, John Quincy Adams, promulgated the Monroe Doctrine in 1823, declaring against foreign colonization or intervention in the Americas. He died in New York City on July 4, 1831, the third president to die on the anniversary of Independence.

JOHN QUINCY ADAMS was born on July 11, 1767, at Braintree (now Quincy), Mass., the son of John Adams, the second President. He spent his early years in Europe with his father, graduated from Harvard, and entered law practice. His anti-Jeffersonian newspaper articles won him political attention. In 1794, he became minister to the Netherlands, the first of several diplomatic posts that occupied him until his return to Boston in 1801. In 1797, he married Louisa Catherine Johnson.

In 1803, Adams was elected to the Senate, nominally as a Federalist, but his repeated displays of independence on such issues as the Louisiana Purchase and the embargo caused his party to demand his resignation and ostracize him socially. In 1809, Madison rewarded him for his support of Jefferson by appointing him minister to St. Petersburg. He helped negotiate the Treaty of Ghent in 1814, and in 1815 became minister to London. In 1817 Monroe appointed him Secretary of State where he served with great distinction, gaining Florida from Spain without hostilities and playing an equal part with Monroe in formulating the Monroe Doctrine.

When no presidential candidate received a majority of electoral votes in 1824, Adams, with the support of Henry Clay, was elected by the House in 1825 over Andrew Jackson, who had the original plurality. Adams had ambitious plans of government activity to foster internal improvements and promote the arts and sciences, but congressional obstructionism, combined with his own unwillingness or inability to play the role of a politician, resulted in little being accomplished. After being defeated for re-election by Jackson in 1828, he successfully ran for the House of Representatives in 1830. There though nominally a Whig, he pursued as ever an independent course. He led the fight to force Congress to receive antislavery petitions and fathered the Smithsonian Institution.

Stricken on the floor of the House, he died on Feb. 23, 1848. His long and detailed *Diary* gives a unique picture of the personalities and politics of the times.

ANDREW JACKSON was born on March 15, 1767, in what is now generally agreed to be Waxhaw, S.C. After a turbulent boyhood as an orphan and a British prisoner, he moved west to Tennessee, where he soon qualified for law practice but found time for such frontier pleasures as horse racing, cockfighting, and dueling. His marriage to Rachel Donelson Robards in 1791 was complicated by subsequent legal uncertainties about the status of her divorce. During the 1790s, Jackson served in the Tennessee Constitutional Convention, the United States House of Representatives and Senate, and on the Tennessee Supreme Court.

After some years as a country gentleman, living at the Hermitage near Nashville, Jackson in 1812 was given command of Tennessee troops sent against the Creeks. He defeated the Indians at Horseshoe Bend in 1814; subsequently he became a major general and won the Battle of New Orleans over veteran British troops, though after the treaty of peace had been signed at Ghent. In 1818, Jackson invaded Florida, captured Pensacola, and hanged two Englishmen named Arbuthnot and Ambrister, creating an international incident. A presidential boom began for him in 1821, and to foster it, he returned to the Senate (1823–25). Though he won a plurality of electoral votes in 1824, he lost in the House when Clay threw his strength to Adams. Four years later, he easily defeated Adams.

As President, Jackson greatly expanded the power and prestige of the presidential office and carried through an unprecedented program of domestic reform, vetoing the bill to extend the United States Bank, moving toward a hard-money currency policy, and checking the program of federal internal improvements. He also vindicated federal authority against South Carolina with its doctrine of nullification and against France on the question of debts. The support given his policies by the workingmen of the East as well as by the farmers of the East, West, and South resulted in his triumphant re-election in 1832 over Clay.

After watching the inauguration of his handpicked successor, Martin Van Buren, Jackson retired to the Hermitage, where he maintained a lively interest in national affairs until his death on June 8, 1845.

MARTIN VAN BUREN was born on Dec. 5, 1782, at Kinderhook, N.Y. After graduating from the village school, he became a law clerk, entered practice in 1803, and soon became active in state politics as state senator and attorney general. In 1820, he was elected to the United States Senate. He threw the support of his efficient political organization, known as the Albany Regency, to William H. Crawford in 1824 and to Jackson in 1828. After leading the opposition to Adams's administration in the Senate, he served briefly as governor of New York (1828–29) and resigned to become Jackson's Secretary of State. He was soon on close personal terms with Jackson and played an important part in the Jacksonian program.

In 1832, Van Buren became vice president; in 1836, President. The Panic of 1837 overshadowed his term. He attributed it to the overexpansion of the credit and favored the establishment of an independent treasury as repository for the federal funds. In 1840, he established a 10-hour day on public works. Defeated by Harrison in 1840, he was the leading contender for the Democratic nomination in 1844 until he publicly opposed immediate annexation of Texas, and was subsequently beaten by the Southern delegations at the Baltimore convention. This incident increased his growing misgivings about the slave power.

After working behind the scenes among the anti-slavery Democrats, Van Buren joined in the movement that led to the Free-Soil Party and became its candidate for President in 1848. He subsequently returned to the Democratic Party while continuing to object to its pro-Southern policy. He died in Kinder-

hook on July 24, 1862. His *Autobiography* throws valuable sidelights on the political history of the times.

His wife, Hannah Hoes, whom he married in 1807, died in 1819.

WILLIAM HENRY HARRISON was born in Charles City County, Va., on Feb. 9, 1773. Joining the army in 1791, he was active in Indian fighting in the Northwest, became secretary of the Northwest Territory in 1798 and governor of Indiana in 1800. He married Anna Symmes in 1795. Growing discontent over white encroachments on Indian lands led to the formation of an Indian alliance under Tecumseh to resist further aggressions. In 1811, Harrison won a nominal victory over the Indians at Tippecanoe and in 1813 a more decisive one at the Battle of the Thames, where Tecumseh was killed.

After resigning from the army in 1814, Harrison had an obscure career in politics and diplomacy, ending up 20 years later as a county recorder in Ohio. Nominated for President in 1835 as a military hero whom the conservative politicians hoped to be able to control, he ran surprisingly well against Van Buren in 1836. Four years later, he defeated Van Buren but caught penumonia and died in Washington on April 4, 1841, a month after his inauguration. Harrison was the first president to die in office.

JOHN TYLER was born in Charles City County, Va., on March 29, 1790. A William and Mary graduate, he entered law practice and politics, serving in the House of Representatives (1817–21), as governor of Virginia (1825–27), and as senator (1827–36). A strict constructionist, he supported Crawford in 1824 and Jackson in 1828, but broke with Jackson over his United States Bank policy and became a member of the Southern state-rights group that co-operated with the Whigs. In 1836, he resigned from the Senate rather than follow instructions from the Virginia legislature to vote for a resolution expunging censure of Jackson from the Senate record.

Elected vice president on the Whig ticket in 1840, Tyler succeeded to the presidency on Harrison's death. His strict-constructionist views soon caused a split with the Henry Clay wing of the Whig party and a stalemate on domestic questions. Tyler's more considerable achievements were his support of the Webster-Ashburton Treaty with Britain and his success in bringing about the annexation of Texas.

After his presidency he lived in retirement in Virginia until the outbreak of the Civil War, when he emerged briefly as chairman of a peace convention and then as delegate to the provisional Congress of the Confederacy. He died on Jan. 18, 1862. He married Letitia Christian in 1813 and, two years after her death in 1842, Julia Gardiner.

JAMES KNOX POLK was born in Mecklenburg County, N.C., on Nov. 2, 1795. A graduate of the University of North Carolina, he moved west to Tennessee, was admitted to the bar, and soon became prominent in state politics. In 1825, he was elected to the House of Representatives, where he opposed Adams and, after 1829, became Jackson's floor leader in the fight against the Bank. In 1835, he became Speaker of the House. Four years later, he was elected governor of Tennessee, but was beaten in tries for re-election in 1841 and 1843.

The supporters of Van Buren for the Democratic

nomination in 1844 counted on Polk as his running mate; but, when Van Buren's stand on Texas alienated Southern support, the convention swung to Polk on the ninth ballot. He was elected over Henry Clay, the Whig candidate. Rapidly disillusioning those who thought that he would not run his own administration, Polk proceeded steadily and precisely to achieve four major objectives—the acquisition of California, the settlement of the Oregon question, the reduction of the tariff, and the establishment of the independent treasury. He also enlarged the Monroe Doctrine to exclude all non-American intervention in American affairs, whether forcible or not, and he forced Mexico into a war that he waged to a successful conclusion.

His wife, Sarah Childress, whom he married in 1824, was a woman of charm and ability. Polk died in Nashville, Tenn., on June 15, 1849.

ZACHARY TAYLOR was born at Montebello, Orange County, Va., on Nov. 24, 1784. Embarking on a military career in 1808, Taylor fought in the War of 1812, the Black Hawk War, and the Seminole War, meanwhile holding garrison jobs on the frontier or desk jobs in Washington. A brigadier general as a result of his victory over the Seminoles at Lake Okeechobee (1837), Taylor held a succession of Southwestern commands and in 1846 established a base on the Rio Grande, where his forces engaged in hostilities that precipitated the war with Mexico. He captured Monterrey in September 1846 and, disregarding Polk's orders to stay on the defensive, defeated Santa Anna at Buena Vista in February 1847, ending the war in the northern provinces.

Though Taylor had never cast a vote for president, his party affiliations were Whiggish and his availability was increased by his difficulties with Polk. He was elected president over the Democrat Lewis Cass. During the revival of the slavery controversy, which was to result in the Compromise of 1850, Taylor began to take an increasingly firm stand against appeasing the South; but he died in Washington on July 9, 1850, during the fight over the Compromise. He married Margaret Mackall Smith in 1810. His bluff and simple soldierly qualities won him the name Old Rough and Ready.

MILLARD FILLMORE was born at Locke, Cayuga County, N.Y., on Jan. 7, 1800. A lawyer, he entered politics with the Anti-Masonic Party under the sponsorship of Thurlow Weed, editor and party boss, and subsequently followed Weed into the Whig Party. He served in the House of Representatives (1833–35 and 1837–43) and played a leading role in writing the tariff of 1842. Defeated for governor of New York in 1844, he became State comptroller in 1848, was put on the Whig ticket with Taylor as a concession to the Clay wing of the party, and became president upon Taylor's death in 1850.

As president, Fillmore broke with Weed and William H. Seward and associated himself with the pro-Southern Whigs, supporting the Compromise of 1850. Defeated for the Whig nomination in 1852, he ran for president in 1856 as candidate of the American, or Know-Nothing Party, which sought to unite the country against foreigners in the alleged hope of diverting it from the explosive slavery issue. Fillmore opposed Lincoln during the Civil War. He died in Buffalo on March 8, 1874.

He was married in 1826 to Abigail Powers, who died in 1853, and in 1858 to Caroline Carmichael McIntosh.

FRANKLIN PIERCE was born at Hillsboro, N.H., on Nov. 23, 1804. A Bowdoin graduate, lawyer, and Jacksonian Democrate, he won rapid political advancement in the party, in part because of the prestige of his father, Gov. Benjamin Pierce. By 1831 he was Speaker of the New Hampshire House of Representatives; from 1833 to 1837, he served in the federal House and from 1837 to 1842 in the Senate. His wife, Jane Means Appleton, whom he married in 1834, disliked Washington and the somewhat dissipated life led by Pierce; in 1842 Pierce resigned from the Senate and began a successful law practice in Concord, N.H. During the Mexican War, he was a brigadier general.

Thereafter Pierce continued to oppose antislavery tendencies within the Democratic Party. As a result, he was the Southern choice to break the deadlock at the Democratic convention of 1852 and was nominated on the 49th ballot. In the election, Pierce overwhelmed Gen. Winfield Scott, the Whig candidate.

As president, Pierce followed a course of appeasing the South at home and of playing with schemes of territorial expansion abroad. The failure of his foreign and domestic policies prevented his renomination; and he died in Concord on Oct. 8, 1869, in relative obscurity.

JAMES BUCHANAN was born near Mercersburg, Pa., on April 23, 1791. A Dickinson graduate and a lawyer, he entered Pennsylvania politics as a Federalist. With the disappearance of the Federalist Party, he became a Jacksonian Democrat. He served with ability in the House (1821–31), as minister to St. Petersburg (1832–33), and in the Senate (1834–45), and in 1845 became Polk's Secretary of State. In 1853, Pierce appointed Buchanan minister to Britain, where he participated with other American diplomats in Europe in drafting the expansionist Ostend Manifesto.

He was elected president in 1856, defeating John C. Frémont, the Republican candidate, and former President Millard Fillmore of the American Party. The growing crisis over slavery presented Buchanan with problems he lacked the will to tackle. His appeasement of the South alienated the Stephen Douglas wing of the Democratic Party without reducing Southern militancy on slavery issues. While denying the right of secession, Buchanan also denied that the federal government could do anything about it. He supported the administration during the Civil War and died in Lancaster, Pa., on June 1, 1868.

The only president to remain a bachelor throughout his term, Buchanan used his charming niece, Harriet Lane, as White House hostess.

ABRAHAM LINCOLN was born in Hardin (now Larue) County, Ky., on Feb. 12, 1809. His family moved to Indiana and then to Illinois, and Lincoln gained what education he could along the way. While reading law, he worked in a store, managed a mill, surveyed, and split rails. In 1834, he went to the Illinois legislature as a Whig and became the party's floor leader. For the next 20 years he practiced law in Springfield, except for a single term (1847–49) in Congress, where he denounced the Mexican War. In 1855, he was a candidate for senator annd the next year he joined the new Republican Party.

A leading but unsuccessful candidate for the vice-presidential nomination with Frémont, Lincoln gained national attention in 1858 when, as Republican candidate for senator from Illinois, he engaged in a series of debates with Stephen A. Douglas, the Democratic candidate. He lost the election, but continued to prepare the way for the 1860 Republican convention and was rewarded with the presidential nomination on the third ballot. He won the election over three opponents.

From the start, Lincoln made clear that, unlike Buchanan, he believed the national government had the power to crush the rebellion. Not an abolitionist, he held the slavery issue subordinate to that of preserving the Union, but soon perceived that the war could not be brought to a successful conclusion without freeing the slaves. His administration was hampered by the incompetence of many Union generals, the inexperience of the troops, and the harassing political tactics both of the Republican Radicals, who favored a hard policy toward the South, and the Democratic Copperheads, who desired a negotiated peace. The Gettysburg Address of Nov. 19, 1863, marks the high point in the record of American eloquence. Lincoln's long search for a winning combination finally brought Generals Ulysses S. Grant and William T. Sherman on the top; and their series of victories in 1864 dispelled the mutterings from both Radicals and Peace Democrats that at one time seemed to threaten Lincoln's re-election. He was re-elected in 1864, defeating Gen. George B. McClellan, the Democratic candidate. His inaugural address urged leniency toward the South: "With malice toward none, with charity for all . . . let us strive on to finish the work we are in; to bind up the nation's wounds . . ." This policy aroused growing opposition on the part of the Republican Radicals, but before the matter could be put to the test, Lincoln was shot by the actor John Wilkes Booth at Ford's Theater, Washington, on April 14, 1865. He died the next morning.

Lincoln's marriage to Mary Todd in 1842 was often unhappy and turbulent, in part because of his wife's pronounced instability.

ANDREW JOHNSON was born at Raleigh, N.C., on Dec. 29, 1808. Self-educated, he became a tailor in Greeneville, Tenn., but soon went into politics, where he rose steadily. He served in the House of Representatives (1843–54), as governor of Tennessee (1853–57), and as a senator (1857–62). Politically he was a Jacksonian Democrat and his specialty was the fight for a more equitable land policy. Alone among the Southern Senators, he stood by the Union during the Civil War. In 1862, he became war governor of Tennessee and carried out a thankless and difficult job with great courage. Johnson became Lincoln's running mate in 1864 as a result of an attempt to give the ticket a nonpartisan and nonsectional character. Succeeding to the presidency on Lincoln's death, Johnson sought to carry out Lincoln's policy, but without his political skill. The result was a hopeless conflict with the Radical Republicans who dominated Congress, passed measures over Johnson's vetoes, and attempted to limit the power of the executive concerning appointments and removals. The conflict culminated with Johnson's impeachment for attempting to remove his disloyal Secretary of War in defiance of the Tenure of Office Act which required senatorial concurrence for such dismissals. The opposition failed by one vote to get the two thirds necessary for conviction.

After his presidency, Johnson maintained an interest in politics and in 1875 was again elected to the Senate. He died near Carter Station, Tenn., on July 31, 1875. He married Eliza McCardle in 1827.

ULYSSES SIMPSON GRANT was born (as Hiram Ulysses Grant) at Point Pleasant, Ohio, on April 27, 1822. He graduated from West Point in 1843 and served without particular distinction in the Mexican War. In 1848 he married Julia Dent. He resigned from the army in 1854, after warnings from his commanding officer about his drinking habits, and for the next six years held a wide variety of jobs in the Middle West. With the outbreak of the Civil War, he sought a command and soon, to his surprise, was made a brigadier general. His continuing successes in the western theaters, culminating in the capture of Vicksburg, Miss., in 1863, brought him national fame and soon the command of all the Union armies. Grant's dogged, implacable policy of concentrating on dividing and destroying the Confederate armies brought the war to an end in 1865. The next year, he was made full general.

In 1868, as Republican candidate for president, Grant was elected over the Democrat, Horatio Seymour. From the start, Grant showed his unfitness for the office. His Cabinet was weak, his domestic policy was confused, many of his intimate associates were corrupt. The notable achievement in foreign affairs was the settlement of controversies with Great Britain in the Treaty of London (1871), negotiated by his able Secretary of State, Hamilton Fish.

Running for re-election in 1872, he defeated Horace Greeley, the Democratic and Liberal Republican candidate. The Panic of 1873 graft scandals close to the presidency created difficulties for his second term.

After retiring from office, Grant toured Europe for two years and returned in time to accede to a third-term boom, but was beaten in the convention of 1880. Illness and bad business judgment darkened his last years, but he worked steadily at the *Personal Memoirs*, which were to be so successful when published after his death at Mount McGregor, near Saratoga, N.Y., on July 23, 1885.

RUTHERFORD BIRCHARD HAYES was born in Delaware, Ohio, on Oct. 4, 1822. A graduate of Kenyon College and the Harvard Law School, he practiced law in Lower Sandusky (now Fremont) and then in Cincinnati. In 1852 he married Lucy Webb. A Whig, he joined the Republican party in 1855. During the Civil War he rose to major general. He served in the House of Representatives from 1865 to 1867 and then confirmed a reputation for honesty and efficiency in two terms as Governor of Ohio (1868–72). His election to a third term in 1875 made him the logical candidate for those Republicans who wished to stop James G. Blaine in 1876, and he was nominated.

The result of the election was in doubt for some time and hinged upon disputed returns from South Carolina, Louisiana, Florida, and Oregon. Samuel J. Tilden, the Democrat, had the larger popular vote but was adjudged by the strictly partisan decisions of the Electoral Commission to have one fewer electoral vote, 185 to 184. The national acceptance of this result was due in part to the general understanding that Hayes would pursue a conciliatory policy toward the South. He withdrew the troops from the South, took a conservative position on financial and labor issues, and urged civil service reform.

Hayes served only one term by his own wish and

spent the rest of his life in various humanitarian endeavors. He died in Fremont on Jan. 17, 1893.

JAMES ABRAM GARFIELD, the last president to be born in a log cabin, was born in Cuyahoga County, Ohio, on Nov. 19, 1831. A Williams graduate, he taught school for a time and entered Republican politics in Ohio. In 1858, he married Lucretia Rudolph. During the Civil War, he had a promising career, rising to major general of volunteers; but he resigned in 1863, having been elected to the House of Representatives, where he served until 1880. His oratorical and parliamentary abilities soon made him the leading Republican in the House, though his record was marred by his unorthodox acceptance of a fee in the DeGolyer paving contract case and by suspicions of his complicity in the Crédit Mobilier scandal.

In 1880, Garfield was elected to the Senate, but instead became the presidential candidate on the 36th ballot as a result of a deadlock in the Republican convention. In the election, he defeated Gen. Winfield Scott Hancock, the Democratic candidate. Garfield's administration was barely under way when he was shot by Charles J. Guiteau, a disappointed office seeker, in Washington on July 2, 1881. He died in Elberton, N.J., on Sept. 19.

CHESTER ALAN ARTHUR was born at Fairfield, Vt., on Oct. 5, 1830. A graduate of Union College, he became a successful New York lawyer. In 1859, he married Ellen Herndon. During the Civil War, he held administrative jobs in the Republican state administration and in 1871 was appointed collector of the Port of New York by Grant. This post gave him control over considerable patronage. Though not personally corrupt, Arthur managed his power in the interests of the New York machine so openly that President Hayes in 1877 called for an investigation and the next year Arthur was suspended.

In 1880 Arthur was nominated for vice president in the hope of conciliating the followers of Grant and the powerful New York machine. As president upon Garfield's death, Arthur, stepping out of his familiar role as spoilsman, backed civil service reform, reorganized the Cabinet, and prosecuted political associates accused of post office graft. Losing machine support and failing to gain the reformers, he was not nominated for a full term in 1884. He died in New York City on Nov. 18, 1886.

STEPHEN GROVER CLEVELAND was born at Caldwell, N.J., on March 18, 1837. He was admitted to the bar in Buffalo, N.Y., in 1859 and lived there as a lawyer, with occasional incursions into Democratic politics, for more than 20 years. He did not participate in the Civil War. As mayor of Buffalo in 1881, he carried through a reform program so ably that the Democrats ran him successfully for governor in 1882. In 1884 he won the Democratic nomination for president. The campaign contrasted Cleveland's spotless public career with the uncertain record of James G. Blaine, the Republican candidate, and Cleveland received enough Mugwump (independent Republican) support to win.

As president, Cleveland pushed civil service reform, opposed the pension grab and attacked the high tariff laws. While in the White House, he married Frances Folsom in 1886. Renominated in 1888, Cleveland was defeated by Benjamin Harrison, polling more popular but fewer electoral votes. In 1892, he was elected over Harrison. When the Panic of 1893 burst upon the country, Cleveland's attempts to solve it by sound-money measures alienated the free-silver wing of the party, while his tariff policy alienated the protectionists. In 1894, he sent troops to break the Pullman strike. In foreign affairs, his firmness caused Great Britain to back down in the Venezuela border dispute.

In his last years Cleveland was an active and much-respected public figure. He died in Princeton, N.J., on June 24, 1908.

BENJAMIN HARRISON was born in North Bend, Ohio, on Aug. 20, 1833, the grandson of William Henry Harrison, the ninth president. A graduate of Miami University in Ohio, he took up the law in Indiana and became active in Republican politics. In 1853, he married Caroline Lavinia Scott. During the Civil War, he rose to brigadier general. A sound-money Republican, he was elected senator from Indiana in 1880. In 1888, he received the Republican nomination for President on the eighth ballot. Though behind on the popular vote, he won over Grover Cleveland in the electoral college by 233 to 168.

As President, Harrison failed to please either the bosses or the reform element in the party. In foreign affairs he backed Secretary of State Blaine, whose policy foreshadowed later American imperialism. Harrison was renominated in 1892 but lost to Cleveland. His wife died in the White House in 1892 and Harrison married her niece, Mary Scott (Lord) Dimmick, in 1896. After his presidency, he resumed law practice. He died in Indianapolis on March 13, 1901.

WILLIAM McKINLEY was born in Niles, Ohio, on Jan. 29, 1843. He taught school, then served in the Civil War, rising from the ranks to become a major. Subsequently he opened a law office in Canton, Ohio, and in 1871 married Ida Saxton. Elected to Congress in 1876, he served there until 1891, except for 1883–85. His faithful advocacy of business interests culminated in the passage of the highly protective McKinley Tariff of 1890. With the support of Mark Hanna, a shrewd Cleveland businessman interested in safeguarding tariff protection, McKinley became governor of Ohio in 1892 and Republican presidential candidate in 1896. The business community, alarmed by the progressivism of William Jennings Bryan, the Democratic candidate, spent considerable money to assure McKinley's victory.

The chief event of McKinley's administration was the war with Spain, which resulted in our acquisition of the Philippines and other islands. With imperialism an issue, McKinley defeated Bryan again in 1900. On Sept. 6, 1901, he was shot at Buffalo, N.Y., by Leon F. Czolgosz, an anarchist, and he died there eight days later.

THEODORE ROOSEVELT was born in New York City on Oct. 27, 1858. A Harvard graduate, he was early interested in ranching, in politics, and in writing picturesque historical narratives. He was a Republican member of the New York Assembly in 1882–84, an unsuccessful candidate for mayor of New York in 1886, a U.S. Civil Service Commissioner under Benjamin Harrison, Police Commissioner of New York City in 1895, and Assistant Secretary of the Navy under McKinley in 1897. He resigned in 1898 to help organize a volunteer regiment, the Rough Riders, and take a more direct part in the war with Spain. He was elected governor of New York in 1898 and vice president in 1900, in spite of lack of enthusiasm on the part of the bosses.

Assuming the presidency of the assassinated McKinley in 1901, Roosevelt embarked on a wide-ranging program of government reform and conservation of natural resources. He ordered antitrust suits against several large corporations, threatened to intervene in the anthracite coal strike of 1902, which prompted the operators to accept arbitration, and, in general, championed the rights of the "little man" and fought the "malefactors of great wealth." He was also responsible for such progressive legislation as the Elkins Act of 1901, which outlawed freight rebates by railroads; the bill establishing the Department of Commerce and Labor; the Hepburn Act, which gave the I.C.C. greater control over the railroads; the Meat Inspection Act; and the Pure Food and Drug Act.

In foreign affairs, Roosevelt pursued a strong policy, permitting the instigation of a revolt in Panama to dispose of Colombian objections to the Panama Canal and helping to maintain the balance of power in the East by bringing the Russo-Japanese War to an end, for which he won the Nobel Peace Prize, the first American to achieve a Nobel prize in any category. In 1904, he decisively defeated Alton B. Parker, his conservative Democratic opponent.

Roosevelt's increasing coldness toward his successor, William Howard Taft, led him to overlook his earlier disclaimer of third-term ambitions and to re-enter politics. Defeated by the machine in the Republican convention of 1912, he organized the Progressive Party (Bull Moose) and polled more votes than Taft, though the split brought about the election of Woodrow Wilson. From 1915 on, Roosevelt strongly favored intervention in the European war. He became deeply embittered at Wilson's refusal to allow him to raise a volunteer division. He died in Oyster Bay, N.Y., on Jan. 6, 1919. He was married twice: in 1880 to Alice Hathaway Lee, who died in 1884, and in 1886 to Edith Kermit Carow.

WILLIAM HOWARD TAFT was born in Cincinnati on Sept. 15, 1857. A Yale graduate, he entered Ohio Republican politics in the 1880s. In 1886 he married Helen Herron. From 1887 to 1890, he served on the Ohio Superior Court; 1890–92, as solicitor general of the United States; 1892–1900, on the federal circuit court. In 1900 McKinley appointed him president of the Philippine Commission and in 1901 governor general. Taft had great success in pacifying the Filipinos, solving the problem of the church lands, improving economic conditions, and establishing limited self-government. His period as Secretary of War (1904–08) further demonstrated his capacity as administrator and conciliator, and he was Roosevelt's hand-picked successor in 1908. In the election, he polled 321 electoral votes to 162 for William Jennings Bryan, who was running for the presidency for the third time.

Though he carried on many of Roosevelt's policies, Taft got into increasing trouble with the progressive wing of the party and displayed mounting irritability and indecision. After his defeat in 1912, he became professor of constitutional law at Yale. In 1921 he was appointed Chief Justice of the United States. He died in Washington on March 8, 1930.

THOMAS WOODROW WILSON was born in Staunton, Va., on Dec. 28, 1856. A Princeton graduate, he turned from law practice to post-graduate work in political science at Johns Hopkins University, receiving his Ph.D. in 1886. He taught at Bryn Mawr, Wesleyan, and Princeton, and in 1902 was made president of Princeton. After an unsuccessful attempt to democratize the social life of the university, he welcomed an invitation in 1910 to be the Democratic gubernatorial candidate in New Jersey, and was elected. His success in fighting the machine and putting through a reform program attracted national attention.

In 1912, at the Democratic convention in Baltimore, Wilson won the nomination on the 46th ballot and went on to defeat Roosevelt and Taft in the election. Wilson proceeded under the standard of the New Freedom to enact a program of domestic reform, including the Federal Reserve Act, the Clayton Antitrust Act, the establishment of the Federal Trade Commission, and other measures designed to restore competition in the face of the great monopolies. In foreign affairs, while privately sympathetic with the Allies, he strove to maintain neutrality in the European war and warned both sides against encroachments on American interests.

Re-elected in 1916 as a peace candidate, he tried to mediate between the warring nations; but when the Germans resumed unrestricted submarine warfare in 1917, Wilson brought the United States into what he now believed was a war to make the world safe for democracy. He supplied the classic formulations of Allied war aims and the armistice of Nov. 11, 1918 was negotiated on the basis of Wilson's Fourteen Points. In 1919 he strove at Versailles to lay the foundations for enduring peace. He accepted the imperfections of the Versailles Treaty in the expectation that they could be remedied by action within the League of Nations. He probably could have secured ratification of the treaty by the Senate if he had adopted a more conciliatory attitude toward the mild reservationists; but his insistence on all or nothing eventually caused the diehard isolationists and diehard Wilsonites to unite in rejecting a compromise.

In September 1919 Wilson suffered a paralytic stroke that limited his activity. After leaving the presidency he lived on in retirement in Washington, dying on Feb. 3, 1924. He was married twice—in 1885 to Ellen Louise Axson, who died in 1914, and in 1915 to Edith Bolling Galt.

WARREN GAMALIEL HARDING was born in Morrow County, Ohio, on Nov. 2, 1865. After attending Ohio Central College, Harding became interested in journalism and in 1884 bought the *Marion* (Ohio) *Star.* In 1891 he married a wealthy widow, Florence Kling De Wolfe. As his paper prospered, he entered Republican politics, serving as state senator (1899–1903) and as lieutenant governor (1904–06). In 1910, he was defeated for governor, but in 1914 was elected to the Senate. His reputation as an orator made him the keynoter at the 1916 Republican convention.

When the 1920 convention was deadlocked between Leonard Wood and Frank O. Lowden, Harding became the dark-horse nominee on his solemn affirmation that there was no reason in his past that he should not be. Straddling the League question, Harding was easily elected over James M. Cox, his Democratic opponent. His Cabinet contained some able men, but also some manifestly unfit for public office. Harding's own intimates were mediocre when they were not corrupt. The impending disclosure of the Teapot Dome scandal in the Interior Department and illegal practices in the Justice Department and Veterans' Bureau, as well as political setbacks, profoundly worried him. On his return from Alaska in 1923, he died unexpectedly in San Francisco on Aug. 2.

JOHN CALVIN COOLIDGE was born in Plymouth, Vt., on July 4, 1872. An Amherst graduate, he went into law practice at Northampton, Mass., in 1897. He married Grace Anna Goodhue in 1905. He entered Republican state politics, becoming successively mayor of Northampton, state senator, lieutenant governor and, in 1919, governor. His use of the state militia to end the Boston police strike in 1919 won him a somewhat undeserved reputation for decisive action and brought him the Republican vice-presidential nomination in 1920. After Harding's death Coolidge handled the Washington scandals with care and finally managed to save the Republican Party from public blame for the widespread corruption.

In 1924, Coolidge was elected without difficulty, defeating the Democrat, John W. Davis, and Robert M. La Follette running on the Progressive ticket. His second term, like his first, was characterized by a general satisfaction with the existing economic order. He stated that he did not choose to run in 1928.

After his presidency, Coolidge lived quietly in Northampton, writing an unilluminating *Autobiography* and conducting a syndicated column. He died there on Jan. 5, 1933.

HERBERT CLARK HOOVER was born at West Branch, Iowa, on Aug. 10, 1874, the first president to be born west of the Mississippi. A Stanford graduate, he worked from 1895 to 1913 as a mining engineer and consultant throughout the world. In 1899, he married Lou Henry. During World War I, he served with distinction as chairman of the American Relief Committee in London, as chairman of the Commission for Relief in Belgium, and as U.S. Food Administrator. His political affiliations were still too indeterminate for him to be mentioned as a possibility for either the Republican or Democratic nomination in 1920, but after the election he served Harding and Coolidge as Secretary of Commerce.

In the election of 1928, Hoover overwhelmed Gov. Alfred E. Smith of New York, the Democratic candidate and the first Roman Catholic to run for the presidency. He soon faced the worst depression in the nation's history, but his attacks upon it were hampered by his devotion to the theory that the forces that brought the crisis would soon bring the revival and then by his belief that there were too many areas in which the federal government had no power to act. In a succession of vetoes, he struck down measures proposing a national employment system or national relief, he reduced income tax rates, and only at the end of his term did he yield to popular pressure and set up agencies such as the Reconstruction Finance Corporation to make emergency loans to assist business.

After his 1932 defeat, Hoover returned to private business. In 1946, President Truman charged him

with various world food missions; and from 1947 to 1949 and 1953 to 1955, he was head of the Commission on Organization of the Executive Branch of the Government. He died in New York City on Oct. 20, 1964.

FRANKLIN DELANO ROOSEVELT was born in Hyde Park, N.Y., on Jan. 30, 1882. A Harvard graduate, he attended Columbia Law School and was admitted to the New York bar. In 1910, he was elected to the New York State Senate as a Democrat. Reelected in 1912, he was appointed Assistant Secretary of the Navy by Woodrow Wilson the next year. In 1920, his radiant personality and his war service resulted in his nomination for vice president as James M. Cox's running mate. After his defeat, he returned to law practice in New York. In August 1921, Roosevelt was stricken with infantile paralysis while on vacation at Campobello, New Brunswick. After a long and gallant fight, he recovered partial use of his legs. In 1924 and 1928, he led the fight at the Democratic national conventions for the nomination of Gov. Alfred E. Smith of New York, and in 1928 Roosevelt was himself induced to run for governor of New York. He was elected, and was re-elected in 1930.

In 1932, Roosevelt received the Democratic nomination for president and immediately launched a campaign that brought new spirit to a weary and discouraged nation. He defeated Hoover by a wide margin. His first term was characterized by an unfolding of the New Deal program, with greater benefits for labor, the farmers, and the unemployed, and the progressive estrangement of most of the business community.

At an early stage, Roosevelt became aware of the menace to world peace posed by totalitarian fascism, and from 1937 on he tried to focus public attention on the trend of events in Europe and Asia. As a result, he was widely denounced as a warmonger. He was re-elected in 1936 over Gov. Alfred M. Landon of Kansas by the overwhelming electoral margin of 523 to 8, and the gathering international crisis prompted him to run for an unprecedented third term in 1940. He defeated Wendell L. Willkie.

Roosevelt's program to bring maximum aid to Britain and, after June 1941, to Russia was opposed, until the Japanese attack on Pearl Harbor restored national unity. During the war, Roosevelt shelved the New Deal in the interests of conciliating the business community, both in order to get full production during the war and to prepare the way for a united acceptance of the peace settlements after the war. A series of conferences with Winston Churchill and Joseph Stalin laid down the bases for the postwar world. In 1944 he was elected to a fourth term, running against Gov. Thomas E. Dewey of New York.

On April 12, 1945, Roosevelt died of a cerebral hemorrhage at Warm Springs, Ga., shortly after his return from the Yalta Conference. His wife, Anna Eleanor Roosevelt, whom he married in 1905, was a woman of great ability who made significant contributions to her husband's policies.

HARRY S. TRUMAN was born on a farm near Lamar, Mo., on May 8, 1884. During World War I, he served in France as a captain with the 129th Field Artillery. He married Bess Wallace in 1919. After engaging briefly and unsuccessfully in the haberdashery business in Kansas City, Mo., Truman entered local politics. Under the sponsorship of Thomas Pendergast, Democratic boss of Missouri, he held a number of local offices, preserving his personal honesty in the midst of a notoriously corrupt political machine. In 1934, he was elected to the Senate and was re-elected in 1940. During his first term he was a loyal but quiet supporter of the New Deal, but in his second term, an appointment as head of a Senate committee to investigate war production brought out his special qualities of honesty, common sense, and hard work, and he won widespread respect.

Elected vice president in 1944, Truman became president upon Roosevelt's sudden death in April 1945 and was immediately faced with the problems of winding down the war against the Axis and preparing the nation for postwar adjustment.

The years 1947–48 were distinguished by civil-rights proposals, the Truman Doctrine to contain the spread of Communism, and the Marshall Plan to aid in the economic reconstruction of war-ravaged nations. Truman's general record, highlighted by a vigorous Fair Deal campaign, brought about his unexpected election in 1948 over the heavily favored Thomas E. Dewey.

Truman's second term was primarily concerned with the Cold War with the Soviet Union, the implementing of the North Atlantic Pact, the United Nations police action in Korea, and the vast rearmament program with its accompanying problems of economic stabilization.

On March 29, 1952, Truman announced that he would not run again for the presidency. After leaving the White House, he returned to his home in Independence, Mo., to write his memoirs. He further busied himself with the Harry S. Truman Library there. He died in Kansas City, Mo., on Dec. 26, 1972.

DWIGHT DAVID EISENHOWER was born in Denison, Tex., on Oct. 14, 1890. His ancestors lived in Germany and emigrated to America, settling in Pennsylvania, early in the 18th century. His father, David, had a general store in Hope, Kan., which failed. After a brief time in Texas, the family moved to Abilene, Kan.

After graduating from Abilene High School in 1909, Eisenhower did odd jobs for almost two years. He won an appointment to the Naval Academy at Annapolis, but was too old for admittance. Then he received an appointment in 1910 to West Point, from which he graduated as a second lieutenant in 1915.

He did not see service in World War I, having been stationed at Fort Sam Houston, Tex. There he met Mamie Geneva Doud, whom he married in Denver on July 1, 1916, and by whom he had two sons: Doud Dwight (died in infancy) and John Sheldon Doud.

Eisenhower served in the Philippines from 1935 to 1939 with Gen. Douglas MacArthur. Afterward, Gen. George C. Marshall, the Army Chief of Staff, brought him into the War Department's General Staff and in 1942 placed him in command of the invasion of North Africa. In 1944, he was made Supreme Allied Commander for the invasion of Europe.

After the war, Eisenhower served as Army Chief of Staff from November 1945 until February 1948, when he was appointed president of Columbia University.

In December 1950, President Truman recalled Eisenhower to active duty to command the North Atlantic Treaty Organization forces in Europe. He held his post until the end of May 1952.

At the Republican convention of 1952 in Chicago, Eisenhower won the presidential nomination on the first ballot in a close race with Senator Robert A. Taft of Ohio. In the election, he defeated Gov. Adlai E. Stevenson of Illinois.

Through two terms, Eisenhower hewed to moderate domestic policies. He sought peace through Free World strength in an era of new nationalisms, nuclear missiles, and space exploration. He fostered alliances pledging the United States to resist Red aggression in Europe, Asia, and Latin America. The Eisenhower Doctrine of 1957 extended commitments to the Middle East.

At home, the popular president lacked Republican Congressional majorities after 1954, but he was re-elected in 1956 by 457 electoral votes to 73 for Stevenson.

While retaining most Fair Deal programs, he stressed "fiscal responsibility" in domestic affairs. A moderate in civil rights, he sent troops to Little Rock, Ark., to enforce court-ordered school integration.

With his wartime rank restored by Congress, Eisenhower returned to private life and the role of elder statesman, with his vigor hardly impaired by a heart attack, an ileitis operation, and a mild stroke suffered while in office. He died in Washington on March 28, 1969.

JOHN FITZGERALD KENNEDY was born in Brookline, Mass., on May 29, 1917. His father, Joseph P. Kennedy, was Ambassador to Great Britain from 1937 to 1940.

Kennedy was graduated from Harvard University in 1940 and joined the Navy the next year. He became skipper of a PT boat that was sunk in the Pacific by a Japanese destroyer. Although given up for lost, he swam to a safe island, towing an injured enlisted man.

After recovering from a war-aggravated spinal injury, Kennedy entered politics in 1946 and was elected to Congress. In 1952, he ran against Senator Henry Cabot Lodge, Jr., of Massachusetts, and won.

Kennedy was married on Sept. 12, 1953, to Jacqueline Lee Bouvier, by whom he had three children: Caroline, John Fitzgerald, Jr., and Patrick Bouvier (died in infancy).

In 1957 Kennedy won the Pulitzer Prize for a book he had written earlier, *Profiles in Courage*.

After strenuous primary battles, Kennedy won the Democratic presidential nomination on the first ballot at the 1960 Los Angeles convention. With a plurality of only 118,574 votes, he carried the election over Vice President Richard M. Nixon and became the first Roman Catholic president.

Kennedy brought to the White House the dynamic idea of a "New Frontier" approach in dealing with problems at home, abroad, and in the dimensions of space. Out of his leadership in his first few months in office came the 10-year Alliance for Progress to aid Latin America, the Peace Corps, and accelerated programs that brought the first Americans into orbit in the race in space.

Failure of the U.S.-supported Cuban invasion in April 1961 led to the entrenchment of the Communist-backed Castro regime, only 90 miles from United States soil. When it became known that Soviet offensive missiles were being installed in Cuba in 1962, Kennedy ordered a naval "quarantine" of the island and moved troops into position to eliminate this threat to U.S. security. The world seemed on the brink of a nuclear war until Soviet Premier Khrushchev ordered the removal of the missiles.

A sudden "thaw," or the appearance of one, in the cold war came with the agreement with the Soviet Union on a limited test-ban treaty signed in Moscow on Aug. 6, 1963.

In his domestic policies, Kennedy's proposals for medical care for the aged, expanded area redevelopment, and aid to education were defeated, but on minimum wage, trade legislation, and other measures he won important victories.

Widespread racial disorders and demonstrations led to Kennedy's proposing sweeping civil rights legislation. As his third year in office drew to a close, he also recommended an $11-billion tax cut to bolster the economy. Both measures were pending in Congress when Kennedy, looking forward to a second term, journeyed to Texas for a series of speeches.

While riding in a procession in Dallas on Nov. 22, 1963, he was shot to death by an assassin firing from an upper floor of a building. The alleged assassin, Lee Harvey Oswald, was killed two days later in the Dallas city jail by Jack Ruby, owner of a strip-tease place.

At 46 years of age, Kennedy became the fourth president to be assassinated and the eighth to die in office.

LYNDON BAINES JOHNSON was born in Stonewall, Tex., on Aug. 27, 1908. On both sides of his family he had a political heritage mingled with a Baptist background of preachers and teachers. Both his father and his paternal grandfather served in the Texas House of Representatives.

After his graduation from Southwest Texas State Teachers College, Johnson taught school for two years. He went to Washington in 1932 as secretary to Rep. Richard M. Kleberg. During this time, he married Claudia Alta Taylor, known as "Lady Bird." They had two children: Lynda Bird and Luci Baines.

In 1935, Johnson became Texas administrator for the National Youth Administration. Two years later, he was elected to Congress as an all-out supporter of Franklin D. Roosevelt, and served until 1949. He was the first member of Congress to enlist in the armed forces after the attack on Pearl Harbor. He served in the Navy in the Pacific and won a Silver Star.

Johnson was elected to the Senate in 1948 after he had captured the Democratic nomination by only 87 votes. He was 40 years old. He became the Senate Democratic leader in 1953. A heart attack in 1955 threatened to end his political career, but he recovered fully and resumed his duties.

At the height of his power as Senate leader, Johnson sought the Democratic nomination for president in 1960. When he lost to John F. Kennedy, he surprised even some of his closest associates by accepting second place on the ticket.

Johnson was riding in another car in the motorcade when Kennedy was assassinated in Dallas on Nov. 22, 1963. He took the oath of office in the presidential jet on the Dallas airfield.

With Johnson's insistent backing, Congress finally adopted a far-reaching civil-rights bill, a voting-rights bill, a Medicare program for the aged, and measures to improve education and conservation. Congress also began what Johnson described as "an all-out war" on poverty.

Amassing a record-breaking majority of nearly 16 million votes, Johnson was elected president in his own right in 1964, defeating Senator Barry Goldwater of Arizona.

The double tragedy of a war in Southeast Asia and urban riots at home marked Johnson's last two years in office. Faced with disunity in the nation and challenges within his own party, Johnson surprised the country on March 31, 1968, with the announcement that he would not be a candidate for re-election. He died of a heart attack suffered at his LBJ Ranch on Jan. 22, 1973.

RICHARD MILHOUS NIXON was born in Yorba Linda, Calif., on Jan. 9, 1913, to Midwestern-bred parents, Francis A. and Hannah Milhous Nixon, who raised their five sons as Quakers.

Nixon was a high school debater and was undergraduate president at Whittier College in California, where he was graduated in 1934. As a scholarship student at Duke University Law School in North Carolina, he graduated third in his class in 1937.

After five years as a lawyer, Nixon joined the Navy in August 1942. He was an air transport officer in the South Pacific and a legal officer stateside before his discharge in 1946 as a lieutenant commander.

Running for Congress in California as a Republican in 1946, Nixon defeated Rep. Jerry Voorhis. As a member of the House Un-American Activities Committee, he made a name as an investigator of Alger Hiss, a former high State Department official, who was later jailed for perjury. In 1950, Nixon defeated Rep. Helen Gahagan Douglas, a Democrat, for the Senate. He was criticized for portraying her as a Communist dupe.

Nixon's anti-Communism, his Western base, and his youth figured in his selection in 1952 to run for vice president on the ticket headed by Dwight D. Eisenhower. Demands for Nixon's withdrawal followed disclosure that California businessmen had paid some of his Senate office expenses. He televised rebuttal, known as "the Checkers speech" (named for a cocker spaniel given to the Nixons), brought him support from the public and from Eisenhower. The ticket won easily in 1952 and again in 1956.

Eisenhower gave Nixon substantive assignments, including missions to 56 countries. In Moscow in 1959, Nixon won acclaim for his defense of U.S. interests in an impromptu "kitchen debate" with Soviet Premier Nikita S. Khrushchev.

Nixon lost the 1960 race for the presidency to John F. Kennedy.

In 1962, Nixon failed in a bid for California's governorship and seemed to be finished as a national candidate. He became a Wall Street lawyer, but kept his old party ties and developed new ones through constant travels to speak for Republicans.

Nixon won the 1968 Republican presidential nomination after a shrewd primary campaign, then made Gov. Spiro T. Agnew of Maryland his surprise choice for vice president. In the election, they edged out the Democratic ticket headed by Vice President Hubert H. Humphrey by 510,314 votes out of 73,212,065 cast.

Committed to wind down the U.S. role in the Vietnamese War, Nixon pursued "Vietnamization"—training and equipping South Vietnamese to do their own fighting. American ground combat forces in Vietnam fell steadily from 540,000 when Nixon took office to none in 1973 when the military draft was ended. But there was heavy continuing use of U.S. air power.

Nixon improved relations with Moscow and reopened the long-closed door to mainland China with a good-will trip there in February 1972. In May of that year, he visited Moscow and signed agreements on arms limitation and trade expansion and approved plans for a joint U.S.-Soviet space mission in 1975.

Inflation was a campaign issue for Nixon, but he failed to master it as president. On Aug. 15, 1971, with unemployment edging up, Nixon abruptly announced a new economic policy: a 90-day wage-price freeze, stimulative tax cuts, a temporary 10% tariff, and spending cuts. A second phase, imposing guidelines on wage, price and rent boosts, was announced October 7.

The economy responded in time for the 1972 campaign, in which Nixon played up his foreign-policy achievements. Played down was the burglary on June 17, 1972, of Democratic national headquarters in the Watergate apartment complex in Washington. The Nixon-Agnew re-election campaign cost a record $60 million and swamped the Democratic ticket headed by Senator George McGovern of South Dakota with a plurality of 17,999,528 out of 77,718,554 votes. Only Massachusetts, with 14 electoral votes, and the District of Columbia, with 3, went for McGovern.

In January 1973, hints of a cover-up emerged at the trial of six men found guilty of the Watergate burglary. With a Senate investigation under way, Nixon announced on April 30 the resignations of his top aides, H. R. Haldeman and John D. Ehrlichman, and the dismissal of White House counsel John Dean III. Dean was the star witness at televised Senate hearings that exposed both a White House cover-up of Watergate and massive illegalities in Republican fund-raising in 1972.

The hearings also disclosed that Nixon had routinely tape-recorded his office meetings and telephone conversations.

On Oct. 10, 1973, Agnew resigned as vice president, then pleaded no-contest to a negotiated federal charge of evading income taxes on alleged bribes. Two days later, Nixon nominated the House minority leader, Rep. Gerald R. Ford of Michigan, as the new vice president. Congress confirmed Ford on Dec. 6, 1973.

In June 1974, Nixon visited Israel and four Arab nations. Then he met in Moscow with Soviet leader Leonid I. Brezhnev and reached preliminary nuclear arms limitation agreements.

But, in the month after his return, Watergate ended the Nixon regime. On July 24 the Supreme Court ordered Nixon to surrender subpoenaed tapes. On July 30, the Judiciary Committee referred three impeachment articles to the full membership. On August 5, Nixon bowed to the Supreme Court and released tapes showing he halted an FBI probe of the Watergate burglary six days after it occurred. It was in effect an admission of obstruction of justice, and impeachment appeared inevitable.

Nixon resigned on Aug. 9, 1974, the first president ever to do so. A month later, President Ford issued an unconditional pardon for any offenses Nixon might have committed as president, thus forestalling possible prosecution.

In 1940, Nixon married Thelma Catherine (Pat) Ryan. They had two daughters, Patricia (Tricia) Cox and Julie, who married Dwight David Eisenhower II, grandson of the former president.

He died on April 22, 1994, in New York City of a massive stroke.

GERALD RUDOLPH FORD was born in Omaha, Neb., on July 14, 1913, the only child of Leslie and Dorothy Gardner King. His parents were divorced in 1915. His mother moved to Grand Rapids, Mich., and married Gerald R. Ford. The boy was renamed for his stepfather.

Ford captained his high school football team in Grand Rapids, and a football scholarship took him to the University of Michigan, where he starred as varsity center before his graduation in 1935. A job as assistant football coach at Yale gave him an opportunity to attend Yale Law School, from which he graduated in the top third of his class in 1941.

He returned to Grand Rapids to practice law, but entered the Navy in April 1942. He saw wartime service in the Pacific on the light aircraft carrier *Monterey* and was a lieutenant commander when he returned to Grand Rapids early in 1946 to resume law practice and dabble in politics.

Ford was elected to Congress in 1948 for the first of his 13 terms in the House. He was soon assigned to the influential Appropriations Committee and rose to become the ranking Republican on the subcommittee on Defense Department appropriations and an expert in the field.

As a legislator, Ford described himself as "a moderate on domestic issues, a conservative in fiscal affairs, and a dyed-in-the-wool internationalist." He carried the ball for Pentagon appropriations, was a hawk on the war in Vietnam, and kept a low profile on civil-rights issues.

He was also dependable and hard-working and popular with his colleagues. In 1963, he was elected chairman of the House Republican Conference. He served in 1963–64 as a member of the Warren Commission that investigated the assassination of John F. Kennedy. A revolt by dissatisfied younger Republicans in 1965 made him minority leader.

Ford shelved his hopes for the Speakership on Oct. 12, 1973, when Nixon nominated him to fill the vice presidency left vacant by Agnew's resignation under fire. It was the first use of the procedures for filling vacancies in the vice presidency laid down in the 25th Amendment to the Constitution, which Ford had helped enact.

Congress confirmed Ford as vice president on Dec. 6, 1973. Once in office, he said he did not believe Nixon had been involved in the Watergate scandals, but criticized his stubborn court battle against releasing tape recordings of Watergate-related conversations for use as evidence.

The scandals led to Nixon's unprecedented resignation on Aug. 9, 1974, and Ford was sworn in immediately as the 38th president, the first to enter the White House without winning a national election.

Ford assured the nation when he took office that "our long national nightmare is over" and pledged "openness and candor" in all his actions. He won a warm response from the Democratic 93rd Congress when he said he wanted "a good marriage" rather than a honeymoon with his former colleagues. In December 1974 Congressional majorities backed his choice of former New York Gov. Nelson A. Rockefeller as his successor in the again-vacant vice presidency.

The cordiality was chilled by Ford's announcement on Sept. 8, 1974, that he had granted an unconditional pardon to Nixon for any crimes he might have committed as president. Although no formal charges were pending, Ford said he feared "ugly passions" would be aroused if Nixon were brought to trial. The pardon was widely criticized.

To fight inflation, the new president first proposed fiscal restraints and spending curbs and a 5% tax surcharge that got nowhere in the Senate and House. Congress again rebuffed Ford in the spring of 1975 when he appealed for emergency military aid to help the governments of South Vietnam and Cambodia resist massive Communist offensives.

In November 1974, Ford visited Japan, South Korea, and the Soviet Union, where he and Soviet leader Leonid I. Brezhnev conferred in Vladivostok and reached a tentative agreement to limit the number of strategic offensive nuclear weapons. It was Ford's first meeting as president with Brezhnev, who planned a return visit to Washington in the fall of 1975.

Politically, Ford's fortunes improved steadily in the first half of 1975. Badly divided Democrats in Congress were unable to muster votes to override his vetoes of spending bills that exceeded his budget. He faced some right-wing opposition in his own party, but moved to pre-empt it with an early announcement—on July 8, 1975—of his intention to be a candidate in 1976.

Early state primaries in 1976 suggested an easy victory for Ford despite Ronald Reagan's bitter attacks on administration foreign policy and defense programs. But later Reagan primary successes threatened the President's lead. At the Kansas City convention, Ford was nominated by the narrow margin of 1,187 to 1,070. But Reagan had moved the party to the right, and Ford himself was regarded as a caretaker president lacking in strength and vision. He was defeated in November by Jimmy Carter.

In 1948, Ford married Elizabeth Anne (Betty) Bloomer. They had four children, Michael Gerald, John Gardner, Steven Meigs, and Susan Elizabeth.

JAMES EARL CARTER, JR., was born in the tiny village of Plains, Ga., Oct. 1, 1924, and grew up on the family farm at nearby Archery. Both parents were fifth-generation Georgians. His father, James Earl Carter, was known as a segregationist, but treated his black and white workers equally. Carter's mother, Lillian Gordy, was a matriarchal presence in home and community and opposed the then-prevailing code of racial inequality. The future President was baptized in 1935 in the conservative Southern Baptist Church and spoke often of being a "born again" Christian, although committed to the separation of church and state.

Carter married Rosalynn Smith, a neighbor, in 1946. Their first child, John William, was born a year later in Portsmouth, Va. Their other children are James Earl III, born in Honolulu in 1950; Donnel Jeffrey, born in New London, Conn., in 1952, and Amy Lynn, born in Plains in 1967.

In 1946 Carter was graduated from the U.S. Naval Academy at Annapolis and served in the nuclear-submarine program under Adm. Hyman G. Rickover. In 1954, after his father's death, he resigned from the Navy to take over the family's flourishing warehouse and cotton gin, with several thousand acres for growing seed peanuts.

Carter was elected to the Georgia Senate in 1962. In 1966 he lost the race for Governor, but was elected in 1970. His term brought a state government reorganization, sharply reduced agencies, increased economy and efficiency, and new social programs, all with no general tax increase. In 1972 the peanut farmer-politician set his sights on the Presidency and in 1974 built a base for himself as he criss-crossed the country as chairman of the Democratic Campaign Committee, appealing for revival and reform. In 1975 his image as a typical Southern white was erased when he won support of most of the old Southern civil-rights coalition after endorsement by Rep. Andrew Young, black Democrat from Atlanta, who had been the closest aide to the Rev. Martin Luther King, Jr. At Carter's 1971 inauguration as Governor he had called for an end to all forms of racial discrimination.

In the 1976 spring primaries, he won 19 out of 31 with a broad appeal to conservatives and liberals, black and white, poor and well-to-do. Throughout his campaigning Carter set forth his policies in his soft Southern voice, and with his electric-blue stare faced down skeptics who joked about "Jimmy Who?" His toothy smile became his trademark. He was nominated on the first roll-call vote of the 1976 Bicentennial Democratic National Convention in New York, and defeated Gerald R. Ford in November. Likewise, in 1980 he was renominated on the first ballot after vanquishing Senator Edward M. Kennedy of Massachusetts in the primaries. At the convention he defeated the Kennedy forces in their attempt to block a party rule that bound a large majority of pledged delegates to vote for Carter. In the election campaign, Carter attacked his rivals, Ronald Reagan and John B. Anderson, independent, with the warning that a Reagan Republican victory would heighten the risk of war and impede civil rights and economic opportunity. In November Carter lost to Reagan, who won 489 Electoral College votes and 51% of the popular tally, to 49 electoral votes and 41% for Carter.

In his one term, Carter fought hard for his programs against resistance from an independent-minded Democratic Congress that frustrated many pet projects although it overrode only two vetoes. Many of his difficulties were traced to his aides' brusqueness in dealing with Capitol Hill and insensitivity to Congressional feelings and tradition. Observers generally viewed public dissatisfaction with the "stagflation" economy as a principal factor in his defeat. Others included his jittery performance in the debate Oct. 28 with Reagan and the final uncertainties in the negotiations for freeing the Iranians' hostages, along with earlier staff problems, friction with Congress, long gasoline lines, and the months-long Iranian crisis, including the abortive sally in April 1980 to free the hostages. The President, however, did deflect criticism resulting from the activities of his brother, Billy. Yet, assessments of his record noted many positive elements. There was, for one thing, peace throughout his term, with no American combat deaths and with a brake on the advocates of force. Regarded as perhaps his greatest personal achievements were the Camp David accords between Israel and Egypt and the resulting treaty—the first between Israel and an Arab neighbor. The treaty with China and the Panama Canal treaties were also major achievements. Carter worked for nuclear-arms control. His concern for international human rights was credited with saving lives and reducing torture, and he supported the British policy that ended internecine warfare in Rhodesia, now Zimbabwe. Domestically, his environmental record was a major accomplishment. His judicial appointments won acclaim; the Southerner who had forsworn racism made 265 choices for the Federal bench that included minority members and women. On energy, he ended by price decontrols the practice of holding U.S. petroleum prices far below world levels.

—*Arthur P. Reed, Jr.*

RONALD WILSON REAGAN rode to the Presidency in 1980 on a tide of resurgent right-wing sentiment among an electorate battered by winds of unwanted change, longing for a distant, simpler era.

He left office in January 1989 with two-thirds of the American people approving his performance during his two terms. It was the highest rating for any retiring President since World War II. In his farewell speech, Reagan exhorted the nation to cling to the revival of patriotism that he had fostered. And he spoke proudly of the economic recovery during his Administrations, although regretting the huge budget deficit, for which, in part, many blamed his policies.

Reagan had retained the public's affection as he applied his political magic to policy goals. His place in history will rest, perhaps, on the short- and intermediate-range missile treaty consummated on a cordial visit to the Soviet Union that he had once reviled as an "evil empire." Its provisions, including a ground-breaking agreement on verification inspection, were formulated in four days of summit talks in Moscow in May 1988 with the Soviet leader, Mikhail S. Gorbachev.

And Reagan can point to numerous domestic achievements: sharp cuts in income tax rates, sweeping tax reform; creating economic growth without inflation, reducing the unemployment rate, among others. He failed, however, to win the "Reagan Revolution" on such issues as abortion and school prayer, and he seemed aloof from "sleazy" conduct by some top officials.

In his final months Reagan campaigned aggressively to win election as President for his two-term Vice President, George Bush.

Reagan's popularity with the public dipped sharply in 1986 when the Iran-Contra scandal broke, shortly after the Democrats gained control of the Senate. Observers agreed that Reagan's presidency had been weakened, if temporarily, by the two unrelated events. Then the weeks-long Congressional hearings in the summer of 1987 heard an array of Administration officials, present and former, tell their tales of a White House riven by deceit and undercover maneuvering. Yet no breath of illegality touched the President's personal reputation; on Aug. 12, 1987, he told the nation that he had not known of questionable activities but agreed that he was "ultimately accountable."

Ronald Reagan, actor turned politician, New Dealer turned conservative, came to the films and politics from a thoroughly Middle-American background—middle class, Middle West and small town. He was born in Tampico, Ill., Feb. 6, 1911, the second son of John Edward Reagan and Nelle Wilson Reagan, and the family later moved to Dixon, Ill. The father, of Irish descent, was a shop clerk and merchant with Democratic sympathies. It was an impoverished family; young Ronald sold homemade popcorn at high school games and worked as a lifeguard to earn money for his college tuition. When the father got a New Deal WPA job, the future President became an ardent Roosevelt Democrat.

Reagan won a B.A. degree in 1932 from Eureka (Ill.) College, where a photographic memory aided in his studies and in debating and college theatricals. In a Depression year, he was making $100 a week as a sports announcer for radio station WHO in Des Moines, Iowa, from 1932 to 1937. His career as a film and TV actor stretched from 1937 to 1966, and his salary climbed to $3,500 a week. As a World War II captain in Army film studios, Reagan recoiled from what he saw as the laziness of Civil Service workers, and moved to the Right. As president of the Screen Actors Guild, he resisted what he considered a Communist plot to subvert the film industry. With advancing age, Reagan left leading-man roles and became a television spokesman for the General Electric Company at $150,000.

With oratorical skill his trademark, Reagan became an active Republican. At the behest of a small group of conservative Southern California businessmen, he ran for governor with a pledge to cut spending, and was elected by almost a million votes over the political veteran, Democratic Gov. Edmund G. Brown, father of the later governor.

In the 1980 election battle against Jimmy Carter, Reagan broadened his appeal by espousing moderate policies, gaining much of his support from disaffected Democrats and blue-collar workers. The incoming Administration immediately set out to "turn the government around" with a new economic program. Over strenuous Congressional opposition, Reagan triumphed on his "supply side" theory to stimulate production and control inflation through tax cuts and sharp reductions in government spending.

The President won high acclaim for his nomination of Sandra Day O'Connor as the first woman on the Supreme Court. His later nominations met increasing opposition but did much to tilt the Court's orientation to the Right.

In 1982, the President's popularity had slipped as the economy declined into the worst recession in 40 years, with persistent high unemployment and interest rates. Initial support for "supply side" economics faded but the President won crucial battles in Congress.

Internationally, Reagan confronted numerous critical problems in his first term. The successful invasion of Grenada accomplished much diplomatically. But the intervention in Lebanon and the withdrawal of Marines after a disastrous terrorist attack were regarded as military failures.

The popular President won reelection in the 1984 landslide, with the economy improving and inflation under control. Domestically, a tax reform bill that Reagan backed became law. But the constantly growing budget deficit remained a constant irritant, with the President and Congress persistently at odds over priorities in spending for defense and domestic programs. His foreign policy met stiffening opposition, with Congress increasingly reluctant to increase spending for the Nicarguan "Contras" and the Pentagon and to expand the development of the MX missile. But even severe critics praised Reagan's restrained but decisive handling of the crisis following the hijacking of an American plane in Beirut by Moslem extremists. The attack on Libya in April 1986 galvanized the nation, although it drew scathing disapproval from the NATO alliance.

Barely three months into his first term, Reagan was the target of an assassin's bullet; his courageous comeback won public admiration.

Reagan is devoted to his wife, Nancy, whom he married after his divorce from the screen actress Jane Wyman. The children of the first marriage are Maureen, his daughter by Miss Wyman, and Michael, an adopted son. In the present marriage the children are Patricia and Ron.

—Arthur P. Reed, Jr.

GEORGE H. BUSH became President on January 20, 1989, with his theme harmony and conciliation after the often-turbulent Reagan years. With his calm and unassuming manner, he emerged from his subordinate Vice-Presidential role with an air of quiet authority. His Inaugural address emphasized "A new breeze is blowing, and the old bipartisanship must be made new again."

In his first months, the President, the nation's 41st, established himself as his own man and all but erased memories of what many had regarded as his fiercely abrasive Presidential election campaign of 1988 and questionable tactics against his Democratic opponent. People liked his easy style and readiness to compromise even as he remained a staunch conservative, although that readiness had disconcerted some conservatives.

Bush's early Cabinet choices reflected a pragmatic desire for an efficient nonideological Government. And with his usual cautious instinct, in 1990 he nominated to the Supreme Court the scholarly David H. Souter, with broadly conservative views. Souter was confirmed without a bruising battle.

In his first year, Bush, a World War II hero, had won plaudits at home and abroad for his confident, competent conduct at the NATO 40th anniversary summit meeting in Brussels, the Paris economic conference, on his tour of Eastern Europe, and at the Malta conference with Gorbachev. Grave challenges in that year were the Lebanese hostage crisis and the ongoing war on the drug traffic.

Domestically, Bush had to cope with such issues as the *Exxon Valdez* oil spill in Alaska and the dispute over flag-burning restrictions, which was resolved, if only for a time, in mid-1990.

But in his second year, 1990, the President confronted a mounting array of problems, the most critical being on the domestic side. Chief among them were the staggering and mushrooming budget deficit and the savings and loan crisis. Other vexing issues were the question of cutting defense expenditures with consequent economic dislocation, the war on drugs and environmental matters.

At home, the President's popularity dipped sharply from its near-record public approval following the invasion of Panama in late 1989. This plunge followed Bush's recantation of his campaign "no new taxes" pledge as he sat down with Congressional leaders to tame the budge deficit and deal with a faltering economy.

In 1991, the 67-year-old President emerged as the leader of an international coalition of Western democracies, Japan, and even some Arab states that freed invaded Kuwait and vanquished, at least for a time, Iraq's President Saddam Hussein and his armies.

A nation grateful at feeling the end of the "Vietnam syndrome" gave the President an over-all rating of 89 percent in a Gallup poll in March after the end of the war. The approval rate fell as the year went on, but a solid majority continued to approve the President's performance, although with growing concern about the faltering economy and other domestic problems. And there were nagging doubts about the Persian Gulf war, its motives and conduct, and about the ensuing refugee crisis.

A major Bush accomplishment in 1991 was the Strategic Arms Reduction Treaty (Start), signed in July with Soviet President Mikhail S. Gorbachev at their fourth summit conference, marking the end of the long weapons buildup. Succeeding events in the Soviet Union and the apparent disintegration of the Communist empire could only enhance his status.

The year also saw the President undergoing treatment for Graves' disease, a thyroid disorder, from which he suffered serious side effects.

Bush, scion of an aristocratic New England family, came to the White House after a long career in public service, in which he held top positions in national and international organizations. As Vice President, he avoided the appearance of direct involvement in the Iran-Contra affair while not seeming to shy away from the President.

Earlier, in the 1960s, Bush won two contests for a Texas Republican seat in the House of Representatives, but lost two bids for a Senate seat and one for the Presidency. After his second race for the Senate, President Nixon appointed him U.S. delegate to the United Nations with the rank of Ambassador and he later became Republican National Chairman. He headed the United States liaison office in Beijing before becoming Director of Central Intelligence.

In 1980 Bush became Reagan's running mate despite earlier criticism of Reagan "voodoo economics" and by the 1984 election had won acclaim for devotion to Reagan's conservative agenda despite his own reputation as somewhat more liberally inclined. Nevertheless, die-hard right-wingers could find satisfaction in Bush's war record and his Government service, particularly with the C.I.A. Throughout he remained influential in White House decisions, particularly in foreign affairs.

In the 1988 campaign, Bush's choice of Senator Dan Quayle of Indiana for Vice President surprised his friends and provoked criticism and ridicule that continued even after the Administration was established in office. Nonetheless Bush strongly defended his choice.

In the 1992 Presidential election, Bush was defeated by Gov. Bill Clinton of Arkansas.

The future President joined the Navy after war broke out and at 18 became the Navy's youngest commissioned pilot, serving from 1942 to 1945. The man later derided by some as a "wimp" fought the Japanese on 58 missions and was shot down once. He won the Distinguished Flying Cross.

Throughout his whole career, Bush had the backing of an established family, headed by his father, the autocratic and wealthy Prescott Bush, who was elected to the Senate from Connecticut in 1952. And his family helped the young patrician became established in his early business ventures, a rich uncle raising most of the capital required for founding a new oil company in Texas.

George Herbert Walker Bush was born June 12, 1924, in Milton, Mass., to Prescott and Dorothy Bush. The family later moved to Connecticut. The youth studied at the elite Phillips Academy in Andover, Mass., before entering the Navy.

After the war, Bush earned an economics degree and a Phi Beta Kappa key in two and a half years at Yale University. While there he captained the baseball team and was initiated into "Skull and Bones," the prestigious Yale secret society.

In 1945 Bush married Barbara Pierce of Rye, N.Y., daughter of a magazine publisher. With his bride, Bush moved to Texas instead of entering his father's investment banking business. There he founded his oil company and in 1980 reported an estimated wealth of $1.4 million.

The Bushes have lived in 17 cities and more than a score of homes and have traveled in as many countries. In her husband's frequent absences during the early years, Mrs. Bush was often matriarch of a family of four boys and a girl. Bush is close to his immediate family and to 10 grandchildren, a sister, and three brothers.

After the Clinton inauguration in January, the Bushes flew to Houston, Texas, where they had rented a home. —*Arthur P. Reed, Jr.*

WILLIAM J. CLINTON was born William Jefferson Blythe III in Hope, Ark., on August 19, 1946. He was named for his father, who was killed in an automobile accident before Clinton's birth. Virginia Kelly, his mother, set an example of hard work and perseverance. She eventually married Roger Clinton, a car dealer, whose name the future governor later adopted.

In high school in Hot Springs, Ark., Clinton considered becoming a doctor, but politics beckoned after a meeting with President John F. Kennedy in Washington on a Boys' Nation trip. He earned a B.S. in international affairs in 1968 at Georgetown University, having spent his junior year working for Arkansas Senator J. William Fulbright. He was a Rhodes scholar at Oxford 1968–70. He then attended Yale Law School, where he met his future wife, Hillary Rodham, a Wellesley graduate. The couple has one child, Chelsea, 16.

Clinton taught at the University of Arkansas (1974–1976), was elected state attorney general (1976), and in 1979 became the nation's youngest governor. But he was defeated for re-election by voters irate at a rise in the state's automobile license fees. In 1982 he was elected again. This time he reined in liberal tendencies to accommodate the conservative bent of the voters.

Clinton became the 42nd U.S. President following a turbulent political campaign. He overcame vigorous personal attacks on his character and on his actions during the Vietnam war, which he actively opposed. The "character issue" stemmed from allegations of infidelity, which Clinton ultimately refuted in a television interview in which he and Hillary avowed their relationship was solid. Throughout his term in office, Clinton was dogged by allegations in connection with the Whitewater real estate deal in which he and Hillary were involved prior to the 1992 election. Though Clinton himself was never accused of any wrongdoing, his partners in the venture, including the governor of Arkansas, Jim Guy Tucker, were convicted of fraud and conspiracy in a trial in 1996.

The problems faced by the new president were as daunting as they were varied. Almost immediately after his inauguration in January 1993 he became embroiled with the military leadership over a politically sensitive issue—his campaign pledge to allow homosexuals to serve openly in the armed services. He ultimately agreed to a compromise, dubbed the "don't ask, don't tell" policy. This controversy was soon supplanted by a series of blunders in appointments to fill positions in his administration.

Early in his tenure, the new President encountered a major defeat when Congress rejected his proposed economic stimulus package. He later won approval for his budget, but it barely survived the criticism of conservatives in Congress, including Democrats, who demanded more spending cuts, fewer taxes, and caps on entitlement programs. In his second year, Clinton faced persistent troubles on the domestic front, with acrimonious battles raging over health care, welfare reform, crime prevention, and White House personnel problems. Clinton appointed his wife to craft a health care reform package, but after months of effort the plan failed to garner sufficient support. Clinton had to reduce his objectives from massive overhaul to incremental reform. Though the health care reform was soundly defeated, Clinton won a major victory with the passage of the North American Free Trade Agreement (NAFTA) and the Global Agreement on Tariffs and Trade (GATT). Congress also approved Clinton's deficit reduction bill, rules allowing abortion counseling in federally funded clinics, a waiting period for handgun purchases (the "Brady bill," named for Reagan Press Secretary Jim Brady), and a national service program.

Foreign affairs, once a weak point for a man elected on a domestic economic agenda, became a proving ground for the former Arkansas governor. With issues erupting around the world, in places as disparate as Bosnia, Somalia, Rwanda, Haiti, and Cuba, Clinton was able to capitalize on several opportunities to improve his international image. The Israel-Jordan peace agreement was signed at the White House in the summer of 1994 by Israeli Prime Minister Yitzhak Rabin and Jordan's King Hussein. In the fall of that year, the administration succeeded in restoring Haiti's ousted president, Jean-Bertrand Aristide, to power. Clinton scored again by bolstering Russian president Boris Yeltsin's popularity with promises of economic aid.

But the problems in Eastern Europe put an end to his winning streak. Though Clinton wanted desperately to end the brutal "ethnic cleansing" in Bosnia and offer security to the 2 million refugees scrambling from one U.N. safe haven to another, he did not want to commit American ground troops to do so. A peace accord, which included provisions for American troops in a peacekeeping role, was ultimately constructed by Richard Holbrook and signed in Dayton, Ohio, in November 1995. The peace accord, however tenuous, greatly improved Clinton's standing in the eyes of the international community.

Foreign affairs continued to plague Clinton's presidency in 1996. In Russia, Clinton's support for Yeltsin drew criticism as the war for Chechen independence erupted. Challenges in the Middle East resurfaced in the form of continuing Israeli-Palestinian disputes and Iraq's invasion of Kurdish territory. Clinton responded to the Iraqi aggression by ordering missile attacks on Iraqi planes and ground forces.

The Republican sweep of the 1994 elections resulted in a Republican-controlled Congress, and 1995 was largely a tug-of-war between the White House and Capitol Hill over budget-balancing and other key points of the G.O.P.'s "Contract with America," crafted by Speaker of the House Newt Gingrich. Government operations shut down repeatedly as the funds allocated in successive continuing resolutions dried up, and the President and Congress were unable to pass budget legislation.

In 1996 Clinton approved several major legislative measures, including a welfare-reform bill reversing several decades of federal policy, which Clinton signed reluctantly and for which he was sharply criticized by liberals. He also enacted measures to improve access to health care, to raise the minimum wage by 90 cents per hour to $5.15, and to impose sanctions on companies that do business with Iran and Libya. In a move to discourage teenage smoking, Clinton approved a series of curbs on cigarette advertising, and introduced plans for the FDA to regulate nicotine as a controlled substance.

In his acceptance speech for renomination at the 1996 Democratic Convention in Chicago, the president vowed to protect programs for young people and the elderly, and to create a bridge to the twenty-first century, built on a commitment to funding technological innovation and education within a balanced budget. Clinton's strengths as a politician lie in his abilities to empathize and to compromise. His core beliefs in programs for social welfare blended with fiscal responsibility and economic growth are often clouded by his tendency to shape his rhetoric to the situation at hand. As he ended his first term in office, Clinton reflected on his successes and made a case for his reelection in November, making it clear that he still believes in a place called Hope.

—Arthur P. Reed, Jr.

Milestones in the Gay Rights Movement

Source: Excerpted from *The Reader's Companion to American History.*
Copyright © 1991 by Houghton Mifflin Company.

Late in the [19th] century, as large cities allowed for greater anonymity, as wage labor apart from family became common, and as more women were drawn out of the home, evidence of a new pattern of homosexual expression surfaced. . . .

At first, these individuals developed ways of meeting one another and institutions to foster a sense of identity. . . . By 1915, one participant in this new gay world was referring to it as "a community distinctly organized." For the most part hidden from view because of social hostility, an urban gay subculture had come into existence by the 1920s and 1930s.

World War II served as a critical divide in the social history of homosexuality. Large numbers of the young left families, small towns, and closely knit ethnic neighborhoods to enter a sex-segregated military or to migrate to larger cities for wartime employment. . . .

After the war, many of them made choices designed to support their gay identities. Pat Bond, a woman from Iowa who first met other lesbians while in the military, decided to stay in San Francisco after her discharge. [Donald] Vining remained in New York City rather than return to his small hometown in New Jersey. They, along with countless others, sustained a vibrant gay subculture that revolved around bars and friendship networks. Many cities saw their first gay bars during the 1940s. . . .

This new visibility provoked latent cultural prejudices. . . . Firings from government jobs and purges from the military intensified in the 1950s. President Dwight D. Eisenhower issued an executive order in 1953 barring gay men and lesbians from all federal jobs. Many state and local governments and private corporations followed suit. The FBI began a surveillance program against homosexuals.

The lead taken by the federal government encouraged local police forces to harass gay citizens. Vice officers regularly raided gay bars, sometimes arresting dozens of men and women on a single night. . . . Under these conditions, some gays began to organize politically. In November 1950 in Los Angeles, a small group of men led by Harry Hay and Chuck Rowland met to form what would become the Mattachine Society. Mostly male in membership, it was joined in 1955 by a lesbian organization in San Francisco, the Daughters of Bilitis, founded by Del Martin and Phyllis Lyon. In the 1950s these organizations remained small, but they established chapters in several cities and published magazines that were a beacon of hope to the readers.

In the 1960s, influenced by the model of a militant black civil rights movement, the "homophile movement," as the participants dubbed it, became more visible. Activists, such as Franklin Kameny and Barbara Gittings, picketed government agencies in Washington to protest discriminatory employment policies. In San Francisco, Martin, Lyon, and others targeted police harassment. By 1969, perhaps fifty homophile organizations existed in the United States, with memberships of a few thousand.

Then, on Friday evening, June 27, 1969, the police in New York City raided a Greenwich Village gay bar, the Stonewall Inn. Contrary to expectations, the patrons fought back, provoking three nights of rioting in the area accompanied by the appearance of "gay power" slogans on the buildings. Almost overnight, a massive grassroots gay liberations movement was born. Owing much to the radical protest of blacks, women, and college students in the 1960s, gays challenged all forms of hostility and punishment meted out by society. Choosing to "come out of the closet" and publicly proclaim their identity, they ushered in a social change movement that has grown substantially. By 1973, there were almost eight hundred gay and lesbian organizations in the United States; by 1990, the number was several thousand. By 1970, 5,000 gay men and lesbians marched in New York City to commemorate the first anniversary of the Stonewall Riots; in October 1987, over 600,000 marched in Washington, to demand equality.

The changes were far-reaching. Over the next two decades, half the states decriminalized homosexual behavior, and police harassment was sharply contained. Many large cities included sexual orientation in their civil rights statutes, as did Wisconsin and Massachusetts, first among the states to do so. . . . [In 1975] the Civil Service Commission eliminated the ban on the employment of homosexuals in most federal jobs. Many of the nation's religious denominations engaged in spirited debates about the morality of homosexuality, and some, like Unitarianism and Reformed Judaism, opened their doors to gay and lesbian ministers and rabbis. The lesbian and gay world was no longer an underground subculture but, in larger cities especially, a well-organized community, with businesses, political clubs, social service agencies, community centers, and religious congregations bringing people together. In a number of places, openly gay candidates ran for elective office and won.

These changes spawned opposition. In 1977 the singer Anita Bryant led a campaign to repeal a gay rights ordinance in Dade County, Florida. Her success encouraged others, and by the early 1980s, a well-organized conservative force had materialized to target the gay rights movement. Politicians, such as Senator Jesse Helms of North Carolina, and fundamentalist ministers, such as Jerry Falwell of Lynchburg, Virginia, who formed Moral Majority, Inc., joined forces to slow the progress of the gay movement.

The onset of the AIDS epidemic in the 1980s, although it intensified the antigay rhetoric of the New Right, also stimulated further organizing within the gay community. AIDS made political mobilization a matter of life and death. With a large majority of the cases striking male homosexuals, the gay community in short order created a host of organizations, such as the Gay Men's Health Crisis in New York City, to provide services and assistance to those infected. Local and national gay civil rights groups also grew in size and number, as the community sought to increase funding for research and education and to win protection against discrimination. A personal and social tragedy of immense proportions, AIDS paradoxically strengthened the political arm of the gay movement. □

Firsts in America

This selection is based on our editorial judgment. Other sources may list different firsts.

Admiral in U.S. Navy: David Glasgow Farragut, 1866.

Air–mail route, first transcontinental: Between New York City and San Francisco, 1920.

Assembly, representative: House of Burgesses, founded in Virginia, 1619.

Bank established: Bank of North America, Philadelphia, 1781.

Birth in America to English parents: Virginia Dare, born Roanoke Island, N.C., 1587.

Black newspaper: *Freedom's Journal*, 1827, edited by John B. Russworm.

Black U.S. diplomat: Ebenezer D. Bassett, 1869, minister-resident to Haiti.

Black elected governor of a state: L. Douglas Wilder, Virginia, 1990.

Black elected to U.S. Senate: Hiram Revels, 1870, Mississippi.

Black elected to U.S. House of Representatives: Jefferson Long, Georgia, 1870.

Black associate justice of U.S. Supreme Court: Thurgood Marshall, Oct. 2, 1967.

Black U.S. cabinet minister: Robert C. Weaver, 1966, Secretary of the Department of Housing and Urban Development.

Botanic garden: Established by John Bartram in Philadelphia, 1728 and is still in existence in its original location.

Cartoon, colored: "The Yellow Kid," by Richard Outcault, in *New York World*, 1895.

College: Harvard, founded 1636.

College to confer degrees on women: Oberlin (Ohio) College, 1841.

College to establish coeducation: Oberlin (Ohio) College, 1833.

Electrocution of a criminal: William Kemmler in Auburn Prison, Auburn, N.Y., Aug. 6, 1890.

Five and Dime Store: Founded by Frank Woolworth, Utica, N.Y., 1879 (moved to Lancaster, Pa., same year).

Fraternity, Greek-letter: Phi Beta Kappa; founded Dec. 5, 1776, at College of William and Mary.

Gay and lesbian civil rights advocacy organization: National Gay and Lesbian Task Force, founded in New York City, 1973.

Gay Power: Rioting following police raid on NYC gay bar, the Stonewall Inn, mobilizes gay community and leads to birth of gay liberation movement, June 27, 1969.

Homosexual, acknowledged, elected to high local office: Harvey Milk, 1977, San Francisco Board of Supervisors.

Law to be declared unconstitutional by U.S. Supreme Court: Judiciary Act of 1789. Case: *Marbury* v. *Madison*, 1803.

Library, circulating: Philadelphia, 1731.

Newspaper, illustrated daily: *New York Daily Graphic*, 1873.

Newspaper published daily: *Pennsylvania Packet and General Advertiser*, Philadelphia, Sept., 1784.

Newspaper published over a continuous period: *The Boston News–Letter*, April, 1704.

Newsreel: Pathé Frères of Paris, in 1910, circulated a weekly issue of their *Pathé Journal*.

Oil well, commercial: Titusville, Pa., 1859.

Panel quiz show on radio: *Information Please*, May 17, 1938.

Postage stamps issued: 1847.

Public School: Boston Latin School, Boston, 1635.

Radio station licensed: KDKA, Pittsburgh, Pa., Oct. 27, 1920.

Railroad, transcontinental: Central Pacific and Union Pacific railroads, joined at Promontory, Utah, May 10, 1869.

Savings bank: The Provident Institute for Savings, Boston, 1816.

Science museum: Founded by Charleston (S.C.) Library Society, 1773.

Skyscraper: Home Insurance Co., Chicago, 1885 (10 floors, 2 added later).

Slaves brought into America: At Jamestown, Va., 1619, from a Dutch ship.

Sorority: Kappa Alpha Theta, at De Pauw University, 1870.

State to abolish capital punishment: Michigan, 1847.

State to enter Union after original 13: Vermont, 1791.

Steam–heated building: Eastern Hotel, Boston, 1845.

Steam railroad (carried passengers and freight): Baltimore & Ohio, 1830.

Strike on record by union: Journeymen Printers, New York City, 1776.

Subway: Opened in Boston, 1897.

"Tabloid" picture newspaper: *The Illustrated Daily News* (now *The Daily News*), New York City, 1919.

Vaudeville theater: Gaiety Museum, Boston, 1883.

Woman astronaut to ride in space: Dr. Sally K. Ride, 1983.

Woman astronaut to walk in space: Dr. Kathryn D. Sullivan, 1984.

Woman cabinet member: Frances Perkins, Secretary of Labor, 1933.

Woman candidate for President: Victoria Claflin Woodhull, nominated by National Woman's Suffrage Assn. on ticket of Nation Radical Reformers, 1872.

Woman candidate for Vice–President: Geraldine A. Ferraro, nominated on a major party ticket, Democratic Party, 1984.

Woman doctor of medicine: Elizabeth Blackwell; M.D. from Geneva Medical College of Western New York, 1849.

Woman elected governor of a state: Nellie Tayloe Ross, Wyoming, 1925.

Woman elected to U.S. Senate: Hattie Caraway, Arkansas; elected Nov., 1932.

Woman graduate of law school: Ada H. Kepley, Union College of Law, Chicago, 1870.

Woman member of U.S. House of Representatives: Jeannette Rankin; elected Nov., 1916.

Woman member of U.S. Senate: Rebecca Latimer Felton of Georgia; appointed Oct. 3, 1922.

Woman member of U.S. Supreme Court: Sandra Day O'Connor; appointed July 1981.

Woman suffrage granted: Wyoming Territory, 1869.

Written constitution: *Fundamental Orders of Connecticut*, 1639.

NATIVE AMERICANS

Major Pre-Columbian Indian Cultures in the United States

Years ago	Culture or event	Comments
c. 15,000 near the end of the Ice Age.[1]	First migration of Paleo-indians in North America by people of Beringian subcontinent.	Nomadic hunters from northeast Asia are believed to have crossed Bering Strait land bridge (that scientists call Beringia) into present-day Alaska.
c. 11,200	Clovis Culture	Known for invention of superbly crafted grooved or fluted stone projectiles (Clovis points) first found near Clovis, New Mexico, in 1932. Clovis points have been found throughout the Americas. Hunted big game, notably mammoths.
c. 10,900	Folsom Culture	Named for site found near Folsom, New Mexico, 1926. Developed a smaller, thinner, fluted spear point than Clovis type. Hunted big game, notably the huge bison ancestor of the modern buffalo. First used a spear-throwing device called an atlatl (an Aztec word for "spear-thrower"). Discovery of Folsom point in 1927 gave first proof of Glacial Man in America.
c. 10,500	Plano or Plainview Culture	Named after the site in Plainview, Texas. They are associated primarily with the Great Plains area. Were bison hunters. Developed a delicately flaked spear point that lacked fluting. Adopted mass-hunting technique (jump–kill) to drive animal herds off a cliff. Preserved meat in the form of pemmican. First to use grinding stones to grind seeds and meat.
c. 8,500	Northwest Coast Indians. Some modern descendants are the Tlingit, Haida, Kwakiutl, Nootka, and Makah tribes.	Settled along the shores, rivers, and creeks of southeastern Alaska to northern California. A maritime culture, were expert canoe builders. Salmon fishing was important. Some tribes hunted whales and other sea mammals. Developed a high culture without the benefit of agriculture, pottery, or influence of ancient Mexican civilizations. Tribes lived in large, complex communities, constructed multifamily cedar plank houses. Evolved a caste system of chiefs, commoners, and slaves. Were highly skilled in crafts and woodworking which reached their height after European contact which provided them steel tools. Placed an inordinate value on accumulated wealth and property. Held lavish feasts (called *potlatches*) to display their wealth and social status. Important site: Ozette, WA (a Makah village).
c. 500 B.C.–A.D. 200	Adena Culture	Named for the estate called Adena near Chilicothe, Ohio, where their earthwork mounds were first found. Culture was centered in present southern Ohio, but also lived in Pennsylvania, Indiana, Kentucky, and West Virginia. Were the pioneer mound builders in the U.S. and constructed spectacular burial and effigy mounds. Settled in villages of circular post-and-wattle houses. Primarily hunter-gatherers, they farmed corn, tobacco, squash, pumpkins, and sunflowers at an early date. Important sites: The Adena Mound, OH; Grave Creek Mound, WV; Monks Mound, IL is the largest mound. May have built the Great Serpent Mound in Ohio.
c. A.D. 300–1300	Hohokam people (a Pima Indian word meaning "The Vanished Ones"). Believed to be ancestors of the modern Papago (Tohono O'odham) and Pima (Akimel O'odham) Indian groups.	Settled in present-day Arizona. Were desert farmers. Cultivated corn. Were first to grow cotton in the southwest. Wove cotton fabrics. Built pit houses and later multistoried buildings (pueblos). Constructed vast network of irrigation systems. Major canals were over 30 miles long. Built ball courts and truncated pyramids similar to those found in Middle America. First in world known to master etching (etched shells with fermented Saguaro juice). Traded with Mesoamerican Toltecs. Important sites: Pueblo Grande, AZ; Snaketown, AZ; Casa Grande, AZ.

Years ago	Culture or event	Comments
c. 300 B.C.–A.D. 1100	Mogollon Culture	Were highland farmers but also hunters in what is now eastern Arizona and southwestern New Mexico. Named after cluster of mountain peaks along Arizona–New Mexico border. They developed pit houses, later dwelt in pueblos. Were accomplished stoneworkers. Are famous for magnificent black on white painted pottery (Minbres Valley pottery), the finest North American native ceramics. Important settlements: Casa Malpais, AZ (first ancient catacombs in U.S., discovered there 1990), Gila Cliff, NM; Galaz, NM. Casa Grandes in Mexico was largest settlement.
c. 300 B.C.–A.D. 1300	Anasazi (a Navajo word meaning "The Ancient Ones"). Their descendents are the Hopi and other Pueblo Indians.	Inhabited Colorado Plateau "four corners," where Arizona, New Mexico, Utah, and Colorado meet. Were an agricultural society. Cultivated cotton, wove cotton fabrics. The early Anasazi are known as the Basketmaker People for their extraordinary basketwork. Were skilled workers in stone. Carved stone Kachina dolls. Built pit houses, later apartment-like pueblos. Constructed road networks. Were avid astronomers. Used a Solar calendar. Traded with Mesoamerican Toltecs. Important sites: Chaco Canyon, NM; Mesa Verde, CO; Canyon de Chelly, AZ; Bandelier, NM; Betatkin, NM. The Acoma Pueblo, NM, build c. A.D. 1300 and still occupied, may be the oldest continuously inhabited village in the U.S.
c. 100 B.C.–A.D. 500	Hopewell Culture. May be ancestors of present-day Zuni Indians.	Named after site in southern Ohio. Lived in Ohio valley, central Mississippi, and Illinois River Valleys. Were both hunter-gatherers and farmers. Villages were built along rivers, characterized by large conical or dome-shaped burial mounds and elaborate earthen walls enclosing large oval or rectangular areas. Were highly skilled craftsmen in pottery, stone, sculpture, and metalworking, especially copper. Engaged in widespread trade all over northern America extending west to the Rocky Mountains. Important sites: Newark Mound, OH; Great Serpent Mound, OH; Crooks Mound, LA.
A.D. c. 700–European contact.	Mississippi Culture. Major tribes of the southeast are their modern descendents.	Extended from Mississippi Valley into Alabama, Georgia, and Florida. Constructed large flat-topped earthen mounds on which were built wooden temples and meeting houses and residences of chiefs and priests. (They were also known as Temple Mound Builders.) Built huge cedar pole circles ("woodhenges") for astronomical observations. Were highly skilled hunters with bow and arrow. Practiced large-scale farming of corn, beans, and squash. Were skilled craftsmen. Falcon and Jaguar were common symbols in their art. Had clear ties with Mexico. The largest Mississippian center and largest of all mounds (Monk's Mound) was at Cahokia, IL. Other great temple centers were at Spiro, OK; Moundville, AL; and Etowah, GA.

NOTE: Dates may vary according to different sources. 1. There is no consensus when people first migrated to the Americas. Estimates vary between 12,000 and 50,000 years ago. However, archaeologists have established that humans already lived in rock shelters and other sites at the southern tip of Argentina (Tierra del Fuego) between 11,500 and 10,000 years ago.

American Indians Today

Population

The 1890 census counted 248,000 American Indians throughout the country. In the first half of this century, their numbers increased slowly until 1950 when a rapid growth began reaching 1,878,285 in 1990. More than half the American Indian population lived in just six states—Oklahoma, California, Arizona, New Mexico, Alaska, and Washington. Projections show that the American Indian population will reach 4.6 million by 2050.

The 1990 census showed that nearly two million American Indians, Eskimos, and Aleuts lived in the United States. Of these, 437,079 American Indians, 182 Eskimos, and 97 Aleuts lived on reservations and trust lands.

In 1990, 39% of the American Indian, Eskimo, and Aleut population was under 20 years old compared with 29% of the rest of the Nation. About eight percent of all American Indians were 60 years old and over in 1990, about half the proportion (17%) for the total population.

Female Householder Families

Among the Nation's 442,000 American Indian families in 1990, only six in ten were married-couple families compared with about eight in ten of the Nation's 64.5 million families. Consistent with the national trend, the number of American Indian families maintained by a woman without a husband present increased during the last decade and reached 27% in 1990. This is considerably higher than the national figure of 17%.

The Sioux (36%) and the Chippewa (33.1%) had the largest proportions of families maintained by women without husbands.

Male Householder Families

The proportions of American Indian families maintained by men without wives for the ten largest tribes were: Navajo (10.3%), Sioux (9.8%), Pueblo (9.6%), Chippewa (8.5%), Apache (8.4%), Lumbee (7.6%), Iroquois (7.0%), Cherokee (6.1%), Choctaw (4.8%), and Creek (4.5%).

Educational Attainment

The educational attainment levels of American Indians, Eskimos, and Aleuts improved significantly during the 1980s. Sixty-six percent of American Indians 25 years old and over were high school graduates or higher in 1990 compared with only 56% in 1980. The total U.S. figure was 75%. About nine percent completed a bachelor's degree or higher compared with 20% for the total U.S. population.

The Creek (73.2%), Iroquois (71.9%), Pueblo (71.5%), Choctaw (70.3%), Chippewa (69.7%), Sioux (69.7%), and Cherokee (68.2%) all had about the same percentage of high school graduates, followed by the Apache (63.8%), Lumbee (51.6%), and Navajo (51.0%).

More than ten percent of the American Indian population had college degrees in four of the ten largest tribes—Choctaw (13.3%), Creek (12.7%), Iroquois (11.3%), and Cherokee (11.1%).

Labor Force

Sixty-two percent, including Eskimos and Aleuts, 16 years old and over were in the labor force in 1990, three percentage points below the 65% for the total population. Sixty-nine percent of American Indian males 16 years old and over were in the labor force compared with more than 74% for all U.S. males.

American Indian women have shared in the national trend of increased labor force participation by women. Their numbers in the work force grew from 48% in 1980 to 55% in 1990 compared with 57% for all women in 1990.

Occupations

The census reported that 729,000 American Indians, including Eskimos and Aleuts, were employed. They had fewer jobs in managerial and professional specialty occupations than that of the total population. This was also true for technical, sales, and administrative support jobs.

A larger proportion of American Indians than the overall population were employed in service occupations; farming, forestry, and fishing; precision production, craft, and repair occupations; or as operators, fabricators, and laborers.

Income

In 1990, the median family income in the U.S. was $35,225. The median family income of American Indians, Eskimos, and Aleuts was $21,750. Stated another way, for every $100 that U.S. families received, American Indian families received $62. The median income of American Indian married-couple families was $28,287, or 71% of the $39,584 median for all married-couple families.

Twenty-seven percent of all American Indian families were maintained by a female householder with no husband present. The median income for these families was $10,742, about 62% of the $17,414 median for all families maintained by women without husbands.

The tribe with the highest median family income in 1989 was the Iroquois ($27,025), and the Navajo had the lowest at $13,940, according to a November 1994 census report.

Ten Largest American Indian Tribes: 1990
(Thousands)

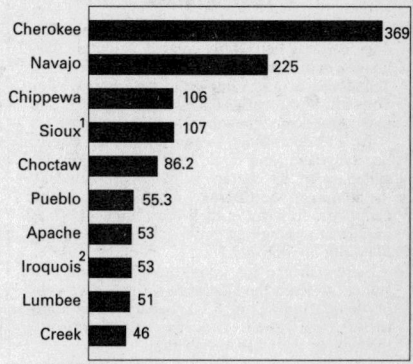

Tribe	Value
Cherokee	369
Navajo	225
Chippewa	106
Sioux[1]	107
Choctaw	86.2
Pueblo	55.3
Apache	53
Iroquois[2]	53
Lumbee	51
Creek	46

1. Any entry with the spelling "Siouan" was miscoded to Sioux in North Carolina. 2. Reporting and/or processing problems have affected the data for this tribe. *Source:* U.S. Department of Commerce, Bureau of the Census.

The report also showed that the Iroquois ($10,568) and the Cherokee ($10,469) tribes had the highest per capita incomes, and the Navajo ($4,788) had the lowest.

Poverty

Fifty-one percent of those residing on reservations and trust lands were living below the poverty level in 1989. The Hopi, Blackfeet, Zuni Pueblo, and Fort Apache Reservations had the lowest percentages of American Indians in poverty, about 50%.

Overall, about 603,000, or 31% were living below the poverty level compared to the national poverty rate of about 13% for the same period. Twenty-seven percent, or 125,000 American Indian families, were in poverty in 1989 compared with ten percent of all families.

Fifty percent of American Indian families maintained by females with no husband percent lived in poverty vs. 31% for all families maintained by women without husbands.

According to the 1990 census, the Navajo (48.8%) and the Sioux (44.4%) tribes had the highest proportions of people living in poverty, while the Iroquois had the lowest at 20.1 percent.

The tribes with the largest percentage of poor families were the Navajo (47.3%) and Lumbee (20.2%), and the Creek at 19.0 percent. The Iroquois had the lowest percent of poor families (17.3%).

Reservations and Trust Lands

Twenty-two percent, or 437,431, of all American Indians including Eskimos and Aleuts lived on reservations and trust lands in 1990. Reservations and trust lands are areas with boundaries established by treaty, statute, and/or executive or court order.

The per capita income in 1989 was about $4,478 for American Indians residing on all reservations and trust lands. On the ten largest reservations it ranged from $3,113 to $4,718. Blackfeet and Hopi had the highest per capita incomes, $4,718 and $4,566, respectively.

Ten percent of the total American Indian population lived in the Tribal Jurisdiction Statistical Areas in Oklahoma. Seven of the ten reservations and trust lands with the largest American Indian populations were entirely or partially located in Arizona.

First Native American Newspaper

Sequoyah (c. 1770–1843) was a Cherokee Indian cultural hero who created a written language for his people. He was born in Taskigi, Tennessee, and was known to the Cherokees as Sogwali. Missionaries called him Sequoyah, and most Americans knew him as George Guess.

He was determined to create a written Cherokee language, and circa 1821, he developed a syllabary of 85 characters that represented all the sounds in the Cherokee tongue and allowed Cherokees to write in their own language. (It is important to note that Sequoyah created a *syllabary*, not an alphabet.)

Sequoyah and his young daughter—the first student to learn the Cherokee script—gave public demonstrations of his syllabary. After some initial resistance, literacy spread rapidly throughout the Cherokee Nation.

His invention was used to publish *The Cherokee Phoenix*, the first newspaper by Native Americans. On Feb. 21, 1828, its four-page inaugural issue was printed in both Cherokee and English.

The sequoia tree is named after him.

School Enrollment

Overall, more than 31% of American Indians three years old and over living on reservations and trust lands were enrolled in elementary or high school. The enrollment rates for all American Indians three years old and over was 25%, higher than the U.S. population rate of 18%.

The proportion of adults 25 years old and older with high school diplomas or higher on the ten largest reservations and trust lands ranged from 37% to 66%. Overall, 54% of the adults were high school graduates or higher. Blackfeet and Hopi had the greatest proportions (66.3% and 62.6%) of high school graduates or higher.

ALASKA NATIVES

Population

The population rose by more than 50,000 persons (153%) between 1950 and 1990 and numbered 85,698 in 1990. The census reported that more than half of all Alaska Natives were Eskimos, about 36% were American Indians, and about 12% were Aleuts. The two main Eskimo groups, Inupiat and Yupik, are distinguished by their language and geography. The former live in the north and northwest parts of Alaska and speak Inupiaq, while the latter live in the south and southwest and speak Yupik.

The American Indian tribes are the Alaskan Athabaskan (11,696) in the central part of the State and the Tlingit (9,448), Tsimshian (1,653) and the Haida (1,083) in the southeast. The Aleuts (10,052) live mainly in the Aleutian Islands.

The median age of Alaska Natives was 24 years, compared with 29 years for the total State population and 33 years for the entire United States. About 44% were under 20 years old and seven percent were 60 years old and over.

Female Householder Families

Alaska Natives had proportionately fewer married-couple families and more families with a female householder and no husband present than the State as a whole. Only 58% of Alaska's 16,432 Native families consisted of a husband and wife compared with 80% of all families in Alaska. The Aleuts had the largest percentage of married-couple families among Alaska Natives.

The proportion of families with a female householder and no husband present was twice as high among Alaska Natives as Alaska's total population.

Thirty-one percent of American Indian families, 28% of Eskimo families, and 26% of Aleut families are maintained by female householders with no husband present compared with 14% of all Alaska's families.

Education

Although Alaska Natives have made great strides in education during this century, they remain less likely to have high school diplomas and bachelor's degrees or higher than other Alaskans.

Sixty-three percent, 25 years old and over, had completed high school or higher compared with 87% statewide. Four percent were college graduates with a bachelor's degree or higher, while the statewide total was 23%.

Labor Force

Just 56% of the 54,614 Alaska Natives 16 years old and over were in the labor force compared with 75% of the State's total population. Fifty-one percent of all Alaska females 16 years old and over were in the labor force compared to 66% of all females in Alaska. Similarly, 61% of all Alaska Native males 16 years old and over were in the labor force in 1990 compared with 82% of all males in the State.

American Indians had the highest labor force participation rate of the three Alaska Native groups; this may be because they were more likely to live in urban areas where job opportunities were greater. Aleuts and Eskimos, who tend to live in rural areas, had lower rates.

Employment

Twenty percent of those 16 years old and over were in managerial and professional occupations compared with 30% of all workers in the State. However, Alaska Natives were as likely as the State's total population to work in technical, sales, and administrative jobs. About three of every ten workers in each population held such jobs. They were also more likely than the statewide population to be in service jobs and to be operators, fabricators, or laborers.

Income

Alaska, with a median family income of $46,581, had the highest income of any state in 1990. However, the median family income for Alaska natives was only $26,695. Aleut families earned an average of $36,472 followed by American Indians ($29,339) and Eskimos ($23,257). Among married-couple families, median income levels were $52,022 for the State and $37,406 for Alaska Natives.

Poverty

In 1989, 23% of Alaska Natives were poor compared with nine percent for the State as a whole. Twenty-eight percent of Eskimos lived in poverty compared with 20% of American Indians and 13% of Aleuts. Twenty-one percent of Native families and seven percent of families statewide lived below the poverty level. □

LOCATIONS OF LARGEST AMERICAN INDIAN TRIBES AND SELECTED RESERVATIONS

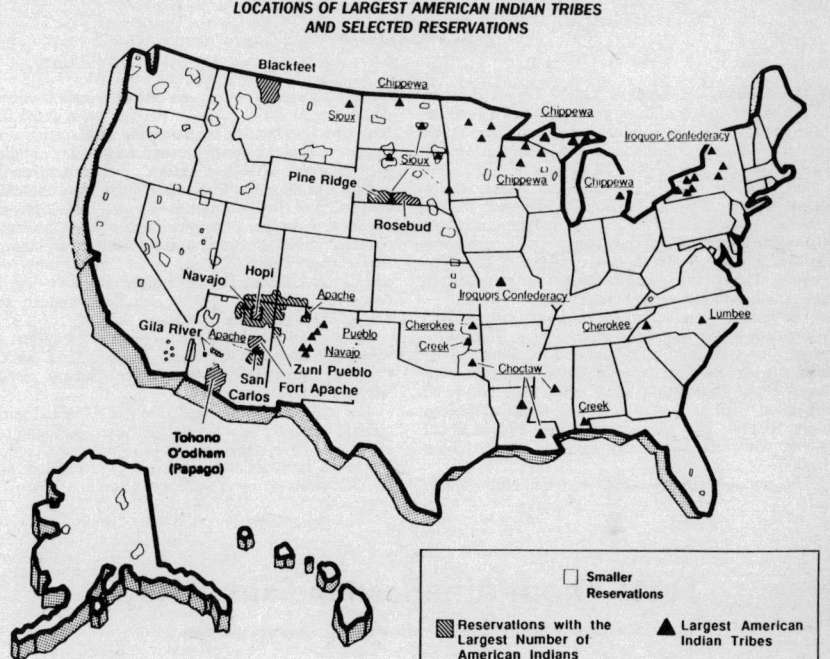

Population of Native Americans By State, 1990

States	American Indian	Eskimo	Aleut	States	American Indian	Eskimo	Aleut
Alabama	16,312	105	89	Montana	47,524	106	49
Alaska	31,245	44,401	10,052	Nebraska	12,344	38	28
Arizona	203,009	284	234	Nevada	19,377	156	104
Arkansas	12,641	80	52	New Hampshire	2,075	45	14
California	236,078	2,552	3,534	New Jersey	14,500	201	269
Colorado	27,271	297	208	New Mexico	134,097	162	96
Connecticut	6,472	83	99	New York	60,855	754	1,042
Delaware	1,982	19	18	North Carolina	79,825	152	178
D.C.	1,432	14	20	North Dakota	25,870	38	9
Florida	35,461	431	443	Ohio	19,859	230	269
Georgia	12,926	223	199	Oklahoma	252,089	202	129
Hawaii	4,738	155	206	Oregon	37,443	545	508
Idaho	13,594	132	54	Pennsylvania	14,210	264	259
Illinois	20,970	414	452	Rhode Island	3,987	42	42
Indiana	12,453	170	97	South Carolina	8,049	106	91
Iowa	7,217	67	65	South Dakota	50,501	62	12
Kansas	21,767	114	84	Tennessee	9,859	96	84
Kentucky	5,614	82	73	Texas	64,349	721	807
Louisiana	18,361	92	88	Utah	24,093	116	74
Maine	5,945	34	19	Vermont	1,650	32	14
Maryland	12,601	169	202	Virginia	14,893	200	189
Massachusetts	11,857	210	174	Washington	77,627	1,791	2,065
Michigan	55,131	253	282	West Virginia	2,385	36	37
Minnesota	49,392	235	282	Wisconsin	38,986	181	220
Mississippi	8,435	50	40	Wyoming	9,426	37	16
Missouri	19,508	173	154	**United States**	**1,878,285**	**57,152**	**23,797**

Source: U.S. Department of Commerce, Bureau of the Census.

Eskimos

The Eskimos are the most widely dispersed group in the world still leading a partly aboriginal way of life. They live in a region that spans more than 3,500 miles, including Greenland, the northern fringe of North America, and a sector of eastern Siberia.

Eskimos are racially distinct from American Indians, and are not, as previously believed, merely "Indians transformed." In fact, the Eskimos are most closely related to the Mongolian peoples of eastern Asia. Eskimos consider themselves to be "Inuit" (The People). The Eskimo-Aleut languages are unrelated to any American Indian language groups.

The Eskimo population was approximately 50,000 at the time of the first widespread contact with Europeans. An estimated 2,000 Siberian Eskimos lived near the Bering Strait, the Alaskan Eskimos numbered about 25,000, and the Central Eskimos (who inhabited what is now northern Canada) numbered about 10,000. The Labrador Eskimos totaled about 3,000, while the Greenland Eskimos totaled about 10,000.

The popular conception of the Eskimos—whale hunters dressed in heavy fur clothing and living in dome-shaped ice lodges—is derived from the Eskimos who live farthest north, on the Arctic islands of Canada and along northwestern Greenland. In reality, these northern Arctic dwellers formed a minority among Eskimos as a whole. No single environmental adaptation existed throughout the area of Eskimo occupancy. Eskimos along the Pacific coast probably obtained much of their food by fishing for salmon, while the Central Eskimos of Canada subsisted mainly on caribou. Eskimo groups lived in various types of shelters, including semi-subterranean sod houses and tents made of caribou skins.

At no time did the Eskimos possess a national or even well-defined tribal sense. The emphasis was on the local and familial group rather than on associations of land and territory.

The overall Eskimo population has remained fairly constant over the past several centuries, although not all groups have remained stable in number. According to the 1990 census, there are 57,152 Eskimos and 23,797 Aleuts living in the United States. □

Facts About American Indians Today

Source: U.S. Department of the Interior, Bureau of Indian Affairs.

Reservations. The number of Indian land areas in the U.S. administered as Federal Indian Reservations total 287. The largest is the Navajo Reservation of some 16 million acres of land in Arizona, New Mexico, and Utah. Many of the smaller reservations are less than 1,000 acres with the smallest less than 100 acres. On some reservations, a high percentage of the land is owned and occupied by non-Indians. Some 140 reservations have entirely tribally-owned land.

Indians do not have to live on reservations and are free to move about like all other Americans. Indians also have the right to buy and hold title to land purchased with their own funds. Over half of the total U.S. Indian and Alaska Native population now lives away from reservations. Many return home to participate in family and tribal life and sometimes to retire.

Indian Tribes. There are over 550 Federally recognized tribes in the United States, including about 226 village groups in Alaska. "Federally-recognized" means these tribes and groups have a special, legal relationship to the U.S. government and its agent, The Bureau of Indian Affairs (BIA).

A number of Indian tribes and groups in the U.S. do not have a federally-recognized status, although some are state-recognized. The Bureau of Indian Affairs has a special program to work with those seeking federal recognition status.

Who is an Indian? No single federal or tribal criterion establishes a person's identity as an Indian. Government agencies use differing criteria to determine who is an Indian eligible to participate in their programs. Tribes also have varying eligibility criteria for membership. To be eligible for Bureau of Indian Affairs services, an Indian must (1) be a member of a tribe recognized by the federal government and (2) must, for some purposes, be of one-fourth or more Indian ancestry. By legislative and administrative decision, the Aleuts, Eskimos, and Indians of Alaska are eligible for BIA services.

Tribal membership. A tribe sets up its own criteria, although the U.S. Congress can also establish tribal membership criteria. Becoming a member of a particular tribe requires meeting its membership rules, including adoption. Except for adoption, the amount of blood quantum needed varies, with some tribes requiring only a trace of Indian blood (of the tribe) while others require as much as one-half.

What is an Indian tribe? Originally, an Indian tribe was a body of people bound together by blood ties who were socially, politically, and religiously organized, who lived together in a defined territory, and who spoke a common language or dialect. The establishment of the reservation system created some new tribal groupings when two or three tribes were placed on one reservation, or when members of one tribe were spread over two or three reservations.

Taxes. Indians pay the same taxes as other citizens with the exceptions applying to those Indians living on federal reservations: (1) federal income taxes are not levied on income from trust lands held for them by the United States; (2) state income taxes are not paid on income earned on a federal reservation; (3) state sales taxes are not paid on transactions made on a federal reservation, and (4) local property taxes are not paid on reservation or trust land.

Citizenship. Indians are U.S. citizens and have the same right to vote as other Americans. They also have the right to hold federal, state, and local government offices. Ben Nighthorse Campbell, a member of the Northern Cheyenne Tribe of Montana, was elected to the U.S. House of Representatives in 1986 from the Third District of Colorado and served a third term in 1992. □

PEOPLE

Many public figures not listed here may be found elsewhere in the *Information Please Almanac.*

40 Governors	929 Sports Personalities
633 Presidents	651 Supreme Court Justices
635 Presidents' Wives	633 Vice Presidents
33 Senators	

A name in parentheses is the original name or form of name. Localities are places of birth. Country name in parenthesis is the present-day name. Dates of birth appear as month/day/year. **Boldface** years in parentheses are dates of **(birth-death)**.

Information has been gathered from many sources, including the individuals themselves. However, the *Information Please Almanac* cannot guarantee the accuracy of every individual item.

A

Aalto, Alvar (architect); Kuortane, Finland **(1898-1976)**

Abbado, Claudio (orchestra conductor); Milan, Italy, 1933

Abbott, Bud (William) (comedian); Asbury Park, N.J. **(1898-1974)**

Abbott, George (stage producer); Forestville, N.Y. **(1887–1995)**

Abelard, Peter (theologian); nr. Nantes, France **(1079-1142)**

Abernathy, Ralph (civil rights leader); Linden, Ala., **(1926-1990)**

Abraham, F(ahrid) Murray (actor); Pittsburgh, Pa., 10/24/39

Achebe, Chinua (writer); Ogidi, Nigeria, 11/16/30

Acheson, Dean (statesman); Middletown, Conn. **(1893-1971)**

Acuff, Roy Claxton (musician); nr. Maynardsville, Tenn. **(1903-1992)**

Adams, Abigail (First Lady, writer); Weymouth, Mass. **(1744–1818)**

Adams, Charles Francis (diplomat); Boston **(1807-1886)**

Adams, Don (actor); New York City, 4/19/26

Adams, Edie (Edie Enke) (actress); Kingston, Pa., 4/16/29

Adams, Franklin Pierce (columnist, author); Chicago **(1881-1960)**

Adams, Gerry (political leader); West Belfast, Northern Ireland, 10/6/48

Adams, Henry Brooks (historian); Boston **(1838-1918)**

Adams, Joey (comedian); New York City, 1/6/11

Adams, Maude (Maude Kiskadden) (actress); Salt Lake City **(1872-1953)**

Adams, Samuel (American Revolutionary patriot); Boston **(1722-1803)**

Adams, Scott (cartoonist); Catskill, N.Y., 6/8/57

Adamson, Joy (naturalist); Troppau, Silesia **(1910-1980)**

Addams, Charles (cartoonist); Westfield, N.J., **(1912-1988)**

Addams, Jane (social worker); Cedarville, Ill. **(1860-1935)**

Adderley, Julian "Cannonball" (jazz saxophonist); Tampa, Fla. **(1928-1975)**

Ade, George (humorist); Kentland, Ind. **(1866-1944)**

Adenauer, Konrad (statesman); Cologne, Germany **(1876-1967)**

Adler, Alfred (psychoanalyst); Vienna **(1870-1937)**

Adler, Larry (musician); Baltimore, 2/10/14

Adler, Richard (songwriter); New York City, 8/3/21

Aeschylus (dramatist); Eleusis (Greece) **(525-456** B.C.)

Aesop (fabulist); birthplace unknown **(lived c. 600** B.C.)

Aherne, Brian (actor); King's Norton, England **(1902-1986)**

Aiello, Danny (actor); New York City, 6/20/33

Aiken, Conrad (poet); Savannah, Ga. **(1889-1973)**

Ailey, Alvin (choreographer); Rogers, Tex., **(1931-1989)**

Akhmatova, Anna (poet); Odessa, Ukraine **(1889–1966)**

Akihito, Tsugunomiya (Emperor of Japan); Tokyo, 12/23/33

Albanese, Licia (operatic soprano); Bari, Italy, 7/22/13

Albee, Edward (playwright); Washington, D.C., 3/12/28

Albers, Josef (painter); Bottrop, Germany **(1888-1976)**

Albert, Eddie (Edward Albert Heimberger) (actor); Rock Island, Ill., 4/22/08

Albert, Edward (actor); Los Angeles, 2/20/51

Albertson, Jack (actor); Malden, Mass. **(1910?-1981)**

Albright, Lola (actress); Akron, Ohio, 7/20/25

Alcott, Louisa May (novelist); Germantown, Pa. **(1832-1888)**

Alda, Alan (actor); New York City, 1/28/36

Alda, Robert (Alphonso d'Abruzzo) (actor); New York City **(1914-1986)**

Alden, John (American Pilgrim); England **(1599?-1687)**

Alexander, Jane (Quigley) (actress); Boston, 10/28/39

Alexander the Great (monarch, conqueror); Pella, Macedonia (Greece) **(356-323** B.C.)

Alger, Horatio (author); Revere, Mass. **(1834-1899)**

Algren, Nelson (novelist); Detroit **(1909-1981)**

Allen, Debbie (dancer-choreographer, actress); Houston, Tex., 1/16/50

Allen, Ethan (American Revolutionary soldier); Litchfield, Conn. **(1738-1789)**

Allen, Fred (John Florence Sullivan) (comedian); Cambridge, Mass. **(1894-1956)**

Allen, Gracie (Grace Ethel Cecile Rosalie Allen) (comedienne); San Francisco **(1906-1964)**

Allen, Mel (Melvin Israel) (sportscaster); Birmingham, Ala. **(1913–1996)**

Allen, Peter (actor, songwriter); Tenterfield, Australia **(1944-1992)**

Allen, Steve (TV entertainer); New York City, 12/26/21

Allen, Woody (Allen Stewart Konigsberg) (actor, writer, director); Brooklyn, N.Y., 12/1/35

Allende, Isabel (novelist); Lima, Peru, 8/2/42

Alley, Kirstie (actress); Wichita, Kan., 1/12/55

Allison, Fran (actress); LaPorte City, Iowa **(1908?-1989)**

Allman, Gregg (singer); Nashville, Tenn., 12/8/47

Allyson, June (Jan Allyson) (actress); New York City, 10/7/23

Alonso, Alicia (ballerina); Havana, 12/21/21(?)

Alpert, Herb (band leader); Los Angeles, 3/31/35(?)

Alsop, Joseph W., Jr. (journalist); Avon, Conn., **(1910-1989)**

Alsop, Stewart (journalist); Avon, Conn. **(1914-1974)**

Altman, Robert (film director); Kansas City, Mo., 2/20/25

Amanpour, Christiane (broadcast journalist); London, 1958

Amati, Nicola (violin maker); Cremona, Italy **(1596-1684)**

Ambler, Eric (suspense writer); London, 6/28/09

Ameche, Don (Dominic Amici) (actor); Kenosha, Wis. **(1908–1993)**

Amis, Kingsley (novelist); London **(1922–1995)**

Amory, Cleveland (writer, conservationist); Nahant, Mass., 9/2/17

Amos (Freeman F. Gosden) (radio comedian); Richmond, Va. **(1899-1982)**

Amos, John (actor); Newark, N.J., 12/27/41

Amsterdam, Morey (actor); Chicago, 12/14/14

Andersen, Hans Christian (author of fairy-tales); Odense, Denmark **(1805-1875)**

Anderson, Eddie. *See* Rochester

Anderson, Gillian (actress); Chicago, 8/9/68

Anderson, Harry (actor); Newport, R.I., 10/14/52

Anderson, Ib (ballet dancer); Copenhagen, 12/14/54

Anderson, Jack (journalist); Long Beach, Calif., 10/19/22

Anderson, Dame Judith (actress); Adelaide, Australia **(1898-1992)**

Anderson, Lindsay (Gordon) (director); Bangalore, India **(1923–1994)**

Anderson, Loni (actress); St. Paul, Minn., 8/5/45

Anderson, Lynn (singer); Grand Forks, N.D., 9/26/47

Anderson, Marian (contralto); Philadelphia **(1897-1993)**

Anderson, Maxwell (dramatist); Atlantic, Pa. **(1888-1959)**

Anderson, Richard Dean (actor); Minneapolis, Minn., 1/23/50

Anderson, Robert (playwright); New York City, 4/28/17

Anderson, Sherwood (novelist); Camden, Ohio **(1876–1941)**

Andersson, Bibi (actress); Stockholm, 11/11/35

Andress, Ursula (actress); Switzerland, 3/19/38

Andrews, Dana (actor); Collins, Miss. **(1909-1992)**

Andrews, Julie (Julia Wells) (actress, singer); Walton-on-Thames, England, 10/1/35

Andrews, La Verne (singer); Minneapolis **(1916-1967)**

Andrews, Maxene (singer); Minneapolis **(1918–1995)**

Andrews, Patti (singer); Minneapolis, 2/16/20

Andy (Charles J. Correll) (radio comedian); Peoria, Ill. **(1890-1972)**

Angeles, Victoria de los (Victoria Gamez Cima) (operatic soprano); Barcelona, 11/1/24

Angelico, Fra (Guido di Pietro; Giovanni de Fiesole) (painter); nr. Florence **(c. 1400–1455)**

Angelou, Maya (poet, novelist); St. Louis, Mo., 4/4/28

Anka, Paul (singer, composer); Ottawa, 7/30/41

Ann-Margret (Ann-Margret Olsson) (actress); Valsjobyn, Sweden, 4/28/41

Anouilh, Jean (playwright); Bordeaux, France **(1910-1987)**

Anthony, Susan Brownell (woman suffragist); Adams, Mass. **(1820-1906)**

Antonioni, Michelangelo (director); Ferrara, Italy, 9/29/12

Antony, Mark (Marcus Antonius) (statesman); Rome **(83?-30** B.C.)

Anuszkiewicz, Richard (painter); Erie, Pa., 5/23/30

Apollinaire, Guillaume (writer); Rome **(1880–1918)**

Aquinas, St. Thomas (philosopher); nr. Aquino (Italy) **(1225?-1274)**

Arafat, Yasir (Mohammed Abdel-Raouf Arafat al Qudwa al Husseini) (Chairman of the Palestine Liberation Organization); Cairo, Egypt, 8/24/29

681

Arbuckle, Roscoe "Fatty" (actor, director); San Jose, Calif. (1887-1933)
Archimedes (physicist, mathematician); Syracuse, Sicily (287?-212 B.C.)
Archipenko, Alexandre (sculptor); Kiev, Ukraine (1887-1964)
Arden, Elizabeth (Florence Nightingale Graham) (cosmetics executive); Woodbridge, Canada (1891-1966)
Arden, Eve (Eunice Quedens) (actress); Mill Valley, Calif. (1907–1990)
Arendt, Hannah (historian); Hannover, Germany (1906-1975)
Aristophanes (dramatist); Athens (448?-380 B.C.)
Aristotle (philosopher); Stagirus, Macedonia (384-322 B.C.)
Arkin, Alan (actor, director); New York City, 3/26/34
Arledge, Roone (TV executive); Forest Hills, N.Y., 7/8/31
Arlen, Harold (Hyman Arluck) (composer); Buffalo, N.Y. (1905-1986)
Arlen, Richard (actor); Charlottesville, Va. (1900-1976)
Arliss, George (actor); London (1868-1946)
Armstrong, Louis ("Satchmo") (musician); New Orleans (1900-1971)
Armstrong-Jones, Anthony. *See* Snowdon, Earl of
Arnaz, Desi (Desiderio) (actor, producer); Santiago, Cuba (1917-1986)
Arness, James (James Aurness) (actor); Minneapolis, 5/26/23
Arno, Peter (cartoonist); New York City (1904-1968)
Arnold, Benedict (American Revolutionary War general, charged with treason); Norwich, Conn. (1741-1801)
Arnold, Eddy (singer); Henderson, Tenn., 5/15/18
Arnold, Matthew (poet, critic); Laleham, England (1822-1888)
Arp, Jean (sculptor, painter); Strasbourg (France) (1887-1966)
Arpino, Gerald (choreographer); Staten Island, N.Y., 1/14/28
Arquette, Cliff ("Charley Weaver") (actor); Toledo, Ohio (1905-1974)
Arquette, Rosanna (actress); New York City, 8/10/59
Arrau, Claudio (pianist); Chillán, Chile (1903–1991)
Arroyo, Martina (soprano); New York City, 2/2/40
Arthur, Bea (Bernice Frankel) (actress); New York City, 5/13/26(?)
Arthur, Jean (Gladys Greene) (actress); New York City (1900–1991)
Ashcroft, Dame Peggy (actress); Croydon, England (1907–1991)
Ashkenazy, Vladimir (concert pianist); Gorki, U.S.S.R., 7/6/37
Ashley, Elizabeth (actress); Ocala, Fla., 8/30/39
Ashton, Sir Frederick William Mallandaine (choreographer); Guayaquil, Ecuador (1904-1988)
Asimov, Isaac (author); Petrovichi, Russia (1920-1992)
Asner, Edward (actor); Kansas City, Mo., 11/15/29
Astaire, Fred (Frederick Austerlitz) (dancer, actor); Omaha, Neb. (1899-1987)
Astin, John (actor, director); Baltimore, Md., 3/30/30
Astor, John Jacob (financier); Waldorf (Germany) (1763-1848)
Astor, Mary (Lucile Langhanke) (actress); Quincy, Ill. (1906-1987)
Ataturk, Kemal (Mustafa Kemal) (Turkish soldier, statesman); Salonika (Greece) (1881-1938)
Atkins, Chet (guitarist); nr. Luttrell, Tenn., 6/20/24
Atkinson, Brooks (drama critic); Melrose, Mass. (1894-1984)
Attenborough, Richard (actor, director); Cambridge, England, 8/29/23
Attila (King of Huns, called "Scourge of God") (406?-453)
Attucks, Crispus (American Revolutionary Patriot); Boston (1723?-1770)
Atwill, Lionel (actor); Croydon, England (1885-1946)
Auberjonois, Rene (actor); New York City, 6/1/40
Auchincloss, Louis (author); Lawrence, N.Y., 9/27/17
Auden, W(ystan) H(ugh) (poet); York, England (1907-1973)
Audubon, John James (naturalist, painter); Haiti (1785-1851)
Auer, Leopold (violinist, teacher); Veszprém, Hungary (1845-1930)
Augustine, Saint (Aurelius Augustinus) (theologian); Tagaste, Numidia (Algeria) (354-430)
Augustus (Gaius Octavius) (Roman emperor); Rome (63 B.C.-A.D. 14)
Aung San Suu Kyi (human rights activist); Rangoon, Burma, 6/19/45
Austen, Jane (novelist); Steventon, England (1775-1817)
Autry, Gene (singer, actor); Tioga, Tex., 9/29/07
Avalon, Frankie (singer); Philadelphia, 9/18/40
Avedon, Richard (photographer); New York City, 5/15/23
Avery, Milton (painter); Altmar, N.Y. (1893-1965)
Ax, Emanuel (pianist); Lvov, Ukraine, 6/8/49
Axelrod, George (playwright); New York City, 6/9/22
Ayckbourn, Alan (playwright); London, 4/12/39
Aykroyd, Dan (actor); Ottawa, Ont., Canada, 7/1/52
Ayres, Lew (actor); Minneapolis, 12/28/08
Aznavour, Charles (singer, composer); Paris, France, 5/22/24

B

Bacall, Lauren (Betty Joan Perske) (actress); New York City, 9/16/24
Bach, Carl Phillipp Emanuel (composer); Weimar, Germany (1714-1788)
Bach, Johann Sebastian (composer); Eisenach, Germany (1685-1750)
Bacharach, Burt (songwriter); Kansas City, Mo., 5/12/29
Backus, Jim (actor); Cleveland (1913-1989)
Bacon, Francis (philosopher, essayist); London (1561-1626)
Bacon, Francis (painter); Dublin (1910-1992)
Bacon, Roger (philosopher, scientist); Ilchester, England (1214?-1294)

Baez, Joan (folk singer); Staten Island, N.Y., 1/9/41
Bailey, F. Lee (lawyer); Waltham, Mass., 6/10/33
Bailey, Pearl (singer); Newport News, Va. (1918-1990)
Bain, Conrad (actor); Lethbridge, Alberta, Canada, 2/4/23
Baio, Scott (actor); Brooklyn, N.Y., 9/22/61
Baird, Bil (William B.) (puppeteer); Grand Island, Neb. (1904-1987)
Baker, Anita (singer); Toledo, Ohio, 1958
Baker, Carroll (actress); Johnstown, Pa., 5/28/31
Baker, Josephine (singer, dancer); St. Louis (1906-1975)
Baker, Russell (columnist); Loudoun County, Va., 8/14/25
Balanchine, George (choreographer); St. Petersburg, Russia (1904-1983)
Balboa, Vasco Nuñez de (explorer); Jerez de los Caballeros (Spain) (1475-1517)
Baldwin, James (novelist); New York City (1924-1987)
Balenciaga, Cristóbal (fashion designer); Guetaria, Spain (1895-1972)
Ball, Lucille (Désirée) (actress, producer); Celoron (nr. Jamestown), N.Y. (1911-1989)
Ballard, Kaye (Catherine Gloria Balotta) (actress); Cleveland, 11/20/26
Balmain, Pierre (fashion designer); St.-Jean-de-Maurienne, France (1914-1982)
Balsam, Martin (actor); New York City (1919–1996)
Balzac, Honoré de (novelist); Tours, France (1799-1850)
Bancroft, Anne (Annemarie Italiano) (actress); New York City, 9/17/31
Bankhead, Tallulah (actress); Huntsville, Ala. (1903-1968)
Banneker, Benjamin (mathematician, astronomer); Endicott, Md. (1731–1806)
Banting, Fredrick Grant (physiologist); Alliston, Ont., Canada (1891-1941)
Bara, Theda (Theodosia Goodman) (actress); Cincinnati (1890-1955)
Baraka, Imamu Amiri (LeRoi Jones) (playwright); Newark, N.J., 10/7/34
Barber, Red (Walter Lanier) (sportscaster); Columbus, Miss. (1908-1992)
Barber, Samuel (composer); West Chester, Pa. (1910-1981)
Barbie, Klaus (Nazi, "The Butcher of Lyon"); Bad Godesberg, Germany (1913–1991)
Bardot, Brigitte (actress); Paris, 1935
Barenboim, Daniel (concert pianist, conductor); Buenos Aires, 11/15/42
Barker, Bob (host); Darrington, Wash., 12/12/23
Barnard, Christiaan N. (heart surgeon); Beauford West, South Africa, 1923
Barnum, Phineas Taylor (showman); Bethel, Conn. (1810-1891)
Barrie, Sir James Matthew (author); Kirriemuir, Scotland (1860-1937)
Barrie, Wendy (actress); Hong Kong (1913-1978)
Barry, Gene (Eugene Klass) (actor); New York City, 6/14/21
Barry, John (naval officer); County Wexford, Ireland (1745-1803)
Barrymore, Diana (actress); New York City (1921-1960)
Barrymore, Ethel (Ethel Blythe) (actress); Philadelphia (1879-1959)
Barrymore, Georgiana Drew (actress); Philadelphia (1856-1893)
Barrymore, John (John Blythe) (actor); Philadelphia (1882-1942)
Barrymore, Lionel (Lionel Blythe) (actor); Philadelphia (1878-1954)
Barrymore, Maurice (Herbert Blythe) (actor, playwright); Agra, India (1847-1905)
Barth, John (novelist); Cambridge, Md., 5/27/30
Barthelme, Donald (novelist); Philadelphia (1931-1989)
Barthelmess, Richard (actor); New York City (1897-1963)
Bartholomew, Freddie (actor); London (1924-1992)
Bartók, Béla (composer); Nagyszentmiklos (Hungary, now Romania) (1881-1945)
Barton, Clara (founder of American Red Cross); Oxford, Mass. (1821-1912)
Baruch, Bernard Mannes (statesman); Camden, S.C. (1870-1965)
Baryshnikov, Mikhail Nikolayevich (ballet dancer, artistic director); Riga, Latvia, 1/27/48
Basehart, Richard (actor); Zanesville, Ohio (1914-1984)
Basie, Count (William) (band leader); Red Bank, N.J. (1904-1984)
Basinger, Kim (actress); Athens, Ga., 12/8/53
Bassett, Angela (actress); New York City, 8/16/58
Bassey, Shirley (singer); Cardiff, Wales, 1/8/37
Batchelor, Clarence Daniel (political cartoonist); Osage City, Kan. (1888-1977)
Bateman, Jason (actor); Rye, N.Y. 1/14/69
Bateman, Justine (actress); Rye, N.Y., 2/19/66
Bates, Alan (actor); Allestree, England, 2/17/34
Bates, Kathy (Kathleen Doyle Bates) (actress); Memphis, Tenn., 6/28/48
Battle, Kathleen (soprano); Portsmouth, Ohio, 8/13/48
Baudelaire, Charles Pierre (poet); Paris (1821-1867)
Baxter, Anne (actress); Michigan City, Ind. (1923-1985)
Baxter, Meredith (actress); Los Angeles, 6/21/47
Bean, Orson (Dallas Frederick Burrows) (actor); Burlington, Vt., 7/22/28
Beardsley, Aubrey Vincent (illustrator); Brighton, England (1872-1898)
Beaton, Cecil (photographer, designer); London (1904-1980)

Botticelli, Sandro (Alessandro di Mariano dei Filipepi) (painter); Florence, Italy **(1444?-1510)**
Bottoms, Timothy (actor); Santa Barbara, Calif., 8/30/50
Boulez, Pierre (conductor); Montbrison, France, 3/26/25
Bourke-White, Margaret (photographer); New York City **(1906-1971)**
Boutros–Ghali, Boutros (Secretary General of the U.N.); Cairo, Egypt, 11/14/22
Bow, Clara (actress); Brooklyn, N.Y. **(1905-1965)**
Bowen, Catherine Drinker (biographer); Haverford, Pa. **(1897-1973)**
Bowes, Edward (radio show director); San Francisco **(1874-1946)**
Bowie, David (David Robert Jones) (actor, musician); London, 1/8/47(?)
Bowie, James (soldier); Burke County, Ga. **(1799-1836)**
Bowles, Chester (diplomat); Springfield, Mass. **(1901-1986)**
Boxleitner, Bruce (actor); Elgin, Ill., 5/12/50
Boyce, William (composer); London? **(1710-1779)**
Boyd, Bill (William) ("Hopalong Cassidy") (actor); Cambridge, Ohio **(1898-1972)**
Boyd, Stephen (Stephen Millar) (actor); Belfast, Northern Ireland **(1928-1977)**
Boyer, Charles (actor); Figeac, France **(1899-1978)**
Boy George (George Alan O'Dowd) (singer); London, 1961
Boyle, Peter (actor); Philadelphia, 10/18/33
Boyle, Robert (scientist); Lismore Castle, Munster, Ireland **(1627-1691)**
Bracken, Eddie (actor); Astoria, Queens, N.Y., 2/7/20
Bradbury, Ray Douglas (science-fiction writer); Waukegan, Ill., 8/22/20
Bradlee, Benjamin C. (editor); Boston, 8/26/21
Bradley, Ed (broadcast journalist); Philadelphia, Pa., 6/22/41
Bradley, Omar N. (5-star general); Clark, Mo. **(1893-1981)**
Bradley, Thomas (mayor of Los Angeles); Calvert, Tex., 12/29/17
Brady, Mathew (early photographer); Warren Co., N.Y. **(c. 1823–1896)**
Brahe, Tycho (astronomer); Knudstrup, Denmark **(1546-1601)**
Brahms, Johannes (composer); Hamburg **(1833-1897)**
Braille, Louis (teacher of blind); Coupvray, France **(1809-1862)**
Brailowsky, Alexander (pianist); Kiev, Ukraine **(1896-1976)**
Bramante, Donato D'Agnolo (architect); Monte Asdrualdo (now Fermignano, Italy) **(1444-1514)**
Brancusi, Constantin (sculptor); Pestisani, Romania **(1876-1957)**
Brando, Marlon (actor); Omaha, Neb., 4/3/24
Brandt, Willy (Herbert Frahm) (ex-Chancellor); Lübeck, Germany **(1913-1992)**
Braque, Georges (painter); Argenteuil, France **(1882-1963)**
Brazelton, T(homas) Berry II (pediatrician, writer); Waco, Tex., 5/10/18
Brazzi, Rossano (actor); Bologna, Italy **(1916–1994)**
Brecht, Bertolt (dramatist, poet); Augsburg, Bavaria **(1898-1956)**
Brel, Jacques (singer, composer); Brussels **(1929-1978)**
Brennan, Walter (actor); Lynn, Mass. **(1894-1974)**
Breslin, Jimmy (journalist); Jamaica, Queens, N.Y., 10/17/30
Breton, André (writer); Tinchebray, France **(1896–1966)**
Breuer, Marcel (architect, designer); Pécs, Hungary **(1902-1981)**
Brewster, Kingman, Jr. (ex-president of Yale); Longmeadow, Mass. **(1919-1988)**
Brezhnev, Leonid I. (Communist Party Secretary); Dneprodzerzhinsk, Ukraine **(1906-1982)**
Brice, Fanny (Fannie Borach) (comedienne); New York City **(1892-1951)**
Bridges, Beau (actor); Los Angeles, 12/9/41
Bridges, Jeff (actor); Los Angeles, 12/4/49
Bridges, Lloyd (actor); San Leandro, Calif. 1/15/13
Brinkley, David (TV newscaster); Wilmington, N.C., 7/10/20
Britten, Benjamin (composer); Lowestoft, England **(1913-1976)**
Brodsky, Joseph Alexandrovitch (poet); St. Petersburg, Russia **(1940–1996)**
Brody, Jane (journalist); Brooklyn, N.Y., 5/19/41
Brokaw, Tom (TV newscaster); Webster, S.D., 2/6/40
Brolin, James (actor); Los Angeles, 7/18/40
Bromfield, Louis (novelist); Mansfield, Ohio **(1896-1956)**
Bronson, Charles (Charles Buchinsky) (actor); Ehrenfield, Pa., 11/3/22(?)
Brontë, Charlotte (novelist); Thornton, England **(1816-1855)**
Brontë, Emily Jane (novelist); Thornton, England **(1818-1848)**
Bronzino, Agnolo (painter); Monticelli (Italy) **(1503-1572)**
Brook, Peter (director); London, 3/21/25
Brooke, Rupert (poet); Rugby, England **(1887-1915)**
Brooks, Geraldine (Geraldine Stroock) (actress); New York City **(1925-1977)**
Brooks, Gwendolyn (poet); Topeka, Kan., 6/7/17
Brooks, Mel (Melvin Kaminsky) (writer, film director); Brooklyn, N.Y., 1926(?)
Brosnan, Pierce (actor); County Meath, Ireland, 5/16/52
Brothers, Joyce (Bauer) (psychologist, author, radio-TV personality); New York City, 1927(?)
Broun, Matthew Heywood Campbell (journalist); Brooklyn, N.Y. **(1888-1939)**
Brown, Charles Brockden (novelist); Philadelphia **(1771-1810)**
Brown, Helen Gurley (author); Green Forest, Ark., 2/18/22

Brown, James (singer); Augusta, Ga., 5/3/34
Brown, Joe E. (comedian); Holgate, Ohio **(1892-1973)**
Brown, John (abolitionist); Torrington, Conn. **(1800-1859)**
Brown, John Mason (critic); Louisville, Ky. **(1900-1969)**
Brown, Les (band leader); Reinerton, Pa., 1912
Brown, Margaret Wise (children's author); Brooklyn, N.Y. **(1910–1952)**
Browne, Jackson (singer, guitarist); Heidelberg, Germany, 10/9/48
Browning, Elizabeth Barrett (poet); Durham, England **(1806-1861)**
Browning, Robert (poet); London **(1812-1889)**
Brubeck, Dave (musician); Concord, Calif., 12/6/20
Bruce, Lenny (comedian); Long Island, N.Y. **(1926-1966)**
Bruce, Nigel (actor); Ensenada, Mexico **(1895-1953)**
Brueghel, Pieter (painter; nr. Breda, Flanders (Netherlands) **(1520?-1569)**
Bruhn, Erik (Belton Evers) (ballet dancer); Copenhagen **(1928-1986)**
Brunelleschi, Filippo (architect); Florence, Italy **(1377-1446)**
Bruno, Giordano (philosopher); Nola, Italy **(1548-1600)**
Brutus, Marcus Junius (Roman politician); **(85?-42** B.C.**)**
Bryan, William Jennings (orator, politician); Salem, Ill. **(1860-1925)**
Bryant, Anita (singer); Barnsdall, Okla., 3/25/40
Bryant, William Cullen (poet, editor); Cummington, Mass. **(1794-1878)**
Brynner, Yul (Taidje Khan) (actor); Sakhalin Island, Russia **(1920-1985)**
Brzezinski, Zbigniew (ex-presidential adviser); Warsaw, 3/28/28
Buber, Martin (philosopher, theologian); Vienna **(1878-1965)**
Buchanan, Edgar (actor); Humansville, Mo. **(1903-1979)**
Buchanan, Pat (politician); Washington, D.C., 11/2/38
Buchholz, Horst (actor); Berlin, 12/4/33
Büchner, Georg (dramatist); Goddelau, Germany **(1813–1837)**
Buchwald, Art (Arthur) (columnist); Mount Vernon, N.Y., 10/20/25
Buck, Pearl S(ydenstricker) (author); Hillsboro, W. Va. **(1892-1973)**
Buckley, William F., Jr. (journalist); New York City, 11/24/25
Buddha. *See* Gautama Buddha
Buffalo Bill (William Frederick Cody) (scout); Scott County, Iowa **(1846-1917)**
Bujold, Genevieve (actress); Montreal, 7/1/42
Bujones, Fernando (ballet dancer); Miami, Fla., 3/9/55
Bulgakov, Mikhail (novelist); Kiev, Ukraine **(1891–1940)**
Bullins, Ed (playwright); Philadelphia, 7/2/35
Bullock, Jim J. (actor); Casper, Wyom., 2/9/?
Bumbry, Grace (mezzo-soprano); St. Louis, 1/4/37
Bunche, Ralph J. (statesman); Detroit **(1904-1971)**
Bundy, McGeorge (educator); Boston, 3/30/19
Bundy, William Putnam (editor); Washington, D.C., 9/24/17
Buñuel, Luis (film director); Calanda, Spain **(1900-1983)**
Bunyan, John (preacher, author); Elstow, England **(1628-1688)**
Burbank, Luther (horticulturist); Lancaster, Mass. **(1849-1926)**
Burke, Adm. Arleigh A. (ex-Chief of Naval Operations); Boulder, Colo. **(1901–1996)**
Burke, Billie (actress, comedienne); Washington, D.C. **(1885-1970)**
Burke, Delta (actress); Orlando, Fla., 7/30/56
Burke, Edmund (statesman); Dublin **(1729-1797)**
Burne-Jones, Edward Coley (painter); Birmingham, England **(1833-1898)**
Burnett, Carol (comedienne); San Antonio, 4/26/33
Burney, Fanny (Frances) (writer); King's Lynn, England **(1752-1840)**
Burns, George (Nathan Birnbaum) (comedian); New York City **(1896-1996)**
Burns, Ken (documentary filmmaker); Brooklyn, N.Y., 7/29/53
Burns, Robert (poet); Alloway, Scotland **(1759-1796)**
Burr, Aaron (political leader); Newark, N.J. **(1756-1836)**
Burr, Raymond (William Stacey Burr) (actor); New Westminster, British Columbia, Canada **(1917–1993)**
Burroughs, Edgar Rice (novelist); Chicago **(1875-1950)**
Burrows, Abe (playwright, director); New York City **(1910-1985)**
Burstyn, Ellen (Edna Rae Gillooly) (actress); Detroit, 12/7/32
Burton, LeVar (actor); Landsthul, Germany, 2/16/57
Burton, Richard (Richard Jenkins) (actor); Pontrhydfen, Wales **(1925-1984)**
Burton, Tim (filmmaker); Burbank, Calif., 1958
Butkus, Dick (actor); Chicago, 12/9/42
Butler, Samuel (author); Langar, England **(1835-1902)**
Butterworth, Charles (actor); South Bend, Ind. **(1896-1946)**
Buttons, Red (Aaron Chwatt) (actor); New York City, 2/5/19
Buzzi, Ruth (comedienne); Wequetequock, Conn., 7/24/36
Byrd, Richard Evelyn (polar explorer); Winchester, Va. **(1888-1957)**
Byron, George Gordon (6th Baron Byron) (poet); London **(1788-1824)**

C

Caan, James (actor); The Bronx, N.Y., 3/26/39
Caballé, Montserrat (soprano); Barcelona, Spain, 4/12/33
Cabot, John (Giovanni Caboto) (navigator); Genoa (?) **(1450-1498)**
Cabot, Sebastian (navigator); Venice **(1476?-1557)**
Cadmus, Paul (painter, etcher); New York City, 12/17/04

Caesar, Gaius Julius (statesman); Rome **(100?-44 B.C.)**
Caesar, Sid (comedian); Yonkers, N.Y., 9/8/22
Cage, Nicholas (Nicolas Coppola) (actor); Long Beach, Calif., 1/7/64
Cagney, James (actor); New York City **(1899-1986)**
Cahn, Sammy (songwriter); New York City **(1913-1993)**
Caine, Michael (Maurice J. Micklewhite) (actor); London, 3/14/33
Calder, Alexander (sculptor); Lawnton, Pa. **(1898-1976)**
Calderón del al Barca, Pedro (dramatist); Madrid **(1600-1681)**
Caldwell, Erskine (novelist); White Oak, Ga. **(1903-1987)**
Caldwell, Sarah (opera director, conductor); Maryville, Mo., 1928
Caldwell, Taylor (novelist); Manchester, England **(1900-1985)**
Caldwell, Zoe (actress); Hawthorn, Australia, 9/14/33
Calhern, Louis (Carl Henry Vogt) (actor); Brooklyn, N.Y. **(1895-1956)**
Calhoun, John Caldwell (statesman); nr. Calhoun Mills, S.C. **(1782-1850)**
Calisher, Hortense (novelist); New York City, 12/20/11
Callas, Maria (Maria Calogeropoulos) (dramatic soprano); New York City **(1923-1977)**
Calloway, Cab (Cabell) (band leader); Rochester, N.Y. **(1907—1994)**
Calvin, John (Jean Chauvin) (religious reformer); Noyon, Picardy **(1509-1564)**
Cambridge, Godfrey (comedian); New York City **(1933-1976)**
Cameron, Rod (Rod Cox) (actor); Calgary, Alberta, Canada **(1912-1983)**
Campbell, Glen (singer); nr. Delight, Ark., 4/22/38
Campbell, Joseph (writer); New York City **(1904—1987)**
Campbell, Mrs. Patrick (Beatrice Stella Tanner) (actress); London **(1865-1940)**
Camus, Albert (author); Mondovi, Algeria **(1913-1960)**
Canaletto, (Giovanni Antonio Canale); (painter) Venice **(1697-1768)**
Candy, John (actor, comedian); Toronto, Ont., Canada **(1950—1994)**
Caniff, Milton (cartoonist); Hillsboro, Ohio **(1907-1988)**
Cannon, Dyan (actress); Tacoma, Wash., 1/4/37
Canova, Judy (comedienne); Jacksonville, Fla. **(1916-1983)**
Cantinflas (Mario Moreno) (comedian); Mexico City **(1911-1993)**
Cantor, Eddie (Edward Iskowitz) (actor); New York City **(1892-1964)**
Capone, Al(fonse) (gangster); Naples, Italy **(1899—1947)**
Capote, Truman (novelist); New Orleans **(1924-1984)**
Capp, Al (Alfred Gerald Caplin) (cartoonist); New Haven, Conn. **(1909-1979)**
Capra, Frank (film producer, dramatist); Palermo, Italy **(1897—1991)**
Caputo, Phil (Philip Joseph) (author, journalist); Chicago, 6/10/41
Caravaggio, Michelangelo Merisi da (painter); Caravaggio (Italy) **(1573-1610)**
Cardin, Pierre (fashion designer); nr. Venice, 7/7/22
Cardinale, Claudia (actress); Tunis, Tunisia, 1939
Carey, Harry (actor); New York City **(1878-1947)**
Carey, Macdonald (actor); Sioux City, Iowa **(1913–1994)**
Carlin, George (comedian); Bronx, N.Y., 5/12/37
Carlisle, Kitty (singer, actress); New Orleans, 9/3/15
Carlyle, Thomas (essayist, historian); Ecclefechan, Scotland **(1795-1881)**
Carmichael, Hoagy (Hoagland Howard) (songwriter); Bloomington, Ind. **(1899-1981)**
Carne, Judy (Joyce Botterill) (singer); Northampton, England, 1939
Carnegie, Andrew (industrialist); Dunfermline, Scotland **(1835-1919)**
Carney, Art (actor); Mt. Vernon, N.Y., 11/4/18
Caron, Leslie (actress); Paris, 7/1/31
Carr, Vikki (singer); El Paso, 7/19/42
Carracci, Annibale (painter); Bologna, Italy **(1560-1609)**
Carracci, Lodovico (painter); Bologna, Italy **(1555-1619)**
Carradine, David (actor); Hollywood, Calif., 12/8/36
Carradine, John (actor); New York City **(1906-1988)**
Carradine, Keith (actor); San Mateo, Calif., 8/8/49
Carreras, José (tenor); Barcelona, Spain, 12/5/46
Carroll, Diahann (Carol Diahann Johnson) (singer, actress); Bronx, N.Y., 7/17/35
Carroll, Leo G. (actor); Weedon, England **(1892-1972)**
Carroll, Lewis (Charles Lutwidge Dodgson) (author, mathematician); Daresbury, England **(1832-1898)**
Carson, Jack (actor); Carmen, Man., Canada **(1910-1963)**
Carson, Johnny (entertainer); Corning, Iowa, 10/23/25
Carson, Kit (Christopher) (scout); Madison County, Ky. **(1809-1868)**
Carson, Rachel (biologist); Springdale, Pa. **(1907-1964)**
Carter, Dixie (actress); McLemoresville, Tenn., 5/25/39
Carter, Jack (comedian); New York City, 1923
Carter, Lynda (actress); Phoenix, Ariz., 7/24/51
Cartier, Jacques (explorer); Saint-Malo, Brittany (France) **(1491-1557)**
Cartier-Brisson, Henri (photographer); Chanteloup, France, 8/22/08
Cartland, Barbara (author); England, 7/9/01
Caruso, Enrico (Errico) (tenor); Naples, Italy **(1873-1921)**
Carver, George Washington (botanist); Diamond Grove, Mo. **(1864-1943)**
Cary, Arthur Joyce Lunel (novelist); Londonderry, Ireland **(1888-1957)**
Casals, Pablo (cellist); Vendrell, Spain **(1876-1973)**
Casanova de Seingalt, Giovanni Jacopo (adventurer); Venice **(1725-1798)**
Cash, Johnny (singer); nr. Kingsland, Ark., 2/26/32
Cass, Peggy (comedienne); Boston, 5/21/24

Cassatt, Mary (painter); Allegheny, Pa. **(1844-1926)**
Cassavetes, John (actor, director); New York City **(1929-1989)**
Cassidy, David (singer); New York City, 4/12/50
Cassidy, Jack (actor); Richmond Hill, Queens, N.Y. **(1927-1976)**
Cassidy, Shaun (actor); Los Angeles, 9/27/58
Cassini, Oleg (Oleg Lolewski-Cassini) (fashion designer); Paris, 4/11/13
Castagno, Andrea del (painter); San Martino a Corella (Italy) **(c.1421-1457)**
Castellano, Richard (actor); New York City **(1934-1988)**
Castle, Irene (Irene Foote) (actress, dancer); New Rochelle, N.Y. **(1893-1969)**
Castle, Vernon Blythe (dancer, aviator); Norwich, England **(1887-1918)**
Castro Ruz, Fidel (Premier); Mayari, Oriente, Cuba, 8/13/26
Cather, Willa Sibert (novelist); Winchester, Va. **(1876-1947)**
Cato, Marcus Porcius (called Cato the Elder) (statesman); Tusculum (Italy) **(234-149 B.C.)**
Catt, Carrie Chapman Lane (woman suffragist); Ripon, Wis. **(1859-1947)**
Catton, Bruce (historian); Petoskey, Mich. **(1899-1978)**
Catullus, Gaius Valerius (poet); Verona **(c. 84–c. 54 B.C.)**
Cavallaro, Carmen (band leader); New York City **(1913-1989)**
Cavett, Dick (Richard) (TV entertainer); Gibbon, Neb., 11/19/36
Ceausescu, Nicolae (Romanian head of state); Scornicesti, Romania **(1918–1989)**
Céline, Louis Ferdinand (pseud. of Louis Fuch Destouches) (novelist); Paris **(1894—1961)**
Cellini, Benvenuto (goldsmith, sculptor); Florence, Italy **(1500-1571)**
Cervantes Saavedra, Miguel de (novelist); Alcalá de Henares, Spain **(1547-1616)**
Cézanne, Paul (painter); Aix-en-Provence, France **(1839-1906)**
Chagall, Marc (painter); Vitebsk, Russia, **(1887-1985)**
Chaliapin, Feodor Ivanovitch (operatic basso); Kazan, Russia **(1873-1938)**
Chamberlain, Arthur Neville (statesman); Edgbaston, England **(1869-1940)**
Chamberlain, Richard (actor); Los Angeles, 3/31/35(?)
Champion, Gower (choreographer); Geneva, Ill. **(1921-1980)**
Champion, Marge (actress, dancer); Los Angeles, 9/2/23
Champlain, Samuel de (explorer); nr. Rochefort, France **(1567?-1635)**
Chancellor, John (TV commentator); Chicago **(1927–1996)**
Chandler, Jeff (actor); Brooklyn, N.Y. **(1918-1961)**
Chandler, Raymond (writer); Chicago **(1883-1959)**
Chanel, "Coco" (Gabriel Bonheur) (fashion designer); Issoire, France **(1883-1971)**
Chaney, Lon (actor); Colorado Springs, Colo. **(1883-1930)**
Channing, Carol (actress); Seattle, 1/31/23
Channing, Stockard (actress); New York City, 2/13/44
Chaplin, Geraldine (actress); Santa Monica, Calif., 7/31/44
Chaplin, Sir Charles (actor); London **(1889-1977)**
Charisse, Cyd (Tula Finklea) (dancer, actress); Amarillo, Tex., 3/8/23
Charlemagne (Holy Roman Emperor); birthplace unknown **(742-814)**
Charles, Ray (Ray Charles Robinson) (pianist, singer, songwriter); Albany Ga., 9/23/30
Charo (Maria Rosario Pilar Martinez) (actress); Murcia, Spain 1/15/51
Chase, Chevy (Cornelius Crane Chase) (comedian); New York City, 10/8/43
Chase, Lucia (founder Ballet Theatre [now American Ballet Theatre]); Waterbury, Conn. **(1907-1986)**
Chateaubriand, François René de (writer, statesman); St. Malo, France **(1768–1848)**
Chaucer, Geoffrey (poet); London **(1340?-1400)**
Chávez, Carlos (composer); nr. Mexico City **(1899-1978)**
Chavez, Cesar (labor leader); nr. Yuma, Ariz. **(1927-1993)**
Chayefsky, Paddy (Sidney) (playwright); New York City **(1923-1981)**
Checker, Chubby (Ernest Evans) (performer); Philadelphia, 10/3/41
Cheever, John (novelist); Quincy, Mass. **(1912-1982)**
Chekhov, Anton Pavlovich (dramatist, short-story writer); Taganrog, Russia **(1860-1904)**
Cher (Cherilyn LaPiere) (actress, singer); El Centro, Calif., 5/20/46
Cherubini, Luigi (composer); Florence **(1760-1842)**
Chesterton, Gilbert Keith (author); Kensington, England **(1874-1936)**
Chestnutt, Charles Waddell (author); Cleveland, Ohio **(1858–1932)**
Chevalier, Maurice (entertainer); Paris **(1888-1972)**
Chiang Kai-shek (Chief of State); Feng-hwa, China **(1887-1975)**
Child, Julia (food expert); Pasadena, Calif., 8/15/12
Chippendale, Thomas (cabinet-maker); Otley, England **(1718?-1779)**
Chirico, Giorgio de (painter); Vólos, Greece **(1888-1978)**
Chisholm, Shirley Anita St. Hill (U.S. Representative); Brooklyn, N.Y. 11/30/24
Chomsky, (Avram) Noam (linguist, educator, activist); Philadelphia, 12/7/28
Chopin, Frédéric François (composer); nr. Warsaw **(1810-1849)**
Chopin, Kate O'Flaherty (author); St. Louis, Mo. **(1851–1904)**
Chou En-lai. *See* Zhou Enlai
Christie, Agatha (mystery writer); Torquay, England **(1890-1976)**

Christie, Julie (actress); Chukua, India, 4/14/41

Christopher, Warren M. (U.S. Secretary of State); Scranton, N.D., 10/27/25

Chung, Connie (broadcast journalist); Washington, D.C., 8/20/46

Churchill, Sir Winston Leonard Spencer (statesman); Blenheim Palace, Oxfordshire, England (1874-1965)

Cicero, Marcus Tullius (orator, statesman); Arpinum (Italy) (106-43 B.C.)

Cid, El (Rodrigo (or Ruy) Díez de Bivar) (Spanish national hero); nr. Burgos, Spain (1040?-1099)

Cilento, Diane (actress); Queensland, Australia, 10/5/33

Cimabue, Giovanni (painter); Florence, Italy (c.1240-c.1302)

Cimino, Michael (film director); New York City, 1943(?)

Clair, René (René Chomette) (film director); Paris (1898-1981)

Clapton, Eric (singer, guitarist); Ripley, England, 3/30/45

Clark, Dick (TV personality); Mt. Vernon, N.Y., 11/30/29

Clark, Mark W. (general); Madison Barracks, N.Y. (1896-1984)

Clark, Mary Higgins (writer); New York City, 12/24/29

Clark, Petula (singer); Epsom, England, 11/15/34

Clark, Roy (country music artist); Meherrin, Va., 4/15/33

Clark, William (explorer); Caroline County, Va. (1770-1838)

Clarke, Arthur C. (science fiction writer); Minehead, England, 12/16/17

Clary, Robert (actor); Paris, France, 3/1/26

Claude Lorrain (Claude Gellée) (painter); Champagne, France (1600-1682)

Clausewitz, Karl von (military strategist); Burg (East Germany) (1780-1831)

Clay, Henry (statesman); Hanover County, Va. (1777-1852)

Clay, Lucius D. (banker, ex-general); Marietta, Ga. (1897-1978)

Clayburgh, Jill (actress); New York City, 4/30/44

Cleary, Beverly (Beverly Atlee Bunn) (children's author); McMinnville, Ore., 1916

Cleaver, Eldridge (Leroy) (author, activist); Wabbaseka, Ark., 1935

Cleese, John (writer, actor); Weston-super-Mare, England, 10/27/39

Clemenceau, Georges (statesman); Mouilleron-en-Pareds, Vondée, France (1841-1929)

Clemens, Samuel L. *See* Mark Twain

Cleopatra (Queen of Egypt); Alexandria, Egypt (69-30 B.C.)

Cliburn, Van (Harvey Lavan Cliburn, Jr.) (concert pianist); Shreveport, La., 7/12/34

Clift, Montgomery (actor); Omaha, Neb. (1920-1966)

Cline, Patsy (singer); Winchester, Va. (1933-1963)

Clooney, Rosemary (singer); Maysville, Ky., 5/23/28

Close, Glenn (actress); Greenwich, Conn., 3/19/47

Clurman, Harold (stage producer); New York City (1901-1980)

Cobb, Irvin Shrewsbury (humorist); Paducah, Ky. (1876-1944)

Cobb, Lee J. (Leo Jacob) (actor); New York City (1911-1976)

Coburn, Charles Douville (actor); Savannah, Ga. (1877-1961)

Coburn, James (actor); Laurel, Neb., 8/31/28

Coca, Imogene (comedienne); Philadelphia, 11/18/08

Cocker, Joe (John Robert Cocker) (singer); Sheffield, England, 5/20/44

Coco, James (actor); New York City (1929-1987)

Cocteau, Jean (author); Maison-Lafitte, France (1891-1963)

Cody, W. F. *See* Buffalo Bill

Cohan, George Michael (actor, dramatist); Providence, R.I. (1878-1942)

Cohn, Mindy (actress); Los Angeles, 5/20/66

Colbert, Claudette (Lily Chauchoin) (actress); Paris (1903-1996)

Cole, Nat "King" (singer); Montgomery, Ala. (1919-1965)

Cole, Natalie (singer); Los Angeles, 2/6/50

Cole, Thomas (painter); Lancashire, England (1801-1848)

Coleman, Dabney (actor); Corpus Christi, Tex., 1/2/32

Coleman, Gary (actor); Zion, Ill., 2/8/68

Coleridge, Samuel Taylor (poet); Ottery St. Mary, England (1772-1834)

Colette (Sidonie-Gabrielle Colette) (novelist); St.-Sauveur, France (c.1873-1954)

Collingwood, Charles (TV commentator); Three Rivers, Mich. (1917-1985)

Collins, Joan (actress); London 5/23/33

Collins, Judy (singer); Seattle, 5/1/39

Colman, Ronald (actor); Richmond, England (1891-1958)

Colonna, Jerry (comedian); Boston (1905-1986)

Coltrane, John (jazz musician); Hamlet, N.C. (1926-1967)

Columbo, Russ (singer, bandleader); San Francisco (1908-1934)

Columbus, Christopher (Cristoforo Colombo) (explorer); Genoa (Italy) (1451-1506)

Comden, Betty (writer); New York City, 5/3/19

Comenius, Johann Amos (educational reformer); Nivnice, Moravia (Czech Republic) (1592-1670)

Commager, Henry Steele (historian); Pittsburgh, 10/25/02

Como, Perry (Pierino) (singer); Canonsburg, Pa., 5/18/12

Compton, Karl Taylor (physicist); Wooster, Ohio (1887-1954)

Comte, Auguste (philosopher); Montpellier, France (1798-1857)

Conant, James B. (educator, statesman); Dorchester, Mass. (1893-1978)

Condon, Eddie (jazz musician); Goodland, Ind. (1905-1973)

Confucius (K'ung Fu-tzu) (philosopher); Shantung province, China (c.551-479 B.C.)

Congreve, William (dramatist); nr. Leeds, England (1670-1729)

Connelly, Marc (playwright); McKeesport, Pa. (1890-1980)

Connery, Sean (actor); Edinburgh, Scotland, 8/25/30

Conniff, Ray (band leader); Attleboro, Mass., 11/6/16

Connors, Chuck (actor); Brooklyn, N.Y. (1921-1992)

Connors, Mike (Krekor Ohanian) (actor); Fresno, Calif., 8/15/25

Conrad, Joseph (Teodor Jozef Konrad Korzeniowski) (novelist); Berdichev, Ukraine (1857-1924)

Conrad, Robert (Conrad Robert Falk) (actor); Chicago, 3/1/35

Conrad, William (actor); Louisville, Ky. (1920-1994)

Conried, Hans (Frank Foster) (actor); Baltimore (1915-1982)

Conroy, Pat (author); Atlanta, Ga., 10/26/45

Constable, John (painter); East Bergholt, Suffolk, England (1776-1837)

Constantine II (ex-king); Athens, 6/2/40

Constantine, Michael (actor); Reading, Pa., 5/22/27

Conte, Richard (actor); New York City (1916-1975)

Conti, Tom (actor); Paisley, Scotland, 11/22/41

Convy, Bert (actor, host); St. Louis, Mo. (1933-1991)

Conway, Tim (comedian); Chagrin Falls, Ohio, 12/15/33

Coogan, Jackie (actor); Los Angeles (1914-1984)

Cook, Peter (actor, writer); Torquay, England (1937-1995)

Cooke, Alistair (Alfred Alistair); (TV narrator, journalist); Manchester, England, 11/20/08

Cooley, Denton A(rthur) (heart surgeon); Houston, Tex., 8/22/20

Coolidge, Rita (singer); Nashville, Tenn., 1944

Cooper, Alice (Vincent Furnier) (rock musician); Detroit, 2/4/48

Cooper, Gary (Frank James Cooper) (actor); Helena, Mont. (1901-1961)

Cooper, Dame Gladys (actress); Lewisham, England (1898-1971)

Cooper, Jackie (actor, director); Los Angeles, 9/15/22

Cooper, James Fenimore (novelist); Burlington, N.J. (1789-1851)

Cooper, Peter (industrialist, philanthropist); New York City (1791-1883)

Copernicus, Nicolaus (Mikolaj Kopernik) (astronomer); Thorn, Poland (1473-1543)

Copland, Aaron (composer); Brooklyn, N.Y. (1900-1990)

Copley, John Singleton (painter); Boston, Mass. (1738-1815)

Copperfield, David (illusionist); Matuchen, N.J., 9/16/56

Coppola, Francis Ford (film director); Detroit, 4/7/39

Corelli, Arcangelo (composer); Fusignano, Italy (1653-1713)

Corelli, Franco (operatic tenor); Ancona, Italy, 4/8/23

Corneille, Pierre (dramatist); Rouen, France (1606-1684)

Cornell, Katharine (actress); Berlin (1893-1974)

Coret, Jean Baptiste Camille (painter); Paris (1796-1875)

Correggio, Antonio Allegri da (painter); Correggio (Italy) (1494-1534)

Corsaro, Frank (opera director); New York harbor, 12/22/24

Cortés (or Cortez), Hernando (explorer); Medellin, Spain (1485-1547)

Cosby, Bill (actor); Philadelphia, 7/12/37

Cosell, Howard (Howard Cohen) (sportscaster); Winston-Salem, N.C. (1918-1995)

Costa-Gavras, Henri (Kostantinos Gavras) (film director); Athens, 1933

Costello, Elvis (Declan Patrick McManus) (singer, musician, songwriter); London, 1954

Costello, Lou (comedian); Paterson, N.J. (1908-1959)

Costner, Kevin (actor); Los Angeles, 1/18/55

Cotten, Joseph (actor); Petersburg, Va. (1905-1994)

Couperin, François (composer); Paris (1668-1733)

Courbet, Gustave (painter); Ornans, France (1819-1877)

Courtenay, Tom (actor); Hull, England, 2/25/37

Cousins, Norman (publisher); Union Hill, N.J. (1915-1990)

Cousteau, Jacques-Yves (marine explorer); St. André-de-Cubzac, France, 6/11/10

Coward, Sir Noel (playwright, actor); Teddington, England (1899-1973)

Cowles, Gardner, Jr. (newspaper publisher); Algona, Iowa (1903-1985)

Cowper, William (poet); Great Berkhamstead, England (1731-1800)

Cox, Archibald (Watergate prosecutor); Plainfield, N.J., 5/17/12

Cox, Wally (actor); Detroit, Mich. (1924-1973)

Cozzens, James Gould (novelist); Chicago (1903-1978)

Crabbe, Buster (Clarence) (actor); Oakland, Calif. (1908-1983)

Cranach, Lucas, the elder (painter); Kronach (Germany) (1472-1553)

Crane, Hart (poet); Garrettsville, Ohio (1899-1932)

Crane, Stephen (novelist, poet); Newark, N.J. (1871-1900)

Cranmer, Thomas (churchman); Aslacton, England (1489-1556)

Crawford, Broderick (actor); Philadelphia (1911-1986)

Crawford, Cheryl (stage producer); Akron, Ohio (1902-1986)

Crawford, Joan (Lucille LeSueur) (actress, business executive); San Antonio (1908-1977)

Crazy Horse (Lakota Indian leader); nr. Bear Butte (S.D.) (1840?-1877)

Crenna, Richard (actor); Los Angeles, 11/30/27

Crespin, Régine (operatic soprano); Marseilles, France, 2/23/29

Crichton, (John) Michael (novelist); Chicago, 10/23/42

Crisp, Donald (actor); London (1880-1974)

Croce, Benedetto (philosopher); Peseasseroli, Aquila, Italy (1866-1952)

Croce, Jim (singer); Philadelphia (1942-1973)

Crockett, Davy (David) (frontiersman); Greene County, Tenn. (1786-1836)

Cromwell, Oliver (statesman); Huntingdon, England **(1599-1658)**
Cronin, A. J. (Archibald J. Cronin) (novelist); Cardross, Scotland **(1896-1981)**
Cronkite, Walter (TV newscaster); St. Joseph, Mo., 11/4/16
Cronyn, Hume (actor); London, Ontario, Canada, 7/18/11
Crosby, Bing (Harry Lillis) (singer, actor); Tacoma, Wash. **(1904-1977)**
Crosby, Bob (musician); Spokane, Wash. **(1913-1993)**
Crosby, Cathy Lee (actress); Los Angeles, 12/2/48
Crosby, Norm (comedian); Boston, 9/15/27
Cross, Ben (Bernard) (actor); Paddington, England, 12/16/47
Cross, Milton (opera commentator); New York City **(1897-1975)**
Crouse, Russel (playwright); Findlay, Ohio **(1893-1966)**
Cruise, Tom (actor); Syracuse, N.Y., 7/3/62
Crystal, Billy (comedian, actor); Long Beach, L.I., N.Y., 3/14/47
Cugat, Xavier (band leader); Barcelona, Spain **(1900–1990)**
Cukor, George (film director); New York City **(1899-1983)**
Cullen, Bill (William Lawrence Cullen) (radio and TV entertainer); Pittsburgh **(1920-1990)**
Cullen, Countee (poet); New York City **(1903–1946)**
Culp, Robert (actor); Berkeley, Calif., 8/16/30
Cummings, E. E. (Edward Estlin Cummings) (poet); Cambridge, Mass. **(1894-1962)**
Cummings, Robert (actor); Joplin, Mo. **(1908–1990)**
Cunningham, Merce (choreographer); Centralia, Wash., 4/16/19
Curie, Marie (Marja Sklodowska) (physical chemist); Warsaw **(1867-1934)**
Curie, Pierre (physicist); Paris **(1859-1906)**
Curtin, Jane (actress); Cambridge, Mass., 9/6/47
Curtin, Phyllis (soprano); Clarksburg, W.Va., 12/3/27
Curtis, Jamie Lee (actress); Los Angeles, 11/22/58
Curtis, Tony (Bernard Schwartz) (actor); Bronx, N.Y., 6/3/25
Curzon, Clifford (concert pianist); London **(1907-1982)**
Custer, George Armstrong (army officer); New Rumley, Ohio **(1839-1876)**

D

da Gama, Vasco (explorer); Sines, Portugal **(1460-1524)**
Daguerre, Louis (photographic pioneer); nr. Paris **(1787-1851)**
Dahl, Arlene (actress); Minneapolis, 8/11/28
Dailey, Dan (actor, dancer); New York City **(1917-1978)**
Dale, Jim (actor, singer, songwriter); Rothwell, England, 8/15/35
Daley, Richard J. (Mayor of Chicago); Chicago **(1902-1976)**
Dali, Salvador (painter); Figueras, Spain **(1904-1989)**
Dalton, John (chemist); nr. Cockermouth, England **(1766-1844)**
Daly, Tyne (actress); Madison, Wis. 2/21/46
d'Amboise, Jacques (ballet dancer); Dedham, Mass., 7/28/34
Damone, Vic (Vito Farinola) (singer); Brooklyn, N.Y., 6/12/28
Damrosch, Walter Johannes (orchestra conductor); Breslau (Poland) **(1862-1950)**
Dana, Charles Anderson (editor); Hinsdale, N.H. **(1819-1897)**
Dandridge, Dorothy (actress); Cleveland **(1923-1965)**
Dangerfield, Rodney (comedian); Babylon, L.I., N.Y., 1921
Daniels, Bebe (Virginia Daniels) (actress); Dallas **(1901-1971)**
Daniels, William (actor); Brooklyn, N.Y., 3/31/27
Danilova, Alexandra (ballerina); Peterhof, Russia, 1/20/04
Dannay, Frederic (novelist, pseudonym Ellery Queen); Brooklyn, N.Y. **(1905-1982)**
Danner, Blythe (actress); Philadelphia, 1944(?)
D'Annunzio, Gabriele (soldier, author); Francaville at Mare, Pescara, Italy **(1863-1938)**
Danson, Ted (actor); San Diego, Calif., 12/29/47
Dante (or Durante) Alighieri (poet); Florence, Italy **(1265-1321)**
Danton, Georges Jacques (French Revolutionary leader); Arcis-sur-Aube, France **(1759-1794)**
Danza, Tony (actor); Brooklyn, N.Y., 4/21/51
Darnell, Linda (actress); Dallas **(1921-1965)**
Darren, James (actor); Philadelphia, 6/8/36
Darrow, Clarence Seward (lawyer); Kinsman, Ohio **(1857-1938)**
Darwell, Jane (actress); Palmyra, Mo. **(1879-1967)**
Darwin, Charles Robert (naturalist); Shrewsbury, England **(1809-1882)**
daSilva, Howard (actor); Cleveland **(1909-1986)**
Dassin, Jules (film director); Middletown, Conn., 12/18/11
Daumier, Honoré (caricaturist); Marseilles, France **(1808-1879)**
David, Jacques-Louis (painter); Paris **(1748-1825)**
David (King of Israel and Judah) (died c. 973 B.C.)
Davidson, John (singer, actor); Pittsburgh, 12/13/41
Davies, Marion (Marion Douras) (actress); New York City **(1898?-1961)**
Davies, (William) Robertson (writer); Thamesville, Ontario, Canada **(1913–1996)**
da Vinci, Leonardo (painter, scientist); Vinci, Tuscany (Italy) **(1452-1519)**
Davis, Angela (social activist); Birmingham, Ala., 1/26/44
Davis, Ann B. (actress); Schenectady, N.Y., 5/5/26
Davis, Lt. Gen. Benhamin O., Jr. (Air Force general); Washington,

D.C., 12/18/12
Davis, Brig. Gen. Benjamin O., Sr. (US Army general); Washington, D.C. **(1877–1970)**
Davis, Bette (actress); Lowell, Mass. **(1908-1989)**
Davis, Jefferson (President of the Confederacy); Christian (now Todd) County, Ky. **(1808-1889)**
Davis, Judy (actress); Perth, Australia, 1955
Davis, Mac (singer); Lubbock, Tex., 1/21/42
Davis, Miles (jazz trumpeter); Alton, Ill. **(1926-1991)**
Davis, Ossie (actor, writer); Cogdell, Ga., 12/18/17
Davis, Sammy, Jr. (actor, singer); New York City **(1925-1990)**
Davis, Skeeter (Mary Francis Penick) (singer); Dry Ridge, Ky., 12/30/31
Davis, Stuart (painter); Philadelphia **(1894-1964)**
Dawber, Pam (actress); Farmington Hills, Mich., 10/18/51
Dawson, Richard (actor, host); Gosport, Hampshire, England, 11/20/32
Day, Doris (Doris von Kappelhoff) (singer, actress); Cincinnati, 4/3/24
Dayan, Moshe (ex-Defense Minister of Israel); Dagania, Palestine **(1915-1981)**
Dean, James (actor); Marion, Ind. **(1931-1955)**
Dean, Jimmy (singer); Seth Ward, nr. Plainview, Tex., 8/10/28
De Bakey, Michael E. (heart surgeon); Lake Charles, La., 9/7/08
de Beauvoir, Simone (novelist, philosopher); Paris **(1908-1986)**
Debs, Eugene Victor (Socialist leader); Terre Haute, Ind. **(1855-1926)**
Debussy, Claude Achille (composer); St. Germain-en-Laye, France **(1862-1918)**
DeCamp, Rosemary (actress); Prescott, Ariz., 11/14/14(?)
De Carlo, Yvonne (Peggy Yvonne Middleton) (actress); Vancouver, B.C., Canada, 9/1/24
de Chirico, Giorgio (painter); Volos, Greece, **(1888-1978)**
Dee, Ruby (actress); Cleveland, Ohio, 10/27/23(?)
Dee, Sandra (Alexandra Zuck) (actress); Bayonne, N.J., 4/23/42
Defoe, Daniel (novelist); London **(1659?-1731)**
Degas, Hilaire Germain Edgar (painter); Paris **(1834-1917)**
de Gaulle, Charles André Joseph Marie (soldier, statesman); Lille, France **(1890-1970)**
de Havilland, Olivia (actress); Tokyo, 7/1/16
de Kooning, Willem (painter); Rotterdam, 4/24/04
Delacroix, Eugène (painter); Charenton-St. Maurice, France **(1798-1863)**
de la Renta, Oscar (fashion designer); Santo Domingo, Dominican Republic, 7/22/32
Delaunay, Robert (painter); Paris **(1885-1941)**
De Laurentiis, Dino (film producer); Torre Annunziata, Bay of Naples, Italy, 8/8/19
della Robbia, Andrea (sculptor) Florence **(1435-1525)**
della Robbia, Luca (sculptor); Florence **(1400-1482)**
Delon, Alain (actor); Sceaux, France, 11/8/35
DeLuise, Dom (comedian); Brooklyn, N.Y., 8/1/33
Demarest, William (actor); St. Paul **(1892-1983)**
de Mille, Agnes (choreographer); New York City **(1905–1993)**
De Mille, Cecil Blount (film director); Ashfield, Mass. **(1881-1959)**
Demosthenes (orator); Athens **(385?-322** B.C.)
Deneuve, Catherine (actress); Paris, 10/22/43
De Niro, Robert (actor); New York City, 8/17/43
Dennehy, Brian (actor); Bridgeport, Conn., 7/9/40
Denning, Richard (actor); Poughkeepsie, N.Y., 3/27/14
Dennis, Sandy (actress); Hastings, Neb. **(1937-1992)**
Denny, Reginald (actor); Richmond, England **(1891-1967)**
Denver, John (Henry John Deutschendorf, Jr.) (singer); Roswell, N.M., 12/31/43
De Palma, Brian (film director); Newark, N.J., 9/11/40
Derain, André (painter); Chatou, Seine-et-Oise, France **(1880-1954)**
Derek, John (actor, director); Los Angeles, 8/12/26
Dern, Bruce (actor); Chicago, 6/4/36
Dershowitz, Alan (lawyer); Brooklyn, N.Y., 9/1/38
Derrida, Jacques (philosopher); El-Biar, Algeria, 7/15/30
Descartes, René (philosopher, mathematician); La Haye, France **(1596-1650)**
De Seversky, Alexander P. (aviator); Tiflis (Georgia) **(1894-1974)**
De Sica, Vittorio (film director); Sora, Italy **(1901-1974)**
Desmond, Johnny (composer); Detroit **(1921-1985)**
Desmond, William (actor); Dublin **(1878-1949)**
De Soto, Hernando (explorer); Barcarrota, Spain **(1500?-1542)**
De Valera, Eamon (ex-President of Ireland); New York City **(1882-1975)**
Devane, William (actor); Albany, N.Y., 9/5/39
Devine, Andy (actor); Flagstaff, Ariz. **(1905-1977)**
DeVito, Danny (Daniel Michael); (actor, director); Neptune, N.J., 11/17/44
De Vries, Peter (novelist); Chicago **(1910–1993)**
de Waart, Edo (conductor); Amsterdam, the Netherlands, 6/1/41
Dewey, George (admiral); Montpelier, Vt. **(1837-1917)**
Dewey, John (philosopher, educator); Burlington, Vt. **(1859-1952)**
Dewey, Thomas E. (politician); Owosso, Mich. **(1902-1971)**
Dewhurst, Colleen (actress); Montreal **(1924–1991)**
DeWitt, Joyce (actress); Wheeling, W.Va., 4/23/49

De Wolfe, Billy (actor); Wollaston, Mass. **(1907-1974)**
Dey, Susan (actress); Pekin, Ill., 12/10/52
Diaghilev, Sergei (ballet impressario); Novgorod, Russia **(1872–1929)**
Diamond, Neil (singer); Brooklyn, N.Y., 1/24/41
Diana (Diana Frances Spencer) (Princess of Wales); Sandringham, England, 7/1/61
Dichter, Misha (pianist); Shanghai, 9/27/45
Dickens, Charles John Huffam (novelist); Portsea, England **(1812-1870)**
Dickey, James (poet); Atlanta, 2/2/23
Dickinson, Angie (Angeline Brown) (actress); Kulm, N.D., 9/30/32
Dickinson, Emily Elizabeth (poet); Amherst, Mass. **(1830-1886)**
Diddley, Bo (Elias McDaniel) (guitarist); McComb, Miss., 12/30/28
Diderot, Denis (encyclopedist); Langres, France **(1713-1784)**
Dietrich, Marlene (Maria Magdalena von Losch) (actress); Berlin **(1901-1992)**
Diller, Phyllis (Phyllis Driver) (comedienne); Lima, Ohio, 7/17/17
Dine, Jim (painter); Cincinnati, 6/16/35
Dinesen, Isak (Karen Blixen) (author); Rungsted, Denmark **(1885–1962)**
Dinkins, David (ex-mayor of New York City); Trenton, N.J., 7/10/27
Diogenes (philosopher); Sinope (Turkey) **(412?-323** B.C.)
Dion (Dion DiMucci) (singer); Bronx, N.Y., 7/18/39
Dior, Christian (fashion designer); Granville, France **(1905-1957)**
Disney, Walt(er) Elias (film animator, producer); Chicago **(1901-1966)**
Disraeli, Benjamin (Earl of Beaconsfield) (statesman); London **(1804-1881)**
Dix, Dorothea (civil rights reformer); Hampden, Me. **(1802-1887)**
Dixon, Jeane (Jeane Pinckert) (seer); Medford, Wis., 1918
Dobbs, Mattiwilda (soprano); Atlanta, Ga., 7/11/25
Doctorow, E(dgar) L(aurence) (novelist); New York City, 1/6/31
Dodgson, C. L. *See* Carroll, Lewis.
Dole, Elizabeth (public official); Salisbury, N.C., 7/29/36
Dole, Robert (politician); Russell, Kan., 7/22/23
Dolin, Anton (dancer); Slinfold, England **(1904-1983)**
Domingo, Placido (tenor); Madrid, 1/21/41
Domino, Fats (Antoine) (musician); New Orleans, 2/26/28
Donahue, Phil (TV personality); Cleveland, 12/21/35
Donahue, Troy (actor); New York City, 1/27/36(?)
Donaldson, Sam (broadcast journalist); El Paso, Texas, 3/11/34
Donat, Robert (actor); Withington, England **(1905-1958)**
Donatello (Donato Niccolò di Betto Bardi) (sculptor); Florence **(c.1386-1466)**
Donlevy, Brian (actor); Portadown, Ireland **(1899-1972)**
Donne, John (poet); London **(1573-1631)**
Donovan (Donovan Leitch) (singer, songwriter); Glasgow, Scotland, 2/10/46
Doolittle, James H. (ex-Air Force general); Alameda, Calif. **(1896–1993)**
Dorati, Antal (orchestra conductor); Budapest **(1906-1988)**
Dorris, Michael (anthropologist, writer); Louisville, Ky., 1/30/45
Dorsey, Jimmy (band leader); Shenandoah, Pa. **(1904-1957)**
Dorsey, Tommy (band leader); Mahanoy Plane, Pa. **(1905-1956)**
Dos Passos, John (author); Chicago **(1896-1970)**
Dostoevski, Fyodor Mikhailovich (novelist); Moscow **(1821-1881)**
Dotrice, Roy (actor); Guernsey, Channel Islands, England, 5/26/23
Douglas, Aaron (painter); Topeka, Kan. **(1900–1979)**
Douglas, Helen Gahagan (ex-Representative); Boonton, N.J. **(1900-1980)**
Douglas, Kirk (Issur Danielovitch) (actor); Amsterdam, N.Y., 12/9/16
Douglas, Melvyn (Melvyn Hesselberg) (actor); Macon, Ga., **(1901-1981)**
Douglas, Michael (actor, movie producer); New Brunswick, N.J., 9/25/44
Douglas, Mike (Michael D. Dowd, Jr.) (TV personality); Chicago, 8/11/25
Douglas, Stephen Arnold (politician); Brandon, Vt. **(1813-1861)**
Douglass, Frederick (abolitionist, author, orator); Tuckahoe, Md. (1817–1895)
Down, Lesley-Anne (actress); London, England, 3/17/54
Downs, Hugh (TV entertainer); Akron, Ohio, 2/14/21
Doyle, Sir Arthur Conan (novelist, spiritualist); Edinburgh, Scotland (1859-1930)
Doyle, David (actor); Lincoln, Neb., 12/1/29
Drake, Sir Francis (navigator); Tavistock, England (1545-1596)
Dreiser, Theodore (writer); Terre Haute, Ind. (1871-1945)
Dreyfus, Alfred (French army officer); Mulhouse, France (1859-1935)
Dreyfuss, Richard (actor); Brooklyn, N.Y., 10/29/47
Drury, Allen (novelist); Houston, 9/2/18
Dryden, John (poet); Northamptonshire, England (1631-1700)
Dryer, Fred (actor); Hawthorne, Calif., 7/6/46
Dubček, Alexander (ex-President of Czechoslovakia); Uhroved, former Czechoslovakia (1921-1992)
Dubinsky, David (David Dobnievski) (labor leader); Brest-Litovsk (U.S.S.R.) (1892-1982)
Du Bois, W(illiam) E(dward) B(urghardt) (scholar, activist); Great Barrington, Mass. (1868–1963)
Duchamp, Marcel (painter); Blainville, France **(1887-1968)**

Duchin, Eddy (pianist, bandleader); Cambridge, Mass. **(1909-1951)**
Duchin, Peter (pianist, band leader); New York City, 7/28/37
Duchovny, David (actor); New York City, 8/7/60
Dufay, Guillaume (composer); Cambrai, France **(c. 1400-1474)**
Duff, Howard (actor); Bremerton, Wash. **(1917-1990)**
Duffy, Julia (actress); Minneapolis, Minn., 6/27/50
Dufy, Raoul (painter); Le Havre, France **(1877-1953)**
Dukakis, Olympia (actress); Lowell, Mass., 6/20/31
Duke, James B. (industrialist); nr. Durham, N.C. **(1856-1925)**
Duke, Patty (Anna Marie Duke) (actress); New York City, 12/14/46
Dullea, Keir (actor); Cleveland, 5/30/36(?)
Dulles, Allen Welsh (ex-Director of CIA); Watertown, N.Y. **(1893-1969)**
Dulles, John Foster (statesman); Washington, D.C. **(1888-1959)**
Dumas, Alexandre (called Dumas fils) (novelist); Paris **(1824-1895)**
Dumas, Alexandre (called Dumas père) (novelist); Villers-Cotterets, France **(1802-1870)**
du Maurier, Daphne (novelist); London **(1907-1989)**
du Maurier, George Louis Palmella Busson (novelist); Paris **(1834-1896)**
Dumont, Margaret (actress); **(1889-1965)**
Dunaway, Faye (actress); Bascom, Fla., 1/14/41
Dunbar, Paul Laurence (poet, novelist); Dayton, Ohio **(1872–1906)**
Duncan, Isadora (dancer); San Francisco **(1878-1927)**
Duncan, Sandy (actress); Henderson, Tex., 2/20/46
Dunham, Katherine (dancer, choreographer); Chicago, 1914
Dunne, Irene (actress); Louisville, Ky. **(1901?-1990)**
Duns Scotus, John (theologian); Duns, Scotland **(1265-1303)**
Du Pont, Pierre S. (economist); Paris **(1739-1817)**
Durante, Jimmy (comedian); New York City **(1893-1980)**
Duras, Marguerite (Donnadieu) (novelist, dramatist); Gia Dinh (Vietnam) **(1914–1996)**
Durbin, Deanna (Edna Mae) (actress); Winnipeg, Canada, 12/4/22
Dürer, Albrecht (painter, engraver); Nürnberg (Germany) **(1471-1528)**
Durning, Charles (actor); Highland Falls, N.Y., 2/28/23
Durrell, Lawrence George (novelist); Julundur, India **(1912–1990)**
Duse, Eleonora (actress); Chioggia, Italy **(1859-1924)**
Dussault, Nancy (actress); Pensacola, Fla., 6/30/36
Duvall, Robert (actor); San Diego, Calif., 1931
Duvall, Shelley (actress); Houston, Tex., 1950
Dvořák, Antonin (composer); Nelahozeves, former Czechoslovakia **(1841-1904)**
Dylan, Bob (Robert Zimmerman) (folk singer and composer); Duluth, Minn., 5/24/41
Dysart, Richard (actor); Brighton, Mass., 3/30/?

E

Eakins, Thomas (painter, sculptor); Philadelphia **(1844-1916)**
Earhart, Amelia (aviator); Atchison, Kan. **(1898-1937)**
Earp, Wyatt Berry Stapp (sheriff, gunfighter); Monmouth, Ill. **(1848–1929)**
Eastman, George (inventor); Waterville, N.Y. **(1854-1932)**
Eastwood, Clint (actor, director); San Francisco, 5/31/30
Ebert, Roger (film critic); Urbana, Ill., 6/18/42
Ebsen, Buddy (Christian Ebsen, Jr.) (actor); Belleville, Ill., 4/2/08
Eckstine, Billy (singer); Pittsburgh **(1914-1993)**
Eddy, Mary Baker (founder of Christian Science Church); Bow, N.H. **(1821-1910)**
Eddy, Nelson (baritone and actor); Providence, R.I. **(1901-1967)**
Edelman, Marian Wright (social activist); Bennettsville, S.C., 6/6/39
Eden, Sir Anthony (Earl of Avon) (ex-Prime Minister); Durham, England **(1897-1977)**
Eden, Barbara (actress); Tucson, Ariz., 8/23/34
Edison, Thomas Alva (inventor); Milan, Ohio **(1847-1931)**
Edwards, Anthony (actor); Santa Barbara, Calif., 7/?
Edwards, Blake (film writer, producer); Tulsa, Okla. 7/26/22
Edwards, Jonathan (theologian); East Windsor, Conn. **(1703-1758)**
Edwards, Ralph (TV and radio producer); Merino, Colo., 1913
Edwards, Vincent (Vincent Edward Zoino) (actor); Brooklyn, N.Y. **(1928–1996)**
Eglevsky, André (ballet dancer); Moscow **(1917-1977)**
Ehrlich, Paul (bacteriologist); Strzelin (Poland) **(1854-1915)**
Eichmann, (Karl) Adolf (Nazi, mass murderer); Solingen, Germany **(1906–1962)**
Eikenberry, Jill (actress); New Haven, Conn., 1/21/47
Einstein, Albert (physicist); Ulm, Germany **(1879-1955)**
Eisenhower, Milton S. (educator); Abilene, Kan. **(1899-1985)**
Eisenstaedt, Alfred (photographer, photojournalist); Dirschau (Prussia, now Tczew, Poland) **(1898–1995)**
Ekberg, Anita (actress); Malmö, Sweden, 9/29/31
Ekland, Britt (Britt-Marie) (actress); Stockholm, Sweden, 1942
Elders, Joycelyn (Minnie Joycelyn Jones) (ex-U.S. Surgeon General); Schaal, Ark., 8/13/33

Elgar, Sir Edward (composer); Worcester, England **(1857-1934)**
Elgart, Larry (band leader); New London, Conn., 3/20/22
El Greco (Domenicos Theotocopoulos) (painter); Candia, Crete (Greece) **(c.1541-1614)**
Eliot, George (Mary Ann Evans) (novelist); Chilvers Coton, England **(1819-1880)**
Eliot, Thomas Stearns (poet); St. Louis **(1888-1965)**
Ellington, Duke (Edward Kennedy) (jazz musician); Washington, D.C. **(1899-1974)**
Elliot, "Mama" Cass (Ellen Naomi Cohen) (singer); Baltimore **(1941-1974)**
Elliott, Sam (actor); California, 8/9/44
Ellison, Ralph (novelist); Oklahoma City, Okla. **(1914–1994)**
Ellsberg, Daniel (activist); Chicago, 1931
Elman, Mischa (violinist); Stalnoye, Ukraine **(1891-1967)**
Emerson, Ralph Waldo (philosopher, poet); Boston **(1803-1882)**
Enesco, Georges (composer); Dorohoi, Romania **(1881-1955)**
Engels, Friedrich (Socialist writer); Barmen (Germany) **(1820-1895)**
Englund, Robert (actor); Glendale, Calif., 6/6/49
Entremont, Philippe (concert pianist); Rheims, France, 6/7/34
Ephron, Nora (writer); New York City, 5/19/41
Epicurus (philosopher); Samos (Greece) **(341-270** B.C.)
Epstein, Sir Jacob (sculptor); New York City **(1880-1959)**
Erasmus, Desiderius (Gerhard Gerhards) (scholar); Rotterdam **(1466?-1536)**
Erdrich, (Karen) Louise (writer); Little Falls, Minn., 7/6/54
Erickson, Leif (actor); Alameda, Calif. **(1911-1986)**
Erikson, Erik H. (psychoanalyst); Frankfurt, Germany **(1902–1994)**
Ernst, Max (painter); Bruhl, Germany **(1891-1976)**
Erté (Romain de Tirtoff) (artist, designer); St. Petersburg, Russia **(1892-1990)**
Estrada, Erik (actor); New York City, 3/16/49
Euclid (mathematician); Megara (Greece) **(c. 300** B.C.)
Euler, Leonhard (mathematician); Basel, Switzerland **(1707-1783)**
Euripides (dramatist); Salamis (Greece) **(c.484-407** B.C.)
Evans, Dale (Frances Butts) (actress, singer); Uvalde, Tex., 10/31/12
Evans, Dame Edith (actress); London **(1888-1976)**
Evans, Linda (actress); Hartford, Conn., 11/18/42
Evans, Maurice (actor); Dorchester, England **(1901-1989)**
Everett, Chad (actor); (Raymon Lee Cramton) South Bend, Ind., 6/11/36
Evers, Charles (civil rights leader); Decatur, Miss., 9/14/23(?)
Evers, Medgar (civil rights leader); Decatur, Miss. **(1925-1963)**
Evers-Williams, Myrlie (civil rights leader); Vicksburg, Miss., 3/17/33
Evigan, Greg (actor); South Amboy, N.J., 10/14/53

F

Fabares, Shelley (actress); Santa Monica, Calif., 1/19/44
Fabian (Fabian Anthony Forte) (singer); Philadelphia, 2/6/43
Fabray, Nanette (Nanette Fabarés) (actress); San Diego, Calif., 10/27/22
Fadiman, Clifton (literary critic); Brooklyn, N.Y., 5/15/04
Fahrenheit, Gabriel (German physicist); Danzig (Poland); **(1686-1736)**
Fairbanks, Douglas (Douglas Ulman) (actor); Denver **(1883-1939)**
Fairbanks, Douglas, Jr. (actor); New York City, 12/9/09
Fairchild, Morgan (actress); Dallas, Tex., 2/3/50
Faith, Percy (conductor); Toronto **(1908-1976)**
Falk, Peter (actor); New York City, 9/16/27
Falla, Manuel de (composer); Cadiz, Spain **(1876-1946)**
Faludi, Susan (journalist, writer); New York City, 4/18/59
Falwell, Jerry (fundamentalist preacher); Lynchburg, Va., 8/11/33
Faraday, Michael (physicist); Newington, England **(1791-1867)**
Farentino, James (actor); Brooklyn, N.Y., 2/24/38
Farmer, Frances (actress); Seattle, Wash. **(1913-1970)**
Farmer, James (civil rights leader); Marshall, Tex., 1/12/20
Farr, Jamie (actor); Toledo, Ohio, 7/1/34
Farrar, Geraldine (soprano, actress); Melrose, Mass. **(1882-1967)**
Farrell, Eileen (operatic soprano); Willimantic, Conn., 2/13/20
Farrell, James T. (novelist); Chicago **(1904-1979)**
Farrell, Mike (actor); St. Paul, Minn., 2/6/39
Farrell, Suzanne (Roberta Sue Ficker) (ballerina); Cincinnati, 8/16/45
Farrow, Mia (actress); Los Angeles, 2/9/46
Fasanella, Ralph (painter); New York City, 9/2/14
Fassbinder, Rainer Werner (film, stage director); Bad Wörishofen, (Germany) **(1946-1982)**
Fast, Howard (novelist); New York City, 11/11/14
Faubus, Orval E(ugene) (governor of Arkansas); Combs, Ark. **(1910–1994)**
Faulkner, William (novelist); New Albany, Miss. **(1897-1962)**
Fauré, Gabriel Urbain (composer); Pamiers, France **(1845-1924)**
Fawcett, Farrah (actress); Corpus Christi, Tex., 2/2/47(?)
Faye, Alice (Ann Leppert) (actress); New York City, 5/5/12
Feiffer, Jules (cartoonist); New York City, 1/26/29
Feininger, Lyonel (painter); New York City **(1871-1956)**

Feldman, Marty (actor, screenwriter, director); London **(1938-1982)**
Feldon, Barbara (actress); Pittsburgh, 3/12/41
Feliciano, José (singer); Larez, Puerto Rico, 9/10/45
Felker, Clay S. (editor, publisher); St. Louis, 10/2/25(?)
Fell, Norman (actor); Philadelphia, 3/24/23
Fellini, Federico (film director); Rimini, Italy **(1920–1993)**
Fender, Freddie (Baldemar Huerta) (singer); San Benito, Tex., 1937
Ferber, Edna (novelist); Kalamazoo, Mich. **(1885-1968)**
Ferguson, Maynard (jazz trumpeter); Verdun, Quebec, Canada, 5/4/28
Ferlinghetti, Lawrence (poet, writer, translator); Yonkers, N.Y., 3/24/19
Fermi, Enrico (atomic physicist); Rome **(1901-1954)**
Fernandel (Fernand Joseph Desire Contandin) (actor); Marseilles, France **(1903-1971)**
Ferraro, Geraldine Anne (political figure); New York City, 8/26/35
Ferrer, José (actor, director); Santurce, Puerto Rico **(1912-1992)**
Ferrer, Mel (actor); Elberon, N.J., 8/25/17
Ferrigno, Lou (actor); Brooklyn, N.Y., 11/9/52
Fetchit, Stepin (Lincoln Theodore Perry) (comedian); Key West, Fla. **(1902-1985)**
Fiedler, Arthur (conductor); Boston **(1894-1979)**
Field, Eugene (poet); St. Louis **(1850-1895)**
Field, Marshall (merchant); nr. Conway, Mass. **(1834-1906)**
Field, Sally (actress); Pasadena, Calif., 11/6/46
Fielding, Henry (novelist); nr. Glastonbury, England **(1707-1754)**
Fields, Gracie (comedienne); Rochdale, England **(1898-1979)**
Fields, Totie (comedienne); Hartford, Conn. **(1931-1978)**
Fields, W. C. (William Claude Dukenfield) (comedian); Philadelphia **(1880-1946)**
Fierstein, Harvey (Forbes) (playwright, actor); Brooklyn, 6/6/54
Filene, Edward A. (merchant); Boston **(1860-1937)**
Finch, Peter (actor); Kensington, England **(1916-1977)**
Finney, Albert (actor); Salford, England, 5/9/36
Firkusny, Rudolf (pianist); Napajedia, former Czechoslovakia **(1912–1994)**
Fischer-Dieskau, Dietrich (baritone); Berlin, 5/28/25
Fisher, Carrie (actress); Los Angeles, 10/21/56
Fisher, Eddie (Edwin) (singer); Philadelphia, 8/10/28
Fitzgerald, Barry (William Joseph Shields) (actor); Dublin **(1888-1961)**
Fitzgerald, Ella (singer); Newport News, Va. **(1918–1996)**
Fitzgerald, F. Scott (Francis Scott Key) (novelist); St. Paul, Minn. **(1896-1940)**
Fitzgerald, Geraldine (actress); Dublin, 11/24/14
Fitzgerald, Pegeen (radio broadcaster); Norcatur, Kan. **(1910-1989)**
Flack, Roberta (singer); Black Mountain, N.C., 2/10/40
Flagstad, Kirsten (Wagnerian soprano); Hamar, Norway **(1895-1962)**
Flatt, Lester Raymond (bluegrass musician); Overton County, Tenn. **(1914-1979)**
Flaubert, Gustave (novelist); Rouen, France **(1821-1880)**
Fleming, Sir Alexander (bacteriologist); Lochfield, Scotland **(1881-1955)**
Fleming, Rhonda (Marilyn Louis) (actress); Los Angeles, 8/10/23
Fletcher, John (dramatist); Rye? England **(1579-1625)**
Flynn, Errol (actor); Hobart, Tasmania **(1909-1959)**
Fodor, Eugene (violinist); Turkey Creek, Colo., 3/5/50
Fokine, Michel (dancer, choreographer); St. Petersburg, Russia **(1880-1942)**
Fonda, Henry (actor); Grand Island, Neb. **(1905-1982)**
Fonda, Jane (actress); New York City, 12/21/37
Fonda, Peter (actor); New York City, 2/23/39
Fontaine, Frank (singer, comedian); Cambridge, Mass. **(1920-1979)**
Fontaine, Joan (Joan de Havilland) (actress); Tokyo, 10/22/17
Fontanne, Lynn (actress); London **(1887-1983)**
Fonteyn, Dame Margot (Margaret Hookham) (ballerina); Reigate, England **(1919–1991)**
Foote, Shelby (historian); Greenville, Miss., 11/17/16
Forbes, Malcolm S(tevenson) (publisher, sportsman); Brooklyn, N.Y. **(1919-1990)**
Forbes, Steve (Malcolm Stevenson Forbes, Jr.) (publisher, presidential candidate); Morristown, N.J., 7/18/47
Ford, Glenn (Gwyllyn Ford) (actor); Quebec, 5/1/16
Ford, Harrison (actor); Chicago, 7/13/42
Ford, Henry (industrialist); Greenfield, Mich. **(1863-1947)**
Ford, John (film director); Cape Elizabeth, Me. **(1895-1973)**
Ford, Tennessee Ernie (Ernie Jennings Ford) (singer); Bristol, Tenn. **(1919-1991)**
Forrester, Maureen (contralto); Montreal, 7/25/30
Forsythe, John (actor); Penn's Grove, N.J., 1/29/18
Fosdick, Harry Emerson (clergyman); Buffalo, N.Y. **(1878-1968)**
Fosse, Bob (Robert Louis) (choreographer, director); Chicago **(1927-1987)**
Foster, Jodie (actress); Bronx, N.Y., 1963
Foster, Stephen Collins (composer); nr. Pittsburgh **(1826-1864)**
Fox, Michael J. (actor); Edmonton, Alta., Canada, 6/9/61

Foxx, Redd (John Elroy Sanford) (actor, comedian); St. Louis **(1922-1991)**

Foy, Eddie, Jr. (dancer, actor); New Rochelle, N.Y. **(1905-1983)**

Fracci, Carla (ballerina); Milan, Italy, 8/20/36

Fragonard, Jean Honoré (painter); Grasse, France **(1732-1806)**

Frampton, Peter (rock musician); Beckenham, England, 4/20/50

France, Anatole (Jacques Anatole François Thibault) (author); Paris **(1844-1924)**

Francescatti, Zino (violinist); Marseilles, France **1902—1991)**

Franciosa, Anthony (Anthony Papaleo) (actor); New York City, 10/25/28

Francis, Anne (actress); Ossining, N.Y., 7/16/30

Francis, Arlene (Arlene Francis Kazanjian) (actress); Boston, 10/20/08

Francis, Connie (Concetta Franconero) (singer); Newark, N.J., 12/12/38

Francis, Genie (actress); Englewood, N.J., 5/26/62

Francis of Assisi, Saint (Giovanni Francesco Barnardone) (founder of Franciscans); Assisi (Italy) **(1182-1226)**

Franck, César Auguste (composer); Liège (Belgium) **(1822-1890)**

Franco Bahamonde, Francisco (Chief of State); El Ferrol, Spain **(1892-1975)**

Frankenthaler, Helen (artist); New York City, 12/12/28

Franklin, Aretha (singer); Memphis, Tenn., 3/25/42

Franklin, Benjamin (statesman, scientist); Boston **(1706-1790)**

Franklin, Bonnie (actress); Santa Monica, Calif., 1/6/44

Franklin, John Hope (historian); Rentiesville, Okla., 1/2/15

Frann, Mary (actress); St. Louis, Mo., 2/27/43

Frazer, Sir James George (anthropologist); Glasgow, Scotland **(1854-1941)**

Freeman, Morgan (actor); Memphis, Tenn., 6/1/37

Freud, Sigmund (psychoanalyst); Moravia, Czech Republic **(1856-1939)**

Frick, Henry Clay (industrialist); Westmoreland Co., Pa. **(1849-1919)**

Friedan, Betty (Betty Naomi Goldstein) (feminist); Peoria, Ill., 2/4/21

Fromm, Erich (psychoanalyst); Frankfurt-am-Main, Germany **(1900-1980)**

Frost, David (TV entertainer); Tenterden, England, 4/7/39

Frost, Robert Lee (poet); San Francisco **(1874-1963)**

Fry, Christopher (playwright); Bristol, England, 12/18/07

Fugard, Athol (playwright); Middleburg, South Africa, 6/11/32

Fulbright, J. William (politician); Sumner, Mo. **(1905—1995)**

Fuller, Charles (playwright); Philadelphia, 3/5/39

Fuller, R(ichard) Buckminster (Jr.) (architect, educator); Milton, Mass. **(1895-1983)**

Fulton, Robert (inventor); Lancaster County, Pa. **(1765-1815)**

Funicello, Annette (actress); Utica, N.Y., 10/22/42

Funt, Allen (TV producer); Brooklyn, N.Y., 9/16/14

G

Gabin, Jean (actor); Paris **(1904-1976)**

Gable, (William) Clark (actor); Cadiz, Ohio **(1901-1960)**

Gabo, Naum (sculptor); Briansk, Russia **(1890-1977)**

Gabor, Eva (actress); Budapest **(1926?—1995)**

Gabor, Zsa Zsa (Sari) (actress); Budapest, 2/6/19(?)

Gabrieli, Giovanni (composer); Venice **(c.1557-1612)**

Gaddis, William (novelist); New York City, 1922

Gainsborough, Thomas (painter); Sudbury, Suffolk, England **(1727-1788)**

Galbraith, John Kenneth (economist); Iona Station, Ontario, Canada, 10/15/08

Galilei, Galileo (astronomer, physicist); Pisa, Italy **(1564-1642)**

Gallico, Paul (novelist); New York City **(1897-1976)**

Gallup, George H. (poll taker); Jefferson, Iowa **(1901-1984)**

Galsworthy, John (novelist, dramatist); Coombe, England **(1867-1933)**

Galway, James (flutist); Belfast, Northern Ireland, 12/8/39

Gambling, John A. (radio broadcaster); New York City, 1930

Gandhi, Indira (Indira Nehru) (Prime Minister); Allahabad, India **(1917-1984)**

Gandhi, Mohandas Karamchand (called Mahatma Gandhi) (Hindu leader); Porbandar, India **(1869-1948)**

Gannett, Frank E. (editor, publisher); **(1876-1957)**

Garagiola, Joe (Joseph Henry) (sportscaster); St. Louis, 2/12/26

Garbo, Greta (Greta Gustafsson) (actress); Stockholm **(1905-1990)**

Garcia, Jerry (rock musician); San Francisco **(1942—1995)**

García Lorca, Federico (poet, dramatist); Fuente Vaqueros, Spain **(1898-1936)**

Garden, Mary (soprano); Aberdeen, Scotland **(1874-1967)**

Gardenia, Vincent (actor); Naples, Italy **(1922-1992)**

Gardner, Ava (actress); Smithfield, N.C. **(1922-1990)**

Gardner, Erle Stanley (novelist); Malden, Mass. **(1889-1970)**

Garfield, John (Jules Garfinkle) (actor); New York City **(1913-1952)**

Garfunkel, Art (Arthur) (singer); Newark, N.J., 11/5/41

Garibaldi, Giuseppe (Italian nationalist leader); Nice, France **(1807-1882)**

Garland, Judy (Frances Gumm) (actress, singer); Grand Rapids, Minn. **(1922-1969)**

Garner, Erroll (jazz pianist); Pittsburgh **(1921-1977)**

Garner, James (James Bumgarner) (actor); Norman, Okla., 4/7/28

Garner, Peggy Ann (actress); Canton, Ohio **(1932-1984)**

Garr, Teri (actress); Lakewood, Ohio, 12/11/49

Garrison, William Lloyd (abolitionist); Newburyport, Mass. **(1805-1879)**

Garroway, Dave (TV host); Schenectady, N.Y. **(1913-1982)**

Garson, Greer (actress); County Down, Northern Ireland **(1903—1996)**

Garvey, Marcus Moziah (black nationalist leader); Jamaica **(1887—1940)**

Gassman, Vittorio (film actor, director); Genoa, Italy, 9/1/22

Gates, Bill (William Henry III) (software pioneer); Seattle, Wash., 10/28/55

Gates, Henry Louis, Jr. (scholar); Keyser, W. Va., 9/16/50

Gaudí, Antonio (architect); Reus, Spain **(1852-1926)**

Gauguin, Eugène Henri Paul (painter); Paris **(1848-1903)**

Gautama Buddha (Prince Siddhartha) (philosopher); Kapilavastu (India) **(563?-?483** B.C.)

Gavin, John (actor, diplomat); Los Angeles, 4/8/35

Gaye, Marvin (singer); Washington, D.C. **(1939—1984)**

Gayle, Crystal (Brenda Gayle Webb) (singer); Paintsville, Ky., 1/9/51

Gaynor, Janet (actress); Philadelphia **(1906-1984)**

Gaynor, Mitzi (Francesca Mitzi Marlene de Czanyi von Gerber) (actress); Chicago, 9/4/31

Gazzara, Ben (Biago Anthony Gazzara) (actor); New York City, 8/28/30

Gedda, Nicolai (tenor); Stockholm, Sweden, 7/11/25

Geddes, Barbara Bel (actress); New York City, 10/31/22

Genet, Jean (playwright); Paris **(1910-1986)**

Genghis Khan (Temujin) (conqueror); nr. Lake Baikal, Russia **(1162-1227)**

Gentry, Bobbie (Roberta Streeter) (singer); Chickasaw Co., Miss., 7/27/44

George, David Lloyd (statesman); Manchester, England **(1863-1945)**

George, Henry (economist, reformer); Philadelphia **(1839—1897)**

Gere, Richard (actor); Philadelphia, 1950

Gericault, Jean Louis (painter); Rouen, France **(1791-1824)**

Geronimo (Goyathlay) (Apache chieftain); Arizona **(1829-1909)**

Gershwin, George (composer); Brooklyn, N.Y. **(1898-1937)**

Gershwin, Ira (lyricist); New York City **(1896-1983)**

Getty, J. Paul (oil executive); Minneapolis **(1892-1976)**

Getz, Stan (saxophonist); Philadelphia **(1927—1991)**

Ghiberti, Lorenzo (goldsmith, sculptor); Florence **(1378-1455)**

Ghostley, Alice (actress); Eve, Mo., 8/14/26

Giacometti, Alberto (sculptor); Switzerland **(1901-1966)**

Giannini, Giancarlo (actor); La Spezia, Italy, 8/1/42

Gibbon, Edward (historian); Putney, England **(1737-1794)**

Gibson, Charles Dana (illustrator); Roxbury, Mass. **(1867-1944)**

Gibson, Henry (actor, comedian); Germantown, Pa., 9/21/35

Gibson, Mel (actor); Peekskill, N.Y., 1/3/56

Gide, André (author); Paris **(1869-1951)**

Gielgud, Sir John (actor); London, 4/14/04

Gilbert, Melissa (actress); Los Angeles, 5/8/64

Gilbert, Sir William Schwenck (librettist); London **(1836-1911)**

Gilels, Emil (concert pianist); Odessa, Ukraine **(1916-1985)**

Gillespie, Dizzy (John Birks Gillespie) (jazz trumpeter); Cheraw, S.C. **(1917-1993)**

Gimbel, Bernard F. (merchant); Vincennes, Ind. **(1885-1966)**

Gingold, Hermione (actress, comedienne); London **(1897-1987)**

Gingrich, Newt (politician); Harrisburg, Pa., 6/17/43

Ginsberg, Allen (poet); Newark, N.J., 6/3/26

Giordano, Luca (painter); Naples, Italy **(1632-1705)**

Giorgione (painter); Castelfranco, (Italy) **(c.1477-1510)**

Giotto di Bondone (painter); Vespignano (Italy) **(c.1266-1337)**

Giovanni, Nikki (poet); Knoxville, Tenn., 6/7/43

Giroud, Françoise (French government official); Geneva, 9/21/16

Gish, Dorothy (actress); Massillon, Ohio **(1898-1968)**

Gish, Lillian (Lillian de Guiche) (actress); Springfield, Ohio **(1893-1993)**

Givenchy, Hubert (fashion designer); Beauvais, France, 2/21/27

Gladstone, William Ewart (statesman); Liverpool, England **(1809-1898)**

Glaser, Paul Michael (actor, director); Cambridge, Mass., 3/25/43

Glass, Philip (composer); Baltimore, 1/31/37

Gleason, Jackie (comedian); Brooklyn, N.Y. **(1916-1987)**

Gless, Sharon (actress); Los Angeles, 5/31/43

Glover, Danny (actor); San Francisco, 7/22/47

Gluck, Christoph Willibald (composer); Erasbach (Germany) **(1714-1787)**

Gobel, George (comedian); Chicago **(1920–1991)**
Godard, Jean Luc (film director); Paris, 12/3/30
Goddard, Paulette (Marion Levy) (actress); Great Neck, N.Y. **(1911?-1990)**
Goddard, Robert Hutchings (father of modern rocketry); Worcester, Mass. **(1882-1945)**
Godfrey, Arthur (entertainer); New York City **(1903-1983)**
Goebbels, Joseph Paul (Nazi leader); Rheydt, Germany **(1897-1945)**
Goering, Hermann (Nazi leader); Rosenheim, Germany **(1893-1946)**
Goethals, George Washington (engineer); Brooklyn, N.Y. **(1858-1928)**
Goethe, Johann Wolfgang von (poet, playwright, novelist); Frankfurt-am-Main, Germany **(1749-1832)**
Gogol, Nikolai Vasilievich (novelist); nr. Mirgorod, Ukraine **(1809-1852)**
Goldberg, Rube (cartoonist); San Francisco **(1883-1970)**
Goldberg, Whoopi (actress); New York City, 1949 (?)
Goldblum, Jeff (actor); Pittsburgh, Pa., 10/22/52
Golden, Harry (Harry Goldhurst) (author); New York City **(1902-1981)**
Goldman, Emma (anarchist); Kovno, Lithuania **(1869-1940)**
Goldsmith, Oliver (dramatist, poet); County Longford, Ireland **(1728-1774)**
Goldwyn, Samuel (Samuel Goldfish) (film producer); Warsaw **(1882-1974)**
Gompers, Samuel (labor leader); London **(1850-1924)**
Goodall, Jane (Baroness van Lawick-Goodall) (ethologist); London, 4/3/34
Goodman, Benny (clarinetist); Chicago **(1909-1986)**
Goodwin, Doris (Helen) Kearns (historian); Rockville Centre, N.Y., 1/4/43
Goodyear, Charles (inventor); New Haven, Conn. **(1800-1860)**
Gorbachev, Mikhail Sergeyevich (Soviet leader); Privolnoye (Russia), 3/2/31
Gordimer, Nadine (novelist, short-story writer); Springs, South Africa, 12/20/23
Gordon, Dexter (jazz musician); Los Angeles **(1923-1990)**
Gordon, Ruth (actress); Wollaston, Mass. **(1896-1985)**
Gordy, Berry, Jr. (record company executive); Detroit, 11/28/29
Goren, Charles H. (bridge expert); Philadelphia **(1901-1991)**
Gorey, Edward (St. John) (illustrator, author); Chicago, 2/22/25
Gorki, Maxim (Alexei Maximovich Peshkov) (author); Nizhni Novgorod, Russia **(1868-1936)**
Gorky, Arshile (painter); Armenia **(1904-1948)**
Gormé, Eydie (singer); Bronx, N.Y., 8/16/32
Gorshin, Frank (actor); Pittsburgh, 4/5/34
Gosden, Freeman F. *See* Amos
Gossett, Louis, Jr. (actor); Brooklyn, N.Y., 5/27/36
Gottschalk, Louis Moreau (pianist, composer); New Orleans, La. **(1829-1869)**
Gould, Chester (cartoonist); Pawnee, Okla. **(1900-1985)**
Gould, Elliott (Elliott Goldstein) (actor); Brooklyn, N.Y., 8/29/38
Gould, Glenn (concert pianist); Toronto **(1932-1982)**
Gould, Morton (composer); Richmond Hill, Queens, N.Y. **(1913–1996)**
Gould, Stephen Jay (paleontologist, science writer); New York City, 9/10/41
Goulet, Robert (singer); Lawrence, Mass., 11/26/33
Gounod, Charles François (composer); Paris **(1818-1893)**
Goya y Lucientes, Francisco José de (painter); Fuendetodos, Spain **(1746-1828)**
Grable, Betty (actress); St. Louis **(1916-1973)**
Grace, Princess of Monaco (Grace Kelly) (ex-actress); Philadelphia **(1929-1982)**
Graham, Bill (Wolfgang Grajonca) (rock impresario); Berlin **(1930–1991)**
Graham, Billy (William F.) (evangelist); Charlotte, N.C., 11/7/18
Graham, Katharine Meyer (newspaper publisher); New York City, 6/16/17
Graham, Martha (choreographer); Pittsburgh **(1894–1991)**
Grahame, Gloria (Gloria Hallward) (actress); Los Angeles **(1929-1981)**
Grainger, Percy Aldridge (pianist, composer); Melbourne, Australia **(1882-1961)**
Gramm, Donald (Grambach) (bass-baritone); Milwaukee **(1927-1983)**
Grammer, Kelsey (actor); St. Thomas, V.I., 2/21/55
Granger, Stewart (James Stewart) (actor); London **(1913-1993)**
Grant, Cary (Alexander Archibald Leach) (actor); Bristol, England **(1904-1986)**
Grant, Lee (Lyova Haskell Rosenthal) (actress); New York City, 10/31/30
Grass, Günter (novelist); Danzig (Poland), 10/16/27
Graves, Nancy (Stevenson) (artist); Pittsfield, Mass. **(1940–1996)**
Graves, Peter (Peter Arness) (actor); Minneapolis, 3/18/26
Graves, Robert (writer); London **(1895-1985)**
Gray, Linda (actress); Santa Monica, Calif., 9/12/40
Gray, Thomas (poet); London **(1716-1771)**
Greco, José (dancer); Montorio nei Frentani, Italy, 12/23/18
Greeley, Horace (journalist, politician); Amherst, N.H. **(1811-1872)**

Green, Adolph (actor, lyricist); New York City, 12/2/15
Green, Al (singer); Forrest City, Ark., 4/13/46
Greene, Graham (novelist); Berkhamsted, England **(1904–1991)**
Greene, Lorne (actor); Ottawa **(1915-1987)**
Greene, Michele (actress); Las Vegas, Nev., 2/3/?
Greene, Shecky (comedian, actor); Chicago, 4/8/25
Greenstreet, Sydney (actor); Sandwich, England **(1879-1954)**
Greer, Germaine (feminist); Melbourne, 1/29/39
Gregory, Cynthia (ballerina); Los Angeles, 7/8/46
Gregory, Dick (comedian); St. Louis, 1932
Gregory, Lady (Isabella) Augusta (playwright); Roxborough, Ireland **(1852–1932)**
Greuze, Jean-Baptiste (painter); Tournus, France **(1725-1805)**
Grey, Joel (Joel Katz) (actor); Cleveland, 4/11/32
Grey, Zane (author); Zanesville, Ohio **(1875-1939)**
Grieg, Edvard Hagerup (composer); Bergen, Norway **(1843-1907)**
Griffin, Merv (TV entertainer); San Mateo, Calif., 7/6/25
Griffith, Andy (actor); Mount Airy, N.C., 6/1/26
Griffith, David Lewelyn Wark (film producer); La Grange, Ky. **(1875-1948)**
Griffith, Melanie (actress); New York City, 8/9/57
Grigorovich, Yuri (choreographer); Leningrad, 1/1/27
Grimes, Tammy (actress); Lynn, Mass., 1/30/34
Grimm, Jacob (author of fairy tales); Hanau (Germany) **(1785-1863)**
Grimm, Wilhelm (author of fairy tales); Hanau (Germany) **(1786-1859)**
Gris, Juan (José Victoriano González) (painter); Madrid **(1887-1927)**
Grisham, John (attorney, aurhor); Arkansas, 1955
Grodin, Charles (actor); Pittsburgh, Pa., 4/21/35
Gromyko, Andrei A. (diplomat); Starye Gromyki, Russia **(1909-1989)**
Gropius, Walter (architect); Berlin **(1883-1969)**
Gropper, William (painter, illustrator); New York City **(1897-1977)**
Gross, Michael (actor); Chicago, 6/21/47
Grosz, George (painter); Germany **(1893-1959)**
Grünewald, Matthias (Mathis Gothart Nithart) (painter); Würzburg, Germany **(c. 1470–1528)**
Guggenheim, Meyer (business executive); Langnau, Switzerland **(1828-1905)**
Guillaume, Robert (actor); St. Louis, Mo., 11/30/27
Guinness, Sir Alec (actor); London, 4/2/14
Guitry, Sacha (Alexandre) (actor, film director); St. Petersburg, Russia **(1885-1957)**
Gumbel, Bryant Charles (TV newscaster); New Orleans, 9/29/48
Gunther, John (author); Chicago **(1901-1970)**
Gutenberg, Johannes (printer); Mainz (Germany) **(1400?-?1468)**
Guthrie, Arlo (singer); New York City, 7/10/47
Guthrie, Woody (folk singer, composer); Okemah, Okla. **(1912-1967)**
Gwenn, Edmund (actor); London **(1875-1959)**
Gwynne, Fred (actor); New York City **(1926-1993)**

H

Hackett, Bobby (trumpeter); Providence, R.I. **(1915-1976)**
Hackett, Buddy (Leonard Hacker) (comedian, actor); Brooklyn, N.Y., 8/31/24
Hackman, Gene (actor); San Bernardino, Calif., 1/30/31
Hagen, Uta (actress); Göttingen, Germany, 6/12/19
Haggard, Merle (songwriter); Bakersfield, Calif., 4/6/37
Hagman, Larry (actor); Weatherford, Tex., 1931
Haig, Alexander Meigs, Jr. (ex-Secretary of State, ex-general); Bala-Cynwyd, Pa., 12/2/24
Haile Selassie (Ras Tafari Makonnen) (ex-Emperor); Ethiopia **(1892-1975)**
Hailey, Arthur (novelist); Luton, England, 4/5/20
Halberstam, David (journalist); New York City, 4/10/34
Hale, Alan (actor, director); Washington, D.C. **(1892-1950)**
Hale, Barbara (actress); DeKalb, Ill., 4/18/21
Hale, Edward Everett (clergyman, author); Boston **(1822-1909)**
Hale, Nathan (American Revolutionary officer); Coventry, Conn. **(1755-1776)**
Halevi, Judah (Jewish poet); Toledo (Spain) **(1085-1140)**
Haley, Alex (writer); Ithaca, N.Y. **(1921-1992)**
Haley, Jack (actor); Boston **(1899-1979)**
Hall, Arsenio (comedian, talk show host); Cleveland, Ohio, 2/12/?
Hall, Donald (Andrew, Jr.) (poet) New Haven, Conn., 9/20/28
Hall, Huntz (actor); New York City, 1920
Hall, Monty (TV personality); Winnipeg, Canada, 1923
Halley, Edmund (astronomer); London **(1656-1742)**
Hals, Frans (painter); Antwerp (Netherlands) **(1580?-1666)**
Halsey, William Frederick, Jr. (naval officer); Elizabeth, N.J. **(1882-1959)**
Hamel, Veronica (actress); Philadelphia, Pa., 11/20/43
Hamill, Pete (journalist); Brooklyn, N.Y., 6/24/35
Hamilton, Alexander (statesman); Nevis, British West Indies **(1757?-1804)**

rt, Al (trumpeter); New Orleans, 11/7/22
tchcock, Alfred J. (film director); London **(1899-1980)**
tler, Adolf (German dictator); Braunau, Austria **(1889-1945)**
tzig, William Maxwell (physician); Austria, 12/15/04
bbes, Thomas (philosopher); Westport, England **(1588-1679)**
bson, Laura Z. (Laura K. Zametkin) (novelist); New York City **(1900-1986)**
Chi Minh (Nguyen That Tranh) (Vietnamese nationalist leader); Kim Lien (Vietnam) **(1890-1969)**
ckney, David (artist); Bradford, England, 7/9/37
ffa, James R(iddle) (labor leader); Brazil, Ind. **(1913-75?)**; presumed murdered.
ffman, Dustin (actor, director); Los Angeles, 8/8/37
fmann, Hans (painter); Germany **(1880-1966)**
fstadter, Richard (historian); Buffalo, N.Y. **(1916-1970)**
gan, Paul (actor); Lightning Ridge, NSW, Australia, 1941 (?)
garth, William (painter, engraver); London **(1697-1764)**
kusai, Katauhika (artist); Yedo, Japan **(1760-1849)**
lbein, Hans (the Elder) (painter); Augsburg (Germany) **(1465?-1524)**
lbein, Hans (the Younger) (painter); Augsburg (Germany) **(1497?-1543)**
lbrook, Hal (actor); Cleveland, 2/17/25
lden, William (William Franklin Beedle, Jr.) (actor); O'Fallon, Ill. **(1918-1981)**
lder, Geoffrey (dancer); Port-of-Spain, Trinidad, 8/1/30
liday, Billie (Eleanora Fagan) (jazz-blues singer); Baltimore **(1915-1959)**
lliday, Judy (Judith Tuvim) (comedienne); New York City **(1922-1965)**
lliday, Polly (actress); Jasper, Ala., 7/2/37
lliman, Earl (actor); Delhi, La., 9/11/28
lloway, Sterling (actor); Cedartown, Ga. **(1905-1992)**
lly, Buddy (singer); Lubbock, Tex. **(1936-1959)**
lm, Celeste (actress); New York City, 4/29/19
lmes, Oliver Wendell (jurist); Boston **(1841-1935)**
lt, Tim (actor); Beverly Hills, Calif. **(1918-1973)**
me, Lord (Alexander Frederick Douglas-Home) (diplomat); London **(1903-1995)**
mer, Winslow (painter); Boston, Mass. **(1836-1910)**
mer (Greek poet) **(c.850 B.C.?)**
molka, Oscar (actor); Vienna **(1898-1978)**
negger, Arthur (composer); Le Havre, France **(1892-1955)**
ok, Sidney (philosopher); New York City **(1902-1989)**
oker, John Lee (blues guitarist, singer, songwriter); Clarksdale, Miss., 8/22/20
over, J. Edgar (FBI director); Washington, D.C. **(1895-1972)**
pe, Bob (Leslie Townes Hope) (comedian); London, 5/29/03
pkins, Sir Anthony (actor); Port Talbot, Wales, 12/31/37
pkins, Gerald Manley (poet); Stratford, England **(1844-1899)**
pkins, Johns (financier); Anne Arundel County, Md. **(1795-1873)**
pper, Dennis (actor); Dodge City, Kan., 5/17/36
pper, Edward (painter); Nyack, N.Y. **(1882-1967)**
race (Quintus Horatius Flaccus) (poet); Venosa (Italy) **(65-8 B.C.)**
rne, Lena (singer); Brooklyn, N.Y., 6/30/17
rne, Marilyn (mezzo-soprano); Bradford, Pa., 1/16/34
rowitz, Vladimir (pianist); Kiev, Ukraine **(1903-1989)**
rsley, Lee (actor); Muleshoe, Tex., 5/15/55
rton, Edward Everett (comedian); Brooklyn, N.Y. **(1887-1970)**
skins, Bob (actor); Bury St. Edmunds, England, 10/26/42
udini, Harry (Ehrich Weiss) (magician); Appleton, Wis. **(1874-1926)**
useman, John (Jacques Haussmann) (producer, director, actor); Bucharest **(1902-1988)**
usman, A(lfred) E(dward) (poet); Fockburg, England **(1859-1936)**
uston, Charles Hamilton (civil rights lawyer); Washington, D.C. **(1895-1950)**
uston, Samuel (political leader); Rockbridge County, Va. **(1793-1863)**
uston, Whitney (singer); Newark, N.J., 8/9/63
ward, Ken (actor); El Centro, Calif., 3/28/44
ward, Leslie (Leslie Stainer) (actor); London **(1893-1943)**
ward, Ron (actor, producer, director); Duncan, Okla., 3/1/54
ward, Trevor (actor); Kent, England **(1916-1988)**
we, Elias (inventor); Spencer, Mass. **(1819-1867)**
we, Irving (literary critic); New York City **(1920-1993)**
we, Julia Ward (poet, reformer); New York City **(1819-1910)**
dson, Henry (English navigator) **(?-1611)**
dson, Rock (born Roy Scherer, Jr.; took Roy Fitzgerald as legal name) (actor); Winnetka, Ill. **(1925-1985)**
ggins, Nathan Irvin (historian); Chicago **(1927-1989)**
ghes, Barnard (actor); Bedford Hills, N.Y., 7/16/15
ghes, Charles Evans (jurist); Glens Falls, N.Y. **(1862-1948)**
ghes, Howard (industrialist, film producer); Houston **(1905-1976)**
ghes, Langston (poet); Joplin, Mo. **(1902-1967)**
go, Victor Marie (author); Besançon, France **(1802-1885)**

Hulce, Tom (actor); Detroit, Mich., 12/6/53
Hume, David (philosopher); Edinburgh, Scotland **(1711-1776)**
Humperdinck, Engelbert (composer); Siegburg (Germany) **(1854-1921)**
Humperdinck, Engelbert (Arnold Dorsey) (singer); Madras, India, 5/2/36
Hunt, Marsha (actress); Chicago, 10/17/17
Hunter, Holly (actress); Atlanta, Ga., 3/20/58
Hunter, Kim (Janet Cole) (actress); Detroit, 11/12/22
Hunter, Tab (Arthur Andrew Gelien) (actor); New York City, 7/11/31
Hunter-Gault, Charlayne (activist, broadcast journalist); Due West, S.C., 2/27/42
Huntley, Chet (TV newscaster); Cardwell, Mont. **(1911-1974)**
Hurok, Sol (Solomon) (impresario); Pogar, Russia **(1884-1974)**
Hurst, Fannie (novelist); Hamilton, Ohio **(1889-1968)**
Hurston, Zora Neale (author); Eatonville, Fla. **(1891?-1960)**
Hurt, John (actor); Shirebrook, England, 1/22/40
Hurt, William (actor); Washington, D.C., 3/20/50
Hus, Jan (Bohemian religious reformer); Husinetz, nr. Budweis (Czech Republic) **(c.1369-1415)**
Hussein I (King); Jordan, 11/14/35
Hussein, Saddam (al-Tikriti) (Iraqi President); Tikrit, Iraq, 4/28/37
Huston, Anjelica (actress); Los Angeles, 7/8/51
Huston, John (actor, director, writer); Nevada, Mo. **(1906-1987)**
Huston, Walter (Walter Houghston) (actor); Toronto **(1884-1950)**
Hutchins, Robert M. (educator); Brooklyn, N.Y. **(1899-1977)**
Hutton, Barbara (Woolworth heiress); New York City **(1912-1979)**
Hutton, Betty (Betty Thornburg) (actress); Battle Creek, Mich., 2/26/21
Hutton, Lauren (actress, model); Charleston, S.C., 11/17/43
Hutton, Timothy (actor); Los Angeles, 8/16/60
Huxley, Aldous (author); Godalming, England **(1894-1963)**
Huxley, Sir Julian S. (biologist, author); London **(1887-1975)**
Huxley, Thomas Henry (biologist); Ealing, England **(1825-1895)**

I

Iacocca, Lee (Lido Anthony) (business executive); Allentown, Pa., 10/15/24
Ian, Janis (singer); New York City, 5/7/51
Ibsen, Henrik (dramatist); Skien, Norway **(1828-1906)**
Inge, William (playwright); Independence, Kan. **(1913-1973)**
Ingres, Jean Auguste Dominique (painter); Montauban, France **(1780-1867)**
Inness, George (painter); nr. Newburgh, N.Y. **(1825-1894)**
Ionesco, Eugene (playwright); Slatina, Romania **(1912-1994)**
Ireland, Jill (actress); London **(1936-1990)**
Ireland, John (actor); Vancouver, B.C., Canada **(1914-1992)**
Ireland, Patricia (feminist, social activist); Oak Park, Ill., 10/19/45
Irons, Jeremy (actor); Cowes, Isle of Wight, England, 9/19/48
Irving, Amy (actress); Palo Alto, Calif., 9/10/53
Irving, John (Winslow) (writer); Exeter, N.H., 3/2/42
Irving, Washington (author); New York City **(1783-1859)**
Isherwood, Christopher (novelist, playwright); nr. Dilsey and High Lane, England **(1904-1986)**
Iturbi, José (concert pianist); Valencia, Spain **(1895-1980)**
Ives, Burl (Icle Ivanhoe) (singer); Hunt, Ill. **(1909-1995)**
Ives, Charles E(dward) (composer); Danbury, Conn. **(1874-1954)**
Ivins, Molly (journalist); Monterey, Calif., 8/30/44

J

Jackson, Anne (actress); Millvale, Pa., 9/3/26
Jackson, Glenda (actress); Hoylake, England, 1937(?)
Jackson, Gordon (actor); Glasgow, Scotland **(1923-1990)**
Jackson, Janet (singer); Gary, Ind., 5/16/66
Jackson, Rev. Jesse (civil rights leader); Greenville, S.C., 10/8/41
Jackson, Kate (actress); Birmingham, Ala., 10/29/49
Jackson, Mahalia (gospel singer); New Orleans **(1911-1972)**
Jackson, Maynard (mayor of Atlanta); Dallas, Tex., 3/23/38
Jackson, Michael (singer); Gary, Ind., 8/29/58
Jackson, Thomas Jonathan ("Stonewall") (general); Clarksburg, Va. (now W. Va.) **(1824-1863)**
Jacobi, Derek (actor); Leytonstone, England, 10/22/38
Jacobi, Lou (actor); Toronto, 12/26/13
Jacobs, Jane (urbanologist); Scranton, Pa., 5/1/16
Jaffe, Sam (actor); New York City **(1891-1984)**
Jagger, Dean (actor); Lima, Ohio **(1903-1991)**
Jagger, Mick (Michael Phillip) (singer); Dartford, England, 7/26/43
James, Harry (trumpeter); Albany, Ga. **(1916-1983)**
James, Henry (novelist); New York City **(1843-1916)**
James, Jesse Woodson (outlaw); Clay County, Mo. **(1847-1882)**
James, William (psychologist); New York City **(1842-1910)**

Jameson, (Margaret) Storm (novelist); Whitby, England **(1897-1986)**
Janis, Byron (pianist); McKeesport, Pa., 3/24/28
Janis, Conrad (actor, musician); New York City, 2/11/28
Jannings, Emil (actor); Brooklyn, N.Y. **(1886-1950)**
Janssen, David (David Meyer) (actor); Naponee, Neb. **(1930-1980)**
Jaworski, Leon (Watergate special prosecutor); Waco, Tex. **(1905–1982)**
Jay, John (statesman, jurist); New York City **(1745-1829)**
Jeanmaire, Renée (dancer); Paris, 4/29/24
Jemison, Mae C. (astronaut, physician); Decatur, Ala., 10/17/56
Jenner, Edward (physician); Berkeley, England **(1749-1823)**
Jennings, Waylon (singer); Littlefield, Tex., 1937
Jessel, George (entertainer); New York City **(1898-1981)**
Jessup, Philip C. (diplomat); New York City **(1897-1986)**
Jillian, Ann (actress); Cambridge, Mass., 1/29/51
Joan of Arc (Jeanne d'Arc) (saint, patriot); Domremy-la-Pucelle, France **(1412-1431)**
Jobs, Steven Paul (computer industry pioneer); San Francisco, 1955
Joel, Billy (singer); New York City, 5/9/49
Joffrey, Robert (Abdullah Jaffa Bey Khan) (choreographer); Seattle **(1930-1988)**
John, Elton (Reginald Kenneth Dwight) (singer, pianist); Pinner, England, 3/25/47
Johns, Jasper (painter, sculptor); Augusta, Ga., 5/15/30
Johnson, Don (actor); Flatt Creek, Mo., 12/15/49
Johnson, James Weldon (author, educator); Jacksonville, Fla. **(1871-1938)**
Johnson, Philip Cortalyou (architect); Cleveland, Ohio, 7/8/06
Johnson, Samuel (lexicographer, author); Lichfield, England **(1709-1784)**
Johnson, Van (actor); Newport, R.I., 8/20/16
Johnson, Virginia (human sexuality expert); Springfield, Mo., 2/11/25
Joliot-Curie, Frédéric (physicist); Paris **(1900-1958)**
Joliot-Curie, Irène (Irène Curie) (physicist); France **(1897-1956)**
Jolliet (or Joliet), Louis (explorer); Beaupré, Canada **(1645-1700)**
Jolson, Al (Asa Yoelson) (actor, singer); St. Petersburg, Russia **(1886-1950)**
Jones, Allan (singer, actor); Old Forge, Pa. **(1908-1992)**
Jones, Buck (Charles Frederick Gebhart) (actor); Vincennes, Ind. **(1889-1942)**
Jones, Carolyn (singer, actress); Amarillo, Tex., **(1933-1983)**
Jones, Dean (actor); Morgan County, Ala., 1/25/35
Jones, George (singer); Saratoga, Tex., 9/12/31
Jones, Inigo (architect); London **(1573-1652)**
Jones, James (novelist); Robinson, Ill. **(1921-1977)**
Jones, James Earl (actor); Arkabutla, Miss., 1/17/31
Jones, Jennifer (Phyllis Isley) (actress); Tulsa, Okla., 3/2/19
Jones, John Paul (John Paul) (naval officer); Scotland **(1747-1792)**
Jones, Quincy (composer); Chicago, 3/14/33
Jones, Shirley (singer, actress); Smithtown, Pa., 3/31/34
Jones, Spike (host, orchestra leader); Long Beach, Calif. **(1911-1965)**
Jones, Tom (Thomas Jones Woodward) (singer); Pontypridd, Wales, 6/7/40
Jones, Tommy Lee (actor); San Saba, Tex., 9/15/46
Jong, Erica (writer); New York City, 3/26/42
Jonson, Ben (Benjamin) (poet, dramatist); Westminster, England **(1572-1637)**
Joplin, Janis (singer); Port Arthur, Tex. **(1943-1970)**
Joplin, Scott (ragtime pianist, composer); Texarkansas, Tex. **(1868-1917)**
Jordan, Barbara (U.S. Representative); Houston, Tex. **(1936–1996)**
Jordan, James Edward (radio actor-Fibber McGee); Peoria, Ill. **(1896-1988)**
Jordan, Marian (radio actress-Molly of Fibber McGee and Molly); Peoria, Ill. **(1898-1961)**
Joseph (Chief Joseph) (Nez Perce Indian leader); (eastern Ore.) **(1841–1904)**
Josquin des Prés (usually known as Josquin) (composer); Conde-sur-L'Escaut?, Hainaut (France or Belgium) **(c.1445-1521)**
Jourdan, Louis (Louis Gendre) (actor); Marseilles, France, 6/19/20
Joyce, James (novelist); Dublin **(1882-1941)**
Juárez, Benito Pablo (statesman); Guelatao, Mexico **(1806-1872)**
Julia, Raul (Raúl Rafael Carlos Julia y Arcelay) (actor); San Juan, Puerto Rico **(1940–1994)**
Jung, Carl Gustav (psychoanalyst); Basel, Switzerland **(1875-1961)**
Jurado, Katy (actress); Guadalajara, Mexico, 1927

K

Kabalevsky, Dmitri (composer); St. Petersburg, Russia **(1904-1987)**
Kafka, Franz (author); Prague **(1883-1924)**
Kádár, János (Communist Party leader); Hungary **(1912-1989)**

Kahn, Gus (songwriter); Coblenz, Germany **(1886-1941)**
Kahn, Louis I. (architect); Oesel Island, Estonia **(1901-1974)**
Kahn, Madeline (actress); Boston, 9/29/42
Kandinsky, Wassily (painter); Moscow **(1866-1944)**
Kanin, Garson (playwright); Rochester, N.Y., 11/24/12
Kant, Immanuel (philosopher); Königsberg (Kaliningrad, Russia) **(1724-1804)**
Kantor, MacKinlay (novelist); Webster City, Iowa **(1904-1977)**
Kaplan, Gabe (Gabriel) (actor); Brooklyn, N.Y., 3/31/45
Kaplan, Justin (writer, editor); New York City, 9/5/25
Karan, Donna (fashion designer); Forest Hills, N.Y. 10/2/48
Karloff, Boris (William Henry Pratt) (actor); London **(1887-1969)**
Kasem, Casey (disc jockey); Detroit, Mich., 4/27/32
Katt, William (actor); Los Angeles, 2/16/50
Kaufman, George S. (playwright); Pittsburgh **(1889-1961)**
Kavner, Julie (actress); Los Angeles, 9/7/51
Kaye, Danny (David Daniel Kominski) (comedian); Brooklyn, N.Y. **(1913-1987)**
Kaye, Sammy (band leader); Cleveland **(1910-1987)**
Kazan, Elia (director); Constantinople, Turkey, 9/7/09
Kazan, Lainie (Levine) (singer); New York City, 5/15/40
Kazantzakis, Nikos (writer); Herakleion, Crete **(1883-1957)**
Keach, Stacy (actor); Savannah, Ga., 6/2/41
Kean, Edmund (actor); London **(1787-1833)**
Keaton, Buster (Joseph Frank Keaton) (comedian); Piqua, Kan. **(1896-1966)**
Keaton, Diane (actress); Los Angeles, 1/5/46
Keaton, Michael (Michael Douglas) (actor); Robinson Township, Pa., 9/9/51
Keats, John (poet); London **(1795-1821)**
Keel, Howard (singer and actor); Gillespie, Ill., 4/13/19
Keeler, Ruby (Lehy Keeler) (actress, dancer); Halifax, Nova Scotia, Canada **(1910-1993)**
Kefauver, Estes (legislator); Madisonville, Tenn. **(1903-1963)**
Keith, Brian (actor); Bayonne, N.J., 11/14/21
Keller, Helen Adams (author, educator); Tuscumbia, Ala. **(1880-1968)**
Kellerman, Sally (actress); Long Beach, Calif., 6/2/38
Kelley, DeForest (actor); Atlanta, Ga., 1/20/20
Kelly, Emmett (clown); Sedan, Kan. **(1898-1979)**
Kelly, Gene (dancer, actor); Pittsburgh **(1912–1996)**
Kelly, Grace. See Grace, Princess of Monaco.
Kelly, Patsy (actress, comedienne); Brooklyn, N.Y. **(1910-1981)**
Kelly, Walt (cartoonist); Philadelphia **(1913-1973)**
Kemal Ataturk (Mustafa Kemal) (Turkish soldier, statesman); Salonika (Greece) **(1881–1938)**
Kempis, Thomas à (mystic); Kempis, Prussia (Germany) **(1380-1471)**
Kennan, George F. (diplomat); Milwaukee, 2/16/04
Kennedy, George (actor); New York City, 2/18/25
Kennedy, Jacqueline. See Onassis, Jacqueline
Kennedy, John F., Jr. (publisher); Washington, D.C., 11/25/60
Kennedy, Joseph P. (financier); Boston **(1888-1969)**
Kennedy, Robert Francis (legislator); Brookline, Mass. **(1925-1968)**
Kennedy, Rose Fitzgerald (President's mother); Boston **(1890–1995)**
Kent, Allegra (ballerina); Santa Monica, Calif., 8/11/38
Kent, Rockwell (painter); Tarrytown Heights, N.Y. **(1882-1971)**
Kenton, Stan (Stanley Newcomb) (jazz musician); Wichita, Kan. **(1912-1979)**
Kepler, Johannes (astronomer); Weil (Germany) **(1571-1630)**
Kercheval, Ken (actor); Wolcottville, Ind., 7/15/35
Kerensky, Alexander Fedorovich (statesman); Simbirsk, Russia **(1881-1970)**
Kern, Jerome David (composer); New York City **(1885-1945)**
Kerns, Joanna (actress); San Francisco, 2/12/53
Kerr, Deborah (actress); Helensburgh, Scotland, 9/30/21
Kettering, Charles F. (engineer, inventor); nr. Loudonville, Ohio **(1876-1958)**
Key, Francis Scott (lawyer, author of national anthem); Frederic (now Carroll) County, Md. **(1779-1843)**
Keyes, Frances Parkinson (novelist); Charlottesville, Va. **(1885-1970)**
Keynes (1st Baron of Tilton) (John Maynard Keynes) (economist); Cambridge, England **(1883-1946)**
Khachaturian, Aram (composer); Tiflis (Georgia) **(1903-1978)**
Khomeini, Ayatollah Ruhollah (Islamic religious leader); Iran **(1900–1989)**
Khrushchev, Nikita S. (Soviet leader); Kalinovka, nr. Kursk, Ukraine **(1894-1971)**
Kidd, Michael (choreographer); Brooklyn, N.Y., 1917
Kidd, William (called Captain Kidd) (pirate); Greenock, Scotland **(1645?-1701)**
Kidder, Margot (actress); Yellowknife, N.W.T., Canada, 10/17/48
Kiepura, Jan (tenor); Sosnowiec, Poland **(1904(?)-1966)**
Kieran, John (writer); New York City **(1892-1981)**
Kierkegaard, Sören Aalys (philosopher); Copenhagen **(1813-1855)**
Kiesinger, Kurt Georg (diplomat); Ebingen, Germany **(1904-1988)**

Kiley, Richard (actor, singer); Chicago, 3/31/22
Kilmer, Alfred Joyce (poet); New Brunswick, N.J. **(1886-1918)**
King, Alan (Irwin Alan Kniberg) (entertainer); Brooklyn, N.Y., 12/26/27
King, B.B. (Riley King) (guitarist); Itta Bena, Miss., 9/16/25
King, Carole (singer, songwriter); Brooklyn, N.Y., 2/9/41
King, Coretta Scott (civil rights leader); Marion, Ala., 4/27/27
King, Martin Luther, Jr. (civil rights leader); Atlanta **(1929-1968)**
King, Stephen (writer); Portland, Maine, 9/21/47
Kingsley, Ben (Krishna Bhanji) (actor); Snainton, England, 12/31/43
Kingsley, Sidney (Sidney Kirschner) (playwright); New York City **(1906-1995)**
Kingsolver, Barbara (writer); Annapolis, Md., 4/8/55
Kingston, Maxine Hong (novelist); Stockton, Calif., 10/27/40
Kinsey, Alfred Charles (human sexuality expert); Hoboken, N.J. **(1894-1956)**
Kinski, Nastassja (Nastassja Nakszynski) (actress); Berlin, 1/24/61
Kipling, Rudyard (author); Bombay **(1865-1936)**
Kipnis, Alexander (basso); Ukraine, **(1891-1978)**
Kirby, George (comedian); Chicago, 1923(?)
Kirchner, Ernst Ludwig (painter); Aschaffenburg, Germany **(1880-1938)**
Kirk, Grayson (educator); Jeffersonville, Ohio, 10/12/03
Kirkland, Gelsey (ballerina); Bethlehem, Pa., 12/29/52
Kirkpatrick, Jeane Jordan (educator-public affairs); Duncan, Okla., 11/19/26
Kirkpatrick, Ralph (harpsichordist); Leominster, Mass. **(1911-1984)**
Kirstein, Lincoln (dance, theater executive); Rochester, N.Y. **(1907-1996)**
Kirsten, Dorothy (soprano); Montclair, N.J. **(1910-1992)**
Kissinger, Henry (Heinz Alfred Kissinger) (ex-Secretary of State); Furth, Germany, 5/27/23
Kitt, Eartha (singer); North, S.C., 1/26/28
Klee, Paul (painter); Münchenbuchsee, nr. Bern, Switzerland **(1879-1940)**
Klein, Calvin (fashion designer); Bronx, N.Y., 11/19/42
Klein, Robert (comedian); New York City, 2/8/42
Kleist, Henrich von (poet); Frankfurt an der Oder (Germany) **(1777-1811)**
Klemperer, Otto (conductor); Breslau (Poland) **(1885-1973)**
Klemperer, Werner (actor); Cologne, Germany, 3/22/20
Klimt, Gustav (painter); Vienna **(1862-1918)**
Kline, Kevin (actor); St. Louis, Mo., 10/24/47
Klugman, Jack (actor); Philadelphia, 4/27/22
Knight, Gladys (singer); Atlanta, 5/28/44
Knight, Ted (Tadeus Wladyslaw Konopka) (actor); Terryville, Conn., **(1923-1986)**
Knight, John S. (publisher); Bluefield, W. Va. **(1894-1981)**
Knopf, Alfred A. (publisher); New York City, **(1892-1984)**
Knotts, Don (actor); Morgantown, W.Va., 7/21/24
Knox, John (religious reformer); Haddington, East Lothian, Scotland **(1505-1572)**
Koch, Robert (physician); Klausthal (Germany) **(1843-1910)**
Koestler, Arthur (novelist); Budapest **(1905-1983)**
Kokoschka, Oskar (painter); Pöchlarn Austria **(1886-1980)**
Kollwitz, Käthe (graphic artist, sculptor); Königsberg, (Russia) **(1867-1945)**
Koop, C. Everett (ex-Surgeon General); Brooklyn, N.Y., 10/14/16
Kooper, Al (singer, pianist); Brooklyn, N.Y., 2/5/44
Kopell, Bernie (actor); New York City, 6/21/33
Koppel, Ted (broadcast journalist); Lancashire, England, 2/8/40
Korman, Harvey (actor); Chicago, 2/15/27
Kosciusko, Thaddeus (Tadeusz Andrzej Bonawentura Kosciuszko) (military officer); Grand Duchy of Lithuania **(1746-1817)**
Kossuth, Lajos (patriot); Monok, Hungary **(1802-1894)**
Kostelanetz, André (orchestra conductor); St. Petersburg, Russia **(1901-1980)**
Kosygin, Aleksei N. (Premier); St. Petersburg, Russia **(1904-1980)**
Koussevitzky, Serge (Sergei) Alexandrovitch (orchestra conductor); Vishni Volochek, Tver, Russia **(1874-1951)**
Kovacs, Ernie (comedian); Trenton, N.J. **(1919-1962)**
Kramer, Stanley E. (film producer, director); New York City, 9/29/13
Kraus, Lili (pianist); Budapest **(1905-1986)**
Kreisler, Fritz (violinist); Vienna **(1875-1962)**
Kresge, S. S. (merchant); Bald Mount, Pa. **(1867-1966)**
Krips, Josef (orchestra conductor); Vienna **(1902-1974)**
Kristofferson, Kris (singer); Brownsville, Tex., 6/22/36
Krupa, Gene (drummer); Chicago **(1909-1973)**
Krupp, Alfred (munitions magnate); Essen, Germany **(1812-1887)**
Kubelik, Rafael (conductor); Bychory, former Czechoslovakia **(1914-1996)**
Kublai Khan (Mongol conqueror) **(1216-1294)**
Kubrick, Stanley (producer and director); New York City, 7/26/28
Kuralt, Charles (TV journalist); Wilmington, N.C., 9/10/34
Kurosawa, Akira (film director); Tokyo, 3/23/10

Kurtz, Efrem (conductor); St. Petersburg, Russia **(1900-1995)**
Kurtz, Swoosie (actress); Omaha, Neb., 9/6/44

L

LaBelle, Patti (singer, actress); Philadelphia, Pa., 5/24/44
Ladd, Alan (actor); Hot Springs, Ark. **(1913-1964)**
Ladd, Cheryl (Cheryl Stoppelmoor) (actress); Huron, S.D., 7/12/51
Ladd, Diane (actress); Meridian, Miss., 11/29/32
Lafayette, Marquis de (Marie Joseph Paul Yves Roch Gilbert du Motier) (military officer); Auvergne, France **(1757-1834)**
Lafitte, Jean (pirate); Bayonne? France **(1780-1826)**
La Follette, Robert Marin (politician); Primrose, Wis. **(1855-1925)**
La Fontaine, Jean de (poet); Château-Thierry, France **(1621-1695)**
La Guardia, Fiorello Henry (Mayor of New York); New York City **(1882-1947)**
Lahr, Bert (Irving Lahrheim) (comedian); New York City **(1895-1967)**
Laine, Frankie (Frank Paul LoVecchio) (singer); Chicago, 3/30/13
Laird, Melvin (ex-Secretary of Defense); Omaha, Neb., 9/1/22
Lake, Veronica (actress); Brooklyn, N.Y. **(1919-1973)**
Lamarck, Chevalier de (Jean Baptiste Pierre Antoine de Monet) (naturalist); Bazantin, France **(1744-1829)**
Lamarr, Hedy (Hedwig Kiesler) (actress); Vienna, 1915
Lamas, Fernando (actor); Buenos Aires, **(1915-1982)**
Lamas, Lorenzo (actor); Los Angeles, 1/20/58
Lamb, Charles (Elia) (essayist); London **(1775-1834)**
L'Amour, Louis (author); Jamestown, N.D. **(1908-1988)**
Lamour, Dorothy (Dorothy Kaumeyer) (actress); New Orleans, 10/10/14
Lancaster, Burt (actor); New York City **(1913-1994)**
Lanchester, Elsa (Elsa Sullivan) (actress); London **(1902-1986)**
Landau, Martin (actor); Brooklyn, N.Y., 1934
Landers, Ann (columnist); Sioux City, Iowa, 7/4/18
Landon, Michael (Eugene Maurice Orowitz) (actor); Forest Hills, Queens, N.Y. **(1936-1991)**
Lane, Abbe (singer); New York City, 1933
Lang, Fritz (film director); Vienna **(1890-1976)**
Lang, Paul Henry (music critic); Budapest **(1901-1991)**
Lange, Hope (actress); Redding Ridge, Conn., 11/28/33
Lange, Jessica (actress); Cloquet, Minn., 4/20/49
Langella, Frank (actor); Bayonne, N.J., 1/1/40
Langford, Frances (singer); Lakeland, Fla., 4/4/13
Langmuir, Irving (chemist); Brooklyn, N.Y. **(1881-1957)**
Langtry, Lillie (Emily Le Breton) (actress); Island of Jersey **(1852-1929)**
Lansbury, Angela (actress); London, 10/16/25
Lansing, Robert (Robert Howell Brown) (actor); San Diego, Calif. **(1928-1994)**
Lanza, Mario (Alfred Arnold Cocozza) (singer, actor); Philadelphia **(1921-1959)**
Lao-Tzu (or Lao-Tse) (Li Erh) (philosopher); Honan Province, China (c. 604-531 B.C.)
Lardner, Ring (Ringgold Wilmar Lardner) (story writer); Niles, Mich. **(1885-1933)**
La Rouchefoucauld, Francois duc de (author); Paris **(1613-1680)**
Larroquette, John (actor); New Orleans, 11/25/47
Larson, Gary (cartoonist); Tacoma, Wash., 8/14/50
La Salle, Sieur de (Robert Cavelier) (explorer); Rouen, France **(1643-1687)**
Lasch, Christopher (historian, social critic); Omaha, Neb. **(1932-1994)**
Lasser, Louise (actress); New York City, 1940(?)
La Tour, Georges de (painter); Vic-sur-Seille, France **(1593-1652)**
Lauder, Sir Harry (Harry MacLennan) (singer); Portobello, Scotland **(1870-1950)**
Laughton, Charles (actor); Scarborough, England **(1899-1962)**
Lauper, Cyndi (singer); New York City, 6/20/53
Laurel, Stan (Arthur Jefferson) (comedian); Ulverston, England **(1890-1965)**
Laurents, Arthur (playwright); New York City, 7/14/18
Laurie, Piper (Rosetta Jacobs) (actress); Detroit, 1/22/32
Lavin, Linda (actress); Portland, Me., 10/15/37
Lavoisier, Antoine-Laurent (chemist); Paris **(1743-1794)**
Lawford, Peter (actor); London **(1923-1984)**
Lawrence, David Herbert (novelist); Nottingham, England **(1885-1930)**
Lawrence, Gertrude (Gertrud Klasen) (actress); London **(1900-1952)**
Lawrence, Jacob (painter); Atlantic City, N.J., 9/7/17
Lawrence, Steve (Sidney Leibowitz) (singer); Brooklyn, N.Y., 7/8/35
Lawrence of Arabia (Thomas Edward Lawrence, later changed to Shaw) (author, soldier); Tremadoc, Wales **(1888-1935)**
Lawrence, Vicki (actress); Inglewood, Calif., 3/26/49

Leach, Penelope (Balchin) (child psychologist, writer); London, 11/19/37

Leach, Robin (host, producer); London, c.1941

Leachman, Cloris (actress); Des Moines, Iowa, 4/30/26(?)

Leadbelly (Huddie Ledbetter) (blues singer, guitarist); Mooringsport, La. **(1885–1949)**

Leakey, Louis Seymour Bazett (anthropologist); Kabete, Kenya **(1903–1972)**

Leakey, Richard (paleoanthropologist, wildlife conservationist); Kenya, 12/19/44

Lean, David (film director); Croydon, England **(1908–1991)**

Lear, Edward (nonsense poet); London **(1812–1888)**

Lear, Evelyn (Shulman) (soprano); Brooklyn, N.Y., 1/8/29(?)

Lear, Norman (TV producer); New Haven, Conn., 7/27/22

Learned, Michael (actress); Washington, D.C., 4/9/39

Leary, Timothy (psychologist, LSD advocate); Springfield, Mass. **(1920–1996)**

le Carré, John (David John Moore Cornwell) (novelist); Poole, England, 10/19/31

Le Corbusier (Charles Edouard Jeanneret) (architect); La Chaux-de-Fonds, Switzerland **(1887-1965)**

Lee, Christopher (actor); London, 5/27/22

Lee, Gypsy Rose (Rose Louise Hovick) (entertainer); Seattle **(1914-1970)**

Lee, Manfred B. (novelist, pseudonym Ellery Queen); Brooklyn, N.Y. **(1905-1971)**

Lee, Michele (actress, singer); Los Angeles, 6/24/42

Lee, Peggy (Norma Engstrom) (singer); Jamestown, N.D., 5/26/20

Lee, Robert Edward (Confederate general); Stratford Estate, Va. **(1807-1870)**

Leeuwenhoek, Anton van (zoologist); Delft (Netherlands) **(1632-1723)**

Le Gallienne, Eva (actress); London **(1899–1991)**

Lehár Franz (composer); Komárom (Hungary) **(1870-1948)**

Lehman, Herbert H. (Governor, Senator); New York City **(1878-1963)**

Lehmann, Lotte (soprano); Perleberg (Germany) **(1888-1976)**

Lehrer, Jim (TV newscaster); Wichita, Kan., 5/19/34

Leibniz, Gottfried W. von (scientist); Leipzig (Germany) **(1646-1716)**

Leibovitz, Annie (photographer); Westbury, Conn., 10/2/49

Leigh, Janet (Jeanette Morrison) (actress); Merced, Calif., 7/6/27

Leigh, Jennifer Jason (Jennifer Morrow) (actress); Los Angeles, Calif., 2/5/62

Leigh, Vivien (Vivien Mary Hartley) (actress); Darjeeling, India **(1913-1967)**

Leinsdorf, Erich (conductor); Vienna **(1912–1993)**

Lemmon, Jack (actor); Boston, 2/8/25

Lenin, Vladimir (Vladimir Ilich Ulyanov) (Soviet leader); Simbirsk, Russia **(1870-1924)**

Lennon, John (singer, songwriter); Liverpool, England **(1940-1980)**

Leno, Jay (comedian, TV host); New Rochelle, N.Y., 4/28/50

Lenya, Lotte (Karoline Blamauer) (singer, actress); Vienna, Austria **(1898-1981)**

Leonard, Sheldon (actor, producer); New York City, 2/22/07

Lerner, Alan Jay (lyricist); New York City **(1918-1986)**

Lerner, Max (columnist); Minsk, Russia **(1902-1992)**

Le Roy, Mervyn (film producer); San Francisco **(1900-1987)**

Lessing, Doris (novelist); Kermanshah, Iran, 10/22/19

Letterman, David (TV personality); Indianapolis, 1947

Levant, Oscar (pianist); Pittsburgh **(1906-1972)**

Levene, Sam (actor); New York City **(1905-1980)**

Levenson, Sam (humorist); New York City **(1911-1980)**

Levi, Carlo (novelist); Turin, Italy **(1902-1975)**

Levine, James (music director, Metropolitan Opera); Cincinnati, 6/23/43

Levine, Joseph E. (film producer); Boston **(1905-1987)**

Lewis, C(live) S(taples) (author); Belfast, Northern Ireland **(1898–1963)**

Lewis, Jerry (Joseph Levitch) (comedian, film director); Newark, N.J., 3/16/26

Lewis, Jerry Lee (singer); Ferriday, La., 9/29/35

Lewis, John Llewellyn (labor leader); Lucas, Iowa **(1880-1969)**

Lewis, Meriwether (explorer); Albemarle Co., Va. **(1774-1809)**

Lewis, (Percy) Wyndham (artist, writer); Bay of Fundy, Maine (at sea) **(1884–1957)**

Lewis, Shari (Shari Hurwitz) (puppeteer); New York City, 1/17/34

Lewis, Sinclair (novelist); Sauk Centre, Minn. **(1885-1951)**

Ley, Willy (science writer); Berlin **(1906-1969)**

Liberace (Wladziu Liberace) (pianist); West Allis, Wis. **(1919-1987)**

Lichtenstein, Roy (painter); New York City, 10/27/23

Lie, Trygve Halvdan (first U.N. Secretary-General); Oslo **(1896-1968)**

Light, Judith (actress); Trenton, N.J., 2/9/49

Lightfoot, Gordon (singer, songwriter); Orillia, Ontario, Canada, 11/17/38

Lillie, Beatrice (Lady Peel) (actress, comedienne); Toronto **(1898-1989)**

Limbaugh, Rush (political commentator); Cape Girardeau, Mo., 1/51

Lin, Maya (architect, sculptor); Athens, Ohio, 10/5/59

Lin Yutang (author); Changchow, China **(1895-1976)**

Lind, Jenny (Johanna Maria Lind) (soprano); Stockholm **(1820-1887)**

Lindbergh, Anne Morrow (author); Englewood, N.J., 6/22/06

Lindbergh, Charles A. (aviator); Detroit **(1902-1974)**

Linden, Hal (Harold Lipshitz) (actor); New York City, 3/20/31

Lindsay, Howard (playwright); Waterford, N.Y. **(1889- 1968)**

Lindstrom, Pia (TV newscaster); Stockholm, 11/?/38

Linkletter, Art (radio-TV personality); Moose Jaw, Saskatchewan, Canada, 7/17/12

Linnaeus, Carolus (Carl von Linné (botanist); Råshult, Sweden **(1707-1778)**

Lipchitz, Jacques (sculptor); Druskieniki, Latvia **(1891-1973)**

Lippi, Fra Filippo (painter); Florence **(1406-1469)**

Lippmann, Walter (columnist, author, political analyst); New York City **(1889-1974)**

Lister, (1st Baron of Lyme Regis) (Joseph Lister) (surgeon); Upton, England **(1827-1912)**

Liszt, Franz (composer, pianist); Raiding (Hungary) **(1811-1886)**

Lithgow, John (actor); Rochester, N.Y., 6/6/45

Little, Cleavon (actor, comedian); Chickasha, Okla. **(1939-1992)**

Little, Rich (impressionist); Ottawa, 11/26/38

Livingstone, David (missionary, explorer); Lanarkshire, Scotland **(1813-1873)**

Livingstone, Mary (Sadye Marks) (comedienne); Seattle **(1909-1983)**

Llewellyn, Richard (novelist); St. David's, Wales **(1906-1983)**

Lloyd, Harold (comedian); Burchard, Neb. **(1894-1971)**

Lloyd George, David (Earl of Dwyfor) (statesman); Manchester, England **(1863-1945)**

Lloyd Webber, Andrew (composer); London, England, 3/22/48

Locke, Alain L. (philosopher); Philadelphia **(1886–1954)**

Locke, John (philosopher); Somersetshire, England **(1632-1704)**

Lockhart, June (actress); New York City, 6/25/25

Lockwood, Margaret (actress); Karachi (Pakistan) **(1916-1990)**

Lodge, Henry Cabot (legislator); Boston **(1850-1924)**

Lodge, Henry Cabot, Jr. (diplomat); Nahant, Mass. **(1902-1985)**

Loesser, Frank (composer); New York City **(1910-1969)**

Loewe, Frederick (composer); Vienna **(1901-1988)**

Logan, Joshua (director, producer); Texarkana, Tex. **(1908-1988)**

Lollobrigida, Gina (actress); Subiaco, Italy, 1928

Lombard, Carole (Carol Jane Peters) (actress); Ft. Wayne, Ind. **(1908-1942)**

Lombardo, Guy (band leader); London, Ontario, Canada **(1902-1977)**

London, George (baritone); Montreal **(1920-1985)**

London, Jack (John Griffith London) (novelist); San Francisco **(1876-1916)**

Long, Huey Pierce (politician); Winnfield, La. **(1893-1935)**

Long, Shelley (actress); Fort Wayne, Ind., 8/23/49

Longfellow, Henry Wadsworth (poet); Portland, Me. **(1807-1882)**

Longworth, Alice Roosevelt (social figure); New York City **(1884-1980)**

Loos, Anita (novelist); Sissons, Calif. **(1888-1981)**

Lopez, Trini (singer); Dallas, Tex., 5/15/37

Lopez, Vincent (band leader); Brooklyn, N.Y. **(1895-1975)**

Lord, Jack (John Joseph Ryan) (actor); New York City, 12/30/30

Loren, Sophia (Sofia Scicolone) (actress); Rome, 9/20/34

Lorenz, Konrad (ethologist); Vienna **(1903–1989)**

Lorre, Peter (Laszlo Löewenstein) (actor); Rosenberg, former Czechoslovakia **(1904-1964)**

Loudon, Dorothy (actress, singer); Boston, 9/17/33

Louise, Tina (actress); New York City, 2/11/37

Love, Susan (surgeon, oncologist, activist); Long Branch, N.J., 2/9/4

Lovecraft, Howard Phillips (author); Providence, R.I., **(1890-1937)**

Lowell, Amy (poet); Brookline, Mass. **(1874-1925)**

Lowell, James Russell (poet); Cambridge, Mass. **(1819-1891)**

Lowell, Robert (poet); Boston **(1917-1977)**

Loy, Myrna (Myrna Williams) (actress); nr. Helena, Mon **(1905–1993)**

Loyola, St. Ignatius (of (Iñigo de Oñez y Loyola) (founder of Jesuits Gúipuzcoa Province, Spain **(1491-1556)**

Lubitsch, Ernst (film director); Berlin **(1892-1947)**

Lucas, George (film director); Modesto, Calif., 5/14/44

Lucci, Susan (actress); Scarsdale, N.Y., 12/23/48

Luce, Clare Boothe (playwright, former Ambassador); New York City **(1903-1987)**

Luce, Henry Robinson (editor, publisher); Tengchow, China **(1898-1967)**

Ludlum, Robert (author); New York City, 5/25/27

Lugosi, Bela (Bela Lugosi Blasko) (actor); Logos, Hungar **(1888-1956)**

Lully, Jean Baptiste (French composer); Florence **(1639-1687)**

Lumet, Sidney (director); Philadelphia, 6/25/24

Lunden, Joan (TV host); Fair Oaks, Calif., 9/19/50

Lunt, Alfred (actor); Milwaukee **(1892-1977)**

Lupino, Ida (actress, director); London **(1918–1995)**

Pone, Patti (actress, singer); Northport, N.Y., 4/21/49
ther, Martin (religious reformer); Eisleben, (Germany) **(1483-1546)**
nde, Paul (comedian); Mt. Vernon, Ohio **(1926-1982)**
nn, Loretta (singer); Butcher's Hollow, Ky., 4/14/35

M

a, Yo-Yo (cellist); Paris, 10/7/55
aazel, Lorin (conductor); Neuilly, France, 3/5/30
acArthur, Charles (playwright); Scranton, Pa. **(1895-1956)**
acArthur, Douglas (five-star general); Little Rock Barracks, Ark. **(1880-1964)**
acArthur, James (actor); Los Angeles, 12/8/37
acaulay, Thomas Babington (author); Rothley Temple, England **(1800-1859)**
acDermot, Galt (composer); Montreal, 12/19/28
acDonald, James Ramsay (statesman); Lossiemouth, Scotland **(1866-1937)**
acDonald, Jeanette (actress, soprano); Philadelphia **(1907-1965)**
acdonald, Ross (Kenneth Millar) (mystery writer); Los Gatos, Calif. **(1915-1983)**
acDowell, Edward Alexander (composer); New York City **(1861-1908)**
acGraw, Ali (actress); New York City, 4/1/39
achaut, Guillaume de (composer); Marchault, France **(1300-1377)**
achiavelli, Niccolò (political philosopher); Florence, Italy **(1469-1527)**
ack, Ted (TV personality); Greeley, Colo. **(1904-1976)**
acke, Bob (designer); Monterey Park, Calif., 3/24/40
acLaine, Shirley (Shirley MacLean Beatty) (actress); Richmond, Va., 4/24/34
acLeish, Archibald (poet); Glencoe, Ill. **(1892-1982)**
acmillan, Harold (ex-Prime Minister); London **(1894-1986)**
acMurray, Fred (actor); Kankakee, Ill. **(1908-1991)**
acNeil, Cornell (baritone); Minneapolis, 1925
acNeil, Robert (TV newscaster); Montreal, Que., Canada, 1/19/31
acRae, Gordon (singer); East Orange, N.J. **(1921-1986)**
acRae, Sheila (comedienne); London, 9/24/24
adison, Guy (Robert Moseley) (actor); Bakersfield, Calif., **(1922–1996)**
adonna (Madonna Louise Ciccone) (singer); Bay City, Mich., 8/16/58
aeterlinck, Count Maurice (author); Ghent, Belgium **(1862-1949)**
agellan, Ferdinand (Fernando de Magalhaes) (navigator); Sabrosa, Portugal **(1480?-1521)**
agliozzi, Ray (host of "Car Talk" on NPR); Cambridge, Mass., 3/30/49
agliozzi, Tom (host of "Car Talk" on NPR); Cambridge, Mass., 6/28/37
agnani, Anna (actress); Rome **(1908-1973)**
agritte, René (painter); Belgium **(1898-1967)**
agsaysay, Ramón (statesman); Iba, Luzon, Philippines **(1907-1957)**
ahan, Alfred Thayer (naval historian); West Point, N.Y. **(1840-1914)**
ahler, Gustav (composer, conductor); Kalischt (Czechoslovakia) **(1860-1911)**
ailer, Norman (novelist); Long Branch, N.J., 1/31/23
ailloi, Aristide (sculptor); Banyuls-sur-Mer, Rousillion, France **(1861-1944)**
aimonides, Moses (Jewish philosopher); Cordoba, Spain **(1135-1204)**
ain, Marjorie (Mary Tomlinson Krebs) (actress); Acton, Ind. **(1890-1975)**
ainbocher (Main Rousseau Bocher) (fashion designer); Chicago **(1891-1976)**
ajors, Lee (actor); Wyandotte, Mich., 4/23/40
akarova, Natalia (ballerina); Leningrad, 11/21/40
akeba, Miriam (singer); Johannesburg, South Africa, 3/4/32
alamud, Bernard (novelist); Brooklyn, N.Y., **(1914-1986)**
alcolm X (Malcolm Little; el Hajj Ma ● lik el-Shabazz) (Black nationalist, religious leader); Omaha, Neb. **(1925–1965)**
alden, Karl (Miaden Sekulovich) (actor); Chicago, 3/22/13
alkovich, John (actor); Christopher, Ill., 12/9/53
allarmé, Stephane (poet, essayist); Paris **(1842–1898)**
alle, Louis (director); Thumeries, France **(1932–1995)**
alone, Dorothy (actress); Chicago, 1/30/25
alraux, André (author); Paris **(1901-1976)**
althus, Thomas Robert (economist); nr. Dorking, England **(1766-1834)**
amet, David (playwright); Chicago, 11/30/47
anchester, Melissa (singer); Bronx, N.Y., 2/15/51
anchester, William (writer); Attleboro, Mass., 4/1/22
ancini, Henry (composer, conductor); Cleveland **(1924–1994)**
andela, Nelson (Rolihlahla) (South African political activist)

Umtata, Transkei, 1918
Mandela, Winnie (Nomzamo) (South African political activist); Pondoland district of the Transkei, 1936(?)
Mandrell, Barbara (singer); Houston, 12/25/48
Manet, Edouard (painter); Paris **(1832-1883)**
Mangano, Silvana (actress); Rome **(1930-1989)**
Mangione, Chuck (hornist, pianist, composer); Rochester, N.Y., 11/29/40
Manilow, Barry (singer); Brooklyn, N.Y., 6/17/46
Mankiewicz, Frank F. (columnist); New York City, 5/16/24
Mankiewicz, Joseph L. (film writer, director); Wilkes-Barre, Pa. **(1909-1993)**
Mann, Horace (educator); Franklin, Mass. **(1796-1859)**
Mann, Thomas (novelist); Lübeck, Germany **(1875-1955)**
Mannes, Marya (writer); New York City, 11/14/04
Mansfield, Jayne (Jayne Palmer) (actress); Bryn Mawr, Pa. **(1932-1967)**
Mansfield, Katherine (story writer); Wellington, New Zealand **(1888-1923)**
Mantegna, Andrea (painter); Isola di Carturo, Italy **(1431–1506)**
Mantovani, Annunzio (conductor); Venice **(1905-1980)**
Mao Zedong (Tse-tung) (Chinese leader); Shao Shan, China **(1893-1976)**
Mapplethorpe, Robert (photographer); Floral Park, Queens, N.Y. **(1946-1989)**
Marat, Jean Paul (French revolutionist); Boudry, Neuchâtei, Switzerland **(1743-1793)**
Marceau, Marcel (mime); Strasbourg, France, 3/22/23
March, Fredric (Frederick Bickel) (actor); Racine, Wis. **(1897-1975)**
Marchand, Nancy (actress); Buffalo, N.Y., 6/19/28
Marconi, Guglielmo (inventor); Bologna, Italy **(1874-1937)**
Marcus Aurelius (Marcus Annius Verus) (Roman emperor); Rome **(121-180)**
Marcuse, Herbert (philosopher); Berlin, **(1898-1979)**
Margaret Rose (Princess); Glamis Castle, Angus, Scotland, 8/21/30
Margrethe II (Queen); Copenhagen, 4/16/40
Marie Antoinette (Josephe Jeanne Marie Antoinette) (Queen of France); Vienna **(1755-1793)**
Marisol (sculptor); Venezuela, 1930
Markham, Edwin (poet); Oregon City, Ore. **(1852-1940)**
Markova, Dame Alicia (Lilian Alice Marks) (ballerina); London 12/1/10
Marley, Bob (reggae singer, songwriter); Kingston, Jamaica **(1945-1981)**
Marlowe, Christopher (dramatist); Canterbury, England **(1564-1593)**
Marquand, J(ohn) P(hillips) (novelist); Wilmington, Del. **(1893-1960)**
Marquette, Jacques (missionary, explorer); Laon, France **(1637-1675)**
Marriner, Neville (conductor); Lincoln, England, 4/15/24
Marsalis, Wynton (musician); New Orleans, La., 10/18/61
Marsh, Jean (actress); Stoke Newington, England, 7/1/34
Marshall, E.G. (actor); Owatonna, Minn., 6/18/10
Marshall, George Catlett (general); Uniontown, Pa. **(1880-1959)**
Marshall, John (jurist); nr. Germantown, Va. **(1755-1835)**
Marshall, Penny (actress); New York City, 10/15/42
Marshall, Thurgood (U.S. Supreme Court justice); Baltimore, Md. **(1908–1993)**
Martin, Dean (Dino Crocetti) (singer, actor); Steubenville, Ohio, **(1917–1995)**
Martin, Mary (singer, actress); Weatherford, Tex. **(1913–1990)**
Martin, Steve (comedian); Waco, Tex., 1945(?)
Martin, Tony (Alvin Morris) (singer); San Francisco, 12/25/13
Martinelli, Giovanni (tenor); Montagnana, Italy **(1885-1969)**
Martins, Peter (dancer, choreographer); Copenhagen, 10/27/45
Marvell, Andrew (poet); Winestead, England **(1621-1678)**
Marvin, Lee (actor); New York City **(1924-1987)**
Marx, Chico (Leonard) (comedian); New York City **(1891-1961)**
Marx, Groucho (Julius) (comedian); New York City **(1890-1977)**
Marx, Harpo (Arthur) (comedian); New York City **(1893-1964)**
Marx, Karl (Socialist writer); Treves (Germany) **(1818-1883)**
Marx, Zeppo (Herbert) (comedian); New York City **(1901-1979)**
Mary Stuart (Queen of Scotland); Linlithgow, Scotland **(1542-1587)**
Masaccio (Tommaso di Giovanni di Simone Cassai) (painter); San Giovanni Valdarno, Tuscany **(1401–c. 1428)**
Masaryk, Jan Garrigue (statesman); Prague (Czech Republic) **(1886-1948)**
Masaryk, Thomas Garrigue (statesman); Hodonin (Czechoslovakia) **(1850-1937)**
Masefield, John (poet); Ledbury, England **(1878-1967)**
Masekela, Hugh (trumpeter); Wilbank, South Africa, 4/4/39
Mason, Jackie (comedian); Sheboygan, Wis., 6/9/30(?)
Mason, James (actor); Huddersfield, England **(1909-1984)**
Mason, Marsha (actress); St. Louis, Mo., 4/3/42
Massenet, Jules Emile Frédéric (composer); Montaud, France **(1842-1912)**
Massey, Raymond (actor); Toronto **(1896-1983)**

Massine, Léonide (choreographer); Moscow **(1895-1979)**
Masters, Edgar Lee (poet); Garnett, Kan. **(1869-1950)**
Masters, William (human sexuality expert); Cleveland, 12/27/15
Mastroianni, Marcello (actor); Fontana Liri, Italy, 9/28/24
Mather, Cotton (clergyman); Boston **(1663-1728)**
Mathis, Johnny (singer); San Francisco, 9/30/35
Matisse, Henri (painter); Le Cateau, France **(1869-1954)**
Matthau, Walter (Walter Matuschanskayasky) (actor); New York City, 10/1/20
Mature, Victor (actor); Louisville, Ky., 1/19/16
Maugham, W(illiam) Somerset (author); Paris **(1874-1965)**
Mauldin, Bill (political cartoonist); Mountain Park, N.M., 10/29/21
Maupassant, Henri René Albert Guy de (story writer); Normandy, France **(1850-1893)**
Maurois, André (Emile Herzog) (author); Elbauf, France **(1885-1967)**
Maximilian (Ferdinand Maximilian Joseph) (Emperor of Mexico); Vienna **(1832-1867)**
Maxwell, James Clerk (physicist); Edinburgh, Scotland **(1831-1879)**
Maxwell, (Ian) Robert (publisher); Selo Slatina, Czechoslovakia **(1923–1991)**
May, Elaine (Elaine Berlin) (entertainer, writer); Philadelphia, 4/21/32
May, Rollo (psychologist); Ada, Ohio **(1909–1994)**
Mayall, John (singer, songwriter); Manchester, England, 11/29/33
Mayer, Louis B. (motion picture executive); Minsk, Russia **(1885-1957)**
Mayo, Charles H. (surgeon); Rochester, Minn. **(1865-1939)**
Mayo, Charles W. (surgeon); Rochester, Minn. **(1898-1968)**
Mayo, Virginia (Jones) (actress); St. Louis, 1920
Mayo, William J. (surgeon); Le Sueur, Minn. **(1861-1939)**
Mayron, Melanie (actress); Philadelphia, 10/20/52
Mazzini, Giuseppe (patriot); Genoa **(1805-1872)**
McBride, Patricia (ballerina); Teaneck, N.J., 8/23/42
McCallum, David (actor); Glasgow, Scotland, 9/19/33
McCambridge, Mercedes (actress); Joliet, Ill., 3/17/18
McCarthy, Eugene J. (ex-Senator); Watkins, Minn., 3/29/16
McCarthy, Joseph Raymond (Senator); Grand Chute, Wis. **(1908-1957)**
McCarthy, Kevin (actor); Seattle, 2/15/14
McCarthy, Mary (novelist); Seattle **(1912-1989)**
McCartney, Paul (singer, songwriter); Liverpool, England, 6/18/42
McClanahan, Rue (actress); Healdton, Okla., 2/21/35
McClellan, George Brinton (general); Philadelphia **(1826-1885)**
McClintock, Barbara (geneticist); Hartford, Conn. **(1902–1992)**
McCloy, John J. (lawyer, banker); Philadelphia **(1895-1989)**
McClure, Doug (actor); Glendale, Calif. **(1938–1995)**
McCormack, John (tenor); Athlone, Ireland **(1884-1945)**
McCormack, John W. (ex-Speaker of House); Boston **(1891-1980)**
McCormick, Cyrus Hall (inventor); Rockbridge County, Va. **(1809-1884)**
McCracken, James (dramatic tenor); Gary, Ind. **(1926-1988)**
McCrea, Joel (actor); Los Angeles **(1905–1990)**
McCullers, Carson (novelist); Columbus, Ga. **(1917-1967)**
McDaniel, Hattie (actress); Wichita, Kan. **(1895-1952)**
McDowall, Roddy (actor); London, 9/17/28
McDowell, Malcolm (actor); Leeds, England, 6/19/43
McFarland, Spanky (George Emmett) (actor); Fort Worth, Tex. **(1928-1993)**
McGavin, Darren (actor); San Joaquin, Calif., 5/7/22
McGinley, Phyllis (poet, writer); Ontario, Ore. **(1905-1978)**
McGoohan, Patrick (actor); Astoria, Queens, N.Y., 1928
McGovern, Maureen (singer); Youngstown, Ohio, 7/27/49
McGuire, Dorothy (actress); Omaha, Neb. 6/14/19
McKellen, Ian (actor); Burnley, England, 5/25/39
McKenna, Siobhan (actress); Belfast, Northern Ireland **(1923-1986)**
McKuen, Rod (singer, composer); Oakland, Calif., 4/29/33
McLaglen, Victor (actor); Tunbridge Wells, Kent, England **(1886-1959)**
McLaughlin, John (guitarist); Yorkshire, England, 1942
McLean, Don (singer, songwriter); New Rochelle, N.Y., 10/2/45
McLuhan, Marshall (Herbert Marshall) (communications writer); Edmonton, Canada **(1911-1980)**
McMahon, Ed (TV personality); Detroit, 3/6/23
McMurtry, Larry (novelist); Wichita Falls, Tex., 6/3/36
McQueen, Butterfly (Thelma) (actress); Tampa, Fla. **(1911–1995)**
McQueen, Steve (Terence Stephen McQueen) (actor); Indianapolis **(1930-1980)**
McRaney, Gerald (actor); Collins, Miss., 8/19/47
Mead, Margaret (anthropologist); Philadelphia **(1901-1978)**
Meadows, Audrey (actress); Wu Chang, China **(1924-1996)**
Meadows, Jayne (actress); Wu Chang, China 9/27/26
Meany, George (labor leader); New York City **(1894-1980)**
Meara, Anne (actress); New York City, 1929
Medici, Lorenzo de' (called Lorenzo the Magnificent) (Florentine ruler); Florence, Italy **(1449-1492)**
Meek, Donald (actor); Glasgow, Scotland **(1880-1946)**
Meeker, Ralph (Ralph Rathgeber) (actor); Minneapolis **(1920-1988)**

Mehta, Zubin (conductor); Bombay, 4/29/36
Meir, Golda (Golda Myerson, nee Mabovitz) (ex-Premier of Israel); Kiev (Ukraine) **(1898-1978)**
Melanie (Melanie Safka) (singer, songwriter); New York City, 2/3/47
Melba, Dame Nellie (Helen Porter Mitchell) (soprano); nr. Melbourne **(1861-1931)**
Melchior, Lauritz (Lebrecht Hommel) (heroic tenor); Copenhagen **(1890-1973)**
Mellon, Andrew William (financier); Pittsburgh **(1855-1937)**
Melville, Herman (novelist); New York City **(1819-1891)**
Mencken, Henry Louis (writer); Baltimore **(1880-1956)**
Mendel, Gregor Johann (geneticist); Heinzendorf, Austrian Silesia **(1822-1884)**
Mendeleyev, Dmitri Ivanovich (chemist); Tobolsk, Russia **(1834-1907)**
Mendelssohn-Bartholdy, Jakob Ludwig Felix (composer); Hamburg **(1809-1847)**
Mendès-France, Pierre (ex-Premier); Paris **(1905-1982)**
Mengele, Josef (Nazi, "Angel of Death"); Günzberg, Germany **(1911–1979)**
Menjou, Adolphe (actor); Pittsburgh **(1890-1963)**
Mennin, Peter (Peter Mennini) (composer); Erie, Pa. **(1923-1983)**
Menninger, William C. (psychiatrist); Topeka, Kan. **(1899-1966)**
Menotti, Gian Carlo (composer); Cadegliano, Italy, 7/7/11
Menuhin, Yehudi (violinist, conductor); New York City, 4/22/16
Menzies, Robert Gordon (ex-Prime Minister); Jeparit, Australia **(1894-1978)**
Mercer, Johnny (songwriter); Savannah, Ga. **(1909-1976)**
Mercer, Mabel (singer); Burton-on-Trent, England **(1900-1984)**
Mercer, Marian (actress, singer); Akron, Ohio, 11/26/35
Merchant, Ismail (Ismail Noormohamed Abdul Rehman) (film producer); Bombay, India, 12/25/36
Mercouri, Melina (actress); Athens **(1925–1994)**
Meredith, Burgess (actor); Cleveland, 11/16/08
Merman, Ethel (Ethel Zimmerman) (singer, actress); Astoria, Queens, N.Y. **(1909-1984)**
Merrick, David (David Margulois) (stage producer); St. Louis, 11/27/12
Merrill, Dina (actress); New York City, 12/9/25
Merrill, Gary (actor); Hartford, Conn. **(1915-1990)**
Merrill, Robert (baritone); Brooklyn, N.Y., 6/4/19
Merton, Thomas (clergyman, writer); France **(1915-1968)**
Mesmer, Franz Anton (physician); Itzmang, nr. Constance (Germany) **(1733-1815)**
Mesta, Perle (social figure); Sturgis, Mich. **(1889-1975)**
Metacom (King Philip) (Wampanoag Indian sachem); (southeastern Mass.) **(1640–1676)**
Metternich, Prince Klemens Wenzel Nepomuk Lothar von (statesman); Coblenz (Germany) **(1773-1859)**
Mfume, Kweisi (Frizzell Gray) (politician, NAACP leader); Baltimore, Md., 10/24/48
Michelangelo Buonarroti (painter, sculptor, architect); Capres (Italy) **(1475-1564)**
Michener, James A. (novelist); New York City, 2/3/07
Mickiewicz, Adam (Polish poet); Zozie, Belorussia (Belarus) **(1798-1855)**
Midler, Bette (singer); Honolulu, 1945
Mielziner, Jo (stage designer); Paris **(1901-1976)**
Mies van der Rohe, Ludwig (architect, designer); Aachen, Germany **(1886-1969)**
Mikoyan, Anastas I. (diplomat); Sanain, Armenia **(1895-1978)**
Miles, Sarah (actress); Essex, England, 12/31/43
Miles, Sylvia (actress); New York City, 9/9/32
Miles, Vera (Vera Ralston) (actress); nr. Boise City, Okla., 8/23/30
Milhaud, Darius (composer); Aix-en-Provence, France **(1892-1974)**
Mill, John Stuart (philosopher); London, **(1806-1873)**
Milland, Ray (Reginald Truscott-Jones) (actor); Neath, Wales **(1907-1986)**
Millay, Edna St. Vincent (poet); Rockland, Me. **(1892-1950)**
Miller, Ann (Lucille Ann Collier) (dancer, actress); Cherino, Tex. 4/12/23
Miller, Arthur (playwright); New York City, 10/17/15
Miller, Glenn (band leader); Clarinda, Iowa **(1904-1944)**
Miller, Henry (novelist); New York City **(1891-1980)**
Miller, Jason (John Miller) (playwright); New York City, 1939(?)
Miller, Mitch (Mitchell) (musician); Rochester, N.Y., 7/4/11
Miller, Roger (singer); Fort Worth **(1936-1992)**
Millet, Jean François (painter); Gruchy, France **(1814-1875)**
Millett, Kate (feminist); St. Paul, 9/14/34
Millikan, Robert A. (physicist); Morrison, Ill. **(1869-1953)**
Mills, Donna (actress); Chicago, 12/11/41
Mills, Hayley (actress); London, 4/18/46
Mills, John (actor); Felixstowe, England, 2/22/08
Mills, Juliet (actress); London, 11/21/41
Milne, A(lan) A(lexander) (author); London **(1882-1956)**

N

Nation, Carry Amelia (temperance leader); Garrard County, Ky. **(1846-1911)**
Natwick, Mildred (actress); Baltimore **(1905–1994)**
Neal, Patricia (actress); Packard, Ky., 1/20/26
Neeson, Liam (William John) (actor); Ballymena, Northern Ireland, 6/7/52
Neff, Hildegarde (actress); Ulm, Germany, 12/28/25
Nehru, Jawaharlal (first Prime Minister of India); Allahabad, India **(1889-1964)**
Nelligan, Kate (actress); London, Ont., Canada, 3/16/51
Nelson, Barry (Neilsen) (actor); San Francisco, 1920
Nelson, David (actor); New York City, 10/24/36
Nelson, Harriet Hilliard (Peggy Lou Snyder) (actress); Des Moines, Iowa **(1909–1994)**
Nelson, Ozzie (Oswald) (actor); Jersey City, N.J. **(1907-1975)**
Nelson, Ricky (Eric) (singer, actor); Teaneck, N.J. **(1940-1985)**
Nelson, Viscount Horatio (naval officer); Burnham Thorpe, England **(1758-1805)**
Nelson, Willie (singer); Waco, Texas, 4/30/33
Nenni, Pietro (Socialist leader); Faenza, Italy **(1891-1980)**
Nero (Nero Claudius Caesar Drusus Germanicus) (Roman emperor); Antium (Italy) **(37-68)**
Nero, Peter (pianist); New York City, 5/22/34
Netanyahu, Benjamin (Binyamin) (Israeli Prime Minister); Tel Aviv, Israel, 10/21/49
Nevelson, Louise (sculptor); Kiev, Russia **(1899-1988)**
Newhart, Bob (entertainer); Chicago, 9/5/29
Newhouse, Samuel I. (publisher); New York City **(1895-1979)**
Newley, Anthony (actor, song writer); London, 9/24/31
Newman, Edwin (news commentator); New York City, 1/25/19
Newman, John Henry (prelate); London **(1801-1890)**
Newman, Paul (actor, director); Cleveland, 1/26/25
Newman, Randy (singer); Los Angeles, 11/28/43
Newton, Huey (black activist); New Orleans **(1942-1989)**
Newton, Sir Isaac (mathematician, scientist); nr. Grantham, England **(1642-1727)**
Newton, Wayne (singer); Norfolk, Va., 4/3/42
Newton-John, Olivia (singer); Cambridge, England, 9/26/48
Nichols, Mike (Michael Peschkowsky) (stage and film director); Berlin, 11/6/31
Nicholson, Jack (actor); Neptune, N.J., 4/22/37
Nietzsche, Friedrich Wilhelm (philosopher); nr. Lützen Saxony (Germany) **(1844-1900)**
Nightingale, Florence (nurse); Florence, Italy **(1820-1910)**
Nijinsky, Vaslav (ballet dancer); Warsaw **(1890-1950)**
Nilsson, Birgit (soprano); West Karup, Sweden, 5/17/23
Nilsson, Harry (singer, songwriter); Brooklyn, N.Y. **(1941–1994)**
Nimitz, Chester W. (naval officer); Fredericksburg, Tex. **(1885-1966)**
Nimoy, Leonard (actor); Boston, 3/26/31
Nin, Anais (author, diarist); Neuilly, France **(1903-1977)**
Niven, David (actor); Kirriemuir, Scotland **(1910-1983)**
Nizer, Louis (lawyer, author); London **(1902–1994)**
Nobel, Alfred Bernhard (industrialist); Stockholm **(1833-1896)**
Noguchi, Isamu (sculptor); Los Angeles **(1904-1988)**
Nolan, Lloyd (actor); San Francisco **(1902-1985)**
Nolte, Nick (actor); Omaha, Neb., 1942
Norell, Norman (Norman Levinson) (fashion designer); Noblesville, Ind. **(1900-1972)**
Norman, Jessye (soprano); Augusta, Ga., 9/15/45
Norman, Marsha (Marsha Williams) (playwright); Louisville, Ky., 9/21/47
Normand, Mabel (actress); Boston **(1894-1930)**
Norstad, Gen. Lauris (ex-commander of NATO forces); Minneapolis **(1907-1988)**
North, John Ringling (circus director); Baraboo, Wis. **(1903-1985)**
North, Oliver (ex-military officer); San Antonio, Tex., 10/7/43
Norton, Eleanor Holmes (U.S. Representative); Washington, D.C., 6/13/37
Nostradamus (Michel de Notredame) (astrologer); St. Rémy, France **(1503-1566)**
Novaes, Guiomar (pianist); São João de Boa Vista, Brazil **(1895-1979)**
Novak, Kim (Marilyn Novak) (actress); Chicago, 2/13/33
Novarro, Ramon (Ramon Samaniegoes) (actor); Durango, Mexico **(1899-1968)**
Novello, Ivor (actor, playwright, composer); Cardiff, Wales **(1893-1951)**
Nugent, Elliott (actor, director); Dover, Ohio, **(1899-1980)**
Nureyev, Rudolf (ballet dancer); Siberia **(1938-1993)**
Nyro, Laura (singer, songwriter); Bronx, N.Y., 1947

O

Oakie, Jack (actor); Sedalia, Mo. **(1903-1978)**
Oakley, Annie (Phoebe Anne Oakley Mozee) (markswoman); Darke County, Ohio **(1860-1926)**
Oates, Joyce Carol (novelist); Lockport, N.Y., 6/16/38
Oberon, Merle (Estelle Merle O'Brien Thompson) (actress); Calcutta, India **(1911-1979)**
Oberth, Hermann (rocketry and space flight pioneer); Hermannstadt, Romania **(1894-1989)**
O'Brian, Hugh (Hugh J. Krampe) (actor); Rochester, N.Y., 4/19/30
O'Brien, Edmond (actor); New York City **(1915-1985)**
O'Brien, Margaret (Angela Maxine O'Brien) (actress); San Diego, Calif., 1/15/37
O'Brien, Pat (William Joseph O'Brien, Jr.) (actor); Milwaukee **(1899-1983)**
O'Casey, Sean (playwright); Dublin **(1881-1964)**
Ochs, Adolph Simon (publisher); Cincinnati **(1858-1935)**
O'Connor, Carroll (actor); New York City, 8/2/24
Odets, Clifford (playwright); Philadelphia **(1906-1963)**
Odetta (Odetta Holmes) (folk singer, actress); Birmingham, Ala., 12/31/30
Offenbach, Jacques (composer); Cologne, Germany **(1819-1880)**
O'Hara, John (novelist); Pottsville, Pa. **(1905-1970)**
O'Hara, Maureen (Maureen FitzSimons) (actress); Dublin, 8/17/21
Ohlsson, Garrick (pianist); Bronxville, N.Y., 4/3/48
Ohrbach, Jerry (actor, singer); Bronx, N.Y., 10/20/35
Oistrakh, David (concert violinist); Odessa, Russia **(1908-1974)**
O'Keeffe, Georgia (painter); Sun Prairie, Wis. **(1887-1986)**
Oland, Warner (actor); Umea, Sweden **(1880-1938)**
Oldenburg, Claes (painter); Stockholm, Sweden, 1/28/29
Oliphant, Patrick B. (editorial cartoonist); Adelaide, Australia, 7/24/35
Oliver, Edna May (actress); Malden, Mass. **(1883-1942)**
Olivier, Lord (Laurence) (actor); Dorking, England **(1907-1989)**
Olmsted, Frederick Law (landscape architect); Hartford, Conn **(1822-1903)**
Olsen, Ole (John Sigvard Olsen) (comedian); Peru, Ind. **(1892-1963)**
Omar Khayyam (poet, astronomer); Nishapur (Iran) **(died c. 1123)**
Onassis, Aristotle (shipping executive); Smyrna, Turkey **(1906-1975)**
Onassis, Christina (shipping executive); New York City **(1950-1988)**
Onassis, Jacqueline Kennedy (Jacqueline Bouvier) (President's widow); Southampton, N.Y. **(1929–1994)**
O'Neal, Ryan (Patrick) (actor); Los Angeles, 4/20/41
O'Neal, Tatum (actress); Los Angeles, 11/5/63
O'Neill, Eugene Gladstone (playwright); New York City **(1888-1953)**
O'Neill, Jennifer (actress); Rio de Janeiro, 2/20/49
Oppenheimer, J. Robert (nuclear physicist); New York City **(1904-1967)**
Orff, Carl (composer); Munich, Germany **(1895-1982)**
Orlando, Tony (Michael Anthony Orlando Cassavitis) (singer); New York City, 4/3/44
Ormandy, Eugene (conductor); Budapest **(1899-1985)**
Orozco, José Clemente (painter); Zapotlán, Jalisco, Mexico **(1883-1949)**
Orwell, George (Eric Arthur Blair) (British author); Motihari, Indi **(1903-1950)**
Osborn, Paul (playwright); Evansville, Ind. **(1901-1988)**
Osborne, John (playwright); London **(1929–1994)**
Osler, Sir William (physician); Bondhead, Ontario, Canada **(1849-1919)**
Osmond, Donny (singer); Ogden, Utah, 12/9/57
Osmond, Marie (singer); Ogden, Utah, 1959
O'Sullivan, Maureen (actress); County Roscommon, Ireland, 5/17/11
Oswald, Lee Harvey (presumed assassin); New Orleans **(1939–196**
Otis, Elisha (inventor); Halifax, Vt. **(1811-1861)**
O'Toole, Peter (actor); Connemara, Ireland, 8/2/33
Ovid (Publius Ovidius Naso) (poet); Sulmona (Italy) **(43 B.C.-?A.D. 17**
Owens, Buck (Alvis Edgar Owens) (singer); Sherman, Tex., 8/12/2
Ozawa, Seiji (orchestra conductor); Fentian (Shenyan), Manchuri 7/1/35

P

Paar, Jack (TV personality); Canton, Ohio, 5/1/18
Pacino, Al (Alfred) (actor); New York City, 4/25/40
Packard, Vance (author); Granville Summit, Pa., 5/22/14
Paderewski, Ignace Jan (pianist, statesman); Kurylowka, Russi Podolia **(1860-1941)**
Paganini, Nicolò (violinist); Genoa, Italy **(1782-1840)**
Page, Geraldine (actress); Kirksville, Mo. **(1924-1987)**
Page, Patti (Clara Ann Fowler) (singer, entertainer); Claremo Okla., 11/8/27
Pagels, Elaine Hiesey (religious scholar); Palo Alto, Calif., 2/13/4
Paglia, Camille (writer, social critic); Endicott, N.Y., 4/2/47
Paine, Thomas (political philosopher); Thetford, England **(1737-180**
Palance, Jack (Walter Palanuik) (actor); Lattimer, Pa., 2/18/20

Palestrina, Giovanni Pierluigi da (composer); Palestrina, (Italy) **(1526-1594)**
Paley, William S. (broadcasting executive); Chicago **(1901–1990)**
Palladio, Andrea (architect); Padua or Vicenza, Italy **(1508-1580)**
Palmerston, Henry John Templeton (3rd Viscount) (statesman); Broadlands, England **(1784-1865)**
Papanicolaou, George N. (physician); Coumi, Greece **(1883-1962)**
Papas, Irene (actress); Chiliomodion, Greece, 1929
Papp, Joseph (Joseph Papirofsky) (stage producer, director); Brooklyn, N.Y. **(1921-1991)**
Paracelaus, Philippus (Aureolus Theophrastus Bombastus von Hohenheim) (physican); Einsiedeln, Switzerland **(1493-1541)**
Park, Chung Hee (President of South Korea); Sangmo-ri, Korea **(1917-1979)**
Parker, Charlie "Bird" (jazz musician); Kansas City, Kan. **(1920–1955)**
Parker, Dorothy (Dorothy Rothschild) (author); West End, N.J. **(1893-1967)**
Parker, Fess (actor); Fort Worth, Tex., 1925
Parker, Suzy (model, actress); San Antonio, 10/28/33
Parkinson, C(yril) Northcote (historian); Durham, England **(1909-1993)**
Parkman, Francis (historian); Boston **(1823–1893)**
Parks, Bert (Bert Jacobson) (entertainer); Atlanta **(1914-1992)**
Parks, Gordon (film director); Ft. Scott, Kan., 11/30/12
Parks, Rosa (civil rights activist); Tuskegee, Ala., 2/4/13
Parnell, Charles Stewart (statesman); Avondale, Ireland **(1846-1891)**
Parnis, Mollie (Mollie Parnis Livingston) (fashion designer); New York City **(1905(?)-1992)**
Parsons, Estelle (actress); Marblehead, Mass., 11/20/27
Parton, Dolly (singer); Locust Ridge, Tenn. 1/19/46
Pascal, Blaise (philosopher); Clermont, France **(1623-1662)**
Pasternak, Boris Leonidovich (author); Moscow **(1890-1960)**
Pasternak, Joseph (film producer); Silagy-Somlyo, Romania **(1901–1991)**
Pasteur, Louis (chemist); Dôle, France **(1822-1895)**
Pastor, Tony (Antonio) (actor, theater manager); New York City **(1837-1908)**
Pater, Walter (Horatio) (writer); London **(1839–1894)**
Paton, Alan (author); Pietermaritzburg, South Africa **(1903-1988)**
Patti, Adelina (soprano); Madrid **(1843-1919)**
Patton, George Smith, Jr. (general); San Gabriel, Calif. **(1885-1945)**
Paul, Alice (feminist, woman suffragist); Moorestown, N.J. **(1885–1977)**
Paul, Les (Lester William Polfus) (guitarist); Waukesha, Wis., 6/9/15
Paul VI (Giovanni Battista Montini) (Pope); Concesio, nr. Brescia, Italy **(1897-1978)**
Pauley, Jane (TV newscaster); Indianapolis, 10/31/50
Pauling, Linus Carl (chemist); Portland, Ore. **(1901–1994)**
Pavarotti, Luciano (tenor); Modena, Italy, 10/12/35
Pavlov, Ivan Petrovich (physiologist); Ryazan district, Russia **(1849-1936)**
Pavlova, Anna (ballerina); St. Petersburg, Russia **(1885-1931)**
Peale, Norman Vincent (clergyman); Bowersville, Ohio **(1898–1993)**
Pearl, Minnie (Sarah Ophelia Colley Cannon) (comedienne, singer); Centerville, Tenn. **(1912–1996)**
Pears, Peter (tenor); Farnham, England **(1910-1986)**
Pearson, Drew (Andrew Russel Pearson) (columnist); Evanston, Ill. **(1897-1969)**
Pearson, Lester B. (statesman); Toronto **(1897-1972)**
Peary, Robert Edwin (explorer); Cresson, Pa. **(1856-1920)**
Peck, Gregory (actor); La Jolla, Calif., 4/5/16
Peckinpah, Sam (film director); Fresno, Calif. **(1925-1984)**
Peerce, Jan (tenor); New York City **(1904-1984)**
Pegler, (James) Westbrook (columnist); Minneapolis **(1894-1969)**
Pei, I(eoh) M(ing) (architect); Canton, China, 4/26/17
Penn, Arthur (stage and film director); Philadelphia, 9/27/22
Penn, Sean (actor, filmmaker); Los Angeles, 8/17/60
Penn, William (American colonist); London **(1644-1718)**
Penney, James C. (merchant); Hamilton, Mo. **(1875-1971)**
Peppard, George (actor); Detroit **(1929–1994)**
Pepys, Samuel (diarist); Bampton, England **(1633-1703)**
Perelman, S(idney) J(oseph) (writer); Brooklyn, N.Y. **(1904-1979)**
Pergolesi, Giovanni Battista (composer); Jesi, (Italy) **(1710-1736)**
Pericles (statesman); Athens **(died 429 B.C.)**
Perkins, Anthony (actor); New York City **(1932–1992)**
Perkins, Frances (social reformer); Boston **(1882–1965)**
Perlman, Itzhak (violinist); Tel Aviv, Israel, 8/31/45
Perlman, Rhea (actress); Brooklyn, N.Y., 3/31/48
Perón, Isabel (María Estela Martínez Cartas) (former chief of state); La Rioja, Argentina, 2/4/31
Perón, Juan D. (statesman); nr. Lobos, Argentina **(1895-1974)**
Perón, Maria Eva Duarte de (political leader); Los Toldos, Argentina **(1919-1952)**
Perot, H. Ross (business executive); Texarkana, Tex., 6/27/30
Perrine, Valerie (actress, dancer); Galveston, Tex., 9/3/43
Pershing, John Joseph (general); Linn County, Mo. **(1860-1948)**

Pestalozzi, Johann (educator); Zurich, Switzerland **(1746-1827)**
Peters, Bernadette (Bernadette Lazzara) (actress); New York City, 2/28/48
Peters, Brock (actor, singer); New York City, 7/2/27
Peters, Jean (actress); Canton, Ohio, 10/15/26
Peters, Roberta (Roberta Peterman) (soprano); New York City, 5/4/30
Petit, Roland (choreographer, dancer); Villemombe, France, 1924
Petrarch (Francesco Petrarca) (poet); Arezzo (Italy) **(1304-1374)**
Pfeiffer, Michelle (actress); Santa Ana, Calif., 4/29/58
Philip. see Metacom
Philip (Philip Mountbatten) (Duke of Edinburgh); Corfu, Greece, 6/10/21
Piaf, Edith (Edith Gassion) (chanteuse); Paris **(1916-1963)**
Piatigorsky, Gregor (cellist); Ekaterinoslav, Russia **(1903-1976)**
Piazza, Marguerite (soprano); New Orleans, 5/6/26
Picasso, Pablo (painter, sculptor); Málaga, Spain **(1881-1973)**
Pickett, Wilson (singer); Prattville, Ala., 3/18/41
Pickford, Mary (Gladys Mary Smith) (actress); Toronto **(1893-1979)**
Picon, Molly (actress); New York City **(1898-1992)**
Pidgeon, Walter (actor); East St. John, New Brunswick, Canada **(1898-1984)**
Pinter, Harold (playwright); London, 10/10/30
Pinza, Ezio (basso); Rome **(1892-1957)**
Pirandello, Luigi (dramatist, novelist); nr. Girgenti, Italy **(1867-1936)**
Piranesi, Giambattista (artist); Mestre (Italy) **(1720-1778)**
Pissaro, Camille Jacob (painter); St. Thomas (U.S. Virgin Islands) **(1830-1903)**
Piston, Walter (composer); Rockland, Me. **(1894-1976)**
Pitman, Sir (Isaac) James (educator, publisher); Bath, England, 8/14/01
Pitt, William ("Younger Pitt") (statesman); nr. Bromley, England **(1759-1806)**
Pitts, ZaSu (actress); Parsons, Kan. **(1898-1963)**
Pius XII (Eugenio Pacelli) (Pope); Rome **(1876-1958)**
Pizarro, Francisco (explorer); Trujillo, Spain **(1470?-1541)**
Planck, Max (physicist); Kiel, Germany **(1858-1947)**
Plath, Sylvia (poet); Boston **(1932–1963)**
Plato (Aristocies) (philosopher); Athens (?) **(427?-347 B.C.)**
Pleasence, Donald (actor); Worksop, England **(1919–1995)**
Pleshette, Suzanne (actress); New York City, 1/31/37
Plimpton, George (author); New York City, 3/18/27
Plisetskaya, Maya (ballerina); Moscow, 11/20/25
Plowright, Joan (actress); Brigg, England, 10/28/29
Plummer, Christopher (actor); Toronto, 12/13/29
Plutarch (biographer); Chaeronea (Greece) **(46?-?120)**
Pocahontas (Matoaka) (American Indian princess); Virginia (?) **(1595?-1617)**
Podhoretz, Norman (author); Brooklyn, N.Y., 1/16/30
Poe, Edgar Allan (poet, story writer); Boston, Mass. **(1809-1849)**
Poitier, Sidney (film actor, director); Miami, Fla., 2/20/27
Polanski, Roman (film director); Paris, 8/18/33
Pollard, Michael J. (actor); Passaic, N.J., 5/30/39
Pollock, Jackson (painter); Cody, Wyo. **(1912-1956)**
Polo, Marco (traveler); Venice **(1254?-?1324)**
Pol Pot (Cambodian political leader); Kompong Thom, Cambodia, 5/19/28
Pompadour, Mme. de (Jeanne Antoinette Poisson) (courtesan); Versailles **(1721-1764)**
Pompey (Gnaeus Pompeius Magnus) (general); Rome (?) **(106-48 B.C.)**
Ponce de León, Juan (explorer); Servas, Spain **(1460?-1521)**
Pons, Lily (coloratura soprano); Cannes, France **(1904-1976)**
Ponselle, Rosa (soprano); Meriden, Conn. **(1897-1981)**
Ponti, Carlo (director); Milan, Italy, 12/11/13
Pontormo, Jacopo da (painter); Pontormo, Italy **(1492–1557)**
Pope, Alexander (poet); London **(1688-1744)**
Porter, Cole (songwriter); Peru, Ind. **(1891-1964)**
Porter, Katherine Anne (novelist); Indian Creek, Tex. **(1891-1980)**
Post, Wiley (aviator); Grand Plain, Tex. **(1900-1935)**
Poston, Tom (actor); Columbus, Ohio, 10/17/27
Potëmkin, Grigori Aleksandrovich, Prince (statesman); Khizovo (Khizov, Belarus) **(1739-1791)**
Potok, Chaim (author); New York City, 2/17/29
Potter, (Helen) Beatrix (author, illustrator); South Kensington, Middlesex, England **(1866–1943)**
Poulenc, Francis (composer); Paris **(1899-1963)**
Pound, Ezra (poet); Hailey, Idaho **(1885-1972)**
Poussin, Nicolas (painter); Villers, France **(1594-1665)**
Powell, Adam Clayton, Jr. (Congressman); New Haven, Conn. **(1908-1972)**
Powell, Colin L. (retired general); New York City, 4/5/37
Powell, Dick (actor); Mt. View, Ark. **(1904-1963)**
Powell, Eleanor (actress, tap dancer); Springfield, Mass. **(1912-1982)**
Powell, Jane (Suzanne Burce) (actress, singer); Portland, Ore., 4/1/29

Powell, William (actor); Pittsburgh (1892-1984)
Power, Tyrone (actor); Cincinnati, Ohio (1914-1958)
Powers, Stephanie (Taffy Paul) (actress); Hollywood, Calif., 11/12/42
Praxiteles (sculptor); Athens (c.370-c.330 B.C.)
Preminger, Otto (film director, producer); Vienna (1906-1986)
Prentiss, Paula (Paula Ragusa) (actress); San Antonio, 1939
Presley, Elvis (singer, actor); Tupelo, Miss. (1935-1977)
Presley, Priscilla (actress); Brooklyn, N.Y., 5/24/45
Preston, Robert (Robert Preston Meservey) (actor); Newton Highlands, Mass (1918-1987)
Previn, André (conductor); Berlin, 4/6/29
Previn, Dory (singer); Rahway, N.J., 10/22/29(?)
Price, Leontyne (Mary) (soprano); Laurel, Miss., 2/10/27
Price, Ray (country music artist); Perryville, Tex., 1/12/26
Price, Vincent (actor); St. Louis (1911–1993)
Pride, Charley (singer); Sledge, Miss., 3/18/38(?)
Priestley, J. B. (John B.) (author); Bradford, England (1894-1984)
Priestley, Joseph (chemist); nr. Leeds, England (1733-1804)
Primrose, William (violist); Glasgow, Scotland (1904-1982)
Prince (Prince Roger Nelson) (singer); Minneapolis, 6/7/58
Prince, Harold (stage producer); New York City, 1/30/28
Principal, Victoria (actress); Fukuoka, Japan, 1/3/45(?)
Prinze, Freddie (actor); New York City (1954-1977)
Pritchett, V(ictor) S(awdon) (literary critic); Ipswich, England, 12/16/00
Procter, William (scientist); Cincinnati (1872-1951)
Prokofiev, Sergei Sergeevich (composer); St. Petersburg, Russia (1891-1953)
Proulx, E. Annie (novelist); Norwich, Conn., 8/22/35
Proust, Marcel (novelist); Paris (1871-1922)
Provine, Dorothy (actress); Deadwood, S. Dak., 1/20/37
Prowse, Juliet (actress); Bombay, 9/25/36
Pryor, Richard (comedian); Peoria, Ill., 12/1/40
Ptolemy (Claudius Ptolemaeus) (astronomer, geographer); Ptolemais Hermii (Egypt) (2nd century A.D.)
Pucci, Emilio (Marchese di Barsento) (fashion designer); Naples, Italy (1914-1992)
Puccini, Giacomo (composer); Lucca, Italy (1858-1924)
Puente, Tito (band leader); New York City, 4/20/23
Pulaski, Casimir (military officer); Podolia, Poland (1748-1779)
Pulitzer, Joseph (publisher); Makó (Hungary) (1847-1911)
Pullman, George (inventor); Brockton, N.Y. (1831-1897)
Purcell, Henry (composer); London (1658-1695)
Pusey, Nathan M. (educator); Council Bluffs, Iowa, 4/4/07
Pushkin, Alexander Sergeevich (poet, dramatist); Moscow (1799-1837)
Puzo, Mario (novelist); New York City, 10/15/21
Pyle, Ernest Taylor (journalist); Dana, Ind. (1900-1945)
Pythagoras (mathematician, philosopher); Samos (Greece) (6th century B.C.)

Q

Qaddafi, Muammar al- (Libyan leader); Libya, 1942
Quaid, Dennis (actor); Houston, Tex., 4/9/54
Quaid, Randy, (actor); Houston, Texas, 10/1/50
Quayle, Anthony (actor); Ainsdale, England (1913-1989)
Queen, Ellery: pen name of the late Frederic Dannay and the late Manfred B. Lee
Queler, Eve (conductor); New York City, 1/1/36
Quennell, Sir Peter Courtney (biographer); Bromley, England (1905–1993)
Quindlen, Anna (writer); Philadelphia, 7/8/53
Quinn, Anthony (actor); Chihuahua, Mexico, 4/21/16

R

Rabe, David (playwright); Dubuque, Iowa, 3/10/40
Rabelais, François (satirist); nr. Chinon, France (1494?-1553)
Rabi, I(sidor) I(saac) (physicist); Rymanow (Poland) (1898-1988)
Rabin, Yitzhak (former Israeli Prime Minister); Jerusalem (1922–1995)
Rachmaninoff, Sergei Wassilievitch (pianist, composer); Oneg Estate, Novgorod, Russia (1873-1943)
Racine, Jean Baptiste (dramatist); La Ferté-Milon, France (1639-1699)
Radner, Gilda (comedienne); Detroit (1946-1989)
Raft, George (actor); New York City (1895-1980)
Rainier III (Prince); Monaco, 5/31/23
Rains, Claude (actor); London (1889-1967)
Raitt, Bonnie (singer); Burbank, Calif., 11/8/49
Raitt, John (actor, singer); Santa Ana, Calif., 1/29(?)/17
Raleigh, Sir Walter (courtier, navigator); London (1552?-1618)
Rambeau, Marjorie (actress); San Francisco (1889-1970)
Rameau, Jean-Philippe (composer); Dijon? France (1683-1764)

Rampal, Jean-Pierre (Louis) (flutist); Marseilles, France, 7/1/22
Rand, Ayn (novelist, philosopher); St. Petersburg, Russia (1905–1982)
Randall, Tony (Leonard Rosenberg) (actor); Tulsa, Okla., 2/26/20
Randolph, A(sa) Philip (labor leader); Crescent City, Fla. (1889-1979)
Rankin, Jeannette (pacifist); Missoula, Mont. (1880–1973)
Raphael (Raffaello Santi) (painter, architect); Urbino, Italy (1483-1520)
Rasputin, Grigori Efimovich (monk); Tobolsk Province, Russia (1871?-1916)
Rathbone, Basil (actor); Johannesburg, South Africa (1892-1967)
Rather, Dan (TV newscaster); Wharton, Tex., 10/31/31
Rattigan, Terence (playwright); London (1911-1977)
Rauschenberg, Robert (painter); Port Arthur, Tex., 10/22/25
Ravel, Maurice Joseph (composer); Ciboure, France (1875-1937)
Ray, Aldo (DaRe) (actor); Pen Argyl, Pa. (1926–1991)
Ray, Gene Anthony (actor, dancer); Harlem, N.Y., 5/24/63
Ray, Man (painter); Philadelphia (1890-1976)
Ray, Satyajat (film director); Calcutta (1921-1992)
Rayburn, Gene (TV personality); Christopher, Ill., 12/22/17
Raye, Martha (Margie Yvonne Reed) (comedienne, actress); Butte, Mont. (1916–1994)
Reasoner, Harry (TV commentator); Dakota City, Iowa (1923–1991)
Redding, Otis (singer); Dawson, Ga. (1941-1967)
Reddy, Helen (singer); Melbourne, 10/25/41
Redford, Robert (Charles Robert Redford, Jr.) (actor); Santa Monica, Calif. 8/18/37
Redgrave, Lynn (actress); London, 3/8/43
Redgrave, Sir Michael (actor); Bristol, England (1908-1985)
Redgrave, Vanessa (actress); London, 1/30/37
Redon, Odilon (artist); Bordeaux, France (1840–1916)
Reed, Donna (actress); Denison, Iowa (1921-1986)
Reed, Rex (critic); Ft. Worth, 10/2/40
Reed, Walter (army surgeon); Belroi, Va. (1851-1902)
Reese, Della (Deloreese Patricia Early) (singer); Detroit, 7/6/32
Reeve, Christopher (actor); New York City, 9/25/52
Reeves, Jim (singer); Panola County, Tex. (1923-1964)
Reich, Robert (U.S. Secretary of Labor); Scranton, Pa., 6/24/46
Reich, Steve (composer); New York City, 10/3/36
Reiner, Carl (actor); New York City, 3/20/22
Reiner, Fritz (conductor); Budapest (1888-1963)
Reiner, Robert (actor); Bronx, N.Y., 1945
Reinhardt, Max (Max Goldmann) (theater producer); nr. Vienna (1873-1943)
Remarque, Erich Maria (novelist); Osnabrück, Germany (1898-1970)
Rembrandt (Rembrandt Harmensz van Rijn) (painter); Leyden (Netherlands) (1605-1669)
Remick, Lee (Ann) (actress); Boston (1935–1991)
Rennert, Günther (opera director, producer); Essen, Germany, 4/1/11
Rennie, Michael (actor); Bradford, England (1909-1971)
Reno, Janet (U.S. Attorney General); Miami, Fla., 7/21/38
Renoir, Jean (film director, writer); Paris, (1894-1979)
Renoir, Pierre Auguste (painter); Limoges, France (1841-1919)
Resnais, Alain (film director); Vannes, France, 6/3/22
Resnik, Regina (mezzo-soprano); New York City, 8/30/22
Respighi, Ottorino (composer); Bologna, Italy (1879-1936)
Reston, James (journalist); Clydebank, Scotland (1909–1995)
Reuther, Walter (labor leader); Wheeling, W. Va. (1907-1970)
Revere, Paul (silversmith, hero of famous ride); Boston (1735-1818)
Revson, Charles (business executive); Boston (1906-1975)
Reynolds, Burt (actor); Lansing, Mich., 2/11/36
Reynolds, Debbie (Marie Frances Reynolds) (actress); El Paso, 4/1/32
Reynolds, Sir Joshua (painter); nr. Plymouth, England (1723-1792)
Reynolds, Marjorie (Goodspeed) (actress); Buhl, Idaho, 8/12/21
Rhodes, Cecil John (South African statesman); Bishop Stortford, England (1853-1902)
Rice, Anne (novelist); New Orleans, 10/14/41
Rice, Elmer (playwright); New York City (1892-1967)
Rice, Grantland (sports writer); Murfreesboro, Tenn. (1880-1954)
Rich, Buddy (Bernard) (drummer); Brooklyn, N.Y. (1917-1987)
Rich, Charlie (singer); Colt, Ark. (1932–1995)
Richards, Ann (Dorothy Ann Willis) (ex-governor of Texas); Lakeview, Tex., 9/1/33
Richards, Keith (rock singer); Dartford, England, 12/18/43
Richardson, Elliot L. (ex-Cabinet member); Boston, 7/20/20
Richardson, Sir Ralph (actor); Cheltenham, England (1902-1983)
Richardson, Tony (director); Shipley, England (1928-1991)
Richelieu, Duc de (Armand Jean du Plessis) (cardinal); Paris (1585-1642)
Richie, Lionel (singer-songwriter); Tuskegee, Ala., 1949 (?)
Richter, Charles Francis (seismologist); Hamilton, Canada (1900-1985)
Richter, Sviatosiav (pianist); Zhitomir, Ukraine, 3/20/14
Rickenbacker, Edward V. (aviator); Columbus, Ohio (1890-1973)
Rickey, Branch (baseball executive); Stockdale, Ohio (1881–1965)
Rickles, Don (comedian); New York City, 5/8/26
Rickover, Vice Admiral Hyman G. (atomic energy expert); Russia (1900-1986)

Riddle, Nelson (composer); Hackensack, N.J. **(1921-1985)**

Ride, Sally K(risten) (astronaut, astrophysicist); Encino, Calif., 5/26/51

Ridgway, General Matthew B. (ex-Army Chief of Staff); Ft. Monroe, Va. **(1895-1993)**

Riemenschneider, Tilman (sculptor); Osterode, Germany **(c. 1460–1531)**

Rigg, Diana (actress); Doncaster, England, 7/20/38

Riley, James Whitcomb (poet); Greenfield, Ind. **(1849-1916)**

Rilke, Rainer Maria (poet); Prague **(1875–1926)**

Rimbaud, (Jean Nicolas) Arthur (poet); Charleville, France **(1854–1891)**

Rimsky-Korsakov, Nikolai Andreevich (composer); Tikhvin, Russia **(1844-1908)**

Rinehart, Mary (née Roberts) (novelist); Pittsburgh **(1876-1958)**

Ritchard, Cyril (actor, director); Sydney, Australia **(1898-1977)**

Ritter, John (Jonathan) (actor); Burbank, Calif., 9/17/48

Ritter, Tex (Woodward Maurice Ritter) (singer); Panola County, Tex., **(1905-1973)**

Ritter, Thelma (actress); Brooklyn, N.Y. **(1905-1969)**

Rivera, Chita (Dolores Conchita Figuero del Rivero) (dancer, actress, singer); Washington, D.C. 1/23/33

Rivera, Diego (painter); Guanajuato, Mexico **(1886-1957)**

Rivera, Geraldo (Miguel) (TV host); New York City, 7/3/43

Rivers, Joan (comedienne); Brooklyn, N.Y., 6/8/33

Rivers, Larry (Yitzroch Loiza Grossberg) (painter); New York City, 8/17/23

Roach, Hal (film producer); Elmira, N.Y. **(1892–1992)**

Robards, Jason, Jr. (actor); Chicago, 7/26/22

Robards, Jason, Sr. (actor); Hillsdale, Mich. **(1892-1963)**

Robbins, Harold (Harold Rubin) (novelist); New York City, 5/21/16

Robbins, Jerome (Jerome Rabinowitz) (choreographer); New York City, 10/11/18

Robbins, Marty (singer); Glendale, Ariz., **(1925-1982)**

Robbins, Tim (Timothy Francis) (actor, director); West Covina, Calif., 10/16/58

Roberts, Cokie (Mary Martha Corinne Morrison Claiborne Boggs) (broadcast journalist); New Orleans, 12/27/43

Roberts, Eric (actor); Bilox, Miss., 4/18/56

Roberts, Julia (actress); Smyrna, Ga., 10/28/67

Roberts, (Granville) Oral (evangelist, publisher); nr. Ada, Okla., 1/24/18

Robertson, Cliff (actor); La Jolla, Calif., 9/9/25

Robertson, Dale (Dayle) (actor); Oklahoma City, 7/14/23

Robeson, Paul (singer, actor); Princeton, N.J. **(1898-1976)**

Robespierre, Maximilien François Marie Isidore de (French Revolutionist); Arras, France **(1758-1794)**

Robinson, Bill "Bojangles" (Luther) (dancer); Richmond, Va. **(1878-1949)**

Robinson, Edward G. (Emanuel Goldenberg) (actor); Bucharest **(1893-1973)**

Robinson, Edwin Arlington (poet); Head Tide, Me. **(1869-1935)**

Robinson, Smokey (singer, songwriter); Detroit, 2/19/40

Rochester (Eddie Anderson) (actor); Oakland, Calif. **(1905-1977)**

Rockefeller, David (banker); New York City, 6/12/15

Rockefeller, John Davison (business executive); Richford, N.Y. **(1839-1937)**

Rockefeller, John Davison, Jr. (industrialist); Cleveland **(1874-1960)**

Rockefeller, John D., 3rd (philanthropist); New York City **(1906-1978)**

Rockefeller, Laurance S. (conservationist); New York City, 5/26/10

Rockwell, Norman (painter, illustrator); New York City **(1894-1978)**

Rodgers, Jimmie (singer); Meridian, Miss. **(1897-1933)**

Rodgers, Richard (composer); New York City **(1902-1979)**

Rodin, François Auguste René (sculptor); Paris **(1840-1917)**

Rodzinski, Artur (conductor); Spalato, Dalmatia **(1894-1958)**

Roeg, Nicolas (film director); London, 8/15/28

Roentgen, Wilhelm Konrad (physicist); Lennep, Prussia **(1845-1923)**

Roethke, Theodore (poet); Saginaw, Mich. **(1908–1963)**

Rogers, Buddy (Charles) (actor); Olathe, Kan., 8/13/04

Rogers, Carl (psychologist); Oak Park, Ill. **(1902-1987)**

Rogers, Fred (TV producer, host); Latrobe, Pa., 3/20/28

Rogers, Ginger (Virginia McMath) (dancer, actress); Independence, Mo. **(1911–1995)**

Rogers, Kenny (singer); Houston, 1939(?)

Rogers, Roy (Leonard Slye) (actor); Cincinnati, 11/5/12

Rogers, Wayne (actor); Birmingham, Ala. 4/7/33

Rogers, Will (William Penn Adair Rogers) (humorist); Oologah, Okla. **(1879-1935)**

Rogers, William P. (ex-Secretary of State); Norfolk, N.Y., 6/23/13

Roland, Gilbert (actor); Juarez, Mexico **(1905-1994)**

Rolland, Romain (author); Clamecy, France **(1866-1944)**

Rollins, Sonny (saxophonist); New York City, 9/7/30

Romberg, Sigmund (composer); Szeged (Hungary) **(1887-1951)**

Rome, Harold (composer); Hartford, Conn. **(1908–1993)**

Romero, Cesar (actor); New York City **(1907–1994)**

Romney, George W. (automobile executive, governor); Chihuahua,

Mexico **(1907–1995)**

Romulo, Carlos P. (diplomat, educator); Manila **(1899-1985)**

Ronsard, Pierre de (poet); La Possonnière nr. Couture (Couture-sur-Loire, France) **(1524-1585)**

Ronstadt, Linda (singer); Tucson, Ariz., 7/30/46

Rooney, Andy (TV personality); Albany, N.Y., 1/14/19

Rooney, Mickey (Joe Yule, Jr.) (actor); Brooklyn, N.Y., 9/23/20

Roosevelt, Anna Eleanor (reformer, humanitarian); New York City **(1884-1962)**

Rorem, Ned (composer); Richmond, Ind., 10/23/23

Rose, Billy (showman); New York City **(1899-1966)**

Rose, Leonard (concert cellist); Washington, D.C. **(1918-1984)**

Roseanne (Barr) (actress); Salt Lake City, 11/3/52

Rosenberg, Ethel (spy); New York City **(1915–1953)**

Rosenberg, Julius (spy); New York City **(1918–1953)**

Ross, Betsy (Betsey Griscom) (flagmaker); Philadelphia **(1752-1836)**

Ross, Diana (singer); Detroit, 3/26/44

Ross, Katharine (actress); Hollywood, Calif., 1/29/43

Rossellini, Isabella (model, actress); Rome, Italy, 6/18/52

Rossellini, Roberto (film director); Rome **(1906-1977)**

Rossetti, Christina Georgina (poet); London **(1830–1894)**

Rossetti, Dante Gabriel (painter, poet); London **(1828-1882)**

Rossini, Gioacchino Antonio (composer); Pesaro, Italy **(1792-1868)**

Rostand, Edmond (dramatist); Marseilles, France **(1868-1918)**

Rostow, Walt Whitman (economist); New York City, 10/7/16

Rostropovich, Mstislav (cellist, conductor); Baku, (Azerbaijan), 3/27/27

Roth, Henry (writer); Tysmenica (Ukraine) **(1906–1995)**

Roth, Philip (novelist); Newark, N.J., 3/19/33

Rothko, Mark (Marcus Rothkovich) (painter); Russia **(1903-1970)**

Rouault, Georges (painter); Paris **(1871-1958)**

Roundtree, Richard (actor); New Rochelle, N.Y., 9/7/42

Rousseau, Henri (painter); Laval, France **(1844-1910)**

Rousseau, Jean Jacques (philosopher); Geneva **(1712-1778)**

Rovere, Richard H. (journalist); Jersey City, N.J., 5/5/15

Rowan, Carl Thomas (journalist); Ravenscroft, Tenn., 8/11/25

Rowan, Dan (comedian); Beggs, Okla. **(1922-1987)**

Rowlands, Gena (actress); Cambria, Wis., 6/19/36(?)

Rubens, Sir Peter Paul (painter); Siegen (Germany) **(1577-1640)**

Rubinstein, Arthur (concert pianist); Lódz (Poland) **(1887-1982)**

Rubinstein, Helena (cosmetics executive); Krakow (Poland) **(1882?-1965)**

Rubinstein, John (actor, composer); Los Angeles, 12/8/46

Rudel, Julius (conductor); Vienna, 3/6/21

Ruffo, Titta (baritone); Italy **(1878-1953)**

Runyon, (Alfred) Damon (journalist); Manhattan, Kan. **(1884-1945)**

Rushdie, (Ahmed) Salman (novelist); Bombay, India, 6/19/47

Rusk, Dean (ex-Sec. of State); Cherokee County, Ga. **(1909–1994)**

Ruskin, John (art critic); London **(1819-1900)**

Russell, Lord Bertrand (Arthur William) (mathematician, philosopher); Trelleck, Wales **(1872-1970)**

Russell, Jane (actress); Bemidji, Minn., 6/21/21

Russell, Ken (film director); Southhampton, England, 4/3/27

Russell, Leon (pianist, singer); Lawton, Okla., 4/2/41

Russell, Lillian (Helen Louise Leonard) (soprano); Clinton, Iowa **(1861-1922)**

Russell, Mark (satirist); Buffalo, N.Y., 8/23/32

Russell, Nipsy (comedian); Atlanta, 1924(?)

Russell, Rosalind (actress); Waterbury, Conn. **(1912-1976)**

Rustin, Bayard (civil rights leader); West Chester, Pa. **(1910-1987)**

Rutherford, Dame Margaret (actress); London **(1892-1972)**

Ryan, Robert (actor); Chicago **(1909-1973)**

Rydell, Bobby (singer); Philadelphia, 1942

Ryder, Winona (Winona Horowitz) (actress); Winona, Minn., 10/29/71

Rysanek, Leonie (dramatic soprano); Vienna, 11/14/28

S

Saarinen, Eero (architect); Finland **(1910-1961)**

Sabin, Albert B. (polio researcher); Bialystok (Poland) **(1906-1993)**

Sabu (Dastagir) (actor); Karapur, India **(1924-1963)**

Sacagawea (Shoshone Indian guide); Lemhi River valley, (Id.) **(1786?-1812?)**

Sachs, Jeffrey D. (economist, educator); Michigan, 1954

Sadat, Anwar el- (President); Egypt **(1918-1981)**

Sade, Marquis de (Donatien Alphonse Francois, Comte de Sade) (libertine, writer); Paris **(1740-1814)**

Safer, Morley (TV newscaster); Toronto, 11/8/31

Sagan, Carl (Edward) (astronomer, astrophysicist); New York City, 11/9/34

Sagan, Françoise (novelist); Cajarc, France, 6/21/35

Sahl, Mort (Morton Lyon Sahl) (comedian); Montreal, 5/11/27

Saint, Eva Marie (actress); Newark, N.J., 7/4/24

Shriver, Maria (TV co-host); Chicago, 11/6/55
Shriver, Sargent (Robert Sargent Shriver, Jr.) (business executive); Westminster, Md., 11/9/15
Shulman, Max (novelist); St. Paul **(1919-1988)**
Sibelius, Jean (Johann Julius Christian Sibelius) (composer); Tavastehus (Finland) **(1865-1957)**
Sidney, Sir Philip (poet); Penshurst, England **(1554-1586)**
Sidney, Sylvia (actress); New York City, 8/8/10
Siepi, Cesare (basso); Milan, Italy, 2/10/23
Signoret, Simone (Simone Kaminker) (actress); Wiesbaden, Germany **(1921-1985)**
Sihanouk, Norodom (King of Cambodia); Cambodia, 10/31/22
Sikorsky, Igor I. (inventor); Kiev, Ukraine **(1889-1972)**
Sills, Beverly (Belle Silverman) (soprano, opera director); Brooklyn, N.Y., 5/25/29
Sills, Milton (actor); Chicago **(1882-1930)**
Silone, Ignazio (Secondo Tranquilli) (novelist); Pescina del Marsi, Italy **(1900-1978)**
Silverman, Fred (broadcasting executive); New York City, 9/13/37
Silver, Ron (actor); New York City, 7/2/46
Silvers, Phil (Philip Silversmith) (comedian); Brooklyn, N.Y. **(1912-1985)**
Sim, Alastair (actor); Edinburgh, Scotland **(1900-1976)**
Simenon, Georges (Georges Sim) (mystery writer); Liège, Belgium **(1903-1989)**
Simmons, Jean (actress); Crouch Hill, London, 1/31/29
Simon, Carly (singer, songwriter); New York City, 6/25/45
Simon, Neil (playwright); Bronx, N.Y., 7/4/27
Simon, Norton (business executive); Portland, Ore. **(1907-1993)**
Simon, Paul (singer, songwriter); Newark, N.J., 11/5/42
Simon, Simone (actress); Marseilles, France, 4/23/14
Simone, Nina (Eunice Kathleen Waymoa) (singer, pianist); Tryon, N.C., 2/21/33
Sinatra, Frank (Francis Albert) (singer, actor); Hoboken, N.J., 12/12/15
Sinclair, Upton Beall (novelist); Baltimore **(1878-1968)**
Singer, Isaac Bashevis (novelist); Radzymin (Poland) **(1904-1991)**
Siqueiros, David (painter); Chihuahua, Mexico **(1896-1974)**
Sisley, Alfred (painter); Paris **(1839-1899)**
Sitting Bull (Prairie Sioux Indian Chief); on Grand River, S.D. **(c. 1835-1890)**
Skelton, Red (Richard) (comedian); Vincennes, Ind., 7/18/13
Skinner, B(urrhus) F(rederic) (psychologist); Susquehanna, Pa. **(1904-1990)**
Skinner, Otis (actor); Cambridge, Mass. **(1858-1942)**
Slatkin, Leonard (conductor); Los Angeles, 9/1/44
Sloan, Alfred P., Jr. (industrialist); New Haven, Conn. **(1875-1965)**
Sloan, John (painter); Lock Haven, Pa. **(1871-1951)**
Smetana, Bedrich (composer); Litomysl (Czech Republic) **(1824-1884)**
Smith, Adam (economist); Kirkaldy, Scotland **(1723-1790)**
Smith, Alexis (actress); Penticon, Canada **(1921-1993)**
Smith, Alfred Emanuel (politician); New York City **(1873-1944)**
Smith, Bessie (blues singer); Chattanooga, Tenn. **(1894-1937)**
Smith, Sir C. Aubrey (actor); London **(1863-1948)**
Smith, David (sculptor); Decatur, Ind. **(1906-1965)**
Smith, Harry (TV co-anchor); Hammond, Ind., 8/21/51
Smith, Howard K. (TV commentator); Ferriday, La., 5/12/14
Smith, Jaclyn (actress); Houston, 10/26/47
Smith, John (American colonist); Willoughby, Lincolnshire, England **(1580-1631)**
Smith, Joseph (religious leader); Sharon, Vt. **(1805-1844)**
Smith, Kate (Kathryn) (singer); Greenville, Va. **(1909-1986)**
Smith, Dame Maggie (actress); Ilford, England, 12/28/34
Smith, Patti Lee (singer, songwriter); Chicago, 12/30/46
Smith, Red (Walter) (sports columnist); Green Bay, Wis. **(1905-1982)**
Smits, Jimmy (actor); New York City, 7/9/58
Smollet, Tobias (novelist); Dalquhurn, Scotland **(1721-1771)**
Smothers, Dick (Richard) (comedian); Governors Island, New York City, 11/20/39
Smothers, Tom (Thomas) (comedian); Governors Island, New York City, 2/2/37
Snow, Lord (Charles Percy) (author); Leicester, England **(1905-1980)**
Snowdon, Earl of (Anthony Armstrong-Jones) (photographer); London, 3/7/30
Snyder, Tom (TV personality); Milwaukee, 5/12/36
Socrates (philosopher); Athens (469-399 B.C.)
Solomon (King of Israel); Jerusalem (?) **(died c. 933** B.C.**)**
Solon (lawgiver); Salamis (Greece) **(638?-559** B.C.**)**
Solti, Sir Georg (conductor); Budapest, 10/21/12
Solzhenitsyn, Aleksandr (novelist); Kislovodsk, Russia, 12/11/18
Somers, Suzanne (Suzanne Mahoney) (actress); San Bruno, Calif., 10/16/46
Somes, Michael (ballet dancer); Horsley, England **(1917-1994)**
Sommer, Elke (Elke Schletz) (actress); Berlin, 11/5/42

Sondheim, Stephen (composer); New York City, 3/22/30
Sontag, Susan (author, film director); New York City, 1/28/33
Sophocles (dramatist); nr. Athens **(467-406** B.C.**)**
Sothern, Ann (Harriette Lake) (actress); Valley City, N.D., 1/22/09
Soul, David (David Solberg) (actor); Chicago, 8/28/(?)
Sousa, John Philip (composer); Washington, D.C. **(1854-1932)**
Soyer, Raphael (painter); Borisoglebsk, Russia **(1899-1987)**
Spaak, Paul-Henri (statesman); Brussels **(1899-1972)**
Spacek, Sissy (Mary Elizabeth) (actress); Quitman, Tex., 12/25/49
Spark, Muriel (novelist); Edinburgh, Scotland, 2/1/18
Spector, Phil (rock producer); Bronx, N.Y., 12/25/40
Spencer, Herbert (philosopher); Derby, England **(1820-1903)**
Spender, Stephen (poet); nr. London **(1909-1995)**
Spengler, Oswald (philosopher); Blankenburg (Germany) **(1880-1936)**
Spenser, Edmund (poet); London **(1552?-1599)**
Spewack, Bella (playwright); Hungary **(1899-1990)**
Spiegel, Sam (producer); Jaroslaw (Poland) **(1901-1985)**
Spielberg, Steven (film director); Cincinnati, 12/18/47
Spillane, Mickey (Frank Spillane) (mystery writer); Brooklyn, N.Y., 3/9/18
Spinoza, Baruch (philosopher); Amsterdam (Netherlands) **(1632-1677)**
Spitalny, Phil (orchestra leader); **(1890-1970)**
Spivak, Lawrence (TV producer); Brooklyn, N.Y. **(1900-1994)**
Spock, Benjamin (pediatrician); New Haven, Conn., 5/2/03
Springsteen, Bruce (singer, songwriter); Freehold, N.J., 9/23/49
Sproul, Robert G. (educator); San Francisco **(1891-1975)**
Squanto (Wampanoag Indian emissary); Patuxet (Plymouth Bay, Mass.) **(c. 1590-1622)**
St. Denis, Ruth (dancer, choreographer); Newark, N.J. **(1878-1968)**
St. James, Susan (Susan Miller) (actress); Los Angeles, 8/14/46
St. John, Jill (actress); Los Angeles, 8/19/40
St. Johns, Adela Rogers (journalist, author); Los Angeles **(1894-1988)**
Stack, Robert (actor); Los Angeles, 1/13/19
Stafford, Jo (singer); Coalinga, Calif., 1918
Stahl, Lesley (broadcast journalist); Lynn, Mass., 12/16/41
Stalin, Joseph Vissarionovich (Iosif V. Dzhugashvili) (Soviet leader); nr. Tiflis (Georgia) **(1879-1953)**
Stallone, Sylvester (actor, writer); New York City, 7/6/46
Stamp, Terrence (actor); London, 1938
Stander, Lionel (actor); New York City **(1908-1994)**
Stanislavski (Konstantin Sergeevich Alekseev) (stage producer); Moscow **(1863-1938)**
Stanley, Sir Henry Morton (John Rowlands) (explorer); Denbigh, Wales **(1841-1904)**
Stanley, Kim (Patricia Reid) (actress); Tularosa, N.M., 2/11/25
Stans, Maurice H. (ex-Secretary of Commerce); Shakope, Minn., 3/22/08
Stanton, Elizabeth Cady (woman suffragist); Johnstown, N.Y. **(1815-1902)**
Stanton, Frank (broadcasting executive); Muskegon, Mich., 3/20/08
Stanwyck, Barbara (Ruby Stevens) (actress); Brooklyn, N.Y. **(1907-1990)**
Stapleton, Jean (Jeanne Murray) (actress); New York City, 1/19/23
Stapleton, Maureen (actress); Troy, N.Y., 6/21/25
Starker, Janós (cellist); Budapest, 7/5/26
Starr, Kay (Starks) (singer); Dougherty, Okla., 7/21/22
Starr, Ringo (Richard Starkey) (singer, songwriter); Liverpool, England, 7/7/40
Stassen, Harold E. (ex-government official); West St. Paul, Minn., 4/13/07
Steber, Eleanor (soprano); Wheeling, W. Va., 7/17/16
Steegmuller, Francis (biographer); New Haven, Conn. **(1906-1994)**
Steele, Tommy (singer); London, 12/17/36
Stegner, Wallace (Earle) (novelist, critic); Lake Mills, Iowa **(1909-1993)**
Steichen, Edward Jean (photographer, artist); Luxembourg **(1879-1973)**
Steiger, Rod (Rodney) (actor); Westhampton, N.Y., 4/14/25
Stein, Gertrude (author); Allegheny, Pa. **(1874-1946)**
Steinbeck, John Ernst (novelist); Salinas, Calif. **(1902-1968)**
Steinberg, David (comedian); Winnipeg, Manitoba, Canada, 8/19/42
Steinberg, William (conductor); Cologne, Germany **(1899-1978)**
Steinem, Gloria (feminist); Toledo, Ohio, 3/25/34
Steinmetz, Charles (electrical engineer); Breslau (Poland) **(1865-1923)**
Stendhal (Marie Henri Beyle) (novelist); Grenoble, France **(1783-1842)**
Stern, Isaac (concert violinist); Kreminlecz, Russia, 7/21/20
Sterne, Laurence (novelist); Clonmel, Ireland **(1713-1768)**
Stevens, Cat (Steven Georgiou) (singer, songwriter); London, 7/?/47
Stevens, Connie (Concetta Ingolia) (singer); Brooklyn, N.Y., 8/8/38
Stevens, George (film director); Oakland, Calif. **(1905-1975)**
Stevens, Risë (mezzo-soprano); New York City, 6/11/13

Stevens, Wallace (poet); Reading, Pa. **(1879–1955)**
Stevenson, Adlai Ewing (statesman); Los Angeles **(1900-1965)**
Stevenson, McLean (actor); Bloomington, Ill. **(1929–1996)**
Stevenson, Parker (actor); Philadelphia, Pa., 6/4/52
Stevenson, Robert Louis Balfour (novelist, poet); Edinburgh, Scotland **(1850-1894)**
Stewart, James (actor); Indiana, Pa., 5/20/08
Stewart, Patrick (actor); Mirfield, England, 7/13/49
Stewart, Rod (Roderick David) (singer); London, 1/10/45
Stieglitz, Alfred (photographer); Hoboken, N.J. **(1864-1946)**
Stiers, David Ogden (actor); Peoria, Ill., 10/31/42
Stiller, Jerry (actor); Brooklyn, N.Y., 6/8/29
Stills, Stephen (singer, songwriter); Dallas, 1/3/45
Sting (Gordon Matthew Sumner) (singer, composer); Wallsend, England, 10/2/51
Stockwell, Dean (actor); North Hollywood, Calif., 3/5/36
Stokes, Carl (TV newscaster); Cleveland, 6/21/27
Stokowski, Leopold (conductor); London **(1882-1977)**
Stone, Edward Durell (architect); Fayetteville, Ark. **(1902-1978)**
Stone, I(sidor) F(einstein) (journalist); Philadelphia **(1907-1989)**
Stone, Irving (Irving Tennenbaum) (novelist); San Francisco **(1903-1989)**
Stone, Lucy (woman suffragist); nr. West Brookfield, Mass. **(1818-1893)**
Stone, Robert (novelist); Brooklyn, N.Y. 8/21/37
Stone, Sharon (actress); Meadville, Pa., 3/10/58
Stone, Sly (Sylvester) (rock musician); 1944
Stooges, The Three (comedy team); Moe Howard, Brooklyn, N.Y. **(1897–1975)**; Shemp (Samuel) Howard, Brooklyn **(1900–1955)**; Larry Fine, Philadelphia **(1911–1974)**; later Curly (Jerome) Howard, Brooklyn **(1906–1952)**
Stoppard, Tom (Thomas Straussler) (playwright); Zlin (Slovakia), 7/3/37
Stout, Rex (mystery writer); Noblesville, Ind. **(1886-1975)**
Stowe, Harriet Elizabeth Beecher (novelist); Litchfield, Conn. **(1811-1896)**
Strachey, (Giles) Lytton (biographer); London **(1880–1932)**
Stradivari, Antonio (violinmaker); Cremona, Italy **(1644-1737)**
Straight, Beatrice (actress); Old Westbury, N.Y., 8/2/16(?)
Strasberg, Lee (stage director); Budanov, Austria **(1901-1982)**
Strasberg, Susan (actress); New York City, 5/22/38
Stratas, Teresa (soprano); Toronto, Ont., Canada, 5/26/38
Straus, Oskar (composer); Vienna **(1870-1954)**
Strauss, Johann (composer); Vienna **(1825-1899)**
Strauss, Lewis L. (naval officer, scientist); Charleston, W. Va. **(1896-1974)**
Strauss, Peter (actor); New York City, 2/20/47
Strauss, Richard (composer); Munich, Germany **(1864-1949)**
Stravinsky, Igor (composer); Orlenbaum, Russia **(1882-1971)**
Streep, Meryl (Mary Louise) (actress); Summit, N.J., 6/22/49
Streisand, Barbra (singer, actress); Brooklyn, N.Y., 4/24/42
Strindberg, (Johan) August (dramatist); Stockholm **(1849–1912)**
Stritch, Elaine (actress); Detroit, 2/2/25(?)
Struthers, Sally Ann (actress); Portland, Ore., 7/28/48
Stuart, Gilbert Charles (painter); Rhode Island **(1755-1828)**
Stuart, James Ewell Brown (known as Jeb) (Confederate army officer); Patrick County, Va. **(1833-1864)**
Sturges, Preston (director, screenwriter, playwright); Chicago **(1898-1959)**
Stuyvesant, Peter (Governor of New Amsterdam); West Friesland (Netherlands) **(1592-1672)**
Styne, Jule (Julius Kerwin Stein) (songwriter); London, 12/31/05
Styron, William (William Clark Styron, Jr.) (novelist); Newport News, Va., 6/11/25
Suharto (President of Indonesia); Sedaju-Godean, Java, 2/20/21
Sukarno (Indonesian leader); Surabaja, Java **(1901–1970)**
Sullavan, Margaret Brooke (actress); Norfolk, Va. **(1911-1960)**
Sullivan, Sir Arthur Seymour (composer); London **(1842-1900)**
Sullivan, Barry (Patrick Barry) (actor); New York City **(1912–1994)**
Sullivan, Ed (columnist, TV personality); New York City **(1901-1974)**
Sullivan, Frank (Francis John) (humorist); Saratoga Springs, N.Y. **(1892-1976)**
Sullivan, Louis Henry (architect); Boston, Mass. **(1856-1924)**
Sulzberger, Arthur Ochs (newspaper publisher); New York City, 2/5/26
Sumac, Yma (singer); Ichocan, Peru, 9/10/27
Summer, Donna (La Donna Andrea Gaines) (singer); Boston, 12/31/48
Sun Tzu (writer, military strategist); China **(fl. c. 500–320 B.C.)**
Sun Yat-sen (statesman); nr. Macao **(1866-1925)**
Susann, Jacqueline (novelist); Philadelphia **(1926?-1974)**
Susskind, David (TV producer); New York City **(1920-1987)**
Sutherland, Donald (actor); St. John, N.B., Canada, 7/17/34
Sutherland, Joan (soprano); Sydney, Australia, 11/7/26
Suzuki, Pat (actress); Cressey, Calif., 1931
Swados, Elizabeth (composer, playwright); Buffalo, N.Y., 2/5/51
Swanson, Gloria (Gloria May Josephine Svensson) (actress); Chicago **(1899-1983)**
Swarthout, Gladys (soprano); Deepwater, Mo. **(1904-1969)**
Swayze, John Cameron (news commentator); Wichita, Kan.

(1906–1995)
Swayze, Patrick (actor, dancer); Houston, Tex., 8/18/54
Swendenborg, Emanuel (scientist, philosopher, mystic); Stockholm **(1688-1772)**
Swift, Jonathan (satirist); Dublin **(1667-1745)**
Swinburne, Algernon Charles (poet); London **(1837-1909)**
Swit, Loretta (actress); Passaic, N.J., 11/4/37
Swope, Herbert Bayard (journalist); St. Louis **(1882-1958)**
Sydow, von, Max (Carl Adolf von Sydow) (actor); Lund, Sweden, 4/10/29
Symons, Arthur (poet, critic); Milford Haven, Wales **(1865–1945)**
Synge, John Millington (dramatist); nr. Dublin **(1871-1909)**
Szilard, Leo (physicist); Budapest **(1898-1964)**

T

Taft, Robert Alphonso (legislator); Cincinnati **(1889-1953)**
Tagore, Sir Rabindranath (poet); Calcutta **(1861-1941)**
Tallchief, Maria (ballerina); Fairfax, Okla., 1/24/25
Talleyrand-Périgord, Charles Maurice de (statesman); Paris **(1754-1838)**
Talmadge, Norma (actress); Niagara Falls, N.Y. **(1897-1957)**
Talvela, Martti (basso); Hiitola, Finalnd **(1935-1989)**
Tamerlane (Timur) (Mongol conqueror); nr. Samarkand (Turkestan) **(1336?-1405)**
Tamiroff, Akim (actor) Baku (Azerbaijan) **(1899-1972)**
Tan, Amy (novelist); Oakland, Calif., 2/19/52
Tandy, Jessica (actress); London **(1909–1994)**
Tarbell, Ida Minerva (author, biographer); Erie Co., Pa. **(1857–1944)**
Tarkington, (Newton) Booth (novelist); Indianapolis **(1869-1946)**
Tate, Allen (John Orley) (poet, critic); Winchester, Ky., **(1899-1979)**
Tate, Sharon (actress); Dallas **(1943-1969)**
Tati, Jacques (Jacques Tatischeff) (actor); Pecq, France **(1908-1982)**
Taylor, Deems (composer); New York City **(1885-1966)**
Taylor, Elizabeth (actress); London, 2/27/32
Taylor, Harold (educator); Toronto, 9/28/14
Taylor, James (singer, songwriter); Boston, 3/12/48
Taylor, (Joseph) Deems (composer); New York City **(1885-1966)**
Taylor, Laurette (Laurette Cooney) (actress); New York City **(1884-1946)**
Taylor, Gen. Maxwell D. (former Army Chief of Staff); Keytesville, Mo. **(1901-1987)**
Taylor, Paul (choreographer); Wilkinsburg, Pa., 7/29/30
Taylor, Robert (Spangler Arlington Brugh) (actor); Filley, Neb. **(1911-1969)**
Tchaikovsky, Peter (Pëtr) Ilich (composer); Votkinsk, Russia **(1840-1893)**
Teasdale, Sara (poet); St. Louis **(1884-1933)**
Tebaldi, Renata (lyric soprano); Pesaro, Italy, 1/2/22
Tecumseh (Shawnee Indian chief); nr. Springfield, Ohio **(1768?-1813)**
Te Kanawa, Kiri (soprano); Gisborne, New Zealand, 1946(?)
Telemann, Georg Philipp (composer); Magdeburg (Germany) **(1681-1767)**
Teller, Edward (atomic physicist); Budapest, 1/15/08
Temple, Shirley. *See* Black, Shirley Temple
Templeton, Alec Andrew (pianist, composer); Cardiff, Wales **(1910-1963)**
Tennille, Toni (singer); Montgomery, Ala., 5/8/43
Tennyson, Alfred (1st Baron Tennyson) (poet); Somersby, England **(1809-1892)**
Tenskwatawa (Shawnee prophet); Old Piqua, Ohio **(1775?–1836?)**
Terhune, Albert Payson (novelist, journalist); Newark, N.J. **(1872-1942)**
Terkel, Studs (writer, interviewer); New York City, 5/16/12
Terry, Ellen Alicia (actress); Coventry, England **(1848-1928)**
Terry-Thomas (Thomas Terry Hoar Stevens) (actor); London **(1911-1990)**
Tesla, Nikola (electrical engineer, inventor); Smiljan (former Yugo-slavia) **(1856-1943)**
Thackeray, William Makepeace (novelist); Calcutta **(1811-1863)**
Thalberg, Irving G. (producer); Brooklyn, N.Y. **(1899-1936)**
Thant, U (U.N. statesman); Pantanaw (Burma) **(1909-1974)**
Tharp, Twyla (dancer, choreographer); Portland, Ind., 7/1/41(?)
Thatcher, Margaret (Prime Minister); Grantham, England, 10/13/25
Thebom, Blanche (mezzo-soprano); Monessen, Pa., 9/19/19
Theodorakis, Mikis (composer); Chios, Greece, 7/29/25
Thicke, Alan (actor); Kirland Lake, Ont., Canada, 3/1/47
Thieu, Nguyen Van (ex-President of South Vietnam); Trithuy (Vietnam) 4/5/23
Thomas, Danny (Amos Jacobs) (entertainer, TV producer); Deer-field, Mich. **(1912–1991)**
Thomas, Dylan Marials (poet); Carmarthenshire, Wales **(1914-1953)**
Thomas, Lowell (explorer, commentator); Woodington, Ohio **(1892-1981)**
Thomas, Marlo (actress); Detroit, 11/21/43
Thomas, Michael Tilson (conductor); Hollywood, Calif., 12/21/44
Thomas, Norman Mattoon (Socialist leader); Marion, Ohio **(1884-1968)**
Thomas, Philip Michael (actor); Columbus, Ohio, 5/26/49

Thomas, Richard (actor); New York City, 6/13/51
Thompson, Dorothy (writer); Lancaster, N.Y. **(1894-1961)**
Thompson, Emma (actress); London, 4/15/59
Thompson, Hunter (Stockton) (writer); Louisville, Ky., 7/18/39
Thompson, Sada (actress); Des Moines, Iowa, 9/27/29
Thomson, Virgil (Garnett) (composer); Kansas City, Mo. **(1896-1989)**
Thoreau, Henry David (naturalist, author); Concord, Mass. **(1817-1862)**
Thorndike, Dame Sybil (actress); Gainsborough, England **(1882-1976)**
Thurber, James Grover (author, cartoonist); Columbus, Ohio **(1894-1961)**
Thurmond, (James) Strom (U.S. Senator); Edgefield, S.C., 12/5/02
Tibbett, Lawrence (baritone); Bakersfield, Calif. **(1896-1960)**
Tiegs, Cheryl (model, actress); Minnesota, 9/25/47
Tierney, Gene (actress); Brooklyn, N.Y. **(1920-1991)**
Tillich, Paul (philosopher, theologian); Starzeddel, Germany **(1886–1965)**
Tillstrom, Burr (puppeteer); Chicago **(1917-1985)**
Tintoretto, Il (Jacopo Robusti) (painter); Venice **(1518-1594)**
Tiny Tim (Herbert Khaury) (entertainer); New York City, 1923(?)
Tiomkin, Dmitri (composer); St. Petersburg, Russia **(1894-1979)**
Titian (Tiziano Vecelli) (painter); Pieve di Cadore (Italy) **(1477-1576)**
Tito (Josip Broz or Brozovich) (President of Yugoslavia); Croatia (former Yugoslavia) **(1892-1980)**
Tocqueville, Alexis de (writer); Verneuil, France **(1805-1859)**
Todd, Michael (producer); Minneapolis, Minn. **(1907-1958)**
Todd, Richard (actor); Dublin, Ireland, 6/11/19
Todd, Thelma (actress); Lawrence, Mass. **(1905-1935)**
Tolkien, J(ohn) R(onald) R(euel) (fantasy writer); Bloemfontein, South Africa **(1892–1973)**
Tolstoi, Count Leo (Lev) Nikolaevich (novelist); Tula Province, Russia **(1828-1910)**
Tomlin, Lily (comedienne); Detroit, 1939(?)
Tone, Franchot (actor); Niagara Falls, N.Y. **(1905-1968)**
Tormé, Mel (Melvin) (singer); Chicago, 9/13/25
Torn, Rip (Elmore Torn, Jr.) (actor, director); Temple, Tex., 2/6/31
Torquemada, Tomásde (Spanish Inquisitor); Valladolid, Spain **(1420-1498)**
Toscanini, Arturo (orchestra conductor); Parma, Italy **(1867-1957)**
Totenberg, Nina (broadcast journalist); New York City, 1/14/44
Toulouse-Lautrec (Henri Marie Raymond de Toulouse-Lautrec Monfa) (painter); Albi, France **(1864-1901)**
Toynbee, Arnold J. (historian); London **(1889-1975)**
Tracy, Spencer (actor); Milwaukee **(1900-1967)**
Traubel, Helen (Wagnerian soprano); St. Louis **(1903-1972)**
Travanti, Daniel J. (actor); Kenosha, Wis., 3/7/40
Travolta, John (actor); Englewood, N.J., 2/18/54
Treacher, Arthur (actor); Brighton, England **(1894-1975)**
Tree, Sir Herbert Beerbolm (actor, manager); London **(1853-1917)**
Trevor, Claire (actress); New York City, 1911
Trigère, (Pauline (fashion designer); Paris, 11/4/12
Trilling, Lionel (author, educator); New York City **(1905-1975)**
Trollope, Anthony (novelist); London **(1815–1882)**
Trotsky, Leon (Lev Davidovich Bronstein) (statesman); Elisavetgrad, Russia **(1879-1940)**
Troyanos, Tatiana (mezzo-soprano); New York City **(1938-1993)**
Trudeau, Garry (cartoonist); New York City, 1948
Trudeau, Pierre Elliott (former Prime Minister); Montreal, 10/18/19
Truffaut, François (film director); Paris **(1932-1984)**
Trujillo y Molina, Rafael Leonidas (Dominican Republic dictator); San Cristóbal, Dominican Republic **(1891-1961)**
Truman, Margaret (author); Independence, Mo., 2/17/24
Trump, Donald (business executive); New York City, 1946
Truth, Sojourner (Isabella) (preacher, abolitionist); Ulster Co., N.Y. **(1797?–1883)**
Tryon, Thomas (actor, novelist); Hartford, Conn. **(1926–1991)**
Tsiolkovsky, Konstantin E. (father of cosmonautics); Izhevskoye, Russia **(1857-1935)**
Tubman, Harriet (Araminta) (abolitionist); Dorchester Co., Md. **(1820?–1913)**
Tuchman, Barbara (Wertheim) (historian, author); New York City **(1912-1989)**
Tucker, Forrest (actor); Plainfield, Ind. **(1919-1986)**
Tucker, Richard (tenor); New York City **(1914-1975)**
Tucker, Sophie (Sophie Abuza) (singer); Europe **(1884?-1966)**
Tudor, Antony (choreographer); London **(1909-1987)**
Tune, Tommy (dancer, choreographer); Wichita Falls, Tex., 2/28/39
Turgenev, Ivan Sergeevich (novelist); Orel, Russia **(1818-1883)**
Turner, Frederick J. (historian); Portage, Wis. **(1861–1932)**
Turner, Ike (singer); Clarksdale, Miss., 11/?/31
Turner, Janine (actress); Lincoln, Neb., 12/6/62
Turner, Joseph M.W. (painter); London **(1775-1851)**
Turner, Kathleen (actress); Springfield, Mo., 1956 (?)
Turner, Lana (Julia Jean Mildred Frances Turner) (actress); Wallace, Idaho **(1920–1995)**
Turner, Nat (civil rights leader); Southampton County, Va. **(1800-1831)**
Turner, Ted (business executive); Cincinnati, 11/19/38

Turner, Tina (Annie Mae Bullock) (singer); Nut Bush, nr. Brownsville, Tenn., 11/26/39
Turpin, Ben (comedian); New Orleans **(1874-1940)**
Twain, Mark (Samuel Langhorne Clemens) (author); Florida, Mo. **(1835-1910)**
Tweed, William Marcy (politician); New York City **(1823-1878)**
Twiggy (Leslie Hornby) (model); London, 9/19/49
Twining, Gen. Nathan F. (former Air Force Chief of Staff); Monroe, Wis. **(1897-1982)**
Twitty, Conway (Harold Lloyd Jenkins) (singer, guitarist); Friars Point, Miss. **(1933-1993)**
Tyson, Cicely (actress); New York City, 12/19/39(?)

U

Uccello, Paolo (painter); Florence **(1397–1475)**
Udall, Stewart L. (ex-Secretary of the Interior); St. Johns, Ariz., 1/31/20
Uggams, Leslie (singer, actress); New York City, 5/25/43
Ulanova, Galina (ballerina); St. Petersburg, Russia, 1/10/10
Ullman, Tracey (actress, singer); Slough, England, 12/30/59
Ullmann, Liv (actress); Tokyo, 12/16/39
Untermeyer, Louis (anthologist, poet); New York City **(1885-1977)**
Updike, John (novelist); Shillington, Pa., 3/18/32
Urey, Harold C. (physicist); Walkerton, Ind. **(1893-1981)**
Uris, Leon (novelist); Baltimore, 8/3/24
Ustinov, Peter (actor, producer); London, 4/16/21
Utrillo, Maurice (painter); Paris **(1883-1955)**

V

Vaccaro, Brenda (actress); Brooklyn, N.Y., 11/18/39
Vadim, Roger (Roger Vadim Plemiannikov) (film director); Paris, 1/26/28
Valentine, Karen (actress); Santa Rosa, Calif., 1947
Valentino, Rudolph (Rodolpho d'Antonguolla) (actor); Castellaneta, Italy **(1895-1926)**
Valentino (Valentino Garavani) (fashion designer); nr. Milan, Italy, 5/11/32
Valéry, Paul (Ambroise Toussaint Jules) (poet, critic); Sète, France **(1871–1945)**
Vallee, Rudy (Hubert Prior Rudy Vallée) (band leader, singer); Island Pond, Vt. **(1901-1986)**
Valli, Frankie (Frank Castellaccio) (singer); Newark, N.J., 5/3/37
Van Allen, James Alfred (space physicist); Mt. Pleasant, Iowa, 9/7/14
Van Buren, Abigail (Mrs. Morton Phillips) (columnist); Sioux City, Iowa, 7/4/18
Vance, Vivian (actress); Cherryvale, Kan. **(1912-1979)**
Vanderbilt, Alfred G. (sportsman); London, 9/22/12
Vanderbilt, Cornelius (financier); Port Richmond, N.Y. **(1794-1877)**
Vanderbilt, Gloria (fashion designer) New York City, 2/20/24
Van Doren, Carl (writer, educator); Hope, Ill. **(1885-1950)**
Van Doren, Mamie (actress); Rowena, S.D., 2/6/33
Van Dyke, Dick (actor); West Plains, Mo., 12/13/25
Vandyke (or Van Dyck), Sir Anthony (painter); Antwerp (Belgium) **(1599-1641)**
Van Eyck, Jan (painter); Maeseyck (Belgium) **(c. 1390-1441)**
Van Fleet, Jo (actress); Oakland, Calif. **(1915–1996)**
van Gogh, Vincent (painter); Groot Zundert, Brabant (Belgium) **(1853-1890)**
van Hamel, Martine (ballerina); Brussels, 11/16/45
Van Heusen, Jimmy (Edward Chester Babcock) (songwriter); Syracuse, N.Y. **(1913-1990)**
Van Patten, Dick (actor); Richmond Hill, N.Y., 12/9/28
Van Peebles, Melvin (playwright); Chicago, 9/21/32
Vasari, Giorgio (art historian); Arezzo, Italy **(1511–1574)**
Vaughan, Sarah (singer); Newark, N.J. **(1924-1990)**
Vaughan Williams, Ralph (composer); Down Ampney, England **(1872-1958)**
Vaughn, Robert (actor); New York City, 11/22/32
Veblen, Thorstein (economist, social critic); Cato Township, Wis. **(1857–1929)**
Veidt, Conrad (actor); Potsdam, Germany **(1893-1943)**
Velázquez, Diego Rodriguez de Silva y (painter); Seville, Spain **(1599-1660)**
Venturi, Robert (Charles) (architect); Philadelphia, 6/25/25
Verdi, Giuseppe (composer); Roncole (Italy) **(1813-1901)**
Verdon, Gwen (actress); Culver City, Calif., 1/13/25
Vereen, Ben (actor, singer); Miami, Fla., 10/10/46
Verlaine, Paul (poet); Metz, France **(1844–1896)**
Vermeer, Jan (or Jan van der Meer van Delft) (painter); Delft (Netherlands) **(1632-1675)**

Verne, Jules (author); Nantes, France (1828-1905)
Veronese, Paolo (Paolo Cagliari) (painter); Verona (1528-1588)
Verrazano, Giovanni da (navigator); Florence, Italy (1485?-1528)
Verrett, Shirley (mezzo-soprano); New Orleans, 5/31/33
Vesalius, Andreas (anatomist); Brussels, Belgium (1515-1564)
Vespucci, Amerigo (navigator); Florence, Italy (1454-1512)
Vickers, Jon (tenor); Prince Albert, Sask, Canada, 10/29/26
Vico, Giovanni Battista (philosopher); Naples, Italy (1668-1744)
Vidal, Gore (novelist); West Point, N.Y., 10/3/25
Vidor, King (film director, producer); Galveston, Tex. (1895-1982)
Vigoda, Abe (actor); New York City, 2/24/21
Villa, Pancho (Doroteo Arango) (revolutionary); Hacienda de Rio Grande, San Juan del Rio, Mexico (1877-1923)
Villella, Edward (ballet dancer); Bayside, Queens, N.Y., 10/1/36
Villon, François (François de Montcorbier) (poet); Paris (1431-1463)
Vinton, Bobby (singer); Canonsburg, Pa., 4/16/35(?)
Virgil (or Vergil) (Publius Vergilius Maro) (poet); nr. Mantua (Italy) (70-19 B.C.)
Vishnevskaya, Galina (soprano); St. Petersburg (Russia), 10/25/26
Vivaldi, Antonio (composer); Venice (1678-1741)
Vlaminck, Maurice de (painter); Paris (1876-1958)
Voight, Jon (actor); Yonkers, N.Y., 12/29/38
Volta, Alessandro (scientist); Como (Italy) (1745-1827)
Voltaire (François Marie Arouet) (author); Paris (1694-1778)
von Aroldingen, Karin (Karin Awny Hannelore Reinbold von Aroedingen and Eltzinger) (ballet dancer); Greiz (Germany) 7/9/41
von Braun, Wernher (rocket scientist); Wirsitz, Germany (1912-1977)
von Furstenberg, Betsy (Elizabeth Caroline Maria Agatha Felicitas Therese von Furstenberg-Hedringen) (actress); Nelheim-Heusen, Germany, 8/16/35
von Fürstenberg, Diane (Diane Simone Michelle Halfin) (fashion designer); Brussels, 12/31/46
von Hindenburg, Paul (statesman); Posen (Poland) (1847-1934)
von Karajan, Herbert (conductor); Salzburg (Austria) (1908-1989)
Vonnegut, Kurt, Jr. (novelist); Indianapolis, 11/11/22
Von Stade, Frederica (mezzo-soprano); Somerville, N.J., 1945
Von Stroheim, Erich Oswald Hans Carl Maria von Nordenwall (film actor, director); Vienna (1885-1957)
Von Zell, Harry (announcer); Indianapolis, Ind. (1906-1981)
Vreeland, Diana (Diana Da Iziel) (fashion journalist, museum consultant); Paris (1903?-1989)

W

Wagner, Lindsay (actress); Los Angeles, 6/22/49
Wagner, Robert (actor); Detroit, 2/10/30
Wagner, Robert F. (ex-Mayor of New York City); New York City (1910-1991)
Wagner, Wilhelm Richard (composer); Leipzig (Germany) (1813-1883)
Waits, Tom (blues singer); Pomona, Calif., 12/7/49
Waldheim, Kurt (ex-U.N. Secretary-General); St. Andrae-Wörden, Austria, 12/21/18
Walesa, Lech (Polish labor leader and ex-president); Popowo, Poland, 9/29/43
Walker, Alice (novelist, poet); Eatonon, Ga., 2/9/44
Walker, Nancy (Ann Myrtle Swoyer); (actress, comedienne); Philadelphia (1922-1992)
Walker, Robert (actor); Salt Lake City, Utah (1918-1951)
Walker, T-Bone (blues singer); Linden, Tex., 5/28/10
Wallace, DeWitt (publisher); St. Paul (1889-1981)
Wallace, George C. (ex-govenor); Clio, Ala., 8/25/19
Wallace, Irving (novelist); Chicago (1916-1990)
Wallace, Mike (Myron Wallace) (TV interviewer, commentator); Brookline, Mass., 5/9/18
Wallach, Eli (actor); Brooklyn, N.Y., 12/7/15
Wallenstein, Alfred (conductor); Chicago (1898-1983)
Waller, Thomas "Fats" (pianist); New York City (1904-1943)
Wallis, Hal (film producer); Chicago (1899-1986)
Walpole, Horace (statesman, novelist); London (1717-1797)
Waltari, Mika (novelist); Helsinki, Finland, (1903-1979)
Walter, Bruno (Bruno Walter Schlesinger) (orchestra conductor); Berlin (1876-1962)
Walters, Barbara (TV commentator); Boston, 9/25/31
Walton, Izaak (author); Stafford, England (1593-1683)
Wambaugh, Joseph (author, screenwriter); East Pittsburgh, Pa., 1/22/37
Wanamaker, John (merchant); Philadelphia (1838-1922)
Wanamaker, Sam (actor, director); Chicago (1919-1993)
Ward, Barbara (economist); York, England (1914-1981)
Warhol, Andy (artist, producer); Pennsylvania (1928(?)-1987)
Waring, Fred (band leader); Tyrone, Pa. (1900-1984)
Warner, H. B. (Henry Bryan Warner Lickford) (actor); London (1876-1958)

Warren, Lesley Ann (actress); New York City, 8/16/46
Warren, Robert Penn (novelist); Guthrie, Ky. (1905-1989)
Warrick, Ruth (actress) St. Joseph, Mo., 6/29/15
Warwick, Dionne (singer); East Orange, N.J., 1941
Washington, Booker Taliaferro (educator); Franklin County, Va. (1856-1915)
Washington, Denzel (actor); Mt. Vernon, N.Y., 12/28/54
Washington, Harold (ex-mayor of Chicago); Chicago, (1922-1987)
Waters, Ethel (actress, singer); Chester, Pa. (1896-1977)
Waters, Muddy (McKinley Morganfield) (singer, guitarist); Rolling Fork, Miss. (1915-1983)
Waterson, Sam (actor); Cambridge, Mass., 11/15/40
Watson, Thomas John (industrialist); Campbell, N.Y. (1874-1956)
Watt, James (inventor); Greenock, Scotland (1736-1819)
Watteau, Jean-Antoine (painter); Valanciennes, France (1684-1721)
Wattleton, Faye (family planning advocate); St. Louis, Mo., 7/8/43
Watts, André (concert pianist); Nuremberg, Germany, 6/20/46
Waugh, Alec (Alexander Raban Waugh) (novelist); London (1898-1981)
Waugh, Evelyn (satirist); London (1903-1966)
Wayne, Anthony (military officer); Waynesboro (family farm), nr. Paoli, Pa. (1745-1796)
Wayne, David (David McMeekan) (actor); Traverse City, Mich. (1914-1995)
Wayne, John (Marion Michael Morrison) (actor); Winterset, Iowa (1907-1979)
Weaver, Dennis (actor); Joplin, Mo., 6/4/25
Weaver, Fritz (actor); Pittsburgh, Pa., 1/19/26
Weaver, Sigourney (actress); New York City, 10/8/49
Webb, Clifton (Webb Parmelee Hollenbeck) (actor); Indianapolis (1893-1966)
Webb, Jack (film actor, producer); Santa Monica, Calif. (1920-1982)
Weber, Karl Maria Friedrich Ernst von (composer); nr. Lübeck (Germany) (1786-1826)
Webster, Daniel (statesman); Salisbury, N.H. (1782-1852)
Webster, Margaret (producer, director, actress); New York City (1905-1973)
Webster, Noah (lexicographer); West Hartford, Conn. (1758-1843)
Weill, Kurt (composer); Dessau, (Germany) (1900-1950)
Weir, Peter (film director); Sydney, Australia, 8/21/44
Weizmann, Chaim (statesman); Grodno Province, Russia (1874-1952)
Welch, Raquel (Raquel Tejada) (actress); Chicago, 9/5/40
Weld, Tuesday (Susan) (actress); New York City, 8/27/43
Welk, Lawrence (band leader); Strasburg, N.D. (1903-1992)
Welles, Orson (actor, producer); Kenosha, Wis. (1915-1985)
Wellington, Duke of (Arthur Wellesley) (statesman); Ireland (1769-1852)
Wells, H(erbert) G(eorge) (author); Bromley, England (1866-1946)
Wells, Ida Bell (Barnett) (journalist); Holly Springs, Miss. (1862-1931)
Welty, Eudora (novelist); Jackson, Miss., 4/13/09
Wenner, Jann (publisher); New York City, 1/7/46
Werfel, Franz (novelist); Prague (1890-1945)
Werner, Oskar (Josef Schliessmayer) (film actor, director); Vienna (1922-1984)
Wertheimer, Linda (radio journalist); Carlsbad, N.M., 3/19/43
Wertmuller, Lina (film director); Rome, 1926(?)
Wesley, John (religious leader); Epworth Rectory, Lincolnshire, England (1703-1791)
West, Benjamin (painter); Springfield, Pa. (1738-1820)
West, Dame Rebecca (Cicily Fairfield) (novelist); County Kerry, Ireland (1892-1983)
West, Jessamyn (novelist); nr. North Vernon, Ind. (1902-1984)
West, Mae (actress); Brooklyn, N.Y. (1893-1980)
West, Nathanael (Nathan Weinstein) (novelist); New York City (1902-1940)
Westheimer, Ruth (Karola Ruth Siegel) (psychologist, author, broadcaster); Frankfurt, Germany, 1928
Westinghouse, George (inventor); Central Bridge, N.Y. (1846-1914)
Westmoreland, William Childs (ex-Army Chief of Staff); Saxon, S.C. 3/26/14
Weyden, Roger van der (painter); Tournai (Belgium) (c. 1400-1464)
Wharton, Edith Newbold (née Jones) (novelist); New York City (1862-1937)
Wheatley, Phyllis (poet); Senegal (1753?-1784)
Wheeler, Bert (Albert Jerome Wheeler) (comedian); Paterson, N.J. (1895-1968)
Whistler, James Abbott McNeill (painter, etcher); Lowell, Mass. (1834-1903)
White, Betty (actress); Oak Park, Ill., 1/17/24(?)
White, Edmund (writer); Cincinnati, Ohio, 1/13/40
White, E(lwyn) B(rooks) (author); Mt. Vernon, N.Y. (1899-1985)
White, Pearl (actress); Green Ridge, Mo. (1889-1938)
White, Stanford (architect); New York City (1853-1906)

White, Theodore H. (historian); Boston **(1915-1986)**
White, Vanna (TV personality); Conway, S.C., 2/18/57
White, William Allen (journalist); Emporia, Kan. **(1868-1944)**
Whitehead, Alfred North (mathematician, philosopher); Isle of Thanet, England **(1861-1947)**
Whiteman, Paul (band leader); Denver **(1891-1967)**
Whiting, Margaret (singer, actress); Detroit, Mich., 7/22/24
Whitman, Walt (Walter) (poet); West Hills, N.Y. **(1819-1892)**
Whitmore, James (actor); White Plains, N.Y., 10/1/21
Whitney, Cornelius Vanderbilt (sportsman); New York City **(1899-1992)**
Whitney, Eli (inventor); Westboro, Mass. **(1765-1825)**
Whitney, John Hay (publisher); Ellsworth, Me. **(1904-1982)**
Whittier, John Greenleaf (poet); Haverhill, Mass. **(1807-1892)**
Wideman, John Edgar (writer); Washington, D.C., 6/14/41
Widmark, Richard (actor); Sunrise, Minn., 12/26/14
Wiesel, Elie (Eliezer) (author); Signet, Romania, 9/30/28
Wiesenthal, Simon (Nazi hunter); Buchach (Ukraine), 12/31/08
Wilde, Cornel (film actor, producer); New York City **(1915-1989)**
Wilde, Oscar Fingal O'Flahertie Wills (author); Dublin **(1854-1900)**
Wilder, Billy (film producer, director); Vienna, 6/22/06
Wilder, Gene (Jerome Silberman) (actor); Milwaukee, 6/11/35(?)
Wilder, Thornton (author); Madison, Wis. **(1897-1975)**
Wilding, Michael (actor); Westcliff, England **(1912-1979)**
Wilkins, Roy (civil rights leader); St. Louis **(1901-1981)**
Williams, Andy (singer); Wall Lake, Iowa, 12/3/30
Williams, Billy Dee (actor); New York City, 4/6/37
Williams, Cindy (actress); Van Nuys, Calif., 8/22/(?)
Williams, Edward Bennett (lawyer); Hartford, Conn. **(1920-1988)**
Williams, Emlyn (actor, playwright); Mostyn, Wales **(1905-1987)**
Williams, Esther (actress); Los Angeles, 8/8/23
Williams, Gluyas (cartoonist); San Francisco **(1888-1982)**
Williams, Hank, Sr. (Hiram King Williams) (singer); Georgiana, Ala. **(1923-1953)**
Williams, Joe (singer); Cordele, Ga., 12/12/18
Williams, John T. (composer, conductor); Queens, N.Y., 2/8/32
Williams, Paul (singer, composer, actor); Omaha, Neb., 9/19/40
Williams, Robin (comedian); Chicago, 7/?/52
Williams, Roger (clergyman); London **(1603?-1683)**
Williams, Tennessee (Thomas L. Williams) (playwright); Columbus, Miss. **(1911-1983)**
Williams, William Carlos (physician, poet); Rutherford, N.J. **(1883-1963)**
Williamson, Nicol (actor); Hamilton, Scotland, 9/14/38
Willkie, Wendell Lewis (lawyer); Elwood, Ind. **(1892-1944)**
Willis, Bruce (actor); Germany, 3/19/55
Willson, Meredith (composer); Mason City, Iowa **(1902-1984)**
Wilson, August (poet, writer, playwright); Pittsburgh, Pa., 1945
Wilson, Don (radio and TV announcer); Lincoln, Neb. **(1900-1982)**
Wilson, Dooley (actor, musician); Tyler, Tex. **(1894-1953)**
Wilson, Edmund (literary critic, author); Red Bank, N.J. **(1895-1972)**
Wilson, Flip (Clerow) (comedian); Jersey City, N.J., 12/8/33
Wilson, Harold (ex-Prime Minister); Huddersfield, England **(1916–1995)**
Wilson, Nancy (singer); Chillicothe, Ohio, 2/20/37
Wilson, Sloan (novelist); Norwalk, Conn., 5/8/20
Winchell, Walter (columnist); New York City **(1897-1972)**
Windsor, Duchess of (Bessie Wallis Warfield); Blue Ridge Summit, Pa. **(1896-1986)**
Windsor, Duke of (formerly King Edward VIII of England); Richmond Park, England **(1894-1972)**
Winfrey, Oprah (talk show hostess, actress); Kosciusko, Miss., 1/29/54
Winger, Debra (actress); Cleveland, Ohio, 1955
Winkler, Henry (actor); New York City, 10/30/45
Winningham, Mare (actress); Phoenix, Ariz., 5/16/59
Winter, Johnny (guitarist); Leland, Miss., 2/23/44
Winters, Jonathan (comedian); Dayton, Ohio, 11/11/25
Winters, Shelley (Shirley Schrift) (actress); East St. Louis, Ill., 8/18/22
Winthrop, John (first Governor, Massachusetts Bay Colony); Suffolk, England **(1588-1649)**
Wise, Stephen Samuel (rabbi); Budapest **(1874-1949)**
Withers, Jane (actress); Atlanta, 1927
Wittgenstein, Ludwig (Josef Johann) (philosopher); Vienna **(1889-1951)**
Wodehouse, P(elham) G(renville) (novelist); Guildford, England **(1881-1975)**
Wolfe, Thomas Clayton (novelist); Asheville, N.C. **(1900-1938)**
Wolfe, Tom (journalist); Richmond, Va., 3/2/31
Wolff, Tobias (author); Birmingham, Ala., 6/19/45
Wolsey, Thomas (prelate, statesman); Ipswich, England **(1475?-1530)**
Wonder, Stevie (Steveland Judkins, later Steveland Morris) (singer, songwriter); Saginaw, Mich., 5/13/50
Wong, Anna May (Lu Tsong Wong) (actress); Los Angeles **(1907-1961)**
Wood, Grant (painter); Anamosa, Iowa **(1892-1942)**
Wood, Natalie (Natasha Gurdin) (film actress); San Francisco **(1938-1981)**

Woodhouse, Barbara (Blackburn) (dog trainer, author, TV personality); Rathfarnham, Ireland **(1910-1988)**
Woodson, Carter G. (historian); New Canton, Va. **(1875–1950)**
Woodward, Edward (actor); Croydon, England, 6/1/30
Woodward, Joanne (film actress); Thomasville, Ga., 2/27/30
Woolf, Adeline Virginia (née Stephens) (novelist); London **(1882-1941)**
Woollcott, Alexander (author, critic); Phalanx, N.J. **(1887-1943)**
Woolley, Monty (Edgar Montillion Woolley) (actor); New York City **(1888-1963)**
Woolworth, Frank (merchant); Rodman, N.Y. **(1852-1919)**
Wopat, Tom (actor); Lodi, Wis., 9/9/50
Wordsworth, William (poet); Cockermouth, England **(1770-1850)**
Wouk, Herman (novelist); New York City, 5/27/15
Wovoka (Jack Wilson) (Paiute Indian religious leader); (western Nev.) **(c. 1858–1932)**
Wray, Fay (actress); Alberta, Canada, 1907
Wren, Sir Christopher (architect); East Knoyle, England **(1632-1723)**
Wright, Frank Lloyd (architect); Richland Center, Wis. **(1869-1959)**
Wright, Martha (singer); Seattle, Wash., 3/23/26
Wright, Orville (inventor); Dayton, Ohio **(1871-1948)**
Wright, Richard (novelist); nr. Natchez, Miss. **(1908-1960)**
Wright, Wilbur (inventor); Millville, Ind. **(1867-1912)**
Wyatt, Jane (film actress); Campgaw, N.J., 8/12/12
Wycliffe, John (church reformer); Hipswell, England **(1320-1384)**
Wyeth, Andrew (painter); Chadds Ford, Pa., 7/12/17
Wyler, William (film director); Mulhouse (France), **(1902-1981)**
Wyman, Jane (Sarah Jane Fulks) (actress); St. Joseph, Mo., 1/4/14
Wynette, Tammy (Wynette Pugh) (singer); Tupelo, Miss. 5/5/42
Wynn, Ed (Isaiah Edwin Leopold) (comedian); Philadelphia **(1886-1966)**
Wynn, Keenan (actor); New York City **(1916-1986)**

X

Xavier, St. Francis (Jesuit missionary); Pamplona, Navarre (Spain) **(1506-1552)**
Xenophon (soldier, historian, essayist); Athens, Greece **(434(?)-355(?)** B.C.)
Xerxes, the Great (king): Persian Empire **(519(?)-465** B.C.)

Y

Yeats, William Butler (poet); nr. Dublin **(1865-1939)**
Yevtushenko, Yevgeny (poet); Zima (Russia), 7/18/33
York, Alvin Cullun (Sergeant York, World War I hero): Tennessee **(1887-1964)**
York, Michael (actor); Fulmer, England, 3/27/42
York, Susannah (Fletcher) (actress); London, 1/9/42
Yorty, Samuel W. (ex-Mayor of Los Angeles); Lincoln, Neb., 10/1/09
Yothers, Tina (actress); Whittier, Calif., 5/5/73
Young, Alan (actor); North Shield, England, 11/19/19
Young, Andrew (civil rights leader); New Orleans, 3/12/32
Young, Brigham (religious leader); Whitingham, Vt. **(1801-1877)**
Young, Gig (Byron Barr) (actor); St. Cloud, Minn. **(1917-1978)**
Young, Loretta (Gretchen Young) (actress); Salt Lake City, Utah, 1/6/13
Young, Neil (singer, songwriter); Toronto, 11/12/45
Young, Robert (actor); Chicago, 2/22/07
Youngman, Henny (comedian); Whitechapel, London, England, 3/16/06

Z

Zanuck, Darryl F. (film producer); Wahoo, Neb. **(1902-1979)**
Zappa, Frank (Francis Vincent Zappa, Jr.) (singer, songwriter); Baltimore **(1940–1993)**
Zeffirelli, Franco (director); Florence, Italy, 2/12/23
Zenger, John Peter (printer, journalist); (Germany) **(1697-1746)**
Zhou Enlai (Premier); Hualyin, China **(1898-1976)**
Ziegfeld, Florenz (theatrical producer); Chicago **(1869-1932)**
Zimbalist, Efrem (concert violinist); Rostov-on-Don, Russia **(1889-1985)**
Zimbalist, Efrem, Jr. (actor); New York City, 11/30/23
Zimbalist, Stephanie (actress); New York City, 10/8/56
Zola, Emile (novelist); Paris **(1840-1902)**
Zoroaster (religious leader); Persian Empire **(c. 6th century** B.C.)
Zukerman, Pinchas (violinist); Tel Aviv, Israel, 7/16/48
Zukor, Adolph (film executive); Risce, Hungary **(1873-1976)**
Zurbarán, Francisco de (painter); Fuentes de Cantos, Spain **(1598–1664)**
Zweig, Stefan (author); Vienna **(1881-1942)**
Zwingli, Huldrych (humanist); Wildaus, Switzerland **(1484-1531)**

AWARDS

Nobel Prizes

The Nobel prizes are awarded under the will of Alfred Bernhard Nobel, Swedish chemist and engineer, who died in 1896. The interest of the fund is divided annually among the persons who have made the most outstanding contributions in the fields of physics, chemistry, and physiology or medicine, who have produced the most distinguished literary work of an idealist tendency, and who have contributed most toward world peace.

In 1968, a Nobel Prize of economic sciences was established by Riksbank, the Swedish bank, in celebration of its 300th anniversary. The prize was awarded for the first time in 1969.

The prizes for physics and chemistry are awarded by the Swedish Academy of Science in Stockholm, the one for physiology or medicine by the Caroline Medical Institute in Stockholm, that for literature by the academy in Stockholm, and that for peace by a committee of five elected by the Norwegian Storting. The distribution of prizes was begun on December 10, 1901, the anniversary of Nobel's death. The amount of each prize varies with the income from the fund and currently is about $190,000. No Nobel prizes were awarded for 1940, 1941, and 1942; prizes for Literature were not awarded for 1914, 1918, and 1943. (See p. 1019 for 1996 winners.)

PEACE

1901 Henri Dunant (Switzerland); Frederick Passy (France)
1902 Elie Ducommun and Albert Gobat (Switzerland)
1903 Sir William R. Cremer (England)
1904 Institut de Droit International (Belgium)
1905 Bertha von Suttner (Austria)
1906 Theodore Roosevelt (U.S.)
1907 Ernesto T. Moneta (Italy) and Louis Renault (France)
1908 Klas P. Arnoldson (Sweden) and Frederik Bajer (Denmark)
1909 Auguste M. F. Beernaert (Belgium) and Baron Paul H.B.B. d'Estournelles de Constant de Rebecque (France)
1910 Bureau International Permanent de la Paix (Switzerland)
1911 Tobias M. C. Asser (Holland) and Alfred H. Fried (Austria)
1912 Elihu Root (U.S.)
1913 Henri La Fontaine (Belgium)
1915 No award
1916 No award
1917 International Red Cross
1919 Woodrow Wilson (U.S.)
1920 Léon Bourgeois (France)
1921 Karl H. Branting (Sweden) and Christian L. Lange (Norway)
1922 Fridtjof Nansen (Norway)
1923 No award
1924 No award
1925 Sir Austen Chamberlain (England) and Charles G. Dawes (U.S.)
1926 Aristide Briand (France) and Gustav Stresemann (Germany)
1927 Ferdinand Buisson (France) and Ludwig Quidde (Germany)
1928 No award
1929 Frank B. Kellogg (U.S.)
1930 Lars O. J. Söderblom (Sweden)
1931 Jane Addams and Nicholas M. Butler (U.S.)
1932 No award
1933 Sir Norman Angell (England)
1934 Arthur Henderson (England)
1935 Karl von Ossietzky (Germany)
1936 Carlos de S. Lamas (Argentina)
1937 Lord Cecil of Chelwood (England)
1938 Office International Nansen pour les Réfugiés (Switzerland)
1939 No award
1944 International Red Cross
1945 Cordell Hull (U.S.)
1946 Emily G. Balch and John R. Mott (U.S.)
1947 American Friends Service Committee (U.S.) and British Society of Friends' Service Council (England)
1948 No award
1949 Lord John Boyd Orr (Scotland)

1950 Ralph J. Bunche (U.S.)
1951 Léon Jouhaux (France)
1952 Albert Schweitzer (French Equatorial Africa)
1953 George C. Marshall (U.S.)
1954 Office of U.N. High Commissioner for Refugees
1955 No award
1956 No award
1957 Lester B. Pearson (Canada)
1958 Rev. Dominique Georges Henri Pire (Belgium)
1959 Philip John Noel-Baker (England)
1960 Albert John Luthuli (South Africa)
1961 Dag Hammarskjöld (Sweden)
1962 Linus Pauling (U.S.)
1963 Intl. Comm. of Red Cross; League of Red Cross Societies (both Geneva)
1964 Rev. Dr. Martin Luther King, Jr. (U.S.)
1965 UNICEF (United Nations Children's Fund)
1966 No award
1967 No award
1968 René Cassin (France)
1969 International Labour Organization
1970 Norman E. Borlaug (U.S.)
1971 Willy Brandt (West Germany)
1972 No award
1973 Henry A. Kissinger (U.S.); Le Duc Tho (North Vietnam)[1]
1974 Eisaku Sato (Japan); Sean MacBride (Ireland)
1975 Andrei D. Sakharov (U.S.S.R.)
1976 Mairead Corrigan and Betty Williams (both Northern Ireland)
1977 Amnesty International
1978 Menachem Begin (Israel) and Anwar el-Sadat (Egypt)
1979 Mother Teresa of Calcutta (India)
1980 Adolfo Pérez Esquivel (Argentina)
1981 Office of the United Nations High Commissioner for Refugees
1982 Alva Myrdal (Sweden) and Alfonso García Robles (Mexico)
1983 Lech Walesa (Poland)
1984 Bishop Desmond Tutu (South Africa)
1985 International Physicians for the Prevention of Nuclear War
1986 Elie Wiesel (U.S.)
1987 Oscar Arias Sánchez (Costa Rica)
1988 U.N. Peacekeeping Forces
1989 Dalai Lama (Tibet)
1990 Mikhail S. Gorbachev (U.S.S.R.)
1991 Daw Aung San Suu Kyi (Myanmar)
1992 Rigoberta Menchú (Guatemala)
1993 F.W. de Klerk and Nelson Mandela (both South Africa)
1994 Yasir Arafat (Palestine) and Yitzhak Rabin (Israel)

1. Le Duc Tho refused prize, charging that peace had not yet been really established in South Vietnam.

995 Joseph Rotblat and Pugwash Conference on Science and World Affairs (England)

LITERATURE

901 René F. A. Sully Prudhomme (France)
902 Theodor Mommsen (Germany)
903 Björnstjerne Björnson (Norway)
904 Frédéric Mistral (France) and José Echegaray (Spain)
905 Henryk Sienkiewicz (Poland)
906 Giosuè Carducci (Italy)
907 Rudyard Kipling (England)
908 Rudolf Eucken (Germany)
909 Selma Lagerlöf (Sweden)
910 Paul von Heyse (Germany)
911 Maurice Maeterlinck (Belgium)
912 Gerhart Hauptmann (Germany)
913 Rabindranath Tagore (India)
915 Romain Rolland (France)
916 Verner von Heidenstam (Sweden)
917 Karl Gjellerup (Denmark) and Henrik Pontoppidan (Denmark)
919 Carl Spitteler (Switzerland)
920 Knut Hamsun (Norway)
921 Anatole France (France)
922 Jacinto Benavente (Spain)
923 William B. Yeats (Ireland)
924 Wladyslaw Reymont (Poland)
925 George Bernard Shaw (Ireland)
926 Grazia Deledda (Italy)
927 Henri Bergson (France)
928 Sigrid Undset (Norway)
929 Thomas Mann (Germany)
930 Sinclair Lewis (U.S.)
931 Erik A. Karlfeldt (Sweden)
932 John Galsworthy (England)
933 Ivan G. Bunin (Russia)
934 Luigi Pirandello (Italy)
935 No award
936 Eugene O'Neill (U.S.)
937 Roger Martin du Gard (France)
938 Pearl S. Buck (U.S.)
939 Frans Eemil Sillanpää (Finland)
944 Johannes V. Jensen (Denmark)
945 Gabriela Mistral (Chile)
946 Hermann Hesse (Switzerland)
947 André Gide (France)
948 Thomas Stearns Eliot (England)
949 William Faulkner (U.S.)
950 Bertrand Russell (England)
951 Pär Lagerkvist (Sweden)
952 François Mauriac (France)
953 Sir Winston Churchill (England)
954 Ernest Hemingway (U.S.)
955 Halldór Kiljan Laxness (Iceland)
956 Juan Ramón Jiménez (Spain)
957 Albert Camus (France)
958 Boris Pasternak (U.S.S.R.) (declined)
959 Salvatore Quasimodo (Italy)
960 St-John Perse (Alexis St.-Léger Léger) (France)
961 Ivo Andric (Yugoslavia)
962 John Steinbeck (U.S.)
963 Giorgios Seferis (Seferiades) (Greece)
964 Jean-Paul Sartre (France) (declined)
965 Mikhail Sholokhov (U.S.S.R.)
966 Shmuel Yosef Agnon (Israel) and Nelly Sachs (Sweden)
967 Miguel Angel Asturias (Guatemala)
968 Yasunari Kawabata (Japan)
969 Samuel Beckett (Ireland)
970 Aleksandr Solzhenitsyn (U.S.S.R.)
971 Pablo Neruda (Chile)
972 Heinrich Böll (Germany)
973 Patrick White (Australia)

1974 Eyvind Johnson and Harry Martinson (both Sweden)
1975 Eugenio Montale (Italy)
1976 Saul Bellow (U.S.)
1977 Vicente Aleixandre (Spain)
1978 Isaac Bashevis Singer (U.S.)
1979 Odysseus Elytis (Greece)
1980 Czeslaw Milosz (U.S.)
1981 Elias Canetti (Bulgaria)
1982 Gabriel García Márquez (Colombia)
1983 William Golding (England)
1984 Jaroslav Seifert (Czechoslovakia)
1985 Claude Simon (France)
1986 Wole Soyinka (Nigeria)
1987 Joseph Brodsky (U.S.)
1988 Naguib Mahfouz (Egypt)
1989 Camilo José Cela (Spain)
1990 Octavio Paz (Mexico)
1991 Nadine Gordimer (South Africa)
1992 Derek Walcott (Trinidad)
1993 Toni Morrison (U.S.)
1994 Kenzaburo Oe (Japan)
1995 Seamus Heaney (Ireland)

PHYSICS

1901 Wilhelm K. Roentgen (Germany), for discovery of Roentgen rays
1902 Hendrik A. Lorentz and Pieter Zeeman (Netherlands), for work on influence of magnetism upon radiation
1903 A. Henri Becquerel (France), for work on spontaneous radioactivity; and Pierre and Marie Curie (France), for study of radiation
1904 John Strutt (Lord Rayleigh) (England), for discovery of argon in investigating gas density
1905 Philipp Lenard (Germany), for work with cathode rays
1906 Sir Joseph Thomson (England), for investigations on passage of electricity through gases
1907 Albert A. Michelson (U.S.), for spectroscopic and metrologic investigations
1908 Gabriel Lippmann (France), for method of reproducing colors by photography
1909 Guglielmo Marconi (Italy) and Ferdinand Braun (Germany), for development of wireless
1910 Johannes D. van der Waals (Netherlands), for work with the equation of state for gases and liquids
1911 Wilhelm Wien (Germany), for his laws governing the radiation of heat
1912 Gustaf Dalén (Sweden), for discovery of automatic regulators used in lighting lighthouses and light buoys
1913 Heike Kamerlingh-Onnes (Netherlands), for work leading to production of liquid helium
1914 Max von Laue (Germany), for discovery of diffraction of Roentgen rays passing through crystals
1915 Sir William Bragg and William L. Bragg (England), for analysis of crystal structure by X rays
1916 No award
1917 Charles G. Barkla (England), for discovery of Roentgen radiation of the elements
1918 Max Planck (Germany), discoveries in connection with quantum theory
1919 Johannes Stark (Germany), discovery of Doppler effect in Canal rays and decomposition of spectrum lines by electric fields
1920 Charles E. Guillaume (Switzerland), for discoveries of anomalies in nickel steel alloys
1921 Albert Einstein (Germany), for discovery of the law of the photoelectric effect
1922 Niels Bohr (Denmark), for investigation of structure of atoms and radiations emanating from them
1923 Robert A. Millikan (U.S.), for work on elementary charge of electricity and photoelectric phenomena

1924 Karl M. G. Siegbahn (Sweden), for investigations in X-ray spectroscopy

1925 James Franck and Gustav Hertz (Germany), for discovery of laws governing impact of electrons upon atoms

1926 Jean B. Perrin (France), for work on discontinuous structure of matter and discovery of the equilibrium of sedimentation

1927 Arthur H. Compton (U.S.), for discovery of Compton phenomenon; and Charles T. R. Wilson (England), for method of perceiving paths taken by electrically charged particles

1928 In 1929, the 1928 prize was awarded to Sir Owen Richardson (England), for work on the phenomenon of thermionics and discovery of the Richardson Law

1929 Prince Louis Victor de Broglie (France), for discovery of the wave character of electrons

1930 Sir Chandrasekhara Raman (India), for work on diffusion of light and discovery of the Raman effect

1931 No award

1932 In 1933, the prize for 1932 was awarded to Werner Heisenberg (Germany), for creation of the quantum mechanics

1933 Erwin Schrödinger (Austria) and Paul A. M. Dirac (England), for discovery of new fertile forms of the atomic theory

1934 No award

1935 James Chadwick (England), for discovery of the neutron

1936 Victor F. Hess (Austria), for discovery of cosmic radiation; and Carl D. Anderson (U.S.), for discovery of the positron

1937 Clinton J. Davisson (U.S.) and George P. Thomson (England), for discovery of diffraction of electrons by crystals

1938 Enrico Fermi (Italy), for identification of new radioactivity elements and discovery of nuclear reactions effected by slow neutrons

1939 Ernest Orlando Lawrence (U.S.), for development of the cyclotron

1943 Otto Stern (U.S.), for detection of magnetic momentum of protons

1944 Isidor Isaac Rabi (U.S.), for work on magnetic movements of atomic particles

1945 Wolfgang Pauli (Austria), for work on atomic fissions

1946 Percy Williams Bridgman (U.S.), for studies and inventions in high-pressure physics

1947 Sir Edward Appleton (England), for discovery of layer which reflects radio short waves in the ionosphere

1948 Patrick M. S. Blackett (England), for improvement on Wilson chamber and discoveries in cosmic radiation

1949 Hideki Yukawa (Japan), for mathematical prediction, in 1935, of the meson

1950 Cecil Frank Powell (England), for method of photographic study of atom nucleus, and for discoveries about mesons

1951 Sir John Douglas Cockcroft (England) and Ernest T. S. Walton (Ireland), for work in 1932 on transmutation of atomic nuclei

1952 Edward Mills Purcell and Felix Bloch (U.S.), for work in measurement of magnetic fields in atomic nuclei

1953 Fritz Zernike (Netherlands), for development of "phase contrast" microscope

1954 Max Born (England), for work in quantum mechanics; and Walther Bothe (Germany), for work in cosmic radiation

1955 Polykarp Kusch and Willis E. Lamb, Jr. (U.S.), for atomic measurements

1956 William Shockley, Walter H. Brattain, and John Bardeen (U.S.), for developing electronic transistor

1957 Tsung Dao Lee and Chen Ning Yang (China), for disproving principle of conservation of parity

1958 Pavel A. Cherenkov, Ilya M. Frank, and Igor E. Tamm (U.S.S.R.), for work resulting in development of co mic-ray counter

1959 Emilio Segre and Owen Chamberlain (U.S.), for demonstrating the existence of the anti-proton

1960 Donald A. Glaser (U.S.), for invention of "bub-b chamber" to study subatomic particles

1961 Robert Hofstadter (U.S.), for determination of shape ar size of atomic nucleus; Rudolf Mössbauer (German for method of producing and measuring recoil-free gar ma rays

1962 Lev D. Landau (U.S.S.R.), for his theories about co densed matter

1963 Eugene Paul Wigner, Maria Goeppert Mayer (bo U.S.), and J. Hans D. Jensen (Germany), for researc on structure of atom and its nucleus

1964 Charles Hard Townes (U.S.), Nikolai G. Basov, ar Aleksandr M. Prochorov (both U.S.S.R.), for develop ing maser and laser principle of producing high-inte sity radiation

1965 Richard P. Feynman, Julian S. Schwinger (both U.S.), ar Shinichiro Tomonaga (Japan), for research in quantu electrodynamics

1966 Alfred Kastler (France), for work on energy levels i side atom

1967 Hans A. Bethe (U.S.), for work on energy productic of stars

1968 Luis Walter Alvarez (U.S.), for study of subatomi particles

1969 Murray Gell-Mann (U.S.), for study of subatomic pa ticles

1970 Hannes Alfvén (Sweden), for theories in plasma physic and Louis Néel (France), for discoveries in antiferromag netism and ferrimagnetism

1971 Dennis Gabor (England), for invention of holographi method of three-dimensional imagery

1972 John Bardeen, Leon N. Cooper, and John Rober Schrieffer (all U.S.), for theory of superconductivit where electrical resistance in certain metals va nishes above absolute zero temperature

1973 Ivar Giaever (U.S.), Leo Esaki (Japan), and Brian l Josephson (U.K.), for theories that have advance and expanded the field of miniature electronics

1974 Antony Hewish (England), for discovery of pulsar Martin Ryle (England), for using radiotelescopes t probe outer space with high degree of precision

1975 James Rainwater (U.S.) and Ben Mottelson an Aage N. Bohr (both Denmark), for showing that th atomic nucleus is asymmetrical

1976 Burton Richter and Samuel C. C. Ting (both U.S.), fc discovery of subatomic particles known as J and ps

1977 Philip W. Anderson and John H. Van Vleck (both U.S and Nevill F. Mott (U.K.), for work underlying con puter memories and electronic devices

1978 Arno A. Penzias and Robert W. Wilson (both U.S.), fc work in cosmic microwave radiation; Piotr L. Kapits (U.S.S.R.), for basic inventions and discoveries i low-temperature physics

1979 Steven Weinberg and Sheldon L. Glashow (both U.S and Abdus Salam (Pakistan), for de-veloping theor that electromagnetism and the "weak" forc which causes radioactive decay in some atomic nucle are facets of the same phenomenon

1980 James W. Cronin and Val L. Fitch (both U.S.), for wo concerning the assymetry of subatomic particles

1981 Nicolaas Bloembergen and Arthur L. Schawlov (both U.S.) and Kai M. Siegbahn (Sweden), for deve oping technologies with lasers and other devices t probe the secrets of complex forms of matter

1982 Kenneth G. Wilson (U.S.), for analysis of changes i matter under pressure and temperature

1983 Subrahmanyam Chandrasekhar and William A. Fowler (both U.S.) for complementary research on processes involved in the evolution of stars

1984 Carlo Rubbia (Italy) and Simon van der Meer (Netherlands), for their role in discovering three subatomic particles, a step toward developing a single theory to account for all natural forces

1985 Klaus von Klitzing (Germany), for developing an exact way of measuring electrical conductivity

1986 Ernst Ruska, Gerd Binnig (both Germany) and Heinrich Rohrer (Switzerland) for work on microscopes

1987 K. Alex Müller (Switzerland) and J. Georg Bednorz (Germany) for their discovery of high-temperature superconductors.

1988 Leon M. Lederman, Melvin Schwartz, and Jack Steinberger (all U.S.) for research that improved the understanding of elementary particles and forces.

1989 Norman F. Ramsey (U.S.), for work leading to development of the atomic clock, and Hans G. Dehmelt (U.S.) and Wolfgang Paul (Germany) for developing methods to isolate atoms and subatomic particles.

1990 Richard E. Taylor (Canada) and Jerome I. Friedman and Henry W. Kendall (both U.S.), for their "breakthrough in our understanding of matter" which confirmed the reality of quarks.

1991 Pierre-Gilles de Gennes (France) for his discoveries about the ordering of molecules in substances ranging from "super" glue to an exotic form of liquid helium.

1992 George Charpak (France), for his inventions of particle detectors.

1993 Joseph H. Taylor and Russell A. Hulse (U.S.) for their discovery of a binary pulsar.

1994 Clifford G. Shull (U.S.) and Bertram N. Brockhouse (Canada), for adapting beams of neutrons as probes to explore the atomic structure of matter.

1995 Martin L. Perl and Frederick Reines (U.S.), for their discoveries of "two of nature's most remarkable subatomic particles"—the tau and the neutrino.

CHEMISTRY

1901 Jacobus H. van't Hoff (Netherlands), for laws of chemical dynamics and osmotic pressure in solutions

1902 Emil Fischer (Germany), for experiments in sugar and purin groups of substances

1903 Svante A. Arrhenius (Sweden), for his electrolytic theory of dissociation

1904 Sir William Ramsay (England), for discovery and determination of place of inert gaseous elements in air

1905 Adolf von Baeyer (Germany), for work on organic dyes and hydroaromatic combinations

1906 Henri Moissan (France), for isolation of fluorine, and introduction of electric furnace

1907 Eduard Buchner (Germany), discovery of cell-less fermentation and investigations in biological chemistry

1908 Sir Ernest Rutherford (England), for investigations into disintegration of elements

1909 Wilhelm Ostwald (Germany), for work on catalysis and investigations into chemical equilibrium and reaction rates

1910 Otto Wallach (Germany), for work in the field of alicyclic compounds

1911 Marie Curie (France), for discovery of elements radium and polonium

1912 Victor Grignard (France), for reagent discovered by him; and Paul Sabatier (France), for methods of hydrogenating organic compounds

1913 Alfred Werner (Switzerland), for linking up atoms within the molecule

1914 Theodore W. Richards (U.S.), for determining atomic weight of many chemical elements

1915 Richard Willstätter (Germany), for research into coloring matter of plants, especially chlorophyll

1916 No award

1917 No award

1918 Fritz Haber (Germany), for synthetic production of ammonia

1919 No award

1920 Walther Nernst (Germany), for work in thermochemistry

1921 Frederick Soddy (England), for investigations into origin and nature of isotopes

1922 Francis W. Aston (England), for discovery of isotopes in nonradioactive elements and for discovery of the whole number rule

1923 Fritz Pregl (Austria), for method of microanalysis of organic substances discovered by him

1924 No award

1925 In 1926, the 1925 prize was awarded to Richard Zsigmondy (Germany), for work on the heterogeneous nature of colloid solutions

1926 Theodor Svedberg (Sweden), for work on disperse systems

1927 In 1928, the 1927 prize was awarded to Heinrich Wieland (Germany), for investigations of bile acids and kindred substances

1928 Adolf Windaus (Germany), for investigations on constitution of the sterols and their connection with vitamins

1929 Sir Arthur Harden (England) and Hans K. A. S. von Euler-Chelpin (Sweden), for research of fermentation of sugars

1930 Hans Fischer (Germany), for work on coloring matter of blood and leaves and for his synthesis of hemin

1931 Karl Bosch and Friedrich Bergius (Germany), for invention and development of chemical high-pressure methods

1932 Irving Langmuir (U.S.), for work in realm of surface chemistry

1933 No award

1934 Harold C. Urey (U.S.), for discovery of heavy hydrogen

1935 Frédéric and Irène Joliot-Curie (France), for synthesis of new radioactive elements

1936 Peter J. W. Debye (Netherlands), for investigations on dipole moments and diffraction of X rays and electrons in gases

1937 Walter N. Haworth (England), for research on carbohydrates and Vitamin C; and Paul Karrer (Switzerland), for work on carotenoids, flavins, and Vitamins A and B

1938 Richard Kuhn (Germany), for carotinoid study and vitamin research (declined)

1939 Adolf Butenandt (Germany), for work on sexual hormones (declined the prize); and Leopold Ruzicka (Switzerland), for work with polymethylenes

1943 Georg De Heves (Hungary), for work on use of isotopes as indicators

1944 Otto Hahn (Germany), for work on atomic fission

1945 Arttuuri Illmari Virtanen (Finland), for research in the field of conservation of fodder

1946 James B. Sumner (U.S.), for crystallizing enzymes; John H. Northrop and Wendell M. Stanley (U.S.), for preparing enzymes and virus proteins in pure form

1947 Sir Robert Robinson (England), for research in plant substances

1948 Arne Tiselius (Sweden), for biochemical discoveries and isolation of mouse paralysis virus

1949 William Francis Giauque (U.S.), for research in thermodynamics, especially effects of low temperature

1950 Otto Diels and Kurt Alder (Germany), for discovery of diene synthesis enabling scientists to study structure of organic matter

1951 Glenn T. Seaborg and Edwin H. McMillan (U.S.), for discovery of plutonium

1952 Archer John Porter Martin and Richard Laurence Millington Synge (England), for development of partition chromatography

1953 Hermann Staudinger (Germany), for research in giant molecules

1954 Linus C. Pauling (U.S.), for study of forces holding together protein and other molecules

1955 Vincent du Vigneaud (U.S.), for work on pituitary hormones

1956 Sir Cyril Hinshelwood (England) and Nikolai N. Semenov (U.S.S.R.), for parallel research on chemical reaction kinetics

1957 Sir Alexander Todd (England), for research with chemical compounds that are factors in heredity

1958 Frederick Sanger (England), for determining molecular structure of insulin

1959 Jaroslav Heyrovsky (Czechoslovakia), for development of polarography, an electrochemical method of analysis

1960 Willard F. Libby (U.S.), for "atomic time clock" to measure age of objects by measuring their radioactivity

1961 Melvin Calvin (U.S.), for establishing chemical steps during photosynthesis

1962 Max F. Perutz and John C. Kendrew (England), for mapping protein molecules with X-rays

1963 Carl Ziegler (Germany) and Giulio Natta (Italy), for work in uniting simple hydrocarbons into large molecule substances

1964 Dorothy Mary Crowfoot Hodgkin (England), for determining structure of compounds needed in combating pernicious anemia

1965 Robert B. Woodward (U.S.), for work in synthesizing complicated organic compounds

1966 Robert Sanderson Mulliken (U.S.), for research on bond holding atoms together in molecule

1967 Manfred Eigen (Germany), Ronald G. W. Norrish, and George Porter (both Eng land), for work in high-speed chemical reactions

1968 Lars Onsager (U.S.), for development of system of equations in thermodynamics

1969 Derek H. R. Barton (England) and Odd Hassel (Norway), for study of organic molecules

1970 Luis F. Leloir (Argentina), for discovery of sugar nucleotides and their role in biosynthesis of carbohydrates

1971 Gerhard Herzberg (Canada), for contributions to knowledge of electronic structure and geometry of molecules, particularly free radicals

1972 Christian Boehmer Anfinsen, Stanford Moore, and William Howard Stein (all U.S.), for pioneering studies in enzymes

1973 Ernst Otto Fischer (W. Germany) and Geoffrey Wilkinson (U.K.), for work that could solve problem of automobile exhaust pollution

1974 Paul J. Flory (U.S.), for developing analytic methods to study properties and molecular structure of long-chain molecules

1975 John W. Cornforth (Australia) and Vladimir Prelog (Switzerland), for research on structure of biological molecules such as antibiotics and cholesterol

1976 William N. Lipscomb, Jr. (U.S.), for work on the structure and bonding mechanisms of boranes

1977 Ilya Prigogine (Belgium), for contributions to non-equilibrium thermodynamics, particularly the theory of dissipative structures

1978 Peter Mitchell (U.K.), for contributions to the understanding of biological energy transfer

1979 Herbert C. Brown (U.S.) and Georg Wittig (West Germany), for developing a group of substances that facilitate very difficult chemical reactions

1980 Paul Berg and Walter Gilbert (both U.S.) and Frederick Sanger (England), for developing methods to map the structure and function of DNA, the substance that controls the activity of the cell

1981 Roald Hoffmann (U.S.) and Kenichi Fukui (Japan), for applying quantum-mechanics theories to predict the course of chemical reactions

1982 Aaron Klug (U.K.), for research in the detailed structures of viruses and components of life

1983 Henry Taube (U.S.), for research on how electrons transfer between molecules in chemical reactions

1984 R. Bruce Merrifield (U.S.) for research that revolutionized the study of proteins

1985 Herbert A. Hauptman and Jerome Karle (both U.S.) for their outstanding achievements in the development of direct methods for the determination of crystal structures

1986 Dudley R. Herschback, Yuan T. Lee (both U.S.), and John C. Polanyi (Canada) for their work on "reaction dynamics"

1987 Donald J. Cram and Charles J. Pedersen (both U.S.) and Jean-Marie Lehn (France), for wide-ranging research that has included the creation of artificial molecules that can mimic vital chemical reactions of the processes of life.

1988 Johann Deisenhofer, Robert Huber, and Hartmut Michel (all West Germany) for unraveling the structure of proteins that play a crucial role in photosynthesis.

1989 Thomas R. Cech and Sidney Altman (both U.S.) for their discovery, independently, that RNA could actively aid chemical reactions in the cells.

1990 Elias James Corey (U.S.) for developing new ways to synthesize complex molecules ordinarily found in nature.

1991 Richard R. Ernst (Switzerland) for refinements he developed in nuclear magnetic resonance spectroscopy.

1992 Rudolph A. Marcus (U.S.), for his mathematical analysis of how the overall energy in a system of interacting molecules changes and induces an electron to jump from one molecule to another.

1993 Kary B. Mullis (U.S.) and Michael Smith (Canada) for their contributions to the science of genetics.

1994 George A. Olah (U.S.), University of Southern California in Los Angeles, for research that opened new ways to break apart and rebuild compounds of carbon and hydrogen.

1995 F. Sherwood Rowland and Mario Molina (U.S.) and Paul Crutzen (The Netherlands), for their pioneering work in explaining the chemical processes that deplete the earth's ozone shield.

PHYSIOLOGY OR MEDICINE

1901 Emil A. von Behring (Germany), for work on serum therapy against diptheria

1902 Sir Ronald Ross (England), for work on malaria

1903 Niels R. Finsen (Denmark), for his treatment of lupus vulgaris with concentrated light rays

1904 Ivan P. Pavlov (U.S.S.R.), for work on the physiology of digestion

1905 Robert Koch (Germany), for work on tuberculosis

1906 Camillo Golgi (Italy) and Santiago Ramón y Cajal (Spain), for work on structure of the nervous system

1907 Charles L. A. Laveran (France), for work with protozoa in the generation of disease

1908 Paul Ehrlich (Germany), and Elie Metchnikoff (U.S.S.R.), for work on immunity

1909 Theodor Kocher (Switzerland), for work on the thyroid gland

1910 Albrecht Kossel (Germany), for achievements in the chemistry of the cell

1911 Allvar Gullstrand (Sweden), for work on the dioptrics of the eye

1912 Alexis Carrel (France), for work on vascular ligature and grafting of blood vessels and organs

1913 Charles Richet (France), for work on anaphylaxy

1914 Robert Bárány (Austria), for work on physiology and pathology of the vestibular system

1915-1918 No award

1919 Jules Bordet (Belgium), for discoveries in connection with immunity

1920 August Krogh (Denmark), for discovery of regulation of capillaries' motor mechanism

1921 No award

1922 In 1923, the 1922 prize was shared by Archibald V. Hill (England), for discovery relating to heat-production in muscles; and Otto Meyerhof (Germany), for correlation between consumption of oxygen and production of lactic acid in muscles

1923 Sir Frederick Banting (Canada) and John J. R. Macleod (Scotland), for discovery of insulin

1924 Willem Einthoven (Netherlands), for discovery of the mechanism of the electrocardiogram

1925 No award

1926 Johannes Fibiger (Denmark), for discovery of the Spiroptera carcinoma

1927 Julius Wagner-Jauregg (Austria), for use of malaria inoculation in treatment of dementia paralytica

1928 Charles Nicolle (France), for work on typhus exanthematicus

1929 Christiaan Eijkman (Netherlands), for discovery of the antineuritic vitamins; and Sir Frederick Hopkins (England), for discovery of growth-promoting vitamins

1930 Karl Landsteiner (U.S.), for discovery of human blood groups

1931 Otto H. Warburg (Germany), for discovery of the character and mode of action of the respiratory ferment

1932 Sir Charles Sherrington (England) and Edgar D. Adrian (U.S.), for discoveries of the function of the neuron

1933 Thomas H. Morgan (U.S.), for discoveries on hereditary function of the chromosomes

1934 George H. Whipple, George R. Minot, and William P. Murphy (U.S.), for discovery of liver therapy against anemias

1935 Hans Spemann (Germany), for discovery of the organizer-effect in embryonic development

1936 Sir Henry Dale (England) and Otto Loewi (Germany), for discoveries on chemical transmission of nerve impulses

1937 Albert Szent-Györgyi von Nagyrapolt (Hungary), for discoveries on biological combustion

1938 Corneille Heymans (Belgium), for determining importance of sinus and aorta mechanisms in the regulation of respiration

1939 Gerhard Domagk (Germany), for antibacterial effect of prontocilate

1943 Henrik Dam (Denmark) and Edward A. Doisy (U.S.), for analysis of Vitamin K

1944 Joseph Erlanger and Herbert Spencer Gasser (U.S.), for work on functions of the nerve threads

1945 Sir Alexander Fleming, Ernst Boris Chain, and Sir Howard Florey (England), for discovery of penicillin

1946 Herman J. Muller (U.S.), for hereditary effects of X-rays on genes

1947 Carl F. and Gerty T. Cori (U.S.), for work on animal starch metabolism; Bernardo A. Houssay (Argentina), for study of pituitary

1948 Paul Mueller (Switzerland), for discovery of insect-killing properties of DDT

1949 Walter Rudolf Hess (Switzerland), for research on brain control of body; and Antonio Caetano de Abreu Freire Egas Moniz (Portugal), for development of brain operation

1950 Philip S. Hench, Edward C. Kendall (both U.S.), and Tadeus Reichstein (Switzerland), for discoveries about hormones of adrenal cortex

1951 Max Theiler (South Africa), for development of anti-yellow-fever vaccine

1952 Selman A. Waksman (U.S.), for co-discovery of streptomycin

1953 Fritz A. Lipmann (Germany-U.S.) and Hans Adolph Krebs (Germany-England), for studies of living cells

1954 John F. Enders, Thomas H. Weller, and Frederick C. Robbins (U.S.), for work with cultivation of polio virus

1955 Hugo Theorell (Sweden), for work on oxidation enzymes

1956 Dickinson W. Richards, Jr., André F. Cournand (both U.S.), and Werner Forssmann (Germany), for new techniques in treating heart disease

1957 Daniel Bovet (Italy), for development of drugs to relieve allergies and relax muscles during surgery

1958 Joshua Lederberg (U.S.), for work with genetic mechanisms; George W. Beadle and Edward L. Tatum (U.S.), for discovering how genes transmit hereditary characteristics

1959 Severo Ochoa and Arthur Kornberg (U.S.), for discoveries related to compounds within chromosomes, which play a vital role in heredity

1960 Sir Macfarlane Burnet (Australia) and Peter Brian Medawar (England), for discovery of acquired immunological tolerance

1961 Georg von Bekesy (U.S.), for discoveries about physical mechanisms of stimulation within cochlea

1962 James D. Watson (U.S.), Maurice H. F. Wilkins, and Francis H. C. Crick (England), for determining structure of deoxyribonucleic acid (DNA)

1963 Alan Lloyd Hodgkin, Andrew Fielding Huxley (both England), and Sir John Carew Eccles (Australia), for research on nerve cells

1964 Konrad E. Bloch (U.S.) and Feodor Lynen (Germany), for research on mechanism and regulation of cholesterol and fatty acid metabolism

1965 François Jacob, André Lwolff, and Jacques Monod (France), for study of regulatory activities in body cells

1966 Charles Brenton Huggins (U.S.), for studies in hormone treatment of cancer of prostate; Francis Peyton Rous (U.S.), for discovery of tumor-producing viruses

1967 Haldan K. Hartline, George Wald, and Ragnar Granit (U.S.), for work on human eye

1968 Robert W. Holley, Har Gobind Khorana, and Marshall W. Nirenberg (U.S.), for studies of genetic code

1969 Max Delbruck, Alfred D. Hershey, and Salvador E. Luria (U.S.), for study of mechanism of virus infection in living cells

1970 Julius Axelrod (U.S.), Ulf S. von Euler (Swed-en), and Sir Bernard Katz (England), for studies of how nerve impulses are transmitted within the body

1971 Earl W. Sutherland, Jr. (U.S.), for research on how hormones work

1972 Gerald M. Edelman (U.S.), and Rodney R. Porter (U.K.), for research on the chemical structure and nature of antibodies

1973 Karl von Frisch and Konrad Lorenz (Austria), and Nikolaas Tinbergen (Netherlands), for their studies of individual and social behavior patterns

1974 George E. Palade and Christian de Duve (both U.S.) and Albert Claude (Belgium), for contributions to understanding inner workings of living cells

1975 David Baltimore, Howard M. Temin, and Renato Dulbecco (all U.S.), for work in interaction between tumor viruses and genetic material of the cell

1976 Baruch S. Blumberg and D. Carleton Gajdusek (U.S.), for discoveries concerning new mechanisms for the origin and dissemination of infectious diseases

1977 Rosalyn S. Yalow, Roger C. L. Guillemin, and Andrew V. Schally (all U.S.), for research in role of hormones in chemistry of the body

1978 Daniel Nathans and Hamilton Smith (both U.S.) and Werner Arber (Switzerland), for discovery of restriction enzymes and their application to problems of molecular genetics

1979 Allan McLeod Cormack (U.S.) and Godfrey Newbold Hounsfield (England), for developing computed axial tomography (CAT scan) X-ray technique

1980 Baruj Benacerraf and George D. Snell (both U.S.) and Jean Dausset (France), for discoveries that explain how the structure of cells relates to organ transplants and diseases

1981 Roger W. Sperry and David H. Hubel (both U.S.) and Torsten N. Wiesel (Sweden), for studies vital to understanding the organization and functioning of the brain

1982 Sune Bergstrom and Bengt Samuelsson (Sweden) and John R. Vane (U.K.), for research in prostaglandins, a hormonelike substance involved in a wide range of illnesses

1983 Barbara McClintock (U.S.), for her discovery of mobile genes in the chromosomes of a plant that change the future generations of plants they produce

1984 Cesar Milstein (U.K./Argentina) Georges J.F. Kohler (West Germany), and Niels K. Jerne (U.K./Denmark) for their work in immunology

1985 Michael S. Brown and Joseph L. Goldstein (both U.S.) for their work which has drastically widened our understanding of the cholesterol metabolism and increased our possibilities to prevent and treat atherosclerosis and heart attacks

1986 Rita Levi-Montalcini (dual U.S./Italy) and Stanley Cohen (U.S.) for their contributions to the understanding of substances that influence cell growth

1987 Susumu Tonegawa (Japan), for his discoveries of how the body can suddenly marshal its immunological defenses against millions of different disease agents that it has never encountered before.

1988 Gertrude B. Elion, George H. Hitchings (both U.S.) and Sir James Black (U.K.) for their discoveries of important principles for drug treatment.

1989 J. Michael Bishop and Harold E. Varmus (both U.S.) for their unifying theory of cancer development.

1990 Joseph E. Murray and E. Donnall Thomas (both U.S.), for their pioneering work in transplants.

1991 Erwin Neher and Bert Sakmann (both Germany) for their research, particularly for the development of a technique called patch clamp.

1992 Edmond H. Fischer and Edwin G. Kerbs (U.S.), for their discovery of a regulatory mechanism affecting almost all cells.

1993 Phillip A. Sharp (U.S.) and Richard J. Roberts (U.K.), for their independent discovery in 1977 of "split genes."

1994 Alfred G. Gilman and Martin Rodbell (both U.S.), for discovery of G-proteins that help cells respond to outside signals.

1995 Edward B. Lewis and Eric F. Wieschaus (U.S.) and Christiane Nüsslein-Volhard (Germany), for studies of the fruit fly that will help explain congenital malformations in humans.

ECONOMIC SCIENCE

1969 Ragnar Frisch (Norway) and Jan Tinbergen (Netherlands), for work in econometrics (application of mathematics and statistical methods to economic theories and problems)

1970 Paul A. Samuelson (U.S.), for efforts to raise the level of scientific analysis in economic theory

1971 Simon Kuznets (U.S.), for developing concept of using a country's gross national product to determine its economic growth

1972 Kenneth J. Arrow (U.S.) and Sir John R. Hicks (U.K.), for theories that help to assess business risk and government economic and welfare policies

1973 Wassily Leontief (U.S.), for devising the input–output technique to determine how different sectors of an economy interact

1974 Gunnar Myrdal (Sweden) and Friedrich A. von Hayek (U.K.), for pioneering analysis of the interdependence of economic, social and institutional phenomena

1975 Leonid V. Kantorovich (U.S.S.R.) and Tjalling C. Koopmans (U.S.), for work on the theory of optimum allocation of resources

1976 Milton Friedman (U.S.), for work in consumption analysis and monetary history and theory, and for demonstration of complexity of stabilization policy

1977 Bertil Ohlin (Sweden) and James E. Meade (U.K.), for contributions to theory of international trade and international capital movements

1978 Herbert A. Simon (U.S.), for research into the decision-making process within economic organizations

1979 Sir Arthur Lewis (England) and Theodore Schultz (U.S.), for work on economic problems of developing nations

1980 Lawrence R. Klein (U.S.), for developing models for forecasting economic trends and shaping policies to deal with them

1981 James Tobin (U.S.), for analyses of financial markets and their influence on spending and saving by families and businesses

1982 George J. Stigler (U.S.), for work on government regulation in the economy and the functioning of industry

1983 Gerard Debreu (U.S.), in recognition of his work on the basic economic problem of how prices operate to balance what producers supply with what buyers want.

1984 Sir Richard Stone (U.K.), for his work to develop the systems widely used to measure the performance of national economics

1985 Franco Modigliani (U.S.) for his pioneering work in analyzing the behavior of household savers and the functioning of financial markets

1986 James M. Buchanan (U.S.) for his development of new methods for analyzing economic and political decision-making

1987 Robert M. Solow (U.S.), for seminal contributions to the theory of economic growth.

1988 Maurice Allais (France) for his pioneering development of theories to better understand market behavior and the efficient use of resources.

1989 Trygve Haavelmo (Norway) for his pioneering work in methods for testing economic theories.

1990 Harry M. Markowitz, William F. Sharpe, and Merton H. Miller (all U.S.), whose work provided new tools for weighing the risks and rewards of different investments and for valuing corporate stocks and bonds.

1991 Ronald Coase (U.S.) for his pioneering work in how property rights and the cost of doing business affect the economy.

1992 Gary S. Becker (U.S.), for "having extended the domain of economic theory to aspects of human behavior which had previously been dealth with—if at all—by other social science disciplines."

1993 Robert W. Fogel and Douglass C. North (U.S.), for their work in economic history.

1994 John F. Nash and John C. Harsanyi (both U.S.), and Reinhard Selten (Germany), for their pioneering work in game theory.

1995 Robert E. Lucas, Jr. (U.S.), who has had the greatest influence on macroeconomic research since 1970.

Motion Picture Academy Awards (Oscars)

1928

Picture: *Wings,* Paramount
Director: Frank Borzage, *Seventh Heaven;* Lewis Milestone, *Two Arabian Nights*
Actress: Janet Gaynor, *Seventh Heaven, Street Angel, Sunrise*
Actor: Emil Jannings, *The Way of All Flesh, The Last Command*

1929

Picture: *The Broadway Melody,* MGM
Director: Frank Lloyd, *The Divine Lady*
Actress: Mary Pickford, *Coquette*
Actor: Warner Baxter, *In Old Arizona*

1930

Picture: *All Quiet on the Western Front,* Universal
Director: Lewis Milestone, *All Quiet on the Western Front*
Actress: Norma Shearer, *The Divorcee*
Actor: George Arliss, *Disraeli*

1931

Picture: *Cimarron:* RKO Radio
Director: Norman Taurog, *Skippy*
Actress: Marie Dressler, *Min and Bill*
Actor: Lionel Barrymore, *A Free Soul*

1932

Picture: *Grand Hotel,* MGM
Director: Frank Borzage, *Bad Girl*
Actress: Helen Hayes, *The Sin of Madelon Claudet*
Actor: Fredric March, *Dr. Jekyll and Mr. Hyde,* and Wallace Beery, *The Champ*

1933

Picture: *Cavalcade,* Fox
Director: Frank Lloyd, *Cavalcade*
Actress: Katharine Hepburn, *Morning Glory*
Actor: Charles Laughton, *The Private Life of Henry VIII*

1934

Picture: *It Happened One Night,* Columbia
Director: Frank Capra, *It Happened One Night*
Actress: Claudette Colbert, *It Happened One Night*
Actor: Clark Gable, *It Happened One Night*

1935

Picture: *Mutiny on the Bounty,* MGM
Director: John Ford, *The Informer*
Actress: Bette Davis, *Dangerous*
Actor: Victor McLaglen, *The Informer*

1936

Picture: *The Great Ziegfeld,* MGM
Director: Frank Capra, *Mr. Deeds Goes to Town*
Actress: Luise Rainer, *The Great Ziegfeld*
Actor: Paul Muni, *The Story of Louis Pasteur*
Supporting Actress: Gale Sondergaard, *Anthony Adverse*
Supporting Actor: Walter Brennan, *Come and Get It*

1937

Picture: *The Life of Emile Zola,* Warner Bros.
Director: Leo McCarey, *The Awful Truth*
Actress: Luise Rainer, *The Good Earth*
Actor: Spencer Tracy, *Captains Courageous*
Supporting Actress: Alice Brady, *In Old Chicago*
Supporting Actor: Joseph Schildkraut, *The Life of Emile Zola*

1938

Picture: *You Can't Take It with You,* Columbia
Director: Frank Capra, *You Can't Take It with You*
Actress: Bette Davis, *Jezebel*
Actor: Spencer Tracy, *Boys Town*
Supporting Actress: Fay Bainter, *Jezebel*

Supporting Actor: Walter Brennan, *Kentucky*

1939

Picture: *Gone with the Wind,* Selznick, MGM
Director: Victor Fleming, *Gone with the Wind*
Actress: Vivien Leigh, *Gone with the Wind*
Actor: Robert Donat, *Goodbye, Mr. Chips*
Supporting Actress: Hattie McDaniel, *Gone with the Wind*
Supporting Actor: Thomas Mitchell, *Stagecoach*

1940

Picture: *Rebecca,* Selznick–UA
Director: John Ford, *The Grapes of Wrath*
Actress: Ginger Rogers, *Kitty Foyle*
Actor: James Stewart, *The Philadelphia Story*
Supporting Actress: Jane Darwell, *The Grapes of Wrath*
Supporting Actor: Walter Brennan, *The Westerner*

1941

Picture: *How Green Was My Valley,* 20th CenturyFox
Director: John Ford, *How Green Was My Valley*
Actress: Joan Fontaine, *Suspicion*
Actor: Gary Cooper, *Sergeant York*
Supporting Actress: Mary Astor, *The Great Lie*
Supporting Actor: Donald Crisp, *How Green Was My Valley*

1942

Picture: *Mrs. Miniver,* MGM
Director: William Wyler, *Mrs. Miniver*
Actress: Greer Garson, *Mrs. Miniver*
Actor: James Cagney, *Yankee Doodle Dandy*
Supporting Actress: Teresa Wright, *Mrs. Miniver*
Supporting Actor: Van Heflin, *Johnny Eager*

1943

Picture: *Casablanca,* Warner Bros.
Director: Michael Curtiz, *Casablanca*
Actress: Jennifer Jones, *The Song of Bernadette*
Actor: Paul Lukas, *Watch on the Rhine*
Supporting Actress: Katina Paxinou, *For Whom the Bell Tolls*
Supporting Actor: Charles Coburn, *The More the Merrier*

1944

Picture: *Going My Way,* Paramount
Director: Leo McCarey, *Going My Way*
Actress: Ingrid Bergman, *Gaslight*
Actor: Bing Crosby, *Going My Way*
Supporting Actress: Ethel Barrymore, *None But the Lonely Heart*
Supporting Actor: Barry Fitzgerald, *Going My Way*

1945

Picture: *The Lost Weekend,* Paramount
Director: Billy Wilder, *The Lost Weekend*
Actress: Joan Crawford, *Mildred Pierce*
Actor: Ray Milland, *The Lost Weekend*
Supporting Actress: Anne Revere, *National Velvet*
Supporting Actor: James Dunn, *A Tree Grows in Brooklyn*

1946

Picture: *The Best Years of Our Lives,* Goldwyn–RKO Radio
Director: William Wyler, *The Best Years of Our Lives*
Actress: Olivia de Havilland, *To Each His Own*
Actor: Fredric March, *The Best Years of Our Lives*
Supporting Actress: Anne Baxter, *The Razor's Edge*
Supporting Actor: Harold Russell, *The Best Years of Our Lives*

1947

Picture: *Gentleman's Agreement,* 20th CenturyFox
Director: Elia Kazan, *Gentleman's Agreement*
Actress: Loretta Young, *The Farmer's Daughter*
Actor: Ronald Colman, *A Double Life*

Supporting Actress: Celeste Holm, *Gentleman's Agreement*
Supporting Actor: Edmund Gwenn, *Miracle on 34th Street*

1948

Picture: *Hamlet,* Rank—Two Cities—UI
Director: John Huston, *Treasure of Sierra Madre*
Actress: Jane Wyman, *Johnny Belinda*
Actor: Laurence Olivier, *Hamlet*
Supporting Actress: Claire Trevor, *Key Largo*
Supporting Actor: Walter Huston, *Treasure of Sierra Madre*

1949

Picture: *All the King's Men,* Rossen—Columbia
Director: Joseph L. Mankiewicz, *A Letter to Three Wives*
Actress: Olivia de Havilland, *The Heiress*
Actor: Broderick Crawford, *All the King's Men*
Supporting Actress: Mercedes McCambridge, *All the King's Men*
Supporting Actor: Dean Jagger, *Twelve O'Clock High*

1950

Picture: *All About Eve,* 20th Century—Fox
Director: Joseph L. Mankiewicz, *All About Eve*
Actress: Judy Holliday, *Born Yesterday*
Actor: José Ferrer, *Cyrano de Bergerac*
Supporting Actress: Josephine Hull, *Harvey*
Supporting Actor: George Sanders, *All About Eve*

1951

Picture: *An American in Paris,* MGM
Director: George Stevens, *A Place in the Sun*
Actress: Vivien Leigh, *A Streetcar Named Desire*
Actor: Humphrey Bogart, *The African Queen*
Supporting Actress: Kim Hunter, *A Streetcar Named Desire*
Supporting Actor: Karl Malden, *A Streetcar Named Desire*

1952

Picture: *The Greatest Show on Earth,* DeMille—Paramount
Director: John Ford, *The Quiet Man*
Actress: Shirley Booth, *Come Back, Little Sheba*
Actor: Gary Cooper, *High Noon*
Supporting Actress: Gloria Grahame, *The Bad and the Beautiful*
Supporting Actor: Anthony Quinn, *Viva Zapata!*

1953

Picture: *From Here to Eternity,* Columbia
Director: Fred Zinnemann, *From Here to Eternity*
Actress: Audrey Hepburn, *Roman Holiday*
Actor: William Holden, *Stalag 17*
Supporting Actress: Donna Reed, *From Here to Eternity*
Supporting Actor: Frank Sinatra, *From Here to Eternity*

1954

Picture: *On the Waterfront,* Horizon—American Corp., Columbia
Director: Elia Kazan, *On the Waterfront*
Actress: Grace Kelly, *The Country Girl*
Actor: Marlon Brando, *On the Waterfront*
Supporting Actress: Eva Marie Saint, *On the Waterfront*
Supporting Actor: Edmond O'Brien, *The Barefoot Contessa*

1955

Picture: *Marty,* Hecht and Lancaster, United Artists
Director: Delbert Mann, *Marty*
Actress: Anna Magnani, *The Rose Tattoo*
Actor: Ernest Borgnine, *Marty*
Supporting Actress: Jo Van Fleet, *East of Eden*
Supporting Actor: Jack Lemmon, *Mister Roberts*

1956

Picture: *Around the World in 80 Days,* Michael Todd Co., Inc.—U.A.

Director: George Stevens, *Giant*
Actress: Ingrid Bergman, *Anastasia*
Actor: Yul Brynner, *The King and I*
Supporting Actress: Dorothy Malone, *Written on the Wind*
Supporting Actor: Anthony Quinn, *Lust for Life*

1957

Picture: *The Bridge on the River Kwai,* Horizon Picture, Columbia
Director: David Lean, *The Bridge on the River Kwai*
Actress: Joanne Woodward, *The Three Faces of Eve*
Actor: Alec Guinness, *The Bridge on the River Kwai*
Supporting Actress: Miyoshi Umeki, *Sayonara*
Supporting Actor: Red Buttons, *Sayonara*

1958

Picture: *Gigi,* Arthur Freed Productions, Inc., MGM
Director: Vincente Minnelli, *Gigi*
Actress: Susan Hayward, *I Want to Live!*
Actor: David Niven, *Separate Tables*
Supporting Actress: Wendy Hiller, *Separate Tables*
Supporting Actor: Burl Ives, *The Big Country*

1959

Picture: *BenHur,* MGM
Director: William Wyler, *BenHur*
Actress: Simone Signoret, *Room at the Top*
Actor: Charlton Heston, *BenHur*
Supporting Actress: Shelley Winters, *The Diary of Anne Frank*
Supporting Actor: Hugh Griffith, *BenHur*

1960

Picture: *The Apartment,* Mirisch Co., Inc., United Artists
Director: Billy Wilder, *The Apartment*
Actress: Elizabeth Taylor, *Butterfield 8*
Actor: Burt Lancaster, *Elmer Gantry*
Supporting Actress: Shirley Jones, *Elmer Gantry*
Supporting Actor: Peter Ustinov, *Spartacus*

1961

Picture: *West Side Story,* Mirisch Pictures, Inc., and B and P Enterprises, Inc., United Artists
Director: Robert Wise and Jerome Robbins, *West Side Story*
Actress: Sophia Loren, *Two Women*
Actor: Maximillian Schell, *Judgment at Nuremberg*
Supporting Actress: Rita Moreno, *West Side Story*
Supporting Actor: George Chakiris, *West Side Story*

1962

Picture: *Lawrence of Arabia,* Horizon Pictures, Ltd.—Columbia
Director: David Lean, *Lawrence of Arabia*
Actress: Anne Bancroft, *The Miracle Worker*
Actor: Gregory Peck, *To Kill a Mockingbird*
Supporting Actress: Patty Duke, *The Miracle Worker*
Supporting Actor: Ed Begley, *Sweet Bird of Youth*

1963

Picture: *Tom Jones,* A Woodfall Production, UA—Lopert Pictures
Director: Tony Richardson, *Tom Jones*
Actress: Patricia Neal, *Hud*
Actor: Sidney Poitier, *Lilies of the Field*
Supporting Actress: Margaret Rutherford, *The V.I.P.s*
Supporting Actor: Melvyn Douglas, *Hud*

1964

Picture: *My Fair Lady,* Warner Bros.
Director: George Cukor, *My Fair Lady*
Actress: Julie Andrews, *Mary Poppins*
Actor: Rex Harrison, *My Fair Lady*
Supporting Actress: Lila Kedrova, *Zorba the Greek*
Supporting Actor: Peter Ustinov, *Topkapi*

1965

Picture: *The Sound of Music,* Argyle Enterprises Production, 20th Century Fox

Director: Robert Wise, *The Sound of Music*
Actress: Julie Christie, *Darling*
Actor: Lee Marvin, *Cat Ballou*
Supporting Actress: Shelley Winters, *A Patch of Blue*
Supporting Actor: Martin Balsam, *A Thousand Clowns*

1966

Picture: *A Man for All Seasons*, Highland Films, Ltd., Production, Columbia
Director: Fred Zinnemann, *A Man for All Seasons*
Actress: Elizabeth Taylor, *Who's Afraid of Virginia Woolf?*
Actor: Paul Scofield, *A Man for All Seasons*
Supporting Actress: Sandy Dennis, *Who's Afraid of Virginia Woolf?*
Supporting Actor: Walter Matthau, *The Fortune Cookie*

1967

Picture: *In the Heat of the Night,* Mirisch Corp. Productions, United Artists
Director: Mike Nichols, *The Graduate*
Actress: Katharine Hepburn, *Guess Who's Coming to Dinner*
Actor: Rod Steiger, *In the Heat of the Night*
Supporting Actress: Estelle Parsons, *Bonnie and Clyde*
Supporting Actor: George Kennedy, *Cool Hand Luke*

1968

Picture: *Oliver!,* Columbia Pictures
Director: Sir Carol Reed, *Oliver!*
Actress: Katharine Hepburn, *The Lion in Winter* and Barbra Streisand, *Funny Girl*
Actor: Cliff Robertson, *Charly*
Supporting Actress: Ruth Gordon, *Rosemary's Baby*
Supporting Actor: Jack Albertson, *The Subject Was Roses*

1969

Picture: *Midnight Cowboy,* Jerome Hellman-John Schlesinger Production, United Artists
Director: John Schlesinger, *Midnight Cowboy*
Actress: Maggie Smith, *The Prime of Miss Jean Brodie*
Actor: John Wayne, *True Grit*
Supporting Actress: Goldie Hawn, *Cactus Flower*
Supporting Actor: Gig Young, *They Shoot Horses Don't They?*

1970

Picture: *Patton,* Frank McCarthy–Franklin J. Schaffner Production, 20th Century Fox
Director: Franklin J. Schaffner, *Patton*
Actress: Glenda Jackson, *Women in Love*
Actor: George C. Scott, *Patton*
Supporting Actress: Helen Hayes, *Airport*
Supporting Actor: John Mills, *Ryan's Daughter*

1971

Picture: *The French Connection,* D'Antoni Productions, 20th Century Fox
Director: William Friedkin, *The French Connection*
Actress: Jane Fonda, *Klute*
Actor: Gene Hackman, *The French Connection*
Supporting Actress: Cloris Leachman, *The Last Picture Show*
Supporting Actor: Ben Johnson, *The Last Picture Show*

1972

Picture: *The Godfather,* Albert S. Ruddy Production, Paramount
Director: Bob Fosse, *Cabaret*
Actress: Liza Minnelli, *Cabaret*
Actor: Marlon Brando, *The Godfather*
Supporting Actress: Eileen Heckart, *Butterflies Are Free*
Supporting Actor: Joel Grey, *Cabaret*

1973

Picture: *The Sting,* Universal-Bill-Phillips-George Roy Hill Production, Universal

Director: George Roy Hill, *The Sting*
Actress: Glenda Jackson, *A Touch of Class*
Actor: Jack Lemmon, *Save the Tiger*
Supporting Actress: Tatum O'Neal, *Paper Moon*
Supporting Actor: John Houseman, *The Paper Chase*

1974

Picture: *The Godfather, Part II,* Coppola Co. Production, Paramount
Director: Francis Ford Coppola, *The Godfather, Part II*
Actress: Ellen Burstyn, *Alice Doesn't Live Here Anymore*
Actor: Art Carney, *Harry and Tonto*
Supporting Actress: Ingrid Bergman, *Murder on the Orient Express*
Supporting Actor: Robert De Niro, *The Godfather, Part II*

1975

Picture: *One Flew Over the Cuckoo's Nest,* Fantasy Films Production, United Artists
Director: Milos Forman, *One Flew Over the Cuckoo's Nest*
Actress: Louise Fletcher, *One Flew Over the Cuckoo's Nest*
Actor: Jack Nicholson, *One Flew Over the Cuckoo's Nest*
Supporting Actress: Lee Grant, *Shampoo*
Supporting Actor: George Burns, *The Sunshine Boys*

1976

Picture: *Rocky,* Robert Chartoff–Irwin Winkler Production, United Artists
Director: John G. Avildsen, *Rocky*
Actress: Faye Dunaway, *Network*
Actor: Peter Finch, *Network*
Supporting Actress: Beatrice Straight, *Network*
Supporting Actor: Jason Robards, *All the President's Men*

1977

Picture: *Annie Hall,* Jack Rollins–Charles H. Joffe Production, United Artists
Director: Woody Allen, *Annie Hall*
Actress: Diane Keaton, *Annie Hall*
Actor: Richard Dreyfuss, *The Goodbye Girl*
Supporting Actress: Vanessa Redgrave, *Julia*
Supporting Actor: Jason Robards, *Julia*

1978

Picture: *The Deer Hunter,* Michael Cimino Film Production, Universal
Director: Michael Cimino, *The Deer Hunter*
Actress: Jane Fonda, *Coming Home*
Actor: Jon Voight, *Coming Home*
Supporting Actress: Maggie Smith, *California Suite*
Supporting Actor: Christopher Walken, *The Deer Hunter*

1979

Picture: *Kramer vs. Kramer,* Stanley Jaffe Production, Columbia Pictures
Director: Robert Benton, *Kramer vs. Kramer*
Actress: Sally Field, *Norma Rae*
Actor: Dustin Hoffman, *Kramer vs. Kramer*
Supporting Actress: Meryl Streep, *Kramer vs. Kramer*
Supporting Actor: Melvyn Douglas, *Being There*

1980

Picture: *Ordinary People,* Wildwood Enterprises Production, Paramount
Director: Robert Redford, *Ordinary People*
Actress: Sissy Spacek, *Coal Miner's Daughter*
Actor: Robert De Niro, *Raging Bull*
Supporting Actress: Mary Steenburgen, *Melvin and Howard*
Supporting Actor: Timothy Hutton, *Ordinary People*

1981

Picture: *Chariots of Fire,* Enigma Productions, Ladd Company/Warner Bros.

Director: Warren Beatty, *Reds*
Actress: Katharine Hepburn, *On Golden Pond*
Actor: Henry Fonda, *On Golden Pond*
Supporting Actress: Maureen Stapleton, *Reds*
Supporting Actor: John Gielgud, *Arthur*

1982

Picture: *Gandhi,* Indo–British Films Production/Columbia
Director: Richard Attenborough, *Gandhi*
Actress: Meryl Streep, *Sophie's Choice*
Actor: Ben Kingsley, *Gandhi*
Supporting Actress: Jessica Lange, *Tootsie*
Supporting Actor: Louis Gossett, Jr., *An Officer and a Gentleman*

1983

Picture: *Terms of Endearment,* Paramount
Director: James L. Brooks, *Terms of Endearment*
Actress: Shirley MacLaine, *Terms of Endearment*
Actor: Robert Duvall, *Tender Mercies*
Supporting Actress: Linda Hunt, *The Year of Living Dangerously*
Supporting Actor: Jack Nicholson, *Terms of Endearment*

1984

Picture: *Amadeus,* Orion Pictures
Director: Milos Forman, *Amadeus*
Actress: Sally Field, *Places in the Heart*
Actor: F. Murray Abraham, *Amadeus*
Supporting Actress: Dame Peggy Ashcroft, *A Passage to India*
Supporting Actor: Haing S. Ngor, *The Killing Fields*

1985

Picture: *Out of Africa,* Universal
Director: Sydney Pollack, *Out of Africa*
Actress: Geraldine Page, *The Trip to Bountiful*
Actor: William Hurt, *Kiss of the Spider Woman*
Supporting Actress: Anjelica Huston, *Prizzi's Honor*
Supporting Actor: Don Ameche, *Cocoon*

1986

Picture: *Platoon,* Orion Pictures
Director: Oliver Stone, *Platoon*
Actress: Marlee Matlin, *Children of a Lesser God*
Actor: Paul Newman, *The Color of Money*
Supporting Actress: Dianne Wiest, *Hannah and Her Sisters*
Supporting Actor: Michael Caine, *Hannah and Her Sisters*

1987

Picture: *The Last Emperor,* Columbia Pictures
Director : Bernardo Bertolucci, *The Last Emperor*
Actress: Cher, *Moonstruck*
Actor: Michael Douglas, *Wall Street*
Supporting Actress: Olympia Dukakis, *Moonstruck*
Supporting Actor: Sean Connery, *The Untouchables*

1988

Picture: *Rain Man,* United Artists
Director: Barry Levinson, *Rain Man*
Actress: Jodie Foster, *The Accused*
Actor: Dustin Hoffman, *Rain Man*
Supporting Actress: Geena Davis, *The Accidental Tourist*
Supporting Actor: Kevin Kline, *A Fish Called Wanda*

1989

Picture: *Driving Miss Daisy,* Warner Brothers
Director: Oliver Stone, *Born on the Fourth of July*
Actress: Jessica Tandy, *Driving Miss Daisy*
Actor: Daniel Day-Lewis, *My Left Foot*
Supporting Actress: Brenda Fricker, *My Left Foot*
Supporting Actor: Denzel Washington, *Glory*

1990

Picture: *Dances With Wolves,* Orion
Director: Kevin Costner, *Dances With Wolves*
Actress: Kathy Bates, *Misery*
Actor: Jeremy Irons, *Reversal of Fortune*
Supporting Actress: Whoopi Goldberg, *Ghost*
Supporting Actor: Joe Pesci, *Goodfellas*

1991

Picture: *The Silence of the Lambs,* Orion
Director: Jonathan Demme, *The Silence of the Lambs*
Actress: Jodie Foster, *The Silence of the Lambs*
Actor: Anthony Hopkins, *The Silence of the Lambs*
Supporting Actress: Mercedes Ruehl, *The Fisher King*
Supporting Actor: Jack Palance, *City Slickers*

1992

Picture: *Unforgiven,* Warner Brothers
Director: Clint Eastwood, *Unforgiven*
Actress: Emma Thompson, *Howards End*
Actor: Al Pacino, *Scent of a Woman*
Supporting Actress: Marisa Tomei, *My Cousin Vinny*
Supporting Actor: Gene Hackman, *Unforgiven*

1993

Picture: *Schindler's List,* Universal
Director: Steven Spielberg, *Schindler's List*
Actress: Holly Hunter, *The Piano*
Actor: Tom Hanks, *Philadelphia*
Supporting Actress: Anna Paquin, *The Piano*
Supporting Actor: Tommy Lee Jones, *The Fugitive*

1994

Picture: *Forrest Gump,* Paramount
Director: Robert Zemeckis, *Forrest Gump*
Actress: Jessica Lange, *Blue Sky*
Actor: Tom Hanks, *Forrest Gump*
Supporting Actress: Dianne Wiest, *Bullets Over Broadway*
Supporting Actor: Martin Landau, *Ed Wood*

1995

Picture: *Braveheart,* Paramount
Director: Mel Gibson, *Braveheart*
Actress: Susan Sarandon, *Dead Man Walking*
Actor: Nicolas Cage, *Leaving Las Vegas*
Supporting Actress: Mira Sorvino, *Mighty Aphrodite*
Supporting Actor: Kevin Spacey, *The Usual Suspects*

Other Academy Awards for 1995

Art Direction: Eugenio Zanetti, *Restoration*
Cinematography: John Toll, *Braveheart*
Costume Design: James Acheson, *Restoration*
Documentary (feature): Jon Blair, *Anne Frank Remembered;* **(short subject):** Kary Antholis, *One Survivor Remembers*
Editing: Mike Hill, Dan Hanley, *Apollo 13*
Foreign-language film: *Antonia's Line,* The Netherlands
Makeup: Peter Frampton, Paul Pattison, and Lois Burwell, *Braveheart*
Music (original musical or comedy score): Alan Menken, Stephen Schwartz, *Pocahontas;* **(original dramatic score)** Luis Bacalov, *The Postman;* **(original song):** Alan Menken and Stephen Schwartz, *Colors of the Wind, Pocahontas*
Screenplay, Original: Christopher McQuarrie, *The Usual Suspects*
Screenplay, Adapted: Emma Thompson, *Sense and Sensibility*
Short subject (live action): Christine Lahti and Jana Sue Memel, *Lieberman in Love;* **(animated):** Nick Park, *A Close Shave*

Sound: Rick Dior, Steve Pederson, Scott Millan, and David MacMillan, *Apollo 13*
Sound effects editing: Lon Bender and Per Hallberg, *Braveheart*
Visual effects: Scott E. Anderson, Charles Gibson, Neal Scanlan, and John Cox, *Babe*

Gordon E. Sawyer Award: Donald C. Rogers, for his contribution to motion picture sound technology
Lifetime Achievement Award: Kirk Douglas
Special Achievement Award: John Lasseter, computer-animator
Honorary Award: Chuck Jones, animator

National Society of Film Critics Awards, 1995

Best Film: *Babe*
Best Actress: Elisabeth Shue, *Leaving Las Vegas*
Best Actor: Nicolas Cage, *Leaving Las Vegas*
Best Supporting Actress: Joan Allen, *Nixon*
Best Supporting Actor: Don Cheadle, *Devil in a Blue Dress*
Best Director: Mike Figgis, *Leaving Las Vegas*
Best Screenwriter: Amy Heckerling, *Clueless*

Best Cinematography: Tak Fujimoto, *Devil in a Blue Dress*
Best Documentary: *Crumb*, Terry Zwigoff
Best Foreign Film: *Wild Reeds*, André Techiné
Experimental Work: *Latcho Drom*, Tony Gatlif
Special Archival Award: *I Am Cuba*, Mikhail Kalatozov's 1964 film

George Foster Peabody Awards for Broadcasting, 1995

Radio

WJR, Detroit: *Blind Justice: Who Killed Janie Fray?*
CBC, Toronto: *Kevin's Sentence.*
Minnesota Public Radio, St. Paul: *St. Paul Sunday.*
Oscar Brand, WNYC, New York: For helping preserve folk music.
National Public Radio, Washington and Sony Classical Film and Video for PBS: *Wynton Marsalis: Making the Music/Marsalis on Music.*

Television

CBS News: Coverage of the assassination of Prime Minister Yitzhak Rabin.
KWTV, KOCO, KFOR, Oklahoma City: Coverage of the terrorist bombing.
ABC News: Barbara Walters interview with Christopher Reeve.
Oprah Winfrey: For her work on talk shows.
PBS: *Hoop Dreams.*
NBC: Prime time entertainment series *Homicide.*
WFAA, Dallas: *The Peavy Investigation.*
ABC News 20/20: *Truth on Trial.*
WXYZ, Detroit: *Target Seven: Armed and Angry.*
WCBS, New York: *New York City School Corruption.*
Television Broadcasts Ltd., Kowloon, Hong Kong: *50 Years After the War.*

Cinemax Reel Life Presentation of a Lauderdale Production for Channel 4, London, and Cinemax, New York: *The Dying Rooms.*
Public Policy Productions Inc., in association with Thirteen/WNET, New York, presented on PBS: *Road Scholar.*
WGBH–TV, Boston and BBC Bristol: *Rock–and–Roll.*
ABC News: *Peter Jennings Reporting: Hiroshima: Why the Bomb Was Dropped.*
Discovery Channel, Bethesda, Md., and Brian Lapping Associates for BBC London: *Yugoslavia: Death of a Nation*, a Discovery Journal Special.
CBS News: *CBS Reports: In the Killing Fields of America.*
P.O.V./Deborah Hoffman, New York, presented on PBS: *Complaints of a Dutiful Daughter.*
Turner Original Productions, Tollin/Robbins and Mundy Lane in association with Television Production Partners: *Hank Aaron: Chasing the Dream.*
Turner Original Productions and BBC Natural History, London: *The Private Life of Plants.*
Deep Focus Productions, Los Angeles, presented on PBS: *Coming Out Under Fire.*
Aardman Animations in association with Wallace & Gromit Ltd., BBC Children's International, BBC Bristol and BBC Lionheart: *Wallace and Gromit.*
WGBH–TV, Boston: *Frontline: Waco: The Inside Story.*

Pulitzer Prize Awards

(For years not listed, no award was made.)
Source: Columbia University.

Pulitzer Prizes in Journalism

MERITORIOUS PUBLIC SERVICE

1918 *New York Times;* also special award to Minna Lewinson and Henry Beetle Hough
1919 *Milwaukee Journal*
1921 *Boston Post*
1922 *New York World*
1923 *Memphis Commercial Appeal*
1924 *New York World*
1926 *Columbus* (Ga.) *Enquirer Sun*
1927 *Canton* (Ohio) *Daily News*
1928 *Indianapolis Times*
1929 *New York Evening World*
1931 *Atlanta Constitution*
1932 *Indianapolis News*
1933 *New York World-Telegram*
1934 *Medford* (Ore.) *Mail Tribune*
1935 *Sacramento Bee*
1936 *Cedar Rapids* (Iowa) *Gazette*
1937 *St. Louis Post-Dispatch*
1938 *Bismarck* (N.D.) *Tribune*
1939 *Miami Daily News*
1940 *Waterbury* (Conn.) *Republican* and *American*
1941 *St. Louis Post-Dispatch*
1942 *Los Angeles Times*
1943 *Omaha World-Herald*
1944 *New York Times*
1945 *Detroit Free Press*
1946 *Scranton* (Pa.) *Times*
1947 *Baltimore Sun*
1948 *St. Louis Post-Dispatch*
1949 (Lincoln) *Nebraska State Journal*
1950 *Chicago Daily News;* and *St. Louis Post-Dispatch*
1951 *Miami Herald;* and *Brooklyn Eagle*
1952 *St. Louis Post-Dispatch*
1953 *Whiteville* (N.C.) *News Reporter;* and *Tabor City* (N.C.) *Tribune*
1954 *Newsday* (Garden City, L.I.)
1955 *Columbus* (Ga.) *Ledger* and *Sunday Ledger-Enquirer*
1956 *Watsonville* (Calif.) *Register-Pajaronian*
1957 *Chicago Daily News*

1958	(Little Rock) *Arkansas Gazette*
1959	*Utica* (N.Y.) *Observer Dispatch* and *Utica Daily Press*
1960	*Los Angeles Times*
1961	*Amarillo* (Tex.) *Globe-Times*
1962	*Panama City* (Fla.) *News-Herald*
1963	*Chicago Daily News*
1964	*St. Petersburg* (Fla.) *Times*
1965	*Hutchinson* (Kan.) *News*
1966	*Boston Globe*
1967	*Louisville Courier-Journal* and *Milwaukee Journal*
1968	*Riverside* (Calif.) *Press-Enterprise*
1969	*Los Angeles Times*
1970	*Newsday* (Garden City, L.I.)
1971	*Winston-Salem* (N.C.) *Journal and Sentinel*
1972	*New York Times*
1973	*Washington Post*
1974	*Newsday* (Garden City, L.I.)
1975	*Boston Globe*
1976	*Anchorage* (Alaska) *Daily News*
1977	*Lufkin* (Tex.) *News*
1978	*Philadelphia Inquirer*
1979	*Point Reyes* (Calif.) *Light*
1980	*Gannett News Service*
1981	*Charlotte* (N.C.) *Observer*
1982	*Detroit News*
1983	*Jackson* (Miss.) *Clarion-Ledger*
1984	*Los Angeles Times*
1985	*The Fort Worth Star-Telegram*
1986	*Denver Post*
1987	Andrew Schneider and Matthew Brelis, *Pittsburgh Press*
1988	*Charlotte* (N.C.) *Observer*
1989	*Anchorage Daily News*
1990	*Philadelphia Inquirer* and *Washington* (N.C.) *Daily News*
1991	*Des Moines Register*, reporting by Jane Schorer
1992	*Sacramento Bee* for "The Sierra in Peril" series by Tom Knudson
1993	*Miami Herald*
1994	*The Akron* (Ohio) *Beacon Journal*
1995	*The Virgin Islands Daily News*
1996	*The News and Observer* (Raleigh, N.C.)

EDITORIAL

1917	*New York Tribune*
1918	*Louisville Courier-Journal*
1920	Harvey E. Newbranch *(Omaha Evening World-Herald)*
1922	Frank M. O'Brien *(New York Herald)*
1923	William Allen White *(Emporia* [Kan.] *Gazette)*
1924	*Boston Herald* (Frank Buxton); special prize: Frank I. Cobb *(New York World)*
1925	*Charleston* (S.C.) *News and Courier*
1926	*New York Times* (Edward M. Kingsbury)
1927	*Boston Herald* (F. Lauriston Bullard)
1928	Grover Cleveland Hall *(Montgomery* [Ala.] *Advertiser)*
1929	Louis Isaac Jaffe *(Norfolk Virginian-Pilot)*
1931	Charles S. Ryckman *(Fremont* [Neb.] *Tribune)*
1933	*Kansas City* (Mo.) *Star*
1934	E. P. Chase *(Atlantic* [Iowa] *News Telegraph)*
1936	Felix Morley *(Washington Post);* George B. Parker (Scripps-Howard Newspapers)
1937	John W. Owens *(Baltimore Sun)*
1938	W. W. Waymack *(Des Moines Register and Tribune)*
1939	Ronald G. Callvert *(Portland Oregonian)*
1940	Bart Howard *(St. Louis Post-Dispatch)*
1941	Reuben Maury *(New York Daily News)*
1942	Geoffrey Parsons *(New York Herald Tribune)*
1943	Forrest W. Seymour *(Des Moines Register and Tribune)*
1944	*Kansas City* (Mo.) *Star* (Henry J. Haskell)
1945	George W. Potter *(Providence* [R.I.] *Journal-Bulletin)*
1946	Hodding Carter ([Greenville, Miss.] *Delta Democrat-Times)*
1947	William H. Grimes *(Wall Street Journal)*
1948	Virginius Dabney *(Richmond Times-Dispatch)*

1949	John H. Crider *(Boston Herald);* Herbert Elliston *(Washington Post)*
1950	Carl M. Saunders *(Jackson* [Mich.] *Citizen Patriot)*
1951	William H. Fitzpatrick *(New Orleans States)*
1952	Louis LaCoss *(St. Louis Globe-Democrat)*
1953	Vermont C. Royster *(Wall Street Journal)*
1954	*Boston Herald* (Don Murray)
1955	*Detroit Free Press* (Royce Howes)
1956	Lauren K. Soth *(Des Moines Register and Tribune)*
1957	Buford Boone *(Tuscaloosa* [Ala.] *News)*
1958	Harry S. Ashmore *(Arkansas Gazette)*
1959	Ralph McGill *(Atlanta Constitution)*
1960	Lenoir Chambers *(Virginian-Pilot)*
1961	William J. Dorvillier *(San Juan* [P.R.] *Star)*
1962	Thomas M. Storke *(Santa Barbara* [Calif.] *News-Press)*
1963	Ira B. Harkey, Jr. *(Pascagoula* [Miss.] *Chronicle)*
1964	Hazel Brannon Smith *(Lexington* [Miss.] *Advertiser)*
1965	John R. Harrison *(Gainesville* [Fla.] *Daily Sun)*
1966	Robert Lasch *(St. Louis Post-Dispatch)*
1967	Eugene Patterson *(Atlanta Constitution)*
1968	John S. Knight (Knight Newspapers)
1969	Paul Greenberg *(Pine Bluff* [Ark.] *Commercial)*
1970	Phillip L. Geyelin *(Washington Post)*
1971	Horance G. Davis, Jr. *(Gainesville* [Fla.] *Sun)*
1972	John Strohmeyer *(Bethlehem* [Pa.] *Globe Times)*
1973	Roger Bourne Linscott (*Berkshire Eagle* [Pittsfield, Mass.])
1974	F. Gilman Spencer *(Trenton* [N.J.] *Trentonian)*
1975	John Daniell Maurice *(Charleston* [W. Va.] *Daily Mail)*
1976	Philip P. Kerby *(Los Angeles Times)*
1977	Warren L. Lerude, Foster Church and Norman F. Cardoza *(Reno* [Nev.] *Gazette* and *Nevada State Journal)*
1978	Meg Greenfield *(Washington Post)*
1979	Edwin M. Yoder, Jr. *(Washington Star)*
1980	Robert L. Bartley *(Wall Street Journal)*
1981	Not awarded
1982	Jack Rosenthal *(New York Times)*
1983	*Miami Herald*
1984	Albert Scardino *(Georgia Gazette)*
1985	Richard Aregood *(Philadelphia Daily News)*
1986	Jack Fuller *(Chicago Tribune)*
1987	Jonathan Freedman *(San Diego Tribune)*
1988	Jane E. Healy *(Orlando Sentinel)*
1989	Lois Wille *(Chicago Tribune)*
1990	Thomas J. Hylton *(Pottstown* [Pa.] *Mercury)*
1991	Ron Casey, Harold Jackson, and Joey Kennedy *(Birmingham* [Ala.] *News)*
1992	Maria Henson *(Lexington* [Ky.] *Herald-Leader)*
1994	R. Bruce Dold *(Chicago Tribune)*
1995	Jeffrey Good *(St. Petersburg* (Fla.] *Times)*
1996	Robert B. Semple, Jr. *(New York Times)*

CORRESPONDENCE

1929	Paul Scott Mowrer *(Chicago Daily News)*
1930	Leland Stowe *(New York Herald Tribune)*
1931	H. R. Knickerbocker *(Philadelphia Public Ledger* and *New York Evening Post)*
1932	Walter Duranty *(New York Times);* Charles G. Ross *(St. Louis Post-Dispatch)*
1933	Edgar Ansel Mowrer *(Chicago Daily News)*
1934	Frederick T. Birchall *(New York Times)*
1935	Arthur Krock *(New York Times)*
1936	Wilfred C. Barber *(Chicago Tribune)*
1937	Anne O'Hare McCormick *(New York Times)*
1938	Arthur Krock *(New York Times)*
1939	Louis P. Lochner (Associated Press)
1940	Otto D. Tolischus *(New York Times)*
1941	Group award[1]
1942	Carlos P. Romulo *(Philippines Herald)*
1943	Hanson W. Baldwin *(New York Times)*

1. For the public services and the individual achievements of American news reporters in the war zones.

1944 Ernie Pyle (Scripps-Howard Newspaper Alliance)
1945 Harold V. (Hal) Boyle (Associated Press)
1946 Arnaldo Cortesi *(New York Times)*
1947 Brooks Atkinson *(New York Times)*
1948 Discontinued

EDITORIAL CARTOONING

1922 Rollin Kirby *(New York World)*
1924 Jay Norwood Darling *(New York Tribune)*
1925 Rollin Kirby *(New York World)*
1926 D. R. Fitzpatrick *(St. Louis Post-Dispatch)*
1927 Nelson Harding *(Brooklyn Eagle)*
1928 Nelson Harding *(Brooklyn Eagle)*
1929 Rollin Kirby *(New York World)*
1930 Charles R. Macauley *(Brooklyn Eagle)*
1931 Edmund Duffy *(Baltimore Sun)*
1932 John T. McCutcheon *(Chicago Tribune)*
1933 H. M. Talburt *(Washington Daily News)*
1934 Edmund Duffy *(Baltimore Sun)*
1935 Ross A. Lewis *(Milwaukee Journal)*
1937 C. D. Batchelor *(New York Daily News)*
1938 Vaughn Shoemaker *(Chicago Daily News)*
1939 Charles G. Werner (*Daily Oklahoman*[Oklahoma City])
1940 Edmund Duffy *(Baltimore Sun)*
1941 Jacob Burck *(Chicago Times)*
1942 Herbert L. Block (NEA Service)
1943 Jay Norwood Darling *(New York Herald Tribune)*
1944 Clifford K. Berryman *(Washington Evening Star)*
1945 Bill Mauldin (United Features Syndicate)
1946 Bruce Alexander Russell *(Los Angeles Times)*
1947 Vaughn Shoemaker *(Chicago Daily News)*
1948 Reuben L. Goldberg *(New York Sun)*
1949 Lute Pease *(Newark Evening News)*
1950 James T. Berryman *(Washington Evening Star)*
1951 Reg (Reginald W.) Manning (*Arizona Republic*[Phoenix])
1952 Fred L. Packer *(New York Mirror)*
1953 Edward D. Kuekes *(Cleveland Plain Dealer)*
1954 Herbert L. Block *(Washington Post* and *Times-Herald)*
1955 Daniel R. Fitzpatrick *(St. Louis Post-Dispatch)*
1956 Robert York *(Louisville Times)*
1957 Tom Little *(Nashville Tennessean)*
1958 Bruce M. Shanks *(Buffalo Evening News)*
1959 Bill Mauldin *(St. Louis Post-Dispatch)*
1961 Carey Orr *(Chicago Tribune)*
1962 Edmund S. Valtman *(Hartford Times)*
1963 Frank Miller *(Des Moines Register)*
1964 Paul Conrad (formerly of *Denver Post,* later on *Los Angeles Times)*
1966 Don Wright *(Miami News)*
1967 Patrick B. Oliphant *(Denver Post)*
1968 Eugene Gray Payne *(Charlotte* [N.C.] *Observer)*
1969 John Fischetti *(Chicago Daily News)*
1970 Thomas F. Darcy *(Newsday* [Garden City, L.I.])
1971 Paul Conrad *(Los Angeles Times)*
1972 Jeffrey K. MacNelly *(Richmond* [Va.] *News Leader)*
1974 Paul Szep *(Boston Globe)*
1975 Garry Trudeau (Universal Press Syndicate)
1976 Tony Auth *(Philadelphia Inquirer)*
1977 Paul Szep *(Boston Globe)*
1978 Jeffrey K. MacNelly *(Richmond* [Va.] *News Leader)*
1979 Herbert L. Block *(Washington Post)*
1980 Don Wright *(Miami News)*
1981 Mike Peters *(Dayton* [Ohio] *Daily News)*
1982 Ben Sargent *(Austin* [Tex.] *American-Statesman)*
1983 Richard Locher *(Chicago Tribune)*
1984 Paul Conrad *(Los Angeles Times)*
1985 Jeff MacNelly *(Chicago Tribune)*
1986 Jules Feiffer *(Village Voice)*
1987 Berke Breathed *(Washington Post* Writers Group)
1988 Doug Marlette *(Atlanta Constitution* and *Charlotte* [N.C.] *Observer)*
1989 Jack Higgins *(Chicago Sun-Times)*

1990 Tom Toles *(Buffalo News)*
1991 Jim Borgman *(Cincinnati Inquirer)*
1992 Signe Wilkinson, *(Philadelphia Daily News)*
1993 Stephen R. Benson *(Arizona Republic)*
1994 Michael P. Ramirez *(The Commercial Appeal,* Memphis)
1995 Mike Luckovich *(The Atlanta Constitution)*
1996 Jim Morin *(The Miami Herald)*

NEWS PHOTOGRAPHY

1942 Milton Brooks *(Detroit News)*
1943 Frank Noel (Associated Press)
1944 Frank Filan (Associated Press); Earle L. Bunker *(Omaha World-Herald)*
1945 Joe Rosenthal (Associated Press)
1947 Arnold Hardy
1948 Frank Cushing *(Boston Traveler)*
1949 Nat Fein *(New York Herald Tribune)*
1950 Bill Crouch *(Oakland Tribune)*
1951 Max Desfor (Associated Press)
1952 John Robinson and Don Ultang *(Des Moines Register & Tribune)*
1953 William M. Gallagher *(Flint* [Mich.] *Journal)*
1954 Mrs. Walter M. Schau
1955 John L. Gaunt, Jr. *(Los Angeles Times)*
1956 *New York Daily News*
1957 Harry A. Trask *(Boston Traveler)*
1958 William C. Beall *(Washington Daily News)*
1959 William Seaman *(Minneapolis Star)*
1960 Andrew Lopez (United Press International)
1961 Yasushi Nagao (Mainichi Newspapers, Tokyo)
1962 Paul Vathis (Harrisburg [Pa.] bureau of Associated Press)
1963 Hector Rondon (*La Republica,* Caracas, Venezuela)
1964 Robert H. Jackson *(Dallas Times Herald)*
1965 Horst Faas (Associated Press)
1966 Kyoichi Sawada (United Press International)
1967 Jack R. Thornell (Associated Press)
1968 News: Rocco Morabito *(Jacksonville* [Fla.] *Journal);* features: Toshio Sakai (United Press International)
1969 Spot news: Edward T. Adams (Associated Press); features: Moneta Sleet, Jr.
1970 Spot news: Steve Starr (Associated Press); features: Dallas Kinney *(Palm Beach Post)*
1971 Spot news: John Paul Filo (*Valley Daily News* and *Daily Dispatch* [Tarentum and New Kensington, Pa.]); features: Jack Dykinga *(Chicago Sun-Times)*
1972 Spot news: Horst Faas and Michel Laurent (Associated Press); features: Dave Kennerly (United Press International)
1973 Spot news: Huynh Cong Ut *(Associated Press);* features: Brian Lanker *(Topeka Capital-Journal)*
1974 Spot news: Anthony K. Roberts (Associated Press); features: Slava Veder (Associated Press)
1975 Spot news: Gerald H. Gay *(Seattle Times);* features: Matthew Lewis *(Washington Post)*
1976 Spot news: Stanley J. Forman *(Boston Herald-American);* features: photographic staff of *Louisville Courier-Journal* and *Times*
1977 Spot news: Neal Ulevich (Associated Press) and Stanley J. Forman *(Boston Herald-American);* features: Robin Hood *(Chattanooga News-Free Press)*
1978 Spot news: John Blair, freelance, Evansville, Ind.; features: J. Ross Baughman (Associated Press)
1979 Spot news: Thomas J. Kelly, 3rd *(Pottstown* [Pa.] *Mercury);* features: photographic staff of *Boston Herald-American*
1980 Features: Erwin H. Hagler *(Dallas Times Herald)*
1981 Spot news: Larry C. Price *(Fort Worth Star-Telegram);* features: Taro M. Yamasaki *(Detroit Free Press)*
1982 Spot news: Ron Edmonds (Associated Press); features: John H. White *(Chicago Sun-Times)*
1983 Spot news: Bill Foley (Associated Press); features: James B. Dickman *(Dallas Times Herald)*

1984 Spot news: Stan Grossfeld *(Boston Globe);* features: Anthony Suau *(Denver Post)*

1985 Spot news: photographic staff of *Register,* Santa Ana, Calif.; features: Stan Grossfeld (*Boston Globe*)

1986 Spot news: Michel duCille and Carol Guzy *(Miami Herald);* features: Tom Gralish *(Philadelphia Inquirer)*

1987 Spot news: Kim Komenich *(San Francisco Examiner);* features: David Peterson *(Des Moines Register)*

1988 Spot news: Scott Shaw *(Odessa* [Texas] *American);* features: Michel duCille *(Miami Herald)*

1989 Spot news: Ron Olshwanger *(St. Louis Post-Dispatch);* features: Manny Crisostomo *(Detroit Free Press)*

1990 Spot news: *Oakland Tribune;* features: David C. Turnley *(Detroit Free Press)*

1991 Spot news: Greg Marinovich (Associated Press); features: William Snyder *(Dallas Morning News)*

1992 Spot news: Associated Press staff; features: John Kaplan *(Herald* [Monterey, Calif.] and *Pittsburgh Post-Gazette)*

1993 Spot news: William Snyder and Ken Geiger *(Dallas Morning News);* features: Associated Press

1994 Spot news: Paul Watson *(Toronto Star);* features: Kevin Carter, freelance for *New York Times*

1995 Spot news: Carol Guzy *(Washington Post);* features: Associated Press Staff

1996 Spot news: Charles Porter IV, freelance photographer for Associated Press; features: Stephanie Welsh, freelance photographer for Newhouse News Service

NATIONAL TELEGRAPHIC REPORTING

1942 Louis Stark *(New York Times)*
1944 Dewey L. Fleming *(Baltimore Sun)*
1945 James Reston *(New York Times)*
1946 Edward A. Harris *(St. Louis Post-Dispatch)*
1947 Edward T. Folliard *(Washington Post)*

NATIONAL REPORTING

1948 Bert Andrews *(New York Herald Tribune);* Nat S. Finney *(Minneapolis Tribune)*
1949 C. P. Trussell *(New York Times)*
1950 Edwin O. Guthman *(Seattle Times)*
1952 Anthony Leviero *(New York Times)*
1953 Don Whitehead (Associated Press)
1954 Richard Wilson (Cowles Newspapers)
1955 Anthony Lewis *(Washington Daily News)*
1956 Charles L. Bartlett *(Chattanooga Times)*
1957 James Reston *(New York Times)*
1958 Relman Morin (Associated Press) and Clark Mollenhoff *(Des Moines Register & Tribune)*
1959 Howard Van Smith *(Miami News)*
1960 Vance Trimble (Scripps-Howard Newspaper Alliance)
1961 Edward R. Cony *(Wall Street Journal)*
1962 Nathan G. Caldwell and Gene S. Graham *(Nashville Tennessean)*
1963 Anthony Lewis *(New York Times)*
1964 Merriman Smith (United Press International)
1965 Louis M. Kohlmeier *(Wall Street Journal)*
1966 Haynes Johnson *(Washington Evening Star)*
1967 Stanley Penn and Monroe Karmin *(Wall Street Journal)*
1968 Howard James *(Christian Science Monitor);* Nathan K. (Nick) Kotz *(Des Moines Register* and *Minneapolis Tribune)*
1969 Robert Cahn *(Christian Science Monitor)*
1970 William J. Eaton *(Chicago Daily News)*
1971 Lucinda Franks and Thomas Powers (United Press International)
1972 Jack Anderson *(United Feature Syndicate)*
1973 Robert Boyd and Clark Hoyt *(Knight Newspapers)*
1974 Jack White *(Providence* [R.I.] *Journal-Bulletin);* and James R. Polk *(Washington Star-News)*
1975 Donald L. Barlett and James B. Steele *(Philadelphia Inquirer)*
1976 James Risser *(Des Moines Register)*
1977 Walter Mears (Associated Press)

1978 Gaylord D. Shaw *(Los Angeles Times)*
1979 James Risser *(Des Moines Register)*
1980 Bette Swenson Orsini and Charles Stafford *(St. Petersburg Times)*
1981 John M. Crewdson *(New York Times)*
1982 Rick Atkinson *(Kansas City* [Mo.] *Times)*
1983 *Boston Globe*
1984 John N. Wilford *(New York Times)*
1985 Thomas J. Knudson *(Des Moines Register)*
1986 Craig Flournoy and George Rodrigue *(Dallas Morning News)* and Arthur Howe *(Philadelphia Inquirer)*
1987 *Miami Herald,* staff; *New York Times,* staff
1988 Tim Weiner *(Philadelphia Inquirer)*
1989 Donald L. Barlett and James B. Steele *(Philadelphia Inquirer)*
1990 Ross Anderson, Bill Dietrich, Mary Ann Gwinn, and Eric Nalder *(Seattle Times)*
1991 Marjie Lundstrom and Rochelle Sharpe (Gannett News Service)
1992 Jeff Taylor and Mike McGraw *(Kansas City Star)*
1993 David Maraniss *(Washington Post)*
1994 Eileen Welsome *(Albuquerque* (N.M.) *Tribune)*
1995 Tony Horwitz *(Wall Street Journal)*
1996 Alix M. Freedman *(Wall Street Journal)*

INTERNATIONAL TELEGRAPHIC REPORTING

1942 Laurence Edmund Allen (Associated Press)
1943 Ira Wolfert (North American Newspaper Alliance, Inc.)
1944 Daniel De Luce (Associated Press)
1945 Mark S. Watson *(Baltimore Sun)*
1946 Homer W. Bigart *(New York Herald Tribune)*
1947 Eddy Gilmore (Associated Press)

INTERNATIONAL REPORTING

1948 Paul W. Ward *(Baltimore Sun)*
1949 Price Day *(Baltimore Sun)*
1950 Edmund Stevens *(Christian Science Monitor)*
1951 Keyes Beech and Fred Sparks *(Chicago Daily News);* Homer Bigart and Marguerite Higgins *(New York Herald Tribune);* Relman Morin and Don Whitehead (Associated Press)
1952 John M. Hightower (Associated Press)
1953 Austin C. Wehrwein *(Milwaukee Journal)*
1954 Jim G. Lucas (Scripps-Howard Newspapers)
1955 Harrison E. Salisbury *(New York Times)*
1956 William Randolph Hearst, Jr. and Frank Conniff (Hearst Newspapers) and Kingsbury Smith (INS)
1957 Russell Jones (United Press)
1958 *New York Times*
1959 Joseph Martin and Philip Santora *(New York Daily News)*
1960 A. M. Rosenthal *(New York Times)*
1961 Lynn Heinzerling (Associated Press)
1962 Walter Lippmann (New York Herald Tribune Syndicate)
1963 Hal Hendrix *(Miami News)*
1964 Malcolm W. Browne (Associated Press) and David Halberstam *(New York Times)*
1965 J. A. Livingston *(Philadelphia Bulletin)*
1966 Peter Arnett (Associated Press)
1967 R. John Hughes *(Christian Science Monitor)*
1968 Alfred Friendly *(Washington Post)*
1969 William Tuohy *(Los Angeles Times)*
1970 Seymour M. Hersh (Dispatch News Service)
1971 Jimmie Lee Hoagland *(Washington Post)*
1972 Peter R. Kann *(Wall Street Journal)*
1973 Max Frankel *(New York Times)*
1974 Hedrick Smith *(New York Times)*
1975 William Mullen and Ovie Carter *(Chicago Tribune)*
1976 Sydney H. Schanberg *(New York Times)*
1978 Henry Kamm *(New York Times)*
1979 Richard Ben Cramer *(Philadelphia Inquirer)*
1980 Joel Brinkley and Jay Mather *(Louisville Courier-Journal)*

1981 Shirley Christian *(Miami Herald)*
1982 John Darnton *(New York Times)*
1983 Thomas L. Friedman *(New York Times)*
1984 Karen E. House *(Wall Street Journal)*
1985 Josh Friedman, Dennis Bell, and Ozier Muhammad *(Newsday)*
1986 Lewis M. Simons, Pete Carey, and Katherine Ellison *(San Jose Mercury News)*
1987 Michael Parks *(Los Angeles Times)*
1988 Thomas L. Friedman *(New York Times)*
1989 Bill Keller *(New York Times)*; Glenn Frankel *(Washington Post)*
1990 Nicholas D. Kristof and Sheryl WuDunn *(New York Times)*
1991 Caryle Murphy *(Washington Post)* and Serge Schmemann *(New York Times)*
1992 Patrick J. Sloyan *(Newsday)*
1993 John F. Burns *(New York Times)* and Roy Gutman *(Newsday)*
1994 *Dallas Morning News,* team
1995 Mark Fritz (Associated Press)
1996 David Rohde *(Christian Science Monitor)*

REPORTING

1917 Herbert B. Swope *(New York World)*
1918 Harold A. Littledale *(New York Evening Post)*
1920 John J. Leary, Jr. *(New York World)*
1921 Louis Seibold *(New York World)*
1922 Kirke L. Simpson (Associated Press)
1923 Alva Johnston *(New York Times)*
1924 Magner White *(San Diego Sun)*
1925 James W. Mulroy and Alvin H. Goldstein *(Chicago Daily News)*
1926 William Burke Miller *(Louisville Courier-Journal)*
1927 John T. Rogers *(St. Louis Post-Dispatch)*
1929 Paul Y. Anderson *(St. Louis Post-Dispatch)*
1930 Russell D. Owen *(New York Times)*; special award: W. O. Dapping *(Auburn* [N.Y.] *Citizen)*
1931 A. B. MacDonald *(Kansas City* [Mo.] *Star)*
1932 W. C. Richards, D. D. Martin, J. S. Pooler, F. D. Webb, J. N. W. Sloan (all of *Detroit Free Press)*
1933 Francis A. Jamieson (Associated Press)
1934 Royce Brier *(San Francisco Chronicle)*
1935 William H. Taylor *(New York Herald Tribune)*
1936 Lauren D. Lyman *(New York Times)*
1937 John J. O'Neill *(New York Herald Tribune)*; William Leonard Laurence *(New York Times)*; Howard W. Blakeslee (Associated Press); Gobind Behari Lal (Universal Service); David Dietz (Scripps-Howard Newspapers)
1938 Raymond Sprigle *(Pittsburg Post-Gazette)*
1939 Thomas L. Stokes *(New York World-Telegram)*
1940 S. Burton Heath *(New York World-Telegram)*
1941 Westbrook Pegler *(New York World-Telegram)*
1942 Stanton Delaplane *(San Francisco Chronicle)*
1943 George Weller *(Chicago Daily News)*
1944 Paul Schoenstein and associates *(New York Journal-American)*
1945 Jack S. McDowell *(San Francisco Call-Bulletin)*
1946 William Leonard Laurence *(New York Times)*
1947 Frederick Woltman *(New York World-Telegram)*
1948 George E. Goodwin *(Atlanta Journal)*
1949 Malcolm Johnson *(New York Sun)*
1950 Meyer Berger *(New York Times)*
1951 Edward S. Montgomery *(San Francisco Examiner)*
1952 George de Carvalho *(San Francisco Chronicle)*
1953 Editorial staff *(Providence Journal and Evening Bulletin)*;[1] Edward J. Mowery *(New York World-Telegram and Sun)*[2]
1954 *Vicksburg* (Miss.) *Sunday Post-Herald*;[1] Alvin Scott McCoy *(Kansas City* [Mo.] *Star)*[2]
1955 Mrs. Caro Brown *(Alice* [Tex.] *Daily Echo)*;[1] Roland Kenneth Towery *(Cuero* [Tex.] *Record)*[2]

1956 Lee Hills *(Detroit Free Press)*;[1] Arthur Daley *(New York Times)*[2]
1957 *Salt Lake Tribune*;[1] Wallace Turner and William Lambert *(Portland Oregonian)*[2]
1958 *Fargo* [N.D.] *Forum*;[1] George Beveridge *(Washington* [D.C.] *Evening Star)*[2]
1959 Mary Lou Werner *(Washington* [D.C.] *Evening Star)*;[1] John Harold Brislin *(Scranton* [Pa.] *Tribune & Scrantonian)*[2]
1960 Jack Nelson *(Atlanta Constitution)*;[1] Miriam Ottenberg *(Washington Evening Star)*[2]
1961 Sanche de Gramont *(New York Herald Tribune)*;[1] Edgar May *(Buffalo Evening News)*[2]
1962 Robert D. Mullins *(Deseret News,* Salt Lake City);[1] George Bliss *(Chicago Tribune)*[2]
1963 Sylvan Fox, Anthony Shannon, and William Longgood *(New York World-Telegram and Sun)*;[1] Oscar Griffin, Jr. (former editor of *Pecos* [Tex.] *Independent and Enterprise,* now on staff of *Houston Chronicle)*[2]

1. Reporting under pressure of edition deadlines. 2. Reporting not under pressure of edition deadlines.

GENERAL LOCAL REPORTING

1964 Norman C. Miller *(Wall Street Journal)*
1965 Melvin H. Ruder *(Hungry Horse News,* Columbia Falls, Mont.)
1966 Staff of *Los Angeles Times*
1967 Robert V. Cox *(Chambersburg* [Pa.] *Public Opinion)*
1968 Staff of *Detroit Free Press*
1969 John Fetterman *(Louisville Times* and *Courier-Journal)*
1970 Thomas Fitzpatrick *(Chicago Sun-Times)*
1971 Staff of *Akron* (Ohio) *Beacon*
1972 Richard Cooper and John Machacek *(Rochester* [N.Y.] *Times-Union)*
1973 *Chicago Tribune*
1974 Arthur M. Petacque and Hugh F. Hough *(Chicago Sun-Times)*
1975 *Xenia* (Ohio) *Daily Gazette*
1976 Gene Miller *(Miami Herald)*
1977 Margo Huston *(Milwaukee Journal)*
1978 Richard Whitt *(Louisville Courier-Journal)*
1979 Staff of *San Diego* (Calif.) *Evening Tribune*
1980 Staff of *Philadelphia Inquirer*
1981 *Longview* (Wash.) *Daily News*
1982 *Kansas City* (Mo.) *Star* and *Kansas City* (Mo.) *Times*
1983 *Fort Wayne* (Ind.) *News-Sentinel*
1984 *Newsday*

GENERAL NEWS REPORTING

1985 Thomas Turcol *(Virginian-Pilot and Ledger-Star)*
1986 Edna Buchanan *(Miami Herald)*
1987 *Akron Beacon Journal,* staff
1988 *Alabama Journal* (Montgomery), staff, *Lawrence* (Mass.) *Eagle-Tribune,* staff
1989 *Louisville Courier-Journal* staff
1990 *San Jose* (Calif.) *Mercury News*

SPOT NEWS REPORTING

1991 *Miami Herald* staff
1992 *New York Newsday* staff
1993 *Los Angeles Times* staff
1994 *New York Times* staff
1995 *Los Angeles Times* staff
1996 Robert D. McFadden *(New York Times)*

SPECIAL LOCAL REPORTING

1964 James V. Magee, Albert V. Gaudiosi, and Frederick A. Meyer *(Philadelphia Bulletin)*
1965 Gene Goltz *(Houston Post)*
1966 John A. Frasca *(Tampa Tribune)*
1967 Gene Miller *(Miami Herald)*
1968 J. Anthony Lukas *(New York Times)*
1969 Albert L. Delugach and Denny Walsh *(St. Louis Globe-Democrat)*

1970 Harold Eugene Martin *(Montgomery Advertiser)*
1971 William Hugh Jones *(Chicago Tribune)*
1972 Timothy Leland, Gerard N. O'Neill, Stephen A. Kurkjian, and Ann DeSantis *(Boston Globe)*
1973 Sun Newspapers of Omaha, Neb.
1974 William Sherman *(New York Daily News)*
1975 *Indianapolis Star*
1976 *Chicago Tribune*
1977 Acel Moore and Wendell Rawls, Jr. *(Philadelphia Inquirer)*
1978 Anthony R. Dolan *(Stamford* [Conn.] *Advocate)*
1979 Gilbert M. Gaul and Elliot G. Jaspin *(Pottsville* [Pa.] *Republican)*
1980 Nils J. Bruzelius, Alexander B. Hawes, Jr., Stephen A. Kurkjian, Robert M. Porterfield, and Joan Vennochi *(Boston Globe)*
1981 Clark Hallas and Robert B. Lowe *(Arizona Daily Star,* Tucson)
1982 Paul Henderson *(Seattle Times)*
1983 Loretta Tofani *(Washington Post)*
1984 *Boston Globe*

INVESTIGATIVE REPORTING

1985 Lucy Morgan and Jack Reed *(St. Petersburg* [Fla.] *Times)* and William K. Marimow *(Philadelphia Inquirer)*
1986 Jeffrey A. Marx and Michael M. York *(Lexington* [Ky.] *Herald Leader)*
1987 Daniel R. Biddle, H.G. Bissinger, and Fredric N. Tulsky *(Philadelphia Inquirer)*
1988 Dean Baquet, William C. Gaines, and Ann Marie Lipinski *(Chicago Tribune)*
1989 Bill Dedman *(Atlanta Journal and Constitution)*
1990 Lou Kilzer and Chris Ison *(Minneapolis-St. Paul Star Tribune)*
1991 Joseph T. Hallinan and Susan M. Headden *(Indianapolis Star)*
1992 Lorraine Adams and Dan Malone *(Dallas Morning News)*
1993 Jeff Brazil and Steve Berry *(Orlando* [Fla.] *Sentinel)*
1994 *Providence* (R.I.) *Journal-Bulletin* staff
1995 Stephanie Saul and Brian Donovan *(Newsday)*
1996 *Orange County Register* staff (Santa Ana, Calif.)

FEATURE WRITING

1979 Jon D. Franklin *(Baltimore Evening Sun)*
1980 Madeleine Blais *(Miami Herald)*
1981 Teresa Carpenter *(Village Voice,* New York)
1982 Saul Pett (Associated Press)
1983 Nan Robertson *(New York Times)*
1984 Peter M. Rinearson *(Seattle Times)*
1985 Alice Steinbach *(Baltimore Sun)*
1986 John Camp *(St. Paul Pioneer Press and Dispatch)*
1987 Steve Twomey *(Philadelphia Inquirer)*
1988 Jacqui Banaszynski *(St. Paul Pioneer Press Dispatch)*
1989 David Zucchino *(Philadelphia Inquirer)*
1990 Dave Curtin *(Colorado Springs Gazette Telegraph)*
1991 Sheryl James, *(St. Petersburg* [Fla.] *Times)*
1992 Howell Raines *(New York Times)*
1993 George Lardner, Jr. *(Washington Post)*
1994 Isabel Wilkerson *(New York Times)*
1995 Ron Suskind *(Wall Street Journal)*
1996 Rick Bragg *(New York Times)*

COMMENTARY

1970 Marquis W. Childs *(St. Louis Post-Dispatch)*
1971 William A. Caldwell *(Record* [Hackensack, N.J.])
1972 Mike Royko *(Chicago Daily News)*
1973 David S. Broder *(Washington Post)*
1974 Edwin A. Roberts, Jr. *(National Observer)*
1975 Mary McGrory *(Washington Star)*
1976 Walter W. (Red) Smith *(New York Times)*
1977 George F. Will *(Washington Post* Writers Group)
1978 William Safire *(New York Times)*
1979 Russell Baker *(New York Times)*

1980 Ellen H. Goodman *(Boston Globe)*
1981 Dave Anderson *(New York Times)*
1982 Art Buchwald *(Los Angeles Times* Syndicate)
1983 Claude Sitton *(Raleigh* [N.C.] *News & Observer)*
1984 Vermont Royster *(Wall Street Journal)*
1985 Murray Kempton *(Newsday)*
1986 Jimmy Breslin *(New York Daily News)*
1987 Charles Krauthammer *(Washington Post* Writers Group)
1988 Dave Barry *(Miami Herald)*
1989 Clarence Page *(Chicago Tribune)*
1990 Jim Murray *(Los Angeles Times)*
1991 Jim Hoagland *(Washington Post)*
1992 Anna Quindlen *(New York Times)*
1993 Liz Balmaseda *(Mami Herald)*
1994 William Raspberry *(Washington Post)*
1995 Jim Dwyer *(New York Newsday)*
1996 E.R. Shipp *(New York Daily News)*

CRITICISM

1970 Ada Louise Huxtable *(New York Times)*
1971 Harold C. Schonberg *(New York Times)*
1972 Frank Peters, Jr. *(St. Louis Post-Dispatch)*
1973 Ronald Powers *(Chicago Sun-Times)*
1974 Emily Genauer (Newsday Syndicate)
1975 Roger Ebert *(Chicago Sun-Times)*
1976 Alan M. Kriegsman *(Washington Post)*
1977 William McPherson *(Washington Post)*
1978 Walter Kerr *(New York Times)*
1979 Paul Gapp *(Chicago Tribune)*
1980 William A. Henry, 3rd *(Boston Globe)*
1981 Jonathan Yardley *(Washington Star)*
1982 Martin Bernheimer *(Los Angeles Times)*
1983 Manuela Hoelterhoff *(Wall Street Journal)*
1984 Paul Goldberger *(New York Times)*
1985 Howard Rosenberg *(Los Angeles Times)*
1986 Donal Henahan *(New York Times)*
1987 Richard Eder *(Los Angeles Times)*
1988 Tom Shales *(Washington Post)*
1989 Michael Skube *(News and Observer,* Raleigh, N.C.)
1990 Allan Temko *(San Francisco Chronicle)*
1991 David Shaw *(Los Angeles Times)*
1993 Michael Dirda *(Washington Post)*
1994 Lloyd Schwartz *(The Boston Phoenix)*
1995 Margo Jefferson *(New York Times)*
1996 Robert Campbell *(Boston Globe)*

EXPLANATORY JOURNALISM

1985 Jon Franklin *(Baltimore Evening Sun)*
1986 *New York Times*
1987 Jeff Lyon and Peter Gorner *(Chicago Tribune)*
1988 Daniel Hertzberg and James B. Stewart *(Wall Street Journal)*
1989 David Hanners, William Snyder, and Karen Blessen *(Dallas Morning News)*
1990 David A. Vise and Coll *(Washington Post)*
1991 Susan C. Faludi *(Wall Street Journal)*
1992 Robert S. Capers and Eric Lipton *(Hartford Courant)*
1993 Mike Toner *(Atlanta Journal–Constitution)*
1994 Ronald Kotulak *(Chicago Tribune)*
1995 Leon Dash and Lucian Perkins *(Washington Post)*
1996 Laurie Garrett *(Newsday* [Long Island, N.Y.])

SPECIALIZED REPORTING

1985 Randall Savage and Jackie Crosby *(Macon* [Ga.] *Telegraph and News)*
1986 Andrew Schneider and Mary Pat Flaherty *(Pittsburgh Press)*
1987 Alex S. Jones *(New York Times)*
1988 Walt Bogdanich *(Wall Street Journal)*
1989 Edward Humes *(Orange County Register)*
1990 Tamar Stieber *(Albuquerque* (N.M.) *Journal)*

BEAT REPORTING

1991 Natalie Angier *(New York Times)*
1992 Deborah Blum *(Sacramento Bee)*

1993 Paul Ingrassia and Joseph B. White, *(Wall Street Journal)*
1994 Eric Freedman and Jim Mitzelfeld *(Detroit News)*
1995 David M. Shribman *(Boston Globe)*
1996 Bob Keeler *(Newsday* [Long Island, N.Y.])

SPECIAL CITATIONS

1938 *Edmonton* (Alberta) *Journal,* special bronze plaque for editorial leadership in defense of freedom of press in Province of Alberta.
1941 *New York Times* for the public educational value of its foreign news report.
1944 Byron Price, Director of the Office of Censorship, for the creation and administration of the newspaper and radio codes. Mrs. William Allen White, for her husband's interest and services during the past seven years as a member of the Advisory Board of the Graduate School of Journalism, Columbia University. Richard Rodgers and Oscar Hammerstein II for their musical *Oklahoma!*
1945 The cartographers of the American press for their war maps.
1947 (Pulitzer centennial year.) Columbia University and the Graduate School of Journalism for their efforts to maintain and advance the high standards governing the Pulitzer Prize awards. The *St. Louis Post-Dispatch* for its unswerving adherence to the public and professional ideals of its founder and its leadership in American journalism.
1948 Dr. Frank D. Fackenthal for his interest and service.
1951 Cyrus L. Sulzberger *(New York Times)* for his exclusive interview with Archbishop Stepinac in a Yugoslav prison.
1952 *Kansas City Star* for coverage of 1951 floods; Max

Kase *(New York Journal-American)* for exposures of bribery in college basketball.
1953 *New York Times* for its 17-year publication of "News of the Week in Review"; and Lester Markel, its founder.
1957 Kenneth Roberts for his historical novels.
1958 Walter Lippmann *(New York Herald Tribune)* for his "wisdom, perception and high sense of responsibility" in his commentary on national and international affairs.
1960 Garrett Mattingly, for *The Armada.*
1961 *American Heritage Picture History of the Civil War,* as distinguished example of American book publishing.
1964 Gannett Newspapers, Rochester, N.Y.
1973 James Thomas Flexner for his biography *George Washington.*
1974 Roger Sessions for his "life's work in music."
1976 John Hohenberg for "services for 22 years as administrator of the Pulitzer Prizes"; Scott Joplin for his contributions to American music.
1977 Alex Haley for his novel, *Roots.*
1978 E.B. White of *New Yorker* magazine and Richard L. Strout of *Christian Science Monitor.*
1982 Milton Babbitt, "for his life's work as a distinguished and seminal American composer."
1984 Theodor Seuss Geisel (Dr. Seuss) for "books full of playful rhymes, nonsense words and strange illustrations."
1985 William H. Schuman for "more than a half century of contribution to American music as a composer and educational leader."
1987 Joseph Pulitzer Jr., "for extraordinary services to American journalism and letters during his 31 years as chairman of the Pulitzer Prize Board and for his accomplishments as an editor and publisher."
1996 Herb Caen *(San Francisco Chronicle)* "for his extraordinary and continuing contribution as a voice and conscience of the city."

Pulitzer Prizes in Letters

FICTION[1]

1918 *His Family.* Ernest Poole
1919 *The Magnificent Ambersons.* Booth Tarkington
1921 *The Age of Innocence.* Edith Wharton
1922 *Alice Adams.* Booth Tarkington
1923 *One of Ours.* Willa Cather
1924 *The Able McLaughlins.* Margaret Wilson
1925 *So Big.* Edna Ferber
1926 *Arrowsmith.* Sinclair Lewis
1927 *Early Autumn.* Louis Bromfield
1928 *The Bridge of San Luis Rey.* Thornton Wilder
1929 *Scarlet Sister Mary.* Julia Peterkin
1930 *Laughing Boy.* Oliver La Farge
1931 *Years of Grace.* Margaret Ayer Barnes
1932 *The Good Earth.* Pearl S. Buck
1933 *The Store.* T. S. Stribling
1934 *Lamb in His Bosom.* Caroline Miller
1935 *Now in November.* Josephine Winslow Johnson
1936 *Honey in the Horn.* Harold L. Davis
1937 *Gone With the Wind.* Margaret Mitchell
1938 *The Late George Apley.* John Phillips Marquand
1939 *The Yearling.* Marjorie Kinnan Rawlings
1940 *The Grapes of Wrath.* John Steinbeck
1942 *In This Our Life.* Ellen Glasgow
1943 *Dragon's Teeth.* Upton Sinclair
1944 *Journey in the Dark.* Martin Flavin
1945 *A Bell for Adano.* John Hersey
1947 *All the King's Men.* Robert Penn Warren
1948 *Tales of the South Pacific.* James A. Michener
1949 *Guard of Honor.* James Gould Cozzens
1950 *The Way West.* A. B. Guthrie, Jr.
1951 *The Town.* Conrad Richter
1952 *The Caine Mutiny.* Herman Wouk
1953 *The Old Man and the Sea.* Ernest Hemingway

1. Before 1948, award was for novels only.

1955 *A Fable.* William Faulkner
1956 *Andersonville.* MacKinlay Kantor
1958 *A Death in the Family.* James Agee
1959 *The Travels of Jaimie McPheeters.* Robert Lewis Taylor
1960 *Advise and Consent.* Allen Drury
1961 *To Kill a Mockingbird.* Harper Lee
1962 *The Edge of Sadness.* Edwin O'Connor
1963 *The Reivers.* William Faulkner
1965 *The Keepers of the House.* Shirley Ann Grau
1966 *Collected Stories of Katherine Anne Porter.* Katherine Anne Porter
1967 *The Fixer.* Bernard Malamud
1968 *The Confessions of Nat Turner.* William Styron
1969 *House Made of Dawn.* N. Scott Momaday
1970 *Collected Stories.* Jean Stafford
1972 *Angle of Repose.* Wallace Stegner
1973 *The Optimist's Daughter.* Eudora Welty
1975 *The Killer Angels.* Michael Shaara
1976 *Humboldt's Gift.* Saul Bellow
1978 *Elbow Room.* James Alan McPherson
1979 *The Stories of John Cheever.* John Cheever
1980 *The Executioner's Song.* Norman Mailer
1981 *A Confederacy of Dunces.* John Kennedy Toole
1982 *Rabbit Is Rich.* John Updike
1983 *The Color Purple.* Alice Walker
1984 *Ironweed.* William Kennedy
1985 *Foreign Affairs,* Alison Lurie
1986 *Lonesome Dove,* Larry McMurtry
1987 *A Summons to Memphis,* Peter Taylor
1988 *Beloved,* Toni Morrison
1989 *Breathing Lessons,* Anne Tyler
1990 *The Mambo Kings Play Songs of Love,* Oscar Hijuelos
1991 *Rabbit at Rest,* John Updike
1992 *A Thousand Acres,* Jane Smiley

1993	*A Good Scent From a Strange Mountain*, Robert Olen Butler
1994	*The Shipping News*, E. Annie Proulx
1995	*The Stone Diaries*, Carol Shields
1996	*Independence Day*, Richard Ford

DRAMA

1918 *Why Marry?* Jesse Lynch Williams
1920 *Beyond the Horizon.* Eugene O'Neill
1921 *Miss Lulu Bett.* Zona Gale
1922 *Anna Christie.* Eugene O'Neill
1923 *Icebound.* Owen Davis
1924 *Hell-Bent Fer Heaven.* Hatcher Hughes
1925 *They Knew What They Wanted.* Sidney Howard
1926 *Craig's Wife.* George Kelly
1927 *In Abraham's Bosom.* Paul Green
1928 *Strange Interlude.* Eugene O'Neill
1929 *Street Scene.* Elmer L. Rice
1930 *The Green Pastures.* Marc Connelly
1931 *Alison's House.* Susan Glaspell
1932 *Of Thee I Sing.* George S. Kaufman, Morrie Ryskind, and Ira Gershwin
1933 *Both Your Houses.* Maxwell Anderson
1934 *Men in White.* Sidney Kingsley
1935 *The Old Maid.* Zöe Akins
1936 *Idiot's Delight.* Robert E. Sherwood
1937 *You Can't Take It With You.* Moss Hart and George S. Kaufman
1938 *Our Town.* Thornton Wilder
1939 *Abe Lincoln in Illinois.* Robert E. Sherwood
1940 *The Time of Your Life.* William Saroyan
1941 *There Shall Be No Night.* Robert E. Sherwood
1943 *The Skin of Our Teeth.* Thornton Wilder
1945 *Harvey.* Mary Chase
1946 *State of the Union.* Russel Crouse and Howard Lindsay
1948 *A Streetcar Named Desire.* Tennessee Williams
1949 *Death of a Salesman.* Arthur Miller
1950 *South Pacific.* Richard Rodgers, Oscar Hammerstein II, and Joshua Logan
1952 *The Shrike.* Joseph Kramm
1953 *Picnic.* William Inge
1954 *The Teahouse of the August Moon.* John Patrick
1955 *Cat on a Hot Tin Roof.* Tennessee Williams
1956 *The Diary of Anne Frank.* Frances Goodrich and Albert Hackett
1957 *Long Day's Journey Into Night.* Eugene O'Neill
1958 *Look Homeward, Angel.* Ketti Frings
1959 *J.B.* Archibald MacLeish
1960 *Fiorello!* George Abbott, Jerome Weidman, Jerry Bock, and Sheldon Harnick
1961 *All the Way Home.* Tad Mosel
1962 *How to Succeed in Business Without Really Trying.* Frank Loesser and Abe Burrows
1965 *The Subject Was Roses.* Frank D. Gilroy
1967 *A Delicate Balance.* Edward Albee
1969 *The Great White Hope.* Howard Sackler
1970 *No Place to Be Somebody.* Charles Gordone
1971 *The Effect of Gamma Rays on Man-in-the-Moon Marigolds.* Paul Zindel
1973 *That Championship Season.* Jason Miller
1975 *Seascape.* Edward Albee
1976 *A Chorus Line.* Conceived by Michael Bennett
1977 *The Shadow Box.* Michael Cristofer
1978 *The Gin Game.* Donald L. Coburn
1979 *Buried Child.* Sam Shepard
1980 *Talley's Folly.* Lanford Wilson
1981 *Crimes of the Heart.* Beth Henley
1982 *A Soldier's Play.* Charles Fuller
1983 *'Night, Mother.* Marsha Norman
1984 *Glengarry Glen Ross.* David Mamet
1985 *Sunday in the Park with George.* Stephen Sondheim and James Lapine
1987 *Fences.* August Wilson

1988 *Driving Miss Daisy.* Alfred Uhry
1989 *The Heidi Chronicles,* Wendy Wasserstein
1990 *The Piano Lesson,* August Wilson
1991 *Lost in Yonkers,* Neil Simon
1992 *The Kentucky Cycle,* Robert Schenkkan
1993 *Angels in America: Millennium Approaches,* Tony Kushner
1994 *Three Tall Women,* Edward Albee
1995 *The Young Man from Atlanta,* Horton Foote
1996 *Rent,* Jonathan Larson

HISTORY OF UNITED STATES

1917 *With Americans of Past and Present Days.* J. J. Jusserand, Ambassador of France to United States
1918 *A History of the Civil War, 1861–1865.* James Ford Rhodes
1920 *The War With Mexico.* Justin H. Smith
1921 *The Victory at Sea.* William Sowden Sims in collaboration with Burton J. Hendrick
1922 *The Founding of New England.* James Truslow Adams
1923 *The Supreme Court in United States History.* Charles Warren
1924 *The American Revolution—A Constitutional Interpretation.* Charles Howard McIlwain
1925 *A History of the American Frontier.* Frederic L. Paxson
1926 *The History of the United States.* Edward Channing
1927 *Pinckney's Treaty.* Samuel Flagg Bemis
1928 *Main Currents in American Thought.* Vernon Louis Parrington
1929 *The Organization and Administration of the Union Army, 1861–1865.* Fred Albert Shannon
1930 *The War of Independence.* Claude H. Van Tyne
1931 *The Coming of the War: 1914.* Bernadotte E. Schmitt
1932 *My Experiences in the World War.* John J. Pershing
1933 *The Significance of Sections in American History.* Frederick J. Turner
1934 *The People's Choice.* Herbert Agar
1935 *The Colonial Period of American History.* Charles McLean Andrews
1936 *The Constitutional History of the United States.* Andrew C. McLaughlin
1937 *The Flowering of New England.* Van Wyck Brooks
1938 *The Road to Reunion, 1865–1900.* Paul Herman Buck
1939 *A History of American Magazines.* Frank Luther Mott
1940 *Abraham Lincoln: The War Years.* Carl Sandburg
1941 *The Atlantic Migration, 1607–1860.* Marcus Lee Hansen
1942 *Reveille in Washington.* Margaret Leech
1943 *Paul Revere and the World He Lived In.* Esther Forbes
1944 *The Growth of American Thought.* Merle Curti
1945 *Unfinished Business.* Stephen Bonsal
1946 *The Age of Jackson.* Arthur M. Schlesinger, Jr.
1947 *Scientists Against Time.* James Phinney Baxter, 3rd
1948 *Across the Wide Missouri.* Bernard DeVoto
1949 *The Disruption of American Democracy.* Roy Franklin Nichols
1950 *Art and Life in America.* Oliver W. Larkin
1951 *The Old Northwest, Pioneer Period 1815–1840.* R. Carlyle Buley
1952 *The Uprooted.* Oscar Handlin
1953 *The Era of Good Feelings.* George Dangerfield
1954 *A Stillness at Appomattox.* Bruce Catton
1955 *Great River: The Rio Grande in North American History.* Paul Horgan
1956 *The Age of Reform.* Richard Hofstadter
1957 *Russia Leaves the War: Soviet-American Relations, 1917–1920.* George F. Kennan
1958 *Banks and Politics in America: From the Revolution to the Civil War.* Bray Hammond
1959 *The Republican Era: 1869–1901.* Leonard D. White, assisted by Jean Schneider
1960 *In the Days of McKinley.* Margaret Leech
1961 *Between War and Peace: The Potsdam Conference.* Herbert Feis

1962 *The Triumphant Empire, Thunder-Clouds Gather in the West.* Lawrence H. Gipson
1963 *Washington, Village and Capital, 1800–1878.* Constance McLaughlin Green
1964 *Puritan Village: The Formation of a New England Town.* Sumner Chilton Powell
1965 *The Greenback Era.* Irwin Unger
1966 *Life of the Mind in America.* Perry Miller
1967 *Exploration and Empire: The Explorer and Scientist in the Winning of the American West.* William H. Goetzmann
1968 *The Ideological Origins of the American Revolution.* Bernard Bailyn
1969 *Origins of the Fifth Amendment.* Leonard W. Levy
1970 *Present at the Creation: My Years in the State Department.* Dean Acheson
1971 *Roosevelt: The Soldier of Freedom.* James McGregor Burns
1972 *Neither Black Nor White. Slavery and Race Relations in Brazil and the United States.* Carl N. Degler
1973 *People of Paradox: An Inquiry Concerning the Origin of American Civilization.* Michael Kammen
1974 *The Americans: The Democratic Experience, Vol. 3.* Daniel J. Boorstin
1975 *Jefferson and His Time.* Dumas Malone
1976 *Lamy of Santa Fe.* Paul Horgan
1977 *The Impending Crisis: 1841–1861.* David M. Potter (posth)
1978 *The Invisible Hand: The Managerial Revolution in American Business.* Alfred D. Chandler, Jr.
1979 *The Dred Scott Case: Its Significance in Law and Politics.* Don E. Fehrenbacher
1980 *Been in the Storm So Long.* Leon F. Litwack
1981 *American Education: The National Experience; 1783–1876.* Lawrence A. Cremin
1982 *Mary Chestnut's Civil War.* C. Vann Woodward, editor
1983 *The Transformation of Virginia, 1740–1790.* Rhys L. Isaac
1985 *The Prophets of Regulation.* Thomas K. McCraw
1986 *. . . the Heavens and the Earth: A Political History of the Space Age.* Walter A. McDougall
1987 *Voyagers to the West: A Passage in the Peopling of America on the Eve of the Revolution.* Bernard Bailyn
1988 *The Launching of Modern American Science 1846–1876.* Robert V. Bruce
1989 *Parting the Waters,* Taylor Branch; *Battle Cry of Freedom,* James M. McPherson
1990 *In Our Image: America's Empire in the Philippines,* Stanley Karnow
1991 *A Midwife's Tale: The Life of Martha Ballard, Based on Her Diary 1785–1812,* Laurel Thatcher Ulrich
1992 *The Fate of Liberty: Abraham Lincoln and Civil Liberties,* Mark E. Neely, Jr.
1993 *The Radicalism of the American Revolution,* Gordon S. Wood
1995 *No Ordinary Time: Franklin and Eleanor Roosevelt: The Home Front in World War II,* Doris Kearns Goodwin
1996 *William Cooper's Town: Power and Persuasion on the Frontier of the Early American Republic,* Alan Taylor

BIOGRAPHY OR AUTOBIOGRAPHY

1917 *Julia Ward Howe.* Laura E. Richards and Maude Howe Elliott, assisted by Florence Howe Hall
1918 *Benjamin Franklin, Self-Revealed.* William Cabell Bruce
1919 *The Education of Henry Adams.* Henry Adams
1920 *The Life of John Marshall.* Albert J. Beveridge
1921 *The Americanization of Edward Bok.* Edward Bok
1922 *A Daughter of the Middle Border.* Hamlin Garland
1923 *The Life and Letters of Walter H. Page,* Burton J. Hendrick
1924 *From Immigrant to Inventor.* Michael Idvorsky Pupin
1925 *Barrett Wendell and His Letters.* M. A. DeWolfe Howe
1926 *The Life of Sir William Osler.* Harvey Cushing

1927 *Whitman.* Emory Holloway
1928 *The American Orchestra and Theodore Thomas.* Charles Edward Russell
1929 *The Training of an American. The Earlier Life and Letters of Walter H. Page.* Burton J. Hendrick
1930 *The Raven.* Marquis James
1931 *Charles W. Eliot.* Henry James
1932 *Theodore Roosevelt.* Henry F. Pringle
1933 *Grover Cleveland.* Allan Nevins
1934 *John Hay.* Tyler Dennett
1935 *R. E. Lee.* Douglas S. Freeman
1936 *The Thought and Character of William James.* Ralph Barton Perry
1937 *Hamilton Fish.* Allan Nevins
1938 *Pedlar's Progress.* Odell Shepard; *Andrew Jackson.* Marquis James
1939 *Benjamin Franklin.* Carl Van Doren
1940 *Woodrow Wilson. Life and Letters,* Vols. VII and VIII. Ray Stannard Baker
1941 *Jonathan Edwards.* Ola E. Winslow
1942 *Crusader in Crinoline.* Forrest Wilson
1943 *Admiral of the Ocean Sea.* Samuel Eliot Morison
1944 *The American Leonardo: The Life of Samuel F. B. Morse.* Carleton Mabee
1945 *George Bancroft: Brahmin Rebel.* Russel Blaine Nye
1946 *Son of the Wilderness.* Linnie Marsh Wolfe
1947 *The Autobiography of William Allen White.*
1948 *Forgotten First Citizen: John Bigelow.* Margaret Clapp
1949 *Roosevelt and Hopkins.* Robert E. Sherwood
1950 *John Quincy Adams and the Foundations of American Foreign Policy.* Samuel Flagg Bemis
1951 *John C. Calhoun: American Portrait.* Margaret Louise Coit
1952 *Charles Evans Hughes.* Merlo J. Pusey
1953 *Edmund Pendleton, 1721–1803.* David J. Mays
1954 *The Spirit of St. Louis.* Charles A. Lindbergh
1955 *The Taft Story.* William S. White
1956 *Benjamin Henry Latrobe.* Talbot F. Hamlin
1957 *Profiles in Courage.* John F. Kennedy
1958 *George Washington.* Douglas Southall Freeman (Vols. 1–6) and John Alexander Carroll and Mary Wells Ashworth (Vol. 7)
1959 *Woodrow Wilson, American Prophet.* Arthur Walworth
1960 *John Paul Jones.* Samuel Eliot Morison
1961 *Charles Sumner and the Coming of the Civil War.* David Donald
1963 *Henry James: Vol. II, The Conquest of London, 1870–1881; Vol. III, The Middle Years, 1881–1895.* Leon Edel
1964 *John Keats.* Walter Jackson Bate
1965 *Henry Adams* (3 Vols.). Ernest Samuels
1966 *A Thousand Days.* Arthur M. Schlesinger, Jr.
1967 *Mr. Clemens and Mark Twain.* Justin Kaplan
1968 *Memoirs, 1925–1950.* George F. Kennan
1969 *The Man From New York.* B. L. Reid
1970 *Huey Long.* T. Harry Williams
1971 *Robert Frost: The Years of Triumph, 1915–1938.* Lawrence Thompson
1972 *Eleanor and Franklin: The Story of Their Relationship Based on Eleanor Roosevelt's Private Papers.* Joseph P. Lash
1973 *Luce and His Empire.* W. A. Swanberg
1974 *O'Neill, Son and Artist.* Louis Sheaffer
1975 *The Power Broker: Robert Moses and the Fall of New York.* Robert A. Caro
1976 *Edith Wharton: A Biography.* Richard W. B. Lewis
1977 *A Prince of Our Disorder.* John E. Mack
1978 *Samuel Johnson.* Walter Jackson Bate
1979 *Days of Sorrow and Pain: Leo Baeck and the Berlin Jews.* Leonard Baker
1980 *The Rise of Theodore Roosevelt.* Edmund Morris
1981 *Peter the Great.* Robert K. Massie
1982 *Grant: A Biography.* William S. McFeely

1983 *Growing Up.* Russell Baker
1984 *Booker T. Washington.* Louis R. Harlan
1985 *The Life and Times of Cotton Mather,* Kenneth Silverman
1986 *Louise Bogan: A Portrait,* Elizabeth Frank
1987 *Bearing the Cross: Martin Luther King Jr. and the Southern Christian Leadership Conference,* David J. Garrow
1988 *Look Homeward: A Life of Thomas Wolfe.* David Herbert Donald
1989 *Oscar Wilde.* Richard Ellmann
1990 *Machiavelli in Hell,* Sebastian de Grazia
1991 *Jackson Pollock: An American Saga,* Steven Naifeh and Gregory White Smith
1992 *Fortunate Son: The Healing of a Vietnam Vet,* Lewis B. Puller, Jr.
1993 *Truman,* David McCullough
1994 *W.E.B. Du Bois: Biography of a Race, 1868–1919,* David Levering Lewis
1995 *Harriet Beecher Stowe: A Life,* Joan D. Hedrick
1996 *God: A Biography,* Jack Miles

POETRY[1]

1918 *Love Songs.* Sara Teasdale
1919 *Old Road to Paradise.* Margaret Widdemer; *Corn Huskers.* Carl Sandburg
1922 *Collected Poems.* Edwin Arlington Robinson
1923 *The Ballad of the Harp-Weaver; A Few Figs from Thistles;* eight sonnets in *American Poetry, 1922, A Miscellany.* Edna St. Vincent Millay
1924 *New Hampshire: A Poem With Notes and Grace Notes.* Robert Frost
1925 *The Man Who Died Twice.* Edwin Arlington Robinson
1926 *What's O'Clock.* Amy Lowell
1927 *Fiddler's Farewell.* Leonora Speyer
1928 *Tristram.* Edwin Arlington Robinson
1929 *John Brown's Body.* Stephen Vincent Benét
1930 *Selected Poems.* Conrad Aiken
1931 *Collected Poems.* Robert Frost
1932 *The Flowering Stone.* George Dillon
1933 *Conquistador.* Archibald MacLeish
1934 *Collected Verse.* Robert Hillyer
1935 *Bright Ambush.* Audrey Wurdemann
1936 *Strange Holiness.* Robert P. T. Coffin
1937 *A Further Range.* Robert Frost
1938 *Cold Morning Sky.* Marya Zaturenska
1939 *Selected Poems.* John Gould Fletcher
1940 *Collected Poems.* Mark Van Doren
1941 *Sunderland Capture.* Leonard Bacon
1942 *The Dust Which Is God.* William Rose Benét
1943 *A Witness Tree.* Robert Frost
1944 *Western Star.* Stephen Vincent Benét
1945 *V-Letter and Other Poems.* Karl Shapiro
1947 *Lord Weary's Castle.* Robert Lowell
1948 *The Age of Anxiety.* W. H. Auden
1949 *Terror and Decorum.* Peter Viereck
1950 *Annie Allen.* Gwendolyn Brooks
1951 *Complete Poems.* Carl Sandburg
1952 *Collected Poems.* Marianne Moore
1953 *Collected Poems, 1917–1952.* Archibald MacLeish
1954 *The Waking.* Theodore Roethke
1955 *Collected Poems.* Wallace Stevens
1956 *Poems—North & South.* Elizabeth Bishop
1957 *Things of This World.* Richard Wilbur
1958 *Promises: Poems, 1954–1956.* Robert Penn Warren
1959 *Selected Poems, 1928–1958.* Stanley Kunitz
1960 *Heart's Needle.* William Snodgrass
1961 *Times Three: Selected Verse From Three Decades.* Phyllis McGinley
1962 *Poems.* Alan Dugan
1963 *Pictures From Breughel.* William Carlos Williams

1. The poetry prize was established in 1922. The 1918 and 1919 awards were made from gifts provided by the Poetry Society.

1964 *At the End of the Open Road.* Louis Simpson
1965 *77 Dream Songs.* John Berryman
1966 *Selected Poems.* Richard Eberhart
1967 *Live or Die.* Anne Sexton
1968 *The Hard Hours.* Anthony Hecht
1969 *Of Being Numerous.* George Oppen
1970 *Untitled Subjects.* Richard Howard
1971 *The Carrier of Ladders.* William S. Merwin
1972 *Collected Poems.* James Wright
1973 *Up Country.* Maxine Winokur Kumin
1974 *The Dolphin.* Robert Lowell
1975 *Turtle Island.* Gary Snyder
1976 *Self-Portrait in a Convex Mirror.* John Ashbery
1977 *Divine Comedies.* James Merrill
1978 *Collected Poems.* Howard Nemerov
1979 *Now and Then: Poems, 1976–1978.* Robert Penn Warren
1980 *Selected Poems.* Donald Rodney Justice
1981 *The Morning of the Poem.* James Schuyler
1982 *The Collected Poems.* Sylvia Plath
1983 *Selected Poems.* Galway Kinnell
1984 *American Primitive.* Mary Oliver
1985 *Yin,* Carolyn Kizer
1986 *The Flying Change,* Henry Taylor
1987 *Thomas and Beulah,* Rita Dove
1988 *Partial Accounts: New and Selected Poems.* William Meredith
1989 *New and Collected Poems.* Richard Wilbur
1990 *The World Doesn't End,* Charles Simic
1991 *Near Changes,* Mona Van Duyn
1992 *Selected Poems,* James Tate
1993 *The Wild Iris,* Louise Gluck
1994 *Neon Vernacular,* Yusef Komunyakaa
1995 *Simple Truth,* Philip Levine
1996 *The Dream of the Unified Field,* Jorie Graham

GENERAL NONFICTION

1962 *The Making of the President, 1960.* Theodore H. White
1963 *The Guns of August.* Barbara W. Tuchman
1964 *Anti-Intellectualism in American Life.* Richard Hofstadter
1965 *O Strange New World.* Howard Mumford Jones
1966 *Wandering Through Winter.* Edwin Way Teale
1967 *The Problem of Slavery in Western Culture.* David Brion Davis
1968 *Rousseau and Revolution.* Will and Ariel Durant
1969 *So Human an Animal.* Rene Jules Dubos; *The Armies of the Night.* Norman Mailer
1970 *Gandhi's Truth.* Erik H. Erikson
1971 *The Rising Sun.* John Toland
1972 *Stilwell and the American Experience in China, 1911–1945.* Barbara W. Tuchman
1973 *Fire in the Lake: The Vietnamese and the Americans in Vietnam.* Frances FitzGerald; and *Children of Crisis* (Vols. 1 and 2). Robert M. Coles
1974 *The Denial of Death.* Ernest Becker
1975 *Pilgrim at Tinker Creek.* Annie Dillard
1976 *Why Survive? Being Old in America.* Robert N. Butler
1977 *Beautiful Swimmers: Watermen, Crabs and the Chesapeake Bay.* William W. Warner
1978 *The Dragons of Eden.* Carl Sagan
1979 *On Human Nature.* Edward O. Wilson
1980 *Gödel, Escher, Bach: An Eternal Golden Braid.* Douglas R. Hofstadter
1981 *Fin-de-Siecle Vienna: Politics and Culture.* Carl E. Schorske
1982 *The Soul of a New Machine.* Tracy Kidder
1983 *Is There No Place on Earth for Me?* Susan Sheehan
1984 *Social Transformation of American Medicine.* Paul Starr
1985 *The Good War: An Oral History of World War II,* Studs Terkel
1986 *Move Your Shadow: South Africa, Black and White,* Joseph Lelyveld; *Common Ground: A Turbulent Decade in the Lives of Three American Families,* J. Anthony Lukas

1987 *Arab and Jew: Wounded Spirits in a Promised Land,* David K. Shipler	**1963** *Piano Concerto No. 1.* Samuel Barber
1988 *The Making of the Atomic Bomb.* Richard Rhodes	**1966** *Variations for Orchestra.* Leslie Bassett
1989 *A Bright Shining Lie.* Neil Sheehan	**1967** *Quartet No. 3.* Leon Kirchner
1990 *And Their Children After Them,* Dale Maharidge and Michael Williamson	**1968** *Echoes of Time and the River.* George Crumb

1987 *Arab and Jew: Wounded Spirits in a Promised Land,* David K. Shipler
1988 *The Making of the Atomic Bomb.* Richard Rhodes
1989 *A Bright Shining Lie.* Neil Sheehan
1990 *And Their Children After Them,* Dale Maharidge and Michael Williamson
1991 *The Ants,* Bert Holldobler and Edward O. Wilson
1992 *The Prize: The Epic Quest for Oil, Money and Power,* Daniel Yergin
1993 *Lincoln at Gettysburg: The Words That Remade America,* Garry Wills
1994 *Lenin's Tomb: The Last Days of the Soviet Empire,* David Remick
1995 *The Beak of the Finch: A Story of Evolution in Our Time,* Jonathan Weiner
1996 *The Haunted Land: Facing Europe's Ghosts After Communism,* Tina Rosenberg

PULITZER PRIZES IN MUSIC

1943 *Secular Cantata No. 2, A Free Song.* William Schuman
1944 *Symphony No. 4* (Op. 34). Howard Hanson
1945 *Appalachian Spring.* Aaron Copland
1946 *The Canticle of the Sun.* Leo Sowerby
1947 *Symphony No. 3.* Charles Ives
1948 *Symphony No. 3.* Walter Piston
1949 *Louisiana Story* music. Virgil Thomson
1950 *The Consul.* Gian Carlo Menotti
1951 Music for opera *Giants in the Earth.* Douglas Stuart Moore
1952 *Symphony Concertante.* Gail Kubik
1954 *Concerto for Two Pianos and Orchestra.* Quincy Porter
1955 *The Saint of Bleecker Street.* Gian Carlo Menotti
1956 *Symphony No. 3.* Ernst Toch
1957 *Meditations on Ecclesiastes.* Norman Dello Joio
1958 *Vanessa.* Samuel Barber
1959 *Concerto for Piano and Orchestra.* John La Montaine
1960 *Second String Quartet.* Elliott Carter
1961 *Symphony No. 7.* Walter Piston
1962 *The Crucible.* Robert Ward

1963 *Piano Concerto No. 1.* Samuel Barber
1966 *Variations for Orchestra.* Leslie Bassett
1967 *Quartet No. 3.* Leon Kirchner
1968 *Echoes of Time and the River.* George Crumb
1969 *String Quartet No. 3.* Karel Husa
1970 *Time's Encomium.* Charles Wuorinen
1971 *Synchronisms No. 6 for Piano and Electronic Sound.* Mario Davidowsky
1972 *Windows.* Jacob Druckman
1973 *String Quartet No. 3.* Elliott Carter
1974 *Notturno.* Donald Martino
1975 *From the Diary of Virginia Woolf.* Dominick Argento
1976 *Air Music.* Ned Rorem
1977 *Visions of Terror and Wonder.* Richard Wernick
1978 *Déjà Vu for Percussion Quartet and Orchestra.* Michael Colgrass
1979 *Aftertones of Infinity.* Joseph Schwantner
1980 *In Memory of a Summer Day.* David Del Tredici
1981 Not awarded
1982 *Concerto for Orchestra.* Roger Sessions
1983 *Three Movements for Orchestra.* Ellen T. Zwilich
1984 *Canti del Sole.* Bernard Rands
1985 *Symphony RiverRun,* Stephen Albert
1986 *Wind Quintet IV,* George Perle
1987 *The Flight Into Egypt,* John Harbison
1988 *12 New Etudes for Piano.* William Bolcom
1989 *Whispers Out of Time,* Roger Reynolds
1990 *Duplicates: A Concerto for Two Pianos and Orchestra,* Mel Powell
1991 *Symphony,* Shulamit Ran
1992 *The Face of the Night, The Heart of the Dark,* Wayne Peterson
1993 *Trombone Concerto,* Christopher Rouse
1994 *Of Reminiscences and Reflections,* Gunther Schuller
1995 *Stringmusic,* Morton Gould
1996 *Lilacs,* George Walker

SPECIAL AWARD

1992 *Maus,* Art Spiegelman

Winners of Bollingen Prize in Poetry

($5,000[1] award is given biennially. It is administered by Yale University and the Bollingen Foundation.)

1949	Ezra Pound	1967	Robert Penn Warren
1950	Wallace Stevens	1969	John Berryman and Karl Shapiro
1951	John Crowe Ransom	1971	Richard Wilbur and Mona Van Duyn
1952	Marianne Moore	1973	James Merrill
1953	Archibald MacLeish and William Carlos Williams	1975	Archie Randolph Ammons
1954	W. H. Auden	1977	David Ignatow
1955	Léonie Adams and Louise Bogan	1979	W. S. Merwin
1956	Conrad Aiken	1981	Howard Nemerov and May Swenson
1957	Allen Tate	1983	Anthony Hecht and John Hollander
1958	E.E. Cummings	1985	John Ashbery and Fred Chappell
1959	Theodore Roethke	1987	Stanley Kunitz
1960	Delmore Schwartz	1989	Edgar Bowers
1961	Yvor Winters	1991	Laura Riding Jackson and Donald Justin
1962	John Hall Wheelock and Richard Eberhart	1993	Mark Strand
1963	Robert Frost	1995	Kenneth Koch
1965	Horace Gregory		

1. Beginning 1989 award increased to $10,000. It now stands at $25,000.

1996 Bancroft Prizes in American History

Walt Whitman's America: A Cultural Biography, by David S. Reynolds (Alfred A. Knopf)

William Cooper's Town: Power and Persuasion on the Frontier of the Early American Republic, by Alan Taylor (Alfred A. Knopf)

New York Drama Critics' Circle Awards

1935–36
Winterset, Maxwell Anderson
1936–37
High Tor, Maxwell Anderson
1937–38
Of Mice and Men, John Steinbeck
Shadow and Substance, Paul Vincent Carroll[1]
1938–39
(No award) *The White Steed,* Paul Vincent Carroll[1]
1939–40
The Time of Your Life, William Saroyan
1940–41
Watch on the Rhine, Lillian Hellman
The Corn Is Green, Emlyn Williams[1]
1941–42
(No award) *Blithe Spirit,* Noel Coward[1]
1942–43
The Patriots, Sidney Kingsley
1943–44
(No award) *Jacobowsky and the Colonel.* Franz Werfel and S. N. Behrman[1]
1944–45
The Glass Menagerie, Tennessee Williams
1945–46
(No award) *Carousel,* Richard Rodgers and Oscar Hammerstein II[2]
1946–47
All My Sons, Arthur Miller
No Exit, Jean-Paul Sartre[1]
Brigadoon, Alan Jay Lerner and Frederick Loewe[2]
1947–48
A Streetcar Named Desire, Tennessee Williams
The Winslow Boy, Terence Rattigan[1]
1948–49
Death of a Salesman, Arthur Miller
The Madwoman of Chaillot, Jean Giraudoux and Maurice Valency[1]
South Pacific, Richard Rodgers, Oscar Hammerstein II, and Joshua Logan[2]
1949–50
The Member of the Wedding, Carson McCullers
The Cocktail Party, T. S. Eliot[1]
The Consul, Gian Carlo Menotti[2]
1950–51
Darkness at Noon, Sidney Kingsley[3]
The Lady's Not for Burning, Christopher Fry[1]
Guys and Dolls, Abe Burrows, Jo Swerling, and Frank Loesser[2]
1951–52
I Am a Camera, John Van Druten[4]
Venus Observed, Christopher Fry[1]
Pal Joey, Richard Rodgers, Lorenz Hart, and John O'Hara[2]
Don Juan in Hell, George B. Shaw[5]
1952–53
Picnic, William Inge *The Love of Four Colonels,* by Peter Ustinov[1]
Wonderful Town, Joseph Fields, Jerome Chodorov, Betty Comden, Adolph Green, and Leonard Bernstein[2]
1953–54
The Teahouse of the August Moon, John Patrick
Ondine, Jean Giraudoux[1]
The Golden Apple, John Latouche and Jerome Moross[2]
1954–55
Cat on a Hot Tin Roof, Tennessee Williams
Witness for the Prosecution, Agatha Christie[1]
The Saint of Bleecker Street, Gian Carlo Menotti[2]
1955–56
The Diary of Anne Frank, Frances Goodrich and Albert Hackett
Tiger at the Gates, Jean Giraudoux and Christopher Fry[1]

My Fair Lady, Frederick Loewe and Alan Jay Lerner[2]
1956–57
Long Day's Journey Into Night, Eugene O'Neill
Waltz of the Toreadors, Jean Anouilh[1]
The Most Happy Fella, Frank Loesser[2 6]
1957–58
Look Homeward, Angel, Ketti Frings[7]
Look Back in Anger, John Osborne[1]
The Music Man, Meredith Willson[2]
1958–59
A Raisin in the Sun, Lorraine Hansberry
The Visit, Friedrich Duerrenmatt-Maurice Valency[1]
La Plume de ma Tante, Robert Dhery and Gerard Calvi[2]
1959–60
Toys in the Attic, Lillian Hellman
Five Finger Exercise, Peter Shaffer[1]
Fiorello!, Jerome Weidman, George Abbott, Jerry Bock, and Sheldon Harnick[2]
1960–61
All the Way Home, Tad Mosel[3]
A Taste of Honey, Shelagh Delaney[1]
Carnival, Michael Stewart[2]
1961–62
The Night of the Iguana, Tennessee Williams
A Man for All Seasons, Robert Bolt[1]
How to Succeed in Business Without Really Trying, Abe Burrows, Jack Weinstock, Willie Gilbert, and Frank Loesser[2 9]
1962–63
Who's Afraid of Virginia Woolf?, Edward Albee
Beyond the Fringe, Alan Bennett, Peter Cook, Jonathan Miller, and Dudley Moore[10]
1963–64
Luther, John Osborne
Hello, Dolly!, Michael Stewart and Jerry Herman[2 11]
The Trojan Women, Euripides[10 12]
1964–65
The Subject Was Roses, Frank D. Gilroy
Fiddler on the Roof, Joseph Stein, Jerry Bock, and Sheldon Harnick[2 13]
1965–66
The Persecution and Assassination of Marat as Performed by the Inmates of the Asylum of Charenton Under the Direction of the Marquis de Sade, Peter Weiss
The Man of La Mancha, Dale Wasserman, Mitch Leigh, and Joe Darion
1966–67
The Homecoming, Harold Pinter
Cabaret, Joe Masteroff, John Kander, and Fred Ebb[2 14]
1967–68
Rosencrantz and Guildenstern Are Dead, Tom Stoppard
Your Own Thing, Donald Driver, Hal Hester, and Danny Apolinar[2]
1968–69
The Great White Hope, Howard Sackler
1776, Sherman Edwards and Peter Stone[2]
1969–70
Borstal Boy, Frank McMahon[15]
The Effect of Gamma Rays on Man-in-the-Moon Marigolds, Paul Zindel[16]
Company, George Furth and Stephen Sondheim[2]
1970–71
Home, David Storey
The House of Blue Leaves, John Guare[16]
Follies, James Goldman and Stephen Sondheim[2]
1971–72
That Championship Season, Jason Miller
Two Gentlemen of Verona, adapted by John Guare and Mel Shapiro[2]

The Screens, Jean Genet[1]
1972–73
The Changing Room, David Storey
The Hot l Baltimore, by Lanford Wilson[16]
A Little Night Music, Hugh Wheeler and Stephen Sondheim[2]
1973–74
The Contractors, David Storey
Short Eyes, Miguel Piñero[16]
Candide, Leonard Bernstein, Hugh Wheeler, and Richard Wilbur[2]
1974–75
Equus, Peter Shaffer
The Taking of Miss Janie, Ed Bullins[16]
A Chorus Line, James Kirkwood and Nicholas Dante[2]
1975–76
Travesties, Tom Stoppard
Streamers, David Rabe[16]
Pacific Overtures, Stephen Sondheim, John Weidman, and Hugh Wheeler[2]
1976–77
Otherwise Engaged, Simon Gray
American Buffalo, David Mamet[16]
Annie, Thomas Meehan, Charles Strouse, and Martin Charnin[2]
1977–78
Da, Hugh Leonard
Ain't Misbehavin', conceived by Richard Maltby, Jr.[2]
1978–79
The Elephant Man, Bernard Pomerance
Sweeney Todd, Hugh Wheeler and Stephen Sondheim[2]
1979–80
Talley's Folly, Lanford Wilson
Evita,[2] Andrew Lloyd Webber and Tim Rice
Betrayal, Harold Pinter[1]
1980–81
A Lesson From Aloes, Athol Fugard
Crimes of the Heart, Beth Henley[16]
1981–82
The Life and Adventures of Nicholas Nickleby, adapted by David Edgar
A Soldier's Play, Charles Fuller[16]
1982–83
Brighton Beach Memoirs, Neil Simon
Plenty, David Hare[1]
Little Shop of Horrors, Alan Menken and Howard Ashman[2] [17]
1983–84
The Real Thing, Tom Stoppard
Glengarry Glen Ross, David Mamet[16]
Sunday in the Park with George, Stephen W Sondheim and James Lapine[2]
1984–85
Ma Rainey's Black Bottom, August Wilson
(No award for best musical or foreign play)
1985–86
Lie of the Mind, Sam Shepard
Benefactors, Michael Frayn[1]
The Search for Signs of Intelligent Life in the Universe, Lily Tomlin and Jane Wagner[10]
(No award for best musical)

1986–87
Fences, August Wilson
Les Liaisons Dangereuses, Christopher Hampton[1]
Les Miserables, Claude-Michel Schonberg and Alain Boublil[2]
1987–88
Joe Turner's Come and Gone, August Wilson
The Road to Mecca, Athol Fugard[1]
Into the Woods, Stephen Sondheim and James Lapine[2]
1988–89
The Heidi Chronicles, Wendy Wasserstein
Aristocrats, Brian Friel[1]
Largely New York, Bill Irwin[10]
(No award for best musical)
1989–90
The Piano Lesson, August Wilson
Privates on Parade, Peter Nichols[1]
City of Angels, Larry Gelbart, Cy Coleman, and David Zippel[2]
1990–91
Six Degrees of Separation, John Guare
Our Country's Good, Timberlake Wertenbaker[1]
The Will Rogers Follies, Cy Coleman, Peter Stone, Betty Comden, and Adolph Green[2]
Eileen Atkins, *A Room of One's Own*[10]
1991–92
Dancing at Lughnasa, Brian Friel
Two Trains Running, August Wilson[16]
(No award for best musical)
1992-93
Angels in America: Millennium Approaches, Tony Kushner
Someone Who'll Watch Over Me, Frank McGuinness[1]
Kiss of the Spider Woman, John Kander, Fred Ebb and Terrence McNally[2]
1993–94
Three Tall Women, Edward Albee
Twilight: Los Angeles, 1992, Anna Deavere Smith, writer/actress, a special award "for unique contribution to theatrical form."
(No award for best foreign play or best musical)
1994–95
Arcadia, Tom Stoppard
Love! Valour! Compassion! Terrence McNally
Signature Theater Company for outstanding achievement.
(No award for best musical or best foreign play)
1995–96
Seven Guitars, August Wilson
Rent, Jonathan Larson[2]
Molly Sweeney, Brian Friel[1]

1. Citation for best foreign play. 2. Citation for best musical. 3. Based on a novel by Arthur Koestler. 4. Based on Christopher Isherwood's *Berlin Stories.* 5. For "distinguished and original contribution to the theater." 6. Based on Sidney Howard's *They Knew What They Wanted.* 7. Based on a novel by Thomas Wolfe. 8. Based on James Agee's *A Death in the Family.* 9. Based on a book by Shepherd Mead. 10. Special citation. 11. Based on Thornton Wilder's *The Matchmaker.* 12. Translated by Edith Hamilton. 13. Based on Sholem Aleichem's Tevye stories, translated by Arnold Perl. 14. Based on John Van Druten's *I Am a Camera,* which won the award for the best play in 1951–52. 15. Based on Brendan Behan's autobiography. 16. Citation for best American play. 17. Based on a story by Roger Corman.

1996 Obie Award Winners

Best New American Play: Adrienne Kennedy, *June and Jean in Concert,* and *Sleep Deprivation Chamber* (with Adam Kennedy)

Performance: Gerry Bamman, *Nixon's Nixon;* Lisa Gay Hamilton, *Valley Song;* Terri Klausner, *Bed and Sofa;* Tom McGowan, *The Food Chain;* Mark Nelson, *Picasso at the Lapin Agile;* Adina Porter, *Venus;* Virginia Rambal, *Troya de America* and *La Dama Duende;* Rose the Dog (Julie Archer and Barbara Pollitt), *Epidog;* Rocco Sisto, *Quills;*

Steven Skybell, *Antigone in New York;* Derek Smith, *The Green Bird;* James Urbaniak, *The Universe;* Mary Louise Wilson, *Full Gallop*

Playwriting: Ain Gordon, *Wally's Ghost;* Donald Margulies, *The Model Apartment;* Suzan-Lori Parks, *Venus;* Doug Wright, *Quills*

Direction: Doug Hughes, *The Grey Zone*

Sustained Achievement: Uta Hagen

Antoinette Perry (Tony) Awards, 1996

Play: *Master Class,* Terrence McNally
Musical: *Rent*
Actor, leading (play): George Grizzard, *A Delicate Balance*
Actress, leading (play): Zoe Caldwell, *Master Class*
Actor, leading (musical): Nathan Lane, *A Funny Thing Happened on the Way to the Forum*
Actress, leading (musical): Donna Murphy, *The King and I*
Actor, featured (play): Ruben Santiago-Hudson, *Seven Guitars*
Actress, featured (play): Audra McDonald, *Master Class*
Actor, featured (musical): Wilson Jermaine Heredia, *Rent*
Actress, featured (musical): Ann Duquesnay, *Bring in da Noise, Bring In da Funk*
Director (play): Gerald Gutierrez, *A Delicate Balance*

Director (musical): George C. Wolfe, *Bring In da Noise, Bring In da Funk*
Book of a musical: *Rent*
Original score: *Rent*
Play revival: *A Delicate Balance*
Musical revival: *The King and I*
Scenic design: Brian Thomson, *The King and I*
Costume design: Roger Kirk, *The King and I*
Lighting design: Jules Fisher and Peggy Eisenhauer, *Bring In da Noise, Bring In da Funk*
Choreography: Savion Glover, *Bring In da Noise, Bring In da Funk*
Regional theater: Alley Theater, Houston

1996 National Magazine Awards

Feature writing: *GQ* (Gentlemen's Quarterly) for an article about a man who raped children by Philip Junod
Fiction: *Harper's* for three stories by Mark Slouka, George Saunders, and Tova Reich
Reporting: *The New Yorker* for "The Politics of Perception" by Connie Bruck
Essays and criticism: *The New Yorker* for essays and art criticism by Simon Schama
Public interest: *Texas Monthly* for an article about a doctor battling the health care system
Special-interest: *Saveur* for an article on Cajun food

Personal service: *Smart Money*
Single-topic issue: *Bon Appetit* on Mediterranean food
Design: *Wired*
Photography: *Saveur*
General excellence: (for magazines with a circulation of more than one million): *Business Week;* (for magazines with a circulation of 400,000 to one million): *Outside;* (for magazines with a circulation of 100,000 to 400,000): *Civilization;* (for magazines with a circulation of under 100,000): *The Sciences*

Alfred I. du Pont-Columbia University Broadcast News Awards

(For work broadcast between July 1, 1994, and June 30, 1995)

Gold Baton Award: Daniel Schorr for a 40-year career as a television and radio news correspondent at CBS News, CNN, and National Public Radio.
Silver Baton Awards: ABC News: its news magazine "Turning Point" for a report on contemporary slavery and its "World News Tonight" for reports on Republican legislative efforts to reverse environmental policies. PBS's "Frontline" won for a report examining issues of race and education in a California high school and its "The American Experience" was honored for "The Battle of the Bulge," "F.D.R.," and "The Way West." The Discovery Channel won for its five-hour documentary series "Watergate." WXYZ-TV in Detroit won for a three-part series on the citizens' militia movement in

Michigan and WTVJ-TV in Miami and its reporter Kerry Sanders won for coverage of political events in Haiti. Three independent television productions were honored: "Blackside Inc.," for its five-hour series "America's War on Poverty"; Deborah Hoffmann and the PBS Series "P.O.V." for "Complaints of a Dutiful Daughter," on the effects of Alzheimer's disease on family members; and Billy Golfus and David E. Simpson for a documentary "When Billy Broke His Head . . . And Other Tales of Wonder," about living with physical disabilities. Radio awards went to WMAL-AM Washington for its coverage of plans by the Disney Company to built a history theme park in Virginia and National Public Radio for political coverage on several of its regular programs.

1996 Christopher Awards

Adult Books

Amazing Grace: The Lives of Children and the Conscience of a Nation, by Jonathan Kozol (Crown)
Bound to Forgive: The Pilgrimage to Reconciliation of a Beirut Hostage, by Lawrence Martin Jenco, O.S.M. (Ave Maria Press)
Lincoln, by David Herbert Donald (Simon & Schuster)
Love Letters From Cell 92: The Correspondence Between Dietrich Bonhoeffer and Maria von Wedemeyer 1943–45, edited by Ruth–Alice von Bismarck and Ulrich Kabitz; translated by John Brownjohn (Abingdon)
Not By the Sword: How the Love of a Cantor and His Family Transformed a Klansman, by Kathryn Watterson (Simon & Schuster)
One Small Sparrow, by Jeff Leeland (Multnomah Books)
The Railway Man: A POW's Searing Account of War, Brutality and Forgiveness, by Eric Lomax (Norton)

Young People's Books

The Christmas Miracle of Jonathan Toomey, by Susan Wojciechowski, illustrated by P.J. Lynch (Candlewich Press)

Been to Yesterdays: Poems of a Life, by Lee Bennett Hopkins, illustrated by Charlene Rendeiro (Wordsong/Boyds Mills Press)
Mother Jones: One Woman's Fight for Labor, by Betsy Harvey Kraft (Clarion Books)
Parallel Journeys, by Eleanor Ayer, with Helen Waterford and Alfons Heck (Young Adult, Atheneum)

Television Specials

The Christmas Box (CBS)
Discovering Women (WGBH/PBS)
If Someone Had Known (NBC)
Living on the Edge (PBS *Frontline* Series)
The More You Know (NBC)
The Piano Lesson (CBS)

Films

Apollo 13 (Universal Pictures)
Cry, The Beloved Country (Miramax)
Dead Man Walking (Gramercy Pictures)

Life Achievement Award

David Brinkley: Host of the ABC TV news program, *This Week with David Brinkley,* for outstanding broadcast journalism for the past five decades.

National Book Awards, 1995

Established by Association of American Publishers

(American Book Awards 1980–86. Reverted to original name in 1987.)

Fiction: *Sabbath's Theater,* by Philip Roth (Houghton Mifflin)

Nonfiction: *The Haunted Land: Facing Europe's Ghosts After Communism,* by Tina Rosenberg (Random House)

Poetry: *Passing Through: The Later Poems, New and Selected,* by Stanley Kunitz (W.W. Norton)

The National Book Foundation Medal for Distinguished Contribution to American Letters: David McCullough, author of works of history and biography.

National Book Critics Circle Awards, 1996

Fiction: *Mrs. Ted Bliss* by Stanley Elkin (Hyperion)

General nonfiction: *A Civil Action* by Jonathan Harr (Random House)

Poetry: *Time & Money* by William Matthews (Houghton Mifflin)

Criticism: *The Forbidden Best-Sellers of Pre-Revolutionary France* by Robert Darnton (W.W. Norton)

Biography/Autobiography: *Savage Art: A Biography of Jim Thompson* by Robert Polito (Alfred A. Knopf)

The Nona Balakian Excellence in Reviewing Award: Laurie Stone

Iva Sandrof Award for Lifetime Achievement in Publishing: Alfred Kazin and Elizabeth Hardwick

American Library Association Awards for Children's Books, 1996

(For books published in 1995)

John Newbery Medal for best book: *The Midwife's Apprentice,* Karen Cushman (Clarion Books)

Newbery Honor Books: *What Jamie Saw,* Carolyn Coman (Front Street); *The Watsons Go to Birmingham: 1963,* Christopher Paul Curtis (Delacorte Press); *Yolanda's Genius,* Carol Fenner (Margaret K. McElderry Books/Simon & Schuster); and *The Great Fire,* Jim Murphy (Scholastic)

Randolph Caldecott Medal for best picture book: *Officer Buckle and Gloria,* Peggy Rathmann (G.P. Putnam's Sons)

Caldecott Honor Books: *Alphabet City,* Stephen T. Johnson (Viking); *Zin! Zin! Zin! A Violin,* illustrated by Marjorie Priceman, written by Lloyd Moss (Simon & Schuster Books for Young Readers); *The Faithful Friend,* illustrated by Brian Pinkney, written by Robert D. Sans Souci (Simon & Schuster Books for Young Readers); *Tops & Bottoms,* Janet Stevens (Harcourt Brace)

The Coretta Scott King Award: *Her Stores,* Virginia Hamilton, illustrated by Bonnie Verberg (Scholastic)

The Mildred L. Batchelder Award, for the most outstanding book originally published in a foreign language: *The Lady With the Hat,* Uri Orlev, translated from the Hebrew by Hillel Halkin (Houghton Mifflin)

Margaret A. Edwards Award for Outstanding Literature for Young Adults: Judy Blume, a lifetime achievement award.

Kingsley Tufts Poetry Prize

$50,000 award given to a poet for a book published in the previous year. Established 1992, it is administered by the Claremont (California) Graduate School.

1993 Susan Mitchell, *Rapture*
1994 Yusef Komunyakaa, *Neon Vernacular*
1995 Thomas Lux, *Split Horizon*
1996 Deborah Digges, *Rough Music*

Poets Laureate of the United States

The post was established in 1985. Appointment is for a one-year term, but is renewable.

Robert Penn Warren	1986–1987	Joseph Brodsky	1991–1992
Richard Wilbur	1987–1988	Mona Van Duyn	1992–1993
Howard Nemerov	1988–1990	Rita Dove	1993–1995
Mark Strand	1990–1991	Robert Hass	1995–1997

Poets Laureate of England

Edmund Spenser	1591–1599	Laurence Eusden	1718–1730	Alfred Lord Tennyson	1850–1892
Samuel Daniel	1599–1619	Colley Cibber	1730–1757	Alfred Austin	1896–1913
Ben Jonson	1619–1637	William Whitehead	1757–1785	Robert Bridges	1913–1930
William Davenant	1638–1668	Thomas Warton	1785–1790	John Masefield	1930–1967
John Dryden[1]	1670–1689	Henry James Pye	1790–1813	C. Day Lewis	1967–1972
Thomas Shadwell	1689–1692	Robert Southey	1813–1843	Sir John Betjeman	1972–1984
Nahum Tate	1692–1715	William Wordsworth	1843–1850	Ted Hughes	1984–
Nicholas Rowe	1715–1718				

1. First to bear the title officially. *Source: Encyclopaedia Britannica.*

1996 MacArthur Foundation Awards

James Roger Prior Angel, 55, astronomer; Tucson, Ariz.
Joaquin G. Avila, 48, litigator; Fremont, Calif.
Allan Bérubé, 49, social historian; San Francisco, Calif.
Barbara Block, 38, marine animal physiologist; Monterey, Calif.
Joan Breton Connelly, 42, archaeologist and art historian; New York, N.Y.
Thomas L. Daniel, 41, biologist; Seattle, Wash.
Martin Daniel Eakes, 41, community organizer; Durham, N.C.
Rebecca Goldstein, 46, novelist; Highland Park, N.J.
Robert Greenstein, 50, public policy analyst; Washington, D.C.
Richard Howard, 66, poet, translator, critic, and editor; New York, N.Y.

John Jesurun, 45, theater director and writer; New York, N.Y.
Richard E. Lenski, 39, biologist; East Lansing, Mich.
Louis Massiah, 42, documentary film maker; Philadelphia, Pa.
Vonnie C. McLoyd, 45, developmental psychologist; Durham, N.C.
Thylias Moss, 42, poet; Ann Arbor, Mich.
Eiko Otake, 44, and **Koma Otake,** 47, dancers; New York, N.Y.
Nathan Seiberg, 39, theoretical physicist; Princeton, N.J.
Anna Deavere Smith, 45, performer and playwright; San Francisco, Calif.
Dorothy Stoneman, 54, educator; Belmont, Mass.
William Strickland, 48, community organizer; Pittsburgh, Pa.

Presidential Medal of Freedom

The nation's highest civilian award, the Presidential Medal of Freedom, was established in 1963 by President John F. Kennedy to continue and expand presidential recognition of meritorious service which, since 1945, had been granted as the Medal of Freedom. NOTE: An asterisk following a year denotes a posthumous award.

AWARDED BY PRESIDENT CLINTON

Arthur Ashe, Jr. (athlete, tennis)	1993 *
Herbert Block (cartoonist)	1994
William J. Brennan, Jr. (jurist)	1993
Peggy Charren (children's television advocate)	1995
Cesar Chavez (labor leader)	1994 *
William Thaddeus Coleman, Jr. (public servant and civil rights advocate)	1995
Joan Ganz Cooney (children's television advocate)	1995
Marjory Stoneman Douglas (conservationist)	1993
Arthur Flemming (government servant)	1994
John Hope Franklin (historian)	1995
J. William Fulbright (public servant)	1993
James Grant (Executive Director, UNICEF)	1994
Dorothy Height (civil rights leader)	1994
A. Leon Higginbotham, Jr. (jurist and civil rights advocate)	1995
Frank M. Johnson, Jr. (jurist)	1995

Barbara Jordan (public servant)	1994
Lane Kirkland (labor leader)	1994
C. Everett Koop (public health worker)	1995
Thurgood Marshall (jurist)	1993 *
Robert H. Michel (public servant)	1994
Gaylord A. Nelson (public servant and conservationist)	1995
General Colin L. Powell[1] (soldier)	1993
Joseph L. Raugh, Jr. (civil rights and labor activist)	1993 *
Martha Raye (entertainer)	1993
Walter P. Reuther (labor leader)	1995
James W. Rouse (urban planner)	1995
R. Sargent Shriver (government servant)	1994
William C. Velasquez (voting rights advocate)	1995 *
Lew R. Wasserman (media executive)	1995
John Minor Wisdom (public servant)	1993

1. With Distinction.

Enrico Fermi Award

Named in honor of Enrico Fermi, the atomic pioneer, the $100,000 award is given in recognition of "exceptional and altogether outstanding" scientific and technical achievement in atomic energy.

1954 Enrico Fermi	1972 Manson Benedict	1986 Ernest D. Courant and M. Stanley Livingston
1956 John von Neumann	1976 William L. Russell	
1957 Ernest O. Lawrence	1978 Harold M. Agnew and Wolfgang K.H. Panofsky	1987 Luis W. Alvarez and Gerald F. Tape
1958 Eugene P. Wigner		
1959 Glenn T. Seaborg	1980 Alvin M. Weinberg and Rudolf E. Peirls	1988 Richard B. Setlow and Victor F. Weisskopf
1961 Hans A. Bethe		
1962 Edward Teller	1981 W. Bennett Lewis	1989 Award not given
1963 J. Robert Oppenheimer	1982 Herbert Anderson and Seth Neddermeyer	1990 George A. Cowan and Robley D. Evans
1964 Hyman G. Rickover		
1966 Otto Hahn, Lise Meitner, and Fritz Strassman	1983 Alexander Hollaender and John Lawrence	1991 Award not given
1968 John A. Wheeler	1984 Robert R. Wilson and Georges Vendryès	1992 Leon M. Lederman, Harold Brown, and John S. Foster, Jr.
1969 Walter H. Zinn		
1970 Norris E. Bradbury	1985 Norman C. Rasmussen and Marshall N. Rosenblath	1993 Freeman J. Dyson and Liane B. Russell
1971 Shields Warren and Stafford L. Warren		1994 Award not given
		1995 Ugo Fano and Martin Kamen

Recipients of Kennedy Center Honors

The Kennedy Center for the Performing Arts in Washington, D.C., created its Honors awards in 1978 to recognize the achievements of five distinguished contributors to the performing arts. Following are the recipients:

1978: Marian Anderson (contralto), Fred Astaire (dancer-actor), Richard Rodgers (Broadway composer), Arthur Rubinstein (pianist), George Balanchine (choreographer).

1979: Ella Fitzgerald (jazz singer), Henry Fonda (actor), Martha Graham (dancer-choreographer), Tennessee Williams (playwright), Aaron Copland (composer).

1980: James Cagney (actor), Leonard Bernstein (composer-conductor), Agnes de Mille (choreographer), Lynn Fontanne (actress), Leontyne Price (soprano).

1981: Count Basie (jazz composer-pianist), Cary Grant (actor), Helen Hayes (actress), Jerome Robbins (choreographer), Rudolf Serkin (pianist).

1982: George Abbott (Broadway producer), Lillian Gish (actress), Benny Goodman (jazz clarinetist), Gene Kelly (dancer-actor), Eugene Ormandy (conductor).

1983: Katherine Dunham (dancer-choreographer), Elia Kazan (director-author), James Stewart (actor), Virgil Thomson (music critic-composer), Frank Sinatra (singer).

1984: Lena Horne (singer), Danny Kaye (comedian-actor), Gian Carlo Menotti (composer), Arthur Miller (playwright), Isaac Stern (violinist).

1985: Merce Cunningham (dancer-choreographer), Irene Dunne (actress), Bob Hope (comedian), Alan Jay Lerner (lyricist-playwright), Frederick Loewe (composer), Beverly Sills (soprano and opera administrator).

1986: Lucille Ball (comedienne), Ray Charles (musician), Yehudi Menuhin (violinist), Antony Tudor (choreographer), Hume Cronyn and Jessica Tandy (husband-and-wife acting team).

1987: Perry Como (singer), Bette Davis (actress), Sammy Davis Jr. (entertainer), Nathan Milstein (violinist), Alwin Nikolais (choreographer).

1988: Alvin Ailey (choreographer), George Burns (comedian-actor), Myrna Loy (actress), Alexander Schneider (violinist), Roger L. Stevens (theatrical producer and the Kennedy Center's founding chairman).

1989: Harry Belafonte (singer-actor), Claudette Colbert (actress), Alexandra Danilova (ballerina-teacher), Mary Martin (actress), William Schuman (composer)

1990: Dizzy Gillespie (jazz trumpeter), Katharine Hepburn (actress), Risë Stevens (mezzo-soprano), Jule Styne (composer), Billy Wilder (director-author).

1991: Roy Acuff (country songwriter and singer), Betty Comden and Adloph Green (co-authors of books and lyrics of musicals), the brothers Fayard and Harold Nicholas (dancers), Gregory Peck (actor), Robert Shaw (choral director).

1992: Lionel Hampton (jazz musician), Paul Newman (actor), Joanne Woodward (actress), Ginger Rogers (dancer–actress), Mstislav Rostropovich (cellist–conductor), Paul Taylor (dancer–choreographer).

1993: Johnny Carson (talk show host), Arthur Mitchell (dancer and choreographer), Georg Solti (conductor), Stephen Sondheim (composer and lyricist), Marion Williams (gospel singer).

1994: Kirk Douglas (actor), Aretha Franklin (singer), Morton Gould (composer), Harold Prince (producer and director), Pete Seeger (folk singer and songwriter).

1995: Jacques D'Amboise (choreographer), Marilyn Horne (mezzo soprano), B.B. King (blues singer), Sidney Poitier (actor), Neil Simon (playwright).

The Spingarn Medal

The Spingarn Medal is awarded annually by the National Association for the Advancement of Colored People (NAACP) for outstanding achievement by a black American.

1915	Ernest E. Judd	1943	William H. Hastie	1969	Clarence M. Mitchell, Jr.
1916	Charles Young	1944	Charles Drew	1970	Jacob Lawrence
1917	Harry T. Burleigh	1945	Paul Robeson	1971	Leon Howard Sullivan
1918	William Stanley Braithwaite	1946	Thurgood Marshall	1972	Gordon Parks
1919	Archibald H. Grimke	1947	Percy Julian	1973	Wilson C. Riles
1920	W. E. B. Du Bois	1948	Channing H. Tobias	1974	Damon Keith
1921	Charles S. Gilpin	1949	Ralph J. Bunche	1975	Hank Aaron
1922	Mary B. Talbert	1950	Charles Hamilton Houston	1976	Alvin Ailey
1923	George Washington Carver	1951	Mabel Keaton Staupers	1977	Alex Haley
1924	Roland Hayes	1952	Harry T. Moore	1978	Andrew Young
1925	James Weldon Johnson	1953	Paul R. Williams	1979	Rosa L. Parks
1926	Carter G. Woodson	1954	Theodore K. Lawless	1980	Rayford W. Logan
1927	Anthony Overton	1955	Carl Murphy	1981	Coleman Young
1928	Charles W. Chesnutt	1956	Jackie Robinson	1982	Benjamin E. Mays
1929	Mordecai Wyatt Johnson	1957	Martin Luther King, Jr.	1983	Lena Horne
1930	Henry A. Hunt	1958	Daisy Bates and the	1984	Tom Bradley
1931	Richard Berry Harrison		Little Rock Nine	1985	Bill Cosby
1932	Robert Russa Moton	1959	Edward Kennedy (Duke)	1986	Benjamin L. Hooks
1933	Max Yergan		Ellington	1987	Percy Ellis Sutton
1934	William T. B. Williams	1960	Langston Hughes	1988	Frederick Douglass Patterson
1935	Mary McLeod Bethune	1961	Kenneth B. Clark	1989	Jesse Jackson
1936	John Hope	1962	Robert C. Weaver	1990	L. Douglas Wilder
1937	Walter White	1963	Medgar Evers	1991	Colin L. Powell
1938	No award	1964	Roy Wilkins	1992	Barbara Jordan
1939	Marian Anderson	1965	Leontyne Price	1993	Dorothy Irene Height
1940	Louis T. Wright	1966	John H. Johnson	1994	Maya Angelou
1941	Richard Wright	1967	Edward W. Brooke III	1995	John Hope Franklin
1942	A. Philip Randolph	1968	Sammy Davis, Jr.	1996	A. Leon Higginbotham, Jr.

Major Grammy Awards for Recording in 1995

Source: National Academy of Recording Arts and Sciences.

Record: "Kiss From a Rose," Seal
Album: "Jagged Little Pill," Alanis Morissette
Song: "Kiss From a Rose"
New Artist: Hootie and the Blowfish
Pop Vocalists: (Female) Annie Lennox, "No More 'I Love You's' "; (Male) Seal, "Kiss From a Rose"
Pop Duo or Group: Hootie and the Blowfish, "Let Her Cry"
Traditional Pop: "Duets II," Frank Sinatra
Rock Vocalists: (Female) Alanis Morissette, "You Oughta Know"; (Male) Tom Petty, "You Don't Know How It Feels"
Rock Duo or Group: Blues Traveler, "Run-Around"
Rock Instrumental: "Jessica," The Allman Brothers Band
Hard Rock: Pearl Jam, "Spin The Black Circle"
Metal: Nine Inch Nails, "Happiness Is Slavery"
Rhythm-and-Blues Vocalists: (Female) Anita Baker, "Apologize"; (Male) Stevie Wonder, "For Your Love"
Rhythm-and-Blues Duo or Group: T.L.C., "Creep"
Rhythm-and-Blues Song: "For Your Love," Stevie Wonder
Traditional Blues Album: "Chill Out," John Lee Hooker
Contemporary Blues Album: "Slipping In," Buddy Guy
Rap Solo: Coolio, "Gangsta's Paradise"
Rap Duo or Group: Method Man and Mary J. Blige, "I'll Be There For You/You're All I Need To Get By"
Contemporary Jazz Album: Pat Metheny Group, "We Live Here"
Jazz Vocalist: Lena Horne, "An Evening With Lena Horne"
Jazz Instrumentalists: (Solo) Michael Brecker, "Impressions"; (Individual or Group) McCoy Tyner Trio and Michael Brecker, "Infinity"
Large Jazz Ensemble Album: "All Blues," G.R.P. All-Star Big Band and Tom Scott
Country Vocalists: (Female) Alison Krauss, "Baby, Now That I've Found You"; (Male) Vince Gill, "Go Rest High on That Mountain"
Country Duo or Group: The Mavericks, "Here Comes the Rain"
Country Instrumental: "Hightower," Asleep at the Wheel
Country Song: "Go Rest High on That Mountain," Vince Gill
Rock Gospel Album: "Lesson of Love," Ashley Cleveland
Pop-Contemporary Gospel Album: "I'll Lead You Home," Michael W. Smith
Southern, Country, or Bluegrass Gospel Album: "Amazing Grace: A Country Salute to Gospel," various artists
Traditional Soul Gospel Album: "Shirley Caesar Live . . . He Will Come," Shirley Caesar
Contemoprary Soul Gospel Album: "Alone in His Presence," CeCe Winans
Gospel Album, Choir or Chorus: "Praise Him . . . Live!" Carol Cymbala, choir director
Latin Pop: Jon Secada, "Amor"
Tropical Latin: Gloria Estefan, "Abriendo Puertas"
Mexican-American: Flaco Jimenez, "Flaco Jimenez"
Traditional Folk: Ramblin' Jack Elliott, "South Coast"

Contemporary Folk: Emmylou Harris, "Wrecking Ball"
Polka Album: "I Love To Polka," Jimmy Sturr.
Reggae Album: "Boombastic," Shaggy
For Children: (Musical) "Sleepy Time Lullabys," J. Aaron Brown and David R. Lehman; (Spoken) "Prokofiev: Peter and the Wolf," Dan Broatman and Martin Sauer
Comedy: Jonathan Winters, "Crank Calls"
Spoken Word or Nonmusical: "Phenomenal Woman," Maya Angelou
Musical Show Album: "Smokey Joe's Cafe: The Songs of Leiber and Stoller"
Instrumental Composition: "A View From the Side," Bill Holman
Instrumental Composition Written for a Motion Picture or Television: "Crimson Tide," Hans Zimmer
Instrumental Arrangement: "Lament" (from "Tangence"), Robert Farnon
Music Video—Short Form: "Scream," Michael Jackson and Janet Jackson
Music Video—Long Form: "Secret World Live," Peter Gabriel
Historical Album: "The Heifetz Collection," Jascha Heifetz and various artists
Classical Album: "Debussy: 'La Mer'; Nocturnes; 'Jeux,' etc.," Pierre Boulez, Cleveland Orchestra
Classical Recording, Opera: "Berlioz: 'Les Troyens,' " Charles Dutoit, Montreal Symphony Orchestra
Classical Soloist With Orchestra: Itzhak Perlman,, "The American Album (Works of Bernstein, Barber, Foss)"; **Without Orchestra:** Radu Lupu, "Schubert: Piano Sonatas (B Flat Major and A Major)"
Chamber Music: "Brahms/Beethoven/Mozart: Clarinet Trios," Emanuel Ax, Yo-Yo Ma, and Richard Stoltzman
Classical Vocal Performance: Sylvia McNair, "The Echoing Air: The Music of Henry Purcell"
Classical Choral: "Brahms: 'Ein Deutsches Requiem,' " Herbert Blomstedt, San Francisco Symphony, San Francisco Symphony Choir and various artists
Contemporary Classical Composition: "Concert à Quatre," Olivier Messiaen
Producer: Non-Classical: Babyface; **Classical:** Steven Epstein
Engineers: Non-Classical: Dave Bianco, Richard Dodd, Stephen McLaughlin, and Jim Scott, "Wildflowers"; **Classical:** Michael Mailes and Jonathan Stokes, "Bartok: Concerto For Orchestra; 'Kossuth'; 'Symphonic Poem' "
Lifetime Achievement: Stevie Wonder, George Martin, and Dave Brubeck

TV Daytime Emmy Awards, 1996

Drama Series: *General Hospital*
Game Show: *The Price Is Right*
Pre-School Children's Series: *Sesame Street*
Talk Show: *The Oprah Winfrey Show*
Leading Actress: Erica Slezak, *One Life To Live*
Leading Actor: Charles Keating, *Another World*
Supporting Actress: Anna Holbrook, *Another World*
Supporting Actor: Jerry Ver Dorn, *Guiding Light*

Younger Actress: Kimberly McCullough, *General Hospital*
Younger Actor: Kevin Mambo, *Guiding Light*
Performer in a Children's Series: Shari Lewis, *Lamb Chop's Play-Along*
Outstanding Talk Show Host: Montel Williams
Directing Team: *The Young and the Restless*
Writing Team: *All My Children*

For Primetime Emmy Awards, see p. 1018.

ENTERTAINMENT & CULTURE

U.S. Symphony Orchestras and Their Music Directors

(With expenses over $1,050,000)

Source: American Symphony Orchestra League.

American Composers Orchestra: Dennis Russell Davies
American Symphony Orchestra: Leon Botstein
Atlanta Symphony: Yoel Levi
Austin Symphony: Sung Kwak
Baltimore Symphony: David Zinman
Baton Rouge Symphony: James Paul
Boston Symphony: Seiji Ozawa
Brooklyn Philharmonic: Robert Spano
Buffalo Philharmonic: Maximiano Valdes
Cedar Rapids Symphony: Christian Tiemeyer
Charleston Symphony: David Stahl
Charlotte Symphony: Peter McCoppin
Chattanooga Symphony & Opera Assn.: Robert Bernhardt
Chicago Symphony: Daniel Barenboim
Cincinnati Symphony: Jesus Lopez-Cobos
Cleveland Orchestra: Christoph von Dohnanyi
Colorado Springs Symphony: Yaacov Bergman[5]
Colorado Symphony (Denver): Marin Alsop
Columbus Symphony: Alessandro Siciliani
Dallas Symphony: Andrew Litton
Dayton Philharmonic: Neal Gittleman
Delaware Symphony: Stephen Gunzenhauser
Detroit Symphony: Neeme Jarvi
Florida Orchestra: Jahja Ling
Florida Philharmonic Orchestra: James Judd
Florida Symphonic Pops: Derek Stannard[3]
Florida West Coast Symphony Orchestra: Paul C. Wolfe[3]
Fort Wayne Philharmonic: Edvard Tchivzhel
Fort Worth Symphony: John Giordano
Grand Rapids Symphony: Catherine Comet
Grant Park Symphony (Chicago): Hugh Wolff[2]
Hartford Symphony: Michael Lankester
Houston Symphony: Christopher Eschenbach
Hudson Valley Philharmonic (Poughkeepsie): Randall Craig Fleischer
Indianapolis Symphony: Raymond Leppard
Jacksonville Symphony: Roger Nierenberg
Kansas City Symphony: William McGlaughlin
Knoxville Symphony: Kirk Trevor
Long Beach Symphony: JoAnn Falletta
Long Island Philharmonic: Marin Alsop
Los Angeles Chamber Orchestra: Christof Perick[2]
Los Angeles Philharmonic: Esa-Pekka Salonen
Louisville Orchestra: Max Bragado-Darman[4]
Memphis Symphony: Alan Balter
Milwaukee Symphony: Neal Gittleman[7]
Minnesota Orchestra: Eiji Oue[5]
Mississippi Symphony: Colman Pearce
Music of the Baroque: Thomas S. Wikman
Naples Philharmonic: Christopher Seaman
Nashville Symphony: Kenneth D. Schermerhorn

National Symphony (D.C.): Leonard Slatkin[5]
New Haven Symphony: Michael Palmer
New Jersey Symphony: Zdenek Macal[1]
New Mexico Symphony: David Lockington
New West Symphony: Boris Brott[3]
New World Symphony (Fla.): Michael Tilson Thomas[1]
New York Chamber Symphony of the 92nd St. Y: Gerard Schwarz
New York Philharmonic: Kurt Masur
New York Pops: Skitch Henderson
North Carolina Symphony: Gerhardt Zimmerman
Ohio Chamber Orchestra: David Lockington
Oklahoma City Philharmonic: Joel A. Levine
Omaha Symphony: Victor Yampolsky[1]
Oregon Symphony: James DePreist
Pacific Symphony (Calif.): Carl St. Clair
Philadelphia Orchestra: Wolfgang Sawallisch
Philharmonia Baroque Orchestra: Nicholas McGegan
Phoenix Symphony: James Sedares
Pittsburgh Symphony: Lorin Maazel
Portland Symphony: Toshiyuki Shimada
Puerto Rico Symphony: Eugene Kohn[6]
Rhode Island Philharmonic: Zuohuang Chen
Richmond Symphony: George Manahan
Rochester Philharmonic: Robert Bernhardt[2]
Sacramento Symphony: Geoffrey Simon
St. Louis Symphony: Hans Vonk
St. Paul Chamber Orchestra: Hugh Wolff
San Antonio Symphony: Christopher Wilkins
San Diego Symphony: Yoav Talmi
San Francisco Symphony: Michael Tilson Thomas
San Jose Symphony: Leonid Grin
Santa Barbara Symphony Orchestra: Gisele Ben-Dor
Savannah Symphony: Philp B. Greenberg
Seattle Symphony: Gerard Schwarz
Shreveport Symphony: Peter Leonard
Spokane Symphony: Fabio Mechetti
Springfield Symphony (Mass.): Mark Russell Smith
Syracuse Symphony: Fabio Mechetti
Toledo Symphony: Andrew Massey
Tucson Symphony: Robert E. Bernhardt
Tulsa Philharmonic: Bernard Rubenstein
Utah Symphony: Joseph Silverstein
Virginia Symphony: JoAnn Falletta
West Virginia Symphony: Thomas B. Conlin[1]
Wichita Symphony: Zuohuang Chen
Winston-Salem Symphony Assn.: Peter J. Perret

1. Artistic Director. 2. Principal conductor. 3. Conductor. 4. Artistic Adviser. 5. Music Director Designate. 6. Music conductor. 7. Resident conductor.

U.S. Opera Companies

(Budgets $2,000,000 and over)

Arizona Opera Company (Tucson), Glynn Ross, Gen. Dir.

Baltimore Opera Company (Md.), Michael Harrison, Gen. Dir.

Boston Lyric Opera Company (Mass.), Janice Mancini Del Sesto, Gen. Dir.

Central City Opera House Association (Colo.), Daniel R. Rule, Gen. Dir.

Cincinnati Opera Association (Ohio), James de Blasis, Art. Dir.

Civic Light Opera (Pittsburgh), Charles Gray, Exec. Dir. & Gen. Mgr.

Cleveland Opera (Ohio), David Bamberger, Gen. Dir.

Dallas Opera, The (Texas), Plato S. Karayanis, Gen. Dir.

Florentine Opera Company (Milwaukee), Dennis W. Hanthorne, Gen. Dir.

Florida Grand Opera (Miami), Robert M. Heuer, Gen. Mgr. & CEO

Gimmerglass Opera (Cooperstown, N.Y.), Paul Kellogg, Art. Dir.

Goodspeed Opera House (East Haddan, Conn.), Michael Price, Exec. Dir.

Hawaii Opera Theatre (Honolulu), J. Mario Ramos, Gen. Dir.

Houston Grand Opera Association (Texas), R. David Gockley, Gen. Dir.

Kentucky Opera (Louisville), Thomson Smillie, Gen. Dir.

Long Beach Civic Light Opera (Calif.), Barry Brown, Producer & CEO

Los Angeles Music Center Opera (Calif.), Peter Hemmings, Gen. Dir.

Lyric Opera of Chicago (Ill.), Ardis Krainik, Gen. Dir.

Lyric Opera of Kansas City (Mo.), Russell Patterson, Gen. & Art. Dir.

Metro Lyric Opera, (Allenhurst, N.J.), Era M. Tognoli, Gen. & Art. Dir.

Metropolitan Opera Association (N.Y.), James Levine, Art. Dir.

Michigan Opera Theatre (Detroit), David di Chiera, Gen. Dir.

Minnesota Opera, The (Minneapolis), Kevin Smith, President & Gen. Dir.

New York City Opera (N.Y.), Paul Kellogg, Gen. Art. Dir.

Ohio Light Opera (Wooster), James Stuart, Art. Dir.

Opera Colorado (Denver), Nathaniel Merrill, President & Gen. Dir.

Opera Company of Philadelphia (Pa.), Robert B. Driver, Gen. Dir.

Opera Pacific (Costa Mesa, Calif.), David Di Chiera, Gen. Dir.

Opera Theater Center (Aspen), Robert Hirth, President & CEO

Opera Theatre of St. Louis (Mo.), Charles MacKay, Gen. Dir.

Palm Beach Opera Inc. (Fla.), Herbert P. Benn, Gen. Dir.

Pittsburgh Opera, Inc. (Pa.), Tito Capobianco, Gen. Dir.

Portland Opera Association (Ore.), Robert Bailey, Gen. Dir.

San Diego Civic Light Opera Association (Calif.), Leon Drew, Gen. Mgr.

San Diego Opera (Calif.), Ian D. Campbell, Gen. Dir.

San Jose Civic Light Opera (Calif.), Dianna Schuster, Art. Dir.

San Francisco Opera (Calif.), Lotfi Mansouri, Gen. Dir.

San Francisco Opera Center (Calif.), Christopher Hahn, Dir.

Santa Barbara Civic Light Opera (Calif.), Paul Jannacone, Exec. Prod.

Santa Fe Opera (N.M.), John Crosby, Gen. Dir.

Sarasota Opera Association (Fla.), Deane Carroll Allyn, Exec. Dir.

Seattle Opera Association (Wash.), Speight Jenkins, Gen. Dir.

Virginia Opera (Norfolk), Peter Mark, Gen. Dir.

Utah Opera Company (Salt Lake City), Anne Ewers, Gen. Dir.

Washington Opera, The (D.C.), Martin Feinstein, Gen. Dir.

U.S. Dance Companies

(Figure in parentheses is year of founding)

Alvin Ailey American Dance Theatre (1958): Art. Dir. Judith Jamison

American Ballet Theatre (1940): Art. Dir. Kevin McKenzie

Atlanta Ballet Company (1929): Art. Dir. John McFall

Ballet West (1968[2]): Art. Dir. John Hart

Boston Ballet (1964): Art. Dir. Bruce Marks

Lucinda Childs Dance Co. (1973): Art. Dir. Lucinda Childs

Cincinnati Ballet (1955): Art. Dir. Peter Anastos

Cleveland Ballet (1976): Art. Dir. Dennis Nahat

Colorado Ballet (1961): Art. Dir. Martin Fredmann

Merce Cunningham Dance Company (1952): Dir. Merce Cunningham

Dance Theater of Harlem (1968): Art. Dir. Arthur Mitchell

Garth Fagan Dance (1970): Art. Dir. Garth Fagan

Feld Ballet New York (1974): Dir. Eliot Feld

Martha Graham Dance Company (1927): Gen. Dir. Ron Protas

Erick Hawkins Dance Co. (1951): Art. Dir. Todd Rosenleib

Houston Ballet (1968): Art. Dir. Ben Stevenson

Hubbard Street Dance Chicago (1977): Art. Dir. Lou Conte

Joffrey Ballet of Chicago[1] (1954): Art. Dir. Gerald Arpino

Bill T. Jones/Arnie Zane Dance Co. (1982): Art. Dir. Bill T. Jones

Miami City Ballet (1986): Art. Dir. Edward Villella

Milwaukee Ballet (1970): Art. Dir. Basil Thompson

Elisa Monte Dance Co. (1981): Art. Dir. Elisa Monte

Mark Morris Dance Co. (1980): Art. Dir. Mark Morris

New York City Ballet (1948): Peter Martin, Ballet Master in Chief

Ocheami-Afrikan Dance Company (1978): Art. Dir. Kofe Anag

Pacific Northwest Ballet (1972): Art. Dirs. Kent Stowell and Francia Russell

The Parsons Dance Co. (1987): Art. Dir. David Parsons

Pennsylvania Ballet (1963): Gen. Mgr. Ellen C. Moran

Pilobolus Dance Theater (1971): Art. Dirs. Robby Barnett, Alison Chase, Michael Tracy, Jonathan Wolken

Pittsburgh Ballet Theater (1970): Art. Dir. Patricia Wilde

San Francisco Ballet (1933): Art. Dir. Helgi Tomasson

Paul Taylor Dance Company (1954): Dir. Paul Taylor

Twyla Tharp Dance Co. (1965): Art. Dir. Twyla Tharp

Washington Ballet (1962): Art. Dir. Mary Day

1. Formerly Joffrey Ballet. Name changed in 1995. 2. Prior company founded 1963, name changed to Ballet West in 1968.

Bestselling Books, 1995

Source: Publishers Weekly

Hardcover Fiction

1. *The Rainmaker,* John Grisham
2. *The Lost World,* Michael Crichton
3. *Five Days in Paris,* Danielle Steel
4. *The Christmas Box,* Richard Paul Evans
5. *Lightning,* Danielle Steel
6. *The Celestine Prophecy,* James Redfield
7. *Rose Madder,* Stephen King
8. *Silent Night,* Mary Higgins Clark
9. *Politically Correct Holiday Stories,* James Finn Garner
10. *The Horse Whisperer,* Nicholas Evans

Trade Paperbacks

1. *2nd Helping of Chicken Soup for the Soul,* Jack Canfield and Mark Hansen, eds.
2. *The Calvin and Hobbes Tenth Anniversary Book,* Bill Watterson
3. *The Far Side Gallery 5,* Gary Larson
4. *Ten Stupid Things Women Do To Mess Up Their Lives,* Laura Schlessinger
5. *What to Expect the Toddler Years,* A. Eisenberg, H. Murfoff, S. Hathaway
6. *The Stone Diaries,* Carol Shields
7. *Microsoft Windows 95 Resource Kit,* Microsoft
8. *Aladdin Factor,* Jack Canfield and Mark Victor Hansen
9. *The Promise,* Thomas Nelson
10. *Snow Falling on Cedars,* David Guterson

Hardcover Nonfiction

1. *Men Are from Mars, Women Are from Venus,* John Gray
2. *My American Journey,* Colin Powell with Joseph Persico
3. *Miss America,* Howard Stern
4. *The Seven Spiritual Laws of Success,* Deepak Chopra
5. *The Road Ahead,* Bill Gates
6. *Charles Kuralt's America,* Charles Kuralt
7. *Mars and Venus in the Bedroom,* John Gray
8. *To Renew America,* Newt Gingrich
9. *My Point . . . and I Do Have One,* Ellen DeGeneres
10. *The Moral Compass,* William J. Bennett

Mass Market Paperbacks

1. *The Chamber,* John Grisham
2. *Tom Clancy's Op-Center,* Tom Clancy and Steve Pieczenik
3. *Accident,* Danielle Steel
4. *Wings,* Danielle Steel
5. *Debt of Honor,* Tom Clancy
6. *Insomnia,* Stephen King
7. *Tom Clancy's Op-Center II: Mirror Image,* Tom Clancy and Steve Pieczenik
8. *Nothing Lasts Forever,* Sidney Sheldon
9. *Remember Me,* Mary Higgins Clark
10. *Icebound,* Dean Koontz

All-Time Children's Bestsellers

From the date of publication (in parentheses) through the end of 1995. *Source: Publishers Weekly*

Hardcovers

1. *The Poky Little Puppy,* Janette Sebring Lowrey (1942)
2. *The Tale of Peter Rabbit,* Beatrix Potter (1902)
3. *Tootle,* Gertrude Crampton (1945)
4. *Saggy Baggy Elephant,* Kathryn and Byron Jackson (1955)
5. *Scuffy the Tugboat,* Gertrude Crampton (1955)
6. *Pat the Bunny,* Dorothy Kunhardt (1940)
7. *Green Eggs and Ham,* Dr. Seuss (1960)
8. *The Cat in the Hat,* Dr. Seuss (1957)
9. *The Littlest Angel,* Charles Tazewell (1946)
10. *One Fish, Two Fish, Red Fish, Blue Fish,* Dr. Seuss (1960)

Paperbacks

1. *Charlotte's Web,* E.B. White, illus. by Garth Williams (1974)
2. *The Outsiders,* S.E. Hinton (1968)
3. *Tales of a Fourth Grade Nothing,* Judy Blume (1976)
4. *Shane,* Jack Schaeffer (1983)
5. *Are You There, God? It's Me, Margaret,* Judy Blume (1972)
6. *Where the Red Fern Grows,* Wilson Rawls (1974)
7. *A Wrinkle in Time,* Madeleine L'Engle (1973)
8. *Island of the Blue Dolphins,* Scott O'Dell (1971)
9. *Little House on the Prairie,* Laura Ingalls Wilder, illus. by Garth Williams (1971)
10. *Little House in the Big Woods,* Laura Ingalls Wilder, illus. by Garth Williams (1971)

Longest Broadway Runs[1]

1.	A Chorus Line (M) (1975–90)	6,137	14.	Oklahoma (M) (1943–48)	2,377
2.	Oh, Calcutta (M) (1976–89)	5,959	15.	Man of La Mancha (M) (1965–71)	2,328
3.	Cats (M) (1982–)	5,772	16.	Abie's Irish Rose (1922–27)	2,327
4.	Les Miserables (M) (1987–)	3,861	17.	Miss Saigon (M) (1991–)	2,212
5.	Phantom of the Opera (1988–)	3,558	18.	Pippin (M) (1971–77)	1,994
6.	42nd Street (M) (1980–89)	3,486	19.	South Pacific (M) (1949–54)	1,925
7.	Grease (M) (1972–80)	3,388	20.	Magic Show (M) (1974–78)	1,920
8.	Fiddler on the Roof (M) (1964–72)	3,242	21.	Deathtrap (1978–82)	1,792
9.	Life with Father (1939–47)	3,224	22.	Gemini (1977–81)	1,788
10.	Tobacco Road (1933–41)	3,182	23.	Harvey (1944–49)	1,775
11.	Hello, Dolly! (M) (1964–71)	2,844	24.	Dancin' (M) (1978–82)	1,774
12.	My Fair Lady (M) (1956–62)	2,717	25.	Cage aux Folles (M) (1983–87)	1,761
13.	Annie (M) (1977–83)	2,377			

1. As of Aug. 4, 1996. M = musical. Years are those of opening and closing.

Major City Public Libraries

City (branches)	Volumes	Circulation	Budget (in millions)	City (branches)	Volumes	Circulation	Budget (in millions)
*Akron–Summit County, Ohio (17)	1,198,257	3,397,585	$15.5	Los Angeles County (88)	6,945,353[10]	15,100,000[11]	55.8[11]
Albuquerque, N.M. (15)	1,534,121	2,913,328	8.1	Louisville, Ky. (16)	975,850[4]	2,990,840	11.7
Annapolis, Md. (15)	1,301,625	5,156,920	11.5	Madison, Wis. (8)	714,200	2,548,463	7.2
*Atlanta–Fulton County (31)	1,960,000	2,704,000	19.5	Memphis, Tenn. (21)	1,720,046	3,737,834	14.2
Austin, Tex. (17)	1,098,586	2,433,992	10.5	Miami–Dade County, Fla. (31)[8]	3,863,700	10,015,492	32.9
Baltimore (29)	2,290,042[1]	1,556,009[2]	20.8[2]	Milwaukee (12)	2,759,494	3,070,767	17.2
Baton Rouge, La. (9)	1,040,392	2,484,339	11.1	Minneapolis (14)	2,088,309	2,815,702	16.9
*Birmingham, Ala. (19)	906,590	1,701,817	10.0	Nashville–Davidson County, Tenn. (18)	704,160[10]	1,831,200	11.3[12]
Boston (25)	6,581,736	3,500,000	30.1	*Newark, N.J. (11)	1,400,000	1,400,000	9.4
Buffalo–Erie County, N.Y. (53)	3,559,310[3]	8,559,556	24.5	New Orleans (15)	926,109	1,125,227	5.6
Charleston–Kanawha County, W.Va. (8)[2]	612,435	1,040,000	4.8	*New York City:*			
Charlotte, N.C. (22)	1,430,257	5,571,572	16.4	New York Public Library			
Chicago (80)	6,122,556[4]	7,585,960	68.2	Branches (82)	6,211,816	11,509,390	96.0
Cincinnati (41)	4,561,725	12,167,290	38.5	Research	12,485,183	—	78.6
Cleveland (27)	2,896,977	5,124,164	39.0	Brooklyn Public Library (60)	6,134,045	9,219,814	42.1
Columbus Metropolitan, Ohio (21)	2,310,808	11,158,107	32.0	Queens Borough Public Library (62)	7,963,171	14,829,837	55.0
Dallas (21)	2,298,094	4,180,638	17.2	Norfolk, Va. (11)	1,001,243[13]	558,898	4.5
Dayton–Montgomery County, Ohio (20)	1,633,332	6,206,420	16.0	Oklahoma City–County (12)	866,405	4,331,000	9.6
Denver (21)	4,005,430	6,177,555	21.7	Omaha, Neb. (9)	656,860	2,067,603	8.6[14]
Des Moines, Iowa (5)	548,495	1,406,799	4.8	Philadelphia (52)	7,881,335	6,374,491	40.0
Detroit (24)	2,718,469	1,644,486	25.5	Phoenix, Ariz. (11)	1,839,946[15]	6,505,372[15]	16.0[16]
D.C. (27)	2,163,321[4]	1,803,599	19.7	Pittsburgh (20)	2,025,316	2,903,062	16.7
*El Paso (10)	1,277,003[5]	1,731,820	6.6[6]	Portland–Multnomah County, Ore. (14)	1,458,576	7,614,507	21.3
Erie, Pa. (6)	573,103	1,634,880	3.5	Providence, R.I. (9)	1,004,746	708,405	5.0
Evansville–Vanderburgh Ind. (7)	801,618	1,485,055	5.5	Richmond, Va. (10)	814,723	814,752	3.7
Fairfax County, Va. (23)	2,100,000	9,200,000	18.4	Rochester, N.Y. (10)	2,000,000	1,582,730	10.6
Fort Wayne–Allen County, Ind. (14)	3,325,392[7]	3,986,405	4.6	Sacramento, Calif. (22)	1,659,985	3,365,822	15.4
Fort Worth (10)	1,995,760[8]	4,231,620[8]	6.9[8]	St. Louis (15)	4,895,532	2,196,246	16.5
Grand Rapids, Mich. (5)	976,640	1,084,540	6.2[8]	St. Paul (12)	1,050,555[17]	2,400,918	7.8
Greenville City–County, S.C. (11)	922,729	1,778,809	7.3	St. Petersburg, Fla. (6)	448,938	1,107,342	3.2
Hawaii State Public Library System (49)[9]	3,466,974[4]	7,499,485	20.8	Salt Lake County, Utah (15)	1,497,700	5,779,659	14.9
Houston (34)	4,237,033	6,136,811	26.7	San Antonio (18)	1,690,734[8]	3,264,013[18]	14.3
Independence, Mo. (29)	2,427,623	6,182,957	19.5	San Diego, Calif. (33)	2,465,162	6,442,096	28.2
Indianapolis–Marion County (21)	1,962,213	8,099,430	24.9	San Francisco, Calif. (26)	1,900,000	3,629,428	37.4
Jackson–Hinds County, Miss. (15)	583,324	820,523	2.9	San Jose, Calif. (18)	1,469,482[19]	4,816,079	16.9
Jacksonville, Fla. (18)	2,542,317	3,634,753	12.1	Seattle (22)	2,357,651[20]	4,498,501	23.5[21]
Kansas City, Mo. (9)	2,041,160	2,266,247	10.9	Springfield, Mass. (8)	695,733	867,979	4.5
Knoxville, Tenn. (16)	719,956	1,966,233	5.4	Tampa, Fla. (17)	1,792,812	2,968,936	15.4[22]
Lincoln, Neb. (7)	655,135	2,000,012	4.4	Tucson, Ariz. (19)	1,162,000	4,900,000	13.4
Long Beach, Calif. (11)	1,110,068	2,617,541	11.7	Tulsa City–County, Okla. (21)	1,006,413	3,772,531	10.2[8]
				Wichita, Kan. (12)	949,466	1,791,385	4.8
				Winston-Salem–Forsyth County, N.C. (9)	400,000	2,100,000	6.0
				Worcester, Mass. (9)	569,957	561,504	3.1
				Youngstown–Mahoning County, Ohio (22)	684,908	1,761,850	9.0

1. As of 6/30/95. 2. 7/1/94–6/30/95. 3. Includes books and audio material. 4. Book collection only. 5. Includes books, periodicals, records, films, government documents (collection weeded). 6. Budget included both general and bonded funds. 7. Includes government documents, bound periodicals, bound serials. 8. FY 1994–95. 9. State-wide system. 10. Includes books and audiovisual materials; excludes microforms. 11. Estimated 1995–96. 12. Operating budget for 1994–95, not including capital improvements and bond funds. 13. As of July 1, 1995. 14. Includes benefits, indirect costs, and county funding. 15. Projected for 1995–96 fiscal year. 16. Projected for 1996–97 budget. 17. Includes books, audiovisual materials, government documents, and musical scores. 18. As of 3/31/96. 19. Includes all library materials. 20. As of 12/31/95; includes print and nonprint materials. 21. Through Dec. 1996. 22. Plus $6.5 million building fund.

Glossary of Art Movements

Abstract Expressionism. American art movement of the 1940s that emphasized form and color within a nonrepresentational framework. Jackson Pollock initiated the revolutionary technique of splattering the paint directly on canvas to achieve the subconscious interpretation of the artist's inner vision of reality.

Art Deco. A 1920s style characterized by setbacks, zigzag forms, and the use of chrome and plastic ornamentation. New York's Chrysler Building is an architectural example of the style.

Art Nouveau. An 1890s style in architecture, graphic arts, and interior decoration characterized by writhing forms, curving lines, and asymmetrical organization. Some critics regard the style as the first stage of modern architecture.

Ashcan School. A group of New York realist artists, formed in 1908, who abandoned decorous subject matter and portrayed the more common as well as the sordid aspects of city life.

Assemblage (Collage). Forms of modern sculpture and painting utilizing readymades, found objects, and pasted fragments to form an abstract composition. Louise Nevelson's boxlike enclosures, each with its own composition of assembled objects, illustrate the style in sculpture. Pablo Picasso developed the technique of cutting and pasting natural or manufactured materials to a painted or unpainted surface.

Barbizon School (Landscape Painting). A group of painters who, around the middle of the 19th century, reacted against classical landscape and advocated a direct study of nature. They were influenced by English and Dutch landscape masters. Theodore Rousseau, one of the principal figures of the group, led the fight for outdoor painting. In this respect, the school was a forerunner of Impressionism.

Baroque. European art and architecture of the 17th and 18th centuries. Giovanni Bernini, a major exponent of the style, believed in the union of the arts of architecture, painting, and sculpture to overwhelm the spectator with ornate and highly dramatized themes. Although the style originated in Rome as the instrument of the Church, it spread throughout Europe in such monumental creations as the Palace of Versailles.

Beaux Arts. Elaborate and formal architectural style characterized by symmetry and an abundance of sculptured ornamentation. New York's old Custom House at Bowling Green is an example of the style.

Black or African-American Art. The work of American artists of African descent produced in various styles characterized by a mood of protest and a search for identity and historical roots.

Classicism. A form of art derived from the study of Greek and Roman styles characterized by harmony, balance, and serenity. In contrast, the Romantic Movement gave free rein to the artist's imagination and to the love of the exotic.

Constructivism. A form of sculpture using wood, metal, glass, and modern industrial materials expressing the technological society. The mobiles of Alexander Calder are examples of the movement.

Cubism. Early 20th-century French movement marked by a revolutionary departure from representational art. Pablo Picasso and Georges Bracque penetrated the surface of objects, stressing basic abstract geometric forms that presented the object from many angles simultaneously.

Dada. A product of the turbulent and cynical post-World War I period, this anti-art movement extolled the irrational, the absurd, the nihilistic, and the nonsensical. The reproduction of Mona Lisa adorned with a mustache is a famous example. The movement is regarded as a precursor of Surrealism. Some critics regard HAPPENINGS as a recent development of Dada. This movement incorporates environment and spectators as active and important ingredients in the production of random events.

Expressionism. A 20th-century European art movement that stresses the expression of emotion and the inner vision of the artist rather than the exact representation of nature. Distorted lines and shapes and exaggerated colors are used for emotional impact.

Vincent Van Gogh is regarded as the precursor of this movement.

Fauvism. The name "wild beasts" was given to the group of early 20th-century French painters because their work was characterized by distortion and violent colors. Henri Matisse and Georges Rouault were leaders of this group.

Futurism. This early 20th-century movement originating in Italy glorified the machine age and attempted to represent machines and figures in motion. The aesthetics of Futurism affirmed the beauty of technological society.

Genre. This French word meaning "type" now refers to paintings that depict scenes of everyday life without any attempt at idealization. Genre paintings can be found in all ages, but the Dutch productions of peasant and tavern scenes are typical.

Impressionism. Late 19th-century French school dedicated to defining transitory visual impressions painted directly from nature, with light and color of primary importance. If the atmosphere changed, a totally different picture would emerge. It was not the object or event that counted but the visual impression as caught at a certain time of day under a certain light. Claude Monet and Camille Pissarro were leaders of the movement.

Mannerism. A mid-16th century movement, Italian in origin, although El Greco was a major practitioner of the style. The human figure, distorted and elongated, was the most frequent subject.

Neoclassicism. An 18th-century reaction to the excesses of Baroque and Rococo, this European art movement tried to recreate the art of Greece and Rome by imitating the ancient classics both in style and subject matter.

Neoimpressionism. A school of painting associated with George Seurat and his followers in late 19th-century France that sought to make Impressionism more precise and formal. They employed a technique of juxtaposing dots of primary colors to achieve brighter secondary colors, with the mixture left to the eye to complete (pointillism).

Op Art. The 1960s movement known as Optical Painting is characterized by geometrical forms that create an optical illusion in which the eye is required to blend the colors at a certain distance.

Pop Art. In this return to representational art, the artist returns to the world of tangible objects in a reaction against abstraction. Materials are drawn from the everyday world of popular culture—comic strips, canned goods, and science fiction.

Realism. A development in mid-19th-century France lead by Gustave Courbet. Its aim was to depict the customs, ideas, and appearances of the time using scenes from everyday life.

Rococo. A French style of interior decoration developed during the reign of Louis XV consisting mainly of asymmetrical arrangements of curves in paneling, porcelain, and gold and silver objects. The characteristics of ornate curves, prettiness, and gaiety can also be found in the painting and sculpture of the period.

Surrealism. A further development of Collage, Cubism, and Dada, this 20th-century movement stresses the weird, the fantastic, and the dreamworld of the subconscious.

Symbolism. As part of a general European movement in the latter part of the 19th century, it was closely allied with Symbolism in literature. It marked a turning away from painting by observation to transforming fact into a symbol of inner experience. Gauguin was an early practitioner.

Top 10 Classical Albums, 1995

1. **The 3 Tenors in Concert 1994,** Jose Carreras, Placido Domingo, Luciano Pavarotti (Mehta) (Atlantic)
2. **Chant,** Benedictine Monks of Santo Domingo De Silos (Angel)
3. **Immortal Beloved,** Soundtrack (Sony Classical)
4. **Chant Noel,** Benedictine Monks of Santo Domingo De Silos (Angel)
5. **In Concert,** Jose Carreras, Placido Domingo, Luciano Pavarotti (Mehta) (London)
6. **Mozart Portraits,** Cecilia Bartoli (London)
7. **Officium,** Jan Garbarek/Hilliard Ensemble (ECM)
8. **Vivaldi: The Four Seasons,** Gil Shaham (DG)
9. **Paper Music,** Saint Paul Chamber Orchestra (McFerrin) (Sony Classical)
10. **A Carnegie Hall Xmas Concert,** Kathleen Battle, Frederica Von Stade, Wynton Marsalis (Previn) (Sony Classical)

Source: © 1995 BPI Communications Inc. Used with permission from *Billboard*/SoundScan, Inc.

Artists of the Year, 1995

Single of the Year: Gangsta's Paradise (from "Dangerous Minds"), Coolio, featuring L.V.
Album of the Year: Cracked Rear View, Hootie & The Blowfish
Female Artist of the Year: Mariah Carey
Male Artist of the Year: Garth Brooks
Group of the Year: Hootie & The Blowfish
New Artist of the Year: Real McCoy
County Artist of the Year: John Michael Montgomery
Rhythm & Blues Artist of the Year: TLC
Adult Contemporary Artist of the Year: Hootie & The Blowfish
Jazz Artist of the Year: Tony Bennett
Classical Artist of the Year: Benedictine Monks of Santo Domingo De Silos

Source: © 1995 BPI Communications Inc. Used with permission from *Billboard*/Broadcast Data Systems/SoundScan Inc.

Top 10 Country Single Recordings, 1995

1. **Sold (The Grundy County Auction Incident),** John Michael Montgomery (Atlantic)
2. **Any Man of Mine,** Shania Twain (Mercury Nashville)
3. **I Like It, I Love It,** Tom McGraw (Curb)
4. **Summer's Comin',** Clint Black (RCA)
5. **I Can Love You Like That,** John Michael Montgomery (Atlantic)
6. **Thinkin' About You,** Trisha Yearwood (MCA)
7. **This Woman and This Man,** Clay Walker (Giant)
8. **You Better Think Twice,** Vince Gill (MCA)
9. **They're Playin' Our Song,** Neal McCoy (Atlantic)
10. **If the World Had a Front Porch,** Tracy Lawrence (Atlantic)

Source: © 1995 BPI Communications Inc. Used with permission from *Billboard*/Broadcast Data Systems/SoundScan, Inc.

Manufacturers' Dollar[1] Shipments of Recordings
(in millions, net after returns)

	1986	1990	1994	1995
CD	930.1	3,451.6	8,464.5	9,401.7
CD single	n.a.	6.0	56.1	88.6
Cassette	2,499.5	3,472.4	2,976.4	2,303.6
Cassette single	n.a.	257.9	274.9	236.3
LP/EP	983.0	86.5	17.8	25.1
Vinyl single	228.1	94.4	47.2	46.7
Music video	n.a.	172.3	231.1	220.3

1. List price value. *Source:* Recording Industry Association of America, Inc.

Top 10 Pop Albums, 1995

1. **Cracked Rear View,** Hootie & The Blowfish (Atlantic)
2. **The Hits,** Garth Brooks (Capitol Nashville)
3. **II,** Boyz II Men (Motown)
4. **Hell Freezes Over,** Eagles (Geffen)
5. **Crazysexycool,** TLC (LaFace)
6. **Vitalogy,** Pearl Jam (Epic)
7. **Dookie,** Green Day (Reprise)
8. **Throwing Copper,** Live (Radioactive)
9. **Miracles: The Holiday Album,** Kenny G (Arista)
10. **The Lion King,** Soundtrack (Walt Disney)

Source: © 1995 BPI Communications Inc. Used with permission from *Billboard*/Broadcast Data Systems/SoundScan, Inc.

Top 10 Pop Single Recordings, 1995

1. **Gangsta's Paradise** (from "Dangerous Minds"), Coolio Featuring L.V. (MCA Soundtracks)
2. **Waterfalls,** TLC (LaFace)
3. **Creep,** TLC (LaFace)
4. **Kiss from a Rose** (from "Batman Forever"), Seal (ZTT/Sire)
5. **On Bended Knee,** Boyz II Men (Motown)
6. **Another Night,** Real McCoy (Arista)
7. **Fantasy,** Mariah Carey (Columbia)
8. **Take a Bow,** Madonna (Maverick/Sire)
9. **Don't Take It Personal (Just One of Dem Days),** Monica (Rowdy)
10. **This Is How We Do It,** Montell Jordan (PMP/RAL)

Source: © 1995 BPI Communications Inc. Used with permission from *Billboard*/Broadcast Data Systems/SoundScan, Inc.

Top 10 Rhythm & Blues Single Recordings, 1995

1. **Creep,** TLC (LaFace)
2. **This Is How We Do It,** Montell Jordan (PMP/RAL)
3. **One More Change/Stay With Me,** The Notorious B.I.G. (Bad Boy)
4. **If You Love Me,** Brownstone (MJJ)
5. **Candy Rain,** Soul for Real (Uptown)
6. **Don't Take It Personal (Just One of Dem Days),** Monica (Rowdy)
7. **Freak Like Me,** Adina Howard (Mecca Don/East West)
8. **Before I Let You Go,** Blackstreet (Interscope)
9. **Boombastic/In the Summertime,** Shaggy (Virgin)
10. **Baby,** Brandy (Atlantic)

Source: © 1995 BPI Communications Inc. Used with permission from *Billboard*/Broadcast Data Systems/SoundScan, Inc.

Top 10 Videocassettes
Sales, 1995

1. **The Lion King** (Buena Vista Home Video)
2. **Forrest Gump** (Paramount Home Video)
3. **Speed** (FoxVideo)
4. **Jurassic Park** (Uni Dist. Corp.)
5. **The Mask** (Turner Home Entertainment)
6. **Playboy: The Best of Pamela Anderson** (Uni Dist. Corp.)
7. **Snow White and The Seven Dwarfs** (Buena Vista Home Video)
8. **The Crow** (Buena Vista Home Video)
9. **Pink Floyd: Pulse** (Sony Music Video)
10. **Yanni: Live at the Acropolis** (BMG Video)

Source: © 1996 BPI Communications Inc. Used with permission from *Billboard.*

Top 10 Music Videocassettes, 1995

1. **Barbra: The Concert**, Barbra Streisand (Sony Music Video)
2. **Live at the Acropolis**, Yanni (BMG Video)
3. **Hell Freezes Over**, Eagles (Uni Dist. Corp.)
4. **The 3 Tenors in Concert 1994**, Carreras, Domingo, Pavarotti (WarnerVision Entertainment)
5. **Pulse**, Pink Floyd (Sony Music Video)
6. **Video Greatest Hits—History**, Michael Jackson (Sony Music Video)
7. **Live! Tonight! Sold Out!!**, Nirvana (Uni Dist. Corp.)
8. **Murder Was the Case**, Snoop Doggy Dogg (WarnerVision Entertainment)
9. **Woodstock '94**, Various Artists (PolyGram Video)
10. **You Might Be a Redneck If . . .**, Jeff Foxworthy (Warner Reprise Video)

Source: © 1996 BPI Communications Inc.. Used with permission from *Billboard.*

Top 10 Kid Videocassettes, 1995

1. **Snow White and The Seven Dwarfs** (Buena Vista Home Video)
2. **The Lion King** (Buena Vista Home Video)
3. **Aladdin** (Buena Vissta Home Video)
4. **Disney's Sing Along Songs: Circle of Life** (Buena Vista Home Video)
5. **The Land Before Time II** (Uni Dist. Corp.)
6. **The Pagemaster** (FoxVideo)
7. **Beavis & Butt-Head: There Goes the Neighborhood** (Sony Music Video)
8. **The Return of Jafar** (Buena Vista Home Video)
9. **The Adventures of Mary-Kate & Ashley: The Case of Sea World** (WarnerVision Entertainment)
10. **Beavis & Butt-Head: Work Sucks!** (Sony Music Video)

Source: © 1996 BPI Communication Inc.. Used with permission from *Billboard.*

Top 10 Videocassettes Rentals, 1995

1. **The Shawshank Redemption** (Columbia TriStar Home Video)
2. **True Lies** (FoxVideo)
3. **Disclosure** (Warner Home Video)
4. **Speed** (FoxVideo)
5. **The Client** (Warner Home Video)
6. **Clear and Present Danger** (Paramount Home Video)
7. **When a Man Loves a Woman** (Buena Vista Home Video)
8. **Dumb and Dumber** (Turner Home Entertainment)
9. **Just Cause** (Warner Home Video)
10. **Outbreak** (Warner Home Video)

Source: © 1996 BPI Communications Inc. Used with permission from *Billboard.*

Top 10 Classical Crossover
Albums, 1995

1. **Vision: Music of Hildegard Von Bingen,** Germaine Fritz/Emily Van Evera (Angel)
2. **The Piano,** Michael Nyman (Virgin)
3. **Schindler's List,** John Williams/Itzhak Perlman (MCA)
4. **Pavarotti & Friends 2,** Various Artists (London)
5. **The Magical Music of Disney,** Cincinnati Pops (Kunzel) (Telarc)
6. **Bach Variations,** Various Artists (Windham Hill)
7. **The Violin Player,** Vanessa-Mae (Angel)
8. **De Mi Alma Latina,** Placido Domingo (Angel)
9. **Wind of Change,** James Galway (RCA Victor)
10. **Pavarotti & Friends,** Various Artists (London)

Source: © 1995 BPI Communications Inc. Used with permission from *Billboard*/SoundScan, Inc.

15 Top-Grossing Concerts
(Dec. 1994–Nov. 1995)

1. **The Rolling Stones,** $27,613,380, Tokyo Dome, Tokyo, Japan, March 6, 8–9, 12, 14, 16–17.
2. **The Rolling Stones, Las Pelotas, Ratones Paranoicas,** $19,796,750, River Plate Stadium, Buenos Aires, Argentina, Feb. 9, 11–12, 14, 16.
3. **The Rolling Stones, Caifanes,** $11,784,755, Hermanos Rodriguez Autodromo, Mexico City, Mexico, Jan. 14, 16, 18, 20.
4. **The Rolling Stones, The Black Crowes,** $8,666,640, Wembley Stadium, London, England, July 11, 15–16.
5. **The Rolling Stones, Bon Jovi, Eric Lapointe,** $8,612,247, Longchamps Racetrack, Paris, France, June 30–July 1.
6. **The Rolling Stones, The Tragically Hip,** $6,222,222, Festival Site, Werchter, Belgium, June 24–25.
7. **The Rolling Stones,** $5,879,683, Cricket Ground, Melbourne, Australia, March 27–28.
8. **The Rolling Stones, The Black Crowes,** $5,561,673, St. Jakob Stadium, Basel, Switzerland, July 29–30.
9. **The Rolling Stones,** $5,237,710, Cricket Ground, Sydney, Australia, April 1–2.
10. **The Rolling Stones, Robert Cray Band,** $5,152,429, Park De Goffert, Nijmegen, The Netherlands, June 13–14.
11. **R.E.M, Blur, The Cranberries, Radiohead,** $4,796,364, National Bowl, Milton Keynes, England, July 29–30.
12. **The Rolling Stones, Mango Groove,** $4,588,405, Ellis Park Stadium, Johannesburg, South Africa, Feb. 24–25.
13. **The Rolling Stones, Runrig, Rudiger Hoffmann, Big Country, Jimmy Barnes,** $4,584,171, Festival Site, Schuttorf, Germany, Aug. 12.
14. **The Rolling Stones, Red Baron, Rita Lee, Spin Doctors,** $4,527,556, Pacaembu Stadium, São Paulo, Brazil, Jan. 27, 28, 30.
15. **Elton John/Billy Joel,** $4,385,725, Joe Robbie Stadium, Miami, Fla., April 13–14.

Source: © 1995, BPI Communications Inc. Used with permission from *Amusement Business.*

Top 15 Regularly Scheduled Network Programs, 1995–96[1]

Rank	Program name (network)	Total percent of TV households
1.	E.R. (NBC)	22.0
2.	Seinfeld (NBC)	21.2
3.	Friends (NBC)	18.7
4.	Caroline in the City (NBC)	17.9
5.	NFL Monday Night Football (ABC)	17.1
6.	Single Guy (NBC)	16.7
7.	Home Improvement (ABC)	16.2
8.	Boston Common (NBC)	15.6
9.	60 Minutes (CBS)	14.2
10.	NYPD Blue (ABC)	14.1
11.	Frasier (NBC)	13.6
11.	20/20 (ABC)	13.6
13.	Grace Under Fire (ABC)	13.2
14.	Coach (ABC)	12.9
14.	NBC Monday Night Movies (NBC)	12.9
Total U.S. TV households 95,900,000		

1. Sept. 8, 1995–May 22, 1996. NOTE: Percentages are calculated from average audience viewings, 5 minutes or longer and 2 or more telecasts. *Source:* Nielsen Media Research. Copyright 1996, Nielsen Media Research.

Top 15 Syndicated TV Programs 1995–96 Season

Rank	Program	Rating (% U.S.)[1]
1.	Wheel of Fortune	12.5
2.	Jeopardy	10.3
3.	Home Improvement	9.2
4.	Oprah Winfrey Show	8.0
5.	Seinfeld	7.3
6.	ESPN NFL—Regular Season	7.1
7.	National Geographic on Assignment	6.9
8.	Entertainment Tonight	6.7
9.	Star Trek: Deep Space Nine	6.3
9.	Wheel of Fortune (Weekend)	6.3
11.	Buena Vista I	6.2
12.	Simpsons	6.1
13.	Journeys of Hercules	5.9
13.	Inside Edition	5.9
15.	Home Improvement (Weekend)	5.7

1. Sept. 8–May 22, 1996. *Source:* Nielsen Syndication Service National TV Ratings. Copyright 1996, Nielsen Media Research.

Top Sports Shows 1995–96[1]

Rank	Program name (network)	Description	Rating (% of TV households)
1.	Super Bowl XXX (NBC)	Dallas vs. Pittsburgh	46.0
2.	Super Bowl XXX Kickoff (NBC)	Dallas vs. Pittsburgh	35.5
3.	Super Bowl XXX Post Game (NBC)	Dallas vs. Pittsburgh	35.0
4.	Fox NFC Championship (Fox)	Green Bay at Dallas	33.3
5.	AFC Championship Game (NBC)	Indianapolis at Pittsburgh	27.1
6.	Fox NFC Playoff (Fox)	Philadelphia at Dallas	25.4
6.	NFL Playoff Game (NBC)	Indianapolis at Kansas City	25.4
8.	Fox NFC Playoff (Fox)	Green Bay at San Francisco	22.2
9.	World Series, Game #5 (ABC)	Atlanta at Cleveland	21.6
10.	Super Bowl XXX Pre-Kickoff (NBC)	Dallas vs. Pittsburgh	21.0

1. Sept. 18, 1995–May 22, 1996. *Source:* Nielsen Media Research. Copyright 1996, Nielsen Media Research.

Top Rated Movies 1995–96[1]

Rank	Program name (network)	Rating (% of TV households)
1.	Home Alone (NBC)	14.5
2.	Dennis the Menace (NBC)	10.9
3.	Rookie of the Year (Fox)	10.8
4.	Cagney and Lacey: True Conviction (CBS)	9.5
4.	Rockford Files: Friends/Foul Play (CBS)	9.5
6.	The Innocent (NBC)	9.2
7.	Father of the Bride (ABC)	9.0
7.	The Mighty Ducks (NBC)	9.0
9.	Beethoven (Fox)	8.8
9.	The Sound of Music (NBC)	8.8

1. Sept. 18, 1995–May 22, 1996. *Source:* Nielsen Media Research. Copyright 1996, Nielsen Media Research.

Top Specials 1995–96[1]

Rank	Program name (network) [first telecast]	Rating (% of TV households)
1.	Academy Awards (ABC) [3/25/96]	30.3
2.	Friends Special (NBC) [11/21/95]	24.9
3.	Frasier Special (NBC) [11/30/95]	17.8
4.	Beatles Anthology, Pt. 1 (ABC) [11/19/95]	17.4
5.	Frasier Special (NBC) [3/14/96]	16.7

1. Sept. 18, 1995–May 22, 1996. *Source:* Nielsen Media Research. Copyright 1996, Nielsen Media Research.

Hours of TV Usage Per Week by Household Income

	Under $30,000	$30,000+	$40,000+	$50,000+	$60,000+
Nov. 1993	53 h 35 min	50 h 34 min	50 h 24 min (includes $50,000+)		47 h 13 min
Nov. 1994	53 h 46 min	52 h 05 min	50 h 04 min (includes $50,000+)		46 h 42 min
Nov. 1995	52 h 25 min	51 h 44 min	48 h 53 min		46 h 02 min

Source: Nielsen Media Research, copyright 1996, Nielsen Media Research.

Television Set Ownership
(May 1996)

Homes with	Number	Percent
Color TV sets	94,941,000	99.0
B&W only	959,000	01.0
2 or more sets	70,007,000	73.0
One set	25,893,000	27.0
Cable	62,335,000	65.0
Total TV households	**95,900,000**	**98.0**

Source: Nielsen Media Research, copyright 1996, Nielsen Media Research.

Persons Viewing Prime Time[1]
(in millions)

	Total persons
Monday	94.5
Tuesday	93.2
Wednesday	85.2
Thursday	88.8
Friday	79.2
Saturday	77.6
Sunday	92.8
Total average	**87.2**

1. Average minute audiences May 1996. NOTE: Prime time is 8–11 p.m. (EST) except Sun. 7–11 pm. *Source:* Nielsen Media Research. Copyright 1996, Nielsen Media Research.

Average Hours of Household TV Usage
(In hours and minutes per day)

	Yearly average	February	July
1985–86	7 h 10 min	7 h 48 min	6 h 37 min
1986–87	7 h 05 min	7 h 35 min	6 h 32 min
1987–88	6 h 55 min	7 h 38 min	6 h 31 min
1988–89	7 h 02 min	7 h 32 min	6 h 27 min
1989–90	6 h 55 min	7 h 16 min	6 h 24 min
1990–91	6 h 56 min	7 h 30 min	6 h 26 min
1991–92	7 h 04 min	7 h 32 min	6 h 39 min
1992–93	7 h 17 min	7 h 41 min	6 h 47 min
1993–94	7 h 21 min	7 h 51 min	6 h 53 min
1994–95	7 h 20 min	7 h 39 min	6 h 46 min

Source: Nielsen Media Research, copyright 1996, Nielsen Media Research.

Weekly TV Viewing by Age
(in hours and minutes)

	Time per week	
	Nov. 1995	Nov. 1994
Women 18–24 years old	24 h 52 min	26 h 23 min
Women 25–54	31 h 45 min	30 h 55 min
Women 55 and over	42 h 20 min	44 h 11 min
Men 18–24	21 h 20 min	22 h 41 min
Men 25–54	28 h 23 min	27 h 13 min
Men 55 and over	37 h 58 min	38 h 38 min
Female Teens	19 h 59 min	20 h 20 min
Male Teens	20 h 38 min	21 h 59 min
Children 6–11	21 h 40 min	21 h 30 min
Children 2–5	24 h 52 min	24 h 42 min

Source: Nielsen Media Research, copyright 1996, Nielsen Media Research.

Audience Composition by Selected Program Type[1]
(Average Minute Audience)

	General drama	Suspense and mystery drama	Situation comedy	Informational[2] 6-7 p.m.	Feature films	All regular network programs 7–11 p.m.
Women (18 and over)	7,170,000	8,410,000	8,130,000	6,250,000	7,900,000	7,750,000
Men (18 and over)	4,530,000	5,930,000	5,310,000	4,880,000	5,220,000	5,630,000
Teens (12–17)	870,000	480,000	1,270,000	280,000	1,010,000	1,000,000
Children (2–11)	1,030,000	680,000	1,780,000	500,000	1,270,000	1,330,000
Total persons (2+)	**13,600,000**	**15,490,000**	**16,490,000**	**11,890,000**	**15,410,000**	**15,700,000**

1. All figures are estimated for the period Nov. 1995. 2. Multiweekly viewing. *Source:* Nielsen Media Research, copyright 1996, Nielsen Media Research.

Source of Household Viewing—Prime Time
Pay Cable, Basic Cable, and Non-Cable Households
(Mon.-Sun. 8–11 pm)

	Nov. 1995			Nov. 1994			Nov. 1993		
	Pay cable	Basic cable	Non-cable	Pay cable	Basic cable	Non-cable	Pay cable	Basic cable	Non-cable
% TV Usage	67.2	60.9	54.4	67.0	61.2	58.1	68.7	61.3	57.2
Pay Cable	9.2	—	—	9.3	—	—	9.2	—	—
Cable-originated programming	25.9	23.6	—	22.1	20.5	—	21.0	20.2	—
Other-on-air stations	6.9	5.4	9.3	7.2	7.8	12.7	7.2	7.1	11.4
Network affiliated stations	38.1	37.5	44.3	41.6	40.7	50.6	44.4	40.7	50.3
Network share	(57)	(62)	(81)	(62)	(67)	(87)	(65)	(66)	(88)

Source: Nielsen Media Research, copyright 1996, Nielsen Media Research.

Motion Picture Revenues
(As of January 2, 1996)

All-Time Top Box Office Grosses[1]		Top Box Office Grosses 1995	
1. E.T. The Extra-Terrestrial (Universal, 1982)	$399,804,539	1. Batman Forever (Warner Brothers)	$183,997,904
2. Jurassic Park (Universal, 1993)	356,839,725	2. Apollo 13 (Universal)	172,036,360
3. Forrest Gump (Paramount, 1994)	329,690,974	3. Toy Story (Buena Vista)	150,004,917
4. Star Wars (20th Century-Fox, 1977)	322,740,142	4. Pocahontas (Buena Vista)	141,539,152
5. The Lion King (Buena Vista, 1994)	312,855,561	5. Ace Ventura 2 When Nature Calls	
6. Home Alone (20th Century-Fox, 1990)	285,016,000	(Warner Brothers)	104,355,781
7. Return of the Jedi (20th Century-Fox, 1983)	263,734,642	6. Casper (Universal)	100,280,870
8. Jaws (Universal, 1975)	260,000,000	7. Die Hard With a Vengeance (20th	
9. Batman (Warner Brothers, 1989)	251,188,924	Century-Fox)	100,003,359
10. Raiders of the Lost Ark (Paramount, 1981)	242,374,454	8. Goldeneye (MGM)	93,211,105
11. Beverly Hills Cop (Paramount, 1984)	234,760,478	9. Crimson Tide (Buena Vista)	91,381,194
12. The Empire Strikes Back (20th Century-		10. Waterworld (Universal)	88,214,660
Fox, 1980)	222,674,266	11. Seven (New Line Cinema)	87,046,142
13. Ghostbusters (Columbia, 1984)	220,858,490	12. Dangerous Minds (Buena Vista)	84,268,691
14. Mrs. Doubtfire (20th Century-Fox, 1993)	219,194,773	13. While You Were Sleeping (Buena Vista)	81,052,361
15. Ghost (Paramount, 1990)	217,631,306	14. Congo (Paramount)	81,012,319
16. Aladdin (Buena Vista, 1992)	217,350,219	15. Mortal Kombat (New Line Cinema)	70,373,848
17. Back to the Future (Universal, 1985)	210,609,762	16. The Bridges of Madison County	
18. Terminator 2 (TriStar, 1991)	204,446,562	(Warner Brothers)	70,067,649
19. Indiana Jones and the Last Crusade		17. Nine Months (20th Century-Fox)	69,689,009
(Paramount, 1989)	197,171,806	18. Get Shorty (MGM)	68,798,612
20. Gone With the Wind (MGM/United Artists/		19. Outbreak (Warner Brothers)	67,598,303
(TEC, 1939)	193,597,756	20. Braveheart (Paramount)	67,019,456
21. Snow White (RKO/Buena Vista, 1937)	184,925,486	21. Bad Boys (Sony/Columbia)	65,654,432
22. Dances With Wolves (Orion, 1990)	184,208,848	22. Species (MGM)	60,000,401
23. Batman Forever (Warner Brothers, 1995)	183,997,904	23. Jumanji (Sony/TriStar)	57,500,265
24. The Fugitive (Warner Brothers, 1993)	183,752,965	24. Babe (Universal)	56,780,755
25. Indiana Jones and the Temple of Doom		25. Clueless (Paramount)	56,461,210
(Paramount, 1984)	179,870,271		

1. Including reissues. *Source:* Exhibitor Relations Co. Inc.

Miss America Winners

1921 Margaret Gorman, Washington, D.C.	1965 Vonda Kay Van Dyke, Phoenix, Ariz.
1922-23 Mary Campbell, Columbus, Ohio	1966 Deborah Irene Bryant, Overland Park, Kan.
1924 Ruth Malcolmson, Philadelphia, Pa.	1967 Jane Anne Jayroe, Laverne, Okla.
1925 Fay Lamphier, Oakland, Calif.	1968 Debra Dene Barnes, Moran, Kan.
1926 Norma Smallwood, Tulsa, Okla.	1969 Judith Anne Ford, Belvidere, Ill.
1927 Lois Delaner, Joliet, Ill.	1970 Pamela Anne Eldred, Birmingham, Mich.
1933 Marion Bergeron, West Haven, Conn.	1971 Phyllis Ann George, Denton, Texas
1935 Henrietta Leaver, Pittsburgh, Pa.	1972 Laurie Lea Schaefer, Columbus, Ohio
1936 Rose Coyle, Philadelphia, Pa.	1973 Terry Anne Meeuwsen, DePere, Wis.
1937 Bette Cooper, Bertrand Island, N.J.	1974 Rebecca Ann King, Denver, Colo.
1938 Marilyn Meseke, Marion, Ohio	1975 Shirley Cothran, Fort Worth, Texas
1939 Patricia Donnelly, Detroit, Mich.	1976 Tawney Elaine Godin, Yonkers, N.Y.
1940 Frances Marie Burke, Philadelphia, Pa.	1977 Dorothy Kathleen Benham, Edina, Minn.
1941 Rosemary LaPlanche, Los Angeles, Calif.	1978 Susan Perkins, Columbus, Ohio
1942 JoCaroll Dennison, Tyler, Texas	1979 Kylene Baker, Galax, Va.
1943 Jean Bartel, Los Angeles, Calif.	1980 Cheryl Prewitt, Ackerman, Miss.
1944 Venus Ramey, Washington, D.C.	1981 Susan Powell, Elk City, Okla.
1945 Bess Myerson, New York, N.Y.	1982 Elizabeth Ward, Russellville, Ark.
1946 Marilyn Buferd, Los Angeles, Calif.	1983 Debra Maffett, Anaheim, Calif.
1947 Barbara Walker, Memphis, Tenn.	1984 Vanessa Williams, Milwood, N.Y.[1]
1948 BeBe Shopp, Hopkins, Minn.	Suzette Charles, Mays Landing, N.J.
1949 Jacque Mercer, Litchfield, Ariz.	1985 Sharlene Wells, Salt Lake City, Utah
1951 Yolande Betbeze, Mobile, Ala.	1986 Susan Akin, Meridian, Miss.
1952 Coleen Kay Hutchins, Salt Lake City, Utah	1987 Kellye Cash, Memphis, Tenn.
1953 Neva Jane Langley, Macon, Ga.	1988 Kaye Lani Rae Rafko, Toledo, Ohio
1954 Evelyn Margaret Ay, Ephrata, Pa.	1989 Gretchen Elizabeth Carlson, Anoka, Minn.
1955 Lee Meriwether, San Francisco, Calif.	1990 Debbye Turner, Mexico, Mo.
1956 Sharon Ritchie, Denver, Colo.	1991 Marjorie Judith Vincent, Oak Park, Ill.
1957 Marian McKnight, Manning, S.C.	1992 Carolyn Suzanne Sapp, Honolulu, Hawaii
1958 Marilyn Van Derbur, Denver, Colo.	1993 Leanza Cornett, Jacksonville, Fla.
1959 Mary Ann Mobley, Brandon, Miss.	1994 Kimberly Clarice Aiken, Columbia, S.C.
1960 Lynda Lee Mead, Natchez, Miss.	1995 Heather Whitestone, Birmingham, Ala.
1961 Nancy Fleming, Montague, Mich.	1996 Shawntel Smith, Muldrow, Okla.
1962 Maria Fletcher, Asheville, N.C.	1997 (*See* Current Events)
1963 Jacquelyn Mayer, Sandusky, Ohio	
1964 Donna Axum, El Dorado, Ark.	1. Resigned July 23, 1984.

States and Territories

Sources for state populations, populations under 18, over 65, median age, largest cities and counties, and population by race are latest data provided by the U.S. Census Bureau. NOTE: Persons of Hispanic origin can be of any race. The population counts set forth herein by the Census Bureau are subject to possible correction for undercount or overcount. They include Armed Forces residing in each state. 1995 State populations are for July 1, 1995. Largest cities include incorporated places only, as defined by the U.S. Census Bureau. They do not include adjacent or suburban areas as do the Metropolitan Statistical Areas found in the "U.S. Statistics" section of this Almanac. For secession and readmission dates of the former Confederate states, *see* Index. For lists of Governors, Senators, and Representatives, *see* Index. For additional state information, *see* the sections on "Business and the Economy," "Elections," "Taxes," and "U.S. Statistics."

ALABAMA

Capital: Montgomery
Governor: Fob James, Jr., R (to Jan. 1999)
Lieut. Governor: Don Siegelman, D (to Jan. 1999)
Secy. of State: Jim Bennett, D (to Jan. 1999)
Treasurer: Lucy Baxley, D (to Jan. 1999)
Atty. General: Jeff Sessions, R (to Jan. 1999)
Auditor: Pat Duncan, R (to Jan. 1999)
Organized as territory: March 3, 1817
Entered Union & (rank): Dec. 14, 1819 (22)
Present constitution adopted: 1901
Motto: *Audemus jura nostra defendere* (We dare defend our rights)
STATE SYMBOLS: flower, Camellia (1959); **bird,** Yellowhammer (1927); **song,** "Alabama" (1931); **tree,** Southern pine (longleaf) (1949); **salt water fish,** Tarpon (1955); **fresh water fish,** Largemouth bass (1975); **horse,** Racking horse (1975); **mineral,** Hematite (1967); **rock,** Marble (1969); **game bird,** Wild turkey (1980); **dance,** Square dance (1981); **nut,** Pecan (1982); **fossil,** species *Basilosaurus Cetoides* (1984); **butterfly,** Eastern Tiger Swallowtail (1989); **insect,** Monarch butterfly (1989); **reptile,** Alabama red-bellied turtle (1990); **gemstone,** Star Blue Quartz (1990); **shell,** Scaphella junonia johnstoneae (1990).
Nickname: Yellowhammer State
Origin of name: May come from Choctaw meaning "thicket-clearers" or "vegetation-gatherers"
10 largest cities (1990 census): Birmingham, 265,968; Mobile, 196,278; Montgomery, 187,106; Huntsville, 159,789; Tuscaloosa, 77,759; Dothan, 53,589; Decatur, 48,761; Gadsden, 42,523; Hoover, 39,788; Florence, 36,426
Land area & (rank): 50,750 sq mi. (131,443 sq km) (28)
Geographic center: In Chilton Co., 12 mi. SW of Clanton
Number of counties: 67
Largest county: Baldwin (1,590 sq mi.)
Most populous county (1990 census): Jefferson, 651,525
State forests: 21 (48,000 ac.)
State parks: 22 (45,614 ac.)
1995 resident population est.: 4,253,000
1990 census population (rank): 4,040,587 (22). **Male:** 1,936,162; **Female:** 2,104,425. **White:** 2,975,797 (73.6%); **Black:** 1,020,705 (25.3%); **American Indian, Eskimo, or Aleut:** 16,506 (0.4%); **Asian or Pacific Islander:** 21,797 (0.5%); **Other race:** 5,782 (0.1%); **Hispanic:** 24,629 (0.6%). **1990 percent population under 18:** 26.2; **65 and over:** 12.9; **median age:** 33.0.

Spanish explorers are believed to have arrived at Mobile Bay in 1519, and the territory was visited in 1540 by the explorer Hernando de Soto. The first permanent European settlement in Alabama was founded by the French at Fort Louis de la Mobile in 1702. The British gained control of the area in 1763 by the Treaty of Paris, but had to cede almost all the Alabama region to the U.S. after the American Revolution. The Confederacy was founded at Montgomery in February 1861 and, for a time, the city was the Confederate capital.

During the last part of the 19th century, the economy of the state slowly improved. At Tuskegee Institute, founded in 1881 by Booker T. Washington, Dr. George Washington Carver carried out his famous agricultural research.

In the 1950s and '60s, Alabama was the site of such landmark civil-rights actions as the bus boycott in Montgomery (1955–56) and the "Freedom March" from Selma to Montgomery (1965).

Today paper, chemicals, rubber and plastics, apparel and textiles, and primary metals comprise the leading industries of Alabama. Continuing as a major manufacturer of coal, iron, and steel, Birmingham is also noted for its world-renowned medical center, especially for heart surgery. The state ranks high in the production of poultry, soybeans, milk, vegetables, livestock, wheat, cattle, cotton, peanuts, fruits, hogs, and corn.

Points of interest include the Helen Keller birthplace "Ivy Green" at Tuscumbia, the Space and Rocket Center at Huntsville, the White House of the Confederacy, the restored state Capitol, the Civil Rights Memorial, and Shakespeare Festival Theater Complex in Montgomery, the Civil Rights Institute in Birmingham, the Russell Cave near Bridgeport, and Bellingrath Gardens at Theodore, the U.S.S. Alabama at Mobile, Mound State Monument near Tuscaloosa, and the Gulf Coast area.

Famous natives and residents: Hank Aaron, baseball player; Ralph Abernathy, civil rights activist; Tallulah Bankhead, actress; Hugo L. Black, jurist; George Washington Carver, educator, agricultural chemist; Nat "King" Cole, entertainer; Marva Collins, educator; Kenneth Gibson, first black mayor of major eastern city (Newark); Lionel Hampton, jazz musician; W.C. Handy, composer; Kate Jackson, actress; Helen Keller, author and educator; Coretta Scott King, civil rights leader; Harper Lee, writer; Joe Louis, boxer; Willie Mays, baseball player; Jim Nabors, actor; Jesse Owens, athlete; Rosa Parks, civil rights activist; Wayne Rogers, actor; Tuscaloosa, Choctaw chief; George Wallace, ex-governor; William Weatherford (Red Eagle), Creek leader

ALASKA

Capital: Juneau
Governor: Tony Knowles, D (to Dec. 1998)
Lieut. Governor: Fran Ulmer, D (to Dec. 1998)
Commissioner of Administration: Mark Boyer
Atty. General: Bruce M. Botelho, D

Organized as territory: 1912
Entered Union & (rank): Jan. 3, 1959 (49)
Constitution ratified: April 24, 1956
Motto: North to the Future
STATE SYMBOLS: flower, Forget-me-not (1949); **tree,** Sitka spruce (1962); **bird,** Willow ptarmigan (1955); **fish,** King salmon (1962); **song,** "Alaska's Flag" (1955); **gem,** Jade (1968); **marine mammal,** Bowhead Whale (1983); **fossil,** Woolly Mammoth (1986); **mineral,** Gold (1968); **sport,** Dog Mushing (1972)
Nickname: The state is commonly called "The Last Frontier" or "Land of the Midnight Sun"
Origin of name: Corruption of Aleut word meaning "great land" or "that which the sea breaks against"
Largest cities[1]: Anchorage, 248,296; Fairbanks, 33,281; Juneau, 29,078; Sitka, 9,052; Ketchikan, 8,846; Kodiak, 7,428; Kenai, 6,813
Land area & (rank): 570,374 sq mi. (1,477,267 sq km) (1)
Geographic center: 60 mi. NW of Mt. McKinley
Number of boroughs: 16
Largest borough (1994): Fairbanks North Star Borough, 82,428
State forests: None
State parks: 5; 59 waysides and areas (3.3 million ac.)
1995 resident population: 604,000
1990 resident census population (rank): 550,043 (49).
　Male: 289,867; **Female:** 260,176. **White:** 415,492 (75.5%); **Black:** 22,451 (4.1%); **American Indian, Eskimo, or Aleut:** 85,698 (15.6%); **Asian or Pacific Islander:** 19,728 (3.6%); **Other race:** 6,675 (1.2%); **Hispanic:** 17,803 (3.2%). **1990 percent population under 18:** 31.3; **65 and over:** 4.1; **median age:** 29..4

1. *Source:* 1995 mailing to Alaska State Library.

Vitus Bering, a Dane working for the Russians, and Alexei Chirikov discovered the Alaskan mainland and the Aleutian Islands in 1741. The tremendous land mass of Alaska—equal to one fifth of the continental U.S.—was unexplored in 1867 when Secretary of State William Seward arranged for its purchase from the Russians for $7,200,000. The transfer of the territory took place on Oct. 18, 1867. Despite a price of about two cents an acre, the purchase was widely ridiculed as "Seward's Folly." The first official census (1880) reported a total of 33,426 Alaskans, all but 430 being of aboriginal stock. The Gold Rush of 1898 resulted in a mass influx of more than 30,000 people. Since then, Alaska has contributed billions of dollars' worth of products to the U.S. economy.

In 1968, a large oil and gas reservoir near Prudhoe Bay on the Arctic Coast was found. The Prudhoe Bay reservoir, with an estimated recoverable 10 billion barrels of oil and 27 trillion cubic feet of gas, is twice as large as any other oil field in North America. The Trans-Alaska pipeline was completed in 1977 at a cost of $7.7 billion. On June 20, oil started flowing through the 800-mile-long pipeline from Prudhoe Bay to the port of Valdez.

Other industries important to Alaska's economy are fisheries, wood and wood products, furs, and tourism.

Denali National Park and Mendenhall Glacier in North Tongass National Forest are of interest, as is the large totem pole collection at Sitka National Historical Park. The Katmai National Park includes the "Valley of Ten Thousand Smokes," an area of active volcanoes.

Famous natives and residents: Clarence L. Andrews, author; Alexander Baranov, first governor of Russian America; Margaret Elizabeth Bell, author; Benny Benson, designed state flag at age 13; Vitus Bering, explorer; Charles E. Bunnell, educator; Susan Butcher, sled-dog racer; William A. Egan, first state governor; Carl Ben Eielson, pioneer pilot; Henry E. Gruennig, political leader; B. Frank Heintzleman, territorial governor; Walter J. Hickel, ex-governor; Sheldon Jackson, educator and missionary; Joe Juneau, prospector; Austin Lathrop, industrialist; Sydney Lawrence, painter; Ray Mala, actor; Virgil F. Partch, cartoonist; Joe Redington, Sr., sled-dog musher and promoter; Peter Trinble Rowe, first Episcopal bishop; Ivan Popov-Veniaminov (St. Innocent), Russian Orthodox missionary; Ferdinand Wrangel, educator; Samuel Hall Young, founder of first American church

ARIZONA

Capital: Phoenix
Governor: Fife Symington, R (to Jan. 1999)
Secy. of State: Jane Dee Hull, R (to Jan. 1999)
Atty. General: Grant Woods, R (to Jan. 1999*)
State Treasurer: Tony West, R (to Jan. 1999)
Organized as territory: Feb. 24, 1863
Entered Union & (rank): Feb. 14, 1912 (48)
Present constitution adopted: 1911
Motto: *Ditat Deus* (God enriches)
STATE SYMBOLS: flower: Flower of saguaro cactus (1931); **bird:** Cactus wren (1931); **colors:** Blue and old gold (1915); **song:** "Arizona March Song" (1919); **tree:** Palo Verde (1954); **neckwear,** Bolo tie (1973); **fossil,** Petrified wood (1988); **gemstone,** Turquoise (1974); **animals, mammal,** Ringtail; **reptile,** Arizona ridgenose rattlesnake; **fish,** Arizona trout; **amphibian,** Arizona tree frog (1986)
Nickname: Grand Canyon State
Origin of name: From the Indian "Arizonac," meaning "little spring" or "young spring"
10 largest cities (1990 census): Phoenix, 983,403; Tucson, 405,390; Mesa, 288,091; Glendale, 148,134; Tempe, 141,865; Scottsdale, 130,069; Chandler, 90,533; Yuma, 54,923; Peoria, 50,618; Flagstaff, 45,857
Land area & (rank): 114,000 sq mi. (296,400 sq km) (6)
Geographic center: In Yavapai Co., 55 mi. ESE of Prescott
Number of counties: 15
Largest county (1990 census): Maricopa, 2,122,101; (1995 est.): 2,454,525
State forests: None
State parks: 24
1995 resident population est.: 4,218,000
1990 resident census population (rank): 3,665,228 (24).
　Male: 1,810,691; **Female:** 1,854,537. **White:** 2,963,186 (80.8%); **Black:** 110,524 (3.0%); **American Indian, Eskimo, or Aleut:** 203,527 (5.6%); **Asian or Pacific Islander:** 55,206 (1.5%); **Other race:** 332,785 (9.1%); **Hispanic:** 688,338 (18.8%). **1990 percent population under 18:** 26.8; **65 and over:** 13.1; **median age:** 32.2

*Ran unopposed

Marcos de Niza, a Spanish Franciscan friar, was the first European to explore Arizona. He entered the area in 1539 in search of the mythical Seven Cities of Gold. Although he was followed a year later by another gold seeker, Francisco Vásquez de Coronado, most of the early settlement was for missionary purposes. In 1775 the Spanish established Fort Tucson. In 1848, after the Mexican War, most of the Arizona territory became part of the U.S., and the southern portion of the territory was added by the Gadsden Purchase in 1853.

In 1973 one of the world's most massive dams, the New Cornelia Tailings, was completed near Ajo.

Arizona history is rich in legends of America's Old West. It was here that the great Indian chiefs Geronimo and Cochise led their people against the frontiersmen. Tombstone, Ariz., was the site of the West's most famous shoot-out—the gunfight at the O.K. Corral. Today, Arizona has the largest U.S. Indian population; more than 14 tribes are represented on 20 reservations.

Manufacturing has become Arizona's most important industry. Principal products include electrical, communications, and aeronautical items. The state produces over half the country's copper. Agriculture is also important to the state's economy.

State attractions include such famous scenery as the Grand Canyon, the Petrified Forest, and the Painted Desert. Hoover Dam, Lake Mead, Fort Apache, and the reconstructed London Bridge at Lake Havasu City are of particular interest.

Famous natives and residents: Apache Kid, Indian outlaw; Cesar Chavez, labor leader; Cochise, Apache chief; Joan Ganz Cooney, children's television executive; Lewis W. Douglas, public official; Max Ernst, painter; Geronimo (Goyathlay), Apache chief; Barry Goldwater, politician; Carl Trumbull Hayden, politician; George Wylie Hunt, first state governor; Helen Hull Jacobs, tennis champion, writer; Ulysses S. Kay, composer; Eusebio Kino, missionary; Percival Lowell, astronomer; Frank Luke, Jr., WWI fighter ace; Charles Mingus, jazz musician, composer; Carlos Montezuma, doctor and Indian spokesman; William O'Neill, frontier sheriff; Alexander M. Patch, general; William H. Pickering, astronomer; Linda Ronstadt, singer; Clyde W. Tombaugh, astronomer; Stewart Udall, ex-Secretary of the Interior; Pauline Weaver, frontier person

ARKANSAS

Capital: Little Rock
Governor: Mike Huckabee, R (to Jan. 1998)
Lieut. Governor: (vacant[1])
Secy. of State: Sharon Priest, D (to Jan. 1998)
Atty. General: Winston Bryant, D (to Jan. 1998)
Auditor of State: Gus Wingfield, D (to Jan. 1998)
Treasurer of State: Jimmie Lou Fisher, D (to Jan. 1998)
Land Commissioner: Charles Daniels, D (to Jan. 1998)
Organized as territory: March 2, 1819
Entered Union & (rank): June 15, 1836 (25)
Present constitution adopted: 1874
Motto: *Regnat populus* (The people rule)
STATE SYMBOLS: flower, Apple Blossom (1901); **tree,** Pine (1939); **bird,** Mockingbird (1929); **insect,** Honeybee (1973); **song,** "Arkansas" (1963)
Nickname: Land of Opportunity
Origin of name: From the Quapaw Indians
10 largest cities (1990 census): Little Rock, 175,795; Fort Smith, 72,798; North Little Rock, 61,741; Pine Bluff, 57,140; Jonesboro, 46,535; Fayetteville, 42,099; Hot Springs, 32,462; Springdale, 29,941; Jacksonville, 29,101; West Memphis, 28,259
Land area & (rank): 52,075 sq mi. (134,875 sq km) (27)
Geographic center: In Pulaski Co., 12 mi. NW of Little Rock
Number of counties: 75
Largest county (1990 census): Pulaski, 349,660
State forests: None
State parks: 44
1995 resident population est.: 2,484,000
1990 resident population (rank): 2,350,725 (33). **Male:** 1,133,076; **Female:** 1,217,649. **White:** 1,944,744 (82.7%); **Black:** 373,912 (15.9%); **American Indian, Eskimo, or Aleut:** 12,773 (0.5%); **Asian or Pacific Islander:** 12,530 (0.5%); **Other race:** 6,766 (0.3%); **Hispanic:** 19,876 (0.8%). **1990 percent population under 18:** 26.4; **65 and over:** 14.9; **median age:** 33.8.

1. Until Nov. 1996 election.

Hernando de Soto, in 1541, was among the early European explorers to visit the territory. It was a Frenchman, Henri de Tonti, who in 1686 founded the first permanent white settlement—the Arkansas Post. In 1803 the area was acquired by the U.S. as part of the Louisiana Purchase.

Food products are the state's largest employing sector, with lumber and wood products a close second. Arkansas is also a leader in the production of cotton, rice, and soybeans. It also has the country's only active diamond mine; located near Murfreesboro, it is operated as a tourist attraction.

Hot Springs National Park, and Buffalo National River in the Ozarks are major state attractions.

Blanchard Springs Caverns, the Arkansas Territorial Restoration at Little Rock, and the Arkansas Folk Center in Mountain View are of interest.

Famous natives and residents: G.M. "Broncho Billy" Anderson, actor; Maya Angelou, author, poet; Katharine Susan Anthony, author; Helen Gurley Brown, author; Glen Campbell, singer; Hattie Caraway, first elected woman senator; Johnny Cash, singer; Eldridge Cleaver, Black activist; William Jefferson Clinton, 42nd President; Dizzy Dean, baseball player; Orval Faubus, ex-governor; John Gould Fletcher, writer; James W. Fulbright, ex-senator; John H. Johnson, publisher; Alan Ladd, actor; Douglas MacArthur, 5-star general; John Paul McConnell, U.S. Air Force officer; Ben Murphy, actor; Frank Pace, Jr., public official; Ben Piazza, actor; Albert Pike, pioneer teacher, lawyer; Dick Powell, actor; Opie P. Read, writer; Jenny D. Rice-Meyrowitz, painter; Brehon Burke Somervell, World Wars I and II U.S. Army officer; Mary Steenburgen, actress; Edward Durrell Stone, architect; Sam Walton, Wal-Mart founder; William C. Warfield, concert singer, actor

CALIFORNIA

Capital: Sacramento
Governor: Pete Wilson, R (to Jan. 1999)
Lieut. Governor: Gray Davis, D (to Jan. 1999)
Secy. of State: Bill Jones, R, (to Jan. 1999)
Controller: Cathleen Connell, D (to Jan. 1999)
Atty. General: Dan Lungren, R (to Jan. 1999)
Treasurer: Matt Fong, R (to Jan. 1999)
Supt. of Public Instruction: David Meaney
Entered Union & (rank): Sept. 9, 1850 (31)
Present constitution adopted: 1879
Motto: *Eureka* (I have found it)
STATE SYMBOLS: flower, Golden poppy (1903); **tree,** California redwoods (*Sequoia sempervirens & Sequoia gigantea*) (1937 % 1953); **bird,** California valley quail (1931); **animal,** California grizzly bear (1953); **fish,** California golden trout (1947); **colors,** Blue and gold (1951); **song,** "I Love You, California" (1951)
Nickname: Golden State
Origin of name: From a book, *Las Sergas de Esplandián*, by Garcia Ordóñez de Montalvo, c. 1500
10 largest cities (1990 census): Los Angeles, 3,485,398; San Diego, 1,110,549; San Jose, 782,248; San Francisco, 723,959; Long Beach, 429,433; Oakland, 372,242; Sacramento, 369,365; Fresno, 354,202; Santa Ana, 293,742; Anaheim, 266,406
Land area & (rank): 155,973 sq mi. (403,970 sq km) (3)
Geographic center: In Madera Co., 35 mi. NE of Madera
Number of counties: 58
Largest county (1990 census): Los Angeles, 8,863,164
State forests: 8 (70,283 ac.)
State parks and beaches: 180 (723,000 ac.)
1995 resident population est.: 31,589,000

1990 resident population (rank): 29,760,021 (1). **Male:** 14,897,627; **Female:** 14,862,394. **White:** 20,524,327 (69.9%); **Black:** 2,208,801 (7.4%); **American Indian, Eskimo, or Aleut:** 242,164 (0.8%); **Asian or Pacific Islander,** 2,845,659 (9.6%); **Other race:** 3,939,070 (13.2%); **Hispanic,** 7,687,938 (25.8%). **1990 percent population under 18:** 26.0; **65 and over:** 10.5; **median age:** 31.5.

Although California was sighted by Spanish navigator Juan Rodríguez Cabrillo in 1542, its first Spanish mission (at San Diego) was not established until 1769. California became a U.S. Territory in 1847 when Mexico surrendered it to John C. Frémont. On Jan. 24, 1848, James W. Marshall discovered gold at Sutter's Mill, starting the California Gold Rush and bringing settlers to the state in large numbers.

In 1964, the U.S. Census Bureau estimated that California had become the most populous state, surpassing New York. California also leads the country in personal income and consumer expenditures.

Leading industries include manufacturing (transportation equipment, machinery, and electronic equipment), agriculture, biotechnology, and tourism. Principal natural resources include timber, petroleum, cement, and natural gas.

More immigrants settle in California than any other state—more than one-third of the nation's total in 1994. Asian-Pacific Islanders led the influx.

Death Valley, in the southeast, is 282 feet below sea level, the lowest point in the nation; and Mt. Whitney (14,491 ft) is the highest point in the contiguous 48 states. Lassen Peak is one of two active U.S. volcanoes outside of Alaska and Hawaii; its last eruptions were recorded in 1917. The General Sherman Tree in Sequoia National Park is estimated to be about 3,500 years old and a stand of bristlecone pine trees in the White Mountains may be over 4,000 years old.

Other points of interest include Yosemite National Park, Disneyland, Hollywood, the Golden Gate bridge, San Simeon State Park, and Point Reyes National Seashore.

Famous natives and residents: Gertrude Atherton, author; David Belasco, playwright and producer; Shirley Temple Black, actress, ambassador; Dave Brubeck, musician; Luther Burbank, horticulturalist; Julia Child, chef; Joe DiMaggio, baseball player; James H. Doolittle, Air Force general; Isadora Duncan, dancer; John Frémont, explorer; Robert Frost, poet; Henry George, economist; Richard "Pancho" Gonzales, tennis player; George E. Hale, astronomer; Bret Harte, writer; William Randolph Hearst, publisher; Sidney Howard, playwright; Collis Potter Huntington, financier; Helen Hunt Jackson, writer; Robinson Jeffers, poet; Anthony M. Kennedy, jurist; Jack London, author; James W. Marshall, first discovered gold; Aimee Semple McPherson, evangelist; Marilyn Monroe, actress; John Muir, naturalist; Richard M. Nixon, President; Isamu Noguchi, sculptor; Frank Norris, novelist; Kathleen Norris, novelist; George S. Patton, Jr, general; Robert Redford, actor; Sally K. Ride, astronaut; William Saroyan, author; Junípero Serra, missionary; Upton Sinclair, novelist; Leland Stanford, railroad magnate; Lincoln Steffens, journalist, author; John Steinbeck, author; Adlai Stevenson, statesman; Johann Sutter, pioneer; Michael Tilson Thomas, conductor; Earl Warren, jurist

COLORADO

Capital: Denver
Governor: Roy Romer, D (to Jan. 1999)
Lieut. Governor: Gail Schoettler, D (to Jan. 1999)

Secy. of State: Vikki Buckley, R (to Jan. 1999)
Treasurer: Bill Owens, R (to Jan. 1999)
Controller: Cliff Hall, R (appointed)
Atty. General: Gale Norton, R (to Jan. 1999)
Organized as territory: Feb. 28, 1861
Entered Union & (rank): Aug. 1, 1876 (38)
Present constitution adopted: 1876
Motto: *Nil sine Numine* (Nothing without Providence)
STATE SYMBOLS: flower, Rocky Mountain columbine (1899); **tree,** Colorado blue spruce (1939); **bird,** Lark bunting (1931); **animal,** Rocky Mountain bighorn sheep (1961); **gemstone,** Aquamarine (1971); **colors,** Blue and white (1911); **song,** "Where the Columbines Grow" (1915); **fossil,** Stegosaurus (1991)
Nickname: Centennial State
Origin of name: From the Spanish, "ruddy" or "red"
10 largest cities (1990 census): Denver, 467,610; Colorado Springs, 281,140; Aurora, 222,103; Lakewood, 126,481; Pueblo, 98,640; Arvada, 89,235; Fort Collins, 87,758; Boulder, 83,312; Westminster, 74,625; Greeley, 60,536
Land area & (rank): 103,730 sq mi. (268,660 sq km) (8)
Geographic center: In Park Co., 30 mi. NW of Pikes Peak
Number of counties: 63
Largest county (1990 census): Denver, 467,610
State forests: 1 (71,000 ac.)
State parks: 44
1995 resident population est.: 3,747,000
1990 resident census population (rank): 3,294,394 (26). **Male:** 1,631,295; **Female:** 1,663,099. **White:** 2,095,474 (88.2%); **Black:** 133,146 (4.0%); **American Indian, Eskimo, or Aleut:** 27,776 (0.8%); **Asian or Pacific Islander,** 59,862 (1.8%); **Other race:** 168,136 (5.1%); **Hispanic:** 424,302 (12.9%). **1990 percent population under 18:** 26.1; **65 and over:** 10.0; **median age:** 32.5

First visited by Spanish explorers in the 1500s, the territory was claimed for Spain by Juan de Ulibarri in 1706. The U.S. obtained eastern Colorado as part of the Louisiana Purchase in 1803, the central portion in 1845 with the admission of Texas as a state, and the western part in 1848 as a result of the Mexican War.

Colorado has the highest mean elevation of any state, with more than 1,000 Rocky Mountain peaks over 10,000 feet high and 54 towering above 14,000 feet. Pikes Peak, the most famous of these mountains, was discovered by U.S. Army Lieut. Zebulon M. Pike in 1806.

Once primarily a mining and agricultural state, Colorado's economy is now driven by the service-producing industries, which provide jobs for approximately 82.4% of the state's non-farm work force. Tourism expenditures in the state total approximately 6 billion dollars annually. Tourist expenditures on the ski industry account for 1.8 billion dollars annually, approximately 1/3 of the total tourist expenditures. The main tourist attractions in the state include Rocky Mountain National Park, Curecanti National Recreation Area, Mesa Verde National Park, the Great Sand Dunes and Dinosaur National Monuments, Colorado National Monument, and the Black Canyon of the Gunnison National Monument.

The two primary facets of Colorado's manufacturing industry are food and kindred products, and printing and publishing.

The mining industry, which includes oil and gas, coal, and metal mining, was important to Colorado's economy, but it now employs only 1.2 percent of the state's workforce. Denver is home to companies that control half of the nation's gold production. The farm industry, which is primarily concentrated in livestock, is also an important element of the state's economy. The primary crops in Colorado are corn, hay, and wheat.

Famous natives and residents: William E. Barrett, writer; William Bent, fur trader and pioneer; Charles F. Brannan, lawyer and public official; M. Scott Carpenter, astronaut; Lon Chaney, actor; Mary Coyle Chase, playwright; Jack Dempsey, boxer; Ralph Edwards, entertainer; John Evans, physician, educator; Douglas Fairbanks, actor; John Thomas Fante, writer; Eugene Fodor, violinist; Gene Fowler, writer; Erick Hawkins, choreographer; Homer Lea, soldier, writer; Ted Mack, TV host; Jaye P. Morgan, singer; Peg Murray, actress; Ouray, Ute Indian chief; Anne Parrish, writer; Barbara Rush, actress; Horace A. Tabor, silver king, Lieut.-Governor; Lowell Thomas, commentator and author; Dalton Trumbo, screenwriter, novelist; Byron R. White, jurist; Paul Whiteman, conductor; Don Wilson, announcer

CONNECTICUT

Capital: Hartford
Governor: John G. Rowland, R (to Jan. 1999)
Lieut. Governor: M. Jodi Rell, R (to Jan. 1999)
Secy. of State: Miles S. Rapoport, D (to Jan. 1999)
Comptroller: Nancy Wyman, D (to Jan. 1999)
Treasurer: Christopher B. Burnham, R (to Jan. 1999)
Atty. General: Richard Blumenthal, D (to Jan. 1999)
Entered Union & (rank): Jan. 9, 1788 (5)
Present constitution adopted: Dec. 30, 1965
Motto: *Qui transtulit sustinet* (He who transplanted still sustains)
STATE SYMBOLS: flower, Mountain Laurel (1907); **tree,** White Oak (1947); **animal,** Sperm Whale (1975); **bird,** American Robin (1943); **hero,** Nathan Hale (1985); **insect,** Praying Mantis (1977); **mineral,** Garnet (1977); **song,** "Yankee Doodle" (1978); **ship,** USS Nautilus (SSN571) (1983); **shellfish,** Eastern Oyster (1989); **fossil,** Eubrontes Giganteus (1991)
Official designation: *Constitution State* (1959)
Nickname: Nutmeg State
Origin of name: From an Indian word (Quinnehtukqut) meaning "beside the long tidal river"
10 largest cities (1990 census): Bridgeport, 141,686; Hartford, 139,739; New Haven, 130,474; Waterbury, 108,961; Stamford, 108,056; Norwalk, 78,331; New Britain, 75,491; Danbury, 65,585; Bristol, 60,640; Meriden, 59,479
Land area & (rank): 4,845 sq mi. (12,550 sq km) (48)
Geographic center: In Hartford Co., at East Berlin
Number of counties: 8
Largest town (1990 census): West Hartford 60,110
State forests: 28 (144,464 ac.)
State parks: 92 (31,597 ac.)
1995 resident population est.: 3,275,000
1990 resident population (rank): 3,287,116 (27). **Male:** 1,592,873; **Female:** 1,694,243. **White:** 2,859,353 (87.0%); **Black:** 274,269 (8.3%); **American Indian, Eskimo, or Aleut:** 6,654 (0.2%); **Asian or Pacific Islander:** 50,698 (1.5%); **Other race:** 96,142 (2.9%); **Hispanic:** 213,116 (6.5%). **1990 percent population under 18:** 22.8; **65 and over:** 13.6; **median age:** 34.4.

The Dutch navigator, Adriaen Block, was the first European of record to explore the area, sailing up the Connecticut River in 1614. In 1633, Dutch colonists built a fort and trading post near present-day Hartford, but soon lost control to English Puritans migrating south from the Massachusetts Bay Colony.

English settlements, established in the 1630s at Windsor, Wethersfield, and Hartford, united in 1639 to form the Connecticut Colony and adopted the *Fundamental Orders*, considered the world's first written constitution.

The colony's royal charter of 1662 was exceptionally liberal. When Gov. Edmund Andros tried to seize it in 1687, it was hidden in the Hartford Oak, commemorated in Charter Oak Place.

Connecticut played a prominent role in the Revolutionary War, serving as the Continental Army's major supplier. Sometimes called the "Arsenal of the Nation," the state became one of the most industrialized in the nation.

Today, Connecticut factories produce weapons, sewing machines, jet engines, helicopters, motors, hardware and tools, cutlery, clocks, locks, ball bearings, silverware, and submarines. Hartford, which has the oldest U.S. newspaper still being published—the *Hartford Courant*, established 1764—is the insurance capital of the nation.

Poultry, fruit, and dairy products account for the largest portion of farm income, and Connecticut's shade-grown tobacco is acknowledged to be the state's most valuable crop per acre.

Connecticut is a popular resort area with its 250-mile Long Island Sound shoreline and many inland lakes. Among the major points of interest are Yale University's Gallery of Fine Arts and Peabody Museum. Other famous museums include the P.T. Barnum, Winchester Gun, and American Clock and Watch. The town of Mystic features a recreated 19th-century New England seaport and the Mystic Marinelife Aquarium.

Famous natives and residents: Dean Acheson, statesman; Ethan Allan, American Revolutionary soldier; Benedict Arnold, American Revolutionary general; Wadsworth Atheneum; P.T. Barnum, showman; Henry Ward Beecher, clergyman; John Brown, abolitionist; Oliver Ellsworth, jurist; Eileen Farrell, soprano; Charles Goodyear, inventor; Nathan Hale, American Revolutionary officer; Dorothy Hamill, ice skater; Katharine Hepburn, actress; Charles Ives, composer; Edwin H. Land, inventor; John Pierpont Morgan, financier; Frederick Law Olmsted, landscape planner; Rosa Ponselle, soprano; Adam Clayton Powell, Jr., congressman; Benjamin Spock, pediatrician; Harriet Beecher Stowe, author; Morris R. Waite, jurist; Noah Webster, lexicographer

DELAWARE

Capital: Dover
Governor: Thomas R. Carper, D (to Jan. 1997)
Lieut. Governor: Ruth Ann Minner, D (to Jan. 1997)
Secy. of State: Edward J. Freel, D (Pleasure of Governor)
State Treasurer: Janet C. Rzewnicki, R (to Jan. 1996)
Atty. General: M. Jane Brady, R (to Jan. 1998)
Entered Union & (rank): Dec. 7, 1787 (1)
Present constitution adopted: 1897
Motto: Liberty and independence
STATE SYMBOLS: colors, Colonial blue and buff; **flower,** Peach blossom (1895); **tree,** American holly (1939); **bird,** Blue Hen chicken (1939); **insect,** Ladybug (1974); **fish,** Weakfish, *Cynoscion regalis* (1981); **song,** "Our Delaware"
Nicknames: Diamond State; First State; Small Wonder
Origin of name: From Delaware River and Bay; named in turn for Sir Thomas West, Lord De La Warr
Largest cities (1994 est.,)[1]: Wilmington, 72,799; Dover, 28,876; Milford, 6,680; Seaford, 6,254; Elsmere, 5,542; New Castle, 5,131; Georgetown, 4,196; Middletown, 4,129
Land area & (rank): 1,982 sq mi. (5,153 sq km) (49)
Geographic center: In Kent Co., 11 mi. S of Dover

Number of counties: 3
Largest county (1990 census): New Castle, 441,946
State forests: 3 (6,149 ac.)
State parks: 12
1995 resident population est.: 717,000
1990 resident census population (rank): 666,168 (46).
Male: 322,968; **Female:** 343,200. **White:** 535,094
(80.3%); **Black:** 112,460 (16.9%); **American Indian,
Eskimo, or Aleut:** 2,019 (0.3%); **Asian or Pacific Islander:** 9,057 (1.4%); **Other race:** 7,538 (1.1%); **Hispanic:** 15,820 (2.4%). **1990 percent population under 18:**
24.5; **65 and over:** 12.1; **median age:** 32.9.

1. Bureau of the Census.

Henry Hudson, sailing under the Dutch flag, is
credited with Delaware's discovery in 1609. The following year, Capt. Samuel Argall of Virginia named
Delaware for his colony's governor, Thomas West,
Baron De La Warr. An attempted Dutch settlement
failed in 1631. Swedish colonization began at Fort
Christina (now Wilmington) in 1638, but New Swed-
en fell to Dutch forces led by New Netherlands' Gov.
Peter Stuyvesant in 1655.

England took over the area in 1664 and it was
transferred to William Penn as the southern Three
Counties in 1682. Semiautonomous after 1704, Delaware fought as a separate state in the American Revolution and became the first state to ratify the constitution in 1787.

During the Civil War, although a slave state, Delaware did not secede from the Union.

In 1802, Éleuthère Irénée du Pont established a
gunpowder mill near Wilmington that laid the foundation for Delaware's huge chemical industry. Delaware's manufactured products now also include vul-
canized fiber, textiles, paper, medical supplies, metal
products, machinery, machine tools, and automobiles.

Delaware also grows a great variety of fruits and
vegetables and is a U.S. pioneer in the food-canning
industry. Corn, soybeans, potatoes, and hay are important crops. Delaware's broiler chicken farms supply the big Eastern markets, fishing and dairy products are other important industries.

Points of interest include the Fort Christina Monument, Hagley Museum, Holy Trinity Church (erected
in 1698, the oldest Protestant church in the United
States still in use), and Winterthur Museum, in and
near Wilmington; central New Castle, an almost unchanged late 18th-century capital; and the Delaware
Museum of Natural History.

Popular recreation areas include Cape Henlopen,
Delaware Seashore, Trapp Pond State Park, and Re-
hoboth Beach.

Famous natives and residents: Richard Allen, founder
of African Methodist Episcopal Church; Valerie Berti-
nelli, actress; Robert Montgomery Bird, playwright
and novelist; Henry S. Canby, editor and author; Annie
Jump Cannon, astronomer; Elizabeth Margaret Chandler, author; Felix Darley, artist; John Dickinson,
statesman; E.I. du Pont, industrialist; Oliver Evans, inventor; Thomas Garrett, abolitionist; Henry Heimlich,
surgeon, inventor; Wilham Julius "Judy" Johnson,
basketball player; J.P. Marquand, novelist; Howard
Pyle, artist and author; George Read, jurist, signer of
Declaration of Independence; Jay Saunders Redding,
educator and author; Caesar Rodney, patriot, signer of
Declaration of Independence; Frank Stephens, sculptor; Estelle Taylor, actress; George Alfred Townsend,
journalist and author

DISTRICT OF COLUMBIA

*See listing at end of 50 Largest Cities of the United
States.*

FLORIDA

Capital: Tallahassee
Governor: Lawton Chiles, D (to Jan. 1999)
Lieut. Governor: Buddy McKay, D (to Jan. 1999)
Secy. of State: Sandra B. Mortham, R (to Jan. 1999)
Comptroller: Bob Milligan, R (to Jan. 1999)
Commissioner of Agriculture: Bob Crawford, D (to Jan.
1999)
Atty. General: Bob Butterworth, D (to Jan. 1999)
Organized as territory: March 20, 1822
Entered Union & (rank): March 3, 1845 (27)
Present constitution adopted: 1969
Motto: In God we trust (1868)
STATE SYMBOLS: flower, Orange blossom (1909); **bird,**
Mockingbird (1927); **song,** "Suwannee River" (1935)
Nickname: Sunshine State (1970)
Origin of name: From the Spanish, meaning "feast of
flowers" (Easter)
10 largest cities (1990 census): Jacksonville (CC[1]),
672,971; Miami, 358,548; Tampa, 280,015; St. Peters-
burg, 238,629; Hialeah, 188,004; Orlando, 164,693; Fort
Lauderdale, 149,377; Tallahassee, 124,773; Hollywood,
121,697; Clearwater, 98,784
Land area & (rank): 53,997 sq mi. (139,852 sq km) (26)
Geographic center: In Hernando Co., 12 mi. NNW of
Brooksville
Number of counties: 67
Largest county (1990 census): Dade, 1,937,094
State forests: 3 (306,881 ac.)
State parks: 105 (215,820 ac.)
1995 resident population est.: 14,166,000
1990 resident census population (rank): 12,937,926 (4).
Male: 6,261,719; **Female:** 6,676,207. **White:** 10,749,285
(83.1%); **Black:** 1,759,534 (13.6%); **American Indian,
Eskimo, or Aleut:** 36,335 (0.3%); **Asian or Pacific Is-
lander:** 154,302 (1.2%); **Other race:** 238,470 (1.8%);
Hispanic: 1,574,143 (12.2%). **1990 percent population
under 18:** 22.2; **65 and over:** 18.3; **median age:** 36.4.

1. Consolidated City (Coextensive with Duval County).

In 1513, Ponce De Leon, seeking the mythical
"Fountain of Youth," discovered and named Florida,
claiming it for Spain. Later, Florida would be held at
different times by Spain and England until Spain finally sold it to the United States in 1819. (Incidentally, France established a colony named Fort Caroline
in 1564 in the state that was to become Florida.)

Florida's early 19th-century history as a U.S. territory was marked by wars with the Seminole Indians
that did not end until 1842, although a treaty was actually never signed.

One of the nation's fastest-growing states, Florida's
population has gone from 2.8 million in 1950 to more
than 12.9 million in 1990.

Florida's economy rests on a solid base of tourism
(in 1992 the state entertained more than 40.5 million
visitors from all over the world), manufacturing, agriculture, and international trade.

In recent years, oranges, grapefruit and tomatoes
lead Florida's crop list, followed by vegetables, potatoes, melons, strawberries, sugar cane, dairy products,
cattle and calves, and forest products.

Major tourist attractions are Miami Beach, Palm
Beach, St. Augustine (founded in 1565, thus the oldest permanent city in the U.S.), Daytona Beach, and
Fort Lauderdale on the East Coast. West Coast resorts
include Sarasota, Tampa, Key West and St. Petersburg. The Orlando area, where Disney World is located on a 27,000-acre site, is Florida's most popular
tourist destination.

Also drawing many visitors are the NASA Kennedy Space Center's Spaceport USA, located in the town of Kennedy Space Center, Everglades National Park, and the Epcot Center.

Famous natives and residents: Julian "Cannonball" Adderley, jazz saxophonist; Pat Boone, singer; Fernando Bujones, ballet dancer; Steve Carlton, baseball player; Fay Dunaway, actress; Stepin Fetchit (Lincoln Theodore Perry), comedian; Lue Gim Gong, horticulturist; Dwight Gooden, baseball player; James Weldon Johnson, author and educator; Frances Langford, singer; Butterfly McQueen, actress; Jim Morrison, singer; Osceola, Seminole Indian leader; Sidney Poitier, actor; A. Philip Randolph, labor leader; Marjorie Kinnan Rawlings, author; Charles and John Ringling, circus entrepreneurs; Joseph W. Stilwell, army general; Ben Vereen, actor

GEORGIA

Capital: Atlanta
Governor: Zell Miller, D (to Jan. 1999)
Lieut. Governor: Pierre Howard, D (to Jan. 1999)
Secy. of State: Lewis A. Massey, D (to Jan. 1999)
Insurance Commissioner: John Oxendine, D (to Jan. 1999)
Atty. General: Michael J. Bowers, R (to Jan. 1999)
Entered Union & (rank): Jan. 2, 1788 (4)
Present constitution adopted: 1977
Motto: Wisdom, justice, and moderation
STATE SYMBOLS: flower, Cherokee rose (1916); **tree,** Live oak (1937); **bird,** Brown thrasher (1935); **song,** "Georgia on My Mind" (1922)
Nicknames: Peach State, Empire State of the South
Origin of name: In honor of George II of England
10 largest cities (1990 census): Atlanta, 394,017; Columbus[1], 179,278; Savannah, 137,560; Macon, 106,612; Albany, 78,122; Roswell, 47,923; Athens, 45,734; Augusta, 44,639; Marietta, 44,129; Warner Robins, 43,726.
Land area & (rank): 57,919 sq mi. (150,010 sq km) (21)
Geographic center: In Twiggs Co., 18 mi. SE of Macon
Number of counties: 159
Largest county (1990 census): Fulton, 648,951
State forests: 25,258,000 ac. (67% of total state area)
State parks: 53 (42,600 ac.)
1995 resident population est.: 7,201,000
1990 resident census population (rank): 6,478,216 (11).
  Male: 3,144,503; **Female:** 3,333,713. **White:** 4,600,148 (71.0%); **Black:** 1,746,565 (27.0%); **American Indian, Eskimo, or Aleut:** 13,348 (0.2%); **Asian or Pacific Islander:** 75,781 (1.2%); **Other race:** 42,374 (0.7%); **Hispanic:** 108,922 (1.7%). **1990 percent population under 18:** 26.7; **65 and over:** 10.1; **median age:** 31.6.

1. Consolidated City (Coextensive with Muscogee County).

Hernando de Soto, the Spanish explorer, first traveled parts of Georgia in 1540. British claims later conflicted with those of Spain. After obtaining a royal charter, Gen. James Oglethorpe established the first permanent settlement in Georgia in 1733 as a refuge for English debtors. In 1742, Oglethorpe defeated Spanish invaders in the Battle of Bloody Marsh.

A Confederate stronghold, Georgia was the scene of extensive military action during the Civil War. Union General William T. Sherman burned Atlanta and destroyed a 60-mile wide path to the coast where he captured Savannah in 1864.

The largest state east of the Mississippi, Georgia is typical of the changing South with an ever-increasing industrial development. Atlanta, largest city in the state, is the communications and transportation center for the Southeast and the area's chief distributor of goods.

Georgia leads the nation in the production of paper and board, tufted textile products, and processed chicken. Other major manufactured products are transportation equipment, food products, apparel, and chemicals.

Important agricultural products are corn, cotton, tobacco, soybeans, eggs, and peaches. Georgia produces twice as many peanuts as the next leading state. From its vast stands of pine come more than half the world's resins and turpentine and 74.4% of the U.S. supply. Georgia is also a leader in the production of marble, kaolin, barite, and bauxite.

Principal tourist attractions in Georgia include the Okefenokee National Wildlife Refuge; Andersonville Prison Park and National Cemetery; Chickamauga and Chattanooga National Military Park; the Little White House at Warm Springs where Pres. Franklin D. Roosevelt died in 1945; Sea Island; the enormous Confederate Memorial at Stone Mountain; Kennesaw Mountain National Battlefield Park; and Cumberland Island National Seashore.

Famous natives and residents: Conrad Aiken, poet; James Bowie, soldier; James Brown, singer; Jim Brown, actor and athlete; Erskine Caldwell, writer; James E. Carter, ex-President; Ray Charles, singer; Lucius D. Clay, banker, ex-general; Ty Cobb, baseball player; Ossie Davis, actor & writer; James Dickey, poet; Mattiwilda Dobbs, soprano; Melvyn Douglas, actor; Rebecca Latimer Felton, first appointed woman U.S. senator; Roosevelt Grier, entertainer and ex-athlete; Oliver Hardy, comedian; Joel Chandler Harris, journalist and author; Larry Holmes, boxer; Miriam Hopkins, actress; Harry James, trumpeter; Jasper Johns, painter and sculptor; Bobby Jones, golfer; Stacy Keach, actor; DeForest Kelley, actor; Martin Luther King, Jr., civil rights leader; Gladys Knight, singer; Joseph R. Lamar, jurist; Juliette Gordon Low, U.S. Girl Scouts founder; Carson McCullers, novelist; Johnny Mercer, songwriter; Margaret Mitchell, novelist; Elijah Muhammad, religious leader; Jessye Norman, soprano; Otis Redding, singer; Burt Reynolds, actor; Jackie Robinson, baseball player; Dean Rusk, ex-Secretary of State; Nipsey Russell, comedian; Alice Walker, author; Joanne Woodward, actress

HAWAII

Capital: Honolulu (on Oahu)
Governor: Benjamin Cayetano, D
Lieut. Governor: Mazie Hirono, D
Comptroller: Sam Callejo
Atty. General: Margery Bronster
Organized as territory: 1900
Entered Union & (rank): Aug. 21, 1959 (50)
Motto: Ua Mau Ke Ea O Ka Aina I Ka Pono (The life of the land is perpetuated in righteousness)
STATE SYMBOLS: flower, Hibiscus (yellow) 1988); **song,** "Hawaii Ponoi" (1967); **bird,** Nene (hawaiian goose) (1957); **tree,** Kukui (Candlenut) (1959)
Nickname: Aloha State (1959)
Origin of name: Uncertain. The islands may have been named by Hawaii Loa, their traditional discoverer. Or they may have been named after Hawaii or Hawaiki, the traditional home of the Polynesians.
10 largest cities[1] (1990 census): Honolulu, 377,059; Hilo, 37,808; Kailua, 36,818; Kaneohe, 35,448; Waipahu, 31,435; Pearl City, 30,993; Waimalu, 29,967; Mililani Town, 29,359; Schofield Barracks, 19,597; Wahiawa, 17,386
Land area & (rank): 6,423.4 sq mi. (16,636.5 sq km) (47)

Geographic center: Between islands of Hawaii and Maui
Number of counties: 4 plus one non-functioning county (Kalawao)
Largest county (1990 census): Honolulu, 836,231
State parks and historic sites: 70
1995 resident population est.: 1,187,000
1990 resident census population (rank): 1,108,229 (40).
   Male: 563,891; **Female:** 544,338. **White:** 369,616 (33.4%); **Black:** 27,195 (2.5%); **American Indian, Eskimo, or Aleut:** 5,099 (0.5%); **Asian or Pacific Islander:** 685,236 (61.8%); **Other race:** 21,083 (1.9%); **Hispanic:** 81,390 (7.3%). **1990 percent population under 18:** 25.3; **65 and over:** 11.3; **median age:** 32.6

1. Census Designated Place. There are no political boundaries to Honolulu or any other place, but statistical boundaries are assigned under state law.

First settled by Polynesians sailing from other Pacific islands between 300 and 600 A.D., Hawaii was visited in 1778 by British Captain James Cook who called the group the Sandwich Islands.

Hawaii was a native kingdom throughout most of the 19th century when the expansion of the vital sugar industry (pineapple came after 1898) meant increasing U.S. business and political involvement. In 1893, Queen Liliuokalani was deposed and a year later the Republic of Hawaii was established with Sanford B. Dole as president. Then, following its annexation in 1898, Hawaii became a U.S. Territory in 1900.

The Japanese attack on the naval base at Pearl Harbor on Dec. 7, 1941, was directly responsible for U.S. entry into World War II.

Hawaii, 2,397 miles west-southwest of San Francisco, is a 1,523-mile chain of islets and eight main islands—Hawaii, Kahoolawe, Maui, Lanai, Molokai, Oahu, Kauai, and Niihau. The Northwestern Hawaiian Islands, other than Midway, are administratively part of Hawaii.

The temperature is mild and Hawaii's soil is fertile for tropical fruits and vegetables. Cane sugar and pineapple are the chief products. Hawaii also grows coffee, bananas and nuts. The tourist business is Hawaii's largest source of outside income.

Hawaii's highest peak is Mauna Kea (13,796 ft.). Mauna Loa (13,679 ft.) is the largest volcanic mountain in the world in cubic content.

Among the major points of interest are Hawaii Volcanoes National Park (Hawaii), Haleakala National Park (Maui), Puuhonua o Honaunau National Historical Park (Hawaii), Polynesian Cultural Center (Oahu), the U.S.S. *Arizona* Memorial at Pearl Harbor, and Iolani Palace (the only royal palace in the U.S.), Bishop Museum, and Waikiki Beach (all in Honolulu).

Famous natives and residents: George Ariyoshi, first Japanese-American elected governor; Hiram Bingham, missionary; Charles R. Bishop, banker and philanthropist; Tia Carrere, singer, actress; Samuel N. Castle, missionary, founder of Castle & Cooke Ltd. with Amos S. Cooke, missionary and educator; Father Damien, leper colony worker; Sanford B. Dole, territorial governor; Jean Erdman, dancer, choreographer; Hiram L. Fong, first Chinese-American senator; Don Ho, entertainer; Daniel K. Inouye, senator; Gerrit P. Judd, advisor of Hawaiian king; Keahumanu, female chief; Duke Paoa Kahanamoku, Olympic swimming champion; Kamehameha I, first Hawaiian king; Kamehameha V, last of the dynasty; George Parsons Lathrop, journalist and poet; Liliuokalani, queen, last Hawaiian monarch; Bette Midler, singer; Ellison Onizuka, astronaut; Kawaipuna Prejean, Hawaiian activist, proponent of Hawaiian sovereignty; Chad Rowan, Yokozuna, sumo wrestler; Harold Sakata, actor; Carolyn Suzanne Sapp, 1991 Miss America; James Shigeta, actor; Claus Spreckels, developer of Hawaiian sugar industry; Don Stroud, actor

IDAHO

Capital: Boise
Governor: Philip E. Batt, R (to Jan. 1999)
Lieut. Governor: C. L. "Butch" Otter, R (to Jan. 1999)
Secy. of State: Pete T. Cenarrusa, R (to Jan. 1999)
State Auditor: J.D. Williams, D (to Jan. 1999)
Atty. General: Alan G. Lance, R (to Jan. 1999)
Treasurer: Lydia Justice Edwards, R (to Jan. 1999)
Organized as territory: March 3, 1863
Entered Union & (rank): July 3, 1890 (43)
Present constitution adopted: 1890
Motto: *Esto perpetua* (It is forever)
STATE SYMBOLS: flower, Syringa (1931); **tree,** White pine (1935); **bird,** Mountain bluebird (1931); **horse,** Appaloosa (1975); **gem,** Star garnet (1967); **song,** "Here We Have Idaho"; **folk dance,** Square Dance; **fish,** Cutthroat trout (1990); **fossil,** Hagerman horse fossil (1988)
Nicknames: Gem State; Spud State; Panhandle State
Origin of name: Unknown. It is an invented name whose meaning, if any, is unknown.
10 largest cities (1994 est.): Boise, 145,987; Pocatello, 50,588; Idaho Falls, 49,928; Nampa, 35,333; Twin Falls, 31,568 Lewiston, 30,097; Coeur d'Alene, 28,457; Caldwell, 23,970; Moscow, 18,909; Meridian, 14,566
Land area & (rank): 82,751 sq mi. (214,325 sq km) (11)
Geographic center: In Custer Co., at Custer, SW of Challis
Number of counties: 44, plus small part of Yellowstone National Park
Largest county (1994 est.): Ada, 243,337
State forests: 881,000 ac.
State parks: 22 (44,177 ac.)
1995 resident population est.: 1,163,000
1990 resident census population (rank): 1,006,749 (42).
   Male: 500,956; **Female:** 505,793. **White:** 950,451 (94.4%); **Black:** 3,370 (0.3%); **American Indian, Eskimo, or Aleut:** 13,780 (1.4%); **Asian or Pacific Islander:** 9,365 (0.9%); **Other race:** 29,783 (3.0%); **Hispanic:** 52,927 (5.3%). **1990 percent population under 18:** 30.6; **65 and over:** 12.0; **median age:** 31.5.

After its acquisition by the U.S. as part of the Louisiana Purchase in 1803, the region was explored by Meriwether Lewis and William Clark in 1805–06 Northwest boundary disputes with Great Britain were settled by the Oregon Treaty in 1846 and the first permanent U.S. settlement in Idaho was established by the Mormons at Franklin in 1860.

After gold was discovered on Orofino Creek in 1860, prospectors swarmed into the territory, but left little more than a number of ghost towns.

In the 1870s, growing white occupation of Indian lands led to a series of battles between U.S. forces and the Nez Percé, Bannock, and Sheepeater tribes.

Mining, lumbering, and irrigation farming have been important for years. Idaho produces more than one fifth of all the silver mined in the U.S. It also ranks high among the states in antimony, lead, cobalt, garnet phosphate rock, vanadium, zinc, mercury, and gold.

Idaho's most impressive growth began when World War II military needs made processing agricultural products a big industry, particularly the dehydrating and freezing of potatoes. The state produces about one fourth of the nation's potato crop, as well a wheat, apples, corn, barley, sugar beets, and hops.

With the growth of winter sports, tourism now out ranks mining in dollar revenue. Idaho's many stream and lakes provide fishing, camping, and boating sites The nation's largest elk herds draw hunters from all ove the world and the famed Sun Valley resort attracts thou sands of visitors to its swimming and skiing facilities.

Other points of interest are the Craters of the Moon National Monument; Nez Percé National Historic Park, which includes many sites visited by Lewis and Clark; and the State Historical Museum in Boise.

Famous natives and residents: Joe Albertson, grocery chain founder; Cecil Andrus, ex-governor; T.H. Bell, educator; Ezra Taft Benson, Eisenhower's Secretary of Agriculture, pres. LDS church, marketing specialist; William E. Borah, ex-senator; Gutzon Borglum, Mt. Rushmore sculptor; Carol R. Brink, author; Frank F. Church, ex-senator; Fred Dubois, ex-senator; Vardis Fisher, novelist; Lawrence H. Gipson, historian; Ernest Hemingway, author; Mariel Hemingway, actress; Chief Joseph, Nez Percé chief; Harmon Killebrew, baseball player; Jerry Kramer, football player, author; Ezra Pound, poet; Sacagawea, Shoshonean guide; J.R. Simplot, industrialist; Robert E. Smylie, political leader; Henry Spalding, missionary; Frank Steunenberg, ex-governor; Picabo Street, skier; David Tompson, founded first trading post; Lana Turner, actress

ILLINOIS

Capital: Springfield
Governor: Jim Edgar, R (to Jan. 1999)
Lieut. Governor: Bob Kustra, R (to Jan. 1999)
Atty. General: Jim Ryan, R (to Jan. 1999)
Secy. of State: George H. Ryan, R (to Jan. 1999)
Comptroller: Loleta Didrickson, R (to Jan. 1999)
Treasurer: Judith Baar Topinka, R (to Jan. 1999)
Organized as territory: Feb. 3, 1809
Entered Union & (rank): Dec. 3, 1818 (21)
Present constitution adopted: 1970
Motto: State sovereignty, national union
STATE SYMBOLS: flower, Violet (1908); **tree,** White oak (1973); **bird,** Cardinal (1929); **animal,** White-tailed deer (1982); **fish,** Bluegill (1987); **insect,** Monarch butterfly (1975); **song,** "Illinois" (1925); **mineral,** Fluorite (1965)
Nickname: Prairie State
Origin of name: From an Indian word and French suffix meaning "tribe of superior men"
10 largest cities (1990 census): Chicago, 2,783,726; Rockford, 139,426; Peoria, 113,504; Springfield, 105,227; Aurora, 99,581; Naperville, 85,351; Decatur, 83,885; Elgin, 77,010; Joliet, 76,836; Arlington Heights Village, 75,460
Land area & (rank): 55,593 sq mi. (143,987 sq km) (24)
Geographic center: In Logan County 28 mi. NE of Springfield
Number of counties: 102
Largest county (1990 census): Cook, 5,105,067
Public use areas: 187 (275,000 ac.), incl. state parks, memorials, forests and conservation areas
1995 resident population est.: 11,830,000
1990 resident census population (rank): 11,430,602 (6).
Male: 5,552,233; **Female:** 5,878,369. **White:** 8,952,978 (78.3%); **Black:** 1,694,273 (14.8%);
American Indian, Eskimo, or Aleut: 21,836 (0.2%);
Asian or Pacific Islander: 285,311 (2.5%); **Other race:** 476,204 (4.2%); **Hispanic:** 904,446 (7.9%). **1990 percent population under 18:** 25.8; **65 and over:** 12.6; **median age:** 32.8.

French explorers Marquette and Joliet, in 1673, were the first Europeans of record to visit the region. In 1699 French settlers established the first permanent settlement at Cahokia, near present-day East St. Louis.

Great Britain obtained the region at the end of the French and Indian War in 1763. The area figured prominently in frontier struggles during the Revolutionary War and in Indian wars during the early 19th century.

Significant episodes in the state's early history include the growing migration of Eastern settlers following the opening of the Erie Canal in 1825; the Black Hawk War, which virtually ended the Indian troubles in the area; and the rise of Abraham Lincoln from farm laborer to President.

Today, Illinois stands high in manufacturing, coal mining, agriculture, and oil production. The sprawling Chicago district (including a slice of Indiana) is a great iron and steel producer, meat packer, grain exchange, and railroad center. Chicago is also famous as a Great Lakes port.

Illinois ranks third in the nation in export of agricultural products, first in corn and soybeans, and third in hog production. An important dairy state, Illinois is also a leader in corn, oats, wheat, barley, rye, truck vegetables, and the nursery products.

The state manufactures a great variety of industrial and consumer products: railroad cars, clothing, furniture, tractors, liquor, watches, and farm implements are just some of the items made in its factories and plants.

Central Illinois is noted for shrines and memorials associated with the life of Abraham Lincoln. In Springfield are the Lincoln Home, the Lincoln Tomb, and the restored Old State Capitol. Other points of interest are the home of Mormon leader Joseph Smith in Nauvoo and, in Chicago: the Art Institute, Field Museum, Museum of Science and Industry, Shedd Aquarium, Adler Planetarium, Merchandise Mart, and Chicago Portage National Historic Site.

Famous natives and residents: Franklin Pierce Adams, author; Jane Addams, social worker; Mary Astor, actress; Jack Benny, comedian; Black Hawk, Sauk Indian chief; Harry A. Blackmun, jurist; Ray Bradbury, author; William Jennings Bryan, orator and politician; Edgar Rice Burroughs, novelist; Gower Champion, choreographer; John Chancellor, TV commentator; Raymond Chandler, writer; Jimmy Connors, tennis champion; James Gould Cozzens, novelist; Richard J. Daley, ex-mayor of Chicago; Miles Davis, musician; Peter DeVries, novelist; Walt Disney, film animator and produceer; John Dos Passos, author; James T. Farrell, novelist; Betty Friedan, feminist; Benny Goodman, musician; John Gunther, author; Ernest Hemingway, author; Charlton Heston, actor; Wild Bill Hickok, scout; William Holden, actor; Rock Hudson, actor; Burl Ives, singer; James Jones, novelist; John Jones, civil rights leader; Quincy Jones, composer; Keokuk (Watchful Fox), chief of the Sac and Fox Indians; Walter Kerr, drama critic; Archibald MacLeish, poet; David Mamet, playwright; Robert A. Millikan, physicist; Sherrill Milnes, baritone; Bill Murray, actor; Bob Newhart, actor, comedian; William S. Paley, broadcasting executive; Drew Pearson, columnist; Richard Pryor, comedian, actor; Ronald Reagan, ex-President; Carl Sandburg, poet; Sam Shepard, playwright; William L. Shirer, author and historian; John Paul Stevens, jurist; McLean Stevenson, actor; Preston Sturges, director; Gloria Swanson, actress; Carl Van Doren, writer and educator; Melvin Van Peebles, playwright; Irving Wallace, novelist; Alfred Wallenstein, conductor; Raquel Welch, actress; Florenz Ziegfeld, theatrical producer

INDIANA

Capital: Indianapolis
Governor: Birch Evans Bayh III, D (to Jan. 1997)
Lieut. Governor: Frank O'Bannon, D (to Jan. 1997)
Secy. of State: Sue Anne Gilroy, R (to Feb. 1999)
Treasurer: Joyce Brinkman, R (to Feb. 1999)
Atty. General: Pamela Carter, D (to Jan. 1997)
Auditor: Morris Wooden, R (to Dec. 1998)
Organized as territory: May 7, 1800
Entered Union & (rank): Dec. 11, 1816 (19)
Present constitution adopted: 1851

Motto: The Crossroads of America
STATE SYMBOLS: flower: Peony (1957); **tree,** Tulip tree (1931); **bird,** Cardinal (1933); **song,** "On the Banks of the Wabash, Far Away" (1913); **river,** Wabash
Official language: English
Nickname: Hoosier State
Origin of name: Meaning "land of Indians"
10 largest cities (1990 census): Indianapolis, 731,327; Fort Wayne, 173,072; Evansville, 126,272; Gary, 116,646; South Bend, 105,511; Hammond, 84,236; Muncie, 71,035; Bloomington, 60,633; Anderson, 59,459; Terre Haute, 57,483
Land area & (rank): 35,870 sq mi. (92,904 sq km) (38)
Geographic center: In Boone Co., 14 mi. NNW of Indianapolis
Number of Counties: 92
Largest county (1990 census): Marion, 797,159
State parks: 20 (56,806 ac.)
State memorials: 16 (941.977 ac.)
1995 resident population est.: 5,803,000
1990 census population (rank): 5,544,159 (14). **Male:** 2,688,281; **Female:** 2,855,878. **White:** 5,020,700 (90.6%); **Black:** 432,092 (7.8%); **American Indian, Eskimo, or Aleut:** 12,720 (0.2%); **Asian or Pacific Islander:** 37,617 (0.7%); **Other race:** 41,030 (0.7%); **Hispanic:** 98,788 (1.8%). **1990 percent population under 18:** 26.3; **65 and over:** 12.6; **median age:** 32.8.

First explored for France by La Salle in 1679–80, the region figured importantly in the Franco-British struggle for North America that culminated with British victory in 1763.

George Rogers Clark led American forces against the British in the area during the Revolutionary War and, prior to becoming a state, Indiana was the scene of frequent Indian uprisings until the victory of Gen. William Henry Harrison at Tippecanoe in 1811.

Indiana's 41-mile Lake Michigan waterfront—one of the world's great industrial centers—turns out iron, steel, and oil products. Products include automobile parts and accessories, mobile homes and recreational vehicles, truck and bus bodies, aircraft engines, farm machinery, and fabricated structural steel. Phonograph records, wood office furniture, and pharmaceuticals are also manufactured.

The state is a leader in agriculture with corn the principal crop. Hogs, soybeans, wheat, oats, rye, tomatoes, onions, and poultry also contribute heavily to Indiana's agricultural output. Much of the building limestone used in the U.S. is quarried in Indiana, which is also a large producer of coal.

Wyandotte Cave, one of the largest in the U.S., is located in Crawford County in southern Indiana, and West Baden and French Lick are well known for their mineral springs. Other attractions include Indiana Dunes National Lakeshore, Indianapolis Motor Speedway, Lincoln Boyhood National Memorial, and the George Rogers Clark National Historical Park.

Famous natives and residents: George Ade, humorist; Leon Ames, actor; Anne Baxter, actress; Albert J. Beveridge, political leader; Larry Bird, basketball player; Bill Blass, fashion designer; Frank Borman, astronaut; Hoagy Carmichael, songwriter; James Dean, actor; Eugene V. Debs, Socialist leader; Lloyd C. Douglas, author; Theodore Dreiser, writer; Bernard F. Gimbel, merchant; Virgil Grissom, astronaut; Phil Harris, actor and band leader; John Milton Hay, statesman; James R. Hoffa, labor leader; Michael Jackson, singer; Buck Jones, actor; Alfred C. Kinsey, zoologist; David Letterman, TV host, comedian; Eli Lilly, pharmaceuticals manufacturer; Carole Lombard, actress; Shelley Long, actress; Marjorie Main, actress; James McCracken, tenor; Joaquin Miller, poet; Paul Osborn, playwright; Cole Porter, songwriter; Gene Stratton Porter, naturalist and author; Ernest Taylor Pyle, journalist; James

Whitcomb Riley, poet; Knute Rockne, football coach; Ned Rorem, composer; Red Skelton, comedian; Rex Stout, mystery writer; Booth Tarkington, author; Twyla Tharp, dancer and choreographer; Forrest Tucker, actor; Harold C. Urey, physicist; Kurt Vonnegut, Jr., author; Jessamyn West, novelist; Wendell Willkie, lawyer; Wilbur Wright, inventor

IOWA

Capital: Des Moines
Governor: Terry E. Branstad, R (to Jan. 1999)
Lieut. Governor: Joy Corning, R (to Jan. 1999)
Secy. of State: Paul Pate, R (to Jan. 1999)
Treasurer: Michael L. Fitzgerald, D (to Jan. 1999)
Atty. General: Tom Miller, D (to Jan. 1999)
Organized as territory: June 12, 1838
Entered Union & (rank): Dec. 28, 1846 (29)
Present constitution adopted: 1857
Motto: Our liberties we prize and our rights we will maintain
STATE SYMBOLS: flower, Wild rose (1897); **bird,** Eastern goldfinch (1933); **colors,** Red, white, and blue (in state flag); **song,** "Song of Iowa"
Nickname: Hawkeye State
Origin of name: Probably from an Indian word meaning "I-o-w-a, this is the place," or "The Beautiful Land"
10 largest cities (1992 est.): Des Moines, 194,540; Cedar Rapids, 111,659; Davenport, 97,509; Sioux City, 81,907; Waterloo, 67,124; Iowa City, 59,313; Dubuque, 58,575; Council Bluffs, 54,884; Ames, 46,672; Cedar Falls, 35,094
Land area & (rank): 55,875 sq mi. (144,716 sq km) (23)
Geographic center: In Story Co., 5 mi. NE of Ames
Number of counties: 99
Largest county (1992 est.): Polk, 338,261
State forests: 5 (28,000 ac.)
State parks: 84 (49,237)
1995 resident population est.: 2,842,000
1990 resident census population (rank): 2,776,755 (30). **Male:** 1,344,802; **Female:** 1,431,953. **White:** 2,683,090 (96.6%); **Black:** 48,090 (1.7%); **American Indian, Eskimo, or Aleut:** 7,349 (0.3%); **Asian or Pacific Islander:** 25,476 (0.9%); **Other race:** 12,750 (0.5%); **Hispanic:** 32,647 (1.2%). **1990 percent population under 18:** 25.9; **65 and over:** 15.3; **median age:** 34.0

The first Europeans to visit the area were the French explorers, Father Jacques Marquette and Louis Joliet in 1673. The U.S. obtained control of the area in 1803 as part of the Louisiana Purchase.

During the first half of the 19th century, there was heavy fighting between white settlers and Indians. Lands were taken from the Indians after the Black Hawk War in 1832 and again in 1836 and 1837.

When Iowa became a state in 1846, its capital was Iowa City; the more centrally located Des Moines became the new capital in 1857. At that time, the state's present boundaries were also drawn.

Although Iowa produces a tenth of the nation's food supply, the value of Iowa's manufactured products is twice that of its agriculture. Major industries are food and associated products, non-electrical machinery, electrical equipment, printing and publishing, and fabricated products.

Iowa stands in a class by itself as an agricultural state. Its farms sell over $10 billion worth of crops and livestock annually. Iowa leads the nation in all corn, soybeans, livestock, and hog marketings, with about 25% of the pork supply and 6% of the grain-fed cattle. Iowa's forests produce hardwood lumber, particularly walnut, and its mineral products include cement, limestone, sand, gravel, gypsum, and coal.

Tourist attractions include the Herbert Hoover birthplace and library near West Branch; the Amana Colonies; Fort Dodge Historical Museum, Fort, and Stockade; the Iowa State Fair at Des Moines in August; and the Effigy Mounds National Monument at Marquette, a prehistoric Indian burial site.

Famous natives and residents: Bix Beiderbecke, jazz musician; Norman Borlang, plant pathologist and geneticist, Nobel Peace Prize winner; William "Buffalo Bill" F. Cody, scout; Johnny Carson, TV entertainer; Gardner Cowles, Jr., publisher; Simon Estes, bass-baritone; William Frawley, actor; George H. Gallup, poll taker; Susan Glaspell, writer; Herbert Hoover, ex-President; MacKinlay Kantor, novelist; Charles A. Kettering, inventor; Ann Landers, columnist; Cloris Leachman, actress; John L. Lewis, labor leader; Glenn L. Martin, aviator, manufacturer; Elsa Maxwell, writer; Frederick L. Maytag, inventor and manufacturer; Glenn Miller, bandleader; Harriet Nelson, actress; Nathan M. Pusey, educator; David Rabe, playwright; Harry Reasoner, TV commentator; Donna Reed, actress; Lillian Russell, soprano; Robert Schiller, evangelist; Wallace Stegner, novelist and critic; Billy Sunday, evangelist; James A. Van Allen, space physicist; Abigail Van Buren, columnist; Henry A. Wallace, statesman and ex-vice president; John Wayne, actor; Andy Williams, singer; Meredith Willson, composer; Grant Wood, painter

KANSAS

Capital: Topeka
Governor: Bill Graves, R (to Jan. 1999)
Lieut. Governor: Sheila Frahm, R (to Jan. 1999)
Secy. of State: Ron Thornburgh, R (to Jan. 1999)
Treasurer: Sally Thompson, D (to Jan. 1999)
Atty. General: Carla Stovall, R (to Jan. 1999)
Commission of Insurance: Kathleen Sebelius, D (to Jan. 1999)
Organized as territory: May 30, 1854
Entered Union & (rank): Jan. 29, 1861 (34)
Present constitution adopted: 1859
Motto: *Ad astra per aspera* (To the stars through difficulties)
STATE SYMBOLS: flower, Sunflower (1903); **tree,** Cottonwood (1937); **bird,** Western meadowlark (1937); **animal,** Buffalo (1955); **song,** "Home on Range" (1947)
Nicknames: Sunflower State; Jayhawk State
Origin of name: From a Sioux word meaning "people of the south wind"
10 largest cities (1990 census): Wichita, 304,011; Kansas City, 149,767; Topeka, 119,883; Overland Park, 111,790; Lawrence, 65,608; Olathe, 63,352; Salina, 42,303; Hutchinson, 39,308; Leavenworth, 38,495; Shawnee, 37,993
Land area & (rank): 81,823 sq mi. (211,922 sq km) (13)
Geographic center: In Barton Co., 15 mi. NE of Great Bend
Number of counties: 105
Largest county (1990 census): Sedgwick, 403,662
State parks: 22 (14,394 ac.)
1995 resident population est.: 2,565,000
1990 resident census population (rank): 2,477,574 (32). **Male:** 1,214,645; **Female:** 1,262,929. **White:** 2,231,986 (90.1%); **Black:** 143,076 (5.8%); **American Indian, Eskimo, or Aleut:** 21,965 (0.9%); **Asian or Pacific Islander:** 31,750 (1.3%); **Other race:** 48,797 (2.0%); **Hispanic:** 93,670 (3.8%). **1990 percent population under 18:** 26.7; **65 and over:** 13.8; **median age:** 32.9.

Spanish explorer Francisco de Coronado, in 1541, is considered the first European to have traveled this region. La Salle's extensive land claims for France (1682) included present-day Kansas. Ceded to Spain by France in 1763, the territory reverted back to France in 1800 and was sold to the U.S. as part of the Louisiana Purchase in 1803.

Lewis and Clark, Zebulon Pike, and Stephen H. Long explored the region between 1803 and 1819. The first permanent settlements in Kansas were outposts—Fort Leavenworth (1827), Fort Scott (1842), and Fort Riley (1853)—established to protect travelers along the Santa Fe and Oregon Trails.

Just before the Civil War, the conflict between the pro- and anti-slavery forces earned the region the grim title "Bleeding Kansas."

Today, wheat fields, oil well derricks, herds of cattle, and grain storage elevators are chief features of the Kansas landscape. A leading wheat-growing state, Kansas also raises corn, sorghums, oats, barley, soy beans, and potatoes. Kansas stands high in petroleum production and mines zinc, coal, salt, and lead. It is also the nation's leading producer of helium.

Wichita is one of the nation's leading aircraft manufacturing centers, ranking first in production of private aircraft. Kansas City is an important transportation, milling, and meat-packing center.

Points of interest include the Kansas Museum of History at Topeka, the Eisenhower boyhood home and the new Eisenhower Memorial Museum and Presidential Library at Abilene, John Brown's cabin at Osawatomie, recreated Front Street in Dodge City, Fort Larned (once the most important military post on the Santa Fe Trail), and Fort Leavenworth and Fort Riley.

Famous natives and residents: Roscoe "Fatty" Arbuckle, actor; Clarence D. Batchelor, political cartoonist; Gwendolyn Brooks, poet; Walter P. Chrysler, auto manufacturer; Clark M. Clifford, ex-Secretary of Defense; John Steuart Curry, painter; Amelia Earhart, aviator; Milton S. Eisenhower, educator; Gary Hart, politician; William Inge, playwright; Walter Johnson, baseball pitcher; Osa L. Johnson, documentary film producer; Buster Keaton, comedian; Emmett Kelly, clown; Stan Kenton, jazz musician; James Lehrer, broadcast journalist; Edgar Lee Masters, poet; Mary McCarthy, actress; Hattie McDaniel, actress; William C. Menninger, psychiatrist; Gordon Parks, film director; Zasu Pitts, actress; Samuel Ramey, opera singer; Charles Robinson, statesman and first governor; Charles (Buddy) Rogers, actor; Damon Runyon, journalist; Eugene W. Smith, photojournalist; Milburn Stone, actor; John Cameron Swayze, news commentator; William Allen White, journalist; Charles E. Whittaker, jurist; Jess Willard, boxer

KENTUCKY

Capital: Frankfort
Governor: Paul E. Patton, D (to Dec. 1999)
Lieut. Governor: Stephen L. Henry, D (to Dec. 1999)
Secy. of State: John Y. Brown III, D (to Dec. 1999)
State Treasurer: Ed Hatchett, D (to Dec. 1999)
State Auditor: John Kennedy Hamilton, D (to Dec. 1999)
Atty. General: A.B. Chandler III, D (to Dec. 1999)
Entered Union & (rank): June 1, 1792 (15)
Present constitution adopted: 1891
Motto: United we stand, divided we fall
STATE SYMBOLS: tree, Tulip poplar (1994); **flower,** Goldenrod; **bird,** Kentucky cardinal; **song,** "My Old Kentucky Home"
Nickname: Bluegrass State
Origin of name: From an Iroquoian word "Ken-tah-ten" meaning "land of tomorrow"

10 largest cities (1990 census): Louisville, 269,063; Lexington-Fayette, 225,366; Owensboro, 53,549; Covington, 43,264; Bowling Green, 40,641; Hopkinsville, 29,809; Paducah, 27,256; Frankfort, 25,968; Henderson, 25,945; Ashland, 23,622

Land area & (rank): 39,732 sq mi. (102,907 sq km) (36)

Geographic center: In Marion Co., 3 mi. NNW of Lebanon

Number of counties: 120

Largest county (1990 census): Jefferson, population 664,937

State forests: 9 (44,173 ac.)

State parks: 43 (40,574 ac.)

1995 resident population est.: 3,860,000

1990 resident census population (rank): 3,685,296 (23). **Male:** 1,785,235; **Female:** 1,900,061. **White:** 3,391,832 (92.0%); **Black:** 262,907 (7.1%); **American Indian, Eskimo, or Aleut:** 5,769 (0.2%); **Asian or Pacific Islander:** 17,812 (0.5%); **Other race:** 6,976 (0.2%); **Hispanic:** 21,984 (0.6%). **1990 percent population below age 18:** 25.9; **65 and over:** 12.7; **median age:** 33.0.

Kentucky was the first region west of the Allegheny Mountains settled by American pioneers. James Harrod established the first permanent settlement at Harrodsburg in 1774; the following year Daniel Boone, who had explored the area in 1767, blazed the Wilderness Trail and founded Boonesboro.

Politically, the Kentucky region was originally part of Virginia, but early statehood was gained in 1792.

During the Civil War, as a slaveholding state with a considerable abolitionist population, Kentucky was caught in the middle of the conflict, supplying both Union and Confederate forces with thousands of troops.

In recent years, manufacturing has shown important gains particularly in automotive assembly and parts manufacturing. Kentucky also prides itself on producing some of the nation's best tobacco, horses, and whiskey. Corn, soybeans, wheat, fruit, hogs, cattle, and dairy farming are among the agricultural items produced.

Among the manufactured items produced in the state are motor vehicles, furniture, aluminum ware, brooms, apparel, lumber products, machinery, textiles, and iron and steel products. Kentucky also produces significant amounts of petroleum, natural gas, fluorspar, clay, and stone. However, coal accounts for 90% of the total mineral income.

Louisville, the largest city, famed for the Kentucky Derby at Churchill Downs, is also the location of a large state university, whiskey distilleries, and cigarette factories. The Bluegrass country around Lexington is the home of some of the world's finest race horses. Other attractions are Mammoth Cave, the George S. Patton, Jr., Military Museum at Fort Knox, and Old Fort Harrod State Park.

Famous natives and residents: John Adair, pioneer and political leader; Muhammad Ali, boxer; Alben W. Barkley, ex-vice president; Louis D. Brandeis, jurist; John Mason Brown, critic; Kit Carson, scout; Champ Clark, politician; Rosemary Clooney, singer; Irvin S. Cobb, humorist; Jefferson Davis, president of Confederacy; Irene Dunne, actress; Crystal Gayle, singer; David W. Griffith, film producer; John M. Harlan, jurist; Elizabeth Hardwick, writer; Casey Jones, celebrated locomotive engineer; Abraham Lincoln, ex-President; Loretta Lynn, singer; Carry Amelia Nation, temperance leader; Patricia Neal, actress; George Reeves, actor; Wiley B. Rutledge, jurist; Diane Sawyer, broadcast journalist; Phil Simms, football player; Adlai Stevenson, ex-vice president; Allen Tate, poet and critic; Hunter Thompson, writer; Frederick M. Vinson, jurist; Robert Penn Warren, novelist

LOUISIANA

Capital: Baton Rouge

Governor: Murphy J. "Mike" Foster, R (to Jan. 2000)

Lieut. Governor: Kathleen Blanco, D (to Jan. 2000)

Secy. of State: W. Fox McKeithen, R (to Jan. 2000)

Treasurer: Ken Duncan, D (to Jan. 2000)

Atty. General: Richard P. Ieyoub, D (to Jan. 2000)

Organized as territory: March 26, 1804

Entered Union & (rank): April 30, 1812 (18)

Present constitution adopted: 1974

Motto: Union, justice, and confidence

STATE SYMBOLS: flower, Magnolia (1900); **tree,** Bald cypress (1963); **bird,** Pelican (1958); **songs,** "Give Me Louisiana" and "You Are My Sunshine"

Nicknames: Pelican State; Sportsman's Paradise; Creole State; Sugar State

Origin of name: In honor of Louis XIV of France

10 largest cities (1990 census): New Orleans, 496,938; Baton Rouge, 219,531; Shreveport, 198,525; Lafayette, 94,440; Kenner, 72,033; Lake Charles, 70,580; Monroe, 54,909; Bossier City, 52,721; Alexandria, 49,188; New Iberia, 31,828

Land area & (rank): 43,566 sq mi. (112,836 sq km) (33)

Geographic center: In Avoyelles Parish, 3 mi. SE of Marksville

Number of parishes (counties): 64

Largest parish (1990 census): Jefferson, 448,306

State forests: 1 (8,000 ac.)

State parks: 30 (13,932 ac.)

1995 resident population est.: 4,342,000

1990 resident census population (rank): 4,219,973 (21). **Male:** 2,031,386; **Female:** 2,188,587. **White:** 2,839,138 (67.3%); **Black:** 1,299,281 (30.8%); **American Indian, Eskimo, or Aleut:** 18,541 (0.4%); **Asian or Pacific Islander:** 41,099 (1.0%); **Other race:** 21,914 (0.5%); **Hispanic:** 93,044 (2.2%). **1990 percent population under 18:** 29.1; **65 and over:** 11.1; **median age:** 31.0.

Louisiana has a rich, colorful historical background. Early Spanish explorers were Piñeda, 1519; Cabeza de Vaca, 1528; and de Soto in 1541. La Salle reached the mouth of the Mississippi and claimed all the land drained by it and its tributaries for Louis XIV of France in 1682.

Louisiana became a French crown colony in 1731, was ceded to Spain in 1763, returned to France in 1800, and sold by Napoleon to the U.S. as part of the Louisiana Purchase (with large territories to the north and northwest) in 1803.

In 1815, Gen. Andrew Jackson's troops defeated a larger British army in the Battle of New Orleans, neither side aware that the treaty ending the War of 1812 had been signed.

As to total value of its mineral output, Louisiana is a leader in natural gas, salt, petroleum, and sulfur production. Much of the oil and sulfur comes from offshore deposits. The state also produces large crops of sweet potatoes, rice, sugar cane, pecans, soybeans, corn, and cotton.

Leading manufactures include chemicals, processed food, petroleum and coal products, paper, lumber and wood products, transportation equipment, and apparel.

Louisiana marshes supply most of the nation's muskrat fur as well as that of opossum, raccoon, mink, and otter, and large numbers of game birds.

Major points of interest include New Orleans with its French Quarter and Superdome, plantation homes near Natchitoches and New Iberia, Cajun country in the Mississippi delta region, Chalmette National Historical Park, and the state capital at Baton Rouge.

Famous natives and residents: Louis Armstrong, musician; Geoffrey Beene, fashion designer; Truman Capote, writer; Kitty Carlisle, singer and actress; Van Cliburn, concert pianist; Michael De Bakey, heart surgeon; Fats Domino, musician; Louis Moreau Gottschalk, pianist, composer; Bryant Gumbel, TV newscaster; Lillian Hellman, playwright; Al Hirt, trumpeter; Mahalia Jackson, gospel singer; Jean Laffite, privateer; Dorothy Lamour, actress; John A. Lejeune, Marine Corps general; Elmore Leonard, author; Jerry Lee Lewis, singer; Huey P. Long, politician; Wynton Marsalis, musician; Jelly Roll Morton, jazz musician and composer; Huey Newton, black activist; Marguerite Piazza, soprano; Paul Prudhomme, chef; Howard K. Smith, TV commentator; Ben Turpin, comedian; Ray Walston, actor; Edward Douglas White, jurist

MAINE

Capital: Augusta
Governor: Angus S. King, Jr., I (to Jan. 1999)
Secy. of State: G. William Diamond, D (to Jan. 1999)
Controller: Carol Whitney, R (to Jan. 1999)
Atty. General: Andrew Ketterer, D (to Jan. 1999)
Entered Union & (rank): March 15, 1820 (23)
Present constitution adopted: 1820
Motto: *Dirigo* (I lead)
STATE SYMBOLS: flower, White pine cone and tassel (1895); **tree,** White pine tree (1945); **bird,** Chickadee (1927); **fish,** Landlocked salmon (1969); **mineral,** Tourmaline (1971); **song,** "State of Maine Song" (1937); **animal,** Moose (1979); **cat,** Maine Coon Cat (1985); **fossil,** Pertica quadrifaria (1985); **insect,** Honeybee (1975)
Nickname: Pine Tree State
Origin of name: First used to distinguish the mainland from the offshore islands. It has been considered a compliment to Henrietta Maria, Queen of Charles I of England. She was said to have owned the province of Mayne in France.
10 largest cities (1990 census): Portland, 64,358; Lewiston, 39,757; Bangor, 33,181; Auburn, 24,309; South Portland, 23,163; Augusta, 21,325; Biddeford, 20,710; Waterville, 17,173; Westbrook, 16,121; Saco, 15,181
Land area & (rank): 30,865 sq mi. (79,939 sq km) (39)
Geographic center: In Piscataquis Co., 18 mi. N of Dover–Foxcroft
Number of counties: 16
Largest town (1990 census): Brunswick, 20,906
State forests: 1 (21,000 ac.)
State parks: 26 (247,627 ac.)
State historic sites: 18 (403 ac.)
1995 resident population est.: 1,241,000
1990 resident census population (rank): 1,227,928 (38). **Male:** 597,850; **Female:** 630,078. **White:** 1,208,360 (98.4%); **Black:** 5,138 (0.4%); **American Indian, Eskimo, or Aleut:** 5,998 (0.5%); **Asian or Pacific Islander:** 6,683: (0.5%); **Other race:** 1,749 (0.1%); **Hispanic:** 6,829 (0.6%).

John Cabot and his son, Sebastian, are believed to have visited the Maine coast in 1498. However, the first permanent English settlements were not established until more than a century later, in 1623.

The first naval action of the Revolutionary War occurred in 1775 when colonials captured the British sloop *Margaretta* off Machias on the Maine coast. In that same year, the British burned Falmouth (now Portland).

Long governed by Massachusetts, Maine became the 23rd state as part of the Missouri Compromise in 1820.

Maine produces 98% of the nation's low-bush blueberries. Farm income is also derived from apples, potatoes, dairy products, and vegetables, with poultry and eggs the largest items.

The state is one of the world's largest pulp-paper producers. It ranks second in boot-and-shoe manufacturing. With almost 89% of its area forested, Maine turns out wood products from boats to toothpicks.

Maine leads the world in the production of the familiar flat tins of sardines, producing more than 75 million of them annually. Lobstermen normally catch 51% of the nation's total of lobsters. The 1995 catch was 36.5 million pounds, the second largest lobster catch in history.

A scenic seacoast, beaches, lakes, mountains, and resorts make Maine a popular vacationland. There are more than 2,500 lakes and 5,000 streams, plus 26 state parks, to attract hunters, fishermen, skiers, and campers.

Major points of interest are: Bar Harbor, Allagash National Wilderness Waterway, the Wadsworth-Longfellow House in Portland, Roosevelt Campobello International Park, and the St. Croix Island National Monument.

Famous natives and residents: F. Lee Bailey, defense attorney; Charles F. Browne (Artemus Ward), humorist; Cyrus Curtis, publisher; Dorothea Dix, civil rights reformer; John Ford, film director; Melville Fuller, jurist; Marsden Hartley, painter; Henry Wadsworth Longfellow, poet; Sarah Orne Jewett, author; Stephen King, writer; Linda Lavin, actress; Edna St. Vincent Millay, poet; Marston Morse, mathematician; Frank Munsey, publisher; Walter Piston, composer; George Putnam, publisher; Kenneth Roberts, historical novelist; Edwin Arlington Robinson, poet; Margaret Chase Smith, politician; Samantha Smith, peacemaker, actress; John Hay Whitney, publisher

MARYLAND

Capital: Annapolis
Governor: Parris N. Glendening, D (to Jan. 1999)
Lieut. Gov.: Kathleen Kennedy Townsend, D (to Jan. 1999)
Secy. of State: John T. Willis, D (to Jan. 1999)
Comptroller of the Treasury: Louis L. Goldstein, D (to Jan. 1999)
Treasurer: Lucille Maurer, D (to Jan. 1999)
Atty. General: J. Joseph Curran, Jr., D (to Jan. 1999)
Entered Union & (rank): April 28, 1788 (7)
Present constitution adopted: 1867
Motto: *Fatti maschii, parole femine* (Manly deeds, womanly words)
STATE SYMBOLS: bird, Baltimore oriole (1947); **boat,** Skipjack (1985); **crustacean,** Maryland Blue Crab (1989); **dog,** Chesapeake Bay retriever (1964); **flower,** Black-eyed susan (1918); **tree,** White oak (1941); **fish,** Rockfish (1965); **folk dance,** Square dancing (1994); **fossil shell,** Ecphora gardnerae gardnerae (Wilson) (1994); **insect,** Baltimore checkerspot butterfly (1973); **song,** "Maryland! My Maryland!" (1939); **sport,** Jousting (1962)
Nicknames: Free State; Old Line State
Origin of name: In honor of Henrietta Maria (Queen of Charles I of England)
10 largest cities (1990 census): Baltimore, 736,014; Rockville, 44,835; Frederick, 40,148; Gaithersburg, 39,542; Bowie, 37,589; Hagerstown, 35,445; Annapolis, 33,187; Cumberland, 23,706; College Park, 21,927; Greenbelt, 21,096
Land area & (rank): 9,775 sq mi. (25,316 sq km) (42)
Geographic center: In Prince Georges Co., 4 1/2 mi. NW of Davidsonville
Number of counties: 23, and 1 independent city
Largest county (1990 census): Montgomery, 757,027
State forests: 13 (132,944 ac.)
State parks: 47 (87,670 ac.)

1995 resident population est.: 5,042,000
1990 resident census population (rank): 4,781,468 (19).
Male: 2,318,671; **Female:** 2,462,797. **White:** 3,393,964 (71.0%); **Black:** 1,189,899 (24.9%);
American Indian, Eskimo, or Aleut: 12,972 (0.3%);
Asian or Pacific Islander: 139,719 (2.9%); **Other race:** 44,914 (0.9%); **Hispanic:** 125,102 (2.6%). **1990 percent population under 18:** 24.3; **65 and over:** 10.8; **median age:** 33.0

Maryland was inhabited by Indians as early as c. 10,000 B.C., and permanent Indian villages were established by c. 1,000 A.D.

In 1608, Capt. John Smith explored Chesapeake Bay. Charles I granted a royal charter for Maryland to Cecil Calvert, Lord Baltimore, in 1632, and English settlers, many of whom were Roman Catholic, landed on St. Clement's (now Blakistone) Island in 1634. Religious freedom, granted all Christians in the Toleration Act passed by the Maryland assembly in 1649, was ended by a Puritan revolt, 1654–58.

From 1763 to 1767, Charles Mason and Jeremiah Dixon surveyed Maryland's northern boundary line with Pennsylvania. In 1791, Maryland ceded land to form the District of Columbia.

In 1814, when the British unsuccessfully tried to capture Baltimore, the bombardment of Fort McHenry inspired Francis Scott Key to write *The Star Spangled Banner.*

The Baltimore clipper ship trade developed during the 19th century. During the Civil War, Maryland remained a Union state even while the battles of South Mountain (1862), Antietam (1862), and Monocacy (1864) were fought on her soil.

In 1904, the Great Fire of Baltimore occurred. In 1937, the City of Greenbelt, a New Deal model community, was chartered.

Maryland's Eastern Shore and Western Shore embrace the Chesapeake Bay, and the many estuaries and rivers create one of the longest waterfronts of any state. The Bay produces more seafood—oysters, crabs, clams, fin fish—than any comparable body of water. Important agricultural products, in order of cash value, are greenhouse and nursery products, chickens, dairy products, soy beans, corn, eggs, vegetables, melons and wheat. Maryland is a leader in vegetable canning. Stone, coal, sand, gravel, cement, and clay are the chief mineral products.

Manufacturing industries produce food and kindred products, instruments, chemicals, printing and publishing, transportation equipment, and primary metals. Baltimore, home of The Johns Hopkins University and Hospital, ranks as the nation's second port in foreign tonnage. Annapolis, site of the U.S. Naval Academy, has one of the earliest state houses (1772–79) still in regular use by a State government.

Among the popular attractions in Maryland are the Fort McHenry National Monument; Harpers Ferry and Chesapeake and Ohio Canal National Historic Parks; Antietam National Battlefield; National Aquarium, USS *Constellation,* and Maryland Science Center at Baltimore's Inner Harbor; Historic St. Mary's City; Jefferson Patterson Historical Park and Museum at St. Leonard; U.S. Naval Academy in Annapolis; Goddard Space Flight Center at Greenbelt; Assateague Island National Park Seashore; Ocean City beach resort; and Catoctin Mountain, Fort Frederick, and Piscataway parks.

Famous natives and residents: Benjamin Banneker, almanacker, mathetmatician-astronomer; John Barth, writer; Eubie Blake, musician; John Wilkes Booth, actor, Lincoln assassin; Francis X. Bushman, actor; James M. Cain, writer; Samuel Chase, jurist; Frederick Douglass, abolitionist; John Hurst Fletcher, Methodist bishop and educator; Christopher Gist, frontiersman; Philip Glass, composer; Matthew Henson, reached North Pole with Peary; Billie Holiday, jazz-blues singer; Johns Hopkins, financier; Reverdy Johnson, lawyer and statesman; Thomas Johnson, political leader; Francis Scott Key, laywer, author of National Anthem; Thurgood Marshall, jurist; H.L. Mencken, writer; Hezekiah Niles, journalist; Charles Wilson Peale, painter; Frank Perdue, farmer, businessman; James R. Randall, journalist, wrote state song; Babe Ruth, baseball player; Upton Sinclair, novelist; Roger B. Taney, jurist; George Alfred Townsend (Gath), journalist; Harriet Tubman, abolitionist; Leon Uris, novelist; Frank Zappa, singer

MASSACHUSETTS

Capital: Boston
Governor: William F. Weld, R (to Jan. 1999)
Lieut. Governor: A. Paul Cellucci, R (to Jan. 1999)
Secy. of the Commonwealth: William F. Galvin (to Jan. 1999)
Treasurer & Receiver-General: Joseph D. Malone, R (to Jan. 1999)
Auditor of the Commonwealth: A. Joseph DeNucci, D (to Jan. 1999)
Atty. General: L. Scott Harshbarger, D (to Jan. 1999)
Present constitution drafted: 1780 (oldest U.S. state constitution in effect today)
Entered Union & (rank): Feb. 6, 1788 (6)
Motto: *Ense petit placidam sub libertate quietem* (By the sword we seek peace, but peace only under liberty)
STATE SYMBOLS: flower, Mayflower (1918); **tree.** American elm (1941); **bird,** Chickadee (1941); **song,** "All Hail to Massachusetts" (1966); **beverage,** Cranberry juice (1970); **insect,** Ladybug (1974); **muffin,** corn muffin
Nicknames: Bay State; Old Colony State
Origin of name: From two Indian words meaning "Great mountain place"
10 largest cities (1990 census): Boston, 574,283; Worcester, 169,759; Springfield, 156,983; Lowell, 103,439; New Bedford, 99,922; Cambridge, 95,802; Brockton, 92,788; Fall River, 92,703; Quincy, 84,985; Newton, 82,585
Land area & (rank): 7,838 sq mi. (20,300 sq km) (45)
Geographic center: In Worcester Co., in S part of city of Worcester
Number of counties: 14
Largest county (1990 census): Middlesex, 1,398,468
State forests and parks: 129 (242,000 ac.)[1]
1995 resident population est.: 6,074,000
1990 resident census population (rank): 6,016,425 (13). **Male:** 2,888,745; **Female:** 3,127,680. **White:** 5,405,374 (89.8%); **Black:** 300,130 (5.0%); **American Indian, Eskimo, or Aleut:** 12,241 (0.2%); **Asian or Pacific Islander:** 143,392 (2.4%); **Other race:** 155,288 (2.6%); **Hispanic:** 287,549 (4.8%). **1990 percent population under 18:** 22.5; **65 and over:** 13.6; **median age:** 33.6.

1. The Metropolitan District Commission, an agency of the Commonwealth serving municipalities in the Boston area, has about 14,000 acres of parkways and reservations under its jurisdiction.

Massachusetts has played a significant role in American history since the Pilgrims, seeking religious freedom, founded Plymouth Colony in 1620.

As one of the most important of the 13 colonies, Massachusetts became a leader in resisting British oppression. In 1773, the Boston Tea Party protested unjust taxation. The Minute Men started the American Revolution by battling British troops at Lexington and Concord on April 19, 1775.

During the 19th century, Massachusetts was famous for the vigorous intellectual activity of famous writers and educators and for its expanding commercial fishing, shipping, and manufacturing interests.

Massachusetts pioneered in the manufacture of textiles and shoes. Today, these industries have been replaced in importance by activity in the electronics and communications equipment fields.

The state's cranberry crop is the nation's largest. Also important are dairy and poultry products, nursery and greenhouse produce, vegetables, and fruit.

Tourism has become an important factor in the economy of the state because of its numerous recreational areas and historical landmarks.

Cape Cod has summer theaters, water sports, and an artists' colony at Provincetown. Tanglewood, in the Berkshires, features the summer concerts of the Boston Symphony.

Among the many other points of interest are Old Sturbridge Village in Sturbridge in central Massachusetts, Minute Man National Historical Park between Lexington and Concord, and, in Boston: Old North Church, Old State House, Faneuil Hall, the USS *Constitution* and the John F. Kennedy Library and Museum.

Famous natives and residents: John Adams, ex-president; John Quincy Adams, ex-president; Samuel Adams, patriot; Horatio Alger, novelist; Susan B. Anthony, woman suffragist; Clara Barton, American Red Cross founder; Leonard Bernstein, conductor; George Bush, ex-president; William Cullen Bryan, poet and editor; Luther Burbank, horticulturalist; John Cheever, novelist; John Singleton Copley, painter; E.E. Cummings, poet; Jacques d'Amboise, ballet dancer; Bette Davis, actress; Cecil B. DeMille, film director; Emily Dickinson, poet; Ralph Waldo Emerson, philosopher and poet; Geraldine Farrar, soprano, actress; Benjamin Franklin, statesman and scientist; Buckminster Fuller, architect and educator; Robert Goddard, father of modern rocketry; John Hancock, statesman; Nathaniel Hawthorne, novelist; Oliver Wendell Holmes, jurist; Winslow Homer, painter; Elias Howe, inventor; John F. Kennedy, ex-president; Amy Lowell, poet; James Russell Lowell, poet; Robert Lowell, poet; Horace Mann, educator; Cotton Mather, clergyman; Samuel F.B. Morse, painter and inventor; Edgar Allan Poe, writer; Paul Revere, silversmith, hero of ride; Dr. Seuss (Theodore Geisel), author and illustrator; David Souter, jurist; Lucy Stone, woman suffragist; Louis Henry Sullivan, architect; Henry David Thoreau, author; Barbara Walters, TV commentator; James McNeill Whistler, painter; Eli Whitney, inventor; John Greenleaf Whittier, poet

MICHIGAN

Capital: Lansing
Governor: John M. Engler, R (to Jan. 1999)
Lieut. Governor: Connie Binsfeld, R (to Jan. 1999)
Secy. of State: Candice S. Miller, R (to Jan. 1999)
Atty. General: Frank J. Kelley, D (to Jan. 1999)
Organized as territory: Jan. 11, 1805
Entered Union & (rank): Jan. 26, 1837 (26)
Present constitution adopted: April 1, 1963, (effective Jan. 1, 1964)
Motto: *Si quaeris peninsulam amoenam circumspice* (If you seek a pleasant peninsula, look around you)
STATE SYMBOLS: flower, Apple blossom (1897); **bird,** Robin (1931); **fishes,** Trout (1965), Brook trout (1988); **gem,** Isle Royal Greenstone (Chlorastrolite) (1972); **stone,** Petoskey Stone (1965); **tree,** White pine (1955); **soil,** Kalkaska Soil series (1990); **reptile,** Painted turtle (1996); **flag,** "Blue charged with the arms of the state" (1911)
Nickname: Wolverine State
Origin of name: From Indian word "Michigana" meaning

"great or large lake"
10 largest cities (1990 census): Detroit, 1,027,974; Grand Rapids, 189,126; Warren, 144,864; Flint, 140,761; Lansing, 127,321; Sterling Heights, 117,810; Ann Arbor, 109,592; Livonia, 100,850; Dearborn, 89,286; Westland, 84,724
Land area & (rank): 56,809.2 sq mi. (151,086 sq km) (22)
Geographic center: In Wexford Co., 5 mi. NNW of Cadillac
Number of counties: 83
Largest county (1990 census): Wayne, 2,111,687
State parks and recreation areas: 82 (250,000 ac.)
1995 resident population est.: 9,549,000
1990 resident census population (rank): 9,295,297 (8). **Male:** 4,512,781; **Female:** 4,787,516. **White:** 7,756,086 (83.4%); **Black:** 1,291,706 (13.9%); **American Indian, Eskimo, or Aleut:** 55,638 (0.6%); **Asian or Pacific Islander:** 104,983 (1.1%); **Other race:** 86,884 (0.9%); **Hispanic:** 201,596 (2.2%). **1990 percent population under 18:** 26.5; **65 and over:** 11.9; **median age:** 32.6.

Indian tribes were living in the Michigan region when the first European, Etienne Brulé of France, arrived in 1618. Other French explorers, including Marquette, Joliet, and La Salle, followed, and the first permanent settlement was established in 1668 at Sault Ste. Marie. France was ousted from the territory by Great Britain in 1763, following the French and Indian War.

After the Revolutionary War, the U.S. acquired most of the region, which remained the scene of constant conflict between the British and U.S. forces and their respective Indian allies through the War of 1812.

Bordering on four of the five Great Lakes, Michigan is divided into Upper and Lower Peninsulas by the Straits of Mackinac, which link Lakes Michigan and Huron. The two parts of the state are connected by the Mackinac Bridge, one of the world's longest suspension bridges. To the north, connecting Lakes Superior and Huron are the busy Sault Ste. Marie Canals.

While Michigan ranks first among the states in production of motor vehicles and parts, it is also a leader in many other manufacturing and processing lines including prepared cereals, machine tools, airplane parts, refrigerators, hardware, steel springs, and furniture.

The state produces important amounts of iron, copper, iodine, gypsum, bromine, salt, lime, gravel, and cement. Michigan's farms grow apples, cherries, beans, pears, grapes, potatoes, and sugar beets. Michigan's forests contribute significantly to the state's economy. Forest-based industries (wood product industry, tourism, and recreation) support nearly 180,000 jobs and contribute over $18 billion to the state economy. With 10,083 inland lakes and 3,288 miles of Great Lakes' shoreline, Michigan is a prime area for both commercial and sport fishing.

Points of interest are the automobile plants in Dearborn, Detroit, Flint, Lansing, and Pontiac; Mackinac Island; Pictured Rocks and Sleeping Bear Dunes National Lakeshores, Greenfield Village in Dearborn; and the many summer resorts along both the inland and Great Lakes.

Famous natives and residents: Nelsen Algren, novelist; Ralph J. Bunche, statesman; Ellen Burstyn, actress; Bruce Catton, historian; Roger Chaffee, astronaut; Francis Ford Coppola, film director; Thomas E. Dewey, politician; Edna Ferber, novelist; Henry Ford, industrialist; Ali Haji-Sheikh, football player; Julie Harris, actress; Earvin "Magic" Johnson, basketball player; Ring Lardner, story writer; Charles A. Lindbergh, aviator; Madonna, singer; Dick Martin, comedian; Terry McMillan, author; John N. Mitchell, former Attorney General; Gilda Radner, comedienne; Della Reese, singer; Jason Robards, Sr., actor; Diana Ross, singer; Thomas Schippers, conductor; Potter Stewart, jurist; Danny Thomas, entertainer; Margaret Whiting, singer; Stevie Wonder, singer

MINNESOTA

Capital: St. Paul
Governor: Arne Carlson, R (to Jan. 1999)
Lieut. Governor: Joanne Benson, R (to Jan. 1999)
Secy. of State: Joan Anderson Growe, D (to Jan. 1999)
State Auditor: Judi Dutcher, R (to Jan. 1999)
Atty. General: Hubert H. Humphrey III, D (to Jan. 1999)
State Treasurer: Michael McGrath, D (to Jan. 1999)
Organized as territory: March 3, 1849
Entered Union & (rank): May 11, 1858 (32)
Present constitution adopted: 1858
Motto: L'Etoile du Nord (The North Star)
STATE SYMBOLS: flower, Showy lady slipper (1902);
tree, Red (or Norway) pine (1953); **bird,** Common loon
(also called Great Northern Diver) (1961); **song,** "Hail
Minnesota" (1945); **fish,** Walleye (1965); **mushroom,**
Morel (1984)
Nicknames: North Star State; Gopher State; Land of
10,000 Lakes
Origin of name: From a Dakota Indian word meaning
"sky-tinted water"
10 largest cities (1991 est. population): Minneapolis,
368,993; St. Paul, 272,537; Bloomington, 86,453; Duluth,
85,382; Rochester, 72,480; Brooklyn Park, 57,359; Coon
Rapids, 54,518; Plymouth, 52,492; Burnsville, 51,743; St.
Cloud, 49,350
Land area & (rank): 79,617 sq mi. (206,207 sq km) (14)
Geographic center: In Crow Wing Co., 10 mi. SW of
Brainerd
Number of counties: 87
Largest county (1991 est. population): Hennepin,
1,039,099
State forests: 56 (3,200,000+ ac.)
State parks: 66 (226,000 ac.)
1995 resident population est.: 4,610,000
1990 resident census population (rank): 4,375,099 (20).
Male: 2,145,183; **Female:** 2,229,916. **White:** 4,130,395
(94.4%); **Black:** 94,944 (2.2%); **American Indian, Eskimo, or Aleut:** 49,909 (1.1%); **Asian or Pacific Islander:**
77,886 (1.8%); **Other race:** 21,965 (0.5%); **Hispanic:**
53,884 (1.2%). **1990 percent population under 18:** 26.7;
65 and over: 12.5; **median age:** 32.5.

Following the visits of several French explorers,
fur traders, and missionaries, including Marquette and
Joliet and La Salle, the region was claimed for Louis
XIV by Daniel Greysolon, Sieur Duluth, in 1679.

The U.S. acquired eastern Minnesota from Great
Britain after the Revolutionary War and 20 years later
bought the western part from France in the Louisiana
Purchase of 1803. Much of the region was explored
by U.S. Army Lt. Zebulon M. Pike before the northern strip of Minnesota bordering Canada was ceded
by Britain in 1818.

The state is rich in natural resources. A few square
miles of land in the north in the Mesabi, Cuyuna, and
Vermillion ranges, produce more than 75% of the nation's iron ore. The state's farms rank high in yields of
corn, wheat, rye, alfalfa, and sugar beets. Other leading farm products include butter, eggs, milk, potatoes,
green peas, barley, soy beans, oats, and livestock.

Minnesota's factory production includes nonelectri-
cal machinery, fabricated metals, flour-mill products,
plastics, electronic computers, scientific instruments,
and processed foods. It is also one of the nation's
leaders in the printing and paper products industries.

Minneapolis is the trade center of the Northwest;
and the headquarters of the world's largest super
computer and grain distributor. St. Paul is the nation's
biggest publisher of calendars and law books. These
"twin cities" are the nation's third largest trucking
center. Duluth has the nation's largest inland harbor
and now handles a significant amount of foreign
trade. Rochester is the home of the Mayo Clinic, an
internationally famous medical center.

Today, tourism is a major revenue producer in Minnesota, with arts, fishing, hunting, water sports, and
winter sports bringing in millions of visitors each year.

Among the most popular attractions are the St.
Paul Winter Carnival; the Tyrone Guthrie Theatre, the
Institute of Arts, Walker Art Center, and Minnehaha
Park, in Minneapolis; Boundary Waters Canoe Area;
Voyageurs National Park; North Shore Drive; and the
Minnesota Zoological Gardens and the state's more
than 10,000 lakes.

Famous natives and residents: LaVerne, Maxene, and
Patti Andrews, singers; Warren E. Burger, jurist; William
E. Colby, ex-director of CIA; William Demarest, actor;
William O. Douglas, jurist; Bob Dylan, singer and composer; F. Scott Fitzgerald, novelist; Judy Garland, singer
and actress; J. Paul Getty, oil executive; Cass Gilbert,
architect; Duane Hanson, sculptor; Hubert H. Humphrey, former senator and vice-president; Jessica
Lange, actress; Sinclair Lewis, novelist; Cornell Mac-
Neil, baritone; Roger Maris, baseball player; E.G. Marshall, actor; Charles H. Mayo, surgeon; William J. Mayo,
surgeon; Eugene J. McCarthy, ex-senator; Kate Millett,
feminist; Gen. Lauris Norstad, ex-commander of NATO
forces; Westbrook Pegler, columnist; John Sargent Pills-
bury, flour milling; Marion Ross, actress; Jane Russell,
actress; Harrison E. Salisbury, journalist; Charles M.
Schulz, cartoonist; Max Shulman, novelist; Maurice H.
Stans, ex-secretary of commerce; Harold E. Stassen,
ex-government official; Michael Todd, producer; Frederick Weyerhaeuser, lumbering; Gig Young, actor

MISSISSIPPI

Capital: Jackson
Governor: Kirk Fordice, R (to Jan. 2000)
Lieut. Governor: Ronnie Musgrove, D (to Jan. 2000)
Secy. of State: Eric Clark, D (to Jan. 2000)
Treasurer: Marshall Bennett, D (to Jan. 2000)
Atty. General: Mike Moore, D (to Jan. 2000)
Organized as Territory: April 7, 1798
Entered Union & (rank): Dec. 10, 1817 (20)
Present constitution adopted: 1890
Motto: *Virtute et armis* (By valor and arms)
STATE SYMBOLS: flower, Flower or bloom of the mag-
nolia or evergreen magnolia (1952); **tree,** Magnolia
(1938); **bird,** Mockingbird (1944); **song,** "Go, Mississip-
pi" (1962); **stone,** Petrified wood (1976); **fish,** Largemouth or black bass (1974); **insect,** Honeybee (1980);
shell, Oyster shell (1974); **water mammal,** Bottle-
nosed dolphin or porpoise (1974); **fossil,** Prehistoric
whale (1981); **land mammal,** White-tailed deer (1974);
waterfowl, Wood duck (1974); **beverage,** Milk (1984)
Nickname: Magnolia State
Origin of name: From an Indian word meaning "Father of
Waters"
10 largest cities (1990 census): Jackson, 196,637; Biloxi,
46,319; Greenville, 45,226; Hattiesburg, 41,882; Meridian, 41,036; Gulfport, 40,775; Tupelo, 30,685; Pascagou-
la, 25,899; Columbus, 23,799; Clinton, 21,847
Land area & (rank): 46,914 sq mi. (121,506 sq km) (31)
Geographic center: In Leake Co., 9 mi. WNW of Cart-
hage
Number of counties: 82
Largest county (1990 census): Hinds, 254,441
State forests: 1 (1,760 ac.)
State parks: 27 (16,763 ac.)
1995 resident population est.: 2,697,000

1990 resident census population (rank): 2,573,216 (31). **Male:** 1,230,617; **Female:** 1,342,599. **White:** 1,633,461 (63.5%); **Black:** 915,057 (35.6%); **American Indian, Eskimo, or Aleut:** 8,525 (0.3%); **Asian or Pacific Islander:** 13,016 (0.5%); **Other race:** 3,157 (0.1%); **Hispanic:** 15,931 (0.6%). **1990 percent population under 18:** 29.0; **65 and over:** 12.5; **median age:** 31.2.

First explored for Spain by Hernando de Soto who discovered the Mississippi River in 1540, the region was later claimed by France. In 1699, a French group under Sieur d'Iberville established the first permanent settlement near present-day Ocean Springs.

Great Britain took over the area in 1763 after the French and Indian War, ceding it to the U.S. in 1783 after the Revolution. Spain did not relinquish its claims until 1798, and in 1810 the U.S. annexed West Florida from Spain, including what is now southern Mississippi.

For a little more than one hundred years, from shortly after the state's founding through the Great Depression, cotton was the undisputed king of Mississippi's largely agrarian economy. Over the last half-century, however, Mississippi has progressively deepened its commitment to diversification by balancing agricultural output with increased industrial activity.

Today, agriculture continues as a major segment of the state's economy. While the most acreage is devoted to soybeans, cotton is the largest cash crop—Mississippi remains third in the nation in cotton production. The state's farmlands yield important harvests of corn, peanuts, pecans, rice, sugar cane, sweet potatoes, soybeans and food grains as well as poultry, eggs, meat animals, dairy products, feed crops and horticultural crops. Mississippi remains the world's leading producer of pond-raised catfish. Mississippi boasts 100,000 of the 140,000 total acres nationwide of catfish ponds.

The state abounds in historical landmarks and is the home of the Vicksburg National Military Park. Other National Park Service areas are Brices Cross Roads National Battlefield Site, Tupelo National Battlefield, and part of Natchez Trace National Parkway. Pre-Civil War mansions are the special pride of Natchez, Oxford, Columbus, Vicksburg, and Jackson.

Famous natives and residents: Red Barber, sportscaster; Jimmy Buffet, singer, songwriter; Craig Claiborne, columnist and restaurant critic; Bo Diddley, guitarist; Charles Evers, civil rights leader; Medgar Evers, civil rights leader; William Faulkner, novelist; John Grisham, novelist; Beth Henley, playwright and actress; Jim Henson, puppeteer; James Earl Jones, actor; B.B. King, guitarist; Mary Ann Mobley, actress; Willie Morris, writer; Elvis Presley, singer and actor; Leontyne Price, soprano; Jerry Rice, football player; Jimmie Rodgers, singer; Sela Ward, actress; Muddy Waters, singer and guitarist; Eudora Welty, novelist; Tennessee Williams, playwright; Oprah Winfrey, talk show host and actress; Richard Wright, novelist; Tammy Wynette, country music star; Zig Ziglar, speaker, author

MISSOURI

Capital: Jefferson City
Governor: Mel Carnahan, D (to Jan. 1997)
Lieut. Governor: Roger Wilson, D (to Jan. 1997)
Secy. of State: Rebecca McDowell "Bekki" Cook, D (to Jan. 1997)
Auditor: Margaret Kelly, R (to Jan. 1999)
Treasurer: Bob Holden, D (to Jan. 1997)
Atty. General: Jeremiah W. "Jay" Nixon, D (to Jan. 1997)
Organized as territory: June 4, 1812

Entered Union & (rank): Aug. 10, 1821 (24)
Present constitution adopted: 1945
Motto: *Salus populi suprema lex esto* (The welfare of the people shall be the supreme law)
STATE SYMBOLS: floral emblem, Hawthorn (1923); **bird,** Bluebird (1927); **song,** "Missouri Waltz" (1949); **fossil,** Crinoid (1989); **musical instrument,** Fiddle (1987); **rock,** Mozarkite (1967); **mineral,** Galena (1967); **insect,** Honeybee (1985); **tree,** Flowering dogwood (1955); **tree nut,** Eastern black walnut (1990); **animal,** Mule (1995); **dance,** Square dance (1995); **Missouri Day,** third Wednesday in October (1915)
Nickname: Show-me State
Origin of name: Named after a tribe called Missouri Indians. "Missouri" means "town of the large canoes."
10 largest cities (1990 census): Kansas City, 435,146; St. Louis, 396,685; Springfield, 140,494; Independence, 112,301; St. Joseph, 71,852; Columbia, 69,101; St. Charles, 54,555; Florissant, 51,206; Lee's Summit, 46,418; St. Peter's, 45,779
Land area & (rank): 68,945 sq mi. (178,446 sq km) (18)
Geographic center: In Miller Co., 20 mi. SW of Jefferson City
Number of counties: 114, plus 1 independent city
Largest county (1990 census): St. Louis, 993,529
Conservation areas[1]: 518 (704,311 ac.)
Conservation accesses: 240 (10,619 ac.)
State parks and historic sites: 79 (134,496 ac.)
1995 resident population est.: 5,324,000
1990 resident census population (rank): 5,117,073 (15). **Male:** 2,464,315; **Female:** 2,652,758. **White:** 4,486,228 (87.7%); **Black:** 548,208 (10.7%); **American Indian, Eskimo, or Aleut:** 19,835 (0.4%); **Asian or Pacific Islander:** 41,277 (0.8%); **Other race:** 21,525 (0.4%); **Hispanic:** 61,702 (1.2%). **1990 percent population under 18:** 25.7; **65 and over:** 14.0; **median age:** 33.5.

1. Includes wildlife areas, natural history areas, state forests, and tower sites.

De Soto visited the Missouri area in 1541. France's claim to the entire region was based on La Salle's travels in 1682. French fur traders established Ste. Genevieve in 1735 and St. Louis was first settled in 1764.

The U.S. gained Missouri from France as part of the Louisiana Purchase in 1803, and the territory was admitted as a state following the Missouri Compromise of 1820. Throughout the pre-Civil War period and during the war, Missourians were sharply divided in their opinions about slavery and in their allegiances, supplying both Union and Confederate forces with troops. However, the state itself remained in the Union.

Historically, Missouri played a leading role as a gateway to the West, St. Joseph being the eastern starting point of the Pony Express, while the much-traveled Santa Fe and Oregon Trails began in Independence. Now a popular vacationland, Missouri has 11 major lakes and numerous fishing streams, springs, and caves. Bagnell Dam, across the Osage River in the Ozarks, completed in 1931, created one of the largest man-made lakes in the world, covering 65,000 acres of surface area.

Missouri's economy relies on a diversified industrial base. Service industries provide more income and jobs than any other segment, and include a growing tourism and travel sector. Wholesale and retail trade, manufacturing and agriculture also play significant roles in the state's economy. Missouri is a leading producer of transportation equipment (including automobile manufacturing and auto parts), beer and beverages, and defense and aerospace technology.

Food processing is the state's fastest-growing industry, well-suited to the state's blend of agricultural, natural, energy and transportation resources. Missouri mines also produce 90% of the nation's principal (non-recycled) lead supply.

Missouri's largest corporate employers include McDonnell-Douglas, Wal-Mart, Trans World Airlines and Southwestern Bell. The state's top agricultural products include: grain, sorghum, hay, corn, soybeans, wheat, oats, barley, tobacco and rice. A well-established grape and wine program brings together aspects of agriculture, manufacturing and tourism to support a vibrant vintner industry.

Tourism draws hundreds of thousands of visitors to a number of Missouri points of interest: the country-music shows of Branson; Bass Pro Shops national headquarters (Springfield); the Gateway Arch at the Jefferson National Expansion (St. Louis); Mark Twain's boyhood home and cave (Hannibal); the Harry S Truman home and library (Independence); the scenic beauty of the Ozark National Scenic Riverways; and the Pony Express and Jesse James museums (St. Joseph). The state's different lakes regions also attract fishermen and sun-seekers from throughout the Midwest.

Famous natives and residents: Robert Altman, film director; Burt Bacharach, songwriter; Josephine Baker, singer and dancer; Wallace Beery, actor; Robert Russell Bennett, composer; Yogi Berra, baseball player; Thomas Hart Benton, painter; Susan Elizabeth Blow, educator; Bill Bradley, basketball player and ex-N.J. senator; Omar N. Bradley, 5-star general; Grace Bumbry, soprano; William Burroughs, writer; Sarah Caldwell, opera director and conductor; Martha Jane Canary (Calamity Jane), frontierswoman; George Washington Carver, scientist; Walter Cronkhite, TV newscaster; Robert Cummings, actor; Jane Darwell, actress; Walt Disney, artist; Jeanne Eagels, actress; T.S. Eliot, poet; Eugene Field, poet; Redd Foxx, actor and comedian; Betty Grable, actress; Dick Gregory, comic and activist; Jean Harlow, actress; George Hearn, actor; Al Hirschfeld, artist; Edwin Hubble, astronomer; Langston Hughes, poet; John Huston, film director; Jesse James, outlaw; Scott Joplin, composer; Bernarr MacFadden, physical culturist; Mary Margaret McBride, TV hostess; Marianne Moore, poet; Geraldine Page, actress; James C. Penney, merchant; Marlin Perkins, TV host, zoo director; John Joseph Pershing, general; Vincent Price, actor; Joseph Pulitzer, journalist; Doris Roberts, actress; Ginger Rogers, dancer and actress; Sacajawea, Indian guide for Lewis and Clark; Ted Shawn, dancer and choreographer; Casey Stengel, baseball player; Gladys Swarthout, soprano; Sara Teasdale, poet; Virgil Thomson, composer; Harry S Truman, ex-president; Mark Twain, author; Dick Van Dyke, actor; Ruth Warrick, actress; Dennis Weaver, actor; Pearl White, actress; Mary Wickes, actress; Laura Ingalls Wilder, author; Roy Wilkins, civil rights leader

MONTANA

Capital: Helena
Governor: Marc Racicot, R (to Jan. 1997)
Lieut. Governor: Dennis R. Rehberg, R (to Jan. 1997)
Secy. of State: Mike Cooney, D (to Jan. 1997)
Auditor: Mark O'Keefe, D (to Jan. 1997)
Atty. General: Joe Mazurek, D (to Jan. 1997)
Organized as territory: May 26, 1864
Entered Union & (rank): Nov. 8, 1889 (41)
Present constitution adopted: 1972
Motto: *Oro y plata* (Gold and silver)
STATE SYMBOLS: flower, Bitterroot (1895); **tree,** Ponderosa pine (1949); **stones,** Sapphire and agate (1969); **bird,** Western meadowlark (1981); **song,** "Montana" (1945)
Nickname: Treasure State

Origin of name: Chosen from Latin dictionary by J. M. Ashley. It is a Latinized Spanish word meaning "mountainous."
10 largest cities (1990 census): Billings, 81,151; Great Falls, 55,097; Missoula, 42,918; Butte-Silver Bow[1], 33,941; Helena, 24,569; Bozeman, 22,660; Kalispell, 11,917; Anaconda-Deer Lodge County, 10,278; Havre, 10,201; Miles City, 8,461
Land area & (rank): 145,556 sq mi. (376,991 sq km) (4)
Geographic center: In Fergus Co., 12 mi. W of Lewistown
Number of counties: 56, plus small part of Yellowstone National Park
Largest county (1990 census): Yellowstone, 113,419
State forests: 7 (214,000 ac.)
State parks and recreation areas: 110 (18,273 ac.)
1995 resident population est.: 870,000
1990 resident census population (rank): 799,065 (44). **Male:** 395,769; **Female:** 403,296. **White:** 741,111 (92.7%); **Black:** 2,381 (0.3%); **American Indian, Eskimo, or Aleut:** 47,679 (6.0%); **Asian or Pacific Islander:** 4,259 (0.5%); **Other race:** 3,635 (0.5%); **Hispanic:** 12,174 (1.5%). **1990 percent population under 18:** 27.8; **65 and over:** 13.3; **median age:** 33.8.

1. Consolidated City.

First explored for France by François and Louis-Joseph Verendrye in the early 1740s, much of the region was acquired by the U.S. from France as part of the Louisiana Purchase in 1803. Before western Montana was obtained from Great Britain in the Oregon Treaty of 1846, American trading posts and forts had been established in the territory.

The major Indian wars (1867–1877) included the famous 1876 Battle of the Little Big Horn, better known as "Custer's Last Stand," in which Cheyennes and Sioux killed George A. Custer and more than 200 of his men in southeastern Montana.

Much of Montana's early history was concerned with mining with copper, lead, zinc, silver, coal, and oil as principal products.

Butte is the center of the area that once supplied half of the U.S. copper.

Fields of grain cover much of Montana's plains; it ranks high among the states in wheat and barley, with rye, oats, flaxseed, sugar beets, and potatoes other important crops. Sheep and cattle raising make significant contributions to the economy.

Tourist attractions include hunting, fishing, skiing, and dude ranching. Glacier National Park, on the Continental Divide, is a scenic and vacation wonderland with 60 glaciers, 200 lakes, and many streams with good trout fishing.

Other major points of interest include the Custer Battlefield National Monument, Virginia City, Yellowstone National Park, Museum of the Plains Indians at Browning, and the Fort Union Trading Post and Grant-Kohr's Ranch National Historic Sites.

Famous natives and residents: Dorothy Baker, author; Dirk Benedict, actor; W.A. (Tony) Boyle, labor union official; Gary Cooper, actor; John Cowan, prospector and founder of Last Chance Gulch (now Helena); Alfred Bertram Guthrie, Pulitzer Prize-winning author; Chet Huntley, TV newscaster; Will James, writer and artist; Dorothy Johnson, author; Evel Knievel, daredevil motorcyclist; Myrna Loy, actress; David Lynch, filmmaker; Mike Mansfield, ex-senator; George Montgomery, actor; Jeannette Rankin, first woman elected to Congress; Martha Raye, actress; Charles M. Russell, Old West painter; Michael Smuin, choreographer; Lester C. Thurow, economist, educator

NEBRASKA

Capital: Lincoln
Governor: Ben Nelson, D (to Jan. 1999)
Lieut. Governor: Kim Robak, D (to Jan. 1999)
Secy. of State: Scott Moore, R (to Jan. 1999)
Atty. General: Don Stenberg, R (to Jan. 1999)
Auditor: John Breslow, R (to Jan. 1999)
Treasurer: David Heineman, R (to Jan. 1999)
Organized as territory: May 30, 1854
Entered Union & (rank): March 1, 1867 (37)
Present constitution adopted: Oct. 12, 1875 (extensively amended 1919–20)
Motto: Equality before the law
STATE SYMBOLS: flower, Goldenrod (1895); **tree,** Cottonwood (1972); **bird,** Western meadowlark (1929); **insect,** Honeybee (1975); **gemstone,** Blue agate (1967); **rock,** Prairie agate (1967); **fossil;** Mammoth (1967); **song,** "Beautiful Nebraska" (1967); **soil,** Typic Arguistolls, Holdrege Series (1979); **mammal,** Whitetail deer (1981); **grass:** Little Bluesteve (1969)
Nicknames: Cornhusker State (1945); Beef State; The Tree Planter State (1895)
Origin of name: From an Oto Indian word meaning "flat water"
10 largest cities (1990 census): Omaha, 335,795; Lincoln, 191,972; Grand Island, 39,386; Bellevue, 30,982; Kearney, 24,396; Fremont, 23,680; Hastings, 22,837; North Platte, 22,605; Norfolk, 21,476; Columbus, 19,480
Land area & (rank): 76,878 sq mi. (199,113 sq km) (15)
Geographic center: In Custer Co., 10 mi. NW of Broken Bow
Number of counties: 93
Largest county (1990 census): Douglas, 416,444
State forests: None
State parks: 86 areas, historical and recreational; 8 major areas
1995 resident population est.: 1,637,000
1990 resident census population (rank): 1,578,385 (36). **Male:** 769,439; **Female:** 808,946. **White:** 1,480,558 (93.8%); **Black:** 57,404 (3.6%); **American Indian, Eskimo, or Aleut:** 12,410 (0.8%); **Asian or Pacific Islander:** 12,422 (0.8%); **Other race:** 15,591 (1.0%); **Hispanic:** 36,969 (2.3%). **1990 percent population under 18:** 27.2; **65 and over:** 14.1; **median age:** 33.0.

French fur traders first visited Nebraska in the early 1700s. Part of the Louisiana Purchase in 1803, Nebraska was explored by Lewis and Clark in 1804–06.

Robert Stuart pioneered the Oregon Trail across Nebraska in 1812–13 and the first permanent white settlement was established at Bellevue in 1823. Western Nebraska was acquired by treaty following the Mexican War in 1848. The Union Pacific began its transcontinental railroad at Omaha in 1865. In 1937, Nebraska became the only state in the Union to have a unicameral (one-house) legislature. Members are elected to it without party designation.

Nebraska is a leading grain-producer with bumper crops of grain sorghum, corn, and wheat. More varieties of grass, valuable for forage, grow in this state than in any other in the nation.

The state's sizable cattle and hog industries make Dakota City and Lexington among the nation's largest meat-packing centers.

Manufacturing has become diversified in Nebraska, strengthening the state's economic base. Firms making electronic components, auto accessories, pharmaceuticals, and mobile homes have joined such older industries as clothing, farm machinery, chemicals, and transportation equipment. Oil was discovered in 1939 and natural gas in 1949.

Among the principal attractions are Agate Fossil Beds, Homestead, and Scotts Bluff National Monuments; Chimney Rock National Historic Site; a recreated pioneer village at Minden; SAC Museum at Bellevue; the Stuhr Museum of the Prairie Pioneer with 57 original 19th-century buildings near Grand Island; the Sheldon Memorial Art Gallery at the University of Nebraska in Lincoln; the Lied Center for the Performing Arts located on the University of Nebraska campus in Lincoln; the Henry Doorly Zoo in Omaha; and the University of Nebraska State Museum in Lincoln.

Famous natives and residents: Grace Abbott, social worker; Fred Astaire, dancer and actor; Max Baer, boxer; Bil Baird, puppeteer; George Beadle, geneticist; Marlon Brando, actor; Dick Cavett, TV entertainer; Richard B. Cheney, ex-secretary of defense; Montgomery Clift, actor; James Coburn, actor; Sandy Dennis, actress; Mignon Eberhart, author; Ruth Etting, singer, actress; Henry Fonda, actor; Gerald Ford, ex-president; Bob Gibson, baseball player; Hoot Gibson, actor; Howard Hanson, conductor; Leland Hayward, producer; Susette La Flesche, Omaha Indian artist; Francis La Flesche, ethnologist; Melvin Laird, politician, ex-secretary of defense; Frank W. Leahy, football coach; Harold Lloyd, actor; David Janssen, actor; Irish McCalla, actress; Dorothy McGuire, actress; Julius Sterling Morton, politician, journalist, originated Arbor Day; Nick Nolte, actor; Inga Swenson, actress; Robert Taylor, actor; Paul Williams, singer, composer, actor; Julie Wilson, singer and actress; Daryl F. Zanuck, film producer

NEVADA

Capital: Carson City
Governor: Robert J. Miller, D (to Jan. 1999)
Lieut. Governor: Lonnie L. Hammargren, R (to Jan. 1999)
Secy. of State: Dean Heller, R (to Jan. 1999)
Treasurer: Bob Seale, R (to Jan. 1999)
Controller: Darrel R. Daines, R (to Jan. 1999)
Atty. General: Frankie Sue Del Papa, D (to Jan. 1999)
Organized as territory: March 2, 1861
Entered Union & (rank): Oct. 31, 1864 (36)
Present constitution adopted: 1864
Motto: All for Our Country
STATE SYMBOLS: flower, Sagebrush (1959); **trees,** Single-leaf pinon (1953) and Bristlecone pine (1987); **bird,** Mountain bluebird (1967); **animal,** Desert bighorn sheep (1973); **colors,** Silver and blue (1983); **song,** "Home Means Nevada" (1933); **rock,** Sandstone (1987); **precious gemstone,** Virgin Valley Black Fire Opal (1987); **semiprecious gemstone,** Nevada Turquoise (1987); **grass,** Indian Ricegrass (1977); **metal,** Silver (1977); **fossil,** Ichthyosaur (1977); **fish,** Lahontan Cutthroat Trout (1981); **reptile,** Desert tortoise (1989); **state artifact:** Tule duck decoy (1995)
Nicknames: Sagebrush State; Silver State; Battle Born State
Origin of name: Spanish: "snowcapped"
10 largest cities (1990 census): Las Vegas, 258,295; Reno, 133,850; Henderson, 64,942; Sparks, 53,367; North Las Vegas, 47,707; Carson City, 40,443; Elko, 14,736; Boulder City, 12,567; Fallon, 6,438; Winnemucca, 6,134
Land area & (rank): 109,806 sq mi. (284,397 sq km) (7)
Geographic center: In Lander Co., 26 mi. SE of Austin
Number of counties: 16, plus 1 independent city
Largest county (1990 census): Clark, 741,459
State forests: None
State parks: 20 (150,000 ac., including leased lands)
1995 resident population est.: 1,530,000
1990 resident census population (rank): 1,201,833 (39). **Male:** 611,880; **Female:** 589,953. **White:** 1,012,695 (84.3%); **Black:** 78,771 (6.6%); **American Indian, Eskimo, or Aleut:** 19,637 (1.6%); **Asian or Pacific Islander:** 38,127 (3.2%); **Other race:** 52,603 (4.4%); **Hispanic:** 124,419 (10.4%). **1990 percent population under 18:** 24.7; **65 and over:** 10.6; **median age:** 33.3.

Trappers and traders, including Jedediah Smith, and Peter Skene Ogden, entered the Nevada area in the 1820s. In 1843–45, John C. Fremont and Kit Carson explored the Great Basin and Sierra Nevada.

In 1848 following the Mexican War, the U.S. obtained the region and the first permanent settlement was a Mormon trading post near present-day Genoa.

The driest state in the nation with an average annual rainfall of only about 7 inches,[1] much of Nevada is uninhabited, sagebrush-covered desert.

Nevada was made famous by the discovery of the fabulous Comstock Lode in 1859 and its mines have produced large quantities of gold, silver, copper, lead, zinc, mercury, barite, and tungsten. Oil was discovered in 1954. Gold now far exceeds all other minerals in value of production.

In 1931, the state created two industries, divorce and gambling. For many years, Reno and Las Vegas were the "divorce capitals of the nation." More liberal divorce laws in many states have ended this distinction, but Nevada is the gambling and entertainment capital of the U.S. State gambling taxes account for 40.1% of general fund tax revenues. Although Nevada leads the nation in per capita gambling revenue, it ranks only fourth in total gambling revenue.

Near Las Vegas, on the Colorado River, stands Hoover Dam, which impounds the waters of Lake Mead, one of the world's largest artificial lakes.

The state's agricultural crop consists mainly of hay, alfalfa seed, barley, wheat, and potatoes.

Nevada manufactures gaming equipment; lawn and garden irrigation devices; titanium products; seismic and machinery monitoring devices; and specialty printing.

Major resort areas flourish in Lake Tahoe, Reno, and Las Vegas. Recreation areas include those at Pyramid Lake, Lake Tahoe, and Lake Mead and Lake Mohave, both in Lake Mead National Recreation Area. Among the other attractions are Hoover Dam, Virginia City, and Great Basin National Park (includes Lehman Caves).

Famous natives and residents: Eva Adams, ex-director of U.S. Mint; Andre Agassi, tennis player; Raymond T. Baker, ex-director of U.S. Mint; Helen Delich Bentley, government official, newspaperwoman; Robert Caples, painter; Walter Van Tilburg Clark, writer; Henry Comstock, prospector of "Comstock Lode" fame; Abby Dalton, actress; Michele Greene, actress; Sarah Winnemucca Hopkins, Paiute interpreter and peacemaker, author; Jack Kramer, tennis player; Paul Laxalt, politician; William Lear, aviation inventor; Robert C. Lynch, surgeon; John W. Mackay, benefactor, one of Big Four of Comstock Lode; Emma Nevada, opera singer; Thelma "Pat" Nixon, First Lady; James W. Nye, territory governor, ex-senator; Lute Pease, cartoonist, Pulitzer Prize winner; Edna Purviance, actress; Patty Sheehan, golfer; Jack Wilson, Paiute Indian prophet; George Wingfield, mining millionaire

1. Wettest part of state receives about 40 inches of precipitation per year, while driest spot has less than four inches per year.

NEW HAMPSHIRE

Capital: Concord
Governor: Stephen E. Merrill, R (to Jan. 1997)
Treasurer: Georgie A. Thomas, R (to Dec. 1996)
Secy. of State: William M. Gardner, D (to Dec. 1996)
Commissioner: Patrick Duffy
Atty. General: Jeffrey R. Howard, R (to Mar. 1997)
Entered Union & (rank): June 21, 1788 (9)
Present constitution adopted: 1784

Motto: Live free or die
STATE SYMBOLS: flower, Purple lilac (1919); **tree,** White birch (1947); **bird,** Purple finch (1957); **songs,** "Old New Hampshire" (1949) and "New Hampshire, My New Hampshire" (1963)
Nickname: Granite State
Origin of name: From the English county of Hampshire
10 largest cities (1990 census): Manchester, 99,567; Nashua, 79,662; Concord, 36,006; Rochester, 26,630; Portsmouth, 25,925; Dover, 25,042; Keene, 22,430; Laconia, 15,743; Claremont, 13,902; Lebanon, 12,183
Land area & (rank): 8,969 sq mi. (23,231 sq km) (44)
Geographic center: In Belknap Co., 3 mi. E of Ashland
Number of counties: 10
Largest county (1990 census): Hillsborough, 336,073
State forests & parks: 210 (156,398 ac.)
1995 resident population est.: 1,148,000
1990 resident census population (rank): 1,109,252 (41). **Male:** 543,544; **Female:** 565,708. **White:** 1,087,433 (98.0%); **Black:** 7,198 (0.6%); **American Indian, Eskimo, or Aleut:** 2,134 (0.2%); **Asian or Pacific Islander:** 9,343 (0.8%); **Other race:** 3,144 (0.3%); **Hispanic:** 11,333 (1.0%). **1990 percent population under 18:** 25.1; **65 and over:** 11.3; **median age:** 32.8.

Under an English land grant, Capt. John Smith sent settlers to establish a fishing colony at the mouth of the Piscataqua River, near present-day Rye and Dover, in 1623. Capt. John Mason, who participated in the founding of Portsmouth in 1630, gave New Hampshire its name.

After a 38-year period of union with Massachusetts, New Hampshire was made a separate royal colony in 1679. As leaders in the revolutionary cause, New Hampshire delegates received the honor of being the first to vote for the Declaration of Independence on July 4, 1776. New Hampshire is the only state that ever played host at the formal conclusion of a foreign war when, in 1905, Portsmouth was the scene of the treaty ending the Russo-Japanese War.

Abundant water power early turned New Hampshire into an industrial state and manufacturing is the principal source of income in the state. The most important industrial products are electrical and other machinery, textiles, pulp and paper products, and stone and clay products.

Dairy and poultry farming and growing fruit, truck vegetables, corn, potatoes, and hay are the major agricultural pursuits.

Tourism, because of New Hampshire's scenic and recreational resources, now brings over $3.5 billion into the state annually.

Vacation attractions include Lake Winnipesaukee, largest of 1,300 lakes and ponds; the 724,000-acre White Mountain National Forest; Daniel Webster's birthplace near Franklin; Strawbery Banke, restored building of the original settlement at Portsmouth; and the famous "Old Man of the Mountain" granite head profile, the state's official emblem, at Franconia.

Famous natives and residents: Sherman Adams, ex-governor and presidential advisor; Salmon P. Chase, jurist; Charles Anderson Dana, editor; Mary Baker Eddy, founder of Christian Science Church; Dustin Farnum, actor; Thomas Green Fessenden, journalist and satirical poet; Daniel Chester French, sculptor; Horace Greeley, journalist and politician; Sarah J. Hale, editor; John Irving, writer; Benjamin F. Keith, theater entrepreneur; Jackson Hall Kelly, promoter of Oregon settlement; John Langdon, political leader; Sharon Christa McAuliffe, teacher and astronaut; Franklin Pierce, ex-president; Augustus Saint-Gaudens, sculptor; Alan Shepard, astronaut; Harlan F. Stone, jurist; Daniel Webster, statesman; Henry Wilson, politician and ex-vice president; Noah Worcester, clergyman and pacifist

NEW JERSEY

Capital: Trenton
Governor: Christine Todd Whitman, R (to Jan. 1998)
Secy. of State: Lonna R. Hooks, R (to Jan. 1998)
Treasurer: Bryan W. Clymer, R (to Jan. 1998)
Atty. General: Deborah T. Poritz, R (to Jan. 1998)
Entered Union & (rank): Dec. 18, 1787 (3)
Present constitution adopted: 1947
Motto: Liberty and prosperity
STATE SYMBOLS: flower, Purple violet (1913); **bird,** Eastern goldfinch (1935); **insect,** Honeybee (1974); **tree,** Red oak (1950); **animal,** Horse (1977); **colors,** Buff and blue (1965)
Nickname: Garden State
Origin of name: From the Channel Isle of Jersey
10 largest cities (1990 census)[1]: Newark, 275,221; Jersey City, 228,537; Paterson, 140,891; Elizabeth, 110,002; Edison[2], 88,680; Trenton, 88,675; Camden, 87,492; East Orange, 73,552; Clifton, 71,742; Cherry Hill[2], 69,319
Land area & (rank): 7,419 sq mi. (19,215 sq km) (46)
Geographic center: In Mercer Co., 5 mi. SE of Trenton
Number of counties: 21
Largest county (1990 census): Bergen, 825,380
State forests: 11
State parks: 35 (67,111 ac.)
1995 resident population est.: 7,945,000
1990 resident census population (rank): 7,730,188 (9). **Male:** 3,735,685; **Female:** 3,994,503. **White:** 6,130,465 (79.3%); **Black:** 1,036,825 (13.4%); **American Indian, Eskimo, or Aleut:** 14,970 (0.2%); **Asian or Pacific Islander:** 272,521 (3.5%); **Other race:** 275,407 (3.6%); **Hispanic:** 739,861 (9.6%). **1990 percent population under 18:** 23.3; **65 and over:** 13.4; **median age:** 34.5.

1. These are the official 1990 census largest cities. However, the townships of Woodbridge, 93,086, and Hamilton, 86,553, are also legal municipalities or cities. 2. Census Designated Place.

New Jersey's early colonial history was involved with that of New York (New Netherlands), of which it was a part. One year after the Dutch surrender to England in 1664, New Jersey was organized as an English colony under Gov. Philip Carteret.

In the late 1600s the colony was divided between Carteret and William Penn; later it would be administered by the royal governor of New York. Finally, in 1738, New Jersey was separated from New York under its own royal governor, Lewis Morris.

Because of its key location between New York City and Philadelphia, New Jersey saw much fighting during the American Revolution.

Today, New Jersey, an area of wide industrial diversification, is known as the Crossroads of the East. Products from over 15,000 factories can be delivered overnight to almost 60 million people, representing 12 states and the District of Columbia. The greatest single industry is chemicals and New Jersey is one of the foremost research centers in the world. Many large oil refineries are located in northern New Jersey and other important manufactures are pharmaceuticals, instruments, machinery, electrical goods, and apparel.

Of the total land area, 37% is forested. Farmland is declining. In 1991 there were about 8,300 farms, with over 880,000 acres under harvest. The state ranks high in production of almost all garden vegetables. Tomatoes, asparagus, corn, and blueberries are important crops, and poultry and dairy farming make significant contributions to the state's economy.

Tourism is the second largest industry in New Jersey. The state has numerous resort areas on 127 miles of Atlantic coastline. In 1977, New Jersey voters approved legislation allowing legalized casino gambling in Atlantic City. Points of interest include the Delaware Water Gap, the Edison National Historic Site in West Orange, Princeton University, Liberty State Park, Jersey City, and the N.J. State Aquarium in Camden (opened 1992).

Famous natives and residents: Bud Abbott, comedian; Charles Addams, cartoonist; Edwin Aldrin, astronaut; Count Basie, band leader; Joan Bennett, actress; Jon Bon Jovi, musician; William J. Brennan, jurist; Aaron Burr, political leader; James Fenimore Cooper, novelist; Lou Costello, comedian; Stephen Crane, writer; Helen Gahagan Douglas, ex-Representative; Allen Ginsberg, poet; William Frederick Halsey, Jr., admiral; Alfred Joyce Kilmer, poet; Ernie Kovacs, comedian; Jerry Lewis, comedian, film director; Anne Morrow Lindbergh, author; Norman Mailer, novelist; Patricia McBride, ballerina; Richard Nixon, ex-president; Dorothy Parker, author; Joe Piscopo, comedian, actor; Paul Robeson, singer and actor; Philip Roth, novelist; Ruth St. Denis, dancer and choreographer; Antonin Scalia, jurist; H. Norman Schwarzkopf, general; Frank Sinatra, singer and actor; Bruce Springsteen, musician; Alfred Stieglitz, photographer; Albert Payson Terhune, journalist and novelist; Sarah Vaughan, singer; William Carlos Williams, physician and poet; Edmund Wilson, literary critic and author

NEW MEXICO

Capital: Santa Fe
Governor: Gary Johnson, R (to Jan. 1998)
Lieut. Governor: Walter Bradley, R (to Jan. 1998)
Secy. of State: Stephanie Gonzales, D (to Jan. 1998)
Atty. General: Tom Udall, D (to Jan. 1998)
State Auditor: Robert E. Vigil, D (to Jan. 1998)
State Treasurer: Michael A. Montoya, D (to Jan. 1998)
Commissioner of Public Lands: Ray Powell, D (to Jan. 1998)
Organized as territory: Sept. 9, 1850
Entered Union & (rank): Jan. 6, 1912 (47)
Present constitution adopted: 1911
Motto: *Crescit eundo* (It grows as it goes)
STATE SYMBOLS: flower, Yucca (1927); **tree,** Pinon (1949); **animal,** Black bear (1963); **bird,** Roadrunner (1949); **fish,** Cutthroat trout (1955); **vegetables,** Chili and frijol (1965); **gem,** Turquoise (1967); **colors,** Red and yellow of old Spain (1925); **song,** "O Fair New Mexico" (1917); **Spanish language song,** "Asi Es Nuevo Méjico" (1971); **poem,** A Nuevo México (1991); **grass,** Blue gramma; **fossil,** Coelophysis; **cookie,** Bizcochito (1989); **insect,** Tarantula hawk wasp (1989)
Nicknames: Land of Enchantment; Sunshine State
Origin of name: From the country of Mexico
10 largest cities (1990 census): Albuquerque, 384,736; Las Cruces, 62,126; Santa Fe, 55,859; Roswell, 44,654; Farmington, 33,997; Rio Rancho, 32,505; Clovis, 30,954; Hobbs, 29,115; Alamogordo, 27,596; Carlsbad, 24,952
Land area & (rank): 121,365 sq mi. (314,334 sq km) (5)
Geographic center: In Torrance Co., 12 mi. SSW of Willard
Number of counties: 33
Largest county (1990 census): Bernalillo, 480,577
State-owned forested land: 933,000 ac.
State parks: 29 (105,012 ac.)
1995 resident population est.: 1,685,000
1990 resident census population (rank): 1,515,069 (37). **Male:** 745,253; **Female:** 769,816. **White:** 1,146,028 (75.6%); **Black:** 30,210 (2.0%); **American Indian, Eskimo, or Aleut:** 134,355 (8.9%); **Asian or Pacific Islander:** 14,124 (0.9%); **Other race:** 190,352 (12.6%); **Hispanic:** 579,224 (38.2%). **1990 percent population under 18:** 29.5; **65 and over:** 10.8; **median age:** 31.3.

Francisco Vásquez de Coronado, Spanish explorer searching for gold, traveled the region that became New Mexico in 1540–42. In 1598 the first Spanish settlement was established on the Rio Grande River by Juan de Onate and in 1610 Santa Fe was founded and made the capital of New Mexico.

The U.S. acquired most of New Mexico in 1848, as a result of the Mexican War, and the remainder in the 1853 Gadsden Purchase. Union troops captured the territory from the Confederates during the Civil War. With the surrender of Geronimo in 1886, the Apache Wars and most of the Indian troubles in the area were ended.

Since 1945, New Mexico has been a leader in energy research and development with extensive experiments conducted at Los Alamos Scientific Laboratory and Sandia Laboratories in the nuclear, solar, and geothermal areas.

Minerals are the state's richest natural resource and New Mexico is one of the U.S. leaders in output of uranium and potassium salts. Petroleum, natural gas, copper, gold, silver, zinc, lead, and molybdenum also contribute heavily to the state's income.

The principal manufacturing industries include food products, chemicals, transportation equipment, lumber, electrical machinery, and stone-clay-glass products. More than two thirds of New Mexico's farm income comes from livestock products, especially sheep. Cotton, pecans, and sorghum are the most important field crops. Corn, peanuts, beans, onions, chile, and lettuce are also grown.

Tourist attractions in New Mexico include the Carlsbad Caverns National Park, Inscription Rock at El Morro National Monument, the ruins at Fort Union, Billy the Kid mementos at Lincoln, the White Sands and Gila Cliff Dwellings National Monuments, and the Chaco Culture National Historical Park.

Famous natives and residents: Ernest L. Blumenshein, artist; William "Billy the Kid" Bonney, outlaw; Bruce Cabot, actor; Kit Carson, Army scout and trapper; Dennis Chavez, ex-representative; John Chisum, cattle king; Mangus Coloradas, Apache leader; Edward Condon, physicist; John Denver, singer; Patrick Garrett, lawman; William Hanna, animator; Carl Hatch, ex-senator; Conrad Hilton, hotel executive; Peter Hurd, artist; Preston Jones, playwright, actor; Ralph Kiner, baseball player, sportscaster; Nancy Lopez, golfer; Maria Martínez, San Ildefonso Pueblo potter; Bill Mauldin, political cartoonist; Popé, San Juan Pueblo medicine man, leader; Harrison Schmitt, astronaut; Kim Stanley, actress; Slim Summerville, actor; Al Unser, Bobby Unser, auto racers; Victorio, Apache chief; Kathy Whitworth, golfer

NEW YORK

Capital: Albany
Governor: George Pataki, R (to Jan. 1999)
Lieut. Governor: Elizabeth McCaughey, R (to Jan. 1999)
Secy. of State: Alexander Treadwell, R (to Jan. 1999)
Comptroller: Carl McCall, D (to Jan. 1999)
Atty. General: Dennis Vacco, R (to Jan. 1999)
Entered Union & (rank): July 26, 1788 (11)
Present constitution adopted: 1777 (last revised 1938)
Motto: *Excelsior* (Ever upward)
STATE SYMBOLS: animal, Beaver (1975); **fish,** Brook trout (1975); **gem,** Garnet (1969); **flower,** Rose (1955); **tree,** Sugar maple (1956); **bird,** Bluebird (1970); **insect,** Ladybug (1989); **song,** "I Love New York" (1980)
Nickname: Empire State
Origin of name: In honor of the English Duke of York
10 largest cities (1990 census): New York, 7,322,564;

Buffalo, 328,123; Rochester, 231,636; Yonkers, 188,082; Syracuse, 163,860; Albany, 101,082; Utica, 68,637; New Rochelle, 67,265; Mount Vernon, 67,153; Schenectady, 65,566
Land area & (rank): 47,224 sq mi. (122,310 sq km) (30)
Geographic center: In Madison Co., 12 mi. S of Oneida and 26 mi. SW of Utica
Number of counties: 62
Largest county (1990 census): Kings, 2,300,664
State forest preserves: Adirondacks, 2,500,000 ac., Catskills, 250,000 ac.
State parks: 150 (250,000 ac.)
1995 resident population est.: 18,136,000
1990 resident census population (rank): 17,990,455 (2). **Male:** 8,625,673; **Female:** 9,364,782. **White:** 13,385,255 (74.4%); **Black:** 2,859,055 (15.9%); **American Indian, Eskimo, or Aleut:** 62,651 (0.3%); **Asian or Pacific Islander:** 693,760 (3.9%); **Other race:** 989,734 (5.5%); **Hispanic:** 2,214,026 (12.3%). **1990 percent population under 18:** 23.7; **65 and over:** 13.1; **median age:** 33.9,.

Giovanni da Verrazano, Italian-born navigator sailing for France, discovered New York Bay in 1524. Henry Hudson, an Englishman employed by the Dutch, reached the bay and sailed up the river now bearing his name in 1609, the same year that northern New York was explored and claimed for France by Samuel de Champlain.

In 1624 the first permanent Dutch settlement was established at Fort Orange (now Albany); one year later Peter Minuit is said to have purchased Manhattan Island from the Indians for trinkets worth about $24 and founded the Dutch colony of New Amsterdam (now New York City), which was surrendered to the English in 1664.

For a short time, New York City was the U.S. capital and George Washington was inaugurated there as first President on April 30, 1789.

New York's extremely rapid commercial growth may be partly attributed to Governor De Witt Clinton, who pushed through the construction of the Erie Canal (Buffalo to Albany), which was opened in 1825. Today, the 559-mile Governor Thomas E. Dewey Thruway connects New York City with Buffalo and with Connecticut, Massachusetts, and Pennsylvania express highways. Two toll-free superhighways, the Adirondack Northway (linking Albany with the Canadian border) and the North-South-Expressway (crossing central New York from the Pennsylvania border to the Thousand Islands) have been opened.

New York, with the great metropolis of New York City, is the spectacular nerve center of the nation. It is a leader in manufacturing, foreign trade, commercial and financial transactions, book and magazine publishing, and theatrical production.

New York City is not only a national but an international leader. A leading seaport, its John F. Kennedy International Airport is one of the busiest airports in the world. It is the largest manufacturing center in the country and its apparel industry is the city's largest manufacturing employer, with printing and publishing second.

Nearly all the rest of the state's manufacturing is done on Long Island, along the Hudson River north to Albany and through the Mohawk Valley, Central New York, and Southern Tier regions to Buffalo. The St. Lawrence seaway and power projects have opened the North Country to industrial expansion and have given the state a second seacoast.

The state ranks third in the nation in manufacturing with 1,057,100 employees in 1991. The principal industries are apparel, printing and publishing, leather products, instruments and electronic equipment.

The convention and tourist business is one of the state's most important sources of income.

New York farms are famous for raising cattle and calves, producing corn for grain, poultry, and the raising of vegetables and fruits. The state is a leading wine producer.

Among the major points of interest are Castle Clinton, Fort Stanwix, and Statue of Liberty National Monuments; Niagara Falls; U.S. Military Academy at West Point; National Historic Sites that include homes of Franklin D. Roosevelt at Hyde Park and Theodore Roosevelt in Oyster Bay and New York City; National Memorials, including Grant's Tomb and Federal Hall in New York City; Fort Ticonderoga; the Baseball Hall of Fame in Cooperstown; and the United Nations, skyscrapers, museums, theaters, and parks in New York City.

Famous natives and residents: Kareem Abdul-Jabbar, basketball player; Lucille Ball, actress; Humphrey Bogart, actor; James Cagney, actor; Maria Callas, soprano; Benjamin N. Cardozo, jurist; Paddy Chayefsky, playwright; Peter Cooper, industrialist and philanthropist; Aaron Copland, composer; Sammy Davis, Jr., actor and singer; Agnes de Mille, choreographer; Eamon De Valera, ex-president of Ireland; George Eastman, inventor; Millard Fillmore, ex-president; Lou Gehrig, baseball player; George Gershwin, composer; Learned Hand, jurist; Edward Hopper, painter; Julia Ward Howe, poet and reformer; Charles Evans Hughes, jurist; Washington Irving, author; Henry James, novelist; John Jay, jurist; Michael Jordan, basketball player; Jerome Kern, composer; Rockwell Kent, painter; Vince Lombardi, football coach; Chico, Groucho, Harpo, Zeppo Marx, comedians; Herman Melville, author; Ethel Merman, singer and actress; Ogden Nash, poet; Eugene O'Neill, playwright; Red Jacket, Seneca chief; John D. Rockefeller, industrialist; Norman Rockwell, painter and illustrator; Mickey Rooney, actor; Anna Eleanor Roosevelt, reformer and humanitarian; Franklin D. Roosevelt, ex-president; Theodore Roosevelt, ex-president; Jonas Salk, polio researcher; Margaret Sanger, birth control leader; Barbara Stanwyck, actress; Risë Stevens, mezzo-soprano; Richard Tucker, tenor; Martin Van Buren, ex-president; Mae West, actress; Walt Whitman, poet; Edith Wharton, novelist

NORTH CAROLINA

Capital: Raleigh
Governor: James B. Hunt, Jr., D (to Jan. 1997)
Lieut. Governor: Dennis A. Wicker, D (to Jan. 1997)
Secy. of State: Janice Faulkner, D (to Jan. 1997)
Treasurer: Harlan E. Boyles, D (to Jan. 1997)
Auditor: Ralph Campbell, D (to Jan. 1997)
Atty. General: Michael Easley, D (to Jan. 1997)
Entered Union & (rank): Nov. 21, 1789 (12)
Present constitution adopted: 1971
Motto: *Esse quam videri* (To be rather than to seem)
STATE SYMBOLS: flower, Dogwood (1941); **tree,** Pine (1963); **bird,** Cardinal (1943); **mammal,** Gray squirrel (1969); **insect,** Honeybee (1973); **reptile,** Eastern box turtle (1979); **gemstone,** Emerald (1973); **shell,** Scotch bonnet (1965); **historic boat,** Shad Boat (1987); **beverage,** Milk (1987); **rock,** Granite (1979); **dog,** Plott Hound (1989); **song,** "The Old North State" (1927); **colors,** Red and blue (1945)
Nickname: Tar Heel State
Origin of name: In honor of Charles I of England
10 largest cities (1990 census): Charlotte, 395,934; Raleigh, 207,951; Greensboro, 183,521; Winston-Salem, 143,485; Durham, 136,611; Fayetteville, 75,695; High Point, 69,496; Asheville, 61,607; Wilmington, 55,530; Gastonia, 54,732

Land area & (rank): 48,718 sq mi. (126,180 sq km) (29)
Geographic center: In Chatham Co., 10 mi. NW of Sanford
Number of counties: 100
Largest county (1990 census): Mecklenburg, 511,433
State forests: 1
State parks: 30 (125,000 ac.)
1995 resident population est.: 7,195,000
1990 resident census population (rank): 6,628,637 (10). **Male:** 3,214,290; **Female:** 3,414,347. **White:** 5,008,491 (75.6%); **Black:** 1,456,323 (22.0%); **American Indian, Eskimo, or Aleut:** 80,155 (1.2%); **Asian or Pacific Islander:** 52,166 (0.8%); **Other race:** 31,502 (0.5%); **Hispanic:** 76,726 (1.2%). **1990 percent population under 18:** 24.2; **65 and over:** 12.1; **median age:** 33.1.

English colonists, sent by Sir Walter Raleigh, unsuccessfully attempted to settle Roanoke Island in 1585 and 1587. Virginia Dare, born there in 1587, was the first child of English parentage born in America.

In 1653 the first permanent settlements were established by English colonists from Virginia near the Roanoke and Chowan Rivers.

The region was established as an English proprietary colony in 1663–65 and its early history was the scene of Culpepper's Rebellion (1677), the Quaker-led Cary Rebellion of 1708, the Tuscarora Indian War in 1711–13, and many pirate raids.

During the American Revolution, there was relatively little fighting within the state, but many North Carolinians saw action elsewhere. Despite considerable pro-Union, anti-slavery sentiment, North Carolina joined the Confederacy.

North Carolina is the nation's largest furniture, tobacco, brick, and textile producer. It holds second place in the Southeast in population and first place in the value of its industrial and agricultural production. This production is highly diversified, with metalworking, chemicals, and paper constituting enormous industries. Tobacco, corn, cotton, hay, peanuts, and truck and vegetable crops are of major importance. It is the country's leading producer of mica and lithium.

Tourism is also important, with travelers and vacationers spending more than $1 billion annually in North Carolina. Sports include year-round golfing, skiing at mountain resorts, both fresh and salt water fishing, and hunting.

Among the major attractions are the Great Smoky Mountains, the Blue Ridge National Parkway, the Cape Hatteras and Cape Lookout National Seashores, the Wright Brothers National Memorial at Kitty Hawk, Guilford Courthouse and Moores Creek National Military Parks, Carl Sandburg's home near Hendersonville, and the Old Salem Restoration in Winston-Salem.

Famous natives and residents: David Brinkley, TV newscaster; Howard Cosell, sportscaster; Virginia Dare, first person born in America to English parents; James B. Duke, industrialist; Roberta Flack, singer; Ava Gardner, actress; Richard Gatling, inventor; Billy Graham, evangelist; Kathryn Grayson, singer and actress; Jesse Helms, politician; O. Henry, story writer; Barbara Howar, broadcaster, writer; Andrew Johnson, ex-president; Charles Kuralt, TV journalist; Sugar Ray Leonard, boxer; Dolley Madison, ex-first lady; Ronni Milsap, country music singer; Theolonious Monk, pianist and composer; Alfred Moore, jurist; Edward R. Murrow, commentator and government official; Walter Hines Page, journalist and ambassador; Floyd Patterson, boxer; Richard Petty, auto racer; James K. Polk, ex-president; Soupy Sales, comedian; Earl Scruggs; bluegrass musician; Randy Travis, musician; John Scott Trotter, orchestra leader; Thomas Wolfe, novelist

NORTH DAKOTA

Capital: Bismarck
Governor: Edward T. Schafer, R (to Dec. 15, 1996)
Lieut. Governor: Rosemarie Myrdal, R (to Dec. 15, 1996)
Secy. of State: Alvin A. Jaeger, R (to Dec. 31, 1996)
Auditor: Robert W. Peterson, R (to Dec. 31, 1996)
State Treasurer: Kathi Gilmore, D (to Dec. 31, 1996)
Atty. General: Heidi Heitkamp, D (to Dec. 31, 1996)
Organized as territory: March 2, 1861
Entered Union & (rank): Nov. 2, 1889 (39)
Present constitution adopted: 1889
Motto: Liberty and union, now and forever: one and inseparable
STATE SYMBOLS: tree, American elm (1947); **bird,** Western meadowlark (1947); **song,** "North Dakota Hymn" (1947); **fish,** Northern Pike (1969); **grass,** Western wheatgrass (1977); **fossil,** Teredo petrified wood (1967); **beverage,** milk (1983); **state march,** Spirit of the Land (1975); **flower,** Wild prairie rose (1907); **state language,** English (1987); **honorary equine,** Nokota horse (1993); **state dance,** square dance (1995)
Nickname: Sioux State; Flickertail State, Peace Garden State
Origin of name: From the Sioux tribe, meaning "allies"
10 largest cities (1992 estimate): Fargo, 77,052; Grand Forks, 49,332; Bismarck, 51,319; Minot, 34,446; Dickinson, 16,264; Jamestown, 15,295; Mandan, 15,254; Williston, 13,033; West Fargo, 12,660; Wahpeton, 8,719
Land area & (rank): 68,994 sq mi. (178,695 sq km) (17)
Geographic center: In Sheridan Co., 5 mi. SW of McClusky
Number of counties: 53
Largest county (1990 census): Cass, 102,874
State forests: None
State parks: 14 (14,922.6 ac.)
1995 resident population est.: 641,000
1990 resident census population (rank): 638,800 (47). **Male:** 318,201; **Female:** 320,599. **White:** 604,142 (94.6%); **Black:** 3,524 (0.6%); **American Indian, Eskimo, or Aleut:** 25,917 (4.1%); **Asian or Pacific Islander:** 3,462 (0.5%); **Other race:** 1,755 (0.3%); **Hispanic:** 4,665 (0.7%). **1990 percent population under 18:** 27.5; **65 and over:** 14.3; **median age:** 32.4.

North Dakota was explored in 1738–40 by French Canadians led by La Verendrye. In 1803, the U.S. acquired most of North Dakota from France in the Louisiana Purchase. Lewis and Clark explored the region in 1804–06 and the first settlements were made at Pembina in 1812 by Scottish and Irish families while this area was still in dispute between the U.S. and Great Britain.

In 1818, the U.S. obtained the northeastern part of North Dakota by treaty with Great Britain and took possession of Pembina in 1823.

North Dakota is the most rural of all the states, with farms covering more than 90% of the land. North Dakota ranks first in the nation's production of spring and durum wheat, and the state's coal and oil reserves are plentiful.

Other agricultural products include barley, rye, sunflowers, dry edible beans, honey, oats, flaxseed, sugar beets, and hay; beef cattle, sheep, and hogs.

Recently, manufacturing industries have grown, especially food processing and farm equipment. The state also produces natural gas, lignite, salt, clay, sand, and gravel.

The Garrison Dam on the Missouri River provides extensive irrigation and produces 400,000 kilowatts of electricity for the Missouri Basin areas.

Known for its waterfowl, grouse, and deer hunting and bass, trout, and northern pike fishing, North Dakota has 20 state parks and recreation areas. Points of interest include the International Peace Garden near Dunseith, Fort Union Trading Post National Historic Site, the State Capitol at Bismarck, the Badlands, Theodore Roosevelt National Park, and Fort Lincoln, now a state park, from which Gen. George Custer set out on his last campaign in 1876.

Famous natives and residents: Lynn Anderson, singer; Maxwell Anderson, playwright; Dr. Robert H. Bahmer, U.S. archivist; Elizabeth Bodine, humanitarian; Dr. Anne Carlsen, educator; Ronald N. Davies, jurist; Angie Dickinson, actress; Ivan Dmitre, artist; Phyllis Frelich, actress; Bertin C. Gamble, founder of Gamble-Skogmo; William H. Gass, writer, philosopher; Rev. Richard C. Halverson, U.S. Senate chaplain; Phil D. Jackson, basketball player, coach; Dr. Leon O. Jacobson, researcher, educator; Harold K. Johnson, ex-army general; David C. Jones, army general; Louis L'Amour, author; Peggy Lee, singer; William Lemke, ex-representative; Roger Maris, baseball player; Marquis de Mores, cattleman, established Medora; Gerald P. Nye, ex-senator; Casper Oimoen, skier; Arthur Peterson, radio and TV actor; Cliff (Fido) Purpur, hockey player, coach; James Rosenquist, paitner; Harold Schafer, founder of Gold Seal Co.; Eric Sevareid, TV commentator; Ann Sothern, actress; Dorothy Stickney, actress; Edward K. Thompson, Life magazine editor; Era Bell Thompson, Ebony magazine editor; Tommy Tucker, band leader; Lawrence Welk, band leader; Larry Woiwode, writer

OHIO

Capital: Columbus
Governor: George V. Voinovich, R (to Jan. 1999)
Lieut. Governor: Nancy Putnam-Hollister, R (to Jan. 1999)
Secy. of State: Bob Taft, R (to Jan. 1999)
Auditor: Jim Petro, R (to Jan. 1999)
Treasurer: J. Kenneth Blackwell, R (to Jan. 1999)
Atty. General: Betty D. Montgomery, R (to Jan. 1999)
Entered Union & (rank): March 1, 1803 (17)
Present constitution adopted: 1851
Motto: With God, all things are possible
STATE SYMBOLS: flower, Scarlet carnation (1904); **tree,** Buckeye (1953); **bird,** Cardinal (1933); **insect,** Ladybug (1975); **gemstone,** Flint (1965); **song,** "Beautiful Ohio" (1969); **drink,** Tomato juice (1965)
Nickname: Buckeye State
Origin of name: From an Iroquoian word meaning "great river"
10 largest cities (1992): Columbus, 642,987; Cleveland, 505,616; Cincinnati, 364,040; Toledo, 332,943; Akron, 223,019; Dayton, 182,044; Youngstown, 95,732; Parma, 87,876; Canton, 84,161; Lorain, 71,245
Land area & (rank): 40,953 sq mi. (106,067 sq km) (35)
Geographic center: In Delaware Co., 25 mi. NNE of Columbus
Number of counties: 88
Largest county (1990 census): Cuyahoga, 1,412,140
State forests: 19 (172,744 ac.)
State parks: 71 (198,027 ac.)
1995 resident population est.: 11,151,000
1990 resident census population (rank): 10,847,115 (7). **Male:** 5,226,340; **Female:** 5,620,775. **White:** 9,521,756 (87.8%); **Black:** 1,154,826 (10.6%); **American Indian, Eskimo, or Aleut:** 20,358 (0.2%); **Asian or Pacific Islander:** 91,179 (0.8%); **Other race:** 58,996 (0.5%); **Hispanic:** 139,696 (1.3%). **1990 percent population under 18:** 25.8; **65 and over:** 13.0; **median age:** 33.3.

First explored for France by La Salle in 1669, the Ohio region became British property after the French and Indian War. Ohio was acquired by the U.S. after the Revolutionary War in 1783 and, in 1788, the first permanent settlement was established at Marietta, capital of the Northwest Territory.

The 1790s saw severe fighting with the Indians in Ohio; a major battle was won by Maj. Gen. Anthony Wayne at Fallen Timbers in 1794. In the War of 1812, Commodore Oliver H. Perry defeated the British in the Battle of Lake Erie on Sept. 10, 1813.

Ohio is one of the nation's industrial leaders, ranking third in the value of manufactured products. Important manufacturing centers are located in or near Ohio's major cities. Akron is known for rubber; Canton for roller bearings; Cincinnati for jet engines and machine tools; Cleveland for auto assembly and parts, refining, and steel; Dayton for office machines, refrigeration, and heating and auto equipment; Youngstown and Steubenville for steel; and Toledo for glass and auto parts.

The state's thousands of factories almost overshadow its importance in agriculture and mining. Its fertile soil produces soybeans, corn, oats, grapes, and clover. More than half of Ohio's farm receipts come from dairy farming and sheep and hog raising. Ohio is the top state in lime production and among the leaders in coal, clay, salt, sand, and gravel. Petroleum, gypsum, cement, and natural gas are also important.

Tourism is a valuable revenue producer, bringing in $8.5 billion in 1992, and ranking 10th among the 50 states. Attractions include the Indian burial grounds at Mound City Group National Monument, Perry's Victory International Peace Memorial, the Pro Football Hall of Fame at Canton, and the homes of Presidents Grant, Taft, Hayes, Harding, and Garfield.

Famous natives and residents: Neil Armstrong, astronaut; Kathleen Battle, soprano; George Bellows, painter and lithographer; Ambrose Bierce, journalist; Erma Bombeck, columnist; Bill Boyd (Hopalong Cassidy), actor; Milton Caniff, cartoonist; Hart Crane, poet; George Armstrong Custer, army officer; Dorothy Dandridge, actress; Doris Day, singer and actress; Clarence Darrow, lawyer; Ruby Dee, actress; Rita Dove, ex-U.S. Poet Laureate; Hugh Downs, TV broadcaster; Thomas A. Edison, inventor; Clark Gable, actor; James A. Garfield, ex-president; Lillian Gish, actress; John Glenn, astronaut and senator; Ulysses S. Grant, ex-president; Warren G. Harding, ex-president; Rutherford Hayes, ex-president; Benjamin Harrison, ex-president; William Dean Howells, novelist and critic; Zane Grey, author; Robert Henri, painter; Kenisaw Mountain Landis, first baseball commissioner; Dean Martin, singer and actor; William McKinley, ex-president; Paul Newman, actor; Jack Nicklaus, golfer; Annie Oakley, markswoman; Norman Vincent Peale, clergyman; Tyrone Power, actor; Judith Resnik, astronaut; Eddie Rickenbacker, aviator; Arthur M. Schlesinger, Jr., historian; William Tecumseh Sherman, army general; Gloria Steinem, feminist; William H. Taft, ex-president; Tecumseh, Shawnee Indian chief; Lowell Thomas, explorer and commentator; James Thurber, author and cartoonist; Orville and Wilbur Wright, inventors; Cy Young, baseball player

OKLAHOMA

Capital: Oklahoma City
Governor: Frank Keating, R (to Jan. 1999)
Lieut. Governor: Mary Fallin, R (to Jan. 1999)
Secy. of State: Tom Cole, R (to Jan. 1999)
Treasurer: Robert Butkin, D (to Jan. 1999)
Atty. General: Drew Edmondson, D (to Jan. 1999)
Organized as territory: May 2, 1890
Entered Union & (rank): Nov. 16, 1907 (46)
Present constitution adopted: 1907
Motto: *Labor omnia vincit* (Labor conquers all things)
STATE SYMBOLS: flower, Mistletoe (1893); **tree,** Redbud (1937); **bird,** Scissor-tailed flycatcher (1951); **animal,** Bison (1972); **reptile,** Mountain boomer lizard (1969);

stone, Rose Rock (barite rose) (1968); **colors,** Green and white (1915); **song,** "Oklahoma" (1953)
Nickname: Sooner State
Origin of name: From two Choctaw Indian words meaning "red people"
10 largest cities (1990 census): Oklahoma City, 444,719; Tulsa, 367,302; Lawton, 80,561; Norman, 80,071; Broken Arrow, 58,043; Edmond, 52,315; Midwest City, 52,267; Enid, 45,309; Moore, 40,318; Muskogee, 37,708
Land area & (rank): 68,679 sq mi. (177,877 sq km) (19)
Geographic center: In Oklahoma Co., 8 mi. N of Oklahoma City
Number of counties: 77
Largest county (1990 census): Oklahoma, 599,611
State forests: None
State parks: 36 (57,487 ac.)
1995 resident population est.: 3,278,000
1990 resident census population (rank): 3,145,585 (28). **Male:** 1,530,819; **Female:** 1,614,766. **White:** 2,583,512 (82.1%); **Black:** 233,801 (7.4%); **American Indian, Eskimo, or Aleut:** 252,420 (8.0%); **Asian or Pacific Islander:** 33,563 (1.1%); **Other race:** 42,289 (1.3%); **Hispanic:** 86,160 (2.7%). **1990 percent population under 18:** 26.6; **65 and over:** 13.5; **median age:** 33.2.

Francisco Vásquez de Coronado first explored the region for Spain in 1541. The U.S. acquired most of Oklahoma in 1803 in the Louisiana Purchase from France; the Western Panhandle region became U.S. territory with the annexation of Texas in 1845.

Set aside as Indian Territory in 1834, the region was divided into Indian Territory and Oklahoma Territory on May 2, 1890. The two were combined to make a new state, Oklahoma, on Nov. 16, 1907.

On April 22, 1889, the first day homesteading was permitted, 50,000 people swarmed into the area. Those who tried to beat the noon starting gun were called "Sooners," hence the state's nickname.

Oil made Oklahoma a rich state, but natural gas production has now surpassed it. Oil refining, meat packing, food processing, and machinery manufacturing (especially construction and oil equipment) are important industries.

Other minerals produced in Oklahoma include helium, gypsum, zinc, cement, coal, copper, and silver.

Oklahoma's rich plains produce bumper yields of wheat, as well as large crops of sorghum, hay, cotton, and peanuts. More than half of Oklahoma's annual farm receipts are contributed by livestock products, including cattle, dairy products, and broilers.

Tourist attractions include the National Cowboy Hall of Fame in Oklahoma City, the Will Rogers Memorial in Claremore, the Cherokee Cultural Center with a restored Cherokee village, the restored Fort Gibson Stockade near Muskogee, and the Lake Texoma recreation area, Pari-Mutual horse racing at Remington Park in Oklahoma City, and Blue Ribbon Downs in Sallisaw.

Famous natives and residents: Johnny Bench, baseball player; John Berryman, poet; Iron Eyes Cody, Cherokee actor; L. Gordon Cooper, astronaut; Ralph Ellison, writer; James Garner, actor; Chester Gould, cartoonist; Woody Guthrie, singer and composer; Roy Harris, composer; Paul Harvey, broadcaster; Van Heflin, actor; Ron Howard, actor and director; Ben Johnson, actor; Jennifer Jones, actress; Jeane Kirkpatrick, educator and public affairs spokesperson; Wilma P. Mankiller, Principal Chief of Cherokee Nation of Oklahoma; Mickey Mantle, baseball player; Bill Moyers, journalist; Daniel Patrick Moynihan, N.Y. Senator; Patti Page, singer; Mary Kay Place, actress and writer; Tony Randall, actor; Oral Roberts, evangelist; Dale Robertson, actor; Will Rogers, humorist; Dan Rowan, comedian; Maria Tallchief, ballerina; Jim Thorpe, athlete; Alfre Woodard, actress

OREGON

Capital: Salem
Governor: John A. Kitzhaber, D (to Jan. 1999)
Secy. of State: Phil Keisling, D (to Jan. 1999)
Treasurer: James A. Hill, D (to Jan. 1999)
Atty. General: Theodore R. Kulongoski, D (to Jan. 1999)
Organized as territory: Aug. 14, 1848
Entered Union & (rank): Feb. 14, 1859 (33)
Present constitution adopted: 1859
Motto: "Alis volat Propriis" ("She flies with her own wings") (1987)
STATE SYMBOLS: flower, Oregon grape (1899); **tree,** Douglas fir (1939); **animal,** Beaver (1969); **bird,** Western meadowlark (1927); **fish,** Chinook salmon (1961); **rock,** Thunderegg (1965); **colors,** Navy blue and gold (1959); **song,** "Oregon, My Oregon" (1927); **insect,** Swallowtail butterfly (1979); **dance,** Square dance (1977); **nut,** Hazelnut (1989); **gemstone,** Sunstone (1987)
Nickname: Beaver State
Poet Laureate: William E. Stafford (1974) [deceased]
Origin of name: Unknown. However, it is generally accepted that the name, first used by Jonathan Carver in 1778, was taken from the writings of Maj. Robert Rogers, an English army officer.
10 largest cities (1993 pop. est.): Portland, 471,328; Eugene, 119,235; Salem, 113,325; Gresham, 73,185; Beaverton, 60,000; Medford, 51,215; Springfield, 46,715; Corvallis, 46,260; Hillsboro, 42,280; Albany, 34,350
Land area & (rank): 96,003 sq mi. (248,647 sq km) (10)
Geographic center: In Crook Co., 25 mi. SSE of Prineville
Number of counties: 36
Largest county (1993 pop. est.): Multnomah, 615,000
State forests: 820,000 ac.
State parks: 240 (93,330 ac.)
1995 resident population est.: 3,141,000
1990 resident census population (rank): 2,842,321 (29). **Male:** 1,397,073; **Female:** 1,445,248. **White:** 2,636,787 (92.8%); **Black:** 46,178 (1.6%); **American Indian, Eskimo, or Aleut:** 38,496 (1.4%); **Asian or Pacific Islander:** 69,269 (2.4%); **Other race:** 51,591 (1.8%); **Hispanic:** 112,707 (4.0%). **1990 percent population under 18:** 25.5; **65 and over:** 13.8; **median age:** 34.5.

Spanish and English sailors are believed to have sighted the Oregon coast in the 1500s and 1600s. Capt. James Cook, seeking the Northwest Passage, charted some of the coastline in 1778. In 1792, Capt. Robert Gray, in the *Columbia*, discovered the river named after his ship and claimed the area for the U.S.

In 1805 the Lewis and Clark expedition explored the area and John Jacob Astor's fur depot, Astoria, was founded in 1811. Disputes for control of Oregon between American settlers and the Hudson Bay Company were finally resolved in the 1846 Oregon Treaty in which Great Britain gave up claims to the region.

Oregon has a $3.3 billion lumber and wood products industry, and an $859 millioon paper and allied manufacturing industry. Its salmon-fishing industry is one of the world's largest.

In agriculture, the state leads in growing peppermint, cover seed crops, blackberries, boysenberries, loganberries, black raspberries, and hazelnuts. It is second in raising hops, raspberries, sweet cherries, prunes, snap beans and onions. Oregon has the only nickel smelter in the United States.

With the low-cost electric power provided by Bonneville Dam, McNary Dam, and other dams in the Pacific Northwest, Oregon has developed steadily as a manufacturing state. Leading manufactures are lumber and plywood, metalwork, machinery, aluminum, chemicals, paper, food packing, and electronic equipment.

Crater Lake National Park, Mount Hood, and Bonneville Dam on the Columbia are major tourist attractions. Oregon Dunes National Recreation Area has been established near Florence. Other points of interest include the Oregon Caves National Monument, Cape Perpetua in Siuslaw National Forest, Columbia River Gorge between The Dalles and Troutdale, Hells Canyon, Newberry Volcanic National Monument, and John Day Fossil Beds National Monument.

Famous natives and residents: James Beard, food expert; Raymond Carver, writer, poet; Homer C. Davenport, political cartoonist; David Douglas, botanist; Abigail Scott Duniway, women's suffrage advocate; John E. Frohnmeyer, ex-chairman National Endowment of the Arts; Robert Gray, sea captain, discoverer of Columbia River; Matt Groening, cartoonist; Mark Hatfield, senator; Donald P. Hodel, ex-secretary of the interior; Chief Joseph, Nez Percé chief; Dave Kingman, baseball player; Ursula LeGuin, writer; Edwin Markham, poet; Phyllis McGinley, author; Linus Pauling, chemist; Jane Powell, actress and singer; John Reed, poet and author; Harvey W. Scott, editor; Doc Severinsen, band leader; Norton Simon, business executive; Paul M. Simon, Illinois senator; William E. Stafford, poet; Sally Struthers, actress

PENNSYLVANIA

Capital: Harrisburg
Governor: Tom Ridge, R (to Jan. 1999)
Lieut. Governor: Mark Schweiker, R (to Jan. 1999)
Secy. of the Commonwealth: Yvette Kane, R (at the pleasure of the governor)
Auditor General: Barbara Hafer, R (to Jan. 1997)
Atty. General: Thomas W. Corbett, Jr., R (to Jan. 1997)
Entered Union & (rank): Dec. 12, 1787 (2)
Present constitution adopted: 1968
Motto: Virtue, liberty, and independence
STATE SYMBOLS: flower, Mountain laurel (1933); **tree,** Hemlock (1931); **bird,** Ruffed grouse (1931); **dog,** Great Dane (1965); **colors,** Blue and gold (1907); **song,** "Pennsylvania" (1990)
Nickname: Keystone State
Origin of name: In honor of Adm. Sir William Penn, father of William Penn. It means "Penn's Woodland."
10 largest cities (1990 census): Philadelphia, 1,585,577; Pittsburgh, 369,879; Erie, 108,718; Allentown, 105,090; Scranton, 81,805; Reading, 78,380; Bethlehem, 71,428; Lancaster, 55,551; Harrisburg, 52,376; Altoona, 51,881
Land area & (rank): 44,820 sq mi. (116,083 sq km) (32)
Geographic center: In Centre Co., 2 1/2 mi. SW of Bellefonte
Number of counties: 67
Largest county (1990 census): Allegheny, 1,336,449
State forests: 1,991,526 ac.
State parks: 114 (277,164.18 ac.)
1995 resident population est.: 12,072,000
1990 resident census population (rank): 11,881,643 (5). **Male:** 5,694,265; **Female:** 6,187,378. **White:** 10,520,201 (88.5%); **Black:** 1,089,795 (9.2%); **American Indian, Eskimo, or Aleut:** 14,733 (0.1%); **Asian or Pacific Islander:** 137,438 (1.2%); **Other race:** 119,476 (1.0%); **Hispanic:** 232,262 (2.0%). **1990 percent population under 18:** 23.5; **65 and over:** 15.4; **median age:** 35.

Rich in historic lore, Pennsylvania territory was disputed in the early 1600s among the Dutch, the Swedes, and the English. England acquired the region in 1664 with the capture of New York and in 1681 Pennsylvania was granted to William Penn, a Quaker, by King Charles II.

Philadelphia was the seat of the federal government almost continuously from 1776 to 1800; there the Declaration of Independence was signed in 1776 and the U.S. Constitution drawn up in 1787. Valley

Forge, of Revolutionary War fame, and Gettysburg, the turning-point of the Civil War, are both in Pennsylvania. The Liberty Bell is located in a glass pavilion across from Independence Hall in Philadelphia.

With the decline of the coal, steel and railroad industries, Pennsylvania's industry has diversified, though the state still leads the country in the production of specialty steel. Pennsylvania is a leader in the production of chemicals, food, and electrical machinery and produces 10% of the nations's cement. Also important are brick and tiles, glass, limestone, and slate. Data processing is also increasingly important.

Pennsylvania's nine million agricultural acres (6 million acres for crops and pasture, 3 million acres in farm woodlands) produce a wide variety of crops and its 55,535 farms are the backbone of the state's economy. Leading products are milk, poultry and eggs, a variety of fruits, sweet corn, potatoes, mushrooms, cheese, beans, hay, maple syrup, and even Christmas trees.

Pennsylvania has the largest rural population in the nation. The state's farmers sell more than $3.3 billion in crops and livestock annually and agribusiness and food-related industries account for another $35 billion in economic activity annually.

Tourists now spend approximately $6 billion in Pennsylvania annually. Among the chief attractions: the Gettysburg National Military Park, Valley Forge National Historical Park, Independence National Historical Park in Philadelphia, the Pennsylvania Dutch region, the Eisenhower farm near Gettysburg, and the Delaware Water Gap National Recreation Area.

Famous natives and residents: Louisa May Alcott, novelist; Marian Anderson, contralto; Maxwell Anderson, dramatist; Samuel Barber, composer; John Barrymore, actor; Donald Barthelme, author; Stephen Vincent Benet, poet and story writer; Daniel Boone, frontiersman; Ed Bradley, TV anchorman; James Buchanan, ex-president; Alexander Calder, sculptor; Rachel Carson, biologist and author; Mary Cassatt, painter; Henry Steele Commager, historian; Bill Cosby, actor; Stuart Davis, painter; Jimmy & Tommy Dorsey, band leaders; W.C. Fields, comedian; Stephen Foster, composer; Robert Fulton, inventor; Grace, Princess of Monaco; Martha Graham, choreographer; Alexander Haig, ex-Secretary of State; Marilyn Horne, mezzo-soprano; Lee Iacocca, auto executive; Reggie Jackson, baseball player; Gene Kelly, dancer and actor; Gelsey Kirkland, ballerina; S.S. Kresge, merchant; Mario Lanza, actor and singer; George C. Marshall, 5-star general; George McClellan, ex-general; Margaret Mead, anthropologist; Andrew Mellon, financier; Tom Mix, actor; Arnold Palmer, golfer; Robert E. Peary, explorer; Man Ray, painter; Mary Roberts Rinehart, novelist; Betsy Ross, flagmaker; B.F. Skinner, psychologist; John Sloan, painter; Gertrude Stein, author; James Stewart, actor; John Updike, novelist; Honus Wagner, baseball player; Fred Waring, band leader; Ethel Waters, singer and actress; Anthony Wayne, military officer; August Wilson, poet, writer, and playwright; Duchess of Windsor (Wallis Warfield); Andrew Wyeth, painter

RHODE ISLAND

Capital: Providence
Governor: Lincoln Almond, R (to Jan. 1999)
Lieut. Governor: Robert A. Weygand, D (to Jan. 1999)
Secy. of State: Jim Langevin, D (to Jan. 1999)
Atty. General: Jeffery B. Pine, D (to Jan. 1999)
General Treasurer: Nancy J. Mayer, D (to Jan. 1999)
Entered Union & (rank): May 29, 1790 (13)
Present constitution adopted: 1843
Motto: Hope
STATE SYMBOLS: flower, Violet (unofficial) (1968); **tree,** Red maple (official) (1964); **bird,** Rhode Island Red

(official) (1954); **shell,** Quahog (official); **mineral,** Bowenite; **stone,** Cumberlandite; **colors,** Blue, white, and gold (in state flag); **song,** "Rhode Island" (1946)
Nickname: The Ocean State
Origin of name: From the Greek Island of Rhodes
10 largest cities (1990 census): Providence, 160,728; Warwick, 85,427; Cranston, 70,060; Pawtucket, 72,644; East Providence, 50,380; Woonsocket, 43,877; Newport, 28,227; Central Falls, 17,637
Land area & (rank): 1,045 sq mi. (2,706 sq km) (50)
Geographic center: In Kent Co., 1 mi. SSW of Crompton
Number of counties: 5
Largest town (1990 census): North Providence, 32,090
State forests: 11 (20,900 ac.)
State parks: 17 (8,200 ac.)
1995 resident population est.: 990,000
1990 resident census population (rank): 1,003,464 (43). **Male:** 481,496; **Female:** 521,968. **White:** 917,375 (91.4%); **Black:** 38,861 (3.9%); **American Indian, Eskimo, or Aleut:** 4,071 (0.4%); **Asian or Pacific Islander:** 18,325 (1.8%); **Other race:** 24,832 (2.5%); **Hispanic:** 45,752 (4.6%). **1990 percent population under 18:** 22.5; **65 and over:** 15.0; **median age:** 34.

From its beginnings, Rhode Island has been distinguished by its support for freedom of conscience and action, started by Roger Williams, who was exiled by the Massachusetts Bay Colony Puritans in 1636, and was the founder of the present state capital, Providence. Williams was followed by other religious exiles who founded Pocasset, now Portsmouth, in 1638 and Newport in 1639.

Rhode Island's rebellious, authority-defying nature was further demonstrated by the burnings of the British revenue cutters *Liberty* and *Gaspee* prior to the Revolution, by its early declaration of independence from Great Britain in May 1776, its refusal to participate actively in the War of 1812, and by Dorr's Rebellion of 1842, which protested property requirements for voting.

Rhode Island, smallest of the fifty states, is densely populated and highly industrialized. It is a primary center for jewelry manufacturing in the United States. Electronics, metal, plastic products, and boat and ship construction are other important industries. Non-manufacturing employment includes research in health, medicine, and the ocean environment. Providence is a wholesale distribution center for New England.

Two of New England's fishing ports are at Galilee and Newport. Rural areas of the state support small-scale farming including grapes for local wineries, turf grass and nursery stock.

Tourism is one of Rhode Island's largest industries, generating over a billion dollars a year in revenue.

Newport became famous as the summer capital of society in the mid-19th century. Touro Synagogue (1763) is the oldest in the U.S. Other points of interest include the Roger Williams National Memorial in Providence, Samuel Slater's Mill in Pawtucket, the General Nathanael Greene Homestead in Coventry and Block Island.

Famous natives and residents: Harry Anderson, actor; George M. Cohan, actor and dramatist; Eddie Dowling, actor and stage producer; Nelson Eddy, baritone and actor; Ann Smith Franklin, printer and almanac publisher; Charles Gorham, silversmith; Spalding Gray, writer, performance artist; Bobby Hackett, trumpeter; David Hartman, TV newscaster; Ruth Hussey, actress; Anne Hutchinson, religious leader; Thomas H. Ince, film producer; Wilbur John, Quaker leader; Van Johnson, actor; Clarence King, first director of the U.S. Geological Survey; Galway Kinnell, poet; Oliver LaFarge, writer; Irving

R. Levine, news correspondent; H.P. Lovecraft, author; Ida Lewis, lighthouse keeper; John McLaughlin, political commentator, broadcaster; Dana C. Munro, educator and historian; Matthew C. Perry, naval officer; Oliver Hazard Perry, naval officer; King Philip (Metacomet), Indian leader; Gilbert Stuart, painter; Sarah Helen (Power) Whitman, poet; Jemima Wilkinson, religious leader; Roger Williams, clergyman and founder of Rhode Island; Leonard Woodcock, labor union official

SOUTH CAROLINA

Capital: Columbia
Governor: David M. Beasley, R (to Jan. 1999)
Lieut. Governor: Robert L. Peeler, R (to Jan. 1999)
Secy. of State: Jim Miles, R (to Jan. 1999)
Comptroller General: Earle E. Morris, Jr., D (to Jan. 1999)
Atty. General: Charles M. Condon, R (to Jan. 1999)
Entered Union & (rank): May 23, 1788 (8).
Present constitution adopted: 1895
Mottoes: *Animis opibusque parati* (Prepared in mind and resources) and *Dum spiro spero* (While I breathe, I hope)
STATE SYMBOLS: flower, Carolina yellow jessamine (1924); **tree,** Palmetto tree (1939); **bird,** Carolina wren (1948); **song,** "Carolina" (1911)
Nickname: Palmetto State
Origin of name: In honor of Charles I of England
10 largest cities (1990 census): Columbia, 98,052; Charleston, 80,414; North Charleston, 70,218; Greenville, 58,282; Spartanburg, 43,467; Sumter, 41,943; Rock Hill, 41,643; Mount Pleasant Town, 30,108; Florence, 29,813; Anderson, 26,184
Land area & (rank): 30,111 sq mi. (77,988 sq km) (40)
Geographic center: In Richland Co., 13 mi. SE of Columbia
Number of counties: 46
Largest county (1990 census): Greenville, 320,167
State forests: 4 (124,052 ac.)
State parks: 50 (61,726 ac.)
1995 resident population est.: 3,673,000
1990 resident census population (rank): 3,486,703 (25). **Male:** 1,688,510; **Female:** 1,798,193. **White:** 2,406,974 (69.0%); **Black:** 1,039,884 (29.8%); **American Indian, Eskimo, or Aleut:** 8,246 (0.2%); **Asian or Pacific Islander:** 22,382 (0.6%); **Other race:** 9,217 (0.3%); **Hispanic:** 30,551 (0.9%) **1990 percent population under 18:** 26.4; **65 and over:** 11.4; **median age: 32.0**

Following exploration of the coast in 1521 by De Gordillo, the Spanish tried unsuccessfully to establish a colony near present-day Georgetown in 1526 and the French also failed to colonize Parris Island near Fort Royal in 1562.

The first English settlement was made in 1670 at Albemarle Point on the Ashley River, but poor conditions drove the settlers to the site of Charleston (originally called Charles Town). South Carolina, officially separated from North Carolina in 1729, was the scene of extensive military action during the Revolution and again during the Civil War. The Civil War began in 1861 as South Carolina troops fired on federal Fort Sumter in Charleston Harbor and the state was the first to secede from the Union.

Once primarily agricultural, South Carolina has built so many large textile and other mills that today its factories produce eight times the output of its farms in cash value. Charleston makes asbestos, wood, pulp, and steel products; chemicals, machinery, and apparel are also important.

Farms have become fewer but larger in recent years. South Carolina grows more peaches than any other state except California; it ranks fifth in overall tobacco pro-

duction. Other farm products include cotton, peanuts, sweet potatoes, soybeans, corn, and oats. Poultry and dairy products are also important revenue producers.

Points of interest include Fort Sumter National Monument, Fort Moultrie, Fort Johnson, and aircraft carrier USS *Yorktown* in Charleston Harbor; the Middleton, Magnolia, and Cypress Gardens in Charleston; Cowpens National Battlefield; and the Hilton Head resorts.

Famous natives and residents: Bernard Baruch, statesman; Mary McLeod Bethune, educator; James F. Byrnes, senator, jurist, Secretary of State; John C. Calhoun, statesman; Mark Clark, general; Joe Frazier, prize fighter; Althea Gibson, tennis champion; Dizzy Gillespie, jazz trumpeter; DuBose Heyward, poet, playwright, novelist; Andrew Jackson, ex-president; Jesse Jackson, civil rights leader; Eartha Kitt, singer; Francis Marion "Swamp Fox," Revolutionary general; Ronald McNair, astronaut; John Rutledge, jurist; Strom Thurmond, politician; Charles Townes, physicist; William Westmoreland, ex-Army Chief of Staff; Vanna White, television personality

SOUTH DAKOTA

Capital: Pierre
Governor: William J. Janklow, R (to Jan. 1999)
Lieut. Governor: Carole Hillard, R (to Jan. 1999)
Atty. General: Mark Barnett, R (to Jan. 1999)
Secy. of State: Joyce Hazeltine, R (to Jan. 1999)
State Auditor: Vern Larson, R (to Jan. 1999)
State Treasurer: Richard Butler, D (to Jan. 1999)
Organized as territory: March 2, 1861
Entered Union & (rank): Nov. 2, 1889 (40)
Present constitution adopted: 1889
Motto: Under God the people rule
STATE SYMBOLS: flower, American pasqueflower (1903); **grass,** Western wheat grass (1970); **soil,** Houdek (1990); **tree,** Black Hills spruce (1947); **bird,** Ring-necked pheasant (1943); **insect,** Honeybee (1978); **animal,** Coyote (1949); **mineral stone,** Rose quartz (1966); **gemstone,** Fairburn agate (1966); **colors,** Blue and gold (in state flag); **song,** "Hail! South Dakota" (1943); **fish,** Walleye (1982); **musical instrument,** Fiddle (1989); **soil,** Houdek soil (1990)
Nicknames: Mount Rushmore State; Coyote State
Origin of name: From the Sioux tribe, meaning "allies"
10 largest cities (1990 census): Sioux Falls, 100,814; Rapid City, 54,523; Aberdeen, 24,927; Watertown, 17,592; Brookings, 16,270; Mitchell, 13,798; Pierre, 12,906; Yankton, 12,703; Huron, 12,448; Vermillion, 10,034
Land area & (rank): 75,898 sq mi. (196,575 sq km) (16)
Geographic center: In Hughes Co., 8 mi. NE of Pierre
Number of counties: 67 (64 county governments)
Largest county (1990 census): Minnehaha, 123,809
State forests: None[1]
State parks: 13 plus 39 recreational areas (87,269 ac.)[2]
1995 resident population est.: 729,000
1990 resident census population (rank): 696,004 (45). **Male:** 342,498; **Female:** 353,506. **White:** 637,515 (91.6%); **Black:** 3,258 (0.5%); **American Indian, Eskimo, or Aleut:** 50,575 (7.3%); **Asian or Pacific Islander:** 3,123 (0.4%); **Other race:** 1,533 (0.2%); **Hispanic:** 5,252 (0.8%). **1990 percent population under 18:** 28.5; **65 and over:** 14.7; **median age: 32.5.**

1. No designated state forests; about 13,000 ac. of state land is forestland. 2. Acreage includes 39 recreation areas and 80 roadside parks, in addition to 12 state parks.

Exploration of this area began in 1743 when Louis-Joseph and François Verendrye came from France in search of a route to the Pacific.

The U.S. acquired the region as part of the Louisiana Purchase in 1803 and it was explored by Lewis and Clark in 1804–06. Fort Pierre, the first permanent settlement, was established in 1817 and, in 1831, the first Missouri River steamboat reached the fort.

Settlement of South Dakota did not begin in earnest until the arrival of the railroad in 1873 and the discovery of gold in the Black Hills the following year.

South Dakota's economy in recent years has benefitted from an expanding and diversifying industrial base. Agriculture is a cultural and economic mainstay, but it no longer leads the state in employment or share of gross state product. Durable goods manufacturing and private services have evolved as the drivers of the economy. Tourism is also a booming industry in the state.

South Dakota is the nation's second leading producer of gold and the Homestake Mine is the richest in the U.S. Other minerals produced include berylium, bentonite, granite, silver, petroleum, and uranium.

The Black Hills are the highest mountains east of the Rockies. Mt. Rushmore, in this group, is famous for the likenesses of Washington, Jefferson, Lincoln, and Theodore Roosevelt, which were carved in granite by Gutzon Borglum. A memorial to Crazy Horse is also being carved in granite near Custer.

Other tourist attractions include the Badlands; the World's Only Corn Palace in Mitchell; and the city of Deadwood where Wild Bill Hickok was killed in 1876 and where gambling was recently legalized to truly recapture the city's Old West flavor.

Famous natives and residents: Sparky Anderson, baseball manager; Gertrude Bonnin (Zitkala-Sa), Sioux writer and pan-Indian activist; Tom Brokaw, TV newscaster; Robert Casey, writer; Myron Floren, accordionist; Joseph J. Foss, WW II Marine fighter ace; Mary Hart, host; Crazy Horse, Oglala chief; Oscar Howe, Sioux artist; Hubert H. Humphrey, ex-vice president; Cheryl Ladd, actress; Ernest Orlando Lawrence, physicist; Russell Means, American Indian activist; George McGovern, politician; Arthur C. Mellette, first governor; Dorothy Provine, actress; Rain-in-the-Face, Hunkpapa Sioux chief; Red Cloud, chief of the Oglala Sioux; Ben Reifel, Brulé Sioux Congressman; Ole Edvart Rölvaag, writer; Sitting Bull, Chief of Hunkpappa Sioux; Norm Van Brocklin, football player; Mamie Van Doren, actress

TENNESSEE

Capital: Nashville
Governor: Don Sundquist, R (to Jan. 1999)
Lieut. Governor: John S. Wilder, D (to Jan. 1997)
Secy. of State: Riley C. Darnell, D (to Jan. 1997)
Atty. General: Charles W. Burson, D (to Aug. 1998)
State Treasurer: Steve Adams, D (to Jan. 1997)
Entered Union & (rank): June 1, 1796 (16)
Present constitution adopted: 1870; amended 1953, 1960, 1966, 1972, 1978
Motto: "Agriculture and Commerce" (1987)
Slogan: "Tennessee—America at its best!" (1965)
STATE SYMBOLS: flower, Iris (1933); **tree,** Tulip poplar (1947); **bird,** Mockingbird (1933); **horse,** Tennessee walking horse; **animal,** Raccoon (1971); **wild flower,** Passion flower (1973); **songs,** "Tennessee Waltz" (1965); My Homeland, Tennessee (1925); When It's Iris Time in Tennessee (1935); My Tennessee (1955); Rocky Top (1982); Tennessee (1992)
Nickname: Volunteer State
Origin of name: Of Cherokee origin; the exact meaning is unknown
10 largest cities (1990 census): Memphis, 610,337; Nashville-Davidson (CC[1]), 510,784; Knoxville, 165,121; Chattanooga, 152,466; Clarksville, 75,494; Johnson City, 49,381; Jackson, 48,949; Murfreesboro, 44,922; Kingsport, 36,365; Germantown, 32,893
Land area & (rank): 41,220 sq mi. (106,759 sq km) (34)

Geographic center: In Rutherford Co., 5 mi. NE of Murfreesboro
Number of counties: 95
Largest county (1990 census): Shelby, 826,330
State forests: 13 (155,000 ac.)
State parks: 50 (133,000 ac.)
1995 resident population est.: 5,256,000
1990 resident census population (rank): 4,877,185 (17). **Male:** 2,348,928; **Female:** 2,528,257. **White:** 4,048,068 (83.0%); **Black:** 778,035 (16.0%); **American Indian, Eskimo, or Aleut:** 10,039 (0.2%); **Asian or Pacific Islander:** 31,839 (0.7%); **Other race:** 9,204 (0.2%); **Hispanic:** 32,741 (0.7%). **1990 percent population under 18:** 24.9; **65 and over:** 12.7; **median age:** 33.6.

1. Consolidated City.

First visited by the Spanish explorer de Soto in 1540, the Tennessee area would later be claimed by both France and England as a result of the 1670s and 1680s explorations of Marquette and Joliet, La Salle, and the Englishmen James Needham and Gabriel Arthur.

Great Britain obtained the region following the French and Indian War in 1763 and it was rapidly occupied by settlers moving in from Virginia and the Carolinas.

During 1784–87, the settlers formed the "state" of Franklin, which was disbanded when the region was allowed to send representatives to the North Carolina legislature. In 1790 Congress organized the territory south of the Ohio River and Tennessee joined the Union in 1796.

Although Tennessee joined the Confederacy during the Civil War, there was much pro-Union sentiment in the state, which was the scene of extensive military action.

The state is now predominantly industrial; the majority of its population lives in urban areas. Among the most important products are chemicals, textiles, apparel, electrical machinery, furniture, and leather goods. Other lines include food processing, lumber, primary metals, and metal products. The state is known as the U.S. hardwood-flooring center and ranks first in the production of marble, zinc, pyrite, and ball clay.

Tennessee is one of the leading tobacco-producing states in the nation; its farming income is derived from livestock and dairy products, as well as corn, cotton, and soybeans.

With six other states, Tennessee shares the extensive federal reservoir developments on the Tennessee and Cumberland River systems. The Tennessee Valley Authority operates a number of dams and reservoirs in the state.

Among the major points of interest: the Andrew Johnson National Historic Site at Greenville, American Museum of Atomic Energy at Oak Ridge, Great Smoky Mountains National Park, The Hermitage (home of Andrew Jackson near Nashville), Rock City Gardens near Chattanooga, and three National Military Parks.

Famous natives and residents: James Agee, writer; Eddy Arnold, singer; Chet Atkins, guitarist; Julian Bond, Georgia legislator; Davy Crockett, frontiersman; David G. Farragut, first American admiral; Lester Flatt, bluegrass musician; Tennessee Ernie Ford, singer; Abe Fortas, jurist; Aretha Franklin, singer; Nikki Giovanni, poet; Al Gore, Jr., vice president; Red Grooms, artist; Isaac Hayes, composer; Benjamin L. Hooks, civil rights activist; Cordell Hull, ex-Sec. of State; Andrew Jackson, ex-president; Andrew Johnson, ex-president; Estes Kefauver, legislator; Anita Kerr, singer; Grace Moore, soprano; Dolly Parton, singer; Minnie Pearl, singer and comedienne; James K. Polk, ex-president; Grantland Rice, sportswriter; Carl Rowan, journalist; Wilma Rudolph, sprinter; Sequoia, Cherokee scholar and educator; Cybil Shepherd, actress; Dinah Shore, actress, singer; Tina Turner, singer; Alvin York, World War I hero

TEXAS

Capital: Austin
Governor: George W. Bush, R (to Jan. 1999)
Lieut. Governor: Bob Bullock, D (to Jan. 1999)
Secy. of State: Tony Garza, R (Apptd. by Gov.)
Treasurer: Martha Whitehead, R (to Jan. 1999)
Comptroller: John Sharp, D (to Jan. 1999)
Atty. General: Dan Morales, D (to Jan. 1999)
Entered Union & (rank): Dec. 29, 1845 (28)
Present constitution adopted: 1876
Motto: Friendship
STATE SYMBOLS: flower, Bluebonnet (1901); **tree,** Pecan (1919); **bird,** Mockingbird (1927); **song,** "Texas, Our Texas" (1929); **fish,** Guadalupe bass (1989); **seashell,** Lightning whelk (1987); **dish,** Chili (1977); **folk dance,** Square dance (1991); **fruit,** Texas Red grapefruit (1993); **gem,** Texas blue topaz (1969); **gemstone cut,** Lone Star Cut (1977); **grass,** Sideoats grama (1971); **reptile,** Horned lizard (1993); **stone,** Petrified palmwood (1969); **plant,** Prickly pear cactus; **insect:** Monarch butterfly; **pepper,** Jalapeño pepper; **mammal,** Longhorn; **small mammal,** Armadillo; **flying mammal,** Mexican free-tailed bat
Nickname: Lone Star State
Origin of name: From an Indian word meaning "friends"
10 largest cities (1990 census): Houston, 1,630,553, 1993: 1,630,864; Dallas, 1,006,877, 1993: 1,007,617; San Antonio, 935,933; El Paso, 515,342; Austin, 465,622; Fort Worth, 447,619; Arlington, 261,721; Corpus Christi, 257,453; Lubbock, 186,206; Garland, 180,650
Land area & (rank): 261,914 sq mi. (678,358 sq km) (2)
Geographic center: In McCulloch Co., 15 mi. NE of Brady
Number of counties: 254
Largest county (1995 est.): Harris, 3,043,400
State forests: 5 (7,609 ac.)
State parks: 218 (206 developed)
1995 resident population est.: 18,724,300
1990 resident census population (rank): 16,986,510 (3). **Male:** 8,365,963; **Female:** 8,620,547. **White:** 12,774,762 (75.2%); **Black:** 2,021,632 (11.9%); **American Indian, Eskimo, or Aleut:** 65,877 (0.4%); **Asian or Pacific Islander:** 319,459 (1.9%); **Other race:** 1,804,780 (10.6%); **Hispanic:** 4,339,905 (25.5%). **1990 percent population under 18:** 28.5; **65 and over:** 10.1; **median age:** 30.8.

Spanish explorers, including Cabeza de Vaca and Coronado, were the first to visit the region in the 16th and 17th centuries, settling at Ysleta near El Paso in 1682. In 1685, La Salle established a short-lived French colony at Matagorda Bay.

Americans, led by Stephen F. Austin, began to settle along the Brazos River in 1821 when Texas was controlled by Mexico, recently independent from Spain. In 1836, following a brief war between the American settlers in Texas and the Mexican government, the Independent Republic of Texas was proclaimed with Sam Houston as president. This war was famous for the battles of the Alamo and San Jacinto.

After Texas became the 28th U.S. state in 1845, border disputes led to the Mexican War of 1846–48.

Today, Texas, second only to Alaska in land area, leads all other states in such categories as oil, cattle, sheep, and cotton. Possessing enormous natural resources, Texas is a major agricultural state and an industrial giant.

Sulfur, salt, helium, asphalt, graphite, bromine, natural gas, cement, and clays give Texas first place in mineral production. Chemicals, oil refining, food processing, machinery, and transportation equipment are among the major Texas manufacturing industries.

Texas ranches and farms produce beef cattle, poultry, rice, pecans, peanuts, sorghum, and an extensive variety of fruits and vegetables.

Millions of tourists spend well over $20.6 billion annually visiting more than 70 state parks, recreation areas, and points of interest such as the Gulf Coast resort area, the Lyndon B. Johnson Space Center in Houston, the Alamo in San Antonio, the state capital in Austin, and the Big Bend and Guadalupe Mountains National Parks.

Famous natives and residents: Alvin Ailey, choreographer; Mary Kay Ash, cosmetics entrepreneur; Steven Fuller Austin, founding father of Texas; Gene Autry, singer and actor; Carol Burnett, comedienne; Cyd Charisse, actress and dancer; Denton A. Cooley, heart surgeon; Joan Crawford, actress; Dwight David Eisenhower, ex-president, general; A.J. Foyt, auto racer; Ben Hogan, golfer; Howard Hughes, industrialist and film producer; Jack Johnson, boxer; Lyndon B. Johnson, ex-president; George Jones, singer; Tommy Lee Jones, actor; Scott Joplin, composer; Trini Lopez, singer; Mary Martin, singer and actress; Spanky McFarland, actor; Audie Murphy, actor and war hero; Chester Nimitz, admiral; Sandra Day O'Connor, jurist; Buck Owens, singer; Katherine Anne Porter, novelist; Wiley Post, aviator; Dan Rather, TV newscaster; Robert Rauschenberg, painter; Tex Ritter, singer; Rip Torn, actor and director; Tommy Tune, dancer and choreographer; Dooley Wilson, actor and musician; Babe Didrikson Zaharias, athlete, golfer

UTAH

Capital: Salt Lake City
Governor: Michael O. Leavitt, R (to Jan. 1997)
Lieut. Governor: Olene Walker, R (to Jan. 1997)
Atty. General: Jan Graham, D (to Jan. 1997)
Organized as territory: Sept. 9, 1850
Entered Union & (rank): Jan. 4, 1896 (45)
Present constitution adopted: 1896
Motto: Industry
STATE SYMBOLS: flower, Sego lily (1911); **tree,** Blue spruce (1933); **bird,** California gull (1955); **emblem,** Beehive (1959); **song,** "Utah, We Love Thee" (1953); **gem,** Topaz; **animal,** Rocky Mountain Elk (1971); **fish,** Rainbow trout (1971); **insect,** Honeybee (1983); **grass,** Indian rice grass (1990); **fossil,** Allosaurus (1988)
Nickname: Beehive State
Origin of name: From the Ute tribe, meaning "people of the mountains"
10 largest cities (1990 census): Salt Lake City, 159,936; West Valley City, 86,976; Provo, 86,835; Sandy, 75,058; Orem, 67,561; Ogden, 63,909; Taylorsville-Bennion, 52,351; West Jordan, 42,892; Layton, 41,784; Bountiful, 36,659
Land area & (rank): 82,168 sq mi. (212,816 sq km) (12)
Geographic center: In Sanpete Co., 3 mi. N. of Manti
Number of counties: 29
Largest county (1990 census): Salt Lake, 725,956
National parks: 5
National monuments: 6
State parks/forests: 44 (64,097 ac.)
1995 resident population est.: 1,951,000
1990 resident census population (rank): 1,722,850 (35). **Male:** 855,759; **Female:** 867,091. **White:** 1,615,845 (93.8%); **Black:** 11,576 (0.7%); **American Indian, Eskimo, or Aleut:** 24,283 (1.4%); **Asian or Pacific Islander:** 33,371 (1.9%); **Other race:** 37,775 (2.2%); **Hispanic:** 84,597 (4.9%). **1990 percent population under 18:** 36.4; **65 and over:** 8.7; **median age:** 26.2.

The region was first explored for Spain by Franciscan friars, Escalante and Dominguez in 1776. In 1824 the famous American frontiersman Jim Bridger discovered the Great Salt Lake.

Fleeing the religious persecution encountered in eastern and middle-western states, the Mormons reached the Great Salt Lake in 1847 and began to build Salt Lake City. The U.S. acquired the Utah region in the treaty ending the Mexican War in 1848 and the first transcontinental railroad was completed with the driving of a golden spike at Promontory Summit in 1869.

Mormon difficulties with the federal government about polygamy did not end until the Mormon Church renounced the practice in 1890, six years before Utah became a state.

Rich in natural resources, Utah has long been a leading producer of copper, gold, silver, lead, zinc, and molybdenum. Oil has also become a major product. Utah shares rich oil shale deposits with Colorado and Wyoming. Utah also has large deposits of low sulphur coal.

Ranked eighth among the states in number of sheep in 1989, Utah also produces large crops of alfalfa, winter wheat, and beans.

Utah's traditional industries of agriculture and mining are complemented by increased tourism business and growing aerospace, biomedical, and computer-related businesses. Utah is home to computer software giant Novell.

Utah is a great vacationland with 11,000 miles of fishing streams and 147,000 acres of lakes and reservoirs. Among the many tourist attractions are Arches, Bryce Canyon, Canyonlands, Capitol Reef, and Zion National Parks; Dinosaur, Natural Bridges, and Rainbow Bridge National Monuments; the Mormon Tabernacle in Salt Lake City; and Monument Valley. Salt Lake City will be the site of the 2002 Winter Olympics.

Famous natives and residents: Maude Adams, actress; Roseanne, actress; Frank Borzage, film director and producer; John M. Browning, inventor; Butch Cassidy, outlaw; Laraine Day, actress; Bernard De Voto, writer; Avard Fairbanks, sculptor; Philo Farnsworth, television pioneer; Jake Garn, ex-senator; John Gilbert, actor; J, Willard Marriott, restaurant and hotel chain founder; Peter Skene Ogden, fur trader, trapper; Merlin Olsen, football player; Donny Osmond, Marie Osmond, singers; Ivy Baker Priest, ex-U.S. treasurer; Lee Greene Richards, painter; Leroy Robertson, composer; Brent Scowcroft, business executive, consultant; Reed Smoot, first Morman elected to U.S. Senate; Mack Swain, actor; Everett Thorpe, painter; Robert Walker, actor; James Woods, actor; Brigham Young, territory governor and religious leader; Loretta Young, actress

VERMONT

Capital: Montpelier
Governor: Howard B. Dean, D (to Jan. 1997)
Lieut. Governor: Barbara W. Snelling, R (to Jan. 1997)
Secy. of State: James F. Milne, R (to Jan. 1997)
Treasurer: James H. Douglas, R (to Jan. 1997)
Auditor of Accounts: Edward S. Flanagan D (to Jan. 1997)
Atty. General: Jeffrey L. Amestoy, R (to Jan. 1997)
Entered Union & (rank): March 4, 1791 (14)
Present constitution adopted: 1793
Motto: Vermont, Freedom, and Unity
STATE SYMBOLS: flower, Red clover (1894); **tree,** Sugar maple (1949); **bird,** Hermit thrush (1941); **animal,** Morgan horse (1961); **insect,** Honeybee (1978); **song,** "Hail, Vermont!" (1938)
Nickname: Green Mountain State
Origin of name: From the French "vert mont," meaning "green mountain"

10 largest cities (1990 census): Burlington, 39,127; Rutland, 18,230; South Burlington, 12,809; Barre, 9,482; Essex Junction, 8,396; Montpelier, 8,247; St. Albans, 7,339; Winooski, 6,649; Newport, 4,434; Bellows Falls, 3,313
Land area & (rank): 9,249 sq mi. (23,956 sq km) (43)
Geographic center: In Washington Co., 3 mi. E of Roxbury
Number of counties: 14
Largest county (1990 census): Chittenden, 131,761
State forests: 34 (113,953 ac.)
State parks: 45 (31,325 ac.)
1995 resident population est.: 585,000
1990 resident census population (rank): 562,758 (48).
Male: 275,492; **Female:** 287,266. **White:** 555,088 (98.6%); **Black:** 1,951 (0.3%); **American Indian, Eskimo, or Aleut:** 1,696 (0.3%); **Asian or Pacific Islander:** 3,215 (0.6%); **Other race:** 808 (0.1%); **Hispanic:** 3,661 (0.7%). **1990 percent population under 18:** 25.4; **65 and over:** 11.8; **median age:** 33.0.

The Vermont region was explored and claimed for France by Samuel de Champlain in 1609 and the first French settlement was established at Fort Ste. Anne in 1666. The first English settlers moved into the area in 1724 and built Fort Drummer on the site of present-day Brattleboro. England gained control of the area in 1763 after the French and Indian War.

First organized to drive settlers from New York out of Vermont, the Green Mountain Boys, led by Ethan Allen, won fame by capturing Fort Ticonderoga from the British on May 10, 1775, in the early days of the Revolutionary War.

In 1777 Vermont adopted its first constitution abolishing slavery and providing for universal male suffrage without property qualifications. In 1791 Vermont became the fourteenth state to join the Union.

Vermont leads the nation in the production of monument granite, marble, and maple syrup. It is also a leader in the production of talc.

Vermont's rugged, rocky terrain discourages extensive agricultural farming, but is well suited to raising fruit trees, and to dairy and truck farming. Vermont has the highest proportion of dairy cows to humans in the nation.

Principal industrial products include electrical equipment, fabricated metal products, printing and publishing, and paper and allied products.

Tourism is a major industry in Vermont. Vermont's many ski areas include Stowe, Killington, Mt. Snow, Bromley, Jay Peak, and Sugarbush. Hunting and fishing also attract many visitors to Vermont each year. Among the many points of interest are the Green Mountain National Forest, Bennington Battle Monument, the Calvin Coolidge Homestead at Plymouth, and the Marble Exhibit in Proctor.

Famous natives and residents: Chester A. Arthur, ex-president; Orson Bean, actor; Calvin Coolidge, ex-president; George Dewey, admiral; John Dewey, philosopher and educator; Stephen A. Douglas, politician; James Fisk, financial speculator; Wilbur Fisk, clergyman and educator; Richard Morris Hunt, architect; William Morris Hunt, painter; Elisha Otis, inventor; Moses Pendleton, choreographer; Joseph Smith, religious leader; Ernest Thompson, actor, writer; Rudy Vallee, singer and band leader; Henry Wells, pioneer entrepreneur (Wells Fargo & Co.); Brigham Young, religious leader

VIRGINIA

Capital: Richmond
Governor: George Allen, R (to Jan. 1998)
Lieut. Governor: Donald S. Beyer, Jr., D (to Jan. 1998)
Secy. of the Commonwealth: Betsy David Beamer (apptd. by governor)

Comptroller: William E. Landsdile (apptd. by governor)
Atty. General: James S. Gilmore, III, R (to Jan. 1998)
Entered Union & (rank): June 25, 1788 (10)
Present constitution adopted: 1970
Motto: *Sic semper tyrannis* (Thus always to tyrants)
STATE SYMBOLS: flower, American dogwood (1918);
  bird, Cardinal (1950); **dog,** American foxhound (1966);
  shell, Oyster shell (1974); **song,** "Carry Me Back to
  Old Virginia" (1940)
Nicknames: The Old Dominion; Mother of Presidents
Origin of name: In honor of Elizabeth "Virgin Queen" of
  England
10 largest cities (1990 census): Virginia Beach, 393,069;
  Norfolk, 261,229; Richmond, 203,056; Newport News,
  170,045; Chesapeake, 151,976; Hampton, 133,793; Alex-
  andria, 111,183; Portsmouth, 103,907; Roanoke, 96,907;
  Lynchburg, 66,049
Land area & (rank): 39,598 sq mi. (102,558 sq km) (37)
Geographic center: In Buckingham Co., 5 mi. SW of
  Buckingham
Number of counties: 95, plus 41 independent cities
Largest county (1990 census): Fairfax, 818,384
State forests: 11 (50,636 ac.)
State parks and recreational parks: 28 (63,000 ac.)[1]
1995 resident population est.: 6,618,000
1990 resident census population (rank): 6,618,358 (12).
  Male: 3,033,974; **Female:** 3,153,384. **White:** 4,791,739
  (77.4%); **Black:** 1,162,994 (18.8%); **American Indian,
  Eskimo, or Aleut:** 15,282 (0.2%); **Asian or Pacific Islander:** 159,053 (2.6%); **Other race:** 58,290 (0.9%); **Hispanic:** 160,288 (2.6%). **1990 percent population under
  18:** 24.3; **65 and over:** 10.7; **median age:** 32.6.

1. Does not include portion of Breaks Interstate Park
(Va.-Ky.), 1,200 ac.) which lies in Virginia.

The history of America is closely tied to that of
Virginia, particularly in the Colonial period. Jamestown, founded in 1607, was the first permanent English settlement in North America and slavery was introduced there in 1619. The surrenders ending both
the American Revolution (Yorktown) and the Civil
War (Appomattox) occurred in Virginia. The state is
called the "Mother of Presidents" because eight chief
executives of the United States were born there.

Today, Virginia has a large number of diversified
manufacturing industries including transportation
equipment, textiles, food processing and printing. Other
important lines are electronic and other electric equipment, chemicals, apparel, lumber and wood products,
furniture, and industrial machinery and equipment.

Agriculture remains an important sector in the Virginia economy and the state ranks among the top 10
in the U.S. in tomatoes, tobacco, peanuts, summer
potatoes, turkeys, apples, broilers, and sweet potatoes. Other crops include corn, vegetables, and
barley. Famous for Smithfield hams, Virginia also has
a large dairy industry.

Coal mining accounts for roughly 75% of Virginia's mineral output, and lime, kyanite, and stone are
also mined.

Points of interest include Mt. Vernon and other places
associated with George Washington; Monticello, home
of Thomas Jefferson; Stratford, home of the Lees; Richmond, capital of the Confederacy and of Virginia; and
Williamsburg, the restored Colonial capital.

The Chesapeake Bay Bridge-Tunnel spans the
mouth of Chesapeake Bay, connecting Cape Charles
with Norfolk. Consisting of a series of low trestles,
two bridges and two mile-long tunnels, the complex
is 18 miles (29 km) long. It was opened in 1964.

Other attractions are the Shenandoah National
Park, Fredericksburg and Spotsylvania National Mili-

tary Park, the Booker T. Washington birthplace near
Roanoke, Arlington House (the Robert E. Lee Memo-
rial), the Skyline Drive, and the Blue Ridge National
Parkway.

Famous natives and residents: Richard Arlen, actor
Arthur Ashe, tennis player; Pearl Bailey, singer; Russell
Baker, columnist; Warren Beatty, actor; George Bing-
ham, painter; Richard E. Byrd, polar explorer; Willa
Cather, novelist; Roy Clark, country music artist; Wil-
liam Clark, explorer; Henry Clay, statesman; Joseph
Cotten, actor; Ella Fitzgerald, singer; William H. Harri-
son, ex-president; Patrick Henry, statesman; Sam
Houston, political leader; Thomas Jefferson, ex-presi-
dent; Robert E. Lee, Confederate general; Meriwether
Lewis, explorer; Shirley MacLaine, actress; James
Madison, ex-president; John Marshall, jurist; Cyrus
McCormick, inventor; James Monroe, ex-president
Opechancanough, Powhatan leader; John Payne, actor; Walter Reed, army surgeon; Matthew Ridgway, ex-
Army Chief of Staff; Bill "Bojangles" Robinson,
dancer; George C. Scott, actor; Sam Snead, golfer
James "Jeb" Stuart, Confederate army officer; Zachary Taylor, ex-president; Nat Turner, civil rights leader; John Tyler, ex-president; Booker T. Washington,
educator; George Washington, first president; Woodrow Wilson, ex-president; Tom Wolfe, journalist

WASHINGTON

Capital: Olympia
Governor: Mike Lowry, D (to 1997)
Lieut. Governor: Joel Pritchard, R (to 1997)
Secy. of State: Ralph Munro, R (to 1997)
State Treasurer: Daniel K. Grimm, D (to 1997)
Atty. General: Christine Gregoire, D (to 1997)
Organized as territory: March 2, 1853
Entered Union & (rank): Nov. 11, 1889 (42)
Present constitution adopted: 1889
Motto: *Al-Ki* (Indian word meaning "by and by")
STATE SYMBOLS: flower, Coast Rhododendron (1949);
  tree, Western hemlock (1947); **bird,** Willow goldfinch
  (1951); **fish,** Steelhead trout (1969); **gem,** Petrified
  wood (1975); **colors,** Green and gold (1925); **song,**
  "Washington, My Home" (1959); **folk song,** "Roll On
  Columbia, Roll On" (1987); **dance,** Square dance (1979)
Nicknames: Evergreen State; Chinook State
Origin of name: In honor of George Washington
10 largest cities (1990 census): Seattle, 516,259; Spokane, 177,196; Tacoma, 176,664; Bellevue, 86,874; Ever-
  ett, 69,961; Yakima, 54,827; Bellingham, 42,155; Renton
  41,688
Land area & (rank): 66,582 sq mi. (172,447 sq km) (20)
Geographic center: In Chelan Co., 10 mi. WSW of We-
  natchee
Number of counties: 39
Largest county (1991 census): King, 1,542,300
State forest lands: 1,922,880 ac.
State parks: 215 (231,861 ac.)[1]
1995 resident population est.: 5,431,000
1990 resident census population (rank): 4,866,692 (18).
  Male: 2,413,747; **Female:** 2,452,945. **White:** 4,308,937
  (88.5%); **Black:** 149,801 (3.1%); **American Indian, Eskimo, or Aleut:** 81,483 (1.7%); **Other race:** 115,513 (2.4%)
  Hispanic: 214,570 (4.4%). **1990
  percent population under 18:** 25.9; **65 and over:** 11.8;
  median age: 33.1.

1. Parks and undeveloped areas administered by State
Parks and Recreation Commission. Dept. of Wildlife administers wildlife and recreation areas totaling 428,989.
acres.

As part of the vast Oregon Country, Washington
territory was visited by Spanish, American, and Brit-

ish explorers—Bruno Heceta for Spain in 1775, the American Capt. Robert Gray in 1792, and Capt. George Vancouver for Britain in 1792–94. Lewis and Clark explored the Columbia River region and coastal areas for the U.S. in 1805–06.

Rival American and British settlers and conflicting territorial claims threatened war in the early 1840s. However, in 1846 the Oregon Treaty set the boundary at the 49th parallel and war was averted.

Washington is a leading lumber producer. Its rugged surface is rich in stands of Douglas fir, hemlock, ponderosa and white pine, spruce, larch, and cedar. The state holds first place in apples, lentils, dry edible peas, hops, pears, red raspberries, spearmint oil, and sweet cherries, and ranks high in apricots, asparagus, grapes, peppermint oil, and potatoes. Livestock and livestock products make important contributions to total farm revenue and the commercial fishing catch of salmon, halibut, and bottomfish makes a significant contribution to the state's economy.

Manufacturing industries in Washington include aircraft and missiles, shipbuilding and other transportation equipment, lumber, food processing, metals and metal products, chemicals, and machinery.

The Columbia River contains one third of the potential water power in the U.S., harnessed by such dams as the Grand Coulee, one of the greatest power producers in the world. Washington has over 1,000 dams built for a variety of purposes including irrigation, power, flood control, and water storage. Its abundance of electrical power makes Washington one of the nation's major producers of refined aluminum.

Among the major points of interest: Mt. Rainier, Olympic, and North Cascades. In 1980, Mount St. Helens, a peak in the Cascade Range in Southwestern Washington erupted on May 18th. Also of interest are National Parks; Whitman Mission and Fort Vancouver National Historic Sites; and the Pacific Science Center and Space Needle in Seattle.

Famous natives and residents: Bob Barker, TV host; Dyan Cannon, actress; Carol Channing, actress; Judy Collins, singer; Bing Crosby, singer, actor; Bob Crosby, musician; Merce Cunningham, choreographer; Howard Duff, actor; Frances Farmer, actress; Bill Gates, software executive; Jimi Hendrix, guitarist; Frank Herbert, writer; Robert Joffrey, choreographer; Gypsy Rose Lee, entertainer; Hank Ketcham, cartoonist; Mary McCarthy, novelist; Guthrie McClintic, theatrical producer and director; John McIntire, actor; Robert Motherwell, artist; Patrice Munsel, soprano; Ella Raines, actress; Jimmy Rogers, singer; Francis Scobee, astronaut; Seattle, Dwamish, Suquamish chief; Jeff Smith, TV cook; Smohalla, Indian prophet and chief; Adam West, actor; Martha Wright, singer; Audrey Wurdemann, poet

WEST VIRGINIA

Capital: Charleston
Governor: Gaston Caperton, D (to Jan. 1997)
Secy. of State: Ken Heckler, D (to Jan. 1997)
State Auditor: Glen Gainer (to Jan. 1997)
Atty. General: Darrell McGraw, D (to Jan. 1997)
Entered Union & (rank): June 20, 1863 (35)
Present constitution adopted: 1872
Motto: *Montani semper liberi* (Mountaineers are always free)
STATE SYMBOLS: flower, Rhododendron (1903); **tree,** Sugar maple (1949); **bird,** Cardinal (1949); **animal,** Black bear (1973); **colors,** Blue and gold (official) (1863); **songs,** "West Virginia, My Home Sweet Home," "The West Virginia Hills," and "This Is My West Virginia" (adopted by Legislature in 1947, 1961, and 1963 as official state songs)

Nickname: Mountain State
Origin of name: In honor of Elizabeth "Virgin Queen" of England
10 largest cities (1990 census): Charleston, 57,287; Huntington, 54,844; Wheeling, 34,882; Parkersburg, 33,862; Morgantown, 25,879; Weirton, 22,124; Fairmont, 20,210; Beckley, 18,296; Clarksburg, 18,059; Martinsburg, 14,073
Land area & (rank): 24,087 sq mi. (62,384 sq km) (41)
Geographic center: In Braxton Co., 4 mi. E of Sutton
Number of counties: 55
Largest county (1990 census): Kanawha, 207,619
State forests: 9 (79,502 ac.)
State parks: 35 (74,508 ac.)
1995 resident population est.: 1,828,000
1990 resident census population (rank): 1,793,477 (34). **Male:** 861,536; **Female:** 931,941. **White:** 1,725,523 (96.2%); **Black:** 56,295 (3.1%); **American Indian, Eskimo, or Aleut:** 2,458 (0.1%); **Asian or Pacific Islander:** 7,459 (0.4%); **Other race:** 1,742 (0.1%); **Hispanic:** 8,489 (0.5%). **1990 percent population under 18:** 24.7; **65 and over:** 15.0; **median age:** 35.4.

West Virginia's early history from 1609 until 1863 is largely shared with Virginia, of which it was a part until Virginia seceded from the Union in 1861. Then the delegates of 40 western counties formed their own government, which was granted statehood in 1863.

First permanent settlement dates from 1731 when Morgan Morgan founded Mill Creek. In 1742 coal was discovered on the Coal River, an event that would be of great significance in determining West Virginia's future.

The state usually ranks 3rd in total coal production with about 15% of the U.S. total. It also is a leader in steel, glass, aluminum, and chemical manufactures; natural gas, oil, quarry products, and hardwood lumber.

Major cash farm products are poultry and eggs, dairy products, apples, and feed crops. Nearly 75% of West Virginia is covered with forests.

Tourism is increasingly popular in mountainous West Virginia and visitors spent $2.475 billion in 1990. More than a million acres have been set aside in 35 state parks and recreation areas and in 9 state forests, and national forests.

Major points of interest include Harpers Ferry and New River Gorge National River, The Greenbrier and Berkeley Springs resorts, the scenic railroad at Cass, and the historic homes in the Eastern Panhandle.

Famous natives and residents: George Brett, baseball player; Pearl S. Buck, author; Phyllis Curtin, soprano; Martin R. Delany, first Black Army major; Billy Dixon, frontiersman and scout; Joanne Dru, actress; Thomas "Stonewall" Jackson, Confederate general; John S. Knight, publisher; Don Knotts, actor; Peter Marshall, TV host; Kathy Mattea, country music superstar; Whitney D. Morrow, banker and diplomat; Mary Lou Retton, gymnast; Walter Reuther, labor leader; Eleanor Steber, soprano; Lewis L. Strauss, naval officer and scientist; Cyrus Vance, government official; William Lyne Wilson, legislator and university president; Chuck Yeager, test pilot and Air Force general

WISCONSIN

Capital: Madison
Governor: Tommy G. Thompson, R (to Jan. 1999)
Lieut. Governor: Scott McCallum, R (to Jan. 1999)
Secy. of State: Douglas J. La Follette, D (to Jan. 1999)
State Treasurer: Jack C. Voight, R (to Jan. 1999)
Atty. General: James E. Doyle, D (to Jan. 1999)
Superintendent of Public Instruction: John Benson Nonpartisan (to July 1997)

Organized as territory: July 4, 1836
Entered Union & (rank): May 29, 1848 (30)
Present constitution adopted: 1848
Motto: Forward
STATE SYMBOLS: flower, Wood violet (1949); **tree,** Sugar maple (1949); **grain,** corn (1990); **bird,** Robin (1949); **animal,** Badger; **"wild life" animal,** White-tailed deer (1957); **"domestic" animal,** Dairy cow (1971); **insect,** Honeybee (1977); **fish,** Musky (Muskellunge) (1955); **song,** "On Wisconsin"; **mineral,** Galena (1971); **rock,** Red Granite (1971); **symbol of peace:** Mourning Dove (1971); **soil,** Antigo Silt Loam (1983); **fossil,** Trilobite (1985); **dog,** American Water Spaniel (1986); **beverage,** Milk (1988); **grain,** Corn (1990); **dance,** Polka (1994)
Nickname: Badger State
Origin of name: French corruption of an Indian word whose meaning is disputed
10 largest cities (1990 census): Milwaukee, 628,088; Madison, 191,262; Green Bay, 96,466; Racine, 84,298; Kenosha, 80,352; Appleton, 65,695; West Allis, 63,221; Waukesha, 56,958; Eau Claire, 56,856; Oshkosh, 55,006
Land area & (rank): 54,314 sq mi. (140,673 sq km) (25)
Geographic center: In Wood Co., 9 mi. SE of Marshfield
Number of counties: 72
Largest county (1990 census): Milwaukee, 959,275
State forests: 9 (476,004 ac.)
State parks & scenic trails: 45 parks, 14 trails (66,185 ac.)
1995 resident population est.: 5,123,000
1990 resident census population (rank): 4,891,769 (16). **Male:** 2,392,935; **Female:** 2,498,834. **White:** 4,512,523 (92.2%); **Black:** 244,539 (5.0%); **American Indian, Eskimo, or Aleut:** 39,387 (0.8%); **Asian or Pacific Islander:** 53,583 (1.1%); **Other race:** 41,737 (0.9%); **Hispanic:** 93,194 (1.9%). **1980 percent population under 18:** 26.4; **65 and over:** 13.3; **median age:** 32.9.

The Wisconsin region was first explored for France by Jean Nicolet, who landed at Green Bay in 1634. In 1660 a French trading post and Roman Catholic mission were established near present-day Ashland.

Great Britain obtained the region in settlement of the French and Indian War in 1763; the U.S. acquired it in 1783 after the Revolutionary War. However, Great Britain retained actual control until after the War of 1812. The region was successively governed as part of the territories of Indiana, Illinois, and Michigan between 1800 and 1836, when it became a separate territory.

Wisconsin is a leading state in milk and cheese production. In 1994 the state ranked first in the number of milk cows (1,500,000) and produced 30% of the nation's total output of cheese. Other important farm products are peas, beans, beets, corn, potatoes, oats, hay, and cranberries.

The chief industrial products of the state are automobiles, machinery, furniture, paper, beer, and processed foods. Wisconsin ranks second among the 47 paper-producing states.

Wisconsin is a pioneer in social legislation, providing pensions for the blind (1907), aid to dependent children (1913), and old-age assistance (1925). In labor legislation, the state was the first to enact an unemployment compensation law (1932) and the first in which a workman's compensation law actually took effect. Wisconsin had the first state-wide primary-election law and the first successful income-tax law. In April 1984, Wisconsin became the first state to adopt the Uniform Marital Property Act. The act took effect on January 1, 1986.

The state has over 14,000 lakes, of which Winnebago is the largest. Water sports, ice-boating, and fishing are popular, as are skiing and hunting. Public parks and forests take up one seventh of the land,

with 45 state parks, 9 state forests, 14 state trails, 3 recreational areas, and 2 national forests.

Among the many points of interest are the Apostle Islands National Lakeshore; Ice Age National Scientific Reserve; the Circus World Museum at Baraboo; the Wolf, St. Croix, and Lower St. Croix national scenic riverways; and the Wisconsin Dells.

Famous natives and residents: Don Ameche, actor; Ray Chapman Andrews, naturalist and explorer; Walter Annenberg, media tycoon and philanthropist; Carrie Catt, woman suffragist; John R. Commons, economist; Tyne Daly, actress; August Derleth, author; Jeanne Dixon, seer; Zona Gale, novelist; Eric Heiden, skater; Woody Herman, band leader; Hildegarde, singer; Harry Houdini, magician; Hans V. Kaltenborne, journalist; Pee Wee King, singer; George F. Kennan, diplomat; Robert La Follette, politician; William D. Leahy, Fleet Admiral; Liberace, pianist; Charles Litel, actor; Allen Ludden, TV host; Alfred Lunt, actor; Frederic March, actor; Jackie Mason, comedian; John Ringling North, circus director; Pat O'Brien, actor; Georgia O'Keeffe, painter; Charlotte Rae, actress; William H. Rehnquist, jurist; Gena Rowlands, actress; Tom Snyder, newscaster; Spencer Tracy, actor; Thorstein Veblen, economist; Orson Welles, actor and producer; Thornton Wilder, author; Charles Winninger, actor; Frank Lloyd Wright, architect.

WYOMING

Capital: Cheyenne
Governor: Jim Geringer, R (to Jan. 1999)
Secy. of State: Diana Ohman, R (to Jan. 1999)
Auditor: Dave Ferrari, R (to Jan. 1999)
Supt. of Public Instruction: Judy Catchpole, R (to Jan. 1999)
Treasurer: Stanford S. Smith, R (to Jan. 1999)
Atty. General: Bill Hill, R (apptd. by Governor)
Organized as territory: May 19, 1869
Entered Union & (rank): July 10, 1890 (44)
Present constitution adopted: 1890
Motto: Equal rights (1955)
STATE SYMBOLS: flower, Indian paintbrush (1917); **tree,** Cottonwood (1947); **bird,** Meadowlark (1927); **gemstone,** Jade (1967); **insignia,** Bucking horse (unofficial); **song,** "Wyoming" (1955)
Nickname: Equality State
Origin of name: From the Delaware Indian word, meaning "mountains and valleys alternating"; the same as the Wyoming Valley in Pennsylvania
10 largest cities (1990 census): Cheyenne, 50,008; Casper, 46,742; Laramie, 26,687; Rock Springs, 19,050; Gillette, 17,635; Sheridan, 13,900; Green River, 12,711; Evanston, 10,903; Rawlins, 9,380; Riverton, 9,202
Land area & (rank): 97,105 sq mi. (251,501 sq km) (9)
Geographic center: In Fremont Co., 58 mi. ENE of Lander
Number of counties: 23, plus Yellowstone National Park
Largest county (1990 census): Laramie, 73,142
State forests: None
State parks and historic sites: 23 (58,498 ac.)
1995 resident population est.: 480,000
1990 resident census population (rank): 453,588 (50). **Male:** 227,007; **Female:** 226,581. **White:** 427,061 (94.2%); **Black:** 3,606 (0.8%); **American Indian, Eskimo, or Aleut:** 9,479 (2.1%); **Asian or Pacific Islander:** 2,806 (0.6%); **Other race:** 10,636 (2.3%); **Hispanic:** 25,751 (5.7%). **1990 percent population under 18:** 29.9 **65 and over:** 10.4; **median age:** 32.0.

The U.S. acquired the land comprising Wyoming from France as part of the Louisiana Purchase in 1803. John Colter, a fur-trapper, is the first white man known to have entered present Wyoming. In 1807 he explored the Yellowstone area and brought back news of its geysers and hot springs.

Robert Stuart pioneered the Oregon Trail across Wyoming in 1812–13 and, in 1834, Fort Laramie, the first permanent trading post in Wyoming, was built. Western Wyoming was obtained by the U.S. in the 1846 Oregon Treaty with Great Britain and as a result of the treaty ending the Mexican War in 1848.

When the Wyoming Territory was organized in 1869 Wyoming women became the first in the nation to obtain the right to vote. In 1925 Mrs. Nellie Tayloe Ross was elected first woman governor in the United States.

Wyoming's towering mountains and vast plains provide spectacular scenery, grazing lands for sheep and cattle, and rich mineral deposits.

Mining, particularly oil and natural gas, is the most important industry. Wyoming has the world's largest sodium carbonate (natrona) deposits and has the nation's second largest uranium deposits.

Wyoming ranks second among the states in wool production. In January 1995, it ranked third in sheep and lambs, exceeded only by Texas and California; it also had 1,390,000 cattle and calves. Principal crops include wheat, oats, sugar beets, corn, potatoes, barley, and alfalfa.

Second in mean elevation to Colorado, Wyoming has many attractions for the tourist trade, notably Yellowstone National Park. Cheyenne is famous for its annual "Frontier Days" celebration. Flaming Gorge, the Fort Laramie National Historic Site, and Devils Tower and Fossil Butte National Monuments are other points of interest.

Famous natives and residents: James Bridger, trapper, guide, storyteller; Dick Cheney, ex-Secretary of Defense; Buffalo Bill Cody; John Colter, trader and first white man to enter Wyoming; June E. Downey, educator; Thomas Fitzpatrick, mountain man and guide; Curt Gowdy, sportscaster; Tom Horn, detective; Isabel Jewell, actress; Velma Linford, writer; Esther Morris, first woman judge; Ted Olson, writer; John "Portugee" Phillips, frontiersman; Jackson Pollock, painter; Nellie Tayloe Ross, first woman elected governor of a state; Alan K. Simpson, senator; Jedediah S. Smith, mountain man and first American to reach California from the East; Alan Swallow, publisher, author; Willis Van Devanter, Supreme Court justice; Francis E. Warren, first state governor; Chief Washakie, chief of the Shoshone; James G. Watt, ex-Secretary of the Interior

U.S. Territories and Outlying Areas

PUERTO RICO

(Commonwealth of Puerto Rico)
Governor: Pedro Rosselló, New Progressive Party (to 1997)
Capital: San Juan
Land area: 3,459 sq mi. (8,959 sq km)
Song: "La Borinqueña"
1990 census population: 3,522,037
1996 est. population: 3,819,023
Languages: Spanish and English
Literacy rate: 90%
Labor force (1995): 1,219,000; 24% services, 22% government, 20% commerce, 16% manufacturing, 6% communications and transportation, 5% construction, 3% agriculture, 4% other.
Ethnic divisions: Almost entirely Hispanic.
10 largest municipalities (1990 census): San Juan, 437,745; Bayamón, 220,262; Ponce, 187,749; Carolina, 177,806; Caguas, 133,447; Mayagüez, 100,371; Arecibo, 93,385; Guaynabo, 92,886; Toa Baja, 89,454; Trujillo Alto, 61,120
Gross product (FY 1995): $28.4 billion; per capita $7,662; real growth rate 3.4%
Land use: 13% cropland, 41% meadows and pastures, 20% forest and woodland, 26% other.
Environment: Subtropical marine climate; high central mountain range circled by coastal plains; abundant agricultural production and foliage fostered by natural irrigation in all regions except relatively arid south coast.

The Commonwealth of Puerto Rico is located in the Caribbean Sea, about 1,000 miles east southeast of Miami, Florida. A possession of the United States, it consists of the island of Puerto Rico—smallest of the Greater Antilles, measuring about 100 miles from east to west and 35 miles across—plus the adjacent islets of Vieques, Culebra and Mona.

Discovered by Christopher Columbus in 1493, Puerto Rico subsequently became the only New World colony of Spain that never waged a war for independence. Despite this lack of animosity toward Madrid, however, Puerto Ricans warmly welcomed invading United States troops during the Spanish-American War of 1898. Since then, Puerto Rico has remained an unincorporated U.S. territory. Its people were granted American citizenship in 1917; were permitted to elect their own governor, beginning in 1948; and now fully administer their internal affairs under a constitution approved by the U.S. Congress in 1952.

From 1940 to 1968, Puerto Rican politics was dominated by a party advocating voluntary association with the U.S. Since then, a party favoring U.S. statehood has won four of seven gubernatorial elections—including that of 1992.

Puerto Rican voters have twice had the opportunity to express themselves directly on political status alternatives. In 1967, the outcome was commonwealth 60%; statehood 39%; independence 1%. In 1993, commonwealth dropped to 48.6%; statehood rose to 46.3%; independence polled 4.4%; and 0.6% of the ballots were blank or spoiled.

Under the commonwealth formula, residents of Puerto Rico lack voting representation in Congress and the right to participate in Presidential elections. Also, funding caps limit their access to several key Federal programs. As U.S. citizens, Puerto Ricans are subject to military service and most Federal laws. Residents of the Commonwealth pay no Federal income tax on locally-generated earnings, but Puerto Rico government income tax rates are set at a level that closely parallels Federal-plus-state levies on the mainland.

Puerto Rico is a major hub of Caribbean commerce, finance, tourism, and communications. San Juan is one of the world's busiest cruise ship ports, and Puerto Rico hosts hundreds of modern manufacturing facilities. Its population's standard of living is among the highest in the hemisphere.

Famous natives and residents: Deborah Carthy-Deu, Miss Universe 1985; José Cabranes, U.S. appeals court judge; Pablo Casals, cellist; Roberto Clemente, baseball player; Angel Cordero, jockey; Justino Diaz, opera singer; Beatriz "Gigi" Fernández, U.S. Olympic tennis gold medalist; Luis Ferré, political leader, philanthropist; José Ferrer, actor; José Luis González, writer; Gabriel Guerra-Mondragón, U.S. Ambassador to Chile; Raúl Juliá, actor; Marisol Malaret, Miss Universe 1970; Jacobo Morales, filmmaker; Rita Moreno, actress; Luis Muñoz-Marín, political leader; Antonia Novello, ex-Surgeon General; Miguel Piñero, dramatist; Tito Puente, Latin jazz artist; Chita Rivera, actress; Juan "Chi Chi" Rodríguez, golfer; José Serrano, (D-NY), member of Congress; Dayanara Torres, Miss Universe 1993; Juan Torruella, chief judge of U.S. First Circuit Court of Appeals.

GUAM

(Territory of Guam)
Governor: Carl T.C. Gutierrez (Nov. 1994)
Capital: Agaña (1990) 1,139
Land area: 209 sq mi. (541 sq km)
1990 census population: 133,152
1996 est. population: 156,974; **Average annual rate of natural increase:** 2.04%; birth rate: 24.2/1000; infant mortality rate: 15.17/1000; **density per square mi.:** 751
1993 est. net migration: 3 migrants per 1,000 population
Ethnic divisions: Chamorro, 47%; Filipino, 25%; Caucasian, 10%; Chinese, Japanese, Korean, and other 18%
Language: English and Chamorro, most residents bilingual; Japanese also widely spoken
Literacy rate: 96%
Labor force (1994): 66,460; 30.6% government, 69.4% private
Gross national product (1994 est.): $3 billion, per capita $20,000; inflation, 11% (1993); unemployment, 7.3% (Dec. 1994) **Industries:** U.S. military, tourism, transshipment services, concrete products, printing and publishing, food processing, textiles.

Guam, the largest of the Mariana Islands, is independent of the trusteeship assigned to the U.S. in 1947. It was acquired by the U.S. from Spain in 1898 (occupied 1899) and was placed under the Navy Department.

In World War II, Guam was seized by the Japanese on Dec. 11, 1941; but on July 21, 1944, it was once more in U.S. hands.

On Aug. 1, 1950, President Truman signed a bill which granted U.S. citizenship to the people of Guam and established self-government. However, the people do not vote in national elections. In November 1970, Guam elected its first Governor. In 1972 Guam elected its first delegate to the U.S. Congress. The Executive Branch of the Guam government is under the general supervision of the U.S. Secretary of the Interior.

Currently, Guam is an unincorporated, organized territory of the United States. It is "unincorporated" because not all of the provisions of the U.S. constitution apply to the territory. It is an "organized" territory because the Congress provided the territory with an Organic Act in 1950 which organized the government much as a constitution would.

Guam's economy is based on two main sources of revenue: tourism and U.S. military spending (U.S. Naval and Air Force bases on Guam). Federal expenditures (FY94): $1,048 million; $457 million for wages and salaries and $295 million for purchases in the local economy.

The tourist industry has grown rapidly over the past 20 years. Visitors numbered about 1,361,830 in 1995. About 60% of the labor force works in the private sector and the rest for government.

U.S. VIRGIN ISLANDS

(Virgin Islands of the United States)
Governor: Dr. Roy L. Schneider (Jan. 1995)
Capital: Charlotte Amalie (on St. Thomas), population 1990: 12,331
1990 population: 101,809 (St. Croix, 50,139; St. Thomas, 48,166; St. John, 3,504)
Population (est. 1996): 97,120; average annual rate of natural increase: 1.24; birth rate: 17.57/1000; infant mortality rate: 12.5/1000; density per sq mi.: 735.8
Land area: 132 sq mi (342 sq km): St. Croix, 84 sq. mi. (218 sq km), St. Thomas, 32 sq mi (83 sq km), St. John, 20 sq mi. (52 sq km)
Ethnic divisions: West Indian, 74% (45% born in the Virgin Islands and 29% born elsewhere in the West Indies), U.S. mainland, 13%; Puerto Rican, 5%; other, 8%; black, 80%, white, 15%, other, 5%; 14% of Hispanic origin.
Language: English (official), but Spanish and various dialects are widely spoken
Literacy rate: 90%
Labor force (1992): 48,620
Gross domestic product (1989): $1.34 billion, per capita $11,052
Economic summary: Exports $2.8 billion (f.o.b. 1990), refined petroleum products. Imports $3.3 billion (c.i.f. 1990), crude oil, foodstuffs, consumer goods, building materials. Major trading partners: U.S., Puerto Rico.

The Virgin Islands, consisting of nine main islands and some 75 islets, were discovered by Columbus in 1493. Since 1666, England has held six of the main islands; the other three (St. Croix, St. Thomas, and St. John), as well as about 50 of the islets, were eventually acquired by Denmark, which named them the Danish West Indies. In 1917, these islands were purchased by the U.S. from Denmark for $25 million.

Congress granted U.S. citizenship to Virgin Islanders in 1927; and, in 1931, administration was transferred from the Navy to the Department of the Interior. Universal suffrage was given in 1936 to all persons who could read and write the English language. The Governor was elected by popular vote for the first time in 1970; previously he had been appointed by the President of the U.S. A unicameral 15-person legislature serves the Virgin Islands, and Congressional legislation gave the islands a non-voting Representative in Congress.

The "Constitution" of the Virgin Islands is the Revised Organic Act of 1954 in which the U.S. Congress defines the three branches of the territorial government, i.e., the Executive Branch, the Legislative Branch, and the Judicial Branch. Residents of the islands substantially enjoy the same rights as those enjoyed by mainlanders with one important exception: citizens of the U.S. Virgin Islands who are residents may not vote in presidential elections.

Tourism is the primary economic activity, accounting for more than 70% of the GDP and 70% of employment. Tourist expenditures are estimated to be over $791.5 million annually. In 1992, 1,963,800 tourists arrived in the Virgin Islands; about two-thirds were day visitors on cruise ships. The manufacturing sector consists of textile, electronics, pharmaceutical and watch assembly plants. The agricultural sector is small with most food imported. International business and financial services are a small but growing component of the economy. The world's largest petroleum refinery is at St. Croix.

AMERICAN SAMOA

(Territory of American Samoa)
Governor: A.P. Lutali
Lieut. Governor: Tauese Pita Sunia
Capital: Pago Pago, population 1990: 3,519
Population (est. July 1994): 55,223; average rate of natural increase: 3.86%; birth rate 36.6/1000; infant mortality rate: 18.7/1000; density per sq mi.: 717.1
Ethnic divisions: Samoan (Polynesian) 89%; Caucasian, 2%; Tongan 4%; other 6%
Language: Samoan (closely related to Hawaiian and other Polynesian languages) and English; most people are bilingual
Literacy rate: 99%

Labor force (1990): 13,250
Land area: 77 sq mi (199 sq km)
Gross domestic product (1991): $128 million; per capita, $2,600; real growth rate: n.a.; inflation: 7%
Aid (1991): $21.0 million in operational funds and $1,227,000 in construction for capital-improvement projects from the U.S. Department of Interior.

American Samoa, a group of five volcanic islands and two coral atolls located some 2,600 miles south of Hawaii in the South Pacific Ocean, is an unincorporated, unorganized territory of the U.S., administered by the Department of the Interior.

By the Treaty of Berlin, signed Dec. 2, 1899, and ratified Feb. 16, 1900, the U.S. was internationally acknowledged to have rights extending over all the islands of the Samoa group east of longitude 1715 west of Greenwich. On April 17, 1900, the chiefs of Tutuila and Aunu'u ceded those islands to the U.S. In 1904, the King and chiefs of Manu'a ceded the islands of Ofu, Olosega and Tau (composing the Manu'a group) to the U.S. Swains Island, some 214 miles north of Samoa, was included as part of the territory by Act of Congress March 4, 1925; and on Feb. 20, 1929, Congress formally accepted sovereignty over the entire group and placed the responsibility for administration in the hands of the President. From 1900 to 1951, by Presidential direction, the Department of the Navy governed the territory. On July 1, 1951, administration was transferred to the Department of the Interior. The first Constitution for the territory was signed on April 27, 1960, and was revised in 1967.

Congress has provided for a non-voting delegate to sit in the House of Representatives in 1981.

The people of American Samoa are U.S. nationals, not U.S. citizens. Like U.S. citizens, they owe allegiance to the United States.

Economic activity is strongly linked to the U.S., with which American Samoa does 80–90% of its foreign trade. Tuna fishing and tuna processing plants are the backbone of the private sector, with canned tuna the primary export. The tuna canneries and the government are by far the two largest employers. Other economic activities include a slowly developing tourist industry. Transfers from the U.S. government add substantially to American Samoa's economic well-being.

BAKER, HOWLAND, AND JARVIS ISLANDS

These Pacific islands were not to play a role in the extraterritorial plans of the U.S. until May 13, 1936. President F. D. Roosevelt, at that time, placed them under the control and jurisdiction of the Secretary of the Interior for administration purposes.

The three islands have a tropical climate with scant rainfall, constant wind, and a burning sun.

Baker Island is a saucer-shaped atoll with an area of approximately one square mile. It is about 1,650 miles from Hawaii.

Howland Island, 36 miles to the northwest, is approximately one and a half miles long and half a mile wide. It is a low-lying, nearly level, sandy, coral island surrounded by a narrow fringing reef.

Howland Island is related to the tragic disappearance of Amelia Earhart and Fred J. Noonan during the round-the-world flight in 1937. They left New Guinea on July 2, 1937, for Howland, but were never seen again.

Jarvis Island is several hundred miles to the east and is approximately one and three quarter miles long by one mile wide. It is a sandy coral island surrounded by a a narrow fringing reef.

Baker, Howland, and Jarvis have been uninhabited since 1942. In 1974, these islands became part of the National Wildlife Refuge System, administered by the U.S. Fish & Wildlife Service, Department of the Interior.

JOHNSTON ATOLL

Population (est. July 1995): 327
Land area: 1.08 sq. mi. (2.8 sq km); density per sq mi.: 302.7

Johnston is a coral atoll about 700 miles southwest of Hawaii. It consists of four small islands—Johnston Island, Sand Island, Hikina Island, and Akau Island—which lie on a reef about 9 miles long in a northeast-southwest direction.

The atoll was discovered by Capt. Charles James Johnston of *H.M.S. Cornwallis* in 1807. In 1858 it was claimed by Hawaii, and later became a U.S. possession.

Johnston Atoll is a Naval Defensive Sea Area and Airspace Reservation and is closed to the public. The airspace entry control has been suspended but is subject to immediate reinstatement without notice. The administration of Johnston Atoll is under the jurisdiction of the Defense Nuclear Agency, Commander, Johnston Atoll (FCDNA), APO San Francisco, CA 96305.

The Atoll is managed cooperatively by the Defense Nuclear Agency and the Fish and Wildlife Service of the U.S. Department of the Interior as part of the National Wildlife Refuge system.

KINGMAN REEF

Kingman Reef, located about 1,000 miles south of Hawaii, was discovered by Capt. E. Fanning in 1798, but named for Capt. W. E. Kingman, who rediscovered it in 1853. The reef, drying only on its northeast, east and southeast edges, is of atoll character. The reef is triangular in shape, with its apex northward; it is about 9.5 miles long, east and west, and 5 miles wide, north and south, within the 100-fathom curve. The island is uninhabited.

A United States possession, Kingman Reef is a Naval Defensive Sea Area and Airspace Reservation, and is closed to the public. The Airspace Entry Control has been suspended, but is subject to immediate reinstatement without notice. No vessel, except those authorized by the Secretary of the Navy, shall be navigated in the area within the 3-mile limit.

MIDWAY ISLANDS

Midway Islands, lying about 1,150 miles west-northwest of Hawaii, were discovered by Captain N. C. Brooks of the Hawaiian bark *Gambia* on July 5, 1859, in the name of the United States. The atoll was formally declared a U.S. possession in 1867, and in 1903 Theodore Roosevelt made it a naval reservation. The island was renamed "Midway" by the U.S. Navy in recognition of its geographic location on the route between California and Japan.

Midway Islands consist of a circular atoll, 6 miles in diameter, and enclosing two islands. Eastern Island, on its southeast side, is triangular in shape, and about 1.2 miles long. Sand Island, on its south side, is about 2.25 miles long in a northeast-southwest direction.

A National Wildlife Refuge was set up on Midway under an agreement with the Fish and Wildlife Service of the U.S. Dept. of the Interior.

The Midway Islands are within a Naval Defensive Sea Area. The Navy Department maintains an installation and has jurisdiction over the atoll. Permission to enter the Naval Defensive Sea Area must be obtained in advance from the Commander Third Fleet (N31), Pearl Harbor, HI 96860.

Midway has no indigenous population. It is currently populated with U.S. military personnel—(July 1995 est.): 453 U.S. military personnel.

WAKE ISLAND

Total area: 2.5 sq mi. (6.5 sq km)
Comparative size: about 11 times the size of the Mall in Washington, D.C.
Population (1995 est.): no indigenous population; 302 U.S. military personnel and civilian contractors.
Economy: The economic activity is limited to providing services to U.S. military personnel and contractors on the island. All food and manufactured goods must be imported.

Wake Island, about halfway between Midway and Guam, is an atoll comprising the three islets of Wilkes, Peale, and Wake. They were discovered by the British in 1796 and annexed by the U.S. in 1899. The entire area comprises 3 square miles and has no native population. In 1938, Pan American Airways established a seaplane base and Wake Island has been used as a commercial base since then. On Dec. 8, 1941, it was attacked by the Japanese, who finally took possession on Dec. 23. It was surrendered by the Japanese on Sept. 4, 1945.

The President, acting pursuant to the Hawaii Omnibus Act, assigned responsibility for Wake to the Secretary of the Interior in 1962. The Department of Transportation exercised civil administration of Wake through an agreement with the Department of the Interior until June 1972, at which time the Department of the Air Force assumed responsibility for the Territory.

The government of Wake Island has been administered by the U.S. Army and Strategic Defense Command since Oct. 1, 1994.

CAROLINE ISLANDS

The Caroline Islands, east of the Philippines and south of the Marianas, include the Yap, Truk, and the Palau groups and the islands of Ponape and Kusqie, as well as many coral atolls.

The islands are composed chiefly of volcanic rock, and their peaks rise 2,000 to 3,000 feet above sea level. Chief exports of the islands are copra, fish products, and handicrafts.

Formerly members of the U.S. Trust Territory of the Pacific, all of the group but Palau joined the Federated States of Micronesia.

MARIANA ISLANDS

(The Commonwealth of The Northern Mariana Islands)

Governor: Frolian C. Tenorio (Jan. 1994)
Lieut. Governor: Jesus Borja
Total area: 184.17 sq mi. (477 sq km)
Population (est. 1996): 52,284; growth rate: 3.04%; birth rate: 33/1000; infant mortality: 37.9/1000; density per sq mi.: 284. The population of the Commonwealth of the Northern Mariana Islands (CNMI) is concen-trated on the three largest inhabited islands: Saipan, the government seat and commerce center; Rota; and Tinian.
Language: English is the official language, but Chamorro and Carolinian are the spoken native tongues. Japanese is also spoken in many of the hotels and shops, reflecting a heavy tourism industry.
Literacy rate: 97%
Economy: The government of the CNMI benefits substantially from U.S. financial assistance. Gross national product (1994 est.): $524 million; GNP reflects U.S. spending. Per capita: $10,500; exports: $263.4 million (f.o.b. 1991 est.): manufactured goods, garments, bread, pastries, concrete blocks, light iron work. Imports: $392.4 million (c.i.f. 1991 est.): food, construction equipment, materials.

The Mariana Islands, east of the Philippines and south of Japan, include the islands of Guam, Rota, Saipan, Tinian, Pagan, Guguan, Agrihan, and Aguijan. Guam, the largest, is independent of the trusteeship, having been acquired by the U.S. from Spain in 1898. (For more information, *see* the entry on Guam in this section.) The remaining islands, referred to as the Commonwealth of the Northern Mariana Islands (CNMI) became part of the United States pursuant to P.L. 94-241 as of November 3, 1986.

Tourism is the leading employer, affecting about 50% of the work force. Seventy-five percent of the tourists are Japanese.

Agricultural products are coconuts, fruits, cattle, vegetables.

Minor Islands

NAVASSA ISLAND

Total area: 2 sq mi. (5.2 sq km)
Comparative size: About nine times the size of The Mall in Washington, D.C.

Navassa Island is strategically located in the Caribbean Sea, 99.4 miles (160 km) south of the U.S. Naval Base at Guantanamo, Cuba, between Cuba, Haiti, and Jamaica. It is an unincorporated territory of the United States, administered by the U.S. Coast Guard. The U.S. is responsible for its defense.

The island's terrain consists of a raised coral and limestone plateau, flat to undulating, and ringed by vertical cliffs, 30 to 50 feet (9 to 15 meters) high.

Navassa is uninhabited and transient Haitian fishermen and others camp there.

PALMYRA ATOLL

Total area: 4.6 sq mi. (11.9 sq km)
Comparative size: About 20 times the size of The Mall in Washington, D.C.

Palmyra Atoll is an unincorporated territory of the U.S., privately owned, but administered by the Office of Territorial and International Affairs, U.S. Department of the Interior. The U.S. is responsible for its defense.

It is located in the North Pacific Ocean, 994 miles (1,600 kilometers) south–southwest of Honolulu, almost halfway between Hawaii and American Samoa. The Atoll consists of about 50 islets covered with dense vegetation, coconut trees, and balsa-like trees almost 100 feet (30 meters) high. Palmyra Atoll is uninhabited.

Tabulated Data on State Governments

State	Governor Term, years	Governor Annual salary	Legislature[1] Membership U[3]	Legislature[1] Membership L[4]	Legislature[1] Term, U[3]	Legislature[1] yrs. L[4]	Legislature[1] Salaries of members[5]		Highest Court[2] Members	Highest Court[2] Term, years	Highest Court[2] Annual salary
Alabama	4[10]	$87,643	35	105	4	4	$10	per diem[21]	9	6	$115,695[6]
Alaska	4	81,648	20	40	4	2	24,012[25]	per annum	5	(8)	99,996[6]
Arizona	4	75,000	30	60	2	2	15,000	per annum	5	6	101,130[6]
Arkansas	4	60,000	35	100	4	2	12,500	per annum	7	8	95,216[6]
California	4	114,000	40	80	2	37	72,500	per annum	7	12	127,276[6]
Colorado	4	70,000	35	65	4	2	17,500	per annum	7	10	91,000[6]
Connecticut	4	78,000	36	151	2	2	16,760	per annum	7	8	113,042[6]
Delaware	4[9]	95,000	21	41	4	2	27,000[5]	per annum	5	12	111,500[6]
Florida	4[10]	104,817	40	120	4	2	24,180	per annum	7	6	116,244
Georgia[10]	4	103,074	56	180	2	2	11,125.	per annum	7	6	114,932
Hawaii	4	94,780	25	51	4	2	32,000	per year	5	10	93,780[6]
Idaho	4	85,000	35	70	2	2	12,360[35]	per annum[5]	5	6	83,142
Illinois	4	110,537	59	118	4-2	2	42,265	per annum	7	10	112,124
Indiana	4[10]	77,200	50	100	4	2	11,600	per annum	5	(24)	81,000
Iowa	4	98,200	50	100	4	2	18,800	per annum	9	8	96,700[6]
Kansas	4	76,091	40	125	4	2	119	per diem[22]	7	6	82,005[6]
Kentucky	4	90,919	38	100	4	2	110	per diem[36]	7	8	94,095[6]
Louisiana	4	95,000	39	105	4	4	16,800[5]	per annum	7	10	85,000
Maine	4	70,000[16]	35	151	2	2	18,000[37]	per annum[16]	7	7	80,392
Maryland	4[10]	120,000	47	141	4	4	29,700	per annum	7	10	107,300[6]
Massachusetts	4	90,000	40	160	2	2	46,410	per annum	7	(13)	95,880[6]
Michigan	4	121,166[16]	38	110	4	2	50,629[38]	per annum	7	8	118,758
Minnesota	4	114,000	67	134	4[32]	2	27,979[5]	per annum[16]	7	6	83,494
Mississippi	4	83,160	52	122	4	4	10,000	per session[5]	9	8	90,800[6]
Missouri	4[9]	98,345	34	163	4[39]	2	25,285[5]	per annum	7	12	99,733[6]
Montana	4	59,310	50	100	4	2	55	per diem[16]	7	8	68,874
Nebraska	4[10]	65,000	49[11]	—	4[11]	—	12,000	per annum	7	6	88,157
Nevada	4	90,000	21	42	4	2	7,800[5]	per biennium	5	6	107,600
New Hampshire	2	86,235	24	(12)	2	2	200	per biennium	5	(13)	95,628[6]
New Jersey	4[10]	130,000	40	80	4[14]	2	35,000[30]	per annum	7	7[15]	112,000
New Mexico	4[40]	90,000	42	70	4	2	75	per diem	5	8	77,250[6]
New York	4	130,000	61	150	2	2	57,500	per annum[16]	7	14	120,000[6]
North Carolina	4[41]	91,938[16]	50	120	2	2	13,026	per annum[16]	7	8	89,532[6]
North Dakota	4	71,042[29]	49	98	4	2	90	per diem[16][23]	5	10	77,448[6][29]
Ohio	4	115,752	33	99	4	2	42,427	per annum	7	6	101,150[6]
Oklahoma	4	70,000	48	101	4	2	32,000[16]	per annum	(19)	6	87,700[6]
Oregon	4[10]	80,000	30	60	4	2	1,092[42]	per month	7	6	83,700
Pennsylvania	4[10]	125,000	50	203	4	2	47,000	per annum	7	10	119,750[6]
Rhode Island	2	69,900	50	100	2	2	5[17]	per diem[17]	5	(18)	104,403
South Carolina	4	106,078	46	124	4	2	10,400	per annum	5	10	92,986[6]
South Dakota	4[10]	82,271	35	70	2	2	8,000	per biennium	5	3[26]	76,469[6]
Tennessee	4	85,000	33	99	4	2	16,500	per annum	5	8	101,820
Texas	4	99,122	31	150	4	2	7,200[5]	per annum	(20)	6	94,686[6]
Utah	4	85,200	29	75	4	2	100	per diem[16]	5	(33)	98,500[6]
Vermont	2	93,122	30	150	2	2	480[16][28]	per week[28]	5	6	80,031[6]
Virginia	4[7]	110,000	40	100	4	2	17,640[31]	per annum	7	12	107,373[6]
Washington	4[43]	121,000	49	98	4[44]	2	25,900	per annum	9	6	107,200
West Virginia	4[10]	72,000	34	100	4	2	15,000[16]	per annum	5	12	72,000
Wisconsin	4	101,861	33	99	4	2	39,211	per annum	7	10	100.690
Wyoming	4	95,000	30	60	4	2	125[16][27]	per diem	5	8	85,000

1. Known as *General Assembly* in Ark., Colo., Conn., Del., Ga., Ill., Iowa, Ind., Ky., Md., Mo., N.C., Ohio, Pa., R.I., S.C., Tenn., Vt., Va.; *Legislative Assembly* in N.D., Ore.; *General Court* in Mass.; *Legislature* in other states. Meets biennially in Calif., Ky., Me., Mont., Nev., N.J., N.D., Ore., Pa., Texas. Wyoming Legislature has regular general session on odd numbered years and a budget session on even numbered years. Arkansas General Assembly meets every other year for 60 days in odd numbered years. Ohio General Assembly meets when deemed necessary. Legislative bodies meet annually in other states. 2. Known as *Court of Appeals* in Md., N.Y.; *Supreme Court of Virginia* in Va.; *Supreme Judicial Court* in Me., Mass.; *Supreme Court* in other states. 3. Upper house: *Senate* in all states except Neb., which has a single-house legislative body, "the Legislature." 4. Lower house: *Assembly* in Calif., Nev., N.Y., Wis.; *House of Delegates* in Md., Va., W.Va.; *General Assembly* in N.J.; *House of Representatives* in other states. 5. Base salary. Does not include additional payments for expenses, mileage, special sessions, etc., or additional per diem payments. 6. Chief Justice receives a higher salary. 7. Cannot succeed himself. 8. Appointed for 3 years; thereafter subject to approval or rejection on a nonpartisan ballot for 10-year term. 9. May serve only 2 terms, consecutive or otherwise. 10. May not serve 3rd consecutive term. 11. Unicameral legislature. 12. Constitutional number: 375-400. 13. Until 70 years old. 14. When term begins in Jan. of 2nd year following U.S. census, term shall be 2 years. 15. 2nd term receive tenure, mandatory retirement at 70. 16. Plus expense allowance. 17. For current legislators or $10,000 per year without a pension. Future legislators must take the $10,000. 18. Term of good behavior. 19. Nine members in Supreme Court, highest in civil cases; five in Court of Criminal Appeals. 20. Nine members in Supreme Court, highest in civil cases; nine in Court of Criminal Appeals. 21. Plus $50 per diem expenses up to $2,280 per month when they are in session. 22. When in session, plus

$600/mo. when not in session. 23. When in session, plus $180 per month for each month of term. 24. Appointed for 2 years; thereafter elected popularly for 10-year term. 25. Senate President and House Speaker receive an additional $500 per year. 26. Subsequent terms, 8 years. 27. $125 per annum. 28. To limit of $13,000 per biennium; $100 per diem for Special Session. 29. As of July 1, 1996, governor's salary jumps to $71,042 and the judges to $77,448. 30. Each legislator receives $80,000 annually for appointment of personal staff aides. 31. Senate $18,000. 32. Every 10 years (the year after census) term is only for 2 years. 33. Appointed by governor. Up for re-election at first general election that takes place at least 3 years after appointment. After that, face a retention election every 10 years. 34. Senator's salary higher. 35. $3,000 additional for speaker and president pro tem of the senate. 36. When in session, plus $950 a month when not in session. 37. For the 2-year term. 38. Expense accounts. 39. Legislators may serve only eight years in each house, 16 combined. 40. May serve two terms in office; after that ineligible to be governor until one term has expired. 41. May only serve two consecutive terms. 42. Plus $75 per day for expenses during session. 43. No person is eligible who would have served during eight of the previous 14 years. 44. Have term limitations. NOTE: Salaries are rounded to nearest dollar. Source: Information Please questionnaires to the states.

Land and Water Area of States, 1990

(in square miles)

State	Rank (total area)	Land[1] area	Water[2] area	Total area	State	Rank (total area)	Land[1] area	Water[2] area	Total area
Alabama	30	50,750.23	1,672.71	52,422.94	Montana	4	145,556.34	1,489.82	147,046.16
Alaska	1	570,373.55	86,050.59	656,424.14	Nebraska	16	76,877.73	480.67	77,358.40
Arizona	6	113,642.26	364.00	114,006.26	Nevada	7	109,805.89	761.02	110,566.91
Arkansas	29	52,075.29	1,107.07	53,182.36	New Hampshire	46	8,969.36	381.57	9,350.93
California	3	155,973.09	7,734.06	163,707.15	New Jersey	47	7,418.84	1,303.11	8,721.95
Colorado	8	103,729.54	370.78	104,100.32	New Mexico	5	121,364.54	233.69	123,598.23
Connecticut	48	4,845.39	698.26	5,543.65	New York	27	47,223.85	7,250.71	54,474.56
Delaware	49	1,954.62	534.76	2,489.38	North Carolina	28	48,718.08	5,103.27	53,821.35
Dist. of Columbia—		61.41	6.95	68.36	North Dakota	19	68,994.24	1,709.59	70,703.83
Florida	22	53,997.08	11,761.00	65,758.08	Ohio	34	40,952.59	3,874.94	44,827.53
Georgia	24	57,918.73	1,522.49	59,441.22	Oklahoma	20	68,678.57	1,224.33	69,902.90
Hawaii	43	6,423.34	4,508.24	10,931.58	Oregon	9	96,002.58	2,383.17	98,385.75
Idaho	14	82,750.93	822.84	83,573.77	Pennsylvania	33	44,819.61	1,238.63	46,058.24
Illinois	25	55,593.29	2,324.55	57,917.84	Rhode Island	50	1,044.98	500.12	1,545.10
Indiana	38	35,870.18	549.91	36,420.09	South Carolina	40	30,111.12	1,895.99	32,007.11
Iowa	26	55,874.90	400.64	56,275.54	South Dakota	17	75,897.74	1,223.72	77,121.46
Kansas	15	81,823.02	458.98	82,282.00	Tennessee	36	41,219.52	926.49	42,146.01
Kentucky	37	39,732.31	678.93	40,411.24	Texas	2	261,914.26	6,686.70	268,600.96
Louisiana	31	43,566.03	8,277.44	51,843.47	Utah	13	82,168.15	2,735.97	84,904.12
Maine	39	30,864.55	4,522.78	35,387.33	Vermont	45	9,249.33	365.67	9,615.00
Maryland	42	9,774.65	2,632.80	12,407.45	Virginia	35	39,597.79	3,171.09	42,768.88
Massachusetts	44	7,837.98	2,716.81	10,554.79	Washington	18	66,581.95	4,720.70	71,302.65
Michigan	11	56,809.18	40,001.04	96,810.22	West Virginia	41	24,086.55	144.89	24,231.44
Minnesota	12	79,616.66	7,326.05	86,942.71	Wisconsin	23	54,313.71	11,189.50	65,503.21
Mississippi	32	46,913.64	1,519.95	48,433.59	Wyoming	10	97,104.55	713.56	97,818.11
Missouri	21	68,898.01	810.80	69,708.81	U.S. Total		3,536,341.73	251,083.35	3,787,425.08

1. Dry land and land temporarily or partially covered by water, such as marshland, swamps, etc.; streams and canals under one-eighth statute mile wide; and lakes, reservoirs, and ponds under 40 acres. 2. Permanent inland water surface, such as lakes, reservoirs, and ponds having an area of 40 acres or more; streams, sloughs, estuaries, and canals one-eighth statute mile or more in width; deeply indented embayments and sounds, and other coastal waters behind or sheltered by headlands or islands separated by less than 1 nautical mile of water, and islands under 40 acres in area. Excludes areas of oceans, bays, sounds, etc. lying within U.S. jurisdiction but not defined as inland water. *Source:* Department of Commerce, Bureau of the Census.

"Go West!"

Source: Census and You, March 1996

The five states whose populations grew the fastest between July 1994 and July 1995 were all in the West. Nevada was the fastest-growing state, expanding by 4.7%, followed by Arizona (3.4%), Idaho (2.5%), Colorado (2.3%), and Utah (2.2%). The region as a whole grew 1.3 percent. The increased population in these states was the result of significant inflows of residents from other states, as well as new births to existing residents.

There were also increases among the most populous states, California and Texas, though at slower rates. California grew at 0.6% for the second straight year, continuing a three-year trend of growing at less than the national average of 0.9 percent. Approximately 383,000 people left California last year for other states; these people were replaced by 234,000 international immigrants, and a natural increase (births minus deaths) of 343,000. Net migration out of the state was the primary factor in California's slower-than-average growth rate. The Texas population grew 1.7% as a result of natural increase, and both domestic and international migration.

In contrast to these (albeit modest) growth rates, New York's population decreased slightly for the first time since the 1970s. New York lost approximately 17,000 people (or 0.1% of its population) between July 1994 and July 1995, largely through migration to other states, and partly through a decline in inflows from international immigration.

U.S. CITIES

50 Largest Cities of the United States

(According to 1994 Census data)

Data supplied by Bureau of the Census and by the cities in response to *Information Please* questionnaires. Ranking of 50 largest cities based on July 1, 1994, census estimates. Per capita personal income data is given for the Metropolitan Statistical Area (MSA), the Primary Metropolitan Statistical Area (PMSA), or the Consolidated Metropolitan Statistical Area (CMSA), as noted, and is for 1992, unless otherwise noted. Average daily temperature data is from *County and City Data Book*. NOTE: Persons of Hispanic origin may be of any race.

ALBUQUERQUE, N.M.

Mayor: Martin J. Chavez
1994 est. population (rank): 411,994 (26)
1990 census population (rank): 384,736 (38); **% change,** 15.6; **Male,** 186,584; **Female,** 198,152; **White,** 301,010; **Black,** 11,484 (3.0%); **American Indian, Eskimo, or Aleut,** 11,708 (3.0%); **Asian or Pacific Islander,** 6,660 (1.7%); **Other race,** 53.874; **Hispanic origin,** 132,706 (34.5%). **1990 percent population under 18:** 25.0%; **65 and over:** 11.1%; **median age:** 32.5.
Land area: 163 sq mi. (422 sq km); **Alt.:** 4,958 ft.
Avg. daily temp.: Jan., 34.8° F; July, 78.8° F
Churches: 211; **City-owned parks:** 189; **Radio stations:** 43 (AM, 17; FM, 26); **Television stations:** 11
CIVILIAN LABOR FORCE: 224,003; **Unemployed:** 10,305, **Percent:** 4.6; **Per capita personal income (MSA) 1992:** $17,758
Chamber of Commerce: Greater Albuquerque Chamber of Commerce, 401 2nd St., N.W., Albuquerque, N.M. 87102. Albuquerque Hispanic Chamber of Commerce, 1520 Central Ave., S.E., Albuquerque, N.M. 87106

Albuquerque is the largest city in New Mexico and the seat of Bernalillo county. It is situated in west central New Mexico on the upper Rio Grande River. Early Spanish settlers arrived there in the mid-1600s. The old town was founded in 1706 by Don Francisco Cuervo y Valdés, the Governor of New Mexico, and named after the Duke of Alburquerque, the viceroy of New Spain. During the Civil War, Confederate forces briefly occupied the city in 1862. The new town section was founded in 1880. In 1883, Albuquerque became the county seat and was incorporated as a city in 1891.

The city is noted as a center for health and medical services in the region, and government agencies, nuclear research, banking, and tourism are important to the economy. There is a growing high-tech center in Albuquerque and Intel Corp.'s largest manufacturing facility is located there.

Famous natives: Erna Fergusson, author; Annabeth Gish, actress; Fred Haney, baseball player, executive; Ernie Pyle, WWII war correspondent; Slim Summerville, actor; Al and Bobby Unser, auto racers

ATLANTA, GA.

Mayor: Bill Campbell (to Jan. 1998)
1994 est. population (rank): 396,052 (37)
1990 census population (rank): 394,017 (36); **% change,** −7.3; **Male,** 187,877; **Female,** 206,140; **White,** 122,327; **Black,** 264,262 (67.1%); **American Indian, Eskimo, or Aleut,** 563 (0.1%); **Asian or Pacific Islander,** 3,498 (0.9%); **Other race,** 3,367; **Hispanic origin,** 7,525 (1.9%). **1990 percent population under 18:** 24.1; **65 and over:** 11.3; **median age:** 31.5.
City land area: 136 sq mi. (352.2 sq km); **Alt.:** Highest, 1,050 ft; lowest, 940
Avg. daily temp.: Jan., 41.9° F; July, 78.6° F

Churches (20-county area): 1,500; **City-owned parks:** 277 (3,178 ac.); **Radio stations (20-county area):** AM, 7; FM, 20; **Television stations (20-county area):** 8 commercial; 2 PBS
CIVILIAN LABOR FORCE (1995): 1,880,106; **Unemployed:** 81,256, **Percent:** 4.7; **Per capita personal income (MSA) 1992:** $21,849
Chamber of Commerce: Metro Atlanta Chamber of Commerce, 235 International Blvd., Atlanta, Ga. 30301-1740; Information is gathered on the 20-county MSA

Atlanta, the largest city and capital of Georgia, is the seat of Fulton county. It is situated in the northwest part of the state at the base of the Blue Ridge Mountains near the Chattahoochee River. The first European settler was Hardy Ivy who built a cabin there in 1833.

The town was founded as Terminus in 1837 as the end of the Georgia railroad line (Western and Atlantic Railroad) and became incorporated as Marthasville in 1843 in honor of ex-governor Lumpkin's daughter Martha. It was renamed Atlanta in 1845 and incorporated as a city in 1847. Its name was suggested by the railroad's chief engineer, J. Edgar Thomson, and was derived from its location at the end of the Georgia and Atlantic railroad line. The city later became the capital of Georgia in 1868.

During the Civil War, the city was burned and almost completely destroyed by General W.T. Sherman in November 1864. It was quickly rebuilt after the war and it grew rapidly due to the expansion of the railroads in the southwest. Atlanta's diverse economy is led by the service, communications, retail trade, manufacturing, and finance and insurance industries. The convention business is also important, and the 1996 Summer Olympic Games were held there.

Famous natives: Hank Aaron, baseball player; Arrested Development, recording artists; Jimmy Carter, former president; Ray Charles, singer; James Dickey, poet; Mattivilda Dobbs, soprano; Walt Frazier, basketball player; Oliver Hardy, comedian; Evander Holyfield, boxer; Allan Jackson, singer; Bobby Jones, golfer; DeForest Kelley, actor; Martin Luther King, Jr., civil rights leader, Nobel Peace Prize winner; Gladys Knight, singer; Kriss Kross, recording artists; Margaret Mitchell, novelist; Bert Parks, entertainer; Eric Roberts, actor; Julia Roberts, actress; Ferroll Sams, author; Doug Stone, singer; Pamela Stone, comedienne; Gwen Torrence, Olympic athlete; Lee Tracy, actor; Travis Tritt, singer; Ted Turner, TBS, CNN founder; Jane Withers, actress; Joanne Woodward, actress; Andrew Young, civil rights activist

AUSTIN, TEX.

Mayor: Bruce Todd (to May 1997)
1994 est. population (rank): 514,013 (23)
1990 census population (rank): 465,622 (27); **% change,** 34.6; **Male,** 232,473; **Female,** 233,149; **White,** 328,542; **Black,** 57,868 (12.4%); **American Indian, Eskimo, or Aleut:,** 1,756 (0.4%); **Asian or Pacific Islander,** 14,141

(3.0%); **Other race,** 63,315; **Hispanic origin,** 106,868 (23.0%). **1990 percent population under 18:** 23.1%; **65 and over:** 7.4%; **median age:** 28.9
Land area: 116 sq mi. (300 sq km); **Alt.:** From 425 ft. to over 1000 ft. elevation
Avg. daily temp.: Jan., 49.1° F; July, 84.7° F
Churches: 353 churches, representing 45 denominations; **City-owned parks and playgrounds:** 169 (11,800 ac.); **Radio stations:** AM, 6; FM, 12; **Television stations:** 3 commercial; 1 PBS; 1 independent
CIVILIAN LABOR FORCE (1995): 616,300; **Unemployed:** 20,338, **Percent:** 3.3; **Per capita personal income:** $18,770, Austin-San Marcos (MSA)
Chamber of Commerce: Greater Austin Chamber of Commerce, P.O. Box 1967, Austin, Tex. 78767

Austin, the capital and seat of Travis county, is the fifth largest city in Texas. It is situated in the south central part of the state on the Colorado River. The site was called Waterloo in 1838 and in 1839 was incorporated as a city and chosen to become the capital of the independent Republic of Texas. Waterloo was renamed Austin in honor of Stephen F. Austin, the founder of the Texas Republic. It became the permanent capital of the state of Texas in 1870.

Austin's growth was spurred by several developments after the Civil War—the railroads reached the city in the 1870s; it was crossed by the important Chisholm cattle trail, and it became the seat of the state university in 1883.

Austin has a growing commercial and diversified manufacturing sector. Civilian government employment is 28% of the labor force and is important to the economy. As home to the University of Texas, Austin is a major research and development, and nationally recognized high-technology center. The city has a new convention center downtown.

Famous natives: Don Baylor, baseball player; manager; Earl Campbell, football player; Liz Carpenter, author; Dabney Coleman, actor; Ben Crenshaw, golfer; Michael Dell, founder Dell Computer Corp.; Tobe Hooper, film director; Lady Bird Johnson, former First Lady; Tom Kite, golfer; James Michener, author; Willie Nelson, musician; Amado Pena, artist; Darrell Royal, legendary UT football coach; Zachary Scott, actor; Jerry Jeff Walker, musician; Dalhart Windberg, artist

BALTIMORE, MD.

Mayor: Kurt L. Schmoke (to Dec. 1995)
1994 est. population (rank): 702,979 (14)
1990 census population (rank): 702,979 (12); **% change,** −6.4; **Male,** 343,513; **Female,** 392,501; **White,** 287,753; **Black,** 435,768 (59.2%); **American Indian, Eskimo, or Aleut,** 2,555 (0.3%); **Asian or Pacific Islander,** 7,942 (1.1%); **Other race:** 1,996; **Hispanic origin:** 7,602 (1.0%). **1990 percent population under 18:** 24.4; **65 and over:** 13.7; **Median age:** 32.6.
Land area: 80.3 sq mi. (208 sq km); **Alt.:** Highest, 490 ft; lowest, sea level
Avg. daily temp.: Jan., 35.5° F; July, 79.9° F
Churches: Roman Catholic, 72; Jewish, 50; Protestant and others, 344; **City-owned parks:** 347 park areas and tracts (6,314 ac.); **Radio stations:** AM, 10; FM, 11; **Television stations:** 7 (including Home Shopping Network)
CIVILIAN LABOR FORCE: 333,043; **Unemployed:** 35,531, **Percent:** 10.7; **Per capita personal income (PMSA)** 1992: $22,412
Chamber of Commerce: Greater Baltimore Committee, 111 S. Calvert St., Ste. 1500, Baltimore, Md. 21202

Baltimore is the largest city in Maryland and is situated in the northern part of the state on the Pataps-

co River estuary, an arm of Chesapeake Bay. The city is independent and is in no county.

The site was settled in the early 17th century and founded as a town in 1729. The town was named after Lord Baltimore, the founder of Maryland, and was incorporated as a city in 1797. It has an excellent harbor and has been a principal port since the 18th century. Baltimore was a pioneer ship-building center and the Baltimore clipper was one of the best sailing ships of its day and was used extensively in world trade. It ranks today as the nation's second port in foreign tonnage.

Baltimore's economy is focused on manufacturing, in steel, heavy and light industries, ship construction, and scientific research and development.

Famous natives: Larry Adler, musician; John Astin, actor; Eubie Blake, pianist; Francis X. Bushman, actor; Charlie Chase, actor; Hans Conried, actor; Mildred Dunnock, actress; "Mama" Cass Elliot, singer; Barry Farber, broadcaster; Paul Ford, actor; Philip Glass, composer; Billy Holiday, singer; Barry Levinson, director; H.L. Mencken, writer; Babe Ruth, baseball player; Upton Sinclair, novelist; Leon Uris, novelist; Frank Zappa, musician

BOSTON, MASS.

Mayor: Thomas Menino (to Dec. 1997)
1994 est. population (rank): 547,725 (21)
1990 census population (rank): 574,283 (20); **% change,** 2.0; **Male,** 275,972; **Female,** 298,311; **White,** 360,875; **Black,** 146,945 (25.6%); **American Indian, Eskimo, or Aleut,** 1,884 (0.3%); **Asian or Pacific Islander,** 30,388 (5.3%); **Other race,** 34,191; **Hispanic origin,** 61,955 (10.8%). **1990 percent population under 18:** 19.1; **65 and over:** 11.5; **median age:** 30.3.
Land area: 47.2 sq mi. (122 sq km); **Alt.:** Highest, 330 ft; lowest, sea level
Avg. daily temp.: Jan., 29.6° F; July, 73.5° F
Churches: Protestant, 187; Roman Catholic, 72; Jewish, 28; others, 100; **City-owned parks, playgrounds, etc.:** 2,276.36 ac.; **Radio stations:** AM, 9; FM, 12; **Television stations:** 10
CIVILIAN LABOR FORCE (1995): 284,448; **Unemployed:** 14,036, **Percent:** 4.9; **Per capita personal income (NECMA)** 1992: $24,109[1]
Chamber of Commerce: Boston Chamber of Commerce, 600 Atlantic Ave., Boston, Mass. 02210
1. Boston-Lawrence-Salem-Lowell-Brockton NECMA.

Boston is the state capital, seat of Suffolk county, and the largest city in Massachusetts. It is located in the eastern part of the state at the head of Boston Bay. It was incorporated as a city in 1822. No city in the U.S. is richer in historical associations than Boston, and no city has retained more of its original buildings as memorials to America's past.

Puritans from England settled at Boston in 1630, only ten years after the Pilgrims had landed at Plymouth in 1620. They named their new town Boston, after the former home of many of the Pilgrims in Lincolnshire, England. Fourteen years later, the pioneer Bostonians set aside the first public park in the U.S.—the Boston Common. The following year, 1635, they opened the first free public school in America. Today, the Boston metropolitan area is home to 68 colleges and universities.

Boston is a major industrial, financial, and educational hub and has one of the finest ports in the world. The port of Boston ships more than $8.5 billion worth of goods each year.

Although the city's banking and financial services, insurance, and real estate sectors declined in the early '90s, other industries continue to grow, especially in the health care field. Boston has 25 medical research institutions, more than any other U.S. city, and its health care industry is growing at a rate of about 3% a year. The city's unique cultural and historic heritage makes it a center of tourism and its hotel industry ranks first in the nation in occupancy. Boston's other businesses are in high-technology, biotechnology, software, and electronics.

Famous natives: Samuel Adams, patriot; John Singleton Copley, painter; Ralph Waldo Emerson, philosopher and poet; Arthur Fiedler, conductor; Benjamin Franklin, statesman, scientist; Edward Everett Hale, clergyman, author; Oliver Wendell Holmes, jurist; Winslow Homer, painter; Joseph P. and Rose Fitzgerald Kennedy; Jack Lemmon, actor; Robert Lowell, poet; Edgar Allan Poe, writer; Paul Revere, patriot, silversmith; John L. Sullivan, boxer; Barbara Walters, TV journalist

CHARLOTTE, N.C.

Mayor: Pat McCrory (to Nov. 1999)
1994 est. population (rank): 437,797 (32)
1990 census population (rank): 395,934 (35); **% change,** 25.5; **Male,** 188,088; **Female,** 207,846; **White,** 259,760; **Black,** 125,827 (31.8%); **American Indian, Eskimo, or Aleut:** 1,425 (0.4%); **Asian or Pacific Islander:** 7,211 (1.8%); **Other race,** 1,711; **Hispanic origin,** 5,571 (1.4%). **1990 percent population under 18:** 24.2%; **65 and over:** 9.8%; **median age:** 32.1.
Land area: 209 sq mi. (541.3 sq km); **Alt.:** 765 ft
Avg. daily temp.: Jan., 40.5° F; July, 78.5° F
Churches: Protestant, over 400; Roman Catholic, 8; Jewish, 3; Greek Orthodox, 1; **City-owned parks and parkways:** 130; **Radio stations:** AM, 7; FM, 13; **Television stations:** 4 commercial; 2 PBS
CIVILIAN LABOR FORCE (1995): 329,360; **Unemployed:** 8,860, **Percent:** 2.6; **Per capita personal income (MSA) 1992:** $19,884[1]
Chamber of Commerce: Charlotte Chamber, P.O. Box 32785, Charlotte, N.C., 28232
1. Charlotte-Gastonia Rock Hill, N.C.–S.C.

Charlotte, North Carolina's largest city and seat of Mecklenburg county, is located in the southern part of the state near the South Carolina border. It was named for King George III of England's wife, Charlotte Sophia of Mecklenburg-Strelitz.

Settled about 1750, Charlotte was incorporated as a city in 1768 and made the county seat in 1774. Charlotte was a leading Confederate city during the Civil War and was the last meeting place of the full Confederate cabinet.

From 1800 to 1848, Charlotte was the center of U.S. gold production and a branch of the U.S. mint operated from there from 1837 to 1913.

The city has a highly diversified economy and is a foremost center for distribution, retailing, technology, and manufacturing. It is the second largest banking center in the U.S. It is the seat of the University of North Carolina at Charlotte.

Famous natives: Romare Bearden, artist; Richard G. Darman, government official; Billy Graham, evangelist; Charles Gwathmey, architect; Hamilton Jordan, government official; Donald Schollander, swimmer; Randolph Scott, actor

CHICAGO, ILL.

Mayor: Richard M. Daley (to April 1999)
1994 est. population (rank): 2,731,743 (3)
1990 census population (rank): 2,783,726 (3); **% change,** –7.4; **Male,** 1,334,705; **Female,** 1,449,021; **White,** 1,263,524; **Black,** 1,087,711 (39.1%); **American Indian,** Eskimo, or Aleut, 7,064 (0.3%); **Asian or Pacific Islander,** 104,118 (3.7%); **Other race,** 321,309; **Hispanic origin,** 545,852 (19.6%). **1990 percent population under 18:** 26.0%; **65 and over:** 11.9%; **median age:** 31.3.
Land area: 228.469 sq mi. (592 sq km); **Alt.:** Highest, 672 ft; lowest, 578.5
Avg. daily temp.: Jan., 21.4° F; July, 73.0° F
Churches: Protestant, 850; Roman Catholic, 252; Jewish, 51; **City-owned parks:** 552; **Radio stations:** AM, 15; FM, 24; **Television stations:** 14
CIVILIAN LABOR FORCE: 1,356,716; **Unemployed:** 124,195, **Percent:** 9.2; **Per capita personal income (PMSA) 1992:** $23,891
Chamber of Commerce: Chicagoland Chamber of Commerce, 200 N. LaSalle, Chicago, Ill. 60601

Chicago is the largest city in Illinois and the seat of Cook county. Built directly on a lake front, it stretches for 22 miles along the southwestern shore of Lake Michigan.

The first white men known to have visited Chicago were Joliet and Father Marquette in 1673. The first permanent white settler in the area was John Kinzie, sometimes called the father of Chicago, who took over a trading post in 1796 that had been established 1791 by Jean Baptiste Point Sable, a French-speaking black fur trapper. Fort Dearborn, a blockhouse and stockade, was built in 1804, but was evacuated in 1812, with more than half of its garrison massacred at what is now the foot of 18th Street. Not until 1830 was the town laid out. The name Chicago is thought to come from the Algonquian Indian word Chicagou meaning "strong" or "powerful." Some early Frenchmen believed that the name was derived from the Algonquian word for "onion place" because wild onions grew there.

Forty-one years later it was destroyed in the great Chicago fire of 1871. Chicago was incorporated as a village in 1833 and as a city in 1837.

Chicago is a major Great Lakes port and the commercial, financial, industrial, and cultural center of the Midwest. The manufacturing industries dominate the wholesale and retail trade, and trade in agricultural commodities is important to the economy. The Chicago Mercantile Exchange is the largest in the world.

Famous natives: Jack Benny, comedian; Edgar Rice Burroughs, author; Raymond Chandler, author; Hillary Rodham Clinton, lawyer, First Lady; Michael Crichton, author; Walt Disney, filmmaker; John Dos Passos, author; Bobby Fischer, chess player; Bob Fosse, choreographer, director; Benny Goodman, clarinetist; Dorothy Hamill, figure skater; Quincy Jones, composer; Gene Krupa, drummer; Dorothy Malone, actress; David Mamet, playwright; Bob Newhart, comedian; Kim Novak, actress; Donald O'Connor, actor; William L. Shirer, journalist, historian; Preston Sturges, film director; Gloria Swanson, actress; Melvin Van Peebles, playwright; Alfred Wallenstein, conductor; Robin Williams, comedian, actor; Robert Young, actor

CINCINNATI, OHIO

Mayor: Roxanne Qualls (to Nov. 1997)
City Manager: John F. Shirey
1994 est. population (rank): 358,170 (46)
1990 census population (rank): 364,040 (45); **% change,** –5.5; **Male,** 169,305; **Female,** 194,735; **White,** 220,285; **Black,** 138,1312 (37.9%); **American Indian, Eskimo, or Aleut,** 660 (0.2%); **Asian or Pacific Islander,** 4,030 (1.1%); **Other race,** 933; **Hispanic origin,** 2,386 (0.7%). **1990 percent population under 18:** 25.1%; **65 and over:** 13.9%; **median age:** 30.9.
Land area: 78.1 sq mi. (202 sq km); **Alt.:** Highest, 960 ft; lowest, 441

Avg. daily temp.: Jan., 30.3° F; July, 76.1° F
Churches: 850; **City-owned parks:** 96 (4,345 ac.); **Radio stations:** AM, 10; FM, 15 (Greater Cincinnati); **Television stations:** 8
CIVILIAN LABOR FORCE: 188,161; **Unemployed:** 14,318, **Percent:** 7.6; **Per capita personal income (PMSA) 1992:** $20,517[1]
Chamber of Commerce: Cincinnati Chamber of Commerce, 441 Vine St. Suite 300, Cincinnati, Ohio 45202
1. OH–KY–IN.

Cincinnati is the third largest city in Ohio and the seat of Hamilton county. It is located on the Ohio River.

Cincinnati began as part of the Miami Purchase of 1788. The first settlement, Columbia, was begun by Benjamin Stites that same year. The town of Losantiville was founded in 1788 on a plateau above the Ohio River by Mathias Denman, Robert Patterson, and Israel Ludlow. Its strategic location in the Western Territory led to the building of Ft. Washington, the most ambitious military establishment in the territory. The community of Losantiville that grew up around the fort was renamed Cincinnati in 1790 by Gen. Arthur St. Clair, Commander of Ft. Washington and first governor of the Northwest Territory, after the Revolutionary officers' Society of the Cincinnati, founded by George Washington. It was incorporated as a village in 1802 and chartered as a city in 1819.

The city began to flourish as a commercial hub with the arrival of the first steamboat in 1811, the completion of the Miami and Erie Canal in 1827, and the coming of the first railroad in 1843.

Cincinnati is a port of entry and more than 46 million tons pass through each year. The city has a diverse economy and is a major center for manufacturing, wholesaling, and retailing, as well as insurance and finance companies and health services. Prominent manufacturing groups include: transportation equipment, which includes aircraft engines and auto parts; food and kindred products; metal working; general industrial machinery; chemicals; fabricated metal products; printing and publishing.

Famous natives: Eddie Arcaro, jockey; Theda Bara, actress; Doris Day, actress; Jim Dine, painter; Suzanne Farrell, ballerina; Robert Henri, painter; James Levine, music director; Adolph Ochs, publisher; Tyrone Power, actor; William Procter, scientist; Roy Rogers, actor; Pete Rose, baseball player; Steven Spielberg, filmmaker; Roger Staubach, football player; Robert A. Taft, legislator; William Howard Taft, ex-president

CLEVELAND, OHIO

Mayor: Michael R. White (to Dec. 1997)
1994 est. population (rank): 492,901 (26)
1990 census population (rank): 505,616 (23); **% change,** –11.9; **Male,** 237,211; **Female,** 268,405; **White,** 250,234; **Black,** 235,405 (46.6%); **American Indian, Eskimo, or Aleut,** 1,562 (0.3%); **Asian or Pacific Islander,** 5,115 (1.0%); **Other race,** 13,300; **Hispanic origin,** 23,197 (4.6%). **1990 percent population under 18:** 26.9; **65 and over:** 14.0; **median age:** 31.9.
Land area: 79 sq mi. (205 sq km); **Alt.:** Highest, 1048 ft.; lowest, 573
Avg. daily temp.: Jan., 25.5° F; July, 71.6° F
Churches: [1] Protestant, 980; Roman Catholic, 187; Jewish, 31; Eastern Orthodox, 22; **City-owned parks:** 41 (1,930 ac.); **Radio stations:** AM, 15; FM, 17; **Television stations:** 7
CIVILIAN LABOR FORCE: 219,836; **Unemployed:** 27,583, **Percent:** 12.5; **Per capita personal income (PMSA) 1992:** $21,533[1]

Chamber of Commerce: Greater Cleveland Growth Association, 200 Tower City Center, Cleveland, Ohio 44113
1. Cleveland–Lorain–Elyria.

Cleveland is the second largest city in Ohio and the seat of Cuyahoga county. It is located in the northeastern part of the state on Lake Erie. In the Colonial era, the Cleveland area was known as the Connecticut Western Reserve, part of a land grant made to Connecticut by King Charles II in 1662. The city was founded in 1796 by Gen. Moses Cleaveland, who was the head surveyor of the Connecticut Land Company. This company had bought three million acres in what is now northern Ohio. A permanent settlement was founded in 1799, named after the General, and the spelling was shortened to Cleveland. The city was incorporated in 1836.

Cleveland's industrial growth was stimulated by the opening of the Ohio and Erie Canals in 1832 and, later, the advent of the Civil War with the corresponding demand for machinery, railroad equipment, ships, and other items.

The port of Cleveland is the largest overseas general cargo port on Lake Erie. Greater Cleveland has long been famous as a diversified durable goods manufacturing area. Following the national trend, Cleveland has been shifting to a more services-based economy. Greater Cleveland is a world corporate center for leading national and multinational companies in industries ranging from transportation, insurance, retailing, and utilities, to commercial banking and finance.

Famous natives: Jim Backus, actor; Dorothy Dandridge, actress; Ruby Dee, actress; Phil Donahue, talk show host; Joel Grey, actor; Arsenio Hall, talk show host; Margaret Hamilton, actress; Philip Johnson, architect; Henry Mancini, composer; Burgess Meredith, actor; Paul Newman, actor; Carl Stokes, judge; Andy Warhol, artist

COLUMBUS, OHIO

Mayor: Gregory S. Lashutka (to Jan. 1996)
1994 est. population (rank): 635,913 (16)
1990 census population (rank): 632,910 (16); **% change,** 12.0; **Male,** 305,574; **Female,** 327,336; **White,** 471,025; **Black,** 142,748 (22.6%); **American Indian, Eskimo, or Aleut,** 1,469 (0.2%); **Asian or Pacific Islander,** 14,993 (2.4%); **Other race,** 2,675; **Hispanic origin,** 6,741 (1.1%). **1990 percent population under 18:** 23.7; **65 and over:** 9.2; **median age:** 29.4.
Land area: 203.269 sq mi. (526.47 sq km); **Alt.:** Highest, 902 ft; lowest, 702
Avg. daily temp.: Jan., 27.1° F; July, 73.8° F
Churches: Protestant, 436; Roman Catholic, 62; Jewish, 5; Other, 8; **City-owned parks:** 203 (12,891 ac.); **Radio stations:** AM, 10; FM, 16; **Television stations:** 9 commercial, 3 PBS
CIVILIAN LABOR FORCE (1995): 554,733; **Unemployed:** 18,233, **Percent:** 3.3; **Per capita personal income:** $13,151
Chamber of Commerce: Columbus Area Chamber of Commerce, P.O. Box 1527, Columbus, Ohio 43216

Columbus, the largest city in Ohio, is the state capital and seat of Franklin county and is located in central Ohio on the Scioto River.

The first structures near downtown Columbus were earthen mounds constructed by Indian tribes known as the Mound Builders. The Indians lived alone

Central Ohio until the 1700s when the first explorers entered the Midwest. The first permanent settlement was founded by a surveyor from Kentucky, Lucas Sullivant, in 1797 and was named Franklinton. The site was laid out as the state capital in 1812 and named to honor Christopher Columbus and became the capital in 1816. Columbus was chartered as a city in 1834 and annexed Franklinton in 1870. The city's growth was stimulated by the development of transportation facilities—a feeder to the Ohio Canal completed in 1832, the National Road in 1833, and the arrival of the railroad in 1850.

Columbus is a port of entry and a major industrial, commercial, manufacturing, and cultural center. It is the seat of Ohio State University. The city has enjoyed steady growth over the years due to its economic diversity—there is no single activity that dominates the economy.

Famous natives: Warner Baxter, actor; George Bellows, painter; Michael Feinstein, singer, pianist; Eileen Heckart, actress; Jack Nicklaus, golfer; Tom Poston, actor; Eddie Rickenbacker, aviator; Arthur M. Schlesinger, historian; James Thurber, writer; Nancy Wilson, singer

DALLAS, TEX.

Mayor: Ron Kirk
City Manager: John Ware (apptd. Nov. 1993)
1994 est. population (rank): 1,022,830 (8)
1990 census population (rank): 1,006,877 (8); **% change,** 11.3; **Male,** 495,141; **Female,** 511,736; **White,** 556,760; **Black,** 296,994 (29.5%); **American Indian, Eskimo, or Aleut,** 4,792 (0.5%); **Asian or Pacific Islander,** 21,952 (2.2%); **Other race,** 126,379; **Hispanic origin,** 210,240 (20.9%). **1990 percent population under 18:** 25.0; **65 and over:** 9.7; **median age:** 30.6.
Land area: 378 sq mi. (979 sq km); **Alt.:** Highest, 750 ft; lowest, 375
Avg. daily temp.: Jan., 45.0° F; July, 86.3° F
Churches: 1,974 (in Dallas Co.); **City-owned parks:** 296 (47,025 ac.); **Radio stations:** AM, 19; FM, 30; **Television stations:** 10 commercial, 1 PBS
CIVILIAN LABOR FORCE: 570,661; **Unemployed:** 50,526, **Percent:** 8.9; **Per capita personal income (PMSA) 1992:** $22,424
Chamber of Commerce: Dallas Chamber of Commerce, 1201 Elm, Dallas, Tex. 75270

Dallas is the second largest city in Texas and is the seat of Dallas county. It is situated 185 miles northeast of Austin on the Trinity River near the junction of its three forks. It was first settled by Tennessee lawyer John Neely Bryan as a trading post on the Trinity River in 1841. Many historians believe that John Neely Bryan named the city after George Mifflin Dallas, vice president under James K. Polk, but there is no official agreement on this. It was incorporated as a town in 1856 and a city in 1871. The city developed as a cotton market in the 1870s and became the chief cotton producing region of Texas.

The economy is highly diversified and the city is the leading commercial, marketing, and industrial center of the southwest. The insurance business is important, and the service sector has experienced rapid growth. Dallas is also a popular tourist and convention city.

Famous natives: Tex Avery, animator, director; Robby Benson, actor; Ernie Banks, baseball player; Bebe Daniels, actress; Linda Darnell, actress; Lee Elder, golfer; Morgan Fairchild, actress; Trini Lopez, singer; Aaron Spelling, producer; Stephen Stills, singer; Sharon Tate, actress; Lee Trevino, golfer

DENVER, COLO.

Mayor: Wellington Webb (to July 1997)
1994 est. population (rank): 493,559 (25)
1990 census population (rank): 467,610 (26); **% change,** −5.1; **Male,** 227,517; **Female,** 240,093; **White,** 337,198; **Black,** 60,046 (12.8%); **American Indian, Eskimo, or Aleut,** 5,381 (1.2%); **Asian or Pacific Islander,** 11,005 (2.4%); **Other race,** 53,980; **Hispanic origin,** 107,382 (23.0%). **1990 percent population under 18:** 22.0; **65 and over:** 13.9; **median age:** 33.9
Land area: 154.63 sq mi. (400.5 sq km); **Alt.:** Highest, 5,494 ft; lowest, 5,140
Avg. daily temp.: Jan., 29.5° F; July, 73.3° F
Churches:[1] Protestant, 859; Roman Catholic, 60; Jewish, 13; **City-owned parks:** 205 (4,166 ac.); **City-owned mountain parks:** 40 (13,600 ac.); **Radio stations:** AM, 23; FM, 20[1] **Television stations:** 17[1]
CIVILIAN LABOR FORCE: 245,495[2]; **Unemployed:** 17,527[2]; **Percent:** 7.1[2]; **Per capita personal income (PMSA) 1992:** $22,930
Chamber of Commerce: Greater Denver Chamber of Commerce, 1445 Market Street, Denver, Colo. 80202
1. Metropolitan area. 2. Denver City/County.

Denver is the largest city and capital of Colorado, and the seat of Denver county. It lies at the foot of the Rocky Mountains and is situated at the junction of the South Platte River and Cherry Creek. The city was born in 1858 when gold was discovered in the sands of Cherry Creek, and it began as a tough village of cabins, shacks, and tents. It was incorporated as a city in 1861 and became the territorial capital in 1867. The city is named for James W. Denver, governor of the Kansas Territory which included part of Colorado. The city prospered from the famous gold and silver mines of the 1870s and the 1880s.

Denver International Airport, the first major new airport to be opened in the U.S. in 21 years, opened to passenger traffic on Feb. 28, 1995, at a cost of $4.9 billion. At 53 square miles, it is the largest airport in North America.

Denver is an important cultural, industrial, transportation, tourist, and marketing center. It is also a regional center for many federal government agencies and a leader in the development of western energy resources.

Denver's fastest growing industries include contract construction, real estate, retail trade, and federal government.

Famous natives: Tim Allen, comedian, actor; Ward Bond, actor; Douglas Fairbanks, Sr., actor; John Hart, newsman; Pat Hingle, actor; Ted Mack, TV host; Barbara Rush, actress; Alan K. Simpson, senator; Paul Whiteman, bandleader; Don Wilson, announcer

DETROIT, MICH.

Mayor: Dennis W. Archer
1994 est. population (rank): 992,038 (10)
1990 census population (rank): 1,027,974 (7); **% change,** −14.6; **Male,** 476,814; **Female,** 551,160; **White,** 222,316; **Black,** 777,916 (75.7%); **American Indian, Eskimo, or Aleut,** 3,655 (0.4%); **Asian or Pacific Islander,** 8,461 (0.8%); **Other race,** 15,626; **Hispanic origin,** 28,473 (2.8%). **1990 percent population under 18:** 29.4; **65 and over:** 12.2; **median age:** 30.8.
Land area: 143 sq mi. (370 sq km); **Alt.:** Highest, 685 ft; lowest, 574
Avg. daily temp.: Jan., 23.4° F; July, 71.9° F
Churches:[1] Protestant, 1,165; Roman Catholic, 89; Jewish, 2; **City-owned parks:** 56 parks (3,843 ac.); 393 sites (5,838 ac.); **Radio stations:** AM, 27; FM, 30 (includes 3 in Windsor, Ont.); **Television stations:** 8[2] (includes 1 in Windsor, Ont.)

CIVILIAN LABOR FORCE (1995): 393,083; **Unemployed:** 33,900, **Percent:** 8.9; **Per capita personal income:** $21,000
Chamber of Commerce: Greater Detroit Chamber of Commerce, 622 W. Lafayette, Detroit, Mich. 48226
1. Six-county metropolitan area. 2. Within four counties of Metro Detroit.

Detroit, the largest city in Michigan, is situated in the southeastern part of the state on the Detroit River. It is the seat of Wayne county. Detroit was incorporated as a city in 1815 and reincorporated in 1824.

Detroit is the oldest city of any size west of the seaboard colonies, having been founded by Antoine de la Mothe Cadillac on July 24, 1701, more than a century before Chicago was founded. The French were the first settlers and they gave the city its name from their word meaning "straight," referring to the 27-mile-long Detroit River which connects Lake Erie and Lake St. Clair. The river forms part of the international boundary, and marks the only point where Canada lies directly south of U.S. territory.

Because of its strategic location, Detroit was fought over by the French, the British, and the Indians. It was the headquarters for the British forces in the Northwest during the American Revolutionary War.

The first steam vessel, the *Walk-in-the-Water*, made its appearance on the Great Lakes in 1818, and Detroit was the western terminus for most of its voyages from Buffalo. Its link to all the important cities on the Great Lakes made it a major exporting port.

Detroit is one of the largest manufacturing cities in the U.S. and is the center of the automobile manufacturing industry, which has experienced a decline to foreign competition in the past decade. The health and medical care sector is important to the economy, and employment in the finance, insurance, and real estate industries has inched up in the Detroit metropolitan area since 1991.

Famous natives: Ralph Bunche, statesman; Francis Ford Coppola, director; Charles Lindbergh, aviator; Madonna, singer; John Mitchell; ex-U.S. attorney general; George Peppard, actor; Gilda Radner, comedian; Della Reese, singer; Sugar Ray Robinson, boxer; Diana Ross, singer; Tom Selleck, actor; Margaret Whiting, singer

EL PASO, TEX.

Mayor: Larry Francis
1994 est. population (rank): 579,307 (19)[2]
1990 census population (rank): 515,342 (22); **% change,** 21.2; **Male,** 247,163; **Female,** 268,179; **White,** 396,122; **Black,** 17,708 (3.4%); **American Indian, Eskimo, or Aleut,** 2,239 (0.4%); **Asian or Pacific Islander,** 5,956 (1.2%); **Other race,** 93,317; **Hispanic origin,** 355,669 (69.0%). **1990 percent population under 18:** 31.9; **65 and over:** 8.7; **median age:** 28.7
1995 population (est.): 652,225
Land area: 247.4 sq mi. (641 sq km); **Alt.:** 4,000 ft
Avg. daily temp.: Jan., 44.2° F; July, 82.5° F
Churches: Protestant, 320; Roman Catholic, 39; Jewish, 3; others, 20; **City-owned parks:** 116[1] (1,180 ac.); **Radio Stations:** AM, 18; FM, 17; **Television stations:** 6
CIVILIAN LABOR FORCE (1995): 285,100; **Unemployed:** 31,100, **Percent:** 10.9; **Per capita personal income:** $12,790
Chamber of Commerce: El Paso Chamber of Commerce and El Paso Hispanic Chamber of Commerce, 10 Civic Center Plaza, El Paso, Tex. 79944
1. Includes 109 developed and 7 undeveloped parks. 2. 1996 est. population: 583,421.

El Paso, the fourth largest city in Texas and the seat of El Paso county, is located in the far western part of the state on the north bank of the Rio Grande River opposite the Mexican city of Ciudad Juárez on the south bank.

In 1581, Spanish explorers came through the Pass of the North to test the missionary and mining possibilities of New Mexico. The area had been inhabited for centuries by various Indian groups. On April 30, 1598, Juan de Onate took formal possession of the area for King Philip II of Spain and subsequently crossed the Rio Grande river near a site west of the present downtown El Paso which he called "El Paso del Rio del Norte," meaning the crossing of the river—the first use of the name "El Paso." In 1659, the mission of Nuestra Senora de Guadalupe was founded on a site that is present-day downtown Ciudad Juárez; the mission is still in use today. In 1682, Spanish colonists from Mexico founded the settlement of Ysleta within the site of the present-day city. However, it wasn't until 1827 that the first permanent settlement at El Paso was established by Juan María Ponce de León. The city's real growth started with the arrival of the Southern Pacific Railroad in 1881. El Paso was incorporated as a city in 1873.

In 1888, Mexico changed the name of Paso del Norte to Ciudad Juárez in honor of Benito Juárez. Later in 1967, the United States agreed to cede a long disputed part of El Paso to Mexico due to changes in the course of the Rio Grande which form the international boundary between the two countries. El Paso and its sister city of Ciudad Juárez across the U.S./Mexico border are inexorably joined by culture and economy. El Paso and Juárez make up the largest international metroplex in the world.

El Paso is an important port of entry to the U.S. from Mexico. The apparel industry plays a major role in the El Paso area. The high technology, medical device manufacturing, plastics, refining, automotive food processing, and defense-related industries are important to the economy. El Paso's service sector has experienced the healthiest growth since 1983. El Paso is also a major tourist resort.

Famous natives: Manuel Acosta, artist; Don Bluth, animation director; Vicki Carr, singer; Sam Donaldson, newsman; Judith Ivey, actress; Guy Kibbee, actor; Sandra Day O'Connor, Supreme Court justice; Debbie Reynolds, actress; Irene Ryan, actress

FORT WORTH, TEX.

Mayor: Kenneth Barr (to May 1997)
City Manager: Bob Terrell
1994 est. population (rank): 451,814 (29)
1990 census population (rank): 447,619 (28); **% change,** 16.2; **Male,** 220,268; **Female,** 227,351; **White,** 285,549; **Black,** 98,532 (22.0%); **American Indian, Eskimo, or Aleut,** 1,914 (0.4%); **Asian or Pacific Islander,** 8,910 (2.0%); **Other race,** 52,714; **Hispanic origin,** 87,345 (19.5%). **1990 percent population under 18:** 26.6; **65 and over:** 11.2; **median age:** 30.3.
Land area: 295.301 sq mi. (765 sq km); **Alt.:** Highest, 780 ft; lowest, 520
Avg. daily temp.: Jan., 44.2° F; July, 82.5° F
Churches: 941, representing 72 denominations; **City-owned parks:** 171 (8,189 ac.; 3,500 ac. in Nature Center); **Radio stations:** AM, 5; FM, 20; **Television stations:** 15 (9 local)
CIVILIAN LABOR FORCE: 235,212; **Unemployed:** 21,653, **Percent:** 9.2; **Per capita personal income (MSA) 1992:** $20,250[1]
1. Fort Worth–Arlington.

Chamber of Commerce: Fort Worth Chamber of Commerce, 777 Taylor Street, Suit 900, Fort Worth, Tex. 76102

Fort Worth, seat of Tarrant county, is situated in the north central part of Texas on the Trinity River.

The city was founded by Major Ripley Arnold in 1849 as a military outpost on the Trinity River to protect settlers moving westward from frequent Indian attacks. It was named after Gen. William J. Worth, the commander of the Texas army. Fort Worth was incorporated in 1873. Its growth was stimulated in the 1870s by the proximity to the Chisholm cattle trail. It prospered as a meat packing and shipping center when the Texas and Pacific Railway arrived in 1876, and later experienced a new boom when oil was discovered nearby in 1917. The establishment of military installations in the area during both world wars also spurred the economy.

Ft. Worth has traditionally been a diverse center of manufacturing and is not dependent on the oil or financial sectors. The city's industries range from clothing and food products to jet fighters, helicopters, computers, pharmaceuticals, and plastics. Ft. Worth is a national leader in aviation products, electronic equipment, and refrigeration equipment. It is home to a multitude of major corporate headquarters, office, and distribution centers.

Famous natives: Robert Bass, financier; Kate Capshaw, actress; Sandra Heynie, golfer; Patricia Highsmith, writer; Spanky McFarland, actor; R. Bruce Merrifield, Nobelist in chemistry; Roger Miller, singer; Fess Parker, actor; Rex Reed, critic; Johnny Rutherford, auto racer; Liz Smith, columnist

FRESNO, CALIF.

Mayor: Jim Patterson (to May 1997)
City Manager: Michael A. Bierman
1994 est. population (rank): 386,551 (38)
1990 census population (rank): 354,202 (47); **% change,** 62.9; **Male,** 172,241; **Female,** 181,961; **White,** 209,604; **Black,** 29,409 (8.3%); **American Indian, Eskimo, or Aleut,** 3,729 (1.1%); **Asian or Pacific Islander,** 44,358 (12.5%); **Other race,** 67,102; **Hispanic origin,** 105,787 (29.9%). **1990 percent population under 18:** 31.7; **65 and over:** 10.1; **median age:** 28.4.
Land area: 99.38 sq mi. (257.39 sq km); **Alt.:** 328 ft
Avg. daily temp.: Jan., 45.5° F; July, 81.0° F
Churches: 450 (approximate); **City-owned parks:** 38 (690 ac.); **Radio stations:** AM 11[1]; FM 13[1]; Bilingual 1; **Television stations:** 8[1]
CIVILIAN LABOR FORCE: 174,496; **Unemployed:** 22,708, **Percent:** 13.0; **Per capita personal income (MSA) 1992:** $16,376
Chamber of Commerce: Fresno County and City Chamber of Commerce, P.O. Box 1469, 2331 Fresno St., Fresno, CA 93716
1. Metropolitan area.

Fresno is located in central California, 184 miles southeast of San Francisco and 222 miles northwest of Los Angeles. It is the seat of Fresno county and was incorporated as a city in 1885.

Fresno began as a station for the Central Pacific Railroad in 1872 and was made the seat of Fresno county in 1874. The city's name is Spanish for the ash trees that the early explorers found in the area.

Fresno is the world capital of the agri-business with 250 different crops produced by 7,500 farmers on 1.9 million irrigated acres, worth $3 billion a year. Fresno county's top five crops are grapes, cotton, tomatoes, cattle and calves, and turkeys. The city is also a trade, financial, media, and commercial center. Its diverse industries include agricultural chemicals, farm equipment, canned fruit and vegetables, clothing, computer software, electric wire, pumps, glass, and plastic products.

Famous natives: Mike Connors, actor; Maynard Dixon, painter; Bruce Furniss, swimmer; Jon Hall, actor; Daryle Lamonica, football player; Sam Peckinpah, director; William Saroyan, novelist; Tom Seaver, baseball player

HONOLULU, HAWAII

Mayor: Jeremy Harris (to Jan. 1997)
1994 est. population (rank): 385,881 (39)
1990 census population (rank): 377,059 (39)[1]; **% change,** 0.1; **Male,** 180,357; **Female,** 184,915; **White,** 97,527; **Black,** 4,821 (1.3%); **American Indian, Eskimo, or Aleut,** 1,126 (0.3%); **Asian or Pacific Islander,** 257,552 (70.5%); **Other race,** 4,246; **Hispanic origin,** 16,704 (4.6%). **1990 percent population under 18:** 19.1; **65 and over:** 16.0; **median age:** 36.9.
Land area: 600 sq mi. (1,554 sq km)[2]; **Alt.:** Highest, 4,025 ft; lowest, sea level
Avg. daily temp.: Jan., 72.6° F; July, 81° F
Churches: Roman Catholic, 34; Buddhist, 35; Jewish, 2; Protestant and others, 329; **City-owned parks:** 6,053 ac.; **Radio stations:** AM, 8; FM, 4; **Television stations:** 10
CIVILIAN LABOR FORCE (1994 avg.): 423,900[2]; **Unemployed:** 19,923[2], **Percent:** 4.7[2]; **Per capita personal income (1992):** $23,864
Chamber of Commerce: Chamber of Commerce of Hawaii, 1132 Bishop St., Suite 200, Honolulu, Hawaii 96813
1. City only. 2. City and county. The census bureau does not include the entire city and county in its census of Honolulu. If it did, the 1990 census and rank would be 836,231 (12).

Honolulu is the capital (on Oahu) and largest city in Hawaii. It is also the seat of Honolulu county. The city and county of Honolulu include the entire island of Oahu, the major island of the state of Hawaii. It is situated in the central Pacific Ocean 2,397 miles westsouthwest of San Francisco. Honolulu's name means "sheltered harbor" and derives from the native words hono meaning "a bay" and lulu meaning "sheltered."

Honolulu's early history was one of turbulence and conflict. One of the last areas on the globe to be discovered and exploited (visited by British Captain James Cook 1778), Hawaii was subject to strong pressures from many forces, including American missionaries who arrived in 1820, and opportunistic whalers. These whalers were among those who built Honolulu originally, bringing trade, commerce, and prosperity that led to expansion into the sugar and pineapple industries.

As early as 1814, Russia tried to move in and Russian soldiers built a bastion at the harbor's edge. The British flag was raised in 1843 and French forces occupied Honolulu in 1849. Each time control was given back to the independent kingdom without bloodshed. In 1898, a group of Americans completed a project attempted at intervals during the previous 65 years—annexation to the United States. Honolulu was incorporated as a city in 1907.

Honolulu was bombed by Japan in a surprise attack on the unprepared U.S. naval base at Pearl Harbor on Dec. 7, 1941. This action forced the United States to enter World War II and "Remember Pearl Harbor," became a famous American wartime slogan.

Hawaiian statehood in 1959 and the arrival of fast jet air travel to the island brought boom times to Honolulu. Tourism is the city's principal industry, followed by federal defense expenditures and agricultural exports (chiefly sugar and pineapples).

Famous natives: Hiram Bingham, explorer; Jean Erdman, dancer, choreographer; Hiram Fong, senator; Daniel Inouye, senator; Duke Kahanamoku, surfer, Olympian swimmer; Bette Midler, actress, singer; Kelly Preston, actress; Louise Morgan Sill, author; Don Stroud, actor; Merlin D. Tuttle, biologist, wildlife photographer

HOUSTON, TEX.

Mayor: Robert C. Lanier (to Dec. 1997)
1994 est. population (rank): 1,702,086 (4)
1990 census population (rank): 1,630,553 (4); **% change,** 2.2; **Male,** 809,048; **Female,** 821,505; **White,** 859,069; **Black,** 457,990 (28.1%); **American Indian, Eskimo, or Aleut,** 4,126 (0.3%); **Asian or Pacific Islander,** 67,113 (4.1%); **Other race,** 242,255; **Hispanic origin,** 450,483 (27.6%). **1990 percent population under 18:** 26.7; **65 and over:** 8.3; **median age:** 30.4.
Land area: 594.03 sq mi. (1,521 sq km); **Alt.:** Highest, 120 ft; lowest, sea level
Avg. daily temp.: Jan., 51.4° F; July, 83.1° F
Churches: 1,750[2]; **City-owned parks:** 307 (32,598 ac.); **Radio stations:** AM, 22; FM, 32[1]; **Television stations:** 13 commercial, 1 PBS
CIVILIAN LABOR FORCE: 979,931; **Unemployed:** 65,315, **Percent:** 6.7; **Per capita personal income (PMSA) 1992:** $21,737
Chamber of Commerce: Greater Houston Partnership, 1200 Smith, Suite 700, Houston, Tex. 77002
1. Includes annexations since 1970. 2. Harris County.

Houston, the largest city in Texas and seat of Harris county, is located in the southeastern part of the state near the Gulf of Mexico.

Sam Houston was the commander in chief of the Texas troops who fought a successful war of rebellion against the domination by Mexico, which had been in possession of Texas. On April 21, 1836, Houston's men won a decisive victory in which the Mexican dictator, Gen. Santa Anna, was taken prisoner, and signed the treaty which launched the Republic of Texas. In September, a constitution was ratified, and Houston was elected president. The Texas Republic was recognized by the U.S. and by the major European powers. The present city of Houston was incorporated in 1837 and named after Sam Houston. This was its first capital.

The port of Houston leads the U.S. in foreign tonnage handled. The city is a major business, financial, science, and technology center. Houston is outstanding in oil and natural gas production and is the energy capital of the world. It is the home of one of the largest medical facilities in the world—the Texas Medical Center—and the focus of the aerospace industry. The Lyndon B. Johnson Space Center is the nation's headquarters for manned spaceflight.

Famous natives: Debbie Allen, choreographer; Lance Alworth, football player; Denton Cooley, heart surgeon; Jim Demaret, golfer; Allen Drury, novelist; Shelly Duvall, actress; A.J. Foyt, auto racer; Howard Hughes, industrialist; Barbara C. Jordan, educator, lawyer, politician; Barbara Mandrell, singer; Annette O'Toole, actress; Dennis and Randy Quaid, actors; Kenny Rogers, singer; Patrick Swayze, actor, dancer

INDIANAPOLIS, IND.

Mayor: Stephen Goldsmith (to Dec. 31, 1999)
1994 est. population (rank): 752,279 (12)
1990 census population (rank)[2]: 731,311 (13); **% change,** 4.3; **Male,** 352,309; **Female,** 389,643; **White,** 564,447; **Black,** 166,031 (22.4%); **American Indian, Eskimo, or Aleut,** 1,580 (0.2%); **Asian or Pacific Islander,** 6,943 (0.9%); **Other race,** 2,951; **Hispanic origin,** 7,790

(1.0%). **1990 percent population under 18:** 25.6%; **65 and over:** 11.5; **median age:** 31.8.
Land area: 352 sq mi. (912 sq km); **Alt.:** Highest, 840 ft; lowest, 700
Avg. daily temp.: Jan., 26.0 F; July, 75.1° F
Churches: 1,200[1]; **City-owned parks:** 130 (9,375 ac.); **Radio stations:** AM, 8[3]; FM, 17[3]; **Television stations:** 7[1]
CIVILIAN LABOR FORCE: 441,780[1], **Unemployed:** 20,820[1] **Percent:** 4.7[1]; **Per capita personal income (MSA) 1992:** $20,992
Chamber of Commerce: Indianapolis Chamber of Commerce, 320 N Meridian St., Indianapolis, Ind. 46204
1. Marion County. 2. Consolidated city. 3. Metropolitan area.

Indianapolis, the largest city in Indiana and seat of Marion county, is located in the central part of the state on the West Fork of the White River. Its name derives from combining "Indiana" with "polis," the Greek word for city.

Indianapolis was settled in 1820 and, in 1825, its site was chosen as the state capital and it was incorporated as a city in 1832 and reincorporated in 1838. The city's growth began when the railroad reached it in 1847. Toward the end of the 19th century, the discovery of nearby natural gas and the start of the automobile industry hastened its industrial expansion. On Jan. 1, 1970, Indianapolis merged with the surrounding Marion county.

Indianapolis is an important center of a rich agricultural region and a major grain and livestock market. It is also a focal point of commerce, transportation, and manufacturing for the region. Some leading industries are electronics, pharmaceuticals, and food processing. The financial sector, and service and insurance industries are growing rapidly.

Indianapolis is the site of the world-famous 500-mile automobile race and the Indiana State Fair.

Famous natives: Monte Blue, actor; David Letterman, TV host; Steve McQueen, actor; Jane Pauley, TV newscaster; Booth Tarkington, author; Kurt Vonnegut, Jr., author; Harry Von Zell, announcer; Clifton Webb, actor

JACKSONVILLE, FLA.

Mayor: John Delaney (to June 30, 1999)
1994 est. population (rank): 665,070 (15)
1990 census population (rank)[1]: 681,126 (15); **% change,** 17.9; **Male,** 328,737; **Female,** 344,234; **White,** 489,604; **Black,** 163,902 (24.4%); **American Indian, Eskimo, or Aleut,** 1,904 (0.3%); **Asian or Pacific Islander,** 12,940 (1.9%); **Other race,** 4,621; **Hispanic origin,** 17,333 (2.6%). **1990 percent population under 18:** 25.9; **65 and over:** 10.7; **median age:** 31.5.
Land area: 759.6 sq mi. (1,967 sq km); **Alt.:** Highest, 71 ft; lowest, sea level
Avg. daily temp.: Jan., 53.2° F; July, 81.3° F
Churches: Protestant, 794; Roman Catholic, 21; Jewish, 5; others, 22; **City-owned parks and playgrounds:** 134 (1,522 ac.); **Radio stations:** AM, 14; FM, 16; **Television stations:** 6 commercial, 1 PBS, 1 religious
CIVILIAN LABOR FORCE: 328,211; **Unemployed:** 24,051, **Percent:** 7.3; **Per capita personal income (MSA) 1992:** $19,146
Chamber of Commerce: Jacksonville Area Chamber of Commerce, Jacksonville, Fla. 32202
1. Consolidated city.

Jacksonville, Florida's largest city, is located in Duval county in the northeast corner of Florida on the banks of the St. Johns River and adjacent to the Atlantic Ocean. It is the largest metropolitan area in northeast Florida and southeast Georgia.

Starting in the 16th century, French, Spanish, and English explorers and colonists were attracted to the region by the St. Johns River. The site was settled by Lewis Hogans in 1816. Jacksonville was laid out in 1822 and was named after Gen. Andrew Jackson, the first military governor of Florida. It was incorporated as a city in 1832.

During the Civil War, much of the city was destroyed by Union forces who occupied Jacksonville four times. The city was rebuilt and, following the development of its harbor and the railroads, fast became the transportation hub and leading industrial city in Florida by the 1880s. In 1968, Jacksonville annexed Duval county.

Jacksonville is the transportation hub and distribution focal point in the state. The strength of the city's economy lies in its broad diversification. The area's economy is balanced among distribution, financial services, biomedical, consumer goods, information services, manufacturing, and other industries. Jacksonville has the largest deepwater port in the South Atlantic and is the leading port in the U.S. for automobile imports.

Famous natives: Mae Axton, songwriter; Pat Boone, singer; Judy Canova, comedian; Harold Carmichael, football player; Merion C. Cooper, producer, director; Billy Daniels, vocalist; Storm Davis, athlete; Bob Hayes, athlete; Wanda Hendrix, actress; James Weldon Johnson, author, educator; John Rosamond Johnson, musician, composer; Mark McCumber, pro golfer; Ray Mercer, boxer; Charles "Hoss" Singleton, songwriter; Bill Terry, Baseball Hall of Fame; Donnie Van Zant, rock musician; Ronnie Van Zant, rock musician; Leeroy Yarbrough, auto racer

KANSAS CITY, MO.

Mayor: Emanuel Cleaver II (to April 1999)
City Manager: Larry J. Brown (apptd. Nov. 1993)
1994 est. population (rank): 443,878 (31)
1990 census population (rank): 434,829 (31); **% change:** −2.9; **Male,** 206,965; **Female,** 228,181; **White,** 290,572; **Black,** 128,768 (29.6%); **American Indian, Eskimo, or Aleut,** 2,144 (0.5%); **Asian or Pacific Islander,** 5,239 (1.2%); **Other race,** 8,423; **Hispanic origin,** 17,017 (3.9%). **1990 percent population under 18:** 24.8; **65 and over:** 12.9; **median age:** 32.8.
Land area: 317 sq mi. (821 sq km); **Alt.:** Highest, 1,014 ft; lowest, 722
Avg. daily temp.: Jan., 28.4° F; July, 80.9 F
Churches: 1,100 churches of all denominations[1];
City-owned parks and playgrounds: 189 (10,647 ac.); **Radio stations:** AM, 14; FM, 19[1]; **Television stations:** 7[1]
CIVILIAN LABOR FORCE: 239,600; **Unemployed:** 15,400, **Percent:** 6.4; **Per capita personal income (MSA) 1992:** $20,948[2]
Chamber of Commerce: Chamber of Commerce of Greater Kansas City, 911 Main St., Kansas City, Mo. 64105
1. Metropolitan area. 2. Kansas City, Mo.–Kan.

Kansas City is the largest city in Missouri. It is located in the western part of the state, at the junction of the Missouri and Kansas Rivers. Kansas City is located in Jackson, Clay, Platte, and Cass counties.

In 1821, the year Missouri entered the Union, French trader François Chouteau came from St. Louis to establish a trading post on the site of the present city to take advantage of the growing fur trade with the Kansa, Osage, Wyandotte, and other tribes. In 1833, a settlement was laid out by John Calvin McCoy and developed, called the town of Westport

Landing. The community became the Town of Kansas and was incorporated as a city in 1850 and renamed Kansas City in 1889. The city's name reflects its Native American heritage—its site was within the territory of the Kansa or Kaw Indians.

The city grew rapidly in the mid-1880s as the starting point for gold prospectors and settlers heading westward. The coming of the Missouri-Pacific railroad in 1865 and the spanning of the Missouri River by the Hannibal Bridge in 1869 also contributed to the city's growth, and it prospered as a center for the nation's cattle business.

The Kansas City metropolitan area once known primarily for agriculture and manufacturing, has expanded its economic base to include strong growth in areas of telecommunications, banking and finance, and the service industry. A transportation hub since the 1800s, the area enjoys a national and regional prominence as a distribution and manufacturing center. Kansas City ranks nationally as first in greeting card publishing, frozen food storage and distribution, and first in hard winter wheat marketing, second in wheat flour production, and third in auto and truck assembly. The area is one of ten federal regional centers and employs over 25,000 in local, state, and federal government. The city is also a regional center for health care, employing over 55,000 in this industry.

Famous natives: Robert Altman, director; Edward Asner, actor; Burt Bacharach, composer; Noah and Wallace Beery, actors; Robert Russell Bennett, composer; Jeanne Eagels, actress; Jean Harlow, actress; Ted Shawn, dancer, choreographer; Casey Stengel, baseball player; Virgil Thompson, composer; Tom Watson, golfer

LAS VEGAS, NEV.

Mayor: Jan Jones
1994 est. population (rank): 327,878 (49).[1]
1990 census population (rank): 358,295 (63); **% change,** 56.9; **Male,** 130,981; **Female,** 127,314; **White,** 202,549 (78.4%); **Black,** 29,529 (11.4%); **American Indian, Eskimo, or Aleut,** 2,282 (0.9%); **Asian or Pacific Islander,** 9,325 (3.6%); **Other race,** 14,610; **Hispanic origin,** 32,369 (12.5%); **1990 percent population under 18:** 25.0; **65 and over:** 10.3; **median age:** 32.5.
Land area: 83.3 sq mi. (1,215.7 sq km); **elevation:** 1,174 ft.
Max., Min. daily temp: Jan., 34–57° F; July, 76–106° F
Churches: over 500 churches and synagogues; **Radio stations:** AM 12, FM 21; **Television stations:** 7
CIVILIAN LABOR FORCE: (1990 census): 131,001; **Unemployed:** 19,043, **Percent:** 4.9; **Per capita personal income (MSA) 1992:** $19,994
Chamber of Commerce: 711 East Desert Inn Road, Las Vegas, Nev. 89109–2797

1. 1995 est. population: 371,809

Las Vegas, seat of Clark County in southeastern Nevada, is the largest city in the state and one of the fastest growing cities in the United States. Between April 1990 and July 1994, the Las Vegas metropolitan area population increased by 26%, growing from 852,646 to 1,076,267.

The area was discovered by Spanish explorers in 1829. The site of Las Vegas ("The Meadows" in Spanish) was originally a watering place for travelers on their way to southern California. It was first settled by Mormons in 1855, who were attracted by its artesian springs. They abandoned their settlement two years later in 1857 and the U.S. Army established Fort Baker there in 1864. In 1867, Las Vegas was detached from the Arizona Territory and joined Nevada.

The town was established in 1905 and started to grow with the arrival of the San Pedro, Los Angeles, and Salt Lake Railroad in 1905. However, its growth did not really begin until shortly after 1931, when the Nevada legislature legalized gambling in an effort to lift the state from the Great Depression. The construction of nearby Hoover Dam economically aided the area as well.

The Las Vegas that we know today basically began after World War II when the idea of large hotels along the brand new "Strip" was developed.

Las Vegas is the Marriage Capital of America. There are 50 wedding chapels in the city. Tourism and the convention industry is the city's major source of income. In addition, manufacturing, government, warehousing, and trucking are major sources of employment. Many high technology companies are also located there. Three of the reasons for that are the city's proximity to sophisticated military technology centers like Nellis Air Force Base, the top-secret Nuclear Testing Grounds, and the College of Engineering at the University of Nevada, Las Vegas.

Las Vegas has a favorable business climate: taxes are relatively low, and there are neither city nor state income taxes. This is because gambling and sales taxes, paid by tourists, have allowed the city and state governments to avoid personal and corporate income taxes.

Popular nearby tourist attractions are Hoover Dam and Lake Mead (largest man-made lake in U.S.), Lake Mojave, the Mt. Charleston Recreation Area, Red Rock Canyon, and the Death Valley National Monument.

Famous natives and residents: Andre Agassi, tennis player; Clara Bow, actress; Howard Hughes, industrialist and film producer; B.B. King, blues singer, guitarist; Jack Kramer, tennis player; Phyllis McGuire, singer; Benjamin Siegel, hotel-casino promoter; Orson Welles, actor, producer; Joe Williams, jazz singer.

LONG BEACH, CALIF.

Mayor: Beverly O'Neill (to April 1998)
City Manager: James C. Hankla
1994 est. population (rank): 433,852 (34)
1990 census population (rank): 429,433 (32); **% change,** 18.8; **Male,** 216,685; **Female,** 212,748; **White,** 250,716; **Black,** 58,761 (13.7%); **American Indian, Eskimo, or Aleut,** 2,781 (0.6%); **Asian or Pacific Islander,** 58,266 (13.6%); **Other race,** 58,909; **Hispanic origin,** 101,419 (23.6%). **1990 percent population under 18:** 25.5; **65 and over:** 10.8; **median age:** 30.0.
Land area: 49.8 sq mi. (129 sq km); **Alt.:** Highest, 170 ft; lowest, sea level
Avg. daily temp.: Jan., 55.2 F; July, 72.8° F
Churches: 236; **City-owned parks:** 48 (2,000 ac.); **Radio stations:** AM, 2; FM, 2; **Television stations:** 8 (metro area)
CIVILIAN LABOR FORCE: 201,900; **Unemployed:** 15,100, **Percent:** 7.5; **Per capita personal income (PMSA) 1992:** $21,434[1]
Chamber of Commerce: Long Beach Area Chamber of Commerce, One World Trade Center, Suite 350, Long Beach, CA 90831-0350
1. Los Angeles-Long Beach.

Long Beach is the fifth largest city in California and is situated on San Pedro Bay, south of Los Angeles, in Los Angeles county.

The town was laid out and settled in 1881 by developer W.E. Willmore who sold lots in the site as a seaside resort community called Willmore City. It was renamed Long Beach for its 8 1/2-mi. beach in 1884. The city was incorporated in 1888 and reincorporated in 1897. Long Beach is a major industrial port. The services

and manufacturing industries together account for over 50% of the local economy. Retail trade and government are the next largest sectors, accounting for an additional 30% of employment. Tourism is also important to the economy. Minor industries include transportation, communication and utilities, wholesale trade, finance, insurance, and real estate. Long Beach's economy has been adversely affected by cutbacks in the defense and aircraft production industries.

Famous natives: Jack Anderson, journalist; Jennifer Bartlett, artist; Barbara Britton, actress; Nicholas Cage, actor; Spike Jones, orchestra leader; Sally Kellerman, actress; Billie Jean King, tennis player; Martha Rae Watson, track; Heather Watts, dancer

LOS ANGELES, CALIF.

Mayor: Richard Riordan (to June 1997)
1994 est. population (rank): 3,448,613 (2)
1990 census population (rank): 3,485,398 (2); **% change,** 17.4; **Male,** 1,750,055; **Female,** 1,735,343; **White,** 1,841,182; **Black,** 487,674 (14.0%); **American Indian, Eskimo, or Aleut,** 16,379 (0.5%); **Asian or Pacific Islander,** 341,807 (9.8%); **Other race,** 798,356; **Hispanic origin,** 1,391,411 (39.9%). **1990 percent population under 18:** 24.8; **65 and over:** 10.0; **median age:** 30.7.
Land area: 467.4 sq mi. (1,210.57 sq km); **Alt.:** Highest, 5,081 ft; lowest, sea level
Avg. daily temp.: Jan., 57.2° F; July, 74.1° F
Churches: 2,000 of all denominations; **City-owned parks:** 355 (15,357 ac.); **Radio stations:** AM, 35; FM, 53; **Television stations:** 19
CIVILIAN LABOR FORCE: 1,827,505; **Unemployed:** 198,626, **Percent:** 10.9; **Per capita personal income (PMSA) 1992:** $21,434[1]
Chamber of Commerce: Los Angeles Chamber of Commerce, 404 S Bixel St., Los Angeles, Calif. 90017
1. Los Angeles-Long Beach.

Los Angeles is the largest city in California and the second largest urban area in the nation. It is located in the southern part of the state on the Pacific Ocean. It is the seat of Los Angeles county. Geographically, it extends more than 40 miles from the mountains to the sea.

The Spanish explorer, Gaspar de Portolá visited the site in 1769. On Sept. 4, 1781, the Mexican Provincial Governor, Filipe de Neve, founded "El Pueblo de Nuestra Señora la Reina de Los Angeles"—meaning "The Village of Our Lady, the Queen of the Angels." The pueblo became the capital of the Mexican province, Alta California, and it was the last place to surrender to the U.S. at the time of the American occupation in 1847. By the Treaty of Guadalupe Hidalgo in 1848, Mexico ceded California to the United States and Los Angeles was incorporated as a city in 1850.

The city's phenomenal growth was brought about primarily by its equable climate, which attracted people and industry from all parts of the nation; the development of its citrus-fruit industry; the discovery of oil in the area during the early 1890s; the development of its man-made harbor—its port is one of the busiest in the U.S.; and the growth of the motion picture industry in the early 20th century. Today, Hollywood is a suburb of Los Angeles.

Los Angeles is a major hub of shipping, manufacturing, industry, and finance, and is world renowned in the entertainment and communications fields. It is a favorite vacation destination and attracts millions of tourists to the area each year from all over the world.

Los Angeles county is the nation's largest manufacturing center, surpassing Chicago, New York, and Detroit. The ports of Los Angeles and Long Beach are second only to New York as the largest customs district in the United States.

Major employers in the Los Angeles Five-County area are in the business and management sector. Growth in the key wholesale industries—apparel and textiles, furniture, jewelry, and toys—and a boom in industrial trade have been forecast for the region. Other important sectors are health services and international trade and investment. The aerospace and technology industries have declined due to defense cutbacks but are still expected to be a viable part of the region's economy.

Famous natives: Busby Berkeley, choreographer, director; Marge Champion, dancer, choreographer; Jackie Coogan, actor; Jackie Cooper, actor; Linda Fratianne, figure skater; Jodie Foster, actress, director; John Gavin, actor, diplomat; Pancho Gonzalez, tennis player; Cynthia Gregory, ballerina; Jerome Hines, basso; Dustin Hoffman, actor; Theodore Harold Maiman, laser inventor; Marilyn Monroe, actress; Isamu Noguchi, sculptor; Leonard Slotkin, conductor; Duke Snider, baseball player; Adlai E. Stevenson, statesman; Madeleine Stowe, actress; Darryl Strawberry, baseball player

MEMPHIS, TENN.

Mayor: W.W. Herenton (to Dec. 1999)
1994 est. population (rank): 614,289 (18)
1990 census population (rank): 610,337 (18); **% change,** −5.6; **Male,** 285,010; **Female,** 325,327; **White,** 268,600; **Black,** 334,737 (54.8%); **American Indian, Eskimo, or Aleut,** 960 (0.2%); **Asian or Pacific Islander,** 4,805 (0.8%); **Other race,** 1,235; **Hispanic origin,** 4,455 (0.7%). **1990 percent population under 18:** 26.9; **65 and over:** 12.2; **median age:** 31.5.
Land area: 277 sq mi. (702 sq km); **Alt.:** Highest, 417 ft
Avg. daily temp.: Jan., 39.6° G; July, 82.1° F
Churches: 2000+; **Parks and playgrounds:** 230 (13,291 ac.); **Radio stations:** AM, 14; FM, 15; **Television stations:** 6
CIVILIAN LABOR FORCE: 292,819; **Unemployed:** 25,640, **Percent:** 8.8; **Per capita personal income (MSA)** 1992: $19,517
Chamber of Commerce: Memphis Area Chamber of Commerce, P.O. Box 224, Memphis, Tenn. 38103

Memphis, the largest city in Tennessee and the seat of Shelby county, is located in the southwestern corner of the state, on the Mississippi River.

The first settlers of Memphis were the Chickasaw Indians, who had a village named Chisca there on the bluffs overlooking the Mississippi River. Hernando DeSoto, in 1541, is said to have had his first glimpse of the Mississippi from the site of Memphis; and in the next century, Joliet and Marquette stopped there to trade with the Indians. The French explorer Sieur de La Salle tried to claim the region for France in 1682 and built Fort Prudhomme there. The area was ceded to the United States by the Chickasaw Indians in 1818. Memphis was officially established in 1819 by three enterprising businessmen from Nashville, James Winchester, John Overton, and future president Andrew Jackson. Jackson named it after the ancient Egyptian city because of its Nilelike site on the Mississippi River. Memphis was incorporated as a city in 1826 and became an important Mississippi River port.

During the Civil War, Memphis was a Confederate military center. In 1862, Federal forces won a gunboat battle on the river at Memphis and General Sherman was enabled to take the city.

Memphis's population was devastated by several yellow-fever epidemics during the 1870s and the city did not recover its prosperity until the end of the 19th century.

Memphis is one of the country's largest inland ports and is known as "America's Distribution Center" serving the northeast, southeast, and southwest regions of the country. Memphis is a leader in agribusiness, cultivating soybeans, rice, grain sorghum, winter wheat, corn, and livestock raising. The city is the world's largest trading center for spot cotton, handling over 40% of the nation's spot cotton crops annually. It is the largest hardwood lumber trading and processing center in the world and is estimated to be the nation's third largest total food processor.

Health care and related activities such as medical education and biomedical research is Memphis's largest industry bringing over $2.5 billion a year to the local economy. Also important are high tech communications.

Famous natives: Kathy Bates, actress; Dixie Carter, actress; Rosalind Cash, singer; Aretha Franklin, singer; Morgan Freeman, actor; Al Green, singer; George Hamilton, actor; Anfernee "Penny" Hardaway, basketball player; Isaac Hayes, singer; Hal Holbrook, actor; Benjamin Hooks, organization official; B.B. King, singer; Hal Needham, director; Charlie Rich, singer; Cybill Shepherd, actress; Robert Siodmak, director; Fred Smith, business executive; Rufus Thomas, singer; Kemmons Wilson, business executive

MIAMI, FLA.

Mayor: Joe Carollo (to Nov. 1997)
City manager: Cesar Odio (apptd. Dec. 1985)
1994 est. population (rank): 373,024 (42)
1990 census population (rank): 358,548 (46); **% change,** 3.4; **Male,** 173,223; **Female,** 185,325; **White,** 235,358; **Black,** 98,207 (27.4%); **American Indian, Eskimo, or Aleut,** 545 (0.2%); **Asian or Pacific Islander,** 2,272 (0.6%); **Other race,** 22,166; **Hispanic origin,** 223,964 (62.5%). **1990 percent population under 18:** 23.0; **65 and over,** 16.6; **median age,** 36.0.
Land area: 34.3 sq mi. (89 sq km); **Water area:** 19.5 sq mi.; **Alt.:** Average, 12 ft
Avg. daily temp.: Jan., 67.1° F; July, 82.4° F
Churches (Dade County): Protestant, 850; Roman Catholic, 61; Jewish, 64; **City-owned parks (Miami):** 109; **Radio stations (Dade County):** 29; **Television stations (Dade County):** 9 TV, 1 Cable
CIVILIAN LABOR FORCE: 181,684; **Unemployed:** 21,348, **Percent:** 11.8; **Per capita personal income (PMSA)** 1992: $17,124
Chamber of Commerce: Greater Miami Chamber of Commerce, 1601 Biscayne Blvd., Miami, Fla. 33132

Miami, the second largest city in Florida and seat of Dade county, is located in the southeastern part of the state, on Biscayne Bay.

The area was once the home of the Tequesta Indians until they were nearly wiped out by European diseases and warfare brought on by two centuries of Spanish control of Florida. Miami was founded in 1870 near the site of Ft. Dallas built in 1835 during the Seminole Indian wars. The city's name is probably derived from "Mayaimi," the Indian word for "big water."

Miami is the only U.S. city to have been conceived by a woman. Julia Tuttle, a Clevelander, arrived there in 1891 and bought several hundred acres on the bank of the Miami River. She convinced New York financier Henry M. Flagler of the area's vast potential and persuaded him to extend his Florida East Coast Railroad to Miami in 1896, the year the city was incorporated. Flagler dredged Miami harbor, built the renowned Royal Palm Hotel which opened Jan. 1, 1897, and promoted the area as a winter playground. Tourists flocked there and, by 1910, the city was a thriving recreational area. Miami survived the collapse of a land speculation boom in the 1920s and severe hurricanes in 1926 and 1935 and continued to grow in the aftermath of these disasters.

Miami experienced one of its most monumental population boosts during the 1960s when about 260,000 Cuban refugees arrived on its shore seeking freedom. They made a great impact on Miami, now a bilingual metropolis, and spurred economic growth.

Miami is an international banking and finance center and the city has the greatest concentration of international and Edge Act banks[1] in North America which constitute a major employment base. Greater Miami[2] has a highly diversified economy with over 170 multinational Miami-based companies, a bevy of Fortune 500 companies, and a rapidly growing manufacturing and distribution center. Miami ranks number one in Florida for total manufacturing income, employment, and number of manufacturing establishments. Greater Miami is the nation's leader in biomedical technology and the health care sector is a major industry. It is also part of an area known as the Computer Coast of Florida, and its growing technologies include computers, electrical engineering, and plastics manufacturing.

Miami is one of the world's leading year-round resort centers with tourism contributing over 60% of the area's economy. The city is a major transportation hub and the port of Miami is the world's largest cruise port and a major seaport for cargo. The famous island resort of Miami Beach, incorporated in 1915, is part of Greater Miami and is connected to Miami by four causeways.

1. Edge Act banks may make only foreign loans and accept foreign deposits. 2. Greater Miami is made up of 27 municipalities of which the City of Miami is the largest.

Famous natives: Fernando Bujones, dancer; Steve Carlton, baseball player; Debbie Harry, singer; Dick Howser, baseball player and manager; Sidney Poitier, actor; Janet Reno, Attorney General of the U.S.; Ben Vereen, actor; Ellen Zwilich, composer

MILWAUKEE, WIS.

Mayor: John O. Norquist (to April 2000)
1994 est. population (rank): 617,044 (17)
1990 census population (rank): 628,088 (17); **% change,** −1.3; **Male,** 296,837; **Female,** 331,251; **White,** 398,033; **Black,** 191,255 (30.5%); **American Indian, Eskimo, or Aleut,** 5,858 (0.9%); **Asian or Pacific Islander,** 11,817 (1.9%); **Other race,** 21,125; **Hispanic origin,** 39,409 (6.3%). **1990 percent population under 18:** 27.4; **65 and over:** 12.4; **median age:** 30.3.
Land area: 95.8 sq mi. (248 sq km); **Alt.:** 580.60 ft
Avg. daily temp.: Jan., 18.7° F; July, 70.5° F
Churches: 411; **County-owned parks:** 14,785 ac.; **Radio stations:** AM, 13; FM, 15; **Television stations:** 10
CIVILIAN LABOR FORCE (1995): 296,700; **Unemployed:** 14,900, **Percent:** 5.0; **Per capita personal income (PMSA) 1992:** $21,797
Chamber of Commerce: Metropolitan Milwaukee Association of Commerce, 828 N. Broadway, Milwaukee, Wis. 53202; Milwaukee Minority Chamber of Commerce, 2821 N. 4th St., Milwaukee, Wis. 53212; Hispanic Chamber of Commerce, 1125 W. National Ave., Milwaukee, Wis. 53204

Milwaukee, the largest city in Wisconsin and seat of Milwaukee county, is located in the southeastern part of the state on Lake Michigan.

French missionaries visited the site of Milwaukee in the seventeenth century, but it was not until 1795 that Jacques Vieau established a fur-trading post there. The first permanent white settler, Vieau's son-

in-law, Solomon Juneau, an agent of the American Fur Company, made his home there in 1818. The settlement merged with several neighboring villages in 1838 to form Milwaukee, and the city was incorporated in 1846. Its name is derived from an Algonquian Indian word Milo-aki meaning "beautiful land." A large wave of German immigrants arrived after 1848 and contributed greatly to the city's political, economic, and cultural development.

Milwaukee is one of the great industrial centers in the country and one of the largest Great Lakes ports. Currently, port commerce runs over 3.3 million tons per year.

Its economy was forged by heavy industries but is now diversified. Manufacturing remains strong and Milwaukee manufacturers are national leaders in lithographic commercial printing and the production of medical diagnostic instruments, small gasoline engines, malt beverages, iron and steel forgings, mining and construction machinery, robotics, speed changers and drives, and electronic controls. Milwaukee's high-tech manufacturing community is the ninth-largest among the nation's 31 major metropolitan areas. Once known as a "beer town," less than one percent of Milwaukee's workforce is involved in beer production. However, beer still plays an important role and almost 11% of the nation's malt beverage is produced there.

Tourism is important to the economy and about 5 million people visit Milwaukee every year.

Famous natives: Donald Gramm, bass-baritone; Woody Herman, band leader; Al Jarreau, singer; George F. Kennan, diplomat; Alfred Lunt, actor; Douglas MacArthur, army general; Pat O'Brien, actor; Tom Snyder, TV personality; Speech, member of rap group, "Arrested Development"; Spencer Tracy, actor; Gene Wilder, actor; Jerry and David Zucker, film producers.

MINNEAPOLIS, MINN.

Mayor: Sharon Sayles-Belton (to Jan. 1998)
1994 est. population (rank): 354,590 (47)
1990 census population (rank): 368,383 (43); **% change,** −0.7; **Male,** 178,671; **Female,** 189,712; **White,** 288,967; **Black,** 47,948 (13.0%); **American Indian, Eskimo, or Aleut,** 12,335 (3.3%); **Asian or Pacific Islander,** 15,723 (4.3%); **Other race,** 3,410; **Hispanic origin,** 7,900 (2.1%). **1990 percent population under 18:** 20.6; **65 and over:** 13.0; **median age:** 31.7
Land area: 58.7 sq mi. (143 sq km); **Alt.:** Highest, 945 ft; lowest, 695
Avg. daily temp.: Jan., 11.2° F; July, 73.1° F
Churches: 419; **City-owned parks:** 153; **Radio stations:** AM, 17; FM, 15 (metro area); **Television stations:** 6 (metro area)
CIVILIAN LABOR FORCE: 204,477; **Unemployed:** 9,905, **Percent:** 4.8; **Per capita personal income (MSA) 1992:** $23,284[1]
Chamber of Commerce: Greater Minneapolis Chamber of Commerce, Young Quinlan Building, 81 S. Ninth Street, Suite 200, Minneapolis, Minn. 55402-3223
1. Minneapolis-St. Paul Minn.–Wis.

Minneapolis, the largest city in Minnesota and seat of Hennepin county, is located in the southeast central part of the state on the Mississippi River. It is adjacent to its "twin city" of St. Paul. The Minneapolis-St. Paul Standard Metropolitan Statistical Area is the 15th largest in the United States.

In 1680, Father Louis Hennepin visited the future site of Minneapolis and gave the Falls of St. Anthony their name. Lieutenant Zebulon Pike made a treaty with the Sioux Indians in 1805–06 by which they ceded to the whites land including the Falls of St. Anthony and the site of Minneapolis. Fort Snelling was built in 1819–20 and, in 1823, the government built a lumber and flour mill. Flour milling became the major industry of early Minneapolis and made the city the milling capital of the world. The town of St. Anthony was established on the east bank of the Mississippi in 1848 and the town of Minneapolis grew up on the opposite bank of the river. The name Minneapolis is a combination of the Dakota Sioux word "minna" for water and the Greek word "polis" for city. Minneapolis was incorporated as a city in 1867 and, in 1872, the city of St. Anthony (chartered in 1860) was annexed to it. After the spread of the railroads in the 1870s, Minneapolis became the gateway to the Northern Great Plains.

Minneapolis is a center of industry and commerce serving a large agricultural region. During the 20th century, manufacturing, food processing, milling, computers, health services, and graphic arts developed as Minneapolis's major industries. Sixteen Fortune 500 industrial and 17 Fortune service companies are headquartered there. The city is the home of the world's largest cash grain market and is the headquarters of the Ninth Federal Reserve Bank.

Famous natives: La Verne, Maxene, Patti Andrews, singers; James Arness, actor; Lew Ayres, actor; Patty Berg, golfer; Virginia Bruce, actress; J. Paul Getty, oil executive; Peter Graves, actor; George Roy Hill, director; Cornell MacNeil, baritone; Ralph Meeker, actor; Westbrook Pegler, columnist; Prince, singer; Harrison Salisbury, journalist; Charles Schulz, cartoonist; Anne Tyler, writer; Bud Wilkinson, football player; David Winfield, baseball player

NASHVILLE-DAVIDSON, TENN.

Mayor: Philip N. Bredesen
1994 est. population (rank): 504,505 (24)
1990 census population (rank)[1]: 488,366 (25); **% change,** 6.9; **Male,** 242,492; **Female,** 268,292; **White,** 381,740; **Black,** 119,273 (23.4%); **American Indian, Eskimo, or Aleut,** 1,162 (0.2%); **Asian or Pacific Islander,** 7,081 (1.4%); **Other race,** 1,528; **Hispanic origin,** 4,775 (0.9%). **1900 percent population under 18:** 22.8; **65 and over:** 11.6; **median age:** 32.6.
Land area: 533 sq mi. (1,380 sq km); **Altitude:** Highest, 1,100 ft; lowest, approx. 400 ft
Avg. daily temp.: Jan., 36.7° F; July, 76.6° F
Churches: Protestant, 781; Roman Catholic, 18; Jewish, 3; **City-owned parks:** 76 (6,650 ac.); **Radio stations:** AM, 11; FM, 8; **Television stations:** 7
CIVILIAN LABOR FORCE (1995): 311,410; **Unemployed:** 9,480, **Percent:** 3.0; **Per capita personal income (1995):** $23,655
Chamber of Commerce: Nashville Area Chamber of Commerce, 161 Fourth Ave. North, Nashville, Tenn. 37219
1. Consolidated city.

The consolidated city of Nashville–Davidson is the capital and second largest city in Tennessee and is located in the north central part of the state on the Cumberland River. It is the seat of Davidson county.

During the winter of 1779–80, James Robertson and John Donelson founded a settlement at Big Salt Lick by the Cumberland River at the present site of the city. They built forts on both sides of the river naming one of them Fort Nashborough in honor of Francis Nash, a Revolutionary War general. In 1784, the town was named Nashville and was incorporated as a city in 1806.

Nashville became the capital of Tennessee in 1843 and was the seat of Davidson county until 1963 when it merged with the county to become Nashville–Davidson.

Nashville's best known industries are recording, publishing, and the distribution of music, especially country music. The city is a port of entry and an important industrial and commercial center serving the Upper South. Its diverse economy includes chemicals, apparel, publishing, insurance, and banking. Auto manufacturing and health care management are also important industries. Nashville is the home of several religious organizations and is a major tourist attraction and convention center.

Famous natives: Gregg Allman, singer; Rita Coolidge, singer; Al Gore, vice president; Red Grooms, artist; Barbara Howar, hostess, writer; Minnie Pearl, comedienne; Annie Potts, actress; Paula Robeson, flutist; Dinah Shore, actress, singer

NEW ORLEANS, LA.

Mayor: Marc H. Morial
1994 est. population (rank): 484,149 (27)
1990 census population (rank): 496,938 (24); **% change,** –10.9; **Male,** 230,883; **Female,** 266,055; **White,** 173,554; **Black,** 307,728 (61.9%); **American Indian, Eskimo, or Aleut,** 759 (0.2%); **Asian or Pacific Islander,** 9,678 (1.9%); **Other race,** 5,219; **Hispanic origin,** 17,238 (3.5%). **1990 percent population under 18:** 27.5; **65 and over,** 13.0; **median age,** 31.6.
Land area: 199.4 sq mi. (516 sq km); **Alt.:** Highest, 15 ft; lowest, –4
Avg. daily temp.: Jan., 52.4° F; July, 77° F
Churches: 712; **City-owned parks:** 165 (299 ac.); **Radio stations:** AM, 12; FM, 14; **Television stations:** 7
CIVILIAN LABOR FORCE: 205,610[1]; **Unemployed:** 15,055[1], **Percent:** 7.3[1]; **Per capita personal income (MSA) 1992:** $18,087
Chamber of Commerce: The Chamber/New Orleans and the River Region, 301 Camp Street, New Orleans, La. 70130
1. New Orleans City/Orleans Parish.

New Orleans, the largest city in Louisiana and seat of Orleans Parish, is located in the southeastern part of the state, between the Mississippi River and Lake Ponchartrain.

One of the few cities of the nation that has been under three flags, New Orleans has belonged to Spain, France, and the U.S. The French founded it in 1718 and named it in honor of the Duke of Orleans. In 1762, France ceded the city and the territory to Spain. In 1800, the territory was returned to France, but government authorities did not take over until 1803, only 20 days before the region became part of the U.S. in the Louisiana Purchase.

New Orleans is famous for its French Quarter, which attracts both tourists and gourmets. The Mardi Gras—a week of carnival held in New Orleans before the beginning of Lent—is the most spectacular festival in the U.S., and is a popular tourist attraction.

New Orleans is one of the world's greatest international ports, the second largest in the nation, and it is a major focus of the city's economy. New Orleans is home to the corporate offices of oil companies with major offshore operations in the Gulf of Mexico, as well as the distribution and service centers of offshore equipment suppliers and fabricators. The manufacturing industry is a significant part of the economy, with petroleum, petrochemical, shipbuilding, and aerospace industries all playing a role. The New Orleans region also functions as a mining, processing, and transportation center for other minerals, principally sulfur. Service industries are playing a larger role, with health care and telecommunications leading the way. The information services sector is one of the fastest-growing, and the New Orleans region is widely regarded as a leading center of medicine and health care in the South.

Tourism has grown rapidly in recent years and New Orleans hosts more than seven million visitors annually.

Famous natives: Louis Armstrong, musician; Truman Capote, author; Fats Domino, musician; Louis Gottschalk, pianist, composer; Bryant Gumbel, TV personality; Lillian Hellman, playwright, author; Al Hirt, musician; Mahalia Jackson, singer; Dorothy Lamour, actress; Wynton Marsalis, musician; Huey Newton, activist; Marguerite Piazza, soprano; Rusty Staub, baseball player; Ben Turpin, comedian; Shirley Verrett, mezzo-soprano; Carl Weathers, actor; Del Williams, football player

NEW YORK, N.Y.

Mayor: Rudolph W. Guiliani (to Dec. 1997)
Borough Presidents: Bronx, Fernando Ferrer; Brooklyn, Howard Golden; Manhattan, Ruth W. Messinger; Queens, Claire Shulman; Staten Island, Guy V. Molinari
1994 est. population (rank): 7,333,153 (1)
1990 census population (rank): 7,322,564 (1): **% change,** 3.5; **Male,** 3,437,687; **Female,** 3,884,877; **White,** 3,827,088; **Black,** 2,102,512 (28.7%); **American Indian, Eskimo, or Aleut,** 27,531 (0.4%); **Asian or Pacific Islander,** 512,719 (7.0%); **Other race,** 852,714; **Hispanic origin,** 1,783,511 (24.4%).[1] **1990 percent population under 18:** 23.0; **65 and over:** 13.0; **median age:** 33.7.
Land area: 321.8 sq mi. (826.68 sq km) (Queens, 112.1; Brooklyn, 81.8; Staten Island, 60.2; Bronx, 44.0 Manhattan, 23.7); **Alt.:** Highest, 410 ft; lowest, sea level
Avg. daily temp.: Jan., 31.8° F; July, 76.7° F
Churches: Protestant, 1,766; Jewish, 1,256; Roman Catholic, 437; Orthodox, 66; **City-owned parks:** 1,701 (26,369 ac.); **Radio stations:** AM, 13; FM, 18; **Television stations:** 6 commercial, 1 public
CIVILIAN LABOR FORCE: 3,311,000; **Unemployed:** 359,000, **Percent:** 10.8; **Per capita personal income (PMSA) 1992:** $27,039
Chamber of Commerce: New York Chamber of Commerce and Industry, 65 Liberty St., New York, N.Y. 10005
1. Race breakdown figures according to N.Y.C. Dept. of City Planning: White, non-Hispanic, 3,163,125; Black, non-Hispanic, 1,847,049; American Indian, Eskimo and Aleut, non-Hispanic, 17,871; Asian and Pacific Islander, non-Hispanic, 489,157; Hispanic, 1,783,511.

New York City is the largest city in the United States. It is located in the southern part of New York State, at the mouth of the Hudson River (also known as North River as it passes Manhattan Island).

In 1609, Henry Hudson, who worked for the Dutch East India Company, sailed up the river that now bears his name and went as far as Albany. Five years later, a permanent settlement was established at what is now New York, but it was originally called New Amsterdam by the Dutch governors. One of them, Peter Minuit, was said to have bought Manhattan Island from the Indians for $24 worth of beads, buttons, and trinkets. In 1664, Great Britain's Duke of York sent a fleet which quietly seized the settlement from the Dutch, without bloodshed, and rechristened the colony in honor of the Duke.

Control of New York passed to the young U.S. at the end of the Revolutionary War, and George Washington was inaugurated President in New York's old City Hall. Congress met in New York from 1785 to 1790.

In 1898, when Greater New York was chartered, the city expanded to include the following five boroughs which are also counties in New York State: Manhattan (New York county); Brooklyn (Kings county); Bronx (Bronx county); Queens (Queens county); and Staten Island (Richmond county).

There is a growing effort among Staten Island residents to separate from Greater New York and become an independent city of Staten Island.

Today, the Big Apple is the most populous city in the United States, a major world capital, and the world leader in finance, the arts, and communications. The city is also the center of advertising, fashion, publishing, and radio broadcasting in the United States. New York has innumerable museums, art galleries, and educational institutions. The port of New York is one of the finest in the world. The city is the home of the United Nations and is headquarters for some of the world's largest corporations.

Famous natives: Kareem Abdul-Jabbar, basketball player; Woody Allen, actor, director; Robert Anderson, playwright; Martina Arroyo, soprano; Jean Arthur, actress; Lauren Bacall, actress; James Baldwin, novelist; Harry Belafonte, singer, actor; Humphrey Bogart, actor; James Cagney, actor; Maria Callas, soprano; Paddy Chayefsky, playwright; Aaron Copland, composer; Sammy Davis, Jr., singer, actor; Agnes de Mille, choreographer; Robert De Niro, actor; Eamon De Valera, ex-president of Ireland; Gertrude Elion, Nobel Prize in medicine; Lou Gehrig, baseball player; George Gershwin, composer; Ira Gershwin, lyricist; Jackie Gleason, actor; Hank Greenberg, baseball player; Rita Hayworth, actress; Lena Horne, singer; Julia Ward Howe, poet, reformer; Washington Irving, author; Henry James, novelist; John Jay, statesman, jurist; Michael Jordan, basketball player; Jerome Kern, composer; Sandy Koufax, baseball player; Michael Landon, actor; Roy Lichtenstein, painter; Vince Lombardi, football player, coach; Chico, Groucho, Harpo, Zeppo Marx, comedians; Herman Melville, novelist; Yehudi Menuhin, violinist; Ethel Merman, singer, actress; James Michener, novelist; Arthur Miller, playwright; Eugene O'Neill, playwright; J. Robert Oppenheimer, nuclear physicist; Al Pacino, actor; Jan Peerce, tenor; Roberta Peters, soprano; Elmer Rice, playwright; Jerome Robbins, choreographer; Norman Rockwell, painter, illustrator; Eleanor Roosevelt, reformer, humanitarian; Theodore Roosevelt, ex-president; Jonas Salk, polio researcher; Beverly Sills, soprano; Neil Simon, playwright; Risë Stevens, mezzo-soprano; Barbra Streisand, singer, actress; Ed Sullivan, TV personality; Fats Waller, pianist; Mae West, actress; Edith Wharton, novelist; Rosalyn Yalow, Nobel Prize in medicine

OAKLAND, CALIF.

Mayor: Elihu Mason Harris (to Jan. 1998)
City Manager: Craig Kocian (apptd. July 1994)
1994 est. population (rank): 366,926 (44)
1990 census population (rank): 372,242 (40); **% change,** 9.7; **Male,** 178,824; **Female,** 193,418; **White,** 120,849; **Black,** 163,335 (43.9%); **American Indian, Eskimo, or Aleut,** 2,371 (0.6%); **Asian or Pacific Islander,** 54,931 (14.8%); **Other race,** 30,756; **Hispanic origin,** 51,711 (13.9%). **1990 percent population under 18,** 24.9; **65 and over,** 12.0; **median age:** 32.7.
Land area: 53.9 sq mi. (140 sq km); **Alt.:** Highest, 1,700 ft; lowest, sea level
Avg. daily temp.: Jan., 49.0° F; July, 63.7° F
Churches: 374, representing over 78 denominations in the City; over 500 churches in Alameda County; **City-owned parks:** 2,196 ac.; **Radio stations:** AM, 1; **Television stations:** 1 commercial
CIVILIAN LABOR FORCE: 180,624; **Unemployed:** 18,148, **Percent:** 10.0; **Per capita personal income (PMSA) 1992:** $24,359
Chamber of Commerce: Oakland Chamber of Commerce, 475 Fourteenth St., Oakland, Calif. 94612-1903

Oakland is located in the west central part of California on the east side of San Francisco Bay. It is the seat of Alameda county.

Don Luis Peralta first settled the site of Oakland in 1820 when he established the Rancho San Antonio. The gold rush of 1849 attracted more people to the area and the city's population continued to grow after a ferry service to San Francisco was started in 1851. Oakland was incorporated as a town in 1852 and as a city in 1854. It was named after the numerous oak trees found in the area. Oakland became the western terminus of the Central Pacific Railroad in 1869 and the seat of Alameda county in 1873.

During the latter part of the 19th century and also in 1910, additional territory was annexed to Oakland and the city assumed its present size. In 1906, thousands of people fled to Oakland in the aftermath of the San Francisco earthquake and settled there permanently, furthering the city's growth. Oakland's economic development continued to rise with the opening of the San Francisco–Oakland Bay Bridge in 1936.

Oakland is a major center of culture and commerce. It is an important container shipping port and the terminus of three transcontinental railroads. Oakland's industries include shipbuilding, food processing, chemicals, pharmaceuticals, electrical and high technology manufacturing. Oakland is also a leading importer of foreign cars. The city is the headquarters of many national and international corporations.

Famous natives: Buster Crabbe, actor; Frederick Cottrell, inventor; Dennis Eckersley, athlete; Hammer, singer, dancer, songwriter; Rod McKuen, singer, composer; Russ Meyer, producer, director; Eddie (Anderson) Rochester, actor; George Stevens, director; Amy Tan, writer; Jo Van Fleet, actress

OKLAHOMA CITY, OKLA.

Mayor: Ron Norick (to April 1998)
City Manager: Don Bown
1994 est. population (rank): 463,201 (29)
1990 census population (rank): 444,719 (29); **% change,** 10.1; **Male,** 214,466; **Female,** 230,253; **White,** 332,539; **Black,** 71,064 (16.0%); **American Indian, Eskimo, or Aleut,** 18,794 (4.2%); **Asian or Pacific Islander,** 10,491 (2.4%); **Other race,** 11,831; **Hispanic origin,** 22,033 (5.0%). **1990 percent population under 18:** 26.0; **65 and over:** 11.9; **median age:** 32.4.
Land area: 608.2 sq mi. (1,575 sq km); **Alt.:** Highest, 1,320 ft; lowest, 1,140
Avg. daily temp.: Jan., 35.9° F; July, 82.1° F
Churches: Roman Catholic, 25; Jewish, 2; Protestant and others, 741; **City-owned parks:** 138 (3,944 ac.); **Television stations:** 8; **Radio stations:** AM, 10; FM, 14
CIVILIAN LABOR FORCE: 230,226; **Unemployed:** 13,059, **Percent:** 5.7; **Per capita personal income (MSA) 1992:** $17,645
Chamber of Commerce: Oklahoma City Chamber of Commerce, 123 Park Ave., Oklahoma City, Okla. 73102

Oklahoma City, the state capital and seat of Oklahoma county, is the largest city in Oklahoma. It is located in the central part of the state on the North Canadian River.

Oklahoma City sprang into being almost overnight. On April 22, 1889, the government threw open the territory for settlement, and there was a classic rush across the line to stake claims. Within a short time, a prawling tent city sprang up near the Santa Fe railroad railroad tracks and Oklahoma City was a bustling town of 10,000. The city was incorporated in 1890 and replaced Guthrie as the state capital in 1910. Oil was discovered in the city in 1928 and petroleum production became a mainstay of the city's economy.

Oklahoma City is the wholesale and distributing center for the state, and the city's stockyards are the largest stocker and feeder cattle market in the world. Following the decline of the energy sector, Oklahoma City is fostering a private entrepreneurial environment and a more diversified economy. Within the service sector, health services are projected to grow, followed by retail trade and business services. Aerospace, distribution, and telecommunications have been targeted for business attraction. Nearby Tinker Air Force Base, one of the world's largest air depots, is a major city employer.

Famous natives: Johnny Bench, baseball; Lon Chaney, Jr., actor; Ralph Ellison, writer; Kay Francis, actress; Dale Robertson, actor; Ted Shackleford, actor; Pamela Tiffin, actress

OMAHA, NEB.

Mayor: Hal Daub (to June 1997)
1994 est. population (rank): 345,033 (48)
1990 census population (rank): 335,795 (48); **% change,** 7.0; **Male,** 160,392; **Female,** 175,403; **White,** 281,603; **Black,** 43,989 (13.1%); **American Indian, Eskimo, or Aleut,** 2,274 (0.7%); **Asian or Pacific Islander,** 3,412 (1.0%); **Other race,** 4,517; **Hispanic origin,** 10,288 (3.1%). **1990 percent population under 18:** 25.4; **65 and over:** 12.9; **median age:** 32.2.
Land area: 109 sq mi. (282.4 sq km); **Alt.:** Highest, 1,270 ft
Avg. daily temp.: Jan., 20.2° F; July, 77.7° F
Churches: Protestant, 246; Roman Catholic, 44; Jewish, 4; **City-owned parks:** 164 (over 7,400 ac.); **Radio stations:** AM, 7; FM, 13; **Television stations:** 4
CIVILIAN LABOR FORCE: 177,387; **Unemployed:** 8,298, **Percent:** 4.7; **Per capita personal income (MSA) 1992:** $20,242[1]
Chamber of Commerce: Omaha Chamber of Commerce, 1301 Harney St., Omaha, Neb. 68102
1. Omaha, Neb.–Iowa.

Omaha, the largest city in Nebraska and the seat of Douglas county, is located in the eastern part of the state on the west bank of the Missouri River opposite Council Bluffs, Iowa.

The area was visited by the Lewis and Clark expedition in 1804, and the U.S. Army built Ft. Atkinson nearby in 1819. Pierre Cabanne established a fur-trading post at the site in 1825. The first Mormon migrants wintered here in 1846–47 on their way to Utah. The city grew rapidly as the most northerly supply point for overland wagons to the Far West.

The city was officially founded in 1854 after the Nebraska Territory was opened for settlement. It was named for the Omaha Indians living nearby, whose tribal name means "those who go upstream or against the current." Omaha was incorporated as a city in 1857 and was the capital of the Nebraska Territory from 1855 to 1867. The city continued to thrive as a point of entry and a major transportation center when the Union Pacific trans-continental railroad arrived in 1869.

Omaha is a major market for food processing, telecommunications, and insurance. Other important industries include electrical equipment, finance, as well as printing and publishing.

Famous natives: Fred Astaire, dancer, actor; Max Baer, boxer; Ronald Boone, former NBA professional; Robert Boozer, former NBA professional; Marlon Brando, actor; Montgomery Clift, actor; Gerald Ford, ex-president; Bob Gibson, baseball player; Swoosie Kurtz, actress; Melvin Laird, ex-Secretary of Defense; Dorothy McGuire, actress; Nick Nolte, actor; Gale Sayers, football; Malcolm X, political activist; Paul Williams, singer, composer

PHILADELPHIA, PA.

Mayor: Edward G. Rendell (to June 2000)
1994 est. population (rank): 1,524,249 (5)
1990 census population (rank): 1,585,577 (5); % change, −6.1; **Male,** 737,763; **Female,** 847,814; **White,** 848,586; **Black,** 631,936 (39.9%); **American Indian, Eskimo, or Aleut,** 3,454 (0.2%); **Asian or Pacific Islander,** 43,522 (2.7%); **Other race,** 58,079; **Hispanic origin,** 89,193 (5.6%). **1990 percent population under 18:** 23.9; **65 and over:** 15.2; **median age:** 33.2.
Land area: 136 sq mi. (352 sq km); **Alt.:** Highest, 440 ft; lowest, sea level
Avg. daily temp.: Jan., 31.2° F; July, 76.5° F
Churches: Roman Catholic, 133; Jewish, 55; Protestant and others, 830; **City-owned parks:** 630 (10,252 ac.); **Radio stations:** AM, 40[1]; FM, 43[1]; **Television stations:** 14[1]
CIVILIAN LABOR FORCE: 699,391[1]; **Unemployed:** 61,403[1], **Percent:** 8.8[1]; **Per capita personal income (PMSA) 1992:** $23,397
Chamber of Commerce: Philadelphia Chamber of Commerce, 1234 Market Street, Suite 1800, Philadelphia, Pa. 19107

1. . Philadelphia City/County.

Philadelphia, the largest city in Pennsylvania and seat of Philadelphia county (coterminous), is located in the southeastern part of the state at the junction of the Schuylkill and Delaware Rivers.

Philadelphia, the "City of Brotherly Love," was settled in 1681 by Capt. William Markham, who, with a small band of colonists, was sent out by his cousin, William Penn. Penn arrived the following year.

In the period before the American Revolution, the city outstripped all others in the colonies in education, arts, science, industry, and commerce. In 1774–76, the First and Second Continental Congresses met in Philadelphia; and, from 1781–83, the city was the capital of the U.S. under the Articles of Confederation. In 1790, it became the nation's capital under the Constitution and remained so until the seat of the federal government moved to Washington in 1800.

Within a half-century of the founding of the nation at Independence Hall, Philadelphia had emerged as the "world's greatest workshop." The steam locomotives and hat factories of the 19th century have been replaced by diverse manufacturing specialties such as chemicals (including pharmaceuticals), medical devices, transportation equipment, and printing and publishing. In the services sector, Philadelphia is a major net "exporter" in subsectors such as health services, insurance carriers, legal services, and architecture and engineering services.

The city abounds in landmarks of early American history, including Independence Hall and the Liberty Bell.

Famous natives: Marian Anderson, contralto; John, Lionel, and Ethel Barrymore, actors; Wilt Chamberlain, basketball player; Bill Cosby, actor; Stuart Davis, painter; Thomas Eakins, painter, sculptor; W.C. Fields, comedian; Stan Getz, saxophonist; Grace (Kelly), Princess of Monaco; Walt Kelly, cartoonist; Jack Klugman, actor; Mario Lanza, singer, actor; George McClellan, general; Margaret Mead, anthropologist; Anna Quindlen, writer, Pulitzer Prize winner; Man Ray, painter; Betsy Ross, flagmaker; Jacqueline Susann, novelist; Robert Venturi, architect

PHOENIX, ARIZ.

Mayor: Skip Rimsza (to Oct. 1999)
City Manager: Frank Fairbanks (appt. May 1990)
1994 est. population (rank): 1,048,949 (7)[1]

1990 census population (rank): 983,403 (9); % change, 24.5; **Male,** 487,589; **Female,** 495,814; **White,** 803,332; **Black,** 51,053 (5.2%); **American Indian, Eskimo, or Aleut,** 18,225 (1.9%); **Asian or Pacific Islander,** 16,303 (1.7%); **Other race,** 94,490; **Hispanic origin,** 197,103 (20.0%). **1990 percent population under 18:** 27.2; **65 and over,** 9.7; **median age,** 31.1.
Land area: 456.702 sq mi. (1,182.85 sq km); **Alt.:** Highest, 2,740 ft.; lowest, 1,017
Avg. daily temp.: Jan., 53.6° F; July, 93.5° F
City-owned parks: 200 (30,412 ac.); **Radio stations:** AM, 20; FM, 20; **Television stations:** 9 commercial; 1 PBS
CIVILIAN LABOR FORCE: 618,497; **Unemployed:** 25,593, **Percent:** 4.1; **Per capita personal income (MSA) 1992:** $19,018
Chamber of Commerce: Phoenix Chamber of Commerce, 201 N. Central, Phoenix, Ariz. 85073

1. 1995 est. population: 1,071,045.

Phoenix, the capital of Arizona and seat of Maricopa county, is the largest city in the state. It is located in the center of Arizona on the Salt River.

The prehistoric Hohokam Indians first settled the area about 300 B.C. and dug a system of extensive irrigation canals for farming. The Indian culture mysteriously broke up in the 1400s. The site was permanently resettled again by Jack Swilling and "Lord Darrell" Duppa about 1867. Because the city was founded on the ruins of the ancient civilization, it was named Phoenix after the legendary Phoenix bird that could regenerate itself. The irrigation canals were restored for farming, and ranching and prospecting began in the surrounding area. The city quickly grew as an important trading center.

Phoenix was incorporated as a city in 1881 and was made the territorial capital in 1889. It became the state capital when Arizona was admitted to the Union in 1912.

Phoenix is a center of agriculture and commerce. Major industries include government, agricultural products, aerospace technology, electronics, air-conditioning, leather goods, and Indian arts and crafts. The city of Phoenix is renowned as a leader in local government management and received the 1993 Bertelsmann Foundation award for the best managed city in the world.

Famous natives: Lynda Carter, actress; Joan Ganz Cooney, TV executive; Alice Cooper, musician; Arthur A. Fletcher, government official; Barry Goldwater, politician; Stevie Nicks, musician; Charles S. Robb, politician; Mare Winningham, actress

PITTSBURGH, PA.

Mayor: Tom Murphy (to Jan. 1998)
1994 est. population (rank): 358,883 (45)
1990 census population (rank): 369,879 (40); % change, −12.8; **Male,** 171,722; **Female,** 198,157; **White,** 266,791; **Black,** 95,362 (25.8%); **American Indian, Eskimo, or Aleut,** 671 (0.2%); **Asian or Pacific Islander,** 5,937 (1.6%); **Other race,** 1,118; **Hispanic origin,** 3,468 (0.9%). **1990 percent population under 18:** 19.8; **65 and over,** 17.9; **median age:** 34.6.
Land area: 55.5 sq mi. (144 sq km); **Alt.:** Highest, 1,240 ft; lowest, 715
Avg. daily temp.: Jan., 26.7° F; July, 72.0° F
Churches: Protestant, 348; Roman Catholic, 86; Jewish, 28; Orthodox, 26; **City-owned parks and playgrounds:** 270 (2,572 ac.); **Radio stations:** AM, 12; FM, 20; **Television stations:** 8
CIVILIAN LABOR FORCE: 176,754; **Unemployed:** 11,613, **Percent:** 6.6; **Per capita personal income (MSA) 1992:** $21,175

Chamber of Commerce: The Chamber of Commerce of Greater Pittsburgh, 3 Gateway Center, Pittsburgh, Pa. 15222

Pittsburgh, the second largest city in Pennsylvania and seat of Allegheny county, is located in the southwestern part of the state at the junction where the Allegheny and Monongahela Rivers join to form the Ohio River.

Some of the first inhabitants of the area were the Shawnee, Seneca, Delaware, and Iroquois Indians who had left the area by 1754. That year a detachment of troops from Virginia put a fort on the site of present Pittsburgh (Ft. Prince George) considering it a strategic spot. Following the original Virginia settlers, the French seized the spot and named it Ft. Duquesne; and, in 1758, the British took it away from the French. The British built a new fort and named it after the British Prime Minister, William Pitt. A town developed around the fort and was incorporated as the City of Pittsburgh in 1816.

By the late 1800s, Pittsburgh had become a world leader in iron and steelmaking, and it remained so for nearly a century. In the early 1980s, the country's domestic steel industry collapsed causing major upheavals in Pittsburgh's manufacturing sector.

The Pittsburgh region underwent a successful diversified economic transition, shifting from heavy industries to light manufacturing, advanced technologies such as industrial automation, advanced materials, software engineering and biomedical technology, medicine, education, finance, and corporate services. Pittsburgh is a national leader in health care services and is the world's leading center for organ transplantation. The city is a hub of international business and ranks fifth as a major corporate headquarters center.

Pittsburgh is also a major U.S. transportation center and is the nation's largest inland port in terms of tonnage.

Famous natives: Rachel Carson, ecologist; Henry Steele Commager, historian; Bill Cullen, radio and TV entertainer; John Davidson, singer, actor; Billy Eckstine, singer; Erroll Garner, jazz pianist; Scott Glenn, actor; Martha Graham, dancer, choreographer; George S. Kaufman, playwright; Michael Keaton, actor; Gene Kelly, actor, dancer; Oscar Levant, pianist; Andrew Mellon, financier; Adolphe Menjou, actor; William Powell, actor; Mary Roberts Rinehart, novelist; Peter Sellars, theater director; David O. Selznick, producer; Joseph Wambaugh, novelist; August Wilson, playwright

PORTLAND, ORE.

Mayor: Vera Katz (to Jan. 1997)
1994 est. population (rank): 450,777 (30)
1990 census population (rank): 437,319 (30); **% change,** 18.8; **Male,** 211,914; **Female,** 225,405; **White,** 370,135; **Black,** 33,530 (7.7%); **American Indian, Eskimo, or Aleut,** 5,399 (1.2%); **Asian or Pacific Islander,** 23,185 (5.3%); **Other race,** 5,070; **Hispanic origin,** 13,874 (3.2%). **1990 percent population under 18:** 21.9; **65 and over,** 14.6; median age: 34.5.
Land area: 137.8 sq mi. (357 sq km.); **Alt.:** Highest, 1073 ft; lowest, sea level
Avg. daily temp.: Jan., 38.9° F; July, 67.7° F
Churches: Protestant, 450; Roman Catholic, 48; Jewish, 9; Buddhist, 6; other, 190; **City-owned parks:** 200 (over 9,400 ac.); **Radio stations:** AM: 14, FM: 14; **Television stations:** 5 commercial, 1 public
CIVILIAN LABOR FORCE: 248,724; **Unemployed:** 18,372, **Percent:** 7.4; **Per capita personal income (PMSA) 1992:** $20,681
Chamber of Commerce: Portland Chamber of Commerce, 221 NW 2nd Ave., Portland, Ore. 97209

Portland, the largest city in Oregon and seat of Multnomah county, is located in the northwestern part of the state on the Willamette River.

Lewis and Clark camped at the site of Portland in 1805 on their expedition across the continent. Portland was founded in 1845 and was almost called Boston after the city in Massachusetts. Its two founders, Amos Lovejoy from Massachusetts and Francis Pettygrove from Maine, flipped a coin to decide the name of the new town. Pettygrove won the toss and named the place Portland after his hometown in Maine. Portland was incorporated as a city in 1851.

Portland's growth was stimulated during the 1850s as a supply base for the California gold rush, the development of its salmon and lumber industries, and by the arrival of the railroad in 1883. The city continued to grow during 1879 to 1900 as a supply point for the Alaska gold rush and as the site of the Lewis and Clark Centennial Exposition in 1905.

The port of Portland leads the west in grain exports and is among the top five auto import centers in the United States. The port ranks third in overall volume behind Los Angeles and Long Beach.

Portland has a diverse economy with a broad base of manufacturing, distribution, wholesale and retail trade, regional government, and business services. Major manufacturing industries include machinery, electronics, metals, transportation equipment, and lumber and wood products. High technology is a thriving part of Portland's economy with over 500 high tech companies located in the metropolitan area. Tourism is also important to Portland's economy.

Famous natives: James Beard, food expert; Pietro Belluschi, architect; Richard Fosbury, high jumper; Matt Groening, cartoonist; Margaux Hemingway, actress; Phil Knight, founder of Nike; Terrance Knox, actor; Jeff Lorber, jazz musician; Linus Pauling, chemist; Jane Powell, singer, actress; Ahmad Rashad, football player, sportscaster; Susan Ruttan, actress; Pat Schroeder, congressperson; Doc Severinson, band leader; Norton Simon, business executive; Sally Ann Struthers, actress; Gus Van Sant, film director; Lindsay Wagner, actress; Mitch Williams, baseball pitcher

SACRAMENTO, CALIF.

Mayor: Joe Serna, Jr. (to March 2000)
1994 est. population (rank): 373,964 (41)[1]
1990 census population (rank): 369,365 (42); **% change,** 34.0; **Male,** 178,737; **Female,** 190,628; **White,** 221,963; **Black,** 56,521 (15.3%); **American Indian, Eskimo, or Aleut,** 4,561 (1.2%); **Asian or Pacific Islander,** 55,426 (15.0%); **Other race,** 30,894; **Hispanic origin,** 60,007 (16.2%). **1990 percent population under 18:** 26.2; **65 and over,** 12.1; median age: 31.8.
Land area: 98 sq mi. (254 sq km);
Avg. daily temp.: Jan., 47.1° F; July, 76.6° F
City park & recreational facilities: 134+ (1,427+ ac.); **Television stations:** 7
CIVILIAN LABOR FORCE: 185,283 (1994); **Unemployed:** 16,418, **Percent:** 7.7; **Per capita personal income: (PMSA) 1992** $20,398
Chamber of Commerce: Sacramento Chamber of Commerce, 917 7th St., Sacramento, Calif. 95814; West Sacramento Chamber of Commerce, 834-C Jefferson Blvd., Sacramento, Calif. 95691

1. 1995 est. population: 396,032

Sacramento is the capital and seventh largest city in California and is the seat of Sacramento county. It is located in the north central part of the state at the confluence of the Sacramento and American Rivers.

In 1839, German-born Swiss citizen John Augustus Sutter obtained a grant from the Mexican governor to establish a colony for fellow Swiss emigrants on a large tract of land in the vicinity which he named New Helvetia (New Switzerland) and established Fort Sutter there as a trading post.

After gold was discovered on Sutter's property in 1848, the settlement rapidly expanded as the prominent supply point for gold prospectors coming from the East. Sacramento was laid out in 1848 and named after the principal river in California which ran beside it. The river's name in Spanish honors the Holy Sacrament. It became incorporated as a city in 1849 and was made the state capital in 1854. Sacramento was the terminus of the first railroad in 1856 and the western terminus of the Pony Express in 1860.

The city has always been a hub of river transportation and is a major deep-water port connected to the Pacific Ocean. Sacramento's economy is highly diversified and, along with state government and military installations, its industries include aerospace, high technology, furniture, chemicals, pharmaceuticals, meat packing, and food processing of crops from the Central Valley.

The defense sector of the economy declined and Mather Air Force Base and the Army Depot were closed in 1995.

Famous natives: Joan Didion, author; Mark Goodson, TV producer; Tom Hanks, actor; Henry Hathaway, director; Anthony M. Kennedy, Supreme Court justice; Molly Ringwald, actress

ST. LOUIS, MO.

Mayor: Freeman Bosley, Jr. (to April 1997)
1994 est. population (rank): 368,215 (43)
1990 census population (rank): 396,685 (34); % change, –12.4; **Male,** 180,680; **Female,** 216,005; **White,** 202,085; **Black,** 188,408 (47.5%); **American Indian, Eskimo, or Aleut,** 950 (0.2%); **Asian or Pacific Islander,** 3,733 (0.9%); **Other race,** 1,509; **Hispanic origin,** 5,124 (1.3%). **1990 percent population under 18:** 25.2; **65 and over:** 16.6; median age: 32.8.
Land area: 61.4 sq mi. (159 sq km); **Alt.:** Highest, 616 ft; lowest, 413
Avg. daily temp.: Jan., 28.8° F; July, 78.9° F
Churches: 900[1]; **City-owned parks:** 89 (2,639 ac.); **Radio stations:** AM, 21; FM 27[1]; **Television stations:** 6 commercial; 1 PBS
CIVILIAN LABOR FORCE: 179,278; **Unemployed:** 14,379, **Percent:** 8.0; **Per capita personal income (MSA) 1992:** $22,700[2]
Chamber of Commerce: St. Louis Regional Commerce and Growth Association, 100 S. Fourth St., Ste. 500, St. Louis, Mo. 63102

1. Metropolitan area. 2. St. Louis, Mo.–Ill.

St. Louis, the second largest city in Missouri, is located in the east central part of the state on the Mississippi River. The city is independent and is in no county.

St. Louis was founded by the French in 1764 when Auguste Chouteau established a fur-trading post and Pierre Laclède Liguest, a New Orleans merchant, founded a town in February 1764 at the present site. They named it after King Louis XV of France and his patron saint, Louis IX. From 1770 to 1803, St. Louis was a Spanish possession and retroceded to France in 1803 in accordance with the Treaty of San Ildefonso (1800), only to be acquired by the U.S. as part of the Louisiana purchase that year.

The town was incorporated in 1809. From 1812 to 1821, St. Louis was the capital of the Missouri Territory and was incorporated as a city in 1822.

John Jacob Astor opened the Western branch of the American Fur Company in 1819 and the city prospered during the early part of the 19th century as a center for the transportation of the fur trade. St. Louis's commercial growth continued as a major transportation hub with the development of steamboat traffic and the later expansion of the railroads in the 1850s. The world-famous Louisiana Purchase Exposition was held here in 1904.

Manufacturing is important to the city's economy, and its highly developed industries include automobiles, aircraft and space technology, metal fabrication, beer, steelmaking, chemicals, food processing, and storage and distribution.

The giant stainless steel Gateway Arch, 630 feet high, standing on the banks of the Mississippi symbolizes St. Louis as the Gateway to the West.

Famous natives: Josephine Baker, singer; Yogi Berra, baseball player; Grace Bumbry, mezzo-soprano; Morris Carnovsky, actor; T.S. Eliot, poet; Eugene Field, poet; Redd Foxx, comedian; Joe Garagiola, baseball player; John Goodman, actor; Betty Grable, actress; Dick Gregory, comedian; Al Hirschfeld, cartoonist; Kevin Kline, actor; David Merrick, producer; Vincent Price, actor; Judy Rankin, golfer; Leon Spinks, boxer; Herbert Bayard Swope, journalist; Sara Teasdale, poet; Helen Traubel, soprano; Roy Wilkins, civil rights leader

SAN ANTONIO, TEX.

Mayor: William E. Thornton (to May 1997)
City Manager: Alexander E. Briseno (apptd. April 27, 1990)
1994 est. population (rank): 998,905 (9)
1990 census population (rank): 935,933 (10); % change, 19.1; **Male,** 450,695; **Female,** 485,238; **White,** 676,082; **Black,** 65,884 (7.0%); **American Indian, Eskimo, or Aleut,** 3,303 (0.4%); **Asian or Pacific Islander,** 10,703 (1.1%); **Other race,** 179,961; **Hispanic origin,** 520,282 (55.6%). **1990 percent population under 18:** 29.0; **65 and over:** 10.5; median age: 29.8.
Land area: 360 sq mi. (933.4 sq km); **Alt.:** 700 ft
Avg. daily temp.: Jan., 51.2° F; July, 86.1° F
City-owned parks: 6,717 ac.; **Radio stations:** AM, 20; FM, 22; **Television stations:** 9
CIVILIAN LABOR FORCE: 695,110; **Unemployed:** 32,177, **Percent:** 4.6; **Per capita personal income (MSA) 1992:** $17,282
Chamber of Commerce: Greater San Antonio Chamber of Commerce, P.O. Box 1628, 602 E Commerce, San Antonio, Tex. 78296

San Antonio, the third largest city in Texas and seat of Bexar county, is located in the south central part of the state, on the San Antonio River.

The site of San Antonio was first visited in 1691 by a Franciscan friar on the feast day of St. Anthony and was named San Antonio de Padua in his honor. San Antonio was permanently settled on May 1, 1718, when the Spanish governor of Coahuila and Texas, Martin de Alarcón, founded the presidio (a fort) of San Antonio de Bejar (Bexar) and the mission of San Antonio de Valero (later called the Alamo[1]) on the site of a Coahuiltecan Indian village. San Antonio remained almost continuously under Spanish rule until 1812 when Mexico won its independence from Spain.

During the outbreak of the Texas revolution (1835) against the tyranny of Mexican dictator General Santa Anna, San Antonio was captured by a small band of rebels who occupied the fortified mission of the Alamo in December 1835. The historic battle of the Alamo was fought there (Feb. 24 to March 6, 1836) an its 183 besieged defenders were massacred by Santa Anna's troops. Their heroism aroused the anger and fighting spirit of Texans to shout their famous battle cry "Remember the Alamo!" and defeat the Mexicans six weeks later (April 21, 1836) at the battle of San Jacinto. Texas became an independent republic in 1836 and San Antonio was incorporated as a city on Jan. 5, 1837.

After the Civil War, San Antonio prospered as a major shipping point for cattle with the arrival of the railroad in 1877. The city has been an important military center since World War II and is the home to five of the largest military installations in the nation, including Fort Sam Houston constructed in 1876. San Antonio is a leading livestock center and one of the largest produce exchange markets. The city's industries are highly diversified and tourism is important to the economy.

1. Spanish for the cottonwood tree.

Famous natives: Carol Burnett, comedienne; Cody Carlson, football player; Henry G. Cisneros, Secretary HUD; Joan Crawford, actress; Cito Gaston, baseball manager; Ann Harding, actress; Jesse James Leija, boxer; Emilio Navaira, Tejano music singer; Oliver North, military officer, government official; Suzy Parker, model, actress; Paula Prentiss, actress; Kyle Rote, football player; David R. Scott, astronaut; John Silber, university president; Patsy Torres, Tejano music singer; Edward H. White, astronaut

SAN DIEGO, CALIF.

Mayor: Susan Golding (to Dec. 2000)
City Manager: Jack McGrory (apptd. April 1991)
1994 est. population (rank): 1,151,977 (6)[1]
1990 census population (rank): 1,110,549 (6); **% change,** 26.8; **Male,** 566,464; **Female,** 544,085; **White,** 745,406; **Black,** 104,261 (9.4%); **American Indian, Eskimo, or Aleut,** 6,800 (0.6%); **Asian or Pacific Islander,** 130,945 (11.8%); **Other race,** 123,137; **Hispanic origin,** 229,519 (20.7%). **1990 percent population under 18:** 23.1; **65 and over:** 10.2; **median age:** 30.5.
Land area: 330.7 sq miles (857 sq km); **Alt.:** Highest, 1,591 ft; lowest, sea level
Avg. daily temp.: Jan., 56.8° F; July, 70.3° F
Churches: Roman Catholic, 39; Jewish, 9; Protestant, 334; Eastern Orthodox, 8; other, 18; **City park and recreation facilities:** 164 (17,207 ac.); **Radio stations:** AM, 8; FM, 18; **Television stations:** 9
CIVILIAN LABOR FORCE: 548,687; **Unemployed:** 41,301, **Percent:** 7.5; **Per capita personal income (MSA) 1992:** $20,384

Chamber of Commerce: San Diego Chamber of Commerce, 402 West Broadway, Suite 1000, San Diego, Calif. 92101

1. 1995 population (Jan. 95): 1,197,676

San Diego is the second largest city in California. It is located in the southwestern part of the state, on San Diego Bay.

Portuguese navigator Juan Rodríguez Cabrillo discovered the bay in 1542 and claimed the area for Spain. The site was named San Miguel by Cabrillo. On Nov. 12, 1602, Don Sebastian de Viscaíno came ashore with his party on the day of St. Didacus (San Diego in Spanish) and celebrated a mass in the saint's honor. By coincidence, Viscaíno's flagship was named *San Diego.* He renamed the place San Diego after the 15th century saint.

In 1769, Franciscan Father Junípero Serra established the first California mission there—San Diego del Alcala. In 1822, Mexico won control of the town after it declared its independence from Spain. In 1846, during the Mexican War, San Diego was seized by the

United States and incorporated into a city in 1850 after California joined the Union that same year.

Today, San Diego's excellent natural harbor is a busy commercial port and a hub of U.S. naval operations. However, the naval training center at San Diego is slated to be closed due to defense cutbacks. Other leading industries are electronics, aerospace and missiles, medical and scientific research, oceanography, and agriculture. Its magnificent climate and proximity to Mexico have made tourism a significant part of the city's economy.

Famous natives: Billy Casper, golfer; Florence Chadwick, swimmer; Dennis Conner, yacht racer; Ted Danson, actor; Robert Duvall, actor; Nanette Fabray, actress; Robert Lansing, actor; Margaret O'Brien, actress; Carol Vaness, soprano; Ted Williams, baseball player; Mickey Wright, golfer

SAN FRANCISCO, CALIF.

Mayor: Willie L. Brown, Jr. (to Jan. 2000)
1994 est. population (rank): 734,676 (13)
1990 census population (rank): 723,959 (14); **% change,** 6.6; **Male,** 362,497; **Female,** 361,462; **White,** 387,783; **Black,** 79,039 (10.9%); **American Indian, Eskimo, or Aleut,** 3,456 (0.5%); **Asian or Pacific Islander,** 210,876 (29.1%); **Other race,** 42,805; **Hispanic origin,** 100,717 (13.9%). **1990 percent population under 18:** 16.1; **65 and over:** 14.6; **median age:** 35.8.
Land area: 46.1 sq mi. (120 sq km); **Alt.:** Highest, 925 ft; lowest, sea level
Avg. daily temp.: Jan., 48.5° F; July, 62.2° F
Churches: 540 of all denominations; **City-owned parks and squares:** 225; **Radio stations:** 29; **Television stations:** 10
CIVILIAN LABOR FORCE (1995): 398,000[1]; **Unemployed (S.F. residents):** 26,000[1], **Percent:** 6.4[1]; **Per capita personal income (PMSA) 1992:** $31,262

Chamber of Commerce: Greater San Francisco Chamber of Commerce, 465 California St., San Francisco, Calif. 94104

1. San Francisco City/County.

San Francisco, the fourth largest city in California, is coextensive with San Francisco county. It is located in the northern part of the state between the Pacific Ocean and San Francisco Bay. A narrow arm of land embraces San Francisco Bay, the largest landlocked harbor in the world, and shelters it from the Pacific Ocean. On this arm of land is San Francisco, a city on hills, almost surrounded by water.

A Franciscan father who was sailing with Sebastián Rodríguez Cermeño named the bay San Francisco on Nov. 7, 1595. In 1776, the Spaniards established a presidio, or military post, and a Franciscan mission on the end of the beautiful peninsula. In the following year, a little town called Yerba Buena, Spanish for "Good Herb," because mint grew in abundance, was founded around the mission.

In 1846, during the Mexican War, Yerba Buena was taken over by the United States. It was renamed San Francisco in 1847 and became incorporated as a city in 1850.

When gold was discovered in California in 1848, the city's population jumped to 10,000, and it experienced turbulent years until order was established by Vigilance Committees, first in 1851, and again in 1856. Then followed a period of more orderly growth and the foundations of the great commerce and industry of today were laid.

In 1906, San Francisco experienced the nation's worst earthquake which, together with the fire that followed, practically destroyed the city. The city was quickly rebuilt and grew rapidly as a leading transportation, industrial, and cultural center. In the 19th century, the American explorer and soldier, John C. Frémont, known as The Pathfinder, named the entrance to the bay, the Golden Gate, and the famous bright orange Golden Gate Bridge was dedicated in May 1937.

Not just where the city meets the bay, but a vital part of the economic and cultural fabric of northern California, the port of San Francisco covers 7 1/2 miles of waterfront as diverse and changing as the city itself. The port is home to a broad range of commercial, maritime, and public activities including ship repair, passenger cruising, ferry and excursion boats, commercial and sport fishing, and public parks. Its major shipping terminals serve shipping lines from around the world. The port also manages over 23 million sq. ft. of commercial real estate including office, retail, industrial, parking, and warehouse facilities. Fisherman's Wharf, Alcatraz, Hyde St. Pier, and Pier 39 all make the port of San Francisco one of the world's leading visitor destinations.

San Francisco inspires entrepreneurs to start their own businesses, and small businesses have a very important place in the economy. More than 80% of the city's 33,800 businesses have fewer than 15 employees. The high-tech industries of electronics and biotechnology are well represented throughout the Bay Area. With nearly 30% of the worldwide biotechnology labor force, and 360 biotech firms, the Bay Area has been appropriately called "Bionic Bay." Tourism is one of San Francisco's largest industries and the largest employer of city residents. Nearly 13.4 million persons visit San Francisco each year, and annual visitor spending is $231 million, providing 66,400 jobs.

The military has played an important role in the San Francisco and the Bay Area's economy, but its impact will decline due to defense cutbacks.

San Francisco is also the banking and financial center of the West and is home to a Federal Reserve Bank and a United States Mint. More than 60 foreign banks maintain offices there.

Famous natives: Gracie Allen, comedienne; Luis Walter Alvarez, Nobel Prize in physics; David Belasco, dramatist, producer; Mel Blanc, actor, voice specialist; Rosemary Casals, tennis player; Isadora Duncan, dancer; Clint Eastwood, actor; Robert Frost, poet; Rube Goldberg, cartoonist; William Randolph Hearst, publisher; Bruce Lee, actor; Mervyn LeRoy, director; Jack London, novelist; Johnny Mathis, singer; Lloyd Nolan, actor; O.J. Simpson, football player; Robert G. Sproul, educator; Irving Stone, novelist; Natalie Wood, actress

SAN JOSE, CALIF.

Mayor: Susan Hammer (to Dec. 31, 1998)
City Manager: Regina V.K. Williams (apptd. Nov. 1994)
1994 est. population (rank): 816,884 (11)[1]
1990 census population (rank): 782,248 (11); **% change,** 24.3; **Male,** 397,709; **Female,** 384,539; **White,** 491,280; **Black,** 36,790 (4.7%); **American Indian, Eskimo, or Aleut,** 5,416 (0.7%); **Asian or Pacific Islander,** 152,815 (19.5%); **Other race,** 95,947; **Hispanic origin,** 208,388 (26.6%). **1990 percent population under 18:** 26.7; **65 and over:** 7.2; **median age:** 30.4.
Land area: 180.8 sq mi. (468.27 sq km), **Alt.:** Highest, 4,372 ft.; lowest, sea level
Avg. daily temp.: Jan., 49.5° F; July, 68.8° F

Churches: 403; **City-owned parks and playgrounds:** 152 (3,136 ac.); **Radio stations:** 14; **Television stations:** 4
CIVILIAN LABOR FORCE: 420,686; **Unemployed:** 33,484, **Percent:** 8.0; **Per capita personal income (PMSA) 1992:** $25,924
Chamber of Commerce: San Jose Chamber of Commerce, One Paseo de San Antonio, San Jose, Calif. 95113

1. **1996 est. population:** 849,400

San Jose, the third largest city in California and seat of Santa Clara county, is located in the northern part of the state in the Santa Clara Valley near San Francisco Bay, 50 miles south of downtown San Francisco.

San Jose was founded on Nov. 29, 1777, by Spanish colonizers who named the settlement Pueblo de San José de Guadalupe in honor of Saint Joseph and after the Guadalupe River on which the pueblo (town) was situated. The town was the first city to be established in California.

After California became a U.S. territory in 1847, San Jose became the first state capital from December 1849 to 1852 and was incorporated as a city in 1850. The city developed commercially as a supply base for gold prospectors and, when the railroad connected it with San Francisco in 1864, it became the distribution point for agricultural products from the Santa Clara Valley.

Today, the city continues to be the distribution and food-processing center for the surrounding rich agricultural region producing seasonal fruits and grapes. More than 50 wineries grace the Valley.

Computers are big business here and San Jose is the capital of Silicon Valley (Santa Clara), the nation's center of high technology where more than 3,000 high tech companies are located. Silicon Valley is also one of the world's leading centers for medical treatment and research. Heart transplants, gene splicing, and transportable baby incubators were developed there.

San Jose has healthy retail, transportation, and tourism industries as well, and is the primary center for real estate and industrial development in the area.

Famous natives: "Fatty" Arbuckle, actor; Chuck Berry, singer, guitarist; Cesar Chavez, labor leader; Peggy Fleming, figure skater; Farley Granger, actor; Edmund Lowe, actor; Jim Plunkett, football player

SEATTLE, WASH.

Mayor: Norman B. Rice (to Dec. 31, 1997)
1994 est. population (rank): 520,947 (22)
1990 census population (rank): 516,259 (21); **% change,** 4.5; **Male,** 252,042; **Female,** 264,217; **White,** 388,858 (75.3%); **Black,** 51,948 (10.1%); **American Indian, Eskimo, or Aleut,** 7,326 (1.4%); **Asian or Pacific Islander,** 60,819 (11.8%); **Other race,** 7,308 (1.4%); **Hispanic origin,** 18,349 (3.6%). **1990 percent population under 18:** 16.5; **65 and over:** 15.2; **median age:** 34.9.
Land area: 144.6 sq mi. (375 sq km); **Alt.:** Highest, 521 ft; lowest, sea level
Avg. daily temp.: Jan., 46.4° F; July, 67.0° F
Churches: Roman Catholic, 33; Jewish, 12; Protestant and others, 497; **City-owned parks, playgrounds, etc.:** 397 (6,000+ ac.); **Radio stations:** AM, 21; FM, 23; **Television stations:** 6 commercial; 1 educational
CIVILIAN LABOR FORCE (1995): (3 counties) 1,084,050; **Unemployed:** 50,950, **Percent:** 4.7; **Per capita personal income:** (4 counties) $27,741
Chamber of Commerce: Greater Seattle Chamber of Commerce, 1301 5th Ave., Suite 2400, Seattle, Wash. 98101

Seattle is the largest city in Washington and the seat of King county. A city of steep hills, Seattle lies in western Washington between two bodies of water—Puget Sound on the west and Lake Washington on the east. Its fine land-locked harbor has made Seattle one of the major ports in the United States.

Seattle was first settled by five pioneer families from Illinois at Alki Point at the south end of Elliott Bay in 1851. They moved in 1852 to the eastern shore of the bay and laid out a town in 1853. It was named Seattle after a friendly Suquamish Indian Chief (Seattle is only an approximation of his name).

Seattle successfully withstood an Indian attack in 1856 and was incorporated as a city in 1869. A disastrous fire almost destroyed the entire business district in 1889. When the Great Northern Railway arrived in 1893, the city became a major rail terminus and it grew rapidly. It was a boom town during the Alaska gold rush of 1897 and continued to prosper as a major Pacific port of entry with the opening of the Panama Canal in 1914.

Seattle is the region's commercial and transportation hub and the center of manufacturing, trade, and finance. Its important diversified industries include aircraft, lumber and forest products, fishing, high technology, food processing, boat building, machinery, fabricated metals, chemicals, pharmaceuticals, and apparel.

Famous natives: Chester Carlson, Xerox inventor; Carol Channing, actress; Judy Collins, singer; Fred Couples, golfer; Gail Devers, athlete; Frances Farmer, actress; William Gates, Microsoft founder; June Havoc, actress; Jimi Hendrix, guitarist; Robert Joffrey, choreographer; Gypsy Rose Lee, entertainer; Mary Livingstone, comedienne; Kevin McCarthy, actor; Mary McCarthy, novelist; Jeff Smith, food expert; Martha Wright, singer

TOLEDO, OHIO

Mayor: Carlton Finkbeiner (to Jan. 1998)
1994 est. population (rank): 322,550 (50)
1990 census population (rank): 332,943 (49); **% change,** −6.1; **Male,** 157,941; **Female,** 175,002; **White,** 256,239; **Black,** 65,598 (19.7%); **Americn Indian, Eskimo, or Aleut,** 920 (0.3%); **Asian or Pacific Islander,** 3,487 (1.0%); **Other race,** 6,699; **Hispanic origin,** 13,207 (4.0%). **1990 percent population under 18:** 26.2; **65 and over:** 13.6; **median age:** 31.7.
Land area: 84.2 sq mi. (218 sq km); **Alt.:** 630 ft
Avg. daily temp.: Jan., 25.2° F; July, 74.6° F
Churches: Protestant, 301; Roman Catholic, 55; Jewish, 4; others, 98; **City-owned parks and playgrounds:** 134 (2,650.90 ac.); **Radio stations:** AM, 8; FM, 8; **Television stations:** 6
CIVILIAN LABOR FORCE (1995): 158,200, **Unemployed:** 9,400, **Percent:** 5.6; **Per capita personal income (MSA) 1992:** $19,166
Chamber of Commerce: Toledo Area Chamber of Commerce, 300 Madison Ave., Ste. 200, Toledo, Ohio 43604

Toledo, the fourth largest city in Ohio and seat of Lucas county, is located in the northwestern part of the state on the Maumee River at Lake Erie.

The first European to visit the area was the French explorer Étienne Brulé in 1615. The first white settlement in the area was at Fort Industry built by Gen. "Mad Anthony" Wayne in 1794, after he defeated the Indians at the Battle of Fallen Timbers fought nearby. The village of Port Lawrence was established next to the fort in 1817 and the village of Vistula was estab-

lished nearby in 1832. The two villages were united in 1833 and named Toledo after the city in Spain. They became incorporated as a city in 1837.

Both Michigan and Ohio claimed the Toledo area which at the time was part of Michigan Territory. The bloodless dispute (Toledo War of 1835) was settled by Congress which awarded the city to Ohio. In return, Michigan received the Upper Peninsula and admission to the Union.

The city developed as a transportation center with the arrival of the railroad in 1836 and the opening of canals in the 1840s. It continued to prosper with the development of the Ohio coalfields, the tapping of gas and oil deposits, and the establishment of the glassworks by Edward Libbey in 1888.

Toledo is a leading commercial and manufacturing center and a major Great Lakes port. Total annual tonnage through the Port of Toledo ranges from 10 to 15 million tons and includes three distinct types of cargo: coal and iron ore, grain, and a wide range of general cargoes.

Toledo is the home of numerous major corporate headquarters and has 13 financial institutions in the area. Major diversified manufacturing industries include Jeeps, glass and plastic containers, fiberglass, automotive components, petroleum refining, coal products, and natural gas distribution. Other important industries are printing and publishing, food products, furniture, and fabricated metal products.

Famous natives: Cliff Arquette, actor; Anita Baker, singer; Teresa Brewer, singer; Jamie Farr, actor; Otto Kruger, actor; Herb Shriner, humorist; Gloria Steinem, feminist

TUCSON, ARIZ.

Mayor: George Miller (to Dec. 1999)
1994 est. population (rank): 434,726 (33)
1990 census population (rank): 405,390 (33); **% change,** 22.6; **Male,** 197,319; **Female,** 208,071; **White,** 305,055; **Black,** 17,366 (4.3%); **American Indian, Eskimo, or Aleut,** 6,464 (1.6%); **Asian or Pacific Islander,** 8,901 (2.2%); **Other race,** 67,604; **Hispanic origin,** 118,595 (29.3%). **1990 percent population under 18:** 24.5; **65 and over:** 12.6; **median age:** 30.6.
Land area: 156.04 sq mi. (404 sq km); **Alt.:** 2,400 ft
Avg. daily temp.: Jan., 51.1° F; July, 86.2° F
Churches: Protestant, 340; Roman Catholic, 42; other, 150; **City-owned parks and parkways:** (25,349 ac.); **Radio stations:** AM, 16; FM, 11; **Television stations:** 3 commercial; 1 educational; 3 other
CIVILIAN LABOR FORCE (Dec. '95): 375,900; **Unemployed:** 11,100, **Percent:** 3.2; **Per capita personal income (1995):** $18,684
Chamber of Commerce: Tucson Metropolitan Chamber of Commerce, P.O. Box 991, Tucson, Ariz. 85702

Tucson is the second largest city in Arizona and the seat of Pima county. It is located in the southeastern part of the state on the Santa Cruz River.

The site was originally settled by the prehistoric Hohokam Indians (300 B.C.–1400s A.D.). The first Europeans to visit the area were Spanish missionaries in the 17th century. In 1700, the Jesuit missionary explorer Father Eusebio Francisco Kino founded the mission of San Xavier del Bac close by the Papago Indian village of Stjukshon (later called Tucson). Stjukshon is an Indian word meaning "village of the dark spring at the foot of the mountain." The Papago Indians are descendants of the ancient Hohakam peoples.

In 1776, Spanish colonists from Mexico constructed a presidio (fort) at Tucson as protection against the hostile Apache Indians and also established the mission of San Jose de Tucson nearby. Tucson remained a military outpost under Spanish rule and later Mexican control until the area was sold to the United States as part of the Gadsden Purchase in 1853. Tucson was the capital of the Arizona Territory from 1867 to 1877. It was incorporated as a city in 1877. The town grew rapidly when the Southern Pacific Railroad arrived in 1880 and silver and copper deposits were discovered nearby.

Tucson is a popular vacation and health resort due to its sunny, mild, and dry climate and unique desert location. Tourism is important to the city's economy. Major industries are aerospace and missile production, high technology, and electronics. Tucson is also the commercial center for the surrounding area's agriculture and mining industries.

Famous natives: Rose E. Bird, jurist; Dennis De Concini, senator; Barbara Eden, actress; Linda Ronstadt, singer

TULSA, OKLA.

Mayor: M. Susan Savage (to May 1998)
1994 est. population (rank): 374,851 (40)
1990 census population (rank): 367,302 (44); **% change,** 1.8; **Male,** 175,538; **Female,** 191,764; **White,** 291,444; **Black,** 49,825 (13.6%); **American Indian, Eskimo, or Aleut,** 17,091 (4.7%); **Asian or Pacific Islander,** 5,133 (1.4%); **Other race,** 3,809; **Hispanic origin,** 9,564 (2.6%). **1990 percent population under 18:** 24.4; **65 and over:** 12.7; **median age:** 33.1.
Land area: 192.24 sq mi. (499 sq km); **Alt.:** 674 ft
Avg. daily temp.: Jan., 35.2° F; July, 83.2° F
Churches: Protestant, 593; Roman Catholic, 32; Jewish, 2; others, 4; **City parks and playgrounds:** 121 (6,050 ac.); **Radio stations:** AM, 9; FM, 21; **Television stations:** 7 commercial; 1 PBS; 1 cable
CIVILIAN LABOR FORCE (1995): 381,400; **Unemployed:** 14,493, **Percent:** 3.8; **Per capita personal income (1995):** $20,479
Chamber of Commerce: Metropolitan Tulsa Chamber of Commerce, 616 S Boston, Tulsa, Okla. 74119

Tulsa, the second largest city in Oklahoma and seat of Tulsa county, is located in the northeastern part of the state on the Arkansas River.

Tulsa was settled in the 1830s by Creek Indians from Alabama who were forcibly sent to the area (then part of Indian Territory) under the Indian Removal Act of 1830. Creek medicine-men planted ashes from their old home at the new site and the Creeks named their new village "Tulsy" meaning old town in memory of their former home in Tallassee, Alabama. In time, the village became the town of Tulsa.

The coming of the first railroad in 1882 attracted white settlers to Tulsa and the town developed into a cattle shipping center. When enormous oil deposits were discovered at nearby Red Fork in 1901 and at Glenn Pool in 1905, the city experienced rapid growth as a center of a booming petroleum industry. Tulsa was incorporated as a city in 1898 and chartered in 1908.

Tulsa is the center of the state's petroleum industry and has a diversified economy. Important industries include aerospace, chemicals, computer parts, automobile glass, fabricated metals, and industrial machinery. The city became a major inland port when the Tulsa Port of Catoosa opened in 1971. It is the

national headquarters of the U.S. Junior Chamber of Commerce (Jaycees).

Famous natives: Garth Brooks, singer; Blake Edwards, director; Paul Harvey, commentator; Jennifer Jones, actress; Henry R. Kravis, investment banker; Daniel Patrick Moynihan, senator; Tony Randall, actor; Alfre Woodard, actress; Judy Woodruff, journalist

VIRGINIA BEACH, VA.

Mayor: Meyera E. Obendorf (to June 2000)
1994 est. population (rank): 430,295 (35)
1990 census population (rank): 393,069 (37); **% change,** 49.9; **Male,** 199,571; **Female,** 193,498; **White,** 316,408; **Black,** 54,671 (13.9%); **American Indian, Eskimo, or Aleut,** 1,384 (0.4%); **Asian or Pacific Islander,** 17,025 (4.3%); **Other race,** 3,581; **Hispanic origin,** 12,137 (3.1%); **1990 percent population under 18:** 28.0; **65 and over:** 5.9; **median age:** 28.9.
Land area: 258.7 sq mi. (670 sq km); **Alt.:** 12 ft
Avg. daily temp.: Jan., 39.9° F; July, 78.4° F
Churches: Protestant, 159; Catholic, 8; Jewish, 4; **City-owned parks:** 182 (1,748 ac.); **Radio stations:** AM 18, FM 26; **Television stations:** 4 commercial, 1 PBS, 1 cable
CIVILIAN LABOR FORCE: 194,579; **Unemployed:** 11,541, **Percent:** 5.9; **Per capita personal income (MSA) 1992:** $18,077[1]
Chamber of Commerce: Hampton Roads Chamber of Commerce, 4512 Virginia Beach Blvd., Virginia Beach, Va., 23456

1. Norfolk-Virginia Beach-Newport News.

Virginia Beach, the largest city in Virginia, is located in the southeasternmost portion of the state on the Atlantic coastline. It is independent and is not part of any county.

The first English settlers to set foot in America landed at Cape Henry at the tip of Virginia Beach on April 29, 1607. They were led by John Smith on his way to establishing Jamestown. The first permanent settlement within the city limits was made at Lynnhaven Bay in 1621. Cape Henry became an important port for British merchant ships calling on America, and it was here that the French Fleet led by Admiral Comte de Grasse blockaded the British Fleet during the American Revolution.

Virginia Beach gained its reputation as a famous vacation resort in the 19th century, following the building of a railroad connecting its oceanfront with Norfolk and the construction of its first hotel in 1883. Virginia Beach was incorporated as a town in 1906 and as a city in 1952. In 1963, Princess Anne County and Virginia Beach merged and gave the present city an area of 310 square miles of oceanfront.

Tourism is the mainstay of the economy and 2.5 million people visit Virginia Beach overnight each year. Virginia Beach's economy is supported by four nearby military bases and diverse industries, including agriculture (165 farms), computer software, engineering, and technical services.

Famous natives and residents: V.C. Andrews, novelist; Raymond Brian Buckland, occult writer; Edgar Cayce, psychic; Ann Woodruff Compton, news correspondent; D.J. Dozier, football and baseball player; George Eastman, inventor; Scott McKenzie, singer; Juice Newton, singer; Kenneth S. Reightler, Jr., astronaut; Pat Robertson, evangelist; Grace Sherwood, accused witch; Henry Walke, naval officer in Mexican and Civil Wars; Pernell "Sweet Pea" Whitaker, boxer; Skip Wilkins, wheelchair athlete

WASHINGTON, D.C.

Created municipal corporation: Feb. 21, 1871
Mayor: Marion Barry (to Jan. 1999)
Motto: *Justitia omnibus* (Justice to all)
Flower: American beauty rose; **Tree:** Scarlet oak
1994 est. population (rank): 567,094 (20)
1990 census population (rank): 606,900 (19); **% change,** -4.9;
  Male, 282,970; **Female,** 323,930; **White,** 179,667; **Black,**
  399,604 (65.8%); **American Indian, Eskimo, or Aleut,** 1,466
  (0.2%); **Asian or Pacific Islander,** 11,214 (1.8%); **Other**
  race, 14,949; **Hispanic origin,** 32,710 (5.4%)
Land area: 68.25 sq mi. (177 sq km); **Alt.:** Highest, 420 ft;
  lowest, sea level
Avg. daily temp.: Jan., 35.2° F; July, 78.9° F
Churches: Protestant, 610; Roman Catholic, 132; Jewish, 9;
  City parks: 753 (7,725 ac.); **Radio stations:** AM, 9; FM,
  38; **Television stations:** 19
CIVILIAN LABOR FORCE: 276,000; Unemployed: 23,000,
  Percent: 8.4; **Per capita personal income (PMSA)**
  1992: $26,817[1]
Board of Trade: Greater Washington Board of Trade,
  1129 20th Street, N.W., Washington, D.C. 20036
Chamber of Commerce: D.C. Chamber of Commerce,
  1319 F St., NW, Washington, D.C. 20004
1. Washington, D.C.–Md.–Va.–WVa.

The District of Columbia—identical with the City of
Washington—is the capital of the United States and
the first carefully planned capital in the world. It is
located between Virginia and Maryland on the Potomac River. The district is named after Columbus.

D.C. history began in 1790 when Congress directed
selection of a new capital site, 100 miles square, along
the Potomac. When the site was determined, it included
30.75 square miles on the Virginia side of the river.
In 1846, however, Congress returned that area to Virginia, leaving the 68.25 square miles ceded by Maryland in 1788. The seat of government was transferred
from Philadelphia to Washington on Dec. 1, 1800,
and President John Adams became the first resident
in the White House.

The city was planned and partly laid out by Major
Pierre Charles L'Enfant, a French engineer. This work
was perfected and completed by Major Andrew Ellicott
and Benjamin Banneker, a freeborn black man, who
was an astronomer and mathematician. In 1814, during
the War of 1812, a British force fired the capital including the White House.

Until Nov. 3, 1967, the District of Columbia was administered by three commissioners appointed by the
president. On that day, a government consisting of a
mayor-commissioner and a 9-member Council, all appointed by the president with the approval of the Senate,
took office. On May 7, 1974, the citizens of the District
of Columbia approved a Home Rule Charter, giving
them an elected mayor and 13-member council—their
first elected municipal government in more than a century. The District also has one non-voting member in
the House of Representatives and an elected Board of
Education.

On Aug. 22, 1978, Congress passed a proposed constitutional amendment to give Washington, D.C., voting representation in the Congress. The amendment
had to be ratified by at least 28 state legislatures within seven years to become effective. As of 1985 it died.

A petition asking for the District's admission to the
Union as the 51st State was filed in Congress on September 9, 1983. The District is continuing this drive
for statehood.

The federal government and tourism are the main-
stays of the city's economy, and many unions, business, professional and nonprofit organizations are
headquartered there.

Famous natives: Edward Albee, playwright; Billie
Burke, comedienne; Ina Claire, actress; John Foster
Dulles, statesman; Duke Ellington, musician; Jane
Greer, actress; Goldie Hawn, actress; Helen Hayes, ac-
tress; J. Edgar Hoover, ex-director F.B.I.; William Hurt,
actor; Noor al-Hussein, Queen of Jordan; Michael
Learned, actress; Roger Mudd, newscaster; Eleanor
Holmes Norton, government official; Chita Rivera,
dancer, actress; Leonard Rose, cellist; John Philip Sou-
sa, composer; Frances Sternhagen, actress

State-Administered Lottery Funds: 1994
(Thousand dollars)

	Income—ticket sales excluding commissions	Prizes	Proceeds available from ticket sales		Income—ticket sales excluding commissions	Prizes	Proceeds available from ticket sales
Total	26,588,320	15,296,376	9,749,087	Minnesota	311,691	192,254	60,288
Arizona	233,355	123,767	83,878	Missouri	329,970	189,288	112,680
California	1,816,321	966,351	686,680	Montana	35,417	18,149	9,283
Colorado	269,355	167,749	74,184	Nebraska	52,853	26,682	14,092
Connecticut	523,746	309,072	191,422	New Hampshire	104,423	61,136	37,587
Delaware	95,890	53,409	35,140	New Jersey	1,353,623	708,722	602,436
Florida	2,043,587	1,071,087	853,702	New York	2,176,356	1,107,476	1,004,879
Georgia	1,010,159	550,493	370,291	Ohio	1,803,079	1,115,020	592,892
Idaho	72,515	41,333	17,201	Oregon	703,437	440,657	108,546
Illinois	1,373,554	794,716	525,875	Pennsylvania	1,462,426	782,974	628,108
Indiana	526,800	311,545	185,840	Rhode Island	167,711	109,803	54,740
Iowa	185,653	116,502	47,222	South Dakota	92,290	17,722	67,707
Kansas	144,448	79,390	48,073	Texas	2,471,555	1,532,407	927,334
Kentucky	448,982	291,266	122,693	Vermont	49,856	29,016	16,625
Louisiana	324,655	174,741	126,412	Virginia	854,889	465,630	304,723
Maine	145,191	79,873	51,042	Washington	314,580	167,790	102,582
Maryland	932,327	507,473	386,331	West Virginia	131,452	75,860	41,429
Massachusetts	2,306,091	1,659,338	578,132	Wisconsin	470,160	273,690	165,224
Michigan	1,249,917	683,995	513,814				

Source: U.S. Census Bureau, Economics & Statistics Administration.

Top 50 Cities in the U.S. by Estimated 1994 Population and Rank

City and state	April 1, 1990 (census)	July 1, 1994 (estimate)	Change, 1990–94 Number	Change, 1990–94 Percent	City rank Population 1990	City rank Population 1994	Percent change 1990–94
New York, NY	7,322,564	7,333,253	10,689	0.1	1	1	149
Los Angeles, CA	3,485,557	3,448,613	−36,944	−1.1	2	2	170
Chicago, IL	2,783,726	2,731,743	−51,983	−1.9	3	3	179
Houston, TX	1,630,864	1,702,086	71,222	4.4	4	4	82
Philadelphia, PA	1,585,577	1,524,249	−61,328	−3.9	5	5	194
San Diego, CA	1,110,623	1,151,977	41,354	3.7	6	6	93
Phoenix, AZ	984,309	1,048,949	64,640	6.6	9	7	60
Dallas, TX	1,007,618	1,022,830	15,212	1.5	8	8	127
San Antonio, TX	935,393	998,905	63,512	6.8	10	9	55
Detroit, MI	1,027,974	992,038	−35,936	−3.5	7	10	191
San Jose, CA	782,224	816,884	34,660	4.4	11	11	81
Indianapolis (remainder), IN[1]	731,311	752,279	20,968	2.9	13	12	101
San Francisco, CA	723,959	734,676	10,717	1.5	14	13	128
Baltimore, MD	736,014	702,979	−33,035	−4.5	12	14	195
Jacksonville (remainder), FL[1]	635,230	665,070	29,840	4.7	15	15	77
Columbus, OH	632,945	635,913	2,968	0.5	16	16	143
Milwaukee, WI	628,088	617,044	−11,044	−1.8	17	17	176
Memphis, TN	618,652	614,289	−4,363	−0.7	18	18	162
El Paso, TX	515,342	579,307	63,965	12.4	22	19	22
Washington, DC	606,900	567,094	−39,806	−6.6	19	20	205
Boston, MA	574,283	547,725	−26,558	−4.6	20	21	196
Seattle, WA	516,259	520,947	4,688	0.9	21	22	135
Austin, TX	465,648	514,013	48,365	10.4	27	23	30
Nashville–Davidson (remainder), TN[1]	488,366	504,505	16,139	3.3	25	24	97
Denver, CO	467,610	493,559	25,949	5.5	26	25	68
Cleveland, OH	505,616	492,901	−12,715	−2.5	23	26	185
New Orleans, LA	496,938	484,149	−12,789	−2.6	24	27	186
Oklahoma City, OK	444,724	463,201	18,477	4.2	29	28	89
Fort Worth, TX	447,619	451,814	4,195	0.9	28	29	134
Portland, OR	438,802	450,777	11,975	2.7	30	30	104
Kansas City, MO	434,829	443,878	9,049	2.1	31	31	115
Charlotte, NC	395,934	437,797	41,863	10.6	35	32	28
Tucson, AZ	408,754	434,726	25,972	6.4	33	33	63
Long Beach, CA	429,321	433,852	4,531	1.1	32	34	133
Virginia Beach, VA	393,089	430,295	37,206	9.5	37	35	33
Albuquerque, NM	384,619	411,994	27,375	7.1	38	26	50
Atlanta, GA	393,929	396,052	2,123	0.5	36	37	140
Fresno, CA	354,091	386,551	32,460	9.2	47	38	37
Honolulu CDP, HI[2]	377,059	385,881	8,822	2.3	39	39	109
Tulsa, OK	367,302	374,851	7,549	2.1	44	40	116
Sacramento, CA	369,365	373,964	4,599	1.2	42	41	131
Miami, FL	358,648	373,024	14,376	4.0	46	42	90
St. Louis, MO	396,685	368,215	−28,470	−7.2	34	43	206
Oakland, CA	372,242	366,926	−5,316	−1.4	40	44	173
Pittsburgh, PA	369,879	358,883	−10,996	−3.0	41	45	188
Cincinnati, OH	364,114	358,170	−5,944	−1.6	45	46	175
Minneapolis, MN	368,383	354,590	−13,793	−3.7	43	47	193
Omaha, NE	335,719	345,033	9,314	2.8	48	48	102
Las Vegas, NV	258,204	327,878	69,674	27.0	63	49	4
Toledo, OH	332,943	322,550	−10,393	−3.1	49	50	189

1. The term "remainder" following a city name indicates that it is part of a consolidated city-county government and that the populations of other incorporated places in the county have been excluded from the population totals shown here. 2. Honolulu CDP (census designated place) is not incorporated as a city but is recognized for census purposes as a large urban place. Honolulu CDP is coextensive with Honolulu Judicial District within the City and County of Honolulu. NOTE: These estimates are consistent with the population as enumerated in the 1990 census, and have not been adjusted for census coverage errors. Source: U.S. Bureau of the Census.

Urban and Rural: The Historical View

In 1790, only 5 percent of the U.S. population lived in urban areas. As our nation grew, so did our cities. In 1920, for the first time, more than half the population lived in urban areas. By 1990, 75 percent lived in areas classified as urban.

In 1790, the U.S. had less than five people per square mile and a land area of 891,364 square miles. By 1990, we had 70 people per square mile and a land area of 3,536,338 square miles.

Tabulated Data on City Governments

City	Mayor			Council or Commission			
	Term, years	Salary[1]	City manager's salary[2]	Name	Members	Term, years	Salary[3]
Albuquerque, N.M.	4	$73,500	—	Council	9	4	$7,028
Atlanta	4	100,000	—	Council	16	4	22,000 [27]
Austin, Tex.	3	35,000	$125,000	Council	7 [2]	3	30,000
Baltimore	4	90,000	—	Council	19	4	36,000 [21]
Boston	4	110,000	—	Council	13	2	54,500
Charlotte, N.C.	2	28,400	123,684	Council	11	2	12,000
Chicago	4	170,000	—	Council	50	4	75,000
Cincinnati	2	48,762	139,500	Council	9	2	45,262
Cleveland	4	98,336	—	Council	21	4	45,048
Columbus, Ohio	4	98,000	—	Council	7	4	25,000 [15]
Dallas	2	50 [6]	164,000	Council	15	2	50 [6]
Denver	4	97,812	—	Council	13	4	43,000 [28]
Detroit	4	130,000	—	Council	9	4	60,000 [29]
El Paso	2	25,000	—	Council	8 [7]	2	15,000
Fort Worth	2	75 [8]	112,000	Council	8	2	75 [8]
Fresno, Calif.	4	99,000	120,000	Council	7 [7]	4	28,800 [23]
Honolulu	4	100,000	95,000 [9]	Council	9	4	38,500
Houston	6	133,005	—	Council	14	2	36,614
Indianapolis	4	83,211	—	Council	29	4	14,705 [10]
Jacksonville, Fla.	2	110,000	105,000 [11]	Council	19	4	24,000
Kansas City, Mo.	4	59,400	125,000	Council	13 [7]	4	26,400
Las Vegas	4	75,800	112,499	Council	4	4	33,480
Long Beach, Calif.	4	84,545	155,786 [25]	Council	9	4	21,135
Los Angeles	4	1 [41]	169,880 [4]	Council	15	4	98,070
Memphis, Tenn.	4	110,000	90,000 [4]	Council	13	4	6,000
Miami, Fla.	4	5,000 [13]	116,887 [39]	Commission	5	4	5,000
Milwaukee	4	112,362	—	Council	17	4	52,528
Minneapolis	4	75,533	102,390 [40]	Council	13	4	56,621
Nashville, Tenn.	4	75,000	8,900 [14]	Council	41	4	6,900
New Orleans	4	106,872	82,980 [38]	Council	7	4	42,500
New York	4	165,000	112,000 [14]	Council	51	4	70,500 [26]
Oakland, Calif.	4	97,740	147,090 [42]	Council	9 [7]	4	47,880 [37, 42]
Oklahoma City	4	2,000	100,000	Council	8	4	20 [17]
Omaha, Neb.	4	80,911	—	Council	7	4	23,436
Philadelphia	4	110,000	95,000 [18]	Council	17	4	65,000 [16]
Phoenix, Ariz.	4	37,500	143,500	Council	9 [7]	4	35,000
Pittsburgh	4	76,559	—	Council	9	4	44,526
Portland, Ore.	4	83,416	—	Council	4	4	70,261
Sacramento	4	2,175 [30]	119,012	Council	9 [12]	4	1,825 [31]
St. Louis	4	71,266	—	Board of Aldermen	29	4	18,500 [32]
San Antonio	2	3,000 [19]	115,000	Council	11 [7]	2	20 [20]
San Diego, Calif.	4	65,300	132,792	Council	8	4	49,000
San Francisco	4	138,669	137,521 [33]	Bd. of Suprvrs.	11	4	23,924
San Jose, Calif.	4	85,000 [34]	145,000 [34]	Council	10	4	56,000 [34]
Seattle	4	112,731	—	Council	9	4	73,377
Toledo, Ohio	4	75,000	—	Council	12 [12]	4	18,500 [36]
Tucson, Ariz.	4	32,000	120,000	Council	7 [7]	4	18,000
Tulsa, Okla.	4	70,000	—	Council	9	2	12,000
Virginia Beach, Va.	4	20,000	108,000 [24]	Council	11	4	18,000
Washington, D.C.	4	90,705	115,700 [35]	Council	13	4	71,885 [22]

1. Annual salary unless otherwise indicated. 2. Annual salary. City Manager's term is indefinite and at will of Council (or Mayor). 3. Annual salary unless otherwise indicated. In some cities, President of Council receives a higher salary. 4. City Administrative Officer appointed by Mayor, approved by Council. 5. For 9 District Councilmen; 4 years for President and 3 Councilmen-at-Large. 6. Per Council meeting; not over $2,600 per year. 7. Including Mayor. 8. Per week and per Council meeting. 9. Managing Director appointed by Mayor; Council approval required. 10. $9,985 base plus $112 per council meeting (20 scheduled); $62 per committee meeting at a maximum of 40 meetings. President gets $1,982 extra, majority and minority leaders get $1,320 extra and the Committee Chairmen get $797 extra. 11. Chief Administrative Officer appointed by Mayor; not subject to Council confirmation. 12. Including the Council President. 13. Plus $2,500 expense account. 14. No City Manager; salary is for Deputy Mayors. 15. Per member. President earns $30,000. 16. Per member. President earns $80,000. 17. Per Council meeting; not to exceed 5 meetings a month. 18. Appointed by Mayor, with title of Managing Director. 19. Plus Council pay. 20. Per Council meeting; not over $1,040 per year. 21. Per member. President earns $53,000. 22. Council Chairman receives $81,885. 23. Mayor Pro Tempore, $31,200. 24. Plus $4,000 in travel expenses. 25. Plus $1,200 per month expense account. 26. Public Advocate receives $125,000. 27. Council President earns $25,000. 28. Council President receives $48,000. 29. Council President receives $63,000. 30. Per month; plus $560 in benefits; includes $150 monthly entertainment allowance. 31. Per month; plus $560 in benefits. 32. For 12 Aldermen $18,500, 16 Aldermen $21,460. 33. Chief Administrative Officer. 34. Plus $4,200 annual vehicle expense allowance for Mayor/Council and $6,000 for City Manager. 35. City Administrator. 36. Members of Council get $1,200 per year expense account. 37. Council also serves as the Redevelopment Agency for which there is additional compensation. 38. Minimum entrance base salary reported. 39. Approx. 40. City Coordinator. 41.At mayor's request; limited to 2 terms. 42. Denotes average based on range. Source: *Information Please* questionnaires to the cities.

U.S. Telephone Area Codes and Time Zones

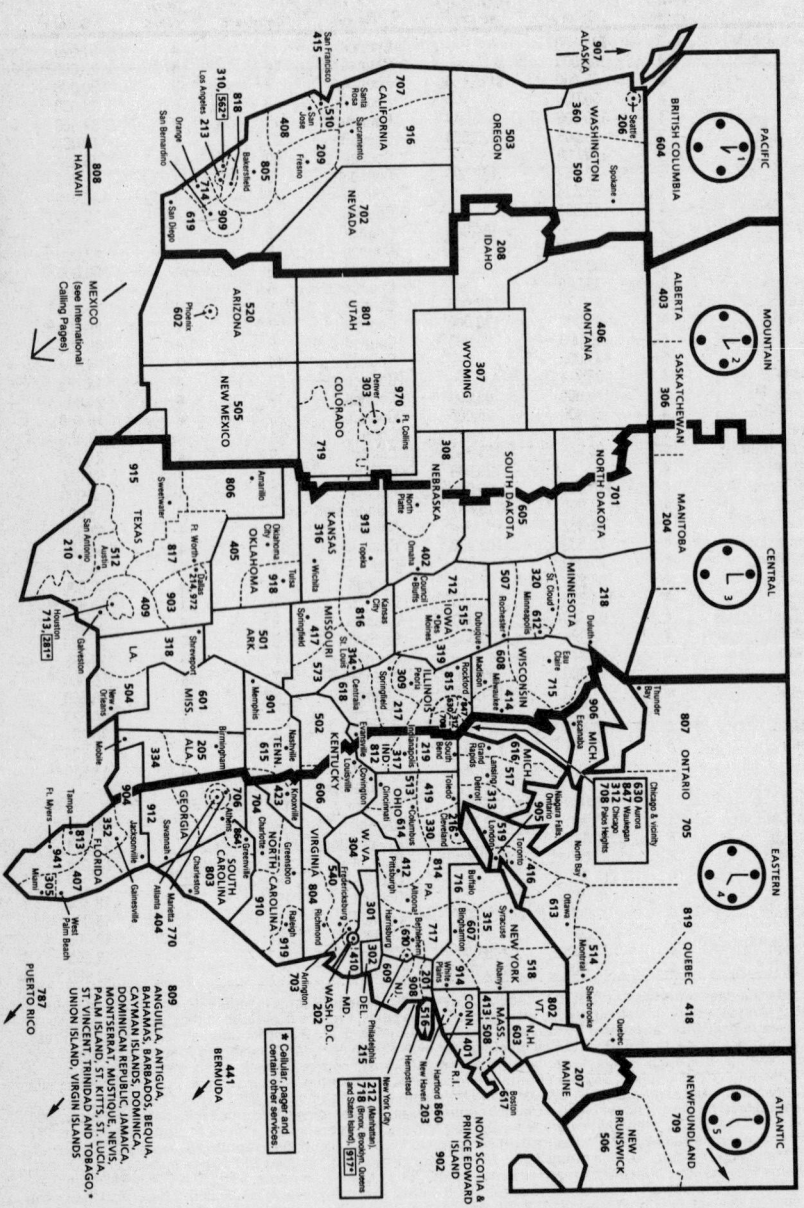

U.S. Cities Over 25,000 Population

Asterisk denotes more than one ZIP code for a city and refers to Postmaster. To find the ZIP code for a particular address, consult the ZIP code directory available in every post office. The ZIP codes printed herein were obtained either from the "National Five-Digit Zip Code & Post Office Directory," published by the U.S. Postal Service or from phone calls made to the postmaster in the areas where they were not listed in the Directory. We have tried to accurately list all the pertinent ZIP codes that were available. If there are any questions regarding the exact ZIP code for a particular street address, you should contact your local post office. NOTE: Census Designated Place (CDP)—A statistical area comprising a densely settled concentration of population that is not incorporated but which resembles an incorporated place in that local people can identify it with a name.

City and major zip code	1990 census	1990 rank
ALABAMA		
Anniston city (36201*)	26,623	1210
Auburn city (36830*)	33,830	904
Bessemer city (35020*)	33,497	921
Birmingham city (35203*)	265,968	60
Decatur city (35601*)	48,761	575
Dothan city (36302*)	53,589	496
Florence city (35630*)	36,426	828
Gadsden city (35902*)	42,523	685
Hoover city (35203*)	39,788	748
Huntsville city (35813*)	159,789	110
Mobile city (36601*)	196,278	79
Montgomery city (36119*)	187,106	86
Phenix City city (36867*)	25,312	1281
Prichard city (36610)	34,311	886
Tuscaloosa city (35401*)	77,759	287
ALASKA		
Anchorage city (99501*)	226,338	69
Fairbanks city (99701*)	30,843	1023
Juneau city (99801*)	26,751	1204
ARIZONA		
Chandler city (85225*)	90,533	230
Flagstaff city (86004*)	45,857	627
Gilbert town (85234)	29,188	1090
Glendale city (85301*)	148,134	119
Mesa city (85201*)	288,091	53
Peoria city (85345*)	50,618	547
Phoenix city (85026*)	983,403	9
Prescott city (86301*)	26,455	1220
Scottsdale city (85251*)	130,069	141
Sierra Vista city (85635*)	32,983	938
Sun City CDP (85351*)	38,126	784
Tempe city (85282*)	141,865	124
Tucson city (85726*)	405,390	33
Yuma city (85364*)	54,923	471
ARKANSAS		
Conway city (72032)	26,481	1218
Fayetteville city (72701*)	42,099	694
Fort Smith city (72917*)	72,798	316
Hot Springs city (71901)	32,462	955
Jacksonville city (72076)	29,101	1096
Jonesboro city (72401)	46,535	613
Little Rock city (72231*)	175,795	96
North Little Rock city (72114*)	61,741	403
Pine Bluff city (71601*)	57,140	446
Springdale city (72764*)	29,941	1059
West Memphis city (72301*)	28,259	1132
CALIFORNIA		
Alameda city (94501)	76,459	292
Alhambra city (91715*)	82,106	271
Altadena CDP (91001*)	42,658	680
Anaheim city (92803*)	266,406	59
Antioch city (94509*)	62,195	395
Apple Valley town (92307*)	46,079	623
Arcadia city (91006*)	48,290	589
Arden-Arcade CDP (95825*)	92,040	228
Azusa city (91702)	41,333	710
Bakersfield city (93380*)	174,820	97
Baldwin Park city (91706)	69,330	343

City and major zip code	1990 census	1990 rank
Bell city (90201)	34,365	885
Bellflower city (90706*)	61,815	401
Bell Gardens city (90201)	42,355	687
Berkeley city (94704*)	102,724	194
Beverly Hills city (90210*)	31,971	974
Brea city (92622*)	32,873	945
Buena Park city (90622*)	68,784	347
Burbank city (91505*)	93,643	221
Burlingame city (94010*)	26,801	1201
Camarillo city (93010*)	52,303	519
Campbell city (95008*)	36,048	839
Carlsbad city (92008*)	63,126	391
Carmichael CDP (95608*)	48,702	579
Carson city (90745*)	83,995	266
Casa de Oro-Mount Helis CDP (91977*)	30,727	1030
Castro Valley CDP (94546)	48,619	582
Cathedral City city (92234*)	30,085	1053
Ceres city (95307)	26,314	1227
Cerritos city (90703)	53,240	503
Chico city (95926*)	40,079	742
Chino city (91710*)	59,682	423
Chino Hills CDP (91710)	27,608	1164
Chula Vista city (92010*)	135,163	133
Citrus Heights CDP (95621)	107,439	183
Claremont city (91711)	32,503	954
Clovis city (93612)	50,323	552
Colton city (92324)	40,213	735
Compton city (90221*)	90,454	231
Concord city (94520*)	111,348	167
Corona city (91720*)	76,095	294
Coronado city (92118*)	26,540	1215
Costa Mesa city (92628*)	96,357	212
Covina city (91722*)	43,207	669
Culver City city (90230*)	38,793	769
Cupertino city (95014*)	40,263	734
Cypress city (90630*)	42,655	681
Daly City city (94015*)	92,311	227
Dana Point city (92629)	31,896	978
Danville city (94526*)	31,306	999
Davis city (95616*)	46,209	619
Diamond Bar city (91765*)	53,672	494
Downey city (90241*)	91,444	229
East Los Angeles CDP (90055)	126,379	146
El Cajon city (92020*)	88,693	236
El Centro city (92244*)	31,384	997
El Monte city (91731*)	106,209	186
El Toro CDP (92630)	62,685	393
Encinitas city (92024*)	55,386	463
Escondido city (92025*)	108,635	180
Eureka city (95501*)	27,025	1193
Fairfield city (94533)	77,211	289
Fair Oaks CDP (95628)	26,867	1198
Florence-Graham CDP (90052*)	57,147	445
Fontana city (92335*)	87,535	241
Foster City city (94404)	28,176	1137
Fountain Valley city (92708*)	53,691	493
Fremont city (94537*)	173,339	98
Fresno city (93706*)	354,202	47
Fullerton city (92634*)	114,144	160
Folsom city (95630)	29,802	1066

City and major zip code	1990 census	1990 rank	City and major zip code	1990 census	1990 rank
Gardena city (90247*)	49,847	557	Pacifica city (94044)	37,670	802
Garden Grove city (92642*)	142,050	122	Palmdale city (93550*)	68,842	346
Gilroy city (95020*)	31,487	994	Palm Springs city (92263*)	40,181	736
Glendale city (92109*)	180,038	92	Palo Alto city (94303*)	55,900	458
Glendora city (91740)	47,828	593	Paradise town (95969*)	25,408	1276
Hacienda Heights CDP (91745)	52,354	515	Paramount city (90723)	47,669	595
Hanford city (93230*)	30,897	1020	Parkway-South Sacramento CDP (95823*)	31,903	977
Hawthorne city (90250*)	71,349	327	Pasadena city (91109*)	131,591	139
Hayward city (94544*)	111,498	166	Petaluma city (94952*)	43,184	671
Hemet city (92343*)	36,094	838	Pico Rivera city (90660)	59,177	429
Hesperia city (92345)	50,418	550	Pittsburg city (94565)	47,564	597
Highland city (92346)	34,439	881	Placentia city (92670)	41,259	711
Huntington Beach city (92647*)	181,519	90	Pleasant Hill city (94523)	31,585	992
Huntington Park city (90255)	56,065	456	Pleasanton city (94566*)	50,553	548
Imperial Beach city (92032)	26,512	1216	Pomona city (91768*)	131,723	138
Indio city (92201*)	36,793	821	Porterville city (93257*)	29,563	1073
Inglewood city (90311*)	109,602	173	Poway city (92064)	43,516	665
Irvine city (92713*)	110,330	171	Rancho Cordova CDP (95670*)	48,731	577
Laguna Hills CDP (92654*)	46,731	610	Rancho Cucamonga city (91739*)	101,409	196
Laguna Niguel city (92607)	44,400	650	Rancho Palos Verdes city (90274)	41,659	706
La Habra city (90631*)	51,266	535	Redding city (96049*)	66,462	366
Lakeside CDP (92040)	39,412	754	Redlands city (92373*)	60,394	417
Lakewood city (90714*)	73,557	311	Redondo Beach city (92077*)	60,167	418
La Mesa city (92041*)	52,931	509	Redwood City city (94063*)	66,072	368
La Mirada city (90638*)	40,452	729	Rialto city (92376*)	72,388	319
Lancaster city (93534*)	97,291	209	Richmond city (94802*)	87,425	243
La Puente city (91744*)	36,955	816	Ridgecrest city (93555*)	27,725	1154
La Verne city (91750)	30,897	1020	Riverside city (92517*)	226,505	68
Lawndale city (90260)	27,331	1180	Rohnert Park city (94928*)	36,326	831
Livermore city (94550*)	56,741	451	Rosemead city (91770)	51,638	528
Lodi city (95240*)	51,874	526	Roseville city (95678*)	44,685	645
Lompoc city (93436*)	37,649	803	Rowland Heights CDP (91748)	42,647	682
Long Beach city (90809*)	429,433	32	Sacramento city (95813*)	369,365	41
Los Altos city (94022*)	26,303	1228	Salinas city (93907*)	108,777	177
Los Angeles city (90052*)	3,485,398	2	San Bernardino city (92403*)	164,164	106
Los Gatos town (95030*)	27,357	1176	San Bruno city (94066)	38,961	765
Lynwood city (90262)	61,945	397	San Buenaventura (Ventura) city (93001*)	92,575	226
Madera city (93638*)	29,281	1084	San Carlos city (94070)	26,167	1241
Manhattan Beach city (90266)	32,063	970	San Clemente city (92674*)	41,100	714
Manteca city (95336)	40,773	723	San Diego city (92199*)	1,110,549	6
Marina city (93933)	26,436	1222	San Dimas city (91773)	32,397	957
Martinez city (94553)	31,808	983	San Francisco city (94188*)	723,959	14
Maywood city (90270)	27,850	1151	San Gabriel city (91776*)	37,120	812
Menlo Park city (94025*)	28,040	1146	San Jose city (95101*)	782,248	11
Merced city (95340*)	56,216	454	San Juan Capistrano city (92690*)	26,183	1240
Milpitas city (95035*)	50,686	544	San Leandro city (94577*)	68,223	351
Mission Viejo city (92690*)	72,820	315	San Luis Obispo city (93401*)	41,958	698
Modesto city (95350*)	164,730	104	San Marcos city (92069)	38,974	764
Monrovia city (91016*)	35,761	844	San Mateo city (94402*)	85,486	254
Montclair city (91763)	28,434	1124	San Pablo city (94806)	25,158	1287
Montebello city (90640)	59,564	425	San Rafael city (94901*)	48,404	587
Monterey city (93940*)	31,954	975	San Ramon city (94583)	35,303	861
Monterey Park city (91754)	60,738	411	Santa Ana city (92799*)	293,742	52
Moorpark city (93021)	25,494	1273	Santa Barbara city (93102*)	85,571	252
Moreno Valley city (92388*)	118,779	155	Santa Clara city (95050*)	93,613	222
Mountain View city (94041*)	67,460	357	Santa Clarita city (91380*)	110,642	170
Napa city (94558*)	61,842	399	Santa Cruz city (95060*)	49,040	570
National City city (92050)	54,249	486	Santa Maria city (93454*)	61,284	408
Newark city (94560)	37,861	792	Santa Monica city (90406*)	86,905	246
Newport Beach city (92658*)	66,643	363	Santa Paula city (93060)	25,062	1294
North Highlands CDP (95660)	42,105	693	Santa Rosa city (95402*)	113,313	162
Norwalk city (90650*)	94,279	220	Santee city (92071*)	52,902	510
Novato city (94947*)	47,585	596	Saratoga city (95070*)	28,061	1145
Oakland city (94615*)	372,242	39	Seal Beach city (90740)	25,098	1289
Oceanside city (92054*)	128,398	143	Seaside city (93955)	38,901	768
Oildale CDP (93308*)	26,553	1214	Simi Valley city (93065*)	100,217	200
Ontario city (91761*)	133,179	136	South Gate city (90280)	86,284	250
Orange city (92613*)	110,658	169	South San Francisco city (94080*)	54,312	484
Orangevale CDP (95662)	26,266	1233	South Whittier CDP (90601*)	49,514	561
Oxnard city (93030*)	142,216	123	Spring Valley CDP (92078)	55,331	465

City and major zip code	1990 census	1990 rank
Stanton city (90680)	30,491	1042
Stockton city (95213*)	210,943	74
Sunnyvale city (94086*)	117,229	157
Temecula city (92390)	27,099	1189
Temple City city (91780)	31,100	1005
Thousand Oaks city (91359*)	104,352	190
Torrance city (90510*)	133,107	137
Tracy city (95376*)	33,558	918
Tulare city (93274*)	33,249	930
Turlock city (95380*)	42,198	689
Tustin city (92681*)	50,689	543
Union City city (94587)	53,762	491
Upland city (91786*)	63,374	388
Vacaville city (95687*)	71,479	325
Vallejo city (94590*)	109,199	175
Victorville city (92392*)	40,674	725
Visalia city (93277*)	75,636	300
Vista city (92083*)	71,872	321
Walnut city (91789*)	29,105	1095
Walnut Creek city (94596*)	60,569	414
Watsonville city (95076*)	31,099	1006
West Covina city (91790*)	96,086	214
West Hollywood city (90046)	36,118	837
Westminster city (92684*)	78,118	286
Westmont CDP (90250*)	31,044	1008
West Sacramento city (95691)	28,898	1101
Whittier city (90605*)	77,671	288
Willowbrook CDP (90223)	32,772	949
Woodland city (31365*)	39,802	747
Yorba Linda city (92686*)	52,422	513
Yuba City city (95991*)	27,437	1175
Yucaipa city (92399)	32,824	948

COLORADO

City and major zip code	1990 census	1990 rank
Arvada city (80001*)	89,235	235
Aurora city (80010*)	222,103	72
Boulder city (80302*)	83,312	268
Colorado Springs city (80910*)	281,140	54
Denver city (80201*)	467,610	26
Englewood city (80110*)	29,387	1079
Fort Collins city (80521*)	87,758	240
Grand Junction city (81501*)	29,034	1099
Greeley city (80631*)	60,536	416
Lakewood city (80215*)	126,481	145
Littleton city (80120*)	33,685	912
Longmont city (80501*)	51,555	529
Loveland city (80538*)	37,352	809
Northglenn city (80233*)	27,195	1186
Pueblo city (81003*)	98,640	207
Southglenn CDP (80122*)	43,087	672
Thornton city (80229*)	55,031	468
Westminster city (80030)	74,625	309
Wheat Ridge city (80033*)	29,419	1078

CONNECTICUT

City and major zip code	1990 census	1990 rank
Bridgeport city (06602*)	141,686	125
Bristol city (06010*)	60,640	412
Central Manchester CDP (06040*)	30,934	1018
Danbury city (06810*)	65,585	374
East Hartford CDP (06118*)	50,452	549
East Haven CDP (06512)	26,144	1242
Hartford city (06101*)	139,739	129
Meriden city (06450)	59,479	426
Middletown city (06457)	42,762	678
Milford city (remainder) (06460)	48,168	590
Naugatuck borough (06770)	30,625	1034
New Britain city (06050*)	75,491	302
New Haven city (06511*)	130,474	140
Newington CDP (06111*)	29,208	1086
New London city (06320)	28,540	1122
Norwalk city (06856*)	78,331	284
Norwich city (06360)	37,391	808
Shelton city (06484)	35,418	856
Stamford city (06910*)	108,056	181
Stratford CDP (06497)	49,389	565
Torrington city (06790)	33,687	911
Trumbull CDP (06611)	32,000	972
Waterbury city (06701*)	108,961	176
West Hartford CDP (06107*)	60,110	419
West Haven city (06516)	54,021	489
Wethersfield CDP (06109*)	25,651	1265

DELAWARE

City and major zip code	1990 census	1990 rank
Dover city (19901*)	27,630	1160
Newark city (19711*)	25,098	1289
Wilmington city (19850*)	71,529	324

DISTRICT OF COLUMBIA

City and major zip code	1990 census	1990 rank
Washington city (20066*)	606,900	19

FLORIDA

City and major zip code	1990 census	1990 rank
Altamonte Springs city (32714*)	34,879	871
Boca Raton city (33431*)	61,492	405
Boynton Beach city (33436*)	46,194	620
Bradenton city (34206*)	43,779	658
Brandon CDP (33511*)	57,985	438
Cape Coral city (33990)	74,991	306
Carol City CDP (33055)	53,331	500
Clearwater city (34618*)	98,784	206
Coconut Creek city (33063)	27,485	1173
Coral Gables city (33114)	40,091	740
Coral Springs city (33075)	79,443	282
Davie town (33329)	47,217	601
Daytona Beach city (32114*)	61,921	398
Deerfield Beach city (33441*)	46,325	617
Delray Beach city (33444*)	47,181	603
Deltona CDP (32725*)	50,828	541
Dunedin city (34698*)	34,012	896
Ferry Pass CDP (32501*)	26,301	1230
Fort Lauderdale city (33310*)	149,377	118
Fort Myers city (33907*)	45,206	637
Fort Pierce city (34950*)	36,830	819
Gainesville city (32602*)	84,770	258
Golden Glades CDP (33054*)	25,474	1274
Hallandale city (33010*)	30,996	1010
Hialeah city (33010*)	188,004	85
Hollywood city (33022*)	121,697	152
Homestead city (33030*)	26,866	1199
Jacksonville city (32203*)	635,230	15
Kendale Lakes CDP (33152*)	48,524	584
Kendall CDP (33256)	87,271	244
Kissimmee city (34744*)	30,050	1054
Lakeland city (33805*)	70,576	334
Lakeside CDP	29,137	1092
Lake Worth city (33461*)	28,564	1121
Largo city (34640*)	65,674	372
Lauderdale Lakes city (33152*)	27,341	1178
Lauderhill city (33152*)	49,708	559
Margate city (33063)	42,985	673
Melbourne city (32901*)	59,646	424
Merritt Island CDP (32953*)	32,886	944
Miami city (33152*)	358,548	46
Miami Beach city (33119)	92,639	225
Miramar city (33023)	40,663	726
North Fort Myers CDP (33903)	30,027	1056
North Lauderdale city (33060*)	26,506	1217
North Miami city (33261)	49,998	556
North Miami Beach city (33160)	35,359	857
Oakland Park city (33334*)	26,326	1226
Ocala city (32678*)	42,045	695
Olympia Heights CDP (33265)	37,792	797

City and major zip code	1990 census	1990 rank
Orlando city (32862*)	164,693	105
Ormond Beach city (32176*)	29,721	1070
Palm Bay city (32901*)	62,632	394
Palm Harbor CDP (34683*)	50,256	553
Panama City city (32401*)	34,378	884
Pembroke Pines city (33084)	65,452	376
Pensacola city (32501*)	58,165	434
Pine Hills CDP (32862*)	35,322	858
Pinellas Park city (34665*)	43,426	667
Plantation city (33318)	66,692	361
Pompano Beach city (33060*)	72,411	318
Port Charlotte CDP (33949)	41,535	708
Port Orange city (32129)	35,317	859
Port St. Lucie city (34985)	55,866	459
Riviera Beach city (33419)	27,639	1158
St. Petersburg city (33730*)	238,629	65
Sanford city (32771*)	32,387	959
Sarasota city (34230*)	50,961	539
South Miami Heights CDP (33152*)	30,030	1055
Spring Hill CDP (34606*)	31,117	1004
Sunrise city (33322)	64,407	381
Tallahassee city (32301*)	124,773	149
Tamarac city (33320)	44,822	643
Tamiami CDP (33144)	33,845	901
Tampa city (33630*)	280,015	55
Titusville city (32780*)	39,394	756
Town 'n' Country CDP (33685)	60,946	409
Westchester CDP (33165)	29,883	1063
West Little River CDP (33152*)	33,575	916
West Palm Beach city (33406*)	67,643	354

GEORGIA

City and major zip code	1990 census	1990 rank
Albany city (31706*)	78,122	285
Athens city (30601*)	45,734	629
Atlanta city (30304*)	394,017	36
Augusta city (30901*)	44,639	648
Candler-McAfee CDP (30304*)	29,491	1075
Columbus city (remainder) (31908*)	178,681	93
Dunwoody CDP (30304*)	26,302	1229
East Point city (30304*)	34,402	883
La Grange city (30240*)	25,597	1268
Mableton CDP (30059)	25,725	1262
Macon city (31201*)	106,612	185
Marietta city (30060*)	44,129	653
Martinez CDP (30907)	33,731	908
North Atlanta CDP (30319)	27,812	1152
Rome city (30161*)	30,326	1045
Roswell city (30075*)	47,923	591
Sandy Springs CDP (30304*)	67,842	353
Savannah city (31402*)	137,560	131
Smyrna city (30080*)	30,981	1014
South Augusta CDP (30901*)	55,998	457
Tucker CDP (30084*)	25,781	1260
Valdosta city (31603*)	39,806	746
Warner Robins city (31088*)	43,726	661
West Augusta CDP (30901*)	27,637	1159

HAWAII

City and major zip code	1990 census	1990 rank
Hilo CDP (96720*)	37,808	796
Honolulu CDP (96820*)	365,272	44
Kailua CDP (96734)	36,818	820
Kaneohe CDP (96744)	35,448	854
Mililani Town CDP (96789)	29,359	1080
Pearl City CDP (96782)	30,993	1011
Waimalu CDP (96701)	29,967	1058
Waipahu CDP (96797)	31,435	996

IDAHO

City and major zip code	1990 census	1990 rank
Boise City city (83708*)	125,738	148
Idaho Falls city (83401*)	43,929	654
Lewiston city (83501)	28,082	1144

City and major zip code	1990 census	1990 rank
Nampa city (83651*)	28,365	1127
Pocatello city (83201*)	46,080	622
Twin Falls city (83301*)	27,591	1167

ILLINOIS

City and major zip code	1990 census	1990 rank
Addison village (60101)	32,058	971
Alton city (62002)	32,905	941
Arlington Heights village (60005*)	75,460	303
Aurora city (60505*)	99,581	203
Belleville city (62220*)	42,785	677
Berwyn city (60402)	45,426	633
Bloomington city (61701*)	51,972	524
Bolingbrook village (60440)	40,843	720
Buffalo Grove village (60089)	36,427	827
Burbank city (60459)	27,600	1165
Calumet City city (60409)	37,840	793
Carbondale city (62901*)	27,033	1192
Carol Stream village (60188)	31,716	987
Champaign city (61820*)	63,502	387
Chicago city (60607*)	2,783,726	3
Chicago Heights city (60411)	33,072	936
Cicero town (60650)	67,436	358
Danville city (61832*)	33,828	905
Decatur city (62523*)	83,885	267
De Kalb city (60115)	34,925	869
Des Plaines city (60018*)	53,223	504
Downers Grove village (60515*)	46,858	608
East St. Louis city (62201*)	40,944	718
Elgin city (60120*)	77,010	290
Elk Grove Village village (60007*)	33,429	924
Elmhurst city (60126)	42,029	696
Evanston city (60201*)	73,233	313
Freeport city (61032)	25,840	1258
Galesburg city (61401*)	33,530	919
Glendale Heights village (60139)	27,973	1147
Glenview village (60025)	37,093	813
Granite City city (62040)	32,862	946
Hanover Park village (60103)	32,895	942
Harvey city (60426)	29,771	1067
Highland Park city (60035)	30,575	1037
Hoffman Estates village (60195)	46,561	612
Joliet city (60436*)	76,836	291
Kankakee city (60901)	27,575	1168
Lansing village (60438)	28,086	1143
Lombard village (60148)	39,408	755
Maywood village (60153)	27,139	1187
Moline city (61265)	43,202	670
Mount Prospect village (60056)	53,170	505
Naperville city (60540*)	85,351	256
Niles village (60648)	28,284	1131
Normal town (61761)	40,023	744
Northbrook village (60062*)	32,308	963
North Chicago city (60064)	34,978	868
Oak Forest city (60452)	26,203	1238
Oak Lawn village (60455*)	56,182	455
Oak Park village (60301*)	53,648	495
Orland Park village (60462)	35,720	846
Palatine village (60067*)	39,253	760
Park Ridge city (60068)	36,175	835
Pekin city (61554*)	32,254	965
Peoria city (61601*)	113,504	161
Quincy city (62301*)	39,681	751
Rockford city (61125*)	139,426	130
Rock Island city (61201*)	40,552	728
Schaumburg village (60194*)	68,586	349
Skokie village (60077*)	59,432	428
Springfield city (62703*)	105,227	188
Streamwood village (60107)	30,987	1012
Tinley Park village (60477)	37,121	811
Urbana city (61801)	36,344	830
Waukegan city (60085*)	69,392	342

City and major zip code	1990 census	1990 rank
Wheaton city (60187*)	51,464	530
Wheeling village (60090)	29,911	1061
Wlimette village (60091)	26,690	1207
Woodridge village (60517)	26,256	1235
INDIANA		
Anderson city (46011*)	59,459	427
Bloomington city (47408*)	60,633	413
Carmel city (46032)	25,380	1279
Columbus city (47201*)	31,802	984
East Chicago city (46312)	33,892	899
Elkhart city (46515*)	43,627	663
Evansville city (47708*)	126,272	147
Fort Wayne city (46802*)	173,072	99
Gary city (46401*)	116,646	158
Greenwood city (46142*)	26,265	1234
Hammond city (46320*)	84,236	263
Indianapolis city (46206*)	731,327	13
Kokomo city (46902*)	44,962	640
Lafayette city (47901*)	43,764	659
Lawrence city (46226)	26,763	1203
Marion city (46952*)	32,618	951
Merrillville town (46410)	27,257	1183
Michigan City city (46360)	33,822	907
Mishawaka city (46544*)	42,608	684
Muncie city (47302*)	71,035	330
New Albany city (47150*)	36,322	832
Portage city (46368)	29,060	1097
Richmond city (47374*)	38,705	772
South Bend city (46624*)	105,511	187
Terre Haute city (47808*)	57,483	442
West Lafayette city (47906*)	25,907	1252
IOWA		
Ames city (50010)	47,198	602
Bettendorf city (52722)	28,132	1141
Burlington city (52601)	27,208	1185
Cedar Falls city (50613)	34,298	887
Cedar Rapids city (52401*)	108,751	178
Clinton city (52732)	29,201	1089
Council Bluffs city (51501*)	54,315	483
Davenport city (52802*)	95,333	218
Des Moines city (50318*)	193,187	80
Dubuque city (52001*)	57,546	441
Fort Dodge city (50501)	25,894	1254
Iowa City city (52240*)	59,738	421
Marshalltown city (50158)	25,178	1286
Mason City city (50401)	29,040	1098
Sioux City city (51101*)	80,505	276
Waterloo city (50703*)	66,467	365
West Des Moines city (50265)	31,702	988
KANSAS		
Emporia city (66801)	25,512	1272
Hutchinson city (67501*)	39,308	759
Kansas City city (66106*)	149,767	116
Lawrence city (66044*)	65,608	373
Leavenworth city (66048)	38,495	775
Lenexa city (66215)	34,034	895
Manhattan city (66502)	37,712	800
Olathe city (66061*)	63,352	389
Overland Park city (66204)	111,790	165
Salina city (67401*)	42,303)	688
Shawnee city (66203)	37,993	788
Topeka city (66603*)	119,883	153
Wichita city (67276*)	304,011	51
KENTUCKY		
Bowling Green city (42101*)	40,641	727
Covington city (41011*)	43,264	668
Frankfort city (40601*)	25,968	1249
Henderson city (42420)	25,945	1250

City and major zip code	1990 census	1990 rank
Hopkinsville city (42240*)	29,809	1065
Lexington-Fayette (40511*)	225,366	70
Louisville city (40231*)	269,063	58
Owensboro city (42301*)	53,549	497
Paducah city (42003*)	27,256	1184
Pleasure Ridge Park CDP (40268)	25,131	1288
LOUISIANA		
Alexandria city (71301*)	49,188	569
Baton Rouge city (70821*)	219,531	73
Bossier City city (71111*)	52,721	511
Chalmette CDP (70043*)	31,860	979
Houma city (70360*)	30,495	1041
Kenner city (70062*)	72,033	320
Lafayette city (70501*)	94,440	219
Lake Charles city (70601*)	70,580	333
Marerro CDP (70072*)	36,671	825
Metairie (70009*)	149,428	117
Monroe city (71203*)	54,909	472
New Iberia city (70560*)	31,828	981
New Orleans city (70113*)	496,938	24
Shreveport city (71102*)	198,525	77
MAINE		
Bangor city (04401*)	33,181	932
Lewiston city (04240*)	39,757	749
Portland city (04101*)	64,358	382
MARYLAND		
Annapolis city (21401*)	33,187	931
Aspen Hill CDP (20916)	45,494	632
Baltimore city (21233*)	736,014	12
Bel Air South CDP (21014*)	26,421	1223
Bethesda CDP (20814*)	62,936	392
Bowie city (20715*)	37,589	804
Carney CDP (21234)	25,578	1269
Catonsville CDP (21228)	35,233	863
Chillum CDP (20783)	31,309	998
Columbia CDP (21045*)	75,883	297
Dundalk CDP (21222*)	65,800	370
Ellicott City CDP (21043)	41,396	709
Essex CDP (21221)	40,872	719
Frederick city (21701*)	40,148	739
Gaithersburg city (20877*)	39,542	752
Germantown CDP (20874*)	41,145	713
Glen Burnie CDP (21061*)	37,305	810
Hagerstown city (21740*)	35,445	855
Lochearn CDP (21207)	25,240	1285
Montgomery Village CDP (20886)	32,315	961
North Bethesda CDP (20850)	29,656	1072
Oxon Hill-Glassmanor (20790*)	35,794	843
Parkville CDP (21234)	31,617	990
Potomac CDP (20859)	45,634	630
Randallstown CDP (21133)	26,277	1231
Rockville city (20850*)	44,835	642
St. Charles CDP (20601)	28,717	1111
Severna Park CDP (21146)	25,879	1255
Silver Spring CDP (20907*)	76,046	296
South Gate CDP (21061)	27,564	1169
Suitland-Silver Mill (20790*)	35,111	865
Towson CDP (21285)	49,445	563
Wheaton-Glenmont CDP (20915)	53,720	492
Woodlawn CDP (21207)	32,907	940
MASSACHUSETTS		
Arlington CDP (02174)	44,630	649
Attleboro city (02703)	38,383	777
Beverly city (01915)	38,195	779
Boston city (02205*)	574,283	20
Braintree CDP (02184)	33,836	903
Brockton city (02402*)	92,788	223

City and major zip code	1990 census	1990 rank
Brookline CDP (02147*)	54,718	479
Cambridge city (02139*)	95,802	215
Chelmsford CDP (01824)	32,388	958
Chelsea city (02150)	28,710	1113
Chicopee city (01020*)	56,632	452
Everett city (02149)	35,701	849
Fall River city (02720*)	92,703	224
Fitchburg city (01420)	41,194	712
Framingham CDP (01701)	64,994	379
Gloucester city (01930*)	28,716	1112
Haverhill city (01830*)	51,418	532
Holyoke city (01040*)	43,704	662
Lawrence city (01842*)	70,207	338
Leominster city (01453)	38,145	782
Lexington CDP (02173)	28,974	1100
Lowell city (01853*)	103,439	193
Lynn city (10901*)	81,245	273
Malden city (02148)	53,884	490
Marlborough city (01752)	31,813	982
Medford city (02155)	57,407	443
Melrose city (02176)	28,150	1139
Milton CDP (02186)	25,725	1262
Needham CDP (02194*)	27,557	1170
New Bedford city (02740*)	99,922	201
Newton city (02164*)	82,585	269
Northampton city (01060*)	29,289	1083
Norwood CDP (02062)	28,700	1115
Peabody city (01960*)	47,039	605
Pittsfield city (01201*)	48,622	581
Quincy city (02369*)	84,985	257
Randolph CDP (02368)	30,093	1052
Revere city (02151)	42,786	676
Salem city (01970*)	48,091	786
Saugus CDP (01906)	25,549	1271
Somerville city (02143*)	76,210	293
Springfield city (01101*)	156,983	112
Taunton city (02780)	49,832	558
Waltham city (02154)	57,878	439
Watertown CDP (02172)	33,284	929
Wellesley CDP (02181)	26,615	1211
Westfield city (01085*)	38,372	778
West Springfield CDP (01089*)	27,537	1172
Weymouth CDP (02188*)	54,063	487
Woburn city (01801)	35,943	841
Worcester city (01613*)	169,759	102

MICHIGAN

City and major zip code	1990 census	1990 rank
Allen Park city (48101)	31,092	1007
Ann Arbor city (48103*)	109,592	174
Battle Creek city (49016*)	53,540	498
Bay City city (48707*)	38,936	766
Bloomfield Township CDP (48302)	42,137	692
Burton city (48529*)	27,617	1162
Canton CDP (48185*)	57,047	447
Clinton city (48043)	85,866	251
Dearborn city (48120*)	89,286	234
Dearborn Heights city (48127*)	60,838	410
Detroit city (48283*)	1,027,974	7
East Detroit city (48021)	35,283	862
East Lansing city (48823*)	50,677	545
Farmington Hills city (48333*)	74,652	308
Ferndale city (48220)	25,084	1292
Flint city (48502*)	140,761	127
Garden City city (48135)	31,846	980
Grand Rapids city (49501*)	189,126	83
Holland city (49423*)	30,745	1028
Inkster city (48141)	30,772	1025
Jackson city (49201*)	37,446	806
Kalamazoo city (49001*)	80,277	279
Kentwood city (49518)	37,826	794
Lansing city (48924*)	127,321	144

City and major zip code	1990 census	1990 rank
Lincoln Park city (48146)	41,832	702
Livonia city (48150*)	100,850	198
Madison Heights city (48071)	32,196	967
Midland city (48640*)	38,053	787
Muskegon city (49440*)	40,283	733
Novi city (48376*)	32,998	937
Oak Park city (48237)	30,462	1043
Pontiac city (48343*)	71,166	329
Portage city (49081)	41,042	715
Port Huron city (48061*)	33,694	910
Redford CDP (48231*)	54,387	482
Rochester Hills city (48309)	61,766	402
Roseville city (48066)	51,412	533
Royal Oak city (48068*)	65,410	377
Saginaw city (48605*)	69,512	340
St. Clair Shores city (48080*)	68,107	352
Shelby CDP (48318*)	48,655	580
Southfield city (48037*)	75,728	298
Southgate city (48195)	30,771	1026
Sterling Heights city (48311*)	117,810	156
Taylor city (48180)	70,811	331
Troy city (48099*)	72,884	314
Warren city (48090*)	144,864	120
Waterford CDP (48329*)	66,692	361
West Bloomfield Township (48343*)	54,843	475
Westland city (48185)	84,724	259
Wyandotte city (48192)	30,938	1017
Wyoming city (49509)	63,891	384

MINNESOTA

City and major zip code	1990 census	1990 rank
Apple Valley city (55124)	34,598	876
Blaine city (55434)	38,975	763
Bloomington city (55431*)	86,335	249
Brooklyn Center city (55429*)	28,887	1102
Brooklyn Park city (55429*)	56,381	453
Burnsville city (55337)	51,288	534
Coon Rapids city (55433)	52,978	508
Duluth city (55806*)	85,493	253
Eagan city (55121)	47,409	599
Eden Prairie city (55344*)	39,311	758
Edina city (55424)	46,070	624
Fridley city (55432)	28,335	1128
Mankato city (56001*)	31,477	995
Maple Grove city (55369)	38,736	770
Maplewood city (55109)	30,954	1015
Minneapolis city (55401*)	368,383	42
Minnetonka city (55345)	48,370	588
Moorhead city (56560*)	32,295	964
Plymouth city (55441*)	50,889	540
Richfield city (55423)	35,710	847
Rochester city (55901*)	70,745	332
Roseville city (55113)	33,485	922
St. Cloud city (56301*)	48,812	574
St. Louis Park city (55426)	43,787	657
St. Paul city (55101*)	272,235	57
Winona city (55987)	25,399	1278

MISSISSIPPI

City and major zip code	1990 census	1990 rank
Biloxi city (39530*)	46,419	618
Greenville city (38701*)	45,226	635
Gulfport city (39503*)	40,775	722
Hattiesburg city (39402*)	41,882	700
Jackson city (39205*)	196,637	78
Meridian city (39301*)	41,036	716
Pascagoula city (39567*)	25,899	1253
Tupelo city (38801*)	30,685	1033

MISSOURI

City and major zip code	1990 census	1990 rank
Blue Springs city (64015*)	40,153	738
Cape Girardeau city (63701*)	34,438	882
Chesterfield city (63017*)	37,991	789

City and major zip code	1990 census	1990 rank
Columbia city (65201*)	69,101	345
Florissant city (63033*)	51,206	536
Gladstone city (64108*)	26,243	1236
Independence city (64050*)	112,301	164
Jefferson City city (65101*)	35,481	853
Joplin city (64801*)	40,961	717
Kansas City city (64108*)	435,146	31
Kirkwood city (63122)	27,291	1182
Lee's Summit city (64063*)	46,418	615
Maryland Heights city (64043)	25,407	1277
Mehlville CDP (63129)	27,557	1170
Oakville CDP (63129)	31,750	985
Raytown city (64108*)	30,601	1035
St. Charles city (63301*)	54,555	480
St. Joseph city (64501*)	71,852	322
St. Louis city (63155*)	396,685	34
St. Peters city (63376)	45,779	628
Springfield city (65801*)	140,494	128
University City city (63130)	40,087	741

MONTANA

Billings city (59101*)	81,151	274
Butte-Silver Bow (remainder) (59701*)	33,336	928
Great Falls city (59401*)	55,097	466
Missoula city (59801*)	42,918	674

NEBRASKA

Bellevue city (68005)	30,982	1013
Grand Island city (68802*)	39,386	757
Lincoln city (68501*)	191,972	81
Omaha city (68108*)	335,795	48

NEVADA

Carson City (89701*)	40,443	730
Henderson city (89015*)	64,942	380
Las Vegas city (89199*)	258,295	63
North Las Vegas city (89030*)	47,707	594
Paradise CDP (89109*)	124,682	150
Reno city (89510*)	133,850	134
Sparks city (89431*)	53,367	499
Spring Valley CDP (89117*)	51,726	527
Sunrise Manor CDP (89110*)	95,362	217

NEW HAMPSHIRE

Concord city (03301*)	36,006	840
Dover city (03820)	25,042	1295
Manchester city (03103*)	99,567	204
Nashua city (03060*)	79,662	281
Portsmouth city (03801*)	25,925	1251
Rochester city (03867*)	26,630	1209

NEW JERSEY

Atlantic City city (08401*)	37,986	790
Bayonne city (07002)	61,444	406
Belleville CDP (07109)	34,213	890
Bloomfield CDP (07003)	45,061	638
Brick Township CDP (08723*)	66,473	364
Camden city (08101*)	87,492	242
Cherry Hill CDP (08034*)	69,319	344
Clifton city (07015*)	71,742	323
East Brunswick CDP (08816)	43,548	664
East Orange city (07019*)	73,552	312
Edison CDP (08818*)	88,680	237
Elizabeth city (07207*)	110,002	172
Ewing CDP (08650*)	34,185	892
Fair Lawn borough (07410)	30,548	1038
Fort Lee borough (07024)	31,997	973
Garfield city (07026)	26,727	1205
Hackensack city (07602*)	37,049	815
Hoboken city (07030)	33,397	926
Irvington CDP (07111)	59,774	420
Jersey City city (07303*)	228,537	67

City and major zip code	1990 census	1990 rank
Kearny town (07032)	34,874	872
Lakewood CDP (08701)	26,095	1243
Linden city (07036)	36,701	823
Livingston CDP (07039)	26,609	1212
Long Branch city (07740)	28,658	1117
Mercerville-Hamilton Square CDP (08619)	26,873	1197
Millville city (08332)	25,992	1248
Montclair CDP (07042*)	37,729	799
Newark city (07102*)	275,221	56
New Bunswick city (08901*)	41,711	704
North Bergen CDP (07047)	48,414	586
North Brunswick Township (08902)	31,287	1001
Nutley CDP (07110)	27,099	1189
Orange CDP (07051*)	29,925	1060
Paramus borough (07652*)	25,067	1293
Parsippany-Troy Hill (07054)	48,478	585
Passaic city (07055)	58,041	436
Paterson city (07510*)	140,891	126
Pennsauken CDP (08110)	34,733	874
Perth Amboy city (08861*)	41,967	697
Plainfield city (07061*)	46,567	611
Rahway city (07065)	25,325	1280
Sayreville borough (08872*)	34,986	867
Teaneck CDP (07666)	37,825	795
Trenton city (08650*)	88,675	238
Union CDP (07083)	50,024	554
Union City city (07087)	58,012	437
Vineland city (08360)	54,780	477
Wayne CDP (07470*)	47,025	606
Westfield town (07091*)	28,870	1103
West Milford CDP (07480)	25,430	1275
West New York town (07093)	38,125	785
West Orange CDP (07052)	39,103	762
Willingboro CDP (08046)	36,291	833

NEW MEXICO

Alamogordo city (88310*)	27,596	1166
Albuquerque city (87101*)	384,736	38
Clovis city (88101*)	30,954	1015
Farmington city (87401*)	33,997	897
Hobbs city (88240*)	29,115	1094
Las Cruces city (88001*)	62,126	396
Rio Rancho city (87124)	32,505	953
Roswell city (88201*)	44,654	647
Santa Fe city (87501*)	55,859	460
South Valley CDP (87101*)	35,701	849

NEW YORK

Albany city (12288*)	101,082	197
Auburn city (13021*)	31,258	1003
Binghamton city (13902*)	53,008	507
Brentwood CDP (11717)	45,218	636
Brighton CDP (14610)	34,455	880
Buffalo city (14240*)	328,123	50
Centereach CDP (11720)	26,720	1206
Central Islip CDP (11722)	26,028	1245
Cheektowaga CDP (14225)	84,387	261
Commack CDP (11725)	36,124	836
Coram CDP (11727)	30,111	1049
Deer Park CDP (11729)	28,840	1105
Dix Hills CDP (11746)	25,849	1257
East Meadow CDP (11554)	36,909	818
Elmira city (14901*)	33,724	909
Elmont CDP (11003)	28,612	1119
Franklin Square CDP (11010)	28,205	1136
Freeport village (11520)	39,894	745
Hempstead village (11551*)	49,453	562
Hicksville CDP (11805*)	40,174	737
Holbrook CDP (11741)	25,273	1284
Huntington Station CDP (11746)	28,247	1133
Irondequoit CDP (14617)	52,322	517

City and major zip code	1990 census	1990 rank
Ithaca city (14850*)	29,541	1074
Jamestown city (14701*)	34,681	875
Levittown CDP (11756)	53,286	502
Lindenhurst village (11757)	26,879	1196
Long Beach city (11561)	33,510	920
Mount Vernon city (10551*)	67,153	360
Newburgh city (12550*)	26,454	1221
New City CDP (10956)	33,673	913
New Rochelle city (10802*)	67,265	359
New York City (10199*)	7,322,564	1
Brooklyn (11256*)	2,300,664	
Bronx (10451*)	1,203,789	
Manhattan (10199*)	1,487,536	
Queens	1,951,598	
Staten Island (10314*)	378,977	
Niagara Falls city (14302*)	61,840	400
North Tonawanda city (14120)	34,989	866
Oceanside CDP (11572)	32,423	956
Plainview CDP (11803)	26,207	1237
Poughkeepsie city (12601*)	28,844	1104
Rochester city (14692*)	231,636	66
Rome city (13440)	44,350	652
Saratoga Springs city (12866)	25,001	1296
Schenectady city (12305*)	65,566	375
Smithtown CDP (11787)	25,638	1266
Syracuse city (13220*)	163,860	107
Tonawanda CDP (14150*)	65,284	378
Troy city (12180*)	54,269	485
Utica city (13504*)	68,637	348
Valley Stream village (11582*)	33,946	898
Watertown city (13601*)	29,429	1077
West Babylon CDP (11707)	42,410	686
West Islip CDP (11795)	28,419	1125
West Seneca CDP (14224)	47,866	592
White Plains city (10602*)	48,718	578
Yonkers city (10702*)	188,082	84

NORTH CAROLINA

Asheville city (28810*)	61,607	404
Burlington city (27215*)	39,498	753
Camp Lejeune Central (28542)	36,716	822
Cary town (27511*)	43,858	656
Chapel Hill town (27514*)	38,719	771
Charlotte city (28228*)	395,934	35
Concord city (28025*)	27,347	1177
Durham city (27701*)	136,611	132
Fayetteville city (28302*)	75,695	299
Fort Bragg CDP (28307)	34,744	873
Gastonia city (28052*)	54,732	478
Goldsboro city (27530*)	40,709	724
Greensboro city (27420*)	183,521	88
Greenville city (27834*)	44,972	639
Hickory city (28603*)	28,301	1130
High Point city (27260*)	69,496	341
Jacksonville city (28540*)	30,013	1057
Kannapolis city (28081*)	29,696	1071
Kinston city (28501*)	25,295	1282
Raleigh city (27611*)	207,951	75
Rocky Mount city (27801*)	48,997	571
Wilmington city (28402*)	55,530	462
Wilson city (27893*)	36,930	817
Winston-Salem city (27102*)	143,485	121

NORTH DAKOTA

Bismarck city (58501*)	49,256	568
Fargo city (58102*)	74,111	310
Grand Forks city (58201*)	49,425	564
Minot city (58701*)	34,544	878

OHIO

Akron city (44309*)	223,019	71
Austintown CDP (44515)	32,371	960

City and major zip code	1990 census	1990 rank
Barberton city (44203)	27,623	1161
Beavercreek city (45430*)	33,626	914
Boardman CDP (44512*)	38,596	774
Bowling Green city (43402)	28,176	1137
Brunswick city (44212)	28,230	1134
Canton city (44711*)	84,161	264
Cincinnati city (45234*)	364,040	45
Cleveland city (44101*)	505,616	23
Cleveland Heights city (44118)	54,052	488
Columbus city (43216*)	632,910	16
Cuyahoga Falls city (44222*)	48,950	572
Dayton city (45401*)	182,044	89
East Cleveland city (44112)	33,096	935
Elyria city (44035*)	56,746	450
Euclid city (44117)	54,875	473
Fairborn city (45324)	31,300	1000
Fairfield city (45014)	39,729	750
Findlay city (45840*)	35,703	848
Gahanna city (43230)	27,791	1153
Garfield Heights city (44125)	31,739	986
Hamilton city (45011*)	61,368	407
Huber Heights city (45424)	38,696	773
Kent city (44240)	28,835	1106
Kettering city (45429)	60,569	414
Lakewood city (44107)	59,718	422
Lancaster city (43130)	34,507	879
Lima city (45802*)	45,549	631
Lorain city (44052*)	71,245	328
Mansfield city (44901*)	50,627	546
Maple Heights city (44137)	27,089	1191
Marion city (43302*)	34,075	894
Massillon city (44646*)	31,007	1009
Mentor city (44060*)	47,358	600
Middletown city (45042*)	46,022	625
Newark city (43055*)	44,389	651
North Olmsted city (44070)	34,204	891
Parma city (44129)	87,876	239
Reynoldsburg city (43068)	25,748	1261
Sandusky city (44870*)	29,764	1068
Shaker Heights city (44120)	30,831	1024
Springfield city (45501*)	70,487	335
Stow city (44224)	27,702	1155
Strongsville city (44136)	35,308	860
Toledo city (43601*)	332,943	49
Upper Arlington city (43221)	34,128	893
Warren city (44481*)	50,793	542
Westerville city (43081)	30,269	1046
Westlake city (44145)	27,018	1194
Youngstown city (44501*)	95,732	216
Zanesville city (43701*)	26,778	1202

OKLAHOMA

Bartlesville city (74003*)	34,256	889
Broken Arrow city (74012*)	58,043	435
Edmond city (73034*)	52,315	518
Enid city (73701*)	45,309	634
Lawton city (73501*)	80,561	275
Midwest City city (73125*)	52,267	520
Moore city (73125*)	40,318	732
Muskogee city (74401*)	37,708	801
Norman city (73069*)	80,071	280
Oklahoma City city (73125*)	444,719	29
Ponca City city (74601*)	26,359	1225
Shawnee city (74801*)	26,017	1246
Stillwater city (74074*)	36,676	824
Tulsa city (74103*)	367,302	43

OREGON

Albany city (97321)	29,462	1076
Aloha CDP (97006*)	34,284	888
Beaverton city (97005*)	53,310	501
Corvallis city (97333*)	44,757	644

City and major zip code	1990 census	1990 rank
Eugene city (97401*)	112,669	163
Gresham city (97030*)	68,235	350
Hillsboro city (97123*)	37,520	805
Lake Oswego city (97034*)	30,576	1036
Medford city (97501*)	46,951	607
Portland city (97208*)	437,319	30
Powellhurst-Centennial CDP (97208*)	28,756	1109
Salem city (97301*)	107,786	182
Springfield city (97477)	44,683	646
Tigard city (97208*)	29,344	1081
PENNSYLVANIA		
Allentown city (18101*)	105,090	189
Altoona city (16601*)	51,881	525
Bethel Park borough (15102)	33,823	906
Bethlehem city (18016*)	71,428	326
Chester city (19013*)	41,856	701
Drexel Hill CDP (19026)	29,744	1069
Easton city (18042*)	26,276	1232
Erie city (16515*)	108,718	179
Harrisburg city (17107*)	52,376	514
Johnstown city (15901*)	28,134	1140
Lancaster city (17604*)	55,551	461
Levittown CDP (19053*)	55,362	464
McCandless Township CDP (15237*)	28,781	1107
McKeesport city (15134*)	26,016	1247
Mount Lebanon CDP (15228)	33,362	927
Municipality of Monroeville borough (15146*)	29,169	1091
New Castle city (16108*)	28,334	1129
Norristown borough (19401*)	30,749	1027
Penn Hills CDP (15235)	51,430	531
Philadelphia city (19104*)	1,585,577	5
Pittsburgh city (15290*)	369,879	40
Plum borough (15239)	25,609	1267
Radnor Township CDP (19087)	28,705	1114
Reading city (19612*)	78,380	283
Ross Township CDP (15290*)	33,482	923
Scranton city (18505*)	81,805	272
Shaler Township CDP (15290*)	30,533	1040
State College borough (16801*)	38,923	767
Wilkes-Barre city (18701*)	47,523	598
Williamsport city (17701*)	31,933	976
York city (17405*)	42,192	690
RHODE ISLAND		
Cranston city (02920*)	76,060	295
East Providence city (02914)	50,380	551
Newport city (02840)	28,227	1135
Pawtucket city (02860*)	72,644	317
Providence city (02904*)	160,728	108
North Providence CDP (02908)	32,090	969
Warwick city (02886*)	85,427	255
West Warwick CDP (02886*)	29,268	1085
Woonsocket city (02895)	43,877	655
SOUTH CAROLINA		
Anderson city (29621*)	26,184	1239
Charleston city (29423*)	80,414	277
Columbia city (29292*)	98,052	208
Florence city (29501*)	29,813	1064
Greenville city (29602*)	58,282	433
Mount Pleasant town (29464*)	30,108	1050
North Charleston city (29406*)	70,218	337
Rock Hill city (29730*)	41,643	707
St. Andrews CDP (29407*)	25,692	1264
Spartanburg city (29301*)	43,467	666
Sumter city (29150*)	41,943	699
SOUTH DAKOTA		
Rapid City city (57701*)	54,523	481

City and major zip code	1990 census	1990 rank
Sioux Falls city (57101*)	100,814	199
TENNESSEE		
Bartlett town (38101*)	26,989	1195
Chattanooga city (37421*)	152,466	114
Clarksville city (37040*)	75,494	301
Cleveland city (37311*)	30,354	1044
Columbia city (38401*)	28,583	1120
Germantown city (38183)	32,893	943
Hendersonville city (37075*)	32,188	968
Jackson city (38301*)	48,949	573
Johnson City city (37601*)	49,381	566
Kingsport city (37660*)	36,365	829
Knoxville city (37950*)	165,121	103
Memphis city (38101*)	610,337	18
Murfreesboro city (37130*)	44,922	641
Nashville-Davidson (37229*)	488,374	25
Oak Ridge city (37830*)	27,310	1181
TEXAS		
Abilene city (79604*)	106,654	184
Amarillo city (79120*)	157,615	111
Arlington city (76010*)	261,721	61
Austin city (78710*)	465,622	27
Baytown city (77520*)	63,850	385
Beaumont city (77707*)	114,323	159
Bedford city (76021*)	43,762	660
Brownsville city (78520*)	98,962	205
Bryan city (77801*)	55,002	470
Carrollton city (75006*)	82,169	270
Channelview CDP (77530)	25,564	1270
College Station city (77840*)	52,456	512
Conroe city (77301*)	27,610	1163
Corpus Christi city (78469*)	257,453	64
Dallas city (75260*)	1,006,877	8
Deer Park city (77536)	27,652	1157
Del Rio city (78840*)	30,705	1032
Denton city (76201*)	66,270	367
DeSoto city (75115)	30,544	1039
Duncanville city (75138*)	35,748	845
Edinburg city (78539*)	29,885	1062
El Paso city (79910*)	515,342	22
Euless city (76039*)	38,149	781
Fort Hood CDP (76541*)	35,580	851
Fort Worth city (76161*)	447,619	28
Galveston city (77550*)	59,070	430
Garland city (75040*)	180,650	91
Grand Prairie city (75051*)	99,616	202
Grapevine city (96051*)	29,202	1088
Haltom City city (76117)	32,856	947
Harlingen city (78550*)	48,735	576
Houston city (77201*)	1,630,553	4
Huntsville city (77340*)	27,925	1149
Hurst city (76053*)	33,574	917
Irving city (75015*)	155,037	113
Killeen city (76541*)	63,535	386
Kingsville city (78363*)	25,276	1283
Kingwood CDP (77338*)	37,397	807
La Porte city (77571*)	27,910	1150
Laredo city (78041*)	122,899	151
League City city (77573*)	30,159	1048
Lewisville city (75067*)	46,521	614
Longview city (75602*)	70,311	336
Lubbock city (79402*)	186,206	87
Lufkin city (75901*)	30,206	1047
McAllen city (78501*)	82,021	265
Mesquite city (75149*)	101,484	195
Midland city (79711*)	89,443	233
Mission city (78572)	28,653	1118
Missouri City city (77489*)	36,176	834
Nacogdoches city (75961*)	30,872	1022

City and major zip code	1990 census	1990 rank
New Braunfels city (78130*)	27,334	1179
North Richland Hills city (76182)	45,895	626
Odessa city (79761*)	89,699	232
Pasadena city (77501*)	119,363	154
Pharr city (78577)	32,921	939
Plano city (75075*)	128,713	142
Port Arthur city (77640*)	58,724	431
Richardson city (75080*)	74,840	307
Round Rock city (78681*)	30,923	1019
San Angelo city (76902*)	84,474	260
San Antonio city (78284*)	935,933	10
San Marcos city (78666*)	28,743	1110
Sherman city (75090*)	31,601	991
Spring CDP (77373*)	33,111	933
Temple city (76501*)	46,109	621
Texarkana city (75501*)	31,656	989
Texas City city (77590*)	40,822	721
The Woodlands CDP (77373*)	29,205	1087
Tyler city (75712*)	75,450	304
Victoria city (77901*)	55,076	467
Waco city (76702*)	103,590	192
Wichita Falls city (76307*)	96,259	213

UTAH

Bountiful city (84010*)	36,659	826
Cottonwood Heights CDP (84121)	28,766	1108
Kearns CDP (84118)	28,374	1126
Layton city (84041*)	41,784	703
Logan city (84321)	32,762	950
Millcreek CDP (84109)	32,230	966
Murray city (84199*)	31,282	1002
Ogden city (84401*)	63,909	383
Orem city (84057*)	67,561	355
Provo city (84601*)	86,835	248
St. George city (84770*)	28,502	1123
Salt Lake City city (84199*)	159,936	109
Sandy city (84070*)	75,058	305
Taylorsville-Bennion (84107*)	52,351	516
West Jordan city (84084*)	42,892	675
West Valley City city (84199*)	86,976	245

VERMONT

Burlington city (05401*)	39,127	761

VIRGINIA

Alexandria city (22313*)	111,183	168
Annandale CDP (22003)	50,975	538
Arlington CDP (22210*)	170,936	100
Blacksburg town (24060*)	34,590	877
Burke CDP (22015)	57,734	440
Centreville CDP (22020)	26,585	1213
Chantilly CDP (22030*)	29,337	1082
Charlottesville city (22906*)	40,341	731
Chesapeake city (23320*)	151,976	115
Dale City CDP (22191*)	47,170	604
Danville city (24541*)	53,056	506
Hampton city (23670*)	133,793	135
Harrisonburg city (22801)	30,707	1031
Jefferson CDP (22030*)	25,782	1259
Lynchburg city (24506*)	66,049	369
Manassas city (22110*)	27,957	1148
McLean CDP (22101*)	38,168	780
Mount Vernon CDP (22121)	27,485	1173
Newport News city (23607*)	170,045	101
Norfolk city (23501*)	261,229	62
Petersburg city (23804*)	38,386	776
Portsmouth city (23707*)	103,907	191
Reston CDP (22090)	48,556	583
Richmond city (23232*)	203,056	76
Roanoke city (24022*)	96,397	211
Suffolk city (23434*)	52,141	522

City and major zip code	1990 census	1990 rank
Tuckahoe CDP (23232*)	42,629	683
Virginia Beach city (23450*)	393,069	37
West Springfield CDP (22152)	28,126	1142
Woodbridge CDP (22191*)	26,401	1224

WASHINGTON

Auburn city (98002*)	33,102	934
Bellevue city (98009*)	86,874	247
Bellingham city (98225*)	52,179	521
Bremerton city (98310*)	38,142	783
Burien CDP (98166)	25,089	1291
Cascade-Fairwood CDP	30,107	1051
East Hill-Meridian CDP	42,696	679
Edmonds city (98020*)	30,744	1029
Everett city (98201*)	69,961	339
Inglewood-Finn Hill (98011*)	29,132	1093
Federal Way CDP (98063)	67,554	356
Kennewick city (99336*)	42,155	691
Kent city (98031*)	37,960	791
Kirkland city (98033*)	40,052	743
Lakewood CDP (98259)	58,412	432
Longview city (98632)	31,499	993
Lynnwood city (98036*)	28,695	1116
Olympia city (98501*)	33,840	902
Redmond city (98052*)	35,800	842
Renton city (98058*)	41,688	705
Richland city (99352)	32,315	961
Richmond Heights CDP (98177)	26,037	1244
Seattle city (98109*)	516,259	21
Spokane city (99210*)	177,196	94
Tacoma city (98413*)	176,664	95
University Place CDP	27,701	1156
Vancouver city (98661*)	46,380	616
Walla Walla city (99362)	26,748	1219
Yakima city (98903*)	54,827	476

WEST VIRGINIA

Charleston city (25301*)	57,287	444
Huntington city (25704*)	54,844	474
Morgantown city (26505*)	25,879	1255
Parkersburg city (26101*)	33,862	900
Wheeling city (26003)	34,882	870

WISCONSIN

Appleton city (54911*)	65,695	371
Beloit city (53511*)	35,573	852
Brookfield city (53045*)	35,184	864
Eau Claire city (54703*)	56,856	449
Fond du Lac city (54935*)	37,757	798
Green Bay city (54303*)	96,466	210
Greenfield city (53220)	33,403	925
Janesville city (53545*)	52,133	523
Kenosha city (53140*)	80,352	278
La Crosse city (54601*)	51,003	537
Madison city (53714*)	191,262	82
Manitowoc city (54220*)	32,520	952
Memomonee Falls village (53051*)	26,840	1200
Milwaukee city (53203*)	628,088	17
New Berlin city (53186*)	33,592	915
Oshkosh city (54901*)	55,006	469
Racine city (53403*)	84,298	262
Sheboygan city (53081*)	49,676	560
Superior city (54836)	27,134	1188
Waukesha city (53186*)	56,958	448
Wausau city (54401*)	37,060	814
Wauwatosa city (53213*)	49,366	567
West Allis city (53214)	63,221	390

WYOMING

Casper city (82601*)	46,742	609
Cheyenne city (82001*)	50,008	555
Laramie city (82070)	26,687	1208

U.S. STATISTICS

Profile of the United States

This Profile was created by the editors of *Information Please* from many data sources. Most figures are approximate. For additional details about the United States, please refer to the appropriate sections of the *Information Please Almanac*. NOTE: figures given are latest available at presstime.

GEOGRAPHY

Number of states: 50
Land area (1990): 3,536,341. Share of world land area (1990): 6.2%
Northernmost point: Point Barrow, Alaska
Easternmost point: West Quoddy Head, Maine
Southernmost point: Ka Lae (South Cape), Hawaii
Westernmost point: Cape Wrangell, Alaska[1]
Geographic center: in Butte County, S.D. (44" 58' N. lat., 103" 46' W. long.)

1. The extreme points are measured from the geographic center of the United States (incl. Alaska and Hawaii), west of Castle Rock, S.D. 44° 58' N. lat., 103° 46' W. long. If measured from the prime meridian in Greenwich, England Cape Wrangell, Alaska would be the easternmost point.

POPULATION

Total[1] (est. June 17, 1996): 265,089,998
Center of population (1990): 9.7 miles northwest of Steelville in Crawford County, Missouri.
Males (1996): 129,540,000
Females (1996): 135,645,000
White (July 1, 1996): 219,655,000
Black (July 1, 1996): 33,618,000
Hispanic origin (can be of any race) (July 1, 1996): 27,937,000
American Indian, Eskimo, Aleut (July 1, 1996): 2,275,000
Asian and Pacific Islanders (July 1, 1996): 9,638,000
Median age (1996): 34.6
Baby boomers (Nov. 1992): 77,000,000
Rural population (1990): 66,964,000
Metropolitan population (1990): 192,725,741
Families (March 1994): 68,490,000
Average family size (March 1994): 2.67
Home ownership (1993): 61,252,000
Married couples (March 1994): 54,251,000
Unmarried couples (1994): 3,661,000
Single parents (1990): female, 6,599,000; male, 1,153,000
Widows (1990): 11,477,000
Widowers (1990): 2,333,000

1. Resident population of the U.S. plus Armed Forces overseas.

VITAL STATISTICS

Births (1995): 3,892,000
Deaths (1995): 2,309,000
Marriages (1995): 2,336,000
Divorces (1995): 1,169,000
Infant Mortality Rate (1995): 7.6 per 1,000
Legal abortions (1992): 1,528,930
Life Expectancy (1993): White men, 73.1; white women, 79.5; all other men, 67.3; all other women, 75.5

CIVILIAN LABOR FORCE

All (July 1996): 126,884,000 (5.3% are unemployed)
Males (June 1996): 72,121,000 (5.3% are unemployed)
Females (June 1996): 61,548,000 (5.2% are unemployed)

Work at home (telecommuters, est. 1993): 7.6 million
Farms (1995 preliminary): 2,073,320; total acres (1995 preliminary): 972,253,000. Farm population (1994): 5,024,000; percent of civilian population, 1.8%.

INCOME AND CREDIT

Gross Domestic Product (1995): $7,245.8 billion
Federal budget (est. 1996): total receipts, $1,415.5 billion; total outlays, $1,612.1 billion; total deficit, $196.6 billion
Personal income per capita (1995): $23,193
Median family income (1993): $36,950
Individual shareholders (1992): 51,300,000
Number below poverty level (1994): white, 25,379,000; black, 10,196,000; Hispanic, 8,416,000

EDUCATION

Public elementary pupils, Grades 1–8 (1995): 28,383,000
Public secondary pupils, Grades 9–12 (1995): 13,751,000
Private elementary pupils, Grades 1–8 (1995): 3,430,000
Private secondary pupils, Grades 9–12 (1995): 1,213,000
College enrollment, public (1995): 11,371,000
College enrollment, private (1995): 3,342,000
College graduates (1994–95): 1,179,000
Money spent on public elementary and secondary education (1992–93): $248,496,276
Projected public school teachers (1994): 2,550,000; elementary, 1,536,000; secondary, 1,014,000; private elementary and secondary school teachers (1994): 370,000
Average salary for public school teachers (1995): $37,436

CONVENIENCES

Radio stations (standard and FM, July 1996): 12,077
Television stations (July 1996): 1,550
Registered automobiles (est. 1995): 134,981,000
Newspaper circulation (morning and evening, Sept. 30, 1995): 58,193,391
Cable TV subscribers (est. May 1996): 62,335,000
Total TV homes (est. May 1996): 95,900,000
TV Homes with VCRs (est. 1993): 80%
Households with computers (1993): 22,605,000

CRIME

Total arrests (est. 1994): 14,648,700; Males, 9,090,567; Under 18, 1,573,567; Females, 2,251,018; Under 18, 503,582
Child neglect and abuse cases (1993): 1,936,242
Prisoners under sentence of death (1993): 2,716
Law enforcement officers killed (1993): 129
Total murder victims (1994): 22,276
Households touched by crime (1994): 14,000,000
Violent crime (1993): 1,924,188
Theft (1993): 7,820,909

Demographic State of the Nation: 1996

Source: U.S. Bureau of the Census, *Current Population Reports,* Series P23–191, February 1996.

Divorced Persons

In 1994, there were 75 million unmarried[1] adults in the Nation, compared with 38 million in 1970. Unmarried persons represented 39% of all adults (ages 18 and older) in 1994, up from 28% in 1970.

Divorced persons were the fastest growing segment of the unmarried population: their number quadrupled from 4 million in 1970 to 17 million in 1994. Divorced persons who had not remarried represented 9% of all adults in 1994.

Never-married persons, who represented the largest segment of the unmarried population in 1994 (59%), more than doubled from 21 million in 1970 to 44 million in 1994. In fact, during this period, the proportion of persons ages 30 to 34 who had never married tripled from 6 to 20% for women and from 9 to 30% for men. Never-married persons represented 23% of all adults in 1994.

In 1994, the estimated median age at first marriage was 24.5 years for women and 26.7 years for men. The median age at first marriage has risen more than three years for men and women since 1975.

Immigrants

Foreign-born persons[2] (i.e., immigrants) represented 9% (23 million) of the United States population in 1994. During this century, the percentage of people born outside the U.S. has ranged from a high of 15% in 1910 to a low of 5% in 1970. Since 1970, however, this percentage has steadily increased. In the past five years, on average, more immigrants came to the United States per year than came per year during the entire 1980s.

Among the foreign born in 1994, 68% were white, 7% were black, and 21% were Asian and Pacific Islander. Nearly half (46%) of all immigrants were Hispanic.[3] Mexicans comprised the largest group of immigrants (6 million) and Filipinos the second largest (1 million).

California was the state with the largest immigrant population in 1994 (8 million). These immigrants comprised over one-third of all immigrants to the United States and nearly one-fourth of all California residents. The states with the second and third largest immigrant populations were New York (3 million) and Florida (2 million).

Mobility

Between March 1993 and March 1994, 43 million Americans, or 17% of persons one year old and over, moved from one residence to another. This was not significantly different from the 1992–93 mobility rate, but was well below the mobility rate of 20% during 1984–85.

Local movers (persons who moved within the same county) numbered 27 million, representing 62% of all movers between March 1993 and March 1994. Longer-distance movers (persons who moved from one county to another within the United States) amounted to 15 million, representing 35% of all movers. Among the longer-distance movers, 8 million moved between counties in the same state, and 7 million moved from one state to another. Movers into the United States from abroad numbered 1 million.

Typically, among persons 20 years and over, as age increases moving rates decline. In 1994, the highest moving rate was for persons ages 20 to 24 (36%). The lowest moving rate was for persons ages 75 to 84 (5%), but this was not significantly different from the rate for persons ages 85 and older (6%).

Moving rates also varied by race and Hispanic origin. Whites had lower overall moving rates (16%) than either blacks (20%) or Hispanics (22%). The age structure of these populations contributed to these differences. The median age of blacks (28.6) and Hispanics (26.4) was lower than that for whites (34.9).

Health Insurance

In 1994, 40 million persons, or 15% of the population, did not have some type of health insurance. The proportion of poor persons without coverage (29%) was almost double that of the total population.

Seventy percent of all persons were covered by a private insurance plan for some or all of calendar year 1994. Insured persons also were covered by Medicaid (12%), Medicare (13%), or military health care (4%). Since many persons carry coverage from more than one type of health insurance plan, the figures for the insured add up to more than the 85% of the population that are, in fact, covered by some health insurance.

In 1994, 20% of part-time workers did not have health insurance coverage, compared with 16% of full-time workers and 13% of persons who did not work. Full-time workers were more likely than part-time workers to be covered through their employer; nonworkers were more likely than workers to be covered by government health programs such as Medicaid and Medicare. For each of these groups, the percent uninsured was much higher for poor persons.

Child Care

In fall 1993, there were 9.9 million children under age five who needed child care while their mothers worked.[4] Families paid an average of $74 per week for child care for their preschool-age children in 1993 (8% of their monthly family income).

Single-parent families spent about $61 per week on child care for their preschoolers, compared with $78 for married-couple families. Single-parent families, however, spent a larger share of their family income on child care (12%) than married-couple families (7%). Similarly, poor families paid less per week for child care than nonpoor families ($50 versus $76), but they spent a larger proportion of their income on child care (18% versus 7%).

---

1. "Unmarried" includes those who have never married plus those who are currently divorced or widowed.
2. Natives are persons born in the United States, Puerto Rico, or an outlying area of the United States, such as Guam or the U.S. Virgin Islands, and persons who were born in a foreign country but who had at least one parent who was a U.S. citizen. Foreign-born persons are all others born outside of the United States.
3. Persons of Hispanic origin may be of any race. These data do not include persons living in Puerto Rico

Care for these preschoolers was provided primarily by relatives (41%); organized facilities, such as nursery schools and preschools (30%); and family day care providers[5] (17%). The average weekly cost per arrangement paid by families was $42 for relatives, about $65 for in-home babysitters and organized facilities, and $52 for family day care providers.

Child Support

In spring 1992, there were 12 million custodial parents of children under age 21 (whose other parent was not living in the household)—10 million were custodial mothers and 2 million were custodial fathers. As of the survey date (spring 1992), child support was awarded to more than 6 million (54%) of these custodial parents. A larger proportion of custodial mothers had child support awards than custodial fathers (56% compared with 41%).

Of the 6 million custodial parents with child support awards in 1992, 5 million were supposed to receive child support payments in 1991. About 76% of the women and 63% of the men received full or partial payment; only about one-half (52% of mothers and 43% of fathers) received the full amount due.

On average, custodial mothers received $3,011 in child support in 1991, constituting 17% of their income. The comparable figure for custodial fathers was $2,292, comprising only 7% of their income. Although child support payments to mothers were larger on average than payments to fathers, mothers had lower average incomes ($18,144 versus $33,579) and higher poverty rates (35 versus 13%) than fathers.

Median Household Income

Median household income[6] was $32,264 in 1994, not different in real terms from 1993 ($32,041), but about $2,200 less than the 1989 prerecessionary median income of $34,445 (in 1994 dollars). The South experienced a 2.9 percent increase in real median household income from $29,169 in 1993 to $30,021 in 1994 (the first annual increase since 1986). Even with this increase, the South still had the lowest median of the four regions in 1994. The median income for households was $34,926 in the Northeast; $32,505 in the Midwest; and $34,452 in the West.[7]

From 1993 to 1994, the real median earnings from males ages 15 and older who worked year-round, full-time declined from $31,186 to $30,854. This was the second consecutive year that real median earnings for men declined. Median earnings for comparable females was $22,205 in 1994, unchanged from 1993.

In 1994, the share of aggregate household income received by the top quintile[8] was 49.1%, up from 43.5% in 1974 (but not different from 1993). Since

1974, the share of aggregate household income received by the four lower quintiles has declined.

Poverty

The number of persons below the official government poverty level dropped from 39.3 million in 1993 to 38.1 million in 1994. In addition, the poverty rate decreased from 15.1 to 14.5%. This is the first time since 1983–84 that both the number and the percentage of poor persons declined from one year to the next.

The number and percentage of poor persons varied by race and Hispanic origin. While the number of poor Hispanics increased from 8.1 million in 1993 to 8.4 million in 1994, the number of poor blacks decreased from 10.9 to 10.2 million. The number of poor whites and poor Asians and Pacific Islanders, however, showed no change (25.4 million and 974,000, respectively). The poverty rate decreased for whites and blacks, but did not change significantly for Hispanics[9] and Asians and Pacific Islanders during this period.

The poverty rate for related children under age six varied widely by type of family. Overall, the poverty rate for these children was 24.5% in 1994. However, almost two-thirds (63.7%) of related children under age six in families maintained by women with no husband present were poor, compared with only 12.3% of comparable children in married-couple families.

Home Ownership

In 1994, 64% of occupied housing units were owner occupied, unchanged from the revised 1993 rate. The homeownership rate ranged from a low of 15% for householders under age 25, to a high of about 80% for householders ages 60 to 74.[10] For persons ages 75 and older, the rate was 74%.

Married-couple families were much more likely to own their own homes than other types of family or nonfamily households. The homeownership rate for married-couple families in 1994 was 79%, compared with 53% for male householders (no wife present) and 44% for female householders (no husband present).

In 1994, about 50% of one-person households owned their own homes. Among persons living alone, the homeownership rate was 43% for men and 55% for women.

There were 111 million housing units in the United States in 1994; 63 million were owner occupied; 36 million were renter occupied, and 12 million were vacant.

Housing

In 1993, the median age of the nation's housing units was 28 years, an increase of six years since 1973. In 1993, our housing units were more likely to have complete kitchen facilities than in 1973 (99 versus 98%), complete plumbing facilities (98 versus 96%), central heat (90 versus 85%), and central air conditioning (44 versus 17%). They were less likely to be crowded (3 versus 6% having more than one person per room), to have peeling paint (4 versus 5%), and to have open cracks (5 versus 6%).

In 1973, 55% of occupied homes were heated by piped gas, 25% by fuel oil, and 10% by electricity. By 1993, gas still heated most homes (51%), but a higher percentage of homes were heated by electricity (27%) than by fuel oil (12%). The installation of heat pumps in many homes is the main reason for this reversal.

Housing also has become less affordable. Median family income (in 1993 dollars) of homeowners, for example, declined 2% to $36,500 from 1973 to 1993; at the same time, home values rose 10% to $86,500.[11] Renters experienced the same patterns in their family incomes and monthly gross rents.

11. Family income is shown because data for household income were not available from the American Housing Survey in 1973.

Singles in the United States

The ratio of unmarried men per 100 unmarried women in U.S. Metro Areas, 1990

Highest Ratio Men to Women

Rank	Metro Area	Ratio
1	Jacksonville, NC MSA	223.64
2	Killeen–Temple, TX MSA	122.75
3	Fayetteville, NC MSA	117.66
4	Brazoria, TX PMSA	116.71
5	Lawton, OK MSA	115.63
6	State College, PA MSA	112.98
7	Clarksville–Hopkinsville, TN–KY MSA	112.71
8	Anchorage, AK MSA	112.45
9	Salinas–Seaside–Monterey, CA MSA	112.01
10	Bryan–College Station, TX MSA	111.40
11	Bremerton, WA MSA	108.30
12	San Diego, CA MSA	105.33
13	Honolulu, HI MSA	105.22
14	Las Vegas, NV MSA	104.65
15	Yuma, AZ MSA	104.64
16	Grand Forks, ND MSA	104.19
17	San Jose, CA PMSA	103.63
18	Reno, NV MSA	103.52
19	Lafayette–West Lafayette, IN MSA	102.01
20	Fort Walton Beach, FL MSA	101.70
21	Vallejo–Fairfield–Napa, CA PMSA	101.68
22	Lake County, IL PMSA	101.56
23	Champaign–Urbana–Rantoul, IL MSA	101.33
24	Jackson, MI MSA	101.24
25	Colorado Springs, CO MSA	99.42

Lowest Ratio Men to Women

Rank	Metro Area	Ratio
1	Sarasota, FL MSA	65.57
2	Bradenton, FL MSA	68.41
3	Altoona, PA MSA	69.42
4	Springfield, IL MSA	69.63
5	Jacksonville, TN, MSA	69.72
6	Gadsden, AL MSA	69.86
7	Wheeling, WV–OH MSA	70.48
8	Charleston, WV MSA	70.65
9	St. Joseph, MO MSA	70.93
10	Lynchburg, VA MSA	71.04
11	Roanoke, VA MSA	71.09
12	Asheville, NC MSA	71.14
13	Shreveport, LA MSA	71.54
14	Birmingham, AL MSA	71.63
15	Danville, VA MSA	71.72
16	Pittsburgh, PA PMSA	72.04
17	Monroe, LA MSA	72.06
18	Owensboro, KY MSA	72.14
19	Pittsburgh–Beaver Valley, PA CMSA	72.16
20	Florence, AL MSA	72.20
21	Sherman–Denison, TX MSA	72.27
22	Florence, SC MSA	72.32
23	Huntington–Ashland, WV–KY–OH MSA	72.67
24	Cumberland, MD–WV MSA	72.73
25	Steubenville–Weirton, OH–WV MSA	72.87

NOTE: Unmarried includes never-married, widowed, and divorced persons, 15 years or older. Metro Areas as defined June 30, 1990. The presence of a military base, college or university, etc. in a metropolitan area may have a significant impact on the size of the ratio. MSA—Metropolitan Statistical Area. CMSA—Consolidated Metropolitan Statistical Area. PMSA—Primary Metropolitan Statistical Area. *Source:* U.S. Bureau of the Census.

Persons Below Poverty Level

Race and Hispanic Origin, Age, and Region, 1994

	Number	Percent		Number	Percent
Total[1]	38,059	14.5%	45 to 54 years	2,381	7.8%
White	25,379	11.7	55 to 59 years	1,129	10.4
Black	10,196	30.6	60 to 64 years	1,129	11.4
Asian and Pacific Islander	974	14.6	65 and over	3,663	11.7
Hispanic origin[2]	8,416	30.7			
			Northeast	6,597	12.9
Under 18 years	15,289	21.8	Midwest	7,965	13.0
18 to 24 years	4,538	18.0	South	14,729	16.1
25 to 44 years	9,930	11.9	West	8,768	15.3

1. Includes races not shown separately. 2. Persons of Hispanic origin may be of any race. *Source:* Income, Poverty, and Valuation of Noncash Benefits: Current Population Reports, U.S. Census Bureau.

Population

National Censuses[1]

Year	Resident population[2]	Land area, sq mi.	Pop. per sq mi.	Year	Resident population[2]	Land area, sq mi.	Pop. per sq mi.
1790	3,929,214	864,746	4.5	1900	75,994,575	2,969,834	25.6
1800	5,308,483	864,746	6.1	1910	91,972,266	2,969,565	31.0
1810	7,239,881	1,681,828	4.3	1920	105,710,620	2,969,451	35.6
1820	9,638,453	1,749,462	5.5	1930	122,775,046	2,977,128	41.2
1830	12,866,020	1,749,462	7.4	1940	131,669,275	2,977,128	44.2
1840	17,069,453	1,749,462	9.8	1950	150,697,361	2,974,726	50.7
1850	23,191,876	2,940,042	7.9	1960	179,323,175	3,540,911	50.6
1860	31,443,321	2,969,640	10.6	1970	203,302,031	3,540,023	57.4
1870	39,818,449	2,969,640	13.4	1980	226,545,805	3,539,289	64.0
1880	50,155,783	2,969,640	16.9	1990	248,709,873	3,536,278	70.3
1890	62,947,714	2,969,640	21.2				

1. Beginning with 1960, figures include Alaska and Hawaii. 2. Excludes armed forces overseas. *Source:* Department of Commerce, Bureau of the Census.

Population Distribution by Age, Race, Nativity, and Sex

			Age				Race and Nativity				
								White[1]			
Year	Total	Under 5	5–19	20–44	45–64	65 and over	Total	Native born	Foreign born	Black	Other races[1]
PERCENT DISTRIBUTION											
1860[2]	100.0	15.4	35.8	35.7	10.4	2.7	85.6	72.6	13.0	14.1	0.3
1870[2]	100.0	14.3	35.4	35.4	11.9	3.0	87.1	72.9	14.2	12.7	0.2
1880[2]	100.0	13.8	34.3	35.9	12.6	3.4	86.5	73.4	13.1	13.1	0.3
1890[3]	100.0	12.2	33.9	36.9	13.1	3.9	87.5	73.0	14.5	11.9	0.3
1900	100.0	12.1	32.3	37.7	13.7	4.1	87.9	74.5	13.4	11.6	0.5
1910	100.0	11.6	30.4	39.0	14.6	4.3	88.9	74.4	14.5	10.7	0.4
1920	100.0	10.9	29.8	38.4	16.1	4.7	89.7	76.7	13.0	9.9	0.4
1930	100.0	9.3	29.5	38.3	17.4	5.4	89.8	78.4	11.4	9.7	0.5
1940	100.0	8.0	26.4	38.9	19.8	6.8	89.8	81.1	8.7	9.8	0.4
1950	100.0	10.7	23.2	37.6	20.3	8.1	89.5	82.8	6.7	10.0	0.5
1960	100.0	11.3	27.1	32.2	20.1	9.2	88.6	83.4	5.2	10.5	0.9
1970[2]	100.0	8.4	29.5	31.7	20.6	9.8	87.6	83.4	4.3	11.1	1.4
1980	100.0	7.2	24.8	37.1	19.6	11.3	83.1	n.a.	n.a.	11.7	5.2
1990	100.0	7.6	21.3	40.1	18.6	12.5	83.9	n.a.	n.a.	12.3	3.8
MALES PER 100 FEMALES											
1860[2]	104.7	102.4	101.2	107.9	111.5	98.3	105.3	103.7	115.1	99.6	260.8
1870[2]	102.2	102.9	101.2	99.2	114.5	100.5	102.8	100.6	115.3	96.2	400.7
1880[2]	103.6	103.0	101.3	104.0	110.2	101.4	104.0	102.1	115.9	97.8	362.2
1890[3]	105.0	103.6	101.4	107.3	108.3	104.2	105.4	102.9	118.7	99.5	165.2
1900	104.4	102.1	100.9	105.8	110.7	102.0	104.9	102.8	117.4	98.6	185.2
1910	106.0	102.5	101.3	108.1	114.4	101.1	106.6	102.7	129.2	98.9	185.6
1920	104.0	102.5	100.8	102.8	115.2	101.3	104.4	101.7	121.7	99.2	156.6
1930	102.5	103.0	101.4	100.5	109.1	100.5	102.9	101.1	115.8	97.0	150.6
1940	100.7	103.2	102.0	98.1	105.2	95.5	101.2	100.1	111.1	95.0	140.5
1950	98.6	103.9	102.5	96.2	100.1	89.6	99.0	98.8	102.0	93.7	129.7
1960	97.1	103.4	102.7	95.6	95.7	82.8	97.4	97.6	94.2	93.3	109.7
1970[2]	94.8	104.0	103.3	95.1	91.6	72.1	95.3	95.9	83.8	90.8	100.2
1980	94.5	104.7	104.0	98.1	90.7	67.6	94.8	n.a.	n.a.	89.6	100.3
1990	95.1	104.8	105.0	99.8	92.5	67.2	95.9	n.a.	n.a.	89.8	96.5

1. The 1980 and 1990 census data for white and other races categories are not directly comparable to those shown for the preceding years because of the changes in the way some persons reported their race, as well as changes in procedures relating to racial classification. 2. Excludes persons for whom age is not available. 3. Excludes persons enumerated in the Indian Territory and on Indian reservations. NOTES: Data exclude Armed Forces overseas. Beginning in 1960, includes Alaska and Hawaii. n.a. = not available. *Source:* Department of Commerce, Bureau of the Census.

Colonial Population Estimates (in round numbers)

Year	Population	Year	Population	Year	Population	Year	Population
1610	350	1660	75,100	1710	331,700	1760	1,593,600
1620	2,300	1670	111,900	1720	466,200	1770	2,148,100
1630	4,600	1680	151,500	1730	629,400	1780	2,780,400
1640	26,600	1690	210,400	1740	905,600		
1650	50,400	1700	250,900	1750	1,170,800		

Estimated 1992 Population of Metro Areas Over One Million

Metropolitan statistical area (MSA) Consolidated metropolitan statistical area (CMSA)	July 1, 1992
New York–Northern New Jersey–Long Island, NY–NJ–CT–PA CMSA	19,670,175
Los Angeles–Riverside–Orange County, CA CMSA	15,047,772
Chicago–Gary–Kenosha, IL–IN–WI CMSA	8,410,402
Washington–Baltimore, DC–MD–VA–WV CMSA	6,919,572
San Francisco–Oakland–San Jose, CA CMSA	6,409,891
Philadelphia–Wilmington–Atlantic City, PA–NJ–DE–MD CMSA	5,938,528
Boston–Worcester–Lawrence, MA–NH–ME–CT CMSA	5,438,815
Detroit–Ann Arbor–Flint, MI CMSA	5,245,906
Dallas–Fort Worth, TX CMSA	4,214,532
Houston–Galveston–Brazoria, TX CMSA	3,962,365
Miami–Fort Lauderdale, FL CMSA	3,309,246
Atlanta, GA MSA	3,142,857
Seattle–Tacoma–Bremerton, WA CMSA	3,131,392
Cleveland–Akron, OH CMSA	2,890,402
Minneapolis–St. Paul, MN–WI MSA	2,617,973
San Diego, CA MSA	2,601,055
St. Louis, MO–IL MSA	2,518,528
Pittsburgh, PA MSA	2,406,452
Phoenix–Mesa, AZ MSa	2,330,353
Tampa–St. Petersburg–Clearwater, FL MSA	2,107,271
Denver–Boulder–Greeley, CO CMSA	2,089,321
Portland–Salem, OR–WA CMSA	1,896,895
Cincinnati–Hamilton, OH–KY–IN CMSA	1,865,002
Milwaukee–Racine, WI CMSA	1,629,420
Kansas City, MO–KS MSA	1,616,930
Sacramento–Yolo, CA CMSA	1,563,374
Norfolk–Virginia Beach–Newport News, VA–NC MSA	1,496,672
Indianapolis, IN MSA	1,424,050
Columbus, OH MSA	1,394,067
San Antonio, TX MSA	1,378,619
Orlando, FL MSA	1,304,700
New Orleans, LA MSA	1,302,697
Charlotte–Gastonia–Rock Hill, NC–SC MSA	1,212,393
Buffalo–Niagara Falls, NY MSA	1,193,901
Hartford, CT MSA	1,155,725
Providence–Fall River–Warwick, RI–MA MSA	1,131,135
Salt Lake City–Ogden, UT MSA	1,128,121
Rochester, NY MSA	1,081,244
Greensboro–Winston-Salem–High Point, NC MSA	1,078,377
Memphis, TN–AR–MS MSA	1,033,813
Nashville, TN MSA	1,023,315

Source: U.S. Bureau of the Census. Areas defined by the Office of Management and Budget as of June 30, 1993. NOTE: These estimates are consistent with the population as enumerated in the 1990 census, and have not been adjusted fo census coverage errors.

Getting to Work in the City

Travel-to-work characeristics for the 15 largest cities by population in the United States: 1990

City of residence	Total workers 16 years and over	Means of transportation (%)				Average travel time to work (min.)
		Drove alone	Car-pool	Public transit	Other means[1]	
New York, NY	3,183,088	24.0%	8.5%	53.4%	14.0%	36.5
Los Angeles, CA	1,629,096	65.2	15.4	10.5	8.9	26.5
Chicago, IL	1,181,677	46.3	14.8	29.7	9.2	31.5
Houston, TX	772,957	71.7	15.5	6.5	6.3	24.7
Philadelphia, PA	640,577	44.7	13.2	28.7	13.5	27.4
San Diego, CA	560,913	70.7	12.8	4.2	12.2	20.4
Detroit, MI	325,054	67.8	16.1	10.7	5.3	24.7
Dallas, TX	500,566	72.5	15.2	6.7	5.7	24.0
Phoenix, AZ	473,966	73.7	15.1	3.3	7.9	23.0
San Antonio, TX	395,551	73.4	15.5	4.9	6.2	21.7
San Jose, CA	400,932	76.9	14.6	3.5	5.1	25.5
Indianapolis, IN	362,777	78.0	13.4	3.3	5.2	20.8
Baltimore, MD	307,679	50.9	16.8	22.0	10.2	26.0
San Francisco, CA	382,309	38.5	11.5	33.5	16.5	26.9
Jacksonville, FL	312,958	75.5	14.2	2.7	7.6	21.6

1. Includes commuting by motorcycle, bicycle, walking, and all other means. Also includes those who worked at home NOTE: May not add due to rounding. *Source:* U.S. Census Bureau, Department of Commerce.

Population by State

State	1990	Percent change, 1980–90	Pop. per sq mi., 1990	Pop. rank, 1990	1980	1950	1900	1790
Alabama	4,040,587	+3.8	79.6	22	3,893,888	3,061,743	1,828,697	—
Alaska	550,403	+36.9	1.0	49	401,851	128,643	63,592	—
Arizona	3,665,228	+34.8	32.3	24	2,718,215	749,587	122,931	—
Arkansas	2,350,725	+2.8	45.1	33	2,286,435	1,909,511	1,311,564	—
California	29,760,021	+25.7	190.4	1	23,667,902	10,586,223	1,485,053	—
Colorado	3,294,394	+14.0	31.8	26	2,889,964	1,325,089	539,700	—
Connecticut	3,287,116	+5.8	674.7	27	3,107,576	2,007,280	908,420	237,946
Delaware	666,168	+12.1	344.8	46	594,338	318,085	184,735	59,096
D.C.	606,900	−4.9	—	—	638,333	802,178	278,718	—
Florida	12,937,926	+32.7	238.9	4	9,746,324	2,771,305	528,542	—
Georgia	6,478,216	+18.6	109.9	11	5,463,105	3,444,578	2,216,331	82,548
Hawaii	1,108,229	+14.9	172.5	41	964,691	499,794	154,001	—
Idaho	1,006,749	+6.7	12.2	42	943,935	588,637	161,772	—
Illinois	11,430,602	0.0	205.4	6	11,426,518	8,712,176	4,821,550	—
Indiana	5,544,159	+1.0	154.2	14	5,490,224	3,934,224	2,516,462	—
Iowa	2,776,755	−4.7	49.6	30	2,913,808	2,621,073	2,231,853	—
Kansas	2,477,574	+4.8	30.3	32	2,363,679	1,905,299	1,470,495	—
Kentucky	3,685,296	+0.7	92.9	23	3,660,777	2,944,806	2,147,174	73,677
Louisiana	4,219,973	+0.3	94.8	21	4,205,900	2,683,516	1,381,625	—
Maine	1,227,928	+9.2	39.6	38	1,124,660	913,774	694,466	96,540
Maryland	4,781,468	+13.4	486.0	19	4,216,975	2,343,001	1,188,044	319,728
Massachusetts	6,016,425	+4.9	768.9	13	5,737,037	4,690,514	2,805,346	378,787
Michigan	9,295,297	+0.4	163.2	8	9,262,078	6,371,766	2,420,982	—
Minnesota	4,375,099	+7.3	55.0	20	4,075,970	2,982,483	1,751,394	—
Mississippi	2,573,216	+2.1	54.5	31	2,520,638	2,178,914	1,551,270	—
Missouri	5,117,073	+4.1	74.2	15	4,916,686	3,954,653	3,106,665	—
Montana	799,065	+1.6	5.5	44	786,690	591,024	243,329	—
Nebraska	1,578,385	+0.5	20.6	36	1,569,825	1,325,510	1,066,300	—
Nevada	1,201,833	+50.1	10.9	39	800,493	160,083	42,335	—
New Hampshire	1,109,252	+20.5	123.3	40	920,610	533,242	411,588	141,885
New Jersey	7,730,188	+5.0	1,035.1	9	7,364,823	4,835,329	1,883,669	184,139
New Mexico	1,515,069	+16.3	12.5	37	1,302,894	681,187	195,310	—
New York	17,990,455	+2.5	379.7	2	17,558,072	14,830,192	7,268,894	340,120
North Carolina	6,628,637	+12.7	135.7	10	5,881,766	4,061,929	1,893,810	393,751
North Dakota	638,800	−2.1	9.0	47	652,717	619,636	319,146	—
Ohio	10,847,115	+0.5	264.5	7	10,797,630	7,946,627	4,157,545	—
Oklahoma	3,145,585	+4.0	45.8	28	3,025,290	2,233,351	790,391[1]	—
Oregon	2,842,321	+7.9	29.5	29	2,633,105	1,521,341	413,536	—
Pennsylvania	11,881,643	+0.1	264.7	5	11,863,895	10,498,012	6,302,115	434,373
Rhode Island	1,003,464	+5.9	951.1	43	947,154	791,896	428,556	68,825
South Carolina	3,486,703	+11.7	115.4	25	3,121,820	2,117,027	1,340,316	249,073
South Dakota	696,004	+0.8	9.1	45	690,768	652,740	401,570	—
Tennessee	4,877,185	+6.2	118.5	17	4,591,120	3,291,718	2,020,616	35,691
Texas	16,986,510	+19.4	64.8	3	14,229,191	7,711,194	3,048,710	—
Utah	1,722,850	+17.9	20.9	35	1,461,037	688,862	276,749	—
Vermont	562,758	+10.0	60.7	48	511,456	377,747	343,641	85,425
Virginia	6,187,358	+15.7	155.8	12	5,346,818	3,318,680	1,854,184	747,610 [2]
Washington	4,866,692	+17.8	73.1	18	4,132,156	2,378,963	518,103	—
West Virginia	1,793,477	−8.0	73.8	34	1,949,644	2,005,552	958,800	—
Wisconsin	4,891,769	+4.0	89.9	16	4,705,767	3,434,575	2,069,042	—
Wyoming	453,588	−3.4	4.7	50	469,557	290,529	92,531	—
Total U.S.	248,709,873	+9.8	—	—	226,545,805	151,325,798	76,212,168	3,929,214

1. Includes population of Indian Territory: 1900, 392,960. 2. Until 1863, Virginia included what is now West Virginia.
Source: Department of Commerce, Bureau of the Census.

Communications Craze

Source: Census and You, Volume 31, No. 7, July 1996

For those of us who have ever said "instant gratification takes too long," the emergence of two growth industries will come as no surprise. The U.S. obsession with instant access to information and communications has led to 24-hour news and sports channels available through cable providers, and has telephone companies clamoring to sell you cellular phone services. According to the U.S. Census Bureau, cable television revenues surpassed those of broadcast television in 1994, climbing to a total of $31.5 billion versus $24.8 billion, the result of an astounding 36% growth rate from 1990 to 1994. Those who just can't afford to be unreachable are attracted to the plethora of pagers, beepers, and cellular phone services ready to take their money in exchange for a promise to keep them connected. Revenues from cellular and other radiotelephone services have leaped more than 30% each year from 1991 to 1994, reaching $15.9 billion in 1994. Though a small proportion of total industry revenues (less than 10%), this segment accounted for nearly one-third of the industry's growth. ☐

Territorial Expansion

Accession	Date	Area[1]
United States	—	3,536,278
Territory in 1790	—	891,364
Louisiana Purchase	1803	831,321
Florida	1819	69,866
Texas	1845	384,958
Oregon	1846	283,439
Mexican Cession	1848	530,706
Gadsden Purchase	1853	29,640
Alaska	1867	591,004
Hawaii	1898	6,471
Other territory	—	4,664
Philippines	1898	115,600[2]
Puerto Rico	1899	3,426
Guam	1899	209
American Samoa	1900	77
Canal Zone[3]	1904	553
Virgin Islands of U.S.	1917	134
Trust Territory of Pacific Islands	1947	177[4]
All other		14
Total, 1990	**—**	**3,540,315**

1. Total land and water area in square miles. 2. Became independent in 1946. 3. Reverted to Panama. 4. Land area only; Palau only Trust Territory remaining. *Source:* Department of Commerce, Bureau of the Census.

Total Population

Area	1990	1980	1970
50 states of U.S.	248,709,873	226,545,805	203,302,031
48 conterminous	247,051,601	225,179,263	202,229,535
Alaska	550,043	401,851	302,583
Hawaii	1,108,229	964,691	769,913
American Samoa	46,773	32,297	27,159
Canal Zone	(1)	(1)	44,198
Corn Islands	—	—	(2)
Guam	133,152	105,979	84,996
Johnston Atoll	n.a.	327	1,007
Midway	(3)	453	2,220
Puerto Rico	3,522,037	3,196,520	2,712,033
Swan Islands	n.a.	n.a.	22
Trust Ter. of Pac. Is.	15,122[5]	132,929[4]	90,940
Virgin Is. of U.S.	101,809	96,569	62,468
Wake Island	(3)	302	1,647
Population abroad	922,819	995,546	1,737,836
Armed forces	910,611	515,408	1,057,776
Total	**253,451,585**	**231,106,727**	**208,066,557**

1. Reverted to Panama. 2. Returned to Nicaragua April 25, 1971. 3. No indigenous population. 4. Includes Northern Mariana Islands. 5. Palau only Trust Territory remaining. NOTE: n.a. = not available. *Source:* Department of Commerce, Bureau of the Census.

Resident Population, by Age Group, Race, and Hispanic Origin, 1995

(in thousands)

Age	White	Black	Hispanic origin[1]	American Indian, Eskimo & Aleut	Asian & Pacific Islanders	All persons
Under 5	15,451	3,100	3,212	207	833	19,591
5–9	15,237	3,025	2,661	228	731	19,220
10–14	15,040	2,877	2,428	234	764	18,915
15–19	14,362	2,822	2,278	201	680	18,065
20–24	14,317	2,638	2,334	185	743	17,882
25–29	15,403	2,594	2,500	180	828	19,005
30–34	17,984	2,825	2,533	186	872	21,868
35–39	18,458	2,788	2,156	177	825	22,249
40–44	16,930	2,390	1,725	156	743	20,219
45–49	14,858	1,855	1,311	125	611	17,449
50–54	11,725	1,381	961	93	430	13,630
55–59	9,541	1,138	762	72	334	11,085
60–64	8,724	988	634	58	276	10,046
65–69	8,726	920	542	47	235	9,928
70–74	7,918	697	404	37	179	8,831
75–79	6,039	510	255	25	107	6,681
80–84	4,069	318	169	16	60	4,464
85–89	2,125	164	22	9	23	2,321
90–94	897	81	11	5	9	991
95–99	237	22	3	1	3	263
100 and over	45	7	2	1	1	53
All ages	**218,086**	**33,140**	**26,903**	**2,243**	**9,287**	**262,756**
16 and over	169,364	23,537	18,226	1,528	6,811	201,240
65 and over	30,055	2,719	1,501	141	617	33,532
Mean age	36.7	31.2	28.2	29.5	31.5	35.8

1. Persons of Hispanic origin may be of any race. Data does not include residents of Puerto Rico. *Source:* U.S. Bureau of the Census.

Empty Nests

As baby boomers age, we should expect to see fewer traditional families and more households composed of people living alone and in families without children. According to Census Bureau projections, by 2010 approximately 72% of all households will be childless. By then, boomers will range in age from their late 40s to their early 60s, which means that even the youngest of these women will have moved beyond their child-bearing years. The combination of more families with no children present and more people living alone could mean shrinking households (projected to decline from 2.62 to 2.53 people, on average) and shrinking families (3.5 to 3.05). With fewer young adults to form new households, the rate of growth for new households is also expected to decline over the next 15 years.

Immigrants to U.S. by Country of Origin

(Figures are totals, not annual averages, and were tabulated as follows: 1820–67, alien passengers arrived; 1868–91 and 1895–97, immigrant aliens arrived; 1892–94 and 1898 to present, immigrant aliens admitted. From 1989 totals include legalized immigrants. (Data before 1906 relate to country whence alien came; 1906–80, to country of last permanent residence; 1981 to present data based on country of birth.)

Countries	1995	1820–1995	1981–90	1971–80	1961–70	1951–60	1941–50	1820–1940
Europe: Albania[1]	1,420	8,223	479	329	98	59	85	2,040
Austria[2]	518	2,664,174	4,636	9,478	20,621	67,106	24,860	2,534,617
Belgium	569	212,243	5,706	5,329	9,192	18,575	12,189	158,205
Bulgaria[3]	1,797	75,963	2,342	1,188	619	104	375	65,856
Former Czechoslovakia[1]	1,174	155,459	11,500	6,023	3,273	918	8,347	120,013
Denmark	551	373,679	5,380	4,439	9,201	10,984	5,393	335,025
Estonia[1]	n.a.	1,974	137	91	163	185	212	506
Finland[1]	476	39,713	3,265	2,868	4,192	4,925	2,503	19,593
France	2,505	792,180	23,124	25,069	45,237	51,121	38,809	594,998
Germany[2]	6,237	7,098,553	70,111	74,414	190,796	477,765	226,578	6,021,951
Greece	1,309	703,227	29,130	92,369	85,969	47,608	8,973	430,608
Hungary[2]	900	166,688	9,764	6,550	5,401	36,637	3,469	1,609,158
Ireland	5,315	4,779,160	32,823	11,490	32,966	48,362	14,789	4,580,557
Italy	2,231	5,350,712	32,894	129,368	214,111	185,491	57,661	4,719,223
Latvia[1]	651	5,567	359	207	510	352	361	1,192
Lithuania[1]	767	6,887	482	248	562	242	683	2,201
Luxembourg[1]	n.a.	3,252	234	307	556	684	820	565
Netherlands	1,196	380,686	11,958	10,492	30,606	52,277	14,860	253,759
Norway[4]	420	756,094	3,901	3,941	15,484	22,935	10,100	697,095
Poland[5]	13,824	734,895	97,390	37,234	53,539	9,985	7,571	414,755
Portugal	2,615	514,987	40,020	101,710	76,065	19,588	7,423	256,044
Romania[6]	4,871	241,459	39,963	12,393	2,531	1,039	1,076	156,945
Spain	1,321	288,020	15,698	39,141	44,659	7,894	2,898	170,123
Sweden[4]	976	1,397,480	10,211	6,531	17,116	21,697	10,665	1,325,208
Switzerland	881	362,115	7,076	8,235	18,453	17,675	10,547	295,680
United Kingdom	12,427	5,183,493	142,123	137,374	213,822	202,824	139,306	4,266,561
Former U.S.S.R.[7]	54,494	3,747,189	84,081	38,961	2,465	671	571	3,343,361
Former Yugoslavia[3]	8,307	156,529	19,182	30,540	20,381	8,225	1,576	56,787
Other Europe	433	62,270	2,661	4,049	4,904	9,799	3,447	36,060
Total Europe	128,185	36,262,871	705,630	800,368	1,123,492	1,325,727	621,147	32,468,776
Asia: China[8]	35,463	1,207,634	388,686	124,326	34,764	9,657	16,709	382,173
India	34,748	658,480	261,841	164,134	27,189	1,973	1,761	9,873
Israel	2,523	149,347	36,353	37,713	29,602	25,476	476	—
Japan[9]	4,837	492,322	43,248	49,775	39,988	46,250	1,555	277,591
Turkey	2,947	421,944	20,843	13,399	10,142	3,519	798	361,236
Other Asia	187,413	4,802,869	2,042,025	1,198,831	285,957	66,374	15,729	44,053
Total Asia[10]	267,931	7,732,596	2,066,455	1,588,178	427,642	153,249	37,028	1,074,926
America: Canada and Newfoundland[11]	12,932	4,332,716	119,204	169,939	413,310	377,952	171,718	3,005,728
Central America	31,814	1,108,928	458,753	134,640	101,330	44,751	21,665	49,154
Mexico[12]	89,932	5,262,820	1,653,250	640,294	453,937	299,811	60,589	778,255
South America	45,666	1,526,639	455,977	295,741	257,954	91,628	21,831	121,302
West Indies	96,788	3,255,915	892,392	741,126	470,213	123,091	49,725	446,971
Other America[12]	60	117,523	1,352	995	19,630	59,711	29,276	56
Total America	277,192	15,604,541	3,580,928	1,982,735	1,716,374	996,944	354,804	4,401,466
Africa	42,456	508,680	192,212	80,779	28,954	14,092	7,367	26,060
Australia and New Zealand	2,478	158,120	20,169	23,788	19,562	11,506	13,805	54,437
Pacific Islands[13]	2,217	63,034	21,041	17,454	5,560	1,470	746	11,089
Countries not specified[14]	2	272,249	196	12	93	12,491	142	253,689
Total all countries	720,461	60,602,091	7,338,062	4,493,314	3,321,677	2,515,479	1,035,039	38,290,443

1. Countries established since beginning of World War I are included with countries to which they belonged. 2. Data for Austria–Hungary not reported until 1861. Austria and Hungary recorded separately after 1905, Austria included with Germany 1938–45. 3. Bulgaria, Serbia, Montenegro first reported in 1899. Bulgaria reported separately since 1920. In 1920, separate enumeration for Kingdom of Serbs, Croats, Slovenes; since 1922, recorded as Yugoslavia. 4. Norway included with Sweden 1820–68. 5. Included with Austria–Hungary, Germany, and Russia 1899–1919. 6. No record of immigration until 1880. 7. From 1931–63, the U.S.S.R. was broken down into European U.S.S.R. and Asian U.S.S.R. Since 1964, total U.S.S.R. has been reported in Europe. 8. Beginning in 1957, China includes Taiwan. 9. No record of immigration until 1861. 10. From 1934, Asia included Philippines; before 1934, recorded in separate tables as insular travel. 11. Includes all British North American possessions, 1820–98. 12. No record of immigration, 1886–93. 13. Included with "Countries not specified" prior to 1925. 14. Includes 32,897 persons returning in 1906 to their homes in U.S. *Source:* Department of Justice, Immigration and Naturalization Service. NOTE: Data are latest available.

The Foreign Born Population in the United States: 1990 and 1980

25 Largest Places of Birth

1990 Rank	Place of Birth	Number	Percent	1980 Rank	Place of Birth	Number	Percent
	United States	**19,767,316**	**100.0**		**United States**	**14,079,906**	**100.0**
1	Mexico	4,298,014	21.7	1	Mexico	2,199,221	15.6
2	Philippines	912,674	4.6	2	Germany	849,384	6.0
3	Canada	744,830	3.8	3	Canada	842,859	6.0
4	Cuba	736,971	3.7	4	Italy	831,922	5.9
5	Germany	711,929	3.6	5	United Kingdom	669,149	4.8
6	United Kingdom	640,145	3.2	6	Cuba	607,814	4.3
7	Italy	580,592	2.9	7	Philippines	501,440	3.6
8	Korea	568,397	2.9	8	Poland	418,128	3.0
9	Vietnam	543,262	2.7	9	Soviet Union	406,022	2.9
10	China	529,837	2.7	10	Korea	289,885	2.1
11	El Salvador	465,433	2.4	11	China	286,120	2.0
12	India	450,406	2.3	12	Vietnam	231,120	1.6
13	Poland	388,328	2.0	13	Japan	221,794	1.6
14	Dominican Republic	347,858	1.8	14	Portugal	211,614	1.5
15	Jamaica	334,140	1.7	15	Greece	210,998	1.5
16	Soviet Union	333,725	1.7	16	India	206,087	1.5
17	Japan	290,128	1.5	17	Ireland	197,817	1.4
18	Colombia	286,124	1.4	18	Jamaica	196,811	1.4
19	Taiwan	244,102	1.2	19	Dominican Republic	169,147	1.2
20	Guatemala	225,739	1.1	20	Yugoslavia	152,967	1.1
21	Haiti	225,393	1.1	21	Austria	145,607	1.0
22	Iran	210,941	1.1	22	Hungary	144,368	1.0
23	Portugal	210,122	1.1	23	Colombia	143,508	1.0
24	Greece	177,398	0.9	24	Iran	121,505	0.9
25	Laos	171,577	0.9	25	France	120,215	0.9

Source: U.S. Bureau of the Census, 1993.

Ancestry of U.S. Population by Rank, 1990 Census

(Over one million)

1990 Rank	Ancestry group	Number	Percent	1990 Rank	Ancestry group	Number	Percent
	Total population	**248,709,873**	**100.0**	17	French Canadian	2,167,127	0.9
1	German	57,947,873	23.3	18	Welsh	2,033,893	0.8
2	Irish	38,735,539	15.6	19	Spanish	2,024,004	0.8
3	English	32,651,788	13.1	20	Puerto Rican	1,955,323	0.8
4	Afro American	23,777,098	9.6	21	Slovak	1,882,897	0.8
5	Italian	14,664,550	5.9	22	White	1,799,711	0.7
6	American	12,395,999	5.0	23	Danish	1,634,669	0.7
7	Mexican	11,586,983	4.7	24	Hungarian	1,582,302	0.6
8	French	10,320,935	4.1	25	Chinese	1,505,245	0.6
9	Polish	9,366,106	3.8	26	Filipino	1,450,512	0.6
10	American Indian	8,708,220	3.5	27	Czech	1,296,411	0.5
11	Dutch	6,227,089	2.5	28	Portuguese	1,153,351	0.5
12	Scotch-Irish	5,617,773	2.3	29	British	1,119,154	0.4
13	Scottish	5,393,581	2.2	30	Hispanic	1,113,259	0.4
14	Swedish	4,680,863	1.9	31	Greek	1,110,373	0.4
15	Norwegian	3,869,395	1.6	32	Swiss	1,045,495	0.4
16	Russian	2,952,987	1.2	33	Japanese	1,004,645	0.4

NOTE: Data are based on a sample and subject to sampling variability. Since persons who reported multiple ancestries were included in more than one group, the sum of the persons reporting the ancestry is greater than the total; for example, a person reporting "English-French" was tabulated in both the "English" and "French" categories. Ancestry groups with fewer than 2,000 persons were not included in this report. *Source:* U.S. Bureau of the Census, 1993.

A Quarter of Nation's Foreign Born Arrived Since 1985

Nearly one-fourth of the United States' nearly 20 million foreign-born residents entered the country between 1985 and 1990, according to tabulations from the 1990 census.

The listing shows that the number of foreign-born persons entering the United States has increased steadily since the early 1960s, from 1.5 million in 1960–64, to a peak of 5.6 million in 1985–90.

About 7.9 percent of the nation's population was foreign born in 1990, the highest proportion in the past four decades.

California was home to one-third of the nation's foreign-born population. Other states with large concentrations include New York, 14 percent; Florida and Texas, 8 percent each; and New Jersey and Illinois, 5 percent each.

Spanish Leads Foreign Languages Spoken by U.S. Residents

According to the latest census studies released in April 1993, over 31.8 million people—14% of the nation's population five years or over—spoke a language other than English in 1990, compared with 23.1 million (or 11%) in 1980. After English, Spanish was the most common language spoken. About 4.5 million Americans spoke an Asian or Pacific Island language and nearly 332,000 spoke a Native North American language.

More than half of all non-English language speakers in 1990 lived in three states: California (8.6 million), New York (3.9 million), and Florida (4 million). New Mexico had the largest percentage of non-English language speakers at 36%, followed by California with 32 percent.

Spanish was the prevailing language in 39 states and the District of Columbia. The next most widely used language varied by region—Italian and German in the Northeast and Midwest, and French and Chinese in the South and West. French was most used in Louisiana, Maine, New Hampshire, and Vermont; and German in Montana, Minnesota, and North and South Dakota. In Rhode Island, Portuguese was first; in Alaska, it was Yupik; and in Hawaii, Japanese was the language of most non-English language speakers. □

Non-English Language Speaking Americans, 1990

Top languages spoken at home, ranked for persons five years old and over

Language	1990 Population 5 years and over	1980 Population 3 years and over	Percent change	Language	1990 Population 5 years and over	1980 Population 3 years and over	Percent change
United States	230,445,777	216,384,403	6.5	Navaho	148,530	123,169	20.6
Total	31,844,979	23,711,574	34.3	Hungarian	147,902	180,083	−17.9
Spanish	17,339,172	11,549,333	50.1	Hebrew	144,292	99,166	45.4
French	1,702,176	1,572,275	8.3	Dutch	142,684	146,429	−2.6
German	1,547,099	1,606,743	−3.7	Mon-Khmer[2]	127,441	16,417	676.3
Italian	1,308,648	1,633,279	−19.9	Gujarathi[3]	102,418	36,865	177.8
Chinese	1,249,213	631,737	97.7	Ukrainian	96,568	122,300	−21.0
Tagalog[1]	843,251	451,962	86.6	Czech	92,485	123,059	−24.8
Polish	723,483	826,150	−12.4	Pennsylvania Dutch	83,525	68,202	22.5
Korean	626,478	275,712	127.2	Miao[4]	81,877	16,189	405.8
Vietnamese	507,069	203,268	149.5	Norwegian	80,723	113,227	−28.7
Portuguese	429,860	361,101	19.0	Slovak	80,388	87,941	−8.6
Japanese	427,657	342,205	25.0	Swedish	77,511	100,886	−23.2
Greek	388,260	410,462	−5.4	Serbocroatian	70,964	83,216	−14.7
Arabic	355,150	225,597	57.4	Kru[5]	65,848	24,506	168.7
Hindi and related	331,484	129,968	155.1	Rumanian	65,265	32,502	100.8
Russian	241,798	174,623	38.5	Lithuanian	55,781	73,234	−23.8
Yiddish	213,064	320,380	−33.5	Finnish	54,350	69,386	−21.7
Thai	206,266	89,052	131.6	Panjabi	50,005	19,298	159.1
Persian	201,865	109,293	84.7	Formosan	46,044	13,661	237.0
French Creole	187,658	24,885	654.1	Croatian	45,206	42,479	6.4
Armenian	149,694	102,301	46.3	Turkish	41,876	27,459	52.5

NOTE: The data for 1980 in this table are for the population 3 years old and over; for 1990 they are for persons 5 years and over. *Source:* Census data published April 1993. 1. Filipino language of Manila and adjacent provinces. 2. Language spoken in southeast Asia, mostly in Cambodia. 3. Language of Gujarat region of western India. 4.Language of Hmong people of mountainous regions of southern China and adjacent areas of Vietnam, Laos, and Thailand. 5. Language spoken in Western Africa, chiefly in Liberia.

Immigrant and Nonimmigrant Aliens Admitted to U.S.

Period[1]	Immigrants	Non–immigrants[2]	Total	Period[1]	Immigrants	Non–immigrants[2]	Total
1901–10	8,795,386	1,007,909	9,803,295	1986	601,708	10,471,024	11,072,732
1911–20	5,735,811	1,376,271	7,112,082	1988	643,025	14,591,735	15,234,760
1921–30	4,107,209	1,774,896	5,882,090	1989	1,090,924[3]	16,144,576	17,235,500
1931–40	528,431	1,574,071	2,102,502	1990	1,536,483[3]	17,145,680	18,682,163
1941–50	1,035,039	2,461,359	3,496,398	1991	1,827,167[3]	18,962,520	20,789,687
1951–60	2,515,479	7,113,023	9,628,502	1992	973,977[3]	20,793,847	21,767,824
1961–70	3,321,677	24,107,224	27,428,901	1993	904,292[3]	21,446,993	22,351,285
1971–77	2,797,209	45,236,597	48,033,806	1994	804,416	22,118,706	22,923,122
1984	543,903	9,426,759	9,970,662	1995	720,461	22,640,539	23,361,000

1. Fiscal year ending June 30 prior to 1977. After 1977 for fiscal year ending Sept. 30. 2. Nonimmigrant aliens include visitors for business or pleasure, students, foreign government officials, and others temporarily in the U.S. 3. Includes immigrants and legalized immigrants. *Source:* Department of Justice, Immigration and Naturalization Service.

Immigration to the United States in Fiscal Year 1995

By State of Intended Residence and Birthplace

State Birthplace	# of Immigrants	Percent of state	State Birthplace	# of Immigrants	Percent of state
California	**166,483**	**100.0%**	**Texas**	**49,963**	**100.0**
Mexico	34,416	20.7	Mexico	22,792	45.6
Philippines	22,584	13.6	Vietnam	4,251	8.5
Vietnam	16,755	10.1	India	2,400	4.8
China	10,256	6.2	Philippines	1,997	4.0
India	6,646	4.0	El Salvador	1,656	3.3
El Salvador	4,914	3.0	China	1,002	2.0
Korea	4,789	2.9	Canada	987	2.0
Taiwan	4,650	2.8	Nigeria	906	1.8
Iran	4,547	2.7	Pakistan	799	1.6
Hong Kong	3,339	2.0	United Kingdom	716	1.4
Other	53,586	32.2	Other	12,457	24.9
New York	**128,406**	**100.0%**	**New Jersey**	**39,729**	**100.0**
Dominican Republic	21,471	16.7	Dominican Republic	4,136	10.4
China	11,254	8.8	India	3,958	10.0
Jamaica	6,884	5.4	Philippines	2,626	6.6
Ukraine	6,428	5.0	Colombia	1,881	4.7
Guyana	5,132	4.0	Poland	1,651	4.2
India	4,859	3.8	Peru	1,534	3.9
Russia	4,111	3.2	Haiti	1,306	3.3
Haiti	3,508	2.7	Jamaica	1,294	3.3
Bangladesh	3,386	2.6	Ecuador	1,221	3.1
Philippines	3,216	2.5	Egypt	1,159	2.9
Other	58,157	45.3	Other	18,963	47.7
Florida	**62,023**	**100.0**	**Illinois**	**33,898**	**100.0**
Cuba	15,112	24.4	Mexico	6,500	19.2
Haiti	5,869	9.5	Poland	4,982	14.7
Jamaica	4,261	6.9	India	3,051	9.0
Colombia	2,819	4.5	Philippines	2,690	7.9
Dominican Republic	2,090	3.4	Ukraine	1,504	4.4
Nicaragua	2,042	3.3	China	986	2.9
Mexico	1,922	3.1	Russia	797	2.4
Philippines	1,806	2.9	Iraq	715	2.1
Canada	1,620	2.6	Pakistan	705	2.1
Peru	1,607	2.6	Bosnia-Herzegovina	641	1.9
Other	22,875	36.9	Other	11,327	33.4

Source: Department of Justice, Immigration and Naturalization Services.

Marital Status and Household Characteristics

Marriages and Divorces

1900–1995

Year	Marriage Number	Marriage Rate[2]	Divorce[1] Number	Divorce[1] Rate[2]	Year	Marriage Number	Marriage Rate[2]	Divorce[1] Number	Divorce[1] Rate[2]
1900	709,000	9.3	55,751	.7	1983	2,444,000	10.5	1,179,000	5.
1910	948,166	10.3	83,045	.9	1984	2,487,000	10.5	1,155,000	4.
1920	1,274,476	12.0	170,505	1.6	1985	2,425,000	10.2	1,187,000	5.
1930	1,126,856	9.2	195,961	1.6	1986	2,400,000	10.0	1,159,000	4.
1940	1,595,879	12.1	264,000	2.0	1987	2,421,000	9.9	1,157,000	4.
1950	1,667,231	11.1	385,144	2.6	1988	2,389,000	9.7	1,183,000	4.
1960	1,523,000	8.5	393,000	2.2	1989	2,404,000	9.7	1,163,000	4.
1965	1,800,000	9.3	479,000	2.5	1990	2,448,000	9.8	1,175,000	4.
1970	2,158,802	10.6	708,000	3.5	1991	2,371,000	9.4	1,187,000	4.
1975	2,152,662	10.1	1,036,000	4.9	1992	2,362,000	9.3	1,215,000	4.
1980	2,406,708	10.6	1,182,000	5.2	1993	2,334,000	9.0	1,187,000	4.
1981	2,438,000	10.6	1,219,000	5.3	1994	2,362,000	9.1	1,191,000	4.
1982	2,495,000	10.8	1,180,000	5.1	1995	2,336,000	8.9	1,169,000	4.

1. Includes annulments. 2. Per 1,000 population. Divorce rates for 1941–46 are based on population including armed forces overseas. Marriage rates are based on population excluding armed forces overseas. NOTE: Marriage and divorce figures for most years include some estimated data. Alaska is included beginning 1959, Hawaii beginning 1960. *Source:* Department of Health and Human Services, National Center for Health Statistics.

Percent of Population Never Married

Age group	All races			White			Black		
	1995	1980	1970	1995	1980	1970	1995	1980	1970
Males: 20 to 24	80.7	68.8	54.6	79.1	67.0	54.5	90.5	79.3	56.1
25 to 29	51.0	33.1	19.1	48.6	31.4	17.8	65.0	44.2	28.4
30 to 34	28.2	15.9	9.4	25.4	14.2	9.2	40.0	30.0	9.2
35 to 39	20.3	7.8	7.2	18.2	6.6	6.1	35.1	18.5	15.8
40 to 44	14.0	7.1	6.3	12.5	6.7	5.7	25.1	10.8	11.2
45 to 54	8.1	6.1	7.5	7.1	5.6	7.1	17.6	11.7	10.4
55 to 64	5.0	5.3	7.8	4.3	5.2	7.6	12.7	5.9	9.1
65 and over	4.2	4.9	7.5	3.9	4.8	7.4	6.7	5.5	5.7
Females: 20 to 24	66.7	50.2	35.8	63.7	47.2	34.6	83.9	68.5	43.5
25 to 29	35.3	20.9	10.5	30.8	18.3	9.2	68.6	37.2	18.8
30 to 34	19.0	9.5	6.2	15.7	8.1	5.5	40.1	19.0	10.8
35 to 39	12.6	6.2	5.4	9.7	5.2	4.6	30.6	12.2	12.1
40 to 44	8.7	4.8	4.9	6.7	4.3	4.8	21.8	9.0	6.9
45 to 54	8.1	4.7	4.9	5.1	4.4	4.9	14.2	7.7	4.4
55 to 64	4.3	4.5	6.8	3.8	4.4	7.0	9.3	5.7	4.7
65 and over	4.2	5.9	7.7	4.0	6.1	8.0	6.3	4.5	4.2

Source: U.S. Bureau of the Census.

Persons Living Alone, by Sex and Age
(numbers in thousands)

Sex and Age[1]	1995		1994		1990		1980		1970	
	Number	Percent	Number	Percent	Number	Percent	Number	Percent	Number	Percent
BOTH SEXES										
15 to 24 years	1,223	4.9	1,126	4.8	1,210	5.3	1,726	9.4	556	5.1
25 to 44 years	7,334	29.6	7,235	30.6	7,110	30.9	4,729	25.8	1,604	14.8
45 to 64 years	6,386	25.7	5,967	25.3	5,502	23.9	4,514	24.7	3,622	33.4
65 years and over	9,862	39.8	9,285	39.3	9,176	39.9	7,328	40.1	5,071	46.7
Total, 15 years and over	**24,805**	**100.0**			**22,999**	**100.0**	**18,296**	**100.0**	**10,851**	**100.0**
MALE										
15 to 24 years	632	6.2	570	6.0	674	7.4	947	13.6	274	2.5
25 to 44 years	4,486	44.1	4,359	46.2	4,231	46.8	2,920	41.9	933	8.6
45 to 64 years	2,793	27.5	2,473	26.2	2,203	24.3	1,613	23.2	1,152	10.6
65 years and over	2,255	22.2	2,037	21.6	1,942	21.5	1,486	21.3	1,174	10.8
Total, 15 years and over	**10,166**	**100.0**			**9,049**	**100.0**	**6,966**	**100.0**	**3,532**	**32.5**
FEMALE										
15 to 24 years	591	4.0	557	3.9	536	3.8	779	6.9	282	2.6
25 to 44 years	2,845	19.5	2,872	20.3	2,881	20.7	1,809	16.0	671	6.2
45 to 64 years	3,594	24.5	3,493	24.6	3,300	23.7	2,901	25.6	2,470	22.8
65 years and over	7,607	52.0	7,248	51.1	7,233	51.8	5,842	51.6	3,897	35.9
Total, 15 years and over	**14,640**	**100.0**	**14,171**	**100.0**	**13,950**	**100.0**	**11,330**	**100.0**	**7,319**	**67.5**

1. Prior to 1980, data are for persons 14 years and older. NOTE: Details may not add because of rounding. *Source:* Department of Commerce, Bureau of the Census.

Characteristics of Unmarried-Couple Households, 1995
(number in thousands)

Characteristics	Number	Percent	Characteristics	Number	Percent
Unmarried-couple households	3,668	100.0	Presence of children:		
			No children under 15 years	2,349	64.0
Age of householders:			Some children under 15 years	1,319	36.0
Under 25 years	742	20.2			
25–44 years	2,188	59.7	Sex of householders:		
45–64 years	558	15.2	Male	2,076	56.6
65 years and over	180	4.9	Female	1,593	43.4

Source: U.S. Bureau of the Census.

Households, Families, and Married Couples

Date	Households Number	Average population per household	Families Number	Average population per family	Maried couple Number
June 1890	12,690,000	4.93	—	—	
April 1930	29,905,000	4.11	—	—	25,174,00
April 1940	34,949,000	3.67	32,166,000	3.76	28,517,00
March 1950	43,554,000	3.37	39,303,000	3.54	36,091,00
April 1955	47,874,000	3.33	41,951,000	3.59	37,556,00
March 1960[1]	52,799,000	3.33	45,111,000	3.67	40,200,00
March 1965	57,436,000	3.29	47,956,000	3.70	42,478,00
March 1970	63,401,000	3.14	51,586,000	3.58	45,373,00
March 1975	71,120,000	2.94	55,712,000	3.42	47,547,00
March 1980	80,776,000	2.76	59,550,000	3.29	49,714,00
March 1985	86,789,000	2.69	62,706,000	3.23	51,114,00
March 1990	93,347,000	2.63	66,090,000	3.17	53,256,00
March 1995	98,990,000	2.65	69,305,000	3.19	54,944,00

1. First year in which figures for Alaska and Hawaii are included. *Source:* Department of Commerce, Bureau of the Census.

Families Maintained by Women, with No Husband Present
(numbers in thousands)

	1995 Number	Percent	1990 Number	Percent	1980 Number	Percent	1970 Number	Percent	1960 Number	Percen
Age of women:										
Under 35 years	4,089	33.5	3,699	34.0	3,015	34.6	1,364	24.4	796	17.
35 to 44 years	3,502	28.7	2,929	26.9	1,916	22.0	1,074	19.2	940	20.
45 to 64 years	3,094	25.3	2,790	25.6	2,514	28.9	2,021	36.1	1,731	38.
65 years and over	1,536	12.6	1,471	13.5	1,260	14.5	1,131	20.2	1,027	22.
Median age	40.4	—	40.7	—	41.7	—	48.5	—	50.1	—
Presence of children:										
No own children under 18 years	4,606	37.7	4,290	39.4	3,260	37.4	2,665	47.7	2,397	53.
With own children under 18 years	7,615	62.3	6,599	60.6	5,445	62.6	2,926	52.3	2,097	46.
Total own children under 18 years	13,419	—	11,378	—	10,204	—	6,694	—	4,674	—
Average per family	1.10	—	1.04	—	1.17	—	1.20	—	1.04	—
Average per family with children	1.76	—	1.72	—	1.87	—	2.29	—	2.24	—
Race:										
White	8,031	65.7	7,306	67.1	6,052	69.5	4,165	74.5	3,547	78.
Black[1]	3,716	30.4	3,275	30.1	2,495	28.7	1,382	24.7	947	21.
Other	473	3.9	309	2.8	158	1.8	44	0.8	n.a.	n.a
Marital status:										
Married, husband absent	2,160	17.7	1,947	17.9	1,769	20.3	1,326	23.7	1,099	24.
Widowed	2,283	18.7	2,536	23.3	2,570	29.5	2,396	42.9	2,325	51.
Divorced	4,537	37.1	3,949	36.3	3,008	34.6	1,259	22.5	694	15.
Never married	3,240	26.5	2,457	22.6	1,359	15.6	610	10.9	376	8.
Total	**12,220**	**100.0**	**10,890**	**100.0**	**8,705**	**100.0**	**5,591**	**100.0**	**4,494**	**100.**

1. Includes other races in 1960. NOTE: n.a. = not available. (—) as shown in this table, means "not applicable." *Source:* Department of Commerce, Bureau of the Census.

Median Age at First Marriage

Year	Males	Females	Year	Males	Females	Year	Males	Females	Year	Males	Females
1900	25.9	21.9	1930	24.3	21.3	1960	22.8	20.3	1990	26.1	23.9
1910	25.1	21.6	1940	24.3	21.5	1970	23.2	20.8	1993	26.5	24.5
1920	24.6	21.2	1950	22.8	20.3	1980	24.7	22.0	1994	26.7	24.5

Source: Department of Commerce, Bureau of the Census.

Selected Family Characteristics

Characteristics[1]	1994 Number (000s)	1994 Median income	Characteristics[1]	1994 Number (000s)	1994 Median income
ALL RACES			Male householder, no wife present	2,507	$32,227
All households	98,990	$32,264	Female householder, no husband present	8,031	22,605
Age of householder					
Under 65 years	77,625	37,247			
15 to 24 years	5,444	19,340	Number of earners		
25 to 34 years	19,453	33,151	No earners	18,065	13,412
35 to 44 years	22,914	41,667	1 earner	27,018	27,775
45 to 54 years	17,590	47,261	2 earners or more	38,654	51,998
55 to 64 years	12,224	35,232	2 earners	30,389	48,934
65 years and over	21,365	18,095	3 earners	6,219	61,697
65 to 74 years	11,803	21,422	4 earners or more	2,046	74,832
75 years and over	9,562	14,731	Size of household		
			1 person	21,000	16,818
Region			2 persons	27,988	35,279
Northeast	19,593	34,926	3 persons	13,931	43,541
Midwest	23,683	32,505	4 persons	12,841	49,293
South	34,766	30,021	5 persons	5,312	47,990
West	20,948	34,452	6 persons	1,751	45,786
			7 persons or more	913	39,018
Type of household					
Family households	69,305	31,390	**BLACK**		
Married-couple family	53,858	45,041	All households	11,655	21,027
Male householder, no wife present	3,226	30,472	Age of householder		
			Under 65 years	9,830	23,363
Female householder, no husband present	12,220	19,872	15 to 24 years	833	11,765
			25 to 34 years	2,674	20,348
Number of earners			35 to 44 years	2,950	25,943
No earners	21,404	12,175	45 to 54 years	2,046	31,432
1 earner	32,973	26,210	55 to 64 years	1,325	22,577
2 earners or more	44,614	51,093	65 years and over	1,825	12,510
2 earners	34,986	47,734	65 to 74 years	1,086	14,504
3 earners	7,257	60,421	75 years and over	739	10,269
4 earners or more	2,370	74,276			
Size of household					
1 person	24,732	16,222	Region		
2 persons	31,834	33,955	Northeast	2,029	23,257
3 persons	16,827	41,043	Midwest	2,285	17,963
4 persons	15,321	46,757	South	6,284	20,603
5 persons	6,616	44,135	West	1,057	25,716
6 persons	2,279	42,683			
7 persons or more	1,382	36,622	Type of household		
			Married-couple family	3,842	40,432
WHITE			Male householder, no wife present	536	23,073
All households	83,737	34,028	Female householder, no husband present	3,716	14,650
Age of householder					
Under 65 years	64,558	39,852			
15 to 24 years	4,365	20,769	Number of earners		
25 to 34 years	15,845	35,518	No earners	2,800	6,949
35 to 44 years	18,978	44,397	1 earner	4,731	18,609
45 to 54 years	14,796	50,019	2 earners or more	4,123	42,831
55 to 64 years	10,574	36,817	2 earners	3,251	39,752
65 years and over	19,179	18,670	3 earners	706	49,717
65 to 74 years	10,479	22,122	4 earners or more	166	71,191
75 years and over	8,700	15,084	Size of household		
			1 person	3,109	11,700
Region			2 persons	3,012	22,637
Northeast	16,962	36,477	3 persons	2,216	25,789
Midwest	20,950	34,103	4 persons	1,728	29,055
South	27,721	32,095	5 persons	920	26,990
West	18,103	35,063	6 persons	362	30,185
Type of household			7 persons or more	308	27,761
Married-couple family	47,899	45,555			

Characteristics[1]	1994 Number (000s)	1994 Median income
HISPANIC ORIGIN OF HOUSEHOLDER[2]		
All households	7,735	$23,421
Age of householder		
Under 65 years	6,846	24,949
15 to 24 years	674	16,713
25 to 34 years	2,237	23,780
35 to 44 years	1,950	28,225
45 to 54 years	1,232	29,208
55 to 64 years	755	24,536
65 years and over	889	13,121
65 to 74 years	607	13,776
75 years and over	282	12,068
Region		
Northeast	1,291	19,021
Midwest	495	29,482
South	2,589	22,620
West	3,360	24,389
Type of household		
Married-couple family	4,235	29,915

Characteristics[1]	1994 Number (000s)	1994 Median income
Male householder, no wife present	479	25,59
Female householder, no husband present	1,485	13,20
Number of earners		
No earners	1,333	7,42
1 earner	2,771	17,72
2 earners or more	3,630	37,08
2 earners	2,632	34,67
3 earners	730	42,01
4 earners or more	268	54,17
Size of household		
1 person	1,156	11,59
2 persons	1,674	21,82
3 persons	1,494	25,15
4 persons	1,582	26,72
5 persons	960	26,80
6 persons	476	31,55
7 persons or more	392	29,68

1. Household data as of March 1995. 2. Persons of Hispanic origin may be of any race. *Source:* Department of Commerce, Bureau of the Census Current Population Reports, Series P60-188, "Money Income of Households, Families, and Persons in the United States: 1994." NOTE: Data are the latest available.

Births
Live Births and Birth Rates

Year	Births[1]	Rate[2]	Year	Births[1]	Rate[2]	Year	Births[1]	Rate[2]
1910	2,777,000	30.1	1961[3]	4,268,326	23.3	1978	3,333,279	15.3
1915	2,965,000	29.5	1962[3]	4,167,362	22.4	1979	3,494,398	15.9
1920	2,950,000	27.7	1963[3]	4,098,020	21.7	1980	3,612,258	15.9
1925	2,909,000	25.1	1964[3]	4,027,490	21.0	1982	3,680,537	15.9
1930	2,618,000	21.3	1965[3]	3,760,358	19.4	1983	3,638,933	15.5
1935	2,377,000	18.7	1966[3]	3,606,274	18.4	1984	3,669,141	15.5
1940	2,559,000	19.4	1967[4]	3,520,959	17.8	1985	3,760,561	15.8
1945	2,858,000	20.4	1968[3]	3,501,564	17.5	1986	3,731,000	15.5
1950	3,632,000	24.1	1969[3]	3,600,206	17.8	1987	3,829,000	15.7
1952[3]	3,913,000	25.1	1970[3]	3,731,386	18.4	1988	3,913,000	15.9
1953[3]	3,965,000	25.1	1971[3]	3,555,970	17.2	1989	4,021,000	16.2
1954[3]	4,078,000	25.3	1972	3,258,411	15.6	1990	4,179,000	16.7
1955	4,104,000	25.0	1973	3,136,965	14.9	1991	4,111,000	16.2
1956[3]	4,218,000	25.2	1974	3,159,958	14.9	1992	4,084,000	16.0
1957[3]	4,308,000	25.3	1975	3,144,198	14.8	1993	4,039,000	15.7
1958[3]	4,255,000	24.5	1976	3,167,788	14.8	1994	3,979,000	15.3
1959[3]	4,295,000	24.3	1977	3,326,632	15.4	1995	3,892,000	14.8
1960[3]	4,257,850	23.7						

1. Figures through 1959 include adjustment for underregistration; beginning 1960, figures represent number registered. For comparison, the 1959 registered count was 4,245,000. 2. Rates are per 1,000 population estimated as of July 1 for each year except 1940, 1950, 1960, 1970, and 1980, which are as of April 1, the census date; for 1942–46 based on population including armed forces overseas. 3. Based on 50% sample of births. 4. Based on a 20 to 50% sample of births. NOTE: Alaska is included beginning 1959; Hawaii beginning 1960. Since 1972, based on 100% of births in selected states and on 50% sample in all other states. *Sources:* Department of Health and Human Services, National Center for Health Statistics.

Unmarried Mothers

The proportion of children born out of wedlock in the U.S. was 26% in 1994, not statistically different from the 1990 figure. About 22.7 million (38%) women 15 to 44 years old in 1994 had never been married, and 20% of these had given birth to at least one child by the time of the Census Bureau survey. Despite the increasing attention paid to teenage pregnancies, only about 7% of never-married teenagers had borne a child, while about 40% of women in their thirties had borne a child out of wedlock.

The prevalence of births to unmarried women in the U.S., 30%, is roughly comparable to levels reported by other countries, such as Canada (29%), the United Kingdom (31%), and France (33%). These numbers were significantly lower than those reported in Denmark and Sweden, however, where almost one half of all children were born to women outside of marriage. In contrast, only 1% of the children born in 1992 in Japan were out of wedlock.

Live Births by Age of Mother and Race

Year[1]/race	Total	Under 15	15–19	20–24	25–29	30–34	35–39	40–44	45+
					Age of Mother				
1940	2,558,647	3,865	332,667	799,537	693,268	431,468	222,015	68,269	7,558
1945	2,858,449	4,028	298,868	832,746	785,299	554,906	296,852	78,853	6,897
1950	3,631,512	5,413	432,911	1,155,167	1,041,360	610,816	302,780	77,743	5,322
1955	4,014,112	6,181	493,770	1,290,939	1,133,155	732,540	352,320	89,777	5,430
1960	4,257,850	6,780	586,966	1,426,912	1,092,816	687,722	359,908	91,564	5,182
1965	3,760,358	7,768	590,894	1,337,350	925,732	529,376	282,908	81,716	4,614
1970	3,731,386	11,752	644,708	1,418,874	994,904	427,806	180,244	49,952	3,146
1975	3,144,198	12,642	582,238	1,093,676	936,786	375,500	115,409	26,319	1,628
1980	3,612,258	10,169	552,161	1,226,200	1,108,291	550,354	140,793	23,090	1,200
1985	3,760,561	10,220	467,485	1,141,320	1,201,350	696,354	214,336	28,334	1,162
1990	4,158,212	11,657	521,826	1,093,730	1,277,108	886,063	317,583	48,607	1,638
1994	3,952,767	12,901	505,488	1,001,418	1,088,845	906,498	371,608	63,502	2,507
White	3,121,004	5,978	348,081	764,085	889,581	754,871	305,291	51,192	1,925
Black	636,391	6,465	140,968	197,841	142,355	99,155	42,029	7,339	239
American Indian[2]	37,740	211	7,705	12,158	9,010	5,738	2,435	461	22
Asian or Pacific Islander	157,632	247	8,734	27,334	47,899	46,734	21,853	4,510	321

1. Data for 1940–55 are adjusted for underregistration. Beginning 1960, only registered births are shown. Data for 1960–70 based on a 50% sample of births. For 1972–84, based on 100% of births in selected states and on 50% sample in all other states. Beginning 1989, births are tabulated by race of mother; previously based on race of child. 2. Includes births to Aleuts and Eskimos. NOTE: Data refer only to births occurring within the U.S. *Source:* Department of Health and Human Services, National Center for Health Statistics.

Births to Unmarried Women
(in thousands, except as indicated)

Age and race	1993	1990	1985	1980	1975	1970	1965	1960	1950
By age of mother:									
Under 15 years	11.5	10.7	9.4	9.0	11.0	9.5	6.1	4.6	3.2
15–19 years	357.4	350.0	270.9	262.8	222.5	190.4	123.1	87.1	56.0
20–24 years	438.5	403.9	300.4	237.3	134.0	126.7	90.7	68.0	43.1
25–29 years	233.8	230.0	152.0	99.6	50.2	40.6	36.8	32.1	20.9
30–34 years	132.3	118.2	67.3	41.0	19.8	19.1	19.6	18.9	10.8
35–39 years	55.6	44.1	24.0	13.2	8.1	9.4	11.4	10.6	6.0
40 years and over	11.1	8.5	4.1	2.9	2.3	3.0	3.7	3.0	1.7
By race:[1]									
White	742.1	669.7	433.0	320.1	186.4	175.1	123.7	82.5	53.5
Black	452.5	495.7	395.2	345.7	261.6	223.6	167.5	141.8	88.1
Total of above births	**1,194.6**	**1,165.4**	**828.2**	**665.8**	**447.9**	**398.7**	**291.2**	**224.3**	**141.6**
Percent of all births[2]	31.0	28.0	22.0	18.4	14.2	10.7	7.7	5.3	3.9
Rate[3]	45.3	43.8	32.8	29.4	24.8	26.4	23.4	21.8	14.1

1. For 1988 and prior years births were tabulated by race of child. Beginning 1989, births are tabulated by race of mother. 2. Through 1955, based on data adjusted for underregistration; thereafter, registered births. 3. Rate per 1,000 unmarried (never married, widowed, and divorced) women, 15–44 years old. *Source:* Department of Health and Human Services, National Center for Health Statistics. NOTE: Data are latest available.

Live Births by Sex and Sex Ratio[1]

Year	Male	Female	Males per 1,000 females	Male	Female	Males per 1,000 females	Male	Female	Males per 1,000 females
	Total[2]			**White[3]**			**Black[3]**		
1983[4]	1,865,553	1,773,380	1,052	1,492,385	1,411,865	1,057	297,011	289,016	1,028
1984[4]	1,879,490	1,789,651	1,050	1,500,326	1,423,176	1,054	300,951	291,794	1,031
1985	1,927,983	1,832,578	1,052	1,536,646	1,454,727	1,056	308,575	299,618	1,030
1986	1,924,868	1,831,679	1,051	1,523,914	1,446,525	1,053	315,788	305,433	1,034
1987	1,951,153	1,858,241	1,050	1,535,517	1,456,971	1,054	325,259	316,308	1,028
1988	2,002,424	1,907,086	1,050	1,562,675	1,483,487	1,053	341,441	330,535	1,033
1989	2,069,490	1,971,468	1,050	1,606,757	1,525,234	1,053	360,131	349,264	1,031
1990	2,129,495	2,028,717	1,050	1,654,928	1,570,415	1,054	367,455	357,121	1,029
1991	2,101,518	2,009,389	1,046	1,659,077	1,582,196	1,049	346,455	336,147	1,031
1992	2,082,097	1,982,917	1,050	1,641,811	1,559,867	1,053	342,726	330,907	1,036
1993	2,048,861	1,951,379	1,050	1,616,332	1,533,501	1,054	333,984	324,891	1,028

1. Excludes births to nonresidents of U.S. 2. Includes races other than white and black. 3. Race of child through 1990. Race of mother from 1991. 4. Based on 100% of births for selected states and 50% sample in all others. *Source:* Department of Health and Human Services, National Center for Health Statistics. NOTE: Data are latest available.

Live Births and Birth Rates

State	1993[1] number	1993[1] rate	1992 number	1992 rate	State	1993[1] number	1993[1] rate	1992 number	1992 rate
Alabama	61,706	14.8	62,260	15.0	Montana	11,365	13.5	11,472	14.
Alaska	11,073	18.5	11,726	20.0	Nebraska	23,224	14.4	23,397	14.
Arizona	69,056	17.5	68,829	18.0	Nevada	22,403	16.2	22,374	16.
Arkansas	34,289	14.1	34,820	14.5	New Hampshire	15,436	13.7	15,990	14.
California	585,324	18.8	601,730	19.5	New Jersey	117,686	15.0	119,909	15.
Colorado	54,022	15.2	54,535	15.7	New Mexico	27,852	17.2	27,922	17.
Connecticut	46,700	14.2	47,573	14.5	New York	282,392	15.6	287,887	15.
Delaware	10,568	15.1	10,656	15.4	North Carolina	101,357	14.6	103,967	15.
D.C.	10,629	18.4	10,960	18.7	North Dakota	8,690	13.6	8,811	13.
Florida	192,537	14.0	191,713	14.2	Ohio	158,793	14.4	162,247	14.
Georgia	110,622	16.0	111,116	16.4	Oklahoma	46,243	14.3	47,557	14.
Hawaii	19,593	16.8	19,864	17.2	Oregon	41,576	13.7	42,035	14.
Idaho	17,440	15.8	17,362	16.3	Pennsylvania	160,762	13.4	164,625	13.
Illinois	190,788	16.3	191,396	16.5	Rhode Island	13,976	14.0	14,500	14.
Indiana	83,949	14.7	84,140	14.9	South Carolina	53,835	14.8	56,192	15.
Iowa	37,826	13.4	38,469	13.7	South Dakota	10,719	15.0	11,018	15.
Kansas	37,406	14.8	38,027	15.1	Tennessee	73,017	14.3	73,614	14.
Kentucky	53,000	14.0	53,840	14.3	Texas	322,071	17.9	320,845	18.
Louisiana	69,402	16.2	70,707	16.5	Utah	37,127	20.0	37,200	20.
Maine	15,065	12.2	16,057	13.0	Vermont	7,457	13.0	7,737	13.
Maryland	74,988	15.1	77,815	15.8	Virginia	94,944	14.7	97,198	15.
Massachusetts	84,668	14.1	87,231	14.6	Washington	78,645	15.0	79,450	15.
Michigan	139,855	14.8	144,089	15.3	West Virginia	21,792	12.0	22,170	12.
Minnesota	64,648	14.3	65,607	14.7	Wisconsin	69,767	13.8	70,670	14.
Mississippi	42,149	16.0	42,681	16.3	Wyoming	6,555	14.0	6,723	14.
Missouri	75,253	14.4	76,301	14.7	**Total**	**4,000,240**	**15.5**	**4,065,014**	**15.**

1. Revised. NOTE: Data by place of residence. Rates are per 1,000 population. *Source:* Department of Health and Human Services, National Center for Health Statistics.

Selected Characteristics of Births, by Race of Mother

United States, 1994

Characteristic	All races	White	Black	American Indian[1]	Asian or Pacific Islander
Percentage of mothers who:					
Had prenatal care beginning in the first trimester	80.2	82.8	68.3	65.2	79.7
Had late or no prenatal care	4.4	3.6	8.2	9.8	4.1
Were tobacco users[2]	14.6	15.6	11.4	21.0	3.6
Were alcohol users[3]	1.7	1.5	2.5	5.1	0.5
Gained <16 lbs[4]	10.4	9.1	16.5	13.8	9.4
Caesarean delivery rate	21.2	21.2	21.8	18.0	18.7
Percentage of infants who:					
Were born prior to 37 full weeks	11.0	9.6	18.1	12.1	10.1
Weighed less than 1,500 grams (3 lb 4 oz.)	1.3	1.0	3.0	1.1	0.9
Weighed less than 2,500 grams (5 lb 8 oz.)	7.3	6.1	13.2	6.4	6.8
Weighed 4,000 grams (8 lb 4 oz) or more	10.4	11.7	5.3	12.5	6.1
Had 5-minute Apgar scores of less than 7[5]	1.4	1.2	2.5	1.5	1.0
Had 1-minute Apgar scores of less than 7[5]	8.4	7.9	10.7	8.7	6.6

1. Includes births to Aleuts and Eskimos. 2. Excludes data for Calif., Ind., N.Y. (but includes NYC), and S.D., which did not report tobacco use on birth certificate. 3. Excludes data for Calif. and S.D., which did not report alcohol use on birth certificate. 4. Excludes data for Calif., which did not report weight gain on birth certificate. 5. Excludes data for Calif. and Tex., which did not report Apgar scores on birth certificate. Apgar scores are derived from evaluations of five major signs at one minute and five minutes after birth. Each sign is given a score of 0–2 for a total of ten possible points; score of 7–10 are considered normal, 4–7 may require resuscitative measures, and 0–3 require immediate resuscitation. The signs and scores (0–1–2) are as follows: **A**ctivity or muscle tone (absent–arms and legs flexed–active movement); **P**ulse (absent–below 100 bpm–above 100 bpm); **G**rimace or reflex irritability (no response–grimace–sneeze, cough, pull away); **A**ppearance or skin color (blue-gray, pale all over–normal, except for extremities–normal over entire body); **R**espiration (absent–slow, irregular–good, crying). *Source:* U.S. Department of Health and Human Services.

Abortions and Abortion Rates

State	Number of Abortions			Abortion occurrence rate[1]			Change 1988–92
	1992	1991	1988	1992	1991	1988	
Alabama	17,450	17,400	18,220	18.2	18.2	18.7	−3
Alaska	2,370	2,400	2,390	16.5	16.9	18.2	−10
Arizona	20,600	19,690	23,070	24.1	23.2	28.8	−16
Arkansas	7,130	7,150	6,250	13.5	13.6	11.6	16
California	304,230	320,960	311,720	42.1	44.4	45.9	−8
Colorado	19,880	21,010	18,740	23.6	25.3	22.4	6
Connecticut	19,720	20,530	23,630	26.2	26.7	31.2	−16
Delaware	5,730	5,720	5,710	35.2	34.9	35.7	−1
District of Columbia	21,320	21,510	26,120	138.4	136.1	163.3	−15
Florida	84,680	84,570	82,850	30.0	29.9	31.5	−5
Georgia	39,680	39,720	36,720	24.0	24.2	23.5	2
Hawaii	12,190	12,130	11,170	46.0	45.9	43.0	7
Idaho	1,710	1,740	1,920	7.2	7.5	8.2	−12
Illinois	68,420	64,990	72,570	25.4	24.1	26.4	−4
Indiana	15,840	15,940	15,760	12.0	12.1	11.9	1
Iowa	6,970	7,200	9,420	11.4	11.7	14.6	−22
Kansas	12,570	12,770	11,440	22.4	22.9	20.1	11
Kentucky	10,000	8,270	11,520	11.4	9.5	13.0	−12
Louisiana	13,600	13,930	17,340	13.4	13.7	16.3	−18
Maine	4,200	4,210	4,620	14.7	14.7	16.2	−9
Maryland	31,260	33,000	32,670	26.4	27.5	28.6	−8
Massachusetts	40,660	44,150	43,720	28.4	30.2	30.2	−6
Michigan	55,580	55,800	63,410	25.2	25.1	28.5	−11
Minnesota	16,180	16,880	18,580	15.6	16.3	18.2	−14
Mississippi	7,550	8,160	5,120	12.4	13.5	8.4	48
Missouri	13,510	15,770	19,490	11.6	13.5	16.4	−29
Montana	3,330	3,680	3,050	18.2	20.6	16.5	11
Nebraska	5,580	6,230	6,490	15.7	17.5	17.7	−11
Nevada	13,300	14,450	10,190	44.2	49.0	40.3	10
New Hampshire	3,890	4,260	4,710	14.6	15.7	17.5	−17
New Jersey	55,320	55,800	63,900	31.0	30.9	35.1	−12
New Mexico	6,410	6,190	6,810	17.7	17.2	19.1	−7
New York	195,390	190,410	183,980	46.2	44.5	43.3	7
North Carolina	36,180	37,210	39,720	22.4	23.2	25.4	−12
North Dakota	1,490	1,600	2,230	10.7	11.4	14.9	−28
Ohio	49,520	52,030	53,400	19.5	20.4	21.0	−7
Oklahoma	8,940	9,130	12,120	12.5	12.8	16.2	−23
Oregon	16,000	16,580	15,960	23.9	24.9	23.9	0
Pennsylvania	49,740	51,780	51,830	18.6	19.2	18.9	−2
Rhode Island	6,990	7,500	7,190	30.0	31.5	30.6	−2
South Carolina	12,190	13,520	14,160	14.2	15.8	16.7	−15
South Dakota	1,040	980	900	6.8	6.4	5.7	19
Tennessee	19,060	19,840	22,090	16.2	16.9	18.9	−14
Texas	97,400	95,930	100,690	23.1	23.0	24.8	−7
Utah	3,940	4,250	5,030	9.3	10.4	12.8	−27
Vermont	2,900	3,110	3,580	21.2	22.7	25.8	−18
Virginia	35,020	35,170	35,420	22.7	22.8	23.7	−5
Washington	33,190	32,640	31,220	27.7	27.6	27.6	0
West Virginia	3,140	2,590	3,270	7.7	6.3	7.5	2
Wisconsin	15,450	15,510	18,040	13.6	13.6	16.0	−15
Wyoming	460	520	600	4.3	4.9	5.1	−16
Total	**1,528,930**	**1,556,510**	**1,590,750**	**25.9**	**26.3**	**27.3**	**−5**

1. Rate per 1,000 women aged 15–44. NOTE: Number of abortions are rounded to nearest 10. *Source:* Reproduced with the permission of The Alan Guttmacher Institute from Stanley K. Henshaw and Jennifer Van Vort, "Abortion Services in the United States, 1991 and 1992," *Family Planning Perspectives*, Volume 26, Number 3, May/June 1994.

Medical Abortion Becomes a New Option for American Women

In September of 1996, Planned Parenthood announced that it would participate in a clinical trial for drugs to medically induce abortions. Women seeking an early term abortion (no more than 49 days) will be offered the option of taking two drugs, methotrexate and misprostol, to abort the fetus.

Medical abortions have been offered in France since 1988 using mifepristone (RU 486), but the U.S. has been slow to investigate the alternatives to surgical abortion. In 1989, the FDA banned import of RU 486 for personal use. Leading scientists testified before Congress in 1990 that the ban has hindered research on the potential medical benefits of mifepristone (RU 486), including use as a possible treatment for breast cancer, AIDS, brain tumors, Cushing's disease, and diabetes. In 1993, President Clinton issued an executive order directing the Department of Health and Human Services to investigate the potential benefits of mifepristone, and in 1996 the FDA granted conditional approval of RU 486 for early-term abortions.

Attendance[1] at Arts Activities, 1992
As a % of population 18 and over

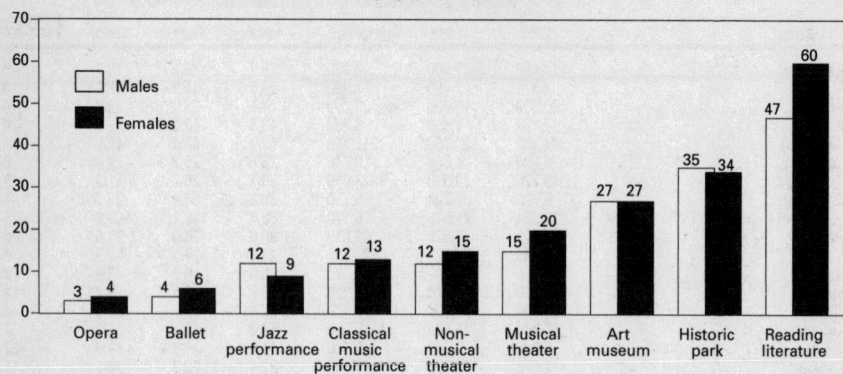

1. Attendance includes at least one event in prior 12 months; excludes elementary and high school performances. *Source:* U.S. National Endowment for the Arts, *Arts Participation in America: 1982 to 1992.*

Funding for the Arts in 1992
Budget for the National Endowment of the Arts, by Program Area
(in millions of dollars)

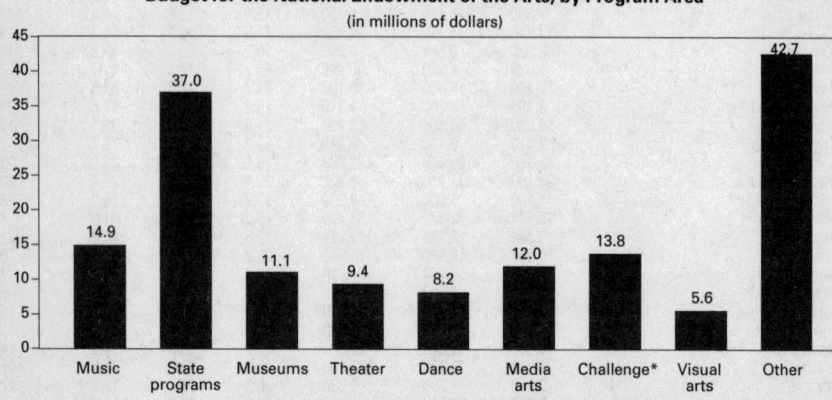

*Program designed to stimulate new sources and higher levels of giving to institutions for the purpose of guaranteeing long-term stability and financial independence. *Source:* U.S. National Endowment for the Arts *Annual Report.*

Travel by U.S. Residents
(in millions)

Characteristic	1985	1990	1992	1993
# of trips whose purpose was:				
To visit friends and relatives	206.8	246.0	195.2	194.5
Other pleasure	177.6	214.5	221.3	226.9
Business or convention	133.3	155.6	208.2	207.4
Other	40.7	45.0	26.0	19.4
# of trips whose transportation was:				
Auto, truck, or recreation vehicle	376.1	483.9	462.0	453.7
Airplane	140.5	144.9	169.2	168.5
Other	41.8	32.3	19.5	25.9

Characteristic	1985	1990	1992	1993
Total # of trips:	**558.4**	**661.1**	**650.7**	**648.**
Travelers to foreign countries:	**34.7**	**44.6**	**43.9**	**44.**
Canada	11.6	12.3	11.8	12.
Mexico	10.5	16.4	16.1	15.
Total overseas	12.7	16.0	16.0	17.
Europe	6.8	8.0	7.1	7.
Latin America	3.6	4.7	5.3	5.
Other	2.3	3.2	3.5	3.

Mortality
Death Rates for Selected Causes

Cause of death	Death rates per 100,000							
	1994[1]	1993	1990	1980	1950	1945–49	1920–24[4]	1900–04[4]
Typhoid fever	n.a.	n.a.	*	0.0	0.1	0.2	7.3	26.7
Communicable diseases of childhood	—	—	—	0.0	1.3	2.3	33.8	65.2
Measles	*	*	0.0	0.0	0.3	0.6	7.3	10.0
Scarlet fever	n.a.	n.a.	*	0.0	0.2	0.1	4.0	11.8
Whooping cough	*	*	*	0.0	0.7	1.0	8.9	10.7
Diphtheria	n.a.	n.a.	*	0.0	0.3	0.7	13.7	32.7
Pneumonia and influenza	31.5	32.1	32.8	23.3	31.3	41.3	140.3	184.3
Influenza	0.5	0.4	0.8	1.1	4.4	5.0	34.8	22.8
Pneumonia	31.0	31.7	31.1	22.0	26.9	37.2	105.5	161.5
Tuberculosis	0.6	0.6	0.7	0.8	22.5	33.3	96.7	184.7
Cancer	206.0	205.6	203.2	182.5	139.8	134.0	86.9	67.7
Diabetes mellitus	21.2	20.9	19.2	15.0	16.2	24.1	17.1	12.2
Major cardiovascular diseases	362.6	367.8	368.3	434.5	510.8	493.1	369.9	359.5
Diseases of the heart	281.6	288.4	289.5	335.2	356.8	325.1	169.8	153.0
Cerebrovascular diseases	59.2	58.2	57.9	74.6	104.0	93.8	93.5	106.3
Nephritis and nephrosis	9.1	9.0	8.3	7.6	16.4	48.4	81.5	84.3
Syphilis	*	1.0	0.0	0.1	5.0	8.4	17.6	12.9
Appendicitis	0.1	0.1	0.2	0.3	2.0	3.5	14.0	9.4
Accidents, all forms	34.6	35.1	37.0	46.0	60.6	67.6	70.8	79.2
Motor vehicle accidents	16.2	16.3	18.8	23.0	23.1	22.3	12.9	n.a.
Infant mortality[2]	n.a.	n.a.	9.2	12.5	29.2	33.3	76.7	n.a.
Neonatal mortality[2]	n.a.	n.a.	5.8	8.4	20.5	22.9	39.7	n.a.
Fetal mortality[3]	n.a.	n.a.	n.a.	9.2	19.2	21.6	n.a	n.a.
Maternal mortality[2]	0.1	0.1	8.2	0.1	0.8	1.4	6.9	n.a.
All causes	876.9	879.3	863.8	883.4	960.1	1,000.6	1,157.4	1,621.6

1. Provisional, based on a 10% sample of deaths. 2. Rates per 1,000 live births. 3. Ratio per 1,000 births. 4. Includes only deaths occurring within the registration areas. Beginning with 1933, area includes the entire United States; Alaska included beginning in 1959 and Hawaii in 1960. Rates per 100,000 population residing in areas, enumerated as of April 1 for 1940, 1950, and 1980 and estimated as of July 1 for all other years. Due to changes in statistical methods, death rates are not strictly comparable. Beginning in 1989 an asterisk is shown in place of a rate based on fewer than 20 deaths for final data and on 100 or fewer estimated deaths for provisional data. n.a. = not available. *Source:* Department of Health and Human Services, National Center for Health Statistics.

Accident Rates, 1994

Class of accident		One every	Class of accident		One every
All accidents	Deaths	6 minutes	Workers off-job	Deaths	15 minutes
	Injuries	2 seconds		Injuries	6 seconds
Motor-vehicle	Deaths	12 minutes	Home	Deaths	20 minutes
	Injuries	15 seconds		Injuries	5 seconds
Work	Deaths	105 minutes	Public non-motor-	Deaths	27 minutes
	Injuries	9 seconds	vehicle	Injuries	5 seconds

NOTE: Data are latest available. *Source:* National Safety Council.

Improper Driving as Factor in Accidents

Kind of improper driving	Fatal accidents		Injury accidents		All accidents	
	1994	1993	1994	1993	1994	1993
Improper driving	63.7	57.7	65.7	72.7	67.2	68.6
Speed too fast or unsafe	19.5	16.5	11.2	13.5	11.9	12.2
Right of way	15.1	12.7	24.1	25.0	21.3	20.6
Failed to yield	*9.1*	*7.8*	*15.0*	*17.3*	*14.5*	*15.1*
Passed stop sign	*2.6*	*2.7*	*3.1*	*2.7*	*2.5*	*2.0*
Disregarded signal	*3.4*	*2.2*	*6.0*	*5.0*	*4.3*	*3.5*
Drove left of center	9.4	7.6	2.5	2.1	2.3	1.8
Improper overtaking	1.6	1.2	1.2	1.0	1.4	1.3
Made improper turn	2.6	2.9	2.9	3.4	4.1	4.5
Followed too closely	0.5	0.5	5.9	6.2	5.6	5.5
Other improper driving	15.0	16.3	17.9	21.5	20.6	22.7
No improper driving stated	36.3	42.3	34.3	27.3	32.8	31.4
Total	100.0%	100.0%	100.0%	100.0%	100.0%	100.0%

Source: Motor-vehicle reports from 11 (1993) and 17 (1994) state traffic authorities to National Safety Council. NOTE: Figures are latest available.

Motor-Vehicle Deaths by Type of Accident

				Deaths from collisions with—				
Year	Pedestrians	Other motor vehicles	Railroad trains	Pedalcycles[1]	Animal-drawn vehicle, animal, or streetcars	Fixed objects[1]	Deaths from non-collision accidents[1]	Total deaths[2]
1980	9,700	23,000	739	1,200	100	3,700	14,700	53,172
1985	8,300	19,900	500	1,100	100	2,800	12,900	45,600
1990	7,400	19,400	600	1,000	100	12,900	4,900	46,300
1991	7,000	18,500	500	800	100	12,100	4,500	43,500
1992	6,500	17,400	500	700	100	10,900	4,200	40,300
1993	6,200	17,900	600	800	100	11,900	4,500	42,000
1994	5,600	19,300	500	800	100	12,400	4,300	43,000

1. Estimates for 1990 and later are not comparable to earlier years. 2. Totals do not equal sums of various types because totals are estimated. NOTE: Figures are latest available. *Source:* National Safety Council.

Accidental Deaths by Principal Types

Year	Motor vehicle	Falls	Drowning[1]	Fire burns[2]	Ingestion of food or object	Firearms	Poison (solid, liquid)	Poison by gas
1987	48,700	11,300	5,300	4,800	3,200	1,400	4,400	1,000
1988	49,000	12,000	5,000	5,000	3,600	1,400	5,300	1,000
1989	46,900	12,400	4,600	4,400	3,900	1,600	5,600	900
1990	46,300	12,400	5,200	4,300	3,200	1,400	5,700	800
1991	43,500	12,200	4,600	4,200	2,900	1,400	5,600	800
1992	40,300	12,400	4,300	4,000	2,700	1,400	5,200	700
1993	42,000	13,500	4,800	4,000	2,900	1,600	6,500	700
1994	43,000	13,300	4,000	4,200	3,000	1,500	8,000	700

1. Includes drowning in water transport accidents. 2. Includes burns by fire and deaths resulting from conflagration regardless of nature of injury. NOTE: Figures are latest available. *Source:* National Safety Council.

Deaths and Death Rates

	Total deaths		Motor vehicle traffic deaths			Total deaths		Motor vehicle traffic deaths	
State	1993 number	1993 rate[1]	1993 number	1993 rate	State	1993 number	1993 rate[1]	1993 number	1993 rate
Alabama	41,272	987.2	1,108	26.5	Montana	7,472	888.5	186	22.1
Alaska	2,383	398.6	110	18.4	Nebraska	15,026	931.4	273	16.9
Arizona	33,321	844.7	797	20.2	Nevada	11,173	808.5	222	16.1
Arkansas	26,531	1,093.7	597	20.2	New Hampshire	8,856	787.7	111	9.9
California	221,989	711.1	4,460	14.3	New Jersey	72,705	925.1	834	10.6
Colorado	23,746	666.4	599	16.8	New Mexico	11,731	726.1	409	25.3
Connecticut	29,037	885.8	371	11.3	New York	171,232	943.3	1,966	10.8
Delaware	6,150	880.5	101	14.5	North Carolina	62,486	898.8	1,404	20.2
Dist. of Col.	7,191	1,241.8	70	12.1	North Dakota	5,825	914.8	93	14.6
Florida	146,699	1,068.8	2,660	19.4	Ohio	102,696	928.4	1,491	13.5
Georgia	56,099	812.8	1,420	20.6	Oklahoma	32,422	1,002.9	709	21.9
Hawaii	7,329	628.8	136	11.7	Oregon	27,602	909.2	512	16.9
Idaho	8,395	762.9	248	22.5	Pennsylvania	126,911	1,051.3	1,637	13.6
Illinois	107,193	917.3	1,577	13.5	Rhode Island	9,786	979	85	8.5
Indiana	52,311	916.8	939	16.5	South Carolina	31,963	880.5	837	23.1
Iowa	27,973	991.5	469	16.6	South Dakota	6,782	947.1	140	19.6
Kansas	23,631	932.2	470	18.5	Tennessee	49,249	966.8	1,198	23.5
Kentucky	36,869	971.8	883	23.3	Texas	134,664	747.2	3,216	17.8
Louisiana	39,593	922.8	911	21.2	Utah	10,465	562.7	337	18.1
Maine	11,695	943.3	183	14.8	Vermont	4,957	861.1	98	17.0
Maryland	40,373	814.3	669	13.5	Virginia	51,538	796.2	883	13.6
Massachusetts	55,634	924.5	549	9.1	Washington	40,473	769.6	730	13.9
Michigan	82,570	872.9	1,458	15.4	West Virginia	20,404	1,122.1	439	24.1
Minnesota	36,450	805.6	607	13.4	Wisconsin	44,506	882.3	753	14.9
Mississippi	26,399	1,000.0	868	32.9	Wyoming	3,490	743	108	23.0
Missouri	53,746	1,026.6	962	18.4	**Total**	**2,268,553**	**44,992**	**43,226**	**883.4**

1. Rates per 100,000 population. *Source:* Monthly Vital Statistics Report, Feb. 1996.

Annual Death Rates

Year	Rate	Year	Rate	Year	Deaths	Rate
1900	17.2	1948	9.9	1972	1,963,944	9.4
1905	15.9	1949	9.7	1973	1,973,003	9.3
1910	14.7	1950	9.6	1974	1,934,388	9.1
1915	13.2	1951	9.7	1975	1,892,879	8.8
1920	13.0	1952	9.6	1976	1,909,440	8.8
1925	11.7	1953	9.6	1977	1,899,597	8.6
1930	11.3	1954	9.2	1978	1,927,788	8.7
1931	11.1	1955	9.3	1979	1,913,841	8.5
1932	10.9	1956	9.4	1980	1,989,841	8.7
1933	10.7	1957	9.6	1982	1,974,797	8.5
1934	11.1	1958	9.5	1983	2,019,201	8.6
1935	10.9	1959	9.4	1984	2,039,369	8.6
1936	11.6	1960	9.5	1985	2,086,440	8.7
1937	11.3	1962	9.5	1986	2,099,000	8.7
1938	10.6	1963	9.6	1987	2,127,000	8.7
1939	10.6	1964	9.4	1988	2,171,000	8.8
1940	10.8	1965	9.4	1989	2,155,000	8.7
1941	10.5	1966	9.5	1990	2,162,000	8.6
1942	10.3	1967	9.4	1991	2,165,000	8.5
1943	10.9	1968	9.7	1992	2,177,000	8.5
1944	10.6	1969	9.5	1993	2,268,000	8.8
1945	10.6	1970[1]	9.5	1994	2,286,000[2]	8.8
1946	10.0	1971	9.3	1995	2,309,000	8.8
1947	10.1					

1. First year for which deaths of nonresidents are excluded. 2. Provisional. NOTE: Includes only deaths occurring within the registration states. Beginning with 1933, area includes entire U.S.; with 1959 includes Alaska, and with 1960 includes Hawaii. Excludes fetal deaths. Rates per 1,000 population residing in area, as of April 1 for 1940, 1950, 1960, 1970, and 1980, and estimated as of July 1 for all other years. *Sources:* Department of Health and Human Services, National Center for Health Statistics.

Death Rates by Age, Race, and Sex

Age	1993	1992	1990	1980	1970[1]	1960	1993	1992	1990	1980	1970[1]	1960
	White males						**White females**					
Under 1 year	7.7	7.8	9.0	12.3	21.1	26.9	6.2	6.2	7.0	9.6	16.1	20.1
1–4	0.4	0.4	0.5	0.7	0.8	1.0	0.3	0.3	0.4	0.5	0.8	0.9
5–14	0.3	0.2	0.3	0.4	0.5	0.5	0.2	0.2	0.2	0.2	0.3	0.3
15–24	1.2	1.2	1.3	1.7	1.7	1.4	0.4	0.4	0.5	0.5	0.6	0.5
25–34	1.8	1.8	1.8	1.7	1.8	1.6	0.6	0.6	0.6	0.7	0.8	0.9
35–44	2.8	2.8	2.7	2.6	3.4	3.3	1.2	1.2	1.2	1.2	1.9	1.9
45–54	5.3	5.3	5.5	7.0	8.8	9.3	3.0	2.9	3.1	3.7	4.6	4.6
55–64	13.9	14.0	14.7	17.3	22.0	22.3	8.1	8.0	8.2	8.8	10.1	10.8
65–74	33.1	32.9	34.0	40.4	48.1	48.5	19.4	19.1	19.2	20.7	24.7	27.8
75–84	76.0	74.4	78.4	88.3	101.0	103.0	48.4	47.0	48.4	54.0	67.0	77.0
85 and over	184.4	179.6	183.0	191.0	185.5	217.5	145.6	140.2	144.0	149.8	159.8	194.8
	All other males						**All other females**					
Under 1 year	15.9	16.2	18.1	23.5	40.2	51.9	12.8	13.3	15.0	19.4	31.7	40.7
1–4	0.7	0.7	0.8	1.0	1.4	2.1	0.6	0.6	0.6	0.8	1.2	1.7
5–14	0.4	0.4	0.4	0.4	0.6	0.8	0.3	0.2	0.3	0.3	0.4	0.5
15–24	2.4	0.2	2.2	2.0	3.0	2.1	0.7	0.6	0.6	0.7	1.1	1.1
25–34	3.5	3.2	3.5	3.6	5.0	3.9	1.4	1.3	1.3	1.4	2.2	2.6
35–44	5.8	5.4	5.6	5.9	8.7	7.3	2.6	2.5	2.4	2.9	4.9	5.5
45–54	10.0	9.8	10.2	13.1	16.5	15.5	5.2	5.1	5.4	6.9	9.8	11.4
55–64	2.1	20.9	22.2	26.1	30.5	31.5	17.7	12.0	13.0	14.2	18.9	24.1
65–74	41.6	41.4	43.4	47.5	54.7	56.6	24.9	24.7	26.0	28.6	36.8	39.8
75–84	82.2	79.0	83.2	86.9	89.8	86.6	54.2	51.0	53.1	58.6	63.9	67.1
85 and over	165.2	157.2	160.8	157.7	114.1	152.4	129.0	126.3	129.0	119.2	102.9	128.7

1. Beginning 1970 excludes deaths of nonresidents of U.S. NOTE: Excludes fetal deaths. Rates are per 1,000 population in each group, enumerated as of April 1 for 1960, 1970, and 1980, and estimated as of July 1 for all other years. *Sources:* Department of Health and Human Services, National Center for Health Statistics.

Expectation of Life

Expectation of Life by Sex, 1850–1993

Calendar period	Age								
	0	10	20	30	40	50	60	70	80
WHITE MALES									
1850[1]	38.3	48.0	40.1	34.0	27.9	21.6	15.6	10.2	5.9
1890[1]	42.50	48.45	40.66	34.05	27.37	20.72	14.73	9.35	5.40
1900–1902[2]	48.23	50.59	42.19	34.88	27.74	20.76	14.35	9.03	5.10
1909–1911[2]	50.23	51.32	42.71	34.87	27.43	20.39	13.98	8.83	5.09
1919–1921[3]	56.34	54.15	45.60	37.65	29.86	22.22	15.25	9.51	5.47
1929–1931	59.12	54.96	46.02	37.54	29.22	21.51	14.72	9.20	5.26
1939–1941	62.81	57.03	47.76	38.80	30.03	21.96	15.05	9.42	5.38
1949–1951	66.31	58.98	49.52	40.29	31.17	22.83	15.76	10.07	5.88
1959–1961[5]	67.55	59.78	50.25	40.98	31.73	23.22	16.01	10.29	5.89
1969–1971[6]	67.94	59.69	50.22	41.07	31.87	23.34	16.07	10.38	6.18
1979–1981	70.82	61.98	52.45	43.31	34.04	25.26	17.56	11.35	6.76
1990	72.7	63.5	54.0	44.7	35.6	26.7	18.7	12.1	7.1
1992	73.2	64.0	54.3	45.1	36.0	27.1	19.1	12.4	7.2
1993	73.1	63.8	54.2	44.9	35.9	27.0	18.9	12.3	7.1
WHITE FEMALES									
1850[1]	40.5	47.2	40.2	35.4	29.8	23.5	17.0	11.3	6.4
1890[1]	44.46	49.62	42.03	35.36	28.76	22.09	15.70	10.15	5.75
1900–1902[2]	51.08	52.15	43.77	36.42	29.17	21.89	15.23	9.59	5.50
1909–1911[2]	53.62	53.57	44.88	36.96	29.26	21.74	14.92	9.38	5.35
1919–1921[3]	58.53	55.17	46.46	38.72	30.94	23.12	15.93	9.94	5.70
1929–1931	62.67	57.65	48.52	39.99	31.52	23.41	16.05	9.98	5.63
1939–1941	67.29	60.85	51.38	42.21	33.25	24.72	17.00	10.50	5.88
1949–1951	72.03	64.26	54.56	45.00	35.64	26.76	18.64	11.68	6.59
1959–1961[5]	74.19	66.05	56.29	46.63	37.13	28.08	19.69	12.38	6.67
1969–1971[6]	75.49	66.97	57.24	47.60	38.12	29.11	20.79	13.37	7.59
1979–1981	78.22	69.21	59.44	49.76	40.16	30.96	22.45	14.89	8.65
1990	79.4	70.1	60.3	50.6	41.0	31.6	23.0	15.4	9.0
1992	79.8	70.4	60.6	50.9	41.2	31.9	23.2	15.6	9.2
1993	79.5	70.1	60.3	50.6	41.0	31.7	23.0	15.3	8.9
ALL OTHER MALES[4]									
1900–1902[2]	32.54	41.90	35.11	29.25	23.12	17.34	12.62	8.33	5.12
1909–1911[2]	34.05	40.65	33.46	27.33	21.57	16.21	11.67	8.00	5.53
1919–1921[3]	47.14	45.99	38.36	32.51	26.53	20.47	14.74	9.58	5.83
1929–1931	47.55	44.27	35.95	29.45	23.36	17.92	13.15	8.78	5.42
1939–1941	52.33	48.54	39.74	32.25	25.23	19.18	14.38	10.06	6.46
1949–1951	58.91	52.96	43.73	35.31	27.29	20.25	14.91	10.74	7.07
1959–1961[5]	61.48	55.19	45.78	37.05	28.72	21.28	15.29	10.81	6.87
1969–1971[6]	60.98	53.67	44.37	36.20	28.29	21.24	15.35	10.68	7.57
1979–1981	65.63	57.40	47.87	39.13	30.64	22.92	16.54	11.36	7.22
1990	67.0	58.5	49.0	40.3	31.9	23.9	17.0	11.4	7.0
1992	67.7	59.0	49.6	40.9	32.4	24.5	17.5	11.7	7.2
1993	67.3	58.6	49.2	40.6	32.2	24.3	17.3	11.5	6.9
ALL OTHER FEMALES[4]									
1900–1902[2]	35.04	43.02	36.89	30.70	24.37	18.67	13.60	9.62	6.48
1909–1911[2]	37.67	42.84	36.14	29.61	23.34	17.65	12.78	9.22	6.05
1919–1921[3]	46.92	44.54	37.15	31.48	25.60	19.76	14.69	10.25	6.58
1929–1931	49.51	45.33	37.22	30.67	24.30	18.60	14.22	10.38	6.90
1939–1941	55.51	50.83	42.14	34.52	27.31	21.04	16.14	11.81	8.00
1949–1951	62.70	56.17	46.77	38.02	29.82	22.67	16.95	12.29	8.15
1959–1961[5]	66.47	59.72	50.07	40.83	32.16	24.31	17.83	12.46	7.66
1969–1971[6]	69.05	61.49	51.85	42.61	33.87	25.97	19.02	13.30	9.01
1979–1981	74.00	65.64	55.88	46.39	37.16	28.59	20.49	14.44	9.17
1990	75.2	66.6	56.8	47.3	38.1	29.2	21.3	14.5	8.8
1992	75.7	67.0	57.2	47.7	38.4	29.6	21.7	14.8	8.9
1993	75.5	66.7	56.9	47.4	38.2	29.5	21.4	14.5	8.7

1. Massachusetts only; white and nonwhite combined, the latter being about 1% of the total. 2. Original Death Registration States. 3. Death Registration States of 1920. 4. Data for periods 1900–1902 to 1929–1931 relate to blacks only. 5. Alaska and Hawaii included beginning in 1959. 6. Deaths of nonresidents of the United States excluded starting in 1970. *Sources:* Department of Health and Human Services, National Center for Health Statistics.

Expectation of Life, 1993

		Expectation of life in years			
	Total persons	White		All other	
Age		Male	Female	Male	Female
0	75.5	73.1	79.5	67.3	75.5
1	75.2	72.6	79.0	67.3	75.4
2	74.2	71.7	78.0	66.4	74.5
3	73.3	70.7	77.0	65.5	73.5
4	72.3	69.7	76.1	64.5	72.6
5	71.3	68.8	75.1	63.5	71.6
6	70.3	67.8	74.1	62.6	70.6
7	69.3	66.8	73.1	61.6	69.7
8	68.4	65.8	72.1	60.6	68.7
9	67.4	64.8	71.1	59.6	67.7
10	66.4	63.8	70.1	58.6	66.7
11	65.4	62.8	69.1	57.6	65.7
12	64.4	61.8	68.2	56.6	64.7
13	63.4	60.9	67.2	55.7	63.8
14	62.4	59.9	66.2	54.7	62.8
15	61.5	58.9	65.2	53.7	61.8
16	60.5	58.0	64.2	52.8	60.8
17	59.5	57.0	63.2	51.9	59.8
18	58.6	56.1	62.3	51.0	58.9
19	57.7	55.1	61.3	50.1	57.9
20	56.7	54.2	60.3	49.2	56.9
21	55.8	53.3	59.4	48.4	56.0
22	54.8	52.4	58.4	47.5	55.0
23	53.9	51.4	57.4	46.7	54.1
24	52.9	50.5	56.4	45.8	53.1
25	52.0	49.6	55.5	44.9	52.2
26	51.1	48.6	54.5	44.1	51.2
27	50.1	47.7	53.5	43.2	50.3
28	49.2	46.8	52.5	42.3	49.3
29	48.3	45.9	51.6	41.4	48.4
30	47.3	44.9	50.6	40.6	47.4
31	46.4	44.0	49.6	39.7	46.5
32	45.5	43.1	48.7	38.9	45.6
33	44.5	42.2	47.7	38.0	44.6
34	43.6	41.3	46.7	37.2	43.7
35	42.7	40.4	45.8	36.3	42.8
36	41.8	39.5	44.8	35.5	41.9
37	40.8	38.6	43.9	34.6	41.0
38	39.9	37.7	42.9	33.8	40.1
39	39.0	36.8	41.9	33.0	39.1
40	38.1	35.9	41.0	32.2	38.2
41	37.2	35.0	40.0	31.4	37.3
42	36.3	34.1	39.1	30.6	36.4
43	35.4	33.2	38.1	29.8	35.6
44	34.5	32.3	37.2	29.0	34.7
45	33.6	31.4	36.3	28.2	33.8
46	32.7	30.5	35.3	27.4	32.9
47	31.8	29.6	34.4	26.6	32.0
48	30.9	28.7	33.5	25.8	31.2
49	30.0	27.9	32.6	25.1	30.3
50	29.2	27.0	31.7	24.3	29.5
51	28.3	26.2	30.7	23.6	28.6
52	27.4	25.3	29.9	22.8	27.8
53	26.6	24.5	29.0	22.1	26.9
54	25.7	23.6	28.1	21.4	26.1
55	24.9	22.8	27.2	20.6	25.3
56	24.1	22.0	26.3	20.0	24.5
57	23.3	21.2	25.5	19.3	23.7
58	22.5	20.5	24.6	18.6	23.0
59	21.7	19.7	23.8	17.9	22.2
60	20.9	18.9	23.0	17.3	21.4
61	20.2	18.2	22.2	16.7	20.7
62	19.5	17.5	21.4	16.0	20.0
63	18.7	16.8	20.6	15.4	19.2
64	18.0	16.1	19.8	14.8	18.5
65	17.3	15.4	19.0	14.3	17.8
66	16.6	14.8	18.3	13.7	17.1

| | | Expectation of life in years | | | |
| | | White | | All other | |
Age	Total persons	Male	Female	Male	Female
67	15.9	14.1	17.5	13.1	16.4
68	15.3	13.5	16.8	12.6	15.8
69	14.6	12.9	16.1	12.0	15.1
70	14.0	12.3	15.3	11.5	14.5
71	13.3	11.7	14.6	11.0	13.8
72	12.7	11.1	14.0	10.5	13.2
73	12.1	10.6	13.3	10.0	12.6
74	11.5	10.0	12.6	9.6	12.0
75	10.9	9.5	12.0	9.1	11.5
76	10.4	9.0	11.3	8.7	10.9
77	9.8	8.5	10.7	8.2	10.3
78	9.3	8.0	10.1	7.8	9.8
79	8.8	7.5	9.5	7.3	9.2
80	8.3	7.1	8.9	6.9	8.7
81	7.8	6.7	8.4	6.5	8.2
82	7.3	6.2	7.8	6.1	7.7
83	6.8	5.9	7.3	5.8	7.2
84	6.4	5.5	6.8	5.4	6.8
85	6.0	5.2	6.4	5.1	6.3

Source: Department of Health and Human Services, National Center for Health Statistics.

Living Arrangements of the Elderly, 1992
(in thousands, noninstitutional population)

Living arrangements and age	All races			White			Black		
	Total	Men	Women	Total	Men	Women	Total	Men	Women
65 years and over	30,779	12,736	18,043	27,580	11,469	16,111	2,510	978	1,532
Living:									
Alone	9,285	2,037	7,248	8,387	1,828	6,560	783	181	602
With spouse	16,954	9,564	7,390	15,572	8,740	6,832	1,039	617	422
With relatives	3,832	790	3,042	3,022	631	2,391	604	120	484
With nonrelatives only	708	345	363	598	270	328	84	60	24
65 to 74 years	18,087	7,924	10,163	16,082	7,116	8,966	1,558	620	937
Living:									
Alone	4,199	1,031	3,168	3,706	921	2,785	428	99	329
With spouse	11,499	6,174	5,324	10,545	5,630	4,915	714	405	309
With relatives	1,953	466	1,488	1,482	375	1,107	350	65	284
With nonrelatives only	436	253	183	349	190	159	66	51	15
75 years and over	12,692	4,812	7,880	11,499	4,353	7,146	952	358	595
Living:									
Alone	5,086	1,006	4,080	4,681	906	3,775	355	82	272
With spouse	5,456	3,389	2,066	5,027	3,111	1,917	324	211	113
With relatives	1,878	325	1,554	1,541	255	1,285	255	57	200
With nonrelatives only	272	92	180	250	81	169	18	8	10

Source: U.S. Bureau of the Census, Current Population Reports, Series P-20, No. 484, *Marital Status and Living Arrangements: March 1994.*

Rental Properties Owned Largely by Individuals

In 1991, individual investors—including single people, married couples, and the estates of deceased people—owned 92% of the nation's rental properties. For properties with 1 to 4 units (76% of available rental housing), individual investors accounted for 92.5% of the properties. As the number of units went up, the percentage owned by individual investors declined. For properties with 5 to 49 units (4% of available rental housing), individual investors accounted for 74.8% of the properties. For properties with 50 or more units (less than 1% of the total), the ownership was primarily through partnerships (40.8%) or Real Estate Investment Trusts (15.5%). Individual investors also owned the overwhelming majority of rental housing in condominiums (90.5%) and mobile homes (97.2%).

Half of all rental properties were financed with a mortgage, with fixed-rate amortized mortgages accounting for 70% of such mortgages. Adjustable-rate mortgages were also popular, accounting for another 22% of mortgages. A higher proportion (88%) of 5-to-49-unit properties were financed with a mortgage, and the fixed-rate mortgages (amortized and short-term combined) accounted for 84% of the mortgages for this type of property. Mobile homes were least likely (only 20%) to have mortgages, and were most likely (84%) to have fixed-rate amortized mortgages when there was a mortgage.

LAW ENFORCEMENT & CRIME

Characteristics of Hate Crimes in 1994

Source: U.S. Department of Justice, *Uniform Crime Reports*

Bias-motivated crime is a phenomenon that touches all segments of society. It exacts an immeasurable toll on its victims who are targeted solely because of hatred toward their race, religion, ethnicity, or sexual orientation.

Preliminary figures show 5,852 hate crime incidents were reported to the FBI during 1994. The incidents were reported by more than 7,200 law enforcement agencies in 43 states and the District of Columbia. Participating agencies covered 58 percent of the U.S. population.

Sixty percent of the incidents were motivated by racial bias, 18 percent by religious bias, 12 percent by sexual-orientation bias, and 11 percent by ethnicity/national origin bias. The 5,852 incidents involved 7,144 separate offenses, 7,187 victims, and 6,189 known offenders.

Crimes against persons accounted for 72 percent of hate crime offenses reported. Intimidation was the single most frequently reported hate crime, accounting for 39 percent of the total. Damage, destruction, or vandalism of property constituted 24 percent; simple assault, 18 percent; and aggravated assault, 14 percent. Thirteen persons were murdered in hate-motivated incidents.

As in previous years, hate crimes in 1994 were most frequently directed at individuals. Individuals

Known Offenders by Race, 1994

Suspected Offender's Race	Number of Known Offenders
Total	6,189
White	3,504
Black	1,854
American Indian/Alaskan Native	29
Asian/Pacific Islander	76
Multi-Racial Group	285
Unknown	441

Source: U.S. Department of Justice, *Uniform Crime Reports.*

comprised 84 percent of all reported bias crime victims for the year. Businesses, religious organizations, and varied other targets comprised the remaining 16 percent.

Law enforcement agencies reported the number of known offenders for 61 percent of hate crimes coming to their attention in 1994. Among the 6,189 known offenders reported to be associated with hate crime incidents, 57 percent were white, and 30 percent were black. The remaining offenders were of other or multi-racial groups. ☐

Summary of Hate Crime Statistics, 1994

	Number of incidents	Number of offenses	Number of victims	Number of known offenders
BIAS MOTIVATION				
Race:	**3,505**	**4,387**	**4,408**	**4,315**
Anti-White	993	1,253	1,268	1,786
Anti-Black	2,154	2,668	2,666	2,120
Anti-American Indian/Alaskan Native	23	26	27	31
Anti-Asian/Pacific Islander	209	267	270	248
Anti-Multi-Racial Group	126	173	177	130
Ethnicity/National Origin:	**619**	**745**	**758**	**694**
Anti-Hispanic	324	407	415	448
Anti-Other Ethnicity/National Origin	295	338	343	246
Religion:	**1,051**	**1,232**	**1,229**	**407**
Anti-Jewish	908	1,080	1,074	346
Anti-Catholic	15	17	18	11
Anti-Protestant	28	30	29	5
Anti-Islamic	16	16	16	4
Anti-Other Religious Group	67	72	75	37
Anti-Multi-Religious Group	14	14	14	3
Anti-Atheism/Agnosticism/etc.	3	3	3	1
Sexual Orientation:	**677**	**780**	**792**	**773**
Anti-Male Homosexual	497	561	567	615
Anti-Female Homosexual	99	119	119	86
Anti-Homosexual	61	77	82	54
Anti-Heterosexual	14	16	15	13
Anti-Bisexual	6	7	9	5
Total	**5,852**	**7,144**	**7,187**	**6,189**

Source: U.S. Department of Justice, *Uniform Crime Reports.*

Serious Crime Continues to Drop

Serious crimes reported to the nation's law enforcement agencies decreased 2 percent in 1995 as compared to 1994, according to preliminary Uniform Crime Reporting Program figures released on May 5, 1996 by the FBI. It was the fourth consecutive yearly decrease in reported crime.

Serious crime is measured by an index consisting of violent and property crimes. Violent crime fell 4 percent last year, and property crime dropped 1 percent.

In the violent crime category, murder showed the greatest decline in 1995—8 percent. Decreases for the other violent offenses were 7 percent for robbery 6 percent for forcible rape, and 3 percent for aggravated assault. Among the property crimes, motor vehicle theft was down 6 percent, and both burglary and arson decreased 5 percent. Larceny-theft was the only offense to show an increase from 1994 to 1995 up 1 percent.

Cities with over a million inhabitants showed the largest decline, 6 percent. A 1-percent increase was experienced in cities with populations from 500,000 to 999,999 and in those with fewer than 25,000 inhabitants. For the 2-year period, the suburban counties showed a 1-percent decrease in their crime level, while the rural counties reported a 3-percent increase.

Murder Victims by Weapons Used

Year	Murder victims, total	Guns		Cutting or stabbing	Blunt object[1]	Strangulation, hands, fists, feet or pushing	Arson[3]	All other[2]
		Total	Percent					
1965	8,773	5,015	57.2	2,021	505	894	226	112
1970	13,649	9,039	66.2	2,424	604	1,031	353	198
1975	18,642	12,061	64.7	3,245	1,001	1,646	193	496
1980	21,860	13,650	62.0	4,212	1,094	1,666	291	947
1985	17,545	10,296	58.7	3,694	972	1,491	243	849
1989	18,954	11,832	62.4	3,458	1,128	1,416	234	886
1990	20,045	12,847	64.1	3,503	1,075	1,424	287	909
1991	21,505	14,265	66.3	3,405	1,082	1,519	194	1,040
1992	22,540	15,377	68.2	3,265	1,029	1,434	203	1,232
1993	23,271	16,189	69.6	2,957	1,024	1,493	217	1,391
1994	22,076	15,456	70.0	2,801	912	1,452	196	1,259

1. Refers to club, hammer, etc. 2. Includes poison, explosives, unknown, drowning, asphyxiation, narcotics, other means, and weapons not stated. 3. Before 1973, includes drowning. *Source:* Department of Justice, Federal Bureau of Investigation, *Uniform Crime Reports for the United States, 1994,* released December 1995.

Full–Time Law Enforcement Employees, 1994

City	Officers	Civilians	Total	1993 Total	City	Officers	Civilians	Total	1993 Total
Atlanta	1,534	438	1,972	2,104	Milwaukee	2,055	456	2,511	2,48
Baltimore	3,065	570	3,635	3,500	Minneapolis	858	163	1,021	1,03
Birmingham, Ala.	758	249	1,007	999	New Orleans	1,465	402	1,867	1,86
Boston	1,978	675	2,653	2,604	Newark, N.J.	1,182	152	1,334	1,29
Chicago	12,971	2,255	15,226	14,196	New York	30,135	9,818	39,953	39,44
Cincinnati	975	228	1,203	1,155	Norfolk, Va.	663	98	761	75
Cleveland	1,751	211	1,962	1,863	Oakland, Calif.	671	335	1,006	1,08
Columbus, Ohio	1,507	366	1,873	1,900	Oklahoma City	1,012	300	1,312	1,28
Dallas	2,777	658	3,435	3,535	Philadelphia	6,101	876	6,977	6,96
Denver	1,378	190	1,568	1,569	Phoenix, Ariz.	2,088	756	2,844	2,65
Detroit	3,855	526	4,381	4,398	Pittsburgh	1,172	25	1,197	1,15
El Paso	967	239	1,206	1,053	Portland, Ore.	1,013	255	1,268	1,13
Fort Worth	1,060	313	1,373	1,390	St. Louis	1,563	664	2,227	2,14
Honolulu	1,790	486	2,276	2,370	St. Paul	549	180	729	67
Houston	4,935	2,057	6,992	6,700	San Antonio	1,696	387	2,083	2,02
Indianapolis	962	379	1,341	1,329	San Diego, Calif.	1,972	699	2,641	2,61
Jacksonville, Fla.	1,306	935	2,241	2,200	San Francisco	1,823	406	2,229	2,19
Kansas City, Mo.	1,156	537	1,693	1,758	San Jose, Calif.	1,209	384	1,593	1,62
Las Vegas, Nev.	1,513	717	2,230	2,102	Seattle	1,264	495	1,759	1,74
Lincoln, Neb.	265	88	353	340	Tampa, Fla.	797	270	1,067	1,04
Long Beach, Calif.	795	322	1,117	1,203	Toledo, Ohio	706	67	773	70
Los Angeles	7,869	2,875	10,744	10,099	Tucson, Ariz.	772	247	1,019	1,00
Louisville, Ky.	632	199	831	843	Tulsa, Okla.	738	113	851	85
Memphis, Tenn.	1,382	396	1,778	1,810	Virginia Beach, Va.	653	239	892	82
Miami, Fla.	1,077	292	1,369	1,495	Washington, D.C.	4,106	654	4,760	5,20

NOTE: As of Oct. 31, 1994. *Source:* Department of Justice, Federal Bureau of Investigation, *Uniform Crime Reports for the United States, 1994,* released December 1995.

Estimated Arrests, 1994[1]

Murder and non–negligent manslaughter	22,100	Weapons—carrying, possession, etc.	259,400
Forcible rape	36,610	Prostitution and commercial vice	98,800
Robbery	172,290	Sex offenses, except forcible rape	
Aggravated assault	547,760	and prostitution	100,700
Burglary	396,100	Drug abuse violations	1,351,400
Larceny—theft	1,514,500	Gambling	18,500
Motor vehicle theft	200,000	Offenses against family and children	117,200
Arson	20,900	Driving under the influence	1,384,600
Total violent crime	778,730	Liquor laws	541,800
Total property crime	2,131,700	Drunkenness	713,200
Other assaults	1,223,600	Disorderly conduct	746,200
Forgery and counterfeiting	115,300	Vagrancy	25,300
Fraud	419,800	All other offenses, except traffic	3,743,200
Embezzlement	14,300	Curfew and loitering law violations	128,400
Stolen property—buying, receiving, possessing	164,700	Runaways	248,800
Vandalism	323,300	**Total**[2]	**14,648,700**

1. Arrest totals based on all reporting agencies and estimates for unreported areas. 2. Because of rounding, items may not add to totals. *Source:* Department of Justice, Federal Bureau of Investigation, *Uniform Crime Reports for the United States, 1994,* released December 1995.

Reported Arrests by Sex and Age

	Male				Female			
	Total		Under 18		Total		Under 18	
Offense	1994	1993	1994	1993	1994	1993	1994	1993
Murder[1]	16,156	17,249	2,838	2,930	1,766	1,778	178	175
Forcible rape	28,299	30,146	4,555	4,952	317	394	93	88
Robbery	130,617	133,683	42,010	37,899	13,355	12,824	4,258	3,695
Aggravated assault	359,857	352,296	54,875	52,836	71,788	65,916	12,523	11,311
Burglary—breaking or entering	274,910	286,972	100,110	99,294	32,346	32,089	10,568	10,691
Larceny—theft	790,790	782,140	268,385	251,142	395,078	379,980	126,949	114,419
Motor vehicle theft	141,759	143,610	61,299	62,846	19,922	19,086	9,919	9,769
Arson	13,599	12,895	7,769	6,574	2,346	2,250	924	938
Violent crime[2]	534,929	533,374	104,278	98,617	87,226	80,912	17,052	15,269
Other assaults	777,871	733,675	121,580	108,000	178,284	160,820	43,612	37,950
Forgery and counterfeiting	56,921	53,864	4,254	3,895	31,444	28,472	2,436	2,105
Fraud	192,984	181,030	13,514	9,747	124,598	125,365	4,751	3,658
Embezzlement	6,517	6,141	508	352	4,632	4,230	282	243
Stolen property—buying, receiving, possessing	111,792	109,779	30,703	30,454	17,216	16,026	3,913	3,800
Vandalism	216,181	211,968	104,738	99,697	31,911	29,687	12,033	10,738
Weapons—carrying, possessing, etc.	190,241	192,761	46,363	45,568	16,666	16,107	4,062	3,941
Prostitution and commercialized vice	33,131	31,025	510	429	52,652	55,478	487	523
Sex offenses, except forcible rape and prostitution	71,641	75,764	12,741	14,171	6,739	7,289	1,063	1,408
Drug abuse violations	907,050	769,242	112,327	79,442	179,348	150,070	14,898	9,924
Gambling	13,226	12,272	1,390	1,041	2,284	2,029	73	50
Offenses against family and children	67,468	65,532	2,450	2,240	17,915	15,620	1,373	1,216
Driving under the influence	871,064	911,524	8,583	7,737	143,795	149,057	1,407	1,310
Liquor laws	324,917	307,325	63,124	58,698	78,276	72,744	25,421	23,326
Drunkenness	477,806	499,438	11,746	10,958	62,145	62,198	2,290	2,146
Disorderly conduct	446,974	438,764	99,481	86,142	118,331	114,723	30,274	25,411
Vagrancy	16,461	21,230	2,913	2,530	4,371	2,921	672	504
All other offenses, except traffic	2,414,760	2,136,012	257,226	227,722	527,354	465,638	72,619	62,214
Curfew and loitering law violations	72,382	57,224	72,382	57,224	29,434	22,098	29,434	22,098
Runaways	65,193	60,893	65,193	60,893	86,706	81,400	86,706	81,400
Total	**9,090,567**	**8,634,459**	**1,573,567**	**1,425,413**	**2,251,018**	**2,096,289**	**503,382**	**445,051**

1. Includes non–negligent manslaughter. 2. Violent crimes are offenses of murder, forcible rape, robbery, and aggravated assault. NOTE: 9,059 agencies reporting; 1994 estimated population 197,160,000. *Source:* Department of Justice, Federal Bureau of Investigation, *Uniform Crime Reports for the United States, 1994,* released December 1995.

Arrests by Race, 1994

Offense	White	Black	Other[1]	Total	Offense	White	Black	Other[1]	Total
Murder[2]	7,705	10,420	350	18,475	Sex offenses, except forcible rape and prostitution	62,300	17,637	1,813	81,750
Forcible rape	16,683	12,419	657	29,759					
Robbery	55,055	89,232	2,506	146,793					
Aggravated assault	264,466	176,062	8,651	449,179	Drug abuse violation	677,025	429,479	10,819	1,117,322
Burglary	215,363	97,867	6,236	319,466	Gambling	7,845	7,247	751	15,843
Larceny–theft	796,212	407,231	31,573	1,235,016	Offenses against family and children	58,427	30,242	2,861	91,530
Motor vehicle theft	95,216	66,544	4,359	166,119					
Arson	12,555	3,853	319	16,727	Driving under the influence	932,802	107,347	23,342	1,063,491
Violent crimes[3]	343,909	288,132	12,164	644,206	Liquor laws	352,683	57,575	13,366	423,624
Property crimes[4]	1,119,346	575,495	42,487	1,737,328	Drukenness	460,300	96,200	14,504	571,004
Other assaults	625,689	341,941	22,024	989,654	Disorderly conduct	390,326	199,094	10,925	600,345
Forgery and counterfeiting	59,127	32,001	1,818	92,946	Vagrancy	12,298	8,635	474	21,407
Fraud	205,362	120,640	4,303	330,305	All other offenses except traffic	1,891,312	1,092,034	59,541	3,042,887
Embezzlement	7,600	3,816	193	11,609					
Stolen property— buying, receiving, possessing	77,709	54,601	2,384	134,694	Suspicion	5,643	5,635	93	11,371
Vandalism	193,538	59,083	6,439	259,060	Curfew and loitering law violations	80,319	22,177	3,285	105,781
Weapons— carrying, possession, etc.	121,834	87,531	3,714	213,079	Runaways	155,201	38,310	7,352	200,863
Prostitution and commercial vice	53,819	30,860	2,054	86,733	**Total**	7,894,414	3,705,713	301,357	11,901,484

1. Includes American Indian, Alaskan Native, and Asian or Pacific Islander. 2. Includes non–negligent manslaughter. 3. Violent crimes are offenses of murder, forcible rape, robbery, and aggravated assault. 4. Property crimes are offenses of burglary, larceny-theft, motor vehicle theft. NOTE: Figures represent arrests reported by 10,648 agencies serving a total 1994 estimated population of 207,569,000. *Source:* Department of Justice, Federal Bureau of Investigation, *Uniform Crime Reports for the United States, 1994,* released December 1995.

Total Arrests, by Age Groups, 1994

Age	Arrests	Age	Arrests	Age	Arrests	Age	Arrests	Age	Arrests
Under 15	780,979	18	520,831	22	419,027	30–34	1,713,145	50–54	227,419
15	428,967	19	505,122	23	420,909	35–39	1,298,615	55 and	
16	489,089	20	459,948	24	406,399	40–49	796,890	over	270,494
17	510,640	21	433,449	25–29	761,357	45–49	433,908	**Total**	11,877,188

NOTE: Based on reports furnished to the FBI by 10,654 agencies covering a 1994 estimated population of 207,624,000. *Source:* Department of Justice, Federal Bureau of Investigation, *Uniform Crime Reports for the United States, 1994,* released December 1995.

Federal Prosecutions of Public Corruption: 1983 to 1992

(Prosecution of persons who have corrupted public office in violation of Federal Criminal Statutes. As of Dec. 31, 1992)

Prosecution status	1992	1991	1990	1989	1988	1987	1986	1985	1984	1983
Total:[1] Indicted	1,189	1,452	1,176	1,349	1,274	1,340	1,192	1,182	936	1,073
Convicted	1,081	1,194	1,084	1,444	1,067	1,075	1,027	997	934	972
Awaiting trial	380	346	300	375	288	368	246	256	269	222
Federal officials: Indicted	624	803	615	695	629	651	596	563	408	460[2]
Convicted	532	665	583	610	529	545	523	470	429	424[2]
Awaiting trial	139	149	103	126	86	118	83	90	77	58
State officials: Indicted	84	115	96	71	66	102	88	79	58	81
Convicted	92	77	79	54	69	76	71	66	52	65
Awaiting trial	24	42	28	18	14	26	24	20	21	26
Local officials: Indicted	232	242	257	269	276	246	232	248	203	270
Convicted	211	180	225	201	229	204	207	221	196	226
Awaiting trial	277	91	88	98	122	79	55	49	74	61

1. Includes individuals who are either public officials nor employees, but who were involved with public officials or employees in violating the law, now shown separately. 2. Increases in the number indicted and convicted between 1982 and 1983 resulted from a greater focus on federal corruption nationwide and more consistent reporting of cases involving lower–level employees. NOTE: Figures are latest available. *Source:* U.S. Department of Justice, *Report to Congress on the Activities and Operations of the Public Integrity Section,* annual, from *Statistical Abstract of the United States, 1995.*

Crime Rates for Selected Large Cities: 1993

(Offenses known to the police per 100,000 population.)

City ranked by population size, 1992[1]	Violent crime				Property crime		
	Murder	Forcible rape	Robbery	Aggravated assault	Burglary	Larceny–theft	Motor vehicle theft
New York, NY	26.5	38.4	1,171	854	1,350	3,200	1,531
Los Angeles, CA	30.5	50.3	1,090	1,204	1,425	3,378	1,695
Chicago, IL	30.3	(2)	1,262	1,425	1,637	4,350	1,450
Houston, TX	25.9	64.3	625	739	1,567	3,571	1,596
Philadelphia, PA	28.1	50.3	739	437	969	2,512	1,525
San Diego, CA	11.5	34.1	401	714	1,257	3,262	1,665
Dallas, TX	30.4	95.9	712	905	2,012	5,197	1,675
Phoenix, AZ	15.2	42.7	331	757	1,984	4,655	1,498
Detroit, MI	56.8	(2)	1,332	1,274	2,264	4,198	2,751
San Antonio, TX	22.3	56.1	302	302	1,813	6,219	1,197
San Jose, CA	5.1	48.3	147	457	743	2,643	496
Indianapolis, IN	18.0	136.9	543	968	2,020	3,808	1,384
San Francisco, CA	17.5	49.0	1,148	600	1,515	4,693	1,501
Baltimore, MD	48.2	91.1	1,689	1,166	2,442	5,655	1,449
Jacksonville, FL	18.6	104.0	536	1,040	2,250	4,750	1,344
Columbus, OH	16.2	101.7	601	386	2,018	4,491	1,093
Milwaukee, WI	25.2	68.0	646	226	1,324	4,101	1,704
Memphis, TN	32.0	117.1	867	618	2,474	3,786	2,147
Washington, DC	78.5	56.1	1,230	1,558	1,995	5,444	1,395
Boston, MA	17.7	86.7	737	1,117	1,441	4,477	2,154
El Paso, TX	8.5	50.7	282	761	1,018	5,309	1,000
Seattle, WA	12.6	67.0	503	818	1,741	7,374	1,284
Cleveland, OH	33.0	164.9	850	596	1,588	2,668	2,011
Nashville-Davidson, TN	16.9	112.3	527	1,127	1,781	6,319	921
Austin, TX	7.4	54.0	310	229	1,684	7,101	868
New Orleans, LA	80.3	60.6	1,054	845	2,275	4,479	1,942
Denver, CO	14.8	78.9	374	586	1,832	3,583	1,516
Fort Worth, TX	28.7	109.4	594	775	2,267	5,678	1,296
Oklahoma City, OK	17.5	112.6	377	910	2,186	6,409	1,211
Portland, OR	12.8	105.3	507	1,232	1,725	5,939	1,860
Long Beach, CA	28.4	45.1	839	693	1,530	3,183	1,720
Kansas City, MO	35.1	118.3	894	1,470	2,780	5,423	1,949
Virginia Beach, VA	5.2	42.8	149	98	770	3,499	282
Charlotte, NC	28.9	84.2	763	1,424	2,528	6,236	703
Tucson, AZ	10.3	73.6	210	730	1,727	7,524	1,206
Albuquerque, NM	12.3	63.6	381	1,187	2,013	5,046	879
Atlanta, GA	50.4	122.1	1,501	2,368	3,269	7,757	2,288
St. Louis, MO	69.0	82.4	1,608	2,116	3,204	6,969	2,600
Sacramento, CA	22.0	43.2	597	592	2,089	4,828	2,039
Fresno, CA	22.9	56.8	758	613	2,230	3,821	3,443
Tulsa, OK	14.3	89.6	302	895	1,902	3,381	1,175
Oakland, CA	40.8	93.6	1,209	1,258	2,216	5,037	2,061
Honolulu, HI	3.5	32.7	124	126	1,062	4,586	509
Miami, FL	34.1	54.8	1,901	1,903	3,296	8,556	3,001
Pittsburgh, PA	21.7	61.3	756	377	1,251	3,533	1,766
Cincinnati, OH	10.6	123.6	636	765	1,680	4,663	564
Minneapolis, MN	15.8	(2)	867	744	2,552	5,442	1,274
Toledo, OH	13.6	107.7	481	361	1,660	4,602	1,363
Buffalo, NY	23.4	90.8	892	853	2,339	3,914	1,699
Wichita, KS	15.3	84.5	423	352	1,865	5,186	919
Mesa, AZ	2.0	36.4	135	593	1,531	4,736	892
Colorado Springs, CO	6.2	87.0	128	290	1,197	4,399	334
Las Vegas, NV	12.7	60.6	498	444	1,364	3,325	1,038
Santa Ana, CA	26.8	26.5	648	395	1,014	3,084	1,360
Tampa, FL	14.9	85.5	1,026	2,120	3,111	6,416	2,933
Arlington, TX	2.5	51.9	252	496	1,414	4,093	872
Anaheim, CA	11.9	25.3	328	339	1,423	3,302	1,302
Louisville, KY	13.5	49.3	509	424	1,537	2,952	850
St. Paul, MN	8.1	(2)	352	548	1,483	4,177	858
Newark, NJ	35.6	95.2	2,183	1,474	2,549	3,861	4,073
Corpus Christi, TX	12.5	71.4	187	548	1,693	6,964	616
Birmingham, AL	45.0	110.5	635	1,694	2,466	5,554	1,319

1. Crime data are not available for Omaha, NE, in 1993. 2. The rate for forcible rape is not shown because the forcible rape figures were not in accordance with national Uniform Crime Reporting guidelines. *Source: Statistical Abstract of the United States, 1995.*

Justifiable Homicide by Weapon, Law Enforcement,[1] 1990–1994

Year	Total	Total firearms	Handguns	Rifles	Shotguns	Firearms type not specified	Knives or other cutting instruments	Other dangerous weapons	Personal weapons
1990	385	382	345	8	19	10	—	2	1
1991	367	361	319	10	25	7	1	3	2
1992	418	411	357	22	21	11	4	1	2
1993	455	451	391	22	26	12	—	2	2
1994	463	461	405	21	29	6	—	1	1

1. The killing of a felon by a law enforcement officer in the line of duty.

Justifiable Homicide by Weapon, Private Citizen,[1] 1990–1994

Year	Total	Total firearms	Handguns	Rifles	Shotguns	Firearms type not specified	Knives or other cutting instruments	Other dangerous weapons	Personal weapons
1990	328	276	210	20	39	7	39	9	4
1991	331	296	243	15	25	13	29	4	2
1992	351	311	264	20	24	3	31	5	4
1993	357	313	254	15	33	11	28	9	7
1994	353	316	260	17	29	10	19	13	5

1. The killing of a felon, during the commission of a felony, by a private citizen. *Source: Crime in the United States 1994, Uniform Crime Reports,* Federal Bureau of Investigation.

Child Abuse and Neglect Cases, 1993

State	Reports: Number of reports[1]	Reports: Number of children	Number of children substantiated[2]	State	Reports: Number of reports[1]	Reports: Number of children	Number of children substantiated[2]
Alabama	26,758	40,388	19,130	Montana	9,005	13,713	4,827
Alaska	9,920[3]	9,920	6,917	Nebraska	8,439	17,481	5,726
Arizona	29,747	51,068	30,729	Nevada	12,568	12,568	7,085
Arkansas	17,489	25,624	10,336	New Hampshire	6,225	7,234	928
California	342,537	455,526	161,612	New Jersey	65,102[3]	65,102	10,510
Colorado	33,287	33,287	7,892	New Mexico	24,984[3]	24,984	6,880
Connecticut	17,871	27,710	23,069	New York	139,468	230,916	59,311
Delaware	5,386	9,635	2,271	North Carolina	58,376	92,739	29,809
District of Columbia	5,669	12,773	3,327	North Dakota	4,884	8,252	4,010
Florida	105,468	161,686	81,982	Ohio	93,144	147,106	51,850
Georgia	52,519	85,118	55,516	Oklahoma	26,349[3]	26,349	8,359
Hawaii	5,412[3]	5,412	2,297	Oregon	25,227	25,227	n.a.
Idaho	12,494	24,759	6,892	Pennsylvania	24,909[3]	24,909	7,814
Illinois	72,101	126,960	43,519	Rhode Island	8,278	13,065	3,130
Indiana	40,263	59,481	29,136	South Carolina	21,227	40,147	11,263
Iowa	20,866	30,776	8,834	South Dakota	10,284[3]	10,284	2,368
Kansas	24,797[3]	24,797	12,327	Tennessee	32,739[3]	32,739	12,136
Kentucky	36,901	57,706	25,282	Texas	110,973	177,328	58,304
Louisiana	27,218	46,170	15,253	Utah	16,168	27,485	10,976
Maine	4,286	9,567	4,955	Vermont	2,732	3,190	1,305
Maryland	29,412	29,412	n.a.	Virginia	36,257	55,937	14,066
Massachusetts	31,833	51,941	24,186	Washington	40,075	55,689	41,602
Michigan	53,302	126,601	19,522	West Virginia	12,932	12,932	n.a.
Minnesota	17,427	26,778	10,535	Wisconsin	49,152[3]	49,152	19,189
Mississippi	17,606	27,568	8,812	Wyoming	3,908	5,080	1,702
Missouri	52,268	85,323	20,472	**Total**	1,936,242	2,825,594	1,007,953

1. Except as noted, reports are on incident/family-based basis or based on the number of reported incidents regardless of the number of children involved. 2. Type of investigation disposition that determines that there is sufficient evidence under State law to conclude that maltreatment occurred or that the child is at risk of maltreatment. 3. Child-based report that enumerates each child who is a subject of the report. NOTE: Based on reports that were referred for investigation by the child protective services agency in each state. The majority of states were unable to provide unduplicated counts except for Alaska, Hawaii, Michigan, Montana, Ohio, Oregon, South Carolina, Vermont, and Washington. Excludes the Armed Forces. n.a. = not available. *Source: Statistical Abstract of the United States, 1995.*

Law Enforcement Officers Killed or Assaulted: 1984 to 1993

(Covers officers killed feloniously and accidentally in line of duty; includes federal officers. 1988 excludes Florida and Kentucky.)

	1993	1992	1991	1990	1989	1988	1987	1986	1985	1984
Northeast	12	16	7	13	23	17	24	15	19	21
Midwest	27	15	20	20	22	18	31	19	23	22
South	57	68	29	68	68	77	51	62	64	69
West	22	23	7	23	23	39	40	29	29	32
Puerto Rico	11	6	7	8	8	1	1	6	10	3
Outlying areas, foreign countries	—	—	1	—	1	4	—	—	3	—
Total killed	**129**	**128**	**70**	**132**	**146**	**155**	**147**	**131**	**148**	**147**
Assaults										
Population (1,000)[1]	210,658	217,997	191,397	199,065	189,641	186,418	190,025	196,030	198,935	195,794
Number of—										
Agencies	9,809	10,682	9,263	9,483	9,023	8,866	8,957	9,755	9,906	10,002
Police officers	454,105	460,430	405,069	412,314	380,232	369,743	378,977	380,249	389,808	372,268
Firearm	66,975	4,455	3,532	3,662	3,154	2,759	2,789	2,852	2,793	2,654
Knife or cutting instrument	4,002	2,095	1,493	1,641	1,379	1,367	1,561	1,614	1,715	1,662
Other dangerous weapon	7,551	8,604	7,014	7,390	5,778	5,573	5,685	5,721	5,263	5,148
Hands, fists, feet, etc.	53,848	66,098	50,813	59,101	51,861	49,053	53,807	54,072	51,953	50,689
Total assaulted	**66,975**	**81,252**	**62,852**	**71,794**	**62,172**	**58,752**	**63,842**	**64,259**	**61,724**	**60,153**

1. Represents the number of persons covered by agencies shown. NOTE: Data are latest available. *Source: Statistical Abstract of the United States, 1995.*

Crime Index by State, 1994

State	Crime index total	Rate per 100,000 inhabitants	Violent crime	Property crime	Murder and non-negligent man-slaughter	State	Crime index total	Rate per 100,000 inhabitants	Violent crime	Property crime	Murder and non-negligent man-slaughter
Ala.	206,859	4,903.0	28,844	178,015	501	Mont.[2]	42,961	5,018.8	1,516	41,445	28
Alas.	34,591	5,708.1	4,644	29,947	38	Neb.	72,068	4,440.0	6,322	65,746	51
Ariz.	322,926	7,924.6	28,653	294,273	426	Nev.	97,290	6,677.4	14,597	82,693	170
Ark.	117,713	4,798.7	14,598	103,115	294	N.H.	31,165	2,741.0	1,328	29,837	16
Calif.	1,940,497	6,173.8	318,395	1,622,102	3,703	N.J.	368,400	4,660.9	48,544	319,856	396
Coo.	194,440	5,318.4	18,632	175,808	199	N.M.	102,346	6,187.8	14,708	87,638	177
Conn.	148,946	4,548.0	14,916	134,030	215	N.Y.	921,278	5,070.6	175,433	745,845	2,016
Del.	29,282	4,147.6	3,961	25,321	33	N.C.	397,705	5,625.2	46,308	351,397	772
D.C.[1]	63,186	11,085.3	15,177	48,009	399	N.D.	17,455	2,735.9	522	16,933	1
Fla.	1,151,121	8,250.0	160,016	991,105	1,165	Ohio	495,310	4,461.4	53,930	441,380	662
Ga.	424,029	6,010.3	47,103	376,926	703	Okla.	181,475	5,570.1	21,225	160,250	226
Hi.	78,763	6,680.5	3,091	75,672	50	Ore.	194,307	6,294.4	16,067	178,240	150
Idaho	46,192	4,077.0	3,238	42,954	40	Pa.	394,326	3,271.9	51,425	342,901	712
Ill.[2]	661,150	5,625.9	112,928	548,222	1,378	P.R.[3]	116,248	n.a.	25,385	90,863	980
Ind.	264,180	4,592.8	30,205	233,975	453	R.I.	41,067	4,119.1	3,744	37,323	41
Iowa	103,389	3,654.6	8,914	94,475	47	S.C.	219,870	6,000.8	37,756	182,114	353
Kan.[2]	124,987	4,893.8	13,226	112,761	149	S.D.	22,367	3,102.2	1,641	20,726	10
Ky.	133,890	3,498.6	23,165	110,725	244	Tenn.	264,952	5,119.8	38,705	226,247	482
La.	287,857	6,671.1	42,369	245,488	856	Tex.	1,079,225	5,872.4	129,838	949,387	2,022
Me.	40,582	3,272.7	1,611	38,971	28	Utah	101,142	5,300.9	5,810	95,332	56
Md.	306,496	6,122.6	47,457	259,039	579	Vt.	18,852	3,250.3	562	18,290	6
Mass.	268,281	4,441.0	42,749	225,532	214	Va.	265,200	4,047.6	23,437	241,763	571
Mich.	517,076	5,445.2	72,751	444,325	927	Wash.	322,051	6,027.5	27,317	294,734	294
Minn.	198,253	4,341.0	16,397	181,856	147	W.Va.	46,067	2,528.4	3,931	42,136	99
Miss.	129,101	4,827.1	13,177	115,924	409	Wis.	200,452	3,944.4	13,748	186,704	227
Mo.	280,138	5,307.7	39,240	240,898	554	Wyo.	20,419	4,289.7	1,297	19,122	16

Source: F.B.I. Uniform Crime Reports for the United States, 1994, published December 1995. NOTE: The Crime Index is composed of the violent and property crime categories. In 1994, 13% of the Index offenses reported to law enforcement agencies were violent crimes and 87% were property crimes. Violent crimes are murder, forcible rape, robbery, and aggravated assault. Property crimes are burglary, larceny–theft, and auto–theft. Data are not included for the property crime of arson. 1. Includes offenses reported by the Zoological Police. 2. Complete data were not available for the states of Illinois, Kansas, and Montana; therefore it was necessary that their crime counts be estimated. 3. n.a. = not available. The 1994 Bureau of Census population for Puerto Rico was not available, therefore no rates per 100,000 inhabitants are provided.

Prisoners Under Sentence of Death[1]

Characteristic	1993	1992	1991	Characteristic	1993	1992	1991
White	1,566	1,519	1,450	Marital status:			
Black and other	1,150	1,075	1,016	Never married	1,222	1,141	1,071
Under 20 years	13	12	14	Married	671	665	663
20–24 years	211	189	179	Divorced or separated[2]	823	788	746
25–34 years	1,066	1,088	1,087	Time elapsed since sentencing:			
35–54 years	1,330	1,220	1,129	Less than 12 months	262	265	252
55 years and over	96	85	73	12–47 months	716	731	718
				48–71 months	422	450	441
Schooling completed:				72 months and over	1,316	1,148	1,071
7 years or less	185	182	173	Legal status at arrest:			
8 years	183	182	181	Not under sentence	1,562	1,493	1,415
9–11 years	885	841	810	On parole or probation[3]	754	704	615
12 years	887	840	783	In prison or escaped	102	101	102
More than 12 years	244	234	222	Unknown	298	296	321
Unknown	332	315	313	**Total**	**2,716**	**2,594**	**2,466**

1. For 1991 revisions to the total number of prisoners were not carried to the characteristics except for race. 2. Includes widows, widowers, and unknown. 3. Includes persons on mandatory conditional release, work release, leave, AWOL, or bail. Covers 29 in 1991 and 1992. NOTE: As of Dec. 31. Excludes prisoners under sentence of death confined in local correctional systems pending appeal or who had not been committed to prison. *Source:* U.S. Bureau of Justice Statistics, *Capital Punishment,* annual, from *Statistical Abstract of the United States, 1995.*

Methods of Execution[1]

State	Method	State	Method
Alabama	Electrocution	Nevada	Lethal injection
Alaska	No death penalty	New Hampshire	Lethal injection
Arizona	Lethal injection[8]	New Jersey	Lethal injection[4]
Arkansas	Lethal injection	New Mexico	Lethal injection
California	Lethal gas	New York	Lethal injection
Colorado	Lethal injection	North Carolina	Lethal gas or injection
Connecticut	Lethal injection	North Dakota	No death penalty
Delaware	Lethal injection[2]	Ohio	Electrocution
D.C.	No death penalty	Oklahoma	Lethal injection
Florida	Electrocution	Oregon	Lethal injection[4]
Georgia	Electrocution	Pennsylvania	Lethal injection
Hawaii	No death penalty	Rhode Island	No death penalty
Idaho	Lethal injection[7]	South Carolina	Electrocution or lethal injection
Illinois	Lethal injection	South Dakota	Lethal injection
Indiana	Lethal injection	Tennessee	Electrocution
Iowa	No death penalty	Texas	Lethal injection
Kansas	Lethal injection	Utah	Firing squad or lethal injection
Kentucky	Electrocution	Vermont	No death penalty
Louisiana	Lethal injection	Virginia	Electrocution or lethal injection[9]
Maine	No death penalty	Washington[5]	Hanging or lethal injection
Maryland	Lethal injection	West Virginia	No death penalty
Massachusetts	No death penalty	Wisconsin	No death penalty
Michigan	No death penalty	Wyoming	Lethal injection
Minnesota	No death penalty	U.S. (Fed. Govt.)	([3])
Mississippi	Lethal injection[6]	American Samoa	No death penalty
Missouri	Lethal injection	Guam	No death penalty
Montana	Hanging, or lethal injection[5]	Puerto Rico	No death penalty
Nebraska	Electrocution	Virgin Islands	No death penalty

1. On July 1, 1976, by a 7–2 decision, the U.S. Supreme Court upheld the death penalty as not being "cruel or unusual." However, in another ruling the same day, the Court, by a 5–4 vote, stated that states may not impose "mandatory" capital punishment on every person convicted of murder. These decisions left uncertain the fate of condemned persons throughout the U.S. On Oct. 4, the Court refused to reconsider its July ruling, which allows some states to proceed with executions of condemned prisoners. The first execution in this country since 1967 was in Utah on Jan. 17, 1977. Gary Mark Gilmore was executed by shooting. 2. Prisoners originally sentenced to death prior to June 1986 may opt instead to hang. Those sentenced after June 1986 have no choice but lethal injection. 3. The method of execution of federal prisoners is lethal injection; for offenses under the Violent Crime Control and Law Enforcement Act of 1994, the method is that of the state in which the conviction took place. 4. Death penalty has been passed, but not been used. 5. Defendant may choose between hanging and a lethal injection. 6. Prisoners sentenced prior to July 1, 1984, shall be executed by lethal gas. 7. If the director of the Idaho Department of Corrections finds it impractical to carry out a lethal injection, he may instead use a firing squad. 8. Defendant sentenced to death for an offense committed before Nov. 23, 1992, shall choose either lethal injection or lethal gas. 9. Beginning January 1995 inmates may choose lethal injection instead of electrocution. *Source: Information Please* questionnaires to the states.

Motor Vehicle Laws, 1996

State	Age for license		Age for driver's license[1]			Driver's license duration	Fee	Annual safety inspection required
	Motor-cycle	Moped	Regular	Learner's	Restrictive			
Alabama	14	14	16	15[5]	14[11]	4 yrs.	$20.00	no[15]
Alaska	16	14	16	14	14[6, 11]	4	15.00	no[15]
Arizona	16	16	18	15 7 mo.[5, 6]	16[6]	Until 60	10/25.00	no[16, 18]
Arkansas	16	10[10]	16	14–16[5]	14[6, 9]	4	14.00	yes
California	18[19]	16[19]	18	15[4, 7, 8]	16[4]	4	12.00	no[18]
Colorado	16	16	21	15 6 mo.[6, 9]	15 1/4[6, 8, 9]	5	15.00	no[18]
Connecticut	16	16	16[4]	16[4]		4	28.50/43.50	no
Delaware	18[19]	16	18	15 10 mo.[4]	16[4, 6]	5	12.50	yes
D.C.	16	16	18	(5, 7)	16[6]	4	20.00	yes[21]
Florida	15	15	16	15[5]	15[6]	4 or 6	20.00	no[18]
Georgia	16	15	16	15	16[6]	4	15.00	no[18]
Hawaii	15	15	18	15[5,7]	15[6]	4[12]	6/12.00	yes
Idaho	16[19]	16[19]	17	15[4, 5, 7]	15[3, 4]	4	20.50	no
Illinois	18	16[19]	18	(5)	16[4, 6]	4 or 5	10.00	no[18]
Indiana	16	15	18	16[7, 8]	16 1 mo.[4, 6]	4[13]	6.00	no[18]
Iowa	16[19]	14		14	14[4, 6]	4[2]	8/16.00	no[15]
Kansas	14	14	16	(5)	14	4	8/14.00	no[15]
Kentucky	16	16	18	(5)	16[6]	4	10.00	no
Louisiana	15	15	14[27]	14[6]	17[3]	4	18.00	yes[21]
Maine	16[4]	15[4]	17	15[4,7]	16[4]	6	30.00	yes
Maryland	18[19]	16	18[28]	15 9 mo.[5, 9]	16[4, 6]	5	30.00	no[18, 20]
Massachusetts	17	16	17	(5)	16 1/2[3, 4, 6]	5	33.75	yes[21]
Michigan	18[19]	15	16	15[4, 6, 7]	16[4, 6]	2 or 4	6/12.00	no[31]
Minnesota	18[22]	15	18	(5)	16[4]	4	18.50/37.50	no[15]
Mississippi	15	15	16	(5)		4[29]	20.00	yes
Missouri	15.5[4]	16	16	15 1/2[23]	15 1/2[23]	3	7.50	yes[18]
Montana	15[4]	15[4]	18	(5)	15[4, 6]	8[30]	16.00/32.00	no
Nebraska	16	16	16	15[7]	14	4	15.00	no
Nevada	16	15.5	16	15 1/2[5, 6, 9]	14[3, 6]	4	15.50/20.50	no[18]
New Hampshire	18[19]	16[4]	18		16[4]	4	32.00	yes[21]
New Jersey	17	15	17		16	4	16./17.50	yes
New Mexico	16	13	16	15[4]	14[9]	4	13.00	no
New York	17	16	17[4]	16	16[6]	4	22.25	yes
North Carolina	18	16	16	15[4, 6, 9]	16	5	10.00	yes
North Dakota	16	14	16	(5)	14[4, 6]	4	10.00	no[15]
Ohio	18	14	18	16[5, 6]	14[11]	4	10.75	no[18]
Oklahoma	16		16	(8)	15 1/2[4]	4	18.00	yes
Oregon	16[19]	16	16	15[6, 9]	14	4	26.25	no[15]
Pennsylvania	16	16	16	16[6, 7]	16[6]	4	27.00	yes
Rhode Island	16	16	16	(5)	16[4]	5	30.00	yes
South Carolina	16	14	16	15[9]	15	5	12.50	yes
South Dakota	16	14	16	14[7]	14[3]	5	8.00	no
Tennessee	16	14	16	15[7]	14	5	19.50	no
Texas	18[19]	15	16[4]	15	15[4, 7]	4	16.00	yes
Utah	16	16	16[4, 6]	16	15 9 mo.[8, 9]	5	15/20.00	yes
Vermont	18	16	16	15[5, 9]	16[7]	2 or 4	12/20.00	yes
Virginia	18[19]	16	18	15[5, 6, 7]	16[4, 6]	5	12.00	yes
Washington	18[19]	16	18	15[8]	16[4]	4	14.00	no[14]
West Virginia	18[19]	16	18	15[9]	16	4	10.50	yes
Wisconsin	18[19]	16	18	15 1/2[5]	16[4, 6]	4	15.00	no[31]
Wyoming	18	15[22]	16	15[6, 7]	15[6, 7]	4	20.00	no

1. Full driving privileges at age given in "Regular" column. A license restricted or qualified in some manner may be obtained at age given in "Restricted" column. 2. 2 years if under 18 or over 70. 3. Hours of operation restricted. 4. Must have completed approved driver education course. 5. Learner's permit required. 6. Guardian's or parental consent required. 7. Driver with learner's permit must be accompanied by locally licensed operator 18 years or older. 8. Must be enrolled in driver education course. 9. Driver with learner's permit must be accompanied by locally licensed operator 21 years or older. 10. Up to 50 cc. 11. Restricted to mopeds. 12. 2 years if 15–24 or over 65. 13. 3 years if over 75. 14. Individual inspection upon reasonable grounds. 15. State troopers are authorized to inspect at their discretion. 16. Arizona emission inspection fee $5.40. 17. Annual emissions test in some counties. 18. Annual emissions test. 19. 18; 16, if approved driver training course completed. 20. All used vehicles upon resale or transfer. 21. Required on out–of–state or salvaged vehicles. Emissions tested in some counties. 22. May obtain instruction permit with motorcycle endorsement. 23. Driver with learner's permit must be accompanied by a licensed parent or guardian. 24. Emission test every two years in Bernalillo County. 25. Biennial emission inspection in the Portland metro area and Rogue Valley. 26. Emission test required in some areas. 27. All first-time new licensees must complete state-approved pre-licensing course. 28. All new drivers must complete 3-hour alcohol-awareness program. 29. 1 year if under 18. 30. 4 years if under 21 or over 75. 31. Some counties have an additional 1 to 2.75 county tax. NOTES: A driver's license is required in every state. All states have an *implied consent* Chemical Test Law for alcohol. *Source:* Reprinted with permission of the American Automobile Association, Heathrow, Fla.

EDUCATION

University Degrees on the Internet

By John Bear, Ph.D.

Nearly two centuries ago, the University of London "invented" the idea of distance learning, or home study, leading to degrees. People living anywhere in the world could (and indeed still can) earn useful degrees of all kinds (Bachelor's, Master's, and Doctorates) by working at their own pace and in their own home or office. In those ancient times, and indeed until the mid 1980s, distance learning took place using the quaint, old-fashioned methods of printed textbooks, and the postal service.

With the rise of personal computers and the growth of the Internet, it is now possible to take thousands of different courses and earn almost any degree, literally without getting up from your desk. Students typically use their computer to "attend" classes on a regular basis, interact with other students and with faculty, join interactive on-line discussion groups and conferences, receive assignments, submit papers, and even take examinations (although the latter is more often done in a supervised session at a local school).

What You Need to Begin

1. A computer or other device that can connect you to the Internet via your phone line. 2. A telephone line. 3. The electronic addresses of some schools. 4. And the will to begin. The first three are easy. For most people, the fourth is the tough one, but more and more people are taking the plunge. My all-time favorite is a 94-year-old man who bought his first computer and began his Ph.D. studies at home. He earned his degree at 97. If he can do it, what's your excuse? Here is a small sampling of what is available, and the list grows every hour.

Bachelor's Degrees

• University of the State of New York, telephone (518) 464–8778. Dean Douglas Whitney can be Emailed at DWhit 9490@aol.com. No faculty. No campus. No courses. No library. No football team. Just widely accepted, accredited Associate's and Bachelor's in a wide variety of subjects (and one Master's program), based on prior course work, exams, correspondence courses and/or assessment of nonschool learning experiences. On-line courses from dozens of other schools can earn credit for the Regents degree.

• Thomas Edison State College (New Jersey), telephone (609) 292–6317. Internet location: http://www.tesc.edu/ This state-run college offers nonresident Associate's and Bachelor's degrees (and one Master's), with an ever-growing list of courses available through its On-Line Computer Classroom. On-line courses done through other universities may also be applied to the Edison Bachelor's degrees.

• Western Illinois University, Internet location http://www.ccnet/users/miebis/index.html This state-run university offers the Bachelor's degree entirely through distance learning. At least 15 semester hours must be earned after enrolling, and these can be done entirely over the Internet, where about thirty different courses are available, ranging from fire science to Shakespeare to managerial economics.

Master's Degrees

• Edinburgh Business School (Scotland). A measure of the power of this approach is that this little-known Scottish school, a part of Heriot–Watt University, has the largest Master's program in the world: the MBA entirely through home study (no Bachelor's is required), using a computer, or just textbooks, or a combination of the two. Email to heriotwatt@aol.com or phone (800) 622–9661. Internet location: http://www.ebs.hw.ac.uk

• City University (Washington). This university in the Seattle area offers a wide variety of degrees at the Bachelor's and Master's level through their Internet site. Subjects include business, public administration, education, fire science, and health care management. Telephone (800) 426–5596; Internet location: http://www.city.edu/inroads/

• California State University Dominguez Hills. This campus of the California State University system offers the M.A. in Humanities entirely through home study, using the computer for some, most, or all the necessary interactions. Students can specialize in history, philosophy, art, music, or religion. The web page is at http://dolphin.csudh.edu/~huxindex.html. Email to huxonline@dhvx20.csudh.edu. Phone (310) 516–3743.

Doctorates

• Walden University (Minnesota). Walden offers accredited Master's and Ph.D. programs in administration and management, education, human services, and health services, with a short residency (several weeks) on campus in Minnesota, and all additional work done electronically over the Internet. Phone: (800) 444–6795; Internet site: http://www.waldenu.edu

• Union Institute (Ohio). Union's accredited Ph.D. can be earned in almost any field of study, with attendance at several short (2 to 5 day, typically) workshops or colloquia, given at various locations around the country, and the balance by distance learning. Phone (800) 543–0366; Internet location: http://www.unioninstitute.edu/

• The Graduate School of America (Minnesota). TGSA offers the Master's and Doctorate in education, human services, organization and management, and interdisciplinary studies, based on guided independent study, plus a short intensive residency in Minneapolis. TGSA is a candidate for accreditation. Phone (800) 987–1133; Internet address: http://www.minn.net/tgsa.index.html

Sources of Information

• *Bears' Guide,* described at the bottom of this article, is a comprehensive source of information on all the ways and means of earning degrees: Internet, correspondence, independent study, by examination, and so on, and, as a warning (the author was the FBI's phony school consultant for 13 years) a list of more than 200 fake schools is included.

• *The Internet University* is a comprehensive printed guide to hundreds of courses offered electronically by thirty major universities and colleges. The publisher's Email address is books@caso.com.

• *Information on line:* The publishers of *The Internet University* make their entire database (list of courses) available without charge on the Internet. The address is http://www.caso.com/

• *Research using Internet:* For doing any kind of academic research using the thousands of Internet sources, there is no better starting point than "Dr. E's Eclectic Compendium of Electronic Resources for Adult/Distance Education," available without any charge at (URL to come).

Consumer Alert:
Five Things To Do Before Sending Any Money to Any School

1. Check out the degree with any relevant decision makers. If a degree will help with job advancement, salary increments, state licensing, graduate school ad-

mission, etc., be certain that the degree in question will meet that need. Don't rely on assurances from the schools.

2. Check out the school with the agency in its state that oversees higher education (typically the Department of Education, in the state capital), and with the Better Business Bureau in its city.

3. If an accreditation claim is made, independently verify that it is correct and that the accrediting agency is one recognized either by the U.S. Department of Education or the Council on Recognition of Postsecondary Accreditation, both in Washington. There are more than 100 accrediting agencies, including at least 20 unrecognized ones, set up by schools for the purpose of accrediting themselves.

4. Check with experts on-line. You will find experts on distance learning of all kinds on the Internet news group called alt.education.distance.

5. Check with the schools themselves. Any legitimate school should be willing to answer questions about their licensing, number of students, credentials of faculty and administration and similar factors, and give you the names and phone numbers of current and former students (who have agreed to be called). ☐

John Bear has been researching and writing about ways and means of earning degrees the old-fashioned way in 1966 at Michigan State University. He is co-author (with his daughter Mariah) of the standard reference book in this field, *Bears' Guide to Earning College Degrees Nontraditionally,* available in bookstores (distributed by Ten Speed Press) or directly from the authors at P.O. Box 7070, Berkeley, CA 94707, phone (800) 835–8535, or by Email at johbbear@aol.com.

High School and College Graduates

School Year	High School			College[1]		
	Men	Women	Total	Men	Women	Total
1900	38,075	56,808	94,883	22,173	5,237	27,410
1910	63,676	92,753	156,429	28,762	8,437	37,199
1920	123,684	187,582	311,266	31,980	16,642	48,622
1929–30	300,376	366,528	666,904	73,615	48,869	122,484
1939–40	578,718	642,757	1,221,475	109,546	76,954	186,500
1949–50	570,700	629,000	1,199,700	328,841	103,217	432,058
1959–60	898,000	966,000	1,864,000	254,063	138,377	392,440
1969–70	1,433,000	1,463,000	2,896,000	484,174	343,060	827,234
1974–75	1,541,000	1,599,000	3,140,000	533,797	425,052	978,849
1978–79	1,531,800	1,602,400	3,134,200	529,996	460,242	990,238
1979–80	1,500,000	1,558,000	3,058,000	526,327	473,221	999,548
1980–81	1,483,000	1,537,000	3,020,000	470,000	465,000	935,000
1981–82	1,474,000	1,527,000	3,001,000	473,000	480,000	953,000
1982–83	1,437,000	1,451,000	2,888,000	479,140	490,370	969,510
1983–84	n.a.	n.a.	2,767,000	482,319	491,990	974,309
1984–85	n.a.	n.a.	2,677,000	482,528	496,949	979,477
1985–86	n.a.	n.a.	2,643,000	485,923	501,900	987,823
1986–87	n.a.	n.a.	2,694,000	480,854	510,485	991,339
1987–88	n.a.	n.a.	2,773,000	477,203	517,626	994,829
1988–89	n.a.	n.a.	2,727,000	483,346	535,409	1,018,755
1989–90	n.a.	n.a.	2,588,000	491,696	559,648	1,051,344
1990–91	n.a.	n.a.	2,503,000	504,045	590,493	1,094,538
1991–92	n.a.	n.a.	2,482,000[2]	520,811	615,742	1,136,553
1992–93	n.a.	n.a.	2,490,000[2]	532,881[2]	632,297[2]	1,165,178[2]
1993–94[3]	n.a.	n.a.	2,479,000[2]	526,000[4]	638,000[4]	1,165,000[4]
1994–95[3]	n.a.	n.a.	2,553,000	528,000[4]	651,000[4]	1,179,000[4]

1. Bachelors's degrees. Includes first-professional degrees for years 1900–1960. 2. Revised from previously published data. 3. Public high school graduates based on state estimates. 4. Projected. n.a. = not available. NOTE: Includes graduates from public and private schools. Beginning in 1959–60, figures include Alaska and Hawaii. Because of rounding, details may not add to totals. Most recent data available. *Source:* Department of Education, Center for Education Statistics.

School Enrollment, October 1995

(in thousands)

Age	White Enrolled	White Percent	Black Enrolled	Black Percent	Hispanic origin[1] Enrolled	Hispanic origin[1] Percent	Total Enrolled	Total Percent
3 and 4 years	3,205	49.6	657	47.5	503	36.9	4,042	48.7
5 and 6 years	6,211	96.2	1,305	95.5	1,159	9.9	7,901	96.0
7 to 9 years	9,088	98.9	1,867	97.7	1,560	98.5	11,555	98.7
10 to 13 years	12,208	99.0	2,441	99.2	2,060	99.2	15,448	99.1
14 and 15 years	6,008	98.8	1,223	99.0	977	98.9	7,651	98.9
16 and 17 years	5,484	93.7	1,127	92.9	778	88.2	6,997	93.6
18 and 19 years	3,379	59.3	631	57.4	467	46.1	4,274	59.4
20 and 21 years	2,483	46.2	363	37.4	268	27.1	3,025	44.9
22 to 24 years	2,033	23.1	309	19.9	250	15.6	2,545	23.2
25 to 29 years	1,783	11.5	254	10.0	172	7.1	2,216	11.6
30 to 34 years	979	5.5	217	7.8	120	4.7	1,284	6.0
Total	**52,862**	**53.2**	**10,395**	**56.1**	**8,313**	**49.7**	**66,939**	**53.7**

1. Persons of Hispanic origin may be of any race. NOTE: Figures include persons enrolled in nursery school, kindergarten, elementary school, high school, and college. *Source:* Department of Commerce, Bureau of the Census.

Persons Not Enrolled in School, October 1995

(in thousands)

Age	Population	Total not enrolled Number	Total not enrolled Percent	High school graduate Number	High school graduate Percent	Not high school graduate (dropouts)[1] Number	Not high school graduate (dropouts)[1] Percent
14 and 15 years	7,738	87	1.1	1	—	86	1.1
16 and 17 years	7,479	481	6.4	233	3.1	406	5.4
18 and 19 years	7,198	2,924	40.6	4,974	69.1	51	14.6
20 and 21 years	6,736	3,711	55.1	5,723	85.0	929	13.8
22 to 24 years	10,966	8,421	76.8	9,428	86.0	1,491	13.6

1. Persons who are not enrolled in school and who are not high school graduates are considered dropouts. *Source:* Department of Commerce, Bureau of the Census.

School Enrollment by Grade, Control, and Race

(in thousands)

Grade level and type of control	White Oct. 1995[3]	White Oct. 1990[3]	White Oct. 1980[4]	Black Oct. 1995[3]	Black Oct. 1990[3]	Black Oct. 1980[4]	All races[1] Oct. 1995[3]	All races[1] Oct. 1990[3]	All races[1] Oct. 1980[4]
Nursery school: Public	1,435	896	432	478	283	180	2,012	1,212	633
Private	2,117	1,961	1,205	185	148	115	2,387	2,188	1,354
Kindergarten: Public	2,440	2,609	2,172	563	574	440	3,174	3,322	2,690
Private	592	472	423	89	62	50	704	567	486
Grades 1–8: Public	22,009	20,997	19,743	4,845	4,431	4,058	28,383	26,615	24,398
Private	2,953	2,359	2,768	339	199	202	3,430	2,676	3,051
Grades 9–12: Public	10,575	9,429	12,056[2]	2,370	1,937	2,200[2]	13,751	11,911	14,556[2]
Private	1,043	810	—	111	65	—	1,213	906	—
College: Public	9,311	9,049	8,875[2]	1,352	1,120	1,007[2]	11,371	10,754	10,180[2]
Private	2,712	2,439	—	420	274	—	3,342	2,869	—
Total: Public	45,770	42,954	—	9,608	8,344	—	58,691	53,823	—
Private	9,416	8,041	—	1,144	748	—	11,077	9,204	—
Grand Total	**55,186**	**50,995**	**47,673**	**10,752**	**9,092**	**8,251**	**69,768**	**63,027**	**57.348**

1. Includes persons of Hispanic origin. 2. Total public and private. Breakdown not available. 3. Estimates controlled to 1990 census base. 4. Estimates controlled to 1970 census base. *Source:* Department of Commerce, Bureau of the Census.

State Compulsory School Attendance Laws, March 1994

State	Enactment[1]	Age limits	State	Enactment[1]	Age limits
Alabama	1915	7–16	Montana[7]	1883	7–16
Alaska[2]	1929	7–16	Nebraska	1887	7–16
Arizona[3]	1899	6–16	Nevada	1873	7–17
Arkansas	1909	5–17	New Hampshire	1871	6–16
California	1874	6–18	New Jersey	1875	6–16
Colorado	1889	7–16	New Mexico	1891	5–16
Connecticut	1872	7–16	New York[8]	1874	6–16
Delaware	1907	5–16	North Carolina	1907	7–16
D. C.	1864	7–17	North Dakota	1883	7–16
Florida	1915	6–16	Ohio	1877	6–18
Georgia	1916	7–16	Oklahoma	1907	5–18
Hawaii	1896	6–18	Oregon	1889	7–18
Idaho	1887	7–16	Pennsylvania	1895	8–17
Illinois	1883	7–16	Rhode Island	1883	6–16
Indiana[4]	1897	7–16	South Carolina[9]	1915	5–17
Iowa	1902	6–16	South Dakota[7]	1883	6–16
Kansas	1874	7–16	Tennessee	1905	7–17
Kentucky[5]	1896	6–16	Texas	1915	6–17
Louisiana	1910	7–17	Utah	1890	6–18
Maine	1875	7–17	Vermont	1867	7–16
Maryland	1902	5–16	Virginia	1908	5–18
Massachusetts	1852	6–16	Washington[10]	1871	8–18
Michigan[6]	1871	6–16	West Virginia	1897	6–16
Minnesota[6]	1885	7–16	Wisconsin[11]	1879	6–18
Mississippi	1918	6–16	Wyoming	1876	7–16
Missouri	1905	7–16			

1. Date of enactment of first compulsory attendance law. 2. Ages 7 to 16 or high school graduation. 3. Ages 6 to 16 or tenth grade completion. 4. Students between 16 and 18 are required to submit to an exit interview and have written parental approval before leaving high school. 5. Must have parental signature for leaving school between ages of 16 and 18. 6. Will change to 7 to 18 in year 2000. 7. May leave after completion of eighth grade. 8. The ages are 6 to 17 for New York City and Buffalo. 9. Permits parental waiver of kindergarten at age 5. 10. Or can exit if age 15 and has completed grade 8, has a useful occupation, has met graduation requirements, or has certificate of education competency. 11. Ages 6 to 18 or high school graduation. *Source:* Department of Education, National Center for Educational Statistics, which prepared this table August 1994.

Major U.S. College and University Libraries—1994–95

(Top 50 based on number of volumes in library)

Institution	Volumes	Microforms[1]	Institution	Volumes	Microforms[1]
Harvard	13,143,330	7,558,615	Pennsylvania State	3,632,652	3,318,822
Yale	9,599,371	5,044,263	U of Pittsburgh	3,627,100	3,366,693
Illinois–Urbana	8,665,814	4,387,714	Rutgers	3,480,920	4,996,144
U of California–Berkeley	8,242,196	5,563,213	New York	3,385,458	3,880,821
U of Texas	7,176,889	5,196,391	U of Kansas	3,379,453	2,898,833
U of Michigan	6,774,515	5,281,831	U of Southern California	3,303,938	5,466,844
Columbia	6,664,748	4,994,833	U of Georgia	3,303,268	5,373,412
U of California–Los Angeles	6,606,361	5,716,979	U of Florida	3,174,460	5,864,399
Stanford	6,549,725	4,494,781	Johns Hopkins	3,118,765	3,386,609
U of Chicago	5,854,014	2,178,083	Arizona State	3,101,920	6,355,681
Cornell	5,835,235	6,773,020	Washington U–St. Louis	3,095,313	2,705,557
Indiana	5,677,326	3,623,090	SUNY–Buffalo	2,937,786	4,565,039
U of Wisconsin	5,652,885	4,280,297	Wayne State	2,904,641	3,374,190
U of Washington	5,471,784	6,255,761	Rochester	2,882,023	4,060,725
Princeton	5,292,949	3,612,712	U of Hawaii	2,854,225	5,565,078
U of Minnesota	5,241,590	5,083,218	Louisiana State	2,831,957	4,967,768
Ohio State	4,864,522	4,005,131	Syracuse	2,826,295	3,514,142
Duke	4,415,525	3,181,567	California–Davis	2,807,863	3,568,949
U of Pennsylvania	4,324,225	2,911,876	Brown	2,762,196	1,508,020
North Carolina	4,263,684	3,898,477	U of Missouri	2,730,756	5,810,794
U of Arizona	4,225,022	4,785,963	South Carolina	2,714,060	4,186,737
U of Virginia	4,165,805	4,386,052	U of Massachusetts	2,696,692	2,131,229
Michigan State	3,972,396	4,993,512	U of Colorado	2,624,243	5,389,160
Northwestern	3,775,526	3,130,069	U of Kentucky	2,590,061	5,454,233
Iowa	3,665,496	5,613,778	U of Connecticut	2,546,979	3,669,956

1. Includes reels of microfilm and number of microcards, microprint sheets, and microfiches. *Source:* Association of Research Libraries.

College and University Endowments, 1994–95
(top 75 in millions of dollars)

Institution	Endowment (market value)	Voluntary support[1]	Expen- ditures[2]	Institution	Endowment (market value)	Voluntary support[1]	Expen- ditures[2]
Harvard Univ.	$7,045.9	$323.4	$1,470.2	Princeton Theol. Sem.	536.8	5.4	25.0
Yale Univ.	3,967.8	199.6	854.2	Swarthmore Col.	536.4	25.8	60.9
Stanford Univ.	3,601.8	240.8	931.0	Wellesley Col.	525.5	21.9	89.0
Princeton Univ.	3,532.5	103.8	356.2	Smith Col.	502.2	26.8	107.9
Columbia Univ.	2,221.4	151.8	1,075.5	Boston Col.	500.7	22.1	237.4
Massachusetts Inst. of Tech.	2,093.2	107.9	776.5	Macalester Col.	494.7	4.1	45.7
Washington Univ.	2,014.2	61.0	777.6	Texas Christian Univ.	487.0	17.9	89.7
Texas A&M Univ.	1,987.8	74.8	773.2	Southern Methodist Univ.	483.0	31.4	161.9
Northwestern Univ.	1,788.6	101.0	685.1	Grinnell Col.	478.4	11.2	41.7
Pennsylvania, Univ. of	1,676.7	135.3	983.8	Williams Col.	460.9	20.6	66.8
Cornell Univ.	1,569.2	198.7	1,078.8	Carnegie-Mellon Univ.	453.5	42.0	327.3
William Marsh Rice Univ.	1,530.0	44.4	174.4	Indiana Univ.	451.4	109.7	1,025.7
Chicago, Univ. of	1,378.0	99.1	542.5	Pittsburgh, Univ. of	444.5	39.4	652.5
Michigan, Univ. of	1,355.2	145.8	1,270.4	Richmond, Univ. of	443.9	18.9	88.6
Mayo Foundation	1,080.2	60.0	221.9	Pomona Col.	438.9	15.5	52.3
Dartmouth Col.	993.7	81.7	269.4	Delaware, Univ. of	435.1	22.8	315.7
Vanderbilt Univ.	952.8	82.5	506.0	Wake Forest Univ.	421.7	35.6	361.0
Notre Dame, Univ. of	909.0	70.2	254.9	Georgetown Univ.	414.8	43.2	426.6
Ca., Univ. of–Berkeley	895.6	103.1	849.2	Wisconsin, Univ. of–Madison	407.7	164.3	1,022.4
Southern California, Univ. of	883.8	138.4	861.1	Washington and Lee Univ.	403.6	34.8	53.1
Johns Hopkins Univ.	838.2	94.7	515.7	Amherst Col.	396.9	15.4	55.8
Minnesota, Univ. of	824.7	131.6	1,272.1	Tulsa, Univ. of	396.5	6.4	87.3
Duke Univ.	790.6	155.2	642.2	Berea Col.	390.4	15.0	34.9
Texas, Univ. of–Austin	763.8	61.5	746.1	Boston Univ.	390.1	37.7	737.5
New York Univ.	762.8	91.8	1,046.0	St. Louis Univ.	388.0	15.8	259.2
Rochester, Univ. of	733.8	40.3	439.7	Kansas, Univ. of	385.2	37.9	284.1
Virginia, Univ. of	730.5	78.5	473.7	Lehigh Univ.	380.2	26.7	166.9
California Inst. of Tech.	695.6	69.0	266.9	Loyola Univ. of Chicago	377.0	18.2	270.2
Brown Univ.	688.3	102.5	257.3	Middlebury Col.	373.0	14.2	70.8
Case Western Reserve Univ.	620.0	62.7	335.4	George Washington Univ.	369.5	23.4	390.2
Rush–Presby.–St. Luke's Med. Center	609.9	17.0	n.a.	Trinity Univ.	367.4	7.6	50.2
Rockefeller Univ.	607.1	44.9	95.7	Pennsylvania St. Univ.	364.3	82.8	1,076.4
Purdue Univ.	582.5	76.2	678.7	Wesleyan Univ.	351.5	10.9	86.5
Ca., Univ. of–Los Angeles	565.3	98.2	1,170.6	Vassar Col.	350.7	27.2	70.8
Ohio St. Univ.	555.7	92.9	979.0	Tennessee, Univ. of	348.0	46.0	768.8
NC at Chapel Hill, Univ. of	554.8	87.4	704.8	Baylor Univ.	340.8	23.6	130.4
Cincinnati, Univ. of	554.0	43.1	484.5	Iowa, Univ. of	336.7	60.1	563.5
				Ca., Univ. of–San Francisco	335.7	108.1	695.0

1. Gifts from alumni, other individuals, corporations, foundations, and other private organizations. 2. Figure represents about 80% of typical operating budget. *Source:* Council for Aid to Education.

Institutions of Higher Education—Average Salaries and Fringe Benefits for Faculty Members, 1970–1994[1]
(in thousands of dollars)

Control and Acadmic Rank	1994	1993	1992	1991	1990	1989	1988	1985	1980	1975	1970
Average Salaries											
Public: All ranks	47.3	46.0	45.3	44.0	41.6	39.6	37.2	31.2	22.1	16.6	13.1
Professor	59.8	58.4	57.4	55.8	53.2	50.1	47.2	39.6	28.8	21.7	17.3
Associate professor	45.3	44.1	43.4	42.2	40.3	37.9	35.6	30.2	21.9	16.7	13.2
Assistant professor	38.0	37.0	36.3	35.2	33.5	31.7	29.6	25.0	18.0	13.7	10.9
Instructor	28.8	27.8	27.2	26.3	25.0	23.9	22.2	19.5	14.8	11.2	9.1
Private:[2] All ranks	53.8	51.6	50.0	47.0	45.1	42.4	39.7	33.0	22.1	16.6	13.1
Professor	71.2	68.7	66.1	61.6	59.6	55.9	52.2	44.1	30.1	22.4	17.8
Associate professor	48.5	46.9	45.6	43.2	41.2	38.8	36.6	30.9	21.0	16.0	12.6
Assistant professor	40.1	38.6	37.8	35.5	34.0	31.9	28.3	23.7	13.0	10.3	
Instructor	30.2	28.3	28.5	26.2	26.0	24.1	22.7	19.0	13.3	10.9	8.6
Average Fringe Benefits—All Ranks Combined											
Public	12.0	11.5	11.0	10.5	9.8	9.0	8.2	7.0	3.9	2.5	1.9
Private[2]	13.9	13.1	12.4	11.6	10.9	10.0	9.2	7.2	4.1	2.8	2.2

1. Figures are for 9 months teaching for full-time faculty members in four-year colleges and universities. 2. Excludes church-related colleges and universities. *Source:* American Association of University Professors. Washington, D.C. *AAUP Annual Report on the Economic Status of the Profession.* From *Statistical Abstract of the United States: 1995.* NOTE: Data are latest available.

Average Monthly Earnings by Field of Degree, Spring 1993

Field of degree	Mean earnings	Field of degree	Mean earnings
Medicine/dentistry	$5,049	Police science/law enforcement	$2,178
Law	4,353	Biology	2,118
Economics	3,330	Social science	1,970
Engineering	3,117	Religion/theology	1,963
Agriculture/forestry	2,973	Nursing/pharmacy/technical health	1,889
Mathematics/statistics	2,583	Education	1,884
Business/management	2,426	Liberal arts/humanities	1,733
Physical/earth sciences	2,357	Vocational/technical studies	1,713
English/journalism	2,331	Home economics	1,165
Psychology	2,236	**Overall**	**$2,339**

Source: Census Bureau, *Current Population Reports*, December 1995.

Average Monthly Income by Educational Attainment, Sex, and Race, Spring 1993

Educational attainment	Total, both sexes	Total, male	Total female	White, both sexes	Black, both sexes	Hispanic, both sexes
Overall	$1,687	$2,230	$1,186	$1,756	$1,192	$1,126
Doctorate	4,328	4,421	4,020	4,449	(B)	(B)
Professional	5,534	6,312	3,530	5,590	(B)	(B)
Master's	3,411	4,298	2,505	3,478	2,834	2,605
Bachelor's	2,625	3,430	1,809	2,682	2,333	2,186
Associate	1,985	2,561	1,544	2,021	1,746	2,069
Vocational	1,736	2,318	1,373	1,768	1,428	1,329
Some college, no degree	1,579	2,045	1,139	1,649	1,222	1,239
High school graduate	1,380	1,812	1,008	1,422	1,071	1,106
Not a high school graduate	906	1,211	621	951	713	786

B = Basis is < 200,000 people. *Source:* Census Bureau, *Current Population Reports*, Series P20–476.

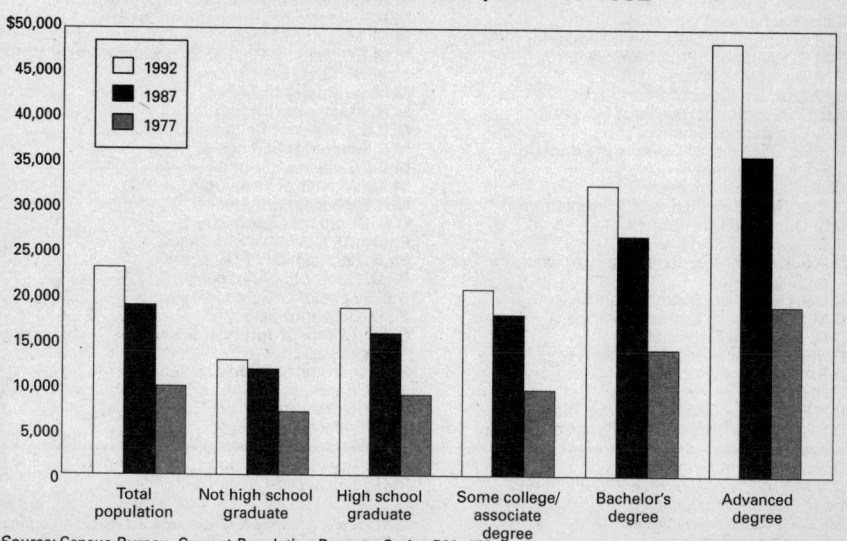

Mean Earnings of Workers 18 Years and Over by Educational Attainment, 1977 to 1992

Source: Census Bureau, *Current Population Reports*, Series P20–476.

Funding for Public Elementary and Secondary Education, 1986–87 to 1992–93
(In thousands except percent)

School year	Total	Federal	State	Local[1]	% Federal	% State	% Local[1]
1986–87	158,523,693	10,146,013	78,830,437	69,547,243	6.4	49.7	43.9
1987–88	169,561,974	10,716,687	84,004,415	74,840,873	6.3	49.5	44.1
1988–89	191,210,310	11,872,419	91,158,363	88,179,529	6.2	47.4	46.1
1989–90	207,752,932	12,700,784	98,238,633	96,813,516	6.1	47.3	46.6
1990–91	223,340,537	13,776,066	105,324,533	104,239,939	6.2	47.2	46.7
1991–92[2]	234,588,732	15,493,330	108,783,449	110,311,953	6.6	46.4	47.0
1992–93	248,496,276	17,267,351	113,396,992	117,831,933	6.9	45.6	47.4

1. Includes a relatively small amount from nongovernmental sources (gifts and tuition and transportation fees from patrons). 2. Revised from previously published figures. *Source:* U.S. Department of Education, National Center for Education Statistics, which prepared this table May 1995.

Selected Degree Abbreviations

A.B. Bachelor of Arts
AeEng. Aeronautical Engineer
A.M.T. Master of Arts in Teaching
B.A. Bachelor of Arts
B.A.E. Bachelor of Arts in Education, or Bachelor of Art Education, Aeronautical Engineering, Agricultural Engineering, or Architectural Engineering
B.Ag. Bachelor of Agriculture
B.A.M. Bachelor of Applied Mathematics
B.Arch. Bachelor of Architecture
B.B.A. Bachelor of Business Administration
B.C.E. Bachelor of Civil Engineering
B.Ch.E. Bachelor of Chemical Engineering
B.C.L. Bachelor of Canon Law
B.D. Bachelor of Divinity
B.E. Bachelor of Education or Bachelor of Engineering
B.E.E. Bachelor of Electrical Engineering
B.F. Bachelor of Forestry
B.F.A. Bachelor of Fine Arts
B.J. Bachelor of Journalism
B.L.S. Bachelor of Liberal Studies or Bachelor of Library Science
B.Lit. Bachelor of Literature
B.M. Bachelor of Medicine or Bachelor of Music
B.M.S. Bachelor of Marine Science
B.N. Bachelor of Nursing
B.Pharm. Bachelor of Pharmacy
B.R.E. Bachelor of Religious Education
B.S. Bachelor of Science
B.S.Ed. Bachelor of Science in Education
C.E. Civil Engineer
Ch.E. Chemical Engineer
D.B.A. Doctor of Business Administration
D.C. Doctor of Chiropractic
D.D. Doctor of Divinity[1]
D.D.S. Doctor of Dental Surgery or Doctor of Dental Science
D.L.S. Doctor of Library Science
D.M.D. Doctor of Dental Medicine
D.O. Doctor of Osteopathy
D.M.S. Doctor of Medical Science
D.P.A. Doctor of Public Administration[2]
D.P.H. Doctor of Public Health
D.R.E. Doctor of Religious Education
D.S.W. Doctor of Social Welfare or Doctor of Social Work
D.Sc. Doctor of Science[3]
D.V.M. Doctor of Veterinary Medicine
Ed.D. Doctor of Education[2]
Ed.S. Education Specialist
E.E. Electrical Engineer

E.M. Engineer of Mines
E.Met. Engineer of Metallurgy
I.E. Industrial Engineer or Industrial Engineering
J.D. Doctor of Laws[2]
J.S.D. Doctor of Juristic Science
L.H.D. Doctor of Humane Letters[3]
Litt.B. Bachelor of Letters
Litt.M. Master of Letters[4]
LL.B. Bachelor of Laws
LL.D. Doctor of Laws[3]
LL.M. Master of Laws
M.A. Master of Arts
M.Aero.E. Master of Aeronautical Engineering
M.B.A. Master of Business Administration
M.C.E. Master of Christian Education or Master of Civil Engineering
M.C.S. Master of Computer Science
M.D. Doctor of Medicine
M.Div. Master of Divinity
M.E. Master of Engineering
M.Ed. Master of Education
M.Eng. Master of Engineering
M.F.A. Master of Fine Arts
M.H.A. Master of Hospital Administration
M.L.S. Master of Library Science
M.M. Master of Music
M.M.E. Master of Mechanical Engineering or Master of Music Education
M.Mus. Master of Music
M.N. Master of Nursing
M.R.E. Master of Religious Education
M.S. Master of Science
M.S.W. Master of Social Work
M.Th. Master of Theology
Nuc.E. Nuclear Engineer
O.D. Doctor of Optometry
Pharm.D. Doctor of Pharmacy[2]
Ph.B. Bachelor of Philosophy
Ph.D. Doctor of Philosophy
S.B. Bachelor of Science
Sc.D. Doctor of Science[3]
S.J.D. Doctor of Juridical Science or Doctor of the Science of Law
S.Sc.D. Doctor of Social Science
S.T.B. Bachelor of Sacred Theology
S.T.D. Doctor of Sacred Theology
S.T.M. Master of Sacred Theology
Th.B. Bachelor of Theology
Th.D. Doctor of Theology
Th.M. Master of Theology

1. Honorary. 2. Earned and honorary. 3. Usually honorary. 4. Sometimes honorary.

Accredited U.S. Senior Colleges and Universities, 1996–97

Source: The Guidance Information System (trademark), a product of The Riverside Publishing Company, a Houghton Mifflin company.

Schools listed are four-year institutions that offer at least a Bachelor's degree and are fully accredited by one of the institutional and professional accrediting associations. Included are accredited colleges outside the U.S.

Tuition, room, and board listed are average annual figures (including fees) subject to fluctuation, usually covering two semesters, two out of three trimesters, or three out of four quarters, depending on the school calendar.

For further information, write to the Registrar of the school concerned.

NOTE: n.a. = information not available. — = does not apply. Enrollment figures are approximate, and are coeducational unless otherwise noted: (M) = primarily for men, (W) = primarily for women.

Control: P = private, Pub = public

Institution and location	Enrollment	Control	Tuition ($) Res.	Tuition ($) Nonres.	Rm/Bd ($)
Abilene Christian University; Abilene, Tex. 79699	4,436	P	8,220	8,220	3,630
Academy of Art College; San Francisco, Calif. 94108–3893	2,156	P	9,200	9,200	4,900
Academy of the New Church College; Bryn Athyn, Pa. 19009	116	P	4,440	4,440	3,729
Adams State College; Alamosa, Colo. 81102	2,179	Pub	1,839	5,481	3,900
Adelphi University; Garden City, N.Y. 11530	3,835	P	13,360	13,360	6,500
Adrian College; Adrian, Mich. 49221	994	P	12,250	12,250	3,880
Aeronautics, College of; Flushing, N.Y. 11371	1,070	P	7,200	7,200	n.a.
Agnes Scott College; Decatur, Ga. 30030	600 (W)	P	14,325	14,325	3,020
Akron, University of; Akron, Ohio 44325-2001	22,755	Pub	3,192	7,954	3,844
Alabama A&M University; Normal, Ala. 35762	3,901	Pub	2,022	3,808	2,810
Alabama State University; Montgomery, Ala. 36101-0271	5,117	Pub	1,650	3,250	3,100
Alabama, University of; Tuscaloosa, Ala. 35487-0132	14,995	Pub	2,470	6,268	3,680
Alabama, University of-Birmingham; Birmingham, Ala. 35294	11,658	Pub	4,348	8,696	3,454
Alabama, University of-Huntsville; Huntsville, Ala. 35899	5,512	Pub	2,480	4,960	3,500
Alaska Bible College; Glennallen, Alas. 99588	43	P	3,300	3,300	3,400
Alaska Pacific University; Anchorage, Alas. 99508	307	P	7,560	7,560	4,120
Alaska, University of Anchorage; Anchorage, Alas. 99508	19,624	Pub	1,886	5,342	2,650
Alaska, University of Fairbanks; Fairbanks, Alas. 99701	7,393	Pub	2,490	7,114	3,690
Alaska, University of Southeast; Juneau, Alas. 99801	833 [1]	Pub	1,800	5,968	4,100
Albany College of Pharmacy; Albany, N.Y. 12208	682	P	9,550	9,550	4,600
Albany State College; Albany, Ga. 31705	3,151	Pub	1,899	5,109	3,045
Albertson College; Caldwell, Idaho 83605	604	P	14,600	14,600	3,225
Albertus Magnus College; New Haven, Conn. 06511–1189	915	P	12,350	12,350	5,664
Albion College; Albion, Mich. 49224	1,641	P	16,000	16,000	4,890
Albright College; Reading, Pa. 19612-5234	1,291	P	16,575	16,575	4,620
Alcorn State University; Lorman, Miss. 39096	3,244	Pub	2,400	4,600	2,160
Alderson-Broaddus College; Philippi, W. Va. 26416	760	P	11,650	11,650	3,866
Alfred University; Alfred, N.Y. 14802	1,984	P	7,652	10,624	5,716
Alice Lloyd College; Pippa Passes, Ky. 41844	548	P	460	3,800	2,960
Allegheny College; Meadville, Pa. 16335	1,854	P	18,020	18,020	4,550
Allentown College of St. Francis de Sales; Center Valley, Pa. 18034-9568	1,044	P	10,990	10,990	5,260
Alma College; Alma, Mich. 48801-1599	1,447	P	13,690	13,690	4,905
Alvernia College; Reading, Pa. 19607–1799	1,354	P	10,200	10,200	4,600
Alverno College; Milwaukee, Wis. 53234-3922	2,457 (W)	P	9,288	9,288	3,890
Ambassador College; Big Sandy, Tex. 75755	1,111	P	3,650	3,650	3,000
Amber University; Garland, Tex. 75041	722	P	3,200	3,200	n.a.
American Baptist College; Nashville, Tenn. 37207	200	P	4,384	4,384	2,654
American College for the Applied Arts, The; Los Angeles, Calif. 90024	472	P	10,230	10,230	3,825
American College of Switzerland; Switzerland	70	P	23,372	23,372	7,954
American Conservatory of Music; Chicago, Ill. 60602–4792	n.a.	P	11,200	11,200	n.a.
American International College; Springfield, Mass. 01109	1,350	P	9,824	9,824	5,062
American University; Washington, D.C. 20016	5,041	P	16,890	16,890	6,698
American University in Cairo; New York, N.Y. 10017	3,084	P	9,014	9,014	5,540
American University of Beirut; Beirut, Lebanon	4,371	Pub	4,860	4,860	2,860
American University of Paris; 75007 Paris, France	791	P	16,300	16,300	8,200
American Universtity of Puerto Rico; Bayamon, P.R. 00621	4,208	P	3,070	3,070	n.a.
Amherst College; Amherst, Mass. 01002	1,608	P	20,710	20,710	5,560
Anderson College; Anderson, SC 29621	932	P	8,821	8,821	4,145
Anderson University; Anderson, Ind. 46012	2,097	P	11,840	11,840	3,980
Andrews University; Berrien Springs, Mich. 49104	1,835	P	10,896	10,896	3,360
Angelo State University; San Angelo, Tex. 76909	6,106	Pub	1,820	5,984	4,048
Anna Maria College; Paxton, Mass. 01612	777	P	11,230	11,230	5,028

Institution and location	Enrollment	Control	Tuition ($) Res.	Tuition ($) Nonres.	Rm/Bd ($)
Antillian Adventist University; Mayaguez, P.R. 00709	854	P	2,850	2,850	2,150
Antioch College; Yellow Springs, Ohio 45387	649	P	17,376	17,376	3,436
Antioch School for Adult & Experiential Learning; Yellow Springs, Ohio 45387	231	P	6,660	6,660	n.a.
Antioch Seattle; Seattle, Wash. 98121	176	P	11,620	11,620	n.a.
Antioch–Southern California at Los Angeles; Marina Del Rey, Calif. 90292	264	P	9,600	9,600	n.a.
Antioch–Southern California at Santa Barbara; Santa Barbara, Calif. 93101	107	P	8,550	8,550	n.a.
Appalachian Bible College; Bradley, W. Va. 25818	254	P	5,320	5,320	2,880
Appalachian State University; Boone, N.C. 28608	10,171	Pub	1,673	8,358	2,750
Aquinas College; Grand Rapids, Mich. 49506–1799	1,951	P	11,852	11,852	4,124
Arizona College of the Bible; Phoenix, Ariz. 85021	90	P	6,500	6,500	7,500
Arizona State University; Tempe, Ariz. 85287-0112	31,212	Pub	1,884	7,912	4,287
Arizona, University of; Tucson, Ariz. 85721	26,468	Pub	1,950	7,978	4,190
Arkansas Baptist College; Little Rock, Ark. 72202	331	P	2,000	2,000	6,200
Arkansas State University; State University, Ark. 72467	8,657	Pub	1,950	3,600	2,580
Arkansas Tech. University; Russellville, Ark. 72801–2222	4,159	Pub	1,865	3,685	2,660
Arkansas, Univ. of; Fayetteville, Ark. 72701	14,692	Pub	2,184	5,746	3,780
Arkansas, Univ. of-Little Rock; Little Rock, Ark. 72204	11,035	Pub	2,262	5,832	2,435
Arkansas, Univ. of-Monticello; Monticello, Ark. 71655	2,398	Pub	1,762	5,218	4,000
Arkansas, Univ. of-Pine Bluff; Pine Bluff, Ark. 71601–2799	3,709	Pub	1,818	3,822	2,464
Arlington Baptist College; Arlington, Tex. 76012	179	P	1,795	1,795	3,100
Armstrong State College; Savannah, Ga. 31419	4,839	Pub	1,719	4,929	3,026
Armstrong University; Berkeley, Calif. 94704	172	P	6,060	6,060	n.a.
Art Academy of Cincinnati; Cincinnati, Ohio 45202	230	P	9,990	9,990	n.a.
Art Center College of Design; Pasadena, Calif. 91103	1,158	P	7,300	7,300	n.a.
Art Institute of Southern California; Laguna Beach, Calif. 92651	140	P	10,200	10,200	n.a.
Arts, University of the; Philadelphia, Pa. 19102	1,213	P	13,850	13,850	3,980
Asbury College; Wilmore, Ky. 40390	1,159[1]	P	10,470	10,470	2,984
Ashland University; Ashland, Ohio 44805	2,692	P	12,494	12,494	4,832
Assumption College; Worcester, Mass. 01615-0005	1,689	P	13,700	13,700	5,980
Athens State College; Athens, Ala. 35611	2,770	Pub	3,750	7,500	4,900
Atlanta Christian College; East Point, Ga. 30344	169	P	4,320	4,320	3,030
Atlanta College of Art; Atlanta, Ga. 30309	420[1]	P	10,500	10,500	3,350
Atlantic Union College; South Lancaster, Mass. 01561	938	P	11,150	11,150	3,600
Atlantic, College of the; Bar Harbor, Maine 04609	246	P	15,150	15,150	4,800
Auburn University; Auburn University, Ala. 36849	18,106	Pub	2,250	6,750	4,098
Auburn University-Montgomery; Montgomery, Ala. 36117–3596	5,503	Pub	1,905	5,715	4,050
Audrey Cohen College; New York, N.Y. 10013	1,052	P	8,240	8,840	n.a.
Augsburg College; Minneapolis, Minn. 55454	1,617	P	13,286	13,286	4,794
Augusta College; Augusta, Ga. 30904–2200	5,759	Pub	1,710	4,920	n.a.
Augustana College; Rock Island, Ill. 61201	2,002	P	13,968	13,968	4,257
Aurora University; Aurora, Ill. 60506	1,847	P	10,800	10,800	4,134
Austin College; Sherman, Tex. 75090–4440	1,095	P	12,195	12,195	4,524
Austin Peay State University; Clarksville, Tenn. 37044	7,556	Pub	1,946	6,076	2,800
Averett College; Danville, Va. 24541-3692	2,734	P	10,800	10,800	4,150
Avila College; Kansas City, Mo. 64145	1,119	P	10,100	10,100	4,150
Azusa Pacific University; Azusa, Calif. 91702-7000	1,975	P	12,416	12,416	4,460
Babson College; Wellesley, Mass. 02157	1,679	P	18,115	18,115	7,275
Baker College of Flint; Flint, Mich. 48507	4,179	P	6,000	6,000	1,650
Baker University; Baldwin City, Kan. 66006	860[1]	P	10,300	10,300	4,400
Baldwin-Wallace College; Berea, Ohio 44017	4,087	P	12,270	12,270	4,635
Ball State University; Muncie, Ind. 47306	2,171	Pub	3,048	7,824	3,768
Baltimore Hebrew University; Baltimore, Md. 21215	255	P	3,300	3,300	n.a.
Baltimore, University of; Baltimore, Md. 21201–5779	2,261	Pub	3,480	8,046	n.a.
Baptist Bible College; Springfield, Mo. 65803	793	P	2,466	2,466	2,812
Baptist Bible College of Pennsylvania; Clarks Summit, Pa. 18411	562	P	6,528	6,528	4,070
Barat College; Lake Forest, Ill. 60045	731	P	11,970	11,970	4,820
Barber-Scotia College; Concord, N.C. 28025	704	P	5,369	5,369	3,070
Barclay College; Haviland, Kan. 67059	106	P	4,265	4,265	2,700
Bard College; Annandale-on-Hudson, N.Y. 12504	1,249	P	20,684	20,684	6,520
Barnard College of Columbia University; New York, N.Y. 10027	2,190 (W)	P	19,452	19,452	8,172
Barry University; Miami Shores, Fla. 33161	4,410[1]	P	11,990	11,990	5,980
Bartlesville Wesleyan College; Bartlesville, Okla. 74006	452	P	7,400	7,400	3,600
Barton College; Wilson, N.C. 27893	1,256	P	8,984	8,984	3,916
Bassist College; Portland, Ore. 97201	103	P	8,900	8,900	3,005
Bates College; Lewiston, Maine 04240	1,550[1]	P	26,300	26,300	n.a.
Bay Path College; Longmeadow, Ma. 01106	586 (W)	P	10,700	10,700	6,350
Baylor University; Waco, Tex. 76798-7008	10,421	P	8,990	8,990	4,139
Beaver College; Glenside, Pa. 19038	1,525	P	13,690	13,690	5,750
Belhaven College; Jackson, Miss. 39202	1,109	P	1,890	1,890	3,100
Bellarmine College; Louisville, Ky. 40205–0671	2,359	P	10,200	10,200	3,480

Institution and location	Enrollment	Control	Tuition ($)		Rm/Bd ($)
			Res.	Nonres.	
Bellevue University; Bellevue, Neb. 68005	2,040	P	4,000	4,000	n.a.
Bellin College of Nursing; Green Bay, Wis. 54305-3400	299	P	8,025	8,025	n.a.
Belmont Abbey College; Belmont, N.C. 28012	916	P	9,360	9,360	5,044
Belmont University; Nashville, Tenn. 37212	2,636	P	9,250	9,250	4,080
Beloit College; Beloit, Wis. 53511	1,246	P	17,544	17,544	3,846
Bemidji State University; Bemidji, Minn. 56601	4,813	Pub	3,311	5,936	2,798
Benedict College; Columbia, S.C. 29204	1,266	P	6,196	6,196	3,210
Benedictine College; Atchison, Kan. 66002	1,200	P	10,600	10,600	4,350
Benedictine University; Lisle, Ill. 60532	1,640	P	11,640	11,640	4,618
Bennett College; Greensboro, N.C. 27401–3239	620 (W)	P	7,290	7,290	3,334
Bennington College; Bennington, Vt. 05201	373	P	21,700	21,700	4,100
Bentley College; Waltham, Mass. 02254	3,389	P	15,650	15,650	6,490
Berklee College of Music; Boston, Mass. 02215	2,686	P	12,390	12,390	7,190
Berry College; Mount Berry, Ga. 30149	1,714	P	9,216	9,216	3,662
Beth–El College of Nursing; Colorado Springs, Colo. 80917	459	Pub	4,295	4,295	n.a.
Bethany Bible College; Scotts Valley, Calif. 95066–2898	589	P	7,300	7,300	3,644
Bethany College; Lindsborg, Kan. 67456	685	P	9,875	9,875	3,535
Bethel College; McKenzie, Tenn. 38201	470	P	6,990	6,990	3,660
Bethel College; Mishawaka, Ind. 46545	1,200	P	9,750	9,750	3,100
Bethel College; North Newton, Kan. 67117	644	P	9,270	9,270	3,800
Bethel College; St. Paul, Minn. 55112	1,832	P	12,260	12,260	4,460
Bethune-Cookman College; Daytona Beach, Fla. 32015	2,345	P	6,458	6,458	3,522
Biola University; La Mirada, Calif. 90639	2,114 [1]	P	12,652	12,652	4,932
Birmingham-Southern College; Birmingham, Ala. 35254	1,669	P	11,660	11,660	4,350
Black Hills State University; Spearfish, S.D. 57799	2,736	Pub	2,597	5,029	2,466
Blackburn College; Carlinville, Ill. 62626	443	P	6,585	6,585	2,700
Bloomfield College; Bloomfield, N.J. 07003	2,174	P	8,850	8,850	4,500
Bloomsburg University of Pennsylvania; Bloomsburg, Pa. 17815	6,632	Pub	3,694	8,452	2,948
Blue Mountain College; Blue Mountain, Miss. 38610	440 (W)	P	4,090	4,090	2,190
Bluefield College; Bluefield, Va. 24605	850	P	8,200	8,200	4,610
Bluefield State College; Bluefield, W. Va. 24701	2,504	Pub	1,916	4,576	n.a.
Bluffton College; Bluffton, Ohio 45817	899	P	10,620	10,620	4,377
Bob Jones University; Greenville, S.C. 29614	3,629	P	5,230	5,230	3,900
Boise State University; Boise, Idaho 83725	12,357	Pub	1,964	7,310	3,370
Boricua College; New York, N.Y. 10032	1,039	P	5,900	5,900	n.a.
Boston Architecture Center; Boston, Mass. 02115	675	P	4,990	4,990	n.a.
Boston College; Chestnut Hill, Mass. 02167	9,079	P	18,356	17,356	7,270
Boston Conservatory; Boston, Mass. 02215	309	P	13,400	13,400	6,280
Boston University; Boston, Mass. 02215	14,334	P	19,420	19,420	7,100
Bowdoin College; Brunswick, Me. 04011	1,489	P	20,230	20,230	5,945
Bowie State University; Bowie, Md. 20715	2,965	Pub	3,019	6,161	4,136
Bowling Green State University; Bowling Green, Ohio 43403	15,532	Pub	4,054	8,612	3,522
Bradford College; Bradford, Mass. 01835	630	P	15,380	15,380	6,590
Bradley University; Peoria, Ill. 61625	5,061	P	11,410	11,410	4,620
Brandeis University; Waltham, Mass. 02254	2,998	P	20,470	20,470	6,950
Brenau University; Gainesville, Ga. 30501	2,225 (W)	P	10,350	10,350	6,330
Brescia College; Owensboro, Ky. 42301	730	P	7,800	7,800	3,400
Brewton-Parker College; Mount Vernon, Ga. 30445	2,250	P	4,770	4,770	2,400
Briar Cliff College; Sioux City, Iowa 51104-2100	1,144	P	11,280	11,280	4,017
Bridgeport, University of; Bridgeport, Conn. 06601	2,084	P	13,700	13,700	6,810
Bridgewater College; Bridgewater, Va. 22812	1,007	P	11,925	11,925	4,975
Bridgewater State College; Bridgewater, Mass. 02325	8,393	Pub	1,338	5,542	4,204
Brigham Young University; Provo, Utah 84602	2,216	P	2,450	3,674	3,740
Brigham Young University-Hawaii; Laie, Oahu, Hawaii 96762	2,032	P	2,970	2,970	3,700
Brooklyn College. *See* New York, City University of					
Brooks Institute of Photography; Santa Barbara, Calif. 93108	450	P	14,100	14,100	n.a.
Brown University; Providence, R.I. 02912	5,718	P	21,128	21,128	6,212
Bryan College; Dayton, Tenn. 37321	421	P	9,500	9,500	3,950
Bryant College; Smithfield, R.I. 02917	2,744	P	13,100	13,100	6,500
Bryn Mawr College; Bryn Mawr, Pa. 19010	1,169 (W)	P	19,250	19,250	7,085
Bucknell University; Lewisburg, Pa. 17837	3,298	P	19,470	19,470	4,925
Buena Vista University; Storm Lake, Iowa 50588	43	P	14,458	14,458	4,125
Burlington College; Burlington, Vt. 05401	184	P	6,276	6,276	n.a.
Butler University; Indianapolis, Ind. 46208	2,739	P	14,000	14,000	5,500
Cabrini College; Radnor, Pa. 19087–3699	1,552	P	11,655	11,655	6,695
Caldwell College; Caldwell, N.J. 07006	1,612	P	9,500	9,500	4,900
California Baptist College; Riverside, Calif. 92504	1,136	P	8,800	8,800	4,464
California College of Arts and Crafts; San Francisco, Calif. 94107	1,111	P	14,995	14,995	4,696
California Institute of Technology; Pasadena, Calif. 91125	912	P	17,370	17,370	5,283
California Institute of the Arts; Valencia, Calif. 91355	659	P	15,450	15,450	5,500
California Lutheran University; Thousand Oaks, Calif. 91360	1,661	P	17,355	17,355	5,640
California Maritime Academy; Vallejo, Calif. 94590	424	Pub	3,596	10,976	5,020

Institution and location	Enrollment	Control	Tuition ($) Res.	Tuition ($) Nonres.	Rm/Bd ($)
California Polytechnic State University; San Luis Obispo, Calif. 93407	15,440	Pub	2,033	7,937	4,877
California State Polytechnic University-Pomona; Pomona, Calif. 91768	14,890	Pub	1,783	1,783	4,824
California State University-Bakersfield; Bakersfield, Calif. 93311-1099	4,134	Pub	1,584	7,851	3,857
California State University-Chico; Chico, Calif. 95929	13,798	Pub	2,006	9,386	4,740
California St. Univ.-Dominguez Hills; Carson, Calif. 90747	6,929	Pub	1,786	6,214	4,022
California State Univ.-Fresno; Fresno, Calif. 93740	15,279	Pub	1,600	5,042	5,227
California State Univ.-Fullerton; Fullerton, Calif. 92634	3,751	Pub	1,622	8,860	5,176
California State Univ.-Hayward; Hayward, Calif. 94542	9,888	Pub	1,776	4,528	4,345
California State Univ.-Long Beach; Long Beach, Calif. 90840	21,424	Pub	1,551	7,856	5,533
California State Univ.-Los Angeles; Los Angeles, Calif. 90032	13,882	Pub	1,710	6,606	2,805
California State Univ.-Northridge; Northridge, Calif. 91330–8207	6,825	Pub	1,970	7,874	3,540
California State Univ.-Sacramento; Sacramento, Calif. 95819	18,401	Pub	1,926	9,240	5,475
California State Univ.-San Bernardino; San Bernardino, Calif. 92407-2397	9,192	Pub	1,128	8,508	4,108
California State Univ.–San Marcos; San Marcos, Calif. 92096	1,998	Pub	1,800	7,704	n.a.
California State Univ.-Stanislaus; Turlock, Calif. 95382	5,972	Pub	1,905	8,547	5,650
California Univ. of Pennsylvania; California, Pa. 15419-1394	5,212	Pub	3,224	8,198	3,890
California, University of; Berkeley, Calif. 94720:					
UC-Berkeley; Berkeley, Calif. 94720	21,841	Pub	4,354	7,699	6,466
UC-Davis; Davis, Calif. 95616	17,273	Pub	4,230	8,394	5,283
UC-Irvine; Irvine, Calif. 92717	17,281	Pub	4,324	11,748	5,824
UC-Los Angeles; Los Angeles, Calif. 90095	23,649 [1]	Pub	3,900	12,300	5,859
UC-Riverside; Riverside, Calif. 92521	8,904	Pub	4,402	12,103	5,575
UC-San Diego; La Jolla, Calif. 92093	14,846	Pub	4,200	7,698	6,877
UC-Santa Barbara; Santa Barbara, Calif. 93106	15,525	Pub	4,098	11,797	5,901
UC-Santa Cruz; Santa Cruz, Calif. 95064	9,923	Pub	4,109	12,083 [1]	6,081
Calumet College of St. Joseph; Whiting, Ind. 46394	1,086	P	4,130	4,130	n.a.
Calvary Bible College; Kansas City, Mo. 64147	297 [1]	P	3,924	3,924	2,950
Calvin College; Grand Rapids, Mich. 49546	3,999	P	11,655	11,655	4,160
Cameron University; Lawton, Okla. 73505	5,988	Pub	1,297	2,430	2,947
Campbell University; Buies Creek, N.C. 27506	4,803 [1]	P	8,850	8,850	3,350
Campbellsville College; Campbellsville, Ky. 42718	1,260	P	6,420	6,420	3,210
Canisius College; Buffalo, N.Y. 14208	3,323	P	11,650	11,650	5,500
Capital University; Columbus, Ohio 43209	1,776	P	13,700	13,700	4,000
Capitol College; Laurel, Md. 20708	679	P	8,781	8,781	4,412
Cardinal Stritch College; Milwaukee, Wis. 53217	1,096	P	8,960	8,960	3,880
Carleton College; Northfield, Minn. 55057	1,752	P	26,300	26,300	4,125
Carlow College; Pittsburgh, Pa. 15213	2,177 (W)	P	10,730	10,730	4,692
Carnegie Mellon University; Pittsburgh, Pa. 15213	4,327	P	18,160	18,160	5,700
Carroll College; Helena, Mont. 59625	1,412	P	10,574	10,574	4,190
Carroll College; Waukesha, Wis. 53186	2,342	P	13,340	13,340	4,000
Carson-Newman College; Jefferson City, Tenn. 37760	2,207	P	9,000	9,000	3,980
Carthage College; Kenosha, Wis. 53140–1994	2,165	P	14,600	14,600	4,195
Cascade College; Portland, Ore. 97216	250	P	6,750	6,750	3,300
Case Western Reserve University; Cleveland, Ohio 44106	3,658	P	17,100	17,100	4,860
Castleton State College; Castleton, Vt. 05735	1,724	Pub	4,026	8,538	4,794
Catawba College; Salisbury, N.C. 28144	1,087	P	10,726	10,726	4,250
Catholic University of America; Washington, D.C. 20064	2,364	P	15,062	15,062	6,614
Cayey University College. *See* Puerto Rico, University of					
Cazenovia College; Cazenovia, N.Y. 13035	1,080	P	9,900	9,900	5,500
Cedar Crest College; Allentown, Pa. 18104-6196	1,342 (W)	P	14,770	14,770	5,365
Cedarville College; Cedarville, Ohio 45314	2,378	P	7,872	7,872	4,572
Centenary College; Hackettstown, N.J. 07840	343	P	11,100	11,100	5,500
Centenary College of Louisiana; Shreveport, La. 71104	780	P	9,800	9,800	3,690
Center for Creative Studies, College of Art and Design; Detroit, Mich. 48202	850	P	13,110	13,110	5,000
Central Arkansas, University of; Conway, Ark. 72032	8,525	Pub	2,000	3,586	2,600
Central Baptist College; Conway, Ark. 72032	307	P	3,792	3,792	2,880
Central Bible College; Springfield, Mo. 65803	969	P	4,200	4,200	2,930
Central Christian College of the Bible; Moberly, Mo. 65270	116	P	3,424	3,424	2,500
Central College; Pella, Iowa 50219	1,453	P	12,152	12,152	3,808
Central Connecticut State University; New Britain, Conn. 06050	6,088	Pub	3,266	8,358	4,952
Central Florida, University of; Orlando, Fla. 32816	26,174	Pub	1,840	6,742	4,490
Central Methodist College; Fayette, Mo. 65248	1,002	P	9,430	9,430	3,600
Central Michigan University; Mt. Pleasant, Mich. 48859	14,582	Pub	3,050	7,818	4,036
Central Missouri State University; Warrensburg, Mo. 64093	9,239	Pub	2,460	4,920	3,538
Central Oklahoma, University of; Edmond, Okla. 73034-0172	12,042	Pub	1,518	3,580	2,391
Central State University; Wilberforce, Ohio 45384	3,263	Pub	2,895	6,432	4,575
Central Texas, University of; Killeen, Tex. 76540	988	P	3,160	3,160	4,698

Institution and location	Enrollment	Control	Tuition ($) Res.	Nonres.	Rm/Bd ($)
Central Washington University; Ellensburg, Wash. 98926–7463	8,512	Pub	2,343	8,289	3,996
Central Wesleyan College; Central, S.C. 29630	1,349	P	8,882	8,882	3,234
Centre College; Danville, Ky. 40422–1394	970	P	13,000	13,000	4,300
Chadron State College; Chadron, Neb. 69337	2,371	Pub	1,459	2,419	2,814
Chaminade University of Honolulu; Honolulu, Hawaii 96816	800	P	10,600	10,600	3,225
Chapman University; Orange, Calif. 92666	2,204	Pub	17,976	17,976	6,454
Charleston Southern University; Charleston, S.C. 29423–8087	3,562	P	8,724	8,724	3,360
Charleston, College of; Charleston, S.C. 29424	7,821	Pub	3,190	6,380	3,690
Charleston, University of; Charleston, W. Va. 25304	1,382	P	10,400	10,400	5,910
Charter Oak State College; Newington, Conn. 06111	1,216[1]	Pub	585	765	n.a.
Chatham College; Pittsburgh, Pa. 15232	725 (W)	P	14,040	14,040	5,440
Chestnut Hill College; Philadelphia, Pa. 19118-2695	728 (W)	P	11,825	11,825	5,445
Cheyney University of Pennsylvania; Cheyney, Pa. 19319	1,084	Pub	3,591	6,128	3,906
Chicago State University; Chicago, Ill. 60628	6,542	Pub	2,336	6,272	4,990
Chicago, University of—The College; Chicago, Ill. 60637	3,447[1]	P	20,378	20,378	7,258
Chowan College; Murfreesboro, N.C. 27855	816	P	9,200	9,200	3,660
Christendom College; Front Royal, Va. 22630	178	P	9,994	9,994	3,600
Christian Brothers University; Memphis, Tenn. 38104	1,085	P	10,000	10,000	3,500
Christian Heritage College; El Cajon, Calif. 92019	454	P	9,240	9,240	4,120
Christian Life College; Stockton, Calif. 95210	173[1]	P	2,475	2,475	2,500
Christopher Newport University; Newport News, Va. 23606-2998	4,788	Pub	3,350	7,946	4,750
Cincinnati Bible College; Cincinnati, Ohio 45204	609	P	4,770	4,770	3,450
Cincinnati College of Mortuary Science; Cincinnati, Ohio 45224–1428	82	P	7,875	7,875	n.a.
Cincinnati, University of; Cincinnati, Ohio 45221–0091	13,231	Pub	3,918	9,873	4,881
Circleville Bible College; Circleville, Ohio 43113	186	P	4,028	4,028	3,628
Citadel-The Military College of South Carolina; Charleston, S.C. 29409	2,000[1]	Pub	10,170	14,164	3,690
City University; Bellevue, Wash. 98004	1,442	P	4,082[1]	4,082[1]	n.a.
City College (NYC). *See* New York, City University of					
Claflin College; Orangeburg, S.C. 29115	756[1]	P	4,412	4,412	2,460
Claremont Colleges:					
Claremont McKenna College; Claremont, Calif. 91711-6420	877	P	17,700	17,790	6,000
Harvey Mudd College; Claremont, Calif. 91711-5990	616	P	18,100	18,100	6,920
Pitzer College; Claremont, Calif. 91711	750	P	19,360	19,360	6,274
Pomona College; Claremont, Calif. 91711	1,402	P	19,530	19,530	7,860
Scripps College; Claremont, Calif. 91711	684 (W)	P	18,180	18,180	7,500
Clarion University of Pennsylvania; Clarion, Pa. 16214	5,860	Pub	3,224	8,198	2,976
Clark Atlanta University; Atlanta, Ga. 30314	3,914	P	8,300	8,300	5,670
Clark University; Worcester, Mass. 01610–1477	2,100	P	19,600	19,600	4,250
Clarke College; Dubuque, Iowa 52001	1,020	P	11,966	11,966	4,480
Clarkson College; Omaha, Neb. 68131–2739	450	P	6,000	6,000	3,450
Clarkson University; Potsdam, N.Y. 13699	2,249	P	17,500	17,500	6,064
Clayton State College; Morrow, Ga. 30260–1221	4,896	Pub	2,256	6,336	n.a.
Clearwater Christian College; Clearwater, Fla. 34619–9997	451	P	6,500	6,500	3,400
Cleary College; Ypsilanti, Mich. 48197	940[1]	P	3,734	3,734	n.a.
Clemson University; Clemson, S.C. 29634–5124	12,302	Pub	3,162	8,366	3,770
Cleveland College of Jewish Studies; Beachwood, Ohio 44122	400	P	3,960	3,960	n.a.
Cleveland Institute of Art; Cleveland, Ohio 44106	48	P	11,900	11,900	4,510
Cleveland Institute of Music; Cleveland, Ohio 44106	201[1]	P	15,726	15,726	4,855
Cleveland State University; Cleveland, Ohio 44115	11,966	Pub	3,336	6,671	2,784
Clinch Valley College. *See* Virginia, University of					
Coastal Carolina University; Conway, S.C. 29526	4,468	Pub	2,880	7,470	2,720
Coe College; Cedar Rapids, Iowa 52402	1,359	P	15,410	15,410	4,455
Cogswell College; Sunnyvale, Calif. 94089	230	P	7,320	7,320	n.a.
Cogswell College North; Kirkland, Wash. 98033	200	P	12,780	12,780	n.a.
Coker College; Hartsville, S.C. 29550	894	P	12,182	12,182	4,516
Colby College; Waterville, Me. 04901	1,650	P	20,990	20,990	5,650
Colby-Sawyer College; New London, N.H. 03257	675	P	15,530	15,530	5,950
Coleman College; La Mesa, Calif. 92041	180	P	6,000	6,000	n.a.
Colgate University; Hamilton, N.Y. 13346	2,740	P	20,500	20,500	5,765
College Misericordia; Dallas, Pa. 18612	1,614	P	12,200	12,200	6,000
Colorado Christian University; Lakewood, Colo. 80226	1,718	P	7,555	7,555	3,710
Colorado College; Colorado Springs, Colo. 80903–3298	19	P	18,084	18,084	4,562
Colorado School of Mines; Golden, Colo. 80401	2,207	Pub	4,392	13,134	4,400
Colorado State University; Fort Collins, Colo. 80523	17,800	Pub	2,779	9,387	4,920
Colorado Technical University; Colorado Springs, Colo. 80907	1,459	P	6,075	6,075	n.a.
Colorado, University of: Boulder, Colo. 80309:					
U. of Colorado-Boulder; Boulder, Colo. 80309	20,407	Pub	2,270	13,338	2,081
U. of Colorado-Colorado Springs; Colorado Springs, Colo. 80933	5,906	Pub	3,318	8,422	5,400
U. of Colorado-Denver; Denver, Colo. 80204	6,128	Pub	2,265	9,759	n.a.
Columbia College–Chicago; Chicago, Ill. 60605	7,308 (W)	P	7,310	7,310	4,350
Columbia College; Columbia, S.C. 29203	1,311 (W)	P	11,535	11,535	4,160
Columbia College-Hollywood; Los Angeles, Calif. 90038	4	P	5,820	5,820	n.a.
Columbia International University; Columbia, S.C. 29230	473	P	7,300	7,300	3,970

Institution and location	Enrollment	Control	Tuition ($) Res.	Tuition ($) Nonres.	Rm/Bd ($)
Columbia Union College; Takoma Park, Md. 20912	979	P	10,995	10,995	3,990
Columbia University; New York, N.Y. 10027	1,000	P	16,884	16,884	7,664
Columbia University-Columbia College; New York, N.Y. 10027	3,573	P	19,730	19,730	6,864
Columbus College; Columbus, Ga. 31907–5645	4,832	Pub	1,740	4,950	3,486
Columbus College of Art and Design; Columbus, Ohio 43215	1,695	P	10,300	10,300	5,700
Conception Seminary College; Conception, Mo. 64433	84 (M)	P	6,742	6,742	3,174
Concord College; Athens, W. Va. 24712	2,623	Pub	2,150	2,325	3,382
Concordia College; Ann Arbor, Mich. 48105	611	P	11,210	11,210	4,650
Concordia College; Bronxville, N.Y. 10708	620	P	11,400	11,400	5,310
Concordia College; Moorhead, Minn. 56562	2,958	P	11,570	11,570	3,400
Concordia College; Portland, Ore. 97211	976	P	11,030	11,030	3,530
Concordia College; St. Paul, Minn. 55104	1,187	P	11,355	11,355	4,200
Concordia College; Seward, Neb. 68434	919	P	9,480	9,480	3,470
Concordia Lutheran College; Austin, Tex. 78705	800	P	7,380	7,380	3,800
Concordia University; Irvine, Calif. 92715	926	P	12,250	12,250	4,920
Concordia University at Austin; Austin, Texas 78705	700	P	8,000	8,000	4,050
Concordia University Wisconsin; Mequon, Wis. 53092	2,091 [1]	P	10,000	10,000	3,600
Concordia University; River Forest, Ill. 60305	1,316	P	9,888	9,888	4,443
Connecticut College; New London, Conn. 06320	1,600	P	26,325	26,325	n.a.
Connecticut, University of; Storrs, Conn. 06269	11,386	Pub	4,810	12,800	5,124
Conservatory of Music of Puerto Rico; Hato Rey, P.R. 00918	283	Pub	670	670	n.a.
Converse College; Spartanburg, S.C. 29301	659 (W)	P	13,150	13,150	3,825
Cooper Union; New York, N.Y. 10003	960	P	8,300	8,300	5,015
Coppin State College; Baltimore, Md. 21216	2,638	Pub	2,749	5,963	4,640
Corcoran School of Art; Washington, D.C. 20006	268	P	11,550	11,550	7,150
Cornell College; Mt. Vernon, Iowa 52314	1,133 [1]	P	17,220	17,220	4,670
Cornell University; Ithaca, N.Y. 14853	13,228	P	20,066	20,066	6,762
Cornish College of the Arts; Seattle, Wash. 98102	603	P	10,540	10,540	5,000
Covenant College; Lookout Mountain, Ga. 30750	707	P	11,450	11,450	3,960
Creighton University; Omaha, Neb. 68178	6,370	P	11,562	11,562	4,548
Crichton College; Memphis, Tenn. 38175-7830	358 [1]	P	5,640	5,640	3,200
Crown College; St. Bonifacius, Minn. 55375-9001	620	P	8,340	8,340	3,920
Culver-Stockton College; Canton, Mo. 63435	1,001	P	8,800	8,800	4,000
Cumberland College; Williamsburg, Ky. 40769	1,505	P	7,898	7,898	3,676
Cumberland University of Tennessee; Lebanon, Tenn. 37087	980	P	7,150	7,150	3,220
Curry College; Milton, Mass. 02186	1,722	P	14,804	14,804	5,740
C. W. Post. *See* Long Island Univ. Center					
D'Youville College; Buffalo, N.Y. 14201	1,433	P	9,510	9,510	4,600
Daemen College; Amherst, N.Y. 14226	1,855	P	9,720	9,720	4,900
Dakota State University; Madison, S.D. 57042	1,356	Pub	2,480	4,608	2,640
Dakota Wesleyan University; Mitchell, S.D. 57301	704	P	7,992	7,992	2,925
Dallas Baptist University; Dallas, Tex. 75211	2,989	P	7,110	7,110	3,413
Dallas Christian College; Dallas, Tex. 75234	99	P	3,400	3,400	2,700
Dallas, University of; Irving, Tex. 75062	1,103	P	11,380	11,380	4,830
Dana College; Blair, Neb. 68008-1099	661	P	10,500	10,500	3,630
Daniel Webster College; Nashua, N.H. 03063–1300	474	P	12,292	12,292	4,934
Dartmouth College; Hanover, N.H. 03755	4,286	P	21,846	21,846	6,129
Davenport College; Grand Rapids, Mich. 49503	4,077	P	4,128	4,128	3,625
David Lipscomb University; Nashville, Tenn. 37204-3951	2,346	P	6,818	6,818	3,450
Davidson College; Davidson, N.C. 28036	1,614	P	18,626	18,626	5,364
Davis and Elkins College; Elkins, W. Va. 26241	782	P	10,580	10,580	4,890
Dayton, University of; Dayton, Ohio 45469–1611	6,435	P	12,350	12,350	4,360
Defiance College, The; Defiance, Ohio 43512	965	P	12,950	12,950	3,800
Delaware State University; Dover, Del. 19901	3,292	Pub	2,390	5,872	4,310
Delaware Valley College; Doylestown, Pa. 18901	1,350 [1]	P	13,208	13,208	5,290
Delaware, University of; Newark, Del. 19716	14,870	P	3,860	10,730	4,420
Delta State University; Cleveland, Miss. 38733	3,887	Pub	2,294	4,888	2,180
Denison University; Granville, Ohio 43023	1,995	P	18,570	18,570	5,160
Denver, University of; Denver, Colo. 80208	2,996	P	16,740	16,740	5,304
The Women's College; Denver, Colo. 80220	420 [1](W)	P	7,830	7,830	n.a
DePaul University; Chicago, Ill. 60604	9,783	P	8,892	8,892	5,000
DePauw University; Greencastle, Ind. 46135	2,102	P	15,175	15,175	5,245
Deree College-Division of the American College of Greece; Athens, Greece GR-153 42	4,182	P	1,456	1,456	n.a.
Design Institute of San Diego; San Diego, Calif. 92121	195	P	8,500	8,500	n.a.
Detroit College of Business; Dearborn, Mich. 48126	5,111 [1]	P	3,936	3,936	n.a.
Detroit Mercy, University of; Detroit, Mich. 48221	4,628	P	6,268	6,268	6,054
DeVry Institute of Technology; Addison, Ill. 60101–6106	3,116	P	6,560	6,560	n.a.
DeVry Institute of Technology; Chicago, Ill. 60618-5994	2,915	P	6,560	6,560	n.a.
DeVry Institute of Technology; Columbus, Ohio 43209-2764	2,585	P	6,560	6,560	n.a.
DeVry Institute of Technology; Decatur, Ga. 30030-2198	2,971	P	6,560	6,560	n.a.
DeVry Institute of Technology; Irving, Tex. 75063-2440	2,315	P	6,280	6,280	n.a.
DeVry Institute of Technology; Kansas City, Mo. 64131-3626	1,965	P	6,560	6,560	n.a.
DeVry Institute of Technology; Long Beach, Calif. 90806	971,	P	6,560	6,560	n.a.

Institution and location	Enrollment	Control	Tuition ($) Res.	Tuition ($) Nonres.	Rm/Bd ($)
DeVry Institute of Technology; Phoenix, Ariz. 85021–2995	2,714	P	6,560	6,560	n.a.
DeVry Institute of Technology University Center; Pomona, Calif. 91768–2642	2,988	P	6,560	6,560	n.a.
Dickinson College; Carlisle, Pa. 17013	2,916	P	19,750	19,750	5,270
Dickinson State University; Dickinson, N.D. 58601	1,591	Pub	1,890	4,732	2,250
Dillard University; New Orleans, La. 70122–3097	1,580	P	7,000	7,000	3,750
District of Columbia, Univ. of the; Washington, D.C. 20008	10,599	Pub	1,118	4,142	1,046
Divine Word College; Epworth, Iowa 52045	71 (M)	P	7,000	7,000	1,200
Doane College; Crete, Neb. 68333	885	P	10,410	10,410	3,165
Dominican College of Blauvelt; Orangeburg, N.Y. 10962	1,786	P	8,940	8,940	5,740
Dominican College of San Rafael; San Rafael, Calif. 94901–2298	936	P	14,380	14,380	6,700
Dominican School of Philosophy and Theology; Berkeley, Calif. 94709	8	P	6,360	6,360	n.a.
Dordt College; Sioux Center, Iowa 51250	1,209	P	10,800	10,800	2,900
Dowling College; Oakdale, N.Y. 11769	3,666	P	10,300	10,300	3,100
Drake University; Des Moines, Iowa 50311	3,802	P	14,380	14,380	5,100
Drew University-College of Liberal Arts; Madison, N.J. 07940	1,290	P	19,638	19,638	5,883
Drexel University; Philadelphia, Pa. 19104	7,269	P	13,305	13,305	4,851
Drury College; Springfield, Mo. 65802	1,110	P	9,391	9,391	3,696
Dubuque, University of; Dubuque, Iowa 52001	880	P	11,680	11,680	4,340
Duke University; Durham, N.C. 27706	6,264	P	20,520	20,520	6,605
Duquesne University; Pittsburgh, Pa. 15282	9,285	P	12,578	12,578	5,580
Dyke College; Cleveland, Ohio 44115	360	P	5,760	5,760	n.a.
Earlham College; Richmond, Ind. 47374	1,017	P	17,362	17,362	4,412
East Carolina University; Greenville, N.C. 27858–4353	14,342	Pub	840	7,682	3,420
East Central University; Ada, Okla. 74820-6899	4,478	Pub	1,490	3,553	2,068
East Stroudsburg University of Pennsylvania; East Stroudsburg, Pa. 18301	4,558	Pub	7,465	12,439	3,448
East Tennessee State University; Johnson City, Tenn. 37614	11,291	Pub	1,888	6,018	3,320
East Texas Baptist University; Marshall, Tex. 75670	1,204 [1]	P	6,260	6,260	3,000
East Texas State University; Commerce, Tex. 75429	5,485	Pub	1,424	4,856	3,384
East-West University; Chicago, Ill. 60605	238	P	6,880	6,880	n.a.
Eastern College; St. Davids, Pa. 19087-3696	1,536	P	11,750	11,750	5,036
Eastern Connecticut State Univ.; Willimantic, Conn. 06226	2,695	Pub	3,202	8,294	5,248
Eastern Illinois University; Charleston, Ill. 61920	842	Pub	2,778	6,716	3,244
Eastern Kentucky University; Richmond, Ky. 40475	3,288	Pub	1,900	5,260	3,460
Eastern Mennonite College; Harrisonburg, Va. 22801	947	P	11,200	11,200	4,200
Eastern Michigan University; Ypsilanti, Mich. 48197	19,563 [1]	Pub	2,730	7,110	4,272
Eastern Nazarene College; Quincy, Mass. 02170	664	P	10,160	10,160	3,600
Eastern New Mexico University; Portales, N.M. 88130	3,296	Pub	1,575	5,817	2,911
Eastern Oregon State College; La Grande, Ore. 97850	1,931	Pub	2,900	2,900	3,800
Eastern Washington University; Cheney, Wash. 99004	7,041	Pub	7,572	15,524	5,560
Eastman School of Music; Rochester, N.Y. 14604	493	P	17,000	17,000	6,730
Eckerd College; St. Petersburg, Fla. 33711	1,366	P	15,975	15,975	4,325
Edgewood College; Madison, Wis. 53711	1,690 [1]	P	9,500	9,500	3,500
Edinboro University of Pennsylvania; Edinboro, Pa. 16444	6,762	Pub	3,224	8,198	3,578
Edward Waters College; Jacksonville, Fla. 32209	773 [1]	P	4,400	4,400	4,500
Electronic Data Processing College of Puerto Rico; Hato Rey, P.R. 00918	1,176	P	2,640	2,640	n.a.
Elizabeth City State University; Elizabeth City, N.C. 27909	1,694	Pub	1,360	7,710	3,264
Elizabethtown College; Elizabethtown, Pa. 17022	1,753	P	16,040	16,040	4,700
Elmhurst College; Elmhurst, Ill. 60126-3296	1,604	P	10,264	10,264	4,390
Elmira College; Elmira, N.Y. 14901	1,104	P	17,550	17,550	5,880
Elms College; Chicopee, Mass. 01013-2839	1,093 (W)	P	12,450	12,450	5,000
Elon College; Elon College, N.C. 27244	3,479	P	10,477	10,477	4,170
Embry-Riddle Aeronautical Univ.; Prescott, Ariz. 86301	1,381	P	8,610	8,610	4,080
Emerson College; Boston, Mass. 02116	2,087	P	15,936	15,936	7,850
Emmanuel College; Boston, Mass. 02115	1,421	P	13,700	13,700	6,525
Emmanuel College; Franklin Springs, Ga. 30639	527	P	5,300	5,300	3,950
Emory and Henry College; Emory, Va. 24327	844	P	10,260	10,260	4,502
Emory University; Atlanta, Ga. 30322	5,100	P	19,000	19,000	6,220
Emporia State University; Emporia, Kan. 66801	4,476	Pub	1,758	5,776	3,220
Endicott College; Beverly, Mass. 01915	1,063 (W)	P	12,475	12,475	6,625
Erskine College; Due West, S.C. 29639	546	P	11,156	11,156	4,086
Esther Boyer College of Music; Philadelphia, Pa. 19122	350 [1]	Pub	5,389	5,389	5,282
ETI Technical College; Cleveland, Ohio 44114	361	P	6,192	6,192	3,850
Eugene Bible College; Eugene, Ore. 97405	261	P	4,977	4,977	3,048
Eureka College; Eureka, Ill. 61530	525 [1]	P	13,066	13,066	4,142
Evangel College; Springfield, Mo. 65802	1,420	P	7,300	7,300	3,170
Evansville, University of; Evansville, Ind. 47722	3,185	P	12,990	12,990	4,710
Evergreen State College; Olympia, Wash. 98505	3,250 [1]	Pub	2,256	7,974	4,000
Fairfield University; Fairfield, Conn. 06430	2,901	P	16,340	16,340	6,600
Fairhaven College; Bellingham, Wash. 98225–9118	400	Pub	2,721	8,290	4,500

Institution and location	Enrollment	Control	Tuition ($) Res.	Tuition ($) Nonres.	Rm/Bd ($)
Fairleigh Dickinson Univ.-Madison; Madison, N.J. 07940	2,501	P	11,610	11,610	5,550
Fairleigh Dickinson Univ.-Rutherford; Rutherford, N.J. 07070	1,505	P	11,081	11,081	5,900
Fairleigh Dickinson Univ.-Teaneck; Teaneck, N.J. 07666	4,557	P	11,610	11,610	5,550
Fairmont State College; Fairmont, W. Va. 26554–2491	6,547	Pub	1,858	4,328	3,360
Faith Baptist Bible College; Ankeny, Iowa 50021	222	P	5,800	5,800	3,160
Faulkner University; Montgomery, Ala. 36109–3398	2,363 [1]	P	6,240	6,240	3,400
Fayetteville State University; Fayetteville, N.C. 28301	3,251	Pub	1,560	8,402	3,000
Felician College; Lodi, N.J. 07644	1,068	P	8,550	8,550	n.a.
Ferris State University; Big Rapids, Mich. 49307	9,991	Pub	3,532	7,153	4,499
Ferrum College; Ferrum, Va. 24088	1,124	P	9,950	9,950	4,550
Findlay, University of; Findlay, Ohio 45840	3,190 [1]	P	12,500	12,500	5,210
Fisk University; Nashville, Tenn. 37208	900 [1]	P	6,990	6,990	3,948
Fitchburg State College; Fitchburg, Mass. 01420	4,500	Pub	1,408	5,542	3,870
Five Towns College; Dix Hills, N.Y. 11746–6055	684	P	8,100	8,100	4,800
Flagler College; St. Augustine, Fla. 32085	1,426	P	5,530	5,530	3,460
Florida Agriculture and Mechanical University; Tallahassee, Fla. 32307	9,879	Pub	2,651	6,669	3,289
Florida Atlantic University; Boca Raton, Fla. 33431-0991	12,211	Pub	1,788	6,693	3,950
Florida Baptist Theological College; Graceville, Fla. 32440	535	P	2,880	2,880	3,000
Florida Christian College; Kissimmee, Fla. 34744	152	P	2,952	2,952	2,820
Florida Institute of Technology; Melbourne, Fla. 32901–6975	1,780	P	14,111	14,111	4,264
Florida International University; Miami, Fla. 33199	18,636	Pub	1,448	5,360	3,647
Florida Memorial College; Miami, Fla. 33054	1,500	P	4,940	4,940	3,190
Florida Southern College; Lakeland, Fla. 33801	1,760 [1]	P	9,350	9,350	5,100
Florida State University; Tallahassee, Fla. 32306	22,554	Pub	1,800	6,700	4,500
Florida, University of; Gainesville, Fla. 32611–8140	28,479	Pub	1,830	7,100	5,430
Fontbonne College; St. Louis, Mo. 63105	1,532	P	9,040	9,040	4,460
Fordham University; Bronx, N.Y. 10458	6,393	P	14,900	14,900	7,473
Forsyth School for Dental Hygienists; Boston, Mass. 02115	108 [1]	P	11,860	11,860	8,010
Fort Hays State University; Hays, Kan. 67601	4,266	Pub	1,902	6,169	3,172
Fort Lauderdale College; Fort Lauderdale, Fla. 33304	427	P	4,428	4,428	6,280 [1]
Fort Lewis College; Durango, Colo. 81301	4,300	Pub	1,558	7,118	2,789
Fort Valley State College; Fort Valley, Ga. 31030	2,549	Pub	1,920	5,130	2,805
Framingham State College; Framingham, Mass. 01701	3,106	Pub	3,394	6,578	3,719
Francis Marion University; Florence, S.C. 29501–0547	3,550	Pub	2,920	5,840	3,138
Franciscan University of Steubenville; Steubenville, Ohio 43952	1,533	P	10,230	10,230	4,500
Franklin and Marshall College; Lancaster, Pa. 17604-3003	1,866	P	21,940	21,940	4,460
Franklin College; Franklin, Ind. 46131	909	P	10,950	10,950	4,210
Franklin College; Switzerland	240	P	16,900	16,900	7,000
Franklin Pierce College; Rindge, N.H. 03461	1,164	P	13,935	13,935	4,900
Franklin University; Columbus, Ohio 43215-5399	3,990	P	5,644	5,644	n.a.
Free Will Baptist Bible College; Nashville, Tenn. 37205	346	P	4,544	4,544	3,955
Freed-Hardeman University; Henderson, Tenn. 38340	1,504	P	6,208	6,208	3,780
Fresno Pacific College; Fresno, Calif. 93702	488	P	10,500	10,500	3,500
Friends University; Wichita, Kan. 67213	2,138	P	9,505	9,505	3,140
Friends World Program; Southampton, N.Y. 11968	n.a.	P	12,500	12,500	5,000
Frostburg State University; Frostburg, Md. 21532	4,950	Pub	3,280	6,990	5,292
Furman University; Greenville, S.C. 29613–0645	2,417	P	15,360	15,360	4,304
Gallaudet University; Washington, D.C. 20002	1,486	P	6,650	6,650	6,270
Gannon University; Erie, Pa. 16541	3,095	P	11,410	11,410	4,710
Gannon University–Villa Marie Campus; Erie, Pa. 16505	2,632 (W)	P	10,350	10,350	4,560
Gardner-Webb College; Boiling Springs, N.C. 28017	1,460 [1]	P	8,990	8,990	4,460
General Motors Institute. See GMI Engineering and Management Institute					
Geneva College; Beaver Falls, Pa. 15010	1,579	P	10,700	10,700	4,600
George Fox College; Newberg, Ore. 97132	1,251	P	14,300	14,300	4,640
George Mason University; Fairfax, Va. 22030	13,510	Pub	4,212	11,604	5,050
George Washington University, The; Washington, D.C. 20052	5,900	P	19,032	19,032	6,590
Georgetown College; Georgetown, Ky. 40324	1,153	P	9,540	9,540	4,050
Georgetown University; Washington, D.C. 20057	6,229	P	19,230	19,230	7,100
Georgia Baptist College of Nursing; Atlanta, Ga. 30312-1239	415 (W)	P	6,048	6,048	4,739
Georgia College; Milledgeville, Ga. 31061	4,551	Pub	1,922	5,801	3,345
Georgia Institute of Technology; Atlanta, Ga. 30332	9,240	Pub	2,457	7,638	4,896
Georgia Southern University; Statesboro, Ga. 30458	12,245 [1]	Pub	1,965	5,175	3,546
Georgia Southwestern College; Americus, Ga. 31709	2,607	Pub	1,926	5,136	2,940
Georgia State University; Atlanta, Ga. 30303	17,161	Pub	2,000	7,200	n.a.
Georgia, University of; Athens, Ga. 30602	22,832 [1]	Pub	2,542	6,829	3,820
Georgian Court College; Lakewood, N.J. 08701–2697	1,843 (W)	P	9,750	9,750	4,150
Gettysburg College; Gettysburg, Pa. 17325–1484	2,100	P	20,800	20,800	4,522
Glenville State College; Glenville, W. Va. 26351	2,417	Pub	1,800	4,200	3,300
GMI Engineering & Management Institute; Flint, Mich. 48504	2,367 [1]	P	12,480	12,480	3,502
God's Bible School and College; Cincinnati, Ohio 45210	184	P	3,560	3,560	2,550
Goddard College; Plainfield, Vt. 05667	466	P	14,632	14,362	5,084
Golden Gate University; San Francisco, Calif. 94105	2,027	P	6,360	6,360	n.a.
Goldey Beacom College; Wilmington, Del. 19808	1,757	P	6,780	6,780	3,135

Institution and location	Enrollment	Control	Tuition ($)		Rm/Bd ($)
			Res.	Nonres.	
Gonzaga University; Spokane, Wash. 99258	2,938	P	13,957	13,957	4,800
Gordon College, Wenham, Mass 01984	1,229	P	14,060	14,060	4,760
Goshen College; Goshen, Ind. 46526	1,081	P	10,900	10,900	3,880
Goucher College; Baltimore, Md. 21204	909	P	16,530	16,530	6,360
Governors State University; University Park, Ill. 60466	2,912	Pub	3,147	9,051	n.a.
Grace Bible College; Grand Rapids, Mich. 49509	153	P	5,000	5,000	3,400
Grace College; Winona Lake, Ind. 46590	688	P	9,500	9,500	4,070
Grace University; Omaha, Neb. 68108	414[1]	P	4,950	4,950	2,850
Graceland College; Lamoni, Iowa 50140	1,058	P	9,760	9,760	3,200
Grambling State University; Grambling, La. 71245	188	Pub	2,088	4,038	2,636
Grand Canyon University; Phoenix, Ariz. 85017	1,641	P	8,250	8,250	3,260
Grand Rapids Baptist College; Grand Rapids, Mich. 49505	777	P	6,520	6,520	4,082
Grand Valley State University; Allendale, Mich. 49401-9401	13,887	Pub	2,780	6,462	4,180
Grand View College; Des Moines, Iowa 50316	1,477	P	10,470	10,470	3,500
Gratz College; Melrose Park , Pa. 19126	65	P	6,400	6,400	n.a.
Great Falls, College of; Great Falls, Mont. 59405	1,237	P	5,170	5,170	1,780
Great Lakes Christian College; Lansing, Mich. 48917	190	P	5,440	5,440	3,200
Green Mountain College; Poultney, Vt. 05764	494	P	13,180	13,180	2,920
Greensboro College; Greensboro, N.C. 27401–1875	1,017	P	9,150	9,150	3,840
Greenville College; Greenville, Ill. 62246	781	P	10,950	10,950	4,750
Grinnell College; Grinnell, Iowa 50112	1,243	P	16,636	16,636	4,782
Grove City College; Grove City, Pa. 16127	2,302	P	6,478	6,478	3,652
Guam, University of; Mangilao, Guam 96913	2,626	Pub	1,500	2,528	2,905
Guilford College; Greensboro, N.C. 27410	1,187	P	14,390	14,390	5,270
Gustavus Adolphus College; St. Peter, Minn. 56082	2,361	P	15,350	15,350	3,900
Gwynedd-Mercy College; Gwynedd Valley, Pa. 19437	1,837	P	11,450	11,450	5,800
Hahnemann University School of Health Sciences and Humanities; Philadelphia, Pa. 19102	917	P	8,800	8,800	4,600
Hamilton College; Clinton, N.Y. 13323	1,710[1]	P	21,500	21,500	5,450
Hamline University; St. Paul, Minn. 55104	1,491	P	13,808	13,808	4,342
Hampden-Sydney College; Hampden-Sydney, Va. 23943	970 (M)	P	14,336	14,336	5,176
Hampshire College; Amherst, Mass. 01002	1,073	P	22,600	22,600	5,990
Hampton University; Hampton, Va. 23668	5,582	P	7,764	7,764	3,518
Hannibal-LaGrange College; Hannibal, Mo. 63401	949	P	6,880	6,880	2,610
Hanover College; Hanover, Ind. 47243	1,086	P	9,250	9,250	3,915
Hardin-Simmons University; Abilene, Tex. 79698	1,802	P	5,760	5,760	3,200
Harding University; Searcy, Ark. 72149	4,081	P	6,825	6,825	3,900
Harrington Institute of Interior Design; Chicago, Ill. 60605	396	P	9,424	9,424	n.a.
Harris Stowe State College; St. Louis, Mo. 63103	1,480[1]	Pub	1,671	3,240	n.a.
Hartford College for Women; Hartford, Conn. 06105	214 (W)	P	13,600	13,600	6,740
Hartford, University of; West Hartford, Conn. 06117	5,222	P	15,600	15,600	6,580
Hartwick College; Oneonta, N.Y. 13820	1,522	P	18,975	18,975	5,310
Harvard and Radcliffe Colleges; Cambridge, Mass. 02138	6,643	P	18,838	18,838	6,710
Harvey Mudd College. *See* Claremont Colleges					
Hastings College; Hastings, Neb. 68901	1,089	P	9,754	9,754	3,472
Haverford College; Haverford, Pa. 19041-1392	1,115	P	20,692	20,692	6,810
Hawaii Pacific University; Honolulu, Hawaii 96813	8,016	P	7,100	7,100	6,900
Hawaii Pacific University–Hawaii Loa Campus; Kaneohe, Hawaii 96744	6,975	P	6,700	6,700	6,500
Hawaii, Univ. of-Hilo; Hilo, Hawaii 96720-4091	2,670	Pub	504	3,096	4,914
Hawaii, University of-Manoa; Honolulu, Hawaii 96822	13,225	Pub	1,558	4,558	4,400
Hawaii, University of-West Oahu; Pearl City, Hawaii 96782	744	Pub	1,392	5,763	n.a.
Health Sciences, University of-The Chicago Medical School; North Chicago, Ill. 60064	77	P	29,106	29,106	n.a.
Hebrew Theological College; Skokie, Ill. 60077	218	P	6,370	6,370	4,625
Heidelberg College; Tiffin, Ohio 44883	1,167	P	14,606	14,606	4,674
Hellenic College; Brookline, Mass. 02146	5	P	7,280	7,280	5,360
Henderson State University; Arkadelphia, Ark. 71923	3,442	Pub	1,824	3,648	2,680
Hendrix College; Conway, Ark. 72023	953	P	9,453	9,453	3,500
Henry Cogswell College; Kirkland, Wash. 98033	200	P	8,520	8,520	n.a.
Herbert H. Lehman College. *See* New York, City University of					
Heritage College; Toppenish, Wash. 98948	517	P	7,919	7,919	n.a.
High Point University; High Point, N.C. 27262-3598	2,516	P	9,880	9,880	4,570
Hillsdale College; Hillsdale, Mich. 49242	1,162	P	12,110	12,110	5,180
Hillsdale Free Will Baptist College; Moore, Okla. 73153	152	P	3,270	3,270	3,400
Hiram College; Hiram, Ohio 44234	847	P	15,000	15,000	4,722
Hobart and William Smith Colleges; Geneva, N.Y. 14456	1,808	P	20,393	20,393	6,075
Hofstra University; Hempstead, N.Y. 11550	7,662	P	11,710	11,710	5,920
Hollins College; Roanoke, Va. 24020	882 (W)	P	14,234	14,234	5,745
Holy Apostles College and Seminary; Cromwell, Conn. 06416	70	P	4,290	4,290	6,150
Holy Cross, College of the; Worcester, Mass. 01610	2,742	P	18,355[1]	18,355[1]	6,300
Holy Family College; Philadelphia, Pa. 19114	2,278	P	10,120	10,120	n.a.
Holy Names College; Oakland, Calif. 94619	603	P	12,000	12,000	4,080
Hong Kong Baptist College; Kowloon, Hong Kong	3,652	Pub	2,200	2,200	n.a.
Hood College; Frederick, Md 21701	1,099 (W)	P	14,780	14,780	6,400
Hope College, Holland, Mich. 49423	2,825	P	13,234	13,234	4,516

Institution and location	Enrollment	Control	Tuition ($) Res.	Nonres.	Rm/Bd ($)
Houghton College; Houghton, N.Y. 14744	1,357	P	10,890	10,890	3,720
Houston Baptist University; Houston, Tex. 77074	1,700	P	7,200	7,200	2,580
Houston, Univ. of; Houston, Tex. 77204-2161	30,757	Pub	1,462	6,598	4,405
Houston, Univ. of-Clear Lake; Houston, Tex. 77058	3,613	Pub	1,881	6,261	n.a.
Houston, Univ. of-Downtown; Houston, Tex. 77002	7,676	Pub	840	5,130	n.a.
Houston, Univ. of-Victoria; Victoria, Tex. 77901–4450	749	Pub	1,608	6,744	n.a.
Howard Payne University; Brownwood, Tex. 76801–2794	1,469	P	5,940	5,940	3,494
Howard University; Washington, D.C. 20059	7,092	P	7,700	7,700	3,983
Humboldt State University; Arcata, Calif. 95521	6,245	Pub	1,860	1,860	4,768
Humphreys College; Stockton, Calif. 95207	873	P	5,460	5,460	3,345
Hunter College. *See* New York, City University of					
Huntingdon College; Montgomery, Ala. 36194	645	P	9,250	9,250	4,410
Huntington College; Huntington, Ind. 46750	531	P	10,450	10,450	4,470
Huron University; Huron, S.D. 57350	403	P	7,878	7,878	3,298
Husson College; Bangor, Me. 04401	1,832	P	8,140	8,140	4,300
Huston-Tillotson College; Austin, Tex. 78702	611	P	5,544	5,544	3,878
Idaho State University; Pocatello, Idaho 83209	9,638	Pub	1,570	7,000	3,100
Idaho, University of; Moscow, Idaho 83844–3133	4,027	Pub	1,620	7,000	3,680
Illinois College; Jacksonville, Ill. 62650	986	P	8,600	8,600	4,000
Illinois Institute of Technology; Chicago, Ill. 60616	2,546	P	15,840	15,840	4,620
Illinois State University; Normal, Ill. 61761	16,663	Pub	3,713	9,404	3,920
Illinois Wesleyan University; Bloomington, Ill. 61702	1,809	P	15,510	15,510	4,290
Illinois, Univ. of, at Chicago; Chicago, Ill. 60680–5220	16,206	Pub	3,974	8,894	5,188
Illinois, Univ. of, at Urbana-Champaign; Urbana, Ill. 61801	29,673	Pub	3,150	8,172	4,560
Immaculata College; Immaculata, Pa. 19345	1,550 (W)	P	10,880	10,880	5,678
Incarnate Word College; San Antonio, Tex. 78209	2,282	P	9,655	9,655	4,337
Indiana Institute of Technology; Fort Wayne, Ind. 46803	477	P	8,960	8,960	3,970
Indiana State University; Terre Haute, Ind. 47809	10,033	Pub	3,000	7,225	3,725
Indiana University of Pennsylvania; Indiana, Pa. 15705	12,825	Pub	3,891	8,865	3,258
Indiana University-Bloomington; Bloomington, Ind. 47405	25,773	Pub	3,472	10,660	4,465
Indiana University-East; Richmond, Ind. 47374	2,387	Pub	3,998	5,184	n.a.
Indiana University-Kokomo; Kokomo, Ind. 46904–9003	3,442[1]	Pub	2,000	5,200	n.a.
Indiana University-Northwest; Gary, Ind. 46408	5,029	Pub	1,999	5,184	n.a.
Indiana University-Purdue University at Fort Wayne; Fort Wayne, Ind. 46805	11,513	Pub	3,156	7,067	n.a.
Indiana University-Purdue University at Indianapolis; Indianapolis, Ind. 46202-5143	26,939	Pub	4,149[1]	12,735[1]	3,400[1]
Indiana University-South Bend; South Bend, Ind. 46634	6,125	Pub	2,027	5,540	n.a.
Indiana University-Southeast; New Albany, Ind. 47150	5,388	Pub	2,000	5,184	n.a.
Indiana Wesleyan University; Marion, Ind. 46953	5,069	P	9,726	9,726	3,932
Indianapolis, University of; Indianapolis, Ind. 46227	3,095	P	11,730	11,730	4,200
Industrial Engineering College of Chicago; Chicago, Ill. 60607	240	P	4,800	4,800	n.a.
Insurance, College of; New York, N.Y. 10007	611	P	12,730	12,730	8,100
Inter-American University of Puerto Rico-Arecibo Campus; Arecibo, P.R. 00614–4050	4,489	P	2,520	2,520	4,416
International College of The Cayman Islands; British West Indies	200	P	2,813	2,813	1,688
International Institute of A.C.E.; Lewisville, Tex. 75067	75	P	2,000	2,000	2,800
International School of the Cayman Islands; British West Indies	n.a.	P	281	281	168
Iona College; New Rochelle, N.Y. 10801	4,626[1]	P	11,330	11,330	6,800
Iowa State University; Ames, Iowa 50011–2010	20,312	Pub	2,470	8,284	3,508
Iowa Wesleyan College; Mount Pleasant, Iowa 52641	829	P	11,300	11,300	3,840
Iowa, University of; Iowa City, Iowa 52242	18,740	Pub	2,470	9,068	3,688
Ithaca College; Ithaca, N.Y. 14850–7020	5,559	P	16,130	16,130	6,990
ITT Technical Institute; West Covina, Calif. 91790-2767	800	P	7,824	7,824	n.a.
Jackson State University; Jackson, Miss. 39217	6,346	Pub	2,430	4,664	3,816
Jacksonville State University; Jacksonville, Ala. 36265-9982	7,697	Pub	1,740[1]	,2,610	2,675
Jacksonville University; Jacksonville, Fla. 32211	2,064	P	10,080	10,080	4,598
James Madison University; Harrisonburg, Va. 22807	10,152	Pub	4,104	8,580	4,884
Jamestown College; Jamestown, N.D. 58405	1,000	P	7,970	7,970	3,080
Jarvis Christian College; Hawkins, Tex. 75765	497	P	6,085	6,085	3,485
Jersey City State College; Jersey City, N.J. 07305	6,035	Pub	3,156	4,446	4,800
Jewish Theological Seminary of America; New York, N.Y. 10027	112 (M)	P	7,000	7,000	6,400
John Brown University; Siloam Springs, Ark. 72761	1,177	P	8,308	8,308	4,224
John Carroll University; University Heights, Ohio 44118	3,469	P	12,390	12,390	5,550
John F. Kennedy University; Orinda, Calif. 94563	327	P	8,976	8,976	n.a.
John Jay Coll. of Criminal Justice. *See* New York, City Univ. of					
John Wesley College; High Point, N.C. 27265	130	P	4,540	4,540	1,600
Johns Hopkins University; Baltimore, Md. 21218	3,297	P	19,750	19,750	6,955
School of Nursing; Baltimore, Md. 21205	214	P	20,480	20,480	n.a.
The Peabody Institute; Baltimore, Md. 21202–2397	269	P	18,230	18,230	7,910
Johnson and Wales University; Providence, R.I. 02903	7,365	P	10,900	10,900	5,100
Johnson Bible College; Knoxville, Tenn. 37998	384	P	4,475	4,475	3,125
Johnson C. Smith University; Charlotte, N.C. 28216	1,278	P	7,128	7,128	3,040
Johnson State College; Johnson, Vt. 05656	1,562	Pub	4,040	8,552	4,794

Institution and location	Enrollment	Control	Tuition ($) Res.	Tuition ($) Nonres.	Rm/Bd ($)
Jones College—Jacksonville; Jacksonville, Fla. 32211	1,700 [1]	P	5,220	5,220	n.a.
Judson College; Elgin, Ill. 60123	605 (W)	P	5,644	5,644	4,690
Judson College; Marion, Ala. 36756	648 [1] (W)	P	5,780	5,780	3,600
Juilliard School; New York, N.Y. 10023	505	P	13,600	13,600	6,300
Juniata College; Huntingdon, Pa. 16652	1,038	P	15,740	15,740	4,620
Kalamazoo College; Kalamazoo, Mich. 49006-3295	1,241	P	16,713	16,713	5,262
Kansas City Art Institute; Kansas City, Mo. 64111	574	P	15,820	15,820	4,470
Kansas City College and Bible School; Overland Park, Kan. 66204	53	P	2,400	2,400	2,780
Kansas Newman College; Wichita, Kan. 67213	1,954	P	8,100	8,100	5,116
Kansas State University; Manhattan, Kan. 66506	16,992	Pub	1,733 [1]	7,344 [1]	3,490
Kansas Wesleyan University; Salina, Kan. 67401	619	P	9,220	9,220	3,600
Kansas, University of; Lawrence, Kan. 66045	18,657	Pub	1,890	7,950	3,640
Kean College of New Jersey; Union, N.J. 07083	10,066	Pub	2,810	3,906	4,142
Keene State College; Keene, N.H. 03435-2604	3,830	Pub	3,604	9,094	4,350
Kendall College; Evanston, Ill. 60201	371	P	8,931	8,931	4,998
Kendall College of Art and Design; Grand Rapids, Mich. 49503	520	P	10,500	10,500	n.a.
Kennesaw College; Marietta, Ga. 30061	11,670	Pub	1,776	4,986	n.a.
Kent State University; Kent, Ohio 44242-0001	19,324	Pub	4,084	8,168	3,834
Kentucky Christian College; Grayson, Ky. 41143	515	P	5,504	5,504	3,708
Kentucky State University; Frankfort, Ky. 40601	2,579	Pub	1,860	5,220	2,984
Kentucky Wesleyan College; Owensboro, Ky. 42301	654	P	8,950	8,950	4,400
Kentucky, University of; Lexington, Ky. 40506	17,658	Pub	2,676	7,356	3,198
Kenyon College; Gambier, Ohio 43022	1,522	P	22,010	22,010	3,820
Keuka College; Keuka Park, N.Y. 14478	921	P	9,960	9,960	4,780
King College; Bristol, Tenn. 37620	589	P	10,280	10,280	3,444
King's College; Wilkes-Barre, Pa 18711	2,176	P	12,260	12,260	5,500
King's College, The; Briarcliff Manor, N.Y. 10510	413	P	8,500 [1]	8,500 [1]	3,920 [1]
Knox College; Galesburg, Ill. 61401	991	P	16,692	16,692	4,257
Knoxville College; Knoxville, Tenn. 37921	846	P	5,400	5,400	3,450
Kutztown University; Kutztown, Pa. 19530	6,960	Pub	3,698	8,552	3,000
L.I.F.E. Bible College; San Dimas, Calif. 91773–3298	405	P	4,560	4,560	2,600
L.I.F.E. Bible College East; Christiansburg, V.A. 24073	105	P	2,760	2,760	2,300
La Grange College; La Grange, Ga. 30240	999	P	8,262	8,262	3,825
La Roche College; Pittsburgh, Pa. 15237	1,469	P	9,286	9,286	5,022
La Salle University; Philadelphia, Pa. 19141	4,078	P	13,160	13,160	6,000
La Sierra University; Riverside, Calif. 92515	1,511	P	13,320	13,320	3,990
La Verne, University of; La Verne, Calif 91750	1,489	P	14,220	14,220	4,500
Laboratory Institute of Merchandising; New York, N.Y. 10022	180	P	10,450	10,450	n.a.
Lafayette College; Easton, Pa. 18042	2,027	P	19,546	19,546	6,000
Lake Erie College; Painesville, Ohio 44077	525	P	12,450	12,450	4,905
Lake Forest College; Lake Forest, Ill. 60045–2399	964	P	18,750	18,750	4,400
Lake Superior State University; Sault Ste. Marie, Mich. 49783	3,157	Pub	3,426	6,612	4,332
Lakeland College; Sheboygan, Wis. 53082	3,600	P	10,820	10,820	4,220
Lakeview College of Nursing; Danville, Ill. 61832	125	P	6,000	6,000	n.a.
Lamar University; Beaumont, Tex. 77710	11,488	Pub	1,484	4,988	3,338
Lambuth College; Jackson, Tenn. 38301	1,227	P	5,600	5,600	4,570
Lancaster Bible College; Lancaster, Pa. 17601	625	P	7,850	7,850	3,650
Lander University; Greenwood S.C. 29649	2,378 [1]	Pub	3,400	5,026	3,350
Lane College; Jackson, Tenn. 38301	664	P	4,796	4,796	3,202
Langston University; Langston, Okla. 73050	4,100	Pub	4,337	6,542	2,580 [1]
Laredo State University; Laredo, Tex. 78040-9960	794	Pub	1,030	4,294	3,380
Lasell College; Newton, Mass. 02166	620 (W)	P	12,700	12,700	6,300
Lawrence Technological University; Southfield, Mich. 48075	4,159	P	8,690	8,690	3,216
Lawrence University; Appleton, Wis. 54912–0599	1,216	P	18,744	18,744	4,213
Le Moyne College; Syracuse, N.Y. 13214-1399	2,177	P	12,390	12,390	5,390
Lebanese American University; Beirut, Lebanon	2,634	P	10,500	10,500	4,500
Lebanon Valley College; Annville, Pa. 17003	1,163	P	14,785	14,785	4,940
Lee College; Cleveland, Tenn. 37311	2,197 [1]	P	4,992	4,992	3,720
Lee College at the University of Judaism; Los Angeles, Calif. 90077	93	P	12,040	12,040	6,300
Lehigh University; Bethlehem, Pa. 18015	4,357	P	19,650	19,650	6,020
Lenoir-Rhyne College; Hickory, N.C. 28603	1,429	P	10,980	10,980	4,760
Lesley College; Cambridge, Mass. 02138-2790	535 (W)	P	12,900	12,900	6,075
LeTourneau University; Longview, Tex. 75607	1,833	P	4,715	4,715	2,220
Lewis and Clark College; Portland, Ore. 97219–7899	1,837	P	17,740	17,740	5,780
Lewis Clark State College; Lewiston, Idaho 83501	2,316	Pub	1,478	6,000	3,230
Lewis University; Romeoville, Ill. 60441	3,378	P	8,256	8,256	5,000
Liberty University; Lynchburg, Va. 24506	3,603 [1]	P	7,350	7,350	4,800
Limestone College; Gaffney, S.C. 29340	326	P	8,200	8,200	3,700
Lincoln Christian College; Lincoln, Ill. 62656	528	P	4,288	4,288	3,100
Lincoln Memorial University; Harrogate, Tenn. 37752	912	P	6,550	6,550	3,250
Lincoln University; San Francisco, Calif. 94118	185	P	10,510	10,510	n.a.
Lincoln University; Jefferson City, Mo. 65101	3,149	Pub	2,216	4,232	2,728
Lincoln University; Lincoln University, Pa. 19352	1,279	Pub	4,431	6,618	3,750

Institution and location	Enrollment	Control	Tuition ($) Res.	Tuition ($) Nonres.	Rm/Bd ($)
Lindenwood College; St. Charles, Mo. 63301–4949	2,143	P	14,700	14,700	4,800
Lindsey Wilson College; Columbia, Ky. 42728	1,327	P	7,128	7,128	3,820
Linfield College; McMinnville, Ore. 97128	1,582	P	14,270	14,270	4,380
Livingstone College; Salisbury, N.C. 28144	683	P	9,200	9,200	5,800
Lock Haven University of Pennsylvania; Lock Haven, Pa. 17745	3,515	Pub	3,224	8,198	3,856
Long Island University:					
Brooklyn Campus; Brooklyn, N.Y. 11201	6,279	P	10,483	10,483	4,620
C.W. Post Campus; Greenvale, N.Y. 11548	4,447	P	12,990	12,990	5,880
Southampton Campus; Southampton, N.Y. 11968	1,266	P	13,030	13,030	6,340
Longwood College; Farmville, Va. 23909	2,999	Pub	4,370	9,842	4,222
Loras College; Dubuque, Iowa 52001	1,907	P	11,826	11,826	4,370
Louisiana College; Pineville, La. 71359	983	P	5,810	5,810	2,940
Louisiana State Univ. and A&M Coll.; Baton Rouge, La. 70803	19,972	Pub	2,645	5,948	3,550
Louisiana State University-Shreveport; Shreveport, La. 71115	4,233	Pub	2,080	5,010	n.a.
Louisiana Tech University; Ruston, La. 71272	8,471	Pub	2,262	4,257	2,385
Louisville, University of; Louisville, Ky, 40292	14,660	Pub	2,470	6,990	3,900
Lourdes College; Sylvania, Ohio 43560	4,496	P	5,888	5,888	n.a.
Loyola College; Baltimore, Md. 21210	3,236	P	15,200	15,200	6,720
Loyola Marymount University; Los Angeles, Calif. 90045–8170	3,934	P	14,640	14,640	6,190
Loyola University; New Orleans, La. 70118	3,602	P	12,031	12,031	5,660
Loyola University of Chicago; Chicago, Ill. 60611	5,236	P	14,400	14,400	6,500
Lubbock Christian University; Lubbock, Tex. 79407	1,147	P	7,742	7,742	3,080
Luther College; Decorah, Iowa 52101	2,368	P	15,400	14,900	3,650
Lutheran Bible Institute of Seattle; Issaquah, Wash. 98029-9299	177	P	4,000	4,000	3,950
Lycoming College; Williamsport, Pa. 17701	1,469	P	15,400	14,400	4,500
Lynchburg College; Lynchburg, Va. 24501	1,646	P	14,080	14,080	4,400
Lyndon State College; Lyndonville, Vt. 05851	1,201	Pub	3,432	7,944	4,854
Lynn University; Boca Raton, Fla. 33431–5598	1,449	P	15,450	15,450	6,250
Lyon College; Batesville, Ark. 72503	586	P	8,990	8,990	4,076
Macalester College; St. Paul, Minn. 55105	1,712	P	16,686	16,686	4,975
MacMurray College; Jacksonville, Ill. 62650	693	P	10,940	10,940	4,000
Madonna University; Livonia, Mich. 48150	4,055	P	5,770	5,770	4,168
Maharishi International University; Fairfield, Iowa 52557-1155	259	P	13,976	13,976	3,728
Maine College of Art; Portland, Maine 04101	296	P	13,860	13,860	6,060
Maine Maritime Academy—The Ocean College; Castine, Maine 04420	660[1]	Pub	4,100	7,325	4,895
Maine, Univ. of, at Augusta; Augusta, Maine 04330	5,320	Pub	2,940	6,600	n.a.
Maine, Univ. of, at Farmington; Farmington, Maine 04938	2,250	Pub	2,940	7,170	4,050
Maine, Univ. of, at Fort Kent; Fort Kent, Maine 04743-1292	641	Pub	2,760	6,720	3,600[1]
Maine, Univ. of, at Machias; Machias, Maine 04654	948[1]	Pub	2,875	6,535	3,680
Maine, Univ. of, at Orono; Orono, Maine 04469	10,206	Pub	3,150	8,910	4,700
Maine, Univ. of, at Presque Isle; Presque Isle, Maine 04769	1,511[1]	Pub	2,430	5,598	3,704
Malone College; Canton, Ohio 44709	1,820	P	10,620	10,620	4,020
Manchester College; North Manchester, Ind. 46962	1,010	P	11,470	11,470	4,080
Manhattan Christian College; Manhattan, Kan. 66502	233	P	5,300	5,300	3,094
Manhattan College; Riverdale, N.Y. 10471	2,300	P	13,000	13,000	7,150
Manhattan School of Music; New York, N.Y. 10027	438	P	15,800	15,800	9,000
Manhattanville College; Purchase, N.Y. 10577	898	P	16,100	16,100	7,680
Mankato State University; Mankato, Minn. 56001	11,048	Pub	2,719	5,649	2,923
Mannes College of Music; New York, N.Y. 10024	96	P	13,850	13,850	7,900
Mansfield University of Pennsylvania; Mansfield, Pa. 16933	3,000	Pub	3,224	8,198	3,438
Marian College; Indianapolis, Ind. 46222	1,350	P	10,700	10,700	4,024
Marian College of Fond du Lac; Fond du Lac, Wis. 54935	1,785	P	10,560	10,560	4,300
Marietta College; Marietta, Ohio 45750	1,327	P	15,290	15,290	4,410
Marist College; Poughkeepsie, N.Y. 12601	3,846	P	12,000	12,000	6,400
Marlboro College; Marlboro, Vt. 05344	268	P	19,100	19,100	6,400
Marquette University; Milwaukee, Wis. 53201–1881	10,781	P	14,700	14,700	5,600
Mars Hill College; Mars Hill, N.C. 28754	1,076	P	8,500	8,500	3,550
Marshall University; Huntington, W. Va. 25755	10,303	Pub	3,826	5,696	3,920
Martin Luther College; New Ulm, Minn. 56073–3965	772	P	4,225	4,225	2,100
Martin University; Indianapolis, Ind. 46218	530	P	6,900	6,900	n.a.
Mary Baldwin College; Staunton, Va. 24401	950 (W)	P	12,200	12,200	7,400
Mary Hardin-Baylor, University of; Belton, Tex. 76513	2,244	P	5,850	5,850	3,890
Mary Washington College; Fredericksburg, Va. 22401	3,637	Pub	3,300	8,190	5,024
Mary, University of; Bismarck, N.D. 58504	1,545	P	7,230	7,230	2,890
Marygrove College; Detroit, Mich. 48221	1,090	P	8,496	8,496	2,080
Maryland Institute-College of Art; Baltimore, Md. 21217	814	P	14,950	14,950	5,050
Maryland, Univ. of-Baltimore County; Baltimore, Md. 21228	8,808	Pub	3,852	8,680	4,474
Maryland, Univ. of-College Park; College Park, Md. 20742	22,163	Pub	3,794	9,738	5,146
Maryland, Univ. of-Eastern Shore; Princess Anne, Md. 21853	2,266	Pub	2,855	7,536	4,030
Maryland, Univ. of, University College; College Park, Md. 20742	10,488	Pub	5,220	5,850	n.a.
Marylhurst College; Marylhurst, Ore. 97036	1,048	P	9,087	9,087	n.a.
Marymount College; Tarrytown, N.Y. 10591	1,005 (W)	P	13,500	13,500	6,750
Marymount Manhattan College; New York, N.Y. 10021	1,896	P	11,650	11,650	6,656
Marymount Univ.; Arlington, Va. 22207	2,066	P	11,900	11,900	5,470

Institution and location	Enrollment	Control	Tuition ($)		Rm/Bd ($)
			Res.	Nonres.	
Maryville College; Maryville, Tenn. 37804	843	P	12,096	12,096	4,378
Maryville University of St. Louis; St. Louis, Mo. 63141–7299	2,859	P	10,280	10,280	4,900
Marywood College; Scranton, Pa. 18509	1,780	P	12,640	12,640	5,200
Massachusetts College of Art; Boston, Mass. 02115	2,057	Pub	4,034	9,278	5,763
Massachusetts College of Pharmacy and Allied Health Sciences; Boston, Mass. 02115	1,235	P	12,336	12,336	6,900
Massachusetts Institute of Technology; Cambridge, Mass. 02139	4,520	P	21,000	21,000	6,150
Massachusetts Maritime Academy; Buzzards Bay, Mass. 02532	686	Pub	4,340	9,299	3,680
Massachusetts, Univ. of–Amherst; Amherst, Mass. 01003	17,504	Pub	5,514	11,860	4,188
Massachusetts, Univ. of–Boston; Boston, Mass. 02125-3393	9,595	Pub	4,520	8,568	n.a.
Massachusetts, Univ. of–Dartmouth; North Dartmouth, Mass. 02747	4,876	Pub	1,836	6,919	4,854
Massachusetts, Univ. of–Lowell; Lowell, Mass. 01854	11,325	Pub	4,735	9,879	4,496
Master's College, The; Newhall, Calif. 91322	819	P	9,992	9,992	4,314
Mayville State University; Mayville, N.D. 58257	716	Pub	1,920	4,726	2,572
McKendree College; Lebanon, Ill. 62258	1,618	P	9,600	9,600	4,050
McMurry College; Abilene, Tex. 79697	1,384	P	7,200	7,200	3,767
McNeese State University; Lake Charles, La. 70609	7,658	Pub	2,008	5,208	2,310
McPherson College; McPherson, Kan. 67460	459	P	8,600	8,600	3,750
Medaille College; Buffalo, N.Y. 14214	1,144 [1]	P	9,360	9,360	4,400
Medcenter One College of Nursing; Bismarck, N.D. 58501	83	Pub	2,480	2,480	2,380
Medical College of Georgia; Augusta, Ga. 30912	859	Pub	1,995	6,282	2,749
Medical University of South Carolina; Charleston, S.C. 29425	847	Pub	4,010	11,655	3,460 [1]
Memphis College of Art; Memphis, Tenn. 38104–2764	188	P	9,900	9,900	4,300
Memphis State University; Memphis, Tenn. 38152	15,767	Pub	2,130	6,264	3,140
Menlo College; Atherton, Calif. 94027-4185	560	P	16,975	16,975	6,200
Mercer University; Macon, Ga. 31207	2,224	P	12,987	12,987	4,365
Mercy College; Dobbs Ferry, N.Y. 10522	6,128	P	7,650	7,650	4,000
Mercyhurst College; Erie, Pa. 16546	2,259	P	11,010	11,010	4,251
Meredith College; Raleigh, N.C. 27607-5298	2,274 (W)	P	7,420	7,420	3,570
Merrimack College; North Andover, Mass. 01845	2,732	P	13,350	13,350	6,600
Mesa State College; Grand Junction, Colo. 81502	4,638	Pub	1,872	5,642	4,100
Messiah College; Grantham, Pa. 17027	2,428	P	11,800	11,800	5,400
Methodist College; Fayetteville, N.C. 28311-1499	1,655 [1]	P	10,005	10,005	3,975
Metropolitan State College of Denver; Denver, Colo. 80204	17,461	Pub	1,729	6,198	n.a.
Metropolitan State University; St. Paul, Minn. 55106	5,444	Pub	1,830	3,979	7,182
Miami University; Oxford, Ohio 45056	16,104	Pub	4,612	9,728	3,960
Miami, University of; Coral Gables, Fla. 33124	8,046	P	17,700	17,700	6,852
Michigan Christian College; Rochester Hills, Mich. 48307	65	P	6,020	6,020	3,500
Michigan State University; East Lansing, Mich. 48824	31,329	Pub	3,983	10,838	3,828
Michigan Technological University; Houghton, Mich. 49931	5,450	Pub	3,717	8,607	4,136
Michigan, Univ. of–Ann Arbor; Ann Arbor, Mich. 48109	23,088 [1]	Pub	5,666	17,671	4,898
Michigan, Univ. of–Dearborn; Dearborn, Mich. 48128	7,111	Pub	5,175	12,183	n.a.
Michigan, Univ. of–Flint; Flint, Mich. 48502	6,312	Pub	3,184	9,454	n.a.
Mid-America Bible College; Oklahoma City, Okla. 73170	421	P	4,098	4,098	3,196
Mid-America Nazarene College; Olathe, Kan. 66062	1,270	P	7,878	7,878	3,928
Middlebury College; Middlebury, Vt. 05753–6002	1,950	P	27,020	27,020	—
Middle Tennessee State University; Murfreesboro, Tenn. 37132	17,424	Pub	1,664	5,794	1,215
Middlebury College; Middlebury; Vt. 05753–6002	2,040	P	28,040	28,040	n.a.
Midland Lutheran College; Fremont, Neb. 68025	1,019	P	10,990	10,990	3,060
Midway College; Midway, Ky. 40347	930 (W)	P	8,100	8,100	4,250
Midwestern State University; Wichita Falls, Tex. 76308	5,129	Pub	1,602	5,700	3,500
Miles College; Birmingham, Ala. 35208	1,215	P	4,350	4,350	2,700
Millersville University of Pennsylvania; Millersville, Pa. 17551-0302	6,701	Pub	4,100	9,074	4,038
Milligan College; Milligan College, Tenn. 37682	866	P	8,800	8,800	3,500
Millikin University; Decatur, Ill. 62522	1,863	P	13,290	13,290	4,850
Mills College; Oakland, Calif. 94613	891 (W)	P	15,260	15,260	6,480
Millsaps College; Jackson, Miss. 39210	1,252	P	12,700	12,700	4,770
Milwaukee Institute of Art and Design; Milwaukee, Wis. 53202	525	P	13,700	13,700	5,800
Milwaukee School of Engineering; Milwaukee, Wis. 53202-3109	2,654	P	13,305	13,305	3,650
Minneapolis Coll. of Art and Design; Minneapolis, Minn. 55404	528	P	13,870	13,870	3,600
Minnesota Bible College; Rochester, Minn. 55902	99	P	4,839	4,839	3,045
Minnesota, Univ. of–Crookston; Crookston, Minn. 56716	1,729	Pub	3,060	8,865	3,570
Minnesota, Univ. of–Duluth; Duluth, Minn. 55812	7,052	Pub	3,418	9,904	3,612
Minnesota, Univ. of–Morris; Morris, Minn. 56267–2199	1,952	Pub	3,858	11,205	3,474
Minnesota, Univ. of–Twin Cities; Minneapolis, Minn. 55455-0213	23,762	Pub	3,857	10,344	4,085
Minot State University; Minot, N.D. 58707	3,761	Pub	1,960	4,953	2,049
Mississippi College; Clinton, Miss. 39058	2,015	P	4,975 [1]	4,975 [1]	3,040
Mississippi State University; Mississippi State, Miss. 39762	13,577	Pub	2,591	5,411	4,100
Mississippi University for Women; Columbus, Miss. 39701	3,071	Pub	2,244	6,630	2,367
Mississippi Valley State University; Itta Bena, Miss. 38941	2,169	Pub	2,278	4,780	2,300
Mississippi, University of; University, Miss. 38677	10,181	Pub	2,546	5,366	3,500
Mississippi, Univ. of, Medical Center; Jackson, Miss. 39216	472	Pub	7,955	13,955	n.a.
Missouri Baptist College; St. Louis, Mo. 63141	1,429	P	7,370	7,370	3,550

Institution and location	Enrollment	Control	Tuition ($) Res.	Tuition ($) Nonres.	Rm/Bd ($)
Missouri Southern State College; Joplin, Mo. 64801	5,511	Pub	1,995	3,990	3,172
Missouri Valley College; Marshall, Mo. 65340	1,212	P	9,700	9,700	5,000
Missouri Western State College; St. Joseph, Mo. 64507	5,167	Pub	2,258	4,028	2,994
Missouri, Univ. of-Columbia; Columbia, Mo. 65211	16,439	Pub	3,538	9,720	3,619
Missouri, Univ. of-Kansas City; Kansas City, Mo. 64110	5,319	Pub	3,100	8,405	3,875
Missouri, Univ. of-Rolla; Rolla, Mo. 65401	4,487	Pub	3,954	10,136	3,735
Missouri, Univ. of-St. Louis; St. Louis, Mo. 63121	9,464	Pub	3,630	10,851	4,800
Mobile College; Mobile, Ala. 36613	2,156	P	6,510	6,510	3,680
Molloy College; Rockville Centre, N.Y. 11570	2,481	P	8,736	8,736	n.a.
Monmouth College; Monmouth, Ill. 61462	1,000	P	13,965	13,965	4,275
Monmouth University; West Long Branch, N.J. 07764	2,826	P	13,140	13,140	5,860
Montana Bible College; Bozeman, Mont. 59771	n.a.	P	2,700	2,700	3,200
Montana State University-Billings; Billings, Mont. 59101	3,767	Pub	2,304	6,316	2,960
Montana State University; Bozeman, Mont. 59717	10,072	Pub	2,378	6,796	3,858
Montana Tech of the University of Montana; Butte, Mont. 59701	1,827	Pub	2,317	6,745	3,456
Montana, University of; Missoula, Mont. 59812	11,753	Pub	2,400	2,400	3,700
Montclair State College; Upper Montclair, N.J. 07043-1624	10,349	Pub	2,390	3,374	5,060
Monterey Institute of Intl. Studies; Monterey, Calif. 93940	714	P	16,200	16,200	n.a.
Montevallo, University of; Montevallo, Ala. 35115	2,769	Pub	2,520	5,040	2,407
Montreat College; Montreat, N.C. 28757	817	P	9,600	9,600	3,700
Montserrat College of Art; Beverly, Mass. 01915	312	P	10,272	10,272	4,500
Moore College of Art and Design; Philadelphia, Pa. 19103	440[1] (W)	P	14,400	14,400	5,143
Moorhead State University; Moorhead, Minn. 56563	8,268	Pub	2,355	5,473	2,958
Moravian College; Bethlehem, Pa. 18018	1,247	P	15,700	15,700	4,950
Morehead State University; Morehead, Ky. 40351	7,049	Pub	2,000	5,200	2,950
Morehouse College; Atlanta, Ga. 30314	3,005 (M)	P	8,930	8,930	5,374
Morgan State University; Baltimore, Md. 21239	5,709	Pub	2,832	6,462	4,840
Morningside College; Sioux City, Iowa 51106	1,207	P	11,050	11,050	4,070
Morris Brown College; Atlanta, Ga. 30314	1,877	P	7,244	7,244	4,750
Morrison College/Reno Business College; Reno, Nev. 89503	279	P	6,210	6,210	n.a.
Mount Aloysius College; Cresson, Pa. 16630	1,958	P	8,360	8,360	3,760
Mount Holyoke College; South Hadley, Mass. 01075	100 (W)	P	21,250	21,250	6,250
Mount Ida College; Newton Centre, Mass. 02159	2,000	P	11,128	11,128	7,718
Mount Marty College; Yankton, S.D. 57078	958	P	7,988	7,988	3,470
Mount Mary College; Milwaukee, Wis. 53222	1,324[1]	P	9,950	9,950	3,322
Mount Mercy College; Cedar Rapids, Iowa 52402	1,235	P	11,020	11,020	3,687
Mount Olive College; Mount Olive, N.C. 28365	970	P	8,265	8,265	3,215
Mount Saint Mary College; Newburgh, N.Y. 12550	1,800	P	8,610	8,610	5,000
Mount Saint Mary's College; Emmitsburg, Md. 21727	1,390 (M)	P	14,120	14,120	6,250
Mount Senario College; Ladysmith, Wis. 54848	1,057	P	8,980	8,980	3,250
Mount St. Clare College; Clinton, Iowa 52732	411	P	10,380	10,380	3,800
Mount St. Joseph, College of; Cincinnati, Ohio 45233-9314	2,214	P	11,300	11,300	4,950
Mount St. Mary's College; Los Angeles, Calif. 90049	1,156 (W)	P	13,347	13,347	6,842
Mount St. Vincent, College of; New York, N.Y. 10471	1,100	P	12,580	12,580	5,944
Mount Union College; Alliance, Ohio 44601-3993	1,693	P	13,880	13,880	3,760
Mount Vernon College; Washington, D.C. 20007	245[1] (W)	P	14,350	14,350	7,200
Mount Vernon Nazarene College; Mount Vernon, Ohio 43050	1,458	P	8,590	8,590	3,576
Muhlenberg College; Allentown, Pa. 18104	1,636	P	17,550	17,550	4,728
Multnomah School of the Bible; Portland, Ore. 97220	530	P	7,100	7,100	3,390
Murray State University; Murray, Ky. 42071	8,166	Pub	1,800	5,020	3,340
Museum Art School, Portland. See Pacific Northwest College of Art					
Muskingum College; New Concord, Ohio 43762	1,113	P	14,240	14,240	4,090
NAES College; Chicago, Ill. 60659	80	P	4,410	4,410	n.a.
Naropa Institute; Boulder, Colo. 80302	140	P	7,920	7,920	n.a.
Nathaniel Hawthorne College. See Hawthorne College					
National College; Rapid City, S.D. 57709	502	P	7,920	7,920	3,360
National College-Albuquerque; Albuquerque, N.M. 87110	122	P	5,680	5,680	n.a.
National College, Colorado Springs Branch; Colorado Springs, Colo. 80909	350	P	5,760	5,760	n.a.
National University; San Diego, Calif. 92108-4194	3,966	P	6,255	6,255	n.a.
National-Louis University; Evanston, Ill. 60201	2,934	P	8,280	8,280	4,821
Nazarene Bible College; Colorado Springs, Colo. 80935	1,400[1]	P	4,000	4,000	n.a.
Nazareth College of Rochester; Rochester, N.Y. 14618	1,755	P	11,450	11,450	5,300
Nebraska Christian College; Norfolk, Neb. 68701	139	P	4,000	4,000	2,660
Nebraska Methodist College of Nursing and Allied Health; Omaha, Neb. 68114	363	P	7,800	7,800	2,960
Nebraska Wesleyan University; Lincoln, Neb. 68504	1,610	P	10,284	10,284	3,520
Nebraska, University of-Kearney; Kearney, Neb. 68849	6,467	Pub	1,770	3,315	4,038
Nebraska, University of-Lincoln; Lincoln, Neb. 68588-0415	19,746	Pub	2,004	4,476	3,350
Nebraska, University of-Medical Center; Omaha, Neb. 68198-4230	918	Pub	2,765	7,534	n.a.
Nebraska, University of-Omaha; Omaha, Neb. 68182	15,216	Pub	1,966	5,161	n.a.
Neumann College; Aston, Pa. 19014	1,214	P	13,540	13,540	n.a.
Nevada, University of-Las Vegas; Las Vegas, Nev. 89154	20,190	Pub	1,930	7,020	5,400
Nevada, University of-Reno; Reno, Nev. 89557	12,137[1]	Pub	5,100	5,100	4,945

Institution and location	Enrollment	Control	Tuition ($) Res.	Tuition ($) Nonres.	Rm/Bd ($)
New England College; Henniker, N.H. 03242	690	P	14,226	14,226	5,620
New England Conservatory of Music; Boston, Mass. 02115	376	P	15,300	15,300	7,300
New England Institute of Technology; Warwick, R.I. 02886	1,950 [1]	P	9,875	9,875	n.a.
New England, University of; Biddeford, Me. 04005	801	P	11,450	11,450	5,070
New Hampshire College; Manchester, N.H. 03104	1,048	P	11,142	11,142	4,884
New Hampshire, University of; Durham, N.H. 03824	10,620	Pub	5,054	13,724	4,150
New Hampshire, Univ. of at Manchester; Manchester, N.H. 03102	543	Pub	3,390	10,130	n.a.
New College of California; San Francisco, Calif. 94110	180	P	7,500	7,500	n.a.
New College of the University of South Florida; Sarasota, Fla. 34243-2197	586	Pub	2,066	7,953	3,847
New Haven, University of; West Haven, Conn. 06516	3,404	P	11,400	11,400	4,860
New Jersey Institute of Technology; Newark, N.J. 07102–1982	4,973	Pub	4,361	8,722	3,840
New Mexico Highlands University; Las Vegas, N.M. 87701	2,839	Pub	1,506	6,582	3,150
New Mexico Inst. of Mining & Technology; Socorro, N.M. 87801	1,494	Pub	1,407	5,814	3,426
New Mexico State University–Main Campus; Las Cruces, N.M. 88003-0001	13,097	Pub	2,088	6,798	3,210
New Mexico, University of; Albuquerque, N.M. 87131	18,998	Pub	1,997	7,542	4,176
New Orleans, University of; New Orleans, La. 70148	11,672	Pub	2,362	5,154	3,116
New Rochelle, College of; New Rochelle, N.Y. 10805-2308	3,860 (W)	P	4,152	4,152	5,500
New School for Social Research Eugene Lang College; New York, N.Y. 10011	350	P	16,119	16,119	8,132
New York City Technical Coll. *See* New York, City Univ. of					
New York Institute of Technology; Old Westbury, N.Y. 11568	3,390	P	9,190	9,190	n.a.
New York Institute of Technology Central Islip Campus; Central Islip, N.Y. 11722	1,303	P	9,700	9,700	5,600
New York Institute of Technology, Manhattan Campus; New York, N.Y. 10023	1,587	P	9,190	9,190	n.a.
New York School of Interior Design; New York, N.Y. 10021	650	P	9,360	9,360	n.a.
New York University; New York, N.Y. 10011	15,335	P	20,756	20,756	7,856
New York, City University of; New York, N.Y. 10021:					
Baruch College; New York, N.Y. 10010	12,730	Pub	3,200	6,800	n.a.
Brooklyn College; Brooklyn, N.Y. 11210	11,326	Pub	3,200	6,800	n.a.
City College; New York, N.Y. 10031	11,541	Pub	3,200	6,800	n.a.
College of Staten Island; Staten Island, N.Y. 10314	10,972	Pub	3,200	6,800	n.a.
Hunter College; New York, N.Y. 10021	14,934	Pub	2,557	5,157	3,440
John Jay College of Criminal Justice; New York, N.Y. 10019	7,918	Pub	2,400	5,050	n.a.
Lehman College; Bronx, N.Y. 10468	8,802	Pub	2,760	3,002	n.a.
Medgar Evers College; Brooklyn, N.Y. 11225–2201	2,823 [1]	Pub	2,352	2,811	n.a.
New York City Technical College; Brooklyn, N.Y. 11201–2983	10,757 [1]	Pub	2,504	5,104	n.a.
Queens College; Flushing, N.Y. 11367	14,478	Pub	1,600	3,400	n.a.
York College; Jamaica, N.Y. 11451	6,869	Pub	135	285	3,200
New York, State University of; Albany, N.Y. 12246:					
SUNY-Albany; Albany, N.Y. 12222	10,947	Pub	3,400	8,300	5,050
SUNY-Binghamton; Binghamton, N.Y. 13902-6001	9,273	Pub	3,400	8,300	4,654
SUNY-Buffalo; Buffalo, N.Y. 14260	16,411	Pub	3,400	8,300	5,300
SUNY-College at Brockport; Brockport, N.Y. 14420	7,170	Pub	3,400	8,300	4,660
SUNY-College at Buffalo; Buffalo, N.Y. 14222	9,555	Pub	3,400	8,300	4,240
SUNY-College at Cortland; Cortland, N.Y. 13045	5,262	Pub	3,400	8,300	5,020
SUNY-College at Fredonia; Fredonia, N.Y. 14063	4,374	Pub	3,400	8,300	4,670
SUNY-College at Geneseo; Geneseo, N.Y. 14454-1471	5,334	Pub	3,400	8,300	4,500
SUNY-College at New Paltz; New Paltz, N.Y. 12561–2499	6,009	Pub	3,400	8,300	4,990
SUNY-College at Old Westbury; Old Westbury, N.Y. 11568	4,111	Pub	3,350	7,250	4,808
SUNY-College at Oneonta; Oneonta, N.Y. 13820	5,400	Pub	3,350	7,250	4,606
SUNY-College at Oswego; Oswego, N.Y. 13126	7,611 [1]	Pub	3,350	7,250	4,640
SUNY-College at Plattsburgh; Plattsburgh, N.Y. 12901	5,275	Pub	3,350	7,250	4,220
SUNY-College at Potsdam; Potsdam, N.Y. 13676	3,946	Pub	3,350	7,250	4,450
SUNY-College of Agriculture and Life Sciences at Cornell University; Ithaca, N.Y. 14853	3,098	Pub	8,440	15,600	6,238
SUNY-College of Environmental Science and Forestry; Syracuse, N.Y. 13210	1,169	Pub	3,350	7,250	6,000
SUNY-College of Human Ecology at Cornell University; Ithaca, N.Y. 14853	1,330	Pub	8,556	16,526	6,557
SUNY-College of Technology-Farmingdale; Farmingdale, N.Y. 11735	293	Pub	3,400	8,300	5,491
SUNY-Empire State College; Saratoga Springs, N.Y. 12866	6,063	Pub	3,350	7,250	n.a.
SUNY-Fashion Institute of Technology; New York, N.Y. 10001-5992	4,253	Pub	3,495	6,910	4,754
SUNY-Health Science Center at Syracuse; Syracuse, N.Y. 13210	404	Pub	3,350	7,250	4,816
SUNY-Institute of Technology at Utica/Rome; Utica, N.Y. 13504-3050	2,271 [1]	Pub	3,350	7,250	4,650
SUNY-Maritime College; Throggs Neck, N.Y. 10465	655	Pub	3,400	8,300	5,300
SUNY-Purchase; Purchase, N.Y. 10577	3,512	Pub	3,400	8,300	4,872
SUNY-School of Industrial and Labor Relations at Cornell University; Ithaca, N.Y. 14853	628	Pub	8,440	15,600	6,238
SUNY-Stony Brook; Stony Brook, N.Y. 11794	10,759	Pub	3,350	7,250	4,768

Institution and location	Enrollment	Control	Tuition ($) Res.	Tuition ($) Nonres.	Rm/Bd ($)
New York, University of the State of, Regents College					
Degrees; Albany, N.Y. 12203	17,269	P	565	565	n.a.
Newberry College; Newberry, S.C. 29108	630	P	10,950	10,950	2,600
Niagara University; Niagara University, N.Y. 14109	2,274	P	11,560	11,560	5,084
Nicholls State University; Thibodaux, La. 70310	6,775	Pub	1,986	4,578	2,700
Nichols College; Dudley, Mass. 01570	1,691	P	10,232	10,232	5,904
Norfolk State University; Norfolk, Va. 23504	7,252	Pub	2,865	6,392	3,720
North Adams State College; North Adams, Mass. 01247	1,650	Pub	3,529	7,917	4,602
North Alabama, University of; Florence, Ala. 35632	4,665 [1]	Pub	1,800	3,600	3,400
North Carolina Agricultural and Technical State					
University; Greensboro, N.C. 27411	7,054 [1]	Pub	840	7,682	3,180
North Carolina Central University; Durham, N.C. 27707	4,070	Pub	1,474	7,540	4,530
North Carolina School of the Arts; Winston-Salem, N.C. 27117-2189	456	Pub	1,308	9,159	3,706
North Carolina State University-Raleigh; Raleigh, N.C. 27695-7103	22,483	Pub	2,086	10,248	3,856
North Carolina Wesleyan College; Rocky Mount, N.C. 27804	762	P	6,600	6,600	4,500
North Carolina, Univ. of-Asheville; Asheville, N.C. 28804	3,176	Pub	1,780	8,634	3,726
North Carolina, Univ. of-Chapel Hill; Chapel Hill, N.C. 27599-2200	15,702	Pub	1,380	9,918	4,500
North Carolina, Univ. of-Charlotte; Charlotte, N.C. 28223	12,972	Pub	1,457	7,941	3,620
North Carolina, Univ. of-Greensboro; Greensboro, N.C. 27412	9,931	Pub	1,868	9,824	3,500
North Carolina, Univ. of-Pembroke; Pembroke, N.C. 28372	2,674	Pub	1,467	8,621	2,856
North Carolina, Univ. of-Wilmington; Wilmington, N.C. 28403	8,107	Pub	1,664	8,506	3,910
North Central Bible College; Minneapolis, Minn. 55404	1,055	P	6,360	6,360	3,550
North Central College; Naperville, Ill. 60566-7063	2,479	P	13,074	13,074	4,854
North Dakota State University; Fargo, N.D. 58105	9,269 [1]	Pub	2,355	5,879	2,854
North Dakota, University of; Grand Forks, N.D. 58202	9,550 [1]	Pub	2,110	5,634	2,871
North Florida, University of; Jacksonville, Fla. 32224	8,662	Pub	1,748	6,990	4,360
North Georgia College; Dahlonega, Georgia 30597	2,515 [1]	Pub	1,827	5,037	2,868
North Park College; Chicago, Illinois 60625	977	P	13,990	13,990	4,780
North Texas, University of; Denton, Tex. 76203	18,654	Pub	1,322	4,538	3,658
Northeast Louisiana University; Monroe, La. 71209	10,214	Pub	1,926	4,086	2,200
Northeast Missouri State University; Kirksville, Mo. 63501	6,061	Pub	2,872	5,152	3,624
Northeastern Illinois University; Chicago, Ill. 60625	10,386	Pub	2,040	6,120	n.a.
Northeastern State Univ.; Tahlequah, Okla. 74464	9,374	Pub	1,620	3,945	3,150
Northeastern University; Boston, Mass. 02115	20,146	P	14,241	14,241	7,710
Northern Arizona University; Flagstaff, Ariz. 86011	20,131	Pub	1,950	7,176	3,400
Northern Colorado, University of; Greeley, Colo. 80639	8,599	Pub	1,872	8,070	4,270
Northern Illinois University; De Kalb, Ill. 60115	16,423	Pub	3,730	7,460	3,316
Northern Iowa, University of; Cedar Falls, Iowa 50614	12,802	Pub	2,650	6,868	3,130
Northern Kentucky University; Highland Heights, Ky. 41099–7010	10,827	Pub	1,960	5,320	4,000
Northern Michigan University; Marquette, Mich. 49855	7,895 [1]	Pub	2,848	5,248	4,100
Northern Montana College; Havre, Mont. 59501	1,742	Pub	3,373	6,565	3,800
Northern State University; Aberdeen, S.D. 57401	2,895 [1]	Pub	2,368	4,629	2,250
Northland College; Ashland, Wis. 54806	813	P	10,870	10,870	3,900
Northwest Christian College; Eugene, Ore. 97401	438	P	9,990	9,990	4,310
Northwest College; Kirkland, Wash. 98083-0579	824	P	8,415	8,415	3,990
Northwest Missouri State University; Maryville, Mo. 64468	5,168 [1]	Pub	2,280	3,975	3,290
Northwest Nazarene College; Nampa, Idaho 83686	1,095	P	11,145	11,145	3,105
Northwestern College; Orange City, Iowa 51041	1,198	P	10,850	10,850	3,250
Northwestern College; St. Paul, Minn. 55113	1,242	P	11,985	11,985	3,960
Northwestern Oklahoma State University; Alva, Okla. 73717	1,812	Pub	1,672	4,024	2,036
Northwestern State Univ. of Louisiana; Natchitoches, La. 71497	9,040	Pub	2,067	4,497	2,216
Northwestern University; Evanston, Ill. 60201-3060	7,615	P	17,184	17,184	5,781
Northwood University; Cedar Hill, Tex. 75104	359	P	10,350	10,350	4,709
Northwood University of Florida; West Palm Beach, Fla. 33409	224	P	9,948	9,948	5,883
Northwood University of Michigan; Midland, Mich. 48640	1,343	P	10,350	10,350	4,734
Norwich University; Northfield, Vt. 05663	2,249	P	14,634	14,634	5,436
Notre Dame College; Manchester, N.H. 03104	788	P	10,690	10,690	5,050
Notre Dame College of Ohio; South Euclid, Ohio 44121	653 (W)	P	11,000	11,000	4,095
Notre Dame of Maryland, College of; Baltimore, Md. 21210	645 (W)	P	11,740	11,740	5,845
Notre Dame, College of; Belmont, Calif. 94002–1997	961	P	14,400	14,400	6,100
Notre Dame, University of; Notre Dame, Ind. 46556	7,820	P	18,850	18,850	4,850
Nova University; Ft. Lauderdale, Fla. 33314	3,509	P	9,150	9,150	4,890
Nyack College; Nyack, N.Y. 10960	554	P	9,450	9,450	4,130
O'More College of Design; Franklin, Tenn. 37604	147	P	7,300	7,300	n.a.
Oakland City College; Oakland City, Ind. 47660	1,054	P	7,800	7,800	3,156
Oakland University; Rochester, Mich. 48309–4401	13,600	Pub	3,000	7,194	4,165
Oakwood College; Huntsville, Ala. 35896	1,344 [1]	P	7,064	7,064	3,680
Oberlin College; Oberlin, Ohio 44074	2,823	P	21,425	21,425	6,174
Oblate College; Washington, D.C. 20017	4	P	5,000	5,000	n.a.
Occidental College; Los Angeles, Calif. 90041–3393	1,677	P	17,666	17,666	5,660
Oglala Lakota College; Kyle, S.D. 57752	1,009	Pub	1,260	1,260	n.a.
Oglethorpe University; Atlanta, Ga. 30319	1,146	P	13,950	13,950	4,800
Ohio Dominican College; Columbus, Ohio 43219	1,736	P	8,490	8,490	4,450
Ohio Northern University; Ada, Ohio 45810	2,997	P	17,970	17,970	4,500

Institution and location	Enrollment	Control	Tuition ($) Res.	Tuition ($) Nonres.	Rm/Bd ($)
hio State University–Columbus; Columbus, Ohio 43210	36,166	Pub	3,087	9,315	5,100
hio State University-Lima; Lima, Ohio 45804	1,244	Pub	3,156	6,540	n.a. [1]
hio State University-Mansfield; Mansfield, Ohio 44906	1,327	Pub	2,976	9,204	n.a. [1]
hio State University-Marion; Marion, Ohio 43302	1,011	Pub	3,156	9,696	n.a.
hio State University-Newark; Newark, Ohio 43055	1,626	Pub	3,156	9,696	n.a.
hio University; Athens, Ohio 45701	15,949	Pub	3,861	8,100	4,260
hio University-Chillicothe; Chillicothe, Ohio 45601-0629	1,917	Pub	2,796	6,831	n.a.
hio University-Lancaster; Lancaster, Ohio 43130	1,554	Pub	3,552	7,629	4,095
hio University-Zanesville; Zanesville, Ohio 43701	1,111	Pub	2,796	6,831	n.a.
hio Valley College; Parkersburg, W.Va. 26101	334	P	5,600	5,600	3,280
hio Wesleyan University; Delaware, Ohio 43015	1,732	P	18,228	18,228	5,996
klahoma Baptist University; Shawnee, Okla. 74801	2,412	P	6,525	6,525	3,210
klahoma Christian University of Science and Arts; Oklahoma City, Okla. 73136-1100	1,480	P	7,000	7,000	3,840
klahoma City University; Oklahoma City, Okla. 73106	2,400	P	8,050	8,050	3,990
klahoma Panhandle State University; Goodwell, Okla. 73939	1,236	Pub	3,706	5,911	600
klahoma State University; Stillwater, Okla. 74078	19,125	Pub	2,148	5,838	3,864
klahoma, University of-Health Sciences Center; Oklahoma City, Okla. 73190	1,143	Pub	1,575	4,016	n.a.
klahoma, University of-Norman; Norman, Okla. 73019	15,088	Pub	1,450	4,043	3,808
ld Dominion University; Norfolk, Va. 23529-0050	11,624	Pub	4,104	9,192	4,676
livet College; Olivet, Mich. 49076	791	P	11,580	11,580	3,860
livet Nazarene University; Kankakee, Ill. 60901	1,532	P	10,026	10,026	4,460
ral Roberts University; Tulsa, Okla. 74171	3,163	P	9,392	9,392	4,653
regon Health Sciences University; Portland, Ore. 97201	373	Pub	4,005	10,200	4,857
regon Institute of Technology; Klamath Falls, Ore. 97601	2,478 [1]	Pub	3,150	9,336	3,804
regon State University; Corvallis, Ore. 97331	11,258 [1]	Pub	3,312	10,113	4,000
regon, University of; Eugene, Ore. 97403	17,138	Pub	3,511	11,635	4,325
rlando College; Orlando, Fla. 32810	2,600	P	4,140	4,140	n.a.
tis College of Art and Design; Los Angeles, Calif. 90057	687	P	13,946	13,946	4,300
ttawa University; Ottawa, Kan. 66067	532	P	7,960	7,960	3,570
ttawa University-Phoenix Center; Phoenix, Ariz. 85021	900	P	4,080	4,080	n.a.
tterbein College; Westerville, Ohio 43081	2,488	P	13,611	13,611	4,569
uachita Baptist University; Arkadelphia, Ark. 71998-0001	1,467	P	7,070	7,070	2,900
ur Lady of Holy Cross College; New Orleans, La. 70131-7399	1,279	P	3,800	3,800	n.a.
ur Lady of the Lake-University of San Antonio; San Antonio, Tex. 78207–4689	2,295	P	9,000	9,000	4,200
zark Christian College; Joplin, Mo. 64801	574	P	3,515	3,515	2,980
zarks, College of the; Point Lookout, Mo. 65726	1,527	P	100	100	1,900
zarks, University of the; Clarksville, Ark. 72830	570	P	6,540	6,540	3,300
ace University; New York, N.Y. 10038	5,614	P	11,800	11,800	5,250
ace University-College of White Plains; White Plains, N.Y. 10603	1,121	P	11,800	11,800	5,000
ace University-Pleasantville-Briarcliff; Pleasantville, N.Y. 10570	3,651	P	11,800	11,800	5,240
acific Christian College; Fullerton, Calif. 92631	500	P	8,515	8,515	4,000
acific Lutheran University; Tacoma, Wash. 98447	2,964	P	14,560	14,560	4,690
acific Northwest College of Art; Portland, Ore. 97205	257	P	10,072	10,072	n.a.
acific Oaks College; Pasadena, Calif. 91103	150	P	10,500	10,500	n.a.
acific States University; Los Angeles, Calif. 90006	300 [1]	P	7,200	7,200	n.a.
acific Union College; Angwin, Calif. 94508	1,578	P	12,360	12,360	3,945
acific University; Forest Grove, Ore. 97116	1,115	P	15,368	15,368	4,514
acific, University of the; Stockton, Calif. 95211	3,560	P	17,910	17,910	5,526
aier College of Art, Inc.; Hamden, Conn. 06511	253 [1]	P	9,980	9,980	n.a.
aine College; Augusta, Ga. 30910	812	P	6,220	6,220	3,020
alm Beach Atlantic College; West Palm Beach, Fla. 33416–4708	1,953	P	8,600	8,600	3,750
ark College; Parkville, Mo. 64152	490	P	4,200	4,200	4,220
arks College of St. Louis University; Cahokia, Ill. 62206	1,070	P	9,560	9,560	4,400
arsons School of Design; New York, N.Y. 10011	1,964 [1]	P	16,070	16,070	9,200
atten College; Oakland, Calif. 94601	636	P	6,672	6,672	2,300
aul Quinn College; Waco, Tex. 75241	509	P	3,400	3,400	3,000
ennsylvania State Erie –The Behrend College; Erie, Pa. 16563	3,208	Pub	5,188	11,240	4,300
ennsylvania State Harrisburg–The Capital College; Middletown, Pa. 17057	3,334	Pub	5,188	11,240	4,300
ennsylvania State University Park; University Park, Pa. 16802	31,732	Pub	5,188	11,240	4,300
ennsylvania, University of; Philadelphia, Pa. 19104	9,917	P	19,898	19,898	7,500
epperdine University School of Business and Management; Culver City, Calif. 90230	451	P	18,000	18,000	n.a.
epperdine University-Seaver College; Malibu, Calif. 90263-4392	2,661	P	19,200	19,200	7,080
eru State College; Peru, Neb. 68421	1,688	Pub	1,575	3,000	2,844
feiffer College; Misenheimer, N.C. 28109	653	P	8,990	8,990	3,950
hiladelphia College of Bible; Langhorne, Pa. 19047	864	P	8,290	8,290	4,630
hiladelphia College of Pharmacy and Science; Philadelphia, Pa. 19104	1,920	P	12,250	12,250	5,000

Institution and location	Enrollment	Control	Tuition ($) Res.	Tuition ($) Nonres.	Rm/Bd ($)
Philadelphia College of Textiles and Science; Philadelphia, Pa. 19144	1,829	P	12,240	12,240	5,676
Philander Smith College; Little Rock, Ark. 72202	956	P	3,192	3,192	2,604
Phillips University; Enid, Okla. 73701	808	P	6,600	6,600	3,904
Phoenix, University of; Phoenix, Ariz. 85040	20,000 [1]	P	5,850	5,850	n.a.
Piedmont Bible College; Winston-Salem, N.C. 27101	337	P	4,590	4,590	2,990
Piedmont College; Demorest, Ga. 30535	922	P	6,360	6,360	3,850
Pikeville College; Pikeville, Ky. 41501	800	P	6,000	6,000	3,000
Pillsbury Baptist Bible College; Owatonna, Minn. 55060	338	P	5,490	5,490	2,800
Pine Manor College; Chestnut Hill, Mass. 02167	400 (W)	P	15,650	15,650	6,660
Pittsburg State University; Pittsburg, Kan. 66762	4,927	Pub	1,806	5,788	3,188
Pittsburgh, University of; Pittsburgh, Pa. 15260	16,721	Pub	5,184	11,240 [1]	4,700
Pittsburgh, University of-Bradford; Bradford, Pa. 16701-2898	1,200	Pub	5,390	6,330	4,240
Pittsburgh, University of-Greensburg; Greensburg, Pa. 15601	1,377	Pub	5,184	11,270	3,870
Pittsburgh, University of-Johnstown; Johnstown, Pa. 15904	3,151	Pub	5,656	11,742	4,100
Pitzer College. See Claremont Colleges.					
Plymouth State College; Plymouth, N.H. 03264–1595	3,500	Pub	3,382	8,662	4,024
Point Loma Nazarene College; San Diego, Calif. 92106	2,103	P	11,584	11,584	4,730
Point Park College; Pittsburgh, Pa. 15222	2,317	P	10,522	10,522	5,072
Polytechnic University; Brooklyn, N.Y. 11201	1,124	P	17,335	17,335	4,700
Polytechnic University-Long Island Campus; Farmingdale, N.Y. 11735-3995	358	P	17,335	17,335	4,700
Pomona College. See Claremont Colleges.					
Pontifical Catholic University of Puerto Rico; Ponce, P.R. 00731-6382	11,805	P	2,784	2,784	2,660
Pontifical College Josephinum; Columbus, Ohio 43235-1498	53 (M)	P	5,896	5,896	4,044
Portland State University; Portland, Ore. 97207–0751	10,216	Pub	3,183	9,816	4,365
Portland, University of; Portland, Ore. 97203–5798	2,163	P	13,200	13,200	4,240
Potsdam Coll. of Arts & Science. See New York, State Univ. of					
Prairie View A&M University; Prairie View, Tex. 77446	6,000	Pub	1,744	6,124	3,620
Pratt Institute; Brooklyn, N.Y. 11205	1,979	P	15,194	15,194	6,326
Presbyterian College; Clinton, S.C. 29325	1,186	P	12,512	12,512	4,776
Prescott College; Prescott, Ariz. 86301	387	P	9,950	9,950	n.a.
Presentation College; Anerdeen, S.D. 57401	486	P	6,694	6,694	3,000
Princeton University; Princeton, N.J. 08544–0430	4,524	P	20,960	20,960	6,016
Principia College; Elsah, Ill. 62028	543	P	13,047	13,047	5,424
Providence College; Providence, R.I. 02918	4,533	P	15,800	15,800	6,670
Puerto Rico, University of-Arecibo Campus; Arecibo, P.R. 00613	4,585	Pub	1,238	2,400	n.a.
Puerto Rico, University of-Cayey University College; Cayey, P.R. 00633	3,243	Pub	1,080	1,080	n.a.
Puerto Rico, University of-Humacao University College; Humacao, P.R. 00791	4,228	Pub	1,638	1,638	3,500
Puerto Rico, University of-Mayaguez Campus; Mayaguez, P.R. 00681	9,594	Pub	1,240	1,240	n.a.
Puerto Rico, University of-Medical Science Campus; San Juan, P.R. 00936	996	Pub	1,080	1,080	n.a.
Puerto Rico, University of-Ponce Technological University College; Ponce, P.R. 00732	2,192	Pub	1,560	1,560	n.a.
Puerto Rico, University of-Rio Piedras Campus; Rio Piedras, P.R. 00931	15,668	Pub	1,286	n.a.	2,100
Puget Sound Christian College; Edmonds, Wash. 98020	125	P	5,280	5,280	3,870
Puget Sound, University of; Tacoma, Wash. 98416	2,786	P	18,030	18,030	4,800
Purdue University; West Lafayette, Ind. 47907–1080	30,785	Pub	3,056	10,128	4,310
Purdue University-Calumet; Hammond, Ind. 46323	8,974	Pub	2,700	6,062	n.a.
Purdue University-North Central; Westville, Ind. 46391	3,551	Pub	1,998	5,028	n.a.
Queens College; Charlotte, N.C. 28274	1,213	P	12,310	12,310	5,380
Queens College (NYC). See New York, City University of					
Quincy University; Quincy, Ill. 62301	1,164	P	11,240	11,240	4,370
Quinnipiac College; Hamden, Conn. 06518	5,119	P	13,430	13,430	6,450
Rabbinical College of America; Morristown, N.J. 07960	230 [1](M)	P	7,000	7,000	6,500
Rabbinical Seminary of America; Forest Hills, N.Y. 11375	120 [1](M)	P	4,000	4,000	2,000
Radcliffe College. See Harvard and Radcliffe Colleges					
Radford University; Radford, Va. 24142	8,110	Pub	3,114	7,688	4,250
Ramapo College of New Jersey, Mahwah, N.J. 07430	4,545	Pub	3,621	4,978	5,300
Randolph-Macon College; Ashland, Va. 23005–5505	1,118	P	15,255	15,255	3,995
Randolph-Macon Woman's College; Lynchburg, Va. 24503	709 (W)	P	21,420	21,420	3,165
Ray College of Design; Chicago, Ill. 60654	580	P	8,880	8,880	n.a.
Redlands, University of; Redlands, Calif. 92373-0999	1,500	P	17,860	17,860	6,640
Reed College; Portland, Ore. 97202	1,230	P	20,760	20,760	5,750
Reformed Bible College; Grand Rapids, Mich. 49505-9749	196	P	6,530	6,530	3,350
Regis College; Weston, Mass. 02193	1,202 (W)	P	14,500	14,500	6,600
Regis University; Denver, Colo. 80221–1099	1,143	P	14,100	14,100	5,700
Reinhardt College; Waleska, Ga. 30183	652	P	4,890	4,890	4,050
Rensselaer Polytechnic Institute; Troy, N.Y. 12180	4,398	P	18,565	18,565	6,155

Institution and location	Enrollment	Control	Tuition ($) Res.	Tuition ($) Nonres.	Rm/Bd ($)
Research College of Nursing; Kansas City, Mo. 64110-2508	268	P	11,000	11,000	4,350
Rhode Island College; Providence, R.I. 02908	6,394	Pub	2,476	6,996	5,600
Rhode Island School of Design; Providence, R.I. 02903	2,011 [1]	P	17,600	17,600	6,618
Rhode Island, University of; Kingston, R.I. 02881	10,670	Pub	4,404	4,242 [1]	5,872
Rhode Island, University of, College of Continuing Education; Providence, R.I. 02908-5090	4,400 [1]	Pub	3,204	10,692	n.a.
Rhodes College; Memphis, Tenn. 38112	1,469	P	15,762	15,762	4,912
Rice University; Houston, Tex. 77251	2,610	P	12,000	12,000	5,900
Richard Stockton College of New Jersey; The; Pomona, N.J. 08240	5,601	Pub	3,152	3,968	4,556
Richmond College, The American International University in London; Richmond, Surrey, TW10 6JP England	915 [1]	P	12,413	12,413	6,279
Richmond, University of; Richmond, Va. 23173	3,501	P	16,570	16,570	3,595
Rider College; Lawrenceville, N.J. 08648-3099	3,670	P	14,400	14,400	6,030
Ringling School of Art and Design; Sarasota, Fla. 34234	823	P	12,300	12,300	6,300
Rio Grande College of Sul Ross State University; Eagle Pass, Texas 78852	827	Pub	1,471	3,000	n.a.
Rio Grande, University of; Rio Grande, Ohio 45674	2,024	P	2,976	2,976	4,221
Ripon College; Ripon, Wis. 54971	800	P	16,780	16,780	4,400
Rivier College; Nashua, N.H. 03060	995	P	11,010	11,010	5,250
Roanoke Bible College; Elizabeth City, N.C. 27909	141 [1]	P	4,000	4,000	2,930
Roanoke College; Salem, Va. 24153	1,694	P	14,100	14,100	4,640
Robert Morris College; Coraopolis, Pa. 15108	4,749	P	7,824	7,824	4,554
Roberts Wesleyan College; Rochester, N.Y. 14624	1,154	P	10,826	10,826	3,744
Rochester Institute of Technology; Rochester, N.Y. 14623	10,286	P	14,937	14,937	5,898
Rochester, University of; Rochester, N.Y. 14627	4,985	P	19,165	19,165	6,730
Rockford College; Rockford, Ill. 61108–2393	1,468	P	14,100	14,100	4,400
Rockhurst College; Kansas City, Mo. 64110–2561	1,936	P	10,200	10,200	4,200
Rocky Mountain College; Billings, Mont. 59102	804	P	9,994	9,994	3,822
Roger Williams College; Bristol, R.I. 02809	2,111	P	15,900	15,900	6,660
Rollins College; Winter Park, Fla. 32789	1,422	P	17,995	17,995	5,555
Roosevelt University; Chicago, Ill. 60605	4,519	P	8,000	8,000	5,000
Rosary College; River Forest, Ill. 60305-1099	906	P	11,550	11,550	4,600
Rose-Hulman Institute of Technology; Terre Haute, Ind. 47803	1,320 [1](M)	P	15,700	15,700	4,700
Rosemont College; Rosemont, Pa. 19010	482 (W)	P	12,460	12,460	6,500
Rowan College of N.J.; Glassboro, N.J. 08028–1701	6,380	Pub	3,096	5,109	4,900
Rush University Colleges of Nursing and Health Sciences; Chicago, Ill. 60612	276	P	13,148	13,148	4,800
Russell Sage College; Troy, N.Y. 12180	1,118 (W)	P	13,400	13,400	5,670
Rust College; Holly Springs, Miss. 38635	1,129	P	4,635	4,635	2,175
Rutgers, The State University of New Jersey–Camden College of Arts and Sciences; Camden, N.J. 08102	2,420	Pub	3,786	7,707	4,936
Rutgers, The State University of New Jersey–College of Engineering; New Brunswick, N.J. 08903–2101	2,260	Pub	4,202	8,550	4,936
Rutgers, The State University of New Jersey–College of Nursing-Newark; Newark, N.J. 07102	372	Pub	3,786	7,707	4,936
Rutgers, The State University of New Jersey–College of Pharmacy; New Brunswick, N.J. 08903–2101	889	Pub	4,202	8,550	4,936
Rutgers, The State Universit of New Jersey–Cook College; New Brunswick, N.J. 08903–2101	3,010	Pub	4,202	8,550	4,936
Rutgers, The State University of New Jersey–Douglass College; New Brunswick, N.J. 08903–2101	2,986 (W)	Pub	3,786	7,707	4,936
Rutgers, The State University of New Jersey–Livingston College; New Brunswick, N.J. 08903–2101	3,273	Pub	3,786	7,707	4,936
Rutgers, The State University of New Jersey–Mason Gross School of the Arts; New Brunswick, N.J. 08903–2101	418	Pub	3,786	7,707	4,936
Rutgers, The State University of New Jersey–Newark College of Arts and Sciences; Newark, N.J. 07102	3,724	Pub	3,786	7,707	4,936
Rutgers, The State University of New Jersey–Rutgers College; New Brunswick, N.J. 08903–2101	8,908	Pub	3,786	7,707	4,936
Rutgers, The State University of New Jersey–University College–Camden; Camden, N.J. 08102	764	Pub	3,922	7,762	n.a.
Rutgers, The State University of New Jersey–University College–New Brunswick; New Brunswick, N.J. 08903	3,132	Pub	3,864	7,704	n.a.
Rutgers, The State University of New Jersey–University College–Newark; Newark, N.J. 07102	1,865	Pub	3,876	7,716	n.a.
Sacred Heart Major Seminary; Detroit, Mich. 48206	220	P	4,820	4,820	4,160
Sacred Heart University; Fairfield, Conn. 06432	1,912	P	12,005	12,005	6,065
Sacred Heart, Univ. of the; Santurce, P.R. 00924	4,753 [1]	P	3,190	3,190	3,000
Saginaw Valley State University; University Center, Mich. 48710	5,680 [1]	Pub	2,317	4,731	3,990
Saint Anselm College; Manchester, N.H. 03102	1,834	P	13,720	13,720	5,550
Saint Joseph's College; Rensselaer, Ind. 47978	973	P	11,900	11,900	4,500
Saint Joseph's University; Philadelphia, Pa. 19131	2,500	P	13,700	13,700	6,200
Saint Leo College; Saint Leo, Fla. 33574	819	P	10,190	10,190	5,240
Saint Mary College; Leavenworth, Kan. 66048	839	P	8,736	8,736	4,120
Saint Meinrad College; St. Meinrad, Ind. 47577	105 (M)	P	6,725	6,725	4,226

Institution and location	Enrollment	Control	Tuition ($) Res.	Tuition ($) Nonres.	Rm/Bd ($)
Saint Michael's College; Colchester, Vt. 05439	1,796	P	13,810	13,810	6,375
Saint Paul's College; Lawrenceville, Va. 23868	672	P	7,418	7,418	3,834
Saint Peter's College; Jersey City, N.J. 07306	3,217	P	11,035[1]	11,035[1]	5,440
Saint Rose, College of; Albany, N.Y. 12203	894	P	10,735	10,735	5,646
Saint Thomas University; Miami, Fla. 33054	1,373	P	10,200	10,200	4,600
Saint Vincent College; Latrobe, Pa. 15650	1,237[1]	P	12,400	12,400	4,410
Salem College; Winston-Salem, N.C. 27108	760 (W)	P	11,260	11,260	6,640
Salem State College; Salem, Mass. 01970	5,468	Pub	3,208	7,332	3,672
Salem-Teikyo University; Salem, W.Va. 26426	855	P	11,658	11,658	3,952
Salisbury State University; Salisbury, Md. 21801	5,398	Pub	3,364	6,478	4,940
Salve Regina University; Newport, R.I. 02840-4192	1,730[1]	P	14,650	14,650	6,700
Sam Houston State University; Huntsville, Tex. 77341	10,837	Pub	1,638	7,398	3,450
Samford University; Birmingham, Ala. 35229	3,231	P	8,648	8,648	3,844
Samuel Merritt College; Oakland, Calif. 94609	323	P	13,865	13,865	4,410
San Diego State University; San Diego, Calif. 92182	22,240	Pub	1,902	1,902	6,192
Imperial Valley Campus; Calexico, Calif. 92231	253	Pub	1,558	7,380	n.a.
San Diego, University of; San Diego, Calif. 92110	3,914	P	14,220	14,220	7,600
San Francisco Art Institute; San Francisco, Calif. 94133	513	P	15,486	15,486	n.a.
San Francisco Conservatory of Music; San Francisco, Calif. 94122	143	P	14,500	14,500	n.a.
San Francisco State Univ.; San Francisco, Calif. 94132	19,902	Pub	1,838	9,218	5,245
San Francisco, University of; San Francisco, Calif. 94117	3,482	P	14,920	14,920	6,934
San Jose Christian College; San Jose, Calif. 95108	300	P	6,300	6,300	3,246
San Jose State University; San Jose, Calif. 95192-0009	24,700	Pub	1,970	6,656	5,100
Sangamon State University; Springfield, Ill. 62708	2,608	Pub	1,766	6,117	3,500
Santa Clara University; Santa Clara, Calif. 95053	4,079	P	14,604	14,604	6,500
Santa Fe, College of; Santa Fe, N.M. 87505	1,368	P	12,714	12,714	4,566
Sarah Lawrence College; Bronxville, N.Y. 10708	1,035	P	20,430	20,430	6,838
Savannah College of Art and Design; Savannah, Ga. 31401	2,090	P	10,800	10,800	3,600
Savannah State College; Savannah, Ga. 31404	3,187	Pub	1,965	5,175	4,665
Schiller International University; 6900 Heidelberg, Germany	1,280	P	11,440	11,440	5,950
School for International Training; Brattleboro, Vt. 05301	650	P	12,200	12,200	4,623
School for Lifelong Learning; Concord, N.H. 03301	1,686	Pub	3,144	3,480	n.a.
School of the Art Institute of Chicago; Chicago, Ill. 60603	1,422	P	15,300	15,300	4,880
School of the Museum of Fine Arts; Boston, Mass. 02115	n.a.	P	13,995	n.a.	n.a.
School of Visual Arts; New York, N.Y. 10010	2,745	P	12,600	12,600	4,800
Schreiner College; Kerrville, Tex. 78028	676	P	9,315	9,315	6,130
Science and Arts, University of, of Oklahoma; Chickasha, Okla. 73018	1,613	Pub	1,218	2,982	1,980
Scranton, University of; Scranton, Pa. 18510-4699	4,215	P	12,480	12,480	6,074
Scripps College. See Claremont Colleges.					
Seattle Pacific University; Seattle, Wash. 98119	2,646	P	13,479	13,479	5,169
Seattle University; Seattle, Wash. 98122	3,420	P	14,265	14,265	5,283
Seaver College. See Pepperdine University					
Selma University; Selma, Ala. 36701	206	P	4,150	4,150	3,700
Seton Hall University; South Orange, N.J. 07079	5,084	P	12,250	12,250	6,588
Seton Hill College; Greensburg, Pa. 15601	923 (W)	P	11,775	11,775	4,435
Shaw University; Raleigh, N.C. 27611	2,432	P	5,716	5,716	3,476
Shawnee State University; Portsmouth, Ohio 45662	3,185	Pub	2,814	4,830	3,630
Sheldon Jackson College; Sitka, Alaska 99835	269	P	9,000	9,000	4,500
Shenandoah University; Winchester, Va. 22601-9986	1,201	P	11,470	11,470	4,800
Shepherd College; Shepherdstown, W. Va. 25443	3,648	Pub	2,064	4,694	3,970
Shimer College; Waukegan, Ill. 60085-0500	120	P	12,600	12,600	4,100
Shippensburg University of Pennsylvania; Shippensburg, Pa. 17257	5,576	Pub	3,244	8,198	3,600
Shorter College; Rome, Ga. 30165	752	P	7,860	7,860	4,050
Siena College; Loudonville, N.Y. 12211	3,492	P	11,840	11,840	5,435
Siena Heights College; Adrian, Mich. 49221	2,139	P	9,970	9,970	4,220
Sierra Nevada College; Incline Village, Nev. 89450	415	P	9,000	9,000	5,150
Silver Lake College; Manitowoc, Wis. 54220	829	P	8,950	8,950	3,700
Simmons Bible College; Louisville, Ky. 40210	109[1]	P	930	930	n.a.
Simmons College; Boston, Mass. 02115	1,352 (W)	P	17,472	17,472	7,228
Simon's Rock of Bard College; Great Barrington, Mass. 01230	318	P	19,770	19,770	5,860
Simpson College; Indianola, Iowa 50125	1,685	P	12,530	12,530	4,145
Simpson College; Redding, Calif. 96003-8606	1,034	P	7,600	7,600	3,800
Sinte Gleska College; Rosebud, S.D. 57570	748	P	1,800	1,800	n.a.
Sioux Falls College; Sioux Falls, S.D. 57105	842	P	9,490	9,490	3,260
Skidmore College; Saratoga Springs, N.Y. 12866	2,128	P	19,945	19,945	5,890
Slippery Rock Univ. of Pennsylvania; Slippery Rock, Pa. 16057	7,162	Pub	4,025	9,075	3,374
Smith College; Northampton, Mass. 01063	2,631 (W)	P	20,380	20,380	6,920
Sojourner-Douglass College; Baltimore, Md. 21205	243	P	3,420	3,420	n.a.
Sonoma State University; Rohnert Park, Calif. 94928	5,536	Pub	2,090	3,205	5,455
South Alabama, University of; Mobile, Ala. 36688	10,159	Pub	2,541	3,591	3,153
South Carolina State University; Orangeburg, S.C. 29117–0001	4,626	Pub	2,500	5,030	3,000
South Carolina, University of; Columbia, S.C. 29208	16,028	Pub	3,278	8,282	3,589

Institution and location	Enrollment	Control	Tuition ($) Res.	Tuition ($) Nonres.	Rm/Bd ($)
South Carolina, Univ. of-Aiken; Aiken, S.C. 29801	3,235	Pub	2,500	6,250	3,175
South Carolina, Univ. of-Coastal Carolina; Myrtle Beach, S.C. 29578	4,023	Pub	3,082	7,180	3,890
South Carolina, Univ. of-Spartanburg; Spartanburg, S.C. 29303	3,270	Pub	2,500	6,250	2,062
South College; Savannah, Ga. 31406	548	P	5,085	5,085	n.a.
South Dakota School of Mines and Technology; Rapid City, S.D. 57701	2,177	Pub	2,866	5,524	3,200
South Dakota State University; Brookings, S.D. 57007	9,326	Pub	1,648	4,480	2,246
South Dakota, University of; Vermillion, S.D. 57069	5,952	Pub	2,191	2,191	2,757
South Florida, University of; Tampa, Fla. 33620	23,622	Pub	1,860	6,760	4,420
South, University of the; Sewanee, Tenn. 37383-1000	1,242	P	16,790	16,790	4,460
Southampton College. *See* Long Island Univ. Center					
Southeast Missouri State Univ.; Cape Girardeau, Mo. 63701	6,151	Pub	2,208	3,984	3,735
Southeastern Baptist College; Laurel, Miss. 39440	83	P	2,220	2,220	1,800
Southeastern Bible College; Birmingham, Ala. 35243	153	P	4,620	4,620	2,900
Southeastern College; Lakeland, Fla. 33801	1,065	P	3,990	3,990	3,134
Southeastern Louisiana University; Hammond, La. 70402	12,623	Pub	2,030	4,262	2,470
Southeastern Oklahoma State Univ.; Durant, Okla. 74701	3,650	Pub	1,676	4,001	2,619
Southeastern University; Washington, D.C. 20024	220[1]	P	6,910	6,910	n.a.
Southern Arkansas University; Magnolia, Ark. 71753	2,761	Pub	1,738	2,616	n.a.
Southern California College; Costa Mesa, Calif. 92626	988	P	10,800	10,800	4,752
Southern California Institute of Architecture; Los Angeles, Calif. 90066	420[1]	P	12,750	12,750	n.a.
Southern California, Univ. of; Los Angeles, Calif. 90089-0911	14,601	P	18,422	18,422	6,524
Southern College of Seventh-Day Adventists; Collegedale, Tenn. 37315-0370	1,652	P	8,880	8,880	3,642
Southern College of Technology; Marietta, Ga. 30060-2896	3,840	Pub	1,761	4,971	3,825
Southern Colorado, University of; Pueblo, Colo. 81001	4,508	Pub	2,066	7,866	4,100
Southern Connecticut State Univ.; New Haven, Conn. 06515	7,705	Pub	3,425	8,517	5,061
Southern Illinois Univ. at Carbondale; Carbondale, Ill. 62901	18,712	Pub	3,338	8,138	3,369
Southern Illinois Univ. at Edwardsville; Edwardsville, Ill. 62026	11,047	Pub	1,928	5,784	3,838
Southern Indiana, University of; Evansville, Ind. 47712	7,443	Pub	1,734	4,224	3,400
Southern Maine, University of; Gorham, Me. 04038	8,624	Pub	3,180	9,000	4,494
Southern Methodist University; Dallas, Tex. 75275	5,247	P	13,510	13,510	5,206
Southern Mississippi, Univ. of; Hattiesburg, Miss. 39406	9,456[1]	Pub	2,468	5,288	2,520
Southern Nazarene Univ.; Bethany, Okla. 73008	1,425	P	7,128	7,128	3,810
Southern Oregon State College; Ashland, Ore. 97520	4,530	Pub	3,100	9,100	4,015
Southern University at New Orleans; New Orleans, La. 70126	4,500	Pub	1,662	3,426	n.a.
Southern University-Baton Rouge; Baton Rouge, La. 70813	9,502	Pub	2,228	4,550	2,952
Southern Utah State University; Cedar City, Utah 84720	5,159	Pub	1,386	5,238	1,845
Southern Vermont College; Bennington, Vt. 05201	743[1]	P	9,810	9,810	4,650
Southwest Baptist University; Bolivar, Mo. 65613	3,136[1]	P	7,466	7,446	2,500
Southwest Missouri State Univ.; Springfield, Mo. 65804	15,577	Pub	2,576	4,946	3,104
Southwest State University; Marshall, Minn. 56258	2,362	Pub	2,745	5,370	2,900
Southwest Texas State Univ.; San Marcos, Tex. 78666-4615	17,886	Pub	900	6,660	3,676
Southwest, College of the; Hobbs, N.M. 88240	365	P	3,120	3,120	1,358
Southwestern Adventist College; Keene, Tex. 76059	971	P	7,728	7,728	3,812
Southwestern Assemblies of God College; Waxahachie, Tex. 75165	761	P	3,354	3,354	3,190
Southwestern College; Phoenix, Ariz. 85032	198	P	6,000	6,000	2,450
Southwestern College; Winfield, Kan. 67156	738[1]	P	7,850	7,850	3,692
Southwestern Louisiana, University of; Lafayette, La. 70504	15,413	Pub	1,898	4,898	2,196
Southwestern Oklahoma State Univ.; Weatherford, Okla. 73096	4,623	Pub	1,305	3,630	2,016
Southwestern University; Georgetown, Tex. 78626	1,261	P	13,400	13,400	5,042
Spalding University; Louisville, Ky. 40203	967	P	9,696	9,696	2,800
Spelman College; Atlanta, Ga. 30314	1,943 (W)	P	8,625	8,625	5,890
Spring Arbor College; Spring Arbor, Mich. 49283	888	P	10,280	10,280	4,070
Spring Hill College; Mobile, Ala. 36608	1,362	P	12,489	12,489	4,788
Springfield College; Springfield, Mass. 01109	2,047[1]	P	11,900[1]	11,900[1]	5,400
St. Ambrose University; Davenport, Iowa 52803	1,819	P	12,180	12,180	4,400
St. Andrews Presbyterian College; Laurinburg, N.C. 28352	721	P	11,440	11,440	5,050
St. Augustine's College; Raleigh, N.C. 27610-2298	1,737[1]	P	5,872	5,872	3,708
St. Benedict, College of; St. Joseph, Minn. 56374-2099	1,787 (W)	P	13,089	13,089	4,370
St. Bonaventure University; St. Bonaventure, N.Y. 14778-2284	1,900	P	11,084	11,084	4,932
St. Catherine, College of; St. Paul, Minn. 55105	2,270 (W)	P	12,960	12,960	4,282
St. Cloud State University; St. Cloud, Minn. 56301-4498	15,958	Pub	2,738	5,522	2,937
St. Edward's University; Austin, Tex. 78704	2,650	P	9,950	9,950	4,280
St. Elizabeth, College of; Convent Station, N.J. 07960-6989	1,504 (W)	P	11,900	11,900	5,600
St. Francis College; Brooklyn Heights, N.Y. 11201	2,166	P	6,650	6,650	n.a.
St. Francis College; Fort Wayne, Ind. 46808	738	P	9,820	9,820	4,070
St. Francis College; Loretto, Pa. 15940	1,136	P	9,660	9,660	5,350
St. Francis Medical Center College of Nursing; Peoria, Ill. 61603	156	P	7,656	7,656	1,400
St. Francis, College of; Joliet, Ill. 60435	1,041	P	10,790	10,790	4,340
St. Hyacinth College and Seminary; Granby, Mass. 01033	24[1](M)	P	4,000	4,000	4,500
St. John Fisher College; Rochester, N.Y. 14618	2,009	P	11,760	11,760	6,060
St. John Vianney College Seminary; Miami, Fla. 33165	40 (M)	P	6,500	6,500	4,000
St. John's College; Annapolis, Md. 21404	419	P	19,850	19,850	5,950

Institution and location	Enrollment	Control	Tuition ($)		Rm/B ($)
			Res.	Nonres.	
St. John's College; Santa Fe, N.M. 87501	391	P	18,180[1]	18,180[1]	5,995[1]
St. John's College; Springfield, Ill. 62702	107	P	6,360	6,360	3,112
St. John's Seminary College; Camarillo, Calif. 93012	80 [1](M)	P	6,100	6,100	1,200
St. John's Seminary College of Liberal Arts; Brighton, Mass. 02135	42 (M)	P	5,200	5,200	2,600
St. John's University; Collegeville, Minn. 56321	1,812 (M)	P	13,094	13,094	4,736
St. John's University; Jamaica, N.Y. 11439	13,881	P	10,450[1]	10,450[1]	n.a.
St. Joseph College; West Hartford, Conn. 06117	1,200 (W)	P	13,020	13,020	4,810
St. Joseph College of Nursing; Joliet, Ill. 60435	170	P	7,884	7,884	n.a.
St. Joseph in Vermont, College of; Rutland, Vt. 05701	378 [1]	P	9,070	9,070	5,100
St. Joseph Seminary College; St. Benedict, La. 70457	58 (M)	P	5,650	5,650	4,550
St. Joseph's College; Brooklyn, N.Y. 11205	1,343	P	7,817	7,817	n.a.
St. Joseph's College-Suffolk; Patchogue, N.Y. 11772	2,438	P	8,024	8,024	n.a.
St. Joseph's College; Standish, Maine 04084–5263	1,087	P	10,990	10,990	5,380
St. Lawrence University; Canton, N.Y. 13617	2,006	P	20,465	20,465	6,130
St. Louis Christian College; Florissant, Mo. 63033	137	P	3,017	3,017	2,650
St. Louis College of Pharmacy; St. Louis, Mo. 63110	851	P	11,000	11,000	4,850
St. Louis University; St. Louis, Mo. 63103	5,409	P	13,900	13,900	5,110
St. Martin's College; Lacey, Wash. 98503–1297	577	P	12,490	12,490	4,590
St. Mary's College of California; Moraga, Calif. 94575	2,580 [1]	P	14,250	14,250	6,608
St. Mary's College of Maryland; St. Mary's City, Md. 20686	1,510	Pub	5,435	8,735	4,970
St. Mary's College–Notre Dame; Notre Dame, Ind. 46556	1,579 (W)	P	13,494	13,494	4,785
St. Mary's College–Orchard Lake; Orchard Lake, Mich. 48324	269	P	6,300	6,300	4,300
St. Mary's College of Minnesota; Winona, Minn. 55987	1,386	P	11,700	11,700	3,920
St. Mary's University of San Antonio; San Antonio, Tex. 78228–8503	4,212	P	9,328	9,328	3,698
St. Mary, College of; Omaha, Neb. 68124	1,172 (W)	P	10,994	10,994	4,080
St. Mary-of-the-Woods Coll.; St. Mary-of-the-Woods, Ind. 47876	1,014 (W)	P	11,940	11,940	4,570
St. Norbert College; De Pere, Wis. 54115	2,097	P	13,700	13,700	4,845
St. Olaf College; Northfield, Minn. 55057	3,015	P	15,000	15,000	3,850
St. Scholastica, College of; Duluth, Minn. 55811	1,551	P	12,459	12,459	3,807
St. Thomas Aquinas College; Sparkill, N.Y. 10976	2,100	P	9,900	9,900	6,050
St. Thomas, University of; Houston, Tex. 77006	1,403	P	9,840	9,840	4,060
St. Thomas, University of; St. Paul, Minn. 55105	4,916	P	13,106	13,106	4,374
St. Xavier University; Chicago, Ill. 60655	2,406	P	11,490	11,490	4,800
Stanford University; Stanford, Calif. 94305	6,561	P	19,695	19,695	7,054
Staten Island, Coll. of (NYC). *See* New York, City Univ. of					
Stephen F. Austin State Univ. Nacogdoches, Tex. 75962	11,758	Pub	1,906	7,606	3,800
Stephens College; Columbia, Mo. 65215	889 (W)	P	14,830	14,830	5,540
Sterling College; Sterling, Kan. 67579	550	P	9,000	9,000	3,500
Stetson University; DeLand, Fla. 32720	2,045	P	13,110	13,110	5,390
Stevens Institute of Technology; Hoboken, N.J. 07030	1,280	P	20,218	20,218	5,950
Stillman College; Tuscaloosa, Ala. 35403	953	P	5,200	5,200	3,100
Stonehill College; North Easton, Mass. 02357	1,943	P	13,329	13,329	6,350
Strayer College Arlington Campus; Arlington, Va. 22204	5,784	P	6,075	6,075	n.a.
Suffolk University; Boston, Mass. 02108-2770	2,904	P	12,046	12,046	7,850
Sul Ross State University; Alpine, Texas 79832	3,212	Pub	1,596	7,416	3,160
Sullivan College; Louisville, Ky. 40232	1,914	P	8,545	8,545	2,700
Susquehanna University; Selinsgrove, Pa. 17870–1001	1,608	P	17,080	17,080	4,900
Swarthmore College; Swarthmore, Pa. 19081	1,269	P	20,186	20,186	6,880
Sweet Briar College; Sweet Briar, Va. 24595	609 (W)	P	14,990	14,990	6,385
Syracuse University; Syracuse, N.Y. 13244	10,097	P	16,710	16,710	7,210
Tabor College; Hillsboro, Kan. 67063	433	P	9,000	9,000	3,600
Talladega College; Talladega, Ala. 35160	912	P	5,666	5,666	2,964
Tampa College; Tampa, Fla. 33614	1,440	P	5,472	5,472	n.a.
Tampa, University of; Tampa, Fla. 33606–1490	2,521	P	13,424	13,424	4,640
Tarleton State University; Stephenville, Tex. 76402	5,576	Pub	960	5,760	3,180
Taylor University; Upland, Ind. 46989	1,817	P	11,914	11,914	4,150
Taylor University–Fort Wayne; Fort Wayne, Ind. 46807	426	P	10,560	10,560	3,910
Teikyo Marycrest University; Davenport, Iowa 52804	1,032	P	10,280	10,280	3,790
Teikyo Post College; Waterbury, Conn. 06723-2540	1,794 [1]	P	12,000	12,000	5,600
Teikyo Westmar University; Le Mars, Iowa 51031	761	P	10,100	10,100	4,100
Temple University; Philadelphia, Pa. 19122	19,529	Pub	5,464	10,246	5,426
Temple University-Ambler; Ambler, Pa. 19002	5,000	Pub	5,314	10,096	5,400
Tennessee State University; Nashville, Tenn. 37209	8,464	Pub	1,866	5,996	3,120
Tennessee Technological Univ.; Cookeville, Tenn. 38505	7,158	Pub	2,558	6,688	3,360
Tennessee Temple University; Chattanooga, Tenn. 37404	653	P	5,240	5,240	3,990
Tennessee Wesleyan College; Athens, Tenn. 37303	632	P	6,200	6,200	3,700
Tennessee, Univ. of-Chattanooga; Chattanooga, Tenn. 37403	7,015	Pub	1,932	6,062	4,322
Tennessee, Univ. of-Knoxville; Knoxville, Tenn. 37996-0230	25,251	Pub	2,164	6,294	3,418
Tennessee, Univ. of-Martin; Martin, Tenn. 38238	5,361	Pub	1,900	5,832	3,040
Tennessee, Univ. of-Memphis; Memphis, Tenn. 38163	417	Pub	8,700	8,700	3,500
Texas A&M University; College Station, Tex. 77843	34,278 [1]	Pub	900	6,660	3,699
Texas A&M University–Corpus Christi; Corpus Christi, Tex. 78412	3,907	Pub	1,588	5,818	2,385
Texas A&M University-Galveston; Galveston, Tex. 77553	1,241	Pub	960	7,380	3,652
Texas A&M University–Kingsville; Kingsville, Tex. 78363	5,302	Pub	1,442	6,050	3,484
Texas Christian University; Fort Worth, Tex. 76129	7,050	P	9,420	9,420	3,500

Institution and location	Enrollment	Control	Tuition ($) Res.	Tuition ($) Nonres.	Rm/Bd ($)
Texas College; Tyler, Tex. 75702–2404	328	P	5,020	5,020	2,430
Texas Lutheran College; Seguin, Tex. 78155	1,091	P	8,626	8,626	3,806
Texas Southern University; Houston, Tex. 77004	6,113	Pub	1,130	4,562	3,320
Texas Tech University; Lubbock, Tex. 79409–5005	19,652	Pub	2,616	9,036	4,084
Texas Wesleyan University; Fort Worth, Tex. 76105–1536	1,493	P	6,900	6,900	3,484
Texas Woman's University; Denton, Tex. 76204	5,319 (W)	Pub	1,396	4,900	3,162
Texas; University of-Arlington; Arlington, Tex. 76019	17,897	Pub	768	5,904	2,820
Texas, University of-Austin; Austin, Tex. 78712	34,746	Pub	1,815	6,105	3,528
Texas, University of-Dallas; Richardson, Tex. 75083-0688	5,013	Pub	2,093	8,513	5,102
Texas, University of-El Paso; El Paso, Tex. 79968	14,746	Pub	1,681	5,911	3,200
Texas, University of-Health Science Center-San Antonio; San Antonio, Tex. 78284	843	Pub	900	6,660	n.a.
Texas, University of, Medical Branch-Galveston; Galveston, Tex. 77555-1305	972	Pub	1,550	6,626	1,956
Texas, University of–Pan American; Edinburg, Tex. 78539	12,733 [1]	Pub	1,400	3,300	2,880
Texas, University of-Permian Basin; Odessa, Tex. 79762–0001	1,578	Pub	1,830	7,590	3,995
Texas, University of-San Antonio; San Antonio, Tex. 78249-0616	14,663	Pub	1,754	6,362	4,800
Texas, University of, Southwestern Medical Center at Dallas; Dallas, Tex. 75235	379	Pub	859	5,083	n.a.
Texas, University of-Tyler; Tyler, Tex. 75701	2,590	Pub	1,222	4,654	3,850
Thiel College; Greenville, Pa. 16125–2181	1,008	P	11,722	11,722	4,958
Thomas Aquinas College; Santa Paula, Calif. 93060	232	P	13,900	13,900	5,300
Thomas College; Thomasville, Ga. 31792–7499	746	P	4,125	4,125	n.a.
Thomas College; Waterville, Me. 04901	450	P	9,720	9,720	4,825
Thomas Edison State College, Trenton, N.J. 08608-1176	8,619	Pub	458	811	n.a.
Thomas Jefferson University, College of Allied Health Sciences; Philadelphia, Pa. 19107	1,066	P	14,920	14,920	5,205
Thomas More College; Crestview Hills, Ky. 41017	1,268	P	10,084	10,084	3,966
Tiffin University; Tiffin, Ohio 44883	1,023	P	8,200	8,200	4,000
Toccoa Falls College; Toccoa Falls, Ga. 30598	903	P	6,376	6,376	3,708
Toledo, University of; Toledo, Ohio 43606	21,162	Pub	3,396	8,145	3,717
Tougaloo College; Tougaloo, Miss. 39174	1,153	P	5,690	5,690	2,279
Touro College; New York, N.Y. 10001-4103	7,704	P	8,780	8,780	6,600
Towson State University; Towson, Md. 21204-7097	13,404	Pub	3,530	6,932	2,360
Transylvania University; Lexington, Ky. 40508-1797	974	P	8,200	8,200	3,040
Trenton State College; Trenton, N.J. 08650–4700	6,067	Pub	4,241	6,658	5,600
Trevecca Nazarene College; Nashville, Tenn. 37210–2877	1,537	P	7,456	7,456	3,410
Tri-State University; Angola, Ind. 46703	1,097	P	10,407	10,407	4,350
Trinity Bible College; Ellendale, N.D. 58436–7150	347	P	5,170	5,170	3,084
Trinity Christian College; Palos Heights, Ill. 60463	624	P	10,700	10,700	4,200
Trinity College of Florida; New Port Richey, Fla. 34655	125	P	3,260	3,260	1,995
Trinity College of Vermont; Burlington, Vt. 05401	1,084 (W)	P	12,120	12,120	6,012
Trinity College–Hartford; Hartford, Conn. 06106	1,944	P	19,690	19,690	6,130
Trinity College–Washington; Washington, D.C. 20017	1,000 (W)	P	11,750	11,750	6,490
Trinity International University–Deerfield; Deerfield, Ill. 60015	869	P	11,918	11,918	4,560
Trinity International University; Miami, Fla. 33101	381	P	3,595	3,595	n.a.
Trinity University; San Antonio, Tex. 78212–7200	2,226	P	13,044	13,044	5,350
Troy State University; Troy, Ala. 36082	5,068	Pub	1,920	3,330	2,895
Troy State University-Dothan; Dothan, Ala. 36303	1,707 [1]	Pub	1,920	3,456	n.a.
Troy State University-Montgomery; Montgomery, Ala. 36103-4419	2,718	Pub	1,887	374	n.a.
Tufts University; Medford, Mass. 02155	4,432	P	22,686	22,686	6,250
Tulane University; New Orleans, La. 70118	6,327	P	20,226	20,226	5,950
Tulsa, University of; Tulsa, Okla. 74104	3,369	P	12,300	12,300	4,074
Tusculum College; Greeneville, Tenn. 37743	1,018	P	9,500	9,500	3,850
Tuskegee University; Tuskegee, Ala. 36088	3,191	P	8,020	8,020	4,104
Union College; Barbourville, Ky. 40906	1,100	P	8,200	8,200	3,040
Union College; Lincoln, Neb. 68506	574	P	9,225	9,225	2,900
Union College; Schenectady, N.Y. 12308	2,009	P	20,995	20,995	6,330
Union Institute, The; Cincinnati, Ohio 45206–1947	482	P	7,776	7,776	n.a.
Union University; Jackson, Tenn. 38305	1,838	P	7,050	7,050	2,940
United States International University; San Diego, Calif. 92131	347	P	10,800	10,800	4,530
United States Merchant Marine Academy; Kings Point, N.Y. 11024	980	Pub	4,464 [1]	4,464 [1]	n.a. [1]
Unity College; Unity, Me. 04988	489	P	10,330	10,330	5,050
Universidad de las Américas—Puebla; Puebla, Mexico 72820	5,481	P	3,400	3,400	3,000
Universidad Politecnica de Puerto Rico; Hato Rey, San Juan, P.R. 00918	4,322	P	3,310	3,310	n.a.
Upper Iowa University; Fayette, Iowa 52142	3,804	P	9,372	9,372	3,560
Urbana Univ.; Urbana, Ohio 43078-2091	1,000	P	8,976	8,976	4,350
Ursinus College; Collegeville, Pa. 19426	1,113	P	15,835	15,835	5,330
Ursuline College; Pepper Pike, Ohio 44124	1,448	P	9,810	9,810	4,339
Utah State University; Logan, Utah 84322	19,861	Pub	1,992	6,042	3,525
Utah, University of; Salt Lake City, Utah 84112	21,756	Pub	2,508	7,707	6,318
Utica College of Syracuse University; Utica, N.Y. 13502	1,762	P	14,116	14,116	5,380
Valdosta State College; Valdosta, Ga. 31698	6,730 [1]	Pub	1,887	5,097	3,225
Valley City State University; Valley City, N.D. 58072	986	Pub	1,680	4,486	2,410
Valley Forge Christian College; Phoenixville, Pa. 19460	510	P	5,680	5,680	3,280

Institution and location	Enrollment	Control	Tuition ($) Res.	Tuition ($) Nonres.	Rm/B ($)
Valparaiso University; Valparaiso, Ind. 46383	2,795	P	13,510	13,510	3,450
Vanderbilt University; Nashville, Tenn. 37203	5,652	P	21,065	21,065	6,656
Vandercook College of Music; Chicago, Ill. 60616	82	P	9,300	9,300	4,600
Vassar College; Poughkeepsie, N.Y. 12601	2,250	P	20,330	20,330	6,150
Vennard College; University Park, Iowa 52595	143	P	5,696	5,696	3,700
Vermont, University of; Burlington, Vt. 05401-3596	7,925	Pub	6,909	16,605	5,292
Villa Julie College; Stevenson, Md. 21153	1,858 [1]	P	8,200	8,200	4,600
Villanova University; Villanova, Pa. 19085–1672	7,643	P	17,500	17,500	6,500
Virgin Islands, University of the; St. Thomas, V.I. 00802	2,668	Pub	1,650	4,950	4,850
Virginia Commonwealth University; Richmond, Va. 23284-2526	12,604	Pub	4,071	11,996	4,352
Virginia Intermont College; Bristol, Va. 24201-4298	747	P	9,975	9,975	4,250
Virginia Military Institute; Lexington, Va. 24450	1,196	Pub	3,655	9,875	3,310
Virginia Polytechnic Institute and State University; Blacksburg, Va. 24061–0202	19,229	Pub	4,087	10,739	3,120
Virginia State University; Petersburg, Va. 23806	4,260	Pub	3,356	7,365	4,845
Virginia Union University; Richmond, Va. 23220	1,209	P	8,100	8,100	3,780
Virginia Wesleyan College; Norfolk-Virginia Beach, Va. 23502	1,513	P	11,650	11,650	5,200
Virginia, University of; Charlottesville, Va. 22906	11,502	Pub	4,614	14,006	3,846
Virginia, University of—Clinch Valley College; Wise, Va. 24293	1,840	Pub	3,200	7,524	3,902
Visual Arts, College of; St. Paul, Minn. 55102–2199	200	P	8,960	8,960	4,500
Viterbo College; La Crosse, Wis. 54601	1,548	P	9,850	9,850	3,750
Voorhees College; Denmark, S.C. 29042	723	P	8,900	8,900	5,084
Wabash College; Crawfordsville, Ind. 47933	770 [1](M)	P	13,700	13,700	4,405
Wadhams Hall Seminary—College; Ogdensburg, N.Y. 13669-9308	31 [1]	P	4,120	4,120	4,115
Wagner College; Staten Island, N.Y. 10301	1,248	P	14,450	14,450	5,800
Wake Forest University; Winston-Salem, N.C. 27109	3,746	P	14,750	14,750	4,585
Walla Walla College; College Place, Wash. 99324	1,620	P	11,475	11,475	4,245
Walsh College of Accountancy and Business Administration; Troy, Mich. 48007–7006	1,552	P	6,150	6,150	n.a.
Walsh University; North Canton, Ohio 44720	1,356	P	9,900	9,900	4,700
Warner Pacific College; Portland, Ore. 97215	692	P	8,940	8,940	4,340
Warner Southern College; Lake Wales, Fla. 33853	581	P	7,200	7,200	3,700
Warren Wilson College; Asheville, N.C. 28815	523	P	11,165	11,165	3,152
Wartburg College; Waverly, Iowa 50677	1,433	P	12,870	12,870	3,990
Warwick, University of; Coventry, CV4 7AL, England	6,706 [1]	Pub	4,748	4,748	3,806
Washburn University; Topeka, Kan. 66621	5,477	Pub	6,120	9,240	3,410
Washington and Jefferson College; Washington, Pa. 15301	1,104	P	17,190	17,190	4,205
Washington and Lee University; Lexington, Va. 24450	1,617	P	14,750	14,750	4,935
Washington Bible College; Lanham, Md. 20706	315	P	4,680	4,680	3,800
Washington College; Chestertown, Md. 21620-9926	881	P	16,800	16,800	5,740
Washington State University; Pullman, Wash. 99164	16,123	Pub	3,124	9,758	4,200
Washington University; St. Louis, Mo. 63130	4,962	P	20,000	20,000	6,284
Washington, University of; Seattle, Wash. 98195–5840	24,592	Pub	3,256	9,872	4,455
Wayland Baptist University; Plainview, Tex. 79072	3,217	P	5,400	5,400	3,021
Wayne State College; Wayne, Neb. 68787	3,192	Pub	1,575	3,000	2,740
Wayne State University; Detroit, Mich. 48202	20,865 [1]	Pub	2,850	6,306	5,839
Waynesburg College; Waynesburg, Pa. 15370	1,267	P	9,800	9,800	4,050
Webber College; Babson Park, Fla. 33827	370 [1]	P	6,540	6,540	3,000
Weber State University; Ogden, Utah 84408	13,996	Pub	1,860	5,547	5,076
Webster University; St. Louis, Mo. 63119	3,709 [1]	P	9,700	9,700	4,384
Wellesley College; Wellesley, Mass. 02181	2,271 [1](W)	P	19,610	19,610	6,200
Wells College; Aurora, N.Y. 13026	400 (W)	P	16,800	16,800	5,800
Wentworth Institute of Technology; Boston, Mass. 02115	2,489	P	10,500	10,500	6,050
Wesley College; Dover, Del. 19901	1,280	P	10,954	10,954	4,674
Wesleyan College; Macon, Ga. 31297	445 (W)	P	13,200	13,200	5,100
Wesleyan University; Middletown, Conn. 06457	2,724	P	20,820	20,820	5,810
West Alabama, The University of; Livingston, Ala. 35470	1,954	Pub	2,010	2,010	2,436
West Chester Univ. of Pennsylvania; West Chester, Pa. 19383	9,274	Pub	3,224	8,198	4,232
West Coast University; Los Angeles, Calif. 90020-1765	500	P	10,200	10,200	n.a.
West Florida, University of; Pensacola, Fla. 32514	6,408	Pub	1,542	7,334	4,134
West Georgia College; Carrollton, Ga. 30118	8,650	Pub	1,884	5,094	2,973
West Liberty State College; West Liberty, W. Va. 26074	2,435	Pub	1,960	5,300	3,000
West Los Angeles, University of; Inglewood, Calif. 90301	235	P	5,070	5,070	n.a.
West Suburban College of Nursing; Oak Park, Ill. 60302	241	P	10,110	10,110	n.a.
West Texas State University; Canyon, Tex. 79016	4,813 [1]	Pub	1,586	5,966	2,716
West Virginia Institute of Technology; Montgomery, W. Va. 25136	3,027	Pub	2,270	4,940	3,940
West Virginia State College; Institute, W. Va. 25112	4,896	Pub	5,188	7,816	3,200
West Virginia University; Morgantown, W. Va. 26506-6009	15,383	Pub	2,100	6,792	4,425
West Virginia University at Parkersburg; Parkersburg, W. Va. 26101-9577	3,726	Pub	1,164	3,564	n.a.
West Virginia Wesleyan College; Buckhannon, W. Va. 26201	1,620	P	14,975	14,975	3,975
West Virginia, The College of; Beckley, W. Va. 25802	2,051	P	3,240	3,240	3,500
Westbrook College; Portland, Me. 04103	387	P	11,650	11,650	4,900
Western Baptist College; Salem, Ore. 97301	749	P	10,490	10,490	4,550
Western Carolina University; Cullowhee, N.C. 28723	5,948	Pub	1,695	8,503	2,516
Western Connecticut State University; Danbury, Conn. 06810	4,679	Pub	3,214	3,214	5,080

Institution and location	Enrollment	Control	Tuition ($) Res.	Tuition ($) Nonres.	Rm/Bd ($)
Western Illinois University; Macomb, Ill. 61455-1390	12,115	Pub	2,810	6,890	3,613
Western International University; Phoenix, Ariz. 85021	1,169	P	3,650	3,650	n.a.
Western Kentucky University; Bowling Green, Ky. 42101	10,676	Pub	1,901	5,270	3,450
Western Maryland College; Westminster, Md. 21157	1,266	P	16,125	16,125	5,365
Western Michigan University; Kalamazoo, Mich. 49008	19,499	Pub	2,549	5,825	4,100
Western Montana College; Dillon, Mont. 59725	1,176	Pub	2,000	6,000	3,400
Western New England College; Springfield, Mass. 01119	1,673	P	9,980	9,980	5,914
Western New Mexico University; Silver City, N.M. 88061	2,001 [1]	Pub	1,486	5,454	2,158
Western Oregon State College; Monmouth, Ore. 97361	3,975	Pub	2,820	7,809	3,631
Western State College of Colorado; Gunnison, Colo. 81230	2,662	Pub	1,993	6,739	4,279
Western Washington University; Bellingham, Wash. 98225–9009	9,858 [1]	Pub	2,613	8,796	4,478
Westfield State College; Westfield, Mass. 01086	3,162 [1]	Pub	3,338	7,473	4,100
Westminster College; Fulton, Mo. 65251	609	P	11,350[1]	11,350[1]	4,660
Westminster College; New Wilmington, Pa. 16172	1,543	P	12,810	12,810	3,980
Westminster Coll. of Salt Lake City; Salt Lake City, Utah 84105	947	P	9,600	9,600	4,190
Westmont College; Santa Barbara, Calif. 93108	1,280	P	17,150	17,150	5,748
Wheaton College; Norton, Mass. 02766	1,319	P	19,740	19,740	6,250
Wheaton College; Wheaton, Ill. 60187-5593	2,304	P	13,100	13,100	4,550
Wheeling Jesuit College; Wheeling, W. Va. 26003	1,365	P	12,000	12,000	4,670
Wheelock College; Boston, Mass. 02215	725	P	14,784	14,784	5,916
White Plains, Coll. of, of Pace Univ. *See* Pace Univ.					
Whitman College; Walla Walla, Wash. 99362	1,373	P	18,650	18,650	5,420
Whittier College; Whittier, Calif. 90608	1,330	P	17,800	17,800	6,047
Whitworth College; Spokane, Wash. 99251	1,577	P	13,620	13,620	4,900
Wichita State University; Wichita, Kan. 67208	11,504	Pub	2,346	8,099	3,465
Widener University; Chester, Pa. 19013	2,350 [1]	P	12,950	12,950	5,650
Wilberforce University; Wilberforce, Ohio 45384	850	P	7,145	7,145	3,760
Wiley College; Marshall, Tex. 75670	505	P	3,660	3,660	2,872
Wilkes University; Wilkes-Barre, Pa. 18766	2,408	P	12,478	12,478	5,410
Willamette University; Salem, Ore. 97301	1,701	P	16,490	16,490	4,800
William and Mary, College of; Williamsburg, Va. 23185	5,402	Pub	4,738	14,428	4,372
William Carey College; Hattiesburg, Miss. 39401	1,885 [1]	P	5,340	5,340	2,335
William Jewell College; Liberty, Mo. 64068	1,182	P	10,864	10,864	3,270
William Paterson College; Wayne, N.J. 07470	8,044 [1]	Pub	3,000	3,952	4,500
William Penn College; Oskaloosa, Iowa 52577	693	P	10,940	10,940	3,490
William Smith College. *See* Hobart and William Smith Colleges					
William Tyndale College; Farmington Hills, Mich. 45018	542	P	4,746	4,746	4,170
William Woods College; Fulton, Mo. 65251	823 [1](W)	P	11,300	11,300	4,700
Williams Baptist College; Walnut Ridge, Ark. 72476	605	P	4,800	4,800	2,722
Williams College; Williamstown, Mass. 01267	1,985	P	20,790	20,790	5,990
Wilmington College; New Castle, Del. 19720	1,773	P	5,700	5,700	n.a.
Wilmington College of Ohio; Wilmington, Ohio 45177	1,006	P	11,050	11,050	4,200
Wilson College; Chambersburg, Pa. 17201-1285	238 (W)	P	11,999	11,999	5,338
Wingate College; Wingate, N.C. 28174	1,276	P	8,800	8,800	3,600
Winona State University; Winona, Minn. 55987	7,000 [1]	Pub	2,500	5,500	3,200
Winston-Salem State University; Winston-Salem, N.C. 27110	2,817	Pub	1,262	6,994	3,048
Winthrop University; Rock Hill, S.C. 29733	5,308	Pub	3,716	6,672	3,488
Wisconsin Lutheran College; Milwaukee, Wis. 53226	393	P	11,000	11,000	4,160
Wisconsin, University of-Eau Claire; Eau Claire, Wis. 54701	9,778	Pub	2,447	7,581	2,800
Wisconsin, University of-Green Bay; Green Bay, Wis. 54302	5,305	Pub	2,427	7,562	2,900
Wisconsin, University of-La Crosse; La Crosse, Wis. 54601	8,005	Pub	2,512	7,648	2,510
Wisconsin, University of-Madison; Madison, Wis. 53706	26,207	Pub	2,730	9,050	4,290
Wisconsin, University of-Milwaukee; Milwaukee, Wis. 53201	17,667	Pub	2,947	9,398	3,500
Wisconsin, University of-Oshkosh; Oshkosh, Wis. 54901	9,098	Pub	2,300	7,435	2,400
Wisconsin, University of-Parkside; Kenosha, Wis. 53141–2000	4,828	Pub	2,420	7,495	3,600
Wisconsin, University of-Platteville; Platteville, Wis. 53818	4,381	Pub	2,485	7,560	3,600
Wisconsin, University of-River Falls; River Falls, Wis. 54022	5,400 [1]	Pub	2,445	7,580	2,776
Wisconsin, University of-Stevens Point; Stevens Point, Wis. 54481	7,983 [1]	Pub	2,395	7,422	3,150
Wisconsin, University of-Stout; Menomonie, Wis. 54751	7,072	Pub	2,043	7,178	2,818
Wisconsin, University of-Superior; Superior, Wis. 54880	2,402 [1]	Pub	2,335	7,470	2,996
Wisconsin, University of-Whitewater; Whitewater, Wis. 53190	9,234	Pub	2,474	7,608	2,500
Wittenberg University; Springfield, Ohio 45501	2,279	P	17,696	17,696	4,536
Wofford College; Spartanburg, S.C. 29303-3663	1,113	P	14,675	14,675	4,185
Woodbury University; Burbanks, Calif. 91510-7846	1,096	P	13,275	13,275	5,685
Wooster, College of; Wooster, Ohio 44691	1,785 [1]	P	17,600	17,600	4,640
Worcester Polytechnic Institute; Worcester, Mass. 01609	2,786	P	18,060	18,060	5,940
Worcester State College; Worcester, Mass. 01602–2597	3,600	Pub	2,653	6,187	3,800
Wright State University; Dayton, Ohio 45435	16,488	Pub	3,429	6,858	4,100
Wyoming, University of; Laramie, Wyo. 82071	11,361	Pub	2,005	2,005	3,520
Xavier University; Cincinnati, Ohio 45207	3,756	P	12,950	12,950	5,480
Xavier University of Louisiana; New Orleans, La. 70125	3,467	P	7,700	7,700	4,500
Yale University; New Haven, Conn. 06520–8234	5,166	P	22,000	22,000	6,680
Yeshiva University; New York, N.Y. 10033-3299	1,852	P	13,650	13,650	6,550
York College of Pennsylvania; York, Pa. 17405	4,911	P	5,525	5,525	4,100
Youngstown State Univ.; Youngstown, Ohio 44555	12,833	Pub	3,366	4,986	4,200

SPORTS

THE OLYMPIC GAMES

(W)—Site of Winter Games. (S)—Site of Summer Games

1896	Athens	1948	St. Moritz (W)	1976	Montreal (S)
1900	Paris	1948	London (S)	1980	Lake Placid (W)
1904	St. Louis	1952	Oslo (W)	1980	Moscow (S)
1906	Athens	1952	Helsinki (S)	1984	Sarajevo, Yugoslavia (W)
1908	London	1956	Cortina d'Ampezzo, Italy (W)	1984	Los Angeles (S)
1912	Stockholm	1956	Melbourne (S)	1988	Calgary, Alberta (W)
1920	Antwerp	1960	Squaw Valley, Calif. (W)	1988	Seoul, South Korea (S)
1924	Chamonix (W)	1960	Rome (S)	1992	Albertville, France (W)
1924	Paris (S)	1964	Innsbruck, Austria (W)	1992	Barcelona, Spain (S)
1928	St. Moritz (W)	1964	Tokyo (S)	1994	Lillehammer, Norway (W)
1928	Amsterdam (S)	1968	Grenoble, France (W)	1996	Atlanta, Ga. (S)
1932	Lake Placid (W)	1968	Mexico City (S)	1998	Nagano, Japan (W)
1932	Los Angeles (S)	1972	Sapporo, Japan (W)	2000	Sydney, Australia (S)
1936	Garmisch–Partenkirchen (W)	1972	Munich (S)	2002	Salt Lake City (W)
1936	Berlin (S)	1976	Innsbruck, Austria (W)		

The first Olympic Games of which there is record were held in 776 B.C., and consisted of one event, a great foot race of about 200 yards held on a plain by the River Alpheus (now the Ruphia) just outside the little town of Olympia in Greece. It was from that date the Greeks began to keep their calendar by "Olympiads," the four–year spans between the celebrations of the famous games.

The modern Olympic Games, which started in Athens in 1896, are the result of the devotion of a French educator, Baron Pierre de Coubertin, to the idea that, since young people and athletics have gone together through the ages, education and athletics might go hand–in–hand toward a better international understanding.

The principal organization responsible for the staging of the Games is the International Olympic Committee (IOC). Other important roles are played by the National Olympic Committees in each participating country, international sports federations, and the orga-nizing committee of the host city.

Beginning in 1994, the IOC decided to change the format of having both the Summer and Winter Games in the same year. Summer and Winter Olympics now alternate every two years. In 1994, the Winter Games were staged in Lillehammer, Norway, just two years after they'd been in Albertville, France. The Winter Games will next be held in Nagano, Japan, in 1998. The next Summer Olympics will be 1996 in Atlanta, Ga.

The headquarters of the 89–member International Olympic Committee are in Lausanne, Switzerland. The president of the IOC is Juan Antonio Samaranch of Spain.

The Olympic motto is "Citius, Altius, Fortius," "Faster, Higher, Stronger." The Olympic symbol is five interlocking circles colored blue, yellow, black, green, and red, on a white background, representing the five continents. At least one of those colors appears in the national flag of every country.

1996 Summer Games

TRACK AND FIELD–MEN

100–Meter Dash

1896	Thomas Burke, United States	12s
1900	Francis W. Jarvis, United States	10.8s
1904	Archie Hahn, United States	11s
1906	Archie Hahn, United States	11.2s
1908	Reginald Walker, South Africa	10.8s
1912	Ralph Craig, United States	10.8s
1920	Charles Paddock, United States	10.8s
1924	Harold Abrahams, Great Britain	10.6s
1928	Percy Williams, Canada	10.8s
1932	Eddie Tolan, United States	10.3s
1936	Jesse Owens, United States	10.3s [1]
1948	Harrison Dillard, United States	10.3s
1952	Lindy Remigino, United States	10.4s
1956	Bobby Morrow, United States	10.5s
1960	Armin Hary, Germany	10.2s
1964	Robert Hayes, United States	10s
1968	James Hines, United States	9.9s
1972	Valery Borzow, U.S.S.R.	10.14s
1976	Hasely Crawford, Trinidad and Tobago	10.06s
1980	Allan Wells, Britain	10.25s
1984	Carl Lewis, United States	9.99s
1988	Carl Lewis, United States	9.92s
1992	Linford Christie, Great Britain	09.96s
1996	Donovan Bailey, Canada	9.84s

1. Wind assisted. 2. Lewis was awarded the gold medal when Ben Johnson of Canada, the original winner, 09.79s, was stripped of the medal after testing positive for steroid use. 3. World record.

200–Meter Dash

1900	John Tewksbury, United States	22.2s
1904	Archie Hahn, United States	21.6s
1908	Robert Kerr, Canada	22.6s
1912	Ralph Craig, United States	21.7s
1920	Allan Woodring, United States	22s
1924	Jackson Scholz, United States	21.6s
1928	Percy Williams, Canada	21.8s
1932	Eddie Tolan, United States	21.2s
1936	Jesse Owens, United States	20.7s
1948	Melvin E. Patton, United States	21.1s
1952	Andrew Stanfield, United States	20.7s
1956	Bobby Morrow, United States	20.6s

1960	Livio Berruti, Italy	20.5s
1964	Henry Carr, United States	20.3s
1968	Tommie Smith, United States	19.8s
1972	Vallery Borzov, U.S.S.R.	20s
1976	Don Quarrie, Jamaica	20.23s
1980	Pietro Mennea, Italy	20.19s
1984	Carl Lewis, United States	19.80s
1988	Joe DeLoach, United States	19.75s
1992	Mike Marsh, United States	20.01s
1996	Michael Johnson, United States	19.32s [1]
1. World record.		

400–Meter Dash

1896	Thomas Burke, United States	54.2s
1900	Maxwell Long, United States	49.4s
1904	Harry Hillman, United States	49.2s
1906	Paul Pilgrim, United States	53.2s
1908	Wyndham Halswelle, Great Britain (walkover)	50s
1912	Charles Reidpath, United States	48.2s
1920	Bevil Rudd, South Africa	49.6s
1924	Eric Liddell, Great Britain	47.6s
1928	Ray Barbuti, United States	47.8s
1932	William Carr, United States	46.2s
1936	Archie Williams, United States	46.5s
1948	Arthur Wint, Jamaica, B.W.I.	46.2s
1952	George Rhoden, Jamaica, B.W.I.	45.9s
1956	Charles Jenkins, United States	46.7s
1960	Otis Davis, United States	44.9s
1964	Mike Larrabee, United States	45.1s
1968	Lee Evans, United States	43.8s
1972	Vincent Matthews, United States	44.66s
1976	Alberto Juantorena, Cuba	44.26s
1980	Viktor Markin, U.S.S.R.	44.60s
1984	Alonzo Babers, United States	44.27s
1988	Steve Lewis, United States	43.87s
1992	Quincy Watts, United States	43.50s
1996	Michael Johnson, United States	43.49s

800–Meter Run

1896	Edwin Flack, Australia	2m11s
1900	Alfred Tysoe, Great Britain	2m1.4s
1904	James Lightbody, United States	1m56s
1906	Paul Pilgrim, United States	2m1.2s
1908	Mel Sheppard, United states	1m52.8s
1912	Ted Meredith, United States	1m51.9s
1920	Albert Hill, Great Britain	1m53.4s
1924	Douglas Lowe, Great Britain	1m52.4s
1928	Douglas Lowe, Great Britain	1m51.8s
1932	Thomas Hampson, Great Britain	1m49.8s
1936	John Woodruff, United States	1m52.9s
1948	Malvin Whitfield, United States	1m49.2s
1952	Malvin Whitfield, United States	1m49.2s
1956	Tom Courtney, United States	1m47.7s
1960	Peter Snell, New Zealand	1m46.3s
1964	Peter Snell, New Zealand	1m45.1s
1968	Ralph Doubell, Australia	1m44.3s
1972	David Wottle, United States	1m45.9s
1976	Alberto Juantorena, Cuba	1m43.5s
1980	Steve Ovett, Britain	1m45.4s
1984	Joaquin Cruz, Brazil	1m43.0s
1988	Paul Ereng, Kenya	1m43.45s
1992	WilliamTanui, Kenya	1m43.66s
1996	Vebjoern Rodal, Norway	1m42.58s

1,500–Meter Run

1896	Edwin Flack, Australia	4m33.2s
1900	Charles Bennett, Great Britain	4m6s
1904	James Lightbody, United States	4m5.4s
1906	James Lightbody, United States	4m12s
1908	Mel Sheppard, United States	4m3.4s
1912	Arnold Jackson, Great Britain	3m56.8s
1920	Albert Hill, Great Britain	4m1.8s
1924	Paavo Nurmi, Finland	3m53.6s
1928	Harry Larva, Finland	3m53.2s

1932	Luigi Becali, Italy	3m51.2s
1936	Jack Lovelock, New Zealand	3m47.8s
1948	Henri Eriksson, Sweden	3m49.8s
1952	Joseph Barthel, Luxembourg	3m45.2s
1956	Ron Delany, Ireland	3m41.2s
1960	Herb Elliott, Australia	3m35.6s
1964	Peter Snell, New Zealand	3m38.1s
1968	Kipchoge Keino, Kenya	3m34.9s
1972	Pekka Vasala, Finland	3m36.3s
1976	John Walker, New Zealand	3m39.17s
1980	Sebastian Coe, Britain	3m38.4s
1984	Sebastian Coe, Britain	3m32.53s
1988	Peter Rono, Kenya	3m35.96s
1992	Fermin Cacho Ruiz, Spain	3m40.12s
1996	Noureddine Morceli, Algeria	3m35.78s

5,000-Meter Run

1912	Hannes Kolehmainen, Finland	14m36.6s
1920	Joseph Guillemot, France	14m55.6s
1024	Paavo Nurmi, Finland	14m31.2s
1928	Willie Ritola, Finland	14m38s
1932	Lauri Lehtinen, Finland	14m30s
1936	Gunnar Hockert, Finland	14m22.2s
1948	Gaston Reiff, Belgium	14m17.6s
1952	Emil Zatopek, Czechoslovakia	14m6.6s
1956	Vladimir Kuts, U.S.S.R.	13m39.6s
1960	Murray Halberg, New Zealand	13m43.4s
1964	Bob Schul, United States	13m48.8s
1968	Mohamed Gammoudi, Tunisia	14m.05s
1972	Lasse Viren, Finland	13m26.4s
1976	Lasse Viren, Finland	13m24.76s
1980	Miruts Yifter, Ethiopia	13m21s
1984	Saud Aouita, Morocco	13m5.59s
1988	John Ngugi, Kenya	13m11.70s
1992	Dieter Baumann, Germany	13m12.52s
1996	Venuste Niyongabo, Burundi	13m07.96

10,000–Meter Run

1912	Hannes Kolehmainen, Finland	31m20.8s
1920	Paavo Nurmi, Finland	31m45.8s
1924	Willie Ritola, Finland	30m23.2s
1928	Paavo Nurmi, Finland	30m18.8s
1932	Janusz Kusocinski, Poland	30m11.4s
1936	Ilmari Salminen, Finland	30m15.4s
1948	Emil Zatopek, Czechoslovakia	29m59.6s
1952	Emil Zatopek, Czechoslovakia	29ml7s
1956	Vladimir Kuts, U.S.S.R.	28m45.6s
1960	Peter Bolotnikov, U.S.S.R.	28m32.2s
1964	Billy Mills, United States	28m24.4s
1968	Nartali Temu, Kenya	29m27.4s
1972	Lasse Viren, Finland	27m38.4s
1976	Lasse Viren, Finland	27m40.38s
1980	Miruts Yifter, Ethiopia	27m42.7s
1984	Alberto Cova, Italy	27m47.5s
1988	Mly Brahim Boutaib, Morocco	27m21.46s
1992	Khalid Skah, Morocco	27m47.70s
1996	Haile Gebrselassie, Ethiopia	27m07.34s

Marathon

1896	Spiridon Loues, Greece	2h58m50s
1900	Michel Teato, France	2h59m45s
1904	Thomas Hicks, United States	3h28m53s
1906	William J. Sherring, Canada	2h51m23.65s
1908	John J. Hayes, United States	2h55m18.4s
1912	Kenneth McArthur, South Africa	2h36m54.8s
1920	Hannes Kolehmainen, Finland	2h32m35.8s
1924	Albin Stenroos, Finland	2h41m22.6s
1928	A.B. El Ouafi, France	2h32m57s
1932	Juan Zabala, Argentina	2h31m36s
1936	Kitei Son, Japan	2h29m19.2s
1948	Delfo Cabrera, Argentina	2h34m51.6s
1952	Emil Zatopek, Czechoslovakia	2h23m3.2s
1956	Alain Mimoun, France	2h25m

1960	Abebe Bikila, Ethiopia	2h15m16.2s
1964	Abebe Bikila, Ethiopia	2h12m11.2s
1968	Mamo Wold, Ethiopia	2h20m26.4s
1972	Frank Shorter, United States	2h12m19.8s
1976	Walter Cierpinski, East Germany	2h09m55s
1980	Walter Cierpinski, East Germany	2h11m3s
1984	Carlos Lopes, Portugal	2h9m.55s
1988	Gelindo Bordin, Italy	2hr10m47s
1992	Hwang Young-Cho, South Korea	2h13m23s
1996	Josia Thugwane, South Africa	2h12m36s

110–Meter Hurdles

1896	Thomas Curtis, United States	17.6s
1900	Alvin Kraenzlein, United States	15.4s
1904	Frederick Schule, United States	16s
1906	R.G. Leavitt, United States	16.2s
1908	Forrest Smithson, United States	15s
1912	Frederick Kelly, United States	15.1s
1920	Earl Thomson, Canada	14.8s
1924	Daniel Kinsey, United States	15s
1928	Sydney Atkinson, South Africa	14.8s
1932	George Saling, United States	14.6s
1936	Forrest Towns, United States	14.2s
1948	William Porter, United States	13.9s
1952	Harrison Dillard, United States	13.7s
1956	Lee Calhoun, United States	13.5s
1960	Lee Calhoun, United States	13.8s
1964	Hayes Jones, United States	13.6s
1968	Willie Davenport, United States	13.3s
1972	Rodney Milburn, United States	13.24s
1976	Guy Drut, France	13.30s
1980	Thomas Munkett, East Germany	13.20s
1984	Roger Kingdom, United States	13.20s
1988	Roger Kingdom, United States	12.98s
1992	Mark McCoy, Canada	13.12s
1996	Allen Johnson, United States	12.95s

200–Meter Hurdles

1900	Alvin Kraenzlein, United States	25.4s
1904	Harry Hillman, United States	24.6s

400–Meter Hurdles

1900	John Tewksbury, United States	57.6s
1904	Harry Hillman, United States	53s
1908	Charles Bacon, United States	55s
1920	Frank Loomis, United States	54s
1924	F. Morgan Taylor, United States	52.6s
1928	Lord David Burghley, Great Britain	53.4s
1932	Robert Tisdall, Ireland	51.8s [1]
1936	Glenn Hardin, United States	52.4s
1948	Roy Cochran, United States	51.1s
1952	Charles Moore, United States	50.8s
1956	Glenn Davis, United States	50.1s
1960	Glenn Davis, United States	49.3s
1964	Rex Cawley, United States	49.6s
1968	David Hemery, Great Britain	48.1s
1972	John Akii–Bua, Uganda	47.8s
1976	Edwin Moses, United States	47.64s
1980	Volker Beck, East Germany	48.70s
1984	Edwin Moses, United States	47.75s
1988	Andre Phillips, United States	47.19s
1992	Kevin Young, United States	46.78s
1996	Derrick Adkins, United States	47.54s

1. Record not allowed.

2,500–Meter Steeplechase

1900	George Orton, United States	7m34s
1904	James Lightbody, United States	7m39.6s

3,000–Meter Steeplechase

1920	Percy Hodge, Great Britain	10m0.4s
1924	Willie Ritola, Finland	9m33.6s
1928	Toivo Loukola, Finland	9m21.8s

1932	Volmari Iso–Hollo, Finland	10m33.4s [1]
1936	Volmari Iso–Hollo, Finland	9m3.8s
1948	Thure Sjoestrand, Sweden	9m4.6s
1952	Horace Ashenfelter, United States	8m45.4s
1956	Chris Brasher, Great Britain	8m41.2s
1960	Zdzislaw Krzyskowiak, Poland	8m34.2s
1964	Gaston Roelants, Belgium	8m30.8s
1968	Amos Biwott, Kenya	8m51s
1972	Kipchoge Keino, Kenya	8m23.6s
1976	Anders Gardervd, Sweden	8m08.02s
1980	Bronislaw Malinowski, Poland	8m09.7s
1984	Julius Korir, Kenya	8m11.80s
1988	Julius Karluki, Kenya	8m05.51s
1992	Matthew Birir, Kenya	8m08.84s
1996	Joseph Keter, Kenya	8m07.12s

1. About 3,450 meters–extra lap by error.

10,000–Meter Walk

1912	George Goulding, Canada	46m28.4s
1920	Ugo Frigerio, Italy	48m6.2s
1924	Ugo Frigerio, Italy	47m49s
1948	John Mikaelsson, Sweden	45m13.2s
1952	John Mikaelsson, Sweden	45m2.8s

20,000–Meter Walk

1956	Leonid Spirin, U.S.S.R.	1h31m27.4s
1960	Vladimir Golubnichy, U.S.S.R.	1h34m7.2s
1964	Ken Mathews, Great Britain	1h29m34s
1968	Vladimir Golubnichy, U.S.S.R.	1h33m58.4s
1972	Peter Frenkel, East Germany	1h26m42.4s
1976	Daniel Bautista, Mexico	1h24m40.6s
1980	Maurizio Damiliano, Italy	1h23m35.5s
1984	Ernesto Conto, Mexico	1m23.13s
1988	Jozef Pribilinec, Czechoslovakia	1h19m57s
1992	Daniel Plaza, Spain	1h21m45s
1996	Jefferson Perez, Ecuador	1h20m7s

50,000–Meter Walk

1932	Thomas W. Green, Great Britain	4h50m10s
1936	Harold Whitlock, Great Britain	4h30m41.1s
1948	John Ljunggren, Sweden	4h41m52s
1952	Giuseppe Dordoni, Italy	4h28m7.8s
1956	Norman Read, New Zealand	4h30m42.8s
1960	Donald Thompson, Great Britain	4h25m30s
1964	Abdon Pamich, Italy	4h11m12.4s
1968	Christoph Hohne, East Germany	4h20m13.6s
1972	Bern Kannernberg, West Germany	3h56m11.6s
1980	Hartwig Guader, East Germany	3h49m24s
1984	Raul Gonzalez, Mexico	3hr37m26s
1988	Viacheslau Ivanenko, U.S.S.R.	3h438m29s
1992	Andrei Perlov, Unified Team	3h50m13s
1996	Robert Korzeniowski, Poland	3h43m30s

400–Meter Relay (4x100)

1912	Great Britain	42.4s
1920	United States	42.2s
1924	United States	41s
1928	United States	41s
1932	United States	40s
1936	United States	39.8s
1948	United States	40.6s
1952	United States	40.1s
1956	United States	39.5s
1960	Germany	39.5s
1964	United States	39s
1968	United States	38.2s
1972	United States	38.19s
1976	United States	38.33s
1980	U.S.S.R.	38.26s
1984	United States	37.83s
1988	U.S.S.R.	38.19s
1992	United States	37.40s [1]
1996	Canada	37.69s

1. World record.

1,600–Meter Relay (4x400)

1912	United States	3m16.6s
1920	Great Britain	3m22.2s
1924	United States	3m16s
1928	United States	3m14.2s
1932	United States	3m8.2s
1936	Great Britain	3m9s
1948	United States	3m10.4s
1952	Jamaica, B.W.I.	3m3.9s
1956	United States	3m4.8s
1960	United States	3m2.2s
1964	United States	3m0.7s
1968	United States	2m56.1s
1972	Kenya	2m59.8s
1976	United States	2m58.65s
1980	U.S.S.R.	3m01.1s
1984	United States	2m57.91s
1988	United States	2m56.16s
1992	United States	2m55.74s [1]
1996	United States	2m55.99s

1. World record.

Team Race

		Pts
1900	Great Britain (5,000 meters)	26
1904	United States (4 miles)	27
1908	Great Britain (3 miles)	6
1912	United States (3,000 meters)	9
1920	United States (3,000 meters)	10
1924	Finland (3,000 meters)	9

Standing High Jump

1900	Ray Ewry, United States	5 ft 5 in.
1904	Ray Ewry, United States	4 ft. 11 in.
1906	Ray Ewry, United States	5 ft 1 5/8 in.
1908	Ray Ewry, United States	5 ft 2 in.
1912	Platt Adams, United States	5 ft 4 1/8 in.

Running High Jump

1896	Ellery Clark, United States	5 ft 11 1/4 in.
1900	Irving Baxter, United States	6 ft 2 3/4 in.
1904	Samuel Jones, United States	5 ft 11 in.
1906	Con Leahy, Ireland	5 ft 9 7/8 in.
1908	Harry Porter, United States	6 ft 3 in.
1912	Alma Richards, United States	6 ft 4 in.
1920	Richmond Landon, United States	6 ft 4 1/4 in.
1924	Harold Osborn, United States	6 ft 5 15/16 in.
1928	Robert W. King, United States	6 ft 4 3/8 in.
1932	Duncan McNaughton, Canada	6 ft 5 5/8 in.
1936	Cornelius Johnson, United States	6 ft 7 15/16 in.
1948	John Winter, Australia	6 ft 6 in.
1952	Walter David, United States	6 ft 8 5/16 in.
1956	Charles Dumas, United States	6 ft 11 1/4 in.
1960	Robert Shavlakadze, U.S.S.R.	7 ft 1 in.
1964	Valeri Brumel, U.S.S.R.	7 ft 1 3/4 in.
1968	Dick Fosbury, United States	7 ft 4 1/4 in.
1972	Yuri Tarmak, U.S.S.R.	7 ft 3 3/4 in.
1976	Jacek Wszola, Poland	(2.25m) 7 ft 4 1/2 in.
1980	Gerd Wessig, East Germany	7 ft 8 3/4 in.
1984	Dietmar Mogenburg, West Germany	7 ft 8 1/2 in.
1988	Guennadi Avdeenko, U.S.S.R.	7 ft 9 1/2 in.
1992	Javier Sotomayor, Cuba	7 ft 8 1/4 in.
1996	Charles Austin, United States	7 ft 10 in.

Long Jump

1896	Ellery Clark, United States	20 ft 9 3/4 in.
1900	Alvin Kraenzlein, United States	23 ft 6 7/8 in.
1904	Myer Prinstein, United States	24 ft 1 in.
1906	Myer Prinstein, United States	23 ft 7 1/2 in.
1908	Frank Irons, United States	24 ft 6 1/2 in.
1912	Albert Gutterson, United States	24 ft 11 1/4 in.
1920	William Petterssen, Sweden	23 ft 5 1/2 in.
1924	DeHart Hubbard, United States	24 ft 5 1/8 in.
1928	Edward B. Hamm, United States	25 ft 4 3/4 in.

1932	Edward Gordon, United States	25 ft 3/4 in.
1936	Jesse Owens, United States	26 ft 5 5/16 in.
1948	Willie Steele, United States	25 ft 8 in.
1952	Jerome Biffle, United States	24 ft 10 in.
1956	Gregory Bell, United States	25 ft 8 1/4 in.
1960	Ralph Boston, United States	26 ft 7 3/4 in.
1964	Lynn Davies, Great Britain	26 ft 5 3/4 in.
1968	Bob Beamon, United States	29 ft 2 1/2 in.
1972	Randy Williams, United States	27 ft 1/4 in.
1976	Arnie Robinson, United States (8.35m)	24 ft 7 3/4 in.
1980	Lutz Dombrowski, E. Germany	28 ft 1/4 in.
1984	Carl Lewis, United States	28 ft 1/4 in.
1988	Carl Lewis, United States	28 ft 7 1/4 in.
1992	Carl Lewis, United States	28 ft 5 1/2 in.
1996	Carl Lewis, United States	27 ft 10 3/4 in.

Triple Jump

1896	James B. Connolly, United States	45 ft
1900	Myer Prinstein, United States	47 ft 4 1/4 in.
1904	Myer Prinstein, United States	47 ft
1906	P.G. O'Connor, Ireland	46 ft 2 in.
1908	Timothy Ahearne, Great Britain	48 ft 11 1/4 in.
1912	Gustaf Lindblom, Sweden	48 ft 5 1/8 in.
1920	Vilho Tuulos, Finland	47 ft 6 7/8 in.
1924	Archie Winter, Australia	50 ft 11 1/8 in.
1928	Mikio Oda, Japan	49 ft 10 13/16 in.
1932	Chuhei Nambu, Japan	51 ft 7 in.
1936	Naoto Tajima, Japan	52 ft 5 7/8 in.
1948	Arne Ahman, Sweden	50 ft 6 1/4 in.
1952	Adhemar da Silva, Brazil	53 ft 2 1/2 in.
1956	Adhemar da Silva, Brazil	53 ft 7 1/2 in.
1960	Jozef Schmidt, Poland	55 ft 1 3/4 in.
1964	Jozef Schmidt, Poland	55 ft 3 1/4 in.
1968	Viktor Saneyev, U.S.S.R.	57 ft 3/4 in.
1972	Viktor Saneyev, U.S.S.R.	56 ft 11 in.
1976	Viktor Saneyev, U.S.S.R. (17.29m)	56 ft 8 3/4 in.
1980	Jaak Uudmae, U.S.S.R.	56 ft 11 1/8 in.
1984	Al Joyner, United States	56 ft 7 1/2 in.
1988	Hristo Markov, Bulgaria	57 ft 9 1/4 in.
1992	Mike Conley, United States	59 ft 7 1/2 in.
1996	Kenny Harrison, United States	59 ft 4 1/4 in.

Pole Vault

1896	William Hoyt, United States	10 ft 9 3/4 in.
1900	Irving Baxter, United States	10 ft 9 7/8 in.
1904	Charles Dvorak, United States	11 ft 6 in.
1906	Fernand Gouder, France	11 ft 6 in.
1908	Alfred Gilbert, United States, and Edward Cook, United States (tie)	12 ft 2 in.
1912	Harry Babcock, United States	12 ft 11 1/2 in.
1920	Frank Foss, United States	13 ft 5 9/16 in.
1924	Lee Barnes, United States	12 ft 11 1/2 in.
1928	Sabin W. Carr, United States	13 ft 9 3/8 in.
1932	William Miller, United States	14 ft 1 7/8 in.
1936	Earle Meadows, United States	14 ft 3 1/4 in.
1948	Guinn Smith, United States	14 ft 1 1/4 in.
1952	Robert Richards, United States	14 ft 11 1/8 in.
1956	Robert Richards, United States	14 ft 11 1/2 in.
1960	Don Bragg, United States	15 ft 5 1/8 in.
1964	Fred Hansen, United States	16 ft 8 3/4 in.
1968	Bob Seagren, United States	17 ft 8 1/2 in.
1972	Wolfgang Nordwig, East Germany	18 ft 1/2 in.
1976	Tadeusz Slusarski, Poland (5.50m)	18 ft 1/2 in.
1980	Wladyslaw Kozakiewics, Poland	18 ft 11 1/2 in.
1984	Pierre Quinon, France	18 ft 10 1/4 in.
1988	Sergei Bubka, U.S.S.R.	18 ft 4 1/4 in.
1992	Maxim Tarassov, Unified Team	19 ft 0 1/4 in.
1996	Jean Galfione, France	19 ft 5 1/4 in.

16–lb Shot–Put

1896	Robert Garrett, United States	36 ft 9 3/4 in.
1900	Richard Sheldon, United States	46 ft 3 1/8 in.
1904	Ralph Rose, United States	48 ft 7 in.
1906	Martin Sheridan, United States	40 ft 4 4/5 in.

1908	Ralph Rose, United States	46 ft 7 1/2 in.
1912	Pat McDonald, United States	50 ft 4 in.
1920	Ville Porhola, Finland	48 ft 7 1/8 in.
1924	Clarence Houser, United States	49 ft 2 1/2 in.
1928	John Kuck, United States	52 ft 11 11/16 in.
1932	Leo Sexton, United States	52 ft 6 3/16 in.
1936	Hans Woellke, Germany	53 ft 1 3/4 in.
1948	Wilbur Thompson, United States	56 ft 2 in.
1952	Parry O'Brien, United States	57 ft 1 1/2 in.
1956	Parry O'Brien, United States	60 ft 11 in.
1960	Bill Nieder, United States	64 ft 6 3/4 in.
1964	Dallas Long, United States	66 ft 8 1/4 in.
1968	Randy Matson, United States	67 ft 4 3/4 in.
1972	Wladyslaw Komar, Poland	69 ft 6 in.
1976	Udo Beyer, East Germany	(21.05m) 69 ft 3/4 in.
1980	Vladmir Klselyov, U.S.S.R.	70 ft 1/2 in.
1984	Alessandro Andrei, Italy	69 ft 9 in.
1988	Uhf Timmerman, East Germany	73 ft 8 3/4 in.
1992	Michael Stulze, United States	71 ft 2 1/2 in.
1996	Randy Barnes, United States	70 ft 11 1/4 in.

Discus Throw

1896	Robert Garrett, United States	95 ft 7 1/2 in.
1900	Rudolf Bauer, Hungary	118 ft 2 7/8 in.
1904	Martin Sheridan, United States	128 ft 10 1/2 in.
1906	Martin Sheridan, United States	136 ft 1/3 in.
1908	Martin Sheridan, United States	134 ft 2 in.
1912	Armas Taipale, Finland	145 ft 9/16 in.
1920	Elmer Niklander, Finland	146 ft 7 in.
1924	Clarence Houser, United States	151 ft 5 1/4 in.
1928	Clarence Houser, United States	155 ft 2 4/5 in.
1932	John Anderson, United States	162 ft 4 7/8 in.
1936	Ken Carpenter, United States	165 ft 7 3/8 in.
1948	Adolfo Consolini, Italy	173 ft 2 in.
1952	Simeon Iness, United States	180 ft 6 1/2 in.
1956	Al Oerter, United States	184 ft 10 1/2 in.
1960	Al Oerter, United States	194 ft 2 in.
1964	Al Oerter, United States	200 ft 1 1/2 in.
1968	Al Oerter, United States	212 ft 6 in.
1972	Ludvik Danek, Czechoslovakia	211 ft 3 in.
1976	Mac Wilkins, United States	(67.5m) 221 ft 5 in.
1980	Viktor Rashchupkin, U.S.S.R.	218 ft 8 in.
1984	Rolf Dannenberg, West Germany	218 ft 6 in.
1988	Jurgen Schult, East Germany	225 ft 9 1/4 in.
1992	Romas Ubartas, Lithuania	213 ft 7 3/4 in.
1996	Lars Riedel, Germany	227 ft 8 in.

Javelin Throw

1906	Eric Lemming, Sweden	175 ft 6 in.
1908	Eric Lemming, Sweden	179 ft 10 1/2 in.
1912	Eric Lemming, Sweden	198 ft 11 1/4 in.
1920	Jonni Myyra, Finland	215 ft 9 3/4 in.
1924	Jonni Myyra, Finland	206 ft 6 3/4 in.
1928	Eric Lundquist, Sweden	218 ft 6 1/8 in.
1932	Matti Jarvinen, Finland	238 ft 7 in.
1936	Gerhard Stoeck, Germany	235 ft 8 5/16 in.
1948	Kaj Rautavaara, Finland	228 ft 10 1/2 in.
1952	Cy Young, United States	242 ft 3/4 in.
1956	Egil Danielsen, Norway	281 ft 2 1/4 in.
1960	Viktor Tsibuelnko, U.S.S.R.	277 ft 8 3/8 in.
1964	Pauli Nevala, Finland	271 ft 2 1/4 in.
1968	Janis Lusis, U.S.S.R.	295 ft 7 in.
1972	Klaus Wolfermann, West Germany	296 ft 10 in.
1976	Miklos Nemeth, Hungary	(94.58m) 310 ft 4 in.
1980	Dainis Kula, U.S.S.R.	299 ft 2 3/8 in.
1984	Arto Haerkoenen, Finland	284 ft 8 in.
1988	Tapio Korjus, Finland	276 ft 6 in.
1992	Jan Zelezny, Czechoslovakia	294 ft 2 in.
1996	Jan Zelezny, Czech Republic	289 ft 3 in.

16–lb Hammer Throw

1900	John Flanagan, United States	167 ft 4 in.
1904	John Flanagan, United States	168 ft 1 in.
1908	John Flanagan, United States	170 ft 4 1/4 in
1912	Matt McGrath, United States	179 ft 7 1/8 in
1920	Pat Ryan, United States	173 ft 5 5/8 in
1924	Fred Tootell, United States	174 ft 10 1/4 in
1928	Patrick O'Callaghan, Ireland	168 ft 7 1/2 in
1932	Patrick O'Callaghan, Ireland	176 ft 11 1/8 in
1936	Karl Hein, Germany	185 ft 4 in
1948	Imre Nemeth, Hungary	183 ft 11 1/2 in
1952	Jozsef Csermak, Hungary	197 ft 11 9/16 in
1956	Harold Connolly, United States	207 ft 2 3/4 in
1960	Vasily Rudenkov, U.S.S.R.	220 ft 1 5/8 in
1964	Romuald Klim, U.S.S.R.	228 ft 9 1/2 in
1968	Gyula Zsivotzky, Hungary	240 ft 8 in
1972	Anatoly Bondarchuk, U.S.S.R.	247 ft 8 1/2 in
1976	Yuri Sedykh, U.S.S.R.	(77.52m)254 ft 4 in
1980	Yuri Sedykh, U.S.S.R.	(81.80m 268 ft 4 1/2 in
1984	Juha Tiainen, Finland	256 ft 2 in
1988	Sergei Litvinov, U.S.S.R.	278 ft 2 1/2 in
1992	Andrey Abduvaliyev, Unified Team	270 ft 9 1/2 in
1996	Balasz Kiss, Hungary	266 ft 6 in.

Decathlon

1912	Jim Thorpe, United States	—
	Hugo Wieslander, Sweden	—
1920	Helge Lovland, Norway	6,804.35 pts.
1924	Harold Osborn, United States	7,710.775 pts.
1928	Paavo Yrjola, Finland	8,053.29 pts.
1932	James Bausch, United States	8,462.23 pts.
1936	Glenn Morris, United States	7,900 pts. [1]
1948	Robert B. Mathias, United States	7,139 pts.
1952	Robert B. Mathias, United States	7,887 pts.
1956	Milton Campbell, United States	7,937 pts.
1960	Rafer Johnson, United States	8,392 pts.
1964	Willi Holdorf, Germany	7,887 pts. [1]
1968	Bill Toomey, United States	8,193 pts.
1972	Nikolai Avilov, U.S.S.R.	8,454 pts.
1976	Bruce Jenner, United States	8,618 pts.
1980	Daley Thompson, Britain	8,495 pts.
1984	Daley Thompson, Britain	8,797 pts.
1988	Christian Schenk, East Germany	8,488 pts.
1992	Robert Zmelik, Czechoslovakia	8,611 pts.
1996	Dan O'Brien, United States	8,824 pts.

1. Point system revised.

TRACK AND FIELD–WOMEN

100–Meter Dash

1928	Elizabeth Robinson, United States	12.2s
1932	Stella Walsh, Poland	11.9s
1936	Helen Stephens, United States	11.5s
1948	Fanny Blankers–Koen, Netherlands	11.9s
1952	Marjorie Jackson, Australia	11.5s
1956	Betty Cuthbert, Australia	11.5s
1960	Wilma Rudolph, United States	11s
1964	Wyomia Tyus, United States	11.4s
1968	Wyomia Tyus, United States	11s
1972	Renate Stecher, East Germany	11.07s
1976	Annegret Richter, West Germany	11.08s
1980	Lyudmila Kondratyeva, U.S.S.R.	11.06s
1984	Evelyn Ashford, United States	10.97s
1988	Florence Griffith–Joyner, United States	10.54s
1992	Gail Devers, United States	10.82s
1996	Gail Devers, United States	10.94s

200–Meter Dash

1948	Fanny Blankers–Koen, Netherlands	24.4s
1952	Marjorie Jackson, Australia	23.7s
1956	Betty Cuthbert, Australia	23.4s
1960	Wilma Rudolph, United States	24s
1964	Edith McGuire, United States	23s
1968	Irena Szewinska, Poland	22.5s
1972	Renate Stecher, East Germany	22.4s
1976	Baerbel Eckert, East Germany	22.37s

1980	Barbara Wockel, East Germany	22.03s
1984	Valerie Brisco–Hooks, United States	21.81s
1988	Florence Griffith–Joyner, United States	21.34s
1992	Gwen Torrence, United States	21.81s
1996	Marie-Jose Perec, France	22.12s

400–Meter Dash

1964	Betty Cuthbert, Australia	52s
1968	Colette Besson, France	52s
1972	Monika Zehrt, East Germany	51.08s
1976	Irena Szewinska, Poland	49.29s
1980	Marita Koch, East Germany	48.88s
1984	Valerie Brisco–Hooks, United States	48.83s
1988	Olga Bryzguina, U.S.S.R.	48.65s
1992	Marie-Jose Perec, France	48.83s
1996	Marie-Jose Perec, France	48.25s

800–Meter Run

1928	Lina Radke, Germany	2m16.8s
1960	Ljudmila Shevcova, U.S.S.R.	2m4.3s
1964	Ann Packer, Great Britain	2m1.1s
1968	Madeline Manning, United States	2m0.9s
1972	Hildegard Falck, West Germany	1m58.6s
1976	Tatiana Kazankina, U.S.S.R.	1m54.94s
1980	Nadezhda Olizarenko, U.S.S.R.	1m53.5s
1984	Doina Melinte, Romania	1m57.60s
1988	Sigrun Wodars, East Germany	1m56.10s
1992	Ellen Van Langen, Netherlands	1m55.54s
1996	Svetlana Masterkova, Russia	1m57.73s

1,500–Meter Run

1972	Ludmila Bragina, U.S.S.R.	4m01.4s
1976	Tatiana Kazankina, U.S.S.R.	4m05.48s
1980	Tatiana Kazankina, U.S.S.R.	3m56.6s
1984	Gabriella Dorio, Italy	4m03.25s
1988	Paula Ivan, Romania	3m53.96s
1992	Hassiba Boulmerka, Algeria	3m55.30s
1996	Svetlana Masterkova, Russia	4m00.83s

3,000–Meter Run

1984	Maricica Puica, Romania	8m35.96s
1988	Tatiana Samolenko, U.S.S.R.	8m26.53s
1992	Elena Romanova, Unified Team	8m46.04s

5,000–Meter Run

1996	Wang Junxia, China	14m59.88s

10,000-Meter Run

1992	Derartu Tulu, Ethiopia	31m6.02s
1996	Fernanda Ribeiro, Portugal	31m01.63s

80–Meter Hurdles

1932	Mildred Didrikson, United States	11.7s
1936	Trebisonda Valla, Italy	11.7s
1948	Fanny Blankers–Koen, Netherlands	11.2s
1952	Shirley S. de la Hunty, Australia	10.9s
1956	Shirley S. de la Hunty, Australia	10.7s
1960	Irina Press, U.S.S.R.	10.8s
1964	Karin Balzer, Germany	10.5s [1]
1968	Maureen Caird, Australia	10.3s

1. Wind assisted.

100–Meter Hurdles

1972	Annelie Ehrhardt, East Germany	12.59s
1976	Johanna Schaller, East Germany	12.77s
1980	Vera Komisova, U.S.S.R.	12.56s
1984	Benita Fitzgerald–Brown, United States	12.84s
1988	Jordanka Donkova, Bulgaria	12.38s
1992	Paraskevi Patoulidou, Greece	12.64s
1996	Ludmila Engquist, Sweden	12.58s

400–Meter Hurdles

1984	Nawai El Moutawakel, Morocco	54.61s
1988	Debra Flintoff–King, Australia	53.17s
1992	Sally Gunnell, Great Britain	53.23s
1996	Deon Hemmings, Jamaica	52.82s

400–Meter Relay

1928	Canada	48.4s
1932	United States	47s
1936	United States	46.9s
1948	Netherlands	47.5s
1952	United States	45.9s
1956	Australia	44.5s
1960	United States	44.5s
1964	Poland	43.6s
1968	United States	42.8s
1972	West Germany	42.81s
1976	East Germany	42.55s
1980	East Germany	41.60s
1984	United States	41.65s
1988	United States	41.98s
1992	United States	42.11s
1996	United States	41.95s

1,600–Meter Relay

1972	East Germany	3m23s
1976	East Germany	3m19.23s
1980	U.S.S.R.	3m20.2s
1984	United States	3m18.29s
1988	U.S.S.R.	3m15.18s
1992	Unified Team	3m20.20s
1996	United States	3m20.91s

10,000-Meter Walk

1992	Chen Yueling, China	44m32s
1996	Yelena Nikolayeva, Russia	41m49s

Marathon

1984	Joan Benoit, United States	2h24m52s
1988	Rose Mota, Portugal	2h25m40s
1992	Valentina Yegorova, Unified Team	2h32m41s
1996	Fatuma Roba, Ethiopia	2h26m05s

Running High Jump

1928	Ethel Catherwood, Canada	5 ft 3 in.
1932	Jean Shiley, United States	5 ft 5 1/4 in.
1936	Ibolya Csak, Hungary	5 ft 3 in.
1948	Alice Coachman, United States	5 ft 6 1/8 in.
1952	Ester Brand, South Africa	5 ft 5 3/4 in.
1956	Mildred McDaniel, United States	5 ft 9 1/4 in.
1960	Iolanda Balas, Romania	6 ft 3/4 in.
1964	Iolanda Balas, U.S.S.R.	6 ft 2 3/4 in.
1968	Miloslava Rezkova, Czechoslovakia	5 ft 11 3/4 in.
1972	Ulrike Meyfarth, West Germany	6 ft 3 5/8 in.
1976	Rosemarie Ackerman, E. Germany	(1.93m) 6 ft 4 in.
1980	Sara Simeoni, Italy	6 ft 5 1/2 in.
1984	Ulrike Meyfarth, West Germany	6 ft 7 1/2 in.
1988	Louise Ritter, United States	6 ft 8 in.
1992	Heike Henkel, Germany	6 ft 7 1/2 in.
1996	Stefka Kostadinova, Bulgaria	6 ft 8 3/4 in.

Long Jump

1948	Olga Gyarmati, Hungary	18 ft 8 1/4 in.
1952	Yvette Williams, New Zealand	20 ft 5 3/4 in.
1956	Elzbieta Krzesinska, Poland	20 ft 9 3/4 in.
1960	Vera Krepkina, U.S.S.R.	20 ft 10 3/4 in.
1964	Mary Rand, Great Britain	22 ft 2 in.
1968	Viorica Ciscopoleanu, Romania	22 ft 4 1/2 in.
1972	Heidemarie Rosendahl, West Germany	22 ft 3 in.
1976	Angela Voigt, East Germany	(6.72m) 22 ft 1/2 in.
1980	Tatiana Kolpakova, U.S.S.R.	23 ft 2 in.

1984	Anisoara Stanciu, Romania	22 ft 10 in.
1988	Jackie Joyner–Kersee, United States	24 ft 3 1/2 in.
1992	Heike Drechsler, Germany	23 ft 5 1/4 in.
1996	Chioma Ajunwa, Nigeria	23 ft 4 1/2 in.

Triple Jump

1996	Inessa Kravets, Ukraine	50 ft 3 1/2 in.

Shot–Put

1948	Micheline Ostermeyer, France	45 ft 1 1/2 in.
1952	Galina Zybina, U.S.S.R.	50 ft 1 1/2 in.
1956	Tamara Tishkyevich, U.S.S.R.	54 ft 5 in.
1960	Tamara Press, U.S.S.R.	56 ft 9 7/8 in.
1964	Tamara Press, U.S.S.R.	59 ft 6 in.
1968	Margitta Gummel, East Germany	64 ft 4 in.
1972	Nadezhda Chizhova, U.S.S.R.	69 ft
1976	Ivanka Christova, Bulgaria	(21.16m) 69 ft 5 in.
1980	Ilona Sluplanek, East Germany	73 ft 6 in.
1984	Claudia Losch, West Germany	67 ft 2 1/4 in.
1988	Natalya Lisovskaya, U.S.S.R.	72 ft 11 1/2 in.
1992	Svetlana Kriveleva, Unified Team	69 ft 1 1/4 in.
1996	Astrid Kumbernuss, Germany	67 ft 5 1/2 in.

Discus Throw

1928	Helena Konopacka, Poland	129 ft 11 7/8 in.
1932	Lillian Copeland, United States	133 ft 2 in.
1936	Gisela Mauermayer, Germany	156 ft 3 3/16 in.
1948	Micheline Ostermeyer, France	137 ft 6 1/2 in.
1956	Olga Fikotova, Czechoslovakia	176 ft 1 1/2 in.
1960	Nina Ponomareva, U.S.S.R.	180 ft 8 1/4 in.
1964	Tamara Press, U.S.S.R.	187 ft 10 3/4 in.
1968	Lia Manoliu, Romania	191 ft 2 1/2 in.
1972	Faina Melnik, U.S.S.R.	218 ft 7 in.
1976	Evelin Schlaak, East Germany	(69.0m) 226 ft 4 in.
1980	Evelin Jahl, East Germany	229 ft 6 1/2 in.
1984	Ria Stalman, Netherlands	214 ft 5 in.
1988	Martina Hellmann, East Germany	237 ft 2 1/4 in.
1992	Maritza Marten, Cuba	229 ft 10 1/4 in.
1996	Ilke Wyludda, Germany	228 ft 6 1/2 in.

Javelin Throw

1932	Mildred Didrikson, United States	143 ft 4 in.
1936	Tilly Fleischer, Germany	148 ft 2 3/4 in.
1948	Herma Bauma, Austria	149 ft 6 in.
1952	Dana Zatopek, Czechoslovakia	165 ft 7 in.
1956	Inessa Janzeme, U.S.S.R.	176 ft 8 in.
1960	Elvira Ozolina, U.S.S.R.	183 ft 8 in.
1964	Mihaela Penes, Romania	198 ft 7 1/2 in.
1968	Angela Nemeth, Hungary	198 ft 0 in.
1972	Ruth Fuchs, East Germany	209 ft 7 in.
1976	Ruth Fuchs, East Germany	(65.94m) 216 ft 4 in.
1980	Maria Colon, Cuba	224 ft 5 in.
1984	Tessa Sanderson, Britain	228 ft 2 in.
1988	Petra Felke, East Germany	245 ft
1992	Silke Renke, Germany	224 ft 2 1/2 in.
1996	Heli Rantanen, Finland	222 ft 11 in.

Pentathlon

1964	Irina Press, U.S.S.R.	5,246 pts.
1968	Ingrid Becker, West Germany	5,098 pts.
1972	Mary Peters, Britain	4,801 pts.
1976	Siegrun Siegl, East Germany	4,745 pts.
1980	Nadyeszhda Tkachenko, U.S.S.R.	5,083 pts.
1984	Daniele Masala, Italy	5,469 pts.
1988	Jackie Joyner–Kersee, United States	7,291 pts.

Heptathlon

1992	Jackie Joyner-Kersee, United States	7,044 pts.
1996	Ghada Shouaa, Syria	6,780 pts.

SWIMMING–MEN

50 Meter Freestyle

1988	Matt Biondi, United States	22.14s
1992	Alexandre Popov, Unified Team	21.91s
1996	Alexander Popov, Russia	22.13s

100 Meter Freestyle

1896	Alfred Hajos, Hungary	1m22.2s
1904	Zoltan de Halmay, Hungary	1m2.8s [1]
1906	Charles Daniels, United States	1m13s
1908	Charles Daniels, United States	1m5.6s
1912	Duke P. Kahanamoku, United States	1m3.4s
1920	Duke P. Kahanamoku, United States	1m1.4s
1924	John Weissmuller, United States	59s
1928	John Weissmuller, United States	58.6s
1932	Yasuji Miyazaki, Japan	58.2s
1936	Ferenc Csik, Hungary	57.6s
1948	Walter Ris, United States	57.3s
1952	Clarke Scholes, United States	57.4s
1956	Jon Henricks, Australia	55.4s
1960	John Devitt, Australia	55.2s
1964	Don Schollander, United States	53.4s
1968	Michael Wenden, Australia	52.2s
1972	Mark Spitz, United States	51.22s
1976	Jim Montgomery, United States	49.99s
1980	Jorg Woithe, East Germany	50.40s
1984	Rowdy Gaines, United States	49.80s
1988	Matt Biondi, United States	48.63s
1992	Alexander Popov, Unified Team	49.02s
1996	Alexander Popov, Russia	48.74s

1. 100 yards.

200–Meter Freestyle

1900	Frederick Lane, Australia	2m25.2s
1904	Charles Daniels, United States	2m44.2s [1]
1968	Michael Wenden, Australia	1m55.2s
1972	Mark Spitz, United States	1m52.78s
1976	Bruce Furniss, United States	1m50.29s
1980	Sergei Kopiliakov, U.S.S.R.	4m49.81s
1984	Michael Gross, West Germany	1m47.44s
1988	Duncan Armstrong, Australia	1m47.25s
1992	Evgueni Sadovyi, Unified Team	1m46.70s
1996	Danyon Loader, New Zealand	1m47.63s

1. 220 yards

400–Meter Freestyle

1896	Paul Neumann, Austria	8m12.6s [1]
1904	Charles Daniels, United States	6m16.2s [2]
1906	Otto Sheff, Austria	6m23.8s
1908	Henry Taylor, Great Britain	5m36.8s
1912	George Hodgson, Canada	5m24.4s
1920	Norman Ross, United States	5m26.8s
1926	John Weissmuller, United States	5m4.2s
1928	Albert Zorilla, Argentina	5m1.6s
1932	Clarence Crabbe, United States	4m48.4s
1936	Jack Medica, United States	4m44.5s
1948	William Smith, United States	4m41s
1952	Jean Boiteux, France	4m30.7s
1956	Murray Rose, Australia	4m27.3s
1960	Murray Rose, Australia	4m18.3s
1964	Don Schollander, United States	4m12.2s
1968	Mike Burton, United States	4m9s
1972	Bradford Cooper, Australia	4m00.27s [3]
1976	Brian Goodell, United States	3m51.93s
1980	Vladimir Salnikov, U.S.S.R.	3m51.31s
1984	George DiCarlo, United States	3m51.23s
1988	Uwe Dassier, East Germany	3m46.95s
1992	Evgueni Sadovyi, Unified Team	3m45.00s [4]
1996	Danyon Loader, New Zealand	3m47.97s

1. 500 meters. 2. 440 yards. 3. Rich DeMont, United States, won but was disqualified following day for medical reasons. 4. World record.

1,500 Meter Freestyle

1904	Emil Rausch, Germany	27m18.2s [1]
1906	Henry Taylor, Great Britain	28m28s [2]
1908	Henry Taylor, Great Britain	22m48.4s
1912	George Hodgson, Canada	22m
1920	Norman Ross, United States	22m23.2s
1924	Andrew Charlton, Australia	20m6.6s
1928	Arne Borg, Sweden	19m51.8s
1932	Kusuo Kitamura, Japan	19m12.4s
1936	Noboru Terada, Japan	19m13.7s
1948	James McLane, United States	19m18.5s
1952	Ford Konno, United States	18m30s
1956	Murray Rose, Australia	17m58.9s
1960	Jon Konrads, Australia	17m19.6s
1964	Robert Windle, Australia	17m1.7s
1968	Michael Burton, United States	16m38.9s
1972	Michael Burton, United States	15m52.58s
1976	Brian Goodell, United States	15m02.4s
1980	Vladimir Salnikov, U.S.S.R.	14m58.27s
1984	Michael O'Brien, United States	15m05.2s
1988	Vladimir Salnikov, U.S.S.R.	15m00.4s
1992	Kieren Perkins, Australia	14m43.48s
1996	Kieren Perkins, Australia	14m56.4s

1. One mile. 2. 1,600 meters

100-Meter Backstroke

1904	Walter Brack, Germany	1m16.8s [1]
1908	Arno Bieberstein, Germany	1m24.6s
1912	Harry Hebner, United States	1m21.2s
1920	Warren Kealoha, United States	1m15.2s
1924	Warren Kealoha, United States	1m13.2s
1928	George Kojac, United States	1m8.2s
1932	Masaji Kiyokawa, Japan	1m8.6s
1936	Adolph Kiefer, United States	1m5.9s
1948	Allen Stack, United States	1m6.4s
1952	Yoshinobu Oyakawa, United States	1m5.4s
1956	David Thiele, Australia	1m2.2s
1960	David Thiele, Australia	1m1.9s
1968	Roland Matthes, East Germany	58.7s
1972	Roland Matthes, East Germany	56.58s
1976	John Naber, United States	55.49s
1980	Bengt Baron, Sweden	56.53s
1984	Rick Carey, United States	55.79s
1988	Daichi Suzuki, Japan	55.05s
1992	Mark Tewksbury, Canada	53.98s
1996	Jeff Rouse, United States	54.10s

1. 100 yards

200-Meter Backstroke

1900	Ernst Hoppenberg, Germany	2m47s
1964	Jed Graef, United States	2m10.3s
1968	Roland Matthes, East Germany	2m9.6s
1972	Roland Matthes, East Germany	2m2.82s
1976	John Naber, United States	1m59.19s
1980	Sandor Wladar, Hungary	2:01.93s
1984	Rick Carey, United States	2m00.23s
1988	Igor Polianski, U.S.S.R.	1m59.37s
1992	Martin Lopez Zubero, Spain	1m58.47s
1996	Brad Bridgewater, United States	1m58.54s

100-Meter Breaststroke

1968	Donald McKenzie, United States	1m7.7s
1972	Nobutaka Taguchi, Japan	1m4.94s
1976	John Hencken, United States	1m03.11s
1980	Duncan Goodhew, Britain	1m03.34s
1984	Steve Lindquist, United States	1m01.65s
1988	Adrian Moorhouse, Great Britain	1m02.04s
1992	Nelson Diebel, United States	1m01.50s
1996	Fred Deburghgraeve, Belgium	1m00.60s [1]

World record.

200-Meter Breaststroke

1908	Frederick Holman, Great Britain	3m9.2s
1912	Walter Bathe, Germany	3m1.8s
1920	Haken Malmroth, Sweden	3m4.4s
1924	Robert Skelton, United States	2m56.6s
1928	Yoshiyuki Tsuruta, Japan	2m48.8s
1932	Yoshiyuki Tsuruta, Japan	2m45.4s
1936	Tetsuo Hamuro, Japan	2m41.5s
1948	Joseph Verdeur, United States	2m39.3s
1952	John Davies, Australia	2m34.4s
1956	Masaru Furukawa, Japan	2m34.7s
1960	Bill Muliken, United States	2m37.4s
1964	Ian O'Brien, Australia	2m27.8s
1968	Felipe Munoz, Mexico	2m28.7s
1972	John Hencken, United States	2m21.55s
1976	David Willkie, Britain	2m15.11s
1980	Robertas Zulpa, U.S.S.R.	2m15.85s
1984	Victor Davis, Canada	2m13.34s
1988	Jozef Szabo, Hungary	2m13.52s
1992	Mike Barrowman, United States	2m10.16s
1996	Norbert Rozsa, Hungary	2m12.57s

100-Meter Butterfly

1968	Douglas Russell, United States	55.9s
1972	Mark Spitz, United States	54.27s
1976	Matt Vogel, United States	54.35s
1980	Par Arvidsson, Sweden	54.92s
1984	Michael Gross, West Germany	53.08s
1988	Anthony Nesty, Surinam	53.0s
1992	Pablo Morales, United States	53.32s
1996	Denis Pankratov, Russia	52.27s [1]

1. World record.

200-Meter Butterfly

1956	Bill Yorzyk, United States	2m19.3s
1960	Mike Troy, United States	2m12.8s
1964	Kevin Berry, Australia	2m6.6s
1968	Carl Robie, United States	2m8.7s
1972	Mark Spitz, United States	2m00.7s
1976	Mike Bruner, United States	1m59.23s
1980	Sergei Fesenko, U.S.S.R.	1m59.76s
1984	Jon Sieben, Australia	1m57.0s
1988	Michael Gross, East Germany	1m56.94s
1992	Mel Stewart, United States	1m56.26s
1996	Denis Pankratov, Russia	1m56.51s

200-Meter Individual Medley

1968	Charles Hickcox, United States	2m12s
1972	Gunnar Larsson, Sweden	2m7.17s
1988	Tamas Darnyi, Hungary	2m0.17s
1992	Tamas Darnyi, Hungary	2m00.76s
1996	Attila Czene, Hungary	1m59.91s

400-Meter Individual Medley

1964	Dick Roth, United States	4m45.4s
1968	Charles Hickcox, United States	4m48.4s
1972	Gunnar Larsson, Sweden	4m31.98s
1976	Rod Strachan, United States	4m23.68s
1980	Aleksandr Sidorenko, U.S.S.R.	4m22.8s
1984	Alex Baumann, Canada	4m17.41s
1988	Tamas Darnyi, Hungary	4m14.75s
1992	Tamas Darnyi, Hungary	4m14.23s
1996	Tom Dolan, United States	4m14.90s

400-Meter Freestyle Relay

1964	United States	3m32.2s
1968	United States	3m31.7s
1972	United States	3m26.42s
1988	United States	3m16.52s
1992	United States	3m16.74s
1996	United States	3m15.41s

800–Meter Freestyle Relay

Year		Time
1908	Great Britain	10m55.6s
1912	Australia	10m11.2s
1920	United States	10m4.4s
1924	United States	9m53.4s
1928	United States	9m36.2s
1932	Japan	8m58.4s
1936	Japan	8m51.5s
1948	United States	8m46.1s
1952	United States	8m31.1s
1956	Australia	8m23.6s
1960	United States	8m10.2s
1964	United States	7m52.1s
1968	United States	7m52.3s
1972	United States	7m35.78s
1976	United States	7m23.22s
1980	U.S.S.R.	7m23.50s
1984	United States	7m16.59s
1988	United States	7m12.51s
1992	Unified Team	7m11.95s
1996	United States	7m14.84s

400–Meter Medley Relay

Year		Time
1960	United States	4m5.4s
1964	United States	3m58.4s
1968	United States	3m54.9s
1972	United States	3m48.16s
1976	United States	3m42.22s
1980	Australia	3m45.70s
1984	United States	3m39.30s
1988	United States	3m36.93s
1992	United States	3m36.93s [1]
1996	United States	3m34.84s [1]

1. World record.

Springboard Dive

Year		Points
1908	Albert Zuerner, Germany	85.5
1912	Paul Guenther, Germany	79.23
1920	Louis Kuehn, United States	675
1924	Albert White, United States	696.4
1928	Pete Desjardins, United States	185.04
1932	Michael Galitzen, United States	161.38
1936	Richard Degener, United States	163.57
1948	Bruce Harlan, United States	163.64
1952	David Browning, United States	205.59
1956	Robert Clotworthy, United States	159.56
1960	Gary Tobian, United States	170.00
1964	Ken Sitzberger, United States	159.90
1968	Bernard Wrightson, United States	170.15
1972	Vladimir Vasin, U.S.S.R.	594.09
1976	Phil Boggs, United States	619.05
1980	Alexsandr Portnov, U.S.S.R.	905.02
1984	Greg Louganis, United States	754.41
1988	Greg Louganis, United States	730.80
1992	Mark Lenzi, United States	676.53
1996	Xiong Ni, China	701.46

Platform Dive

Year		Points
1904	G.E. Sheldon, United States	12.75
1906	Gottlob Walz, Germany	156
1908	Hialmar Johansson, Sweden	83.75
1912	Erik Adlerz, Sweden	73.94
1920	Clarence Pinkston, United States	100.67
1924	Albert White, United States	487.3
1928	Pete Desjardins, United States	98.74
1932	Harold Smith, United States	124.80
1936	Marshall Wayne, United States	113.58
1948	Samuel Lee, United States	130.05
1952	Samuel Lee, United States	156.28
1956	Joaquin Capilla, Mexico	152.44
1960	Bob Webster, United States	165.56
1964	Bob Webster, United States	148.58
1968	Klaus Dibiasi, Italy	164.18

1972	Klaus Dibiasi, Italy	504.12
1976	Klaus Dibiasi, Italy	600.51
1980	Falk Hoffman, E. Germany	835.65
1984	Greg Louganis, United States	710.91
1988	Greg Louganis, United States	638.61
1992	Sun Shuwei, China	677.3
1996	Dmitri Saoutine, Russia	692.34

SWIMMING–WOMEN

50–Meter Freestyle

1988	Kristin Otto, East Germany	25.49
1992	Yang Wenyi, China	24.79s
1996	Amy Van Dyken, United States	24.87

100–Meter Freestyle

1912	Fanny Durack, Australia	1m22.2
1920	Ethelda Bleibtrey, United States	1m13.6
1924	Ethel Lackie, United States	1m12.4
1928	Albina Osipowich, United States	1m11s
1932	Helene Madison, United States	1m6.8
1936	Hendrika Mastenbroek, Netherlands	1m5.9
1948	Greta Andersen, Denmark	1m6.3
1952	Katalin Szoke, Hungary	1m6.8
1956	Dawn Fraser, Australia	1m2
1960	Dawn Fraser, Australia	1m1.2
1964	Dawn Fraser, Australia	59.5
1968	Marge Jan Henne, United States	1m
1972	Sandra Neilson, United States	58.59
1976	Kornelia Ender, East Germany	55.65
1980	Barbara Krause, East Germany	54.79
1984	Carrie Steinseifer, United States	55.92
1988	Kristin Otto, East Germany	54.93
1992	Zhuang Yong, China	54.64
1996	Le Jingyi, China	54.5

200–Meter Freestyle

1968	Debbie Meyer, United States	2m10.5
1972	Shane Gould, Australia	2m3.56
1976	Kornelia Ender, East Germany	1m59.26
1980	Barbara Krause, East Germany	1m58.33
1984	Mary Wayle, United States	1m59.23
1988	Heike Friedrich, East Germany	1m57.65
1992	Nicole Haislett, United States	1m57.90
1996	Claudia Poll, Costa Rica	1m58.16

400–Meter Freestyle

1920	Ethelda Bleibtrey, United States	4m34s
1924	Martha Norelius, United States	6m2.2s
1928	Martha Norelius, United States	5m42.8s
1932	Helene Madison, United States	5m28.5s
1936	Hendrika Mastenbroek, Netherlands	5m26.4s
1948	Ann Curtis, United States	5m17.8s
1952	Valerie Gyenge, Hungary	5m12.1s
1956	Lorraine Crapp, Australia	4m54.6s
1960	Chris von Saltza, United States	4m50.6s
1964	Ginny Duenkel, United States	4m43.3s
1968	Debbie Meyer, United States	4m31.8s
1972	Shane Gould, Australia	4m19.04s
1976	Petra Thumer, East Germany	4m09.89s
1980	Ines Diers, East Germany	4m08.76s
1984	Tiffany Cohen, United States	4m07.10s
1988	Janet Evans, United States	4m03.85s
1992	Dagmar Hase, Germany	4m07.18s
1996	Michelle Smith, Ireland	4m07.25s

1. 300 meters.

800–Meter Freestyle

1968	Debbie Meyer, United States	9m24
1972	Keena Rothhammer, United States	8m53.68
1976	Petra Thumer, East Germany	8m37.14
1980	Michelle Ford, Australia	8m28.9s

1984	Tiffany Cohen, United States	8m24.95s
1988	Janet Evans, United States	8m20.20s
1992	Janet Evans, United States	8m25.52s
1996	Brooke Bennett, United States	8m27.89s

100–Meter Backstroke

1924	Sybil Bauer, United States	1m23.2s
1928	Marie Braun, Netherlands	1m22s
1932	Eleanor Holm, United States	1m19.4s
1936	Dina Senff, Netherlands	1m18.9s
1948	Karen Harup, Denmark	1m14.4s
1952	Joan Harrison, South Africa	1m14.3s
1956	Judy Grinham, Great Britain	1m12.9s
1960	Lynn Burke, United States	1m9.3s
1964	Cathy Ferguson, United States	1m7.7s
1968	Kaye Hall, United States	1m6.2s
1972	Melissa Belote, United States	1m5.78s
1976	Ulrike Richter, East Germany	1m01.83s
1980	Rica Reinisch, East Germany	1m00.86s
1984	Theresa Andrews, United States	1m02.55s
1988	Kristin Otto, East Germany	1m0.89s
1992	Kristina Egerszegi, Hungary	1m0.68s
1996	Beth Botsford, United States	1m01.19s

200–Meter Backstroke

1968	Pokey Watson–United States	2m24.8s
1972	Melissa Belote, United States	2m19.19s
1976	Ulrike Richter, East Germany	2m13.43s
1980	Rica Reinisch, East Germany	2m11.77s
1984	Jolanda DeRover, Netherlands	2m12.38s
1988	Krisztina Egerszegi, Hungary	2m09.29s
1992	Krisztina Egerszegi, Hungary	2m07.06s
1996	Krisztina Egerszegi, Hungary	2m07.83s

100–Meter Breaststroke

1968	Djurdjica Bjedov, Yugoslavia	1m15.8s
1972	Catherine Carr, United States	1m13.58s
1976	Hannelore Anke, East Germany	1m11.16s
1980	Ute Geweniger, East Germany	1m10.22s
1984	Petra Van Staveren, Netherlands	1m09.88s
1988	Tainia Dangalakova, Bulgaria	1m07.95s
1992	Elena Roudkovskaia, Unified Team	1m08.00s
1996	Penny Heyns, South Africa	1m07.73s

200–Meter Breaststroke

1924	Lucy Morton, Great Britain	3m33.2s
1928	Hilde Schrader, Germany	3m12.6s
1932	Clare Dennis, Australia	3m6.3s
1936	Hideko Maehata, Japan	3m3.6s
1948	Nel van Vliet, Netherlands	2m57.2s
1952	Eva Szekely, Hungary	2m51.7s
1956	Ursala Happe, Germany	2m53.1s
1960	Anita Lonsbrough, Great Britain	2m49.5s
1964	Galina Prozumenschikova, U.S.S.R.	2m46.4s
1968	Sharon Wichman, United States	2m44.4s
1972	Beverly Whitfield, Australia	2m41.71s
1976	Marina Koshevaia, U.S.S.R.	2m33.35s
1980	Lina Kachushite, U.S.S.R.	2m29.54s
1984	Anne Ottenbrite, Canada	2m30.38s
1988	Silke Hoerner, East Germany	2m26.71s
1992	Kyoko Iwasaki, Japan	2m26.65s
1996	Penny Heyns, South Africa	2m25.41s

100–Meter Butterfly

1956	Shelley Mann, United States	1m11s
1960	Carolyn Schuler, United States	1m9.5s
1964	Sharon Stouder, United States	1m4.7s
1968	Lynn McClements, Australia	1m5.5s
1972	Mayumi Aoki, Japan	1m3.34s
1976	Kornelia Ender, East Germany	1m00.13s
1980	Caren Metschuck, East Germany	1m00.42s
1984	Mary Meagher, United States	59.26s
1988	Kristin Otto, East Germany	59s
1992	Qian Hong, China	58.62s
1996	Amy Van Dyken, United States	59.13s

200–Meter Butterfly

1968	Ada Kok, Netherlands	2m24.7s
1972	Karen Moe, United States	2m15.57s
1976	Andrea Pollack, East Germany	2m11.41s
1980	Ines Geissler, East Germany	2m10.44s
1984	Mary Meagher, United States	2m06.90s
1988	Kathleen Nord, East Germany	2m09.51s
1992	Summer Sanders, United States	2m06.67s
1996	Susan O'Neill, Australia	2m07.76s

200–Meter Individual Medley

1968	Claudia Kolb, United States	2m24.7s
1972	Shane Gould, Australia	2m23.07s
1984	Tracy Caulkins, United States	2m12.64s
1988	Daniela Hunger, East Germany	2m12.59s
1992	Lin Lee, China	2m11.55s [1]
1996	Michelle Smith, Ireland	2m13.93s

1. World record.

400–Meter Individual Medley

1964	Donna de Varona, United States	5m18.7s
1968	Claudia Kolk, United States	5m8.5s
1972	Gail Neall, Australia	5m2.97s
1976	Ulrike Tauber, East Germany	4m42.77s
1980	Petra Schneider, East Germany	4m36.29s
1984	Tracy Caulkins, United States	4m39.21s
1988	Janet Evans, United States	4m37.76s
1992	Krisztina Egerszegi, Hungary	4m36.54s
1996	Michelle Smith, Ireland	4m39.18s

400–Meter Freestyle Relay

1912	Great Britain	5m52.8s
1920	United States	5m11.6s
1924	United States	4m58.8s
1928	United States	4m47.6s
1932	United States	4m38s
1936	Netherlands	4m36s
1948	United States	4m29.2s
1952	Hungary	4m24.4s
1956	Australia	4m17.1s
1960	United States	4m8.9s
1964	United States	4m3.8s
1968	United States	4m2.5s
1972	United States	3m55.19s
1976	United States	3m44.82s
1980	East Germany	3m42.71s
1984	United States	3m44.43s
1988	East Germany	3m40.63s
1992	United States	3m39.46s [1]
1996	United States	3m39.29s

1. World record.

800–Meter Freestyle Relay

1996	United States	7m59.87s

400–Meter Medley Relay

1960	United States	4m41.1s
1964	United States	4m33.9s
1968	United States	4m28.3s
1972	United States	4m20.75s
1976	East Germany	4m07.95s
1980	East Germany	4m06.67s
1984	United States	4m08.34s
1988	East Germany	4m03.74s
1992	United States	4m02.54s [1]
1996	United States	4m02.88

1. World record.

Springboard Dive	Points
1920 Aileen Riggin, United States	539.90
1924 Elizabeth Becker, United States	474.5
1928 Helen Meany, United States	78.62
1932 Georgia Coleman, United States	87.52
1936 Marjorie Gestring, United States	89.27
1948 Victoria M. Draves, United States	108.74
1952 Patricia McCormick, United States	147.30
1956 Patricia McCormick, United States	142.36
1960 Ingrid Kramer, Germany	155.81
1964 Ingrid Kramer Engel, Germany	145.00
1968 Sue Gossick, United States	150.77
1972 Micki King, United States	450.03
1976 Jennifer Chandler, United States	506.19
1980 Irina Kalinina, U.S.S.R.	725.91
1984 Sylvie Bernier, Canada	530.70
1988 Gao Min, China	580.23
1992 Gao Min, China	572.40
1996 Fu Mingxia, China	547.68

Platform Dive	Points
1912 Greta Johansson, Sweden	39.9
1920 Stefani Fryland, Denmark	34.60
1924 Caroline Smith, United States	166
1928 Elizabeth B. Pinkston, United States	31.60
1932 Dorothy Poynton, United States	40.26
1936 Dorothy Poynton Hill, United States	33.92
1948 Victoria M. Draves, United States	68.87
1952 Patricia McCormick, United States	79.37
1956 Patricia McCormick, United States	84.85
1960 Ingrid Kramer, Germany	91.28
1964 Lesley Bush, United States	99.80
1968 Milena Duchkova, Czechoslovakia	109.59
1972 Ulrika Knape, Sweden	390.00
1976 Elena Vaytsekhovskaia, U.S.S.R.	406.59
1980 Martina Jaschke, East Germany	596.25
1984 Zhou Jihong, China	435.51
1988 Xu Yanmei, China	445.20
1992 Fu Mingxia, China	461.43
1996 Fu Mingxia, China	521.58

BASKETBALL–MEN

1904	United States	1972	U.S.S.R.
1936	United States	1976	United States
1948	United States	1980	Yugoslavia
1952	United States	1984	United States
1956	United States	1988	U.S.S.R.
1960	United States	1992	United States
1964	United States	1996	United States
1968	United States		

DISTRIBUTION OF MEDALS—1996 SUMMER GAMES

Country	Gold	Silver	Bronze	Total	Country	Gold	Silver	Bronze	Total
United States	44	32	25	101	Ethiopia	2	0	1	3
Germany	20	18	27	65	Algeria	2	0	1	3
Russia	26	21	16	63	Iran	1	1	1	3
China	16	22	12	50	Slovakia	1	1	1	3
Australia	9	9	23	41	Argentina	0	2	1	
France	15	7	15	37	Austria	0	1	2	
Italy	13	10	12	35	Armenia	1	1	0	
South Korea	7	15	5	27	Croatia	1	1	0	
Cuba	9	8	8	25	Portugal	1	0	1	
Ukraine	9	2	12	23	Thailand	1	0	1	
Canada	3	11	8	22	Namibia	0	2	0	
Hungary	7	4	10	21	Slovenia	0	2	0	
Romania	4	7	9	20	Malaysia	0	1	1	
Netherlands	4	5	10	19	Moldova	0	1	1	
Poland	7	5	5	17	Uzbekistan	0	1	1	
Spain	5	6	6	17	Georgia	0	0	2	
Britain	1	8	7	16	Morocco	0	0	2	
Bulgaria	3	7	5	15	Trinidad & Tobago	0	0	2	
Belarus	1	6	8	15	Burundi	1	0	0	
Brazil	3	2	10	15	Costa Rica	1	0	0	
Japan	3	6	5	14	Ecuador	1	0	0	
Czech Republic	4	3	4	11	Hong Kong	1	0	0	
Kazakhstan	3	4	4	11	Syria	1	0	0	
Greece	4	4	0	8	Azerbaijan	0	1	0	
Sweden	2	4	2	8	Bahamas	0	1	0	
Kenya	1	4	3	8	Latvia	0	1	0	
Switzerland	4	3	0	7	Phillipines	0	1	0	
Norway	2	2	3	7	Taiwan	0	1	0	
Denmark	4	1	1	6	Tonga	0	1	0	
Turkey	4	1	1	6	Zambia	0	1	0	
New Zealand	3	2	1	6	India	0	0	1	
Belgium	2	2	2	6	Israel	0	0	1	
Nigeria	2	1	3	6	Lithuania	0	0	1	
Jamaica	1	3	2	6	Mexico	0	0	1	
South Africa	3	1	1	5	Mongolia	0	0	1	
North Korea	2	1	2	5	Mozambique	0	0	1	
Ireland	3	0	1	4	Puerto Rico	0	0	1	
Finland	1	2	1	4	Tunisia	0	0	1	
Indonesia	1	1	2	4	Uganda	0	0	1	
Yugoslavia	1	1	2	4					

BASKETBALL–WOMEN

1976	U.S.S.R.	1988	United States
1980	U.S.S.R.	1992	Unified Team
1984	United States	1996	United States

BOXING

(U.S. winners only)

(U.S. boycotted Olympics in 1980)

Flyweight–112 pounds (51 kilograms)

1904	George v. Finnegan	1952	Nate Brooks
1920	Frank De Genaro	1976	Leo Randolph
1924	Fidel La Barba	1984	Steve McCrory

Bantamweight–119 (54 kg)

1904	O.L. Kirk	1988	Kennedy McKinney

Featherweight–126 pounds (57 kg)

1904	O.L. Kirk	1984	Meldrick Taylor
1924	Jackie Fields		

Lightweight–132 pounds (60 kg)

1904	H.J. Spanger	1976	Howard Davis
1920	Samuel Mosberg	1984	Pernell Whitaker
1968	Ronnie Harris	1992	Oscar De La Hoya

Light Welterweight–140 pounds (63.5 kg)

1952	Charles Adkins	1976	Ray Leonard
1972	Ray Seales	1984	Jerry Page

Welterwight–148 pounds (67 kg)

1904	Al Young	1984	Mark Breland
1932	Edward Flynn		

Light Middleweight–157 pounds (71 kg)

1960	Wilbert McClure	1996	David Reid
1984	Frank Tate		

Middleweight–165 pounds (75 kg)

1904	Charles Mayer	1960	Eddie Cook
1932	Carmen Barth	1976	Michael Spinks
1952	Floyd Patterson		

Light Heavyweight–179 pounds (81 kg)

1920	Edward Eagan	1960	Cassius Clay
1952	Norvel Lee	1976	Leon Spinks
1956	James Boyd	1988	Andrew Maynard

Heavyweight–201 pounds

1904	Sam Berger	1968	George Foreman
1952	Edward Sanders	1984	Henry Tilman
1956	Pete Rademacher	1988	Ray Mercer
1964	Joe Frazier		

Super Heavyweight (unlimited)

1984	Tyrell Biggs

Other 1996 Summer Olympic Games Champions

Archery

Women's individual—Kim Kyung Wook, South Korea
Women's team—South Korea
Men's individual—Justin Huish, United States
Men's team—United States

Badminton

Men's singles—Poul-Erik Hoyer-Larsen, Denmark
Men's doubles—Indonesia (Rexy Mainaky, Ricky Subagja)
Women's singles—Bang Soo-Hyun, South Korea
Women's doubles—China (Ge Fei, Gu Jun)
Mixed doubles—South Korea (Gil Young-ah, Kim Dong-moon)

Baseball

Men—Cuba

Beach Volleyball

Women—Jackie Silva/Sandra Pires, Brazil
Men—Karch Kiraly/Kent Steffes, United States

Canoe–Kayak—Men

Canoe single slalom—Michal Martikan, Slovakia
Canoe slalom pairs—France
Kayak slalom singles—Oliver Fix, Germany
Canoe singles 500m—Martin Doktor, Czech Republic
Canoe singles 1000m—Martin Doktor, Czech Republic
Canoe pairs 500m—Csaba Horvath/

Gyorgy Kolonics, Hungary
Canoe pairs 1000m—Andreas Dittmer/Gunar Kirchbach, Germany
Kayak singles 500m—Antonio Rossi, Italy
Kayak singles 1000m—Knut Holmann, Norway
Kayak pairs 500m—Kay Bluhm/Torsten Gutsche, Germany
Kayak pairs 1000m—Antonio Rossi/Daniele Scarpa, Italy
Kayak fours 1000m—Germany

Kayak—Women

Single slalom—Stepnka Hilgertova, Czech Republic
500m singles—Rita Koban, Hungary
500m pairs—Agneta Andersson/Susanne Gunnarsson, Sweden
500m pairs—Germany

Cycling—Men

Individual road race—Pascal Richard, Switzerland
1 km time trial—Florian Rousseau, France
Individual pursuit—Andrea Collinelli, Italy
Individual spring—Jens Fiedler, Germany
Individual point race—Silvio Martinello, Italy
Team pursuit—France
Cross country—Bart Jan Brentjens, Netherlands
Individual time trial—Miguel Indurain, Spain

Cycling—Women

Individual road race—Jeannie Longo-Ciprelli, France

Track sprint—Felicia Ballanger, france
Individual pursuit—Antonella Bellutti, Italy
Point race—Nathalie Lancien, France
Cross country—Paola Pezzo, Italy
Individual time trial—Zulfiya Zabirova, Russia

Equestrian

Three-day team event—Australia
Individual three-day—Blyth Tait, New Zealand
Team dressage—Germany
Individual dressage—Isabell Werth, Germany
Team jumping—Germany
Show jumping—Ulrich Kirchhoff, Germany

Fencing—Men

Individual epee—Aleksandr Beketov, Russia
Individual sabre—Stanislav Pozydnakov, Russia
Individual foil—Alessandro Puccini, Italy
Team epee—Italy
Team sabre—Russia
Team foil—Russia

Fencing—Women

Individual epee—Laura Flessel, France
Individual foil—Laura Badea, Romania
Team epee—France
Team foil—Italy

Field Hockey
Women—Australia
Men—Netherlands

Gymnastics—Men
Team—Russia
All-around—Li Xiaoshuang, China
Floor exercise—Ioannis Melissanidis, Greece
Vault—Alexei Nemov, Russia
Parallel bars—Rustam Sharipov, Ukraine
High bar—Andreas Wecker, Germany
Pommel horse—Li Donghua, Switzerland
Rings—Yuri Chechi, Italy

Gymnastics—Women
Team—United States
All-around—Lilia Podkopayeva, Ukraine
Balance beam—Shannon Miller, United States
Floor exercise—Lilia Podkopayeva, Ukraine
Uneven bars—Svetlana Chorkina, Russia
Vault—Simona Amanar, Romania

Judo—Men
Extra-lightweight—Tadahiro Nomura, Japan
Half-lightweight—Udo Quellmalz, Germany
Lightweight—Kenzo Nakamura, Japan
Half-middleweight—Djamel Bouras, France
Middleweight—Jeon Ki Young, South Korea
Light-heavyweight—Pawel Nastula, Poland
Heavyweight—David Douillet, France

Judo—Women
Extra-lightweight—Sun Kye, North Korea
Half-lightweight—Marie-Claire Restoux, France
Lightweight—Driulis Gonzalez, Cuba
Half-middleweight—Yuko Emoto, Japan
Middleweight—Cho Min Sun, South Korea
Light-heavyeight—Ulla Werbrouck, Belgium
Heavyweight—Sun Fuming, China

Modern Pentathlon
Individual—Aleksandr Parygin, Kazakstan

Rhythmic Gymnastics
Team—Spaing
Individual—Ekaterina Serebryanskaya, Ukraine

Rowing—Men
Coxless pairs—Great Britain
Coxless four—Australia
Single sculls—Xeno Müller, Switzerland

Double sculls—Italy
Lightweight double sculls—Switzerland
Eight—Netherlands
Quaduple sculls—Germany
Lightweight coxless four—Denmkar

Rowing—Women
Coxless pairs—Australia
Single sculls—Yekaterina Khodotovich, Belarus
Double sculls—Canada
Eight—Romania
Quadruple sculls—Germany
Lightweight double sculls—Romania

Shooting—Women
10m air rifle—Renata Mauer, Poland
10m air pistol—Olga Klochneva, Russia
Double trap—Kim Rhode, United States
Rifle three position—Aleksandra Ivosev, Yugoslavia
24m sport pistol—Li Duihong, China

Shooting—Mem
10m air pistol—Roberto Di Donna, Italy
Trap—Michael Diamond, Australia
Air rifle—Artem Khadzhibekov, Russia
50m free pistol—Boris Kokorev, Russia
Double trap—Russell Mark, Australia
25m rapid fire pistol—Ralf Schumann, Germany
50m rifle prone—Christian Klees, Germany
Running game target—Yank Ling, China
50m free rifle 3-position—Jean-Pierre Amat, France
Skeet shooting—Ennio Falco, Italy

Soccer
Women—United States
Men—Nigeria

Softball
United States

Synchronized Swimming
Team—United States

Table Tennis
Women's singles—Deng Yaping, China
Women's doubles—China (Deng Yaping, Qiao Hong)
Men's singles—Liu Guoliang, China
Men's doubles—China (Kong Linghui, Liu Guoliang)

Team Handball
Women—Denmark
Men—Croatia

Tennis
Men's singles—Andre Agassi, United States

Men's doubles—Todd Woodbridge and Mark Woodforde, Australia
Women's singles—Lindsay Davenport, United States
Women's doubles—Gigi Fernandez and Mary Joe Fernandez, United States

Volleyball
Women—Cuba
Men—Netherlands

Water Polo
Spain

Weightlifting
119 lb—Halil Mutlu, Turkey
130 lb—Tang Lingshen, China
141 lb—Naim Suleymanoglu, Turkey
154 lb—Zhan Xugang, China
161.5 lb—Pablo Lara, Cuba
183 lb—Pyrros Dias, Greece
200.5 lb—Aleksey Petrov, Russia
218 lb—Akakide Kakiashvilis, Greece
238 lb—Timur Taimazov, Ukraine
238 + lb—Andrei Chemerkin, Russia

Wrestling—Greco-Roman
105.5 lb—Sim Kwon-Ho, South Korea
114.5 lb—Armen Nazaryan, Armenia
125.5 lb—Yuri Melnichenko, Kazakhstan
136.5 lb—Wlodzimierz Zwadzki, Poland
149.5 lb—Ryszard Wolny, Poland
163 lb—Feliberto Ascuy Aquilera, Cuba
180.5 lb—Hamza Yerlikiya, Turkey
198 lb—Vyacheslav Oleynyk, Uklraine
220 lb—Andrzej Wronski, Poland
286 lb—Aleksandr Karelin, Russia

Wrestling—Freestyle
105.5 lb—Kim Il, North Korea
114.5 lb—Valentin Jordanov, Bulgaria
125.5 lb—Kendall Cross, United States
136.5 lb—Tom Brands, United States
149.5 lb—Vadim Bogiev, Russia
163 lb—Bouvaisa Satiev, Russia
180.5 lb—Khadzhimurad Magomedov, Russia
198 lb—Rsaul Khadem, Iran
220 lb—Kurt Angle, United States
286 lb—Mahmut Demir, Turkey

Yachting
Men's Mistral—Nikolaos Kaklamanakis, Greece
Men's 470—Ukraine
Men's Finn—Mateusz Kusznierewicz, Poland
Women's Mistral—Lee Lai-Shan, Hong Kong
Women's Europe—Kristine Rough, Denmark
Women's 470—Spain
Open Laser—Robert Scheidt, Brazil
Open Tornado—Spain
Open Soling—Germany
Open Star—Brazil

Winter Games

FIGURE SKATING–MEN

1908	Ulrich Salchow, Sweden	
1920	Gillis Grafstrom, Sweden	
1924	Gillis Grafstrom, Sweden	
1928	Gillis Grafstrom, Sweden	
1932	Karl Schaefer, Austria	
1936	Karl Schaefer, Austria	
1948	Richard Button, United States	
1952	Richard Button, United States	
1956	Hayes Alan Jenkins, United States	
1960	David Jenkins, United States	
1964	Manfred Schnelldorfer, Germany	
1968	Wolfgang Schwartz, Austria	
1972	Ondrej Nepela, Czechoslovakia	
1976	John Curry, Great Britain	
1980	Robin Cousins, Great Britain	
1984	Scott Hamilton, United States	
1988	Brian Boitano, United States	
1992	Viktor Petrenko, Unified Team*	
1994	Alexei Urmanov, Russia	

*Former Soviet Union team.

FIGURE SKATING–WOMEN

1908	Madge Syers, Britain
1920	Magda Julin–Maurey, Sweden
1924	Herma Szabo–Planck, Austria
1928	Sonja Henie, Norway
1932	Sonja Henie, Norway
1936	Sonja Henie, Norway
1948	Barbara Ann Scott, Canada
1952	Jeannette Altwegg, Great Britain
1956	Tenley Albright, United States
1960	Carol Heiss, United States
1964	Sjoukje Dijkstra, Netherlands
1968	Peggy Fleming, United States
1972	Beatrix Schuba, Austria
1976	Dorothy Hamill, United States
1980	Anett Poetzsch, East Germany
1984	Katarina Witt, East Germany
1988	Katarina Witt, East Germany
1992	Kristi Yamaguchi, United States
1994	Oksana Baiul, Ukraine

SPEED SKATING–MEN

(U.S. winners only)

500 Meters

1924	Charles Jewtraw	44.0
1932	John A. Shea	43.4
1952	Kenneth Henry	43.2
1964	Terrence McDermott	40.1
1980	Eric Heiden	38.03

1,000 Meters

1976	Peter Mueller	1:19.32
1980	Eric Heiden	1:15.18
1994	Dan Jansen	1:12.43[1]

1. World Record

1,500 Meters

1932	John A. Shea	2:57.5
1980	Eric Heiden	1:55.44

5,000 Meters

1932	Irving Jaffee	9:40.8
1980	Eric Heiden	7:02.29

10,000 Meters

1932	Irving Jaffee	19:13.6
1980	Eric Heiden	14:28.13

SPEED SKATING–WOMEN

500 Meters

1972	Anne Henning	43.33
1976	Sheila Young	42.76
1988	Bonnie Blair	39.10
1992	Bonnie Blair	40.33
1994	Bonnie Blair	39.25

1,000 Meters

1992	Bonnie Blair	1:21.90
1994	Bonnie Blair	1:18.74

1,500 Meters

1972	Dianne Holum	2:20.85

SKIING, ALPINE–MEN

Downhill

1948	Henri Oreiller, France	2m55.0s
1952	Zeno Colo, Italy	2m30.8s
1956	Anton Sailer, Austria	2m52.2s
1960	Jean Vuarnet, France	2m06.2s
1964	Egon Zimmermann, Austria	2m18.16s
1968	Jean–Claude Killy, France	1m59.85s
1972	Bernhard Russi, Switzerland	1m51.43s
1976	Franz Klammer, Austria	1m45.72s
1980	Leonhard Stock, Austria	1m45.50s
1984	Bill Johnson, United States	1m45.59s
1988	Pirmin Zurbriggen, Switzerland	1m59.63s
1992	Patrick Ortlieb, Austria	1m50.37s
1994	Tommy Moe, United States	1m45.75s

Slalom

1948	Edi Reinalter, Switzerland	2m10.3s
1952	Othmar Schneider, Austria	2m00.0s
1956	Anton Sailer, Austria	194.7 pts.
1960	Ernst Hinterseer, Austria	2m08.9s
1964	Josef Stiegler, Austria	2m10.13
1968	Jean–Claude Killy, France	1m39,73s
1972	Francisco Fernandez Ochoa, Spain	1m49.27s
1976	Piero Gros, Italy	2m03.29s
1980	Integmar Stenmark, Sweden	1m44.26s
1984	Phil Mahre, United States	1m39.41s
1988	Alberto Tomba, Italy	1m39.47s
1992	Finn Christian, Norway	1m44.39s
1994	Thomas Stangassinger, Austria	2m2.02s

Giant Slalom

1952	Stein Eriksen, Norway	2m25.0s
1956	Anton Sailer, Austria	3m00.1s
1960	Roger Staub, Switzerland	1m48.3s
1964	François Bonlieu, France	1m46.71s
1968	Jean-Claude Killy, France	3m29.28s
1972	Gustavo Thoeni, Italy	3m09.52s
1976	Heini Hemmi, Switzerland	3m26.97s
1980	Ingemar Stenmark, Sweden	2m40.74s
1984	Max Julen, Switzerland	1m20.54s
1988	Alberto Tomba, Italy	2m06.37s
1992	Alberto Tomba, Italy	2m06.98s
1994	Markus Wasmeier, Germany	2m52.46s

SKIING, ALPINE–WOMEN

Downhill

1948	Hedi Schlunegger, Switzerland	2m28.3s
1952	Trude Jochum–Beiser, Austria	1m47.1s
1956	Madeleine Berthod, Switzerland	1m40.1s
1960	Heidi Biebl, Germany	1m37.6s
1964	Christi Haas, Austria	1m55.39s
1968	Olga Pall, Austria	1m40.87s
1972	Marie–Therese Nadig, Switzerland	1m36.68s
1976	Rosi Mittermeier, West Germany	1m46.16s
1980	Annemarie Proell Moser, Austria	1m37.52s
1984	Michela Figini, Switzerland	1m13.36s
1988	Marina Kiehl, West Germany	1m25.86s
1992	Kerrin Lee-Gartner, Canada	1m52.55s
1994	Katja Seizinger, Germany	1m35.93s

Slalom

1948	Gretchen Fraser, United States	1m57.2s
1952	Andrea Mead Lawrence, United States	2m10.6s
1956	Renee Colliard, Switzerland	112.3 pts.
1960	Anne Heggtveigt, Canada	1m49.6s
1964	Christine Goitschel, France	1m29.86s
1968	Marielle Goitschel, France	1m25.86s
1972	Barbara Cochran, United States	1m31.24s
1976	Rosi Mittermeier, West Germany	1m30.54s
1980	Hanni Wenzel, Liechtenstein	1m25.09s
1984	Paoletta Magoni, Italy	1m36.47s
1988	Vreni Schneider, Switzerland	1m36.69s
1992	Petra Kronberger, Austria	1m32.68s
1994	Vreni Schneider, Switzerland	1m56.01s

Giant Slalom

1952	Andrea M. Lawrence, United States	2m06.8s
1956	Ossi Reichert, Germany	1m56.5s
1960	Yvonne Ruegg, Switzerland	1m39.9s
1964	Marielle Goitschel, France	1m52.24s
1968	Nancy Greene, Canada	1m51.97s
1972	Marie–Therese Nadig, Switzerland	1m29.90s
1976	Kathy Kreiner, Canada	1m29.13s
1980	Hanni Wenzel, Liechtenstein	2m41.66s
1984	Debbie Armstrong, United States	2m20.98s
1988	Vreni Schneider, Switzerland	2m06.49s
1992	Pernilla Wiberg, Sweden	2m12.74s
1994	Deborah Compagnoni, Italy	2m30.97s

1994 UNITED STATES MEDALISTS

Figure Skating

Women—SILVER—Nancy Kerrigan, Stoneham, Mass.

Alpine Skiing

Men's Downhill—GOLD—Tommy Moe, Palmer, Alaska.

Men's Super Giant Slalom—SILVER—Tommy Moe, Palmer, Alaska.

Women's Downhill—SILVER—Picabo Street, Sun Valley, Idaho.

Women's Super Giant Slalom—GOLD—Diann Roffe-Steinrotter, Potsdam, N.Y.

Freestyle Skiing

Women's Moguls—SILVER—Liz McIntyre, Winter Park, Colo.

Speedskating

Women's 500 meters—GOLD—Bonnie Blair, Milwaukee, Wis.

Women's 1,000 meters—GOLD—Bonnie Blair, Milwaukee, Wis.

Men's 1,000 meters—GOLD—Dan Jansen, Greenfield, Wis.

DISTRIBUTION OF MEDALS 1994 WINTER GAMES

(Lillehammer, Norway)

	Gold	Silver	Bronze	Total
Norway	10	11	5	26
Germany	9	7	8	24
Russia	11	8	4	23
Italy	7	5	8	20
United States	6	5	2	13
Canada	3	6	4	13
Austria	3	3	4	10
Switzerland	2	4	2	8
South Korea	4	1	1	6
Finland	0	1	5	6
Japan	1	2	2	5
France	0	1	4	5
Netherlands	0	1	3	4
Sweden	2	1	0	3
Kazakhstan	1	2	0	3
China	0	1	2	3
Slovenia	0	0	3	3
Ukraine	1	0	1	2
Belarus	0	2	0	2
Britain	0	0	2	2
Uzbekistan	1	0	0	1
Australia	0	0	1	1

Short Track Speedskating

Women's 3,000 meter relay—BRONZE—United States (Karen Cashman, Quincy Mass.; Amy Peterson, Maplewood, Minn.; Cathy Turner, Hilton, N.Y.; Nicole Ziegelmayer, Milwaukee, Wis.)

Women's 500 meters—GOLD—Cathy Turner, Hilton, N.Y.—BRONZE—Amy Peterson, Maplewood, Minn.

Men's 5,000 meter relay—SILVER—United States (Randy Bartz, Milwaukee, Wis.; John Coyle, Milwaukee, Wis.; Eric Flaim, Hyde Park, Mass.; Andy Gabel, Northbrook, Ill.)

ICE HOCKEY

1920	Canada	1964	U.S.S.R.
1924	Canada	1968	U.S.S.R.
1928	Canada	1972	U.S.S.R.
1932	Canada	1976	U.S.S.R.
1936	Great Britain	1980	United States
1948	Canada	1984	U.S.S.R.
1952	Canada	1988	U.S.S.R.
1956	U.S.S.R.	1992	Unified Team*
1960	United States	1994	Sweden

*Former Soviet Union team.

FINAL 1994 OLYMPIC HOCKEY STANDINGS

Group A

	W	L	T	GF	GA
Finland	5	0	0	25	4
Germany	3	2	0	11	14
Czech Republic	3	2	0	16	11
Russia	3	2	0	20	14
Austria	1	4	0	13	28
Norway	0	5	0	5	19

Group B

	W	L	T	GF	GA
Slovakia	3	0	2	26	14
Canada	3	1	1	17	11
Sweden	3	1	1	23	13
United States	1	1	3	21	17
Italy	1	4	0	15	31
France	0	4	1	11	30

Championship
Sweden 3, Canada 2 (Shootout)
Bronze Medal
Finland 4, Russia 0
Fifth Place
Czech Republic 7, Slovakia 1
Seventh Place
Germany 4, United States 3

Other 1994 Winter Olympic Games Champions

Biathlon
Men's 10–kilometer—Sergei Tchepikov, Russia
Men's 20-kilometer—Sergei Tarasov, Russia
Men's 4 × 7.5 kilometer relay—Germany
Women's 7.5-kilometer—Myriam Bedard, Canada
Women's 15-kilometers—Myriam Bedard, Canada
Women's 4×7.5 kilometer relay—Russia

Bobsledding
2–man—Switzerland I
4–man—Germany II

Figure Skating
Men's singles—Alexei Urmanov, Russia
Women's singles—Oksana Baiul, Ukraine
Pairs—Ekaterina Gordeeva and Sergei Grinkov, Russia
Ice dancing—Oksana Gritschuk and Evgeni Platov, Russia

Speed Skating–Men
500m—Aleksandr Golubev, Russia
1,000m—Dan Jansen, United States
1,500m—Johann Olav Koss, Norway
5,000m—Johann Olav Koss, Norway
10,000m—Johann Olav Koss, Norway

Speed Skating–Women
500m—Bonnie Blair, United States
1,000m—Bonnie Blair, United States

1,500m—Emese Hunyady, Austria
3,000m—Svetlana Bazhanova, Russia
5,000m—Claudia Pechstein, Germany

Luge
Men's singles—Georg Hackl, Germany
Men's doubles—Kurt Brugger and Wilfried Huber, Italy
Women's singles—Gerda Weissensteiner, Italy

Skiing, Nordic–Men
Combined team—Japan
Combined—Fred Borre Lundberg, Norway
90-meter jump—Espen Bredesen, Norway
120-meter jump—Jens Weissflog, Germany
Team 120-meter jump—Germany
10-kilometer classical—Bjorn Dahlie, Norway
15-kilometer free pursuit—Bjorn Dahlie, Norway
30-kilometer freestyle—Thomas Alsgaard, Norway
50-kilometer classical—Vladimir Smirnov, Kazakhstan
4 × 10 kilometer relay—Italy

Skiing, Nordic–Women
5–kilometer classical—Lyubov Egorova, Russia
10-kilometer free pursuit—Lyubov Egorova, Russia
15-kilometer freestyle—Manuela Di Centa, Italy
30-kilometer classical—Manuela Di Centa, Italy
4×5 kilometer relay—Russia

Norway Wins Medals Race, United States Best-Ever 13 Medals at 1994 Winter Olympics

The names Nancy Kerrigan and Tonya Harding dominated the 1994 Winter Olympics in Lillehammer, Norway. While Kerrigan won a silver medal and Harding none at all, the pre-Olympics attack on Kerrigan's knee, in which associates of Harding and even Harding herself were implicated, kept the spotlight on figure skating as soap opera rather than sport.

The on-ice big name for the United States, as it won a Winter Games record 13 medals, was Bonnie Blair of Milwaukee, Wis. Blair won gold in both the 500-meter and 1,000-meter speed skating races, giving her a career total of five gold medals. That's one more than any American woman had ever won, winter or summer. With one gold medal at Calgary in 1988, two at Albertville in 1992, and two at Lillehammer, Blair passed diver Pat McCormack, swimmer Janet Evans, and sprinter Evelyn Ashford.

Only speedskater Eric Heiden, the hero of the Lake Placid Winter Games in 1980, has won as many winter golds for the United States.

The United States ice hockey team's poor showing—1–1–3 in preliminary competition and an eighth place finish in the medal round—was the only mark on an otherwise stellar winter games for the Americans.

The U.S. won a surprising four medals in Alpine skiing, two by Tommy Moe of Palmer, Alaska, and one each by Diann Roffe-Steinrotter and Picabo Street.

The most emotional moment of the 1994 Winter Games for the American team came when Dan Jansen, in his final attempt, finally took the long-awaited gold medal in the 1,000-meter speedskating event. He not only won it, but did so in world record time.

Aside from Kerrigan's silver, the U.S. figure skating team came up empty.

Norway won the medals race with 26, two ahead of Germany with 24. Russia was third with 23, and Italy a surprising fourth with 20.

FOOTBALL

The pastime of kicking around a ball goes back beyond the limits of recorded history. Ancient savage tribes played football of a primitive kind. There was a ball-kicking game played by Athenians, Spartans, and Corinthians 2500 years ago, which the Greeks called *Episkuros*. The Romans had a somewhat similar game called *Harpastum* and are supposed to have carried the game with them when they invaded the British Isles in the First Century, B.C.

Undoubtedly the game known in the United States as Football traces directly to the English game of Rugby, though the modifications have been many. Informal football was played on college lawns well over a century ago, and an annual Freshman-Sophomore series of "scrimmages" began at Yale in 1840. The first formal intercollegiate football game was the Princeton-Rutgers contest at New Brunswick, N.J. on Nov. 6, 1869, with Rutgers winning by 6 goals to 4.

In those days, games were played with 25, 20, 15, or 11 men on a side. In 1880, there was a convention at which Walter Camp of Yale persuaded the delegates to agree to a rule calling for 11 players on a side.

The first professional game was played in 1895 at Latrobe, Pa. The National Football League was founded in 1921. The All-American Conference went into action in 1946. At the end of the 1949 season the two circuits merged, retaining the name of the older league. In 1960, the American Football League began operations. In 1970, the leagues merged. The United States Football League played its first season in 1983, from March to July. It suspended spring operations after the 1985 season, and planned a 1986 move to fall, but suspended operations again.

In 1991, another effort at spring football was launched, but this time it had the backing of the National Football League. The World League of American Football debuted in March 1991 with 10 teams. Three of them were in Europe. The other seven were in North America, including the Montreal Machine in Canada. With television contracts signed with ABC and USA Cable Network, the league seemed to be on sound footing from the beginning. But after just two seasons, it was suspended. In the summer of 1994 the NFL announced the league would be back in 1995, but only with six teams in Europe.

College Football

NATIONAL COLLEGE FOOTBALL CHAMPIONS

The "National Collegiate A.A. Football Guide" recognizes as unofficial national champion the team selected each year by press association polls. If the Associated Press Poll (of writers) did not agree with the United Press International poll (of coaches) through 1991 or the USA Today–CNN poll from 1992, the guide lists both teams selected.

1937	Pittsburgh	1952	Mich. State	1963	Texas	1974	Oklahoma and
1938	Texas Christian	1953	Maryland	1964	Alabama		So. California
1939	Texas A & M	1954	Ohio State	1965	Alabama and	1975	Oklahoma
1940	Minnesota		and U.C.L.A.		Mich. State	1976	Pittsburgh
1941	Minnesota	1955	Oklahoma	1966	Notre Dame	1977	Notre Dame
1942	Ohio State	1956	Oklahoma	1967	So. California	1978	Alabama and
1943	Notre Dame	1957	Auburn and	1968	Ohio State		So. California
1944	Army		Ohio State	1969	Texas	1979	Alabama
1945	Army	1958	Louisiana	1970	Texas and	1980	Georgia
1946	Notre Dame		State		Nebraska	1981	Clemson
1947	Notre Dame	1959	Syracuse	1971	Nebraska	1982	Penn State
1948	Michigan	1960	Minnesota	1972	So. California	1983	Miami
1949	Notre Dame	1961	Alabama	1973	Notre Dame	1984	Brigham Young
1950	Oklahoma	1962	So. California		and U. of Ala.	1985	Oklahoma
1951	Tennessee						

1986	Penn State
1987	Miami
1988	Notre Dame
1989	Miami
1990	Colorado and
	Georgia Tech
1991	Miami and
	Washington
1992	Alabama
1993	Florida State
1994	Nebraska
1995	Nebraska

RECORD OF ANNUAL MAJOR COLLEGE FOOTBALL BOWL GAMES

Rose Bowl

(At Pasadena, Calif.)

1902	Michigan 49, Stanford 0	1931	Alabama 24, Wash. State 0	1950	Ohio State 17, California 14
1916	Washington State 14, Brown 0	1932	So. California 21, Tulane 12	1951	Michigan 14, California 6
1917	Oregon 14, Pennsylvania 0	1933	So. California 35, Pittsburgh 0	1952	Illinois 40, Stanford 7
1918	Mare Island Marines 19, Camp Lewis 7	1934	Columbia 7, Stanford 0	1953	So. California 7, Wisconsin 0
		1935	Alabama 29, Stanford 13	1954	Michigan State 28, U.C.L.A. 20
1919	Great Lakes 17, Mare Island Marines 0	1936	Stanford 7, So. Methodist 0	1955	Ohio State 20, So. California 7
		1937	Pittsburgh 21, Washington 0	1956	Michigan State 17, U.C.L.A. 14
1920	Harvard 7, Oregon 6	1938	California 13, Alabama 0	1957	Iowa 35, Oregon State 19
1921	California 28, Ohio State 0	1939	So. California 7, Duke 3	1958	Ohio State 10, Oregon 7
1922	Washington and Jefferson 0, California 0	1940	So. California 14, Tennessee 0	1959	Iowa 38, California 12
		1941	Stanford 21, Nebraska 13	1960	Washington 44, Wisconsin 8
1923	So. California 14, Penn State 3	1942	Oregon State 20, Duke 16[1]	1961	Washington 17, Minnesota 7
1924	Navy 14, Washington 14	1943	Georgia 9, U.C.L.A. 0	1962	Minnesota 21, U.C.L.A. 3
1925	Notre Dame 27, Stanford 10	1944	So. California 29, Washington 0	1963	So. California 42, Wisconsin 37
1926	Alabama 20, Washington 19	1945	So. California 25, Tennessee 0	1964	Illinois 17, Washington 7
1927	Alabama 7, Stanford 7	1946	Alabama 34, So. California 14	1965	Michigan 34, Oregon State 7
1928	Stanford 7, Pittsburgh 6	1947	Illinois 45, U.C.L.A. 14	1966	U.C.L.A. 14, Michigan State 12
1929	Georgia Tech 8, California 7	1948	Michigan 49, So. California 0	1967	Purdue 14, So. California 13
1930	So. California 47, Pittsburgh 14	1949	Northwestern 20, California 14	1968	So. California 14, Indiana 3

1969	Ohio State 27, So. California 16	
1970	So. California 10, Michigan 3	
1971	Stanford 27, Ohio State 17	
1972	Stanford 13, Michigan 12	
1973	So. California 42, Ohio State 17	
1974	Ohio State 42, So. California 21	
1975	So. California 18, Ohio State 17	
1976	U.C.L.A. 23, Ohio State 10	
1977	So. California 14, Michigan 6	
1978	Washington 27, Michigan 20	
1979	So. California 17, Michigan 10	
1980	So. California 17, Ohio State 16	
1981	Michigan 23, Washington 6	
1982	Washington 28, Iowa 0	
1983	U.C.L.A. 24, Michigan 14	
1984	U.C.L.A. 45, Illinois 9	
1985	USC 20, Ohio St. 17	
1986	U.C.L.A. 45, Iowa 28	
1987	Arizona State 22, Michigan 15	
1988	Michigan State 20, USC 17	
1989	Michigan 22, So. California 14	
1990	USC 17, Michigan 10	
1991	Washington 46, Iowa 34	
1992	Washington 34, Michigan 14	
1993	Michigan 38, Washington 31	
1994	Wisconsin 21, UCLA 16	
1995	Penn State 38, Oregon 20	
1996	So. California 41, Northwestern 32	

1. Played at Durham, N.C.

Orange Bowl
(At Miami)

1933	Miami (Fla.) 7, Manhattan 0
1934	Duquesne 33, Miami (Fla.) 7
1935	Bucknell 26, Miami (Fla.) 0
1936	Catholic 20, Mississippi 19
1937	Duquesne 13, Mississippi State 12
1938	Auburn 6, Michigan State 0
1939	Tennessee 17, Oklahoma 0
1940	Georgia Tech 21, Missouri 7
1941	Mississippi State 14, Georgetown 7
1942	Georgia 40, Texas Christian 26
1943	Alabama 37, Boston College 21
1944	Louisiana State 19, Texas A&M 14
1945	Tulsa 26, Georgia Tech 12
1946	Miami (Fla.) 13, Holy Cross 6
1947	Rice 8, Tennessee 0
1948	Georgia Tech 20, Kansas 14
1949	Texas 41, Georgia 28
1950	Santa Clara 21, Kentucky 13
1951	Clemson 15, Miami (Fla.) 14
1952	Georgia Tech 17, Baylor 14
1953	Alabama 61, Syracuse 6
1954	Oklahoma 7, Maryland 0
1955	Duke 34, Nebraska 7
1956	Oklahoma 20, Maryland 6
1957	Colorado 27, Clemson 21
1958	Oklahoma 48, Duke 21
1959	Oklahoma 21, Syracuse 6
1960	Georgia 14, Missouri 0
1961	Missouri 21, Navy 14
1962	Louisiana State 25, Colorado 7
1963	Alabama 17, Oklahoma 0
1964	Nebraska 13, Auburn 7
1965	Texas 21, Alabama 17
1966	Alabama 39, Nebraska 28
1967	Florida 27, Georgia Tech 12
1968	Oklahoma 26, Tennessee 24
1969	Penn State 15, Kansas 14

1970	Penn State 10, Missouri 3
1971	Nebraska 17, Louisiana State 12
1972	Nebraska 38, Alabama 6
1973	Nebraska 40, Notre Dame 6
1974	Penn State 16, Louisiana State 9
1975	Notre Dame 13, Alabama 11
1976	Oklahoma 14, Michigan 6
1977	Ohio State 27, Colorado 10
1978	Arkansas 31, Oklahoma 6
1979	Oklahoma 31, Nebraska 24
1980	Oklahoma 24, Florida State 7
1981	Oklahoma 18, Florida State 17
1982	Clemson 22, Nebraska 15
1983	Nebraska 21, Louisiana State 20
1984	Miami 31, Nebraska 30
1985	Washington 28, Oklahoma 17
1986	Oklahoma 25, Penn St. 10
1987	Oklahoma 42, Arkansas 8
1988	Miami 20, Oklahoma 14
1989	Miami 23, Nebraska 3
1990	Notre Dame 21, Colorado 6
1991	Colorado 10, Notre Dame 9
1992	Miami 22, Nebraska 0
1993	Florida State 27, Nebraska 14
1994	Florida State 18, Nebraska 16
1995	Nebraska 24, Miami 17
1996	Florida State 31, Notre Dame 26

Sugar Bowl
(At New Orleans)

1935	Tulane 20, Temple 14
1936	Texas Christian 3, Louisiana State 2
1937	Santa Clara 21, Louisiana State 14
1938	Santa Clara 6, Louisiana State 0
1939	Texas Christian 15, Carnegie Tech 7
1940	Texas A & M 14, Tulane 13
1941	Boston College 19, Tennessee 13
1942	Fordham 2, Missouri 0
1943	Tennessee 14, Tulsa 7
1944	Georgia Tech 20, Tulsa 18
1945	Duke 29, Alabama 26
1946	Oklahoma A & M 33, St. Mary's (Calif.) 13
1947	Georgia 20, North Carolina 10
1948	Texas 27, Alabama 7
1949	Oklahoma 14, North Carolina 6
1950	Oklahoma 35, Louisiana State 0
1951	Kentucky 13, Oklahoma 7
1952	Maryland 28, Tennessee 13
1953	Georgia Tech 24, Mississippi 7
1954	Georgia Tech 42, West Virginia 19
1955	Navy 21, Mississippi 0
1956	Georgia Tech 7, Pittsburgh 0
1957	Baylor 13, Tennessee 7
1958	Mississippi 39, Texas 7
1959	Louisiana State 7, Clemson 0
1960	Mississippi 21, Louisiana State 0
1961	Mississippi 14, Rice 6
1962	Alabama 10, Arkansas 3
1963	Mississippi 17, Arkansas 13
1964	Alabama 12, Mississippi 7
1965	Louisiana State 13, Syracuse 10
1966	Missouri 20, Florida 18
1967	Alabama 34, Nebraska 7
1968	Louisiana State 20, Wyoming 13
1969	Arkansas 16, Georgia 2
1970	Mississippi 27, Arkansas 22
1971	Tennessee 34, Air Force Academy 13

1972	Oklahoma 40, Auburn 22
1973	Oklahoma 14, Penn State 0
1974	Notre Dame 24, Alabama 23
1975	Nebraska 13, Florida 10
1976	Alabama 13, Penn State 6
1977	Pittsburgh 27, Georgia 3
1978	Alabama 35, Ohio State 6
1979	Alabama 14, Penn State 7
1980	Alabama 24, Arkansas 9
1981	Georgia 17, Notre Dame 10
1982	Pittsburgh 24, Georgia 20
1983	Penn State 27, Georgia 23
1984	Auburn 9, Michigan 7
1985	Nebraska 28, LSU 10
1986	Tennessee 35, Miami, Fla. 7
1987	Nebraska 30, Louisiana State 15
1988	Syracuse 16, Auburn 16 (tie)
1989	Florida State 13, Auburn 7
1990	Miami 33, Alabama 25
1991	Tennessee 23, Virginia 22
1992	Notre Dame 39, Florida 28
1993	Alabama 34, Miami 13
1994	Florida 41, West Virginia 7
1995	Florida State 23, Florida 17
1996	Virginia Tech 28, Texas 10

Cotton Bowl
(At Dallas)

1937	Texas Christian 16, Marquette 6
1938	Rice 28, Colorado 14
1939	St. Mary's (Calif.) 20, Texas Tech. 13
1940	Clemson 6, Boston College 3
1941	Texas A & M 13, Fordham 12
1942	Alabama 29, Texas A & M 21
1943	Texas 14, Georgia Tech 7
1944	Randolph Field 7, Texas 7
1945	Oklahoma A & M 34, Texas Christian 0
1946	Texas 40, Missouri 27
1947	Louisiana State 0, Arkansas 0
1948	So. Methodist 13, Penn State 13
1949	So. Methodist 21, Oregon 13
1950	Rice 27, North Carolina 13
1951	Tennessee 20, Texas 14
1952	Kentucky 20, Texas Christian 7
1953	Texas 16, Tennessee 0
1954	Rice 28, Alabama 6
1955	Georgia Tech 14, Arkansas 6
1956	Mississippi 14, Texas Christian 13
1957	Texas Christian 28, Syracuse 27
1958	Navy 20, Rice 7
1959	Air Force 0, Texas Christian 0
1960	Syracuse 23, Texas 14
1961	Duke 7, Arkansas 6
1962	Texas 12, Mississippi 7
1963	Louisiana State 13, Texas 0
1964	Texas 28, Navy 6
1965	Arkansas 10, Nebraska 7
1966	Louisiana State 14, Arkansas 7
1967	Georgia 24, So. Methodist 9
1968	Texas A & M 20, Alabama 16
1969	Texas 36, Tennessee 13
1970	Texas 21, Notre Dame 17
1971	Notre Dame 24, Texas 11
1972	Penn State 30, Texas 6
1973	Texas 17, Alabama 13
1974	Nebraska 19, Texas 3
1975	Penn State 41, Baylor 20
1976	Arkansas 31, Georgia 10
1977	Houston 30, Maryland 21
1978	Notre Dame 38, Texas 10

1979	Notre Dame 35, Houston 34	1955	Auburn 33, Baylor 13	1980	North Carolina 17, Michigan 15
1980	Houston 17, Nebraska 14	1956	Vanderbilt 25, Auburn 13	1981	Pittsburgh 37, South Carolina 9
1981	Alabama 30, Baylor 2	1957	Georgia Tech 21, Pittsburgh 14	1982	North Carolina 31, Arkansas 27
1982	Texas 14, Alabama 12	1958	Tennessee 3, Texas A & M 0	1983	Florida State 31, West Virginia 12
1983	So. Methodist 7, Pittsburgh 3	1959	Mississippi 7, Florida 3		
1984	Georgia 10, Texas 9	1960	Arkansas 14, Georgia Tech 7	1984	Florida 14, Iowa 6
1985	Boston College 45, Houston 28	1961	Florida 13, Baylor 12	1985	Oklahoma St. 21, South Carolina 14
1986	Texas A & M 36, Auburn 16	1962	Penn State 30, Georgia Tech 15		
1987	Ohio State 28, Texas A & M 12	1963	Florida 17, Penn State 7	1986	Florida State 34, Oklahoma St. 23
1988	Texas A & M 35, Notre Dame 10	1964	No. Carolina 35, Air Force 0		
1989	UCLA 17, Arkansas 3	1965	Florida State 36, Oklahoma 19	1987	Clemson 27, Stanford 21
1990	Tennessee 31, Arkansas 27	1966	Georgia Tech 31, Texas Tech 21	1988	LSU 30, South Carolina 13
1991	Miami 46, Texas 3	1967	Tennessee 18, Syracuse 12	1989	Georgia 34, Michigan St. 27
1992	Florida State 10, Texas A&M 2	1968	Penn State 17, Florida State 17	1990	Clemson 27, West Virginia 7
1993	Notre Dame 28, Texas A&M 3	1969	Missouri 35, Alabama 10	1991	Michigan 35, Mississippi 3
1994	Notre Dame 24, Texas A&M 21	1970	Florida 14, Tennessee 13	1992	Oklahoma 38, Virginia 14
1995	Southern California 55, Texas Tech 14	1971	Auburn 35, Mississippi 28	1993	Florida 27, No. Carolina St. 10
		1972	Georgia 7, North Carolina 3	1994	Alabama 24, No. Carolina 10
1996	Colorado 38, Oregon 6	1973	Auburn 24, Colorado 3	1995	Tennessee 45, Virginia Tech 23
		1974	Texas Tech 28, Tennessee 19	1996	Syracuse 41, Clemson 0
		1975	Auburn 27, Texas 3		
		1976	Maryland 13, Florida 0		
Gator Bowl		1977	Notre Dame 20, Penn State 9		
(At Jacksonville, Fla.)		1978	Pittsburgh 34, Clemson 3		
1953	Florida 14, Tulsa 13	1979	Clemson 17, Ohio State 15		
1954	Texas Tech 35, Auburn 13				

RESULTS OF OTHER 1995 SEASON BOWL GAMES

Alamo (San Antonio, Texas, Dec. 28, 1995)—Texas A&M 22, Michigan 20

Aloha (Honolulu, Hawaii, Dec. 25, 1995)—Kansas 51, UCLA 30

Carquest Classic (Miami, Fla., Dec. 30, 1995)—North Carolina 20, Arkansas 10

Citrus (Orlando, Fla., Jan. 1, 1996)—Tennessee 20, Ohio State 14

Copper (Tucson, Ariz., Dec. 27, 1995)—Texas Tech 55, Air Force 41

Fiesta (Tempe, Ariz., Jan. 2, 1996)—Nebraska 62, Florida 24

Heritage (Atlanta, Ga., Dec. 29, 1995)—Southern University 30, Florida A&M 25

Holiday (San Diego, Calif., Dec. 29, 1995)—Kansas State 54, Colorado State 21

Independence (Shreveport, La., Dec. 29, 1995)—Louisiana State 45, Michigan State 26

Las Vegas (Las Vegas, Nev., Dec. 14, 1995)—Toledo 40, Nevada 37

Liberty (Memphis, Tenn., Dec. 30, 1995)—East Carolina 29, Stanford 13

Outback (Tampa, Fla., Jan. 1, 1996)—Penn State 43, Auburn 14

Peach (Atlanta, Ga., Dec. 30, 1995)—Virginia 34, Georgia 27

Sun (El Paso, Tex., Dec. 29, 1995)—Iowa 38, Washington 18

HEISMAN MEMORIAL TROPHY WINNERS

The Heisman Memorial Trophy is presented annually by the Downtown Athletic Club of New York City to the nation's outstanding college football player, as determined by a poll of sportswriters and sportscasters.

1935	Jay Berwanger, Chicago	1957	John Crow, Texas A & M	1978	Billy Sims, Oklahoma
1936	Larry Kelley, Yale	1958	Pete Dawkins, Army	1979	Charles White, Southern California
1937	Clinton Frank, Yale	1959	Billy Cannon, Louisiana State		
1938	Davey O'Brien, Texas Christian	1960	Joe Bellino, Navy	1980	George Rogers, South Carolina
		1961	Ernie Davis, Syracuse		
1939	Nile Kinnick, Iowa	1962	Terry Baker, Oregon State	1981	Marcus Allen, Southern California
1940	Tom Harmon, Michigan	1963	Roger Staubach, Navy		
1941	Bruce Smith, Minnesota	1964	John Huarte, Notre Dame	1982	Hershel Walker, Georgia
1942	Frank Sinkwich, Georgia	1965	Mike Garrett, Southern California	1983	Mike Rozier, Nebraska
1943	Angelo Bertelli, Notre Dame			1984	Doug Flutie, Boston College
1944	Leslie Horvath, Ohio State	1966	Steve Spurrier, Florida	1985	Bo Jackson, Auburn
1945	Felix Blanchard, Army	1967	Gary Beban, U.C.L.A.	1986	Vinnie Testeverde, Miami
1946	Glenn Davis, Army	1968	O.J. Simpson, Southern California	1987	Tim Brown, Notre Dame
1947	Johnny Lujack, Notre Dame			1988	Barry Sanders, Oklahoma State
1948	Doak Walker, So. Methodist	1969	Steve Owens, Oklahoma		
1949	Leon Hart, Notre Dame	1970	Jim Plunkett, Stanford	1989	Andre Ware, Houston
1950	Vic Janowicz, Ohio State	1971	Pat Sullivan, Auburn	1990	Ty Detmer, Brigham Young
1951	Dick Kazmaier, Princeton	1972	Johnny Rodgers, Nebraska	1991	Desmond Howard, Michigan
1952	Billy Vessels, Oklahoma	1973	John Cappelletti, Penn State	1992	Gino Torretta, Miami
1953	Johnny Lattner, Notre Dame	1974–75	Archie Griffin, Ohio State	1993	Charlie Ward, Florida State
1954	Alan Ameche, Wisconsin	1976	Tony Dorsett, Pittsburgh	1994	Rashaan Salaam, Colorado
1955	Howard Cassady, Ohio State	1977	Earl Campbell, Texas	1995	Eddie George, Ohio State
1956	Paul Hornung, Notre Dame				

1995 N.C.A.A. CHAMPIONSHIP PLAYOFFS

DIVISION I-AA

Quarterfinals
(Dec. 2, 1995)

Marshall 41, Northern Iowa 21
Montana 45, Georgia Southern 0
Stephen F. Austin 27, Appalachian
State 17
McNeese State 52, Delaware 18

Semifinals
(Dec. 9, 1995)

Montana 70, Stephen F. Austin 14
Marshall 25, McNeese State 13

Championship
(Dec. 16, 1995)

Montana 22, Marshall 20

DIVISION II

Quarterfinals
(Nov. 25, 1995)

Ferris State, Mich. 17, New Haven,
Conn. 9
Pittsburg St., Kan. 9, N. Dakota State 7
Texas A&M–Kingsville 30, Portland St. 3
North Alabama 28, Carson–Newman,
Tenn. 7

Semifinals
(Dec. 2, 1995)

North Alabama 45, Ferris State, Mich. 7
Pittsburg State, Kan. 28, Texas A&M–
Kingsville 25 (OT)

Championship
(Dec. 9, 1995)

North Alabama 27, Pittsburg, Kan. 7

DIVISION III

Quarterfinals
(Nov. 25, 1995)

Rowan, N.J. 38, Union, N.Y. 7
Washington & Jefferson, Pa. 48, Ly-
coming, Pa. 0
Mount Union, Ohio 40, Wheaton, Ill. 14
Wis.–LaCrosse 28, Wis.–River Falls 14

Semifinals
(Dec. 2, 1995)

Wis.–LaCrosse 20, Mt. Union, Ohio 17
Rowan, N.J. 28, Washington & Jefferson, Pa. 15

Championship
(Dec. 9, 1995)

Wis.–LaCrosse 36, Rowan, N.J. 7

1995 NATIONAL ASSOCIATION OF INTERCOLLEGIATE ATHLETICS CHAMPIONSHIPS

DIVISION I

Semifinals
(Nov. 25, 1995)

Northeastern State, Okla. 17, Alabama–Pine Bluff 14
Central State, Ohio 49, Western Montana 21

Championship
(Dec. 2, 1995)

Central State, Ohio 37, Northeastern State, Okla. 7

DIVISION II

Quarterfinals
(Dec. 2, 1995)

Findlay, Ohio 15, Malone, Ohio 7
Lambuth, Tenn. 63, Bethany, Kan. 28
Central Washington 40, Hardin–Simmons, Texas 20
Mary, N.D. 42, Sioux Falls 17

Semifinals
(Dec. 9, 1995)

Findlay, Ohio 63, Lambuth, Tenn. 13
Central Washington 48, Mary, N.D. 7

Championship
(Dec. 16, 1995)

Findlay, Ohio 21, Central Washington 21 (TIE—
Co–Champions)

COLLEGE FOOTBALL HALL OF FAME

(P.O. Box 11146, South Bend, Indiana) (Date given is player's last year of competition)

Players

Abell, Earl—Colgate, 1915
Agase, Alex—Purdue/Illinois, 1946
Agganis, Harry—Boston Univ., 1952
Albert, Frank—Stanford, 1941
Aldrich, Chas. (Ki)—T.C.U., 1938
Aldrich, Malcolm—Yale, 1921
Alexander, John—Syracuse, 1920
Alworth, Lance—Arkansas, 1961
Ameche, Alan (Horse)—Wisconsin, 1954
Amling, Warren—Ohio State, 1946
Anderson, Dick—Colorado, 1967
Anderson, Donny—Texas Tech, 1965
Anderson, H. (Hunk)—Notre Dame, 1921
Atkins, Doug—Tennessee, 1952
Babich, Bob—Miami–Ohio, 1968
Bacon, C. Everett—Wesleyan, 1912
Bagnell, Francis (Reds)—Penn, 1950
Baker, Hobart (Hobey)—Princeton, 1913
Baker, John—So. Calif., 1931
Baker, Terry—Oregon State, 1962
Ballin, Harold—Princeton, 1914
Banker, Bill—Tulane, 1929
Banonis, Vince—Detroit, 1941
Barnes, Stanley—S. California, 1921
Barrett, Charles—Cornell, 1915
Baston, Bert—Minnesota, 1916
Battles, Cliff—W. Va. Wesleyan, 1931
Baugh, Sammy—Texas Christian U., 1936
Baughan, Maxie—Georgia Tech, 1959
Bausch, James—Kansas, 1930
Beagle, Ron—Navy, 1955
Beban, Gary—UCLA, 1967
Bechtol, Hub—Texas Tech, 1946
Beckett, John—Oregon, 1913
Bednarik, Chuck—Pennsylvania 1948
Behm, Forrest—Nebraska, 1940
Bell, Bobby—Minnesota, 1962
Bellino, Joe—Navy, 1960

Below, Marty—Wisconsin, 1923
Benbrook, A.—Michigan, 1911
Bertelli, A.—Notre Dame, 1943
Berry, Charlie—Lafayette, 1924
Berwanger, John (Jay)—Chicago, 1935
Bettencourt, Larry—St. Mary's, 1927
Biletnikoff, Fred—Florida State, 1964
Blanchard, Felix (Doc)—Army, 1946
Bock, Ed—Iowa State, 1938
Bomar, Lynn—Vanderbilt, 1924
Bomeisler, Doug (Bo)—Yale, 1913
Booth, Albie–Yale, 1931
Borries, Fred—Navy, 1934
Bosely, Bruce—West Virginia, 1955
Bosseler, Don—Miami, Fla., 1956
Bottari, Vic—California, 1939
Boynton, Ben—Williams, 1920
Bozis, Al—Georgetown, 1941
Bradshaw, Terry—Louisiana Tech, 1969
Brewer, Charles—Harvard, 1895
Bright, John—Drake, 1951
Brodie, John—Stanford, 1956
Brooke, George—Pennsylvania, 1895
Brown, Bob—Nebraska, 1963
Brown, George—Navy, San Diego St., 1947
Brown, Gordon—Yale, 1900
Brown, Jim—Syracuse, 1956
Brown, John, Jr.—Navy, 1913
Brown, Johnny Mack—Alabama, 1925
Brown, Raymond (Tay)—So. Calif., 1932
Buchanan, Buck—Grambling State, 1962
Bunker, Paul—Army, 1902
Burford, Chris—Stanford, 1959
Burton, Ron—Northwestern, 1956
Butkus, Dick—Illinois, 1964
Butler, Robert—Wisconsin, 1912
Cafego, George—Tennessee, 1939
Cagle, Chris—SW La. / Army, 1929
Cain, John—Alabama, 1932

Cameron, Eddie—Wash. & Lee, 1924
Campbell, David C.—Harvard, 1901
Campbell, Earl—Texas, 1977
Cannon, Billy—L.S.U., 1959
Cannon, Jack—Notre Dame, 1929
Cappelletti, John—Penn State, 1973
Carideo, Frank—Notre Dame, 1930
Caroline, J.C.—Illinois, 1954
Carney, Charles—Illinois, 1921
Carpenter, Bill—Army, 1959
Carpenter, C. Hunter—VPI, 1905
Carroll, Charles—Washington, 1928
Casanova, Tommy—Louisiana State, 1971
Casey, Edward L.—Harvard, 1919
Cassady, Howard—Ohio State, 1955
Chamberlain, Guy—Nebraska, 1915
Chapman, Sam—Cal.–Berkeley, 1938
Chappuis, Bob—Michigan, 1947
Christman, Paul—Missouri, 1940
Clark, Earl (Dutch)—Colo. College, 1929
Cleary, Paul—USC, 1947
Clevenger, Zora—Indiana, 1903
Cloud, Jack—William & Mary, 1948
Cochran, Gary—Princeton, 1895
Cody, Josh—Vanderbilt, 1920
Coleman, Don—Mich. State, 1951
Conerly, Chuck—Mississippi, 1947
Connor, George—Notre Dame, 1947
Corbin, W.—Yale, 1888
Corbus, William—Stanford, 1933
Cowan, Hector—Princeton, 1889
Coy, Edward H. (Tad)—Yale, 1909
Crawford, Fred—Duke, 1933
Crow, John D.—Texas A&M, 1957
Crowley, James—Notre Dame, 1924
Csonka, Larry—Syracuse, 1967
Cutter, Slade—Navy, 1934
Czarobski, Ziggie—Notre Dame, 1947
Dale, Carroll—Virginia Tech, 1959

Michaels, Lou—Kentucky, 1957
Michels, John—Tennessee, 1952
Mickal, Abe—La. State U., 1935
Miller, Creighton—Notre Dame, 1943
Miller, Don—Notre Dame, 1925
Miller, Edgar (Rip)—Notre Dame, 1924
Miller, Eugene—Penn State, 1913
Miller, Fred—Notre Dame, 1928
Millner, Wayne—Notre Dame, 1935
Milstead, Century—Wabash, Yale, 1923
Minds, John—Pennsylvania, 1897
Minisi, Anthony—Navy, Pennsylvania, 1947
Modzelewski, Dick—Maryland, 1952
Moffatt, Alex—Princeton, 1884
Molinski, Ed—Tennessee, 1940
Montgomery, Cliff—Columbia, 1933
Montgomery, Wilbert—Abilene
  Christian, 1976
Moomaw, Donn—U.C.L.A., 1952
Morley, William—Columbia, 1903
Morris, George—Georgia Tech, 1952
Morris, Larry—Georgia Tech., 1954
Morton, Craig—California, 1964
Morton, William—Dartmouth, 1931
Moscrip, Monk—Stanford, 1935
Muller, Harold (Brick)—Calif., 1922
Nagurski, Bronko—Minnesota, 1929
Nevers, Ernie—Stanford, 1925
Newell, Marshall—Harvard, 1893
Newman, Harry—Michigan, 1932
Newsome, Ozzie—Alabama, 1977
Nielsen, Gifford—Brigham Young, 1976
Nobis, Tommy—Texas, 1965
Nomellini, Leo—Minnesota, 1949
Oberland, Andrew—Dartmouth, 1925
O'Brien, Davey—Texas Chrtist. U., 1938
O'Dea, Pat—Wisconsin, 1899
Odell, Robert—Pennsylvania, 1943
O'Hearn, J.—Cornell, 1915
Olds, Robin—Army, 1942
Oliphant, Elmer—Purdue/Army, 1917
Olsen, Merlin—Utah State, 1961
Onkotz, Dennis—Penn State, 1969
Oosterbaan, Ben—Michigan, 1927
O'Rourke, Charles—Boston College, 1940
Orsi, John—Colgate, 1931
Osgood, W.D.—Cornell/Penn, 1895
Osmanski, William—Holy Cross, 1938
Owen, George—Harvard, 1922
Owens, Jim—Oklahoma, 1949
Owens, Steve—Oklahoma, 1969
Page, Alan—Notre Dame, 1966
Pardee, Jack—Texas A&M, 1956
Parilli, Vito (Babe)—Kentucky, 1951
Parker, Clarence (Ace)—Duke, 1936
Parker, Jackie—Miss. State, 1953
Parker, James—Ohio State, 1956
Payton, Walter—Jackson State, 1974
Pazzetti, V.J.—Wes./Lehigh, 1912
Peabody, Endicott—Harvard, 1941
Peck, Robert—Pittsburgh, 1916
Pellegrini, Bob—Maryland, 1955
Pennock, Stanley B.—Harvard, 1914
Pfann, George—Cornell, 1923
Phillips, H.D.—U. of South, 1904
Phillips, Loyd—Arkansas, 1966
Pingel, John—Michigan State, 1938
Pihos, Pete—Indiana, 1945
Pinckert, Ernie—So. California, 1931
Plunkett, Jim—Stanford, 1970
Poe, Arthur—Princeton, 1899
Pollard, Fritz—Brown, 1916
Poole, Barney—Miss./Army, 1947
Powell, Marvin—Southern California, 1976
Pregulman, Merv—Michigan, 1943
Price, Eddie—Tulane, 1949
Pund, Henry—Georgia Tech, 1928
Ramsey, Gerrard—Wm. & Mary, 1942
Reasons, Gary—Northwestern State
  (La.), 1983
Redman, Rick—Washington, 1964
Reeds, Claude—Oklahoma, 1913
Reid, Mike—Penn St., 1970
Reid, Steve—Northwestern, 1936
Reid, William—Harvard, 1900

Renfro, Mel—Oregon, 1963
Rentner, Ernest—Northwestern, 1932
Reynolds, Robert—Nebraska, 1952
Reynolds, Robert—Stanford, 1935
Richter, Les—California, 1951
Richter, Pat—Wisconsin, 1962
Riley, John—Northwestern, 1931
Rinehart, Charles—Lafayette, 1897
Roberts, J.D.—Oklahoma, 1953
Robeson, Paul—Rutgers, 1918
Robinson, Jerry—UCLA, 1978
Rodgers, Ira—West Virginia, 1919
Rogers, Edward L.—Minnesota, 1903
Romig, Joe—Colorado, 1961
Rosenberg, Aaron—So. California, 1934
Rote, Kyle—So. Methodist, 1950
Routt, Joe—Texas A&M, 1937
Salmon, Louis—Notre Dame, 1904
Sauer, George—Nebraska, 1933
Savitsky, George—Pennsylvania, 1947
Saxton, Jimmy—Texas, 1961
Sayers, Gale—Kansas, 1964
Scarbath, Jack—Maryland, 1952
Scarlett, Hunter—Pennsylvania, 1909
Schloredt, Bob—Washington, 1960
Schoonover, Wear—Arkansas, 1929
Schreiner, Dave—Wisconsin, 1942
Schultz, Adolf (Germany)—Mich., 1908
Schwab, Frank—Lafayette, 1922
Schwartz, Marchmont—Notre Dame, 1931
Schwegler, Paul—Washington, 1931
Scott, Clyde—Arkansas, 1949
Scott, Richard—Navy, 1947
Scott, Tom—Virginia, 1953
Seibels, Henry—Sewanee, 1899
Sellers, Ron—Florida State, 1968
Selmon, Lee Roy—Oklahoma, 1975
Shakespeare, Bill—Notre Dame, 1935
Shelton, Murray—Cornell, 1915
Shevlin, Tom—Yale, 1905
Shively, Bernie—Illinois, 1926
Simons, Claude—Tulane, 1934
Sims, Billy—Oklahoma, 1979
Simpson, O.J.—So. Calif., 1968
Singletary, Mike—Baylor, 1977–80
Sington, Fred—Alabama, 1930
Sinkwich, Frank—Georgia, 1942
Sitko, Emil—Notre Dame, 1949
Skladany, Joe—Pittsburgh, 1933
Slater, F.F. (Duke)—Iowa, 1921
Smith, Bruce—Minnesota, 1941
Smith, Bubba—Michigan State, 1966
Smith, Ernie—So. California, 1932
Smith, Harry—So. California, 1939
Smith, Jim Ray—Baylor, 1954
Smith, John (Clipper)—Notre Dame, 1927
Smith, Riley—Alabama, 1935
Smith, Vernon—Georgia, 1931
Snow, Neil—Michigan, 1901
Sparlis, Al—U.C.L.A., 1945
Spears, Clarence W.—Dartmouth, 1915
Spears, W.D.—Vanderbilt, 1927
Sprackling, William—Brown, 1911
Sprague, M. (Bud)—Texas/Army, 1928
Spurrier, Steve—Florida, 1966
Stafford, Harrison—Texas, 1932
Stagg, Amos Alonzo—Yale, 1889
Starcevich, Max—Washington, 1936
Staubach, Roger—Navy, 1963
Steffen, Walter—Chicago, 1908
Steffy, Joe—Army, 1947
Stein, Herbert—Pittsburgh, 1921
Steuber, Robert—Missouri, 1943
Stevens, Mal—Yale, 1923
Stevenson, Vincent—Pennsylvania, 1905
Stillwagon, Jim—Ohio State, 1970
Stinchcomb, Gaylord—Ohio State, 1920
Strom, Brock—Air Force, 1959
Strong, Ken—New York Univ., 1928
Strupper, George—Georgia Tech, 1917
Stuhldreher, Harry—Notre Dame, 1924
Stydahar, Joe—West Virginia, 1935
Suffridge, Robert—Tennessee, 1940
Suhey, Steve—Pennsylvania State, 1947

Sullivan, Pat—Auburn, 1971
Sundstrom, Frank—Cornell, 1923
Swann, Lynn—USC, 1973
Swanson, Clarence—Nebraska, 1921
Swiacki, Bill—Holy Cross/Colombia, 1947
Swink, Jim—Texas Christian, 1956
Taliaferro, George—Indiana, 1948
Tarkenton, Fran—Georgia, 1960
Tavener, John—Indiana, 1944
Taylor, Charles—Stanford, 1942
Thomas, Aurelius—Ohio St., 1957
Thompson, Joe—Pittsburgh, 1907
Thorne, Samuel B.—Yale, 1906
Thorpe, Jim—Carlisle, 1912
Ticknor, Ben—Harvard, 1930
Tigert, John—Vanderbilt, 1904
Tinsley, Gaynell—La. State U., 1936
Tipton, Eric—Duke, 1938
Tonnemaker, Clayton—Minnesota, 1949
Torrey, Robert—Pennsylvania, 1906
Travis, Ed Tarkio—Missouri, 1920
Trippi, Charles—Georgia, 1946
Tryon, J. Edward—Colgate, 1922
Tubbs, Jerry—Oklahoma, 1956
Utay, Joe—Texas A&M, 1907
Van Brocklin, Norm—Oregon, 1948
Van Sickel, Dale—Florida, 1929
Van Surdam, Henderson—Wesleyan, 1905
Very, Dexter—Penn Stste, 1912
Vessels, Billy—Oklahoma, 1952
Vick, Ernie—Michigan, 1921
Wagner, Huber—Pittsburgh, 1913
Walker, Doak—So. Methodist, 1949
Wallace, Bill—Rice, 1935
Walsh, Adam—Notre Dame, 1924
Warburton, I. (Cotton)—So. Calif., 1934
Ward, Robert (Bob)—Maryland, 1951
Warner, William—Cornell, 1903
Washington, Ken—U.C.L.A., 1939
Weatherall, Jim—Oklahoma, 1951
Webster, George—Michigan St., 1966
Wedemeyer, Herman J.—St. Mary's, 1947
Weekes, Harold—Columbia, 1902
Weiner, Art—North Carolina, 1949
Weir, Ed—Nebraska, 1925
Welch, Gus—Carlisle, 1914
Weller, John—Princeton, 1935
Wendell, Percy—Harvard, 1913
West, D. Belford—Colgate, 1919
Westfall, Bob—Michigan, 1941
Weyand, Alex—Army, 1915
Wharton, Charles—Pennsylvania, 1896
Wheeler, Arthur—Princeton, 1894
White, Byron (Whizzer)—Colorado, 1937
White, Charles—USC, 1979
White, Randy—Maryland, 1974
Whitmire, Don—Alabama/Navy, 1944
Wickhorst, Frank—Navy, 1926
Widseth, Ed—Minnesota, 1936
Wildung, Richard—Minnesota, 1942
Williams, Bob—Notre Dame, 1950
Williams, James—Rice, 1949
Willis, William—Ohio State, 1945
Wilson, George—Washington, 1925
Wilson, George—Lafayette, 1928
Wilson, Harry—Penn State/Army, 1923
Wilson, Marc—BYU, 1979
Wistert, Albert A.—Michigan, 1942
Wistert, Al—Michigan, 1942
Wistert, Frank (Whitey)—Mich., 1933
Wood, Barry—Harvard, 1931
Wojciechowicz, Alex—Fordham, 1936
Wyant, Andrew—Bucknell/Chicago, 1894
Wyatt, Bowden—Tennessee, 1938
Wyckoff, Clint—Cornell, 1896
Yarr, Tom—Notre Dame, 1931
Yary, Ron—USC, 1968
Yoder, Lloyd—Carnegie Tech, 1926
Young, Claude (Buddy)—Illinois, 1946
Young, Harry—Wash. & Lee, 1916
Young, Walter—Oklahoma, 1938
Youngblood, Jack—Florida, 1970
Youngblood, Jim—Tennessee Tech, 1972
Zarnas, Gus—Ohio State, 1937

Coaches

Bill Alexander	Michael Donohue	Thomas (Tad) Jones	William Murray	Clark Shaughnessy
Dr. Ed Anderson	Vince Dooley	Ralph (Shug) Jordan	Ed (Hooks) Mylin	Buck Shaw
Ike Armstrong	Gus Dorais	Andy Kerr	Earle (Greasy) Neale	Edgar Sherman
Earl Banks	Bill Edwards	Frank Kush	Jess Neely	Andrew L. Smith
Harry Baujan	Charles (Rip) Engle	Frank Leahy	David Nelson	Carl Snavely
Matty Bell	Don Faurot	George E. Little	Robert Neyland	Amos A. Stagg
Hugo Bezdek	Jake Gaither	Lou Little	Homer Norton	Gilbert Steinke
Dana X. Bible	Sid Gillman	El (Slip) Madigan	Frank (Buck) O'Neill	Jock Sutherland
Bernie Bierman	Ernest Godfrey	Dave Maurer	Bennie Owen	James Tatum
Bob Blackman	Ray Graves	Charley McClendon	Ara Parseghian	Frank W. Thomas
Earl (Red) Blaik	Andy Gustafson	Herbert McCracken	Doyt LPerry	Lee Tressell
Frank Broyles	Jack Harding	Daniel McGugin	James Phalea	Thad Vann
Paul (Bear) Bryant	Edward K. Hall	John McKay	Tommy Prothro	John H. Vaught
Harold Burry	Richard Harlow	Allyn McKeen	John Ralston	Wallace Wade
Charles W. Caldwell	Jesse Harper	DeOrmond (Tuss)	E.N. Robinson	Lynn Waldorf
Walter Camp	Percy Haughton	McLaughry	Knute Rockne	Glenn (Pop) Warner
Len Casanova	Woody Hayes	John Merritt	E.L. (Dick) Romney	E.E. (Tad) Wieman
Frank Cavanaugh	John W. Heisman	L.R. (Dutch) Meyer	William W. Roper	John W. Wilce
Richard Colman	R.A. (Bob) Higgins	Bernie Moore	Darrell Royal	Bud Wilkinson
Fritz Crisler	Orin E. Hollingberry	Scrappy Moore	Henry (Red) Sanders	Henry L. Williams
Duffy Daugherty	Frank Howard	Jack Mollenkopf	George F. Sanford	George W. Woodruff
Bob Devaney	William Ingram	Ray Morrison	Bo Schembechler	Warren Woodson
Dan Devine	Morley Jennings	George A. Munger	Francis A. Schmidt	Fielding H. Yost
Gil Dobie	Howard Jones	Clarence Munn	Floyd (Ben) Schwartz-	Robert Zuppke
Bobby Dodd	L. (Biff) Jones	Frank Murray	walder	

Professional Football

NATIONAL FOOTBALL LEAGUE FINAL STANDINGS 1995

AMERICAN FOOTBALL CONFERENCE

Eastern Division

	W	L	T	Pct	Pts	Op
Buffalo Bills[1]	10	6	0	.625	350	335
Indianapolis Colts[2]	9	7	0	.563	331	316
Miami Dolphins[2]	9	7	0	.563	398	332
New England Patriots	6	10	0	.375	294	377
New York Jets	3	13	0	.187	233	384

Central Division

	W	L	T	Pct	Pts	Op
Pittsburgh Steelers[1]	11	5	0	.687	407	327
Houston Oilers	7	9	0	.437	348	324
Cincinnati Bengals	7	9	0	.437	349	374
Cleveland Browns	5	11	0	.313	289	356
Jacksonville Jaguars	4	12	0	.250	275	404

Western Division

	W	L	T	Pct	Pts	Op
Kansas City Chiefs[1]	13	3	0	.812	358	241
San Diego Chargers[2]	9	7	0	.563	321	323
Denver Broncos	8	8	0	.500	388	345
Seattle Seahawks	8	8	0	.500	363	366
Oakland Raiders	8	8	0	.500	348	332

1. Division champion. 2. Wild card qualifier for playoffs. Playoffs: Buffalo 37, Miami 22; Indianapolis 35, San Diego 20; Pittsburgh 40, Buffalo 21; Indianapolis 10, Kansas City 7; Pittsburgh 20, Indianapolis 16.

NATIONAL FOOTBALL CONFERENCE

Eastern Division

	W	L	T	Pct	Pts	Op
Dallas Cowboys[1]	12	4	0	.750	435	291
Philadelphia Eagles[2]	10	6	0	.625	318	338
Washington Redskins	6	10	0	.375	326	359
New York Giants	5	11	0	.313	290	340
Arizona Cardinals	4	12	0	.250	275	422

Central Division

	W	L	T	Pct	Pts	Op
Green Bay Packers[1]	11	5	0	.687	404	314
Detroit Lions[2]	10	6	0	.625	436	336
Chicago Bears	9	7	0	.563	392	360
Minnesota Vikings	8	8	0	.500	412	385
Tampa Bay Buccaneers	7	9	0	.437	238	335

Western Division

	W	L	T	Pct	Pts	Op
San Francisco 49ers[1]	11	5	0	.687	457	258
Atlanta Falcons[2]	9	7	0	.563	362	349
St. Louis Rams	7	9	0	.437	309	418
Carolina Panthers	7	9	0	.437	289	325
New Orleans Saints	7	9	0	.437	319	348

1. Division champion. 2. Wild card qualifier for playoffs. Playoffs: Philadelphia 58, Detroit 37; Green Bay 37, Atlanta 20; Green Bay 27, San Francisco 17; Dallas 30, Philadelphia 11; Dallas 38, Green Bay 27.

LEAGUE CHAMPIONSHIP–SUPER BOWL XXX

(January 28, 1996, Sun Devil Stadium, Tempe, Ariz. Attendance: 76,347, no shows: 0. Time: 3:24.)

Scoring

	1st Q	2nd Q	3rd Q	4th Q	Final
Dallas Cowboys	10	3	7	7	27
Pittsburgh Steelers	0	7	0	10	17

First Quarter: Dallas—(2:55)—Chris Boniol 42 yard FIELD GOAL. Dallas—(9:37)—Jay Novacek 3 yard TD PASS from Troy Aikman. Dallas—(9:37)—Chris Boniol EXTRA POINT.

Second Quarter: Dallas—(8:57)—Chris Boniol 35 yard FIELD GOAL. Pittsburgh—(14:47)—Yancey Thigpen 6 yard TD PASS from Neil O'Donnell. Pittsburgh—(14:47)—Norm Johnson EXTRA POINT.

Third Quarter: Dallas—(8:18)—Emmitt Smith 1 yard TD RUN. Dallas—(8:18)—Chris Boniol EXTRA POINT.

Fourth Quarter: Pittsburgh—(3:40)—Norm Johnson 46 yard

FIELD GOAL. Pittsburgh—(8:24)—Bam Morris 1 yard TD RUN. Pittsburgh—(8:24)—Norm Johnson EXTRA POINT. Dallas—(11:17)—Emmitt Smith 4 yard TD RUN. Dallas—(11:17)—Chris Boniol EXTRA POINT.

Statistics of the Game

	Cowboys	Steelers
First Downs	15	25
Rushes–Yards	25–56	31–103
Passing Yards	198	207
Return Yards	88	18
Comp–Att–Int	15–23–0	28–49–3
Sacks–Yards Lost	2–11	4–32
Fumbles–Lost	0–0	2–0
Penalties–Yards	4–25	2–15
Time of Possession	26:11	33:49

Individual Statistics
Rushing: DALLAS: Emm. Smith 18–49, Dar. Johnston 2–8, Kev. Williams 1–2, Tro. Aikman 4–3; PITTSBURGH: Bam. Morris 19–73, Err. Pegram 6–15, Kor. Stewart 4–15, Neil O'Donnell 1–0, Joh. Williams 1–0.
Passing: DALLAS: Tro. Aikman 15–23–0–209; PITTSBURGH: Nei. O'Donnell 28–49–3–239.

Receiving: DALLAS: Mic. Irvin 5–76, Jay Novacek 5–50, Kev. Williams 2–29, Dei. Sanders 1–47, Dar. Johnston 1–4, Emm. Smith 1–3; PITTSBURGH: And. Hastings 10–98, Ern. Mills 8–78, Yan. Thigpen 3–19, Bam Morris 3–18, Cor. Holliday 2–19, Joh. Williams 2–7.
Missed Field Goals: DALLAS: None. PITTSBURGH: None.

SUPER BOWLS I–XXX

Game	Date	Winner	Loser	Site	Attendance
XXX	Jan. 28, 1996	Dallas (NFC) 27	Pittsburgh (AFC) 17	Sun Devil Stadium, Tempe, Ariz.	76,347
XXIX	Jan. 29, 1995	San Francisco (NFC) 49	San Diego (AFC) 26	Joe Robbie Stadium, Miami, Fla.	74,107
XXVIII	Jan. 30, 1994	Dallas (NFC) 30	Buffalo (AFC) 13	Georgia Dome, Atlanta, Ga.	72,817
XXVII	Jan. 31, 1993	Dallas (NFC) 52	Buffalo (AFC) 17	Rose Bowl, Pasadena, Calif.	98,374
XXVI	Jan. 26, 1992	Washington (NFC) 37	Buffalo (AFC) 24	Metrodome, Minneapolis, Minn.	63,130
XXV	Jan. 27, 1991	Giants (NFC) 20	Buffalo (AFC) 19	Tampa Stadium, Tampa, Fla.	73,813
XXIV	Jan. 28, 1990	San Francisco (NFC) 55	Denver (AFC) 10	Superdome, New Orleans	72,919
XXIII	Jan. 22, 1989	San Francisco (NFC) 20	Cincinnati (AFC) 16	Joe Robbie Stadium, Miami, Fla.	75,179
XXII	Jan. 31, 1988	Washington (NFC) 42	Denver (AFC) 10	Jack Murphy Stadium, San Diego, Calif.	73,302
XXI	Jan. 25, 1987	Giants (NFC) 39	Denver (AFC) 20	Rose Bowl, Pasadena, Calif.	101,063
XX	Jan. 26, 1986	Chicago (NFC) 46	New England (AFC) 10	Superdome, New Orleans	73,818
XIX	Jan. 20, 1985	San Francisco (NFC) 38	Miami (AFC) 16	Stanford Stadium, Palo Alto, Calif.	84,059
XVIII	Jan. 22, 1984	Los Angeles Raiders (AFC) 38	Washington (NFC) 9	Tampa Stadium, Tampa, Fla.	72,920
XVII	Jan. 30, 1983	Washington (NFC) 27	Miami (AFC) 17	Rose Bowl, Pasadena, Calif.	103,667
XVI	Jan. 24, 1982	San Francisco (NFC) 26	Cincinnati (AFC) 21	Silverdome, Pontiac, Mich.	81,270
XV	Jan. 25, 1981	Oakland (AFC) 27	Philadelphia (NFC) 10	Superdome, New Orleans	75,500
XIV	Jan. 20, 1980	Pittsburgh (AFC) 31	Los Angeles (NFC) 19	Rose Bowl, Pasadena	103,985
XIII	Jan. 21, 1979	Pittsburgh (AFC) 35	Dallas (NFC) 31	Orange Bowl, Miami	79,484
XII	Jan. 15, 1978	Dallas (NFC) 27	Denver (AFC) 10	Superdome, New Orleans	75,583
XI	Jan. 9, 1977	Oakland (AFC) 32	Minnesota (NFC) 14	Rose Bowl, Pasadena	103,424
X	Jan. 18, 1976	Pittsburgh (AFC) 21	Dallas (NFC) 17	Orange Bowl, Miami	80,187
IX	Jan. 12, 1975	Pittsburgh (AFC) 16	Minnesota (NFC) 6	Tulane Stadium, New Orleans	80,997
VIII	Jan. 13, 1974	Miami (AFC) 24	Minnesota (NFC) 7	Rice Stadium, Houston	71,882
VII	Jan. 14, 1973	Miami (AFC) 14	Washington (NFC) 7	Memorial Coliseum, Los Angeles	90,182
VI	Jan. 16, 1972	Dallas (NFC) 24	Miami (AFC) 3	Tulane Stadium, New Orleans	81,591
V	Jan. 17, 1971	Baltimore (AFC) 16	Dallas (NFC) 13	Orange Bowl, Miami	79,204
IV	Jan. 11, 1970	Kansas City (AFL) 23	Minnesota (NFL) 7	Tulane Stadium, New Orleans	80,562
III	Jan. 12, 1969	New York (AFL) 16	Baltimore (NFL) 7	Orange Bowl, Miami	75,389
II	Jan. 14, 1968	Green Bay (NFL) 33	Oakland (AFL) 14	Orange Bowl, Miami	75,546
I	Jan. 15, 1967	Green Bay (NFL) 35	Kansas City (AFL) 10	Memorial Coliseum, Los Angeles	61,946

NOTE: Super Bowls I to IV were played before the American Football League and National Football League merged into the NFL, which was divided into two conferences, the NFC and AFC.

NATIONAL LEAGUE CHAMPIONS

Year	Champion (W–L–T)
1921	Chicago Bears (Staley's) (10–1–1)
1922	Canton Bulldogs (10–0–2)
1923	Canton Bulldogs (11–0–1)
1924	Cleveland Indians (7–1–1)
1925	Chicago Cardinals (11–2–1)
1926	Frankford Yellow Jackets!(14–1–1)
1927	New York Giants (11–1–1)
1928	Providence Steamrollers (8–1–2)
1929	Green Bay Packers (12–0–1)
1930	Green Bay Packers (10–3–1)
1931	Green Bay Packers (12–2–0)
1932	Chicago Bears (7–1–6)

Year	Eastern Conference winners (W–L–T)	Western Conference winners (W–L–T)	League champion playoff results
1933	New York Giants (11–3–0)	Chicago Bears (10–2–1)	Chicago Bears 23, New York 21
1934	New York Giants (8–5–0)	Chicago Bears (13–0–0)	New York 30, Chicago Bears 13
1935	New York Giants (9–3–0)	Detroit Lions (7–3–2)	Detroit 26, New York 7
1936	Boston Redskins (7–5–0)	Green Bay Packers (10–1–1)	Green Bay 21, Boston 6
1937	Washington Redskins (8–3–0)	Chicago Bears (9–1–1)	Washington 28, Chicago Bears 21
1938	New York Giants (8–2–1)	Green Bay Packers (8–3–0)	New York 23, Green Bay 17
1939	New York Giants (9–1–1)	Green Bay Packers (9–2–0)	Green Bay 27, New York 0
1940	Washington Redskins (9–2–0)	Chicago Bears (8–3–0)	Chicago Bears 73, Washington 0
1941	New York Giants (8–3–0)	Chicago Bears (10–1–1)[2]	Chicago Bears 37, New York 9
1942	Washington Redskins (10–1–1)	Chicago Bears (11–0–0)	Washington 14, Chicago Bears 6

Year	Eastern Conference winners (W–L–T)	Western Conference winners (W–L–T)	League champion playoff results
1943	Washington Redskins (6–3–1)[2]	Chicago Bears (8–1–1)	Chicago Bears 41, Washington 21
1944	New York Giants (8–1–1)	Green Bay Packers (8–2–0)	Green Bay 14, New York 7
1945	Washington Redskins (8–2–0)	Cleveland Rams (9–1–0)	Cleveland 15, Washington 14
1946	New York Giants (7–3–1)	Chicago Bears (8–2–1)	Chicago Bears 24, New York 14
1947	Philadelphia Eagles (8–4–0)[2]	Chicago Cardinals (9–3–0)	Chicago Cardinals 28, Philadelphia 21
1948	Philadelphia Eagles (9–2–1)	Chicago Cardinals (11–1–0)	Philadelphia 7, Chicago Cardinals 0
1949	Philadelphia Eagles (11–1–0)	Los Angeles Rams (8–2–2)	Philadelphia 14, Los Angeles 0
1950[1]	Cleveland Browns (10–2–0)[2]	Los Angeles Rams (9–3–0)[2]	Cleveland 30, Los Angeles 28
1951[1]	Cleveland Browns (11–1–0)	Los Angeles Rams (8–4–0)	Los Angeles 24, Cleveland 17
1952[1]	Cleveland Browns (8–4–0)	Detroit Lions (9–3–0)[2]	Detroit 17, Cleveland 7
1953	Cleveland Browns (11–1–0)	Detroit Lions (10–2–0)	Detroit 17, Cleveland 16
1954	Cleveland Browns (9–3–0)	Detroit Lions (9–2–1)	Cleveland 56, Detroit 10
1955	Cleveland Browns (9–2–1)	Los Angeles Rams (8–3–1)	Cleveland 38, Los Angeles 14
1956	New York Giants (8–3–1)	Chicago Bears (9–2–1)	New York 47, Chicago Bears 7
1957	Cleveland Browns (9–2–1)	Detroit Lions (8–4–0)[2]	Detroit 59, Cleveland 14
1958	New York Giants (9–3–0)[2]	Baltimore Colts (9–3–0)	Baltimore 23, New York 17[3]
1959	New York Giants (10–2–0)	Baltimore Colts (9–3–0)	Baltimore 31, New York 16
1960	Philadelphia Eagles (10–2–0)	Green Bay Packers (8–4–0)	Philadelphia 17, Green Bay 13
1961	New York Giants (10–3–1)	Green Bay Packers (11–3–0)	Green Bay 37, New York 0
1962	New York Giants (12–2–0)	Green Bay Packers (13–1–0)	Green Bay 16, New York 7
1963	New York Giants (11–3–0)	Chicago Bears (11–1–2)	Chicago 14, New York 10
1964	Cleveland Browns (10–3–1)	Baltimore Colts (12–2–0)	Cleveland 27, Baltimore 0
1965	Cleveland Browns (11–3–0)	Green Bay Packers (11–3–1)[2]	Green Bay 23, Cleveland 12
1966	Dallas Cowboys (10–3–1)	Green Bay Packers (12–2–0)	Green Bay 34, Dallas 27
1967	Dallas Cowboys (9–5–0)[2]	Green Bay Packers (9–4–1)[2]	Green Bay 21, Dallas 17
1968	Cleveland Browns (10–4–0)[2]	Baltimore Colts (13–1–0)[2]	Baltimore 34, Cleveland 0
1969	Cleveland Browns (10–3–1)2	Minnesota Vikings (12–2–0)[2]	Minnesota 27, Cleveland 7

1. League was divided into American and National Conferences, 1950–52 and again in 1970, when leagues merged. 2. Won divisional playoff. 3. Won at 8:15 of sudden death overtime period.

NATIONAL CONFERENCE CHAMPIONS

Year	Eastern Division	Central Division	Western Division	Champion
1970	Dallas Cowboys (10–4–0)	Minnesota Vikings (12–2–0)	San Francisco 49ers (10–3–1)	Dallas
1971	Dallas Cowboys (11–3–0)	Minnesota Vikings (11–3–0)	San Francisco 49ers (9–5–0)	Dallas
1972	Washington Redskins (11–3–0)	Green Bay Packers (10–4–0)	San Francisco 49ers (8–5–1)	Washington
1973	Dallas Cowboys (10–4–0)	Minnesota Vikings (12–2–0)	Los Angeles Rams (12–2–0)	Minnesota
1974	St. Louis Cardinals (10–4–0)	Minnesota Vikings (10–4–0)	Los Angeles Rams (10–4–0)	Minnesota
1975	St. Louis Cardinals (11–3–0)	Minnesota Vikings (12–2–0)	Los Angeles Rams (10–4–0)	Dallas
1976	Dallas Cowboys (11–3–0)	Minnesota Vikings (11–2–1)	Los Angeles Rams (10–3–1)	Minnesota
1977	Dallas Cowboys (12–2–0)	Minnesota Vikings (9–5–0)	Los Angeles Rams (10–4–0)	Dallas
1978	Dallas Cowboys (12–4–0)	Minnesota Vikings (8–7–1)	Los Angeles Rams (12–4–0)	Dallas
1979	Dallas Cowboys (11–5–0)	Tampa Bay Buccaneers (10–6–0)	Los Angeles Rams (9–7–0)	Los Angeles
1980	Philadelphia Eagles (12–4–0)	Minnesota Vikings (9–7–0)	Atlanta Falcons (12–4–0)	Philadelphia
1981	Dallas Cowboys (12–4–0)	Tampa Bay Buccaneers (9–7–0)	San Francisco 49ers (13–3–0)	San Francisco
1982*	Washington Redskins won conference title and also had best regular–season record (8–1–0)			
1983	Washington Redskins (14–2–0)	Detroit Lions (8–8–0)	San Francisco 49ers (10–6–0)	Washington
1984	Washington Redskins (11–5–0)	Chicago Bears (10–6–0)	San Francisco 49ers (15–1–0)	San Francisco
1985	Dallas Cowboys (10–6–0)	Chicago Bears (15–1–0)	Los Angeles Rams (11–5–0)	Chicago
1986	New York Giants (14–2–0)	Chicago Bears (14–2–0)	San Francisco 49ers (10–5–1)	New York
1987	Washington Redskins (11–4–0)	Chicago Bears (11–4–0)	San Francisco 49ers (13–2–0)	Washington
1988	Philadelphia Eagles (10–6–0)	Chicago Bears (12–4–0)	San Francisco 49ers (10–6–0)	San Francisco
1989	New York Giants (12–4–0)	Minnesota Vikings (10–6–0)	San Francisco 49ers (14–2–0)	San Francisco
1990	New York Giants (13–3–0)	Chicago Bears (11–5–0)	San Francisco 49ers (14–2–0)	New York
1991	Washington (14–2–0)	Detroit Lions (12–4–0)	New Orleans Saints (11–5–0)	Washington
1992	Dallas (13–3–0)	Minnesota (11–5–0)	San Francisco (14–2–0)	Dallas
1993	Dallas (12–4–0)	Detroit (10–6–0)	San Francisco (10–6–0)	Dallas
1994	Dallas (12–4–0)	Minnesota (10–6–0)	San Francisco (13–3–0)	San Francisco
1995	Dallas (12–4–0)	Green Bay (11–5–0)	San Francisco (11–5–0)	Dallas

*Schedule reduced to 9 games from usual 16, with no standings kept in Eastern, Central, and Western Divisions, because of 57–day player strike.

AMERICAN LEAGUE CHAMPIONS

Year	Eastern Division (W–L–T)	Western Division (W–L–T)	League champion, playoff results
1960	Houston Oilers (10–4–0)	Los Angeles Chargers (10–4–0)	Houston 24, Los Angeles 16
1961	Houston Oilers (10–3–1)	San Diego Chargers (12–2–0)	Houston 10, San Diego 3
1962	Houston Oilers (11–3–0)	Dallas Texans (11–3–0)	Dallas 20, Houston 17[1]
1963	Boston Patriots (8–6–1)[2]	San Diego Chargers (11–3–0)	San Diego 51, Boston 10
1964	Buffalo Bills (12–2–0)	San Diego Chargers (8–5–1)	Buffalo 20, San Diego 7
1965	Buffalo Bills (10–3–1)	San Diego Chargers (9–2–3)	Buffalo 23, San Diego 0
1966	Buffalo Bills (9–4–1)	Kansas City Chiefs (11–2–1)	Kansas City 31, Buffalo 7
1967	Houston Oilers (9–4–1)	Oakland Raiders (13–1–0)	Oakland 40, Houston 7
1968	New York Jets (11–3–0)	Oakland Raiders (12–2–0)[2]	New York 27, Oakland 23
1969	New York Jets (10–4–0)	Oakland Raiders (12–1–1)	Kansas City 17, Oakland 7[3]

1. Won at 2:45 of second sudden death overtime period. 2. Won divisional playoff. 3. Kansas City defeated New York, 13–6, and Oakland defeated Houston, 56–7, in interdivisional playoffs.

AMERICAN CONFERENCE CHAMPIONS

Year	Eastern Division	Central Division	Western Division	Champion
1970	Baltimore Colts (11–2–1)	Cincinnati Bengals (8–6–0)	Oakland Raiders (8–4–2)	Baltimore
1971	Miami Dolphins (10–3–1)	Cleveland Browns (9–5–0)	Kansas City Chiefs (10–3–1)	Miami
1972	Miami Dolphins (14–0–0)	Pittsburgh Steelers (11–3–0)	Oakland Raiders (10–3–1)	Miami
1973	Miami Dolphins (12–2–0)	Cincinnati Bengals (10–4–0)	Oakland Raiders (9–4–1)	Miami
1974	Miami Dolphins (11–3–0)	Pittsburgh Steelers (10–3–1)	Oakland Raiders (12–2–0)	Pittsburgh
1975	Baltimore Colts (10–4–0)	Pittsburgh Steelers (12–2–0)	Oakland Raiders (12–2–0)	Pittsburgh
1976	Baltimore Colts (11–3–0)	Pittsburgh Steelers (10–4–0)	Oakland Raiders (13–1–0)	Oakland
1977	Baltimore Colts (10–4–0)	Pittsburgh Steelers (9–5–0)	Denver Broncos (12–2–0)	Denver
1978	New England Patriots (11–5–0)	Pittsburgh Steelers (14–2–0)	Denver Broncos (10–6–0)	Pittsburgh
1979	Miami Dolphins (10–6–0)	Pittsburgh Steelers (12–4–0)	San Diego Chargers (12–4–0)	Pittsburgh
1980	Buffalo Bills (11–5–0)	Cleveland Browns (11–5–0)	San Diego Chargers (11–5–0)	Oakland
1981	Miami Dolphins (11–4–1)	Cincinnati Bengals (12–4–0)	San Diego Chargers (10–6–0)	Cincinnati
1982*	Miami Dolphins won the conference title, but the Los Angeles Raiders had best regular–season record (8–1–0).			
1983	Miami (12–4–0)	Pittsburgh (10–6–0)	Los Angeles Raiders (12–4–0)	Los Angeles
1984	Miami (14–2–0)	Pittsburgh (9–7–0)	Denver (13–3–0)	Miami
1985	Miami (12–4–0)	Cleveland (8–8)	Los Angeles Raiders (12–4–0)	New England
1986	New England (11–5–0)	Cleveland (12–4–0)	Denver (11–5–0)	Denver
1987	Indianapolis Colts (9–6–0)	Cleveland Browns (10–5–0)	Denver Broncos (10–4–1)	Denver
1988	Buffalo Bills (12–4–0)	Cincinnati Bengals (12–4–0)	Seattle Seahawks (9–7–0)	Cincinnati
1989	Buffalo Bills (9–7–0)	Cleveland Browns (9–6–1)	Denver Broncos (11–5–0)	Denver
1990	Buffalo Bills (13–3–0)	Cincinnati Bengals (9–7–0)	Los Angeles Raiders (12–4–0)	Buffalo
1991	Buffalo Bills (13–3–0)	Houston Oilers (11–5–0)	Denver Broncos (12–4–0)	Buffalo
1992	Miami Dolphins (11–5–0)	Pittsburgh Steelers (11–5–0)	San Diego Chargers (11–5–0)	Buffalo
1993	Buffalo (12–4–0)	Houston (12–4–0)	Kansas City (11–5–0)	Buffalo
1994	Miami Dolphins (10–6–0)	Pittsburgh Steelers (12–4–0)	San Diego Chargers (11–5–0)	San Diego
1995	Buffalo (10–6–0)	Pittsburgh (11–5–0)	Kansas City (13–3–0)	Pittsburgh

*Schedule reduced to 9 games from usual 16, with no standings kept in Eastern, Central, and Western Divisions, because of 57–day player strike.

PRO FOOTBALL HALL OF FAME

(National Football Museum, Canton, Ohio)

Teams named are those with which player is best identified; figures in parentheses indicate number of playing seasons.

Adderley, Herb, defensive back, Packers, Cowboys (12)	1961–72
Alworth, Lance, wide receiver, Chargers, Cowboys (12)	1962–72
Atkins, Doug, defensive end, Browns, Bears, Saints (17)	1953–69
Badgro, Morris, end, N.Y. Yankees, Giants, Bklyn. Dodgers (8)	1927, 1930–36
Barney, Lem, defensive back, Lions (11)	1967–78
Battles, Cliff, back, Redskins (6)	1932–37
Baugh, Sammy, quarterback, Redskins (16)	1936–52
Bednarik, Chuck, center–lineback, Eagles (14)	1949–62
Bell, Bert, N.F.L. founder, Eagles and Steelers, N.F.L. Commissioner	1946–59
Bell, Bobby, linebacker, Chiefs (12)	1963–74
Berry, Raymond, end, Colts (13)	1955–67
Bidwell, Charles W., owner Chicago Cardinals	1933–47
Biletnikoff, Fred, wide receiver, Raiders (14)	1965–1978
Blanda, George, quarterback–kicker, Bears, Oilers, Raiders (27)	1949–75
Blount, Mel, cornerback, Pittsburgh Steelers (14)	1970–83
Bradshaw, Terry, quarterback, Pittsburgh Steelers (14)	1970–83
Brown, Jim, fullback, Browns (9)	1957–65
Brown, Paul E., coach, Browns (1946–62), Bengals (1968–75)	1946–75
Brown, Roosevelt, tackle, Giants (13)	1953–65
Brown, Willie, cornerback, Broncos, Raiders (16)	1963–78
Buchanan, Buck, tackle, Chiefs (11)	1963–73
Butkus, Dick, linebacker, Bears (9)	1965–73
Campbell, Earl, running back, Oilers, Saints (8)	1978–85
Canadeo, Tony, back, Packers (11)	1941–52
Carr, Joe, president N.F.L. (18)	1921–39
Chamberlin, Guy, end 4 teams (9)	1919–27
Christiansen, Jack, defensive back, Lions (8)	1951–58
Clark, Earl (Dutch), Qback, Spartans, Lions (7)	1931–38
Connor, George, tackle, linebacker, Bears (8)	1948–55
Conzelman, Jimmy, Qback 5 teams (10), owner	1921–48
Creekmur, Lou, offensive tackle/guard, Lions (10)	1950–59
Csonka, Larry, back, Dolphins, Giants (11)	1968–79
Davis, Al, owner, Raiders, coach, general manager	1963–present
Davis, Willie, defensive end, Packers (10)	1960–69
Dawson, Len, quarterback, Steelers, Browns, Texans, Chiefs (19)	1957–75
Dierdorf, Dan, tackle/center, Cardinals (13)	1971–83
Ditka, Mike, tight end, Bears, Eagles, Cowboys (12)	1961–72
Donovan, Art, defensive tackle, Colts (12)	1950–61
Dorsett, Tony, running back, Cowboys, Broncos (12)	1977–88

N.F.L. INDIVIDUAL LIFETIME, SEASON, AND GAME RECORDS

(American Football League records were incorporated into N.F.L. records after merger of the leagues) Players listed in boldface were active during the 1995 season. Players listed in capital letters are members of the Pro Football Hall of Fame. The All-America Football Conference (AAFC) existed from 1946 to 1949. The 49ers, Browns, and Colts merged with the NFL in 1949.

All-Time Leading Touchdown Scorers
(Through 1995)

Rank	Player	Yrs	Rush.	Rec.	Returns	TD
1.	Jerry Rice	11	9	146	1	156
2.	JIM BROWN	9	106	20	0	126
3.	WALTER PAYTON	13	110	15	0	125
4.	Marcus Allen	14	103	21	1	125
5.	JOHN RIGGINS	14	104	12	0	116
6.	LENNY MOORE	12	63	48	2	113
7.	DON HUTSON	11	3	99	3	105
8.	STEVE LARGENT	14	1	100	0	101
9.	Emmitt Smith	6	96	4	0	100
9.	FRANCO HARRIS	13	91	9	0	100
11.	Eric Dickerson	11	90	6	0	96
12.	JIM TAYLOR	10	83	10	0	93
13.	TONY DORSETT	12	77	13	1	91
13.	BOBBY MITCHELL	11	18	65	8	91
15.	LEROY KELLY	10	74	13	3	90
15.	CHARLEY TAYLOR	13	11	79	0	90

All-Time Leading Receivers
(Through 1995)

Rank	Player	Yrs	No.	Yds.	Avg.	TD
1.	Jerry Rice	11	942	15,123	16.1	146
2.	Art Monk	16	940	12,721	13.5	68
3.	STEVE LARGENT	14	819	13,089	16.0	100
4.	James Lofton	16	764	14,004	18.3	75
5.	Charlie Joiner	18	750	12,146	16.2	65
6.	Henry Ellard	13	723	12,163	16.8	59
7.	Andre Reed	11	700	9,848	14.1	69
8.	Gary Clark	11	699	10,856	15.5	65
9.	Ozzie Newsome	13	662	7,980	12.1	47
10.	CHARLEY TAYLOR	13	649	9,110	14.0	79
11.	Drew Hill	15	634	9,831	15.5	60
12.	DON MAYNARD	15	633	11,834	18.7	88
13.	RAYMOND BERRY	13	631	9,275	14.7	68
14.	Sterling Sharpe	7	595	8,134	13.7	65
15.	Harold Carmichael	14	590	8,985	15.2	79

All-Time Leading Passers
(Minimum 1,500 attempts. Through 1995)

Rank	Player	Yrs	Att.	Comp.	Pct. Comp.	Yds.	TD	Int.	Avg. Gain	Rating
1.	Steve Young	11	2,876	1,845	64.2	23,069	160	79	8.02	96.1
2.	Joe Montana	15	5,391	3,409	63.2	40,551	273	139	7.52	92.3
3.	Dan Marino	13	6,531	3,913	59.9	48,841	352	200	7.48	88.4
4.	Brett Favre	5	2,150	1,342	62.4	14,825	108	66	6.90	86.8
5.	Jim Kelly	10	4,400	2,652	60.3	32,657	223	156	7.42	85.4
6.	Troy Aikman	7	2,713	1,704	62.8	19,607	98	85	7.23	83.5
7.	ROGER STAUBACH	11	2,958	1,685	57.0	22,700	153	109	7.67	83.4
8.	Neil Lomax	8	3,153	1,817	57.6	22,771	136	90	7.22	82.7
9.	SONNY JURGENSEN	18	4,262	2,433	57.1	32,224	255	189	7.56	82.63
10.	LEN DAWSON	19	3,741	2,136	57.1	28,711	239	183	7.67	82.56
11.	Dave Krieg	16	4,911	2,866	58.4	35,668	247	187	7.26	81.88
12.	Ken Anderson	16	4,475	2,654	59.3	32,838	197	160	7.34	81.86
13.	Jeff Hostetler	10	1,792	1,036	57.8	12,983	66	47	7.24	81.80
14.	Neil O'Donnell	6	1,871	1,069	57.1	12,867	68	37	6.88	81.78
15.	Danny White	13	2,950	1,761	59.7	21,959	155	132	7.44	81.7

All-Time Leading Scorers
(Through 1995)

Rank	Player	Yrs	TD	FG	PAT	Pts
1.	GEORGE BLANDA	26	9	335	943	2,002
2.	JAN STENERUD	19	0	373	580	1,699
3.	Nick Lowery	17	0	366	536	1,634
4.	Eddie Murray	16	0	325	498	1,473
5.	Pat Leahy	18	0	304	558	1,470
6.	Gary Anderson	14	0	331	448	1,441
7.	Morten Andersen	14	0	333	441	1,440
8.	Jim Turner	16	1	304	521	1,439
9.	Matt Bahr	17	0	300	522	1,422
10.	Mark Moseley	16	0	300	482	1,382
11.	Jim Bakken	17	0	282	534	1,380
12.	Fred Cox	15	0	282	519	1,365
13.	LOU GROZA	17	1	234	641	1,349
14.	Norm Johnson	14	0	277	515	1,346
15.	Jim Breech	14	0	243	517	1,246

All-Time Leading Rushers
(Through 1995)

Rank	Player	Yrs	Att.	Yds	Avg	TDs
1.	WALTER PAYTON	13	3,838	16,726	4.4	110
2.	Eric Dickerson	11	2,996	13,259	4.4	90
3.	TONY DORSETT	12	2,936	12,739	4.3	77
4.	JIM BROWN	9	2,359	12,312	5.2	106
5.	FRANCO HARRIS	13	2,949	12,120	4.1	91
6.	JOHN RIGGINS	14	2,916	11,352	3.9	104
7.	O.J. SIMPSON	11	2,404	11,236	4.7	61
8.	Marcus Allen	14	2,692	10,908	4.1	103
9.	Ottis Anderson	14	2,562	10,273	4.0	81
10.	Barry Sanders	7	2,077	10,172	4.9	73
11.	Thurman Thomas	8	2,285	9,729	4.3	54
12.	EARL CAMPBELL	8	2,187	9,407	4.3	74
13.	Emmitt Smith	6	2,007	8,956	4.5	96
14.	JIM TAYLOR	10	1,941	8,597	4.4	83
15.	JOE PERRY	14	1,737	8,378	4.8	53

Scoring

Most points scored, lifetime—2,002, George Blanda, Chicago Bears, 1949–58; Baltimore, 1950; Houston, 1960–66; Oakland, 1967–75 (9tds, 943 pat, 335 fgs).

Most points, season—176, Paul Hornung, Green Bay, 1960 (15 td, 41 pat, 15 fg).

Most points, game—40, Ernie Nevers, Chicago Cardinals, 1929 (6 td, 4 pat).

Most points, per quarter—29, Don Hutson, Green Bay, 1945 (4 td, 5 pat).

Most touchdowns, lifetime—146, Jerry Rice, San Francisco, 1985–95.

Most touchdowns, season—25, Emmitt Smith, Dallas, 1995.

Most touchdowns, game—6, Ernie Nevers, Chicago Cardinals, 1929; William Jones, Cleveland, 1951; Gale Sayers, Chicago Bears, 1965.

Most points after touchdown, lifetime—959, George Blanda, Chicago Bears, 1949–58; Baltimore, 1950; Houston, 1960–66; Oakland, 1967–75.

Most points after touchdown, game—10, Charlie Gogolak, Washington, vs. N.Y. Giants, 1966

Most consecutive points after touchdown—234, Tommy Davis, San Francisco, 1959–65.

Most points after touchdown, no misses, season—56, Danny Villanueva, Dallas, 1966; Ray Wersching, San Francisco, 1984; Chip Lohmiller, Washington, 1991.

Most field goals, lifetime—373, Jan Stenerud, Kansas City Chiefs, 1967–79; Green Bay Packers, 1980–83; Minnesota Vikings, 1984–85.

Most field goals, season—35, Ali Haji–Sheikh, N.Y. Giants, 1983; Jeff Jaeger, L.A. Raiders, 1993.

Most field goals, game—7, Jim Bakken, St. Louis, 1967; and Rick Karlis, Minnesota, 1989.

Longest field goal—63 yards, Tom Dempsey, New Orleans, 1970.

Rushing

Most yards gained, lifetime—16,726, Walter Payton, Chicago Bears, 1975–1987.

Most yards gained, season—2,105, Eric Dickerson, Los Angeles, 1984.

Most yards gained, game—275, Walter Payton, Chicago, 1977.

Most touchdowns, lifetime—110, Walter Payton, Chicago, 1975–1987.

Most touchdowns, season—25, Emmitt Smith, Dallas, 1995.

Most touchdowns, game—6, Ernie Nevers, Chicago Cardinals, 1929; Dub Jones, Cleveland Browns, 1951; Gale Sayers, Chicago Bears, 1968.

Longest run from scrimmage—99 yards, Tony Dorsett, Dallas, Jan. 3, 1983.

Passing

Most touchdown passes, lifetime—352, Dan Marino, Miami, 1983– .

Most touchdown passes, season—48, Dan Marino, Miami, 1984.

Most touchdown passes, game—7, Sid Luckman, Chicago Bears, 1943; Adrian Burk, Philadelphia, 1954; George Blanda, Houston, 1961; Y.A. Tittle, New York Giants, 1963; Joe Kapp, Minnesota, 1969.

Most consecutive games, touchdown passes—47, John Unitas, Baltimore, 1956–60.

Most consecutive passes attempted, none intercepted—308, Bernie Kosar, Cleveland, 1990–91.

Longest pass completion—99 yards, Frank Filchock (to Andy Farkas), Washington, 1939; George Izo (to Bob Mitchell), Washington, 1963; Karl Sweetan (to Pat Studstill), Detroit, 1966; Sonny Jurgensen (to Gerry Allen), Washington, 1968; Jim Plunkett (to Cliff Branch) L.A. Raiders, 1985; Ron Jaworksi (to Mike Quick), Philadelphia, 1985; Stan Humphries (to Tony Martin), San Diego, 1994; Brett Favre (to Robert Brooks), Green Bay, 1995.

Receiving

Most pass receptions, lifetime—942, Jerry Rice, San Francisco, 1985– .

Most pass receptions, season—123, Herman Moore, Detroit, 1995.

Most pass receptions, game—18, Tom Fears, Los Angeles, 1950.

Most consecutive games, pass receptions—180, Art Monk, Washington, 1980–93; N.Y. Jets, 1994.

Most yards gained, pass receptions, lifetime—15,123, Jerry Rice, San Francisco, 1985– .

Most yards gained receptions, season—1,746, Charley Hennigan, Houston, 1961.

Most yards gained receptions, game—336, Willie Anderson, Los Angeles Rams, Nov. 26, 1989 vs. New Orleans.

Most touchdown receptions, lifetime—131, Jerry Rice, San Francisco, 1985–94.

Most touchdown pass receptions, season—22, Jerry Rice, San Francisco 49ers, 1987.

Most touchdown pass receptions, game—5, Bob Shaw, Chicago Cards, 1950; Kellen Winslow, San Diego Chargers, 1981; Jerry Rice, San Francisco 49ers, 1990.

Most consecutive games, touchdown pass receptions—13, Jerry Rice, San Francisco 49ers, 1986–87.

Interceptions

Most pass interceptions, lifetime—81, Paul Krause, Washington, 1964–67; Minnesota, 1968–79.

Most pass interceptions, season—14, Richard (Night Train) Lane, Los Angeles, 1952.

Most pass interceptions, game—4, by 17 players.

Longest pass interception return—103 yards, Vencie Glenn, San Diego, vs. Denver, Nov. 29, 1987.

Kicking

Longest punt—98 yrds, Steve O'Neal, New York Jets, 1969.

Highest average punting, lifetime—45.16 yards, Sammy Baugh, Washington, 1937–52.

Longest punt return—103 yards, Robert Bailey, L.A. Rams, 1994.

Longest kick-off return—106 yards, Roy Green, St. Louis, 1979; Al Carmichael, Green Bay, 1956; Noland Smith, Kansas City, 1967.

Most punts lifetime—1,154, Dave Jennings, N.Y. Giants 1974–84; N.Y. Jets, 1985–87.

Passing

Most passes completed, lifetime—3,913, Dan Marino, Miami, 1983– .

Most passes completed, season—404, Warren Moon, 1991.

Most passes completed, game—45, Drew Bledsoe, New England, 1994.

Most consecutive passes completed—22, Joe Montana, San Francisco, 1987.

Most yards gained, lifetime—48,841, Dan Marino, Miami, 1983– .

Most yards gained, season—5,084, Dan Marino, Miami, 1984.

Most yards gained, game—554, Norm Van Brocklin, Los Angeles, 1951.

NFL GOVERNMENT

Paul Tagliabue, Commissioner; Neil Austrian, President; Jay Moyer, Executive Vice President and League Counsel; Harold Henderson, Executive Vice President for Labor Relations/Chairman NFLMC; Joe Browne, Vice President of Communications & Development; Val Pinchbeck, Jr., Vice President of Broadcasting & Productions; Tom Sullivan, Vice President–Internal Audit; Jim Steeg, Executive Director for Special Events; Roger Goodell, Executive Director for Club Relations and International Development; Dennis Curran, General Counsel/Management Council; Pete Abitante, Director of Information; Greg Aiello, Director of Communications; Phil Ayoub, Comptroller; Nancy Behar, Assistant Director of Broadcasting and Productions; Joel Bussert, Director of Player Personnel; John Buzzeo, Director of Administration; David Cornwell, Director of Equal Emploument and Assistant Counsel; Joe Ellis, Assistant Director of Club Administration; Bill Granholm, Director of Special Projects; Leslie Hammond, Director of Information, AFC; Charlie Jackson, Assistant Director of Security; John Jones, Director of Labor Relations; Dick Maxwell, Director of Broadcasting Services; Susan McCann Minogue, Assistant Director of Special Events; Jack Reader, Assistant Director of Officiating; Reggie Roberts, Director of Information, NFC; Peter Ruocco, Director of Planning for Player Employment; Jerry Seeman, Director of Officiating; Jan Van Duser, Director of Game Operations; Don Weiss, Director of Planning; Warren Welsh, Director of Security.

BASKETBALL

Basketball may be the one sport whose exact origin is definitely known. In the winter of 1891–92, Dr. James Naismith, an instructor in the Y.M.C.A. Training College (now Springfield College) at Springfield, Mass., deliberately invented the game of basketball in order to provide indoor exercise and competition for the students between the closing of the football season and the opening of the baseball season. He affixed peach baskets overhead on the walls at opposite ends of the gymnasium and organized teams to play his new game in which the purpose was to toss an association (soccer) ball into one basket and prevent the opponents from tossing the ball into the other basket. The game is fundamentally the same today, though there have been improvements in equipment and some changes in rules.

Because Dr. Naismith had eighteen available players when he invented the game, the first rule was: "There shall be nine players on each side." Later the number of players became optional, depending upon the size of the available court, but the five-player standard was adopted when the game spread over the country. United States soldiers brought basketball to Europe in World War I, and it soon became a worldwide sport.

College Basketball

NATIONAL COLLEGIATE A.A. CHAMPIONS

1939	Oregon	1953	Indiana	1967–73	U.C.L.A.	1986	Louisville
1940	Indiana	1954	La Salle	1974	No. Carolina State	1987	Indiana
1941	Wisconsin	1955	San Francisco	1975	U.C.L.A.	1988	Kansas
1942	Stanford	1956	San Francisco	1976	Indiana	1989	Michigan
1943	Wyoming	1957	North Carolina	1977	Marquette	1990	Nevada–Las Vegas
1944	Utah	1958	Kentucky	1978	Kentucky	1991	Duke
1945	Oklahoma A & M	1959	California	1979	Michigan State	1992	Duke
1946	Oklahoma A & M	1960	Ohio State	1980	Louisville	1993	North Carolina
1947	Holy Cross	1961	Cincinnati	1981	Indiana	1994	Arkansas
1948	Kentucky	1962	Cincinnati	1982	North Carolina	1995	U.C.L.A.
1949	Kentucky	1963	Loyola (Chicago)	1983	North Carolina State	1996	Kentucky
1950	C.C.N.Y.	1964	U.C.L.A.				
1951	Kentucky	1965	U.C.L.A.	1984	Georgetown		
1952	Kansas	1966	Texas Western	1985	Villanova		

NATIONAL INVITATION TOURNAMENT (NIT) CHAMPIONS

1939	Long Island U.	1955	Duquesne	1969	Temple	1983	Fresno State
1940	Colorado	1956	Louisville	1970	Marquette	1984	Michigan
1941	Long Island U.	1957	Bradley	1971	North Carolina	1985	U.C.L.A.
1942	West Virginia	1958	Xavier (Cincinnati)	1972	Maryland	1986	Ohio State
1943–44	St. John's (N.Y.C.)	1959	St. John's (N.Y.C.)	1973	Virginia Tech	1987	So. Mississippi
1945	DePaul	1960	Bradley	1974	Purdue	1988	Connecticut
1946	Kentucky	1961	Providence	1975	Princeton	1989	St. John's (N.Y.C.)
1947	Utah	1962	Dayton	1976	Kentucky	1990	Vanderbilt
1948	St. Louis	1963	Providence	1977	St. Bonaventure	1991	Stanford
1949	San Francisco	1964	Bradley	1978	Texas	1992	Virginia
1950	C.C.N.Y.	1965	St. John's (N.Y.C.)	1979	Indiana	1993	Minnesota
1951	Brigham Young	1966	Brigham Young	1980	Virginia	1994	Villanova
1952	La Salle	1967	So. Illinois	1981	Tulsa	1995	Virginia Tech
1953	Seton Hall	1968	Dayton	1982	Bradley	1996	Nebraska
1954	Holy Cross						

N.C.A.A. MAJOR COLLEGE INDIVIDUAL SCORING RECORDS

Single Season Averages

Player, Team	Year	G	FG	FT	Pts	Avg
Pete Maravich, Louisiana State	1969–70	31	522 [1]	337	1381 [1]	44.5 [1]
Pete Maravich, Louisiana State	1968–69	26	433	282	1148	44.2
Pete Maravich, Louisiana State	1967–68	26	432	274	1138	43.8
Frank Selvy, Furman	1953–54	29	427	355 [1]	1209	41.7
Johnny Neumann, Mississippi	1970–71	23	366	191	923	40.1
Freeman Williams, Portland State	1976–77	26	417	176	1010	38.8
Billy McGill, Utah	1961–62	26	394	221	1009	38.8
Calvin Murphy, Niagara	1967–68	24	337	242	916	38.2
Austin Carr, Notre Dame	1969–70	29	444	218	1106	38.1

1. Record.

N.C.A.A. CAREER SCORING TOTALS

Division I

Player, Team	Last year	G	FG	FT	Pts	Avg
Pete Maravich, Louisiana State	1970	83	1387 [1]	893 [1]	3667 [1]	44.2 [1]
Austin Carr, Notre Dame	1971	74	1017	526	2560	34.6
Oscar Robertson, Cincinnati	1960	88	1052	869	2973	33.8
Calvin Murphy, Niagara	1970	77	947	654	2548	33.1
Dwight Lamar [2]	1973	57	768	326	1862	32.7
Frank Selvy, Furman	1954	78	922	694	2538	32.5
Rick Mount, Purdue	1970	72	910	503	2323	32.3
Darrel Floyd, Furman	1956	71	868	545	2281	32.1
Nick Werkman, Seton Hall	1964	71	812	649	2273	32.0

1. Record. 2. Also played two seasons in college division.

Division II

Player, Team	Last year	G	FG	FT	Pts	Avg
Travis Grant, Kentucky State	1972	121	1760 [1]	525	4045 [1]	33.4 [1]
John Rinka, Kenyon	1970	99	1261	729	3251	32.8
Florindo Vieira, Quinnipiac	1957	69	761	741	2263	32.8
Willie Shaw, Lane	1964	76	960	459	2379	31.3
Mike Davis, Virginia Union	1969	89	1014	730	2758	31.0
Henry Logan, Western Carolina	1968	107	1263	764	3290	30.7
Willie Scott, Alabama State	1969	103	1277	601	3155	30.6
Gregg Northington, Alabama State	1972	75	894	403	2191	29.2
Bob Hopkins, Grambling	1956	126	1403	953	3759	29.8

1. Record.

TOP SINGLE-GAME SCORING MARKS

Player, Team (Opponent)	Yr	Pts	Player, Team (Opponent)	Yr	Pts
Selvy, Furman (Newberry)	1954	100 [1]	Maravich, LSU (Alabama)	1970	69
Arizin, Villanova (Phi. NAMC)	1949	85	Murphy, Niagara (Syracuse)	1969	68
Williams, Portland State (Rocky Mtn.)	1978	81	Floyd, Furman (Morehead)	1955	67
Mlkvy, Temple (Wilkes)	1951	73	Maravich, LSU (Tulane)	1969	66
Bradshaw, U.S. International (Loyola–CA)	1991	72	Handlan, W & L (Furman)	1951	66
Williams, Portland State (So. Oregon)	1977	71	Roberts, Oral Roberts (N.C. A&T)	1977	66

1. Record.

MEN'S N.C.A.A. BASKETBALL CHAMPIONSHIPS—1996

DIVISION I

First Round—East
Massachusetts 92, Central Florida 70
Stanford 66, Bradley 58
Arkansas 86, Penn State 80
Marquette 68, Monmouth 44
North Carolina 83, New Orleans 62
Texas Tech 74, Northern Illinois 73
New Mexico 69, Kansas State 48
Georgetown 93, Miss. Valley State 56

First Round—Southeast
Connecticut 68, Colgate 59
Eastern Michigan 75, Duke 60
Miss. State 58, Va. Commonwealth 51
Princeton 43, UCLA 41
Boston College 64, Indiana 51
Georgia Tech 90, Austin Peay 79
Temple 61, Oklahoma 43
Cincinnati 66, North Carolina–
Greensboro 61

First Round—Midwest
Kentucky 110, San Jose State 72
Virginia Tech 61, Wis.–Green Bay 48
Iowa State 74, California 64
Utah 72, Canisius 43
Louisville 82, Tulsa 80 (OT)
Villanova 92, Portland 58
Texas 80, Michigan 76
Wake Forest 62, Northeast Louisiana 50

First Round—West
Purdue 73, Western Carolina 71
Georgia 81, Clemson 74

Drexel 75, Memphis 63
Syracuse 88, Montana State 55
Iowa 81, George Washington 79
Arizona 90, Valparaiso 51
Santa Clara 91, Maryland 79
Kansas 92, South Carolina State 54

Second Round—East
Massachusetts 79, Stanford 74
Arkansas 65, Marquette 56
Texas Tech 92, North Carolina 73
Georgetown 73, New Mexico 62

Second Round—Southeast
Connecticut 95, Eastern Michigan 81
Mississippi State 63, Princeton 41
Georgia Tech 103, Boston College 89
Cincinnati 78, Temple 65

Second Round—Midwest
Kentucky 84, Virginia Tech 60
Utah 73, Iowa State 67
Louisville 68, Villanova 64
Wake Forest 65, Texas 62

Second Round—West
Georgia 76, Purdue 69
Syracuse 69, Drexel 55
Arizona 87, Iowa 73
Kansas 76, Santa Clara 51

Third Round—East
Massachusetts 79, Arkansas 63
Georgetown 98, Texas Tech 90

Third Round—Southeast
Mississippi State 60, Connecticut 55

Cincinnati 87, Georgia Tech 70

Third Round—Midwest
Kentucky 101, Utah 70
Wake Forest 60, Louisville 59

Third Round—West
Syracuse 83, Georgia 81 (OT)
Kansas 83, Arizona 80

Regional Finals
East—Mass. 86, Georgetown 62
Southeast—Miss. State 73, Cinncinati 63
Midwest—Kentucky 83, Wake Forest 63
West—Syracuse 60, Kansas 57

National Semifinals
March 30, 1996, East Rutherford, N.J.
Kentucky 81, Massachusetts 74
Syracuse 77, Mississippi State 69

National Final
April 1, 1996, East Rutherford, N.J.
Kentucky 76, Syracuse 67

DIVISION II

Semifinals
Fort Hays State 76, California, Pa. 56
Northern Kentucky 68, Virginia Union 66

Championship
Ft. Hays State 70, Northern Kentucky 63

DIVISION III

Semifinals
Rowan, N.J. 79, Illinois Wesleyan 77
Hope, Mich. 76, Franklin & Marshall 57

Championship
Rowan, N.J. 100, Hope, Mich. 93

WOMEN'S N.C.A.A. BASKETBALL CHAMPIONSHIPS—1996

DIVISION I

First Round—East
Tennessee 97, Radford 56
Ohio State 97, Memphis 75
Texas 75, Southwest Missouri 55
Kansas 72, Middle Tennessee 57
George Washington 83, Maine 67
Virginia 100, Manhattan 55
Toledo 65, Mississippi 53
Old Dominion 83, Holy Cross 66

First Round—Mideast
Connecticut 94, Howard 63
Mich. State 60, Massachusetts 57 (OT)
San Francisco 68, Florida 61
Duke 85, James Madison 53
Wisconsin 74, Oregon 60
Vanderbilt 100, Harvard 83
DePaul 96, Southern Methodist 82
Iowa 72, Butler 67

First Round—Midwest
Louisiana Tech 98, Central Florida 41
Southern Mississippi 74, Utah 66
Notre Dame 73, Purdue 60
Texas Tech 78, Portland 61
S.F. Austin 67, Oregon State 65
Clemson 79, Austin Peay 52
Oklahoma State 90, Rhode Island 82
Georgia 98, St. Francis 66

First Round—West
Stanford 82, Grambling 43
Colorado State 66, Nebraska 62
North Carolina State 77, Montana 68
Alabama 95, Appalachian State 56
Auburn 73, Hawaii 53

Colorado 83, Tulane 75
Kent 72, Texas A&M 68
Penn State 94, Youngstown State 74

Second Round—East
Tennessee 97, Ohio State 65
Old Dominion 72, Toledo 66
Virginia 62, George Washington 43
Kansas 77, Texas 70

Second Round—Mideast
Vanderbilt 96, Wisconsin 82
Iowa 72, DePaul 71
San Francisco 64, Duke 60
Connecticut 88, Michigan State 68

Second Round—Midwest
Louisiana Tech 84, So. Mississippi 46
Texas Tech 82, Notre Dame 67
S.F. Austin 93, Clemson 88 (OT)
Georgia 83, Oklahoma State 55

Second Round—West
Stanford 94, Colorado State 63
Alabama 88, North Carolina State 68
Auburn 68, Colorado 61 (OT)
Penn State 86, Kent 59

Third Round—East
Tennessee 92, Kansas 71
Virginia 72, Old Dominion 60

Third Round—Mideast
Connecticut 72, San Francisco 44
Vanderbilt 74, Iowa 63

Third Round—Midwest
Georgia 78, S.F. Austin 64
Louisiana Tech 66, Texas Tech 55

Third Round—West
Stanford 78, Alabama 76 (OT)
Auburn 75, Penn State 69

Regional Finals
East—Tennessee 52, Virginia 46
Mideast—Connecticut 67, Vanderbilt 57
Midwest—Georgia 90, Louisiana Tech 76
West—Stanford 71, Auburn 57

National Semifinals
March 29, 1996, Charlotte, N.C.
Tennessee 88, Connecticut 83 (OT)
Georgia 86, Stanford 76

National Championship
March 31, 1996, Charlotte, N.C.
Tennessee 83, Georgia 65

DIVISION II

Semifinals
Shippensburg 84, Abilene Christian 81
North Dakota State 93, Delta State 72

Championship
No. Dakota State 104, Shippensburg 78

DIVISION III

Semifinals
Wisconsin–Oshkosh 62, New York
    University 37
Mount Union 71, St. Thomas, Minn. 57

Championship
Wisconsin–Oshkosh 66, Mount Union 50

LEADING N.C.A.A. SCORERS—1995–96

DIVISION I

	TFG	3FG	FT	Pts	Avg
1. Kevin Granger, Texas So.	194	30	230	648	27.0
2. Marcus Brown, Murray St.	254	74	185	767	26.4
3. Bubba Wells, Austin Peay	312	34	131	789	26.3
4. JaFonde Williams, Hampton	220	83	146	669	25.7
5. Bonzi Wells, Ball St.	269	31	143	712	25.4
6. Anquell McCollum, W. Carolina	257	99	138	751	25.0
7. Allen Iverson, Georgetown	312	87	215	926	25.0
8. Eddie Benton, Vermont	187	69	193	636	24.5
9. Matt Alosa, New Hamp.	199	76	150	624	24.0
10. Ray Allen, Connecticut	292	115	119	818	23.4
11. Michael Hart, Tenn.–Martin	246	1	123	616	22.8
12. Tunji Awojobi, Boston, U.	253	3	149	658	22.7
13. Darren McLinton, James Mad.	213	122	132	680	22.7
14. Reggie Elliott, Mercer	226	54	150	656	22.6
15. Jeff Nordgaard, Wis.–Gr. Bay	277	8	93	655	22.6
16. Reggie Freeman, Texas	237	87	134	695	22.4
17. Anthony Harris, Hawaii	219	24	164	626	22.4
18. Jason Daisy, North. Iowa	208	68	119	603	22.3
19. Chris McGuthrie, Mt. St. Mary	229	102	87	647	22.3
20. John Wallace, Syracuse	293	37	222	845	22.2
21. Curtis McCants, Geo. Mason	200	39	155	594	22.0
22. Sam Bowie, Southeastern La.	208	59	115	590	21.9
23. Craig Thames, Toledo	216	59	208	699	21.8
24. Ronnie Henderson, LSU	183	49	87	502	21.8
25. Marcus Mann, Miss. Valley	251	1	126	629	21.7

NATIONAL ASSOCIATION OF INTERCOLLEGIATE ATHLETICS—1996

MEN'S TOURNAMENT

DIVISION I
Semifinals
Georgetown, Kentucky 97, Lipscomb, Tennessee 84
Oklahoma City 80, Belmont, Tennessee 77

Championship
Oklahoma City 85, Georgetown, Kentucky 80

DIVISION II
Semifinals
Albertson, Idaho 92, Walsh, Ohio 79
Whitworth, Washington 87, William Jewell, Missouri 83

Championship
Albertson, Idaho 82, Whitworth, Washington 71 (OT)

WOMEN'S TOURNAMENT

DIVISION I
Semifinals
Southeast Oklahoma 84, Lipscomb, Tennessee 75
Southern Nazarene 70, Union, Tennessee 69

Championship
Southern Nazarene 80, Southeast Oklahoma 79

DIVISION II
Semifinals
Western Oregon 65, Evangel, Missouri 59
Huron, South Dakota 77, Doane, Nebraska 75

Championship
Western Oregon 80, Huron, South Dakota 77

NATIONAL INVITATION TOURNAMENT (N.I.T.)—1996

Semifinals

March 26, 1996, Madison Square Garden, N.Y.

Nebraska 90, Tulane 78
St. Joseph's, Pennsylvania 74, Alabama 69 (OT)

Championship

March 28, 1996, Madison Square Garden, N.Y.

Nebraska 60, St. Joseph's, Pennsylvania 55

Consolation Game

Tulane 87, Alabama 76

FINAL 1995–96 N.C.A.A. REBOUNDING LEADERS

	Games	No.	Avg
1. Marcus Mann, Mississippi Val.	29	394	13.6
2. Malik Rose, Drexel	31	409	13.2
3. Adonal Foyle, Colgate	29	364	12.6
4. Tim Duncan, Wake Forest	32	395	12.3
5. Scott Farley, Mercer	29	349	12.0
6. Chris Ensminger, Valparaiso	32	368	11.5
7. Thaddeous DeLaney, Chas. (S.C.)	29	330	11.4
8. Alan Tomidy, Marist	29	329	11.3
9. Quadre Lollis, Montana St.	30	340	11.3
10. Kyle Snowden, Harvard	26	289	11.1
11. Tim Moore, Houston	21	228	10.9
12. Tunji Awojobi, Boston U.	29	314	10.8
13. Curtis Fincher, Eastern Kentucky	27	292	10.8
14. Greg Logan, Maine	28	300	10.7
15. Monte O'Quinn, NE Illinois	27	285	10.6
16. Lorenzen Wright, Memphis	30	313	10.4
17. James Harper, South Florida	28	291	10.4
18. H.L. Coleman, Wyoming	29	301	10.4
19. Terrence Brandon, Georgia St.	24	249	10.4
20. Stanley Caldwell, Tennessee St.	22	228	10.4
21. Harry Harrison, Idaho	25	258	10.3
22. Zendon Hamilton, St. John's (N.Y.)	27	277	10.3
23. Jason Winningham, SE Louisiana	27	276	10.2
24. Will Johnson, St. Joseph's (Pa.)	32	326	10.2
25. Ernie Abercrombie, Oklahoma	30	304	10.1

LACROSSE

NATIONAL INTERCOLLEGIATE CHAMPIONS

1946	Navy	1962–66	Navy	1983	Syracuse
1947–48	Johns Hopkins	1967	Johns Hopkins, Maryland, Navy	1984	Johns Hopkins
1949	Johns Hopkins, Navy	1968	Johns Hopkins	1985	Johns Hopkins
1950	Johns Hopkins	1969	Army, Johns Hopkins	1986	North Carolina
1951	Army, Princeton	1970	Johns Hopkins, Navy, Virginia	1987	Johns Hopkins
1952	Virginia, R.P.I.	1971[1]	Cornell	1988	Syracuse
1953	Princeton	1972	Virginia	1989	Syracuse
1954	Navy	1973	Maryland	1990	Syracuse
1955–56	Maryland	1974	Johns Hopkins	1991	North Carolina
1957	Johns Hopkins	1975	Maryland	1992	Princeton
1958	Army	1976–77	Cornell	1993	Syracuse
1959	Army, Johns Hopkins, Maryland	1978–80	Johns Hopkins	1994	Princeton
1960	Navy	1981	North Carolina	1995	Syracuse
1961	Army, Navy	1982	North Carolina	1996	Princeton

1. First year of N.C.A.A. Championship Tournaments.

1996 N.C.A.A. LACROSSE

DIVISION I
Men's Championship
May 27, 1996, at College Park, Md.
Princeton 13, Virginia 12 (OT)

DIVISION II
Men's Championship
May 11 at C.W. Post
C.W. Post 15, Adelphi 10

National Collegiate Women's Championship
May 19, 1996, at Lehigh University
Maryland 10, Virginia 5

DIVISION III CHAMPIONSHIP
Men
May 26 at University of Maryland
Nazareth 11, Washington 10 (OT)

Women
May 19 at Bethlehem, Pa.
Trenton State (N.J.) 15, Middlebury 8

Professional Basketball

NATIONAL BASKETBALL ASSOCIATION CHAMPIONS

Source: National Basketball Association.

The National Basketball Association was originally the Basketball Association of America. It took its current name in 1949 when it merged with the National Basketball League.

Season	Eastern Conference (W–L)	Western Conference (W–L)	Playoff Champions[1]
1946–47	Washington Capitols (49–11)	Chicago Stags (39–22)	Philadelphia Warriors
1947–48	Philadelphia Warriors (27–21)	St. Louis Bombers (29–19)	Baltimore Bullets
1948–49	Washington Capitols (38–22)	Rochester Royals (45–15)	Minneapolis Lakers
1949–50	Syracuse Nationals (51–13)	Indianapolis Olympians (39–25)	Minneapolis Lakers
1950–51	Philadelphia Warriors (40–26)	Minneapolis Lakers (44–24)	Rochester Royals
1951–52	Syracuse Nationals (40–26)	Rochester Royals (41–25)	Minneapolis Lakers
1952–53	New York Knickerbockers (47–23)	Minneapolis Lakers (48–22)	Minneapolis Lakers
1953–54	New York Knickerbockers (44–28)	Minneapolis Lakers (46–26)	Minneapolis Lakers
1954–55	Syracuse Nationals (43–29)	Ft. Wayne Pistons (43–29)	Syracuse Nationals
1955–56	Philadelphia Warriors (45–27)	Ft. Wayne Pistons (37–35)	Philadelphia Warriors
1956–57	Boston Celtics (44–28)	St. Louis Hawks (38–34)	Boston Celtics
1957–58	Boston Celtics (48–23)	St. Louis Hawks (41–31)	St. Louis Hawks
1958–59	Boston Celtics (52–20)	St. Louis Hawks (49–23)	Boston Celtics
1959–60	Boston Celtics (59–16)	St. Louis Hawks (46–29)	Boston Celtics
1960–61	Boston Celtics (57–22)	St. Louis Hawks (51–28)	Boston Celtics
1961–62	Boston Celtics (60–20)	Los Angeles Lakers (54–26)	Boston Celtics
1962–63	Boston Celtics (58–22)	Los Angeles Lakers (53–27)	Boston Celtics
1963–64	Boston Celtics (59–21)	San Francisco Warriors (48–32)	Boston Celtics
1964–65	Boston Celtics (62–18)	Los Angeles Lakers (49–31)	Boston Celtics
1965–66	Philadelphia 76ers (55–25)	Los Angeles Lakers (45–35)	Boston Celtics
1966–67	Philadelphia 76ers (68–13)	San Francisco Warriors (44–37)	Philadelphia 76ers
1967–68	Philadelphia 76ers (62–20)	St. Louis Hawks (56–26)	Boston Celtics
1968–69	Baltimore Bullets (57–25)	Los Angeles Lakers (55–27)	Boston Celtics
1969–70	New York Knickerbockers (60–22)	Atlanta Hawks (48–34)	New York Knicks
1970–71	Baltimore Bullets (42–40)	Milwaukee Bucks (66–16)	Milwaukee Bucks
1971–72	New York Knickerbockers (48–34)	Los Angeles Lakers (69–13)	Los Angeles Lakers
1972–73	New York Knickerbockers (57–25)	Los Angeles Lakers (60–22)	New York Knicks
1973–74	Boston Celtics (56–26)	Milwaukee Bucks (59–23)	Boston Celtics
1974–75	Washington Bullets (60–22)	Golden State Warriors (48–34)	Golden State Warriors
1975–76	Boston Celtics (54–28)	Phoenix Suns (42–40)	Boston Celtics
1976–77	Philadelphia 76ers (50–32)	Portland Trail Blazers (49–33)	Portland Trail Blazers
1977–78	Washington Bullets (44–38)	Seattle SuperSonics (47–35)	Washington Bullets
1978–79	Washington Bullets (54–28)	Seattle SuperSonics (52–30)	Seattle Super Sonics
1979–80	Philadelphia 76ers (59–23)	Los Angeles Lakers (60–22)	Los Angeles Lakers
1980–81	Boston Celtics (62–20)	Houston Rockets (40–42)	Boston Celtics
1981–82	Philadelphia 76ers (58–24)	Los Angeles Lakers (57–25)	Los Angeles Lakers
1982–83	Philadelphia 76ers (65–17)	Los Angeles Lakers (58–24)	Philadelphia 76ers
1983–84	Boston Celtics (56–26)	Los Angeles Lakers (58–24)	Boston Celtics
1984–85	Boston Celtics (63–19)	Los Angeles Lakers (62–20)	Los Angeles Lakers
1985–86	Boston Celtics (67–15)	Houston Rockets (51–31)	Boston Celtics
1986–87	Boston Celtics (59–23)	Los Angeles Lakers (65–17)	Los Angeles Lakers
1987–88	Detroit Pistons (54–28)	Los Angeles Lakers (62–20)	Los Angeles Lakers
1988–89	Detroit Pistons (63–18)	Los Angeles Lakers (57–25)	Detroit Pistons
1989–90	Detroit Pistons (59–23)	Portland Trail Blazers (59–23)	Detroit Pistons
1990–91	Chicago Bulls (61–21)	Los Angeles Lakers (58–24)	Chicago Bulls
1991–92	Chicago Bulls (67–15)	Portland Trail Blazers (57–25)	Chicago Bulls
1992–93	Chicago Bulls (57–25)	Phoenix Suns (62–20)	Chicago Bulls
1993–94	New York Knicks (57–25)	Houston Rockets (58–24)	Houston Rockets
1994–95	Orlando Magic (57–25)	Houston Rockets (47–35)	Houston Rockets
1995–96	Chicago Bulls (72–10)	Seattle SuperSonics (64–18)	Chicago Bulls

1. Playoffs may involve teams other than conference winners.

INDIVIDUAL N.B.A. SCORING CHAMPIONS

Season	Player, Team	G	FG	FT	Pts	Avg
1953–54	Neil Johnston, Philadelphia Warriors	72	591	577	1759	24.4
1954–55	Neil Johnston, Philadelphia Warriors	72	521	589	1631	22.7
1955–56	Bob Pettit, St. Louis Hawks	72	646	557	1849	25.7
1956–57	Paul Arizin, Philadelphia Warriors	71	613	591	1817	25.6
1957–58	George Yardley, Detroit Pistons	72	673	655	2001	27.8
1958–59	Bob Pettit, St. Louis Hawks	72	719	667	2105	29.2
1959–60	Wilt Chamberlain, Philadelphia Warriors	72	1065	577	2707	37.6

Season	Player, Team	G	FG	FT	Pts	Avg
1960–61	Wilt Chamberlain, Philadelphia Warriors	79	1251	531	3033	38.4
1961–62	Wilt Chamberlain, Philadelphia Warriors	80	1597	835	4029	50.4
1962–63	Wilt Chamberlain, San Francisco Warriors	80	1463	660	3586	44.8
1963–64	Wilt Chamberlain, San Francisco Warriors	80	1204	540	2948	36.9
1964–65	Wilt Chamberlain, San Francisco Warriors–Phila. 76ers	73	1063	408	2534	34.7
1965–66	Wilt Chamberlain, Philadelphia 76ers	79	1074	501	2649	33.5
1966–67	Rick Barry, San Francisco Warriors	78	1011	753	2775	35.6
1967–68	Dave Bing, Detroit Pistons	79	835	472	2142	27.1
1968–69	Elvin Hayes, San Diego Rockets	82	930	467	2327	28.4
1969–70	Jerry West, Los Angeles Lakers	74	831	647	2309	31.2
1970–71	Lew Alcindor,[1] Milwaukee Bucks	82	1063	470	2596	31.7
1971–72	Kareem Abdul-Jabbar, Milwaukee Bucks	81	1159	504	2822	34.8
1972–73	Nate Archibald, Kansas City–Omaha Kings	80	1028	663	2719	34.0
1973–74	Bob McAdoo, Buffalo Braves	74	901	459	2261	30.8
1974–75	Bob McAdoo, Buffalo Braves	82	1095	641	2831	34.5
1975–76	Bob McAdoo, Buffalo Braves	78	934	559	2427	31.1
1976–77	Pete Maravich, New Orleans Jazz	73	886	501	2273	31.1
1977–78	George Gervin, San Antonio Spurs	82	864	504	2232	27.2
1978–79	George Gervin, San Antonio Spurs	80	947	471	2365	29.6
1979–80	George Gervin, San Antonio Spurs	78	1024	505	2585	33.1
1980–81	Adrian Dantley, Utah Jazz	80	909	632	2452	30.7
1981–82	George Gervin, San Antonio Spurs	79	993	555	2551	32.3
1982–83	Alex English, Denver Nuggets	82	959	406	2326	28.4
1983–84	Adrian Dantley, Utah Jazz	79	802	813	2418	30.6
1984–85	Bernard King, New York Knicks	55	691	426	1809	32.9
1985–86	Dominique Wilkins, Atlanta Hawks	78	888	527	2366	30.3
1986–87	Michael Jordan, Chicago Bulls[2]	82	1098	833	3041	37.1
1987–88	Michael Jordan, Chicago Bulls[3]	82	1069	723	2868	35.0
1988–89	Michael Jordan, Chicago Bulls[4]	81	966	674	2633	32.5
1989–90	Michael Jordan, Chicago Bulls[5]	82	1034	593	2753	33.6
1990–91	Michael Jordan, Chicago Bulls[6]	82	990	571	2580	31.5
1991–92	Michael Jordan, Chicago Bulls[7]	80	943	491	2404	30.1
1992–93	Michael Jordan, Chicago Bulls[8]	78	992	476	2541	32.6
1993–94	David Robinson, San Antonio Spurs[9]	80	840	693	2383	29.8
1994–95	Shaquille O'Neal, Orlando Magic[10]	79	930	455	2315	29.3
1995–96	Michael Jordan, Chicago Bulls[11]	82	916	548	2491	30.4

1. (Kareem Abdul-Jabbar). 2. Also had 12 3-point field goals. 3. Also had 7 3-point field goals. 4. Also had 27 3-point field goals. 5. Also had 92 3-point field goals. 6. Also had 29 3-point-field goals. 7. Also had 27 3-pt field goals in 1991–92. 8. Also had 81 3-pt field goals in 1992–93. 9. Also had 10 3-pt field goals in 1993–94. 10. O'Neal scored no 3-point field goals in 1994–95. 11. Also had 111 3-pt field goals in 1995–96.

N.B.A. LIFETIME LEADERS

(Through 1995–96 season)
NBA and ABA records combined

Most Games Played

Robert Parish[1]	1,568	Alex English	1,193
Kareem Abdul-Jabbar	1,560	Buck Williams[1]	1,192
Moses Malone	1,455	James Edwards[1]	1,168
Elvin Hayes	1,303	Tree Rollins	1,156
John Havlicek	1,270	Hal Greer	1,122
Paul Silas	1,254		

Free Throw Percentage

(1,200 free throws made, minimum)

	FTA	FTM	Pct
Mark Price[1]	2,088	1,893	.907
Rick Barry	4,243	3,818	.900
Calvin Murphy	3,864	3,445	.892
Scott Skiles	1,731	1,540	.890
Larry Bird	4,471	3,960	.886
Bill Sharman	3,559	3,143	.883
Reggie Miller[1]	4,122	3,616	.877
Ricky Pierce[1]	3,664	3,207	.875
Kiki Vandeweghe	3,997	3,484	.872
Jeff Malone[1]	3,383	2,947	.871

Blocked Shots

Hakeem Olajuwon[1]	3,190	Patrick Ewing[1]	2,327
Kareem Abdul-Jabbar	3,189	Manute Bol	2,086
Mark Eaton	3,064	George T. Johnson	2,082
Tree Rollins	2,542	Larry Nance	2,027
Robert Parish[1]	2,342	Elvin Hayes	1,771

1. Still active going into 1996–97 season.

Scoring Average

(400 games or 10,000 points minimum)

	G	Pts	Avg
Michael Jordan[1]	766	24,489	32.0
Wilt Chamberlain	1045	31,419	30.1
Elgin Baylor	846	23,149	27.4
Jerry West	932	25,192	27.0
Bob Pettit	792	20,880	26.4
George Gervin	791	20,708	26.2
Karl Malone[1]	898	23,343	26.0
Dominique Wilkins	984	25,389	25.8
Oscar Robertson	1040	26,710	25.7
David Robinson[1]	557	14,260	25.6

Steals

John Stockton[1]	2,365
Maurice Cheeks	2,310
Michael Jordan[1]	2,025
Clyde Drexler[1]	1,962
Alvin Robertson	1,946
Isiah Thomas	1,861
Derek Harper[1]	1,749
Magic Johnson	1,698
Lafayette Lever	1,666
Gus Williams	1,638

Rebounds

Wilt Chamberlain	23,924
Bill Russell	21,620
Kareem Abdul-Jabbar	17,440
Elvin Hayes	16,279
Moses Malone	16,212
Robert Parish[1]	14,626
Nate Thurmond	14,464
Walt Bellamy	14,241
Wes Unseld	13,769
Jerry Lucas	12,942

Field Goal Percentage
(2,000 field goals made, minimum)

	FGA	FGM	Pct
Artis Gilmore	9,570	5,732	.599
Shaquille O'Neal[1]	5,522	3,208	.581
Mark West[1]	4,084	2,391	.575
Steve Johnson	4,965	2,841	.572
Darryl Dawkins	6,079	3,477	.572
James Donaldson	5,442	3,105	.571
Jeff Ruland	3,734	2,105	.564
Kareem Abdul-Jabbar	28,307	15,837	.559
Otis Thorpe[1]	10,368	5,735	.553
Charles Barkley[1]	13,445	7,393	.550

1. Active going into 1996–97 season.

Assists

John Stockton[1]	11,310
Magic Johnson	9,921
Oscar Robertson	9,887
Isiah Thomas	9,061
Maurice Cheeks	7,392
Len Wilkens	7,211
Bob Cousy	6,955
Guy Rodgers	6,917
Nate Archibald	6,476
John Lucas	6,454

Points

Kareem Abdul-Jabbar	38,387
Wilt Chamberlain	31,419
Moses Malone	27,409
Elvin Hayes	27,313
Oscar Robertson	26,710
John Havlicek	26,395
Alex English	25,613
Dominique Wilkins	25,389
Jerry West	25,192
Adrian Dantley	23,177

NATIONAL BASKETBALL ASSOCIATION
FINAL STANDINGS—1995–96

EASTERN CONFERENCE
Atlantic Division

	W	L	Pct	Games behind
x–Orlando Magic	60	22	.732	—
x–New York Knicks	47	35	.573	13
x–Miami Heat	42	40	.512	18
Washington Bullets	39	43	.476	21
Boston Celtics	33	49	.402	27
New Jersey Nets	30	52	.366	30
Philadelphia 76ers	18	64	.220	42

Central Division

	W	L	Pct	Games behind
x–Chicago Bulls	72	10	.878	—
x–Indiana Pacers	52	30	.634	20
x–Cleveland Cavaliers	47	35	.573	25
x–Atlanta Hawks	46	36	.561	26
x–Detroit Pistons	46	36	.561	26
Charlotte Hornets	41	41	.500	31
Milwaukee Bucks	25	57	.305	47
Toronto Raptors	21	61	.256	51

x—Clinched playoff berth.

WESTERN CONFERENCE
Midwest Division

	W	L	Pct	Games behind
x–San Antonio Spurs	59	23	.720	—
x–Utah Jazz	55	27	.671	4
x–Houston Rockets	48	34	.585	11
Denver Nuggets	35	47	.427	24
Dallas Mavericks	26	56	.317	33
Minnesota Timberwolves	26	56	.317	33
Vancouver Grizzlies	15	67	.183	44

Pacific Division

	W	L	Pct	Games behind
x–Seattle SuperSonics	64	18	.780	—
x–L.A. Lakers	53	29	.646	11
x–Portland Trail Blazers	44	38	.537	20
x–Phoenix Suns	41	41	.500	23
x–Sacramento Kings	39	43	.476	25
Golden St. Warriors	36	46	.439	28
L.A. Clippers	29	53	.354	35

N.B.A. PLAYOFFS—1996

EASTERN CONFERENCE

First Round
(Best 3 out of 5)

Chicago defeated Miami, 3 games to 0
Orlando defeated Detroit, 3 games to 0
Atlanta defeated Indiana, 3 games to 2
New York defeated Cleveland, 3 games to 0

Second Round
Chicago defeated New York, 4 games to 1
Orlando defeated Atlanta, 4 games to 1

Conference Finals
Chicago defeated Orlando, 4 games to 0
  May 19—CHICAGO 121, Orlando 83
  May 21—CHICAGO 93, Orlando 88
  May 25—Chicago 86, ORLANDO 67
  May 27—Chicago 106, ORLANDO 101

CHAMPIONSHIP
Chicago Bulls defeated Seattle SuperSonics, 4 games to 2
  June 5—CHICAGO 107, Seattle 90
  June 7—CHICAGO 92, Seattle 88
  June 9—Chicago 108, SEATTLE 86
  June 12—SEATTLE 107, Chicago 86
  June 14—SEATTLE 89, Chicago 78
  June 16—CHICAGO 87, Seattle 75

NOTE: All caps denotes home team

WESTERN CONFERENCE

First Round
(Best 3 out of 5)

Seattle defeated Sacramento, 3 games to 1
San Antonio defeated Phoenix, 3 games to 1
Utah defeated Portland, 3 games to 2
Houston defeated L.A. Lakers, 3 games to 1

Second Round

Seattle defeated Houston, 4 games to 1
Utah defeated San Antonio, 4 games to 2

Conference Finals

Seattle defeated Utah, 4 games to 3
  May 18—SEATTLE 102, Utah 72
  May 20—SEATTLE 91, Utah 87
  May 24—UTAH 96, Seattle 76
  May 26—Seattle 88, UTAH 86
  May 28—Utah 98, SEATTLE 95 (OT)
  May 30—UTAH 118, Seattle 83
  June 2—SEATTLE 90, Utah 86

N.B.A. INDIVIDUAL RECORDS
(Through 1995–96 season)

Most points, game—100, Wilt Chamberlain, Philadelphia vs. New York at Hershey, Pa. 1962

Most points, quarter—33, George Gervin, San Antonio, 1978

Most points, half—59, Wilt Chamberlain, Philadelphia, 1962

Most free throws, game—28, Wilt Chamberlain, Philadelphia vs. New York at Hershey, Pa. 1962; 28, Adrian Dantley, Utah vs. Houston, 1984

Most free throws, quarter—14, Rick Barry, San Francisco, 1966

Most free throws, half—19, Oscar Robertson, Cincinnati, 1964

Most field goals, game—36, Wilt Chamberlain, Philadelphia, 1962

Most consecutive field goals, game—18, Wilt Chamberlain, San Franciscco, 1963; Wilt Chamberlain, Philadelphia, 1967

Most assists, game—30, Scott Skiles, Orlando vs. Denver, 1990

Most rebounds, game—55, Wilt Chamberlain, Philadelphia vs. Boston, 1960

Most 3-pt. field goals, game—10, Brian Shaw, Miami vs. Milwaukee, 1993

N.B.A. MOST VALUABLE PLAYERS

1956	Bob Pettit	1973	Dave Cowens	1984	Larry Bird, Boston
1957	Bob Cousy	1974	Kareem Abdul–Jabbar, Milwaukee	1985	Larry Bird, Boston
1958	Bill Russell			1986	Larry Bird, Boston
1959	Bob Pettit	1975	Bob McAdoo, Buffalo	1987	Earvin Johnson, Los Angeles
1960	Wilt Chamberlain	1976–77	Kareem Abdul–Jabbar, Los Angeles	1988	Michael Jordan, Chicago
1961–63	Bill Russell			1989	Earvin Johnson, Los Angeles
1964	Oscar Robertson	1978	Bill Walton, Portland	1990	Earvin Johnson, Los Angeles
1965	Bill Russell	1979	Moses Malone, Houston	1991	Michael Jordan, Chicago
1966–68	Wilt Chamberlain	1980	Kareem Abdul–Jabbar, Los Angeles	1992	Michael Jordan, Chicago
1969	Wes Unseld			1993	Charles Barkley, Phoenix
1970	Willis Reed	1981	Julius Erving, Philadelphia	1994	Hakeem Olajuwon, Houston
1971–72	Lew Alcindor (Kareem Abdul–Jabbar)	1982	Moses Malone, Houston	1995	David Robinson, San Antonio
		1983	Moses Malone, Philadelphia	1996	Michael Jordan, Chicago

N.B.A. TEAM RECORDS

Most points, game—186, Detroit vs. Denver, 3 overtimes, 1983

Most points, quarter—58, Buffalo vs. Boston, 1968

Most points, half—97, Atlanta vs. San Diego, 1970

Most points, overtime period—22, Detroit vs. Cleveland, 1973

Most field goals, game—74, Detroit, 1983

Most field goals, quarter—23, Boston, 1959; Buffalo, 1972

Most field goals, half—40, Boston, 1959; Syracuse, 1963; Atlanta, 1979

Most assists, game—53, Milwaukee, 1978

Most rebounds, game—109, Boston, 1960

Most points, both teams, game—370 (Detroit 186, Denver 184)

3 overtimes, Denver, December 13, 1983

Most points, both teams, quarter—96 (Boston 52, Minneapolis 44), 1959; (Detroit 53, Cincinnati 43), 1972

Most points, both teams, half—170 (Philadelphia 90, Cincinnati 80), Philadelphia, 1971

Longest winning streak—33, Los Angeles, 1971–72

Longest losing streak—20, Philadelphia, 1973

Longest winning streak at home—36, Philadelphia, 1966–67

Most games won, season—69, Los Angeles, 1971–72

Most games lost, season—73, Philadelphia, 1972–73

Highest average points per game—126.5, Denver, 1981–82

LEADING SCORERS—1995–1996
Minimum of 49 games played or 1,344 points scored

	GP	Pts	Avg
Michael Jordan, Chicago	82	2,491	30.4
Hakeem Olajuwon, Houston	72	1,936	26.9
Shaquille O'Neal, Orlando	54	1,434	26.6
Karl Malone, Utah	82	2,106	25.7
David Robinson, San Antonio	82	2,051	25.0
Charles Barkley, Phoenix	71	1,649	23.2
Alonzo Mourning, Miami	70	1,623	23.2
Mitch Richmond, Sacramento	81	1,872	23.1
Patrick Ewing, New York	76	1,711	22.5
Juwan Howard, Washington	81	1,789	22.1
Penny Hardaway, Orlando	82	1,780	21.7
Glen Rice, Charlotte	79	1,710	21.7
Cedric Ceballos, L.A. Lakers	78	1,656	21.2
Reggie Miller, Indiana	76	1,606	21.1
Vin Baker, Milwaukee	82	1,729	21.1
Clifford Robinson, Portland	78	1,644	21.1
Larry Johnson, Charlotte	81	1,660	20.5
Glenn Robinson, Milwaukee	82	1,660	20.2
Grant Hill, Detroit	80	1,618	20.2
Sean Elliott, San Antonio	77	1,537	20.0
Allan Houston, Detroit	82	1,617	19.7
Dino Radja, Boston	53	1,043	19.7

STEALS LEADERS—1995–1996
Minimum of 49 games played or 120 steals

	GP	Stl	Avg
Gary Payton, Seattle	80	228	2.9
Mookie Blaylock, Atlanta	80	209	2.6
Alvin Robertson, Toronto	76	166	2.2
Michael Jordan, Chicago	81	176	2.2
Jason Kidd, Dallas	80	172	2.2
Penny Hardaway, Orlando	81	166	2.1
Clyde Drexler, Houston	52	105	2.0
Eric Murdock, Vancouver	72	133	1.9
Hersey Hawkins, Seattle	81	149	1.8
Eddie Jones, L.A. Lakers	69	124	1.8
Tom Gugliotta, Minnesota	78	139	1.8
Scottie Pippen, Chicago	76	132	1.7
Terrell Brandon, Cleveland	74	128	1.7
Nate McMillan, Seattle	55	95	1.7
John Stockton, Utah	82	140	1.7
Greg Anthony, Vancouver	68	115	1.7
Karl Malone, Utah	82	138	1.7
Robert Horry, Houston	71	116	1.6
Kenny Anderson, Charlotte	68	111	1.6
Tim Hardaway, Miami	79	128	1.6
Latrell Sprewell, Golden State	77	125	1.6

ASSISTS LEADERS—1995–1996

Minimum of 49 games played or 384 assists

	GP	Ast	Avg
John Stockton, Utah	82	916	11.2
Jason Kidd, Dallas	81	783	9.7
Avery Johnson, San Antonio	82	789	9.6
Rod Strickland, Portland	67	640	9.6
Damon Stoudamire, Toronto	70	653	9.3
Kevin Johnson, Phoenix	56	517	9.2
Kenny Anderson, Charlotte	69	575	8.3
Tim Hardaway, Miami	80	640	8.0
Mark Jackson, Indiana	81	635	7.8
Gary Payton, Seattle	81	608	7.5
Penny Hardaway, Orlando	82	582	7.1
Chris Childs, N.J. Nets	78	548	7.0
Greg Anthony, Vancouver	69	476	6.9
Nick Van Exel, L.A. Lakers	74	509	6.9
Grant Hill, Detroit	80	548	6.9
Mahmoud Abdul-Rauf, Denver	57	389	6.8
Terrell Brandon, Cleveland	75	487	6.5
Jalen Rose, Denver	80	495	6.2
Tyus Edney, Sacramento	80	491	6.1
Mookie Blaylock, Atlanta	81	478	5.9

FREE-THROW PERCENTAGE LEADERS—1995–1996

Minimum of 120 free throws made

	GP	FTM	FTA	Pct
Mahmoud Abdul-Rauf, Denver	57	146	157	.930
Jeff Hornacek, Utah	82	259	290	.893
Terrell Brandon, Cleveland	75	338	381	.887
Dana Barros, Boston	80	130	147	.884
Brent Price, Washington	81	167	191	.874
Hersey Hawkins, Seattle	82	247	283	.873
Mitch Richmond, Sacramento	81	425	491	.866
Reggie Miller, Indiana	76	430	498	.863
Tim Legler, Washington	77	132	153	.863
Spud Webb, Minnesota	77	125	145	.862
Kevin Johnson, Phoenix	56	342	398	.859
Magic Johnson, L.A. Lakers	32	172	201	.856
Chris Mullin, Golden State	55	137	160	.856
Dell Curry, Charlotte	82	146	171	.854
Dee Brown, Boston	65	135	158	.854

BLOCKED–SHOT LEADERS—1995–1996

Minimum of 49 games played or 96 block shots

	GP	No.	Avg
Dikembe Mutombo, Denver	74	332	4.5
Shawn Bradley, N.J. Nets	79	288	3.7
David Robinson, San Antonio	82	271	3.3
Hakeem Olajuwon, Houston	72	207	2.9
Alonzo Mourning, Miami	70	189	2.7
Elden Campbell, L.A. Lakers	82	212	2.6
Patrick Ewing, N.Y. Knicks	76	184	2.4
Gheorghe Muresan, Washington	76	172	2.3
Shaquille O'Neal, Orlando	54	115	2.1
Jim McIlvaine, Washington	80	166	2.1
Oliver Miller, Toronto	76	143	1.9
Lorenzo Williams, Dallas	65	122	1.9
Andrew Lang, Minnesota	71	126	1.8
Vlade Divac, L.A. Lakers	79	131	1.7
Kevin Garnett, Minnesota	80	131	1.6
Joe Smith, Golden State	82	134	1.6
Shawn Kemp, Seattle	79	127	1.6
Ervin Johnson, Seattle	81	129	1.6
Theo Ratliff, Detroit	75	116	1.6
Robert Horry, Houston	71	109	1.5

REBOUND LEADERS—1995–1996

Minimum of 49 games played or 768 rebounds

	GP	Reb	Avg
Dennis Rodman, Chicago	64	952	14.9
David Robinson, San Antonio	82	1000	12.2
Dikembe Mutombo, Denver	74	871	11.8
Charles Barkley, Phoenix	71	821	11.6
Shawn Kemp, Seattle	79	904	11.4
Shaquille O'Neal, Orlando	54	596	11.0
Hakeem Olajuwon, Houston	72	784	10.9
Popeye Jones, Dallas	68	737	10.8
Patrick Ewing, N.Y. Knicks	76	806	10.6
Alonzo Mourning, Miami	70	727	10.4
Loy Vaught, L.A. Clippers	80	808	10.1
Jayson Williams, N.J. Nets	80	803	10.0
Vin Baker, Milwaukee	82	808	9.9
Dino Radja, Boston	53	522	9.9
Karl Malone, Utah	82	804	9.8
Grant Hill, Detroit	80	783	9.8
Clarence Weatherspoon, Phila.	78	753	9.7
Grant Long, Atlanta	82	788	9.6
Gheorghe Muresan, Washington	76	728	9.6
Olden Polynice, Sacramento	81	764	9.4

FIELD GOAL PERCENTAGE LEADERS—1995–1996

Minimum of 288 field goals made

	GP	FGM	FGA	Pct
Gheorghe Muresan, Wash.	76	466	798	.584
Chris Gatling, Miami	71	326	567	.575
Shaquille O'Neal, Orlando	54	592	1033	.573
Anthony Mason, N.Y. Knicks	82	449	798	.563
Shawn Kemp, Seattle	79	526	937	.561
Dale Davis, Indiana	78	334	599	.558
Arvydas Sabonis, Portland	73	394	723	.545
Brian Williams, L.A. Clippers	65	416	766	.543
Chucky Brown, Houston	82	300	555	.541
John Stockton, Utah	82	440	818	.538
Matt Geiger, Charlotte	77	357	666	.536
Cedric Ceballos, L.A. Lakers	78	638	1203	.530
Otis Thorpe, Detroit	82	452	853	.530
Olden Polynice, Sacramento	81	431	818	.527
Oliver Miller, Toronto	76	418	795	.526

3–POINT FIELD GOAL LEADERS 1995–1996

Minimum of 82 3-point field goals made

	GP	3FG	3FA	Pct
Tim Legler, Washington	77	128	246	.520
Steve Kerr, Chicago	82	122	237	.515
Hubert Davis, N.Y. Knicks	74	127	267	.476
B.J. Armstrong, Golden State	82	98	207	.473
Jeff Hornacek, Utah	82	104	223	.466
Brent Price, Washington	81	139	301	.462
Bobby Phills, Cleveland	72	93	211	.441
Terry Dehere, L.A. Clippers	82	139	316	.440
Mitch Richmond, Sacramento	81	225	515	.437
Allan Houston, Detroit	82	191	447	.427
Michael Jordan, Chicago	82	111	260	.427
David Wesley, Boston	82	116	272	.426
Dennis Scott, Orlando	82	267	628	.425
Glen Rice, Charlotte	79	171	403	.424
Tracy Murray, Toronto	82	151	358	.422
John Stockton, Utah	82	95	225	.422

Sports Personalities

A name in parentheses is the original name or form of name. Localities are places of birth. Dates of birth appear as month/day/year. **Boldface** years in parentheses are dates of **(birth–death)**.
Information has been gathered from many sources, including the individuals themselves. However, the *Information Please Almanac* cannot guarantee the accuracy of every individual item.

Aaron, Hank (Henry) (baseball); Mobile, Ala., 2/5/34
Abbott, Jim (baseball); Flint, Mich., 9/19/67
Abdul–Jabbar, Kareem (Lewis Ferdinand Alcindor, Jr.) (basketball); New York City, 4/16/47
Adderly, Herbert A. (football); Philadelphia, 6/8/39
Affleck, Francis (auto racing) **(1951–1985)**
Agassi, Andre (tennis); Las Vegas, Nev., 4/29/70
Aikman, Troy (football); Henryetta, Okla., 11/21/66
Alcindor, Lew. *See* Abdul–Jabbar.
Ali, Muhammad (Cassius Clay) (boxing); Louisville, Ky., 1/18/42
Allen, Dick (Richard Anthony) (baseball); Wampum, Pa., 3/8/42
Allen, George (football) **(1918–1990)**
Allison, Bobby (Robert Arthur) (auto racing); Hueytown, Ala., 12/3/37
Allison, Davey (auto racing); Hueytown, Ala. **(1961–1993)**
Alston, **Walter** (baseball); Venice, Ohio **(1911–1984)**
Alworth, Lance (football); Houston, 8/3/40
Ameche, Alan (football); Houston, Tex., **(1933–1988)**
Anderson, Ken (football); Batavia, Ill., 2/15/49
Anderson, Sparky (George) (baseball); Bridgewater, S.D., 2/22/34
Andretti, Mario (auto racing); Montona, Trieste, Italy, 2/28/40
Anthony, Earl (bowling); Kent, Wash., 4/27/38
Appling, Luke (baseball); High Point, N.C **(1907–1990)**
Arcaro, Eddie (George Edward) (jockey); Cincinnati, 2/19/16
Ashe, Arthur (tennis); Richmond, Va. **(1943–1993)**
Ashford, Evelyn (track & field); Shreveport, La., 4/15/57
Austin, Tracy (tennis); Rolling Hills, Calif., 12/2/62
Averill, Earl (baseball); Everett, Wash. **(1915–1983)**
Babashoff, Shirley (swimming); Whittier, Calif., 1/31/57
Baer, Max (boxing); Omaha, Neb. **(1909–1959)**
Bagwell, Jeff (baseball); Boston, Mass., 5/17/68
Banks, Ernie (baseball); Dallas, 1/31/31
Bannister, Roger (runner); Harrow, England, 3/24/29
Barkley, Charles (basketball); Leeds, Ala., 2/20/63
Barry, Rick (Richard) (basketball); Elizabeth, N.J., 3/28/44
Bauer, Hank (Henry) (baseball); East St. Louis, Ill., 7/31/22
Baugh, Sammy (football); Temple, Tex., 3/17/14
Bayi, Filbert (runner); Karratu, Tanganyika, 6/23/53
Baylor, Elgin (basketball); Washington, D.C., 9/16/34
Beamon, Bob (long jumper); New York City, 8/2/46
Becker, Boris (tennis); Leiman, W. Germany, 11/22/67
Bee, Clair (basketball); Cleveland, Ohio **(1896–1983)**
Beliveau, Jean (hockey); Three Rivers, Quebec, Canada, 8/31/31
Bell, Rickey (football); Inglewood, Calif. **(1949–1984)**
Belle, Albert (baseball); Shreveport, La., 8/25/66
Beman, Deane (golf); Washington, D.C., 4/22/38
Bench, Johnny (Johnny Lee) (baseball); Oklahoma City, 12/7/47
Berg, Patty (Patricia Jane) (golf); Minneapolis, 2/13/18
Berra, Yogi (Lawrence) (baseball); St. Louis, 5/12/25
Biletnikoff, Frederick (football); Erie, Pa., 2/23/43
Bing, Dave (basketball); Washington, D.C., 11/24/43
Bird, Larry (basketball); French Lick, Ind., 12/7/56
Blaik, Earl H. (football); Detroit **(1897–1989)**
Blanda, George Frederick (football); Youngwood, Pa., 9/17/27
Bledsoe, Drew (football); Walla Walla, Wash., 2/14/72
Blue, Vida (baseball); Mansfield, La., 7/28/49
Bodine, Brett (auto racing); Chemung, N.Y., 1/11/59
Bodine, Geoff (auto racing); Chemung, N.Y., 4/18/49
Boggs, Wade (baseball); Omaha, Neb., 6/15/58
Bonds, Barry (baseball); Riverside, Calif., 7/24/64
Borg, Björn (tennis); Stockholm, 6/6/56
Boros, Julius (golf); Fairfield, Conn., 3/3/20
Bossy, Mike (hockey); Montreal, 1/22/57
Boston, Ralph (long jumper); Laurel, Miss., 5/9/39
Bourque, Ray (hockey); Montreal, Que., 12/28/60
Bradley, Bill (William Warren) (basketball); Crystal City, Mo., 7/28/43
Bradley, Pat (golf); Westford, Mass., 3/24/51
Bradshaw, Terry (football); Shreveport, La., 9/2/48
Brathwaite, Chris (track); Eugene, Ore. **(1949–1984)**
Breedlove, Craig (Norman) (speed driving); Los Angeles, 3/23/38
Brett, George (baseball); Glendale, W. Va., 5/15/53
Brock, Louis Clark (baseball); El Dorado, Ark., 6/18/39
Brown, Jimmy (football); St. Simon Island, Ga., 2/17/36
Brumel, Valeri (high jumper); Tolbuzino, Siberia, 4/14/42
Bryant, Paul "Bear" (football); Tuscaloosa, Ala., **(1913–1983)**
Bryant, Rosalyn Evette (track); Chicago, 1/7/56

Burton, Michael (swimming); Des Moines, Iowa, 7/3/47
Butkus, Dick (Richard Marvin) (football); Chicago, 12/9/42
Calipari, John (basketball); Moon, Pa., 2/10/59
Campanella, Roy (baseball); Homestead, Pa. **(1921–1993)**
Campbell, Earl (football); Tyler, Tex., 3/29/55
Canseco, Jose (baseball); Havana, Cuba, 7/2/64
Caponi, Donna Maria (golf); Detroit, 1/29/45
Cappelletti, Gino (football); Keewatin, Minn., 3/26/34
Carew, Rod (Rodney Cline) (baseball); Gatun, Panama, 10/1/45
Carlos, John (sprinter); New York City, 6/5/45
Carlton, Steven Norman (baseball); Miami, Fla., 12/22/44
Carner, Joanne Gunderson, Mrs. Don (golf); Kirkland, Wash., 3/4/39
Casals, Rosemary (tennis); San Francisco, 9/16/48
Casper, Billy (golf); San Diego, Calif., 6/24/31
Caulkins, Tracy (swimming); Winona, Minn., 1/11/63
Cauthen, Steve (jockey); Covington, Ky., 5/1/60
Chamberlain, Wilt (Wilton) (basketball); Philadelphia, 8/21/36
Chandler, A.B. (Happy) (baseball); Louisville, Ky. **(1899–1991)**
Chandler, Spud (baseball); Commerce, Ga., **(1907–1990)**
Chapot, Frank (equestrian); Camden, N.J., 2/24/34
Chinaglia, Giorgio (soccer); Carrara, Italy, 1/24/47
Clarke, Bobby (Robert Earle) (hockey); Flin Flon, Manitoba, Canada, 8/13/49
Clay, Cassius. *See* Ali, Muhammad
Clemens, Roger (baseball); Dayton, Ohio, 8/4/62
Clemente, Roberto Walker (baseball); Carolina, Puerto Rico **(1934–1972)**
Cobb, Ty (Tyrus Raymond) (baseball); Narrows, Ga., **(1886–1961)**
Cochran, Barbara Ann (skiing); Claremont, N.H., 1/14/51
Cochran, Marilyn (skiing); Burlington, Vt., 2/7/50
Cochran, Robert (skiing); Claremont, N.H., 12/11/51
Coe, Sebastian Newbold (track); London, England, 9/29/56
Coffey, Paul (hockey); Weston, Ont., 6/1/61
Colavito, Rocky (Rocco Domenico) (baseball); New York City, 8/10/33
Coleman, Derrick (basketball); Mobile, Ala., 6/21/67
Comaneci, Nadia (gymnast); Onesti, Romania, 11/12/61
Conigliaro, Tony (baseball); Revere, Mass., **(1945–1990)**
Connors, Jimmy (James Scott) (tennis); East St. Louis, Ill., 9/2/52
Cordero, Angel (jockey); Santurce, Puerto Rico, 5/8/42
Cosell, Howard (broadcaster); Winston–Salem, N.C. **(1918–1995)**
Courier, Jim (tennis); Sanford, Fla., 8/17/70
Cournoyer, Yvan Serge (hockey); Drummondville, Quebec, Canada, 11/22/43
Court, Margaret Smith (tennis); Albury, New South Wales, Australia, 7/16/42
Cousy, Bob (basketball); New York City, 8/9/28
Crabbe, Buster (swimming); Scottsdale, Ariz. **(1908–1983)**
Crenshaw, Ben (golf); Austin, Tex., 1/11/52
Cronin, Joe (baseball executive); San Francisco, **(1906–1984)**
Cruyff, Johan (soccer); Amsterdam, Netherlands, 4/25/47
Csonka, Larry (Lawrence Richard) (football); Stow, Ohio, 12/25/46
Dancer, Stanley (harness racing); New Egypt, N.J., 7/25/27
Dantley, Adrian (basketball); Washington, D.C., 2/28/56
Dark, Alvin (baseball); Comanche, Okla., 1/7/22
Davenport, Willie (track); Troy, Ala., 6/6/43
Dawson, Andre (baseball); Miami, Fla., 7/10/54
Dawson, Leonard Ray (football); Alliance, Ohio, 6/20/35
Dean, Dizzy (Jay Hanna) (baseball); Lucas, Ark. **(1911–1974)**
DeBusschere, Dave (basketball); Detroit, 10/16/40
Delvecchio, Alex Peter (hockey); Fort William, Ontario, Canada, 12/4/31
Demaret, Jim (golf); Houston **(1910–1983)**
Dempsey, Jack (William H.) (boxing); Manassa, Colo. **(1895–1983)**
DeVicenzo, Roberto (golf); Buenos Aires, 4/14/23
Dibbs, Edward George (tennis); Brooklyn, New York, 2/23/51
Dietz, James W. (rowing); New York, N.Y., 1/12/49
DiMaggio, Joe (baseball); Martinez, Calif., 11/25/14
Dionne, Marcel (hockey); Drummondville, Quebec, Canada, 8/3/51
Dominguin, Luis Miguel (matador); Madrid, 12/9/26
Dorsett, Tony (football); Rochester, Pa., 4/7/54
Dryden, Kenneth (hockey); Hamilton, Ontario, Canada, 8/4/47
Drysdale, Don (baseball); Van Nuys, Calif. **(1936–1993)**
Duran, Roberto (boxing); Panama City, 6/16/51
Durocher, Leo (baseball); West Springfield, Mass. **(1906–1991)**
Durr, Francois (tennis); Algiers, Algeria, 12/25/42

Eckersley, Dennis (baseball); Oakland, Calif., 10/3/54
El Cordobés, (Manuel Benitez Pérez) (matador); Palma del Rio, Córdoba, Spain, 5/4/36(?)
Elder, Lee (golf); Dallas, 7/14/34
Elway, John (football); Port Angeles, Wash., 6/28/60
Emerson, Roy (tennis); Kingsway, Australia, 11/3/36
Ender, Kornelia (swimming); Plauen, East Germany, 10/25/58
Erving, "Dr. J" (Julius) (basketball); Roosevelt, N.Y., 2/22/50
Esposito, Phil (Philip Anthony) (hockey); Sault Ste. Marie, Ontario, Canada, 2/20/42
Evans, Lee (runner); Mandena, Calif., 2/25/47
Everett, Chris (tennis); Fort Lauderdale, Fla., 12/21/54
Ewbank, Weeb (football); Richmond, Ind., 5/6/07
Ewing, Patrick (basketball); Kingston, Jamaica, 8/5/62
Feller, Robert (Bobby) (baseball); Van Meter, Iowa, 11/3/18
Feuerbach, Allan Dean (track); Preston, Iowa, 1/10/49
Finley, Charles O. (sportsman); Ensley, Ala., 2/22/18
Fischer, Bobby (chess); Chicago, 3/9/43
Fitzsimmons, Bob (Robert Prometheus) (boxing); Cornwall, England (1862–1917)
Fleming, Peggy Gale (ice skating); San Jose, Calif., 7/27/48
Ford, Whitey (Edward) (baseball); New York City, 10/21/28
Foreman, George (boxing); Marshall, Tex., 1/10/49
Fosbury, Richard (high jumper); Portland, Ore., 3/6/47
Fox, Nellie (Jacob Nelson) (baseball); St. Thomas, Pa. (1927–1975)
Foxx, James Emory (baseball); Sudlersville, Md. (1907–1967)
Foyt, A. J. (auto racing); Houston, 1/16/35
Fratianne, Linda (figure skating); Los Angeles, 8/2/60
Frazier, Joe (boxing); Beauford, S.C., 1/17/44
Frazier, Walt (basketball); Atlanta, 3/29/45
Frick, Ford C. (baseball); Wawaka, Ind. (1894–1978)
Furillo, Carl (baseball); Stony Creek Mills, Pa. (1922–1989)
Furniss, Bruce (swimming); Fresno, Calif., 5/27/57
Gable, Dan (wrestling); Waterloo, Iowa, 10/25/45
Gabriel, Roman (football); Wilmington, N.C., 8/5/40
Gallagher, Michael Donald (skiing); Yonkers, N.Y., 10/3/41
Garms, Debs (baseball); Glen Rose, Tex. (1908–1984)
Garvey, Steve (baseball); Tampa, Fla., 12/22/48
Gehrig, Lou (Henry Louis) (baseball); New York City (1903–1941)
Gehringer, Charlie (baseball); Fowlerville, Mich., 5/11/03
Geoffrion, "Boom Boom" (Bernie) (hockey); Montreal, 2/14/31
Gerulaitis, Vitas (tennis); Brooklyn, N.Y. (1954–1994)
Gervin, George (basketball); Long Beach, Calif., 4/27/52
Giacomin, Ed (hockey); Sudbury, Ontario, Canada, 6/6/39
Giamatti, A. Bartlett (baseball); South Hadley, Mass. (1938–1989)
Gibson, Bob (baseball); Omaha, Neb., 11/9/35
Gifford, Frank (football); Santa Monica, Calif., 8/16/30
Gilbert, Rod (Rodrique) (hockey); Montreal, 7/1/41
Giles, Warren (baseball executive); Tiskilwa, Ill. (1896–1979)
Gilmore, Artis (basketball); Chipley, Fla., 9/21/49
Glance, Harvey (track); Phenix City, Ala., 3/28/57
Gonzalez, Pancho (tennis); Los Angeles (1928–1995)
Goodell, Brian Stuart (swimming); Stockton, Calif., 4/2/59
Gooden, Dwight (baseball); Tampa, Fla., 11/16/64
Goodrich, Gail (basketball); Los Angeles, 4/23/43
Goolagong, Cawley, Evonne (tennis); Griffith, Australia, 7/31/51
Gordon, Jeff (auto racing); Vallejo, Calif. 8/4/71
Gossage, "Goose" (Rich) (baseball); Colorado Springs, Colo., 4/5/51
Gottfried, Brian (tennis); Baltimore, Md., 1/27/52
Graf, Steffi (tennis); Mannheim, W. Germany, 6/14/69
Graham, David (golf); Windson, Australia, 5/23/46
Graham, Otto Everett (football); Waukegan, Ill., 12/6/21
Grange, Red (Harold) (football); Forksville, Pa. (1904–1991)
Green, Hubert (golf); Birmingham, Ala., 12/28/46
Greene, Charles E. (sprinter); Pine Bluff, Ark., 3/21/45
Greene, "Mean" (Joe) (football); Temple, Tex., 9/24/46
Gretzky, Wayne (hockey); Brantford, Ont., 1/26/61
Griese, Bob (Robert Allen) (football); Evansville, Ind., 2/3/45
Griffey, Ken, Jr. (baseball); Donora, Pa., 11/21/69
Groebli, "Mr. Frick" (Werner) (ice skating); Basil, Switzerland, 4/21/15
Grove, Lefty (Robert Moses) (baseball); Lonaconing, Md., (1900–1975)
Groza, Lou (football); Martins Ferry Ohio, 1/25/24
Guidry, Ronald Ames (baseball); Lafayette, La., 8/28/50
Gunter, Nancy Richey (tennis); San Angelo, Tex., 8/23/42
Gwynn, Tony (baseball); Los Angeles, Calif., 5/9/60
Halas, George (football); Chicago (1895–1983)
Hall, Gary (swimming); Fayetteville, N.C., 8/7/51
Hamill, Dorothy (figure skating); Chicago, 1956(?)
Hamilton, Scott (figure skating); Bowling Green, Ohio, 8/28/58
Hammond, Kathy (runner); Sacramento, Calif., 11/2/51
Hardaway, Anfernee (basketball); Memphis, Tenn., 7/18/72
Harris, Franco (football); Ft. Dix, N.J., 3/7/50

Hartack, William, Jr. (jockey); Colver, Pa., 12/9/32
Hasek, Dominik (hockey); Pardubice, Czechoslovakia, 1/29/65
Haughton, William (harness racing); Gloversville, N.Y. (1923–1986)
Havlicek, John (basketball); Martins Ferry, Ohio, 4/8/40
Hayes, Elvin (basketball); Rayville, La., 11/17/45
Hayes, Woody (football); Upper Arlington, Ohio (1913–1987)
Haynie, Sandra (golf); Fort Worth, 6/4/43
Heiden, Eric (speed skating); Madison, Wis., 6/14/58
Hencken, John (swimming); Culver City, Calif., 5/29/54
Henderson, Rickey (baseball); Chicago, 12/25/58
Henie, Sonja (ice skater); Oslo (1912–1969)
Herman, Floyd Caves (Babe) (baseball); Buffalo, N.Y. (1903–1987)
Hernandez, Keith (baseball); San Francisco, 10/20/53
Hershiser, Orel (baseball); Buffalo, N.Y., 9/16/58
Hickcox, Charles (swimming); Phoenix, Ariz., 2/6/47
Hines, James (sprinter); Dumas, Ark., 9/10/46
Hodges, Gil (baseball); Princeton, Ind. (1924–1972)
Hogan, Ben (golf); Dublin, Tex., 8/13/12
Holmes, Larry (boxing); Cuthert, Ga., 11/3/49
Hornsby, Rogers (baseball); Winters, Tex. (1896–1963)
Hornung, Paul (football); Louisville, Ky., 12/23/35
Houk, Ralph (baseball); Lawrence, Kan., 8/9/19
Howard, Elston (baseball); St. Louis (1929–1980)
Howe, Gordon (hockey); Floral, Sask., Canada, 3/31/28
Howell, Jim Lee (football); Lonoke, Ark. (1914–1995)
Howser, Dick (baseball); Miami, Fla. (1937–1987)
Hubbell, Carl (baseball); Carthage, Mo. (1903–1988)
Huff, Sam (Robert Lee) (football); Morgantown, W. Va., 10/4/34
Hull, Bobby (hockey); Point Anne, Ontario, Canada, 1/3/39
Hunter, "Catfish" (Jim) (baseball); Hertford, N.C., 4/8/46
Huntley, Joni (track); McMinnville, Ore., 8/4/56
Hutson, Donald (football); Pine Bluff, Ark., 1/31/13
Insko, Del (harness racing); Amboy, Minn., 7/10/31
Irwin, Hale (golf); Joplin, Mo., 6/3/45
Jackson, Reggie (baseball); Wyncote, Pa., 5/18/46
Jagr, Jaromir (hockey); Kladno, Czechoslovakia, 2/15/72
Jeffries, James J. (boxing); Carroll, Ohio (1875–1953)
Jenkins, Ferguson Arthur (baseball); Chatham, Ontario, Canada, 12/13/43
Jenner, (W.) Bruce (track); Mt. Kisco, N.Y., 10/28/49
Jezek, Linda (swimming); Palo Alto, Calif., 3/10/60
Johnson, "Magic" (Earvin) (basketball); E. Lansing, Mich., 8/14/59
Johnson, Anthony (rowing); Washington, D.C., 11/16/40
Johnson, Jack (John Arthur) (boxing); Galveston, Tex. (1876–1946)
Johnson, Jimmy (football); Port Arthur, Tex., 8/14/43
Johnson, Rafer (decathlon); Hillsboro, Tex., 8/13/35
Johnson, Randy (baseball); Walnut Creek, Calif., 9/10/63
Johnson, Wilham Julius (Judy) (baseball); Wilmington, Del. (1899–1989)
Jones, Deacon (David) (football); Eatonville, Fla., 12/9/38
Jordan, Michael (basketball); Brooklyn, N.Y. 2/17/63
Joyner, Florence Griffith (sprinter); Mojave Desert, Calif., 12/21/59
Joyner-Kersee, Jackie (track); East St. Louis, Ill., 3/3/62
Juantoreno, Alberto (track); Santiago, Cuba, 12/3/51
Jurgensen, Sonny (football); Wilmington, N.C., 8/23/34
Justice, Dave (baseball); Cincinnati, Ohio, 4/14/66
Kaat, Jim (baseball); Zeeland, Mich., 11/7/38
Kaline, Al (Albert) (baseball); Baltimore, 12/19/34
Keino, Kipchoge (runner); Kapchemoiymo, Kenya 1/?/40
Kelly, Leroy (football); Philadelphia, 5/20/42
Kelly, Red (Leonard Patrick) (hockey); Simcoe, Ontario, Canada, 7/9/27
Killebrew, Harmon (baseball); Payette, Idaho, 6/29/36
Killy, Jean–Claude (skiing); Saint–Cloud, France, 8/30/43
Kilmer, Bill (William Orland) (football); Topeka, Kan., 9/5/39
King, Bille Jean (Bille Jean Moffitt) (tennis); Long Beach, Calif., 11/22/43
Kinsella, John (swimming); Oak Park, Ill. 8/26/52
Kluszeewski, Ted (baseball); Argo, Ill. (1924–1988)
Kodes, Jan (tennis); Prague, 3/1/46
Kolb, Claudia (swimming); Hayward, Calif., 12/19/49
Koosman, Jerry Martin (baseball); Appleton, Minn., 12/23/42
Korbut, Olga (gymnast); Grodno, Byelorussia, U.S.S.R., 5/16/55
Koufax, Sandy (Sanford) (baseball); Brooklyn, N.Y., 12/30/35
Kramer, Jack (tennis); Las Vegas, Nev., 8/1/21
Kramer, Jerry (football); Jordan, Mont., 1/23/36
Kuenn, Harvey (baseball); West Allis, Wis. (1930–1988)
Kuhn, Bowie Kent (baseball); Takoma Park, Md., 10/28/26
Kwalik, Ted (Thaddeus John) (football); McKees Rocks, Pa., 4/15/47
Lafleur, Guy Damien (hockey); Thurson, Quebec, Canada, 8/20/51
Laird, Ronald (walker); Louisville, Ky., 5/31/35
Lamonica, Daryle (football); Fresno, Calif., 7/17/41
Landis, Kenesaw Mountain (1st baseball commissioner); Millville, Ohio (1866–1944)

Landry, Tom (football); Mission, Tex., 9/11/24
Landy, John (runner); Australia, 4/4/30
Larrieu, Francie (track); Palo Alto, Calif., 11/28/52
La Russa, Tony (baseball); Tampa, Fla., 10/4/44
Lasorda, Tom (baseball); Norristown, Pa., 9/22/27
Laver, Rod (tennis); Rockhampton, Australia, 8/9/38
Layne, Bobby (football); Lubbock, Texas **(1927–1986)**
Leetch, Brian (hockey); Corpus Christi, Tex., 3/3/68
Lemieux, Mario (hockey); Montreal, Quebec, Canada, 10/5/65
Lendl, Ivan (tennis); Prague, 3/7/60
Leonard, Benny (Benjamin Leiner) (boxing); New York City **(1896–1947)**
Leonard, Sugar Ray (boxing); Wilmington, N.C., 5/17/56
Lewis, Carl (track); Willingboro, N.J., 7/1/61
Lindros, Eric (hockey); London, Ont., 2/28/73
Liquori, Marty (runner); Montclair, N.J., 9/11/49
Little, Lou (football); Leominster, Mass., **(1893–1979)**
Littler, Gene (golf); La Jolla, Calif., 7/21/30
Lobo, Rebecca (basketball); Southwick, Mass., 10/6/73
Lombardi, Vince (football); Brooklyn, N.Y. **(1913–1970)**
Longden, Johnny (horse racing); Wakefield, England, 2/14/07
Lopat, Eddie (baseball); New York, N.Y. **(1918–1992)**
Lopez, Al (baseball); Tampa, Fla., 8/20/08
Lopez, Nancy (golf); Torrance, Calif., 1/6/57
Louis, Joe (Joe Louis Barrow) (boxing); Lafayette, Ala. **(1914–1981)**
Lukas, D. Wayne (horses); Antigo, Wis., 9/2/35
Lynn, Frederic Michael (baseball); Chicago, Ill., 2/3/52
Lynn, Janet (figure skating); Rockford, Ill., 4/6/53
Mack, Connie (Cornelius Alexander McGillicuddy) (baseball executive); East Brookfield, Mass. **(1862–1956)**
Mackey, John (football); New York City, 9/24/41
Maddux, Greg (baseball); San Angelo, Texas, 4/15/67
Mahovlich, Frank (Francis William) (hockey); Timmins, Ontario, Canada, 1/10/38
Mahre, Phil (skiiing); White Pass, Wash., 5/10/57
Malone, Karl (basketball); Summerfield, La., 7/24/63
Malone, Moses (basketball); Petersburg, Va., 3/23/55
Mandlikova, Hana (tennis); Prague, Czechoslovakia, 2/62
Mann, Carol (golf); Buffalo, N.Y., 2/3/41
Manning, Madeline (runner); Cleveland, 1/11/48
Mantle, Mickey Charles (baseball); Spavinaw, Okla. **(1931–1995)**
Maravich, "Pistol Pete" (Peter); Aliquippa, Pa. **(1948–1988)**
Marble, Alice (tennis); Palm Springs, Calif. **(1913–1990)**
Marciano, Rocky (boxing); Brockton, Mass. **(1923–1969)**
Marichal, Juan (baseball); Laguna Verde, Monteeristi, Dominican Republic, 10/20/37
Marino, Dan (football); Pittsburgh, Pa., 9/15/61
Maris, Roger (baseball); Hibbing, Minn. **(1934–1985)**
Martin, Billy (Alfred Manuel) (baseball); Berkeley, Calif. **(1928–1989)**
Martin, Rick (Richard Lionel) (hockey); Verdun, Quebec, Canada, 7/26/51
Mathews, Ed (Edwin) (baseball); Texarkana, Tex., 10/13/31
Mattingly, Don (baseball); Evansville, Ind., 4/20/61
Matson, Randy (shot putter); Kilgore, Tex., 3/5/45
Mays, Willie (baseball); Westfield, Ala., 5/6/31
McAdoo, Bob (basketball); Greensboro, N.C., 9/25/51
McCarthy, Joe (Joseph Vincent) (baseball); Philadelphia **(1887–1978)**
McCovey, Willie Lee (baseball); Mobile, Ala., 1/10/38
McDonald, Lanny (hockey); Hanna, Alberta, Canada, 2/16/53
McDowell, Jack (baseball); Van Nuys, Calif., 1/16/66
McEnroe, John Patrick, Jr. (tennis); Wiesbaden, Germany, 2/16/59
McGraw, John Joseph (baseball); Truxton, N.Y. **(1873–1934)**
McGwire, Mark (baseball); Pomona, Calif., 10/1/63
McLain, Dennis (baseball); Chicago, 3/24/44
McMillan, Kathy Laverne (track); Raeford, N.C., 11/7/57
Merrill, Janice (track); New London, Conn., 6/18/62
Messier, Mark (hockey); Edmonton, Alberta, Canada, 1/18/61
Meyer, Deborah (swimming); Haddonfield, N.J., 8/14/52
Meyers, Anne (basketball); San Diego, Calif., 3/26/55
Middlecoff, Cary (golf); Halls, Tenn., 1/6/21
Mikita, Stan (hockey); Sokolce, Czechoslovakia, 5/20/40
Milburn, Rodney, Jr. (hurdler); Opelousas, La., 5/18/50
Miller, Cheryl (basketball); Riverside, Calif., 1/3/64
Miller, Johnny (golf); San Francisco, 4/29/47
Miller, Reggie (basketball); Riverside, Calif., 8/24/65.
Montana, Joe (football); New Eagle, Pa., 6/11/56
Montgomery, Jim (swimming); Madison, Wis., 1/24/55
Moore, Archie (boxing); Benoit, Miss., 12/13/16
Morgan, Joe Leonard (baseball); Bonham, Tex., 9/19/43
Morrall, Earl (football); Muskegon, Mich., 5/17/34
Morton, Craig L. (football); Flint, Mich., 2/5/43
Mosconi, Wilie (pocket billiards); Philadelphia, 6/27/13

Moser, Annemarie. See Proell, Annemarie.
Moses, Edward Corley (track); Dayton, Ohio, 8/31/58
Mungo, Van Lingo (baseball); Pageland, S.C. **(1911–1985)**
Munson, Thurman (baseball); Akron, Ohio **(1947–1979)**
Murphy, Calvin (basketball); Norwalk, Conn., 5/9/48
Murray, Eddie (baseball); Los Angeles, Calif., 2/24/56
Musial, Stan (baseball); Donora, Pa., 11/21/20
Myers, Linda (archery); York, Pa., 6/19/47
Naber, John (swimming); Evanston, Ill., 1/20/56
Namath, Joe (Joseph William) (football); Beaver Falls, Pa., 5/31/43
Nastase, Ilie (tennis); Bucharest, 7/19/46
Navratilova, Martina (tennis); Prague, 10/18/56
Nehemiah, Renaldo (track); Newark, N.J., 3/24/59
Nelson, Cindy (skiing); Lutsen, Minn., 8/19/55
Newcombe, John (tennis); Sydney, Australia, 5/23/43
Niekro, Phil (baseball); Lansing, Ohio, 4/1/39
Nicklaus, Jack (golf); Columbus, Ohio, 1/21/40
Norman, Gregory (golf); Mount Isa, Australia, 2/10/55
Oerter, Al (discus thrower); New York City, 9/19/36
Olajuwon, Hakeem (basketball); Lagos, Nigeria, 1/21/63
Oldfield, Barney (racing driver); Fulton County, Ohio **(1878–1946)**
Oliva, Tony (Pedro) (baseball); Pinar Del Rio, Cuba, 7/20/40
Olsen, Merlin Jay (football); Logan, Utah, 9/15/40
O'Malley, Walter (baseball executive); New York City **(1903–1979)**
O'Neal, Shaquille (basketball); Newark, N.J., 3/6/72
Orantes, Manuel (tennis); Granada, Spain, 2/6/49
Orr, Bobby (hockey); Parry Sound, Ontario, Canada, 3/20/48
Ovett, Steve (track); Brighton, England, 10/9/55
Owens, Jesse (track); Decatur, Ala. **(1914–1980)**
Paige, Satchell (Leroy) (baseball); Mobile, Ala. **(1906–1982)**
Palmer, Arnold (golf); Latrobe, Pa., 9/10/29
Palmer, James Alvin (baseball); New York City, 10/15/45
Parent, Bernard Marcel (hockey); Montreal, 4/3/45
Park, Brad (Douglas Bradford) (hockey); Toronto, Ontario, Canada 7/6/48
Parseghian, Ara (football); Akron, Ohio, 5/21/23
Pasarell, Charles (tennis); San Juan, Puerto Rico, 2/12/44
Patterson, Floyd (boxing); Waco, N.C., 1/4/35
Peete, Calvin (golf); Detroit, Mich., 7/18/43
Pelé (Edson Arantes do Nascimento) (soccer); Tres Coracoes, Brazil, 10/23/40
Perry, Gaylord (baseball); Williamston, N.C., 9/15/38
Perry, Jim (baseball); Williamston, N.C., 10/30/36
Petrovic, Drazen (basketball); Yugoslavia **(1965–1993)**
Pettit, Bob (basketball); Baton Rouge, La., 12/12/32
Petty, Richard Lee (auto racing); Randleman, N.C., 7/2/37
Pincay, Laffit, Jr. (jockey); Panama City, Panama, 12/29/46
Plager, Barclay (ice hockey); Kirkland Lake, Ontario **(1941–1988)**
Plante, Jacques (hockey); Sahwinigan Falls, Quebec, Canada, 1/17/29
Player, Gary (golf); Johannesburg, South Africa, 11/1/35
Plunkett, Jim (football); San Jose, Calif., 12/5/47
Potvin, Denis Charles (hockey); Hull, Quebec, Canada, 10/29/53
Powell, Boog (John) (baseball); Lakeland, Fla., 8/17/41
Powell, Mike (track); Philadelphia, 11/10/63
Prefontaine, Steve Roland (runner); Coos Bay, Ore. **(1951–1975)**
Prince, Bob (baseball announcer); Pittsburgh **(1917–1985)**
Proell, Annemarie Moser (Alpine skier); Kleinarl, Austria, 3/27/53
Ralston, Dennis (tennis); Bakersfield, Calif., 7/27/42
Rankin, Judy Torluemke (golf); St. Louis, Mo., 2/18/45
Raschi, Vic (baseball); West Springfield, Mass. **(1919–1988)**
Ratelle, Jean (Joseph Gilbert Yvon Jean) (hockey); St. Jean, Quebec, Canada, 10/29/53
Rawls, Betsy (Elizabeth Earle) (golf); Spartanburg, S.C., 5/4/28
Reed, Willis (basketball); Hico, La., 6/25/42
Reese, Pee Wee (Harold) (baseball); Ekron, Ky., 7/23/19
Resch, Glenn "Chico" (hockey); Moose Jaw, Saskatchewan, Canada, 7/10/48
Rice, Jerry (football); Crawford, Miss., 10/13/62
Richard, Maurice (hockey); Montreal, 8/14/24
Riessen, Martin (tennis); Hinsdale, Ill., 12/4/41
Rigney, William (baseball); Alameda, Calif., 1/29/18
Ripken, Cal, Jr. (baseball); Havre de Grace, Md., 8/24/60
Rizzuto, Phil (baseball); New York City, 9/25/18
Roark, Helen Willis Moody (tennis); Centerville, Calif., 10/6/06
Robertson, Oscar (basketball); Charlotte, Tenn., 11/24/38
Robinson, Arnie (track); San Diego, Calif., 4/7/48
Robinson, Brooks (baseball); Little Rock, Ark., 5/18/37
Robinson, Dave (basketball); Key West, Fla., 8/6/65
Robinson, Frank (baseball); Beaumont, Texas, 8/31/35
Robinson, Jackie (baseball); Cairo, Ga. **(1919–1972)**
Robinson, Larry Clark (hockey); Marvelville, Ontario, Canada, 6/2/51
Robinson, "Sugar" Ray (boxing); Detroit **(1920–1989)**
Rockne, Knute Kenneth (football); Voss, Norway **(1888–1931)**

Rockwell, Martha (skiing); Providence, R.I., 4/26/44
Rono, Harry (track); Kiptaragon, Kenya, 2/12/52
Rooney, Art (football); Pittsburgh, Pa. (1901–1988)
Rose, Pete (Peter Edward) (baseball); Cincinnati, 4/14/42
Rosenbloom, Maxie (boxing); New York City (1904–1976)
Rosewall, Ken (tennis); Sydney, Australia, 11/2/34
Rote, Kyle (football); San Antonio, 10/27/28
Roush, Edd (baseball); Oakland City, Ind. (1893–1988)
Rozelle, Pete (Alvin Ray) (commissioner of National Football
    League); South Gate, Calif., 3/1/26
Rudolph, Wilma Glodean (sprinter); St. Bethlehem, Tenn.
    (1940–1994)
Russell, Bill (basketball); Monroe, La., 2/12/34
Ruth, Babe (George Herman Ruth) (baseball); Baltimore
    (1895–1948)
Rutherford, Johnny (auto racing); Fort Worth, 3/12/38
Ryan, Nolan (Lynn Nolan, Jr.) (baseball); Refugio, Tex., 1/31/47
Ryon, Luann (archery); Long Beach, Calif., 1/13/53
Ryun, Jim (runner); Wichita, Kan., 4/29/47
Salazar, Alberto (track); Havana, 8/7/58
Sampras, Pete (tennis); Washington, D.C., 8/12/71
Samuels, Howard (horse racing soccer); New York City
    (1920–1984)
Sanders, Barry (football); Wichita, Kan., 7/16/68
Sanders, Deion (baseball/football); Ft. Myers, Fla., 8/9/67
Santana, Manuel (Manuel Santana Martinez) (tennis); Chamartin,
    Spain, 5/10/38
Sayers, Gale (football); Wichita, Kan., 5/30/43
Schmidt, Mike (baseball); Dayton, Ohio, 9/27/49
Schoendienst, Al (Albert) (baseball); Germantown, Ill., 2/2/23
Schollander, Donald (swimming); Charlotte, N.C., 4/30/46
Seagren, Bob (Robert Lloyd) (pole vaulter); Pomona, Calif.,
    10/17/46
Seau, Junior (football); Oceanside, Calif., 1/19/69
Seaver, Tom (baseball); Fresno, Calif., 11/17/44
Seidler, Maren (track); Brooklyn, N.Y., 6/11/62
Selke, Frank (ice hockey); Canada (1893–1985)
Sewell, Joe (baseball); Titus, Ala., (1898–1990)
Shepherd, Lee (auto racing) (1945–1985)
Shero, Fred (hockey); Camden, N.J. (1945–1990)
Shoemaker, Willie (jockey); Fabens, Tex., 8/19/31
Shorter, Frank (runner); Munich, Germany, 10/31/47
Shriver, Pam (tennis); Baltimore, 7/4/62
Shula, Don (Donald Francis) (football); Grand River, Ohio, 1/4/30
Silvester, Jay (discus thrower); Tremonton, Utah, 2/27/37
Simpson, O.J. (Orenthal James) (football); San Francisco, 7/9/47
Sims, Billy (football); St. Louis, 9/18/55
Smith, Bubba (Charles Aaron) (football); Orange, Tex., 2/28/45
Smith, Emmitt (football); Escambia, Fla., 5/15/69
Smith, Ozzie (baseball); Mobile, Ala., 12/26/54
Smith, Ronnie Ray (sprinter); Los Angeles, 3/28/49
Smith, Stanley Roger (tennis); Pasadena, Calif., 12/14/46
Smith, Tommie (sprinter); Clarksville, Tex., 6/5/44
Smoke, Marcia Jones (canoeing); Oklahoma City, 7/18/41
Sneva, Tom (auto racing); Spokane, Wash., 6/1/48
Snider, Duke (Edwin) (baseball); Los Angeles, 9/19/26
Solomon, Harold (tennis); Washington, D.C., 9/17/52
Spahn, Warren (baseball); Buffalo, N.Y., 4/23/21
Speaker, Tristram (baseball); Hubbard City, Tex. (1888–1958)
Spencer, Brian (ice hockey); Fort St. James, British Columbia
    (1949–1988)
Spinks, Leon (boxing); St. Louis, 7/11/53
Spitz, Mark (swimming); Modesto, Calif., 2/10/50
Stabler, Kenneth (football); Foley, Ala., 12/25/45
Stagg, Amos Alonzo (football); West Orange, N.J. (1862–1965)
Stargell, Willie (Wilver Dornell) (baseball); Earlsboro, Okla., 3/6/41
Starr, Bart (football); Montgomery, Ala., 1/9/34
Staub, "Rusty" (Daniel) (baseball); New Orleans, 4/4/44
Staubach, Roger (football); Cincinnati, 2/5/42
Steinkraus, William C. (equestrian); Cleveland, 10/12/25
Stenerud, Jan (football); Fetsund, Norway, 11/26/42
Stengel, Casey (Charles Dillon) (baseball); Kansas City, Mo.
    (1891–1975)
Stenmark, Ingemar (Alpine skier); Tarnaby, Sweden, 3/18/56
Stevens, Scott (hockey); Completon, New Brunswick, 5/4/66
Stockton, Richard LaClede (tennis); New York City, 2/18/51

Stones, Dwight Edwin (track); Los Angeles, 12/6/53
Strawberry, Darryl (baseball); Los Angeles, 3/12/62
Sullivan, John Lawrence (boxing); Boston (1858–1918)
Summitt, Pat (basketball); Henrietta, Tenn., 6/14/52
Sutton, Don (Donald Howard) (baseball); Clio, Ala., 4/2/45
Swann, Lynn (football); Alcoa, Tenn., 3/7/52
Tanner, Leonard Roscoe III (tennis); Chattanooga, Tenn., 10/15/51
Tarkenton, Fran (Francis) (football); Richmond, Va., 2/3/40
Tebbetts, Birdie (George R.) (baseball); Nashua, N.H., 11/10/14
Theismann, Joe (football); New Brunswick, N.J., 9/9/46
Thomas, Frank (baseball); Columbus, Ga., 5/27/68
Thomas, Isiah (basketball); Chicago, Ill., 4/30/61
Thomas, Thurman (football); Houston, Texas, 5/16/66
Thompson, David (basketball); Shelby, N.C., 7/13/54
Thorpe, Jim (James Francis) (all–around athlete); nr. Prague,
    Okla. (1888–1953)
Tilden, William Tatem II (tennis); Philadelphia (1893–1953)
Tittle, Y. A. (Yelberton Abraham) (football); Marshall, Tex., 10/24/26
Toomey, William (decathlon); Philadelphia, 1/10/39
Trevino, Lee (golf); Dallas, 12/1/39
Trottier, Bryan (hockey); Val Marie, Sask., Canada, 7/17/56
Tunney, Gene (James J.) (boxing); New York City (1898–1978)
Tyus, Wyomia (runner); Griffin, Ga. 8/29/45
Ueberroth, Peter (baseball); Evanston, Ill., 9/2/37
Unitas, John (football); Pittsburgh, 5/7/33
Unser, Al (auto racing); Albuquerque, N. Mex., 5/29/39
Unser, Bobby (auto racing); Albuquerque, N. Mex., 2/20/34
Valenzuela, Fernando (baseball); Sonora, Mexico, 11/1/60
Valvano, Jim (basketball); New York, N.Y. (1946–1993)
Van Brocklin, Norm (football); Eagle Butte, S. Dak. (1926–1983)
Vaughn, Mo (baseball); Norwalk, Conn., 12/15/67
Vilas, Guillermo (tennis); Mar del Plata, Argentina, 8/17/52
Viola, Frank (baseball); Hempstead, N.Y., 4/19/60
Viren, Lasse (track); Myrskyla, Finland, 7/12/49
Vitale, Dick (basketball); E. Rutherford, N.J., 6/9/39
Wade, Virginia (tennis); Bournemouth, England, 7/10/45
Wagner, Honus (John Peter Honus) (baseball); Carnegie, Pa.
    (1867–1955)
Waitz, Grete (Andersen) (running); Oslo, Norway, 10/1/53
Walcott, Jersey Joe (Arnold Cream) (boxing); Merchantville, N.J.
    (1914–1994)
Wallace, Rusty (auto racing); St. Louis, Mo., 8/14/56
Walsh, Adam (football) (1902–1985)
Walton, Bill (basketball); La Mesa, Calif., 11/5/52
Waterfield, Bob (football); Burbank, Calif. (1921–1983)
Watson, Martha Rae (track); Long Beach, Calif., 8/19/46
Watson, Tom (golf); Kansas City, Mo., 9/4/49
Weaver, Earl (baseball); St. Louis, 8/14/30
Weiskopf, Tom (golf); Massillon, Ohio, 11/9/42
Weiss, George (baseball executive); New Haven, Conn.
    (1895–1972)
Weissmuller, Johnny (swimmer and actor); Windber, Pa.
    (1904–1984)
West, Jerry (basketball); Cheylan, W. Va., 5/28/38
White, Reggie (football); Chattanooga, Tenn., 12/19/61
White, Willye B. (long jumper); Money, Miss., 1/1/36
Whitworth, Kathy (golf); Monahans, Tex., 9/27/39
Wilkens, Mac Maurice (track); Eugene, Ore., 11/15/50
Wilkins, Lennie (basketball); 11/25/37
Wilkinson, Bud (football); Minneapolis, 4/23/16
Williams, Dick (baseball); St. Louis, 5/7/29
Williams, Ted (baseball); San Diego, Calif., 8/30/18
Wills, Maury (baseball); Washington, D.C., 10/2/32
Winfield, Dave (baseball); St. Paul, Minn., 10/3/51
Wohlhuter, Richard C. (runner); Geneva, Ill., 12/23/45
Wood, "Smokey" (Joseph) (baseball); Kansas City, Mo.
    (1890–1985)
Woodhead, Cynthia (swimming); Riverside, Calif., 2/7/64
Wottle, David James (runner); Canton, Ohio, 8/7/50
Wright, Mickey (Mary Kathryn) (golf); San Diego, Calif., 2/14/35
Yarborough, Cale (William Caleb) (auto racing); Timmonsville,
    S.C., 3/27/39
Yarbrough, Leeroy (auto racing); Jacksonville, Fla. (1938–1984)
Yastrzemski, Carl (baseball); Southampton, N.Y., 8/22/39
Young, Cy (Denton True) (baseball); Gilmore, Ohio (1867–1955)
Young, Shelia (speed skater, bicycle racer); Detroit, 10/14/50
Young, Steve (football); Salt Lake City, Utah, 10/11/61
Zaharias, Babe Didrikson (golf); Port Arthur, Tex. (1913–1956)

HOCKEY

Ice hockey, by birth and upbringing a Canadian game, is an offshoot of field hockey. Some historians say that the first ice hockey game was played in Montreal in December 1879 between two teams composed almost exclusively of McGill University students, but others assert that earlier hockey games took place in Kingston, Ontario, or Halifax, Nova Scotia. In the Montreal game of 1879, there were fifteen players on a side, who used an assortment of crude sticks to keep the puck in motion. Early rules allowed nine men on a side, but the number was reduced to seven in 1886 and later to six.

The first governing body of the sport was the Amateur Hockey Association of Canada, organized in 1887. In the winter of 1894–95, a group of college students from the United States visited Canada and saw hockey played. They became enthused over the game and introduced it as a winter sport when they returned home. The first professional league was the International Hockey League, which operated in northern Michigan in 1904–06.

Until 1910, professionals and amateurs were allowed to play together on "mixed teams," but this arrangement ended with the formation of the first "big league," the National Hockey Association, in eastern Canada in 1910. The Pacific Coast League was organized in 1911 for western Canadian hockey. The league included Seattle and later other American cities. The National Hockey League replaced the National Hockey Association in 1917. Boston, in 1924, was the first American city to join that circuit. The league expanded to include western cities in 1967. The Stanley Cup was competed for by "mixed teams" from 1894 to 1910, thereafter by professionals. It was awarded to the winner of the N.H.L. playoffs from 1926–67 and now to the league champion. The World Hockey Association was organized in October 1972 and was dissolved after the 1978–79 season when the N.H.L. absorbed four of the teams.

The National Hockey League Players Association staged a 10-day strike near the end of the 1991–92 season, the first strike in the league's 75-year history.

The agreement which settled the strike extended the regular season from 80 to 84 games beginning with the 1992–93 season, with owners and players sharing revenues from the final two games on a partnership basis.

The agreement also increased the players' playoff fund from $7.5 million to $9 million and the minimum salary to $100,000.

In addition, free agency for the players was made less restrictive and owners' contributions to the pension fund increased.

Shortly after the 1992 Stanley Cup playoffs concluded, John Ziegler, president of the NHL since 1977, resigned under pressure from the league's owners. Gil Stein was named as interim president and a search began to name the league's first commissioner.

The search ended in 1993 when Gary Bettman, longtime assistant to National Basketball Association Commissioner David Stern, was named to the position. Hopes were that Bettman would bring with him the same ideas and savvy marketing strategies that brought a burst of popularity to the NBA in the 1980s and early '90s.

After a successful debut season in 1993–94, Bettman suffered through a rocky second, as witnessed by the 1994–95 lockout that lasted 103 days, canceled the All-Star game and shortened the season from 82 games to 48.

By the conclusion of the 1995–96 hockey season, it appears Bettman has the league moving in the right direction. Rule changes have been implemented to steer the league from its violent reputation in order to better showcase the world's most talented stars.

The NHL has expanded to 26 teams under the Bettman regime and topped the 17 million mark in attendance for the first time in history.

Hockey, once considered a cold-weather sport, has taken major strides in increasing its fan base to the southern and western part of the United States as well. Florida and Colorado battled in the 1995–96 Stanley Cup Finals, the San Jose Sharks sold out all 41 of their home games, and the second team in two years (Winnipeg) migrated from Canada to the Southwest region of the U.S.

STANLEY CUP WINNERS

Emblematic of World Professional Championship; N.H.L. Championship after 1967

1894	Montreal A.A.A.	1925	Victoria Cougars	1956–60	Montreal Canadiens
1895	Montreal Victorias	1926	Montreal Maroons	1961	Chicago Black Hawks
1896	Winnipeg Victorias	1927	Ottawa Senators	1962–64	Toronto Maple Leafs
1897–99	Montreal Victorias	1928	N.Y. Rangers	1965–66	Montreal Canadiens
1900	Montreal Shamrocks	1929	Boston Bruins	1967	Toronto Maple Leafs
1901	Winnipeg Victorias	1930–31	Montreal Candiens	1968–69	Montreal Canadiens
1902	Montreal A.A.A.	1932	Toronto Maple Leafs	1970	Boston Bruins
1903–05	Ottawa Silver Seven	1933	N.Y. Rangers	1971	Montreal Canadiens
1906	Montreal Wanderers	1934	Chicago Black Hawks	1972	Boston Bruins
1907	Kenora Thistles[1]	1935	Montreal Maroons	1973	Montreal Canadiens
1907	Mont. Wanderers[2]	1936–37	Detroit Red Wings	1974–75	Philadelphia Flyers
1908	Montreal Wanderers	1938	Chicago Black Hawks	1976–79	Montreal Canadiens
1909	Ottawa Senators	1939	Boston Bruins	1980–83	New York Islanders
1910	Montreal Wanderers	1940	N.Y. Rangers	1984	Edmonton Oilers
1911	Ottawa Senators	1941	Boston Bruins	1985	Edmonton Oilers
1912–13	Quebec Bulldogs	1942	Toronto Maple Leafs	1986	Montreal Canadiens
1914	Toronto	1943	Detroit Red Wings	1987	Edmonton Oilers
1915	Vancouver Millionaires	1944	Montreal Canadiens	1988	Edmonton Oilers
1916	Montreal Canadiens	1945	Toronto Maple Leafs	1989	Calgary Flames
1917	Seattle Metropolitans	1946	Montreal Canadiens	1990	Edmonton Oilers
1918	Toronto Arenas	1947–49	Toronto Maple Leafs	1991	Pittsburgh Penguins
1919	No champion	1950	Detroit Red Wings	1992	Pittsburgh Penguins
1920–21	Ottawa Senators	1951	Toronto Maple Leafs	1993	Montreal Canadiens
1922	Toronto St. Patricks	1952	Detroit Red Wings	1994	N.Y. Rangers
1923	Ottawa Senators	1953	Montreal Canadiens	1995	N.J. Devils
1924	Montreal Canadiens	1954–55	Detroit Red Wings	1996	Colorado Avalanche

1. January. 2. March.

NATIONAL HOCKEY LEAGUE YEARLY TROPHY WINNERS

The Hart Trophy—Most Valuable Player

1924	Frank Nighbor, Ottawa
1925	Billy Burch, Hamilton
1926	Nels Stewart, Montreal Maroons
1927	Herb Gardiner, Montreal Canadiens
1928	Howie Morenz, Montreal Canadiens
1929	Roy Worters, N.Y. Americans
1930	Nels Stewart, Montreal Maroons
1931–32	Howie Morenz, Montreal Canadiens
1933	Eddie Shore, Boston
1934	Aurel Joliat, Montreal Canadiens
1935–36	Eddie Shore, Boston
1937	Babe Siebert, Montreal Canadiens
1938	Eddie Shore, Boston
1939	Toe Blake, Montreal Canadiens
1940	Eddie Goodfellow, Detroit
1941	Bill Cowley, Boston
1942	Tom Anderson, N.Y. Americans
1943	Bill Cowley, Boston
1944	Babe Pratt, Toronto
1945	Elmer Lach, Montreal Canadiens
1946	Max Bentley, Chicago
1947	Maurice Richard, Montreal Canadiens
1948	Buddy O'Connor, N.Y. Rangers
1949	Sid Abel, Detroit
1950	Chuck Rayner, N.Y. Rangers
1951	Milt Schmidt, Boston
1952–53	Gordon Howe, Detroit
1954	Al Rollins, Chicago
1955	Ted Kennedy, Toronto
1956	Jean Belveau, Montreal Canadiens
1957–58	Gordon Howe, Detroit
1959	Andy Bathgate, N.Y. Rangers
1960	Gordon Howe, Detroit
1961	Bernie Geoffrion, Montreal Canadiens
1962	Jacques Plante, Montreal Canadiens
1963	Gordon Howe, Detroit
1964	Jean Beliveau, Montreal Canadiens
1965–66	Bobby Hull, Chicago
1967–68	Stan Mikita, Chicago
1969	Phil Esposito, Boston
1970–72	Bobby Orr, Boston
1973	Bobby Clarke, Philadelphia
1974	Phil Esposito, Boston
1975–76	Bobby Clarke, Philadelphia
1977–78	Guy Lafleur, Montreal
1979	Bryan Trottier, N.Y. Islanders
1980	Wayne Gretzky, Edmonton
1981	Wayne Gretzky, Edmonton
1982	Wayne Gretzky, Edmonton
1983	Wayne Gretzky, Edmonton
1984	Wayne Gretzky, Edmonton
1985	Wayne Gretzky, Edmonton
1986	Wayne Gretzky, Edmonton
1987	Wayne Gretzky, Edmonton
1988	Mario Lemieux, Pittsburgh
1989	Wayne Gretzky, Los Angeles
1990	Mark Messier, Edmonton
1991	Brett Hull, St. Louis
1992	Mark Messier, N.Y. Rangers
1993	Mario Lemieux, Pittsburgh
1994	Sergei Fedorov, Detroit
1995	Eric Lindros, Philadelphia
1996	Mario Lemieux, Pittsburgh

Vezina Trophy—Leading Goalkeeper

1956–60	Jacques Plante, Montreal
1961	Johnny Bower, Toronto
1962	Jacques Plante, Montreal
1963	Glenn Hall, Chicago
1964	Charlie Hodge, Montreal
1965	Terry Sawchuk—Johnny Bower, Toronto
1966	Lorne Worsley—Charlie Hodge, Montreal
1967	Glen Hall—Denis DeJordy, Chicago
1968	Lorne Worsley—Rogatien Vachon, Montreal
1969	Glen Hall—Jacques Plante, St. Louis
1970	Tony Esposito, Chicago
1971	Ed Giacomin—Gilles Villemure, New York
1972	Tony Esposito—Gary Smith, Chicago
1973	Ken Dryden, Montreal
1974	Bernie Parent, Philadelphia and Tony Esposito, Chicago
1975	Bernie Parent, Philadelphia
1976	Ken Dryden, Montreal
1977–79	Ken Dryden—Michel Larocque, Montreal
1980	Bob Sauve—Don Edwards, Buffalo
1981	Richard Sevigny, Denis Herron and Michel Larocque, Montreal
1982	Billy Smith, New York Islanders
1983	Pete Peeters, Boston
1984	Tom Barrasso, Buffalo
1985	Pelle Lindbergh, Philadelphia
1986	John Vanbiesbrouck, New York Rangers
1987	Ron Hextall, Philadelphia
1988	Grant Fuhr, Edmonton
1989	Patrick Roy, Montreal
1990	Patrick Roy, Montreal
1991	Ed Belfour, Chicago
1992	Patrick Roy, Montreal
1993	Ed Belfour, Chicago
1994	Dominik Hasek, Buffalo
1995	Dominik Hasek, Buffalo
1996	Jim Carey, Washington

James Norris Trophy—Defenseman

1954	Red Kelly, Detroit
1955–58	Doug Harvey, Montreal
1959	Tom Johnson, Montreal
1960–62	Doug Harvey, Montreal; New York (62)
1963–65	Pierre Pilote, Chicago
1966	Jacques Laperriere, Montreal
1967	Harry Howell, New York
1968–75	Bobby Orr, Boston
1976	Denis Potvin, N.Y. Islanders
1977	Larry Robinson, Montreal
1978–79	Denis Potvin, N.Y. Islanders
1980	Larry Robinson, Montreal
1981	Randy Carlyle, Pittsburgh
1982	Doug Wilson, Chicago
1983–84	Rod Langway, Washington
1985	Paul Coffey, Edmonton
1986	Paul Coffey, Edmonton
1987	Ray Bourque, Boston
1988	Ray Bourque, Boston
1989	Chris Chelios, Montreal
1990	Ray Bourque, Boston
1991	Ray Bourque, Boston
1992	Brian Leetch, N.Y. Rangers
1993	Chris Chelios, Chicago
1994	Ray Bourque, Boston
1995	Paul Coffey, Detroit
1996	Chris Chelios, Chicago

Lady Byng Trophy—Sportsmanship

1960	Don McKenney, Boston
1961	Red Kelly, Detroit
1962–63	Dave Keon, Toronto
1964	Ken Wharram, Chicago
1965	Bobby Hull, Chicago
1966	Alex Delvecchio, Detroit
1967–68	Stan Mikita, Chicago
1969	Alex Delvecchio, Detroit
1970	Phil Goyette, St. Louis
1971	John Bucyk, Boston
1972	Jean Ratelle, New York
1973	Gil Perrault, Buffalo
1974	John Bucyk, Boston
1975	Marcel Dionne, Detroit
1976	Jean Ratelle, N.Y. Rangers–Boston
1977	Marcel Dionne, Los Angeles
1978	Butch Goring, Los Angeles
1979	Bob MacMillan, Atlanta
1980	Wayne Gretzky, Edmonton
1981	Rick Kehoe, Pittsburgh
1982	Rick Middleton, Boston
1983–84	Mike Bossy, N.Y. Islanders
1985	Jari Kurri, Edmonton
1986	Mike Bossy, N.Y. Islanders
1987	Joe Mullen, Calgary
1988	Mats Naslund, Montreal
1989	Joe Mullen, Calgary
1990	Brett Hull, St. Louis
1991	Wayne Gretzky, Los Angeles
1992	Wayne Gretzky, Los Angeles
1993	Pierre Turgeon, N.Y. Islanders
1994	Wayne Gretzky, Los Angeles
1995	Ron Francis, Pittsburgh
1996	Paul Kariya, Anaheim

Calder Trophy—Rookie

1962	Bobby Rousseau, Montreal
1963	Kent Douglas, Toronto
1964	Jacques Laperriere, Montreal
1965	Roger Crozier, Detroit
1966	Brit Selby, Toronto
1967	Bobby Orr, Boston
1968	Derek Sanderson, Boston
1969	Danny Grant, Minnesota
1970	Tony Esposito, Chicago
1971	Gilbert Perrault, Buffalo
1972	Ken Dryden, Montreal
1973	Steve Vickers, N.Y. Rangers

1974	Denis Potvin, N.Y. Islanders	1992	Pavel Bure, Vancouver	1969	Phil Esposito, Boston
1975	Eric Vail, Atlanta	1993	Teemu Selanne, Winnipeg	1970	Bobby Orr, Boston
1976	Bryan Trottier, N.Y. Islanders	1994	Martin Brodeur, New Jersey	1971–74	Phil Esposito, Boston
1977	Willi Plett, Atlanta	1995	Peter Forsberg, Quebec	1975	Bobby Orr, Boston
1978	Mike Bossy, N.Y. Islanders	1996	Daniel Alfredsson, Ottawa	1976–78	Guy Lafleur, Montreal
1979	Bobby Smith, Minnesota			1979	Bryan Trottier, N.Y. Islanders
1980	Ray Bourque, Boston		**Art Ross Trophy—Leading scorer**	1980	Marcel Dionne, Los Angeles
1981	Peter Stastny, Quebec	1955	Bernie Geoffrion, Montreal	1981–87	Wayne Gretzky, Edmonton
1982	Dale Hawerchuk, Winnipeg	1956	Jean Beliveau, Montreal	1988	Mario Lemieux, Pittsburgh
1983	Steve Larmer, Chicago	1957	Gordie Howe, Detroit	1989	Mario Lemieux, Pittsburgh
1984	Tom Barrasso, Buffalo	1958–59	Dickie Moore, Montreal	1990	Wayne Gretzky, Los Angeles
1985	Mario Lemieux, Pittsburgh	1960	Bobby Hull, Chicago	1991	Wayne Gretzky, Los Angeles
1986	Gary Suter, Calgary	1961	Bernie Geoffrion, Montreal	1992	Mario Lemieux, Pittsburgh
1987	Luc Robitaille, Los Angeles	1962	Bobby Hull, Chicago	1993	Mario Lemieux, Pittsburgh
1988	Joe Niewendyk, Calgary	1963	Gordie Howe, Detroit	1994	Wayne Gretzky, Los Angeles
1989	Brian Leetch, N.Y. Rangers	1964–65	Stan Mikita, Chicago	1995	Jaromir Jagr, Pittsburgh
1990	Sergei Makarov, Calgary	1966	Bobby Hull, Chicago	1996	Mario Lemieux, Pittsburgh
1991	Ed Belfour, Chicago	1967–68	Stan Mikita, Chicago		

N.H.L. CHAMPIONS

		Eastern Division		1989	Montreal		1978–79	N.Y. Islanders
		1968–69	Montreal	1990	Boston		1980	Philadelphia
Wales Trophy		1970	Chicago	1991	Pittsburgh		1981	New York Islanders
1939	Boston	1971	Boston	1992	Pittsburgh		1982	Edmonton
1940	Boston	1972	Boston	1993	Montreal		1983	Edmonton
1941	Boston	1973	Montreal	1994	N.Y. Rangers		1984	Edmonton
1942	New York	1974	Boston	1995	Quebec		1985	Edmonton
1943	Detroit			1996	Florida		1986	Calgary
1944–47	Montreal	**Eastern Conference[1]**					1987	Edmonton
1948	Toronto	1975	Buffalo	**CAMPBELL BOWL**			1988	Edmonton
1948–55	Detroit	1976–79	Montreal	**Western Division**			1989	Calgary
1956	Montreal	1980	Buffalo	1968	Philadelphia		1990	Edmonton
1957	Detroit	1981	Montreal	1969	St. Louis		1991	Minnesota
1958–62	Montreal	1982	New York Islanders	1970	St. Louis		1992	Chicago
1963	Toronto	1983	New York Islanders	1971–73	Chicago		1993	Los Angeles
1964	Montreal	1984	New York Islanders	1974	Philadelphia		1994	Detroit
1965	Detroit	1985	Philadelphia	**Western Conference[2]**			1995	Detroit
1966	Montreal	1986	Montreal	1975	Philadelphia		1996	Colorado
1967	Chicago	1987	Philadelphia	1976–77	Philadelphia			
		1988	Boston					

1. Prior to 1994 was the Wales Conference. 2. Prior to 1994 was the Campbell Conference.

Stanley Cup Playoffs—1996

EASTERN CONFERENCE

Quarterfinals
Philadelphia Flyers defeated Tampa Bay Lightning, 4 games to 2
Pittsburgh Penguins defeated Washington Capitals, 4 games to 2
New York Rangers defeated Montreal Canadiens, 4 games to 2
Florida Panthers defeated Boston Bruins, 4 games to 1

Semifinals
Florida Panthers defeated Philadelphia Flyers, 4 games to 2
Pittsburgh Penguins defeated New York Rangers, 4 games to 1

Finals
Florida Panthers defeated Pittsburgh Penguins, 4 games to 3
  May 18—Florida 5, PITTSBURGH 1
  May 20—PITTSBURGH 3, Florida 2
  May 24—FLORIDA 5, Pittsburgh 2
  May 26—Pittsburgh 2, FLORIDA 1
  May 28—PITTSBURGH 3, Florida 0
  May 30—FLORIDA 4, Pittsburgh 3
  June 1—Florida 3, PITTSBURGH 1

WESTERN CONFERENCE

Quarterfinals
Detroit Red Wings defeated Winnipeg Jets, 4 games to 2
Colorado Avalanche defeated Vancouver Canucks, 4 games to 2
Chicago Black Hawks defeated Calgary Flames, 4 games to
St. Louis Blues defeated Toronto Maple Leafs, 4 games to 2

Semifinals
Detroit Red Wings defeated St. Louis Blues, 4 games to 3
Colorado Avalanche defeated Chicago Black Hawks, 4 games to 2

Finals
Colorado Avalanche defeated Detroit Red Wings, 4 games to 2
  May 19—Colorado 3, DETROIT 2 (OT)
  May 21—Colorado 3, DETROIT 0
  May 23—Detroit 6, COLORADO 4
  May 25—COLORADO 4, Detroit 2
  May 27—DETROIT 5, Colorado 2
  May 29—COLORADO 4, Detroit 1

NOTE: Home teams are in capitals.

STANLEY CUP CHAMPIONSHIP FINALS

Colorado Avalanche defeated Florida Panthers, 4 games to 0

June 4—COLORADO 3, Florida 1
June 6—COLORADO 8, Florida 1
June 8—Colorado 3, FLORIDA 2
June 10—Colorado 1, FLORIDA 0 (3OT)

Conn Smythe Award for most valuable player in the playoffs:
Joe Sakic, Colorado Avalanche

OTHER N.H.L. AWARDS—1996

Frank Selke Trophy (top defensive forward)—Sergei Fedorov, Detroit
King Clancy Trophy (Humanitarian community involvement)—Kris King, Winnipeg
Jack Adams Trophy (Coach of the Year)—Scotty Bowman, Detroit
Bill Masterton Trophy (Sportsmanship)—Gary Roberts, Calgary

NATIONAL HOCKEY LEAGUE
FINAL STANDINGS OF THE CLUBS—1995–96

EASTERN CONFERENCE
Atlantic Division

	W	L	T	GF	GA	Pts
Philadelphia Flyers	45	24	13	282	208	103
New York Rangers	41	27	14	272	237	96
[2,3] Florida Panthers	41	31	10	254	234	92
Washington Capitals	39	32	11	234	204	89
Tampa Bay Lightning	38	32	12	238	248	88
New Jersey Devils	37	33	12	215	202	86
New York Islanders	22	50	10	229	315	54

Northeast Division

	W	L	T	GF	GA	Pts
[2] Pittsburgh Penguins	49	29	4	362	284	102
Boston Bruins	40	31	11	282	269	91
Montreal Canadiens	40	32	10	265	248	90
Hartford Whalers	34	39	9	237	259	77
Buffalo Sabres	33	42	7	247	262	73
Ottawa Senators	18	59	5	191	291	41

WESTERN CONFERENCE
Central Division

	W	L	T	GF	GA	Pts
[1,2] Detroit Red Wings	62	13	7	325	181	131
[1] Chicago Black Hawks	40	28	14	273	220	94
[1] Toronto Maple Leafs	34	36	12	247	252	80
[1] St. Louis Blues	32	34	16	219	248	80
[1] Winnipeg Jets	36	40	6	275	291	78
Dallas Stars	26	42	14	227	280	66

Pacific Division

	W	L	T	GF	GA	Pts
[1,2,3] Colorado Avalanche	47	25	10	326	240	104
[1] Calgary Flames	34	37	11	241	240	79
[1] Vancouver Canucks	32	35	15	278	278	79
Anaheim Mighty Ducks	35	39	8	234	247	78
Edmonton Oilers	30	44	8	240	304	68
Los Angeles Kings	24	40	18	256	302	66
San Jose Sharks	20	55	7	252	357	47

1. Clinched Playoff berth. 2. Clinched Division title. 3. Clinched Conference title.

N.H.L. LEADING GOALTENDERS—1995–96

	Gm	Min	GAA	Record (W–L–T)
Ron Hextall, Philadelphia	53	3102	2.166	31–13–7
Chris Osgood, Detroit	50	2933	2.168	39–6–5
Jim Carey, Washington	71	4069	2.260	35–24–9
Mike Vernon, Detroit	32	1855	2.260	21–7–2
Martin Brodeur, New Jersey	77	4434	2.340	34–30–12
Jeff Hackett, Chicago	35	2000	2.400	18–11–4
Darren Puppa, Tampa Bay	57	3189	2.460	29–16–9
John Vanbiesbrouck, Florida	57	3178	2.680	26–20–7
Mike Richter, N.Y. Rangers	41	2396	2.680	24–13–3
Ed Belfour, Chicago	50	2956	2.740	27–17–10

N.H.L. LEADING SCORERS—1995–96

	Team	GP	G	A	Pts
Mario Lemieux	Pittsburgh	70	69	92	161
Jaromir Jagr	Pittsburgh	82	62	87	149
Joe Sakic	Colorado	82	51	69	120
Ron Francis	Pittsburgh	77	27	92	119
Peter Forsberg	Colorado	82	30	86	116
Eric Lindros	Philadelphia	73	47	68	115
Paul Kariya	Anaheim	82	50	58	108
Teemu Selanne	Wpg–Ana	79	40	68	108
Alexander Mogilny	Vancouver	79	55	52	107
Sergei Fedorov	Detroit	78	39	68	107
Doug Weight	Edmonton	82	25	79	104
Wayne Gretzky	L.A.–Stl	80	23	79	102
Mark Messier	N.Y. Rangers	74	47	52	99
Petr Nedved	Pittsburgh	80	45	54	99
Keith Tkachuk	Winnipeg	76	50	48	98
John Leclair	Philadelphia	82	51	46	97

N.H.L. CAREER SCORING LEADERS

(Through 1995–96 season)

		Yrs	Games	G	A	Pts
1.	Wayne Gretzky[1]	17	1,253	837	1,771	2,608
2.	Gordie Howe	26	1,767	801	1,049	1,850
3.	Marcel Dionne	18	1,348	731	1,040	1,771
4.	Phil Esposito	18	1,282	717	873	1,590
5.	Mark Messier[1]	17	1,201	539	929	1,468
6.	Stan Mikita	22	1,394	541	926	1,467
7.	Bryan Trottier	18	1,279	524	901	1,425
8.	Paul Coffey[1]	16	1,154	372	1,038	1,410
9.	Dale Hawerchuk	15	1,137	506	869	1,375
10.	Mario Lemieux[1]	11	669	563	809	1,372
11.	John Bucyk	23	1,540	556	813	1,369
12.	Guy Lafleur	17	1,126	560	793	1,353
13.	Jari Kurri	15	1,099	583	758	1,341
14.	Gilbert Perreault	17	1,191	512	814	1,326
15.	Ray Bourque[1]	17	1,228	343	970	1,313
16.	Denis Savard[1]	16	1,132	464	847	1,311
17.	Alex Delvecchio	24	1,549	456	825	1,281
18.	Jean Ratelle	21	1,281	491	776	1,267
19.	Ron Francis[1]	15	1,085	376	881	1,257
20.	Steve Yzerman[1]	13	942	517	738	1,255
21.	Mike Gartner[1]	17	1,290	664	581	1,245
22.	Peter Stastny	15	977	450	789	1,239
23.	Norm Ullman	20	1,410	490	739	1,229
24.	Jean Beliveau	20	1,125	507	712	1,219
25.	Bobby Clarke	15	1,144	358	852	1,210
26.	Bobby Hull	16	1,063	610	560	1,170
27.	Michel Goulet	15	1,089	548	604	1,152
28.	Bernie Nicholls[1]	15	992	457	677	1,134
29.	Bernie Federko	14	1,000	369	761	1,130
30.	Mike Bossy	10	752	573	553	1,126

1. Still active entering 1996–97 season.

BOWLING

The game of bowling in the United States is an indoor development of the more ancient outdoor game that survives as lawn bowling. The outdoor game is prehistoric in origin and probably goes back to primitive man and round stones that were rolled at some target. It is believed that a game something like nine-pins was popular among the Dutch, Swiss and Germans as long ago as A.D. 1200 at which time the game was played outdoors with an alley consisting of a single plank 12 to 18 inches wide along which was rolled a ball toward three rows of three pins each placed at the far end of the alley. When the first indoor alleys were built and how the game was modified over time are matters of dispute.

It is supposed that the early Dutch settlers of New Amsterdam (New York City) brought their two bowling games with them. About a century ago the game of nine-pins was flourishing in the United States but so corrupted by gambling on matches that it was barred by law in New York and Connecticut. Since the law specifically barred "nine-pins," it was eventually evaded by adding another pin and thus legally making it a new game.

Various organizations were formed to make rules for bowling and supervise competition in the United States but none was successful until the American Bowling Congress, organized Sept. 9, 1895, became the ruling body.

AMERICAN BOWLING CONGRESS CHAMPIONS

Year	Singles	All–events	Year	Singles	All–events
1959	Ed Lubanski	Ed Lubanski	1979	Rick Peters	Bob Basacchi
1960	Paul Kulbaga	Vince Lucci	1980	Mike Eaton	Steve Fehr
1961	Lyle Spooner	Luke Karen	1981	Rob Vital	Rod Toft
1962	Andy Renaldo	Billy Young	1982	Bruce Bohm	Rich Wonders
1963	Fred Delello	Bus Owalt	1983	Rick Kendrick	Tony Cariello
1964	Jim Stefanich	Les Zikes, Jr.	1984	Bob Antczak and	
1965	Ken Roeth	Tom Hathaway		Neal Young (tie)	Bob Goike
1966	Don Chapman	John Wilcox	1985	Glen Harbison	Barry Asher
1967	Frank Perry	Gary Lewis	1986	Jess Mackey	Ed Marazka
1968	Wayne Kowalski	Vince Mazzanti	1987	Terry Taylor	Ryan Schafer
1969	Greg Campbell	Eddie Jackson	1988	Steve Hutkowski	Rick Steelsmith
1970	Jake Yoder	Mike Berlin	1989	Paul Tetreault	George Hall
1971	Al Cohn	Al Cohn	1990	Bob Hochrein	Mike Neumann
1972	Bill Pointer	Mac Lowry	1991	Ed Deines	Tom Howery
1973	Ed Thompson	Ron Woolet	1992	Bob Youker and	
1974	Gene Krause	Bob Hart		Gary Blatchford (tie)	Mike Tucker
1975	Jim Setser	Bobby Meadows	1993	Dan Bock	Jeff Nimke
1976	Mike Putzer	Jim Lindquist	1994	John Weltzien	Thomas Holt
1977	Frank Gadaleto	Bud Debenham	1995	Matt Surina	Jeff Kwiatkowski
1978	Rich Mersek	Chris Cobus	1996	Donald Scudder, Jr.	Scott Kurtz

PROFESSIONAL BOWLERS ASSOCIATION

National Championship Tournament

1960	Don Carter	1970	Mike McGrath	1980	Johnny Petraglia	1990	Jim Pencak
1961	Dave Soutar	1971	Mike Lemongello	1981	Earl Anthony	1991	Mike Miller
1962	Carmen Salvino	1972	Johnny Guenther	1982	Earl Anthony	1992	Eric Forkel
1963	Billy Hardwick	1973	Earl Anthony	1983	Earl Anthony	1993	Ron Palombi
1964	Bob Strampe	1974	Earl Anthony	1984	Bob Chamberlain	1994	David Traber
1965	Dave Davis	1975	Earl Anthony	1985	Mike Aulby	1995	Scott Alexander
1966	Wayne Zahn	1976	Paul Colwell	1986	Tom Crites	1996	Butch Soper
1967	Dave Davis	1977	Tommy Hudson	1987	Randy Pedersen		
1968	Wayne Zahn	1978	Warren Nelson	1988	Brian Voss		
1969	Mike McGrath	1979	Mike Aulby	1989	Pete Weber		

BOWLING PROPRIETORS' ASSOCIATION OF AMERICA—MEN[2]

United States Open[1]

1971	Mike Lemongello	1978	Nelson Burton, Jr.	1985	Marshall Holman	1992	Robert Lawrence
1972	Don Johnson	1979	Joe Berardi	1986	Steve Cook	1993	Del Ballard, Jr.
1973	Mike McGrath	1980	Steve Martin	1987	Del Ballard	1994	Justin Hromek
1974	Larry Laub	1981	Marshall Holman	1988	Pete Weber	1995	Dave Husted
1975	Steve Neff	1982	Dave Husted	1989	Mike Aulby		
1976	Paul Moser	1983	Gary Dickinson	1990	Ron Palumbi, Jr.		
1977	Johnny Petraglia	1984	Mark Roth	1991	Pete Weber		

1. Replaced All-Star tournament and is rolled as part of B.P.A. tour. 2. The 1996 tournament was scheduled to be held after IPA went to press.

WOMEN'S INTERNATIONAL BOWLING CONGRESS CHAMPIONS

Year	Singles	All–events	Year	Singles	All–events
1959	Mae Bolt	Pat McBride	1980	Betty Morris	Cheryl Robinson
1960	Marge McDaniels	Judy Roberts	1981	Virginia Norton	Virginia Norton
1961	Elaine Newton	Evelyn Teal	1982	Gracie Freeman	Aleta Rzepecki
1962	Martha Hoffman	Flossie Argent	1983	Aleta Rzepecki	Virginia Norton
1963	Dot Wilkinson	Helen Shablis	1984	Freida Gates	Shinobu Saitoh
1964	Jean Havlish	Jean Havlish	1985	Polly Schwarzel	Aleta Sill
1965	Doris Rudell	Donna Zimmerman	1986	Dana Stewart	Robin Romeo
1966	Gloria Bouvia	Kate Helbig			Maria Lewis (tie)
1967	Gloria Paeth	Carol Miller	1987	Regi Junak	Leanne Barrette
1968	Norma Parks	Susie Reichley	1988	Michelle Meyer–Welty	Lisa Wagner
1969	Joan Bender	Helen Duval	1989	Lorraine Anderson	Nancy Fehn
1970	Dorothy Fothergill	Dorothy Fothergill	1990	Dana Miller–Mackie	
1971	Mary Scruggs	Lorrie Nichols		and Paula Carter	Carol Norman
1972	D. D. Jacobson	Mildred Martorella	1991	Debbie Kuhn	Debbie Kuhn
1973	Bobby Buffaloe	Toni Calvery	1992	Patty Ann	Mitsuko Tokimoto
1974	Shirley Garms	Judy C. Soutar	1993	Karen Collura and	Bertha Blackshur
1975	Barbara Leicht	Virginia Norton		Kari Murph (tie)	and Sharon Davis (tie)
1976	Bev Shonk	Betty Morris	1994	Vicki Fifield	Wendy Macpherson–
1977	Akiko Yamaga	Akiko Yamaga			Papanos
1978	Mae Bolt	Annese Kelly	1995	Beth Owen	Beth Owen
1979	Betty Morris	Betty Morris	1996	Cindy Berlanga	Lorrie Nichols

BOWLING PROPRIETORS' ASSOCIATION OF AMERICA—WOMEN[1]

United States Open

1971	Paula Carter	1978	Donna Adamek	1985	Pat Mercatanti	1992	Tish Johnson
1972	Lorrie Nichols	1979	Diana Silva	1986	Wendy MacPherson	1993	Dede Davidson
1973	Mildred Martorella	1980	Pat Costello (Calif.)	1987	Carol Nurman	1994	Aleta Sill
1974	Pat Costello (Calif.)	1981	Donna Adamek	1988	Lisa Wagner	1995	Tish Johnson
1975	Paula Carter	1982	Shinobu Saitoh	1989	Robin Romeo		
1976	Patty Costello (Pa.)	1983	Dana Miller	1990	Dana Miller–Mackie		
1977	Betty Morris	1984	Karen Ellingsworth	1991	Anne Marie Duggan		

The 1996 tournament was scheduled to be held after IPA went to press.

WIBC QUEENS TOURNAMENT CHAMPIONS

1961	Janet Harman	1970	Mildred Martorella	1979	Donna Adamek	1988	Wendy McPherson
1962	Dorothy Wilkinson	1971	Mildred Martorella	1980	Donna Adamek	1989	Carol Gianotti
1963	Irene Monterosso	1972	Dorothy Fothergill	1981	Katsuko Sugimoto	1990	Patty Ann
1964	D.D. Jacobson	1973	Dorothy Fothergill	1982	Katsuko Sugimoto	1991	Dede Davidson
1965	Betty Kuczynski	1974	Judy Soutar	1983	Aleta Rzepecki	1992	Cindy Coburn-Carroll
1966	Judy Lee	1975	Cindy Powell	1984	Kazue Inahashi	1993	Jan Schmidt
1967	Mildred Martorella	1976	Pamela Buckner	1985	Aleta Sill	1994	Anne Marie Duggan
1968	Phyllis Massey	1977	Dana Stewart	1986	Cora Fiebig	1995	Sandy Postma
1969	Ann Feigel	1978	Loa Boxberger	1987	Cathy Almeida	1996	Lisa Wagner

PROFESSIONAL BOWLERS ASSOCIATION CHAMPIONSHIP—1996

(Toledo, Ohio, June 8, 1996)

Winner—Butch Soper defeated Walter Ray Williams, Jr., 226–210 in title match
2. Walter Ray Williams, Jr., Stockton, Calif.
3. Justin Hromek, Andover, Kan.
4. Tim Criss, Bel Air, Md.
5. Mark Williams, Beaumont, Texas

WOMEN'S INTERNATIONAL BOWLING CONGRESS TOURNAMENT—1996

(April 4–June 2, 1996, Buffalo, N.Y.)

Singles—Cindy Berlanga, San Antonio		723
Doubles—Mandy Wilson and Linda Kelly,		
Dayton, Ohio		1,410
Events—Lorrie Nichols, Algonquin, Ill.		1,985
Team—The Naecarato Group, Tacoma, Wash.		3,184

AMERICAN BOWLING CONGRESS TOURNAMENT—1996

(Feb. 10–June 12, Salt Lake City)

Regular Division

Singles—Donald Scudder, Jr., Cincinnati, Ohio	823
Doubles—Jamie Burke, Loveland, Ohio, and Drew Hauck, Finytown, Ohio	1,508
All Events—Scott Kurtz, Somerset, N.J.	2,224
Team—Trout's Minnows, Spokane, Wash.	3,473

Booster Division

Team—Canterbury Lanes #4, Oak Grove, Okla.	2,829

AMERICAN BOWLING CONGRESS MASTERS TOURNAMENT—1996

(April 30–May 4, 1996, Salt Lake City)

Ernie Schlegel, Vancouver, Wash., defeated Mike Aulby, Indianapolis, Ind. 236–200 in final match.

SKIING

HISTORY OF SKIING IN THE UNITED STATES

Skis were devised for utility, to aid those who had to travel over snow. The Norwegians, Swedes, Lapps, and other inhabitants of northern lands used skis for many centuries before skiing became a sport. Emigrants from these countries brought skis to the United States with them. The first skier of record in the United States was a mailman by the name of "Snow-shoe" Thompson, born and raised in Telemarken, Norway, who came to the United States and, beginning in 1850, used skis through 20 successive winters in carrying mail from Northern California to Carson Valley, Idaho.

Ski clubs sprang up over 100 years ago when there were Norwegian and Swedish settlers in Wisconsin and Minnesota and ski contests were held in that territory in 1886. On Feb. 21, 1904, at Ishpeming, Mich., a small group of skiers organized the National Ski Association. In 1961 it was renamed the United States Ski Association.

ALPINE WORLD CUP OVERALL WINNERS

Year	Men	Women	Team
1967	Jean–Claude Killy, France	Nancy Greene, Canada	France
1968	Jean–Claude Killy, France	Nancy Greene, Canada	France
1969	Karl Schranz, Austria	Gertrude Gabl, Austria	Austria
1970	Karl Schranz, Austria	Michel Jacot, France	France
1971	Gustavo Thoeni, Italy	Annemarie Proell, Austria	France
1972	Gustavo Thoeni, Italy	Annemarie Proell, Austria	France
1973	Gustavo Thoeni, Italy	Annemarie Proell Moser, Austria	Austria
1974	Piero Gros, Italy	Annemarie Proell Moser, Austria	Austria
1975	Gustavo Thoeni, Italy	Annemarie Proell Moser, Austria	Austria
1976	Ingemar Stenmark, Sweden	Rosi Mittermaier, West Germany	Austria
1977	Ingemar Stenmark, Sweden	Lise–Marie Morerod, Switzerland	Austria
1978	Ingemar Stenmark, Sweden	Hanni Wenzel, Liechtenstein	Austria
1979	Peter Luescher, Switzerland	Annemarie Proell Moser, Austria	Austria
1980	Andreas Wenzel, Liechtenstein	Hanni Wenzel, Liechtenstein	Liechtenstein
1981	Phil Mahre, United States	Marie–Theres Nadig, Switzerland	Switzerland
1982	Phil Mahre, United States	Erika Hess, Switzerland	Austria
1983	Phil Mahre, United States	Tamara McKinney, United States	Switzerland
1984	Pirmin Zurbriggen, Switzerland	Erika Hess, Switzerland	Switzerland
1985	Marc Girardelli, Luxembourg	Michela Figini, Switzerland	Switzerland
1986	Marc Girardelli, Luxembourg	Maria Walliser, Switzerland	Switzerland
1987	Pirmin Zubriggen, Switzerland	Maria Walliser, Switzerland	Switzerland
1988	Pirmin Zubriggen, Switzerland	Michela Figini, Switzerland	Switzerland
1989	Marc Girardelli, Luxembourg	Vreni Schneider, Switzerland	Switzerland
1990	Pirmin Zubriggen, Switzerland	Petra Kronberger, Austria	Austria
1991	Marc Girardelli, Luxembourg	Petra Kronberger, Austria	Austria
1992	Paul Accola, Switzerland	Petra Kronberger, Austria	Switzerland
1993	Marc Girardelli, Luxembourg	Anita Wachter, Austria	Austria
1994	Kjetil Andre Aamodt, Norway	Anita Wachter, Austria	Austria
1995	Alberto Tomba, Italy	Vreni Schneider, Switzerland	Austria
1996	Lasse Kjus, Norway	Katja Seizinger, Germany	Austria

1996 UNITED STATES ALPINE CHAMPIONSHIPS

Women's Slalom
1. Kristina Koznick, U.S.A.
2. Carrie Sheinberg, U.S.A.
3. Sarah Schleper, U.S.A.
4. Tatum Skoglund, U.S.A.
5. Taylor Watts, U.S.A.

Women's Giant Slalom
1. Jennifer Collins, U.S.A.
2. Kirsten Clark, U.S.A.
3. Jonna Mendes, U.S.A.
4. Tatum Skoglund, U.S.A.
5. Carrie Sheinberg, U.S.A.

Women's Downhill
1. Picabo Street, U.S.A.
2. Megan Gerety, U.S.A.
3. Kjersti Bjorn-Roli, U.S.A.
4. Shannon Nobis, U.S.A.
5. Kirsten Clark, U.S.A.

Women's Combined
1. Kirsten Clark, U.S.A.
2. Jonna Mendes, U.S.A.

Men's Slalom
1. Chip Knight, U.S.A.
2. Casey Puckett, U.S.A.
3. Bode Miller, U.S.A.
4. Stanley Hayer, Canada
5. Sacha Gros, U.S.A.

Men's Giant Slalom
1. Daron Rahlves, U.S.A.
2. Chris Puckett, U.S.A.
3. Kyle Rasmussen, U.S.A.
4. Chip Knight, U.S.A.
5. Cary Mullen, Canada

Men's Downhill
1. Chad Fleischer, U.S.A.
2. Chris Puckett, U.S.A.
3. Tommy Moe, U.S.A.
4. Mike Makar, U.S.A.
5. Daron Rahlves, U.S.A.

Men's Combined
1. Chris Puckett, U.S.A.
2. Casey Puckett, U.S.A.

1996 ALPINE WORLD CUP CHAMPIONS

Men	**Pts**
Overall—Lasse Kjus, Norway	1,216
Downhill—Luc Alphand, France	577
Super G—Atle Skaardal, Norway	312
Giant Slalom—Michael Von Gruenigen, Switzerland	738
Slalom—Sebastien Amiez, France	539

Women	
Overall—Katja Seizinger, Germany	1,472
Downhill—Picabo Street, United States	640
Super G—Katja Seizinger, Germany	545
Giant Slalom—Martina Ertl, Germany	485
Slalom—Elfi Eder, Austria	580

1996 NATIONS CUP STANDINGS

Overall		**Men**	
1. Austria	10,844	1. Austria	5,729
2. Switzerland	6,959	2. Switzerland	3,800
3. Italy	6,214	3. Italy	3,558
4. Germany	4,539	4. Norway	3,263
5. Norway	4,370	5. France	2,451
6. France	3,717		
7. Sweden	2,764	**Women**	
8. Slovenia	2,364	1. Austria	5,115
9. United States	1,809	2. Germany	3,932
10. Canada	982	3. Switzerland	3,159
		4. Italy	2,656
		5. Sweden	1,842

1996 WORLD CUP SKI JUMPING

1. Primoz Peterka, Slovakia
2. Adam Malysz, Poland
3. Jens Weissflog, Germany
4. Takanobu Okabe, Japan
5. Didier Mollard, France
5. Andreas Widhoelzl, Austria

1996 FREESTYLE SKIING WORLD CUP

Women
Acro-Ski—Elena Batalova, Russia
Moguls—Donna Weinbrecht, United States
Aerials—Colette Brand, Switzerland

Men
Acro-Ski—Heini Baumgartner, Switzerland
Moguls—Jean-Luc Brassard, Canada
Aerials—Sébastien Foucras, France

1996 CROSS COUNTRY WORLD CUP

Women	
1. Manuela Di Centa, Italy	1,004
2. Elena Välbe, Russia	945
3. Larissa Lazutina, Russia	732
4. Nina Gavriljuk, Russia	717
5. Ljubov Jegorova, Russia	690

Men	
1. Björn Dählie, Norway	1,110
2. Vladimir Smirnov, Kazakhstan	1,034
3. Jari Isometsä, Finland	617
4. Aleksei Prokurorov, Russia	544
5. Silvio Fauner, Italy	508

UNITED STATES SKI JUMPING CHAMPIONSHIPS—1996

1. Randy Weber	230.9
2. Casey Colby	222.6
3. Matt Kuusinen	218.0
4. Brendan Doran	211.4
5. Taylor Hoffman	154.3

1996 U.S. EXTREME SKIING CHAMPIONSHIPS

Men	
1. Peter Bowers	1,524
2. Seth Morrison	1,482
3. Brant Moles	1,435
4. Shane McConkey	1,414
5. Dave Bluestein,	1,388

Women	
1. Jill Sickels-Matlock	1,309
2. Alison Gannett	1,256
3. Wendy Fischer	1,252
4. Asia Jenkins	1,198
5. Kasha Rigby	1,175

FREESTYLE NATIONS CUP

	Men	Women	Total
1. United States	6,188	4,868	11,056
2. Canada	5,944	4,644	10,588
3. France	3,764	1,772	5,536
4. Switzerland	2,244	2,980	5,224
5. Russia	1,056	4,048	5,104

CURLING

UNITED STATES CHAMPIONSHIPS—1996

	Site	Winner's Home Club	Skip
Men's	Bemidji, Minn.	Superior, Wis.	Tim Somerville
Women's	Bemidji, Minn.	Madison, Wis.	Lisa Schoeneberg
Junior Men's	Schenectady, N.Y.	Seattle, Wash.	Travis Way
Junior Women's	Schenectady, N.Y.	Omaha, Neb.	Amy Becher

WORLD CHAMPIONSHIPS—1996

	Site	Winner's Country	Skip
Men's	Hamilton, Canada	Canada	Jeff Stoughton
Women's	Hamilton, Canada	Canada	Marilyn Bodogh
Junior Men's	Reed Deer, Alberta	Scotland	James Dryburgh
Junior Women's	Reed Deer, Alberta	Canada	Heather Godberson

SPEED SKATING

U.S. OUTDOOR CHAMPIONS (LONG TRACK)

Men

1959–60	Ken Bartholomew	1986	Eric Klein	1970–71	Sheila Young
1961	Ed Rudolph	1987	Dave Paulicic	1972	Ruth Moore, Nancy Thorne
1962	Floyd Bedbury	1988	Patrick Wentland	1973	Nancy Class
1963	Tom Gray	1989	Matt Trimble	1974	Kris Garbe
1964	Neil Blatchford	1990	Andy Zak	1975	Nancy Swider
1965–66	Rich Wurster	1991	Pat Seltsam	1976	Connie Carpenter
1967	Mike Passarella	1992	Dan Jansen	1977	Liz Crowe
1968–70	Peter Cefalu	1993	Brian Smith	1978	Paula Class, Betsy Davis
1971	Jack Walters	1994	K.C. Boutiette	1979	Gretchen Byrnes
1972	Barth Levy	1995	David Tamburrino	1980	Shari Miller
1973	Mike Woods	1996	K.C. Boutiette	1981–82	Lisa Merrifield
1974	Leigh Barczewski, Mike			1983–84	Janet Hainstock
	Passarella	**Women**		1985	Betsy Davis
1975	Rich Wurster	1960	Mary Novak	1986	Deb Perkins
1976	John Wurster	1961	Jean Ashworth	1987	Laura Zuckerman
1977	Jim Chapin	1962	Jean Omelenchuk	1988	Elise Brinich
1978	Bill Heinkel	1963	Jean Ashworth	1989	Liza Merrifield
1979	Erik Henriksen	1964	Diane White	1990	Jane Eickhoff
1980	Greg Oly	1965	Jean Omelenchuk	1991	Liza Dennehy
1981	Tom Grannes	1966	Diane White	1992	Hilary Mills
1982	Greg Oly	1967	Jean Ashworth	1993	Chantal Bailey
1983–84	Michael Ralston	1968	Helen Lutsch	1994–96	Moira D'Andrea
1985	Andy Gabel	1969	Sally Blatchford		

WORLD SPEED SKATING RECORDS (LONG TRACK)

Men

Distance	Time	Skater	Place	Year
500m	35.39	Hiroyasu Shimizu, Japan	Calgary, Canada	1996
1000m	1:11.67	Manabu Horii, Japan	Calgary, Canada	1996
1500m	1:50.61	Hiroyuki Noake, Japan	Calgary, Canada	1996
3000m	3:53.06	Bob de Jong, Netherlands	Calgary, Canada	1996
5000m	6:34.96	Johann Olav Koss, Norway	Lillehammer, Norway	1994
10,000m	13:30.55	Johann Olav Koss, Norway	Lillehammer, Norway	1994

Women

500m	0:38.69	Bonnie Blair, United States	Calgary, Canada	1995
1000m	1:17.65	Christa Rothenburger, Germany	Calgary, Canada	1988
1500m	1:59.30	Karin Kania, Germany	Medeo, U.S.S.R.	1986
3000m	4:09.32	Gunda Niemann, Germany	Calgary, Canada	1994
5000m	7:03.26	Gunda Niemann, Germany	Calgary, Canada	1994

U.S. SPRINT CHAMPIONSHIPS—1996

(Dec. 22–23, 1995, Milwaukee, Wis.)

Men

	Time
500m—Casey FitzRandolph	36.76
1000m—Casey FitzRandolph	1:14.52
Overall standings:	**Points**
1. Casey FitzRandolph	148.245
2. Patrick Kelly	151.330
3. Cory Carpenter	151.685

Women

	Time
500m—Christine Witty	40.60
1000m—Christine Witty	1:20.74
Overall standings:	**Points**
1. Christine Witty	161.935
2. Becky Sundstrom	165.560
3. Moira D'Andrea	165.855

U.S. ALL-AROUND CHAMPIONSHIPS—1996

(Dec. 30–31, 1995, Milwaukee, Wis.)

Men

	Time
500m—Casey FitzRandolph	37.43
1500m—K.C. Boutiette	1:54.86
5000m—K.C. Boutiette	7:03.43
10000m—K.C. Boutiette	14:48.02
Overall—K.C. Boutiette	163.400 pts

Women

	Time
500m—Christine Witty	41.30
1500m—Tama Sundstrom	2:08
3000m—Christine Witty	4:37.45
5000m—Kirstin Holum	8:01.12
Overall—Moira D'Andrea	180.662 pts

U.S. SHORT TRACK CHAMPIONSHIPS—1996

(Feb. 17–18, 1996, Saratoga Springs, N.Y.)

Women

	Time
9 Lap Time Trial—Julie Goskowicz	1:36.50
500m—Amy Peterson	46.63
1000m—Erin Porter	1:40.25
1500m—Erin Porter	2:34.51
3000m—Amy Peterson	6:13.31

Overall ranking—1. Amy Peterson. 2. Erin Porter. 3. Julie Goskowicz.

Men

	Time
9 Lap Time Trial—Tony Goskowicz	1:29.80
500m—Andy Gabel	43.55
1000m—Tony Goskowicz	1:30.47
1500m—Tony Goskowicz	2:21.70
3000m—Tony Goskowicz	5:07.32

Overall ranking—1. Tony Goskowicz. 2. Andy Gabel. 3. J.P. Shilling.

WORLD CHAMPIONSHIPS—1996
(Feb. 17–18, 1996, Heerenveen, Netherlands)

Men	Time	Women	Time
500m—Hiroyasu Shimizu, Japan	39.95	500m—Catriona Lemay, Canada	39.96
1000m—Sergei Klevchenja, Russia	1:13.10	1000m—Christine Witty, United States	1:19.97
Overall standings:	Points	Overall standings:	Points
1. Sergei Klevchenja, Russia	145.655	1. Christine Witty, United States	161.170
2. Hiroyasu Shimizu, Japan	146.135	2. Edel Therese Hoiseth, Norway	161.350
3. Manabu Horii, Japan	147.300	3. Franziska Schenk, Germany	162.270

FIGURE SKATING

WORLD CHAMPIONS

Men

1960	Alain Giletti, France
1961	No competition
1962	Donald Jackson, Canada
1963	Don McPherson, Canada
1964	Manfred Schnelldorfer, West Germany
1965	Alain Calmat, France
1966–68	Emmerich Danzer, Austria
1969–70	Tim Wood, United States
1971–73	Ondrej Nepela, Czechoslovakia
1974	Jan Hoffman, East Germany
1975	Sergei Yolkov, U.S.S.R.
1976	John Curry, Britain
1977	Vladimir Kovalev, U.S.S.R.
1978	Charles Tickner, United States
1979	Vladimir Kovalev, U.S.S.R.
1980	Jan Hoffman, East Germany
1981–84	Scott Hamilton, United States
1985	Alexandr Fadeev, U.S.S.R.
1986	Brian Boitano, United States
1987	Brian Orser, Canada
1988	Brian Boitano, United States
1989–91	Kurt Browning, Canada
1992	Viktor Petrenko, Unified Team
1993	Kurt Browning, Canada
1994	Elvis Stoyko, Canada
1995	Elvis Stoyko, Canada
1996	Todd Eldredge, United States

Women

1956–60	Carol Heiss, United States
1961	No competition
1962–64	Sjoukje Dijkstra, Netherlands
1965	Petra Burka, Canada
1966–68	Peggy Fleming, United States
1969–70	Gabriele Seyfert, East Germany
1971–72	Beatrix Schuba, Austria
1973	Karen Magnusson, Canada
1974	Christine Errath, East Germany
1975	Dianne de Leeuw, Netherlands
1976	Dorothy Hamill, United States
1977	Linda Fratianne, United States
1978	Anett Poetzsch, East Germany
1979	Linda Fratianne, United States
1980	Anett Poetzsch, East Germany
1981	Denise Beillmann, Switzerland
1982	Elaine Zayak, United States
1983	Rosalynn Sumners, United States
1984–85	Katarina Witt, East Germany
1986	Debi Thomas, United States
1987–88	Katarina Witt, East Germany
1989	Midori Ito, Japan
1990	Jill Trenary, United States
1991–92	Kristi Yamaguchi, United States
1993	Oksana Baiul, Ukraine
1994	Yuka Sato, Japan
1995	Chen Lu, China
1996	Michelle Kwan, United States

U.S. CHAMPIONS

Men

1946–52	Richard Button
1953–56	Hayes Jenkins
1957–60	David Jenkins
1961	Bradley Lord
1962	Monty Hoyt
1963	Tommy Liz
1964	Scott Allen
1965	Gary Visconti
1966	Scott Allen
1967	Gary Visconti
1968–70	Tim Wood
1971	John M. Petkevich
1972	Ken Shelley
1973–75	Gordon McKellen
1976	Terry Kubicka
1977–80	Charles Tickner
1981–84	Scott Hamilton
1985–88	Brian Boitano
1989	Christopher Bowman
1990–91	Todd Eldredge
1992	Christopher Bowman
1993–94	Scott Davis
1995	Todd Eldredge
1996	Rudy Galindo

Women

1943–48	Gretchen Merrill
1949–50	Yvonne Sherman
1951	Sonya Klopfer
1952–56	Tenley Albright
1957–60	Carol Heiss
1961	Laurence Owen
1962	Barbara Roles Pursley
1963	Lorraine Hanlon
1964–68	Peggy Fleming
1969–73	Janet Lynn
1974–76	Dorothy Hamill
1977–80	Linda Fratianne
1981	Elaine Zayak
1982–84	Rosalynn Sumners
1985	Tiffany Chin
1986	Debi Thomas
1987	Jill Trenary
1988	Debi Thomas
1989–90	Jill Trenary
1991	Tonya Harding
1992	Kristi Yamaguchi
1993	Nancy Kerrigan
1994	Tonya Harding
1995	Nicole Bobek
1996	Michelle Kwan

1996 WORLD CHAMPIONSHIPS

Men's singles—Gold: Todd Eldredge, United States
  Silver: Ilia Kulik, Russia
  Bronze: Rudy Galindo, United States
Women's singles—Gold: Michelle Kwan, United States
  Silver: Lu Chen, China
  Bronze: Irina Slutskaya, Russia
Pairs—Gold: Marina Eltsova and Andrei Bushkov, Russia
  Silver: Mandy Wotzel and Ingo Steuer, Germany
  Bronze: Jenni Meno and Todd Sand, United States
Dance—Gold: Oksana Gritschuk and Evgeny Platov, Russia
  Silver: Anjelica Krylova and Oleg Ovsiannikov, Russia
  Bronze: Shae-Lynn Bourne and Victor Kraatz, Canada

1996 UNITED STATES CHAMPIONSHIPS

Senior men—Rudy Galindo, San Jose, Calif.

Senior women—Michelle Kwan, Torrance, Calif.

Senior pairs—Jenni Meno, Westlake, Ohio, and Todd Sand, Thousand Oaks, Calif.

Senior dance—Elizabeth Punsalan, Syracuse, N.Y., and Jerod Swallo, Ann Arbor, Mich.

SWIMMING

WORLD RECORDS—MEN

(Through September 1, 1996)
Approved by the International Swimming Federation (F.I.N.A.)
(F.I.N.A. discontinued acceptance of records in yards in 1968)
Source: United States Swim Team

Distance	Record	Holder	Country	Date
Freestyle				
50 meters	0:21.81	Tom Jager	United States	March 24, 1990
100 meters	0:48.21	Alexander Popov	Russia	June 18, 1994
200 meters	1:46.69	Georgio Lamberti	Italy	Aug. 15, 1989
400 meters	3:43.80	Kieren Perkins	Australia	Sept. 9, 1994
800 meters	7:46.00	Kieren Perkins	Australia	Aug. 24, 1994
1,500 meters	14:41.66	Kieren Perkins	Australia	Aug. 24, 1994
Backstroke				
100 meters	53.86	Jeff Rouse	United States	July 31, 1992
200 meters	1:56.57	Martin Zubero	Spain	Nov. 23, 1991
Breaststroke				
100 meters	1:00.60	Fred de Burghgraeve	Belgium	July 20, 1996
200 meters	2:10.16	Mike Barrowman	United States	July 29, 1992
Butterfly				
100 meters	0:52.27	Denis Pankratov	Russia	July 24, 1996
200 meters	1:55.22	Denis Pankratov	Russia	June 14, 1995
Individual Medley				
200 meters	1:58.16	Jani Sievinen	Finland	Sept. 11, 1994
400 meters	4:12.30	Tom Dolan	United States	Sept. 6, 1994
Medley Relay				
400 meters	3:34.84	United States	Olympic Team	July 26, 1996
Freestyle Relay				
400 meters	3:15.11	United States	Pan Pacific Team	Aug. 12, 1995
800 meters	7:11.95	Unified Team	Former Soviet Union	July 27, 1992

WORLD RECORDS—WOMEN

Distance	Record	Holder	Country	Date
Freestyle				
50 meters	0:24.51	Jingyi Le	China	Sept. 11, 1994
100 meters	0:54.01	Jingyi Le	China	Sept. 5, 1994
200 meters	1:56.78	Franziska van Almsick	Germany	Sept. 6, 1994
400 meters	4:03.85	Janet Evans	United States	Sept. 22, 1988
800 meters	8:16.22	Janet Evans	United States	Aug. 20, 1989
1,500 meters	15:52.10	Janet Evans	United States	March 26, 1988
Backstroke				
100 meters	1:00.16	Cihong He	China	Sept. 10, 1994
200 meters	2:06.62	Krisztina Egerszegi	Hungary	Aug. 26, 1991
Breaststroke				
100 meters	1:07.02	Penny Heyns	South Africa	July 21, 1996
200 meters	2:24.76	Rebecca Brown	Australia	March 16, 1994
Butterfly				
100 meters	0:57.93	Mary T. Meagher	United States	Aug. 16, 1981
200 meters	2:05.96	Mary T. Meagher	United States	Aug. 13, 1981
Individual Medley				
200 meters	2:11.65	Lin Li	China	July 30, 1992
400 meters	4:36.10	Petra Schneider	East Germany	Aug. 1, 1982
Medley Relay				
400 meters	4:01.67	China	National Team	Sept. 10, 1994
Freestyle Relay				
400 meters	3:37.91	China	National Team	Sept. 7, 1994
800 meters	7:55.47	East Germany	National Team	Aug. 18, 1987

AMERICAN SWIMMING RECORDS
(As of September 1, 1996)

Distance	Holder	Record	Date
MEN			
Freestyle			
50 meters	Tom Jager	0:21.81	March 24, 1990
100 meters	Matt Biondi	0:48.42	Aug. 10, 1988
200 meters	Matt Biondi	1:47.72	Aug. 8, 1988
400 meters	Matt Cetlinski	3:48.06	Aug. 11, 1988
800 meters	Sean Killion	7:52.45	July 27, 1987
1500 meters	George DiCarlo	15:01.51	June 30, 1984
Backstroke			
100 meters	Jeff Rouse	0:53.86	July 31, 1992
200 meters	Tripp Schwenk	1:58.33	Aug. 1, 1995
Breaststroke			
100 meters	Jeremy Linn	1:00.77	July 20, 1996
200 meters	Mike Barrowman	2:10.16	July 29, 1992
Butterfly			
100 meters	Pablo Morales	0:52.84	June 23, 1986
200 meters	Melvin Stewart	1:55.69	Jan. 12, 1991
Individual Medley			
200 meters	David Wharton	2:00.11	Aug. 20, 1989
400 meters	Tom Dolan	4:12.30	Sept. 6, 1994
Medley Relay			
400 meters	US Olympic Team	3:34.84	July 26, 1996
Freestyle Relay			
400 meters	US Pan Pacific Team	3:15.11	Aug. 12, 1995
800 meters	US Olympic Team	7:12.51	Sept. 21, 1988

Distance	Holder	Record	Date
WOMEN			
Freestyle			
50 meters	Amy Van Dyken	0:24.87	July 26, 1996
100 meters	Jenny Thompson	0:54.48	March 1, 1992
200 meters	Nicole Haislett	1:57.90	July 27, 1992
400 meters	Janet Evans	4:03.85	Sept. 22, 1988
800 meters	Janet Evans	8:16.22	Aug. 20, 1989
1500 meters	Janet Evans	15:52.10	March 26, 1988
Backstroke			
100 meters	Lea Loveless	1:00.82	July 30, 1992
200 meters	Betsy Mitchell	2:08.60	June 27, 1986
Breaststroke			
100 meters	Amanda Beard	1:08.09	July 21, 1996
200 meters	Anita Nall	2:25.35	March 3, 1992
Butterfly			
100 meters	Mary T. Meagher	0:57.93	Aug. 16, 1981
200 meters	Mary T. Meagher	2:05.96	Aug. 13, 1981
Individual Medley			
200 meters	Summer Sanders	2:11.91	July 28, 1992
400 meters	Summer Sanders	4:37.58	July 26, 1992
Medley Relay			
400 meters	US Olympic Team	4:02.54	July 30, 1992
Freestyle Relay			
400 meters	US Olympic Team	3:39.46	July 28, 1992
800 meters	US Olympic Team	8:02.12	Aug. 22, 1986

N.C.A.A. SWIMMING AND DIVING CHAMPIONSHIPS—1996

Women

(March 21–23, 1996, University of Michigan)

50-yard freestyle—Nicole deMan, Tennessee	0:22.59
100-yard freestyle—Claudia Franco, Stanford	0:49.04
200-yard freestyle—Martina Moravcova, Southern Methodist	1:44.64
500-yard freestyle—Lindsay Benko, Southern California	4:42.46
1650-yard freestyle—Mimosa McNerney, Florida	16:06.23
100-yard backstroke—Jessica Tong, Stanford	0:54.40
200-yard backstroke—Lindsay Benko, Southern California	1:55.78
100-yard breaststroke—Penny Heyns, Nebraska	1:00.27
200-yard breaststroke—Kristine Quance, Southern California	2:09.57
100-yard butterfly—Lisa Coole, Georgia	0:54.21
200-yard butterfly—Annette Salmeen, UCLA	1:55.84
200-yard individual medley—Kristine Quance, Southern California	1:57.58
400-yard individual medley—Kristine Quance, Southern California	4:06.60
200-yard medley relay—Stanford	1:40.90
400-yard medley relay—Southern Methodist	3:37.76
200-yard freestyle relay—Arizona	1:31.09
400-yard freestyle relay—Stanford	3:18.28
800-yard freestyle relay—Stanford	7:11.28
1-meter springboard dive—Kimiko Hirai, Indiana	443.35
3-meter springboard dive—Michelle Rojohn, Kansas	567.95
10-meter platform dive—Becky Ruehl, Cincinnati	636.05

Team standings: 1. Stanford, 478; 2. SMU, 397; 3. Michigan, 363.5

Men

(March 28–30, 1996, University of Texas at Austin)

50-yard freestyle—Francisco Sanchez, Arizona St.	0:19.35
100-yard freestyle—Ricky Busquets, Tennessee	0:42.64
200-yard freestyle—Bela Szabados, Florida	1:34.33
500-yard freestyle—Tom Dolan, Michigan	4:12.77
1650-yard freestyle—Tom Dolan, Michigan	14:38.37
100-yard backstroke—Ryan Berube, Southern Methodist	0:46.15
200-yard backstroke—Ryan Berube, Southern Methodist	1:41.23
100-yard breaststroke—Jeremy Linn, Tennessee	0:53.04
200-yard breaststroke—Matthew Buck, Georgia	1:56.62
100-yard butterfly—Martin Pepper, Arizona	0:46.74
200-yard butterfly—Urug Taner, California	1:43.22
200-yard individual medley—Ryan Berube, Southern Methodist	1:44.85
400-yard individual medley—Tom Dolan, Michigan	3:41.44
200-yard freestyle relay—Texas	1:17.90
400-yard freestyle relay—Auburn	2:52.87
800-yard freestyle relay—Michigan	6:20.89
200-yard medley relay—Tennessee	1:25.85
400-yard medley relay—Tennessee	3:09.97
1-meter springboard dive—P.J. Bogart, Minnesota	564.90
3-meter springboard dive—Chris Mantilla, Miami	648.00
10-meter platform dive—Bryan Gillooly, Miami (Fla.)	789.75

Team standings: 1. Texas, 479.0; 2. Auburn, 443.5; 3. Michigan, 358.0

PHILLIPS 66 NATIONAL SWIMMING CHAMPIONSHIPS—1996

(February 8–11, 1996, Orlando, Florida)

Men

50-meter freestyle—David Fox, Raleigh, N.C.	0:22.73
100-meter freestyle—David Fox, Raleigh, N.C.	0:50.66
200-meter freestyle—Josh Davis, San Antonio, Texas	1:50.47
400-meter freestyle—Josh Davis, San Antonio, Texas	3:55.63
800-meter freestyle—Yann deFabrique, France	8:19.40
1500-meter freestyle—Peter Wright, Delran, N.J.	15:31.97
100-meter backstroke—Tripp Schwenk, Sarasota, Fla.	0:56.39
200-meter backstroke—Tripp Schwenk, Sarasota, Fla.	2:02.57
100-meter breaststroke—Seth Van Neerden, Ft. Lauderdale, Fla.	1:03.24
200-meter breaststroke—Norbert Rozsa, Hungary	2:16.65
100-meter butterfly—Peter Horvath, Hungary	0:54.59
200-meter butterfly—Attila Czene, Hungary	1:59.47
200-meter individual medley—Ron Karnaugh, Maplewood, N.J.	2:03.13
400-meter individual medley—Eric Namesnik, Butler, Pa.	4:23.06
4 x 100 medley relay—Budapest Sport, Hungary	3:47.09
4 x 100 free relay—Ft. Lauderdale, Florida	3:31.13
4 x 200 free relay—Bolles School, United States	7:44.07

Women

50-meter freestyle—Angel Martino, Americus, Ga.	0:25.45
100-meter freestyle—Angel Martino, Americus, Ga.	0:55.39
200-meter freestyle—Suzu Chiba, Japan	1:59.80
400-meter freestyle—Brooke Bennett, Tampa, Fla.	4:12.66
800-meter freestyle—Brooke Bennett, Tampa, Fla.	8:30.54
1500-meter freestyle—Brooke Bennett, Tampa, Fla.	16:37.94
100-meter backstroke—Whitney Hedgepeth, Rocky Mount, N.C.	1:02.36
200-meter backstroke—Whitney Hedgepeth, Rocky Mount, N.C.	2:13.10
100-meter breaststroke—Jilen Siroky, Charlotte, N.C.	1:11.45
200-meter breaststroke—Riley Mants, Canada	2:31.78
100-meter butterfly—Richelle DePold, Scotia, N.Y.	1:01.10
200-meter butterfly—Lauren Stinnett, Reston, Va.	2:13.52
200-meter individual medley—Shannon Cullen, Redlands, Calif.	2:18.61
400-meter individual medley—Corrie Murphy, Seattle, Wash.	4:50.75
4 x 100 medley relay—Mecklenburg	4:21.96
4 x 100 free relay—Phoenix Swim Club	3:52.12
4 x 200 free relay—Phoenix Swim Club	8:19.27

PHILLIPS 66 NATIONAL DIVING CHAMPIONSHIPS—1996

MEN	Points
1-meter springboard—Dean Panaro, Ft. Lauderdale, Fla.	416.61
3-meter springboard—Mark Lenzi, Bloomington, Ind.	692.67
3-meter springboard synchronized—Kent Ferguson, Miami Beach, Fla., and David Pichler, Ft. Lauderdale, Fla.	326.97
10-meter platform—David Pichler, Ft. Lauderdale, Fla.	622.50
10-meter platform synchronized—Mark Ruiz and Kongzheng Li, Orlando, Fla.	293.13

WOMEN	Points
1-meter springboard—Reyne Borup, Ft. Lauderdale, Fla.	267.66
3-meter springboard—Jenny Keim, Ft. Lauderdale, Fla.	497.97
3-meter springboard synchronized—Kim Stanfield, Long Beach, Calif., and Kristen Walls, San Diego, Calif.	268.80
10-meter platform—Becky Ruehl, Lakeside Park, Ky.	485.13
10-meter platform synchronized—Patty Armstrong, The Woodlands, Texas, and Laura Wilkinson, Spring, Texas	264.06

BOXING

Whether it be called pugilism, prize fighting or boxing, there is no tracing "the Sweet Science" to any definite source. Tales of rivals exchanging blows for fun, fame or money go back to earliest recorded history and classical legend. There was a mixture of boxing and wrestling called the "pancratium" in the ancient Olympic Games and in such contests the rivals belabored one another with hands fortified with heavy leather wrappings that were sometimes studded with metal. More than one Olympic competitor lost his life at this brutal exercise.

There was little law or order in pugilism until Jack Broughton, one of the early champions of England, drew up a set of rules for the game in 1743. Broughton, called "the father of English boxing," also is credited

with having invented boxing gloves. However, these gloves—or "mufflers" as they were called—were used only in teaching "the manly art of self-defense" or in training bouts. All professional championship fights were contested with "bare knuckles" until 1892, when John L. Sullivan lost the heavyweight championship of the world to James J. Corbett in New Orleans in a bout in which both contestants wore regulation gloves.

The Broughton rules were superseded by the London Prize Ring Rules of 1838. The 8th Marquis of Queensberry, with the help of John G. Chambers, put forward the "Queensberry Rules" in 1866, a code that called for gloved contests. Amateurs took quickly to the Queensberry Rules, the professionals slowly.

HISTORY OF WORLD HEAVYWEIGHT CHAMPIONSHIP FIGHTS
(Bouts in which a new champion was crowned)

Date	Where held	Winner, weight (age)	Loser, weight, age	Rounds	Referee
Sept. 7, 1892	New Orleans, La.	James J. Corbett, 178 (26)	John L. Sullivan, 212 (33)	21	Prof. John Duffy
March 17, 1897	Carson City, Nev.	Bob Fitzsimmons, 167 (34)	James J. Corbett, 183 (30)	KO 14	George Siler
June 9, 1899	Coney Island, N.Y.	James J. Jeffries, 206 (24)[1]	Bob Fitzsimmons, 167 (37)	KO 11	George Siler
Feb. 23, 1906	Los Angeles	Tommy Burns, 180 (24)[2]	Marvin Hart, 188 (29)	20	James J. Jeffries
Dec. 26, 1908	Sydney, N.S.W.	Jack Johnson, 196 (30)	Tommy Burns, 176 (27)	KO 14	Hugh McIntosh
April 5, 1915	Havana, Cuba	Jess Willard, 230 (33)	Jack Johnson, 205 1/2 (37)	KO 26	Jack Welch
July 4, 1919	Toledo, Ohio	Jack Dempsey, 187 (24)	Jess Willard, 245 (37)	KO 3	Ollie Pecord
Sept. 23, 1926	Philadelphia	Gene Tunney, 189 (28)[3]	Jack Dempsey, 190 (31)	10	Pop Reilly
June 12, 1930	New York	Max Schmeling, 188 (24)	Jack Sharkey, 197 (27)	WF 4	Jim Crowley
June 21, 1932	Long Island City	Jack Sharkey, 205 (29)	Max Schmeling, 188 (26)	15	Gunboat Smith
June 29, 1933	Long Island City	Primo Carnera, 260 1/2 (26)	Jack Sharkey, 201 (30)	KO 6	Arthur Donovan
June 14, 1934	Long Island City	Max Baer, 209 1/2 (25)	Primo Carnera, 263 1/4 (27)	KO 11	Arthur Donovan
June 13, 1935	Long Island City	Jim Braddock, 193 3/4 (29)	Max Baer, 209 1/2 (26)	15	Jack McAvoy
June 22, 1937	Chicago	Joe Louis, 197 1/4 (23)	Jim Braddock, 197 (31)	KO 8	Tommy Thomas
June 22, 1949	Chicago	Ezzard Charles, 181 3/4 (27)[4]	Joe Walcott, 195 1/2 (35)	15	Davey Miller
Sept. 27, 1950	New York	Ezzard Charles, 184 1/2 (29)[5]	Joe Louis, 218 (36)	15	Mark Conn
July 18, 1951	Pittsburgh	Joe Walcott, 194 (37)	Ezzard Charles, 182 (30)	KO 7	Buck McTiernan
Sept. 23, 1952	Philadelphia	Rocky Marciano, 184 (29)[6]	Joe Walcott, 196 (38)	KO 13	Charley Daggert
Nov. 30, 1956	Chicago	Floyd Patterson, 182 1/4 (21)	Archie Moore, 187 3/4 (42)	KO 5	Frank Sikora
June 26, 1959	New York	Ingemar Johansson, 196 (26)	Floyd Patterson, 182 (24)	KO 3	Ruby Goldstein
June 20, 1960	New York	Floyd Patterson, 190 (25)	Ingemar Johansson, 194 3/4 (27)	KO 5	Arthur Mercante
Sept. 25, 1962	Chicago	Sonny Liston, 214 (28)	Floyd Patterson, 189 (27)	KO 1	Frank Sikora
Feb. 25, 1964	Miami Beach, Fla.	Cassius Clay, 210 (22)[7]	Sonny Liston, 218 (30)	KO 7	Barney Felix
March 4, 1968	New York	Joe Frazier, 204 1/2 (24)[8]	Buster Mathis, 243 1/2 (23)	KO 11	Arthur Mercante
April 27, 1968	Oakland, Calif.	Jimmy Ellis, 197 (28)[9]	Jerry Quarry, 195 (22)	15	Elmer Costa
Feb. 16, 1970	New York	Joe Frazier, 205 (26)[10]	Jimmy Ellis, 201 (29)	KO 5	Tony Perez
Jan. 22, 1973	Kingston, Jamaica	George Foreman, 217 1/2 (24)	Joe Frazier, 214 (29)	KO 2	Arthur Mercante
Oct. 30, 1974	Kinshasa, Zaire	Muhammad Ali, 216 1/2 (32)	George Foreman, 220 (26)	KO 8	Zack Clayton
Feb. 15, 1978	Las Vegas, Nev.	Leon Spinks, 197 (25)	Muhammad Ali, 224 1/2 (36)	15	Howard Buck
June 9, 1978	Las Vegas, Nev.	Larry Holmes, 212 (28)[11]	Ken Norton, 220 (32)	15	Mills Lans
Sept. 15, 1978	New Orleans	Muhammad Ali, 221 (36)[12]	Leon Spinks, 201 (25)	15	Lucien Joubert
Oct. 20, 1979	Pretoria, S. Africa	John Tate, 240 (24)[13]	Gerrie Coetzee, 222 (24)	15	Carlos Berrocal
March 31, 1980	Knoxville, Tenn.	Mike Weaver, 207 1/2 (27)	John Tate, 232 (25)	KO 15	Ernesto Magana Ansorena
Dec. 10, 1982	Las Vegas, Nev.	Michael Dokes, 216 (24)	Mike Weaver, 209 1/2 (30)	KO 1	Joey Curtis
Sept. 23, 1983	Richfield, Ohio	Gerrie Coetzee, 215 (28)	Michael Dokes, 217 (25)	KO 10	Tony Perez
March 9, 1984	Las Vegas, Nev.	Tim Witherspoon, 220 1/2 (26)[14]	Greg Page, 239 1/2 (25)	12	Mills Lane
August 31, 1984	Las Vegas, Nev.	Pinklon Thomas, 216 (26)	Tim Witherspoon, 217 (26)	12	Richard Steele
Nov. 9, 1984	Las Vegas, Nev.	Larry Holmes, 221 1/2 (35)[15]	James Smith 227 (31)	KO 12	Dave Pearl
Dec. 1, 1984	Sun City, S. Africa	Greg Page, 236 (25)[16]	Gerry Coetzee, 217 (29)	KO 8	unavailable
April 29, 1985	Buffalo, N.Y.	Tony Tubbs, 229 (26)[16]	Greg Page, 239 1/2 (26)	15	unavailable.
Sept. 21, 1985	Las Vegas, Nev.	Michael Spinks, 200 (29)	Larry Holmes, 221 (35)	15	Carlos Padilla
Jan. 17, 1986	Atlanta, Ga.	Tim Witherspoon, 227 (28)	Tony Tubbs, 229 (27)	15	unavailable
Nov. 23, 1986	Las Vegas, Nev.	Mike Tyson, 217 (20)[17]	Trevor Berbick, 220 (29)	KO 2	unavailable
Dec. 12, 1986	New York, N.Y.	James Smith, 230 (33)[16]	Tim Witherspoon, 217 (25)	KO 1	unavailable
March 7, 1987	Las Vegas, Nev.	Mike Tyson, 217 (20)[16]	James Smith, 230 (33)	12	unavailable
Feb. 10, 1990	Tokyo	James "Buster" Douglas,[18] 231 1/2 (29)	Mike Tyson (220) (23)	KO 10	Octavio Meyrom
Oct. 25, 1990	Las Vegas, Nev.	Evander Holyfield, 208 (28)	James "Buster" Douglas, 246 (30)	KO 3	Mills Lane
Nov. 13, 1992	Las Vegas, Nev.	Riddick Bowe,[19] 235 (25)	Evander Holyfield, 205 (30)	12	Joe Cortez

Date	Where held	Winner, weight (age)	Loser, weight, age	Rounds	Referee
Nov. 6, 1993	Las Vegas, Nev.	Evander Holyfield, 217 (30)	Riddick Bowe, 246 (26)	12	Mills Lane
April 22, 1994	Las Vegas, Nev.	Michael Moorer, 214 (26)	Evander Holyfield[20], 214 (31)	12	unavailable
Sept. 24, 1994	London, England	Oliver McCall,[21] 228 (29)	Lennox Lewis, 238	2	Lupe Garcia
Nov. 5, 1994	Las Vegas, Nev.	George Foreman,[22] 250 (45)	Michael Moorer, 222 (26)	10	unavailable
April 8, 1995	Las Vegas, Nev.	Bruce Seldon,[23] 232 (28)	Tony Tucker, 238 (36)	7	unavailable
Dec. 9, 1995	Stuttgart, Ger.	Frans Botha[24], 227 (28)	Axel Schulz, 222 (27)	12	unavailable
March 16, 1996	Las Vegas, Nev.	Mike Tyson[25], 220 (29)	Frank Bruno, 247 (34)	3	Mills Lane
June 22, 1996	Dortmund, Ger.	Michael Moorer, 222 (28)	Axel Schulz, 222 (27)	12	unavailable

1. Jeffries retired as champion in March 1905. He named Marvin Hart and Jack Root as leading contenders and agreed to referee their fight in Reno, Nev., on July 3, 1905, with the stipulation that he would term the winner the champion. Hart 190 (28), knocked out Root, 171 (29), in the 12th round. 2. Burns claimed the title after defeating Hart. 3. Tunney retired as champion after defeating Tom Heeney on July 26, 1928. 4. After Louis announced his retirement as champion on March 1, 1949, Charles won recognition from the National Boxing Association as champion by defeating Walcott. 5. Charles gained undisputed recognition as champion by defeating Louis, who came out of retirement. 6. Retired as champion April 27, 1956. 7. The World Boxing Association later withdrew its recognition of Clay as champion and declared the winner of a bout between Ernie Terrell and Eddie Machen would gain its version of the title. Terrell, 199 (25), won a 15–round decision from Machen, 192 (32), in Chicago on March 5, 1965. Clay, 212 1/4 (25) and Terrell, 212 1/2 (27) met in Houston on Feb. 6, 1967, Clay winning a 15–round decision. 8. Winner recognized by New York, Massachusetts, Maine, Illinois, Texas and Pennsylvania to fill vacated title when Clay was stripped of championship for failing to accept U. S. Induction. 9. Bout was final of eight–man tournament to fill Clay's place and is recognized by World Boxing Association. 10. Bout settled controversy over title. 11. Holmes won World Boxing Council title after WBC had withdrawn recognition of Spinks, March 18, 1978, and awarded its title to Norton. WBC said Spinks had reneged on agreement to fight Norton. 12. Ali regained World Boxing Association championship. 13. Tate won WBA title after Ali retired and left it vacant. 14. Tim Witherspoon and Greg Page fought for the WBC heavyweight title vacated by Larry Holmes, who could not come to agreement on a deal to fight Page, the No. 1 contender. Holmes declared he would fight under the banner of the International Boxing Federation. Several dates were set and postponed for fights between Holmes and Gerry Coetzee, the WBA champ, the latest being Nov. 16, 1984. 15. First fight under banner of International Boxing Federation. 16. New W.B.A. champion. 17. New W.B.C. champion. 18. New undisputed champion. 19. The W.B.C. stripped Bowe of its recognition of the title in December 1992 and named Lennox Lewis champion. 20. After the loss, Holyfield retired. 21. New WBC champion. Lennox Lewis had been named champion in 1992 and had won three title defenses before losing to McCall. 22. For combined WBA/IBF titles. Later WBA stripped Foreman of title for failing to fight no. 1 contender Tony Tucker. IBF also stripped Foreman on June 29, 1995. 23. New WBA champion. 24. Botha later tested positive for steroids and was stripped of the title. 25. New WBC champ. 26. New IBF champ.

OTHER WORLD BOXING TITLEHOLDERS

(Through June 25, 1996)

Light Heavyweight
1903	Jack Root, George Gardner
1903–05	Bob Fitzsimmons
1905–12	Philadelphia Jack O'Brien[1]
1912–16	Jack Dillon
1916–20	Battling Levinsky
1920–22	Georges Carpentier
1923	Battling Siki
1923–25	Mike McTigue
1925–26	Paul Berlenbach
1926–27	Jack Delaney[2]
1927	Mike McTigue
1927–29	Tommy Loughran
1930	Jimmy Slattery
1930–34	Maxie Rosenbloom
1934–35	Bob Olin
1935–39	John Henry Lewis
1939	Melio Bettina
1939–41	Billy Conn[2]
1941	Anton Christoforidis (NBA)
1941–48	Gus Lesnevich
1948–50	Freddie Mills
1950–52	Joey Maxim
1952–61	Archie Moore[3]
1961–63	Harold Johnson
1963–65	Willie Pastrano
1965–66	José Torres
1966–67	Dick Tiger
1968	Dick Tiger, Bob Foster
1969–70	Bob Foster
1971	Vicente Rondon (WBA), Bob!Foster (WBC)
1972-73	Bob Foster (WBA, WBC)
1974	John Conteh (WBC), Bob Foster (WBC)[1,4]
1975–76	Victor Galindez (WBA), John Conteh (WBC)

1977	Victor Galindez (WBA), John Conteh (WBC)[4] Miguel Cuello (WBC)
1978	Victor Galindez (WBA), Mike Rossman (WBA), Miguel Cuello (WBC) Mate Parlov (WBC), Marvin Johson (WBC)
1979	Mike Rossman (WBA), Victor Galindez (WBA), Marvin Johnson (WBC), Matthew (Franklin) Saad Muhammad (WBC)
1980	Matthew Saad Muhammad (WBC), Marvin Johnson (WBA), Eddie (Gregory), Mustafa Muhammad (WBA)
1981	Matthew Saad Muhammad (WBC), Eddie Mustafa Muhammad (WBA), Michael Spinks (WBA), Dwight Braxton (WBC)
1982	Dwight Braxton (WBC), Michael Spinks (WBA)
1983	Michael Spinks (undisputed)
1984	Michael Spinks (undisputed)
1985	Michael Spinks (undisputed)[5]
1986	Marvin Johnson (WBA) Dennis Andries (WBC)
1987	Thomas Hearns (WBC), Virgil Hill (WBA), Bobby Czyz (IBF)
1988	Charles Williams (IBF), Virgil Hill (WBA),

	Donny LaLonde (WBC), Sugar Ray Leonard (WBC)
1989	Dennis Andries (WBC), Virgil Hill (WBA), Charles Williams (IBF), Jeff Harding (WBC)
1990	Virgil Hill (WBA), Charles Williams (IBF), Jeff Harding (WBC), Dennis Andries (WBC)
1991	Virgil Hall (WBA), Thomas Hearns (WBA), Dennis Andries (WBC), Charles Williams (IBF)
1992	Charlie Williams (IBF), James Waring (IBF), Jeff Harding (WBC)
1993	Virgil Hill (WBA), Jeff Harding (WBC), Henry Maske (IBF)
1994	Virgil Hill (WBA), Mike McCallum (WBC), Henry Maske (IBF)
1995	Virgil Hill (WBA), Fabrice Tiozzo (WBC), Henry Maske (IBF)
1996	Virgil Hill (WBA), Fabrice Tiozzo (WBC), Henry Maske (IBF)

1. Retired. 2. Abandoned title. 3. NBA withdrew recognition in 1961, New York Commission in 1962; recognized thereafter only by California and Europe. 4. WBC withdrew recognition. 5. Spinks relinquished title in 1985 to fight for heavyweight title.

Middleweight

1867–72 Tom Chandler
1872–81 George Rooke
1881–82 Mike Donovan[1]
1884–91 Jack (Nonpareil) Dempsey
1891–97 Bob Fitzsimmons[2]
1908 Stanley Ketchel, Billy Papke
1908–10 Stanley Ketchel[3]
1913 Frank Klaus
1913–14 George Chip
1914–17 Al McCoy
1917–20 Mike O'Dowd
1920–23 Johnny Wilson
1923–26 Harry Greb
1926 Tiger Flowers
1926–31 Mickey Walker[2]
1931–41 Gorilla Jones, Ben Jeby, Marcel Thil, Lou Brouillard, Vince Dundee, Teddy Yarosz, Babe Risko, Freddy Steele, Al Hostak, Solly Kreiger, Fred Apostoli, Ceferino Garcia, Ken Overlin, Billy Soose, Tony Zale[4]
1941–47 Tony Zale
1947–48 Rocky Graziano
1948 Tony Zale
1948–49 Marcel Cerdan
1949–51 Jake LaMotta
1952 Ray Robinson, Randy Turpin
1951–52 Ray Robinson[1]
1953–55 Carl Olson
1955–57 Ray Robinson[5]
1957 Gene Fullmer, Ray Robinson
1957–58 Carmen Basilio
1958–60 Ray Robinson[6]
1960–61 Paul Pender[7]
1959–62 Gene Fullmer (NBA)
1961–62 Terry Downes[1]
1962 Paul Pender[1]
1962–63 Dick Tiger
1963–65 Joey Giardello
1965–66 Dick Tiger
1966 Emile Griffith
1967 Nino Benvenuti, Emile Griffith
1968 Emile Griffith, Nino Benvenuti
1969 Nino Benvenuti
1970 Nino Benvenuti, Carlos Monzon
1971–73 Carlos Monzon
1974–75 Carlos Monzon (WBA), Rodrigo Valdez (WBC)
1976 Carlos Monzon (WBA, WBC), Rodrigo Valdez (WBC)
1977 Carlos Monzon (WBA,WBC)[1], Rodrigo Valdez (WBA, WBC)
1978 Rodrigo Valdez, Hugo Corro
1979 Hugo Corro, Vito Antuofermo
1980 Vito Antuofermo, Alan Minter, Marvin Hagler
1981 Marvin Hagler
1982–86 Marvelous Marvin Hagler (undisputed)
1987 Marvin Hagler (undisputed) Sugar Ray Leonard (undisputed)
1988 Sumbu Kalambay (WBA), Thomas Hearns (WBC), Iran Barkley (WBC), Frank Tate (IBF), Michael Nunn (IBF), James Kinchen (NABF)

1989 Michael Nunn (IBF), Mike McCallum (WBA), Iran Barkley (WBC), Roberto Duran (WBC)
1990 Michael McCallum (WBA), Michael Nunn (IBF), Iran Barkley (WBC)
1991 Michael Nunn (IBF), James Toney (IBF), Michael McCallum (WBA)
1992 James Toney (IBF), Julian Jackson (WBC), Reggie Johnson (WBA)
1993 Reggie Johnson (WBA), Gerald McClellan (WBC), Roy Jones (IBF)
1994 Julian Jackson (WBA), Gerald McClellan (WBC), Roy Jones (IBF)
1995 Jorge Castro (WBA), Julian Jackson (WBC), Bernard Hopkins (IBF)
1996 William Joppy (WBA), Keith Holmes (WBC), Bernard Hopkins (IBF)

1. Retired. 2. Abandoned title. 3. Died. 4. National Boxing Association and New York Boxing Commission disagreed on champions. Those listed were accepted by one or the other until Zale gained world–wide recognition. 5. Ended retirement in 1954. 6. NBA withdrew recognition. 7. Recognized by New York, Massachusetts, and Europe.

Welterweight

1892–94 Mysterious Billy Smith
1894–96 Tommy Ryan
1896 Kid McCoy[2]
1896–
1900 Mysterious Billy Smith
1900 Rube Ferns
1900–01 Matty Matthews
1901 Ruby Ferns
1901–04 Joe Walcott
1904 Dixie Kid[2]
1904–06 Joe Walcott
1906–07 Honey Mellody
1907 Mike (Twin) Sullivan[2]
1915–19 Ted Lewis
1919–22 Jack Britton
1922–26 Mickey Walker
1926–27 Pete Latzo
1927–29 Joe Dundee
1929–30 Jackie Fields
1930 Young Jack Thompson
1930–31 Tommy Freeman
1931 Young Jack Thompson
1931–32 Lou Brouillard
1932–33 Jackie Fields
1933 Young Corbett 3rd
1933–34 Jimmy McLarnin, Barney Ross
1934–35 Jimmy McLarnin
1935–38 Barney Ross
1938–40 Henry Armstrong
1940–41 Fritzie Zivic
1941–46 Freddie Cochrane
1946 Marty Servo[1]
1946–51 Ray Robinson[2]
1951 Johnny Bratton (NBA)
1951–54 Kid Gavilan
1954–55 Johnny Saxton
1955 Tony DeMarco
1955–56 Carmen Basilio

1956 Johnny Saxton
1956–57 Carmen Basilio[2]
1958 Virgil Akins
1959–60 Don Jordan
1960–61 Benny (Kid) Paret
1961 Emile Griffith
1961–62 Benny (Kid) Paret
1962–63 Emile Griffith, Luis Rodriguez
1963–66 Emile Griffith[2]
1966-69 Curtis Cokes
1969 Curtis Cokes, José Napoles
1970 José Napoles, Billy Backus
1971 Billy Backus, José Napoles
1972–74 José Napoles
1975 José Napoles (WBA, WBC),[3] Angel Espada (WBA), John Stracey (WBC)
1976 Angel Espada (WBA), José Cuevas (WBA), John Stracey (WBC), Carlos Palomino
1977–78 José Cuevas (WBA), Carlos Palomino (WBC)
1979 José Cuevas (WBA), Carlos Palomino (WBC), Wilfredo Benitez (WBC)
1980 José Cuevas (WBA), Ray Leonard (WBC), Roberto Duran (WBC), Thomas Hearns (WBA)
1981 Ray Leonard (WBC), Thomas Hearns (WBA), Ray Leonard (WBC,WBA)
1982 Ray Leonard
1983–85 Donald Curry (WBA)
1983–85 Milton McCrory (WBC)
1985–86 Donald Curry (undisputed)
1987 Mark Breland (WBA) Marlon Starling (WBA) Lloyd Honeychan (IBF)
1988 Marlon Starling (WBA), Tomas Molinares (WBA), Lloyd Honeyghan (WBC), Simon Brown (IBF)
1989 Mark Breland (WBA), Marlon Starling (WBC), Simon Brown (IBF)
1990 Mark Breland (WBA), Aaron Davis (WBA), Simon Brown (IBF), Marlon Starling (WBC), Maurice Blocker (WBC)
1991 Meldrick Taylor (WBA), Simon Brown (IBF, WBC)
1992 Meldrick Taylor (WBA), James "Buddy" McGirt (WBC), Maurice Blocker (IBF)
1993 Cristianto Espana (WBA), Pernell Whitaker (WBC), Felix Trinidad (IBF)
1994 Ike Quartey (WBA), Pernell Whitaker (WBC), Felix Trinidad (IBF)
1995 Ike Quartey (WBA), Pernell Whitaker (WBC), Felix Trinidad (IBF)
1996 Ike Quartey (WBA), Pernell Whitaker (WBC), Felix Trinidad (IBF)

1. Retired. 2. Abandoned title. 3. WBA withdrew recognition.

Lightweight
1869–99 Kid Lavigne
1899–
1902　Frank Erne
1902–08 Joe Gans
1908–10 Battling Nelson
1910–12 Ad Wolgast
1912–14 Willie Ritchie
1914–17 Freddy Welsh
1917–25 Benny Leonard[1]
1925　Jimmy Goodrich
1925–26 Rocky Kansas
1926–30 Sammy Mandell
1930　Al Singer
1930–33 Tony Canzoneri
1933–35 Barney Ross[2]
1935–36 Tony Canzoneri
1936–38 Lou Ambers
1938–39 Henry Armstrong
1939–40 Lou Ambers
1940–41 Lew Jenkins
1941–42 Sammy Angott[1]
1943–47 Beau Jack (N.Y.), Bob Montgomery (N.Y.), Sammy Angott (NBA), Juan Zurita (NBA), Ike Williams (NBA)
1947–51 Ike Williams
1951–52 James Carter
1952　Lauro Salas
1952–54 James Carter
1954　Paddy DeMarco
1954–55 James Carter
1955–56 Wallace Smith
1956–62 Joe Brown
1962–65 Carlos Ortiz
1965　Ismael Laguna
1965–68 Carlos Ortiz
1968　Teo Cruz
1969　Teo Cruz, Mando Ramos
1970　Mando Ramos, Ismael Laguna, Ken Buchanan
1971　Ken Buchanan (WBA), Mando Ramos (WBC), Pedro Carrasco (WBC)
1972　Ken Buchanan (WBA), Roberto Duran (WBA), Pedro Carrasco (WBC), Mando Ramos (WBC), Chango Carmona (WBC), Rodolfo Gonzalez (WBC)
1973　Roberto Duran (WBA), Rodolfo Gonzalez (WBC)
1974　Roberto Duran (WBA), Rodolfo Gonzalez (WBC), Guts Ishimatsu (WBC)
1975　Roberto Duran (WBA), Guts Ishimatsu (WBC)
1976　Roberto Duran (WBA), Guts Ishimatsu (WBC), Esteban!De Jesus (WBC)
1977　Roberto Duran (WBA), Esteban De Jesus (WBC)
1978　Roberto Duran (WBA, WBC)
1979　Roberto Duran[2], Jim Watt (WBC), Ernesto Espana (WBA)
1980　Ernesto Espana (WBA), Hilmer Kenty (WBA), Jim Watt (WBC)
1981　Hilmer Kenty (WBA), Sean O'Grady (WBA), James Watt (WBC), Alexis Arguello (WBC), Arturo Frias

1982　Arturo Frias (WBA), Ray Mancini (WBA), Alexis Arguello (WBC)
1983　Edwin Rosario (WBC), Ray Mancini (WBA)
1984　Edwin Rosario (WBC), Livingstone Bramble (WBA)
1985　Jose Luis Ramirez (WBC) Hector Camacho (WBC) Livingstone Bramble (WBA)
1986　Hector Camacho (WBC) Livingstone Bramble (WBA) Jim Paul (IBF)
1987　Edwin Rosario (WBA) Jose Luis Ramirez (WBC), Greg Haugen (IBF)
1988　Jose Luis Ramirez (WBC), Julio Cesar Chavez (WBA), Greg Haugen (IBF), Julius Cesar Chavez (WBC & WBA title unified)
1989　Pernell Whitaker (IBF, WBC), Edwin Rosario
1990　Pernell Whitaker (IBF, WBC) Juan Nazario (WBA)
1991　Pernell Whitaker (IBF, WBA, WBC)
1992　Pernell Whitaker (IBF, WBA, WBC)[3], Joey Gamache (WBA).
1993　Dingaan Thobela (WBA), Angel Gonzalez (WBC), Freddie Pendleton (IBF)
1994　Orzubek Nazarov (WBA), Angel Gonzalez (WBC), Rafael Ruelas (IBF)
1995　Orzubek Nazarov (WBA), Angel Gonzalez (WBC), Oscar de la Hoya (IBF)
1996　Gusshie Nazarov (WBA), Jean Baptiste Mendy (WBC), Phillip Holiday (IBF)

1. Retired. 2. Abandoned title. 3. Moving up in weight class, so resigned titles.

Featherweight
1889　Dal Hawkins[1]
1890　Billy Murphy
1892–
1900　George Dixon
1900–01 Terry McGovern
1901　Young Corbett[1]
1901–12 Abe Attell
1912–23 Johnny Kilbane
1923　Eugene Criqui
1923–25 Johnny Dundee[1]
1925–27 Louis (Kid) Kaplan[1]
1927–28 Benny Bass
1928　Tony Canzoneri
1928–29 Andre Routis
1929–32 Battling Battalino[1]
1932　Tommy Paul (NBA), Kid Chocolate (N.Y.)
1933–36 Freddie Miller
1936–37 Petey Sarron
1937–38 Henry Armstrong[1]
1938–40 Joey Archibald
1940–41 Harry Jefra, Joey Archibald
1941–42 Chalky Wright
1942–48 Willie Pep

1949–50 Willie Pep
1950–57 Sandy Saddler
1957–59 Kid Bassey
1959–63 Davey Moore
1963–64 Sugar Ramos
1964–67 Vicente Saldivar[2]
1968　Howard Winstone, José Legra,[3] Paul Rojas (WBA), Sho Saijo (WBA)
1969　Sho Saijo (WBA), Johnny Famechon[3]
1970　Sho Saijo (WBA), Johnny Famechon,[3] Vicente Salvidar,[3] Kuniaki Shibata[3]
1971　Sho Saijo (WBA), Antonio Gomez (WBA), Kuniaki Shibata (WBC)
1972　Antonio Gomez (WBA), Ernesto Marcel (WBA), Kuniaki Shibata (WBC), Clemente Sanchez (WBC), José Legra (WBC)
1973　Ernesto Marcel (WBA), José Legra (WBC), Eder Jofre (WBC)
1974　Ernesto Marcel (WBA)[2], Ruben Olivares (WBA), Alexis Arguello (WBA), Eder Jofre (WBC), Bobby Chacon (WBC)
1975　Alexis Arguello (WBA), Bobby Chacon (WBC), Ruben Olivares (WBC), David Kotey (WBC)
1976　Alexis Arguello (WBA),[2] David Kotey (WBC), Danny Lopez (WBC)
1977　Rafael Ortega (WBA), Danny Lopez (WBC)
1978　Rafael Ortega (WBA), Cecilio Lastra (WBA), Eusebio Pedroza (WBA), Danny Lopez (WBC)
1979　Eusebio Pedroza (WBA), Danny Lopez (WBC)
1980　Eusebio Pedroza (WBA), Danny Lopez (WBC), Salvador Sanchez (WBC)
1981　Eusebio Pedroza (WBA), Salvador Sanchez (WBC)
1982　Eusebio Pedroza (WBA), Salvador Sanchez (WBC)[4]
1983　Juan Laporte (WBC), Eusebio Pedroza (WBA)
1984　Wilfred Gomez (WBC), Eusebio Pedroza (WBA)
1985　Eusebio Pedroza (WBA) Barry McGuigan (WBA) Azumah Nelson (WBC)
1986　Barry McGuigan (WBA) Stevie Cruz (WBA) Azumah Nelson (WBC)
1987　Azumah Nelson (WBC) Antonio Esparragoza (WBA)
1988　Calvin Grove (IBF), Jorge Paez (IBF), Antonio Esparragoza (WBA), Jeff Fenech (WBC)
1989　Jorge Paez (IBF), Antonio Esparragoza (WBA), Jeff Fenech (WBC)
1990　Marcos Villasana (WBC), Antonio Esparragoza

1991	Park Young-Kyun (WBA), Troy Dorsey (IBF), Marcos Villagana (WBC)
1992	Paul Hodkinson (WBC), Manuel Medina (IBF), Yung Kyun Park (WBA)
1993	Yung-Kyun Park (WBA), Goyo Vargas (WBC), Tom Johnson (IBF)
1994	Eloy Rojas (WBA), Kevin Kelley (WBC), Tom Johnson (IBF)
1995	Elroy Rojas (WBA), Alejandro Gonzalez (WBC), Tom Johnson (IBF)
1996	Wilfredo Vázquez (WBA), Luisito Espinosa (WBC), Tom Johnson (IBF)

1. Abandoned title. 2. Retired. 3. Recognized in Europe, Mexico, and Orient. 4. Killed in auto accident.

Bantamweight

1890–92	George Dixon[1]
1894–99	Jimmy Barry[2]
1899–	
1900	Terry McGovern[1]
1901	Harry Harris[1]
1902–03	Harry Forbes
1903–04	Frankie Neil
1904	Joe Bowker[1]
1905–07	Jimmy Walsh[1]
1910–14	Johnny Coulon
1914–17	Kid Williams
1917–20	Pete Herman
1920	Joe Lynch
1920–21	Joe Lynch, Pete Herman, Johnny Buff
1922	Johnny Buff, Joe Lynch
1923	Joe Lynch
1924	Joe Lynch, Abe Goldstein
1924	Abe Goldstein, Eddie (Cannonball) Martin
1925	Eddie (Cannonball) Martin, Charlie (Phil) Rosenberg[3]
1927–28	Bud Taylor (NBA)[1]
1929–34	Al Brown
1935	Al Brown, Baltazar Sangchili
1936	Baltazar Sangchili, Tony Marino, Sixto Escobar
1937	Sixto Escobar, Harry Jeffra
1938	Harry Jeffra, Sixto Escobar
1939–40	Sixto Escobar[2]
1940–42	Lou Salica
1942–46	Manuel Ortiz
1947	Manuel Ortiz, Harold Dade
1948–50	Manuel Ortiz
1950–52	Vic Toweel
1952–54	Jimmy Carruthers[2]
1954–55	Robert Cohen
1956	Robert Cohen, Mario D'Agata, Raul Macias (NBA)
1957	Mario D'Agata, Alphonse Halimi
1958–59	Alphonse Halimi
1959–60	Jose Becerra[2]
1960–61	Alphonse Halimi[4]
1961–62	Johnny Caldwell[4]
1961–65	Eder Jofre
1965–68	Masahika (Fighting) Harada
1968	Masahika (Fighting) Harada, Lionel Rose

1969	Lionel Rose, Ruben Olivares
1970	Ruben Olivares, Chucho Castillo
1971	Chucho Castillo, Ruben Olivares
1972	Ruben Olivares, Rafael Herrera, Enrique Pinder
1973	Enrique Pinder (WBA), Romeo Anaya (WBA), Arnold Taylor (WBA), Rodolfo Martinez (WBC), Rafael Herrera
1974	Arnold Taylor (WBA), Soo Hwan Hong (WBA), Rafael Herrera (WBC), Rodolfo Martinez (WBC)
1975	Soo Hwan Hong (WBA), Alfonso Zamora (WBA), Rodolfo Martinez (WBC)
1976	Alfonso Zamora (WBA), Rodolfo Martinez (WBC), Carlos Zarate (WBC)
1977	Alfonso Zamora (WBA), Jorge Lujan (WBA), Carlos Zarate (WBC)
1978	Jorge Lujan (WBA), Carlos Zarate (WBC)
1979	Jorge Lujan (WBA), Carlos Zarate (WBC), Lupe Pintor (WBC)
1980	Jorge Lujan (WBA), Lupe Pintor (WBC), Julian Solis (WBA), Jeff Chandler (WBA)
1981	Lupe Pintor (WBC), Jeff Chandler (WBA)
1982	Lupe Pintor (WBC), Jeff Chandler (WBA)
1983	Jeff Chandler (WBA), Albert Dauila (WBC)
1984	Richie Sandqual (WBA), Albert Dauila (WBC)
1985	Richard Sandoval (WBA) Daniel Zaragoza (WBC) Miguel Lora (WBC)
1986	Richard Sandoval (WBA) Bernardo Pinango (WBA) Jeff Fenech (IBF)
1987	Bernardo Pinango (WBA) Takuya Muguruma (WBA) Miguel Lora (WBC)
1988	Wilfred Vasquez (WBA), Jibaro Perez (WBC), Moon Sung–gil (WBA) Orlando Canizales (IBF)
1989	Jibaro Perez (WBC), Moon Sung–gil (WBA), Orlando Canizales (IBF) Kaokor Galaxy (WBA), Luis Espinosa (WBA)
1990	Orlando Canizales (IBF), Jibaro Perez (WBC), Luis Espinosa (WBA)
1991	Greg Richardson (WBC), Orlando Canizales (IBF), Luis Espinosa (WBA)
1992	Joichiro Tatsuyoshi (WBC), Victor Manuel Rabanales (WBC), Eddie Cook (WBA), Orlando Gonzales (IBF)
1993	Jorge Julio (WBA), Byun-Jong-il (WBC), Orlando Canizales (IBF)

1994	John Michael Johnson (WBA), Yasuei Yakushiji (WBC), Orlando Canizales (IBF)
1995	Daorun Chuwatang (WBA), Yasuei Yakushiji (WBC), Mbulelo Botile (IBF)
1996	Nana Konadu (WBA), Wayne McCullough (WBC), Mbulelo Bottle (IBF)

1. Abandoned title. 2. Retired. 3. Deprived of title for failing to make weight. 4. Recognized in Europe.

Flyweight

1916–23	Jimmy Wilde
1923–25	Pancho Villa[1]
1925	Frankie Genaro
1925–27	Fidel La Barba[2]
1927–31	Corporal Izzy Schwartz, Frankie Genaro, Emile (Spider) Pladner, Midget Wolgast, Young Perez[3]
1932–35	Jackie Brown
1935–38	Bennie Lynch[4]
1939	Peter Kane[4]
1943–47	Jackie Paterson[1]
1947–50	Rinty Monaghan[2]
1950	Terry Allen
1950–52	Dado Marino
1952–54	Yoshio Shirai
1954–60	Pascual Perez
1960–62	Pone Kingpetch
1962–63	Masahika (Fighting) Harada
1963–64	Hiroyuki Ebihara
1964–65	Pone Kingpetch
1965–66	Salvatore Burrini
1966	Walter McGown, Chartchai Chionoi
1966–68	Charchai Chionoi
1969	Bernabe Villacampa, Efran Torres (WBA)
1970	Bernabe Villacampa, Chartchai Chionoi, Erbito Salavarria, Berkrerk Chartvanchai (WBA) Masao Ohba (WBA)
1971	Masao Ohba (WBA), Erbito Salavarria (WBC)
1972	Masao Ohba (WBA), Erbito Salavarria (WBC), Betulio Gonzalez (WBC), Venice Borkorsor (WBC)
1973	Masao Ohba (WBA), Chartchai Chionoi (WBA), Venice Borkorsor (WBC), Betulio Gonzalez (WBC)
1974	Chartchai Chionoi (WBA), Susumu Hanagata (WBA), Betulio Gonzalez (WBC), Shoji Oguma (WBC)
1975	Susumu Hanagata (WBA), Erbito Salavarria (WBA), Shoji Oguma (WBC), Miguel Canto (WBC)
1976	Erbito Salavarria (WBA), Alfonso Lopez (WBA), Guty Espadas (WBA), Miguel Canto (WBC)
1977	Guty Espadas (WBA), Miguel Canto (WBC)

1978	Guty Espadas (WBA), Betulio Gonzalez (WBA), Miguel Canto (WBC)	
1979	Betulio Gonzalez (WBA), Miguel Canto (WBC), Park Chan–Hee (WBC)	
1980	Luis Ibarra (WBA), Kim Tae Shik (WBA), Park Chan–Hee (WBC), Shoji Oguma (WBC)	
1983	Frank Cedeno (WBC), Santos Lacia (WBA)	
1984	Koji Kobayashy (WBA), Gabriel Bernal (WBC), Santos Laciar (WBA)	
1985	Sot Chitlada (WBC) Santos Laciar (WBA)	
1986	Hilario Zapata (WBA) Julio Cesar–Chevez (WBC)	
1987	Shin Hi Sop (IBF) Chang Ho Choi (IBF) Sot Chitlada (WBC)	

1988 Sot Chitlada (WBC), Kim Young Kang (WBC), Duke McKenzie (IBF), Fidel Bassa (WBA)
1989 Kim Young–gang (WBC), Sot Chitlada (WBC), Lee Yol–woo (WBA), Duke McKenzie (IBF), Dave McAuley (IBF) Jesus Rojas (WBA)
1990 Sot Chitlada (WBC), Kim Bong–Jung (WBA), Lee Yul–woo (IBF), Dave McAuley (IBF), Leopard Tamakuma (WBA)
1991 Muangchai Kittasem (WBC), Kim–Young-Kang (WBC), Elvis Alvarez (WBA), Dave McAuley (IBF)

1992 Kim Young-Kang (WBA), Yuri Arbachakov (WBC), Rodolfo Blanco (IBF)
1993 David Griman (WBA), Yuri Arbachakov (WBC), P. Sitbangprachan (IBF)
1994 Saen Sor Ploenchit (WBA), Yuri Arbachakov (WBC), Humberto Gonzalez (IBF)
1995 Saen Sor Ploenchit (WBA), Yuri Arbachakov (WBC), Humberto Gonzalez (IBF)
1996 Saen Sor Ploenchit (WBA), Yuri Arbachakov (WBC), Mark Johnson (IBF)

1. Died. 2. Retired. 3. Claimants to NBA and New York Commission titles. 4. Abandoned title.

WEIGHTLIFTING

U.S. WEIGHTLIFTING FEDERATION

MEN'S NATIONAL CHAMPIONSHIPS
(March 1–3, 1996, Shreveport, La.)

	Snatch	C&J[1]	Total[2]
54 kg—Chad Ikei	97.5	125.0	222.5
59 kg—LeGrand Sakamaki	105.0	127.5	232.5
64 kg—Thanh Nguyen	115.0	157.5	272.5
70 kg—Tim McRae	140.0	170.0	310.0
76 kg—David Santillo	135.0	170.0	305.0
83 kg—Dean Goad	135.0	177.5	312.5
91 kg—Tom Gough	160.0	190.0	350.0
99 kg—Pete Kelley	162.5	190.0	352.5
108 kg—Robert Wentlejewski	140.0	182.5	322.5
108+ kg—Mark Henry	180.0	220.0	400.0

1. Clean and jerk. 2. All results in kilograms.

WOMEN'S NATIONAL CHAMPIONSHIPS
(March 1–3, 1996, Shreveport, La.)

	Snatch	C&J[1]	Total
46 kg—Sibby Flowers	60.0	80.0	140.0
50 kg—Tara Nott	50.0	77.5	127.5
54 kg—Robin Goad	77.5	90.0	167.5
59 kg—Christina Wilson	72.5	95.0	167.5
64 kg—Lea Rentmeester	85.0	107.5	192.5
70 kg—Kerri Hanebrink	85.0	100.0	185.0
76 kg—Stacey Ketchum	85.0	112.5	197.5
83 kg—Decia Stenzel	92.5	107.5	200.0
83+ kg—Vikki Scaffe	87.5	105.0	192.5

WRESTLING

N.C.A.A. CHAMPIONSHIPS—1996

Division I
118 lb—Sheldon Thomas, Clarion dec. Jason Nurre, Iowa State, 6–4
126 lb—Sanshiro Abe, Penn State, dec. Dwight Hinson, Iowa State, 6–5
134 lb—Cary Kolat, Lock Haven, dec. Steve St. John, Arizona State, 5–2
142 lb—Bill Zadick, Iowa, dec. John Hughes, Penn State, 4–2
150 lb—Chris Bono, Iowa State, dec. Charlie Becks, Ohio State, 6–3
158 lb—Joe Williams, Iowa, dec. Ernest Benion, Ill., 9–8
167 lb—Daryl Weber, Iowa, inj. Mark Branch, Oklahoma State, 2:30
177 lb—Les Gutches, Oregon State, dec. Reese Andy, Wyoming, 8–2
190 lb—John Kading, Oklahoma, dec. Paschal Duru, California–Bakersfield, 7–3
275 lb—Jeff Walter, Wisconsin, dec. Justin Harty, North Carolina, 3–2

Team Standings
1. Iowa, 122.50; 2. Iowa State, 78.50; 3. California–Bakersfield, 66.00; 4. Penn State, 65.00; 5. Nebraska, 61.00

WORLD WRESTLING CHAMPIONSHIPS—1995*
(Aug. 10–13, 1995, Atlanta, Ga.)

Freestyle
105.5 lb (48 kg)—Vugar Orudjev, Russia
114.5 lb (52 kg)—Valentin Jordanov, Bulgaria
125.5 lb (57 kg)—Terry Brands, United States
136.5 lb (62 kg)—Elbrus Tedeev, Ukraine
149.5 lb (68 kg)—Arayik Gevorkian, Armenia
163.0 lb (74 kg)—Buvaisa Saitev, Russia
180.5 lb (82 kg)—Kevin Jackson, United States
198.0 lb (90 kg)—Rasoul Khadem, Iran
220.0 lb (100 kg)—Kurt Angle, United States
286 lb (130 kg)—Bruce Baumgartner, United States
Team
1. United States, 71; 2. Iran, 59; 3. Russia, 58; 4. Turkey, 35; 5 Cuba, 34.
*Not held in 1996.

HORSE RACING

Ancient drawings on stone and bone prove that horse racing is at least 3000 years old, but Thoroughbred Racing is a modern development. Practically every thoroughbred in training today traces its registered ancestry back to one or more of three sires that arrived in England about 1728 from the Near East and became known, from the names of their owners, as the Byerly Turk, the Darley Arabian, and the Godolphin Arabian. The Jockey Club (English) was founded at Newmarket in 1750 or 1751 and became the custodian of the Stud Book as well as the court of last resort in deciding turf affairs.

Horse racing took place in this country before the Revolution, but the great lift to the breeding industry came with the importation in 1798, by Col. John Hoomes of Virginia, of Diomed, winner of the Epsom Derby of 1780. Diomed's lineal descendants included

such famous stars of the American turf as American Eclipse and Lexington. From 1800 to the time of the Civil War there were race courses and breeding establishments plentifully scattered through Virginia, North Carolina, South Carolina, Tennessee, Kentucky, and Louisiana.

The oldest stake event in North America is the Queen's Plate, a Canadian fixture that was first run in the Province of Quebec in 1836. The oldest stake event in the United States is The Travers, which was first run at Saratoga in 1864. The gambling that goes with horse racing and trickery by jockeys, trainers, owners, and track officials caused attacks on the sport by reformers and a demand among horse racing enthusiasts for an honest and effective control of some kind, but nothing of lasting value to racing came of this until the formation in 1894 of The Jockey Club.

"TRIPLE CROWN" WINNERS IN THE UNITED STATES[1]
(Kentucky Derby, Preakness and Belmont Stakes)

Year	Horse	Owner	Year	Horse	Owner
1919	Sir Barton	J. K. L. Ross	1946	Assault	Robert J. Kleberg
1930	Gallant Fox	William Woodward	1948	Citation	Warren Wright
1935	Omaha	William Woodward	1973	Secretariat	Meadow Stable
1937	War Admiral	Samuel D. Riddle	1977	Seattle Slew	Karen Taylor
1941	Whirlaway	Warren Wright	1978	Affirmed	Louis Wolfson
1943	Count Fleet	Mrs. John Hertz			

KENTUCKY DERBY
Churchill Downs; 3-year-olds; 1 1/4 miles.

Year	Winner	Jockey	Wt.	Win val.	Year	Winner	Jockey	Wt.	Win val.
1875	Aristides	O. Lewis	100	$2,850	1910	Donau	F. Herbert	117	$4,850
1876	Vagrant	R. Swim	97	2,950	1911	Meridian	G. Archibald	117	4,850
1877	Baden Baden	W. Walker	100	3,300	1912	Worth	C. H. Shilling	117	4,850
1878	Day Star	J. Carter	100	4,050	1913	Donerail	R. Goose	117	5,475
1879	Lord Murphy	C. Schauer	100	3,550	1914	Old Rosebud	J. McCabe	114	9,125
1880	Fonso	G. Lewis	105	3,800	1915	Regret	J. Notler	112	11,450
1881	Hindoo	J. McLaughlin	105	4,410	1916	George Smith	J. Loftus	117	9,750
1882	Apollo	B. Hurd	102	4,560	1917	Omar Khayyam	C. Borel	117	16,600
1883	Leonatus	W. Donohue	105	3,760	1918	Exterminator	W. Knapp	114	14,700
1884	Buchanan	I. Murphy	110	3,990	1919	Sir Barton	J. Loftus	1121/2	20,825
1885	Joe Cotton	E. Henderson	110	4,630	1920	Paul Jones	T. Rice	126	30,375
1886	Ben Ali	P. Duffy	118	4,890	1921	Behave Yourself	C. Thompson	126	38,450
1887	Montrose	I. Lewis	118	4,200	1922	Morvich	A. Johnson	126	46,775
1888	Macbeth II	G. Covington	115	4,740	1923	Zev	E. Sande	126	53,600
1889	Spokane	T. Kiley	118	4,970	1924	Black Gold	J. D. Mooney	126	52,775
1890	Riley	I. Murphy	118	5,460	1925	Flying Ebony	E. Sande	126	52,950
1891	Kingman	I. Murphy	122	4,680	1926	Bubbling Over	A. Johnson	126	50,075
1892	Azra	A. Clayton	122	4,230	1927	Whiskery	L. McAtee	126	51,000
1893	Lookout	E. Kunze	122	4,090	1928	Reigh Count	C. Lang	126	55,375
1894	Chant	F. Goodale	122	4,020	1929	Clyde Van Dusen	L. McAtee	126	53,950
1895	Halma	J. Perkins	122	2,970	1930	Gallant Fox	E. Sande	126	50,725
1896	Ben Brush	W. Simms	117	4,850	1931	Twenty Grand	C. Kurtsinger	126	48,725
1897	Typhoon H	F. Garner	117	4,850	1932	Burgoo King	E. James	126	52,350
1898	Plaudit	W. Simms	117	4,850	1933	Brokers Tip	D. Meade	126	48,925
1899	Manuel	F. Taral	117	4,850	1934	Cavalcade	M. Garner	126	28,175
1900	Lieut. Gibson	J. Boland	117	4,850	1935	Omaha	W. Saunders	126	39,525
1901	His Eminence	J. Winkfield	117	4,850	1936	Bold Venture	I. Hanford	126	37,725
1902	Alan-a-Dale	J. Winkfield	117	4,850	1937	War Admiral	C. Kurtsinger	126	52,050
1903	Judge Himes	H. Booker	117	4,850	1938	Lawrin	E. Arcaro	126	47,050
1904	Elwood	F. Prior	117	4,850	1939	Johnstown	J. Stout	126	46,350
1905	Agile	J. Martin	122	4,850	1940	Gallahadion	C. Bierman	126	60,150
1906	Sir Huon	R. Troxler	117	4,850	1941	Whirlaway	E. Arcaro	126	61,275
1907	Pink Star	A. Minder	117	4,850	1942	Shut Out	W. D. Wright	126	64,225
1908	Stone Street	A. Pickens	117	4,850	1943	Count Fleet	J. Longden	126	60,725
1909	Wintergreen	V. Powers	117	4,850	1944	Pensive	C. McCreary	126	64,675

Year	Winner	Jockey	Wt.	Win val.	Year	Winner	Jockey	Wt.	Win val.
1945	Hoop Jr.	E. Arcaro	126	$64,850	1972	Riva Ridge	R. Turcotte	126	$140,300
1946	Assault	W. Mehrtens	126	96,400	1973	Secretariat	R. Turcotte	126	155,050
1947	Jet Pilot	E. Guerin	126	92,160	1974	Cannonade	A. Cordero, Jr.	126	274,000
1948	Citation	E. Arcaro	126	83,400	1975	Foolish Pleasure	J. Vasquez	126	209,600
1949	Ponder	S. Brooks	126	91,600	1976	Bold Forbes	A. Cordero, Jr.	126	165,200
1950	Middleground	W. Boland	126	92,650	1977	Seattle Slew	J. Cruguet	126	214,700
1951	Count Turf	C. McCreary	126	98,050	1978	Affirmed	S. Cauthen	126	186,900
1952	Hill Gail	E. Arcaro	126	96,300	1979	Spectacular Bid	R. Franklin	126	228,650
1953	Dark Star	H. Moreno	126	90,050	1980	Genuine Risk	J. Vasquez	126	250,550
1954	Determine	R. York	126	102,050	1981	Pleasant Colony	J. Velasquez	126	317,200
1955	Swaps	W. Shoemaker	126	108,400	1982	Gato del Sol	E. Delahoussaye	126	417,600
1956	Needles	D. Erb	126	123,450	1983	Sunny's Halo	E. Delahoussaye	126	426,000
1957	Iron Liege	W. Hartack	126	107,950	1984	Swale	L. Pincay, Jr.	126	537,400
1958	Tim Tam	I. Valenzuela	126	116,400	1985	Spend a Buck	A. Cordero, Jr.	126	406,800
1959	Tomy Lee	W. Shoemaker	126	119,650	1986	Ferdinand	W. Shoemaker	126	609,400
1960	Venetian Way	W. Hartack	126	114,850	1987	Alysheba	C. McCarron	126	618,600
1961	Carry Back	J. Sellers	126	120,500	1988	Winning Colors	Gary Stevens	126	611,200
1962	Decidedly	W. Hartack	126	119,650	1989	Sunday Silence	Patrick Valen-		
1963	Chateauguay	B. Baeza	126	108,900			zuela	126	574,200
1964	Northern Dancer	W. Hartack	126	114,300	1990	Unbridled	Craig Perret	126	581,000
1965	Lucky Debonair	W. Shoemaker	126	112,000	1991	Strike the Gold	Chris Antley	126	655,800
1966	Kauai King	D. Brumfield	126	120,500	1992	Lil E. Tee	P. Day	126	724,800
1967	Proud Clarion	R. Ussery	126	119,700	1993	Sea Hero	Jerry Bailey	126	735,900
1968	Forward Pass[1]	I. Valenzuela	126	122,600	1994	Go For Gin	Chris McCarron	126	628,800
1969	Majestic Prince	W. Hartack	126	113,200	1995	Thunder Gulch	Gary Stevens	126	707,400
1970	Dust Commander	M. Manganello	126	127,800	1996	Grindstone	Jerry Bailey	126	869,800
1971	Canonero II	G. Avila	126	145,500					

1. Dancer's Image finished first but was disqualified after traces of drug were found in system.

PREAKNESS STAKES

Pimlico; 3-year-olds; 1 3/16 miles; first race 1873.

Year	Winner	Jockey	Wt.	Win val.	Year	Winner	Jockey	Wt.	Win val.
1919	Sir Barton	J. Loftus	126	$24,500	1964	Northern Dancer	W. Hartack	126	$124,200
1930	Gallant Fox	E. Sande	126	51,925	1965	Tom Rolfe	R. Turcotte	126	128,100
1931	Mate	G. Ellis	126	48,225	1966	Kauai King	D. Brumfield	126	129,000
1932	Burgoo King	E. James	126	50,375	1967	Damascus	W. Shoemaker	126	141,500
1933	Head Play	C. Kurtsinger	126	26,850	1968	Forward Pass	I. Valenzuela	126	142,700
1934	High Quest	R. Jones	126	25,175	1969	Majestic Prince	W. Hartack	126	129,500
1935	Omaha	W. Saunders	126	25,325	1970	Personality	E. Belmonte	126	151,300
1936	Bold Venture	G. Woolf	126	27,325	1971	Canonero II	G. Avila	126	137,400
1937	War Admiral	C. Kurtsinger	126	45,600	1972	Bee Bee Bee	E. Nelson	126	135,300
1938	Dauber	M. Peters	126	51,875	1973	Secretariat	R. Turcotte	126	129,900
1939	Challedon	G. Seabo	126	53,710	1974	Little Current	M. Rivera	126	156,000
1940	Bimelech	F.A. Smith	126	53,230	1975	Master Derby	D. McHargue	126	158,100
1941	Whirlaway	E. Arcaro	126	49,365	1976	Elocutionist	J. Lively	126	129,700
1942	Alsab	B. James	126	58,175	1977	Seattle Slew	J. Cruguet	126	138,600
1943	Count Fleet	J. Longden	126	43,190	1978	Affirmed	S. Cauthen	126	136,200
1944	Pensive	C. McCreary	126	60,075	1979	Spectacular Bid	R. Franklin	126	165,300
1945	Polynesian	W.D. Wright	126	66,170	1980	Codex	A. Cordero	126	180,600
1946	Assault	W. Mehrtens	126	96,620	1981	Pleasant Colony	J. Velasquez	126	270,800
1947	Faultless	D. Dodson	126	98,005	1982	Aloma's Ruler	J. Kaenel	126	209,900
1948	Citation	E. Arcaro	126	91,870	1983	Deputed Testi-			
1949	Capot	T. Atkinson	126	79,985		mony	D. Miller	126	251,200
1950	Hill Prince	E. Arcaro	126	56,115	1984	Gate Dancer	A. Cordero	126	243,600
1951	Bold	E. Arcaro	126	83,110	1985	Tank's Prospect	Pat Day	126	423,200
1952	Blue Man	C. McCreary	126	86,135	1986	Snow Chief	A. Solis	126	411,900
1953	Native Dancer	E. Guerin	126	65,200	1987	Alysheba	C. McCarron	126	421,100
1954	Hasty Road	J. Adams	126	91,600	1988	Risen Star	E. Delahoussaye	126	413,700
1955	Nashua	E. Arcaro	126	67,550	1989	Sunday Silence	P. Valenzuela	126	438,230
1956	Fabius	W. Hartack	126	84,250	1990	Summer Squall	Pat Day	126	445,900
1957	Bold Ruler	E. Arcaro	126	65,250	1991	Hansel	Jerry Bailey	126	432,770
1958	Tim Tam	I. Valenzuela	126	97,900	1992	Pine Bluff	C. McCarron	126	484,120
1959	Royal Orbit	W. Harmatz	126	136,200	1993	Prairie Bayou	Mike Smith	126	471,835
1960	Bally Ache	R. Ussery	126	121,000	1994	Tabasco Cat	Pat Day	126	447,720
1961	Carry Back	J. Sellers	126	126,200	1995	Timber Country	Pat Day	126	446,810
1962	Greek Money	J. Rotz	126	135,800	1996	Louis Quatorze	Pat Day	126	458,120
1963	Candy Spots	W. Shoemaker	126	127,500					

BELMONT STAKES

Belmont Park; 3–year–olds; 1 1/2 miles.

Run at Jerome Park 1867 to 1890; at Morris Park 1890–94; at Belmont Park 1905–62; at Aqueduct 1963–67. Distance 1 5/8 miles prior to 1874; reduced to 1 1/2 miles, 1874; reduced to 1 1/4 miles, 1890; reduced to 1 1/8 miles, 1893; increased to 1 1/4 miles, 1895; increased to 1 3/8 miles, 1896; reduced to 1 1/4 miles in 1904; increased to 1 1/2 miles, 1926.

Year	Winner	Jockey	Wt.	Win val.	Year	Winner	Jockey	Wt.	Win val.
1919	Sir Barton	J. Loftus	126	$11,950	1965	Hail to All	J. Sellers	126	$104,150
1930	Gallant Fox	E. Sande	126	66,040	1966	Amberoid	W. Boland	126	117,700
1931	Twenty Grand	C. Kurtsinger	126	58,770	1967	Damascus	W. Shoemaker	126	104,950
1932	Faireno	T. Malley	126	55,120	1968	Stage Door			
1933	Hurryoff	M. Garner	126	49,490		Johnny	H. Gustines	126	117,700
1934	Peace Chance	W.D. Wright	126	43,410	1969	Arts and Letters	B. Baeza	126	104,050
1935	Omaha	W. Saunders	126	35,480	1970	High Echelon	J. Rotz	126	115,000
1936	Granville	J. Stout	126	29,800	1971	Pass Catcher	R. Blum	126	97,710
1937	War Admiral	C. Kurtsinger	126	38,020	1972	Riva Ridge	R. Turcotte	126	93,540
1938	Pasteurized	J. Stout	126	34,530	1973	Secretariat	R. Turcotte	126	90,120
1939	Johnstown	J. Stout	126	37,020	1974	Little Current	M. Rivera	126	101,970
1940	Bimelech	F.A. Smith	126	35,030	1975	Avatar	W. Shoemaker	126	116,160
1941	Whirlaway	E. Arcaro	126	39,770	1976	Bold Forbes	A. Cordero, Jr.	126	117,000
1942	Shut Out	E. Arcaro	126	44,520	1977	Seattle Slew	J. Cruguet	126	109,080
1943	Count Fleet	J. Longden	126	35,340	1978	Affirmed	S. Cauthen	126	110,580
1944	Bounding Home	G.L. Smith	126	55,000	1979	Coastal	R. Hernandez	126	161,400
1945	Pavot	E. Arcaro	126	56,675	1980	Temperence Hill	E. Maple	126	176,220
1946	Assault	W. Mehrtens	126	75,400	1981	Summing	G. Martens	126	170,580
1947	Phalanx	R. Donoso	126	78,900	1982	Conquistador			
1948	Citation	E. Arcaro	126	77,700		Cielo	L. Pincay, Jr.	126	159,720
1949	Capot	T. Atkinson	126	60,900	1983	Caveat	L. Pincay, Jr.	126	215,100
1950	Middleground	W. Boland	126	61,350	1984	Swale	L. Pincay, Jr.	126	310,020
1951	Counterpoint	D. Gorman	126	82,000	1985	Creme Fraiche	Eddie Maple	126	307,740
1952	One Count	E. Arcaro	126	82,400	1986	Danzig Connec-			
1953	Native Dancer	E. Guerin	126	82,500		tion	C. McCarron	126	338,640
1954	High Gun	E. Guerin	126	89,000	1987	Bet Twice	C. Perret	126	329,160
1955	Nashua	E. Arcaro	126	83,700	1988	Risen Star	E. Delahoussaye	126	303,720
1956	Needles	D. Erb	126	83,600	1989	Easy Goer	P. Day	126	413,520
1957	Gallant Man	W. Shoemaker	126	77,300	1990	Go And Go	Michael Kinane	126	411,600
1958	Cavan	P. Anderson	126	73,440	1991	Hansel	Jerry Bailey	126	417,480
1959	Sword Dancer	W. Shoemaker	126	93,525	1992	A.P. Indy	E. Delahoussay	126	458,880
1960	Celtic Ash	W. Hartack	126	96,785	1993	Colonial Affair	Julie Krone	126	444,450
1961	Sherluck	B. Baeza	126	104,900	1994	Tabasco Cat	Pat Day	126	392,280
1962	Jaipur	W. Shoemaker	126	109,550	1995	Thunder Gulch	Gary Stevens	126	415,440
1963	Chateauguay	B. Baeza	126	101,700	1996	Editor's Note	R. Douglas	126	437,880
1964	Quadrangle	M. Ycaza	126	110,850					

TRIPLE CROWN RACES—1996

Kentucky Derby (Churchill Downs, Louisville, Ky., May 4, 1996). Gross purse: $1,169,800. Distance: 1 1/4 miles. Order of finish: 1. Grindstone (Bailey), mutuel returns: $13.80, $6.00, $4.00. 2. Cavonnier (McCarron) $6.20, $4.40. 3. Prince of Thieves (Day) $4.60. 4. Halo's Sunshine (Perret). 5. Unbridled's Song (Smith). 6. Editors Note (Stevens). 7. Blow Out (Johnson). 8. Alyrob (Nakatani). 9. Diligence (Desormeaux). 10. Victory Speech (Santos). 11. Corker (Black). 12. Skip Away (Sellers). 13. Zarb's Magic (Ardoin). 14. Semoran (Baze). 15. In Contention (Black). 16. Louis Quatorze (Antley). 17. Matty G (Solis). 18. Honour and Glory (Gryder). 19. BuiltforPleasure (Velazquez). Winner's purse: $869,800. Margin of victory: nose. Time of race: 2:01.

Preakness Stakes (Pimlico, Md., May 18, 1996). Gross purse: $704,800. Distance: 1 3/16 miles. Order of finish: 1. Louis Quatorze (Day), mutuel returns: $19.00, $7.80, $5.20. 2. Skip Away (Sellers) $5.60, $4.60. 3. Editor's Note (Stevens) $5.00. 4. Cavonnier (McCarron). 5. Victory Speech (Douglas). 6. In Contention (Solis). 7. Prince of Thieves (Bailey). 8. Allied Forces (Migliore). 9. Secreto de Estado (C. Valesquez). 10. Tour's Big Red (Bravo). 11. Mixed Count (Prado). 12. Feather Box (J. Velasquez). Winner's purse: $458,120. Margin of victory: 3 1/4 lengths. Time of race: 1:53 2/5.

Belmont Stakes (Elmont, N.Y., June 8, 1996). Gross purse: $729,800. Distance: 1 1/2 miles. Order of finish: 1. Editor's Note (Douglas), mutuel returns: $13.60, $6.50, $4.30. 2. Skip Away (Santos) $8.20, $6.20. 3. My Flag (Smith) $5.50. 4. Louis

Quatorze (Day). 5. Prince of Thieves (Bailey). 6. Rocket Flash (Maple). 7. Natural Selection (Romero). 8. Jamies First Punch (Velazquez). 9. In Contention (Bravo). 10. Traffic Circle (Chavez). 11. Saratoga Dandy (Davis). 12. Appealing Skier (Migliore). 13. South Salem (Krone). 14. Cavonnier (McCarron). Winner's purse: $437,880. Margin of victory: 1 length. Time of race: 2:28 4/5.

ECLIPSE AWARDS—1995

(Presented Feb. 9, 1996)

Horse of the Year	Cigar
4-year-old and up colt, horse, or gelding	Cigar
3-year-old colt or gelding	Thunder Gulch
3-year-old filly	Serena's Song
4-year-old and up filly or mare	Inside Information
Jockey	Jerry Bailey
Trainer	William Mott
Breeder	Juddmonte Farm
Owner	Allen Paulson
Apprentice jockey	Ramon B. Perez
2-year-old colt or gelding	Maria's Mon
2-year-old filly	Golden Attraction
Sprinter	Not Surprising
Male turf horse	Northern Spur
Female turf horse	Possibly Perfect
Steeplechase	Lonesome Glory

(Based on vote by the Thoroughbred Racing Associations, the *Daily Racing Form*, and the National Turf Writers Association.)

TRACK AND FIELD

WORLD RECORDS—MEN
(Through Sept. 20, 1996)

Recognized by the International Athletic Federation.
The I.A.A.F. decided late in 1976 not to recognize records in yards except for the one–mile run.
The I.A.A.F. also requires automatic timing for all records for races of 400 meters or less.

Event	Record	Holder	Home Country	Where Made	Date
Running					
100 m	0:09.84	Donovan Bailey	Canada	Atlanta, Ga.	July 27, 1996
200 m	0:19.32	Michael Johnson	United States	Atlanta, Ga.	Aug. 1, 1996
400 m	0:43.29	Harry Reynolds	United States	Zurich, Switzerland	Aug. 17, 1988
800 m	1:41.73	Sebastian Coe	England	Florence, Italy	June 10, 1981
1,000 m	2:12.18	Sebastian Coe	England	Oslo, Norway	July 11, 1981
1,500 m	3:27.37	Noureddine Morceli	Algeria	Nice, France	July 12, 1995
1 mile	3:44.39	Noureddine Morceli	Algeria	Rieti, Italy	Sept. 5, 1993
2,000 m	4:47.88	Noureddine Morceli	Algeria	Paris, France	July 3, 1995
3,000 m	7:20.67	Daniel Komen	Kenya	Rieti, Italy	Sept. 1, 1996
3,000 m steeplechase	7:59.18	Moses Kiptanui	Kenya	Zurich, Switzerland	Aug. 16, 1995
5,000 m	12:44.39	Haile Gebrselassie	Ethiopia	Zurich, Switzerland	Aug. 16, 1995
10,000 m	26:38.08	Salah Hissou	Morroco	Brussels, Belgium	Aug. 23, 1996
25,000 m	1:13:55.80	Toshihiko Seko	Japan	Christchurch, N.Z.	March 22, 1981
30,000 m	1:29:18.80	Toshihiko Seko	Japan	Christchurch, N.Z.	March 22, 1981
20,000 m	56:55.60	Arturo Barrios	Mexico	La Fleche, France	March 30, 1991
1 hour	21,101 m	Arturo Barrios	Mexico	La Fleche, France	March 30, 1991
Marathon	2:06.50	Belayneh Densimo	Ethiopia	Rotterdam, Netherlands	April 17, 1988
Walking					
20,000 m	1:17:25.60	Bernardo Segura	Mexico	Bergen, Norway	May 7, 1994
2 hours	29,572 m	Maurizio Damilano	Italy	Cuneo, Italy	Oct. 3, 1992
30,000 m	2:01:44.10	Maurizio Damilano	Italy	Cuneo, Italy	Oct. 3, 1992
50,000 m	3:41.28.20	Rene Piller	France	Bergen, Norway	May 7, 1994
Hurdles					
110 m	0:12.91	Colin Jackson	Great Britain	Stuttgart, Germany	Aug. 20, 1993
400 m	0:46.78	Kevin Young	United States	Barcelona, Spain	Aug. 6, 1992
Relay Races					
400 m (4 × 100)	0:37.40	United States		Stuttgart, Germany	Aug. 21, 1993
800 m (4 × 200)	1:18.68	Santa Monica T.C.	United States	Walnut, Calif.	April 17, 1994
1,600 m (4 × 400)	2:54.29	United States		Stuttgart, Germany	Aug. 22, 1993
3,200 m (4 × 800)	7:03.89	National Team	Britain	London, England	Aug. 30, 1982
		(Peter Elliot, Garry Cook, Steve Cram, Sebastian Coe)			
Field Events					
High Jump	2.45 m	Javier Sotomayor	Cuba	Salamanca, Spain	July 27, 1993
Long jump	8.95 m	Mike Powell	United States	Tokyo, Japan	Aug. 30, 1991
Triple Jump	18.29 m	Jonathan Edwards	Great Britain	Gothenburg, Sweden	Aug. 7, 1995
Pole vault	6.14 m	Sergey Bubka	Ukraine	Sestriere, Italy	July 31, 1994
Shot put	23.12 m	Randy Barnes	United States	Los Angeles, Calif.	May 20, 1990
Discus throw	74.08 m	Jürgen Schult	East Germany	Neubrandenburg, East Germany	June 6, 1986
Hammer throw	86.74 m	Yuriy Sedykh	U.S.S.R.	Stuttgart, Germany	Aug. 30, 1986
Javelin throw	98.48 m	Ján Zelezny	Czech Republic	Jena, Germany	May 25, 1996
Decathlon	8,891 pts.	Dan O'Brien	United States	Talence, France	Sept. 4–5, 1992

WORLD RECORDS—WOMEN
(Through Sept. 20, 1996)

Event	Record	Holder	Home Country	Where Made	Date
Running					
100 m	0:10.49	Florence Griffith-Joyner	United States	Indianapolis, Ind.	July 16, 1988
200 m	0:21.34	Florence Griffith-Joyner	United States	Seoul, South Korea	Sept. 29, 1988
400 m	0:47.60	Martina Koch	East Germany	Canberra, Australia	Oct. 6, 1985
800 m	1:53.28	Jarmila Kratochvilova	Czechoslovakia	Munich, W. Germany	July 26, 1983
1,000 m	2:28.98	Svetlana Masterkova	Russia	Brussels, Belgium	Aug. 23, 1996
1,500 m	3:50.46	Qu Yunxia	China	Beijing, China	Sept. 11, 1993
1 mile	4:12.56	Svetlana Masterkova	Russia	Zurich, Switzerland	Aug. 14, 1996
3,000 m	8:06.11	Wang Junxia	China	Beijing, China	Sept. 13, 1993
5,000 m	14:36.45	Fernanda Ribeiro	Portugal	Hechtel, Belgium	July 22, 1995

10,000 m	29:31.78	Wang Junxia	China	Beijing, China	Sept. 8, 1993
20,000 m	1:06:48.80	Izumi Maki	Japan	Amagasaki, Japan	Sept. 19, 1993
25,000 m	1:29:29.20	Karolina Szabó	Hungary	Budapest, Hungary	April 22, 1988
30,000 m	1:47:05.60	Karolina Szabó	Hungary	Budapest, Hungary	April 22, 1988
Marathon	2:21:06.00	Ingrid Kristiansen	Norway	London, England	April 21, 1985

Walking

| 5,000 m | 20:07.52 | Beate Anders | East Germany | Rostock, East Germany | June 23, 1990 |
| 10,000 m | 41:37.90 | Gao Hongmiao | China | Beijing, China | April 7, 1994 |

Hurdles

| 100 m | 0:12.21 | Yordanka Donkova | Bulgaria | Stara Zagora, Bulgaria | Aug. 20, 1988 |
| 400 m | 0:52.61 | Kim Batten | United States | Goteborg, Sweden | Aug. 11, 1995 |

Relay Races

400 m (4 × 100)	0:41.53	East Germany	E. Germany	Berlin, East Germany	July 31, 1983
800 m (4 × 200)	1:28.15	East Germany	E. Germany	Jena, East Germany	Aug. 9, 1980
1,600 m (4 × 400)	3:15.18	Soviet Union	Soviet Union	Seoul, South Korea	Oct. 1, 1988
3,200 m (4 × 800)	7:52.30	U.S.S.R.	U.S.S.R.	Podolsk, U.S.S.R.	Aug. 16, 1976

Field Events

High jump	2.09 m	Stefka Kostadinova	Bulgaria	Rome, Italy	Aug. 30, 1987
Pole vault	4.45 m	Emma George	Australia	Sapporo, Japan	July 14, 1996
Long jump	7.52 m	Galina Chistyakova	Soviet Union	Leningrad, U.S.S.R.	June 11, 1988
Triple jump	15.50 m	Inessa Kravets	Ukraine	Göteborg, Sweden	Aug. 10, 1995
Shot put	22.63 m	Natalya Lisovskaya	U.S.S.R.	Moscow, U.S.S.R.	June 7, 1987
Discus throw	76.80 m	Gabriele Reinsch	East Germany	Neubrandenburg, E. Ger.	July 9, 1988
Hammer throw	69.42 m	Mihaela Melinte	Russia	Cluj, Romania	May 12, 1996
Javelin throw	80.00 m	Petra Felke	East Germany	Potsdam, E. Germany	Sept. 9, 1988
Heptathlon	7,291 pts	Jackie Joyner-Kersee	United States	Seoul, South Korea	Sept. 23–24, 1988

AMERICAN RECORDS—MEN

(Through Sept. 20, 1996)

Event	Record	Holder	Where Made	Date
Running				
100 m	0:09.85	Leroy Burrell	Lausanne, Switzerland	July 6, 1994
200 m	0:19.32	Michael Johnson	Atlanta, Ga.	Aug. 1, 1996
400 m	0:43.29	Harry Reynolds	Zurich, Switzerland	Aug. 17, 1988
800 m	1:42.60	Johnny Gray	Koblenz, West Germany	Aug. 29, 1985
1,000 m	2:13.90	Richard Wohlhuter	Oslo, Norway	July 30, 1974
1,500 m	3:29.77	Sydney Maree	Cologne, West Germany	Aug. 25, 1985
1 mile	3:47.69	Steve Scott	Oslo, Norway	July 7, 1982
2,000 m	4:54.71	Steve Scott	Ingelhelm, West Germany	Aug. 31, 1982
3,000 m	7:31.69	Bob Kennedy	Brussels, Belgium	Aug. 23, 1996
5,000 m	12:58.21	Bob Kennedy	Zurich, Switzerland	Aug. 14, 1996
10,000 m	27:20.56	Mark Nenow	Brussels, Belgium	Sept. 5, 1986
20,000 m	58:15.00	Bill Rodgers	Boston, Mass.	Aug. 9, 1977
25,000 m	1:14:11.80	Bill Rodgers	Saratoga, Cal.	Feb. 21, 1979
30,000 m	1:31:49.00	Bill Rodgers	Saratoga, Cal.	Feb. 21, 1979
1 hour	12 mi., 1351 yds	Bill Rodgers	Boston, Mass.	Aug. 9, 1977
3,000–m steeplechase	8:09.17	Henry Marsh	Koblenz, West Germany	Aug. 29, 1985
Hurdles				
110 m	0:12.92	Roger Kingdom	Berlin, Germany	Aug. 16, 1989
		Allen Johnson	Brussels, Belgium	Aug. 23, 1996
400 m	0:46.78	Kevin Young	Barcelona, Spain	Aug. 6, 1992
Relay Races				
400 m (4 × 100)	0:37.40	USA National Team	Stuttgart, Germany	Aug. 21, 1993
800 m (4 × 200)	1:18.68	Santa Monica T.C.	Walnut, Calif.	April 17, 1994
1,600 m (4 × 400)	2:54.29	USA National Team	Stuttgart, Germany	Aug. 22, 1993
3,200 m (4 × 800)	7:06.50	Santa Monica T.C.	Walnut, Calif.	April 26, 1986
Field Events				
High jump	7 ft 10 1/2 in.	Charles Austin	Zurich, Switzerland	Aug. 7, 1991
Long jump	29 ft 4 1/2 in.	Mike Powell	Tokyo, Japan	Aug. 30, 1991
Triple jump	59 ft 4 in.	Kenny Harrison	Atlanta, Ga.	July 27, 1996
Pole vault	19 ft 7 1/2 in.	Lawrence Johnson	Knoxville, Tenn.	May 25, 1996
Shot put	74 ft 10 in.	Randy Barnes	Los Angeles, Calif.	May 20, 1990
Discus throw	237 ft 4 in.	Ben Plucknett	Stockholm, Sweden	July 7, 1981
Javelin throw	285 ft 1 in.	Tom Pukstys	Sheffield, England	Aug. 25, 1996
Hammer throw	270 ft 9 in.	Lance Deal	Milan, Italy	July 9, 1996
Decathlon	8,891 pts	Dan O'Brien	Talence, France	Sept. 4–5, 1992

AMERICAN RECORDS—WOMEN
(Through Sept. 20, 1996)

Event	Record	Holder	Where Made	Date
Running				
100 m	0:10.49	Florence Griffith–Joyner	Indianapolis, Ind.	July 16, 1988
200 m	0:21.56	Florence Griffith–Joyner	Seoul, South Korea	Oct. 1, 1988
400 m	0:48.83	Valerie Brisco–Hooks	Los Angeles, California	Aug. 6, 1984
800 m	1:56.90	Mary Decker Slaney	Bern, Switzerland	Aug. 16, 1985
1,500 m	3:57.12	Mary Decker Slaney	Stockholm, Sweden	July 26, 1983
1000 m	2:34.80	Mary Decker Slaney	Eugene, Oregon	July 4, 1985
1 mile	4:16.71	Mary Decker Slaney	Zurich, Switzerland	Aug. 21, 1985
3,000 m	8:29.69	Mary Decker Slaney	Cologne, W. Germany	Aug. 25, 1985
5,000 m	14:56.04	Amy Rudolph	Stockholm, Sweden	July 8, 1996
10,000 m	31:28.92	Francie L. Smith	Austin, Texas	April 4, 1991
Hurdles				
100 m hurdles	0:12.46	Gail Devers	Stuttgart, Germany	Aug. 20, 1993
400 m hurdles	0:52.61	Kim Batten	Gothenburg, Sweden	Aug. 11, 1995
Relay Races				
400 m (4 × 100)	0:41.49	U.S. National Team	Stuttgart, Germany	Aug. 22, 1993
800 m (4 × 200)	1:32.57	Louisiana State	Des Moines, Iowa	April 28, 1989
800 m (4 × 200)	1:32.57	Louisiana State	Philadelphia, Pa.	April 30, 1994
1,600 m (4 × 400)	3:15.51	U.S. Olympic Team	Seoul, South Korea	Oct. 1, 1988
Field Events				
Pole vault	13 ft 9 in.	Stacey Dragila		1996
High jump	6 ft 8 in.	Louise Ritter	Austin, Texas	July 9, 1988
Long jump	24 ft 7 in.	Jackie Joyner–Kersee	New York, N.Y.	May 22, 1994
Triple jump	47 ft 3 1/2 in.	Sheila Hudson	Stockholm, Sweden	July 8, 1996
Shot–put	66 ft 2 1/2 in.	Ramon Pagel	San Diego, California	June 25, 1988
Discus throw	216 ft 10 in.	Carol Cady	San Jose, California	May 31, 1986
Javelin throw	227 ft 5 in.	Kate Schmidt	Furth, W. Germany	Sept. 10, 1977
Hammer throw	199 ft	Paulette Mitchell	Lincoln, Nebraska	May 20, 1996
Heptathlon	7,291 pts	Jackie Joyner–Kersee	Seoul, South Korea	Sept. 23–24, 1988

HISTORY OF THE RECORD FOR THE MILE RUN
Source: USA Track & Field

Time	Athlete	Country	Year	Location
4:36.5	Richard Webster	England	1865	England
4:29.0	William Chinnery	England	1868	England
4:28.8	Walter Gibbs	England	1868	England
4:26.0	Walter Slade	England	1874	England
4:24.5	Walter Slade	England	1875	London, England
4:23.2	Walter George	England	1880	London, England
4:21.4	Walter George	England	1882	London, England
4:18.4	Walter George	England	1884	Birmingham, England
4:18.2	Fred Bacon	Scotland	1894	Edinburgh, Scotland
4:17.0	Fred Bacon	Scotland	1895	London, England
4:15.6	Thomas Conneff	United States	1895	Travers Island, N.Y.
4:15.4	John Paul Jones	United States	1911	Cambridge, Mass.
4:14.4	John Paul Jones	United States	1913	Cambridge, Mass.
4:12.6	Norman Taber	United States	1915	Cambridge, Mass.
4:10.4	Paavo Nurmi	Finland	1923	Stockholm, Sweden
4:09.2	Jules Ladoumegue	France	1931	Paris, France
4:07.6	Jack Lovelock	New Zealand	1933	Princeton, N.J.
4:06.8	Glenn Cunningham	United States	1934	Princeton, N.J.
4:06.4	Sydney Wooderson	England	1937	London, England
4:06.2	Gundar Hägg	Sweden	1942	Göteborg, Sweden
4:06.2	Arne Andersson	Sweden	1942	Stockholm, Sweden
4:04.6	Gunder Hägg	Sweden	1942	Stockholm, Sweden
4:02.6	Arne Andersson	Sweden	1943	Göteborg, Sweden
4:01.6	Arne Andersson	Sweden	1944	Malmo, Sweden
4:01.4	Gunder Hägg	Sweden	1945	Malmo, Sweden
3:59.4	Roger Bannister	England	1954	Oxford, England
3:58.0	John Landy	Australia	1954	Turku, Finland
3:57.2	Derek Ibbotson	England	1957	London, England
3:54.5	Herb Elliott	Australia	1958	Dublin, Ireland
3:54.4	Peter Snell	New Zealand	1962	Wanganui, N.Z.
3:54.1	Peter Snell	New Zealand	1964	Auckland, N.Z.
3:53.6	Michel Jazy	France	1965	Rennes, France
3:51.3	Jim Ryun	United States	1966	Berkeley, Calif.
3:51.1	Jim Ryun	United States	1967	Bakersfield, Calif.

3:51.0	Filbert Bayi	Tanzania	1975	Kingston, Jamaica
3:49.4	John Walker	New Zealand	1975	Goteborg, Sweden
3:49.0	Sebastian Coe	England	1979	Oslo, Norway
3:48.8	Steve Ovett	England	1980	Oslo, Norway
3:48.53	Sebastian Coe	England	1981	Zurich, Switzerland
3:48.40	Steve Ovett	England	1981	Koblenz, W. Ger.
3:47.33	Sebastian Coe	England	1981	Brussels, Belgium
3:46.31	Steve Cram	England	1985	Oslo, Norway
3:44.39	Noureddine Morceli	Algeria	1993	Rieti, Italy

TOP TEN WORLD'S FASTEST OUTDOOR MILES

Source: USA Track & Field

Time	Athlete	Country	Date	Location
3:44.39	Noureddine Morceli	Algeria	Sept. 5, 1993	Rieti, Italy
3:46.31	Steve Cram	England	July 27, 1985	Oslo, Norway
3:47.33	Sebastian Coe	England	Aug. 28, 1981	Brussels, Belgium
3:47.69	Steve Scott	United States	July 7, 1982	Oslo, Norway
3:47.79	Jose Gonzalez	Spain	July 27, 1985	Oslo, Norway
3:48.40	Steve Ovett	England	Aug. 26, 1981	Koblenz, W. Germany
3:48.53	Sebastian Coe	England	Aug. 19, 1981	Zurich, Switzerland
3:48.53	Steve Scott	United States	June 26, 1982	Oslo, Norway
3:48.8	Steve Ovett	England	July 1, 1980	Oslo, Norway
3:48.83	Sydney Maree	United States	Sept. 9, 1981	Rieti, Italy

NOTE: Professional marks not included.

TOP TEN WORLD'S FASTEST INDOOR MILES

Source: USA Track & Field

Time	Athlete	Country	Date	Location
3:49.78	Eamonn Coghlan	Ireland	Feb. 27, 1983	East Rutherford, N.J.
3:50.6	Eamonn Coghlan	Ireland	Feb. 20, 1981	San Diego, California
3:50.7	Noureddine Morceli	Algeria	Feb. 20, 1993	Birmingham, England
3:50.94	Marcus O'Sullivan	Ireland	Feb. 13, 1988	East Rutherford, N.J.
3:51.2	Ray Flynn[1]	Ireland	Feb. 27, 1983	East Rutherford, N.J.
3:51.66	Marcus O'Sullivan	Ireland	Feb. 10, 1989	East Rutherford, N.J.
3:51.8	Steve Scott[1]	United States	Feb. 20, 1981	San Diego, California
3:52.28	Steve Scott[2]	United States	Feb. 27, 1983	East Rutherford, N.J.
3:52:30	Frank O'Mara	Ireland	Feb. 1986	New York, New York
3:52.37	Eamonn Coghlan	Ireland	Feb. 9, 1985	East Rutherford, N.J.

1. Finished second. 2. Finished third.

IAAF GRAND PRIX—1996

(Milan, Italy, Sept. 7, 1996)

Men's Events

100 m—Dennis Mitchell, United States	09.91
200 m—Michael Johnson, United States	44.53
800 m—Norberto Tellez, Cuba	1:44.70
1,500 m—Hicham El Guerroudjk, Morroco	3:38.80
5,000 m—Daniel Komen, Kenya	12:52.38
3,000 m steeplechase—John Kosgei, Kenya	8:05.68
400 m hurdles—Derrick Adkins, United States	48.63
Triple jump—Jonathan Edwards, Great Britain	17.59 m
High jump—Patrik Sjoberg, Sweden	2.33 m
Pole vault—Maksim Tarasov, Russia	5.90 m
Shot put—John Godina, United States	21.18 m
Hammer throw—Lance Deal, United States	82.52 m

Women's Events

100 m—Merlene Ottey, Jamaica	10.74
400 m—Cathy Freeman, Australia	49.60
1,500 m—Svetlana Masterkova, Russia	4:11.42
5,000 m—Roberta Brunet, Italy	14:54.54
100 m hurdles—Ludmila Engquist, Sweden	12.61
Long jump—Inessa Kravets, Ukraine	7.07 m
Discus—Ilke Wyludda, Germany	67.74 m
Javelin—Tanja Damaske, Germany	66.28 m

IAAF GRAND PRIX OVERALL WINNERS

Men

1985	Doug Padilla, United States
1986	Said Aouita, Morocco
1987	Tonie Campbell, United States
1988	Said Aouita, Morocco
1989	Said Aouita, Morocco
1990	Leroy Burrell, United States
1991	Sergey Bubka, Ukraine
1992	Kevin Young, United States
1993	Sergey Bubka, Ukraine
1994	Noureddine Morceli, Morocco
1995	Moses Kiptanui, Kenya
1996	Daniel Komen, Kenya

Women

1985	Mary Decker Slaney, United States
1986	Yordanka Donkova, Bulgaria
1987	Merlene Ottey, Jamaica
1988	Paula Ivan, Romania
1989	Paula Ivan, Romania
1990	Merlene Ottey, Jamaica
1991	Heike Henkel, Germany
1992	Heike Drechsler, Germany
1993	Sandra Farmer-Patrick, United States
1994	Jackie Joyner-Kersee, Unitaed States
1995	Maria Mutola, Mozambique
1996	Ludmila Engquist, Sweden

USATF INDOOR CHAMPIONSHIPS

(March 1–2, 1996, Atlanta, Ga.)

Men's Events

60 m—Donovan Powell	6.55
200 m—Kevin Little	20.46
400 m—Michael Johnson	44.66
800 m—Brandon Rock	1:48.71
Mile—Steve Holman	3:57.72
3,000 m—Khalid Kairouani	7:46.77
60 m hurdles—Courtney Hawkins	7.46
5,000 m walk—Allen James	20:02.59
4 x 400 Relay—Ohio State	3:09.19
High jump—Charles Austin	7 ft 9 1/4 in.
Pole vault—Pat Manson	18 ft 8 1/4 in.
Long jump—Erick Walder	26 ft 7 in.
Triple jump—LaMark Carter	56 ft 2 in.
Shot put—John Godina	66 ft 9 3/4 in.
Weight throw—Lance Deal	83 ft 7 1/4 in.

Team standings—1. Nike, 25; 2. Powerade AC, 20; 3. Reebok, 17; 4. NYAC, 14; 5. Adidas, 10

Women's Events

60 m—Gwen Torrence	7.05
200 m—Gwen Torrence	22.33
400 m—Maicel Malone	51.49
800 m—Joetta Clark	2:00.90
Mile—Stephanie Best	4:34.67
3,000 m—Joan Nesbit	8:56.01
60 m hurdles—Michelle Freeman	7.91
3,000 m walk—Michelle Rohl	12:55.90
High jump—Tisha Waller	6 ft 6 1/4 in.
Long jump—Shana Williams	22 ft 3 1/2 in.
Triple jump—Sheila Hudson	46 ft 7 1/2 in.
Shot put—Connie Price-Smith	61 ft 9 in.
Weight throw—Dawn Ellerbe	65 ft 1 1/4 in.

Team standings—1. Reebok RC, 29; 2. Nike, 18; 3. Mizuno TC, 11; 4. Powerade AC, 9; 5. South Carolina, 8

NCAA DIVISION I OUTDOOR FINALS

(May 20–June 2, 1996, Eugene, Ore.)

Men's Events

100 m—Ato Boldon, UCLA	9.92
110 m hurdles—Dominique Arnold, Washington State	13.46
200 m—Rohsaan Griffin, Louisiana State	20.24
400 m—Davian Clarke, Miami (Fla.)	45.29
1,500 m—Marko Koers, Illinois	3:37.57
1,600 relay—Baylor	3:01.25
5,000 m—Alan Culpepper, Colorado	13:47.26
Triple jump—Robert Howard, Arkansas	56 ft 1 in.
Shot put—Andy Bloom, Wake Forest	65 ft 1/2 in.
Decathlon—Victor Houston, Auburn	7,766 pts

Team standings—1. Arkansas, 55; 2. George Mason, 40; 3. UCLA, 37; 4. North Carolina, 30; 5. Texas, 27

Women's Events

100 m—D'Andre Hill, Louisiana State	11.03
100 m hurdles (wind aided)—Kim Carson Louisian State	12.82
200 m—Zundra Feagin, Texas	22.44
400 m—Suziann Reid, Texas	52.16
1,500 m—Miesha Marzell, Georgetown	4:17.92
1,600 relay—Texas	3:27.50
5,000 m—Jennifer Rhines, Villanova	16:05.85
High jump—Amy Acuff, UCLA	6 ft 4 1/4 in.
Hammer throw—Dawn Ellerbe, South Carolina	209 ft 2 in.

Team standings—1. Louisiana State, 81; 2. Texas, 52; 3. Southern Methodist, 50; 4. Illinois, 43; 5. North Carolina, 35

BICYCLING

TOUR DE FRANCE—1996

(June 29–July 21, 1996)

Bjarne Riis, 32, became the first Dane to win the Tour de France with a winning time of 95 hours, 57 minutes, 16 seconds. Only one American, Frankie Andreu, of Dearborn, Michigan, completed the race and came in 111th place, 2:48:46 behind Riis. The final order of finish:

1. Bjarne Riis, Denmark—95 hours, 57 minutes, 16 seconds
2. Jan Ullrich, Germany—1 minute, 41 seconds behind
3. Richard Virenque, France—4:37 behind
4. Laurent Dufaux, Switzerland—5:53 behind
5. Peter Luttenberger, Austria—7:07 behind
6. Luc Leblanc, France—10:03 behind
7. Piotyr Ugrumov, Russia—10:04 behind
8. Fernando Escartin, Spain—10:26 behind
9. Abraham Olano, Spain—11:00 behind
10. Tony Rominger, Switzerland—11:53

EXTREME SPORTS

1996 ESPN EXTREME GAMES

(Providence, Rhode Island, June 24–30, 1996)

In-line Skating
Half-Pipe (Men's)—Gold: Rene Hulgreen; Silver: Tom Fry; Bronze: Chris Edwards
Half-Pipe (Women's)—Gold: Fabiola De Silva; Silver: Jodie Tyler; Bronze: Tasha Hodgson
Best Trick—Gold: Dion Antony; Silver: Ryan Jacklone; Bronze: Eric Schrijn
Street—Gold: Arlo Eisenberg; Silver: Matt Mantz; Bronze: Chris Edwards

Barefoot Waterski Jumping
Gold: Ron Scarpa; Silver: John Kretchman; Bronze: Rael Nurick

Bicycle Stunt
Dirt—Gold: Joey Garcia; Silver: TJ Lavin; Bronze: Brian Foster
Street—Gold: Dave Mirra; Silver: Jay Miron; Bronze: Rob Nolli

Bungee
Gold: Peter Bihun; Silver: Doug Anderson; Bronze: Carolyn Anderson

In-line Downhill
Men's—Gold: Dante Muse; Silver: Derek Parra; Bronze: Jim Weiderhold
Women's—Gold: Gypsy Tidwell; Silver: Jennifer Jones; Bronze: Desly Hill

Skateboarding
Best Trick—Gold: Gershon Mosley; Silver: Chris Senn; Bronze: Brian Patch
Street—Gold: Rodil de Araujo; Silver: Chris Senn; Bronze: Brian Patch
Vert—Gold: Andy MacDonald; Silver: Tony Hawk; Bronze: Tas Pappas

Skysurfing
Gold: Bob Greiner/Cliff Burch; Silver: Troy Hartman/Vic Pappadato; Bronze: Patrick de Gayardon/Joe Jennings

Sport Climbing
Difficulty (Men's)—Gold: Arnaud Petit; Silver: Francois Lombard; Bronze: Cristian Brenna
Difficulty (Women's)—Gold: Katie Brown; Silver: Laurence Guyon; Bronze: Liz Sansoz
Speed (Men's)—Gold: Hans Florine; Silver: Chris Bloch; Bronze: Tim Fairfield
Speed (Women's)—Gold: Cecile Leflem; Silver: Elena Shumilova; Bronze: Natalie Richer

Street Luge
Dual—Gold: Shawn Goulart/Stefan Wagner; Silver: Dennis Derammelaere/Tom Mason; Bronze: Johnnie Mechikoff, Jr./Bob Pereyra

Wakeboarding
Gold: Parks Bonifay; Silver: Jeremy Kovaky; Bronze: Scott Byerly

GYMNASTICS

WORLD CHAMPIONSHIPS—1995
(Sabae, Japan, October 1–10, 1995)

Men	Pts
Floor exercise—1. Vitaly Scherbo, Belarus	9.812
2. Xiaoshuang Li, China	9.775
3. Grigory Misutin, Ukraine	9.762
Pommel horse—1. Donghua Li, Switzerland	9.762
2. Huadong Huang, China	9.737
3. Yoshiaki Hatakeda, Japan	9.737
Still Rings—1. Yuri Chechi, Italy	9.850
2. Dan Burinca, Romania	9.762
3. Jordan Jovtchev, Bulgaria	9.750
Vault—1. Alexei Nemov, Russia	9.756
2. Grigory Misutin, Ukraine	9.756
3. Vitaly Scherbo, Belarus	9.662
Parallel bars—1. Vitaly Scherbo, Belarus	9.812
2. Liping Huang, China	9.750
3. Hikaru Tanaka, Japan	9.725
Horizontal bar—1. Andreas Wecker, Germany	9.812
2. Yoshiaki Hatakeda, Japan	9.775
3. Krasimir Dounev, Bulgaria and	
Jinjing Zhang, China (tie)	9.750
All-Around—1. Xiaoshuang Li, China	57.998
2. Vitaly Scherbo, Belarus	57.499
3. Evgeni Chabaev, Russia	57.248

Women	Pts
Vault—1. Simona Amanar, Romania and	
Lilia Podkopayeva, Ukraine (tie)	9.781
3. Gina Gogean, Romania	9.706
Uneven bars—1. Svetlana Chorkina, Russia	9.900
2. Huilan Mo, China and Lilia Podkopayeva,	
Ukraine (tie)	9.837
4. Alexandra Marinescu, Romania	9.800
Balance beam—1. Huilan Mo, China	9.900
2. Lilia Podkopayeva, Ukraine and Dominique	
Moceanu, United States (tie)	9.837
4. Alexandra Marinescu, Romania and	
Shannon Miller, United States (tie)	9.737
Floor—1. Gina Gogean, Romania	9.825
2. Liya Ji, China	9.675
3. Ludivine Furnon, France	9.625
All-Around—1. Lilia Podkopayeva, Ukraine	39.248
2. Svetlana Chorkina, Russia	39.130
3. Lavinia Milosovici, Romania	39.000

INIDIVIDUAL EVENT WORLD CHAMPIONSHIPS—1996
(San Juan, Puerto Rico, April 15–21, 1996)

Men	Pts
Vault—1. Alexei Nemov, Russia	9.756
2. Yeo Hong-Chul, South Korea, and	
Andrea Massucchi, Italy (tie)	9.743
4. Sergei Fedorchenko, Kazakhstan, and	
Vitaly Scherbo, Belarus (tie)	9.643
Parallel bars—1. Rustam Charipov, Ukraine	9.750
2. Alexei Nemov, Russia, and	
Vitaly Scherbo, Belarus (tie)	9.737
4. Jung Jin-Soo, South Korea, and	
Ivan Ivankov, Belarus (tie)	9.725
High bar—1. Jesus Carballo, Spain	9.800
2. Krasimir Dounev, Bulgaria	9.775
3. Vitaly Scherbo, Belarus	9.762
Floor exercise—1. Vitaly Scherbo, Belarus	9.787
2. Alexei Voropaev, Russia	9.700
3. Grigory Misutin, Ukraine	9.625
Pommel horse—1. Gil Su Pae, North Korea	9.825
2. Donghua Li, Switzerland	9.812
3. Alexei Nemov, Russia	9.787
Still rings—1. Yuri Chechi, Italy	9.825
2. Jordan Jovtchev, Bulgaria, and	
Szilveszter Csollany, Hungary (tie)	9.737
4. Dan Burinca, Romania	9.712

Women	Pts
Balance beam—1. Dina Kochetkova, Russia	9.887
2. Alexandra Marinescu, Romania	9.812
3. Dominique Dawes, United States and	
Xuan Liu, China (tie)	9.800
Floor exercise—1. Gina Gogean, Romania, and	
Kui Yuanyuan, China (tie)	9.850
3. Lavinia Milosovici, Romania, and	
Lyubov Sheremeta, Ukraine (tie)	9.800
Vault—1. Gina Gogean, Romania	9.800
2. Simona Amanar, Romania	9.787
3. Annia Portuondo, Cuba	9.756
Uneven bars—1. Svetlana Chorkina, Russia, and	
Yelena Piskun, Belarus (tie)	9.787
3. Isabelle Severino, France	9.775

NATIONAL CHAMPIONSHIPS—1996
(Knoxville, Tenn., June 5–8, 1996)

Men	Pts
Floor exercise—1. Jay Thornton, Iowa	9.737
2. Josh Stein, Stanford	9.612
3. Steve McCain, UCLA	9.600
Pommel horse—1. Josh Stein, Stanford	9.712
2. Blaine Wilson, Ohio State	9.600
3. John Roethlisberger, Minnesota	9.050
Rings—1. Kip Simons, Ohio State	9.637
2. John Macready, USOTC	9.500
3. Garry Denk, Iowa	9.475
Vault—1. Blaine Wilson, Ohio State	9.537
2. Jay Thornton, Iowa	9.525
3. John Macready, USOTC	9.462
Parallel bars—1. Jair Lynch, Stanford	9.762
2. Kip Simons, Ohio State	9.675
3. Blaine Wilson, Ohio State	9.612

	Pts
High bar—1. Bill Roth, Temple	9.687
2. Aaron Cotter, Iowa	9.662
3. John Macready, USOTC	9.637

Women (Listed with club affiliation)	Pts
Vault—1. Dominique Dawes, Hills	9.800
2. Kerri Strug, Karolyi's	9.793
3. Kristy Powell, Colorado Aerials	9.756
Uneven bars—1. Dominique Dawes, Hills	9.912
2. Katie Teft, Twistars	9.825
3. Monica Flammer, Cypress	9.787
Balance beam—1. Dominique Dawes, Hills	9.862
2. Mohini Bhardwaj, Brown's	9.650
3. Katie Teft, Twistars	9.637
Floor exercise—1. Dominique Dawes, Hills	9.900
2. Kerri Strug, Karolyi's	9.862
3. Jennie Thompson, Dynamo	9.775

TENNIS

Lawn tennis is a comparatively modern modification of the ancient game of court tennis. Major Walter Clopton Wingfield thought that something like court tennis might be played outdoors on lawns, and in December, 1873, at Nantclwyd, Wales, he introduced his new game under the name of *Sphairistike* at a lawn party. The game was a success and spread rapidly, but the name was a total failure and almost immediately disappeared when all the players and spectators began to refer to the new game as "lawn tennis." In the early part of 1874, a young lady named Mary Ewing Outerbridge returned from Bermuda to New York, bringing with her the implements and necessary equipment of the new game, which she had obtained from a British Army supply store in Bermuda. Miss Outerbridge and friends played the first game of lawn tennis in the United States on the grounds of the Staten Island Cricket and Baseball Club in the spring of 1874.

For a few years, the new game went along in haphazard fashion until about 1880, when standard measurements for the court and standard equipment with

in definite limits became the rule. In 1881, the U.S. Lawn Tennis Association (whose name was changed in 1975 to U.S. Tennis Association) was formed and conducted the first national championship at Newport, R.I. The international matches for the Davis Cup began with a series between the British and United States players on the courts of the Longwood Cricket Club, Chestnut Hill, Mass., in 1900, with the home players winning.

Professional tennis, which got its start in 1926 when the French star Suzanne Lenglen was paid $50,000 for a tour, received full recognition in 1968. Staid old Wimbledon, the London home of what are considered the world championships, let the pros compete. This decision ended a long controversy over open tennis and changed the format of the competition. The United States championships were also opened to the pros and the site of the event, long held at Forest Hills, N.Y., was shifted to the National Tennis Center in Flushing Meadows, N.Y., in 1978. Pro tours for men and women became worldwide in play that continued throughout the year.

DAVIS CUP CHAMPIONSHIPS

No matches in 1901, 1910, 1915–18, and 1940–45.

1900	United States 3, British Isles 0	1935	Great Britain 5, United States 0	1969	United States 5, Romania 0
1902	United States 3, British Isles 2	1936	Great Britain 3, Australia 2	1970	United States 5, West Germany 0
1903	British Isles 4, United States 1	1937	United States 4, Great Britain 1		
1904	British Isles 5, Belgium 0	1938	United States 3, Australia 2	1971	United States 3, Romania 2
1905	British Isles 5, United States 0	1939	Australia 3, United States 2	1972	United States 3, Romania 2
1906	British Isles 5, United States 0	1946	United States 5, Australia 0	1973	Australia 5, United States 0
1907	Australasia 3, British Isles 2	1947	United States 4, Australia 1	1974	South Africa (Default by India)
1908	Australasia 3, United States 2	1948	United States 5, Australia 0	1975	Sweden 3, Czechoslovakia 2
1909	Australasia 5, United States 0	1949	United States 4, Australia 1	1976	Italy 4, Chile 1
1911	Australasia 5, United States 0	1950	Australia 4, United States 1	1977	Australia 3, Italy 1
1912	British Isles 3, Australasia 2	1951	Australia 3, United States 2	1978	United States 4, Britain 1
1913	United States 3, British Isles 2	1952	Australia 4, United States 1	1979	United States 5, Italy 0
1914	Australasia 3, United States 2	1953	Australia 3, United States 2	1980	Czechoslovakia 3, Italy 2
1919	Australasia 4, British Isles 1	1954	United States 3, Australia 2	1981	United States 3, Argentina 1
1920	United States 5, Australasia 0	1955	Australia 5, United States 0	1982	United States 3, France 0
1921	United States 5, Japan 0	1956	Australia 5, United States 0	1983	Australia 3, Sweden 2
1922	United States 4, Australasia 1	1957	Australia 3, United States 2	1984	Sweden 4, United States 1
1923	United States 4, Australasia 1	1958	United States 3, Australia 2	1985	Sweden 3, West Germany 2
1924	United States 5, Australasia 0	1959	Australia 3, United States 2	1986	Australia 3, Sweden 2
1925	United States 5, France 0	1960	Australia 4, Italy 1	1987	Sweden 5, Austria 0
1926	United States 4, France 1	1961	Australia 5, Italy 0	1988	West Germany 4, Sweden 1
1927	France 3, United States 2	1962	Australia 5, Mexico 0	1989	West Germany 3, Sweden 2
1928	France 4, United States 1	1963	United States 3, Australia 2	1990	United States 3, Australia 2
1929	France 3, United States 2	1964	Australia 3, United States 2	1991	France 3, United States 1
1930	France 4, United States 1	1965	Australia 4, Spain 1	1992	United States 3, Switzerland 1
1931	France 3, Great Britain 2	1966	Australia 4, India 1	1993	Germany 4, Australia 1
1932	France 3, United States 2	1967	Australia 4, Spain 1	1994	Sweden 4, Russia 1
1933	Great Britain 3, France 2	1968	United States 4, Australia 1	1995	United States 3, Russia 1
1934	Great Britain 4, United States 1				

FEDERATION CUP CHAMPIONSHIPS

World team competition for women conducted by International Lawn Tennis Federation.

1963	United States 2, Australia 1	1971	Australia 3, Britain 0	1979	United States 3, Australia 0
1964	Australia 2, United States 1	1972	South Africa 2, Britain 1	1980	United States 3, Australia 0
1965	Australia 2, United States 1	1973	Australia 3, South Africa 0	1981	United States 3, Britain 0
1966	United States 3, West Germany 0	1974	Australia 2, United States 1	1982	United States 3, West Germany 0
		1975	Czechoslovakia 3, Australia 0		
1967	United States 2, Britain 0	1976	United States 2, Australia 1	1983	Czechoslovakia 2, West Germany 1
1968	Australia 3, Netherlands 0	1977	United States 2, Australia 1		
1969	United States 2, Australia 1	1978	United States 2, Australia 1		
1970	Australia 3, West Germany 0				

1984	Czechoslovakia 2, Australia 1		States 1	1992	Germany 2, Spain 1
1985	Czechoslovakia 2, United	1988	Czechoslovakia 2, Soviet	1993	Spain 3, Australia 0
	States 1		Union 1	1994	Spain 3, United States 0
1986	United States 3,	1989	United States 3, Spain 0	1995	Spain 3, United States 2
	Czechoslovakia 0	1990	United States 2, Soviet Union 1	1996	United Staets 5, Spain 0
1987	West Germany 2, United	1991	Spain 2, United States 1		

U.S. CHAMPIONS

Singles—Men

NATIONAL

1881–87	Richard D. Sears	1926–27	Jean Rene	1956	Ken Rosewall	1974	Jimmy Connors
1888–89	Henry Slocum, Jr.		Lacoste	1957	Mal Anderson	1975	Manuel Orantes
1890–92	Oliver S. Campbell	1928	Henri Cochet	1958	Ashley Cooper	1976	Jimmy Connors
1893–94	Robert D. Wrenn	1929	Bill Tilden	1959–60	Neale Fraser	1977	Guillermo Vilas
1895	Fred H. Hovey	1930	John H. Doeg	1961	Roy Emerson	1978	Jimmy Connors
1896–97	Robert D. Wrenn	1931–32	Ellsworth Vines	1962	Rod Laver	1979	John McEnroe
1898–		1933–34	Fred J. Perry	1963	Rafael Osuna	1980–81	John McEnroe
1900	Malcolm Whitman	1935	Wilmer L. Allison	1964	Roy Emerson	1982	Jimmy Connors
1901–02	William A. Larned	1936	Fred J. Perry	1965	Manuel Santana	1983	Jimmy Connors
1903	Hugh L. Doherty	1937–38	Don Budge	1966	Fred Stolle	1984	John McEnroe
1904	Holcombe Ward	1939	Robert L. Riggs	1967	John Newcombe	1985–87	Ivan Lendl
1905	Beals C. Wright	1940	Donald McNeill	1968	Arthur Ashe	1988	Mats Wilander
1906	William J. Clothier	1941	Robert L. Riggs	1969	Rod Laver	1989	Boris Becker
1907–11	William A. Larned	1942	Fred Schroeder			1990	Pete Sampras
1912–13	Maurice	1943	Joseph Hunt			1991	Stefan Edberg
	McLoughlin[1]	1944–45	Frank Parker	**OPEN**		1992	Stefan Edberg
1914	R. N. Williams II	1946–47	Jack Kramer	1968	Arthur Ashe	1993	Pete Sampras
1915	William Johnston	1948–49	Richard Gonzales	1969	Rod Laver	1994	Andre Agassi
1916	R. N. William II	1950	Arthur Larsen	1970	Ken Rosewall	1995	Pete Sampras
1917–18	R. Lindley	1951–52	Frank Sedgman	1971	Stan Smith	1996	Pete Sampras
	Murray[2]	1953	Tony Trabert	1972	Ilie Nastase		
1919	William Johnston	1954	Vic Seixas	1973	John Newcombe		
1920–25	Bill Tilden	1955	Tony Trabert				

Singles—Women

NATIONAL

1887	Ellen F. Hansel	1908	Maud	1946	Pauline Betz	1973	Margaret Court
1888–89	Bertha Townsend		Bargar–Wallach	1947	Louise Brough	1974	Billie Jean King
1890	Ellen C. Roosevelt	1909–11	Hazel V.	1948–50	Margaret Osborne	1975–78	Chris Evert
1891–92	Mabel E. Cahill		Hotchkiss		duPont	1979	Tracy Austin
1893	Aline M. Terry	1912–14	Mary K. Browne	1951–53	Maureen Connolly	1980	Chris Evert–Lloyd
1894	Helen R. Helwig	1915–18	Molla Bjurstedt	1954–55	Doris Hart	1981	Tracy Austin
1895	Juliette P.	1919	Hazel Hotchkiss	1956	Shirley Fry	1982	Chris Evert–Lloyd
	Atkinson		Wightman	1957–58	Althea Gibson	1983–84	Martina Navratilova
1896	Elisabeth H.	1920–22	Molla Bjurstedt	1959	Maria Bueno	1985	Hana Mandlikova
	Moore			1960–61	Darlene Hard	1986–87	Martina Navratilova
1897–98	Juliette P.	1923–25	Helen N. Wills	1962	Margaret Smith	1988	Steffi Graf
	Atkinson	1926	Molla B. Mallory	1963–64	Maria Bueno	1989	Steffi Graf
1899	Marion Jones	1927–29	Helen N. Wills	1965	Margaret Smith	1990	Grabriela Sabatini
1900	Myrtle McAteer	1930	Betty Nuthall	1966	Maria Bueno	1991	Monica Seles
1901	Elisabeth H.	1931	Helen Wills Moody	1967	Billie Jean King	1992	Monica Seles
	Moore	1932–35	Helen Jacobs	1968–69	Margaret Smith	1993	Steffi Graf
1902	Marion Jones	1936	Alice Marble		Court[3]	1994	Arantxa Sanchez
1903	Elisabeth H.	1937	Anita Lizana				Vicario
	Moore	1938–40	Alice Marble			1995	Steffi Graf
1904	May Sutton	1941	Sarah Palfrey	**OPEN**		1996	Steffi Graf
1905	Elisabeth H.		Cooke	1968	Virginia Wade		
	Moore	1942–44	Pauline Betz	1969–70	Margaret Court		
1906	Helen Homans	1945	Sarah Cooke	1971–72	Billie Jean King		
1907	Evelyn Sears						

Doubles—Men

NATIONAL

1920	Bill Johnston–C. J. Griffin	1942	Gardnar Mulloy–Bill Talbert	1955	Kosei Kamo–Atsushi Miyagi
1921–22	Bill Tilden–Vincent Richards	1943	Jack Kramer—Frank Parker	1956	Lewis Hoad–Ken Rosewall
1923	Bill Tilden–B. I. C. Norton	1944	Don McNeill—Bob	1957	Ashley Cooper–Neale Fraser
1924	H. O. Kinsey–R. G. Kinsey		Falkenburg	1958	Ham Richardson–Alex
1925–26	Vincent Richards—R. N.	1945	Gardnar Mulloy–Bill Talbert		Olmedo
	Williams II	1946	Gardnar Mulloy–Bill Talbert	1959–60	Neale Fraser–Roy Emerson
1927	Bill Tilden—Frank Hunter	1947	Jack Kramer–Fred	1961	Chuck McKinley–Dennis
1928	G. M. Lott, Jr.–V. Hennessy		Schroeder		Ralston
1929–30	G. M. Lott, Jr.–J. H. Doeg	1948	Gardnar Mulloy–Bill Talbert	1962	Rafael Osuna–Antonio
1931	W. L. Allison–John Van Ryn	1949	John Bromwich–William		Palafox
1932	E. H. Vines, Jr.–Keith Gledh		Sidwell	1963–64	Chuck McKinley–Dennis
1933–34	G. M. Lott, Jr.–L. R. Stoefen	1950	John Bromwich–Frank		Ralston
1935	W. L. Allison–John Van Ryn		Sedgman	1965–66	Fred Stolle–Roy Emerson
1936	Don Budge–Gene Mako	1951	Frank Sedgman–Ken	1967	John Newcombe–Tony
1937	G. von Cramm–H. Henkel		McGregor		Roche
1938	Don Budge–Gene Mako	1952	Vic Seixas–Mervyn Rose	1968	Stan Smith–Bob Lutz[3]
1939	A. K. Quist–J. E. Bromwich	1953	Mervyn Rose–Rex Hartwig	1969	Richard Crealy–Allan Stone[3]
1940–41	Jack Kramer–F. R. Schroeder	1954	Vic Seixas–Tony Trabert		

OPEN

1968	Stan Smith–Bob Lutz		Fleming		Sanchez
1969	Fred Stolle–Ken Rosewall	1980	Stan Smith–Bob Lutz	1989	John McEnroe–Mark
1970	Nikki Pilic–Fred Barthes	1981	John McEnroe–Peter		Woodforde
1971	John Newcombe–Roger		Fleming	1990	Pieter Aldrich–Danie Visser
	Taylor	1982	Kevin Curren–Steve Denton	1991	John Fitzgerald–Anders
1972	Cliff Drysdale–Roger Taylor	1983	John McEnroe–Peter		Jarryd
1973	John Newcombe–Owen		Fleming	1992	Jim Grabb–Richey
	Davidson	1984	John Fitzgerald–Tomas		Reneberg
1974	Bob Lutz–Stan Smith		Smid	1993	Ken Flach–Rick Leach
1975	Jimmy Connors–Ilie	1985	Ken Flach–Robert Seguso	1994	Jacco Hingh–Paul Haarhuis
	Nastase	1986	Andres Gomez–Slobodan	1995	Todd Woodbridge–Mark
1976	Marty Riessen–Tom Okker		Zivojinovic		Woodforde
1977	Frew McMillan–Bob Hewitt	1987	Stefan Edberg–Anders	1996	Todd Woodbridge–Mark
1978	Bob Lutz–Stan Smith		Jarryd		Woodforde
1979	John McEnroe–Peter	1988	Sergio Casal–Emilio		

1. Challenge round abandoned in 1912. 2. Patriotic Tournament in 1917. 3. With the inaugural of the Open Tournament in 1968, the United States Lawn Tennis Association held a national championship at Longwood, Chestnut Hill, Mass. which barred contract professionals in 1968 and 1969.

Doubles—Women

NATIONAL

1924	G. W. Wightman–Helen Wills		O. duPont	1970	Margaret Court–Judy Dalton
1925	Mary K. Browne–Helen Wills	1951–54	Doris Hart–Shirley Fry	1971	Rosemary Casals–Judy
1926	Elizabeth Ryan–Eleanor Goss	1955–57	A. Louise Brough–Margaret		Dalton
1927	L. A. Godfree–Ermyntrude		O. duPont	1972	Francoise Durr–Betty Stove
	Harvey	1958–59	Darlene Hard–Jeanne Arth	1973	Margaret Court–Virginia
1928	Hazel Hotchkiss Wightman–	1960	Darlene Hard–Maria Bueno		Wade
	Helen Wills	1961	Darlene Hard–Lesley Turner	1974	Billie Jean King–Rosemary
1929	Phoebe Watson–L. R. C.	1962	Darlene Hard–Maria Bueno		Casals
	Michell	1963	Margaret Smith–Robyn	1975	Margaret Court–Virginia
1930	Betty Nuthall–Sarah Palfrey		Ebbern		Wade
1931	Betty Nuthall–E. B.	1964	Karen Hantze Susman–Billie	1976	Linky Boshoff–Ilana Kloss
	Wittingstall		Jean Moffitt	1977	Martina Navratilova–Betty
1932	Helen Jacobs–Sarah Palfrey	1965	Nancy Richey–Carole		Stove
1933	Betty Nuthall–Freda James		Caldwell Graebner	1978	Billie Jean King–Martina
1934	Helen Jacobs–Sarah Palfrey	1966	Nancy Richey–Maria Bueno		Navratilova
1935	Helen Jacobs–Sarah Palfrey	1967	Billie Jean King–Rosemary	1979	Betty Stove–Wendy Turnbull
	Fabyan		Casals	1980	Billie Jean King–Martina
1936	Marjorie G. Van Ryn–Carolin	1968	Margaret Court–Maria		Navratilova
	Babcock		Bueno[3]	1981	Kathy Jordan–Anne Smith
1937–40	Sarah Palfrey Fabyan–Alice	1969	Margaret Court–Virginia	1982	Rosemary Casals–Wendy
	Marble		Wade[3]		Turnbull
1941	Sarah Palfrey Cooke–			1983–84	Martina Navratilova–Pam
	Margaret Osborne	**OPEN**			Shriver
1942–47	A. Louise Brough–Margaret	1968	Maria Bueno–Margaret	1985	Claudia Khode–Kilsch–
	Osborne		Court		Helena Sukova
1948–50	A. Louise Brough–Margaret	1969	Darlene Hard–Francoise Durr		

1986–87	Martina Navratilova–Pam Shriver	1991	Pam Shriver–Natalia Zvereva	1995	Gigi Fernandez–Natasha Zvereva
1988	Gigi Fernandez–Robin White	1992	Gigi Fernandez–Natalia Zvereva	1996	Gigi Fernandez–Natasha Zvereva
1989	Hana Mandlikova–Martina Navratilova	1993	Arantxa Sanchez Vicario–Helena Sukova		
1990	Gigi Fernandez–Martina Navratilova	1994	Jana Novotna–Arantxa Sanchez Vicario		

1. Challenge round abandoned in 1912. 2. Patriotic Tournament in 1917. 3. With the inaugural of the Open Tournament in 1968, the United States Lawn Tennis Association held a national championship at Longwood, Chestnut Hill, Mass. which barred contract professionals in 1968 and 1969.

BRITISH (WIMBLEDON) CHAMPIONS

(Amateur from inception in 1877 through 1967)

Singles—Men

1908–09	Arthur Gore	1933	J. H. Crawford	1959	Alex Olmedo	1983–84	John McEnroe
1910–13	A. F. Wilding	1934–36	Fred Perry	1960	Neale Fraser	1985–86	Boris Becker
1914	N. E. Brookes	1937–38	Don Budge	1961–62	Rod Laver	1987	Pat Cash
1919	G. L. Patterson	1939	Robert L. Riggs	1963	Chuck McKinley	1988	Stefan Edberg
1920–21	Bill Tilden	1946	Yvon Petra	1964–65	Roy Emerson	1989	Boris Becker
1922	G. L. Patterson	1947	Jack Kramer	1966	Manuel Santana	1990	Stefan Edberg
1923	William Johnston	1948	R. Falkenburg	1967	John Newcombe	1991	Michael Stich
1924	Jean Borotra	1949	Fred Schroeder	1968–69	Rod Laver	1992	Andre Agassi
1925	Rene Lacoste	1950	Budge Patty	1970–71	John Newcombe	1993	Peter Sampras
1926	Jean Borotra	1951	Richard Savitt	1972	Stan Smith	1994	Pete Sampras
1927	Henri Cochet	1952	Frank Sedgman	1973	Jan Kodes	1995	Pete Sampras
1928	Rene Lacoste	1953	Vic Siexas	1974	Jimmy Connors	1996	Richard Krajicek
1929	Jean Cochet	1954	Jaroslav Drobny	1975	Arthur Ashe		
1930	Bill Tilden	1955	Tony Trabert	1976–80	Bjorn Borg		
1931	S. B. Wood	1956–57	Lewis Hoad	1981	John McEnroe		
1932	Ellsworth Vines	1958	Ashley Cooper	1982	Jimmy Connors		

Singles—Women

1919–23	Lenglen	1946	Pauline M. Betz	1966–67	Billie Jean King	1981	Chris Evert–Lloyd
1924	Kathleen McKane	1947	Margaret Osborne	1968	Billie Jean King	1982–87	Martina Navratilova
1925	Lenglen	1948–50	A. Louise Brough	1969	Ann Jones	1988–89	Steffi Graf
1926	Godfree	1951	Doris Hart	1970	Margaret Court	1990	Martina Navratilova
1927–29	Helen Wills	1952–54	Maureen Connolly	1971	Evonne Goolagong	1991	Steffi Graf
1930	Helen Wills Moody	1955	A. Louise Brough	1972–73	Billie Jean King	1992	Steffi Graf
1931	Frl. C. Aussen	1956	Shirley Fry	1974	Chris Evert	1993	Steffi Graf
1932–33	Helen Wills Moody	1957–58	Althea Gibson	1975	Billie Jean King	1994	Conchita Martinez
1934	D. E. Round	1959–60	Maria Bueno	1976	Chris Evert	1995	Steffi Graf
1935	Helen Wills Moody	1961	Angela Mortimer	1977	Virginia Wade	1996	Steffi Graf
1936	Helen Jacobs	1962	Karen Susman	1978–79	Martina Navratilova		
1937	D. E. Round	1963	Margaret Smith	1980	Evonne Goolagong Cawley		
1938	Helen Wills Moody	1964	Maria Bueno				
1939	Alice Marble	1965	Margaret Smith				

Doubles—Men

1953	K. Rosewall–L. Hoad	1972	Bob Hewitt–Frew McMillan		Wilander	
1954	R. Hartwig–M. Rose	1973	Jimmy Connors–Ilie Nastase	1987	Ken Flach–Robert Seguso	
1955	R. Hartwig–L. Hoad	1974	John Newcombe–Tony Roche	1988	Ken Flach–Robert Seguso	
1956	L. Hoad–K. Rosewall	1975	Vitas Gerulaitis–Sandy Mayer	1989	John Fitzgerald–Anders Jarryd	
1957	Gardnar Mulloy–Budge Patty	1976	Brian Gottfried–Raul Ramirez	1990	Rick Leach–Jim Pugh	
1958	Sven Davidson–Ulf Schmidt	1977	Ross Case–Geoff Masters	1991	Anders Jarryd–John Fitzgerald	
1959	Roy Emerson–Neale Fraser	1978	Fred McMillan–Bob Hewitt	1992	John McEnroe–Michael Stich	
1960	Dennis Ralston–Rafael Osuna	1979	Peter Fleming–John McEnroe	1993	Todd Woodbridge–Mark Woodforde	
1961	Roy Emerson–Neale Fraser	1980	Peter McNamara–Paul McNamee			
1962	Fred Stolle–Bob Hewitt	1981	John McEnroe–Peter Fleming	1994	Todd Woodbridge–Mark Woodforde	
1963	Rafael Osuna–Antonio Palafox	1982	Paul McNamee–Peter McNamara	1995	Todd Woodbridge–Mark Woodforde	
1964	Fred Stolle–Bob Hewitt	1983–84	John McEnroe–Peter Fleming	1996	Todd Woodbridge–Mark Woodforde	
1965	John Newcombe–Tony Roche	1985	Heinz Gunthardt–Balazs Taroczy			
1966	John Newcombe–Ken Fletcher	1986	Joakim Nystrom–Mats			
1967	Bob Hewitt–Frew McMillan					
1968–70	John Newcombe–Tony Roche					
1971	Rod Laver–Roy Emerson					

Doubles–Women

1956	Althea Gibson–Angela Buxton		Casals	1982–84	Pam Shriver–Martina
1957	Althea Gibson–Darlene Hard	1972	Billie Jean King–Betty Stove		Navratilova
1958	Althea Gibson–Maria Bueno	1973	Billie Jean King–Rosemary	1985	Kathy Jordan–Elizabeth Smylie
1959	Darlene Hard–Jeanne Arth		Casals	1986	Pam Shriver–Martina
1960	Darlene Hard–Maria Bueno	1974	Evonne Goolagong–Peggy		Navratilova
1961	Karen Hantze–Billie Jean		Michel	1987	Claudia Khode–Kilsch–Helena
	Moffitt	1975	Ann Kiyomura–Kazuko		Sukova
1962	Karen Hantze Susman–Billie		Sawamatsu	1988	Steffi Graf–Gabriela Sabatini
	Jean Moffitt	1976	Chris Evert–Martina	1989	Jana Novotna–Helena Sukova
1963	Darlene Hard–Maria Bueno		Navratilova	1990	Jana Novotna–Helena Sukova
1964	Margaret Smith–Les Turnerley	1977	Helen Cawley–JoAnne Russell	1991	Pam Shriver–Natalia Zvereva
1965	Billie Jean Moffitt–Maria	1978	Wendy Turnbull–Kerry Reid	1992	Gigi Fernandez–Natalia Zvereva
	Bueno	1979	Billie Jean King–Martina	1993	Gigi Fernandez–Natalia Zvereva
1966	Nancy Richey–Maria Bueno		Navratilova	1994	Gigi Fernandez–Natalia Zvereva
1967–68	Billie Jean King–Rosemary	1980	Kathy Jordan–Anne Smith	1995	Jana Novotna–Arantxa
	Casals	1981	Martina Navratilova–Pam		Sanchez Vicario
1969	Margaret Court–Judy Tegart		Shriver	1996	Martina Hingis–Helena Sukova
1970–71	Billie Jean King–Rosemary				

UNITED STATES CHAMPIONS—1996

United States Open
(Flushing Meadow, N.Y., Aug. 26–Sept. 8, 1996)

Men's singles—Pete Sampras defeated Michael Chang, 6–1, 6–4, 7–6 (7–3).

Women's singles—Steffi Graf defeated Monica Seles 7–5, 6–4.

Men's doubles—Mark Woodforde–Todd Woodbridge defeated Jacco Eltingh and Paul Haarhuis, 4–6, 7–6 (7–5), 7–6 (7–2).

Women's doubles—Gigi Fernandez–Natasha Zvereva, defeated Jana Novotna and Arantxa Sanchez Vicario, 1–6, 6–1, 6–4

Mixed doubles—Lisa Raymond and Patrick Galbraith defeated Manon Bollegraf and Rick Leach, 7–6 (8–6), 7–6 (7–4).

OTHER 1996 CHAMPIONS

Wimbledon Open
(Wimbledon, England, June 24–July 7, 1996)

Men's singles—Richard Krajicek defeated MaliVai Washington, 6–3, 6–4, 6–3.

Women's singles—Steffi Graf defeated Arantxa Sanchez Vicario, 6–3, 7–5.

Men's doubles—Mark Woodforde–Todd Woodbridge defeated Byron Black and Grant Connell, 4–6, 6–1, 6–3, 6–2.

Women's doubles—Martina Hingis and Helena Sukova defeated Meredith McGrath and Larisa Neiland, 5–7, 7–5, 6–1.

Mixed doubles—Cyril Suk and Helena Sukova defeated Mark Woodforde and Larisa Neiland, 1–6, 6–3, 6–2.

French Open
(Paris, May 27–June 9, 1996)

Men's singles—Yevgeny Kafelnikov, Russia, defeated Michael Stich, Germany, 7–6 (7–4), 7–5, 7–6 (7–4).

Women's singles—Steffi Graf, Germany, defeated Arantxa Sanchez Vicario, Spain, 6–3, 6–7 (4–7), 10–8.

Men's doubles—Yevgeny Kafelnikov, Russia, and Daniel Vacek, Czech Republic, defeated Guy Forget, France, and Jakob Hlasek, Czech Republic, 6–2, 6–3.

Women's doubles—Lindsay Davenport and Mary Joe Fernandez, United States, defeated Gigi Fernandez, United States, and Natasha Zvereva, Russia, 6–2, 6–1.

Mixed doubles—Patricia Tarabini and Javier Frana, Argentina, defeated Nicole Arendt and Luke Jensen, United States, 6–2, 6–2.

Australian Open
(Melbourne, Australia, Jan. 15–28, 1996)

Men's singles—Boris Becker defeated Michael Chang, 6–2, 6–4, 2–6, 6–2.

Women's singles—Monica Seles defeated Anke Huber, 6–4, 6–1.

Men's doubles—Stefan Edberg and Petr Korda defeated Sebastien Lareau and Alex O'Brien, 7–5, 7–5, 4–6, 6–1.

Women's doubles—Chanda Rubin and Arantxa Sanchez Vicario defeated Lindsay Davenport and MaryJoe Fernandez, 6–4, 2–6, 6–2.

Mixed doubles—Mark Woodforde and Larisa Neiland defeated Luke Jensen and Nicole Arendt, 4–6, 7–5, 6–0.

MEN'S MONEY WINNERS—1995

1.	Pete Sampras	$5,415,066
2.	Goran Ivanisevic	3,777,862
3.	Boris Becker	3,712,358
4.	Andre Agassi	2,975,738
5.	Thomas Muster	2,887,979
6.	Michael Chang	2,655,870
7.	Sergi Bruguera	2,058,044
8.	Yevgeny Kafelnikov	1,841,561
9.	Todd Martin	1,455,558
10.	Wayne Ferreira	1,276,216
11.	Thomas Enqvist	1,229,646
12.	Jim Courier	1,202,769
13.	Paul Haarhuis	1,005,587
14.	Richard Krajicek	853,974
15.	Andrei Medvedev	922,692
16.	Michael Stich	853,974
17.	Magnus Larsson	702,245
18.	Arnaud Boetsch	607,535
19.	Marc Rosset	570,786
20.	Gilbert Schaller	426,568

WOMEN'S MONEY WINNERS—1996

1.	Steffi Graf	$2,538,620
2.	Arantxa Sanchez Vicario	1,456,516
3.	Conchita Martinez	1,266,558
4.	Natasha Zvereva	867,287
5.	Jana Novotna	787,936
6.	Gabriela Sabatini	718,978
7.	Mary Pierce	698,838
8.	Anke Huber	620,969
9.	Kimiko Date	607,113
10.	Brenda Schultz-McCarthy	577,807
11.	Gigi Fernandez	569,428
12.	Mary Joe Fernandez	522,370
13.	Iva Majoli	508,460
14.	Magdalena Maleeva	488,068
15.	Lindsay Davenport	438,682
16.	Monica Seles	397,010
17.	Chanda Rubin	386,365
18.	Larisa Neiland	374,630
19.	Amanda Coetzer	327,481
20.	Lori Mcneil	302,113

ROWING

Rowing goes back so far in history that it cannot be traced to any single source. The oldest rowing race still on the calendar is the "Doggett's Coat and Badge" contest among professional watermen of the Thames (England) that began in 1715. The first Oxford-Cambridge race was held at Henley in 1829. Competitive rowing in the United States began with matches between boats rowed by professional oarsmen of the New York waterfront. They were oarsmen who rowed the small boats that plied as ferries from Manhattan Island to Brooklyn and return, or who rowed salesmen down the harbor to meet ships arriving from Europe. Since the first salesman to meet an incoming ship had some advantage over his rivals, there was keen competition in the bidding for fast boats and the best oarsmen. This gave rise to match races.

Amateur boat clubs sprang up in the United States between 1820 and 1830 and seven students of Yale joined together to purchase a four-oared lap-streak gig in 1843. The first Harvard-Yale race was held Aug. 3, 1852, on Lake Winnepesaukee, N.H. The first time an American college crew went abroad was in 1869 when Harvard challenged Oxford and was defeated on the Thames. There were early college rowing races on Lake Quinsigamond, near Worcester, Mass., and on Saratoga Lake, N.Y., but the Intercollegiate Rowing Association in 1895 settled on the Hudson, at Poughkeepsie, as the setting for the annual "Poughkeepsie Regatta." In 1950 the I.R.A. shifted its classic to Marietta, Ohio, and in 1952 it was moved to Syracuse, N.Y. The National Association of Amateur Oarsmen, organized in 1872, has conducted annual championship regattas since that time.

INTERCOLLEGIATE ROWING ASSOCIATION REGATTA

(Varsity Eight-Oared Shells)

Rowed at 4 miles, Poughkeepsie, N.Y., 1895–97, 1899–1916, 1925–32, 1934–41. Rowed at 3 miles, Saratoga, N.Y., 1898; Poughkeepsie, 1921–24, 1947–49; Syracuse, N.Y., 1952–1963, 1965–67. Rowed at 2 miles, Ithaca, N.Y., 1920; Marietta, Ohio, 1950–51. Suspended 1917–19, 1933, 1942–46. Rowed at 2,000 meters, Syracuse, N.Y., 1964, 1968–1974. Rowed at Camden, N.J., since 1975.

Year	Time	First	Second	Year	Time	First	Second
1895	21:25	Columbia	Cornell	1951	7:50.5	Wisconsin	Washington
1896	19:59	Cornell	Harvard	1952	15:08.1	Navy	Princeton
1897	20:47 4/5	Cornell	Columbia	1953	15:29.6	Navy	Cornell
1898	15:51 1/2	Pennsylvania	Cornell	1954	16:04.4	Navy[1]	Cornell
1899	20:04	Pennsylvania	Wisconsin	1955	15:49.9	Cornell	Pennsylvania
1900	19:44 3/5	Pennsylvania	Wisconsin	1956	16:22.4	Cornell	Navy
1901	18:53 1/5	Cornell	Columbia	1957	15:26.6	Cornell	Pennsylvania
1902	19:03 3/5	Cornell	Wisconsin	1958	17:12.1	Cornell	Navy
1903	18:57	Cornell	Georgetown	1959	18:01.7	Wisconsin	Syracuse
1904	20:22 3/5	Syracuse	Cornell	1960	15:57	California	Navy
1905	20:29	Cornell	Syracuse	1961	16:49.2	California	Cornell
1906	19:36 4/5	Cornell	Pennsylvania	1962	17:02.9	Cornell	Washington
1907	20:02 2/5	Cornell	Columbia	1963	17:24	Cornell	Navy
1908	19:24 1/5	Syracuse	Columbia	1964	6:31.1	California	Washington
1909	19:02	Cornell	Columbia	1965	16:51.3	Navy	Cornell
1910	20:42 1/5	Cornell	Pennsylvania	1966	16:03.4	Wisconsin	Navy
1911	20:10 4/5	Cornell	Columbia	1967	16:13.9	Pennsylvania	Wisconsin
1912	19:31 2/5	Cornell	Wisconsin	1968	6:15.6	Pennsylvania	Washington
1913	19:28 3/5	Syracuse	Cornell	1969	6:30.4	Pennsylvania	Dartmouth
1914	19:37 4/5	Columbia	Pennsylvania	1970	6:39.3	Washington	Wisconsin
1915	19:36 3/5	Cornell	Stanford	1971	6:06	Cornell	Washington
1916	20:15 2/5	Syracuse	Cornell	1972	6:22.6	Pennsylvania	Brown
1920	11:02 3/5	Syracuse	Cornell	1973	6:21	Wisconsin	Brown
1921	14:07	Navy	California	1974	6:33	Wisconsin	M.I.T.
1922	13:33 3/5	Navy	Washington	1975	6:08.2	Wisconsin	M.I.T.
1923	14:03 1/5	Washington	Navy	1976	6:31	California	Princeton
1924	15:02	Washington	Wisconsin	1977	6:32.4	Cornell	Pennsylvania
1925	19:24 4/5	Navy	Washington	1978	6:39.5	Syracuse	Brown
1926	19:28 3/5	Washington	Navy	1979	6:26.4	Brown	Wisconsin
1927	20:57	Columbia	Washington	1980	6:46	Navy	Northeastern
1928	18:35 4/5	California	Columbia	1981	5:57.3	Cornell	Navy
1929	22:58	Columbia	Washington	1982	5:57.5	Cornell	Princeton
1930	21:42	Cornell	Syracuse	1983	6:14.4	Brown	Navy
1931	18:54 1/5	Navy	Cornell	1984	5:54.7	Navy	Pennsylvania
1932	19:55	California	Cornell	1985	5:49.9	Princeton	Brown
1934	19:44	California	Washington	1986	5:50.2	Brown	Pennsylvania
1935	18:52	California	Cornell	1987	6:02.9	Brown	Wisconsin
1936	19:09 3/5	Washington	California	1988	6:14.0	Northeastern	Brown
1937	18:33 3/5	Washington	Navy	1989	5:56.0	Penn	Wisconsin
1938	18:19	Navy	California	1990	5:55.5	Wisconsin	Pennsylvania
1939	18:12 3/5	California	Washington	1991	6:05.2	Northeastern	Pennsylvania
1940	22:42	Washington	Cornell	1992	6:10.5	Dartmouth	Harvard
1941	18:53 3/10	Washington	California	1993	5:59.1	Brown	Pennsylvania
1947	13:59 1/5	Navy	Cornell	1994	5:54.4	Brown	Princeton
1948	14:06 2/5	Washington	California	1995	5:31.3	Brown	Navy
1949	14:42 3/5	California	Washington	1996	5:29.6[2]	Princeton	Washington
1950	8:07.5	Washington	California				

1. Disqualified. 2. New course record.

JAMES E. SULLIVAN MEMORIAL AWARD WINNERS

(Amateur Athlete of Year Chosen in Amateur Athletic Union Poll)

Year	Name	Sport
1930	Robert Tyre Jones, Jr.	Golf
1931	Bernard E. Berlinger	Track and field
1932	James A. Bausch	Track and field
1933	Glenn Cunningham	Track and field
1934	William R. Bonthron	Track and field
1935	W. Lawson Little, Jr.	Golf
1936	Glenn Morris	Track and field
1937	J. Donald Budge	Tennis
1938	Donald R. Lash	Track and field
1939	Joseph W. Burk	Rowing
1940	J. Gregory Rice	Track and field
1941	Leslie MacMitchell	Track and field
1942	Cornelius Warmerdam	Track and field
1943	Gilbert L. Dodds	Track and field
1944	Ann Curtis	Swimming
1945	Felix (Doc) Blanchard	Football
1946	Y. Arnold Tucker	Football
1947	John B. Kelly, Jr.	Rowing
1948	Robert B. Mathias	Track and field
1949	Richard T. Button	Figure skating
1950	Fred Wilt	Track and field
1951	Robert E. Richards	Track and field
1952	Horace Ashenfelter	Track and field
1953	Major Sammy Lee	Diving
1954	Malvin Whitfield	Track and field
1955	Harrison Dillard	Track and field
1956	Patricia McCormick	Diving
1957	Bobby Jo Morrow	Track and Field
1958	Glenn Davis	Track and field
1959	Parry O'Brien	Track and field
1960	Rafer Johnson	Track and field
1961	Wilma Rudolph Ward	Track and field
1962	Jim Beatty	Track and field
1963	John Pennel	Track and field
1964	Don Schollander	Swimming
1965	Bill Bradley	Basketball
1966	Jim Ryun	Track and field
1967	Randy Matson	Track and field
1968	Debbie Meyer	Swimming
1969	Bill Toomey	Decathlon
1970	John Kinsella	Swimming
1971	Mark Spitz	Swimming
1972	Frank Shorter	Marathon
1973	Bill Walton	Basketball
1974	Rick Wohlhuter	Track
1975	Tim Shaw	Swimming
1976	Bruce Jenner	Track and field
1977	John Naber	Swimming
1978	Tracy Caulkins	Swimming
1979	Kurt Thomas	Gymnastics
1980	Eric Heiden	Speed skating
1981	Carl Lewis	Track and field
1982	Mary Decker Tabb	Track and field
1983	Edwin Moses	Track and field
1984	Greg Louganis	Diving
1985	Joan Benoit–Samuelson	Marathon
1986	Jackie Joyner–Kersee	Heptathlon
1987	Jim Abbott	Baseball
1988	Florence Griffith–Joyner	Track and field
1989	Janet Evans	Swimming
1990	John Smith	Wrestling
1991	Mike Powell	Track and field
1992	Bonnie Blair	Speed skating
1993	Charles Ward	Football/basketball
1994	Dan Jansen	Speed skating
1995	Bruce Baumgartner	Wrestling

BADMINTON

1996 THOMAS CUP—MEN'S WORLD TEAM CHAMPIONSHIPS

(Hong Kong, May 16–26, 1996)

Indonesia defeated Denmark, 5–0.

1996 UBER CUP—WOMEN'S WORLD TEAM CHAMPIONSHIPS

(Hong Kong, May 17–26, 1996)

Indonesia defeated China, 4–1

(1997 World Individual Championships, which are held every other year, to be held at Glasgow, Scotland, May 25–June 1, 1997)

(1997 Sudirman Cup—World Mixed Team Championship to be held at Glasgow, Scotland, May 20–24, 1997.)

1996 YONEX U.S. NATIONAL CHAMPIONSHIPS

Men's singles—Steve Butler, Miller Place, N.Y., defeated Kevin Han, Colorado Springs, Colo., 15–2, 15–11.

Women's singles—Tang Yeping, Gaithersburg, Md., defeated Andrea Andersson, Colorado Springs, Colo., 11–6, 11–4.

Men's doubles—Kevin Han and Tom Reidy, Tempe, Ariz., defeated Andy Chong, Miami Lakes, Fla., and Ben Lee, San Jose, Calif., 15–8, 15–13.

Women's doubles—Kathy Zimmerman, Denver, Colo., and Ann French, La Jolla, Calif., defeated Tan Yeping and Andrea Andersson, 15–7, 8–15, 15–9.

Mixed doubles—Andy Chong and Tang Yeping defeated Mike Edstrom, Denver, Colo., and Andrea Andersson, 12–15, 15–8, 15–6.

COLLEGE GOLF

N.C.A.A. DIVISION I CHAMPIONSHIP

(May 29–June 1, 1996, Ooltewah, Tenn.)

Team scores

Arizona State	286–300–295–305	1,186
UNLV	291–296–299–303	1,189
East Tennessee State	303–294–301–306	1,204
Stanford	292–304–303–306	1,205
Arizona	303–301–297–306	1,207
Florida	296–300–312–304	1,212
New Mexico	300–304–302–306	1,212
Oklahoma State	298–308–299–310	1,215
Southern Cal.	303–296–303–314	1,216
San Jose State	302–300–303–315	1,220

Leading individual scorers

Tiger Woods, Stanford	69–67–69–80	285
Rory Sabbatini, Arizona	70–70–74–75	289
Mike Ruiz, UNLV	71–74–74–72	291
Darren Angel, Arizona State	72–74–69–76	291
Tim Clark, North Carolina State	70–77–71–74	292
Brad Elder, Texas	71–68–76–77	292
Lewis Chitengwa, Virginia	77–72–68–76	293
Rob McMillan, New Mexico	75–71–75–73	294
Steve Scott, Florida	75–73–77–70	295
Keith Nolan, East Tennessee St.	76–71–76–72	295

HARNESS RACING

Oliver Wendell Holmes, the famous Autocrat of the Breakfast Table, wrote that the running horse was a gambling toy but the trotting horse was useful and, furthermore, "horse–racing is not a republican institution; horse–trotting is." Oliver Wendell Holmes was a born–and–bred New Englander, and New England was the nursery of the harness racing sport in America. Pacers and trotters were matters of local pride and prejudice in colonial New England, and, shortly after the Revolution, the Messenger and Justin Morgan strains produced many winners in harness racing "matches" along the turnpikes of New York, Connecticut, Rhode Island, Massachusetts, Vermont, and New Hampshire.

There was English thoroughbred blood in Messenger and Justin Morgan, and, many years later, it was blended in Rysdyk's Hambletonian, foaled in 1849. Hambletonian was not particularly fast under harness but his descendants have had almost a monopoly of prizes, titles, and records in the harness racing game. Hambletonian was purchased as a foal with its dam for a total of $124 by William Rysdyk of Goshen, N.Y., and made a modest fortune for the purchaser.

Trotters and pacers often were raced under saddle in the old days, and, in fact, the custom still survives in some places in Europe. Dexter, the great trotter that lowered the mile record from 2:19 3/4 to 2:17 1/4 in 1867, was said to handle just as well under saddle as when pulling a sulky. But as sulkies were lightened in weight and improved in design, trotting under saddle became less common and finally faded out in this country.

WORLD RECORDS

Established in a race or against time at one mile. *Source:* United States Trotting Association

➡ (Through Sept. 25, 1996)

Pacing on Mile Track

Div.	Horse	Driver	Track	Date	Time
2 C	The Big Dog	Joe S. Anderson	Woodbine	8/17/96	1:51.3
	Gothic Dream	John D. Campbell	Woodbine	8/31/96	1:51.3
2 F	Miss Easy	John D. Campbell	Lexington, Ky.	9/25/90	1:51.2
2 G	Hot Chilli Pepper	Andy Ray Miller	Springfield, Ill.	8/15/96	1:52.2
	Wrestling Matt	John D. Campbell	Woodbine	8/30/96	1:52.2
3 C	Jenna's Beach Boy	William R. Fahy	Lexington, Ky.	9/30/95	1:48.4
3 F	Shady Daisy	Michel La Chance	Lexington, Ky.	10/4/91	1:51.0
	Ellamony	Jack G. Moiseyev	Meadowlands	8/12/93	1:51.0
	Immortality	John D. Campbell	Lexington, Ky.	10/7/93	1:51.0
3 G	Gee Gee Digger	Howard G. Parker	Meadowlands	8/10/96	1:49.3
4 H	Jenna's Beach Boy	William R. Fahy	Meadowlands	6/22/96	1:47.3
4 M	Sweetgeorgiabrown	Mark J. Kesmodel	Meadowlands	8/9/96	1:50.1
4 G	Staying Together	William A. O'Donnell	Meadowlands	6/19/93	1:48.2
5+H	Riyadh	William Roy Gale	Woodbine	8/17/96	1:48.4
5+M	Ellamony	Ronald W. Waples	Meadowlands	6/23/95	1:50.3
5"G	Armbro Maestro	Mark J. Kemodel	Meadowlands	6/15/96	1:49.2
	Darth Raider	James A. Morrill, Jr.	Meadowlands	7/6/96	1:49.2

Pacing on Five-Eighths Mile Track

Div.	Horse	Driver	Track	Date	Time
2 C	Artsplace	John D. Campbell	Pompano Park	11/30/90	1:51.1
2 F	Central Park West	John D. Campbell	Pompano Park	11/18/88	1:53.3
	Hardie Hanover	Timothy P. Twaddle	Mohawk	10/24/93	1:53.3
2 G	Nights Journey	Thomas H. Jackson	Rosecroft	6/27/92	1:54.1
3 C	Riyadh	James A. Morrill, Jr.	Ladbroke	8/14/93	1:50.1
3 F	Hardie Hanover	Timothy P. Twaddle	Ladbroke	9/24/94	1:52.1
3 G	Nights Journey	Thomas H. Jackson	Rosecroft	8/14/93	1:52.0
	Duke Duke	David S. Miller	Scioto Downs	7/23/94	1:52.0
4 H	Jenna's Beach Boy	William R. Fahy	Rosecroft	8/31/96	1:49.2
4 M	She's A Great Lady	Kevin M. Sizer	Pocono Downs	8/31/96	1:51.0
4 G	Staying Together	William A. O'Donnell	Greenwood Raceway	8/14/93	1:50.4
5+H	Hi Ho Silverheel's	Richard H. Kuebler	Los Alamitos	4/5/96	1:51.1
	Wynfield Mark	Steven W. Warrington	Rosecroft	6/29/96	1:51.1
	Eicarl	David L. Myers	Scioto Downs	6/15/96	1:51.1
5+M	Camourous	David M. Palone	Ladbroke	11/04/94	1:52.0
5+G	Shadow Dance	Richard A. Wojcio	Pocono Downs	8/24/96	1:51.0

Pacing on Half- Mile Track

Div.	Horse	Driver	Track	Date	Time
2 C	Tooter Scooter	William R. Fahy	Louisville, Ky.	9/01/90	1:54.1
	W R H	John D. Campbell	Delaware, Ohio	9/20/90	1:54.1
	Easter Sun Hanna	Luc R. Ouellette	Freehold	10/3/92	1:54.1
	Mattcando	Sam O. Noble III	Delaware, Ohio	9/22/94	1:54.1
2 F	CR Daniella	Michael Lee Allen	Freehold	10/8/94	1:55.3
2 G	Scotch Baker	Steve J. Brannon	Delaware, Ohio	9/20/89	1:55.3
	Cinder Lane Same	David S. Miller	Delaware, Ohio	9/21/94	1:55.3
	Fortune On Hold	David S. Miller	Delaware, Ohio	9/18/96	1:55.3
3 C	Falcon Seelster	Thomas Gleen Harmer	Delaware, Ohio	9/19/85	1:51.0
3 F	She's A Great Lady	Joe S. Anderson	Maywood	6/17/95	1:51.2
3 G	Nick's Fantasy	John D. Campbell	Delaware, Ohio	9/21/95	1:51.2
4 H	Stand Forever	John D. Campbell	Delaware, Ohio	9/19/96	1:49.2
4 M	She's A Great Lady	John D. Campbell	Delaware, Ohio	9/17/96	1:51.0
4 G	Majestic Osborne	Joseph Adamsky	Northfield Park	6/19/93	1:52.3
	Hotrod Falcon	Richard W. Wojcio	Freehold	8/28/93	1:52.3
5+H	Silver Almahurst	James A. Morrill, Jr.	Yonkers	4/24/93	1:50.4
5+M	Pacific Flight N	Joe S. Anderson	Maywood	6/16/95	1:52.3
5+G	Legal Alien	Richard A. Wojcio	Yonkers	6/17/95	1:52.3

Trotting on a Mile Track

Div.	Horse	Driver	Track	Date	Time
2 C	Mack Lobell	John D. Campbell	Lexington, Ky.	10/3/86	1:55.3
2 F	CR Kay Suzie	Carl E. Allen	Meadowlands	8/3/94	1:55.1
2 G	I'm Impeccable	David A. Rankin	Lexington, Ky.	9/28/89	1:57.2
	Harmony Oaks Royal	Andy Ray Miller	Springfield, Ill.	8/12/95	1:57.2
3 C	Mack Lobell	John D. Campbell	Springfield, Ill.	8/21/87	1:52.1
3 F	Continentalvictory	Michel La Chance	Meadowlands	8/3/96	1:52.1
3 G	Champion On Ice	David R. Magee	Springfield, Ill.	8/12/94	1:53.2
4 H	Pine Chip	John D. Campbell	Meadowlands	8/6/94	1:52.4
4 M	Beat The Wheel	Catello R. Manzi	Meadowlands	7/8/94	1:51.4
4 G	Champion On Ice	David R. Magee	Springfield, Ill.	8/12/95	1:53.1
5+H	Wesgate Crown	Catello R. Manzi	Meadowlands	7/27/96	1:52.3
5+M	Beat The Wheel	Catello R. Manzi	Meadowlands	7/6/95	1:53.3
5+G	Oaklea Count	Ronald W. Waples	Meadowlands	8/3/96	1:52.1

Trotting on a Five-Eighths Mile Track

Div.	Horse	Driver	Track	Date	Time
2 C	King Conch	William Roy Gale	Pompano Park	10/25/91	1:56.2
2 F	CR Kay Suzie	Rodney D. Allen	Rosecroft	9/9/94	1:56.1
2 G	Woodman	William Roy Gale	Mohawk	11/14/93	1:58.4
3 C	Mack Lobell	John D. Campbell	Pompano Park	11/13/87	1:54.1
3 F	Expressway Hanover	Per Henriksen	Pompano Park	10/29/93	1:55.4
3 G	Woodman	J. Douglas McIntosh	Mohawk	10/7/94	1:55.0
4 H	Express Ride	Berndt O. Lindstedt	Sportsman's Park	9/6/87	1:55.0
	Earl	Chris J. Christoforou	Mohawk	5/10/93	1:55.0
4 M	Lifelong Victory	Michel La Chance	Pocono Downs	7/28/96	1:54.2
	Peace Corps	Stig H. Johansson	Pompano Park	11/2/90	1:54.2
4 G	Delray Lobell	Donald Irvine, Jr.	Freestate Raceway	8/20/89	1:55.2
5+H	Earl	Sylvain R. Filion	Hyperdrome de Quebec	8/19/94	1:55.0
5+M	Lifetime Dream	David W. Wall	Mohawk	10/8/94	1:55.3
5+G	Golly Too	Jeffery D. Fout	Scioto Downs	8/31/96	1:54.2

Trotting on a Half-Mile Track

Div.	Horse	Driver	Track	Date	Time
2 C	Royal Troubador	Carl E. Allen	Delaware, Ohio	9/19/89	1:58.1
2 F	CR Kay Suzie	Rodney D. Allen	Freehold	9/21/94	1:56.3
2 G	Armbro Marshall	William Wellwood	Barrie Raceway	10/6/93	1:59.3
3 C	Incredible Abe	John D. Campbell	Delaware, Ohio	9/18/94	1:55.4
3 F	Peace Corps	John D. Campbell	Delaware, Ohio	9/21/89	1:56.0
	CR Kay Suzie	Rodney D. Allen	Yonkers	7/8/95	1:56.0
3 G	Armbro Leader	William A. O'Donnell	Maywood	11/16/93	1:57.0
4 H	Pine Chip	John D. Campbell	Delaware, Ohio	9/18/94	1:54.0
4 M	Lifelong Victory	Ronald D. Piercve	Delaware, Ohio	9/15/96	1:54.4
4 G	Doc Mistake	Donald Irvine, Jr.	Delaware, Ohio	9/15/96	1:55.4
5+H	Six Day War	Raymond W. Schnittker	Yonkers	4/23/93	1:56.4
5+M	Sunbird Groovey	James F. Doherty	Freehold	8/27/93	1:56.4
5+G	Impeccable Image	Walter H. Case, Jr.	Yonkers	4/5/96	1:55.4

HISTORY OF TRADITIONAL HARNESS RACING STAKES

The Hambletonian

Three-year-old trotters. One mile. Guy McKinney won first race at Syracuse in 1926; held at Goshen, N.Y., 1930–1942, 1944–1956; at Yonkers, N.Y., 1943; at Du Quoin, Ill., 1957–1980. Since 1981, the race has been held at The Meadowlands in East Rutherford, N.J.

Year	Winner	Driver	Best time	Total purse
1967	Speedy Streak	Del Cameron	2:00	$122,650
1968	Nevele Pride	Stanley Dancer	1:59 2/5	116,190
1969	Lindy's Pride	Howard Beissinger	1:57 3/5	124,910
1970	Timothy T.	John Simpson, Jr.	1:58 2/5[1]	143,630
1971	Speedy Crown	Howard Beissinger	1:57 2/5	129,770
1972	Super Bowl	Stanley Dancer	1:56 2/5	119,090
1973	Flirth	Ralph Baldwin	1:57 1/5	144,710
1974	Christopher T	Billy Haughton	1:58 3/5	160,150
1975	Bonefish	Stanley Dancer	1:59[2]	232,192
1976	Steve Lobell	Billy Haughton	1:56 2/5	263,524
1977	Green Speed	Billy Haughton	1:55 3/5	284,131
1978	Speedy Somolli	Howard Beissinger	1:55[3]	241,280
1979	Legend Hanover	George Sholty	1:56 1/5	300,000
1980	Burgomeister	Billy Haughton	1:56 3/5	293,570
1981	Shiaway St. Pat	Ray Remmen	2:01 1/5[4]	838,000
1982	Speed Bowl	Tommy Haughton	1:56 4/5	875,750
1983	Duenna	Stanley Dancer	1:57 2/5	1,000,000
1984	Historic Free	Ben Webster	1:56 2/5	1,219,000
1985	Prakas	Bill O'Donnell	1:54 3/5	1,272,000
1986	Nuclear Kosmos	Ulf Thoresen	1:56	1,172,082
1987	Mack Lobell	John Campbell	1:53 3/5	1,046,300
1988	Armbro Goal	John Campbell	1:54 3/5	1,156,800
1989	Park Avenue Joe	Ron Wayples	1:55 3/5	1,131,000
1990	Embassy Lobell	Michel La Chance	1:56 1/5	1,346,000

1991	Giant Victory	Jack Moiseyev	1:54 4/5	1,238,000
1992	Alf Palema	Mickey McNichol	1:56 3/5	1,288,000
1993	American Winner	Ron Pierce	1:53 1/5	1,200,000
1994	Victory Dream	Michel La Chance	1:53 4/5	1,200,000
1995	Tagliabue	John Campbell	1:54 3/5	1,200,000
1996	Continentalvictory	Michel La Chance	1:52 4/5	1,200,000

1. By Formal Notice. 2. By Yankee Bambino. 3. By Speedy Somolli and Florida Pro. 4. By Super Juan.

Little Brown Jug
Three–year–old pacers. One Mile. Raced at Delaware County Fair Grounds, Delaware, Ohio.

Year	Winner	Driver	Best time	Total purse
1967	Best of All	Jim Hackett	1:59[1]	S84,778
1968	Rum Customer	Billy Haughton	1:59 3/5	104,226
1969	Laverne Hanover	Billy Haughton	2:00 2/5	109,731
1970	Most Happy Fella	Stanley Dancer	1:57 1/5	100,110
1971	Nansemond	Herve Filion	1:57 2/5	102,994
1972	Strike Out	Keith Waples	1:56 3/5	104,916
1973	Melvin's Woe	Joe O'Brien	1:57 3/5	120,000
1974	Ambro Omaha	Billy Haughton	1:57	132,630
1975	Seatrain	Ben Webster	1:57[2]	147,813
1976	Keystone Ore	Stanley Dancer	1:56 4/5[3]	153,799
1977	Governor Skipper	John Chapman	1:56 1/5	150,000
1978	Happy Escort	William Popfinger	1:55 2/5[4]	186,760
1979	Hot Hitter	Herve Filion	1:55 3/5	226,455
1980	Niatross	Clint Galbraith	1:54 4/5	207,361
1981	Fan Hanover	Glen Garnsey	1:56[5]	243,799
1982	Merger	John Campbell	1:56 3/5	328,900
1983	Ralph Hanover	Ron Waples	1:55 3/5	358,800
1984	Colt 46	Norman Boring	1:53 3/5	366,717
1985	Nihilator	Bill O'Donnell	1:52 1/5	350,730
1986	Barberry Spur	Bill O'Donnell	1:52 4/5	407,684
1987	Jaguar Spur	Richard Stillings	1:55 3/5	412,330
1988	B.J. Scoot	Michel La Chance	1:52 3/5	486,050
1989	Goalie Jeff	Michel La Chance	1:54 1/5	500,200
1990	Beach Towel	Ray Remmen	1:53 3/5	253,049
1991	Precious Bunny	Jack Moiseyev	1:54 1/5	575,150
1992	Fake Left	Ron Waples	1:54 2/5	556,210
1993	Life Sign	John Campbell	1:52	465,500
1994	Magical Mike	Michel La Chance	1:52 3/5	512,830
1995	Nick's Fantasy	John Campbell	1:51 2/5	543,670
1996	Armbro Operative	Michel La Chance	1:52 3/5	542,220

1. By Nardin's Byrd. 2. By Albert's Star. 3. By Armbro Ranger. 4. By Falcon Almahurst. 5. By Seahawk Hanover.

HARNESS HORSE OF THE YEAR
Chosen in poll conducted by United States Trotting Association in conjunction with the U.S. Harness Writers Assn.

1959	Bye Bye Byrd, Pacer	1975	Savoir, Trotter	1986	Forrest Skipper
1960–61	Adios Butler, Pacer	1976	Keystone Ore, Pacer	1987–88	Mack Lobell
1962	Su Mac Lad, Trotter	1977	Green Speed, Trotter	1989	Matt's Scooter
1963	Speedy Scot, Trotter	1978	Abercrombie, Pacer	1990	Beach Towel
1964–66	Bret Hanover, Pacer	1979–80	Niatross, Pacer	1991	Precious Bunny
1967–69	Nevele Pride, Trotter	1981	Fan Hanover, Pacer	1992	Artsplace
1970	Fresh Yankee, Trotter	1982–83	Cam Fella, Pacer	1993	Staying Together
1971–72	Albatross, Pacer	1984	Fancy Crown, Trotter	1994	Cam's Card Shark
1973	Sir Dalrae, Pacer	1985	Nihilator, Trotter	1995	CR Kay Suzie
1974	Delmonica Hanover, Trotter				

RODEO

A rodeo was originally a contest held after a roundup where the cowboys competed among themselves in contests such as horse racing, steer riding, and calf roping. This display of cowboy skills originated in Mexico and the word "rodeo" comes from the Spanish word *rodear* which means a cattle roundup. The first real rodeo is commonly believed to have been held in Kansas in 1882 and was organized by Col. George Miller of the famous 101 Ranch. Others think that the first organized rodeo was held in Pecos, Texas, in 1883.

PROFESSIONAL RODEO COWBOY ASSOCIATION, ALL AROUND COWBOY

1953	Bill Linderman	1962	Tom Nesmith	1975	Leo Camarillo and	1983	Roy Cooper
1954	Buck Rutherford	1963–65	Dean Oliver		Tom Ferguson	1984	Dee Pickett
1955	Casey Tibbs	1966–70	Larry Mahan	1976–79	Tom Ferguson	1985–87	Lewis Field
1956–59	Jim Shoulders	1971–72	Phil Lyne	1980	Paul Tierney	1988	Dave Appleton
1960	Harry Tompkins	1973	Larry Mahan	1981	Jimmie Cooper	1989–94	Ty Murray
1961	Benny Reynolds	1974	Tom Ferguson	1982	Chris Lybbert	1995	Joe Beaver

NOTE: 1996 Championship scheduled after *Information Please Almanac* went to press.

GOLF

It may be that golf originated in Holland—historians believe it did—but certainly Scotland fostered the game and is famous for it. In fact, in 1457 the Scottish Parliament, disturbed because football and golf had lured young Scots from the more soldierly exercise of archery, passed an ordinance that "futeball and golf be utterly cryit doun and nocht usit." James I and Charles I of the royal line of Stuarts were golf enthusiasts, whereby the game came to be known as "the royal and ancient game of golf."

The golf balls used in the early games were leather–covered and stuffed with feathers. Clubs of all kinds were fashioned by hand to suit individual players. The great step in spreading the game came with the change from the feather ball to the guttapercha ball about 1850. In 1860, formal competition began with the establishment of an annual tournament for the British Open championship. There are records of "golf clubs" in the United States as far back as colo-nial days but no proof of actual play before John Reid and some friends laid out six holes on the Reid lawn in Yonkers, N.Y., in 1888 and played there with golf balls and clubs brought over from Scotland by Robert Lockhart. This group then formed the St. Andrews Golf Club of Yonkers, and golf was established in this country.

However, it remained a rather sedate and almost aristocratic pastime until a 20-year-old ex-caddy, Francis Ouimet of Boston, defeated two great British professionals, Harry Vardon and Ted Ray, in the United States Open championship at Brookline, Mass., in 1913. This feat put the game and Francis Ouimet on the front pages of the newspapers and stirred a wave of enthusiasm for the sport. The greatest feat so far in golf history is that of Robert Tyre Jones, Jr., of Atlanta, who won the British Open, the British Amateur, the U.S. Open, and the U.S. Amateur titles in one year, 1930.

THE MASTERS TOURNAMENT WINNERS

Augusta National Golf Club, Augusta, Ga.

Year	Winner	Score	Year	Winner	Score	Year	Winner	Score
1934	Horton Smith	284	1957	Doug Ford	283	1977	Tom Watson	276
1935	Gene Sarazen[1]	282	1958	Arnold Palmer	284	1978	Gary Player	277
1936	Horton Smith	285	1959	Art Wall, Jr.	284	1979	Fuzzy Zoeller[1]	280
1937	Byron Nelson	283	1960	Arnold Palmer	282	1980	Severiano Ballesteros	275
1938	Henry Picard	285	1961	Gary Player	280	1981	Tom Watson	280
1939	Ralph Guldahl	279	1962	Arnold Palmer[1]	280	1982	Craig Stadler[1]	284
1940	Jimmy Demaret	280	1963	Jack Nicklaus	286	1983	Severiano Ballesteros	280
1941	Craig Wood	280	1964	Arnold Palmer	276	1984	Ben Crenshaw	277
1942	Byron Nelson[1]	280	1965	Jack Nicklaus	271	1985	Bernhard Langer	282
1943–45	No Tournaments		1966	Jack Nicklaus[1]	288	1986	Jack Nicklaus	279
1946	Herman Keiser	282	1967	Gay Brewer, Jr.	280	1987	Larry Mize[1]	285
1947	Jimmy Demaret	281	1968	Bob Goalby	277	1988	Sandy Lyle	281
1948	Claude Harmon	279	1969	George Archer	281	1989	Nick Faldo[1]	283
1949	Sam Snead	282	1970	Billy Casper[1]	279	1990	Nick Faldo	278
1950	Jimmy Demaret	283	1971	Charles Coody	279	1991	Ian Woosnam	277
1951	Ben Hogan	280	1972	Jack Nicklaus	286	1992	Fred Couples	275
1952	Sam Snead	286	1973	Tommy Aaron	283	1993	Bernard Langer	277
1953	Ben Hogan	274	1974	Gary Player	278	1994	Jose Maria Olazabal	279
1954	Sam Snead[1]	289	1975	Jack Nicklaus	276	1995	Ben Crenshaw	274
1955	Cary Middlecoff	279	1976	Ray Floyd	271	1996	Nick Faldo	276
1956	Jack Burke	289						

1. Winner in playoff.

U.S. OPEN CHAMPIONS

Year	Winner	Score	Where played	Year	Winner	Score	Where played
1895	Horace Rawlins	173	Newport	1915	Jerome D. Travers[2]	297	Baltusrol
1896	James Foulis	152	Shinnecock Hills	1916	Charles Evans, Jr.[2]	286	Minikahda
1897	Joe Lloyd	162	Chicago	1917–18	No tournaments[4]		
1898[3]	Fred Herd	328	Myopia	1919	Walter Hagen[2]	301	Brae Burn
1899	Willie Smith	315	Baltimore	1920	Edward Ray	295	Inverness
1900	Harry Vardon	313	Chicago	1921	Jim Barnes	289	Columbia
1901	Willie Anderson[1]	331	Myopia	1922	Gene Sarazen	288	Skokie
1902	Laurie Auchterlonie	307	Garden City	1923	R. T. Jones, Jr.[1 2]	296	Inwood
1903	Willie Anderson[1]	307	Baltusrol	1924	Cyril Walker	297	Oakland Hills
1904	Willie Anderson	303	Glen View	1925	Willie Macfarlane[1]	291	Worcester
1905	Willie Anderson	314	Myopia	1926	R. T. Jones, Jr.[2]	293	Scioto
1906	Alex Smith	295	Onwentsia	1927	Tommy Armour[1]	301	Oakmont
1907	Alex Ross	302	Philadelphia	1928	Johnny Farrell[1]	294	Olympia Fields
1908	Fred McLeod[1]	322	Myopia	1929	R. T. Jones, Jr.[1 2]	294	Winged Foot
1909	George Sargent	290	Englewood	1930	R. T. Jones, Jr.[2]	287	Interlachen
1910	Alex Smith[1]	298	Philadelphia	1931	Billy Burke[1]	292	Inverness
1911	John McDermott[1]	307	Chicago	1932	Gene Sarazen	286	Fresh Meadow
1912	John McDermott	294	Buffalo	1933	John Goodman[2]	287	North Shore
1913	Francis Ouimet[1 2]	304	Brookline	1934	Olin Dutra	293	Merion
1914	Walter Hagen	290	Midlothian	1935	Sam Parks, Jr.	299	Oakmont

Year	Winner	Score	Where played	Year	Winner	Score	Where played
1936	Tony Manero	282	Baltusrol	1969	Orville Moody	281	Champions G. C.
1937	Ralph Guldahl	281	Oakland Hills	1970	Tony Jacklin	281	Hazeltine
1938	Ralph Guldahl	284	Cherry Hills	1971	Lee Trevino[1]	280	Merion
1939	Byron Nelson[1]	284	Philadelphia	1972	Jack Nicklaus	290	Pebble Beach
1940	Lawson Little[1]	287	Canterbury	1973	Johnny Miller	279	Oakmont
1941	Craig Wood	284	Colonial	1974	Hale Irwin	287	Winged Foot
1942–45	No tournaments[5]			1975	Lou Graham[1]	287	Medinah
1946	Lloyd Mangrum[1]	284	Canterbury	1976	Jerry Pate	277	Atlanta A.C.
1947	Lew Worsham[1]	282	St. Louis	1977	Hubert Green	278	Southern Hills
1948	Ben Hogan	276	Riviera	1978	Andy North	285	Cherry Hills
1949	Cary Middlecoff	286	Medinah	1979	Hale Irwin	284	Inverness
1950	Ben Hogan[1]	287	Merion	1980	Jack Nicklaus	272	Baltusrol
1951	Ben Hogan	287	Oakland Hills	1981	David Graham	273	Merion
1952	Julius Boros	281	Northwood	1982	Tom Watson	282	Pebble Beach
1953	Ben Hogan	283	Oakmont	1983	Larry Nelson	280	Oakmont
1954	Ed Furgol	284	Baltusrol	1984	Fuzzy Zoeller[1]	276	Winged Foot
1955	Jack Fleck[1]	287	Olympic	1985	Andy North	279	Oakland Hills
1956	Cary Middlecoff	281	Oak Hill	1986	Ray Floyd	279	Shinnecock Hills
1957	Dick Mayer[1]	298	Inverness	1987	Scott Simpson	277	Olympic Golf Club
1958	Tommy Bolt	283	Southern Hills	1988	Curtis Strange[1]	278	The Country Club
1959	Bill Casper, Jr.	282	Winged Foot	1989	Curtis Strange	278	Oak Hill Country Club
1960	Arnold Palmer	280	Cherry Hills				
1961	Gene Littler	281	Oakland Hills	1990	Hale Irwin[1]	280	Medinah C.C.
1962	Jack Nicklaus[1]	283	Oakmont	1991	Payne Stewart[1]	282	Hazeltine
1963	Julius Boros[1]	293	Country Club	1992	Tom Kite	285	Pebble Beach
1964	Ken Venturi	278	Congressional	1993	Lee Janzen	272	Baltusrol
1965	Gary Player[1]	282	Bellerive	1994	Ernie Els	279	Oakmont
1966	Bill Casper[1]	278	Olympic	1995	Corey Pavin	280	Shinnecock Hills
1967	Jack Nicklaus	275	Baltusrol	1996	Steve Jones	278	Oakland Hills
1968	Lee Trevino	275	Oak Hill				

1. Winner in playoff. 2. Amateur. 3. In 1898, competition was extended to 72 holes. 4. In 1917, Jock Hutchison, with a 292, won an Open Patriotic Tournament for the benefit of the American Red Cross at Whitemarsh Valley Country Club. 5. In 1942, Ben Hogan, with a 271 won a Hale American National Open Tournament for the benefit of the Navy Relief Society and USO at Ridgemoor Country Club.

U.S. AMATEUR CHAMPIONS

1895	Charles B. Macdonald	1923	Max R. Marston	1952	Jack Westland	1975	Fred Ridley
1896–97	H. J. Whigham	1924–25	R. T. Jones, Jr.	1953	Gene Littler	1976	Bill Sander
1898	Findlay S. Douglas	1926	George Von Elm	1954	Arnold Palmer	1977	John Fought
1899	H. M. Harriman	1927–28	R. T. Jones, Jr.	1955–56	Harvie Ward	1978	John Cook
1900–01	Walter J. Travis	1929	H. R. Johnston	1957	Hillman Robbins	1979	Mark O'Meara
1902	Louis N. James	1930	R. T. Jones, Jr.	1958	Charles Coe	1980	Hal Sutton
1903	Walter J. Travis	1931	Francis Ouimet	1959	Jack Nicklaus	1981	Nathaniel Crosby
1904–05	H. Chandler Egan	1932	Ross Somerville	1960	Deane Beman	1982	Jay Sigel
1906	Eben M. Byers	1933	G. T. Dunlap, Jr.	1961	Jack Nicklaus	1983	Jay Sigel
1907–08	Jerome D. Travers	1934–35	Lawson Little	1962	Labron Harris, Jr.	1984	Scott Verplank
1909	Robert A. Gardner	1936	John W. Fischer	1963	Deane Beman	1985	Sam Randolph
1910	W. C. Fownes, Jr.	1937	John Goodman	1964	Bill Campbell	1986	Buddy Alexander
1911	Harold H. Hilton	1938	Willie Turnesa	1965[2]	Robert Murphy, Jr.	1987	Bill Mayfair
1912–13	Jerome D. Travers	1939	Marvin H. Ward	1966	Gary Cowan[1]	1988	Eric Meeks
1914	Francis Ouimet	1940	R. D. Chapman	1967	Bob Dickson	1989	Chris Patton
1915	Robert A. Gardner	1941	Marvin H. Ward	1968	Bruce Fleisher	1990	Phil Mickelson
1916	Charles Evans, Jr.	1946	Ted Bishop	1969	Steven Melnyk	1991	Mitch Voges
1919	S. D. Herron	1947	Robert Riegel	1970	Lanny Wadkins	1992	Justin Leonard
1920	Charles Evans, Jr.	1948	Willie Turnesa	1971	Gary Cowan	1993	John Harris
1921	Jesse P. Guilford	1949	Charles Coe	1972	Vinny Giles 3d	1994	Tiger Woods
1922	Jess W. Sweetser	1950	Sam Urzetta	1973[3]	Craig Stadler	1995	Tiger Woods
		1951	Billy Maxwell	1974	Jerry Pate	1996	Tiger Woods

1. Winner in playoff. 2. Tourney switched to medal play through 1972. 3. Return to match play.

U.S. P.G.A. CHAMPIONS

1916	Jim Barnes	1930	Tommy Armour	1938	Paul Runyan	1946	Ben Hogan
1919	Jim Barnes	1931	Tom Creavy	1939	Henry Picard	1947	Jim Ferrier
1920	Jock Hutchison	1932	Olin Dutra	1940	Byron Nelson	1948	Ben Hogan
1921	Walter Hagen	1933	Gene Sarazen	1941	Victor Ghezzi	1949	Sam Snead
1922–23	Gene Sarazen	1934	Paul Runyan	1942	Sam Snead	1950	Chandler Harper
1924–27	Walter Hagen	1935	Johnny Revolta	1944	Bob Hamilton	1951	Sam Snead
1928–29	Leo Diegel	1936–37	Denny Shute	1945	Byron Nelson	1952	Jim Turnesa

1953	Walter Burkemo	1964	Bobby Nichols	1975	Jack Nicklaus	1986	Bob Tway
1954	Chick Harbert	1965	Dave Marr	1976	Dave Stockton	1987	Larry Nelson
1955	Doug Ford	1966	Al Geiberger	1977	Lanny Wadkins[1]	1988	Jeff Sluman
1956	Jack Burke, Jr.	1967	Don January[1]	1978	John Mahaffey	1989	Payne Stewart
1957	Lionel Hebert	1968	Julius Boros	1979	David Graham[1]	1990	Mac Grady
1958[2]	Dow Finsterwald	1969	Ray Floyd	1980	Jack Nicklaus	1991	John Daly
1959	Bob Rosburg	1970	Dave Stockton	1981	Larry Nelson	1992	Nick Price
1960	Jay Hebert	1971	Jack Nicklaus	1982	Ray Floyd	1993	Paul Azinger[1]
1961	Jerry Barber[1]	1972	Gary Player	1983	Hal Sutton	1994	Nick Price
1962	Gary Player	1973	Jack Nicklaus	1984	Lee Trevino	1995	Steve Elkington
1963	Jack Nicklaus	1974	Lee Trevino	1985	Hubert Green	1996	Mark Brooks

1. Winner in playoff. 2. Switched to medal play.

U.S. WOMEN'S AMATEUR CHAMPIONS

1916	Alexa Stirling	1941	Mrs. Frank Newell		Decker	1978	Cathy Sherk
1919–20	Alexa Stirling	1946	Mildred Zaharias	1962	JoAnne	1979	Carolyn Hill
1921	Marion Hollins	1947	Louise Suggs		Gunderson	1980	Juli Inkster
1922	Glenna Collett	1948	Grace Lenczyk	1963	Anne Quast Welts	1981	Juli Inkster
1923	Edith Cummings	1949	Mrs. D. G. Porter	1964	Barbara McIntire	1982	Juli Inkster
1924	Dorothy Campbell Hurd	1950	Beverly Hanson	1965	Jean Ashley	1983	Joanne Pacillo
		1951	Dorothy Kirby	1966	JoAnne	1984	Deb Richard
1925	Glenna Collett	1952	Jacqueline Pung		Gunderson	1985	Michiko Hattori
1926	Helen Stetson	1953	Mary Lena Faulk	1967	Lou Dill	1986	Kay Cockerill
1927	Mrs. M. B. Horn	1954	Barbara Romack	1968	JoAnne G. Carner	1987	Kay Cockerill
1928–30	Glenna Collett	1955	Patricia Lesser	1969	Catherine LaCoste	1988	Pearl Sinn
1931	Helen Hicks	1956	Marlene Stewart	1970	Martha Wilkinson	1989	Vicki Goetze
1932–34	Virginia Van Wie	1957	JoAnne	1971	Laura Baugh	1990	Pat Hurst
1935	Glenna Collett Vare		Gunderson	1972	Mary Ann Budke	1991	Amy Fruhwirth
1936	Pamela Barton	1958	Anne Quast	1973	Carol Semple	1992	Vicki Goetze
1937	Mrs. J. A. Page, Jr.	1959	Barbara McIntire	1974	Cynthia Hill	1993	Jill McGill
		1960	JoAnne	1975	Beth Daniel	1994	Wendy Ward
1938	Patty Berg		Gunderson	1976	Donna Horton	1995	Kelli Kuehne
1939–40	Betty Jameson	1961	Anne Quast	1977	Beth Daniel	1996	Kelli Kuehne

U.S. WOMEN'S OPEN CHAMPIONS

Year	Winner	Score	Year	Winner	Score	Year	Winner	Score
1946	Patty Berg (match play)	—	1963	Mary Mills	289	1980	Amy Alcott	280
1947	Betty Jameson	295	1964	Mickey Wright[1]	290	1981	Pat Bradley	279
1948	Mildred D. Zaharias	300	1965	Carol Mann	290	1982	Janet Alex	283
1949	Louise Suggs	291	1966	Sandra Spuzich	297	1983	Jan Stephenson	290
1950	Mildred D. Zaharias	291	1967	Catherine LaCoste[2]	294	1984	Hollis Stacy	290
1951	Betsy Rawls	293	1968	Susie Berning	289	1985	Kathy Baker	280
1952	Louise Suggs	284	1969	Donna Caponi	294	1986	Jane Geddes[1]	287
1953	Betsy Rawls[1]	302	1970	Donna Caponi	287	1987	Laura Davies[1]	285
1954	Mildred D. Zaharias	291	1971	JoAnne Carner	288	1988	Liselotte Neumann	277
1955	Fay Crocker	299	1972	Susie Berning	299	1989	Betsy King	278
1956	Katherine Cornelius[1]	302	1973	Susie Berning	290	1990	Betsy King	284
1957	Betsy Rawls	299	1974	Sandra Haynie	295	1991	Meg Mallon	283
1958	Mickey Wright	290	1975	Sandra Palmer	295	1992	Patty Sheehan	280
1959	Mickey Wright	287	1976	JoAnne Carner[1]	292	1993	Lauri Merten	280
1960	Betsy Rawls	291	1977	Hollis Stacy	292	1994	Patty Sheehan	277
1961	Mickey Wright	293	1978	Hollis Stacy	289	1995	Annika Sorenstam	278
1962	Murle Lindstrom	301	1979	Jerilyn Britz	284	1996	Annika Sorenstam	272

1. Winner in playoff. 2. Amateur.

BRITISH OPEN CHAMPIONS

(First tournament, held in 1860, was won by Willie Park, Sr.)

Year	Winner	Score	Year	Winner	Score	Year	Winner	Score
1920	George Duncan	303	1928	Walter Hagen	292	1936	A. H. Padgham	287
1921	Jock Hutchison[1]	296	1929	Walter Hagen	292	1937	Henry Cotton	290
1922	Walter Hagen	300	1930	R. T. Jones, Jr.	291	1938	R. A. Whitcombe	295
1923	A. G. Havers	295	1931	Tommy Armour	296	1939	R. Burton	290
1924	Walter Hagen	301	1932	Gene Sarazen	283	1940	Sam Snead	290
1925	Jim Barnes	300	1933	Denny Shute[1]	292	1947	Fred Daly	294
1926	R. T. Jones, Jr.	291	1934	Henry Cotton	283	1948	Henry Cotton	283
1927	R. T. Jones, Jr.	285	1935	A. Perry	283	1949	Bobby Locke[1]	283

1. Winner in playoff.

Year	Winner	Score	Year	Winner	Score	Year	Winner	Score
1950	Bobby Locke	279	1966	Jack Nicklaus	282	1982	Tom Watson	284
1951	Max Faulkner	285	1967	Roberto de Vicenzo	278	1983	Tom Watson	275
1952	Bobby Locke	287	1968	Gary Player	289	1984	Severiano Ballesteros	276
1953	Ben Hogan	282	1969	Tony Jacklin	280	1985	Sandy Lyle	282
1954	Peter Thomson	283	1970	Jack Nicklaus[1]	283	1986	Greg Norman	280
1955	Peter Thomson	281	1971	Lee Trevino	278	1987	Nick Faldo	279
1956	Peter Thomson	286	1972	Lee Trevino	278	1988	Seve Ballesteros	273
1957	Bobby Locke	279	1973	Tom Weiskopf	276	1989	Mark Calcavecchia	275
1958	Peter Thomson[1]	278	1974	Gary Player	282	1990	Nick Faldo	270
1959	Gary Player	284	1975	Tom Watson[1]	279	1991	Ian Baker-Finch	272
1960	Kel Nagle	278	1976	Johnny Miller	279	1992	Nick Faldo	272
1961	Arnold Palmer	284	1977	Tom Watson	268	1993	Greg Norman	267
1962	Arnold Palmer	276	1978	Jack Nicklaus	281	1994	Nick Price	268
1963	Bob Charles[1]	277	1979	Severiano Ballesteros	283	1995	John Daly	282
1964	Tony Lema	279	1980	Tom Watson	271	1996	Tom Lehman	271
1965	Peter Thomson	285	1981	Bill Rogers	276			

1. Winner in playoff.

OTHER 1996 PGA TOUR WINNERS

(Through Sept. 29, 1996)

Mercedes Championships—Mark O'Meara	$180,000
Nortel Open—Phil Mickelson	225,000
Bob Hope Chrysler Classic—Mark Brooks	234,000
Phoenix Open—Phil Mickelson	234,000
United Airlines Hawaiian Open—Jim Furyk	216,000
Nissan Open—Craig Stadler	216,000
Doral-Ryder Open—Greg Norman	324,000
The Players Championship—Fred Couples	630,000
BellSouth Classic—Paul Stankowski	234,000
MCI Classic—Loren Roberts	252,000
Greater Greensboro Chrysler Classic—Mark O'Meara	324,000
Shell Houston Open—Mark Brooks	270,000
Byron Nelson Classic—Phil Mickelson	270,000
MasterCard Colonial—Corey Pavin	270,000
Kemper Open—Steve Stricker	270,000
Memorial Tournament—Tom Watson	324,000
Buick Classic—Ernie Els	216,000
FedEx St. Jude Classic—John Cook	243,000
Canon Greater Hartford Open—D.A. Weibring	270,000
Motorola Western Open—Steve Stricker	360,000
CVS Charity Classic—John Cook	216,000
Buick Open—Justin Leonard	216,000
Sprint International—Clarence Rose	288,000
Buick Challenge—Michael Bradley	180,000

OTHER 1996 LPGA TOUR WINNERS

(Through Sept. 29, 1996)

Chrysler-Plymouth Tournament of Champions—Liselotte Neumann	$117,500
Cup Noodles Hawaiian Ladies Open—Meg Mallon	90,000
Ping/Welch's Championship—Liselotte Neumann	67,500
Nabisco Dinah Shore—Patty Sheehan	135,000
Twelve Bridges LPGA Classic—Kelly Robbins	75,000
Sara Lee Classic—Meg Mallon	90,000
Sprint Titleholders Championship—Karrie Webb	180,000
McDonald's LPGA Championship—Laura Davies	180,000
LPGA Corning Classic—Rosie Jones	90,000
Oldsmobile Classic—Michelle McGann	90,000
The Edina Realty LPGA Classic—Liselotte Neumann	82,500
Rochester International—Dottie Pepper	90,000
ShopRite LPGA Classic—Dottie Pepper	112,500
Jamie Farr Kroger Classic—Joan Pitcock	86,250
Youngstown-Warren LPGA Classic—Michelle McGann	90,000
Friendly's Classic—Dottie Pepper	75,000
Michelob Light Heartland Classic—Vicki Fergon	82,500
du Maurier Ltd. Classic—Laura Davies	150,000
Ping Welch's Championship—Emilee Klein	75,000
Weetabix Women's British Open—Emilee Klein	127,500
Star Bank LPGA Classic—Laura Davies	82,500

FENCING

1995 WORLD CHAMPIONS

(1996 World Championships not held)

Individual
Men's sabre—Grigori Kirienko, Russia
Men's epee—Eric Srecki, France
Women's epee—Joanna Kakimiuk, Poland
Women's foil—Laura Badea, Romania
Men's foil—Dmitry Chevtchenko, Russia

Team
Women's foil—Italy
Men's sabre—Italy

Wonen's epee—Hungary
Men's foil—Cuba
Men's epee—Germany

1996 UNITED STATES CHAMPIONS

Women's foil—Felicia Zimmerman, Rochester, N.Y.
Women's epee—Leslie Marx, Pittsford, N.Y.
Men's sabre—Adam Skarbonkiewicz, Portland, Ore.
Men's foil—Eric Nick Bravin, New York City
Men's epee—Ben Atkins, New York City

SOFTBALL

Source: Amateur Softball Association.

AMATEUR CHAMPIONS

1959	Aurora (Ill.) Sealmasters	1974	Santa Rosa (Calif.)	1985	Pay 'n Pak, Bellevue, Wash.
1960	Clearwater (Fla.) Bombers	1975	Rising Sun Hotel, Reading, Pa.	1986	Pay 'n Pak, Bellevue, Wash.
1961	Aurora (Ill.) Sealmasters	1976	Raybestos Cardinals,	1987	Pay 'n Pak, Bellevue, Wash.
1962–63	Clearwater (Fla.) Bombers		Stratford, Conn.	1988	TransAire, Elkhart, Ind.
1964	Burch Gage & Tool, Detroit	1977	Billard Barbell, Reading, Pa.	1989	Penn Corp., Sioux City, Iowa
1965	Aurora (Ill.) Sealmasters	1978	Reading, Pa.	1990	Penn Corp., Sioux City, Iowa
1966	Clearwater (Fla.) Bombers	1979	Midland, Mich.	1991	Guanella Brothers, Rohnert
1967	Aurora (Ill.) Sealmasters	1980	Peterbilt Western, Seattle		Park, Calif.
1968	Clearwater (Fla.) Bombers	1981	Archer Daniels Midland,	1992	National Health Care, Sioux
1969–70	Raybestos Cardinals,		Decatur, Ill.		City, Iowa
	Stratford, Conn.	1982	Peterbilt Western, Seattle	1993	National Health Care, Sioux
1971	Welty Way, Cedar Rapids, Iowa	1983	Franklin Cardinals, West		City, Iowa
1972	Raybestos Cardinals, Stratford,		Haven, Conn.	1994	Decatur Pride, Decatur, Ill.
	Conn.	1984	California Coors Kings,	1995	Decatur Pride, Decatur, Ill.
1973	Clearwater (Fla.) Bombers		Merced, Calif.	1996	Green Bay All Car, Green Bay, Wis.

1996 AMATEUR SOFTBALL ASSOCIATION CHAMPIONS

Fast Pitch

Men's Major—Greem Bay All Car, Green Bay, Wis.
Men's Class A—Hy-Line Enterprises, Elkhart, Ind.
Men's Class B—D & R Engine, Odessa, Texas
Men's Class C—Lorain UPC, Lorain, Ohio
Women's Major—California Commotion, Woodland Hills, Calif.
Women's Class A—Diamonds, Montclair, Calif.
Women's Class B—Xplosion, Tampa, Fla.
Women's Class C—Pat McKeown Ford, Charlevoix, Mich.
Men's 40-Over—Knoll Lumber Legends, Mill Creek, Wash.
Men's 45-Over—Colt 45's, Clearwater, Fla.
Men's 23-Under—Junkers, Garden City, Minn.

Slow Pitch

Men's Super—Ritch's Superior—Windsor Locks, Conn.
Men's Major—Bell II/Roberts, Orlando, Fla.
Men's Class A—Reece, Springfield, Ky.
Men's Major Industrial—Sikorsky, Stratford, Conn.
Men's Class A Industrial—Luria Brothers, Ellwood, Pa.
Men's 35-Over—Capital X-Ray, Herndon, Va.
Men's 45-Over—Winchell, Evansville, Ind.
Men's 55-Over—Nothdurft, St. Claire Shore, Mich.
Men's 60-Over—Fairway Ford, Placentia, Calif.
Men's 65-Over—Palm Springs 65's, Westminster, Calif.
Men's Major Church—Olive Baptist, Pensacola, Fla.
Men's Class A Church—Cottage Hill, Mobile, Ala.
Women's Major—Spooks, Anoka, Minn.
Women's Industrial—Denso Mfg., Maryville, Tenn.
Women's Church—North Gadsden, Gadsden, Ala.

Women's Class A—Fletch's Softball Club, Newark, Del.
Women's 35-Over—Don's Softball Crew, Dothan, Ala.

Junior

Girls' Gold Under-18 Fast Pitch—Gordon's Panthers, Cypress, Calif.
Girls' 18-Under Fast Pitch—Orland Park Sparks Red, Orland Park, Ill.
Girls' 16-Under Fast Pitch—Lady Sharks, San Jose, Calif.
Girls' 14-Under Fast Pitch—So. California Stealth, Woodland Hills, Calif.
Girls' 12-Under Fast Pitch—So. California Stealth, Van Nuys, Calif.
Boys' 18-Under Fast Pitch—Red Men Construction, Leroy, Minn.
Boys' 16-Under Fast Pitch—Taco Bell, Sioux Falls, S.D.
Boys' 14-Under Fast Pitch—Sullivan's Sioux Falls, S.D.
Boys' 12-Under Fast Pitch—M.J. Daisin, Sioux Falls, S.D.
Girls' 18-Under Slow Pitch—Lady Panthers, Douglasville, Ga.
Girls' 16-Under Slow Pitch—Bryant Express, Little Rock, Ark.
Girls' 14-Under Slow Pitch—Saints, Muskogee, Okla.
Girls' 12-Under Slow Pitch—Moore Magic, Moore, Okla.
Boys' 18-Under Slow Pitch—Classics, Claxton, Ga.
Boys' 16-Under Slow Pitch—Outlaws, Tifton, Ga.
Boys' 14-Under Slow Pitch—McLean Co. Astros, Normal, Ill.
Boys' 12-Under Slow Pitch—Eastlake Rockets, Eastlake, Ohio

Modified Pitch

Women's Major Modified—Thunderbolts, Keene, N.H.
Men's Major Modified Pitch—CBS, New York City, N.Y.
Class A Modified—Waves, Cecilton, Md.

LITTLE LEAGUE WORLD SERIES CHAMPIONS

Year	Champion	Runner-up	Score	Year	Champion	Runner-up	Score
1947	Williamsport, Pa.	Lock Haven, Pa.	16–7	1972	Taipei, Taiwan	Hammond, Ind.	6–0
1948	Lock Haven, Pa.	St. Petersburg, Fla.	6–5	1973	Tainan City, Taiwan	Tucson, Ariz.	12–0
1949	Hammonton, N.J.	Pensacola, Fla.	5–0	1974	Kao Hsiung, Taiwan	El Cajun, Calif.	7–2
1950	Houston, Tex.	Bridgeport, Conn.	2–1	1975	Lakewood, N.J.	Tampa, Fla.	4–3
1951	Stamford, Conn.	Austin, Tex.	3–0	1976	Tokyo, Japan	Campbell, Calif.	10–3
1952	Norwalk, Conn.	Monongahela, Pa.	4–3	1977	Kao Hsiung, Taiwan	El Cajun, Calif.	7–2
1953	Birmingham, Ala.	Schenectady, N.Y.	1–0	1978	Pin-Tung, Taiwan	Danville, Calif.	11–1
1954	Schenectady, N.Y.	Colton, Calif.	7–5	1979	Hsien, Taiwan	Campbell, Calif.	2–1
1955	Morrisville, Pa.	Merchantville, N.J.	4–3	1980	Hua Lian, Taiwan	Tampa, Fla.	4–3
1956	Roswell, N.M.	Merchantville, N.J.	3–1	1981	Tai-Chung, Taiwan	Tampa, Fla.	4–2
1957	Monterrey, Mex.	LaMesa, Calif.	4–0	1982	Kirkland, Wash.	Hsien, Taiwan	6–0
1958	Monterrey, Mex.	Kankakee, Ill.	10–1	1983	Marietta, Ga.	Barahona, D. Rep.	3–1
1959	Hamtramck, Mich.	Auburn, Calif.	12–0	1984	Seoul, S. Korea	Altamonte Springs, Fla.	6–2
1960	Levittown, Pa.	Ft. Worth, Tex.	5–0	1985	Seoul, S. Korea	Mexicali, Mex.	7–1
1961	El Cajon, Calif.	El Campo, Tex.	4–2	1986	Tainan Park, Taiwan	Tucson, Ariz.	12–0
1962	San Jose, Calif.	Kankakee, Ill.	3–0	1987	Hua Lian, Taiwan	Irvine, Calif.	21–1
1963	Granada Hills, Calif.	Stratford, Conn.	2–1	1988	Tai-Chung, Taiwan	Pearl City, Haw.	10–0
1964	Staten Island, N.Y.	Monterrey, Mex.	4–0	1989	Trumbull, Conn.	Kaohsiung, Taiwan	5–2
1965	Windsor Locks, Conn.	Stoney Creek, Can.	3–1	1990	Taipei, Taiwan	Shippensburg, Pa.	9–0
1966	Houston, Tex.	W. New York, N.J.	8–2	1991	Tai-Chung, Taiwan	San Ramon Valley, Calif.	11–0
1967	West Tokyo, Japan	Chicago, Ill.	4–1	1992*	Long Beach, Calif.	Zamboanga, Phil.	6–0
1968	Osaka, Japan	Richmond, Va.	1–0	1993	Long Beach, Calif.	David Chiriqui, Pan.	3–2
1969	Taipei, Taiwan	Santa Clara, Calif.	5–0	1994	Maracaibo, Venezuela	Northridge, Calif.	4–3
1970	Wayne, N.J.	Campbell, Calif.	2–0	1995	Tainan, Taiwan	Spring, Texas	17–3
1971	Tainan, Taiwan	Gary, Ind.	12–3	1996	Kao-Hsuing City, Taipei	Cranston, R.I.	13–3

*Long Beach declared a 6–0 winner after the international tournament committee determined that Zamboanga City used players that were not within its city limits.

AUTO RACING

INDIANAPOLIS 500

Year	Winner	Car	Time	mph	Second place
1911	Ray Harroun	Marmon	6:42:08	74.59	Ralph Mulford
1912	Joe Dawson	National	6:21:06	78.72	Teddy Tetzloff
1913	Jules Goux	Peugeot	6:35:05	75.93	Spencer Wishart
1914	René Thomas	Delage	6:03:45	82.47	Arthur Duray
1915	Ralph DePalma	Mercedes	5:33:55.51	89.84	Dario Resta
1916[1]	Dario Resta	Peugeot	3:34:17	84.00	Wilbur D'Alene
1919	Howard Wilcox	Peugeot	5:40:42.87	88.05	Eddie Hearne
1920	Gaston Chevrolet	Monroe	5:38:32	88.62	René Thomas
1921	Tommy Milton	Frontenac	5:34:44.65	89.62	Roscoe Sarles
1922	Jimmy Murphy	Murphy Special	5:17:30.79	94.48	Harry Hartz
1923	Tommy Milton	H. C. S. Special	5:29:50.17	90.95	Harry Hartz
1924	L. L. Corum–Joe Boyer	Dusenberg Special	5:05:23.51	98.23	Earl Cooper
1925	Peter DePaolo	Dusenberg Special	4:56:39.45	101.13	Dave Lewis
1926[2]	Frank Lockhart	Miller Special	4:10:14.95	95.904	Harry Hartz
1927	George Souders	Dusenberg Special	5:07:33.08	97.54	Earl DeVore
1928	Louis Meyer	Miller Special	5:01:33.75	99.48	Lou Moore
1929	Ray Keech	Simplex Special	5:07:25.42	97.58	Louis Meyer
1930	Billy Arnold	Miller–Hartz Special	4:58:39.72	100.448	Shorty Cantlon
1931	Louis Schneider	Bowes Special	5:10:27.93	96.629	Fred Frame
1932	Fred Frame	Miller–Hartz Special	4:48:03.79	104.144	Howard Wilcox
1933	Louis Meyer	Tydol Special	4:48:00.75	104.162	Wilbur Shaw
1934	Bill Cummings	Boyle Products Special	4:46:05.20	104.863	Mauri Rose
1935	Kelly Petillo	Gilmore Special	4:42:22.71	106.240	Wilbur Shaw
1936	Louis Meyer	Ring Free Special	4:35:03.39	109.069	Ted Horn
1937	Wilbur Shaw	Shaw–Gilmore Special	4:24:07.80	113.580	Ralph Hepburn
1938	Floyd Roberts	Burd Piston Ring Special	4:15:58.40	117.200	Wilbur Shaw
1939	Wilbur Shaw	Boyle Special	4:20:47.39	115.035	Jimmy Snyder
1940	Wilbur Shaw	Boyle Special	4:22:31.17	114.277	Rex Mays
1941	Floyd Davis–Mauri Rose	Noc–Out Hose Clamp Special	4:20:36.24	115.117	Rex Mays
1946	George Robson	Thorne Engineering Special	4:21:26.71	114.820	Jimmy Jackson
1947	Mauri Rose	Blue Crown Special	4:17:52.17	116.338	Bill Holland
1948	Mauri Rose	Blue Crown Special	4:10:23.33	119.814	Bill Holland
1949	Bill Holland	Blue Crown Special	4:07:15.97	121.327	Johnny Parsons
1950[3]	Johnnie Parsons	Wynn's Friction Proof Special	2:46:55.97	124.002	Bill Holland
1951	Lee Wallard	Belanger Special	3:57:38.05	126.244	Mike Nazaruk
1952	Troy Ruttman	Agajanian Special	3:52:41.88	128.922	Jim Rathmann
1953	Bill Vukovich	Fuel Injection Special	3:53:01.69	128.740	Art Cross
1954	Bill Vukovich	Fuel Injection Special	3:49:17.27	130.840	Jim Bryan
1955	Bob Sweikert	John Zink Special	3:53:59.13	128.209	Tony Bettenhausen
1956	Pat Flaherty	John Zink Special	3:53:28.84	128.490	Sam Hanks
1957	Sam Hanks	Belond Exhaust Special	3:41:14.25	135.601	Jim Rathmann
1958	Jimmy Bryan	Belond A–P Special	3:44:13.80	133.791	George Amick
1959	Rodger Ward	Leader Card 500 Roadster	3:40:49.20	135.857	Jim Rathmann
1960	Jim Rathmann	Ken–Paul Special	3:36:11.36	138.767	Rodger Ward
1961	A. J. Foyt	Bowes Special	3:35:37.49	139.130	Eddie Sachs
1962	Rodger Ward	Leader Card Special	3:33:50.33	140.293	Len Sutton
1963	Parnelli Jones	Agajanian Special	3:29:35.40	143.137	Jim Clark
1964	A. J. Foyt	Sheraton–Thompson Spl.	3:23:35.83	147.350	Rodger Ward
1965	Jim Clark	Lotus–Ford	3:19:05.34	150.686	Parnelli Jones
1966	Graham Hill	Red Ball Lola–Ford	3:27:52.53	144.317	Jim Clark
1967[4]	A. J. Foyt	Sheraton-Thompson Coyote–Ford	3:18:24.22	151.207	Al Unser
1968	Bobby Unser	Rislone Eagle–Offenhauser	3:16:13.76	152.882	Dan Gurney
1969	Mario Andretti	STP Hawk–Ford	3:11:14.71	156.867	Dan Gurney
1970	Al Unser	Johnny Lightning P. J. Colt–Ford	3:12:37.04	155.749	Mark Donohue
1971	Al Unser	Johnny Lightning P. J. Colt–Ford	3:10:11.56	157.735	Peter Revson
1972	Mark Donohue	Sunoco McLaren–Offenhauser	3:04:05.54	162.962	Al Unser
1973[5]	Gordon Johncock	STP Eagle–Offenhauser	2:05:26.59	159.036	Bill Vukovich, Jr.
1974	Johnny Rutherford	McLaren–Offenhauser	3:09:10.06	158.589	Bobby Unser
1975[6]	Bobby Unser	Jorgensen Eagle–Offenhauser	2:54:55.08	149.213	Johnny Rutherford
1976[7]	Johnny Rutherford	Hy-gain McLaren–Offenhauser	1:42:52.48	148.725	A. J. Foyt
1977	A. J. Foyt	Gilmore Coyote–Foyt	3:05:57.16	161.331	Tom Sneva
1978	Al Unser	1st Nat'l City Lola–Cosworth	3:05:54.99	161.363	Tom Sneva
1979	Rick Mears	Gould Penske–Cosworth	3:08:27.97	158.899	A. J. Foyt
1980	Johnny Rutherford	Pennzoil Chaparral–Cosworth	3:29:59.56	142.862	Tom Sneva
1981[8]	Bobby Unser	Norton Penske–Cosworth	3:35:41.78	139.029	Mario Andretti
1982	Gordon Johncock	STP Wildcat–Cosworth	3:05:09.14	162.029	Rick Mears
1983	Tom Sneva	Texaco Star March–Cosworth	3:05:03.06	162.117	Al Unser
1984	Rick Mears	Pennzoil March–Cosworth	3:03:21.00	162.962	Roberto Guerrero
1985	Danny Sullivan	Miller March–Cosworth	3:16:06.069	152.982	Mario Andretti

Year	Winner	Car	Time	mph	Second place
1986	Bobby Rahal	Budweiser March–Cosworth	2:55:43.48	170.722	Kevin Cogan
1987	Al Unser, Sr.	Cummins March–Cosworth	3:04:59.147	162.175	Roberto Guerrero
1988	Rick Mears	Pennzoil Penske P.C.17–Chevrolet	3:27:10.204	144.809	Emerson Fittipaldi
1989	Emerson Fittipaldi	Marlboro Penske–Cosworth	2:59:01.04	167.581	Al Unser, Jr.
1990	Arie Luyendyk	Domino's Pizza Lola–Cosworth	2:41:18.248	185.987	Bobby Rahal
1991	Rick Mears	Marlboro Penske–Cosworth	2:50:01.018	176.460	Michael Andretti
1992	Al Unser, Jr.	Valvoline–Chevrolet	3:43.05.148	134.477	Scott Goodyear
1993	Emerson Fittipaldi	Penske–Chevrolet	3:10:49.860	157.207	Arie Luyendyk
1994	Al Unser, Jr.	Penske–Mercedes	3:06:29.006	160.872	Jacques Villeneuve
1995	Jacques Villeneuve	Reynard–Ford	3:15:17.561	156.616	Christian Fittipaldi
1996	Buddy Lazier	Reynard–Ford	3:22:45.753	147.956	Davy Jones

1. 300 miles. 2. Race ended at 400 miles because of rain. 3. Race ended at 345 miles because of rain. 4. Race, postponed after 18 laps because of rain on May 30, was finished on May 31. 5. Race postponed May 28 and 29 was cut to 332.5 miles because of rain, May 30. 6. Race ended at 435 miles because of rain. 7. Race ended at 255 miles because of rain. 8. Andretti was awarded the victory the day after the race after Bobby Unser, whose car finished first, was penalized one lap and dropped from first place to second for passing other cars illegally under a yellow caution flag. Unser appealed the decision to the U.S. Auto Club and was upheld. A panel ruled the penalty was too severe and instead fined Unser $40,000, but restored the victory to him.

U.S. 500

The U.S. 500 was started by IndyCar, after Indianapolis 500 race officials joined forces with IndyCar\s upstart rivals the Indy Racing League. A disagreement over the number of automatic qualifiers that would be given to IRL drivers spurred IndyCar to stage a Memorial Day race of its own to go head-to-head with the Indy 500.

Year	Winner	Car	Time	mph	Second place
1996	Jimmy Vasser	Reynard–Honda	3:11:48	156.403	Mauricio Gugelmin

NATIONAL ASSOCIATION FOR STOCK CAR AUTO RACING
WINSTON CUP CHAMPIONS

1949	Red Byron	1961	Ned Jarrett	1974–75	Richard Petty	1987	Dale Earnhardt
1950	Bill Rexford	1962–63	Joe Weatherly	1976–78	Cale Yarborough	1988	Bill Elliott
1951	Herb Thomas	1964	Richard Petty	1979	Richard Petty	1989	Rusty Wallace
1952	Tim Flock	1965	Ned Jarrett	1980	Dale Earnhardt	1990	Dale Earnhardt
1953	Herb Thomas	1966	David Pearson	1981	Darrell Waltrip	1991	Dale Earnhardt
1954	Lee Petty	1967	Richard Petty	1982	Darrell Waltrip	1992	Alan Kulwicki[1]
1955	Tim Flock	1968–69	David Pearson	1983	Bobby Allison	1993	Dale Earnhardt
1956–57	Buck Baker	1970	Bobby Isaac	1984	Terry Labonte	1994	Dale Earnhardt
1958–59	Lee Petty	1971–72	Richard Petty	1985	Darrell Waltrip	1995	Jeff Gordon
1960	Rex White	1973	Benny Parsons	1986	Dale Earnhardt		

1. Kulwicki was killed in a plane crash in April 1993.

INDYCAR NATIONAL CHAMPIONS

1910	Ray Harroun	1928–29	Louis Meyer	1954	Jimmy Bryan	1977–78	Tom Sneva
1911	Ralph Mulford	1930	Billy Arnold	1955	Bob Sweikert	1979	Rick Mears (CART)
1912	Ralph DePalma	1931	Louis Schneider	1956–57	Jimmy Bryan		A.J. Foyt (USAC)[1]
1913	Earl Cooper	1932	Bob Carey	1958	Tony Bettenhausen	1980	Johnny Rutherford
1914	Ralph DePalma	1933	Louis Meyer	1959	Rodger Ward	1981–82	Rick Mears
1915	Earl Cooper	1934	Bill Cummings	1960–61	A. J. Foyt	1983	Al Unser
1916	Dario Resta	1935	Kelly Petillo	1962	Rodger Ward	1984	Mario Andretti
1917	Earl Cooper	1936	Mauri Rose	1963–64	A. J. Foyt	1985	Al Unser
1918	Ralph Mulford	1937	Wilbur Shaw	1965–66	Mario Andretti	1986–87	Bobby Rahal
1919	Howard Wilcox	1938	Floyd Roberts	1967	A. J. Foyt	1988	Danny Sullivan
1920	Gaston Chevrolet	1939	Wilbur Shaw	1968	Bobby Unser	1989	Emerson Fittipaldi
1921	Tommy Milton	1940–41	Rex Mays	1969	Mario Andretti	1990	Al Unser Jr.
1922	James Murphy	1946–48	Ted Horn	1970	Al Unser	1991	Michael Andretti
1923	Eddie Hearne	1949	Johnnie Parsons	1971–72	Joe Leonard	1992	Bobby Rahal
1924	James Murphy	1950	Henry Banks	1973	Roger McCluskey	1993	Nigel Mansell
1925	Peter DePaolo	1951	Tony Bettenhausen	1974	Bobby Unser	1994	Al Unser, Jr.
1926	Harry Hartz	1952	Chuck Stevenson	1975	A. J. Foyt	1995	Jacques Villeneuve
1927	Peter DePaolo	1953	Sam Hanks	1976	Gordon Johncock	1996	Jimmy Vasser

1. Two separate series were held in 1979. NOTE: There have been three sanctioning bodies for the series: the Automobile Association of America (1909–1955), the U.S. Auto Club (1956–1979), and the Championship Auto Racing Team (CART), 1979–present.

1996 INDYCAR POINTS LEADERS

1.	Jimmy Vasser	154	6.	Gil de Ferran	104
2.	Michael Andretti	132	7.	Bobby Rahal	102
3.	Alex Zanardi	132	8.	Bryan Herta	86
4.	Al Unser, Jr.	125	9.	Greg Moore	84
5.	Christian Fittipaldi	110	10.	Scott Pruett	82

1995 NASCAR LEADING MONEY WINNERS

1.	Jeff Gordon	$2,430,460
2.	Dale Earnhardt	2,378,300
3.	Sterling Marlin	1,712,155
4.	Mark Martin	1,534,966
5.	Rusty Wallace	1,375,878
6.	Terry Labonte	1,328,295
7.	Bobby Labonte	1,293,200
8.	Dale Jarrett	1,259,224
9.	Ricky Rudd	1,153,874
10.	Ted Musgrave	943,675

1995 WINSTON CUP POINT LEADERS

1.	Jeff Gordon	4,614
2.	Dale Earnhardt	4,580
3.	Sterling Marlin	4,361
4.	Mark Martin	4,320
5.	Rusty Wallace	4,240
6.	Terry Labonte	4,164
7.	Ted Musgrave	3,949
8.	Bill Elliott	3,746
9.	Ricky Rudd	3,734
10.	Bobby Labonte	3,718

WORLD GRAND PRIX DRIVER CHAMPIONS

1950	Giuseppe Farina, Italy, Alfa Romeo		1974	Emerson Fittipaldi, Brazil, McLaren–Ford
1951	Juan Fangio, Argentina, Alfa Romeo		1975	Niki Lauda, Austria, Ferrari
1952	Alberto Ascari, Italy, Ferrari		1976	James Hunt, Britain, McLaren–Ford
1953	Alberto Ascari, Italy, Ferrari		1977	Niki Lauda, Austria, Ferrari
1954	Juan Fangio, Argentina, Maserati, Mercedes–Benz		1978	Mario Andretti, United States, Lotus
1955	Juan Fangio, Argentina, Mercedes–Benz		1979	Jody Scheckter, South Africa, Ferrari
1956	Juan Fangio, Argentina, Lancia–Ferrari		1980	Alan Jones, Australia, Williams–Ford
1957	Juan Fangio, Argentina, Masserati		1981	Nelson Piquet, Brazil, Brabham–Ford
1958	Mike Hawthorn, England, Ferrari		1982	Kiki Rosberg, Finland, Williams–Ford
1959	Jack Brabham, Australia, Cooper		1983	Nelson Piquet, Brazil. Brabham–BMW
1960	Jack Brabham, Australia, Cooper		1984	Nikki Lauda, Austria, McLaren–Porsche
1961	Phil Hill, United States, Ferrari		1985	Alain Prost, France, McLaren–Porsche
1962	Graham Hill, England, BRM		1986	Alain Prost, France, McLaren–Porsche
1963	Jim Clark, Scotland, Lotus–Ford		1987	Nelson Piquet, Brazil, Williams–Honda
1964	John Surtees, England, Ferrari		1988	Aryton Senna, Brazil, McLaren–Honda
1965	Jim Clark, Scotland, Lotus–Ford		1989	Alain Prost, France, McLaren–Honda
1966	Jack Brabham, Australia, Brabham–Repco		1990	Ayrton Senna, Brazil, McLaren–Honda
1967	Denis Hulme, New Zealand, Brabham–Repco		1991	Ayrton Senna, Brazil, McLaren–Honda
1968	Graham Hill, England, Lotus–Ford		1992	Nigel Mansell, Britain, Williams–Renault
1969	Jackie Stewart, Scotland, Matra–Ford		1993	Alain Prost
1970	Jochen Rindt, Austria, Lotus–Ford		1994	Michael Schumacher, Germany, Benetton
1971	Jackie Stewart, Scotland, Tyrrell–Ford		1995	Michael Schumacher, Germany, Benetton Renault
1972	Emerson Fittipaldi, Brazil, Lotus–Ford		1996	Damon Hill, Britain, Williams
1973	Jackie Stewart, Scotland, Tyrrell–Ford			

IDITAROD

24TH IDITAROD TRAIL SLED DOG RACE—1996

(Alaska, March 2–12, 1996)

The annual 1,159-mile race stretches from Anchorage to Nome, Alaska. Begun in 1973, the course follows an old frozen river route and is named after a deserted mining town along the way. The Iditarod also commemorates a famous midwinter emergency mission to get medical supplies to Nome during a 1925 diphtheria epidemic. Men and women mushers compete together.

Course: Anchorage to Nome.

1996 Champion—Jeff King, a 39-year-old former Denali National Park ranger, won the 24th annual Iditarod Trail Sled Dog Race on Mar. 12. King, the 1993 winner, reached Nome and the burled arch finish line of the 1,151-mile course in 9 days, 5 hours, 43 minutes and 13 seconds—the second-fastest time ever. The Iditarod began March 2 in Anchorage. In even-numbered years, the trail follows the 1,151-mile long Northern Route, while in odd-numbered years it takes the slightly different 1,161-mile Southern Route. Rick Swenson,

one of the race favorites and the Idiatord's only five-time winner, was disqualified under the race's controversial new "dead dog" rule after one of his dogs, Ariel, died early in the race. King, who finished the race with six of his original 16 dogs, took home $50,000 and a new pickup. Doug Swingley, the 1995 champion and only non-Alaskan ever to win the race, placed second.

Winning times since 1980: 1980, Joe May, 14 days–7 hours–11 minutes; 1981, Swenson, 12–8–45; 1982, Swenson, 16–4–40; 1983, Rick Mackey, 12–14–10; 1984, Dean Osmar, 12–15–7; 1985, Libby Riddles, 18–00–20; 1986, Butcher, 11–15–6; 1987, Butcher, 11–2–5; 1988, Butcher, 11–11–41; 1989, Joe Runyan, 11–5–24; 1990, Butcher, 11–1–53; 1991, Swenson, 12–16–34; 1992, Martin Buser, 10–19–17; 1993, Jeff King, 10–15–30; 1994, Martin Buser, 10–13–2; 1995, Doug Swingly, 9–2–43; 1996, Jeff King, 9–5–43.

BASEBALL

The popular tradition that baseball was invented by Abner Doubleday at Cooperstown, N.Y., in 1839 has been enshrined in the Hall of Fame and National Museum of Baseball erected in that town, but research has proved that a game called "Base Ball" was played in this country and England before 1839. The first team baseball as we know it was played at the Elysian Fields, Hoboken, N.J., on June 19, 1846, between the Knickerbockers and the New York Nine. The next fifty years saw a gradual growth of baseball and an improvement of equipment and playing skill.

Historians have it that the first pitcher to throw a curve was William A. (Candy) Cummings in 1867. The Cincinnati Red Stockings were the first all–professional team, and in 1869 they played 64 games without a loss. The standard ball of the same size and weight, still the rule, was adopted in 1872. The first catcher's mask was worn in 1875. The National League was organized in 1876. The first chest protector was worn in 1885. The three–strike rule was put on the books in 1887, and the four–ball ticket to first base was instituted in 1889. The pitching distance was lengthened to 60 feet 6 inches in 1893, and the rules have been modified only slightly since that time.

The American League, under the vigorous leadership of B. B. Johnson, became a major league in 1901. Judge Kenesaw Mountain Landis, by action of the two major leagues, became Commissioner of Baseball in 1921. Peter Ueberroth became baseball's fifth commissioner and took office Oct. 1, 1984.

Ueberroth did not seek a new term in 1989 and was succeded by Bart Giamatti who died suddenly on Sept. 1, 1989. Francis T. Vincent, Jr., replaced him on Sept. 13, 1989.

Vincent, under pressure from owners to relinquish some of his powers, resigned in late 1992. Bud Selig, principal owner of the Milwaukee Brewers, headed a baseball executive committee that ruled baseball during the search for a new commissioner.

MAJOR LEAGUE ALL–STAR GAME

Year	Date	Winning league and manager	Runs	Losing league and manager	Runs	Winning pitcher	Losing pitcher	Site	Paid attendance
1933	July 6	A.L. (Mack)	4	N.L. (McGraw)	2	Gomez	Hallahan	Chicago A.L.	47,595
1934	July 10	A.L. (Cronin)	9	N.L. (Terry)	7	Harder	Mungo	New York N.L.	48,363
1935	July 8	A.L. (Cochrane)	4	N.L. (Frisch)	1	Gomez	Walker	Cleveland A.L.	69,831
1936	July 7	N.L. (Grimm)	4	A.L. (McCarthy)	3	J. Dean	Grove	Boston N.L.	25,556
1937	July 7	A.L. (McCarthy)	8	N.L. (Terry)	3	Gomez	J. Dean	Washington A.L.	31,391
1938	July 6	N.L. (Terry)	4	A.L. (McCarthy)	1	Vander Meer	Gomez	Cincinnati N.L.	27,067
1939	July 11	A.L. (McCarthy)	3	N.L. (Hartnett)	1	Bridges	Lee	New York A.L.	62,892
1940	July 9	N.L. (McKechnie)	4	A.L. (Cronin)	0	Derringer	Ruffing	St. Louis N.L.	32,373
1941	July 8	A.L. (Baker)	7	N.L. (McKechnie)	5	E. Smith	Passeau	Detroit A.L.	54,674
1942	July 6	A.L. (McCarthy)	3	N.L. (Durocher)	1	Chandler	Cooper	New York N.L.	34,178
1943	July 13[1]	A.L. (McCarthy)	5	N.L. (Southworth)	3	Leonard	Cooper	Philadelphia A.L.	31,938
1944	July 11[1]	N.L. (Southworth)	7	A.L. (McCarthy)	1	Raffensberger	Hughson	Pittsburgh N.L.	29,589
1946	July 9	A.L. (O'Neill)	12	N.L. (Grimm)	0	Feller	Passeau	Boston A.L.	34,906
1947	July 8	A.L. (Cronin)	2	N.L. (Dyer)	1	Shea	Sain	Chicago N.L.	41,123
1948	July 13	A.L. (Harris)	5	N.L. (Durocher)	2	Raschi	Schmitz	St. Louis A.L.	34,009
1949	July 12	A.L. (Boudreau)	11	N.L. (Southworth)	7	Trucks	Newcombe	Brooklyn N.L.	32,577
1950	July 11	N.L. (Shotton)	4	A.L. (Stengel)	3[3]	Blackwell	Gray	Chicago A.L.	46,127
1951	July 10	N.L. (Sawyer)	8	A.L. (Stengel)	3	Maglie	Lopat	Detroit A.L.	52,075
1952	July 8	N.L. (Durocher)	3	A.L. (Stengel)	2[4]	Rush	Lemon	Philadelphia N.L.	32,785
1953	July 14	N.L. (Dressen)	5	A.L. (Stengel)	1	Spahn	Reynolds	Cincinnati N.L.	30,846
1954	July 13	A.L. (Stengel)	11	N.L. (Alston)	9	Stone	Conley	Cleveland A.L.	68,751
1955	July 12	N.L. (Durocher)	6	A.L. (Lopez)	5[5]	Conley	Sullivan	Milwaukee N.L.	45,643
1956	July 10	N.L. (Alston)	7	A.L. (Stengel)	3	Friend	Pierce	Washington A.L.	28,843
1957	July 9	A.L. (Stengel)	6	N.L. (Alston)	5	Bunning	Simmons	St. Louis N.L.	30,693
1958	July 8	A.L. (Stengel)	4	N.L. (Haney)	3	Wynn	Friend	Baltimore A.L.	48,829
1959[2]	July 7	N.L. (Haney)	5	A.L. (Stengel)	4	Antonelli	Ford	Pittsburgh N.L.	35,277
	Aug. 3	A.L. (Stengel)	5	N.L. (Haney)	3	Walker	Drysdale	Los Angeles N.L.	55,105
1960[2]	July 11	N.L. (Alston)	5	A.L. (Lopez)	3	Friend	Monbouquette	Kansas City A.L.	30,619
	July 13	N.L. (Alston)	6	A.L. (Lopez)	0	Law	Ford	New York A.L.	38,362
1961[2]	July 11	N.L. (Murtaugh)	5	A.L. (Richards)	4[6]	Miller	Wilhelm	San Francisco N.L.	44,115
	July 31	N.L (Murtaugh)	1	A.L. (Richards)	1[7]	—	—	Boston A.L.	31,851
1962[2]	July 10	N.L. (Hutchinson)	3	A.L. (Houk)	1	Marichal	Pascual	Washington A.L.	45,480
	July 30	A.L. (Houk)	9	N.L. (Hutchinson)	4	Herbert	Mahaffey	Chicago N.L.	38,359
1963	July 9	N.L. (Dark)	5	A.L. (Houk)	3	Jackson	Bunning	Cleveland A.L.	44,160
1964	July 7	N.L. (Alston)	7	A.L. (Lopez)	4	Marichal	Radatz	New York N.L.	50,850
1965	July 13	N.L. (March)	6	A.L. (Lopez)	5	Koufax	McDowell	Minnesota N.L.	46,706
1966	July 12	N.L. (Alston)	2	A.L. (Mele)	1[6]	Perry	Rickert	St. Louis N.L.	49,926
1967	July 11	N.L. (Alston)	2	A.L. (Bauer)	1[8]	Drysdale	Hunter	Anaheim A.L.	46,309
1968	July 9	N.L. (Schoendienst)	1	A.L. (Williams)	0	Drysdale	Tiant	Houston N.L.	48,321
1969	July 23	N.L. (Schoendienst)	9	A.L. (M. Smith)	3	Carlton	Stottlemyre	Washington A.L.	45,259
1970	July 14	N.L. (Hodges)	5	A.L. (Weaver)	4	Osteen	Wright	Cincinnati N.L.	51,838
1971	July 13	A.L. (Weaver)	6	N.L. (Anderson)	4	Blue	Ellis	Detroit A.L.	53,559
1972	July 25	N.L. (Murtaugh)	4	A.L. (Weaver)	3[6]	McGraw	McNally	Atlanta N.L.	53,107
1973	July 24[1]	N.L. (Anderson)	7	A.L. (Williams)	1	Wise	Blyleven	Kansas City A.L.	40,849

Year	Date	Winning league and manager	Runs	Losing league and manager	Runs	Winning pitcher	Losing pitcher	Site	Paid attendance
1974	July 23[1]	N.L. (Berra)	7	A.L. (Williams)	2	Brett	Tiant	Pittsburgh N.L.	50,706
1975	July 15[1]	N.L. (Alston)	6	A.L. (Dark)	3	Matlack	Hunter	Milwaukee A.L.	51,540
1976	July 13[1]	N.L. (Anderson)	7	A.L. (D. Johnson)	1	R. Jones	Fidrych	Philadelphia N.L.	63,974
1977	July 19[1]	N.L. (Anderson)	7	A.L. (Martin)	5	Sutton	Palmer	New York A.L.	56,683
1978	July 11[1]	N.L. (Lasorda)	7	A.L. (Martin)	3	Sutter	Gossage	San Diego N.L.	51,549
1979	July 17[1]	N.L. (Lasorda)	7	A.L. (Lemon)	6	Sutter	Kern	Seattle A.L.	58,905
1980	July 8[1]	N.L. (Tanner)	4	A.L. (Weaver)	2	Reuss	John	Los Angeles N.L.	56,088
1981	Aug. 9[1]	N.L. (Green)	5	A.L. (Frey)	4	Blue	Fingers	Cleveland* A.L.	72,086
1982	July 13[1]	N.L. (Lasorda)	4	A.L. (Martin)	1	Rogers	Eckersley	Montreal N.L.	59,057
1983	July 6[1]	A.L. (Kuenn)	13	N.L. (Herzog)	3	Steib	Soto	Chicago A.L.	43,801
1984	July 11[1]	N.L. (Owens)	3	A.L. (Altobelli)	1	Leg	Steib	San Francisco, N.L.	57,756
1985	July 16[1]	N.L. (Williams)	6	A.L. (Anderson)	1	Hoyt	Morris	Minneapolis, A.L.	54,960
1986	July 15[1]	A.L. (Howser)	3	N.L. (Herzog)	2	Clemens	Gooden	Houston, N.L.	45,774
1987	July 14[1]	N.L. (Johnson)	2	A.L. (McNamara)	0	Smith	Howell	Oakland, A.L.	49,671
1988	July 12[1]	A.L. (Kelly)	2	N.L. (Herzog)	1	Viola	Gooden	Cincinnati, N.L.	55,837
1989	July 11[1]	A.L. (LaRussa)	5	N.L. (Lasorda)	3	Ryan	Smoltz	California, A.L.	64,036
1990	July 10[1]	A.L. (LaRussa)	2	N.L. (Craig)	0	Saberhagen	Brantley	Chicago, N.L.	39,071
1991	July 9[1]	A.L. (LaRussa)	4	N.L. (Piniella)	2	Key	Martinez	Toronto, A.L.	52,383
1992	July 14	A.L. (Kelly)	13	N.L. (Cox)	6	Brown	Glavine	San Diego, N.L.	59,372
1993	July 13	A.L. (Gaston)	9	N.L. (Cox)	3	McDowell	Burkett	Baltimore, A.L.	48,147
1994	July 12	N.L. (Fregosi)	8	A.L. (Gaston)	7	Jones	Bere	Pittsburgh, N.L.	59,568
1995	July 11	N.L. (Alou)	3	A.L. (Showalter)	2	Slocumb	Rogers	Texas, A.L.	50,920
1996	July 9	N.L. (Cox)	6	A.L. (Hargrove)	0	Smoltz	Nagy	Philadelphia, N.L.	62,670

1. Night game. 2. Two games. 3. Fourteen innings. 4. Five innings, rain. 5. Twelve innings. 6. Ten innings. 7. Called because of rain after nine innings. 8. Fifteen innings. NOTE: No game in 1945. *Game was originally scheduled for July 14, but was put off because of players' strike.

NATIONAL BASEBALL HALL OF FAME

Cooperstown, N.Y.

Fielders

Member	Active years
Aaron, Henry (Hank)	1954–1976
Anson, Adrian (Cap)	1876–1897
Aparicio, Luis	1956–1973
Appling, Lucius (Luke)	1930–1950
Ashburn, Richie	1948–1962
Averill, H. Earl	1929–1941
Baker, J. Frank (Home Run)	1908–1922
Bancroft, David	1915–1930
Banks, Ernest	1953–1971
Beckley, Jacob	1888–1907
Bell, James (Cool Papa)[1]	1920–1947
Bench, John	1967–1983
Berra, Lawrence (Yogi)	1946–1965
Bottomley, James	1922–1937
Boudreau, Louis	1938–1952
Bresnahan, Roger	1897–1915
Brock, Lou	1961–1980
Brouthers, Dennis	1879–1896
Burkett, Jesse	1890–1905
Campanella, Roy	1948–1957
Carew, Rod	1967–1985
Carey, Max	1910–1929
Chance, Frank	1898–1914
Charleston, Oscar[1]	1915–1954
Clarke, Fred	1894–1915
Clemente, Roberto	1955–1972
Cobb, Tyrus	1905–1928
Cochrane, Gordon (Mickey)	1925–1937
Collins, Edward	1906–1930
Collins, James	1895–1908
Comiskey, Charles	1882–1894
Combs, Earle	1924–1935
Connor, Roger	1880–1897
Crawford, Samuel	1899–1917
Cronin, Joseph	1926–1945
Cuyler, Hazen (Kiki)	1921–1938

Member	Active years
Dandridge, Ray[1]	1933–1953
Delahanty, Edward	1888–1903
Dickey, William	1928–1946
Dihigo, Martin[1]	1923–1945
DiMaggio, Joseph	1936–1951
Doerr, Bobby	1937–1951
Duffy, Hugh	1888–1906
Ewing, William	1880–1897
Eyers, John	1902–1919
Ferrell, Rick	1929–1947
Flick, Elmer	1898–1910
Foxx, James	1925–1945
Frisch, Frank	1919–1937
Gehrig, H. Louis (Lou)	1923–1939
Gehringer, Charles	1924–1942
Gibson, Josh[1]	1929–1946
Goslin, Leon (Goose)	1921–1938
Greenberg, Henry (Hank)	1933–1947
Hafey, Charles (Chick)	1924–1937
Hamilton, William	1888–1901
Hartnett, Charles (Gabby)	1922–1941
Heilmann, Harry	1914–1932
Herman, William	1931–1947
Hooper, Harry	1909–1925
Hornsby, Rogers	1915–1937
Irvin, Monford (Monte)[1]	1939–1956
Jackson, Reggie	1967–1987
Jackson, Travis	1922–1936
Jennings, Hugh	1891–1918
Johnson, William (Judy)[1]	1921–1937
Kaline, Albert W.	1953–1974
Keeler, William (Wee Willie)	1892–1910
Kell, George	1943–1957
Kelley, Joseph	1891–1908
Kelly, George	1915–1932
Kelly, Michael (King)	1878–1893
Killebrew, Harmon	1954–1975

Member	Active years
Kiner, Ralph	1946–1955
Klein, Charles H. (Chuck)	1928–1944
Lajoie, Napoleon	1896–1916
Lazzeri, Tony	1926–1939
Leonard, Walter (Buck)[1]	1933–1955
Lindstrom, Frederick	1924–1936
Lloyd, John Henry[1]	1905–1931
Lombardi, Ernie	1932–1947
Mantle, Mickey	1951–1968
Manush, Henry (Heinie)	1923–1939
Maranville, Walter (Rabbit)	1912–1935
Matthews, Edwin	1952–1968
Mays, Willie	1951–1973
McCarthy, Thomas	1884–1896
McGraw, John J.	1891–1906
McCovey, Willie	1959–1980
Medwick, Joseph (Ducky)	1932–1948
Mize, John (The Big Cat)	1936–1953
Morgan, Joe	1963–1984
Musial, Stanley	1941–1963
O'Rourke, James	1876–1894
Ott, Melvin	1926–1947
Reese, Harold (Pee Wee)	1940–1958
Rice, Edgar (Sam)	1915–1934
Rizzuto, Phil	1941–1956
Robinson, Brooks	1955–1977
Robinson, Frank	1956–1976
Robinson, Jack	1947–1956
Robinson, Wilbert	1886–1902
Roush, Edd	1913–1931
Ruth, Babe	1914–1935
Schalk, Raymond	1912–1929
Schoendienst, Red	1945–1963
Schmidt, Mike	1973–1989
Sewell, Joseph	1920–1933
Simmons, Al	1924–1944
Sisler, George	1915–1930
Slaughter, Enos	1938–1959

Snider, Edwin D. (Duke)	1947–1964	Vaughan, Arky	1932–1948	Wheat, Zachariah	1909–1927
Speaker, Tristram	1907–1928	Wagner, John (Honus)	1897–1917	Williams, Billy	1959–1976
Stargell, Willie	1962–1982	Wallace, Roderick (Bobby)	1894–1918	Williams, Theodore	1939–1960
Terry, William	1923–1936	Waner, Lloyd	1927–1945	Wilson, Lewis R. (Hack)	1923–1934
Thompson, Samuel	1885–1906	Waner, Paul	1926–1945	Yastrzemski, Carl	1961–1983
Tinker, Joseph	1902–1916	Ward, John (Monte)	1878–1894	Youngs, Ross (Pep)	1917–1926
Traynor, Harold (Pie)	1920–1937				

1. Negro League player selected by special committee.

Pitchers

Alexander, Grover	1911–1930	Griffith, Clark	1891–1914	Paige, Leroy (Satchel)[1]	1926–1965
Bender, Charles (Chief)	1903–1925	Grimes, Burleigh	1916–1934	Palmer, Jim	1965–1984
Brown, Mordecai (3–Finger)	1903–1916	Grove, Robert (Lefty)	1925–1941	Pennock, Herbert	1912–1934
Bunning, Jim	1955–1971	Haines, Jesse	1918–1937	Perry, Gaylord	1962–1983
Carlton, Steve	1965–1988	Hoyt, Waite	1918–1938	Plank, Edward	1901–1917
Chesbro, John	1899–1909	Hubbell, Carl	1928–1943	Radbourn, Charles (Hoss)	1880–1891
Clarkson, John	1882–1894	Hunter, Jim (Catfish)	1965–1979	Rixey, Eppa	1912–1933
Coveleski, Stanley	1912–1928	Jenkins, Ferguson	1965–1983	Roberts, Robert (Robin)	1948–1966
Day, Leon[1]	1935–1955	Johnson, Walter	1907–1927	Ruffing, Charles (Red)	1924–1947
Dean, Jerome (Dizzy)	1930–1947	Joss, Adrian	1902–1910	Rusie, Amos	1889–1901
Drysdale, Don	1956–1969	Keefe, Timothy	1880–1893	Seaver, Tom	1967–1986
Faber, Urban (Red)	1914–1933	Koufax, Sanford (Sandy)	1955–1966	Spahn, Warren	1942–1965
Feller, Robert	1936–1956	Lemon, Robert	1946–1958	Vance, Arthur (Dazzy)	1915–1935
Fingers, Rollie	1968–1985	Lyons, Theodore	1923–1946	Waddell, Rube	1897–1910
Ford, Edward (Whitey)	1950–1967	Marichal, Juan	1960–1975	Walsh, Edward	1904–1917
Foster, Andrew (Rube)	1897–1926	Marquard, Richard (Rube)	1908–1924	Welch, Michael (Mickey)	1880–1892
Foster, Bill	1923–1937	Mathewson, Christopher	1900–1916	Wilhelm, Hoyt	1952–1972
Galvin, James (Pud)	1876–1892	McGinnity, Joseph	1899–1908	Willis, Vic	1898–1910
Gibson, Bob	1959–1975	Neuhouser, Hal	1939–1955	Wynn, Early	1939–1963
Gomez, Vernon (Lefty)	1930–1943	Nichols, Charles (Kid)	1890–1906	Young, Denton (Cy)	1890–1911

1. Negro League player selected by special committee.

Officials and Others

Alston, Walter[1]	Cummings, William A.[5]	Huggins, Miller J.[1]	McKechnie, William B.[1]
Barlick, Al[4]	Durocher, Leo[1]	Hulbert, William[2]	Rickey, W. Branch[1,2]
Barrow, Edward[1,2]	Evans, William G.[4,2]	Johnson, B. Bancroft[2]	Spalding, Albert G.[4]
Bulkeley, Morgan G.[2]	Foster, Rube[2]	Klem, William[4]	Stengel, Charles D.[7]
Cartwright, Alexander[2]	Frick, Ford C.[6,2]	Landis, Kenesaw M.[6]	Veeck, Bill[2]
Chadwick, Henry[3]	Giles, Warren C.[2]	Lopez, Alfonso R.[7]	Weaver, Earl[1]
Chandler, A.B.[6]	Hanlon, Ned[1]	Mack, Connie[1,2]	Weiss, George M.[2]
Comiskey, Charles[1]	Harridge, William[2]	MacPhail, Leland S.[2]	Wright, George[5]
Conlan, John[2]	Harris, Stanley R.[7]	McCarthy, Joseph V.[1]	Wright, Harry[5,1]
Connolly, Thomas[4]	Hubbard, R. Calvin[4]	McGowan, Bill[4]	Yawkey, Thomas[2]

1. Manager. 2. Executive. 3. Writer–statistician. 4. Umpire. 5. Early player. 6. Commissioner. 7. Player–manager.

BASEBALL'S PERFECTLY PITCHED GAMES[1]
(no opposing runner reached base)

Lee Richmond—Worcester vs. Cleveland (NL) June 12, 1880	(1–0)	Jim Bunning—Philadelphia vs. New York (NL) June 21, 1964	(6–0
John M. Ward—Providence vs. Buffalo (NL) June 17, 1880	(5–0)	Sandy Koufax—Los Angeles vs. Chicago (NL) Sept. 9, 1965	(1–0
Cy Young—Boston vs. Philadelphia (AL) May 5, 1904	(3–0)	Jim Hunter—Oakland vs. Minnesota (AL) May 8, 1968	(4–0
Addie Joss—Cleveland vs. Chicago (AL) Oct. 2, 1908	(1–0)	Len Barker—Cleveland vs. Toronto (AL) May 15, 1981	(3–0
Ernest Shore[2]—Boston vs. Washington (AL) June 23, 1917	(4–0)	Mike Witt—California vs. Texas (AL) Sept. 30, 1984	(1–0
Charles Robertson—Chicago vs. Detroit (AL) April 30, 1922	(2–0)	Tom Browning—Cincinnati vs. Los Angeles (NL) Sept. 16, 1988	(1–0
Don Larsen[3]—New York (AL) vs. Brooklyn (NL) Oct. 8, 1956	(2–0)	Dennis Martinez—Montreal vs. Los Angeles (NL) July 28, 1991	(2–0
		Kenny Rogers—Texas vs. California (AL) July 28, 1994	(4–0

1. Harvey Haddix, of Pittsburgh, pitched 12 perfect innings against Milwaukee (NL), May 26, 1959 but lost game in 13th on error and hit. 2. Shore, relief pitcher for Babe Ruth who walked first batter before being ejected by umpire, retired 26 batters who faced him and baserunner was out stealing. 3. World Series.

LIFETIME BATTING, PITCHING, AND BASE–RUNNING RECORDS
(Records Through 1995)

Hits (3,000 or more)

Pete Rose	4,256
Ty Cobb	4,189
Hank Aaron	3,771
Stan Musial	3,630
Tris Speaker	3,514
Carl Yastrzemski	3,419
Honus Wagner	3,415
Eddie Collins	3,312
Willie Mays	3,283
Nap Lajoie	3,242
George Brett	3,154
Paul Waner	3,152
Robin Yount	3,142
Dave Winfield	3,110
Eddie Murray	3,071
Rod Carew	3,053
Lou Brock	3,023
Al Kaline	3,007
Roberto Clemente	3,000

Earned Run Average

(Minimum 1,500 innings pitched)

Ed Walsh	1.82
Addie Joss	1.89
Mordecai Brown	2.06
John Ward	2.10
Christy Mathewson	2.13
Rube Waddell	2.16
Walter Johnson	2.17
Orval Overall	2.23
Tommy Bond	2.25
Ed Ruelbach	2.28
Will White	2.28
Jim Scott	2.30
Ed Plank	2.35
Larry Corcoran	2.36
Ed Cicotte	2.38
Ed Killian	2.38
George McQuillan	2.38
Doc White	2.39
Nap Rucker	2.42
Terry Larkin	2.43
Jim McCormick	2.43
Jeff Tesreau	2.43

Runs Scored

Ty Cobb	2,246
Hank Aaron	2,174
Babe Ruth	2,174
Pete Rose	2,165

Willie Mays	2,062
Stan Musial	1,949
Lou Gehrig	1,888
Tris Speaker	1,882
Mel Ott	1,859
Frank Robinson	1,829
Eddie Collins	1,821
Carl Yastrzemski	1,816
Ted Williams	1,798
Charlie Gehringer	1,774
Jimmie Foxx	1,751
Honus Wagner	1,736
Jesse Burkett	1,720
Cap Anson	1,719
Rickey Henderson	1,719
Willie Keeler	1,719
Billy Hamilton	1,690
Bid McPhee	1,678
Mickey Mantle	1,677
Dave Winfield	1,669
Joe Morgan	1,650

Strikeouts, Pitching

Nolan Ryan	5,714
Steve Carlton	4,136
Bert Blyleven	3,701
Tom Seaver	3,640
Don Sutton	3,574
Gaylord Perry	3,534
Walter Johnson	3,509
Phil Niekro	3,342
Ferguson Jenkins	3,192
Bob Gibson	3,117
Jim Bunning	2,855
Mickey Lolich	2,832
Cy Young	2,803
Frank Tanana	2,773
Warren Spahn	2,583
Bob Feller	2,581
Jerry Koosman	2,556
Tim Keefe	2,543
Christy Mathewson	2,502

Home Runs (350 or More)

Hank Aaron	755
Babe Ruth	714
Willie Mays	660
Frank Robinson	586
Harmon Killebrew	573
Reggie Jackson	563

Mike Schmidt	548
Mickey Mantle	536
Jimmie Foxx	534
Willie McCovey	521
Ted Williams	521
Eddie Mathews	512
Mel Ott	511
Lou Gehrig	493
Eddie Murray	479
Stan Musial	475
Willie Stargell	475
Dave Winfield	465
Carl Yastrzemski	452
Dave Kingman	442
Andre Dawson	436
Billy Williams	426
Darrell Evans	414
Duke Snider	407
Al Kaline	399
Dale Murphy	398
Graig Nettles	390
Johnny Bench	389
Dwight Evans	385
Frank Howard	382
Jim Rice	382
Orlando Cepeda	379
Tony Perez	379
Norm Cash	377
Carlton Fisk	376
Rocky Colavito	374
Gil Hodges	370
Ralph Kiner	369
Joe DiMaggio	361
Johnny Mize	359
Yogi Berra	358
Lee May	354
Dick Allen	351

Shutouts

Walter Johnson	110
Pete Alexander	90
Christy Mathewson	79
Cy Young	76
Ed Plank	69
Warren Spahn	63
Nolan Ryan	61
Tom Seaver	61
Bert Blyleven	60
Don Sutton	58

Pud Galvin	57
Ed Walsh	57
Bob Gibson	56
Mordecai Brown	55
Steve Carlton	55
Jim Palmer	53
Gaylord Perry	53
Juan Marichal	52

Strikeouts, Batting

Reggie Jackson	2,597
Willie Stargell	1,936
Mike Schmidt	1,883
Tony Perez	1,867
Dave Kingman	1,816
Bobby Bonds	1,757
Dale Murphy	1,748
Lou Brock	1,730
Mickey Mantle	1,710
Harmon Killebrew	1,699
Dwight Evans	1,697
Dave Winfield	1,686
Lee May	1,570
Dick Allen	1,556
Willie McCovey	1,550
Dave Parker	1,537
Frank Robinson	1,532
Lance Parrish	1,527
Willie Mays	1,526

Walks

Babe Ruth	2,056
Ted Williams	2,019
Joe Morgan	1,865
Carl Yastrzemski	1,845
Mickey Mantle	1,733
Mel Ott	1,708
Eddie Yost	1,614
Darrell Evans	1,605
Stan Musial	1,599
Pete Rose	1,566
Harmon Killebrew	1,559
Rickey Henderson	1,550
Lou Gehrig	1,508
Mike Schmidt	1,507
Eddie Collins	1,499
Willie Mays	1,464
Jimmie Foxx	1,452
Eddie Mathews	1,444
Frank Robinson	1,420
Hank Aaron	1,402

RECORD OF WORLD SERIES GAMES
(Through 1995)

Source: The Book of Baseball Records, published by Seymour Siwoff, New York City.

Figures in parentheses for winning pitchers (WP) and losing pitchers (LP) indicate the game number in the series.

903—Boston A.L. 5 (Jimmy Collins); Pittsburgh N.L. 3 (Fred Clarke). WP—Bos.: Dinneen (2, 6, 8), Young (5, 7); Pitts.: Phillippe (1, 3, 4). LP—Bos.: Young (1), Hughes (3), Dinneen (4); Pitts.: Leever (2, 6), Kennedy (5), Phillippe (7, 8).

904—No series.

905—New York N.L. 4 (John J. McGraw); Philadelphia A.L. 1 (Connie Mack). WP—N.Y.: Mathewson (1, 3, 5); McGinnity (4); Phila.: Bender (2). LP—N.Y.: McGinnity (2); Phila.: Plank (1, 4), Coakley (3), Bender (5).

906—Chicago A.L. 4 (Fielder Jones); Chicago N.L. 2 (Frank Chance). WP—Chi.: A.L.: Altrock (1), Walsh (3, 5), White (6); Chi.: N.L.: Reulbach (2), Brown (4). LP—Chi. A.L.: White (2), Al-

trock. (4); Chi.: N.L.: Brown (1, 6), Pfeister (3, 5).

907—Chicago N.L. 4 (Frank Chance); Detroit A.L. 0 (Hugh Jennings). First game tied 3–3, 12 innings. WP—Pfeister (2), Reulbach (3), Overall (4), Brown (5). LP—Mullin (2, 5), Siever (3), Donovan (4).

908—Chicago N.L. 4 (Frank Chance); Detroit A.L. 1 (Hugh Jennings). WP—Chi.: Brown (1, 4), Overall (2, 5); Det.: Mullin (3). LP—Chi.: Pfeister (3); Det.: Summers (1, 4), Donovan (2, 5).

909—Pittsburgh N.L. 4 (Fred Clarke); Detroit A.L. 3 (Hugh Jennings). WP—Pitts.: Adams (1, 5, 7), Maddox (3); Det.: Donovan (2), Mullin (4, 6). LP—Pitts.: Camnitz (2), Leifield (4), Willis (6); Det.: Mullin (1), Summers (3, 5), Donovan (7).

1910—Philadelphia A.L. 4 (Connie Mack); Chicago N.L. 1 (Frank Chance). WP—Phila.: Bender (1), Coombs (2, 3, 5); Chi.: Brown (4). LP—Phila.: Bender (4); Chi.: Overall (1), Brown (2, 5), McIntyre (3).

1911—Philadelphia A.L. 4 (Connie Mack); New York N.L. 2 (John J. McGraw). WP—Phila.: Plank (2), Coombs (3), Bender (4, 6); N.Y.: Mathewson (1), Crandall (5). LP—Phila.: Bender (1), Plank (5); N.Y.: Marquard (2), Mathewson (3, 4), Ames (6).

1912—Boston A.L. 4 (J. Garland Stahl); New York N.L. 3 (John J. McGraw). Second game tied, 6–6, 11 innings. WP—Bos.: Wood (1, 4, 8), Bedient (5); N.Y.: Marquard (3, 6), Tesreau (7). LP—Bos.: O'Brien (3, 6), Wood (7); N.Y.: Tesreau (1, 4), Mathewson (5, 8).

1913—Philadelphia A.L. 4 (Connie Mack); New York N.L. 1 (John J. McGraw). WP—Phila.: Bender (1, 4), Bush (3), Plank (5); N.Y.: Mathewson (2); LP—Phila.: Plank (2); N.Y.: Marquard (1), Tesreau (3), Demaree (4), Mathewson (5).

1914—Boston N.L. 4 (George Stallings); Philadelphia A.L. 0 (Connie Mack). WP—Rudolph (1, 4), James (2, 3). LP—Bender (1), Plank (2), Bush (3), Shawkey (4).

1915—Boston A.L. 4 (Bill Carrigan); Philadelphia N.L. 1 (Pat Moran). WP—Bos.: Foster (2, 5), Leonard (3), Shore (4); Phila.: Alexander (1). LP—Bos.: Shore (1); Phila.: Mayer (2), Alexander (3), Chalmers (4), Rixey (5).

1916—Boston A.L. 4 (Bill Carrigan); Brooklyn N.L. 1 (Wilbert Robinson). WP—Bos.: Shore (1, 5), Ruth (2), Leonard (4); Bklyn.: Coombs (3). LP—Bos.: Mays (3); Bklyn.: Marquard (1, 4), Smith (2), Pfeffer (5).

1917—Chicago A.L. 4 (Clarence Rowland); New York N.L. 2 (John J. McGraw). WP—Chi.: Cicotte (1), Faber (2, 5, 6); N.Y.: Benton (3), Schupp (4), LP—Chi.: Cicotte (3), Faber (4); N.Y.: Sallee (1), Anderson (2), Benton (6).

1918—Boston A.L. 4 (Ed Barrow); Chicago N.L. 2 (Fred Mitchell). WP—Bos.: Ruth (1, 4), Mays (3, 6); Chi.: Tyler (2), Vaughn (5). LP—Bos.: Bush (2), Jones (5); Chi.: Vaughn (1, 3), Douglas (4), Tyler (6).

1919—Cincinnati N.L. 5 (Pat Moran); Chicago A.L. 3 (William Gleason). WP—Cin.: Ruether (1), Sallee (2), Ring (4), Eller (5, 8); Chi.: Kerr (3, 6), Cicotte (7). LP—Cin.: Fisher (3), Ring (6), Sallee (7); Chi.: Cicotte (1, 4), Williams (2, 5, 8).

1920—Cleveland A.L. 5 (Tris Speaker); Brooklyn N.L. 2 (Wilbert Robinson). WP—Cleve.: Coveleski (1, 4, 7), Bagby (5), Mails (6); Bklyn.: Grimes (2), Smith (3). LP—Cleve.: Bagby (2), Caldwell (3). Bklyn.: Marquard (1), Cadore (4), Grimes (5, 7), Smith (6).

1921—New York N.L. 5 (John J. McGraw); New York A.L. 3 (Miller Huggins). WP—N.Y. N.L.: Barnes (3, 6), Douglas (4, 7), Nehf (8); N.Y. A.L.: Mays (1), Hoyt (2, 5). LP—N.Y. N.L.: Nehf (2, 5), Douglas (1). N.Y. A.L.: Quinn (3), Mays (4, 7), Shawkey (6), Hoyt (8).

1922—New York N.L. 4 (John J. McGraw); New York A.L. 0 (Miller Huggins). Second game tied 3–3, 10 innings. WP—Ryan (1), Scott (3), McQuillan (4), Nehf (5); LP—Bush (1, 5), Hoyt (3), Mays (4).

1923—New York A.L. 4 (Miller Huggins); New York N.L. 2 (John J. McGraw). WP—N.Y. A.L.: Pennock (2, 6), Shawkey (4), Bush (5); N.Y. N.L.: Ryan (1), Nehf (3). LP—N.Y. A.L.: Bush (1), Jones (3); N.Y. N.L.: McQuillan (2), Scott (4), Bentley (5), Nehf (6).

1924—Washington A.L. 4 (Bucky Harris); New York N.L. 3 (John J. McGraw). WP—Wash.: Zachary (2, 6), Mogridge (4), Johnson (7); N.Y.: Nehf (1), McQuillan (3), Bentley (5). LP—Wash.: Johnson (1, 5), Marberry (3); N.Y.: Bentley (2, 7), Barnes (4), Nehf (6).

1925—Pittsburgh N.L. 4 (Bill McKechnie); Washington A.L. 3 (Bucky Harris). WP—Pitts.: Aldridge (2, 5), Kremer (6, 7); Wash.: Johnson (1, 4), Ferguson (3). LP—Pitts.: Meadows (1), Kremer (3), Yde (4); Wash.: Coveleski (2, 5), Ferguson (6), Johnson (7).

1926—St. Louis N.L. 4 (Rogers Hornsby); New York A.L. 3 (Miller Huggins). WP—St. L.: Alexander (2, 6), Haines (3, 7); N.Y.: Pennock (1, 5), Hoyt (4). LP—St. L.: Sherdel (1, 5), Reinhart (4); N.Y.: Shocker (2), Ruether (3), Shawkey (6), Hoyt (7).

1927—New York A.L. 4 (Miller Huggins); Pittsburgh N.L. 0 (Donie Bush). WP—Hoyt (1), Pipgras (2), Pennock (3), Moore (4). LP—Kremer (1), Aldridge (2), Meadows (3), Miljus (4).

1928—New York A.L. 4 (Miller Huggins); St. Louis N.L. 0 (Bill McKechnie). WP—Hoyt (1, 4), Pipgras (2), Zachary (3). LP—Sherdel (1, 4), Alexander (2), Haines (3).

1929—Philadelphia A.L. 4 (Connie Mack); Chicago N.L. 1 (Joe McCarthy). WP—Phila.: Ehmke (1), Earnshaw (2), Rommel (4), Walberg (5); Chi.: Bush (3). LP—Phila.: Earnshaw (3) Chi.: Root (1), Malone (2, 5), Blake (4).

1930—Philadelphia A.L. 4 (Connie Mack); St. Louis N.L. 2 (Gabby Street). WP—Phila.: Grove (1, 5), Earnshaw (2, 6); St. L.: Hallahan (3), Haines (4). LP—Phila.: Walberg (3), Grove (4); St. L.: Grimes (1, 5), Rhem (2), Hallahan (6).

1931—St. Louis N.L. 4 (Gabby Street); Philadelphia A.L. 3 (Connie Mack). WP—St. L.: Hallahan (2, 5), Grimes (3, 7); Phila. Grove (1, 6), Earnshaw (4). LP—St. L.: Derringer (1, 6), Johnson (4); Phila.: Earnshaw (2, 7), Grove (3), Hoyt (5).

1932—New York A.L. 4 (Joe McCarthy); Chicago N.L. 0 (Charlie Grimm). WP—Ruffing (1), Gomez (2), Pipgras (3), Moore (4) LP—Bush (1), Warneke (2), Root (3), May (4).

1933—New York N.L. 4 (Bill Terry); Washington A.L. 1 (Joe Cronin.). WP—N.Y.: Hubbell (1, 4), Schumacher (2), Luque (5); Wash.: Whitehill (3). LP—N.Y.: Fitzsimmons (3); Wash.: Stewart (1), Crowder (2), Weaver (4), Russell (5).

1934—St. Louis N.L. 4 (Frank Frisch); Detroit A.L. 3 (Mickey Cochrane). WP—St. L.: J. Dean (1, 7), P. Dean (3, 6); Det. Rowe (3), Auker (4), Bridges (5). LP—St. L.: W. Walker (2, 4), J. Dean (5); Det.: Crowder (1), Bridges (3), Rowe (6), Auker (7)

1935—Detroit A.L. 4 (Mickey Cochrane); Chicago N.L. 2 (Charles Grimm). WP—Det.: Bridges (2, 6), Rowe (3), Crowder (4); Chi.: Warneke (1, 5); LP—Det.: Rowe (1, 5), Chi.: Root (2), French (3, 6), Carleton (4).

1936—New York A.L. 4 (Joe McCarthy); New York N.L. 2 (Bill Terry). WP—N.Y. A.L.: Gomez (2, 6), Hadley (3), Pearson (4) N.Y. N.L.: Hubbell (1), Schumacher (5); LP—N.Y. A.L.: Ruffing (1), Malone (5); N.Y. N.L.: Schumacher (2), Fitzsimmons (3, 6) Hubbell (4).

1937—New York A.L. 4 (Joe McCarthy); New York N.L. 1 (Bill Terry). WP—N.Y. A.L.: Gomez (1, 5), Ruffing (2), Pearson (3) N.Y. N.L.: Hubbell (4). LP—N.Y. A.L.: Hadley (4); N.Y. N.L. Hubbell (1), Melton (2, 5), Schumacher (3).

1938—New York A.L. 4 (Joe McCarthy); Chicago N.L. 0 (Gabby Hartnett). WP—Ruffing (1, 4), Gomez (2), Pearson (3) LP—Lee (1, 4), Dean (2), Bryant (3).

1939—New York A.L. 4 (Joe McCarthy); Cincinnati N.L. 0 (Bill McKechnie). WP—Ruffing (1), Pearson (2), Hadley (3) Murphy (4). LP—Derringer (1), Walters (2, 4), Thompson (3)

1940—Cincinnati N.L. 4 (Bill McKechnie); Detroit A.L. 3 (Del Baker). WP—Cin.: Walters (2, 6), Derringer (4, 7); Det. Newsom (1, 5), Bridges (3). LP—Cin.: Derringer (1), Turner (2) Thompson (5); Det.: Rowe (2, 6), Trout (4), Newsom (7).

1941—New York A.L. 4 (Joe McCarthy); Brooklyn N.L. 1 (Leo Durocher). WP—N.Y.: Ruffing (1), Russo (3), Murphy (4), Bonham (5); Bklyn: Wyatt (2). LP—N.Y.: Chandler (2); Bklyn: Davis (1) Casey (3, 4), Wyatt (5).

1942—St. Louis N.L. 4 (Billy Southworth); New York A.L. 1 (Joe McCarthy). WP—St. L.: Beazley (2, 5), White (3), Lanier (4); N.Y Ruffing (1). LP—St. L.: Cooper (1); N.Y.: Bonham (2), Chandler (3) Donald (4), Ruffing (5).

1943—New York A.L. 4 (Joe McCarthy); St. Louis N.L. 1 (Billy Southworth). WP—N.Y.: Chandler (1, 5), Borowy (3), Russo (4) St. L.: Cooper (2). LP—N.Y.: Bonham (2); St. L.: Lanier (1), Brazle (3), Brecheen (4), Cooper (5).

1944—St. Louis N.L. 4 (Billy Southworth); St. Louis A.L. 2 (Luke Sewell). WP—St. L. N.L.: Donnelly (2), Brecheen (4), Cooper (5) Lanier (6); St. L. A.L.: Galehouse (1), Kramer (3). LP—St. L. N.L. Cooper (1), Wilks (3); St. L. A.L.: Muncrief (2), Jakucki (4), Galehouse (5), Potter (6).

1945—Detroit A.L. 4 (Steve O'Neill); Chicago N.L. 3 (Charlie Grimm). WP—Det.: Trucks (2), Trout (4), Newhouser (5, 7); Chi. Borowy (1, 6), Passeau (3). LP—Det.: Newhouser (1), Overmire (3), Trout (6); Chi.: Wyse (2), Prim (4), Borowy (5, 7).

1946—St. Louis N.L. 4 (Eddie Dyer); Boston A.L. 3 (Joe Cronin) WP—St. L.: Brecheen (2, 6, 7), Munger (4); Bos.: Johnson (1, 4 Ferriss (3), Dobson (5). LP—St. L.: Pollet (1), Dickson (3), Brazle (5); Bos.: Harris (2, 6), Hughson (4), Klinger (7).

1947—New York A.L. 4 (Bucky Harris); Brooklyn N.L. 3 (Burt Shotton). WP—N.Y.: Shea (1, 5), Reynolds (2), Page (7); Bklyn.: Casey (3, 4), Branca (6). LP—N.Y.: Newsom (3), Bevens (4), Page (6); Bklyn.: Branca (1), Lombardi (2), Barney (5), Gregg (7).

1948—Cleveland A.L. 4 (Lou Boudreau); Boston N.L. 2 (Billy Southworth). WP—Cleve.: Lemon (2, 6), Bearden (4), Gromek (4); Bos.: Sain (1), Spahn (5). LP—Cleve.: Feller (1, 5); Bos.: Spahn (2), Bickford (3), Sain (4), Voiselle (6).

1949—New York A.L. 4 (Casey Stengel); Brooklyn N.L. 1 (Burt Shotton). WP—N.Y.: Reynolds (1), Page (3), Lopat (4), Raschi (5); Bklyn.: Roe (2). LP—N.Y.: Raschi (2); Bklyn.: Newcombe (1, 4), Branca (3), Barney (5).

1950—New York A.L. 4 (Casey Stengel); Philadelphia N.L. 0 (Eddie Sawyer). WP—Raschi (1), Reynolds (2), Ferrick (3), Ford (4). LP—Konstanty (1), Roberts (2), Meyer (3), Miller (4).

1951—New York A.L. 4 (Casey Stengel); New York N.L. 2 (Leo Durocher). WP—N.Y.A.L.: Lopat (2, 5), Reynolds (4), Raschi (6); N.Y. N.L.: Koslo (1), Hearn (3). LP—N.Y.A.L.: Reynolds (1), Raschi (3); N.Y. N.L.: Jansen (2, 5), Maglie (4), Koslo (6).

1952—New York A.L. 4 (Casey Stengel); Brooklyn N.L. 3 (Chuck Dressen). WP—N.Y.: Raschi (2, 6), Reynolds (4, 7); Bklyn.: Black (1), Roe (3), Erskine (5). LP—N.Y.: Reynolds (1), Lopat (3), Sain (5); Bklyn.: Erskine (2), Black (4, 7), Loes (6).

1953—New York A.L. 4 (Casey Stengel); Brooklyn N.L. 2 (Chuck Dressen). WP—N.Y.: Sain (1), Lopat (2), McDonald (5), Reynolds (6); Bklyn.: Erskine (3), Loes (4). LP—N.Y.: Raschi (3), Ford (4); Bklyn.: Labine (1, 6), Roe (2), Podres (5).

1954—New York N.L. 4 (Leo Durocher); Cleveland A.L. 0 (Al Lopez). WP—Grissom (1), Antonelli (2), Gomez (3), Liddie (4). LP—Lemon (1, 4), Wynn (2), Garcia (3).

1955—Brooklyn N.L. 4 (Walter Alston); New York A.L. 3 (Casey Stengel). WP—Bklyn.: Podres (3, 7), Labine (4), Craig (5); N.Y.: Ford (1, 6), Byrne (2). LP—Bklyn.: Newcombe (1), Loes (2), Spooner (6); N.Y.: Turley (3), Larsen (4), Grim (5), Byrne (7).

1956—New York A.L. 4 (Casey Stengel); Brooklyn N.L. 3 (Walter Alston). WP—N.Y.: Ford (3), Sturdivant (4), Larsen (5), Kucks (7); Bklyn.: Maglie (1), Bessent (2), Labine (6). LP—N.Y.: Ford (1), Morgan (2), Turley (6); Bklyn.: Craig (3), Erskine (4), Maglie (5), Newcombe (7).

1957—Milwaukee N.L. 4 (Fred Haney); New York A.L. 3 (Casey Stengel). WP—Mil.: Burdette (2, 5, 7), Spahn (4); N.Y.: Ford (1), Larsen (3), Turley (6). LP—Mil.: Spahn (1), Buhl (3), Johnson (6); N.Y.: Shantz (2), Grim (4), Ford (5), Larsen (7).

1958—New York A.L. 4 (Casey Stengel); Milwaukee N.L. 3 (Fred Haney). WP—N.Y.: Larsen (3), Turley (5, 7), Duren (6); Mil.: Spahn (1, 4), Burdette (2). LP—N.Y.: Duren (1), Turley (2), Ford (4); Mil.: Rush (3), Burdette (5, 7), Spahn (6).

1959—Los Angeles N.L. 4 (Walter Alston); Chicago A.L. 2 (Al Lopez). WP—L.A.: Podres (2), Drysdale (3), Sherry (4, 6); Chi.: Wynn (1), Shaw (5). LP—L.A.: Craig (1), Koufax (5); Chi.: Shaw (2), Donovan (3), Staley (4), Wynn (6).

1960—Pittsburgh N.L. 4 (Danny Murtaugh); New York A.L. 3 (Casey Stengel). WP—Pitts.: Law (1, 4), Haddix (5, 7); N.Y.: Turley (2), Ford (3, 6). LP—Pitts.: Friend (2, 6), Mizell (3); N.Y.: Ditmar (1, 5), Terry (4, 7).

1961—New York A.L. 4 (Ralph Houk); Cincinnati N.L. 1 (Fred Hutchinson). WP—N.Y.: Ford (1, 4), Arroyo (3), Daley (5); Cin.: Jay (2). LP—N.Y.: Terry (2); Cin.: O'Toole (1, 4), Purkey (3), Jay (5).

1962—New York A.L. 4 (Ralph Houk); San Francisco N.L. 3 (Al Dark). WP—N.Y.: Ford (1), Stafford (3), Terry (5, 7); S.F. Sanford (2), Larsen (4), Pierce (6). LP—N.Y.: Terry (2), Coates (4), Ford (6); S.F.: O'Dell (1), Pierce (3), Sanford (5, 7).

1963—Los Angeles N.L. 4 (Walter Alston); New York A.L. 0 (Ralph Houk). WP—Koufax (1, 4), Podres (2), Drysdale (3). LP—Ford (1, 4), Downing (2), Bouton (3).

1964—St. Louis N.L. 4 (Johnny Keane); New York A.L. 3 (Yogi Berra). WP—St. L.: Sadecki (1), Craig (4), Gibson (5, 7); N.Y.: Stottlemyre (2), Bouton (3, 6). LP—St. L.: Gibson (2), Schultz (3), Simmons (6); N.Y.: Ford (1), Downing (4), Mikkelsen (5), Stottlemyre (7).

1965—Los Angeles N.L. 4 (Walter Alston); Minnesota A.L. 3 (Sam Mele). WP—L.A.: Osteen (3), Drysdale (4), Koufax (5, 7); Minn.: Grant (1, 6), Kaat (2). LP—L.A.: Drysdale (1), Koufax (2), Osteen (6); Minn.: Pascual (3), Grant (4), Kaat (5, 7).

1966—Baltimore A.L. 4 (Hank Bauer); Los Angeles N.L. 0 (Walter Alston). WP—Drabowsky (1), Palmer (2), Bunker (3), McNally (4). LP—Drysdale (1, 4), Koufax (2), Osteen (3).

1967—St. Louis N.L. 4 (Red Schoendienst); Boston A.L. 3 (Dick Williams). WP—St. L.: Gibson (1, 4, 7), Briles (3); Bos.: Lonborg (2, 5); Wyatt (6). LP—St. L.: Hughes (2), Carlton (5), Lamabe (6); Bos.: Santiago (1, 4), Bell (3).

1968—Detroit A.L. 4 (Mayo Smith); St. Louis N.L. 3 (Red Schoendienst). WP—Det.: Lolich (2, 5, 7), McLain (6); St. L.: Gibson (1, 4), Washburn (3). LP—Det.: McLain (1, 4), Wilson (3); St. L.: Briles (2), Hoerner (5), Washburn (6), Gibson (7).

1969—New York N.L. 4 (Gil Hodges); Baltimore A.L. 1 (Earl Weaver). WP—N.Y.: Koosman (2, 5), Gentry (3), Seaver (4); Balt.: Cuellar (1). LP—N.Y.: Seaver (1); Balt.: McNally (2), Palmer (3), Hall (4), Watt (5).

1970—Baltimore A.L. 4 (Earl Weaver); Cincinnati N.L. 1 (Sparky Anderson) 1. WP—Balt.: Palmer (1), Phoebus (2), McNally (3), Cuellar (5); Cin.: Carroll (4). LP—Cin.: Nolan (1), Wilcox (2), Cloninger (3), Merritt (5); Balt.: Watt (4).

1971—Pittsburgh N.L. 4 (Danny Murtaugh); Baltimore A.L. 3 (Earl Weaver). WP—Pitts.: Blass (3, 7), Kison (4), Briles (5); Balt.: McNally (1, 6), Palmer (2). LP—Pitts.: Ellis (1), R. Johnson (2), Miller (6); Balt.: Cuellar (3, 7), Watt (4) McNally (5).

1972—Oakland A.L. 4 (Dick Williams); Cincinnati N.L. (Sparky Anderson) 3. WP—Oakland: Holtzman (1), Hunter (2, 7), Fingers (4); Cincinnati: Billingham (3), Grimsley (5, 6). LP—Oakland: Odom (3), Fingers (5), Blue (6); Cincinnati: Nolan (1), Grimsley (2), Carroll (4), Borbon (7).

1973—Oakland A.L. 4 (Dick Williams): New York N.L. 3 (Yogi Berra). WP—Oakland: Holtzman (1, 7), Lindblad (3), Hunter (6). New York: McGraw (2), Matlack (4), Koosman (5). LP—Oakland: Fingers (1), Holtzman (4), Blue (5). New York: Matlack (1, 7) Parker (3), Seaver (6).

1974—Oakland A.L. 4 (Al Dark); Los Angeles N.L. 1 (Walter Alston). WP—Oakland: Fingers (1), Hunter (3), Holtzman (4), Odom (5). Los Angeles: Sutton (2). LP—Oakland: Blue (2), Los Angeles: Messersmith (1, 4), Downing (3), Marshall (5).

1975—Cincinnati N.L. 4 (Sparky Anderson); Boston A.L. 3 (Darrell Johnson). WP—Cincinnati: Eastwick (2, 3), Gullett (5), Carroll (7); Boston: Tiant (1, 4), Wise (6). LP—Cincinnati: Gullett (1), Norman (4), Darcy (6); Boston: Drago (2), Willoughby (3), Cleveland (5), Burton (7).

1976—Cincinnati N.L. 4 (Sparky Anderson); New York A.L. 0 (Billy Martin). WP—Gullett (1), Billingham (2), Zachry (3), Nolan (4). LP—Alexander (1), Hunter (2), Ellis (3), Figueroa (4).

1977—New York A.L. 4 (Billy Martin); Los Angeles N.L. 2 (Tom Lasorda). WP—New York: Lyle (1), Torrez (3, 6), Guidry (4); Los Angeles: Hooton (2), Sutton (5). LP—New York: Hunter (2), Gullett (5); Los Angeles: Rhoden (1), John (3), Rau (4), Hooton (6).

1978—New York A.L. 4 (Bob Lemon), Los Angeles N.L. 2 (Tom Lasorda); WP—New York: Guidry (3), Gossage (4); Beattie (5), Hunter (6); Los Angeles: John (1), Hooton (2). LP—New York: Figueroa (1), Hunter (2); Los Angeles: Sutton (3, 6), Welch (4), Hooton (5).

1979—Pittsburgh N.L. 4 (Chuck Tanner), Baltimore A.L. 3 (Earl Weaver); WP—Pittsburgh: D. Robinson (2), Blyleven (5), Candelaria (6), Jackson (7); Baltimore: Flanagan (1), McGregor (3), Stoddard (4). LP—Pittsburgh: Kison (1), Candelaria (3), Tekulve (4); Baltimore: Stanhouse (2), Flanagan (5), Palmer (6), McGregor (7).

1980—Philadelphia N.L. 4 (Dallas Green), Kansas City A.L. 2 (Jim Frey); WP—Philadelphia: Walk (1), Carlton (2), McGraw (5), Carlton (6); Kansas City: Quisenberry (3), Leonard (4). LP—Philadelphia: McGraw (3), Christenson (4); Kansas City: Leonard (1), Quisenberry (2), Quisenberry (5), Gale (6).

1981—Los Angeles N.L. 4 (Tom Lasorda), New York A.L. 2 (Bob Lemon); WP—Los Angeles: Valenzuela (3), Howe (4), Reuss (5), Hooton (6), Guidry (1), John (2). LP—Los Angeles: Reuss (1), Hooton (2); New York: Frazier (3), Frazier (4), Guidry (5), Frazier (6).

1982—St. Louis N.L. 4 (Whitey Herzog), Milwaukee A.L. 3 (Harvey Kuenn). WP—St. Louis: Sutter (2), Andujar (3), Stuper (6), Andujar (7). Milwaukee: Caldwell (1), Slaton (4), Caldwell (5). LP—St. Louis: Forsch (1), Bair (4), Forsch (5). Milwaukee: McClure (2), Vuckovich (3), Sutton (6), McClure (7).

1983—Baltimore A.L. 4 (Joe Altobelli), Philadelphia N.L. 1 (Paul Owens); WP—Baltimore: Boddicker (2), Palmer (3), Davis (4), McGregor (5). Philadelphia: Denny (1).

1984—Detroit A.L. 4 (Sparky Anderson), San Diego N.L. 1 (Dick Williams); WP—Det.: Morris (1,4), Wilcox (3), Lopez (5), San Diego: Hawkins (2). LP—Det.: Petry (2), San Diego: Thurmond (1), Lollar (3), Show (4), Hawkins (5).

1985—Kansas City A.L. 4 (Dick Howser), St. Louis N.L. 3 (Whitey Herzog); WP—KC: Saberhagen (3,7) Quisenberry (6), Jackson (5). St. Louis: Tudor (1,4) Dayley (2). LP—KC: Jackson (1), Leibrandt (2), Black (4); St. Louis: Andujar (3), Forsch (5), Worrell (6), Tudor (7).

1986—New York N.L. 4 (Dave Johnson); Boston A.L. (John McNamara) 3 WP—N.Y.—Ojeda (3), Darling (4), Aguilera (6), McDowell (7), Bos: Hurst (1), (5), Crawford (2). LP—N.Y. Darling (1), Gooden (2, 5).

1987—Minnesota, A.L. 4 (Tom Kelly); St. Louis N.L. (Whitey Herzog) 3. WP—Minn. Viola (1, 7), Blyleven (2), Schatzeder (6); St. Louis: Tudor (3), Forsch (4), Cox (5). LP—Minn. Berenguer (3), Viola (4), Blyleven (5); St. Louis: Magrane (1), Cox (2, 7), Tudor (6).

1988—Los Angeles N.L. 4 (Tommy Lasorda); Oakland A.L. (Tony LaRussa) 1. WP—Los Angeles: Hershiser (2, 5), Pena (1), Belcher (4); Oakland: Honeycutt (3). LP—Los Angeles: Howell (3); Oakland: Davis (2, 5), Eckersley (1), Stewart (4).

1989—Oakland, A.L. 4 (Tony LaRussa); San Francisco N.L. 0

(Roger Craig). WP—Oakland: Dave Stewart (1, 3), Mike Moore (2, 4). LP—San Francisco: Scott Garrelts (1, 3), Don Robinson (4), Rick Reuschel (2).

1990—Cincinnati N.L. 4 (Lou Piniella); Oakland A.L. 0 (Tony La Russa). WP—Cincinnati: Jose Rijo (1, 4), Rob Dibble (2), Tom Browning (3). LP—Oakland: Dave Stewart (1, 4), Dennis Eckersley (2), Mike Moore (3).

1991—Minnesota, A.L. 4 (Tom Kelly); Atlanta, N.L. 3 (Bobby Cox) WP—Minnesota: Morris (1,7), Tapani (2), Aguilera (6). Atlanta Clancy (3), Stanton (4), Glavine (5). LP—Minnesota: Aguilera (3), Guthrie (4), Tapani (5). Atlanta: Leibrandt (1, 6), Glavine (2) Pena (7).

1992—Toronto, A.L. 4 (Cito Gaston), Atlanta, N.L. 2 (Bobby Cox) WP—Toronto: Ward (2, 3), Key (4, 6). Atlanta: Glavine (1) Smoltz (5). LP—Toronto: Morris (1, 5). Atlanta: Leibrandt (3), Reardon (2), Avery (3), Glavine (4).

1993—Toronto, A.L. 4 (Cito Gaston), Philadelphia, N.L. 2 (Jim Fregosi). WP—Toronto: Leiter (1), Hentgen (3), Castillo (4), Ward (6). Philadelphia: Mullholland (2), Schilling (5). LP—Toronto Stewart (2), Guzman (5). Philadelphia: Schilling (1), Jackson (3) Williams (4,6).

1994—World Series cancelled due to players' strike.

1995—Atlanta, N.L. 4 (Bobby Cox); Cleveland, A.L. 2 (Mike Hargrove). WP—Atlanta: Maddux (1), Glavine (2,6), Avery (4) Cleveland: Mesa (3), Hershiser (5). LP—Atlanta: Pena (3), Maddux (5). Cleveland: Hershiser (1), Martinez (2), Hill (4), Poole (6)

Before the World Series

Source: Information Please Sports Almanac

The NL–American Assn. Series, 1882–90

When the National League met the American League for the first time in the 1903 World Series, it was not the N.L.'s first venture into post–season play.

From 1882–90, the N.L. pennant winner engaged in a championship series with the champion of the American Association. The Nationals won four of the eight series, lost once, and tied three times.

Year	Champion	Loser	Series	Year	Champion	Loser	Series
1882	Chicago (NL) & Cincinnati (AA)	—	1–1	1886	St. Louis (AA)	Chicago (NL)	4–2
1883	No series			1887	Detroit (NL)	St. Louis (AA)	10–5
1884	Providence (NL)	New York (AA)	3–0	1888	New York (NL)	St. Louis (AA)	6–4
1885	Chicago (NL) & St. Louis (AA)	—	3–3–1	1889	New York (NL)	Brooklyn (AA)	6–3
				1890	Brooklyn (NL) & Louisville (AA)	—	3–3–1

Early NL and AL Pennant Winners

The National League had been around 27 years before the 1903 World Series. The AL, however, was only in its third season when the two leagues met. The following lists account for the pennant winners in those pre–World Series years and in 1904 when the NL champion New York Giants refused to play Boston.

NL Pennant Winners, 1876–1902, '04

Year	Winner	Manager	Year	Winner	Manager	Year	Winner	Manager
1876	Chicago	Al Spalding	1885	Chicago	Cap Anson	1895	Baltimore	Ned Hanlon
1877	Boston	Harry Wright	1886	Chicago	Cap Anson	1896	Baltimore	Ned Hanlon
1878	Boston	Harry Wright	1887	Detroit	Bill Watkins	1897	Boston	Frank Selee
1879	Providence	George Wright	1888	New York	Jim Mutrie	1898	Boston	Frank Selee
1880	Chicago	Cap Anson	1889	New York	Jim Mutrie	1899	Brooklyn	Ned Hanlon
1881	Chicago	Cap Anson	1890	Brooklyn	Bill McGunnigle	1900	Brooklyn	Ned Hanlon
1882	Chicago	Cap Anson	1891	Boston	Frank Selee	1901	Pittsburgh	Fred Clarke
1883	Boston	John Morrill	1892	Boston	Frank Selee	1902	Pittsburgh	Fred Clarke
1884	Providence	Frank Bancroft	1893	Boston	Frank Selee	1904	New York	John McGraw
			1894	Baltimore	Ned Hanlon			

AL Pennant Winners, 1901–02, '04

Year	Winner	Manager	Year	Winner	Manager	Year	Winner	Manager
1901	Chicago	Clark Griffith	1902	Philadelphia	Connie Mack	1904	Boston	Jimmy Collins

WORLD SERIES CLUB STANDING
(Through 1995)

	Series	Won	Lost	Pct.		Series	Won	Lost	Pct.
Toronto (A)	2	2	0	1.000	Detroit (A)	9	4	5	.444
Pittsburgh (N)	7	5	2	.714	New York (N–Giants)	14	5	9	.357
New York (A)	33	22	11	.667	Washington (A)	3	1	2	.333
Oakland (A)	6	4	2	.667	Philadelphia (N)	5	1	4	.200
Cleveland (A)	4	2	2	.500	Chicago (N)	10	2	8	.200
Minnesota (A)	3	2	1	.667	Brooklyn (N)	9	1	8	.111
New York (N–Mets)	3	2	1	.667	St. Louis (A)	1	0	1	.000
Philadelphia (A)	8	5	3	.625	San Francisco (N)	2	0	2	.000
St. Louis (N)	15	9	6	.600	Milwaukee (A)	1	0	1	.000
Boston (A)	9	5	4	.550	San Diego (N)	1	0	1	.000
Los Angeles (N)	9	5	4	.550	Atlanta (N)	3	1	2	.333
Cincinnati (N)	9	5	4	.550					
Milwaukee (N)	2	1	1	.500	**Recapitulation**				
Boston (N)	2	1	1	.500					
Chicago (A)	4	2	2	.500					**Won**
Baltimore (A)	6	3	3	.500	American League				52
Kansas City (A)	2	1	1	.500	National League				37

LIFETIME WORLD SERIES RECORDS
(Through 1995)

Most hits—71, Yogi Berra, New York A.L., 1947, 1949–53, 1955–58, 1960–63.

Most runs—42, Mickey Mantle, New York A.L., 1951–53, 1955–58, 1960–64.

Most runs batted in—40, Mickey Mantle, New York A.L., 1951–53, 1955–58, 1960–64.

Most home runs—18, Mickey Mantle, New York A.L., 1951–53, 1955–58, 1960–64.

Most bases on balls—43, Mickey Mantle, New York A.L., 1951–53, 1955–58, 1960–64.

Most strikeouts—54, Mickey Mantle, New York A.L., 1951–53, 1955–58, 1960–64.

Most stolen bases—14, Eddie Collins, Philadelphia A.L. 1910–11, 13–14; Chicago A.L., 1917, 1919. Lou Brock, St. Louis N.L., 1964, 67–68.

Most victories, pitcher—10, Whitey Ford, New York A.L., 1950, 1953, 1955–58, 1960–64.

Most times member of winning team—10, Yogi Berra, New York A.L., 1947, 1949–53, 1956, 1958, 1961–62.

Most victories, no defeats—6, Vernon Gomez, New York A.L., 1932, 1936(2), 1937(2), 1938.

Most shutouts—4, Christy Mathewson, New York N.L., 1905 (3), 1913.

Most innings pitched—146, Whitey Ford, New York A.L., 1950, 1953, 1955–58, 1960–1964

Most consecutive scoreless innings—33 2/3, Whitey Ford, New York A.L., 1960 (18), 1961 (14), 1962 (1 2/3).

Most strikeouts by pitcher—94, Whitey Ford, New York A.L., 1950, 1953, 1955–58, 1960–64.

SINGLE GAME AND SINGLE SERIES RECORDS
(Through 1995)

Most hits game—5, Paul Molitor, Milwaukee A.L., first game vs. St. Louis, N.L., 1982.

Most 4–hit games, series—2, Robin Yount, Milwaukee A.L., first and fifth games vs. St. Louis N.L., 1982.

Most hits inning—2, held by many players.

Most hits series—13 (7 games) Bobby Richardson, New York A.L., 1964; Lou Brock, St. Louis N.L., 1968; 12 (6 games) Billy Martin, New York A.L., 1953; 12 (8 games) Buck Herzog, New York N.L., 1912; Joe Jackson, Chicago A.L., 1919; 10 (4 games) Babe Ruth, New York A.L., 1928; 9 (5 games) held by 8 players.

Most home runs, series—5 (6 games) Reggie Jackson, New York A.L., 1977; 4 (7 games) Babe Ruth, New York A.L., 1926; Duke Snider, Brooklyn N.L., 1952, 1955; Hank Bauer, New York A.L., 1958; Gene Tenace, Oakland A.L., 1972; 4 (4 games) Lou Gehrig, New York A.L., 1928; 3 (6 games) Babe Ruth, New York A.L., 1923; Ted Kluszewski, Chicago A.L., 1959; 3 (5 games) Donn Clendenon, New York Mets N.L., 1969.

Most home runs, game—3, Babe Ruth, New York A.L., 1926 and 1928; Reggie Jackson, New York A.L., 1977.

Most strikeouts, series—12 (6 games) Willie Wilson, Kansas City A.L., 1980; 11 (7 games) Ed Mathews, Milwaukee N.L., 1958; Wayne Garrett, New York N.L., 1973; 10 (8 games) George Kelly, New York N.L., 1921; 9 (6 games) Jim Bottom-

ley, St. Louis N.L., 1930; 9 (5 games) Carmelo Martinez, San Diego, N.L., 1984; Duke Snider, Brooklyn N.L., 1949; 7 (4 games) Bob Muesel, New York A.L., 1927.

Most stolen bases, game—3, Honus Wagner, Pittsburgh N.L., 1909; Willie Davis, Los Angeles N.L., 1965; Lou Brock, St. Louis N.L., 1967 and 1968.

Most strikeouts by pitcher, game—17, Bob Gibson, St. Louis N.L. 1968.

Most strikeouts by pitcher in succession—6, Horace Eller, Cincinnati N.L., 1919; Moe Drabowsky, Baltimore A.L., 1966.

Most strikeouts by pitcher, series—35 (7 games) Bob Gibson, St. Louis N.L., 1968; 28 (8 games) Bill Dinneen, Boston A.L., 1903; 23 (4 games) Sandy Koufax, Los Angeles, 1963; 20 (6 games) Chief Bender, Philadelphia A.L., 1911; 18 (5 games) Christy Mathewson, New York N.L., 1905.

Most bases on balls, series—11 (7 games) Babe Ruth, New York A.L., 1926; Gene Tenace, Oakland A.L., 1973; 9 (6 games) Willie Randolph, New York A.L., 1981; 7 (5 games) James Sheckard, Chicago N.L., 1910; Mickey Cochrane, Philadelphia A.L., 1929; Joe Gordon, New York A.L., 1941; 7 (4 games) Hank Thompson, New York N.L., 1954.

Most consecutive scoreless innings one series—27, Christy Mathewson, New York N.L., 1905.

AMERICAN LEAGUE HOME RUN CHAMPIONS

Year	Player, team	No.
1901	Nap Lajoie, Phila.	13
1902	Ralph Seybold, Phila.	16
1903	Buck Freeman, Bost.	13
1904	Harry Davis, Phila.	10
1905	Harry Davis, Phila.	8
1906	Harry Davis, Phila.	12
1907	Harry Davis, Phila.	8
1908	Sam Crawford, Det.	7
1909	Ty Cobb, Det.	9
1910	J. Garland Stahl, Bost.	10
1911	Franklin Baker, Phila.	9
1912	Franklin Baker, Phila.	10
1913	Franklin Baker, Phila.	12
1914	Franklin Baker, Phila., and Sam Crawford, Det.	8
1915	Robert Roth, Chi.–Cleve.	7
1916	Wally Pipp, N.Y.	12
1917	Wally Pipp, N.Y.	9
1918	Babe Ruth, Bost., and Clarence Walker, Phila.	11
1919	Babe Ruth, Bost.	29
1920	Babe Ruth, N.Y.	54
1921	Babe Ruth, N.Y.	59
1922	Ken Williams, St. L.	39
1923	Babe Ruth, N.Y.	41
1924	Babe Ruth, N.Y.	46
1925	Bob Meusel, N.Y.	33
1926	Babe Ruth, N.Y.	47
1927	Babe Ruth, N.Y.	60
1928	Babe Ruth, N.Y.	54
1929	Babe Ruth, N.Y.	46
1930	Babe Ruth, N.Y.	49
1931	Lou Gehrig, N.Y., and Babe Ruth, N.Y.	46
1932	Jimmy Foxx, Phila.	58
933	Jimmy Foxx, Phila.	48
1934	Lou Gehrig, N.Y.	49
1935	Jimmy Foxx, Phila., and Hank Greenberg, Det.	36
1936	Lou Gehrig, N.Y.	49
1937	Joe DiMaggio, N.Y.	46
1938	Hank Greenberg, Det.	58
1939	Jimmy Foxx, Bost.	35
1940	Hank Greenberg, Det.	41
1941	Ted Williams, Bost.	37
1942	Ted Williams, Bost.	36
1943	Rudy York, Det.	34
1944	Nick Etten, N.Y.	22
1945	Vern Stephens, St. L.	24
1946	Hank Greenberg, Det.	44
1947	Ted Williams, Bost.	32
1948	Joe DiMaggio, N.Y.	39
1949	Ted Williams, Bost.	43
1950	Al Rosen, Cleve.	37
1951	Gus Zernial, Chi.–Phila.	33
1952	Larry Doby, Cleve.	32
1953	Al Rosen, Cleve.	43
1954	Larry Doby, Cleve.	32
1955	Mickey Mantle, N.Y.	37
1956	Mickey Mantle, N.Y.	52
1957	Roy Sievers, Wash.	42
1958	Mickey Mantle, N.Y.	42
1959	Rocky Colavito, Cleve., and Harmon Killebrew, Wash.	42
1960	Mickey Mantle, N.Y.	40
1961	Roger Maris, N.Y.	61
1962	Harmon Killebrew, Minn.	48
1963	Harmon Killebrew, Minn.	45
1964	Harmon Killebrew, Minn.	49
1965	Tony Conigliaro, Bost.	32
1966	Frank Robinson, Balt.	49
1967	Carl Yastrzemski, Bost., and Harmon Killebrew, Minn.	44
1968	Frank Howard, Wash.	44
1969	Harmon Killebrew, Minn.	49
1970	Frank Howard, Wash.	44
1971	Bill Melton, Chicago	33
1972	Dick Allen, Chicago	37
1973	Reggie Jackson, Oak.	32
1974	Dick Allen, Chicago	32
1975	Reggie Jackson, Oak., and George Scott, Mil.	36
1976	Graig Nettles, N.Y.	32
1977	Jim Rice, Boston	39
1978	Jim Rice, Boston	46
1979	Gorman Thomas, Milwaukee	45
1980	Reggie Jackson, N.Y., and Ben Oglivie, Mil.	41
1981*	Tony Armas, Oak., Dwight Evans, Bost., Bobby Grich, Calif., and Eddie Murray, Balt. (tie)	22
1982	Gorman Thomas, Mil., and Reggie Jackson, Calif.	39
1983	Jim Rice, Boston	39
1984	Tony Armas, Boston	43
1985	Darrell Evans, Detroit	40
1986	Jesse Barfield, Toronto	40
1987	Mark McGwire, Oakland	49
1988	Jose Canseco, Oakland	42
1989	Fred McGriff, Toronto	36
1990	Cecil Fielder, Detroit	51
1991	Jose Canseco, Oakland Cecil Fielder, Detroit (tie)	44
1992	Juan Gonzalez, Texas	43
1993	Juan Gonzalez, Texas	46
1994¹	Ken Griffey, Jr., Seattle	40
1995	Albert Belle, Cleveland	50
1996	Mark McGwire, Oakland	52

AMERICAN LEAGUE BATTING CHAMPIONS

Year	Player, team	Avg
1901	Nap Lajoie, Phila.	.422
1902	Ed Delahanty, Wash.	.376
1903	Nap Lajoie, Cleve.	.355
1904	Nap Lajoie, Cleve.	.381
1905	Elmer Flick, Cleve.	.306
1906	George Stone, St. L.	.358
1907	Ty Cobb, Det.	.350
1908	Ty Cobb, Det.	.324
1909	Ty Cobb, Det.	.377
1910	Ty Cobb, Det.	.385
1911	Ty Cobb, Det.	.420
1912	Ty Cobb, Det.	.410
1913	Ty Cobb, Det.	.390
1914	Ty Cobb, Det.	.368
1915	Ty Cobb, Det.	.369
1916	Tris Speaker, Cleve.	.386
1917	Ty Cobb, Det.	.383
1918	Ty Cobb, Det.	.382
1919	Ty Cobb, Det.	.384
1920	George Sisler, St. L.	.407
1921	Harry Heilmann, Det.	.394
1922	George Sisler, St. L.	.420
1923	Harry Heilmann, Det.	.403
1924	Babe Ruth, N.Y.	.378
1925	Harry Heilmann, Det.	.393
1926	Heinie Manush, Det.	.378
1927	Harry Heilmann, Det.	.398
1928	Goose Goslin, Wash.	.379
1929	Lew Fonseca, Cleve.	.369
1930	Al Simmons, Phila.	.381
1931	Al Simmons, Phila.	.390
1932	Dale Alexander, Det.–Bost.	.367
1933	Jimmy Foxx, Phila.	.356
1934	Lou Gehrig, N.Y.	.363
1935	Buddy Myer, Wash.	.349
1936	Luke Appling, Chi.	.388
1937	Charley Gehringer, Det.	.371
1938	Jimmy Foxx, Bost.	.349
1939	Joe DiMaggio, N.Y.	.381
1940	Joe DiMaggio, N.Y.	.352
1941	Ted Williams, Bost.	.406
1942	Ted Williams, Bost.	.356
1943	Luke Appling, Chi.	.328
1944	Lou Boudreau, Cleve.	.327
1945	George Sternweiss, N.Y.	.309
1946	Mickey Vernon, Wash.	.353
1947	Ted Williams, Bost.	.343
1948	Ted Williams, Bost.	.369
1949	George Kell, Det.	.343
1950	Billy Goodman, Bost.	.354
1951	Ferris Fain, Phila.	.344
1952	Ferris Fain, Phila.	.327
1953	Mickey Vernon, Wash.	.337
1954	Bobby Avila, Cleve.	.341
1955	Al Kaline, Det.	.340
1956	Mickey Mantle, N.Y.	.353
1957	Ted Williams, Bost.	.388
1958	Ted Williams, Bost.	.328
1959	Harvey Kuenn, Det.	.353
1960	Pete Runnels, Bost.	.320
1961	Norman Cash, Det.	.361
1962	Pete Runnels, Bost.	.326
1963	Carl Yastrzemski, Bost.	.321
1964	Tony Oliva, Minn.	.323
1965	Tony Oliva, Minn.	.321
1966	Frank Robinson, Balt.	.316
1967	Carl Yastrzemski, Bost.	.326
1968	Carl Yastrzemski, Bost.	.301
1969	Rod Carew, Minn.	.332
1970	Alex Johnson, Calif.	.329
1971	Tony Oliva, Minn.	.337
1972	Rod Carew, Minn.	.318
1973	Rod Carew, Minn.	.350
1974	Rod Carew, Minn.	.364
1975	Rod Carew, Minn.	.359
1976	George Brett, Kansas City	.333
1977	Rod Carew, Minn.	.388

*Split season because of player strike. 1. Season ended on August 12 because of a player's strike.

Year	Player, team	Avg	Year	Player, team	Avg	Year	Player, team	Avg
1978	Rod Carew, Minn.	.333	1985	Wade Boggs, Boston	.368	1991	Julio Franco, Texas	.341
1979	Fred Lynn, Boston	.333	1986	Wade Boggs, Boston	.357	1992	Edgar Martinez, Seattle	.343
1980	George Brett, Kansas City	.390	1987	Wade Boggs, Boston	.363	1993	John Olerud, Toronto	.363
1981*	Carney Lansford, Bost.	.336	1988	Wade Boggs, Boston	.366	1994[1]	Paul O'Neill, New York	.359
1982	Willie Wilson, Kansas City	.332	1989	Kirby Puckett, Minnesota	.339	1995	Edgar Martinez, Seattle	.356
1983	Wade Boggs, Boston	.361	1990	George Brett, Kansas City	.328	1996	Alex Rodriguez, Seattle	.358
1984	Don Mattingly, New York	.343						

NATIONAL LEAGUE HOME RUN CHAMPIONS

Year	Player, team	No.	Year	Player, team	No.	Year	Player, team	No.
1876	George Hall, Phila. Athletics	5	1916	Davis Robertson, N.Y., and Fred Williams, Chi.	12	1953	Ed Mathews, Mil.	47
1877	George Shaffer, Louisville	3	1917	Davis Robertson, N.Y., and Cliff Cravath, Phila.	12	1954	Ted Kluszewski, Cin.	49
1878	Paul Hines, Providence	4	1918	Cliff Cravath, Phila.	8	1955	Willie Mays, N.Y.	51
1879	Charles Jones, Bost.	9	1919	Cliff Cravath, Phila.	12	1956	Duke Snider, Bklyn.	43
1880	James O'Rourke, Bost., and Harry Stovey, Worcester	6	1920	Cy Williams, Phila.	15	1957	Henry Aaron, Mil.	44
1881	Dan Brouthers, Buffalo	8	1921	George Kelly, N.Y.	23	1958	Ernie Banks, Chi.	47
1882	George Wood, Det.	7	1922	Rogers Hornsby, St. L.	42	1959	Ed Mathews, Mil.	46
1883	William Ewing, N.Y.	10	1923	Cy Williams, Phila.	41	1960	Ernie Banks, Chi.	41
1884	Ed Williamson, Chi.	27	1924	Jacques Fournier, Bklyn.	27	1961	Orlando Cepeda, San Fran.	46
1885	Abner Dalrymple, Chi.	11	1925	Rogers Hornsby, St. L.	39	1962	Willie Mays, San Fran.	49
1886	Arthur Richardson, Det.	11	1926	Hack Wilson, Chi.	21	1963	Henry Aaron, Mil., and Willie McCovey, San Fran.	44
1887	Roger Connor, N.Y., and Wm. O'Brien, Wash.	17	1927	Hack Wilson, Chi., and Cy Williams, Phila.	30	1964	Willie Mays, San Fran.	47
1888	Roger Connor, N.Y.	14	1928	Hack Wilson, Chi., and Jim Bottomley, St. L.	31	1965	Willie Mays, San Fran.	52
1889	Sam Thompson, Phila.	20	1929	Chuck Klein, Phila.	43	1966	Henry Aaron, Atlanta	44
1890	Tom Burns, Bklyn., and Mike Tiernan, N.Y.	13	1930	Hack Wilson, Chi.	56	1967	Henry Aaron, Atlanta	39
1891	Harry Stovey, Bost., and Mike Tiernan, N.Y.	16	1931	Chuck Klein, Phila.	31	1968	Willie McCovey, San Fran.	36
1892	Jim Holliday, Cin.	13	1932	Chuck Klein, Phila., and Mel Ott, N.Y.	38	1969	Willie McCovey, San Fran.	45
1893	Ed Delahanty, Phila.	19	1933	Chuck Klein, Phila.	28	1970	Johnny Bench, Cin.	45
1894	Hugh Duffy, Bost., and Robert Lowe, Bost.	18	1934	Mel Ott, N.Y., and Rip Collins, St. L.	35	1971	Willie Stargell, Pitts.	48
1895	Bill Joyce, Wash.	17	1935	Wally Berger, Bost.	34	1972	Johnny Bench, Cin.	40
1896	Ed Delahanty, Phila., and Sam Thompson, Phila.	13	1936	Mel Ott, N.Y.	33	1973	Willie Stargell, Pitts.	44
1897	Nap Lajoie, Phila.	10	1937	Mel Ott, N.Y., and Joe Medwick, St. L.	31	1974	Mike Schmidt, Phila.	36
1898	James Colins, Bost.	14	1938	Mel Ott, N.Y.	36	1975	Mike Schmidt, Phila.	38
1899	John Freeman, Wash.	25	1939	John Mize, St. L.	28	1976	Mike Schmidt, Phila.	38
1900	Herman Long, Bost.	12	1940	John Mize, St. L.	43	1977	George Foster, Cin.	52
1901	Sam Crawford, Con.	16	1941	Dolph Camilli, Bklyn.	34	1978	George Foster, Cin.	40
1902	Tom Leach, Pitts.	6	1942	Mel Ott, N.Y.	30	1979	Dave Kingman, Chicago	48
1903	James Sheckard, Bklyn.	9	1943	Bill Nicholson, Chi.	29	1980	Mike Schmidt, Phila.	48
1904	Harry Lumley, Bklyn.	9	1944	Bill Nicholson, Chi.	33	1981*	Mike Schmidt, Phila.	31
1905	Fred Odwell, Cin.	9	1945	Tommy Holmes, Bost.	28	1982	Dave Kingman, N.Y.	37
1906	Tim Jordan, Bklyn	12	1946	Ralph Kiner, Pitts.	23	1983	Mike Schmidt, Phila.	40
1907	David Brain, Bost.	10	1947	Ralph Kiner, Pitts., and John Mize, N.Y.	51	1984	Mike Schmidt, Phila. and Dale Murphy, Atlanta	36
1908	Tim Jordan, Bklyn.	12	1948	Ralph Kiner, Pitts., and John Mize, N.Y.	40	1985	Dale Murphy, Atlanta	37
1909	John Murray, N.Y.	7	1949	Ralph Kiner, Pitts.	54	1986	Mike Schmidt, Phila.	37
1910	Fred Beck, Bost., and Frank Schulte, Chi.	10	1950	Ralph Kiner, Pitts.	47	1987	Andre Dawson, Chicago	49
1911	Frank Schulte, Chi.	21	1951	Ralph Kiner, Pitts.	42	1988	Darryl Strawberry, N.Y.	39
1912	Henry Zimmerman, Chi.	14	1952	Ralph Kiner, Pitts., and Hank Sauer, Chi.	37	1989	Kevin Mitchell, San Francisco	47
1913	Cliff Cravath, Phila.	19				1990	Ryne Sandberg, Chicago	40
1914	Cliff Cravath, Phila.	19				1991	Howard Johnson, N.Y.	38
1915	Cliff Cravath, Phila.	24				1992	Fred McGriff, San Diego	35
						1993	Barry Bonds, San Francisco	46
						1994[1]	Matt Williams, San Francisco	43
						1995	Dante Bichette, Colorado	40
						1996	Andres Galarraga, Colorado	47

*Split season because of player strike. 1. Season ended on August 12 because of a player's strike.

NATIONAL LEAGUE BATTING CHAMPIONS

Year	Player, team	Avg	Year	Player, team	Avg	Year	Player, team	Avg
1876	Roscoe Barnes, Chicago	.404	1882	Dan Brouthers, Buffalo	.367	1888	Cap Anson, Chicago	.343
1877	Jim White, Boston	.385	1883	Dan Brouthers, Buffalo	.371	1889	Dan Brouthers, Boston	.373
1878	Abner Dalrymple, Mil.	.356	1884	James O'Rourke, Buffalo	.350	1890	John Glasscock, N. Y.	.336
1879	Cap Anson, Chicago	.407	1885	Roger Connor, N. Y.	.371	1891	William Hamilton, Phila.	.338
1880	George Gore, Chicago	.365	1886	King Kelly, Chicago	.388	1892	Dan Brouthers, Bklyn., and Clarence Childs, Cleve.	.335
1881	Cap Anson, Chicago	.399	1887	Cap Anson, Chicago	.421			

Year	Player, team	Avg	Year	Player, team	Avg	Year	Player, team	Avg
1893	Hugh Duffy, Boston	.378	1928	Rogers Hornsby, Boston	.387	1963	Tommy Davis, L. A.	.326
1894	Hugh Duffy, Boston	.438	1929	Lefty O'Doul, Phila.	.398	1964	Roberto Clemente, Pitts.	.339
1895	Jesse Burkett, Cleveland	.423	1930	Bill Terry, N.Y.	.401	1965	Roberto Clemente, Pitts.	.329
1896	Jesse Burkett, Cleveland	.410	1931	Chick Hafey, St. Louis	.349	1966	Matty Alou, Pittsburgh	.342
1897	Willie Keeler, Baltimore	.432	1932	Lefty O'Doul, Brooklyn	.368	1967	Roberto Clemente, Pitts.	.357
1898	Willie Keeler, Baltimore	.379	1933	Chuck Klein, Phila.	.368	1968	Pete Rose, Cincinnati	.335
1899	Ed Delahanty, Phila.	.408	1934	Paul Waner, Pittsburgh	.362	1969	Pete Rose, Cincinnati	.348
1900	Honus Wagner, Pittsburgh	.381	1935	Arky Vaughan, Pittsburgh	.385	1970	Rico Carty, Atlanta	.366
1901	Jesse Burkett, St. Louis	.382	1936	Paul Waner, Pittsburgh	.373	1971	Joe Torre, St. Louis	.363
1902	Clarence Beaumont, Pitts.	.357	1937	Joe Medwick, St. Louis	.374	1972	Billy Williams, Chicago	.333
1903	Honus Wagner, Pittsburgh	.355	1938	Ernie Lombardi, Cin.	.342	1973	Pete Rose, Cincinnati	.338
1904	Honus Wagner, Pittsburgh	.349	1939	John Mize, St. Louis	.349	1974	Ralph Garr, Atlanta	.353
1905	Cy Seymour, Cincinnati	.377	1940	Debs Garms, Pittsburgh	.355	1975	Bill Madlock, Chicago	.354
1906	Honus Wagner, Pittsburgh	.339	1941	Pete Reiser, Brooklyn	.343	1976	Bill Madlock, Chicago	.339
1907	Honus Wagner, Pittsburgh	.350	1942	Ernie Lombardi, Boston	.330	1977	Dave Parker, Pittsburgh	.338
1908	Honus Wagner, Pittsburgh	.354	1943	Stan Musial, St. Louis	.357	1978	Dave Parker, Pittsburgh	.334
1909	Honus Wagner, Pittsburgh	.339	1944	Dixie Walker, Brooklyn	.357	1979	Keith Hernandez, St. Louis	.344
1910	Sherwood Magee, Phila.	.331	1945	Phil Cavarretta, Chicago	.355	1980	Bill Buckner, Chicago	.324
1911	Honus Wagner, Pittsburgh	.334	1946	Stan Musial, St. Louis	.365	1981*	Bill Madlock, Pittsburgh	.341
1912	Henry Zimmerman, Chicago	.372	1947	Harry Walker, St. L.–Phila.	.363	1982	Al Oliver, Montreal	.331
1913	Jake Daubert, Brooklyn	.350	1948	Stan Musial, St. Louis	.376	1983	Bill Madlock, Pittsburgh	.323
1914	Jake Daubert, Brooklyn	.329	1949	Jackie Robinson, Brooklyn	.342	1984	Tony Gwynn, San Diego	.351
1915	Larry Doyle, New York	.320	1950	Stan Musial, St. Louis	.346	1985	Willie McGee, St. Louis	.353
1916	Hal Chase, Cincinnati	.339	1951	Stan Musial, St. Louis	.355	1986	Tim Raines, Montreal	.334
1917	Edd Roush, Cincinnati	.341	1952	Stan Musial, St. Louis	.336	1987	Tony Gwynn, San Diego	.370
1918	Zack Wheat, Brooklyn	.335	1953	Carl Furillo, Brooklyn	.344	1988	Tony Gwynn, San Diego	.313
1919	Edd Roush, Cincinnati	.321	1954	Willie Mays, N. Y.	.345	1989	Tony Gwynn, San Diego	.336
1920	Rogers Hornsby, St. Louis	.370	1955	Richie Ashburn, Phila.	.338	1990	Willie McGee, St. Louis	.335
1921	Rogers Hornsby, St. Louis	.397	1956	Henry Aaron, Mil.	.328	1991	Terry Pendleton, Atlanta	.319
1922	Rogers Hornsby, St. Louis	.401	1957	Stan Musial, St. Louis	.351	1992	Gary Sheffield, San Diego	.330
1923	Rogers Hornsby, St. Louis	.384	1958	Richie Ashburn, Phila.	.350	1993	Andres Galarraga, Colorado	.370
1924	Rogers Hornsby, St. Louis	.424	1959	Henry Aaron, Mil.	.355	1994[1]	Tony Gwynn, San Diego	.394
1925	Rogers Hornsby, St. Louis	.403	1960	Dick Groat, Pittsburgh	.325	1995	Tony Gwynn, San Diego	.368
1926	Gene Hargrave, Cincinnati	.353	1961	Roberto Clemente, Pitts.	.351	1996	Ellis Burks, Colorado	.344
1927	Paul Waner, Pittsburgh	.380	1962	Tommy Davis, L. A.	.346			

1. Season ended on August 12 because of a player's strike.

AMERICAN LEAGUE PENNANT WINNERS

Year	Club	Manager	Won	Lost	Pct	Year	Club	Manager	Won	Lost	Pct
1901	Chicago	Clark C. Griffith	83	53	.610	1931	Philadelphia	Connie Mack	107	45	.704
1902	Philadelphia	Connie Mack	83	53	.610	1932[1]	New York	Joseph V. McCarthy	107	47	.695
1903[1]	Boston	Jimmy Collins	91	47	.659	1933	Washington	Joseph E. Cronin	99	53	.651
1904[2]	Boston	Jimmy Collins	95	59	.617	1934	Detroit	Gordon Cochrane	101	53	.656
1905	Philadelphia	Connie Mack	92	56	.622	1935[1]	Detroit	Gordon Cochrane	93	58	.616
1906[1]	Chicago	Fielder A. Jones	93	58	.616	1936[1]	New York	Joseph V. McCarthy	102	51	.667
1907	Detroit	Hugh A. Jennings	92	58	.613	1937[1]	New York	Joseph V. McCarthy	102	52	.662
1908	Detroit	Hugh A. Jennings	90	63	.588	1938[1]	New York	Joseph V. McCarthy	99	53	.651
1909	Detroit	Hugh A. Jennings	98	54	.645	1939[1]	New York	Joseph V. McCarthy	106	45	.702
1910[1]	Philadelphia	Connie Mack	102	48	.680	1940	Detroit	Delmar D. Baker	90	64	.584
1911[1]	Philadelphia	Connie Mack	101	50	.669	1941[1]	New York	Joseph V. McCarthy	101	53	.656
1912[1]	Boston	J. Garland Stahl	105	47	.691	1942	New York	Joseph V. McCarthy	103	51	.669
1913[1]	Philadelphia	Connie Mack	96	57	.627	1943[1]	New York	Joseph V. McCarthy	98	56	.636
1914	Philadelphia	Connie Mack	99	53	.651	1944	St. Louis	Luke Sewell	89	65	.578
1915[1]	Boston	William F. Carrigan	101	50	.669	1945[1]	Detroit	Steve O'Neill	88	65	.575
1916[1]	Boston	William F. Carrigan	91	63	.591	1946	Boston	Joseph E. Cronin	104	50	.675
1917[1]	Chicago	Clarence H. Rowland	100	54	.649	1947	New York	Stanley R. Harris	97	57	.630
1918[1]	Boston	Ed Barrow	75	51	.595	1948[1]	Cleveland	Lou Boudreau	97	58	.626
1919	Chicago	William Gleason	88	52	.629	1949[1]	New York	Casey Stengel	97	57	.630
1920[1]	Cleveland	Tris Speaker	98	56	.636	1950[1]	New York	Casey Stengel	98	56	.636
1921	New York	Miller J. Huggins	98	55	.641	1951[1]	New York	Casey Stengel	98	56	.636
1922	New York	Miller J. Huggins	94	60	.610	1952[1]	New York	Casey Stengel	95	59	.617
1923[1]	New York	Miller J. Huggins	98	54	.645	1953[1]	New York	Casey Stengel	99	52	.656
1924[1]	Washington	Stanley R. Harris	92	62	.597	1954	Cleveland	Al Lopez	111	43	.721
1925	Washington	Stanley R. Harris	96	55	.636	1955	New York	Casey Stengel	96	58	.623
1926	New York	Miller J. Huggins	91	63	.591	1956[1]	New York	Casey Stengel	97	57	.630
1927[1]	New York	Miller J. Huggins	110	44	.714	1957	New York	Casey Stengel	98	56	.636
1928[1]	New York	Miller J. Huggins	101	53	.656	1958[1]	New York	Casey Stengel	92	62	.597
1929[1]	Philadelphia	Connie Mack	104	46	.693	1959	Chicago	Al Lopez	94	60	.610
1930[1]	Philadelphia	Connie Mack	102	52	.662	1960	New York	Casey Stengel	97	57	.630

Year	Club	Manager	Won	Lost	Pct	Year	Club	Manager	Won	Lost	Pct
1961[1]	New York	Ralph Houk	109	53	.673	1980	Kansas City[9]	Jim Frey	97	65	.599
1962[1]	New York	Ralph Houk	96	66	.593	1981	New York[10]	Gene Michael–			
1963	New York	Ralph Houk	104	57	.646			Bob Lemon	59	48	.551 *
1964	New York	Yogi Berra	99	63	.611	1982	Milwaukee[11]	Harvey Kuenn	95	67	.586
1965	Minnesota	Sam Mele	102	60	.630	1983[1]	Baltimore[12]	Joe Altobelli	98	64	.605
1966[1]	Baltimore	Hank Bauer	97	53	.606	1984[1]	Detroit[13]	Sparky Anderson	104	58	.642
1967	Boston	Dick Williams	92	70	.568	1985[1]	Kansas City[14]	Dick Howser	91	71	.562
1968[1]	Detroit	Mayo Smith	103	59	.636	1986	Boston[11]	John McNamara	95	66	.590
1969	Baltimore[3]	Earl Weaver	109	53	.673	1987	Minnesota[15]	Tom Kelly	85	77	.525
1970[1]	Baltimore[3]	Earl Weaver	108	54	.667	1988	Oakland[16]	Tony LaRussa	104	58	.642
1971	Baltimore[4]	Earl Weaver	101	57	.639	1989	Oakland[17]	Tony LaRussa	99	63	.611
1972[1]	Oakland[5]	Dick Williams	93	62	.600	1990	Oakland[18]	Tony LaRussa	103	59	.636
1973[1]	Oakland[6]	Dick Williams	94	68	.580	1991	Minnesota[19]	Tom Kelly	95	67	.586
1974[1]	Oakland[6]	Alvin Dark	90	72	.556	1992	Toronto[10]	Cito Gaston	96	66	.593
1975	Boston[4]	Darrell Johnson	95	65	.594	1993	Toronto[12]	Cito Gaston	95	67	.586
1976	New York[7]	Billy Martin	97	62	.610	1994	Strike ended season Aug. 11. No playoffs, no pennant winner.				
1977[1]	New York[7]	Billy Martin	100	62	.617						
1978[1]	New York[7]	Billy Martin and				1995	Cleveland[20]	Mike Hargrove	100	44	.694
		Bob Lemon	100	63	.613	1996	New York[21]	Joe Torre	92	70	.568
1979	Baltimore[8]	Earl Weaver	102	57	.642						

*Split season because of player strike. 1. World Series winner. 2. No World Series. 3. Defeated Minnesota, Western Division winner, in playoff. 4. Defeated Oakland, Western Division Leader, in playoff. 5. Defeated Detroit, Eastern Division winner, inplayoff. 6. Defeated Baltimore, Eastern Division winner, in playoff. 7. Defeated Kansas City, Western Division winner, in playoff. 8. Defeated California, Western Division winner, in playoff. 9. Defeated New York, Eastern Division winner, in playoff. 10. Defeated Oakland, Western Division winner, in playoff. 11. Defeated California, Western Division winner, in playoff. 12. Defeated Chicago, Western Division winner in playoff. 13. Defeated Kansas City, Western Division winner, in playoff. 14. Defeated Toronto, Eastern Division winner, in playoff. 15. Defeated Detroit, Eastern winner, in playoff. 16. Defeated Boston, Eastern division winner, in playoff. 17. Defeated Toronto, Eastern Division winner, in playoffs. 18. Defeated Boston, Eastern Division winner, in playoffs. 19. Defeated Toronto, Eastern Division winner, in playoffs. 20. Defeated Seattle Mariners, Western Division winner in playoffs. 21. Defeated Baltimore Orioles, Eastern Division wild-card team, in playoffs.

NATIONAL LEAGUE PENNANT WINNERS

Year	Club	Manager	Won	Lost	Pct	Year	Club	Manager	Won	Lost	Pct
1876	Chicago	Albert G. Spalding	52	14	.788	1908	Chicago[1]	Frank L. Chance	99	55	.643
1877	Boston	Harry Wright	31	17	.646	1909	Pittsburgh[1]	Fred C. Clarke	110	42	.724
1878	Boston	Harry Wright	41	19	.683	1910	Chicago	Frank L. Chance	104	50	.675
1879	Providence	George Wright	55	23	.705	1911	New York	John J. McGraw	99	54	.647
1880	Chicago	Adrian C. Anson	67	17	.798	1912	New York	John J. McGraw	103	48	.682
1881	Chicago	Adrian C. Anson	56	28	.667	1913	New York	John J. McGraw	101	51	.664
1882	Chicago	Adrian C. Anson	55	29	.655	1914	Boston[1]	George T. Stallings	94	59	.614
1883	Boston	John F. Morrill	63	35	.643	1915	Philadelphia	Patrick J. Moran	90	62	.592
1884	Providence	Frank C. Bancroft	84	28	.750	1916	Brooklyn	Wilbert Robinson	94	60	.610
1885	Chicago	Adrian C. Anson	87	25	.777	1917	New York	John J. McGraw	98	56	.636
1886	Chicago	Adrian C. Anson	90	34	.726	1918	Chicago	Fred L. Mitchell	84	45	.651
1887	Detroit	W. H. Watkins	79	45	.637	1919	Cincinnati[1]	Patrick J. Moran	96	44	.686
1888	New York	James J. Mutrie	84	47	.641	1920	Brooklyn	Wilbert Robinson	93	61	.604
1889	New York	James J. Mutrie	83	43	.659	1921	New York[1]	John J. McGraw	94	59	.614
1890	Brooklyn	Wm. H. McGunnigle	86	43	.667	1922	New York[1]	John J. McGraw	93	61	.604
1891	Boston	Frank G. Selee	87	51	.630	1923	New York	John J. McGraw	95	58	.621
1892	Boston	Frank G. Selee	102	48	.680	1924	New York	John J. McGraw	93	60	.608
1893	Boston	Frank G. Selee	86	44	.662	1925	Pittsburgh[1]	Wm. B. McKechnie	95	58	.621
1894	Baltimore	Edward H. Hanlon	89	39	.695	1926	St. Louis[1]	Rogers Hornsby	89	65	.578
1895	Baltimore	Edward H. Hanlon	87	43	.669	1927	Pittsburgh	Donie Bush	94	60	.610
1896	Baltimore	Edward H. Hanlon	90	39	.698	1928	St. Louis	Wm. B. McKechnie	95	59	.617
1897	Boston	Frank G. Selee	93	39	.705	1929	Chicago	Joseph V. McCarthy	98	54	.645
1898	Boston	Frank G. Selee	102	47	.685	1930	St. Louis	Gabby Street	92	62	.597
1899	Brooklyn	Edward H. Hanlon	88	42	.677	1931	St. Louis[1]	Gabby Street	101	53	.656
1900	Brooklyn	Edward H. Hanlon	82	54	.603	1932	Chicago	Charles J. Grimm	90	64	.584
1901	Pittsburgh	Fred C. Clarke	90	49	.647	1933	New York[1]	William H. Terry	91	61	.599
1902	Pittsburgh	Fred C. Clarke	103	36	.741	1934	St. Louis[1]	Frank F. Frisch	95	58	.621
1903	Pittsburgh	Fred C. Clarke	91	49	.650	1935	Chicago	Charles J. Grimm	100	54	.649
1904	New York[2]	John J. McGraw	106	47	.693	1936	New York	William H. Terry	92	62	.597
1905	New York[1]	John J. McGraw	105	48	.686	1937	New York	William H. Terry	95	57	.625
1906	Chicago	Frank L. Chance	116	36	.763	1938	Chicago	Gabby Hartnett	89	63	.586
1907	Chicago[1]	Frank L. Chance	107	45	.704	1939	Cincinnati	Wm. B. McKechnie	97	57	.630

Year	Club	Manager	Won	Lost	Pct	Year	Club	Manager	Won	Lost	Pct
1940	Cincinnati[1]	Wm. B. McKechnie	100	53	.654	1969	New York[1,3]	Gil Hodges	100	62	.617
1941	Brooklyn	Leo E. Durocher	100	54	.649	1970	Cincinnati[4]	Sparky Anderson	102	60	.630
1942	St. Louis[1]	Wm. H. Southworth	106	48	.688	1971	Pittsburgh[1,5]	Danny Murtaugh	97	65	.599
1943	St. Louis	Wm. H. Southworth	105	49	.682	1972	Cincinnati[4]	Sparky Anderson	95	59	.617
1944	St. Louis[1]	Wm. H. Southworth	105	49	.682	1973	New York[6]	Yogi Berra	82	79	.509
1945	Chicago	Charles J. Grimm	98	56	.636	1974	Los Angeles[4]	Walter Alston	102	60	.630
1946	St. Louis[1]	Edwin H. Dyer	98	58	.628	1975	Cincinnati[1,4]	Sparky Anderson	108	54	.667
1947	Brooklyn	Burton E. Shotton	94	60	.610	1976	Cincinnati[7,1]	Sparky Anderson	102	60	.630
1948	Boston	Wm. H. Southworth	91	62	.595	1977	Los Angeles[7]	Tom Lasorda	98	64	.605
1949	Brooklyn	Burton E. Shotton	97	57	.630	1978	Los Angeles[7]	Tom Lasorda	95	67	.586
1950	Philadelphia	Edwin M. Sawyer	91	63	.591	1979[1]	Pittsburgh[6]	Chuck Tanner	98	64	.605
1951	New York	Leo E. Durocher	98	59	.624	1980[1]	Philadelphia[8]	Dallas Green	91	71	.562
1952	Brooklyn	Charles W. Dressen	96	57	.630	1981	Los Angeles[1,9]	Tom Lasorda	63	*47	.573
1953	Brooklyn	Charles W. Dressen	105	49	.682	1982[1]	St. Louis[3]	Whitey Herzog	92	70	.568
1954	New York[1]	Leo E. Durocher	97	57	.630	1983	Philadelphia[11]	Paul Owens	90	72	.556
1955	Brooklyn[1]	Walter Alston	98	55	.641	1984	San Diego[12]	Dick Williams	92	70	.568
1956	Brooklyn	Walter Alston	93	61	.604	1985	St. Louis[11]	Whitey Herzog	101	61	.623
1957	Milwaukee1	Fred Haney	95	59	.617	1986	New York[8]	Dave Johnson	108	54	.667
1958	Milwaukee	Fred Haney	92	62	.597	1987	St. Louis[5]	Whitey Herzog	95	67	.586
1959	Los Angeles[1]	Walter Alston	88	68	.564	1988	Los Angeles[10]	Tom Lasorda	94	67	.584
1960	Pittsburgh[1]	Danny Murtaugh	95	59	.617	1989	San Francisco[12]	Roger Craig	92	70	.568
1961	Cincinnati	Fred Hutchinson	93	61	.604	1990	Cincinnati[4]	Lou Piniella	91	71	.562
1962	San Francisco	Alvin Dark	103	62	.624	1991	Atlanta[4]	Bobby Cox	94	68	.580
1963	Los Angeles[1]	Walter Alston	99	63	.611	1992	Atlanta[4]	Bobby Cox	98	64	.605
1964	St. Louis[1]	Johnny Keane	93	69	.574	1993	Philadelphia[3]	Jim Fregosi	97	65	.599
1965	Los Angeles[1]	Walter Alston	97	65	.599	1994	Strike ended season Aug. 11. No playoffs, no pennant winner.				
1966	Los Angeles	Walter Alston	95	67	.586						
1967	St. Louis[1]	Red Schoendienst	101	60	.627	1995	Atlanta[13]	Bobby Cox	90	54	.625
1968	St. Louis	Red Schoendienst	97	65	.599	1996	Atlanta[14]	Bobby Cox	96	66	.593

*Split season because of player strike. 1. World Series winner. 2. No World Series. 3. Defeated Atlanta, Western Division winner, in playoff. 4. Defeated Pittsburgh, Eastern Division winner, in playoff. 5. Defeated San Francisco, Western Division winner, in playoff. 6. Defeated Cincinnati, Western Division winner, in playoff. 7. Defeated Philadelphia, Eastern Division winner, in playoff. 8. Defeated Houston, Western Division winner, in playoff. 9. Defeated Montreal, Eastern Division winner, in playoff. 10. Defeated New York, Eastern Division winner, in playoff. 11. Defeated Los Angeles, Western Division winner, in playoff. 12. Defeated Chicago, Eastern Division winner, in playoff. 13. Defeated Cincinnati, Central Division winner, in playoff. 14. Defeated St. Louis, Central Division winner, in playoff.

MOST VALUABLE PLAYERS

(Baseball Writers Association selections)

American League

Year	Player
1931	Lefty Grove, Philadelphia
1932–33	Jimmy Foxx, Philadelphia
1934	Mickey Cochrane, Detroit
1935	Hank Greenberg, Detroit
1936	Lou Gehrig, New York
1937	Charlie Gehringer, Detroit
1938	Jimmy Foxx, Boston
1939	Joe DiMaggio, New York
1940	Hank Greenberg, Detroit
1941	Joe DiMaggio, New York
1942	Joe Gordon, New York
1943	Spurgeon Chandler, New York
1944–45	Hal Newhouser, Detroit
1946	Ted Williams, Boston
1947	Joe DiMaggio, New York
1948	Lou Boudreau, Cleveland
1949	Ted Williams, Boston
1950	Phil Rizzuto, New York
1951	Yogi Berra, New York
1952	Bobby Shantz, Philadelphia
1953	Al Rosen, Cleveland
1954–55	Yogi Berra, New York
1956–57	Mickey Mantle, New York
1958	Jackie Jensen, Boston
1959	Nellie Fox, Chicago
1960–61	Roger Maris, New York
1962	Mickey Mantle, New York
1963	Elston Howard, New York
1964	Brooks Robinson, Baltimore
1965	Zoilo Versalles, Minnesota
1966	Frank Robinson, Baltimore
1967	Carl Yastrzemski, Boston
1968	Dennis McLain, Detroit
1969	Harmon Killebrew, Minnesota
1970	John (Boog) Powell, Baltimore
1971	Vida Blue, Oakland
1972	Dick Allen, Chicago
1973	Reggie Jackson, Oakland
1974	Jeff Burroughs, Texas
1975	Fred Lynn, Boston
1976	Thurman Munson, New York
1977	Rod Carew, Minnesota
1978	Jim Rice, Boston
1979	Don Baylor, California
1980	George Brett, Kansas City
1981	Rollie Fingers, Milwaukee
1982	Robin Yount, Milwaukee
1983	Cal Ripken, Jr., Baltimore
1984	Willie Hernandez, Detroit
1985	Don Mattingly, New York
1986	Roger Clemens, Boston
1987	George Bell, Toronto
1988	Jose Canseco, Oakland
1989	Robin Yount, Milwaukee
1990	Rickey Henderson, Oakland
1991	Cal Ripken, Jr., Baltimore
1992	Dennis Eckersley, Oakland
1993	Frank Thomas, Chicago
1994	Frank Thomas, Chicago
1995	Mo Vaughn, Boston

National League

Year	Player
1931	Frank Frisch, St. Louis
1932	Chuck Klein, Philadelphia
1933	Carl Hubbell, New York
1934	Dizzy Dean, St. Louis
1935	Gabby Hartnett, Chicago
1936	Carl Hubbell, New York
1937	Joe Medwick, St. Louis
1938	Ernie Lombardi, Cincinnati
1939	Bucky Walters, Cincinnati
1940	Frank McCormick, Cincinnati
1941	Dolph Camilli, Brooklyn
1942	Mort Cooper, St. Louis
1943	Stan Musial, St. Louis
1944	Marty Marion, St. Louis
1945	Phil Cavarretta, Chicago
1946	Stan Musial, St. Louis
1947	Bob Elliott, Boston
1948	Stan Musial, St. Louis
1949	Jackie Robinson, Brooklyn
1950	Jim Konstanty, Philadelphia
1951	Roy Campanella, Brooklyn
1952	Hank Sauer, Chicago

1953	Roy Campanella, Brooklyn	1969	Willie McCovey, San	1982	Dale Murphy, Atlanta
1954	Willie Mays, New York		Francisco	1983	Dale Murphy, Atlanta
1955	Roy Campanella, Brooklyn	1970	Johnny Bench, Cincinnati	1984	Ryne Sandberg, Chicago
1956	Don Newcombe, Brooklyn	1971	Joe Torre, St. Louis	1985	Willie McGee, St. Louis
1957	Henry Aaron, Milwaukee	1972	Johnny Bench, Cincinnati	1986	Mike Schmidt, Philadelphia
1958–59	Ernie Banks, Chicago	1973	Pete Rose, Cincinnati	1987	Andre Dawson, Chicago
1960	Dick Groat, Pittsburgh	1974	Steve Garvey, Los Angeles	1988	Kirk Gibson, Los Angeles
1961	Frank Robinson, Cincinnati	1975–76	Joe Morgan, Cincinnati	1989	Kevin Mitchell, San Francisco
1962	Maury Wills, Los Angeles	1977	George Foster, Cincinnati	1990	Barry Bonds, Pittsburgh
1963	Sandy Koufax, Los Angeles	1978	Dave Parker, Pittsburgh	1991	Terry Pendleton, Atlanta
1964	Ken Boyer, St. Louis	1979	Willie Stargell, Pittsburgh	1992	Barry Bonds, Pittsburgh
1965	Willie Mays, San Francisco	1979	Keith Hernandez, St. Louis	1993	Barry Bonds, Pittsburgh
1966	Roberto Clemente, Pittsburgh	1980	Mike Schmidt, Philadelphia	1994	Jeff Baswell, Houston
1967	Orlando Cepeda, St. Louis	1981	Mike Schmidt, Philadelphia	1995	Barry Larkin, Cincinnati
1968	Bob Gibson, St. Louis				

CY YOUNG AWARD

1956	Don Newcombe, Brooklyn N.L.	1974	Catfish Hunter, Oakland A.L.; Mike Marshall, Los Angeles N.L.	1985	Bret Saberhagen, Kansas City, A.L.; Dwight Gooden, New York, N.L.
1957	Warren Spahn, Milwaukee N.L.				
1958	Bob Turley, New York A.L.				
1959	Early Wynn, Chicago A.L.	1975	Jim Palmer, Baltimore A.L.; Tom Seaver, New York N.L.	1986	Roger Clemens, Boston, A.L.; Mike Scott, Houston, N.L.
1960	Vernon Law, Pittsburgh, N.L				
1961	Whitey Ford, New York A.L.	1976	Jim Palmer, Baltimore A.L.; Randy Jones, San Diego N.L.	1987	Roger Clemens, Boston, A.L.; Steve Bedrosian, Philadelphia, N.L.
1962	Don Drysdale, Los Angeles N.L.				
1963	Sandy Koufax, Los Angeles N.L.	1977	Sparky Lyle, N.Y., A.L.; Steve Carlton, Philadelphia N.L.	1988	Frank Viola, Minnesota, A.L.; Orel Hershiser, Los Angeles, N.L.
1964	Dean Chance, Los Angeles A.L.	1978	Ron Guidry, N.Y., A.L.; Gaylord Perry, San Diego N.L.		
1965	Sandy Koufax, Los Angeles N.L.	1979	Mike Flanagan, Baltimore, A.L.; Bruce Sutter, Chicago, N.L.	1989	Bret Saberhagen, Kansas City, A.L.; Mark Davis, San Diego, N.L.
1966	Sandy Koufax, Los Angeles N.L.	1980	Steve Stone, Baltimore, A.L.; Steve Carlton, Philadelphia, N.L.	1990	Bob Welch, Oakland, A.L.; Doug Drabek, Pittsburgh, N.L.
1967	Jim Lonborg, Boston A.L.; Mike McCormick, San Francisco N.L.	1981	Rollie Fingers, Milwaukee, A.L.; Fernando Valenzuela, Los Angeles, N.L.	1991	Roger Clemens, Boston, A.L.; Tom Glavine, Atlanta, N.L.
1968	Dennis, McLain, Detroit A.L.; Bob Gibson, St. Louis N.L.	1982	Pete Vuckovich, Milwaukee, A.L.; Steve Carlton, Philadelphia, N.L.	1992	Dennis Eckersley, Oakland, A.L.; Greg Maddux, Chicago, N.L.
1969	Mike Cuellar, Baltimore, and Dennis McLain, Detroit, tied in A.L.; Tom Seaver, N.Y. N.L.	1983	LaMarr Hoyt, Chicago, A.L.; John Denny, Philadelphia, N.L.	1993	Jack McDowell, Chicago, A.L.; Greg Maddux, Atlanta, N.L.
1970	Jim Perry, Minnesota A.L; Bob Gibson, St. Louis N.L.	1984	Willie Hernandez, Detroit, A.L.; Rick Sutcliffe, Chicago, N.L.	1994	David Cone, Kansas City, A.L. Greg Maddux, Atlanta, N.L.
1971	Vida Blue, Oakland A.L.; Ferguson Jenkins, Chicago N.L.			1995	Randy Johnson, Seattle, A.L.; Greg Maddux, Atlanta, N.L.
1972	Gaylord Perry, Cleveland A.L.; Steve Carlton, Phila. N.L.				
1973	Jim Palmer, Baltimore A.L.; Tom Seaver, New York N.L.				

1996 GOLD GLOVE AWARDS

Pitchers
National League: Greg Maddux, Atlanta
American League: Mike Mussina, Baltimore

Catchers
National League: Charles Johnson, Florida
American League: Ivan Rodriguez, Texas

First Basemen
National League: Mark Grace, Chicago
American League: J.T. Snow, California

Second Basemen
National League: Craig Biggio, Houston
American League: Roberto Alomar, Baltimore

Third Basemen
National League: Ken Caminiti, San Diego
American League: Robin Ventura, Chicago

Shortstops
National League: Barry Larkin, Cincinnati
American League: Omar Vizquel, Cleveland

Outfielders
National League: Barry Bonds, San Francisco; Steve Finley, San Diego; Marquis Grisson; Atlanta
American League: Ken Griffey, Jr., Seattle; Jay Buhner, Seattle; Kenny Lofton, Cleveland

MAJOR LEAGUE LIFETIME RECORDS
(Through 1995)

Leading Pitchers—Wins
* Indicates left-handed pitcher.

		Yrs	GS	W	L	Pct
1.	Cy Young	22	815	511	313	.620
2.	Walter Johnson	21	666	416	279	.599
3.	Christy Mathewson	17	551	373	188	.665
	Grover Alexander	20	598	373	208	.642
5.	Warren Spahn*	21	665	363	245	.597
6.	Kid Nichols	15	561	361	208	.634
	Pud Galvin	14	682	361	308	.540
8.	Tim Keefe	14	594	342	225	.603
9.	Steve Carlton*	24	709	329	244	.574
10.	Eddie Plank*	17	527	327	193	.629
11.	John Clarkson	12	518	326	177	.648
12.	Don Sutton	23	756	324	256	.559
13.	Nolan Ryan	27	773	324	292	.539
14.	Phil Niekro	24	716	318	274	.537
15.	Gaylord Perry	22	690	314	265	.542
16.	Old Hoss Radbourn	12	503	311	194	.616
	Tom Seaver	20	647	311	205	.603
18.	Mickey Welch	13	549	308	209	.596
19.	Lefty Grove*	17	456	300	141	.680
	Early Wynn	23	612	300	244	.551
21.	Tommy John*	26	700	288	231	.555
22.	Bert Blyleven	22	685	287	250	.534
23.	Robin Roberts	19	609	286	245	.539
24.	Tony Mullane	13	505	285	220	.564
25.	Ferguson Jenkins	19	594	284	226	.557

Pitchers Active in 1995 Season
(150 or more lifetime victories)

		Yrs	W	L	Pct
1.	Dennis Martinez	20	231	176	.568
2.	Dennis Eckersley	21	192	159	.547
3.	Roger Clemens	12	182	98	.650
4.	Frank Viola*	14	175	147	.543
5.	Mark Langston*	12	166	140	.542
6.	Scott Sanderson	18	163	141	.536
7.	Mike Moore	14	161	176	.478
8.	Fernando Valenzuela*	15	158	133	.543
9.	Jimmy Key*	12	152	93	.620
10.	Greg Maddux	10	150	93	.617
	Orel Hershiser	13	150	108	.581

Leading Batters, by Average
* Indicates left-handed hitter.

		Years	AB	H	Avg
1.	Ty Cobb*	24	11,429	4,191	.367
2.	Rogers Hornsby	23	8,137	2,930	.358
3.	Joe Jackson*	13	4,981	1,774	.356
4.	Ed Delahanty	16	7,502	2,591	.345
5.	Tris Speaker*	22	10,195	3,514	.345
6.	Ted Williams*	19	7,706	2,654	.344
7.	Billy Hamilton*	14	6,284	2,163	.344
8.	Willie Keeler*	19	8,585	2,947	.343
9.	Dan Brouthers*	19	6,711	2,296	.342
10.	Babe Ruth*	22	8,399	2,873	.342
11.	Harry Heilmann	17	7,787	2,660	.342
12.	Pete Browning	13	4,820	1,646	.341
13.	Bill Terry*	14	6,428	2,193	.341
14.	George Sisler*	15	8,267	2,812	.340
15.	Lou Gehrig*	17	8,001	2,721	.340
16.	Jesse Burkett*	16	8,413	2,853	.339
17.	Nap Lajoie	21	9,592	3,244	.338
18.	Riggs Stephenson	14	4,508	1,515	.336
19.	Tony Gwynn*	14	7,144	2,401	.336
20.	Al Simmons	20	8,761	2,927	.334
21.	Wade Boggs*	14	7,599	2,541	.334
22.	Paul Waner*	20	9,459	3,152	.333
23.	Eddie Collins*	25	9,949	3,311	.333
24.	Stan Musial*	22	10,972	3,630	.331
25.	Sam Thompson*	14	6,005	1,986	.331

Players Active in 1995 Season
(600 or more lifetime hits)

		Years	H	Avg
1.	Tony Gwynn*	14	2,401	.336
2.	Wade Boggs*	14	2,541	.334
3.	Frank Thomas	6	893	.323
4.	Kirby Puckett	12	2,304	.318
5.	Edgar Martinez	9	868	.313
6.	Kenny Lofton*	5	673	.312
7.	Hal Morris	8	737	.308
8.	Don Mattingly*	14	2,153	.307
9.	Mark Grace	8	1,333	.306
10.	Jeff Bagwell	5	771	.306

MAJOR LEAGUE INDIVIDUAL ALL-TIME RECORDS
(Through 1995)

Highest Batting Average—.442, James O'Neill, St. Louis, A.A., 1887; .438, Hugh Duffy, Boston, N.L., 1894 (Since 1900—.424, Rogers Hornsby, St. Louis, N.L., 1924; .422, Nap Lajoie, Phil., A.L., 1901)

Most Times at Bat—12,364, Henry Aaron, Milwaukee N.L., 1954–65; Atlanta N.L., 1966–74; Milwaukee A.L., 1975–76.

Most Years Batted .300 or Better—23, Ty Cobb, Detroit A.L., 1906–26, Philadelphia A.L., 1927–28.

Most hits—4,256, Pete Rose, Cincinnati 1963–79, Philadelphia 1980–83, Montreal 1984, Cincinnati 1984–86.

Most Hits, Season—257, George Sisler, St. Louis A.L., 1920.

Most Hits, Game (9 innings)—7, Wilbert Robinson, Baltimore N.L., 6 singles, 1 double, 1892. Rennie Stennett, Pittsburgh N.L., 4 singles, 2 doubles, 1 triple, 1975.

Most Hits, Game (extra innings)—9, John Burnett, Cleveland A.L., 18 innings, 7 singles, 2 doubles, 1932.

Most Hits in Succession—12, Mike Higgins, Boston A.L., in four games, 1938; Walt Dropo, Detroit A.L., in three games, 1952.

Most Consecutive Games Batted Safely—56, Joe DiMaggio, New York A.L., 1941.

Most Runs—2,244, Ty Cobb, Detroit A.L., 1905–26, Philadelphia A.L., 1927–28.

Most Runs, Season—196, William Hamilton, Philadelphia N.L., 1894. (Since 1900—177, Babe Ruth, New York A.L., 1921.)

Most Runs, Game—7, Guy Hecker, Louisville A.A., 1886. (Since 1900—6, by Mel Ott, New York N.L., 1934, 1944; Johnny Pesky, Boston A.L., 1946; Frank Torre, Milwaukee N.L., 1957.)

Most Runs Batted in—2,297, Henry Aaron, Milwaukee N.L., 1954–1965; Atlanta N.L., 1966–74; Milwaukee A.L., 1975–76.

Most Runs Batted in, Season—190, Hack Wilson, Chicago N.L., 1930.

Most Runs Batted In, Game—12, Jim Bottomley, St. Louis N.L., 1924, and Mark Whiten, St. Louis N.L., 1993.

Most Home Runs—755, Henry Aaron, Milwaukee N.L., 1954–1965; Atlanta N.L., 1966–74; Milwaukee A.L., 1975–76.

Most Home Runs, Season—61, Roger Maris, New York A.L., 1961 (162–game season); 60, Babe Ruth, New York A.L., 1927 (154–game season)

Most Home Runs with Bases Filled—23, Lou Gehrig, New York A.L., 1927–39.

Most 2–Base Hits—793, Tris Speaker, Boston A.L., 1907–15, Cleveland A.L., 1916–26, Washington A.L., 1927, Philadelphia A.L., 1928.

Most 2–Base Hits, Season—67, Earl Webb, Boston A.L., 1931.

Most 2–base Hits, Game—4, by many.

Most 3–Base Hits—312, Sam Crawford, Cincinnati N.L., 1899–1902, Detroit A.L., 1903–17.

Most 3–Base Hits, Season—36, Owen Wilson, Pittsburgh N.L., 1912.

Most 3–Base Hits, Game—4, George Strief, Philadelphia A.A., 1885; William Joyce, New York N.L., 1897. (Since 1900—3, by many.)

Most Games Played—3,562, Pete Rose, Cincinnati N.L., Philadelphia N.L., Montreal N.L., 1964–86

Most Consecutive Games Played—2,316, Cal Ripken, Jr., Baltimore Orioles, A.L., 1981– .

Most Bases on Balls—2,056, Babe Ruth, Boston A.L., 1914–19; New York A.L., 1920–34, Boston N.L., 1935.

Most Bases on Balls, Season—170, Babe Ruth, New York A.L., 1923.

Most bases on Balls, Game—6, Jimmy Foxx, Boston A.L., 1938.

Most Strikeouts, Season—189, Bobby Bonds, San Francisco N.L., 1970.

Most Strikeouts, Game (9 innings)—5, by many.

Most Strikeouts, Game (extra innings)—6, Carl Weilman, St. Louis A.L., 15 innings, 1913; Don Hoak, Chicago N.L., 17 innings, 1956; Fred Reichardt, California A.L., 17, innings, 1966; Billy Cowan, California A.L., 20, 1971; Cecil Cooper, Boston A.L., 15, 1974.

Most pinch—hits, lifetime—150, Manny Mota, S.F., 1962; Pitt., 1963–68; Montreal, 1969; L.A., 1969–80, N.L.

Most Pinch–hits, season—25, Jose Morales, Montreal N.L., 1976.

Most consecutive pinch–hits—9, Dave Philley, Phil., N.L., 1958 (8), 1959 (1).

Most pinch–hit home runs, lifetime—18, Gerald Lynch, Pitt.–Cin. N.L., 1957–66.

Most pinch–hit home runs, season—6, Johnny Frederick, Brooklyn, N.L., 1932.

Most stolen bases, lifetime (since 1900)—1,042, Rickey Henderson,* 1979–84 Oakland, 1985–89 New York (A.L.), 1989–92 Oakland

Most stolen bases, season—156, Harry Stovey, Phil., A.A., 1888. Since 1900: 130, Rickey Henderson, Oak., A.L., 1982; 118, Lou Brock, St. Louis, N.L., 1974.

Most stolen bases, game—7, George Gore, Chicago N.L. 1881; William Hamilton, Philadelphia N.L. 1894. (Since 1900—6, Eddie Collins, Philadelphia A.L., 1912.) and Otis Nixon*, Atlanta N.L., 1991.

Most time stealing home, lifetime—35, Ty Cobb, Detroit–Phil. A.L., 1905–28.

MAJOR LEAGUE ALL–TIME PITCHING RECORDS
(Through 1995)

Most Games Won—511, Cy Young, Cleveland N.L., 1890–98, St. Louis N.L., 1899–1900, Boston A.L., 1901–08, Cleveland A.L., 1909–11, Boston N.L., 1911.

Most Games Won, Season—60, Hoss Radbourne, Providence N.L., 1884. (Since 1900—41, Jack Chesbro, New York A.L., 1904.)

Most Consecutive Games Won—24, Carl Hubbell, New York N.L., 1936 (16) and 1937 (8).

Most Consecutive Games Won, Season—19, Tim Keefe, New York N.L., 1888; Rube Marquard, New York N.L., 1912.

Most Years Won 20 or More Games—16, Cy Young, Cleveland N.L., 1891–98, St. Louis N.L., 1899–1900, Boston A.L., 1901–04, 1907–08.

Most Shutouts—110, Walter Johnson, Wash. A.L., 1907–27.

Most Shutouts, Season—16, Grover Alexander, Philadelphia N.L., 1916.

Most Consecutive Shutouts—6, Don Drysdale, Los Angeles, N.L., 1968.

Most Consecutive Scoreless Innings—59, Orel Hershiser, Los Angeles Dodgers, 1988.

Most Strikeouts—5,714, Nolan Ryan, New York N.L., California A.L., Houston N.L., 1968–1988 Texas, 1989–93.

Most Strikeouts, Season—505, Matthew Kilroy, Baltimore A.A., 1886. (Since 1900—383, Nolan Ryan, California, A.L., 1973.)

Most Strikeouts, Game—21, Tom Cheney, Washington A.L., 1962, 16 innings. Nine innings: 20, Roger Clemens, Boston, A.L., 1986; 19, Charles McSweeney, Providence N.L., 1884; Hugh Dailey, Chicago U.A., 1884. (Since 1900—19, Steve Carlton, St. Louis N.L. vs. New York, Sept. 15, 1969; Tom Seaver, New York N.L. vs. San Diego, April 22, 1970; Nolan Ryan, California A.L. vs. Boston, Aug. 12, 1974; David Cone, New York N.L. vs. Philadelphia, Oct. 6, 1991.)

Most Consecutive Strikeouts—10, Tom Seaver, New York N.L. vs. San Diego, April 22, 1970.

Most Games, Season—106, Mike Marshall, Los Angeles, N.L., 1974.

Most Complete Games, Season—74, William White, Cincinnati N.L., 1879. (Since 1900—48, Jack Chesbro, New York A.L., 1904.)

ROOKIE OF THE YEAR
(Baseball Writers Association selections)

American League

1949	Roy Sievers, St. Louis	1965	Curt Blefary, Baltimore	1980	Joe Charboneau, Cleveland
1950	Walt Dropo, Boston	1966	Tommy Agee, Chicago	1981	Dave Righetti, New York
1951	Gil McDougald, New York	1967	Rod Carew, Minnesota	1982	Cal Ripken, Jr., Baltimore
1952	Harry Byrd, Philadelphia	1968	Stan Bahnsen, New York	1983	Ron Kittle, Chicago
1953	Harvey Kuenn, Detroit	1969	Lou Piniella, Kansas City	1984	Alvin Davis, Seattle
1954	Bob Grim, New York	1970	Thurman Munson, New York	1985	Ozzie Guillen, Chicago
1955	Herb Score, Cleveland	1971	Chris Chambliss, Cleveland	1986	Jose Canseco, Oakland
1956	Luis Aparicio, Chicago	1972	Carlton Fisk, Boston	1987	Mark McGwire, Oakland
1957	Tony Kubek, New York	1973	Alonzo Bumbry, Baltimore	1988	Walter Weiss, Oakland
1958	Albie Pearson, Washington	1974	Mike Hargrove, Texas	1989	Gregg Olson, Baltimore
1959	Bob Allison, Washington	1975	Fred Lynn, Boston	1990	Sandy Alomar Jr., Cleveland
1960	Ron Hansen, Baltimore	1976	Mark Fidrych, Detroit	1991	Chuck Knoblauch, Minnesota
1961	Don Schwall, Boston	1977	Eddie Murray, Baltimore	1992	Pat Listach, Milwaukee
1962	Tom Tresh, New York	1978	Lou Whitaker, Detroit	1993	Tim Salmon, California
1963	Gary Peters, Chicago	1979	Alfredo Griffin, Toronto	1994	Bob Hamelin, Kansas City
1964	Tony Oliva, Minnesota	1979	John Castino, Minnesota	1995	Marty Cordova, Minnesota

National League

1949	Don Newcombe, Brooklyn	1966	Tommy Helms, Cincinnati	1981	Fernando Valenzuela, Los Angeles
1950	Sam Jethroe, Boston	1967	Tom Seaver, New York	1982	Steve Sax, Los Angeles
1951	Willie Mays, New York	1968	Johnny Bench, Cincinnati	1983	Darryl Strawberry, New York
1952	Joe Black, Brooklyn	1969	Ted Sizemore, Los Angeles	1984	Dwight Gooden, New York
1953	Jim Gilliam, Brooklyn	1970	Carl Morton, Montreal	1985	Vince Coleman, St. Louis
1954	Wally Moon, St. Louis	1971	Earl Williams, Atlanta	1986	Todd Worrell, St. Louis
1955	Bill Virdon, St. Louis	1972	Jon Matlack, New York	1987	Benito Santiago, San Diego
1956	Frank Robinson, Cincinnati	1973	Gary Matthews, San Francisco	1988	Chris Sabo, Cincinnati
1957	Jack Sanford, Philadelphia	1974	Bake McBride, St. Louis	1989	Jerome Walton, Chicago
1958	Orlando Cepeda, San Francisco	1975	John Montefusco, San Francisco	1990	Dave Justice, Atlanta
1959	Willie McCovey, San Francisco	1976	Pat Zachry, Cincinnati	1991	Jeff Baguell, Houston
1960	Frank Howard, Los Angeles	1976	Bruce Metzger, San Diego	1992	Eric Karros, Los Angeles
1961	Billy Williams, Chicago	1977	Andre Dawson, Montreal	1993	Mike Piazza, Los Angeles
1962	Ken Hubbs, Chicago	1978	Bob Horner, Atlanta	1994	Raul Mondesi, Los Angeles
1963	Pete Rose, Cincinnati	1979	Rick Sutcliffe, Los Angeles	1995	Hideo Nomo, Los Angeles
1964	Richie Allen, Philadelphia	1980	Steve Howe, Los Angeles		
1965	Jim Lefebvre, Los Angeles				

MAJOR LEAGUE ATTENDANCE RECORDS
(Through 1995)

Single game—78,672, San Francisco at Los Angeles (N.L.), April 18, 1958. (At Memorial Coliseum.)

Doubleheader—84,587, New York at Cleveland (A.L.), Sept. 12, 1954.

Night—78,382, Chicago at Cleveland (A.L.), Aug. 20, 1948.

Season, home—4,483,350, Colorado (N.L.), 1993.

Season, league—36,912,502, National League, 1993.

Season, both leagues—70,257,938, 1993.

Season, road—2,461,240, New York (A.L.), 1980.

World Series, single game—92,706, Chicago (A.L.) at Los Angeles (N.L.), Oct. 6, 1959.

World Series, all games (6)—420,784, Chicago (A.L.) and Los Angeles (N.L.), 1959.

MOST HOME RUNS IN ONE SEASON
(45 or More)

HR	Player/Team	Year	HR	Player/Team	Year
61	Roger Maris, New York (AL)	1961	48	Harmon Killebrew, Minnesota (AL)	1962
60	Babe Ruth, New York (AL)	1927	48	Willie Stargell, Pittsburgh (NL)	1971
59	Babe Ruth, New York (AL)	1921	48	Dave Kingman, Chicago (NL)	1979
58	Jimmy Foxx, Philadelphia (AL)	1932	48	Mike Schmidt, Philadelphia (NL)	1980
58	Hank Greenberg, Detroit (AL)	1938	47	Babe Ruth, New York (AL)	1926
56	Hack Wilson, Chicago (NL)	1930	47	Ralph Kiner, Pittsburgh (NL)	1950
54	Babe Ruth, New York (AL)	1920	47	Ed Mathews, Milwaukee (NL)	1953
54	Babe Ruth, New York (AL)	1928	47	Ernie Banks, Chicago (NL)	1958
54	Ralph Kiner, Pittsburgh (NL)	1949	47	Willie Mays, San Francisco (NL)	1964
54	Mickey Mantle, New York (AL)	1961	47	Henry Aaron, Atlanta (NL)	1971
52	Mickey Mantle, New York (AL)	1956	47	Reggie Jackson, Oakland (AL)	1969
52	Willie Mays, San Francisco (NL)	1965	47	George Bell, Toronto (AL)	1987
52	George Foster, Cincinnati (NL)	1977	47	Kevin Mitchell, San Francisco (NL)	1989
51	Ralph Kiner, Pittsburgh (NL)	1947	46	Babe Ruth, New York (AL)	1924
51	John Mize, New York (NL)	1947	46	Babe Ruth, New York (AL)	1929
51	Willie Mays, New York (NL)	1955	46	Babe Ruth, New York (AL)	1931
51	Cecil Fielder (AL)	1990	46	Lou Gehrig, New York (AL)	1931
50	Jimmy Foxx, Boston (AL)	1938	46	Joe DiMaggio, New York (AL)	1937
50	Albert Belle, Cleveland (AL)	1995	46	Ed Mathews, Milwaukee (NL)	1959
49	Babe Ruth, New York (AL)	1930	46	Orlando Cepeda, San Francisco (NL)	1961
49	Lou Gehrig, New York (AL)	1934	46	Jim Rice, Boston (AL)	1978
49	Lou Gehrig, New York (AL)	1936	46	Juan Gonzalez, Texas (AL)	1993
49	Ted Kluszewski, Cincinnati (NL)	1954	46	Barry Bonds, San Francisco (NL)	1993
49	Willie Mays, San Francisco (NL)	1962	45	Harmon Killebrew, Minnesota (AL)	1963
49	Harmon Killebrew, Minnesota (AL)	1964	45	Willie McCovey, San Francisco (NL)	1969
49	Frank Robinson, Baltimore (AL)	1966	45	Johnny Bench, Cincinnati (NL)	1970
49	Harmon Killebrew, Minnesota (AL)	1969	45	Gorman Thomas, Milwaukee (AL)	1979
49	Mark McGwire, Oakland (AL)	1987	45	Mike Schmidt, Philadelphia (NL)	1979
49	Andre Dawson, Chicago (NL)	1987	45	Henry Aaron, Milwaukee (NL)	1962
48	Jimmy Foxx, Philadelphia (AL)	1933	45	Ken Griffey, Jr., Seattle (AL)	1993
48	Frank Howard, Washington (AL)	1969			

MAJOR LEAGUE BASEBALL—1996

AMERICAN LEAGUE
Final Standings—1996

NATIONAL LEAGUE
Final Standings—1996

EASTERN DIVISION

Team	W	L	Pct	GB
New York Yankees	92	70	.568	—
Baltimore Orioles	88	74	.543	4
Boston Red Sox	85	77	.525	7
Toronto Blue Jays	74	88	.457	18
Detroit Tigers	53	109	.327	39

CENTRAL DIVISION

Team	W	L	Pct	GB
Cleveland Indians	99	62	.615	—
Chicago White Sox	85	77	.525	14 1/2
Milwaukee Brewers	80	82	.494	19 1/2
Minnesota Twins	78	84	.481	21 1/2
Kansas City Royals	75	86	.466	24

WESTERN DIVISION

Team	W	L	Pct	GB
Texas Rangers	90	72	.556	—
Seattle Mariners	85	76	.528	4 1/2
Oakland Athletics	78	84	.481	12
California Angels	70	91	.435	19 1/2

EASTERN DIVISION

Team	W	L	Pct	GB
Atlanta Braves	96	66	.593	—
Montreal Expos	88	74	.543	8
Florida Marlins	80	82	.494	16
New York Mets	71	91	.438	25
Philadelphia Phillies	67	95	.414	29

CENTRAL DIVISION

Team	W	L	Pct	GB
St. Louis Cardinals	88	74	.543	—
Houston Astros	82	80	.506	6
Cincinnati Reds	81	81	.500	7
Chicago Cubs	76	86	.469	12
Pittsburgh Pirates	73	89	.451	15

WESTERN DIVISION

Team	W	L	Pct	GB
San Diego Padres	91	71	.562	—
Los Angeles Dodgers	90	72	.556	1
Colorado Rockies	83	79	.512	8
San Francisco Giants	68	94	.420	23

AMERICAN LEAGUE LEADERS—1996

Batting—Alex Rodriguez, Seattle	.358
Runs—Alex Rodriguez, Seattle	141
Hits—Paul Molitor, Minnesota	225
Runs batted in—Albert Belle, Cleveland	148
Triples—Chuck Knoblauch, Minneosta	14
Doubles—Alex Rodriguez, Seattle	54
Home runs—Mark McGwire, Oakland	52
Stolen bases—Kenny Lofton, Cleveland	75
Walks—Tony Phillips, Chicago	125
Slugging percentage—Mark McGwire, Oakland	.730
Strikeouts—Jay Buhner, Seattle	159

A.L. Pitching

Victories—Andrew Pettitte, New York	21
Earned run average—Juan Guzman, Toronto	2.93
Strikeouts—Roger Clemens, Boston	257
Shutouts—Pat Hentgen, Toronto, Ken Hill, Texas, Rich Robertson, Minnesota	3
Complete games—Pat Hentgen, Toronto	10
Saves—John Wetteland, New York	43
Innings pitched—Pat Hentgen, Toronto	265.2

NATIONAL LEAGUE LEADERS—1996

Batting—Ellis Burks, Colorado	.344
Runs—Ellis Burks, Colorado	142
Hits—Lance Johnson, New York	227
Runs batted in—Andres Galarraga, Colorado	150
Triples—Lance Johnson, New York	21
Doubles—Jeff Bagzell, Houston	48
Home runs—Andres Galarraga, Colorado	47
Stolen bases—Eric Young, Colorado	53
Walks—Barry Bonds, San Francisco	151
Slugging percentage—Ellis Burks, Colorado	.639
Strikeouts—Henry Rodriguez, Montreal	160

N.L. Pitching

Victories—John Smoltz, Atlanta	24
Earned run average—Kevin Brown, Florida	1.89
Strikeouts—John Smoltz, Atlanta	276
Shutouts—Kevin Brown, Florida	3
Complete games—Curt Schilling, Philadelphia	8
Saves—Jeff Brantley, Cincinnati	44
Innings pitched—John Smoltz, Atlanta	253.2

AMERICAN LEAGUE DIVISIONAL SERIES

New York Yankees defeated Texas Rangers, 3 games to 1.
  Oct. 1—Texas 6, NEW YORK 2
  Oct. 2—NEW YORK 5, Texas 4 (12 innings)
  Oct. 4—New York 3, TEXAS 2
  Oct. 5—New York 6, TEXAS 4

Baltimore Orioles defeated Cleveland Indians, 3 games to 1.
  Oct. 1—BALTIMORE 10, Cleveland 4
  Oct. 2—BALTIMORE 7, Cleveland 4
  Oct. 4—CLEVELAND 9, Baltimore 4
  Oct. 5—Baltimore 4, CLEVELAND 3 (12 innings)

(HOME TEAM IN CAPS.)

NATIONAL LEAGUE DIVISIONAL SERIES

St. Louis Cardinals defeated San Diego Padres 3 games to 0.
  Oct. 1—ST. LOUIS 3, San Diego 1
  Oct. 3—ST. LOUIS 5, San Diego 4
  Oct. 5—St. Louis 7, SAN DIEGO 5

Atlanta Braves defeated Los Angeles Dodgers, 3 games to 0.
  Oct. 2—Atlanta 2, LOS ANGELES 1 (10 innings)
  Oct. 3—Atlanta 3, LOS ANGELES 2
  Oct. 5—ATLANTA 5, Los Angeles 2

(HOME TEAM IN CAPS.)

AMERICAN LEAGUE AVERAGES—1996

Team Batting

	AB	R	H	HR	RBI	Avg
Cleveland	5,681	952	1,665	218	904	.293
Minnesota	5,673	877	1,633	118	812	.288
New York	5,628	871	1,621	162	830	.288
Seattle	5,668	993	1,625	245	954	.287
Texas	5,703	928	1,622	221	890	.284
Boston	5,756	928	1,631	209	882	.283
Chicago	5,644	898	1,586	195	860	.281
Milwaukee	5,659	894	1,577	178	845	.279
California	5,682	762	1,571	192	727	.276
Baltimore	5,689	949	1,557	257	914	.274
Kansas City	5,543	746	1,477	123	689	.266
Oakland	5,630	861	1,492	243	822	.265
Toronto	5,599	766	1,451	177	712	.259
Detroit	5,530	783	1,413	204	741	.256

Individual Batting
(Based on 300 plate appearances.)

Player/Team	AB	R	H	HR	RBI	Avg
Alex Rodriguez, Sea.	601	141	215	36	123	.358
Frank Thomas, Chi.	527	110	184	40	134	.349
Chuck Knoblauch, Minn.	578	140	197	13	72	.341
Paul Molitor, Minn.	660	99	225	9	113	.341
Rusty Greer, Tex.	542	96	180	18	100	.332
Dave Nilsson, Mil.	453	81	150	17	84	.331
Roberto Alomar, Bal.	588	132	193	22	94	.328
Edgar Martinez, Sea.	499	121	163	26	103	.327
Mo Vaughn, Bos.	635	118	207	44	143	.326
Kevin Seitzer, Cle.	570	85	186	13	78	.326
Jeff Cirillo, Mil.	566	101	184	15	83	.325
Julio Franco, Cle.	432	72	139	14	76	.322
Bob Higginson, Det.	440	75	141	26	81	.320
Kenny Lofton, Cle.	662	132	210	14	67	.317
Juan Gonzalez, Tex.	541	89	170	47	144	.314
Derek Jeter, N.Y.	582	104	183	10	78	.314
Mark McGwire, Oak.	423	104	132	52	113	.312
Harold Baines, Chi.	495	81	154	22	95	.311
Albert Belle, Cle.	602	124	187	48	148	.311
Wade Boggs, N.Y.	501	80	156	2	41	.311

Individual Pitching
(Based on 3 decisions)

Player/Team	IP	H	BB	SO	W	L	ERA
Juan Guzman, Tor.	187.2	158	53	165	11	8	2.93
Pat Hentgen, Tor.	265.2	238	94	177	20	10	3.22
Charles Nagy, Cle.	222.0	217	61	167	17	5	3.41
Alex Fernandez, Chi.	258.0	248	72	200	16	10	3.45
Kevin Appier, Kan.	211.1	192	75	207	14	11	3.62
Ken Hill, Tex.	250.2	250	95	170	16	10	3.63
Roger Clemens, Bos.	242.2	216	106	257	10	13	3.63
Andy Pettitte, N.Y.	221.0	229	72	162	21	8	3.87
Ben McDonald, Mil.	221.0	228	67	146	12	10	3.90
Tim Belcher, Kan.	238.2	262	68	112	15	11	3.92
Chuck Finley, Cal.	238.0	241	94	215	15	16	4.16
Wilson Alvarez, Chi.	217.1	216	97	181	15	10	4.22
Orel Hershiser, Cle.	206.0	238	58	125	15	9	4.24
James Baldwin, Chi.	169.0	168	57	127	11	6	4.42
Brad Radke, Minn.	232.0	231	57	148	11	16	4.46
Kevin Tapani, Chi.	225.1	236	76	150	13	10	4.59
Darren Oliver, Tex.	173.2	190	76	112	14	6	4.66

Team Pitching

	ERA	H	ER	BB	SO	ShO	Sv
Cleveland	4.35	1,530	702	484	1,033	9	46
Chicago	4.53	1,529	735	616	1,039	5	43
Kansas City	4.55	1,563	733	460	925	8	37
Toronto	4.58	1,476	735	610	1,033	7	35
New York	4.65	1,469	744	610	1,139	9	53
Texas	4.66	1,569	750	582	976	6	43
Boston	5.00	1,606	810	722	1,166	5	37
Baltimore	5.15	1,604	841	597	1,047	2	44
Milwaukee	5.17	1,570	831	635	846	5	42
Oakland	5.20	1,638	842	644	884	5	34
Seattle	5.21	1,562	829	605	1,000	4	34
Minnesota	5.30	1,561	848	581	959	5	31
California	5.31	1,546	849	662	1,052	8	38
Detroit	6.38	1,699		784	957	4	22

NATIONAL LEAGUE AVERAGES—1996

Team Batting

	AB	R	H	HR	RBI	Avg
Colorado	5,590	961	1,607	221	909	.287
Atlanta	5,614	773	1,514	197	735	.270
New York	5,618	746	1,515	147	697	.270
St. Louis	5,503	759	1,468	142	711	.267
Pittsburgh	5,665	776	1,509	138	738	.266
San Diego	5,655	771	1,499	147	718	.265
Houston	5,508	753	1,445	129	703	.262
Montreal	5,506	741	1,441	148	696	.262
Florida	5,498	688	1,413	150	650	.257
Cincinnati	5,455	778	1,398	191	733	.256
Philadelphia	5,499	650	1,405	132	604	.256
San Francisco	5,533	752	1,400	153	707	.253
Los Angeles	5,538	703	1,396	150	661	.252
Chicago	5,531	772	1,388	175	725	.251

Individual Batting
(Based on 300 plate appearances.)

Player/Team

	AB	R	H	HR	RBI	Avg
Tony Gwynn, San D.	451	67	158	3	50	.353
Ellis Burks, Col.	613	142	211	40	128	.344
Mike Piazza, L.A.	547	87	184	36	105	.336
Lance Johnson, N.Y.	682	117	227	9	69	.333
Mark Grace, Chi.	547	88	181	9	75	.331
Ken Caminiti, San D.	546	109	178	40	130	.326
Eric Young, Col.	568	113	184	8	74	.324
Bernard Gilkey, N.Y.	571	108	181	30	117	.317
Jeff Bagwell, Hou.	568	111	179	31	120	.315
Gary Sheffield, Fla.	519	118	163	42	120	.314
Dante Bichette, Col.	633	114	198	31	141	.313
Hal Morris, Cin.	528	82	165	16	80	.313
Brian Jordan, St. L.	513	82	159	17	104	.310
Chipper Jones, Atl.	598	114	185	30	110	.309
Barry Bonds, S.F.	517	122	159	42	129	.308
Marquis Grissom, Atl.	671	106	207	23	74	.308
Mark Grudzielanek, Mon.	657	99	201	6	49	.306
Andres Galarraga, Col.	626	119	190	48	150	.304
Vinny Castilla, Col.	629	97	191	40	113	.304
Al Martin, Pitt.	630	101	189	18	72	.300

Individual Pitching
(Based on 10 decisions)

Player/Team	IP	H	BB	SO	W	L	ERA
Kevin Brown, Fla.	233.0	187	33	159	17	11	1.89
Greg Maddux, Atl.	245.0	225	28	172	15	11	2.72
Al Leiter, Fla.	215.1	153	119	200	16	12	2.93
John Smoltz, Atl.	253.2	199	55	276	24	8	2.94
Tom Glavine, Atl.	235.1	222	85	181	15	10	2.98
Steve Trachsel, Chi.	205.0	181	62	132	13	9	3.03
Hideo Nomo, L.A.	228.1	180	85	234	16	11	3.19
Curt Schilling, Phil.	183.1	149	50	182	9	10	3.19
Jeff Fassero, Mon.	231.2	217	55	222	15	11	3.30
Ismael Valdes, L.A.	225.0	219	54	173	15	7	3.32
Ramon Martinez, L.A.	168.2	153	86	133	15	6	3.42
Mark Clark, N.Y.	212.1	217	48	142	14	11	3.43
Pedro Astacio, L.A.	211.2	207	67	130	9	8	3.44
Denny Neagle, Atl.	221.1	226	48	149	16	9	3.50
Donovan Osborne, St. L.	198.2	191	57	134	13	9	3.53
Fernando Valenzuela, S.D.	171.2	177	67	95	13	8	3.62
John Smiley, Cin.	217.1	207	54	171	13	14	3.64
Shane Reynolds, Hou.	239.0	227	44	204	16	10	3.65

Team Pitching

	ERA	H	ER	BB	SO	ShO	Sv		ERA	H	ER	BB	SO	ShO	Sv
Los Angeles	3.48	1,378	567	534	1,213	9	50	Cincinnati	4.33	1,447	695	591	1,089	8	52
Atlanta	3.54	1,372	577	451	1,245	9	46	Chicago	4.36	1,447	705	546	1,027	11	34
San Diego	3.73	1,394	617	506	1,194	11	47	Houston	4.38	1,541	704	539	1,164	4	35
Montreal	3.78	1,352	605	482	1,204	7	43	Philadelphia	4.49	1,463	710	510	1,043	6	42
Florida	3.95	1,385	633	598	1,051	13	41	Pittsburgh	4.64	1,603	749	479	1,046	7	37
St. Louis	3.98	1,380	642	539	1,050	11	43	San Francisco	4.72	1,520	757	570	998	8	35
New York	4.22	1,517	675	532	999	10	41	Colorado	5.60	1,597	885	624	932	5	34

MAJOR LEAGUE BASEBALL—1996

AMERICAN LEAGUE CHAMPIONSHIP SERIES—1996
New York Yankees win series, 4 games to 1

1st Game, at New York, Oct. 9, 1996

Baltimore	011	101	000	00	4	11	1
New York	110	000	110	01	5	11	0

Pitchers—Baltimore: Erickson, Orosco, Benitez, Rhodes, T. Mathews, R. Myers. New York: Pettitte, Nelson, Wetteland, M. Rivera.
Winner: Rivera. Loser: R. Myers. Attendance: 56,495.

2nd Game, at New York, Oct. 10, 1996

Baltimore	002	000	210	—	5	10	0
New York	200	000	100	—	3	11	1

Pitchers—Baltimore: Wells, Mills, Orosco, R. Myers, Benitez. New York: Cone, Nelson, Lloyd, Weathers.
Winner: Wells. Loser: Nelson. Attendance: 56,432.

3rd Game, at Baltimore, Oct. 11, 1996

New York	000	100	040	—	5	8	0
Baltimore	200	000	000	—	2	3	2

Pitchers—New York: Key, Wetteland. Baltimore: Mussina, Orosco, T. Mathews.
Winner: Key. Loser: Mussina. Attendance: 48,635.

4th Game, at Baltimore, Oct. 12, 1996

New York	210	200	030	—	8	9	0
Baltimore	101	200	000	—	4	11	0

Pitchers—New York: Rogers, Weathers, Lloyd, M. Rivera, Wetteland. Baltimore: Coppinger, Rhodes, Mills, Orosco, Benitez, T. Mathews.
Winner: Weathers. Loser: Coppinger. Attendance: 48,974.

5th Game, at Baltimore, Oct. 13, 1996

New York	006	000	000	—	6	11	0
Baltimore	000	001	012	—	4	4	1

Pitchers—New York: Pettitte, Wetteland. Baltimore: Erickson, Rhodes, Mills, R. Myers.
Winner: Pettitte. Loser: Erickson. Attendance: 48,718.

NATIONAL LEAGUE CHAMPIONSHIP SERIES—1996
Atlanta Braves win series, 4 games to 3

1st Game, at Atlanta, Oct. 9, 1996

St. Louis	010	000	100	—	2	5	1
Atlanta	020	000	02x	—	4	9	0

Pitchers—St. Louis: Andy Benes, Petkovsek, Fossas, T.J. Mathews. Atlanta: Smoltz, Wohlers.
Winner: Smoltz. Loser: Petkovsek. Attendance: 48,686.

2nd Game, at Atlanta, Oct. 10, 1996

St. Louis	102	000	500	—	8	11	2
Atlanta	002	001	000	—	3	5	2

Pitchers—St. Louis: Stottlemyre, Petkovsek, Honeycutt, Eckersley. Atlanta: G. Maddux, McMichael, Neagle, Avery.
Winner: Stottlemyre. Loser: G. Maddux. Attendance: 52,067.

3rd Game, at St. Louis, Oct. 12, 1996

Atlanta	100	000	010	—	2	8	1
St. Louis	200	001	00x	—	3	7	0

Pitchers—Atlanta: Glavine, Bielecki, McMichael. St. Louis: Osborne, Petkovsek, Honeycutt, Eckersley.
Winner: Osborne. Loser: Glavine. Attendance: 56,769.

4th Game, at St. Louis, Oct. 13, 1996

Atlanta	010	002	000	—	3	9	1
St. Louis	000	000	31x	—	4	5	0

Pitchers—Atlanta: Neagle, McMichael, Wohlers. St. Louis: Andy Benes, Fossas, T.J. Mathews, Alan Benes, Honeycutt, Eckersley.
Winner: Eckersley. Loser: McMichael. Attendance: 56,764.

5th Game, at St. Louis, Oct. 14, 1996

Atlanta	520	310	012	—	14	22	0
St. Louis	000	000	000	—	0	7	0

Pitchers—Atlanta: Smoltz, Bielecki, Wade, Clontz. St. Louis: Stottlemyre, D. Jackson, Fossas, Petkovsek, Honeycutt.
Winner: Smoltz. Loser: Stottlemyre. Attendance: 56,782.

6th Game, at Atlanta, Oct. 16, 1996

St. Louis	000	000	010	—	1	6	1
Atlanta	010	010	01x	—	3	7	0

Pitchers—St. Louis: Alan Benes, Fossas, Petkovsek, Stottlemyre. Atlanta: G. Maddux, Wohlers.
Winner: G. Maddux. Loser: Alan Benes. Attendance: 52,067.

7th Game, at Atlanta, Oct. 17, 1996

St. Louis	000	000	000	—	0	4	2
Atlanta	600	403	20x	—	15	17	0

Pitchers—St. Louis: Osborne, Andy Benes, Petkovsek, Honeycutt, Fossas. Atlanta: Glavine, Bielecki, Avery.
Winner: Glavine. Loser: Osborne. Attendance: 52,067.

Realignment of Major Leagues

The move by the American and National leagues to three divisions in 1994 doubled the number of teams qualifying for the postseason from four to eight overall. All three divisional winners plus a wild-card team (the non-division winner with the best record) will reach the playoffs, which will expand to two rounds. The first round will be a Best-of-5 series, followed by a Best-of-7 championships series.

American League			National League		
West	**Central**	**East**	**West**	**Central**	**East**
California	Chicago	Baltimore	Colorado	Chicago	Atlanta
Oakland	Cleveland	Boston	Los Angeles	Cincinnati	Florida
Seattle	Kansas City	Detroit	San Diego	Houston	Montreal
Texas	Milwaukee	New York	San Francisco	Pittsburgh	New York
	Minnesota	Toronto		St. Louis	Philadelphia

WORLD SERIES—1996
New York Yankees win series, 4 games to 2

1st Game—New York, Oct. 20
Atlanta 12, New York 1

ATLANTA (N)	AB	R	H	RBI
Grissom cf	5	2	2	1
Lemke 2b	4	0	2	1
C. Jones 3b	4	1	1	3
McGriff 1b	5	2	2	0
Lopez c	4	2	1	0
Perez c	0	0	0	0
Dye rf	5	0	1	0
A. Jones lf	4	3	3	5
Klesko dh	4	1	0	0
Blauser ss	3	1	1	0
Polonia ph	1	0	0	0
Belliard ss	0	0	0	0
Totals	**39**	**12**	**13**	**12**

NEW YORK (A)	AB	R	H	RBI
Jeter ss	3	1	0	0
Boggs 3b	4	0	2	1
B. Williams cf	3	0	0	0
T. Martinez 1b	3	0	1	0
Fielder dh	4	0	0	0
Strawberry lf	3	0	0	0
Raines lf	1	0	0	0
O'Neill rf	2	0	0	0
Aldrete rf	0	0	0	0
Hayes ph	1	0	0	0
Duncan 2b	1	0	0	0
Fox 2b	0	0	0	0
Sojo ph	1	0	0	0
Leyritz c	3	0	1	0
Total	**31**	**1**	**4**	**1**

Atlanta	026		013		000	—	12	13	0
New York	000		010		000	—	1	4	1

E—Duncan (1). LOB—Atlanta 3, New York 8. 2B—Boggs (1). HR—McGriff (1) off Boehringer; A. Jones 2 (2) off Petitte, Boehringer. SB—C. Jones (1). SF—C. Jones.

Atlanta	IP	H	R	ER	BB	SO	ERA
Smoltz (W 1-0)	6	2	1	1	5	4	1.50
McMichael	1	2	0	0	0	1	0.00
Neagle	1	0	0	0	0	0	0.00
Wade	2/3	0	0	0	0	0	0.00
Clontz	1/3	0	0	0	0	0	0.00
New York							
Pettitte (L 0-1)	2 1/3	6	7	7	1	1	27.00
Boehringer	3	5	5	3	0	2	9.00
Weathers	1 2/3	1	0	0	0	0	0.00
Nelson	1	1	0	0	0	1	0.00
Wetteland	1	0	0	0	0	2	0.00

Inherited runners scored—Boehringer 2-2, Weathers 2-1. NP—Smoltz 104, McMichael 13, Neagle 10, Wade 5, Clontz 2, Pettitte 54, Boehringer 71, Weathers 19, Nelson 13, Wetteland 17. Umpires—Home, Evans; First, Tata; Second, Welke; Third, Rippley; Left, Young; Right, Davis. T—3:02. Att.—56,365.

2nd Game—New York, Oct. 21
Atlanta 4, New York 0

ATLANTA (N)	AB	R	H	RBI
Grissom cf	5	1	2	1
Lemke 2b	4	2	2	0
C. Jones 3b	3	0	1	0
McGriff 1b	3	0	2	3
J. Lopez c	4	0	1	0
Dye rf	4	0	1	0
A. Jones lf	3	0	0	0
Pendleton dh	4	1	1	0
Blauser ss	2	0	0	0
Polonia ph	1	0	0	0
Belliard ss	0	0	0	0
Totals	**33**	**4**	**10**	**4**

NEW YORK (A)	AB	R	H	RBI
Raines lf	4	0	2	0
Boggs 3b	4	0	1	0
B. Williams cf	4	0	0	0
T. Martinez 1b	4	0	0	0
Fielder dh	4	0	2	0
Fox pr	0	0	0	0
O'Neill rf	4	0	1	0
Duncan 2b	3	0	0	0
Girardi c	3	0	0	0
D. Jeter ss	2	0	1	0
Totals	**32**	**0**	**7**	**0**

Atlanta	101		011		000	—	4	10	0
New York	000		000		000	—	0	7	1

E—Raines (1). LOB—Atlanta 7, New York 6. 2B—Grissom (1), Lemke (1), C. Jones (1) Pendleton (1), O'Neill (1). CS—Raines (1). S—Lemke. SF—McGriff. DP—Atlanta 1, New York 2. GIDP—J. Lopez, Blauser, Boggs.

Atlanta	IP	H	R	ER	BB	SO	ERA
Maddux (W 1-0)	8	6	0	0	0	2	0.00
Wohlers	1	1	0	0	0	3	0.00

New York
	6	10	4	4	2	0	6.00
Key (L 0-1)	6	10	4	4	2	0	6.00
Lloyd	2/3	0	0	0	0	0	0.00
Nelson	1 1/3	0	0	0	0	2	0.00
M. Rivera	1	0	0	0	0	1	0.00

HBP—by Maddux (D. Jeter), by Key (A. Jones). NP—Maddux 82, Wohlers 18, Key 99, Lloyd 8, Nelson 14, M. Rivera 15. Umpires—Home, Tata; First, Welke; Second, Rippley; Third, Young; Left, Davis; Right, Evans. T—2:44. Att.—56,340.

3rd Game—Atlanta, Oct. 22
New York 5, Atlanta 2

NEW YORK (A)	AB	R	H	RBI
Raines lf	4	1	1	0
Jeter ss	3	1	1	0
B. Williams cf	5	2	2	3
Fielder 1b	3	0	1	0
Fox pr	0	1	0	0
T. Martinez 1b	0	0	0	0
Hayes 3b	5	0	0	0
Strawberry rf	3	0	1	1
Duncan 2b	3	0	1	0
Sojo 2b	1	0	1	1
Girardi c	2	0	0	0
Cone p	2	0	0	0
Leyritz ph	1	0	0	0
M. Rivera p	1	0	0	0
Lloyd p	0	0	0	0
Wetteland p	0	0	0	0
Totals	**33**	**5**	**8**	**5**

ATLANTA (N)	AB	R	H	RBI
Grissom cf	4	1	3	0
Lemke 2b	4	0	1	1
C. Jones 3b	3	0	1	0
McGriff 1b	3	0	0	0
Klesko lf	3	0	0	1
J. Lopez c	4	0	1	0
A. Jones rf	4	0	0	0
Blauser ss	4	0	0	0
Glavine p	1	1	0	0
Polonia ph	1	0	0	0
McMichael p	0	0	0	0
Clontz p	0	0	0	0
Bielecki p	0	0	0	0
Pendleton ph	1	0	0	0
Totals	**31**	**2**	**6**	**2**

New York	100		100		030	—	5	8	1
Atlanta	000		010		010	—	2	6	1

E—Jeter (1), Blauser (1). LOB—New York 9, Atlanta 7. 2B—Fielder (1). 3B—Grissom (1). HR—B. Williams (1) off McMichael. CS—A. Jones (1), Polonia (1). S—Jeter, Girardi. DP—New York 1, Atlanta 1. GIDP—Lemke.

New York	IP	H	R	ER	BB	SO	ERA
Cone (W 1-0)	6	4	1	1	4	3	1.50
M. Rivera	1 1/3	2	1	1	1	1	3.86
Lloyd	2/3	0	0	0	0	1	0.00
Wetteland (S 1)	1	0	0	0	0	2	0.00
Atlanta							
Glavine (L 0-1)	7	4	2	1	3	8	1.29
McMichael	0	3	3	3	0	0	27.00
Clontz	1	1	0	0	1	1	0.00
Bielecki	1	0	0	0	2	2	0.00

McMichael pitched to 3 batters in the 8th. Inherited runners scored—Lloyd 1-0, Clontz 1-1. IBB—off Clontz (Strawberry) 1. NP—Cone 97, M. Rivera 35, Lloyd 6, Wetteland 25, Glavine 110, McMichael 7, Clontz 15, Bielecki 18. Umpires—Home, Welke; First, Rippley; Second, Young; Third, Davis; Left, Evans; Right, Tata. T—3:22. Att.—51,843.

4th Game—Atlanta, Oct. 23
New York 8, Atlanta 6

NEW YORK (A)	AB	R	H	RBI
Raines lf	5	1	0	0
D. Jeter ss	4	2	2	0
B. Williams cf	4	1	0	0
Fielder 1b	4	1	2	1
Boggs ph-3b	0	0	0	1
Hayes 3b-1b	5	1	3	1
Strawberry rf	5	0	2	0
Duncan 2b	5	1	0	0
Girardi c	2	0	0	0
O'Neill ph	1	0	0	0
Leyritz c	2	1	1	3

ATLANTA (N)	AB	R	H	RBI
Grissom cf	5	0	1	2
Lemke 2b	5	0	1	0
C. Jones 3b-ss	3	2	1	0
McGriff 1b	3	1	2	1
J. Lopez c	2	1	0	1
Klesko 1b	1	0	0	0
A. Jones lf	4	1	3	1
Dye rf	4	0	0	0
Blauser ss	3	1	1	1
Polonia ph	1	0	0	0
Pendleton 3b	1	0	0	0

NEW YORK (A) / ATLANTA (N)

NEW YORK (A)	AB	R	H	RBI	ATLANTA (N)	AB	R	H	RBI
Rogers p	1	0	1	0	Neagke p	1	0	0	0
Sojo ph	1	0	1	0	E. Perez c	1	0	0	0
T. Martinez ph	1	0	0	0					
Aldrete ph	1	0	0	0					
Lloyd p	1	0	0	0					
Totals	42	8	12	6	Totals	35	6	9	6

New York   000 003 030 2— 8 12 0
Atlanta   041 010 000 0— 6 9 2

E—Klesko (1), Dye (1). LOB—New York 13, Atlanta 8. 2B—Grissom (2), A. Jones (1). HR—McGriff (2) off Rogers, Leyritz (1) off Wohlers. S—Dye, Neagle. SF—J. Lopez.

New York	IP	H	R	ER	BB	SO	ERA
Rogers	2	5	5	5	2	0	22.50
Boehringer	2	0	0	0	0	3	5.40
Weathers	1	1	1	1	2	2	3.38
J. Nelson	2	0	0	0	1	2	0.00
M. Rivera	1 1/3	2	0	0	1	1	2.45
Lloyd (W 1-0)	1	0	0	0	0	1	0.00
Wetteland (S 2)	2/3	1	0	0	0	0	0.00
Atlanta							
Neagle	5	5	3	2	4	3	3.00
Wade	0	0	0	0	1	0	0.00
Bielecki	2	0	0	0	1	4	0.00
Wohlers	2	6	3	3	0	1	9.00
Avery (L 0-1)	2/3	1	2	1	3	0	13.50
Clontz	1/3	0	0	0	0	1	0.00

Balk—Weathers. NP—Rogers 52, Boehringer 23, Weathers 26, J. Nelson 35, M. Rivera 26, Lloyd 9, Wetteland 10, Neagle 92, Wade 6, Bielecki 34, Wohlers 28, Avery 25, Clontz 7. T—4:17. Att.—51,881.

5th Game—Atlanta, Oct. 24
New York 1, Atlanta 0

NEW YORK (A)	AB	R	H	RBI	ATLANTA (N)	AB	R	H	RBI
D. Jeter ss	4	0	0	0	Grissom cf	3	0	2	0
Hayes 3b	4	1	0	0	Lemke 2b	4	0	0	0
B. Williams cf	4	0	0	0	C. Jones 3b	4	0	1	0
Fielder 1b	4	0	3	1	McGriff 1b	3	0	0	0
T. Martinez 1b	0	0	0	0	J. Lopez c	4	0	0	0
Strawberry lf	3	0	0	0	A. Jones lf	2	0	1	0
O'Neill rf	2	0	0	0	Klesko ph	0	0	0	0
Duncan 2b	4	0	0	0	Dye rf	3	0	0	0
Sojo 2b	0	0	0	0	Polonia ph	1	0	0	0
Leyritz c	2	0	1	0	Blauser ss	3	0	0	0
Pettitte p	4	0	0	0	Smoltz p	2	0	1	0
Wetteland p	0	0	0	0	Mordecai ph	1	0	0	0
					Wohlers p	0	0	0	0
Totals	31	1	4	1	Totals	30	0	5	0

New York   000 100 000 — 1 4 1
Atlanta   000 000 000 — 0 5 1

E—D. Jeter (2), Grissom (1). LOB—New York 8, Atlanta 7. 2B—Fielder (2), C. Jones (2). SB—Duncan (1), Leyritz (1), Grissom (1), A. Jones (1). CS—A. Jones (2). GIDP—C. Jones, J. Lopez. Runners left in scoring position—New York 4 (Duncan 3, Pettitte). Atlanta 4 (Lemke, C. Jones, Dye, Polonia). Runners moved up—B. Williams, O'Neill, Leyritz. DP—New York 2 (Duncan, D. Jeter and Fielder), (Pettitte, Duncan and Fielder), Atlanta 1 (McGriff).

New York	IP	H	R	ER	BB	SO	ERA
Pettitte (W 1-1)	8 1/3	5	0	0	3	4	5.91
Wetteland (S 3)	2/3	0	0	0	1	0	0.00
Atlanta							
Smoltz (L 1-1)	8	4	1	0	3	10	0.64
Wohlers	1	0	0	0	2	0	6.75

Inherited runner scored—Wetteland 1-0. IBB—off Wetteland (Klesko) 1, off Wohlers (Leyritz) 1. WP—Wohlers. NP—Pettitte 95, Wetteland 8, Smoltz 116, Wohlers 16. Umpires—Home, Young; First, Davis; Second, Evans; Third, Tata; Left, Welke; Right, Rippley. T—2:54. Att.—51,881.

6th Game—New York, Oct. 26
New York 3, Atlanta 2

ATLANTA (N)	AB	R	H	RBI	NEW YORK (A)	AB	R	H	RBI
Grissom cf	5	0	2	1	Jeter ss	4	1	1	1
Lemke 2b	5	0	0	0	Boggs 3b	3	0	0	0
C. Jones 3b	4	0	1	0	Hayes 3b	1	0	0	0
McGriff 1b	3	1	0	0	Williams cf	4	0	2	1
Lopez c	3	0	1	0	Fielder dh	4	0	1	0
A. Jones lf-rf	3	0	1	0	Martinez 1b	3	0	0	0
Dye rf	1	0	0	1	Strawberry lf	2	0	0	0
Klesko ph-lf	2	1	1	0	O'Neill rf	3	1	1	0
Pendleton dh	3	0	1	0	Duncan 2b	1	0	0	0
Belliard pr	0	0	0	0	Sojo 2b	2	0	1	0
Blauser ss	3	0	0	0	Girardi c	3	1	2	1
Polonia ph	1	0	0	0					
Totals	33	2	8	2	Totals	30	3	8	3

Atlanta   000 100 001 — 2 8 0
New York   003 000 00x — 3 8 1

E—Duncan (2). LOB—Atlanta 9, New York 4. 2B—C. Jones (3), Blauser (1), O'Neill (2), Sojo (1). 3B—Girardi (1). SB—Jeter (3), Williams (1). CS—Pendleton (1). DP—Atlanta 2, New York 1.

Atlanta	IP	H	R	ER	BB	SO	ERA
Maddux (L 1-1)	7 2/3	8	3	3	1	3	1.72
Wohlers	1/3	0	0	0	0	0	6.23
New York							
Key (W 1-1)	5 1/3	5	1	1	3	1	3.97
Weathers	1/3	0	0	0	1	0	3.00
Lloyd	1/3	0	0	0	0	0	0.00
Rivera	2	0	0	0	1	2	1.59
Wetteland (S 4)	1	3	1	1	0	2	2.08

Inherited runners scored—Wohlers 1-0, Weathers 1-0, Lloyd 2-0. NP—Maddux 103, Wohlers 4, Key 92, Weathers 8, Lloyd 3, Rivera 22, Wetteland 25. Umpires—Home, Davis; First, Evans; Second, Tata; Third, Welke; Left, Rippley; Right, Young. T—2:53. Att.—56,375.

Series MVP—John Wetteland.

JONES YOUNGEST TO HOMER IN WORLD SERIES

Nineteen-year-old Andruw Jones of the Atlanta Braves broke Mickey Mantle's record as the youngest player to hit a home run in the World Series. He did it in his first time at bat in the second inning of the first game of the 1996 World Series, in Yankee Stadium, and he did it on what would have been Mickey Mantle's 65th birthday. In the third inning, Jones hit another homer, driving in three runs. The Curacao native was signed by the Braves at age 16 and joined the Gulf Coast League in 1994. While in the minors he was named the Minor League Player of the Year by USA Today, Baseball Weekly, and Baseball America. Two months before the 1996 World Series, Jones was called up to Atlanta and homered 2 days after joining the team.

WOMEN'S PROFESSIONAL BASKETBALL

The American Basketball League debuted in October 1996 with an eight-team, two-conference league. The league boasts nine 1996 Olympians, including Teresa Edwards and heptathlete Jackie Joyner-Kersee. The teams will play a 40 game schedule, ending with championship playoffs in March.

The National Basketball Association also announced plans for a women's basketball league, the WNBA. The WNBA season is scheduled to begin play in June 1997 with eight teams competing in a 30-game schedule, culminating with the WNBA championship game on August 30.

MEDIA

(Courtesy of *Information Please Sports Almanac.*)

DAILY NEWSPAPER

USA Today
1000 Wilson Blvd., Arlington, Va. 22229
(703) 276-3400. http://www.usatoday.com

WEEKLY MAGAZINE

Sports Illustrated
Time & Life Bldg., Rockefeller Ctr., New York, N.Y. 10020
(212) 586-1212. http://pathfinder.com

TELEVISION

ABC Sports
47 West 66th St., 13th Floor, New York, N.Y. 10023
(212) 887-4867. http://www.abc.com

CBS Sports
51 West 52nd St., 30th Floor, New York, N.Y. 10019
(212) 975-5230. http://www.cbs.com

ESPN
ESPN Plaza, Bristol, Conn. 06010
(203) 585-2000. http://espnet.sportszone.com

HBO Sports
1100 Ave. of the Americas, New York, N.Y. 10036
(212) 512-1000. http://www.hbo.com

NBC Sports
30 Rockefeller Plaza, New York, N.Y. 10112
(212) 664-4444. http://www.nbc.com

Prime Network
5251 Gulfton St., Houston, Texas 77081
(713) 661-0078. http://www.prime-tv.com

SportsChannel
3 Crossways Park West, Woodbury, N.Y. 11797
(516) 921-3764. http://www.sportschannel.com

Turner Sports
One CNN Center, Suite 1300, Atlanta, Ga. 30303
(404) 827-1735. http://www.turner.com

USA Network
1230 Ave. of the Americas, New York, N.Y. 10020
(212) 408-9100. http://www.viacom.com/usa

YACHTING

AMERICA'S CUP RECORD

First race in 1851 around Isle of Wight, Cowes, England. First defense and all others through 1920 held 30 miles off New York Bay. Races since 1930 held 30 miles off Newport, R.I. Conducted as one race only in 1851 and 1870; best four–of–seven basis, 1871; best two–of–three, 1876–1887; best three–of–five, 1893–1901; best four–of–seven, since 1930. Figures in parentheses indicate number of races won.

Year	Winner and owner	Loser and owner
1851	AMERICA (1), John C. Stevens, U.S.	AURORA, T. Le Marchant, England[1]
1870	MAGIC (1), Franklin Osgood, U.S.	CAMBRIA, James Ashbury, England[2]
1871	COLUMBIA (2), Franklin Osgood, U.S.[3] SAPPHO (2), William P. Douglas, U.S.	LIVONIA (1), James Ashbury, England
1876	MADELEINE (2), John S. Dickerson, U.S.	COUNTESS OF DUFFERIN, Chas. Gifford, Canada
1881	MISCHIEF (2), J. R. Busk, U.S.	ATALANTA, Alexander Cuthbert, Canada
1885	PURITAN (2), J. M. Forbes–Gen. Charles Paine, U.S.	GENESTA, Sir Richard Sutton, England
1886	MAYFLOWER (2), Gen. Charles Paine, U.S.	GALATEA, Lt. William Henn, England
1887	VOLUNTEER (2), Gen. Charles Paine, U.S.	THISTLE, James Bell et al., Scotland
1893	VIGILANT (3), C. Oliver Iselin et al., U.S.	VALKYRIE II, Lord Dunraven, England
1895	DEFENDER (3), C. O. Iselin–W. K. Vanderbilt–E. D. Morgan, U.S	.VALKYRIE III, Lord Dunraven–Lord Lonsdale–Lord Wolverton, England
1899	COLUMBIA (3), J. P. Morgan–C. O. Iselin, U.S.	SHAMROCK I, Sir Thomas Lipton, Ireland
1901	COLUMBIA (3), Edwin D. Morgan, U.S.	SHAMROCK II, Sir Thomas Lipton, Ireland
1903	RELIANCE (3), Cornelius Vanderbilt et al., U.S.	SHAMROCK III, Sir Thomas Lipton, Ireland
1920	RESOLUTE (3), Henry Walters et al., U.S.	SHAMROCK IV (2), Sir Thomas Lipton, Ireland
1930	ENTERPRISE (4), Harold S. Vanderbilt et al., U.S.	SHAMROCK V, Sir Thomas Lipton, Ireland
1934	RAINBOW (4), Harold S. Vanderbilt, U.S.	ENDEAVOUR (2), T. O. M. Sopwith, England
1937	RANGER (4), Harold S. Vanderbilt, U.S.	ENDEAVOUR II, T. O. M. Sopwith, England
1958	COLUMBIA (4), Henry Sears et al., U.S.	SCEPTRE, Hugh Goodson et al., England
1962	WEATHERLY (4), Henry D. Mercer et al., U.S.	GRETEL (1), Sir Frank Packer et al., Australia
1964	CONSTELLATION (4), New York Y.C. Syndicate, U.S.	SOVEREIGN (0), J. Anthony Bowden, England
1967	INTREPID (4), New York Y.C. Syndicate, U.S.	DAME PATTIE (0), Sydney (Aust.) Syndicate
1970	INTREPID (4), New York Y.C. Syndicate, U.S.	GRETEL II (1), Sydney (Aust.) Syndicate
1974	COURAGEOUS (4), New York, N.Y. Syndicate, U.S.	SOUTHERN CROSS (0), Sydney (Aust.) Syndicate
1977	COURAGEOUS (4), New York, N.Y. Syndicate, U.S.	AUSTRALIA (0), Sun City (Aust.) Syndicate
1980	FREEDOM (4), New York, N.Y. Syndicate, U.S.	AUSTRALIA (1), Alan Bond et al, Australia
1983	AUSTRALIA II (4) Alan Bond et al., Australia,	LIBERTY (3) New York, N.Y. Syndicate, U.S.
1987	STARS & STRIPES (4), Dennis Conner et al., United States	KOOKABURRA III (0), Iain Murray et al., Australia
1988[4]	STARS & STRIPES, Dennis Conner et al., United States	NEW ZEALAND Michael Fay, et al., New Zealand
1992	AMERICA 3, Bill Koch et al., United States	IL MORO DI VENEZIA, Paul Cayard, et al., Italy
1995	BLACK MAGIC, Peter Blake, et al., New Zealand	YOUNG AMERICA, Dennis Conner, et al., United States

1. Fourteen British yachts started against America; Aurora finished second. 2. Cambria sailed against 23 U.S. yachts and finished tenth. 3. Columbia was disabled in the third race, after winning the first two; Sappho substituted and won the fourth and fifth. 4. Shortly after Dennis Conner and his 60–foot, twin–hulled catamaran easily defeated the challenge of the New Zealand, a 133–foot, single–hulled yacht in the waters off San Diego in September 1988, a New York State Supreme Court judge ruled that the Americans did not live up to the America's Cup Deed of Gift, which means competing boats must be similar. The judge ruled that the Americans had an unfair advantage over the monohulled ship, and awarded the Cup to New Zealand. However, an Appeal awarded the Cup to the United States.

SOCCER

The early history of the sport is uncertain. A form of the game in which a leather ball was dribbled was played in China as early as the 4th century B.C. The Romans played a variation of soccer which eventually spread throughout Europe. British schools and universities played soccer (known as football) during the 1800s, however, each school used different sets of rules and the number of players varied. This difficulty was corrected on Oct. 26, 1863 when the Football Association (FA) was formed in London for the purpose of unifying the rules of the game.

The Federation of International Football Associations (FIFA) was created in 1913 as a world governing body to coordinate all of the national associations in the world. The FIFA held the first World Cup Championship tournament in 1930 in Montevideo, Uruguay. Today, soccer is the world's most popular sport.

WORLD CUP

1930	Uruguay	1950	Uruguay	1970	Brazil	1990	West Germany
1934	Italy	1954	West Germany	1974	West Germany	1994	Brazil
1938	Italy	1958	Brazil	1978	Argentina		
1942	No competition	1962	Brazil	1982	Italy		
1946	No competition	1966	England	1986	Argentina		

WORLD CUP—1994

FINAL GROUP STANDINGS

Group A	W	L	T	GF	GA	Pts
x–Romania	2	1	0	5	5	6
x–Switzerland	1	1	1	5	4	4
x–United States	1	1	1	3	3	4
y–Colombia	1	2	0	4	5	3
Group B						
x–Brazil	2	0	1	6	1	7
x–Sweden	1	0	2	6	4	5
y–Russia	1	2	0	7	6	3
y–Cameroon	0	2	1	3	11	1
Group C						
x–Germany	2	0	1	5	3	7
x–Spain	1	0	2	6	4	5
y–South Korea	0	1	2	4	5	2
y–Bolivia	0	2	1	1	4	1
Group D						
x–Nigeria	2	1	0	6	2	6
x–Bulgaria	2	1	0	6	3	6
x–Argentina	2	1	0	6	3	6
y–Greece	0	3	0	0	10	0
Group E						
x–Mexico	1	1	1	3	3	4
x–Ireland	1	1	1	2	2	4
x–Italy	1	1	1	2	2	4
y–Norway	1	1	1	1	1	4
Group F						
x–Netherlands	2	1	0	4	3	6
x–Saudi Arabia	2	1	0	4	3	6
x–Belgium	2	1	0	2	1	6
y–Morocco	0	3	0	2	4	0

x–Advance to next round. y–Eliminated.

QUARTERFINALS
Italy 2, Spain 1
Brazil 3, Netherlands 2

Bulgaria 2, Germany 1
Sweden 2, Romania 2 (Sweden won 5–4 in shootout)

SEMIFINALS
Italy 2, Bulgaria 1
Brazil 1, Sweden 0

CHAMPIONSHIP
Italy 0, Brazil 0 (Brazil won 3–2 in shootout)

BRAZIL WINS RECORD FOURTH WORLD CUP ON SHOOTOUT

Brazil became the first country to win four World Cup championships and the first ever to win on a penalty kick shootout as the first World Cup tournament ever played in the United States ended on a high note.

The championship, Brazil's first since 1970, when it defeated Italy 4–1 at Mexico City, came as Brazil won the post-game penalty kick shootout, 3–2.

The game ended in a 0–0 tie.

The teams played 90 minutes of regulation and 30 minutes of overtime before the shootout.

Romario, Branco, and Dunga recorded the shootout scores for Brazil. Albergio Evani and Demetrio Albertini converted the penalty kicks for Italy.

With Italy trailing 3–2 and one opportunity left to keep the shootout going, Roberto Baggio's shot sailed over the crossbar, clinching the championship for Brazil.

Brazil had the best scoring opportunity of the game in the second overtime, when Romario found himself alone in front of the goal, having only to beat the Italian goalie Gianluca Pagliuca. But he shanked the ball and the ball rolled slowly wide of the net.

WORLD CUP
All-Time Top 10

	Tourneys	Total Games	Record (W–L–T)	Total Pts
1. Brazil	14	66	44–11–11	99
2. West Germany	12	68	39–14–15	93
3. Italy	12	54	31–11–12	74
4. Argentina	10	48	24–15–9	57
5. England	9	41	18–11–12	48
6. Uruguay	9	37	15–14–8	38
7. Soviet Union	7	31	15–10–6	36
8. France	9	34	15–14–5	35
9. Yugoslavia	8	33	14–12–7	35
10. Hungary	9	32	15–14–3	33
Spain	8	32	13–12–7	33

TOURNAMENT TO EXPAND TO 32 TEAMS IN 1998

Soccer's world governing body, the Federation Internationale de Football Association, voted in 1994 to expand the World Cup from 24 to 32 teams, beginning with the 1998 tournament, to be held in France. The tournament's first round will expand to eight groups of four, with the two top teams in each group advancing to the second round. Previously, there were six groups with the two top teams and the four best third place teams advancing.

U.S. PRO LEAGUES—OUTDOOR

National Professional Soccer League (1967)

Not sanctioned by FIFA, the international soccer federation. The NPSL recruited individual players to fill the rosters of its 10 teams. The leage lasted only one season with the Oakland Clippers beating the Baltimore Bays on the basis of goal differential.

United Soccer Association (1967)

Sanctioned by FIFA. Originally called the North American Soccer League, it became the USA to avoid being confused with the National Professional Soccer League. Instead of recruiting individual players, the USA imported 12 entire teams from Europe to represent its 12 franchises. It, too, only lasted a season. The league champion Los Angeles Wolves were actually Wolverhampton of England and the runner-up Washington Whips were Aberdeen of Scotland.

North American Soccer League (1968–1984)

The NPSL and USA merged to form the NASL in 1968 and the new league lasted until 1985. The NASL championship was known as the Soccer Bowl from 1975–84. One game decided the NASL title every year but five.

NORTH AMERICAN SOCCER LEAGUE CHAMPIONS

1968—Atlanta Chiefs	1973—Philadelphia Atoms	1978—New York Cosmos	1982—New York Cosmos
1969—Kansas City Stars	1974—Los Angeles Aztecs	1979—Vancouver Whitecaps	1983—Tulsa Roughnecks
1970—Rochester Lancers	1975—Tampa Bay Rowdies	1980—New York Cosmos	1984—Chicago Sting
1971—Dallas Tornado	1976—Toronto Metro–Croatia	1981—Chicago Sting	
1972—New York Cosmos	1977—New York Cosmos		

MAJOR LEAGUE SOCCER
1996 Final Standings

Conference champions (*) and playoff qualifiers (+) are noted. SOW refers to shootout wins. Teams receive three points for a win but just one point for a shootout win. SOW are included in W (win) column. The GF and GA columns refer to Goals For and Goals Against in regulation play.

EASTERN CONFERENCE

	W	L	Pts	GF	GA	SOW
*Tampa Bay	20	12	58	66	51	1
+D.C. United	16	16	46	62	56	1
+N.Y./N.J.	15	17	39	45	47	3
+Columbus	15	17	37	59	60	4
New England	15	17	33	43	56	6

Eastern Conference Semifinals
D.C. United defeats New York/New Jersey 2–1
Tampa Bay defeats Columbus 2–1.

Eastern Conference Finals
D.C. United wins series 2–0, advances to MLS Cup.
Oct. 10—at D.C. United 4, Tampa Bay 1
Oct. 12—D.C. United 2, at Tampa Bay 1

WESTERN CONFERENCE

	W	L	Pts	GF	GA	SOW
*Los Angeles	19	13	49	59	49	4
+Dallas	17	15	41	50	48	5
+Kansas City	17	15	41	61	63	5
+San Jose	15	17	39	50	50	3
Colorado	11	21	29	44	59	2

Western Conference Semifinals
Kansas City defeats Dallas 2–1.
Los Angeles defeats San Jose 2–1.

Western Conference Finals
Los Angeles wins series 2–0, advances to MLS Cup.
Oct. 10—at Los Angeles 2, Kansas City 1
Oct. 13—Los Angeles 2, at Kansas City 1

MLS CUP
Oct. 20, Foxboro Stadium, Massachusetts
D.C. United 3, Los Angeles Galaxy 2 (OT)

Los Angeles Galaxy	1	1	0	—	2
D.C. United	0	2	1	—	3

First half—1, Los Angeles, Hurtado (Cienfuegos) 5th minute.
Second half—2, Los Angeles, Armas (unassisted) 56th minute.

3, D.C., Sanneh (Etcheverry) 73rd minute. 4, D.C., Medved (unassisted) 82nd minute. Overtime—5, D.C., Pope (Etcheverry) 94th minute. Goalies—Los Angeles, Campos (7 shots, 4 saves), D.C., Simpson (4 shots, 2 saves). Attendance: 34,643.

1996 REGULAR SEASON

LEADING SCORERS

	Gm	G	A	Pts
Roy Lassiter, Tampa Bay	30	27	5	58
Preki, Kansas City	32	18	13	49
Eduardo Hurtado, Los Angeles	26	21	7	49
Raul Diaz Arce, Washington	28	23	2	48
Brian McBride, Columbus	28	17	3	37
Eric Wynalda, San Jose	27	10	13	33

	Gm	G	A	Pts
Vitalis Takawira, Kansas City	28	13	7	33
Steve Rammel, Washington	26	14	4	32
Paul Bravo, San Jose	31	13	5	31
Jason Kreis, Dallas	31	13	5	31
Giovanni Savarese, New York	26	13	1	27
Marco Etcheverry, Washington	26	4	19	27

GOALS

	G	Pts
Roy Lassiter, Tampa Bay	30	27
Raul Diaz Arce, Washington	28	23
Eduardo Hurtado, Los Angeles	26	21
Preki, Kansas City	32	18
Brian McBride, Columbus	28	17
Steve Rammel, Washington	26	14
Giovanni Savarese, New York	26	13
Vitalis Takawira, Kansas City	28	13
Paul Bravo, San Jose	31	13
Jason Kreis, Dallas	31	13

ASSISTS

	Gm	No
Marco Etcheverry, Washington	26	19
Carlos Valderrama, Tampa Bay	23	17
Eric Wynalda, San Jose	27	13
Preki, Kansas City	32	13
Mauricio Cienfuegos, Los Angeles	28	11
Robert Warzycha, Columbus	20	10
Tab Ramos, New York	25	10
Adrian Paz, Columbus	27	10
Billy Thompson, Columbus	24	9
Mark Chung, Kansas City	32	9

LEADING GOALTENDERS

(Minimum 1,395 mins)

	Gm	Min	Shots	Svs	GAA	W–L
J. Campos, L.A.	24	2,025	131	92	1.20	13–8
T. Meola, N.Y.	29	2,610	198	143	1.31	14–15
M. Dodd, Dal.	31	2,776	240	161	1.46	17–14

	Gm	Min	Shots	Svs	GAA	W–L
M. Dougherty, T.B.	28	2,520	192	117	1.68	17–14
A. Heaney, N.E.	19	1,534	133	90	1.70	8–9
Tom Liner, S.J.	20	1,712	125	74	1.73	7–12
G. Lagerwey, K.C.	23	1,959	140	83	1.75	12–9
C. Woods, Colo.	23	2,070	159	97	1.87	8–15
J. Causey, Wash.	19	1,620	114	69	1.94	9–10

SAVES

	Gm	No
Mark Dodd, Dallas	31	161
Tony Meola, New York	29	143
Mark Dougherty, Tampa Bay	28	117
Chris Woods, Colorado	23	97
Jorge Campos, Los Angeles	24	92
Aidan Heaney, New England	19	90
Garth Lagerwey, Kansas City	23	83
Tom Liner, San Jose	20	74
Jeff Causey, Washington	19	69
Bo Oshoniyi, Colorado	13	64

SHUTOUTS

	Gm	No
Tony Meola, New York	29	9
Mark Dodd, Dallas	31	6
Brad Friedel, Columbus	9	4
Aidan Heaney, New England	19	4
Tom Liner, San Jose	10	4
Jorge Campos, Los Angeles	24	4

Seven tied with three each.

CHESS

WORLD CHAMPIONS

The chess world continued to be divided as the Professional Chess Association (PCA) and the International Chess Association (FIDE) held separate world championship matches in 1995 and 1996, respectively. Efforts to reunite the two titles stalled. In December 1995, Garry Kasparov successfully defended his PCA title against Viswanathan Anand of India. In June–July 1996, Anatoly Karpov retained his FIDE title in a match against Gata Kamsky, a former U.S. champion.

1894–1921	Emanuel Lasker, Germany
1921–27	Jose R. Capablanca, Cuba
1927–35	Alexander A. Alekhine, U.S.S.R.
1935–37	Dr. Max Euwe, Netherlands
1937–46	Alexander A. Alekhine, U.S.S.R.[1]
1948–57	Mikhail Botvinnik, U.S.S.R.
1957–58	Vassily Smyslov, U.S.S.R.
1958–60	Mikhail Botvinnik, U.S.S.R.
1960–61	Mikhail Tal, U.S.S.R.
1961–63	Mikhail Botvinnik, U.S.S.R.
1963–68	Tigran Petrosian, U.S.S.R.
1969–71	Boris Spassky, U.S.S.R.
1972–74	Bobby Fischer, Los Angeles
1975	Bobby Fischer[2], Anatoly Karpov, U.S.S.R.
1976–85	Anatoly Karpov, U.S.S.R.[3]
1985–	Garry Kasparov, Russia[4]
1993–	Anatoly Karpov[5]

1. Alekhine, a French citizen, died while champion. 2. Relinquished title. 3. In 1978, Karpov defeated Viktor Korchnoi 6 games to 5. 4. PCA world champion after 1993. 5. FIDE world champion.

UNITED STATES CHAMPIONS

1909–36	Frank J. Marshall, New York
1936–44	Samuel Reshevsky, New York[1]
1944–46	Arnold S. Denker, New York
1946	Samuel Reshevsky, Boston
1948	Herman Steiner, Los Angeles
1951–52	Larry Evans, New York
1954–57	Arthur Bisguier, New York
1958–61	Bobby Fischer, Brooklyn, N.Y.
1962	Larry Evans, New York
1963–67	Bobby Fischer, New York
1968	Larry Evans, New York
1969–71	Samuel Reshevsky, Spring Valley, N.Y.
1972	Robert Byrne, Ossining, N.Y.
1973	Lubomir Kavalek, Washington; John Grefe, San Francisco
1974–77	Walter Browne, Berkeley, Calif.
1978–79	Lubomir Kavalek, New York
1980	Tie, Walter Browne, Berkeley, Calif. Larry Christiansen, Modesto, Calif. Larry Evans, Reno, Nev.
1981–82[2]	Tie, Walter Browne, Berkeley, Calif. Yasser Seirawan, Seattle, Wash.
1983	Tie, Walter Browne, Berkeley, Calif. Larry Christiansen, Los Angeles, Calif., Roman Dzindzichashvili, Corona, N.Y.
1984–85	Lev Alburt, New York City
1986	Yasser Seirawan, Seattle, Wash.
1987	Tie—Nick Defirmian, San Francisco, and Joel Benjamin, Brooklyn, N.Y.
1988	Michael Wilder, Princeton, N.J.
1989	Tie, Stuart Rachels, Birmingham, Ala. Yasser Seirawan, Seattle, Wash. Roman Dzindzichashvili, New York, N.Y.
1990–91	Lev Alburt, New York, N.Y.
1992	Gata Kamsky, Brooklyn, N.Y. Patrick Wolff, Somerville, Mass.
1993	Alexander Shabalov, Pittsburgh, Pa. and Alex Yermolinsky, Edison, N.J.
1994	Boris Gulko, Fairlawn, N.J.
1995	Patrick Wolff, Somerville, Mass.
1996	Alex Yermolinsky, Cleveland, Ohio

1. In 1942, Isaac I. Kashdan of New York was co-champion for a while because of a tie with Reshevsky in that year's tournament. Reshevsky won the play-off. 2. Championship not contested in 1982.

SPORTS ORGANIZATIONS AND BUREAUS

(Note: Addresses are subject to change. An asterisk after a name indicates that no reply to questionnaire was received.)

Amateur Athletic Union of the U.S. The Walt Disney World Resort, P.O. Box 10,000, Lake Buena Vista, Fla. 32830-1000. (407) 363-6170, fax (407) 363-6171.

Amateur Softball Association/USA Softball. 2801 N.E. 50th St., Oklahoma City, Okla. 73111

American Amateur Racquetball Association/International Racquetball Federation/Pan American Racquetball Confederation. 1685 West Uintah, Colorado Springs, Colo. 80904-2921

American Association of Professional Baseball Clubs. 6801 Miami Ave., Cincinnati, Ohio 45243

American Bowling Congress. 5301 South 76th St., Greendale, Wis. 53129–1127

American Hockey League. 425 Union St., West Springfield, Mass. 01089

American Horse Shows Association. 220 E. 42nd St., New York, N.Y. 10017–5876

American Kennel Club Inc. 51 Madison Ave., New York, N.Y. 10010

American League (baseball). 350 Park Ave., New York, N.Y. 10022

American Sportcasters Association, The. 5 Beekman St., New York, N.Y. 10038

Big Ten Conference, Inc. (1896). 1500 W. Higgins Rd., Park Ridge, Ill. 60068-6300

International Game Fish Association. 1301 E. Atlantic Blvd., Pompano Beach, Fla. 33060

International League of Professional Baseball Clubs, Inc. 55 S. High St., Ste. 202, Dublin, Ohio 43017

International Olympic Committee. Château de Vidy, Case Postale 356, 1001 Lausanne, Switzerland

International Tennis Hall of Fame. National Historic Landmark, Newport Casino, 194 Bellevue Ave., Newport, R.I. 02840. (401) 849-3990.

Little League Baseball. P.O. Box 3485, Williamsport, Pa. 17701

National Archery Association. One Olympic Plaza, Colorado Springs, Colo. 80909-5788. (719) 578-4576, fax (719) 632-4733, e-mail: 102036.3634@compuserve.com

National Association for Stock Car Auto Racing. P.O. Box 2875, Daytona Beach, Fla. 32120-2875

National Association of Intercollegiate Athletics. 6120 South Yale Ave., Ste. 1450, Tulsa, Okla. 74136

National Baseball Congress. P.O. Box 1420, Wichita, Kan. 67201

National Baseball Hall of Fame. P.O. Box 590, Cooperstown, N.Y. 13326-0590

National Collegiate Athletic Association. 6201 College Blvd., Overland Park, Kan. 66211-2422

National Duckpin Bowling Congress. 4991 Fairview Ave., Linthicum, Md. 21090

National Field Archery Association. 31407 Outer I–10, Redlands, Calif. 92373

National Football Foundation and College Hall of Fame Inc. 1865 Palmer Ave., Suite 103, Larchmont, N.Y. 10538.

National Football League. 410 Park Ave., New York, N.Y. 10022

National Hockey League.* 75 International Blvd., Ste. 300, Rexdale, Ont., Canada M9W 6L9

National Horseshoe Pitchers Association. 3085 76th Street, Franksville, Wis. 53126

National Hot Rod Association. P.O. Box 5555, Glendora, Calif. 91740-0750

National Junior College Athletic Association. P.O. Box 7305, Colorado Springs, Colo. 80933-7305

National Rifle Association of America. 11250 Waples Mill Rd., Fairfax, Va. 22030

National Shuffleboard Association. *Summer:* 2508 Westmoor Rd., Findlay, Ohio 45840. *Winter:* 904 52nd Ave. Lane. W., Bradenton, Fla. 34207

National Skeet Shooting Association.* 5931 Roft Rd., San Antonio, Tex. 78253-9261

National Sporting Clays Association. 5931 Roft Rd., San Antonio, Tex. 78253-9261

New York Racing Association, Inc. P.O. Box 90, Jamaica, N.Y. 11417

New York State Athletic Commission (boxing and wrestling). 270 Broadway, New York, N.Y. 10007

PGA Tour, Inc. 112 TPC Blvd., Sawgrass, Ponte Vedra, Fla. 32082

Pro Football Hall of Fame. 2121 George Halas Drive, N.W., Canton, Ohio 44708

Roller Skating Associations. 7301 Georgetown Rd., Ste. 123, Indianapolis, Ind. 46268

Thoroughbred Racing Assns. of N. America. 420 Fair Hill Dr., Ste. 1, Elkton, Md. 21921-2573

United States Amateur Boxing, Inc. One Olympic Plaza, Colorado Springs, Colo. 80909

United States Amateur Confederation of Roller Skating. P.O. Box 6579, Lincoln, Neb. 68506

United States Auto Club. 4910 West 16th St., Speedway, Ind. 46224

United States Sailing Association. P.O. Box 1260, Portsmouth, R.I. 02871

USA Baseball. 2160 Greenwood Ave., Trenton, N.J. 08609

USA Basketball. 5465 Mark Dabling Blvd., Colorado Springs, Colo. 80918-3842

USA Cycling Inc. One Olympic Plaza, Colorado Springs, Colo. 80909

USA Gymnastics. Pan American Plaza, 201 S. Capitol, Ste. 300, Indianapolis, Ind. 46225

USA Hockey, Inc. 4965 N. 30th St., Colorado Springs, Colo. 80919. (719) 549-5500

USA Track & Field. One Hoosier Dome, Ste. 140, Indianapolis, Ind. 46225.

U.S. Chess Federation. 186 Route 9W, New Windsor, N.Y. 12553. (914) 561-2437 (fax)

U.S. Fencing Association. One Olympic Plaza, Colorado Springs, Colo. 80909-5774

U.S. Figure Skating Association. 20 First St., Colorado Springs, Colo. 80906

U.S. Golf Association. Golf House, P.O. Box 708, Far Hills, N.J. 07931–0708. (908) 234-2300

U.S. Handball Association. 2333 N. Tucson Blvd. Tucson, Ariz. 85716. (520) 795-0434

U.S. Olympic Committee. One Olympic Plaza, Colorado Springs, Colo. 80909-5760

U.S. Orienteering Federation. Box 1444, Forest Park, Ga. 30051

US Rowing. Pan American Plaza, 201 S. Capitol Ave., Ste. 400, Indianapolis, Ind. 46225

U.S. Soccer Federation. 1801-1811 S. Prairie Ave., Chicago, Ill. 60616. (312) 808-1300

U.S. Tennis Association. 70 W. Red Oak Lane, White Plains, N.Y. 10604

U.S. Trotting Association. 750 Michigan Ave., Columbus, Ohio 43215

Women's International Bowling Congress. 5301 S. 76th St., Greendale, Wis. 53129-1191

The International Scene

By Arthur P. Reed, Jr.

Elections in Israel, Bosnia, Russia, and India set the political agenda for much of the international arena in 1996. Tenuous peace accords in Bosnia and Chechnya were overshadowed by renewed violence in Israel, Northern Ireland, and Africa.

Israel

Benjamin Netanyahu was elected Prime Minister to succeed Yitzhak Rabin, whose peacemaking efforts were cut short by his November 1995 assassination. Netanyahu and his Likud party capitalized on the growing concern among conservative Israelis that the peace plan pursued by Rabin would exchange land for peace. Orthodox voters were particularly opposed to the vision of a future Israel articulated by Netanyahu's rival Shimon Peres, which they believed would lead to further westernization at the expense of traditional Jewish culture. Though the U.S. had unofficially backed Peres, President Clinton welcomed Netanyahu to the White House in July, and both pledged to continue working toward peace in the Middle East. In September, the opening of a tourist tunnel near Islamic holy sites was perceived by Palestinians as the latest in a series of antagonistic actions by Israel. Skirmishes between Israeli troops and Palestinian police resulted in more than seventy deaths, mostly Palestinian. An emergency summit convened by President Clinton in early October was tainted by an air of mistrust among the parties, who questioned the new Israeli government's commitment to implementing agreements negotiated by previous administrations. The talks ended with no substantive agreements, but Netanyahu promised to resume peace talks with Palestinian leader Yasir Arafat.

Bosnia

Four years of ethnic fighting and atrocities that killed a quarter of a million people, destroyed thousands of homes, and appalled the international community were ended with a peace accord constructed by the U.S.-led contact group. In November 1995, the Balkan leaders—President Slobodan Milosevic of Serbia, Alija Izetbegovic of Bosnia, and Franjo Tudjman of Croatia—met at Wright-Patterson Air Force Base near Dayton, Ohio. After three weeks of talks, the parties agreed to divide Bosnia along ethnic lines, ensuring the survival of Muslims in Bosnia, and to provide some regional autonomy and self-government for the Serbs. The implementation of the plan was to be overseen by 60,000 NATO peacekeeping troops. President Clinton pledged one-third of the total troops to enforce the accord, which he termed a step to "a serious and lasting peace in Bosnia."

As 1996 wore on, attention turned from fighting the war to punishing those responsible for its most flagrant atrocities. In November 1995, Bosnian Serb leaders Radko Mladic and Radovan Karadzic were indicted by the International War Crimes Tribunal for ordering and carrying out a campaign of genocide against Muslims. However, neither man was arrested and concerns mounted throughout 1996 that they would go unpunished in exchange for peace.

Despite concerns voiced by Muslims prior to the September 14 elections that those voting in Serbian territories would be subjected to intimidation, the elections were largely free from incident. The Bosnian Muslim leader, President Alija Izetbegovic, won the majority of votes to become the leader of the three-member presidency specified in the Dayton peace accord.

Russia

Boris N. Yeltsin won an overwhelming majority of the votes in the runoff election held in July, an outcome that belied the underlying divisions that characterized the original election held a month earlier. The June election pitted Yeltsin against Communist Party leader Gennady Zyuganov and an ultra-nationalist, Vladimir Zhirinovsky. Neither Yeltsin nor Zyuganov garnered sufficient votes for a decisive victory, so a runoff election was scheduled for July. The Communist platform called for an end to Yeltsin's market reforms and a return to state-controlled enterprises, though the intent was carefully veiled to allay the fears of non-Communist voters and Western governments. The threat posed by the hard-line candidate was significant: the Communists had won nearly one-third of the seats in Parliament in the December 1995 election, and had formed alliances with the Agrarian Party and the Nationalists, thereby marginalizing the reformers. Yeltsin successfully managed to marshal his own resources, however. He halted hostilities in Chechnya, which had caused divisions within the reform party, and secured endorsements based on his ability to prevent the regression the Communists stood for.

But the war in Chechnya continued to torment Yeltsin. He had failed to recognize the intensity of the ethnic feeling in the region, and had paid the political price when the war erupted and threatened his chances for reelection. He had capitalized on the opportunity presented by the war, however, making its end a key campaign promise. After the June election and before the runoff, Yeltsin appointed Alexander I. Lebed, an army critic of the war and candidate in the 1996 presidential elections, as security chief. Lebed visited Chechnya twice, and late in the summer announced a cease-fire. The parties also agreed to postpone a decision regarding the status of Chechnya until December 31, 2001.

The success of the campaign was soon overshadowed by concerns about Yeltsin's health. Plagued with bouts of depression and insomnia and prone to excessive drinking, Yeltsin, now 65, was also faced with serious heart problems. The August 9 inaugural ceremony was kept short, with Yeltsin speaking for less than a minute. In September, Yeltsin acquiesced to his doctors' recommendations and scheduled coronary bypass surgery. Cardiac specialists from the U.S. and Germany flew to Moscow to offer advice and aid in the surgery, while Yeltsin's political opponents called for him to step down. Prime Minister Viktor Chernomyrdin's role is likely to expand as Yeltsin's health makes it impossible for him to effectively maintain the concentration of power he orchestrated in his first term.

India

More than 590 million eligible voters chose among more than 14,000 candidates in elections that took place between April 27 and May 30, in what was described as the largest democratic exercise in the world. The primary issue was the economy and recent market reforms. The Congress party, beset by recent scandals and architect of the free market reforms, insisted that the reforms have improved the economy and enabled India to better compete. Critics declare that the reforms have westernized the country and have benefited only the upper classes. Fighting by rebel factions seeking independence—Muslim guerrillas in Jammu and Kashmir—was suspended during the elections.

The Hindu nationalist party, the Bharatiya Janata Party or BJP, won a majority of the Parliamentary seats and formed a coalition government with Atal Bihari Vajpayee as prime minister. But Vajpayee was forced to resign 13 days later to avoid certain defeat in a confidence vote. Though they had come in second in the election, the Congress party declared its support of the third-placed United Front, comprising 13 political parties representing socialist and lower-caste voters. The United Front chose Deve Gowda, who was sworn in as Prime Minister on June 1. The new government called for continued economic reform, but at a slower pace, and for investment to improve technology and infrastructure. In a nod toward communist constituents, the leaders called for protectionist policies to discourage international investment in consumer goods. India vetoed the U.N. nuclear test ban treaty, and Gowda declared that India would reserve the right to build nuclear weapons.

Other Global Events

Afghanistan. In September, President Burhanuddin Rabbani and Prime Minister Gulbuddin Hekmatyar were overthrown in a coup by the Taliban militia, a group of fundamentalists who declared their intention to impose strict Islamic rule, including dress codes for men and women, draconian restrictions on the rights of women, and severe corporal punishments for violation of Islamic law. The Talibans hanged former (1987–92) president Mohammad Najibullah, who had been backed by the Kremlin. After taking the capital, the Taliban militia controlled two-thirds of the country; and with the seven ethnically diverse northern regions outside Taliban control, continued fighting seems likely.

Africa. Simmering tensions in Burundi erupted in July in a massacre of more than 300 Tutsis by Hutu extremists. Later that month, a coup led by Tutsi Maj. Pierre Buyoya deposed Hutu President Sylvestre Ntibantung. Buyoya said he had seized power to prevent further ethnic killing, though international agencies refused to recognize the new government. Ethnic fighting between the majority Hutus and the minority Tutsis, who control the military, has erupted recently in the region, which saw more than 500,000 people killed in neighboring Rwanda in 1994 in genocidal conflicts. As millions of refugees fled into surrounding countries, particularly Zaire, resources were scarce and disease rampant. Despite the poor living conditions of the refugee camps, many Hutus refused to return to Rwanda for fear of retaliation from the Tutsi-controlled government. War crimes trials began amidst skepticism that high-level Rwandan officials responsible for inciting genocide would be captured and brought to justice.

Liberia. Two months of warfare in the spring killed more than 3,000 people and largely destroyed the capital, Monrovia. A cease fire was signed in August, allowing aid workers to provide food to refugees who had been hiding during the seven months of factional fighting. More than 150,000 have died since the civil war began in 1989.

Northern Ireland. The IRA broke a seventeen-month cease fire in February, and had not renewed it by September. Peace talks continued throughout the year, but were beset by infighting that stymied negotiators, led by former U.S. Senator George Mitchell. The IRA's political wing, Sinn Fein, has been excluded from negotiations because they refuse to renounce violence in dealing with Britain.

Iraq. Saddam Hussein ordered troops into a Kurdish enclave in northern Iraq in August, provoking the U.S. into launching 44 missiles in two separate strikes directed at Iraqi military installations. Hussein claimed he was responding to a request from one of the Kurdish rebel factions for help in fighting off a rival, Iranian-backed faction. Clinton perceived the move as another in a series of Iraqi maneuvers designed to test U.S. resolve in enforcing the covenants that ended the Gulf War. The U.S. reaction was deemed as overzealous by many Gulf War allies, but was also criticized domestically for being too soft on Iraq.

Guatemala. A final cease-fire ending 36 years of civil war became more likely when guerrilla leaders and army officers signed an agreement in September to reduce the size and budget for the military, and to disband elite squads. Agrarian reforms and rights for indigenous people were top concerns for the rebels, who also called for civilian control of the military. More than 140,000 have died in the war, mostly civilians. A final accord is expected to be signed in Madrid by the end of the year.

The National Scene

By Arthur P. Reed, Jr.

With the specter of a reelection campaign looming before them, the Republican Congress and the Democratic President saw 1996 as the time to make good on previous campaign pledges. Legislation that had lain dormant since the 1994 elections was suddenly revived, debated, and voted upon, with both parties managing to take credit for every bill that passed and was signed into law by the president. Key laws enacted in 1996 that met 1992 campaign promises include welfare reform, an increase in the minimum wage, and health care reform. The political conventions in August gave the parties a forum in which to articulate their agenda, and apart from the disagreements within the Republican party over abortion, both events were carefully scripted to minimize surprises. Speakers were scheduled to maximize the impact of prime-time network coverage, despite low ratings for both conventions.

As promised, the welfare-reform bill ended "welfare as we know it." The law replaced federal payments to impoverished and disabled individuals with lump sum payments to states, who then decide how to distribute the funds and to whom. The main provisions were as follows:

• the head of every welfare family must work within two years or the family loses benefits

• states must maintain their own welfare spending at 75 percent of the 1994 level, or 80 percent if they fail to put sufficient numbers of welfare recipients to work

• future legal immigrants who have not become citizens will be ineligible for most federal welfare benefits and social services during their first five years in the U.S.

• eligibility standards were tightened to exclude many disabled children in low-income families seeking Supplemental Insurance income

• lifetime welfare benefits are limited to five years (though up to 20 percent of families may be exempted due to hardship)

• states generally must deny benefits to anyone convicted of drug felonies (some exceptions)

States anticipate that it will be several months before some provisions are implemented, due to practical considerations such as capacity on computers to track recipients. Though the bill cuts $56 billion in federal expenditures, Clinton signed it only reluctantly because it was more severe than the plan he had envisioned. His decision to sign the bill drew sharp criticism from his fellow Democrats, and Clinton acknowledged that the bill "has serious flaws"; action to remedy these flaws seems likely after the election.

In a show of the power of party unity, and despite opposition from small businesses and many Republicans, Clinton worked with the Democrats to enact a bill to raise the minimum wage by 90 cents per hour to $5.15. The Republicans also claimed victory in this bill, however, having included financial benefits for small businesses and tax breaks for consumers. Known as the Small Business Job Protection Act, it covers many nonwage issues, including a tax credit for adopting children, a phase-out of the special levy on new luxury cars, and a simpler pension plan administration. It also temporarily reinstates tax exemptions for employees who receive education assistance.

The health-care reform bill was not the ambitious overhaul Clinton had promised in his 1992 campaign. Rather, he was forced to accept incremental reform when it was passed by Congress. The Senate voted unanimously to approve the bill, sponsored by Senators Nancy Kassebaum (R-Kansas) and Edward Kennedy (D-Mass.), and the House passed it with only two dissenting votes. The key provisions allow workers to keep health insurance when changing jobs, and prevent insurance companies from denying coverage for those with preexisting conditions.

The costs of treating tobacco users received increased attention this year, with several states suing tobacco companies to recover the money spent to treat smokers who are Medicaid recipients. In an effort to curtail cigarette use among teenagers, President Clinton announced a series of curbs on cigarette advertising directed toward children, and introduced plans for the FDA to regulate nicotine as a controlled substance.

Throughout late 1995 and early 1996, the White House and the Capitol battled over the budget, resulting in two partial government shutdowns when Congress refused to appropriate funds to continue operations. In April 1996, both sides agreed on a stopgap measure to fund government operations. In the "final" agreement, the Republicans achieved their goal of a $23 billion cut in discretionary spending, while the president got $5 billion in additional spending for jobs, education, and health programs.

The Conventions

The Republican National Convention, held in San Diego in early August, nominated former Senate majority leader Bob Dole for president and Jack Kemp for vice president. Dole's nomination, like much of the convention, came as no surprise; it had been guaranteed by a series of victories in the primaries.

Delegates to the convention had threatened a floor battle when, a week before the convention, the platform committee had included a constitutional amendment outlawing all abortions. The public display of party discord was averted, however, when Dole and other Republican leaders agreed to allow dissenters to the platform to publish their views in a platform appendix. The main platform reflected extreme conservative views on issues such as immigration, criminal punishment, civil rights for homosexuals, education, welfare, and the environment.

Dole sought to soft-pedal disputes within the G.O.P. during his acceptance speech, mentioning the abortion issue only briefly. He focused on his life experience (rather than his 35-year career in the House and Senate) and presented himself as "a man of the people who has the maturity to lead." He emphasized that the G.O.P. "is broad and inclusive," and "open to citizens of every race and religion." His assertions were bolstered by endorsements, which ranged from right-wing extremist (and erstwhile opponent) Patrick Buchanan to the more moderate Gov. Pete Wilson of California.

As he opened his campaign, Dole promised to emphasize drugs, crime, and the economy. Dole's economic plan called for a 15 percent tax cut and a balanced budget "as a sure way to restore the promise of America." In a reversal of his earlier skepticism, Dole also espoused Reagan's supply-side economics.

The Democratic National Convention met in Chicago, where tumult and antiwar protests had marked their 1968 convention. As expected, the delegates nominated President Bill Clinton and Vice President Al Gore for re-election. The party emphasized its diversity with its choice of speakers, including Hillary Clinton, Jesse Jackson, and Christopher Reeve, who advocated increased funding for medical research. As the convention awaited Mr. Clinton, Vice President Gore contrasted the president with Bob Dole and Jack Kemp. "In his speech from San Diego, Senator Dole offered himself as a bridge to the past. Tonight, Bill Clinton and I offer ourselves as a bridge to the future."

The president arrived at the convention after a four-day whistle-stop campaign trip throughout the Midwest. In a triumphant climax, he accepted the nomination and continued Gore's theme as he pledged to "build a bridge to the 21st century." He declared that "hope is back in America" and promised to protect programs for children, the elderly, and the environment from Republican budget-cutting. Clinton vowed to create "a strong American community where everyone has a place and plays a role."

Ross Perot staved off a challenge from former Colorado Gov. Richard Lamm to win nomination from the Reform Party that he founded in 1992. Perot's popularity has waned since the 1992 election, however, and his campaign was further hindered when the bipartisan Commission on Presidential Debates decided to exclude Perot. Perot filed suit to appeal the decision, but the decision was upheld.

The Final Days of the 104th Congress

Eager to end the year on a high note before heading home to begin campaigning, the 104th Congress voted on several significant pieces of legislation in September. A law making it legal for states to refuse to recognize same-sex marriages was passed by the Senate and signed quietly by the president. The so-called Defense of Marriage Act was passed overwhelmingly in the House in July. The bill denies homosexual partners federal benefits accorded to spouses, such as Medicare and Social Security. A separate measure outlawing workplace discrimination based on sexual orientation was defeated in the Senate by one vote.

Spending measures were also approved, with little of the acrimonious debate that characterized the earlier budget battles. A bill that provides funding for programs from housing to space exploration also included a provision mandating that insurance companies pay for a minimum 48 hour hospital stay for new mothers. The bill also addressed iniquities in the coverage for mental illness. Finally, a bill meant to curb illegal immigration passed the House in the final week of September.

CURRENT EVENTS

What Happened in 1996

Highlights of the important events of the year from January to October 1996, organized month by month, in three categories for easy reference. For the year's major Supreme Court decisions, see page 653. The Countries of the World section (starting on page 143) covers specific international events, country by country.

JANUARY 1996
International

Bosnian Serbs Accused of Abductions (Jan. 2): Government charges seizure of at least 16 civilians traveling through Sarajevo suburbs. Calls act a violation of Dayton, Ohio, peace agreement. (**Jan. 4**): Under pressure from NATO and U.S., Serbs back down and agree to free the captives.

Bomb Kills Palestinian Terrorist (Jan. 5): "The Engineer," most wanted by Israel, dies in Gaza Strip in explosion of booby-trapped cellular telephone. Believed behind suicide bombings.

Chechens Capture 2,000 Russians (Jan. 9): Storm hospital in southern Russian city of Kizlyar and seize hostages in move to compel Russian troop withdrawal from Chechnya. (**Jan. 18**): In fierce attack, Russian troops overcome remaining rebels and free many hostages.

Appeals Court Panel Rebuffs Clinton (Jan. 9): Rules President cannot delay trial to defend himself against sexual harassment charges by former Arkansas aide.

New Japanese Prime Minister (Jan. 11): Ryutaro Hashimoto pledges "reform and creativity," but names Cabinet likely to continue existing policies.

Peru Sentences American Woman for Treason (Jan. 11): Military court metes life term to Lori Helene Berenson of New York, found guilty of aiding Marxist guerrilla terrorists. U.S. protests proceedings.

Clinton Praises Troops in Bosnia (Jan. 13): On visit to war-torn area, he praises troops as "warriors for peace." He announces new campaign medal for service.

Polish Prime Minister Resigns (Jan. 24): Josef Oleksy, in TV address, declares that he is innocent of charges that he had spied for Moscow for more than a decade.

Yeltsin Appoints Soviet-Era Official (Jan. 25): Names Vladimir V. Kadanikov, industrialist, as top economic executive, in sign of weakening of reforms.

Senate Ratifies Major Arms Treaty (Jan. 26): Approves strategic arms reduction pact three years after signing by President Bush and Russian President Yeltsin. Fate in Russian Parliament uncertain.

Mexico Repaying Part of U.S. Loan (Jan. 26): Announces plan to repay $1.3 billion borrowed in 1995. Economic recovery credited for decision to repay installment.

France Announces End to Nuclear Tests (Jan. 29): Underground blast in South Pacific is last in series protested by allies and many other countries.

Clinton Confident on Russian Reforms (Jan. 30): After meeting with Prime Minister Chernomyrdin, he says he expects market advances to continue.

National

Senate G.O.P. Votes to Reopen Offices (Jan. 2): In break with House, agrees to brief action while President and Congress debate budget balancing.

U.S. Budget Crisis in Fourth Month (Jan. 3): Government shutdown passes 19th day with no sign of resolution in budget-balancing talks with White House. Republicans in Congress divided. (**Jan. 5**): Congress votes to put 760,000 federal workers back on payroll for three weeks. (**Jan. 25**): House passes measure to avert third shutdown. (**Jan. 27**): Senate also approves legislation for reduced spending.

Clinton Approves Return of Workers (Jan. 6): Signs bill to resume many shuttered government operations. Budget negotiations with G.O.P. continue.

Martin Luther King, Jr., Honored (Jan. 15): In Atlanta address, Clinton tells audience King would probably have applauded nation's peace-keeping efforts abroad and progress toward social equality at home.

Clinton Gives State of the Union Address (Jan. 23): Offers own version of limited government and lays out series of challenges to nation, including steps to provide educational opportunities, economic security, and freedom from crime. In G.O.P. response, Dole calls Clinton "almost the last public defender of a discredited status quo."

U.S. Approves Fat Substitute for Snacks (Jan. 24): F.D.A. sanctions Olestra despite possible side effects.

Hillary Clinton Testifies on Records (Jan. 26): Tells federal grand jury in Whitewater inquiry she cannot explain finding of law firm's records.

Oregon Elects Democratic Senator (Jan. 31): In mail ballot, state chooses first Democrat in 34 years, Representative Ron Wyden, liberal.

General

Global Warming Climbs to Record (Jan. 3): Scientists report Earth's average surface temperature rose to a record high in 1995. Fossil fuels blamed.

Retailers Report Bad Shopping Season (Jan. 4): Merchants call December figures worst since recession of 1990–91. Stormy weather called a factor.

Blizzard Cripples Much of East (Jan. 7): Record-breaking storm drives up eastern seaboard with heavy damage. Transportation crippled; thousands stranded. Three feet of snow blankets entire region.

Plane Crash Kills 250 in Zaire (Jan. 8): Cargo aircraft hits crowded market in center of Kinshasa, capital. Most of victims are women and children.

Sheik Sentenced to Life for Bomb Plot (Jan. 17): Blind Omar Abdel Rahman, 57, gets prison term in U.S. court after conviction of conspiring in terrorist acts to force U.S. to end support for Israel and Egypt.

Shuttle Retrieves Japanese Science Satellite (Jan. 20): Space craft *Endeavour* lands at night at Cape Canaveral after nine-day flight covering 3.7 million miles. Crew members took two space walks.

Thousands Flee Floods in Northeast (Jan. 20): Driven from homes by rising waters after blizzard. At least 15 deaths are reported. City of Wilkes–Barre evacuated. Rising rivers wash out roads and bridges from Virginia to New England.

Du Pont Heir Held in Murder (Jan. 28): Pennsylvania police arrest John E. du Pont, 57, on charge of killing David Schultz, a former Olympic wrestling champion. Capture follows a 48-hour stand-off.

Rebels' Blast Kills 53 in Sri Lanka (Jan. 31): Some 1,400 injured as explosive-laden truck rams central bank in Colombo's financial district.

FEBRUARY 1996
International

At Least 73 Dead in Sri Lanka Bombing (Feb. 1): Colombo center recovering from suicide attack linked to Tamil rebels. Two accomplices arrested.

Russian Coal Miners Strike (Feb. 1): Nearly half a million defy President in walkout seeking $200 million in unpaid wages. **(Feb. 3):** Government rushes money to end strike and promises $2.2 million allocation to coal industry this year.

Land Mine Kills U.S. Soldier in Bosnia (Feb. 3): First American serviceman to die since NATO–led peace–keeping mission began. Clinton expresses regret.

New Haitian President Takes Office (Feb. 7): René Préval succeeds Jean-Bertrand Aristide.

China Sale of Atom–Arms Parts Revealed (Feb. 7): U.S. says Beijing secretly sold technology to Pakistan.

Yeltsin Seeks a Second Term (Feb. 15): Russian President says he alone could prevent Communist victory in June election and continue reforms.

Balkan Leaders Reach Accord (Feb. 18): Presidents of Serbia, Croatia, and Bosnia agree in NATO–sponsored conference to recommit regimes to full compliance with all provisions of peace accord.

Bomb Wrecks London Bus; One Dead, Nine Injured (Feb. 18): Irish Republican Army claims responsibility. Dead victim reported to have been carrying bomb.

Defectors From Iraq Slain After Return (Feb. 23): Two sons-in-law of Saddam Hussein killed by family after denunciation as "disappointed traitors."

Clinton Punishes Cuba for Air Attack (Feb. 26): President denounces downing of two private American planes. Suspends all air charter travel and pledges to seek tighter economic sanctions.

Peres Pledges War on Palestinian Terrorists (Feb. 26): In response to deadly suicide bombing, Israeli leader vows to wage a "methodical and incessant" war against Hamas, militant Islamic movement. Whole nation aroused.

Russians Attack Chechen Rebel Stronghold (Feb. 29): Report 170 secessionists killed in fortified town. Doubts cast on Yeltsin pledge to end warfare.

National

Congress Revises Communications Laws (Feb. 1): Both houses vote for measure favored by Clinton, to promote rivalry between local telephone companies, long-distance carriers and cable television operators. **(Feb. 8):** Clinton signs measure.

Unexpected Shortfall in Medicare Fund (Feb. 4): New government data show Hospital Insurance Trust lost money in 1995 for first time since 1972.

Governors Agree on Medicaid Plan (Feb. 5): Conference accepts bipartisan proposal to remove a major stumbling block in Washington budget impasse.

Court Orders Clinton to Testify in Trial (Feb. 5): U.S. judge orders President to appear as defense witness in bank fraud and conspiracy case involving former partners in Whitewater land venture.

Clinton Reluctantly Signs Defense Bill (Feb. 10): Approves $265 billion measure but promises not to enforce "discriminatory" provision that requires Pentagon to discharge troops with AIDS virus.

Opponents Agree on Pollution Rules (Feb. 11): Federal panel including industry and environmental groups reaches consensus that while existing system can be approved it must not be weakened.

Dole and Buchanan Lead in Iowa Caucuses (Feb. 12): Buchanan established as strong contender by taking second place ahead of Lamar Alexander.

Buchanan Wins New Hampshire Primary (Feb. 20): Victory over Senator Dole and other contenders has alarmed many Republicans who consider Buchanan an extremist; they debate how he can be stopped.

Former G.I. Charged With Spying (Feb. 23): Robert Stephan Lipka, 50, arrested and accused of betraying secrets to Soviet Union while working as Army employee at National Security Agency.

Navy Limits F–14 Fighter Pilots After Crashes (Feb. 24): Imposes new restrictions on fliers after three trouble-plagued jets crash in a month, killing four Navy airmen and three civilians.

Clinton Presses School–Pupil Attire (Feb. 24): President orders Federal Education Department to distribute manual telling nation's 16,000 school districts how they can legally enforce dress code.

Federal Judge Upholds Gingrich (Feb. 29): Rules House Speaker's political action committee, Gopac, did not make illegal campaign contributions.

General

Bitter Cold Grips Much of U.S. (Feb. 2): Midwest and South strangled. Temperatures below 60 degrees below zero in Minnesota, breaking 97-year record.

Earthquake in China Kills More Than 200 (Feb. 3): Levels thousands of mud-walled village homes in southern province of Yunnan. **(Feb. 4):** China mobilizes military and appeals for international assistance.

Plane Crash Kills 189 German Tourists in Atlantic (Feb. 6): Boeing 757 plunges into ocean about 13 miles offshore on flight from Dominican Republic. Debris spread over wide area. Many bodies recovered.

New Polish Government Sworn in (Feb. 7): Prime Minister and Cabinet replace regime toppled by allegations that its chief passed state secrets to Moscow.

I.M.F. Approves Loan for Russia (Feb. 8): Sanctions $1.05 billion in aid and expresses satisfaction with Moscow's economic reform progress.

I.R.A. Bomb Wounds 100 in London (Feb. 9): Explodes beneath train station in East London. Blast ending cease-fire imperils Northern Ireland talks. **(Feb. 10):** I.R.A. claims responsibility.

Joan Collins Wins Verdict Over Script (Feb. 13): New York jury rules actress can keep $1.2-million advance from Random House although its editors had deemed the novel unreadable and unpublishable.

Four TV Networks Plan Rating System (Feb. 14 et seq.): Broadcasters seek to meet growing public objection to sex and violence by code similar to Hollywood code for movies. Seek to avoid censorship.

Clinton Tours Flood-Ravaged Areas in West (Feb. 14): President promises speedy relief to victims in Oregon, Washington, and Idaho. Winter storm worst to strike region in 30 years.

Train Crash Kills 11 in Maryland (Feb. 16): Eight job corps members among victims of head-on collision of commuter and Amtrak trains at Silver Spring.

Oklahoma Bombing Trial Moved to Denver (Feb. 20): U.S. judge grants change of venue, ruling that Timothy J. McVeigh and Terry L. Nichols cannot get a fair trial anywhere in Oklahoma.

Tanker Spills Oil Off Welsh Coast (Feb. 21): Vessel refloated after releasing more than 70,000 tons of crude oil in one of Britain's most environmentally sensitive areas. Damage called far greater than 38,000 tons in *Exxon Valdez* disaster in Alaska. Wildlife experts accuse official of giving false estimates of damage.

Leg at Oklahoma Bomb Site Identified (Feb. 23): Found to belong to body of woman already buried, possibly with someone else's limb.

Cambodian Survivor Shot Dead on Coast (Feb. 26): Dr. Haing Ngor, 45–55 (age uncertain) was physician who later won Academy Award for debut acting performance in 1984 film "The Killing Fields."

MARCH 1996
International

European–Asian Partnership Pledged (March 2): Leaders end first economic conference in Thailand with agreement on trade and investment.

Suicide Bombers Kill 59 in Israel (March 4): Fourth attack in nine days strikes at Tel Aviv. Government promises to take war against terrorists into areas under Palestinian control.

Israelis Retaliate Against Palestinians (March 5): Troops weld houses shut and barricade residents in towns and villages in response to four attacks within nine days by terrorist suicide bombers.

Palestinians Arrest Three Hamas Leaders (March 10): Seize top officials of military wing of Hamas movement in response to mounting pressure from Israel after series of terrorist suicide bombings.

Egypt Conference Condemns Violence (March 13): Leaders of 27 nations, including Arabs, condemn wave of suicide bombing attacks in Israel. Vow to cooperate in combating terrorism and promoting Middle East peace.

Britain Alarmed by Deadly Cow Disease (March 20, et seq.): Government says there may be link between "mad cow" ailment and similar fatal brain disease in humans. **(March 27):** Europe orders ban on British exports of beef products. Nations fear deadly cattle disease may have entered human food chain.

U.N. Tribunal Charges War Crimes Against Serbs (March 22): In first such action, indicts three Bosnian Muslims and Bosnian Croat for murdering, torturing, and raping prisoners at detention camp.

Taiwan's President Wins Sweeping Victory (March 23): Lee Teng-hui receives strong mandate from island's voters in first democratic balloting. Result called rebuke to mainland China over independence.

Rabin's Killer Sentenced to Life (March 27): Yigal Amir, 25, found guilty by Israeli court of murder in assassination of Prime Minister Yitzhak Rabin.

Russia Signs Accord With Three Ex-Soviet States (March 29): Yeltsin agrees to closer economic integration with Kazakstan, Kyrgyzstan, and Belarus.

Yeltsin Orders End to War in Chechnya (March 31): Seeks to end unpopular conflict with secessionist republic before presidential election in June.

National

Dole Sweeps Primaries (March 5): Senate leader wins in Massachusetts, Connecticut, Maryland, and leads in Georgia, Maine, Vermont, Colorado, and Rhode Island. Voting is biggest test in G.O.P. primary season.

Televising U.S. Appeals Courts Permitted (March 12): Judicial panel reverses decision and allows courts to televise appellate arguments if they wish.

Dole Victor in Super Tuesday Primaries (March 12): Virtually assured of Republican nomination by winning in seven states, including Florida and Texas, with their heavy lists of convention delegates.

Steve Forbes Quits Presidential Race (March 14): Magazine publishing heir supports Senator Bob Dole.

F.D.A. Speeds Approval of New Anti-AIDS Drug (March 14): Acts quickly on indinavir, third of recently accepted medications that attack AIDS virus.

President Draws up Budget for 1997 (March 18): Clinton calls for some $100 billion in tax cuts over next five years. He amplifies proposals to benefit middle class and close business loopholes.

House Votes to Repeal Assault–Weapons Ban (March 22): Republicans win move to end 1994 restriction on 19 semiautomatic weapons and high-capacity ammunition clips. Two-day battle often furious.

Congress Votes Ban on Abortion Method (March 27): House, 286–129 gives final approval to bill outlawing specific technique called "partial birth abortion."

Congress Approves Borrowing Increase (March 28): Votes to raise U.S. authority to borrow $5.5 trillion in compromise acceptable to G.O.P. and President.

President to Speed Approval of Cancer Drugs (March 29): Plans steps to streamline F.D.A. procedures.

General

G.M. Strike Settled After 16 Days (March 5): Almost 3,500 members of U.A.W. walk out, shutting down two factories that make brake parts in Dayton, Ohio. The effect is to shut down other factories. **(March 21):** General Motors and union reach agreement on hiring policies and other issues. **(March 22):** Workers return after ratifying agreement. Big issues unresolved.

F. Lee Bailey Goes to Jail (March 6): Famed criminal defense lawyer sentenced to six months after refusing to obey judge's order to turn over millions of dollars in assets that a former client, a drug trafficker, had agreed to forfeit to government.

Three Servicemen Convicted in Okinawa Rape (March 7): Japanese court finds Americans guilty in abduction and attack on 12-year-old Japanese girl.

Stock Market Plunges 171.4 Points (March 8): Bonds also fall sharply after report that more jobs were created in February than in any month since 1983.

Dr. Kevorkian Acquitted Second Time (March 8): Michigan jury finds physician not guilty of violating state law banning assisted suicides.

Shuttle *Columbia* Lands in Florida (March 9): Seven-man crew returns to Earth. Difficult 16-day flight was marred by landing-system failure and loss of a tethered satellite for scientific experiment.

Stock Market Rises 110.55 Points (March 11): Dow Jones average recovers after worst percentage decline in four years. Investment fund managers account for strongest gain in almost two years.

Gunman Slays 16 Children in Scottish School (March 13): Also kills teacher as he storms into gym class at Dunblane carrying four handguns. He then kills himself. Twelve children wounded, three critically. Killer identified as avid gun enthusiast, aged 43.

Major Tobacco Companies Break Ranks (March 13): Liggett Group dropped from lawsuit by millions of smokers in return for payments to national quit-smoking campaign and withdrawing from suit against F.D.A.

Man Guilty in Abortion Site Killings (March 18): Court in Massachusetts convicts John C. Salvi III, 24, of murdering two receptionists at clinics. He is sentenced to two life terms in prison without parole.

Nelson Mandela Granted Divorce (March 19): South African President ends 38-year marriage with wife, Winnie. Judge finds no hope of reconciliation.

Disco Fire Kills at Least 150 in Manila (March 19): Flames rage through disco packed with students celebrating end of school year. About 400 persons were in place approved for only 35.

Menendez Brothers Convicted of Killing Parents (March 20): Erik and Lyle found guilty by Los Angeles jury of shotgun murders. They face death penalty.

Space Shuttle *Atlantis* Launched (March 22): Rockets into orbit at Cape Canaveral, Fla., on mission to link up with Russian space station *Mir.*

Brightest Comet in 20 Years Nears Earth (March 24): The Hyakutake reaches closest approach, within 9.3 million miles. Extends across patch of sky several times the size of the full moon.

APRIL 1996

International

North Koreans Invade Buffer Zone (April 7): Heavily armed troops enter sensitive area between North and South in violation of armistice that ended war.

Civil War Rages in Liberia (April 9 et seq.): U.S. evacuates hundreds of Americans and others from West African capital of Monrovia after peace fails.

Bosnian Serbs Boycott Conference (April 11): Refuse to join move to raise funds for rebuilding Bosnia.

U.S. to Give Up Air Base in Okinawa (April 12): Agrees to return to Japan areas on island in move to scale back American military presence.

Cease-Fire in Liberia Broken (April 13): Hastily arranged truce ends as gunfire rings out and sporadic shelling resumes near diplomatic enclave where thousands of Liberian refugees had sought shelter.

$1.23 Billion Aid Pledged for Bosnia (April 13): Nations and international institutions promise additional funds to rebuild shattered areas. Total relief pledges mount to $1.8 billion.

Gunmen Kill 18 Tourists in Egypt (April 18): Wound at least 17 other Greeks in attack on hotel. Officials suspect Islamic fundamentalist group.

Israeli Fire Kills 75 in Lebanon (April 18): Artillery barrage hits U.N. peacekeeping camp at Qana. More than 100 wounded. Israeli calls attack on camp a grave error. Says barrage was a response to rockets and mortar fire by guerrillas near the base.

Italian Left Wins in National Vote (April 22): Former Communists, in breakthrough, and centrist partners share victory in both houses of Parliament.

Chechen Rebel Leader Killed (April 24): Death of Dzhodkhar Dudayev in Russian rocket attack announced. Vice President now heads Russian separatist movement.

P.L.O. Drops Stand Against Jewish State (April 24): Palestinian National Council bows to Yasir Arafat and revokes clauses in 32-year-old charter that call for armed struggle to abolish Israel.

Agreement on Lebanon Fighting Reached (April 26): Israel, Syria, and Lebanon in accord on ending 16 days of rocketing and shelling in northern Israel and southern Lebanon. More than 150 Lebanese killed, and hundreds of thousands in both countries forced to flee homes. Damage in millions of dollars.

Lebanese Refugees Return Home (April 27): As cease-fire takes effect, tens of thousands cart possessions back to villages struck by Israeli bombs.

U.S. Technology to Aid Israel (April 28): White House announced it will help develop a weapons-defense system to shield Israel from ballistic missiles and small rockets fired by Lebanese guerrillas.

National

Commerce Secretary Killed in Plane Crash (April 3): Ronald H. Brown, 54, aboard military plane as it hit mountainside on approach to Dubrovnik Airport on Croatian coast. Several corporate leaders also perish. Mr. Brown and others had been on trip in connection with Bosnian reconstruction.

Court Upholds Clinton Policy on Gay Troops (April 5): Federal Appeals bench in Richmond rules courts cannot tell the President and Congress how to deal with issue of homosexuals in the military.

Clinton Signs Line-Item Veto Bill (April 9): In White House ceremony, President approves measure he says will let presidents fight "special interest boondoggles, loopholes and pure pork."

President Blocks Ban on Late-Term Abortions (April 10): Clinton says women who need procedure for own health "should not become pawns in a larger debate."

Trade Representative Named Commerce Secretary (April 12): President picks Mickey Kantor, a loyal political strategist, to succeed Ronald H. Brown.

Administration Defends Bosnia Arms Decision (April 23): But House inquiry reveals little about the reasons for 1994 decision not to block Iranian shipments to Bosnia despite arms embargo.

Clinton Signs Antiterrorism Legislation (April 25): Approves broad measure providing new tools and penalties for federal law-enforcement officials to use. New law restricts appeals by death row inmates.

Congress Votes 1996 Spending Bill (April 25): Outlay of $160 billion approved by Senate, 88–11, and House, 399–25. Action assures that government will stay open during remaining five months of fiscal year. **(April 26):** Clinton signs measure. With other actions, it will cut domestic spending by $24 billion, or 10 percent. Most of savings come from housing, labor, education, and commerce department programs.

President Plans Oil Sale From Reserves (April 29): Seeks to stem election-year surge in gasoline prices by releasing about 12 million barrels.

General

Two Bell Companies Agree to Merge (April 1): SBC Communications to acquire Pacific Telesis group for $17 billion. Giant communications empire to serve more than 30 million telephone lines in seven states.

British Farmers to Be Recompensed (April 2): European Union agrees to meet 70 percent of cost for farmers whose cattle will be destroyed over five years to eliminate human exposure to "mad cow disease," an often fatal ailment.

F.B.I. Arrests Suspected Unabomber (April 3): Hold Theodore J. Kaczynski, 53, former mathematics professor, living in remote Montana cabin. He is believed responsible for 17-year trail of bombings that killed three and maimed 23 others. **(April 15):** Federal judge unseals inventory of evidence including explosive devices and weapons.

Girl Pilot, 7, Killed in Plane Crash (April 11): Jessica Dubroff of California had sought to become youngest cross-country pilot. Father and flight instructor also die in storm at Cheyenne, Wyo. **(April 12):** Federal inspector says single-engine aircraft was overweight when it left airport.

Two Surrender in Montana Standoff (April 11): Freemen sought by F.B.I. are charged with conspiracy, mail and bank fraud involving millions in bogus checks.

Jury Spares Lives of Menendez Brothers (April 17): Los Angeles panel recommends life sentences for Erik, 25, and Lyle, 28, convicted of murdering parents. Prosecution had asked for death sentence.

F. Lee Bailey Freed From Jail (April 19): Released from Federal confinement in Florida after serving six weeks for contempt of court. Sentenced after missing court deadline to give up client's assets.

Two Big Telephone Companies Merge (April 22): Bell Atlantic and NYNEX agree on one of largest corporate mergers in American history to become second-largest telephone company in U.S., after AT&T.

Lone Gunman Kills 32 in Australia (April 28): Fires randomly at people at popular resort of Tasmania. Captured after setting fire to guesthouse where he had been holding three hostages during standoff with police. **(April 30):** Martin Bryant, 28, in hospital, is formally charged with murder.

Unpublished Alcott Manuscript Discovered (April 30): First novel, written at age 18, found in Houghton Library at Harvard University by two scholars.

MAY 1996
International

Bosnia Detains Two Indicted Muslims (May 2): First former Yugoslav republic to honor arrest warrants from international war crimes tribunal.

New Prime Minister in Spain (May 4): José Maria Aznar, leader of conservative Popular Party, wins vote in Parliament, ending 13 years of Socialist rule.

Israelis Blame Mapping Errors in Shelling (May 5): Army says artillery gunners relied on incorrect maps when they fired on Hezbollah guerillas and instead killed nearly 100 Palestinian refugees in April.

U.S. Reports Chinese Pirating on Increase (May 7): Administration officials find may undisclosed factories producing versions of American software, videos, and music. Retaliatory moves planned.

South Africa Gets New Constitution (May 8): Constitutional Assembly adopts charter officially and peacefully completing transition from centuries of white supremacy to a nonracial democracy.

F.W. de Klerk Party Quits Government (May 9): He says South Africa's first nonracial democracy is now strong enough for him to present a vigorous opposition.

U.S. Bars Punishment of China (May 10): Administration decides against retaliation for sale to Pakistan of nuclear equipment for weapons-grade uranium.

Governing Party Defeated in India's Election (May 10): Returns show devastating rout for Congress Party, which held power for all but four years since independence in 1947. Coalition rule likely.

Iraq and U.N. Agree on Oil Imports (May 20): Iraqis allowed to sell oil for first time since 1990 invasion of Kuwait to pay for needs of civilian population suffering from six years of sanctions.

French Troops End African Mutiny (May 27): Drive rebellious soldiers back to barracks in Bengui, capital of Central African Republic, former colony.

Chechnya Peace Treaty Signed (May 27): Leaders of Russia and separatist republic meet in Moscow to seek end of 18-month conflict that killed 40,000 Chechens and devastated the country. President Yeltsin invited republic's leader, Zelimkhan Yanderbiyev, in move to strengthen presidential campaign imperiled by the war.

New Hindu Government Resigns (May 28): Nationalists leave office ahead of certain defeat in Parliament. Way cleared for coalition of centrists, leftists, and regional parties.

Israel Elects New Prime Minister (May 31): Benjamin Netanyahu, leader of conservative Likud Party, defeats Prime Minister Shimon Peres by narrow margin. He had campaigned on charges that Labor Government had neglected Israel's security.

Croat First to Be Convicted in Balkan War (May 31): Pleads guilty before Hague war crimes tribunal of crimes against humanity for part in massacre of thousands of Muslims at U.N. "safe area."

National

Senate Votes Compromise AIDS Care Bill (May 2): Gives final Congressional approval to measure to extend federal assistance for five years and seek to increase voluntary H.I.V. testing of pregnant women.

President Vetoes Limits on Liability Verdicts (May 2): Rejects measure to limit state and federal courts on punitive damages for faulty products.

Free TV Time for Candidates (May 8): ABC joins other major networks offering each a live one-hour special program on prime time in week before election. PBS, CNN, and cable operators will also allot time.

Clinton Tapes Testimony in Whitewater Trial (May 9): President repeatedly denies that he once asked an Arkansas businessman to make improper loan to his former partners in land venture.

Dole Announces Resignation From Senate (May 15): Says he will abandon 35-year Congressional career to concentrate on his campaign for the presidency.

Navy's Top Admiral Kills Himself (May 16): Adm. Jeremy M. Boorda shoots himself in chest shortly after being told of pending magazine article suggesting he wore two unearned Vietnam War combat decorations.

Air Force General Ousted in Brown Crash (May 30): Two other high officers also relieved of duty in Germany as result of investigation of crash of jetliner in Croatia that killed Commerce Secretary Ronald H. Brown and 34 others.

Rally for Children Held in Washington (May 31): Thousands assemble to demonstrate concern for millions under 18, calling their problems overlooked.

General

Company Rejects Tobacco Billboards (May 2): In setback for cigarette companies, 3M Media announces it will not accept tobacco contracts after 1996.

Experts Call DNA Evidence Reliable (May 2): Committee of National Academy of Sciences cites recent advances in knowledge and technology.

William E. Colby's Body Found (May 6): Former Director of Central Intelligence drowned April 27 in Maryland tributary of Potomac River. Body discovered nine days after he set out on solo canoe trip from weekend home in Rock Point, Md.

Disease Kills 10,000 in West Africa (May 6): Bacterial meningitis infects more than 100,000 in three months, one of worst epidemics in recent memory.

Fourteen Marines Killed as Helicopters Collide (May 10): Two injured as aircraft crash and then plunge into densely forested marsh at Camp Lejeune, N.C.

Jetliner Crashes in Everglades; 110 Perish (May 11): All aboard killed as Valujet DC-9 hits swampy area infested by alligators and snakes. Cause of crash unknown. **(May 15):** Improper cargo, oxygen generators, studied as possible cause. **(May 26):** Police find cockpit voice recorder, second "black box" to be recovered. **(May 27):** Tape reveals warning to pilot of fire in cabin. **(May 30):** Tape reveals unidentified sound and captain's voice stating need to return to Miami Airport.

Tornado Kills Nearly 500 in Bangladesh (May 13): More than 32,000 wounded in half an hour as high winds flatten 80 villages in northern region.

Dr. Jack Kevorkian Acquitted in Suicide Cases (May 14): Michigan jury finds him not guilty of two violations of state's law against assisted death.

Some 500 Dead as Ferry Sinks on Lake Victory (May 21): Tanzania vessel hits rock and capsizes. May of those drowned reported to be teenagers.

Chinese Sought in Arms Smuggling Case (May 22): In sting operation, U.S. agents begin arresting representatives of China's state-owned arms companies accused of importing AK-47 automatic rifles.

Clinton Partners in Arkansas Convicted (May 28): Jury in Little Rock, in first trial of Whitewater investigation, finds Governor and two others guilty of fraud and other crimes for series of bad loans issued by Arkansas savings and loan association.

Shuttle *Endeavour* Lands in Florida (May 29): Glides to earth at Cape Canaveral after ten-day mission. Crew of six astronauts tested inflatable antenna and self-stabilizing satellite.

U.S. Arrests Leaders of Drug Smuggling Ring (May 30): Two heads of multi-million-dollar international group and three workers held in Florida after agents seize 34,000 pounds of hashish.

JUNE 1996
International

Ukraine Finishes Nuclear Disarmament (June 4): Sunflower seeds scattered at 80 underground sites that housed SS–19 missiles aimed at U.S. Defense secretaries of U.S., Russia and Ukraine join in ceremony ending a three-year process.

Wife of Nigerian Opposition Leader Slain (June 4): Kudirat Abiola, 44, shot in capital, Lagos. She had been campaigning for release of her jailed husband.

China Agrees to World Ban on Atomic Tests (June 6): In concession at international disarmament conference, abandons long-standing insistence on right to conduct nuclear explosion for nonmilitary purposes. **(June 8):** China conducts underground nuclear test. Announces there will be just one more test by September before joining international ban.

Russian–Chechen Agreement Signed (June 10): Negotiators sign accords expected to lay groundwork for ending 18-month conflict. Details withheld.

Ex-Senator Heads Northern Ireland Peace Talks (June 12): George J. Mitchell installed in Belfast after surviving attacks by Protestant leaders who feel that, as Roman Catholic, he would be prejudiced.

Bangladesh Party Returns to Power (June 13): Awami League wins general election 21 years after losing office in army massacre. League won nation its independence from Pakistan. New Prime Minister to be named.

Accord on Arms Limits Signed in Balkans (June 14): Bosnian Serbs, Croats, and Muslims, with governments of Croatia and Yugoslavia, agree on sweeping curbs on number and types of weapons each faction can have.

Bomb Injures 200 in Manchester, England (June 15): I.R.A. linked to explosion in parked van in downtown area. Windows shattered for blocks around.

U.S. and China Agree on Piracy Fight (June 17): Decide on measures to stem theft of music, movies, and computer software in China. U.S. scraps plan to impose $2 billion in trade sanctions.

Yeltsin Chooses Rival as Defense Chief (June 18): Names Alexander I. Lebed, retired general defeated in Russian presidential election. Yeltsin dismisses unpopular defense minister Pavel S. Grachev.

New Israeli Cabinet Sworn In (June 18): After battle with political associates, Prime Minister Benjamin Netanyahu and ministers form new government.

Truck Bomb Kills 19 at U.S. Saudi Arabian Base (June 25): Blast injures 150 at apartment complex housing Air Force pilots and other military personnel at eastern city of Dhahran. All victims were Americans. President Clinton vows to bring terrorists to justice. **(June 26):** American and Saudi officials insist attack will not harm close military cooperation.

Islamic Leader Becomes Turkey's Premier (June 28): Necmettin Erbakan, Welfare Party Leader, ends 75-year secular rule. Forms coalition government.

National

Clinton Names New Head of Navy (June 5): Appoints Adm. Jay L. Johnson, 50, as Chief of Naval Operations to succeed Adm. Jeremy M. Boorda, his mentor.

Medicare Funds Reported Running Out (June 5): Hospital Insurance trustees say system is being drained faster than ever. Political attacks erupt.

Health-Care Bill Founders in Congress (June 7): Legislation pressed by Senate leader Bob Dole before retirement blocked by disagreement between Republicans and Democrats over Medical Savings Accounts.

Cover-Up on Vietnam Forces Revealed (June 7): Newly declassified documents show U.S. lied about fate of Vietnamese commandos. Hundreds who had survived torture and imprisonment after carrying out U.S. sabotage missions into North Vietnam were declared dead by U.S. military and their service covered up.

President Apologizes for Use of F.B.I. Files (June 9): White House tells several prominent Republicans confidential material was improperly obtained.

Whitewater Counsel Sifts Transfer of F.B.I. Files (June 10): Kenneth W. Starr seeks to find how White House obtained confidential data on several prominent Republicans. Pentagon aide interviewed.

Senate Whitewater Inquiry Ends (June 11): Panel finishes 14 months of hearings on Arkansas case affecting President. Chairman Alfonse M. D'Amato fails to get immunity for Clinton accuser to testify.

Bob Dole Resigns From Senate (June 11): Majority Leader bids colleagues farewell to campaign as "just a man" for presidency. Clinton praises Senator's service.

Senate Republicans Choose New Leader (June 12): Name Trent Lott of Mississippi to succeed Bob Dole. Congress now headed by southern conservatives.

Woman Flees Genital Mutilation (June 13): U.S. sets precedent by granting political asylum to 19-year-old from Togo who said she fled homeland to escape surgical rite.

F.A.A. Shuts Down Valujet (June 17): Reports "serious difficulties" have turned up in wake of Everglades crash. Administrator says airline had failed to establish "airworthiness" of craft.

Congress Curbs Investments in Iran (June 19): House unanimously votes heavy economic sanctions against companies, splitting with allies.

Clinton to Fight Church Burnings (June 19): Pledges southern governors renewed efforts to prevent arson at black houses of worship. Orders Emergency Management Agency to help community watch programs.

Senate Blocks Campaign Reform (June 25): Republicans follow new leader, Trent Lott, to keep finance legislation measure from coming to vote.

General

Alabama Jury Awards Record $150-Million Damages (June 4): Rules in lawsuit against General Motors involving apparently faulty door latches on vehicles in case brought by driver paralyzed in accident.

Panel Approves Drug to Treat Stroke (June 6): Advisers to F.D.A. recommend that blood clot–dissolving drug, Activase, be accepted. It is expected to revolutionize treatment of strokes.

Arson Destroys 30th Black Church in 18 Months (June 7): Wooden sanctuary, 93 years old, burned down at Charlotte, N.C.

Everglades Crash Search Ended (June 10): Federal investigators declare official finish to search of wreckage of Valujet Flight 592, with 110 dead.

Paratrooper Sentenced to Death in Killing (June 12): Sgt. William Kreutzer, Jr., doomed by court-martial at Fort Bragg, N.C., for slaying officer in sniper attack that also wounded 18 soldiers.

New Heart Operation Developed (June 13): Brazilian surgeon uses unconventional procedure to remove living tissue from enlarged organ and stitch sides together. Physicians predict relief for heart failure victims.

Last of Freemen Surrender in Montana (June 13): Sixteen holdouts hand themselves over to federal agents after 81-day siege at remote ranch. Antigovernment group faces Federal and state charges.

Suspect Indicted on Unabomber Charges (June 18): California federal grand jury names Theodore J. Kaczynski in two counts of death and two injuries. **(June 21):** Suspect moved from Montana to Sacramento to face charges.

Space Shuttle Columbia Blasts Off (June 20): Carries crew of seven from three countries into orbit on mission designed to be longest in space history.

JULY 1996
International

Communists Ousted in Mongolia After 70 Years (July 2): Coalition opposition breaks grip on power by winning 50 of 76 seats in single-chamber parliament.

Yeltsin Wins in Crucial Russian Election (July 3): Voters reject return to Communist past and re-elect him for second term by overwhelming margin over Communist opponent Gennady A. Zyuganov. Yeltsin had played critical role in dissolution of Soviet Union and launching of market-oriented reforms.

Islamic Party Heads Turkish Government (July 8): Parliament, in break with secularist tradition, approves its coalition with center-right organization.

Israeli Prime Minister Confers With Clinton (July 9): Benjamin Netanyahu notes important differences with U.S. on approach to peace in Middle East, with no concessions on settlements and other issues. **(July 10):** Netanyahu uses diplomatic skill in addressing joint session of Congress, meeting key leaders and speaking publicly. Stresses Israeli self-reliance and doubts of Arab intentions.

Bomb Wrecks Luxury Hotel in Northern Ireland (July 14): Explodes minutes after 250 guests and wedding party revelers left. First terrorist blast since cease-fire, it lessens hopes for peace in Ulster.

Truce Broken in Chechen War (July 10): Russian troops launch fiercest attack in months. Dozens of civilians killed in bombardment of two villages.

U.S. Plans Transfer of Force in Saudi Arabia (July 17): Pentagon announces "drastic changes" to protect American troops from chemical and biological weapons and terrorist bombs four or five times as large as weapon that killed 19 American airmen in June.

Bosnian Serb Leader Agrees to Resign (July 19): Radovan Karadzic, political chief in war of ethnic separation, gives up power. He is under indictment by Hague war crimes tribunal for genocide. Action removes obstacle to Bosnia national elections.

I.M.F. Delays Payment to Russia (July 22): For first time, International Monetary Fund holds up $300 million because of Yeltsin government's problems with tax collection. A $10.2 billion three-year loan was contingent on monthly economic reviews.

Deadly Food Infection Strikes Japan (July 24): Seven killed and thousands poisoned by strain of bacteria. Government moves for emergency action.

China Pledges End to Nuclear Tests (July 29): Announces decision after exploding device. China is last acknowledged nuclear weapons power to declare a moratorium on testing. May seek treaty revision.

U.S. Vetoes Iraq Oil-Sale Agreement (July 31): Rejects United Nations plan to allow sales up to $2 billion to pay for six months' food and relief supplies.

National

NASA Picks Builder of Experimental Rocket (July 2): Lockheed Marietta Corporation to construct X-33, the first major new U.S. spacecraft in 25 years.

U.S. Jobless Rate Lowest in 6 Years (July 5): Drop to 5.3 percent for June reported, down from 5.6 percent for May. Sudden signs of inflation appear.

U.S. Revises Meat Inspection System (July 6): President announces first major changes in nearly a century. New rules will impose scientific tests for bacteria.

Senate 74–24, Approves Rise in Minimum Wage (July 9): In victory for Democrats, it approves 90-cents-an-hour increase, to $5.15. Twenty-seven Republicans join all Democrats in favor. Tax provisions benefiting small business included in final version.

U.S. to Penalize Canadian Company on Cuba Dealings (July 10): Clinton warns large mining concern of reprisals under new law. Worldwide protest aroused.

Clinton Tapes Arkansas Testimony (July 19): In testimony played in courtroom, President denies trading patronage jobs for campaign contributions. Speaks as defense witness for two accused bankers.

F.D.A. Advised to Approve Abortion Pill (July 19): Panel recommends that agency accept marketing of RU-486, mifepristone, as safe and effective.

Senate Approves Welfare Changes (July 23): Votes, 74–24, for comprehensive measure to end long-standing federal guarantee of cash assistance for poorest children. Bill would give states lump sums to run own welfare programs with vast new powers.

Christian Coalition Sued on Political Stand (July 30): Federal Election Commission charges nation's largest group of religious conservatives acted illegally to promote prominent Republican candidates.

Clinton Agrees to Sign Welfare Reform Bill (July 31): After long thought, President accepts Congressional measure reversing six decades of policy. Bill would eliminate federal cash guarantees for poorest children and give states new authority over programs.

Safer Whooping Cough Vaccine Approved (July 31): F.D.A. finds Tripedia less likely to cause side effects.

General

Menendez Brothers Sentenced to Life in Prison (July 2): Los Angeles court imposes prison without parole on Erik, 26, and Lyle, 28, convicted of killing parents.

First Hurricane Batters East Coast (July 8): Bertha rips through Caribbean islands with winds at times exceeding 85 miles an hour. **(July 13):** Weakens to tropical storm as it moves up east coast. Death toll placed at 10. Heavy damage reported.

Gains in AIDS Treatment Reported (July 11): Scientists release results of studies at international meeting in Vancouver, B.C. They report combinations of old and new drugs suppress virus for long periods.

Charles and Diana Agree on Divorce (July 12): Prince and Princess of Wales announce divorce terms almost 15 years after fairy-tale wedding. Princess to get large lump-sum payment instead of alimony.

747 Airliner Crashes in Atlantic; 230 Perish (July 17): T.W.A. Flight 800 plunges in flames off Long Island after taking off from J.F.K. Airport for Paris. Cause of crash a mystery. **(July 20):** As weather improves, rescue workers continue removing bodies and seeking bulk of wreckage on ocean floor. Navy sends sophisticated equipment to facilitate operations. **(July 26):** Flight and voice recorder boxes recovered. Radar indicates plane flew 24 seconds after catastrophe.

F.T.C. Favors Broadcasting Merger (July 17): But stipulates that Time Warner Inc. and Turner Broadcasting System Inc. must have the new company's cable-television system carry second news channel as a rival to its own Cable News Network.

Clinton Opens Olympic Games in Atlanta (July 19): Calls U.S. athletes "source of pride" to nation and meets other heads of states. Centennial Summer Olympics opens with more than 10,000 athletes from nearly 200 nations marching into stadium filled with 83,100 spectators. Olympic flame lighted in ceremony.

Hundreds Die in Chinese Floods (July 25 et seq.): Several central provinces ravaged by heavy rainfall and surging Yangtze River. Thousands of villages flooded. Hundreds of thousands of homes destroyed.

Bomb Mars Summer Olympic Games (July 25): Homemade device stuffed with shrapnel of nails and screws explodes at crowded corner of Centennial Olympic Park at Atlanta. Woman killed, 111 wounded. Games go on. **(July 28):** Clinton responds with call for Congress to vote expanded measures against terrorism.

AUGUST 1996

International

Somali Who Opposed U.S. Is Dead (Aug. 2): Mohammed Farah Aidid, clan leader, whose fighters humiliated U.S. forces in 1993 by killing 18 Army Rangers and dragging body of one of them through streets.

Israel Lifts Freeze on Settlements (Aug. 2): New Likud government takes first steps toward reversing predecessors' dovish policies on West Bank and Gaza.

U.S. Allows Oil Sale to Aid Iraqi Civilians (Aug. 7): Lifts last major barrier to sale of Iraqi oil to pay for emergency food, medicine, and other goods to ease hardships from six years of international sanctions imposed after Baghdad's invasion of Kuwait.

Serbia and Croatia Agree to Diplomatic Ties (Aug. 7): Five years after war over breakup of Yugoslavia, presidents reach accord in surprise talks near Athens. Territorial dispute had delayed agreement.

Yeltsin Sworn in at Brief Inauguration (Aug. 9): Takes oath as first democratically elected President of independent Russia. A feeble Yeltsin, 65, speaks for less than a minute in quiet ceremony.

India Vetoes International Nuclear-Test Ban (Aug. 20): Blocks treaty after two years of negotiations, rejecting pleas by U.S. and other nuclear powers.

Russia-Chechnya Peace Accord Signed (Aug. 22): Security chiefs of Russia and secessionist region approve agreement to resolve 20-month conflict. It calls for cease-fire and pullback of Russian troops from Grozny, the capital.

Croatia and Yugoslavia Reach Accord (Aug. 23): Mutual recognition agreement formally ends five years of hostilities and prevents resumption of war in Balkans. Accord will restore full diplomatic relations and resume trade and transportation links.

Russia and Chechnya Agree on Peace Talks (Aug. 30): Kremlin security chief and rebel leaders will seek peace and agree to postpone decision on status of rebel republic until Dec. 31, 2001.

Iraqi Troops Invade Kurd Enclave (Aug. 31): Armored divisions seize a main city in northern Iraq. U.S. warning ignored as President Clinton orders troops on high alert and sends in reinforcements.

National

Two Acquitted in Whitewater Trial (Aug. 1): Federal jury clears Arkansas bankers of charges that they conspired to conceal large cash withdrawals by Bill Clinton's campaign for governor. Verdict is setback to office of Whitewater independent counsel.

Congress Passes Welfare Reform Bill (Aug. 1): Senate, 78–21, completes action on measure to reverse six decades of social policy, eliminating federal guarantees of cash assistance for poorest children. Clinton says he will sign the legislation.

Congress Votes Wages and Health Bills (Aug. 2): Gives final approval to measures to raise federal minimum wage, make drinking water safer, and guarantee workers' health insurance will follow from job to job.

Bob Dole Offers Economic Program (Aug. 5): Probable G.O.P. candidate proposes $548 billion in tax cuts and overhaul of education system, while balancing federal budget within five years. Espouses supply-side economics he had long opposed.

Clinton Signs Clean Water Bill (Aug. 6): Approves measure to help states upgrade municipal water systems and require information to public on contaminants.

TV Programs for Children Required (Aug. 8): F.C.C. orders networks to show three hours each week. Regulation is compromise with broadcasters.

Republicans Convene in San Diego (Aug. 12): Open 36th National Convention, carefully managed to stress unity and inclusiveness. Delegates adopt platform that calls for constitutional amendment to outlaw abortion and takes conservative stand on immigration, crime, civil rights for homosexuals, education, welfare, and the environment. **(Aug. 15):** In forceful address, Bob Dole accepts presidential nomination, and stresses economic program. Jack Kemp accepts vice-presidential nomination.

Ross Perot Nominated by Reform Party (Aug. 18): Texas billionaire, 66, launches presidential campaign at Valley Forge, Pa., convention with attack on two-party system.

Ralph Nader Nominated for White House (Aug. 19): Consumer advocate named by Green Party.

Clinton Friend Sentenced in Whitewater Case (Aug. 20): Susan McDougal, onetime business partner of Clintons, draws two-year term on fraud charges.

Clinton Signs Bill to Raise Minimum Wage (Aug. 20): Approves increase of 90 cents an hour over next year to $5.15. President says 10 million workers will get "a chance to raise stronger families."

President Approves Expanded Access to Health Insurance (Aug. 20): Enacts new law allowing workers to retain coverage when they change jobs and assures coverage for pre-existing medical conditions.

Clinton Approves Welfare Reform Bill (Aug. 22): Signs legislation ending decades of federal policy guaranteeing help to poorest children. Measure requires states to deal more directly with poverty.

Democrats Convene in Chicago (Aug. 26): Return to scene of tumultuous 1968 convention. Delegates, with little dissent, approve platform that holds to "New Democrat" theme of 1992, backing Clinton policies on jobs, education, and crime. Convention speakers tell personal tragedies and triumphs. **(Aug. 28):** President in Chicago after campaign tour. Gore leads speakers contrasting the Administration and opposition. **(Aug. 29):** Clinton and Gore accept renomination. President vows to protect social and environmental programs.

Clinton Adviser Resigns Over Ties to Call Girl (Aug. 29): Dick Morris announces resignation during Democratic convention after tabloid reveals relationship. He was force behind emphasis on family values.

General

Centennial Olympic Games End (Aug. 4): Athletic competitions at Atlanta emphasize feats by women athletes from established and emerging nations. Bomb explosion and commercialism mar 16-day event.

Clues to Primitive Life on Mars Found (Aug. 6): Scientists report identifying organic compounds and minerals on meteorite that fell to Earth as evidence that microbial life existed on Mars long ago.

Stricken Smoker Wins $750,000 Award (Aug. 9): Florida jury grants judgment to lung cancer victim, 66, who had smoked cigarettes for 44 years. Verdict against Brown & Williamson Corporation is second in which tobacco industry had to pay damages.

Crash of Clinton Cargo Plane Kills 9 (Aug. 18): Secret Service and Air Force crew perish as military C-130 rams Wyoming mountain soon after takeoff.

Food Poisoning Kills 52 in India (Aug. 18): Eighteen others gravely ill in town north of Bombay. Investigators uncertain whether cause was accidental or a case of mass murder.

Traces of Explosive Found on Downed Jetliner (Aug. 23): F.B.I. confirms report that crime lab had detected evidence of plastic-explosive residue, PETN, on wreckage of T.W.A. flight 800, downed in Atlantic.

Russian Jetliner Crashes, Killing 140 (Aug. 29): Hits mountain on remote Arctic island of Spitsbergen.

Death Toll in Himalayas Reaches 160 (Aug. 25): Hindu pilgrims and mountain guides perish in Kashmir storm. Disaster toll expected to rise.

SEPTEMBER 1996

International

Iraqis Strike at Kurdish Enclave (Aug. 31): Despite U.S. warnings, armored divisions attack northern area. **(Sept. 1):** Clinton vows to punish Saddam Hussein. U.N. suspends agreement to allow Iraq to sell oil. **(Sept. 2 and 3):** U.S. launches attacks against Iraq's southern air defenses. **(Sept. 5):** Hussein withdraws most of his forces from Kurdish enclaves. **(Sept. 13):** Iraq halts attacks on U.S. jets enforcing flight exclusion zones in north and south. U.S. reconsiders plans to attack Iraq.

Yeltsin Reveals Plans for Heart Surgery (Sept. 5): Russian President breaks silence about condition. Surgeon says bypass operation is certain. **(Sept. 10):** Formally hands national security and law enforcement power to Prime Minister Viktor S. Chernomyrdin.

Bosnians Elect Existing Ethnic Leaders (Sept. 14): Hundreds of thousands cast ballots in heavy turnout with few reports of violence. They chose three-person presidency, a national parliament, regional parliaments, and presidents for Muslim, Serb, and Croat enclaves. Power given to existing leaders of the three major ethnic groups. **(Sept. 29):** Western officials certify results despite accusations of fraud. **(Sept. 30):** Three former enemies hold first meeting as joint presidents.

Guatemala and Rebels Sign Peace Accord (Sept. 19): Government and leftists move to end 35-year war, longest guerrilla conflict in Western Hemisphere. Size and political power of military sharply reduced.

Violence Flares in Jerusalem (Sept. 24): Palestinians protest Israel's opening of tourist tunnel near Al Aqsa Mosque, Islamic holy site. **(Sept. 25):** Two Palestinians dead and hundreds wounded in clash between Palestinian authority police and Israeli troops. **(Sept. 27):** Security forces disperse stone-throwing youths on fourth day of Arab-Israeli disorder. U.S. fails in diplomatic efforts to bring peace. About 70 die in clashes, and hundreds on both sides are wounded.

Islamic Rebels Capture Afghan Capital (Sept. 27): Hang a former president in one of first acts of vengeance. **(Sept. 30):** New rulers impose harsh Islamic code on capital, Kabul. Music and movies banned. Women and girls the most restricted, barred from schools, jobs, and forced to cover entire body, including face, when appearing in public.

National

Jobless Rate Lowest in Seven Years (Sept. 6): Labor Department reports 5.1 percent for August. Hourly earnings show second increase in three months.

Perot Picks Economist for Ticket (Sept. 10): Chooses Pat Choate, Washington economist and author to be election running mate. Choate a political unknown.

Senate Rejects Same-Sex Marriage Bill (Sept. 10): Votes 85–14 against recognizing gay couples' rights with federal benefits. Antidiscrimination bill loses.

Pentagon Criticized in Bombing Deaths (Sept. 12): Two reports find fault with intelligence operations before killing of 19 airmen in Saudi Arabia. **(Sept. 16):** Pentagon report says American commanders ignored repeated warnings of terrorist threats to apartment complex housing American forces. **(Sept. 18):** Defense Secretary Perry accepts some blame for "failure of leadership" in Saudi explosion.

Miss America 1996 Crowned (Sept. 14): Tara Dawn Holland, Miss Kansas, assumes title.

Debate Commission Rules Out Ross Perot (Sept. 17): Rules Texan has no chance of election as president and will not be invited to face Clinton and Dole.

Abortion Drug Clears Hurdle for Sale in U.S. (Sept. 18): F.D.A. gives conditional approval to RU-486, sponsored by Population Council after research.

Senate Fails to Override Abortion Veto (Sept. 26): Vote is eight short on measure to outlaw procedure known as "partial-birth abortion." Vote is 57–41.

Accord reached on 1997 U.S. Budget (Sept. 28): President and Congress settle on deal that yields to Clinton on immigration issues and some spending priorities but retains Republican demands for overall $30 billion cut in government outlays.

General

Storm Kills 22 in Eastern U.S. (Sept. 8): Thousands homeless and without power four days after hurricane Fran hits North Carolina and moves inland, causing flooding and heavy damage in Northeast and Mid-Atlantic states.

New Ford Contract Aids Job Security (Sept. 16): Company and U.A.W. reach accord on layoffs and reliance on outside parts suppliers, a growing trend in industry.

Virginia Military Institute Agrees to Admit Women (Sept. 21): After defying Supreme Court order, V.M.I. decides to transform last single-sex school that is state-supported.

Astronaut Home After 6 Months in Space (Sept. 23): Dr. Shannon W. Lucid, 53, bids farewell to colleagues aboard Russian space station *Mir.* **(Sept. 26):** She steps from shuttle Atlantis at Cape Canaveral, Fla., after shuttle's 10-day mission to exchange cargo and retrieve her. John E.B. Laka, 54, retired Air Force colonel, replaces her on *Mir* for four months.

Valujet Wins Right to Resume Flying (Sept. 26): Transportation Department gives approval three months after safety violations were revealed following May 11 crash of airline's DC-9 in Florida Everglades.

Chrysler and U.A.W. Agree on Contract (Sept. 29): Three-year pact follows pattern of maintaining employment at current levels.

Major Emmy Awards for TV, 1996

(Sept. 8, 1996)

Drama Series: *E.R.* (NBC)
  Actress: Kathy Baker, *Picket Fences*
  Actor: Dennis Franz, *NYPD Blue*
  Supporting actress: Tyne Daly, *Christy*
  Supporting actor: Ray Walston, *Picket Fences*
Comedy series: *Frasier* (NBC)
  Actress: Helen Hunt, *Mad About You*
  Actor: John Lithgow, *3rd Rock From the Sun*
  Supporting actress: Julia Louis-Dreyfus, *Seinfeld*
  Supporting actor: Rip Torn, *The Larry Sanders Show*
Variety, Music or Comedy Series: *Dennis Miller Live* (HBO)
Variety, Music or Comedy Special: *The Kennedy Center Honors* (CBS)
Miniseries or Special: *Gulliver's Travels* (NBC)
  Actress: Helen Mirren, *Prime Suspect: "Scent of Darkness"*
  Actor: Alan Rickman, *Rasputin*
  Supporting actress: Greta Scacchi, *Rasputin*
  Supporting actor: Tom Hulce, *The Heidi Chronicles*
Made for TV Movie: *Truman* (HB)
Individual Performance, Variety or Music Program: Tony Bennett, *Tony Bennett Live by Request: A Valentine Special*

OCTOBER 1996

(Through October 28)

International

Emergency Mideast Summit Inconclusive (Oct. 2): Israeli Prime Minister Benjamin Netanyahu and Palestinian leader Yasir Arafat end two-day summit failing to resolve differences. The Washington summit was hastily arranged by President Clinton in response to violence that erupted the week before in Jerusalem, the West Bank, and the Gaza Strip.

Israeli and Palestinian Negotiators Begin Talks (Oct. 6): Series of on-going talks agreed to at Washington Summit center on the long-delayed withdrawal of Israeli troops from the West Bank town of Hebron. **(Oct. 28):** American mediator Dennis Ross departs after weeks of negotiations falter.

Militant Muslims in Afghanistan Vow to Enforce Harsh Islamic Rule (Oct. 7): In face of international condemnation Taliban cleric Mullah Mutai warns against "an attempt to impose alien principles on our country," contending that Islamic principles have not "changed in the last 1,400 years" and "will remain eternal."

I.R.A. Bomb Wounds 31 in Ulster (Oct. 7): I.R.A. claims responsibility for detonating two bombs wounding 21 soldiers and 10 civilians at the British Army's headquarters in Lisburn, Northern Ireland, the I.R.A.'s first admission of violence since the Sept. 1, 1994, cease-fire.

Ethnic Violence Breaks Out in Zairian Refugee Camps (Oct. 13): Fighting erupts between Zairian soldiers, who support the Hutu refugee camps on their border, and local Tutsi guerrillas, who are resisting orders to leave adopted homeland and return to Rwanda. **(Oct. 21):** About 70 die and more than 220,000 refugees from Rwanda and Burundi abandon their camps as fighting intensifies. **(Oct. 27):** U.N. aid workers evacuate camps as chaos reigns in eastern Zaire; bewildering number of groups clash.

Yeltsin Sacks Political Heir (Oct. 17): Four months after declaring Russian security chief Alexander Lebed his likely successor, President Boris Yeltsin dismisses him for infighting and insubordination.

Nicaraguans Elect Arnoldo Aleman as President (Oct. 21): Choose right-wing leader and former Managuan mayor over former president Daniel Ortega, of the leftist Sandinistas.

National

Uneventful Presidential Debate Focuses on Medicare, Economy, Education, and Tax Cuts (Oct. 6): Bob Dole's performance exceeds expectations, but polls indicate Clinton won Hartford, Conn., debate.

Gore Declared Winner in Polite Vice-Presidential Standoff (Oct. 9): Vice President Al Gore and Republican Jack Kemp debate tax cuts and Medicare in St. Petersburg, Fla.

Second and Final Presidential Debate Held in San Diego, Calif. (Oct. 16): Bob Dole intensified attacks on Bill Clinton's character, while the President ignored charges and emphasized his accomplishments.

General

Peruvian Plane Crash Kills 70 (Oct. 2): Aeroperu Flight 603's navigational equipment malfunctioned shortly after takeoff from Lima, the Peruvian capital, on a flight to Santiago, Chile.

Strike Shuts Down General Motors Operations in Canada (Oct. 3): Largest Canadian manufacturer brought to standstill when 26,300 CAW members walk. Prolonged strike would have significant impact on economy. **(Oct. 22):** Issues still unresolved as strike enters nineteenth day; tens of thousands of workers across North America idled and numerous U.S. plans partially shut down. **(Oct. 23):** Tentative agreement reached.

Dow Jones Industrial Average Surpasses 6,000 Barrier (Oct. 7): In a year where the record was broken dozens of times, DJIA reaches a historic high.

Guatemalan Stadium Disaster Kills More than Eighty (Oct. 16): Spectators were trampled or suffocated in stampede at World Cup qualifying soccer match in Guatemala City, Guatemala.

Anniversary of Million Man March Commemorated (Oct. 16): Nation of Islam leader Louis Farrakhan called the United States a "bully" with "evil policies" in a rally attended by thousands outside of the U.S. headquarters in New York.

1996 Nobel Prize Winners

Peace: Bishop Carlos Filipe Ximenes Belo and José Ramos-Horta (both East Timorese) for their work to end more than two decades of oppression in East Timor, a former Portuguese colony invaded by Indonesia in 1976. Under Indonesian rule, an estimated one-third of the population has died of starvation, epidemics, and human rights abuses.

Literature: Wislawa Szymborska (Polish), poet whose work crystallizes the nature of everyday life and personal relations. Little known outside of Poland, Szymborska is the fifth Polish-born writer to win the literature prize.

Medicine: Dr. Peter C. Doherty (Australian) and Rolf M. Zinkernagel (Swiss) for discoveries about how the immune system recognizes virus-infected cells, which will aid in designing vaccines and in treating cancer, multiple sclerosis, and diabetes.

Economics: Dr. James A. Mirrlees (U.K.) of Cambridge University, and William Vickrey, a Canadian-born professor emeritus of Columbia University, for "their fundamental contributions to the economic theory of incentives." On Oct. 11, 1996, three days after winning the prize, Vickrey, 82, died of a heart attack.

Physics: Dr. David M. Lee (U.S.) and Dr. Robert C. Richardson (U.S.), both of Cornell University, and Dr. Douglas D. Osheroff (U.S.) of Stanford University, for their discovery of superfluidity in helium-3, a breakthrough in low-temperature physics. Their 1972 discovery was so unexpected that a leading journal initially rejected their findings.

Chemistry: Dr. Richard E. Smalley and Dr. Robert F. Curl, Jr. (U.S.), both of Rice University, and Sir Harold W. Kroto (U.K.) of the University of Sussex, England, for their discovery of a new class of carbon molecule. These and similar molecules are called "fullerenes" or "Buckyballs" because their geodesic molecular structure is reminiscent of the architectural domes designed by R. Buckminster Fuller.

Deaths

Agnew, Spiro T., 77: Sharp-tongued conservative political leader. Forced to resign as Richard Nixon's vice president after pleading guilty in a tax-evasion scheme. Sept. 17, 1996.

Allen, Mel, 83: broadcaster of New York Yankee baseball games from 1939 to 1964. June 16, 1996.

Amis, Sir Kingsley, 73: prolific British novelist, poet, and critic famed as moral satirist. One of group known as Britain's Angry Young Men. Oct. 22, 1995.

Andrews, Maxene, 77: one of three singing sisters popular in 1940s and an inspiration for servicemen. Oct. 21, 1995.

Argiris, Spiros, 47: principal conductor and director of operatic and symphonic activities at Spoleto Festival U.S.A. at Charleston, S.C. May 19, 1996.

Belli, Melvin, 88: flamboyant West Coast lawyer who pioneered new legal techniques. Defended Jack Ruby in killing of Lee Harvey Oswald. July 9, 1996.

Boorda, Adm. Jeremy M. "Mike", 57: Chief of Naval Operations. First Navy enlisted man to rise to rank of four-star admiral. May 16, 1996.

Bourdet, Claude, 86: leader in French Resistance in World War II. Later released from Nazi concentration camp and became prominent in non-Communist Left. Mar. 21, 1996.

Boyer, Ernest L., 67: helped shape education as United States Commission of Education and president of Carnegie Foundation for Advancement of Teaching. Dec. 8, 1995.

Brett, Jeremy, 59: British actor who portrayed Sherlock Holmes on long-running "Mystery" series on public television. Oct. 10, 1995.

Brodsky, Joseph, 55: persecuted Russian poet who settled in United States. Won Nobel Prize for Literature in 1987. Jan. 28, 1996.

Brown, Edmund G., 90: former California governor. Fostered state's modern economic boom with vast program of public works and low-cost public universities. Feb. 16, 1996.

Bundy, McGeorge, 77: Foreign policy adviser to Presidents Kennedy and Johnson. Was influential advocate of expanded U.S. role in Vietnam War. Sept. 16, 1996.

Burke, Adm. Arleigh A., 94: Chief of Naval Operations. Much decorated for combat exploits against Japanese in South Pacific. Jan. 1, 1996.

Burns, George, 100: comedian known as best "straight man" of all time in partnership with wife, Gracie Allen. Began solo career in show business when nearly 80. Starred in vaudeville, radio, television, nightclubs, records, books, and movies. Mar. 9, 1996

Casscells, S. Ward, 80: pioneer in arthroscopic surgery who helped revolutionize sports medicine. Feb. 8, 1996.

Chancellor, John, 68: radio and television reporter who covered 20 political conventions, a dozen space shots, and several wars in 41 years at NBC News. July 12, 1996.

Colbert, Claudette, 92: versatile stage and film star. Skill in light comedy cheered audiences in Depression era and for decades afterward. July 30, 1996.

Chukovskaya, Lidiya, 88: Russian writer who risked her life to speak out against horrors of Stalinism and Soviet persecution of dissenters. Feb. 7, 1996.

Colby, William E., 78: as director of Central Intelligence, he helped reveal C.I.A.'s shortcomings and prevented its destruction. Apr. 27, 1996.

Corrigan, Douglas, 88: Depression-era pilot idolized as "wrong-way Corrigan" after landing in Ireland on supposed flight from Brooklyn to Los Angeles. Dec. 9, 1995.

Cowie, Mervyn, 87: British Kenyan who pressed for creation of vast network of East African animal parks. July 19, 1996.

Craven, John, 79: actor with long career on stage and in films and television. Created role in original Broadway production of "Our Town." Nov. 24, 1995.

Davie, Donald, 73: British poet, professor, and literary critic. A major influence on British poetry in the 1950s. Sept. 18, 1995.

Davies, Robertson, 82: novelist and educator, one of first Canadian literary figures to gain international recognition. Dec. 2, 1995.

Delany, Annie Elizabeth (Bessie), 104: younger of two sisters whose wisdom and triumphs were celebrated in a best-selling book and Broadway play, "Having Our Say." Sept. 25, 1995.

Dobrushin, Roland L., 66: Russian mathematician, world famed as pioneer in probability theory. Nov. 12, 1995.

Douglas-Home, Sir Alec (Lord Home of the Hirsel), 92: British aristocrat, prime minister for 12 months in 1963 and 1964. Oct. 9, 1995.

Druckman, Jacob, 67: Pulitzer Prize-winning composer, teacher and conductor. An influential proponent of contemporary music. May 24, 1996.

Elytis, Odysseus, 84: Greek poet, winner of Nobel Prize. Celebrated for lyrical evocations of country's history, myths, and rugged landscape. Mar. 18, 1996.

Erdos, Paul, 83: One of the century's greatest mathematicians; founder of discrete mathematics, the basis of computer science. Sept. 24, 1996.

Fitzgerald, Ella, 79: most celebrated jazz singer of her generation, noted for silvery voice and inventive vocal improvisations. June 15, 1996.

Franey, Pierre, 75: *New York Times* food columnist and cookbook author who helped popularize French cooking in the U.S. Oct. 15, 1996.

Fuchs, Lillian, 91: renowned violinist, teacher, composer, and musical traditionalist. Oct. 6, 1995.

Gellhorn, Walter, 89: Columbia University law professor whose writings, teaching, and public appearances helped shape modern law. Dec. 9, 1995.

Gellner, Ernest, 69: philosopher who was expert on social anthropology, philosophy, and politics at universities in London; Cambridge, England; and Prague. Nov. 5, 1995.

Gould, Morton, 82: American composer and conductor whose compositions erased the line between concert and popular idioms. Feb. 21, 1996.

Graves, Nancy, 54: learned post-minimalist artist. Combined abstraction with exacting naturalism. Oct. 21, 1995.

Grosz, Karoly, 65: former Hungarian Communist leader who unleashed reforms that destroyed system he had believed in. Jan. 6, 1996.

Gucci, Paolo, 64: former design chief in Gucci family empire of choice leather goods and clothing. Oct. 10, 1995.

Hemingway, Margaux, 41: a former leading fashion model and granddaughter of Ernest Hemingway. July 1, 1996

Jordan, Barbara, 59: black Congresswoman and scholar from Texas. Stirred nation with denunciations of Watergate scandal. Jan. 17, 1996.

Kelly, Gene, 83: athletic dancer, director, choreographer, and producer. Starred in lavish Hollywood musicals, including "On the Town" and "Singin' in the Rain." Feb. 2, 1996.

Kirstein, Lincoln, 88: pioneer in spread of ballet in United States, cofounder of New York City Ballet. Poet, novelist, historian, and art critic. Jan. 7, 1996.

Kuhn, Thomas S., 73: scientific philosopher whose theories on scientific revolution exerted profound influence on twentieth century thinking by scientists, economists, historians, sociologists and philosophers. June 17, 1996.

Lacoste, Rene, 92: legendary French tennis player, inventor of the metal racquet, and sportswear designer whose clothing line was famous for its alligator logo. Oct. 12, 1996.

Lamour, Dorothy, 81: Film star of 1930s and '40s. Appeared in "road pictures" with Bob Hope and Bing Crosby. Sept. 22, 1996.

Leary, Timothy, 75: clinical psychologist at Harvard, dabbler in Eastern mysticism and leader in introducing young Americans to LSD in 1960s. May 31, 1996.

Lewis, Henry, 63: first black conductor and music director of a major American orchestra, the New Jersey Symphony. Was first black to conduct at the Metropolitan Opera in New York. Jan. 26, 1996.

Lindfors, Viveca, 74: Swedish actress who starred in dozens of movies and plays. Oct. 25, 1995.

Malle, Louis, 63: French film director famed for varied works on both sides of Atlantic. Works included "Pretty Baby" and "Au Revoir les Enfants." Nov. 23, 1995.

Martin, Dean, 78: pop crooner and actor. With Jerry Lewis formed one of most popular comedy teams in movie history. Dec. 25, 1995.

Maynor, Dorothy, 85: highly acclaimed soprano recitalist whose career opened way for many other black artists. Founded Harlem School of the Arts. Feb. 19, 1996.

McCampbell, Capt. David, 86: naval aviation ace of World War II who shot down 34 Japanese planes and won Medal of Honor. June 30, 1996.

Meadows, Audrey, 71: actress who portrayed working-class housewife in popular television series, "The Honeymooners." Jan. 30, 1996.

Milne, Christopher Robin, 76: Briton immortalized by father, A.A. Milne, as young friend of Winnie the Pooh in children's stories. Apr. 20, 1996.

Mitford, Jessica, 78: British-born writer known for sharp wit in satirical reformist writings. Outstanding work was "The American Way of Death," an indictment of the funeral industry. July 23, 1996.

Mitterand, François, 79: revived France's Socialist Party and as president ended decades of Gaullist rule. Jan. 8, 1996.

Monroe, Bill, 84: Mandolin player, singer, and songwriter who created bluegrass music, which was named after his band, "The Blue Grass Boys." Sept. 9, 1996.

Morgan, William J., 85: psychologist who fought Germans and Japanese behind enemy lines. Outmaneuvered Soviet spies in Cold War. Mar. 2, 1996.

Morini, Erica, 91: violinist noted for musicianship and technique, especially in performance of concerto repertory. Oct. 30, 1995.

Muir, Jean, 85: television, stage and screen actress. Dismissal by NBC from "Aldrich Family" series in 1950 brought to light TV industry's practice of blacklisting suspected Communists. She denied Communist affiliation. July 23, 1996.

Muskie, Edmund S., 81: Maine Democrat who served as state's governor, as United States senator, and briefly as secretary of state. Mar. 26, 1996.

Niarchos, Stavros S., 86: Greek shipping magnate. Apr. 15, 1996.

Papandreou, Andreas, 77: former prime minister of Greece, politically active more than two decades. June 23, 1996.

Patterson, Clair C., 73: geochemist who made first accurate estimate of Earth's age and raised alarm about dangerous levels of lead in environment. Dec. 5, 1995.

Pearl, Minnie, 83: radio, television, and stage personality known as queen of country comedy. Mar. 4, 1996.

Peterson, Roger Tory, 87: ornithologist, author of "Field Guide to the Birds," read by millions of birdwatchers worldwide. July 28, 1996.

Rabin, Yitzak, 73: Prime Minister of Israel and leader of the Labor Party, whose efforts to create peace in the Middle East earned him the Nobel Prize for Peace in 1994. He was assassinated after speaking at a peace rally in Tel Aviv. Nov. 4, 1995.

Reston, James, 86: former columnist, Washington correspondent, and executive editor of *The New York Times.* Famed for contacts in world capitals. Dec. 6, 1995.

Rifkind, Simon H., 94: versatile lawyer who represented major organizations and needy Holocaust survivors. Nov. 14, 1995.

Riggs, Bobby, 77: former Wimbledon tennis champion, known for bragging, beaten later by Billie Jean King. Oct. 25, 1995.

Rosenthal, M.L., 79: poet, teacher and a sharp critic of contemporary poetry in Britain and the United States. July 21, 1996.

Roth, Henry, 89: novelist famed for book *Call It Sleep,* portrait of lives of poor Jewish immigrants in New York. Oct. 13, 1995.

Rouse, James W., 81: visionary developer who built new towns in countrysides, shopping malls in suburbs and such festival places as Faneuil Hall in Boston. Apr. 9, 1996.

Rudolph, Arthur, 89: scientist who developed giant *Saturn 5* rocket for American astronauts to make first manned flight to moon. Dec. 22, 1995.

Schapiro, Dr. Meyer, 91: university professor emeritus at Columbia University. Known as multi-disciplinary historian, critic, and teacher. Was a life-long radical. Mar. 3, 1996.

Schine, G. David, 69: a central figure in McCarthy era's Army-McCarthy hearings. June 19, 1996.

Scribner, Charles, Jr., 74: longtime head of Charles Scribner's Sons book publishing company. Nov. 12, 1995.

Shakur, Tupac, 25: Rap singer and actor, center of controversies. Sept. 13, 1996.

Southern, Terry, 71: novelist and screenwriter. Credits included "Dr. Strangelove" and "Easy Rider." Oct. 29, 1995.

Stokes, Carl B., 68: first black mayor of a major U.S. city, elected in Cleveland in 1967. Apr. 4, 1996.

Takemitsu, Toru, 65: first Japanese composer to become known in the West. Championed by Stravinsky. Feb. 20, 1996.

Tordella, Dr. Louis W., 84: mathematician who helped break German military code in World War II. Later served as deputy director of National Security Agency. Jan. 9, 1996.

Travers, P.L., 96: British woman author, native Australian, who wrote Mary Poppins children's books. Apr. 23, 1996.

Trilling, Diana, 91: public intellectual and cultural critic, best known for her incisive commentary in *The Nation, The Partisan Review, The New Yorker, The Atlantic,* and *Harper's.* Oct. 25, 1996.

Tuttle, Judge Elbert Parr, 98: Chief Judge in former Fifth Circuit U.S. Court of Appeals who ordered integration of University of Georgia. Prominent in extending civil rights to blacks. June 23, 1996.

Vlachos, Helen, 85: Greek publisher who closed newspapers and fled Greece rather than submit to military junta from 1967 to 1974. Oct. 14, 1995.

Volkogonov, Col. Gen. Dmitri, 67: Soviet army historian whose writings helped in overthrow of Communist rule. Dec. 6, 1995.

Waldman, Frederic, 92: innovative musical conductor. In 30 year career presented forgotten works by great composers and contemporary compositions. Dec. 1, 1995.

Wallach, Ira, 82: novelist and writer for films and Broadway theater. Dec. 2, 1995.

Williams, Garth, 84: artist who illustrated scores of children's classics, including E.B. White's "Stuart Little" and "Charlotte's Web." May 8, 1996.

Wisher, Peter B., 84: former athletic coach who choreographed students' hand movements in sign language into choreography for the deaf. Oct. 8, 1995.

POSTAL REGULATIONS

U.S. Postal Rates and Fees

Domestic Rates Effective July 1, 1996

First-Class Mail

Single-Piece Letter/Flat Rates

1st ounce	$0.32
Each additional ounce	0.23

Weight not over (oz.)		Weight not over (oz.)	
1*	$0.32	7	$1.70
2	0.55	8	1.93
3	0.78	9	2.16
4	1.01	10	2.39
5	1.24	11	2.62
6	1.47	Over 11 ounces, see Priority Mail.	

*Nonstandard surcharge may apply to pieces weighing 1 ounce or less based on size.

Card Rates

Single postal card sold by USPS	$0.20
Double postal card sold by USPS	0.40
Single postcard (commercial)	0.20

Postcard Dimensions: Not larger than 4-1/4 by 6 inches by 0.0095 inch thick. Not smaller than 3-1/2 by 5 inches by 0.007 thick.

Periodicals

Only publishers and registered news agents approved for periodicals mailing privileges may mail at periodicals rates. Publications mailed by the public are charged at the applicable Express Mail, Priority Mail, single-piece First-Class, standard "A," or standard "B" rate.

Standard "A"

Used primarily by retailers, catalogers, and other advertisers to promote products and services. See postmaster for details. **Use**—For mailing certain items—circulars, books, catalogs, other printed matter, merchandise, seeds, cuttings, bulbs, and plants—weighing less than 16 ounces.

Single-Piece Rates

Weight not over (oz.)		Weight not over (oz.)	
1	$0.32	8	$1.93
2	0.55	9	2.16
3	0.78	10	2.39
4	1.01	11	2.62
5	1.24	13	2.90
6	1.47	Over 13 but	
7	1.70	under 16	2.95

Express Mail

Express Mail is the Post Office's fastest service. Next day delivery by 12 noon to most destinations. Delivered 365 days a year with no extra charge for Saturday, Sunday, or holiday delivery. All packages must use an Express Mail label. Items may weigh up to 70 pounds and measure up to 108 inches in combined length and girth. Call 1–800–222–1811 for delivery information between ZIP Codes.

Features—Express Mail envelopes, labels, and boxes are available, at no additional charge, at post offices or by calling 1–800–222–1811.

Post Office to Addressee Service

Up to 8 ounces	$10.75
Over 8 ounces, up to 2 pounds	15.00
Up to 3 pounds	17.25
Up to 4 pounds	19.40
Up to 5 pounds	21.55
Up to 6 pounds	25.40
Up to 7 pounds	26.45
Over 7 pounds, see postmaster.	

Flat Rate Envelope—Post Office to Addressee Service

$15.00, regardless of weight or destination for matter sent in a flat rate envelope provided by the Postal Service.

Priority Mail

Priority Mail offers 2-day service to most domestic destinations. Items may weigh up to 70 pounds and measure up to 108 inches in combined length and girth.

Features—Priority Mail envelopes, labels, and boxes are available, at no additional charge, at post offices or by calling 1–800–222–1811.

Single-Piece Rates[1]

Up to 2 pounds	$3.00
Up to 3 pounds	4.00
Up to 4 pounds	5.00
Up to 5 pounds	6.00
Over 5 pounds, see postmaster.	

Flat Rate Envelope

$3.00, regardless of weight or destination, for matter sent in a flat rate envelope provided by the Postal Service.

Standard "B"

For mailing circulars, books, catalogs, other printed matter, and packages weighing 16 ounces or more. Enclosed or attached First-Class Mail is charged at First-Class rates. Packages may weigh up to 70 pounds and measure up to 108 inches in combined length and girth.

Parcel Post Zone Rates

For rates priced by distance and weight, see postmaster.

1. Parcels weighing less than 15 pounds but measuring more than 84 inches in length and girth combined are chargeable with a minimum rate equal to that for a 15-pound parcel for the zone to which it is addressed.

Special Services (Domestic Mail)

Certificate of Mailing

Proves that an item was mailed. Must be purchased at time of mailing. No record kept at the post office.

ee, in addition to postage—$0.55

Certified Mail

Provides a mailing receipt, and a record is kept at the recipient's post office. A return receipt can also be purchased for an additional fee. Available only with First-Class and Priority Mail.

ee, in addition to postage—$1.10

Insurance

Provides coverage against loss or damage. Coverage up to $600.00 for standard "A" and standard "B" mail as well as standard "A" and standard "B" matter mailed at Priority Mail or First-Class Mail rate. Insurance up to $25,000 can be purchased by using Registered Mail. Do not insure a package for more than its value.

Liability			Fee, in addition to postage
.01	to	$50.00	$ .75
50.01	to	$100.00	1.60
100.01	to	$200.00	2.50
200.01	to	$300.00	3.40
300.01	to	$400.00	4.30
400.01	to	$500.00	5.20
500.01	to	$600.00	6.10

Money Orders

Provides safe transmission of money. Available in amounts up to $700.00.

ee, in addition to postage—$0.85

Registered Mail

Provides maximum protection and security for valuables. Available only for Priority Mail and First-Class Mail. May be combined with COD, restricted delivery, or return receipt. Additional postal insurance available.

Value			Fee, in addition to postage	
			With postal insurance	Without postal insurance
$ 0.00	to	$100.00	$4.95	$4.85
100.01	to	500.00	5.40	5.20
500.01	to	1,000.00	5.85	5.55
1,000.01	to	2,000.00	6.30	5.90

or higher values, consult your postmaster.

Restricted Delivery

Available only for Certified Mail, COD, Insured Mail for more than $50.00, or Registered Mail.

ee, in addition to postage—$2.75

Return Receipt

Available only for Express Mail, Certified Mail, COD, Insured Mail for more than $50.00, or Registered Mail.

Requested at time of mailing
Showing to whom (signature) and date delivered—$1.10
Showing to whom (signature), date, and addressee's address—$1.50

Requested after mailing
Showing to whom (signature) and date delivered—$6.60

Special Delivery

Available for all classes except Express Mail. Provides preferential handling to the extent practicable in dispatch, transportation, and expedited delivery at the destination.

Class of mail	Fee, in addition to postage		
	2 lb. or less	Over 2 lb., but not over 10 lb.	Over 10 lb
First–Class & Priority Mail	$ 9.95	$10.35	$11.15
Other classes	10.45	11.25	12.10

Collect on Delivery (COD)

Allows mailers to collect the price of goods and/or postage on merchandise ordered by addressee when it is delivered. Fees include insurance. Maximum amount $600.00; see postmaster for details.

Sizes for Domestic Mail

Mail must meet these standards:
• Thickness—No less than 0.007 inch thick. Pieces that are 1/4 inch thick or less must be at least 3-1/2 inches high, 5 inches long, and rectangular in shape.
• Combined length and girth—No more than 108 inches.
• Weight—No more than 70 pounds.
Keys and identification devices are exempted from these requirements.
Additional standards apply to bulk mail and mail addressed to APOs and FPOs.

The Mail Order Merchandise Rule

The mail order rule adopted by the Federal Trade Commission in October 1975 provides that when you order by mail:
You must receive the merchandise when the seller says you will.
If you are not promised delivery within a certain time period, the seller must ship the merchandise to you no later than 30 days after your order comes in.
If you don't receive it shortly after that 30-day period, you can cancel your order and get your money back.

How the Rule Works

The seller must notify you if the promised delivery date (or the 30-day limit) cannot be met. The seller must also tell you what the new shipping date will be and give you the option to cancel the order and receive a full refund or agree to the new shipping date. The seller must also give you a free way to send back your answer, such as a stamped envelope or a postage-paid postcard. *If you don't answer, it means that you agree to the shipping delay.*
The seller must tell you if the shipping delay is going to be more than 30 days. You then can agree to the delay or, if you do not agree, the seller must return your money by the end of the first 30 days of the delay.
If you cancel a prepaid order, the seller must mail you the refund within seven business days. Where there is a credit sale, the seller must adjust your account within one billing cycle.
It would be impossible, however, for one rule to apply uniformly to such a varied field as mail order merchandising. For example, the rule does not apply to mail order photo finishing, magazine subscriptions, and other serial deliveries (except for the initial shipment); to mail order seeds and growing plants; to COD orders; or to credit orders where the buyer's account is not charged prior to shipment of the merchandise.

International Rates Effective as of July 1995

Letters and Letter Packages—Airmail Rates

All countries except Canada & Mexico

Weight not over (oz.)		Weight not over (oz.)	
0.5	$ 0.60	9.0	7.40
1.0	1.00	9.5	7.80
1.5	1.40	10.0	8.20
2.0	1.80	10.5	8.60
2.5	2.20	11.0	9.00
3.0	2.60	11.5	9.40
3.5	3.00	12.0	9.80
4.0	3.40	12.5	10.20
4.5	3.80	13.0	10.60
5.0	4.20	13.5	11.00
5.5	4.60	14.0	11.40
6.0	5.00	14.5	11.80
6.5	5.40	15.0	12.20
7.0	5.80	15.5	12.60
7.5	6.20	16.0	13.00
8.0	6.60	16.5	13.40
8.5	7.00		

See postmaster for weights up to 4 lb.
Maximum weight: 64 ounces.

Letters and Letter Packages

Weight not over (lbs) (oz.)		Can-ada[1]	Mex-ico	Weight not over (lbs) (oz.)		Can-ada[1]	Mex-ico
0	0.5	$.48	$.40	0	10	2.28	4.06
0	1	.52	.48	0	11	2.47	4.46
0	1.5	.64	.66	0	12	2.66	4.86
0	2	.72	.86	1	0	3.42	6.46
0	3	.95	1.26	1	8	4.30	9.66
0	4	1.14	1.66	2	0	5.18	12.86
0	5	1.33	2.06	2	8	6.06	16.06
0	6	1.52	2.46	3	0	6.94	19.26
0	7	1.71	2.86	3	8	7.82	22.46
0	8	1.90	3.26	4	0	8.70	25.66
0	9	2.09	3.66				

1. A 4-pound maximum applies except for registered items sent to Canada. Canada-bound registered items may weigh up to 66 pounds. For registered items weighing over 4 pounds, the rate is $1.76 for each additional pound up to the 66-pound limit.

Aerogrammes

All countries—$0.50

Postcards and Postal Rates

Canada—$0.40; Mexico—$0.35; All others—$0.50

How to Complain About a Postal Problem

When you have a problem with your mail service, complete a Consumer Service Card which is available from letter carriers and at post offices. This will help your postmaster respond to your problem. If you wish to telephone a complaint, a postal employee will fill out the card for you.

The Consumer Advocate represents consumers at the top management level in the Postal Service. If your postal problems cannot be solved by your local post office, then write to the Consumer Advocate. His staff stands ready to serve you.

Write to: The Consumer Advocate, U.S. Postal Service, Washington, D.C. 20260-6320. Or phone: 1-202-268-2284.

Authorized 2-Letter State Abbreviations

When the Post Office instituted the ZIP Code for mail in 1963, it also drew up a list of two-letter abbreviations for the states which would gradually replace the traditional ones in use. Following is the official list, including the District of Columbia, Guam, Puerto Rico, and the Virgin Islands (note that only capital letters are used):

Alabama	AL	Kentucky	KY	Ohio	OH
Alaska	AK	Louisiana	LA	Oklahoma	OK
Arizona	AZ	Maine	ME	Oregon	OR
Arkansas	AR	Maryland	MD	Pennsylvania	PA
California	CA	Massachusetts	MA	Puerto Rico	PR
Colorado	CO	Michigan	MI	Rhode Island	RI
Connecticut	CT	Minnesota	MN	South Carolina	SC
Delaware	DE	Mississippi	MS	South Dakota	SD
Dist. of Columbia	DC	Missouri	MO	Tennessee	TN
Florida	FL	Montana	MT	Texas	TX
Georgia	GA	Nebraska	NE	Utah	UT
Guam	GU	Nevada	NV	Vermont	VT
Hawaii	HI	New Hampshire	NH	Virginia	VA
Idaho	ID	New Jersey	NJ	Virgin Islands	VI
Illinois	IL	New Mexico	NM	Washington	WA
Indiana	IN	New York	NY	West Virginia	WV
Iowa	IA	North Carolina	NC	Wisconsin	WI
Kansas	KS	North Dakota	ND	Wyoming	WY